Anncated Teacher's Edition

Prentie Hall

LITIRATURE

Timess Voices, Timeless Themes

The Bitish Tradition

ISBN 0-13-434866-4

3 4 5 6 7 8 9 10 02 01 00 99 98

What's special about *PrenticeHall Literature: Timeless Voices, Timeles Themes*?

This exciting new program sets a new standard in quality language arts instructional materials. No other literature program provides a more complete blend of classic and contemporary literature; such an extensive array of motivating, real-world connections; such consistent and comprehensive instruction in communication skills; or such a flexible array of teaching materials.

The program also includes a library of longer works and technology in the form of literature videodiscs, audiocassettes of selections, and CD-ROM software. Use the materials you want in the medium that is most convenient for you to address your students' needs.

A uniquerganization

Prentice Hall Lrature: Timeless Voices, Timeless Themes is the first literaturerogram that lets you emphasize genre and theme withinchronological approach.

Strong rl-world connections make literaturrelevant to students

Prentice Hall erature: Timeless Voices, Timeless Themes provides feaes that make all literature, including the classics, relet to today's students.

A new lel of skills instruction

Prentice Hallerature: Timeless Voices, Timeless Themes is the only prograto provide instruction in all of the following skills with *ey selection*:

Reading Stegies	Literary Elements and Forms
Writing	Vocabulary
Grammand Style	Critical Thinking
Critical Wing	Speaking and Listening

Teachirsupport that you can custome to your needs

A wide ar of print and technology resources make it easy for yto customize instruction to meet the needs of all studs.

A unique organization that highlights relevant themes, historical and cultural connections, and emerging literary forms

The British Tradition volume of *Prentice Hall Literature: Timeless Voices, Timeless Themes* provides a comprehensive overview of British literature, emphasizing the link between historical events and literature. Each unit includes the following:

- A highly visual introduction that identifies the major trends in politics, culture, literature, technology, and language development
- One section devoted to a specific genre important to the period
- A thematic strand that traces through literature the history of Britain
- One or more sections featuring thematically related literature of the time

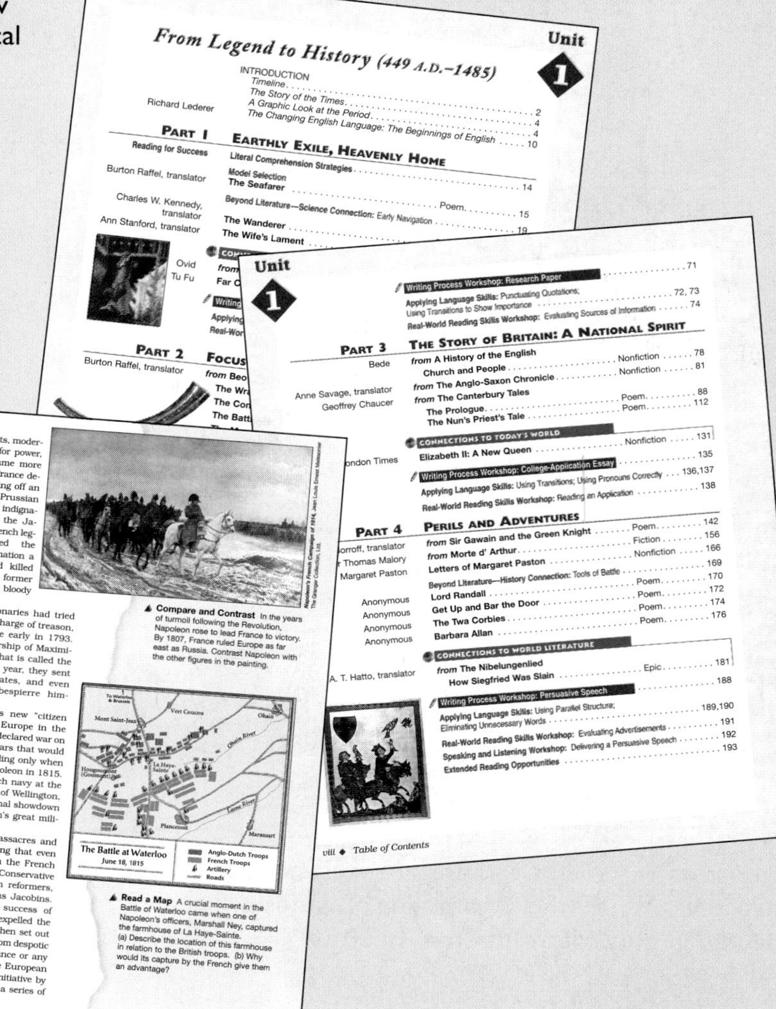

From Legend to History (449 A.D.–1485) — Unit 1

A GRAPHIC LOOK AT THE PERIOD

Declaration of the Rights of Man, 1793, with Robespierre's modifications of the 1789 document

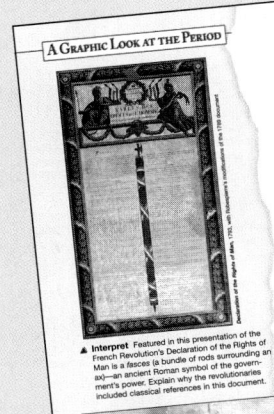

▲ **Interpret** Featured in this presentation of the French Revolution's Declaration of the Rights of Man is a *fasces* (a bundle of rods surrounding an ax)—an ancient Roman symbol of the government's power. Explain why the revolutionaries included classical references in this document.

The Battle of Trafalgar, October 21, 1805, J.M.W. Turner, The Granger Collection, Ltd.

The Story of the Times (1798–1832)

Historical Background

After nearly a century of progress in science and industry, the faith of poets in reason had been eroded. Where eighteenth-century poets had celebrated the power of human understanding—their most bitter satire could say no more than, "humanity is unreasonable"—Wordsworth marked the end of the century with the warning "Our meddling intellect/Misshapes the beauteous forms of things—/We murder to dissect."

In the ensuing period, which was named the Romantic Age by historians during the late 1800's, nearly all the attitudes and tendencies of eighteenth-century classicism and rationalism were redefined or changed dramatically. To understand how these changes occurred, it is necessary to examine not only the impact of events in Britain, but also the effects of the social and political upheaval that began taking place in other parts of the world.

Revolution and Reaction Some of the defining events for British thought and politics at the end of the eighteenth century took place, not in England, but in France. The French Revolution began on July 14, 1789, when a group of French citizens stormed the Bastille, a Paris prison for political prisoners. The revolutionaries placed limits on the powers of King Louis XVI, established a new government, and approved a document called the Declaration of the Rights of Man, affirming the principles of "liberty, equality, and fraternity." France became a constitutional monarchy.

In England, the ruling class felt threatened by the events in France, which seemed to strike at the roots of social order. Most intellectuals, including the most important and influential writers of the Romantic Age, such as William ... supported the rev- ... on which it

he Reign of Terror As royalists, moder- ...tes, and radicals jockeyed for power, ...e French Revolution became more ...d more chaotic. In 1792, France de- ...red war on Austria, touching off an ...asion by Austrian and Prussian ...ps. Fuming with patriotic indigna- ... a radical group called the Ja- ...s gained control of the French leg- ...ve assembly, abolished the ...rchy, and declared the nation a ...lic. Mobs attacked and killed ... prisoners—including former ...rats and priests—in the bloody ...ber massacres."

...in weeks the revolutionaries had tried ...victed Louis XVI on a charge of treason, ...t him to the guillotine early in 1793. ...bins, under the leadership of Maximi- ...spierre, then began what is called the ...Terror. Over the next year, they sent ...00 royalists, moderates, and even ...ncluding finally Robespierre him- ...guillotine.

...same time, France's new "citizen ...making war across Europe in the ...ty. In 1793, France declared war on ... began a series of wars that would ...enty-two years, ending only when ... allies defeated Napoleon in 1815. ...ho broke the French navy at the ...gar, and the Duke of Wellington, ...ish forces in the final showdown ...were two of Britain's great mili- ... the time.

...he September massacres and ...r were so shocking that even ...sympathized with the French ...rned against it. Conservative ... a crackdown on reformers, ...ced as dangerous Jacobins. ...alarm was the success of ... army," which expelled the ... invaders and then set out ...pean nations from despotic ...d not want France or any ...minance on the European ...nce took the initiative by ...n. Thus began a series of

Napoleon's French Campaign of 1814, Jean Louis Ernest Meissonier, The Granger Collection, Ltd.

▲ **Compare and Contrast** In the years of turmoil following the Revolution, Napoleon rose to lead France to victory. By 1807, France ruled Europe as far east as Russia. Contrast Napoleon with the other figures in the painting.

To Waterloo & Brussels
Mont Saint-Jean
Vert Coucou
Ohain
Ohain River
Hougoumont (Goumont)
La Haye-Sainte
Plancenoit
Lasne River
Maransart
The Battle at Waterloo
June 18, 1815
Anglo-Dutch Troops
French Troops
Artillery
Roads

▲ **Read a Map** A crucial moment in the Battle of Waterloo came when one of Napoleon's officers, Marshall Ney, captured the farmhouse of La Haye-Sainte. (a) Describe the location of this farmhouse in relation to the British troops. (b) Why would its capture by the French give them an advantage?

CONNECTIONS TO WORLD LITERATURE

from *Gilgamesh*
Translated by David Ferry

from the *Iliad*
Homer, Translated by Richmond Lattimore

Literary Connection

THE EPIC

If you enjoy watching movies or reading books about heroes battling the forces of evil, you have a lot in common with audiences of thousands of years ago. These audiences would thrill to heroic stories sung and chanted by poet-performers.

Often these heroic tales were **epics**—long narrative poems that celebrated the adventures of legendary heroes. Epics provided not only a roller-coaster ride of nonstop thrills, but also examples of how to behave properly in all kinds of situations. The heroes were role models, and as you read about their exploits today, you can learn about the values and behaviors that ancient societies admired. The legendary fighter who served as a model for the English was Beowulf, whose exploits are described in the poem named for him. (See p. 38.)

Other, even earlier, epics in world literature are the epic of *Gilgamesh*, an ancient Near Eastern poem about 4,000 years old, and the *Iliad*, a Greek poem that is almost 3,000 years old. This section contains the Prologue to *Gilgamesh* and the most famous battle scene from the *Iliad*.

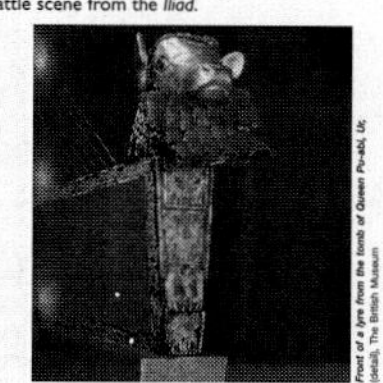

Front of a lyre from the tomb of Queen Pu-abi, Ur, (detail), The British Museum

▲ **Critical Viewing** Music often accompanied the telling of epics, such as *Gilgamesh* and the *Iliad*. Does the appearance of this lyre seem appropriate for the telling of an epic? [Make a Judgment]

GILGAMESH

Gilgamesh is a long narrative poem about a Sumerian king named Gilgamesh who lived between 2700 and 2500 B.C. Unlike modern books, this epic does not have a single author. Stories about King Gilgamesh were told and handed down by Sumerians for hundreds of years after his death. When the Babylonians conquered the Sumerians, they inherited the Sumerian cultural tradition. A Babylonian author, borrowing from some of these tales, created a unified epic about the legendary Sumerian king.

HOMER

The ancient Greeks ascribed the *Iliad* and the *Odyssey*, their two oldest epic poems, to Homer, whom they called "The Poet." Nothing certain is known about Homer's life.

Although Homer's birth and death dates are uncertain, the *Iliad* was probably composed late in the eighth century B.C. The epic tells about a legendary war that occurred hundreds of years earlier, in which Greek forces had attacked the city of Troy in Asia Minor.

Strong connections to contemporary literature and world literature

Each section concludes with a Connection to Today's World feature or with a Connection to World Literature, linking the literature from the time period with high-interest contemporary writings or with literature from other cultures. The program also provides Beyond Literature features that lead students into an exploration of careers, communities, and other subject areas.

Comprehensive skills instruction with every selection

Prentice Hall Literature: Timeless Voices, Timeless Themes is the only literature program to provide instruction in all language arts skills with *every selection*. The following instructional options are provided before, during, and after each selection. Choose the ones that best fit your curricular goals.

Guide for Interpreting

Samuel Pepys (1633–1703)

Samuel Pepys (pēps) is an unusual literary celebrity. Not only does his fame rest on a single work but that work was never intended for publication! The work in question is Pepys's diary, which he wrote in shorthand and in his own private code. Undeciphered until the nineteenth century, the Diary provides a fascinating glimpse of London from 1660 to 1669, when Pepys's failing eyesight forced him to abandon the project.

An Ideal Observer Pepys was in a good position to report on the era. The son of a London tailor, he attended Cambridge University and after graduation became the secretary of his influential cousin, the Earl of Sandwich. In 1660, the year the monarchy was restored, he got his first government post as a clerk for the navy. From there, his rise to fame and fortune was rapid, though not always smooth. Twice his political connections made him a prisoner in the Tower of London, once on charges of treason. Despite these setbacks, Pepys earned a lasting reputation as a man of intelligence and a keen observer.

Daniel Defoe (1660–1731)

"A false, shuffling, prevaricating rascal"— that was how fellow author Joseph Addison described Daniel Defoe. In many ways, Addison was not far wrong. Constantly in debt, Defoe often engaged in shady business deals and declared bankruptcy in 1692, owing a small fortune to his creditors. He was also a sometime government spy and propagandist who even upgraded his own name, originally Foe, by adding an aristocratic De.

An Innovative Novelist Despite all these flaws, we remember Defoe for an important literary achievement. He practically invented the modern realistic novel. He did so with a handful of works published around his sixtieth birthday: *Robinson Crusoe* (1719), his almost documentary narrative of a man marooned on a desert island; *Moll Flanders* (1722), a satirical tale of a lowborn woman seeking respectability; and *A Journal of the Plague Year* (1722), his fictional journal of the great plague that devastated England in 1664–1665, "the plague year."

◆ Background for Understanding

HISTORY: TWIN DISASTERS

In the 1660's, following years of upheaval and a short period of peace, London was struck by twin disasters. The first of these was a plague that began in 1664 and by the next year killed nearly 70,000 Londoners—in a population of about 460,000.

A usually fatal infectious disease, bubonic plague is spread by fleas from an infected host, such as the black rat. Then, in 1666, just as the city was beginning to recover, the Great Fire of London broke out, destroying more than 13,000 buildings.

Like the plague, the Great Fire of London also had a devastating effect on London.

You will read about these disasters in two unusual literary works, a novel about the plague that is written in journal form, and an actual diary that contains an account of the plague and the Great Fire of London.

The Great Fire of London, 1666

460 ◆ A Turbulent Time (1625–1798)

◆ from The Diary ◆
from A Journal of the Plague Year

◆ Literature and Your Life

CONNECT YOUR EXPERIENCE

Despite the best efforts of scientists and doctors, disasters and diseases still threaten us. Although, on average, we may live longer than our ancestors, we're not yet germproof or fireproof. As you read this diary and journal, you will become familiar with two disasters that threatened seventeenth-century England, the bubonic plague and the Great Fire of London.

Journal Writing Jot down in your journal any unfortunate events that you've experienced or seen reported on television.

THEMATIC FOCUS: THE TIES THAT BIND

Although misfortunes strike at human relationships, they may strengthen emotional ties. As you read, look for evidence of compassion on the part of Pepys and the narrator of Defoe's *Journal*.

◆ Reading Strategy

DRAW CONCLUSIONS

You can learn more about a person or a period by using given details to **draw conclusions**. As you read, keep a chart of details from the selections and conclusions that you draw from them.

The Diary	Conclusions
"I had appointed a boat to attend me. . . ."	Pepys was probably fairly rich since he could hire his own boat.

◆ Literary Focus

DIARY OR JOURNAL

A **diary** or **journal** is a daily account of a writer's experiences and reactions. The words *diary* and *journal* are from the Latin (*dies*) and French (*jour*) words for "day" respectively. Most diaries or journals record the small details of a life, but diaries that become literature provide insights into important historical events or periods.

Pepys's *Diary* describes not only his personal life but also historical events that he witnessed, like the bubonic plague and the Great Fire of London. Defoe's *Journal of the Plague Year* is actually a well-researched novel posing as a journal to make it seem more realistic.

◆ Build Vocabulary

PREFIXES: *dis-*

In *A Journal of the Plague Year* you'll see the word *distemper*, a term for an infectious disease. Its prefix *dis-*, which means "apart," combines with *temper*, meaning "balance," to suggest the imbalance of the disease.

WORD BANK

Before you read, preview this list of words from the selections.

apprehensions
abated
lamentable
combustible
malicious
discoursing
distemper
importuning
prodigious

◆ Grammar and Style

GERUNDS

In Pepys's *Diary* and Defoe's *Journal*, you'll find many examples of **gerunds,** verb forms that end in *-ing* and function as nouns. Gerunds can be preceded by articles, as nouns are.

> Church being done, my Lord Bruncker, Sir J. Minnes, and I up to the vestry . . . in order to the *doing* something for the *keeping* of the plague from *growing*.

As you read, note the different ways gerunds are used.

Guide for Interpreting ◆ 461

Before Reading

Engage your students and prepare them to read each selection through the unparalleled prereading support offered in the **Guide for Interpreting**.

- ◆ **An extensive author biography** brings the author to life for students and places the author in historical context.
- ◆ **Build Vocabulary** previews new words and teaches a vocabulary-building strategy.
- ◆ **Grammar and Style** provides instruction in a grammar skill or style point modeled in the selection.
- ◆ **Literature and Your Life** captures students' interest by linking the literature to their own experiences.
- ◆ **Background for Understanding** provides context related to history, science, culture, and more.
- ◆ **Reading Strategy** helps students read more critically and with a higher level of comprehension.
- ◆ **Literary Focus** teaches a literary form or element.

During Reading

To help students through the selection, *Prentice Hall Literature: Timeless Voices, Timeless Themes* offers the following support:

- ◆ **Reading Strategy** prompts support comprehension and guide students in using the strategy introduced before the selection.

> **◆ Reading Strategy**
> What conclusions can you draw about Pepys from the last two sentences?

- ◆ **Literary Focus** prompts help students see how the literary element is illustrated in specific passages.

> **◆ Literary Focus**
> What abbreviated language in this passage is evidence of Pepys's own personal shorthand?

- ◆ **Literature and Your Life** prompts help students connect details in the selection to their lives.

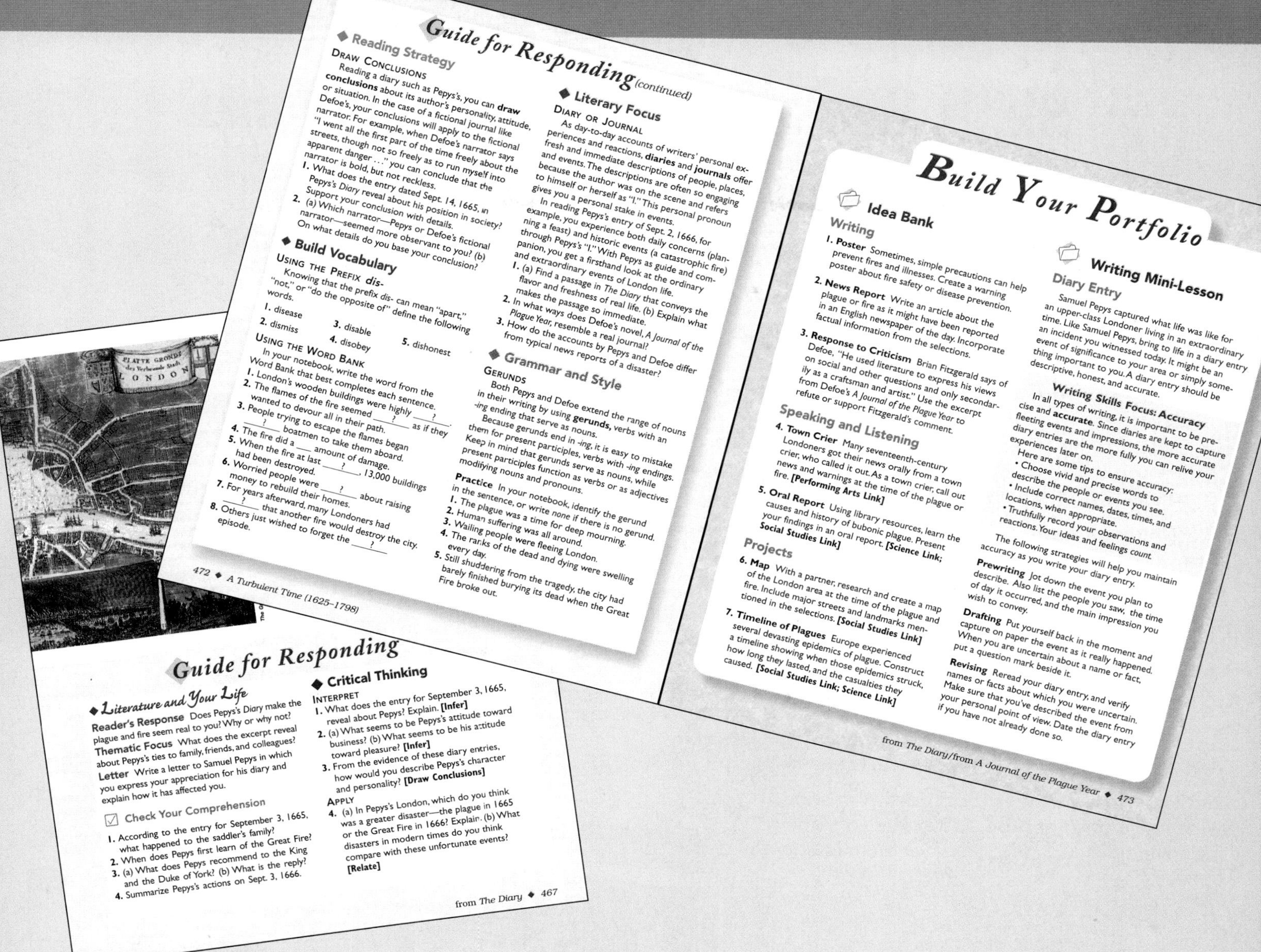

Guide for Responding (continued)

◆ **Reading Strategy**

Draw Conclusions

Reading a diary such as Pepys's, you can **draw conclusions** about its author's personality, attitude, or situation. In the case of a fictional journal like Defoe's, your conclusions will apply to the fictional narrator. For example, when Defoe's narrator says "I went all the first part of the time freely about the streets, though not so freely as to run myself into apparent danger . . ." you can conclude that the narrator is bold, but not reckless.

1. What does the entry dated Sept. 14, 1665, in Pepys's *Diary* reveal about his position in society? Support your conclusion with details.
2. (a) Which narrator—Pepys or Defoe's fictional narrator—seemed more observant to you? (b) On what details do you base your conclusion?

◆ **Build Vocabulary**

Using the Prefix *dis-*

Knowing that the prefix *dis-* can mean "apart," "not," or "do the opposite of" define the following words.

1. disease
2. dismiss
3. disable
4. disobey
5. dishonest

Using the Word Bank

In your notebook, write the word from the Word Bank that best completes each sentence.

1. London's wooden buildings were highly ___?___.
2. The flames of the fire seemed ___?___ as if they wanted to devour all in their path.
3. People trying to escape the flames began ___?___ boatmen to take them aboard.
4. The fire did a ___ amount of damage.
5. When the fire at last ___?___, 13,000 buildings had been destroyed.
6. Worried people were ___?___ about raising money to rebuild their homes.
7. For years afterward, many Londoners had ___?___ that another fire would destroy the city.
8. Others just wished to forget the ___?___ episode.

◆ **Literary Focus**

Diary or Journal

As day-to-day accounts of writers' personal experiences and reactions, **diaries** and **journals** offer fresh and immediate descriptions of people, places, and events. The descriptions are often so engaging because the author was on the scene and refers to himself or herself as "I." This personal pronoun gives you a personal stake in events.

In reading Pepys's entry of Sept. 2, 1666, for example, you experience both daily concerns (planning a feast) and historic events (a catastrophic fire) through Pepys's "I." With Pepys as guide and companion, you get a firsthand look at the ordinary and extraordinary events of London life.

1. (a) Find a passage in *The Diary* that conveys the flavor and freshness of real life. (b) Explain what makes the passage so immediate.
2. In what ways does Defoe's novel, *A Journal of the Plague Year*, resemble a real journal?
3. How do the accounts by Pepys and Defoe differ from typical news reports of a disaster?

◆ **Grammar and Style**

Gerunds

Both Pepys and Defoe extend the range of nouns in their writing by using **gerunds**, verbs with an *-ing* ending that serve as nouns.

Because gerunds end in *-ing*, it is easy to mistake them for present participles, verbs with *-ing* endings. Keep in mind that gerunds serve as nouns, while present participles function as verbs or as adjectives modifying nouns and pronouns.

Practice In your notebook, identify the gerund in the sentence, or write *none* if there is no gerund.

1. The plague was a time for deep mourning.
2. Human suffering was all around.
3. Wailing people were fleeing London.
4. The ranks of the dead and dying were swelling every day.
5. Still shuddering from the tragedy, the city had barely finished burying its dead when the Great Fire broke out.

472 ◆ A Turbulent Time (1625–1798)

Build Your Portfolio

Idea Bank

Writing

1. **Poster** Sometimes, simple precautions can help prevent fires and illnesses. Create a warning poster about fire safety or disease prevention.
2. **News Report** Write an article about the plague or fire as it might have been reported in an English newspaper of the day. Incorporate factual information from the selections.
3. **Response to Criticism** Brian Fitzgerald says of Defoe, "He used literature to express his views on social and other questions and only secondarily as a craftsman and artist." Use the excerpt from Defoe's *A Journal of the Plague Year* to refute or support Fitzgerald's comment.

Speaking and Listening

4. **Town Crier** Many seventeenth-century Londoners got their news orally from a town crier, who called it out. As a town crier, call out news and warnings at the time of the plague or fire. **[Performing Arts Link]**
5. **Oral Report** Using library resources, learn the causes and history of bubonic plague. Present your findings in an oral report. **[Science Link; Social Studies Link]**

Projects

6. **Map** With a partner, research and create a map of the London area at the time of the plague and fire. Include major streets and landmarks mentioned in the selections. **[Social Studies Link]**
7. **Timeline of Plagues** Europe experienced several devasting epidemics of plague. Construct a timeline showing when those epidemics struck, how long they lasted, and the casualties they caused. **[Social Studies Link; Science Link]**

Writing Mini-Lesson

Diary Entry

Samuel Pepys captured what life was like for an upper-class Londoner living in an extraordinary time. Like Samuel Pepys, bring to life in a diary entry an incident you witnessed today. It might be an event of significance to your area or simply something important to you. A diary entry should be descriptive, honest, and accurate.

Writing Skills Focus: Accuracy

In all types of writing, it is important to be precise and **accurate**. Since diaries are kept to capture fleeting events and impressions, the more accurate diary entries are the more fully you can relive your experiences later on.

Here are some tips to ensure accuracy:

- Choose vivid and precise words to describe the people or events you see.
- Include correct names, dates, times, and locations, when appropriate.
- Truthfully record your observations and reactions. Your ideas and feelings count.

The following strategies will help you maintain accuracy as you write your diary entry.

Prewriting Jot down the event you plan to describe. Also list the people you saw, the time of day it occurred, and the main impression you wish to convey.

Drafting Put yourself back in the moment and capture on paper the event as it really happened. When you are uncertain about a name or fact, put a question mark beside it.

Revising Reread your diary entry, and verify names or facts about which you were uncertain. Make sure that you've described the event from your personal point of view. Date the diary entry if you have not already done so.

from The Diary/from A Journal of the Plague Year ◆ 473

Guide for Responding

◆ ***Literature and Your Life***

Reader's Response Does Pepys's *Diary* make the plague and fire seem real to you? Why or why not?

Thematic Focus What does the excerpt reveal about Pepys's ties to family, friends, and colleagues?

Letter Write a letter to Samuel Pepys in which you express your appreciation for his diary and explain how it has affected you.

☑ **Check Your Comprehension**

1. According to the entry for September 3, 1665, what happened to the saddler's family?
2. When does Pepys first learn of the Great Fire?
3. (a) What does Pepys recommend to the King and the Duke of York? (b) What is the reply?
4. Summarize Pepys's actions on Sept. 3, 1666.

◆ **Critical Thinking**

Interpret

1. What does the entry for September 3, 1665, reveal about Pepys? Explain. **[Infer]**
2. (a) What seems to be Pepys's attitude toward business? (b) What seems to be his attitude toward pleasure? **[Infer]**
3. From the evidence of these diary entries, how would you describe Pepys's character and personality? **[Draw Conclusions]**

Apply

4. (a) In Pepys's London, which do you think was a greater disaster—the plague in 1665 or the Great Fire in 1666? Explain. (b) What disasters in modern times do you think compare with these unfortunate events? **[Relate]**

from The Diary ◆ 467

After Reading

Assess students' understanding and **extend** their learning through the **Guide for Responding** after each selection. Additional instruction and practice are provided for all of the skills introduced before the literature.

◆ **Literature and Your Life** promotes reader response and thematic connections.

☑ **Check Your Comprehension** questions assess students' literal understanding of the selection.

◆ **Critical Thinking** questions assess students' ability to use higher level thinking skills to construct meaning.

◆ **Reading Strategy** assesses students' mastery of the reading strategy.

◆ **Build Vocabulary** checks students' mastery of both the vocabulary strategy and the words used in the selection, often in an SAT-style format.

◆ **Literary Focus** reinforces students' understanding of the literary element.

◆ **Grammar and Style** provides reteaching and assessment with practice activities and a writing application.

Build Your Portfolio provides a wealth of activities for students to demonstrate their understanding.

Idea Bank provides:

- Three writing activities keyed to varying performance levels
- Two speaking and listening activities
- Two projects, often linked to cross-curricular topics

Writing Mini-Lesson provides step-by-step writing process instruction and focuses students on developing a specific writing skill.

Skills Workshops provide additional in-depth skills instruction.

Writing Process Workshops provide detailed step-by-step writing process instruction in all modes of writing.

- Provides at least 20 opportunities for extended writing projects
- Linked to the end-of-selection Writing Mini-Lessons through the Writing Skills Focus sections; enables students to build on skills they've already learned

Two **Applying Language Skills** mini-lessons accompany each Writing Process Workshop to provide additional grammar instruction right at point-of-use.

Real-World Reading Skills Workshops help students build reading skills essential to success in future careers and in daily life.

- 20 lessons in each book

Speaking and Listening Workshops provide instruction and practice in real-life communication skills.

Extended Reading Opportunities provide a wide range of suggestions for extended reading, including titles in the *Prentice Hall Literature Library*.

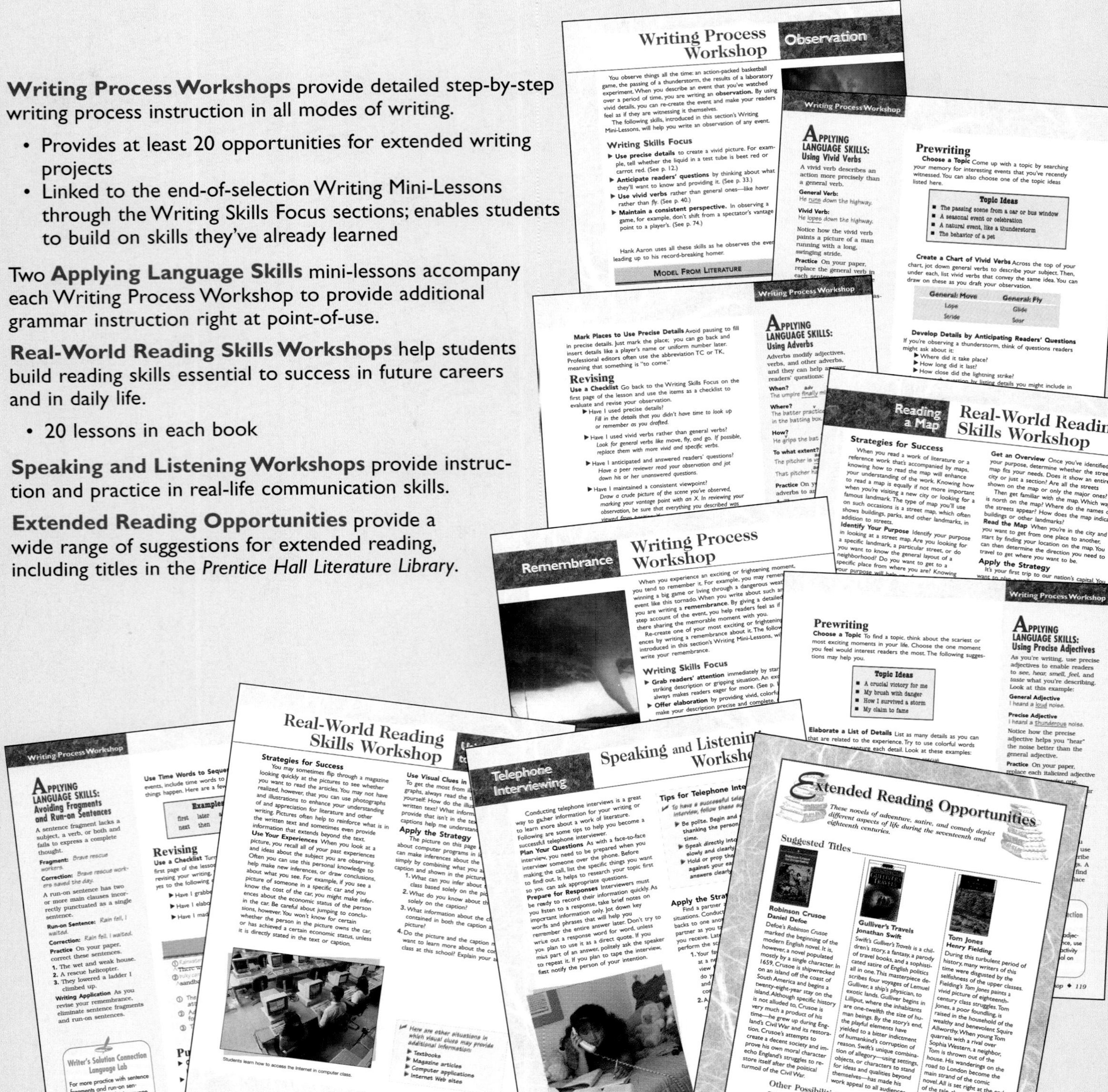

The Annotated Teacher's Edition provides flexible teaching pathways and customized strategies to meet your curricular goals and your students' individual needs.

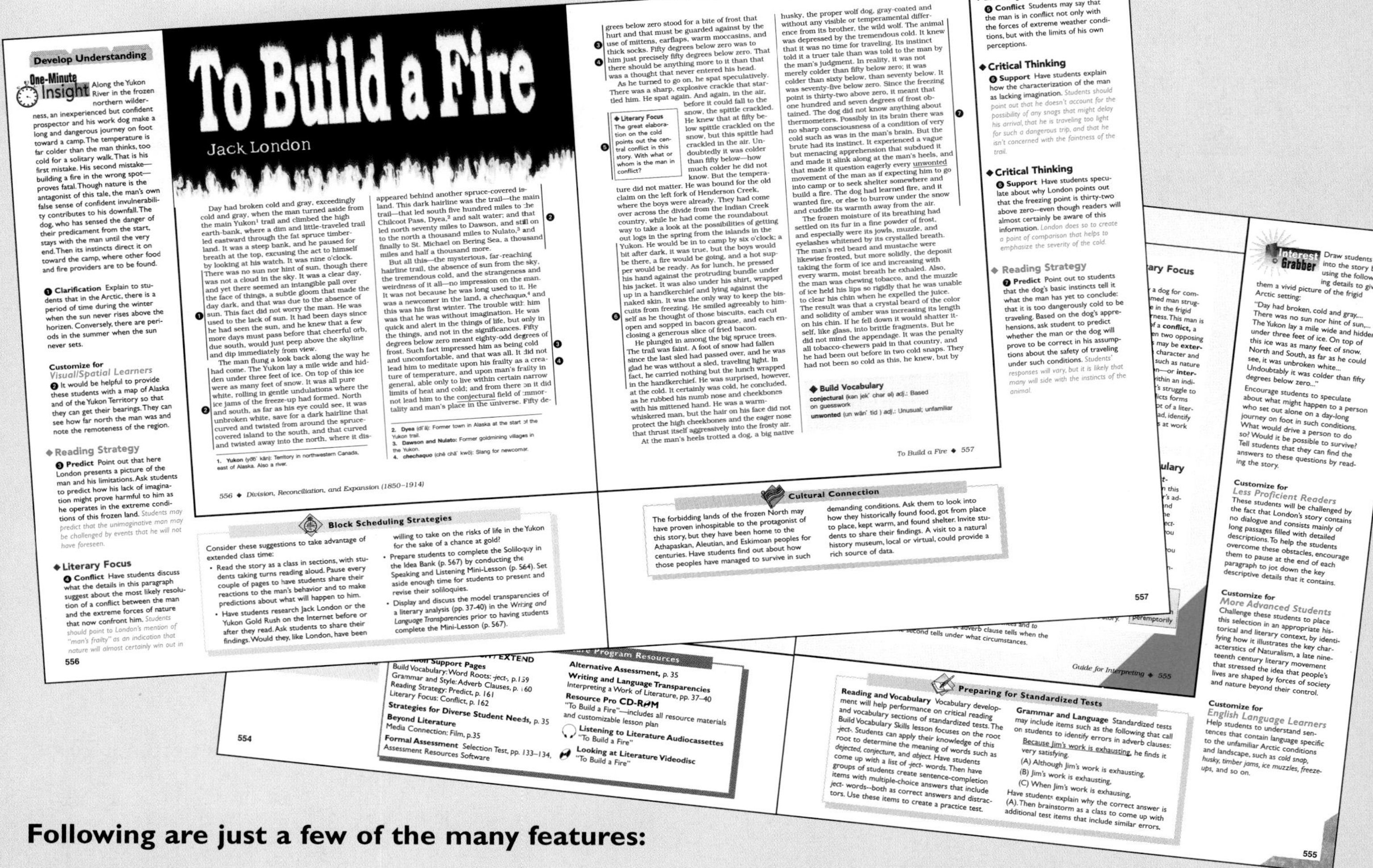

Following are just a few of the many features:

Customize notes provide tips and strategies for addressing the needs of various student populations: Less Proficient Readers, More Advanced Students, English Language Learners, Visual/Spatial Learners, and so on.

Interest Grabber notes at the beginning of every selection provide a quick activity or teaching strategy for piquing students' interest.

One-Minute Insight provides a summary and an explanation of the selection's underlying meaning.

Preparing for Standardized Tests shows you how to connect skills instruction to a standardized test format.

Beyond the Selection notes with every selection provide **Internet Links** to appropriate Web sites.

Other notes include:

- **Humanities Notes**
- **Cross-Curricular Connections**
- **Cultural Connections**
- **Beyond the Classroom (Career and Community Connections; Workplace Skills)**
- **Literary Focus**
- **Reading Strategy**
- **Grammar and Style**
- **Build Vocabulary**
- **Enrichment**
- **Comprehension Check**

A wealth of options for reteaching, extension, and assessment

Teacher Resources

Selection Support: Skills Development

Practice pages reinforce the skills taught with each selection:

- ◆ **Build Vocabulary** includes practice activities in standardized test formats.
- ◆ **Grammar and Style** includes practice activities and a writing application.
- ◆ **Reading Strategy** often provides graphic organizers to aid students as they read the selection.
- ◆ **Literary Focus** reinforces literary concepts.

Beyond Literature

Cross Curricular, Career, and Community Connections

Daily Language Practice

Brief daily activities, ready for easy class presentation

Art Transparencies

20 full-color transparencies

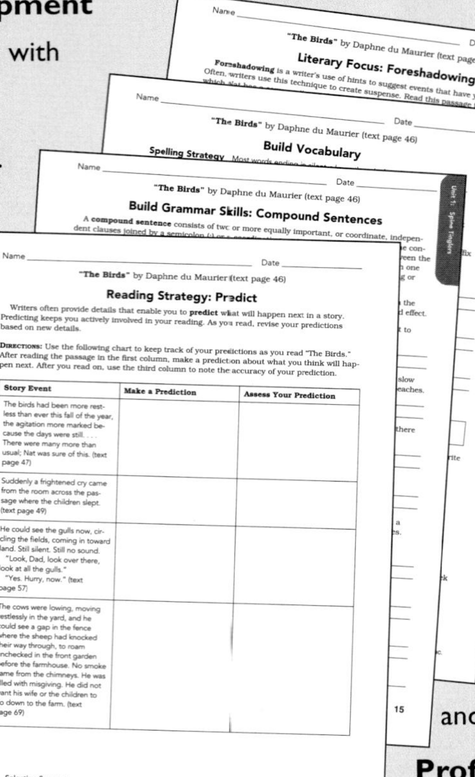

Name ____________ Date ____________

"The Birds" by Daphne du Maurier (text page 46)

Reading Strategy: Predict

Writers often provide details that enable you to **predict** what will happen next in a story. Predicting keeps you actively involved in your reading. As you read, revise your predictions based on new details.

Directions: Use the following chart to keep track of your predictions as you read "The Birds." After reading the passage in the first column, make a prediction about what you think will happen next. After you read on, use the third column to note the accuracy of your prediction.

Story Event	Make a Prediction	Assess Your Prediction
The birds had been more restless than ever this fall of the year, the agitation more marked because the days were still. . . . There were many more than usual; Nat was sure of this. (text page 47)		
Suddenly a frightened cry came from the room across the passage where the children slept. (text page 49)		
He could see the gulls now, circling the fields, coming in toward land. Still silent. Still no sound. "Look, Dad, look over there, look at all the gulls." "Yes. Hurry, now." (text page 57)		
The cows were lowing, moving restlessly in the yard, and he could see a gap in the fence where the sheep had knocked their way through, to roam unchecked in the front garden before the farmhouse. No smoke came from the chimneys. He was filled with misgiving. He did not want his wife or the children to go down to the farm. (text page 69)		

16 Selection Support © Prentice-Hall, Inc.

Formal Assessment

- ◆ **Selection Tests** assess all skills objectives and include essay questions geared to varying performance levels.
- ◆ **Unit Tests** assess mastery of unit skills objectives in a standardized-test format.
- ◆ **Assessment Resources Software** allows you to easily customize tests to performance levels or curricular goals.

Alternative Assessment

Alternative assessment activities, rubrics, portfolio forms, peer and parental assessment support, and much more

Strategies for Diverse Student Needs

Selection summaries in English and Spanish and guided support for every selection

Professional Development

Articles on a wide range of topics promote professional development

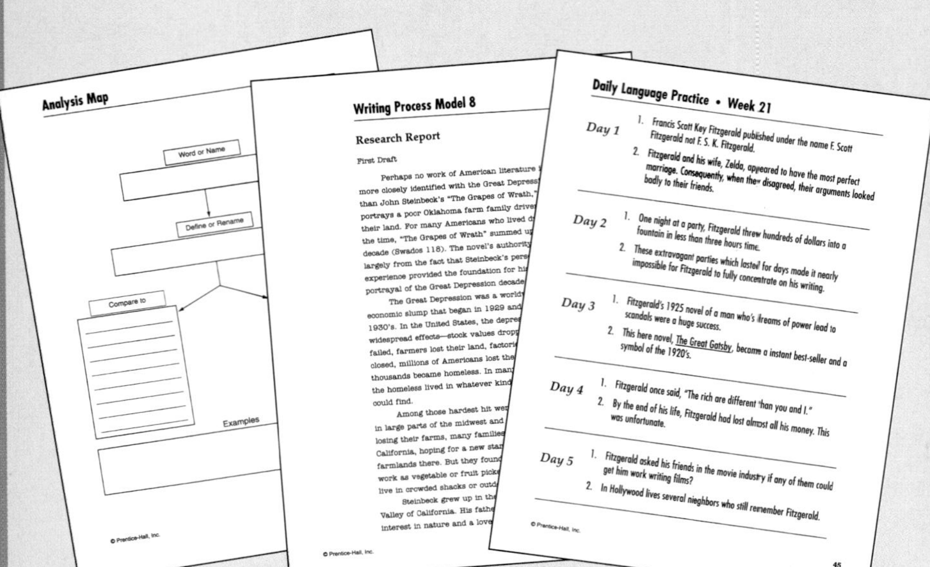

Daily Language Practice • Week 21

Day 1
1. Francis Scott Key Fitzgerald published under the name F. Scott Fitzgerald not F. S. K. Fitzgerald.
2. Fitzgerald and his wife, Zelda, appeared to have the most perfect marriage. Consequently, when they disagreed, their arguments looked badly to their friends.

Day 2
1. One night at a party, Fitzgerald threw hundreds of dollars into a fountain in less than three hours time.
2. These extravagant parties which lasted for days made it nearly impossible for Fitzgerald to fully concentrate on his writing.

Day 3
1. Fitzgerald's 1925 novel of a man who's dreams of power lead to scandals were a huge success.
2. This here novel, The Great Gatsby, became a instant best-seller and a symbol of the 1920's.

Day 4
1. Fitzgerald once said, "The rich are different than you and I."
2. By the end of his life, Fitzgerald had lost almost all his money. This was unfortunate.

Day 5
1. Fitzgerald asked his friends in the movie industry if any of them could get him work writing films?
2. In Hollywood lives several neighbors who still remember Fitzgerald.

© Prentice-Hall, Inc. 45

Writing and Language Transparencies

- ◆ More than 100 transparencies for writing and grammar instruction
- ◆ Complete writing models for various types of writing—ranging from reports to persuasive essays—including rough drafts, revised drafts, and proofread drafts
- ◆ Graphic organizers for support of both writing and reading
- ◆ Daily Language Practice overheads for five-minute activities to improve language skills

Extend your students' appreciation of fine literature.

Prentice Hall Literature Library

- ◆ 24 titles to choose from
- ◆ Special hard covers with a beautiful design for attractiveness and durability
- ◆ Uncut editions so students enjoy complete works
- ◆ Classic novels by honored writers
- ◆ Great drama, including additional Shakespeare offerings
- ◆ Literature collections featuring writings from specific regions, cultures, or genre

Study Guides for each title provide expert teaching support with summaries, teaching strategies, and more.

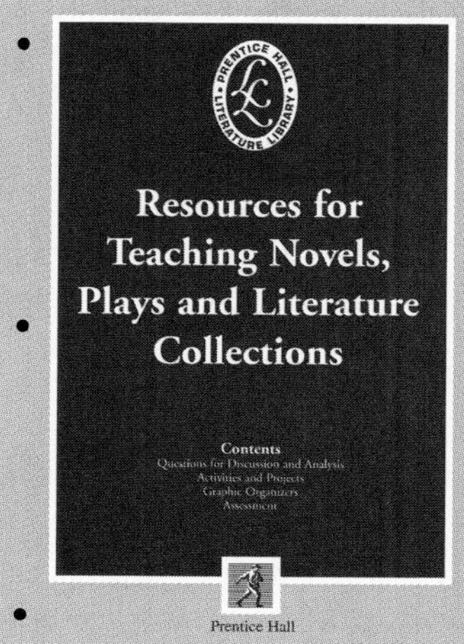

Resources for Teaching Novels, Plays, and Literature Collections provides a wealth of teaching materials and assessment aids for use with any of the titles in our library; includes transparencies, graphic organizers, and tests.

A wide range of quality technology enhances and extends literature instruction.

Listening to Literature Audiocassettes

Use these complete, unabridged recordings of selections in *Prentice Hall Literature: Timeless Voices, Timeless Themes* to bring the literature to life and to meet the diverse needs and learning styles of your students. Includes all of the selections in the program. In addition, an audio CD presents musical selections that support and enhance the literature.

- Motivate auditory learners
- Help less proficient readers
- Aid English language learners

Looking at Literature Videodiscs and Videotapes

Full-motion video segments provide a wide range of support for the literature—from student response to historical context to connections to today's world.

- Motivate students
- Build background
- Establish relevance
- Encourage class discussion of the literature

Resource Pro and Literature Database CD-ROM

Imagine a complete Teaching Resources, a customizable Lesson Planner, and a wide range of additional literature selections that all fit in one hand! With this CD-ROM, you can customize lesson plans at the touch of a button. You can also review, edit, and print an entire year's worth of blackline masters and other teaching support materials. In addition, more than 100 supplemental literature selections are provided for every grade level.

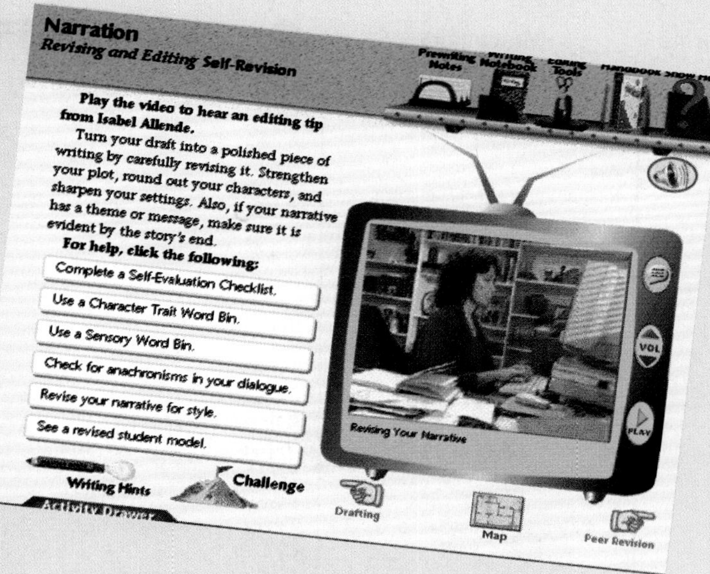

Writer's Solution

Writer's Solution, Prentice Hall's award-winning interactive writing instruction program, has been fully integrated into *Prentice Hall Literature: Timeless Voices, Timeless Themes*. Components include:

- ◆ Writing Lab CD-ROM—provides interactive tutorials on the major modes of writing, including Response to Literature
- ◆ Language Lab CD-ROM—provides self-directed instruction and practice in grammar, usage, and mechanics
- ◆ Writers at Work videodisc and videotape—to bring real writers into the classroom
- ◆ Writer's Toolkit networked software—provides tools and activities for all stages of writing

Formal Assessment CD-ROM

All selection tests and unit tests are available on software so you can customize assessment for your students. The software enables you to:

- ◆ Customize tests to ability levels
- ◆ Customize tests by skills objectives

Literature CD-ROM Library

Multimedia presentations; hyperlinks to glossaries, indexes, and encyclopedias; and complete, on-line testing are just some of the outstanding features on these interactive CD-ROMs. Titles include the following:

- ◆ How to Read and Understand Poetry
- ◆ How to Read and Understand Drama
- ◆ The Time, Life, and Works of Shakespeare
- ◆ The History of American Literature, Part 1
- ◆ The History of American Literature, Part 2
- ◆ Greek Myths and Legends

Internet Home Page

Visit the Prentice Hall Web site at **phschool.com** for features that support *Prentice Hall Literature: Timeless Voices, Timeless Themes:*

- ◆ Visit literary sites through our updated Links.
- ◆ Share ideas through our Faculty Forum electronic bulletin board.
- ◆ Take part in special events, such as electronic dialogues with notable authors.

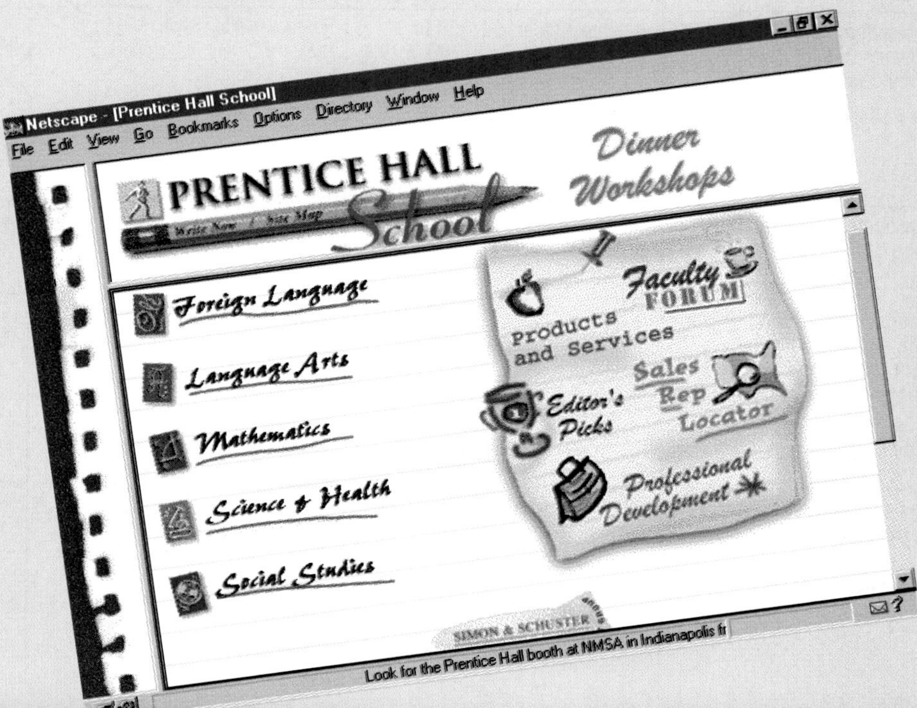

Program Planner Unit 1 From Legend to History (449 A.D.–1485)

Selection	Reading	Literary Elements/Forms	Vocabulary	Grammar
"The Seafarer," translated by **Burton Raffel; "The Wanderer,"** translated by **Charles W. Kennedy; "The Wife's Lament,"** translated by **Ann Stanford,** SE pp. 15, 20, 24 Reading Levels: Average, Easy, Average	• Reading for Success: Literal Comprehension Strategies, SE pp. 14, 26; TR Selection Support, pp. 3–4 • Model, SE pp. 15–19 • Change the Word Order, TR Str. for Diverse St. Needs, p. 1	• Anglo-Saxon Lyrics, SE pp. 13, 19, 23, 25, 26; TR Selection Support, p. 5	• Related Words: Forms of *Grievous,* SE pp. 13, 26; TR Selection Support, p. 1 Word Bank: admonish, sentinel, fervent, rancor, p. 17; compassionate, grievous, p. 21; rapture, redress, p. 23	• Compound Predicates, SE pp. 13, 26; TR Selection Support, p. 2
from ***Tristia,* Ovid; "Far Corners of Earth," Tu Fu,** SE pp. 29, 31 Reading Levels: Challenging, Average			• TR Selection Support, p. 6	
from ***Beowulf,*** translated by **Burton Raffel,** SE p. 40 Reading Level: Average	• Paraphrase, SE pp. 39, 62; TR Selection Support, p. 10 • Monitor What You Know and What You Don't Know, TR Str. for Diverse St. Needs, p. 2	• The Epic, SE pp. 39, 62; TR Selection Support, p. 11	• Word Roots: *-sol-,* SE pp. 39, 62; TR Selection Support, p. 8 Word Bank: reparation, solace, p. 42; purge, p. 47; writhing, p. 49; massive, loathsome, p. 52	• Appositives and Appositive Phrases, SE pp. 39, 62; TR Selection Support, p. 9 • WS Language Lab CD-ROM, Appositives and Appositive Phrases • WS Gram. Pr. Book, p. 28
from ***Gilgamesh,*** translated by **David Ferry;** from **the *Iliad,* Homer,** SE pp. 65, 67 Reading Levels: Average, Challenging			• TR Selection Support, p. 12	
from ***A History of the English Church and People,* Bede;** from ***The Anglo-Saxon Chronicle,* Anne Savage,** SE pp. 78, 81 Reading Levels: Average, Average	• Break Down Sentences, SE pp. 77, 84; TR Selection Support, p. 16 • Organizing Details, TR Str. for Diverse St. Needs, p. 3	• Historical Writing, SE pp. 77, 84; TR Selection Support, p. 17	• Suffixes: *-ade,* SE pp. 77, 84; TR Selection Support, p. 14 Word Bank: promontories, innumerable, p. 79; stranded, barricaded, ravaged, p. 82	• Compound Sentences, SE pp. 77, 84; TR Selection Support, p. 15 • WS Language Lab CD-ROM, Varying Sentence Structure • WS Gram. Pr. Book, p. 13
from ***The Canterbury Tales,* "The Prologue,"** Geoffrey Chaucer, SE p. 88 Reading Level: Average	• Analyze Difficult Sentences, SE pp. 87, 110; TR Selection Support, p. 20 • Analyze a Character, TR Str. for Diverse St. Needs, p. 4	• Characterization, SE pp. 87, 110; TR Selection Support, p. 21	• Suffixes: *-tion,* SE pp. 87, 110; TR Selection Support, p. 18 Word Bank: solicitous, p. 92; garnished, absolution, p. 95; commission, p. 97; sanguine, avouches, p. 98; prevarication, p. 107	• Past and Past Perfect Tenses, SE pp. 87, 110; TR Selection Support, p. 19 • WS Language Lab CD-ROM, Correct and Efficient Use of Verbs • WS Gram. Pr. Book, p. 54
from ***The Canterbury Tales,* "The Nun's Priest's Tale," Geoffrey Chaucer,** SE p. 112 Reading Level: Average	• Context Clues, SE pp. 111, 128; TR Selection Support, p. 24 • Analyze the Story, TR Str. for Diverse St. Needs, p. 5	• Mock-Heroic Style, SE pp. 111, 128; TR Selection Support, p. 25	• Word Roots: *-cap-,* SE pp. 111, 128; TR Selection Support, p. 22 Word Bank: capital, p. 112; timorous, p. 115; derision, p. 119; maxim, p. 121; stringent, p. 123; cant, p. 125	• Pronoun Case, SE pp. 111, 128; TR Selection Support, p. 23 • WS Language Lab CD-ROM, Pronoun Case • WS Gram. Pr. Book, pp. 57, 58, 60
"Elizabeth II: A New Queen," SE p. 131 Reading Level: Average			• TR Selection Support, p. 26	
from ***Sir Gawain and the Green Knight,*** translated by **Marie Borroff;** from ***Morte d'Arthur,* Sir Thomas Malory,** SE pp. 142, 156 Reading Level: Average	• Summarize, SE pp. 141, 162; TR Selection Support, p. 30 • Paraphrase, TR Str. for Diverse St. Needs, p. 6	• Medieval Romance, SE pp. 141, 162; TR Selection Support, p. 31	• Word Roots: *-droit-,* SE pp. 141, 162; TR Selection Support, p. 28 Word Bank: assay, p. 144; adjure, p. 147; feigned, adroitly, p. 152; largesse, p. 155; righteous, entreated, p. 157; peril, p. 159; interred, p. 161	• Comparative and Superlative Forms, SE pp. 141, 162; TR Selection Support, p. 29
Letters of Margaret Paston, Margaret Paston; Four Ballads, SE pp. 166, 170 Reading Levels: Average, Easy	• Understand Dialect, SE pp. 165, 178; TR Selection Support, p. 34 • Tell Who, What, Where, When, and Why, TR Str. for Diverse St. Needs, p. 7	• Understand Dialect, SE pp. 165, 178; TR Selection Support, p. 35	• Word Roots: *-cert-,* SE pp. 165, 178; TR Selection Support, p. 32 Word Bank: alderman, enquiry, succor, certify, remnant, ransacked, asunder, p. 166; assault, p. 168	• Direct Address, SE pp. 165, 178; TR Selection Support, p. 33 • WS Language Lab CD-ROM, Commas

KEY: SE: Student Edition; ATE: Annotated Teacher's Edition; TR: Teaching Resources; LL and WS: Technology

Writing	Speaking and Listening	Projects	Assessment	Technology
• Funeral Oration, Analysis of Theme, Comparison and Contrast, SE p. 27 • Mini-Lesson: Song [Sequence of Events], SE p. 27 • Report, TR Alt. Assess., p. 1	• Demonstration of Caesuras, Oral Interpretation, SE p. 27 • Mini-Lesson: Oral Interpretation, ATE p. 22 • Dream, TR Alt. Assess., p. 1	• Help Wanted, Portrait, SE p. 27 • Drawings; Storyboard, TR Alt. Assess. p. 1	• Selection Test, TR Formal Assessment, pp. 1–3; Assess. Res. Software • Poetry Rubric [for Mini-Lesson], TR Alt. Assess., p. 109 • TR Alt. Assess., p. 1	• "The Seafarer," "The Wanderer," "The Wife's Lament," LL Audiocassettes • WS Writing Lab CD-ROM, Creative Writing Tutorial; Wr. at Work Videodisc, Ch. 6
• Screenplay Treatment, Comparison and Contrast, Symbols of Exile, SE p. 32	• Monologue of an Exile, SE p. 32	• Exile's Map, Time Line, SE p. 32	• Selection Test, TR Formal Assessment, pp. 4–5; Assess. Res. Software	• from *Tristia*, "Far Corners of Earth," LL Audiocassettes
• Memo, Comparison and Contrast, Response to Criticism, SE p. 63 • Mini-Lesson: Press Release for Grendel [Grab Readers' Attention], SE p. 63 • Obituary for Beowulf, TR Alt. Assess., p. 2	• Performance, Speech, SE p. 63 • Mini-Lesson: Performance, ATE p. 48 • Heroic Re-enactment, TR Alt. Assess., p. 2	• Multimedia Presentation, Sculpture, SE p. 63 • Translation Display, TR Alt. Assess., p. 2	• Selection Test, TR Formal Assessment, pp. 9–11; Assess. Res. Software • Persuasion Rubric [for Mini-Lesson], TR Alt. Assess., p. 106 • TR Alt. Assess., p. 2	• from *Beowulf*, LL Audiocassettes • WS Writing Lab CD-ROM, Persuasion Tutorial; Wr. at Work Videodisc, Ch. 4
• Classified Ad, Adventure, Response to Criticism, SE p. 70	• Song for an Epic Hero, SE p. 70	• Comic Book, SE p. 70	• Selection Test, TR Formal Assessment, pp. 12–13; Assess. Res. Software	• from *Gilgamesh,* from the *Iliad*, LL Audiocassettes
• Details That Identify You, Weekly Chronicle, Fantasy History, SE p. 85 • Mini-Lesson: Regional History [Coherence], SE p. 85 • Unbiased Writing, TR Alt. Assess., p. 3	• Interview With Bede, Speech for Alfred the Great, SE p. 85 • Mini-Lesson: Interview, ATE p. 81 • Storytelling,TR Alt. Assess., p. 3	• Tour of a Viking Ship, Evening Newscast From the Tenth Century, SE p. 85 • Making History, TR Alt. Assess., p. 3	• Selection Test, TR Formal Assessment, pp. 17–19; Assess. Res. Software • Research Report/Paper Rubric [for Mini-Lesson], TR Alt. Assess., p. 108 • TR Alt. Assess., p. 3	• from *A History of the English Church and People,* from *The Anglo-Saxon Chronicle,* LL Audiocassettes • WS Writing Lab CD-ROM, Narration Tutorial
• Modern Types, Comparison and Contrast, Response to Criticism, SE p. 110 • Exploring a Character, TR Alt. Assess., p. 4	• Monologue, SE p. 110 • Mini-Lesson: Monologue, ATE p. 107 • Speaking Middle English, TR Alt. Assess., p. 4	• Portraits of the Pilgrims, SE p. 110 • Geography Connection, TR Alt. Assess., p. 4	• Selection Test, TR Formal Assessment, pp. 20–22; Assess. Res. Software • TR Alt. Assess., p. 4	• from *The Canterbury Tales,* "The Prologue," LL Audiocassettes
• Animals as Symbols, Modern Beast Fable, Critical Response, SE p. 129 • Mini-Lesson: Script for an Animated Fable [Using Exaggeration], SE p. 129 • Diary Entry, TR Alt. Assess., p. 5	• Oral Interpretation of a Debate, Mock-Heroic Scene, SE p. 129 • Mini-Lesson: Mock-Heroic Scene, ATE p. 119 • What Did Widowed Women Do?, TR Alt. Assess., p. 5	• Mock-Heroic Comic Book, Pilgrim's Path, SE p. 129 • Illuminate the Text, TR Alt. Assess. p. 5	• Selection Test, TR Formal Assessment, pp. 23–25; Assess. Res. Software • Drama Rubric [for Mini-Lesson], TR Alt. Assess., p. 110 • TR Alt. Assess., p. 5	• from *The Canterbury Tales,* "The Nun's Priest's Tale," LL Audiocassettes • WS Writing Lab CD-ROM, Creative Writing Tutorial
• Symbolic People, Diary of an Unhappy Queen, The Rhetoric of Royalty, SE p. 134	• Crowning Event, SE p. 134	• The Royal Family Tree, SE p. 134	• Selection Test, TR Formal Assessment, pp. 26–27; Assess. Res. Software	• "Elizabeth II: A New Queen," LL Audiocassettes
• T-shirt, Résumé, Response to Criticism, SE p. 163 • Mini-Lesson: Valedictory Speech [Effective Repetition], SE p. 163 • Women's Roles, TR Alt. Assess., p. 6	• Oral Report, Multimedia Presentation, SE p. 163 • Mini-Lesson: Oral Report, ATE p. 146 • Rules of Chivalry, TR Alt. Assess., p. 6	• Musical Presentation, Illuminated Manuscript, SE p. 163 • The Great Hall, TR Alt. Assess., p. 6	• Selection Test, TR Formal Assessment, pp. 31–33; Assess. Res. Software • Summary Rubric [for Mini-Lesson], TR Alt. Assess.; p. 99 • TR Alt. Assess., p. 6	• from *Sir Gawain and the Green Knight,* from *Morte d'Arthur,* LL Audiocassettes • WS Writing Lab CD-ROM, Exposition Tutorial; Wr. at Work Videodisc, Ch. 4
• Casting Call, A Modern Ballad, Critical Response, SE p. 179 • Mini-Lesson: Persuasive Letter [Elaboration to Support an Argument], SE p. 179 • Magazine Article, TR Alt. Assess., p. 7	• Letter vs. Phone Call, Song Translation, SE p. 179 • Mini-Lesson: Song Translation, ATE p. 174 • Dramatic Presentation, TR Alt. Assess., p. 7	• Holidays Chart, An English Manor, SE p. 179 • Medieval Comic Strip TR Alt. Assess., p. 7	• Selection Test, TR Formal Assessment, pp. 34–36; Assess. Res. Software • Persuasion Rubric [for Mini-Lesson], TR Alt. Assess., p. 106 • TR Alt. Assess., p. 7	• Letters of Margaret Paston, Four Ballads, LL Audiocassettes • WS Writing Lab CD-ROM, Persuasion Tutorial; Wr. at Work Videodisc, Ch. 4

Unit 1 From Legend to History (449 A.D.–1485) *(Continued)*

Selection/Feature	Reading	Literary Elements/Forms	Vocabulary	Grammar
from ***The Nibelungenlied,*** **A. T. Hatto,** SE p. 181 Reading Level: Average			• TR Selection Support, p. 36	

Program Planner Unit 2 Celebrating Humanity (1485–1625)

Selection/Feature	Reading	Literary Elements/Forms	Vocabulary	Grammar
Sonnets 1, 35, 75, Edmund Spenser; Sonnets 31, 39, Sir Philip Sidney, SE pp. 209, 210, 211, 212, 213 Reading Levels: Average, Average, Average, Easy, Easy	• Reading for Success: Strategies for Reading Poetry, SE pp. 208, 214; TR Selection Support, pp. 40–41 • Model, SE pp. 209–211 • Explain the Metaphor, TR Str. for Diverse St. Needs, p. 8	• The Sonnet, SE pp. 207, 214; TR Selection Support, p. 42	• Related Words: Forms of *Languished,* SE pp. 207, 214; TR Selection Support, p. 38 Word Bank: deign, p. 209; assay, devise, p. 211; wan, languished, balm, p. 212	• Capitalization of Proper Nouns, SE pp. 207, 214; TR Selection Support, p. 39 • WS Gram. Pr. Book, p. 76
Sonnets 29, 106, 116, 130, William Shakespeare, SE pp. 220, 221, 222, 223 Reading Levels: Average, Average, Easy, Easy	• Relate Structure to Theme, SE pp. 219, 224; TR Selection Support, p. 45 • Using Sentence Structure to Help You Paraphrase, TR Str. for Diverse St. Needs, p. 9	• Shakespearean Sonnet, SE pp. 219, 224; TR Selection Support, p. 46	• Word Roots: *-chron-,* SE pp. 219, 224; TR Selection Support, p. 43 Word Bank: scope, sullen, chronicle, prefiguring, p. 221; impediments, alters, p. 222	• Participles as Adjectives, SE pp. 219, 224; TR Selection Support, p. 44 • WS Language Lab CD-ROM, Recognizing and Using Participles
Sonnets 18, 28, Francesco Petrarch; Sonnets 69, 89, Pablo Neruda, SE pp. 227, 228, 229 Reading Levels: Average, Average, Average, Average			• TR Selection Support, p. 47	
from ***Utopia,*** **Sir Thomas More;** from **"Speech Before Defeating the Spanish Armada," Queen Elizabeth I,** SE pp. 238, 240 Reading Levels: Challenging, Easy	• Summarize, SE pp. 237, 242; TR Selection Support, p. 51 • Identify Supporting Details, TR Str. for Diverse St. Needs, p. 10	• The Monarch as Hero, SE pp. 237, 242; TR Selection Support, p. 52	• Word Roots: *-sequent-,* SE pp. 237, 242; TR Selection Support, p. 49 Word Bank: confiscation, sloth, subsequently, abrogated, forfeited, fraudulent, p. 239; treachery, stead, p. 241	• Complex Sentences, SE pp. 237, 242; TR Selection Support, p. 50 • WS Language Lab CD-ROM, Varying Sentence Structure • WS Gram. Pr. Book, p. 31–33
from ***The King James Bible,*** SE p. 246 Reading Level: Average	• Inferring Meaning, SE pp. 245, 250; TR Selection Support, p. 55 • Identify Author's Purpose, TR Str. for Diverse St. Needs, p. 11	• Psalm, Sermon, and Parable, SE pp. 245, 250; TR Selection Support, p. 56	• Word Roots: *-stat-,* SE pp. 245, 250; TR Selection Support, p. 53 Word Bank: righteousness, stature, p. 246; prodigal, entreated, transgressed, p. 249	• Infinitive Phrases, SE pp. 245, 250; TR Selection Support, p. 54 • WS Language Lab CD-ROM, Recognizing and Using Phrases • WS Gram. Pr. Book, p. 30
from ***A Man for All Seasons,*** **Robert Bolt,** SE p. 253 Reading Level: Easy			• TR Selection Support, p. 57	
The Tragedy of Macbeth, **Act I, William Shakespeare,** SE p. 272 Reading Level: Challenging	• Use Text Aids, SE pp. 271, 292; TR Selection Support, p. 61 • Identify the Chain of Events, TR Str. for Diverse St. Needs, p. 12	• Elizabethan Drama, SE pp. 271, 292; TR Selection Support, p. 62	• Words About Power, SE pp. 271, 292; TR Selection Support, p. 59 Word Bank: valor, p. 274; treasons, imperial, liege, p. 281; sovereign, p. 285	• Action Verbs and Linking Verbs, SE pp. 271, 292; TR Selection Support, p. 60
The Tragedy of Macbeth, **Act II, William Shakespeare,** SE p. 294 Reading Level: Challenging	• Read Verse for Meaning, SE pp. 293, 308; TR Selection Support, p. 65 • Complete a Sequence Chain, TR Str. for Diverse St. Needs, p. 13	• Blank Verse, SE pp. 293, 308; TR Selection Support, p. 66	• Word Roots: *-voc-,* SE pp. 293, 308; TR Selection Support, p. 63 Word Bank: augment, palpable, stealthy, p. 294; multitudinous, equivocate, p. 298; predominance, p. 305	• Commonly Confused Words: *Lie* and *Lay,* SE pp. 293, 308; TR Selection Support, p. 64
The Tragedy of Macbeth, **Act III, William Shakespeare,** SE p. 310 Reading Level: Challenging	• Read Between the Lines, SE pp. 309, 326; TR Selection Support, p. 69 • Envision the Scene, TR Str. for Diverse St. Needs, p. 14	• Conflict, SE pp. 309, 326; TR Selection Support, p. 70	• Prefixes: *mal-,* SE pp. 309, 326; TR Selection Support, p. 67 Word Bank: indissoluble, dauntless, p. 310; jocund, p. 317; infirmity, p. 320; malevolence, p. 325	• Subject and Verb Agreement, SE pp. 309, 326; TR Selection Support, p. 68

KEY: SE: Student Edition; ATE: Annotated Teacher's Edition; TR: Teaching Resources; LL and WS: Technology

Writing	Speaking and Listening	Projects	Assessment	Technology
• Finding Siegfried a Job, A Modern Fable, Hunting the Hunter, Critical Response, SE p. 187	• Dramatizing the Story, Telling the Story With Music, SE p. 187 • Mini-Lesson: Dramatizing the Story, ATE p. 184	• A Map of Medieval Heroes, SE p. 187	• Selection Test, TR Formal Assessment, pp. 37–39; Assess. Res. Software	• from *The Nibelungenlied,* LL Audiocassettes
• Analysis of a Love Song, Response to the Poem, Spenser v. Sidney, SE p. 215 • Mini-Lesson: Paraphrase of a Sonnet [Clear Beginning, Middle, and End], SE p. 215 • Reading Petrarch, TR Alt. Assess., p. 8	• Dialogue Between Man and Woman, Poetry Reading, SE p. 215 • Mini-Lesson: Poetry Reading, ATE p. 211 • Modern Love Songs, TR Alt. Assess., p. 8	• Visual Sonnet, Scientific Paper, SE p. 215 • Design a Valentine, TR Alt. Assess., p. 8	• Selection Test, TR Formal Assessment, pp. 43–45; Assess. Res. Software • TR Alt. Assess., p. 8	• Sonnets 1, 35, 75, Sonnets 31, 39, LL Audiocassettes • WS Writing Lab CD-ROM, Response to Literature Tutorial; Wr. at Work Videodisc, Ch. 7
• Personal Response, Updating, Shakespearean Sonnet, SE p. 225 • Mini-Lesson: Introduction to Shakespeare's Sonnets [Necessary Background], SE p. 225 • Epilogue, TR Alt. Assess., p. 9	• Recitation, Debate, SE p. 225 • Mini-Lesson: Debate, ATE p. 221 • Musical Accompaniment, TR Alt. Assess., p. 9	• Elizabethan Fashions, Elizabethan Music, SE p. 225 • Storyboard, TR Alt. Assess., p. 9	• Selection Test, TR Formal Assessment, pp. 46–48; Assess. Res. Software • TR Alt. Assess., p. 9	• Sonnets 29, 106, 116, 130, LL Audiocassettes • WS Writing Lab CD-ROM, Response to Literature Tutorial
• Advice to the Lovelorn, Essay on Love, Sonnet, SE p. 230	• Role Play, SE p. 230	• Collage, History of Valentine's Day, SE p. 230	• Selection Test, TR Formal Assessment, pp. 49–50; Assess. Res. Software	• Sonnets 18, 28, Sonnets 69, 89, LL Audiocassettes
• Help Wanted, Letter of Support, Updated Utopia, SE p. 243 • Mini-Lesson: Letter to an Editor [Persuasive Tone], SE p. 243 • Character Sketch, TR Alt. Assess., p. 10	• Debate, Oral Interpretation, SE p. 243 • Mini-Lesson: Oral Interpretation, ATE p. 240 • Modern Speeches, TR Alt. Assess., p. 10	• Timeline of Elizabethan England, Movie Review, SE p. 243 • Television Broadcast, TR Alt. Assess., p. 10	• Selection Test, TR Formal Assessment, pp. 54–56; Assess. Res. Software • Persuasion Rubric [for Mini-Lesson], TR Alt. Assess., p. 106 • TR Alt. Assess., p. 10	• from *Utopia,* from "Speech Before Defeating the Spanish Armada," LL Audiocassettes • WS Writing Lab CD-ROM, Persuasion Tutorial
• Letters, Modern Update, Allusion, SE p. 251 • Mini-Lesson: Opening Argument of a Debate [Elaboration], SE p. 251 • Reflection, TR Alt. Assess., p. 11	• Oral Retelling, Sermon, SE p. 251 • Mini-Lesson: Oral Retelling, ATE p. 248 • Psalms, TR Alt. Assess., p. 11	• Compare Translations, Song, SE p. 251 • Illustration, TR Alt. Assess., p. 11	• Selection Test, TR Formal Assessment, pp. 57–59; Assess. Res. Software • Persuasion Rubric [for Mini-Lesson], TR Alt. Assess., p. 106 • TR Alt. Assess., p. 11	• from *The King James Bible,* LL Audiocassettes • WS Writing Lab CD-ROM, Persuasion Tutorial
• Letter to a Monarch, Opening Argument, Continuation, SE p. 258	• Television Interview, SE p. 258	• Visual History, SE p. 258	• Selection Test, TR Formal Assessment, pp. 60–61; Assess. Res. Software	• from *A Man for All Seasons,* LL Audiocassettes
• Speech of Welcome, Comparison and Contrast, SE p. 292 • Journal, TR Alt. Assess., p. 12	• Oral Interpretation, SE p. 292 • Mini-Lesson: Oral Interpretation, ATE p. 290 • Question Game, TR Alt. Assess., p. 12	• Performance, TR Alt. Assess., p. 12	• Selection Test, TR Formal Assessment, pp. 65–67; Assess. Res. Software • TR Alt. Assess., p. 12	• *The Tragedy of Macbeth,* Act I, LL Audiocassettes
• Detective's Journal, Response to Criticism, SE p. 308 •Contrast, TR Alt. Assess., p. 13	• Mock Trial, TR Alt. Assess., p. 13	• Costume Design, SE p. 30 • Nonverbal Communication, TR Alt. Assess., p.13	• Selection Test, TR Formal Assessment, pp. 68–70; Assess. Res. Software • TR Alt. Assess., p. 13	• *The Tragedy of Macbeth,* Act II, LL Audiocassettes
• Diary Entry, Critical Note, SE p. 326 • Posthumous Letter, TR Alt. Assess., p. 14	• Performance, SE p. 326 • Mini-Lesson: Performance, ATE p. 324 • Press Release, TR Alt. Assess., p. 14	• Write a Scene, TR Alt. Assess., p. 14	• Selection Test, TR Formal Assessment, pp. 71–73; Assess. Res. Software • TR Alt. Assess., p. 14	• *The Tragedy of Macbeth,* Act III, LL Audiocassettes

Unit 2 Celebrating Humanity (1485–1625) *(Continued)*

Selection	Reading	Literary Elements/Forms	Vocabulary	Grammar
***The Tragedy of Macbeth,* Act IV, William Shakespeare,** SE p. 328 Reading Level: Challenging	• Use Your Senses, SE pp. 327, 346; TR Selection Support, p. 73 • Create Cartoon Panels, TR Str. for Diverse St. Needs, p. 15	• Imagery, SE pp. 327, 346; TR Selection Support, p. 74	• Word Roots: *-cred-*, SE pp. 327, 346; TR Selection Support, p. 71 Word Bank: pernicious, p. 333; judicious, p. 335; sundry, p. 339; intemperance, avarice, credulous, p. 341	• Possessive Forms: Singular and Plural, SE pp. 327, 346; TR Selection Support, p. 72
***The Tragedy of Macbeth,* Act V, William Shakespeare,** SE p. 348 Reading Level: Challenging	• Infer Beliefs of the Period, SE pp. 347, 362; TR Selection Support, p. 77 • Paraphrase a Conversation, TR Str. for Diverse St. Needs, p. 16	• Shakespearean Tragedy, SE pp. 347, 362; TR Selection Support, p. 78	• Word Roots: *-turb-*, SE pp. 347, 362; TR Selection Support, p. 75 Word Bank: perturbation, p. 348; pristine, p. 354; clamorous, harbingers, p. 357	• Pronouns and Antecedents, SE pp. 347, 362; TR Selection Support, p. 76 • WS Language Lab CD-ROM, Pronouns and Antecedents • WS Gram. Pr. Book, p. 66
from ***Oedipus, the King,* Sophocles,** SE p. 365 Reading Level: Challenging			• TR Selection Support, p. 79	

Program Planner Unit 3 A Turbulent Time (1625–1798)

Selection	Reading	Literary Elements/Forms	Vocabulary	Grammar
Works of John Donne, SE p. 393 Reading Level: Challenging, Average, Average, Average	• Reading for Success: Strategies for Constructing Meaning, SE pp. 392, 402; TR Selection Support, pp. 83–84 • Model, SE pp. 93–95 • Understanding an Argument, TR Str. for Diverse St. Needs, p. 17	• Metaphysical Poetry, SE pp. 391, 402; TR Selection Support, p. 85	• Prefixes: *inter-*, SE pp. 391, 402; TR Selection Support, p. 81 Word Bank: contention, piety, intermit, covetousness, p. 395; profanation, laity, trepidation, breach, p. 399	• Active and Passive Voice, SE pp. 391, 402; TR Selection Support, p. 82 • WS Language Lab CD-ROM, Strengthening Sentences • WS Gram. Pr. Book, p. 56
"On My First Son," "Song: To Celia," "Still to Be Neat," Ben Jonson, SE pp. 406, 407, 408 Reading Levels: Average, Average, Easy	• Hypothesize, SE pp. 405, 410; TR Selection Support, p. 88 • Paraphrase, TR Str. for Diverse St. Needs, p. 18	• Epigrams, SE pp. 405, 410; TR Selection Support, p. 89	• Archaic Words, SE pp. 405, 410; TR Selection Support, p. 86	• The Placement of Only, SE pp. 405, 410; TR Selection Support, p. 87 • WS Language Lab CD-ROM, Sentence Errors and Misplaced and Dangling Modifiers • WS Gram. Pr. Book, p. 45
"To His Coy Mistress," Andrew Marvell; "To the Virgins, to Make Much of Time," Robert Herrick; "Song," Sir John Suckling, SE pp. 414, 416, 417 Reading Levels: Average, Average, Average	• Infer Speakers' Attitudes, SE pp. 413, 418; TR Selection Support, p. 92 • Identify Main Ideas, TR Str. for Diverse St. Needs, p. 19	• *Carpe Diem* Theme, SE pp. 413, 418; TR Selection Support, p. 93	• Related Words: Forms of *Prime,* SE pp. 413, 418; TR Selection Support, p. 90 Word Bank: coyness, amorous, languish, p. 415; prime, p. 416; wan, p. 417	• Irregular Forms of Adjectives, SE pp. 413, 418; TR Selection Support, p. 91 • WS Language Lab CD-ROM, Degrees of Comparison • WS Gram. Pr. Book, p. 68–69
"Freeze Tag," Suzanne Vega; "New Beginning," Tracy Chapman, SE p. 421, 422 Reading Levels: Easy, Easy			• TR Selection Support, p. 94	
"Sonnet VII," "Sonnet XIX," from ***Paradise Lost,* John Milton,** SE pp. 432, 433, 434 Reading Levels: Average, Average, Challenging	• Break Down Sentences, SE pp. 431, 442; TR Selection Support, p. 98 • Summarize Sections, TR Str. for Diverse St. Needs, p. 20	• The Italian Sonnet: Epic Poetry, SE pp. 431, 442; TR Selection Support, p. 99	• Word Roots: *-lum-*, SE pp. 431, 442; TR Selection Support, p. 96 Word Bank: semblance, p. 433; illumine, transgress, guile, obdurate, p. 434; tempestuous, transcendent, p. 437; suppliant, ignominy, p. 438	• Correct Use of *Who* and *Whom,* SE pp. 431, 442; TR Selection Support, p. 97 • WS Language Lab CD-ROM, Using *Who* and *Whom* Correctly • WS Gram. Pr. Book, p. 60
from ***Eve's Apology in Defense of Women,* Amelia Lanier; "To Lucasta, on Going to the Wars," "To Althea, from Prison," Richard Lovelace,** SE pp. 446, 448, 449 Reading Levels: Average, Easy, Average	• Use Historical Context, SE pp. 445, 450; TR Selection Support, p. 102 • Restate Main Ideas, TR Str. for Diverse St. Needs, p. 21	• Tradition and Reform, SE pp. 445, 450; TR Selection Support, p. 103	• Terms with *Breach,* SE pp. 445, 450; TR Selection Support, p. 100 Word Bank: breach, discretion, p. 447; inconstancy, p. 448	• Correlative Conjunctions, SE pp. 445, 450; TR Selection Support, p. 101 • WS Language Lab CD-ROM, Varying Sentence Structure • WS Gram. Pr. Book, p. 13
from ***Light Shining in Buckinghamshire,* Caryl Churchill,** SE p. 453 Reading Levels: Average			• TR Selection Support, p. 104	

KEY: SE: Student Edition; ATE: Annotated Teacher's Edition; TR: Teaching Resources; LL and WS: Technology

Writing	Speaking and Listening	Projects	Assessment	Technology
• Malcolm Wants You!, Plot Analysis, SE p. 346 • Ghost Story, TR Alt. Assess., p. 15	• Role Play, SE p. 346 • Mini-Lesson: Role Play, ATE p. 341 • Imagery Game, TR Alt. Assess., p. 15	• Model, TR Alt. Assess., p. 15	• Selection Test, TR Formal Assessment, pp. 74–76; Assess. Res. Software • TR Alt. Assess., p. 15	• *The Tragedy of Macbeth,* Act IV, LL Audiocassettes
• Independence Day, Dear Diary, Response to Criticism, SE p. 363 • Mini-Lesson: Macbeth: The Film Version? [Precise Details], SE p. 363 • Today's Beliefs, TR Alt. Assess., p. 16	• Performance, Battlefield Report, SE p. 363 • Mini-Lesson: Battlefield Report, ATE p. 356 • Town Crier, TR Alt. Assess., p. 16	• Set Design, Macbeth, the Opera, SE p. 363 • Comic Strip, TR Alt. Assess., p. 16	• Selection Test, TR Formal Assessment, pp. 77–79; Assess. Res. Software • Literary Analysis/Interpretation Rubric [for Mini-Lesson], TR Alt. Assess., p. 113 • TR Alt. Assess., p. 16	• *The Tragedy of Macbeth,* Act V, LL Audiocassettes • WS Writing Lab CD-ROM Response to Literature Tutorial
• Greece's Most Wanted, Journal of a King, The Tragic Flaw, SE p. 371	• Performance, SE p. 371 • Mini-Lesson: Performance, ATE p. 366	• Greek Mask, SE p. 371	• Selection Test, TR Formal Assessment, pp. 80–81; Assess. Res. Software	• from *Oedipus, the King,* LL Audiocassettes
• Journal Entry, The Lady's Turn, Critical Response, SE p. 403 • Mini-Lesson: Speech [Unity], SE p. 403 • Philosophical Argument, TR Alt. Assess., p. 17	• Oral Interpretation, Presentation of a Conceit, SE p. 403 • Mini-Lesson: Oral Interpretation, ATE p. 398 • Oral Report, TR Alt. Assess., p. 17	• Sculpture of a Conceit, Map of the Universe, SE p. 403 • Collection of Paradoxes, TR Alt. Assess., p. 17	• Selection Test, TR Formal Assessment, pp. 86–88; Assess. Res. Software • Persuasion Rubric [for Mini-Lesson], TR Alt. Assess., p. 106 • TR Alt. Assess., p. 17	• Works of John Donne, LL Audiocassettes • WS Writing Lab CD-ROM, Persuasion Tutorial
• T-shirt Saying, Fashion Essay, Literary Analysis, SE p. 411 • Mini-Lesson: Persuasive Letter [Elaboration to Support an Argument], SE p. 411 • Poem, TR Alt. Assess., p. 18	• Love Song, Fashion Debate, SE p. 411 • Mini-Lesson: Debate, ATE p. 408 • Dramatic Presentation, TR Alt. Assess., p. 18	• Sons of Ben, Biographical Report, SE p. 411 • Poetry and Music, TR Alt. Assess., p. 18	• Selection Test, TR Formal Assessment, pp. 89–91; Assess. Res. Software • Persuasion Rubric [for Mini-Lesson], TR Alt. Assess., p. 106 • TR Alt. Assess., p. 18	• "On My First Son," "Song: To Celia," "Still to be Neat," LL Audiocassettes • WS Writing Lab CD-ROM, Persuasion Tutorial
• Persuasive Essay, Advice Column, Comparison and Contrast, SE p. 419 • Mini-Lesson: Witty Poem [Persuasive Tone], SE p. 419 • Counter-Argument, TR Alt. Assess., p. 19	• Phone Conversation, Oral Interpretation, SE p. 419 • Mini-Lesson: Presenting a Skit, ATE p. 415 • Debate, TR Alt. Assess., p. 19	• Wedding Plan, Song, SE p. 419 • One-Act Play, TR Alt. Assess., p. 19	• Selection Test, TR Formal Assessment, pp. 92–94; Assess. Res. Software • Poetry Rubric [for Mini-Lesson], TR Alt. Assess., p. 109 • TR Alt. Assess., p. 19	• "To His Coy Mistress," "To the Virgins, To Make Much of Time," "Song," LL Audiocassettes • WS Writing Lab CD-ROM, Creative Writing Tutorial
• Time Log, Song, Editorial for Teenagers, SE p. 424	• Talk-Show Host, SE p. 424	• Time Experiment, SE p. 424	• Selection Test, TR Formal Assessment, pp. 95–96; Assess. Res. Software	
• Description of a Place, Poem, Response to Criticism, SE p. 443 • Mini-Lesson: Retelling a Story [Consistent Point of View], SE p. 443 • Film Treatment, TR Alt. Assess., p. 20	• Dramatic Readings, Reading Paradise Lost, SE p. 443 • Mini-Lesson: Dramatic Reading, ATE p. 439 • Dramatic Performance, TR Alt. Assess., p. 20	• Illustration for Paradise Lost, Blindness and Creativity, SE p. 443 • Illustration, TR Alt. Assess., p. 20	• Selection Test, TR Formal Assessment, pp. 100–102; Assess. Res. Software • Fictional Narrative Rubric [for Mini-Lesson], TR Alt. Assess., p. 96 • TR Alt. Assess., p. 20	• "Sonnet VII," "Sonnet XIX," from *Paradise Lost,* LL Audiocassettes • WS Writing Lab CD-ROM, Narration Tutorial
• Editorial, Declaration of Parliament, Response to Criticism, SE p. 451 • Mini-Lesson: College Application [Using Dramatic Effects], SE p. 451 • Letter to the Editor, TR Alt. Assess., p. 21	• Ballad, Role Play, SE p. 451 • Using Tradition, TR Alt. Assess., p. 21	• Poster, Civil War, SE p. 451 • Meet the Press, TR Alt. Assess., p. 21	• Selection Test, TR Formal Assessment, pp. 103–105; Assess. Res. Software • Problem-Solution Rubric [for Mini-Lesson], TR Alt. Assess., p. 95 • TR Alt. Assess., p. 21	• from *Eve's Apology in Defense of Women,* "To Lucasta, on Going to the Wars," "To Althea, from Prison," LL Audiocassettes • WS Writing Lab CD-ROM, Exposition Tutorial; Wr. at Work Videodisc, Ch. 3
• Newspaper Article, Press Release, Retelling, SE p. 454	• Panel Discussion, SE p. 454	• Collage, SE p. 454	• Selection Test, TR Formal Assessment, pp. 106–107; Assess. Res. Software	• from *Light Shining in Buckinghamshire,* LL Audiocassettes

Selection/Feature	Reading	Literary Elements/ Forms	Vocabulary	Grammar
from ***The Diary,* Samuel Pepys;** from ***A Journal of the Plague Year,* Daniel Defoe,** SE pp. 462, 468 Reading Levels: Average, Easy:	• Draw Conclusions, SE pp. 461, 472; TR Selection Support, p. 108 • Asking and Answering Questions, TR Str. for Diverse St. Needs, p. 22	• Diary or Journal, SE pp. 461, 472; TR Selection Support, p. 109	• Prefixes: *dis-*, SE pp. 461, 472; TR Selection Support, p. 106 Word Bank: apprehensions, abated, p. 463; lamentable, combustible, p. 465; malicious, discoursing, p. 466; distemper, p. 469; importuning, prodigious, p. 471	• Gerunds, SE pp. 461, 472; TR Selection Support, p. 107 • WS Language Lab CD-ROM, Types of Nouns
from ***Gulliver's Travels,* Jonathan Swift,** SE p. 476 Reading Level: Average	• Interpret, SE pp. 475, 484; TR Selection Support, p. 112 • Complete a Sequence-of-Events Chain, TR Str. for Diverse St. Needs, p. 23	• Satire, SE pp. 475, 484; TR Selection Support, p. 113	• Word Roots: *-jec-*, SE pp. 475, 484; TR Selection Support, p. 110 Word Bank: conjecture, expostulate, schism, p. 477; expedient, p. 479; habituate, p. 481; odious, p. 482	• Correct Use of *Between* and *Among,* SE pp. 475, 484; TR Selection Support, p. 111
from ***The Rape of the Lock,*** from ***An Essay on Man,* Alexander Pope,** SE pp. 488, 498 Reading Levels: Average	• Author's Purpose, SE pp. 487, 500; TR Selection Support, p. 116 • Paraphrase, TR Str. for Diverse St. Needs, p. 24	• Mock Epic, SE pp. 487, 500; TR Selection Support, p. 117	• Related Words: Words About Society, SE pp. 487, 500; TR Selection Support, p. 114 Word Bank: obliquely, p. 489; plebeian, destitute, p. 491; assignations, p. 495; stoic, disabused, p. 498	• Inverted Word Order, SE pp. 487, 500; TR Selection Support, p. 115 • WS Gram. Pr. Book, p. 19
from ***The Preface to A Dictionary of the English Language;*** from ***A Dictionary of the English Language,* Samuel Johnson;** from ***The Life of Samuel Johnson,* James Boswell,** SE pp. 505, 508, 510 Reading Levels: Average, Easy, Average	• Set a Purpose, SE pp. 503, 516; TR Selection Support, p. 120 • Determine the Author's Attitude, TR Str. for Diverse St. Needs, p. 25	• Dictionary; Biography, SE pp. 503, 516; TR Selection Support, p. 121	• Word Roots: *-dict-*, SE pp. 503, 516; TR Selection Support, p. 118 Word Bank: recompense, caprices, adulterations, p. 505; propagators, risible, p. 507; abasement, p. 511; credulity, p. 513; malignity, pernicious, inculcated, p. 515	• Commas With Parenthetical Expressions, SE pp. 503, 516; TR Selection Support, p. 119 • WS Language Lab CD-ROM, Commas • WS Gram. Pr. Book, p. 83
"Elegy Written in a Country Churchyard," Thomas Gray; "A Nocturnal Reverie," Anne Finch, Countess of Winchilsea, SE pp. 520, 526 Reading Levels: Average, Average	• Paraphrase, SE pp. 519, 530; TR Selection Support, p. 124 • Use Your Senses, TR Str. for Diverse St. Needs, p. 26	• Preromantic Poetry, SE pp. 519, 530; TR Selection Support, p. 125	• Prefixes: *circum-*, SE pp. 519, 530; TR Selection Support, p. 122 Word Bank: penury, circumscribed, ingenuous, ignoble, p. 523; nocturnal, temperate, venerable, p. 527; forage, p. 529	• Pronoun-Antecedent Agreement, SE pp. 519, 530; TR Selection Support, p. 123 • WS Language Lab CD-ROM, Nouns and Pronouns • WS Gram. Pr. Book, pp. 64–65
from ***The Analects,* Confucius;** from ***The Declaration of Independence,* Thomas Jefferson,** SE pp. 533, 555 Reading Levels: Easy, Average			• TR Selection Support, p. 126	
"On Spring," Samuel Johnson; from **"The Aims of the Spectator," Joseph Addison,** SE pp. 546, 550 Reading Levels: Average, Average	• Make Inferences, SE pp. 545, 552; TR Selection Support, p. 130 • State the Main Idea, TR Str. for Diverse St. Needs, p. 27	• Essay, SE pp. 545, 552; TR Selection Support, p. 131	• Word Roots: *-spec-*, SE pp. 545, 552; TR Selection Support, p. 128 Word Bank: procured, divert, p. 547; speculation, pp. 549, 551; transient, affluence, contentious, trifles, embellishments, p. 551	• Adjective Clauses, SE pp. 545, 552; TR Selection Support, p. 129 • WS Language Lab CD-ROM, Adjective Clauses • WS Gram. Pr. Book, p. 31
"Homeless," Anna Quindlen, SE p. 555 Reading Level: Easy			• TR Selection Support, p. 132	

KEY: SE: Student Edition; ATE: Annotated Teacher's Edition; TR: Teaching Resources; LL and WS: Technology

Writing	Speaking and Listening	Projects	Assessment	Technology
• Poster, News Report, Response to Criticism, SE p. 473 • Mini-Lesson: Diary Entry [Accuracy], SE p. 473 • Diary Entry, TR Alt. Assess., p. 22	• Town Crier, Oral Report, SE p. 473 • Mini-Lesson: Town Crier, ATE p. 470 • Therapy Session, TR Alt. Assess., p. 22	• Map, Timeline of Plagues, SE p. 473 • Painting/Sculpture, TR Alt. Assess., p. 22	• Selection Test, TR Formal Assessment, pp. 111–113; Assess. Res. Software • Expression Rubric [for Mini-Lesson], TR Alt. Assess., p. 95 • TR Alt. Assess., p. 22	• from *The Diary,* from *A Journal of the Plague Year,* LL Audiocassettes • WS Writing Lab CD-ROM, Description Tutorial
• Imaginary Language, SE p. 485 • Mini-Lesson: Satirical Essay [Appropriateness for Medium], SE p. 485 • Point of View, TR Alt. Assess., p. 23	• Film Conference, Reader's Theater, SE p. 485 • Mini-Lesson: Readers Theater, ATE p. 482 • Classroom Satire, TR Alt. Assess., p. 23	• A New Adventure, Gunpowder Report, SE p. 485 • Measurement, TR Alt. Assess., p. 23	• Selection Test, TR Formal Assessment, pp. 114–116; Assess. Res. Software • Persuasion Rubric [for Mini-Lesson], TR Alt. Assess., p. 106 • TR Alt. Assess., p. 23	• from *Gulliver's Travels,* LL Audiocassettes • WS Writing Lab CD-ROM, Persuasion Tutorial
• Paraphrase, Reply, Comparison and Contrast, SE p. 501 • Mini-Lesson: Imitating an Author's Style [Maintain Consistent Style], SE p. 501 • Description, TR Alt. Assess., p. 24	• Reading and Pantomime, Graduation Speech, ATE p. 501 • Mini-Lesson: Reading and Pantomime, ATE p. 490 • Stage a Scene, TR Alt. Assess., p. 24	• High Society in Pope's Day, Classical Glossary, SE p. 501 • Chart the Action, TR Alt. Assess., p. 24	• Selection Test, TR Formal Assessment, pp. 117–119; Assess. Res. Software • Fictional Narrative or Poetry Rubric [for Mini-Lesson], TR Alt. Assess., pp. 96, 109 • TR Alt. Assess., p. 24	• from *The Rape of the Lock,* from *An Essay on Man,* LL Audiocassettes • WS Writing Lab CD-ROM, Creative Writing Tutorial
• Book Ad, Revised Preface, Response to Criticism, SE p. 517 • Mini-Lesson: Dictionary of New Words [Keeping to a Format], SE p. 517 • Johnsonian Dictionary, TR Alt. Assess., p. 25	• Reenactment, Interpretation of Attitudes, SE p. 517 • Mini-Lesson: Interpretation of Attitudes, ATE p. 514 • Debate, TR Alt. Assess., p. 25	• First-Person Biography, The School of Johnson, SE p. 517 • A Memorial Painting, TR Alt. Assess., p. 25	• Selection Test, TR Formal Assessment, pp. 120–122; Assess. Res. Software • Definition/Classification Rubric [for Mini-Lesson], TR Alt. Assess., p. 100 • TR Alt. Assess., p. 25	• from *The Preface to A Dictionary of the English Language;* from *A Dictionary of the English Language,* from *The Life of Samuel Johnson,* LL Audiocassettes • WS Writing Lab CD-ROM, Research Writing Tutorial
• Diary Entry, Epitaphs, Response to Criticism, SE p. 531 • Mini-Lesson: Reflective Essay [Elaboration to Make Writing Personal], SE p. 531 • Reflection, TR Alt. Assess., p. 26	• Choral Reading, Eulogy, SE p. 531 • Mini-Lesson: Eulogy, ATE p. 526 • Television Commercial, TR Alt. Assess., p. 26	• Nighttime Walk, Brain Study, SE p. 531 • Musical Accompaniment, TR Alt. Assess., p. 26	• Selection Test, TR Formal Assessment, pp. 123–125; Assess. Res. Software • Description Rubric [for Mini-Lesson], TR Alt. Assess., p. 98 • TR Alt. Assess., p. 26	• "Elegy Written in a Country Churchyard," "A Nocturnal Reverie," LL Audiocassettes • WS Writing Lab CD-ROM, Description Tutorial; Wr. at Work Videodisc, Ch. 1
• Yearbook Entry, Analects for Today, Imaginary Correspondence, SE p. 538	• Ask Confucius, SE p. 538	• Charter or Constitution, SE p. 538	• Selection Test, TR Formal Assessment, pp. 126–127; Assess. Res. Software	• from *The Analects,* from *The Declaration of Independence,* LL Audiocassettes
• Advertisement, Seasonal Essay, Letter to the Editor, SE p. 553 • Mini-Lesson: Essay on Human Behavior [Precise Details], SE p. 553 • Reflection, TR Alt. Assess., p. 27	• Monologue, Satiric Monologue, SE p. 553 • Mini-Lesson: Satiric Monologue, ATE p. 550 • Round Table Discussion, TR Alt. Assess., p. 27	• Satirical Cartoons, Press Wars, SE p. 553 • Work of Art, TR Alt. Assess., p. 27	• Selection Test, TR Formal Assessment, pp. 132–134; Assess. Res. Software • Description Rubric [for Mini-Lesson], TR Alt. Assess., p. 98 • TR Alt. Assess., p. 27	• "On Spring," from *The Aims of the Spectator,* LL Audiocassettes • WS Writing Lab CD-ROM, Exposition Tutorial
• Public Service Announcement, Newspaper Column, Response to Criticism, SE p. 557	• Reporter's Interview, SE p. 557	• Newsletter, SE p. 557	• TR Alt. Assess., p. 1 • Selection Test, TR Formal Assessment, pp. 135–136; Assess. Res. Software	• "Homeless," LL Audiocassettes

Program Planner Unit 4 Rebels and Dreamers (1798–1832)

Selection	Reading	Literary Elements/Forms	Vocabulary	Grammar
Introduction to *Frankenstein,* Mary Wollstonecraft Shelley, SE p. 579 Reading Level: Average	• Reading for Success: Interactive Reading Strategies, SE pp. 578, 584; TR Selection Support, pp. 136–137 • Model, SE pp. 579–583 • Identify the Sequence of Events, TR Str. for Diverse St. Needs, p. 28	• The Gothic Tradition, SE pp. 577, 584; TR Selection Support, p. 138	• Related Words: Phantasm and Fantasy, SE pp. 577, 584; TR Selection Support, p. 134 Word Bank: appendage, ungenial, p. 579; acceded, p. 581; platitude, phantasm, incitement, p. 583	• Past Participial Phrases, SE pp. 577, 584; TR Selection Support, p. 135
"To a Mouse," "To a Louse," Robert Burns; "Woo'd and Married and A'," Joanna Baillie, SE pp. 579, 588, 590, 592 Reading Levels: Challenging, Challenging, Average	• Translate Dialect, SE pp. 587, 594; TR Selection Support, p. 141 • Paraphrase, TR Str. for Diverse St. Needs, p. 29	• Dialect, SE pp. 587, 594; TR Selection Support, p. 142	• Words Related to Clothing, SE pp. 587, 594; TR Selection Support, p. 139 Word Bank: dominion, p. 589; impudence, p. 591; winsome, discretion, inconstantly, p. 593	• Interjections, SE pp. 587, 594; TR Selection Support, p. 140
"The Lamb," "The Tyger," "The Chimney Sweeper," "Infant Sorrow," William Blake, SE pp. 598, 599, 600, 601 Reading Levels: Easy, Easy, Average, Easy	• Use Visuals as a Key to Meaning, SE pp. 597, 602; TR Selection Support, p. 145 • Ask and Answer Questions, TR Str. for Diverse St. Needs, p. 30	• Symbols, SE pp. 597, 602; TR Selection Support, p. 146	• Word Roots: *-spir-,* SE pp. 597, 602; TR Selection Support, p. 143 Word Bank: vales, symmetry, aspire, p. 598	• Commonly Confused Words: *Rise* and *Raise,* SE pp. 597, 602; TR Selection Support, p. 144
"The Oval Portrait," Edgar Allan Poe, SE p. 605 Reading Level: Average			• TR Selection Support, p. 147	
Poetry of William Wordsworth, SE pp. 616, 621, 624, 625 Reading Levels: Average, Challenging, Average, Average	• Use Literary Context, SE pp. 615, 626; TR Selection Support, p. 151 • Read Sentence by Sentence, TR Str. for Diverse St. Needs, p. 31	• Romanticism and the Lyric, SE pp. 615, 626; TR Selection Support, p. 152	• Related Words: Forms of *Anatomize,* SE pp. 615, 626; TR Selection Support, p. 149 Word Bank: recompense, p. 619; roused, p. 621; presumption, anatomize, confounded, p. 623; sordid, p. 624; stagnant, p. 625	• Present Participial Phrases, SE pp. 615, 626; TR Selection Support, p. 150 • WS Language Lab CD-ROM, Sentence Errors • WS Gram. Pr. Book, p. 29
"The Rime of the Ancient Mariner," "Kubla Khan," Samuel Taylor Coleridge, SE pp. 630, 652 Reading Levels: Average, Easy	• Poetic Effects, SE pp. 629, 654; TR Selection Support, p. 155 • Replace Unfamiliar Words and Spellings, TR Str. for Diverse St. Needs, p. 32	• Poetic Sound Devices, SE pp. 629, 654; TR Selection Support, p. 156	• Word Roots: *-journ-,* SE pp. 629, 654; TR Selection Support, p. 153 Word Bank: averred, p. 632; sojourn, p. 641; expiated, p. 645; reverence, p. 651; sinuous, tumult, p. 653	• Inverted Word Order, SE pp. 629, 654; TR Selection Support, p. 154 • WS Language Lab CD-ROM, Special Problems in Agreement • WS Gram. Pr. Book, p. 23
"She Walks in Beauty," from ***Childe Harold's Pilgrimage;*** from ***Don Juan,*** **George Gordon, Lord Byron,** SE pp. 658, 660, 663 Reading Levels: Easy, Average, Easy	• Question, SE pp. 657, 666; TR Selection Support, p. 159 • Ask and Answer Questions, TR Str. for Diverse St. Needs, p. 33	• Figurative Language, SE pp. 657, 666; TR Selection Support, p. 160	• Suffixes: *-ous,* SE pp. 657, 666; TR Selection Support, p. 157 Word Bank: arbiter, p. 660; tempests, torrid, fathomless, p. 662; retort, p. 663; insensible, credulous, copious, avarice, p. 665	• Subject and Verb Agreement, SE pp. 657, 666; TR Selection Support, p. 158 • WS Language Lab CD-ROM, Special Problems in Agreement • WS Gram. Pr. Book, p. 61–63
"Ozymandias," "Ode to the West Wind," "To a Skylark," Percy Bysshe Shelley, SE pp. 670, 672, 676 Reading Levels: Average, Average, Easy	• Respond to Imagery, SE pp. 669, 680; TR Selection Support, p. 163 • Determine the Poet's Attitude, TR Str. for Diverse St. Needs, p. 34	• Imagery, SE pp. 669, 680; TR Selection Support, p. 164	• Word Roots: *-puls-,* SE pp. 669, 680; TR Selection Support, p. 161 Word Bank: visage, p. 670; verge, sepulcher, p. 673; impulse, p. 675; blithe, profuse, p. 677; vernal, satiety, p. 678	• Subjunctive Mood, SE pp. 669, 680; TR Selection Support, p. 162 • WS Gram. Pr. Book, p. 55
Poetry of John Keats, SE pp. 684, 685, 686, 690 Reading Levels: Average, Average, Average, Average	• Paraphrase, SE pp. 683, 692; TR Selection Support, p.167 • Identify the Speaker, TR Str. for Diverse St. Needs, p. 35	• Ode, SE pp. 683, 692; TR Selection Support, p. 168	• Suffixes: *-age,* SE pp. 683, 692; TR Selection Support, p. 165 Word Bank: ken, surmise, p. 684; gleaned, teeming, p. 685; vintage, p. 686; requiem, p. 688	• Direct Address, SE pp. 683, 692; TR Selection Support, p. 166 • WS Language Lab CD-ROM, Punctuation • WS Gram. Pr. Book, p. 83

KEY: SE: Student Edition; ATE: Annotated Teacher's Edition; TR: Teaching Resources; LL and WS: Technology

Writing	Speaking and Listening	Projects	Assessment	Technology
• Journal Entry, Physical Description, Gothic Tale, SE p. 585 • Mini-Lesson: Comparison-and-Contrast Essay [Organization], SE p. 585 • Book Review, TR Alt. Assess., p. 28	• Radio Narration, Movie Review, SE p. 585 • Mini-Lesson: Narration, ATE p. 582 • Introduce a Radio Show, TR Alt. Assess., p. 28	• Set Design, Scientific Research, SE p. 585 • Illustration of Shelley's Vision, TR Alt. Assess., p. 28	• Selection Test, TR Formal Assessment, pp. 140–142; Assess. Res. Software • Comparison/Contrast Rubric [for Mini-Lesson], TR Alt. Assess., p. 104 • TR Alt. Assess., p. 28	• Introduction to *Frankenstein,* LL Audiocassettes • WS Writing Lab CD-ROM, Exposition Tutorial
• Advice, Comparison and Contrast, Response, SE p. 595 • Mini-Lesson: Scene With Dialogue [Clear Beginning, Middle, and End], SE p. 595 • Poetic License, TR Alt. Assess., p. 29	• Oral Interpretation, Lecture, SE p. 595 • Mini-Lesson: Lecture, ATE p. 589 • Performing, TR Alt. Assess., p. 29	• Comic Strip, Multimedia Presentation, SE p. 595 • Dramatic Presentation, TR Alt. Assess., p. 29	• Selection Test, TR Formal Assessment, pp. 143–145; Assess. Res. Software • Drama Rubric [for Mini-Lesson], TR Alt. Assess., p. 110 • TR Alt. Assess., p. 29	• "To a Mouse," "To a Louse," "Woo'd and Married and A'," LL Audiocassettes • WS Writing Lab CD-ROM, Creative Writing Tutorial
• Journal Entry, Research Report, Response to Criticism, SE p. 603 • Mini-Lesson: Comparative Analysis [Placement for Emphasis], SE p. 603 • Poetry Review, TR Alt. Assess., p. 30	• Blake Reading, Setting Blake to Music, SE p. 603 • Performing Poetry, TR Alt. Assess., p. 30	• Advertisement, Illuminated Poem, SE p. 603 • News Report, TR Alt. Assess., p. 30	• Selection Test, TR Formal Assessment, pp. 146–148; Assess. Res. Software • Comparison/Contrast Rubric [for Mini-Lesson], TR Alt. Assess., p. 104 • TR Alt. Assess., p. 30	• "The Lamb," "The Tyger," "The Chimney Sweeper," "Infant Sorrow," LL Audiocassettes • WS Writing Lab CD-ROM, Response to Literature Tutorial; Wr. at Work Videodisc, Ch. 7
• Description of a Gothic Setting, Literary Analysis, Response to Criticism, SE p. 608	• Dramatic Recitation, SE p. 608	• Poe on Film, SE p. 608	• Selection Test, TR Formal Assessment, pp. 149–150; Assess. Res. Software	• "The Oval Portrait," LL Audiocassettes
• Literary Analysis, Romantic Travel Brochure, Response to Criticism, SE p. 627 • Mini-Lesson: Public Service Announcement [Adapting the Message to the Medium], SE p. 627 • Interpolation, TR Alt. Assess., p. 31	• Debate, Ask the Poet, SE p. 627 • Mini-Lesson: Debate, ATE p. 624 • Debate, TR Alt. Assess., p. 31	• Ecology and Romanticism, History of Gardening, SE p. 627 • Advertising Poster, TR Alt. Assess., p. 31	• Selection Test, TR Formal Assessment, pp. 154–156; Assess. Res. Software • Persuasion Rubric [for Mini-Lesson], TR Alt. Assess., p. 106 • TR Alt. Assess., p. 31	• Poetry of William Wordsworth, LL Audiocassettes • WS Writing Lab CD-ROM, Persuasion Tutorial
• Utopia, Response to the Poem, Response to the Poet, SE p. 655 • Mini-Lesson: Poem With Sound Effects [Dramatic Effects Through Sound], SE p. 655 • Dramatic Monologue, TR Alt. Assess., p. 32	• Dramatic Reading, Panel Discussion, SE p. 655 • Mini-Lesson: Panel Discussion, ATE p. 645 • Sailors' Superstitions, TR Alt. Assess., p. 32	• Research Project, Illustrated Journey, SE p. 655 • Costume Design, TR Alt. Assess., p. 32	• Selection Test, TR Formal Assessment, pp. 157–159; Assess. Res. Software • Poetry Rubric [for Mini-Lesson], TR Alt. Assess., p. 109 • TR Alt. Assess., p. 32	• "The Rime of the Ancient Mariner," "Kubla Khan," LL Audiocassettes • WS Writing Lab CD-ROM, Creative Writing Tutorial; Wr. at Work Videodisc, Ch. 6
• Health Regimen, Ocean's Response, Response to Criticism, SE p. 667 • Mini-Lesson: Dramatic Monologue [Realistic Speech], SE p. 667 • Satire, TR Alt. Assess., p. 33	• Oral Reading, Eulogy, SE p. 667 • Mini-Lesson: Eulogy, ATE p. 664 • Debate, TR Alt. Assess., p. 33	• Portrait, Music, SE p. 667 • Collage, TR Alt. Assess., p. 33	• Selection Test, TR Formal Assessment, pp. 160–162; Assess. Res. Software • Fictional Narrative Rubric [for Mini-Lesson], TR Alt. Assess., p. 96 • TR Alt. Assess., p. 33	• "She Walks in Beauty," from *Childe Harold's Pilgrimage;* from *Don Juan,* LL Audiocassettes • WS Writing Lab CD-ROM, Narration Tutorial; Wr. at Work Videodisc, Ch. 2
• Direct Address, Comparison and Contrast, Response to Criticism, SE p. 681 • Mini-Lesson: Research Report [Necessary Background], SE p. 681 • Reply from the West Wind, TR Alt. Assess., p. 34	• Role Play, Weather Report, SE p. 681 • Mini-Lesson: Weather Report, ATE p. 695 • Musical Characters, TR Alt. Assess., p. 34	• Observation Journal, Art Presentation, SE p. 681 • West Wind Illustration, TR Alt. Assess., p. 34	• Selection Test, TR Formal Assessment, pp. 163–165; Assess. Res. Software • Research Report/Paper Rubric [for Mini-Lesson], TR Alt. Assess., p. 107 • TR Alt. Assess., p. 34	• "Ozymandias," "Ode to the West Wind," "To a Skylark," LL Audiocassettes • WS Writing Lab CD-ROM, Research Writing Tutorial
• Prose Tribute, Irregular Ode, Response to Criticism, SE p. 693 • Mini-Lesson: Description of a Moment in Time [Precise Details], SE p. 693 • Poetic Response, TR Alt. Assess., p. 35	• Informal Retelling, Oral Report, SE p. 693 • Mini-Lesson: Oral Report, ATE p. 688 • Song or Spoken-word, TR Alt. Assess., p. 35	• Museum Catalog, Science Display, SE p. 693 • Vase Drawing, TR Alt. Assess., p. 35	• Selection Test, TR Formal Assessment, pp. 166–168; Assess. Res. Software • Description Rubric [for Mini-Lesson], TR Alt. Assess., p. 98 • TR Alt. Assess., p. 35	• Poetry of John Keats, LL Audiocassettes • WS Writing Lab CD-ROM, Description Tutorial; Wr. at Work Videodisc, Ch. 1

Unit 4 Rebels and Dreamers (1798–1832) *(Continued)*

Selection/Feature	Reading	Literary Elements/ Forms	Vocabulary	Grammar
"The Lorelei," Heinrich Heine; Haiku by Basho, Yosa Buson, Kobayashi Issa, SE pp. 695, 696, 696, 697 Reading Level: Easy			• TR Selection Support, p. 169	
"Speech to Parliament," George Gordon, Lord Byron; "A Song: 'Men of England,'" Percy Bysshe Shelley; "On the Passing of the Reform Bill," Thomas Babington Macaulay, SE pp. 706, 708, 710 Reading Levels: Average, Average, Average	• Set a Purpose for Reading, SE pp. 705, 712; TR Selection Support, p. 173 • Chart the Information, TR Str. for Diverse St. Needs, p. 36	• Political Commentary, SE pp. 705, 712; TR Selection Support, p. 174	• Word Roots: *-deci-* or *-deca-,* SE pp. 705, 712; TR Selection Support, p. 171 Word Bank: impediments, decimation, efficacious, emancipate, p. 707; balm, p. 708; inauspicious, p. 711	• Correlative Conjunctions, SE pp. 705, 712; TR Selection Support, p. 172
"On Making an Agreeable Marriage," Jane Austen; from ***A Vindication,*** **Mary Wollstonecraft,** SE pp. 716, 720 Reading Levels: Average, Average	• Determine the Writer's Purpose, SE pp. 715, 722; TR Selection Support, p. 177 • Restate and Simplify Key Points, TR Str. for Diverse St. Needs, p. 37	• Social Commentary, SE pp. 715, 722; TR Selection Support, p. 178	• Word Roots: *-fort-,* SE pp. 715, 722; TR Selection Support, p. 175 Word Bank: scruple, p. 716; amiable, p. 718; vindication, solicitude, fastidious, specious, p. 720; fortitude, preponderates, gravity, p. 721	• Commas in a Series, SE pp. 715, 722; TR Selection Support, p. 176 • WS Language Lab CD-ROM
from ***The Sense and Sensibility Screenplay and Diaries,*** **Emma Thompson,** SE pp. 725 Reading Level: Easy			• TR Selection Support, p. 179	

Program Planner Unit 5 Progress and Decline (1833–1901)

Selection/Feature	Reading	Literary Elements/ Forms	Vocabulary	Grammar
from ***In Memoriam, A.H.H.,*** **"The Lady of Shalott," "Ulysses," "Tears, Idle Tears," Alfred, Lord Tennyson,** SE pp. 751, 754, 759, 762 Reading Levels: Average, Easy, Average, Easy	• Reading for Success: Strategies for Reading Critically, SE pp. 750, 764; TR Selection Support, pp. 183–184 • Model, SE pp. 751–753 • Classify the Type of Poem, TR Str. for Diverse St. Needs, p. 38	• The Speaker in Poetry, SE pp. 749, 764; TR Selection Support, p. 185	• Related Words: Medieval Words, SE pp. 749, 764; TR Selection Support, p. 181 Word Bank: diffusive, p. 753; churls, p. 754; waning, p. 757; furrows, p. 761	• Parallel Structure, SE pp. 749, 764; TR Selection Support, p. 182 • WS Language Lab CD-ROM, Developing a Mature Style; Strengthening Sentences • WS Gram. Pr. Book, p. 46
"My Last Duchess," "Love Among the Ruins," "Life in a Love," Robert Browning; Sonnet 43, Elizabeth Barrett Browning, SE pp. 768, 771, 772, 776 Reading Levels: Average, Easy, Average, Easy	• Make Inferences About the Speaker, SE pp. 767, 778; TR Selection Support, p. 188 • Empathize with the Listener, TR Str. for Diverse St. Needs, p. 39	• Dramatic Monologue, SE pp. 767, 778; TR Selection Support, p. 189	• Suffixes: *-ence,* SE pp. 767, 778; TR Selection Support, p. 186 Word Bank: countenance, p. 769; officious, munificence, dowry, p. 770; eludes, p. 771; vestige, p. 773; sublime, minions, p. 775	• The Use of *Like* and *As*, SE pp. 767, 778; TR Selection Support, p. 187
"You Know the Place: Then," Sappho; "Invitation to the Voyage," Charles Baudelaire, SE pp. 781, 782 Reading Levels: Average, Average			• TR Selection Support, p. 190	
"Dover Beach," Matthew Arnold; "Recessional," "The Widow at Windsor," Rudyard Kipling, SE pp. 792, 794, 796 Reading Levels: Average, Average, Average	• Draw Conclusions, SE pp. 791, 798; TR Selection Support, p. 194 • Evaluate Diction, TR Str. for Diverse St. Needs, p. 40	• Mood as a Key to Theme, SE pp. 791, 798; TR Selection Support, p. 195	• Word Roots: *-domi-,* SE pp. 791, 798; TR Selection Support, p. 192 Word Bank: tranquil, cadence, turbid, p. 793; dominion, contrite, p. 795	• Present Tense, SE pp. 791, 798; TR Selection Support, p. 193 • WS Language Lab CD-ROM, Correct and Effective Use of Verbs • WS Gram. Pr. Book, p. 53–54

KEY: SE: Student Edition; ATE: Annotated Teacher's Edition; TR: Teaching Resources; LL and WS: Technology

Writing	Speaking and Listening	Projects	Assessment	Technology
• Japanese "Lorelei," Personality Profile, Response to Criticism, SE p. 698	• Music and Poetry, SE p. 698 • Mini-Lesson: Music and Poetry, ATE p. 695	• Personalities of Poets, SE p. 698	• Selection Test, TR Formal Assessment, pp. 169–170; Assess. Res. Software	• "The Lorelei," Haiku, LL Audiocassettes
• Casting Memo, Letter to the Editor, Response to Criticism, SE p. 713 • Mini-Lesson: News Article on a Political Issue [Elaboration to Give Information], SE p. 713 • Slogan, TR Alt. Assess., p. 36	• Political Speech, Panel Discussion, SE p. 713 • Mini-Lesson: Panel Discussion, ATE p. 708 • Debate, TR Alt. Assess., p. 36	• Political Cartoon, Song, SE p. 713 • Map, TR Alt. Assess., p. 36	• Selection Test, TR Formal Assessment, pp. 175–177; Assess. Res. Software • Summary Rubric [for Mini-Lesson], TR Alt. Assess., p. 99 • TR Alt. Assess., p. 36	• "Speech to Parliament," "A Song: 'Men of England,'" "On the Passing of the Reform Bill," LL Audiocassettes • WS Writing Lab CD-ROM, Exposition Tutorial
• Letter, Comparison and Contrast, Response to Criticism, SE p. 723 • Mini-Lesson: Letter to an Author [Appropriate Language for a Purpose], SE p. 723 • Dear Aunt Jane, TR Alt. Assess., p. 37	• Conversation, Persuasive Speech, SE p. 723 • Mini-Lesson: Persuasive Speech, ATE p. 719 • Speech, TR Alt. Assess., p. 37	• Portrait, Timeline of Women's Rights, SE p. 723 • Song, TR Alt. Assess., p. 37	• Selection Test, TR Formal Assessment, pp. 178–180; Assess. Res. Software • Business Letter/Memo Rubric [for Mini-Lesson], TR Alt. Assess., p. 114 • TR Alt. Assess., p. 37	• "On Making an Agreeable Marriage," from *A Vindication*, LL Audiocassettes • WS Writing Lab CD-ROM, Response to Literature Tutorial
• Letter to the President, Prediction, Social Criticism, SE p. 729	• Interview, SE p. 729	• Historical Account, SE p. 729	• Selection Test, TR Formal Assessment, pp. 181–182; Assess. Res. Software	• from *The Sense and Sensibility Screenplay and Diaries*, LL Audiocassettes
• Song, Literary Analysis, Critical Response, SE p. 765 • Mini-Lesson: Essay of Tribute [Clear Explanation of Cause and Effect], SE p. 765 • Comparison, TR Alt. Assess., p. 38	• Oral Interpretation, Camelot Late-Night News, SE p. 765 • Mini-Lesson: Camelot Late-Night News, ATE p. 757 • Oral Report, TR Alt. Assess., p. 38	• Set Design, Tennyson on Tape, SE p. 765 • Drama, TR Alt. Assess., p. 38	• Selection Test, TR Formal Assessment, pp. 186–188; Assess. Res. Software • Cause-Effect Rubric [for Mini-Lesson], TR Alt. Assess., p. 765 • TR Alt. Assess., p. 38	• from *In Memoriam, A.H.H.*, "The Lady of Shalott," "Ulysses," "Tears, Idle Tears," LL Audiocassettes • WS Writing Lab CD-ROM, Exposition Tutorial
• Profile, Messenger's Report, Response to Criticism, SE p. 779 • Mini-Lesson: Written Recommendation [Cause-and-Effect Transitions], SE p. 779 • Visualization, TR Alt. Assess., p. 39	• Oral Interpretation, Fateful Meeting, SE p. 779 • Mini-Lesson: Oral Interpretation, ATE p. 771 • Enactment, TR Alt. Assess., p. 39	• The Brownings in Media, The Brownings in Italy, SE p. 779 • Art Report, TR Alt. Assess., p. 39	• Selection Test, TR Formal Assessment, pp. 189–191; Assess. Res. Software • Cause-Effect Rubric [for Mini-Lesson], TR Alt. Assess., p. 103 • TR Alt. Assess., p. 39	• "My Last Duchess," "Love Among the Ruins," "Life in a Love," Sonnet 43, LL Audiocassettes • WS Writing Lab CD-ROM, Practical and Technical Tutorial; Wr. at Work Videodisc, Ch. 8
• Invitation, Literary Analysis, Response to Criticism, SE p. 784	• Love Songs, SE p. 784	• Poetry Reading, SE p. 784	• Selection Test, TR Formal Assessment, pp. 192–193; Assess. Res. Software	• "You Know the Place: Then," Sappho; "Invitation to the Voyage," LL Audiocassettes
• Letter to the Editor, Proposal, Literary Analysis, SE p. 799 • Mini-Lesson: World Responsibility Speech [Statistics as a Form of Support], SE p. 799 • Letter, TR Alt. Assess., p. 40	• Address to England, Oral Interpretation, SE p. 700 • Mini-Lesson: Oral Interpretation, ATE p. 793 • Debate, TR Alt. Assess., p. 40	• Film Review, Tour of a Castle, SE p. 799 • Geological Timeline, TR Alt. Assess., p. 40	• Selection Test, TR Formal Assessment, pp. 197–199; Assess. Res. Software • Persuasion Rubric [for Mini-Lesson], TR Alt. Assess., p. 106 • TR Alt. Assess., p. 40	• "Dover Beach," "Recessional," "The Widow at Windsor," LL Audiocassettes • WS Writing Lab CD-ROM Persuasion Tutorial

Unit 5 Progress and Decline (1833–1901) *(Continued)*

Selection/Feature	Reading	Literary Elements/ Forms	Vocabulary	Grammar
"Condition of Ireland," "Progress in Personal Comfort," Sydney Smith, SE pp. 802, 805 Reading Levels: Average, Easy	• Distinguish Emotive and Information Language, SE pp. 801, 808; TR Selection Support, p. 198 • Identifying Evidence, TR Str. for Diverse St. Needs, p. 41	• Journalistic Essay, SE pp. 801, 808; TR Selection Support, p. 199	• The Humors, SE pp. 801, 808; TR Selection Support, p. 196 Word Bank: requisites, sanction, exonerate, melancholy, p. 803; indolence, p. 804; depredation, p. 805	• Coordinating Conjunctions, SE pp. 801, 808; TR Selection Support, p. 197 • WS Gram. Pr. Book, p. 13
"Opening Statement for the Inaugural Session of the Forum for Peace and Reconciliation," Judge Catherine McGuinness, SE p. 811 Reading Level: Average			• TR Selection Support, p. 200	
from ***Hard Times,* Charles Dickens;** from ***Jane Eyre,* Charlotte Brontë,** SE pp. 822, 828 Reading Levels: Average, Easy	• Recognize the Writer's Purpose, SE pp. 821, 834; TR Selection Support, p. 204 • Understand Characters, TR Str. for Diverse St. Needs, p. 42	• The Novel and Social Criticism, SE pp. 821, 834; TR Selection Support, p. 205	• Word Roots: *-mono-*, SE pp. 821, 834; TR Selection Support, p. 202 Word Bank: monotonous, obstinate, p. 822; adversary, p. 825; indignant, approbation, p. 826; obscure, comprised, sundry, p. 829	• Punctuation of Dialogue, SE pp. 821, 834; TR Selection Support, p. 203 • WS Language Lab CD-ROM, Quotation Marks • WS Gram. Pr. Book, p. 86–87
from ***War and Peace,* Leo Tolstoy,** SE p. 837 Reading Level: Average			• TR Selection Support, p. 206	
"Remembrance," Emily Brontë; "The Darkling Thrush," "'Ah, Are You Digging on My Grave?'," Thomas Hardy, SE pp. 848, 850, 852 Reading Levels: Easy, Easy, Easy	• Read Stanzas as Units of Meaning, SE pp. 847, 854; TR Selection Support, p. 210 • Make Inferences About Speaker, TR Str. for Diverse St. Needs, p. 43	• Stanza Structure and Irony, SE pp. 847, 854; TR Selection Support, p. 211	• Word Roots: *-terr(a)-*, SE pp. 847, 854; TR Selection Support, p. 208 Word Bank: languish, rapturous, p. 849; gaunt, terrestrial, p. 851	• Pronoun Case Following *Than* or *As*, SE pp. 847, 854; TR Selection Support, p. 209 • WS Language Lab CD-ROM, Pronoun Case
"God's Grandeur," "Spring and Fall," Gerard Manley Hopkins; "To an Athlete Dying Young," "When I Was One-and-Twenty," A. E. Housman, SE pp. 858, 859, 860, 861 Reading Levels: Easy, Average, Easy, Easy	• Apply Biography, SE pp. 857, 862; TR Selection Support, p. 214 • Use Titles, TR Str. for Diverse St. Needs, p. 44	• Rhythm and Meter, SE pp. 857, 862; TR Selection Support, p. 215	• Coined Words, SE pp. 857, 862; TR Selection Support, p. 212 Word Bank: grandeur, blight, p. 859; rue, p. 861	• Capitalization: Compass Points, SE pp. 857, 862; TR Selection Support, p. 213
"Eternity," Arthur Rimbaud, SE p. 865 Reading Level: Average			• TR Selection Support, p. 216	

KEY: SE: Student Edition; ATE: Annotated Teacher's Edition; TR: Teaching Resources; LL and WS: Technology

Writing	Speaking and Listening	Projects	Assessment	Technology
• Compare Opinions, Fictional Memoir, Journalistic Essay, SE p. 809 • Mini-Lesson: Written Evaluation [Supporting Details], SE p. 809 • Personal Essay, TR Alt. Assess., p. 41	• Comic Monologue, Television Editorial, SE p. 809 • Mini-Lesson: Comic Monologue, ATE p. 805 • Discussion, TR Alt. Assess., p. 41	• History of the Newspaper, Contemporary Famine, SE p. 809 • Newspaper, TR Alt. Assess., p. 41	• Selection Test, TR Formal Assessment, pp. 200–202; Assess. Res. Software • Evaluation/Review Rubric [for Mini-Lesson], TR Alt. Assess., p. 105 • TR Alt. Assess., p. 41	• "Condition of Ireland," "Progress in Personal Comfort," LL Audiocassettes • WS Writing Lab CD-ROM, Exposition Tutorial
• Reporter's Questions, Personal Profile, Guidelines for Conflict Resolution, SE p. 814	• Press Conference, SE p. 814 • Mini-Lesson: Press Conference, ATE p. 811	• Teens Caught Up in Conflicts, SE p. 814	• Selection Test, TR Formal Assessment, pp. 203–204; Assess. Res. Software	• "Opening Statement for the Inaugural Session of the Forum for Peace and Reconciliation," LL Audiocassettes
• Diary Entry, Comparison and Contrast, Response to Criticism, SE p. 835 • Mini-Lesson: Observation of a Person [Using an Incident to Reveal Character], SE p. 835 • Short Story, TR Alt. Assess., p. 42	• Oral Presentation, Dialogue, SE p. 835 • Mini-Lesson: Dialogue, ATE p. 826 • Scene, TR Alt. Assess., p. 42	• Caricature, Exploring Historical Background, SE p. 835 • Imagination Campaign, TR Alt. Assess., p. 42	• Selection Test, TR Formal Assessment, pp. 208–210; Assess. Res. Software • Description Rubric [for Mini-Lesson], TR Alt. Assess., p. 98 • TR Alt. Assess., p. 42	• from *Hard Times,* from *Jane Eyre,* LL Audiocassettes • WS Writing Lab CD-ROM, Description Tutorial; Wr. at Work Videodisc, Ch. 1
• Character Description, Scene from Everyday Life, Essay on Leadership, SE p. 840	• Music as the Messenger, SE p. 840	• Novel Study, SE p. 840	• Selection Test, TR Formal Assessment, pp. 211–212; Assess. Res. Software	• from *War and Peace,* LL Audiocassettes
• Remembrance, Comparison and Contrast, Critical Essay, SE p. 855 • Mini-Lesson: Remembrance [Elaboration to Make Writing Personal], SE p. 855 • Symbol Analysis, TR Alt. Assess., p. 43	• Dramatic Reading, Role-Play, SE p. 855 • Mini-Lesson: Dramatic Reading, ATE p. 852 • Clapping, TR Alt. Assess., p. 43	• Biography, Timeline of the Century, SE p. 855 • Landscape, TR Alt. Assess., p. 43	• Selection Test, TR Formal Assessment, pp. 216–218; Assess. Res. Software • Description Rubric [for Mini-Lesson], TR Alt. Assess., p. 98 • TR Alt. Assess., p. 43	• "Remembrance," "The Darkling Thrush," "'Ah, Are You Digging on My Grave?'," LL Audiocassettes • WS Writing Lab CD-ROM, Description Tutorial
• Tribute, Comparative Analysis, Response to Criticism, SE p. 863 • Mini-Lesson: Literary Analysis [Presenting a Thesis], SE p. 863 • Updated Grandeur, TR Alt. Assess., p. 44	• Victorian Poetry Contest, Newspaper Interview, SE p. 863 • Mini-Lesson: Newspaper Interview, ATE p. 860 • Laurel Report, TR Alt. Assess., p. 44	• Biographical Report, Multimedia Presentation, SE p. 863 • English Money Table, TR Alt. Assess., p. 44	• Selection Test, TR Formal Assessment, pp. 219–221; Assess. Res. Software • Literary Analysis/Interpretation Rubric [for Mini-Lesson], TR Alt. Assess., p. 113 • TR Alt. Assess., p. 44	• "God's Grandeur," "Spring and Fall,""To an Athlete Dying Young," "When I Was One-and-Twenty," LL Audiocassettes • WS Writing Lab CD-ROM, Response to Literature Tutorial; Wr. at Work Videodisc, Ch. 7
• Perfect Place, Dictionary of Abstract Words, Response to Criticism, SE p. 867	• Ask the Poet, SE p. 867	• Past Glory, Multimedia Presentation, SE p. 867	• Selection Test, TR Formal Assessment, pp. 222–223; Assess. Res. Software	• "Eternity," LL Audiocassettes

Program Planner Unit 6 A Time of Rapid Change (1901–Present)

Selection	Reading	Literary Elements/Forms	Vocabulary	Grammar
"The Demon Lover," Elizabeth Bowen, SE p. 889 Reading Level: Average	• Reading for Success: Strategies for Reading and Interpreting Fiction, SE pp. 888, 894; TR Selection Support, pp. 220–221 • Model, pp. 889–893 • Keep Track of Events, TR Str. for Diverse St. Needs, p. 45	• The Ghost Story, SE pp. 887, 894; TR Selection Support, p. 222	• Word Roots: *-loc-*, SE pp. 887, 894; TR Selection Support, p. 218 Word Bank: spectral, dislocation, arboreal, circumscribed, p. 891; aperture, p. 892	• Sentence Beginnings: Participial Phrases, SE pp. 887, 894; TR Selection Support, p. 219 • WS Language Lab CD-ROM, Varying Sentence Structure
Poetry of William Butler Yeats, SE pp. 898, 899, 900, 902, 904 Reading Levels: Easy, Easy, Easy, Average, Average	• Apply Literary Background, SE pp. 897, 906; TR Selection Support, p. 225 • Identify with the Speaker, TR Str. for Diverse St. Needs, p. 46	• Symbolism, SE pp. 897, 906; TR Selection Support, p. 226	• Word Roots: *-ques-*, SE pp. 897, 906; TR Selection Support, p. 223 Word Bank: clamorous, conquest, p. 900; anarchy, conviction, p. 903; paltry, artifice, p. 904	• Noun Clauses, SE pp. 897, 906; TR Selection Support, p. 224 • WS Gram. Pr. Book, p. 33
"Preludes," "Journey of the Magi," "The Hollow Men," T. S. Eliot, SE pp. 910, 912, 914 Reading Levels: Average, Easy, Challenging	• Interpret, SE pp. 909, 920; TR Selection Support, p. 229 • Read the Poem Part by Part, TR Str. for Diverse St. Needs, p. 47	• Modernism, SE pp. 909, 920; TR Selection Support, p. 230	• Word Roots: *-fract-*, SE pp. 909, 920; TR Selection Support, p. 227 Word Bank: galled, refractory, dispensation, p. 912; supplication, 917; tumid, p. 918	• Adjectival Modifiers, SE pp. 909, 920; TR Selection Support, p. 228 • WS Language Lab CD-ROM, Writing Style • WS Gram. Pr. Book, p. 28–32
"In Memory of W. B. Yeats," "Musée des Beaux Arts," W. H. Auden; "Carrick Revisited," Louis MacNeice; "Not Palaces," Stephen Spender, SE pp. 924, 928, 930, 932 Reading Levels: Average, Average, Challenging, Challenging	• Paraphrase, SE pp. 923, 934; TR Selection Support, p. 233 • Interpret the Metaphors, TR Str. for Diverse St. Needs, p. 48	• Theme, SE pp. 923, 934; TR Selection Support, p. 234	• Word Roots: *-top-*, SE pp. 923, 934; TR Selection Support, p. 231 Word Bank: sequestered, p. 926; topographical, affinities, prenatal, p. 930, intrigues, p. 932	• Parallel Structure, SE pp. 923, 934; TR Selection Support, p. 232 • WS Language Lab CD-ROM, Using Parallel Structure • WS Gram. Pr. Book, p. 46
"Shooting an Elephant," George Orwell, SE p. 938 Reading Level: Average	• Recognize the Writer's Attitudes, SE pp. 937, 946; TR Selection Support, p. 237 • Organize the Details, TR Str. for Diverse St. Needs, p. 49	• Irony, SE pp. 937, 946; TR Selection Support, p. 238	• Related Words: Words About Politics, SE pp. 937, 946; TR Selection Support, p. 235 Word Bank: prostrate, imperialism, despotic, squalid, p. 940; dominion, p. 943; senility, p. 944	• Participial Phrases: Restrictive and Nonrestrictive, SE pp. 937, 946; TR Selection Support, p. 236 • WS Language Lab CD-ROM, Using Phrases • WS Gram. Pr. Book, p. 29
"The Diameter of the Bomb," Yehuda Amichai; "Everything Is Plundered," Anna Akhmatova; "Testament," Bei Dao, SE pp. 949, 950, 951 Reading Levels: Average, Average, Average			• TR Selection Support, p. 239	
"The Soldier," Rupert Brooke; "Wirers," Siegfried Sassoon; "Anthem for Doomed Youth," Wilfred Owen; "Birds on the Western Front," Saki, SE pp. 960, 962, 963, 964 Reading Levels: Easy, Easy, Average, Average	• Make Inferences, SE pp. 959, 968; TR Selection Support, p. 243 • Tell Who, What, Where, When, and Why, TR Str. for Diverse St. Needs, p. 50	• Tone, SE pp. 959, 968; TR Selection Support, p. 244	• Word Roots: *-laud-*, SE pp. 959, 968; TR Selection Support, p. 241 Word Bank: stealthy, desolate, mockeries, pallor, p. 962; laudable, requisitioned, p. 965; disconcerted, p. 967	• Use of *Who* and *Whom* in Adjectival Clauses, SE pp.959, 968; TR Selection Support, p. 242 • WS Language Lab CD-ROM, Pronoun Case
"Wartime Speech," Winston Churchill; "Defending Nonviolent Resistance," Mohandas K. Gandhi, SE pp. 972, 975 Reading Levels: Average, Average	• Identify Main Points and Support, SE pp. 971, 980; TR Selection Support, p. 247 • Write a Definition, TR Str. for Diverse St. Needs, p. 51	• Speech, SE pp. 971, 980; TR Selection Support, p. 248	• Word Roots: *-dur-*, SE pp. 971, 980; TR Selection Support, p. 245 Word Bank: intimidated, endurance, formidable, invincible, retaliate, p. 973; disaffection, diabolical, p. 975; extenuating, excrescence, p. 977	• Parallel Structure, SE pp. 971, 980; TR Selection Support, p. 246 • WS Language Lab CD-ROM, Using Parallel Structures

KEY: SE: Student Edition; ATE: Annotated Teacher's Edition; TR: Teaching Resources; LL and WS: Technology

Writing	Speaking and Listening	Projects	Assessment	Technology
• Journal Entry, Critical Evaluation, Response to Criticism, SE p. 895 • Mini-Lesson: Sequel [Clear and Logical Organization], SE p. 895 • TR Alt. Assess., p. 45	• Dramatic Retelling, Ballad, SE p. 895 • Mini-Lesson: Dramatic Retelling, ATE p. 891 • TR Alt. Assess., p. 45	• Portrait of the Demon Lover, Blitz Report, SE p. 895 • TR Alt. Assess., p. 45	• Selection Test, TR Formal Assessment, pp. 227–229; Assess. Res. Software • Fictional Narrative Rubric [for Mini-Lesson], TR Alt. Assess., p. 96 • TR Alt. Assess., p. 45	• "The Demon Lover," LL Audiocassettes • WS Writing Lab CD-ROM, Narration Tutorial
• Description, Essay, Response to Criticism, SE p. 907 • Mini-Lesson: Prediction Essay [Knowledge Level of Readers], SE p. 907 • TR Alt. Assess., p. 46	• Irish Poetry, Music and Swans, SE p. 907 • Mini-Lesson: Irish Poetry, ATE p. 900 • TR Alt. Assess., p. 46	• Yeats Timeline, Byzantium, SE p. 907 • TR Alt. Assess., p. 46	• Selection Test, TR Formal Assessment, pp. 230–232; Assess. Res. Software • Description Rubric [for Mini-Lesson], TR Alt. Assess., p. 98 • TR Alt. Assess., p. 46	• Poetry of William Butler Yeats, LL Audiocassettes • WS Writing Lab CD-ROM, Description Tutorial; Wr. at Work Videodisc, Ch. 1
• Analysis of an Image, Critical Evaluation, Response to Criticism, SE p. 921 • Mini-Lesson: Music Video Treatment [Variety of Sources], SE p. 921 • TR Alt. Assess., p. 47	• Choral Reading, Debate, SE p. 921 • Mini-Lesson: Debate, ATE p. 914 • TR Alt. Assess., p. 47	• Imagism, Modern Dance, SE p. 921 • TR Alt. Assess., p. 47	• Selection Test, TR Formal Assessment, pp. 233–235; Assess. Res. Software • General Rubric [for Mini-Lesson], TR Alt. Assess., p. 94 • TR Alt. Assess., p. 47	• "Preludes," "Journey of the Magi," "The Hollow Men," LL Audiocassettes • WS Writing Lab CD-ROM, Creative Writing Tutorial
• Tribute, Essay, Response to Criticism, SE p. 935 • Mini-Lesson: Poem About Art [Conveying a Main Impression], SE p. 935 • TR Alt. Assess., p. 48	• Museum Guide, Oral Interpretation, SE p. 935 • Mini-Lesson: Museum Guide, ATE p. 931 • TR Alt. Assess., p. 48	• Art Exhibition, Family Background, SE p. 935 • TR Alt. Assess., p. 48	• Selection Test, TR Formal Assessment, pp. 236–238; Assess. Res. Software • Poetry Rubric [for Mini-Lesson], TR Alt. Assess., p. 109 • TR Alt. Assess., p. 48	• "In Memory of W. B. Yeats," "Musée des Beaux Arts," "Carrick Revisited," "Not Palaces," LL Audiocassettes • WS Writing Lab CD-ROM, Creative Writing Tutorial; Wr. at Work Videodisc, Ch. 6
• Profile, Film Treatment, Response to Criticism, SE p. 947 • Mini-Lesson: Police Report [Elaboration to Give Information], SE p. 947 • TR Alt. Assess., p. 49	• Role Play, Debate, SE p. 947 • Mini-Lesson: Debate, ATE p. 943 • TR Alt. Assess., p. 49	• Orwell in Film, Biography, SE p. 947 • TR Alt. Assess., p. 49	• Selection Test, TR Formal Assessment, pp. 239–241; Assess. Res. Software • Technical Description/ Explanation Rubric [for Mini-Lesson], TR Alt. Assess., p. 116 • TR Alt. Assess., p. 49	• "Shooting an Elephant," LL Audiocassettes • WS Writing Lab CD-ROM, Practical and Technical Writing Tutorial
• Narrative Essay, Personal Testament, Response to Criticism, SE p. 952	• Persuasive Speech, SE p. 952	• Historical Context, SE p. 952	• Selection Test, TR Formal Assessment, pp. 242–243; Assess. Res. Software	• "The Diameter of the Bomb," "Everything Is Plundered," "Testament," LL Audiocassettes
• Interview Questions, Veterans Day, Critical Response, SE p. 969 • Mini-Lesson: Historical Letter [Transitions to Show Time], SE p. 969 • TR Alt. Assess., p. 50	• Debate, Skit, SE p. 969 • Mini-Lesson: Skit, ATE p. 965 • TR Alt. Assess., p. 50	• Timeline, Trench Warfare, SE p. 969 • TR Alt. Assess., p. 50	• Selection Test, TR Formal Assessment, pp. 248–250; Assess. Res. Software • Description Rubric [for Mini-Lesson], TR Alt. Assess., p. 98 • TR Alt. Assess., p. 50	• "The Soldier," "Wirers," "Anthem for Doomed Youth," "Birds on the Western Front," LL Audiocassettes • WS Writing Lab CD-ROM, Exposition Tutorial
• Reporting on a Speech, Dialogue, Comparison-and-Contrast Essay, SE p. 981 • Mini-Lesson: Press Release [Anticipating Questions], SE p. 981 • TR Alt. Assess., p. 51	• Speech, Panel Discussion, SE p. 981 • Mini-Lesson: Speech, ATE p. 977 • TR Alt. Assess., p. 51	• Leaders on Film, Gandhi's Legacy, SE p. 981 • TR Alt. Assess., p. 51	• Selection Test, TR Formal Assessment, pp. 251–253; Assess. Res. Software • Summary Rubric [for Mini-Lesson], TR Alt. Assess., p. 99 • TR Alt. Assess., p. 51	• "Wartime Speech," "Defending Nonviolent Resistance," LL Audiocassettes • WS Writing Lab CD-ROM, Exposition Tutorial

Unit 6 A Time of Rapid Change (1901–Present) *(Continued)*

Selection/Feature	Reading	Literary Elements/ Forms	Vocabulary	Grammar
"The Fiddle," Alan Sillitoe, SE p. 984 Reading Level: Average	• Predict Effect of Setting, SE pp. 983, 990; TR Selection Support, p. 251 • Make a Character Map, TR Str. for Diverse St. Needs, p. 52	• Setting and Atmosphere, SE pp. 983, 990; TR Selection Support, p. 252	• Word Origins: *Sublime,* SE pp. 983, 990; TR Selection Support, p. 249 Word Bank: persistent, obliterate, p. 985; sublimity, p. 987; harried, p. 988	• Vary Sentence Beginnings, SE pp. 983, 990; TR Selection Support, p. 250 • WS Language Lab CD-ROM, Varying Sentence Structure • WS Gram. Pr. Book, p. 105
"The Distant Past," William Trevor, SE p. 994 Reading Level: Average	• Cause and Effect, SE pp. 993, 1000; TR Selection Support, p. 255 • Understand Conflict Through Contrast, TR Str. for Diverse St. Needs, p. 53	• Social Conflict, SE pp. 993, 1000; TR Selection Support, p. 256	• Suffixes: *-ity (-ty),* SE pp. 993, 1000; TR Selection Support, p. 253 Word Bank: countenance, adversity, sovereignty, p. 995; anachronism, p. 996; internment, p. 998	• Restrictive and Nonrestrictive Adjective Clauses, SE pp. 993, 1000; TR Selection Support, p. 254 • WS Gram. Pr. Book, p. 31
"Follower," "Two Lorries," Seamus Heaney; "Outside History," Eavan Boland, SE pp. 1004, 1006, 1008 Reading Levels: Easy, Average, Average	• Summarize, SE pp. 1003, 1010; TR Selection Support, p. 259 • Draw Conclusions About the Text, TR Str. for Diverse St. Needs, p. 54	• Diction and Style, SE pp. 1003, 1010; TR Selection Support, p. 260	• Word Roots: *-mort-,* SE pp. 1003, 1010; TR Selection Support, p. 257 Word Bank: furrow, nuisance, p. 1004; inklings, mortal, ordeal, p. 1009	• Concrete and Abstract Nouns, SE pp. 1003, 1010; TR Selection Support, p. 258 • WS Language Lab CD-ROM, Choosing Exact Nouns and Vivid Verbs • WS Gram. Pr. Book, pp. 99–102
"No Witchcraft for Sale," Doris Lessing, SE p. 1014 Reading Level: Easy	• Analyze Cultural Differences, SE pp. 1013, 1020; TR Selection Support, p. 263 • Read Between the Lines, TR Str. for Diverse St. Needs, p. 55	• Cultural Conflict, SE pp. 1013, 1020; TR Selection Support, p. 264	• Related Words: Forms of *Skeptical,* SE pp. 1013, 1020; TR Selection Support, p. 261 Word Bank: reverently, defiantly, p. 1015; efficacy, incredulously, skeptical, p. 1017	• Correct Use of *Like* and *As,* SE pp. 1013, 1020; TR Selection Support, p. 262
"The Rights We Enjoy, the Duties We Owe," Tony Blair, SE p. 1023 Reading Level: Challenging			• TR Selection Support, p. 265	
"The Lagoon," Joseph Conrad; "Araby," James Joyce, SE pp. 1033, 1050 Reading Levels: Average, Average	• Envision Action and Situation, SE pp. 1033, 1050; TR Selection Support, p. 269 • Use Senses to Appreciate Setting, TR Str. for Diverse St. Needs, p. 56	• Plot Devices, SE pp. 1033, 1050; TR Selection Support, p. 270	• Word Roots: *-vinc-,* SE pp. 1033, 1050; TR Selection Support, p. 267 Word Bank: portals, invincible, propitiate, p. 1035; conflagration, p. 1037; august, p. 1039; imperturbable, p. 1045; litanies, garrulous, p. 1047; derided, p. 1049	• Adverb Clauses, SE pp. 1033, 1050; TR Selection Support, p. 268 • WS Gram. Pr. Book, p. 32
"The Lady in the Looking Glass: A Reflection," Virginia Woolf; "The First Year of My Life," Muriel Spark, SE pp. 1054, 1058 Reading Levels: Challenging, Average	• Question, SE pp. 1053, 1064; TR Selection Support, p. 273 • Draw Conclusions, TR Str. for Diverse St. Needs, p. 57	• Point of View: Modern Experiments, SE pp. 1053, 1064; TR Selection Support, p. 274	• Word Roots: *-trans-,* SE pp. 1053, 1064; TR Selection Support, p. 271 Word Bank: suffused, transient, upbraidings, p. 1055; evanescence, reticent, p. 1057; omniscient, authenticity, discerned, p. 1059	• Subject-Verb Agreement in Inverted Sentences, SE pp. 1053, 1064; TR Selection Support, p. 272 • WS Language Lab CD-ROM, Agreement in Number and Special Problems in Agreement • WS Gram. Pr. Book, p. 63
"The Rocking-Horse Winner." D. H. Lawrence; "A Shocking Accident," Graham Greene, SE pp. 1068, 1078 Reading Levels: Average, Average	• Identify With a Character, SE pp. 1067, 1082; TR Selection Support, p. 277 • Identify Causes and Effects, TR Str. for Diverse St. Needs, p. 58	• Theme, SE pp. 1067, 1082; TR Selection Support, p. 278	• Prefixes: *ob-,* SE pp. 1067, 1082; TR Selection Support, p. 275 Word Bank: discreet, p. 1068; brazening, careered, p. 1070; obstinately, p. 1072; uncanny, remonstrated, p. 1075; apprehension, embarked, p. 1078; intrinsically, p. 1080	• Subjunctive Mood, SE pp. 1067, 1082; TR Selection Support, p. 276 • WS Gram. Pr. Book, p. 55
"The Book of Sand," Jorge Luis Borges, SE p. 1085 Reading Level: Easy			• TR Selection Support, p. 279	

KEY: SE: Student Edition; ATE: Annotated Teacher's Edition; TR: Teaching Resources; LL and WS: Technology

Writing	Speaking and Listening	Projects	Assessment	Technology
• Journal Entry, Newspaper Report, Response to Criticism, SE p. 991 • Mini-Lesson: Favorite Setting [Vivid Details], SE p. 991 • TR Alt. Assess., p. 52	• Debate, Music Discussion, SE p. 991 • Mini-Lesson: Debate, ATE p. 988 • TR Alt. Assess., p. 52	• Performing Arts, Coal Mining Report, SE p. 991 • TR Alt. Assess., p. 52	• Selection Test, TR Formal Assessment, pp. 254–256; Assess. Res. Software • Description Rubric [for Mini-Lesson], TR Alt. Assess., p. 98 • TR Alt. Assess., p. 52	• "The Fiddle," LL Audiocassettes • WS Writing Lab CD-ROM, Description Tutorial; Wr. at Work Videodisc, Ch. 1
• Obituary, Poem, Literary Analysis, SE p. 1001 • Mini-Lesson: Persuasive Letter [Brevity and Clarity], SE p. 1001 • TR Alt. Assess., p. 53	• Eulogy, Interview, SE p. 1001 • Mini-Lesson: Eulogy, ATE p. 998 • TR Alt. Assess., p. 53	• Portfolio, A Celebration of Irish Culture, SE p. 1001 • TR Alt. Assess., p. 53	• Selection Test, TR Formal Assessment, pp. 257–259; Assess. Res. Software • Persuasion Rubric [for Mini-Lesson], TR Alt. Assess., p. 106 • TR Alt. Assess., p. 53	• "The Distant Past," LL Audiocassettes • WS Writing Lab CD-ROM, Persuasion Tutorial; Wr. at Work Videodisc, Ch. 4
• Book Blurb, Comparison and Contrast, Response to Criticism, SE p. 1011 • Mini-Lesson: Conflict-Resolution Guidelines [Clear Explanation of Procedures], SE p. 1011 • TR Alt. Assess., p. 54	• Monologue, Oral Interpretation, SE p. 1011 • Mini-Lesson: Monologue, ATE p. 1005 • TR Alt. Assess., p. 54	• Irish Folk Music, The History of the "Troubles," SE p. 1011 • TR Alt. Assess., p. 54	• Selection Test, TR Formal Assessment, pp. 260–262; Assess. Res. Software • How-to/Process Explanation Rubric [for Mini-Lesson], TR Alt. Assess., p. 101 • TR Alt. Assess., p. 54	• "Follower," "Two Lorries," "Outside History," LL Audiocassettes • WS Writing Lab CD-ROM, Practical and Technical Writing Tutorial; Wr. at Work Videodisc, Ch. 8
• Review, Proposal, Critical Response, SE p. 1021 • Mini-Lesson: Problem-and-Solution Essay [Elaboration to Enhance Understanding], SE p. 1021 • TR Alt. Assess., p. 55	• Debate, Dramatic Scene, SE p. 1021 • Mini-Lesson: Debate, ATE p. 1018 • TR Alt. Assess., p. 55	• Book Cover Design, Comparison Report, SE p. 1021 • TR Alt. Assess., p. 55	• Selection Test, TR Formal Assessment, pp. 263–265; Assess. Res. Software • How-to/Process Explanation Rubric [for Mini-Lesson], TR Alt. Assess., p. 101 • TR Alt. Assess., p. 55	• "No Witchcraft for Sale," LL Audiocassettes • WS Writing Lab CD-ROM, Exposition Tutorial
• Campaign Poster, Persuasive Essay, Problem-Solution Essay, SE p. 1026	• Global Village Meeting, SE p. 1026 • Mini-Lesson: Global Village Meeting, ATE p. 1024	• Taking Responsibility, SE p. 1026	• Selection Test, TR Formal Assessment, pp. 266–267; Assess. Res. Software	• "The Rights We Enjoy, the Duties We Owe," LL Audiocassettes
• Recollection, Extending a Story, Essay, SE p. 1051 • Mini-Lesson: Personal Essay [Elaboration to Entertain], SE p. 1051 • TR Alt. Assess., p. 56	• Courtroom, Panel Discussion, SE p. 1051 • Mini-Lesson: Courtroom, Panel Discussion, ATE p. 1042, 1047 • TR Alt. Assess., p. 56	• Poster, Report on Colonialism, SE p. 1051 • TR Alt. Assess., p. 56	• Selection Test, TR Formal Assessment, pp. 271–273; Assess. Res. Software • Narrative Based on Personal Experience Rubric [for Mini-Lesson], TR Alt. Assess., p. 97 • TR Alt. Assess., p. 56	• "The Lagoon," "Araby," LL Audiocassettes • WS Writing Lab CD-ROM, Narration Tutorial
• Letter to the Author, Stream-of-Consciousness Narrative, Res-sponse to Criticism, SE p. 1065 • Mini-Lesson: Narrative From an Unusual Perspective [Suspense], SE p. 1065 • TR Alt. Assess., p. 57	• Poetry Reading, Oral Interpretation, SE p. 1065 • Mini-Lesson: Oral Interpretation, ATE p. 1062 • TR Alt. Assess., p. 57	• Report on World War I, Freudian Psychology and Fiction, SE p. 1065 • TR Alt. Assess., p. 57	• Selection Test, TR Formal Assessment, pp. 274–276; Assess. Res. Software • Fictional Narrative Rubric [for Mini-Lesson], TR Alt. Assess., p. 96 • TR Alt. Assess., p. 57	• "The Lady in the Looking Glass: A Reflection," "The First Year of My Life," LL Audiocassettes • WS Writing Lab CD-ROM, Narration Tutorial; Wr. at Work Videodisc, Ch. 2
• Notes for a Screenplay, Retelling a Passage, Response to Criticism, SE p. 1083 • Mini-Lesson: Product Description [Climax and Resolution], SE p. 1083 • TR Alt. Assess., p. 58	• Soliloquy, Discussion Group, SE p. 1083 • Mini-Lesson: Soliloquy, ATE p. 1080 • TR Alt. Assess., p. 58	• Social Research, Multimedia Travelogue, SE p. 1083 • TR Alt. Assess., p. 58	• Selection Test, TR Formal Assessment, pp. 277–279; Assess. Res. Software • Description Rubric [for Mini-Lesson], TR Alt. Assess., p. 98 • TR Alt. Assess., p. 58	• "The Rocking-Horse Winner," "A Shocking Accident," LL Audiocassettes • WS Writing Lab CD-ROM, Description Tutorial; Wr. at Work Videodisc, Ch. 1
• New Ending, Comparison and Contrast, Response to Criticism, SE p. 1088		• Model of the Book of Sand, Geometry and the Short Story, SE p. 1088	• Selection Test, TR Formal Assessment, pp. 280–281; Assess. Res. Software	• "The Book of Sand," LL Audiocassettes

Selection	Reading	Literary Elements/Forms	Vocabulary	Grammar
"Do Not Go Gentle into That Good Night," "Fern Hill," Dylan Thomas; "The Horses," "The Rain Horse," Ted Hughes, SE pp. 1096, 1098, 1100, 1102 Reading Levels: Average, Easy, Average, Easy	• Judge the Message, SE pp. 1095, 1108; TR Selection Support, p. 283 • Identify Emotive Language, TR Str. for Diverse St. Needs, p. 59	• Voice, SE pp. 1095, 1108; TR Selection Support, p. 284	• Word Roots: *-vol-*, SE pp. 1095, 1108; TR Selection Support, p. 281 Word Bank: grieved, p. 1097; transfiguring, exasperated, nondescript, p. 1103; malevolent, p. 1107	• Sentence Beginnings: Adverb Clauses, SE pp. 1095, 1108; TR Selection Support, p. 282 • WS Language Lab CD-ROM, Varying Sentence Structure • WS Gram. Pr. Book, p. 32
"An Arundel Tomb," "The Explosion," Philip Larkin; "On the Patio," Peter Redgrove; "Not Waving but Drowning," Stevie Smith, SE pp. 1112, 1113, 1114, 1115 Reading Levels: Easy, Average, Average, Easy	• Read in Sentences, SE pp. 1111, 1116; TR Selection Support, p. 287 • Envision, TR Str. for Diverse St. Needs, p. 60	• Free Verse and Meter, SE pp. 1111, 1116; TR Selection Support, p. 288	• Word Roots: *-fid-*, SE pp. 1111, 1116; TR Selection Support, p. 285 Word Bank: effigy, supine, fidelity, p. 1112; larking, p. 1115	• Sequence of Tenses, SE pp. 1111, 1116; TR Selection Support, p. 286 • WS Language Lab CD-ROM, Correct and Effective Use of Verbs • WS Gram. Pr. Book, p. 53
"B. Wordsworth," V. S. Naipaul, SE p. 1120 Reading Level: Average	• Respond to Character, SE pp. 1119, 1126; TR Selection Support, p. 291 • Read Dialect, TR Str. for Diverse St. Needs, p. 61	• First-Person Narrator, SE pp. 1119, 1126; TR Selection Support, p. 292	• Related Words: Forms of Patron, SE pp. 1119, 1126; TR Selection Support, p. 289 Word Bank: rogue, p. 1121; patronize, distill, keenly, p. 1125	• Pronoun Case in Compound Constructions, SE pp. 1119, 1126; TR Selection Support, p. 290 • WS Language Lab CD-ROM, Pronoun Case • WS Gram. Pr. Book, p. 57–58
"The Train from Rhodesia," Nadine Gordimer, SE p. 1130 Reading Level: Easy	• Read Between the Lines, SE pp. 1129, 1134; TR Selection Support, p. 295 • Outline Major Events, TR Str. for Diverse St. Needs, p. 62	• Conflict and Theme, SE pp. 1129, 1134; TR Selection Support, p. 296	• Prefixes: *a-*, SE pp. 1129, 1134; TR Selection Support, p. 293 Word Bank: impressionistic, elongated, p. 1131; segmented, splaying, atrophy, p. 1133	• Absolute Phrases, SE pp. 1129, 1134; TR Selection Support, p. 294 • WS Gram. Pr. Book, p. 29–30
from ***Midsummer, XXIII,*** from ***Omeros,*** from ***Chapter XXVIII,*** **Derek Walcott; "From Lucy: Englan' Lady," James Berry,** SE pp. 1138, 1140, 1142 Reading Levels: Challenging, Average, Average	• Apply Background Information, SE pp. 1137, 1144; TR Selection Support, p. 299 • Identify Figurative Language, TR Str. for Diverse St. Needs, p. 63	• Theme and Context, SE pp. 1137, 1144; TR Selection Support, p. 300	• Word Roots: *-duc-*, SE pp. 1137, 1144; TR Selection Support, p. 297 Word Bank: antic, rancor, eclipse, inducted, p. 1138	• Commonly Confused Words: Affect and Effect, SE pp. 1137, 1144; TR Selection Support, p. 298 • WS Gram. Pr. Book, p. 75
"A Devoted Son," Anita Desai, SE p. 1148 Reading Level: Average	• Evaluate Characters' Decisions, SE pp. 1147, 1156; TR Selection Support, p. 303 • Recognizing Problems and Solutions, TR Str. for Diverse St. Needs, p. 64	• Static and Dynamic Characters, SE pp. 1147, 1156; TR Selection Support, p. 304	• Word Roots: *-fil-*, SE pp. 1147, 1156; TR Selection Support, p. 301 Word Bank: exemplary, filial, encomiums, complaisant, p. 1149; fathom, p. 1150	• Sentence Variety, SE pp. 1147, 1156; TR Selection Support, p. 302 • WS Language Lab CD-ROM, Varying Sentence Structure • WS Gram. Pr. Book, p. 103–105
from **"We'll Never Conquer Space," Arthur C. Clarke,** SE p. 1160 Reading Level: Average	• Challenge the Text, SE pp. 1159, 1166; TR Selection Support, p. 307 • List Reasons, TR Str. for Diverse St. Needs, p. 65	• Prophetic Essay, SE pp. 1159, 1166; TR Selection Support, p. 308	• Suffixes: *-ible* and *-able,* SE pp. 1159, 1166; TR Selection Support, p. 305 Word Bank: ludicrous, irrevocable, p. 1161; instantaneous, enigma, inevitable, p. 1163, zenith, p. 1165	• Linking Verbs and Subject Complements, SE pp. 1159, 1166; TR Selection Support, p. 306 • WS Language Lab CD-ROM, Choosing Exact Nouns and Vivid Verbs • WS Gram. Pr. Book, p. 21

KEY: SE: Student Edition; ATE: Annotated Teacher's Edition; TR: Teaching Resources; LL and WS: Technology

Writing	Speaking and Listening	Projects	Assessment	Technology
• Description, Reflective Essay, Response to Criticism, SE p. 1109 • Mini-Lesson: Nature Journal [Use of Specific Details], SE p. 1109 • TR Alt. Assess., p. 59	• Oral Interpretation, Anecdote, SE p. 1109 • Mini-Lesson: Anecdote, ATE p. 1102 • TR Alt. Assess., p. 59	• The Laureateship, The Voice of Dylan Thomas, SE p. 1109 • TR Alt. Assess., p. 59	• Selection Test, TR Formal Assessment, pp. 285–287; Assess. Res. Software • Description Rubric [for Mini-Lesson], TR Alt. Assess., p. 98 • TR Alt. Assess., p. 59	• "Do Not Go Gentle into That Good Night," "Fern Hill," "The Horses," "The Rain Horse," LL Audiocassettes • WS Writing Lab CD-ROM, Description Tutorial
• Description, Comparison and Contrast, Response to Criticism, SE p. 1117 • Mini-Lesson: How-to Guide for an Interview [Elaboration to Prove a Point], SE p. 1117 • TR Alt. Assess., p. 60	• Eulogy, Poetry Reading, SE p. 1117 • Mini-Lesson: Eulogy, ATE p. 1113 • TR Alt. Assess., p. 60	• Pantomime of a Poem, Film Review, SE p. 1117 • TR Alt. Assess., p. 60	• Selection Test, TR Formal Assessment, pp. 288–290; Assess. Res. Software • How-to/Process Explanation Rubric [for Mini-Lesson], TR Alt. Assess., p. 101 • TR Alt. Assess., p. 60	• "An Arundel Tomb," "The Explosion," "On the Patio," "Not Waving but Drowning," LL Audiocassettes • WS Writing Lab CD-ROM, Exposition Tutorial
• Memorial Plaque, SE p. 1127 • Mini-Lesson: Description of a Person [Types of Support—Details], SE p. 1127 • TR Alt. Assess., p. 61	• Poetry Reading, Music Appreciation, SE p. 1127 • Mini-Lesson: Poetry Reading, Music Appreciation, ATE p. 1122, 1123 • TR Alt. Assess., p. 61	• Exhibit, Fashion Design, SE p. 1127 • TR Alt. Assess., p. 61	• Selection Test, TR Formal Assessment, pp. 291–293; Assess. Res. Software • Description Rubric [for Mini-Lesson], TR Alt. Assess., p. 98 • TR Alt. Assess., p. 61	• "B. Wordsworth," LL Audiocassettes • WS Writing Lab CD-ROM, Description Tutorial
• Letter of Advice, Interpretation, Evaluation, SE p. 1135 • Mini-Lesson: Wedding Speech [Level of Formality], SE p. 1135 • TR Alt. Assess., p. 62	• Debate, Nobel Prize Address, SE p. 1135 • Mini-Lesson: Debate, ATE p. 1131 • TR Alt. Assess., p. 62	• Retelling, African Art, SE p. 1135 • TR Alt. Assess., p. 62	• Selection Test, TR Formal Assessment, pp. 291–293; Assess. Res. Software • Narrative Based on Personal Experience Rubric [for Mini-Lesson], TR Alt. Assess., p. 97 • TR Alt. Assess., p. 62	• "The Train from Rhodesia," LL Audiocassettes • WS Writing Lab CD-ROM, Narration Tutorial
• Personal Letter, Literary Analysis, Response to Criticism, SE p. 1145 • Mini-Lesson: Pro-and-Con Editorial [Transitions to Show Comparisons], SE p. 1145 • TR Alt. Assess., p. 63	• Oral Interpretation of a Dialect, Debate, SE p. 1145 • Mini-Lesson: Debate, ATE p. 1142 • TR Alt. Assess., p. 63	• Black Roots, Caribbean Festival, SE p. 1145 • TR Alt. Assess., p. 63	• Selection Test, TR Formal Assessment, pp. 291–293; Assess. Res. Software • Persuasion Rubric [for Mini-Lesson], TR Alt. Assess., p. 106 • TR Alt. Assess., p. 63	• from *Midsummer, XXIII,* from *Omeros,* from *Chapter XXVIII,* "From Lucy: Englan' Lady," LL Audiocassettes • WS Writing Lab CD-ROM, Persuasion Tutorial; Wr. at Work Videodisc, Ch. 4
• Character Sketch, Memorial Tribute, Response to Criticism, SE p. 1157 • Mini-Lesson: Proposal [Connotations], SE p. 1157 • TR Alt. Assess., p. 64	• Role-Play, Panel Discussion, SE p. 1157 • Mini-Lesson: Panel Discussion, ATE p. 1150 • TR Alt. Assess., p. 64	• India's Public Health, Cross-Cultural Survey, SE p. 1157 • TR Alt. Assess., p. 64	• Selection Test, TR Formal Assessment, pp. 294–296; Assess. Res. Software • Persuasion Rubric [for Mini-Lesson], TR Alt. Assess., p. 106 • TR Alt. Assess., p. 64	• "A Devoted Son," LL Audiocassettes • WS Writing Lab CD-ROM, Persuasion Tutorial
• E-mail Response, Reflective Essay, Literary Analysis, SE p. 1167 • Mini-Lesson: Astronaut's Diary [Consistent Perspective], SE p. 1167 • TR Alt. Assess., p. 65	• Panel Discussion, Introduction, SE p. 1167 • Mini-Lesson: Panel Discussion, ATE p. 1164 • TR Alt. Assess., p. 65	• Film Review, Museum Exhibit, SE p. 1167 • TR Alt. Assess., p. 65	• Selection Test, TR Formal Assessment, pp. 297–299; Assess. Res. Software • Fictional Narrative Rubric [for Mini-Lesson], TR Alt. Assess., p. 96 • TR Alt. Assess., p. 65	• from "We'll Never Conquer Space," LL Audiocassettes • WS Writing Lab CD-ROM, Narration Tutorial

Skills Workshops

Unit	Writing Process Workshops	Applying Language Skills	Real-World Reading Skills Workshops	Speaking and Listening Workshops
From Legend to History	Dramatic Monologue, p. 33	Using Verb Tenses; Punctuating Free Verse, pp. 34, 35	Placing Reading in Time Context, p. 36	Delivering a Persuasive Speech, p. 192
	Research Paper, p. 71	Punctuating Quotations; Using Transitions, pp. 72, 73	Evaluating Sources of Information, p. 74	
	College-Application Essay, p. 135	Using Transitions; Using Pronouns Correctly, pp. 136, 137	Reading a Job Application, p. 138	
	Persuasive Speech, p. 188	Using Parallel Structure; Eliminating Unnecessary Words, pp. 189, 190	Evaluating Advertisements, p. 191	
Celebrating Humanity	Comparative Analysis, p. 231	Using Quotation Marks; Avoiding Ambiguous References, pp. 232, 233	Evaluating Contracts, p. 234	Oral Retelling, p. 376
	Persuasive Speech, p. 259	Using Active Voice; Using Persuasive Language; pp. 260, 261	Evaluating Political Persuasion, p. 262	
	Drama, p. 372	Informal English; Formatting Drama, pp. 373, 374	Following Test Directions, p. 375	
A Turbulent Time	Editorial, p. 425	Avoiding Logical Fallacies; Fixing Misplaced Modifiers, pp. 426, 427	Judging a Writer's Purpose, p. 428	Oral Presentation With Visuals, p. 562
	Autobiographical Incident, p. 455	Agreement With Indefinite Pronouns; Appositive Phrases, pp. 456, 457	Recognizing Bias in Articles, p. 458	
	Multimedia Presentation, p. 539	Using Documentation; Incorporating Media, pp. 540, 541	Reading Visual Information, p. 542	
	Reflective Essay, p. 558	Using Vivid Verbs; Using Modifiers Correctly, pp. 559, 560	Reading to Enrich Your Life, p. 561	
Rebels and Dreamers	Comparison-and-Contrast Essay, p. 609	Using Modifiers; Using Past Participial Phrases, pp. 610, 611	Reading to Find Specific Information, p. 612	Handling a Job Interview, p. 734
	Video Script, p. 699	Special Problems With Agreement; Formatting Scripts, pp. 700, 701	Using Visual Clues, p. 702	
	Job Portfolio, p. 730	Positive Language; Concise Language, pp. 731, 732	Evaluating Perspective in Historical Accounts, p. 733	
Progress and Decline	Cause-and-Effect Essay, p. 785	Revising Stringy Sentences; Using Precise Language, pp. 786, 787	Identifying Main Ideas in an Article, p. 788	Critically Evaluating a News Report, p. 872
	Statistical Report, p. 815	Introducing Statistical Information; Interpreting Statistics, pp. 816, 817	Reading Consumer Reports, p. 818	
	Character Sketch, p. 841	Using Figurative Language; Dangling Modifiers, pp. 842, 843	Reading Novels and Other Extended Works, p. 844	
	Parody, p. 868	Imitate Sentence Types; Avoiding Redundancy, pp. 869, 870	Adjusting Reading Rate, p. 871	
A Time of Rapid Change	Research Paper, 953	Citing Sources; Creating a Bibliography, pp. 954, 955	Evaluating Information on the Internet, p. 956	Conflict Resolution, p. 1172
	How-to Essay, p. 1027	Avoiding Run-on Sentences; Formatting Instructions, pp. 1028, 1029	Following Directions, p. 1030	
	Short Story, p. 1089	Writing Dialogue; Using Active Voice, pp. 1090, 1091	Reading Manuals, p. 1092	
	Critical Evaluation, p. 1168	Avoiding Illogical Comparisons; Avoiding Clichés, pp. 1169, 1170	Using Heads and Text Structure, p. 1171	

Copper
Bronze
Silver
Gold
Platinum
The American Experience
The British Tradition

PROGRAM ADVISORS

The program advisors provided ongoing input throughout the development of Prentice Hall Literature: Timeless Voices, Timeless Themes. *Their valuable insights ensure that the perspectives of teachers throughout the country are represented within this literature series.*

Diane Cappillo
Language Arts Department Chair
Barbara Goleman Senior High School
Miami, Florida
Facilitator at the University of Miami/Dade County Public Schools Summer Writing Institute. Past president of the Dade County Council of Teachers of English.

Anita Clay
English Instructor
Gateway Institute of Technology
St. Louis, Missouri
Former supervisory positions:
Middle School Team Leader Chairman, High School English Department; Coordinator, Effective and Efficient School; Coordinator, Writing Across the Curriculum Project.

Nancy M. Fahner
Language Arts Instructor
Charlotte High School
Charlotte, Michigan
Recipient of Charlotte Teacher of the Year Award 1992. Currently working on School-to-Work Curriculum Development.

Terri Fields
Language Arts and Communication Arts Teacher, Author
Sunnyslope High School
Phoenix, Arizona
Recipient of both Arizona Teacher of the Year and U. S. WEST Outstanding Arizona Teacher awards. Member of the Northern Arizona University Center for Excellence in Education Advisory Council. First place award for educational writing from National Federation of PressWomen.

Argelia Arizpe Guadarrama
Secondary Curriculum Coordinator
Phar-San Juan-Alamo Independent School District
San Juan, Texas
Recognized by Texas Education Agency for work on Texas Assessment of Academic Skills. Recipient of National Recognition of Positive Avenues for Student Success Program.

V. Pauline Hodges, Ph.D.
Teacher and Educational Consultant
Forgan High School
Forgan, Oklahoma
Formerly Language Arts Coordinator
Jefferson County, Colorado
Denver Professor in English Education/Reading, Colorado State University. President-elect of the National Rural Education Association. Recipient of Oklahoma Foundation for Excellence Award for Secondary Teaching 1993 and Outstanding Educator Award from the Colorado Language Arts Society.

Jennifer Huntress
Secondary Language Arts Coordinator
Putnam City Schools
Oklahoma City, Oklahoma
National trainer for writing evaluation, curriculum integration, and alternative assessment strategies. Instructor of language arts methods classes at Oklahoma City University.

Angelique McMath Jordan
English Teacher
Dunwoody High School
Dunwoody, Georgia
Teacher of the Year at Dunwoody High School, 1991.

Nancy L. Monroe
English and Speed Reading Teacher
Bolton High School
Alexandria, Louisiana
Past president of the Rapides Council of Teachers of English and the Louisiana Council of Teachers. National Advanced Placement Consultant.

Rosemary A. Naab
English Chairperson
Ryan High School
Archdiocese of Philadelphia
Philadelphia, Pennsylvania
English Curriculum Committee. Awarded Curriculum Quill Award by the Archdiocese of Philadelphia for the development of effective strategies for the teaching of writing and the integration of technology and writing.

Ann Okamura
English Teacher
Laguna Creek High School
Elk Grove, California
Participant of the College Board Pacesetters Program. Formerly K–12 District Resource Specialist in Writing, Foreign Languages, Lay Readers, District Writing, Competency Assessment, and the Elk Grove Writing Project. A fellow in the San Joaquin Valley Writing Project and California Literature Project.

Jonathan L. Schatz
English Teacher/Team Leader
Tappan Zee High School
Orangeburg, New York
Creator of a literacy program to assist students with reading in all content areas.

John Scott
English Teacher
Hampton High School
Hampton, Virginia
Recipient of the Folger Shakespeare Library Renaissance Forum Award. Master Teacher in Shakespeare who produces workshops for professional development at the local, state, and national level. Selected to participate in four National Endowment for the Humanities teacher programs.

Ken Spurlock
Assistant Principal
Boone County High School
Florence, Kentucky
Former English Teacher at Holmes High School and district writing supervisor. Past president of Kentucky Council of Teachers of English.

MULTICULTURAL REVIEW BOARD

Jocelyn Chadwick-Joshua, Ph.D.
Director of American Studies
The Dallas Institute of Humanities and Culture
Dallas, Texas

Clara M. Chu
Assistant Professor, Department of Library and Information Science
UCLA
Los Angeles, California

Nora A. Little Light Bird
Bilingual Project Director
Lodge Grass Public Schools
Lodge Grass, Montana

K. Tsianina Lomawaima
Associate Professor, American Indian Studies
University of Arizona
Tucson, Arizona

Larry L. Martin
Chair of History, Geography, and International Studies
Coppin State College
Baltimore, Maryland

Sunita Sunder Mukhi
Program Associate
Cultural Programs Division
Asia Society
New York, New York

Julio Noboa Polanco
Professor, Department of Teaching
The University of Northern Iowa, San Antonio Center
San Antonio, Texas

Alfredo Samone
Educational Consultant
Region 4, Education Service Center
Houston, Texas

A. J. Williams-Meyers, Ph.D.
Professor, Black Studies Department
SUNY-College at New Paltz
New Paltz, New York

CONTRIBUTING WRITERS

Amy K. Duer, M.Ed.
Former Teacher, Expert on Special Needs
Palm Beach Lakes High School
West Palm Beach, Florida

Carroll Moulton, M.A., Ph.D.
Former English Teacher
Stoughton High School
Stoughton, Massachusetts

Emily Hutchinson
Former English Teacher
Los Angeles Unified School District
Los Angeles, California

Lois Markham
Former English Teacher
Fort Lee High School
Fort Lee, New Jersey

Eileen Oshinsky
Former ESL Teacher
New York City Public Schools
Brooklyn, New York

Joan Hefele, M.S.
Research Writing Instructor
College of Mount Saint Vincent
Riverdale, New York

Robert McIlwaine, Ph.D.
Instructor of Literature
Duke University
Durham, North Carolina

iv

Prentice Hall

LITERATURE

Timeless Voices, Timeless Themes

The British Tradition

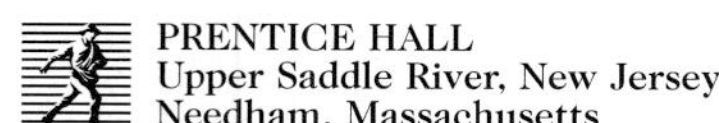

PRENTICE HALL
Upper Saddle River, New Jersey
Needham, Massachusetts

ISBN 0-13-434058-2

2 3 4 5 6 7 8 9 10 02 01 00 99 98

PRENTICE HALL
Simon & Schuster Education Group
A VIACOM COMPANY

STAFF CREDITS FOR PRENTICE HALL LITERATURE

(in alphabetical order)

Advertising and Promotion: Judy Goldstein, Carol Leslie, Rip Odell, Rob Richman, Ann Shea

Business Office: Emily Heins

Design: Laura Jane Bird, Sarah Carroll, Annemarie Franklin, Monduane Harris, Jim O'Shea, AnnMarie Roselli, Gerry Schrenk

Director of Language Arts: Douglas McCollum

Editorial: Ellen Bowler, Pam Cardiff, Megan Chill, Barbara W. Coe, Donna C. DiCuffa, Elisa Mui Eiger, Amy E. Fleming, Philip Fried, Rebecca Z. Graziano, James S. Jeglikowski, Jacqueline M. Regan

Electronic Publishing: Gregory Myers, Cleasta Wilburn

Manufacturing: Katherine Clarke, Rhett Conklin

Market Research: Eileen Friend, Joan McCulley

Marketing: Glenn E. Bell, Jean Faillace, Belinda Loh

Media Resources: Martha Conway, Libby Forsyth, Melanie Jones, Vickie Menanteaux, Maureen Raymond, Melissa Shustyk, Keirsten Wallace

National Language Arts Consultants: Linda Alexander, Kelly Ford, Karen Massey, Gail Witt

Permissions: Doris Robinson

PrePress Production: Kathryn Dix, William J. Hanna

Production: Christina Burghard, Holly Gordon, Elizabeth Torjussen

Technology: Rick Hickox

Art/Photograph Credits begin on p. 1223

ACKNOWLEDGMENTS

Grateful acknowledgment is made to the following for copyrighted material:

Georges Borchardt, Inc.
"The First Year of My Life" from *The Stories of Muriel Spark.* Copyright © 1985 by Copyright Administration. Reprinted by permission of Georges Borchardt, Inc. for the author.

Cambridge University Press
Excerpt from "Letter to Thomas Flower Ellis from Thomas Babington Macaulay on the Passing of the Reform Bill" written in 1831, from *The Selected Letters of Thomas Babington Macaulay,* ed. Thomas Pinney, 5 vols.(Cambridge: Cambridge University Press, 1974–80). Reprinted by permission of the publisher.

(Acknowledgments continue on p. 1219)

Unit 

From Legend to History (449 A.D.–1485)

Unit

Unit 2

Celebrating Humanity (1485–1625)

PART 1 LOVERS AND THEIR LINES

PART 2 THE STORY OF BRITAIN: THE INFLUENCE OF THE MONARCHY

Unit 2

PART 3 — FOCUS ON LITERARY FORMS: DRAMA

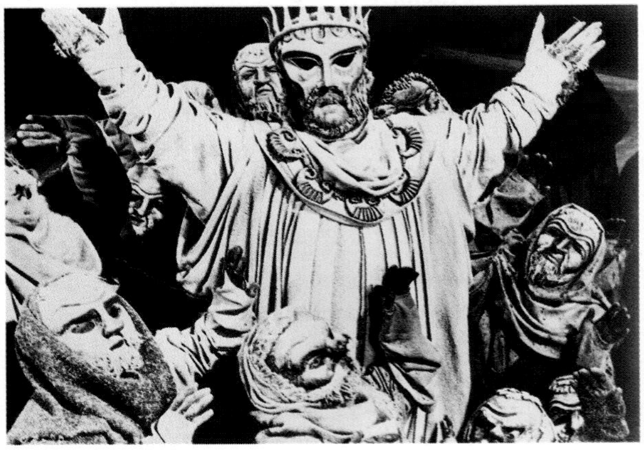

Unit

A Turbulent Time (1625–1798)

Unit

PART 3 THE TIES THAT BIND

PART 4 FOCUS ON LITERARY FORMS: THE ESSAY

Rebels and Dreamers (1798–1832)

Unit

Progress and Decline (1833–1901)

Unit

Unit 6

A Time of Rapid Change (1901–Present)

PART I WAKING FROM THE DREAM

Unit

PART 2 THE STORY OF BRITAIN: CONFLICTS ABROAD AND AT HOME

PART 3 FOCUS ON LITERARY FORMS: THE SHORT STORY

Unit 6

Part 4 From the National to the Global

Planning Instruction and Assessment

Unit Objectives

1. To read selections from the beginnings of the British literary tradition through the Middle Ages
2. To apply a variety of reading strategies, particularly literal comprehension strategies, appropriate for reading these selections
3. To recognize literary elements used in these selections
4. To build vocabulary in context
5. To learn elements of grammar, usage, and style
6. To write in a variety of modes and about situations based on the selections
7. To develop speaking and listening skills, by completing proposed activities

Meeting the Objectives

With each selection, you will find instructional material and portfolio opportunities through which students can meet these objectives. Further, you will find additional practice pages for reading strategies, literary elements, vocabulary, and grammar in the ***Selection Support*** booklet in the Teaching Resources box.

Setting Goals Work with your students at the beginning of the unit to set goals for unit outcomes. Plan what skills and concepts you wish students to acquire. You may individualize these according to students' performance levels or learning modalities.

Portfolios You may have students keep portfolios of their work or of their work in progress. The activities and prompts on the Build Your Portfolio page of each selection provide opportunities for students to apply the concepts presented with the selection.

Sir Gawain and the Green Knight, Bodleian Library, Oxford

Humanities: Art

Gawain Departs Guenivere and Arthur, The Bodleian Library, Oxford.

Explain to students that this picture comes from an illuminated medieval manuscript. (For more on illuminated manuscripts, see the Humanities: Art note at the bottom of page 5.)

Illuminated manuscripts contained pictures and decorations like this one, painted on hand-lettered vellum. Vellum was a fine kind of parchment prepared from calfskin, lambskin, or kidskin, and used in books. This miniature painting shows the knight Sir Gawain departing from King Arthur and his queen, Guenivere. It illustrates a book about the adventures of Sir Gawain. Point out to students the lack of perspective and "realism" that they might naturally assume a painting should have but that came in as a style with the Renaissance.

Use these questions for discussion:

1. What clues reveal that this painting is from a book? *You can see the lettering from the text above the picture.*
2. Would you like to see illustrations like this one in the novels and stories you read? Explain. *Accept reasonable answers.*

UNIT 1

From Legend to History (449–1485)

Who pulleth out this sword of this stone and anvil, is rightwise king born of all England.

—Sir Thomas Malory, from *Morte d'Arthur*

Assessing Student Progress

The following tools are available to measure the degree to which students meet the unit objectives:

Informal Assessment

The questions in the Guide for Responding sections are a first level of response to the concepts and skills presented with the selection. Students' responses are a brief informal measure of their grasp of the material. Their responses on this level can indicate where further instruction and practice are needed. You may then follow up with the practice pages in the ***Selection Support*** booklet.

You will find literature and reading guides in the ***Alternative Assessment*** booklet, which you may give students on an individual basis for informal assessment of their performance.

Formal Assessment

In the ***Formal Assessment*** booklet, you will find selection tests and a part test.

Selection Tests The selection tests measure comprehension and skills acquisition for each selection or group of selections.

Present Test The part test, which calls on students to read a passage of literature they have not previously seen, applies the unit skills on a broader level. The Critical Reading section measures Unit Objectives 1, 2, and 3. The Vocabulary and Grammar section measures Objectives 4 and 5. The Essay section measures Objectives 1 and 6. Both the Critical Reading and Vocabulary and Grammar sections use formats similar to those found on many standardized tests, including the SAT.

Alternative Assessment

Portfolios As you review individual pieces or the collected work in students' portfolios, you will find assessment sheets available in the portfolio section of the ***Alternative Assessment*** booklet.

Scoring Rubrics You will find scoring rubrics for writing modes in the ***Alternative Assessment*** booklet. You can apply these to Writing Mini-Lessons and to Writing Process Workshop lessons.

Speaking and Listening The ***Alternative Assessment*** booklet contains assessment sheets for speaking and listening activities.

Learning Modalities The ***Alternative Assessment*** booklet contains activities that appeal to different learning styles. You may use these too as an alternative measurement of students' growth.

Using the Timeline

The Timeline can serve a number of instructional purposes, as follows:

Getting an Overview Use the Timeline to help students get a quick overview of themes and events of the period. This approach will benefit all students but may be especially helpful for visually oriented students, English language learners, and those less proficient in reading. (For strategies in using the Timeline as an overview, see the bottom of this page.)

Thinking Critically Questions are provided on the facing page. Use these questions to have students review the events, discuss their significance, and examine the *so what* behind the *what happened*.

Connecting to Selections Have students refer to the Timeline when beginning to read individual selections. By consulting the Timeline regularly, they will gain a better sense of the period's chronology. In addition, they will appreciate the world events that gave rise to these works of literature.

Projects Students can use the Timeline as a launching pad for projects like these:

- **Customized Timeline** Have students create a period timeline in their notebooks, adding key dates as they read new selections. They can use dates from this Timeline as a starting framework.
- **Special Reports** Have students scan the Timeline for items that interest them, research these further, and report on them to the class.

Timeline

449–1485

449 | **600** | **900**

British Events

- **449** Anglo-Saxon invasion. ▼

- **597** St. Augustine founds Christian monastery at Canterbury, Kent.
- **664** Synod of Whitby establishes Roman Church in England.
- **731 Bede** completes *A History of the English Church and People.*
- **c. 750** Surviving version of *Beowulf* composed.
- **792** Vikings attack Lindisfarne. ▼

- **843** Scottish ruler Kenneth MacAlprin unites Scots and Picts.
- **871** Alfred the Great becomes King of Wessex. ▼

- **c. 930** Howel the Good unites kingdom of Wales.
- **c. 975** Saxon monks copy Old English poems into *The Exeter Book.*
- **991** English defeated by Danes at Battle of Maldon.
- **1002** Brian Boru unites kingdom of Ireland.
- **1034** Duncan I inherits Scottish throne.
- **1040** Macbeth murders Duncan I.
- **1042** Edward the Confessor becomes king of Saxons.
- **1066** Normans defeat Saxons at Hastings; William the Conqueror becomes king of England. ▼

World Events

- **476** Western Europe: Fall of Western Roman Empire.
- **493** Italy: Theodoric the Great establishes Ostrogothic kingdom.
- **496** France: Clovis, king of Franks, converts to Christianity.
- **542** Constantinople: Plague kills half the population.
- **c. 550** Mexico: Toltecs defeat Mayas.
- **552** Japan: Buddhism introduced. ▶
- **591** China: Beginning of book printing.
- **637** Middle East: Jerusalem conquered by Arabs.
- **641** Egypt: Library at Alexandria destroyed.
- **712** Spain: Seville conquered by Moors.
- **732** France: Charles Martel defeats Moors.
- **771** France: Charlemagne becomes king. ▲
- **800** Peru: Incas build city of Machu Picchu.
- **c. 810** Persia: Algebra devised.
- **c. 830** France: Einhard writes *Life of Charlemagne.*
- **861** North Atlantic: Vikings discover Iceland.
- **c. 882** Russia: Nation founded by Vikings.
- **c. 900** Western Europe: Feudalism develops.
- **911** France: Normans establish Normandy.
- **982** Greenland: Eric the Red establishes first Viking colony.
- **1009** Middle East: Moslems destroy Holy Sepulcher in Jerusalem.
- **c. 1020** America: Viking explorer Leif Ericson explores Canadian coast.
- **1045** Spain: Birth of El Cid, national hero who fought Moors.
- **1053** Italy: Normans conquer Sicily.

Getting an Overview of the Period

Introduction To give students an overview of the period, indicate the span of dates along the top of the Timeline. How much time is covered in this unit? *This unit covers a period of 1,036 years.* Next, point out that the Timeline is divided into specifically British Events (on the top) and World Events (on the bottom). Have them practice scanning the Timeline across, looking both at the British Events and the World Events. Finally, point out that the events in the Timeline often represent beginnings, turning points, and endings (for example, 1096, the beginning of the Crusades).

Key Events Have students identify key political events, like invasions. *In 449, Anglo-Saxons invaded; in 1066, the Normans invaded.* Then have them find events suggesting a growing sense of national identity. *In 597, Christianity was introduced; in 871, Alfred the Great became king; and in 1215, the Magna Carta was signed.* Finally, ask students how the contrast between first and last events on the Timeline suggests a development from legend to history. *The Timeline moves from the chaos of invasions, 449, to developments like the building of the first printing press, 1476.*

1070 | 1220 | 1380 | 1485

British Events

- **1073** Canterbury becomes England's religious center.
- **c. 1075** Construction on Tower of London begins.
- **1100** Henry I becomes king.
- **c. 1130** Oxford becomes a center for learning.
- **1170** Thomas Becket, Archbishop of Canterbury, murdered. ▼

- **1171** Henry II conquers south-eastern Ireland.
- **1180** Glass windows first used in private homes.
- **1215** King John forced to sign Magna Carta.
- **1218** First Newgate prison built in London.
- **c. 1209** Cambridge University founded.
- **1233** First coal mined at Newcastle.
- **1258** First commoners allowed in Parliament.
- **1272** Edward I becomes king.
- **1282** England conquers Wales.
- **1295** Edward I assembles Model Parliament.
- **1337** Beginning of the Hundred Years' War with France.
- **1348** Black Death begins sweeping through England. ▼

- **1361** Bible first translated into English.
- **c. 1375** Surviving version of *Sir Gawain and the Green Knight* written.
- **1381** Peasants' Revolt.
- **1386 Chaucer** begins writing *The Canterbury Tales*. ▶
- **1455** Beginning of the Wars of the Roses.
- **1460** Richard of York killed at Battle of Wakefield.
- **c. 1470 Thomas Malory** writes *Morte d'Arthur*.
- **1476** William Caxton builds first English printing press.

World Events

- **1096** Europe and Middle East: First Crusade begins.
- **c. 1100** France: *Song of Roland* written.
- **c. 1130** Portugal: Alfonso VII defeats Moors.
- **c. 1150** Spain: First paper made.
- **1174** Italy: Tower of Pisa built.
- **1192** Austria: Duke Leopold imprisons Richard I of England.
- **1194** Iceland: *Elder Edda*, a collection of Norse myths and legends, first appears.
- **1214** China: Mongol leader Genghis Khan captures Peking.
- **1221** Italy: First known sonnet appears.
- **1231** Europe: Pope Gregory IX establishes Inquisition.
- **1241** Eastern Europe: Mongols withdraw from Poland and Hungary.
- **1275** China: Marco Polo visits court of Kublai Khan.
- **1291** Europe and Middle East: End of Crusades.
- **1307** Italy: Dante begins writing *The Divine Comedy*.
- **1327** Mexico: Aztecs establish Mexico City and create a dating system with a solar year of 365 days. ▲
- **1332** India: Bubonic plague begins.
- **1341** Italy: Petrarch crowned poet laureate of Rome.
- **1346** France: English defeat French at Crecy.
- **c. 1400** Italy: Beginning of Medici rule.
- **1429** France: Joan of Arc leads French in breaking siege of Orleans. ▼
- **c.1450** North America: Iroquois nations unite.
- **1453** France: Hundred Years' War with England ends.
- **1453** Germany: First Gutenberg Bible printed.
- **1461** France: François Villon writes *Grand Testament*.
- **1483** Portugal: John II refuses to finance Columbus.
- **1484** Italy: Botticelli paints *Birth of Venus*.
- **1485** Peru: Incan empire reaches its zenith.

▶Critical Viewing◀

1. Why might the invaders of Britain (449) have decorated their helmets with horns? **[Infer]** *The invaders probably wore horns to frighten their enemies in battle.*
2. William the Conqueror is being crowned by bishops (1066). What does this suggest about the relations between church and state at this time? **[Infer]** *The Church was viewed as an authority in worldly affairs; the king needed the cooperation of the Church to reign.*
3. Describe the style in which the artist portrays the Black Death (1348). What does this style suggest about the seriousness of this disease? **[Interpret]** *The artist uses gestures to show people's despair and anguish, suggesting that the Black Death was a deadly disease.*
4. Look at the picture of Chaucer's pilgrim (1386). What would it have been like to travel on horseback from London to Canterbury? **[Speculate]** *Students may mention exposure to elements and the need to stop at inns.*

◆Critical Thinking

1. (a) What is the earliest date given for the introduction of Christianity to England? (b) Why is this date important? **[Hypothesize]** *(a) In 597, St. Augustine founded a monastery at Canterbury. (b) Britain eventually became a Christian nation.*
2. (a) When did the Vikings attack a site in Britain? (b) What may have happened to this seafaring, warlike people? **[Infer]** *(a) They attacked Lindisfarne in 792. (b) Reasonable answers include these: the Vikings were defeated by the settled peoples of the area in which they sailed and gave up raiding; the Vikings settled down in the places to which they traveled and were assimilated by the local people.*
3. (a) What important military campaign occurred in France a year after Bede completed his *History*? (b) If those who lost the battle had won it, how might the history of Britain been different? **[Speculate]** *(a) Charles Martel defeated the Moors. (b) Britain too might have fallen to Moorish invaders.*
4. (a) When did the Normans conquer England? (b) Does the Timeline suggest that they were eventually expelled, or that they were assimilated (married local people and eventually lost their distinct identity)? Explain. **[Hypothesize]** *(a) The Normans conquered England in 1066. (b) Since there is no mention of a battle or revolution against the Normans after 1066, the Timeline suggests that they assimilated.*
5. (a) What two dramatic events occurred in Britain in the 1330's and 1340's? (b) How might these events have affected the population of the British isles? **[Infer]** *(a) In 1337, the Hundred Years War began with France. In 1348, the Black Death swept across England. (b) They probably decreased the population dramatically.*

Develop Understanding

Customize for
Less Proficient Readers
Have students preview the art and illustrations in A Graphic Look at the Period and answer the questions about them before reading The Story of the Times.

Customize for
English Language Learners
Have these students use A Graphic Look at the Period, without the questions, to speculate about the era. Also have them glance at the bold heads in The Story of the Times and formulate questions that the sections introduced by these heads might answer.

Customize for
Visual/Spatial Learners
Students with a visual or spatial orientation will benefit by using the map on page 10 to locate the homelands of various peoples named in the Historical Background.

Customize for
More Advanced Students
Challenge more advanced students to use evidence from A Graphic Look at the Period and The Story of the Times to draw conclusions about the daily life of teenagers during this period.

Answers to
A GRAPHIC LOOK

Compare and Contrast These keys somewhat resemble modern keys. However, these keys were probably handcrafted and therefore don't have the standardized look of modern keys, which are manufactured by machine.

Draw Conclusions Judging from the figures' air of concentration and the fact that two are steadying the horse, the trade may have been dangerous. Differences in dress between the smith and the assistants suggest that smiths enjoyed some prestige.

A GRAPHIC LOOK AT THE PERIOD

▲ **Compare and Contrast** How are these housekeys from the Viking era similar to and different from those you use today?

▲ **Draw Conclusions** From looking at the details in this illuminated drawing what conclusions can you draw about the trade of shoeing horses during this era?

The Story of the Times
(A.D. 449–1485)

Historical Background

The Conquest of Britain Between 800 and 600 B.C., two groups of Celts from southern Europe invaded the British Isles. One group, who called themselves Brythons (now spelled "Britons"), settled on the largest island, Britain. The other, known as Gaels, settled on the second largest island, known to us as Ireland.

The Celts were farmers and hunters. They organized themselves into tightly knit clans, each with a fearsome loyalty to its chieftain. When these clans fell into disagreement with one another, they often looked to a class of priests known as Druids to settle their disputes.

The next conquerors of Britain were the far more sophisticated Romans. In 55 B.C. and again the next year, the Roman general Julius Caesar made hasty invasions. The true conquest of Britain, however, occurred nearly one hundred years later. Disciplined Roman legions spread out over the island, establishing camps that soon grew into towns.

Roman rule of Britain lasted for more than 300 years. It ended only when northern European tribes invaded Italy and increased pressure on Rome itself. The last Roman legions departed from Britain to defend Rome in A.D. 407. By that time, the Britons faced a new set of invaders.

The next invaders were the Anglo-Saxons, from what is now Germany. Some Anglo-Saxons appear to have been deep-sea fishermen; others seem to have been farmers, perhaps seeking soil richer than the sandy or marshy land at home. Gradually, the newcomers took over more and more of what today is England.

The Coming of Christianity During the fourth century, the Romans had accepted Christianity and introduced it to Britain. A century later,

Cross-Curricular Connection: Social Studies

The Meaning of Roman Rule To help students understand the importance of Roman rule, ask them if they have ever visited another city in the United States. How did they find their way there? Where did they eat and, if they paid for accommodations, where did they spend the night? Point out factors enabling Americans to leave their homes and travel hundreds of miles with confidence: a uniform currency, restaurant franchises, hotel chains, similar laws.

Explain to students that Rome provided some of the same things. It built roads, fortifications, and aqueducts. Its military defended Britain against alien invasion. Its laws enabled the English to enjoy some of the protections enjoyed by other citizens. Also, the use of Latin throughout the empire guaranteed that traders could be at home in many places around the world. Have students speculate whether our world is moving in the direction of a universal language and currency.

when the Celts fled the Anglo-Saxons, they took their Christian faith with them. Although Rome fell to barbarian tribes in A.D. 476, the Celtic Christian church continued to thrive.

In the late sixth century, a soldier and abbot named Columba, along with some monks, gained converts to Christianity and established monasteries in the north.

In 597, the Roman cleric Saint Augustine (not the early Christian Church father) arrived in southeast England and converted King Ethelbert of Kent to Christianity. Augustine set up a monastery at Canterbury in Kent and began preaching his faith to other rulers as well. By providing counsel to quarreling rulers, the Church promoted peace and helped to unify the English people.

Danish Invasion In the ninth century, the Norse of Norway and the Danes of Denmark were beset with a rising population and took to the seas. These Vikings carried their piracy to the British Isles. The Norse set their sights on Northumbria, Scotland, Wales, and Ireland, whereas the Danes targeted eastern and southern England.

Viking invaders sacked and plundered monasteries, destroyed manuscripts, and stole sacred religious objects. They burned entire communities and put villagers to the sword. Although the English fought back valiantly, the Danes made broad inroads. By the middle of the ninth century, most of northern, eastern, and central England had fallen to the invaders.

In 871, a king ascended to the Wessex throne who would become the only ruler in England's history ever to be honored with the epithet "the Great." His name was Alfred, and he earned the title partly by resisting further Danish encroachment. Under a truce concluded in 886, England was formally divided: the Saxons acknowledged Danish rule in the east and north, but the Danes agreed to respect Saxon rule in the south. Alfred the Great became a national hero.

Alfred's achievements went far beyond the field of battle, however. Not only was he instrumental in preserving the remnants of pre-Danish civilization in Britain, but he encouraged a rebirth of learning and education.

▲ **Analyze Causes and Effects** This map shows the spread of Christianity throughout Europe. What effects might this religious conversion have had on daily life?

Answers to A Graphic Look

Analyze Causes and Effects
Church-going would have become part of people's weekly routines; people may have turned to priests and monks for advice or for help in settling disputes; traditional pagan rituals accompanying planting, harvesting, and other work may have been banned by the Church.

More About Alfred the Great
To make literature and other documents more accessible, Alfred oversaw translations of Bede's *History* and other works from Latin into Anglo-Saxon, the everyday language of the people. In this way he fostered the growth of the English language and its literature. He also began to keep records of English history in the *Anglo-Saxon Chronicle,* one of our principal sources of information on early English life.

Connection to the Literature
- "The Seafarer," p. 15, and "The Wanderer," p. 20, offer piercing, first-person accounts of the loneliness and alienation that sea-roving and warfare could prompt.
- *Beowulf,* p. 40, sets forth the stoic credo of the Anglo-Saxon invaders mentioned in the historical accounts.
- The excerpt from Bede's *A History of the English Church and People,* p. 78, will acquaint students with a work that was translated into English and was made more accessible under the sponsorship of King Alfred the Great.

Humanities: Art

Illuminated Manuscripts.

Use A Graphic Look at the Period to introduce students to illuminated manuscripts. (excerpts from manuscripts appear on page 4, bottom and page 8, top).

Explain how monks, dedicated to copying over precious manuscripts, would devote days to working with paints and gold leaf to adorn the pages of illuminated manuscripts.

Tasks were divided: Some provided paintings to illustrate the story; others adorned with clever designs the borders of the page or the capital letters. (The latter are the original illuminators; the picture-makers were said to "historiate.")

Before the invasions of the Danes, English manuscript art at Lindisfarne, Weymouth, and Jarrow was dominated by the decorative techniques brought by Irish monks.

Ask students whether desktop publishing will introduce a new kind of illuminated manuscript. *They may answer that it will.*

Answers to

A GRAPHIC LOOK

Draw a Conclusion The Normans who arrived in England came prepared to camp, since they brought with them cooking implements such as the tongs and grill shown at the right. This suggests that they were used to military campaign away from home.

Make an Inference The Vikings were metal workers. The sword is long and broad, not thin like a rapier; it is designed for long cross-cuts, not thrusts. This indicates that the Vikings valued physical strength.

More About Edward the Confessor Edward had spent many of his early years in Normandy, a region once settled by Scandinavians and now a part of France. Norman on his mother's side, Edward had developed a close friendship with his cousin William, Normandy's ruler.

More About the Normans Although they descended from the Vikings, the Normans had adopted many French ways over the years. They had become devout Christians. They had accustomed themselves to speaking a dialect of the French language. They had also organized themselves according to the French political and economic system of the times—feudalism.

Art Transparencies Use Art Transparency 2, *Harold Brings News to William*, to give students more of a sense of the Bayeux Tapestry. The transparency is accompanied by a Humanities Note on the tapestry and additional activities.

▲ **Draw a Conclusion** The Bayeux Tapestry is a piece of embroidery (230 feet by 20 inches) that tells the story of King Harold's defeat at Hastings in 1066. This small section of the tapestry shows the Normans preparing a meal after their channel crossing. What conclusions can you draw from this scene about the Normans and their way of life?

▶ **Make an Inference** What can you infer about Viking society and technology by studying this sword?

Toward the close of the tenth century, however, more Danes from Europe attempted to recapture and widen the Danelaw, the eastern and northern sections of England under Danish control. Once they succeeded, they forced the Saxons to select Danish kings.

Then, in 1042, the line of succession returned to a descendant of Alfred the Great. This king, Edward, had gained the title "the Confessor" because he was a deeply religious Christian. His death in 1066 led to the end of the Anglo-Saxon period of history.

The Norman Conquest The Normans, or "north men," were descendants of Vikings who had invaded the coast of France in the ninth century. William, Duke of Normandy, had family ties to Edward the Confessor, the English king. When Edward died in 1066, the Saxon council of elders chose Harold II as king. William of Normandy, meanwhile, claimed that Edward had promised him the throne and he crossed the English Channel to assert his claim by force. At the Battle of Hastings near a seaside village in southern England, Harold was killed, and William emerged victorious.

Over the next five years William suppressed the Anglo-Saxon nobility and confiscated their lands. He saw to it that Normans controlled government and that business was conducted in Norman French or Latin. The Normans gradually remade England along feudal lines.

Feudalism had taken root on the European continent at a time when no central government was strong enough to keep order. The feudal system involved an exchange of property for personal service. In theory, all the land belonged to the king, who parceled out land among his powerful supporters. He gave these supporters noble titles—usually "Baron"—and special privileges. As a vassal of his overlord, each baron paid certain fees, or taxes, and supplied a specified number of knights—professional soldiers—should the king require them. In return for their services, knights usually received smaller parcels of land, called manors. The peasants who worked these manors were the lowest class in the feudal system, the serfs.

Humanities: Art

Bayeux Tapestry.

Using colored thread, medieval French needleworkers stitched the story of William the Conqueror's invasion of England—from the precipitating events through the Battle of Hastings—in more than seventy scenes on a long (231 feet), narrow (19 inches) strip of linen. Their work, known as the Bayeux Tapestry (after the French town in which it was hung), has served as a valuable source of information about these events. Though the tapestry's pictorial style is simple, details are rendered precisely and accurately.

Help students envision the Bayeux Tapestry by marking off 19 inches on the board and asking students to suggest areas that would come close to being 231 feet long (for example, more than three quarters of a football field).

Ask students to examine the detail from the tapestry on this page or on Art Transparency 2. Ask these questions:

1. Describe the style of the pictures, considering the types of lines used and the accuracy of the portrayals. *The artist uses many straight lines but works in graceful curves as well. Figures are not always accurately portrayed.*
2. Name two reasons for creating the tapestry. *It may have been created to celebrate a victory and to make sure that the French version of events was remembered.*

Reign of the Plantagenets Although Norman influence continued for centuries, Norman rule ended in 1154 when Henry Plantagenet, Count of Anjou, came to the throne as Henry II. Henry founded the royal house of Plantagenet and established a record as one of England's ablest kings.

Henry's concern with legal matters led him into direct conflict with the Church. When the archbishop's seat at Canterbury fell vacant, he appointed his friend Thomas Becket to the position, expecting Becket to go along with royal policy. Instead, Becket defied the king and appealed to the Pope. The Pope sided with Becket, provoking Henry to rage.

Some of Henry's knights misunderstood the royal wrath. In 1170, four of them murdered Becket in his cathedral. Henry quickly condemned the crime and tried to atone for it by making a holy journey, or pilgrimage, to Becket's tomb. Thereafter, a pilgrimage to Becket's shrine at Canterbury became a common English means of showing religious devotion.

The Magna Carta The next king, Richard I, spent most of his reign staging military expeditions overseas. His activities proved costly, and his successor, King John, inherited the debts. John tried to raise money by ordering new taxes on the barons. The barons resisted these measures, bringing England to the edge of civil war. To avert further trouble, King John at last agreed to certain of the barons' conditions by putting his seal to the Magna Carta (Latin for "Great Charter").

In this document, the king promised not to tax land without first meeting with the barons. The Magna Carta produced no radical changes in government. Yet many historians believe that the document's restrictions on royal power marked the beginning of constitutional government in England.

The Lancasters, Yorks, and Tudors During the fourteenth and fifteenth centuries, the house of Lancaster replaced the Plantagenets on the throne, only to be replaced in turn by the house of York. The Lancastrian kings were Henry IV, Henry V, and Henry VI, all of whom later became central figures in the historical dramas of Shakespeare.

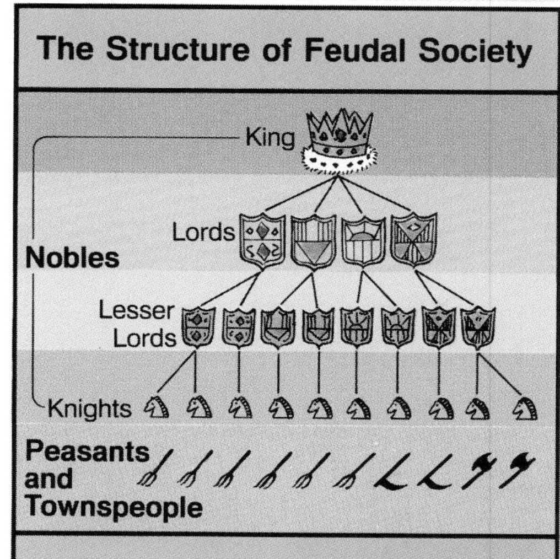

▲ **Relate** What aspects of feudal society, as diagrammed here, are similar to aspects of modern-day America? What class of modern people are equivalent to the class of knights in feudal society?

Answers to A GRAPHIC LOOK

Relate In medieval society, fewer people occupied places of extreme privilege. Modern-day equivalents to the knights of feudal society might include professional soldiers. Those who own or have important managerial authority over a large business could be compared to lords or lesser lords. Today's workers, with the freedom to move from job to job, are not really equivalent to medieval serfs.

More About Feudalism

Explain to students that a peasant's diet was limited to bread and vegetables; meat was a luxury. After 1000, trade began to flourish, agriculture expanded, and money began to circulate. By the 1300's, peasants were renting their land or being paid for their labor. Their old bondage to the land was loosening.

Connection to the Literature

- The ties binding king to lord and lord to peasant in medieval society gave people a firm sense of their place in the social order. For an earlier, affecting lament for the loss of this place—the plight of the exile—refer students to "The Wanderer," beginning on page 20.
- The chart of Feudal Society suggests that medieval society was rigidly hierarchical. However, let students know that Chaucer's *The Canterbury Tales: The Prologue* (p. 88) reveals a colorful diversity of occupations and social types.

Humanities: Music

Gregorian Chant.

Monastic culture, preserver of the Anglo-Saxon epics and histories, also produced the distinctive music of the period: the Gregorian chant. Named for Pope Gregory I (c. A.D. 540–604), these chants are musical settings for the texts used in masses and prayer services. The chants, or plainsongs, feature only one melody line and rarely use more than ten pitches, yet they encompass a variety of styles and structures.

Have students listen to the Gregorian chant on the **Listening to Music** Audio CD: *The British Tradition.* Ask these questions:

1. Does the mood of this chant reflect the life of the time, or does it offer a contrast? Explain. *The chant's peaceful mood may seem to contrast with the violence of the times.*
2. St. Bernard warned against performing the chants as a "vocal display." What does this reveal about the function of the chants? *They had a strictly religious purpose.*

Answers to

A Graphic Look

Deduce The picture shows a woman scything a field. This suggests that intensive manual labor was not judged inappropriate for women of certain classes in the Middle Ages.

Speculate The dancer on the viewer's right appears to be hopping, suggesting that he is dancing to lively music; the dress and poses of the figures suggest that this dance was not meant for a formal court affair but might have formed an entertainment for peasants.

Historical Background

Comprehension Check

1. Who ruled Britain before the coming of the Anglo-Saxons? *The Roman empire ruled Britain before the coming of the Anglo-Saxons.*
2. What important cultural development occured in Britain during the late sixth century? *Roman missionaries began to convert the Anglo-Saxons to Christianity.*
3. Which Anglo-Saxon king is remembered for making peace with the Danes? *Alfred the Great is the Anglo-Saxon king who made peace with the Danes.*
4. Briefly describe the social system the Normans imposed on England. *The Normans imposed feudalism on England. Feudalism was a hierarchical society with distinct classes, based on landownership and loyalty.*

Critical Thinking

1. How was the concept of property under feudalism different from today's ideas of property? **[Compare and Contrast]** *In feudalism, all land was owned, in theory, by the king. In return for the loyalty of his barons, he granted them its use. In the modern idea of property, land is owned by whoever has bought it.*
2. How is the Magna Carta a step on the way to Britain's constitutional monarchy of today? **[Infer]** *It lessened the monarch's power, making it more dependent on his or her subjects' consent.*
3. How did the plague contribute to the birth of capitalism? **[Generalize]** *It led to the introduction of money as the link between lord and serf.*

▲ **Deduce** From the evidence in this picture, what can you deduce about women's duties and chores?

▲ **Speculate** Dance is an important part of most cultures: celebrations, entertainment, and religious rituals usually involve some form of dancing. Speculate about the nature of the medieval dance portrayed in this picture.

The Decline of the Feudal System After the great plague, called the Black Death, swept across England in 1348 and 1349, a massive labor shortage increased the value of a peasant's work. Landowners began paying their farmers in cash, giving these workers a greater sense of freedom. Along with freedom went frustration, as peasants began to complain about discriminatory laws and heavy taxation. Finally, in 1381, peasants in southern England staged a revolt, demanding an end to serfdom. Although the revolt was crushed, many of its causes continued, and so did the peasants' discontent.

The conflicts known as the Wars of the Roses began in 1453, pitting the house of York against the house of Lancaster. Eventually, Henry Tudor, a distant cousin and supporter of the Lancastrian kings, led a rebellion against the unpopular Yorkist king Richard III and killed him. Tudor, crowned Henry VII, later married Richard's niece, uniting the houses of York and Lancaster and ending the Wars of the Roses.

Literature of the Period

Saxon Literature Anglo-Saxon literature began not with books, but with spoken verse and incantations. The reciting of poems often occurred on ceremonial occasions, such as the celebration of military victories.

This early verse falls mainly into two categories: heroic poetry, recounting the achievements of warriors, and elegiac poetry, lamenting the deaths of loved ones and the loss of the past. The long poem *Beowulf* is the most famous example of heroic poetry, and a famous elegiac poem is "The Wanderer."

Beowulf is an epic—a long heroic poem. It tells the story of a great pagan warrior renowned for his courage, strength, and dignity. Because it is the first such work composed in the English language, it is considered the national epic of England.

Before the reign of Alfred the Great, all important prose written in the British Isles was composed in Latin. The monks who transcribed these works regarded the vernacular, the language of the common people, as a "vulgar tongue." The greatest of England's Latin schol-

Cross-Curricular Connection: Science and Technology

Though people sometimes describe the Middle Ages as a time of intellectual darkness and superstition, it was an era that saw significant advances in the technology of agriculture. In at least some parts of western Europe, the plow was no longer a simple blade to scratch the earth. It rode on wheels; a new arrangement of parts ensured that it would actually turn over the soil as it passed. Windmills began to appear, harnessing the power of the wind to grind grain into flour. Even hand tools such as axes were improved during this time.

Ask your students which technological improvements have had the most significant impact on their own lives, and why. Then ask them why improvements in agricultural technology might have made such a difference in the lives of people in the Middle Ages. *What may emerge in the discussion is that, in medieval times, simply producing enough food to live could be a struggle. In modern western countries, improvements in technology no longer make as significant a difference in the margin for survival.*

ars was the Venerable Bede, whose *A History of the English Church and People* gives an account of England from the Roman invasion to his own time (673–735).

Another great work of prose from this time is *The Anglo-Saxon Chronicles*, the name given to a group of historical journals written and compiled in monasteries. Unlike Bede's *History*, these records were written in Old English.

Literature of the English Middle Ages Lyric poems of this period fall into two major categories—secular and religious. The usual topics of secular poetry are love and nature. Another popular poetic form was the ballad, a folk song that told a story. One surviving series of ballads, for example, concerns the exploits of the legendary outlaw Robin Hood.

During early Norman times, the Church often sponsored plays as part of religious services. In time, these plays moved from the church to the churchyard and then to the marketplace. The earliest dramas were miracle plays, or mystery plays, that retold stories from the Bible or dealt with some aspect of the lives of saints.

During the turbulent fifteenth century, a new kind of drama arose: the morality play. Morality plays depicted the life of an ordinary person and taught a moral lesson.

An Emerging National Identity In 1454, a German silversmith, Johann Gutenberg, perfected a process of printing from movable type. Printing then spread rapidly throughout Europe, and, in 1476, William Caxton set up the first movable-type press in England. English literature no longer needed to be hand copied by church scribes.

One of Caxton's first projects was the printing of Geoffrey Chaucer's *The Canterbury Tales*, a series of verse stories told by pilgrims on their way to the tomb of Thomas Becket. Chaucer wrote in Middle English, a language quite close to English as it is spoken today. After centuries of the ebb and flow of conquerors and their languages, the island of England had finally settled on a national identity of its own.

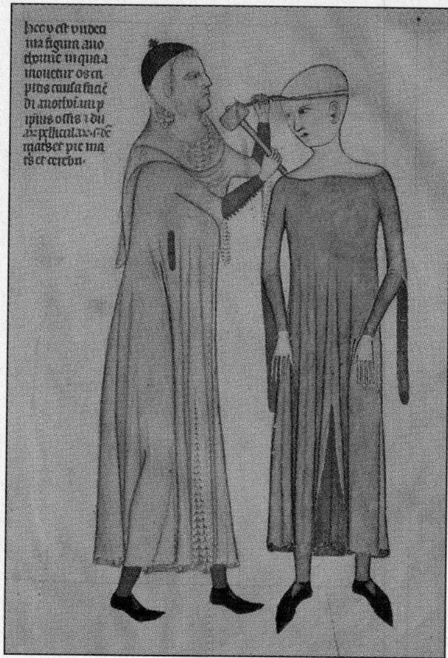

▲ **Infer** During this time, folk medicines were widely used to treat diseases. What does this representation of head surgery suggest about the surgical techniques of the period?

▲ **Speculate** In the late fifteenth century, the movable type press began to play an important role in society. This set of letters and designed border were created by William Caxton's printing device. Speculate about the effect this device had on English society.

Answers to

A Graphic Look

Infer Surgery at the time was crude and did not involve either anesthesia or rigorous hygiene.

Speculate Books were easier to make, so they became more widespread; it became easier to acquire knowledge; more people could learn to read.

Literature of the Period

Comprehension Check

1. How was early Anglo-Saxon literature distributed and passed down? *Early Anglo-Saxon literature was recited, not written down.*
2. In what language was early British prose written? *Early British prose was written in Latin.*
3. (a) What is elegiac poetry? (b) When was it an important form? *(a) Elegiac poetry is poetry of mourning for a loved one or a vanished past. (b) It was an important form during the Anglo-Saxon period.*
4. Who sponsored the first plays, and what were they about? *The first plays were sponsored by the Church, and they concerned religious subjects such as Bible stories and the lives of the saints.*

Critical Thinking

1. Anglo-Saxon heroic poems tell the story of great warriors. Who might have been the audience for such poems? **[Infer]** *Anglo-Saxon nobles and warriors were a likely audience for these heroic poems.*
2. Monks originally wrote in Latin. What conclusions can you draw from the fact that *The Anglo-Saxon Chronicle* was written in Old English? **[Draw Conclusions]** *The English began to take their own, native tradition more seriously.*
3. (a) How is a morality play different from a mystery play? (b) Why might morality plays have emerged during the turmoil of the fifteenth century? **[Analyze Causes and Effects]** *(a) Morality plays had ordinary people as their main characters. Mystery plays used Bible characters. (b) Perhaps during times of trouble, people looked to see their own uncertainties and troubles dramatized on stage.*

Develop Understanding

◆ Critical Thinking

1. What kinds of events caused important changes in early English? **[Generalize]** *Conquest and invasion contributed to the development of early English.*
2. Review the examples of English words with Norman roots. What areas of life do you think the English words adapted from the Normans mostly concern? Explain. **[Draw Conclusions]** *Normans dominated the upper strata of society. They influenced the vocabulary of courtly behavior and etiquette.*

▶Critical Viewing◀

1. Use the map to determine what type of language the Danes brought to England. **[Interpret a Map]** *The Danes brought a Germanic language to England.*
2. Use the map to determine which people who contributed to the English language did not come from the European continent. **[Interpret a Map]** *The Celts who came from Ireland did not come from the Continent.*

Answers to Activities

Students can find the first eighteen lines of "The Prologue" to *The Canterbury Tales* in Chaucer's original Middle English on page 88. The subject of a Middle English sentence, like that of a modern English sentence, generally precedes and adjoins the verb. Common nouns are generally preceded by articles. "Little" words, such as *the* and *and,* appear in identical form in both languages. Many Middle English words, such as *melodyë,* are almost exactly like their modern forms but include a final e. Middle English used the verb form *hath,* no longer current in modern English. In some forms, verbs that otherwise resemble their modern equivalents end in *-en.* A *y* appears at the beginning of some verbs.

The Changing English Language

THE BEGINNINGS OF ENGLISH

by Richard Lederer

English

The rise of English as a planetary language is an unparalleled success story that begins long ago, in the middle of the fifth century A.D. Several large tribes of sea rovers, the Angles, Saxons, and Jutes, lived along the continental North Sea coast, from Denmark to Holland. Around A.D. 449, these Teutonic plunderers sailed across the water and invaded the islands then known as Britannia. (See the map of invasions on this page.) They found the land pleasant and the people easy to conquer, so they remained there. They brought with them a Low Germanic tongue that, in its new setting, became Anglo-Saxon, or Old English. In A.D. 827, King Egbert first named Britannia *Englaland,* "land of the Angles," after the chief people there.

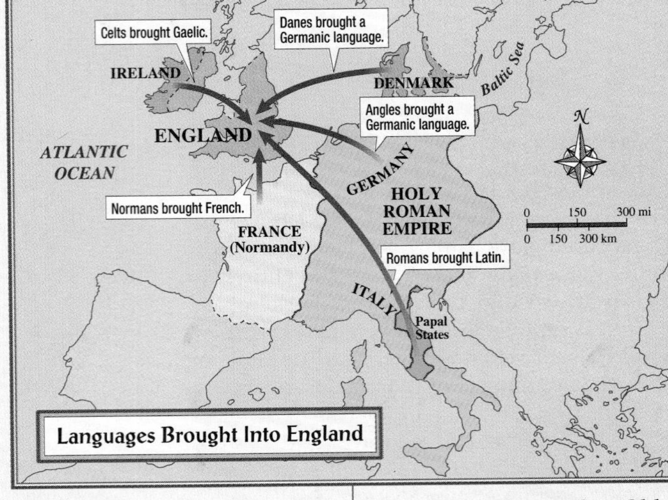

Languages Brought Into England

The language came to be called *Englisc.* Old Englisc differs so much from modern English that it is harder for us to learn than German or Latin. Still, we can recognize a number of Anglo-Saxon words: *bedd, candel, eorth, faederm froendscipe, healf, healp, mann, moder,* and *waeter.*

Middle English

A dramatic evolution in the language came after yet another conquest of England, this one by the Norman French two centuries after the rule of Egbert. The new conquerors came from Normandy, a province of France across the English Channel. These Normans (shortened from *Northmen*) had originally been Viking freebooters from Scandinavia, but they now spoke French and had taken to French customs. Their *triouveurs,* or minstrels, sang the *Song of Roland* and the legends of King Charlemagne.

In 1066, under William, Duke of Normandy, the Normans invaded England. In a bloody battle at Hastings they conquered the Saxons and Danes who resisted them, killed the Saxon king, Harold, and forced the nobles to choose Duke William as king of England.

One result was that Old Englisc changed rapidly as many of the French words used by the Normans flooded the vocabulary of their adopted tongue. Examples include *sir* and *madam; courtesy, honor,* and *chivalry; dine, table,* and *roast;* and *court* and *royal.* From this infusion of French words emerged a tongue that we today call Middle English.

Activities

Examine a passage from Geoffrey Chaucer's *The Canterbury Tales.* In what way do the vocabulary, word forms, and word order resemble Modern English? In what ways are the two languages different?

Listening to Old and Middle English

Have students listen to the readings in Old English (from *Beowulf*) and in Middle English (from "The Prologue" to *The Canterbury Tales*) on the **Listening to Literature Audiocassettes.**

Before playing the reading from *Beowulf,* have students read lines 530–542 of that poem in the Burton Raffel translation on page 40. Knowing the basic meaning of the passage that is read may help them identify words. Ask them what words they recognized. *Students may recognize the words* sweord *(sword) and* mon *(man), among others.*

Have students listen to the Middle English before doing the Activities on page 10. To prepare for the reading, have them scan and sound out the Middle English on page 88. After they hear the recording, ask them whether the Middle English was easier to understand than the Old English. *Most should answer yes.* Ask them how much they understood, and have them use a dictionary to identify words with Anglo-Saxon and French roots. *An Anglo-Saxon word is* droghte *(drought); a word with a French root is* vertu *(virtue).*

PART 1 # *Earthly Exile, Heavenly Home*

Arrival of William at Penvesy (detail from Bayeux Tapestry)

One-Minute Planning Guide

The selections in this section explore the theme of exile in Anglo-Saxon poetry. "The Seafarer" tells the tale of a sailor whose passion for the sea causes him to undertake dangerous, lonely voyages. The plight of a warrior who must find a new place in the world after his lord dies is described in "The Wanderer." In "The Wife's Lament," a woman whose husband has sent her away describes her misfortune. The theme of exile in world literature is examined in the selections from *Tristia* and "Far Corners of Earth."

Customize for
Varying Student Needs

When assigning the selections in this part, keep in mind these factors:

"The Seafarer"
- English language learners and less proficient readers may need assistance with breaking down long sentences
- Cultural context is necessary to understanding

"The Wanderer"
- Long, complex sentences
- Less proficient readers may need coaching in reading in sentences

"The Wife's Lament"
- Students may have difficulty understanding the wife's situation
- The structure of Anglo-Saxon verse may confuse less proficient readers

from *Tristia*
- An understanding of the poet's situation is essential to the understanding of this poem
- Reference to places, people, and gods may need to be clarified

"Far Corners of Earth"
- Very brief
- Simple vocabulary

Humanities: Art

Arrival of William at Penvesy (detail from Bayeux Tapestry).

The Bayeux Tapestry commemorates the conquest of England by William the Conqueror in 1066 and was probably commissioned by William's half-brother Odo, the bishop of Bayeux. The tapestry has embroidered on it over seventy scenes portraying William's arrival in England from Normandy, France, and his victory over the British King Harold in the Battle of Hastings.

Have your students link the art to the focus of this part, "Earthly Exile, Heavenly Home," by answering the following questions:

1. The Bayeux Tapestry shows over seventy details from a historical event. What historical event might be commemorated in such an artwork today? *Sample answers: A contemporary Bayeux Tapestry might show the conquest of space, beginning with the first airplanes; it might show a presidential campaign, beginning with earlier events in the candidates' careers.*
2. This great work about a nonreligious subject was probably commissioned by a bishop and displayed in his cathedral. What do these facts tell you about the role of the Church in the Middle Ages? *These facts suggest that the Church was actively involved in political and international events in the Middle Ages.*

Prepare and Engage

OBJECTIVES

1. To read, comprehend, interpret, and respond to Anglo-Saxon lyric poetry
2. To relate the poems to personal experience
3. To use a variety of literal comprehension strategies to facilitate comprehension
4. To identify characteristics of Anglo-Saxon lyric poetry
5. To build vocabulary in context and learn forms of the word *grievous*
6. To recognize and form compound predicates
7. To retell a story through song, using a specific sequence of events
8. To respond to Anglo-Saxon lyric poetry through writing, speaking and listening, and projects

SKILLS INSTRUCTION

Vocabulary: Related Words: Forms of *Grievous*

Grammar and Style: Compound Predicates

Reading for Success: Literal Comprehension Strategies

Literary Focus: Anglo-Saxon Lyrics

Writing: Sequence of Events

Speaking and Listening: Oral Interpretation (teacher edition)

Critical Viewing: Classify; Evaluate; Hypothesize; Compare and Contrast

PORTFOLIO OPPORTUNITIES

Writing: Funeral Oration; Analysis of Theme; Comparison and Contrast

Writing Mini-Lesson: Song

Speaking and Listening: Demonstration of Caesuras; Oral Interpretation

Project: Help Wanted; Portrait

More About Anglo-Saxon Lyric Poetry

These poems describe difficult lives led in a dark, forbidding world, where earthly comforts are few, and where a person may meet his or her fate at any moment. When the speaker in these poems does recall a pleasure, such as companionship, love, or the mead-hall, he or she sees it as fleeting or lost forever. Yet the longing for something more, usually a spiritual home, in combination with deeply emotional ways of speaking vividly recaptures the experience of exile in the Anglo-Saxon world.

Guide for Interpreting

The Exeter Book

Before *Star Wars* A family gathers with a group of friends to see the latest installment of their favorite drama. The following day, almost everyone in town is discussing the event and reenacting exciting passages. This event may sound to you like the opening of the latest movie thriller, but it also accurately describes a popular form of entertainment during Britain's Anglo-Saxon period.

> ***Anglo-Saxon communities gathered to listen to storytellers weave tales of enchantment, heroes, and the everyday.***

Telling the Story Very few people were able to read during this period. As a result, an oral tradition flourished in which traveling storytellers, known as *scops,* would entertain the masses. Through the years, many stories ceased to be told and were lost. Others, however, have been preserved because they were eventually written down.

The Exeter Book "The Seafarer," "The Wanderer," and "The Wife's Lament" were all discovered in a collection of manuscripts called *The Exeter Book.* The book was probably compiled by monks during the reign of Alfred the Great, between 871 and 899. The history of *The Exeter Book* is a mystery to scholars, but it has evidently survived some rough treatment. The book has a large burn in the manuscript, several stains from a drinking mug, and marks that look almost as if the book had been used as a cutting board! Without *The Exeter Book,* many stories that came out of the oral tradition would have been lost to us forever.

◆ Background for Understanding

CULTURE: THE MEANING OF EXILE

To be in exile is to be forced to leave one's home. We cannot understand what exile meant to Anglo-Saxons until we understand what they meant by "home." While we identify ourselves as citizens of a certain country, an Anglo-Saxon warrior viewed himself as the follower of a particular lord or king. The notion of loyalty toward one's country, called patriotism today, did not exist. It was the lord himself who commanded allegiance: He dispensed bread, fruit, and goods won in raids and skirmishes. Perhaps even more important, he guaranteed the security of his followers in a dangerous and uncertain world.

The most important symbol of home for Anglo-Saxon warriors was the mead-hall (mead was an alcoholic beverage made of honey and water), where the lord and his followers shared the warmth of fire, food and drink, and entertainment such as hearing poetry recited. The pleasures of poetry were especially welcome when the *scop* praised the heroism of the listening warriors. Enlivened with a feeling of fellowship, the mead-hall was smoky, noisy, smelly, and crowded. It was home.

Journal Writing Suppose that you were forced to leave your home. List some of the things that you would miss the most.

Prentice Hall Literature Program Resources

REINFORCE / RETEACH / EXTEND

Selection Support Pages
Build Vocabulary: Related Words: Forms of *Grievous,* p. 1
Grammar and Style: Compound Predicates, p. 2
Reading for Success: Literal Comprehension Strategies, pp. 3–4
Literary Focus: Anglo-Saxon Lyrics, p. 5

Strategies for Diverse Student Needs, p. 1

Beyond Literature
Cross-Curricular Connection: Social Studies, p. 1

Formal Assessment Selection Test, pp. 1–3; Assessment Resources Software

Alternative Assessment, p. 1

Writing and Language Transparencies
Daily Language Practice: Week 1, p. 136

Resource Pro CD-ROM "The Seafarer," "The Wanderer," "The Wife's Lament"—includes all resource material and customizable lesson plan

Listening to Literature Audiocassettes "The Seafarer," "The Wanderer," "The Wife's Lament"

Literature CD-ROM
How to Read and Understand Poetry, Feature 2

MODEL SELECTION

◆ The Seafarer ◆ The Wanderer ◆ The Wife's Lament

◆ Literature and Your Life

CONNECT YOUR EXPERIENCE

You are forced to leave home and live among strangers in another country. You don't know the language or customs, nor do you like the food served in this country. All you dream of is returning home, but you can't.

In the poems you're about to read, three speakers tell the story of how they came to live in exile and how they survived.

THEMATIC FOCUS: EARTHLY EXILE, HEAVENLY HOME

When these poems were written, it was not uncommon for people to lose their family, friends, and home following a great battle. How do you think they coped with such devastating losses?

◆ Build Vocabulary

RELATED WORDS: FORMS OF *GRIEVOUS*

"The Wanderer" contains the word *grievous*, which is related to the verb *grieve*, meaning "to feel deep sorrow or distress." By knowing the meaning of the verb, you can determine that the adjective *grievous* means "causing sorrow" or "hard to bear."

WORD BANK

Before you read, preview this list of words from the poems.

admonish
sentinel
fervent
rancor
compassionate
grievous
rapture
redress
blithe

◆ Grammar and Style

COMPOUND PREDICATES

One characteristic of Anglo-Saxon poetry is the use of **compound predicates**. A predicate is the sentence part that says something about the subject; it includes the verb and its modifiers. When a sentence or poetic line contains more than one verb that has the same subject, it has a compound predicate.

In this example, the subject is *sea*. The three verbs in the compound predicate are in italics. Notice how the compound predicate creates a rolling effect that mirrors the motion of the sea.

> . . . It tells/How the sea *took* me, *swept* me back/And forth in sorrow and fear and pain,/*Showed* me suffering in a hundred ships,/In a thousand ports, and in me. . . .

◆ Literary Focus

ANGLO-SAXON LYRICS

A **lyric poem** expresses the thoughts and feelings of a single speaker, usually by recounting events in the speaker's life. One type of lyric poem is the elegy, in which the loss of someone or something is mourned. All three poems that follow are elegies.

Because **Anglo-Saxon lyrics** sprang from the oral tradition, they were composed in a way that made them easy to memorize. The poems have been translated with an effort to preserve the rhythms and imagery of the original versions.

Most Anglo-Saxon poetry contained lines with regular rhythms, usually four strong beats or stresses to a line. In "The Wanderer" and "The Wife's Lament," a sound break called a **caesura** appears in the middle of each line, indicating a pause for breath in the reading. This caesura was probably a useful device for scops who had to recite hundreds of lines of poetry.

Another notable feature of Anglo-Saxon poetry is the **kenning**, a two-word metaphorical name for something, such as "whales' home" for the sea. Kennings were clever ways of renaming familiar things; for example, a modern kenning might be "bird's nest" for someone's messy hair.

Preparing for Standardized Tests

Reading and Vocabulary The Build Vocabulary lesson focuses on words related to *grieve*, thereby providing a specific example of how affixes produce related nouns, verbs, adjectives, and adverbs. Familiarity with related words provides a cognitive framework that helps students deduce the meaning of unfamiliar words. For additional practice, use the Build Vocabulary page in ***Selection Support***, p. 1.

Grammar and Style Certain questions on standardized tests require students to make choices about improving a flawed paragraph. Such items may draw on an understanding of compound predicates, as in the following:

They boarded the ship. They packed their belongings. They were looking for adventure.

(A) (As it is now)

(B) They boarded the ship, packed their belongings, and looked for adventure.

(C) Looking for adventure, they boarded the ship. They packed their belongings.

For practice with compound predicates, use the Grammar and Style page, p. 2, in ***Selection Support***.

What is exile? Does it happen today? How do people survive it? To make the theme of exile more concrete for students, have them imagine that they are sent away forever from their home, their friends, and their community. Ask each student to imagine a place of exile, such as a foreign country, the wilderness, the sea, or space. Then have students imagine themselves in this place permanently—and without contact with those they love. Ask students to list, in order of importance, things and people they would yearn for and feelings they might have. Also ask students to name the kinds of hopes and dreams that might sustain them.

Customize for
Less Proficient Readers

Draw a who, what, where, when, why organizer on the chalkboard. Model how you would fill it in for "The Seafarer." Encourage students to make and complete a similar organizer for "The Wanderer" and "The Wife's Lament."

Customize for
Visual/Spatial Learners

Invite students to jot down notes about the things they can see in their mind's eye as they read each of the poems. For the poem of their choice, ask whether they were satisfied with the way it was illustrated in the text and, if so, why, or whether they would have selected or drawn other illustrations and, if so, what.

Customize for
English Language Learners

Encourage English language learners to draw meaning from each poem stanza by stanza rather than word by word. These students might record a main idea for each stanza. When they are finished reading, students can use these ideas to summarize the poem.

Customize for
More Advanced Students

Challenge more advanced students to create a paragraph or more of introductory text for each of the poems in which they explain who the speaker is and what the main idea of the poem is. The introduction should also briefly tell what makes the poem special or unique.

Reading for Success

The Reading for Success page in each unit presents a set of problem-solving procedures to help readers understand authors' words and ideas on multiple levels. Good readers develop a bank of strategies from which they can draw as needed.

Unit 1 introduces strategies for literal comprehension. It is important for students to understand a work on its literal level before they apply higher-level critical thinking strategies. These strategies for literal comprehension give readers an approach for attacking text on a surface level—recognize the historical context and the characteristics of the period, reread or read ahead, break down long or confusing sentences, use context clues, and restate for understanding.

These strategies for literal comprehension are modeled with "The Seafarer." Each green box shows an example of the thinking process involved in applying one of these strategies.

How to Use the Reading for Success Page

- Introduce the literal comprehension strategies, presenting each as a problem-solving procedure. Be sure students understand what each strategy involves and under what circumstances to apply it.
- Before students read the story, have them preview it, looking at the annotations in the green boxes that model the strategies.
- To reinforce these strategies after students have read "The Seafarer," have students do the Reading for Success pages in ***Selection Support,*** pp. 3–4. These pages give students an opportunity to read a selection and practice literal comprehension strategies by writing their own annotations.

Reading for Success

Literal Comprehension Strategies

To fully appreciate literature, you first must have a clear understanding of the basics: What's happening and to whom? Where is it happening? Why is it happening? Often the answers to these questions are found in the text of the story, poem, or piece of nonfiction. Successful readers use a few simple strategies to make sense of confusing or difficult passages of literature.

Use one of the following strategies to unlock the meaning of troublesome passages you encounter:

Recognize the historical context and the characteristics of the period.

Knowing about the period from which a work comes will help you comprehend the writer's words and ideas. The introduction to this unit provides background on the period.

Reread or read ahead.

- ▶ Reread a sentence or a paragraph to find the connections among the words or to connect the ideas in several sentences.
- ▶ Read ahead. A confusing detail may become clear further on.

Break down long or confusing sentences.

- ▶ Figure out the subject of the sentence and what the sentence is saying about the subject. You may need to rearrange the parts of a sentence or to take other groups of words out of the way to do this.

Use context clues.

Context refers to the words, phrases, and sentences that surround a word. You can often use clues in the context to figure out the meaning of an unfamiliar word.

> . . . Who could understand / . . . what we others suffer / As the paths of exile stretch endlessly on?

The words "suffer" and "stretch endlessly" provide clues that exile is something that involves long suffering.

Restate for understanding.

- ▶ Paraphrase, or restate a sentence or a paragraph in your own words.
- ▶ Summarize; review and state the main points of what has happened.

As you read "The Seafarer," read the side notes, which demonstrate how to apply these strategies to a work of early English literature.

Reading Strategies: Support and Reinforcement

Appropriate Reading Strategies Students are given a reading strategy to apply in reading each selection. In those selections where surface language may be challenging, students are given one of these literal comprehension strategies. In other selections a strategy is suggested that is appropriate to the selection.

Reading Prompts To encourage application of the given reading strategy, there are occasional prompts, within green boxes, at appropriate and significant points.

In addition, there are red boxes prompting application of the Literary Focus concept and maroon boxes prompting students to connect with their lives.

Using the Boxed Annotations and Prompts The material in the green, red, and maroon boxes along the sides of selections is intended to help students apply the literary element and the reading strategy and to make a connection with their lives. You may use the boxed material in several ways:

- Have students pause when they come to a box and respond to its prompt before they continue reading.
- Urge students to read through the selection ignoring the boxes. After they have read the selection completely, they may go back and review the selection, responding to the prompts.

MODEL

The Seafarer

Translated by Burton Raffel

Ships With Three Men, Fish
Bodleian Library, Oxford

Critical Viewing ▶ Which elements in this picture are true to the seafarer's experience? Which elements are stylized? **[Classify]**

❷ **Read ahead** to understand that the speaker is a sailor who is speaking about his life on the sea.

This tale is true, and mine. It tells
How the sea took me, swept me back
And forth in sorrow and fear and pain,
Showed me suffering in a hundred ships,
In a thousand ports, and in me. It tells
Of smashing surf when I sweated in the cold
Of an anxious watch, perched in the bow
As it dashed under cliffs. My feet were cast ❸

Develop Understanding

One-Minute Insight

Who could be more alone and wretched than the lonely seafarer, drifting in icy waters, far from human companionship? Yet, though the seafarer "drowns in desolation" at sea, he returns to it again and again, for life itself, no matter where it is spent, is exile: The only home is heaven.

◆ Critical Thinking

Speculate Explain that in "The Seafarer," the speaker undertakes ocean voyages despite their loneliness and danger. Show students a map of the British Isles. Ask: Why is the sea a common subject in British poetry? *Since Britain is composed of islands, the sea plays an important role in daily life.*

▶Critical Viewing◀

❶ **Classify** Students may observe that the perspective is flat and that the too-small boat, triangular rigging, many-finned whale, and waves on the water are stylized. The sailors' clothing, the rudder, and sail may be true to the seafarer's experience.

◆ Reading for Success

❷ **Read Ahead** Explain to students that the poem will reveal all the tribulations the seafarer faced at sea. It will conclude with some reason for why he faced them.

◆ Critical Thinking

❸ **Support** Ask students: What are three things in this first stanza that you can see or hear in your imagination? *Possible answers: A ship being tossed in the waves, different ships and different ports, the roar of pounding surf.*

Humanities: Art

Ships With Three Men, Fish, illuminated manuscript.

In this illustration, three men in a boat are confronted by a whale. Although the whale does not seem to threaten the men and is busy feeding on fish, the men seem anxious and intent on navigating their sailboat out of the whale's reach.

The illustration lacks the perspective we take for granted. The sea is interpreted as an abstract shape with linear wave patterns. The shapes representing the boat and fish seem plunked on top of the water. Not only is perspective missing, but so is realism. The whale is so fancifully depicted, with numerous and curling fins, that it seems likely the artist never saw a whale. Yet the size of the whale and its proximity to the boat enable the artist to convey that this is a fearful moment.

Use these questions for discussion:

1. Does this illustration help you to visualize what the seafarer relates? Explain. *Running into a whale is not one of the hardships that the seafarer relates. Also the seafarer was completely alone, whereas three men travel together in this boat.*
2. Do any of the sailors in this illustration seem to share the feelings of the seafarer? Explain. *Possible response: The sailor who is seated seems most like the seafarer because he appears to accept his fate.*

Customize for *Musical/Rhythmic Learners*

❶ Challenge small groups of students to interpret, practice, and perform this very powerful stanza, beginning with the first line of the poem and continuing through line 26. Ask students to re-create not only the rhythm and tone but also some of the background sounds that the seafarer would have experienced.

◆ Reading for Success

❷ **Break Down Long Sentences; Restate for Understanding** Have students break down and restate lines 27–38. *Those who know the pleasures of cities could not believe how often I went back to sea and how the sea called to my soul.*

Customize for *Intrapersonal Learners*

❸ Ask intrapersonal learners to close their eyes and think about what hobbies or activities seem to call to them that perhaps no one else, or very few other people, could understand. Students might record in a journal the reasons why they make the choices they make, and how they are drawn to these choices as the seafarer is drawn to the sea.

Comprehension Check ☑

❹ Ask students: What do things like orchards blooming and lovely fields admonish, or advise, the seafarer not to do? *They warn him not to go back to sea.*

Writing and Language Transparencies To teach grammar and style skills with information about Anglo-Saxons, use the Daily Language Practice, Week 1 (p. 136).

Literature CD-ROM Students can learn more about poetry and the oral tradition by viewing Feature 2 in *How to Read and Understand Poetry.*

In icy bands, bound with frost,
With frozen chains, and hardship groaned
Around my heart. Hunger tore
At my sea-weary soul. No man sheltered
On the quiet fairness of earth can feel
How wretched I was, drifting through winter
On an ice-cold sea, whirled in sorrow,
Alone in a world blown clear of love,
Hung with icicles. The hailstorms flew.
❶ The only sound was the roaring sea,
The freezing waves. The song of the swan
Might serve for pleasure, the cry of the sea-fowl,
The death-noise of birds instead of laughter,
The mewing of gulls instead of mead.[1]
Storms beat on the rocky cliffs and were echoed
By icy-feathered terns and the eagle's screams;
No kinsman could offer comfort there,
To a soul left drowning in desolation.
And who could believe, knowing but
The passion of cities, swelled proud with wine
And no taste of misfortune, how often, how wearily,
I put myself back on the paths of the sea.
Night would blacken; it would snow from the north;
Frost bound the earth and hail would fall,
❷ The coldest seeds. And how my heart
Would begin to beat, knowing once more
The salt waves tossing and the towering sea!
The time for journeys would come and my soul
Called me eagerly out, sent me over
The horizon, seeking foreigners' homes.
But there isn't a man on earth so proud,
So born to greatness, so bold with his youth,
Grown so brave, or so graced by God,
That he feels no fear as the sails unfurl,
❸ Wondering what Fate has willed and will do.
No harps ring in his heart, no rewards,
No passion for women, no worldly pleasures,
Nothing, only the ocean's heave;
But longing wraps itself around him.
Orchards blossom, the towns bloom,
Fields grow lovely as the world springs fresh,
❹ And all these admonish that willing mind
Leaping to journeys, always set
In thoughts traveling on a quickening tide.
So summer's sentinel, the cuckoo, sings

Paraphrase lines 12–17 to clarify their meaning: No landlubber can understand my misery. All winter long I was sailing on the cold sea. I was filled with sorrow and felt alone in a loveless, cold world.

Use **context clues** to figure out the meaning of *terns* (l. 24); "icy-feathered" helps you see that terns are a kind of bird.

Break down and **restate** this long, confusing passage (lines 47–52): The loveliness of one's home in spring serves to scold a person who is always looking for adventure in places other than home.

1. **mead:** Liquor made from fermented honey and water.

Block Scheduling Strategies

Consider these suggestions to take advantage of extended class time:

- Ask students to listen to one or more of the poems on audiocassette. Have them listen for ways in which the performer or reader re-creates the rhythms, breaks the lines in the middle, and brings the tone of the speaker to life. Have students comment on the ways in which listening to the tape enhances their understanding of one of the poems.
- As they read, have students respond individually or in pairs to the Reading for Success prompts.
- Direct students to work in pairs or small groups to complete the Guide for Responding that follows each of the poems (pp. 19, 23, 25).
- Give students an opportunity to plan their approach to the Writing Mini-Lesson (p. 27). Encourage students to discuss their choice of a poem and their ideas for a refrain with one another. Have students share their drafts for their songs with one another and make suggestions.
- Instruct students to work individually or in groups of three to complete the project of their choice in the Idea Bank (p. 27).

In his murmuring voice, and our hearts mourn
As he urges. Who could understand,
In ignorant ease, what we others suffer
As the paths of exile stretch endlessly on?
And yet my heart wanders away,
My soul roams with the sea, the whales'
Home, wandering to the widest corners
Of the world, returning ravenous with desire,
Flying solitary, screaming, exciting me
To the open ocean, breaking oaths
On the curve of a wave. ❺
Thus the joys of God
Are fervent with life, where life itself
Fades quickly into the earth. The wealth
Of the world neither reaches to Heaven nor remains.
No man has ever faced the dawn
Certain which of Fate's three threats
Would fall: illness, or age, or an enemy's ❻
Sword, snatching the life from his soul.
The praise the living pour on the dead
Flowers from reputation: plant
An earthly life of profit reaped
Even from hatred and rancor, of bravery
Flung in the devil's face, and death
Can only bring you earthly praise
And a song to celebrate a place
With the angels, life eternally blessed
In the hosts of Heaven.
The days are gone
When the kingdoms of earth flourished in glory; ❼
Now there are no rulers, no emperors,
No givers of gold, as once there were,
When wonderful things were worked among them
And they lived in lordly magnificence.
Those powers have vanished, those pleasures are dead.
The weakest survives and the world continues,
Kept spinning by toil. All glory is tarnished.
The world's honor ages and shrinks,
Bent like the men who mold it. Their faces
Blanch as time advances, their beards
Wither and they mourn the memory of friends.
The sons of princes, sown in the dust.
The soul stripped of its flesh knows nothing
Of sweetness or sour, feels no pain,
Bends neither its hand nor its brain. A brother
Opens his palms and pours down gold
On his kinsman's grave, strewing his coffin ❽

Recognize the **characteristics of the period** in lines 64–80: Anglo-Saxons were new to Christianity, and religious themes and ideas pervade their literature and philosophy.

Use **historical context.** In lines 81–86, the speaker mourns the passage of a golden era. The Anglo-Saxons lived in a world of confusion and uncertainty.

◆ Build Vocabulary

admonish (ad män´ ish) *v.*: Advise; caution

sentinel (sen´ ti nəl) *n.*: Person or animal that guards or watches over

fervent (fur´ vənt) *adj.*: Having or showing great warmth of feeling

rancor (raŋ´ kər) *n.*: Ill will

◆ Background for Understanding

❺ **Culture** Point out that the exile described in this poem is self-imposed. The seafarer cannot resist the call of the sea, but he does have a home to which he returns from time to time. Nevertheless, his exile seems no less lonely or profound than the exile of a person who has been forced to leave.

◆ Reading for Success

❻ **Recognize the Historical Context and the Characteristics of the Period** Here the speaker talks about the uncertainty of life. In Anglo-Saxon times, life expectancy was so short that a person's existence could easily be cut off in his or her twenties or thirties; also, in a time of marauding armies and bandits, one could easily die by the sword.

◆ Literature and Your Life

❼ Explain to students that the speaker regrets how things have changed, how the present is different from the past. Then ask students to name changes that a modern writer of elegies might mourn. *Students may suggest that the world is more crowded, more polluted, busier, more impersonal, or more insecure than the world of the past.*

◆ Reading for Success

❽ **Reread or Read Ahead** Direct students to reread lines 82–102. Have students explain what is going on in this passage. *The speaker is using a variety of examples here to make his point that the world has lost its meaning, and is leading up to his main idea that all that truly matters is the heavenly home.* Then ask them to explain how rereading improves their comprehension of a passage. *Students may say that rereading helps them remember the ideas in a passage and to see the connections among them.*

Cultural Connection

Explain to students that different cultures have different opinions about the role of fate in people's lives. These opinions can be seen as running along a continuum. At one end are those who believe that there is no free choice whatsoever; at the other end are those who believe that people have responsibility for everything that happens in their lives. The Greeks believed that human life was subject to the whims of the gods, whereas Chaldean Egyptians, who introduced astrology, believed that the position of the planets had a direct influence on people's lives. The Catholic Church suggests that people have free will, while Hinduism combines fate with free will in the concept of karma, the belief that life in the present is determined by actions in past lives but that people are free to improve their character for future lives.

Have students research and compare concepts of fate such as determinism, free will, karma, kismet, reincarnation, and biology as destiny. Ask how these belief systems might affect a person's behavior.

▶Critical Viewing◀

❶ **Evaluate** Students may say that the painting, like the poem, captures the loneliness of the seafarer and the vastness of the sea. Some students may say that the light illuminating the horizon is a sunrise and suggests the hope of heaven; others may say that it is a sunset, a reminder of the inevitability of death.

◆Reading for Success

❷ **Recognize the Historical Context and the Characteristics of the Period** Point out that the Anglo-Saxons would have believed that God quite literally turned the Earth, just as we might wind up an analog watch. When the speaker says, "We all fear God," he is referring to the awe felt toward a great and powerful god, the presence of whom explains all the mysteries that the Anglo-Saxons had not yet developed the science to understand.

◆Grammar and Style

❸ **Compound Predicates** Ask students to identify the verbs in the compound predicate in lines 104–105. *The verbs are* set *and* gave.

Arthur Going to Avalon for "The High Kings" (detail), George Sharp

❶ ▲ **Critical Viewing** How well does this painting capture the theme of exile as it is treated in the poem? **[Evaluate]**

With treasures intended for Heaven, but nothing
Golden shakes the wrath of God
For a soul overflowing with sin, and nothing
Hidden on earth rises to Heaven.
❷ We all fear God. He turns the earth,
He set it swinging firmly in space,
❸ Gave life to the world and light to the sky.
Death leaps at the fools who forget their God.
He who lives humbly has angels from Heaven
To carry him courage and strength and belief.
A man must conquer pride, not kill it,
Be firm with his fellows, chaste for himself,
Treat all the world as the world deserves,
With love or with hate but never with harm,
Though an enemy seek to scorch him in hell,

Paraphrase lines 103–124: We should think about heaven and how we might earn eternal life and happiness, which is given through loving God and living a Christian life.

Humanities: Art

Arthur Going to Avalon (detail), 1983, by George Sharp.

George Sharp is a contemporary British illustrator who began painting professionally in 1975. He studied art at the Nottingham School of Art in England.

Sharp created this painting for Joy Chant's book *The High Kings*, which was published in 1983. Executed in transparent color washes on canvas, this painting has a misty, dreamlike quality.

Use the following questions for discussion:

1. What mood does the painting create? How does the mood of the painting compare to the mood of the poem? *Students may describe the mood of the painting as peaceful, lonely, or sad. Students might observe that the mood of the poem is also lonely, but is far less peaceful with its images of "smashing surf" and "an enemy's/Sword."*
2. Does this contemporary painting technique properly illustrate this poem? Why or why not? *Some students may think that a modern painting is not appropriate for an ancient Anglo-Saxon poem. Other students may express the opinion that any painting that captures the content and mood of a literary work is an appropriate illustration.*

Or set the flames of a funeral pyre
Under his lord. Fate is stronger
And God mightier than any man's mind.
Our thoughts should turn to where our home is,
Consider the ways of coming there,
Then strive for sure permission for us
To rise to that eternal joy,
That life born in the love of God
And the hope of Heaven. Praise the Holy
Grace of Him who honored us,
Eternal, unchanging creator of earth. Amen.

Beyond Literature

Science Connection

Early Navigation "My soul roams with the sea" says the speaker of "The Seafarer." In order to roam the seas, he had to rely upon early navigation techniques. The earliest sailors used landmarks to help guide short trips. For longer ocean voyages, a sailor used the temperature of the wind to determine direction—a cold wind came from the north and a warm wind came from the south. Early sailors also guided themselves by observing celestial bodies, noting the directions of sunrise and sunset, shadows cast by the noon-day sun, and the rising and setting of the night stars. Finally, navigators recorded all their methods of plotting courses, making it possible for others to follow the same routes. When you take a trip, what aids do you use to help you follow your course?

Guide for Responding

◆ Literature and Your Life

Reader's Response Do you agree that "Fate is stronger . . . than any man's mind"? Why or why not?

Thematic Focus In what ways is the seafarer in exile? How do his ideas of heaven compare with his earthly experience?

Draw Comparisons Take a few moments to draw a comparison between the sailor of old and a modern figure who experiences the same need for travel and risk-taking.

☑ Check Your Comprehension

1. To what is the speaker constantly drawn?
2. To what does the speaker compare the relationship of man and the sea?
3. What does the seafarer miss about the days of the past?
4. According to the speaker, what qualities might earn a person a place in heaven?

◆ Critical Thinking

INTERPRET

1. What are three images the poet uses in the first stanza to convey his sense of isolation? **[Support]**
2. How might you explain the mixed feelings about the sea that the poet seems to feel? **[Interpret]**
3. What contrast is implied in lines 80–102? **[Compare and Contrast]**

APPLY

4. Explain how a person can dislike something as much as the seafarer dislikes life at sea and yet keep going back to it. **[Hypothesize]**

◆ Literary Focus

ANGLO-SAXON LYRICS: KENNING

One interesting element in Anglo-Saxon is the **kenning,** a two-word metaphorical name for something, like "summer's sentinel" for "cuckoo." Locate two more kennings in "The Seafarer." Explain how each enhances the poem's meaning.

◆ Reading for Success

❹ **Use Context Clues** Ask students what clues they could use to figure out the meaning of *pyre*. *They might use the word* funeral, *which modifies* pyre; *they might also use the word* flames *or the phrase "under his lord" to infer what a pyre is or where it can be found.*

◆ Critical Thinking

❺ **Hypothesize** Ask students: How do the seafarer's ideas about God and heaven help to explain why he keeps going back to sea? *His ideas about God and heaven seem to suggest that life on Earth is not as important as the heavenly home; where one lives is not the important thing; it is how one lives that matters.*

Reinforce and Extend

Answers

◆ Literature and Your Life

Reader's Response Students should cite specific examples from their lives or from their reading to support their opinions about the relative importance of fate and free will.

Thematic Focus The seafarer is in exile on his ocean voyages because he is far from home, family, and the comforts of life on land. To him, heaven is "eternal joy," whereas his earthly experiences are a detailed catalog of specific miseries.

☑ Check Your Comprehension

1. He is drawn to the sea.
2. He compares it to the relationship between man and God.
3. He misses the glory and strong rulers.
4. These qualities, which are described in lines 106–115, include humility, chastity, fairness, and forgiveness.

◆ Critical Thinking

1. Students may cite the images of loneliness, desolation, and exile in lines 16, 18–19, 25–26, 57, and 59–60.
2. Suggested response: Although the sailor knows the perils and hardships of the sea, he is overpowered by his attachment to seafaring.
3. In these lines the poet contrasts the world of his day and the world of an earlier, heroic time.
4. Suggested response: A person's attraction to something may outweigh any fear of its negative aspects. Despite the negatives, something may be perceived as better than its alternatives.

◆ Literary Focus

The kenning "coldest seeds" (line 33) sharpens the contrast between the icy sea and warm, fruitful land. The kenning "givers of gold" (line 83) provides a vivid image of the generosity and wealth of past rulers.

Develop Understanding

One-Minute Insight The wanderer in this poem has experienced the complete collapse of his entire world: His lord has died. That means he has no more purpose, no more friends, no more hopes of enjoying treasures, no one to feast with, and no one's knee upon which to lay his hand and head and promise loyalty. He is alone, cast out, left to wander in search of a new lord.

Enrichment This poem probably dates to the 700's or earlier, at a time when Scandinavia was in upheaval and many sailors fled ancestral homes there to settle finally in England. The poem might have reminded its northern English audience of the struggles their forebears met before reaching England. Point out that modern immigrants also may recite poems, tell stories, and sing songs about their former homeland. Ask students to describe the ways in which their families or people whom they know keep the traditions of their ancestors.

►Critical Viewing◄

❶ **Hypothesize** Students may suggest that the castle might have been destroyed in war, toppled by an earthquake, or simply abandoned and allowed to fall into ruin.

◆ Reading for Success

❷ **Restate for Understanding** The first sentence of the poem is difficult to read because it has an unexpected word order. Ask students to paraphrase it. *God's love comes often to the wanderer, who is sadly rowing in icy seas.*

The WANDERER

Translated by Charles W. Kennedy

Sketch for Hadleigh Castle, John Constable

❶ ▲ **Critical Viewing** Every picture tells a story. What might have happened in this setting to cause its ruined and desolate condition? **[Hypothesize]**

Oft to the wanderer, weary of exile,
Cometh God's pity, compassionate love,
❷ Though woefully toiling on wintry seas
With churning oar in the icy wave,
Homeless and helpless he fled from fate.
Thus saith the wanderer mindful of misery,
Grievous disasters, and death of kin:

Humanities: Art

Sketch for Hadleigh Castle, c. 1828–1829, by John Constable.

During his own time, Constable (1776–1837) was considered the greatest painter of the English landscape. Although he painted the final versions in his studio, Constable always did his sketches outdoors, not so much in order to capture precise details as to capture the light or the atmosphere surrounding his subject.

Constable's sketches were generally painted in oils on paper about twelve inches wide. In this sketch, the concentration of light becomes as much of a focal point as the ruins of the castle itself. Nevertheless, Constable believed that a landscape painting had to be based on what could be observed; it was not to be fanciful or purely imagined.

Use the following question for discussion: What lines from the poem might be used as a caption for this painting? *Suggested responses: "Walls stand rime-covered and swept by the winds./The battlements crumble, the wine-halls decay . . ."; ". . . these giant-built structures stand empty of life./He who shall muse on these moldering ruins,/And deeply ponder this darkling life,/Must brood on old legends of battle and bloodshed . . ."; "Where now is the warrior? Where is the war horse?/Bestowal of treasure, and sharing of feast?"*

"Oft when the day broke, oft at the dawning,
Lonely and wretched I wailed my woe.
No man is living, no comrade left.
To whom I dare fully unlock my heart.
I have learned truly the mark of a man
Is keeping his counsel and locking his lips,
Let him think what he will! For, woe of heart
Withstandeth not fate: a failing spirit
Earneth no help. Men eager for honor
Bury their sorrow deep in the breast.
"So have I also, often in wretchedness
Fettered[1] my feelings, far from my kin,
Homeless and hapless,[2] since days of old,
When the dark earth covered my dear lord's face,
And I sailed away with sorrowful heart,
Over wintry seas, seeking a gold-lord,
If far or near lived one to befriend me
With gift in the mead-hall and comfort for grief.
"Who bears it, knows what a bitter companion,
Shoulder to shoulder, sorrow can be,
When friends are no more. His fortune is exile,
Not gifts of fine gold; a heart that is frozen,
Earth's winsomeness[3] dead. And he dreams of the hall-men,
The dealing of treasure, the days of his youth,
When his lord bade welcome to wassail[4] and feast.
But gone is that gladness, and never again
Shall come the loved counsel of comrade and king.
"Even in slumber his sorrow assaileth,
And, dreaming he claspeth his dear lord again,
Head on knee, hand on knee, loyally laying,
Pledging his liege[5] as in days long past.
Then from his slumber he starts lonely-hearted,
Beholding gray stretches of tossing sea.
Sea-birds bathing, with wings outspread,
While hailstorms darken, and driving snow.
Bitterer then is the bane of his wretchedness,
The longing for loved one: his grief is renewed.

---

1. **fettered** (fet′ ərd): Chained; restrained.
2. **hapless** (hap′ lis): Unlucky.
3. **winsomeness** (win′ səm nəs): Pleasantness; delightfulness.
4. **wassail** (wäs′ əl): A toast in drinking a person's health, or a celebration at which such toasts are made.
5. **liege** (lēj): Loyalty.

◆ Build Vocabulary

compassionate (kəm pash′ ən it) *adj.*: Sympathizing; pitying
grievous (grēv′ əs) *adj.*: Causing sorrow; hard to bear

◆ Critical Thinking

3 Distinguish Ask students: How are these two lines different from the lines that came before them? *They are in the first person; the speaker has switched from a narrator to the wanderer.*

Customize for
More Advanced Students

4 Challenge students to define the ideal Anglo-Saxon man, based on clues from this poem and other poems in this unit. *Lines 10–20 suggest that the ideal Anglo-Saxon man is tight-lipped and hides his feelings.*

◆ Reading for Success

5 Reread or Read Ahead Explain that students will understand the meaning of "gold-lord" if they read ahead. They will learn that the wanderer seeks a new lord, so that he may experience the "dealing of treasure," or, presumably, gold dealt out by his lord, or "gold-lord."

Customize for
Bodily/Kinesthetic Learners

6 Students can be asked to act out the posture of the wanderer in deference to the lord, as well other moments in the poem that deal with movement.

Enrichment "The Wanderer" is considered the most nearly perfect in form and feeling of all Old English lyrics. This is partly because of the intensity of its emotion and partly because it shows the fewest signs of accidental mutilation or of deliberate tamperings by later copyists.

Cross-Curricular Connection: Social Studies

The Anglo-Saxons When the Anglo-Saxons conquered the area that is now part of England, they came as pagans and farmers. They were immensely skilled sailors who crossed the seas in shallow boats that did not have decks or masts. They used these boats to travel the high seas and also to follow inland rivers into Britain. Carrying spears, wooden shields, and longbows, each followed a chief, or a lord.

Soon after they arrived in England, the Anglo-Saxons fell under the influence of Christianity, which had been established by the Romans. St. Augustine and others drew them in by incorporating some pagan rituals into Christianity, by allowing women to receive communion, and by not punishing those who robbed the churches too heavily. These and other compromises, along with the hope of eternal relief from suffering, soon brought many converts.

◆ Critical Thinking

❶ **Analyze** Ask students: What does the wanderer imagine? *He imagines his comrades before him. The wanderer greets them, but they disappear without returning the greeting.*

◆ Grammar and Style

❷ **Compound Predicates** Ask students to identify the compound predicate in the clause that begins "day by day." *The predicate is "ages and droops unto death."*

❸ **Enrichment** Point out to students that this passage interrupts an intensely concrete and dramatic scene with a homily, a passage that gives general advice pertaining to morals and conduct. Some critics have argued that the homiletic passages in "The Wanderer" must be later additions to a poem that is otherwise remarkably terse, lyrical, intense, concrete, and dramatic. Other critics assert that the homilies are perfectly in character, even when they contradict attitudes expressed in other parts of the poem. In this view, they serve as an ironic device, showing the wanderer's belief in just at those moments when he is most overcome by grief.

◆ Critical Thinking

❹ **Analyze** Ask students what feeling is evoked by the images of the rime-covered walls and crumbling battlements. *Among many possible answers, students may say these images suggest destruction, despair, desolation, or time passing.*

The forms of his kinsmen take shape in the silence:
In rapture he greets them; in gladness he scans
❶ Old comrades remembered. But they melt into air
With no word of greeting to gladden his heart.
Then again surges his sorrow upon him;
And grimly he spurs his weary soul
Once more to the toil of the tossing sea.
"No wonder therefore, in all the world,
If a shadow darkens upon my spirit
When I reflect on the fates of men—
How one by one proud warriors vanish
❷ From the halls that knew them, and day by day
All this earth ages and droops unto death.
No man may know wisdom till many a winter
Has been his portion. A wise man is patient,
Not swift to anger, nor hasty of speech,
Neither too weak, nor too reckless, in war,
❸ Neither fearful nor fain,[6] nor too wishful of wealth,
Nor too eager in vow— ere he know the event.
A brave man must bide[7] when he speaketh his boast
Until he know surely the goal of his spirit.
"A wise man will ponder how dread is that doom
When all this world's wealth shall be scattered and waste
As now, over all, through the regions of earth,
❹ Walls stand rime-covered[8] and swept by the winds.
The battlements crumble, the wine-halls decay;
Joyless and silent the heroes are sleeping
Where the proud host fell by the wall they defended.
Some battle launched on their long, last journey;
One a bird bore o'er the billowing sea:
One the gray wolf slew; one a grieving earl
Sadly gave to the grave's embrace.
The Warden of men hath wasted this world
Till the sound of music and revel is stilled,
And these giant-built structures stand empty of life.
"He who shall muse on these moldering ruins,
And deeply ponder this darkling life,
Must brood on old legends of battle and bloodshed,
And heavy the mood that troubles his heart:
'Where now is the warrior? Where is the war horse?
Bestowal of treasure, and sharing of feast?
Alas! the bright ale-cup, the byrny-clad[9] warrior,
The prince in his splendor— those days are long sped
In the night of the past, as if they never had been!'
And now remains only, for warriors' memorial,
A wall wondrous high with serpent shapes carved.
Storms of ash-spears have smitten the earls,

---

6. **fain** (fān): Archaic word meaning "eager"; In this context it means "too eager."
7. **bide** (bīd): Wait.
8. **rime** (rīm)**-covered:** Covered with frost.
9. **byrny** (bər´ nē)**-clad:** Dressed in a coat of chain-mail armor.

Speaking and Listening Mini-Lesson

Oral Interpretation

This mini-lesson supports the Speaking and Listening activity in the Idea Bank on page 27.

Introduce the Concept Remind students that the *scop* might perform for a large gathering in a mead-hall. Elicit from students that in order to entertain and inspire the audience, the *scop* would have to project his or her voice, use gestures and facial expressions, and speak clearly and with feeling.

Develop Background Once students have selected the poem they will perform, ask them to do the following:

- Practice reading the poem aloud.
- Try out different tones of voice and degrees of loudness and softness.
- Highlight passages by slowing down or adding facial expressions and gestures.
- Assess whether their interpretation would suit the speaker.

Apply the Information Have students perform their oral interpretation for an audience.

Assess the Outcome Have students assess their own oral interpretation, as well as interpretations performed by other individuals, pairs, or groups. You may wish to distribute the Peer Assessment: Dramatic Performance in ***Alternative Assessment,*** p. 121.

Carnage of weapon,   and conquering fate.
"Storms now batter   these ramparts of stone;
Blowing snow   and the blast of winter
Enfold the earth;   night-shadows fall ❺
Darkly lowering,   from the north driving
Raging hail   in wrath upon men.
Wretchedness fills   the realm of earth,
And fate's decrees   transform the world.
Here wealth is fleeting,   friends are fleeting,
Man is fleeting,   maid is fleeting;
All the foundation   of earth shall fail!"
Thus spake the sage   in solitude pondering.
Good man is he   who guardeth his faith.
He must never too quickly   unburden his breast
Of its sorrow, but eagerly   strive for redress;
And happy the man   who seeketh for mercy
From his heavenly Father,   our fortress and strength.

◆ Build Vocabulary

rapture (rap´ chər) *n.*: Expression of joy or pleasure
redress (ri dres´) *n.*: Compensation, as for a wrong

Guide for Responding

◆ Literature and Your Life

Reader's Response In what ways is the wanderer someone to whom you can relate?

Thematic Focus Explain how the wanderer experiences exile, both emotionally and physically. In what ways do his ideas about heaven comfort him?

Group Discussion In a group of four, quickly explore the types of exile a person can experience. For example, exile might be self-imposed; it could be a frame of mind; it could be for a short duration. You can use situations from fiction, television, movies, or real life.

☑ Check Your Comprehension

1. What event causes the wanderer to go into exile?
2. What is the goal of the wanderer's search?
3. What is the wanderer's outlook on life?

◆ Critical Thinking

INTERPRET

1. This poem contains two speakers. Identify the points at which the speaker changes, and explain how the change affects the poem. **[Distinguish]**
2. What images does the poet use to convey isolation and despair? **[Analyze]**
3. Explain the wanderer's attitude toward wisdom. Give details to support your answer. **[Analyze]**
4. What is the message of this poem? **[Draw Conclusions]**

EXTEND

5. For what sort of modern-day profession might the wanderer be suited? **[Career Link]**

◆ Literary Focus

ANGLO-SAXON LYRICS: RHYTHM

Most Anglo-Saxon lyrics contain a distinct **rhythm.** Examine the poetic structure of "The Wanderer."

1. How many strong beats per line are there?
2. What effect might this rhythm have on the listener?

◆ Literary Focus

❺ **Anglo-Saxon Lyrics** Ask students to name characteristics of these lines that make them typical of Anglo-Saxon lyric poetry. *All of these are characteristic: the pattern of beats, the presence of caesuras in each line, and the kenning night-shadows for darkness.*

◆ Literature and Your Life

Invite students to speculate on how the wanderer would fit into modern twentieth-century society. *Students may reasonably argue for or against the possibility that the wanderer would fit in. Students might say that the mead-hall has its equivalent everywhere in modern living, and they might compare it to everything from a community hall to a casino. Students might say the wanderer would enjoy such twentieth-century community gathering places. On the other hand, they might also say that the wanderer would be horrified by a society in which people are not loyal to just one "lord."*

Reinforce and Extend

Answers

◆ Literature and Your Life

Reader's Response Students may relate to the wanderer's search for belonging or his concern about being a good person.

Thematic Focus The wanderer is without a lord, companions, or family. His ideas about God and heaven keep him from feeling completely alone.

☑ Check Your Comprehension

1. His lord died.
2. He is seeking a new lord.
3. Students may say he is sadly resigned to his fate.

◆ Critical Thinking

1. The speaker changes from a narrator to the wanderer at line 8. The change makes the poem more immediate and personal.
2. Students may identify the images in lines 21, 39–42, 47–48, 69–70, and 78–79. Other answers are possible.
3. The wanderer believes that wisdom comes from experience and results in behavior that is never immoderate (lines 58–65).
4. Possible responses include these: A person with faith in God is never completely alone; a wise person is moderate in all things; a person needs a sense of belonging to feel whole.
5. The wanderer might be suited for careers that involve obeying a leader and working with comrades, such as soldier, player in a team sport, dancer, or middle-manager.

◆ Literary Focus

1. There are four strong beats per line.
2. It might give the listener a feeling of order and predictability.

Develop Understanding

One-Minute Insight The speaker of this poem has been sent into exile by her husband. Although she still longs for him, she is bitter and angry about the friendless, lonely, joyless fate she must endure.

Humanities: Art

Susannah Fetching Water (detail from **Susannah in Bath**), 1526, by Albrecht Altdorfer.

One of the most important artists of the German Renaissance, Albrecht Altdorfer was a painter, draftsman, and printmaker.

Although everything he painted seems highly detailed; Altdorfer aimed for the coordination of all details within the space of the picture.

Use this question for discussion: Does this picture expresses the idea of sadness? Would you use it to illustrate the theme of exile? Explain. *Students may say that despite the beauty of the details, the dark colors and the shadows create a dominant impression of detachment. All of these impressions help evoke the state of exile.*

▶Critical Viewing◀

❶ **Compare and Contrast** The woman in this painting is somewhat alone like the speaker in the poem. However, the speaker appears to live in some wretched, lonely, dark place, whereas the woman in this painting lives in or approaches a civilized dwelling, in which the presence of another human being can be detected.

◆ Literary Focus

❷ **Anglo-Saxon Lyrics** Ask students to tell what might be meant by *wave-tumult* and to explain why this phrase is typical of Anglo-Saxon poetry. *"Wave-tumult" is probably the ocean; kennings like this are typical of Anglo-Saxon poetry.*

◆ Reading for Success

❸ **Restate for Understanding** Ask students to restate the sentence that begins "For this . . ." *I am sorry that the man who seemed like my match turned out to be unlucky, grim, and considering murder.*

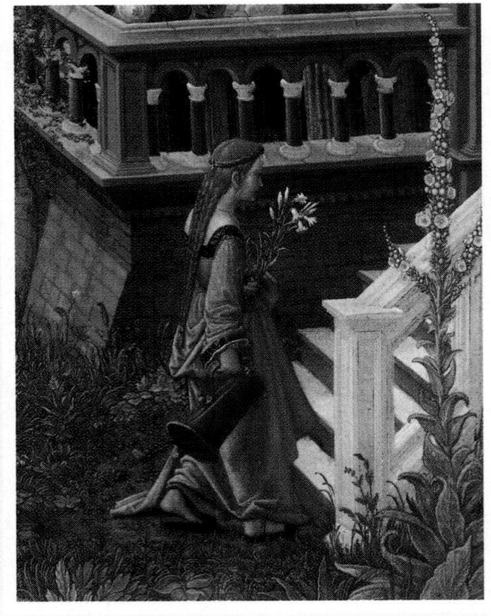

Susannah in Bath, (detail), Albrecht Altdorfer
Wasserholendes Madchen, Munchen, Alte Pinakothek

❶ ▲ **Critical Viewing** Compare the woman in this picture with the speaker in the poem. **[Compare and Contrast]**

The Wife's Lament

Translated by Ann Stanford

I make this song about me full sadly
my own wayfaring. I a woman tell
what griefs I had since I grew up
new or old never more than now.
Ever I know the dark of my exile.

First my lord went out away from his people
over the wave-tumult. I grieved each dawn ❷
wondered where my lord my first on earth might be.
Then I went forth a friendless exile
to seek service in my sorrow's need.
My man's kinsmen began to plot
by darkened thought to divide us two
so we most widely in the world's kingdom
lived wretchedly and I suffered longing.

My lord commanded me to move my dwelling here.
I had few loved ones in this land
or faithful friends. For this my heart grieves:
that I should find the man well matched to me ❸
hard of fortune mournful of mind
hiding his mood thinking of murder.

Blithe was our bearing often we vowed
that but death alone would part us two
naught else. But this is turned round
now . . . as if it never were
our friendship. I must far and near
bear the anger of my beloved.
The man sent me out to live in the woods
under an oak tree in this den in the earth.
Ancient this earth hall. I am all longing.

The valleys are dark the hills high
the yard overgrown bitter with briars
a joyless dwelling. Full oft the lack of my lord
seizes me cruelly here. Friends there are on earth
living beloved lying in bed

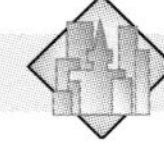

Beyond the Classroom

Career Connection

Psychology and Social Work In modern times, people who have problems in their relationships, like the wife or the husband in this poem, would be likely to seek the help of, or be referred to, someone who could provide them with counseling. They might spend several sessions with a psychologist, a licensed social worker, or a psychiatrist.

Have interested students find out the similarities and differences among these mental-healthcare professionals. Students might research training and education requirements for each field, job outlook, and levels of compensation. They might also learn about the questioning techniques whereby therapists help patients to ask and answer important questions about their own background, behavior, and goals.

while I at dawn   am walking alone
under the oak tree   through these earth halls.
There I may sit   the summerlong day
there I can weep   over my exile
my many hardships.   Hence I may not rest
from this care of heart   which belongs to me ever
nor all this longing   that has caught me in this life.

May that young man   be sad-minded always
hard his heart's thought   while he must wear
a blithe bearing   with care in the breast
a crowd of sorrows.   May on himself depend
❹ all his world's joy.   Be he outlawed far
in a strange folk-land—   that my beloved sits
under a rocky cliff   rimed with frost
a lord dreary in spirit   drenched with water
in a ruined hall.   My lord endures
much care of mind.   He remembers too often
a happier dwelling.   Woe be to them
that for a loved one   must wait in longing.

◆ **Build Vocabulary**

blithe (blīth) *adj.*: Cheerful

Guide for Responding

◆ Literature and Your Life

Reader's Response In what ways do you think the wife is justified in her anger and sorrow?

Thematic Focus Why was a sense of belonging or home important to the Anglo-Saxons? Why was exile such a prominent theme in their stories?

Letter to the Wife Write a brief letter to the wife in which you give advice on how she could overcome her feelings of abandonment, anger, and loss.

☑ Check Your Comprehension

1. To whom does the wife refer as "her lord"?
2. Why is the wife unhappy?
3. Why was the wife commanded to leave her home?

◆ Critical Thinking

INTERPRET

1. What does the wife mean by the phrase "grew up" in line 3? **[Interpret]**
2. What is meant by the line "I must far and near bear the anger of my beloved"? **[Interpret]**
3. If the husband were to return, do you think the wife would be welcoming? **[Make Predictions]**

EVALUATE

4. Does the poem effectively portray the wife as a believable person? **[Evaluate]**

◆ Literary Focus

ANGLO-SAXON LYRICS: THE CAESURA

One feature of Anglo-Saxon poetry is the **caesura,** which divides each line into two parts.

Identify three examples of caesura in "The Wife's Lament." Explain how the caesura makes the poem easier to recite.

Beyond the Selection

FURTHER READING

Other Anglo-Saxon Lyrics

"The Husband's Message"; "The Ruin";
"The Dream of the Rood"; "Deor's Lament";
"The Battle of Maldon"

Other Works About Exile

"Home Thoughts From Abroad," Robert Browning; *One Day in the Life of Ivan Denisovich,* Alexander Solzhenitsyn; "The Watch," Elie Wiesel

We suggest that you preview these works before recommending them to students.

INTERNET

You and your students may find additional information on the Internet at the following sites.

For links on Anglo-Saxon archaeology, literature, and language, go to **http://www.ccc.nottingham.ac.uk/~aczkdc/asresource.html**

Hear Old English at **http://www.georgetown.edu/cball/hwaet/hwaet06.html**

We *strongly recommend* that you preview the sites before you send students to them.

◆ Critical Thinking

❹ **Evaluate** Ask students whether what the wife wishes for her husband here—that he be "outlawed" in a strange land—is more or less than he deserves. *Students may say that it is less than he deserves: The wife has received as much punishment, and she has committed no crime or wrongdoing. The husband, on the other hand, seems to have thought about murder, and he has ruined his wife's life.*

Reinforce and Extend

Answers

◆ Literature and Your Life

Reader's Response Students may say she is justified because her husband sent her away, believing lies rather than her side of the story.

Thematic Focus Students may say that life was harsh in those times, so belonging to a group was a matter of survival. Being exiled was the worst thing that could happen to a person, so the theme of exile was one of intense interest.

☑ Check Your Comprehension

1. She refers to her husband.
2. She has been exiled far from husband, friends, and loved ones.
3. Her husband's kinsmen enacted a successful plot to separate her from her husband's affections. Angry with her, her husband sent her away.

◆ Critical Thinking

1. Suggested response: She means "since [she] became a woman."
2. She carries the knowledge of her husband's anger like a burden wherever she goes.
3. Some students will say that she will because she still longs for him. Others may point out she wishes him ill in lines 42–51, and so would not be welcoming.
4. Students may say that the wife's longing for, and anger with, her husband are believable.

◆ Literary Focus

Caesuras are found in every line. Students may point out that the caesuras in lines 2, 7, 17, 25, 29, 32, 33, 39, 45, 46, 50, 51, and 52 coincide with the end of a sentence, which forms a convenient breaking point and makes the poem easy to recite.

Reinforce and Extend

Answers

◆ Reading for Success

1. Suggested response: The placement of *flourished* in the phrase and its *-ed* suffix show that it is a verb. The meaning of *flourished* can be inferred from the phrase "in glory."
2. Suggested response: Sorrow cannot prevent destiny, and help does not come to those who don't try.
3. Students may say that the description of the castle in lines 69, 79–80, and 90, as well as the phrase "of stone" in line 93, allowed them to decode the word *ramparts*.
4. Possible response: The wife's husband went off to sea. The husband's kinsmen plotted to separate the two, and were successful. The husband exiled his wife to an earthen hall beneath an oak.

◆ Build Vocabulary

Using Forms of *Grievous*

1. b 2. c 3. a 4. d

Using the Word Bank

1. blithe, rapturous; 2. redress; 3. compassionate, grief; 4. admonished, rancor; 5. fervent, sentinel

◆ Literary Focus

1. Suggested response: The seafarer laments the end of a golden era, the wanderer mourns the loss of his lord, and the wife laments her exile and loss of her husband's affection.
2. Students may point out the poems' regular rhythm, caesuras, and logical ordering of images as aids to memory. Students should support their ideas with details from the poems.

◆ Grammar and Style

Practice

1. ages, shrinks; 2. shall muse, ponder; 3. opens, pours; 4. knows, feels, bends; 5. ages, droops

Writing Application

1. She walked to the wharf, watched the ships dock, and scanned faces in the crowd.
2. The lord mounted his horse, ordered a siege on the castle, and claimed victory.

Guide for Responding *(continued)*

◆ Reading for Success

Literal Comprehension Strategies

Review the reading strategies and the notes showing how to comprehend a writer's words and intention. Then apply them to answer the following questions.

1. Explain how context clues help reveal the meaning of *flourished*, in line 82 of "The Seafarer."
2. Paraphrase lines 14–16 from "The Wanderer":

   . . . For, woe of heart
   Withstandeth not fate: a failing spirit
   Earneth no help. . . .
3. What context clues enabled you to decode the meaning of *ramparts* in line 93?
4. Summarize "The Wife's Lament."

◆ Build Vocabulary

Using Forms of *Grievous*

Grievous, which means "causing sorrow" or "hard to bear," is related to a variety of other words that are similar in meaning. Match each form of *grievous* to its definition.

1. grievance	**a.** one in sorrow or distress
2. aggrieved	**b.** a serious complaint
3. griever	**c.** offended or wronged
4. grief	**d.** sorrow

Using the Word Bank

Replace each italicized word with a synonym from the Word Bank. You may change the form of the word.

1. Before being exiled by the king, we were *carefree* and in a state of *bliss*.
2. Being left with nothing, my husband and I sought *compensation*.
3. Our queen was *sympathetic* when she learned of our *distressing* loss.
4. The queen *scolded* the king and, out of *spite,* repealed our banishment.
5. A(An) *ardent* believer in justice, the queen appointed a *guard* to accompany us on our return home.

◆ Literary Focus

Anglo-Saxon Lyrics

All these poems are **lyrics**—poems that express the thoughts and feelings of a single speaker.

1. An **elegy** is a specific type of lyric in which the loss of something or someone is mourned. Explain why each poem is an example of an elegy.
2. All these lyrics sprang from the Anglo-Saxon oral tradition. Find three elements in these poems that would have helped people remember and recite the poems. Explain each example.

◆ Grammar and Style

Compound Predicates

Compound predicates help the writers of these poems provide detailed descriptions of events.

A predicate is a sentence part that contains the verb and states the action or condition of the subject. A **compound predicate** has two or more verbs or verb phrases that relate to the same subject.

Practice In your notebook, write the verbs or verb phrases in the compound predicate in each of the following sentences.

1. The world's honor ages and shrinks, . . .
2. He who shall muse on these moldering ruins, / And deeply ponder this darkling life, / Must brood on old legends of battle and bloodshed. . . .
3. A brother / Opens his palm and pours down gold / On his kinsman's grave, . . .
4. The soul . . . knows nothing / Of sweetness, or sour, feels no pain, / Bends neither its hand nor its brain.
5. All this earth ages and droops unto death.

Writing Application Rewrite each group of sentences as one sentence with a compound predicate.

1. She walked to the wharf. She watched the ships dock. She scanned faces in the crowd.
2. The lord mounted his horse. He ordered a siege on the castle. He claimed victory.

Build Your Portfolio

Idea Bank

Writing

1. Funeral Oration Write a funeral oration, describing the speaker of one of the poems. In your speech, mourn the loss of the speaker.

2. Analysis of Theme Each of these poems deals with the themes of exile and loneliness. Write an analysis of one of the poems, explaining how its theme is conveyed through imagery and symbols.

3. Comparison and Contrast In both "The Seafarer" and "The Wanderer," several religious passages are interwoven with the narrative. Compare and contrast the religious philosophies presented in the two poems.

Speaking and Listening

4. Demonstration of Caesuras With a partner, take turns reading portions of these poems aloud. Then discuss how the caesura—the break within each line—helps readers understand the poem's meaning and helps reciters present the poem to an audience. **[Performing Arts Link]**

5. Oral Interpretation Assume the role of a *scop,* or traveling storyteller, and perform one of these poems for the class. Capture the emotions of the speaker. **[Performing Arts Link]**

Projects

6. Help Wanted The speakers in these poems had ordinary occupations—as a wife, a sailor, and a soldier. Investigate Anglo-Saxon occupations. Then create a Help Wanted page listing the positions to be filled as well as the job requirements. **[Career Link]**

7. Portrait Choose one of the speakers from these poems to portray visually. Display your portrait in the classroom. **[Art Link]**

Writing Mini-Lesson

Song

"The Seafarer," "The Wanderer," and "The Wife's Lament" are all lyric poems that tell of each speaker's misery and loss. Choose one of the speakers' stories to re-create in the form of a song. Include a verse in which a story is told, as well as a refrain, which is repeated throughout the song and captures its essence or theme. You may also include sound devices such as rhyme, rhythm, and alliteration. Keep this strategy in mind as you write.

Writing Skills Focus: Sequence of Events

Because you're retelling a story through song, be specific about the **sequence of events.** Transitions such as *first, then, next,* and *later* clarify the connections among the events. In this passage from "The Wife's Lament," transitions make the sequence of events clear.

Model From the Poem

First my lord went out away . . .
Then I went forth a friendless exile

Prewriting Reread the poem you want to retell and take notes about the sequence of events that led to the speaker's state of misery. Identify a major event or a dominant theme and create a refrain, or chorus, to repeat throughout your song.

Drafting Draft the verses of your song, laying out the speaker's story in its proper sequence. Each verse should tell a part of the story. Alternate the refrain with the verses.

Revising Add transitions such as *then* and *next* wherever necessary to make the sequence of events more clear. Add sound devices like alliteration to make your song more memorable.

✓ ASSESSMENT OPTIONS

Formal Assessment, Selection Test, pp. 1–3, and Assessment Resources Software. The selection test is designed so that it can be easily customized to the performance levels of your students.
Alternative Assessment, p. 1, includes options for less advanced students, more advanced students, intrapersonal learners, verbal/linguistic learners, visual/spatial learners, and bodily/kinesthetic learners.

PORTFOLIO ASSESSMENT
Use the following rubrics in the ***Alternative Assessment*** booklet to assess student writing:
Funeral Oration: Expression Rubric, p. 95
Analysis of Theme: Literary Analysis/Interpretation Rubric, p. 113
Comparison and Contrast: Comparison/Contrast Rubric, p. 104
Writing Mini-Lesson: Poetry Rubric, p. 109

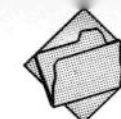

Idea Bank

Customizing for
Performance Levels
Following are suggestions for matching Idea Bank topics with your students' performance levels:
Less Advanced Students: 1, 7
Average Students: 2, 4, 5, 6
More Advanced Students: 3

Customizing for
Learning Modalities
Following are suggestions for matching Idea Bank topics with your students' learning modalities:
Visual/Spatial: 7
Verbal/Linguistic: 1, 2, 3, 4, 5, 6
Interpersonal: 4

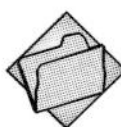

Writing Mini-Lesson

Refer students to the Writing Handbook, page 1189, for instruction on the writing process, and page 1192 for further information on creative writing.

Writer's Solution

Writers at Work Videodisc
Have students view the videodisc segment (Ch. 6) featuring Derek Walcott to hear his views about creative writing. Have students discuss how poetry and music are linked.

Play frames 9291 to 19694

Writing Lab CD-ROM
Have students write their songs using the tutorial on Creative Writing. Follow these steps:

1. View the audio-annotated Literary Models for poetry to see samples of poems that use sound devices.
2. Use the Story Line Diagram to plan and diagram the sequence of events in the poem.
3. Draft on computer.
4. Use the Revision Checkers to find vague words so they can be replaced with more vivid ones.

Sourcebook
Have students use Chapter 6, Creative Writing (pp. 167–195), for additional support. The chapter includes instruction on gathering details (p. 183) and using sound devices (p. 186).

Prepare and Engage

OBJECTIVES

1. To read, comprehend, interpret, and respond to poems about exile
2. To connect *Tristia* and "Far Corners of Earth" to the theme of exile
3. To respond to the poems through writing, speaking and listening, and projects

PORTFOLIO OPPORTUNITIES

Writing: Screenplay Treatment; Comparison and Contrast; Symbols of Exile
Speaking and Listening: Monologue of an Exile
Projects: Exile's Map; Timeline

More About the Authors

Ovid lived in Rome during a time of order, peace, and efficient autocracy. When he was fifty-one years old, he was banished to Tomis, which is in present-day Romania. There this sophisticated, witty poet, who had enjoyed cosmopolitan pleasures, lived on the very outposts of civilization. Although he pleaded directly and indirectly to be allowed to return to his beloved Rome, Ovid died in exile at the age of sixty.

"Far Corners of Earth" was written near the end of **Tu Fu**'s life, probably in 768. In March of that year, during a brief interlude of political stability, Tu Fu and his family began, finally, to return home. After a 250-mile journey, they stopped en route at Chiang-ling where news of yet another invasion reached them, and the family moved again, but not home. Tu Fu died while still traveling in 770.

Play a recording of a song that touches on the theme of exile and wandering. Possibilities include: "Far From the Home I Love" from the musical *Fiddler on the Roof,* the folk songs "By the Waters of Babylon," "500 Miles" by Hedy West, "Englishman in New York" by Sting, and "America" by Paul Simon. Have students discuss the emotions of the person singing the song, then tell them that the poems they are about to read were written by people exiled from their homes.

CONNECTIONS TO WORLD LITERATURE

from Tristia
Ovid

Far Corners of Earth
Tu Fu

Thematic Connection

THE THEME OF EXILE

Exile can be experienced in many ways, in many degrees, and for many reasons. For example, in "The Seafarer," the exile is self-imposed; the seafarer cannot resist the lure of the sea and all its dangers. "The Wanderer," however, experiences exile due to the death in battle of his lord and comrades. In "The Wife's Lament," exile is enforced on the woman by her husband and his conniving relatives.

The following poems also deal with the theme of exile. For Tu Fu, exile is not to be wholly reviled; in some ways, Tu Fu finds himself as a poet when banished from government service.

The same cannot be said of Ovid. For him, exile was perhaps more cruel than death. The verses in *Tristia* echo the deeply felt sorrow and longing he felt for his beloved Rome.

OVID
(43 B.C.–A.D. 17)

Born in Sulmona, Italy, Publius Ovidius Naso, known to us as Ovid, was educated for a career in law. Preferring to be a writer, Ovid became the author of numerous elegies as well as the narrative poem *Metamorphoses*, in which he recounted legends involving miraculous transformations of form since the beginning of time. Ovid lived and wrote chiefly in Rome, a city he loved and in which he was celebrated and favored. In A.D. 8, however, Ovid offended Emperor Augustus with his satires and was banished from Rome to Tomis, near the Black Sea. Despite numerous pleas for forgiveness, Ovid was to remain in exile until his death. *Tristia*, a lament, was written while Ovid was in exile.

TU FU
(712–770)

The son of a prominent scholar and an emperor's great-granddaughter, the poet Tu Fu had connections to people of power and influence. His background appears to be a mix of the traditional and unexpected: Although classically educated, he left home at a very early age to travel alone through China. He eventually ended up in the nation's capital and took a test for government service, failing it several times. He finally passed the exam in 752, and in 755 was granted a position in the palace of the crown-prince. The next few years of Tu Fu's life are a blur of political upheavals: Rebel forces send the emperor into exile; Tu Fu himself is exiled; Tu Fu flees into the country with his family to live in poverty and write; Tu Fu returns to a government position; and so on. The bulk of Tu Fu's poetry was written in the last eleven years of his life, when he left his government position and traveled in poverty with his family through the vast countryside of China.

Thematic Connection

Ovid was sent into exile and kept forever from a homeland he loved; it is therefore not surprising that these lines focus on the differences between that homeland and his new "home." Tu Fu, on the other hand, focuses on the condition of the mobile exile, who is always on the road, always in a strange, cold land.

Customize for
Less Proficient Readers
Paraphrase the opening lines of each poem and encourage students to paraphrase, line by line, as they read.

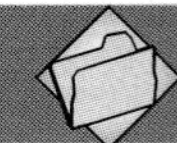

Prentice Hall Literature Program Resources

REINFORCE / RETEACH / EXTEND

Selection Support
Build Vocabulary, p. 6
Thematic Connection: Exile, p. 7

Formal Assessment Selection Test, pp. 4–5, Assessment Resources Software

Resource Pro CD-ROM
Tristia, "Far Corners of Earth"—includes all resource material and customizable lesson plan

Listening to Literature Audiocassettes
Tristia, "Far Corners of Earth"

from TRISTIA

Ovid, Translated by L. R. Lind

CONNECTIONS TO WORLD LITERATURE

Book 10

Since I've been here in the Pontus the Danube has frozen thrice over, ❶
  The waves of the Euxine ocean have hardened as well three times.
And it seems now I've been far from my country just so long a time
  As Dardanian Troy was besieged by the Grecian Army—ten years.
So slowly the time goes you'd think it was standing still in its traces
  And the year takes its way as though it were dragging its footsteps along.
The summer solstice deprives me of nothing at all from the nighttime ❷
  Nor does the winter solstice make shorter each of my days.

Can it be in my case that nature has taken unusual posture
  And does she make everything long as the wearisome length of my cares?
Or does that time common to all pursue its accustomed progress
  While the time that's peculiar to me is simply more harsh in my life,
I whom the shore of the Euxine, the sea that is falsely denoted,
  Holds now and the left (and ill-omened) land of the Scythian strait?

The numberless races around me menace with terrible warfare,
  These people who think it is shameful to live without plundering men;
Nothing beyond me lacks danger; the hill is defended around it
  By the slightest of walls, the strategic position that favors the place.
Whenever you least expect it, like a bird the enemy gathered
  In a dense mass flies past us and, scarce seen, drives its booty along.
Often inside of the walls when the gates have been shut quite securely,
  We have picked up their poisoned arrows flung into the midst of the roads. ❸
It's a rare farmer who dares to till his acres, and he with
  One hand (poor devil) goes plowing, with the other he handles his sword.
Under his helmet the shepherd blows on straws joined with pitch-gum
  And instead of a wolf the trembling sheep stand in dread of war.
We are scarcely defended within the fortress and even within it
  The barbarous crowd mixed with Greeks still inspires our hearts with fear.
In fact, the barbarians live with us without discrimination
  And they possess more than half of the houses which shelter us.
Even though you don't fear them you would hate them all when you see them,
  Their chests covered over with hides and their heads with long hanging hair. ❹
And even those men who're believed to descend from Greek colonizers
  Wear Persian trousers instead of the garments their own nation wears.

Develop Understanding

Like the seafarer, the wanderer, and the exiled wife in the Anglo-Saxon lyrics on pages 15–25, the speaker in *Tristia,* who is the poet Ovid himself, speaks autobiographically, and with profound sadness, of his exile. He has been banished from Rome to a remote outpost of the empire, where his days are unbearably long, where barbarians roam the land and threaten security, and where, because he speaks a different language, he cannot even communicate with others.

Customize for
Visual/Spatial Learners

❶ Ask visual learners to imagine the coldness of frozen countryside and rivers and to predict how such an image of coldness sets the tone for a poem about exile.

Customize for
English Language Learners

❷ Students may be unfamiliar with the term *solstice*. Use a calendar and diagrams of the Earth orbiting the sun to explain the term. Point out that the longest day and shortest night of the year occur during the summer solstice, and the shortest day and longest night occur during the winter solstice. Make sure that students understand that the total length of the day is still twenty-four hours; what differs is the relative lengths of daytime and nighttime.

Comprehension Check ☑

❸ Ask students to describe the dangers among which Ovid now lives. *The place where Ovid lives is not well defended and is constantly being attacked by armies that rob and plunder. Even farmers can't plow their land without a sword in hand.*

◆ Critical Thinking

❹ **Compare and Contrast** Ask students how the description of the barbarians contrasts with the image of a Roman that is conveyed by Ovid's own image on page 28. *Possible answers: The barbarians have "long hanging hair"; the Romans are neatly coifed; the barbarians wear hides and trousers, whereas the Romans wear togas.*

Beyond the Selection

FURTHER READING

Other Works by or About the Authors

Metamorphoses, Ovid
Fasti, Ovid
Tu Fu, China's Greatest Poet, William Hung
Endless River: Li Po and Tu Fu, A Friendship in Poetry, Sam Hamill

We suggest that you preview these works before recommending them to students.

INTERNET

You and your students may find additional information about the authors on the Internet. We suggest the following site. Please be aware that sites may have changed since we published this information.

To see how artists have illustrated Ovid's *Metamorphoses,* go to **http://www.uvm.edu/~hag/ovid/index.html**

We *strongly recommend* that you preview sites before you send students to them.

▶Critical Viewing◀

❶ **Speculate** Students may say that Rome is grand and civilized, citing the temples, statues, and paved streets. Students may say that in addition to being homesick, Ovid may have also missed the amenities that the city could offer.

Customize for
Interpersonal Learners

❷ Have students hypothesize about why the inability to communicate would be such a trial to someone like Ovid. Have them list the many emotions Ovid might feel toward his listeners, himself, and his exile at such utter lack of understanding.

❸ **Clarification** Lachesis (lak´ i sis) is one of the three Fates; she measures the thread that corresponds to the length of a human's life.

Reinforce and Extend

Answers

◆ ***Literature and Your Life***

Reader's Response Ovid has a negative attitude; he thinks that the people in his new home are uncivilized barbarians.

Thematic Focus Students may say that exile is worse than death for the poet, citing lines 45–52 in *Tristia*.

☑ **Check Your Comprehension**

1. The speaker is unhappy because he has been exiled from Rome.
2. He has been in exile for three years.
3. He is living in a half-civilized frontier town that is always being attacked by local peoples that resent the Roman invaders.

◆ Critical Thinking

1. Ovid notes that unlike civilized people, barbarians wear hides, have long hair, wear trousers, and don't speak Latin.
2. Suggested response: Exile cuts him off from the Roman culture that gave his life meaning.
3. Students may cite the way time drags (lines 3–12), the attacks from the enemy (lines 15–26), and Ovid's feelings of alienation (lines 36–38).
4. Suggested response: Ovid might live in New York City, Los Angeles, Paris, or another large city that is perceived as a cultural center.

Roman Forum at the Height of the Empire

◀ **Critical Viewing** Judging from this picture of Rome, why might Ovid have missed it so much while in exile? **[Speculate]** ❶

They carry on their relations by means of their common language
  While I am reduced to communication by making signs.
❷ Here I am the barbarian, and I'm understood by no one,
  And the stupid Getae make fun of the Latin words which I speak;
And openly often they speak ill of me and with perfect freedom,
  Perhaps even holding against me the fact that I'm exiled from Rome.
And as it happens, they think I am crazy when to their jabber
  I nod my head to say "yes" and shake it to signify "no."
Add that an unjust justice is enforced with the rigid sword blade
  And wounds are frequently given in the midst of the market place.

❸ O harsh Lachesis, who gave me, born under a star that's unlucky,
  The threads of a life that were not shorter than those which are mine!
The fact that I lack the sight of my fatherland and of my comrades
  And that I live here among the Scythian race I lament:
Both of these penalties are grave, but I deserved the loss of my City;
  Perhaps I did not deserve to be punished in such a place.
Why do I speak? I'm a madman. I deserved to lose even my life then
  When I did injury to the power of Caesar the god.

Guide for Responding

◆ *Literature and Your Life*

Reader's Response What do you think of the speaker's attitude toward the people who surround him in his new home?

Thematic Focus Which do you think is worse for the poet—death or exile? Explain.

☑ **Check Your Comprehension**

1. Why is the speaker unhappy?
2. How long has the speaker been in exile?
3. Under what conditions is the speaker forced to live?

◆ Critical Thinking

INTERPRET

1. How does Ovid distinguish between a civilized person and a barbarian? **[Distinguish]**
2. What does this passage suggest about the meaning of exile for Ovid? **[Interpret]**

EVALUATE

3. Which details are especially effective in conveying Ovid's distress? Why? **[Criticize]**

APPLY

4. If Ovid were a contemporary writer, where might he live? Why? **[Hypothesize]**

Humanities: Art

Roman Forum at the Height of the Empire, nineteenth-century engraving.

The Roman word *forum* means "marketplace" or "out-of-doors place" and referred in Roman times to any place of assembly. Every city in the empire had a forum.

This engraving shows the original Roman forum, which was built between the Palatine and Capitoline hills and Quirinal Hill.

Among the stately, columned buildings shown here is the Temple of Saturn, which served as the government treasury and housed the state financial records. Characteristic of Roman architecture, with its many tall monuments, temples, and altars, it bespeaks the glory of the empire.

Use this question for discussion:

How does the setting shown in this engraving contrast with the setting Ovid describes in *Tristia*? *Ovid does not allude to any similarity whatsoever between the kind of setting shown in this engraving and what he faces in exile. He is exiled in a rural, uncivilized setting. There is a marketplace, but it scarcely seems organized or safe, since "justice" is given there by the sword.*

FAR CORNERS OF *Earth*

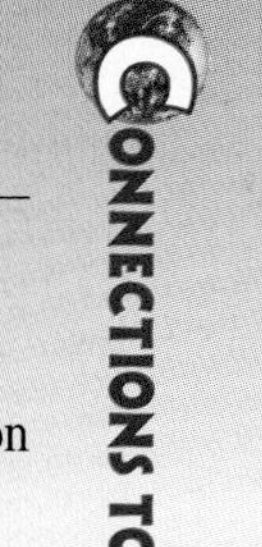

CONNECTIONS TO WORLD LITERATURE

Tu Fu

Translated by David Hinton

Chiang-han mountains looming, impassable,
A cloud drifts over this far corner of earth. ❹
Year after year, nothing familiar, nothing
Anywhere but one further end of the road.

Here, Wang Ts'an found loss and confusion,
And Ch'ü Yüan cold grief. My heart already ❺
Broken in quiet times—and look at me,
Each day wandering a new waste of highway.

▲ **Critical Viewing** In what ways does this painting depict isolation and solitude? **[Analyze]** ❻

Guide for Responding

◆ *Literature and Your Life*

Reader's Response What mood does this poem evoke in you?

Thematic Focus What type of exile does the speaker of this poem experience? How does exile affect the outlook of the speaker?

Additional Stanza Write another stanza to this poem, extending the mood already established by Tu Fu.

☑ Check Your Comprehension

1. As the poem begins, what does the poet see before him?
2. What is the poet doing "Each day"?

◆ Critical Thinking

INTERPRET

1. Explain how details from the landscape contribute to the mood of the poem. **[Analyze]**
2. What seems to be the hardest thing about exile for Tu Fu? Why? **[Interpret]**

EVALUATE

3. What is the intended effect of beginning the poem with a description of the landscape? Explain. **[Criticize]**

APPLY

4. What sort of person in modern life might experience a life similar to Tu Fu's? Explain. **[Relate]**

Develop Understanding

One-Minute Insight In Tu Fu's poem, the unfamiliar landscape is part of the punishment of exile: He is forced to wander in places he does not know, where nothing is familiar, and where one unknown road leads only to another.

◆ Critical Thinking

❹ **Infer** Ask students what Tu Fu means by the phrase "far corner of earth." *He is referring to a place that is so remote from his own sense of place that it seems as if it is in a "far corner of" the world.*

◆ Critical Thinking

❺ **Hypothesize** Ask students to conjecture about who Wang Ts'an and Ch'ü Yüan might be. *Both are poets who were exiled. Students may reasonably suggest that they were well-known people who met with suffering in the region or perhaps died there.*

▶Critical Viewing◀

❻ **Analyze** The painting consists primarily of open, empty sky. The pavilion and rooftops near the bottom are dwarfed into insignificance.

Reinforce and Extend

Answers

◆ *Literature and Your Life*

Reader's Response Students may say that the poem evokes a sad, lonely mood.

Thematic Focus In his exile, the speaker wanders from place to place, never settling down. Students may say that this experience makes the speaker feel sad and lonely.

(Answers continue on page 32.)

Humanities: Art

Evening in Spring Hills, c. 1150–1250.

Chinese landscape painting, one of China's greatest artistic gifts to the world, began to develop during the Tang dynasty, which was the era in which Tu Fu lived. Landscape painting reached its height during the Sung dynasty, which is when this work was created.

Landscapes were typically done in ink, so that they were nearly monochromatic, with variations in the ink subtly re-creating the landscape. Sometimes they had washes of color, but they were never full-color paintings.

In landscape painting, the figures, are usually very small or partly hidden: it is the landscape that is of primary importance. Through intricate brushwork, rocks, mountains, branches, and other elements are all given character and force. Mountains and rivers often stretch forever into the distance, as the mountains do in this landscape.

Use these questions for discussion:

1. In what ways does this painting suggest a "far corner of earth"? *Students may respond that the landscape is large and imposing, the horizon stretches on forever, and the pavilion and the people inside it are tiny and insignificant in relation to he natural world.*
2. What mood does the painting seem to suggest? In what ways does the mood of the painting complement the mood of the poem? *The painting seems to suggest quiet, solitude, and the enormous power of the landscape. The poem focuses more on suffering and frustration but invokes the power of the landscape, with its impassable mountains and drifting clouds.*

Answers

 **Check Your Comprehension**

1. He sees mountains.
2. He wanders down a new road.

◆Critical Thinking

1. The "impassable" mountains and drifting cloud add to the sense of futility, isolation, and lack of purpose.
2. The hardest thing seems to be the lack of familiar places, which compounds his feelings of hopelessness and of not being anywhere.
3. Students may say that the landscape forms both the physical and emotional setting for the poem; the external remoteness mirrors the internal feelings of emptiness.
4. Students may suggest that a refugee or homeless person might experience a similar life.

Thematic Connection

1. Student responses may include the following points: The exiles in *Tristia* and "The Wife's Lament," involve being sent to a specific place of banishment. Both of these poems deal with homesickness and imply that the exile might be ended. In "Far Corners of Earth," the speaker wanders from place to place, rather than being confined to a specific place, and seems more resigned to his fate than the speakers of the other two poems.
2. Current examples of exiles might include the Dalai Lama, refugees from war zones, political dissidents who have defected to the United States, and expatriate artists and writers.
3. Students may cite lines 4–5, 16, 25–26, and 56–57 in "The Seafarer," lines 3–5, 20, 39–40, and 50–51 in "The Wanderer," and lines 3–4 and 8 in "Far Corners of Earth."

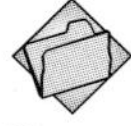 **Idea Bank**

Customizing for
Performance Levels

Following are suggestions for matching Idea Bank topics with your students' performance levels:

Less Advanced Students: 1, 5
Average Students: 2, 4
More Advanced Students: 3

Customizing for
Learning Modalities

Following are suggestions for matching Idea Bank topics with your students' learning modalities:

Verbal/Linguistic: 1, 2, 3, 4
Visual/Spatial: 1, 5

Thematic Connection

The Theme of Exile

Tristia and "Far Corners of Earth" both deal with the theme of exile, or expulsion from home or society. This theme can be found throughout world literature, in just about every era of history.

1. Compare Ovid's treatment of exile with its treatment in "The Wanderer" or "The Wife's Lament." Consider the use of symbols to represent the life of an exile and the speaker's attitude toward exile.
2. Name three current examples of people who live in exile. Draw these examples from the news, from songs, or from books and movies.
3. In Tu Fu's "Far Corners of Earth," the line "Year after year, nothing familiar" gets at the essence of what it's like to be without a home. Show how this same idea is expressed in "The Seafarer" and "The Wanderer." Cite specific passages from the poems to illustrate the points you're making.

Idea Bank

Writing

1. **Screenplay Treatment** Reread the excerpt from *Tristia* and think of a few camera shots you could use to accompany a reading of this poem. For each shot, explain why it would be effective. **[Media Link]**
2. **Comparison and Contrast** *Tristia* is a poem lamenting Ovid's exile from Rome. In the Anglo-Saxon poems, however, the characters are fictional. Choose one of these fictional characters and compare his or her attitudes and emotional state with Ovid's.
3. **Symbols of Exile** A symbol is a person, place, or thing that stands for an idea. In "Far Corners of Earth," for example, the endless highway symbolizes the monotony of a journey never ended or the life of a permanent exile looking for a home. Reexamine the three Anglo-Saxon poems and look for symbols of exile. Analyze each symbol and explain why it is or isn't effective.

Speaking and Listening

4. **Monologue of an Exile** Write a brief monologue for the speaker in Tu Fu's poem. Borrow the situation laid out in "Far Corners of Earth" and expand upon it in the monologue, conveying the sense of despair and monotony that Tu Fu has captured in his poem. Perform your monologue for the class. **[Performing Arts Link]**

Project

5. **Exile's Map** Draw a map that illustrates China in Tu Fu's time or the Roman empire in Ovid's. Use labels to show what Tu Fu's or Ovid's exile meant in geographical terms. **[Social Studies Link; Art Link]**
6. Ovid was exiled from Rome after angering Emperor Augustus. Research other actions by this emperor and create a timeline that shows significant events during his reign. **[Social Studies Link]**

Writing Process Workshop

Dramatic Monologue

The lyric poems in this unit resemble **dramatic monologues**; in the poems, an imaginary character speaks to a silent listener, revealing his or her innermost self, often at a moment of crisis. Similarly, in a dramatic monologue, a character speaks to a silent listener about something that concerns him or her. The character might reflect on life or express fears, beliefs, or desires.

Write a dramatic monologue in which you tell the story of your speaker—a character living during the Anglo-Saxon or medieval periods, or someone from our own time. Your speaker might respond in the monologue to something that has just occurred in his or her life. Use the following skills to bring the speaker of your poem to life.

Writing Skills Focus

- **Follow a sequence of events** to make the speaker's story clear. Decide on the type of conflict that will propel the story. (See p. 27.)
- **Develop your character's personality** through his or her speech patterns and vocabulary.
- **Try free verse form**—verse without a regular rhythm or rhyme scheme—to emphasize the content and mood of your poem.

The following passage from "The Wanderer" contains many elements found in dramatic monologues.

Model From Literature

from "The Wanderer"

① Oft when the day broke, oft at the
dawning,
② Lonely and wretched I wailed my woe.
③ No man is living, no comrade is left,
To whom I dare fully unlock my heart.

① This passage is spoken by the wanderer, the character who's telling the story.

② The speaker begins by telling what's happened in the past.

③ Here, the speaker moves forward in time to reveal his present thoughts.

Cross-Curricular Connection: Social Studies

Dramatic monologues often reveal historical events or information about a certain time period. For example, from Robert Browning's "My Last Duchess," the reader learns about marriage arrangements and the position of women during the time period in which the poem takes place.

Encourage students to research a historical character or time period in which they are interested as a possible topic for their dramatic monologues. Through their poems, they can reveal historical information as well as impressions of characters and daily life during the period.

Prepare and Engage

Establish Writing Guidelines
Before beginning this lesson, review the following key characteristics of a dramatic monologue:

- A dramatic monologue is a part of a poem in which the speaker discloses his or her thoughts to a silent listener.
- Through the monologue, the speaker reveals something of his or her personality, usually at a moment of crisis.
- The speaker's vocabulary, speech patterns, and attitudes provide clues to the speaker's background.

You might work with your students to develop a rubric by which to evaluate their dramatic monologues. You may include the points contained in the rubric on page 35.

Refer students to the Writing Handbook, page 1189, for an overview of the writing process and to page 1192 for tips on a dramatic monologue.

Connection to Literature
To prepare students to write a dramatic monologue, have them look at examples from literature. The section from "The Wanderer" that appears on this page (lines 8–11) is a partial example. For additional examples of dramatic monologues, have students read Alfred, Lord Tennyson's, "Ulysses" on page 759 and Robert Browning's "My Last Duchess" on page 768. Then have students work in groups to identify the key characteristics that make these pieces dramatic monologues.

Writing Lab CD-ROM
If students have access to computers, have them work in the tutorial on Creative Writing to complete all or part of their dramatic monologue. Follow these steps:

1. Have students use the Situation Word Bins and Characters, Conflict, and Setting Wheel to stimulate ideas for a topic.
2. Students can review interactive examples of character developments on which they can model their own characters.
3. Have students use the revision checker for vague words.

Sourcebook
Students can find additional support for prewriting, drafting, and revising in the chapter on Creative Writing, pp. 166–195.

Develop Student Writing

Review with students the selection-related writing ideas that appear on this page. Ask students to share their impressions of the "seafarer," "wanderer," and "the wife" in a class discussion. Have students list impressions and characteristics of each for possible use in their dramatic monologues.

Art Transparencies Place Art Transparency 2, *Harold Brings News to William; Normans Set Fire to a House,* on an overhead projector. Explain to students that the Bayeux Tapestry has survived to the present from approximately 1067–1077. The scenes on it recorded an important historical event—the invasion and conquest of England by William the Conqueror in 1066. This particular scene depicts a messenger bringing news of victory to William. Have students research the historical background of this time and create a dramatic monologue in which William reflects on the news brought to him by the messenger.

Customize for
Visual/Spatial Learners
For those students who works best visually, recommend that they follow the directions for Map Out a Sequence of Events on this page. Also provide copies of the Branching Organizer, page 5 in ***Writing and Language Transparencies.*** Students can use the organizer to develop character as follows: Have them place the name of the speaker on top and then follow with two personality characteristics they would like to reveal in their monologue. They should then place details that establish these characteristics on the lines beneath.

Writer's Solution

Writing Lab
The Word Bins for poetry and drama include rhyming words, sensory details, and character traits that may help students write their dramatic monologues. Have students also review the audio-annotated models of poetry for examples of end rhyme, internal rhyme, alliteration, and repetition.

Applying Language Skills: Using Verb Tenses

Because a dramatic monologue often tells a story, it's important to use correct verb tenses to keep the story events clear and logical. Use the **present tense** to express an action or state of being that is ongoing or taking place now. Use the **past tense** to express an action or state of being that has already happened. Use the **future tense** to express an action or state of being that will happen.

Present: *I am jumping overboard.*

Past: *I jumped overboard.*

Future: *I will jump overboard if the storm continues.*

Practice Identify the tenses of the italicized verbs.

Madness *overtook* me as the ship's captain was swept away. I *shudder* now when I think back on it. Tomorrow, I *will continue* my long journey homeward, over land.

Writer's Solution Connection
Language Lab

For more on using verb tenses, see the Principal Parts of Verbs and Verb Tense lessons in the Sharpening Language Skills section.

Prewriting

Choosing a Topic Whose story would make an interesting monologue? Consider characters from literature or movies, legendary figures, or characters you create yourself.

Selection-Related Writing Ideas

- The "seafarer" debates the merits of life at sea
- The "wanderer" recounts the battle in which his lord was killed, leaving him alone in the world
- The "wife" spills out her anger and fears when her husband finally returns

Map Out a Sequence of Events Create a diagram to illustrate the sequence of events in your dramatic monologue.

Beginning: The husband tells his wife of his journey home after being away for a year.
Middle: He reveals that the ship he was traveling in was battered by a storm and took on water.
High Point: The husband tells how he spotted the shoreline and imagined that his wife was waving a welcome to him.
End: The husband bursts into tears and expresses his love for his wife.

Develop Character Through Speech Choose a manner of speaking that will fit your character. To do this, experiment with different ways of saying the same thing. For example, would your character say "I don't want to go back" or " Wild horses couldn't drag me home"?

Drafting

Let the Character Tell the Story Now that you've sketched out your character's situation and personality, take a moment to "assume your character's identity" and let the character take over as you write.

Draft Free Verse As you draft, rough out the form your poem will take. Break lines by instinct, and let the character you've created and the emotional situation guide the structure of your poem. For example, if your character is angry, you might explore creating short, choppy lines to emphasize that emotion. If your character is recalling a pleasant experience, the lines of your poem could be long, like an uninterrupted dream.

Drafting

Have students first draft their dramatic monologue in free verse as suggested on this page. Tell them not to worry about specific poetic devices such as rhyme scheme, alliteration, and figurative language. They can attend to these points while revising.

Customize for
Less Advanced Students
Have less advanced students draft their dramatic monologues in prose form. Getting their basic ideas written out before struggling with poetic form will help them write a clear and coherent dramatic monologue.

Applying Language Skills

Answers

1. *overtook,* past tense
2. *shudder,* present
3. *will continue,* future

Writer's Solution

For additional instruction on verb tenses, have students use the Correct and Effective Use of Verbs lesson on the **Language Lab CD-ROM.** For more practice, have students complete the practice pages on verb tense in the *Writer's Solution Grammar Practice Book,* pp. 50–54.

Revising

Connect Sequence of Events In the drafting stage, your character took you on a dramatic journey. Now, make sure that your readers can follow along. Insert transitions such as *then, immediately after*, and *before*, to connect the story events.

Strengthen Characterization Read your monologue aloud and replace any words or phrases that seem out of character. Following are tips for strengthening character through speech.

- Choose vocabulary appropriate to the time period and personality of the speaker:
  Draft: I was *devastated* when *my lord exiled* me.
  Revision: I was *depressed* when *my boss fired* me.
- Change complete sentences into fragments wherever it seems natural to do so:
  Draft: The waves broke over my head in a fury.
  Revision: The waves! The fury!

Revise Structure to Enhance a Poem's Meaning
Review the lines of your poem and revise line breaks and line lengths to match the events and emotional content of your dramatic monologue.

In the following example, lines of free verse were revised to mirror the desperate efforts of the speaker's struggle.

Draft

My heart pounded
furiously as I struggled to free myself from the tenacious
grasp of the murderous sea.

Revision

My heart pounded furiously
as I
struggled to free myself
from the
tenacious grasp
of the murderous sea.

Publishing

- **Performing** Read your dramatic monologue aloud to the class.
- **Group Activity** With a group of friends, put on a production of dramatic monologues.
- **Cross-Disciplinary Activity** Draw a portrait of the speaker of your dramatic monologue. Post the portrait and the monologue on a bulletin board.

APPLYING LANGUAGE SKILLS: Punctuating Free Verse

Because free verse contains no consistent structure or rhyme scheme, punctuation takes on added importance. Use commas to indicate short pauses, ellipsis points to indicate breaks in thought, periods to indicate full stops, and dashes to indicate interruptions.

Draft	Revision
Fist of sand	Fist of sand . . .
Waves lapping lapping lapping	Waves lapping, lapping, lapping,
Gently lifting then dropping exhausted legs	Gently lifting, then dropping exhausted legs.

Writing Application Review your dramatic monologue, and then insert or revise punctuation as needed to enhance your poem's meaning or mood.

Writer's Solution Connection
Writing Lab

To help you develop your character, use the Character Trait Word Bin in the Writing Lab tutorial on Creative Writing.

Revising

Students can revise their dialogues as they rehearse. As they say their monologues, they will discover weak spots that need revising. Refer students to the tips in the Speaking and Listening Handbook, pp. 1200–1201, on oral communication.

Writers at Work Videodisc
Play the videodisc section in which Derek Walcott discusses revising and editing and then ask students: When Walcott says "the liberation comes in the discipline," what does he mean?

Play frames 17162 to 19694

Publishing

In addition to the suggestions on this page, encourage those students whose dramatic monologues presented a historical time or character to present it to their history class.

Reinforce and Extend

Review the Writing Guidelines
After students have completed their dramatic monologues, review the key characteristics. Use the rubric below or the one you have created with students to evaluate students' monologues.

Apply Language Skills

Punctuating Free Verse
Review with students the guidelines for punctuating free verse on this page. Have them complete the Writing Application and then review one another's work.

✓ ASSESSMENT		4	3	2	1
PORTFOLIO ASSESSMENT Use this rubric to assess student writing.	**Develop Character's Personality**	The writer reveals significant characteristics of the speaker's personality through the speaker's expressed thoughts.	The writer reveals a few significant characteristics of the speaker's personality through the speaker's expressed thoughts.	The writer does not sufficiently reveal the speaker's personality through the speaker's thoughts.	The writer does not reveal significant characteristics of the speaker's personality.
	Sequence of Events	The events of the dramatic monologue flow smoothly and coherently.	Most of the events of the dramatic monologue flow smoothly and coherently.	Only a few of the events in the dramatic monologue seem to be connected.	The events of the dramatic monologue follow no sequence.

Introduce the Strategy

Explain to students that historical papers and documents reflect the values and beliefs of the time in which they were written. Not only will writers bring unique experiences to their perspectives but they may also use different vocabulary. Let students know that taking the points into consideration will improve their comprehension of historical documents.

Customize for
Verbal/Linguistic Learners
To accommodate students who learn best by hearing information, have students work in pairs in which they read the historical documents on this page to each other, or a student may wish to audiotape him- or herself reading the document and play the reading back.

Apply the Strategy

Answers

Suggested responses:

1. Two terms that suggest this text was written a long time ago are *Albion* and *Gaul*. Because these countries no longer exist, these terms indicate that the text was written long ago.
2. The writer does not assume his readers have any knowledge of Britain, because he provides a detailed description of its location.
3. Possible response: Bede's concept of Europe includes three countries in Europe, one of which no longer exist—Gaul, which is now Belgium and France.

Placing Reading in Time Context

Real-World Reading Skills Workshop

Strategies for Success

In your research and school work, you often read material that was written long ago. In works from a different period, the writer's assumptions, experiences, and vocabulary are probably different from yours. To read this material effectively, you need to place it in the context of its own time, and place yourself in that time context.

Scan the Text A quick scan of the text will help you determine its time period. Look for old-fashioned words or phrases that suggest a different time. Also look for ideas that come from another era and for references to events, people, and places of the time.

Scan Your Own Mind At the same time, scan your own mind for what you know about the period. You may have recently read introductions and background features like the ones in this book. Apply what you know to the text in front of you.

Use Text Aids and Research Tools As you read, increase your knowledge of the time context by using text aids like footnotes, glossaries, and appendixes. Also, don't hesitate to use reference works like historical dictionaries, atlases, almanacs, and encyclopedias to learn even more about how the work fits into its time period.

✔ *When reading the following, it will be helpful to place them in time context:*

- ▶ Historical speeches and documents
- ▶ Advertisements and posters from the past
- ▶ Scripts of old movies

Britain, formerly known as Albion, is an island in the ocean, facing between north and west, and lying at a considerable distance from the coasts of Germany, Gaul, and Spain, which together form the greater part of Europe. . . .

—Bede, from *A History of the English Church and People*

Cotton Ms. Tiberius c II Folio 5 Verso Page of Bede's History

Apply the Strategy

1. Find two terms in this text by Bede that suggest it was written a long time ago. Explain your choices.
2. Does the author assume that his readers are familiar with a land called Britain? Why or why not?
3. In what ways does the author's concept of Europe differ from our concept of it today?

Cross-Curricular Connection: Social Studies

When students learn about history they may not realize that information comes from historical records and documents written during the time they occurred. Students need to realize that the history they learn may reflect the perspective of the historian.

Students should also look beyond the historical facts for information that indicates attitudes and beliefs of the time. By doing so, they be better able to recognize the elements of perspective that might suggest attitudes and beliefs.

PART 2 *Focus on Literary Forms: The Epic*

Beowulf on the Funeral Pyre, Rockwell Kent

From the fifth through fifteenth centuries, England was a place of upheaval and uncertainty. Invasions, plagues, and political battles raged, and people looked for reassurance in the form of heroes who embodied strength, honor, and virtue. This need for heroes is met in epic tales, such as *Beowulf,* which follows.

One-Minute Planning Guide

The selections in this part provide insight into the nature of the epic hero and the conventions of the epic. The primary selection consists of excerpts from *Beowulf,* the most famous epic in the British tradition, and includes the battles with Grendel, Grendel's mother, and the dragon. Epics from ancient times are represented by excerpts from *Gilgamesh* and the *Iliad.* These reveal how the qualities prized in a hero vary across cultures. Gilgamesh is celebrated for his construction of cities and temples. Although the heroes of the *Iliad* have human failings, they are regarded as heroes for their skill as warriors.

Customize for ***Varying Student Needs***

When assigning the selections in this part, keep in mind these factors:

from *Beowulf*
- Very long poem (24 pp.)
- Less proficient readers will need assistance with reading verse
- Action-packed fantasy with monsters and warriors will appeal to most students

from *Gilgamesh*
- Short (30 lines)
- Students may find the riddle-like and mysterious first few lines frustrating

from the *Iliad*
- Knowing the context of the scene improves understanding
- Students may need assistance with the Greek names

Humanities: Art

Beowulf on the Funeral Pyre by Rockwell Kent.

This work depicts the Saxon epic hero Beowulf being cremated in a hero's funeral. Tell students that they will read about Beowulf, an Anglo-Saxon hero who helped the Danish king by slaying the monster Grendel and Grendel's mother but who was himself fatally wounded when he killed a fire-breathing dragon. Point out the contrast between the stylized, shimmering flames in the background and the dark, solid pyre upon which Beowulf's body rests.

Have your students link the painting to Part 2, The Epic, by answering these questions:

1. Even if you did not know the title of this art, what details and elements in the work would lead you to the sense that this man is a hero? *Sample answer: Heroic elements of the work include the unearthly light above the body, the way the pyre is carefully arranged and decorated with shields, the garlands on the pyre and funeral bier, the position of the man—sitting up as if he is still alive, looking upward, holding his sword as if undefeated and ready to fight again.*
2. What does the artist suggest is most noble about Beowulf? *Sample answer: The fact that Beowulf looks almost alive suggests that the artist admired his unquenched willingness to do battle where necessary.*

Prepare and Engage

Guide for Interpreting

About Beowulf

Origins of a Legend Long before there were books, stories and poems were passed along by word of mouth. In Anglo-Saxon England, traveling minstrels known as *scops* captivated audiences with entertaining presentations of long narrative poems. One of these poems was *Beowulf*, which was told and retold to audiences throughout England over hundreds of years. Although the action takes place in sixth-century Scandinavia, *Beowulf* was originally told in Old English. When *Beowulf* was finally written down in the eleventh century, it marked the beginning of English literature.

Beowulf *is not only an important historical record, but also a hair-raising tale that has electrified readers through the centuries.*

Beowulf, a Geat from a region that is today southern Sweden, sets sail from his homeland to try to free Danish King Hrothgar's great banquet hall, Herot, of a monster that has been ravaging it for twelve years. The monster, Grendel, is a terrifying swampland creature of enormous size whose eyes burn "with gruesome light." The struggle between Beowulf, a young adventurer eager for fame, and Grendel, a fierce and bloodthirsty foe, is the first of three mortal battles in the long poem.

From Oral Tradition to Cyberspace The only original manuscript of the complete 3,182-line poem comes to us from Sir Robert Cotton's (1571–1631) collection of medieval manuscripts. In 1731, the manuscript was saved from a fire but did not escape damage—the edges of 2,000 letters crumbled away.

Fortunately, the computer age has made it possible to prevent additional damage to the manuscript. Thanks to an initiative called the Electronic *Beowulf* Project, the manuscript has been preserved and made available electronically. Not only is the legend of *Beowulf* timeless, but the Old English manuscript has proved its adaptability to the computer age.

◆ Background for Understanding

HISTORY: PAGANISM AND CHRISTIANITY

Before Christianity began taking hold of the nation in the seventh century, England was a pagan society. People believed that their lives were completely in the hands of fate, and they told tales of monsters and other shadowy creatures that lurked in the depths of the forest. These pagan beliefs contrasted sharply with the Christian beliefs in a single deity, in the freedom of individuals to determine their own path, and in the clear distinction between good and evil.

At the time when *Beowulf* was written, England was in the process of changing from a pagan culture to a Christian society. Not surprisingly, *Beowulf* reflects both pagan and Christian ideals. For example, Grendel is reminiscent of monsters found in pagan legends, yet the battle of Beowulf and Grendel captures the Christian ideal of good conquering the forces of evil.

OBJECTIVES

1. To read, comprehend, interpret, and respond to an epic
2. To relate an epic to personal experience
3. To paraphrase key ideas and details
4. To identify the elements of an Anglo-Saxon epic poem
5. To build vocabulary in context and learn the root *-sol-*
6. To recognize and use appositives and appositive phrases
7. To write a press release with an attention-grabbing opening
8. To respond to an epic through writing, speaking and listening, and projects

SKILLS INSTRUCTION

Vocabulary: Word Roots: *-sol-*
Grammar and Style: Appositives and Appositive Phrases
Reading Strategy: Paraphrase
Literary Focus: The Epic
Writing: Grab Readers' Attention
Speaking and Listening: Performance; Speech
Critical Viewing: Analyze; Compare and Contrast

PORTFOLIO OPPORTUNITIES

Writing: Memo; Comparison and Contrast; Response to Criticism
Writing Mini-Lesson: Press Release for Grendel
Speaking and Listening: Performance; Speech
Projects: Multimedia Presentation; Sculpture

More About the Author
The Anglo-Saxon *scops* bear some resemblance to the court poets of a later period and to modern poet laureates, but unlike their more recent counterparts, *scops* traveled from court to court. The *scop* was both a composer and storyteller whose status was largely determined by the number of stories he could recite and the skill he employed in telling them. Drawing from the heroic tales of the early Germanic peoples, the *scop* was no doubt expected to celebrate the court or family he was entertaining.

Prentice Hall Literature Program Resources

REINFORCE / RETEACH / EXTEND

Selection Support Worksheets
Build Vocabulary: Word Roots: *-sol-*, p. 8
Grammar and Style: Appositives and Appositive Phrases, p. 9
Reading Strategy: Paraphrase, p. 10
Literary Focus: The Epic, p. 11

Strategies for Diverse Student Needs, p. 2

Beyond Literature
Media Connection, p. 2

Formal Assessment Selection Test, pp. 9–11; Assessment Resources Software

Alternative Assessment, p. 2

Writing and Language Transparencies
Writing Process Model 5, pp. 37–43
Daily Language Practice, Weeks 2 and 3

Resource Pro CD-ROM
Beowulf—includes all resource material and customizable lesson plan

Listening to Literature Audiocassettes
Beowulf

from Beowulf

◆ Literature and Your Life

CONNECT YOUR EXPERIENCE

A defiant hero battles an arch-enemy in a deadly struggle. This ever-popular combination of villain and hero in literature and media can be traced to a poem composed more than twelve hundred years ago. Like the heroes of today, Beowulf fights for the safety of society.

THEMATIC FOCUS: PERILS AND ADVENTURES

The adventures of Beowulf are legendary, whereas the adventures of Charlemagne were actual. What characteristics do actual and legendary adventurers share?

Journal Writing Describe the types of problems that heroes of today's world confront.

◆ Build Vocabulary

WORD ROOTS: *-sol-*

In *Beowulf*, the Danes are unable to find solace from their misfortunes. The word *solace* is built upon the Latin root *-sol-*, which means "to comfort." Solace is an easing of grief, loneliness, or discomfort.

WORD BANK

Before you read, preview this list of words from the story.

reparation
solace
purge
writhing
massive
loathsome

◆ Grammar and Style

APPOSITIVES AND APPOSITIVE PHRASES

Throughout *Beowulf*, the poet uses **appositive phrases**—nouns or pronouns with modifiers that identify, explain, or rename other nouns or pronouns—to provide important information about the characters and setting. In the following lines, an appositive phrase, in italics, gives additional information about Beowulf:

In his far-off home Beowulf, *Higlac's*
Follower and the strongest of the Geats—

As you read *Beowulf*, notice how appositives and appositive phrases provide information without hindering the flow of the story.

◆ Literary Focus

THE EPIC

An **epic** is a long narrative poem, sometimes developed orally, that celebrates the deeds of a legendary or heroic figure. Typically, an epic is presented in a serious manner, often through the use of elevated language. The hero of an epic battles the forces of evil and represents widespread national, cultural, or religious values.

Epics such as *Beowulf* also contain elements of Anglo-Saxon poetry like the **kenning** and **caesura.** (For more about these, see p. 13.) Look for elements of the epic as you read *Beowulf.*

◆ Reading Strategy

PARAPHRASE

Although *Beowulf* has been translated into modern English, its long, involved sentences may be difficult to follow. To aid your understanding, **paraphrase**—identify key ideas and details and restate them in your own words. Look at the following example:

High on a wall a Danish watcher / Patrolling along the cliffs saw / The travelers crossing to the shore, their shields / Raised and shining; . . .

Paraphrased

A Danish guard saw strangers with raised shields come ashore.

Beowulf contains many of the features found in the most popular movies—a superhero who possesses amazing strength and courage; a bizarre, ruthless villain; suspense; and sustained action.

To demonstrate each of these elements of the modern action movie, dramatically read the following passages:

- *Superhero*, lines 506–511
- *Villain*, lines 19–29
- *Suspense*, lines 295–302
- *Sustained Action*, lines 682–688.

Have students speculate on the following question: If a current movie of *Beowulf* were made, what rating do you think it would be given?

Customize for
Less Proficient Readers

Have students read and study the summaries connecting the various parts of the epic and the subtitles for each of the eight parts. Then have students summarize what happens in each of the eight parts.

Customize for
More Advanced Students

Have students select one part of *Beowulf* to present as a radio drama. Allow them latitude in converting text to dialogue and adding sound effects. Tape the performance to play for the class.

Customize for
English Language Learners

The long, often inverted sentences will be difficult for English language learners. Have students mark off the beginning and end of each sentence, then read and summarize each element between commas or semicolons within the longer sentence. Check their understanding of each sentence and clarify any misunderstandings.

Customize for
Bodily/Kinesthetic Learners

Have some students act out one or more scenes from *Beowulf* as a good reader recites the lines. Many scenes lend themselves to this type of presentation: the arrival of Beowulf, Grendel's approach to Herot, the battle with Grendel's mother, and so on.

Preparing for Standardized Tests

Reading and Vocabulary The Reading Strategy lesson focuses on paraphrasing, which requires that students be able to identify main points and to comprehend the ideas in a passage well enough to communicate them in their own words. Because of this, paraphrasing will help students improve their performance on reading-comprehension items and on content-area items, in which students are asked to interpret and analyze historic documents, descriptions of scientific experiments, or hypotheses. For additional practice on paraphrasing, use the Reading Strategy exercise on page 62 and the Reading Strategy page in ***Selection Support,*** p. 8.

Grammar and Language Items on standardized tests may require students to choose the correct punctuation of an appositive, as in the following example:

The epic poem, Beowulf, is a famous work of literature. *(B)*

(A) poem, Beowulf,
(B) poem Beowulf
(C) poem, Beowulf
(D) poem Beowulf,

For practice, use the Grammar and Style page, p. 7, in ***Selection Support.***

Develop Understanding

One-Minute Insight *Beowulf* lays the groundwork for an understanding of English literature. A familiarity with its epic formula is an essential prerequisite for reading major works by Milton and Tennyson as well as light-hearted mock epics by Chaucer and Pope. However, it would be a mistake to view *Beowulf* as a mere footnote to later writers. Its stirring language and compelling action stand on its own merits, and inexorably draw readers into another time and place, a time when Christian values began to mold behavior and a place where monsters dwelled in steamy swamps. In *Beowulf* students should see a character transforming himself from a hero using raw strength to ensure his own fame to a noble leader who willingly dies for the sake of his people.

◆ Critical Thinking

❶ Compare and Contrast Contrast the description of Herot with the dwelling of the monster Grendel. Why do you think the storyteller placed these two descriptions next to each other? *Herot is filled with music and rejoicing while the monster lives down in the darkness and growls with pain. The sharp contrast serves to make the differences seem more dramatic and foreboding.*

◆ Critical Thinking

❷ Evaluate Which words in this description of Grendel's birth are particularly effective in portraying the evil nature of this monster? *Responses could include the following: spawned, slime, murderous, banished, demons, exile, fiends, goblins, and brood.*

from BEOWULF

Translated by Burton Raffel

The selection opens during an evening of celebration at Herot, the banquet hall of the Danish king Hrothgar (hroth′ gär). *Outside in the darkness, however, lurks the monster Grendel, a murderous creature who poses a great danger to the people inside the banquet hall.*

The Wrath of Grendel

A powerful monster, living down
In the darkness, growled in pain, impatient
❶ As day after day the music rang
Loud in that hall,[1] the harp's rejoicing
Call and the poet's clear songs, sung
Of the ancient beginnings of us all, recalling
The Almighty making the earth, shaping
These beautiful plains marked off by oceans,
Then proudly setting the sun and moon
To glow across the land and light it;
The corners of the earth were made lovely with trees
And leaves, made quick with life, with each
Of the nations who now move on its face. And then
As now warriors sang of their pleasure:
So Hrothgar's men lived happy in his hall
Till the monster stirred, that demon, that fiend,
Grendel, who haunted the moors, the wild
Marshes, and made his home in a hell
Not hell but earth. He was spawned in that slime,
Conceived by a pair of those monsters born
Of Cain,[2] murderous creatures banished
❷ By God, punished forever for the crime
Of Abel's death. The Almighty drove
Those demons out, and their exile was bitter,
Shut away from men; they split
Into a thousand forms of evil—spirits
And fiends, goblins, monsters, giants,
A brood forever opposing the Lord's
Will, and again and again defeated.

1. **hall:** Herot.

2. **Cain:** Oldest son of Adam and Eve, who murdered his brother Abel.

Block Scheduling Strategies

Consider these suggestions to take advantage of extended class time:

- Use the Daily Language Practice sentences for Weeks 2 and 3 in the ***Writing and Language Transparencies,*** pp. 137–138. Display the practice sentences on an overhead projector and have students write them correctly.
- Introduce the epic as a form of literature. Have students read the Literary Focus on page 39 and, after reading, answer the Literary Focus questions on page 62. You may follow up with the Literary Focus page from ***Selection Support,*** p. 9
- Students may enjoy using the Internet to find out more about Old English, *Beowulf,* or the Electronic Beowulf Project either before or after they read the poem.
- Encourage students to work in small groups to complete the Literature and Your Life activities on page 61.
- Allow students to work on the writing activities described in the Idea Bank on page 63.
- Have students develop and rehearse a dramatic performance, as described in the Idea Bank, p. 63. This activity is supported by a Speaking and Listening Mini-Lesson on page 48 in this teacher's edition.
- Direct students to work in groups to complete the Media Connection activity in ***Beyond Literature,*** p. 2. Allow interested groups the opportunity to present their proposals for a movie version of the epic to the class.

Grendel (Frontispiece from *Beowulf*), Patten Wilson, The British Library

▲ **Critical Viewing** Analyze the artist's use of details to make Grendel look fearsome. **[Analyze]** ❸

▶Critical Viewing◀

❸ Details that make Grendel look fearsome include the horns, pointed ears, and goatlike beard that are traditionally used in representations of evil characters like demons and devils. The vampiric fangs, bestial fur, and enormous claws also contribute to Grendel's frightening appearance. In addition, the use of dark colors, such as crimson and black, gives the illustration a sinister, threatening mood.

Customize for *More Advanced Students*

As they read this epic poem, have these students note evidence showing the storyteller was familiar with the Bible. These opening lines, for example, make clear references to the creation by the "Almighty" and to the story of Cain and Abel. If practical, have them explain these allusions to the class by retelling the biblical accounts to which they refer.

◆ Background for Understanding

Charles Kennedy, a translator of *Beowulf*, considers the Christian/pagan duality in the story to be extremely important. He writes: "We have seen that the primitive material of *Beowulf* was derived from pagan folk-tale chronicle, and legend, and slowly welded into new unities. It remained for the Old English poet to complete this process of fusion by the conversion, or transmutation, of this material from pagan to Christian. The epic emerges at last as a Christian poem. This mutation, moreover, is not merely a matter of altered phrases, or of interpolated references to the Christian faith, but is a deeply pervasive infusion of Christian spirit coloring thought and judgment, governing motive and action, a continuous and active agent in the process of transformation."

Humanities: Art

Grendel by Patten Wilson.

This portrait of a demonic Grendel was commissioned as the frontispiece for an edition of *Beowulf*.

Use these questions for discussion:

1. Which details in Wilson's drawing of Beowulf are actually mentioned in the epic poem? Which ones are implied, but not specifically mentioned? *Grendel's mighty claws are mentioned several times and are emphasized in the drawing. See lines 33–35 and 319–324. Reference is made to "gleaming eyes" in lines 300–302. Lines 316–319 mention Grendel's "powerful jaws" and "great teeth." The demonic appearance reflected in the horns and pointed ears is implied in the opening, especially lines 15–29, where Grendel is called a demon and evil spirit, much like the biblical devil.*
2. Do you agree with the artist's view of Grendel? Why or why not? *Some students will think that Wilson's view captures the essentially demonic nature of Grendel. Other students will think that Grendel looks too human or too much like the stereotypical devil.*
3. What moment in the narrative is suggested by this drawing? *Possible Response: Grendel appears to be stalking victims in Herot, possibly the night Beowulf was waiting for him.*

Customize for
Less Proficient Readers

❶ Help these students understand this long sentence by having them break it into several shorter sentences. Help them get started by writing these short sentences on the chalkboard:

- He slipped through the door.
- Then he snatched up thirty men.

◆ Grammar and Style

❷ **Appositives and Appositive Phrases** Have students identify the appositive in this line. *The appositive is "their lord."* Point out that the appositive refers to Hrothgar and is set off by commas.

◆ Reading Strategy

❸ **Paraphrase** Have students paraphrase these lines. *Student's paraphrases should include the following points: Grendel, the evil one, had overcome the many forces of good. As a result Herot was deserted for twelve years. This was a time of grief for Hrothgar, the king of the Danes. The story of his misery had spread across the seas. Stories spread about how Grendel's savagery was unstoppable.*

Customize for
More Advanced Students

❹ Have students examine the symbolism in the epic by asking questions such as the following: What had Herot represented in the land? What is the significance of it standing empty? *Students may say that Herot represents goodness, beauty, and the power of the king. The empty hall signifies that the king is not in control of the situation, and goodness and beauty are threatened.*

❺ **Clarification** Anglo-Saxon custom dictated that a person who killed another person, even accidentally, had to pay a "man-price," or wergild, to the dead person's kin or risk deadly retribution. A relative who did not exact wergild from his kin's killer was humiliated. In this darkly cynical passage, the poet notes that the only payment Grendel makes is more murder.

Then, when darkness had dropped, Grendel
Went up to Herot, wondering what the warriors
Would do in that hall when their drinking was done.
He found them sprawled in sleep, suspecting
Nothing, their dreams undisturbed. The monster's
Thoughts were as quick as his greed or his claws:
❶ He slipped through the door and there in the silence
Snatched up thirty men, smashed them
Unknowing in their beds and ran out with their bodies,
The blood dripping behind him, back
To his lair, delighted with his night's slaughter.
At daybreak, with the sun's first light, they saw
How well he had worked, and in that gray morning
Broke their long feast with tears and laments
❷ For the dead. Hrothgar, their lord, sat joyless
In Herot, a mighty prince mourning
The fate of his lost friends and companions,
Knowing by its tracks that some demon had torn
His followers apart. He wept, fearing
The beginning might not be the end. And that night
Grendel came again, so set
On murder that no crime could ever be enough,
No savage assault quench his lust
For evil. Then each warrior tried
To escape him, searched for rest in different
Beds, as far from Herot as they could find,
Seeing how Grendel hunted when they slept.
Distance was safety; the only survivors
Were those who fled him. Hate had triumphed.
❸ So Grendel ruled, fought with the righteous,
One against many, and won; so Herot
Stood empty, and stayed deserted for years,
Twelve winters of grief for Hrothgar, king
Of the Danes, sorrow heaped at his door
By hell-forged hands. His misery leaped
❹ The seas, was told and sung in all
Men's ears: how Grendel's hatred began,
How the monster relished his savage war
On the Danes, keeping the bloody feud
Alive, seeking no peace, offering
No truce, accepting no settlement, no price
❺ In gold or land, and paying the living
For one crime only with another. No one
Waited for reparation from his plundering claws:
That shadow of death hunted in the darkness,
Stalked Hrothgar's warriors, old
And young, lying in waiting, hidden
In mist, invisibly following them from the edge
Of the marsh, always there, unseen.
So mankind's enemy continued his crimes,
Killing as often as he could, coming
Alone, bloodthirsty and horrible. Though he lived

◆ Build Vocabulary

reparation (rep′ə rā′ shən) *n.*: Making up for wrong or injury

solace (säl′ is) *n.*: Comfort; relief

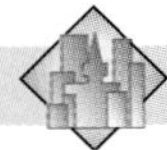

Beyond the Classroom

Career Connection

Archaeologist Much of what we know about the early civilizations that produced epics like *Beowulf* is the result of the work of archaeologists. The artifacts pictured in this unit provide fascinating insights into the people, their lives, and their values. A skilled archaeologist can derive an amazing amount of information from a small relic of the past.

Have interested students find additional photographs of early European and Scandinavian artifacts and summarize the information archaeologists are able to piece together from such remnants of these early people. They might begin by making some conjectures based on the artifacts pictured in the textbook. Have them make a special note of any controversies over the meaning of certain artifacts.

In Herot, when the night hid him, he never
❻ Dared to touch king Hrothgar's glorious
Throne, protected by God—God,
Whose love Grendel could not know. But Hrothgar's
Heart was bent. The best and most noble
Of his council debated remedies, sat
In secret sessions, talking of terror
And wondering what the bravest of warriors could do.
And sometimes they sacrificed to the old stone gods,
Made heathen vows, hoping for Hell's
❼ Support, the Devil's guidance in driving
Their affliction off. That was their way,
And the heathen's only hope, Hell
Always in their hearts, knowing neither God
Nor His passing as He walks through our world, the Lord
Of Heaven and earth; their ears could not hear
His praise nor know His glory. Let them
Beware, those who are thrust into danger,
❽ Clutched at by trouble, yet can carry no <u>solace</u>
In their hearts, cannot hope to be better! Hail
To those who will rise to God, drop off
Their dead bodies and seek our Father's peace!

The Coming of Beowulf

So the living sorrow of Healfdane's son[3]
Simmered, bitter and fresh, and no wisdom
❾ Or strength could break it: that agony hung
On king and people alike, harsh
And unending, violent and cruel, and evil.
In his far-off home Beowulf, Higlac's[4]
Follower and the strongest of the Geats—greater
And stronger than anyone anywhere in this world—
Heard how Grendel filled nights with horror
And quickly commanded a boat fitted out,
Proclaiming that he'd go to that famous king,
❿ Would sail across the sea to Hrothgar,
Now when help was needed. None
Of the wise ones regretted his going, much
As he was loved by the Geats: the omens were good,
And they urged the adventure on. So Beowulf
Chose the mightiest men he could find,
The bravest and best of the Geats, fourteen
In all, and led them down to their boat;
He knew the sea, would point the prow
Straight to that distant Danish shore.
Then they sailed, set their ship
Out on the waves, under the cliffs.
Ready for what came they wound through the currents,
The seas beating at the sand, and were borne
In the lap of their shining ship, lined
With gleaming armor, going safely

3. **Healfdane's** (hā´ alf den´ nəz) **son:** Hrothgar.

4. **Higlac's** (hig´ laks): Higlac was the king of the Geats (gā´ ats) and Beowulf's feudal lord and uncle.

◆ Critical Thinking

❻ **Analyze** Ask students: How does the storyteller establish that the coming battle is not just a battle between a hero and a monster, but a battle between good and evil? *Hrothgar's throne is untouched because it is protected by God, who is unknown to Grendel.*

❼ **Enrichment** Have students identify the Christian and pagan elements in this passage. *Christian elements include the references to Hell, the Devil, and God. Pagan elements include the sacrifices to stone gods.* Ask students to speculate about what this passage reveals about Christian attitudes to pagan practices and about the religious practices of the Danes in the poem. *Students may point out that the Christian attitudes expressed by the poem's speaker are harshly condemning of pagan practices, equating the "old stone gods" with "Hell's support." The behavior of the Danes in the poem and the harshness of the speaker's criticism of them suggest that in times of trouble, people in newly Christianized countries often lapsed back into their pagan practices.*

◆ Build Vocabulary

❽ **The root *-sol-*** Point out that the word *solace* is derived from the Latin word *solare,* meaning "to console." You might wish to mention that the noun form is used in the expression *consolation prize.* A consolation prize goes to the person who does not win. It is intended to "console" the loser.

Customize for *Less Proficient Readers*

❾ These students may have difficulty understanding the inverted word order where adjectives follow the noun they modify. Ask: Which word do the following adjectives modify: *harsh, unending, violent, cruel,* and *evil? All of these adjectives modify the noun agony in line 106.*

◆ Literary Focus

❿ **The Epic** An epic hero embodies the values and ideals of the culture that produces it. Ask students: Based on this initial description of Beowulf, what things did the storytellers of *Beowulf* value? *They valued great physical strength, leadership ability, compassion for others, and bravery.*

Cross-Curricular Connection: Science

The Geats were excellent sailors whom "the wind hurried . . . over the waves" and "through the sea like a bird." Acquiring such sailing skill is not a simple matter; it requires an understanding of the forces of wind, water, and the capabilities of your ship. This is especially true when your destination lies directly into the wind.

Have interested students research the forces at work and the techniques required to sail a ship against the wind. The process of sailing can be diagrammed and demonstrated to the class using a hypothetical island destination that lies a prescribed number of miles upwind from one's present location. The diagram should show the angle of the wind, the position of the sail, and the direction of the various forces that result in forward movement.

◆ **Literary Focus**

❶ **Epic** Most students will probably approve of the kenning *sea-road*. Challenge them to propose additional kennings for the ocean.

Check Comprehension

❷ Have students explain why Hrothgar's lieutenant is concerned. *Although Beowulf and his men have come ashore openly, unlike sneaky pirates or raiders, they are unexpected, and do not have passwords or tokens to show that the king has given them permission to come to Denmark.*

◆ ***Literature and Your Life***

❸ Hrothgar's lieutenant recognizes that Beowulf is a hero because he looks like one and carries noble weapons. Encourage students to draw upon their own experiences and observations to discuss the practice of judging a person from his or her appearance. Ask them about the benefits and dangers of "judging a book by its cover."

In that oak-hard boat to where their hearts took them.
The wind hurried them over the waves,
The ship foamed through the sea like a bird
Until, in the time they had known it would take,
Standing in the round-curled prow they could see
Sparkling hills, high and green
Jutting up over the shore, and rejoicing
In those rock-steep cliffs they quietly ended
Their voyage. Jumping to the ground, the Geats
Pushed their boat to the sand and tied it
In place, mail[5] shirts and armor rattling
As they swiftly moored their ship. And then
They gave thanks to God for their easy crossing.
  High on a wall a Danish watcher
Patrolling along the cliffs saw
The travelers crossing to the shore, their shields
Raised and shining; he came riding down,
Hrothgar's lieutenant, spurring his horse,
Needing to know why they'd landed, these men
In armor. Shaking his heavy spear
In their faces he spoke:
            "Whose soldiers are you,
You who've been carried in your deep-keeled ship
Across the sea-road to this country of mine?
Listen! I've stood on these cliffs longer
❷ Than you know, keeping our coast free
Of pirates, raiders sneaking ashore
From their ships, seeking our lives and our gold.
None have ever come more openly—
And yet you've offered no password, no sign
From my prince, no permission from my people for your landing
Here. Nor have I ever seen,
Out of all the men on earth, one greater
❸ Than has come with you; no commoner carries
Such weapons, unless his appearance, and his beauty,
Are both lies. You! Tell me your name,
And your father's; no spies go further onto Danish
Soil than you've come already. Strangers,
From wherever it was you sailed, tell it,
And tell it quickly, the quicker the better,
I say, for us all. Speak, say
Exactly who you are, and from where, and why."
  Their leader answered him, Beowulf unlocking

5. **mail:** Flexible body armor made of metal.

◆ **Literary Focus**
Is the kenning *sea-road* an effective description of the ocean? Explain. ❶

The Oseberg Ship (Viking artifact, c. A.D. 850)
Viking Ship Museum, Bygdoy, Oslo

Humanities: Art

The Oseberg Ship, Viking artifact, c. A.D. 850.

Perhaps the best-known relic of Viking times is the Oseberg ship shown here. Although this ship dates from the ninth century, its design is so elegant that it has interested modern shipbuilders. (In 1893 a replica of the Oseberg ship actually crossed the Atlantic.) The rudder was at the side, rather than in the stern. The planks at the bottom of the ship are less than one inch thick, while the boat itself is over seventy-two feet long.

Use the following questions for discussion:

1. Does this ship look as though it could cross from Sweden to Denmark the way Beowulf's ship did? Why or why not? *Most students will think that the boat is seaworthy, particularly after learning that a replica crossed the Atlantic.*
2. The Vikings believed that the souls of the dead journeyed on a ship. What does this belief suggest about the relationship between a people's way of life and its ideas about the afterlife? *In general, the afterlife is viewed as being similar to earthly life.*
3. How is the Oseberg ship similar to or different from modern ships? *Modern ships retain a streamlined hull, but lack the elaborate decorations of the Viking ship. Modern ships are made of steel, powered by engines and propellers, and have their rudder in the stern. The Viking ship is made of wood, is powered by sail and oar, and has its rudder at the side.*

Words from deep in his breast:
"We are Geats,
Men who follow Higlac. My father
Was a famous soldier, known far and wide
❹ As a leader of men. His name was Edgetho.
His life lasted many winters;
Wise men all over the earth surely
Remember him still. And we have come seeking
Your prince, Healfdane's son, protector
Of this people, only in friendship: instruct us,
Watchman, help us with your words! Our errand
Is a great one, our business with the glorious king
Of the Danes no secret; there's nothing dark
Or hidden in our coming. You know (if we've heard
The truth, and been told honestly) that your country
Is cursed with some strange, vicious creature
That hunts only at night and that no one
Has seen. It's said, watchman, that he has slaughtered
Your people, brought terror to the darkness. Perhaps
Hrothgar can hunt, here in my heart,
For some way to drive this devil out—
If anything will ever end the evils
Afflicting your wise and famous lord.
Here he can cool his burning sorrow.
Or else he may see his suffering go on
Forever, for as long as Herot towers
High on your hills."
The mounted officer
Answered him bluntly, the brave watchman:
"A soldier should know the difference between words
And deeds, and keep that knowledge clear
In his brain. I believe your words, I trust in
Your friendship. Go forward, weapons and armor
And all, on into Denmark. I'll guide you
Myself—and my men will guard your ship,
Keep it safe here on our shores,
Your fresh-tarred boat, watch it well,
Until that curving prow carries
❻ Across the sea to Geatland a chosen
Warrior who bravely does battle with the creature
Haunting our people, who survives that horror
Unhurt, and goes home bearing our love."
Then they moved on. Their boat lay moored,
Tied tight to its anchor. Glittering at the top
Of their golden helmets wild boar heads gleamed,
❼ Shining decorations, swinging as they marched,
Erect like guards, like sentinels, as though ready
To fight. They marched, Beowulf and his men
And their guide, until they could see the gables
Of Herot, covered with hammered gold
And glowing in the sun—that most famous of all dwellings,
Towering majestic, its glittering roofs

◆ **Reading Strategy**
Paraphrase lines 179–198, giving Beowulf's reasons for coming to the Danish land. ❺

◆ Critical Thinking

❹ **Infer** Ask students what they can infer from this passage about characteristics valued by the Anglo-Saxons. *They valued loyalty to an overlord, military prowess, leadership, having a respected father, and wisdom.*

◆ Reading Strategy

❺ **Paraphrase** Student responses should convey the gist of Beowulf's words: *We seek Hrothgar in friendship and have no evil or secret purpose. We heard about the monster and we can help your people get rid of it.*

Customize for *English Language Learners*

❻ Students may have difficulty following this flowery speech. Guide students to understand that in lines 205–207, the guard promises that his men will guard Beowulf's ship and keep it safe. In lines 208–212, the guard is wishing Beowulf luck. By phrasing this as a declaration of a future event, he expresses his faith that Beowulf will succeed.

❼ **Clarification** The Anglo-Saxons believed that the image of a boar on a helmet would protect the wearer in battle.

Cross-Curricular Connection: Geography

The text speaks of "that distant Danish shore," and setting out "under the cliffs" and seeing high, green hills upon arrival. Scholars believe that Beowulf was traveling from southern Sweden to Denmark.

Have interested students research the geography of that area to determine the possible starting and ending points of the voyage. They might also check what type of seas and currents Beowulf might have encountered on his voyage and how long it might have taken a sailing ship to make the trip.

◆ *Literature and Your Life*

❶ In this passage, Hrothgar, a brave and powerful leader, opens his hall to a neighboring hero who has come to save him. Hrothgar says nothing as Beowulf addresses him. However, he must have had very strong feelings about the situation. Have volunteers recall a time when they needed to accept help with a problem they could not handle or when they had to help someone else.

◆ Critical Thinking

❷ **Comparison and Contrast** Ask students: Would a modern-day hero boast of his achievement the way Beowulf does in these lines? How would you react to someone who tells you of all his or her accomplishments? *Some students will think that Beowulf is excessively boastful. Others will think that he is simply doing the equivalent of presenting his résumé.* How do you think the Anglo-Saxon audience reacted to this hero's boasts? *Anglo-Saxon audiences did not value humility in their heroes as we do today.*

◆ Critical Thinking

❸ **Evaluate** In this passage, Beowulf says he will fight Grendel without using weapons. Ask students what this decision reveals about Beowulf's character. *Students may say that Beowulf is fearless, confident in his abilities, and decisive.* Then ask them what they think of this plan. *Some students may feel that this plan is reasonable, since Beowulf has conquered monsters before and is certain that God is on his side. Other students may think that Beowulf is being foolish.*

Visible far across the land.
Their guide reined in his horse, pointing
To that hall, built by Hrothgar for the best
And bravest of his men; the path was plain,
They could see their way . . .

Beowulf and his men arrive at Herot and are about to be escorted in to see King Hrothgar.

Beowulf arose, with his men
Around him, ordering a few to remain
With their weapons, leading the others quickly
Along under Herot's steep roof into Hrothgar's
Presence. Standing on that prince's own hearth,
Helmeted, the silvery metal of his mail shirt
Gleaming with a smith's high art, he greeted
The Danes' great lord:
"Hail, Hrothgar!
Higlac is my cousin[6] and my king; the days
❶ Of my youth have been filled with glory. Now Grendel's
Name has echoed in our land: sailors
Have brought us stories of Herot, the best
Of all mead-halls,[7] deserted and useless when the moon
Hangs in skies the sun had lit,
Light and life fleeing together.
My people have said, the wisest, most knowing
And best of them, that my duty was to go to the Danes'
Great king. They have seen my strength for themselves,
Have watched me rise from the darkness of war,
Dripping with my enemies' blood. I drove
Five great giants into chains, chased
❷ All of that race from the earth. I swam
In the blackness of night, hunting monsters
Out of the ocean, and killing them one
By one; death was my errand and the fate
They had earned. Now Grendel and I are called
Together, and I've come. Grant me, then,
Lord and protector of this noble place,
A single request! I have come so far,
Oh shelterer of warriors and your people's loved friend,
That this one favor you should not refuse me—
That I, alone and with the help of my men,
May purge all evil from this hall. I have heard,
Too, that the monster's scorn of men
Is so great that he needs no weapons and fears none.
Nor will I. My lord Higlac
Might think less of me if I let my sword
Go where my feet were afraid to, if I hid
❸ Behind some broad linden[8] shield: my hands
Alone shall fight for me, struggle for life
❹ Against the monster. God must decide

Gilt silver brooch from Gotland (Pre-Viking Scandinavia) Statens Historiska Museet, Stockholm

6. **cousin:** Here, used as a general term for relative.

7. **mead-halls:** To reward his thanes, the king in heroic literature would build a hall where mead (a drink made from fermented honey) was served.

8. **linden:** Very sturdy type of wood.

Humanities: Artifact

Gilt-Silver Brooch From Gotland.

Pre-Viking Scandinavia (that is, pre–ninth century) produced many artifacts highly decorated with carving and ornamentation. This so-called barbarian art may have been influenced by forms and patterns of Near Eastern origin; for example, snake forms have been traced to ancient Mesopotamia. Decorated metalwork, like the gilt-silver brooch seen here, was carried westward to England and Ireland by traders and invaders.

Use the following questions for discussion:

1. How do you think the sunlight might have enhanced the appearance of objects like this brooch? *It probably caused the intricate designs to sparkle as they reflected the light in many directions.*
2. What can you infer about ancient Scandinavian society based on decorative objects like this one? *Possible responses: People valued beauty even in utilitarian objects. The society was advanced and wealthy enough to support artisans.*
3. Do we wear jewelry similar to this brooch? Explain. *Students may point out that people still wear decorative brooches today.*

Who will be given to death's cold grip.
Grendel's plan, I think, will be
What it has been before, to invade this hall
And gorge his belly with our bodies. If he can,
If he can. And I think, if my time will have come,
There'll be nothing to mourn over, no corpse to prepare
For its grave: Grendel will carry our bloody
❹ Flesh to the moors, crunch on our bones
And smear torn scraps of our skin on the walls
Of his den. No, I expect no Danes
Will fret about sewing our shrouds, if he wins.
And if death does take me, send the hammered
Mail of my armor to Higlac, return
The inheritance I had from Hrethel, and he
From Wayland.[9] Fate will unwind as it must!"

The Battle with Grendel

That night Beowulf and his men take the places of Hrothgar and the Danes inside Herot. While his men sleep, Beowulf lies awake, eager to meet with Grendel.

Out from the marsh, from the foot of misty
Hills and bogs, bearing God's hatred,
Grendel came, hoping to kill
Anyone he could trap on this trip to high Herot.
He moved quickly through the cloudy night,
Up from his swampland, sliding silently
Toward that gold-shining hall. He had visited Hrothgar's
Home before, knew the way—
But never, before nor after that night,
❻ Found Herot defended so firmly, his reception
So harsh. He journeyed, forever joyless,
Straight to the door, then snapped it open,
Tore its iron fasteners with a touch
And rushed angrily over the threshold.
He strode quickly across the inlaid
Floor, snarling and fierce: his eyes
Gleamed in the darkness, burned with a gruesome
Light. Then he stopped, seeing the hall
Crowded with sleeping warriors, stuffed
With rows of young soldiers resting together.
And his heart laughed, he relished the sight,
Intended to tear the life from those bodies
By morning; the monster's mind was hot
With the thought of food and the feasting his belly
Would soon know. But fate, that night, intended
Grendel to gnaw the broken bones
Of his last human supper. Human

◆ **Reading Strategy** ❺
To follow what happens when Beowulf and Grendel meet, paraphrase lines 264–279, describing their plans of action.

9. Wayland: From Germanic folklore, an invisible blacksmith.

◆ Build Vocabulary

purge (purj) *v.*: Purify; cleanse

◆ Critical Thinking

❹ **Interpret** Ask students: What evidence do you see in these lines of both Christian and a pagan influence on the storyteller? *Initially Beowulf says that God will decide the outcome of the battle, but concludes by saying Fate will decide the matter. This latter reference implies that the outcome is beyond the control of supernatural forces.*

◆ Reading Strategy

❺ **Paraphrase** Paraphrases should resemble this one: *I plan to fight Grendel with my bare hands. Grendel will probably plan to do what he has done before: to invade the hall and eat its inhabitants.*

◆ Critical Thinking

❻ **Evaluate** Read these lines aloud slowly to the class. Then ask: Does the storyteller do a good job of creating a feeling of anticipation and suspense in these lines? How does he achieve this effect? *Words like* marsh, misty, bogs, *and* swampland *slowly create a foreboding picture in the reader's mind. The sounds of the words add to the mood of imminent bloodshed. Note especially the alliterative "trap on this trip to high Herot," and "Up from his swampland, sliding silently."*

Enrichment

Literary historians have pointed out that the themes and style of *Beowulf* owe much to the Germanic heroic tradition. The writers of *The New Encyclopedia Britannica* state the following:

> Beowulf himself seems more altruistic than other Germanic heroes or the heroes of the *Iliad*. It is significant that his three battles are not against men, which would entail the retaliation of the blood feud, but against evil monsters, enemies of the whole community and of civilization itself. Many critics have seen the poem as a Christian allegory, with Beowulf the champion of goodness and light against the forces of evil and darkness. His sacrificial death is not seen as tragic but as the fitting end of a good (some would say "too good") hero's life.

Customize for
Bodily/Kinesthetic Learners

❶ Have two students role-play this arm-wrestling scene while a third student reads the text. Allow them to rehearse it privately before performing it in front of the class. Have the class critique the performance for its adherence to the details of the description.

◆ Literary Focus

❷ **The Epic** Have students identify the kennings in line 325. *The kennings are "shepherd of evil" and "guardian of crime."*

◆ Critical Thinking

❸ **Relate** Have students relate the loving description of the splendor of Herot to the photographs of the Scandinavian artifacts that illustrate this selection. *Students should note that even everyday objects are decorated; objects are valued for their beauty as well as their functionality.*

◆ *Literature and Your Life*

❹ Students may mention specific movies that reflect a similar "final battle" between the forces of good and evil. This scene will no doubt compare favorably to any fight with an exaggerated portrayal of its scope and violence. Have students identify elements of the struggle that seem unrealistic, such as the swaying roof board in line 342. Ask them to compare this to similar exaggerations in movie fights.

Eyes were watching his evil steps,
Waiting to see his swift hard claws.
Grendel snatched at the first Geat
He came to, ripped him apart, cut
His body to bits with powerful jaws,
Drank the blood from his veins and bolted
Him down, hands and feet; death
And Grendel's great teeth came together,
Snapping life shut. Then he stepped to another
Still body, clutched at Beowulf with his claws,
Grasped at a strong-hearted wakeful sleeper
—And was instantly seized himself, claws
Bent back as Beowulf leaned up on one arm.
    That shepherd of evil, guardian of crime,
Knew at once that nowhere on earth
Had he met a man whose hands were harder;
His mind was flooded with fear—but nothing
❶ Could take his talons and himself from that tight
Hard grip. Grendel's one thought was to run
❷ From Beowulf, flee back to his marsh and hide there:
This was a different Herot than the hall he had emptied.
But Higlac's follower remembered his final
Boast and, standing erect, stopped
The monster's flight, fastened those claws
In his fists till they cracked, clutched Grendel
Closer. The infamous killer fought
For his freedom, wanting no flesh but retreat,
Desiring nothing but escape; his claws
Had been caught, he was trapped. That trip to Herot
Was a miserable journey for the writhing monster!
    The high hall rang, its roof boards swayed,
And Danes shook with terror. Down
The aisles the battle swept, angry
And wild. Herot trembled, wonderfully
Built to withstand the blows, the struggling
Great bodies beating at its beautiful walls;
Shaped and fastened with iron, inside
And out, artfully worked, the building
Stood firm. Its benches rattled, fell
To the floor, gold-covered boards grating
❸ As Grendel and Beowulf battled across them.
Hrothgar's wise men had fashioned Herot
To stand forever; only fire,
They had planned, could shatter what such skill had put
Together, swallow in hot flames such splendor
Of ivory and iron and wood. Suddenly
The sounds changed, the Danes started
In new terror, cowering in their beds as the terrible
Screams of the Almighty's enemy sang
In the darkness, the horrible shrieks of pain
And defeat, the tears torn out of Grendel's
Taut throat, hell's captive caught in the arms

◆ *Literature and Your Life*
How does this scene compare with those you have seen in horror movies? ❹

Speaking and Listening Mini-Lesson

Performance
This mini-lesson supports the Speaking and Listening activity in the Idea Bank on page 63.

Introduce the Concept Demonstrate the impact a dramatic reading can have on one's understanding and enjoyment of literature by playing a recording done by a professional. Explain that the Anglo-Saxon *scop* was the professional performer of his time. In addition to keeping the stories of their great heroes alive, he entertained his listeners.

Develop Background Students should begin by analyzing the passage for meaning. Every sentence should be looked at closely, and the subject, verb, and modifiers identified. Students should note the important words and the punctuation. These give important clues to which words to stress and where to pause. Have students identify places of suspense and action and decide on the pace of the reading. It might be helpful to make an enlarged copy of the passage so students can write their notes on delivery right on the page.

Apply the Information Allow students to practice their reading before presenting it to the class.

Assess the Outcome Have students evaluate their own and others' readings using the Peer Assessment: Oral Interpretation page, p. 123, in ***Alternative Assessment.*** Allow them to offer both compliments and constructive criticism of each performance.

Of him who of all the men on earth
Was the strongest.
That mighty protector of men
Meant to hold the monster till its life
Leaped out, knowing the fiend was no use ❺
To anyone in Denmark. All of Beowulf's
Band had jumped from their beds, ancestral
Swords raised and ready, determined
To protect their prince if they could. Their courage
Was great but all wasted: they could hack at Grendel
From every side, trying to open
A path for his evil soul, but their points
Could not hurt him, the sharpest and hardest iron
Could not scratch at his skin, for that sin-stained demon
Had bewitched all men's weapons, laid spells ❻
That blunted every mortal man's blade.
And yet his time had come, his days ❼
Were over, his death near; down
To hell he would go, swept groaning and helpess
To the waiting hands of still worse fiends.
Now he discovered—once the afflictor
Of men, tormentor of their days—what it meant
To feud with Almighty God: Grendel
Saw that his strength was deserting him, his claws
Bound fast, Higlac's brave follower tearing at
His hands. The monster's hatred rose higher,
But his power had gone. He twisted in pain,
And the bleeding sinews deep in his shoulder
Snapped, muscle and bone split
And broke. The battle was over, Beowulf
Had been granted new glory: Grendel escaped,
But wounded as he was could flee to his den,
His miserable hole at the bottom of the marsh,
Only to die, to wait for the end
Of all his days. And after that bloody
Combat the Danes laughed with delight.
He who had come to them from across the sea,
Bold and strong-minded, had driven affliction
Off, purged Herot clean. He was happy,
Now, with that night's fierce work; the Danes
Had been served as he'd boasted he'd serve them; Beowulf,
A prince of the Geats, had killed Grendel,
Ended the grief, the sorrow, the suffering
Forced on Hrothgar's helpless people
By a bloodthirsty fiend. No Dane doubted
The victory, for the proof, hanging high
From the rafters where Beowulf had hung it, was the monster's ❽
Arm, claw and shoulder and all.

◆ Build Vocabulary

writhing (rīth′ iŋ) *adj.*: Making twisting or turning motions

◆ Reading Strategy

❺ **Paraphrase** Have students replace the following words with a simpler or more direct words:

- That mighty protector of men *Beowulf*
- . . . life/Leaped out *died*
- . . . the fiend . . . *Grendel*

◆ Literary Focus

❻ **The Epic** One characteristic of an epic is the involvement of the supernatural in the outcome. Have students look at these lines closely to identify how supernatural forces are involved in this battle. *Grendel has bewitched the weapons of Beowulf's men; Grendel learns he is feuding with "Almighty God."*

◆ Critical Thinking

❼ **Evaluate** Have students revisit their reactions to lines 264–269, in which Beowulf announces he will fight Grendel barehanded, lest his lord Higlac think less of him. How do they evaluate Beowulf's decision in light of the information in lines 371–378? *Some students may say that Beowulf made a good decision. Others may say that Beowulf lucked into the correct course of action; his reasoning was wrong, even if he did end up fighting Grendel in the only way possible.*

◆ Literature and Your Life

❽ Beowulf hangs the arm he tore from Grendel from the rafters as evidence of his victory. Like Beowulf, we also like to display evidence of our achievements. The most obvious examples are the trophies awarded to athletes. Have students think of other contemporary reminders of an achievement. *Examples might include medals and decorations given to military heroes and keys or other forms of jewelry awarded by honor societies.*

Enrichment

There are many kennings in "The Battle With Grendel." These include "shepherd of evil" and "guardian of crime" (line 325), "Higlac's follower" (line 333), "infamous killer" (line 337), "Almighty's enemy" (line 360), and "hell's captive" (line 363). In the original Old English, the primary purpose of kennings was to maintain the alliteration required by Anglo-Saxon verse. According to convention, one of the accented syllables after the caesura has to alliterate with at least one of the accented syllables in the first half of the line.

Use questions like the following to help students examine the form of Anglo-Saxon verse in detail:

1. Copy lines 374–378 on a piece of paper. Mark the accented syllables and the caesura. Underline the appropriate letter in a stressed symbol to show alliteration before and after the caesura. *Suggested response: A páth for his évil sóul ‖ but their póints/Could not húrt him, the shárpest and hárdest íron/Could not scrátch at his skín, ‖ for that sín-stained démon/Had bewítched ‖ all mén's wéapons, laid spélls/That blúnted ‖ every mórtal mán's bláde.*
2. What are the accented syllables in lines 374–378? *Answers should match the student's marked lines. There should be four stresses per line.*
3. Where is the caesura in each line? *Answers should match the student's marked lines.*
4. How well do the lines follow the traditional pattern of alliteration? *They follow it quite closely. Most of the lines in this translation follow the traditional patterns of alliteration.*
5. How does the kenning in line 376 enhance the alliteration in the line? *The kenning "sin-stained demon" alliterates with "scratch" and "skin."*

◆ Reading Strategy

Paraphrase The lengthy monologue in "The Monsters' Lair" (lines 411–448) provides an opportunity for students to paraphrase the key points as they read it, and then to use these notes to deliver Hrothgar's monologue in their own words. *Students will paraphrase the passage in different ways, but should include the following points: Grendel had been spotted with a female monster, his mother; the monsters' lair lies beneath a lake; the place is so fearsome that a hunted deer will not enter the lake so that it can escape by swimming; Hrothgar will reward Beowulf with golden treasure for slaying Grendel's mother.*

◆ Background for Understanding

❶ **History** Point out that this passage, which states that nothing is known about Grendel's ancestry or kin, contradicts lines 17–29. In this passage, Grendel and other monsters like him are said to be descendants of Cain, the first murderer. Explain that these contradictory passages are an example of the inconsistent interweaving of pagan and Christian elements in this epic.

❷ **Enrichment** The eighth-century poet who composed *Beowulf* lived in a civilization that had become Christian only a century or so earlier. It is not surprising, therefore, that he drew upon pagan legends and folk tales for the characters and events in his epic. Grendel and his mother, for example, are derived from the trolls of Scandinavian mythology. Trolls, shadowy creatures that lurked around waterfalls or caves, were dangerous and frightening. However, the author of *Beowulf* used a great deal of imagination and poetic license to transform trolls into mighty opponents worthy of his hero.

Customize for
Visual/Spatial Learners

❸ Encourage students to make a diagram, map, or drawing showing the location of the monsters' lair.

❹ **Enrichment** This passage is one of three closely placed echoes in *Beowulf* of the seventh book of the *Aeneid,* a text known to the scribes and monks of Bede's Golden Age.

Hrothgar and his host celebrate Beowulf's victory over the monster Grendel. That night, however, Grendel's mother kidnaps and kills Hrothgar's closest friend and carries off the claw that Beowulf tore from her child. The next day the horrified king tells Beowulf about the two monsters and their underwater lair.

The Monsters' Lair

"I've heard that my people, peasants working
In the fields, have seen a pair of such fiends
Wandering in the moors and marshes, giant
Monsters living in those desert lands.
And they've said to my wise men that, as well as they could see,
One of the devils was a female creature.
The other, they say, walked through the wilderness
Like a man—but mightier than any man.
They were frightened, and they fled, hoping to find help
In Herot. They named the huge one Grendel:
If he had a father no one knew him,
❶ Or whether there'd been others before these two,
Hidden evil before hidden evil.
They live in secret places, windy
Cliffs, wolf-dens where water pours
From the rocks, then runs underground, where mist
❷ Steams like black clouds, and the groves of trees
Growing out over their lake are all covered
❸ With frozen spray, and wind down snakelike
Roots that reach as far as the water
And help keep it dark. At night that lake
Burns like a torch. No one knows its bottom,
No wisdom reaches such depths. A deer,
Hunted through the woods by packs of hounds,
A stag with great horns, though driven through the forest
❹ From faraway places, prefers to die
On those shores, refuses to save its life
In that water. It isn't far, nor is it
A pleasant spot! When the wind stirs
And storms, waves splash toward the sky,
As dark as the air, as black as the rain
That the heavens weep. Our only help,
Again, lies with you. Grendel's mother
Is hidden in her terrible home, in a place
You've not seen. Seek it, if you dare! Save us,
Once more, and again twisted gold,
Heaped-up ancient treasure, will reward you
For the battle you win!"

Golden horn, National Museet, Copenhagen

Humanities: Artifact

Golden Horn.

This Viking drinking horn was fashioned from a cattle horn and decorated with metal. It was used for drinking beer and mead. Its use required practice, as all of the liquid rushes out at once. The design prevented the horn from being put down until it was empty.

Use these questions for discussion:

1. What do the appearance and limitations of the drinking horn suggest about Viking culture? *Students may say that the Vikings prized beauty and style, sometimes to the detriment of practicality.*
2. How do you think the Vikings would react to someone who was unable to use the horn properly? *Possible response: The Vikings would have ridiculed anyone who could not use the horn and would have considered it unmanly to be unable to consume large amounts of strong drinks.*
3. What role might a horn like this one play in *Beowulf?* *It might be used at the banquet celebrating Beowulf's victory over Grendel or serve as a reward and gift from Hrothgar to Beowulf.*

The Battle With Grendel's Mother

Beowulf resolves to kill the "lady monster." Arriving at the lake under which she lives, Beowulf and his companions see serpents in the water and sea beasts on the rocks. The young hero kills one of the beasts with an arrow and then prepares to fight Grendel's mother.

Then Edgetho's brave son[10] spoke:
"Remember,
Hrothgar, Oh knowing king, now
When my danger is near, the warm words we uttered,
And if your enemy should end my life
Then be, oh generous prince, forever
❺ The father and protector of all whom I leave
Behind me, here in your hands, my beloved
Comrades left with no leader, their leader
Dead. And the precious gifts you gave me,
My friend, send them to Higlac. May he see
In their golden brightness, the Geats' great lord
❻ Gazing at your treasure, that here in Denmark
I found a noble protector, a giver
Of rings whose rewards I won and briefly
Relished. And you, Unferth,[11] let
My famous old sword stay in your hands:
I shall shape glory with Hrunting, or death
Will hurry me from this earth!"
As his words ended
He leaped into the lake, would not wait for anyone's
Answer; the heaving water covered him
❼ Over. For hours he sank through the waves;
At last he saw the mud of the bottom.
And all at once the greedy she-wolf
Who'd ruled those waters for half a hundred
Years discovered him, saw that a creature
From above had come to explore the bottom
Of her wet world. She welcomed him in her claws,
Clutched at him savagely but could not harm him,
Tried to work her fingers through the tight
Ring-woven mail on his breast, but tore
And scratched in vain. Then she carried him, armor
And sword and all, to her home; he struggled
To free his weapon, and failed. The fight
Brought other monsters swimming to see
Her catch, a host of sea beasts who beat at
His mail shirt, stabbing with tusks and teeth
As they followed along. Then he realized, suddenly,
That she'd brought him into someone's battle-hall,

10. Edgetho's brave son: Beowulf. Elsewhere he is identified by such phrases as "the Geats' proud prince" and "the Geats' brave prince." These different designations add variety and interest to the poem.

11. Unferth: Danish warrior who had questioned Beowulf's bravery before the battle with Grendel.

◆ Critical Thinking

❺ **Relate** If students have read "The Wanderer" (pp. 20–23), ask them to discuss how this passage connects to that poem. *This passage, like "The Wanderer," reveals how important it was in Anglo-Saxon culture for a warrior to have a lord. Beowulf is ensuring that his men do not meet the fate of the wanderer by asking Hrothgar to become their lord should Beowulf be killed.*

◆ Literary Focus

❻ **The Epic** Have students identify the kenning in this passage. *The reference to Hrothgar as "a giver of rings" is an example of kenning.*

◆ Literary Focus

❼ **The Epic** The original says that it took Beowulf almost a day to sink to the bottom of the lake. This flair for exaggeration is typical of many epics and other stories about heroes.

Cultural Connection

Mythical Monsters

Most of us are familiar with Frankenstein's monster, King Kong, Godzilla, and other movie monsters. However, monsters go back a lot further in history. Almost all cultures tell stories of fantastic creatures that both frighten and fascinate us.

Many mythical monsters are composites of familiar animals or of humans and animals. The chimera of Greek myth is a combination of a lion, a goat and a snake; the Egyptian deity Horus has the head of a falcon; and the Aztec god Quetzalcoatl is represented by a winged serpent. Other monsters, like King Kong, are simply oversized. The Arabian roc is an immense eagle, the Hawaiian *mo'o* is a giant lizard, and the Norse Midgaard Serpent is a snake big enough to encircle the world. In Jacarilla Apache folk tales, the hero Killer-of-Enemies slays a giant elk and a monster eagle.

Monsters, like Grendel and his mother, may be used to symbolize evil. In medieval Christian art, for example, several saints are depicted as dragon-slayers. Present-day Balinese, who believe that life is a struggle between good and evil spirits, depict battles between monsters in sacred dances in which the good lionlike *barong* clashes with the evil witch-goddess *Rangda.*

Encourage interested students to find out about the monsters in the myths and legends of a culture that interests them. Students may also be interested in finding out more about the field of cryptozoology.

◆ Critical Thinking

Interpret The storyteller adds variety to his tale by referring to people and things with a variety of words. Have students study lines 470–529 to determine who or what is referred to by these terms:

- she-wolf (line 471) *Grendel's mother*
- her guest (line 495) *Beowulf*
- Hrunting (line 497) *Beowulf's sword*
- the Geats'/Proud prince (lines 512–513) *Beowulf*
- Edgetho's son (line 525) *Beowulf*

Writer's Solution

Beowulf is protected from harm by his magical mail shirt in lines 484 and 522–526. Students can learn about the construction of chain-mail armor by viewing the Workplace Writing Model of a How-to Essay in the **Writing Lab CD-ROM** lesson on Exposition. Alternatively, they can refer to the *Sourcebook,* p. 68. Encourage interested students to follow the instructions to produce a piece of chain-mail fabric. The rings can be made by winding wire around a dowel so that successive loops touch, then using wire cutters to snip rings off the resulting coil.

1 Clarification Point out to students that Beowulf's longing only for fame is purely pagan in emphasis. Explain that Beowulf means "bear's son" or possibly "bee-wolf" (bears are notorious for stealing honey from beehives). As the expression "bear hug" suggests, bears were considered to have a remarkable crushing grip. Beowulf lives up to his name by relying on the strength in his arms and hands to wrestle with Grendel (lines 323–392) and with Grendel's mother (lines 498–515).

And there the water's heat could not hurt him.
Nor anything in the lake attack him through
The building's high-arching roof. A brilliant
Light burned all around him, the lake
Itself like a fiery flame.
Then he saw
The mighty water witch and swung his sword,
His ring-marked blade, straight at her head;
The iron sang its fierce song,
Sang Beowulf's strength. But her guest
Discovered that no sword could slice her evil
Skin, that Hrunting could not hurt her, was useless
Now when he needed it. They wrestled, she ripped
And tore and clawed at him, bit holes in his helmet,
And that too failed him; for the first time in years
Of being worn to war it would earn no glory;
It was the last time anyone would wear it. But
Beowulf
Longed only for fame, leaped back
Into battle. He tossed his sword aside,
Angry; the steel-edged blade lay where
He'd dropped it. If weapons were useless he'd use
His hands, the strength in his fingers. So fame
Comes to the men who mean to win it
And care about nothing else! He raised
His arms and seized her by the shoulder; anger
Doubled his strength, he threw her to the floor.
She fell, Grendel's fierce mother, and the Geats'
Proud prince was ready to leap on her. But she rose
At once and repaid him with her clutching claws,
Wildly tearing at him. He was weary, that best
And strongest of soldiers; his feet stumbled
And in an instant she had him down, held helpless.
Squatting with her weight on his stomach, she drew
A dagger, brown with dried blood, and prepared
To avenge her only son. But he was stretched
On his back, and her stabbing blade was blunted
By the woven mail shirt he wore on his chest.
The hammered links held; the point
Could not touch him. He'd have traveled to the bottom of the earth,
Edgetho's son, and died there, if that shining
Woven metal had not helped—and Holy
God, who sent him victory, gave judgment
For truth and right, Ruler of the Heavens,
Once Beowulf was back on his feet and fighting.

Then he saw, hanging on the wall, a heavy
Sword, hammered by giants, strong
And blessed with their magic, the best of all weapons
But so massive that no ordinary man could lift
Its carved and decorated length. He drew it
From its scabbard, broke the chain on its hilt,

Silver pendant showing the helmet of the Vendel
(Early Viking period, 10th century), Statens Historiska Museet, Stockholm

◆ Build Vocabulary

massive (mas´ iv) *adj.*: Big and solid

loathsome (lōth´ səm) *adj.*: Disgusting

Humanities: Artifact

Silver Pendant Showing the Helmet of the Vendel, tenth century.

Warriors and conquerors, the Vikings celebrated courage and skill in battle. Their destruction and piracy were feared throughout Europe. However, Viking culture was sophisticated in many ways and enriched the countries they invaded. Vikings were noted for daring exploration (they colonized parts of North America long before the continent was "discovered" by Columbus), an emphasis on individual freedom, a tradition of storytelling, and skill in carving.

The silver pendant seen here bears a face that is remarkably similar to faces found on Viking helmets, buckles, and other articles of clothing. This face has both realistic and mythical elements.

Use these questions for discussion:

1. How does the helmet on the pendant compare to the way you imagine Beowulf's helmet to be? *Some students may say that they imagine Beowulf in a simple helmet like this one. Others may say that they expect Beowulf to wear a more elaborate helmet, perhaps with a nose-guard and horns or other decorations.*
2. Who do you think might have worn a pendant like this one? Why? *Students may suggest that the pendant may represent a patron deity of warriors, and would have been worn by a warrior to give him luck in battle.*

And then, savage, now, angry
And desperate, lifted it high over his head
And struck with all the strength he had left, ❷
Caught her in the neck and cut it through,
Broke bones and all. Her body fell
To the floor, lifeless, the sword was wet
With her blood, and Beowulf rejoiced at the sight.
   The brilliant light shone, suddenly,
As though burning in that hall, and as bright as Heaven's
Own candle, lit in the sky. He looked
At her home, then following along the wall
Went walking, his hands tight on the sword,
His heart still angry. He was hunting another
Dead monster, and took his weapon with him
For final revenge against Grendel's vicious
Attacks, his nighttime raids, over
And over, coming to Herot when Hrothgar's
Men slept, killing them in their beds,
Eating some on the spot, fifteen
Or more, and running to his loathsome moor
With another such sickening meal waiting
In his pouch. But Beowulf repaid him for those visits,
Found him lying dead in his corner,
Armless, exactly as that fierce fighter ❸
Had sent him out from Herot, then struck off
His head with a single swift blow. The body
jerked for the last time, then lay still.
   The wise old warriors who surrounded Hrothgar,
Like him staring into the monsters' lake,
Saw the waves surging and blood
Spurting through. They spoke about Beowulf,
All the graybeards, whispered together
And said that hope was gone, that the hero
Had lost fame and his life at once, and would never ❹
Return to the living, come back as triumphant
As he had left; almost all agreed that Grendel's
Mighty mother, the she-wolf, had killed him.
The sun slid over past noon, went further
Down. The Danes gave up, left
The lake and went home, Hrothgar with them.
The Geats stayed, sat sadly, watching, ❺
Imagining they saw their lord but not believing
They would ever see him again.
                                        —Then the sword
Melted, blood-soaked, dripping down
Like water, disappearing like ice when the world's
Eternal Lord loosens invisible
Fetters and unwinds icicles and frost ❻
As only He can, He who rules
Time and seasons, He who is truly
God. The monsters' hall was full of
Rich treasures, but all that Beowulf took

Customize for
English Language Learners

❷ This seven-line sentence will be difficult for these students because of its structure and multiple verbs. Diagram the sentence on the chalkboard, showing the subject, "He," on a line with multiple forks to list the predicates. Have students identify the actions and, where applicable, the objects of those actions. *The diagram will include the following predicates:* drew it *(the sword),* broke the chain, lifted it *(the sword),* struck, caught her, cut it *(her neck),* broke bones.

◆ Critical Thinking

❸ Compare and Contrast Beowulf beheads Grendel even though the creature is already dead. Ask students to compare this behavior with those of current heroes. Would such behavior be admired today? What does this tell us about the values at the time of the storyteller? *The desecration of a dead body, even an enemy's dead body is repulsive to current concepts of valor and bravery. However, violent revenge against enemies even to this extreme degree was acceptable in Anglo-Saxon times.*

◆ Grammar and Style

❹ Appositives and Appositive Phrases Have students identify the appositive used to describe "Grendel's/Mighty mother." *She is called the she-wolf.*

◆ Literary Focus

❺ The Epic A recurring motif in Scandinavian heroic legends involves loyal followers waiting faithfully for the return of the hero, while others give up hope and leave. Ask students to explain the popularity of this motif. *Students may say that it adds drama and uncertainty about the fate of the hero, provides a touch of realism, or shows the importance of having faith.*

Enrichment

The popularity of pagan and almost-pagan legends like *Beowulf* was a source of concern and irritation to early Christian leaders. The scholar and monk Alcuin, who was taught by Bede and who created a system of universal education for Charlemagne, wrote a famous letter home in 797. In it, he criticized the English bishop for allowing Christian priests, while dining, to listen to poetry about the pagan king Ingeld—one of the characters in *Beowulf.* Alcuin argued that the poem was inappropriate; holy scripture should be read instead. Luckily for us, the legends continued to be popular for another two centuries, allowing *Beowulf* to be written down at last so that we can still enjoy it today.

◆ Background for Understanding

❻ History Point out that this simile is an example of the pagan/Christian blend in the poem. Have students analyze the simile. *The sword blade is compared to water, specifically, melting ice.* What are the pagan elements in the simile? *Students may say that Grendel's blood melting the sword and the reference to the seasons are pagan elements.*

◆ Critical Thinking

Extend Even today there are those who firmly believe that monsters exist in remote parts of deep lakes. One is the famous Loch Ness monster. Several scientific efforts have been made to determine if such a monster really exists. Invite interested students to research the background of the Loch Ness monster and the scientific efforts to prove or disprove its existence.

◆ Reading Strategy

❶ **Paraphrase** Beowulf swims to shore happily carrying Grendel's head and the hilt of the sword. He and his followers thank God for the victory and leave. The water of the lake thickens with the monsters' blood. Four men carry Grendel's heavy head on a spear to Herot. They enter the hall in glory. Beowulf carries Grendel's head by the hair and presents it to Hrothgar.

◆ *Literature and Your Life*

❷ The Geats have been rewarded for their faith in their prince: Beowulf has triumphed, and the Geats have Grendel's head to prove it. Have students relate the Geats' sense of victory to their own experiences of proving nay-sayers wrong. Perhaps they aced a difficult test, made the cut for a varsity team, obtained a coveted summer internship, or continued to believe in a sports star who eventually came spectacularly out of a slump. Encourage students to describe their experiences and feelings in their journal.

Was Grendel's head and the hilt of the giants'
Jeweled sword; the rest of that ring-marked
Blade had dissolved in Grendel's steaming
Blood, boiling even after his death.
And then the battle's only survivor
Swam up and away from those silent corpses;
The water was calm and clean, the whole
Huge lake peaceful once the demons who'd lived in it
Were dead.
   Then that noble protector of all seamen
Swam to land, rejoicing in the heavy
Burdens he was bringing with him. He
And all his glorious band of Geats
Thanked God that their leader had come back unharmed;
They left the lake together. The Geats
Carried Beowulf's helmet, and his mail shirt.
Behind them the water slowly thickened
As the monsters' blood came seeping up.
They walked quickly, happily, across
Roads all of them remembered, left
The lake and the cliffs alongside it, brave men
Staggering under the weight of Grendel's skull,
Too heavy for fewer than four of them to handle—
Two on each side of the spear jammed through it—
❷ Yet proud of their ugly load and determined
That the Danes, seated in Herot, should see it.
Soon, fourteen Geats arrived
At the hall, bold and warlike, and with Beowulf,
Their lord and leader, they walked on the mead-hall
Green. Then the Geats' brave prince entered
Herot, covered with glory for the daring
Battles he had fought; he sought Hrothgar
To salute him and show Grendel's head.
He carried that terrible trophy by the hair,
Brought it straight to where the Danes sat,
Drinking, the queen among them. It was a weird
And wonderful sight, and the warriors stared.

◆ Reading Strategy
Paraphrase lines 596–622, which describe what happens after Grendel's mother dies. ❶

The Last Battle

After being honored by Hrothgar, Beowulf and his fellow Geats return home. He is welcomed by the king, his uncle Higlac, and later becomes king himself when Higlac and his son have died. Beowulf rules Geatland for fifty years. Then a dragon menaces his kingdom. Although he is an old man, Beowulf determines to slay the beast. Before going into battle, he tells the men who have accompanied him about the history of the royal house and his exploits in its service.

❸ And Beowulf uttered his final boast:
"I've never known fear, as a youth I fought

Enrichment

Although *Beowulf* was probably first written down a thousand years ago, it probably had been created long before. One incident—a raid on the southern Rhine—can be definitely dated and supported by evidence outside the poem as occurring around 520. However, the poem was probably composed about 1,300 years ago during the Northumbrian Golden Age, also called the age of the Venerable Bede. The creation of the poem must have occurred before Viking raids, beginning in 787, destroyed Bede's society.

The Dragon for "The High Kings," George Sharp

In endless battles. I am old, now,
But I will fight again, seek fame still,
If the dragon hiding in his tower dares
To face me."
Then he said farewell to his followers,
Each in his turn, for the last time:
"I'd use no sword, no weapon, if this beast
Could be killed without it, crushed to death
Like Grendel, gripped in my hands and torn
Limb from limb. But his breath will be burning
Hot, poison will pour from his tongue.
I feel no shame, with shield and sword
And armor, against this monster: when he comes to me
I mean to stand, not run from his shooting
Flames, stand till fate decides
Which of us wins. My heart is firm,
My hands calm: I need no hot

▲ **Critical Viewing** What characteristics do this dragon and Grendel have in common? **[Compare and Contrast]**

◆ Critical Thinking

3 Compare and Contrast Have students study Beowulf's monologue; then have them compare and contrast Beowulf's approach to this battle with his approach to his earlier conquests. *As in his approach to the earlier battles, Beowulf boasts of his past deeds and his strength. However, this time he will use a shield and a sword. Also, he speaks of the gold that is to be his after his successful battle. The giants of the last battle had a hall full of "Rich treasures," but Beowulf took only Grendel's head and the hilt of the sword.*

▶Critical Viewing◀

4 Compare and Contrast Students may say that the dragon, like Grendel, is huge, has fearsome claws, and lives in a dark lair. The dragon is reptilian, and the wisps of smoke emerging from his nostrils indicate that he, unlike Grendel, can breathe fire.

Humanities: Art

The Dragon for *The High Kings,* 1983, by George Sharp.

George Sharp is a contemporary British illustrator who began painting professionally in 1975. He studied art at the Nottingham School of Art in England. *The Dragon* was done for the book *The High Kings*, by Joy Chant, published in 1983. Sharp was concerned with authenticity when creating the illustrations for this book. He spent many hours researching the myths and artifacts of ancient England. Sharp paints in a detailed illustrative style and uses transparent washes of color on a white ground. The dragon he portrays is imaginative, and it is as fearsome looking as the dragons portrayed in historic legends.

Use these questions for discussion:

1. What feelings do the various elements of content and color in this illustration create? *Some students may think that the use of light and shadow creates a feeling of foreboding and danger. Others may think that the bright light and vibrant colors of the dragon convey a sense of discovery and excitement.*
2. Is this illustration appropriate for "The Last Battle"? *Some students may think that the enormous, well-fed dragon is a formidable opponent for the aged king Beowulf. Other students may think that the sleeping dragon is not sufficiently menacing.*

◆ Literary Focus

❶ **The Epic** The superhuman courage expressed in this boast is typical of the epic hero. In addition, by waging war on such a monster, he champions the cause of good over evil.

◆ Critical Thinking

❷ **Evaluate** Have students discuss how the storyteller creates a sense of drama and suspense about the approaching battle. Ask students: Do you think this storyteller was able to keep his listeners' interest? *Most students will agree, noting that the vivid, detailed descriptions are riveting.*

◆ Critical Thinking

❸ **Analyze** Point out that this passage can be seen as the turning point of the epic. Ask students: How is this battle different from the others Beowulf has fought? *Fate is against the hero. For the first time, Beowulf knows he is going to lose.* What new aspect does this passage reveal about Beowulf's character? *Suggested response: He is aware of his inevitable fate, but tries his best anyway.* How does the writer evoke sympathy for Beowulf? *Students may suggest that the references to fate and the description of the hero's shield and sword failing him evoke sympathy for Beowulf.*

Words. Wait for me close by, my friends.
We shall see, soon, who will survive
This bloody battle, stand when the fighting
Is done. No one else could do
What I mean to, here, no man but me
Could hope to defeat this monster. No one
Could try. And this dragon's treasure, his gold
And everything hidden in that tower, will be mine
Or war will sweep me to a bitter death!"
Then Beowulf rose, still brave, still strong,
And with his shield at his side, and a mail shirt on his breast,
Strode calmly, confidently, toward the tower, under
The rocky cliffs: no coward could have walked there!
And then he who'd endured dozens of desperate
Battles who'd stand boldly while swords and shields
Clashed, the best of kings, saw
Huge stone arches and felt the heat
Of the dragon's breath, flooding down
Through the hidden entrance, too hot for anyone
To stand, a streaming current of fire
And smoke that blocked all passage. And the Geats'
Lord and leader, angry, lowered
His sword and roared out a battle cry,
A call so loud and clear that it reached through
The hoary rock, hung in the dragon's
Ear. The beast rose, angry,
Knowing a man had come—and then nothing
But war could have followed. Its breath came first.
A steaming cloud pouring from the stone,
Then the earth itself shook. Beowulf
Swung his shield into place, held it
In front of him, facing the entrance. The dragon
Coiled and uncoiled, its heart urging it
Into battle. Beowulf's ancient sword
Was waiting, unsheathed, his sharp and gleaming
Blade. The beast came closer; both of them
Were ready, each set on slaughter. The Geats'
Great prince stood firm, unmoving, prepared
Behind his high shield, waiting in his shining
Armor. The monster came quickly toward him,
Pouring out fire and smoke, hurrying
To its fate. Flames beat at the iron
Shield, and for a time it held, protected
Beowulf as he'd planned; then it began to melt,
And for the first time in his life that famous prince
Fought with fate against him, with glory
Denied him. He knew it, but he raised his sword
And struck at the dragon's scaly hide.
The ancient blade broke, bit into
The monster's skin, drew blood, but cracked
And failed him before it went deep enough, helped him
Less than he needed. The dragon leaped

◆ Literary Focus
In lines 644–649, how does Beowulf show himself to be a true epic hero? ❶

Detail of a dragon head on the Mammen horse collar (Viking artifact, 10th century), National Museum, Denmark

Humanities: Artifact

The Mammen Horse Collar (detail), tenth century.

This gold dragon head comes from a tenth-century horse collar found at the Viking stronghold of Jutland. The Vikings terrified Europe and the British Isles with their coastal raids from the ninth to the eleventh centuries (the Viking Age).

The head reveals the Viking fascination with mythical beasts and intricate designs. Viking artisans could rival any in Europe in the making of decorative carvings like this one and in the production of swords and armor.

Use the following questions for discussion:

1. Why is this artifact an appropriate illustration for *Beowulf?* *Suggested response: It was made at about the same time the epic was popular, and reflects its Scandinavian setting.*
2. How does this figure suggest the skill of Viking artisans? *Its intricate detail and precise geometric lines indicate that it was made by a skilled metalworker.*
3. Why do you think mythical creatures like this dragon fascinated the Vikings? *Students may suggest that the artists enjoyed the opportunity to create imaginary creatures or to represent abstract ideas such as ferocity or evil in their art. Those who wore or used the art may have enjoyed its beauty or respected the ideas it represented.*

With pain, thrashed and beat at him, spouting
Murderous flames, spreading them everywhere.
And the Geats' ring-giver did not boast of glorious
Victories in other wars: his weapon
Had failed him, deserted him, now when he needed it
Most, that excellent sword. Edgetho's
❹ Famous son stared at death,
Unwilling to leave this world, to exchange it
For a dwelling in some distant place—a journey
Into darkness that all men must make, as death
Ends their few brief hours on earth.
Quickly, the dragon came at him, encouraged
As Beowulf fell back; its breath flared,
And he suffered, wrapped around in swirling
Flames—a king, before, but now
A beaten warrior. None of his comrades
Came to him, helped him, his brave and noble
Followers; they ran for their lives, fled
Deep in a wood. And only one of them
Remained, stood there, miserable, remembering,
As a good man must, what kinship should mean.

His name was Wiglaf, he was Wexstan's son
❺ And a good soldier; his family had been Swedish,
Once. Watching Beowulf, he could see
How his king was suffering, burning. Remembering
Everything his lord and cousin had given him,
Armor and gold and the great estates
Wexstan's family enjoyed, Wiglaf's
Mind was made up; he raised his yellow
Shield and drew his sword—an ancient
Weapon that had once belonged to Onela's
Nephew, and that Wexstan had won, killing
The prince when he fled from Sweden, sought safety
With Herdred, and found death.[12] And Wiglaf's father
Had carried the dead man's armor, and his sword,
To Onela, and the king had said nothing, only
Given him armor and sword and all,
Everything his rebel nephew had owned

12. Onela's/Nephew . . . found death: When Onela seized the throne of Sweden, his two nephews sought shelter with the king of Geatland, Herdred. Wiglaf's father, Wexstan, killed the older nephew for Onela.

Gilt bronze winged dragon (Swedish artifact, 8th century), Statens Historiska Museet, Stockholm

◆ *Literature and Your Life*

❹ The storyteller makes it clear that Beowulf faces certain death in this encounter. This somewhat modern depiction of heroism contrasts with the Beowulf of earlier episodes, where he is presented as the strong and unconquerable hero. Have students identify other heroes who acted nobly against some evil force even though they knew it may result in their death. *Possible answers include: Civil rights leaders such as Martin Luther King and Medgar Evers, the leaders of the Warsaw Ghetto uprising during World War II, environmental activists such as Chico Mendes and Ken Saro-Wiwa, and human-rights activists such as Norma Sapién and Chinese dissidents. Numerous saints and martyrs might also be mentioned.*

◆ *Literature and Your Life*

❺ It is common in epics to insert homilies or other digressions just when the action and suspense are reaching the boiling point. Have students relate the *scop's* timing of less-interesting passages to the timing of television commercials. *The first commercial is often delayed until the director feels the audience is deeply absorbed in the story. Commercials are then inserted at moments of high interest so that the audience will not change channels or leave the room for fear of missing the story. Commercials also occur more often toward the end of a long program, such as a movie or miniseries, because the audience has invested time in the program and is determined to hear how it ends.*

Humanities: Artifact

Gilt Bronze Winged Dragon, eighth century.

This example of eighth-century gilt-bronze craftsmanship comes from Sweden, but it is representative of works by other Scandinavian artists who also preferred designs of real or mythical animals to the human figure or plant forms. They were less concerned with accurate representation than with creating complex, abstract patterns. Dragons like this one eventually appeared in Christian art as well.

Use these questions for discussion:

1. How does this artifact suggest that eighth-century Scandinavians were interested in abstract designs? *The artifact is not strongly representational; in fact, it is difficult to tell what it is. The artist was more interested in creating beautiful, flowing lines than in depicting a plausible creature.*
2. Compare the dragon to the one on the previous page. *This dragon is far more abstract than the one on page 56.*
3. Why are artifacts like this one appropriate illustrations for *Beowulf?* *They help a reader envision the setting of the epic and to understand the culture that produced it.*

◆ Critical Thinking

❶ Infer Ask students what they can infer from this passage about Scandinavian and Anglo-Saxon attitudes about arms and armor. *Possible responses: Good swords and armor are extremely valuable and highly prized, making them a suitable reward from a king to a retainer who has done him a great service. Weapons and armor were among the most important items a son inherited from his father. The pedigree of a warrior's sword and armor was almost as important as his own.*

◆ Critical Thinking

❷ Analyze Have students imagine that they are one of Beowulf's men who "ran for their lives" (line 710) when the dragon appeared. Have them analyze Wiglaf's speech. Ask if they would be moved by his words enough to rejoin in battle. Discuss which elements make the strongest appeal. *Some students may say that Wiglaf's strongest point is that Beowulf was good to his men, and they owe it to the king to help him. Other students may find other points more compelling.*

And lost when he left this life. And Wexstan
Had kept those shining gifts, held them
For years, waiting for his son to use them,
❶ Wear them as honorably and well as once
His father had done; then Wexstan died
And Wiglaf was his heir, inherited treasures
And weapons and land. He'd never worn
That armor, fought with that sword, until Beowulf
Called him to his side, led him into war.
But his soul did not melt, his sword was strong;
The dragon discovered his courage, and his weapon,
When the rush of battle brought them together.
   And Wiglaf, his heart heavy, uttered
The kind of words his comrades deserved:
   "I remember how we sat in the mead-hall, drinking
And boasting of how brave we'd be when Beowulf
Needed us, he who gave us these swords
And armor: all of us swore to repay him,
When the time came, kindness for kindness
—With our lives, if he needed them. He allowed us to
   join him,
Chose us from all his great army, thinking
Our boasting words had some weight, believing
Our promises, trusting our swords. He took us
For soldiers, for men. He meant to kill
This monster himself, our mighty king,
Fight this battle alone and unaided,
As in the days when his strength and daring dazzled
❷ Men's eyes. But those days are over and gone
And now our lord must lean on younger
Arms. And we must go to him, while angry
Flames burn at his flesh, help
Our glorious king! By almighty God,
I'd rather burn myself than see
Flames swirling around my lord.
And who are we to carry home
Our shields before we've slain his enemy
And ours, to run back to our homes with Beowulf
So hard-pressed here? I swear that nothing
He ever did deserved an end
Like this, dying miserably and alone,
Butchered by this savage beast: we swore
That these swords and armor were each for us all!"
   Then he ran to his king, crying encouragement
As he dove through the dragon's deadly fumes.

Cultural Connection

Epics

Epics have been used the world over to keep alive traditions and to inspire later generations to value and imitate the often larger-than-life heroes of the past. The epic is therefore a rich resource for tapping the cultural diversity of our world.

Encourage interested students to gather information on these epics and epic heroes and to share their findings with the class.

- Finland: *Kalevala*
- France: *Chanson de Roland*
- India: *Ramayana* and *Mahabharata*
- Italy: *Orlando Furioso*
- Japan: *Heike Monogatari*
- Mali: *Sundiata*
- Norway: *Volsunga Saga*
- Polynesia: *Maui*
- Rome: The *Aeneid*
- Spain: *Poema del Cid*

The Spoils

Together, Wiglaf and Beowulf kill the dragon, but the old king is mortally wounded. As a last request, Beowulf asks Wiglaf to bring him the treasure that the dragon was guarding.

Then Wexstan's son went in, as quickly
As he could, did as the dying Beowulf
Asked, entered the inner darkness
Of the tower, went with his mail shirt and his sword.
Flushed with victory he groped his way,
A brave young warrior, and suddenly saw
Piles of gleaming gold, precious
Gems, scattered on the floor, cups
And bracelets, rusty old helmets, beautifully
Made but rotting with no hands to rub
And polish them. They lay where the dragon left them;
It had flown in the darkness, once, before fighting
Its final battle. (So gold can easily
Triumph, defeat the strongest of men,
No matter how deep it is hidden!) And he saw,
❸ Hanging high above, a golden
Banner, woven by the best of weavers
And beautiful. And over everything he saw
A strange light, shining everywhere,
On walls and floor and treasure. Nothing
Moved, no other monsters appeared;
He took what he wanted, all the treasures
That pleased his eye, heavy plates
And golden cups and the glorious banner,
Loaded his arms with all they could hold.
Beowulf's dagger, his iron blade,
Had finished the fire-spitting terror
That once protected tower and treasures
Alike; the gray-bearded lord of the Geats
Had ended those flying, burning raids
Forever.
Then Wiglaf went back, anxious
To return while Beowulf was alive, to bring him
Treasure they'd won together. He ran,
Hoping his wounded king, weak
And dying, had not left the world too soon.
Then he brought their treasure to Beowulf, and found
His famous king bloody, gasping
For breath. But Wiglaf sprinkled water
Over his lord, until the words
Deep in his breast broke through and were heard.
Beholding the treasure he spoke, haltingly:
"For this, this gold, these jewels, I thank
Our Father in Heaven, Ruler of the Earth—
For all of this, that His grace has given me,
Allowed me to bring to my people while breath

◆ *Literature and Your Life*

What type of rewards do modern heroes receive? ❹

Customize for
Visual/Spatial Learners

❸ Encourage visual/spatial learners to draw a picture, or create a sculpture that shows Wiglaf gathering the dragon's treasure. Direct students to use the details in the description to help them create their artwork.

◆ Literature and Your Life

❹ Modern military heroes and military units are given medals, citations, and other forms of recognition, but not monetary rewards. Heroes in other endeavors, such as sports, may also get a trophy or similar symbol of victory, but they also often receive huge sums of money as well.

Customize for
More Advanced Students

Challenge students to find out how the dragon in *Beowulf* compares to other dragons in mythology, literature, and popular fiction. Have students gather information from books they may have read and from resources in the library. Possible sources of information include J.R.R. Tolkein's *The Hobbit*, Anne McCaffrey's Pern series, and numerous other works of fantasy.

Enrichment

Explain to students that mythographers such as Joseph Campbell (in his book *The Hero With a Thousand Faces*) point out that heroes are usually described in terms of life's peak moments. For example, young Beowulf's initiation into manhood is dramatized—he slays both Grendel and Grendel's mother. His death fighting the dragon is also featured in the epic. However, nothing of his fifty-year reign as king is shown in the poem.

Humanities: Artifact

Oseberg Dragon, c. 850.

This spectacular carved wooden artifact is one of the most impressive finds from the ship burial at Oseberg. The Oseberg Dragon is a post head found among the furniture on the ninth-century Oseberg ship, a royal barge used for the burial of a Norwegian queen. The post is covered with an intricate profusion of "gripping beasts," a classic Viking decorative pattern.

Use these questions for discussion:

1. Where might carving like this be seen in *Beowulf*? *Suggested response: Elaborate carvings may have been found in Herot, in Beowulf's mead-hall, or in the dragon's lair among his other collected treasures.*
2. What does this artifact and the descriptions of Beowulf's funeral tell you about funerary practices in Scandinavian culture? *Students may suggest that important people were often buried with treasure.*

◆ Literary Focus

❶ Ask students: How has your concept of Beowulf as an epic hero changed from your initial impression of him as he arrives at Herot to these dying words? Is he more human and less superhuman? *Beowulf's concern for his people's welfare is a dramatic shift from the boasting hero who seemed to care only for his reputation in the first episode.*

Customize for
More Advanced Students

❷ Have these students analyze the various elements that went into Beowulf's tomb and decide what the purpose of each element might be. Note especially the following:

- It is built on the water's edge, high on a spit of land so sailors can see it.
- Beowulf's ashes are sealed inside.
- The treasures are buried inside.

Ask students to compose an inscription to be written on the tomb that sums up Beowulf's legacy to the Geats.

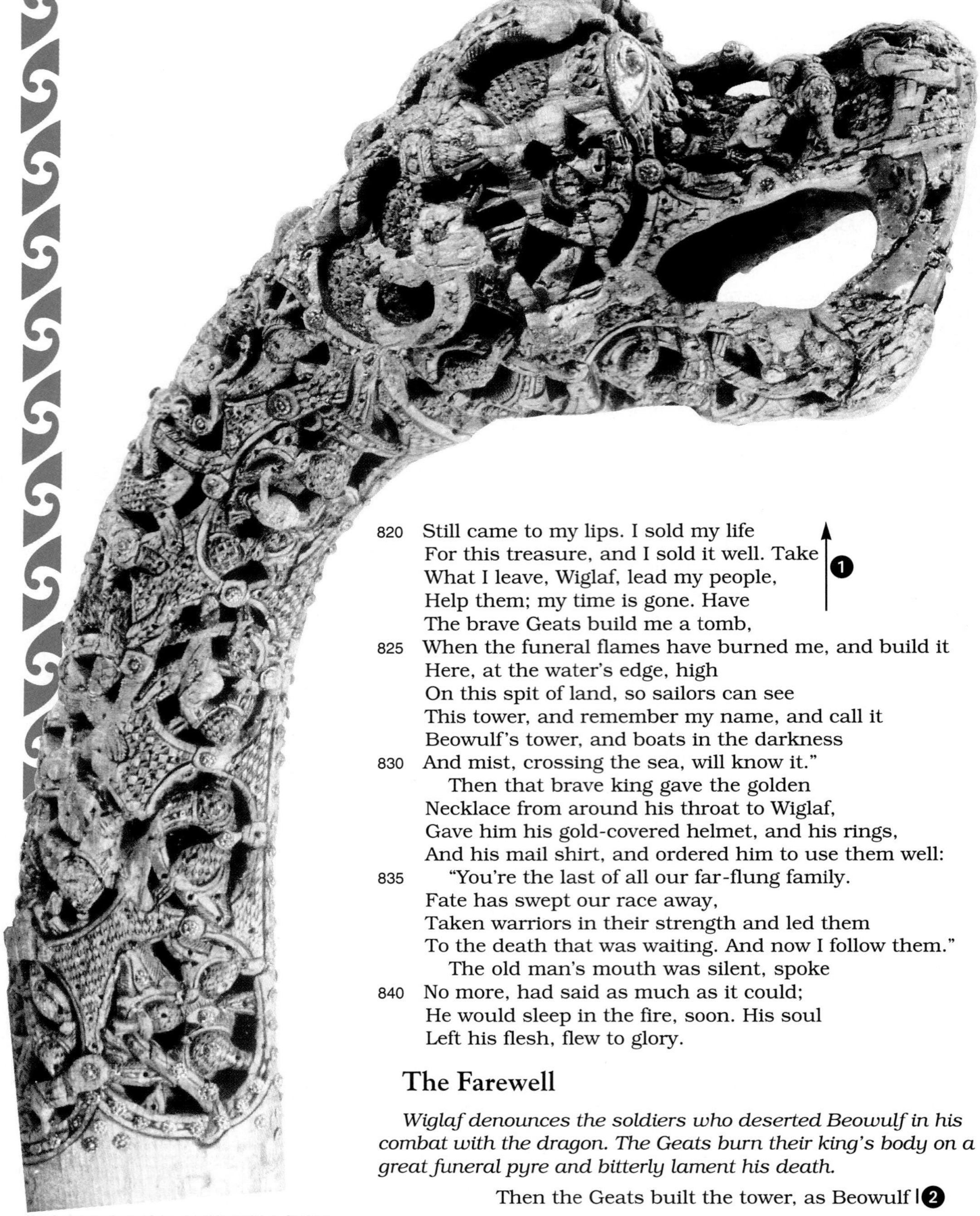

Head of carved post from the ship burial at Oseberg

Still came to my lips. I sold my life
For this treasure, and I sold it well. Take
What I leave, Wiglaf, lead my people, ❶
Help them; my time is gone. Have
The brave Geats build me a tomb,
When the funeral flames have burned me, and build it
Here, at the water's edge, high
On this spit of land, so sailors can see
This tower, and remember my name, and call it
Beowulf's tower, and boats in the darkness
And mist, crossing the sea, will know it."
Then that brave king gave the golden
Necklace from around his throat to Wiglaf,
Gave him his gold-covered helmet, and his rings,
And his mail shirt, and ordered him to use them well:
"You're the last of all our far-flung family.
Fate has swept our race away,
Taken warriors in their strength and led them
To the death that was waiting. And now I follow them."
The old man's mouth was silent, spoke
No more, had said as much as it could;
He would sleep in the fire, soon. His soul
Left his flesh, flew to glory.

The Farewell

Wiglaf denounces the soldiers who deserted Beowulf in his combat with the dragon. The Geats burn their king's body on a great funeral pyre and bitterly lament his death.

Then the Geats built the tower, as Beowulf ❷

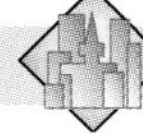

Beyond the Classroom

Community Connection

Local Monuments Like Beowulf's tomb, monuments are an attempt to remind later generations of a person or event. Such reminders might inspire others to imitate certain qualities or simply to keep the memory of a loved one alive. Our nation has built memorials to the veterans of Vietnam, to Abraham Lincoln, and to the sailors on the battleship *Arizona,* lying at the bottom of Pearl Harbor.

Have students identify monuments to local heroes and local events. They might be simple plaques on buildings or elaborate tombs in local cemeteries. Students can prepare a report on one or more such monuments indicating what person or event is being remembered and the purpose of the monument. Some may wish to propose a monument to a local hero. If so, have them design an appropriate monument and specify its purpose.

Had asked, strong and tall, so sailors
Could find it from far and wide; working
For ten long days they made his monument,
Sealed his ashes in walls as straight
And high as wise and willing hands
Could raise them. And the riches he and Wiglaf
Had won from the dragon, rings, necklaces,
Ancient, hammered armor—all
The treasures they'd taken were left there, too,
Silver and jewels buried in the sandy
Ground, back in the earth, again
And forever hidden and useless to men.
And then twelve of the bravest Geats
Rode their horses around the tower,
Telling their sorrow, telling stories
Of their dead king and his greatness, his glory,
Praising him for heroic deeds, for a life
As noble as his name. So should all men
Raise up words for their lords, warm
With love, when their shield and protector leaves
His body behind, sends his soul
On high. And so Beowulf's followers
Rode, mourning their beloved leader,
Crying that no better king had ever
Lived, no prince so mild, no man
So open to his people, so deserving of praise.

❷ ❸

Guide for Responding

◆ Literature and Your Life

Reader's Response What part of the poem did you find most thrilling? Why?

Thematic Focus Explain how Beowulf grows in stature as a hero as he meets peril.

Group Discussion In a small group, list people you consider the heroes of today's world. Compare and contrast each to Beowulf.

☑ Check Your Comprehension

1. What does Grendel do when he first goes to Herot?
2. What is Beowulf's plan for fighting Grendel?
3. How does Grendel die?
4. Describe the battle with Grendel's mother.
5. What happens to Beowulf during his fight with the dragon?

◆ Critical Thinking

❸ **Interpret** Tell students that before Beowulf's funeral, a prophecy in the poem suggests that the Geats as a nation will shortly perish utterly; historically, the Geats had died out before *Beowulf* was composed. Ask students how this fact affects their understanding of the funeral in *Beowulf*. *The funeral enacts a mourning not only for Beowulf but for an entire people.*

Reinforce and Extend

Answers

◆ Literature and Your Life

Reader's Response Some students may prefer the battle with Grendel; others may prefer the battle with Grendel's mother or the battle with the dragon. Students should cite specific details that make their chosen part of the poem thrilling.

Thematic Focus As students formulate their response, have them consider factors such as Beowulf's achievements, attitudes toward others, courage, values, and integrity.

☑ Check Your Comprehension

1. Grendel kills thirty men and makes off with their bodies.
2. Beowulf plans to fight Grendel barehanded.
3. Beowulf tears Grendel's arm off; Grendel escapes to his lair to die.
4. Beowulf plunges into the lake, where he is captured by Grendel's mother, who drags him to her lair. Beowulf's sword is useless against the monster, so he wrestles with her, but she pounces on him and strikes at him with a dagger, from which his armor protects him. Beowulf sees an ancient sword on the wall, seizes it, and beheads Grendel's mother.
5. His shield melts, his sword breaks, and he in engulfed by the dragon's fiery breath.

Beyond the Selection

FURTHER READING

Other Examples of Old English Literature

The Battle of Brunanburg
Caedmon's Hymn

Works Inspired by *Beowulf* and Anglo-Saxon Poetry

Grendel, John Gardner
The Legacy of Heorot, Larry Niven, Jerry Pournelle, and Steven Barnes

We suggest that you preview these works before recommending them to students.

INTERNET

You and your students may find additional information about *Beowulf* on the Internet at the following sites. Please be aware, however, that sites may have changed since we published this information.

To learn about the Electronic Beowulf Project, go to **http://www.bl.uk/diglib/beowulf/**

Many links to resources for studying *Beowulf* can be found at **http://www.georgetown.edu/irvinemj/english016/beowulf/beowulf.html**

We *strongly recommend* that you preview sites.

Guide for Responding *(continued)*

◆ Critical Thinking

Interpret

1. At the beginning of the poem, Hrothgar's warriors are happy, whereas Grendel is consumed by hatred. What causes these differences in attitude? **[Analyze]**

2. What traits of Beowulf and Grendel raise the fight between them to an epic struggle between good and evil? **[Interpret]**

3. Compare and contrast the three battles described in these excerpts. In what ways are all three different versions of the poem's main conflict? **[Compare and Contrast]**

Evaluate

4. Critics have praised the *Beowulf* poet's skill at describing various settings. (a) Find a passage in which the poet displays this skill. (b) Explain what makes the description so effective. **[Evaluate]**

Extend

5. What can you infer about Anglo-Saxon beliefs and life from the poem? Support your answer with details. **[Social Studies Link]**

◆ Build Vocabulary

Using the Word Root *-sol-*

Considering that *solace*, with the root *-sol-*, means "to comfort," answer the following.

1. Which characters in *Beowulf* would receive a *consolation* prize?

2. Which character is *inconsolable* and seeks revenge?

Using the Word Bank

On your paper, write the letter of the word that is the antonym, the word opposite in meaning, to the first word.

1. loathsome: (a) disgusting, (b) delightful, (c) angry

2. massive: (a) tremendous, (b) average, (c) flimsy

3. purge: (a) pollute, (b) purify, (c) complete

4. reparation: (a) renewal, (b) destruction, (c) reimbursement

5. writhing: (a) valor, (b) moving, (c) still

6. solace: (a) comfort, (b) resentment, (c) aggravation

◆ Reading Strategy

Paraphrase

By **paraphrasing**—restating passages in your own words—you can better understand the main events in a work like *Beowulf*.

Paraphrase lines 238–243 from *Beowulf*.

◆ Literary Focus

The Epic

Beowulf is an **epic**—a long narrative poem, presented in an elevated style, that celebrates episodes in a people's heroic tradition. An **epic hero** battles forces of evil as he fights for the good of society.

1. Find three details in lines 109–116 that show Beowulf in a heroic light.

2. Epics usually center on a battle between good and evil. Find evidence in lines 173–198 that indicates Beowulf is battling for the forces of good.

3. Through Beowulf's deeds, you can infer the qualities that make him a hero. In what specific ways does Beowulf demonstrate loyalty and valor?

◆ Grammar and Style

Appositives and Appositive Phrases

An **appositive** is a noun or pronoun placed near another noun or pronoun to identify or explain it. An **appositive phrase** is an appositive with modifiers.

Practice Identify the appositive phrases in the following lines from *Beowulf*.

1. "We are Geats, / Men who follow Higlac. My father / Was a famous soldier, known far and wide"

2. "Grendel escaped. / But wounded as he was could flee to his den, / His miserable hole at the bottom of the marsh . . ."

3. " . . . And we have come seeking / Your prince, Healfdane's son, protector / Of this people, only in friendship: instruct us . . ."

Writing Application Use appositive phrases to combine each set of sentences into one.

1. Hrothgar welcomed Beowulf and his men to Herot. Herot was the strongest hall ever built.

2. Beowulf gave the monster's arm to Hrothgar. Beowulf was a prince of Geats. Hrothgar was king of the Danes.

Answers

◆ Critical Thinking

1. Hrothgar's warriors are celebrating God's creation of the world; Grendel and his forebears have been exiled by God. Grendel's hate is fueled by hearing the joyful warriors.
2. Beowulf is a mighty Christian warrior who has previously rid the Earth of evils such as giants and sea monsters. Grendel is part of a "brood forever opposing the Lord's Will"; he is described as "bearing God's hatred" and "the Almighty's enemy."
3. The battle with Grendel is similar to the one with his mother: While both are monsters, they have some human attributes. By contrast, the enraged dragon is wholly monstrous and animal. All the battles involve fighting the forces of evil, the hero's quest for fame and glory.
4. (a) Students may cite lines 425–443, 485–491, 775–805, or 843–869. (b) In all cases, it is the concrete and specific details that make the description effective.
5. Sample response: The Anglo-Saxons valued loyalty (lines 281–284, 370–371, 596–601, 712–713, 745–768, and 861–865), valor (lines 109–134, 246–254, 399–407, among others), and faith in God (lines 5–14, 269–270, 383–385, 526–529, among others).

◆ Reading Strategy

Sample response: Greetings, Hrothgar! I am a relative of King Higlac's. We've heard about Grendel and how his killings have cause people to desert Herot.

◆ Literary Focus

1. He is "stronger and greater than anyone anywhere in this world," acts decisively to mount an expedition, and sets sail to give help.
2. Suggested response: He is the son of a wise and famous soldier; he seeks Hrothgar only in friendship; he wants to get rid of the monster and end the suffering.
3. He shows loyalty to Higlac by requesting that his armor be sent back should he be killed in his fight with Grendel. Before his fight with Grendel's mother, he requests that his gifts be sent to Higlac and that his warriors be given a place with Hrothgar. Beowulf shows valor in setting himself up as bait for Grendel and in engaging in single combat with Grendel's mother and the dragon.

◆ Build Vocabulary

Using the Word Root *-sol-*

1. Grendel, the dragon, Grendel's mother; 2. Grendel's mother

Using the Word Bank

1. b 2. c 3. a 4. b 5. c 6. c

◆ Grammar and Style

Practice

1. Men who follow Higlac;
2. His miserable hole at the bottom of the marsh . . . ;
3. Healfdane's son, protector of this people. . . .

Writing Application

1. Hrothgar welcomed Beowulf and his men to Herot, the strongest hall ever built.
2. Beowulf, prince of the Geats, gave the monster's arm to Hrothgar, king of the Danes.

Writer's Solution

For additional instruction and practice use the lesson on Recognizing and Using Phrases in the **Language Lab CD-ROM** and the page on Appositives and Appositive Phrases in the *Writer's Solution Grammar Practice Book*, p. 28.

Build Your Portfolio

Idea Bank

Writing

1. **Memo** Write a memo from Beowulf to Hrothgar, reporting on your victory in a businesslike manner. Include the following heads at the top: *To, From, Re* (about), and *Date*. **[Career Link]**

2. **Comparison and Contrast** Choose another courageous hero from literature and compare and contrast that hero with Beowulf.

3. **Response to Criticism** Burton Raffel remarked that "of all the many-sided excellences of *Beowulf*," one of the most satisfying "is the poet's insight into people." Agree or disagree with this observation in a brief paper.

Speaking and Listening

4. **Performance** Present a dramatic reading of "The Battle With Grendel." Create dramatic effects by emphasizing key words. **[Performing Arts Link]**

5. **Speech** Prepare a speech for Hrothgar to read at a ceremony honoring Beowulf. The speech should not only thank Beowulf but also emphasize his value as a role model. Present the speech to the class. **[Performing Arts Link]**

Projects

6. **Multimedia Presentation** Prepare a presentation that follows the history of superheroes. Find illustrations from older comic books and more current computer animation to show how characters have changed. **[Media Link]**

7. **Sculpture** Create a sculpture of Grendel's mother or the dragon. Refer to details in the poem as you create your sculpture. **[Art Link]**

Writing Mini-Lesson

Press Release for Grendel

Give Grendel the opportunity to present the events of this epic poem from his point of view. Prepare a statement that Grendel might read at a press conference to inform the public of his side of the story.

Use the following skill to guide you as you prepare your statement.

Writing Skills Focus: Grab Readers' Attention

Grab your readers' attention by surprising them: Present Grendel with human qualities. For example, in the following passage, Grendel describes his feelings about being left out of the festivities at Herot.

> Every day I listen to the happy noises at Herot and weep alone. Why do they leave me out? What have I ever done to them?

Prewriting Review the scenes that involve Grendel. Choose a scene that your readers would find surprising if presented from the monster's point of view. Jot down what Grendel might be feeling at the time and why you think he feels this way.

Drafting Using your notes, write a rough draft of the statement to be read at the press conference. As Grendel, state your main grievances, and support each one with examples. Remembering your audience (your press) and your purpose (to win sympathy), choose details and examples that will show you in a positive light.

Revising Read your draft to a classmate and ask for his or her response. If at any point the statement does not hold your reader's attention, consider adding details to enhance Grendel's human qualities.

✓ ASSESSMENT OPTIONS

Formal Assessment, Selection Test, pp. 9–11, and assessment Resources Software. The selection test is designed so that it can be easily customized to the performance levels of your students.

Alternative Assessment, p. 2, includes options for less advanced students, more advanced students, bodily/kinesthetic learners, musical/rhythmic learners, verbal/linguistic learners, and visual/spatial learners.

PORTFOLIO ASSESSMENT

Use the following rubrics in the ***Alternative Assessment*** booklet to assess student writing:
Memo: Business Letter/Memo Rubric, p. 114
Comparison and Contrast: Comparison/Contrast Rubric, p. 104
Response to Criticism: Literary Analysis/Interpretation Rubric, p. 113
Writing Mini-Lesson: Persuasion Rubric, p. 106

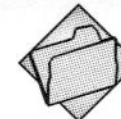

Idea Bank

Customizing for *Performance Levels*

Following are suggestions for matching Idea Bank topics with your students' performance levels:

- Less Advanced Students: 1, 7
- Average Students: 2, 4, 5
- More Advanced Students: 3, 6

Customizing for *Learning Modalities*

Following are suggestions for matching Idea Bank topics with your students' learning modalities:

- Verbal/Linguistic: 1, 2, 3, 4, 5
- Visual/Spatial: 6, 7
- Musical/Rhythmic: 4

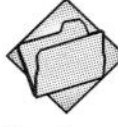

Writing Mini-Lesson

Refer students to the Writing Handbook, page 1189, for instruction on the writing process, and page 1192 for further information on persuasion.

Writer's Solution

Writers at Work Videodisc

Have students view the videodisc segment (Ch. 4) featuring public defender Cary Bricker to see how she uses persuasion to get the best possible outcomes for her clients. Have students discuss how they can use persuasion to change the way people perceive a person—or a monster like Grendel.

Play frames 33218 to 42857

Writing Lab CD-ROM

Have students complete the Tutorial on Persuasion. Follow these steps:

1. Use the interactive instruction on identifying an audience.
2. Arrange details using the Note Cards activity.
3. Draft the press release on computer.
4. Use the Revision Checker to locate and replace overused words.

Allow approximately 90 minutes of class time to complete these steps.

Sourcebook

Have students use Chapter 4, Persuasion (pp. 97–129), for additional support. The chapter includes instruction on considering audience and purpose (pp. 113–114), main idea-and-details-organization (p. 117), and revision (p. 121).

Prepare and Engage

OBJECTIVES

1. To read, comprehend, and interpret epics
2. To explore the literary connections among epics from different cultures
3. To respond to *Gilgamesh* and the *Iliad* through writing, speaking and listening, and a project

PORTFOLIO OPPORTUNITIES

Writing: Classified Ad; Adventure; Response to Criticism
Speaking and Listening: Song for an Epic Hero
Project: Comic Book

More About the Epics

The most commonly read version of the epic *Gilgamesh* was recorded on twelve stone tablets. It was written in Akkadian, the Semitic language of Mesopotamia.

Herotodus, a fifth-century B.C. historian, said that **Homer** was a Greek from Ionia. Homer may have lived on the island of Chios. Traditionally depicted as blind, Homer possibly dictated his poems to someone who then recorded them.

Customize for
Less Proficient Readers
Read through the excerpts with students. Stop at strategic breaking points in the narratives (roughly every two to three stanzas in *Gilgamesh* and every ten to twenty lines in the *Iliad*) and have students summarize or paraphrase what they have read.

Mention a few current popular action-adventure movies. Ask: What are some characteristics of a good action movie? Jot student responses on the chalkboard. Then go over the list and point out that most of the characteristics of a good action movie are shared by epics.

▶Critical Viewing◀

❶ **Make a Judgment** Suggested response: The decorations on this lyre suggest heroic episodes.

CONNECTIONS TO WORLD LITERATURE

from *Gilgamesh*
Translated by David Ferry

from the *Iliad*
Homer, Translated by Richmond Lattimore

Literary Connection

THE EPIC

If you enjoy watching movies or reading books about heroes battling the forces of evil, you have a lot in common with audiences of thousands of years ago. These audiences would thrill to heroic stories sung and chanted by poet-performers.

Often these heroic tales were **epics**—long narrative poems that celebrated the adventures of legendary heroes. Epics provided not only a roller-coaster ride of nonstop thrills, but also examples of how to behave properly in all kinds of situations. The heroes were role models, and as you read about their exploits today, you can learn about the values and behaviors that ancient societies admired. The legendary fighter who served as a model for the English was Beowulf, whose exploits are described in the poem named for him. (See p. 38.)

Other, even earlier, epics in world literature are the epic of *Gilgamesh*, an ancient Near Eastern poem about 4,000 years old, and the *Iliad*, a Greek poem that is almost 3,000 years old. This section contains the Prologue to *Gilgamesh* and the most famous battle scene from the *Iliad*.

Front of a lyre from the tomb of Queen Pu-abi, Ur, (detail), The British Museum

❶ ▲ Critical Viewing Music often accompanied the telling of epics, such as *Gilgamesh* and the *Iliad*. Does the appearance of this lyre seem appropriate for the telling of an epic? **[Make a Judgment]**

GILGAMESH

Gilgamesh is a long narrative poem about a Sumerian king named Gilgamesh who lived between 2700 and 2500 B.C. Unlike modern books, this epic does not have a single author. Stories about King Gilgamesh were told and handed down by Sumerians for hundreds of years after his death. When the Babylonians conquered the Sumerians, they inherited the Sumerian cultural tradition. A Babylonian author, borrowing from some of these tales, created a unified epic about the legendary Sumerian king.

HOMER

The ancient Greeks ascribed the *Iliad* and the *Odyssey,* their two oldest epic poems, to Homer, whom they called "The Poet." Nothing certain is known about Homer's life.

Although Homer's birth and death dates are uncertain, the *Iliad* was probably composed late in the eighth century B.C. The epic tells about a legendary war that occurred hundreds of years earlier, in which Greek forces had attacked the city of Troy in Asia Minor.

Literary Connection

Like the Anglo-Saxon epic *Beowulf*, the heroes of *Gilgamesh* and the *Iliad* embody the values of the people who kept these stories alive. All the key ingredients of the national epic are here—the larger-than-life hero, the providence of the supernatural, the serious tone and elevated language. As in all epics, these stories serve to preserve and transmit a national culture to future generations.

Prentice Hall Literature Program Resources

REINFORCE / RETEACH / EXTEND

Selection Support
Build Vocabulary, p. 12
Thematic Connection: The Epic, p. 13
Formal Assessment Selection Test, pp. 12–13; Assessment Resources Software

Resource Pro CD-ROM
from *Gilgamesh*, from the *Iliad*—includes all resource material and customizable lesson plan

Listening to Literature Audiocassettes
from *Gilgamesh*, from the *Iliad*

from GILGAMESH

The Prologue

Translated by David Ferry

❷

Hero and Animals, Impression from a Sumerian cylinder seal of about 2750 B.C.

The Story
of him who knew the most of all men know;
who made the journey; heartbroken; reconciled;

who knew the way things were before the Flood
the secret things, the mystery; who went

to the end of the earth, and over; who returned,
and wrote the story on a tablet of stone.

❸ He built Uruk.[1] He built the keeping place
of Anu and Ishtar.[2] The outer wall

shines in the sun like brightest copper; the inner
wall is beyond the imagining of kings.

Study the brickwork, study the fortification;
climb the great ancient staircase to the terrace;

❹

study how it is made; from the terrace see
the planted and fallow fields, the ponds and orchards.

1. Uruk (o͞o′ ro͝ok): Ancient Sumerian city.

2. Anu and Ishtar (ä′ no͞o; ish′ tär): Anu is the father of the Babylonian gods and god of the sky; Ishtar is the Babylonian goddess of love.

Develop Understanding

One-Minute Insight These brief excerpts from *Gilgamesh* and the *Iliad* serve to enlarge the concept of the national epic to encompass a world view. The Prologue to *Gilgamesh* offers a summary of the God-hero's achievements. This list includes references to his wisdom and architectural skills, as well as his expected prowess on the battlefield.

Customize for
English Language Learners
The extensive use of pronouns in *Gilgamesh* may pose a problem for English language learners. Have students substitute the name *Gilgamesh* for the pronouns *he, him,* and *who* as they read the selection. Remind them that a semicolon represents the end of a complete thought.

▶Critical Viewing◀

❷ **Infer** This image was formed when a carved cylindrical seal was rolled over soft clay like a rolling pin. Have students study the images of the animals and the hero. Ask students: What can you infer about the traits of a hero in a Sumerian myth? *Possible responses: A hero is strong enough to fight barehanded with bulls and lions; a hero has magical power over animals.*

◆ Literary Focus

❸ **The Epic** Remind students that epics have two purposes: to entertain and to instruct. Ask students to speculate about what a Sumerian or Babylonian child might learn from this passage. *Suggested response: A child might learn that it is important to record adventures or other important events and that building cities and making them beautiful is a task worthy of a hero.*

◆ Critical Thinking

❹ **Infer** The storyteller asks the reader to study the brickwork and other details of Uruk. Ask students what would be revealed by such a close examination based on the information given in the Prologue to *Gilgamesh*. *The details of construction would no doubt reflect the same beauty and ingenuity suggested in the description of the walls in the previous lines.*

◆ Literary Focus

❶ **The Epic** Ask students: How is Gilgamesh similar to Beowulf? *They are both kings and mighty warriors.* How is he different? *Gilgamesh is known for his work during times of peace: building Uruk, laying out fields, opening passes, digging wells, restoring shrines. In Beowulf, nothing is mentioned about what the king accomplished during his peaceful fifty-year reign.* What can you infer about Sumerian and Anglo-Saxon cultures from the differences in their heroes? *Students may say that the Anglo-Saxons prized a leader's military prowess and generosity above all else, whereas the Sumerians placed a high value on a king's ability to plan and carry out large-scale building projects.*

❷ **Clarification** Gilgamesh sought out Utnapishtim, the only person whom the gods had given everlasting life, in order to find out the secret of immortality. Gilgamesh finds Utnapishtim, but fails to earn immortality for himself.

Reinforce and Extend

Answers

◆ *Literature and Your Life*

Reader's Response Students may say that the building of Uruk and the creation of the temple of Anu and Ishtar are Gilgamesh's most important achievements because they are mentioned most often in the excerpt.

Thematic Focus Lines 1–5 and 17–25 hint at Gilgamesh's adventures.

☑ Check Your Comprehension

1. He wrote it on a tablet of lapis lazuli.
2. The Prologue praises the excellence of the structures he built.
3. He knew "the secret things," traveled to the end of the Earth, built Uruk, built the temple of Anu and Ishtar, was a powerful warrior ("the vanguard and rear guard of the army"), opened passes, dug wells, measured the world, and restored the shrines.

This is Uruk, the city of Gilgamesh
the Wild Ox, son of Lugalbanda, son

of the Lady Wildcow Ninsun, Gilgamesh
the vanguard and the rear guard of the army,

❶ Shadow of Darkness over the enemy field,
the Web, the Flood that rises to wash away
❷
the walls of alien cities, Gilgamesh
the strongest one of all, the perfect, the terror.

It is he who opened passes through the mountains;
and he who dug deep wells on the mountainsides;

who measured the world; and sought out Utnapishtim[3]
beyond the world; it is he who restored the shrines;

two-thirds a god, one-third a man, the king.
Go to the temple of Anu and Ishtar:

open the copper chest with the iron locks;
the tablet of lapis lazuli[4] tells the story.

3. **Utnapishtim** (o͞ot nə pēsh´ təm): The Mesopotamian Noah, survivor of the great flood.

4. **lapis lazuli** (lap´ is laz´ yo͞o lī´): An azure-blue, opaque, semiprecious stone.

Guide for Responding

◆ *Literature and Your Life*

Reader's Response Which achievements of King Gilgamesh do you think were most important? Explain.

Thematic Focus What parts of the Prologue hint at the adventures of Gilgamesh?

☑ Check Your Comprehension

1. Where did Gilgamesh write his story?
2. What qualities of Gilgamesh does the Prologue praise?
3. What are Gilgamesh's accomplishments?

◆ Critical Thinking

INTERPRET

1. What does the prologue suggest about the values of ancient Mesopotamia? **[Infer]**
2. Gilgamesh is described as being "two-thirds a god" and "one-third a man." What conflicts might arise from such a combination? **[Infer]**

EVALUATE

3. Does the Prologue help build your anticipation for what is to come? Why or why not? **[Evaluate]**

EXTEND

4. Compare Gilgamesh and Beowulf as protectors of their people. **[Literature Link]**

◆ Critical Thinking

1. Ancient Mesopotamians valued the building of cities.
2. Possible responses: The "god" portion might keep him from sympathizing with ordinary people, and the "man" portion might cause him to make mistakes.
3. Students may say that the Prologue builds their anticipation; they want to find out about the events that are hinted at in the Prologue.
4. Suggested response: Beowulf protects his people against supernatural monsters, whereas Gilgamesh protects his people by building a strong city.

from the ILIAD

Homer, *Translated by Richmond Lattimore*

CONNECTIONS TO WORLD LITERATURE

During the war between the Greeks and the Trojans over Helen of Troy, Achilleus, the greatest warrior of the Greeks, faces Hektor, the best warrior of the Trojans. Hektor has brutally killed Achilleus' friend Patroklos, who was wearing Achilleus' armor. As the scene opens, Hektor and Achilleus meet for battle.

'My brother, it is true our father and the lady our mother, taking
my knees in turn, and my companions about me, entreated
that I stay within, such was the terror upon all of them.
But the heart within me was worn away by hard sorrow for you.
But now let us go straight on and fight hard, let there be no sparing
❸ of our spears, so that we can find out whether Achilleus
will kill us both and carry our bloody war spoils back
to the hollow ships, or will himself go down under your spear.'
So Athene[1] spoke and led him on by beguilement.
Now as the two in their advance were come close together,
first of the two to speak was tall helm-glittering Hektor:
'Son of Peleus, I will no longer run from you, as before this
I fled three times around the great city of Priam, and dared not
❹ stand to your onfall. But now my spirit in turn has driven me
to stand and face you. I must take you now, or I must be taken.
Come then, shall we swear before the gods? For these are the highest
who shall be witnesses and watch over our agreements.
Brutal as you are I will not defile you, if Zeus[2] grants
to me that I can wear you out, and take the life from you.
❺ But after I have stripped your glorious armour, Achilleus,
I will give your corpse back to the Achaians.[3] Do you do likewise.'
Then looking darkly at him swift-footed Achilleus answered:
'Hektor, argue me no agreements. I cannot forgive you.
As there are no trustworthy oaths between men and lions,
nor wolves and lambs have spirit that can be brought to agreement
❻ but forever these hold feelings of hate for each other,
so there can be no love between you and me, nor shall there be
oaths between us, but one or the other must fall before then
to glut with his blood Ares the god who fights under the shield's guard.
Remember every valour of yours, for now the need comes
hardest upon you to be a spearman and a bold warrior.
There shall be no more escape for you, but Pallas Athene
will kill you soon by my spear. You will pay in a lump for all those
sorrows of my companions you killed in your spear's fury.'
So he spoke, and balanced the spear far shadowed, and threw it;

1. **Athene** (ə thē′ nə): Daughter of Zeus. She is associated with victory in war and clever thinking and speaking. She protects the Greeks.

2. **Zeus** (zo͞os): The most powerful of the gods, known as "father of men and gods."

3. **Achaians** (ə kē′ ənz): Greeks.

Develop Understanding

One-Minute Insight Like the Anglo-Saxon *Beowulf,* the *Iliad* reveals a society that perceives itself and its heroes as God's favored people. However, in the *Iliad*, the distinction between the meddlesome and sometimes petty gods and the heroic humans is blurred.

Customize for
More Advanced Students
The dialogue between Achilleus and Hektor plays an important role in revealing character and events in the *Iliad*. Have more advanced students identify key statements by these characters and indicate what is revealed about the character by each statement.

❸ **Clarification** The gods have determined that Hektor is fated to die at the hands of Achilleus and have withdrawn their support of the Trojan hero. This allows the goddess Athene, who is on the side of the Greeks, to encourage Hektor to engage in a fatal battle with Achilleus. To do so, she assumes the form of Hektor's brother Deïphobos. Hektor, tricked into believing that his beloved brother has left safety within the walls of Troy to give him advice, is therefore inclined to do as the devious goddess tells him.

◆ Literary Focus

❹ **The Epic** Have students compare Hektor's attitude toward fate with Beowulf's. *The fatalistic attitude is quite similar in both heroes.*

❺ **Enrichment** The ancient Greeks and Trojans had several options in dealing with a dead opponent. The most generous option was to burn the body in its armor and perform the funeral rites. When Achilleus killed the father of Hektor's wife, he respected the dead man enough to do this. An option acceptable to both sides is the one Hektor proposes: keeping the dead man's armor, but returning the body to his friends and family. However, this course is more merciful than the one Hektor himself followed with Achilleus' best friend, Patroklos. Hektor had stripped Patroklos' body of its armor, which had been borrowed from Achilleus and had belonged to Achilleus' father, Peleus. Hektor then refused to return the corpse, although the Greeks were able to retrieve it after a battle.

◆ Critical Thinking

❻ **Assess** Explain to students that Achilleus is in despair over the death of Patroklos, so that his own life and the warrior's code of honor by which he has lived hold no meaning for him. In another scene, Achilleus says, "In the time before Patroklos came to the day of his destiny/then it was the way of my heart's choice to be sparing/of the Trojans, and many I took alive . . . /Now there is not one who can escape death, if the gods send him against my hands in front of Ilion, not one/of all the Trojans and beyond all others the children of Priam." Ask students to assess Achilleus' character, based on this information. *Most students will still think his attitude excessively harsh, but will agree there are extenuating circumstances.*

◆ Literary Focus

❶ **The Epic** Have students list the main characteristics of an epic. *An epic is a long narrative poem that celebrates the deeds of legendary or heroic figure, typically features a hero with superhuman strength and courage, often depicts the eternal struggle between good and evil, and frequently features supernatural beings or forces that take an active role in events.* Ask: How is this passage characteristic of an epic? *It shows a supernatural being—the goddess Athene—taking an active role in the outcome of events.*

Comprehension Check ☑

❷ Ask students to explain what is going on in this passage. *Hektor discovers that Deïphobos was Athene in disguise. Hektor realizes that he has lost the favor of Zeus and Apollo, and that he is doomed.*

◆ Literary Focus

❸ **The Epic** What might a student in ancient Greece have learned from Hektor's example? *Suggested response: It is important to conduct yourself with honor and valor, even when the situation is hopeless.* Would Beowulf have agreed with this idea? *Suggested response: Yes; Beowulf continued to fight the dragon even though he knew he was going to be killed.*

Customize for *More Advanced Students*

❹ Explain that Greek epics are characterized by *epic similes*, much as Anglo-Saxon epics are characterized by kennings. An epic simile is a long, elaborate comparison between an action in the epic and something with which an audience in ancient Greece would have been familiar. Challenge students to identify another epic simile on this page. *Another epic simile is found in lines 79–82.*

CONNECTIONS TO WORLD LITERATURE

but glorious Hektor kept his eyes on him, and avoided it,
for he dropped, watchful, to his knee, and the bronze spear flew over his shoulder
❶ and stuck in the ground, but Pallas Athene snatched it, and gave it
back to Achilleus, unseen by Hektor shepherd of the people.
But now Hektor spoke out to the blameless son of Peleus:
'You missed; and it was not, o Achilleus like the immortals,
from Zeus that you knew my destiny; but you thought so; or rather
you are someone clever in speech and spoke to swindle me,
to make me afraid of you and forget my valour and war strength.
You will not stick your spear in my back as I run away from you
but drive it into my chest as I storm straight in against you;
if the god gives you that; and now look out for my brazen
spear. I wish it might be taken full length in your body.
And indeed the war would be a lighter thing for the Trojans
if you were dead, seeing that you are their greatest affliction.
  So he spoke, and balanced the spear far shadowed, and threw it,
and struck the middle of Peleïdes' shield, nor missed it,
but the spear was driven far back from the shield, and Hektor was angered
because his swift weapon had been loosed from his hand in a vain cast.
He stood discouraged, and had no other ash spear; but lifting
his voice he called aloud on Deïphobos[4] of the pale shield,
and asked him for a long spear, but Deïphobos was not near him.
And Hektor knew the truth inside his heart, and spoke aloud:
'No use. Here at last the gods have summoned me deathward.
I thought Deïphobos the hero was here close beside me,
❷ but he is behind the wall and it was Athene cheating me,
and now evil death is close to me, and no longer far away,
and there is no way out. So it must long since have been pleasing
to Zeus, and Zeus' son who strikes from afar, this way; though before this
they defended me gladly. But now my death is upon me.
Let me at least not die without a struggle, inglorious,
❸ but do some big thing first, that men to come shall know of it.'
  So he spoke, and pulling out the sharp sword that was slung
at the hollow of his side, huge and heavy, and gathering
himself together, he made his swoop, like a high-flown eagle
❹ who launches himself out of the murk of the clouds on the flat land
to catch away a tender lamb or a shivering hare; so
Hektor made his swoop, swinging his sharp sword, and Achilleus
charged, the heart within him loaded with savage fury.
In front of his chest the beautiful elaborate great shield
covered him, and with the glittering helm with four horns
he nodded; the lovely golden fringes were shaken about it
which Hephaistos[5] had driven close along the horn of the helmet.
And as a star moves among stars in the night's darkening,
Hesper,[6] who is the fairest star who stands in the sky, such
was the shining from the pointed spear Achilleus was shaking
in his right hand with evil intention toward brilliant Hektor.
He was eyeing Hektor's splendid body, to see where it might best
give way, but all the rest of the skin was held in the armour,
brazen and splendid, he stripped when he cut down the strength of Patroklos;[7]
yet showed where the collar-bones hold the neck from the shoulders,
the throat, where death of the soul comes most swiftly; in this place
brilliant Achilleus drove the spear as he came on in fury,

4. **Deïphobos** (dā i fō′ bōs): Son of Priam; powerful Trojan fighter.

5. **Hephaistos** (hē fes′ təs): God of fire and the forge. He made Achilleus' armor.

6. **Hesper** (hes′ pər): The evening star.

7. **Patroklos** (pə träk′ lōs): Companion and henchman to Achilleus.

and clean through the soft part of the neck the spearpoint was driven.
Yet the ash spear heavy with bronze did not sever the windpipe,
so that Hektor could still make exchange of words spoken.
But he dropped in the dust, and brilliant Achilleus vaunted above him:
'Hektor, surely you thought as you killed Patroklos you would be
safe, and since I was far away you thought nothing of me,
o fool, for an avenger was left, far greater than he was,
behind him and away by the hollow ships. And it was I;
and I have broken your strength; on you the dogs and the vultures
shall feed and foully rip you; the Achaians will bury Patroklos.'
❺ In his weakness Hektor of the shining helm spoke to him:
'I entreat you, by your life, by your knees, by your parents,
do not let the dogs feed on me by the ships of the Achaians,
but take yourself the bronze and gold that are there in abundance,
those gifts that my father and the lady my mother will give you,
and give my body to be taken home again, so that the Trojans
and the wives of the Trojans may give me in death my rite of burning.'
But looking darkly at him swift-footed Achilleus answered:
'No more entreating of me, you dog, by knees or parents.
I wish only that my spirit and fury would drive me
to hack your meat away and eat it raw for the things that
you have done to me. So there is no one who can hold the dogs off
from your head, not if they bring here and set before me ten times
and twenty times the ransom, and promise more in addition,
not if Priam son of Dardanos should offer to weigh out
your bulk in gold; not even so shall the lady your mother
who herself bore you lay you on the death-bed and mourn you:
no, but the dogs and the birds will have you all for their feasting.'
Then, dying, Hektor of the shining helmet spoke to him:
'I know you well as I look upon you, I know that I could not
persuade you, since indeed in your breast is a heart of iron.
Be careful now; for I might be made into the gods' curse
❼ upon you, on that day when Paris and Phoibos Apollo[8]
destroy you in the Skaian gates,[9] for all your valour.'
He spoke, and as he spoke the end of death closed in upon him,
and the soul fluttering free of the limbs went down into Death's house
mourning her destiny, leaving youth and manhood behind her.
Now though he was a dead man brilliant Achilleus spoke to him:
'Die: and I will take my own death at whatever time
Zeus and the rest of the immortals choose to accomplish it.'

Shield of Achilles: gold and silver sculpture, John Flaxman

▲ **Critical Viewing** ❻ In what ways is this shield suitable for a great warrior like Achilleus? **[Analyze]**

8. **Paris and Phoibus Apollo** (par´ is; fē´ bəs; ə pôl´ ō): Paris, son of King Priam, and Apollo, the archer god: a god of light and of healing who favors and protects the Trojans.

9. **Skaian gates** (skē´ ən): The northwest gates of Troy.

Guide for Responding

◆ Literature and Your Life

Reader's Response Who do you think acts more heroically—Hektor or Achilleus? Explain.

Thematic Focus Like most epics, the *Iliad* has its roots in historical events. What are the legendary and mythological aspects of the battle scene between Hektor and Achilleus?

☑ Check Your Comprehension

1. Briefly summarize the battle between Hektor and Achilleus.
2. What does Hektor ask of Achilleus after he is mortally wounded? How does Achilleus respond?

❺ **Enrichment** One of the worst threats in the *Iliad*, and among the worst fears people express, is that a corpse will be left unburied, to be eaten by vultures and dogs. In fact, this never actually happens in the poem. The ancient Greeks' great concern about proper burial is also seen in the *Odyssey*, in which the ghost of one of Odysseus' men begs for proper burial and, most famously, in Sophocles' *Antigone*, in which Antigone defies a royal edict in order to bury her brother.

▶Critical Viewing◀

❻ **Analyze** Some students may say that the shield is beautiful, and therefore worthy of a great warrior. Other students may question the practicality of the ornamentation and whether the metal would hold up in battle.

◆ Literary Focus

❼ **The Epic** Ask: In what way is Hektor's warning a lesson about proper behavior? *Suggested response: This passage can be seen as a warning against iron-hearted, merciless behavior, which can anger the gods and so bring about the offender's death.*

Reinforce and Extend

Answers

◆ Literature and Your Life

Reader's Response Students may say that Hektor acts more heroically, even though he loses the battle.

Thematic Focus Legendary and mythical aspects include the running conversation between the two opponents and the intervention of Athene.

☑ Check Your Comprehension

1. Achilleus throws his spear at Hektor and misses, but Athene returns his spear to him. Hektor's spear is deflected by Achilleus' shield. Hektor asks his brother for another spear and, discovering that his brother is not there, realizes that he has been tricked by the gods and must be fated to die. Hektor rushes at Achilleus with his sword, and Achilleus stabs him in the neck with his spear.
2. Hektor asks that his body be returned to his people. Achilleus replies that he intends to leave Hektor's body for the dogs and vultures to eat, and that no amount of ransom will dissuade him.

Answers
◆ Critical Thinking

1. Students may infer that by assisting Achilleus, Athene ensures that the dictates of fate are carried out.
2. Suggested response: He appears more determined to fight, does not attempt to bargain before the battle begins, and cannot be swayed from his intentions.
3. Achilleus' refusal suggests that he has lost all faith in human society and custom. The ideal Greek warrior may be implacable when it comes to killing an opponent, but does not demean himself by taking revenge upon the corpse.
4. Most students will say that Achilleus goes overboard in his lust for revenge.
5. Suggested response: Achilleus would not function well in a modern army, because his desire to take revenge on Hektor's corpse—an unproductive course of action that would be distasteful or demoralizing even to his own people—demonstrates a lack of discipline.

Literary Connection

1. Suggested response: It ensured that the body would not be eaten by scavengers or otherwise defiled.
2. It suggests that it was the duty of a Sumerian king to build cities and temples.
3. Some students may say that Achilleus and Beowulf are too specialized as warriors to be good Sumerian kings. Other students may point out that Beowulf ruled the Geats for fifty years, so he may well have skills in building that are simply not mentioned in the epic.
4. Student responses should reflect a thorough understanding of the heroes they are comparing. Students should discuss similarities as well as differences between the heroes.

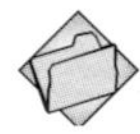

Idea Bank

Customizing for
Performance Levels
Following are suggestions for matching Idea Bank topics with your students' performance levels:

Less Advanced Students: 1
Average Students: 2, 4, 5
More Advanced Students: 3

◆ Critical Thinking

INTERPRET

1. What role does the goddess Athene play in this battle? **[Infer]**
2. In what ways does Achilleus appear more warriorlike than Hektor? Explain. **[Infer]**
3. Hektor pleads with Achilleus not to defile his corpse. What does Achilleus' refusal suggest about the Greek warrior? **[Infer]**

EVALUATE

4. Is Achilleus more brutal than he needs to be, even in avenging the death of a friend? Explain. **[Evaluate]**

EXTEND

5. Would a warrior like Achilleus function well in a modern army? Why or why not? **[Career Link]**

Literary Connection

THE EPIC

Like the English poem *Beowulf, Gilgamesh* and the *Iliad* are examples of **epics**—long narrative poems about the deeds of legendary heroes. You can read these poems not only for their action scenes, but for what they reveal about the societies that created them. Hektor's concern about the fate of his body after death, for example, discloses the importance of burial ceremonies to the ancient Greeks.

1. Why do you think the "rite of burning" was important to ancient Greek warriors? **[Infer]**
2. What does the Prologue to *Gilgamesh* suggest about the duties of a Sumerian king? **[Infer]**
3. Would Beowulf and Achilleus have been successful as Sumerian kings? Explain. **[Speculate]**
4. Compare and contrast an action hero of today with Gilgamesh, Achilleus, or Beowulf. Consider both the deeds and the values of the heroes you're comparing. **[Compare and Contrast]**

Idea Bank

Writing

1. **Classified Ad** As an employer of heroes, create a print advertisement that will attract candidates with the characteristics of Beowulf, Achilleus, or Gilgamesh.
2. **Adventure** Write your own episode for *Gilgamesh*—in prose or in verse—based on the information in the Prologue.
3. **Response to Criticism** N. K. Sandars declared that epic poetry "is a mixture of pure adventure, of mortality, and of tragedy." Respond to this statement by identifying elements of adventure, mortality, and tragedy in the excerpts from *Beowulf, Gilgamesh*, and the *Iliad*.

Speaking and Listening

4. **Song for an Epic Hero** Write a modern song—rock, rap, blues, or any other style—about one of these ancient epic heroes. Compose the music for it or set it to a tune that you already know. Then perform it for the class. **[Performing Arts Link]**

Project

5. **Comic Book** Create a comic book adventure for an epic hero of your own. Illustrate your comic book by drawing pictures, clipping photos from magazines, or using computer graphics. **[Media Link; Art Link]**

Customizing for
Learning Modalities
Following are suggestions for matching Idea Bank topics with your students' learning modalities:

Verbal/Linguistic: 1, 2, 3, 4
Visual/Spatial: 5
Musical/Rhythmic: 4

✓ ASSESSMENT OPTIONS

Formal Assessment, Selection Test, pp. 12–13; Assessment Resources Software.

PORTFOLIO ASSESSMENT
Use the following rubrics in the ***Alternative Assessment*** booklet to assess student writing:
Classified Ad: Persuasion Rubric, p. 106
Adventure: Fictional Narrative Rubric, p. 96; Poetry Rubric, p. 109
Response to Criticism: Literary Analysis/Interpretation Rubric, p. 113

Writing Process Workshop

Research Paper

To defeat his foes, Beowulf may have researched information about their battle techniques and areas of weakness. **Research writing**—writing based on information gathered from outside sources—gives you the power to become an expert on any subject. Researchers are like detectives searching for information that goes beyond common knowledge.

Write a research paper in which you share with your audience what you have learned from your research.

Writing Skills Focus

- ▶ Begin your paper with a startling fact, an anecdote, a question, or a quotation to **grab your readers' attention**. (See p. 63.)
- ▶ Organize the information you have gathered so it has a **clear beginning, middle,** and **end**.
- ▶ **Keep a clear and consistent purpose.** Decide what you want to accomplish in the paper before you begin writing. Then keep to that purpose as you plan, write, and revise your report.

Notice how these skills work together in the following model.

Writing Model

Imagine being judged a "barbarian" because you are wearing pants! ① During the Anglo-Saxon period, trousers distinguished the Germanic settlers from Greeks and Romans, who wore loose, gownlike garments called togas. Also, different styles of trousers—loose or tight, slit at the ankle or with belt loops—were not just a matter of personal taste but often indicated a tribal tradition. By examining the clothing of the Anglo-Saxons, we can learn more about Anglo-Saxon society, especially its various social groups and the types of work done by men and women. ②

① Beginning with a startling fact that grabs readers' attention and makes them want to find out more.

② This thesis statement tells readers what the middle of the report will explore in greater detail and clarifies the writer's purpose.

Beyond the Classroom

Career Connection

News Reporter Tell students that good research skills can benefit them in future employment. Research skills are important in many types of jobs, but particularly if they work for a news provider. Whether reporting the news or writing the articles, news reporters must be well informed, and doing research is the way that reporters become informed. Reporters must be aware of all possible sources and know how to evaluate their usefulness. Have students discuss the many ways news reporters may get information. Lead them to see that interviews, town records, and library resources all provide information.

Prepare and Engage

Establish Writing Guidelines
Before students begin this lesson, review the following elements of an effective research paper:

- A research paper is built around a thesis statement, which presents your position on a topic.
- An effective introduction should grab the readers' attention with, for example, a startling fact or an intriguing question.
- The introduction also includes the thesis statement. The body paragraphs of a research paper develop the thesis, and a conclusion sums up the main idea of the paper.
- The purpose of a research paper is to prove the thesis. Information from research develops and supports the position stated in the thesis.

Before students begin their research paper, distribute the Scoring Rubric for Research Report/Paper (p. 107 in ***Alternative Assessment***) to apprise students of the criteria on which they will be evaluated. See the suggestions on page 73 for customizing the rubric to this assignment.

Writer's Solution

Writers at Work Videodisc
Prepare students for research writing by introducing them to a professional research writer. Show the videodisc segment on Research Writing in which sportswriter Peter Ginsburg defines research writing and its role in his life.

Play frames 3 to 7599

Sourcebook
Students can find additional support including topic ideas, tips on gathering information, models and revision help in the chapter on Research Writing (pp. 131–165).

Develop Student Writing

Prewriting
Have students form groups to brainstorm for possible literature-related research topics. Collect each group's ideas and choose those that seem most appropriate. Then give students the option of choosing one of the topics that you have selected.

Writer's Solution

Writing Lab CD-ROM
If students have access to computers, have them work in the Research Writing tutorial to guide them in researching and writing their papers. Have students follow these steps:

1. Students can review the interactive model of a research paper.
2. Have students use a topic web to narrow their topic.
3. Before students gather information, they should refer to the audio-annotated instruction on using library sources and the interactive instruction on using on-line services.
4. Students can draft their research papers on the computer.
5. Have students use a self-evaluation checklist when revising their paper.

After students have chosen a topic and gathered information, they will need to formulate a thesis statement. Direct students to the annotated instruction on grouping information in the Research Writing tutorial. In addition, have students review the audio-annotated examples of thesis statements. Then have students group their notes into categories and come up with a main idea, or thesis statement.

Customize for
Visual/Spatial Learners
Provide visual/spatial learners with a copy of a Branching organizer, page 95 in ***Writing and Language Transparencies*** to help them arrange their details into subtopics visually.

Applying Language Skills
Punctuating Quotations Explain to students that they must use quotation marks to indicate the use of words or ideas that are not their own. Review these rules with students and have them check their drafts for correct punctuation of quotations.

APPLYING LANGUAGE SKILLS: Punctuating Quotations

When you incorporate quoted material into your research paper, use the following guidelines.

- Use quotation marks to enclose passages taken from another writer. If an end mark is part of a quotation, place it inside the closing quotation marks. Otherwise, place the end mark outside. When using a period, though, always place it inside the closing quotation marks.
- If you introduce a quotation with words like *stated that* or *wrote that,* don't use a comma:
- The professor stated that "advertising is our greatest export."
- When you use a quotation of four lines or more, introduce it with a colon, don't use quotation marks, and set it off from the rest of your report.

Writing Application In your research report, check that you have punctuated quotations correctly.

Writer's Solution Connection
Writing Lab
For more help in using the computer and other research tools to gather information, see the Research Writing tutorial.

Prewriting

Choose a Topic If you aren't interested in a topic, the chances are that your readers won't be either. Find a general topic that interests you, like clothing or sports, and then apply it to the period or discipline about which you're writing.

Selection-Related Ideas

- Beowulf and John Gardner's Grendel
- Anglo-Saxon superstitions about dragons
- The strange fate of the Beowulf manuscript

Identify Your Purpose Identify the goal you want to accomplish with your research paper. Use a K-W-L chart like the one below to help you determine this goal.

Gather Information Before you go to a library or log on to a computer, devise a research plan in which you identify likely sources. Ask questions such as *How far back in time should my sources be dated?* to guide your research.

Formulate a Thesis Statement After organizing your notes according to the topics you will cover in your paper, develop a thesis statement that sums up your main idea.

What I Know	What I Want To Know	What I Learned
I know that clothing indicates a great deal about a person's culture and background.	I want to know what Anglo-Saxon clothing can tell us about that time.	Anglo-Saxon clothing reflected the wearer's social status.

Drafting

Write a Strong Introduction An effective introduction conveys your own interest in your topic. Include your thesis statement and grab readers' attention with an anecdote, a startling fact, a question, or a quotation.

Write Body Paragraphs In the body of your paper, you develop your ideas with facts and details. Each body paragraph should contain a topic sentence and should examine one aspect of your thesis.

Write a Conclusion In your conclusion, restate your main points and leave your readers with a recommendation, a provocative statement, or a question.

Drafting
Have students use their grouped notes to write their research papers. Encourage students to include an anecdote, startling fact, question, or quotation in their introduction. Remind students not to labor over small points, but to get all their ideas on paper in an organized fashion. They can correct grammatical and spelling errors while revising.

Writer's Solution

Writing Lab CD-ROM
For further practice on punctuating quotations, direct students to the interactive instructions on citing and crediting sources in the Research Writing tutorial.

Revising

Use a Writing Skills Checklist Go back to the Writing Skills Focus on page 71 and use the items as a checklist to evaluate and revise your research paper. Make revisions that will

- ▶ Grab readers' attention
- ▶ Make them aware of your purpose
- ▶ Provide a clear beginning, middle, and end of your report

Revision Model

~~Although we may not like to believe that we~~ Do you judge others by their appearance ① ? Most people do and this type of evaluation has been occurring as long as clothing has existed. What was worn ② during the Anglo-Saxon period has provided us with information on the roles the German tribes and Romans and Greeks had in society. ~~Today's clothing is much more interesting than Anglo-Saxon clothing.~~ ③

① The writer begins her concluding paragraph with a question that will grab readers' attention.

② The writer adds a phrase to clarify her meaning.

③ The writer deletes a sentence that distracts readers from her conclusion.

Publishing

- ▶ **Classroom Presentation** Present your paper orally to your classmates. Do not read it directly, but present the key points in a clear and engaging manner. You may opt to use visual prompts to make your report come alive for your peers.
- ▶ **Paper Exchange** Exchange papers with a group of classmates and read one another's work. Then meet for a friendly discussion of your findings.
- ▶ **Internet** Post your report to a message board in a news group about your topic. Be sure to credit all the sources you've used before you post your work.

Applying Language Skills: Using Transitions to Show Importance

Use transitions to show the order of importance among ideas. You can use the following phrases:

First of all, most of all, more importantly, less significantly, primarily, secondarily, best of all, worst of all, the main reason, more outstanding, the most vital

Practice Rewrite the following passage, using order-of-importance transitions.

Space science, medicine, and engineering have been greatly changed by computers. Business and industry have also experienced significant change. Personal home computers also affect people's lives.

Writing Application Review your paper and add transitions to show order-of-importance relationships and to create a smooth, logical flow of ideas.

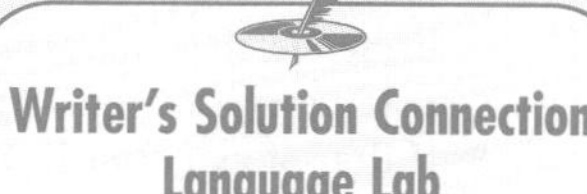

Writer's Solution Connection Language Lab

For more help using transitions in your writing, use the Composition lesson in the Writing Style section.

Revising

Suggest that students work with a peer reviewer to revise their papers. Have students use the revising checklist and the scoring rubric as evaluation tools. Prepare peer reviewers to be sensitive when giving comments to writers.

Writing and Language Transparencies To provide model of the revision process, use Writing Process Model 7, Research Report, pp. 57–72.

Applying Language Skills

Using Transitions to Show Importance Explain to students that order of importance is effective in research papers because it helps to build coherent support for a thesis.

Answers

Suggested Response:

Computers affect people's lives. *First of all*, business and industry have experienced significant change. *Even more significantly*, space science, medicine, and engineering have been greatly changed by computers.

Reinforce and Extend

Self-Evaluation Have students reflect upon what they have learned about research writing by answering questions such as *What part of the research process do you think you learned the most from? Which did you enjoy the most? What did you learn about your topic?*

Connect to Real Life Explain to students that everyday life requires research skills. Every time students comparison shop or look in consumer magazines to check ratings of products, they are researching. Ask students to come up with other areas in their daily lives where research is important.

☑ Assessment

PORTFOLIO ASSESSMENT		4	3	2	1
Use the Scoring Rubric for Research Report in ***Alternative Assessment*** (p. 107) to assess students' writing. Add these criteria to customize the rubric to this assignment.	**Attention-Getting Introduction**	The writer includes a thought-provoking introduction that will interest readers in the paper.	The writer includes information in the introduction that may interest some but is already widely known.	The writer includes information that grabs the readers' attention but it occurs too late in the paper.	The writer did not include any information that would grab a reader's attention.
	Proving the Thesis	The writer provides details that support and prove the thesis of the paper.	The writer provides much support for the thesis but also includes information that does not help prove the thesis.	The paper contains some information that proves the thesis but the majority of information does not relate to it.	The writer does not prove the thesis.

Introduce the Strategy

Students may assume that all sources of information are factual and free of bias. Point out that most information, including television broadcasts and historical documents is presented from a particular point of view and therefore is biased. This lesson gives students an opportunity to assess bias in a political flyer. The strategies they use will help them evaluate all sources of information.

Customize for
Less Advanced Students
Some students may have difficulty recognizing bias. Have these students create a checklist based on the strategies provided. They can use this checklist to detect bias when they are presented with any type of information.

Apply the Strategy

Review with students the following signs of bias:

- emotionally loaded language—language used to provoke a quick, emotional response not a well-thought-out response
- unsupported generalizations—information that might be true for small groups of people but not the quantity claimed
- oversimplified reasoning—when the information presented is reduced to an *either/or* situation that is not necessarily true

Then direct students' attention to the flyer on this page.

Answers
Suggested Responses:

1. The following signs of bias appear in this flyer: emotionally charged language: *Raised taxes, homeowners pay more, maintenance costs may triple, the old library has served the town well;* unsupported generalizations: *Raised taxes, homeowners pay more, maintenance costs may triple;* oversimplified reasoning: *If passed, the bond issue for a new town library will raise your taxes.*
2. The information in the flyer seems incomplete because claims of raised taxes are never supported by statistical or factual information.

Evaluating Sources of Information

Real-World Reading Skills Workshop

Strategies for Success

Computer modems, electronic mail, and satellite television have made it possible to communicate information very quickly. An increase in the speed of communication, however, does not necessarily mean an increase in its quality. When you get information—even from the newest media—you need to evaluate it for bias, accuracy, and completeness.

Look for Bias Bias is a prejudice for or against a person or idea. When you evaluate information, be alert for signs that your source may be biased, rather than balanced and impartial. Signs of bias include emotionally loaded words, personal attacks, unsupported generalizations, and oversimplified either/or reasoning.

Consider *who* is speaking. Does the person or group providing information have an interest in the outcome? If so, that interest may lead to bias.

Consider what the writer does *not* say. Omitting details can slant information in a particular direction. This, too, is a form of bias.

Evaluate the Facts Make sure that the information is accurate and complete. Ask yourself these questions:

- ▶ Am I aware of facts that seem to contradict this information? Are the sources of this information reliable and up-to-date?
- ▶ Is the information complete? Is there evidence that important facts and contradictory opinions were left out?
- ▶ If the information is a statistical sample, is it representative?

VOTE NO!!!

Let's not fool ourselves. If it is passed, the bond issue for a new town library will raise your taxes. Some homeowners will pay a great deal more every year. And that's just the beginning. Hidden maintenance costs may triple the annual tax bite within three to five years. The old library has served the town well and can continue to do so. SAY NO ON OCTOBER 19! VOTE THE SPENDTHRIFT LIBRARY BOND ISSUE DOWN!!

NO

Apply the Strategy

1. List any of the following signs of bias that you find in the flier: emotionally loaded language, unsupported generalizations, and oversimplified reasoning. Explain for each sign you list how the flier exemplifies it.
2. Does the information in the flier seem accurate and complete? Why?

Here are other sources of information that you need to evaluate carefully:

- ▶ Campaign posters and speeches
- ▶ Sales messages in all media
- ▶ News stories in print and on television

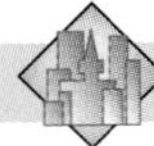

Beyond the Classroom

Workplace Skills
Creating Unbiased Reports Explain to students that being able to identify bias in information they receive and eliminate it from information they distribute will help them establish credibility and a reputation for fairness. Employees are often required to give reports to supervisors. It is important that these reports provide unbiased information because further decisions may be based upon them. For instance, a police officer must create completely unbiased reports. The officer will hear two sides of an argument, each being heavily biased, and must discern which information is relevant to the case and which is personal opinion.

Part 3 A National Spirit

Four Kings of England, British Library, London, Great Britain

Despite invasions by Romans, Vikings, Anglo-Saxons, and Normans, by the fifteenth century, England began to come together as a nation as its peoples expanded their concerns and loyalties beyond the boundaries of villages and towns. The two pieces in this section, Bede's *History* and *The Anglo-Saxon Chronicle,* are both notable documents that capture and preserve the newly developing English identity.

One-Minute Planning Guide

The selections in this section reveal the development of an English national identity. Excerpts from two medieval histories, *A History of the English Church and People* and *The Anglo-Saxon Chronicle,* describe events of the early Middle Ages. The two excerpts from *The Canterbury Tales: The Prologue* reveal much about the structure of fourteenth-century society and also show the development of a national language.

The newspaper article "Elizabeth II: A New Queen" tells of an important event and shows how national identity plays a role in twentieth-century England.

Customize for
Varying Student Needs

When assigning the selections in this part, keep in mind these factors:

from *A History of the English Church and People*
- Brief
- Contains both realistic and fanciful elements

from *The Anglo-Saxon Chronicle*
- Brief
- Less proficient readers may have trouble keeping track of events

from *The Canterbury Tales: The Prologue*
- Long narrative poem (22 pages)
- Vivid, candid, and motivating descriptions of characters

The Nun's Priest's Tale
- Long narrative poem (15 pages)
- Appealing fable

"Elizabeth II: A New Queen"
- High-interest topic: the British royal family
- Connects a twentieth-century monarch to ancestors shown on this page and mentioned in connection with the other selections

Humanities: Art

Four Kings of England.

This page from an illuminated manuscript depicts four successive kings of England. King Henry II (upper left) ruled from 1154 to 1189. He increased the king's authority throughout his reign, a policy that led to the murder of Thomas à Becket. Henry II was succeeded by his son, Richard I (upper right). Richard the Lion-hearted was king until 1199 but spent all but six months of his reign outside of England, fighting in the Crusades. While he was absent, the country was ruled by his brother, John (lower left), who succeeded him in 1199 and ruled until 1216. John was an unpopular king (he is the villainous Prince John of the Robin Hood legend) and is most famous for signing the Magna Carta in 1215. Henry III (lower right), John's son, ascended to the throne in 1216, when he was only nine years old. He ruled until 1272. Like his father, Henry III was an unpopular king who was forced to give away royal authority.

Have your students link the art to Part 3, *The Story of Britain: A National Spirit,* by answering this question:

When this manuscript was created, all important documents were written in Latin, not in English. Why might the use of English for important documents enhance the national identity? *The use of English for important documents would imply that English is as "permanent" or "worthy" as Latin; it shows that the English people have something in common.*

OBJECTIVES

1. To read, comprehend, and interpret historical accounts
2. To relate historical accounts to personal experience
3. To break down sentences to facilitate comprehension
4. To identify historical writing
5. To build vocabulary in context and learn the suffix *-ade*
6. To develop skill in using compound sentences
7. To write a coherent regional history of a local place
8. To respond to historical accounts through writing, speaking and listening, and projects

SKILLS INSTRUCTION

Vocabulary: Suffixes: *-ade*

Grammar and Style: Compound Sentences

Reading Strategy: Break Down Sentences

Literary Focus: Historical Writing

Writing: Coherence

Speaking and Listening: Interview with Bede (teacher edition)

Critical Viewing: Infer; Speculate; Interpret

PORTFOLIO OPPORTUNITIES

Writing: Details That Identify You; Weekly Chronicle; Fantasy History

Writing Mini-Lesson: Regional History

Speaking and Listening: Interview With Bede; Speech for Alfred the Great

Projects: Tour of a Viking Ship; Evening Newscast From the Tenth Century

More About the Author

Bede, who entered the monastery at age seven, had numerous and wide interests. His writings included works on grammar, science, and theology. Bede began the practice of dating historical events from Christ's birth. Other scholars began doing this too, noting whether events occurred B.C. or A.D.

Bede himself was the subject of a history by a former student, Cuthbert, who recorded the details of Bede's last day alive. According to Cuthbert, Bede gave away his few possessions, spoke instructive and comforting words, and then "passed his last day happily until evening . . . upon the floor of his little cell, chanting."

Guide for Interpreting

Bede *(673–735)*

Though he lived all his life in a tiny corner of northeastern England, Bede's influence spread across Europe and down the ages. Born in Wearmouth (now the city of Sunderland), Bede entered the monastic school of Jarrow in northeastern England. He was a diligent student and stayed on at the monastery as a priest and scholar. Bede lived his whole life at Jarrow, but he wrote in Latin, so his work was accessible to scholars throughout the West. His pupils carried his writings to Europe. Famous in his own lifetime for his scholarship, after his death he was honored with the title "the Venerable Bede."

A Respected Historian Modern historians still turn to Bede's book, *A History of the English Church and People,* to learn about England before A.D. 700. To tell the story of England's warring kings and of the spread of Christianity, Bede used not only the documents assembled in his monastery's rich library, but also the learning and research of knowledgeable monks in other parts of England.

The Anglo-Saxon Chronicle

Except for Bede's *History*, the story of Britain's past was fragmentary in the years before the ninth century: a poem passed from one person to another; a parchment listing the names of old kings; a soldier's memories of a battle. During the renaissance of scholarship in King Alfred's reign (A.D. 871–899), a group of monks decided to knit together this fragmentary story. Their efforts resulted in *The Anglo-Saxon Chronicle,* the most important English historical record of the time.

Putting the Pieces Together In writing the *Chronicle,* these monks pulled together parts of Bede's *History,* existing chronologies, royal genealogies (family trees), and other historical documents. They wrote their new manuscript out by hand and sent copies to several other monasteries.

A Letter to the Future For the following two centuries, members of these monasteries added news to the Chronicle—ranging from gossip about a local baron to the battles of kings. *The Anglo-Saxon Chronicle* became a kind of chain letter from one generation to the next.

◆ Background for Understanding

HISTORY: THE FIGHT TO PRESERVE LEARNING

It was as if the lights had gone out. In the fifth century, two hundred years or so before Bede's time, Rome had abandoned Britain. The empire that had been ruled from Rome, Italy, was the most advanced civilization in the West. As part of the Roman empire, Britain had been connected with a larger world of trade and culture; the Roman army had patrolled Britain's borders. With Britain now isolated, threatened by invasion from without and by strife from within, who in Britain would continue the traditions of reading, learning, and teaching?

Monks, particularly in Ireland, kept knowledge alive during these dark times, studying Latin and copying books (which were rare and expensive) during the centuries of Anglo-Saxon rule. Through their work and, later, with the encouragement of King Alfred the Great (849–899), learning endured and prospered.

Prentice Hall Literature Program Resources

REINFORCE / RETEACH / EXTEND

Selection Support Pages
Build Vocabulary: Suffixes: *-ade,* p. 14
Grammar and Style: Compound Sentences, p. 15
Reading Strategy: Break Down Sentences, p. 16
Literary Focus: Historical Writing, p. 17

Strategies for Diverse Students Needs, p. 3

Beyond Literature
Career Connection: Today's Historian, p. 3

Formal Assessment Selection Test, pp. 23–25

Alternative Assessment, p. 3

Writing and Language Transparencies
Research Report, pp. 57–69

Resource Pro CD-ROM
from *A History of the English Church and People,* from *The Anglo-Saxon Chronicle*—includes all resource material and customizable lesson plan

Listening to Literature Audiocassettes
from *A History of the English Church and People,* from *The Anglo-Saxon Chronicle*

from A History of the English Church and People ◆ *from* The Anglo-Saxon Chronicle ◆

◆ Literature and Your Life

CONNECT YOUR EXPERIENCE

What sources might the students of the future use to learn about life in your time? How accurate a picture would those sources give?

Our best sources of information about life in early England include the two histories excerpted here. They were handwritten on parchment and treasured for generations in monasteries.

Journal Writing In a journal entry, list the sources that students of the future might use to learn about the present.

THEMATIC FOCUS: A NATIONAL SPIRIT

How do these works of history reflect a new sense of regional identity?

◆ Literary Focus

HISTORICAL WRITING

Historical writing tells the story of past events using evidence, such as documents from the time, that the writer has evaluated for reliability. Examining the evidence is one way in which writers of history take a step back from the shared beliefs of those around them.

You can sense this special historical "step back" at work in a sentence from Bede's *History:* "Britain, formerly known as Albion, is an island in the ocean. . . ." The moment Bede writes that sentence, he has left behind the tiny corner of England in which he lived his life and entered a wider world. He writes not just for his neighbors, but for those who may never have heard of Britain before.

◆ Grammar and Style

COMPOUND SENTENCES

Bede uses **compound sentences**, which contain two or more independent clauses (groups of words, with subjects and predicates, that can stand alone as sentences). In a compound sentence, the clauses can be joined by *and, or, but,* or a semicolon.

independent clause
There are many land and sea birds of various species, and

independent clause
it is well known for its plentiful springs and rivers abounding in fish.

◆ Reading Strategy

BREAK DOWN SENTENCES

Break down sentences—identify the key part of a sentence—to aid your understanding of long, complex sentences like Bede's.

> As time went on, *Britain received a third nation*, that of the Scots, who migrated from Ireland under their chieftain Reuda, and by a combination of force and treaty, obtained from the Picts the settlements that they still hold.

The independent clause expressing the main action is italicized. Once you have identified this clause, it is easier to see how each of the "leftover" clauses explains the *when, where, how, why,* and *who* of the main action.

◆ Build Vocabulary

SUFFIXES: *-ade*

In *The Anglo-Saxon Chronicle,* a nobleman occupied a large house and "barricaded" its gate against his enemies. Knowing that the suffix *-ade* often means "the act of" or "people involved in," you can figure out that *barricade* means "the act of barring the way."

WORD BANK

Before you read, preview this list of words from the selections.

promontories
innumerable
stranded
barricaded
ravaged

Preparing for Standardized Tests

Reading and Vocabulary Learning to get to the heart of a sentence will help students improve their performance on the reading comprehension portions of standardized tests. It will also help them deal with historical documents, excerpts from scientific literature, and other complex readings in content-area achievement tests. For practice in breaking down sentences, use the Reading Strategy exercise on page 84 and the Reading Strategy page in ***Selection Support,*** p. 16.

Grammar and Language Standardized tests may require students to choose among several options for improving a sentence. For example:

Bede was cannonized in 1899, his feast day is May 25. *(D.) (Option C is grammatically correct, but inappropriately contrasts the two ideas.)*

(A) 1899, his (C) 1899, but his
(B) 1899 and his (D) 1899; his

The Grammar and Style lesson for this selection will help students correctly answer questions that involve compound sentences. For additional practice, use the Grammar and Style page in ***Selection Support,*** p. 15.

Interest Grabber Obtain a paper plate and create a dial or gauge by drawing an arrow along a radius with a colored marker. Draw tick marks along the edge. Tape the dial to a door in the classroom. Inform students that you have built a time machine. Ask students where they would like to travel, and why. Elicit the idea that time travel permits a person to learn about a particular time in history. Point out that, unfortunately, your time machine doesn't work. (You may punctuate this idea by removing the dial and tossing it into a trash can.) Ask: Now what can you do to learn about the past? Elicit the idea that you can learn about the past by reading histories. Point out that the selections they are about to read will allow them to travel in their imaginations more than a thousand years into the past.

Customize for
Less Proficient Readers
To help less proficient readers through the detail-packed text, encourage them to break the text into chunks or paragraphs and read one at a time. After reading a few sentences of each paragraph, have them ask themselves: Does this tell about a place or about people?

Customize for
More Advanced Students
Students might enjoy noting the types of details that are not included in the selection, such as details about food, transportation, or entertainment. Have students consider what these omissions suggest about the writers' knowledge and interests.

Customize for
English Language Learners
This will be a difficult selection for English language learners because of the long sentences and unfamiliar names. To help these students, preview what each paragraph or section is about and then have them read it.

Customize for
Verbal/Linguistic Learners
Have students work in pairs to create and answer *who? what? where? why? when?* and *how?* questions about each paragraph or section. Explain that this is one way to rephrase information and check comprehension.

Develop Understanding

One-Minute Insight Bede's work, which traced English history from the time of the Roman Invasion (54 B.C.) until A.D. 731, was written in Latin but later translated into English, where it reached a wider audience. This excerpt describes the geography and early peoples of Britain.

Bede has been called the father of English history, since he was among the first to use the methods of a historian: He consulted written records, interviewed knowledgeable people, studied letters and documents, and cited sources.

Customize for *More Advanced Students* Challenge students to locate the places that Bede describes and to check the accuracy of his facts.

◆ Grammar and Style

❶ Compound Sentences Have students identify the independent clauses in these compound sentences. *The independent clauses are: "Britain . . . timber," "it . . . animals," "vines . . . localities," "There . . . species," and "it . . . fish."*

◆ Literary Focus

❷ Historical Writing Facts in this passage include: Cockles are abundant, a scarlet dye is obtained from cockles, the country has both salt and hot springs, the land has metals, and jet and amber carry a static charge. Superstitions include: Water is heated by flowing across certain metals and burning jet drives away snakes.

❸ Clarification Bede, like other scholars of his time, believed that the sun moved around the Earth.

from

A History of the English Church and People

Bede

Translated by Leo Sherley-Price

The Situation of Britain and Ireland: *Their Earliest Inhabitants*

Britain, formerly known as Albion, is an island in the ocean, facing between north and west, and lying at a considerable distance from the coasts of Germany, Gaul, and Spain, which together form the greater part of Europe. It extends 800 miles northwards, and is 200 in breadth, except where a number of promontories stretch farther, the coastline round which extends to 3,675 miles. To the south lies Belgic Gaul,[1] from the nearest shore of which travelers can see the city known as Rutubi Portus, which the English have corrupted to Reptacestir.[2] The distance from there across the sea to Gessoriacum,[3] the nearest coast of the Morini, is 50 miles or, as some write it, 450 furlongs.[4] On the opposite side of Britain, which lies open to the boundless ocean, lie the isles of the Orcades.[5] Britain is rich in grain and timber; it has good pasturage for cattle and draft animals,[6] and vines are cultivated in various localities. There are many land and sea birds of various species, and it is well known for its plentiful springs and rivers abounding in fish. ❶ There are salmon and eel fisheries, while seals, dolphins, and sometimes whales are caught. There are also many varieties of shellfish, such as mussels, in which are often found excellent pearls of several colors: red, purple, violet, and green, but mainly white. Cockles[7] are abundant, and a beautiful scarlet dye is extracted from them which remains unfaded by sunshine or rain; indeed, the older the cloth, the more beautiful its color. The country has both salt and hot springs, and the waters flowing from them provide hot baths, in which the people bathe separately according to age and sex. As Saint Basil says: "Water receives its heat when it flows across certain metals, and becomes hot, and even scalding." The land has rich veins of many metals, including copper, iron, lead, and silver. There is also much black jet[8] of fine quality, which sparkles in firelight. When burned, it drives away snakes, and, like amber, when it is warmed by friction, it clings to whatever is applied to it. In old times, the country had twenty-eight noble cities, and innumerable castles, all of which were guarded by walls, towers, and barred gates.

> ◆ **Literary Focus** Find an example of a fact and a superstition in this passage. ❷

Since Britain lies far north toward the pole, the nights are short in summer, and at midnight it is hard to tell whether the evening twilight still lingers or whether dawn is approaching; for in these northern latitudes the sun does not remain long below the horizon at night. Consequently both summer days and winter nights are long, and when the sun withdraws southwards, the winter nights last ❸

1. **Belgic Gaul:** France.
2. **Reptacestir:** Richborough, part of the city of Sandwich.
3. **Gessoriacum:** Boulogne, France.
4. **furlongs:** Units for measuring distance; a furlong is equal to one eighth of a mile.
5. **Orcades:** Orkney Isles.
6. **draft animals:** Animals used for pulling loads.
7. **cockles:** Edible shellfish with two heart-shaped shells.
8. **jet** *n.*: Type of coal.

Block Scheduling Strategies

Consider these suggestions to take advantage of extended class time:

- Instruct students to work individually to complete the journal activity in Literature and Your Life (p.77) and then meet in small groups to compare, contrast, and discuss their entries.
- Encourage students to work together to determine how to pronounce various Anglo-Saxon names (p. 81). Have them practice their skills on passages from the selections.
- Direct students to identify compound sentences as they read the selections. Reinforce the concept with the Grammar and Style activity in the Guide for Responding (p. 84) and the practice page in ***Selection Support*** (p. 15)
- Have students practice and perform their interviews, as suggested in the Idea Bank (p. 85). The Interview With Bede activity is supported by a Speaking and Listening Mini-Lesson (p. 81).
- Students can conduct peer reviews of the items produced for the writing activities in the Idea Bank or for the Writing Mini-Lesson (p. 85). When evaluating one another's regional histories, they should pay particular attention to coherence.

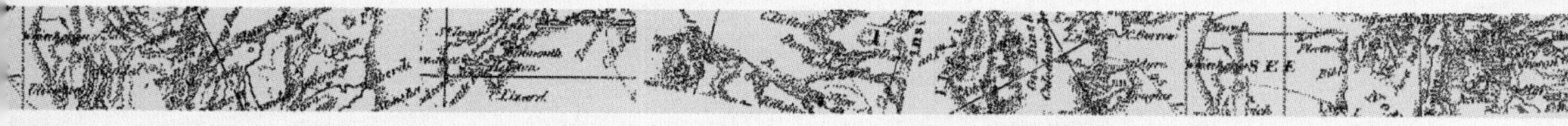

4 eighteen hours. In Armenia,[9] Macedonia,[10] and Italy, and other countries of that latitude, the longest day lasts only fifteen hours and the shortest nine.

At the present time there are in Britain, in harmony with the five books of the divine law, five languages and four nations —English,
5 British, Scots, and Picts. Each of these have their own language, but all are united in their
6 study of God's truth by the fifth, Latin, which has become a common medium through the study of the scriptures. The original inhabitants of the island were the Britons, from whom it takes its name, and who, according to tradition, crossed into Britain from Armorica,[11] and occupied the southern parts. When they had spread northwards and possessed the greater part of the islands, it is said that some Picts from Scythia[12] put to sea in a few long ships and were driven by storms around the coasts of Britain, arriving at length on the north coast of Ireland. Here they found the nation of the Scots, from whom they asked permission to settle, but their request was refused. Ireland is the largest island after Britain, and lies to the west. It is shorter than Britain to the north, but extends far beyond it to the south towards the northern coasts of Spain, although a wide sea separates them. These Pictish seafarers, as I have said, asked for a grant of land to make a settlement. The Scots replied that there was not room for them both, but said: "We can give you good advice. There is another island not far to the east, which we often see in the distance on clear days. Go and settle there if you wish; should you meet resistance, we will come to your help." So the Picts crossed into Britain, and began to settle in the north of the island, since the Britons were in possession of the south. Having no women with them, these Picts asked wives of the Scots, who consented on condition that, when any dispute arose, they should choose a king from the female royal line rather than the male. This custom continues among the Picts to this day. As time went on, Britain received a third nation, that of the Scots, who migrated from Ireland under their chieftain Reuda, and by a combination of force and treaty, obtained from the Picts the settlements that they still hold. From the name of this chieftain, they are still known as Dalreudians, for in their tongue *dal* means a division.

Ireland is broader than Britain, and its mild 9

7 ◆ Reading Strategy
Break down this sentence to find the core ideas.

Cotton Ms Tiberius C II Folio 5 Verso
Page of Bede's *History*, The British Library

▲ Critical Viewing Bede's fellow monks spent years creating books filled with pages such as this one. What can you infer about the values of the society that produced such work? **[Infer]** 8

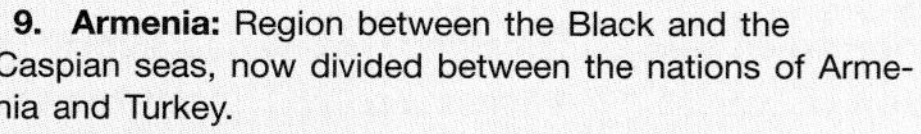

9. **Armenia:** Region between the Black and the Caspian seas, now divided between the nations of Armenia and Turkey.
10. **Macedonia:** Region in the eastern Mediterranean, divided among Greece, Yugoslavia, and Bulgaria.
11. **Armorica:** Brittany, France.
12. **Scythia:** Ancient region in southeastern Europe.

◆ **Build Vocabulary**

promontories (prä′ mən tôr′ ēz) *n.*: Parts of high land sticking out into the sea or other body of water

innumerable (i no͞o′ mər ə bəl) *adj.*: Too many to count

Customize for
Visual/Spatial Learners

4 Have students locate Armenia, Macedonia, Italy, and Britain on a map. What are the latitudes of these parts of the world? *Armenia is at 40.3°N, Macedonia is at 41°N, Italy is at 42.5°N, and Britain is at 54°N.*

5 **Clarification** "British" here refers to the people now called Welsh.

◆ Critical Thinking

6 **Analyze** Ask students how Bede's religious background is revealed by this passage. *He refers to divine law and the study of God's truth.*

◆ Reading Strategy

7 **Break Down Sentences** The independent clause expressing the main action is "it is said . . . coast of Britain." The *who* in this sentence is "Picts from Scythia." What they did was travel around the coasts of Britain and arrive in Ireland. How they traveled was by boat. Where they traveled from was Scythia, and where they traveled to was Britain and Ireland. Why they ended up where they did was because storms drove them. When this happened was after the Britons had spread northward and occupied most of the islands.

►Critical Viewing◄

8 **Infer** Students may say that the society valued learning, literacy, and art; they were willing to invest large amounts of time and resources to preserve knowledge.

9 **Enrichment** Bede probably never went to Ireland, and he believed the geographic assumption of his day that the island extended far south of England.

Humanities: Art

A Page of Bede's *History*, c. ninth century.

This page is from an illuminated, or decorated, manuscript. Such manuscripts were entirely hand-crafted by scribes, who worked in monasteries in rooms called *scriptoriums,* where they spent day after day copying pages from books. Originally, they copied religious works, but later they copied other types of work as well.

Copying a book required a great deal of work. Before scribes could even begin, they had to cut pens from quills or reeds, grind ink, mix paints, and prepare parchment from calf- or lambskin.

In manuscripts such as the one shown, the scribes often created large ornate letters called *versals.* Versals marked the beginnings of books, chapter, verses, and paragraphs. In some manuscripts, real gold was applied to the versals as well as to other parts of the page. Many pages were works of art.

You might discuss the following:

1. Why, do you think, did this artist work so hard to produce this image? *The artist wanted to show the importance of the written word by making it beautiful.*
2. What can you infer about the history of the English people from the artwork? *Suggested response: The knotwork and zoomorphic forms suggest the influence of Anglo-Saxon settlers and Viking invaders.*

▶Critical Viewing◀

❶ **Speculate** Suggested response: Medieval people saw the past and present as having equal importance. Students may say that Bede expresses the sequence of events in the same way that a timeline would.

◆ Literary Focus

❷ **Historical Writing** Ask students what source Bede gives for his information about snakes and snakebites. *He obtained the information from hearsay; has "heard it said."*

◆ Reading Strategy

❸ **Break Down Sentences** What three main ideas does this sentence contain? *The three main ideas are these: Almost everything is immune to poison; snakebite can be cured by drinking water in which leaves of Irish books have been soaked; this stopped the spread of poison and reduced swelling.*

◆ Critical Thinking

❹ **Infer** Why do you think Bede's description of Ireland is so inaccurate? *He probably had never been there, and his sources of information were unreliable.* What can you infer about travel and learning during this period? *Travel was difficult and uncommon. Travelers may have exaggerated their accounts of their travels to make them more interesting and exciting.*

Humanities: Art

The Venerable Bede Writing His Book and Presenting It to the Bishop of Lindisfarne.

This illumination comes from a twelfth-century copy of Bede's Life of Saint Cuthbert. St. Cuthbert is the patron saint of sailors.

1. What do you think was the purpose of this illustration? *Suggested response: The illustration showed the importance of the book and explained the book's history. It served a similar purpose to the photograph of the author and the blurb on the dust jacket of a modern book.*
2. What does this illustration tell you about the attitude of later generations toward Bede? *Bede and his writings were held in high regard centuries after his death.*

Monks, Bodleian Library, Oxford

❶ ▲ Critical Viewing The picture shows two events that occurred at different times. Speculate about medieval ideas of time. In what sense is time like a straight line for Bede? **[Speculate]**

and healthy climate is superior. Snow rarely lies longer than three days, so that there is no need to store hay in summer for winter use or to build stables for beasts. There are no reptiles, and no snake can exist there, for although often brought over from Britain, as soon as the ship nears land, they breathe its scented air and die. In fact, almost everything in this isle enjoys immunity to poison, and I ❷ have heard that folk suffering from snakebite have drunk water in which scrapings from the ❸ leaves of books from Ireland had been steeped, and that this remedy checked the spreading ❹ poison and reduced the swelling. The island abounds in milk and honey, and there is no lack of vines, fish, and birds, while deer and goats are widely hunted. It is the original home of the Scots, who, as already mentioned, later migrated and joined the Britons and Picts in Britain. There is a very extensive arm of the sea, which originally formed the boundary between the Britons and the Picts. This runs inland from the west for a great distance as far as the strongly fortified British city of Alcuith.[13] It was to the northern shores of this firth[14] that the Scots came and established their new homeland.

13. **Alcuith:** Dumbarton, Scotland.
14. **firth:** Narrow arm of the sea.

Guide for Responding

◆ Literature and Your Life

Reader's Response List three details that you found interesting in Bede's history of England.

Thematic Focus Find two details of Bede's account that give a sense of national pride.

☑ Check Your Comprehension

1. (a) In Bede's time, what were the four nations of Britain? (b) What united them?
2. (a) Who were the original inhabitants of Britain? (b) Who were the later settlers?

◆ Critical Thinking

INTERPRET

1. Write down two conclusions that Bede's explanation of scarlet dye suggests to you about the lifestyle of the people of Britain. **[Infer]**
2. Bede states that Britain once "had twenty-eight noble cities guarded by walls, towers, and barred gates." What does this statement suggest about the political situation at the time? **[Interpret]**
3. (a) Why does Bede think learning Latin is important? (b) According to Bede, what factor is most important in uniting people and giving them a common identity? **[Draw Conclusions]**

Reinforce and Extend

Answers

Reader's Response Details may include the colors of pearls, the use of cockles for dye, the qualities of jet, and the Pictish custom of inheritance.

Thematic Focus Students may cite "rich in grain and cattle," "rivers abounding with fish," five languages "in harmony with five books of divine law."

☑ Check Your Comprehension

1. (a) They were English, British, Scots, and Picts. (b) They were united through Latin and Christianity.
2. (a) They were Britons. (b) Picts and Scots followed.

◆ Critical Thinking

1. Possible responses: People liked bright colors; people wore the same clothing for a long time; trade was sufficiently developed to create a market for scarlet dye or cloth.
2. Britain may have consisted of many separate political entities that did not necessarily get along with one another.
3. (a) Latin is used for the study of the scriptures and is common to all four peoples in Britain.
(b) The most important factor is the "study of God's truth"; that is, the shared religion of Christianity.

from *The* Anglo-Saxon Chronicle

Translated by Anne Savage

896 In the summer of this year, the force[1] split up, one part in East Anglia,[2] one part in
❶ Northumbria;[3] and those who were without property got themselves ships and went south over the sea to the Seine.

The force had not, by the grace of God, utterly broken down the English; but they were more greatly broken in those three years by the slaughter of cattle and men, most of all by the fact that many of the king's best thanes[4] in the land had died in those three years. One of them was Swithulf, bishop of Rochester; also Ceolmund, ealdorman[5] in Kent, Beorhtulf, ealdorman in Essex, Wulfred, ealdorman in Hampshire, Ealhheard, bishop of Dorchester, Eadulf, king's thane in Sussex, Beornulf, reeve[6] of Winchester, Ecgulf, king's horse-thane, and many others also, though I have named the most distinguished.

The same year, the forces in East Anglia and Northumbria greatly harassed Wessex along the south coast with raiding bands, most of all with the ash-ships[7] they had built many years before. Then king Alfred commanded longships to be built against the ash-ships. They were nearly twice as long as the others; some had sixty oars, some more. They were both swifter and steadier, also higher than the others; nor were they in the Frisian[8] manner or the Danish, but as he himself thought might be most useful.

As it fell out, at a certain time in the same year, six ships came to the Isle of Wight and did much evil there, both in Devon and everywhere along the sea-coast. Then the king commanded men to go there with nine of the new ships, and they went in front of them at the river's mouth in the open sea. The Danes went out with three ships against them, and three stood higher up the river's mouth, beached on dry land; the men from them had gone inland. The English took two of their three ships at the river's mouth, further out, killed the men, and one ship got away—and also on that all the men were killed but five. They got away because the other ships ran aground. They were very awkwardly aground: three were stranded on the same side of the deep water as the Danish ships, and the others all on the other side. But when the tide

> **◆ Literary Focus** ❷
> Find details in this passage that indicate which side the author favors.

1. **the force:** Danish settlers in England; Vikings.
2. **East Anglia:** Kingdom of Anglo-Saxon England in the East, including modern Norfolk and Suffolk.
3. **Northumbria:** Kingdom of Anglo-Saxon England in the North, including the city of York.
4. **thanes:** Lords in Anglo-Saxon society, ranking below the members of a king's family.
5. **ealdorman:** Official who managed specific areas of a kingdom.
6. **reeve:** Official who collected his subjects' taxes.
7. **ash-ships:** Ships used by Vikings, propelled by oar and sail.
8. **Frisian:** Relating to people originally from Frisia, a region now divided between the Netherlands and Germany.

ANGLO-SAXON PRONUNCIATIONS

General Rules

There are no silent letters in Old English. Most consonants are pronounced as in modern English.

Example: *Eadulf* can be pronounced a´ əd o͞olf´.

H before a vowel is pronounced as it is in modern English. Before a consonant or at the end of a word, it has a "throat-clearing" sound, as in the Scottish *loch.*

Example: *Beorhtulf* was probably pronounced bā´ ōrkh to͞olf´.

Specific Vowel and Consonant Pronunciations

ae = *a* in *ash*
c before or after *i* and *e*, or after *a* = *ch*; otherwise, *c* = *k*
cg = *j*
ea = *a* in *ash* + ə
f between two vowels = *v*
g before or after *i* or *e*, or after *ae* = *y* as in *year*, otherwise, *g* = *g* in *get*
sc = *sh* in *ship*
y = *u* in French *tu* or German *grün*

Develop Understanding

The Anglo-Saxon Chronicle went on to cover the period until 1154. Because the documents in it were written over several centuries, they provide more than just a history of certain events; they also give insight into the development of the English language.

◆ Reading Strategy

❶ Break Down Sentences Remind students that a clause contains both a verb and its subject. Help students to identify the subject and verb of the two clauses in the first sentence. *force . . . split up; those . . . got and went.*

◆ Literary Focus

❷ Historical Writing Details that indicate that the author favors the Anglo-Saxons include the description of the Danish forces as doing "much evil" and the listing of the notable Anglo-Saxon dead.

Cultural Connection

Societies have many ways of recording history, and some methods depend primarily on illustrations rather than on text. For example, Native Americans, the Hmong, and the ancient Mayans used pictures on skins, cloth, or carved into stone. Incas kept records with quipus, knotted colored threads. Many modern alphabets developed from pictographs. Have students discuss advantages and disadvantages of using pictures instead of written words.

Speaking and Listening Mini-Lesson

Interview

This mini-lesson supports the Speaking and Listening activity in the Idea Bank on page 85.

Introduce the Concept Explain that an interview is a method that allows one person to get information from another. The person who asks questions is the interviewer and the person who answers is the subject. Often, a subject provides opinions and insights as well as factual details.

Develop Background Before students begin, have them discuss what an interesting, informative interview would sound like. Lead students to consider these points:

- Answers that are merely yes or no are not interesting and may not be informative.
- Questions that ask *who, what, why,* and *how* are likely to produce more interesting responses.
- Questions should take advantage of the subject's knowledge, interests, or skills.

Apply the Information Students should develop questions and conduct an interview with Bede. Students may enjoy the humorous aspects of having Bede comment on the magic of modern communications.

Assess the Outcome Have students evaluate their own interviews, as well as those of their classmates with these criteria: preparedness, clarity and expression of speech, logical ordering of questions, and appropriateness of answers and follow-up questions.

Customize for
Visual/Spatial Learners
Direct students to trace the events of 896 on the map on page 83. Have them locate the places where the Danish raiders did their damage. *The Isle of Wight and the Devon coast are on the southern coast of Britain.* Ask students: Do you think the Danes who ended up in East Anglia were also hanged? Why or not? *The Danes who managed to get to East Anglia were safe; that area was under Danish rule.*

Customize for
Less Proficient Readers
Focus students' attention on the last syllable of the following names: Aethelhere, Aethelwald, Aethelred, and Aethelwulf. Help them recognize that Aethelwald was the peacebreaker in 903.

Customize for
Less Proficient Readers
❶ Have students summarize the events in this passage. *The incoming tide allowed the Danish ships to escape from where they and the English ships had run aground before the English ships could be freed. The Danish ships were so damaged that two of them were washed ashore. The Danes were taken to Winchester, where the king ordered them hanged. The men on the third Danish ship arrived in East Anglia.* You may want to select other passages throughout this selection for students to summarize or paraphrase.

❷ **Clarification** In medieval times, a date was usually given in terms of a saint's day rather than the day of the month. All Saints' Day is November 1.

Comprehension Check ☑
❸ What does *leave* mean in this context? *It means "permission."*

◆ Reading Strategy
❹ **Break Down Sentences**
Suggested response: Aethelwald lured the East Anglian force into breaking the peace. As a result, they ravaged the land of Mercia. When they came to Cricklade, they crossed the Thames. They seized all they could carry in and around Braydon. Then they headed home.

had ebbed many furlongs[9] from the ships, the Danes went out from their three ships to the other three that were stranded on their side and there fought with them. There were killed Lucumon the king's reeve, Wulfheard the Frisian, Aebbe the Frisian, Aethelhere the Frisian, Athelferth of the king's household, and in all, Frisians and English, sixty-two, and one hundred and twenty of the Danes.

❶ The tide, however, came to the Danish ships before the Christians[10] could shove out, and in this way they rowed out. They were all so damaged that they could not row around Sussex; but there the sea threw two of them to land, and the men were led to Winchester, to the king. He commanded them to be hanged. The men who were on the one ship badly wounded came to East Anglia. The same summer no less than twenty ships perished with men and all along the south coast. The same year Wulfric the king's horse-thane died; he was also the Welsh-reeve.

900 Alfred, son of Aethelwulf, passed away, ❷ six nights before All Saints' Day. He was king over all the English, except for that part which was under Danish rule; and he held that kingdom for one and a half years less than thirty. Then his son Edward received the kingdom. Aethelwald, his father's brother's son, took over the manors at Wimbourne and at ❸ Christchurch, without the leave of the king and his counsellors. Then the king rode with the army until he camped at Badbury Rings near Wimbourne, and Aethelwald occupied the manor with those men who were loyal to him, and had barricaded all the gates against them; he said that he would stay there, alive or dead. Then he stole himself away under the cover of night, and sought the force in Northumbria. The king commanded them to ride after, but he could not be overtaken. They captured the woman he had seized without the king's leave and against the bishop's command, because she was hallowed[11] as a nun.

In the same year, Aethelred passed away, who was an ealdorman in Devon, four weeks before king Alfred.

902 Athelwald came here over the sea with all the ships he could get, and in Essex they submitted to him.

903 Aethelwald lured the East Anglian force into breaking the peace, so that they ravaged over the land of Mercia, until they came to Cricklade, went over the Thames there, seized all they could carry off both in and around Braydon and then went home-ward again. Then king Edward went after them, as quickly as he could gather his army, and ravaged all their land between Devil's Dyke and Fleam Dyke and the Ouse, and everything up to the northern fens.[12] When he meant to leave there, he had it announced to the army that they would all leave together. The Kentish[13] stayed on there against his command and seven messages he had sent to them. The force came upon them there, and they fought; ealdorman Sigulf was killed there, ealdorman Sigelm, Eadwold the king's thane, abbot[14] Cenulf, Sigebriht son of Sigulf, Eadwald son of Acca, and many besides them although I have named the most distinguished. On the Danish side were killed Eohric their king, atheling[15] Aethelwald, who had lured them into peacebreaking, Byrhtsige son of the atheling Beornoth, hold Ysopa, hold Oscytel, and very many besides them we might not now name. On either hand much slaughter was made, and of the Danes there were more killed, though they had the battlefield. Ealhswith

> **◆ Reading Strategy** ❹
> Break down this sentence into smaller sentences to clarify its meaning.

9. **furlongs:** Units for measuring distance; a furlong is equal to one eighth of a mile.
10. **the Christians:** Referring here to the English and Frisian forces, in contrast to the unconverted Danes.
11. **hallowed:** Made holy; given over, in a ceremony, to religious purposes.

12. **Dyke . . . fens:** Dykes are barriers made of earth; fens are areas of peaty land covered with water.
13. **The Kentish:** Inhabitants of Kent, an English kingdom ruled by the kings of Wessex after 825.
14. **abbot:** Leader of a monastery; chief monk.
15. **atheling:** Anglo-Saxon noble, especially one related to the kings of Wessex.

◆ Build Vocabulary
stranded (stranʹ did) *v.*: Forced into shallow water or onto a beach, reef, or other land; left helpless
barricaded (berʹ i kaʹ did) *v.*: Blocked
ravaged (ravʹ ijd) *v.*: Destroyed

Cross-Curricular Connection: Science
Histories such as these have provided astronomers with information about early eclipses and comets. Such information helps scientists predict past and future occurrences.

For example, after noticing that comets in 1531 and 1607 had similar paths, Edmund Halley concluded that they were the same comet. He then predicted when the comet would return. He was correct, and the comet now bears his name. Have students use an almanac to discover what astronomical events are scheduled to happen this year.

5 ▶ **Critical Viewing** Locate on the map the kingdoms of East Anglia, Wessex, and Kent. **[Interpret]**

passed away. That same year was the fight at The Holme between the Kentish and the Danes. Ealdorman Aethelwulf died, brother of Ealhswith, king Alfred's mother; and abbot Virgilus of the Scots, and the mass-priest Grimbold. In the same year a new church in Chester was hallowed, and the relics of St. Judoc[16] brought there.

6 **904** The moon darkened.
905 A comet appeared on October 20th.
906 Alfred died, who was town-reeve at Bath; and in the same year the peace was fastened at Tiddingford, just as king Edward advised, both with the East Anglians and the Northumbrians.

16. **relics of St. Judoc:** Objects associated with Saint Josse, patron of harvests and ships.

Guide for Responding

◆ Literature and Your Life

Reader's Response Was life interesting in the ninth and tenth centuries? Explain.

Thematic Focus In what way do the authors of the *Chronicle* display a national spirit?

Journal Entry Write an account of one of the events in the *Chronicle* from the point of view of the Danes.

☑ Check Your Comprehension

1. Who are the main warring peoples in this excerpt?
2. What technological innovation does Alfred introduce?
3. What part of England did Alfred rule by the end of his reign?
4. How would you characterize relations between Edward and his cousin Aethelwald?
5. What other kinds of events besides battles does the *Chronicle* relate?

◆ Critical Thinking

INTERPRET

1. (a) Judging from this excerpt, how strong was Edward's authority? (b) How united was England under his reign? **[Draw Conclusions]**
2. Some of the king's followers have the title "bishop" or "abbot." What does this suggest about the society of the time? **[Infer]**
3. Not very much is recorded for the years 904 and 905. What does this suggest about the way in which the *Chronicle* was created? **[Infer]**

EVALUATE

4. In what ways does this excerpt succeed as a historical record? What are its shortcomings? **[Make a Judgment]**

EXTEND

5. Name three facts reported by *The Anglo-Saxon Chronicle* and the methods a modern historian might use to check whether or not they are true. **[Social Studies Link]**

▶**Critical Viewing**◀

5 **Interpret** East Anglia is in the east, below the compass rose; Wessex is near the center of the southern coast, and Kent is in the southeasternmost area of the island.

◆ Critical Thinking

6 **Speculate** Ask students: How would you explain why the lunar eclipse and comet are recorded in the *Anglo-Saxon Chronicle*? *Students might suggest that these were noteworthy events, or that they may have been seen as omens of events to come, such as the peace treaty with the East Anglians and Northumbrians.*

Reinforce and Extend

Answers

◆ Literature and Your Life

Reader's Response Based on the years mentioned in the excerpt, the ninth and tenth centuries were very interesting, with invasions, rebellions, and wars.

Thematic Focus Their work celebrates the deeds and people of the nation's past.

☑ Check Your Comprehension

1. They are the Danes and the English.
2. He introduced longships in a new design.
3. He ruled all of England except the part held by the Danes.
4. They are enemies. Aethelwald defies Edward's authority; he is perhaps a rival for Alfred's throne.
5. It records deaths of important personages, religious events such as the hallowing of a church, and astronomical events such as eclipses and comets.

(Answers continue on page 84.)

Beyond the Selection

FURTHER READING

Other Works About Anglo-Saxon Times

An Introduction to Anglo-Saxon England, Peter Hunter Blair
Everyday Life in Roman and Anglo-Saxon Times, Marjorie and C.H.B. Quennell
"Song of the Shield Wall," Debra Doyle and Melissa Williamson

Historical Fiction About Anglo-Saxon Times

The Summer of the Danes, Ellis Peters; *Dawn Wind,* Rosemary Sutcliffe; *Escape to King Alfred,* Geoffrey Trease

We suggest you preview these works before recommending them to students.

INTERNET

You and your students may find additional information about Anglo-Saxon art, literature, and history on the Internet. We suggest the following sites. Please be aware, however, that sites may have changed from the time we published this information.

Glossed versions of two of Bede's works can be found at **http://www.ucalgary.ca/ UofC/eduweb/engl401/texts/**

See also **http://www.bedesworld.co.uk/**

We *strongly recommend* that you preview the sites before you send students to them.

Reinforce and Extend

Answers

◆ Critical Thinking

1. Edward's authority does not appear too strong, and England does not appear entirely united. In 903, Aethelwald is able to persuade the Danes to attack the Anglo-Saxons, and the Kentish ignore Edward's command that they withdraw.
2. The fact that men with the titles of "bishop" and "abbot" went to battle with the king suggests that affairs of church and state mixed.
3. The absence of detailed records for certain years suggests that record-keeping at the time was sporadic; society was probably less stable.
4. It is successful in that it dates events and names participants in them. Its shortcomings include that it is often hazy on details; it assumes that the reader is aware of many of the circumstances of which it tells.
5. Possible answers: Edward succeeded Alfred—a modern historian might look for coins that could be dated back to period. Alfred was responsible for longships—they might look at statues and pictures for representations of such ships before Alfred's times.

◆ Reading Strategy

1. The force split up.
2. It happened in the summer of this year (896).
3. One part stayed in East Anglia. One part stayed in Northumbria. The third group was those without property. They went south to the Seine.

◆ Literary Focus

1. (a) Bede says that the nations are "united in the study of God's truth" by Latin; Bede notes when reptiles breathe Ireland's "scented air" they die; the *Chronicle* notes Aethelwald's seizure of a nun. (b) Bede's opinions about Latin and religion show bias. He presents even incredible stories in Ireland's favor. In the *Chronicle,* peripheral details such as the nun's capture seem included only to discredit Aethelwald.
2. (a), (b) Modern historians would include statistics and descriptions of the economy and of government.

Guide for Responding *(continued)*

◆ Reading Strategy

Break Down Sentences

As you read the sentence in *The Anglo-Saxon Chronicle* introducing "the force," you may have been distracted by unfamiliar place names and secondary information. Look at the sentence again and **break it down** to find a clause that can stand on its own and expresses the main action:

> In the summer of this year, the force split up, one part in East Anglia, one part in Northumbria, and those who were without property got themselves ships and went south over the sea to the Seine.

1. What is the main action of the sentence?
2. When did it happen?
3. Name the three parts of the force that were involved in the main action. Tell where each one went.

◆ Build Vocabulary

Using the Suffix *-ade*

Knowing that the suffix *-ade* means "the act of, the people involved in an action, or the product of a raw material," write the definition of these words (use the clues provided in parentheses):

1. lemonade
2. motorcade
3. cannonade
4. ambuscade (related to the word *ambush*)
5. cavalcade (related to the word *cavalier,* meaning "horseman")

Using the Word Bank

Choose words from the Word Bank to complete the following paragraph:

High on the __?__, the king could see his ships entering the firth. The ships were only a few furlongs away from safety. Suddenly, a fleet of Viking ships appeared and began to __?__ the king's ships. Several of the king's ships were __?__ on the beach. Others tried to sail back out to sea, but the Viking ships had __?__ the mouth of the harbor.

◆ Literary Focus

Historical Writing

Authors of **historical writing** use evidence as they tell the story of past events. Even as they strive to be objective, however, they may reveal their own opinions and biases. For example, when the authors of the *Chronicle* write that the Vikings did not "by the grace of God" defeat the English, they reveal their loyalty to the Anglo-Saxon cause.

1. (a) List three details from either the *Chronicle* or Bede's *A History of the English Church and People* that show the writers' opinions. (b) Explain how each detail indicates the writer's bias.
2. (a) Name three types of details that Bede's *History* or the *Chronicle* leaves out but which a modern historian would have included. (b) Explain your choices.

◆ Grammar and Style

Compound Sentences

The conjunction or punctuation that joins the parts of a **compound sentence** expresses the relationship between the parts.

***and* or a semicolon:** addition; further details or support; sequence; explanation
but: contrast; opposition; exception
or: alternative

A **compound sentence** contains two or more independent clauses joined by *and, or, but,* or a semicolon.

Practice Rewrite the following pairs of sentences as a single compound sentence. Use the conjunction that suggests the indicated relation between ideas.

1. Alfred did not set out to rule England. Events dictated otherwise. [Contrast]
2. Later, Northumbria was taken over by Viking raiders. Bede lived in Northumbria when it was still a center for Anglo-Saxon learning. [Sequence]
3. It is a fact that there are no snakes in Ireland. Bede writes that Ireland has an immunity to poison. [Explanation]
4. We call them Vikings. The Anglo-Saxons referred to them as the Danes. [Contrast]

◆ Build Vocabulary

Using the Suffix *-ade*

(1) a drink produced from lemons; (2) a procession formed of motor vehicles; (3) the sound of several cannons being fired; (4) a group formed by people lying in ambush; (5) a procession formed by people riding horses

Using the Word Bank

promontory; ravage; stranded; barricaded

◆ Grammar and Style

1. Alfred did not start out to rule England, but events dictated otherwise.
2. Bede lived in Northumbria when it was still a center for Anglo-Saxon learning; eventually it was taken over by Viking raiders.
3. Bede writes that Ireland has an immunity to poison; it is a fact that there are no snakes in Ireland.
4. We call them Vikings, but the Anglo-Saxons referred to them as the Danes.

For additional instruction and practice, use the lesson on Varying Sentence Structure in the **Language Lab CD-ROM** and the practice page on Conjunctions, p. 13, in the *Writer's Solution Grammar Practice Book.*

Build Your Portfolio

Idea Bank

Writing

1. **Details That Identify You** Bede gives details that identify the island of Britain. List key details about your hometown and the groups to which you belong.

2. **Weekly Chronicle** Write a "history" of your school week—either from the point of view of students or from the point of view of teachers. **[Social Studies Link]**

3. **Fantasy History** Write a brief history, following Bede's model, of a land of your own invention. Include maps and, if you like, drawings of buildings and people. **[Social Studies Link]**

Speaking and Listening

4. **Interview With Bede** Referring to the details of Bede's history, create a radio interview between a reporter and Bede. With a partner, perform your interview for the class. **[Performing Arts Link]**

5. **Speech for Alfred the Great** Find out more about Alfred the Great. Then write a speech in support of his ideas such as he might have delivered to other Anglo-Saxons. **[Social Studies Link; Performing Arts Link]**

Projects

6. **Tour of a Viking Ship** Research Danish seafaring technology, and construct a set of diagrams of a Viking ship. Once you have "built" your ship, take your class on a tour of it. **[Art Link; Science Link; Social Studies Link]**

7. **Evening Newscast From the Tenth Century** Using information from these selections, write an evening newscast for a day in the tenth century, and present it to your class. **[Media Link]**

Writing Mini-Lesson

Regional History

Like the Anglo-Saxons who appear in Bede's *History* and in *The Anglo-Saxon Chronicle,* the ancestors of most American citizens crossed an ocean to live in a new land. With a new home came a new identity.

Write a history of a place such as a park or a sports arena that has helped define your identity. To help your reader follow the connections, organize your ideas coherently.

Writing Skills Focus: Coherence

Coherence in writing involves tying individual details to general ideas and clearly showing the order in which events occurred. In a coherent essay, paragraphs are arranged according to an obvious plan, with clear connections between ideas. For example, Bede creates coherence by first dealing with Britain's physical characteristics, then discussing the people who inhabit it.

Prewriting Gather facts, examples, quotations, and other details for your history. You may conduct original research by interviewing someone connected with the subject of your paper. Organize your facts before you write, arranging them in outline form.

Drafting Refer to your outline as you write, and use transitions to show: order in time (*before, after, soon*), order in space (*above, below, beside*), order of importance (*first, second, finally*), cause and effect (*because, therefore, so*).

Revising Read your draft critically, making sure that it is coherent. If the links between ideas are unclear as you reread your draft, add transitions to clarify these connections. Also, double-check all your facts for accuracy, and delete any passages in which you display bias or an opinion.

✓ ASSESSMENT OPTIONS

Formal Assessment, Selection Test, pp. 23–25, and Assessment Resources Software. The selection test is designed so that it can be easily customized to the performance levels of your students.
Alternative Assessment, p. 3, includes options for less advanced students, more advanced students, verbal/linguistic learners, visual/spatial learners, and bodily/kinesthetic learners

PORTFOLIO ASSESSMENT
Use the following rubrics in the ***Alternative Assessment*** booklet to assess student writing:
Details That Identify You: Description Rubric, p. 98
Weekly Chronicle: Description Rubric, p. 98
Fantasy History: Technical Description/Explanation Rubric, p. 116
Writing Mini-Lesson: Research Report/Paper Rubric, p. 108

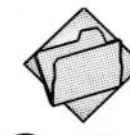

Idea Bank

Customizing for Performance Levels
Following are suggestions for matching Idea Bank topics with your students' performance levels:
Less Advanced Students: 1, 7
Average Students: 2, 4, 6
More Advanced Students: 3, 5

Customizing for Learning Modalities
Following are suggestions for matching Idea Bank topics with your students' learning modalities:
Visual/Spatial: 6, 3
Interpersonal: 4
Verbal/Linguistic: 1, 2, 3, 4, 5, 7

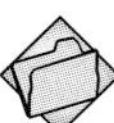

Writing Mini-Lesson

Refer students to the Writing Handbook, page 1189, for instruction on the writing process, and page 1191 for further information on narration.

Writing and Language Transparencies Use Writing Process Model 7: Research Report, pp. 57–69, in order to show students the steps in the writing process that they will use in writing their regional histories.

Writer's Solution

Writing Lab CD-ROM
Have students write their history using the tutorial on Narration. Follow these steps:

1. View the audio-annotated writing models that explore audience and purpose.
2. Use the chain of events to map the sequence of events covered in the regional history.
3. Draft on the computer.
4. Use the transition word bins to clarify the relationships among ideas.
5. While revising, use the revision checkers for transitions and sentence length.

Allow approximately 70 minutes of class time to complete these steps.

Sourcebook
Have students use Chapter 2, Narration (pp. 31–61), for additional support. The chapter includes a model for literature of a historical narrative (p. 37), instruction on organizing a narrative (p. 51), and a proofreading checklist (p. 54).

Prepare and Engage

OBJECTIVES

1. To read, comprehend, interpret, and respond to a narrative poem
2. To relate a narrative poem to personal experience
3. To analyze difficult sentences to facilitate comprehension
4. To distinguish between direct and indirect characterization
5. To build vocabulary in context and learn the suffix *-tion*
6. To recognize and use past and past perfect tenses
7. To respond to the narrative poem through writing, speaking and listening, and projects

SKILLS INSTRUCTION

Vocabulary:
Suffixes: *-tion*

Grammar and Style:
Past and Past Perfect Tenses

Reading Strategy:
Analyze Difficult Sentences

Literary Focus:
Characterization

Speaking and Listening:
Monologue (teacher edition)

Critical Viewing:
Analyze; Compare and Contrast; Infer; Assess

PORTFOLIO OPPORTUNITIES

Writing: Modern Types; Comparison and Contrast; Response to Criticism
Speaking and Listening: Monologue
Project: Portraits of the Pilgrims

Guide for Interpreting

Geoffrey Chaucer *(1343?–1400)*

From Page to Poet Son of a merchant, page in a royal house, soldier, diplomat, and royal clerk, Geoffrey Chaucer saw quite a bit of the medieval world. His varied experiences helped prepare him to write *The Canterbury Tales.* It provides the best contemporary picture we have of fourteenth-century England.

Gathering together characters from different walks of life, Chaucer takes the reader on a journey across medieval society.

The exact date of Geoffrey Chaucer's birth is unknown, but official records furnish many details of his active life. In 1359, while serving in the English army in France, Chaucer was captured and held prisoner. The king paid a £16 (sixteen-pound) ransom for his release (eight times what a simple laborer might make in a year). In 1366, Chaucer married Philippa Pan, a lady-in-waiting to the queen. Their eldest child, Thomas, continued his father's rise in the world, marrying a noblewoman and acquiring great wealth.

The Poet Matures While Chaucer was rising through the ranks of medieval society, he managed to practice and hone his skills as a poet. Chaucer began writing in his twenties and continued into his old age. His early poems were based on the works of European poets. He also wrote translations of French poetry. As he grew older, he developed a mature style of his own. In *Troilus and Criseyde,* a later poem drawn from the Greek legend of the Trojan War, Chaucer displays penetrating insight into human character.

The Canterbury Tales Chaucer wrote *The Canterbury Tales* in his later years. Only 24 of the projected 124 tales were finished, but these 24 stand together as a complete work.

In this masterwork, each character tells a tale on the pilgrimage to the cathedral of Canterbury. Even as the tellers of *The Canterbury Tales* come from the length and breadth of medieval society, the tales themselves take you on a trip through medieval literature: romances and comedies; stories in rhyme and stories in prose; crude humor and religious mysteries.

The Father of English Poetry In his own lifetime, Geoffrey Chaucer was considered the greatest English poet. Since his death, his poems have never gone out of print. Each new generation of poets writing in English has studied Chaucer's work.

Chaucer lies buried in Westminster Abbey. The Abbey's honorary burial area for distinguished writers, the Poet's Corner, was established around his tomb.

◆ Background for Understanding

HISTORY: PILGRIMAGES

In medieval Christianity, pilgrimages—long trips to holy places—were popular. Every year, pilgrims would travel great distances, sometimes as far as Rome or the Holy Land (the modern Middle East), to tombs of saints and other shrines. Some came to ask for divine assistance, such as a miraculous cure, or to give thanks for that already received. Others came to do penance or simply to show devotion.

Canterbury, a town about fifty miles southeast of London, was a major destination for English pilgrims. The cathedral in Canterbury was the site of Archbishop Thomas à Becket's murder in 1170. Days after the murder, and three years before Becket officially was made a saint, people began flocking to the cathedral to pay their respects.

More About the Author

In addition to being a prolific poet, Chaucer earned a comfortable living as a civil servant. Records indicate he was on familiar terms with royalty. King Edward awarded him the gift of a daily pitcher of wine. King Henry IV honored him with a fur-trimmed robe.

His involvement in royal circles has had fortunate consequences for modern readers. In fourteenth-century England, there was no standard English. Instead, English consisted of numerous dialects that could vary widely. Chaucer wrote in the Midland dialect commonly used in the government and diplomatic circles of London. This dialect eventually became the standard. As a result, the Middle English of Chaucer's writings is more readable today than it would have been had he employed some other dialect.

Prentice Hall Literature Program Resources

REINFORCE / RETEACH / EXTEND

Selection Support Pages
Build Vocabulary: Suffixes: *-tion,* p. 18
Grammar and Style: Past and Past Perfect Tenses, p. 19
Reading Strategy: Analyze Difficult Sentences, p. 20
Literary Focus: Characterization, p. 21

Strategies for Diverse Student Needs, p. 4

Beyond Literature
Career Connection: Travel Agent, p. 4

Formal Assessment Selection Test, pp. 20–22; Assessment Resources Software

Alternative Assessment, p. 4

Writing and Language Transparencies
Daily Language Practice, Week 6, p. 141

Resource Pro CD-ROM
from *The Canterbury Tales: The Prologue*—includes all resource material and customizable lession plan

Listening to Literature Audiocassettes
from *The Canterbury Tales: The Prologue*

Literature CD-ROM
The Time, Life and Works of Shakespeare, Presentation 2

from The Canterbury Tales: The Prologue

◆ Literature and Your Life

Connect Your Experience

Trips taken for the purpose of renewal or inspiration, even if they are not religious, can loosely be called pilgrimages. Think about a pilgrimage you've taken or would like to take. The Prologue to *The Canterbury Tales* describes a group of people who are setting out on a pilgrimage.

Journal Writing Briefly describe your fellow "pilgrims" on a "pilgrimage" you have taken.

Thematic Focus: A National Identity

Each of Chaucer's characters represents a different social type—from knights to plowmen. As you read, notice all the different ways of "being English" in Chaucer's day.

◆ Build Vocabulary

Suffixes: *-tion*

One of Chaucer's characters has a gift for *prevarication*. The suffix *-tion*, which means "the action of," gives a clue to the meaning of *prevarication*. To *prevaricate* means "to distort the truth." One way to define *prevarication* is "the act of distorting the truth."

Word Bank

Before you read, preview this list of words from the Prologue to *The Canterbury Tales*.

solicitous
garnished
absolution
commission
sanguine
avouches
prevarication

◆ Grammar and Style

Past and Past Perfect Tenses

Like most storytellers, Chaucer tells his tales in the **past tense,** a verb form showing an action or a condition that began and ended at a given time in the past. Chaucer uses the **past perfect tense** to indicate an action or condition that ended before another past action began. The past perfect tense is formed by using the helping verb *had* before the past participle of the main verb. Here are examples from *The Canterbury Tales*:

Past Tense: It *happened* in that season that one day . . .

Past Perfect Tense: In fifteen mortal battles he *had been* . . . (He had been in these battles before the time of the story.)

◆ Literary Focus

Characterization

Characterization is the act of creating and developing the personality of a character. Authors use **direct characterization** when they make direct statements about characters. They use **indirect characterization** when they reveal a character's personality through his or her actions, thoughts, and words.

Chaucer delighted audiences with his skillful characterizations. For example, when he says the Knight "followed chivalry/Truth, honor . . .", he is describing this character directly. He uses indirect characterization when he says, "he was not gaily dressed," which suggests the man is poor or severe.

◆ Reading Strategy

Analyze Difficult Sentences

When reading works of literature, **analyze difficult sentences** by asking yourself what information they express.

To understand the eighteen-line sentence at the beginning of the Prologue, for example, ask yourself *when, who,* and *what:*

When: in April

Who: people; palmers

What: long to go on pilgrimages

Interest Grabber Many teenagers enjoy fantasy role-playing games or computer adventure games. Have students discuss strategies for winning such games. Elicit the idea that it is vital to pay attention to the surroundings and to the other characters.

Have students imagine that they have just started a new medieval adventure game. Ask what first impressions they might form of these strangers:

- A nun who feeds her dogs meats, milk, and fresh bread
- A well-fed monk wearing fine clothing and riding an excellent horse with a fancy bridle
- A skinny young man in tattered clothes carrying books
- A large, brawny man telling off-color stories and jokes

Record these first impressions and compare them to the impressions students form after studying the characters in this selection.

Customize for
Less Proficient Readers
Have students read along while listening to the audiocassette. Stop the tape at convenient points and have students summarize or rephrase the narrative.

Listening to Literature Audiocassettes

Customize for
More Advanced Students
Occasionally a single line reveals a great deal about a person's character. Have students note and record individual lines that are especially revealing about one or more of the characters.

Customize for
English Language Learners
The occasional use of inverted sentences will be a challenge to these students. To aid them, help them restate difficult sentences in more familiar or conventional sentence patterns.

Customize for
Visual/Special Learners
Have these students preview the illustrations accompanying this selection prior to reading it. Encourage them to share their impression of the characters based on the illustrations.

Preparing for Standardized Tests

Reading and Vocabulary The ability to extract meaning from difficult sentences will enhance student performance on reading-comprehension items on standardized tests such as the SAT. It will also help students on items on achievement tests that require that students answer questions about scientific hypotheses, historical essays, or other documents. Have students practice analyzing difficult sentences by completing the Reading Strategy exercise on page 110. For additional practice, use the Reading Strategy page in ***Selection Support,*** p. 20.

Grammar and Language Questions on some standardized tests require students to use the past and past perfect tenses correctly. Students may be asked to use the correct tense of a verb in a sentence, as the following:

I will read the whole book before I realized I had another week to finish the report. *(D)*

(A) will read (C) have read
(B) be reading (D) had read

For additional practice, use the Build Grammar Skills page in ***Selection Support,*** p. 19.

Develop Understanding

One-Minute Insight The engaging panorama of fourteenth-century life presented in *The Canterbury Tales* marks an important milestone in English literature. Geoffrey Chaucer's work offers a sweeping array of memorable characters. There is nothing vague about these people; they are exact and individual. In fact, it is in the minute detail that the reader sees and understands the character most clearly. Chaucer's collection of heroes and rogues offers a rare snapshot of medieval life and values. Moreover, it provides enduring evidence that while times and circumstances change, human nature changes very little. In Chaucer's characters we see something of ourselves and the people around us.

Customize for
More Advanced Students
❶ Play the recording on **Listening to Literature Audiocassettes** of the first eighteen lines of "The Prologue" in Middle English. Have students compare the Middle English version of these lines with the translated version of the same lines. Then have them create a Middle English–Modern English Dictionary. Each entry should offer a "translation" for any strange or unusual Middle English term.

Customize for
Less Proficient Readers
❷ Have students create a two-column chart to illustrate the cause-effect relationships in lines 1 to 18. Have students list the causes or "when" factors in one column and the effects or "then" factors in another column. *Charts may resemble the following:* When: *April showers arrive; the March drought ends; flowers bloom; the west wind blows; small birds sing.* Then: *People go on pilgrimages; some travel to new lands; many go to Canterbury.*

from
The Canterbury Tales
The Prologue

Geoffrey Chaucer
Translated by Nevill Coghill

Chaucer wrote in what we now call Middle English. The first eighteen lines of the Prologue are presented here in Middle English, followed by the entire Prologue in a modern translation.

Whan that Aprill with his shourës sootë
The droghte of March hath percëd to the rootë
And bathëd every veyne in swich licour
Of which vertu engendrëd is the flour,
Whan Zephirus eek with his sweetë breeth
Inspirëd hath in every holt and heeth
The tendrë croppës, and the yongë sonnë
Hath in the Ram his half cours y-ronnë,
And smalë fowelës maken melodyë
❶ That slepen al the nyght with open eye,
So priketh hem Nature in hir corages,
Than longen folk to goon on pilgrymages,
And palmeres for to seken straungë strondës,
To fernë halwës kouthe in sondry londës.
And specially, from every shirës endë
Of Engelond, to Caunterbury they wendë,
The holy, blisful martir for to seke
That hem hath holpen whan that they were seekë.

When in April the sweet showers fall
And pierce the drought of March to the root, and all
The veins are bathed in liquor of such power
As brings about the engendering of the flower,
❷ When also Zephyrus[1] with his sweet breath
❸ Exhales an air in every grove and heath
Upon tender shoots, and the young sun
His half-course in the sign of the Ram[2] has run,
And the small fowl are making melody
That sleep away the night with open eye

1. **Zephyrus** (zef′ ə rəs): The west wind.
2. **Ram:** Aries, the first sign of the zodiac. The pilgrimage began on April 11, 1387.

Block Scheduling Strategies

Consider these suggestions to take advantage of extended class time:

- Display the Daily Language Practice sentences for Week 6 on the overhead projector. Have students write corrected versions of the sentences.
- Direct students to jot down responses to the boxed prompts as they read.
- Have students work individually or in pairs to answer the Check Your Comprehension and Critical Thinking questions on page 109.
- Allow student to work on their choice of the Writing activities in the Idea Bank on page 110.
- Have students prepare a monologue, as described on page 110. This activity is supported by a Speaking and Listening Mini-Lesson on page 107 in this teacher edition.

The Tabard Inn, Arthur Szyk for *The Canterbury Tales*

4 ▲ **Critical Viewing** In what ways does the rhythm of lines and patterns capture the mood of the poem's opening? **[Analyze]**

(So nature pricks them and their heart engages)
2 Then people long to go on pilgrimages
And palmers[3] long to seek the stranger strands[4]
3 Of far-off saints, hallowed in sundry lands,
And specially, from every shire's end
In England, down to Canterbury they wend
To seek the holy blissful martyr,[5] quick
To give his help to them when they were sick.
  It happened in that season that one day
In Southwark,[6] at The Tabard,[7] as I lay
5 Ready to go on pilgrimage and start
For Canterbury, most devout at heart,
6 At night there came into that hostelry
Some nine and twenty in a company
7 Of sundry folk happening then to fall
In fellowship, and they were pilgrims all
That towards Canterbury meant to ride.
The rooms and stables of the inn were wide;
They made us easy, all was of the best.
And shortly, when the sun had gone to rest,
By speaking to them all upon the trip
I soon was one of them in fellowship
And promised to rise early and take the way
To Canterbury, as you heard me say.
  But nonetheless, while I have time and space,
Before my story takes a further pace,
It seems a reasonable thing to say

3. **palmers:** Pilgrims who wore two crossed palm leaves to show that they had visited the Holy Land.
4. **strands:** Shores.
5. **martyr:** St. Thomas à Becket, the Archbishop of Canterbury, who was murdered in Canterbury Cathedral in 1170.
6. **Southwark** (suth′ ərk): Suburb of London at the time.
7. **The Tabard** (ta′ bərd): An inn.

Humanities: Art

The Tabard Inn, 1946, by Arthur Szyk.

This painting shows the innkeeper standing proudly at the door as the pilgrims arrive. The rich color and detail of Chaucer's narrative are captured in the expressions and body language of the figures seen in the painting.

Arthur Szyk (1894–1951), a Polish-born American artist, studied art at the Academy of Fine Art in Krakow, Poland, and at the Beaux Arts Academy in Paris. This painting, like much of his work, was done as a miniature in the style of a medieval monk illuminating a manuscript.

Use these questions for discussion:

1. Does the humorous nature of this painting reflect the tone of *The Canterbury Tales?* *Like the narrative poem, this painting conveys a humorous and lighthearted mood. Note especially the whimsical look on the animals' faces.*
2. What do the expressions and movements of each character convey? *Students may note the proud stance of the host, the cordial gesture of the monk, and the self-important look of the wife.*

◆ Literature and Your Life

3 Have students note the time of year that these stirrings to make a pilgrimage occur. Ask students if spring brings about similar feelings today. What activities does spring prompt in people today? *Students might use the term spring fever to identify similar feelings. Instead of a pilgrimage, vacation trips or other outdoor activities like baseball and camping trips begin to occur. Students may point to the annual spring break activities associated with the pause in the school year.*

▶Critical Viewing◀

4 **Analyze** The rhythmic pattern of horses' hooves suggest the predictable meter and rhyme of the opening lines. The bright colors and festive air suit the "spring fever" that the poet wryly notes is a reason for pilgrimages, and captures the lighthearted mood of the opening lines.

Customize for *Visual/Spatial Learners*

5 Have students locate Southwark and Canterbury on a map. Why was Southwark a good location from which to start a pilgrimage to Canterbury? *Southwark was a suburb at the southern end of the London Bridge. Since Canterbury lies about 80 miles southeast of London, travelers from the city were likely to pass through Southwark.*

◆ Reading Strategy

6 **Analyze Difficult Sentences** Have students analyze the sentence in lines 19–27. In what circumstances does the speaker find himself? *The narrator is staying at the Tabard Inn, and is about to start on his way to Canterbury, when a group of twenty-nine pilgrims, also destined for Canterbury, arrives at the inn.*

◆ Critical Thinking

7 **Compare and Contrast** Ask students: How does the tone of lines 19–34 compare to that of lines 1–18? *Lines 1–18 are rather formal, impersonal, and lofty; lines 19–34 are direct and informal.*

◆ Critical Thinking

❶ **Speculate** Ask students: What do you expect will follow these lines? *A description of the pilgrims will follow. This description will include information about their profession or standing in the community as well as their clothing and appearance.*

◆ Critical Thinking

❷ **Infer** Have students explain why the Knight is the first pilgrim the narrator describes. *Suggested response: He possesses the highest social standing among the pilgrims.*

❸ **Enrichment** When Chaucer describes the Knight as the epitome of chivalry, he is talking about an ideal from the past. By the 1380's, when Chaucer began *The Canterbury Tales,* feudalism and chivalry, feudalism's social code for the nobility, were all but gone.

◆ Reading Strategy

❹ **Analyze Difficult Sentences** The knight has participated in battles in Lithuania, Russia, Spain, North Africa, Turkey, and various sites in the Mediterranean. He has also won in three jousts, always killing his opponent.

◆ Critical Thinking

❺ **Support** Although the Knight is generally considered admirable and even idealized, lines 65–68 suggest that even this character has his flaws. Have students identify possible shortcomings and back up their observations with details from the passage. *The knight may not be merciful, as he killed rather than spared his jousting opponents. At times, he may have fought for mercenary reasons rather that chivalric ideals, as shown by his assisting one "heathen Turk" against another.*

◆ Literary Focus

❻ **Characterization** Ask students if this line from the poem is a direct or indirect characterization of the knight. *It is direct characterization.* What indirect characterization does Chaucer offer to support this direct characterization of the knight? *The Knight often sat in a place of honor at banquets, participated in fifteen battles and in jousts, was admired, and was modest in speech and action.*

What their condition was, the full array
Of each of them, as it appeared to me
According to profession and degree,
And what apparel they were riding in;
❷ And at a Knight I therefore will begin.
There was a *Knight,* a most distinguished man,
Who from the day on which he first began
To ride abroad had followed chivalry,
Truth, honor, generousness and courtesy.
He had done nobly in his sovereign's war
And ridden into battle, no man more,
As well in Christian as heathen places,
And ever honored for his noble graces.
When we took Alexandria,[8] he was there.
He often sat at table in the chair
Of honor, above all nations, when in Prussia.
In Lithuania he had ridden, and Russia,
No Christian man so often, of his rank.
When, in Granada, Algeciras sank
Under assault, he had been there, and in
North Africa, raiding Benamarin;
In Anatolia he had been as well
And fought when Ayas and Attalia fell,
For all along the Mediterranean coast
He had embarked with many a noble host.
In fifteen mortal battles he had been
And jousted for our faith at Tramissene
Thrice in the lists, and always killed his man.
This same distinguished knight had led the van[9]
Once with the Bey of Balat,[10] doing work
For him against another heathen Turk;
He was of sovereign value in all eyes.
And though so much distinguished, he was wise
And in his bearing modest as a maid.
He never yet a boorish thing had said
In all his life to any, come what might;
❻ He was a true, a perfect gentle-knight.
Speaking of his equipment, he possessed
Fine horses, but he was not gaily dressed.
He wore a fustian[11] tunic stained and dark
With smudges where his armor had left mark;
Just home from service, he had joined our ranks
To do his pilgrimage and render thanks.
He had his son with him, a fine young *Squire,*
A lover and cadet, a lad of fire
With locks as curly as if they had been pressed.
He was some twenty years of age, I guessed.
In stature he was of a moderate length,
With wonderful agility and strength.
He'd seen some service with the cavalry
In Flanders and Artois and Picardy[12]
And had done valiantly in little space

8. Alexandria: Site of one of the campaigns fought by Christians against groups who posed a threat to Europe during the fourteenth century. The place names that follow refer to other battle sites in these campaigns, or crusades.

◆ Reading Strategy
According to lines 56–65, what has the knight done? ❹

9. van: The part of the army that goes before the rest (short for vanguard).
10. Bey of Balat: Pagan leader.

11. fustian (fus′ chən) *n.:* Coarse cloth of cotton and linen.

12. Flanders . . . Picardy: Regions in Belgium and France.

Cultural Connection

The knight is said to have done nobly in "his sovereign's war." Scholars suggest that this is a reference to the campaigns of the Hundred Years' War between England and France. However, based on the other references, the knight must have served some forty years in northeastern Europe, the western Mediterranean, the Turkish empire of the eastern Mediterranean, and north Africa.

Have students trace the travels of the knight and report on the culture and customs of the people occupying these regions today.

Literature CD-ROM Play Presentation 2 on *The Time, Life, and Works of Shakespeare* CD-ROM. This presentation consists of readings from Middle English, including excerpts of "The Prologue" from *The Canterbury Tales* and Chaucer's *Troilus and Criseyde.*

The Yeoman, Arthur Szyk for *The Canterbury Tales*

8 ▶ **Critical Viewing** Compare this portrait with Chaucer's description of the Yeoman. What details did the artist choose to change or omit? **[Compare and Contrast]**

Of time, in hope to win his lady's grace.
He was embroidered like a meadow bright
And full of freshest flowers, red and white.
Singing he was, or fluting all the day;
He was as fresh as is the month of May.
Short was his gown, the sleeves were long and wide;
7 He knew the way to sit a horse and ride.
He could make songs and poems and recite,
Knew how to joust and dance, to draw and write.
He loved so hotly that till dawn grew pale
He slept as little as a nightingale.
Courteous he was, lowly and serviceable,
And carved to serve his father at the table.
There was a *Yeoman*[13] with him at his side,
No other servant; so he chose to ride.
This Yeoman wore a coat and hood of green,
And peacock-feathered arrows, bright and keen
And neatly sheathed, hung at his belt the while
—For he could dress his gear in yeoman style,
His arrows never drooped their feathers low—
And in his hand he bore a mighty bow.
His head was like a nut, his face was brown.
He knew the whole of woodcraft up and down.
A saucy brace[14] was on his arm to ward

13. ***Yeoman*** (yō′ mən) *n.*: Attendant.

14. **brace:** Bracelet.

◆ Literature and Your Life

7 Students may see some similarities to their own youthful behavior in the description of the Squire. Ask students to note some modern equivalents to the squire's apparent concern for his appearance and his attempt to gain the attention of the opposite sex. *Students will describe the latest in teen male fashions. They may compare the squire's skills in riding, poetry, and so on, to currently fashionable skills such as skateboarding, surfing, or playing an electric guitar.*

▶Critical Viewing◀

8 **Compare and Contrast** The Yeoman's arrows are slung over his shoulder rather than hanging at his belt as in Chaucer's description. The artist has also chosen to omit the arm brace, the medal of St. Christopher, and the hunting horn. Some students may dispute whether the coat and hood are green, since only the lining appears to be green. Students may also identify elements in the portrait that Chaucer does not mention, such as the purse and feathered cap.

Humanities: Art

The Yeoman, 1946, by Arthur Szyk.

In this miniature painted in 1946 for *The Canterbury Tales,* the artist shows a fully equipped medieval yeoman. He appears ready for any occurrence in the forest, from the appearance of game to an attack by highwaymen. He is portrayed as a sturdy fellow with a serious expression on his face. In painting these miniatures, Arthur Szyk, with patience and meticulous care, imitates monkish manuscript painters. Through this painstaking effect, he succeeds in capturing the charm and medieval flavor of that art.

Use these questions for discussion:

1. How does Szyk's depiction of the yeoman compare with your image of him? *Some students may say that the art matches their image of the yeoman. Other students may point out ways in which the artist's depiction differs from what they imagine. For many students, the Yeoman will match their images of Robin Hood.*
2. What details of this illustration would you like to change? *Students may suggest ways to make the illustration match Chaucer's description more closely, such as changing the Yeoman's jacket to green, or putting a brace on his arm.*

❶ **Clarification** The fact that he wears a St. Christopher medal does not necessarily mean that the Yeoman is pious. Because St. Christopher was the patron saint of travelers, many medieval travelers wore a medal for luck.

◆ Critical Thinking

❷ **Interpret** Eglantyne is a type of wild rose whose long, thorny stems readily entangle passersby. Not surprisingly, Eglantyne was also the name of several clinging-vine heroines in medieval romances. Have students explain what Chaucer is saying about the Prioress by this seemingly innocuous remark. *Suggested response: He is saying that she is overly dainty and helpless.*

❸ **Clarification** Point out that Chaucer is being mildly critical in noting that the Prioress spoke an imperfect "textbook" French rather than the more refined and natural French of true Parisians.

◆ Critical Thinking

❹ **Draw Conclusions** Ask students if Chaucer's excessive praise for the Prioress's manners should be taken literally. Is he overstating her fastidious behavior in order to achieve some other effect? *Students might conclude that Chaucer is being satirical and in fact poking fun at the Prioress's behavior.*

◆ Literary Focus

❺ **Characterization** Ask students: What kind of characterization is used in line 154? *It is direct characterization.* What did the Prioress do to cause the narrator to reach this conclusion? *Students should point to the following: She wept at the sight of a mouse in a trap, fed costly food to her little pet dogs, and cried when one of them died or if someone hit one of them.*

◆ Reading Strategy

❻ **Analyze Difficult Sentences** Ask students: How large is the Nun? Why does the author use understatement in his description instead of simply saying directly, "She was indeed overgrown"? *By apparently trying to minimize the Nun's size, the reader is amused and assumes she must be quite large.*

It from the bow-string, and a shield and sword
Hung at one side, and at the other slipped
A jaunty dirk,[15] spear-sharp and well-equipped.
❶ A medal of St. Christopher[16] he wore
Of shining silver on his breast, and bore
A hunting-horn, well slung and burnished clean,
That dangled from a baldric[17] of bright green.
He was a proper forester I guess.
  There also was a *Nun*, a Prioress.[18]
Her way of smiling very simple and coy.
Her greatest oath was only "By St. Loy!"[19]
❷ And she was known as Madam Eglantyne.
And well she sang a service,[20] with a fine
Intoning through her nose, as was most seemly,
❸ And she spoke daintily in French, extremely,
After the school of Stratford-atte-Bowe;[21]
French in the Paris style she did not know.
❹ At meat her manners were well taught withal;
No morsel from her lips did she let fall,
Nor dipped her fingers in the sauce too deep;
But she could carry a morsel up and keep
The smallest drop from falling on her breast.
For courtliness she had a special zest,
And she would wipe her upper lip so clean
That not a trace of grease was to be seen
Upon the cup when she had drunk; to eat,
She reached a hand sedately for the meat.
She certainly was very entertaining,
Pleasant and friendly in her ways, and straining
To counterfeit a courtly kind of grace,
A stately bearing fitting to her place,
And to seem dignified in all her dealings.
As for her sympathies and tender feelings,
She was so charitably solicitous
She used to weep if she but saw a mouse
Caught in a trap, if it were dead or bleeding.
And she had little dogs she would be feeding
With roasted flesh, or milk, or fine white bread.
And bitterly she wept if one were dead
Or someone took a stick and made it smart;
❺ She was all sentiment and tender heart.
Her veil was gathered in a seemly way,
Her nose was elegant, her eyes glass-gray;
Her mouth was very small, but soft and red,
Her forehead, certainly, was fair of spread,
Almost a span[22] across the brows, I own;
❻ She was indeed by no means undergrown.
Her cloak, I noticed, had a graceful charm.

15. dirk *n.*: Dagger.
16. St. Christopher: Patron saint of forests and travelers.
17. baldric *n.*: Belt worn over one shoulder and across the chest to support a sword.
18. *Prioress* *n.*: In an abbey, the nun ranking just below the abbess.
19. St. Loy: St. Eligius, patron saint of goldsmiths and courtiers.
20. service: Daily prayer.
21. Stratford-atte-Bowe: Nunnery near London.
22. span: Nine inches.

◆ Build Vocabulary

solicitous (sə lis′ ə təs) *adj.*: Showing care or concern

The Monk
Arthur Szyk for *The Canterbury Tales*

◀ Critical Viewing What can you infer from this picture about the Monk's style of living? List three details supporting your conclusion. **[Infer]**

She wore a coral trinket on her arm,
A set of beads, the gaudies[23] tricked in green,
Whence hung a golden brooch of brightest sheen
On which there first was graven a crowned A,
And lower, *Amor vincit omnia*.[24]
  Another *Nun*, the chaplain at her cell,
Was riding with her, and *three Priests* as well.
  A *Monk* there was, one of the finest sort
Who rode the country; hunting was his sport.
A manly man, to be an Abbot able;
Many a dainty horse he had in stable.

23. gaudies: Large green beads that marked certain prayers on a set of prayer beads.

24. *Amor vincit omnia* (ä môr′ wink′ it ôm′ nē ä): "Love conquers all" (Latin).

▶Critical Viewing◀

7 Infer Students may point to the following: *The monk's size and weight suggest that he eats well. His fur-trimmed clothing and fine purse indicate a degree of wealth. The spurs and sword suggest he rides and possibly hunts or engages in sport. The huge gold cross hanging from his belt reminds the viewer that he is a member of a religious order, but also suggests great wealth.*

◆ Literary Focus

8 Characterization Ask students what Chaucer might be indirectly suggesting about the Nun's character with this ambiguous maxim. Is it a reflection of the golden rule or a suggestion of a more worldly sentiment? *Most students will probably seize upon this as evidence of a worldly nature. Challenge them to support this view of the Nun's character with other evidence in Chaucer's description.*

Humanities: Art

The Monk, 1946, by Arthur Szyk.

In this miniature, Szyk shows the massive and richly robed monk described in the Prologue. His wealth is apparent from his fine fur-trimmed robes, gold brooch, elaborate sword, and tooled wallet. His expression is one of haughty self-satisfaction. Szyk painted the worldly cleric with humor and wit, emphasizing the incongruity between the trappings of wealth and the man's humble vocation.

Use these questions for discussion:

1. How does Szyk's pictorial representation of the monk compare with Chaucer's description? *Although the artist has used his imagination to fill in some details about the monk's clothing, the miniature closely matches Chaucer's description.*
2. Does this depiction look realistic or exaggerated? *Students may say that the depiction is stylized, but contains some realistic details in the obese monk's facial feature and his heavily ornamented clothing.*

◆ Literary Focus

❶ Characterization By comparing the jingling of the Monk's riding bridle with the chapel bell, Chaucer is drawing into sharp contrast the Monk's worldly pursuits and his religious obligations as a Prior.

◆ Critical Thinking

❷ Analyze Ask students what this passage reveals about the Monk's attitude toward the rules of his order. *The Monk does not care about the rules.* What else does the author reveal about the Monk in this passage? *The references to "a plucked hen" and "an oyster" suggest that the Monk is a glutton.*

❸ Clarification Remind students that the narrator is not really Chaucer but an imaginary character.

◆ *Literature and Your Life*

❹ Point out that the narrator might not, in fact, agree with the Monk. The questions in lines 188–191 can be seen as being rhetorical, even sarcastic. What situations can students recall when they or someone they know used the device of a rhetorical question to further an argument? *Students may recall using such questions when arguing with a parent or friend. For example: "Do you mean that I have to wait by the phone on a Saturday night because you can't decide what you want to do?"*

◆ Grammar and Style

❺ Past and Past Perfect Tenses Ask students in what order these two events took place: the shining head and face and the possible greasing of the head and face. Follow up by asking what tense the word *shone* represents and what tense the verb *had greased* is. *The greasing had to occur prior to the appearance of the shining head and face. The verb* shone *is the past tense of shine while the verb* had greased *is in the past perfect tense.*

His bridle, when he rode, a man might hear
Jingling in a whistling wind as clear,
Aye, and as loud as does the chapel bell
Where my lord Monk was Prior of the cell.
The Rule of good St. Benet or St. Maur[25]
As old and strict he tended to ignore;
He let go by the things of yesterday
And took the modern world's more spacious way.
He did not rate that text at a plucked hen
Which says that hunters are not holy men
And that a monk uncloistered is a mere
Fish out of water, flapping on the pier,
That is to say a monk out of his cloister.
That was a text he held not worth an oyster;
And I agreed and said his views were sound;
Was he to study till his head went round
Poring over books in cloisters? Must he toil
As Austin[26] bade and till the very soil?
Was he to leave the world upon the shelf?
Let Austin have his labor to himself.
  This Monk was therefore a good man to horse;
Greyhounds he had, as swift as birds, to course.
Hunting a hare or riding at a fence
Was all his fun, he spared for no expense.
I saw his sleeves were garnished at the hand
With fine gray fur, the finest in the land,
And on his hood, to fasten it at his chin
He had a wrought-gold cunningly fashioned pin;
Into a lover's knot it seemed to pass.
His head was bald and shone like looking-glass;
So did his face, as if it had been greased.
He was a fat and personable priest;
His prominent eyeballs never seemed to settle.
They glittered like the flames beneath a kettle;
Supple his boots, his horse in fine condition.
He was a prelate fit for exhibition,
He was not pale like a tormented soul.
He liked a fat swan best, and roasted whole.
His palfrey[27] was as brown as is a berry.
  There was a *Friar*, a wanton[28] one and merry
A Limiter,[29] a very festive fellow.
In all Four Orders[30] there was none so mellow
So glib with gallant phrase and well-turned speech.
He'd fixed up many a marriage, giving each
Of his young women what he could afford her.
He was a noble pillar to his Order.
Highly beloved and intimate was he
With County folk[31] within his boundary,
And city dames of honor and possessions;
For he was qualified to hear confessions,
Or so he said, with more than priestly scope;
He had a special license from the Pope.

◆ Literary Focus
What does the comparison of the two sounds (lines 173–176) suggest about the Monk?

25. St. Benet or St. Maur: St. Benedict, author of monastic rules, and St. Maurice, one of his followers. Benet and Maur are French versions of Benedict and Maurice.

26. Austin: English version of St. Augustine, who criticized lazy monks.

27. palfrey *n.*: Saddle horse.
28. wanton *adj.*: Jolly.
29. Limiter: Friar who is given begging rights for a certain limited area.
30. Four Orders: There were four orders of friars who supported themselves by begging: Dominicans, Franciscans, Carmelites, and Augustinians.
31. County folk: The phrase refers to rich landowners.

Cultural Connection

In *The Canterbury Tales,* Chaucer introduces a host of people from all classes of medieval society. Though all are on a religious pilgrimage, not all are religious—including some who have religious vocations. Chaucer portrays such figures as the Monk, Friar, Prioress, and Pardoner not as perfect, austere, and devoted servants of God, but as human beings, complete with such recognizable foibles as gluttony, lust, vanity, and hypocrisy. Point out that Chaucer's descriptions of the Monk's love of fine food and hunting and of the Prioress's possession of riches (such as jewelry) are both satiric and realistic.

Point out to students that the roles of religious figures vary from culture to culture. In the Ifugao tribe of the Philippines, priests are not required to embody morality but to act as their people's agents. In contrast, lamas of Tibet are regarded as divine. Eskimo priests are trained from childhood in the sacred lore of the tribe. Shamans in West African tribes inspire both awe and fear. Ask students to find about the roles of clergy and other religious officials in different religions and cultures. Have them relate their findings to the characters in *The Canterbury Tales.*

Sweetly he heard his penitents at shrift[32]
❽ With pleasant absolution, for a gift.
❾ He was an easy man in penance-giving
Where he could hope to make a decent living;
It's a sure sign whenever gifts are given
To a poor Order that a man's well shriven,[33]
And should he give enough he knew in verity
The penitent repented in sincerity.
For many a fellow is so hard of heart
He cannot weep, for all his inward smart.
Therefore instead of weeping and of prayer
One should give silver for a poor Friar's care.
He kept his tippet[34] stuffed with pins for curls,
And pocket-knives, to give to pretty girls.
And certainly his voice was gay and sturdy,
For he sang well and played the hurdy-gurdy.[35]
At sing-songs he was champion of the hour.
His neck was whiter than a lily-flower
But strong enough to butt a bruiser down.
He knew the taverns well in every town
And every innkeeper and barmaid too
Better than lepers, beggars and that crew,
For in so eminent a man as he
It was not fitting with the dignity
Of his position, dealing with a scum
Of wretched lepers; nothing good can come
Of dealings with the slum-and-gutter dwellers,
But only with the rich and victual-sellers.
But anywhere a profit might accrue
Courteous he was and lowly of service too.
⓫ Natural gifts like his were hard to match.
He was the finest beggar of his batch,
And, for his begging-district, payed a rent;
His brethren did no poaching where he went.
For though a widow mightn't have a shoe,
So pleasant was his holy how-d'ye-do
He got his farthing from her just the same
Before he left, and so his income came
To more than he laid out. And how he romped,
Just like a puppy! He was ever prompt
To arbitrate disputes on settling days
(For a small fee) in many helpful ways,
Not then appearing as your cloistered scholar
With threadbare habit hardly worth a dollar,
But much more like a Doctor or a Pope.
Of double-worsted was the semi-cope[36]
Upon his shoulders, and the swelling fold
About him, like a bell about its mold
When it is casting, rounded out his dress.
He lisped a little out of wantonness
To make his English sweet upon his tongue.
When he had played his harp, or having sung,

32. **shrift** *n.*: Confession.

33. **well shriven** *adj.*: Absolved of his sins.

34. **tippet** *n.*: Hood.

35. **hurdy-gurdy:** Stringed instrument played by cranking a wheel.

36. **semi-cope:** Cape.

◆ Literary Focus ❿
In this sentence (lines 244–252), is Chaucer using direct or indirect characterization, or both?

◆ Build Vocabulary

garnished (gär´ nisht) *adj.*: Decorated; trimmed

absolution (ab sə lo͞o´ shən) *n.*: Act of freeing someone of a sin or of a criminal charge

❻ **Clarification** To be fat in the Middle Ages was a status symbol. Only the rich had more than enough to eat; thus, obesity suggested affluence.

❼ **Enrichment** Unlike monks, whose work lay within a monastery, friars were itinerant ecclesiastics whose begging supported schools, hospitals, and other church-related institutions. This Friar exemplifies the corruption to which many in these mendicant orders had sunk by Chaucer's time.

◆ Build Vocabulary

❽ **Suffixes: *-tion*** Point out the word *absolution* contains the suffix *-tion.* This suffix is typically used to change a verb into a noun by adding the meaning "the action of" or "the result of the action of." Ask students: what action causes the result of absolution? *Absolution is the result of the action of absolving. The Friar absolved one of his penitents by granting absolution.*

Comprehension Check ☑

❾ What point is the author making in these lines 226–236? *The author is being sarcastic, asking why a man should repent and pray to be absolved of sin when all he needs to do is make a large donation to a friar.*

◆ Literary Focus

❿ **Characterization** Students should see that Chaucer is using an indirect method of characterization by describing who the Friar knew and where he spent his time.

Comprehension Check ☑

⓫ What special talent does the Friar possess? *He is extremely skillful as a beggar, getting money even from those who have very little.*

◆ Critical Thinking

❶ **Making Inferences** What can you infer about the Merchant from the description of his clothes? Is that inference confirmed or refuted in the lines that follow? *Motley, cloth woven into multicolored designs, was extremely expensive in medieval times, so the Merchant must be rich. The imported beaver hat and buckled shoes also suggest the Merchant is wealthy. However, the reader is told in line 290 the Merchant has concealed the fact that he is in debt.*

◆ Literature and Your Life

❷ The Merchant believes that the government should spare no expense to keep the sea where he does business free from pirates. Have students relate the Merchant's outlook to that of modern lobbyists and politicians. *A lobbyist's job is to convince government officials to use public funds or to create legislation to support a particular special-interest group. Part of a politician's job is to ensure that his or her constituents get as much money or government benefits as possible. Occasionally, special interests or constituencies may benefit at the expense of other groups.*

►Critical Viewing◄

❸ **Infer** Students may conclude that the student likes to read and lives rather frugally. This is suggested by the following details: He is reading. His hose are patched at the knees. He lacks the more luxurious purses, swords, and headgear seen in the pictures of the other pilgrims.

His eyes would twinkle in his head as bright
As any star upon a frosty night.
This worthy's name was Hubert, it appeared.
❶ There was a *Merchant* with a forking beard
And motley dress, high on his horse he sat,
Upon his head a Flemish[37] beaver hat
And on his feet daintily buckled boots.
He told of his opinions and pursuits
In solemn tones, and how he never lost.
❷ The sea should be kept free at any cost
(He thought) upon the Harwich-Holland range,[38]
He was expert at currency exchange.

37. **Flemish:** From Flanders.

38. **Harwich-Holland range:** The North Sea between England and Holland.

The Student
Arthur Szyk for *The Canterbury Tales*

◄ **Critical Viewing** What can you infer from this picture about the Oxford Cleric's style of living? List three details supporting your conclusion. **[Infer]** ❸

Humanities: Art

The Student, 1946, by Arthur Szyk.

In the miniature *The Student,* Szyk cleverly shows the Oxford Cleric's preference for intellectual attainment over worldly matters. His drab tunic and patched knees contrast with his intent expression as he reads his book. He absently gestures with his left hand as if in conversation with himself, unaware of the picture he presents to others. Although not as decorative as the other, more richly dressed characters illustrated by Szyk, the student is detailed with care and skill.

Use these questions for discussion:

1. Do you think Szyk's miniature captures the personality of the Oxford Cleric as Chaucer has portrayed him? *Students will probably say that the miniature captures the Oxford Cleric's "unworldly," studious personality.*
2. Does Szyk's student remind you of any young scholar you have ever seen? *Students may be reminded of classmates or acquaintances whom they characterize as bookworms or nerds.*

This estimable Merchant so had set
His wits to work, none knew he was in debt,
He was so stately in negotiation,
Loan, bargain and commercial obligation.
He was an excellent fellow all the same;
To tell the truth I do not know his name.
An *Oxford Cleric*, still a student though,
One who had taken logic long ago,
Was there; his horse was thinner than a rake,
And he was not too fat, I undertake,
But had a hollow look, a sober stare;
The thread upon his overcoat was bare.
He had found no preferment in the church
And he was too unworldly to make search
For secular employment. By his bed
He preferred having twenty books in red
And black, of Aristotle's[39] philosophy,
To having fine clothes, fiddle or psaltery.[40]
(5) Though a philosopher, as I have told,
He had not found the stone for making gold.[41]
(6) Whatever money from his friends he took
He spent on learning or another book
And prayed for them most earnestly, returning
Thanks to them thus for paying for his learning.
(7) His only care was study, and indeed
He never spoke a word more than was need,
Formal at that, respectful in the extreme,
Short to the point, and lofty in his theme.
The thought of moral virtue filled his speech
And he would gladly learn, and gladly teach.
(8) A *Sergeant at the Law* who paid his calls,
Wary and wise, for clients at St. Paul's[42]
There also was, of noted excellence.
(9) Discreet he was, a man to reverence,
Or so he seemed, his sayings were so wise.
He often had been Justice of Assize
By letters patent, and in full commission.
His fame and learning and his high position
Had won him many a robe and many a fee.
There was no such conveyancer[43] as he;
All was fee-simple[44] to his strong digestion,
Not one conveyance could be called in question.
Nowhere there was so busy a man as he;
But was less busy than he seemed to be.
He knew of every judgment, case and crime
Recorded, ever since King William's time.
He could dictate defenses or draft deeds;

◆ *Literature and Your Life*

Name a modern type of person who resembles the Cleric. (4)

39. **Aristotle's** (ar′ is tät′ əlz): Referring to the Greek philosopher (384–322 B.C.).
40. **psaltery** (sôl′ tər ē): Ancient stringed instrument.
41. **stone . . . gold:** At the time, alchemists believed that a "philosopher's stone" existed that could turn base metals into gold.

42. **St. Paul's:** London cathedral near which lawyers often met to discuss their cases.

43. **conveyancer:** One who draws up documents for transferring ownership of property.
44. **fee-simple:** Unrestricted ownership.

◆ Build Vocabulary

commission (kə mish′ ən) *n.*: Authorization; act of giving authority to an individual

Enrichment

Considering that Chaucer's characters have traveled as widely as they have and experienced the ups and downs of fortune, it is interesting to trace the advances and reversals of the author himself. In a book entitled *The History of English Literature,* Peter Quennell reports the following:

> Between 1370 and 1386, Chaucer undertook a variety of important diplomatic missions. Thus he made an official journey to Italy toward the end of 1372, where he visited Genoa, Pisa, Florence, and remained for over ten months; in 1377 he was dispatched to Flanders and France; in 1378 he returned to France and, soon afterwards, set forth on another errand to Bernabo Visconti, Duke of Milan. His activities were well rewarded—not only with such minor privileges as the right to demand a jug of wine from the pantry of the royal butler, but with the comptrollership of the duties of wool and skins and, later, the comptrollership of the Petty Customs. In 1386 he became a knight for the shire of Kent. But that same year he suffered a temporary disgrace, lost both his comptrollerships and was obliged to borrow money. In 1389, however, he re-entered the civil service and received several lucrative appointments. . . . The closing years of Chaucer's existence seem to have been calm and cheerful.

◆ *Literature and Your Life*

(4) Students will likely classify the Oxford Cleric as a bookworm or egghead whose devotion to learning causes him to care little about his appearance, food, or social life. Some may also associate him with modern-day computer geniuses.

◆ Grammar and Style

(5) **Past and Past Perfect Tenses** Have students identify the verb in the past perfect tense. Have them further indicate which word is the helping verb and which word is the main verb. *The past perfect verb is* had found. *The helping verb is* had *and the main verb is* found.

◆ Background for Understanding

(6) **History** At the time Chaucer wrote *The Canterbury Tales,* movable type had not yet been invented. Consequently, books represented a considerable expense.

(7) **Enrichment** The Oxford Cleric is considered to be one of the handful of idealized characters introduced in the Prologue. He is the model of what a student should be rather than a portrait of what a student generally is. He represents the passion for learning that was already stirring in Europe. The description "he would gladly learn, and gladly teach" is an often-quoted encomium for the dedicated scholar.

Customize for *English Language Learners*

(8) Inverted sentence patterns such as this may confuse students learning English. Have students convert this sentence into several shorter, more conventional sentences. *Students' sentences should be similar to the following: There was also a Sergeant at the Law. He was wary and wise. He met with clients at St. Paul's. He was excellent. He was discreet. He deserved reverence. His sayings were wise.*

(9) **Enrichment** The term "Sergeant at the Law" referred to a member of a small, chosen group of lawyers—one who had at least sixteen years' experience, was the King's legal servant, acted as judge, and was an eminent member of his profession. In Chaucer's day there were about twenty in this exclusive group.

◆ Literary Focus

❶ Characterization Ask students: Is the Sergeant at the Law characterized as skillful and competent? Does Chaucer use direct or indirect characterization? *The Sergeant is indeed skillful and competent. Chaucer uses indirect characterization in these lines.*

◆ Reading Strategy

❷ Analyze Difficult Sentences Have students use the notes beside the text to assist them in determining the meaning of this difficult sentence. Ask students to identify the greatest source of pleasure for the Franklin. *Good food and drink were the Franklin's chief source of pleasure.*

◆ Critical Thinking

❸ Deduce Ask students what they can deduce about the status of tradesmen in Chaucer's time from the description of the Haberdasher, Dyer, Carpenter, Weaver, and Carpetmaker. *The guildsmen are solid members of the middle class. They are financially secure and have upward social mobility.*

Clarification In England the term *haberdasher* means "a dealer in small wares or notions." In the United States, it refers to a dealer in men's furnishings.

No one could pinch a comma from his screeds,[45]
And he knew every statute off by rote.
He wore a homely parti-colored coat
Girt with a silken belt of pin-stripe stuff;
Of his appearance I have said enough.
There was a *Franklin*[46] with him, it appeared;
White as a daisy-petal was his beard.
A sanguine man, high-colored and benign,
He loved a morning sop[47] of cake in wine.
He lived for pleasure and had always done,
For he was Epicurus'[48] very son,
In whose opinion sensual delight
Was the one true felicity in sight.
As noted as St. Julian[49] was for bounty
He made his household free to all the County.
His bread, his ale were the finest of the fine
And no one had a better stock of wine.
His house was never short of bake-meat pies,
Of fish and flesh, and these in such supplies
It positively snowed with meat and drink
And all the dainties that a man could think.
According to the seasons of the year
Changes of dish were ordered to appear.
He kept fat partridges in coops, beyond,
Many a bream and pike were in his pond.
Woe to the cook whose sauces had no sting
Or who was unprepared in anything!
And in his hall a table stood arrayed
And ready all day long, with places laid.
As Justice at the Sessions[50] none stood higher;
He often had been Member for the Shire.[51]
A dagger and a little purse of silk
Hung at his girdle, white as morning milk.
As Sheriff he checked audit, every entry.
He was a model among landed gentry.
A *Haberdasher*, a *Dyer*, a *Carpenter*,
A *Weaver* and a *Carpet-maker* were
Among our ranks, all in the livery
Of one impressive guild-fraternity.[52]
They were so trim and fresh their gear would pass
For new. Their knives were not tricked out with brass
But wrought with purest silver, which avouches
A like display on girdles and on pouches.
Each seemed a worthy burgess,[53] fit to grace
A guild-hall with a seat upon the dais.
Their wisdom would have justified a plan
To make each one of them an alderman;

45. **screeds:** Long, boring speeches or pieces of writing.

46. **Franklin:** Wealthy landowner.

47. **sop:** Piece.

48. **Epicurus'** (ep´ i kyoor´ əs): Referring to a Greek philosopher (342?–270 B.C.) who believed that happiness is the most important goal in life.

49. **St. Julian:** Patron saint of hospitality.

50. **Sessions:** Court sessions.

51. **Member . . . Shire:** Parliamentary representative for the county.

52. **guild-fraternity:** In the Middle Ages, associations of men practicing the same craft or trade, called guilds, set standards for workmanship and protected their members by controlling competition.

53. **burgess:** Member of a legislative body.

◆ Build Vocabulary

sanguine (saŋ´ gwin) *adj.*: Confident; cheerful
avouches (ə vouch´ ez) *v.*: Asserts positively; affirms

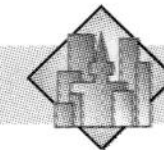

Beyond the Classroom

Career Connection

The Skilled Trades Chaucer includes several skilled tradesmen in his tale. Some, like the carpenter, are still well known today. Others, like the miller, a person who operates a grain mill, have all but disappeared.

Have interested students investigate which skilled trades have disappeared or come into being over the years. You might help them get started by having them look up what a fletcher did for a living and when welding became an important skill.

They had the capital and revenue,
Besides their wives declared it was their due.
And if they did not think so, then they ought;
[4] To be called "*Madam*" is a glorious thought,
And so is going to church and being seen
Having your mantle carried like a queen.
They had a *Cook* with them who stood alone
For boiling chicken with a marrow-bone,
Sharp flavoring-powder and a spice for savor.
He could distinguish London ale by flavor,
[5] And he could roast and seethe and broil and fry,
Make good thick soup and bake a tasty pie.
But what a pity—so it seemed to me,
That he should have an ulcer on his knee.
As for blancmange,[54] he made it with the best.
There was a *Skipper* hailing from far west;
He came from Dartmouth, so I understood.
[6] He rode a farmer's horse as best he could,
In a woolen gown that reached his knee.
A dagger on a lanyard[55] falling free
Hung from his neck under his arm and down.
The summer heat had tanned his color brown,
And certainly he was an excellent fellow.
Many a draught of vintage, red and yellow,
He'd drawn at Bordeaux, while the trader snored.
The nicer rules of conscience he ignored.
If, when he fought, the enemy vessel sank,
He sent his prisoners home; they walked the plank.
As for his skill in reckoning his tides,
Currents and many another risk besides,
Moons, harbors, pilots, he had such dispatch
That none from Hull to Carthage was his match.
Hardy he was, prudent in undertaking;
[7] His beard in many a tempest had its shaking,
And he knew all the havens as they were
From Gottland to the Cape of Finisterre,
And every creek in Brittany and Spain;
The barge he owned was called *The Maudelayne*.
A *Doctor* too emerged as we proceeded;
No one alive could talk as well as he did
On points of medicine and of surgery,
[9] For, being grounded in astronomy,
He watched his patient's favorable star
And, by his Natural Magic, knew what are
The lucky hours and planetary degrees
For making charms and magic effigies.
The cause of every malady you'd got
He knew, and whether dry, cold, moist or hot;[56]
He knew their seat, their humor and condition.
He was a perfect practicing physician.
These causes being known for what they were,

54. **blancmange** (blə mänzh′): At the time, a creamy chicken dish.

55. **lanyard:** Loose rope around the neck.

◆ **Reading Strategy** How does the Doctor attempt to heal patients (lines 421–428)? [8]

56. **The cause . . . hot:** It was believed that the body was composed of four "humors" (cold and dry, hot and moist, hot and dry, cold and moist) and that diseases resulted from a disturbance of one of these "humors."

Customize for
Less Proficient Readers
Help students break down the sentence in lines 421–428 into individual clauses. Have students paraphrase the meaning of each clause. *It turned out that one member of our group was a doctor. He could talk about medicine and surgery better than any other person alive. Because he knew astronomy, he would watch his patient's favorable star. He knew what times of day and planetary positions were needed to make healing charms.*

9 **Clarification** Explain that *astronomy* really means "astrology" here. Astronomy is the scientific study of the universe. Astrology is the divination of the supposed influence of the stars on human events.

◆ Literary Focus

4 **Characterization** Although the guildsmen's wives are not participating in the pilgrimage, the reader gets a strong impression of their character. Ask students what one word they would use to describe the wives. *Students may settle on* vain, conceited, proud, arrogant, egotistical, *or a similar word to describe the wives.* Does Chaucer use direct or indirect characterization to create this impression? *Chaucer's characterization is indirect. He tells about their thoughts and words and allows the reader to form an impression of their character.*

◆ Literature and Your Life

5 Point out that Chaucer heaps praise on the Cook for seven of the nine lines he devotes to this pilgrim, then in two lines (lines 395–396) he completely reverses the reader's impression of this Cook with one very unappetizing suggestion. Ask students to share some positive impressions they have formed of someone only to have their opinion reversed by a single incident or revelation about that person. *Students might mention someone whom they admired, but then learned he or she had cheated or gossiped. They might also mention a sports hero who was arrested for a crime or engaged in an unsportsmanlike act.*

◆ Critical Thinking

6 **Make Inferences** What can you infer about the Skipper's riding ability from this line? Follow by asking why the Skipper might lack skill in riding a horse. *The Skipper lacked riding experience because he spent most of his life at sea.*

7 **Clarification** The breadth of the Skipper's maritime skill is suggested in geographic terms. *From Hull to Carthage* means "from northern England to northern Africa," and from *Gottland to the Cape of Finisterre* means "from Sweden to Spain." The name *Finisterre* means "the end of the earth."

◆ Reading Strategy

8 **Analyze Difficult Sentences** The doctor attempts to use "charms" and "magic effigies." You may want to point out to students that people didn't know about germs until the nineteenth century.

◆ Literature and Your Life

1 Explain that guile is a deceit or sly trick. Ask students: What deceit or sly trick between the Doctor and the apothecaries is suggested here? *Students should recognize that the doctor is prescribing unnecessary drugs in return for a share in the druggists' profits.* How does this compare to problems with modern health care? *Students may have read about scandals involving unnecessary or excessively expensive medication. They may also have read about allegations that needed treatment is being withheld to keep down insurance costs.*

◆ Background for Understanding

2 History Doctors were commonly regarded as irreligious skeptics, especially those who followed the school of the great twelfth-century Arabian physician Averroës. A comparison is often made between this line and the proverb *Ubi tres medici, duo athei*—"Where there are three doctors, two are atheists."

◆ Background for Understanding

3 History The pestilence referred to here may be the Black Death of 1347–1351, an epidemic of plague in both bubonic form and pneumonic forms. About one fourth to one third of the population of Europe died during the Black Death. Additional outbreaks of plague occurred in 1361–1363, 1369–1371, 1374–1375, 1390, and 1400.

◆ Critical Thinking

4 Draw Conclusions Two possible conclusions can be drawn from these lines. Ask students why the Doctor had a "special love of gold." *A few students may say that the Doctor uses the gold for medicinal purposes, to stimulate the heart. Most will perceive that the Doctor is a miser.*

▶Critical Viewing◀

5 Analyze Students say that the Wife's self-assured, bold stance suggests confidence, independence, and even superiority to others on the journey. Her cane, gold buttons, and fur-trimmed attire imply a degree of wealth. Her hat and smiles could be evidence of a flamboyance that is reinforced by Chaucer's description.

He gave the man his medicine then and there.
All his apothecaries[57] in a tribe
(1) Were ready with the drugs he would prescribe,
And each made money from the other's guile;
They had been friendly for a goodish while.
He was well-versed in Esculapius[58] too
And what Hippocrates and Rufus knew
And Dioscorides, now dead and gone,
Galen and Rhazes, Hali, Serapion,
Averroes, Avicenna, Constantine,
Scotch Bernard, John of Gaddesden, Gilbertine.[59]
In his own diet he observed some measure;
There were no superfluities for pleasure,
Only digestives, nutritives and such.
(2) He did not read the Bible very much.
In blood-red garments, slashed with bluish-gray
And lined with taffeta,[60] he rode his way;
Yet he was rather close as to expenses
(3) And kept the gold he won in pestilences.
(4) Gold stimulates the heart, or so we're told.

57. apothecaries (ə päth′ ə ker′ ēz): Persons who prepared medicines.

58. Esculapius (es′ kyoo lā′ pē əs): In Greek mythology, the god of medicine and healing.

59. Hippocrates . . . Gilbertine: Famous physicians and medical authorities.

60. taffeta (taf′ i tə): Fine silk fabric.

The Wife of Bath
Arthur Szyk for *The Canterbury Tales*

◀ **Critical Viewing** What does the Wife of Bath's body language convey about her character? **[Analyze]** (5)

Humanities: Art

The Wife of Bath, 1946, by Arthur Szyk.

In this miniature the artist shows the good Wife of Bath to be an imposing and decorative figure. The provocative posture and bold eyes are in keeping with Chaucer's description of her. The tiny details of dress, such as the gold buttons and the heart pattern on her belt, show the extreme skill of the artist in executing a painting on such a small scale. When discussing this painting with your class, point out the similarities in Szyk's portrait of the Wife of Bath and Chaucer's written account of her.

Use these questions for discussion:

1. What impression of the Wife's personality does the painting express? *Suggested response: She is bold, saucy, and outspoken.*
2. What does Chaucer's description of her convey that the painting does not? *Students may point out physical details that the artist chose not to include, such as her wimple or gap-teeth. Chaucer's description also includes details that cannot be shown in the portrait, such as her deafness, her skill at cloth-making, her anger when others do not defer to her, and her love of traveling.*

(4) He therefore had a special love of gold.
A worthy *woman* from beside Bath[61] city
Was with us, somewhat deaf, which was a pity.
In making cloth she showed so great a bent
She bettered those of Ypres and of Ghent.[62]
(6) In all the parish not a dame dared stir
Towards the altar steps in front of her,
And if indeed they did, so wrath was she
As to be quite put out of charity.
Her kerchiefs were of finely woven ground;[63]
I dared have sworn they weighed a good ten pound,
The ones she wore on Sunday, on her head.
Her hose were of the finest scarlet red
And gartered tight; her shoes were soft and new.
Bold was her face, handsome, and red in hue.
A worthy woman all her life, what's more
She'd had five husbands, all at the church door,
Apart from other company in youth;
No need just now to speak of that, forsooth.
And she had thrice been to Jerusalem,
Seen many strange rivers and passed over them;
She'd been to Rome and also to Boulogne,
St. James of Compostella and Cologne,[64]
And she was skilled in wandering by the way.
(7) She had gap-teeth, set widely, truth to say.
Easily on an ambling horse she sat
(8) Well wimpled[65] up, and on her head a hat
As broad as is a buckler[66] or a shield;
She had a flowing mantle that concealed
Large hips, her heels spurred sharply under that.
In company she liked to laugh and chat
And knew the remedies for love's mischances,
An art in which she knew the oldest dances.
A holy-minded man of good renown
(9) There was, and poor, the *Parson* to a town,
Yet he was rich in holy thought and work.
He also was a learned man, a clerk,
Who truly knew Christ's gospel and would preach it
Devoutly to parishioners, and teach it.
Benign and wonderfully diligent,
And patient when adversity was sent
(For so he proved in great adversity)
He much disliked extorting tithe[67] or fee,
Nay rather he preferred beyond a doubt
Giving to poor parishioners round about
From his own goods and Easter offerings
He found sufficiency in little things.
Wide was his parish, with houses far asunder,
Yet he neglected not in rain or thunder,
In sickness or in grief, to pay a call
On the remotest, whether great or small,
Upon his feet, and in his hand a stave.

61. **Bath:** English resort city.

62. **Ypres** (ē´ prə) **and of Ghent** (gent): Flemish cities known for wool making.

63. **ground:** Composite fabric.

64. **Jerusalem . . . Rome . . . Boulogne . . . St. James of Compostella . . . Cologne:** Famous pilgrimage sites at the time.

65. **wimpled:** Wearing a scarf covering the head, neck, and chin.

66. **buckler:** Small round shield.

67. **tithe** (tīth): One tenth of a person's income, paid as a tax to support the church.

◆ Literature and Your Life

(6) Explain that people approached the altar to make their offerings in the order of their social standing. These lines therefore reveal the fact that the Wife of Bath felt she was superior to all others. What actions by people today reflect a similar "me first" attitude? *Possible answers include pushing ahead in line, seating oneself at the head of a table, and asking to be addressed by a title.*

(7) Enrichment Medieval physiognomists believed there was a connection between character and physical features. A gap between teeth was regarded not only as a sign that a person would be lucky and would travel extensively, but also that this person was bold, false, gluttonous, and lascivious.

(8) Enrichment The traditional garments, or habits, for many orders of nuns are based on medieval dress. While secular styles changed, theirs did not. The cloth covering the hair, ears, and neck is the wimple that all married women wore in the Middle Ages. Nuns were considered married women, the brides of Christ.

◆ Reading Strategy

(9) Analyze Difficult Sentences This inverted sentence with its unusual structure may prove challenging. Have students break it down into sentences with the normal subject-verb-complement order. *Students' sentences should be similar to the following: There was a holy-minded man of good renown. He was the parson to a town. Although he was poor, he was rich in holy thought and work.*

Cross-Curricular Connection: Science

Plague, which is caused by the bacterium *Yersinia pestis,* is primarily a disease of rats and the fleas that feed upon them. Under certain conditions, the fleas bite humans, transmitting the plague-causing bacterium.

There are three forms of plague in humans: bubonic, pneumonic, and septicemic. Bubonic plague is characterized by swellings (buboes) of the lymph nodes, and is transmitted from person to person only by fleas. Pneumonic plague is a severe infection of the lungs that can be transmitted directly from one person to another. Pneumonic plague is extremely contagious and is usually fatal. Septicemic plague causes a massive infection of the blood that causes death before bubonic or pneumonic signs appear. Because of the way plague is transmitted, the most severe epidemics occur in crowded, unsanitary urban areas where people live in close proximity to rats—such as medieval cities.

The Black Death, a severe plague epidemic in the fourteenth century, had an enormous impact on European society, art, and philosophy. Challenge students to find out how the Black Death changed English society and to identify ways in which these changes are seen in *The Canterbury Tales. The Black Death created a shortage of labor that led to increased social mobility, something that the wives of the Haberdasher, Dyer, Carpenter, Weaver, and Carpet-maker are determined to take advantage of. The Black Death also killed off those who ministered to the sick, leaving gaps in the ranks of the clergy that were filled by unfit individuals such as the Monk and Friar.*

◆ Literature and Your Life

❶ Ask students to think of contemporary expressions that express the idea that it is important to set a good example. *Possible axioms include "walk the talk" and "little jugs have big ears," a warning to watch what one says in front of children.* Encourage students to discuss the importance of being a good role model. *Teenagers are quick to condemn hypocrisy. Be prepared to steer students away from discussing specific personal issues or complaints about parents, teachers, classmates, and so on.*

◆ Critical Thinking

❷ **Interpret** Point out that gold does not react readily with other chemicals; it does not rust. Have students explain the logic and literal meaning of the Parson's proverb in line 510. *If gold, which is not subject to corrosion, rusts, then iron, which is susceptible to corrosion, will definitely rust.* Then ask students what the gold and iron symbolize. What is the meaning of the proverb? *The gold represents the clergy, and the iron represents the people. If the clergy fail to set a good example and fall into sin, then the people will certainly fall into sin.* Is there an example of rusting gold in the Prologue? *Students may identify the Prioress, Monk, and Friar.*

◆ Literary Focus

❸ **Characterization** Explain that in this passage Chaucer provides readers an indirect characterization by listing things the Parson did not do. Have students identify some of the things the Parson did not do; then ask if Chaucer might be suggesting that others do these things. Whom might Chaucer have in mind? *Chaucer again seems to bring the Parson into sharp contrast with the wealthy, well-fed Monk, the frivolous Prioress, and the sleazy Friar.*

This noble example to his sheep he gave,
❶ First following the word before he taught it,
And it was from the gospel he had caught it.
This little proverb he would add thereto
That if gold rust, what then will iron do?
For if a priest be foul in whom we trust
No wonder that a common man should rust;
❷ And shame it is to see—let priests take stock—
A soiled shepherd and a snowy flock.
The true example that a priest should give
Is one of cleanness, how the sheep should live.
He did not set his benefice to hire[68]
And leave his sheep encumbered in the mire
Or run to London to earn easy bread
By singing masses for the wealthy dead,
Or find some Brotherhood and get enrolled.
He stayed at home and watched over his fold
So that no wolf should make the sheep miscarry.
He was a shepherd and no mercenary.
Holy and virtuous he was, but then
Never contemptuous of sinful men,
Never disdainful, never too proud or fine,
❸ But was discreet in teaching and benign.
His business was to show a fair behavior
And draw men thus to Heaven and their Savior,
Unless indeed a man were obstinate;
And such, whether of high or low estate,
He put to sharp rebuke to say the least.
I think there never was a better priest.
He sought no pomp or glory in his dealings,
No scrupulosity had spiced his feelings.
Christ and His Twelve Apostles and their lore
He taught, but followed it himself before.
There was a *Plowman* with him there, his brother.
Many a load of dung one time or other
He must have carted through the morning dew.
He was an honest worker, good and true,
Living in peace and perfect charity,
And, as the gospel bade him, so did he,
Loving God best with all his heart and mind
And then his neighbor as himself, repined
At no misfortune, slacked for no content,
For steadily about his work he went
To thrash his corn, to dig or to manure
Or make a ditch; and he would help the poor
For love of Christ and never take a penny
If he could help it, and, as prompt as any,
He paid his tithes in full when they were due
On what he owned, and on his earnings too.
He wore a tabard[69] smock and rode a mare.
There was a *Reeve*,[70] also a *Miller*, there,
A College *Manciple*[71] from the Inns of Court,

68. **set . . . hire:** Pay someone else to perform his parish duties.

69. **tabard:** Loose jacket.

70. ***Reeve*:** Estate manager.

71. ***Manciple*:** Buyer of provisions.

Cross-Curricular Connection: Social Studies

The murder of Thomas à Becket is a well-known, if somewhat mysterious event in English history. A close friend of Henry II, Thomas was Archbishop of Canterbury and Chancellor of England. However, Thomas and the King eventually became engaged in a bitter quarrel over the right of the courts to try members of the clergy accused of crimes. On December 29, 1170, four of the king's knights killed the archbishop in his cathedral at Canterbury. Thomas was canonized in 1173, and the pope took the unusual step of forcing Henry to do public penance. Historians dispute whether Henry gave orders for the assassination. Nevertheless, Thomas à Becket is considered a martyr to the faith, and his murder in the cathedral is the source of literature and legend.

Have students collect the historical facts and issues surrounding the murder of Thomas à Becket. After presenting the historical background, students might discuss how someone like Thomas à Becket could still inspire people 200 years after his death.

Interested students might investigate T. S. Eliot's poetic drama *Murder in the Cathedral.* This work was first performed in 1935 in the Chapter House of the Cathedral, just a few yards from the spot where Thomas à Becket was murdered more than 700 years earlier.

A papal *Pardoner*[72] and, in close consort,
A Church-Court *Summoner*,[73] riding at a trot,
And finally myself—that was the lot.
The *Miller* was a chap of sixteen stone,[74]
A great stout fellow big in brawn and bone.
He did well out of them, for he could go
And win the ram at any wrestling show.
Broad, knotty and short-shouldered, he would boast
❹ He could heave any door off hinge and post,
Or take a run and break it with his head.
❺ His beard, like any sow or fox, was red
And broad as well, as though it were a spade;
❻ And, at its very tip, his nose displayed
A wart on which there stood a tuft of hair.
Red as the bristles in an old sow's ear.
His nostrils were as black as they were wide.
He had a sword and buckler at his side,
His mighty mouth was like a furnace door.
A wrangler and buffoon, he had a store
Of tavern stories, filthy in the main.
His was a master-hand at stealing grain.
He felt it with his thumb and thus he knew
Its quality and took three times his due—
A thumb of gold, by God, to gauge an oat!
He wore a hood of blue and a white coat.
He liked to play his bagpipes up and down
And that was how he brought us out of town.
The *Manciple* came from the Inner Temple;
All caterers might follow his example
In buying victuals; he was never rash
Whether he bought on credit or paid cash.
He used to watch the market most precisely
And go in first, and so he did quite nicely.
Now isn't it a marvel of God's grace
That an illiterate fellow can outpace
The wisdom of a heap of learned men?
His masters—he had more than thirty then—
All versed in the abstrusest legal knowledge,
Could have produced a dozen from their College
Fit to be stewards in land and rents and game
To any Peer in England you could name,
And show him how to live on what he had
Debt-free (unless of course the Peer were mad)
Or be as frugal as he might desire,
And they were fit to help about the Shire
In any legal case there was to try;
And yet this Manciple could wipe their eye.
The *Reeve* was old and choleric and thin;
His beard was shaven closely to the skin,
His shorn hair came abruptly to a stop
Above his ears, and he was docked on top
Just like a priest in front; his legs were lean,

72. *Pardoner*: One who dispenses papal pardons.
73. *Summoner*: One who serves summonses to church courts.
74. sixteen stone: 224 pounds. A stone equals 14 pounds.

◆ **Reading Strategy** How is the Manciple better than his masters (lines 585–604)? ❼

Customize for
Visual/Spatial Learners

❹ Have students search magazines for pictures of people they think resemble the Miller in appearance. Which elements of the pictured individual most resemble the Miller? Which elements are missing? Have students vote on which picture is the best match for the Miller.

❺ **Enrichment** Chaucer devotes considerable space to a physical description of the Miller. Medieval physiognomists would have associated his short-shouldered, stocky figure, his bushy red beard, and his warty nose with the traits of shamelessness, loquacity, belligerence, and lecherousness.

◆ Critical Thinking

❻ **Deduce** Direct students' attention to line 575. Have students name the qualities of a furnace door they think Chaucer wants to evoke in this simile. *Students may mention its size, temperature, and smell.*

◆ Reading Strategy

❼ **Analyze Difficult Sentences** The Manciple possessed practical knowledge and first-hand experience of the marketplace, knowing how and when to buy. His masters, on the other hand, had academic knowledge gained from books and a formal education in the law. Chaucer suggests that the Manciple's practical know-how is far superior to his masters' book learning.

Customize for
Less Proficient Readers

This is a good time to review the characters. Draw a three-column chart on the chalkboard. Label the columns *Positive, Negative,* and *Not Sure.* Name a character, hand a piece of chalk to a student, and have the student write the name of the character in a column and explain his or her decision. Guide the class in discussing whether they agree or disagree with the classification and why. *Students will probably converge on the following classifications.* Positive: *Knight, Squire, Yeoman, Oxford Cleric (Student), Sergeant at the Law, Franklin, Parson, Plowman.* Negative: *Prioress (Nun), Monk (Prior), Friar, Merchant, Skipper, Doctor.* Not Sure: *Narrator, Nun (Chaplain), Priests, Haberdasher, Dyer, Carpenter, Weaver, Carpet-maker, Cook, Wife of Bath.* Have students complete this chart after they have finished reading the Prologue. *Student responses may resemble the following:* Positive: *Manciple, Host.* Negative: *Miller, Summoner, Pardoner.* Not Sure: *Reeve.*

❶ **Support** A reeve was generally a subordinate estate manager. Chaucer's Reeve evidently had greater power and was more like a chief manager or steward. His choleric complexion would have denoted to physiognomists sharpness of wit, irascibility, and wantonness. Which of these traits does his description in the Prologue include? *His sharpness of wit is seen in his meticulous management of his master's grain, livestock, and household accounts. His irascibility might be reflected in the fact that his subordinates not only could not fool him but also feared him.*

❷ **Deduce** It is interesting to note that the Reeve chose his place in the cavalcade farthest away from the Miller, who led the procession. There was a traditional enmity between the two occupations. Why? *Part of a reeve's job is to make sure that he gets the best price possible from a miller and to ensure that the miller doesn't cheat by putting his thumb on the scale as the flour is being weighed.*

◆ Literary Focus

❸ **Characterization** In lavishing such attention on the Summoner's bad complexion, Chaucer implies that the Summoner's personality is similarly unsavory. Have students discuss whether it is fair to judge a person by his or her appearance. *Even though it is not fair to judge someone by his or her appearance, a common practice in fiction and in movies is to equate a person's appearance with his or her personality.*

◆ Reading Strategy

❹ **Analyze Difficult Sentences** Ask students how lines 660–661 serve to summarize the six previous lines. How is the Summoner like a trained bird? *The Summoner speaks Latin, but he merely recites lines he has memorized and does not really speak or understand Latin any more than a trained bird understands what it says.*

Like sticks they were, no calf was to be seen.
He kept his bins and garners[75] very trim;
No auditor could gain a point on him.
And he could judge by watching drought and rain
The yield he might expect from seed and grain.
His master's sheep, his animals and hens,
Pigs, horses, dairies, stores and cattle-pens
❶ Were wholly trusted to his government.
And he was under contract to present
The accounts, right from his master's earliest years.
No one had ever caught him in arrears.
No bailiff, serf or herdsman dared to kick,
He knew their dodges, knew their every trick;
Feared like the plague he was, by those beneath.
He had a lovely dwelling on a heath,
Shadowed in green by trees above the sward.[76]
A better hand at bargains than his lord,
He had grown rich and had a store of treasure
Well tucked away, yet out it came to pleasure
His lord with subtle loans or gifts of goods,
To earn his thanks and even coats and hoods.
When young he'd learnt a useful trade and still
He was a carpenter of first-rate skill.
The stallion-cob he rode at a slow trot
Was dapple-gray and bore the name of Scot.
He wore an overcoat of bluish shade
And rather long; he had a rusty blade
Slung at his side. He came, as I heard tell,
From Norfolk, near a place called Baldeswell.
His coat was tucked under his belt and splayed.
❷ He rode the hindmost of our cavalcade.
 There was a *Summoner* with us in the place
Who had a fire-red cherubinnish face,[77]
For he had carbuncles. His eyes were narrow,
He was as hot and lecherous as a sparrow.
Black, scabby brows he had, and a thin beard.
Children were afraid when he appeared.
❸ No quicksilver, lead ointments, tartar creams,
Boracic, no, nor brimstone, so it seems,
Could make a salve that had the power to bite,
Clean up or curve his whelks of knobby white.
Or purge the pimples sitting on his cheeks.
Garlic he loved, and onions too, and leeks,
And drinking strong wine till all was hazy.
Then he would shout and jabber as if crazy,
And wouldn't speak a word except in Latin
When he was drunk, such tags as he was pat in;
❹ He only had a few, say two or three,
That he had mugged up out of some decree;
❺ No wonder, for he heard them every day.
And, as you know, a man can teach a jay
To call out "Walter" better than the Pope.

75. **garners** *n.*: Buildings for storing grain.

76. **sward** *n.*: Turf.

77. **fire-red . . . face:** In the art of the Middle Ages, the faces of cherubs, or angels, were often painted red.

[4] But had you tried to test his wits and grope
[5] For more, you'd have found nothing in the bag.
Then *"Questio quid juris"*[78] was his tag.
He was a gentle varlet and a kind one,
No better fellow if you went to find one.
He would allow—just for a quart of wine—
Any good lad to keep a concubine
A twelvemonth and dispense it altogether!
Yet he could pluck a finch to leave no feather:
And if he found some rascal with a maid
He would instruct him not to be afraid
In such a case of the Archdeacon's curse
(Unless the rascal's soul were in his purse)
For in his purse the punishment should be.
"Purse is the good Archdeacon's Hell," said he.
But well I know he lied in what he said;
A curse should put a guilty man in dread,
For curses kill, as shriving brings, salvation.
[6] We should beware of excommunication.
Thus, as he pleased, the man could bring duress
On any young fellow in the diocese.
He knew their secrets, they did what he said.
He wore a garland set upon his head
Large as the holly-bush upon a stake
Outside an ale-house, and he had a cake,
A round one, which it was his joke to wield
As if it were intended for a shield.
He and a gentle *Pardoner* rode together,
[7] A bird from Charing Cross of the same feather,
Just back from visiting the Court of Rome.
He loudly sang *"Come hither, love, come home!"*
The Summoner sang deep seconds to this song,
No trumpet ever sounded half so strong.
This Pardoner had hair as yellow as wax,
Hanging down smoothly like a hank of flax.
In driblets fell his locks behind his head
Down to his shoulder which they overspread;
Thinly they fell, like rat-tails, one by one.
He wore no hood upon his head, for fun;
The hood inside his wallet had been stowed,
He aimed at riding in the latest mode;
But for a little cap his head was bare
And he had bulging eyeballs, like a hare.
He'd sewed a holy relic on his cap;
[8] His wallet lay before him on his lap,
Brimful of pardons come from Rome all hot.
He had the same small voice a goat has got.
His chin no beard had harbored, nor would harbor,
Smoother than ever chin was left by barber.
I judge he was a gelding, or a mare.
As to his trade, from Berwick down to Ware
There was no pardoner of equal grace,

78. ***"Questio quid juris"***: "The question is, What is the point of the law?" (Latin)

Customize for
More Advanced Learners

5 Have more advanced students review Chaucer's description of the Nun's ability to speak French (lines 128–130). Have them compare the Nun's ability with French to the Summoner's ability with Latin. What can they infer from this? *Possible answer: Because Chaucer was a well-traveled, multilingual diplomat, one of his pet peeves was people who pretended to know a foreign language and didn't.*

◆ Building Vocabulary

6 Suffixes: *-tion* Point out that the words *salvation* and *excommunication* have the *-tion* suffix. Ask students to identify these words' part of speech. *They are nouns.* From what verb was *excommunication* formed? *Excommunication was formed from the verb excommunicate.*

◆ Critical Thinking

7 Hypothesize Ask students: Based on these two lines, what type of person do you expect the Pardoner to be? *Since Chaucer refers to the Pardoner and the Summoner as birds of a feather, students will expect the Pardoner to be another disreputable cleric.*

◆ Background for Understanding

8 History Explain that according to church doctrine, even sins that have been forgiven merit punishment. This punishment could be pardoned through an indulgence earned by prayer or the adoration of relics. The pardons "from Rome all hot" were such indulgences.

Beyond the Classroom

Community Connection

Local Historic Site Point out that the pilgrims set out to visit the site of an important event in their religious and civic history. Perhaps there are places in your area that people come to visit because of a well-known event that occurred there. It does not have to be something that changed history. It might be something known primarily to people in the area.

Have students decide on such a place in your area and have them create a sign or similar marker to place on the site. The sign should summarize what happened and why it is significant.

Enrichment The physical description of the Pardoner would have suggested to the medieval reader familiar with the pseudoscience of physiognomy that the man was effeminate, deceptive, gluttonous, drunken, and treacherous.

Clarification Pardoners were sellers of papal indulgences. Some were laymen, many wholly unauthorized, and their tricks and abuses were condemned by Church authority. Chaucer's Pardoner seems to have taken at least minor orders.

▶Critical Viewing◀

❶ **Assess** Students may say that the picture matches Chaucer's description quite well. The pardoner has stringy blond hair, lacks a beard, and has relic or pilgrim's medal attached to his cap.

◆ Reading Strategy

❷ **Analyze Difficult Sentences** The Pardoner sells phony relics and pardons.

◆ Build Vocabulary

❸ **Suffixes: *-tion*** Point out that people who *congregate,* or come together, in church constitute a *congregation.* To tell a falsehood is to prevaricate; prevarication is the act of lying. In both cases, the suffix *-tion* is added to a verb to form the noun.

Customize for *More Advanced Students*

❹ These two lines can be understood in one of three ways: (1) as a literal statement of the narrator's belief in the Pardoner's nobility as a man of God; (2) as a sarcastic statement meant to suggest that the Pardoner is anything but a noble man of God; (3) as a criticism of the Church, which considers such a man to be an exemplary man of God. Challenge students to cite examples elsewhere in *The Prologue* to support their interpretation.

The Pardoner
Arthur Szyk for *The Canterbury Tales*

❶ ▶ **Critical Viewing** How well does this picture of the Pardoner match Chaucer's description of him in lines 695–710? **[Assess]**

For in his trunk he had a pillowcase
Which he asserted was Our Lady's veil.
He said he had a gobbet[79] of the sail
Saint Peter had the time when he made bold
To walk the waves, till Jesu Christ took hold.
He had a cross of metal set with stones
And, in a glass, a rubble of pigs' bones.
And with these relics, any time he found
Some poor up-country parson to astound,
On one short day, in money down, he drew
More than the parson in a month or two,
❸ And by his flatteries and <u>prevarication</u>
Made monkeys of the priest and <u>congregation</u>.
❹ But still to do him justice first and last
In church he was a noble ecclesiast.
How well he read a lesson or told a story!
But best of all he sang an Offertory,[80]
For well he knew that when that song was sung
He'd have to preach and tune his honey-tongue

79. gobbet: Piece.

◆ Reading Strategy How does the Pardoner get money (lines 712–726)? ❷

80. Offertory: Song that accompanies the collection of the offering at a church service.

Humanities: Art

The Pardoner, 1946, by Arthur Szyk.

The Pardoner's stringy yellow hair and wallet bulging with relics are straight out of Chaucer. The sanctimonious expression and gesture of forgiveness are from the imagination of Arthur Szyk. This miniature is finely detailed and painted in subtle, glowing colors. In discussing Szyk's miniatures with your students, you may wish to mention that the costumes portrayed are close in style to those actually worn in England in Chaucer's time.

Use these questions for discussion:

1. Does the Pardoner look trustworthy? *Some students may say he looks sneaky. Others may say that he looks like a respectable, highly religious person, which is why he is able to fool country parsons and their congregations.*
2. What is the effect of the cross he carries and the crosses on his wallet and satchel? *Some students may say it enhances the Pardoner's illusion of holiness. Other students may say that the number of religious symbols is suspiciously overdone.*

And (well he could) win silver from the crowd.
That's why he sang so merrily and loud.
Now I have told you shortly, in a clause,
❺ The rank, the array, the number and the cause
Of our assembly in this company
In Southwark, at that high-class hostelry
Known as *The Tabard*, close beside *The Bell*.
And now the time has come for me to tell
How we behaved that evening; I'll begin
After we had alighted at the inn,
Then I'll report our journey, stage by stage,
All the remainder of our pilgrimage.
But first I beg of you, in courtesy,
❻ Not to condemn me as unmannerly
If I speak plainly and with no concealings
And give account of all their words and dealings,
Using their very phrases as they fell.
For certainly, as you all know so well,
He who repeats a tale after a man
Is bound to say, as nearly as he can,
❼ Each single word, if he remembers it,
However rudely spoken or unfit,
Or else the tale he tells will be untrue,
The things invented and the phrases new.
He may not flinch although it were his brother,
If he says one word he must say the other.
And Christ Himself spoke broad[81] in Holy Writ,
And as you know there's nothing there unfit,
And Plato[82] says, for those with power to read,
"The word should be as cousin to the deed."
Further I beg you to forgive it me
If I neglect the order and degree
And what is due to rank in what I've planned.
I'm short of wit as you will understand.
Our *Host* gave us great welcome; everyone
❽ Was given a place and supper was begun.
He served the finest victuals you could think,
The wine was strong and we were glad to drink.
A very striking man our Host withal,
And fit to be a marshal in a hall.
His eyes were bright, his girth a little wide;
There is no finer burgess in Cheapside.[83]
Bold in his speech, yet wise and full of tact,
There was no manly attribute he lacked,
What's more he was a merry-hearted man.
After our meal he jokingly began
To talk of sport, and, among other things
After we'd settled up our reckonings,
He said as follows: "Truly, gentlemen,
You're very welcome and I can't think when
—Upon my word I'm telling you no lie—
I've seen a gathering here that looked so spry,

81. broad: Bluntly.

82. Plato: Greek philosopher (427?–347? B.C.)

83. Cheapside: District in London.

◆ Build Vocabulary

prevarication (pri var′ i kā′ shən) *n.*: Evasion of truth

◆ Critical Thinking

❺ **Draw Conclusions** Ask students whether they think the narrator has accomplished his original intentions in describing the pilgrims. *Most students will feel that Chaucer has amply described the pilgrims.* Ask students what classes of society the narrator criticizes, and why. What classes does he seem to favor? *The narrator is highly critical of religious personnel who are not living up to the standards of their callings. He also does not have a high opinion of tradespeople and professionals because they are social-climbing or engage in shady practices. The narrator seems to favor peasants such as the Plowman, scholars such as the Oxford Cleric, and nobles such as the Knight.*

Comprehension Check ☑

❻ What does Chaucer ask of his readers in these lines? *He asks that they not think ill of him if he reports matters frankly, without euphemisms.*

◆ Reading Strategy

❼ **Analyze Difficult Sentences** This lengthy sentence contains several parenthetical clauses and phrases, which if removed make the meaning more accessible. Have students restate the sentence so that only the central meaning remains. *Suggested response: He who repeats a tale must repeat every word or else the tale is fiction.*

Customize for *Logical/Mathematical Learners*

❽ Ask students to imagine themselves as the Host. How would they arrange the pilgrims at a dinner table? Ask students to recall what they know about each of the pilgrims. Which ones would they avoid placing next to one another? Which would enjoy one another's company? Instruct students to draw the outline of a table on a piece of paper and fill in the seating arrangement they would propose.

Speaking and Listening Mini-Lesson

Monologue

This mini-lesson supports the Speaking and Listening activity in the Idea Bank on page 110.

Introduce the Concept Explain that a monologue is a speech given entirely by one person or one character. A monologue often reveals the speaker's thoughts and attitudes indirectly or unintentionally.

Develop Background Before students begin writing their scripts, have them list the qualities of the character they wish to reveal. Then have them list one direct and one indirect way of conveying that characteristic to the listeners.

Apply the Information Have students use their lists to develop and deliver a monologue by one of the characters in *The Canterbury Tales*. Remind students to include as much detail about the character as possible into the script.

Assess the Outcome Criteria include:

- Could the audience identify the character without being told who it was supposed to be?
- Were the character's words consistent with his or her personality as described by Chaucer?
- Did the performer speak clearly and with feeling?
- Did the performer use gestures, facial expressions and vocal effects to convey or emphasize meaning?

◆ Literary Focus

❶ **Characterization** What a person says indirectly reveals something of his character. Ask students: What can you conclude about he Host's character from what he says to his guests? Does he feel at ease with strangers? Do you think he was a successful innkeeper? *Students may say that the Host is a successful innkeeper—he is friendly, comfortable with strangers, creative, and good at making people feel comfortable.*

◆ *Literature and Your Life*

❷ Students may mention games involving license plates or being the first to spot a target object, such as a car wash, cow, or purple car. They may mention singing rounds or songs with vast numbers of verses.

Customize for *Less Proficient Readers*

❸ Have students study these lines to determine the exact terms of the Host's proposal. Check their comprehension with questions like the following: How many tales is each pilgrim to tell during the course of the trip to Canterbury and back? *Each person is to tell four stories.* What two criteria will be used to determine the best story? *The two criteria are the morality of the story and the pleasure it gives.* What prize does the winner receive? *The prize is dinner at the Tabard Inn.* How is the prize to be purchased? *The other travelers and the host must pay for it.* Who is to be the judge? *The Host will be the judge.*

No, not this year, as in this tavern now.
I'd think you up some fun if I knew how.
And, as it happens, a thought has just occurred
And it will cost you nothing, on my word.
You're off to Canterbury—well, God speed!
❶ Blessed St. Thomas answer to your need!
And I don't doubt, before the journey's done
You mean to while the time in tales and fun.
Indeed, there's little pleasure for your bones
Riding along and all as dumb as stones.
So let me then propose for your enjoyment,
Just as I said, a suitable employment.
And if my notion suits and you agree
And promise to submit yourselves to me
Playing your parts exactly as I say
Tomorrow as you ride along the way,
Then by my father's soul (and he is dead)
If you don't like it you can have my head!
Hold up your hands, and not another word."
    Well, our consent of course was not deferred,
It seemed not worth a serious debate;
We all agreed to it at any rate
And bade him issue what commands he would.
"My lords," he said, "now listen for your good,
And please don't treat my notion with disdain.
This is the point. I'll make it short and plain.
Each one of you shall help to make things slip
By telling two stories on the outward trip
To Canterbury, that's what I intend,
And, on the homeward way to journey's end
Another two, tales from the days of old;
And then the man whose story is best told,
That is to say who gives the fullest measure
❸ Of good morality and general pleasure,
He shall be given a supper, paid by all,
Here in this tavern, in this very hall,
When we come back again from Canterbury.
And in the hope to keep you bright and merry
I'll go along with you myself and ride
All at my own expense and serve as guide.
I'll be the judge, and those who won't obey
Shall pay for what we spend upon the way.
Now if you all agree to what you've heard
Tell me at once without another word,
And I will make arrangements early for it."
    Of course we all agreed, in fact we swore it
Delightedly, and made entreaty too
That he should act as he proposed to do,
Become our Governor in short, and be
Judge of our tales and general referee,
And set the supper at a certain price.
We promised to be ruled by his advice

◆ *Literature and Your Life*

When traveling with friends or family, what games do you play? What songs do you sing? ❷

Beyond the Selection

FURTHER READING

Other Works by Geoffrey Chaucer

Book of the Duchess
House of Fame
Troilus and Criseyde

Works About Chaucer

Chaucer in His Time, Derek Brewer
The Life and Times of Chaucer, J. C. Gardner
The Mind and Art of Chaucer, J. S. Tatlock

We suggest that you preview these works before recommending them to students.

INTERNET

You and your students may find additional information about Chaucer on the Internet. We suggest the following sites. Please be aware, however, that sites may have changed from the time we published this information.

For the complete text in original language, go to **http://www. webgroup.com/mrslong/chaucer.htm**

For images of manuscript, art, maps, and photos related to Chaucer, see **http://lummi.stanford.edu/Media2/ASD/ASd_Homepage/electchaucer.htm**

We *strongly recommend* that you preview the sites before you send students to them.

Come high, come low; unanimously thus
We set him up in judgment over us.
More wine was fetched, the business being done;
We drank it off and up went everyone
To bed without a moment of delay.
   Early next morning at the spring of day
Up rose our Host and roused us like a cock,
Gathering us together in a flock,
And off we rode at slightly faster pace
Than walking to St. Thomas' watering-place;[84]
And there our Host drew up, began to ease
His horse, and said, "Now, listen if you please,
My lords! Remember what you promised me.
If evensong and matins will agree[85]
Let's see who shall be first to tell a tale.
And as I hope to drink good wine and ale
I'll be your judge. The rebel who disobeys,
However much the journey costs, he pays.
Now draw for cut[86] and then we can depart;
The man who draws the shortest cut shall start."

84. St. Thomas' watering-place: A brook two miles from the inn.

85. If evensong . . . agree: If what you said last night holds true this morning.

86. draw for cut: Draw lots, as when pulling straws from a bunch; the person who pulls the short straw is "it."

Guide for Responding

◆ *Literature and Your Life*

Reader's Response Which pilgrim would you most like to meet? Why?

Thematic Focus What modern character types can you match up with the characters in the Prologue? What types would Chaucer not have anticipated?

Casting Call With a small group, discuss several of Chaucer's pilgrims and their personalities. Imagine that you are making a film of the *Tales*. Come up with casting ideas for each of the characters.

☑ Check Your Comprehension

1. What does Chaucer say that people long to do when spring comes?
2. (a) Where does the Prologue take place? (b) Why have people gathered at this place?
3. Briefly describe four of Chaucer's pilgrims.
4. What entertainment does the host propose for the journey?

◆ Critical Thinking

INTERPRET

1. Chaucer pokes gentle fun at some of the pilgrims. What is his opinion of the Nun's singing voice and of her French? **[Deduce]**
2. What are some of the ways in which two of the religious men—the Friar and the Parson—differ?
3. What does Chaucer seem to dislike about (a) the Skipper? (b) the Doctor? **[Infer]**
4. Judging from his pilgrims, do you think Chaucer believes people are basically good? Support your answer with details from the description of three pilgrims. **[Draw Conclusions]**

APPLY

5. If Chaucer were writing *The Canterbury Tales* today, what three kinds of pilgrims might he consider adding to the group? **[Hypothesize]**

EXTEND

6. Most of Chaucer's characters are named after a profession. What does Chaucer's emphasis on social roles suggest to you about medieval society? **[Social Studies Link]**

Reinforce and Extend

Answers

◆ *Literature and Your Life*

Reader's Response Students may want to meet the knight or the Wife of Bath because they have traveled a great deal and have a lot of experiences to share.

Thematic Focus Students should support their opinions with logical reasons. Some character types that Chaucer might not have anticipated might include the technogeek, the movie- or rock-star wannabe, the corporate raider, or the animal-rights activist. Many answers are possible.

☑ Check Your Comprehension

1. They "long to go on pilgrimages."
2. (a) The Prologue takes place at the Tabard, an inn on the route to Canterbury. (b) People have gathered here on their way to the holy shrine at Canterbury. They have stopped at the Tabard for the night.
3. Check student responses for accuracy. Sample response: The Knight is a brave, well-mannered, and honorable soldier. The Prioress is sentimental and pretentious. The Friar is a slick ladies' man and flatterer. The Parson is a humble, pious man, dedicated to his parishioners.
4. The host proposes that each pilgrim tell two tales going and two more on the return. The teller of the best tale shall receive a free dinner.

◆ Critical Thinking

1. Her voice is too nasal. Her French would be incomprehensible to a Parisian.
2. The Friar does not take his religious vows seriously; he prefers worldly pleasures and catering to the wealthy. The Parson is all that a good priest should be.
3. (a) Chaucer dislikes the Skipper because he disregards the rules of conscience—stealing wine and forcing prisoners to walk the plank. (b) The Doctor cares more about gold than about his patients; he and his apothecaries worked together selling drugs at inflated prices. He does not read the Bible.
4. Students' choice of details should support their answers. Chaucer applauds the goodness of the Parson and is scandalized by the Friar's and Summoner's corruptness. Though Chaucer exposes folly and vice in many of the pilgrims, he seems to accept imperfection as part of humanity's fate.
5. Additional pilgrims might include a politician, a sales representative, a mechanic, a computer programmer, a crime boss, or a movie actor. Other answers are possible.
6. In medieval society, people may have been comfortably defined by their profession or social role. Chaucer's pilgrims do not seem the type to ask modern questions such as "Who am I?" and "Who do I want to be?"

Reinforce and Extend

Answers

◆ Reading Strategy

1. A Knight is being described.
2. He rode to battle.
3. He did it during his sovereign's war and at other times.
4. He went to battle in both Christian and heathen places.

◆ Literary Focus

1. The Doctor cares more about gold than about his patients (direct); he and his apothecaries worked together selling drugs at inflated prices (indirect). He does not read the Bible (indirect).
2. Possible responses: (a) Characterizing the Plowman as "an honest worker, good and true" is an instance of direct statement. Characterizing the Reeve as "old and choleric and thin" is an example of the use of physical appearance. Explaining that the Nun "used to weep if she but saw a mouse/ Caught in a trap" is an instance of the use of action. (b) The Reeve's appearance shows that he is shrewd and tough. The Nun's action shows she is foolishly tenderhearted or sentimental.

◆ Build Vocabulary

Using the Suffix *-tion*

1. Narration is the product of the act of narrating; it is a story.
2. Accumulation is the result of the act of accumulating; it is an amount gathered.
3. Elevation is the result of the act of elevating, or lifting up; it is a high place.
4. Oration is the product of orating, or speaking formally; it is a speech.

Using the Word Bank

1. e 2. f 3. d 4. a 5. b 6. c 7. g

◆ Grammar and Style

1. met, had stayed; 2. tricked, had told; 3. made, had earned

Writer's Solution

For additional instruction and practice, use the lesson on Correct and Efficient Use of Verbs in the **Language Lab CD-ROM** and the page on Sequence of Tenses in the *Writer's Solution Grammar Practice Book,* p. 54.

Guide for Responding *(continued)*

◆ Reading Strategy

ANALYZE DIFFICULT SENTENCES

Asking questions like *who, what, when, where, why,* and *how* as you read can help you **analyze difficult sentences.** For example, look again at lines 47–50.

1. *Who* is being described?
2. *What* did this person do?
3. *When* did he do it?
4. *Where* did he do it?

◆ Literary Focus

CHARACTERIZATION

In creating vivid portraits of his pilgrims, Chaucer uses both **direct characterization**—describing their personalities directly—and **indirect characterization**—revealing their personalities by describing their appearance, thoughts, or actions. In your notebook, answer the following:

1. Give three details that Chaucer uses to characterize the Doctor. For each detail, note whether the characterization is direct or indirect.
2. (a) Give one example of each of the following kinds of details in Chaucer's characterizations: direct statement, physical appearance, and action. (b) Explain how your examples of physical appearance and action indirectly characterize the pilgrim concerned.

◆ Build Vocabulary

USING THE SUFFIX *-tion*

Using your knowledge that a word ending in the suffix *-tion* refers to an action or process and its result, define these words in your notebook:

1. narration
2. accumulation
3. elevation
4. oration

USING THE WORD BANK

Match each numbered vocabulary word with its lettered synonym.

1. solicitous	**a.** asserts
2. garnished	**b.** authorization
3. sanguine	**c.** freeing from sin
4. avouches	**d.** confident
5. commission	**e.** caring
6. absolution	**f.** decorated
7. prevarication	**g.** lying

◆ Grammar and Style

PAST AND PAST PERFECT TENSES

Chaucer's use of the **past and past perfect tenses** makes clear to readers which events happened earlier than others.

Writing Application Rewrite these sentences, putting one of the verbs in the past tense and one in the past perfect tense to show a sequence of events.

1. The narrator of the Prologue *meets* the pilgrims the next morning. He *stays* the night at the Tabard Inn.
2. The Pardoner *tricks* a parson into buying a relic. He *tells* him it was part of Saint Peter's sail.
3. The Sergeant at Arms *makes* a success at law. His learning *earns* him many important positions.

Idea Bank

Writing

1. Modern Types Chaucer's Prologue is full of rich characterizations. Write a brief description of a character from the modern world.

2. Comparison and Contrast Chaucer's Prologue contains three figures involved in religion—a friar, a monk, and a nun. Write a paper in which you compare and contrast their characters.

3. Response to Criticism The poet John Dryden referred to Chaucer as the "father of English poetry." Using examples from the Prologue, show why Chaucer deserves this title.

Speaking and Listening

4. Monologue Write a monologue in which you capture the character of one of Chaucer's pilgrims. Then present your monologue to the class. **[Performing Arts Link]**

Project

5. Portraits of the Pilgrims Use Chaucer's verbal portrait of a pilgrim to paint, draw, or sculpt this character. **[Art Link]**

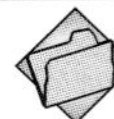

Idea Bank

Customizing for
Performance Levels

Less Advanced Students: 1, 5
Average Students: 2, 4
More Advanced Students: 3

Customizing for
Learning Modalities

Following are suggestions for matching Idea Bank topics with your students' learning modalities:
Visual/Spatial: 5
Verbal/Linguistic: 1, 2, 3, 4

✓ ASSESSMENT OPTIONS

Formal Assessment, Selection Test, pp. 20–22
Alternative Assessment, p. 4, includes options for less advanced students, more advanced students, musical/rhythmic learners, verbal/linguistic learners, and interpersonal learners.

PORTFOLIO ASSESSMENT

Use the following rubrics in the ***Alternative Assessment*** booklet to assess student writing:
Modern Types: Description, p. 98
Comparison and Contrast:
Comparison/Contrast, p. 104
Response to Criticism: Literary Analysis, p. 113

The Nun's Priest's Tale

◆ Review and Anticipate

Each pilgrim from the Prologue agrees to tell a tale on the way to Canterbury. It's of interest that the teller of this tale, the Nun's Priest, is mentioned in the Prologue but not fully described. He reappears suddenly when the Host spots him at a crucial moment: The Knight has objected to the Monk's tragic tale, and it looks as if the storytelling game might end in bitterness.

The Nun's Priest is asked to save the game with a merry tale. Here's a brief description of the new storyteller: He's riding a "jade," an old, filthy cart-horse. Yet he vows to be "merry," and Chaucer describes him as both "sweet" and "goodly."

See if you can use this scanty description to predict the kind of story this character will tell. Then review your prediction when you've finished reading and see whether you were on target.

◆ Build Vocabulary

Word Roots: *-cap-*

In "The Nun's Priest's Tale," Chaucer writes of the widow: "Little she had in capital or rent." *Capital* is formed on the Latin root *-cap-*, from *caput,* meaning "a head," and it refers to money or property that is the chief part of a person's fortune.

Word Bank

Before you read, preview this list of words from "The Nun's Priest's Tale."

capital
timorous
derision
maxim
stringent
cant

◆ Grammar and Style

Pronoun Case

Most personal pronouns have different subject and object forms, or **cases,** which reflect how they are used in a sentence.

Subjective Case Pronouns: *I, he, she, we, they, who*

The subjective case is used for subjects and subject complements.

subject
She had a yard that was enclosed about . . .

Objective Case Pronouns: *me, him, her, us, them, whom*

The objective is used for direct and indirect objects and objects of prepositions.

direct object
. . . apoplexy struck *her* not . . .

◆ Literary Focus

Mock-Heroic Style

In the **mock-heroic style,** a writer uses a style of language usually used for describing heroes in order to describe ordinary characters. This results in a hilarious disparity between content and style.

In "The Nun's Priest's Tale," Chaucer uses heroic language to retell a popular tale about a charming rooster, Chanticleer, and a fox. By mismatching these noble words with barnyard doings, he shows the silly side of heroic tales and of the serious words that he loves. In the end, his affection for his characters rules the day, and Chanticleer triumphs by words alone.

◆ Reading Strategy

Context Clues

When you encounter an unfamiliar word as you read, use **context clues** from the surrounding passage to determine its meaning. Such clues may include synonyms or antonyms of the new word, or examples that clarify its meaning.

In line 14, a phrase may be unfamiliar to you: "There was no *sauce piquante* to spice her veal." You can deduce that if "spice" is similar in meaning to *sauce piquante,* then the phrase must mean "a spicy or sharp-tasting sauce."

Objectives

1. To read, comprehend, and interpret a mock-heroic narrative poem
2. To relate the poem to personal experience
3. To use context clues to determine the meaning of unfamiliar words
4. To recognize the mock-heroic style
5. To build vocabulary in context and learn the word root *-cap-*
6. To distinguish between and correctly use case forms of pronouns
7. To use exaggeration in writing a script for an animated fable
8. To respond to the poem through writing, speaking and listening, and projects

Skills Instruction

Vocabulary: Word Roots: *-cap-*

Grammar and Style: Pronoun Case

Reading Strategy: Context Clues

Literary Focus: Mock-Heroic Style

Writing: Exaggeration

Speaking and Listening: Oral Interpretation of a Debate

Critical Viewing: Speculate; Classify; Interpret; Support; Deduce

Portfolio Opportunities

Writing: Animals as Symbols; Modern Beast Fable; Critical Response

Writing Mini-Lesson: Script for an Animated Fable

Speaking and Listening: Oral Interpretation of a Debate; Mock-Heroic Scene

Projects: Mock-Heroic Comic Book; Pilgrim's Path

Interest Grabber Recruit two actors in your class to play the roles of someone who believes in dreams and someone who doesn't. Ask how many people had a dream last night. Ask Conspirator 1 to describe his dream and what it means. Then ask whether students agree. Call on Conspirator 2, who will argue that dreams don't mean anything. Allow other students to enter the discussion of whether or not dreams can come true.

Tell students that the nun's priest's story begins when the hero has a nightmare. His wife thinks it's indigestion; he thinks it is a warning.

Prentice Hall Literature Program Resources

REINFORCE / RETEACH / EXTEND

Selection Support pages
Build Vocabulary: Word Roots: *-cap-*, p. 22
Grammar and Style: Pronoun Case, p. 23
Reading Strategy: Context Clues, p. 24
Literary Focus: Mock-Heroic Style, p. 25

Strategies for Diverse Student Needs, p. 5

Beyond Literature
Humanities Connection: Details of Daily Life, p. 5

Formal Assessment Selection Test, pp. 23–25; Assessment Resources Software

Alternative Assessment, p. 5

Art Transparencies
Art Transparency 3, p. 15

Writing and Language Transparencies
Dramatic Scene, pp. 25–34
Story Map, p. 127

Listening to Literature Audiocassettes
from *The Canterbury Tales: The Nun's Priest's Tale*

Develop Understanding

One-Minute Insight With the same adeptness employed in "The Prologue," Chaucer holds a magnifying glass up to human nature and lets his readers enjoy the imperfections they see. In the case of Chanticleer, we see a self-important, proud rooster brought low by false flattery. In this tale, amusement and instruction are inextricably combined.

Customize for
Less Proficient Readers
To help less proficient students, have them follow along in the text as they listen to the selection or portions of the selection. At the conclusion of each paragraph, turn off the recording and have them write a brief summary. Review the summaries and fill in any missing elements.

Customize for
English Language Learners
The vocabulary in "The Nun's Priest's Tale" may present a challenge to these students. Guide them in using context clues to determine the meanings of unfamiliar words, which may include *dale, sooty, melancholy, disquiet, gout,* and so on.

◆ Build Vocabulary

❶ **Word Roots: *-cap-*** Point out that the word *capital* has two meanings. In line 7 of "The Nun's Priest's Tale" it means "one's wealth in money." *Capital* can also mean the city or town that is the seat of government.

◆ Critical Thinking

❷ **Interpret** Ask students: What does the author mean by this seemingly unrelated line? *It means that she made do with what she had.*

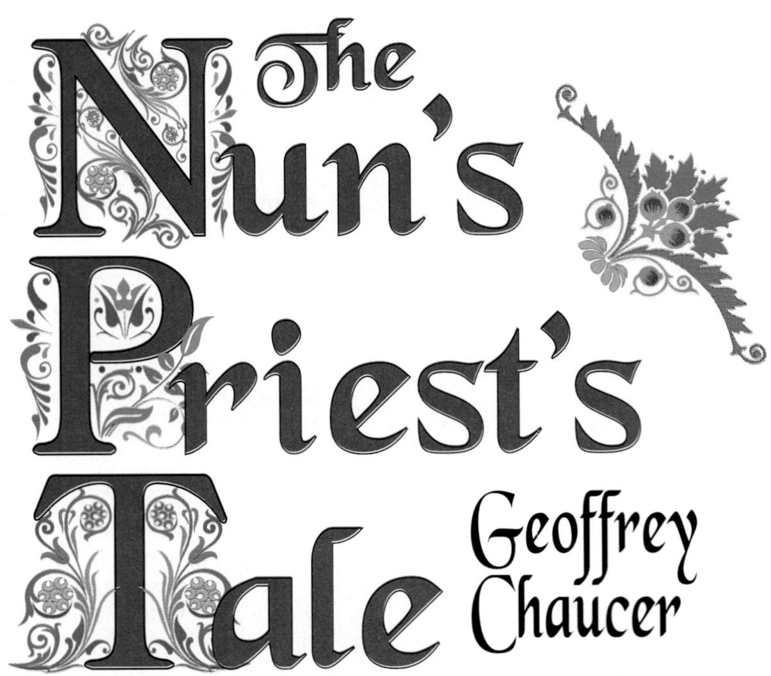

Translated by Nevill Coghill

Once, long ago, there dwelt a poor old widow
In a small cottage, by a little meadow
Beside a grove and standing in a dale.
This widow-woman of whom I tell my tale
Since the sad day when last she was a wife
Had led a very patient, simple life.
❶ Little she had in capital or rent,
But still, by making do with what God sent,
She kept herself and her two daughters going.
Three hefty sows—no more—were all her showing,
Three cows as well; there was a sheep called Molly.
  Sooty her hall, her kitchen melancholy,
And there she ate full many a slender meal;
There was no *sauce piquante*[1] to spice her veal,
No dainty morsel ever passed her throat,
❷ According to her cloth she cut her coat.
Repletion[2] never left her in disquiet
And all her physic was a temperate diet,
Hard work for exercise and heart's content.

1. ***sauce piquante*** (pē´ kәnt): French for a pleasantly sharp sauce, used for fancy and expensive meals.
2. **Repletion** (ri plē´ shәn) *n.*: The state of having eaten too much.

◆ Build Vocabulary

capital (kap´әt 'l) *n.*: Wealth in money or property

Preparing for Standardized Tests

Reading and Vocabulary The use of context clues is an important strategy for improving performance on reading-comprehension items on standardized tests. Similarly, the Build Vocabulary lesson with its focus on the *-cap-* root provides an additional method for unlocking the meaning of unfamiliar words. Have students complete the Reading Strategy and Build Vocabulary exercises on page 128. For additional practice, use ***Selection Support,*** pp. 22 and 24.

Grammar and Language Items on standardized tests may ask students to choose among different ways of correcting a sentence. Choosing the correct answer may depend on a knowledge of pronoun case, as in the following:

Me and her gave them the gift. *(C)*
(A) Me and her gave them
(B) Her and I gave they
(C) She and I gave them
(D) Me and she gave them

For additional practice, use the Grammar and Style exercises on page 128 and the Build Grammar Skills page in ***Selection Support,*** p. 23.

And rich man's gout did nothing to prevent
Her dancing, apoplexy[3] struck her not;
She drank no wine, nor white nor red had got.
Her board was mostly served with white and black,
Milk and brown bread, in which she found no lack;
Broiled bacon or an egg or two were common,
She was in fact a sort of dairy-woman.
She had a yard that was enclosed about
By a stockade and a dry ditch without,
In which she kept a cock called Chanticleer.
❸ In all the land for crowing he'd no peer;
His voice was jollier than the organ blowing
In church on Sundays, he was great at crowing.
Far, far more regular than any clock
Or abbey bell the crowing of this cock.
The equinoctial wheel and its position[4]
At each ascent he knew by intuition;
At every hour—fifteen degrees of movement—
He crowed so well there could be no improvement.
His comb was redder than fine coral, tall
And battlemented like a castle wall,
❹ His bill was black and shone as bright as jet,
Like azure were his legs and they were set
On azure toes with nails of lily white,
Like burnished gold his feathers, flaming bright.
This gentlecock was master in some measure
Of seven hens, all there to do his pleasure.
They were his sisters and his paramours,
Colored like him in all particulars;
She with the loveliest dyes upon her throat
Was known as gracious Lady Pertelote.
Courteous she was, discreet and debonair,
Companionable too, and took such care
In her deportment, since she was seven days old
❺ She held the heart of Chanticleer controlled,
Locked up securely in her every limb;
O such happiness his love to him!
And such a joy it was to hear them sing,
As when the glorious sun began to spring,
In sweet accord *My love is far from land*[5]
—For in those far off days I understand
All birds and animals could speak and sing.
Now it befell, as dawn began to spring,
When Chanticleer and Pertelote and all
His wives were perched in this poor widow's hall
(Fair Pertelote was next him on the perch),
This Chanticleer began to groan and lurch
Like someone sorely troubled by a dream,
And Pertelote who heard him roar and scream
Was quite aghast and said, "O dearest heart,
What's ailing you? Why do you groan and start?
Fie, what a sleeper! What a noise to make!"

3. apoplexy: Old-fashioned term for a stroke.

4. equinoctial . . . position: Chaucer and his contemporaries accounted for changes in the positions of stars and planets by imagining that the heavens circled the Earth once a day, moving fifteen degrees each hour.

5. *My love is far from land:* Refrain of a popular song.

◆ **Reading Strategy** What context clues might help you figure out the meaning of *aghast* in line 69? ❻

◆ Grammar and Style

❸ **Pronoun Case** Have students identify the subjective-case pronouns in these lines. *The pronouns are she (lines 27 and 29) and he (lines 30 and 32).* Have students explain why the subjective case is required in these sentences. *Each one is the subject of a sentence.* Be sure students note that two pronouns are masculine and two are feminine.

Customize for *Visual/Spatial Learners*

❹ Encourage these students to find examples of the colors mentioned in this description. More artistic students may enjoy drawing or painting a picture of Chanticleer using these colors. Point out that bright, rich colors—gold, red, black, and azure—are commonly associated with royalty.

◆ Literary Focus

❺ **Mock-Heroic Style** Point out that lines 49–59 are characteristic of the mock-heroic style. Ask students to identify the details in this description that help create this style. *A grand, lofty, tongue-in-cheek tone is created by the overstatement of Pertelote's appearance and manner and the fact that she is referred to as Lady Pertelote. The description of the two chickens singing together pokes fun at similar passages in serious heroic tales.*

◆ Reading Strategy

❻ **Context Clues** Students may say that context clues that reveal the meaning of *aghast* include Pertelote's expected reaction to Chanticleer's screams and her words of surprise and alarm in lines 70 and 71. The context suggests that aghast means "shocked" or "amazed."

Block Scheduling Strategies

Consider these suggestions to take advantage of extended class time:

- Although being able to use context clues is an important skill for all students, it is particularly vital for English language learners and less proficient readers. Ask students to generate a list of words in the selection that they don't know or that they think others will find difficult. Select suitable words from this list and have students deduce the meaning of the words from their context. Use the Reading Strategy page in ***Selection Support,*** p. 24, for additional practice.
- Encourage students to prepare the role playing activity described in Literature and Your Life (p. 127) for presentation to the class.
- Instruct students to work individually or in pairs to answer the Check Your Comprehension and Critical Thinking questions on page 127.
- Allow students to conduct peer-review conferences on their drafts for the writing activities in the Idea Bank (p. 129), the reports in ***Alternative Assessment*** (p. 5), and the Writing Mini-Lesson (p. 129).
- Display the illustration for the month of March from *Tres Riches Heures du Duc du Berry,* in ***Art Transparencies,*** p. 15. Use the transparency as the basis for a free-writing exercise or for a research report, as described in ***Art Transparencies,*** p. 18.

►Critical Viewing◄

❶ Speculate Some students may say that the pilgrims look too serious to enjoy a mock-heroic fable. Other students may think that the pilgrims would react favorably to the tale because it teaches a moral lesson.

Enrichment Seventeenth-century poet and dramatist John Dryden called Chaucer the "father of English poetry," a ranking still considered valid today. Dryden held Chaucer in the "same degree of veneration as the Grecians held Homer or the Romans held Virgil," and found in his work "a perpetual fountain of good sense." Writing about a hundred years later, poet and essayist Samuel Taylor Coleridge found:

> unceasing delight in Chaucer. His cheerfulness is especially delicious to me in my old age. How exquisitely tender he is, and yet how perfectly free from the least touch of sickly melancholy or morbid drooping. The sympathy of the poet with the subjects of his poetry is particularly remarkable in Shakespeare and Chaucer; but what Shakespeare effects by a strong act of imagination and mental changing, Chaucer does without any effort, merely by the inborn kindly joyousness of his nature. How well we seem to know Chaucer! How absolutely nothing do we know of Shakespeare!

English Travelers Setting Forth, From *The Canterbury Tales*, The British Library

❶ ▲ **Critical Viewing** How do you think these pilgrims would have reacted to "The Nun's Priest's Tale"? **[Speculate]**

Humanities: Art

English Travelers Setting Forth, from *The Canterbury Tales.*

This miniature painting, from an edition of *The Canterbury Tales,* reveals many details of medieval life. The pilgrims ride by a walled city with a cathedral at the center. A large manor house stands at the left. The roadway is unpaved and filled with mud, and the pilgrims wear hooded cloaks and heavy hats. They travel in a group for protection.

The artist has also captured the sense of intimacy and friendship that developed on long pilgrimages. The man in the center, leaning toward the red-hatted man, might be telling a story. He is one of Chaucer's characters, probably the monk whose "bridle jingled in the whistling wind."

By the time this painting was made, the simple decorative style of Chaucer's day had been replaced by a more detailed, realistic technique. Note the careful attention to architecture, landscape, and clothing.

Use the following questions for discussion:

1. What does this picture suggest about medieval life? *Students may suggest that life was more difficult than it is today, but that people have not really changed in essential ways.*
2. Why do you think storytelling was such a popular recreation for pilgrims stopping at inns? *They had few other forms of entertainment available.*

"Madam," he said, "I beg you not to take
Offense, but by the Lord I had a dream
So terrible just now I had to scream;
I still can feel my heart racing from fear.
God turn my dream to good and guard all here.
And keep my body out of durance vile![6]
I dreamt that roaming up and down a while
Within our yard I saw a kind of beast,
A sort of hound that tried or seemed at least
(2) To try and seize me. . . would have killed me dead!
His color was a blend of yellow and red,
His ears and tail were tipped with sable fur
Unlike the rest; he was a russet cur.
Small was his snout, his eyes were glowing bright.
It was enough to make one die of fright.
That was no doubt what made me groan and swoon."
"For shame," she said, "you timorous poltroon![7]
Alas, what cowardice! By God above,
You've forfeited my heart and lost my love.
I cannot love a coward, come what may.
For certainly, whatever we may say,
All women long—and O that it might be!—
For husbands tough, dependable and free,
Secret, discreet, no niggard,[8] not a fool
That boasts and then will find his courage cool
(4) At every trifling thing. By God above,
How dare you say for shame, and to your love,
That anything at all was to be feared?
Have you no manly heart to match your beard?
And can a dream reduce you to such terror?
Dreams are a vanity, God knows, pure error.
Dreams are engendered in the too-replete
From vapors in the belly, which compete
With others, too abundant, swollen tight.
"No doubt the redness in your dream tonight
Comes from the superfluity and force
Of the red choler in your blood. Of course.
That is what puts a dreamer in the dread
Of crimsoned arrows, fires flaming red,
Of great red monsters making as to fight him,
And big red whelps and little ones to bite him;
Just so the black and melancholy vapors
Will set a sleeper shrieking, cutting capers
And swearing that black bears, black bulls as well,
Or blackest fiends are haling him to Hell.
And there are other vapors that I know
That on a sleeping man will work their woe,
But I'll pass on as lightly as I can.
(5) "Take Cato[9] now, that was so wise a man,
Did he not say, 'Take no account of dreams'?
Now, sir," she said, "on flying from these beams,
For love of God do take some laxative;

6. **durance vile:** Long imprisonment.

◆ **Literary Focus**
How does Pertelote's reaction (lines 88–105) lend comedy to this passage? (3)

7. **poltroon** (päl trōōn′) *n.*: Coward.

8. **niggard:** Stingy person.

9. **Cato:** Dionysius Cato, supposed author of a book of maxims used in elementary education.

◆ **Build Vocabulary**
timorous (tim′ ər əs) *adj.*: Timid

◆ Literature and Your Life

2 Ask students if they think that men are still expected to feel no fear. Are men considered to be cowards if they admit to being afraid? Have students explain why this notion persists or why it has changed. *Some students will assert that men still cannot admit to being afraid; that's just the way our culture is and has been. Other students will say that people are now expected to be aware of and express their feelings, so it's acceptable for a man to admit to being afraid.*

◆ Literary Focus

3 Mock-Heroic Style Pertelote overreacts to Chanticleer's explanation, claiming it has destroyed her love for him. Her reaction is comedic because it is completely out of proportion. It also is funny because it comes shortly after an equally exaggerated description of their perfect love for each other.

◆ Critical Thinking

4 Compare and Contrast Ask students: What does Pertelote claim is the measure of a husband's manliness? *Manliness is equated with courage, toughness, and a complete lack of fear.* Compare and contrast Pertelote's attitude to attitudes toward manliness today. *Generally speaking, normal human feelings of fear and tenderness are more tolerated in men today.*

5 Clarification In scholarly debates of the time, it was common to cite ancient philosophers as support for an argument.

Cultural Connection

Dreams

"The Nun's Priest's Tale" revolves around a dream. Tell students that dreams are regarded as oracles in many cultures. A dream lies engraved between the paws of the Great Sphinx at Al Jizah. The Hurons believe that the soul makes its desires known in dreams and that to ignore dreams is to court illness or death.

Encourage students to find out how dreams are interpreted in different cultures. Are dreams regarded as a source of religious knowledge or psychological truth? Are they regarded, as Pertelote suggests in line 104, as simply a product of digestive upset or a symptom of illness?

Customize for
More Advanced Students

Much of the humor in "The Nun's Priest's Tale" is derived from the fact that the reader tends to forget that the principal characters are a rooster and a hen. Details that remind readers that the characters are chickens, such as when Pertelote recommends a diet of worms in line 141, are surprising and funny. Have students identify and record such startling lines.

◆ Reading Strategy

❶ **Context Clues** Pertelote uses the word *purge* in lines 126, 133, and 144. Have students study the contexts in which this word appears and write a definition for the word. *Definitions should suggest removing or cleaning impurities of some kind.*

❷ **Enrichment** Point out that the theory of humors as the cause of illness already existed centuries before Chaucer, but that the use of the word *humor* in line 137 is its first appearance in English. Another word that appears in English for the first time is also found in a work by Chaucer: *Tragedy* appears in *Troilus and Criseyde.*

◆ Literary Focus

❸ **Mock-Heroic Style** Ask students: How does Chaucer remind his readers of the trivial nature of his characters? *Students should note that by having Pertelote prescribe a diet of worms, Chaucer is providing a humorous reminder that these are mere barnyard animals, not learned philosophers, as the previous dialogue might suggest.*

Customize for
Less Proficient Readers

❹ Before beginning Chanticleer's story within the story, remind students that Chanticleer must defend his belief that dreams can serve as a sign of things to come. Have them make some predictions about the story Chanticleer will tell. They should be able to anticipate that it will be a story about a dream that came true.

Upon my soul that's the advice to give
For melancholy choler; let me urge
You free yourself from vapors with a purge.
And that you may have no excuse to tarry
By saying this town has no apothecary,
❶ I shall myself instruct you and prescribe
Herbs that will cure all vapors of that tribe,
Herbs from our very farmyard! You will find
Their natural property is to unbind
And purge you well beneath and well above.
Now don't forget it, dear, for God's own love!
Your face is choleric and shows distension;
Be careful lest the sun in his ascension
❷ Should catch you full of humors,[10] hot and many.
And if he does, my dear, I'll lay a penny
It means a bout of fever or a breath
Of tertian ague.[11] You may catch your death.
"Worms for a day or two I'll have to give
❸ As a digestive, then your laxative.
Centaury, fumitory, caper-spurge
And hellebore will make a splendid purge;
And then there's laurel or the blackthorn berry,
Ground-ivy too that makes our yard so merry;
Peck them right up, my dear, and swallow whole.
Be happy, husband, by your father's soul!
Don't be afraid of dreams. I'll say no more."
"Madam," he said, "I thank you for your lore,
But with regard to Cato all the same,
His wisdom has, no doubt, a certain fame,
❹ But though he said that we should take no heed
Of dreams, by God in ancient books I read
❺ Of many a man of more authority
Than ever Cato was, believe you me,
Who say the very opposite is true
And prove their theories by experience too.
Dreams have quite often been significations
As well of triumphs as of tribulations
That people undergo in this our life.
This needs no argument at all, dear wife,
The proof is all too manifest indeed.
"One of the greatest authors one can read
Says thus: there were two comrades once who went
On pilgrimage, sincere in their intent.
And as it happened they had reached a town
Where such a throng was milling up and down
And yet so scanty the accommodation,
They could not find themselves a habitation,
No, not a cottage that could lodge them both.
And so they separated, very loath,
Under constraint of this necessity
And each went off to find some hostelry,
And lodge whatever way his luck might fall.

10. humors: People in Chaucer's time believed that bodily fluids, called humors, were responsible for one's health and disposition. An excess of the fluid called yellow bile resulted in a choleric, or quick-tempered, personality. In lines 108 and 125, Chaucer seems to use the word *choler* as a synonym for the term *humor.*

11. tertian ague (tʉr′ shən ā′ gyo͞o) Malarial fever.

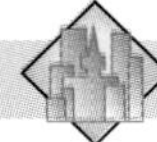

Beyond the Classroom

Workplace Skills

Animal Care The widow and her daughters raised cows, sows, sheep, and chickens. Raising such animals requires careful attention to their diet and health. A proper diet will not only keep the animals healthy, but it will develop the weight and other features that make them marketable. In addition, some animals are susceptible to certain diseases, and steps must be taken to ensure that they are protected.

Have interested students choose one or more of these animals, investigate their unique dietary and health-related needs, and develop a program and schedule of proper feeding and care. It should include the types and amounts of food and water the animals should be fed as well as a plan for regular veterinary visits and necessary vaccinations.

Woman Feeding Chickens, From an Italian manuscript (c. 1385), Osterreichische National Bibliothek, Vienna

◀ **Critical Viewing** What qualities of the animals pictured remind you of human qualities? **[Classify]** ❻

"The first of them found refuge in a stall
Down in a yard with oxen and a plow.
His friend found lodging for himself somehow
Elsewhere, by accident or destiny,
Which governs all of us and equally.
"Now it so happened, long ere it was day,
This fellow had a dream, and as he lay
In bed it seemed he heard his comrade call,
'Help! I am lying in an ox's stall
And shall tonight be murdered as I lie.
Help me, dear brother, help or I shall die!
Come in all haste!' Such were the words he spoke;
The dreamer, lost in terror, then awoke.
But once awake he paid it no attention,
Turned over and dismissed it as invention,
It was a dream, he thought, a fantasy.
And twice he dreamt this dream successively.
"Yet a third time his comrade came again,
Or seemed to come, and said, 'I have been slain.
Look, look! my wounds are bleeding wide and deep,
Rise early in the morning, break your sleep ❼

Customize for
More Advanced Students

❺ Have these students keep track of the types of arguments Chanticleer and Pertelote use in their debate over dreams. For example, Pertelote quotes ancient authorities and cites the humors as the cause of Chanticleer's meaningless dream. Chanticleer begins with a story exemplifying the importance of dreams. Ask them how one might go about proving or disproving the importance of dreams today. *Students should realize that in medieval times, scholars supported their arguments by citing ancient authorities. In modern times, scientists perform experiments and search for verifiable, replicable evidence to support a hypothesis.*

▶Critical Viewing◀

❻ **Classify** Students may say that the crowing rooster reminds them of the human quality of boastfulness, the two roosters facing each other remind students of how people like to converse, the chicken peering from the henhouse represents the quality of caution, and the chicken on top of the henhouse might be displaying individualism.

Customize for
Less Proficient Readers

❼ Help students understand this part of the story by assigning various students to take the parts of the characters below. Then have them read the parts aloud.

- the narrator (Chanticleer)
- the first comrade, who has the dream
- the second comrade, who appears in the dream
- the innkeeper

Have students preview and study the lines they will read.

Humanities: Art

Woman Feeding Chickens, c. 1385.

This painting from an Italian manuscript shows a simply dressed farm woman feeding chickens in front of a chicken coop. The choice of such an earthy subject for a manuscript miniature painting shows how far European tastes had moved toward nonreligious art. The earliest manuscript miniatures were all religious in nature; by the later Middle Ages, treatises on many subjects, including farming and fencing, had fine illustrations, as did poetry, romances, and songs.

This picture, including decoratively placed roosters and hens, accompanies a text on farming and, no doubt, on the tasks of the farm wife. It demonstrates the turn toward realism that began to characterize art after the Middle Ages.

Discuss the following questions with your class:

1. Is this picture realistic? Explain. *In many ways it is realistic. It shows details of ordinary dress and farm life.*
2. How is this picture like depictions of farm life today, and how is it different? What factors explain the similarities and differences? *It is similar in that a person working on a small farm might perform the same action today. Details of clothing are different, and a modern farmer would be likely to have a different chicken coop and perhaps new ways of feeding the birds. These differences are due to changes in fashion and in technology.*

◆ Literary Focus

❶ **Mock-Heroic Style** Ask students: How do these lines fit the definition of the mock-heroic style? *The bombastic appeal to God and the attempt to be deep and philosophical are a humorous exaggeration of the heroic style found in epics such as* Beowulf.

◆ Critical Thinking

❷ **Draw Conclusions** Have students identify the line that summarizes the point of Chanticleer's story of the two comrades. *Line 243 provides the point of the story.*

And go to the west gate. You there shall see
A cart all loaded up with dung,' said he,
'And in that dung my body has been hidden.
Boldly arrest that cart as you are bidden.
It was my money that they killed me for.'
"He told him every detail, sighing sore,
And pitiful in feature, pale of hue.
This dream, believe me, Madam, turned out true;
For in the dawn, as soon as it was light,
He went to where his friend had spent the night
And when he came upon the cattle-stall
He looked about him and began to call.
"The innkeeper, appearing thereupon,
Quickly gave answer, 'Sir, your friend has gone.
He left the town a little after dawn.'
The man began to feel suspicious, drawn
By memories of his dream—the western gate,
The dung-cart—off he went, he would not wait,
Towards the western entry. There he found,
Seemingly on its way to dung some ground,
A dung-cart loaded on the very plan
Described so closely by the murdered man.
So he began to shout courageously
For right and vengeance on the felony,
'My friend's been killed! There's been a foul attack,
He's in that cart and gaping on his back!
Fetch the authorities, get the sheriff down
—Whosever job it is to run the town—
Help! My companion's murdered, sent to glory!'
"What need I add to finish off the story?
People ran out and cast the cart to ground,
And in the middle of the dung they found
The murdered man. The corpse was fresh and new.
"O blessed God, that art so just and true,
Thus thou revealest murder! As we say,
'Murder will out.' We see it day by day.
Murder's a foul, abominable treason,
❶ So loathsome to God's justice, to God's reason,
He will not suffer its concealment. True,
Things may lie hidden for a year or two,
But still 'Murder will out,' that's my conclusion.
"All the town officers in great confusion
Seized on the carter and they gave him hell,
And then they racked the innkeeper as well,
And both confessed. And then they took the wrecks
And there and then they hanged them by their necks.
❷ "By this we see that dreams are to be dreaded.
And in the self-same book I find embedded,
Right in the very chapter after this
(I'm not inventing, as I hope for bliss)
The story of two men who started out
To cross the sea—for merchandise no doubt—

Cross-Curricular Connection: Psychology

Dreams have been the subject of considerable study and speculation in the twentieth century. Freud claimed he could gain insights into the working of the mind through the study of dreams. A dream, he said, was "the life of the mind while asleep." Freud employed psychoanalysis to interpret the dreams of his patients.

Scientific studies in 1953 revealed that rapid eye movement, REM, occurs during a dream. In addition, brain waves and respiration increase. Such a dream state has also been observed in dogs, monkeys, and elephants. Scientists are now beginning to associate dreams with certain physiological features.

Have interested students investigate the status of our scientific knowledge of dreams.

But as the winds were contrary they waited.
It was a pleasant town, I should have stated,
Merrily grouped about the haven-side.
A few days later with the evening tide
The wind veered round so as to suit them best;
They were delighted and they went to rest
Meaning to sail next morning early. Well,
To one of them a miracle befell.
"This man as he lay sleeping, it would seem,
Just before dawn had an astounding dream.
He thought a man was standing by his bed
Commanding him to wait, and thus he said:
'If you set sail tomorrow as you intend
You will be drowned. My tale is at an end.'
"He woke and told his friend what had occurred
And begged him that the journey be deferred
At least a day, implored him not to start.
❸ But his companion, lying there apart,
Began to laugh and treat him to <u>derision</u>.
'I'm not afraid,' he said, 'of any vision,
To let it interfere with my affairs;
A straw for all your dreamings and your scares.
Dreams are just empty nonsense, merest japes;[12]
Why, people dream all day of owls and apes,
All sorts of trash that can't be understood,
Things that have never happened and never could.
But as I see you mean to stay behind
And miss the tide for wilful sloth of mind,
God knows I'm sorry for it, but good day!'
And so he took his leave and went his way.
"And yet, before they'd covered half the trip
—I don't know what went wrong—there was a rip
And by some accident the ship went down,
Her bottom rent,[13] all hands aboard to drown
In sight of all the vessels at her side,
That had put out upon the self-same tide.
"So, my dear Pertelote, if you discern
The force of these examples, you may learn
One never should be careless about dreams,
For, undeniably, I say it seems
That many are a sign of trouble breeding.
"Now, take St. Kenelm's life which I've been reading;
He was Kenulphus' son, the noble King
Of Mercia. Now, St. Kenelm dreamt a thing
Shortly before they murdered him one day.
He saw his murder in a dream, I say.
❹ His nurse expounded it and gave her reasons
On every point and warned him against treasons
But as the saint was only seven years old
All that she said about it left him cold.
He was so holy how could visions hurt?
"By God, I willingly would give my shirt

12. **japes:** Jokes.

13. **rent:** Torn.

◆ Build Vocabulary

derision (di rizh´ ən) *n.*: Contempt or ridicule

◆ Grammar and Style

❸ Pronoun Case Have students point out all the pronouns in the subjective or objective case in these passages and tell why that cases is needed in the sentence. If some students choose the pronoun *his*, explain that *his* is in the possessive case because it shows ownership. *He is in the nominative case because it is the subject of the first sentence. The pronoun* him *is the object of the verb in lines 264, 265, and 267.* I *is the subject of the sentence spoken by the man in the story and therefore in the nominative case.* He *is the subject of the sentence and also in the nominative case.*

◆ Critical Thinking

❹ Analyze Ask students to enumerate the number and type of authorities Chanticleer cites in his arguments. Ask: Does the addition of more and more authorities strengthen his argument? How do you think Pertelote is responding to all of this? Do you think she is gradually beginning to agree with Chanticleer or are her convictions firm? *Chanticleer gets off to a shaky start, since he doesn't remember the name of his authority (line 164) and it can be inferred by Chanticleer's assertion (line 246) that he is not making this up that Pertelote is skeptical. Chanticleer gradually strengthens his argument by citing the life of a saint (line 290–301), Roman history (lines 303–304), the Bible (lines 306–315), and classical myth (lines 317–328), which was regarded during medieval times as genuine history. It is not clear whether Pertelote is convinced or whether she is simply overwhelmed by Chanticleer's incessant talking.*

Speaking and Listening Mini-Lesson

Mock-Heroic Scene

This mini-lesson supports the Speaking and Listening activity on page 129.

Introduce the Concept Review the key characteristics of the mock-heroic style. Explain that an improvisation is a dramatic presentation that is made up as the actors go along. Although an improvisation is traditionally done with no preparation on the part of the participants, assure students that they will be allowed to discuss beforehand what they would like to do.

Develop Background Brainstorm for possible situations and treatments. What truly serious problem might the tiny everyday occurrence be compared to in order to achieve a humorous effect? How can exaggeration and overdramatization be used to make a point? Would it be helpful to have a narrator introduce the story and make connections?

Apply the Information Students should use both dialogue and action to convey their message. Point out that the way the lines are delivered is as important to creating the desired effect as the actual words.

Assess the Outcome Have students evaluate improvisations based on creativity, the appropriateness of the situation for a mock-heroic treatment, the achievement of the mock-heroic style, and the criteria in Peer Assessment: Dramatic Performance, on page 121 in ***Alternative Assessment.***

◆ Critical Thinking

❶ Draw Conclusions Have students discuss what they can tell about Chanticleer's motives for telling Pertelote stories for the past 200 lines of the narrative. *Students may infer that Chanticleer wishes to educate his wife, show off his own learning, win the argument, and, most importantly, distract Pertelote from her plan of dosing him with purges.* How does this passage add humor to the piece? *It makes it clear that a driving force behind all Chanticleer's lofty stories is a desire to keep Pertelote from medicating him—hardly a heroic motivation!*

◆ Literary Focus

❷ Mock-Heroic Style In lines 303–328, using the allusions to epic heroes to bolster an argument over such a trivial matter as a rooster's dream, creates a satirical and humorous effect.

◆ Literary Focus

❸ Mock-Heroic Style Here, Chanticleer resorts to flattery to end the argument and the threat of Pertelote dosing him with purgatives and laxatives. Ask students to explain why this passage is a good illustration of mock-heroic style. *Chanticleer's words to Pertelote resemble a love poem addressed to a courtly lady. However, the word scarlet is ludicrously inappropriate to a woman, though quite suitable to a hen. This one word sends up the whole courtly style into utter hilarity.*

❹ Clarification Chanticleer deliberately mistranslates this Latin proverb. Point out to students that a more accurate translation of the Latin saying is "Woman is man's confusion." The irony in Chanticleer's sly deceitfulness satirizes the courtly lover.

◆ Literary Focus

❺ Mock-Heroic Style Point out to students that Chaucer, having provided the setting of the story in the opening exposition and the complication in the just-concluded debate, now moves to the climax. Ask students: How does Chaucer mock the importance of what is about to happen? *The ponderous, belabored manner in which he presents the time and place of the action mocks the traditional heroic style of the epic and satirizes the importance of what is about to happen.*

To have you read his legend as I've read it;
And, Madam Pertelote, upon my credit,
Macrobius wrote of dreams and can explain us
The vision of young Scipio Africanus,[14]
And he affirms that dreams can give a due
Warnings of things that later on come true.
"And then there's the Old Testament—a manual
Well worth your study; see the *Book of Daniel.*
Did Daniel think a dream was vanity?
Read about Joseph too and you will see
That many dreams—I do not say that all—
Give cognizance of what is to befall.
"Look at Lord Pharaoh, king of Egypt! Look
At what befell his butler and his cook.
Did not their visions have a certain force?
But those who study history of course
Meet many dreams that set them wondering.
"What about Croesus too, the Lydian king,
Who dreamt that he was sitting in a tree,
Meaning he would be hanged? It had to be.
"Or take Andromache, great Hector's wife;[15]
The day on which he was to lose his life
She dreamt about, the very night before,
And realized that if Hector went to war
He would be lost that very day in battle.
She warned him; he dismissed it all as prattle
And sallied forth to fight, being self-willed,
And there he met Achilles and was killed.
The tale is long and somewhat overdrawn,
And anyhow it's very nearly dawn,
So let me say in very brief conclusion
My dream undoubtedly foretells confusion,
❶ It bodes me ill, I say. And, furthermore,
Upon your laxatives I set no store,
For they are venomous. I've suffered by them
Often enough before and I defy them.
"And now, let's talk of fun and stop all this.
Dear Madam, as I hope for Heaven's bliss.
Of one thing God has sent me plenteous grace,
❸ For when I see the beauty of your face,
That scarlet loveliness about your eyes,
All thought of terror and confusion dies.
For it's as certain as the Creed, I know,
Mulier est hominis confusio
❹ (A Latin tag, dear Madam, meaning this:
'Woman is man's delight and all his bliss').
For when at night I feel your feathery side,
Although perforce I cannot take a ride
Because, alas, our perch was made too narrow,
Delight and solace fill me to the marrow
And I defy all visions and all dreams!"
And with that word he flew down from the beams,

14. Scipio Africanus (sip´ē ō af´ ri kā´ nəs): Famous Roman general (237–183 B.C.).

15. Andromache (an dräm´ ə kē) . . . **wife:** The wife of Hector, the greatest warrior in Troy at the time of the Trojan War.

◆ Literary Focus
References to heroes appear often in epics. What effect do the references in this passage have? ❷

For it was day, and down his hens flew all,
And with a chuck he gave the troupe a call
For he had found a seed upon the floor.
Royal he was, he was afraid no more.
He feathered Pertelote in wanton play
And trod her twenty times ere prime of day.
Grim as a lion's was his manly frown
As on his toes he sauntered up and down;
He scarcely deigned to set his foot to ground
And every time a seed of corn was found
He gave a chuck, and up his wives ran all.
Thus royal as a prince who strides his hall
Leave we this Chanticleer engaged on feeding
And pass to the adventure that was breeding.
    Now when the month in which the world began,
March, the first month, when God created man,
Was over, and the thirty-second day
Thereafter ended, on the third of May
It happened that Chanticleer in all his pride,
His seven wives attendant at his side,
5 Cast his eyes upward to the blazing sun,
Which in the sign of *Taurus* then had run
His twenty-one degrees and somewhat more,
And knew by nature and no other lore
That it was nine o'clock. With blissful voice
He crew triumphantly and said, "Rejoice,
Behold the sun! The sun is up, my seven.
Look, it has climbed forty degrees in heaven,
Forty degrees and one in fact, by this.
Dear Madam Pertelote, my earthly bliss,
Hark to those blissful birds and how they sing!
Look at those pretty flowers, how they spring!
Solace and revel fill my heart!" He laughed.
    But in that moment Fate let fly her shaft;
Ever the latter end of joy is woe,
God knows that worldly joy is swift to go.
A rhetorician[16] with a flair for style
Could chronicle this maxim in his file
Of Notable Remarks with safe conviction.
Then let the wise give ear; this is no fiction
My story is as true, I undertake,
As that of good Sir Lancelot du Lake[17]
Who held all women in such high esteem.
Let me return full circle to my theme.
    A coal-tipped fox of sly iniquity[18]
That had been lurking round the grove for three
Long years, that very night burst through and passed
7 Stockade and hedge, as Providence forecast,
Into the yard where Chanticleer the Fair
Was wont, with all his ladies, to repair.
Still, in a bed of cabbages, he lay
Until about the middle of the day

Chaucer Reciting Troilus and Cressida Before a Court Gathering (Frontispiece) Corpus Christi College

▲ Critical Viewing Judging from this scene, what was a storytelling event in Chaucer's time like? **[Interpret]** 

16. rhetorician (ret´ ə rish´ ən) *n.*: Person skilled in public speaking or writing.

17. Sir Lancelot du Lake: The most celebrated of King Arthur's Knights of the Round Table.

18. iniquity (i nik´ wi tē) *n.*: Wickedness.

◆ Build Vocabulary

maxim (maks´ im) *n.*: Briefly expressed general truth or rule of conduct

▶Critical Viewing◀

6 Interpret Storytelling in Chaucer's time was a gala event, involving an assembly of notables in fine clothes appropriate for court functions (and perhaps inappropriate for the quaint, bucolic garden setting in which the poet is giving his reading).

◆ Reading Strategy

7 Context Clues Point out that *repair* (line 402) does not mean "to fix." Have students use context to determine the meaning of *repair* in this sentence. *It means "to go often."*

Customize for
More Advanced Students

Beginning at line 397, with the appearance of the fox, the nun's priest alternates between telling the story and stepping out of the story to comment on the action or one of the characters. Have these students note where these shifts occur and what devices Chaucer uses to signal them.

Customize for
Less Proficient Readers

To help these students follow this part of the story, have them skip over the passages where the narrator comments on the action or the character. You might be able to use the work done by more advanced students in the preceding suggestion. After the less proficient readers have a firm understanding of the story, have them reread this part of the tale in its entirety.

Humanities: Art

Chaucer Reciting *Troilus and Cressida* Before a Court Gathering, c. 1400.

This colorful manuscript illumination is one of the finest surviving English miniature paintings. It is from a manuscript of Chaucer's poem, which is based on the legendary love affair of Troilus and Cressida. As the popularity of tales of courtly love and chivalry spread in late medieval England, poets were in demand at courts and festive gatherings. Chaucer was known to read his poems to perhaps fifteen or twenty people at a time. He is said to have watched their eyes as he progressed from line to line, always ready to stop when he had lost their attention. As this picture suggests, his poems were designed to be recited. The court scene includes a prince (in the golden robe) and, near the castle in the background, a queen and her attendants.

Use the following questions for discussion:

1. Why do you think the artist included a castle and fine clothes in this picture? *People have always been interested in the trappings of royalty; these details reflect the setting.*
2. How can you identify Chaucer? *He is the figure reading the poem.*
3. Why would listeners have been unable to follow along from their own copies of the poem? *Most people could not read, and books were expensive and rare.*

◆ Literary Focus

1 Mock-Epic Style Explain to students that the authors of epics frequently addressed their characters in exactly this way. Chaucer's mockery here is directed at such flowery addresses (called apostrophes) in epics themselves as well as at the pomposity of using such addresses to describe a fox's attack on a chicken coop. Ask students: Is the comparison of the fox to Judas Iscariot and other traitors a reasonable one? *It is not; it is highly exaggerated.* How does Chaucer remind the reader that the story is about a chicken? *He mentions that Chanticleer had been brought "to the yard from [his] high beams."*

◆ Critical Thinking

2 Analyze Explain to students that Chaucer was extremely interested in such philosophical questions as the conflict between God's foreknowledge and man's free will. The Nun's Priest's discussion is an accurate summation of the medieval view of this paradox. Ask students what the effect is of bringing such a lofty philosophical question to bear on the tale he is telling. *Some students may say it makes the philosophical question more accessible. Other students may feel that it pokes fun at the rarefied atmosphere of most philosophical discussions and makes light of the issue.*

▶Critical Viewing◀

3 Support He is gesturing, his eyes appear to be focused one some point in the distance, and he appears to be in the act of speaking. These details suggest that he is telling a story.

Watching the cock and waiting for his cue,
As all these homicides so gladly do
That lie about in wait to murder men.
O false assassin, lurking in thy den!
O new Iscariot, new Ganelon!
And O Greek Sinon,[19] thou whose treachery won
Troy town and brought it utterly to sorrow!
O Chanticleer, accursed be that morrow
That brought thee to the yard from thy high beams!
Thou hadst been warned, and truly, by thy dreams
That this would be a perilous day for thee.
But that which God's foreknowledge can foresee
Must needs occur, as certain men of learning
Have said. Ask any scholar of discerning;
He'll say the Schools are filled with altercation
On this vexed matter of predestination[20]
Long bandied by a hundred thousand men.
How can I sift it to the bottom then?
The Holy Doctor St. Augustine shines
In this, and there is Bishop Bradwardine's
Authority, Boethius'[21] too, decreeing
Whether the fact of God's divine foreseeing
Constrains me to perform a certain act
—And by "constraint" I mean the simple fact
Of mere compulsion by necessity—
Or whether a free choice is granted me
To do a given act or not to do it
Though, ere it was accomplished, God foreknew it.

19. Iscariot . . . Ganeton . . . Sinon: Each of these men was famous for betrayal. Judas Iscariot betrayed Jesus Christ; Ganelon betrayed Charlemagne's greatest knight, Roland; and Sinon convinced King Priam to bring the Trojan horse, filled with Greek troops, into Troy.

20. predestination (prē des′ tə nā′ shən) *n.*: The idea that God arranges beforehand everything that will happen.

21. Bishop Bradwardine's . . . Boethius' (bō ē′ thē əs): Bishop Bradwardine was a well-known theologian of Chaucer's time. Boethius (A.D. 480–524) was a famous Roman philosopher.

The Nun's Priest, Detail from the Ellesmere Manuscript, The Huntington Library, San Marino, California

▶ **Critical Viewing** How do the position and facial expression of the subject of this painting suggest he is telling a story? **[Support]**

Humanities: Art

The Nun's Priest, detail from the Ellesmere Manuscript, c. 1478.

About ninety manuscripts of *The Canterbury Tales* exist, but most of them are not complete. The best of these manuscripts is the Ellesmere Manuscript, which is named for the Ellesmere family, who owned it for many years. This book was printed by William Caxton almost one hundred years after Chaucer began writing these tales.

Even after Gutenberg's invention of the printing press in 1438, manuscripts sometimes included decorations drawn by an illuminator who prepared the bright colors from colored earth and other substances and mixed them with gum so the color would hold fast to the pages.

Use these questions for discussion:

1. Does the pilgrim pictured here look like the man who might have told this tale? Explain. *Most students will be satisfied with the art of the Nun's Priest, saying that although he looks serious, it is believable that he has a sense of humor that would allow him to generate a mock-heroic epic.*
2. How does the illuminator's style differ from the style of Arthur Szyk, who painted the pictures shown in *The Prologue?* Which style do you prefer? *Students may prefer Szyk's style because the faces and postures of Szyk's paintings convey a more human quality and are more suggestive of the painter's attitude toward his subject.*

Or whether Providence is not so stringent
And merely makes necessity contingent.
    But I decline discussion of the matter;
My tale is of a cock and of the clatter
That came of following his wife's advice
To walk about his yard on the precise
Morning after the dream of which I told.
    O woman's counsel is so often cold!
A woman's counsel brought us first to woe,
Made Adam out of Paradise to go
Where he had been so merry, so well at ease.
But, for I know not whom it may displease
5 If I suggest that women are to blame,
Pass over that; I only speak in game.
Read the authorities to know about
What has been said of women; you'll find out
These are the cock's words, and not mine, I'm giving;
I think no harm of any woman living.
    Merrily in her dust-bath in the sand
Lay Pertelote. Her sisters were at hand
Basking in sunlight. Chanticleer sang free,
More merrily than a mermaid in the sea
(For *Physiologus*[22] reports the thing
And says how well and merrily they sing).
And so it happened as he cast his eye
Towards the cabbage at a butterfly
It fell upon the fox there, lying low.
Gone was all inclination then to crow.
"Cok cok," he cried, giving a sudden start,
As one who feels a terror at his heart,
For natural instinct teaches beasts to flee
The moment they perceive an enemy,
Though they had never met with it before.
    This Chanticleer was shaken to the core
And would have fled. The fox was quick to say
However, "Sir! Whither so fast away?
Are you afraid of me, that am your friend?
A fiend, or worse, I should be, to intend
You harm, or practice villainy upon you;
Dear sir, I was not even spying on you!
Truly I came to do no other thing
Than just to lie and listen to you sing.
6 You have as merry a voice as God has given
To any angel in the courts of Heaven;
To that you add a musical sense as strong
As had Boethius who was skilled in song.
My Lord your Father (God receive his soul!),
7 Your mother too—how courtly, what control!—
Have honored my poor house, to my great ease;
And you, sir, too, I should be glad to please.
For, when it comes to singing, I'll say this
(Else may these eyes of mine be barred from bliss),

◆ **Reading Strategy**
Explain what context clues could help you to decode the word *counsel* in line 441. 4

22. ***Physiologus:*** Book on nature written in Latin meter.

◆ **Build Vocabulary**

stringent (strin′ jənt) *adj.*: Strict

Cultural Connection

Fables

Fables have several distinctive characteristics that make them unique and universal. Regardless of the cultural setting in which they originated, fables are always brief tales in prose or verse in which the chief characters are animals. Fables always strongly suggest or openly state a moral. The subject matter of a fable often originates in folklore. The most famous fables are those ascribed to Aesop, a Greek slave living about 600 B.C. Other well-known fables are those of La Fontaine, a seventeenth-century French writer. Others have been written by Lessing, a German, and Krylov, a Russian.

In spite of their clearly defined characteristics, fables can be quite diverse. They range from Rudyard Kipling's *Just So Stories,* to Joel Chandler Harris's *Uncle Remus Stories,* to George Orwell's *Animal Farm.*

Have interested students choose a fable from another culture and report on the common characteristics this fable has with all fables as well as the unique cultural elements found in the story.

◆ Reading Strategy

4 Context Clues Since Eve advised Adam to eat the forbidden fruit and thereby lose Paradise, one can infer that counsel is a synonym for advice.

5 Clarification Point out to students that in this era it was customary for theologians to blame women for all human woe since Eve got Adam to eat the forbidden fruit. However, possibly no male author, ancient or modern, is so remarkably free of sexism as Chaucer and generally so positive in his portrayal of women. Explain that in this passage, Chaucer's humor is based on satirizing the traditional view. The narrator, after all, is a nun's priest—that is, a man assigned to hear that nun's confession. Consequently, the narrator is shown as reluctant to displease anyone (namely, the nun) and blames this whole tirade on Chanticleer.

◆ Literature and Your Life

6 Draw students' attention to the fox's use of flattery to trick Chanticleer. Ask students what experiences they have had in which someone used flattery to achieve some goal. *Students may admit to having complimented a teacher in hopes of getting a better grade, or a parent or friend in order to get a favor or a loan.*

◆ Critical Thinking

7 Compare and Contrast Although the fox is lying about simply being there to hear Chanticleer sing, he may not be lying about his acquaintance with Chanticleer's parents. Contrast what the fox wants Chanticleer to believe with what probably happened in reality. *The fox implies that Chanticleer's parents were guests in his home and sang for him; what probably happened is that the fox stole Chanticleer's parents from the widow's yard and feasted on them.*

◆ Critical Thinking

1 Analyze Ask students: What is it about Chanticleer's character that makes him especially susceptible to flattery? *Chanticleer is vain and accepts all compliments as genuine. He responds to the fox's request in hope of garnering additional praise.*

▶Critical Viewing◀

2 Deduce Students may say that the pilgrims seem realistic, but that the setting and orderly procession of horses seem mythic or fantastic. The artist may have chosen to combine these elements to capture the allegorical aspects of *The Canterbury Tales*.

There never was a singer I would rather
Have heard at dawn than your respected father.
All that he sang came welling from his soul
And how he put his voice under control!
The pains he took to keep his eyes tight shut
In concentration—then the tip-toe strut,
The slender neck stretched out, the delicate beak!
No singer could approach him in technique
Or rival him in song, still less surpass.
I've read the story in *Burnel the Ass*,[23]
Among some other verses, of a cock
Whose leg in youth was broken by a knock
A clergyman's son had given him, and for this
He made the father lose his benefice.
But certainly there's no comparison
Between the subtlety of such an one
And the discretion of your father's art
And wisdom. Oh, for charity of heart,
Can you not emulate your sire and sing?"
    This Chanticleer began to beat a wing
As one incapable of smelling treason,
So wholly had this flattery ravished reason.
1 Alas, my lords! there's many a sycophant[24]
And flatterer that fill your courts with cant
And give more pleasure with their zeal forsooth
Than he who speaks in soberness and truth.
Read what *Ecclesiasticus*[25] records
Of flatterers. 'Ware treachery, my lords!
    This Chanticleer stood high upon his toes,
He stretched his neck, his eyes began to close,
His beak to open; with his eyes shut tight
He then began to sing with all his might.

23. ***Burnel the Ass:*** Twelfth-century poem in which a rooster gains revenge after being mistreated by a priest's son.

24. **sycophant** (sik´ ə fənt) *n.:* Person who seeks favor by flattering influential people.

25. ***Ecclesiasticus:*** Not Ecclesiastes, but a book of proverbs included with the Apocrypha in the Authorized Version of the Bible.

Chaucer's Canterbury Pilgrims, William Blake
The Huntington Library, San Marino, California

2 ▲ **Critical Viewing** Which elements in this etching seem realistic? Which elements seem mythic or fantastic? Why did the artist choose to combine these elements? **[Deduce]**

Humanities: Art

Chaucer's Canterbury Pilgrims, c. 1820, by William Blake.

This nineteenth-century version of Chaucer's pilgrims is by William Blake (1757–1827), the English mystic, artist, and writer. He chose many familiar themes, such as *The Canterbury Tales,* as subject matter. As a boy, Blake was apprenticed to an engraver, and later he studied that subject at the Royal Academy in London. In 1784, he opened a print shop, where he published many of his own books. Blake's books were visually stunning. He invented a unique technique, called "illuminated printing," in which he engraved text and art on the same plate. The pages produced by that method were often hand-colored by Blake and his wife.

Blake first made a painting of the pilgrims in 1809, and it featured prominently in an exhibit of his works. He hoped for success with an engraving (seen here) of the same composition, but it received little notice.

Use the following questions for discussion:

1. Why do you suppose the theme of journeys—in particular, pilgrimages—has frequently been the subject of poetry and art? *Students may suggest that journeys often symbolize life or change or adventure.*
2. How is this picture of Chaucer's pilgrims like the one on page 114? How is it different? *Because the engraving is black and white, students may say that it is more formal and serious. Accept other answers.*

❸ Sir Russel Fox then leapt to the attack,
Grabbing his gorge he flung him o'er his back
And off he bore him to the woods, the brute,
And for the moment there was no pursuit.
O Destiny that may not be evaded!
Alas that Chanticleer had so paraded!
Alas that he had flown down from the beams!
O that his wife took no account of dreams!
And on a Friday too to risk their necks!
O Venus, goddess of the joys of sex,
Since Chanticleer thy mysteries professed
And in thy service always did his best,
And more for pleasure than to multiply
His kind, on thine own day is he to die?
O Geoffrey, thou my dear and sovereign master[26]
Who, when they brought King Richard to disaster
And shot him dead, lamented so his death,
Would that I had thy skill, thy gracious breath,
❹ To chide a Friday half so well as you!
(For he was killed upon a Friday too.)
Then I could fashion you a rhapsody
For Chanticleer in dread and agony.
Sure never such a cry or lamentation
Was made by ladies of high Trojan station,
When Ilium fell and Pyrrhus with his sword
Grabbed Priam by the beard, their king and lord,
And slew him there as the *Aeneid* tells,[27]
As what was uttered by those hens. Their yells
Surpassed them all in palpitating fear
When they beheld the rape of Chanticleer.
Dame Pertelote emitted sovereign shrieks
That echoed up in anguish to the peaks
❺ Louder than those extorted from the wife
Of Hasdrubal,[28] when he had lost his life
And Carthage all in flame and ashes lay.
She was so full of torment and dismay
That in the very flames she chose her part
And burnt to ashes with a steadfast heart.
O woeful hens, louder your shrieks and higher
Than those of Roman matrons when the fire
Consumed their husbands, senators of Rome,
When Nero burnt their city and their home,
Beyond a doubt that Nero was their bale![29]
Now let me turn again to tell my tale;
This blessed widow and her daughters two
Heard all these hens in clamor and halloo
And, rushing to the door at all this shrieking,
They saw the fox towards the covert streaking
And, on his shoulder, Chanticleer stretched flat.
"Look, look!" they cried, "O mercy, look at that!
Ha! Ha! the fox!" and after him they ran,
And stick in hand ran many a serving man,

26. O Geoffrey . . . master: Geoffrey de Vinsauf, twelfth-century author of a book on rhetoric.

27. Sure never . . . *Aeneid* tells: Reference to the destruction of Troy as described in the Roman poet Virgil's *Aeneid.*

28. Hasdrubal (haz′ drōō bəl): Carthaginian general.

29. bale *n.*: Evil; harm.

◆ Build Vocabulary

cant (kant) *n.*: Insincere or meaningless talk

❸ **Enrichment** *Russe* means "red," and thus Russel is an appropriate name for a fox. Chaucer's source for Sir Russel the Fox and Master Chanticleer the Cock is ultimately the French *Roman de Renart* and the German *Reinecke Fuchs.* But in England Russel first appeared as Reynard the Fox, a century before Chaucer, in *The Fox and the Wolf,* a comic satire expressing social unrest. In these tales Reynard represents man preying upon others out of desperation and escaping by his cunning.

◆ Critical Thinking

❹ **Apply** Ask students why this passage is considered ironic. *Chaucer is invoking a pompous writer of the past in a flattering manner. However, Chaucer has thoroughly rejected Vinsauf's artificial and flowery heroic-style methods—except for mock-heroic, satiric pieces like this one.*

◆ Critical Thinking

❺ **Compare and Contrast** Several comparisons are made between the events in the barnyard and events in classical mythology or ancient history. Ask students to list the events being compared. Then ask if these are reasonable comparisons. Conclude by asking what the author hoped to achieve by such unlikely comparisons. *Suggested response: The hens' shrieks are compared to the cries of the women of Troy when their city fell and to the cries of Roman matrons when Nero burned their city; Pertelote's cries are compared to those of the wife of a slain Carthaginian general who threw herself into the flames of her burning city. The comparisons are exaggerated to the point of being ridiculous. By making such comparisons, Chaucer is mocking the heroic style of traditional epics.*

Beyond the Classroom

Career Connection

Conservationist "The Nun's Priest's Tale" takes a light-hearted look at the timeless conflict between a domestic animal, the cock, and a hungry fox. In reality, however, such conflicts can be quite serious and pose a real dilemma in various parts of our nation. Ranchers in large areas of the West and Midwest have lost cattle to attacking wolves, yet in most cases the ranchers are prevented from killing these predators by conservation laws that protect such animals. On the other hand, unrestricted destruction of predators and other "pests" in the past has led to species becoming extinct or endangered and thus has severely damaged the balance of nature. In addition, overly cautious ranchers killed off animals, such as pronghorn antelope, bison, and bald eagles, that later turned out to relatively harmless to domesticated animals.

Have interested students investigate these two legitimate, but conflicting interests and report on the arguments made by both sides of this important issue. Have them include recommendations for conserving our endangered species while recognizing certain human needs and rights.

◆ Critical Thinking

❶ **Interpret** Explain to students that the concept of Fortune as a fickle goddess that ruled human affairs was extremely popular in the medieval period, despite its direct conflict with Christian doctrine. Ask students: Based on these lines, what would you expect to happen next? *There will be a reversal of some kind.*

◆ Critical Thinking

❷ **Compare and Contrast** How is the trick Chanticleer plays on the fox like the one the fox played on Chanticleer? How does it differ? *Both tricks are based on flattery. The fox, however, appeals to Chanticleer's pride in his appearance and voice. Chanticleer appeals to the fox's sense of invincibility and cleverness.*

◆ *Literature and Your Life*

❸ Ask students: What current proverb or saying comes to mind as you read these lines? *A likely response is "Fool me once, shame on you. Fool me twice, shame on me." Other answers are possible.*

◆ Critical Thinking

❹ **Compare and Contrast** Point out that Chanticleer, the fox, and the narrator arrive at slightly different lessons from this experience. Ask students which moral lesson seems most appropriate. How would they restate the morals of this story? *Chanticleer declares that you should "look before you leap," the fox huffs that "loose lips sink ships," and the narrator warns "beware of flatterers." Students should support their choice of morals with evidence from the story and their own experience.*

Ran Coll our dog, ran Talbot, Bran and Shaggy,
And with a distaff in her hand ran Maggie,
Ran cow and calf and ran the very hogs
In terror at the barking of the dogs;
The men and women shouted, ran and cursed,
They ran so hard they thought their hearts would burst,
They yelled like fiends in Hell, ducks left the water
Quacking and flapping as on point of slaughter,
Up flew the geese in terror over the trees,
Out of the hive came forth the swarm of bees;
So hideous was the noise—God bless us all,
Jack Straw and all his followers in their brawl[30]
Were never half so shrill, for all their noise,
When they were murdering those Flemish boys,
As that day's hue and cry upon the fox.
They grabbed up trumpets made of brass and box,
Of horn and bone, on which they blew and pooped,
And therewithal they shouted and they whooped
So that it seemed the very heavens would fall.
    And now, good people, pay attention all.
❶ See how Dame Fortune quickly changes side
And robs her enemy of hope and pride!
This cock that lay upon the fox's back
In all his dread contrived to give a quack
❷ And said, "Sir Fox, if I were you, as God's
My witness, I would round upon these clods
And shout, 'Turn back, you saucy bumpkins all!
A very pestilence upon you fall!
Now that I have in safety reached the wood
Do what you like, the cock is mine for good;
I'll eat him there in spite of every one.'"
    The fox replying, "Faith, it shall be done!"
Opened his mouth and spoke. The nimble bird,
Breaking away upon the uttered word,
Flew high into the tree-tops on the spot.
And when the fox perceived where he had got,
"Alas," he cried, "alas, my Chanticleer,
I've done you grievous wrong, indeed I fear
I must have frightened you; I grabbed too hard
When I caught hold and took you from the yard.
But, sir, I meant no harm, don't be offended,
Come down and I'll explain what I intended;
So help me God I'll tell the truth—on oath!
❸ "No," said the cock, "and curses on us both,
And first on me if I were such a dunce
As let you fool me oftener than once.
Never again, for all your flattering lies,
You'll coax a song to make me blink my eyes;
❹ And as for those who blink when they should look,
God blot them from his everlasting Book!"
"Nay, rather," said the fox, "his plagues be flung
On all who chatter that should hold their tongue."

30. Jack Straw . . . brawl: Jack Straw was one of the leaders of the Peasants' Revolt (1381).

Enrichment

Chaucer was employed as a government official by three successive kings, Edward III, Richard II, and Henry IV. Even during the conflict in which the second was replaced by the third, Chaucer himself was never threatened with the loss of his livelihood. All critics have remarked on his tolerant acceptance of people much as he found them, the good with the bad. He criticized corrupt clergy, for example, but never the church.

In "The Nun's Priest's Tale," however, his genial, open-minded neutrality slips for a moment when he says that those pursuing the fox were more shrill than those who massacred the Flemish boys (lines 579–583). This refers to the first great popular rebellion in English history, called the Peasants' Revolt, led by Wat Tyler. Jack Straw may have been another leader—or only a contemptuous way of referring to Tyler himself.

In any case, the rebels entered London on June 13, 1381, and killed Flemish apprentices in the wood trade for taking jobs away from the English. The rebellion lasted less than a month but eyewitnesses all reported the blood-chilling cruelty of the massacre.

Probably not yet forty years old at the time, Chaucer could quite possibly have looked down on scenes of the rebellion from his rent-free quarters safely perched atop one of the gates in London's encircling wall. When he began to write *The Canterbury Tales* some six or more years later, he must still have remembered the massacre, to judge by his reference to it in this tale.

4 Lo, such it is not to be on your guard
Against the flatterers of the world, or yard,
And if you think my story is absurd,
A foolish trifle of a beast and bird,
A fable of a fox, a cock, a hen,
Take hold upon the moral, gentlemen.
St. Paul himself, a saint of great discerning,
Says that all things are written for our learning;
So take the grain and let the chaff be still.
And, gracious Father, if it be thy will
As saith my Savior, make us all good men,
And bring us to his heavenly bliss.
Amen.

Guide for Responding

◆ Literature and Your Life

Reader's Response In what part of the tale did you find the mismatch between Chaucer's style and the events of the story the funniest? Why?

Thematic Focus In this tale, what members of society might Chaucer be mocking?

Role Play With a partner, role-play a conversation between Chanticleer and Pertelote about the day's events.

☑ Check Your Comprehension

1. Who are Chanticleer and Pertelote?
2. Why is Chanticleer disturbed at the beginning of the story?
3. What is Pertelote's advice to Chanticleer when he tells her his dream?
4. (a) How does the fox capture Chanticleer? (b) How does Chanticleer escape?

◆ Critical Thinking

INTERPRET

1. (a) Name three characteristics of Chanticleer that are realistic. (b) Name three characteristics of Chanticleer that it would be absurd to attribute to a rooster. **[Classify]**
2. Compare and contrast the methods of argument that Pertelote and Chanticleer use to defend their interpretations of dreams. **[Compare and Contrast]**
3. The first story that Chanticleer tells has the three-part structure typical of medieval tales: an exposition describing the characters and setting, a complication or problem, and a climax. Does "The Nun's Priest's Tale" as a whole follow this pattern? Why or why not? **[Analyze]**
4. (a) What is the moral of this fable? (b) How seriously do you think the narrator takes this moral? Explain. **[Interpret]**
5. What does this tale suggest about its teller, the nun's priest? **[Draw Conclusions]**

Beyond the Selection

FURTHER READING

Other Mock-Heroic Works

The Battle of the Books, Jonathan Swift
The Rape of the Lock, Alexander Pope

Other Fables

Fables for Our Times, James Thurber
Animal Farm, George Orwell
Aesop's Fables

We suggest that you preview these works before recommending them to students.

INTERNET

You and your students may find additional information about Chaucer and his times on the Internet. We suggest the following site. Please be aware, however, that sites may have changed from the time we published this information.

To put Chaucer in historical context with a lavishly illustrated history, see **http://www.siue.edu/CHAUCER/14thcent.html**

We *strongly recommend* that you preview the site before you send students to it.

Reinforce and Extend

Answers

Reader's Response Students should support their choice with quotations from the story.

Thematic Focus Possible response: Chaucer might be mocking courtiers and other pompous individuals.

☑ Check Your Comprehension

1. They are the rooster and his wife, the main characters in the story.
2. He has had a bad dream.
3. She tells him to ignore his dream because dreams merely reflect humors caused by overeating. She advises him to eat worms and herbs and to stay out of the sun.
4. The fox flatters Chanticleer's singing and asks to hear a song. As Chanticleer sings with closed eyes, the fox seizes him and carries him off. Chanticleer escapes by advising the fox to turn and taunt his pursuers. When the fox opens his mouth to do so, Chanticleer escapes.

◆ Critical Thinking

1. Suggested response: (a) Chanticleer struts around the yard pecking at seeds; he crows when he sees the sun; he lords it over his hens. (b) Chanticleer reads books; he knows astronomy; he cares about the finer points of philosophy and science.
2. (a) Both quote authorities, but Pertelote outlines the theory of humors, diagnoses Chanticleer's condition, then prescribes precise remedies for it. By contrast, Chanticleer tells long stories without drawing conclusions. (b) Although Pertelote proceeds systematically from theory to prescription, neither she nor Chanticleer offer convincing evidence to back up either argument.
3. Yes, the tale as a whole shows the same pattern. The characters who live in the cottage and yard are presented first, then the argument about the meaning of the dream, then the seizing of Chanticleer by the fox and Chanticleer's escape.
4. Possible response: (a) The moral is "Beware of flatterers." (b) The narrator is quite serious about the moral but seems to believe that our vanity will make most of us vulnerable to flattery.
5. Students may respond that the tale suggests he is learned, humorous, mild-mannered, and skeptical.

Answers

◆ Reading Strategy

1. Students may say that context clues that reveal the meaning of *aghast* include Pertelote's expected reaction to Chanticleer's screams and her words of surprise and alarm in lines 70 and 71. The context suggests that *aghast* means "shocked" or "amazed."
2. The synonym *too abundant* in line 105 provides a clue to the meaning of *superfluidity*.

◆ Literary Focus

1. Possible responses: (a) He claims he has read the books of many authorities greater than Cato (lines 154–156) and is "royal as a prince who strides his hall" (line 364). (b) His pride in his learning is ridiculous because it is quite impossible. The description of his strutting, although greatly exaggerated, still rings true.
2. Words and phrases more suitable for a lady include *gracious, courteous, discreet, debonair, companionable,* and *care in her deportment.*
3. In lines 588–590, when Chanticleer is most helpless, Dame Fortune is invoked.

◆ Build Vocabulary

Using the Word Root: *-cap-*

1. A *capital city* is the chief city of a state or country.
2. A *capital crime* is a crime with the highest penalty given by law.
3. *Per capita income* is income earned by each individual.
4. *Capital that is taxed* is the portion of someone's wealth that is taxed.
5. A *captain of industry* is the head of an important company.
6. *To capitulate* means to bow one's head in defeat.

Using the Word Bank

1. c 2. e 3. b 4. d 5. a 6. f

◆ Grammar and Style

Practice

1. us; objective; 2. he; subjective;
3. they; subjective; 4. us; objective;
5. they; subjective

Writing Application

1. she, S; 2. he, S;
3. him, O; 4. I/he, S.
5. me/us/you/them, O

Guide for Responding *(continued)*

◆ Reading Strategy

Context Clues

Synonyms, antonyms, or examples from the passage in which a word appears often provide **context clues** to its meaning. For instance, when Chaucer says of Chanticleer's feathers that they were "Like burnished gold . . . flaming bright," you can use his description of the effects of burnishing to figure out that *burnished* means "polished."

1. In lines 68–71, use context clues to figure out the meaning of *aghast*.
2. In lines 106–108, show how a synonym helps you figure out the meaning of *superfluity*.

◆ Grammar and Style

Pronoun Case

Pronoun case indicates whether a personal pronoun serves as the subject of a sentence or clause, or whether it is the object of a verb or preposition.

Practice In your notebook, identify the pronoun and its case in each passage.

1. "No," said the cock, "and curses on us both, . . ."
2. Alas that he had flown down from the beams!
3. They saw the fox towards the covert streaking . . .
4. God bless us all, . . .
5. They grabbed up trumpets made of brass and box, . . .

Writing Application In your notebook, write a pronoun in the proper case for each blank. Next to each sentence, write an *S* if you have chosen a subjective pronoun or an *O* if you have chosen an objective one.

1. Chanticleer and ___?___ roamed the barnyard like a king and queen.
2. I've told you that ___?___ was a common character in medieval literature.
3. We know the fox was wily because the clever Chanticleer was tricked by ___?___.
4. It was ___?___, Chanticleer, that the fox abducted.
5. After finishing the tale, he gave ___?___ a blessing.

◆ Literary Focus

Mock-Heroic Style

Chaucer uses the **mock-heroic style** in this description of a rooster, which makes him sound like the hero of an epic: "His comb was redder than fine coral, tall / And battlemented like a castle wall." The subject is only a barnyard animal, but the comparisons of his comb to "coral" and a "castle wall" give the rooster a nobility that is absurd.

1. Epic heroes are often boastful. (a) Give two examples of Chanticleer's boastfulness. (b) Why does this boastfulness seem humorous?
2. Which words and phrases in the description of Pertelote would be more suitable for a noble lady than for a hen?
3. Epics often depict the intervention of gods or goddesses in the affairs of humans. Where does Chaucer imitate this convention?

◆ Build Vocabulary

Using the Word Root *-cap-*

The word root *-cap-* means "head." It also refers to the main, chief, or highest part of living and nonliving things. Use your knowledge of this root to explain these phrases:

1. a capital city
2. a capital crime
3. per capita income
4. capital that is taxed
5. a captain of industry
6. to capitulate

Using the Word Bank

Match each of the words with its definition in the right column.

1. timorous	**a.** idle talk
2. derision	**b.** principle guiding behavior
3. maxim	**c.** fearful
4. stringent	**d.** strict; severe
5. cant	**e.** scorn; ridicule
6. capital	**f.** money or property

Writer's Solution

For additional instruction and practice, use the lesson in the **Language Lab CD-ROM** on Pronoun Case and the practice pages on pronouns in the *Writer's Solution Grammar Practice Book,* pp. 57, 58, 60.

Build Your Portfolio

Idea Bank

Writing

1. **Animals as Symbols** List three animals used to symbolize teams or products, and briefly describe the qualities they represent.

2. **Modern Beast Fable** Write your own beast fable, in which animals are characters, that has some sort of moral or lesson.

3. **Critical Response** Chaucer scholar Michael Hoy says of "The Nun's Priest's Tale": "This is a poem which raises searching questions about the nature of existence and man's response to the human predicament." Find examples from the poem that support or contradict his view.

Speaking and Listening

4. **Oral Interpretation of a Debate** Pertelote and Chanticleer debate the meaning of dreams in the passage beginning with line 89 and ending on line 337. With a partner, perform this debate for the class, using your tone of voice to convey humor. **[Performing Arts Link]**

5. **Mock-Heroic Scene** With a small group, improvise dialogue and actions to make small, everyday occurrences seem like events in a tragedy or a heroic tale. **[Performing Arts Link]**

Projects

6. **Mock-Heroic Comic Book** Using what you know of comic book heroes—their origins, powers, enemies—create a mock-heroic fully illustrated comic book. **[Art Link]**

7. **Pilgrim's Path** Do some research and create a map showing the route pilgrims traveled from London to Canterbury. **[Social Studies Link]**

Writing Mini-Lesson

Script for an Animated Fable

Chaucer does with words what an animated cartoon does with moving pictures and dialogue. In the spirit of "The Nun's Priest's Tale," write a script for your own animated fable. Besides the dialogue your animal characters will speak, include bracketed directions describing their appearance and actions. Remember to exaggerate their traits and problems to create humor.

Writing Skills Focus: Using Exaggeration

Comic writing of all kinds uses **exaggeration,** making little problems seem gigantic and therefore ridiculous. Notice, for example, Chaucer's use of exaggeration in describing a fox as if he were one of the greatest betrayers in history:

Model From Literature

O false assassin, lurking in thy den!
O new Iscariot, new Ganelon!

The following strategies will guide you as you draft your script.

Prewriting To help you add humor to your script, jot down the key events in the plot and how you can exaggerate each.

Drafting Follow your story outline, but allow yourself to invent exaggerated details and situations as you go. Create such details by picturing the actions you describe. Then you can exaggerate each situation.

Revising Check your script to make sure that you've described your characters' exaggerated actions as well as provided their words. If not, add bracketed directions where necessary.

✓ ASSESSMENT OPTIONS

Formal Assessment, Selection Test, pp. 23–25, and Assessment Resources Software. The selection test is designed so that it can be easily customized to the performance levels of your students.

Alternative Assessment, p. 5, includes options for less advanced students, more advanced students, verbal/linguistic learners, visual/spatial learners, and musical/rhythmic learners.

PORTFOLIO ASSESSMENT
Use the following rubrics in the ***Alternative Assessment*** booklet to assess student writing:
Animals as Symbols: Description Rubric, p. 98
Modern Beast Fable: Fictional Narrative Rubric, p. 96
Critical Response: Literary Analysis/Interpretation Rubric, p. 113
Writing Mini-Lesson: Drama Rubric, p. 110

Idea Bank

Customizing for
Performance Levels
Following are suggestions for matching Idea Bank topics with your students' performance levels:

- Less Advanced Students: 1, 4
- Average Students: 2, 5, 6
- More Advanced Students: 3, 7

Customizing for
Learning Modalities
Following are suggestions for matching Idea Bank topics with your students' learning modalities:

- Visual/Spatial: 6, 7
- Bodily/Kinesthetic: 5
- Interpersonal: 4, 5
- Verbal/Linguistic: 1, 2, 3, 4, 5, 6

Writing Mini-Lesson

Refer students to the Writing Handbook, page 1189, for instructions on the writing process, and page 119[illegible] for further information on creative writing.

Writing and Language Transparencies Use Writing Process Model 4: Dramatic Scene, pp. [illegible]5–34, to give students an overview of the process of writing a script.

Display the Story Map, p. 15, on the overhead projector. Instruct students to prepare a story map for their scripts.

Writer's Solution

Writing Lab CD-ROM
Have students write their scripts using the tutorial on Creative Writing. Follow these steps:

1. View the video clip from *Cyrano de Bergerac* to see ways of using details and character traits to create memorable characters.
2. Explore elements of plot with the Story Line Diagram.
3. Draft on computer.
4. Use the revision checker to highlight vague words so that they can be replaced.

Sourcebook
Have students use Chapter 6, Creative Writing (pp. 167–195), for additional support. The chapter includes a model from literature of a video script (p. 173), tips on drafting a play (p. 1[illegible]7), and a revision checklist for drama (p. 188).

Prepare and Engage

OBJECTIVES

1. To read, comprehend, and interpret a contemporary historical account
2. To explore thematic connections between a contemporary historical account and the selections in Part 3
3. To respond to the historical account through writing, speaking and listening, and projects

PORTFOLIO OPPORTUNITIES

Writing: Symbolic People; Diary of an Unhappy Queen; The Rhetoric of Royalty
Speaking and Listening: Crowning Event
Project: The Royal Family Tree

About the London *Times*

Newspapers are relatively modern inventions, appearing in the early seventeenth century. Before that time, individuals or groups might circulate newsletters, but these were not for a wide audience. Today, however, people in Britain love their newspapers, and as a result they have some of the highest readership in the world. *The Times* alone is read by more than 600,000 people.

The Times was founded in 1785 and originally called the *Daily Universal Register*. During the next century, it became the unofficial voice of the government. It suspended publication briefly during the 1970's, primarily over labor disputes. In 1981, it was purchased by an Australian, Rupert Murdoch.

Current and former members of the British royal family are popular tabloid topics. Bring in a copy of a scandal-sheet article or an unauthorized biography. Have students share the gossip they've heard. Ask students why they think the British royal family is of interest to American readers. Discuss how British subjects might feel about such articles. Then ask how the monarch and his or her family might feel. Have students share their opinions about whether public figures, such as royalty or politicians, have a right to privacy. Should people who represent a nation be held to higher standards of behavior?

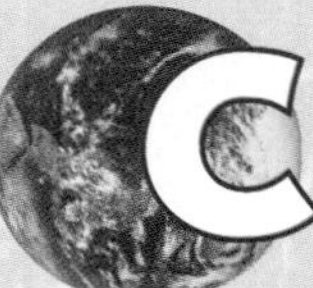

CONNECTIONS TO TODAY'S WORLD

Elizabeth II: A New Queen

Thematic Connection

A NATIONAL SPIRIT

A thousand years ago, the bloody wars of kings and queens defined Britain's national identity in a decisive way. *The Anglo-Saxon Chronicle* tells how Alfred, ninth-century warrior-king of a small kingdom in southern England, fought off the invading Danes and united all of Britain's Anglo-Saxon kingdoms under his rule. The affairs of kings and queens—their births and deaths, marriages and friendships, rivalries and assassinations—continued to govern the nation's destiny for centuries after Alfred's time.

THE NEW ROYALTY

Since the 1640's, though, when the people revolted and executed their king, the real power to govern has shifted to the country's Parliament and prime minister. Modern kings and queens have little to do with running the country. Their official duties are ceremonial—handing out awards or receiving foreign dignitaries. The kings and queens of the twentieth century may seem like shadows compared with the monarchs of the past.

Yet government officials in Britain still act in the name of "Her Majesty." And even while the gossip columns dissect the private lives of the royal family, the appearance of Queen Elizabeth II in public, waving from a car or balcony, still has a thrilling effect on her subjects.

NATIONAL SYMBOLS

A national identity binds together diverse people, most of whom have never met and may have few things in common. To anchor that idea of a nation in their hearts as well as in their minds, people look to emotionally charged symbols of national identity. Britain's monarch remains the foremost symbol of the British nation.

NEWSPAPER ACCOUNTS OF BRITISH ROYALTY

Open any newspaper in Britain and you're bound to find an article about a member of the royal family. Whether opening Parliament, visiting a hospital, or yachting in the Caribbean, the royal family makes the news.

Following is an especially important article about the royal family that appeared in *The London Times* on February 7, 1952. It gives a brief biography of Elizabeth II, Britain's new queen. (The report of George VI's death appears in the same paper.)

Prentice Hall Literature Program Resources

REINFORCE / RETEACH / EXTEND

Selection Support Pages
Build Vocabulary, p. 26
Thematic Connection, p. 27

Formal Assessment Selection Test, pp. 26–27; Assessment Resources Software

Resource Pro CD-ROM
"Elizabeth II: A New Queen"—includes all resource material and customizable lesson plan

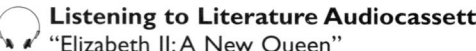

Listening to Literature Audiocassettes
"Elizabeth II: A New Queen"

Elizabeth II: A New Queen

The London Times 2/7/52

DEATH OF THE KING

THE NEW QUEEN EXPECTED IN LONDON TO-DAY

PUBLIC PROCLAMATION TO BE MADE TO-MORROW

It is with profound regret that we announce the death of the King at Sandringham early yesterday.

The following statement was issued from Buckingham Palace:

"It was announced from Sandringham at 10.45 a.m. to-day, February 6, 1952, that the King, who retired to rest last night in his usual health, passed peacefully away in his sleep early this morning."

The London Times 2/7/52

THE NEW QUEEN

AN OUTSTANDING REPRESENTATIVE OF HER GENERATION

Princess Elizabeth Alexandra Mary was
❶ born a little before three o'clock on the morning of April 21, 1926, at No. 17, Bruton Street, the London home of her grandparents, the late Lord and Lady Strathmore. At the age of five weeks she was baptized at Buckingham Palace by the late Lord Lang of Lambeth, then Dr. Cosmo Gordon Lang, Archbishop of York.

At that time the Prince of Wales, though unmarried, was not quite 32; and there was no expectation that the newly born Princess, especially as she might some day have a brother, would ever come very close to the succession. Even if there had been, it would probably not have been allowed to influence her early upbringing, which the Duke and Duchess of York deliberately kept as simple as possible. In infancy her time was divided between her parents' home in Piccadilly and the various country houses of her maternal grandparents in England and Scotland; and Lady Strathmore took charge of her when the Duke and Duchess went to Australia in 1927 to inaugurate the new capital.

King George V was devoted to his grandchild, and at his desire she was sent, at the age of two and a half, to keep him company at Bognor during his convalescence after his dangerous illness in 1928. The birth of her sister in August, 1930, brought her a playmate who was destined to be by far her closest friend until she was fully grown up. Her nursery days, spent mostly in the country and in constant association with horses, dogs, and other pets, may be said to have ended with the death of King George V in ❷ 1936 and the abdication of her uncle at the end of the same year. At this date the family moved from Piccadilly to Buckingham Palace, and the position of the Princess as Heiress-Presumptive took on new importance.

It was not, however, allowed to overshadow her education. She did not go to school but was taught, under the close personal direction of the Queen, by a governess, Miss Marion Crawford, who joined the household in 1933.

The outbreak of war found the Royal Family at Balmoral; but the Princesses were soon moved to Windsor, where the quiet routine of lessons continued through the darkest and most stirring days. Gradually, subjects specially appropriate to a future queen, notably constitutional history, were introduced into the curriculum; and the Provost of Eton took a large part in the Princess's instruction. She became a good musician and singer; and in regular participation in amateur theatricals she not only showed a marked talent for acting but overcame the tendency to shyness which at one time looked like becoming a handicap to her in the great position that lay ahead.

On her sixteenth birthday in 1942 the

Develop Understanding

One-Minute Insight This modern historical account deals with an important aspect of British life: royalty. Like earlier works, it is filled with specific factual details: names, dates, places, and events. It also presupposes an educated British audience that would recognize not only the vocabulary but also the references to the conventions of royalty.

Customize for *English Language Learners*

This will be a difficult selection for English language learners, since it contains unfamiliar names and formal language. To help these students, first explain what section is about and then have them read it. For instance, explain that the first four paragraphs cover Queen Elizabeth's early childhood and education.

Thematic Connection

❶ **A National Spirit** Ask students what people and places mentioned in the text are assumed to be known to the British public. *Readers are expected to understand the significance of titles like* Prince of Wales *and the* Duke and Duchess of York *and places such as* Sandringham *and* Buckingham Palace. Help students realize how such assumptions foster a national spirit. *"Insiders" are bound together by common knowledge and interests.*

❷ **Clarification** After King George V died, his son Edward became King Edward VIII. However, he abdicated—resigned as king—in order to marry an American divorced woman, of whom many disapproved. He is the only British monarch ever to step down by choice.

Humanities: Photography

The Coronation of Elizabeth II, 1953, by Sir Cecil Beaton.

Sir Cecil Beaton (1904–1980) was an English designer, photographer, and writer. Beaton attended school and college in England. During World War II, he worked for Britain's Ministry of Information. Besides taking dramatic portraits of well-known people, Beaton designed the costumes for the stage version of *My Fair Lady* and for the film version of *Gigi.*

When Queen Elizabeth II was crowned on June 2, 1953, she was only twenty-seven. Beaton's photograph is designed to impress viewers with her power and authority as head of church and state. Three symbols of this authority are arranged near the center of the image: the crown, the scepter, and the orb. In the background, viewers see the inside of a cathedral, probably Westminster Abbey, where every British coronation since 1066 has taken place.

Use these questions for discussion:

1. Why, do you think, was a famous photographer such as Beaton chosen for this official picture? *Students may say that he could be expected to do a good job.*
2. What does this picture emphasize, and why? *The photograph emphasizes the trappings of royalty, rather than the young woman wearing the crown; it is meant to emphasize continuity and tradition rather than reveal her personality.*

Customize for
Less Proficient Readers
Suggest that students construct a simple timeline, beginning with the birth of Princess Elizabeth Alexandra Mary and ending with the death of King George VI. Have them read the article looking for the four or five most important milestones along the timeline.

Customize for
Visual/Spatial Learners
Have students find pictures or videotapes of royal events that show the pageantry associated with the British Royal Family. Discuss how such events help bind the nation together.

❶ **Clarification** *A.T.S.* stands for the Auxiliary Territorial Service, a support branch of the military. As a member of the A.T.S., Elizabeth trained as a mechanic to repair military vehicles. Her stint in the A.T.S. did not last long—she joined in March, and World War II ended in Europe in May.

◆ Critical Thinking

❷ **Evaluate** Ask students what tone the writer uses and why. *The tone is positive, almost flattering; the woman is now the queen, and therefore treated with the utmost respect.*

◆ Critical Thinking

❸ **Draw Conclusions** Ask students what conclusions they can draw about the inclusion of details about Philip's parents. *A person's birth and history are important, especially when he or she is marrying a future monarch. Philip's parentage reveals that he is a distant cousin to Elizabeth; his mother was a great-granddaughter of Queen Victoria.*

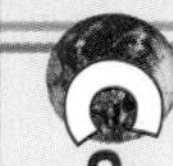

Princess registered for national service, and soon after her eighteenth birthday—when special legislation was passed to qualify her to act as a Counsellor of State in the King's absence from the realm—she was gazetted ❶ to a commission in the A.T.S. This was at her own insistence, the King withdrawing his original ruling that her duties as heir precluded her entry to any of the services. She in fact became an efficient driver in the mechanical transport branch of the A.T.S.

PUBLIC CAREER

Her public career may be said to have begun with her broadcast to the children of the Empire during the Battle of Britain; but it was only when war ended that she began to emerge into full publicity as a leading figure in ceremonial and social life. Naturally most of her appearances were made under the wing of one or both of her parents. But she was accompanied only by members of her own staff—her first lady in waiting had been appointed in July—when she went to Greenock in November 1944, and launched the great battleship H.M.S. Vanguard. The commissioning of this ship was the principal event of her notable visit to Northern Ireland—again without her parents—in the summer of 1946; and it was in the Vanguard that she embarked with the rest of the Royal Family on February 1, 1947, for their tour of South Africa and Rhodesia.

This was the Princess's first journey outside the British Isles, and the beginning of her introduction to those dominions beyond the seas over which, equally with the United Kingdom, she will now reign.

Although she was content to remain somewhat in the background, especially in the early part of the tour, South Africans rapidly became conscious of her as a personality, and her character made a great and favourable impression. A speech at the opening of the graving dock, named after herself, at East London seemed to mark the emergence of a new representative of the ❷ younger generation; and at her coming of age, which she celebrated in Cape Town, she broadcast to the Empire, and especially to the young, in vigorous and vibrant terms which carried the impression farther.

She was already outstandingly qualified to be the representative figure among the girls who came to womanhood with her. She had absorbed an admirably balanced education and entered into the gaieties appropriate to her age, from the racecourse to the ballroom. But she already combined with a capacity for enjoyment a high seriousness which even at that time made her insist upon doing thoroughly everything that her hand found to do, and spare herself nothing that belonged to her preparation for the greater responsibilities that she knew lay ahead. ❷

Soon after the return of the Royal Family from South Africa, the nation learnt with joy on July 9, 1947, that the King had gladly given his consent to the betrothal of the Heiress-Presumptive to Lieutenant Philip Mountbatten, R.N., son of the late Prince Andrew of Greece and Princess Andrew (Princess Alice of Battenberg). ❸ Messages of congratulation to the betrothed couple from the people of the Commonwealth and from all parts of the world showed clearly the affection in which Princess Elizabeth was held, and the four months of their engagement during which preparations for the royal wedding went forward were a period of intense and eager expectation for the nation. The feelings of the nation were expressed by the then Prime Minister, Mr. Attlee, when, on October 22, he moved a congratulatory Address to their Majesties on the occasion of the royal marriage, and said: "Her royal Highness has shown, in the public duties which she has undertaken, the same unerring graciousness and understanding, and the same human simplicity, which has endeared the Royal House to the people of this country," and by Mr. Churchill, who prophesied that millions would welcome the joyous event as a flash of colour on the hard road we had to travel.

On the eve of the wedding came the announcement that Lieutenant Mountbatten had been made Duke of Edinburgh.

MARRIAGE

The marriage was solemnized[1] in Westminster Abbey on November 20, when the royal processions were watched by countless thousands. The ceremony was per-

1. **solemnized:** Done according to ritual or tradition.

Cultural Connection

Royal Succession
Different cultures have different ways of determining who is to be the next monarch. Britain follows the rule of primogeniture, in which the oldest son inherits the position. If there is no son, then the oldest daughter inherits. Elizabeth II succeeded her father because she was his oldest child. In contrast, her namesake, Elizabeth I, ascended the throne after her younger brother, Edward VI, and her older sister, Mary I. Another type of inheritance is described in Bede's *History,* in which he reports that Picts pass down leadership from maternal uncle to nephew. Still other methods exist for determining who gets to rule. Have interested students find out more and present their findings in illustrated reports.

formed by the Archbishop of Canterbury in the presence of three generations of the Royal Family, and was followed by scenes of rich pageantry and of homely greetings from people gathered from all parts of the British Isles as the bride and bridegroom left for Winchester, on their journey to Broadlands, near Romsey, where they spent their honeymoon.

Early in the New Year they set out on their public life together, and in May paid an official visit to Paris, where they were greeted with a welcome of great warmth and spontaneity. Then early in June it was announced that the Princess would soon cancel all her engagements. On November 14 her son, Prince Charles, was born. In 1949 Princess Elizabeth resumed her busy public life and during that year the Duke of Edinburgh returned to sea. He was stationed at Malta and in November was joined there by his wife.

At the end of March, 1950, the Princess paid a second visit to Malta and while there it was announced that her Royal Highness was expecting a baby. Princess Anne was born in August. In November Princess Elizabeth joined the Duke of Edinburgh and together they visited Athens. In the spring of 1951 they went to Rome, where they were received by the Pope, and it was in Rome that her Royal Highness celebrated her twenty-fifth birthday.

Returning to England in time for the opening of the Festival of Britain, she embarked upon a programme of public duties more formidable[2] even than those of the years immediately before. It fell to her more than once on great state occasions to stand in the place of her father and to speak for him.

When, last September, the King underwent an operation, Princess Elizabeth and the Duke of Edinburgh deferred their departure for Canada, but the King's progress enabled them to leave by air on October 7. Their six weeks' tour, probably the most strenuous ever undertaken by royal personages, took them across Canada in a memorable series of visits and ceremonies. Not least successful was their visit to Washington, where they were welcomed by President Truman. Upon their return, a "brilliant mission" accomplished, they were ceremonially received in Liverpool on November 17, and given an official welcome at Guildhall two days later.

After spending Christmas with the Royal Family at Sandringham, the Princess and the Duke left London Airport last Thursday on the first stage of the journey which was to have taken them to Ceylon, Australia, and New Zealand, but which has been so untimely cut short only four days after they reached their hunting lodge at Nyeri, in Kenya. ❹

2. **formidable:** Awe-inspiring in size.

Guide for Responding

◆ Literature and Your Life

Reader's Response Name three things that you would most enjoy about being a monarch.

Thematic Focus Describe the effect of the article's serious treatment of Elizabeth's life.

☑ Check Your Comprehension

1. What is Elizabeth's relation to the king whom she succeeded?
2. Name three public functions that Princess Elizabeth performed after World War II.

◆ Critical Thinking

INTERPRET

1. Name three details that show the new queen's virtues. **[Analyze]**
2. What overall impression of the new queen does the *Times* strive to create? **[Interpret]**

EVALUATE

3. At points, the reader of the *Times* article may suspect that royalty does not have a "real job." (a) Identify two passages that might encourage such suspicions. (b) Explain the implications of these passages. **[Evaluate]**

◆ Critical Thinking

❹ **Interpret** What does the writer mean by the trip being "untimely cut short"? *The King died and Elizabeth had to return.*

Reinforce and Extend

Answers

◆ Literature and Your Life

Reader's Response Students might respond that they would enjoy being the center of attention, being wealthy, and having many different homes.

Thematic Focus Although the article is about Elizabeth, it also creates an effect of awe and admiration for the institution of the monarchy.

☑ Check Your Comprehension

1. She is his oldest child.
2. Possible response: Elizabeth commissioned and launched a battleship; she toured South Africa and Rhodesia; she gave a speech at the opening of a new dock.

◆ Critical Thinking

1. She asserts her independence and willingness to accept responsibility when she insists on joining the British war effort as a driver; her personality makes a good impression on radio and in public appearances; she shows "a high seriousness" and does thoroughly everything she sets her hand to.
2. Elizabeth is serious, hard-working, and independent-minded, and has been aware from an early age of the nature of royal responsibilities. At the same time, she has a human side, and represents the generation of which she is part. She is well suited to be Britain's queen.
3. Elizabeth's program of public duties is "formidable"; her tour of North America is "'brilliant.'" Since the article does not give any hint of what the duties or tour entailed, it seems likely that they involved little of substance. The strong adjectives are justified only because the person concerned is royal.

Answers
Thematic Connection

1. Modern British monarchs do not wield real political power; modern British monarchs reign over a country that is already united, whereas Alfred fought to create a nation.
2. For Bede, a shared religion, Christianity, makes a bond between people deeper than their national differences. For Bede, national identity is a question of revealed truth, not sentiment. For the authors of *The Anglo-Saxon Chronicle,* whose side one fights on in battle seems to be crucial. National identity is a matter of war and self-defense, not sentiment. Chaucer, showing a Britain unified both by a pilgrimage and by a common love of stories, perhaps combines something of Bede and of the contemporary, sentimentalized idea of British identity.

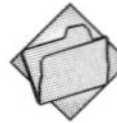

Idea Bank

Customizing for
Performance Levels

Following are suggestions for matching Idea Bank topics with your students' performance levels:

Less Advanced Students: 1
Average Students: 2, 4
More Advanced Students: 3, 5

Customizing for
Learning Modalities

Following are suggestions for matching Idea Bank topics with your students' learning modalities:

Visual/Spatial: 5
Interpersonal: 4
Verbal/Linguistic: 1, 2, 3, 4, 5

Thematic Connection

A National Spirit

The continued presence through the centuries of a monarch on the British throne shows the importance of symbols in creating and nourishing a national identity.

1. Name two respects in which the British monarchy of today has a different relation to England than King Alfred the Great had.
2. The *Times* article implies that common sentiment—a people's ability to mourn their old king and to welcome proudly their new queen—helps to bind the nation of Britain together. Contrast this idea with the sources of Britain's national identity found in *The History of the English Church and People,* in *The Anglo-Saxon Chronicle*, and in Chaucer's *The Canterbury Tales*.

Idea Bank

Writing

1. **Symbolic People** Monarchs symbolize the countries they rule. List people who symbolize things you or others value. Next to each name, write down the qualities the person seems to embody.
2. **Diary of an Unhappy Queen** If you feel unwell at four, it's on the news at six. However, they rarely ask for your opinion on really important matters. Also, for goodness' sake, don't forget to smile, however grumpy you may feel. Being a ceremonial royal ruler must certainly have its drawbacks. Write down the inner thoughts of a royal ruler in diary form.
3. **The Rhetoric of Royalty** Write an essay in which you compare and contrast newspaper or magazine profiles of celebrities in a particular field (professional sports, the movies, rock, politics, or some other field). What virtues (or vices) are commonly discussed in these articles?

Speaking and Listening

4. **Crowning Event** No one expected Elizabeth to become queen because there were others entitled to the throne before her. Research the rules that govern who gets to be the monarch of Britain. Present these rules to your class in dramatic form by assigning roles in the royal family to a number of classmates. Show how a series of choices and events could lead to the choice of one of your classmates as ruler. **[Social Studies Link]**

Project

5. **The Royal Family Tree** Elizabeth II is the latest in a long line of England's Monarchs. Create an annotated family tree of the rulers of Britain—from Alfred the Great to the present. For each ruler, explain how they came to the throne—did they inherit it or fight for it? **[Social Studies Link; Art Link]**

✓ ASSESSMENT OPTIONS

Formal Assessment, Selection Test, pp. 26–27, and Assessment Resources Software. The selection test is designed so that it can be easily customized to the performance levels of your students.

PORTFOLIO ASSESSMENT

Use the following rubrics in the ***Alternative Assessment*** booklet to assess student writing:
Symbolic People: Description Rubric, p. 98
Diary of an Unhappy Queen: Fictional Narrative Rubric, p. 96
The Rhetoric of Royalty: Comparison/Contrast Rubric, p. 104

Writing Process Workshop

College-Application Essay

During the Anglo-Saxon period, writers such as Bede began producing vivid records of key historical events. As you grow older, you may be called on to develop written records of your own personal history. In a **college-application essay,** for instance, you'll be called on to describe key experiences that shaped you as a person and to explain what you gained from these experiences. This type of essay may also require you to outline your achievements and describe your personality.

The following skills, introduced in this section's Writing Mini-Lessons, will help you write an effective college-application essay.

Writing Skills Focus

- Use a clear **organization plan** to ensure that your audience will be able to follow the events and absorb the information you present. Keep in mind that your organization plan should fit your topic.
- Establish **coherence** by making logical connections between sentences so that each idea clearly follows the one before it. (See p. 85.)
- Use **humor** where appropriate to grab your readers' attention and to reveal your personality.

These skills are evident in the following paragraph from a college-application essay.

Writing Model

Can you imagine being angry with your third-grade teacher for offering you encouragement? ① It wasn't until I graduated from elementary school that I realized my teacher, Mrs. Allerton, had become one of the most important people in my life. ② As I waited in line for her to sign my graduation album, ③ I noticed that she seemed to be studying each entry in the albums of others ahead of me.

① The writer begins the application essay with a humorous question. It grabs the reader's attention and indicates that the writer is about to learn a valuable lesson.

② The writer constructs his introduction effectively by beginning with a question that draws the reader in and then follows up with a statement that reveals the focus of the essay.

③ This phrase connects this sentence to the previous one, making the passage coherent.

Beyond the Classroom

Career Connection: Workplace Skill

Presenting a Positive Image Explain to students that one goal of their college-application essays is to present a positive image of themselves as motivated and reliable. Also explain that presenting a positive image should be a goal in the workplace. Let students know that accepting tasks in a positive manner, never belittling or making coworkers feel uncomfortable, and owning up to their mistakes and correcting them are ways to present such an image. Let students know that the way they present themselves at their workplace will greatly influence the way their careers progress.

Prepare and Engage

Establish Writing Guidelines
Review the following suggestions for a college-application essay:

- A college-application essay should follow the format that each college has defined in its application form. The essays should use an organizational plan appropriate for the type of writing required.
- The essay must be coherent; it includes an attention-grabbing introduction, a body that supports the topic, and a memorable conclusion.
- Humor is an excellent way to reveal personality. Using humor will keep readers interested and influence their evaluation of the application.

You may want to give students the Scoring Rubrics for Narration based on Personal Experience, p. 97, and Description, p. 98, in ***Alternative Assessment***. As a class combine these rubrics to determine the criteria on which a college-application essay should be evaluated.

Refer students to the Writing Handbook, page 1189, to review the writing process, and page 1193 for information on writing a college-application essay. You may also want to suggest that students review the College and Career Handbook on pages 1204–1206.

Writing Lab CD-ROM
If students have access to computers, you may have them work in the Practical and Technical Writing tutorial to complete their essays. Suggest that they follow these steps:

1. Review the annotated model of a college-application essay.
2. Determine audience and purpose by using the Audience Profile and Purpose Profile.
3. Draft their papers on the computer.
4. Use a revision checker to pinpoint informal or imprecise language.

Sourcebook
Students can find additional support in the chapter on Practical and Technical Writing, pp. 230–264.

Develop Student Writing

Prewriting

Since a clear organization is an indicator of a student's writing and academic ability, help students concentrate on creating a coherent and unified paper. Consider providing students with any of the following graphic organizers available in ***Writing and Language Transparencies.*** These organizers will help them arrange their information: the Branching Organizer (p. 95), Argument Organizer (p.103), Problem-and-Solution Organizer (p.107), Comparison-and-Contrast Organizer (p.115), Cause-and-Effect Organizer (p. 119), Outline Organizer (p.123).

Customize for
English Language Learners

Many of these students will be planning to attend college. Because they may find it difficult to express themselves in English, have them first draft their essays in their native language and then orally convey what they wrote in English. This process will allow them to gather and organize their thoughts before attempting to write an essay in English.

Writers at Work Videodisc

To give students insight into organizing ideas, play the segment in which Jeff Christian talks about how he organizes his ideas. Then ask students to identify the basic structure he uses to create coherent writing.

Play frames 37727 to 39423

Drafting

As students draft, they should incorporate transitions to make their writing coherent and organized. Point out different transitions shown on this page (in Applying Language Skills) that are useful in the organization they have chosen.

Sourcebook

Suggest that students review page 255 for additional transitions that would work with their organizational plans.

Writing Process Workshop

Applying Language Skills: Using Transitions

Use transitions to indicate relationships among ideas and tighten your organization.

- To indicate **chronological order** use transitions such as *before, as soon as, next, after, then,* and *at that point.*
- To indicate **order of importance** use transitions such as *first, best,* or *least of all.*
- To introduce an **example** use transitional words such as *namely, in other words,* or *such as.*

Writing Application Identify areas in your paper that indicate relationships in time, importance, or where examples are introduced. Add transitions to tie ideas together.

Writer's Solution Connection
Writing Lab

To help you organize details for your college-application essay, use the graphic organizers in the Writing Lab Tutorial on Practical Writing.

Prewriting

Consider Your Audience A college-application essay has a clearly defined audience: the members of the admissions committee. Before you even choose your topic, think carefully about the types of things that might impress this audience. Ask yourself:

- What achievements would catch their interest? What personal qualities would they like to see?
- What experiences have you had in which you exhibited these personal qualities?

Choose Your Topic Use your ideas about what will impress your audience to come up with a topic. You might choose to focus on a single event—such as your most powerful learning experience or your greatest personal experience—or you might focus on a series of events or a relationship with a special person.

Develop a Clear Organization Most likely, your topic will dictate how you organize your essay. For example, if you're describing a series of events, you'll probably want to use a chronological organization. On the other hand, if your essay is outlining your most important personal qualities, you may want to use an order-of-importance organization. Once you've chosen your organization, jot down some details you'll include in your essay and arrange them in the proper order.

Drafting

Maintain Coherence As you draft your paper, create coherence by using transitions to indicate how the ideas and events in your essay fit together. Also, be careful not to include any details that don't fit in with the main points you're making.

Incorporate Humor Using humor to reveal your personality is an excellent way to grab your readers' attention and help them evaluate you as a real person, not just an academic student. For example, you may use exaggeration to emphasize a reaction you had to an absurd or ridiculous situation. As you write, determine the best places in your essay to include humorous events.

Organize As you draft your paper, follow your organizational plan. Stop after each paragraph to double-check the direction in which your essay is headed. You may decide that another type of organization is more suitable.

Writing Lab CD-ROM

Have students use the Transition Word Bins in the drafting section of the tutorial on Practical and Technical Writing.

Applying Language Skills

Using Transitions

After students draft their essays, have them review their papers and highlight all of the transitional words. Then have students add or delete transitions where there are too many or not enough.

Revising

Use the following checklist, which refers to the Writing Skills Focus on page 135, while revising your paper.

- ▶ Did you use transitions to maintain coherence?
  Underline the transitions in your paper and the repetition of key ideas. If you have not used enough of either, add more.
- ▶ Have you kept to the organizational pattern you chose?
  Review your essay and create an outline as you read. Then check the order of details in the outline to ensure that you've used a clear, consistent organization.
- ▶ Is your use of humor effective?
  Read your essay to a friend or family member and ask for their opinions of your humorous descriptions.

Revision Model

Ever since the seventh grade, I've been known as "Indiana Grimes."
① Although my real name is Lois, my friends recognize the longing I have for adventures. ② ~~It~~ This thirst for excitement stemmed from a tubing mishap that left a friend and me stranded on the rocks in the mighty Delaware River. ③ There I learned a great deal about responsibility and a respect for nature.

① The writer adds this statement to begin her discussion of a serious occurrence with a light, humorous tone.
② She adds this phrase to make a clear connection to the previous sentence.
③ To establish the cause-and-effect format of the paper, the writer adds this statement summing up the effect of her adventure.

Publishing

- ▶ **Portfolio** Add your college-application essays to a personal portfolio of other essays you have written.
- ▶ **Classroom** Share your techniques and ideas for college applications with other students. Compile a list of the most effective techniques to help other students prepare their essays.

Applying Language Skills: Using Pronouns Correctly

When using pronouns, avoid confusion by making sure that there is a clear antecedent—the word or group of words to which the pronoun refers. A vague reference will result if an antecedent is not clear.

Unclear: Move the plastic tab to a closed position. This prevents accidental erasure. (*This* has no apparent antecedent.)

Clear: Move the plastic tab to a closed position. This shift prevents accidental erasure. (The meaning is clarified by adding the noun *shift* to the sentence.)

Writing Application Underline the pronouns in your paper. Make sure that they all have clear antecedents.

Writer's Solution Connection Language Lab

For more practice with pronouns, complete the Pronouns and Antecedents lesson in the Sharpening Language Skills section.

Revising

Have students work with peer reviewers who can evaluate whether or not they have used humor effectively in their papers. Have students consider whether humor provides insight into their peer's personality or if it instead seems inappropriate and jarring. If it is not appropriate, the writer should revise or remove it.

Writer's Solution

Writing Lab CD-ROM
Have students use a Peer Evaluation Checklist for evaluating one another's work. Also direct their attention to tips for peer editors.

Publishing

Students may adjust their college-application essay to make it appropriate for a summer job application or for a program they are interested in; or they may also revise it to attach to a résumé.

Reinforce and Extend

Review the Writing Guidelines
Ask students if the rubric that the class established was an effective standard for evaluating their essays.

Applying Language Skills

Using Pronouns Correctly
Stress the importance of clear antecedents in creating a coherent paper. Have students complete the Writing Application and then have a peer review their work.

Writer's Solution

For additional instruction and practice, use the practice pages on Pronouns and Antecedents, pp. 64–67, in the *Writer's Solution Grammar Practice Book.*

✓ ASSESSMENT		4	3	2	1
PORTFOLIO ASSESSMENT Use the rubrics on Personal Narrative and Description in ***Alternative Assessment*** (pp. 97 and 98) or the one you developed as a class, to assess students' writing. Add these criteria to customize the rubric to this assignment.	**Coherence**	The essay is coherent; the writer provides logical connections so that ideas flow smoothly.	The essay needs transitions in a few places to show the connection among ideas.	The essay does not present a tight and coherent organization.	The ideas in the essay are not connected and do not flow smoothly from one to another.
	Revealing the Writer's Personality	The writer successfully reveals his or her personality characteristics and accomplishments to the reader.	The writer reveals many personality characteristics and accomplishments, but should include more.	The writer includes few details that reveal personality characteristics and accomplishments.	The writer does not include details that reveal personality characteristics or accomplishments.

Introduce the Strategy

Students may have already had the experience of filling out applications. Remind them that application forms are often the way in which they introduce themselves and make a first impression on prospective employers or admission counselors.

Often applications for jobs must be completed on the spot. To prepare students for the experience of filling out an application under time pressure, suggest that they interview others about the types of questions they have found in applications. Then have students compile a list of the questions and answer them within their own time frame. They should review this list before completing an application. Also suggest that students do not actually refer to their lists when filling out the application, as this may give employers a wrong impression.

Apply the Strategy

Have students review the application for any parts that might require more thought when answering. Then have them answer the questions.

Answers

Suggested response:

1. A prospective employer asks for an objective because he or she wants to know why someone is applying for a job. The objective indicates motivation and gives the employer an idea about how someone will work. For example, an employer would view an objective stating that someone needs money much differently from an objective indicating a desire to learn about a particular field.
2. The space for comments provides the student with an opportunity to give more information about himself or herself. Availability, background, goals, and special experiences or unique qualifications might be included here.

Reading a Job Application

Real-World Reading Skills Workshop

Strategies for Success

Applications, such as job applications and college applications, are often the main means by which you introduce yourself to people who make decisions that are crucial to your future. To fill out an application clearly and accurately, you must first read and understand the questions.

Identify the Focus of Each Question Make sure you understand what each question on the application is asking. An application blank labeled "Work Experience" is your opportunity to list the jobs you have had. The person who will read your answer is looking for some indication that you can take on responsibility and satisfy an employer, as well as some information about the background and the skills you might have acquired.

Most questions on an application are standard, and you will quickly become familiar with them. Your answers to these questions should be brief and formal. Sometimes, though, applications include open-ended questions. There may be a space for "Comments," for instance. Such questions invite you to tell your interviewer more about your availability, background, or goals.

Looking Beyond the Page Most questions on a job application, or any other kind of application, are pretty direct. Sometimes, though, it pays to look beyond what's right on the page. For instance, you might have little paid work experience. Your prospective employer is asking about your experience, though, to find out whether you can take on responsibility. The unpaid, hard work you've done for a church or social group indicates that you can handle responsibility.

Apply the Strategy

Imagine that a friend has asked you to help him or her with the following job application.

1. Why is the prospective employer asking for your friend's "Objective"? What kind of information would fit the question?
2. Why is there space for "Comments" on the application? What information might be suitable to include here?

APPLICATION FOR EMPLOYMENT

Name: ______________________
(First) (Middle) (Last)

Address: ______________________
(Street and Number, City, State, Zip)

School: ______________________

Date of Birth: ______________________
(Month, Day, Year)

Objective: ______________________

Experience: ______________________

References: ______________________

Comments: ______________________

Here are other situations in which understanding the questions on a form or application is important:

- *Giving a medical history at a doctor's office or hospital*
- *Filling out a college admissions application*
- *Applying for a scholarship or financial aid*

Beyond the Classroom

Career Connection

Employment Agent An employment agent works for many different companies and many prospective employees in an attempt to match the right person with the right job. An agent must evaluate hundreds of applications and résumés. The questions they choose to ask on applications will help them figure out what job would best suit a client and what client would best suit a company. When students are seeking employment, explain that they may provide a résumé to an employment agent. They should then meet with the agent to discuss the type of job they are seeking and their qualifications. Then the agent will evaluate the résumé and client and see if any of the companies seeking employees has a position that would be appropriate. The agent would then send the client on an interview.

PART 4 *Perils and Adventures*

St. George and the Dragon, c.1506, Raphael, National Gallery of Art, Washington, D.C.

One-Minute Insight The selections in this section are full of the perils and adventures that characterize medieval legends. In *Sir Gawain and the Green Knight,* the hero faces challenges that test his courage, loyalty, and honesty—virtues all knights of King Arthur's court should possess. The final showdown between Gawain and the Green Knight will provide thrills for readers as they await the outcome of the challenge.

In *Morte d'Arthur,* King Arthur battles and kills his own son, Mordred. The knights who were with King Arthur during that fateful last day marvel at the wonders and mysteries that surround their king, as Arthur is carried away on a barge to Avilion—his final adventure.

The letters of Margaret Paston provide an insight into the perils of maintaining an estate. The ballads tell of perilous adventures that befell unfortunate individuals.

Customize for
Varying Student Needs

When assigning the selections in this part, keep in mind these factors:

from *Sir Gawain and the Green Knight*

- High-interest long poem that tells of adventure (12 pp.)
- Less proficient readers may have difficulty reading some sections
- Some sections are bloody and graphic; some sections touch on supernatural or magical events

from *Morte d'Arthur*

- Archaic vocabulary may prove difficult to less advanced readers
- Magical and mysterious events
- Graphic battle scene

Letters of Margaret Paston

- Readable despite some archaic phrasing

Four Ballads

- Brief
- Dialect may prove challenging

Humanities: Art

St. George and the Dragon, 1506, by Raphael.

Born Raffaello Sanzio in Urbino, Italy, Raphael (1483–1520) was one of the supreme artists of the High Renaissance in Italy. As a boy Raphael left home to study with the great painter Perugino; later, he was strongly influenced by the work of the older painters Leonardo da Vinci and Michelangelo. Although he did not live long, Raphael was a tremendously successful artist, patronized by rulers and popes.

St. George is the patron saint of England. The most famous legend associated with St. George was his slaying of a dragon and rescue of a princess.

Link the art to "Perils and Adventures," with the following questions:

1. What elements in the painting help add to the heroic stature of St. George? *Sample answer: St. George is a handsome young man in gleaming armor on a beautiful white horse. He has already overmastered the rather small dragon. All eyes in the painting—the dragon's, the horse's, the princess's—are directed at St. George.*
2. Why might St. George be better known for this legend than for his real-life martyrdom for being a Christian? *Sample answer: The dragon might be viewed as a symbol of evil, and St. George's victory over it symbolizes the conquest of evil by good. In real life, St. George was brave but not invincible—he was put to death for his religion.*

Guide for Interpreting

Prepare and Engage

OBJECTIVES

1. To read, comprehend, interpret, and respond to medieval romances
2. To relate medieval romances to personal experience
3. To summarize a story's main ideas
4. To recognize the elements of medieval romances
5. To build vocabulary in context and learn the word root *-droit-*
6. To identify comparative and superlative forms of modifiers
7. To write a valedictory speech, using effective repetition
8. To respond to medieval romances through writing, speaking and listening, and projects

SKILLS INSTRUCTION

Vocabulary:
Word Roots: *-droit-*
Grammar:
Comparative and Superlative Forms
Reading Strategy:
Summarize
Literary Focus:
Medieval Romance
Writing:
Effective Repetition
Speaking and Listening:
Oral Report (teacher edition)
Critical Viewing:
Interpret; Infer; Compare and Contrast; Assess; Draw Conclusions; Deduce

PORTFOLIO OPPORTUNITIES

Writing: T-shirt; Résumé; Response to Criticism
Writing Mini-Lesson: Valedictory Speech
Speaking and Listening: Oral Report; Multimedia Presentation
Projects: Musical Presentation; Illuminated Manuscript

More About the Authors

No one is completely sure who wrote *Sir Gawain and the Green Knight.* Many scholars refer to unknown author as "The Pearl Poet" because they believe that this writer also created three other poems, one of which was called *The Pearl.*

Sir Thomas Malory's life seems as cloaked in mystery and legend as King Arthur's. Scholar P.J.C. Field says of him, "... he had access to very expensive manuscripts, that he knew French and was proud of it, and that he loved hunting, tournaments, and chivalry."

Legendary Knights

The feudal system of medieval Europe grew out of the tradition of warriors swearing an oath of loyalty to a chief who provided for their needs. Medieval nobles carried on this tradition by providing for knights, or mounted warriors, in exchange for their loyalty.

The Code of Chivalry Beginning in the eleventh century, feudal nobles developed a code of conduct called chivalry. This code combined Christian values and the virtues of being a warrior. A knight was expected to be brave, generous, and loyal; to right wrongs; and to defend the helpless without hope of reward.

King Arthur and His Knights The legendary King Arthur and his Knights of the Round Table served as models of chivalrous behavior in countless medieval tales. *Sir Gawain and the Green Knight,* for example, tells how Arthur's nephew Sir Gawain was put to the test. In meeting this test, Sir Gawain is admirable but not invulnerable, which lends psychological truth to this medieval story. As one critic puts it, the hero "gains in human credibility what he loses in ideal perfection."

Sir Thomas Malory

(1405?–1471)

The identity of Sir Thomas Malory is a mystery. Several crimes were attributed to him—such as looting, extorting money, setting an ambush with intent to murder, and raiding cattle. He was even charged with breaking out of jail and once escaped custody by swimming a moat! However, he denied any wrongdoing.

A Prisoner It is generally accepted that during the War of the Roses (the bloody conflict between the two factions of royalty that marred the latter half of the fifteenth century in England), Malory was imprisoned at least once. It is not certain to what extent the criminal charges were justified; nevertheless, Malory spent the greater portion of his later years in prison.

A Book From Behind Bars It is believed that Malory completed *Morte d'Arthur,* his account of King Arthur's life, in prison and may even have died there. His great prose work was given its name and published posthumously in 1485 by William Caxton, the man who established the first printing press in England.

◆ Background for Understanding

History: The Legends of King Arthur

Legends are anonymous traditional stories that reflect the attitudes and values of the society that created them. The heroes of legends, such as Sir Gawain or King Arthur, usually possess qualities that the society considers admirable.

The legend of King Arthur is probably based on the life of a Celtic warrior who fought the Germanic invaders of England in the late fifth and early sixth centuries. His role as a defender of England made him a hero to Britons and led people to invent stories about his miraculous deeds.

Although the legend of Arthur arose in England, it has appealed to people from many different countries. Everywhere, readers are stirred by the story of a wise and noble king who rules from the great castle of Camelot and wields the magical sword Excalibur. They are touched by his death, which seems more like a strange vanishing, and by the notion that he will return one day.

Journal Writing Think about a legend of today—someone who has accomplished difficult or important tasks. Identify this person and briefly describe his or her achievements.

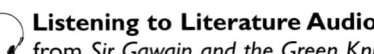

Prentice Hall Literature Program Resources

REINFORCE / RETEACH / EXTEND

Selection Support Pages
Build Vocabulary: Word Roots: *-droit-,* p. 28
Build Grammar Skills: Comparative and Superlative Forms, p. 29
Reading Strategy: Summarize, p. 30
Literary Focus: Medieval Romance, p. 31

Strategies for Diverse Students Needs, p. 6

Beyond Literature
Media Connection: King Arthur, p. 6

Formal Assessment Selection Test, pp. 31–33;
Assessment Resources Software

Alternative Assessment, p. 6

Writing and Language Transparencies
Outline, p. 123

Resource Pro CD-ROM
from *Sir Gawain and the Green Knight;* from *Morte d'Arthur*—includes all resource material and a customizable lesson plan

Listening to Literature Audiocassettes
from *Sir Gawain and the Green Knight;* from *Morte d'Arthur*

from Sir Gawain and the Green Knight ◆ *from* Morte d'Arthur ◆

◆ Literature and Your Life

CONNECT YOUR EXPERIENCE

You may not slay many dragons on an average day. However, if you volunteer at a soup kitchen, defend someone weaker than you, or remain loyal to friends, you are living by a knightly code of behavior called chivalry.

In *Sir Gawain and the Green Knight* and *Morte d'Arthur,* you encounter the legendary men from chivalry's hall of fame: King Arthur and the Knights of the Round Table.

THEMATIC FOCUS: PERILS AND ADVENTURES

As you read these selections, ask yourself why a code of chivalry was especially important in the Middle Ages.

◆ Build Vocabulary

WORD ROOTS: *-droit-*

As you read these selections, you will come across the word *adroitly,* which means "with great skill." This word is built upon the root *-droit-,* meaning "right." The use of "right" to mean "skillful" reflects a historical bias for right-handedness.

WORD BANK

Before you read, preview this list of words.

assay
adjure
feigned
adroitly
largesse
righteous
entreated
peril
interred

◆ Grammar and Style

COMPARATIVE AND SUPERLATIVE FORMS

These selections, like many others, contain comparative and superlative forms of adjectives and adverbs. The **comparative form** compares one thing with another by adding *-er* to short modifiers and using *more* with most modifiers of two or more syllables. The **superlative form** compares more than two things by adding *-est* to one-syllable modifiers and using *most* with modifiers of two or more syllables.

Comparative Form: Grow green as the grass, and *greener* it seemed. Then green fused on gold *more glorious* by far.

Superlative Form: . . . thereupon sat King Arthur in the *richest* cloth of gold that might be made.

◆ Literary Focus

MEDIEVAL ROMANCE

Medieval romances are based on the ideal of chivalry, the code of behavior by which knights lived. Filled with adventure, love, and the supernatural, they featured kings, knights, and damsels in distress.

Of all the medieval romances, the best known are those about King Arthur, a legendary British king of the fifth or sixth century, and his knights. In reading these romances, you will see how they blend realistic elements with supernatural ones.

◆ Reading Strategy

SUMMARIZE

When you **summarize** a passage of a work, you express and keep track of its key ideas or events. As you read, capture key ideas and events in a summary like this:

From *Morte d'Arthur*

"Ah, traitor unto me and untrue," said King Arthur, "now hast thou betrayed me twice. Who would have weened that thou that has been to me so loved and dear, and thou art named a noble knight, and would betray me for the riches of this sword."

Summary: King Arthur's knight lies to him twice about Arthur's sword.

Preparing for Standardized Tests

Reading and Vocabulary The skill of summarizing aids in students' comprehension of a work and helps them to recall a work they've read. Students can apply this skill on standardized tests when they're asked to identify the main events or idea within a passage. The Reading Strategy emphasizes the skill of summarizing. For additional practice with summarizing, use the Reading Strategy page on Summarizing in ***Selection Support,*** p. 20.

Grammar and Language Standardized tests may include sections in which students are expected to select the appropriate form of comparative and superlative modifiers. Students' ability to use the comparative and superlative modifier can be applied in revision passage and in essay tests. The Grammar and Style lesson with these selections reinforces the correct usage of comparative and superlative modifiers and gives examples from the selections of their proper usage. For additional practice, use the Grammar and Style page in ***Selection Support,*** p. 19.

Point out that these selections on Sir Gawain and King Arthur contain many features of popular action-adventure stories: brave heroes, adventure, action, humor, and hints of magic. Have students recall tales from the Arthurian legend and cite instances of these features. Like stories of modern superheroes, these tales also describe powerful individuals who set out to right wrongs.

Customize for
Less Proficient Readers

Less proficient readers may be intimidated by difficult vocabulary, such as *hurtles.* Identify those words and provide students with more familiar synonyms, such as *throws* for *hurtles.* Encourage them to read several lines at a time and to use context to help them understand what is happening. You may also wish to give a synopsis of the story to help them.

Customize for
More Advanced Readers

These students may enjoy looking for poetic sound devices such as alliteration that make *Sir Gawain and the Green Knight* so memorable and vivid.

Customize for
English Language Learners

Explain to students that many of the lines in these selections contain unusual word order. For example, one line reads, "The head of this hostelry Arthur am I," while another says, "Then were they condescended." Model how to rearrange such sentences into more familiar, standard word order. When students encounter such inversions, encourage them to identify the subject, verb, and object and to mentally rearrange them to make sense of the line.

Customize for
Musical/Rhythmic Learners

Direct students to examine the rhythmic structure of the stanzas in *Sir Gawain and the Green Knight.* Have them identify reasons for the shorter quatrains at the end of each stanza.

Develop Understanding

One-Minute Insight The story of the green knight who tests the honesty and bravery of Arthur's knight Gawain remains one of the most popular of the Arthurian legends. Its vivid descriptions, lively language, and dramatic picture of life in medieval times have a timeless appeal for students, and its skillful use of alliteration and rhyme makes it a superb introduction to Arthurian legends.

In the story an enormous green knight bursts into Arthur's hall and challenges King Arthur to deal the first blow in a duel, provided that in a year's time he seek out the green knight's home and allow him to issue the first blow. Gawain, a knight of Arthur's, takes on the challenge in Arthur's behalf and promptly chops off the intruder's head. To his astonishment, the intruder picks up his head, repeats his challenge, and leaves. Gawain, a year from that night, sets out on his adventure, in the course of which his loyalty, honesty and bravery undergo various tests.

◆ Critical Thinking

❶ **Infer** Ask students to use details from this passage to decide whether the horseman exhibits characteristics of a hero or a villain or both. *His vitality and boldness seem heroic, but the word swaggered points to an arrogance that seems appropriate for a villain.*

◆ Literary Focus

❷ **Medieval Romance** Direct students to find elements within this passage that are typical of medieval romances. *There is a mysterious stranger who inspires wonder and dread in the onlookers; the stranger has a strange green coloring like that of a fairy or phantom.*

from Sir Gawain and the Green Knight

Translated by Marie Borroff

The scene begins at the start of a New Year's Eve feast at King Arthur's Court in Camelot. Before anyone has started eating, the festivities are interrupted by an immense green knight who suddenly appears at the hall door. The knight rides a green horse and is armed with a gigantic ax.

This horseman hurtles in, and the hall enters;
Riding to the high dais,[1] recked he no danger;
Not a greeting he gave as the guests he o'erlooked,
Nor wasted his words, but "Where is," he said,
❶ "The captain of this crowd? Keenly I wish
To see that sire with sight, and to himself say my say."
He swaggered all about
To scan the host so gay;
He halted, as if in doubt
Who in that hall held sway.

There were stares on all sides as the stranger spoke,
For much did they marvel what it might mean
That a horseman and a horse should have such a hue,
Grow green as the grass, and greener, it seemed.
❷ Then green fused on gold more glorious by far.
All the onlookers eyed him, and edged nearer,
And awaited in wonder what he would do,
For many sights had they seen, but such a one never,
So that phantom and fairy the folk there deemed it,
Therefore chary[2] of answer was many a champion bold,
And stunned at his strong words stone-still they sat
In a swooning silence in the stately hall.
As all were slipped into sleep, so slackened their speech apace.
Not all, I think, for dread,
But some of courteous grace
Let him who was their head
Be spokesman in that place.

1. **dais** (dā′ is) *n.*: Platform.

2. **chary** (cher′ ē) *adj.*: Not giving freely.

Block Scheduling Strategies

Use any or all of the following suggestions to make use of extended class time:

- Direct students to complete the journal activity in Background for Understanding (p. 140) and discuss their entries with partners.
- Introduce the concept of the medieval romance. Have students read the Literary Focus on page 141. After students have read these selections, have them answer the questions on page 162. You may follow up with the Literary Focus page in ***Selection Support,*** p. 21.
- Working in pairs or small groups, have students develop their arguments for their Response to Criticism essays (p. 163). Encourage them to discuss the points they want to emphasize before writing them.
- Have students work together on the Illuminated Manuscript project described on page 163.
- Locate a recording of medieval music and play it for students.

From ***The Romance of King Arthur and His Knights of the Round Table,*** Arthur Rackham

◀ Critical Viewing
Could this castle be a setting for the opening scene of this tale? Why or why not? **[Interpret]** ❸

Then Arthur before the high dais that entrance beholds,
And hailed him, as behooved, for he had no fear.
And said "Fellow, in faith you have found fair welcome;
The head of this hostelry Arthur am I;
Leap lightly down, and linger, I pray,
And the tale of your intent you shall tell us after."
"Nay, so help me," said the other, "He that on high sits,
To tarry here any time, 'twas not mine errand;
❹ But as the praise of you, prince, is puffed up so high,
And your court and your company are counted the best,
Stoutest under steel-gear on steeds to ride,
Worthiest of their works the wide world over,
And peerless to prove in passages of arms,
And courtesy here is carried to its height,
And so at this season I have sought you out.
You may be certain by the branch that I bear in hand
That I pass here in peace, and would part friends,
For had I come to this court on combat bent,
I have a hauberk[3] at home, and a helm beside,
A shield and a sharp spear, shining bright,
And other weapons to wield, I ween well, to boot,
But as I willed no war, I wore no metal.
But if you be so bold as all men believe,
You will graciously grant the game that I ask by right."
  Arthur answer gave
❻ And said, "Sir courteous knight,
  If contest here you crave,
  You shall not fail to fight."

◆ *Literature and Your Life*
Which of the virtues in lines 36–41 do you find most admirable? ❺

3. **hauberk** (hô´ bərk) *n.*: Coat of armor.

▶Critical Viewing◀

❸ **Interpret** Many students may notice that this castle has only one door, which would make a surprise visit difficult, if not impossible.

◆ Grammar and Style

❹ **Comparative and Superlative Forms** Have students identify the three superlative modifiers and explain who or what is being compared. *The superlative modifiers are* best, stoutest, worthiest; *Arthur's court is being compared to all the others in the world.*

◆ *Literature and Your Life*

❺ Before students answer, you may wish to have them discuss each virtue in turn: strength, skill in fighting, and courtesy.

◆ Critical Thinking

❻ **Infer** Why, do you think, do Arthur and the visitor act so politely toward each other? *Students should infer that they are following the rules of chivalry.*

Humanities: Art

From *The Romance of King Arthur and His Knights of the Round Table* by Arthur Rackham.

Arthur Rackham (1864–1936) was born in London. He studied drawing at the Lambeth School of Art and for most of his life worked as an illustrator of magazines and books. Many of his original drawings are now in the collection of London's prestigious Tate Gallery.

Arthur Rackham's style of drawing reflects his interest in prints of the German Renaissance. Although more modern in approach, his works maintain the detail and angular grace of that school. This illustration of a castle was done for a book entitled *The Romance of King Arthur and His Knights of the Round Table.* Ever a lover of fairy tales and scenes of fantasy, Rackham enjoyed drawing such scenes as this castle.

Use these questions for discussion:

1. Does this castle convey a feeling of hospitality or does it seem forbidding? Explain. *Accept any reasonable response. Most students will feel the clouds and the dark linear appearance make the castle forbidding.*
2. What details of the castle's architecture reflect the needs of the occupants? Which elements seem purely decorative? *The elevated parapets provide a vantage point for observing approaching enemies. The narrow slits provide protection while allowing defenders to release spears or arrows. The Gothic doors and windows are decorative elements.*

❶ **Enrichment** Explain to students that the Beheading Game, described here, is a traditional plot element in early medieval romances. Many authorities believe that the ritual beheadings were originally related to crops. Beheading seed pods is one way of ensuring strong plant growth for the next year, and perhaps this is what the custom reflects.

◆ Reading Strategy

❷ **Summarize** Tell students to summarize what the green knight wants. *He wants someone to play a game. He will allow someone to hit him with an ax, and in a year and a day he will return the blow.*

Customize for
Auditory Learners

❸ Help students make sense of the scene by reading this speech while students listen to the words and the challenging tone.

◆ Critical Thinking

❹ **Make a Judgment** Ask if students think that Arthur has made a wise decision in accepting the green knight's challenge. *Students may respond that by accepting the challenge, Arthur has been unwise and too quick to anger.*

◆ Literary Focus

❺ **Medieval Romance** Elicit the following responses: *The description combines realistic and supernatural elements; the knight challenges their honor.*

"Nay, to fight, in good faith, is far from my thought;
There are about on these benches but beardless children,
Were I here in full arms on a haughty[4] steed,
For measured against mine, their might is puny.
And so I call in this court for a Christmas game,
For 'tis Yule, and New Year, and many young bloods about;
If any in this house such hardihood claims,
Be so bold in his blood, his brain so wild,
As stoutly to strike one stroke for another,
I shall give him as my gift this gisarme[5] noble,
This ax, that is heavy enough, to handle as he likes,
And I shall bide the first blow, as bare as I sit.
If there be one so wilful my words to assay,
❶ Let him leap hither lightly, lay hold of this weapon;
I quitclaim it forever, keep it as his own,
❷ And I shall stand him a stroke, steady on this floor,
So you grant me the guerdon to give him another, sans blame.[6]
  In a twelvemonth[7] and a day
  He shall have of me the same;
  Now be it seen straightway
  Who dares take up the game."

If he astonished them at first, stiller were then
All that household in hall, the high and the low;
The stranger on his green steed stirred in the saddle,
And roisterously his red eyes he rolled all about,
Bent his bristling brows, that were bright green,
Wagged his beard as he watched who would arise.
When the court kept its counsel he coughed aloud,
And cleared his throat coolly, the clearer to speak:
"What, is this Arthur's house," said that horseman then,
"Whose fame is so fair in far realms and wide?
Where is now your arrogance and your awesome deeds,
❸ Your valor and your victories and your vaunting words?
Now are the revel and renown of the Round Table
Overwhelmed with a word of one man's speech,
For all cower and quake, and no cut felt!"
With this he laughs so loud that the lord grieved;
The blood for sheer shame shot to his face, and pride.
  With rage his face flushed red,
❹ And so did all beside.
  Then the king as bold man bred
  Toward the stranger took a stride.

And said, "Sir, now we see you will say but folly,
Which whoso has sought, it suits that he find.
No guest here is aghast of your great words.
Give to me your gisarme, in God's own name,

4. **haughty** (hôt´ ē) *adj.*: Lofty.

5. **gisarme** (gi zärm´) *n.*: Battle-ax.

6. **I . . . blame:** I will stand firm while he strikes me with the ax provided that you reward me with the opportunity to do the same to him without being blamed for it.

7. **twelvemonth:** A year.

◆ Literary Focus
How is this description of the Green Knight (lines 79–86) characteristic of a medieval romance? ❺

◆ Build Vocabulary
assay (as ā´) *v.*: Prove or test

Cross-Curricular Connection: Music

The festivities in Arthur's time might have contained music, but it was different from the music students hear today. Someone might have played a dulcimer or a harp or a fiddle, or perhaps a wandering troubadour sang a song of unrequited love.

Music was changing. Previously, it was primarily monophonic—in other words, it had one melody line. However, the fourteenth century saw the development of polyphonic secular music, in which several melodies were blended in harmony.

Students might enjoy listening to music of the period and discussing how it and its instruments differ from those of modern times.

And the boon you have begged shall straight be granted."
He leaps to him lightly, lays hold of his weapon;
The green fellow on foot fiercely alights.
Now has Arthur his ax, and the haft[8] grips,
And sternly stirs it about, on striking bent.
6 The stranger before him stood there erect,
Higher than any in the house by a head and more;
With stern look as he stood, he stroked his beard,
And with undaunted countenance drew down his coat,
No more moved nor dismayed for his mighty dints
Than any bold man on bench had brought him a drink of wine.

8. **haft** *n.:* Handle of a weapon or tool.

Three Knights Returning From a Tournament

▲ Critical Viewing From this picture, what can you infer about a knight's preparations for challenges of skill, such as tournaments and the Green Knight's challenge? **[Infer]** 

◆ Critical Thinking

6 Predict Ask students to predict what will happen. Discuss reasons why the writer might have stretched out this scene. *Students may predict that Arthur will strike the knight. Help students recognize that stretching out the scene builds suspense.*

▶Critical Viewing◀

7 Infer Students may say that the knights cover themselves from head to toe with armor and brandish large swords. They decorate themselves and their horses.

Customize for *Visual/Spatial Learners*

This selection would make a wonderful comic book. You might wish to have students create a comic strip of the main scenes as a way of summarizing the events.

Humanities: Art

Three Knights Returning From a Tournament.

Medieval art often depicts events from real life, such as this scene of three knights returning from a tournament. In fact, information about customs, clothing, food, and relationships in the Middle Ages often comes from art of the times.

Use these questions for discussion:

1. How do the knights in this illustration compare with the popular image of knights seen in movies and television? *Popular versions tend to glamorize and idealize the knight by giving him shiny armor, a magnificent horse, and similar enhancements. These knights and their horses are rather commonplace.*
2. What details in this illustration suggest that a tournament was more concerned with fashion and appearance than with a serious test of skill? *The knights' tunics and the fancy bridles are more decorative than practical in a tournament.*

Customize for
Less Proficient Readers
Point out to students that the quatrains concluding each stanza sometimes restate what's happened or reveal an important plot event. Encourage these students to look at the quatrains when they become confused.

◆ Critical Thinking

1 Analyze Point out to students that Gawain speaks very humbly to the king and describes himself in strongly negative terms. Ask: Do you think Gawain sincerely believes that he is so inferior to the other knights or is this type of speech an example of chivalry? Explain. *Students may respond that this humble language is part of the chivalric code and that Gawain probably has great confidence in his abilities.*

◆ Grammar and Style

2 Comparative and Superlative Forms Have students identify the comparative and superlative modifiers in lines 126–129. What purpose do the modifiers serve in depicting Gawain's character? What does the use of the modifiers suggest about chivalric ideals? *The superlative modifiers are weakest, feeblest, least. Gawain is comparing himself to all the other knights. The use of negative modifiers suggests that it was considered appropriate to humble oneself before one's peers.*

◆ Reading Strategy

3 Summarize The summary could include the following: *Whatever happens, Gawain will seek out the knight in a year. When Gawain asks the knight's name, the knight says that he will tell Gawain after he has received Gawain's blow. If he can't speak, Gawain can drop the matter.*

Gawain by Guenevere
Toward the king doth now incline:
"I beseech, before all here,
That this melee may be mine."

"Would you grant me the grace," said Gawain to the king,
"To be gone from this bench and stand by you there,
If I without discourtesy might quit this board,
And if my liege lady[9] misliked it not,
I would come to your counsel before your court noble.
For I find it not fit, as in faith it is known,
When such a boon is begged before all these knights,
Though you be tempted thereto, to take it on yourself
While so bold men about upon benches sit,
That no host under heaven is hardier of will,
Nor better brothers-in-arms where battle is joined;
I am the weakest, well I know, and of wit feeblest;
And the loss of my life would be least of any;
That I have you for uncle is my only praise;
My body, but for your blood, is barren of worth;
And for that this folly befits not a king,
And 'tis I that have asked it, it ought to be mine,
And if my claim be not comely let all this court judge in sight."
The court assays the claim,
And in counsel all unite
To give Gawain the game
And release the king outright.

Then the king called the knight to come to his side,
And he rose up readily, and reached him with speed,
Bows low to his lord, lays hold of the weapon,
And he releases it lightly, and lifts up his hand,
And gives him God's blessing, and graciously prays
That his heart and his hand may be hardy both.
"Keep, cousin," said the king, "what you cut with this day,
And if you rule it aright, then readily, I know,
You shall stand the stroke it will strike after."
Gawain goes to the guest with gisarme in hand,
And boldly he bides there, abashed not a whit.
Then hails he Sir Gawain, the horseman in green:
"Recount we our contract, ere you come further.
First I ask and <u>adjure</u> you, how you are called
That you tell me <u>true</u>, so that trust it I may."
"In good faith," said the good knight, "Gawain am I
Whose buffet befalls you,[10] whate'er betide after,
And at this time twelvemonth take from you another
With what weapon you will, and with no man else alive."

9. liege (lēj) **lady:** Guenevere, the wife of the lord, Arthur, to whom Gawain is bound to give service and allegiance.

◆ Reading Strategy Summarize the key points and conditions of the challenge, as described in lines 150–184.

10. Whose . . . you: Whose blow you will receive.

Speaking and Listening Mini-Lesson

Oral Report
This mini-lesson supports the activity in the Idea Bank on page 163.

Introduce the Concept Oral reports often include graphic aids, such as pictures, charts, or diagrams.

Develop Background Explain or review with students the steps needed to create an oral report (research, documentation, drafting, fact-checking, revising). Then direct students to do research to learn about the types of arms carried in medieval battle. Also challenge them to learn whether there's a distinction between the arms of a knight or nobleman and a serf.

As they find information, instruct students to draw or photocopy examples of medieval weapons and to make a notecard describing each weapon's use, manufacture, and effectiveness in battle.

Apply the Information Have students work in small groups or individually to prepare their reports. Students should present their oral reports to the class with props and cue cards. Making eye contact with the audience and gesturing to visual displays will enhance the effectiveness of the presentation.

Assess the Outcome Have students evaluate their own reports, as well as those of their classmates. They may use the Self-Assessment for a Speech and the Peer Assessment for a Speaker/Speech, pp. 122–123 in ***Alternative Assessment.***

The other nods assent:
"Sir Gawain, as I may thrive,
I am wondrous well content
That you this dint[11] shall drive."

"Sir Gawain," said the Green Knight, "By God, I rejoice
That your fist shall fetch this favor I seek,
And you have readily rehearsed, and in right terms,
Each clause of my covenant with the king your lord,
Save that you shall assure me, sir, upon oath,
That you shall seek me yourself, wheresoever you deem
[4] My lodgings may lie, and look for such wages[12]
As you have offered me here before all this host."
"What is the way there?" said Gawain, "Where do you dwell?
I heard never of your house, by Him that made me,
Nor I know you not, knight, your name nor your court.
But tell me truly thereof, and teach me your name,
And I shall fare forth to find you, so far as I may,
And this I say in good certain, and swear upon oath."
"That is enough in New Year, you need say no more,"
Said the knight in the green to Gawain the noble,
"If I tell you true, when I have taken your knock,
And if you handily have hit, you shall hear straightway
Of my house and my home and my own name;
Then follow in my footsteps by faithful accord.
And if I spend no speech, you shall speed the better:
You can feast with your friends, nor further trace my tracks.[13]
Now hold your grim tool steady
And show us how it hacks."
"Gladly, sir; all ready,"
Says Gawain; he strokes the ax.

The Green Knight upon ground girds him with care:
Bows a bit with his head, and bares his flesh:
His long lovely locks he laid over his crown,
Let the naked nape for the need be shown
Gawain grips to his ax and gathers it aloft—
The left foot on the floor before him he set—
Brought it down deftly upon the bare neck,
[5] That the shock of the sharp blow shivered the bones
And cut the flesh cleanly and clove it in twain,[14]
That the blade of bright steel bit into the ground.
The head was hewn off and fell to the floor;
Many found it at their feet, as forth it rolled;
The blood gushed from the body, bright on the green,
Yet fell not the fellow, nor faltered a whit,
But stoutly he starts forth upon stiff shanks,

11. **dint** *n.:* Blow.

12. **wages** *n.:* A blow.

13. **If I tell you . . . tracks:** (lines 178–183): The Green Knight tells Gawain that he will let him know where he lives after he has taken the blow. If he is unable to speak following the blow, there will be no need for Gawain to know.

14. **clove it in twain:** Split it in two.

◆ Build Vocabulary

adjure (ə jo͝or′) *v.:* Appeal earnestly

◆ Literary Focus

4 Medieval Romance Remind students that honor and honesty were important characteristics of medieval knights. Have students locate several phrases within this passage that emphasize the importance of honor and honesty. *The terms* covenant, upon oath, oath, *and* swear upon oath *all emphasize the importance of a knight's word.*

◆ Critical Thinking

5 Evaluate Ask students which details in this stanza are realistic and which are supernatural. *Details from the beheading are realistic; what follows—what the knight does next—is not.*

◆ *Literature and Your Life*

❶ Ask students what kind of movie or television show might have a scene like the one described. Discuss reasons for their answers. *Students might mention horror films, fantasy or adventure films, cartoons, or films that combine live action and animation.*

◆ Literary Focus

❷ **Medieval Romance** Students should mention that Sir Gawain's honor is being put to the test. They may also mention that the dramatic language and action are characteristic of medieval romances.

◆ Critical Thinking

❸ **Extend** Encourage students to think of other characters from literature who are similar to or reminiscent of the Green Knight. *Students may mention the Headless Horseman from "The Legend of Sleepy Hollow" or Mephistopheles from* Dr. Faustus.

◆ Critical Thinking

❹ **Hypothesize** Ask students why Arthur might behave in such a casual manner after witnessing such a scene. *Some students might suggest he wants to be cool, or that he does not want to spoil the festivities. Others might think he does not want to upset Gawain.*

And as all stood staring he stretched forth his hand,
Laid hold of his head and heaved it aloft,
Then goes to the green steed, grasps the bridle,
Steps into the stirrup, bestrides his mount,
And his head by the hair in his hand holds,
And as steady he sits in the stately saddle
As he had met with no mishap, nor missing were his head.
    His bulk about he haled,
    That fearsome body that bled;
    There were many in the court that quailed
    Before all his say was said.

For the head in his hand he holds right up;
Toward the first on the dais directs he the face,
❶ And it lifted up its lids, and looked with wide eyes,
And said as much with its mouth as now you may hear:
"Sir Gawain, forget not to go as agreed,
And cease not to seek till me, sir, you find,
As you promised in the presence of these proud knights.
To the Green Chapel come, I charge you, to take
Such a dint as you have dealt—you have well deserved
That your neck should have a knock on New Year's morn.
The Knight of the Green Chapel I am well-known to many,
❸ Wherefore you cannot fail to find me at last;
Therefore come, or be counted a recreant[15] knight."
With a roisterous rush he flings round the reins,
Hurtles out at the hall door, his head in his hand,
That the flint fire flew from the flashing hooves.
Which way he went, not one of them knew
Nor whence he was come in the wide world so fair.
    The king and Gawain gay
    Make a game of the Green Knight there,
    Yet all who saw it say
    'Twas a wonder past compare.

Though high-born Arthur at heart had wonder,
He let no sign be seen, but said aloud
To the comely queen, with courteous speech,
"Dear dame, on this day dismay you no whit;
Such crafts are becoming at Christmastide,
Laughing at interludes, light songs and mirth,
❹ Amid dancing of damsels with doughty knights.
Nevertheless of my meat now let me partake,
For I have met with a marvel, I may not deny."
He glanced at Sir Gawain, and gaily he said,
"Now, sir, hang up your ax, that has hewn enough,"
And over the high dais it was hung on the wall
That men in amazement might on it look,
And tell in true terms the tale of the wonder.

◆ Literary Focus
How is the description in lines 219–229 characteristic of a medieval romance? ❷

15. Recreant: *adj.* Cowardly.

Cultural Connection

The Green Knight has arrived at a New Year's celebration, at which people are feasting. Although not everyone celebrates the New Year on the same date, cultures throughout the world do celebrate it on some day.

Many New Year's festivities involve traditional foods. Most foods eaten on New Year's are chosen because they are associated with some combination of good luck, wealth, or fertility. The foods are thought to help ensure these in the coming year.

Celebrants in some cultures enjoy sweet foods, such as challah or honey cake eaten by the Jews, and sweet cakes made from rice eaten by Cambodians. Other cultures feature savory foods, such as noodles in Japan; lentils in Italy; and a combination of black-eyed peas and rice eaten by African Americans. Some families avoid meat on New Year's, whereas other families emphasize it.

Invite students to share any New Year's traditions that they know about or enjoy. Discuss reasons why such traditions continue, into modern times.

Sir Gawain and the Green Knight, The Bodleian Library, Oxford

▲ **Critical Viewing** Compare the depiction of Sir Gawain in the picture (center) and in the text. **[Compare and Contrast]** ❺

Then they turned toward the table, those two together,
The good king and Gawain, and made great feast,
With all dainties double, dishes rare,
With all manner of meat and minstrelsy both,
Such happiness wholly had they that day in hold.
  Now take care, Sir Gawain,
  That your courage wax not cold
  When you must turn again
  To your enterprise foretold. ❻

The following November, Sir Gawain sets out to fulfill his promise to the Green Knight. For weeks he travels alone through the cold, threatening woods of North Wales. Then, after he prays for shelter, he comes upon a wondrous castle on Christmas Eve, where he is greeted warmly by the lord of the castle and his lady. Sir Gawain inquires about the location of the Green Chapel, and the lord assures him that it is nearby and promises to provide him with a guide to lead him there on New Year's Day. Before the lord and Sir Gawain retire for the night, they agree to exchange whatever they receive during the next three days. Sir Gawain keeps his pledge for the first two days, but on the third day he does not give the lord the magic green girdle that the lady gives him because she promises that the girdle will protect him from any harm. The next day, Gawain sets out for the Green Chapel. His guide urges him not to proceed, but Gawain refuses to take this advice. He feels that it would be dishonorable not to fulfill his pledge. He is determined to accept his fate; however, he does wear the magic green girdle that the lady had given him.

▶Critical Viewing◀

❺ Compare and Contrast
Students may say that in the story, Gawain is brave, strong, and confident. In the painting, his posture is erect and his facial expression seems thoughtful and prayerful.

◆ Critical Thinking

❻ Analyze Ask students to identify what's different about this quatrain and what effect this difference has on the reader. *The quatrain directly addresses Gawain, warning him not to lose courage. This gives readers a sense of foreboding and suspense.*

Customize for
More Advanced Students
Help students appreciate some of the traditional elements in this story. For example, point out that here and later in the story, an event is repeated three times. Encourage students to take note of the significance of the number three as they read this tale and others from folklore.

Humanities: Art

Sir Gawain and the Green Knight, The Bodleian Library, Oxford.

Medieval illuminated manuscripts were produced in monasteries by cloistered monks and by specially hired laymen. They were painted on hand-lettered vellum manuscripts to decorate and often illustrate a part of the text. Works of both a religious and secular nature were produced. Today, they provide an invaluable literary and visual historic record.

The miniature painting *Gawain Departs Guenivere and Arthur* is from an illuminated manuscript about the adventures of Sir Gawain. This charming painting is executed in the calligraphic, flat style that is typical of medieval art. The format, three separate scenes on a single plane, can be compared to that of today's comic strip. This lively, brightly colored account of the knight's adventures is a welcome message from the past to today's reader of ancient works.

Use these questions for discussion:

1. How does the artist show the King and Queen reacting to Gawain's departure? *The medieval style of the art does not allow for the depiction of strong emotions. However, Gawain's departure seems to be amicable.*
2. What might the artist show in a fourth scene? *Accept any reasonable response.*

◆ Critical Thinking

1 Analyze Ask students to describe how the setting in this passage adds to the story. *Students should observe that the setting mirrors Gawain's mental state and creates suspense.*

◆ Critical Thinking

2 Infer Ask students to infer medieval ideas about religion and superstition from these lines. *Students may reply that medieval people may have believed both in Christianity (chapel, matins, heaven, hell) and in folklore (black midnight, Fiend).*

Comprehension Check ☑

3 What does Gawain see and hear, and how does he react? *He finds only a mound with a hole, and he hears a horrible grinding noise. He worries that his opponent is the devil, but he does not fear the noise.*

He puts his heels to his horse, and picks up the path;
Goes in beside a grove where the ground is steep,
Rides down the rough slope right to the valley;
And then he looked a little about him–the landscape was wild,
And not a soul to be seen, nor sign of a dwelling,
But high banks on either hand hemmed it about,
With many a ragged rock and rough-hewn crag;
The skies seemed scored by the scowling peaks.
Then he halted his horse, and hoved there a space,
1 And sought on every side for a sight of the Chapel,
But no such place appeared, which puzzled him sore,
Yet he saw some way off what seemed like a mound,
A hillock high and broad, hard by the water,
Where the stream fell in foam down the face of the steep
And bubbled as if it boiled on its bed below.
The knight urges his horse, and heads for the knoll;
Leaps lightly to earth; loops well the rein
Of his steed to a stout branch, and stations him there.
He strides straight to the mound, and strolls all about,
Much wondering what it was, but no whit the wiser;
It had a hole at one end, and on either side,
And was covered with coarse grass in clumps all without,
And hollow all within, like some old cave,
Or a crevice of an old crag—he could not discern aright.
"Can this be the Chapel Green?
Alack!" said the man, "Here might
The devil himself be seen
Saying matins[16] at black midnight!"

2

"Now by heaven," said he, "it is bleak hereabouts;
This prayer house is hideous, half covered with grass!
Well may the grim man mantled in green
Hold here his orisons,[17] in hell's own style!
Now I feel it is the Fiend, in my five wits,
That has tempted me to this tryst,[18] to take my life;
This is a Chapel of mischance, may the mischief take it!
As accursed a country church as I came upon ever!"
With his helm on his head, his lance in his hand,
He stalks toward the steep wall of that strange house.
Then he heard, on the hill, behind a hard rock,
Beyond the brook, from the bank, a most barbarous din:
3 Lord! it clattered in the cliff fit to cleave it in two,
As one upon a grindstone ground a great scythe!
Lord! it whirred like a mill-wheel whirling about!
Lord! it echoed loud and long, lamentable to hear!
Then "By heaven," said the bold knight, "That business up there
Is arranged for my arrival, or else I am much misled.

16. matins *n.*: Morning prayers.

17. orisons *n.*: Prayers.

18. tryst (trist) *n.*: Meeting.

Let God work! Ah me!
All hope of help has fled!
Forfeit my life may be
But noise I do not dread."

Then he listened no longer, but loudly he called,
"Who has power in this place, high parley to hold?
For none greets Sir Gawain, or give him good day;
If any would a word with him, let him walk forth
And speak now or never, to speed his affairs."
"Abide," said one on the bank above over his head,
"And what I promised you once shall straightway be given."
Yet he stayed not his grindstone, nor stinted its noise,
But worked awhile at his whetting before he would rest,
And then he comes around a crag, from a cave in the rocks,
Hurtling out of hiding with a hateful weapon,
❺ A Danish ax[19] devised for that day's deed,
With a broad blade and bright, bent in a curve,
Filed to a fine edge—four feet it measured
By the length of the lace that was looped round the haft.
And in form as at first, the fellow all green,
His lordly face and his legs, his locks and his beard,
Save that firm upon two feet forward he strides,
Sets a hand on the ax-head, the haft to the earth;
When he came to the cold stream, and cared not to wade,
He vaults over on his ax, and advances amain
On a broad bank of snow, overbearing and brisk of mood.
Little did the knight incline
When face to face they stood;
Said the other man, "Friend mine,
It seems your word holds good!"

"God love you, Sir Gawain!" said the Green Knight then,
"And well met this morning, man, at my place!
And you have followed me faithfully and found me betimes,
And on the business between us we both are agreed:
Twelve months ago today you took what was yours,
And you at this New Year must yield me the same.
And we have met in these mountains, remote from all eyes:
❻ There is none here to halt us or hinder our sport;
Unhasp your high helm, and have here your wages;
Make no more demur than I did myself
When you hacked off my head with one hard blow."
"No, by God," said Sir Gawain, "that granted me life,
I shall grudge not the guerdon[20] grim though it prove;
And you may lay on as you like till the last of my part be paid."

◆ ***Literature and Your Life***

Think of a time you may have been apprehensive about approaching a situation. Did you react in the same way as Sir Gawain? Explain. ❹

19. Danish ax: Long-bladed ax.

20. guerdon *n.*: Reward.

◆ *Literature and Your Life*

❹ Students may reply that waiting for a doctor's appointment or playing in a big game causes apprehension. Students' reactions will differ.

◆ Literary Focus

❺ **Medieval Romance** Ask students why the ax might be described in such detail. How does this add to the drama? *It is described in detail so the audience can appreciate how frightening and dangerous it is. It underscores Gawain's courage, since such an ax would have scared off a less courageous person.*

◆ Reading Strategy

❻ **Summarize** Ask students to summarize this stanza. *The Green Knight commends Gawain for being honorable, and Gawain bravely sticks out his neck.*

Cross-Curricular Connection: Social Studies

Although Arthurian legends are largely romanticized and fictionalized, most of them contain actual historical information. For example, clues in the text may reveal such things as the social structure, customs, and religious beliefs of medieval Britain.

Lead a discussion with the class about the historical information that can be gleaned by reading *Sir Gawain and the Green Knight.* You may also want to list on the board any questions about medieval history that are unanswered by the selection. Encourage interested students to research to find the answers and report back to the class.

Customize for
Verbal/Linguistic Learners
Read lines 354–359 aloud to help students appreciate the sound and rhythm of the language. Help them appreciate the writer's achievement—putting such an exciting tale into such a format.

◆ Reading Strategy

❶ **Summarize** Summaries should include the fact that Gawain saw the blow falling and winced.

◆ Critical Thinking

❷ **Relate** Ask students how they would have felt in Gawain's place; would they have winced, as well? *Most students will say that they would have been very hesitant about allowing the Green Knight to take his turn.*

◆ Critical Thinking

❸ **Interpret** Ask students if they think the Green Knight's hesitation is deliberate, and if so, why. *Responses may include: Yes, the Green Knight is still testing the courage and honor of Gawain.*

He proffered, with good grace,
His bare neck to the blade,
And feigned a cheerful face:
He scorned to seem afraid.

Then the grim man in green gathers his strength,
Heaves high the heavy ax to hit him the blow.
With all the force in his frame he fetches it aloft,
With a grimace as grim as he would grind him to bits;
Had the blow he bestowed been as big as he threatened,
A good knight and gallant had gone to his grave.
But Gawain at the great ax glanced up aside
❷ As down it descended with death-dealing force,
And his shoulders shrank a little from the sharp iron.
Abruptly the brawny man breaks off the stroke,
And then reproved with proud words that prince among knights.
"You are not Gawain the glorious," the green man said,
"That never fell back on field in the face of the foe,
And now you flee for fear, and have felt no harm:
Such news of that knight I never heard yet!
I moved not a muscle when you made to strike,
Nor caviled[21] at the cut in King Arthur's house;
My head fell to my feet, yet steadfast I stood,
And you, all unharmed, are wholly dismayed—
Wherefore the better man I, by all odds, must be."
Said Gawain, "Strike once more;
I shall neither flinch nor flee;
But if my head falls to the floor
There is no mending me!"

"But go on, man, in God's name, and get to the point!
Deliver me my destiny, and do it out of hand,
For I shall stand to the stroke and stir not an inch
Till your ax has hit home—on my honor I swear it!"
"Have at thee then!" said the other, and heaves it aloft,
And glares down as grimly as he had gone mad.
He made a mighty feint, but marred not his hide;
❸ Withdrew the ax adroitly before it did damage.
Gawain gave no ground, nor glanced up aside,
But stood still as a stone, or else a stout stump
That is held in hard earth by a hundred roots.
Then merrily does he mock him, the man all in green:
"So now you have your nerve again, I needs must strike;
Uphold the high knighthood that Arthur bestowed,
And keep your neck-bone clear, if this cut allows!"
Then was Gawain gripped with rage, and grimly he said,
"Why, thrash away, tyrant, I tire of your threats;
You make such a scene, you must frighten yourself."

◆ Reading Strategy
Summarize Sir Gawain's actions in lines 359–363. ❶

21. caviled: Raised trivial objections.

◆ Build Vocabulary

feigned (fānd) *v.*: Made a false show of; pretended

adroitly (ə droit´ lē) *adv*: Physically or mentally skillful

Said the green fellow, "In faith, so fiercely you speak
That I shall finish this affair, nor further grace allow."
He stands prepared to strike
And scowls with both lip and brow;
No marvel if the man mislike
Who can hope no rescue now.

He gathered up the grim ax and guided it well:
Let the barb at the blade's end brush the bare throat;
He hammered down hard, yet harmed him no whit
Save a scratch on one side, that severed the skin;
The end of the hooked edge entered the flesh,
And a little blood lightly leapt to the earth.
And when the man beheld his own blood bright on the snow,
He sprang a spear's length with feet spread wide,
Seized his high helm, and set it on his head,
Shoved before his shoulders the shield at his back,
[4] Bares his trusty blade, and boldly he speaks—
Not since he was a babe born of his mother
Was he once in this world one half so blithe—
"Have done with your hacking—harry me no more!
I have borne, as behooved, one blow in this place;
If you make another move I shall meet it midway
And promptly, I promise you, pay back each blow with brand.
One stroke acquits me here;
So did our covenant stand
In Arthur's court last year—
Wherefore, sir, hold your hand!"

He lowers the long ax and leans on it there,
Sets his arms on the head, the haft on the earth,
And beholds the bold knight that bides there afoot,
How he faces him fearless, fierce in full arms,
[5] And plies him with proud words—it pleases him well.
Then once again gaily to Gawain he calls,
And in a loud voice and lusty, delivers these words:
"Bold fellow, on this field your anger forbear!
No man has made demands here in manner uncouth,
Nor done, save as duly determined at court.
I owed you a hit and you have it; be happy therewith!
The rest of my rights here I freely resign.
Had I been a bit busier, a buffet, perhaps,
I could have dealt more directly; and done you some harm.
First I flourished with a feint, in frolicsome mood,
And left your hide unhurt—and here I did well
By the fair terms we fixed on the first night;
And fully and faithfully you followed accord:
Gave over all your gains as a good man should.

◆ *Literature and Your Life*

Do you consider Sir Gawain's behavior heroic? [6]

◆ Literary Focus

4 Medieval Romance Have student locate elements of medieval romance within this stanza. *Gawain stays true to his word and lets the Green Knight swing at him. An element of fantasy enters in as the Green Knight "Hammers down hard" but barely scratches Gawain's flesh. As soon as Gawain's promise is fulfilled, however, he leaps backs into his role as adventurer, and he rearms himself and readies again for battle.*

◆ Critical Thinking

5 Infer Elicit from students why the Green Knight may be pleased with Gawain. *Students may point out that the Green Knight is pleased because he wanted Gawain to pass the test and prove his honor all along.*

◆ *Literature and Your Life*

6 Students may reply that Gawain was heroic because he held his end of the bargain.

Cross-Curricular Connection: Art

The colorful characters and events in this story lend themselves to visual representation. Brainstorm with the class about how they envision a character or scene from this work. Then bring those visions to fruition by discussing rough ideas and possible materials with which to work. For example, would modeling clay or metal work better when sculpting the Green Chapel?

Encourage interested students to visit the school's art studio and work with the teacher to create an artistic depiction of a character or scene from this story. Display finished artworks in the classroom.

◆ Critical Thinking

❶ **Draw Conclusions** Ask students, "Who is the Green Knight?" *He is the lord of the wondrous castle.*

◆ Reading Strategy

❷ **Summarize** Students should include the following: Gawain is angry at himself and ashamed; he hands over the girdle with an apology; he asks forgiveness.

▶Critical Viewing◀

❸ **Assess** Students might mention the clarity of details in the woodcut, or the fact that it illustrates a specific scene, rather than giving a general view of the setting or participants. If necessary, point out that the woodcut is far more modern than an illuminated manuscript.

A second feint, sir, I assigned for the morning
You kissed my comely wife—each kiss you restored.
For both of these there behooved but two feigned blows by right.
  True men pay what they owe;
  No danger then in sight.
  You failed at the third throw,
  So take my tap, sir knight.

"For that is my belt about you, that same braided girdle,
My wife it was that wore it; I know well the tale,
❶ And the count of your kisses and your conduct too,
And the wooing of my wife—it was all my scheme!
She made trial of a man most faultless by far
Of all that ever walked over the wide earth;
As pearls to white peas, more precious and prized,
So is Gawain, in good faith, to other gay knights.
Yet you lacked, sir, a little in loyalty there,
But the cause was not cunning, nor courtship either,
But that you loved your own life; the less, then, to blame."
The other stout knight in a study stood a long while,
So gripped with grim rage that his great heart shook.
All the blood of his body burned in his face
As he shrank back in shame from the man's sharp speech.
The first words that fell from the fair knight's lips:
"Accursed be a cowardly and covetous heart!
In you is villainy and vice, and virtue laid low!"
Then he grasps the green girdle and lets go the knot,
Hands it over in haste, and hotly he says:
"Behold there my falsehood, ill hap betide it!
Your cut taught me cowardice, care for my life,
And coveting came after, contrary both
To largesse and loyalty belonging to knights.
Now am I faulty and false, that fearful was ever
Of disloyalty and lies, bad luck to them both! and
  greed.
  I confess, knight, in this place,
  Most dire is my misdeed;
  Let me gain back your good grace,

◆ Reading Strategy Summarize Sir Gawain's response to the Green Knight in lines 459–477. ❷

Gawain Receiving the Green Girdle, Woodcut by Fritz Kredel from Gardner, *The Complete Works of the Gawain Poet,* 1965, The University of Chicago

❸ ▶ **Critical Viewing** Assess the effectiveness of a woodcut like this one in illustrating the poem, as opposed to a painted representation. **[Assess]**

Humanities: Art

Gawain Receiving the Green Girdle by Fritz Kredel.

Fritz Kredel (1900–1973) was a German-born American artist. Kredel worked chiefly in woodcut, prints made from designs cut into wooden blocks. He won many awards both in the United States and in Europe for his book illustrations.

Kredel used medieval techniques to make this woodcut. If Kredel's illustration were compared with a medieval woodcut, it would be difficult to tell, from style alone, which was done in this century.

Kredel made a point of thoroughly studying a text before he illustrated it. He felt that in illustration the artist should strive to glorify the author's work, not to overshadow it. In *Gawain,* the simple lines and sparse detail give an accurate portrayal of the characters without distracting our focus of attention from the poem.

Use these questions for discussion:

1. Are the style and effect of the woodcut well suited to the poem? Explain. *The simple rendering provided by a woodcut runs no risk of overwhelming the story.*
2. Are highly realistic oil or watercolor paintings usually preferable to line drawings or woodcuts such as this? Explain. *An elaborate painting would be inconsistent with the stylized narrative and dialogue of the poem.*

And thereafter I shall take heed."

Then the other laughed aloud, and lightly he said,
"Such harm as I have had, I hold it quite healed.
You are so fully confessed, your failings made known,
And bear the plain penance of the point of my blade,
I hold you polished as a pearl, as pure and as bright
As you had lived free of fault since first you were born. ❹
And I give you sir, this girdle that is gold-hemmed
And green as my garments, that, Gawain, you may
Be mindful of this meeting when you mingle in throng
With nobles of renown—and known by this token
How it chanced at the Green Chapel, to chivalrous knights.
And you shall in this New Year come yet again
And we shall finish out our feast in my fair hall with cheer."

◆ Build Vocabulary

largesse (lär jes′) *n.*: Nobility of spirit

Guide for Responding

◆ Literature and Your Life

Reader's Response If you were King Arthur, would you have allowed Sir Gawain to accept the Green Knight's challenge? Why or why not?

Thematic Focus How does Sir Gawain's concern for his own life lead him into greater danger?

Casting Ideas With a small group, cast the parts of King Arthur, Sir Gawain, the Green Knight, and the lady of the castle for a film version of this story.

☑ Check Your Comprehension

1. The Green Knight's challenge has two parts. (a) What is Sir Gawain to do immediately? (b) What is he to do a year later?
2. What does Sir Gawain get from the lady of the castle, and what is the purpose of this present?
3. What occurs when Sir Gawain and the Green Knight meet at the Chapel Green?
4. Summarize what the Green Knight tells Sir Gawain at the end of the story.

◆ Critical Thinking

INTERPRET

1. Why does the Green Knight laugh at the members of the Round Table in line 92? **[Analyze]**
2. When Sir Gawain sees the Green Chapel, who does he think the Green Knight might be? **[Deduce]**
3. In lines 464–477, why is Sir Gawain upset? **[Interpret]**
4. What do you think Sir Gawain has learned from his second encounter with the Green Knight? **[Draw Conclusions]**

EVALUATE

5. In your opinion, has Sir Gawain failed to live up to his knightly ideals? Explain. **[Make a Judgment]**

EXTEND

6. What modern occupation do you think comes closest to matching the duties and ideals of the Knights of the Round Table? Explain your answer. **[Career Link]**

◆ Critical Thinking

❹ Analyze Direct students to find details in this passage in which Christian and chivalric ideas are similar. Ask them what significance the similarities have. *Students should point out that Gawain's confession and penance lead to his being pure and "as free of guilt since first you were born." Medieval storytellers celebrated their beliefs and values through romances such as these. Therefore, a hero like Gawain embodied the beliefs of the culture, in this case, a Christian one.*

Reinforce and Extend

Answers

◆ Literature and Your Life

Reader's Response Responses may resemble this one: No, I would never let any of my subjects accept challenges on my behalf.

Thematic Focus By accepting the green girdle from the lady of the castle, he displays dishonorable behavior.

☑ Check Your Comprehension

1. (a) Sir Gawain is to strike a blow with an ax at the Green Knight. (b) A year later he is to find the Green Knight and receive a blow from an ax in return.
2. Gawain gets a girdle from the lady. Its purpose is to protect him from harm.
3. Gawain held his part of the bargain, and the Green Knight takes a swing at him with the ax.
4. The Green Knight reveals that he is the lord of the castle and that he knows that Gawain took the girdle and broke his promise to him. However, the Green Knight recognizes that Gawain is penitent, so he gives him the girdle to keep and invites him to his home for a feast the following New Year.

◆ Critical Thinking

1. He laughs insultingly because he finds Arthur's knights cowardly. He may also laugh to taunt them.
2. Sir Gawain thinks the Green Knight might be Satan.
3. He is upset at himself for being false, greedy, cowardly, and disloyal to his code.
4. He may have learned that it's always best to keep your word and act honorably, no matter what fears you may have.
5. Gawain probably feels that he has failed to live up to his knightly ideals because he broke his word to the lord of the castle (the Green Knight).
6. Responses may include soldier, president of the United States, judge.

Develop Understanding

One-Minute Insight No one knows for sure whether King Arthur was real, but his name has popped up since the sixth century, and by the ninth century, he was a folk hero. During the fourteenth and fifteenth centuries, there was a revival of interest in Arthurian legends, mainly due to *Sir Gawain and the Green Knight* and to *Morte d'Arthur*. Unlike the former, written in verse, *Morte d'Arthur* was the first English prose version of King Arthur's life. After reading, students will understand why, with its realistic detail and natural dialogue, it has become a classic.

Customize for
English Language Learners
Students will probably be confused by some of the language here, especially terms like *anon, unto, hither,* and *verily*. Have students skim the pages first, listing words they see that are unfamiliar. Make a master list on the board and define them for students before they begin reading.

◆ Literary Focus

❶ **Medieval Romance** Ask students what elements of medieval romance appear on the first page. *Students may identify a king, a knight, reference to righteous battles.*

◆ Reading Strategy

❷ **Summarize** Have students summarize this paragraph. *Summaries should resemble this one: Because of Gawain's good deeds, God allows him to warn Arthur not to fight Mordred the next day, because Arthur will be slain. Instead, Arthur is told to make a month-long treaty, after which time, Sir Lancelot will rescue Arthur and slay Mordred.*

from Morte d'Arthur

Sir Thomas Malory

This selection begins after King Arthur has traveled to France at the insistence of his nephew, Gawain, to besiege his former friend and knight, Lancelot, for his involvement with Queen Guenevere. However, the king's attempts to punish are halfhearted, and he is soon forced to abandon them altogether when he learns that his nephew, Mordred, has seized control of England. Arthur leads his forces back to England, and Mordred attacks them upon their landing. Gawain is killed in the fighting, but before he dies, he manages to send word to Lancelot that Arthur is in need of assistance.

So upon Trinity Sunday at night King Arthur dreamed a wonderful dream, and in his dream him seemed[1] that he saw upon a chafflet[2] a chair, and the chair was fast to a wheel, and thereupon sat King Arthur in the richest cloth of gold that might be made. And the King thought there was under him, far from him, an hideous deep black water, and therein was all manner of serpents, and worms, and wild beasts, foul and horrible. And suddenly the King thought that the wheel turned upside down, and he fell among the serpents, and
❶ every beast took him by a limb. And then the King cried as he lay in his bed, "Help, help!"

And then knights, squires, and yeomen awaked the King, and then he was so amazed that he wist[3] not where he was. And then so he awaked until it was nigh day, and then he fell on slumbering again, not sleeping nor thoroughly waking. So the King seemed[4] verily that there came Sir Gawain unto him with a number of fair ladies with him. So when King Arthur saw him, he said, "Welcome, my sister's son. I weened ye had been dead. And now I see thee on-live, much am I beholden unto Almighty Jesu. Ah, fair nephew and my sister's son, what been these ladies that hither be come with you?" ❶

"Sir," said Sir Gawain, "all these be ladies for whom I have foughten for when I was man living. And all these are those that I did battle for in righteous quarrels, and God hath given them that grace, at their great prayer, because I did battle for them for their right, that they should bring me hither unto you. Thus much hath given me leave God, for to warn you of your death. For and ye fight as tomorn[5] with Sir Mordred, as ye both have assigned, doubt ye not ye must be slain, and the most party of your people on both parties. And for the great grace ❷
and goodness that Almighty Jesu hath unto you, and for pity of you and many more other good men there shall be slain, God hath sent me to you of his special grace to give you warning that in no wise ye do battle as tomorn, but that ye take a treaty for a month from today. And proffer you largely[6] you so that tomorn ye put in a delay. For within a month shall come Sir Lancelot with all his noble knights and rescue you worshipfully and slay Sir Mordred and all that ever will hold with him."

Then Sir Gawain and all the ladies vanished. And anon the King called upon his knights, squires, and yeomen, and charged them

1. **him seemed:** It seemed to him.
2. **chafflet:** Platform.
3. **wist:** Knew.
4. **the King seemed:** It seemed to the King.
5. **and . . . tomorn:** If you fight tomorrow.
6. **proffer you largely:** Make generous offers.

Beyond the Classroom

Career Connection

Armed Forces In these selections, knights perform the function that the armed forces perform today. Today, many young people consider one of the armed forces as a career. More than a million and a half men and women now serve in the Army, the Air Force, the Navy, the Marine Corps, and the Coast Guard. Each of these services has a four-year academy that provides academic as well as military instruction.

Another military option is the National Guard, which provides back-up for the Army and Air Force. People who join the National Guard are basically civilians with other careers who meet once a month for military training.

Have interested students gather information about the requirements for joining the military, as well as the benefits and responsibilities of being in the military.

Workplace Skills

Leadership Skills Point out to students that the skills that make a good soldier are not the only ones required of a military leader. Discuss and list qualities that good leaders have. For example, students might mention vision, enthusiasm, organizational skills, interpersonal skills, an ability to inspire respect, and self-discipline.

Students may be interested in interviewing leaders of businesses or chiefs of local fire and police departments to learn more about these and related skills.

wightly[7] to fetch his noble lords and wise bishops unto him. And when they were come the King told them of his avision,[8] that Sir Gawain had told him and warned him that, and he fought on the morn, he should be slain. Then the King commanded Sir Lucan the Butler and his brother Sir Bedivere the Bold, with two bishops with them, and charged them in any wise to take a treaty for a month from today with Sir Mordred. ❸ "And spare not: proffer him lands and goods as much as ye think reasonable."

So then they departed and came to Sir Mordred where he had a grim host of an hundred thousand, and there they entreated Sir Mordred long time. And at the last Sir Mordred was agreed for to have Cornwall and Kent by King Arthur's days, and after that, all England, after the days of King Arthur.

Then were they condescended[9] that King Arthur and Sir Mordred should meet betwixt both their hosts, and each of them should bring fourteen persons. And so they came with this word unto Arthur. Then said he, "I am glad that this is done," and so he went into the field.

And when King Arthur should depart, he warned all his host that, and they see any sword drawn, "Look ye come on fiercely and slay that traitor Sir Mordred, for I in no wise trust him." In like wise Sir Mordred warned his host that "And ye see any manner of sword drawn, look that ye come on fiercely, and so slay all that ever before you standeth, for in no wise I will not trust for this treaty." And in the same wise said Sir Mordred unto his host, "For I know well my father will be avenged upon me."

And so they met as their pointment[10] was and were agreed and accorded thoroughly. And wine was fetched and they drank together. Right so came an adder out of a little heathbush, and it stung a knight in the foot. And so when the knight felt him so stung, he looked down and saw the adder. And anon he drew his sword to slay the adder, and thought none other harm. And when the host on both parties saw that sword drawn, then they blew beams,[11] trumpets, horns, and shouted grimly. And so both hosts dressed them together. And King Arthur took his horse and said, "Alas, this unhappy day!" and so rode to his party, and Sir Mordred in like wise.

King Arthur's Round Table and the Holy Grail

❹ ▲ **Critical Viewing** Using your knowledge of chivalry, draw conclusions about King Arthur's decision to set his knights at a round table. **[Draw Conclusions]**

7. **wightly:** Quickly.
8. **avision:** Dream.
9. **condescended:** Agreed.
10. **pointment:** Arrangement.
11. **beams:** Type of trumpet.

◆ Build Vocabulary

righteous (rī′ chəs) *adj.*: Acting in a just, upright manner; doing what is right

entreated (en trēt′ id) *v.*: Made an earnest appeal; pleaded

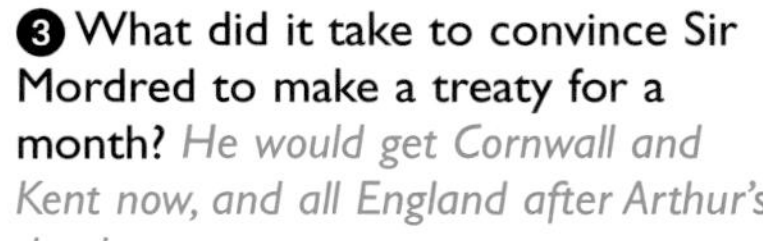

Comprehension Check

❸ What did it take to convince Sir Mordred to make a treaty for a month? *He would get Cornwall and Kent now, and all England after Arthur's death.*

▶Critical Viewing◀

❹ **Draw Conclusions** Students should recognize that a round table has no head and no foot, so all members have equal status.

Humanities: Art

King Arthur's Round Table and the Holy Grail.

Among the most popular subjects in medieval literature, songs, and art was the legendary King Arthur. This painting depicts King Arthur's Round Table, around which were seated his knights.

Use these questions for discussion:

1. Does seating knights at a round table really ensure equality? Are some places, for example, those immediately to the left or right of Arthur, more prestigious than others? *Being seated next to Arthur would surely have been an honor that elevated that knight above others at the table. In fact, the closer one sits to Arthur, the more elevated he would seem to be.*
2. What does this illustration suggest about the status of a knight in Arthur's time? *Their dress and surroundings suggest nobility.*

▶Critical Viewing◀

❶ **Deduce** Students should note that Arthur appears tall in relation to the door or window shown on the right; that his crown and the flag he carries seem to touch the ceiling; that he is bedecked with crowns, which are signs of royalty.

◆ Grammar and Style

❷ **Comparative and Superlative Forms** Have students translate the phrase "never since was there never seen a more dolefuller battle in no Christian land" into modern English. *This was the most doleful (or the saddest) battle ever seen in any Christian land*

◆ Literary Focus

❸ **Medieval Romance** Note the hyperbole in this battle description. In one day, one hundred thousand men are slain. There are three left on Arthur's side and only Mordred on the other. What might be the purpose of such hyperbole in this romance? *The exaggeration heightens the sense of drama. It also focuses attention on the major figures of the narrative.*

The Nine Heroes Tapestries: Christian Heroes: Arthur, Probably Nicolas Bataille, Paris; The Metropolitan Museum of Art

❶ ▲ **Critical Viewing** What can you deduce about King Arthur's heroic stature from his depiction in this tapestry? **[Deduce]**

❷ And never since was there never seen a more dolefuller battle in no Christian land, for there was but rushing and riding, lunging and striking; and many a grim word was there spoken of either to other, and many a deadly stroke. But ever King Arthur rode throughout the battle[12] of Sir Mordred many times and did full nobly, as a noble king should do, and at all times he fainted never. And Sir Mordred did his devoir that day and put himself in great peril.

❸ And thus they fought all the long day, and never stinted[13] till the noble knights were laid to the cold earth. And ever they fought still till it was near night, and by then was there an hundred thousand laid dead upon the down. Then was King Arthur wood-wroth[14] out of measure when he saw his people so slain from him. And so he looked about him and could see no more of all his host, and good knights left no more on-live, but two knights: the t'one was Sir Lucan the Butler and the other his brother Sir Bedivere. And yet they were full sore wounded. ❸

"Jesu, mercy," said the King, "where are all my noble knights become? Alas that ever I should see this doleful day! For now," said King Arthur, "I am come to mine end. But would to God," said he, "that I wist now where were that traitor Sir Mordred that has caused all this mischief."

Then King Arthur looked about and was ware where stood Sir Mordred leaning upon his sword among a great heap of dead men.

12. **battle:** Battalion.
13. **stinted:** Stopped.
14. **wood-wroth:** Wild with rage.

Humanities: Art

Detail from *The Nine Heroes Tapestries.*
Tapestries, woven figured textiles, have been created for more than 5,000 years by people all over the globe. They are used as wall hangings and decorations. European tapestries of the eleventh through the fourteenth centuries primarily showed historical events, characters from stories and legends, and scenes from daily life. Some tapestries provide the best picture we have of the dress and activities of a period.

The Nine Heroes Tapestries, which hang in the Cloisters in New York City, were made in France during the fourteenth century, probably around 1385. This detail was originally part of a set of three large panels, 16 by 21 feet in size. Each panel showed three heroes: One showed three pagans; one showed three Hebrews; and the last showed three Christians. Of the latter, only Arthur remains.

The three crowns shown on Arthur's tunic and banner represent England, Scotland, and Brittany. Use these questions for discussion:

1. What qualities of character are suggested by Arthur's face? *His stern appearance and stare suggest a strong, almost threatening character.*
2. What does the background convey about Arthur? *The cathedral conveys that Arthur is a Christian king; the banners show that he is king of England, Scotland, and Brittany.*

"Now give me my spear," said King Arthur unto Sir Lucan, "for yonder I have espied the traitor that all this woe hath wrought."

4 "Sir, let him be," said Sir Lucan, "for he is unhappy. And if ye pass this unhappy day ye shall be right well revenged upon him. And, good lord, remember ye of your night's dream, and what the spirit of Sir Gawain told you tonight, and yet God of his great goodness hath preserved you hitherto. And for God's sake, my lord, leave off by this, for, blessed be God, ye have won the field: for yet we been here three on-live, and with Sir Mordred is not one on-live. And therefore if ye leave off now, this wicked day of destiny is past."

"Now, tide[15] me death, tide me life," said the King, "now I see him yonder alone, he shall never escape mine hands. For at a better avail shall I never have him."

"God speed you well!" said Sir Bedivere.

Then the King got his spear in both his hands and ran toward Sir Mordred, crying and saying, "Traitor, now is thy deathday come!"

And when Sir Mordred saw King Arthur he ran until him with his sword drawn in his hand, and there King Arthur smote Sir Mordred under the shield, with a thrust of his spear, throughout the body more than a fathom. And when Sir Mordred felt that he had his death's wound, he thrust himself with the might that he had up to the burr[16] of King Arthur's spear, and right so he smote his father King Arthur with his sword holden in both his hands, upon the side of the head, that the sword pierced the helmet and the casing of the brain. And therewith Sir Mordred dashed down stark dead to the earth.

5 ◆ Reading Strategy
Summarize the events leading to the death of Mordred and the mortal wounding of King Arthur.

And noble King Arthur fell in a swough to the earth, and there he swooned oftentimes, and Sir Lucan and Sir Bedivere ofttimes heaved him up. And so, weakly betwixt them, they led him to a little chapel not far from the seaside, and when the King was there, him thought him reasonably eased. Then heard they people cry in the field. "Now go thou, Sir Lucan," said the King, "and do me to wit[17] what betokens that noise in the field."

So Sir Lucan departed, for he was grievously wounded in many places. And so as he walked he saw and harkened by the moonlight how that pillagers and robbers were come into the field to pill and to rob many a full noble knight of brooches and bracelets and of many a good ring and many a rich jewel. And who that were not dead all out there they slew them for their harness and their riches. When Sir Lucan understood this work, he came to the King as soon as he might and told him all what he had heard and seen. "Therefore by my read,"[18] said Sir Lucan, "it is best that we bring you to some town." 6

"I would it were so," said the King, "but I may not stand, my head works so. Ah, Sir Lancelot," said King Arthur, "this day have I sore missed thee. And alas that ever I was against thee, for now have I my death, whereof Sir Gawain me warned in my dream."

Then Sir Lucan took up the King the t'one party[19] and Sir Bedivere the other party; and in the lifting up the King swooned and in the lifting Sir Lucan fell in a swoon that part of his guts fell out of his body, and therewith the noble knight's heart burst. And when the King awoke he beheld Sir Lucan how he lay foaming at the mouth and part of his guts lay at his feet. 7

"Alas," said the King, "this is to me a full heavy sight to see this noble duke so die for my sake, for he would have helped me that had more need of help than I. Alas that he would not complain him for his heart was so set to help me. Now Jesu have mercy upon his soul."

Then Sir Bedivere wept for the death of his brother.

"Now leave this mourning and weeping gentle knight," said the King, "for all this will not avail me. For wit thou well, and might I live myself, the death of Sir Lucan would grieve me evermore. But my time passeth on fast," said the King. "Therefore," said King Arthur unto Sir Bedivere, "take thou here Excalibur my good sword and go with it to yonder water's side;

15. **tide:** Befall.
16. **burr:** Hand guard.
17. **me to wit:** Let me know.
18. **read:** Advice.
19. **party:** Side.

◆ Build Vocabulary

peril (per´ əl) *n.*: Exposure to harm or injury

Customize for
Less Proficient Readers
Focus students' attention on the details that show this was a terrible battle, including the following: "many a grim word," "many a deadly stroke," "put himself in great peril," "an hundred thousand laid dead."

◆ Critical Thinking

4 Make a Judgment Ask students if the advice given to Arthur by Sir Lucan was sound and wise. *Students may respond that the advice was sound, but destined to fall on deaf ears.*

◆ Reading Strategy

5 Summarize Students should mention that everyone on Sir Mordred's side is dead, and Arthur has but two men left. One, Sir Lucan, tries to dissuade Arthur, but the king realizes he will never have a better opportunity, so he attacks Mordred and gives him a mortal wound. As he dies, Mordred strikes King Arthur's head.

◆ Literature and Your Life

6 Draw students' attention to the looters described here, and ask when they have heard of similar events. Discuss reasons why people might act that way. *Looters may rob people who have been victims of floods, hurricanes, or civil disturbances. They take advantage of all the confusion at such a time.*

◆ Literary Focus

7 Medieval Romance Sir Lucan's loyalty to the king cost him his life. Ask students why loyalty might have been such an important virtue, and why the writer might have written such a vivid description of Lucan's death. *Loyalty may have been important because so many people were fighting that leaders wanted to trust their own knights. The vivid description makes the action seem lifelike and immediate. It also adds to the excitement.*

◆ Literature and Your Life

❶ Ask students whether they would be willing to throw a jewel-encrusted sword away. *Students may respond that they'd be willing to throw the sword away if they were bid to do so by the king.*

◆ Critical Thinking

❷ **Analyze** Magic is a common element in medieval romances. Ask students how its use here affects the story. *It adds an element of mystery; it proves to Arthur that Bedivere followed instructions.*

◆ Literary Focus

❸ **Medieval Romance** Students might note the pageantry, the drama, and the symbolism of black hoods.

Customize for
Visual/Spatial Learners
You might wish to create a simple two-column chart. Label one side "Evidence of Arthur's Death" and the other side "Reasons Arthur Might be Alive." Have students find details in the text for each side.

and when thou comest there I charge thee throw my sword in that water and come again and tell me what thou sawest there."

"My lord," said Sir Bedivere, "your commandment shall be done, and I shall lightly[20] bring you word again."

❶ So Sir Bedivere departed. And by the way he beheld that noble sword, that the pommel and the haft[21] was all precious stones. And then he said to himself, "If I throw this rich sword in the water, thereof shall never come good, but harm and loss." And then Sir Bedivere hid Excalibur under a tree. And so, as soon as he might, he came again unto the King and said he had been at the water and had thrown the sword into the water.

"What saw thou there?" said the King.

"Sir," he said, "I saw nothing but waves and winds."

"That is untruly said of thee," said the King. "And therefore go thou lightly again and do my commandment; as thou art to me loved and dear, spare not, but throw it in."

Then Sir Bedivere returned again and took the sword in his hand. And yet him thought sin and shame to throw away that noble sword. And so eft[22] he hid the sword and returned again and told the King that he had been at the water and done his commandment.

"What sawest thou there?" said the King.

"Sir," he said, "I saw nothing but waters wap and waves wan."[23]

"Ah, traitor unto me and untrue," said King Arthur, "now hast thou betrayed me twice. Who would have weened that thou that has been to me so loved and dear, and thou art named a noble knight, and would betray me for the riches of this sword. But now go again lightly, for thy long tarrying putteth me in great jeopardy of my life, for I have taken cold. And but if thou do now as I bid thee, if ever I may see thee I shall slay thee mine own hands, for thou wouldest for my rich sword see me dead."

❷ Then Sir Bedivere departed and went to the sword and lightly took it up, and so he went to the water's side; and there he bound the girdle about the hilts, and threw the sword as far into the water as he might. And there came an arm and an hand above the water and took it and clutched it, and shook it thrice and brandished; and then vanished away the hand with the sword into the water. So Sir Bedivere came again to the King and told him what he saw. ❷

"Alas," said the King, "help me hence, for I dread me I have tarried overlong."

Then Sir Bedivere took the King upon his back and so went with him to that water's side. And when they were at the water's side, even fast[24] by the bank floated a little barge with many fair ladies in it; and among them all was a queen; and all they had black hoods, and all they wept and shrieked when they saw King Arthur.

> **◆ Literary Focus**
> In what ways is the description of King Arthur's death characteristic of medieval romances? ❸

"Now put me into that barge," said the King; and so he did softly. And there received him three ladies with great mourning, and so they set them down. And in one of their laps King Arthur laid his head, and then the queen said, "Ah, my dear brother, why have ye tarried so long from me? Alas, this wound on your head hath caught overmuch cold." And anon they rowed fromward the land, and Sir Bedivere beheld all tho ladies go froward him.

Then Sir Bedivere cried and said, "Ah, my lord Arthur, what shall become of me, now ye go from me and leave me here alone among mine enemies?"

"Comfort thyself," said the King, "and do as well as thou mayest, for in me is no trust for to trust in. For I must into the vale of Avilion[25] to heal me of my grievous wound. And if thou hear nevermore of me, pray for my soul."

But ever the queen and ladies wept and shrieked, that it was pity to hear. And as soon as Sir Bedivere had lost sight of the barge he wept and wailed, and so took the forest and went all that night.

And in the morning he was ware, betwixt two bare woods, of a chapel and an hermitage. Then was Sir Bedivere glad, and thither he went, and when he came into the chapel he saw where lay an hermit groveling on all fours, close thereby a tomb was new dug. When the hermit saw Sir Bedivere he knew him well, for he was but little tofore Bishop of Canterbury,

---

20. **lightly:** Quickly.
21. **pommel . . . haft:** Hilt and hand guard.
22. **eft:** Again.
23. **waters . . . wan:** Waters lap and waves grow dark.
24. **fast:** Close.
25. **Avilion:** Legendary island.

that Sir Mordred put to flight.

"Sirs," said Sir Bedivere, "what man is there here interred that you pray so fast for?"

"Fair son," said the hermit. "I wot not verily but by guessing. But this same night, at midnight, here came a number of ladies and brought here a dead corpse and prayed me to inter him. And here they offered an hundred tapers, and gave me a thousand gold coins."

"Alas," said Sir Bedivere, "that was my lord King Arthur, which lieth here buried in this chapel."

Then Sir Bedivere swooned, and when he awoke he prayed the hermit that he might abide with him still, there to live with fasting and prayers:

"For from hence will I never go," said Sir Bedivere, "by my will, but all the days of my life here to pray for my lord Arthur."

"Sir, ye are welcome to me," said the hermit, "for I know you better than ye think that I do: for ye are Sir Bedivere the Bold, and the full noble duke Sir Lucan the Butler was your brother."

Then Sir Bedivere told the hermit all as you have heard tofore, and so he stayed with the hermit that was beforehand Bishop of Canterbury. And there Sir Bedivere put upon him poor clothes, and served the hermit full lowly in fasting and in prayers.

Thus of Arthur I find no more written in books that been authorized, neither more of the very certainty of his death heard I nor read, but thus was he led away in a ship wherein were three queens; that one was King Arthur's sister, Queen Morgan le Fay, the other was the Queen of North Galis, and the third was the Queen of the Waste Lands.

Now more of the death of King Arthur could I never find, but that these ladies brought him to his grave, and such one was interred there which the hermit bare witness that was once Bishop of Canterbury. But yet the hermit knew not in certain that he was verily the body of **4**
King Arthur; for this tale Sir Bedivere, a knight of the Table Round, made it to be written.

Yet some men say in many parts of England that King Arthur is not dead, but carried by the will of our Lord Jesu into another place; and men say that he shall come again, and he shall win the Holy Cross. Yet I will not say that it shall be so, but rather I would say: here in this world he changed his life. And many men say that there is written upon the tomb this:

HIC IACET ARTHURUS, REX
QUONDAM, REXQUE FUTURUS[26]

26. **Hic . . . futurus:** Here lies Arthur, who was once king and king will be again.

◆ Build Vocabulary

interred (in turd′) *v.*: Buried

Guide for Responding

◆ Literature and Your Life

Reader's Response If King Arthur had asked you to throw his sword into the water, would you have hesitated as Sir Bedivere did? Why or why not?

Thematic Focus Would you classify this tale as one of peril or one of adventure? Explain.

Epitaph for Arthur Write an epitaph, or tomb inscription, that captures King Arthur's magical life.

☑ Check Your Comprehension

1. What warning does King Arthur receive in his dream?
2. (a) How does Arthur slay Mordred? (b) What does Mordred do just before he dies?
3. Summarize what happens when Arthur asks Sir Bedivere to throw Excalibur into the water.

◆ Critical Thinking

4 Evaluate Ask what information Malory provides to make this account seem factual. *He mentions "written in books that been authorized," and he quotes what people say is written on Arthur's tombstone.*

Customize for More Advanced Students

You may wish to point out that the title of the well-known novel *The Once and Future King* was based on the epitaph on Arthur's tomb. Written by T. H. White, the book is a modern retelling of Arthurian stories. In it, Malory appears briefly as a character.

Reinforce and Extend

Answers

◆ Literature and Your Life

Reader's Response Suggested response: No; it's against the code of chivalry to disobey your king.

Thematic Focus Suggested response: This is a story of peril because it's really about betrayal and death.

☑ Check Your Comprehension

1. Arthur is warned not to do battle with Mordred the next day or he will die.
2. (a) Arthur kills him with the thrust of a spear. (b) Mordred hits Arthur on the side of his head with his sword.
3. Sir Bedivere first hid the sword under a tree; then he hid the sword again; the third time, he threw it in the lake as he was told to do.

Beyond the Selection

FURTHER READING

Other Books About King Arthur

The Acts of King Arthur and His Noble Knights, edited by John Steinbeck

King Arthur and His Knights of the Round Table, Antonia Fraser

The Once and Future King, T. H. White

Books About King Arthur's Times

The Search for King Arthur, David Day

We suggest that you preview these works before recommending them to students.

INTERNET

You and your students may find additional information about Arthurian legends on the Internet at the following site. Please be aware, however, that sites may have changed from the time we published this information.

For information about Sir Gawain, go to **http: www.luminarium.org/medlit/gawain.htm**

You may also find related information on King Arthur on the Internet. We *strongly recommend* that you preview the sites before you send students to them.

Guide for Responding (continued)

◆ Critical Thinking

Interpret

1. How are Arthur and Mordred similar and how are they different? **[Compare and Contrast]**

2. What do you think are Sir Bedivere's reasons for twice failing to obey Arthur's request to throw Excalibur into the water? **[Interpret]**

3. How does the ending add to the mysterious, magical quality of the tale? **[Draw Conclusions]**

Apply

4. Why do you think the legend of King Arthur has retained its popularity for so long? **[Generalize]**

◆ Reading Strategy

Summarize

As your read *Sir Gawain and the Green Knight* and *Morte d'Arthur*, you **summarized** passages so you could identify key ideas and events in the stories. Use your summaries to answer these questions:

1. If you were retelling *Sir Gawain and the Green Knight* for an audience of fifth graders, which key events would you emphasize?

2. As Sir Bevidere, summarize for a curious traveler who is visiting your hermitage the events leading up to King Arthur's death.

◆ Literary Focus

Medieval Romances

Most **medieval romances** embody the ideals of chivalry, are set in a remote time or place, and combine supernatural events with realistic ones. They also feature a hero engaged in pure adventure and feature spontaneous, unmotivated fighting and include love as a major part of the story.

1. Which of these characteristics *is not* displayed in this excerpt from *Sir Gawain and the Green Knight*?

2. Does Sir Gawain fit the mold of a medieval hero? Explain.

3. In the excerpt from *Morte d'Arthur*, how do the supernatural events surrounding Arthur's death link the story to the future?

4. King Arthur was supposedly a Briton who fought against the invading Anglo-Saxons. Why do you think Britons kept his memory alive for centuries after their defeat by the Anglo-Saxons?

◆ Build Vocabulary

Using the Word Root *-droit-*

The word root *-droit-*, which means "right," reveals a historical bias toward right-handedness.

1. Knowing that the prefix *mal* means "bad," what might *maladroit* mean?

2. Gauche means the opposite of "socially adroit." Which of these two might it also mean—"left" or "right"?

Using the Word Bank

On your paper, write the letter of the word that best expresses the meaning of the first word.

1. assay: (a) test, (b) deny, (c) ignore

2. adjure: (a) reject, (b) appeal, (c) ask

3. feigned: (a) revealed, (b) refused, (c) pretended

4. largesse: (a) nobility, (b) insignificance, (c) wisdom

5. interred: (a) included, (b) uncovered, (c) buried

6. righteousness: (a) awkwardness, (b) virtuousness, (c) dishonorableness

7. entreated: (a) pleaded, (b) requested, (c) refused

8. peril: (a) safety, (b) security, (c) danger

◆ Grammar and Style

Comparative and Superlative Forms

The world of medieval romances is a world of **comparatives** and **superlatives**. Supernatural wonders are the *most* marvelous ever seen, and one knight is always *braver* or *more* skillful than another.

Practice Identify the comparative and superlative forms of modifiers in the following passages.

	One Syllable	Two Syllables
Comparative Form:	-er	more
Superlative Form:	-est	most

1. She made trial of a man most faultless by far / Of all that ever walked over the wide earth; / As pearls to white peas, more precious and prized,

2. [W]here battle is joined; / I am the weakest, well I know, and of wit feeblest; And the loss of my life would be least of any;

Writing Application In a brief paragraph, use comparative and superlative modifiers to compare and contrast characters from either story.

Answers

◆ Critical Thinking

1. They are both noble and both are great warriors. Arthur, however, is the epitome of the chivalric king; Mordred seems vindictive and insolent.
2. The sword is too beautiful and precious to throw away. Another reason may be that throwing the sword into the lake signifies that Arthur is really gone.
3. The ending is full of mystery and the supernatural, suggesting that perhaps Arthur has not really died.
4. Suggested response: The qualities Arthur represented are still valued today. It's human nature to root for a hero who stands for goodness and valor. *Morte d'Arthur* contains a great hero as well as a terrific battle scene.

◆ Reading Strategy

1. Key events to emphasize would include these: A large Green Knight arrives at Arthur's court and dares anyone there to take a swing at him with an ax while he stands unarmed. The Green Knight will then do the same to Arthur's knight. Sir Gawain takes up the challenge and beheads the knight, who miraculously remains standing and orders Gawain to appear at his home in a year's time to take his turn. A year later, Gawain finds the Green Knight and lets him swing at him. The Green Knight barely scratches him and then he reveals his real identity to Gawain, explaining that he was testing his honor and courage.
2. Arthur and Mordred meet on the battlefield with their armies. King Arthur and Sir Mordred then meet in personal combat. Arthur kills Mordred but is himself grievously wounded. Knowing he is near death, Arthur has Bedivere toss Excalibur, his sword, into the lake, from which a hand emerges and catches the sword. Bedivere then carries Arthur to a barge containing a queen and her ladies. The barge sails off, taking Arthur to Avilion, where his wound may heal. No one ever sees him again.

◆ Literary Focus

1. Love is not a major element in *Sir Gawain and the Green Knight.*
2. Yes, Gawain fits the mold of a medieval hero. He is brave, skilled in fighting, and loyal to his king and to God.
3. Arthur was never laid to rest; he floated off in a ship into the night. Because he was never interred, he never really died, and he is considered the king for all future time.
4. Because heroes embody the culture from which they came, preserving the Arthur legend was one way of preserving the culture of the Britons, who had been defeated by the Anglo-Saxons.

◆ Build Vocabulary

Using the Word Root *-droit-*

1. *Maladroit* means "not right" or "unskilled."
2. *Gauche* means "left."

Using the Word Bank

1. (a) test; 2. (c) ask; 3. (c) pretended; 4. (a) nobility; 5. (c) buried; 6. (b) virtuousness; 7. (a) pleaded; 8. (c) danger

◆ Grammar and Style

1. most faultless (superlative); more precious and prized (comparative)
2. weakest, feeblest, least (all superlative)

Build Your Portfolio

Idea Bank

Writing

1. **T-shirt** Write a message for a T-shirt featuring a legendary character. Include the name and a brief description of his or her accomplishments.

2. **Résumé** Create a résumé that highlights Sir Gawain's skills. Be creative, but arrange the information clearly: name and address on top, job objective, work history, education, and special skills and talents. **[Career Link]**

3. **Response to Criticism** One critic views Sir Gawain and the Green Knight as: "... a rare combination: at once a comedy—even a satire—of manners and a profoundly Christian view of man's character and his destiny." Write a short essay agreeing or disagreeing with this view.

Speaking and Listening

4. **Oral Report** Explore methods of combat in the medieval era. Prepare a brief oral report with illustrations and present it to your class. **[Social Studies Link]**

5. **Multimedia Presentation** Use clips from movies, illustrations, reproductions of fine art, and computer games to give a multimedia presentation on the Arthurian legend. **[Media Link; Social Studies Link]**

Projects

6. **Musical Presentation** Find a piece of instrumental music that matches the tone or mood of *Sir Gawain and the Green Knight.* Play a recording of the music in class.

7. **Illuminated Manuscript** Create one page of an illuminated manuscript for either *Sir Gawain and the Green Knight* or *Morte d'Arthur.* You may choose to depict a certain scene or the entire piece. **[Art Link]**

Writing Mini-Lesson

Valedictory Speech

The final paragraphs of the excerpt from *Morte d'Arthur* sum up the facts of Arthur's death and hint at future events. A valedictory speech at a high-school graduation performs a similar function, summing up the high-school experience and suggesting what the future holds.

Write such a valedictory speech for your own graduation, and follow these hints for using repetition effectively.

Writing Skills Focus: Effective Repetition

Repeated words or phrases can make any piece of writing more memorable. Notice how Malory uses repetition to suggest the return of Arthur:

Model From Literature

Yet some men say in many parts of England that King Arthur is not dead, . . . and *men say* that he shall come again, and he shall win the Holy Cross. . . .

Use the following strategies to guide you as you write.

Prewriting Outline your speech. Then scan your outline for a memorable word or group of words that sums up your whole message. Underline these words so you can refer to them as you write.

Drafting Using your outline, write a rough draft of your speech. Try repeating the word or words you underlined at varying intervals. Also, be sure to use your "refrain" in the final part of your speech.

Revising Read your speech aloud, emphasizing the repeated phrase. If you are overusing the word or words, eliminate some examples of repetition. If the words sound insincere, replace them with a phrase that sounds better.

✓ ASSESSMENT OPTIONS

Formal Assessment, Selection Test, pp. 31–33, and Assessment Resources Software. The selection test is designed so that it can be easily customized to the ability levels of your students.
Alternative Assessment, p. 6, includes options for less advanced students, more advanced students, visual/spatial learners, and auditory learners.

PORTFOLIO ASSESSMENT
Use the following rubrics in the ***Alternative Assessment*** booklet to assess student writing:
Résumé: Résumé, Cover Letter Rubric, p. 115
Response to Criticism: Response to Literature Rubric, p. 111
Oral Report: Research Report Rubric, p. 107
Valedictory Speech: Summary Rubric, p. 99

Idea Bank

Customizing for *Learning Modalities*
Following are suggestions for matching Idea Bank topics with your students' learning modalities:
- Visual/Spatial: 1, 7
- Verbal/Linguistic: 6, 7
- Bodily/Kinesthetic: 5
- Interpersonal: 4, 5

Customizing for *Performance Levels*
Following are suggestions for matching Idea Bank topics with your students' ability levels:
- Less Advanced Students: 1, 7
- Average Students: 2, 4
- More Advanced Students: 3, 5

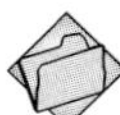

Writing Mini-Lesson

Refer students to the Writing Handbook, page 1189, for instruction on the writing process, and page 1191 for further information on exposition.

Writing and Language Transparencies Use the Outline organizer, p. 123, to help students plan and organize their writing.

Writer's Solution

Writers at Work Videodisc
Play for students the videodisc segment featuring defense attorney Cary Bricker to get tips about public speaking. Following the segment, lead a discussion with the class about what skills contribute to effective public speaking.

Play frames 38700 to 39570

Writing Lab CD-ROM
Direct students to prepare their speeches using the tutorial on Exposition. Follow these steps:
1. Complete the Audience and Purpose Profiles.
2. Use the interactive instruction for gathering details for informative speeches.
3. Create a draft on the computer.
4. Use a Revision Checker for Unity and Coherence.

Sourcebook
Have students complete Chapter 3, Exposition (pp. 63–95), for additional support.

Prepare and Engage

OBJECTIVES

1. To read, comprehend, interpret, and respond to letters and folk ballads
2. To relate the content of the letters and folk ballads to personal experience
3. To understand dialect
4. To identify letters and folk ballads as forms of literature and communication
5. To build vocabulary in context and learn the word root *-cert-*
6. To identify instances of direct address and incorporate direct address in writing
7. To write a persuasive letter supporting an argument through elaboration
8. To respond to letters and folk ballads through writing, speaking and listening, and projects

SKILLS INSTRUCTION

Vocabulary:
Word Roots: *-cert-*

Grammar:
Direct Address

Reading Strategy:
Understand Dialect

Literary Focus:
Letter; Folk Ballad

Writing:
Persuasive Writing

Speaking and Listening:
Song Translation (teacher edition)

Critical Viewing:
Speculate; Infer; Compare and Contrast; Interpret

PORTFOLIO OPPORTUNITIES

Writing: Casting Call; A Modern Ballad; Critical Response
Writing Mini-Lesson: Persuasive Letter
Speaking and Listening: Letter vs. Phone Call; Song Translation
Projects: Holidays Chart; An English Manor

More About the Authors

According to *Women in the Middle Ages,* by Frances and Joseph Gies, **Margaret Paston,** may have been illiterate. This theory comes about because her 104 surviving letters are written in many different hands. This is not conclusive proof, however; she may have disliked writing and preferred to dictate her letters to secretaries.

The **four ballads** in this grouping originated in the wild border country between England and Scotland. As they were sung, these ballads acquired new words and new verses because every balladeer felt free to make alterations.

Guide for Interpreting

Margaret Paston *(1423–1484)*

Brokering deals . . . defending the manor . . . fighting lawsuits . . . hiring staff . . . This description would fit today's top executives, but it could also apply to Margaret Paston, a woman who lived in fifteenth-century England. Margaret Paston, born a Mautby, married John Paston, the son of a well-to-do landowner educated in the law. Because of John Paston's profession, he was frequently called to London on business, leaving Margaret to run the estates, settle rent disputes, and defend their manors against takeovers—which she did admirably.

The Legacy of the Pastons The letters of the Paston family deal with everyday matters. They also deal with scandals, like one daughter's secret marriage to the family's bailiff and the other daughter's marriage to the son of her father's rival.

Sometimes these letters seem like a script for a medieval soap opera.

Numbering in the hundreds, they provide us with a glimpse into life as it really was in the fifteenth century.

Folk Ballads

Long before most people in Britain could read or write, they were familiar with the stories told in ballads. A ballad is a narrative poem meant to be sung.

Much like country western songs of today, these ballads tell stories about characters who face challenges in life and love. Some ballads are very gruesome, however, and show the dark side of love and life.

The Ballad's Origins No one knows when the first folk ballads appeared in England, but it was probably during the twelfth century. Because the ballads were unwritten, they were passed along orally for many centuries. The earliest written ballads we know date from about the fifteenth century, but no one can absolutely identify the original versions of many of them.

In 1765, ballad enthusiast Bishop Thomas Percy published *Reliques of Ancient English Poetry*, an extensive collection of ballads. People began to appreciate the ballads for their literary value as well as for their fascinating glimpses into history. Percy's collection of ballads was based on an old manuscript he rescued from a housemaid who was about to light a fire with it.

◆ Background for Understanding

History: Political Uncertainty

The Hundred Years' War had just come to an end, with the English military suffering defeat. King Henry VI's inability and later senility caused the government to lapse into chaos. In the midst of this upheaval and uncertainty, many families were able to struggle out of poverty by seizing properties to which they had no legal claim.

The Paston family had recently emerged from the upper class of the peasantry and were eager to increase their landholdings and rise in society. Holding onto their estates was not easy: The Pastons were sued, threatened, and bullied over the years by those who wanted to profit from their holdings.

Culture: Perils of Everyday Life

Life was half over by the age of eighteen for most people who lived during the Middle Ages. Living in an uncertain world, where death before the age of thirty-five was the norm, prompted an unsentimental, cynical outlook on life. This view of life was expressed in folk ballads that tell about everyday people and their adventures, loves, jealousies, and disasters.

Throughout the centuries, these ballads changed as the times and language changed. Luckily for us, some of these early ballads have survived the remaining centuries and still give pleasure and entertainment today.

Prentice Hall Literature Program Resources

REINFORCE / RETEACH / EXTEND

Selection Support Pages
Build Vocabulary: Word Roots: *-cert-*, p. 32
Grammar and Style: Direct Address, p. 33
Reading Strategy: Understand Dialect, p. 34
Literary Focus: Letter; Folk Ballad, p. 35

Strategies for Diverse Student Needs, p. 7

Beyond Literature Community Connection, p. 7

Formal Assessment Selection Test, pp. 34–35
Assessment Resources Software

Alternative Assessment, p. 7

Writing and Language Transparencies
Argument Organizer, pp. 103–106
Writing Process Model 5, pp. 37–43

Resource Pro CD-ROM includes all resource material and customizable lesson plan

Listening to Literature Audiocassettes
"The Paston Letters"; "Four Ballads"
Music Cassette: "Barbara Allan"

Looking at Literature Videodisc
Chapters 1 and 2

The Letters of Margaret Paston
◆ Four Ballads ◆

◆ Literature and Your Life

Connect Your Experience

Certain television shows and soap operas hook viewers into eagerly awaiting each episode because they depict the adventure and romance of everyday life.

This appeal of the drama of everyday life is not new. Margaret Paston's letters, written long ago, reveal incredible but true happenings at the Paston manors. Also, folk ballads that are centuries old contain riveting stories of doomed lovers and twisted fates.

Journal Writing Write about the qualities that make a popular song a classic.

Thematic Focus: Perils and Adventures

As you read the following letters and ballads, ask yourself: What were the perils and challenges of medieval life?

◆ Literary Focus

Letter; Folk Ballad

A **letter** is a form of communication that usually contains a date, greeting, body, and closing. Letters range from short news-bearing notes to action-packed narratives.

As you read Margaret Paston's letters, note what they reveal about medieval life.

A **folk ballad** is a narrative poem by an unknown author, which is meant to be sung. Most ballads have four-line stanzas, in which the second and fourth lines rhyme. Many have regularly repeated lines, called a refrain, and contain elements such as dialogue and repetition.

These ballads, from the rugged area near the Scottish-English border, are cynical or darkly humorous.

◆ Grammar and Style

Direct Address

The folk ballads that follow use **direct address,** which is the name, title, or descriptive phrase used when speaking directly to someone or something. For example: "Oh where ha'e ye been, *Lord Randall my son?"*

The person being addressed is Lord Randall. The words "my son" indicate that Lord Randall's mother is addressing him.

◆ Reading Strategy

Understand Dialect

A **dialect** is the form of a language spoken by people in a particular region or group. The ballads that follow are in Scottish-English dialect.

To understand the dialect, follow these strategies:

1. Read the lines aloud. The word sounds and context may lead you to the corresponding current English word. Look at this example:

   The wind *sae cauld* blew.

   The sound of *sae cauld* and the fact that these words describe the wind lead you to recognize their meaning as "so cold."
2. Use the footnotes to get definitions of words no longer in use. For example, you'll see that "twa corbies" are two ravens.

◆ Build Vocabulary

Word Roots: *-cert-*

Margaret Paston uses the phrase, "certify to him the names of. . . ." The root of *certify, -cert-,* comes from the Latin *certus,* which means "sure." Certify means "to make sure," or "to verify."

Word Bank

Before you read, preview this list of words.

aldermen
enquiry
succor
certify
remnant
ransacked
asunder
assault

Preparing for Standardized Tests

Reading and Vocabulary Knowledge of word roots like *-cert-,* the one taught in this lesson will prove invaluable to students as they take various standardized tests. For example, students will be required to identify word meanings through matching questions and by selecting a word's antonym or synonym. For additional practice, use the Build Vocabulary page in ***Selection Support,*** p. 28.

Grammar and Language Some standardized test portions may require students to revise passages. Knowing how to punctuate words of direct address may be beneficial in these test items. For example, students may be asked to punctuate sentences such as the following:

- Kim have you read this letter? *Kim, have*
- Well Carla I hope you're happy. *Well, Carla, I*

The Grammar and Style lesson for this selection focuses on this topic. For additional practice, use the Grammar and Style page on Direct Address, p. 29, in ***Selection Support.***

Interest Grabber The language of these letters and ballads may seem long ago and far away to students, but the characters and themes will not. To help students get beyond the intimidating language and into the lure of the plots, ask them to name a book, movie, or episode from a soap opera or movie in which they've encountered any of the following characters or situations—or something like them:

- a woman left in charge of large estates in a time of plotting, intrigue, and uprising
- a handsome young man mysteriously killed by an enemy
- a husband and wife so intent on squabbling with each other that they seem not to care that they are about to be mugged
- two characters discuss the situation following a man's death
- a woman who is cruel to her love on his death bed

Then tell students that these ballads deal with these very situations.

Customize for
Less Proficient Readers

Inform students that the language of these works will require them to slow down as they read and also to reread. When reading the ballads in this section, suggest that they preview the footnotes first, to familiarize themselves with words particular to the Scottish-English dialect.

Customize for
Musical/Rhythmic Learners

The four ballads lend themselves to rhythmic recitation or other musical treatment. Help students to find a rhythm and beat appropriate to each ballad and lead them to recite or sing each ballad in a way that helps reveal its emotional content and meaning.

Customize for
Verbal/Linguistic Learners

Verbal learners may benefit from reading the four ballads aloud. This will enable them to receive and appreciate the full effect of the musical dialect in which they're written.

Develop Understanding

One-Minute Insight Letters are a way of sharing life's news, and, in the case of Margaret Paston, the news is dramatic, detailed, and very directly stated. Letters can also go a long way toward revealing the personality of the writer. In the first pair of letters, Paston tells her husband that one of their homes, Hellesdon, has been attacked, seized, and ransacked by the Duke of Suffolk. As she details events, her outrage is palpable. The third letter, written almost two years later and warning her son of yet another impending attack, reveals Paston's keen awareness of political turmoil.

By reading these letters students will receive firsthand information about life in the Middle Ages. They will also come to appreciate and respect Margaret Paston herself, a truly remarkable woman.

Looking at Literature Videodisc To introduce students to Margaret Paston's world, play Chapter 1: Life in the Middle Ages. Following the segment, hold a brief discussion with the class about how life was different from and similar to life today.

Chapter 1

◆ Literary Focus

❶ **Letter** Ask students to find three details in this paragraph that indicate that Paston was an observant correspondent. *Paston notes the time, the date, the number of men, and the precise actions of the duke, including the date and time by which names had to be certified.*

Comprehension Check ☑

❷ What does Paston want her husband to tell her? *Paston wants advice from him on how to act or, more specifically, whether she should stay at Caister or come to London.*

Letters of Margaret Paston

Margaret Paston

Hellesdon, one of the Paston manors, was coveted by the Duke of Suffolk. The duke bribed the mayor of Norwich, which lies southeast of London, to assist him in launching a campaign of terror to force the Pastons to surrender their property. Although Margaret Paston, along with a garrison of sixty, successfully repelled the first attacks, Hellesdon eventually was seized and plundered by the duke. In this letter Margaret writes to her husband in London with the news.

Margaret Paston to John Paston
17 October 1465
Norwich

❶ . . . The Duke came to Norwich on Tuesday at 10 o'clock with some 500 men. And he sent for the mayor and aldermen with the Sheriffs, desiring them in the King's name that they should make enquiry of the constables of every ward in the City as to what men had gone to help or succor your men at any time during these gatherings and, if they could find any, that they should take and arrest and correct them, and certify to him the names by 8 o'clock on Wednesday. Which the Mayor did and will do anything that he may for him and his men . . .

I am told that the old Lady [the Dowager Duchess] and the Duke are fiercely set against us on the information of Harleston, the bailiff of Costessey . . . and such other false shrews which would have this matter carried through for their own pleasure . . . And as for Sir John Heveningham, Sir John Wingfield and other worshipful men, they are but made their doggebolds [lackeys], which I suppose will cause their disworship hereafter. I spoke with Sir John Heveningham and informed him of the truth of the matter and of all our demeaning at Drayton, and he said he would that all things were well, and that he would inform my Lord what I told him, but that Harleston had all the influence with the Duke here, and at this time he was advised by him and Dr. Aleyn.

The lodge and the remnant of your place was beaten down on Tuesday and Wednesday and the Duke rode on Wednesday to Drayton and so forth to Costessey while the lodge at Hellesdon was being beaten down. And this night at midnight Thomas Slyforth . . . and others had a cart and fetched away featherbeds and all our stuff that was left at the parson's and Thomas Waters' house to be kept . . . I pray you send me word how I shall act—whether you wish that I abide at Caister or come to you at London . . . ❷

◆ Build Vocabulary

aldermen (ôl´ dər mən) *n.*: Chief officers in a shire, or district

enquiry (en kwīr´ ē) *n.*: Question

succor (suk´ ər) *v.*: Help; aid; relieve

certify (surt´ ə fī´) *v.*: Declare a thing true or accurate; verify; attest

remnant (rem´ nənt) *n.*: What is left over; remainder; residue

ransacked (ran´ sakt´) *v.*: Searched through for plunder; pillaged; robbed

asunder (ə sun´ dər) *adv.*: Into parts or pieces

Block Scheduling Strategies

Consider these suggestions to take advantage of extended class time:

- Have students watch the *Looking at Literature* videodisc segment on Life in the Middle Ages (Letters of Margaret Paston) or "Get Up and Bar the Door" (Four Ballads) to introduce students to the time period or concept of ballads.
- Before students read the ballads, introduce them to the Reading Strategy on page 165. Have them apply the strategies for understanding dialect as they read the ballads. Then have them answer the Reading Strategy questions on page 178.
- Have students read the History Connection in Beyond Literature on page 169 and respond to the question.
- Play the recording of "Barbara Allan," which appears on the **Listening to Literature Audiocassettes.** Hold a discussion about how the music adds to or detracts from the words of the ballad.
- Have students answer the Critical Thinking questions in response to each selection.

Margaret Paston to John Paston
27 October 1465
Norwich

. . . Please you to know that I was at Hellesdon on Thursday last and saw the place there, and, in good faith, nobody would believe how foul and horrible it appears unless they saw it. There come many people daily to wonder at it, both from Norwich and many other places, and they speak of it with shame. The Duke would have been a £1000 better off if it had not happened, and you have the more good will of the people because it was so foully done. They made your tenants of Hellesdon and Drayton, with others, break down the walls of both the place and the lodge—God knows full much against their wills, but they dare not refuse for fear. I have spoken with your tenants of Hellesdon and Drayton and comforted them as well as I can. The Duke's men ransacked the church and bore away all the goods that were left there, both of ours and of the tenants, and even stood upon the high altar and ransacked the images and took away those that they could find, and put the parson out of the church till they had done, and ransacked every man's house in the town five or six times . . . As for lead, brass, pewter, iron, doors, gates and other stuff of the house, men from Costessey and Cawston have it, and what they might not carry away they have hewn asunder in the most spiteful manner . . .

◆ **Literary Focus** How does the detail about the "high altar" show the desperation of the situation? ❸

At the reverence of god, if any worshipful and profitable settlement may be made in your matters, do not forsake it, to avoid our trouble and great costs and charges that we may have and that may grow hereafter . . . ❹

▼ **Critical Viewing** The Pastons' manors were often attacked by their enemies. Using clues from this photograph, what would have made this manor worth fighting over? **[Speculate]** ❺

◆ Literary Focus

❸ **Letter** Accept answers that are similar to the following: *The detail about the "high altar" shows that those who ransacked stopped at nothing. It suggests total disregard for ownership and propriety.*

◆ Critical Thinking

❹ **Connect** Ask students to tell which words or phrases they think best reveal the emotions Margaret feels and the great strain she is under. *The phrase* At the reverence of god *suggests Paston is resorting to the divine and, therefore, nearly begging. Her plea to her husband not to forsake any possibility of making money or a profit also shows she is worried about finances.*

▶Critical Viewing◀

❺ **Speculate** Suggested responses: The manor appears to be large enough to house numerous family members and servants. It also appears to have been built very solidly, making it useful as a fortress in times of battle.

Customize for
Less Proficient Readers
A large number of proper nouns occur in this selection. To help less proficent readers keep people and places straight, encourage students to make a two-column chart in which they list people, such as the Duke, in column 1, and, when possible, the place each is associated with, such as Norwich, in column 2.

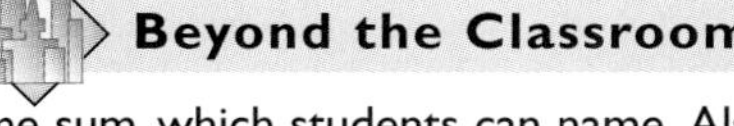

Beyond the Classroom

Career Connection

Accounting Margaret Paston refers to the huge financial losses that resulted from the assault. Although tenants in medieval times were different from tenants of today, the financial stability of the manor often rested on income from tenants.

Have students assume that they manage an apartment building with thirty-two units, each of which is occupied and rents for the same sum, which students can name. Also have them estimate average monthly expenditures per unit for taxes, maintenance, repairs, and other costs, such as insurance. Students can use spreadsheets to display monthly and yearly projected profits and losses based on full tenancy for one year, as well as for periods of total or partial vacancy.

Community Connection

Property Disputes Margaret Paston was kept very busy, defending her family's manors from those who challenged their ownership. Point out to the class, that to this day, legal squabbles about ownership of land and buildings still arise and are sorted out in the court system. Encourage students to visit a local real estate agent to learn more about the process of buying land or property and obtaining the paperwork necessary to prove ownership.

Enrichment Inform students that these letters were composed during the Wars of the Roses. Beginning in 1455, nobles battled one another under emblems of the white rose (House of Lancaster) or the red rose (House of York). The goal was the eventual control of the crown. For thirty years, the noble families of England battled one another. Still, life and culture somehow went on. At almost the same time that Paston was writing her letters, Sir Thomas Malory was composing *Morte d'Arthur* and William Caxton was experimenting with the printing press.

◆ Literature and Your Life

❶ Students may suggest any book, movie, or television plot in which a woman is stranded and asking for help; in which there is a threatened attack and help must be sent; or in which men refuse to take orders from, or even follow the advice of, a woman.

◆ Critical Thinking

❷ **Draw Conclusions** How would you describe Margaret Paston's attitude toward her son at this point? *Suggested answers: From the tone of her letter, she is becoming exasperated and annoyed with her son because he has not responded to her previous requests for assistance.*

Art Transparency 3 As students read the letters of Margaret Paston, show students this transparency depicting life on a manor. Ask students to describe the evidence of daily life they see. Also have students speculate about what the numbers and pictures that appear at the top of the picture mean. *This is part of a calendar, which shows the month of March.*

The following letter was sent to Sir John Paston, Margaret's knighted son. Caister, with many manors and estates, had been willed to the Paston family by Sir John Fastolf, for whom John Paston worked as financial adviser. There followed years of legal wrangles during which the Pastons faced numerous challenges to the will. John Paston having died the year before, Margaret turned to her son Sir John for help defending Caister. Sir John sent his younger brother, also named John, to protect the castle. John failed, however, surrendering the castle after his protector, King Edward IV, was captured during the Wars of the Roses.

Margaret Paston to Sir John Paston
11 July 1467
Norwich

. . . Also this day was brought me word from Caister that Rising of Fritton had heard in divers places in Suffolk that Fastolf of Cowhawe gathers all the strength he may and intends to assault Caister and to enter there if he may, insomuch that it is said that he has five score men ready and daily sends spies to know what men guard the place. By whose power or favour or support he will do this I know not, but you know well that I have been afraid there before this time, when I had other comfort than I had now: I cannot guide nor rule soldiers well and they set not by [do not respect] a woman as they should by a man. Therefore I would that you should send home your brothers or else Daubeney to take control and to bring in such men as are necessary for the safeguard of the place . . . And I have been about my livelode to set a rule therein, as I have written to you, which is not yet all performed after my desire, and I would not go to Caister till I had done. I do not want to spend more days near thereabouts, if I can avoid it; so make sure that you send someone home to keep the place and when I have finished what I have begun I shall arrange to go there if it will do any good—otherwise I had rather not be there . . .

❶ **◆ Literature and Your Life** Of what fictional tales does this true-life adventure remind you?

. . . I marvel greatly that you send me no word how you do, for your enemies begin to grow right bold and that puts your friends in fear and doubt. Therefore arrange that they may have some comfort, so that they be not discouraged, for if we lose our friends, it will be hard in this troublous world to get them again . . . ❷

◆ Build Vocabulary

assault (ə sôlt′) *v.*: Violently attack

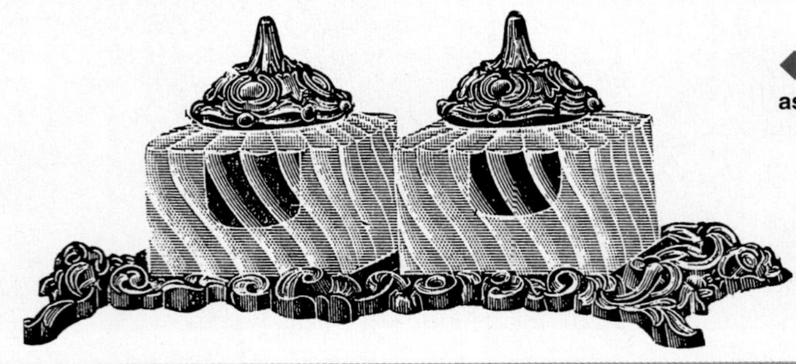

Cross-Curricular Connection: Social Studies

Paston does not appear to be a typical woman of her times. During the 1500's, most women were not allowed to have any part in men's affairs. The lady of the manor typically was limited in her responsibilities to overseeing the housekeeping and perhaps also to keeping the garden, in which she cultivated fruit bushes, kitchen vegetables, medicinal herbs, sweet-smelling herbs (for perfuming the house and clothing), and flowers. Those women who did step outside the narrow boundaries of household affairs, like Joan of Arc, who was burned as a witch, and Queen Margaret of Anjou, who was a contemporary of Paston's and participated in the Wars of the Roses, were often regarded as unnatural—or worse.

Beyond Literature

History Connection

Tools of War Margaret Paston's letters provide insights into daily life in medieval England. One disturbing aspect of medieval life that she documents is the continual battle over land and power. Because warfare was a way of life, many advances in weaponry and armor occurred during this time. Knights, who fought for a feudal lord, originally wore long corsets of chain mail—flexible metal mesh—for protection during battle. Because the holes in the mail did not protect the knights from harm, armor was added—until the mail became a full suit of armor!

Knights were also equipped with a variety of weapons, such as a twelve-foot lance tipped with iron, a shield, and a long sword. Although a knight may have appeared to be untouchable, his horse was vulnerable. If a knight was thrown from a horse, the heavy armor made it virtually impossible for him to remount by himself, and he was at the mercy of foot soldiers. In fact, the use of organized troops of foot soldiers and the invention of the longbow and crossbow, both of which could pierce armor, marked the end of the armored knight.

Activity Can you think of examples in other fields where one type of technology replaced another? Explain.

Guide for Responding

◆ Literature and Your Life

Reader's Response Would you have liked Margaret Paston? Why or why not?

Thematic Focus Do families still have to fight for their property as the Pastons did? Explain.

Continuation of the Adventure As Margaret Paston, write a letter to your husband requesting his aid in still another difficulty.

☑ Check Your Comprehension

1. What does the Duke want?
2. At the end of the second letter, what does Margaret urge John to do?
3. Who is planning to attack Caister? To whom does Margaret appeal for help?

◆ Critical Thinking

INTERPRET

1. Margaret Paston says, "The lodge and the remnant of your place was beaten down." Why do you think she refers to the lodge as John Paston's place and not *our* place? **[Infer]**
2. What attitude does Margaret Paston have toward the tenants of the Paston's lands? Explain. **[Analyze]**
3. What do these letters reveal about Margaret Paston? **[Draw Conclusions]**

APPLY

4. What do these letters suggest about the ease or difficulty of the landowner's life in the fifteenth century? **[Generalize]**

EXTEND

5. What modern careers might suit the abilities of a woman like Margaret Paston? Explain your response. **[Career Link]**

Customize for
Visual/Spatial Learners
Obtain photographs of medieval tools of war and armor and display them for students to help them get a better understanding of what Margaret Paston's world was like.

Reinforce and Extend

Answers

◆ Literature and Your Life

Reader's Response Responses may include these: Yes, I would have liked Margaret Paston because she seemed to be smart and brave. No, she relied too much on others in times of crisis.

Thematic Focus Yes, families still occasionally have to fight legal battles to prove ownership of property.

☑ Check Your Comprehension

1. The Duke wants to wrest ownership of Hellesdon manor from the Paston family.
2. Margaret wants John to settle any disputes now before troubles escalate.
3. Fastolf of Cowhawe is planning to attack Caister. Margaret Paston appeals to her son for help.

◆ Critical Thinking

1. In medieval times, it was not usual for women to own property outright; they were used to all property being legally owned by their husbands.
2. Margaret Paston shows concern for the plight of her tenants, although it is unclear how much the concern is prompted by their woes and how much is caused by the possible loss of income from the land they occupy.
3. The letters reveal that Paston is a capable manager of the family's lands, although she does seek out the advice and assistance of her husband and her son.
4. The letters suggest that land ownership was lucrative in times of peace but that when challenged by others for ownership, it was largely up to the family to defend it as best they could.
5. Modern careers to suit Paston may include office manager, hotel manager, construction foreman.

Develop Understanding

One-Minute Insight

The familiar repeated lyrics of this ballad have been sung throughout the ages. Students may in fact be familiar with a version with the repeated words "my darling young son." What they may not ever have realized, however, is that this is a tune of treachery. The darling young son, also known as the handsome young man, comes home to his mother to die, for he has been poisoned by his "true-love."

By reading this ballad, students will become familiar with one of the most famous (and gruesome) ballads from the Middle Ages.

Customize for
Less Proficient Readers
Have pairs of students work together to read the poem in two voices. Ask them to draw a conclusion about the structure of the poem. *Every stanza has the same structure: the first two lines are spoken by the mother; the last two lines are spoken by the son.*

◆ Reading Strategy

❶ Understand Dialect Ask students to say aloud, listen to, and "translate" the words "Where hae ye been?" *Where have you been? or Where were you?*

◆ Literary Focus

❷ Folk Ballad Ask students what characteristics of a folk ballad this selection exhibits. *It is like a song, with a lot of repetition in the lyrics. Each stanza consists of four lines. All the stanzas repeat the same pattern of near rhymes at the end of each line: Each first line ends with son, each second line ends with man, each third line ends with soon, and each fourth line ends with down.*

"O where hae ye been, Lord Randall, my son? ❶
O where hae ye been, my handsome young man?"
"I hae been to the wild wood; mother, make my bed soon,
For I'm weary wi' hunting, and fain[1] wald[2] lie down."

"Where gat ye your dinner, Lord Randall, my son?
Where gat ye your dinner, my handsome young man?"
"I dined wi' my true-love; mother, make my bed soon,
For I'm weary wi' hunting, and fain wald lie down." ❷

"What gat ye to your dinner, Lord Randall, my son?
What gat ye to your dinner, my handsome young man?"
"I gat eels boil'd in broo;[3] mother, make my bed soon,
For I'm weary wi' hunting, and fain wald lie down."

1. **fain:** Gladly.
2. **wald:** Would.
3. **broo:** Broth.

Cultural Connection

Ballads are part of the oral tradition. Oral literature forms the basis of almost every literary history in every culture. Often, oral literature consists of myths and tales, and in particular, emphasizes creation myths. This is the case in the Native American and African literary traditions. Ballads, which tell stories without much character development, resemble many early myths in which the emphasis is on plot and especially outcome rather than on motivation or any other psychological dimension of human action.

Have students speculate about why literature from the oral tradition reveals so much about the culture from which it sprang.

Noble Hunting With a Falcon in May

◀ **Critical Viewing** Lord Randall tells his mother that he's tired from hunting. What does this painting reveal about the sport? **[Infer]** ❸

"What became of your bloodhounds, Lord Randall, my son?
What became of your bloodhounds, my handsome young man?"
"O they swell'd and they died; mother, make my bed soon,
For I'm weary wi' hunting, and fain wald lie down."

"O I fear ye are poison'd, Lord Randall, my son!
O I fear ye are poison'd, my handsome young man!"
"O yes! I am poison'd; mother, make my bed soon,
For I'm sick at the heart, and I fain wald lie down." ❹

Guide for Responding

◆ Literature and Your Life

Reader's Response Do you think that Lord Randall deserves his fate? Explain.

Thematic Focus In what way is falling in love perilous for Lord Randall?

Bill of Indictment Suppose Lord Randall's "true love" is arrested for her crime. Draw up the indictment by giving her name, address, and a brief description of the crime for which she is being charged.

☑ Check Your Comprehension

1. Who are the two speakers in the ballad?
2. What does Lord Randall say he wants to do?
3. What happens to Lord Randall?

◆ Critical Thinking

INTERPRET

1. What two clues in stanzas three and four foreshadow Lord Randall's fate? **[Infer]**
2. What two meanings can you derive from line 20? **[Infer]**
3. In the poem's fifth stanza, the wording of the repeated line, or refrain, varies. What emotional impact does this have on the reader? **[Interpret]**
4. What underlying message about love is implied in this ballad? Give details from the text to support your answer. **[Draw Conclusions]**

APPLY

5. To make this ballad into a modern rock song, what elements would you change? **[Modify]**

▶Critical Viewing◀

❸ **Infer** Students may suggest any of the following: *Hunting was done on horseback. Trained birds called falcons may have been used to spot or retrieve prey. The hunter had to be a good rider to stay astride the horse and carry the bird. This type of hunting may well have been the leisure of lords and landed gentry.*

◆ Critical Thinking

❹ **Drawing Conclusions** Ask students what Lord Randall means when he says he is "sick at the heart." *Lord Randall may be alluding to his physical state—that he is about to die. Or he may be sick at heart because he is going to die. Most likely, however, Lord Randall is sick at heart because he realizes that the woman he loved poisoned him.*

Reinforce and Extend

Answers

◆ Literature and Your Life

Reader's Response Responses may include: No, Lord Randall was innocent and did not deserve to be poisoned. Yes, Lord Randall should have been smarter in the company he chose to keep.

Thematic Focus Falling in love was perilous for Lord Randall because his love ended up poisoning him.

☑ Check Your Comprehension

1. Lord Randall and his mother are the two speakers.
2. Lord Randall says that he wants to lie down.
3. Lord Randall dies.

◆ Critical Thinking

1. The phrase "eels boil'd in broo" and the bloodhounds' deaths are clues to Lord Randall's fate.
2. The line may mean that Lord Randall is lovesick or that his heart is literally wounded or ailing.
3. This variation signals to the reader that the poem is coming to a tragic end.
4. The poem's underlying message of love may be that it's a foolish and unwise state to be in. The "wild wood" Lord Randall has been to may symbolize love's tangled complications, and the fact that his "true-love" fed him eels boiled in blood also indicates that love is a strange and dangerous emotional state.
5. Students may reply that they'd translate the story into modern English to make it into a rock song.

Develop Understanding

One-Minute Insight Most ballads from this period are tragic and bloody, but this one is humorous, as the husband and wife in this ballad raise bickering to a high art form. In an era when robbers could and did enter homes under the cover of night, this stubborn couple refuses to get up and lock the door. When intruders do come in, the stubbornness of the pair—each refusing to budge—is comical. When the husband finally breaks his silence to confront the robbers, the wife happily announces that she's won the round and that the husband must now lock the door!

This ballad reveals that petty, psychological battles some people engage in have been occuring for literally hundreds of years!

▶Critical Viewing◀

❶ **Infer** Based on the furnishings and the dress, this appears to be a comfortable medieval home, yet luxuries are few. Light comes only from the fire and the candle. Heat comes only from the fire. There is no variety in the food on the table, and there are no utensils. The woman appears to be serving the man.

◆ Grammar and Style

❷ **Direct Address** Remind students that direct address can help them figure out who is speaking to whom. Ask what the use of the appellation *Goodman* tells students in this stanza. *It is a signal that the wife is responding to her husband, the goodman.*

◆ Reading Strategy

❸ **Understand Dialect** Tell students to read this passage aloud, try out different pronunciations, and see whether any of the dialect terms sound like their modern counterpart. *Students should discover that neer = never; wa = would; ane = one.*

Get Up and Bar the Door

A Dinner Scene in January, The Granger Collection

❶ ▶ Critical Viewing What does this painting tell you about domestic life in medieval times? **[Infer]**

It fell about the Martinmas time,[1]
And a gay time it was then,
When our goodwife got puddings to make,
She's boild them in the pan.

The wind sae cauld blew south and north,
And blew into the floor;
Quoth our goodman to our goodwife,
"Gae out and bar the door."

❷ "My hand is in my hussyfskap,[2]
Goodman, as ye may see;
An it should nae be barrd this hundred year,
It's no be barrd for me."[3]

They made a paction[4] tween them twa,
They made it firm and sure,
That the first word whaeer shoud speak,
Shoud rise and bar the door.

Then by there came two gentlemen,
At twelve o'clock at night,
And they could neither see house nor hall,
Nor coal nor candlelight.

"Now whether is this a rich man's house,
Or whether it is a poor?"
❸ But neer a word wad ane o' them[5] speak,
For barring of the door.

1. **Martinmas time:** November 11.
2. **hussyfskap:** Household duties.
3. **"An it should . . . me":** If it has to be barred by me, then it will not be barred in a hundred years.
4. **paction:** Agreement.
5. **them:** The man and his wife.

Humanities: Art

A Dinner Scene in January, The Granger Collection.

This is an illustration from a Flemish Book of Hours, circa 1515. It depicts a household dinner scene in the wintertime. From the man warming his hands in front of the fire to the cat sitting hopefully next to the table, this scene seems timeless in its portrayal of an average household on an average day.

Use this question for discussion:

In what ways does the scene in the picture seem modern? What about it is outmoded? *Students should observe that the basic items for dining, a table, chairs, plates, and such, are still used today. Many households today possess pet cats, like the one shown. Also, the activity of preparing a table for a meal seems to be largely unchanged since the Middle Ages. Differences include a different style of dress, unusal type of chair in front of the fireplace, absence of electric light, use of a candle.*

And first they[6] ate the white puddings,
    And then they ate the black:
Tho muckle[7] thought the goodwife to hersel,
    Yet neer a word she spake.

Then said the one unto the other,
4   "Here, man, take ye my knife;
Do ye tak aff the auld man's beard,
    And I'll kiss the goodwife."

"But there's nae water in the house,
    And what shall we do than?"
"What ails ye at the pudding broo,[8]
    That boils into[9] the pan?"

O up then started our goodman,
5   An angry man was he:
"Will ye kiss my wife before my een,
    And scad[10] me wi pudding bree?"[11]

Then up and started our goodwife,
    Gied three skips on the floor:
6 "Goodman, you've spoken the foremost word;
    Get up and bar the door."

6. **they:** The strangers.
7. **muckle:** Much.
8. **"What . . . broo":** What's the matter with pudding water?
9. **into:** In.
10. **scad:** Scald.
11. **bree:** Broth.

Guide for Responding

◆ *Literature and Your Life*

Reader's Response Whom do you like better—the goodman or the goodwife? Explain.

Thematic Focus This ballad tells of an ordinary adventure that takes place in the home of a bickering couple. What elements of this adventure could happen today?

Advice Column Acting as an advice columnist, help the goodman and goodwife communicate better.

☑ Check Your Comprehension

1. What does the goodman want the goodwife to do? What's the goodwife's reply?
2. How do the goodman and goodwife resolve their problem?
3. Who wins the battle of wills between goodman and goodwife? How?

◆ Critical Thinking

INTERPRET

1. Why does the goodman want the door barred? **[Analyze]**
2. In lines 25–29, the goodwife is thinking to herself. What might she be thinking? **[Infer]**
3. What does the stranger mean when he suggests taking "aff the auld man's beard"? **[Interpret]**
4. What serious point does this humorous ballad make? **[Interpret]**

EVALUATE

5. Which of the two characters in "Get Up and Bar the Door" is more foolish? Why? **[Make a Judgment]**

APPLY

6. Can people be hurt by stubbornness—their own or someone else's? Explain. **[Generalize]**

Looking at Literature Videodisc To enjoy a reading and student response to "Get Up and Bar the Door," play Chapter 2 on the videodisc.

Chapter 2

◆ Critical Thinking

1. The cold wind blows in.
2. Suggested answers: She is angry about the fruits of her labors being consumed by the strangers.
3. The stranger means to cut the man's throat.
4. The message is that stubbornness can have some serious consequences.
5. Suggested responses: The wife is more foolish because she refused to acknowledge the danger they were in; the man is more foolish because he waited too long before challenging the robbers.
6. Students should recognize that stubbornness can lead to irrational or dangerous behavior.

Comprehension Check ☑

4 Ask students how many characters are in the ballad and what each is probably doing at this point. *There are four characters: the goodman, or husband; the goodwife, or wife; and two "gentlemen," who are not gentlemen at all but intruders who have eaten the food and now intend to do harm to the couple. The intruders are up and about, while the goodman and goodwife, hidden by the darkness, are quietly listening to them.*

◆ Literary Focus

5 **Folk Ballad** Ask students to name the characteristics of this stanza that make it typical of a folk ballad. *It has four lines; the last words in the second and the fourth line rhyme; it contains dialogue.*

◆ Critical Thinking

6 **Interpret** What is humorous about the last thing the wife says? *The wife tells the husband that, since he has spoken, he must get up and bar the door. Of course, it's too late. The intruders have entered, and they are thinking about harming the couple. Yet the wife is gleeful that the husband has spoken, and the burden of barring the door is off her shoulders.*

Reinforce and Extend

Answers

◆ *Literature and Your Life*

Reader's Response Students may prefer the goodman because he finally showed common sense at the end.

Thematic Focus Robbers and burglars are perils to society in today's world.

☑ Check Your Comprehension

1. The goodman wants the goodwife to get up and lock the door. The goodwife says that she'll never get up and lock the door.
2. The goodman and goodwife break their impasse only when the goodman confronts the burglars.
3. The goodwife wins the battle of wills by remaining silent even when threatened by the burglars.

Develop Understanding

One-Minute Insight Death by murder or accident is one of the most common themes of ballads. This ballad is no exception: A young knight lies slain, unmourned by his hawk, his hound, or his lady love. What makes this particular ballad distinctive and memorable, however, is that the story unfolds through a conversation between two ravens who look at the whole affair in a matter-of-fact, cold-blooded way.

◆ Reading Strategy

1 Understand Dialect Have students translate this line of dialect into modern English. *"The tane unto the tither" means "one to the other."*

◆ Critical Thinking

2 Interpret What does this stanza reveal about attitudes about youth, beauty, and privilege? *Youth, beauty and privilege mean nothing when you consider that they're all gone when one dies.*

Customize for
Body/Kinesthetic Learners
Suggest that three students take on the roles of the fallen knight and the two ravens and act out the ballad. What does the physicalization of the scene add to the story?

The Twa Corbies[1]

As I was walking all alane,
I heard twa corbies making a mane.[2]
1 The tane unto the tither did say,
"Whar sall we gang and dine the day?"

"In behint yon auld fail dyke,[3]
I wot[4] there lies a new-slain knight;
And naebody kens[5] that he lies there
But his hawk, his hound, and his lady fair.

"His hound is to the hunting gane,
His hawk to fetch the wild-fowl hame,
His lady's ta'en anither mate,
So we may mak our dinner sweet.

2 "Ye'll sit on his white hause-bane,[6]
And I'll pike out his bonny blue e'en;[7]
Wi' ae lock o' his gowden hair
We'll theek[8] our nest when it grows bare.

"Mony a one for him maks mane,
But nane sall ken whar he is gane.
O'er his white banes, when they are bare,
The wind sall blaw for evermair."

1. **Twa Corbies:** Two ravens.
2. **mane:** Moan.
3. **fail dyke:** Bank of earth.
4. **wot:** Know.
5. **kens:** Knows.
6. **hause-bane:** Neck-bone.
7. **e'en:** Eyes.
8. **theek:** Thatch.

Speaking and Listening Mini-Lesson

Song Translation
This mini-lesson supports the Speaking and Listening activity on page 179.

Introduce the Concept The goal of this activity is to translate or paraphrase an old ballad into one that is suited for a modern audience. Students can start by retelling the ballad, word by word, in their own words. They should find synonyms or near-synonyms for the words in the original ballad.

Develop Background Remind students of the characteristics of a ballad. Once students complete their paraphrase, they might take care to create lines of approximately equal length, with four lines per stanza. If possible, they might also make the last words in the second and fourth lines rhyme.

Apply the Information As students re-create the ballad in modern English, have them keep in mind that the ballad is meant to be sung and that the rhythm, or song-like quality, of the ballad is all-important. When the ballads are complete, students have the option of reading or singing them to the class. Encourage students to practice their presentations several times before performing them.

Assess the Outcome Assess students' song translations based on the clarity and effectiveness of modern English and the rhythm and rhyme of the stanzas. They might also consider how their translation changes the original ballad, and whether that change is for the better.

▲ Critical Viewing In what ways do these ravens resemble the ones in the poem? **[Compare and Contrast]** ❸

Guide for Responding

◆ Literature and Your Life

Reader's Response Do you find "The Twa Corbies" amusing or sad? Explain.

Thematic Focus In what ways does this ballad draw a connection between romance and danger? Explain.

Changing Perspectives Briefly retell this ballad from the point of view of the hawk and the hound.

☑ Check Your Comprehension

1. Who are the "twa corbies"?
2. Where is the knight lying?
3. In what condition is the knight?
4. Who knows that the knight lies there?

◆ Critical Thinking

INTERPRET

1. How would you describe the ravens' attitude toward the knight? Cite examples to support your answer. **[Analyze]**
2. What effect would be lost if the incident were described by a human speaker rather than by ravens? **[Infer]**
3. What does the ballad ultimately say about loyalty and love? **[Draw Conclusions]**

EXTEND

4. The hawk, the hound, and the lady seem to be given equal status in this ballad. Why were the hawk and hound so important to a man of the fifteenth century? **[Social Studies Link]**

►Critical Viewing◄

❸ **Compare and Contrast** These ravens resemble the ones in the ballad because they seem to be looking at the same thing. They are different from the ones in the ballad because they cannot hold a conversation.

Reinforce and Extend

Answers

◆ Literature and Your Life

Reader's Response Responses may vary, but most students will find the ballad amusing, but macabre.

Thematic Focus Although it's not revealed how the knight met his death, it's obvious that the beings loved and trusted by the knight—his hawk, his hound, and his lady—were not what they seemed.

☑ Check Your Comprehension

1. The twa corbies are two ravens discussing the slain knight.
2. The knight is lying behind a bank of dirt.
3. The knight is dead.
4. The knight's hawk, hound, and lady love know that he is there.

◆ Critical Thinking

1. The ravens' attitude is pragmatic; they see him as a source for food and nest-making. In the poem, they speak of using his golden hair in nest-making.
2. The poem would lose the objectivity that is so often a part of ballads. It would also lose its strange, haunting quality.
3. The poem suggests that loyalty and love are illusions and not to be counted on from one's companions.
4. Hawks and hounds were important in several ways. Hawks were used in sport and hounds were companions, protectors, and retrievers of game.

Develop Understanding

One-Minute Insight No ballad has generated more adaptations and changes than "Barbara Allan." It has had over a dozen titles and is spoken in countless local accents. A ballad historian found ninety-two versions in Virginia alone!

In this popular ballad, Sir John Graeme lies on his deathbed and calls for the love of his life, Barbara Allan. Instead of murmuring words of love or reassurance, Allan uses her last moments with Graeme to remind him that he slighted her. Yet, when she returns home, it is only to die tomorrow, for her own true love died today.

❶ **Clarification** Be sure students understand that the words that begin "O haste" are spoken by John Graeme's "man," or servant.

◆ Grammar and Style

❷ **Direct Address** Ask students what this example of direct address reveals. *It reveals that she's either unmoved by his condition or that she's suppressing her feelings toward him.*

◆ Critical Thinking

❸ **Infer** What reason might Sir John have for saying this before he dies? *Sir John thinks people will blame Barbara Allan because she refused to reconcile with him, which led him to his early death.*

◆ Critical Thinking

❹ **Criticize** Do you think that Barbara Allan's dying makes sense, or does it seem to come out of nowhere? *It does seem to arise suddenly. Nevertheless, it shows her character, and it is the point of the ballad.* Remind students that ballads told stories; they did not explain motive, or develop characters.

Barbara Allan

It was in and about the Martinmas time,[1]
When the green leaves were a-fallin';
That Sir John Graeme in the West Country
Fell in love with Barbara Allan.

He sent his man down through the town
To the place where she was dwellin':
❶ "O haste and come to my master dear,
Gin[2] ye be Barbara Allan."

O slowly, slowly rase[3] she up,
To the place where he was lyin',
And when she drew the curtain by:
❷ "Young man, I think you're dyin'."

"O it's I'm sick, and very, very sick,
And 'tis a' for Barbara Allan."
"O the better for me ye sal[4] never be,
Though your heart's blood were a-spillin'.

"O dinna ye mind,[5] young man," said she,
"When ye the cups were fillin',
That ye made the healths gae round and round,
And slighted Barbara Allan?"

❸ He turned his face unto the wall,
And death with him was dealin':
"Adieu, adieu, my dear friends all,
And be kind of Barbara Allan."

And slowly, slowly rase she up,
And slowly, slowly left him;
And sighing said she could not stay,
Since death of life had reft[6] him.

She had not gane a mile but twa,[7]
When she heard the dead-bell knellin',
And every jow[8] that the dead-bell ga'ed[9]
It cried, "Woe to Barbara Allan!"

❹ "O mother, mother, make my bed,
O make it soft and narrow:
Since my love died for me today,
I'll die for him tomorrow."

1. **Martinmas time:** November 11.
2. **Gin:** If.
3. **rase:** Rose.
4. **sal:** Shall.
5. **dinna ye mind:** Don't you remember.
6. **reft:** Deprived.
7. **not . . . twa:** Gone but two miles.
8. **jow:** Stroke.
9. **ga'ed:** Made.

Humanities: Art

Veronica Veronese, 1872, by Dante Gabriel Rossetti.

Rossetti said this painting showed a young woman in a "passionate reverie." Her thoughts are clearly far away from the present moment, and the visual details, such as the fluid motion of the arms, the scarf, and the branch in the birdcage, all serve to bring the eye back to the woman's pensive face.

A poet and a painter, Rossetti was a founding member of the Pre-Raphaelite brotherhood, a group of artists who admired and sought to emulate the work of Italian painters who preceded Raphael. The pre-Raphaelite style of painting paid close attention to natural detail and dealt with romantic, moral, and religious subjects.

Use these questions for discussion:

1. Does the woman in the painting seem to have the same strength of character as Barbara Allan has in this ballad? *Students may find this woman more feminine and contemplative than Barbara Allan seems, or they may regard this to be a vividly accurate portrayal of a woman on the verge of lying down to die because her true love has died.*
2. Why do you think this painting was chosen to illustrate this ballad? Do you think it is an apt illustration? *The ballad is about a woman making a difficult decision in a very sad situation. Both the sadness and the deeply considered decision are reflected in the painting's subject and mood.*

Veronica Veronese, Dante Gabriel Rossetti, Delaware Art Museum

◀ **Critical Viewing** How does the artist's choice of color and the posture of the subject suit the description of the fictional Barbara Allan? **[Interpret]** ❺

Guide for Responding

◆ Literature and Your Life

Reader's Response Which character—Sir John or Barbara Allan—do you find more sympathetic? Why?

Thematic Focus This ballad, like many others of its kind, makes a connection between love and death. Why do you think this theme is so predominant in literature and songs of the Middle Ages?

Extra Stanza Add a stanza at any point in this ballad giving more information about the characters, how they met, or the nature of Sir John's illness.

☑ Check Your Comprehension

1. Why does Sir John Graeme send his man to Barbara Allan?
2. What reason does Barbara Allan give for seeming unconcerned about his illness?
3. What does Barbara Allan do after Sir John dies?

◆ Critical Thinking

INTERPRET

1. Why is Sir John sick? **[Infer]**
2. Lines 25 and 26 describe Barbara Allan's reaction to the death of Sir John. What do those lines reveal about her emotional state? **[Analyze]**
3. When Barbara Allan asks her mother to "make my bed . . . soft and narrow" in lines 33 and 34, what kind of "bed" does she mean? **[Infer]**
4. What overall message about love and death is conveyed by "Barbara Allan"? **[Draw Conclusions]**

EVALUATE

5. Do the characters in "Barbara Allan" seem believable or romanticized? Give details from the text to support your ideas. **[Criticize]**

EXTEND

6. Lines 30–32 in "Barbara Allan" refer to a death knell being rung on the church bells to inform the town of the passing of one of its residents. What other uses might people have had for church bells in medieval times? **[Social Studies Link]**

▶**Critical Viewing**◀

❺ **Interpret** The colors suggest a dark and vibrant personality; the posture suggests that the woman is depressed or tired. Barbara Allan seems to have a vibrant personality, one that inspires love in Sir John. At the end of the ballad, Barbara Allan states that she is tired, and it is implied that she is depressed over the loss of Sir John.

Reinforce and Extend

Answers

◆ Literature and Your Life

Reader's Response Students may find Sir John more sympathetic because he just wanted to reconcile with Barbara Allan before he died.

Thematic Focus Responses may include that because living conditions were harsh and life expectancy was short, ideas of love and death were foremost in most people's minds.

☑ Check Your Comprehension

1. Sir John sends his man to ask Barbara Allan to visit him.
2. Barbara Allan says she is unconcerned because Sir John had previously slighted her at a social gathering.
3. Barbara Allan goes home and tells her mother that she'll die tomorrow.

◆ Critical Thinking

1. He is sick because Barbara Allan rejected him.
2. These actions reveal that she is not unaffected by Sir John's death.
3. She is referring to a coffin.
4. "Barbara Allan" suggests that love and death are closely connected, that one can actually die for love.
5. As in most ballads, the characters seem romanticized; details include these: that Sir John is "very, very sick" for the love of Barbara Allan; Sir John fell in love immediately, and just as quickly he died when the love was unreturned.
6. Students may say that church bells were rung to warn of invasion; of natural disasters, like fire or flood; or for happy occasions such as weddings and births.

Beyond the Selection

FURTHER READING

Other Folk Ballads

"Edward"; "The Wife of Usher's Well"; "The Three Ravens"; "Sir Patrick Spens"

More About Margaret Paston

Women in the Middle Ages, Frances and Joseph Gies

We suggest that you preview these works before recommending them to students.

INTERNET

Students may find additional information on the Internet. Sites listed may have changed since publication.

For information about Margaret Paston, go to **http://www.ukans.edu/ftp/pub/history/Europe/Medieval/bibliographies/marriag1.bib**

For a bibliography of folk ballads, go to **http://www.redgum.bendigo.latrobe.edu.au/~warneke/ballads/ballads.html**

We *strongly recommend* that you preview the sites before you send students to them.

Answers

◆ Literary Focus

Letter

1. Possible response: In the first paragraph of the passage from the letter of October 27, Margaret Paston gives a detailed account of the incident at Hellesdon.
2. In the letter dated July 11, Margaret Paston reveals her limitations as battle-chief. This suggests that, although women in medieval times had lots of responsibility, in battle they were not respected.

Folk Ballad

1. Example: Stanza 2 of "Get Up and Bar the Door" contains a four-line stanza, rhyme, and dialogue.
2. Their explanations should include discussion on repetition, refrain, and dialogue. Suggested response: The dialogue and repetition in "Lord Randall" make it suspenseful and thrilling. The refrain makes the ballad easy to remember, and the one time the pattern in the refrain is broken, it increases the reader's interest.
3. Their responses should show how the characters and plot events within the ballad reflect a time of harsh living. Suggested response: "The Twa Corbies" emphasizes that death can come quickly and suddenly, even to someone as handsome and young as the dead knight. The ballad also suggests that love was not given freely, since the knight's hawk, hound, and lady seem unmoved by his death.

◆ Reading Strategy

1. (a) nobody; (b) would one; (c) have you
2. Possible answers from "Barbara Allan": *gin; reft; gane.*

◆ Build Vocabulary

Using the Word Root *-cert-*

1. (c) make certain
2. (a) written form of qualifications
3. (b) sureness

Using the Word Bank

1. (c) officials
2. (g) question
3. (f) assist
4. (d) remainder
5. (a) looted
6. (e) to pieces
7. (b) attack

Guide for Responding *(continued)*

◆ Literary Focus

Letter

The **letters** of Margaret Paston—personal messages to her husband and son—show her to be capable and observant.

1. Find a passage that shows Margaret in the role of an information gatherer and reporter, and explain your choice.
2. (a) In what passage does Margaret indicate her limitations as a battle-chief? (b) What does this passage suggest about the role of women in medieval times?

Folk Ballad

The **folk ballad** "Barbara Allan" contains many elements typical of ballads. Notice the use of the four-line stanza called a quatrain, the rhyme in the second and fourth lines, the repetition of the word *slowly*, and the use of dialogue in the last line:

O slowly, slowly rase she up,
    To the place where he was lyin',
And when she drew the curtain by:
    "Young man, I think you're dyin'."

1. Find examples of these elements in a stanza from one of the other ballads: quatrain, rhyme, repetition, and dialogue.
2. Choose one of the ballads and explain how repetition, refrain, and dialogue make it dramatic.
3. Choose one of these ballads and explain how it reflects the harsher elements of medieval times.

◆ Reading Strategy

Understand Dialect

The **dialect** in these ballads—specialized language of the English-Scots region—made use of variances in word pronunciations and vocabulary.

1. Give the modern English words whose pronunciation is similar to the italicized words:
   a. And *naebody* kens that he lies there . . .
   b. But neer a word *wad ane* o' them speak, . . .
   c. O where *ha'e* ye been, . . .
2. Give three words from the ballads that are particular to the dialect of the time and place.

◆ Build Vocabulary

Using the Word Root *-cert-*

Knowing that the root *-cert-* means "sure," choose the best definition for each word.

1. ascertain: (a) question, (b) sort through, (c) make certain
2. certificate: (a) written proof of qualifications, (b) form showing receipt of goods, (c) application form for a diploma
3. certitude: (a) vagueness, (b) sureness, (c) righteousness

Using the Word Bank

Match each vocabulary word with its definition.

1. aldermen	a. looted
2. enquiry	b. attack
3. succor	c. officials
4. remnant	d. remainder
5. ransacked	e. to pieces
6. asunder	f. assist
7. assault	g. question

◆ Grammar and Style

Direct Address

Terms of **direct address** indicate to whom (or sometimes to what) the speaker or writer is talking. In writing, terms of direct address are set off by commas.

Practice In your notebook, identify each instance of direct address:

1. Here, man, take ye my knife; . . .
2. O dinna ye mind, young man, said she, . . .
3. O mother, mother, make my bed, . . .

Writing Application In your notebook, rewrite the following as dialogue. Use at least three examples of direct address.

Clara called to her raven named Beak to come back home. Beak replied to Clara that his bones were old and cold and that it was time to leave her. Clara ran to her dear mother, crying that Beak was lost and hurt and gone for good. Clara's mother told her that Beak knew best and that when she got older, she'd begin to understand.

◆ Grammar and Style

Practice

1. , man,
2. , young man,
3. O mother, mother,

Writing Application

Possible rewrite:
"Beak, oh Beak, where are you?" called Clara. "Clara, my bones are old and cold, and it's time to leave you," replied Beak. Clara ran to her mother, crying, "Mother dear, my dearest Beak is lost and hurt and gone for good." "Now Clara, my dear, Beak is wise and old and best knows when it's time to go. As you grow older, you'll surely understand, my little one."

For additional instruction and practice punctuating direct address, use the lesson in the **Language Lab CD-ROM** on Commas.

Build Your Portfolio

Idea Bank

Writing

1. Casting Call Reread the letters of Margaret Paston, taking notes about Margaret's personality. Then cast an actress to play her life story. Give reasons for your choice. **[Performing Arts Link]**

2. A Modern Ballad Write a ballad about an everyday person, using language that reflects how he or she really speaks. **[Performing Arts Link]**

3. Critical Response Critic John Fenn writes of the Paston letters: "the distress of private life . . . will present a truer picture of that turbulent period than could be exhibited by the artful pen of a sedate historian." Support or disagree with this opinion in a brief essay.

Speaking and Listening

4. Letter vs. Phone Call Margaret Paston had no phone, fax, or e-mail system to send messages to her husband. With a classmate, improvise a phone conversation between Margaret and John. **[Social Studies Link; Performing Arts Link]**

5. Song Translation Choose one of the ballads in this series to translate into modern English. Perform your translation for the class.

Projects

6. Holidays Chart Research the origins of medieval holidays and festivals such as Martinmas. Make a poster listing each holiday or festival and describing its origins. **[Social Studies Link; Art Link]**

7. An English Manor With a small group, research fifteenth-century manors like those of the Pastons, and create a scale model of one that is typical of the period. **[Social Studies Link; Art Link]**

Writing Mini-Lesson

Persuasive Letter

When Margaret Paston urges her husband to settle a dispute or her son to defend their property, she gives reasons to support her points. Write a persuasive letter in which you convince someone to do something. Like Margaret Paston, use elaboration to support your argument.

Writing Skills Focus: Elaboration to Support an Argument

When writing persuasively, support your argument with examples, anecdotes, statistics, or causes and effects. Notice, for example, how Margaret Paston uses causes and effects to show what will happen if the Pastons do not respond to their enemies' boldness:

Model From Literature

Your enemies begin to grow right bold and that puts your friends in fear and doubt. . . . [F]or if we lose our friends, it will be hard in this troublous world to get them again . . .

Prewriting Decide what you want the recipient of your persuasive letter to think or do. Write a statement expressing your desired outcome. Then list the points or reasons that will convince him or her to agree with you or do what you suggest. Make notes elaborating on each point, with the details you will use to support or explain it.

Drafting Use a standard letter format and write the heading, greeting, body, and closing of your letter. Refer to your prewriting notes as you develop your argument in the body of the letter.

Revising Evaluate the elaboration that you've used to support your arguments. If an argument seems to be weak, consider replacing one type of elaboration with another to strengthen your point. Proofread the heading of the letter carefully.

ASSESSMENT OPTIONS

Formal Assessment, Selection Test, pp. 34–35, and Assessment Resources Software. The selection test is designed so that it can be customized to the ability levels of your students.
Alternative Assessment, p. 7, includes options for less advanced students, more advanced students, visual/spatial learners, and auditory learners.

PORFOLIO ASSESSMENT
Use the following rubrics in the ***Alternative Assessment*** booklet to assess student writing:
Casting Call: Technical Description/Explanation Rubric, p. 116
A Modern Ballad: Poetry Rubric, p. 109
Critical Response: Response to Literature Rubric, p. 111

Idea Bank

Customizing for
Learning Modalities
Following are suggestions for matching Idea Bank topics with your students' learning modalities:
- Visual/Spatial: 6, 7
- Musical/Rhythmic: 2
- Interpersonal: 1, 4
- Verbal/Linguistic: 3, 5

Customizing for
Performance Levels
Following are suggestions for matching Idea Bank topics with your students' ability levels:
- Less Advanced Students: 1, 4, 6
- Average Students: 2, 5, 7
- More Advanced Students: 3

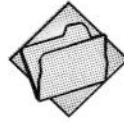

Writing Mini-lesson

Writing Handbook
Refer students to the Writing Handbook, p. 1189, for instruction on the writing process, and p. 1192 for further information on persuasion.

Writing and Language Transparencies Have students use the Argument Organizer, pp. 103–106, as they write their persuasive letters. For more instruction on persuasion, show the class Writing Process Model 5, Persuasive Essay, on pp. 37–43.

Writer's Solution

Writers at Work Videodisc
Have students view the videodisc segment (Ch. 4) featuring public defender Cary Bricker to get tips for writing persuasively. Have students brainstorm for persuasive techniques that they've used or seen used.

Play frames 33218 to 42857

Writing Lab CD-ROM
Have students complete the tutorial on Persuasion. Follow these steps:
1. Listen to the audio-annotated examples of supporting facts with opinions.
2. Complete the interactive instruction on organization.
3. Have students draft their letters on the computer.
4. Use a Revision Checker for Language Variety.

Prepare and Engage

OBJECTIVES

1. To read, comprehend, interpret, and respond to an excerpt from an epic poem told in the form of a story
2. To relate the selection to personal experience
3. To connect "How Siegfried Was Slain" to the theme of perils and adventures
4. To respond to the selection through writing, speaking and listening, and projects

PORTFOLIO OPPORTUNITIES

Writing: Finding Siegfried a Job; A Modern Fable; Hunting the Hunter; Critical Response

Speaking and Listening: Dramatizing the Story; Telling the Story With Music

Project: A Map of Medieval Heroes

More About *The Nibelungenlied*

Siegfried, the hero of *The Nibelungenlied,* is a great warrior from the Netherlands. Early in the epic, he kills two Burgundian chiefs of the Nibelung family and acquires their gold and a magic cape that renders the wearer invisible. He then goes to Worms, the Burgundian capital, to court Kriemhild, who is the sister of Gunther, the king. Siegfried helps Gunther to win Brunhild, Queen of Iceland, in marriage, with the understanding that Gunther will then let him marry Kriemhild. Siegfired invisibly performs all the tasks required by Brunhild of her future husband, while Gunther takes the credit. Gunther marries Brunhild, and Siegfried marries Kriemhild, but Gunther's gratitude is shortlived, as this selection reveals.

The Nibelungenlied does not end with Siegfried's death but instead goes on to recount other adventures, including Kriemhild's marriage to Attila, king of the Huns, as well as her death.

Customize for
Interpersonal Learners
Direct students to form groups to read the story together. Ask the groups to pause at the bottom of every page or two to discuss what has happened and to make and revise predictions about how Siegfried will be slain.

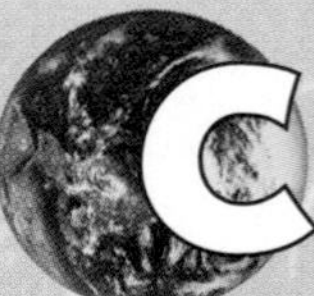

CONNECTIONS TO WORLD LITERATURE

from The Nibelungenlied: How Siegfried Was Slain

Translated by A. T. Hatto

Thematic Connection

THE THEME OF PERILS AND ADVENTURES

Medieval literature might remind you of a television adventure series: Deception and betrayal, power and triumph make for exciting stories—whether written hundreds of years ago or today. From Malory's King Arthur, who combated enemies while seeking to create a better world, to Margaret Paston, who battled real-life thugs to save the manors belonging to her family, perils and adventures seem to be part of medieval life.

Perils and adventures also occurred throughout medieval Europe. The literature of the period highlights the adventures of several warrior heroes: Spain's El Cid, a tremendous warrior, was exiled by King Alfonso VI because other nobles were jealous of his victories; France's Roland, from *The Song of Roland,* was based on an actual warrior who was ambushed by Basques while serving with Charlemagne; and Germany's Siegfried was a brave warrior who risked life and limb to please his king and claim a wife.

THE NIBELUNGENLIED

The epic poem *The Nibelungenlied* is one of the great works of German literature. Composed more than eight hundred years ago by an unknown author, its themes of betrayal, forgiveness, and salvation still ring true.

The Nibelungenlied tells the tale of Kriemhild and Siegfried, a doomed couple who suffer betrayal at the hands of their family. Siegfried falls in love with Kriemhild, a Burgundian princess, when he hears of her great beauty. In order to marry her, he must first help her brother, King Gunther, win the hand of Brunhild, a maiden warrior.

In the course of winning Brunhild's hand for the king, Siegfried steals Brunhild's belt and ring. His mission accomplished, Siegfried marries Kriemhild and suffers the wrath of the jealous Brunhild. When Brunhild accuses Kriemhild of acting like a powerful queen, Kriemhild shows her the tokens that suggest her dishonor. When Brunhild vows revenge, her loyal servant Hagen plots with King Gunther to murder Siegfried. Kriemhild foolishly reveals that Siegfried's vulnerable spot is between his shoulders.

Prentice Hall Literature Program Resources

REINFORCE / RETEACH / EXTEND

Selection Support Pages
Build Vocabulary, p. 36
Thematic Connection, p. 37

Formal Assessment Selection Test, pp. 37–39; Assessment Resources Software

Resource Pro CD-ROM
from *The Nibelungenlied*—includes all resource material and customizable lesson plan

Listening to Literature Audiocassettes
from *The Nibelungenlied*

CONNECTIONS TO WORLD LITERATURE

from *The* Nibelungenlied: How Siegfried *Was* Slain

TRANSLATED BY A. T. HATTO

The fearless warriors Gunther and Hagen treacherously proclaimed a hunt in the forest where they wished to chase the boar, the bear, and the bison—and what could be more daring? Siegfried rode with their party in magnificent style. They took all manner of food with them;
1 and it was while drinking from a cool stream that the hero was to lose his life at the instigation of Brunhild, King Gunther's queen.

Bold Siegfried went to Kriemhild while his and his companions' hunting-gear was being loaded onto the sumpters in readiness to cross the Rhine,[1] and she could not have been more afflicted. "God grant that I may see you well again, my lady," he said, kissing his dear wife, "and that your eyes may see me too. Pass the time pleasantly with your relations who are so kind to you, since I cannot stay with you at home."

Kriemhild thought of what she had told Hagen,
2 but she dared not mention it and began to lament that she had ever been born. "I dreamt last night—and an ill-omened dream it was—" said lord Siegfried's noble queen, weeping with unrestrained passion, "that two boars chased you over the heath and the flowers were dyed with blood! How can I help weeping so? I stand in great dread of some attempt against your life.—What if we have offended any men who have the power to vent their malice on us? Stay away, my lord, I urge you."

"I shall return in a few days time, my darling. I know of no people here who bear me any hatred. Your kinsmen without exception wish me well, nor have I deserved otherwise of 3
them."

"It is not so, lord Siegfried. I fear you will come to grief. Last night I had a sinister dream of how two mountains fell upon you and hid 4
you from my sight! I shall suffer cruelly if you go away and leave me." But he clasped the noble woman in his arms and after kissing and caressing her fair person very tenderly, took his leave and went forthwith. Alas, she was never to see him alive again.

They rode away deep into the forest in pursuit of their sport. Gunther and his men were accompanied by numbers of brave knights, but Gernot and Giselher stayed at home. Ahead of the hunt many horses had crossed the Rhine laden with their bread, wine, meat, fish, and

1. **sumpters . . . Rhine:** Sumpters are pack horses, and the Rhine River flows from eastern Switzerland north through Germany, then west through the Netherlands into the North Sea.

Develop Understanding

One-Minute Insight Composed more than 800 years ago, *The Nibelungenlied* (nē´ bə lo͝oŋ´ ən lēt) is one of the great works of German literature. In this selection, students will encounter an unusual literary combination—an epic tale that contains elements of courtly romance.

Practically a medieval Superman, Siegfried conducts himself with all the good manners of Clark Kent and has no reason to suspect treachery when he receives an invitation to hunt with his brother-in-law, Gunther, and Hagen, Gunther's counselor. Despite reservations of his wife Kriemhild, Siegfried goes boldly off, succeeding roundly in the hunt. Yet despite his prowess and courage, Siegfried later finds himself among the hunted, when Gunther, in an act of supreme treachery and cowardice, stabs him in the back.

◆ Critical Thinking

1 Analyze Ask students: Why might the writer have chosen to reveal the end of the story in the first paragraph? *Possible responses: By revealing the ending first it whets the readers' interest in finding out what caused Siegfried's death to occur.*

◆ Critical Thinking

2 Connect Have student read on to discover why Kriemhild wishes that she had never been born. *She had unwittingly revealed the secret of Siegfried's weakness to his enemy.*

3 Clarification Point out that Kriemhild is Gunther's sister. This explains the reference to "your kinsmen."

◆ Critical Thinking

4 Hypothesize Ask students what Kriemhild's dreams seem to suggest. *Possible response: The dreams suggest that whatever threatens Siegfried's safety comes as a pair. The first dream suggests bloodshed, while the second suggests eternal disappearance.*

On the chalkboard write the heading Tragic Flaws, and engage students in a discussion of heroes and their tragic flaws. Prompt the discussion by asking them to name the tragic flaws (usually an excess of love, hate, or revenge) that expose the weaknesses of the heroes Achilleus (heel) and Samson (hair). Then introduce Siegfried to the class, explaining that he too has a tragic flaw, his excessive love for Kriemhild, that leads to the exposure of his weakness—the spot between his shoulder blades.

Customize for
Less Advanced Readers

Prepare students by identifying the characters in the selection on the board . For example:
Siegfried, a great warrior
Kriemhild, his wife
Gunther, king

Customize for
Visual/Spatial Learners

Scenes from this story lend themselves well to storyboarding. Invite visual learners to recapture one or more scenes in sketches.

▶Critical Viewing◀

❶ **Infer** They may have preferred hunting in groups for companionship or for practical reasons of safety.

◆ Critical Thinking

❷ **Speculate** Ask students whether, judging from this description, they think that hunting parties were everyday occurrences. *Possible answer: This does not appear to be an everyday activity. This appears to be a royal hunt, to which only great personages are invited, and for which lavish preparations have been made. It is probably as fancy and as regal an occasion as any hunt can be.*

◆ Critical Thinking

❸ **Infer** Ask students to infer why Siegfried requests only one tracker. *Siegfried is so confident in his abilities as a hunter that he requires just one great dog, not lots of dogs as the other hunters require.*

◆ *Literature and Your Life*

❹ Point out to students that this type of success in hunting identifies Siegfried as superior. If this story were set in contemporary United States, what sport or game might be substituted for hunting to highlight the abilities of Siegfried? *Responses may include steer wrestling, basketball, or javelin throwing.*

King Konrad "the Younger" of Germany, Hunting With Falcons

❶ ▲ **Critical Viewing** Like Siegfried, Gunther, and his men, the hunters in this picture seem to enjoy the sport as a group activity. What practical reason may they have had for hunting in a group? **[Infer]**

various other provisions such as a King of Gunther's wealth is bound to have with him.

❷ The proud and intrepid hunters were told to set up their lodges on a spacious isle in the river on which they were to hunt, at the skirt of the greenwood over toward the spot where the game would have to break cover. Siegfried, too, had arrived there, and this was reported to the King. Thereupon the sportsmen everywhere manned their relays.[2]

"Who is going to guide us through the forest to our quarry, brave warriors?" asked mighty Siegfried.

"Shall we split up before we start hunting here?" asked Hagen. "Then my lords and I could tell who are the best hunters on this foray into the woods. Let us share the huntsmen and hounds between us and each take the direction he likes—and then all honor to him that hunts best!" At this, the hunters quickly dispersed.

"I do not need any hounds," said lord Siegfried, "except for one tracker so well fleshed that he recognizes the tracks which the game leave through the wood: then we shall not fail to find our quarry." ❸

An old huntsman took a good sleuth-hound and quickly led the lord to where there was game in abundance. The party chased everything that was roused from its lair, as good hunting-men still do today. Bold Siegfried of the Netherlands killed every beast that his hound started, for his hunter was so swift that nothing could elude him. Thus, versatile as he was, Siegfried outshone all the others in that hunt.

The very first kill was when he brought down a strong young tusker,[3] after which he soon chanced on an enormous lion. When his hound had roused it he laid a keen arrow to his bow and shot it so that it dropped in its tracks at the third bound. Siegfried's fellow-huntsmen acclaimed him for this shot. Next, in swift succession, he killed a wisent, an elk, four mighty aurochs,[4] and a fierce and monstrous buck—so well mounted was he that nothing, ❹ be it hart or hind, could evade him. His hound then came upon a great boar, and, as this turned to flee, the champion hunter at once blocked his path, bringing him to bay; and when in a trice the beast sprang at the hero in a fury, Siegfried slew him with his sword, a feat no other hunter could have performed with such ease. After the felling of this boar, the tracker was returned to his leash and Siegfried's splendid bag was made known to the Burgundians.

"If it is not asking too much, lord Siegfried," said his companions of the chase, "do leave some of the game alive for us. You are emptying the hills and woods for us today." At this the brave knight had to smile.

2. **relays:** Fresh horses to relieve tired ones.

3. **tusker** (tusk′ ər): Wild boar.

4. **wisent** (vē′ zant) . . . **aurochs** (ô′ räks′): European bison and wild oxen.

Humanities: Art

King Conrad "the Younger" of Germany, Hunting With Falcons.

Depicted in this scene are two noblemen, a king and a companion, engaged in the sport of hunting with falcons. Falconry dates from ancient times and became very popular with the nobility of Europe. Falcons and other hunting birds were kept in mewses, attended to by a master falconer who was responsible for the long and elaborate training process.

Use these questions for discussion:

1. What clues about falconry can you derive from this picture? *Gloves were worn when handling the birds; the nobility were fond of the sport; horses and dogs were part of the hunting party.*
2. Judging from this picture, would Siegfried have enjoyed hunting with falcons? Explain. *Possible responses: Yes, Siegfried liked all contests and he would have enjoyed hunting with falcons; no, Siegfried was a more physical person and he would have preferred hunting with a bow and arrow.*

5 There now arose a great shouting of men and clamor of hounds on all sides, and the tumult grew so great that the hills and the forest re-echoed with it—the huntsmen had unleashed no fewer than four and twenty packs! Thus, many beasts had to lose their lives there, since each of these hunters was hoping to bring it about that *he* should be given the high honors of the chase. But when mighty Siegfried appeared beside the campfire there was no chance of that.

The hunt was over, yet not entirely so. Those who wished to go to the fire brought the hides of innumerable beasts, and game in plenty—what loads of it they carried back to the kitchen to the royal retainers! And now the noble King had it announced to those fine hunters that he wished to take his repast, and there was one great blast of the horn to tell them that he was back in camp.

At this, one of Siegfried's huntsmen said: "Sir, I have heard a horn-blast telling us to return to our lodges.—I shall answer it." There was much blowing to summon the companions.

"Let us quit the forest, too," said lord Siegfried. His mount carried him at an even pace, and the others hastened away with him but with the noise of their going they started a savage bear, a very fierce beast.

"I shall give our party some good entertainment," he said over his shoulder. "Loose the hound, for I can see a bear which will have to come back to our lodges with us. It will not be able to save itself unless it runs very fast." The hound was unleashed, and the bear made off at speed. Siegfried meant to ride it down but soon found that his way was blocked and his intention thwarted, while the mighty beast fancied it would escape from its pursuer. But the proud knight leapt from his horse and started to chase it on foot, and the animal, quite off its guard, failed to elude him. And so he quickly caught and bound it, without having wounded it at all—nor could the beast use either claws or teeth on the man. Siegfried tied it to his saddle, mounted his horse, and in his high-spirited fashion led it to the campfire in order to amuse the good knights.

And in what magnificent style Siegfried rode! He bore a great spear, stout of shaft and broad of head; his handsome sword reached down to his spurs; and the fine horn which this lord carried was of the reddest gold. Nor have I ever heard tell of a better hunting outfit: he wore a surcoat of costly black silk and a splendid hat of sable,[5] and you should have seen the gorgeous silken tassels on his quiver, which was covered in panther-skin for the sake of its fragrant odor![6] He also bore a bow so strong that apart from Siegfried any who wished to span it would have had to use a rack. His hunting suit was all of otter-skin, 6 varied throughout its length with furs of other kinds from whose shining hair clasps of gold gleamed out on either side of this daring lord of the hunt. The handsome sword that he wore was Balmung, a weapon so keen and with such excellent edges that it never failed to bite when swung against a helmet. No wonder this splendid hunter was proud and gay. And (since I am bound to tell you all) know that his quiver was full of good arrows with gold mountings and heads a span[7] in width, so that any beast they pierced must inevitably soon die.

Thus the noble knight rode along, the very image of a hunting man. Gunther's attendants saw him coming and ran to meet him to take his horse—tied to whose saddle he led a mighty bear! On dismounting, he loosed the bonds from its muzzle and paws, whereupon all the hounds that saw it instantly gave tongue. The beast made for the forest and the people were seized with 7 panic. Affrighted by the tumult, the bear strayed into the kitchen—and how the cooks scuttled from their fire at its approach! Many caldrons were sent flying and many fires were scattered, while heaps of good food lay among the ashes. Lords and retainers leapt from their seats, the bear

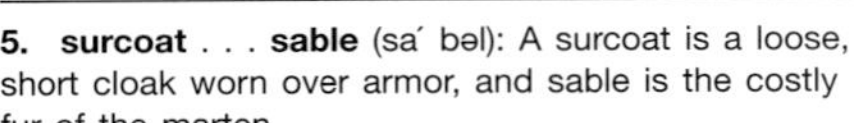

5. surcoat . . . sable (sa´ bəl): A surcoat is a loose, short cloak worn over armor, and sable is the costly fur of the marten.
6. panther-skin . . . odor: The odor of panther skin was supposed to lure other animals and therefore help with the hunt.
7. span: Nine inches.

CONNECTIONS TO WORLD LITERATURE

Customize for
Less Proficient Readers

5 Encourage students to paraphrase as they read. To model the skill, you might paraphrase the first long sentence in this paragraph in the following way: "Now there was a lot of shouting and dogs barking everywhere, and all the commotion echoed in the hills and forest. The hunters had let loose at least twenty-four packs of dogs!"

◆ Critical Thinking

6 Interpret Ask students why so much detail is devoted to Siegfried's appearance. *Siegfried is made all the more heroic and superhuman by means of this regal description.*

◆ Critical Thinking

7 Draw Conclusions Remind students that this tale comes out of the oral tradition. When reciting the tale, storytellers would need to sustain their audience's attention for long periods of time. Based on this information, ask students to draw a conclusion about why the incident with the bear is included. *Suggested answers: It is likely that the bear is here to add excitement, to bring the tale into the setting of the common people (for example, into the kitchen), to show lords and retainers being afraid of the bear, and to develop the characterization of Siegfried as bravest among all the people.*

Humanities: Music

This story has been immortalized in the form of a grand opera by composer Richard Wagner (väg´ nər). *Siegfried* is just one part of the four-part opera cycle known as *The Ring (Der Ring des Nibelungen).*

Encourage interested students to obtain a recording of *Siegfried* and play it for the class, holding a discussion afterward of the how well the music captures the mood and plot of the story. If the recording is in German, provide photocopies of an English translation so students can follow along.

Those students who participate in the school choir or orchestra may want to work in conjunction with their music instructors to rehearse and perform a portion of the music from *Siegfried.*

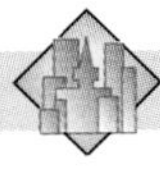

Beyond the Classroom

Career Connection

Music and Theater Point out to students that careers in the arts often come out of great works of literature such as this. Tell students that this story has been made into one of the most-loved operas of all time.

With students, brainstorm for a list of professions that are directly related to opera productions. *Composer, conductor, musician, singer, set designer, costume designer, lighting designer, sound technician, producer, box office manager, advertising and promotion manager, poster designer, and so on.*

Encourage students to choose one of these professions to research. Then hold a "career seminar" in which students staff "booths" and answer questions about each career.

Customize for
Less Proficient Readers

Students may need to have the many changes in setting pointed out to them. So far, Siegfried has been seen at home with his wife, in various settings for the hunt, crashing though the kitchen in pursuit of the bear, and now at table in the meadow.

Customize for
Intrapersonal Learners

Challenge intrapersonal learners to write or record their ideas about the thoughts that are going through the minds of both Siegfried and Gunther.

◆ Critical Thinking

❶ Speculate Ask students to speculate on why, in the midst of so great a feast, the wine is not being poured. *Possible answer: Somehow this relates to the plot to kill Siegfried. Perhaps Gunther is trying to anger Siegfried so that he will do something rash for which he must be punished.*

◆ Critical Thinking

❷ Analyze Ask students to determine whether Siegfried has any character flaws and, if so, what they are. *Possible answer: Siegfried has several traits that could be seen as flaws. He is very proud and very sure of himself. He welcomes every challenge too readily; sometimes he seems to act before he thinks.*

became infuriated, and the King ordered all the hounds on their leashes to be loosed—and if all had ended well they would have had a jolly day! Bows and spears were no longer left idle, for the brave ones ran toward the bear, yet there were so many hounds in the way that none dared shoot. With the whole mountain thundering with people's cries the bear took to flight before the hounds and none could keep up with it but Siegfried, who ran it down and then dispatched it with his sword. The bear was later carried to the campfire, and all who had witnessed this feat declared that Siegfried was a very powerful man.

The proud companions were then summoned to table. There were a great many seated in that meadow. Piles of sumptuous dishes were set before the noble huntsmen, but the butlers who were to pour their wine were very slow to appear. Yet knights could not be better cared for than they and if only no treachery had been lurking in their minds those warriors would have been above reproach.

❶ "Seeing that we are being treated to such a variety of dishes from the kitchen," said lord Siegfried, "I fail to understand why the butlers bring us no wine. Unless we hunters are better looked after, I'll not be a companion of the hunt. I thought I had deserved better attention."

"We shall be very glad to make amends to you for our present lack," answered the perfidious[8] King from his table. "This is Hagen's fault—he wants us to die of thirst."

"My very dear lord," replied Hagen of Troneck, "I thought the day's hunting would be away in the Spessart and so I sent the wine there. If we go without drink today I shall take good care that it does not happen again."

"Those fellows!" said lord Siegfried. "It was arranged that they were to bring along seven panniers of spiced wine and mead[9] for me. Since that proved impossible, we should have been placed nearer the Rhine."

"You brave and noble knights," said Hagen of Troneck, "I know a cool spring nearby—do not be offended!—let us go there."—A proposal which (as it turned out) was to bring many knights into jeopardy.

Siegfried was tormented by thirst and ordered the board to be removed all the sooner in his eagerness to go to that spring at the foot of the hills. And now the knights put their treacherous plot into execution.

Word was given for the game which Siegfried had killed to be conveyed back to Worms on wagons, and all who saw it gave him great credit for it.

Hagan of Troneck broke his faith with Siegfried most grievously, for as they were leaving to go to the spreading lime-tree he said: "I have often been told that no one can keep up with Lady Kriemhild's lord when he cares to show his speed. I wish he would show it us now." ❷

"You can easily put it to the test by racing me to the brook," replied gallant Siegfried of the Netherlands. "Then those who see it shall declare the winner."

"I accept your challenge," said Hagen.

"Then I will lie down in the grass at your feet, as a handicap," replied brave Siegfried, much to Gunther's satisfaction. "And I will tell you what more I shall do. I will carry all my equipment with me, my spear and my shield and all my hunting clothes." And he quickly strapped on his quiver and sword. The two men took off their outer clothing and stood there in their white vests. Then they ran through the clover like a pair of wild panthers. Siegfried appeared first at the brook.

Gunther's magnificent guest who excelled so many men in all things quickly unstrapped his sword, took off his quiver, and after leaning his great spear against a branch of the lime, stood beside the rushing brook. Then he laid down his shield near the flowing water, and although he was very thirsty he most courteously refrained from drinking until the King had drunk. Gunther thanked him very ill for this.

The stream was cool, sweet, and clear. Gunther stooped to its running waters and after drinking stood up and stepped aside.

8. **perfidious** (pər fid′ ē əs) *adj.*: Treacherous.
9. **panniers** (pan′ yərz) . . . **mead** (mēd): Panniers are baskets, and mead is an alcoholic liquor made of fermented honey and water.

Speaking and Listening Mini-Lesson

Dramatizing the Story

This mini-lesson supports the Speaking and Listening activity in the Idea Bank on page 187.

Introduce the Concept A dramatization is a play form of a given story. Interested students can develop the described scene into a dramatic skit to be performed before the class.

Develop Background Have students reread this selection and jot down details of the death of Siegfried. Then have them create a situation in which a knight tells Kriemhild of Siegfried's death. Students may invent details for this scene and invent the conversation, but the knight's narration of the death of Siegfried should be true to the story. Suggest that in writing the script, they follow format and conventions of dramatic scripts: character's name followed by a colon and the character's words; directions for movement and expression in parentheses or brackets.

Apply the Information Students may work in pairs to develop and revise scripts for this scene. Have them practice the skit and make any refinements. Then have the pair present it to the class.

Assess the Outcome Use the Peer Assessment sheet for a Dramatic Performance in ***Alternative Assessment,*** p. 121.

Siegfried in turn would have liked to do the same, but he paid for his good manners. For now Hagen car-
3 ried Siegfried's sword and bow beyond his reach, ran back for the spear, and searched for the sign on the brave man's tunic. Then, as Siegfried bent over the brook and drank, Hagen hurled the spear at the cross, so that the hero's heart's blood leapt from the wound and splashed against Hagen's clothes. No warrior will ever do a darker deed. Leaving the spear fixed in Siegfried's heart, he fled in
4 wild desperation, as he had never fled before from any man.

When lord Siegfried felt the great wound, maddened with rage he bounded back from the stream with the long shaft jutting from his heart. He was hoping to find either his bow or his sword, and, had he succeeded in doing so, Hagen would have had his pay. But finding no sword, the gravely wounded man had nothing but his shield. Snatching this from the bank he ran at Hagen, and King Gunther's vassal was unable to elude him. Siegfried was wounded to death, yet he struck so powerfully that he sent many precious stones whirling from the shield as it smashed to pieces. Gunther's noble guest would dearly have loved to avenge himself. Hagen fell reeling under the weight of the blow and the riverside echoed loudly. Had Siegfried had his sword in his hand it would have been the end of Hagen, so enraged was the wounded man, as indeed he had good cause to be.

The hero's face had lost its color and he was no longer able to stand. His strength had ebbed away, for in the field of his bright countenance he now displayed Death's token. Soon many fair ladies would be weeping for him.

The lady Kriemhild's lord fell among the flowers, where you could see the blood surging from his wound. Then—and he had cause—he rebuked those who had plotted his foul murder. "You vile cowards," he said as he lay dying. "What good has my service done me now that you have slain me? I was always loyal to you, but now I have paid for it. Alas, you have wronged your kinsmen so that all who are born in days to come will be dishonored by your deed. You have cooled your anger on me beyond all measure. You will be held in contempt and stand apart from all good warriors."

Siegfried's Death, Handschriftenabteilung, Staatsbibliothek Preussischer Kulterbesitz, Berlin

▲ **Critical Viewing** What aspects of the scene does the artist emphasize? What did he omit? What conclusion can you draw based on his choices? **[Draw Conclusions]** 5

◆ Critical Thinking

3 Analyze Causes and Effects Ask students why Hagen moves Siegfried's sword and bow beyond his reach. *Possible answer: Hagen is preparing to kill Siegfried, and he wants to make sure that Siegfried can't get to his weapons and fight back with them.*

◆ Critical Thinking

4 Analyze Ask students why Hagen flees "as he had never fled before from any man." *Possible answers: Siegfried is so strong that Hagen fears he will fight back, even with a sword sticking in him; also, his deed is so dark that he may feel a horror that causes him to run so fast.*

▶Critical Viewing◀

5 Draw Conclusions The artist emphasized the murder of Siegried; he omitted the actual scene in which Siegried drinks from the stream. The artist may have chosen to do this so that he could depict both Siegfried's and Hagan's faces.

Customize for *Musical/Rhythmic Learners*

Ask musical learners to imagine that this story is being brought to the screen. Different music must be composed for each change of scene. Ask students to describe the type of music and instruments they think might be used to heighten this scene as well as others in the selection.

Humanities: Art

Siegfried's Death.

Use these questions for discussion:

1. How does this illustration of Siegfried's death compare to the mental image you formed as you read the story? *Students may feel the illustration does not show the blood and gore described in the selection.*
2. Which elements in this scene are realistic? Which are romanticized? Explain. *Suggested reponses: The characters look realistic, but the action of the murder seems stilted or unnatural. The animals seem representational rather than realistic. The artist seems to have crowded as many characters and animals into the scene as possible, making the scene interesting, but improbable.*

◆ Critical Thinking

❶ **Analyze** Ask students why Gunther is lamenting a death which he himself helped to plan and execute. *Possible answers: Gunther is Siegfried's brother-in-law; Siegfried was a very great man who probably did not deserve his death and did not deserve to be killed in this manner.*

◆ Critical Thinking

❷ **Compare and Contrast** Have students compare and contrast Gunther's attitude toward the death with Hagen's attitude. *Hagen is glad that Siegfried is dead, and he is relieved that all threats to the kingdom are now over. He does not feel guilt as Gunther presumably does.*

◆ Critical Thinking

❸ **Compare and Contrast** Ask students to recall Kriemhild's dreams. How do the real events compare with Kriemhild's dream? *Just as Kriemhild envisioned, her husband's blood drenched the flowers. Although Siegfried was not chased by two boars, two powerful men, Gunther and Hagen, acted in a most beastly way toward him.*

Customize for
Interpersonal Learners
Interpersonal learners may enjoy discussing, planning, or enacting either the trial or the memorial service that might follow these events.

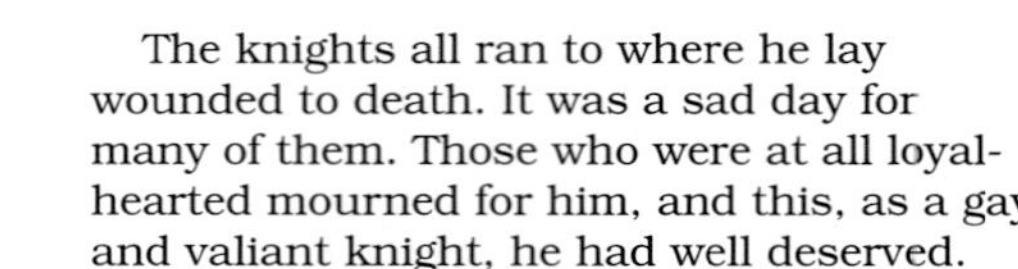

CONNECTIONS TO WORLD LITERATURE

The knights all ran to where he lay wounded to death. It was a sad day for many of them. Those who were at all loyal-hearted mourned for him, and this, as a gay and valiant knight, he had well deserved.

❶ The King of Burgundy too lamented Siegfried's death.

"There is no need for the doer of the deed to weep when the damage is done," said the dying man. "He should be held up to scorn. It would have been better left undone."

❷ "I do not know what you are grieving for," said Hagen fiercely. "All our cares and sorrows are over and done with. We shall not find many who will dare oppose us now. I am glad I have put an end to his supremacy."

"You may well exult," said Siegfried. "But had I known your murderous bent I should easily have guarded my life from you. I am sorry for none so much as my wife, the lady Kriemhild. May God have mercy on me for ever having got a son who in years to come will suffer the reproach that his kinsmen were murderers. If I had the strength I would have good reason to complain. But if you feel at all inclined to do a loyal deed for anyone, noble King," continued the mortally wounded man, "let me commend my dear sweetheart to your mercy. Let her profit from being your sister. By the virtue of all princes, stand by her loyally! No lady was ever more greatly wronged through her dear friend. As to my father and his vassals, they will have long to wait for me."

The flowers everywhere were drenched with blood. Siegfried was at grips with Death, yet not for long, since Death's sword ever was too sharp. And now the warrior who had been so brave and gay could speak no more. ❸

When those lords saw that the hero was dead they laid him on a shield that shone red with gold, and they plotted ways and means of concealing the fact that Hagen had done the deed. "A disaster has befallen us," many of them said. "You must all hush it up and declare with one voice that Siegfried rode off hunting alone and was killed by robbers as he was passing through the forest."

"I shall take him home," said Hagen of Troneck. "It is all one to me if the woman who made Brunhild so unhappy should come to know of it. It will trouble me very little, however much she weeps."

Guide for Responding

◆ *Literature and Your Life*

Reader's Response How would you describe Siegfried?

Thematic Focus Which perils are brought on by Siegfried's character flaws?

Happy Ending Rewrite the ending of the story you've just read so that Siegfried survives the murder plot.

☑ Check Your Comprehension

1. Why doesn't Kriemhild want Siegfried to go hunting?
2. Why does Siegfried become angry at dinner?
3. Why does Hagen challenge Siegfried to a race?

◆ Critical Thinking

INTERPRET

1. What might the two boars in Kriemhild's dream stand for? **[Interpret]**
2. What do you learn about Siegfried's character and judgment from the passage in which Siegfried chases and kills a bear? **[Connect]**
3. What causes Siegfried's downfall? **[Infer]**

APPLY

4. What message might this story send to people your age? **[Relate]**

EXTEND

5. Larger-than-life heroes, like Siegfried, are found throughout literature and across cultures. Name one with whom you're familiar and compare and contrast your choice with Siegfried. **[Literature Link]**

Reinforce and Extend

Answers

◆ *Literature and Your Life*

Reader's Response Students may describe Siegfried as brave, strong and honorable. Some may also point out that he was foolish and too trusting.

Thematic Focus The perils Siegfried encounters—the treachery among his wife's family—are in part able to occur because Siegfried is too blinded by his love for his wife.

Check Your Comprehension

1. Kriemhild had a dream in which Siegfried is killed.
2. Siegfried becomes angry because there is no wine to drink and he's very thirsty.
3. Hagen challenges Siegfried to a race in order to tire him out more and to make him even thirstier.

◆ Critical Thinking

1. The boars may stand for Hagen and Gunther.
2. It suggests that Siegfried is too caught up in the fun of the game to realize possible dangers.
3. Siegfried's downfall is caused by his disregard for his wife's concerns, his over trust in the people he keeps company with, and with his love for competition.
4. The story might serve as a warning against having too much confidence.
5. Responses may include Greece's Achilleus and Rome's Julius Caesar.

Thematic Connection

THE THEME OF PERILS AND ADVENTURES

During the Middle Ages, people faced upheavals and dangers from all sides. The struggles were many and varied: people against their neighbors, countries against invaders, king versus king. These struggles were very much a part of life and were explored in the songs and stories of the time. So, too, were more subtle but equally wrenching struggles, such as winning the love of another.

1. Whom do you find more courageous—Margaret Paston or Siegfried? Explain your choice.
2. In "How Siegfried Was Slain," love comes hand in hand with danger: Brunhild's love for Siegfried provokes her to instigate his murder; Siegfried, in turn, is too blinded by his love for Kriemhild and for adventure to foresee any danger. In medieval ballads, there is also a connection between love and danger. Choose a ballad to compare with "How Siegfried Was Slain." Explore the idea of love and danger in both works.
3. In what ways does Siegfried's stubbornness compare with that of the couple in "Get Up and Bar the Door"?

Idea Bank

Writing

1. **Finding Siegfried a Job** Imagine that Siegfried is looking for a job in contemporary America. Help him out by writing a résumé that lists his accomplishments and skills. **[Career Link]**
2. **A Modern Fable** Rewrite this story as a modern fable with modern dialogue and characters. Keep the theme and message of the original, but revise settings, symbols, and other details as much as you wish.
3. **Hunting the Hunter** In the medieval romance and epic, the hunter often becomes the hunted. In what ways does the hunt scene foreshadow what is to come in the story? How does Siegfried's death become part of the hunting ritual? Explore the answers to these questions in a written analysis. Support your ideas with examples from the story.
4. **Critical Response** The author Robert Service asserts, "Fate has written a tragedy; its name is 'The Human Heart.'" In a written response, explore how this quotation relates to Siegfried; then explain how it relates to life in general.

Speaking and Listening

5. **Dramatizing the Story** Imagine that a knight who was loyal to Siegfried returns to tell Kriemhild what has happened. What details would he give her of the hunt and the death of the hero? How would Kriemhild react? Write your version of the conversation between the knight and Kriemhild. With a classmate, perform the scene for the class. **[Performing Arts Link]**
6. **Telling the Story With Music** *The Nibelungenlied* was set to music by German composer Richard Wagner; it consists of four operas that are frequently performed and recorded. Obtain a recording of the opera *Siegfried* and listen to scenes corresponding with this passage from the story. Then write a review in which you explain how well the essence of the tragedy is captured through music. **[Art Link]**

Project

7. **A Map of Medieval Heroes** Create a map of medieval Europe, labeling things like kingdoms, rivers, centers of religion. Indicate locations of fictional and real-life heroes like Siegfried. Display your map. **[Social Studies Link]**

Beyond the Selection

FURTHER READING

Other Works of Norse Folklore and Siegfried

The Saga of the Volsungs: The Norse Epic of Sigurd the Dragon Slayer, Jesse L. Byock, translator

The Legend of the Nibelungenlied, Heilan Yvette Grimes

Wagner's Siegfried: Its Drama, Its History, and Its Music, P. P. McCreless

INTERNET

You and your students may find additional information about Norse mythology on the Internet at the following site. Please be aware, however, that sites may have changed from the time we published this information.

For information about Norse mythology, go to **http: www. ugcs.caltech.edu/~cherryne/mythology.html**

You may also find other related information on the Internet. We *strongly recommend* that you preview sites before you send students to them.

Thematic Connection

1. Suggested response: Margaret Paston was more courageous because she recognized the dangers surrounding her, yet she battled on.
2. Comparisons should illustrate how love and danger go hand in hand.
3. Siegfried's stubbornness is very like that of the couple in "Get Up and Bar the Door." Siegfried, like the goodwife, probably would not have broken the silence if he were in the same situation.

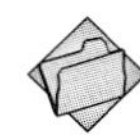

Idea Bank

Customizing for *Learning Modalities*

Following are suggestions for matching Idea Bank topics with your students' learning modalities:

- Visual/Spatial: 7
- Musical/Rhythmic: 6
- Interpersonal: 1, 5
- Verbal/Linguistic: 3, 4, 5

Customizing for *Performance Levels*

Following are suggestions for matching Idea Bank topics with your students' ability levels:

- Less Advanced Students: 1, 2
- Average Students: 3, 5, 7
- More Advanced Students: 4

ASSESSMENT OPTIONS

Formal Assessment, Selection Test, pp. 37–39, and Assessment Resources Software. The selection test is designed so that it can be easily customized to the performance levels of your students.

PORTFOLIO ASSESSMENT

Use the following rubrics in the ***Alternative Assessment*** booklet to assess student writing:
Résumé: Résumé/Cover Letter Rubric, p. 115
Fable: Fictional Narrative Rubric, p. 96
Literary Analysis: Literary Analysis Rubric, p. 113
Critical Response: Response to Literature Rubric, p. 111

Prepare and Engage

Establish Writing Guidelines Prepare students to write a persuasive speech by introducing the following key characteristics:

- A persuasive speech attempts to convince an audience to think or act in a certain way.
- A persuasive speech may include special rhetorical devices such as repetition of key words and ideas.
- A persuasive speech builds its argument through effective organization.
- An effective persuasive speech maintains one consistent viewpoint.

Refer students to the Writing Handbook page 1189 for support with the writing process and page 1192 for more information on persuasive writing.

Connect to Literature Have students review the historical speeches in this book for elements of effective speeches: Queen Elizabeth's *Speech Before the Spanish Armada*, p. 240; Lord Byron's *Speech to Parliament: In Defense of the Lower Classes*, p. 706; Judge Catherine McGuinness's *Opening Statement for the Inaugural Session of the Forum for Peace and Reconciliation*, p. 811, Winston Churchill's *Wartime Speech*, p. 972; and Mohandas K. Gandhi's *Defending Nonviolent Resistance*, p. 975.

Discussion Ask students to think about the many types of persuasive writing and speeches to which they are exposed. Have the class identify common features of persuasive writing. Then have them analyze which are effective. Also have them distinguish those that are sound, based on logical reasoning and sound arguments, from those that are based on faulty reasoning and appeals to emotion. Urge them to incorporate only sound logical arguments into their own persuasive speeches.

Writer's Solution

Writers at Work Videodisc
Show the segment in which Cary Bricker discusses persuasive writing. Point out how Bricker prepares persuasive speeches as part of her job as a public defender. Ask students to evaluate what Bricker says about the significance of word choice in preparing persuasive writing.

Play frames 33218 to 42857

Writing Lab CD-ROM
Allow students to write their persuasive speech on the computer using the tutorial on Persuasion. Have them follow these steps:

1. Choose a topic by reviewing the inspirations for writing.
2. Identify their audience by creating an audience profile.
3. Review research tips from writers before gathering support for their speeches.
4. While drafting, review the interactive instruction on avoiding faulty logic or unreasonable appeals.
5. Use the persuasive word bins while revising their papers.

Sourcebook
Students can find additional support, including topic ideas, and models in Chapter 4, Persuasion (pp. 96–129).

Persuasive Speech — Writing Process Workshop

Persuasive Speech

To convince her husband and family to take certain actions, Margaret Paston used persuasive techniques in her letters. You may encounter similar persuasive techniques when you hear news commentaries or campaign speeches. You probably use them yourself when you ask favors of friends. These modern examples are all forms of **persuasive speech**, in which the speaker tries to influence or change people's views on a topic.

The following skills, introduced in this section's Writing Mini-Lessons, will help you write an effective persuasive speech.

Writing Skills Focus

- **Use effective repetition** to draw attention to the points in your speech that you want listeners to remember. (See p. 163.)
- Maintain a **consistent perspective** so your ideas are unified and your argument is solid. For example, you might discuss an issue from the standpoint of a consumer or from that of all the world's people. (See p. 179.)
- **Build an argument** by using an effective organizational plan, such as order of importance, cause and effect, or pro and con.

This excerpt from a speech by Britain's former prime minister Margaret Thatcher incorporates all these skills.

Model From Literature

from a speech given by Margaret Thatcher

The Soviet collapse has also aggravated the single most awesome threat of modern times: the proliferation of weapons of mass destruction. ① These weapons ② —and the ability to develop and deliver them—are today acquired by middle-income countries with modest populations such as Iraq, Iran, Libya, and Syria; acquired sometimes from other powers like China and North Korea; but most ominously from former Soviet arsenals or unemployed scientists or from organized criminal rings, all via a growing international black market ③.

① Thatcher establishes a cause-and-effect relationship from which she will build her argument.
② She repeats the word *weapons* to emphasize the main idea of her speech: control of weapons.
③ Throughout the passage, Thatcher maintains a consistent perspective by observing the situation from a global standpoint.

Prewriting

Choose a Topic Focus on an issue or idea that you feel strongly about, or choose one of the following topic ideas.

Topic Ideas

- Take a side on an environmental issue
- Compare and contrast going to college and going into the work force
- Create a campaign speech
- Defend an issue on which you feel strongly

Create an Outline Plan the most effective way of building your argument and organizing details—order of importance (from most important to least important, or vice versa), pro and con (list the reasons that support your stand and those against it), and cause and effect (examine various causes of one effect; for example, prohibiting dangerous poisons and enforcing hunting bans might be two **causes** contributing to a desired **effect**—the recovery of the bald eagle). Create an outline that reflects your choice of organization.

List Key Ideas Before drafting, list the points you want to convey in your speech and different ways of phrasing them. Then list key words related to your points. You can later use these lists to incorporate repetition into your speech.

Drafting

Keep a Consistent Perspective Decide upon the point of view from which you will prepare your argument. For example, if you are upset about a company's lack of environmental concern, you may choose to present your speech from the perspective of a consumer who buys that company's products. Then try to match each point to that perspective.

Use Persuasive Language Your choice of wording and use of repetition can make your argument weak or strong. Use positive terms—such as *fine, superior, best*—to make your recommendations more appealing. Use negative terms—such as *bad, appalling, poor, terrible*—to sharpen your criticism.

Read Aloud Read your speech aloud as you draft. Pause at places you want to stress and decide on words you want to emphasize. You may find that you have too many key ideas in one place, detracting from their force.

APPLYING LANGUAGE SKILLS: Using Parallel Structure

Effective persuasion often uses parallel, or similar, grammatical structures to express similar ideas.

Not Parallel: Think of our store when you plan to hike, to bike, or go fishing.

Parallel: Think of our store when you plan to hike, to bike, or to fish.

Practice Rewrite the following sentences so all parts are parallel.

1. She has served on the library board, the school board, and is a town council member.

2. As state senator, she plans to reduce taxes, increase aid to education, and she is concerned about protecting the environment.

Writing Application Review your persuasive speech for constructions that are not parallel. Revise constructions so they are parallel.

Writer's Solution Connection Writing Lab

To help a peer review your paper, use the Peer Evaluation Checklist in the Writing Lab tutorial on Persuasion.

Cross-Curricular Connection: Social Studies

Memorable Speeches in History Point out to students that history is marked by great speeches. For example, Martin Luther King Jr.'s words "I have a dream" still poignantly remind us of the struggles of the civil rights movement. These words were carefully chosen for their persuasive and memorable effects. Advise students to include memorable words and phrases in their speeches. They might also consider repeating these memorable words and phrases. Encourage students to research and review speeches with similar topics to their own topics, such as Winston Churchill's or Abraham Lincoln's speeches, and then use them as models for their own writing.

Develop Student Writing

Prewriting

Have students brainstorm in groups for topics about which they have strong feelings and that impact their lives. Choosing a topic about which they feel strongly will motivate students to create a convincing persuasive speech.

Writing Lab CD-ROM

Remind students that in order to build a successful argument they must use an effective organization. Have students review the various audio-annotated examples of different types of organizations in the Persuasion tutorial. Also suggest that students choose a graphic organizer to help organize details.

Customize for
Visual/Spatial Learners

Help visual/spatial learners organize their speeches by providing them with copies of an Argument Organizer, p. 103, and an Outline Organizer, p. 123, in ***Writing and Language Transparencies.***

Drafting

Remind students to keep a consistent perspective. Tell them to stop after each paragraph and evaluate whether or not they are presenting all details from one consistent perspective.

Applying Language Skills

Parallel Structure Let students know that one of the effective devices that writers of persuasive speeches use is parallel structure. Expressing similar ideas in similar grammatical form sets up a rhythm that makes ideas memorable.

Answers

Suggested response:

1. She has served on the library board, the school board, and the town council.
2. As a state senator, she plans to reduce taxes, increase aid to education, and protect the environment.

For additional practice, use the **Language Lab CD-ROM** lesson Strengthening Sentences and the practice page on faulty parallelism, p. 46, in the *Writer's Solution Grammar Practice Book.*

Revising

Have students use the Revising Checklist to evaluate their work. Have them answer each question on paper. Then have students exchange their speeches and comments with a peer reviewer. Each peer should proofread and evaluate the speech. Students should then compare their evaluations with the peer reviewer to help them identify weaknesses and strengths in their writing.

Writer's Solution

Writers at Work Videodisc

Play the videodisc section in which public defender Cary Bricker describes her revising techniques. Then ask students to evaluate whether they could use some of the same methods.

Play frames 39870 to 40926

Reinforce and Extend

Have students go beyond this assignment by researching speeches on a topic of their choice. Then ask them to evaluate the speeches for effectiveness as based on the criteria presented in this lesson.

Applying Language Skills

Eliminating Unnecessary Words

Writer's Solution

For extra help, have students complete the **Language Lab CD-ROM** lesson on Eliminating Unnecessary Words.

Applying Language Skills: Eliminating Unnecessary Words

Clear, direct writing is more persuasive than writing weighed down with unnecessary words. Use the following tips while writing:

- Eliminate words and phrases that contribute no meaning, such as *due to the fact that*.
- Avoid expressions that repeat meanings unnecessarily, such as *past history*. (All history is past.)
- Replace wordy expressions with shorter words or phrases; for example, replace *at this point in time* with *now*.

Writing Application After you draft your speech, go through it sentence by sentence to find words or phrases that do not add meaning, and eliminate them.

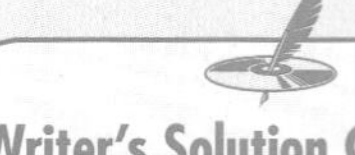

Writer's Solution Connection
Language Lab

To help you identify and eliminate unnecessary words in your persuasive speech, use the Language Lab lesson on Eliminating Unnecessary Words.

Revising

Use the following checklist, which refers to the Writing Skills Focus points on p. 188, while revising your speech.

- ▶ Have I kept a clear and consistent perspective?
  Delete or revise areas in which you stray from your chosen perspective; they weaken your argument.
- ▶ Did I use repetition effectively?
  Underline instances where you have repeated key ideas and phrases. Evaluate their effectiveness by reading your speech to a peer and getting his or her reaction.
- ▶ Have I built my argument effectively?
  Go back through your speech and create an outline of the way you have presented details in your speech. Compare it with the outline you prepared before drafting. Make sure your organization is effective and coherent.

Revision Model

Physical activity is not [just] good for you ① [; it is essential if you are to remain healthy]. ~~As a student I read~~ ② studies ~~that~~ have shown that people who regularly engaged in activities such as walking, climbing stairs, or dancing have lived longer, [healthier] ③ lives.

① The writer added this information so she could begin with a clear cause-and-effect statement on which to build her argument.

② Deleting these words makes the perspective clearer. The writer presents herself as an authority on the subject.

③ By repeating forms of the word *healthy*, the writer focuses on the benefits of exercise.

Publishing

- ▶ **Presentation** Present your speech to your classmates.
- ▶ **Internet** Post your speech to a message board in a news group.
- ▶ **Media Presentation** Either audiotape or videotape yourself giving your speech. Then present it at a school club or town organization where your subject would be relevant.

✓ ASSESSMENT		4	3	2	1
PORTFOLIO ASSESSMENT Use the Scoring Rubric for Persuasion in ***Alternative Assessment*** (p.106) to assess students' writing. In addition, use these criteria to customize the rubric to this assignment.	**Effective Repetition**	The writer effectively repeats key words and phrases for emphasis.	The writer uses some repetition of key words and phrases for emphasis.	The writer repeats words and phrases that are not key.	The writer does not use any type of repetition.
	Consistent Perspective	The writer presents the argument from one consistent perspective.	The writer's perspective occasionally strays.	The writer mixes perspectives from which the argument is presented.	The writer does not maintain any type of perspective.

Real-World Reading Skills Workshop

Evaluating Advertisements

Strategies for Success

Often, people learn of products through advertisements on television and in print. If you have to decide whether or not to buy a product based on advertising, you might want to evaluate just what the ad is conveying.

Evaluate the Message Use these questions as guidelines for evaluating advertisements.

- ▶ Do the ad's statements contain facts or opinions, or are they actually just tough-sounding phrases that mean very little?
- ▶ Are the statements true?
- ▶ How does the writer support each statement?
- ▶ Does the ad give information that sounds as if it supports its claims, but is actually irrelevant?

Relating the Message to Your Life When you have evaluated the message in an ad, you can decide whether or not to accept the ad's claims. Is the message in line with your situation or needs? Only after you evaluate the ad's claims can you make a reasonable decision about whether to buy.

Apply the Strategy

Examine this advertisement for toothpaste. Then answer the following questions.

1. Which statements in the ad lack specific support?
2. What empty phrases does it use?
3. What irrelevant, though potentially persuasive, information does the ad contain?

AT LAST, A TOOTHPASTE THAT HAS IT ALL

- Prevents Cavities
- Counteracts gum disease
- Whitens and brightens
- Freshens your breath

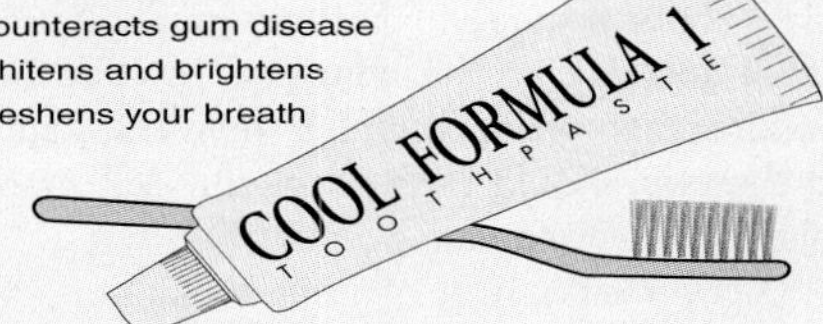

STUDIES HAVE SHOWN THAT COOL FORMULA 1

— is today's most popular toothpaste
— is used by more movie stars and models than any other brand
— gets down between teeth for tougher cleaning
— actually hardens tooth enamel

FOOL YOUR DENTIST. USE COOL

Here are other situations in which it is important to evaluate the persuasive message:

- ▶ Political campaigns
- ▶ Direct mail ads
- ▶ Information on packages

Introduce the Strategy

Students are constantly bombarded by advertisements and tend to be influenced by them. Stress to students that advertisements generally do not provide factual information but are instead developed to persuade them to act a certain way. It is important that students recognize the content for what it is.

Customize for
More Advanced Students
Ask more advanced students to compare the advertisement on this page to the most effective forms of advertisement they have seen. Have students make a list of elements of effective advertising and share it with the rest of the class, explaining how advertisers use these elements to persuade consumers.

Apply the Strategy

Have students look at the advertisement for the same amount of time they would normally give to any advertisement. Then ask students what most impressed them about the ad and why. Finally, have students evaluate the advertisement by applying the strategy.

1. The statements that lack specific support are as follows: the claims that the toothpaste prevents cavities, counteracts gum disease, whitens and brightens, and freshens your breath; and the points that it claims studies have shown.
2. The empty phrases that the advertisement uses are "at last, a toothpaste that has it all" and "Fool your dentist. Use Cool."
3. The irrelevant statement "is used by more movie stars and models than any other brand" is potentially persuasive.

Introduce the Strategy

Tell students that the skills they acquire writing and presenting persuasively will have value in all types of presentations in their life. Whether they are presenting themselves at a college interview, or negotiating the purchase of a car, students will need to hold the attention of others, make effective points, and be memorable.

Activity Have students videotape themselves presenting their speeches. The videotape will show the weaknesses and strengths in their voice and gestures. Have students review tapes in small groups. Group members may offer constructive suggestions for improvement. Caution students against making remarks that are not helpful; it is important that they phrase suggestions tactfully.

Customize for
Non-Interpersonal Learners
Some students will feel uncomfortable presenting a speech in front of a group of people. Provide them with the following tips:

- Point out that eye contact is important, but if looking directly at an audience makes them too nervous, suggest that they fix their eyes on a place on the wall behind the audience. This will keep them from looking at their notes but still avoid direct eye contact.
- Encourage students to use props. Props will take the attention off them and direct it toward a map, chart, etc. Props will also give speakers something to do with their hands.

Remind students that these methods are only temporary solutions and that with practice students will no longer need them.

Apply the Strategy

Answers

1. Possible response: If an editorial is critical of economic policy, a strong authoritative tone would work best.
2. Possible response: Gestures for a speech critical of economic policy may occur when points are being made about how the audience will be affected if policy is passed.

Speaking and Listening Workshop

Delivering a Persuasive Speech

Politicians, actors, and lawyers soon learn: that to make an effective persuasive speech, you must offer your audience more than convincing reasons, examples, and other evidence supporting your viewpoint. The most brilliant arguments may be ignored if the person making a speech does not hold the attention of the audience. *How* you deliver a speech is just as important as *what* you say.

Look at Your Audience Make eye contact with your audience so they know you're addressing them. If you stare at your notes while you give a speech, your audience will automatically feel as if you are not talking to them. They will be easily distracted. Looking at your audience adds persuasive power to your words. Practice your speech often enough so that you are comfortable looking up from your notes.

Adjust Your Tone of Voice As you speak, vary the rate, pitch, and volume of your voice to suit what you are saying. Speaking in a monotone is unappealing, no matter how passionately you believe in your ideas. Try to sound confident, but also courteous.

Use Appropriate Gestures Delivering a speech is usually a more formal act than participating in a conversation. Use gestures to emphasize important points in your speech, but use them sparingly, and make them count. Making a formal speech should not turn you into a statue. Raising your hand, tapping the lectern, visibly shrugging—such gestures allow you to engage your audience's eyes as well as their ears.

Tips for Speaking Persuasively

If you want to convince an audience to adopt your point of view or opinion, follow these strategies:

- Look at your audience directly
- Use a confident but courteous tone of voice
- Make your gestures count for emphasis

Apply the Strategy

In a small group, choose newspaper editorials about a current national or community issue and deliver the editorials as speeches. Before each group member delivers a speech, the group should read all of the editorials and discuss the following points:

1. Consider the content. What tone would work best in a live presentation?
2. At which points would gestures work best for emphasis? What gestures?

Keeping the group's advice in mind, rehearse and deliver your speech.

Beyond the Classroom

Career Connection

Sales Representative A sales representative is a person who sells products or services. When presenting an item or service, a sales representative must provide a memorable and persuasive pitch that will convince a customer to make a purchase. Sales representatives can be memorable and persuasive when they believe in what they are selling and know the product well. Sales representatives' success is often dependent on their honesty and integrity. Whether working for a small retail store or selling large aircraft to millionaires, a sales representative must be an excellent presenter and speaker. Ask students about purchases they have made that relied on the attitude and presentation of a salesperson. Which qualities made them want to buy? Which qualities discouraged them from making a purchase?

Extended Reading Opportunities

The following novels explore the world of monsters, magic and mayhem set in the time when Britain moved from legend to history.

Suggested Titles

Grendel
John Gardner

Once again we meet Beowulf's foe, but this time we get the story from Grendel's point of view. This retelling of the epic poem begins with the monster attacking Hrothgar's meadhall and men, and ends right after his fight with Beowulf, as Grendel is about to die. *Grendel* is a funny, intriguing, and ultimately touching examination of the way we look at monsters, heroes, and the world we create with both.

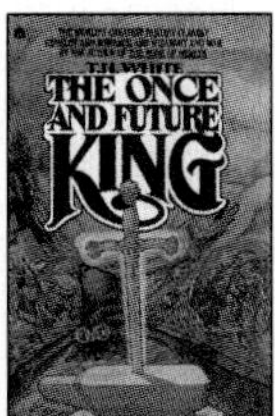

The Once and Future King
T. H. White

This novel is a magical retelling of the legend of King Arthur, from the adventure-filled days of Arthur's youth, to the golden age of Camelot, to the final scene in which the old, broken king lies alone on the battlefield at Salisbury. In this unforgettable tale, the characters of legend step out of the book's pages and into your life as they experience the wonders and horrors of magic, suffer victory and defeat in battle, and grapple with matters of love, betrayal, and honor.

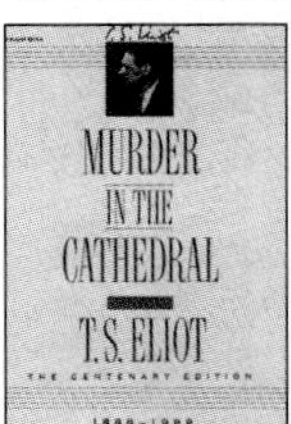

Murder in the Cathedral
T. S. Eliot

This play is a dramatization of the inner struggle of a saint, Thomas à Becket, Archbishop of Canterbury. The first part of the drama provides insight into Becket's struggle to keep faith with his ideals. In the third part of the play, Becket chooses martyrdom when he refuses to take the opportunity to escape from his murderers. The four knights who have murdered Becket then directly address the audience in an attempt to justify their act.

Other Possibilities

British

Ivanhoe	Sir Walter Scott
The Mists of Avalon	Marion Zimmer Bradley
The Lord of the Rings	J.R.R. Tolkien

Planning Students' Extended Reading

The following works extend students' understanding of the theme "From Legend to History." The following information will help you decide which works to assign.

Customize for *Varying Student Needs and Interests*

This information will give you a better idea of which works would best suit your students needs and interests.

- Students should read *Beowulf* before reading the monster's version of events in *Grendel.*
- Both *Grendel* and *The Once and Future King* are high-interest novels that will appeal to most students.
- *Murder in the Cathedral* is a more difficult work. It is best if students have some historical background on the murder of Thomas à Becket, Archbishop of Canterbury. (Some of this information can be found in the Introduction for Unit 1 beginning on page 2.) You might prepare some focus questions for students before they read. These questions should help them identify main points in the play.

Sensitive Issues Each of these works is true to its medieval setting in which fighting, murder, and death were part of life. You may want to use caution in recommending these works due to the inclusion of violent episodes. *The Once and Future King,* being based on the legends of King Arthur, also includes strong language, inappropriate relationships, and magic. On the other hand, it is an excellent novel to help students delve further into the legends of Arthur based on Malory's work.

Resources for Teaching Novels, Plays, and Literature Collections This booklet contains graphic organizers, teaching strategies, and transparencies that will be invaluable in teaching any of these novels.

Planning Instruction and Assessment

Unit Objectives

1. To read selections from the English Renaissance, including the work of William Shakespeare
2. To apply a variety of reading strategies, particularly strategies for reading poetry, appropriate for reading these selections
3. To recognize literary elements used in these selections
4. To build vocabulary in context
5. To learn elements of grammar usage, and style.
6. To write in a variety of modes and about situations based on the selections
7. To develop speaking and listening skills by completing proposed activities

Meeting the Objectives

With each selection, you will find instructional material and portfolio opportunities through which students can meet these objectives. Further, you will find additional practice pages for reading strategies, literary elements, vocabulary, and grammar in the ***Selection Support*** booklet in the Teaching Resources box.

Setting Goals Work with your students at the beginning of the unit to set goals for unit outcomes. Plan what skills and concepts you wish students to acquire. You may individualize these according to students' performance levels or learning modalities.

Portfolios You may have students keep portfolios of their work or of their work in progress. The activities and prompts on the Build Your Portfolio page of each selection provide opportunities for students to apply the concepts presented with the selection.

Wedding Celebration at Bermondsey, England, Joris Hoefnagel

Humanities: Art

Wedding Celebration at Bermondsey, England, c. 1600, by Joris Hoefnagel.

Elizabethans enjoyed weddings so much that Shakespeare included a wedding celebration in most of his comedies, complete with the music-wand dancing that is shown here. The people in the foreground of this painting appear to be servants. Their clothing contrasts with the more formal dress of the group on the right. One explanation for the presence of servants is that the party has been going on for a while, long enough for the servants to join in the celebration.

Have your students link the art to the focus of Unit 2, Celebrating Humanity, by answering the following questions:

1. Weddings celebrate many things: romantic love, family ties, and hope for the future. How does this painting show that weddings also are reasons for the larger community to celebrate? *The painting shows this by including what appear to be different social classes, as well as the buildings of the community—other houses, streets, and the church.*
2. Describe the mood of this painting and find three details that contribute to it. *Students may say that the painting has a joyous mood, citing details like the dancing figures, the musicians, the couples, and the landscape.*

UNIT 2

Celebrating Humanity (1485–1625)

What a piece of work is man! How noble in reason! how infinite in faculty! in form, in moving, how express and admirable! in action how like an angel!

—William Shakespeare, from *Hamlet*

Assessing Student Progress

The following tools are available to measure the degree to which students meet the unit objectives:

Informal Assessment

The questions in the Guide for Responding sections are a first level of response to the concepts and skills presented with the selection. Students' responses are a brief informal measure of their grasp of the material. Their responses on this level can indicate where further instruction and practice are needed. You may then follow up with the practice pages in the ***Selection Support*** booklet.

You will find literature and reading guides in the ***Alternative Assessment*** booklet, which you may give students on an individual basis for informal assessment of their performance.

Formal Assessment

In the ***Formal Assessment*** booklet, you will find selection tests and part tests.

Selection Tests The selection tests measure comprehension and skills acquisition for each selection or group of selections.

Part Tests Each part test, which calls on students to read a passage of literature they have not previously seen, applies the unit skills on a broader level. The Critical Reading section measures Unit Objectives 1, 2, and 3. The Vocabulary and Grammar section measures Objectives 4 and 5. The Essay section measures Objectives 1 and 6. Both the Critical Reading and Vocabulary and Grammar sections use formats similar to those found on many standardized tests, including the SAT.

Alternative Assessment

Portfolios As you review individual pieces or the collected work in students' portfolios, you will find assessment sheets available in the portfolio section of the ***Alternative Assessment*** booklet.

Scoring Rubrics You will find scoring rubrics for writing modes in the ***Alternative Assessment*** booklet. You can apply these to Writing Mini-Lessons and to Writing Process Workshop lessons.

Speaking and Listening The ***Alternative Assessment*** booklet contains assessment sheets for speaking and listening activities.

Learning Modalities The ***Alternative Assessment*** booklet contains activities that appeal to different learning styles. You may use these as an alternative assessment of students' growth.

Using the Timeline

The Timeline can serve a number of instructional purposes, as follows:

Getting an Overview Use the Timeline to help students get a quick overview of themes and events of the period. This approach will benefit all students but may be especially helpful for visually oriented students, English language learners, and those less proficient in reading. (For strategies in using the Timeline as an overview, see the bottom of this page.)

Thinking Critically Questions are provided on the facing page. Use these questions to have students review the events, discuss their significance, and examine the *so what* behind the *what happened.*

Connecting to Selections Have students refer to the Timeline when reading individual selections. By consulting the Timeline regularly, they will gain a better sense of the period's chronology. In addition, they will appreciate what was occurring in the world that gave rise to these works of literature.

Projects Students can use the Timeline as a launching pad for projects like these:

- **Customized Timeline** Have students create a period timeline in their notebooks, adding key dates as they read new selections. They can use dates from this Timeline as a starting framework. If they wish, they can create a specialized timeline for political, scientific, or artistic developments.
- **Report on an Illustration** Have students scan the Timeline for a visual that interests them, research the story behind the picture, and report on their findings to the class.

Timeline
1485–1625

1485 | 1520 | 1550

British Events

- **c. 1500** *Everyman* first performed.
- **1512** First masque performed.
- **1516 Thomas More** publishes *Utopia.*
- **1520** Bowling becomes popular in London.
- **1534** Henry VIII issues Act of Supremacy. ▲
- **1534** Church of England established.
- **1535 Thomas More** executed. ◀
- **1541** John Knox leads Calvinist reformation in Scotland.
- **1547** Henry VIII dies.
- **1549** The *Book of Common Prayer* issued.
- **1558 Elizabeth I** becomes queen. ▶
- **1560** Thomas Tallis publishes English cathedral music.
- **1563** More than 20,000 Londoners die in plague.
- **1564 William Shakespeare** born. ▼

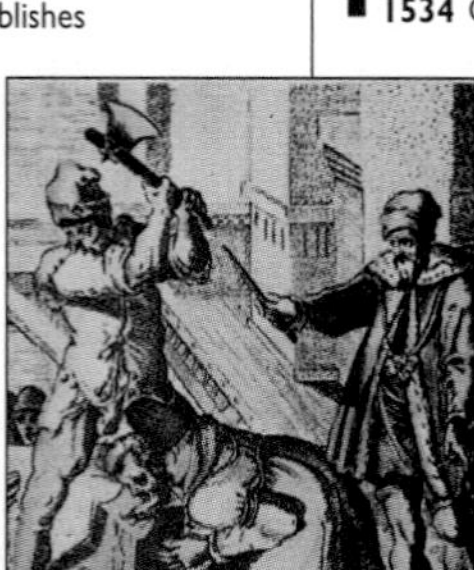

World Events

- **1492** Columbus lands in Western Hemisphere.
- **1497** North America: John Cabot explores northeastern coast.
- **1497** Africa: Vasco da Gama rounds Cape of Good Hope.
- **1503** Italy: Leonardo da Vinci paints *Mona Lisa.* ▲
- **1509** Italy: Michelangelo paints ceiling of Sistine Chapel.
- **1513** North America: Ponce de León explores Florida.
- **1518** Africa: Algiers and Tunisia founded.
- **1519–22** Magellan sails around the world.
- **1521** Italy: Pope Leo X excommunicates Martin Luther.
- **1530** Poland: Copernicus completes treatise on astronomy.
- **1532** Peru: Pizarro conquers Incas. ▶
- **1532** France: Rabelais publishes *Gargantua and Pantagruel,* Book I.
- **1534** Spain: St. Ignatius Loyola founds Jesuit brotherhood.
- **1554** Italy: Cellini completes bronze statue of Perseus.
- **1556** India: Akbar the Great comes to power.
- **1565** Malta: Knights of St. John fight off Turkish invasion.
- **1566** Belgium: Bruegel paints *The Wedding Dance.*
- **1567** South America: 2 million Indians die of typhoid.
- **1567** Brazil: Rio de Janeiro founded by Portuguese.

Getting an Overview of the Period

Introduction To give students an overview of the period, indicate the span of dates in the upper left-hand corner. How much time is covered in this unit? *A period of 140 years is covered.* Next, point out that the Timeline is divided into specifically British Events (on top) and World Events (on bottom). Have them practice scanning the Timeline across, looking both at the British Events and the World Events. Finally, point out that the events in the Timeline often represent beginnings, turning points, and endings (For example, 1558 marks the start of Elizabeth I's reign.).

Key Events Have students identify key political events. *In 1534, the Church of England was established; in 1588, the Spanish Armada was defeated.* Then have them find events suggesting a new cultural excitement and confidence in humanity. *In 1576, Drake circumnavigated the earth; in 1599, the Globe theater opened; in 1623, the first patent laws were passed.* Finally, ask students what these events suggest about England's new place in the world. *England's religious split from Rome, New World explorations, and victory over Spain suggest that it has become a world power.*

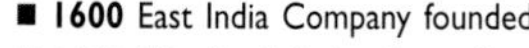

1570 | 1600 | 1610 | 1625

British Events

- **1580** Francis Drake returns from circumnavigating the globe.
- **c. 1582 Sir Philip Sidney** writes *Astrophel and Stella.*
- **1587** Mary, Queen of Scots, executed.
- **1588** English navy defeats Spanish Armada. ▼

- **1590 Edmund Spenser** publishes *The Faerie Queene*, Part I.
- **1594 Shakespeare** writes *Romeo and Juliet.* ▶
- **1599** Globe theater opens.

- **1600** East India Company founded.
- **1603 Elizabeth I** dies; James I becomes king.
- **1605 Shakespeare's** *Macbeth* first performed.
- **1606** Guy Fawkes executed for gun powder plot.
- **1611** King James Bible published. ▼
- **1620** Francis Bacon publishes *Novum Organum*.
- **1623** First patent laws passed.
- **1625** James I dies.

World Events

- **1580** France: Montaigne's *Essays* published.
- **1582** Italy: Pope Gregory XIII introduces new calendar. ▼
- **1595** South America: Sir Walter Raleigh explores Orinoco River.

- **1605** Spain: Cervantes publishes Part I of *Don Quixote.*
- **1607** North America: British colony established at Jamestown.
- **1608** North America: French colony of Quebec established.
- **1609** Italy: Galileo builds first telescope. ▶

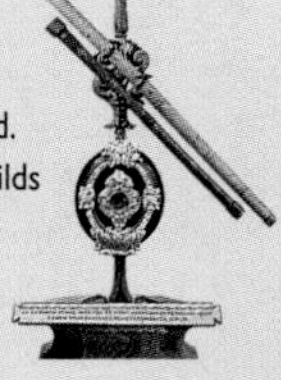

- **1618** Germany: Kepler proposes laws of planetary motion.
- **1620** North America: Pilgrims land at Plymouth Rock. ▼

▶Critical Viewing◀

1. Describe the expression on the Mona Lisa's face (1503). How successfully does it convey the sense that she is a living, individual person? **[Evaluate]** *Her smile is enigmatic and suggests an inner life, which gives a strong sense of her individuality.*
2. (a) How does the artist impress upon us Elizabeth I's power (1558)? (b) Does the overall impression make her seem inhuman? Explain. **[Interpret]** *(a) By showing her in rich clothing, her arms held confidently, the artist stresses her power. (b) Her face is distinctive, preserving a sense of her personality.*
3. Speculate about the design of the antique telescope (1609). (a) Why is it mounted on a spherical support? (b) Why are there two tubes? **[Speculate]** *Possible Response: (a) the "globe" allows the user to track accurately the direction in which the telescope is pointed; (b) one tube is a finder, showing a greater area under less magnification than the other.*
4. What devices do the designers of this edition of the Bible (1611) use to create an effect of seriousness and respect? **[Speculate]** *The title appears set back in a shrine-like space; the bearded figures convey seriousness; the scribe (lower right) appears to expect inspiration.*

◆Critical Thinking

1. (a) What two important religious works were published during this period? (b) What connections might there be between these publications and the creation of the Church of England (1534)? **[Connect]** *(a) The Book of Common Prayer appeared in 1549; the King James Bible appeared in 1611.*
   (b) These books helped establish the authority of the Church of England following its break with the Pope.
2. (a) Name two seafaring exploits during this period. (b) What do these exploits suggest about seafaring and navigation during the period? **[Hypothesize]** *(a) Seafaring exploits include the expeditions of Francis Drake (1576), Vasco da Gama (1497), and Magellan (1519–1522). (b) These exploits indicate that seafaring and navigation had recently reached a new level of proficiency.*
3. (a) Name two disasters, one in Britain and one in the world, that occurred in the period 1550–1570. (b) What do these events suggest about medical science? **[Infer]** *(a) In 1563, more than 20,000 Londoners died in the plague. In 1567, two million Indians died of typhoid in South America. (b) These events suggest that medical science was not very advanced.*
4. (a) Name two events that indicate British presence in the New World. (b) What do these events suggest about the importance of overseas trade to Britain? **[Infer]** *(a) Suggested Answers: the establishment of the East India Company in 1600, Raleigh's explorations in South America (1595), and the establishment of Jamestown (1607). (b) These events indicate Britain's commercial interest in the New World.*
5. Compare the British people who are named in the Timeline for Unit 1 (pages 2 and 3) with the people who are named in this Timeline. (a) What role predominates among those in the earlier Timeline? What new roles appear in this Timeline? (b) What does your comparison suggest about the changing concept of the individual? **[Draw Conclusions]** *(a) Most people named before 1485 are kings. After 1485, explorers, reformers, poets, playwrights, and music compilers are also named. (b) This suggests that later society granted fame and glory for individual achievements in a variety of fields.*

Develop Understanding

Customize for
Less Proficient Readers
Ask students what they know about the colonization of America. Then explain that the period covered in this unit marked the beginnings of European colonization of the Americas. Ask students to look for the "British side" of this story as they read.

Customize for
English Language Learners
Have these students look over A Graphic Look at the Period, then come up with three words they associate somehow with the pictures. Then ask them to see if they can find these words or related ideas in The Story of the Times.

Customize for
Interpersonal Learners
Students with an interpersonal orientation will benefit by discussing the personal dimension of historical events. For example, you might introduce the problems created by Henry VIII's sonless marriage and ask what responsibilities marriage carries for royalty.

Customize for
More Advanced Students
Challenge more advanced students to use A Graphic Look at the Period and The Story of the Times to come up with similarities and differences between trends in the English Renaissance and in modern times.

Answers to
A Graphic Look

Infer The text on the hornbook is the Lord's Prayer, suggesting that religion was an important part of education.

A Graphic Look at the Period

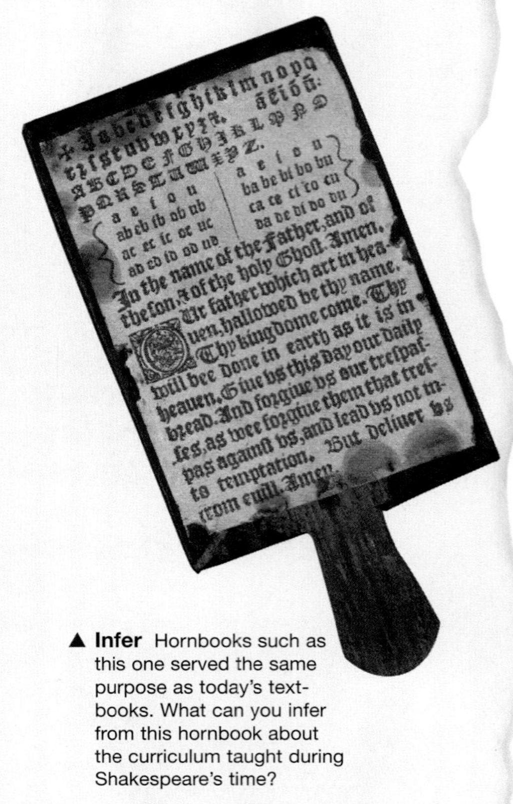

▲ **Infer** Hornbooks such as this one served the same purpose as today's textbooks. What can you infer from this hornbook about the curriculum taught during Shakespeare's time?

The Story of the Times
(1485–1625)

Historical Background

The ending of the Wars of the Roses and the founding of the Tudor dynasty in 1485 opened a new era in English life. Monarchs assured stability by increasing their own power and undercutting the strength of the nobles. At the same time, they dramatically changed England's religious practices and helped to transform England from a small nation into one of the world's great powers.

The Tudors The first Tudor monarch, Henry VII, inherited an England that had been depleted and exhausted by years of civil war. By the time he died in 1509, he had rebuilt the nation's treasury and established law and order. In doing so, he had restored the prestige of the monarchy and had set the stage for his successors.

Henry VII was succeeded by his handsome and athletic son, Henry VIII. Like his father, Henry VIII was a practicing Catholic. He even wrote a book against Martin Luther, for which a grateful Pope granted him the title "Defender of the Faith."

Henry VIII's good relationship with the Pope did not last, however. Because his marriage with Catherine of Aragon had not produced a son, Henry tried to obtain an annulment from the Pope so that he could marry Anne Boleyn. When the Pope refused, Henry remarried anyway. This defiance of papal authority led to an open break with the Roman Catholic Church. Henry seized the Catholic Church's English property and dissolved the powerful monasteries. He even had his former friend and leading advisor, Thomas More, executed because More had refused to renounce his faith.

Henry married six times in all. His first two marriages produced two daughters, Mary and Elizabeth. His third wife, Jane Seymour, bore a son, Edward, who was but a frail child when Henry died in 1547.

Cross-Curricular Connection: Social Studies

The English Reformation Explain to students that the sixteenth-century desire to reform Christian institutions had deep roots. In the 1300's, power struggles and corruption in the Church and the anxieties of the plague encouraged people to look for new inspiration. John Wycliffe argued that the Bible, not the Pope, was the true authority in religious matters. Later, in Germany, Martin Luther attacked the Church's practice of promising salvation for donations. Only faith, he argued, not works, could save souls.

In Henry VIII's England, such radical ideas had won favor even among the respectable. When the Pope, afraid to offend Henry VIII's wife's powerful relatives (Catherine of Aragon was the daughter of Spanish monarchs), denied Henry's request for an annulment, the stage had already been set. Henry took control of the Church of England.

While the Reformation in Europe led to rebellion and prolonged wars, Protestantism took hold in England in a temperate way. Henry left much Church doctrine intact.

In the Reformation, a single undisputed authority was replaced by competing ideas of truth. Ask students to speculate about the long-term effects of this new climate. *The Reformation prompted questions of where to turn for truth. This new climate might cause more sects or splinter groups to form.*

Religious Turmoil Henry VIII's son, Edward VI, became king at the age of nine and died at the age of fifteen. During his brief reign, a series of parliamentary acts dramatically changed the nation's religious practices. English replaced Latin in church ritual, and the Anglican prayer book, the *Book of Common Prayer*, became required in public worship. By Edward's death in 1553, England was well on its way to becoming a Protestant nation.

Roman Catholicism made a turbulent comeback, however, when Edward's half-sister Mary took the throne. Mary I was Catholic, and she restored Roman practices to the Church of England. She also restored the authority of the Pope over the English Church. Ordering the execution of nearly 300 Protestants, Mary I earned the nickname "Bloody Mary" and strengthened anti-Catholic sentiment within England.

Elizabeth I When Mary I died after a five-year reign, her half-sister, Elizabeth I, came to the throne. Strong and clever, Elizabeth was probably England's ablest monarch since William the Conqueror. She had received a Renaissance education and read widely in the Greek and Latin classics. Becoming a great patron of the arts, she gathered around her the best writers of her day.

Elizabeth also put an end to the religious turmoil that had existed during Mary I's reign. She reestablished the monarch's supremacy in the Church of England, restored the *Book of Common Prayer*, and instituted a policy of religious moderation that enjoyed great popular support, although it failed to please many devout Catholics and Protestants.

Elizabeth's one outstanding problem was her Catholic cousin Mary Stuart, queen of Scotland by birth and next in line for the throne of England. Because Catholics did not recognize Henry VIII's marriage to Elizabeth's mother, Anne Boleyn, they considered Mary Stuart the queen of England. Imprisoned by Elizabeth for nineteen years, Mary instigated numerous Catholic plots against Elizabeth. Following the advice of her advisors, Elizabeth stepped up punishment of the Catholics but let her royal cousin live. Finally, Parliament insisted on Mary's execution. Mary was beheaded in 1587, a Catholic martyr.

▲ **Draw Conclusions** This painting depicts a noble family at dinner. From this scene, what conclusions can you draw about family life during the Renaissance?

◄ **Hypothesize** These gold coins were minted during the reigns of Henry VIII and Elizabeth I. Hypothesize about the types of things an Elizabethan might have bought with these coins.

Answers to

A GRAPHIC LOOK

Draw Conclusions The family pictured is large compared to the average American family. In addition to the mother, another woman is present, suggesting that noble mothers had help rearing their children. The children appear to be eating at their own table, separate from the adults.

Hypothesize Possible answer: One of these coins might have bought a supply of food, clothing, or a stay in an inn. (Presumably, money went far in the past, and gold coins could buy much more than smaller denominations.)

Art Transparency Use Art Transparency 5, *The Tower of London With London Bridge Behind,* to give students a sense of England's capital city at the beginning of this period. Students will be able to observe the bustling energy that indicates the nation's feeling of confidence and pride.

Connections to the Literature

- Students will gain greater insight into the conflict between Henry VIII and his leading advisor, Thomas More, as they read the excerpt from More's *Utopia,* p. 238, and the excerpt from Robert Bolt's screenplay, *A Man for All Seasons,* p. 253.
- Queen Elizabeth I's strength and cleverness are evident in her stirring "Speech Before Defeating the Spanish Armada," p. 240.
- As they read work by Edmund Spenser, p. 209; Sir Philip Sidney, p. 212; Christopher Marlowe, p. 217; Sir Walter Raleigh, p. 217; and William Shakespeare, pp. 220 and 272, students will better understand why Elizabeth I was regarded as "a great patron of the arts."

Humanities: Literature

The Book of Common Prayer.

Explain to students that *The Book of Common Prayer,* published in 1549, was a radical departure from the past and would influence English literature in times to come. The new Church of England needed standard texts for prayers and services. The Archbishop of Canterbury, Thomas Cranmer, prepared these texts—in English. The solemn Latin of Catholic Church services had been replaced by the plain, everyday speech of England.

The *Book of Common Prayer* was revised in ensuing years to help smooth over disputes between religious factions. In the meantime, the English language had found a new power: in a simple, serious style, it now embodied people's devotions. Along with the King James Bible (1611), *The Book of Common Prayer* gave writers of future generations a new sense of the weight of their own language.

If students have access to *The Book of Common Prayer*, you might have them analyze its style and present their results to the class. They might focus on memorable phrases, reciting them aloud for the class to demonstrate the new interest in English that the *Book* represents.

Historical Background

Comprehension Check

1. What condition was England in when Henry VII became king? *England had been exhausted by years of civil war.*
2. (a) Over what did Henry VIII quarrel with the Pope? (b) What did Henry do as a result? *(a) They quarreled over the annulment of Henry's marriage to Catherine of Aragon. (b) Henry declared himself, not the Pope, the supreme ruler of the Church of England.*
3. How did Elizabeth I address England's religious difficulties? (b) For what is her rule remembered? *(a) Elizabeth I returned England to Protestantism, but kept a policy of moderation in religion. (b) She is remembered for her strong, tactful rule and her patronage of literature.*
4. What internal conflict marked England during the reign of James I? *James I often quarreled with Parliament over taxes and foreign wars.*
5. (a) To what civilization did Renaissance artists and thinkers turn for inspiration? (b) What culture did they reject? *(a) The artists and thinkers of the Renaissance turned to ancient Greece and Rome for inspiration. (b) They rejected the Middle Ages, dubbing it as the "Dark Ages."*

Critical Thinking

1. How does Henry VIII's desire to re-marry demonstrate the political significance of a monarch's marriage? **[Analyze]** *Henry VIII wanted to re-marry so that he could have a son, presumably to provide England with a ruler.*
2. Mary Stuart, Queen of Scots, plotted against Elizabeth I. Why did Elizabeth I keep her in prison instead of executing her right away? **[Infer]** *Elizabeth I probably thought that Mary's execution would inflame Catholics and lead to civil unrest.*
3. (a) James I was perhaps the first monarch to insist on a "divine right" to rule. Explain how his claim suggests that the monarchy had become weak. (b) What other fact from his reign supports this hypothesis? **[Support]** *(a) The claim suggests that the monarchy was under challenge. (b) The fact that he quarreled with Parliament over taxes and foreign wars suggests that his power was limited by Parliament.*

▲ **Infer** This armor belonged to King Henry VIII. Why do you think medieval ideals of chivalry—associated with such armor—inspired some Elizabethan poets?

▲ **Infer** This picture dates from the nineteenth century, but it portrays the type of pastoral scene that appealed to many Elizabethan poets. Why do you think the lives of shepherds and shepherdesses like these interested court poets?

Stuarts and Puritans The English Renaissance continued after Elizabeth died in 1603, although a new dynasty—the Stuarts—came to the throne of England. Determined to avoid a dispute over the throne and a return of civil strife, Elizabeth named King James VI of Scotland as her successor. James's claim to England's throne rested on his descent from King Henry VII through his mother, Mary Stuart, Elizabeth's old antagonist. Unlike Mary, however, James was a Protestant.

The years of James I's reign are sometimes described as the Jacobean era, from *Jacobus*, the Latin word for James. Like his predecessor, James I was a strong supporter of the arts. He also took measures to further England's position as a world power, sponsoring the establishment of England's first successful American colony—Jamestown, Virginia.

During his reign, however, James and Parliament struggled for power, a conflict that would later erupt into war. Guided by the idea of the "divine right of kings," James I often treated Parliament with contempt, and they quarreled over taxes and foreign wars. James I also persecuted the Puritans, who were strongly represented in the House of Commons. Prompted by James's religious intolerance, a group of Puritans migrated to America and established the Plymouth Colony in 1620.

Philosophy One of the most exciting periods in history, the Renaissance was both a worldly and a religious age. It blossomed first in the Italian city-states (1350–1550), where commerce and a wealthy middle class supported learning and the arts. Slowly, Renaissance ideas spread northward, making possible the English Renaissance (1485–1625). During the Renaissance, scholars reacted against what they saw as the "dark ages" of medieval Europe and revived the learning of ancient Greece and Rome. They thought they were bringing about a rebirth of civilization.

The Age of Exploration The Renaissance thirst for knowledge prompted a great burst of exploration by sea. Navigators ventured far and wide, aided by the development of the compass and by advances in astronomy, which freed them from the need to cling to the shores of the Atlantic.

Humanities: Music

Madrigals

One of the distinctive musical forms of the English Renaissance, madrigals originated in Italy in the fourteenth century. They are songs composed for a number of voices, each carrying its own melody, and often unaccompanied by instruments.

Madrigal composers usually used secular texts, such as Petrarch's sonnets. They considered English sonnets too complex, favoring simpler verse with liberal helpings of *fa-la-la*'s. Often, their subject was pastoral, featuring the "merry lads" and "bonny lasses" of an idealized countryside.

Play Thomas Morley's 1595 madrigal, "Now is the Month of Maying," from the **Listening to Music** Audio CD. Then ask these questions:

1. How does the harmony of the voices reflect the text? *The complicated harmonies, like the text, suggest a world in which "all the pieces fit."*
2. What events of the times might have promoted the spirit reflected in this music? *Possible answers include: Elizabeth's easing of religious turmoil; the success of English explorers; the renewal of creativity in the arts.*

Their explorations culminated in Columbus's arrival in the Western Hemisphere in 1492.

England's participation in the Age of Exploration began in 1497, when the Italian-born explorer John Cabot, sailing for an English company, reached Newfoundland (an island off the east coast of what is now Canada) and perhaps also the mainland. Cabot thus laid the basis for future English claims in North America.

Religion A growing sense of nationalism along with the Renaissance spirit led many Europeans to question the authority of the Roman Catholic Church. Many people had grievances against the Church. Some felt that Church officials were corrupt; others questioned Church teachings and hierarchy.

The great Dutch scholar Desiderius Erasmus's (1466–1536) edition of the New Testament raised serious questions about standard interpretations of the Bible. Through his friendship with such English writers as Thomas More (1478–1535), Erasmus focused attention on issues of morality and religion, which continued as central concerns of the English Renaissance.

Although Erasmus himself remained a Roman Catholic, he helped to pave the way for a split in the Church that began in 1517, when a German monk named Martin Luther (1483–1546) nailed a list of dissenting beliefs to the door of a German church. Luther's protest resulted in dividing the Church and introducing a new Christian denomination known as Lutheranism. The process that Luther started has come to be called the Protestant Reformation.

Literature of the Period

Like painting and sculpture, literature expressed the attitudes of the Renaissance. Narratives, poetry, dramas, and comedies reflected the ideas of the times. They also provided a forum for subtle and satirical criticisms of social institutions such as the monarchy and the Church.

Elizabethan Poetry During the reign of Elizabeth I, English literature came of age. The most significant literary developments came in the area of poetry. Favoring lyric poetry, rather than the narrative poems favored by their medieval predecessors, the Elizabethan poets perfected

▲ **Speculate** These portraits show Queen Elizabeth and Sir Walter Raleigh dressed in elaborate fashions. Speculate about the types of lives led by the people who could afford these clothes.

Answers to

A GRAPHIC LOOK

(from page 200)

Infer Suggested answer: For Renaissance poets, the ways of people in the past had the charm of distance. Chivalry is also an attractive subject, because of the simple and pure ideas of romantic love and valor it embodies.

Infer Suggested answer: The simple lives of shepherds offered a contrast to the busy intrigues of the court.

(from page 201)

Speculate Possible answer: People who wore such clothes must have attended occasions at which display counted for a great deal—the clothing is not designed for comfort or ease of movement. Their wealth probably brought a householdful of servants; they probably did not do work themselves.

More About the Reformation

Fueled by political discontent, the Protestant Reformation swept through much of Europe. It led to frequent wars between European nations whose rulers had opposing religious beliefs. Protestants and Catholics both suffered persecution, depending on where they happened to live and which religion their ruler supported. Protestants themselves were divided, and in Germany the followers of Luther (called Lutherans) persecuted the followers of another Protestant reformer, John Calvin of Geneva. Calvin's ideas (called Calvinism) found a foothold in Switzerland, England, and Scotland, however, and helped bring about the establishment of the Puritan and Presbyterian sects.

Connections to the Literature

- If the Italian Renaissance paved the way for the English Renaissance, the Italian poet Petrarch's use of the sonnet paved the way for the Elizabethan sonnet craze. Students can read the sonnets of Spenser, p. 209; Sir Philip Sidney, p. 212; and Shakespeare, p. 220.
- In reading *Macbeth*, p. 272, students will encounter Shakespeare's flattery of James I.

Humanities: Perfoming Arts

Masques

The life of the court was marked by elaborate courtesy, wit, and finery. This culture of display reached its height in the masque.

Explain to students that a masque was a courtly entertainment in which masked, costumed actors used verse, dance, and music to present characters such as Greek gods or shepherds. Intended for one performance, masques nonetheless involved elaborate stage sets and complicated machinery. Masques were presented at social gatherings, such as weddings. Actors entered in procession, introduced their characters, then mingled with the guests. They exited after a farewell scene.

Elizabeth I helped settle questions about the fitness of women to rule by cultivating an image as the Virgin Queen. The masques presented at her court confirmed and celebrated this image.

Ask students to give examples of semi-theatrical events in modern American politics. *Example answer: The President lights the White House Christmas tree.* For an extended project, students can plan and perform a masque of their own, using thematically linked character types.

Literature of the Period

Check Your Comprehension

1. What type of poetry did Renaissance writers favor? *Renaissance writers favored lyric poetry.*
2. What poetic form was of particular significance during the period? *The sonnet and the sonnet cycle were particularly popular during the time.*
3. What is a sonnet cycle? *A sonnet cycle is a series of sonnets that fit loosely together to form a story.*
4. Who was the first major dramatist of the time? *Christopher Marlowe was the period's first major playwright.*
5. What body of work from the period has had the greatest influence? *Shakespeare's plays continue to be highly valued.*
6. What was the central prose achievement of the period? *The central prose achievement of the period was the King James translation of the Bible into English.*

Critical Thinking

1. Lyric poems were more popular during the Renaissance than narrative poetry. From this fact, what can you deduce about the audience for poetry? **[Deduce]** *Possible answers include: Poetry's audience had become more sophisticated, since they were interested in nuances of feeling or description rather than in the presentation of action.*
2. What evidence can you give that English writers were not just imitating, but were expanding upon Renaissance Italian influences? **[Support]** *Shakespeare adapted the form of the Italian sonnet by changing its rhyme scheme and stanza structure.*
3. Name two major prose works of the period, and explain how each reflects developments of the time. **[Connect]** *Possible answers: The King James Bible reflects the growing concern with matters of religious authority; Sir Francis Bacon's* Novum Organum, *a comprehensive work on knowledge, shows the period's new spirit of enquiry.*

▲ **Speculate** Doctors could do little to stop epidemics of smallpox, measles, influenza, and yellow fever which regularly swept through cities and towns, killing thousands. Study this picture and speculate about the measures taken in epidemics: (a) Why has the door been padlocked? (b) Why is a fire burning before the house?

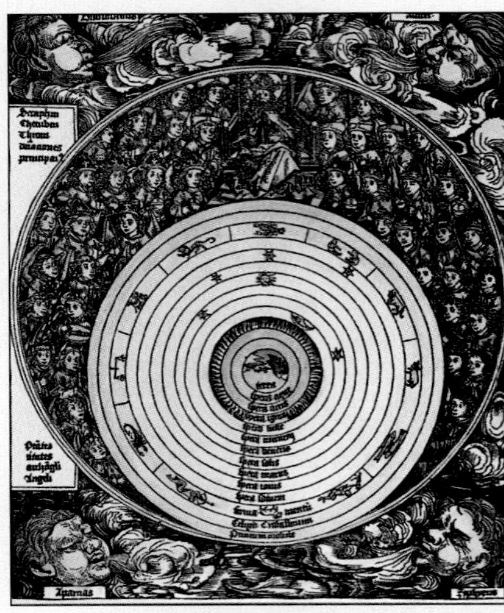

▲ **Compare and Contrast** Ptolemy was an astronomer and mathematician who lived in the second century A.D. Renaissance thinkers believed in his model of the universe with the Earth at the center. Compare and contrast this view of the universe with our view of the universe today.

the sonnet and began experimenting with other poetic forms.

One of the most popular literary forms during the Elizabethan Age was the sonnet cycle, a series of sonnets that fit loosely together to form a story. The first of the great Elizabethan sonnet cycles was *Astrophel and Stella* by Sir Philip Sidney. Sidney also helped to adapt classical verse forms to fit the English language.

Another major Elizabethan poet was Edmund Spenser, who wrote intricate verse filled with rich imagery. His sonnet cycle *Amoretti* is unique for being addressed to the poet's wife.

The brilliant lyric poet William Shakespeare brought the Elizabethan sonnet to new heights. Shakespeare changed the pattern and rhyme scheme of the Petrarchan, or Italian, sonnet, employing a form now known as the English, or Shakespearean, sonnet.

Elizabethan Drama During the Elizabethan Age, playwrights turned away from religious subjects and began writing more complex and sophisticated plays. Drawing upon the classical models of ancient Greece and Rome, playwrights reintroduced tragedies and dramas.

Also a leading poet, Christopher Marlowe became the first major Elizabethan dramatist in the 1580's, writing such plays as *Tamburlaine the Great* and *The Tragical History of Doctor Faustus*. Had Marlowe lived past the age of thirty, he might well have rivaled Shakespeare as England's greatest playwright.

Shakespeare began his involvement with the theater as an actor. By 1592, he was a popular playwright, his works having been performed even at Elizabeth I's court. Shakespeare wrote thirty-seven plays, among them many of the greatest dramas of all time. Filled with powerful and beautiful language, his works display his deep understanding of human nature. Because of their eloquent language and depth, Shakespeare's plays have retained their popularity for centuries. The seventeenth-century writer Ben Jonson said of Shakespeare, "He was not of an age but for all time."

Cross-Curricular Connection: Science

Renaissance Science Explain to students that Renaissance science, like much of Renaissance painting, was born of a new thirst for observation. Yet at the same time, the claims of ancient authorities on people's belief were strong.

The bold explorers of the time had already shaken one Ptolemaic theory: They had discovered a new continent in the West. In 1543, the Polish astronomer Nicolaus Copernicus dealt Ptolemy another blow—the earth, he said, went around the sun. It would take some time before Copernicus' theory caught on.

Ask students to speculate about other links they can see between the exploration of the world and the science of the time. *Answers may include: Exploration required good tools for navigation, including some that could aid astronomical observation.*

Elizabethan and Jacobean Prose Prose took a back seat to poetry and drama in the English Renaissance. Scholars still preferred to write in Latin, and their English prose had a Latin flavor. Because they used long words and ornate sentences, their work is often difficult to read today.

Several Elizabethan poets also contributed major works of prose. Sir Philip Sidney's *Defence of Poesie* (about 1582) is one of the earliest works of English literary criticism. Thomas Nashe's *The Unfortunate Traveler* (1594), a fictional tale, was a forerunner of the novel. *History of the World*, another important work of prose, was written by Sir Walter Raleigh during his imprisonment in the Tower of London.

Perhaps the leading prose writer of the English Renaissance was Sir Francis Bacon, a high government official under James I. "I have taken all knowledge to be my province," Bacon wrote, and his literary output reflects his scholarship in many fields. *Novum Organum* (1620), his greatest work, made major contributions to natural science and philosophy.

The most monumental prose achievement of the entire English Renaissance is undoubtedly the English translation of the Bible commissioned by King James on the advice of Protestant clergymen. Fifty-four scholars labored for seven years to bring this magnificent work to fruition. The King James Bible, or Authorized Version, is among the most widely quoted and influential works in the English language.

The English Renaissance moved England out of its medieval past and into the modern world. No writers since have surpassed the literary achievements of Shakespeare or the majestic language of the King James Bible. They provide the standard against which all English literature has been judged right down to the present time.

▲ **Infer** The English navy gained supremacy of the sea after defeating the Spanish Armada. Examine this painting and infer the types of war tactics used by the English that may have contributed to their success.

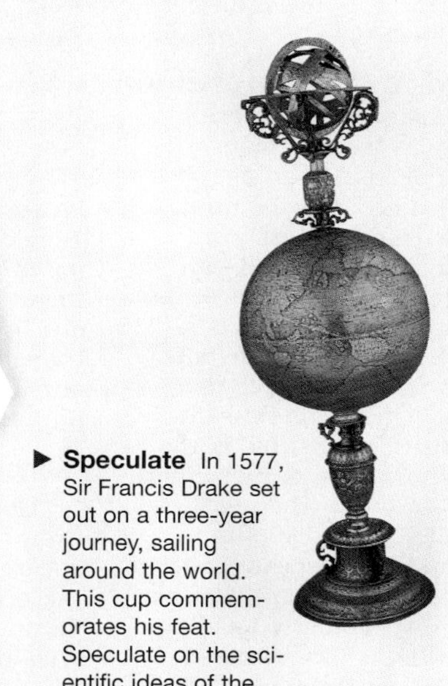

▶ **Speculate** In 1577, Sir Francis Drake set out on a three-year journey, sailing around the world. This cup commemorates his feat. Speculate on the scientific ideas of the time, suggested by the cup.

More About the Spanish Armada
During this period, England supported Protestant Dutch rebels against Catholic Spain, the superpower of the day. Spanish ships returning from the New World loaded with treasure were attacked by English raiders like Sir Francis Drake. Spain finally sent a fleet of 130 battle ships, called the Armada, to invade England in 1588. The smaller, more maneuverable English fleet did well against the ponderous Spanish ships, attacking with cannon and with burning ships filled with gunpowder. Many surviving Spanish ships were wrecked by storms when they fled. England was on its way to ending Spanish naval supremacy.

Answers to A Graphic Look

(from page 202)

Speculate Reasonable answers: (a) The door has been padlocked to prevent people from entering the quarters of a dead or infected person, perhaps to prevent them from stealing, perhaps to prevent them from picking up the disease. (b) The fire burning before the house may have been fueled with compounds that were thought to drive away germs. Perhaps the clothing of the dead is being burned in the hopes of destroying the disease that might linger on it.

Compare and Contrast Modern people believe that the sun, not the Earth, is at the center of the solar system. The whole notion of a "center" of the universe has become problematic (the solar system is near the periphery of the Milky Way). The place and time of the Big Bang is one candidate for such a "center." Judging from the illustration, Ptolemy's universe is limited. Modern scientists hypothesize that the universe is infinite or even that its dimensions are changing.

(from page 203)

Infer The English used explosives or incendiaries in combat; they set ships on fire and sent them towards the enemy fleet.

Speculate People of the time understood that the world was round. They probably divided the world by the Equator and measured position with navigational aids. Their maps were probably more accurate than those of the past.

Activities

1. **Graphic Organization of Events** Give students the Cause and Effect organizer, p. 119, in ***Writing and Language Transparencies.*** Have them use the form to break down one sequence of events described in The Story of the Times.
2. **Monarchs on the Air** Have each of several students assume the identify of a monarch from the The Story of the Times. Then have them appear together on a late-night television discussion show. Have each monarch tell about his or her experiences and discuss with other monarchs the challenges and tribulations of ruling.
3. **Letter From the Future** Ask students to select a figure discussed in The Story of the Times and write a letter to him or her warning of or applauding the future consequences of his or her acts. Students should make an effort to appeal to the values of the person to whom they are writing.
4. **Connect to the Literature** Challenge students to find passages in *Macbeth,* beginning on p. 272, relating to the question of a monarch's authority, its sources, nature, or justification. Then ask them to read these passages aloud to the class and explain how they relate to the career of one of the monarchs in The Story of the Times.

Develop Understanding

◆ Critical Thinking

1. What other factor, besides his innovativeness, might account for the fact that Shakespeare's use of many words was their first appearance in print? *The people of Shakespeare's day may have used some of these words in their speech, but considered them unfit—too ordinary or vulgar—for writing.*
2. Speculate on how the people of Shakespeare's day would have "heard" his style. (Draw evidence from the chart and from the phrases in the Activity.) **[Speculate]** *Some students may speculate that Shakespeare's audience may have found his style difficult to follow because of all the new words he used and his metaphorical style; others may argue that his success proves that his audiences found his style interesting and memorable.*

▶Critical Viewing◀

1. Use the chart to find two very common words introduced by Shakespeare into writing. **[Interpret]** *Possible answers include* bedroom, useless.
2. Use the chart to find two words that Shakespeare probably derived from another language. **[Interpret]** *Possible answers include* assassination, exposure.

Answers to Activities

1. Neither a borrower nor a lender be
2. All the world's a stage.
3. With bated breath
4. Break the ice
5. Come full circle
6. Eaten me out of house and home
7. A foregone conclusion
8. Laugh yourselves into stitches
9. Not budge an inch
10. Too much of a good thing

The Changing English Language

"A Man of Fire—New Words"

by Richard Lederer

The Ageless Bard

Shakespeare's plays, which he wrote in London between approximately 1590 and 1613, have been in almost constant production since their creation. Because the playwright dealt with universal truths and conflicts in human nature, his tragedies, comedies, and history plays continue to draw audiences from all walks of life, just as they did in their own day. Time has proved the truth of what Shakespeare's contemporary, Ben Jonson, said of him: "He was not of an age but for all time."

Word-Maker Supreme

William Shakespeare's words, as well as his works, were not just of an age, but for all time. He was, quite simply, the greatest word maker who ever lived—an often neglected aspect of his genius.

Of the 20,138 different words that Shakespeare employs in his plays, sonnets, and other poems, his is the first known use of more than 1,700 of them. The most verbally innovative of our authors, Shakespeare made up more than 8.5 percent of his written vocabulary. Reading his works is like witnessing the birth of language itself.

"I pitied thee,/Took pains to make thee speak," says Prospero to Caliban in *The Tempest*. "I endow'd thy purposes/With words that made them known." Shakespeare is our Prospero; he dressed our thoughts with words and set our tongue teeming with phrases.

Consider the following list of thirty representative words that, as far as we can tell, Shakespeare was the first to use in writing. So great is his influence on his native tongue that we find it hard to imagine a time when these words did not exist.

aerial	*bedroom*	*critic*	*frugal*
invulnerable	*monumental*	*amazement*	*bump*
dishearten	*generous*	*lapse*	*perusal*
assassination	*castigate*	*dislocate*	*gloomy*
laughable	*pious*	*auspicious*	*countless*
dwindle	*hurry*	*lonely*	*sneak*
baseless	*courtship*	*exposure*	*impartial*
majestic	*useless*		

The striking compound that Shakespeare fashioned to describe Don Adriano de Armando in *Love's Labour's Lost* is an important label for the playwright himself: "a man of fire–new words." No day goes by that we do not speak and hear, and read and write using his legacy.

Activity

Oscar Wilde once quipped, "Now we sit through Shakespeare in order to recognize the quotations." Unrivaled in his invention of words, William Shakespeare is unequaled as a phrasemaker. Complete the following expressions, each of which first saw the light in one of his plays:

1. Neither a _______ nor a _______ be
2. All the world's a _______
3. With bated _______
4. Break the _______
5. Come full _______
6. Eaten me out of house and _______
7. A foregone _______
8. Laugh yourselves into _______
9. Not _______ an inch
10. Too much of a good _______

Cross-Curricular Connection: Science

The Language of Technology Shakespeare flooded our language with new coinages, some invented or derived from other languages. Explain to students that, in our own time, science and technology have become a major source of new words.

From the *sound byte* (a minimal unit of information) to the *fax* (short for *facsimile,* a copy), techno-speak has flooded the language. Traces of technology's influence may also be evident in the brisker, more clipped style of new coinages: *to upgrade,* for instance, or *to impact,* used transitively.

Ask students to give their own examples of techno-speak. *Examples might include: the* red-eye *(an early morning flight);* to e-mail; to crash *(a computer); internal capitalization of trademark names.*

Part 2 The Influence of the Monarchy

King Henry VIII of England, after Hans Holbein

Queen Elizabeth I of England, Unknown Artist

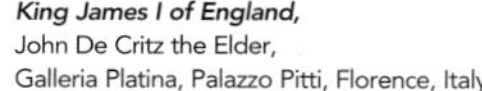

King James I of England, John De Critz the Elder, Galleria Platina, Palazzo Pitti, Florence, Italy

After the Wars of the Roses ended, the Tudors and James I brought a new era to English life. These monarchs increased their own power while undercutting the strength of the nobles. They dramatically changed the country's religious practices and transformed England from a small, insular nation into a world power. As a result, the English people gained a new pride in what Shakespeare called "this earth, this realm, this England."

Humanities: Art

King Henry VIII of England, after Hans Holbein; **Elizabeth I of England,** unknown artist; and **James I of England,** John De Critz the Elder.

These portraits show three monarchs who made their mark on their age and the literature it produced. The elaborate pattern on Henry's clothing is produced by blackwork embroidery, which, ironically, is a style that Catherine of Aragon brought from Spain. The portrait of Elizabeth I shows her in a resplendent costume of gold brocade trimmed lavishly with ermine. James wears white satin trimmed at the collar and cuffs with *punto-in-aria* lace, which is created through a laborious process of embroidery. Like his predecessors, he is richly jeweled.

Use these questions for discussion:

1. Why were royal portraits important? *They allowed people to see what the monarchs looked like, which was important in the days before photography.*
2. Are these portraits completely accurate? What might the artist have changed? *Most students will note that the artist probably glossed over warts, wrinkles, and unpleasant expressions, to show the monarch in the best possible light.*

One-Minute Planning Guide

The selections in this section demonstrate the influence of three British monarchs on the literature of the sixteenth and early seventeenth centuries. Thomas More's *Utopia* was written in response to the excesses of Henry VIII; Robert Bolt's contemporary screenplay *A Man for All Seasons* brings to life the highly charged relationship between More and his king. Elizabeth I's "Speech Before Defeating the Spanish Armada" reveals the public persona of this extremely powerful monarch. A committee appointed by Elizabeth's successor, James I, produced one of the most enduring and influential works of English literature, as shown by the excerpts from the King James Bible.

Customize for Varying Student Needs

When assigning the selections in this part, keep in mind these factors:

From *Utopia*
- Short
- High-level vocabulary may challenge less proficient readers

"Speech Before Defeating the Spanish Armada"
- Short
- Complex and unusual sentence structures may be difficult for English language learners

Psalm 23
- Will be comfortably familiar to many students
- Different Judeo-Christian traditions have different versions of this psalm

from *The Sermon on the Mount*
- May be familiar to many students
- Archaic language may be challenging for English language learners

The Parable of the Prodigal Son
- May be familiar to many students
- English language learners may need assistance with archaic verb forms and pronouns

from *A Man for All Seasons*
- Connection to Academy Award–winning film will interest students
- Familiarity with historical context will improve understanding of the scene

Prepare and Engage

OBJECTIVES

1. To read, comprehend, interpret, and respond to writings about the monarchy
2. To relate writings about the monarchy to personal experience
3. To summarize to keep track of ideas
4. To examine the idea of monarch as hero
5. To build vocabulary in context and learn the word root *-sequent-*
6. To identify and form complex sentences
7. To write a persuasive letter to an editor
8. To respond to writings about the monarchy through writing, speaking and listening, and projects

SKILLS INSTRUCTION

Vocabulary: Word Root: *-sequent-*
Grammar Complex Sentences
Reading Strategy: Summarize
Literary Focus: The Monarch as Hero
Writing: Persuasive Tone
Speaking and Listening: Oral Interpretation (teacher edition)
Critical Viewing: Apply; Interpret

PORTFOLIO OPPORTUNITIES

Writing: Help Wanted; Letter of Support; Updated Utopia
Writing Mini-Lesson: Letter to an Editor
Speaking and Listening: Debate; Oral Interpretation
Projects: Timeline of Elizabethan England; Movie Review

More About the Authors

Sir Thomas More was known for his courtesy, his kindness, and his humor. He retained his grace even when he was found guilty of treason and sentenced to be hanged. He joked with the officer who helped him up the scaffold, and he tried to cheer up the executioner, saying, "Pluck up thy spirits, man, and be not afraid to do thine office."

Following her mother's execution, **Elizabeth I** was sent to live elsewhere and provided with a series of tutors, one of whom described her this way: "Her perseverance is equal to that of a man, and her memory long keeps what it quickly picks up. She talks French and Italian as well as she does English."

Guide for Interpreting

Sir Thomas More *(1478–1535)*

Devoted husband and father, passionate defender of the common citizen, sophisticated legal adviser, and deeply religious man—Sir Thomas More had the respect even of the king who put him to death.

Opposing the King More was an important advisor to King Henry VIII. At different times, however, More's stand on issues made him a friend and then a bitter enemy of the king. More certainly aroused the king's anger when he refused to support Henry's bid to divorce Catherine of Aragon. This divorce went against More's conscience as a Catholic. In the end, More's conscience cost him his life, because the king had him beheaded for his opposition.

An Ideal Kingdom More, however, had a kind of revenge. In his book *Utopia,* about an ideal kingdom (the title means "not a place"), he casts a disapproving eye on the injustices of his time.

Elizabeth I *(1533–1603)*

The only child of Henry VIII and Anne Boleyn, Elizabeth Tudor had a childhood filled with sadness and danger. Her mother was executed by her father when Elizabeth was not even three years old. Then Elizabeth was proclaimed illegitimate by Parliament when Henry's son by Jane Seymour was born. Finally, in 1558, after the death of her half sister, Mary, Elizabeth was crowned queen of England and Ireland.

The Elizabethan Age Today, Elizabeth is regarded as one of the finest monarchs ever to rule England. She was highly intelligent, and her colorful personality made her popular with her subjects. Moreover, her reign was a time of artistic achievement, military success, and expanding industry and trade. As a result of this success, the young girl who grew up in danger gave her name to an era of English history: the Elizabethan Age.

◆ Background for Understanding

History: More, Elizabeth I, and Religious Conflict

The late sixteenth century was a period of religious conflict within England and between England and Spain. England was a Catholic country in 1516 when More wrote *Utopia,* about eleven years before Henry VIII divorced Catherine of Aragon. Henry's divorce led not only to More's execution but to England's permanent break with the Roman Catholic Church, as Henry declared himself the head of an independent Church of England.

Mary I, Henry's daughter and Elizabeth's half sister, brought Catholicism back. Then, when Elizabeth ascended to the throne in 1558, she reestablished the Church of England. During her reign, Roman Catholics tried on several occasions to oust her from the throne. As a result, Elizabeth I stepped up persecution of Catholics. The climax of this persecution came in 1587, when Elizabeth agreed to have her Catholic cousin, Mary, Queen of Scots, executed. This act gave Philip II, the Catholic king of Spain, an excuse to attack England with the Spanish Armada.

Prentice Hall Literature Program Resources

REINFORCE / RETEACH / EXTEND

Selection Support Pages
Build Vocabulary: Word Root: *-sequent-*, p. 49
Grammar and Style: Complex Sentences, p. 50
Reading Strategy: Summarize, p. 51
Literary Focus: The Monarch as Hero, p. 52

Strategies for Diverse Student Needs, p. 10

Beyond Literature
Career Connection: Speechwriter, p. 10

Formal Assessment Selection Test, pp. 54–56; Assessment Resources Software

Alternative Assessment, p. 10

Writing and Language Transparencies
Writing Process Model 5: Persuasive Essay, pp. 37–44

Resource Pro CD-ROM
from *Utopia,* "Speech Before Defeating the Spanish Armada"—includes all resource material and customizable lesson plan

Listening to Literature Audiocassettes
from *Utopia,* "Speech Before Defeating the Spanish Armada"

◆ from Utopia ◆
Speech Before Defeating the Spanish Armada

◆ Literature and Your Life

Connect Your Experience

Just before the start of a big game, when nervous energy is at its greatest, a coach may gather a team together for a "pep talk." Such a talk is similar to Elizabeth's stirring speech to her subjects before the war with Spain. More's text is philosophical, but it is also designed to stir emotions and to promote cooperation.

Thematic Focus: The Influence of the Monarchy

As you read the passage from *Utopia* and Elizabeth's speech, consider what qualities a good ruler must have.

Journal Writing Jot down some ways in which the United States would be different if it were ruled by a monarch rather than governed by a president.

◆ Build Vocabulary

Word Roots: *-sequent-*

In *Utopia,* Thomas More uses the adverb *subsequently*. Knowing that its root *-sequent-* means "following in time or order," you can figure out that *subsequently* means "at a later time."

Word Bank

Before you read, preview this list of words from *Utopia* and Elizabeth's speech.

confiscation
sloth
subsequently
abrogated
forfeited
fraudulent
treachery
stead

◆ Grammar and Style

Complex Sentences

In **complex sentences**—sentences with a main clause and one or more subordinate clauses—the main clause can stand by itself as a sentence, and subordinate clauses are dependent on the main clause. Through its structure, a complex sentence expresses the relationship between a main and subordinate ideas.

The main clause can appear at the beginning, middle, or end of a sentence. In this example from *Utopia*, the main clause appears at the end.

Subordinate clauses: When a ruler enjoys wealth and pleasure while all about him are grieving and groaning,

Main clause: he acts as a jailer rather than as a king.

◆ Literary Focus

The Monarch as Hero

The literature of the English Renaissance (1485–1625) contains many depictions of the **monarch as hero**, the ruler as a perfect or larger-than-life person.

Look for this theme in More's depiction of what a king should be and Elizabeth's presentation of herself as an ideal monarch.

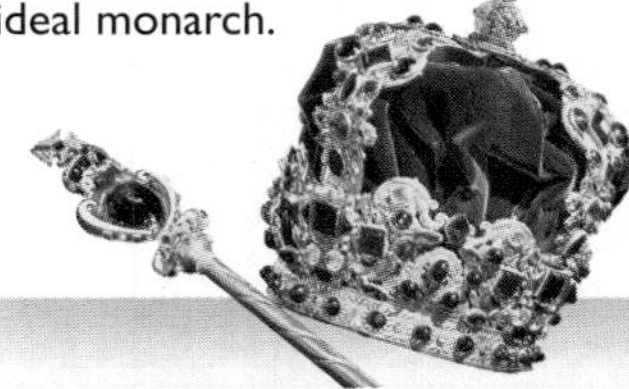

◆ Reading Strategy

Summarize

To keep track of ideas in sentences, you can **summarize** them by restating the main idea.

In reading More's *Utopia* and Elizabeth's speech, identify the main idea of a long or difficult sentence. Then see how the other ideas qualify, explain, or support it.

More's Sentence

Let him curb crime, and by his wise conduct prevent it rather than allow it to increase, only to punish it subsequently.

Summary

The monarch should prevent crime.

Preparing for Standardized Tests

Reading and Vocabulary The reading strategy for this selection, summarizing, helps students to identify the most important ideas in a reading. Quick, accurate identification of main ideas will improve students' performance on tests. For additional practice, use the Reading Strategy page in ***Selection Support,*** p. 51.

Grammar and Language Some standardized tests require students to revise sentences by replacing an underlined section. One choice is usually the same as the original. The others are different. For example:

When a ruler enjoys wealth and pleasure while all about him are grieving and groaning, <u>he acts as a jailer rather than as a king.</u> *(A)*

(A) he acts as a jailer rather than as a king.
(B) he acts as a jailer rather than king.
(C) when he acts as a jailer rather than as a king.

The Grammar and Style lesson for this selection focuses on complex sentences. For additional practice, use the Grammar and Style page, p. 50, in ***Selection Support.***

Interest Grabber When students today think of a monarchy, they probably think of Britain's royal family. Most students will have some knowledge of one or more of its members. Ask students to identify any royalty they know of. Then point out that there is a difference between an institution, such as the monarchy, and the individuals in it. Invite students to consider the monarchy as an institution. Use these questions to focus their thinking:

- What is the role of a good monarch?
- How should that person govern others? What should that person do?
- What qualities should monarchs have?

Explain that the writings they will read address these issues directly.

Customize for
Less Proficient Readers
Point out to students the purpose of each selection: to describe an ideal monarch, and to prepare a nation to enter a war. Since both selections are short, encourage pairs of students to read each piece sentence-by-sentence, agreeing on the meaning of each sentence before going on to the next.

Customize for
More Advanced Students
Students might enjoy trying to translate each speech into modern language, using slang, idioms, and catchphrases. Such translations are not only fun, but also useful for less advanced students.

Customize for
English Language Learners
Help these students break long sentences into shorter parts. You may also want to provide synonyms for unfamiliar words.

Customize for
Musical/Rhythmic Learners
Students may enjoy the sounds of Elizabethan English, which is more rhythmic and complex than contemporary English. Encourage students to read the words as an orator, or speechmaker, might say them, and to "hear" them as they read.

Develop Understanding

One-Minute Insight Although many people have written about utopian communities before and after Thomas More did, his work gave the world the term that most people use today to describe an ideal society. The word comes from the Greek *ou topos*, which means "no place." This passage will provide students with a glimpse of a political ideal—or at least of one man's version of it.

Students might be interested to learn that More's book and others like it encouraged people to try to create their own utopian communities. In the United States, well-known communities included the Oneida Community in New York and New Harmony in Indiana.

◆ Reading Strategy

❶ **Summarize** Students should understand that a people choose a king for their own comfort and safety. Therefore, a good king will put his subjects' happiness before his own.

◆ Critical Thinking

❷ **Infer** Ask students what a good king gains by being good. *He obtains a peaceful, contented populace that likes him and is worthwhile to rule.* What problems are avoided? *Good rule prevents disorder and rebellion.*

◆ Grammar and Style

❸ **Complex Sentences** Have students identify two or more complex sentences. Then have them restate each sentence using shorter sentences. *Example: He should do this because the people's hatred and scorn arise from these faults.*

from Utopia

Sir Thomas More

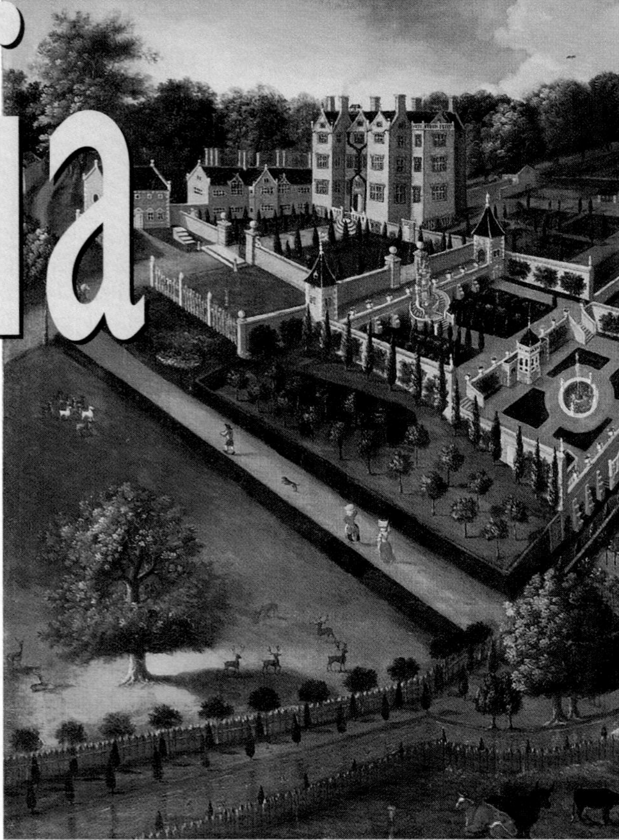

Suppose I should maintain that men choose a king not for his sake, but for theirs, that by his care and efforts they may live comfortably and safely. And that therefore a prince ought to take more care of his people's happiness than of his own, as a shepherd ought to take more care of his flock than of himself. Certainly it is wrong to think that the poverty of the people is a safeguard of public peace. Who quarrel more than beggars do? Who long for a change more earnestly than the dissatisfied? Or who rushes in to create disorders with such desperate boldness as the man who has nothing to lose and everything to gain? If a king is so hated and scorned by his subjects that he can rule them only by insults, ill-usage, confiscation, and impoverishment, it would certainly be better for him to quit his kingdom than to keep the name of authority when he has lost the majesty of kingship through his misrule. It is less befitting the dignity of a king to reign over beggars than over rich and happy subjects. Thus Fabricius, a man of noble and exalted spirit, said he would rather govern rich men than be rich himself. When a ruler enjoys wealth and pleasure while all about him are grieving and groaning, he acts as a jailor rather than as a king. He is a poor physician who cannot cure a disease except by throwing his patient into another. A king who can only rule his people by taking from them the pleasures of life shows that he does not know how to govern free men. He ought to shake off either his sloth or his pride, for the people's hatred and scorn arise from these faults in him. Let him live on his own income without wronging others, and limit his expenses to his revenue. Let him curb crime, and by his wise conduct prevent it rather than allow it to increase, only to punish ❸
it subsequently. Let him not rashly revive laws already abrogated by disuse, especially if they have been long forgotten and never wanted. And let him never seize any property on the ground that it is forfeited as a fine, when a judge would regard a subject as wicked and fraudulent for claiming it.

◆ **Reading Strategy** ❶ Summarize the first two sentences.

❷

Block Scheduling Strategies

Consider these suggestions to take advantage of extended class time:

- Display Art Transparency 5: *The Tower of London With London Bridge Behind,* page 23 in ***Art Transparencies.*** Explain that both of the featured authors were prisoners in the infamous Tower at some point in their lives. Use the art as a springboard for writing about rulers, political prisoners, or other topics of interest.
- Allow students to research Elizabeth I on the Internet or in an on-line encyclopedia. You may wish to have them create a family tree for Henry VIII that shows the relationships among Mary I; Elizabeth I; Mary, Queen of Scots; and James I.
- Students may perform the oral interpretations, as described in the Idea Bank on page 243), in front of the class. This activity is supported by the Speaking and Listening Mini-Lesson on page 240 of this teacher edition.
- Direct students to exchange with a partner the persuasive letters that they write for the Writing Mini-Lesson. Have each partner provide feedback about the most and least persuasive parts of the letters.
- Suggest that students sketch political cartoons about the failings of the monarchy, as suggested in ***Alternative Assessment,*** page 10.

Gardens at Llancerch, Denbighshire, Yale Center for British Art, New Haven, Connecticut

4 ▲ Critical Viewing How does this painting illustrate the order of the well-run kingdom More describes? **[Apply]**

◆ Build Vocabulary

confiscation (kän´ fis kā´ shən) *n.*: Act of seizing private property for the public treasury or for personal gain, usually as a penalty

sloth (slôth) *n.*: Laziness, idleness

subsequently (sub´ si kwənt lī) *adv.*: At a later time

abrogated (ab´rō gāt´ id) *v.*: Repealed; annulled

forfeited (fôr´ fit id) *v.*: Gave up, as a penalty

fraudulent (frô´ jə lənt) *adj.*: Characterized by deceit or trickery

Guide for Responding

◆ Literature and Your Life

Reader's Response Do you think Thomas More's ideas apply to leaders today?

Thematic Focus How much power should a monarch have? What limits should be set on powers of a monarch?

Journal Writing What would More have to say about the responsibilities of a modern-day president of the United States? Write your response in your journal.

☑ Check Your Comprehension

1. What reason does More give for poverty's becoming a threat to peace in a nation?
2. According to More, what is lacking in a king who can govern people only by taking their pleasures away?
3. How does More think a monarch should deal with the problem of crime?

◆ Critical Thinking

INTERPRET

1. How important does More think wealth is to a king? **[Analyze]**
2. From where do you think More draws his examples of a bad ruler? **[Infer]**
3. In general, what is the principle character trait that More thinks makes a good ruler? **[Draw Conclusions]**
4. Is More the kind of person who would say that the ends justify the means? Explain. **[Deduce]**
5. What universal lessons about good leadership are provided by this selection? **[Draw Conclusions]**

EVALUATE

6. How persuasive is More's argument? **[Make a Judgment]**

EXTEND

7. In what ways do More's views of good government resemble modern democratic ideals? **[Social Studies Link]**

Humanities: Art

Gardens at Lianerch, Denbighshire.

This picture clearly emphasizes the garden instead of the house, which is set in the background. The careful arrangement of the elements reflects a love of order and proportion.

In Elizabethan times, a garden was viewed as an extension of the house. If the house had square shapes and straight lines, so did the garden. Furthermore, the garden was placed so that it provided splendid views from the main windows of the house. Most gardens had formal flowers beds, often surrounded by walls or hedges. In addition, most gardens had decorative fountains and sculptures.

Use these questions to spark discussion:

1. What is noteworthy about the trees in this garden? *They are laid out in neat rows with even spacing between them.*
2. Do you think this house and garden is typical? Why? *Most students will notice that the other homes in the picture are not as ornate as the one in the foreground.*

▶Critical Viewing◀

4 **Apply** Everything is neatly maintained. Plants are in precise rows, and even the deer seem to know enough to stay out of the road.

Reinforce and Extend

Answers

◆ Literature and Your Life

Reader's Response Students will say that More's ideas—that a good leader should be just and ensure the well-being of those he or she leads—still apply today.

Thematic Focus Possible response: The power of monarchs should be limited. Those who govern should be subject to clear, well-known, and enforcable laws.

☑ Check Your Comprehension

1. Poverty makes it more likely that people will be quarrelsome, discontented, and disorderly.
2. Such a king lacks the ability to govern free people.
3. A monarch should find ways to prevent crime.

◆ Critical Thinking

1. He thinks that wealth should not be important, noting that Fabricus said he "would rather rule rich men than be rich himself."
2. Suggested response: More draws his examples from his own observations of Henry VIII.
3. Suggested response: A good monarch should be unselfish and "take more care of his people's happiness than his own."
4. Suggested response: No; this is implied by his point that a monarch should prevent crime, rather than allow it to rise and then punish it.
5. Suggested response: A good leader should be responsive to those who are ruled and put the people's needs first.
6. Most students will find More's arguments persuasive; many will think his points are obvious.
7. Suggested response: More's views put the needs and welfare of the people above the desires of those who govern; More thinks that monarchs should behave within the law.

Develop Understanding

One-Minute Insight Part of a leader's job is rallying support for causes that the government proposes. Queen Elizabeth I's speech exemplifies some of the techniques that a persuasive speaker uses, including flattery and rhetorical devices such as repetition and parallel structure.

Humanities: Art

Portrait of Queen Elizabeth I. Many portraits were painted of Elizabeth I, and often, each would emphasize a different aspect of her. This picture, known as the Armada portrait, stresses her victory over Spain.

Use this question for discussion: How does this portrait differ from the one on page 235? *Answers may include: Queen looks older; her costume is far more ornate; she is more bejeweled; she dominates the space in the painting.*

▶Critical Viewing◀

1 Interpret The window on the right shows the orderly formations of the English ships. The window on the left shows the Spanish ships being battered by storms at sea. The queen's hand rests on a globe, which suggests that the world is under her control.

◆ Reading Strategy

2 Summarize What does the queen say about her relationship with her people? *She does not want to distrust her subjects, since they are the source of her strength. She is speaking as one of them when she decides to wage war.*

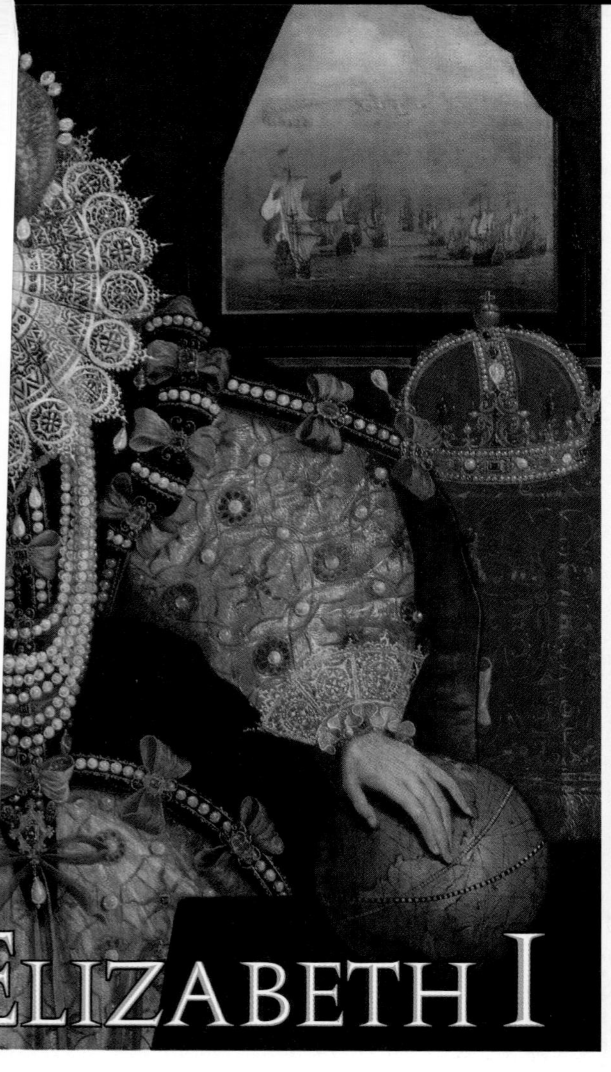

Portrait of Queen Elizabeth I, Anonymous Artist, Private Collection

QUEEN ELIZABETH I

Speech Before Defeating the Spanish Armada

▲ Critical Viewing How does this rendering of Elizabeth symbolize her great success? **[Interpret]** 1

Speaking and Listening Mini-Lesson

Oral Interpretation

This mini-lesson supports the Speaking and Listening activity in the Idea Bank on page 243.

Introduce the Concept Explain that a persuasive speech persuades not only by its content but also by its delivery. The speaker must use her or his voice to convey sincerity, reliability, and strong conviction.

Develop Background Before students begin, ask them to listen to or recall a major political speech. This could include Martin Luther King's "I have a dream" speech, Winston Churchill's "blood, sweat, and tears" speech, or John F. Kennedy's "Ask not what your country can do for you" speech. Discuss these elements:

- The slow, deliberate pace of the speech.
- The use of rising and falling inflection.
- The emphasis given to certain words and phrases.

Apply the Information Encourage students to rehearse their speeches first alone and then with partners. Finally, have them take turns delivering the speech aloud.

Assess the Outcome Ask students to vote on who gave the most effective presentation. Before they vote, ask them to consider the following questions: Who sounded most convincing and sincere? Who voiced each idea clearly? You may also have students use the Peer Assessment page for Oral Interpretation, page 120 in ***Alternative Assessment***.

My loving people, we have been persuaded by some, that are careful of our safety, to take heed how we commit ourselves to armed multitudes, for fear of treachery; but I assure you, I do not desire to live to distrust my faithful and loving people.
2 Let tyrants fear; I have always so behaved myself that, under God, I have placed my chiefest strength and safeguard in the loyal hearts and good will of my subjects. And therefore I am come amongst you at this time, not as for my recreation or sport, but being resolved, in the midst and heat of the battle, to live or die amongst you all; to lay down, for my God, and for my kingdom, and for my people, my honor and my blood, even the dust. I know I have but the body of a weak and feeble woman; but I have the heart of a king, and of a king of England, too; and think foul scorn that Parma or Spain, or any prince of Europe, should dare to invade the borders of my realms: to which, rather than any dishonor should grow by me, I myself will take up arms; I myself will be your general, judge, and rewarder of every one of your virtues in the field. I know already, by your forwardness, that you have deserved rewards and crowns; and we do assure you, on the word of a prince, they shall be duly paid you. In the mean my lieutenant general shall be in my stead, than whom never prince commanded a more noble and worthy subject; not doubting by your obedience to my general, by your concord in the camp, and by your valor in the field, we shall shortly have a famous victory over the enemies of my God, of my kingdom, and of my people.

◆ Literary Focus Make a list of words that Elizabeth uses that make her appear heroic. 3

◆ Build Vocabulary

treachery (trech´ ər ē) *n.*: Betrayal of trust, faith, or allegiance

stead (sted) *n.*: Position of a person as filled by a replacement or substitute

4 ▶ Critical Viewing These *Dangers Averted* medals celebrated the defeat of the Spanish Armada. How do you think those who received this medal were treated by average British citizens? **[Hypothesize]**

Guide for Responding

◆ *Literature and Your Life*

Reader's Response Do you think Elizabeth really intended to reward her subjects in the way she promised? Why or why not?

Thematic Focus What words does Elizabeth use to present herself as a friend of the common man or woman?

☑ Check Your Comprehension

1. What does Queen Elizabeth I say she is willing to risk for her people when they go to war?
2. What does the queen say to assure her subjects that being a woman won't hinder her performance during wartime?
3. What prediction does Elizabeth make about the war's outcome?

◆ Critical Thinking

INTERPRET

1. (a) Name two concerns of her audience that Elizabeth addresses. (b) Indicate how she puts these concerns to rest. **[Interpret]**
2. Do Elizabeth's words mean that she will actually fight and die with her soldiers? Why or why not? **[Interpret]**
3. Name two ways in which Elizabeth appeals to her subjects' patriotism. **[Analyze]**
4. What effect do you think Elizabeth hoped her speech would have? **[Draw Conclusions]**

EVALUATE

5. How effective is Elizabeth's speech as a "pep talk"? **[Evaluate]**

EXTEND

6. What modern leaders have given speeches like this one? Explain. **[Social Studies Link]**

Beyond the Selection

FOR FURTHER READING

Other Utopian Books

Lost Horizon, James Hilton
Erewhon, Samuel Butler

Other Books About Tudor England

The Elizabethan Renaissance, A. L. Rowse
Life in Elizabethan Days, William Stearns Davis

We suggest that you preview these works before recommending them to students.

INTERNET

You and your students may find additional information about Sir Thomas More on the Internet at the following site. For a timeline of More's life, a bibliography, and web links, go to **http://www.orst.edu/instruct/phl302/philosophers/more.html**

We *strongly recommend* that you preview the site before you send students to it.

◆ Literary Focus

3 The Monarch as Hero
Students' lists may include the following words and phrases: *we, resolved, live or die amongst you, my honor, heart of a king, take up arms, be your general, judge, and rewarder, noble and worthy.*

▶Critical Viewing◀

4 Hypothesize Most students will think that those who wore the medals were viewed with respect.

Reinforce and Extend

Answers

◆ *Literature and Your Life*

Reader's Response Students may say that Elizabeth does intend to pay her troops, although probably not as richly as they might hope.

Thematic Focus Students may say that she speaks of her people often and with affection, referring to them as "my faithful and loving people," and says that she intends to stand by them "to live or die amongst you all."

☑ Check Your Comprehension

1. She is willing to risk her honor and her life.
2. She says she has the heart of a king—an English king.
3. She predicts a "famous victory" over "the enemies of my God, of my kingdom, and of my people."

◆ Critical Thinking

1. (a) Two concerns are treachery against the queen and failing to get just rewards. (b) Elizabeth says that she has nothing to fear from her people. She assures her soldiers, on the word of a prince, that they will get their rewards.
2. Students may say that despite her words, Elizabeth will not physically fight alongside her soldiers.
3. She says that she trusts in the loyalty of her subjects and evokes the image of being a "king of England."
4. She hoped her speech would inspire loyalty to her and give her soldiers courage.
5. Most students will find it effective.
6. Students may mention Churchill's "we have nothing to fear but fear itself" speech and Martin Luther King's "I have a dream" speech.

Answers

◆ Reading Strategy

Suggested responses:

1. Main Clause: Let him not rashly revive laws already abrogated by disuse. Paraphrase: He should not foolishly restore laws that are long forgotten.
2. She has come to talk to the soldiers, despite the security risks, because she has faith in her subjects. Although a woman, she has the strength and will of a true king of England. She promises that the soldiers will be properly rewarded. Her lieutenant general will act in her place. She is sure her troops will win.

◆ Literary Focus

1. Suggested response: More expects a ruler to put the people's welfare above his or her own.
2. Suggested response: She shows her generosity by giving her word that the soldiers will be rewarded. She portrays herself as heroic by pointing out that she has come among the troops despite the possible dangers and by stating that she would be willing to take up arms to preserve the honor of her country.

◆ Build Vocabulary

Using the Word Root *-sequent-*

1. d 2. c 3. a 4. b

Using the Word Bank

Students responses should reflect an understanding of the ideas in the two works. Check that students have incorporated all eight of the Word Bank terms into their profile.

◆ Grammar and Style

Practice

1. And . . . fine when . . . it
2. He . . . physician who . . . disease except . . . another
3. we . . . some that . . . safety, to . . . multitudes
4. my . . . stead, than . . . subject
5. I know already, by your forwardness, that . . . crowns

Guide for Responding *(continued)*

◆ Reading Strategy

Summarize

Summarizing passages by restating their main ideas will help you better understand what you read. This sentence from More's *Utopia*, for example, can be boiled down to the statement in the main clause about what a good ruler should do:

> Let him not rashly revive laws already abrogated by disuse, especially if they have been long forgotten and never wanted.

1. Identify the main clause and summarize it in your own words.

2. As a reporter, take notes on the queen's speech. Jot down the key ideas she expresses.

◆ Literary Focus

The Monarch as Hero

In *Utopia* and "Speech Before Defeating the Spanish Armada," the **monarch as hero** is a central idea. More is writing about an ideal ruler, and Elizabeth is talking about herself! However, both writers portray the monarch as a superior person, endowed with courage and generosity.

1. Indicate another way in which More expects a king to be generous.

2. What words does Elizabeth use to portray herself as generous and heroic? Explain.

◆ Build Vocabulary

Using the Word Root *-sequent-*

Knowing that the word root *-sequent-* means "following in time or order," match the number of the *-sequent-* words with the letter of the correct definitions:

1. consequence	**a.** something that doesn't follow
2. sequential	**b.** episode that follows
3. non sequitur	**c.** following in time or order
4. sequel	**d.** result of an action

Using the Word Bank

Use all the words in the Word Bank to write a brief profile of an ideal monarch.

◆ Grammar and Style

Complex Sentences

By using complex sentences, More and Queen Elizabeth I are able to create a tone that is persuasive and full of authority.

> A **complex sentence** contains a main clause with the key idea and one or more subordinate clauses relating to that idea.

Practice On your paper, write the following complex sentences. Underline the main clause once and the subordinate clauses twice.

1. And let him never seize any property on the ground that it is forfeited as a fine, when a judge would regard a subject as wicked and fraudulent for claiming it.

2. He is a poor physician who cannot cure a disease except by throwing his patient into another.

3. . . . we have been persuaded by some, that are careful of our safety, to take heed how we commit ourselves to armed multitudes . . .

4. . . . my lieutenant general shall be in my stead, than whom never prince commanded a more noble and worthy subject . . .

5. . . . I know already, by your forwardness, that you have deserved rewards and crowns . . .

Writing Application On your paper, combine each pair of simple sentences into a complex sentence. (You may use connecting words like *because, although, when,* and *who.*)

1. Sir Thomas More was amazingly self-possessed. He was even able to make a joke at his own execution.

2. More knew what his king wanted him to do. He still insisted on opposing the king's wishes.

3. Elizabeth was a woman in a man's world. She showed the men what a "feeble woman" could do.

4. King Philip II was the ruler of Catholic Spain. He thought he could conquer England.

5. Elizabeth I restored the Church of England. The persecution of Catholics intensified.

242 ◆ Celebrating Humanity (1485–1625)

Writing Application

1. Sir Thomas More was so self-possessed that he was even able to make a joke at his own execution.
2. Although More knew what his king wanted him to do, he still insisted on opposing the king's wishes.
3. Elizabeth was a woman in a man's world, who showed the men what a "feeble woman" could do.
4. King Phillip II, who was the ruler of Catholic Spain, though he could conquer England.
5. When Elizabeth I restored the Church of England, the persecution of Catholics intensified.

Writer's Solution

For additional instruction and practice, use the lesson on Varying Sentence Structure in the **Language Lab CD-ROM** and the pages on Clauses in the *Writer's Solution Grammar Practice Book*, pp. 31–33.

Build Your Portfolio

Idea Bank

Writing

1. Help Wanted Using Thomas More's ideas about a perfect monarch, write a Help Wanted ad for such a ruler.

2. Letter of Support As a loyal subject of Elizabeth I, write her a letter telling why you support her decision to fight the Spanish and pledging your aid. **[Social Studies Link]**

3. Updated Utopia Following More's lead, write a fantasy about an ideal place where all of America's problems have been corrected. **[Social Studies Link]**

Speaking and Listening

4. Debate Form two groups and debate this question: Do Sir Thomas More's ideas about the qualities of a perfect king still apply to today's leaders? **[Social Studies Link]**

5. Oral Interpretation With a partner, take turns delivering Elizabeth's speech. Vary the speed with which you read and the emphasis you place on words to heighten the drama of your delivery. **[Performing Arts Link]**

Projects

6. Timeline of Elizabethan England Research this era of English history. Then create a large, illustrated timeline of the period, indicating its major achievements. **[Art Link; Social Studies Link]**

7. Movie Review Robert Bolt wrote a play and filmscript about Sir Thomas More entitled *A Man for All Seasons*. Rent the video of the movie and review it for your class. (You can read an excerpt from the play on page 253.) **[Media Link; Social Studies Link]**

Writing Mini-Lesson

Letter to an Editor

Sir Thomas More and Elizabeth I waste no time in revealing their opinions to readers and listeners. Reveal your own opinion in a letter to an editor about a political leader in the news. Respond to a particular story about this leader, giving your own perspective on the story and on the leader. Follow these tips to make your arguments convincing.

Writing Skills Focus: Persuasive Tone

In all types of persuasive writing—from letters to the editor to persuasive essays—it is important to maintain a **persuasive tone**. The word *tone* refers to the writer's attitude toward a subject, and a persuasive tone should reflect the writer's sense of conviction. It should also inspire readers to feel that their interests are the same as the writer's.

Notice how Elizabeth I signals her conviction with words like *strength* and *safeguard*, then links herself to listeners with words like *loyal* and *good will:*

> . . . I have always so behaved myself that, under God, I have placed my chiefest strength and safeguard in the loyal hearts and good will of my subjects.

Prewriting Outline your own point of view, and choose words and phrases that reflect it.

Drafting As you write, imagine yourself talking to someone you respect. Draw from your prewriting notes the words and phrases that will convince—not antagonize—this person. Develop the points you want to make by supporting them with specific examples.

Revising Add words and phrases that will bring you and your readers together in a community of concern. Whenever possible, use the pronoun *we* rather than *I*.

✓ ASSESSMENT OPTIONS

Formal Assessment, Selection Test, pp. 54–56, and Assessment Resources Software. The selection test is designed so that it can be easily customized to the performance levels of your students. ***Alternative Assessment,*** p. 10, includes options for less advanced students, more advanced students, intrapersonal learners, bodily/kinesthetic learners, verbal/linguistic learners, and visual/spatial learners.

PORTFOLIO ASSESSMENT
Use the following rubrics in the ***Alternative Assessment*** booklet to assess student writing:
Help Wanted: Description Rubric, p. 98
Letter of Support: Expression Rubric, p. 95
Updated Utopia: Description Rubric, p. 98
Writing Mini-Lesson: Persuasion Rubric, p. 106

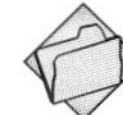

Idea Bank

Customizing for
Performance Levels
Following are suggestions for matching Idea Bank topics with your students' performance levels:
Less Advanced Students: 1, 5
Average Students: 2, 6, 7
More Advanced Students: 3, 4

Customizing for
Learning Modalities
Following are suggestions for matching Idea Bank topics with your students' learning modalities:
Visual/Spatial: 6, 7
Interpersonal: 4, 5
Verbal/Linguistic: 1, 2, 3, 4, 5, 7

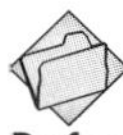

Writing Mini-Lesson

Refer students to the Writing Handbook, page 1189, for instruction on the writing process, and page 1192 for further information on persuasion.

Writer's Solution

Writing Lab CD-ROM
Have students complete the tutorial on Persuasion. Follow these steps:

1. View the Audio-annotated Writing Models that demonstrate writing for an audience.
2. Use the interactive instruction on evaluating facts and opinions.
3. Draft on the computer, using the Persuasive Word Bin for assistance in finding words that will make arguments more effective.
4. Fill out the interactive Self-Evaluation Checklist to identify areas that can be improved by revision.

Allow approximately 70 minutes of class time to complete these steps.

Sourcebook
Have students use Chapter 4, Persuasion (pp. 97–129), for additional support. The chapter includes instruction on audience (pp. 112–113), purpose (p. 114), and persuasive language (p. 119) as well as an annotated student model of a position paper on the British monarchy (pp. 124–125).

Prepare and Engage

OBJECTIVES

1. To read, comprehend, interpret, and respond to a psalm, a sermon, and a parable
2. To relate a psalm, a sermon, and a parable to personal experience
3. To infer meaning to understand the writer's message
4. To distinguish among psalms, sermons, and parables
5. To build vocabulary in context and learn the word root *-stat-*
6. To recognize and correctly use infinitive phrases
7. To write an opening argument of a debate, elaborating on key points
8. To respond to a psalm, a sermon, and a parable through writing, speaking and listening, and projects

SKILLS INSTRUCTION

Vocabulary: Word Roots: *-stat-*

Grammar: Infinitive Phrases

Reading Strategy: Inferring Meaning

Literary Focus: Psalm, Sermon, and Parable

Writing: Elaboration

Speaking and Listening: Oral Retelling (teacher edition)

Critical Viewing: Infer

PORTFOLIO OPPORTUNITIES

Writing: Letters; Modern Update; Allusion

Writing Mini-Lesson: Opening Argument of a Debate

Speaking and Listening: Oral Retelling; Sermon

Projects: Compare Translations; Song

More About the Author

Many people mistakenly believe that King James I actually wrote the bible that bears his name. In fact, it was written by a committee that borrowed heavily from a version written by William Tyndale. If anyone deserves credit as the author, it is Tyndale. More than three-quarters of the King James Bible was based on his work. Tyndale's aim was to create a Bible that would "cause a boy that driveth the plough to know more of the Scriptures" than most clergy of the day. The Church was not pleased to have its power diluted, and its reaction was swift and severe. First, copies of his books were burned. Later, in 1536, Tyndale himself was burned at the stake.

Guide for Interpreting

The King James Bible

(completed 1611)

When King James I ascended the throne, one of the issues he faced was the demand for a uniform English version of the Bible. He commissioned fifty-four scholars and clergymen in 1604 to compare all texts of the Bible and come up with a definitive English edition.

The King James version of the Bible has been called "the only classic ever created by a committee."

Laboring for seven years, the group produced a translation that has been regarded as one of the great works of English literature.

Early Bibles The Bible, a collection of books developed over a period of more than 1,200 years, consists of two main parts—the Old Testament and the New Testament. The Old Testament was originally written in Hebrew; the New Testament, in Greek. In the fourth century A.D., St. Jerome began translating the Bible into Latin. This translation, the Vulgate, remained the standard Bible of the West for centuries.

The reformer John Wycliffe produced the first English translation from Latin in the late 1300's. The Protestant Reformation in the 1500's, and the growing use of Gutenberg's movable type, resulted in an increased demand for a Bible in the vernacular, or common language of the people. William Tyndale, a Protestant chaplain and tutor, decided to prepare such a Bible.

Tyndale's Legacy Faced with clerical opposition at home, Tyndale fled to what is now Germany and there published his English translation of the New Testament. He had translated only part of the Old Testament when he was arrested for heresy and executed near Brussels, Belgium, in 1536.

Ironically, Henry VIII two years before had broken with Rome and established the Church of England. As England became more Protestant, the nation viewed Tyndale not as a heretic but as a hero. Throughout the sixteenth century, many others translated all or part of the Bible into English. However, when the committee appointed by James I began work on what would be called the King James or Authorized Version of the Bible, the magnificent diction and rhythms of Tyndale's translation were followed most closely.

◆ Background for Understanding

HISTORY: THE IMPACT OF THE BIBLE

Up through the Middle Ages, Bibles were painstakingly copied by hand. The resulting manuscripts, though often beautiful to behold, were rare and costly. In 1456, the German inventor Johann Gutenberg used a portion of the Bible to illustrate his newly devised method of printing with movable type. The development of printing made the Bible far more accessible than it had ever been before and also helped spur the demand for vernacular translations.

Still, prior to its translation into English, the Bible could be read only by well-educated members of the upper class who understood Latin. With the publication of the King James Bible, however, the Bible became available to the masses. Generations of people in Great Britain and the United States have grown up reading the King James Bible and adding its wisdom to the common store of knowledge.

Prentice Hall Literature Program Resources

REINFORCE / RETEACH / EXTEND

Selection Support Pages
Build Vocabulary: Word Roots: *-stat-*, p. 53
Grammar and Style: Infinitive Phrases, p. 54
Reading Strategy: Inferring Meaning, p. 55
Literary Focus: Psalm, Sermon, and Parable, p. 56

Strategies for Diverse Student Needs, p. 11

Beyond Literature Cross-Curricular Connection: Performing Arts, p. 11

Formal Assessment Selection Test, pp. 57–59; Assessment Resources Software

Alternative Assessment, p. 11

Writing and Language Transparencies
Argument Organizer, p. 103
Daily Language Practice, Week 11, p. 146

Resource Pro CD-ROM
from *The King James Bible*—includes all resource material and customizable lesson plan

Listening to Literature Audiocassettes
from *The King James Bible*

from The King James Bible

◆ Literature and Your Life

Connect Your Experience

In today's world, it seems that almost every day there are new inventions or developments that make it easier to access information. Think how inventions such as the cellular phone and the personal computer have changed people's lives. Then try to imagine the impact of the publication of the King James Bible on a society where few people ever had access to the information in the Bible.

Journal Writing Jot down your thoughts about how reactions to new methods of communication might be similar to Renaissance reactions to the printing press or a new Bible translation.

Thematic Focus: Influence of the Monarchy

The fact that the King James Bible was commissioned by the king played an important role in contributing to its impact. What does this suggest about the influence of the monarchy?

◆ Build Vocabulary

Word Roots: *-stat-*

The excerpt from the Sermon on the Mount includes the word *stature*, which includes the root *-stat-*, meaning "to stand." The root offers a clue to the word's meaning, "a person's height or standing." The root is also spelled *-stit-*, as in *substitute*.

Word Bank

Preview the list before you read.

righteousness
stature
prodigal
entreated
transgressed

◆ Grammar and Style

Infinitive Phrases

An **infinitive phrase** is a group of words consisting of an infinitive (the base form of a verb preceded by *to*) and its modifiers and complements. An infinitive phrase functions as a noun, adjective, or adverb. The following example from the Bible serves as an adverb modifying *sent.*

He sent him into his fields *to feed swine*.

◆ Literary Focus

Psalm, Sermon, and Parable

A **psalm** is a sacred song or lyric poem in praise of God. The Old Testament's Book of Psalms contains 150 such pieces.

A **sermon** is a speech offering religious or moral instruction. Given by Jesus on a mountainside in Galilee, the Sermon on the Mount contains the basic teachings of Christianity.

A **parable** is a short, simple story from which a moral or religious lesson can be drawn. The most famous parables are those in the New Testament.

◆ Reading Strategy

Inferring Meaning

Although some portions of the Bible are clear and direct, others require you to **make inferences**, or draw conclusions, about the messages they convey. For example, Psalm 23 includes the line "The Lord is my shepherd."

To understand the psalm, you must infer the meaning of this comparison. By considering the role that a shepherd performs, you can infer that the line suggests that, like a shepherd, God watches over his flock and leads them toward a better place.

Preparing for Standardized Tests

Reading and Vocabulary Being able to infer meaning will help students improve their performance on reading-comprehension items on standardized tests. To review and reinforce this skill, instruct students to complete the Reading Strategy exercise in the Guide for Responding on page 250. For additional practice, assign the Reading Strategy page in ***Selection Support***, p. 51.

Grammar and Language Some standardized tests present students with a sentence with one section underlined. The student is given choices for replacing that section. Sentences often include errors in parallel construction, which students may recognize more easily after they have learned to identify infinitive phrases. For example:

The best way to appreciate the King James Bible is reading it aloud. *(C)*
(A) reading it aloud.
(B) having read it aloud.
(C) to read it aloud.

The Grammar and Style lesson for this selection focuses on infinitive phrases. For additional practice, use the Grammar and Style page, p. 50, in ***Selection Support.***

Point out to students that many common expressions today come from the King James Bible. Provide them with these examples: *Let there be light! Am I my brother's keeper? Out of the mouths of babes. Let my people go. Flesh of my flesh. God forbid. Stranger in a strange land. Physician, heal thyself.* If possible, show students books whose titles are based on biblical phrases, such as Robert Heinlein's *Stranger in a Strange Land* or William Barrett's *The Lilies of the Field.*

Explain that before this version of the Bible was written, only highly educated people could read the Bible, since it was written in Latin. This edition made the work accessible to ordinary people. It used language that was then simple English. In addition, the language had a rhythm and beauty that had a profound influence on English literature.

Customize for
Less Proficient Readers
Many students will have heard Psalm 23. Read aloud to them, or play the recording on the ***Listening to Literature Audiocassettes*** before asking them to read it independently. Before they read the sermon and the parable, you may wish to explain that one is a speech giving moral rules and the other is a story that teaches a lesson.

Customize for
English Language Learners
If students are familiar with the Bible in another language, have them first read these selections in that language. Otherwise, ask students to identify religious prayers, stories, or phrases that are common to their cultures. Explain that these three works have influenced many English-speaking people, even ones who are not particularly religious.

Customize for
Intrapersonal Learners
Encourage students to put themselves into the role of each speaker. Under what circumstances would they say the psalm, give the sermon, or tell the parable? Who would be the audience in each case?

Develop Understanding

One-Minute Insight Although the Book of Psalms contains 150 sacred poems, this is undoubtedly the best known. It is recited at funerals, in times of trouble, and when people are in need of comfort.

◆ Critical Thinking

❶ **Analyze** Have students analyze the images used in the psalm. What images convey a sense of peace and well-being? *Students might suggest any of the following: green pastures, still waters, a prepared table, an overflowing cup.*

▶Critical Viewing◀

❷ **Infer** Students may point out that the art gives clues to the content, showing, for example, Moses holding the ten commandments. They may also note that the classical dress that the figures wear suggests dignity and importance.

Customize for
Verbal/Linguistic Learners
Ask students why so many people have memorized this psalm. *It comforts them; it is short; it is musical.*

Psalm 23

from The King James Bible

1 The Lord is my shepherd; I shall not want.

2 He maketh me to lie down in green pastures: he leadeth me beside the still waters.

3 He restoreth my soul: he leadeth me in the paths of righteousness for his name's sake.

❶ 4 Yea, though I walk through the valley of the shadow of death, I will fear no evil: for thou art with me; thy rod and thy staff they comfort me.

5 Thou preparest a table before me in the presence of mine enemies; thou anointest my head with oil; my cup runneth over.

6 Surely goodness and mercy shall follow me all the days of my life: and I will dwell in the house of the Lord forever.

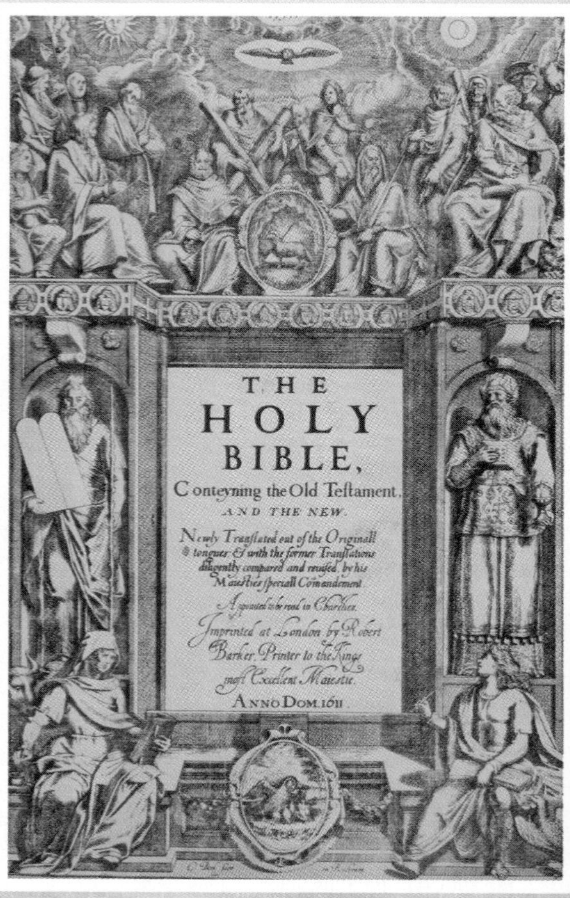

King James Bible, 1611, title page of the New Testament, The Folger Shakespeare Library, Washington, D.C.

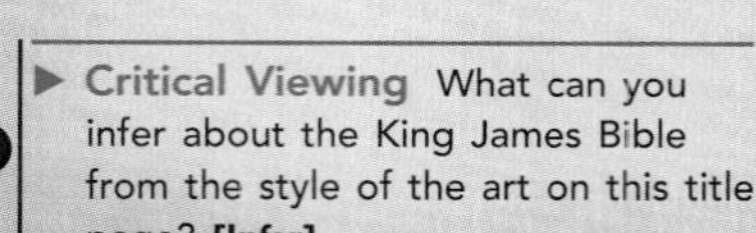
❷ ▶ **Critical Viewing** What can you infer about the King James Bible from the style of the art on this title page? **[Infer]**

Block Scheduling Strategies

Consider these suggestions to take advantage of extended class time:

- Direct students to complete the journal writing activity in Literature and Your Life, p. 245, and discuss their responses in small groups.
- Display the Daily Language Practice for Week 11, page 146 in ***Writing and Language Transparencies,*** on the overhead. Have students write the sentences correctly.
- Familiarize students with the features of psalms, sermons, and parables. As students read, have them identify how the readings match the definitions of these types of writing. After reading, have students complete the Literary Focus page, in ***Selection Support,*** p. 52.
- Allow students time to work on the writing activities in the Idea Bank on page 251.
- Students can rehearse and present oral retellings of a parable, as suggested in the Idea Bank on page 251. This activity is supported by a Speaking and Writing Mini-Lesson on page 248 of this teacher edition.

from the Sermon on the Mount

from THE KING JAMES BIBLE

Matthew 6: 24–30

24 No man can serve two masters:
for either he will hate the one, and
love the other; or else he will hold to
the one, and despise the other. Ye
cannot serve God and mammon.[1]
25 Therefore I say unto you, Take
no thought for your life, what ye shall
❸ eat, or what ye shall drink; nor yet for
your body, what ye shall put on. Is
not the life more than meat, and the
body than raiment?[2]
26 Behold the fowls of the air: for
they sow not, neither do they reap,
nor gather into barns; yet your heavenly Father feedeth them. Are ye not
much better than they?
27 Which of you by taking thought
can add one cubit unto his stature?
28 And why take ye thought for
raiment? Consider the lilies of the
field, how they grow; they toil not,
neither do they spin:
29 And yet I say unto you, That
even Solomon[3] in all his glory was
not arrayed like one of these.
30 Wherefore, if God so clothe the
grass of the field, which to day is, and
to morrow is cast into the oven, *shall
he* not much more *clothe* you, O ye of
little faith?

1. **mammon** (mam´ ən) *n.*: Money personified as a false god.
2. **raiment** (rā´ mənt) *n.*: Clothing; wearing apparel.
3. **Solomon** (säl´ ə mən) *n.*: Tenth-century B.C. king of Israel.

◆ Build Vocabulary

righteousness (rī´ chəs nis) *n.*: Doing what is fair and just

stature (stach´ ər) *n.*: Height of a person standing; development, growth, or level of achievement

Guide for Responding

◆ *Literature and Your Life*

Reader's Response Which words or phrases in Psalm 23 and the excerpt from the Sermon on the Mount are familiar to you?

Thematic Response How do you think the quality of this translation would have reflected on King James?

☑ Check Your Comprehension

1. In the first part of Psalm 23, what images convey the idea of the Lord as a shepherd?
2. What two masters does Jesus say you cannot serve at the same time?
3. What does he point out about the "lilies of the field"?

One-Minute Insight Many people consider the *Sermon on the Mount* to be the single most important teaching in the Bible. Jesus was supposed to have spoken these words to the public and to his disciples. The sermon as a whole teaches the virtues and the actions that are the essence of Christianity.

◆ Literary Focus

Psalm, Sermon, and Parable Ask students what features beside the title help them identify the excerpt from the sermon on the mount as a sermon. *It is a speech, and provides religious instruction.*

Customize for *Less Proficient Readers*
Point out that in some sentences, the words are in an unusual order. Help students restate such sentences in a more familiar order and form.

◆ Reading Strategy

❸ **Inferring Meaning** Ask students to infer what the speaker means in verse 25. Should the words be taken literally? *People should not be overly concerned about their bodies. The advice is not meant to be taken literally, since people would die from starvation.*

Reinforce and Extend

Answers

◆ *Literature and Your Life*

Reader's Response Students' familiarity with the words and phrases will depend on their religious background. Most Christians and Jews will be familiar with Psalm 23.

Thematic Focus It would have enhanced his reputation as a devout king.

☑ Check Your Comprehension

1. Students may point to the direct statement in verse 1 and the images of green pastures and sources of water for sheep.
2. You cannot serve God and mammon (money).
3. They do not work (or care for material things), but God takes care of them and makes them beautiful.

Humanities: Art

King James Bible, title page, 1611.

This frontispiece appeared in the first edition of the English Bible of 1611, which is now known as the King James or Authorized version. The art on this title page was created by an unknown artist who was working for the King's printer, a man named Robert Barker (d. 1645). Barker's position gave him exclusive rights to print English Bibles, prayer books, statutes, and proclamations. Students might enjoy comparing this distinctive page, with its classically garbed figures, with biblical illustrations by other artists, such as Gustave Doré.

Use questions like these for discussion:

1. Why do you think the artist dressed the characters this way? *They are wearing classical clothes; either the artist thought people dressed that way in biblical times or else he wanted to make them seem dignified.*
2. What is emphasized in the illustration? *Suggested response: The illustration emphasizes the word "Holy" and the ideas of beauty and order.*

Develop Understanding

One-Minute Insight Many religions, including Judaism and Zen Buddhism, teach lessons by means of parables. The parables in the New Testament are among the most famous in western literature. In some ways, they are like fables. However, fables often contain fantasy elements, whereas parables involve recognizable humans in situations that listeners can identify with. In this parable, a young man demands his inheritance and leaves home. Later, he returns home in disgrace, but is welcomed back by his father with open arms. This parable symbolizes God's readiness to forgive those who fall from grace.

Cross-Curricular Connection: Science

In the parable, the prodigal son finds himself starving as a result of a famine. Famines have occurred throughout the world, including Africa, Ireland, China, and India. Their causes include pests, weather patterns, and politics. Have students identify some of the major famines that have occurred during the last century. Encourage them to find out what caused each, what happened as a result of each, and what is happening in that location today.

◆ Critical Thinking

❶ **Infer** Ask students if they think the son would have returned home if there had been no famine. Have them give reasons for their answers. *He probably would not have returned home. He only thought about returning after no one gave him food.*

The Parable of the Prodigal Son

from THE KING JAMES BIBLE — Luke 15: 11–32

11 And he said, A certain man had two sons:
12 And the younger of them said to *his* father, Father, give
me the portion of goods that falleth *to me*. And he divided
unto them *his* living.
13 And not many days after the younger son gathered all
together, and took his journey into a far country, and there
wasted his substance with riotous living.
14 And when he had spent all, there arose a mighty
famine in that land; and he began to be in want.
15 And he went and joined himself to a citizen of that
country; and he sent him into his fields to feed swine.
16 And he would fain[1] have filled his belly with the husks
that the swine did eat: and no man gave unto him.
❶ 17 And when he came to himself, he said, How many
hired servants of my father's have bread enough and to
spare, and I perish with hunger!
18 I will arise and go to my father, and will say unto him,
Father, I have sinned against heaven, and before thee,
19 And am no more worthy to be called thy son: make me
as one of thy hired servants.
20 And he arose, and came to his father. But when he was
yet a great way off, his father saw him, and had compassion,
and ran, and fell on his neck, and kissed him.
21 And the son said unto him, Father, I have sinned
against heaven, and in thy sight, and am no more worthy to
be called thy son.
22 But the father said to his servants, Bring forth the best
❷ robe, and put *it* on him; and put a ring on his hand, and
shoes on *his* feet:

1. **fain** *adv.*: Gladly.

Speaking and Listening Mini-Lesson

Oral Retelling

This mini-lesson supports the Speaking and Listening activity in the Idea Bank on page 251.

Introduce the Concept In an oral retelling, a performer presents a story to an audience in a way that is suited to the artistic vision of the performer and matches the interests and needs of the audience. Explain to students that they will be creating their own version of the Parable of the Prodigal Son for an audience of young children.

Develop Background To decide how to present the story, students will need to brainstorm for guidelines that suit their audience. Their lists may include the following:

- Speak slowly and clearly, using simple words and sentences.
- Use broad gestures and exaggerated facial expressions to make meaning clear.
- Make the story brief, simple, and full of action and humor.

Apply the Information Students should develop and rehearse their performances individually or in groups. When they are ready, they can perform for their audience.

Assess the Outcome In addition to using the list generated in Develop Background, students may assess their performances and those of their classmates using the Peer Assessment: Dramatic Performance page, in ***Alternative Assessment,*** p. 121.

❷ 23 And bring hither the fatted calf, and kill *it;* and let us
eat, and be merry:
24 For this my son was dead, and is alive again; he was
lost, and is found. And they began to be merry.
25 Now his elder son was in the field: and as he came and
drew nigh to the house, he heard music and dancing.
26 And he called one of the servants, and asked what
these things meant.
27 And he said unto him, Thy brother is come; and thy father hath killed the fatted calf, because he hath received
him safe and sound.
28 And he was angry, and would not go in: therefore came
his father out, and entreated him.
29 And he answering said to *his* father, Lo, these many
years do I serve thee, neither transgressed I at any time thy
commandment: and yet thou never gavest me a kid, that I
might make merry with my friends:
30 But as soon as this thy son was come, which hath devoured thy living with harlots, thou hast killed for him the
fatted calf.
31 And he said unto him, Son, thou art ever with me, and
all that I have is thine.
32 It was meet[2] that we should make merry, and be glad:
❸ for this thy brother was dead, and is alive again; and was
lost, and is found.

2. **meet** *adj.*: Fitting.

◆ **Build Vocabulary**

prodigal (präd′ i gəl) *adj.:* Addicted to wasteful expenditure

entreated (in trēt′ id) *v.:* Begged; pleaded

transgressed (trans grest′) *v.:* Overstepped or broken (a law or commandment)

Guide for Responding

◆ Literature and Your Life

Reader's Response If you were the elder son, how would you have reacted to the father's response at the end? Why?

Journal Writing Jot down ideas for your own parable about family ties, friendship, or another important human relationship.

☑ Check Your Comprehension

1. What causes the younger son to return home?
2. Summarize the father's reaction to his return.
3. (a) What complaint does the elder son make?
   (b) Summarize the father's response.

Beyond the Selection

FOR FURTHER READING

Other Editions of the Bible

The Jerusalem Bible; The New American Bible; The New Revised Standard Version of the Bible

Books About the Bible and the English Language

The Oxford Companion to the Bible, B. Metzger and M. Coogan

The Mother Tongue, Bill Bryson

We suggest that you preview these works before recommending them to students.

INTERNET

You and your students may find additional information about the King James Bible on the Internet at the following sites. Please be aware, however, that sites may have changed from the time we published this information. For a brief history of the King James bible, go to **http://www.netc.com/~gok/bible20.html**

For a timeline showing revisions of the Bible, go to **http://www.greatsite.com/timeline.htm.**

We *strongly recommend* that you preview the sites before you send students to them.

◆ Literature and Your Life

❷ Encourage students to relate the events in the parable to parties that they have attended or that have been held for them. Ask volunteers to describe extra-special gifts, foods, or activities that they have experienced. Connect the killing of the fatted calf to modern practices like having a gala event at the most expensive restaurant in town.

◆ Reading Strategy

❸ **Inferring Meaning** Explain that as well as showing idealized human behavior, this parable speaks to people's relationship with God. Ask students: What is the religious meaning of this parable? *Students should infer that the father represents God, who is always ready to welcome back a repentant sinner.*

Customize for *Intrapersonal Learners*

Have students consider the parable from each character's point of view. Ask them to imagine, for example, how they would feel if they were the father. Then have them imagine how they would feel if they were the elder son, and finally the younger.

Reinforce and Extend

Answers

◆ Literature and Your Life

Reader's Response Some students will say that they would adopt the father's forgiving and happy outlook. Most students will say that they would still find the situation unfair.

☑ Check Your Comprehension

1. He is starving.
2. The father is happy, excited, welcoming, and not at all critical.
3. (a) He complains that he has been good, and no one has thrown a party for him; his brother, on the other hand, has behaved badly and is being honored with a feast.
   (b) The father says that he always knew he could count on the older brother, but it is a cause for celebration that the younger brother has mended his ways and come home.

Answers

◆ Critical Thinking

1. The rod and staff will protect and guide the speaker.
2. Suggested response: God will protect and guide me.
3. It focuses on choosing between a life of the body and physical comforts and a life of the spirit and faith in God.
4. (a) He contrasts the actions of birds with sowing, reaping, and storing grain and the inaction of lilies with toiling and spinning. (b) Although they do not work for a living, the Lord takes care of them.
5. Suggested response: The older son is reliable and stays at home; the younger son is a spendthrift and leaves home.
6. The parable suggests that we should be forgiving.
7. Students may select the psalm for its strong central image and poetic language, the sermon for its vivid language and parallel structure, or the parable for its accessible, storylike quality.
8. Possible responses: The notion of having someone on one's side is captured in the Beatles' "Let It Be," James Taylor's "You've Got a Friend," and innumerable hymns. George and Ira Gershwin's "Plenty of Nothing" is an example of a song that celebrates letting go of material concerns.

◆ Grammar and Style

1. to take his inheritance, noun; 2. to spend it on riotous living, noun; 3. to avoid starvation, adverb; 4. to feast his son lavishly, adjective; 5. to attend the feast, noun

◆ Reading Strategy

1. It means "I will have a place in heaven"; heaven is God's house.
2. It means "it was as if my son were dead, because I never thought I'd see him again, but now he's come back."

◆ Literary Focus

1. (a) The psalm is formal and lyric. The sermon is also formal, but has a more structured "feel" due to the use of repetition and parallel structure. The parable has an informal, storylike "feel." (b) The lyricism of the poem is suitable for a song of praise. The precise structure of the sermon presents ideas clearly and makes it easy for a listener to follow. The parable presents its message in an appealing way.
2. The central message is that if God cares for birds and weeds, He will certainly take care of people.
3. (a) Suggested response: It is important to forgive people and allow them to make a fresh start. (b) This lesson is directed toward anyone who feels that he or she has been wronged.

◆ Build Vocabulary

Using the Word Root *-stat-*

1. A *statue* is a carved figure that stands on a pedestal.
2. Something that is *stationary* stands still.
3. When you *institute* something, you set it up, or establish it.

Using the Word Bank

1. a 2. b 3. b 4. c 5. a

Writer's Solution

For additional instruction and practice, use the lesson on Recognizing and Using Phrases in the **Language Lab CD-ROM** and the page on Verbals and Verbal Phrases in the *Writer's Solution Grammar Practice Book,* p. 30.

Guide for Responding *(continued)*

◆ Critical Thinking

Interpret

1. In Psalm 23, why is the speaker comforted by the Lord's (shepherd's) rod and staff? **[Analyze]**
2. What is the central message of Psalm 23? Support your answer. **[Draw Conclusions]**
3. On what central choice in life does the passage from the Sermon on the Mount focus? **[Connect]**
4. (a) With what specific human activities does Jesus contrast the fowls' and the lilies' behavior in the Sermon on the Mount? (b) What does he suggest the fowls and lilies have in common? **[Compare and Contrast]**
5. How would you describe the two sons in the Parable of the Prodigal Son? **[Compare and Contrast]**
6. What does the parable suggest about how we should treat others? **[Connect]**

Evaluate

7. Which of these selections conveys its message most effectively? Why? **[Assess]**

Extend

8. What modern poems or songs can you think of that convey a message similar to that of one of these selections? **[Literature Link]**

◆ Grammar and Style

Infinitive Phrases

An **infinitive phrase** consists of an infinitive (the base form of the verb preceded by *to*) and its modifiers and complements. It can function as an adjective, adverb, or noun.

Practice In your notebook, write the infinitive phrases that appear in the following sentences and identify whether they function as adjectives, adverbs, or nouns.

1. The younger son chose to take his inheritance.
2. He began to spend it on riotous living.
3. To avoid starvation he returned to his home.
4. His father made plans to feast his son lavishly.
5. His elder brother did not want to attend the feast.

◆ Reading Strategy

Inferring Meaning

Use details from the selections, along with your prior knowledge, to **make inferences**, or draw conclusions, about the meaning of each of these lines. Explain each answer.

1. "dwell in the house of the Lord forever" (Psalm 23)
2. "my son was dead, and is alive again" (Parable of the Prodigal Son)

◆ Literary Focus

Psalm, Sermon, and Parable

The three selections in this grouping illustrate three literary forms included in the Bible. A **psalm** is a sacred song or lyric poem in praise of God. A **sermon** is a speech giving religious or moral instruction. A **parable** is a short, simple story from which a moral or religious lesson can be drawn.

1. (a) Contrast the styles of the selections. (b) How is the style of each selection appropriate to its function or purpose?
2. What is the central message of this portion of the Sermon on the Mount? Support your answer.
3. (a) What is the chief moral lesson of the Parable of the Prodigal Son? (b) Is this lesson directed only at family members? Explain.

◆ Build Vocabulary

Using the Word Root *-stat-*

The root *-stat-*, sometimes spelled *-stit-*, means "to stand" or "to set up." Define each of the following words, incorporating the idea of standing or setting up.

1. statue **2.** stationary **3.** institute

Using the Word Bank

In your notebook, write the letter of the word that is the best synonym of the first word.

1. righteousness: (a) justness, (b) neatness, (c) error
2. stature: (a) depth, (b) status, (c) interference
3. prodigal: (a) brilliant, (b) wasteful, (c) awful
4. entreated: (a) agreed, (b) financed, (c) begged
5. transgressed: (a) sinned, (b) poached, (c) traveled

Build Your Portfolio

Idea Bank

Writing

1. Letters Write a series of letters that the prodigal son might have written to a friend back home.

2. Modern Update Create an updated version of one of these selections by changing the language, setting, characters, and/or circumstances. Your psalm, sermon, or parable should focus on the same moral lesson as those in the originals.

3. Allusion English speakers often make allusions, or references, to the King James Bible. Write your own poem, story, or essay in which you allude at least once to each of the three Bible selections.

Speaking and Listening

4. Oral Retelling Prepare a retelling of the Parable of the Prodigal Son for an audience of young children. Deliver your modified version to your classmates or to such an audience.

5. Sermon Imagine that you are a member of the clergy and the class is your congregation. Compose and deliver a sermon built around one of the three Bible selections.

Projects

6. Compare Translations The King James version is only one of many English translations of the Bible. Working in a small group, compare two other translations of one of the selections. Share your impressions in a panel discussion. **[Literature Link]**

7. Song Set Psalm 23 to your own original music or to music composed by someone else. Performyour musical version of the psalm live, on audiocassette, or on videotape. **[Music Link]**

Writing Mini-Lesson

Opening Argument of a Debate

Imagine that you are part of a team planning to debate the father's decision in the Parable of the Prodigal Son. One side will defend the father's decision; the other will argue against that decision. You are in charge of preparing a written opening argument for your side of the debate. The following tips on elaboration should help you develop your opening argument.

Writing Skills Focus: Elaboration

In your opening statement, you must do more than simply state your key points. Instead, use these techniques to **elaborate** on your points.

- Support your argument with examples, reasons, and other details.
- Clarify broad information by providing more specific details.
- Anticipate counterarguments and provide information to rebut them.
- Anticipate questions and provide information to answer them.
- Restate your main point in different words.

Use the following strategies to guide you as you write.

Prewriting Taking either side of the argument, write a clear, brief statement of your position and jot down details that support it. Also, anticipate the questions and counterarguments of others and jot down possible answers.

Drafting Organize details so they effectively support your position. Incorporate answers to possible questions and counterarguments. End with a restatement of your main argument.

Revising Practice presenting your opening statement to an audience, using a peer reviewer. Have the reviewer make suggestions about where you could add more support for your arguments.

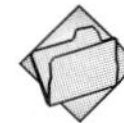

Idea Bank

Customizing for Performance Levels

Following are suggestions for matching Idea Bank topics with your students' performance levels:

Less Advanced Students: 1, 4
Average Students: 2, 5, 7
More Advanced Students: 3, 6

Customizing for Learning Modalities

Following are suggestions for matching Idea Bank topics with your students' learning modalities:

Interpersonal: 4, 5, 6
Verbal/Linguistic: 1, 2, 3, 4, 5, 6
Musical/Rhythmic: 7

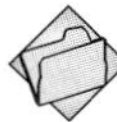

Writing Mini-Lesson

Refer students to the Writing Handbook, page 1189, for instruction on the writing process, and page 1192 for further information on persuasion.

On the overhead, you may wish to display the Argument Organizer in ***Writing and Language Transparencies,*** p. 103. Students organize their ideas for their opening arguments using a format similar to this one.

Writer's Solution

Writing Lab CD-ROM

Have students complete the tutorial on Persuasion. Follow these steps:

1. Complete a Pros and Cons Chart to sort opposing ideas to build an argument for a position.
2. Use the Keyhole Organizer to arrange evidence in main-idea-and-details order.
3. Draft on the computer.
4. Revise and proofread, using the Homonyms checker to help make sure that the right spelling of a word is used.

Allow approximately 70 minutes of class time to complete these steps.

Sourcebook

Have students use Chapter 4, Persuasion (pp. 97–129), for additional support. The chapter includes a workplace writing model of a position paper, in-depth instruction on purpose (p. 114) and a model and discussion of main-idea-and-details organization.

✓ ASSESSMENT OPTIONS

Formal Assessment, Selection Test, pp. 57–59, and Assessment Resources Software. The selection test is designed so that it can be easily customized to the performance levels of your students. ***Alternative Assessment,*** p. 11, includes options for less advanced students, more advanced students, verbal/linguistic learners, musical/rhythmic learners, and visual/spatial learners.

PORTFOLIO ASSESSMENT

Use the following rubrics in the ***Alternative Assessment*** booklet to assess student writing:
Letters: Expression Rubric, p. 95
Modern Update: Poetry Rubric, p. 109; How-To/Process Explanation Rubric, p. 101; Fictional Narrative Rubric, p. 96
Allusion: Poetry Rubric, p. 109; Fictional Narrative Rubric, p. 96;
Writing Mini-Lesson: Persuasion Rubric, p. 106

Prepare and Engage

OBJECTIVES

1. To read, comprehend, and interpret a screenplay
2. To explore the thematic connection between a contemporary screenplay and sixteenth-century and early seventeenth-century writings
3. To respond to the dramatic scene through writing, speaking and listening, and projects

PORTFOLIO OPPORTUNITIES

Writing: Letter to a Monarch; Opening Argument; Continuation
Speaking and Listening: Television Interview
Project: Visual History

More About the Author
Although *A Man for All Seasons* is perhaps Robert Bolt's best-known work, it is not his only story of a historical struggle. *Vivat! Vivat! Regina* examines the conflict between Mary, Queen of Scots, and Elizabeth I; *State of Revolution* focuses on the Russian Revolution and how power affected the personalities of its leaders.

Ahead of time, recruit two students to play "guards" and two students to play the "condemned" in the following scenario: A student approaches you to complain about the grade on a paper. Argue with the student, then thunder "Off with his (her) head." The two guards then drag the protesting student from the room. After a pause, the next student approaches you to explain that the dog has eaten his (or her) homework. After this student is condemned and dragged away, snarl "Okay. Does anyone else have a problem?"

Point out that there are some people you just shouldn't disagree with. Grant a stay of execution to the "condemned," and explain to the class that in the scene they are about to read, Thomas More is trapped into having to choose between acting against his conscience or defying his powerful, unforgiving king.

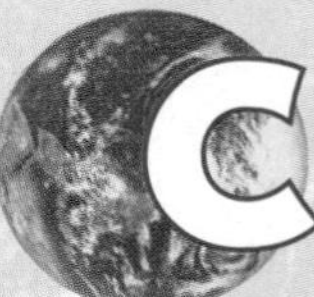

CONNECTIONS TO TODAY'S WORLD

from A Man for All Seasons

Robert Bolt

Thematic Connection

ROYAL PROCLAMATIONS

Imagine waking up tomorrow and finding out that the president has decided that everyone in the country has to drive a station wagon. Although it seems impossible and absurd, for the people of the sixteenth century, living according to the whim of a ruler was a way of life. At that time, monarchs of Europe wielded absolute power. By simply issuing a royal proclamation, a monarch could radically change how people lived their lives.

BATTLE OF POWER

The authority and power of the Church during the Renaissance were also great and far-reaching. The Church was wealthy, and politically and socially powerful. When the Church and monarchy disagreed, the power of the Church usually prevailed, until the reign of Henry VIII. Henry VIII sought an annulment of his marriage to Catherine of Aragon. When his request was denied, King Henry asserted that royal power was greater than the power of the Church. He remarried and formed his own church, the Church of England, of which he was head.

DIMINISHING POWER

Through the centuries, parliamentary authority has grown while royal power has diminished. By the end of World War I, most Western monarchies had ceased to exist. Present-day monarchies are considered "constitutional monarchies," in which a royal figure exists for purposes of tradition and as a symbol of national unity but has no political authority.

Although the power of monarchies has diminished, the influence of the monarchies has had long-reaching effects, such as the present-day use of the King James Bible and fascination with the possibilities of absolute power. The monarchy is still a popular theme in today's literature and movies. For example, the screenplay *A Man for All Seasons* presents a historical struggle with the monarchy. In the following excerpt, King Henry VIII is trying to force Sir Thomas More to choose allegiance to the king over his religious beliefs. More chose to adhere to his personal belief. He was later tried and put to death.

ROBERT BOLT
(1924–1995)

Robert Bolt was a successful British playwright and writer of screenplays. He was born in Manchester and educated at Manchester University. He served three years in the army and air force before trying his hand as a playwright. He was teaching when his first play, *Flowing Cherry,* was produced in London. Its great success led Bolt to leave the classroom for the stage.

Bolt wrote the screenplay for *A Man for All Seasons,* as well as for other successful movies, including *Dr. Zhivago, Lawrence of Arabia,* and *Ryan's Daughter.*

Prentice Hall Literature Program Resources

REINFORCE / RETEACH / EXTEND

Selection Support Pages
Build Vocabulary, p. 57
Thematic Connection, p. 58

Formal Assessment Selection Test, pp. 60–61; Assessment Resources Software

Resource Pro CD-ROM
From *A Man for All Seasons*—includes all resource material and customizable lesson plan

Listening to Literature Audiocassettes
From *A Man for All Seasons*

1

In the following scene, Sir Thomas More, friend and colleague of King Henry VIII, is being forced to chose between his devotion to the Church and respect for its teaching, and his loyalty to his ruler. His strong religious principles prevent him from taking an oath of supremacy, an assertion that papal authority could not supersede the king's authority. This defiance cost him his life.

2

HENRY. I am a fool.

MORE. How so, Your Grace?

HENRY. [*A pause, during which the music fades to silence*] What else but a fool to live in a Court, in a licentious[1] mob—when I have friends, with gardens.

MORE. Your Grace—

2

HENRY. No courtship, no ceremony, Thomas. Be seated. You *are* my friend, are you not? [MORE *sits*]

MORE. Your Majesty.

HENRY. [*Eyes lighting on the chain on the table by* MORE] And thank God I have a friend for my Chancellor.[2] [*Laughingly,*

1. **licentious** (lī sen′ shəs) *adj.*: Disregarding accepted rules and standards.
2. **Chancellor** (chan′ sə lər) *n.*: More's position as an important advisor to the king.

Develop Understanding

This selection illustrates the power of the monarchy at the time of Henry VIII, as well as the personalities of two men involved.

When Henry first came to power, he was handsome, charming, and keen-witted. But unbridled power exposed a cruel streak and a lack of self-control. By 1534, Henry ruled both the church and the government.

Henry demanded that everyone sign a bill acknowledging his supremacy over the Pope. More refused to sign on principle, and Henry had him executed for treason in 1535. Four hundred years later, in 1935, More was canonized for his actions.

Customize for
Bodily/Kinesthetic Learners
Encourage students to act out the roles, using vocal emphasis, gestures, and facial expressions. Deciding how the lines should be said will help students understand the different personalities.

Customize for
English Language Learners
To prevent language barriers from getting in the way of an understanding of this scene, first explain the context of the scene. Then play the recording of this selection on the **Listening to Literature Audiocassettes** or have students view a videocassette recording of this portion of the 1966 movie.

◆ Critical Thinking

1 Hypothesize Tell students that the title refers to More, not to Henry VIII. Have them interpret the title's meaning. *Students may suggest that More was a man who could weather bad times as well as good or who deserves to be admired at all times.*

◆ Critical Thinking

2 Draw Conclusions Ask students who is leading the conversation and who is following. What does this suggest? *Henry leads and More follows. This suggests their status as ruler and advisor.*

◆ Reading Strategy

❶ **Infer** Ask students what the chain might symbolize. *It might show More's status as Chancellor; it might symbolize Henry's control over More.*

❷ **Clarification** Point out that "Wolsey" refers to Thomas Wolsey (1475–1530), a Catholic cardinal and an extremely powerful man who was twice a candidate to be pope. As lord chancellor of England, he dominated the government from 1515 to 1529. He made many enemies, eventually including Henry himself, and was arrested for treason. He died soon after.

◆ Critical Thinking

❸ **Infer** Ask students what they can infer about Henry from this speech. *Students may mention his anger; his vindictiveness; his dislike of the Church; or the way his mind jumps about.*

Clarification When Henry refers to Wolsey failing him "in the one thing that mattered," he is referring to Wolsey's inability to convince the Pope to annul Henry's marriage to Catherine of Aragon.

Customize for ***Visual/Spatial Learners***
Have students study the photograph and share the impression it gives of each man's character. Does the illustration fit the scene or just show the characters? *Students may disagree; some will think that Henry looks too calm and More too agitated for this photograph to be an illustration of this scene.*

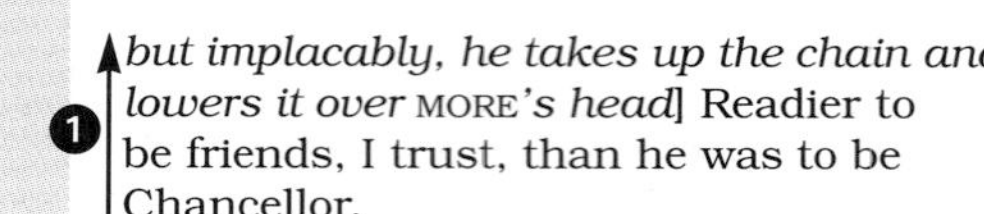

CONNECTIONS TO TODAY'S WORLD

❶ *but implacably, he takes up the chain and lowers it over* MORE*'s head*] Readier to be friends, I trust, than he was to be Chancellor.

MORE. My own knowledge of my poor abilities—

❷ **HENRY.** I will judge of your abilities, Thomas . . . Did you know that Wolsey named you for Chancellor?

MORE. Wolsey!

HENRY. Aye, before he died. Wolsey named you and Wolsey was no fool.

MORE. He was a statesman of incomparable ability, Your Grace.

❸ **HENRY.** Was he? Was he so? [*He rises*] Then why did he fail me? Be seated—it was villainy then! Yes, villainy. I was right to break him; he was all pride, Thomas; a proud man; pride right through. And he failed me! [MORE *opens his mouth*] He failed me in the one thing that mattered! The one thing that matters, Thomas, then or now. And why? He wanted to be Pope! Yes, he wanted to be the Bishop of Rome. I'll tell you something, Thomas, and you can check this for yourself—it was never merry in England while we had Cardinals amongst us. [*He nods significantly at* MORE, *who lowers his eyes*] But look now—[*Walking away*] —I shall forget the feel of that . . . great tiller[3] under my hands . . . I took her down to Dogget's Bank, went about and brought her up in Tilbury Roads. A man could sail clean round the world in that ship.

MORE. [*With affectionate admiration*] Some men could, Your Grace.

3. **tiller** (tilʹ ər) *n.*: Bar or handle for turning a boat's rudder.

Beyond Literature

Media Connection

The Monarchs and the Movies The 1966 movie *A Man for All Seasons* represents the public's fascination with monarchs. The first blockbuster hit about a monarch was 1912's *Elizabeth, Queen of England;* more recently, Mel Gibson's *Braveheart* about Edward I's struggle with Scotland met great success. What is it about the lives of monarchs that lends itself to movie making? Explain.

Humanities: Film

Scene From *A Man for All Seasons.*
A Man for All Seasons has had several incarnations: it was a radio production in 1954; a television production in 1957; a state production in 1960; and a film in 1966. A remake of the film, starring Charleton Heston in the role of Thomas More, was produced for television in 1988.

The original film won numerous awards, including the Academy Award for Best Picture. Actor Paul Scofield won an Academy Award for his portrayal of Thomas More, as did Robert Shaw, who played Henry. Bolt won an Oscar for his screenplay, and the director, Fred Zinnemann, also took one home.

This was Scofield's first major film role. Before, he was known primarily as a fine Shakespearean actor. A film critic of the time, Pauline Kael, wrote that the martyr More was perhaps too perfect in the film. He was the only honorable person on screen, she wrote, and furthermore, he had all the good lines.

Use these questions for discussion:

1. Why, do you think, was a film on such a serious subject so popular? *It was a good film; the oral issue is timeless; people are always interested in films on the monarchy.*
2. What are some other films about important historical events or people? *Answers may include* Schindler's List; Braveheart; Glory; Mandela; and, Gandhi.

4 ▲ **Critical Viewing** How does this movie still illustrate the conflict in this excerpt from *A Man for All Seasons*? **[Support]**

HENRY. [*Offhand*] Touching this matter of my divorce, Thomas; have you thought of it since we last talked?

MORE. Of little else.

HENRY. Then you see your way clear to me?

MORE. That you should put away Queen Catherine, Sire? Oh, alas [*He thumps the chair in distress*] as I think of it I see so clearly that I can *not* come with Your Grace that my endeavor is not to think of it at all. 5

HENRY. Then you have not thought enough! . . . [*With real appeal*] Great God, Thomas, why do you hold out against me in the desire of my heart—the very wick of my heart?

MORE. [*Draws up his sleeve, baring his arm*] There is my right arm. [*A practical proposition*] Take your dagger and saw it from my shoulder, and I will laugh and be thankful, if by that means I can come with Your Grace with a clear conscience. 6

HENRY. [*Uncomfortably pulls at the sleeve*] I know it, Thomas, I know . . .

MORE. [*Rises, formally*] I crave pardon if I offend.

HENRY. [*Suspiciously*] Speak then.

MORE. When I took the Great Seal your Majesty promised not to pursue me on this matter. 7

HENRY. Ha! So I break my word, Master More! No no, I'm joking . . . I joke roughly . . . [*He wanders away*] I often think I'm a rough fellow . . . Yes, a rough young fellow. [*He shakes his head indulgently*] Be seated

▶Critical Viewing◀

4 Support Students may mention More's indecision, shown by his expression and gestures, and the difference between Henry's rich robes and More's simple ones.

Comprehension Check ☑

5 Have students paraphrase More's convoluted and courtly response. *Students' restatement of More's words should be similar to the following: No. I have thought about your divorce from Queen Catherine. When I do so, I see that I cannot agree with you. This is why I try not to think about it at all.*

◆ Critical Thinking

6 Analyze What does this exchange of dialogue reveal about Henry's and More's relationship? *The dialogue reveals that their relationship is complex. One moment they're speaking honestly and informally, the next moment, More addresses the King as a humble, fearful subject.*

◆ Critical Thinking

7 Interpret Why does More remind the King of his promise? *He does not want to be in the position of having to publicly disagree with the King or of being forced to choose between his loyalty to the Church and his loyalty to the king.*

Thematic Connection

❶ **Battle of Power** Have students explain how the battle of power between Church and State is demonstrated in this passage. *The passage shows a conflict between the king and the Church. Henry has convinced himself that he must end his marriage to Catherine, but the Church will not give permission for the marriage to be annulled. Henry's arguments reveal that he is no longer accepting Church authority when it comes to interpreting the Scriptures; he is insisting that religious law be interpreted his way.*

◆ Critical Thinking

❷ **Infer** Ask students why Henry is so determined to get More to agree with him. *Answers may include any of the following: he wanted his approval; More was respected and Henry thought that he could sway public opinion; Henry did not want to feel guilty; Henry sincerely believed that he was right.*

◆ Critical Thinking

❸ **Assess** Ask students if Henry is being truthful when he says he loves truth better than praise. *Most students will say he is not; when More says the music is delightful, Henry drops all pretense of wanting a real evaluation.* Have students describe what they can tell about More from his evaluation of the music. *Suggested response: He is perfectly honest, even when he knows that honesty is not desired by the King and that an honest answer may annoy or anger the king.*

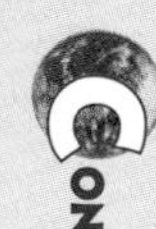

. . . That's a rosebay.[4] We have one like it at Hampton—not so red as that though. Ha—I'm in an excellent frame of mind. [*Glances at the rosebay*] Beautiful. [*Reasonable, pleasant*] You must consider, Thomas, that I stand in peril of my soul. It was no marriage; she was my brother's widow. Leviticus: "Thou shalt not uncover the nakedness of thy brother's wife." Leviticus, Chapter eighteen, Verse sixteen.[5]

MORE. Yes, Your Grace. But Deuteronomy—[6]

HENRY. [*Triumphant*] Deuteronomy's ambiguous!

❶ **MORE.** [*Bursting out*] Your Grace, I'm not fit to meddle in these matters—to me it seems a matter for the Holy See—

HENRY. [*Reprovingly*] Thomas, Thomas, does a man need a Pope to tell him when he's sinned? It was a sin, Thomas; I admit it; I repent. And God has punished me; I have no son . . . Son after son she's borne me, Thomas, all dead at birth, or dead within the month; I never saw the hand of God so clear in anything . . . I have a daughter, she's a good child, a well-set child— But I have no son. [*He flares up*] It is my bounden *duty* to put away the Queen, and all the Popes back to St. Peter shall not come between me and my duty! How is it that you cannot see? Everyone else does.

❷ **MORE.** [*Eagerly*] Then why does Your Grace need my poor support?

HENRY. Because you are honest. What's more to the purpose, you're known to be honest . . . There are those like Norfolk who follow me because I wear the crown, and there are those like Master Cromwell who follow me because they are jackals with sharp teeth and I am their lion, and there is a mass that follows me because it follows anything that moves—and there is you. ❷

MORE. I am sick to think how much I must displease Your Grace.

HENRY. No, Thomas, I respect your sincerity. Respect? Oh, man, it's water in the desert . . . How did you like our music? That air they played, it had a certain—well, tell me what you thought of it.

MORE. [*Relieved at this turn; smiling*] Could it have been Your Grace's own?

HENRY. [*Smiles back*] Discovered! Now I'll never know your true opinion. And that's irksome, Thomas, for we artists, though we love praise, yet we love truth better.

MORE. [*Mildly*] Then I will tell Your Grace truly what I thought of it.

HENRY. [*A little disconcerted*] Speak then.

MORE. To me it seemed—delightful. ❸

HENRY. Thomas—I chose the right man for Chancellor.

MORE. I must in fairness add that my taste in music is reputedly deplorable.[7]

HENRY. Your taste in music is excellent. It exactly coincides with my own. Ah music! Music! Send them back without me, Thomas; I will live here in Chelsea and make music.

---

4. **rosebay** (rōz′ bā) *n.*: Any of the genus (rhododendron) of trees or shrubs with showy flowers of pink, white, or purple.
5. **Leviticus** (lə vit′ i kəs), **Chapter eighteen, Verse sixteen:** Reference to the third book of the Pentateuch in the Bible, containing the laws relating to priests and their assistants, the Levites.
6. **Deuteronomy** (do͞ot′ ər än′ ə mē): Fifth book of the Pentateuch in the Bible, in which the laws of Moses are set down.
7. **deplorable** (dē plôr′ə bəl) *adj.*: Regrettable or wretched.

Enrichment

Henry's desire for a legitimate male heir, perhaps coupled with his growing infatuation with Anne Boleyn, caused him to request an annulment of his marriage to Catherine in 1527. Catherine appealed to the Pope that her marriage was valid because her one-year marriage to Arthur, Henry's older brother, was never consummated. The Pope put off the issue for seven years for both political and religious reasons. Politically, the Pope dared not go against the wishes of Catherine's nephew, the Holy Roman Emperor Charles V, who had kept the Pope a prisoner from 1597 to 1598. Religiously, the Pope would have had to nullify a previous papal decision that had allowed Henry to marry Catherine. As well as calling into question the decision-making of the Church, such a decision would have also caused financial problems. The granting of permissions of the type that allowed Henry to marry Catherine was an important source of revenue.

MORE. My house is at Your Grace's disposal.

HENRY. Thomas, you understand me; we will stay here together and make music.

MORE. Will Your Grace honor my roof after dinner?

HENRY. [*Walking away, blowing moodily on his whistle*] Mm? Yes, I expect I'll bellow for you . . .

MORE. My wife will be more—

HENRY. Yes, yes. [*He turns, his face set*] Touching this other business, mark you, Thomas, I'll have no opposition.

MORE. [*Sadly*] Your Grace?

HENRY. No opposition, I say! No opposition! Your conscience is your own affair; but you are my Chancellor! There, you have my word—I'll leave you out of it. But I
4 don't take it kindly, Thomas, and I'll have no opposition! I see how it will be; the bishops will oppose me. The full-fed, hypocritical, "Princes of the *Church*"! Ha! As for the Pope! Am I to burn in Hell because the Bishop of Rome, with the King of Spain's knife to his throat, mouths me Deuteronomy? Hypocrites! They're all hypocrites! Mind they do not take you in, Thomas! Lie 4
low if you will, but I'll brook no opposition—no noise! No words, no signs, no letters, no pamphlets—Mind that, Thomas —no writings against me!

MORE. Your grace is unjust. I am Your Grace's loyal minister. If I cannot serve Your Grace in this great matter of the Queen—

HENRY. I have no Queen! Catherine is not my wife and no priest can make her so, and they that say she is my wife are not only liars . . . but traitors! Mind it, Thomas!

MORE. Am I a babbler, Your Grace? [*But his voice is unsteady*]

HENRY. You are stubborn . . . [*Wooingly*] If you could come with me, you are the man I would soonest raise—yes, with my own hand.

MORE. [*Covers his face*] Oh, Your Grace overwhelms me!

CONNECTIONS TO TODAY'S WORLD

Guide for Responding

◆ Literature and Your Life

Reader's Response If you were Sir Thomas More, how would you have responded to the king? Explain.

Thematic Focus Aside from government, what other situations can you think of in which it is dangerous for one person to have absolute power? Explain.

☑ Check Your Comprehension

1. What position does More hold in Henry's court?
2. Why does Henry feel he has the right to divorce Queen Catherine?
3. How does More feel about Henry's decision to divorce the queen?

Thematic Connection

4 Royal Proclamations Ask students what role Henry expects More to play and what clues suggest this. *More is supposed to be quiet and not oppose the King; anyone who says Catherine is his wife is a liar and a traitor.* Discuss what they think will happen if More refuses. *More will be seen as a traitor.*

Reinforce and Extend

Answers

◆ Literature and Your Life

Reader's Response Students may say that they might have been more reluctant to defy the king.

Thematic Focus Students may say that its is dangerous for anyone to have absolute power, and may cite examples in business and the military.

☑ Check Your Comprehension

1. He is the Chancellor.
2. He thinks that the marriage is invalid because it violates a commandment in Leviticus. He feels his decision is supported by heaven, because all but one of his children have died in infancy.
3. More does not think the decision, which defies the ruling of the Pope, is correct.

Beyond the Selection

FURTHER READING

More Works by Robert Bolt

The thwarting of Baron Bolligrew
State of Revolution

More Works About King Henry VIII

Henry VIII: Images of a Tudor King, Christopher Lloyd
The Wives of Henry VIII, Lady Antonia Fraser

We suggest that you preview these works before recommending them to students.

INTERNET

You and your students may find additional information about Thomas More on the Internet at the following site. Please be aware, however, that sites may have changed from the time we published this information.

To learn more about Thomas More's life and his works, go to **http://www.luminarium.org/renlit/tmore.htm.**

We *strongly recommend* that you preview the sites before you send students to them.

Reinforce and Extend

Answers

◆ Critical Thinking

1. Wolsey failed to convince the Pope to annul Henry's marriage to Catherine. Henry brings this up as a warning to More not to fail him.
2. Henry does not really care what More thinks, but he will not tolerate any open criticism.
3. Some students will interpret More's gesture as a sign of despair and resignation; he will not openly oppose Henry. Other students may interpret More's despairing gesture as meaning that More realizes that he must now oppose his king.
4. The stage directions convey information about body language that reveal that the king is intimidating and sly, and that More is his subordinate.
5. Students may mention military dictatorships in Africa, Asia, and South and Central America.

Thematic Connection

1. Students may say that Elizabeth I had the most power, because she was supported by the people and thus did not have to expend as much energy crushing her opponents. Elizabeth seems to have used her power for the good of the people, helping them believe that they could defeat the "invincible" Armada, whereas her father appears to have used his power for selfish reasons, such as getting rid of unwanted wives.
2. Students may say that the world would not be as technologically advanced, particularly in the area of communications, because widespread education and the free flow of information tend to undermine absolute authority.
3. Some students may think that voting is extremely important. A few may complain that they are not given the right to participate in government early enough. Other students may think that voting does not confer enough power to the people, and that the country is really run for the benefit of special-interest groups.

◆ Critical Thinking

Interpret

1. Why does Henry think Wolsey failed him? Why do you think the king brings this up to More? **[Interpret]**
2. Henry asked More to critique his music as well as his decision to divorce Catherine. What do his reactions reveal about how he feels about More's opinions? Support your answer. **[Infer]**
3. Judging by More's final gesture of covering his face and his words "Your Grace overwhelms me," what do you think his decision will be? **[Predict]**
4. How do the stage directions add to your understanding of the relationship between Henry and More? **[Explain]**

Extend

5. In which countries in today's world does a ruler have absolute power? **[Social Studies Link]**

Thematic Connection

The Influence of the Monarchy

Bolt's screenplay captures a time when the British monarchy had absolute power. Today, in contrast, the monarchy has little power and serves mostly as a symbol of the nation's unity.

1. Which of the monarchs represented in the selections in this section do you believe had the most power? Which used power for the good of the people? Which used it for selfish reasons? Support your answers.
2. How might the world be different if European monarchies still had absolute authority? Support your answer.
3. Being part of a democracy, we become part of the decision-making process at the age of eighteen. In many countries people are not given the privilege of voting and live by the will of a dictator. How do you feel about having the privilege to vote?

Idea Bank

Writing

1. **Letter to a Monarch** Write a letter to Henry VIII explaining why you agree or disagree with the decision he has made. Provide reasons to support your position.
2. **Opening Argument** The defense lawyer for Sir Thomas More was eventually tried and sentenced to death for opposing Henry VIII. As More's lawyer, write an opening argument.
3. **Continuation** Write a continuation of this scene. Base your dialogue and your depiction of the characters on the portion of the screenplay you've just read.

Speaking and Listening

4. **Television Interview** Team up with fellow students to interview Henry VIII and Thomas More for the evening news. Prepare questions for each character, and write their responses based on what you learned from this excerpt. Stage your interview for the class.

Project

5. **Visual History** Create a visual history of one of the monarchs of England. Using images from books and magazines, or your own drawings, create a timeline that covers the most important events that took place during the reign of that monarch.

Idea Bank

Customizing for *Performance Levels*

Following are suggestions for matching Idea Bank topics with your students' performance levels:

Less Advanced Students: 1
Average Students: 2, 5
More Advanced Students: 3, 4

Customizing for *Learning Modalities*

Following are suggestions for matching Idea Bank topics with your students' learning modalities:

Visual/Spatial: 5
Verbal/Linguistic: 1, 2, 3, 4
Interpersonal: 4

✓ Assessment Options

Formal Assessment, Selection Test, pp. 60–61, and Assessment Resources Software.

PORTFOLIO ASSESSMENT

Use the following rubrics in the ***Alternative Assessment*** booklet to assess student writing:

Letter to a Monarch: Evaluation/Review Rubric, p. 105
Opening Argument: Persuasion Rubric, p. 106
Continuation: Drama Rubric, p. 110

Writing Process Workshop

Persuasive Essay

The selections in this unit—a political statement, a rousing speech, and a sermon—all contain elements of persuasion. You can use persuasion yourself, whenever you try to get someone to see things your way. Put that skill to use in a persuasive essay in which you convince your readers of something. In a persuasive essay, you present an argument in favor of your point and support your argument with unbiased, accurate evidence.

The following skills, introduced in this section's Writing Mini-Lessons, will help you write a persuasive essay.

Writing Skills Focus

- **Use a persuasive tone** to convince readers to adopt a point of view or to take a specific action. Your readers should feel that you have their interests in mind. (See p. 243.)
- **Support your argument** with logical reasons, examples, research, or anecdotal data. (See p. 251.)
- **Maintain coherence** by focusing the elements of the essay on your purpose. Close your essay by summarizing your central position.

Model From Literature

from Queen Elizabeth I's *Speech Before Defeating the Spanish Armada*

I know I have but the body of a weak and feeble woman; but I have the heart of a king, and of a king of England, too: ① and think foul scorn that Parma or Spain, or any prince of Europe, should dare to invade the borders of my realms ② to which rather than dishonor should grow by me, I myself will take arms: I myself ③ will be your general, judge and rewarder of every one of your virtues in the field.

① The Queen begins with an appeal to emotions to set the persuasive tone.

② To support her appeal, the Queen gives a specific example of an invasion that is threatening England.

③ By repeating the pronoun *I*, she maintains coherence and reinforces the personal tone.

Prepare and Engage

Establish Writing Guidelines
Before students begin this lesson, review with them the following key elements of a persuasive essay:

- A persuasive essay is a short piece of writing whose purpose is to convince people to take a certain position or action.
- Logical reasons, statistics, and examples support the recommended action or position of a persuasive essay.
- A persuasive tone—such as a commanding or an urgent tone—strengthens the presentation.
- All elements of the essay support the recommended position.

Distribute the Scoring Rubric for Persuasion (p. 106) in ***Alternative Assessment*** to make students aware of the criteria for a persuasive essay. In addition, see the suggestions for customizing the rubric on page 261.

Review with students the elements of persuasion in Queen Elizabeth's speech. Ask students what elements made the queen's speech effective. How can they use the same elements or techniques in their own essays?

Writing and Language Transparencies To model the writing and revising of a persuasive essay, use Writing Process Model 5: Persuasive Essay, pp. 37–44.

Writing Lab CD-ROM
If students have access to a computer, have them work in the tutorial for Persuasion to complete their essays. Have students follow these steps:

1. Review an annotated model of a persuasive essay.
2. Use a persuasion word bin to help them find a topic.
3. Use the Pros-and-Cons Chart to sort opposing ideas for their topics and organize information for their essays.
4. Use the persuasive word bin while drafting.
5. Have students watch the author video of Cary Bricker to get a tip on revising.

Sourcebook
Students can find additional support for the writing process in Chapter 4: Persuasion, pp. 97–129.

Beyond the Classroom

Career Connection

Presenting a Proposal Explain to students that they may have the opportunity in their careers to present a proposal—a plan for improving or developing something at the workplace—to their employers. Point out that an idea or a proposal should include all the elements of persuasive writing and that a persuasive tone strengthens the presentation of an idea. Let students know that making a strong case for their proposals requires effort and preparation. They should research any possible opposition and address it before presenting their proposals. They should also include statistics, graphs, charts, and facts to support their proposal and give it credibility. Presenting a persuasive proposal that wins the support of coworkers and employers marks an important step in a career.

APPLYING LANGUAGE SKILLS: Using Active Voice

The active voice, in which the subject of the sentence performs the action, is usually more effective than the passive voice, in which the subject of the sentence receives the action. As much as possible, use the active voice in your persuasive essay.

Passive Voice
Pollution was created by people.
[subject receives the action]

Active Voice
People create pollution.
[subject performs the action]

Practice Rewrite each sentence, changing the passive voice to the active voice.

1. Tuition at Levitt University has been raised by its trustees.
2. The fund drive was called off by school officials.
3. The scholarship fund was created by the Garden Club.

Writing Application As you draft your persuasive essay, change the passive voice to the active voice.

Writer's Solution Connection Language Lab

For more practice using the active voice, complete the Active and Passive Voice lesson on the Language Lab CD-ROM.

Prewriting

Choose a Topic Consider issues that personally concern you, such as the rising cost of college tuition or the importance of participating in sports. You may also want to consider as a topic global issues such as pollution, world hunger, or military spending.

Keep these points in mind as you choose a topic:

1. **Scope** Choose a topic you can fully discuss within a short persuasive essay.
2. **Debate** Choose a topic that is subject to debate.
3. **Research** Choose a topic about which sufficient information is available.

Gather Evidence Make use of facts, statistics, reasons, and quotations to support your argument. When gathering evidence, use a variety of current, unbiased sources, such as articles, on-line services, interviews, and nonfiction books.

Organize Evidence Choose one of the following organizational strategies to present your argument effectively.

- ▶ **Main Idea and Details** Make key points, then support them with specific evidence.
- ▶ **Order of Importance** Arrange supporting details from weakest to strongest to build your argument.
- ▶ **Pro and Con** Present the opposition to your position, then refute the argument using your evidence.
- ▶ **Cause and Effect** Arrange key points to show how your audience's action or inaction could affect their lives.

Drafting

Write an Introduction, Body, and Conclusion In the introduction, state your argument in a way that will grab the attention of your audience. State your main points and support each with solid evidence in the body of your essay. In the conclusion, restate your argument and emphasize the action you want your audience to take.

Create a Persuasive Tone A persuasive tone is the manner (pleading, urgent, commanding) in which you get your message across. Decide on a tone that will suit your topic as well as appeal to your audience. Then, as you weave together the facts for your essay, choose words that create that persuasive tone.

Develop Student Writing

Prewriting

Help students brainstorm for topic ideas. Have them discuss issues they find controversial and that affect their lives. List these issues on the chalkboard as possible writing topics. Suggest to students that they consider taking a position on one of these topics for their persuasive essays.

Customize for
More Advanced Students
Challenge these students to write their essays from a viewpoint that is the opposite of what they believe. Writing a persuasive essay from another point of view will give these students additional skills in developing a persuasive case.

Writing and Language Transparencies Review with students the various ways to organize their persuasive essays as shown on this page. Offer students the options of using the Argument Organizer, p. 103, or the Cause-and-Effect Organizer, p. 119.

Writer's Solution

Writing Lab CD-ROM
Students may want to use Organizing Evidence section of the Persuasion tutorial. The Pros-and-Cons Chart, Outliner, Note Cards Activity, Keyhole Organizer, Venn Diagram, or Chain of Events Organizer can help them organize details. In addition, they can view interactive instruction to receive tips on the different types of organization suitable for their persuasive essays.

Community Connection
A good way for students to get a topic for a persuasive essay is to get involved in their community. Suggest that interested students volunteer at a youth center, a home for the elderly, a soup kitchen, or some other community service organization. Suggest that they apply their experiences and write a persuasive essay on how to improve the facility or organization in which they worked.

Drafting

Have students write down the main impression they would like to convey with their essay. Tell them to refer to it as they draft and to choose language and use a tone that will help them to convey that impression.

Applying Language Skills

Using Active Voice Explain to students that verbs in the active voice will make their persuasive essays stronger. Have them practice revising sentences with passive voice to make them active.

Answers

1. The trustees at Levitt University have raised the tuition.
2. The school officials called off the fund drive.
3. The Garden Club created the scholarship fund.

Writer's Solution

For additional practice, have students complete the Active and Passive Voice lesson on the **Language Lab CD-ROM.** Students may also complete the practice pages on Active Voice in the *Writer's Solution Grammar Practice Book,* p. 56.

Revising

Strengthen the Persuasive Tone Make your essay as appealing as possible by strengthening its persuasive tone. To do this, replace any weak, vague words with words that convey urgency, seriousness, or joy, depending on your tone. For example, if your tone is urgent, change the message "Register to vote" to "Don't waste your vote."

Check Support Review the details you use to support your topic. Do they support it strongly, or will they give your opponent an opportunity to point out weaknesses in your argument? Eliminate details that do not support your argument.

Revision Model

It is ~~pretty important~~ crucial ① to practice the guitar every day. Many guitar players gain confidence by practicing daily. ② I was given a guitar for my twelfth birthday. I took lessons and practiced faithfully every day after school. As an adult, I have had many opportunities to play at large parties and gatherings.③ ~~Many musicians are able to earn a small income playing at local events.~~ Remember, you won't become an accomplished musician overnight, but if you keep practicing, you'll find that persistence pays off.

① This wording has been revised to reflect the persuasive tone of the essay, which is serious.

② A personal anecdote supports the persuasive argument.

③ To maintain coherence, the writer deleted a sentence that takes the reader away from the main purpose of the piece.

Publishing

- ▶ **Local Radio Station** Call a local radio talk show and make your persuasive argument before a live audience.
- ▶ **Local Newspaper** Submit your essay as a letter to the editor.
- ▶ **Community** Present a persuasive argument for a community improvement idea before your town or county council.

Applying Language Skills: Using Persuasive Language

Use words that have positive or negative connotations—or associated meanings—to make your argument convincing. The following chart lists words with similar definitions according to their positive or negative connotations.

Positive Connotations	Negative Connotations
visionary	dreamer
challenge	problem
introverted	self-absorbed

Practice Replace the italicized words with ones that have strong positive or negative connotations.

1. The *health farm* was run by *athletes.*
2. Marv's *car* runs on diesel.
3. We had two of Rosa's *small cookies.*

Writing Application As you revise your essay, replace neutral terms with ones that have more positive connotations.

Writer's Solution Connection Writing Lab

To guide your revision, complete the Self-Evaluation Checklist in the Revising and Editing section of the Persuasion tutorial.

Revising

Have students work with a peer to revise their essays. Students should use the Writing Skills Focus points on page 259 and the Rubric for Persuasion as guidelines for reviewing each other's papers.

Writing and Language Transparencies Review the revision model on this page as well as the revising sections of Writing Process Model 5: Persuasive Essay (pp. 41–44). This review will help students identify similar weaknesses in their essays.

Writer's Solution

Writers at Work Videodisc

Play the videodisc section in which Cary Bricker discusses her views on revising and editing. Ask students if they agree with her methods.

Play frames 39870 to 40926

Reinforce and Extend

Review the Writing Guidelines

After students have completed their essays, review the key characteristics of a persuasive essay. Encourage students to come up with additional criteria based on what they have learned by completing the assignment.

Applying Language Skills

Using Persuasive Language

Explain to students that a key effort of their revision should be to replace vague language with language that will create a persuasive tone.

Answers

Suggested responses:

1. The *retirees* ran the *club*.
2. Marv's *limousine* runs on diesel.
3. We had two of Rosa's *petit fours*.

ASSESSMENT		4	3	2	1
PORTFOLIO ASSESSMENT Use the rubric on Persuasion in ***Alternative Assessment*** (p. 106) to assess students' writing. Add these criteria to customize this assignment.	**Active Voice**	The writer uses the active voice to present a strong argument.	The writer uses the active voice most of the time, but occasionally uses the passive voice when the active voice would be more effective.	The writer uses mostly passive voice when active voice would be more effective.	The writer makes no attempt to use the active voice.
	Unity	The essay is unified: all details support the writer's position.	The essay lacks unity because some points stray from the writer's position.	Much of the support provided does not develop the writer's position; therefore, the paper lacks unity.	The writer's position is unclear, and the paper is not unified.

Introduce the Strategy

Most students will turn eighteen this year and will be able to vote. Explain to students that it is important that they learn to evaluate political messages and discern what is factual and what is biased. Have students read the strategies on this page and answer the questions.

Customize for
English Language Learners
Political messages often use charged language, which students learning English might not recognize as such. Have these students write brief summary statements of each idea in the political flier. Then students should review them with a native speaker to see if they have been misled by any of the statements. Students should then work together to answer the questions in Apply the Strategies.

Apply the Strategy

Answers

1. The candidate cannot do what he promises. He alone does not have the power to decide what the state funds and maintains, which is probably decided either by the electorate or by the state legislature.
2. Martin's reasons for voting for the Jennings Bikeway bill should be investigated. Martin's claim that he is a true environmentalist should also be investigated—find out if anything in his background supports or refutes this claim.
3. "For a better and brighter future, Vote Martin!" is a vague and misleading statement.

Evaluating Political Persuasion

Real-World Reading Skills Workshop

Strategies for Success

Political persuasion is a lot like advertising. In fact, it *is* advertising—an attempt to sell a candidate or an issue instead of a product. As with any other kind of advertising, you need to evaluate the information carefully before making any decisions.

Responding to Political Advertisements Remember the sole purpose of a political advertisement is to convince you to vote for a certain candidate. The information in this type of advertising is slanted to give you a specific impression. Before you decide to support a candidate, carefully assess that candidate's political message.

Get All the Information Often political flyers incorporate vague statements and partial truths that create a misleading impression of the candidate. For example, the vague statement "*John Martin supports cutting automobile insurance costs*" could lead you to believe that John Martin consistently fights to lower insurance costs. If you don't question the validity of this statement, you won't find out that John Martin supported only one bill to cut rates, but he voted for three others that increased rates.

When evaluating a political message, use the following questions:

1. Has the advertisement provided all the information?
2. Can the candidate really keep this campaign promise? What might keep him or her from doing so?
3. Is the candidate trying to appeal only to my emotions in order to gain my support?

RE-ELECT JOHN MARTIN TO THE STATE ASSEMBLY.

Assemblyman Martin cares about preserving the beauties of our natural world.

- He voted for the Jennings Bikeway bill to show his support for bikers.
- He will make sure that all state-funded parks will be litter free and bike paths will be well maintained.
- Martin is an environmentalist who will work to conserve resources and ensure the health of our planet.

For a better and brighter future, Vote Martin!

Apply the Strategies

You are going to vote in an upcoming local election. As an avid hiker and biker, you want to elect someone who will help protect the environment. This flyer just arrived in the mail. Answer the following questions as you read it:

1. Does this candidate have the power to do what he promises? Why or why not?
2. What claims does he make that should be investigated? On what subject might you want to do some research?
3. Are any of these statements so vague as to be meaningless?

Here are other instances where you need to evaluate persuasive political tactics:

- Paid political advertisements in newspapers
- Letters from local officeholders
- Campaign posters and billboards

Cross-Curricular Connection: Social Studies

Explain to students that the often deceiving methods of political persuasion are not specific to our time but are part of history. Since the time of President John Adams, political campaigns have been aimed at convincing the public to vote for a certain candidate, which often involves misleading them. In addition, some campaigns take an ugly turn when candidates exploit the weaknesses of their opponents as a way of winning support for themselves. Have students research a presidential campaign of their choice. Ask them to share examples of political persuasion used during the campaign.

PART 3 *Focus on Literary Forms: Drama*

The Globe Theatre, London

"All the world's a stage," exclaims one of Shakespeare's characters, and the audience agreed. Elizabethan England had a dramatic sense of itself as a new power, acting its part on the world's stage. That's why it loved the bold new dramas that playwrights like Marlowe and Shakespeare were creating. In open-air theaters with names like the Globe, these writers let the English language strut and swagger.

One-Minute Planning Guide

William Shakespeare's *The Tragedy of Macbeth* is one of the greatest dramatic tragedies ever staged. *Macbeth* works on many levels: it is a human tragedy wherein the war hero develops a raging lust for power that leads him to commit murder and lose his humanity. It is also an exciting, gruesome tale of greed, murder, and retribution.

The play contains many exciting dramatic elements: the witches and apparitions lend the drama a supernatural, otherworldly atmosphere; there is suspense as the audience waits to see whether Macbeth will give in to his wife's goading and fulfill his foretold fate; there is danger as Duncan, Banquo, Fleance, and the Macduff family are murderously attacked, and there is adventure as the final battle scene rages at Dunsinane.

Customize for *Varying Student Needs*

When assigning the reading of *MacBeth*, keep in mind these factors:

- Long dramatic work that will require weeks of reading
- Blank verse and vocabulary may be difficult for students to read and comprehend
- Supernatural elements appear throughout the drama; murder and treachery propel the plot
- Theme concerning fate versus free will may be of interest to students

Humanities: Art

The Globe Theater, London.

This early drawing of the Globe, the theater in which many of Shakespeare's plays were staged, shows not only the building but also some of Southwark, the part of London in which the Globe was located. It also shows a few audience members lined up to attend a performance—perhaps of *As You Like It* or *Henry V,* two of Shakespeare's plays believed to have been performed in 1600, soon after the theater had been erected.

Use the following questions for discussion:

1. Judging from the appearance of the Globe and the other details in the picture, was going to the theater in Elizabethan England a special event or a commonplace one? *Students may say that because theater stands by itself in a clearing, it looks like a special building. The people lining up may be an indication that going to the theater was a special or exciting event for most Elizabethans.*
2. Using the details in the picture as a guide, what do you imagine the inside of the Globe to have been like? *Students may say that the circular shape of the building leads them to believe that the performances may have been "in the round." The little building on the roof may house stage technicians or other employees of the theater. The lack of windows on the ground floor may indicate that the audience would be seated up high.*

Enrichment

Shakespeare's Globe Theater

Although Shakespeare did not have the advantages of the modern theater to draw on, the theaters of his day must be considered highly sophisticated. The greatest dramas in our language were produced on the sixteenth-century English stage. This fact alone suggests how advanced the theater arts were when Shakespeare was writing his masterpieces.

Most of Shakespeare's plays were performed at the Globe. It was built by Richard and Cuthbert Burbage, sons of James Burbage, who had constructed The Theater, London's first theater. Richard Burgage was multitalented: He was also a leading actor in Shakespeare's acting company!

The foundation of the original Globe was discovered in 1990. The excavation revealed clues about the theater itself as well as the actors and audience. The tiny part of the foundation that was originally uncovered yielded a great number of hazelnut shells. Hazelnuts were the Elizabethan equivalent of popcorn: The audience munched on them throughout the performances.

INTERNET

The Internet provides excellent opportunities for students to learn more about the Globe. Please be aware, however, that sites may have changed from the time we published this information. For information about the Globe, go to Shakespeare and the Globe: Then and Now at this address: **http://shakespeare.eb.com/shakespeare/index2.html**

You may also go to **http://www.rdg.ac.uk/AcaDepts/In/Globe/QuickGuide.html**

You may also find related information on Elizabethan theater and Shakespeare's Globe on the Internet.

We *strongly recommend* that you preview the sites before you send students to them.

THE *Elizabethan Theater*

English drama came of age during the reign of Elizabeth I, developing into a sophisticated and very popular art form. Although playwrights like Shakespeare were mainly responsible for the great theatrical achievements of the time, the importance of actors, audiences, and theater buildings should not be underestimated.

Before the reign of Elizabeth I, theater companies traveled about the country putting on plays wherever they could find an audience, often performing in the open courtyards of inns. Spectators watched either from the ground or from balconies or galleries above.

England's First Playhouse

When Shakespeare was twelve years old, an actor named James Burbage built London's first theater, called simply The Theater, just beyond the city walls in Shoreditch. Actors—even prominent and well-to-do actors like Burbage—occupied a strange place in London society: They were frowned upon by the city fathers but were wildly popular with the common people, who clamored to see them perform in plays. Though actors were considered rogues and vagabonds by some, they were held in sufficient repute to be called on frequently to perform at court. A man like Burbage enjoyed a reputation somewhat like a rock star's today.

The Globe

In 1597, the city fathers closed down The Theater. In late 1598, Richard Burbage (James's son) and his men dismantled it and hauled it in pieces across the Thames to Southwark. It took them six months to rebuild it, and when they did they renamed it the Globe.

Scholars disagree about what the Globe actually looked like, since there are no surviving drawings from the time or detailed written descriptions. Shakespeare refers to the building in *Henry V* as "this wooden O," so we have a sense that it was round or octagonal. It is presumed that an important influence on the design of the theater was the bear-baiting and bull-baiting rings built in Southwark. These "sports" arenas were circular, open to the sky, and had galleries all around.

The building had to have been small enough to ensure that the actors would be heard, but we know that performances could draw audiences as large as 2,500 to 3,000 people. These truly packed houses must have been quite uncomfortable at times, especially when you consider that people didn't bathe or change their clothes very often! Those who paid an admission price of a penny (not an inconsiderable sum of money then) stood throughout the performance. Some of the audience even sat in a gallery behind the performers. Their seats were the second most expensive in the house, and though they saw only the actors' backs and probably couldn't hear very well, they were content to be seen by the other members of the audience.

Actors of the period had none of the elaborate technology that helps modern actors. There were no sets or lighting at the Globe. Plays were performed in the bright afternoon sunlight, and a playwright's words alone had to create moods like the one in the eerie first scene of *Macbeth.* Holding an audience spellbound was made even more difficult by the fact that most were eating and drinking throughout the performance.

Beyond the Classroom

Career Connection

Theater Management Inform students that theater management is an exciting career that combines business skills with the glamour of theater. Brainstorm with the class about the responsibilities and challenges a theater manager might encounter during his or her job (determining which plays to produce, hiring ushers and box office staff, arranging for advertising and posters, holding special fund-raising events, attracting talented directors, balancing a budget, and so on). Encourage interested students to visit a local playhouse or theater and investigate career opportunities.

▲ **Critical Viewing** Would you have preferred standing near the stage or sitting in the galleries to see Shakespeare's plays? Explain. **[Relate]**

The first Globe met its demise in 1613, when a cannon fired as part of a performance of *Henry VIII* ignited the theater's thatched roof. Everyone escaped unharmed, but the Globe burned to the ground. Although the theater was rebuilt, the Puritans had it permanently closed in 1642.

The New Globe

Almost four centuries after the original Globe opened, an actor stood onstage in the replica of the Globe and recited these lines from Shakespeare's *Henry V*: "Can this cockpit hold/The vasty fields of France? Or may we cram/Within this wooden O the very casques/That did affright the air at Agincourt?"

Building a replica of Shakespeare's Globe was American actor Sam Wanamaker's dream. After long years of fund-raising and construction, the theater opened to its first full season on June 8, 1997, with a production of *Henry V*. Like the earlier Globe, this one is made of wood, with a thatched roof and lime plaster covering the walls. The stage and the galleries are covered, but the "bear pit," where the modern-day groundlings stand, is open to the skies, exposing the spectators to the weather.

Perhaps the most striking aspect of seeing Shakespeare's plays performed at the Globe is the immediacy of the action."They are talking to you, asking you questions, involving you in their fears," wrote Benedict Nightingale of the performers in the *Times* of London. At the Globe you are part of the debate. Isn't that what theater is all about?

Humanities: Art

The Globe Theater, London.

This drawing shows Shakespeare's Globe. The stage is surrounded on three sides by seats and standing room for spectators. The "shadow," located over the stage and supported by pillars, protected players from the rain. Behind the stage is an inner recess, called the "tiring house," used for indoor scenes. On the second level is the "chamber," with a balcony, which was used to represent a wall of a castle or town or a bedchamber. On the third level is another chamber, usually used by the musicians. The fourth level is the turret, known as "the heavens," containing a bell and other means of creating sound effects.

Use these questions for discussion:

1. How does this theater compare with theaters of today? *Most theaters of today are buildings with roofs and seats for everyone.*
2. Would you be more likely to stage a grand drama or a lighthearted romance in a space such as this? Why? *Possible response: Most students will say that the Globe is more suited to a grand drama because its stage is big enough for battles to be performed.*

▶Critical Viewing◀

Relate Possible responses: Standing in front is preferable, because you get a head-on view of the action and you can feel like you're actually part of the play; sitting in the gallery is preferable because you're shielded from the weather and more comfortable.

Customize for *For Bodily/Kinesthetic Learners*

To help these students understand the effect the shape of the theater has on a performance, ask several students to take turns reading a speech to the class standing in front of the class. Then have them read the same speech with the class surrounding them on three sides. Discuss how the two arrangements affect such things as movement and eye contact. Also discuss how each arrangement affects what the audience sees and hears.

Enrichment

The New Globe London's new Globe theater is located on the Thames, a short distance from the site of the original. It retains the characteristics of the original—including its circular shape, open center, and thatched roof. Since few details of the original remain, the builders referred to the building contracts that exist for the rival theaters, the Rose and the Fortune, which were built by the same master carpenter who built the Globe.

The new Globe seats 1,000. Because the seats curve around the stage, everyone has a different view of the action. For some the view is blocked by pillars, but no audience member is more than fifty feet from the stage. The yard, or pit, has room for 450 groundlings, some of whom rest their arms on the edge of the stage. As in Elizabethan times, the audience tends to join in the proceedings, commenting on the action.

Plays are performed as they would have been in Shakespeare's time, with little or no scenery, people moving around in the yard, and vendors circulating to sell refreshments. The experience contrasts with performances in modern theaters—even performances of Shakespeare's plays—which take place in a darkened, quiet theater with an attentive and respectful audience.

Enrichment Laurence Olivier played Macbeth in 1937 and 1955. In his book *On Acting,* he discusses the differences between these two productions and the changes in his conception of the role:

The director of my 1937 *Macbeth* was Michel St.-Denis, a star director full of wit and imagination, though on this particular production neither seemed to be on our side. When I told Ralph Richardson I was going down to the Vic, he asked, "What are you going to play?" and when I said "Macbeth," he said, "You'll break your neck, my dear boy. You don't want to play Macbeth at your age; be very, very careful." It was what you might call a stylized production. Everything in godlike proportions. The makeups were masklike. I had a huge false face on, a nose that went down, a stuck-on chin and a putty forehead with vast eyebrows. The idea was to make something real through a highly poetic and unreal approach. . . . I think, in that production Macbeth was nearer my sleeve than my heart. . . .

I was to play [Macbeth] again some years later, at Stratford in 1955, directed by Glen Byam Shaw, with a considerable degree of success. My voice was infinitely stronger and more powerful, and the extra chunk of life experience I had had since I'd first played the part really counted. The first time, I had played age through pure imagination; now I could bring knowledge to bear . . . . I found that it was genuinely possible to make every second of Macbeth human despite all that murdering of children.

Macbeth on Stage

Actors have played Macbeth and Lady Macbeth in a variety of ways—as evil, sympathetic, noble—as these quotations illustrate.

Many Faces of Macbeth

Poetic Murderer John Gielgud portrayed Macbeth as "the most poetic of all murderers." For Gielgud, the key point about Macbeth is that he is able to describe how he feels and what he does in "poetic" language.

Lion-Hearted The director Glen Baym Shaw, who directed Laurence Olivier in the part of Macbeth, describes the role in these words: "A superb leader with the courage of a lion and the imagination of a poet . . . No one would ever dare to slap Macbeth on the back . . ."

Enthusiastic Warrior Following Shaw's direction, Olivier portrayed Macbeth so enthusiastically that one night, he injured the actor playing Macduff in their staged sword fight. On another occasion, with a substitute Macduff, Olivier fought the sword battle so vigorously that his sword broke and flew into the audience.

A Haitian Dictator In 1936 Orson Welles directed a version of *Macbeth* set in Haiti rather than Scotland. In this innovative production with an all black cast, Macbeth was modeled after a famous Haitian dictator.

Humanities: Theater

Producing *Macbeth* Theater buffs will tell you that *Macbeth* is cursed—that all an actor need do is quote from the play in a theater, or just mention its title, and disasters will come flying. Superstitions aside, in three centuries of productions, *Macbeth* has met with some flesh-and-blood difficulties.

When the English theaters reopened in 1660 after years of Puritan rule, Charles II asked William Davenant to produce the play. Davenant liked color—he added dancing, singing, and chanting to the witches' scenes. This was mere tinkering, though; the serious work began when he enlarged Lady Macduff's role. Scenes in which Lady Macbeth goads on Macbeth alternated with scenes in which Lady Macduff warns her husband against ambition. As if to keep up with the Macbeths and their spirit problems, the new, improved Lady Macduff has a run-in with Duncan's ghost. After years of these outrageous productions, in which the original play became almost unrecognizable, actor David Garrick restored Macbeth to something more closely resembling Shakespeare in the mid- to late 1700's.

A play that can return to life after this type of treatment surely has some sort of magic to it. Perhaps that is why its named cannot be mentioned lightly in a theater!

Lady Macbeth:

Ambition Above All Sarah Siddons, who played the role of Lady Macbeth about 200 years ago, declared, "In this astonishing creature one sees a woman in whose bosom the passion of ambition has almost obliterated all the characteristics of human nature . . ."

Essentially Feminine The famous nineteenth-century actress Ellen Terry believed that "Shakespeare's Lady is essentially feminine, even in the urgency of her appeal to her husband, and one strong argument is the very feminine way in which, when all is over—the deed done . . . she faints."

Beauty and Evil Vivien Leigh played Lady Macbeth to bring out the mixture of beauty and evil in her personality. In a striking gesture, for example, Leigh's Lady Macbeth sent Duncan off to bed with a betraying kiss.

A Psychiatric Opinion Dame Judith Anderson consulted psychiatrists to find out why Lady Macbeth sleepwalks in Act V. "In all mental cases you can trace the trouble back to a moment when the disintegration commenced. With Lady Macbeth it was here."

Enrichment Sarah Siddons (1755–1831) was a great English actress known for her portrayal of Lady Macbeth. She played this part a number of times over a span of twenty-seven years, and it was in this role that she gave the farewell performance of her acting career (1812).

Siddons portrayed Lady Macbeth as a strong, manlike woman, chilling in her ruthlessness. Her private notes, however reveal that she saw another side to Lady Macbeth that she was unwilling or unable to communicate in performance. She wrote, for instance, that Lady Macbeth is "fair, feminine, nay, perhaps, even fragile" and "captivating in feminine loveliness."

Enrichment Ellen Terry (1848–1928) was to portray Lady Macbeth to great critical acclaim. Terry tried to express the "feminine" quality of Lady Macbeth in her interpretation of the role. She wrote the following note to herself about the part: "Play with his (Macbeth's) hands and *charm* him."

In a letter to the critic William Winter, she was even clearer about wanting to break away from the traditional Siddons portrayal of Lady Macbeth as a monster:

> Everyone seems to think that Mrs. McB is a *Monstrousness* & I can only see that she's a *woman* —a mistaken woman—& *weak*— not a Dove—of course not—but *first of all* **a wife**—I don't think she's *at all clever* ("Lead Macbeth" *indeed!*—she's not even clever enough to *sleep!*).

Extension Activities
Although *Macbeth* is the one of the shortest of Shakespeare's plays, it is full of spine-tingling soliloquies, supernatural appearances, remarkable characters, and chaotic events. Perhaps that's why it's such a popular play to stage.

Encourage students who are interested in theater to explore *Macbeth* in depth by completing any of the following activities:

- Designing a set for any scene in *Macbeth*
- Holding an informal play reading with a group of peers
- Performing for the class one of the monologues from the play
- Designing costumes for the lead characters in *Macbeth*
- Making a "dream cast" list for a proposed stage production of *Macbeth*

Prepare and Engage

More About the Author
The known facts regarding Shakespeare's life tell us little about him as a person. Born in April 1564, in Stratford-on-Avon, a small, country town, Shakespeare probably attended grammar school there. The principal subject of the Elizabethan grammar school was Latin, so Shakespeare no doubt read the works of Cicero, Ovid, and Virgil. Frequent allusions are made to such classics in his works. In 1582 he married Anne Hathaway. They had three children. Although best known as a playwright, Shakespeare also wrote 154 sonnets and 2 narrative poems, "Venus and Adonis" (1593) and "The Rape of Lucrece" (1594).

Like Chaucer before him, Shakespeare was a gifted storyteller. However, most of the stories portrayed in his dramas had already been told by others. In Shakespeare's hands, however, these stories took on a dramatic new life. His ability to use just the right word or phrase is evident in the many familiar expressions first penned by the Bard of Avon: "Now is the winter of our discontent . . ." *(Richard III)*, ". . . parting is such sweet sorrow . . ." *(Romeo and Juliet)*, ". . . it was Greek to me" *(Julius Caesar)*, "All the world's a stage . . ." *(As You Like It)*. Shakespeare died in Stratford-on-Avon in 1616 and was buried near the altar in the church. His wife died seven years later.

Literature CD-ROM To acquaint students with William Shakespeare's life, use *The Time, Life, and Works of Shakespeare* CD-ROM. In Feature 2, students can learn about Shakespeare's early life. Shakespeare's career as an actor is described in Feature 3. Feature 4 documents Shakespeare's rise as a playwright. Feature 5 focuses on the historical context that shaped Shakespeare's later work, and includes information about the Essex rebellion, the ascent to the throne of James I, other major dramatists of Shakespeare's day, and the publication of the first folio of Shakespeare's plays.

Guide for Interpreting

William Shakespeare

(1564–1616)

Because of his deep understanding of human nature, his compassion for all types of people, and the power and beauty of his language, William Shakespeare is regarded as the greatest writer in the English language. Nearly four hundred years after his death, Shakespeare's plays continue to be read widely and produced throughout the world. They have the same powerful impact on today's audiences as they had when they were first staged.

Timeline of Praise No other English writer has won such universal and enthusiastic praise from critics and fellow writers. Here are just a few samples of that praise, shown on a timeline from Shakespeare's day to our own:

1600 —Ben Jonson (1572–1637)
"He was not of an age, but for all time!"

—John Dryden (1631–1700)
"He was the man who of all modern, and perhaps ancient poets, had the largest and most comprehensive soul."

1700 —Samuel Johnson (1709–1784)
"Shakespeare is, above all writers, at least above all modern writers, the poet of nature: the poet that holds up to his readers a faithful mirror of manners and life."

1800 —Samuel Taylor Coleridge (1772–1834)
"The Englishman, who, without reverence, a proud and affectionate reverence, can utter the name of William Shakespeare, stands disqualified for the office of critic."

1900 —A. C. Bradley (1851–1935)
"Where his power or art is fully exerted, it really does resemble that of nature."

—T. S. Eliot (1888–1965)
"About any one so great as Shakespeare, it is probable that we can never be right . . ."

The Playwright in His Own Time It is a myth that we know absolutely nothing about Shakespeare's life. As critic Irving Ribner attests, "we know more about him than we do about virtually any other of his contemporary dramatists, with the exception of Ben Jonson." Shakespeare was born on April 23, 1564 in Stratford-on-Avon, northwest of London. (The date is based on a record of his baptism on April 26th.) Stratford, with a population of about 2,000 in Shakespeare's day, was the market town for a fertile agricultural region.

Shakespeare's father, John, was a successful glove maker and businessman who held a number of positions in the town government. His mother, whose maiden name was Mary Arden, was the daughter of his father's landlord. Their marriage, therefore, boosted the Shakespeare family's holdings. Nevertheless, there is evidence that in the late 1570's, John Shakespeare began to suffer financial reverses.

Shakespeare's Education No written evidence of Shakespeare's boyhood exists, not even a name on a school attendance list. However, given his father's status, it is highly probable that he attended the Stratford Grammar School, where he acquired a knowledge of Latin.

Although Shakespeare did not go on to study at a university, his attendance at the grammar school from ages seven to sixteen would have provided him with a good education. Discipline at such a school was strict, and the school day lasted from 6:00 A.M. in the summer (7:00 in the winter) until 5:00 P.M. From 11:00 to 1:00, students were dismissed to eat lunch with their families. At 3:00, they were allowed to play for a quarter of an hour!

Shakespeare's Marriage and Family Shakespeare's name enters the official records again in November, 1582, when he receives a license to marry

Enrichment

Holinshed as a Source For *Macbeth* as for many other plays, Shakespeare drew upon Raphael Holinshed's *Chronicles of England, Scotland, and Ireland* (1577). The following is Holinshed's version of Macbeth's encounter with the three witches:

> Shortly after happened a strange and uncouth wonder, which afterward was the case of much trouble in the realm of Scotland, as ye shall after hear. It fortuned as Macbeth and Banquo journeyed toward Forres, where the King then lay, they went sporting by the way together without other company, save only themselves, passing through the woods and fields, when suddenly in the midst of a laund [lawn, open place] there met them three women in strange and wild apparel, resembling creatures of elder world, whom when they attentively beheld, wondering much at the sight, the first of them spake and said: "All hail, Macbeth, Thane of Glammis!" (for he had lately entered into that dignity and office by the death of his father Sinell). The second of them said: "Hail Macbeth, Thane of Cawdor!" But the third said: "All hail, Macbeth, that hereafter shalt be King of Scotland!"

The Tragedy of Macbeth

Anne Hathaway. The couple had a daughter, Susanna, in 1583, and twins, Judith and Hamnet, in 1585. Beyond names and years in which his children were born, we know little about his family life. Some writers have made much of the fact that Shakespeare left his wife and children behind when he went to London not long after his twins were born. However, he visited his family in Stratford regularly during his years as a playwright, and they may have lived with him for a time in London.

His Career as Actor and Playwright

It's uncertain how Shakespeare became connected with the theater in the late 1580's and early 1590's. By 1594, however, he had become a part owner and the principal playwright of the Lord Chamberlain's Men, one of the most successful theater companies in London.

In 1599, the company built the famous Globe theater on the south bank of the Thames river, in Southwark. This is where most of Shakespeare's plays were performed. When James I became king in 1603, following the death of Elizabeth I, he took control of the Lord Chamberlain's Men and renamed the company The King's Men.

Retirement In about 1610, Shakespeare retired to Stratford, though he continued to write plays. He was a prosperous middle-class man, having profited from his share in a successful theater company. Six years later, on April 23, 1616, he died and was buried in Holy Trinity Church in Stratford. Because it was common practice to move bodies after burial to make room for others, Shakespeare wrote the following as his epitaph:

> Good friends, for Jesus' sake forbear
> To dig the dust enclosèd here!
> Blest be the man that spares these stones,
> And curst be he that moves my bones.

His Literary Record Shakespeare did not think of himself as a man of letters. He wrote his plays to be performed and did not bring out editions of them for the reading public. The first published edition of his work, called the First Folio, was issued in 1623 by two members of his theater company, John Heminges and Henry Condell, and contained thirty-six of the thirty-seven plays now attributed to him.

Shakespeare's varied output includes romantic comedies like *A Midsummer Night's Dream* and *As You Like It*; history plays like *Henry IV*, Parts 1 and 2; tragedies like *Romeo and Juliet*, *Hamlet*, *Othello*, *King Lear*, and *Macbeth*; and later romances like *The Tempest*. In addition to his plays, he wrote 154 sonnets and three longer poems.

"Speaking" Shakespeare

You may not realize the extent to which you already "speak" Shakespeare. For example, have you ever used or heard any of these common phrases?

He's full of *the milk of human kindness*. (I, v, 17)
She thinks she's *the be-all and the end-all*. (I, vii, 5)
What *a sorry sight that was*! (II, ii, 20)
Don't worry about it, *what's done is done*! (III, ii, 12)
That will last until *the crack of doom*. (IV, i, 117)
She finished the jobs in *one fell swoop*. (IV, iii, 219)

Shakespeare invented each of these now common phrases, which were unknown in English before their appearance in *Macbeth*. Look for them as you read—their place in the play is indicated in parentheses—and discover if their meanings have changed since Shakespeare's time.

Enrichment

James I and Witchcraft Macbeth was probably performed for King James I and his brother-in-law in the summer of 1606. If so, the king would have found much to interest him in the play. The subject was Scottish, as was the king himself, and the action turned on the prophecies of witches. King James I was an authority on witchcraft, having taken part in a lively controversy about this subject.

While some Elizabethans believed in witches, others were skeptical. Among the skeptics was Reginald Scot, who wrote *Discovery of Witchcraft* (1584) to demonstrate "that the compacts and contracts of witches with all Devils and all Infernal Spirits or Familiars are but erroneous novelties and imaginary conceptions."

The king, when he was still King James VI of Scotland, objected to Scot's "damnable opinions" about witches and wrote a book entitled *Daemonology* (1597) to state his case. King James's strong opinions on this matter came from personal experience. A group of Scottish witches had been accused of plotting against his life. One of the suspects, Agnes Sampson, made such wild statements that James was convinced the whole affair was absurd. At that point, Agnes Sampson spoke to the king in private and "declared unto him the very words which passed between the King's Majesty and his Queen at Upslo in Norway the first night of their marriage; whereat the king wondered greatly and swore by the living God that he believed that all the devils in Hell could not have discovered the same." Sampson's clairvoyance or lucky guess made the king a firm believer in the power of witchcraft.

The sensational news from this trial was fully covered in England, and it is tempting to imagine Shakespeare reading this account and storing it up for future use!

OBJECTIVES

1. To read, comprehend, interpret, and respond to an Elizabethan drama
2. To connect relationships in a drama to personal experience
3. To use text aids to understand and interpret drama
4. To recognize the elements of Elizabethan drama
5. To build vocabulary in context and learn words about power
6. To distinguish between action verbs and linking verbs
7. To respond to Act I of *Macbeth* through writing, speaking and listening, and projects

SKILLS INSTRUCTION

Vocabulary: Words About Power
Grammar: Action Verbs and Linking Verbs
Reading Strategy: Use Text Aids
Literary Focus: Elizabethan Drama
Speaking and Listening: Oral Interpretation (teacher edition)
Critical Viewing: Draw Conclusions; Deduce; Connect; Generalize

PORTFOLIO OPPORTUNITIES

Writing: Speech of Welcome; Comparison and Contrast
Speaking and Listening: Oral Interpretation

Literature CD-ROM To familiarize students with Elizabethan drama, use the CD-ROM *How to Read and Understand Drama,* Feature 4. This video focuses on stage conventions such as soliloquies and asides.

Guide for Interpreting, Act I

◆ Background for Understanding

Literature: Shakespeare's Sources

By Shakespeare's time, the story of the eleventh-century Scottish king Macbeth was a mixture of fact and legend. Shakespeare and his contemporaries, however, probably regarded the account of Macbeth in Raphael Holinshed's *Chronicles of England, Scotland, and Ireland* as completely factual. The playwright drew on the *Chronicles* as a source for the play. Yet he freely adapted the material for his own purposes, as this chart indicates:

Holinshed's Chronicles	Shakespeare's Macbeth
• Macbeth meets the witches.	• Shakespeare uses this account.
• Duncan is slain in an ambush set up by Macbeth and his friends, who are angry at the naming of Malcolm as Prince of Cumberland. Macbeth's claim to the throne has some basis.	• Duncan is slain while he is a guest at Macbeth's castle. Macbeth and his wife are the only conspirators, and Macbeth does not apparently have a legitimate claim to the throne.
• Banquo is Macbeth's accomplice in the slaying, and Lady Macbeth does not have a prominent role in the narrative.	• Banquo is not an accomplice. Using a different story in the Chronicles , in which a wife urges her husband to kill a friend and guest, Shakespeare creates Lady Macbeth.

Although Shakespeare may have consulted other Scottish histories, it is probable that he primarily relied on Holinshed's *Chronicles* for his "facts."

Some scholars have suggested that Shakespeare became aware of Holinshed's account of Macbeth in the summer of 1605. At that time he may have seen, at Oxford, an entertainment titled *Tres Sibyllae* staged for King James. In this pageant, three sibyls—the prophetesses named in the title—predict that the descendants of the Scottish king Banquo would reign over a great kingdom. This was meant to flatter King James because he regarded Banquo as his own mythical ancestor.

History: A Tribute to the King

Macbeth is set in eleventh-century Scotland. However, Shakespeare wrote the play with an eye on seventeenth-century current events. In November 1605, a group of Catholics seeking revenge for the severe anti-Catholic laws of James I plotted to blow up the king and Parliament. With the help of Guy Fawkes, a soldier of fortune, they rented a cellar directly beneath the House of Lords, in which to stockpile barrels of gunpowder. Incredibly, the conspirators succeeded in storing thirty-six barrels of gunpowder in that cellar. To appreciate the magnitude of the threat, imagine a group of terrorists today smuggling tons of high explosives into the Capitol building in Washington, D.C.

The plot was revealed when a lord, who happened to be a brother-in-law of one of the conspirators, was anonymously warned by letter not to attend the opening of Parliament. This warning helped the authorities to break the case, and they arrested Guy Fawkes as he entered the cellar. Fawkes and some of the other chief conspirators were executed. Although their numbers were few, their plan was so frightening that it led, for a time, to increased persecution of all English Catholics. In England, Guy Fawkes day is still commemorated on November 5th each year with fireworks and the burning of dummies representing Guy Fawkes.

In *Macbeth*, Shakespeare capitalized on the sympathy generated for the king by this incident. He chose the Scottish setting for his play, knowing that James's family, the Stuarts, first came to the Scottish throne in the eleventh century. One of the most virtuous characters in the play, Banquo, was thought to be the father of the first of the Stuart kings.

Shakespeare included witches in the play knowing that James I had written a book that argued for the existence of witches.

Journal Writing Think of a play, movie, or novel about a famous political figure. Was it flattering or not? Explain in your journal.

Prentice Hall Literature Program Resources

REINFORCE / RETEACH / EXTEND

Selection Support Pages
Build Vocabulary: Words About Power, p. 59
Grammar and Style: Action Verbs and Linking Verbs, p. 60
Reading Strategy: Use Text Aids, p. 61
Literary Focus: Elizabethan Drama, p. 62

Strategies for Diverse Student Needs, p. 12

Beyond Literature Design a Playbill, p. 12

Formal Assessment Selection Test, pp. 65–67; Assessment Resources Software

Alternative Assessment, p. 12

Writing and Language Transparencies
Daily Language Practice, Week 10, p. 145; Story Map, p. 126

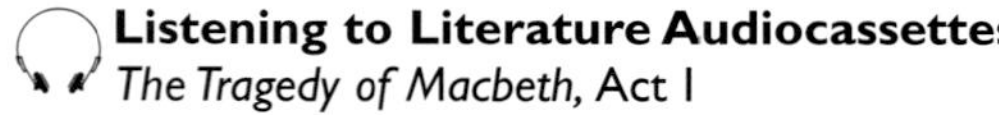

Listening to Literature Audiocassettes
The Tragedy of Macbeth, Act I

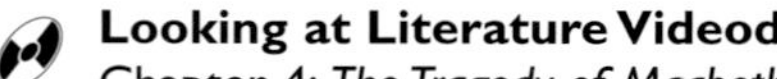

Looking at Literature Videodisc
Chapter 4: *The Tragedy of Macbeth: Shakespeare*

Literature CD-ROM
The Time, Life, and Works of Shakespeare
How to Read and Understand Drama

The Tragedy of Macbeth

◆ Literature and Your Life

CONNECT YOUR EXPERIENCE

If you've ever been elbowed aside by a team member eager for glory, you've experienced the effects of blind and driving ambition. An elbow in the ribs isn't usually fatal. In *Macbeth*, however, blind ambition causes a brave soldier to become an evil plotter who will stop at nothing to accomplish his goal.

THEMATIC FOCUS: THE INFLUENCE OF THE MONARCHY

If Shakespeare were alive today, do you think he would write plays flattering the royal family? Why or why not?

◆ Literary Focus

ELIZABETHAN DRAMA

During the late sixteenth century, **Elizabethan drama** came into full bloom. Playwrights turned away from religious subjects and began writing more sophisticated plays. Drawing on models from ancient Greece and Rome, writers reintroduced tragedies—plays in which disaster befalls a hero or heroine. Dramatists also began writing their plays in carefully crafted unrhymed verse, using rich language and vivid imagery.

Macbeth, like other Shakespearean plays, was performed at the Globe theater. This structure was circular, open to the sky, and lined with galleries. Because the Globe, like other Elizabethan theaters, had no lighting, the plays were performed in broad daylight. Also there were no sets, so the words of the play had to create the illusion of time and place for the audience.

As you read *Macbeth*, Act I, imagine what it would have been like to be watching the play at the Globe.

◆ Grammar and Style

ACTION VERBS AND LINKING VERBS

Shakespeare uses both action verbs and linking verbs. **Action verbs** express physical or mental action. **Linking verbs** connect subjects with a subject complement that either renames or modifies the subject.

Action Verb: "Shipwracking storms and direful thunders *break* . . ." (I, ii, 26)

Linking Verb: ". . . he *seems* rapt withal." (I, iii, 57)

◆ Reading Strategy

USE TEXT AIDS

Like all drama, Shakespeare's plays were meant to be performed, not read in a classroom. Playwrights provide directions for actors that can help readers as well. The stage directions that tell actors where and how to move can help you to picture what is happening on the stage. Pay attention to the stage directions, printed in italics in the text, to help you follow the stage action.

Elizabethan plays prepared for a modern reading audience provide another aid: Notes along the sides of the text lines explain the meanings of words and phrases that are no longer in use. Refer to these notes to clarify unfamiliar language.

◆ Build Vocabulary

WORDS ABOUT POWER

In *Macbeth*, Act I, Shakespeare uses words from the world of politics and power. Two of these words, *liege* and *sovereign*, refer to the role of the king as chief lord in a feudal system (*liege*) and to his supreme power over his subjects (*sovereign* power).

WORD BANK

Before you read, preview this list of words from Act I of *Macbeth*.

valor
treasons
imperial
liege
sovereign

Write *FATE* on the board and elicit from students definitions of the word. Then lead students into a discussion of the role, if any, fate plays in our lives. (Do we cause our destinies, or does fate intervene? Do we make our own fates?)

Explain that in *Macbeth,* they will encounter a man who has brilliantly served in battle, has the favor of the king of Scotland, and has an extremely promising future. When his fate is revealed by three "weird sisters"—the witches—his life begins to change irrevocably.

Customize for
Less Proficient Readers

Emphasize the reading strategy, using the aids provided in the text. Encourage these students to make use of the information provided for them in the text. You might give them the Reading Strategy page, Use Text Aids, page 61 in ***Selection Support,*** to give them practice before they read the selection.

To help less proficient readers follow the action and dialogue, have them follow along in their text as they listen to a recording of the play.

Customize for
More Advanced Students

Explain to students that Shakespeare used rhythm, or meter, to add meaning to his plays. For example, iambic pentameter (five strong beats) is used in most dialogue and for soliloquies; prose is used to indicate dialogue of the peasantry or, in the case of the porter, comic crudeness. Direct students to identify the rhythm or meter of the witches' dialogue and speculate about why Shakespeare made that choice.

Customize for
Musical/Rhythmic Learners

Shakespeare enhances the eeriness of the witches by contrasting their rhythmic, rhyming dialogue with the more stately unrhymed blank verse of the other characters. Have these students read the three parts of the witches, emphasizing the rhythm and rhyme and using vocal tones that reinforce the eerie mood of these scenes.

Preparing for Standardized Tests

Reading and Vocabulary The vocabulary of politics and power may be used in analogy tests. Understanding these words will help students recognize relationships in questions such as this:

SOVEREIGN is to MONARCHY as PRESIDENT is to __________. *(C)*

(A) VICE PRESIDENT
(B) CONGRESS
(C) DEMOCRACY
(D) CITIZEN

Grammar and Language The ability to distinguish between action verbs and linking verbs is important in tests of grammar and usage, when students are asked to choose the correct pronoun following a verb. If students recognize whether the verb is action or linking, they can correctly choose the nominative or objective form of a following pronoun.

For additional practice, use the Grammar and Style page on Action Verbs and Linking Verbs, p. 60 in ***Selection Support.***

Develop Understanding

One-Minute Insight In *The Tragedy of Macbeth,* Act I, the war hero Macbeth returns home and, on the way, encounters three witches who prophesy that he will one day be king of Scotland. Seized by ruthless ambition and spurred on by his wife, Macbeth plans to murder King Duncan when he visits their home, thus setting in motion a series of events that will lead to his eventual downfall.

Customize for
More Advanced Students
Have students observe the recurring juxtaposition of opposites that begins in line 4 (lost/won; fair/foul). Such opposites occur again and again through the play and they help reinforce that idea that things in Macbeth's world are topsy-turvy.

Customize for
Visual/Spatial Learners
Throughout the reading of *Macbeth,* have students refer to the drawing of the Globe on page 265. Suggest that they envision the action as it would take place in the acting areas.

◆ Reading Strategy

❶ **Use Text Aids** Ask students the ways in which the stage directions calling for lightning and thunder help set the mood of the opening scene. *The thunder and lightning make the atmosphere seem dark and threatening or ominous. The approaching storm may symbolize or mirror the storm that is approaching on Macbeth's horizon.*

CHARACTERS

Duncan, King of Scotland	**Seyton,** an officer attending on Macbeth
Malcolm, **Donalbain** } his sons	**Son to Macduff**
Macbeth, **Banquo**, **Macduff**, **Lennox**, **Ross**, **Menteith**, **Angus**, **Caithness** } noblemen of Scotland	**An English Doctor**
	A Scottish Doctor
	A Porter
	An Old Man
	Three Murderers
	Lady Macbeth
	Lady Macduff
	A Gentlewoman attending on Lady Macbeth
Fleance, son to Banquo	**Hecate**
Siward, Earl of Northumberland, general of the English forces	**Witches**
	Apparitions
Young Siward, his son	**Lords, Officers, Soldiers, Attendants, and Messengers**

Setting: Scotland; England

Act I

Scene i. *An open place.*
[*Thunder and lightning. Enter* THREE WITCHES.] ❶

FIRST WITCH. When shall we three meet again?
In thunder, lightning, or in rain?

SECOND WITCH. When the hurlyburly's done,
When the battle's lost and won.

THIRD WITCH. That will be ere the set of sun.

A Critic's Response
"These were not ordinary witches or seeresses. They were great powers of destiny, great ministers of fate."
—George Lyman Kittredge

Block Scheduling Strategies

Consider these suggestions to take advantage of extended class time.

- Have students write responses to the question raised in Thematic Focus: The Influence of the Monarchy, p. 271.
- Introduce the elements of Elizabethan Drama in Literary Focus (p. 271) and hold a class discussion on the differences between dramas and theater then and now.
- Familiarize students with the listing of characters on page 272 before they read Act I.
- Have students work in pairs to prepare and role-play the discussion between Macbeth and Lady Macbeth under Literature and Your Life (page 291).
- Use Daily Language Practice for Week 10, p. 145. You may put the transparency on the overhead projector and have students write the passages correctly, or you may dictate the passages to students for them to write.
- You may have students write the Speech of Welcome or the Comparison and Contrast in the Idea Bank on page 292.
- Have students prepare and deliver the oral interpretation described in Speaking and Listening on page 292. Use the mini-lesson on page 290 for guidance in developing the activity.

▲ Critical Viewing Examine Fuseli's rendering of the witches. Explain how his depiction of the witches makes them appear other-worldly. **[Draw Conclusions]** ❷

FIRST WITCH. Where the place?

SECOND WITCH. Upon the heath.

THIRD WITCH. There to meet with Macbeth.

FIRST WITCH. I come, Graymalkin.[1]

SECOND WITCH. Paddock[2] calls.

THIRD WITCH. Anon![3]

ALL. Fair is foul, and foul is fair.
Hover through the fog and filthy air. 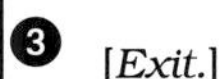 [*Exit.*]

1. **Graymalkin:** First witch's helper, a gray cat.
2. **Paddock:** Second witch's helper, a toad.
3. **Anon:** At once.

▶Critical Viewing◀

❷ **Draw Conclusions** Students might suggest that the ghost-like features of the witches—their pale faces, bony hands, and sheer white clothing—give them an other-worldly appearance.

◆ Critical Thinking

❸ **Analyze** Point out to the class that Shakespeare often used rhyming couplets to end scenes. Ask students: Why might Shakespeare have chosen to end the first scene with these lines? *Responses may include these: The couplet sums ups the mood of the play; the use of alliteration and the rhyme make the couplet memorable.*

Humanities: Art

The Three Witches, 1783, by Henry Fuseli.

Henry Fuseli (1741–1825), a Swiss-born English artist, began as a writer, but with the encouragement of Sir Joshua Reynolds, the head of the Royal Academy of Art, he began to paint. His formal art education consisted of an eight-year residence in Rome, where he studied the art of the Italian master Michelangelo. His style is a combination of romanticism, fantasy, and the grotesque. Throughout his life, Fuseli was influenced by literature, especially the works of William Shakespeare.

The strong composition is enhanced by the rhythm of the three outstretched arms ending in talon-like hands.

Use these questions for discussion:

1. Read Banquo's description of the witches in lines 40–47 of Scene iii. Is Fuseli's painting faithful to this description? *The witches appear to be withered, with choppy fingers and skinny lips, as described by Banquo.*
2. Does this painting give you a better understanding of the fright felt by the characters upon encountering the witches? *Possible responses: Yes, they certainly seem strange; no, they are merely old women, nothing to be afraid of.*

Customize for
Less Proficient Readers
Because blank verse can be daunting for less proficient readers, direct such students to preview long speeches by reading the final word in each line. Often, this will reveal to students the gist of the passage, which they can then read slowly and carefully.

◆ Reading Strategy

❶ **Use Text Aids** Ask students what mental picture these stage directions suggest. *The trumpet call suggests the appearance of royalty. Consequently, a reader can form a mental picture of people dressed in rich clothing and riding fine horses while being attended by servants and flag bearers. This scene stands in stark contrast to the previous scene with the witches.*

◆ Critical Thinking

❷ **Interpret** To what is the captain referring when he says "discomfort swells"? *He is referring to an uprising by the King of Norway, who is challenging the King of Scotland's right to rule.*

Scene ii. *A camp near Forres, a town in northeast Scotland.*
[*Alarum within.*[1] *Enter* KING DUNCAN, MALCOLM, DONALBAIN, LENNOX, *with* ATTENDANTS, *meeting a bleeding* CAPTAIN.] ❶

KING. What bloody man is that? He can report,
As seemeth by his plight, of the revolt
The newest state.

MALCOLM. This is the sergeant[2]
Who like a good and hardy soldier fought
'Gainst my captivity. Hail, brave friend!
Say to the king the knowledge of the broil[3]
As thou didst leave it.

CAPTAIN. Doubtful it stood,
As two spent swimmers, that do cling together
And choke their art.[4] The merciless Macdonwald—
Worthy to be a rebel for to that
The multiplying villainies of nature
Do swarm upon him—from the Western Isles[5]
Of kerns and gallowglasses[6] is supplied;
And fortune, on his damnèd quarrel[7] smiling,
Showed like a rebel's whore:[8] but all's too weak:
For brave Macbeth—well he deserves that name—
Disdaining fortune, with his brandished steel,
Which smoked with bloody execution,
Like valor's minion[9] carved out his passage
Till he faced the slave;
Which nev'r shook hands, nor bade farewell to him,
Till he unseamed him from the nave to th' chops,[10]
And fixed his head upon our battlements.

KING. O valiant cousin! Worthy gentleman!

CAPTAIN. As whence the sun 'gins his reflection[11]
Shipwracking storms and direful thunders break,
So from that spring whence comfort seemed to come
Discomfort swells. Mark, King of Scotland, mark:
No sooner justice had, with valor armed,
Compelled these skipping kerns to trust their heels
But the Norweyan lord,[12] surveying vantage,[13]
With furbished arms and new supplies of men,
Began a fresh assault. ❷

KING. Dismayed not this
Our captains, Macbeth and Banquo?

1. **Alarum within:** Trumpet call offstage.
2. **sergeant:** Officer.
3. **broil:** Battle.
4. **choke their art:** Prevent each other from swimming.
5. **Western Isles:** The Hebrides, off Scotland.
6. **Of kerns and gallowglasses:** With lightly armed Irish foot soldiers and heavily armed soldiers.
7. **damned quarrel:** Accursed cause.
8. **Showed . . . whore:** Falsely appeared to favor Macdonwald.
9. **minion:** Favorite.
10. **unseamed . . . chops:** Split him open from the navel to the jaws.
11. **'gins his reflection:** Rises.
12. **Norweyan lord:** King of Norway.
13. **surveying vantage:** Seeing an opportunity.

◆ Build Vocabulary

valor (val´ ər) *n.*: Marked courage or bravery

Reading Shakespeare
Many students will find Shakespeare's language a challenge. He uses words and structures not familiar to the modern ear. This situation would probably not be a problem in a theater, where actors communicate meanings through their interpretation, but it does pose a problem for readers. Students will need to develop skill in recognizing some Elizabethan language and in untangling unusual sentence structures.

The reading strategies provided for each act of the play support students in reading *Macbeth.* In addition, you may share with students the following insights and tips that will give them an overview and an approach to Shakespeare's language.

Shakespeare's Vocabulary
Some of Shakespeare's words are no longer in use, and some of the words that are still in use have evolved different meanings. Encourage students to refer to the glosses and notes that are provided alongside the text lines. These notes explain many terms or usages that are not recognizable to a modern reader.

Shakespeare's Sentences
Shakespeare frequently plays with the standard English word order of subject-verb-complement. A reader—and especially a novice reader of Shakespeare—may have to go over the lines slowly and carefully, using the notes provided and puzzling out the meaning of

CAPTAIN. Yes;
As sparrows eagles, or the hare the lion.
If I say sooth,[14] I must report they were
As cannons overcharged with double cracks;[15]
So they doubly redoubled strokes upon the foe.
Except[16] they meant to bathe in reeking wounds,
Or memorize another Golgotha,[17]
I cannot tell—
But I am faint; my gashes cry for help.

KING. So well thy words become thee as thy wounds;
They smack of honor both. Go get him surgeons.
[*Exit* CAPTAIN, *attended.*]

[*Enter* ROSS *and* ANGUS.]

Who comes here?

MALCOLM. The worthy Thane[18] of Ross.

LENNOX. What a haste looks through his eyes! So should he look
That seems to[19] speak things strange. (4)

ROSS. God save the king!

KING. Whence cam'st thou, worthy Thane?

ROSS. From Fife, great King;
Where the Norweyan banners flout the sky
And fan our people cold.
Norway[20] himself, with terrible numbers,
Assisted by that most disloyal traitor
The Thane of Cawdor, began a dismal[21] conflict; (5)
Till that Bellona's bridegroom, lapped in proof,[22]
Confronted him with self-comparisons,[23]
Point against point, rebellious arm 'gainst arm,
Curbing his lavish [24] spirit: and, to conclude,
The victory fell on us.

KING. Great happiness!

ROSS. That now
Sweno, the Norways' king, craves composition;[25]
Nor would we deign him burial of his men
Till he disbursed, at Saint Colme's Inch,[26]
Ten thousand dollars to our general use.

(3) ◆ **Literary Focus** What background does this conversation (ll. 1–43) provide?

14. sooth: Truth.
15. cracks: Explosives.
16. except: Unless.
17. memorize . . . Golgotha (gôl′ gə thə): Make the place as memorable for slaughter as Golgotha, the place where Christ was crucified.
18. Thane: Scottish title of nobility.
19. seems to: Seems about to.
20. Norway: King of Norway.
21. dismal: Threatening.
22. Bellona's . . . proof: Macbeth is called the mate of Bellona, the goddess of war, clad in tested armor.
23. self-comparisons: Counter movements.
24. lavish: Insolent.
25. composition: Terms of peace.
26. St. Colme's Inch: Island near Edinburgh, Scotland.

◆ Literary Focus

(3) Elizabethan Drama Shakespeare begins by having Malcolm identify the wounded captain as a participant in the battle against the King of Norway. The captain then supplies detailed information about the battle that occurred offstage.

◆ Critical Thinking

(4) Speculate Why might Shakespeare have Lennox describe the look in the Thane of Ross's eyes? *Possible response: Since the audience was vast and may have had difficulties seeing the stage, Shakespeare gives important clues in the dialogue.*

◆ Critical Thinking

(5) Analyze Cause and Effect Ask students to explain the cause-and-effect relationship of events in this recounting of a battle. *In Fife, supporters of Norway and the Thane of Cawdor rebelled against the rule of the king; as a result, Macbeth led a force to curb their rebellion. Macbeth's forces won.*

the lines. Share the following information and tips with students:

- Look for the placement of the subject and the verb. Shakespeare often places the complement before the subject. He also frequently places the verb before the subject.

  Inverted Subject and Complement: "O, never shall sun tomorrow see."

  Standard Order: "O, tomorrow shall never see the sun."

  Inverted verb and subject: "Know you not he has?"

  Standard Order: "You know not he has?"
- Shakespeare often separates words that belong together in meaning. A number of constructions may separate a verb from a subject or a complement from a verb. For example: *"Will it not be received, /* When we have marked with blood those sleepy two / Of his own chamber, and used their very daggers, / *That they have done 't?"*
- Shakespeare's lines are not necessarily sentences. Remind students to read in sentences as a unit of meaning rather than in lines. A sentence may extend over a number of lines. Students should not stop at the end of a line unless the punctuation dictates a stop.

Enrichment

Classical Tragedy A tragedy in the classical sense is a type of drama in which the major character undergoes a morally significant struggle that ends disastrously. According to Aristotle in the *Poetics,* the purpose of tragedy is to arouse the emotions of pity and fear in the audience and thus to produce a catharsis of these emotions.

Macbeth is a tragic figure in this classical sense. When introduced in Act I, scene iii, Macbeth is flushed with victory after fighting nobly for the king. He is presented in a pleasing light, and the audience is meant to like him and root for him.

◆ Critical Thinking

❶ Draw Conclusions Ask students what they think the first witch means by "I'll do, I'll do, and I'll do." *Possible conclusion: She'll seek to injure the sailor to get revenge on the sailor's wife.*

◆ Grammar and Style

❷ Action Verbs and Linking Verbs Direct students to find the action verbs and the linking verb in this passage. *Action verbs include* dwindle, peak, pine; *the linking verbs are "be" in "it shall be tempest-tossed" and in "bark cannot be lost."*

KING. No more that Thane of Cawdor shall deceive
Our bosom interest:[27] go pronounce his present[28] death,
And with his former title greet Macbeth.

ROSS. I'll see it done.

KING. What he hath lost, noble Macbeth hath won.

[*Exit.*]

Scene iii. *A heath near Forres.*
[*Thunder. Enter the* THREE WITCHES.]

FIRST WITCH. Where hast thou been, sister?

SECOND WITCH. Killing swine.[1]

THIRD WITCH. Sister, where thou?

FIRST WITCH. A sailor's wife had chestnuts in her lap,
And mounched, and mounched, and mounched.
"Give me," quoth I.
"Aroint thee,[2] witch!" the rump-fed ronyon[3] cries.
Her husband's to Aleppo[4] gone, master o' th' Tiger:
But in a sieve[5] I'll thither sail,
And, like a rat without a tail,[6]
I'll do, I'll do, and I'll do. ❶

SECOND WITCH. I'll give thee a wind.

FIRST WITCH. Th' art kind.

THIRD WITCH. And I another.

FIRST WITCH. I myself have all the other;
And the very ports they blow,[7]
All the quarters that they know
I' th' shipman's card.[8]
I'll drain him dry as hay:
Sleep shall neither night nor day
Hang upon his penthouse lid;[9]
He shall live a man forbid:[10]
Weary sev'nights[11] nine times nine
Shall he dwindle, peak,[12] and pine:
Though his bark cannot be lost,
Yet it shall be tempest-tossed. ❷
Look what I have.

27. our bosom interest: My heart's trust.
28. present: Immediate.

1. Killing swine: It was commonly believed that witches killed domestic animals.
2. Aroint thee: Be off.
3. rump-fed ronyon: Fat-rumped, scabby creature.
4. Aleppo: Trading center in Syria.
5. sieve: It was commonly believed that witches often sailed in sieves.
6. rat . . . tail: According to popular belief, witches could assume the form of any animal, but the tail would always be missing.
7. they blow: To which the winds blow.
8. card: Compass.
9. penthouse lid: Eyelid.
10. forbid: Cursed.
11. sev'nights: Weeks.
12. peak: Waste away.

Cross-Curricular Connection: History

Scholars believe that one reason Shakespeare included witches in *Macbeth* is the fact that the king, James I, had openly expressed his belief in witches. Witchcraft was a topic of controversy in seventeenth-century Europe and America. The attitude toward witches and witchcraft varied widely. Some regarded the existence of witches to be nothing more than a harmless superstition. Others felt witches to be real and a source of evil that had to be wiped out. As a result, waves of hysteria over witches and their supposed links to the devil sometimes swept over the land. Between the fifteenth and eighteenth centuries, thousands of people were convicted of being witches and executed. The most famous trials in America occurred in 1692 in Salem, Massachusetts, where nineteen people were convicted of being witches and hanged.

Have interested students learn more about the beliefs of Elizabethans in regard to witchcraft.

SECOND WITCH. Show me, show me.

FIRST WITCH. Here I have a pilot's thumb,
Wracked as homeward he did come.
[*Drum within.*]

THIRD WITCH. A drum, a drum!
Macbeth doth come.

ALL. The weird[13] sisters, hand in hand,
Posters[14] of the sea and land,
Thus do go about, about:
Thrice to thine, and thrice to mine,
And thrice again, to make up nine.
Peace! The charm's wound up. ❸

[*Enter* MACBETH *and* BANQUO.]

MACBETH. So foul and fair a day I have not seen.

BANQUO. How far is 't called to Forres? What are these

13. weird: Destiny-serving.
14. Posters: Swift travelers.

▼ Critical Viewing Which of the two soldiers on the right do you think is Macbeth? Explain your reasoning. **[Deduce]** ❹

Macbeth and the Witches, Clarkson Stanfield, Leicestershire Museums, Art Galleries and Records Service

Enrichment

The Fates In Greek mythology, a person's fate was determined by three women, sometimes called the "weird sisters." They were usually pictured spinning or weaving the fabric of a person's life which was then arbitrarily cut. In fact, the Middle English word *werde* meant "fate."

In *Macbeth,* three witches (also known as the three weird sisters) appear throughout the play to foretell Macbeth's future—and determine his fate.

Customize for *Musical/Rhythmic Learners*

❸ Encourage musical and rhythmic learners to recite this "spell" aloud to appreciate the effect of its rhythm and rhyme.

▶Critical Viewing◀

❹ **Deduce** The soldier on the right appears to be more nobly attired, and his attire seems to match that of the troops, suggesting that this soldier is Macbeth.

Humanities: Art

Macbeth and the Witches by Clarkson Stanfield.

Like Henry Fuseli, Clarkson Stanfield (1793–1867) did not start out as a painter. Stanfield was a sailor who passed time on board ship by painting. Stanfield drew marine scenes and made scenery for the sailors' plays. Upon leaving the navy, Stanfield took a job as a scene painter in a London theater. There he gained an outstanding reputation for his painted scenery.

This watercolor, *Macbeth and the Witches,* was done for a production of Macbeth at one of the theaters in which Stanfield worked. It was painted between 1813 and 1829. This skillfully executed design serves to explain the popularity Stanfield enjoyed in theater circles.

Use these questions for discussion:

1. In what ways does this sketch help you to visualize the impact of this scene on a theater audience? *Possible response: The dimly lit scene with shadows probably made the audiences nervous and anxious.*
2. Does the setting in this picture match the one you envision for this scene? Why or why not? *Possible response: No; this setting is more majestic, with a mountain and low-lying clouds.*

◆ Critical Thinking

❶ **Analyze** Ask students to find the point at which Banquo stops addressing Macbeth and addresses the witches. *In the middle of line 52, Banquo begins to address the witches with the words "I' th' name of truth."*

◆ Literary Focus

❷ **Elizabethan Drama** Sound effects such as thunder could be used to make this scene mysterious. In addition, the witches could be costumed in witch-like robes. Most important, perhaps, would be the manner in which the witches recited their lines. A high-pitched, quavery voice quality can effectively convey a sense of mystery.

◆ Critical Thinking

❸ **Analyze** Tell students that throughout *Macbeth* a series of contradictory and seemingly impossible predictions eventually come to pass. Have students identify these apparent contradictions and the message they send to the audience. *These contradictions, in lines 65–69, foretell and mirror Macbeth's eventual inner conflicts; the contradictions serve to build suspense and interest as the audience strives to understand what the witches mean.*

So withered, and so wild in their attire,
That look not like th' inhabitants o' th' earth,
And yet are on 't? Live you, or are you aught
That man may question? You seem to understand me,
By each at once her choppy[15] finger laying
Upon her skinny lips. You should be women,
And yet your beards forbid me to interpret
That you are so.

MACBETH. Speak, if you can: what are you?

FIRST WITCH. All hail, Macbeth! Hail to thee, Thane of Glamis!

SECOND WITCH. All hail, Macbeth! Hail to thee, Thane of Cawdor!

THIRD WITCH. All hail, Macbeth, that shalt be King hereafter!

BANQUO. Good sir, why do you start, and seem to fear
Things that do sound so fair? I' th' name of truth,
Are you fantastical,[16] or that indeed
Which outwardly ye show? My noble partner
You greet with present grace[17] and great prediction
Of noble having[18] and of royal hope,
That he seems rapt withal:[19] to me you speak not.
If you can look into the seeds of time,
And say which grain will grow and which will not,
Speak then to me, who neither beg nor fear
Your favors nor your hate. ❶

FIRST WITCH. Hail!

SECOND WITCH. Hail!

THIRD WITCH. Hail!

FIRST WITCH. Lesser than Macbeth, and greater.

SECOND WITCH. Not so happy,[20] yet much happier.

THIRD WITCH. Thou shalt get kings, though thou be none.
So all hail, Macbeth and Banquo! ❸

FIRST WITCH. Banquo and Macbeth, all hail!

MACBETH. Stay, you imperfect[21] speakers, tell me more:
By Sinel's[22] death I know I am Thane of Glamis;

15. **choppy:** Chapped.

16. **fantastical:** Imaginary.
17. **grace:** Honor.
18. **having:** Possession.
19. **rapt withal:** Entranced by it.

❷ **◆ Literary Focus** How could Elizabethan actors have made this scene mysterious without help from special lighting effects?

20. **happy:** Fortunate.

21. **imperfect:** Incomplete.
22. **Sinel's** (si´ nəlz): Macbeth's father's.

But how of Cawdor? The Thane of Cawdor lives,
A prosperous gentleman; and to be King
Stands not within the prospect of belief,
No more than to be Cawdor. Say from whence
You owe[23] this strange intelligence?[24] Or why
Upon this blasted heath you stop our way
With such prophetic greeting? Speak, I charge you.
[WITCHES *vanish.*]

BANQUO. The earth hath bubbles as the water has,
And these are of them. Whither are they vanished? ❹

MACBETH. Into the air, and what seemed corporal[25] melted
As breath into the wind. Would they had stayed!

BANQUO. Were such things here as we do speak about?
Or have we eaten on the insane root[26]
That takes the reason prisoner?

MACBETH. Your children shall be kings.

BANQUO. You shall be King. ❺

MACBETH. And Thane of Cawdor too. Went it not so?

BANQUO. To th' selfsame tune and words. Who's here?

[*Enter* ROSS *and* ANGUS.]

ROSS. The King hath happily received, Macbeth,
The news of thy success; and when he reads[27]
Thy personal venture in the rebels' fight,
His wonders and his praises do contend
Which should be thine or his.[28] Silenced with that,
In viewing o'er the rest o' th' selfsame day,
He finds thee in the stout Norweyan ranks,
Nothing afeard of what thyself didst make,
Strange images of death.[29] As thick as tale
Came post with post,[30] and every one did bear
Thy praises in his kingdom's great defense,
And poured them down before him.

ANGUS. We are sent
To give thee, from our royal master, thanks;
Only to herald thee into his sight,
Not pay thee.

23. **owe:** Own.
24. **intelligence:** Information.
25. **corporal:** Real.
26. **insane root:** Henbane or hemlock, believed to cause insanity.
27. **reads:** Considers.
28. **His wonders . . . his:** His admiration contends with his desire to praise you.
29. **Nothing . . . death:** Killing, but not being afraid of being killed.
30. **As thick . . . post:** As fast as could be counted came messenger after messenger.

◆ Reading Strategy

❹ **Use Text Aids** Ask students to use the stage directions as well as the remarks by Banquo and Macbeth to visualize how exactly the witches left the stage. How would their exit be staged today? How might it have been staged at the Globe? *In a modern theater, the witches might disappear in a puff of smoke. In Shakespeare's time they might have left the stage through a trap door located in the floor of the theater.*

◆ Grammar and Style

❺ **Action Verbs and Linking Verbs** Have students identify the linking verb in these two lines and the subject complements following these verbs that rename the subject. *The linking verb, which occurs twice, is "shall be." The subject complements are "kings" and "King"; they rename the subjects "Your children" and "You."*

Enrichment

After centuries of bitter hostility, Scotland and England were joined in 1707 to form Great Britain, a single kingdom. However, the Scots have retained a distinct culture that is deeply embedded in their history and the rugged terrain of the countryside. For example, the steep mountains forced Scottish highlanders to live in small groups called clans. Most clans consisted of people with the same surname, such as MacDonald, MacKinnon, and MacLeod. They developed their own fabric pattern or tartan and displayed it on kilts—short skirts that made it easy to climb hills—and other clothing.

Have interested students do research on the clans and identify their tartans, or plaids, as they are commonly called today. Have them report their findings to the class.

❶ Clarification The use of an aside was a common convention among playwrights of the period to indicate words that were thought or spoken so the audience could hear them but the other characters in the play could not. It is sometimes used, as it is in lines 107 and 116, to reveal a character's secret thoughts. Sometimes an aside is a joke or witty remark at the expense of the other characters. An aside can also indicate a private conversation between two characters outside the hearing of other characters on stage.

Ask students what purpose the aside serves in line 107. *The aside lets the audience hear Macbeth's inner thoughts, which, in this case, reveal his astonishment that the first of the witches' predictions has come true.*

❷ Clarification Ross is not sure whether Cawdor aligned himself with Norway or Macdonwald. In either case, he is being hanged for treason.

Customize for
Visual/Spatial Learners
❸ This series of asides can be confusing to read and comprehend. Cast and stage this portion of the scene for the class, making it clear by Macbeth's body movements whether he is speaking to himself or to another character.

ROSS. And for an earnest[31] of a greater honor,
He bade me, from him, call thee Thane of Cawdor;
In which addition,[32] hail, most worthy Thane!
For it is thine.

BANQUO. [*Aside*] What, can the devil speak true? ❶

MACBETH. The Thane of Cawdor lives: why do you dress me
In borrowed robes?

ANGUS. Who was the thane lives yet,
But under heavy judgment bears that life
Which he deserves to lose. Whether he was combined[33]
With those of Norway, or did line[34] the rebel
With hidden help and vantage,[35] or that with both
He labored in his country's wrack,[36] I know not;
But treasons capital, confessed and proved,
Have overthrown him. ❷

MACBETH. [*Aside*] Glamis, and Thane of Cawdor:
The greatest is behind.[37] [*To* ROSS *and* ANGUS]
Thanks for your pains.
[*Aside to* BANQUO] Do you not hope your children shall be kings,
When those that gave the Thane of Cawdor to me
Promised no less to them?

BANQUO. [*Aside to* MACBETH] That, trusted home,[38] ❸
Might yet enkindle you unto[39] the crown,
Besides the Thane of Cawdor. But 'tis strange:
And oftentimes, to win us to our harm,
The instruments of darkness tell us truths,
Win us with honest trifles, to betray 's
In deepest consequence.
Cousins,[40] a word, I pray you.

MACBETH. [*Aside*] Two truths are told,
As happy prologues to the swelling act
Of the imperial theme.[41]—I thank you, gentlemen.—
[*Aside*] This supernatural soliciting
Cannot be ill, cannot be good. If ill,
Why hath it given me earnest of success,
Commencing in a truth? I am Thane of Cawdor:
If good, why do I yield to that suggestion[42]
Whose horrid image doth unfix my hair
And make my seated[43] heart knock at my ribs,
Against the use of nature?[44] Present fears
Are less than horrible imaginings.
My thought, whose murder yet is but fantastical

31. **earnest:** Pledge.

32. **In which addition:** With this new title.

33. **combined:** Allied.
34. **line:** Support.
35. **vantage:** Assistance.
36. **wrack:** Ruin.

37. **behind:** Still to come.

38. **home:** Fully.
39. **enkindle you unto:** Encourage you to hope for.

40. **Cousins:** Often used as a term of courtesy between fellow noblemen.

41. **swelling . . . theme:** Stately idea that I will be King.

42. **suggestion:** Thought of murdering Duncan.
43. **seated:** Fixed.
44. **Against . . . nature:** In an unnatural way.

Shakes so my single[45] state of man that function
Is smothered in surmise, and nothing is
But what is not.

BANQUO. Look, how our partner's rapt.

MACBETH. [*Aside*] If chance will have me King, why, chance may crown me,
Without my stir. ❹

BANQUO. New honors come upon him,
Like our strange[46] garments, cleave not to their mold
But with the aid of use.

MACBETH. [*Aside*] Come what come may,
Time and the hour runs through the roughest day.

BANQUO. Worthy Macbeth, we stay upon your leisure.[47]

MACBETH. Give me your favor.[48] My dull brain was wrought
With things forgotten. Kind gentlemen, your pains
Are registered where every day I turn
The leaf to read them. Let us toward the King.
[*Aside to* BANQUO] Think upon what hath chanced, and at more time,
The interim having weighed it,[49] let us speak
Our free hearts[50] each to other. ❺

BANQUO. Very gladly.

MACBETH. Till then, enough. Come, friends. [*Exit.*]

45. single: Unaided, weak.

46. strange: New.

47. stay upon your leisure: Await your convenience.

48. favor: Pardon.

49. The interim . . . it: When we have had time to think about it.

50. Our free hearts: Our minds freely.

Scene iv. *Forres. The palace.*
[*Flourish.*[1] *Enter* KING DUNCAN, LENNOX, MALCOLM, DONALBAIN, *and* ATTENDANTS.]

KING. Is execution done on Cawdor? Are not
Those in commission[2] yet returned?

MALCOLM. My liege,
They are not yet come back. But I have spoke
With one that saw him die, who did report
That very frankly he confessed his treasons,
Implored your Highness' pardon and set forth
A deep repentance: nothing in his life
Became him like the leaving it. He died ❻

1. Flourish: Trumpet fanfare.

2. in commission: Commissioned to oversee the execution.

◆ Build Vocabulary

treasons (trē′ zenz) *n.*: Betrayals of one's country or oath of loyalty

imperial (im pir′ ē əl) *adj.*: Of an empire; having supreme authority

liege (lēj) *n.*: Lord or king

◆ Critical Thinking

❹ **Interpret** At what decision does Macbeth seem to have arrived? *He's decided to let chance or fate unfold without actively seeking to make the prophecies come true.*

◆ Literature and Your Life

❺ Ask students: Judging from Macbeth's request and your own experiences, do Banquo and Macbeth share a close relationship? *Possible responses: Yes, Macbeth seems to want to share his inner thoughts with Banquo, so they must be good friends; no, Macbeth just wants Banquo to keep quiet about their encounter until Macbeth can figure out what to do.*

◆ Critical Thinking

❻ **Interpret** According to Malcolm's description, in what manner did Cawdor die? *He confessed his treasons, repented and begged the king's forgiveness. He was more graceful in dying than he had ever been in life.*

Enrichment

Imagery Shakespeare's imagery is a key element of his plays, commenting on and reinforcing such other elements as plot, character, atmosphere, and theme. In *Macbeth,* for instance, one strand of images concerns darkness as a cloak for evil. The murder of Duncan is so horrible a deed that Macbeth wants it to be done in darkness (I.iv.50–51). "Stars, hide your fires; / Let not light see my black and deep desires." The next two lines, even more subtly, indicate that Macbeth wants to darken or blind his own conscience: "The eye wink at the hand; yet let that be / Which the eye fears, when it is done, to see."

These images relate to many other literary elements, hinting at the deed to come (plot), suggesting a conflict within Macbeth (character), evoking a scene of ominous darkness (atmosphere), and revealing the evil that will permeate the play (theme.)

◆ *Literature and Your Life*

❶ Ask students if, like the king, they feel they can judge a person's character by his or her face. *Possible responses: Yes, honest people have open faces and maintain direct eye contact; no, looks can be misleading.*

◆ Literary Focus

❷ **Elizabethan Drama** News of Cawdor's death is important because it confirms Macbeth's receipt of Cawdor's title, as predicted by the witches.

◆ Critical Thinking

❸ **Analyze** Have students identify the use of plants and growing imagery in this passage of dialogue. Ask: Why is this a particularly appropriate image? *Like the seeds of a plant, the offspring of the king grow and eventually replace the dying parent. The witches predicted that Banquo's "seed" will become king, so the king's remark that he will "labor to make thee (Banquo) full of growing" has special significance.*

As one that had been studied[3] in his death,
To throw away the dearest thing he owed[4]
As 'twere a careless[5] trifle.

KING. There's no art
To find the mind's construction[6] in the face: ❶
He was a gentleman on whom I built
An absolute trust.

[*Enter* MACBETH, BANQUO, ROSS, *and* ANGUS.]

O worthiest cousin!
The sin of my ingratitude even now
Was heavy on me: thou art so far before,
That swiftest wing of recompense is slow
To overtake thee. Would thou hadst less deserved,
That the proportion both of thanks and payment
Might have been mine![7] Only I have left to say,
More is thy due than more than all can pay.

MACBETH. The service and the loyalty I owe,
In doing it, pays itself.[8] Your Highness' part
Is to receive our duties: and our duties
Are to your throne and state children and servants;
Which do but what they should, by doing every thing
Safe toward[9] your love and honor.

KING. Welcome hither.
I have begun to plant thee, and will labor
To make thee full of growing. Noble Banquo,
That hast no less deserved, nor must be known
No less to have done so, let me enfold thee
And hold thee to my heart. ❸

BANQUO. There if I grow,
The harvest is your own.

KING. My plenteous joys,
Wanton[10] in fullness, seek to hide themselves
In drops of sorrow. Sons, kinsmen, thanes,
And you whose places are the nearest, know,
We will establish our estate upon
Our eldest, Malcolm,[11] whom we name hereafter
The Prince of Cumberland: which honor must
Not unaccompanied invest him only,
But signs of nobleness, like stars, shall shine
On all deservers. From hence to Inverness,[12]
And bind us further to you.

3. **studied:** Rehearsed.
4. **owed:** Owned.
5. **careless:** Worthless.
6. **mind's construction:** Person's character.

❷ **◆ Literary Focus**
How is the information that Cawdor is dead important in understanding the witches' predictions?

7. **Would . . . mine:** If you had been less worthy, my thanks and payment could have exceeded the rewards you deserve.
8. **pays itself:** Is its own reward.
9. **Safe toward:** With sure regard for.
10. **Wanton:** Unrestrained.
11. **Establish. . . Malcolm:** Make Malcolm the heir to my throne.
12. **Inverness:** Macbeth's castle.

▲ **Critical Viewing** How does this Scottish castle reflect the mood of the play? **[Connect]** ❹

MACBETH. The rest is labor, which is not used for you.[13]
I'll be myself the harbinger,[14] and make joyful
The hearing of my wife with your approach;
So, humbly take my leave.

KING. My worthy Cawdor!

MACBETH. [*Aside*] The Prince of Cumberland! That is a step
On which I must fall down, or else o'erleap,
For in my way it lies. Stars, hide your fires;
Let not light see my black and deep desires:
The eye wink at the hand;[15] yet let that be
Which the eye fears, when it is done, to see. [*Exit.*] ❺

KING. True, worthy Banquo; he is full so valiant,
And in his commendations I am fed;
It is a banquet to me. Let's after him,
Whose care is gone before to bid us welcome.
It is a peerless kinsman. [*Flourish. Exit.*]

13. The rest . . . you: Anything not done for you is laborious.
14. harbinger: Advance representative of the army or royal party who makes arrangements for a visit.

15. wink at the hand: Be blind to the hand's deed.

▶**Critical Viewing**◀

❹ **Connect** The use of blue and white colors conveys an icy, deathlike coldness consistent with the coldblooded murder of the king. The steep walls and surrounding water reflect both isolation and power.

◆ Critical Thinking

❺ **Interpret** What decision has Macbeth reached here? *He has reversed his previous decision to let fate work on its own; here he expresses an active desire to become king, and he views the prince of Cumberland as an obstacle in his path.*

Humanities: Art

This photograph, taken by Anne Van De Vaeken, is of Eilean Donan Castle in Dornie, Scotland. Castles such as this one were places of safety, from which occupants could defend themselves from attack. The castle in this picture is situated on a small island. The only access to the castle is by way of a narrow bridge.

Use these questions for discussion:

1. What might be the drawbacks and advantages of living in a castle such as this one? *Possible responses: Being isolated on an island would make it difficult to escape in case of attack; having only one entrance makes the castle easier to defend.*
2. How does this picture of a castle contrast with the description of Macbeth's castle: "This castle hath a pleasant seat" (Scene vi, line 1)? *The king and Banquo describe Macbeth's castle as a pleasant, inviting place, which contrasts with the cold isolation suggested in the one pictured.*

◆ Reading Strategy

❶ Use Text Aids The stage direction indicates that Lady Macbeth is reading rather than speaking. It becomes apparent that she is reading a letter from Macbeth wherein he relates his experience with the witches.

◆ Critical Thinking

❷ Analyze Ask: What is Lady Macbeth's reaction to the prophecy? *She immediately decides that the prophecy will come true, even if she has to help it along.*

◆ Critical Thinking

❸ Interpret Ask students: What does Lady Macbeth plan to do? *Lady Macbeth plans to begin coaxing Macbeth, persuading him to fulfill his destiny.*

◆ Grammar and Style

❹ Action Verbs and Linking Verbs Challenge students to find the linking verb in this sentence. *Thou'rt is a contraction of thou art. Art is an archaic form of are, the linking verb.*

Scene v. *Inverness.* MACBETH'S *castle.*
[*Enter* MACBETH'S WIFE, *alone, with a letter.*]

LADY MACBETH. [*Reads*] "They met me in the day of success; and I have learned by the perfect'st report they have more in them than mortal knowledge. When I burned in desire to question them further, they made themselves air, into which they vanished. Whiles I stood rapt in the wonder of it, came missives[1] from the King, who all-hailed me 'Thane of Cawdor'; by which title, before, these weird sisters saluted me, and referred me to the coming on of time, with 'Hail, King that shalt be!' This have I thought good to deliver thee,[2] my dearest partner of greatness, that thou mightst not lose the dues of rejoicing, by being ignorant of what greatness is promised thee. Lay it to thy heart, and farewell."

Glamis thou art, and Cawdor, and shalt be
What thou art promised. Yet do I fear thy nature; ❷
It is too full o' th' milk of human kindness
To catch the nearest[3] way. Thou wouldst be great,
Art not without ambition, but without
The illness[4] should attend it. What thou wouldst highly,
That wouldst thou holily; wouldst not play false,
And yet wouldst wrongly win. Thou'dst have, great Glamis,
That which cries "Thus thou must do" if thou have it;
And that which rather thou dost fear to do
Than wishest should be undone.[5] Hie thee hither,
That I may pour my spirits in thine ear,
And chastise with the valor of my tongue
All that impedes thee from the golden round[6] ❸
Which fate and metaphysical aid doth seem
To have thee crowned withal.

[*Enter* MESSENGER.]

What is your tidings?

MESSENGER. The King comes here tonight.

LADY MACBETH. Thou'rt mad to say it! ❹
Is not thy master with him, who, were't so,
Would have informed for preparation?

MESSENGER. So please you, it is true. Our thane is coming.
One of my fellows had the speed of him,[7]
Who, almost dead for breath, had scarcely more
Than would make up his message.

◆ Reading Strategy
❶ Use the stage directions and the footnotes to make sense of Lady Macbeth's speech.

1. **missives:** Messengers.

2. **deliver thee:** Report to you.

3. **nearest:** Quickest.

4. **illness:** Wickedness.

5. **that which . . . undone:** What you are afraid of doing you would not wish undone once you have done it.

6. **round:** Crown.

7. **had . . . him:** Overtook him.

Enrichment

A Writer Responds The supernatural, intrigue, murder, madness—these and other elements in *The Tragedy of Macbeth* have guaranteed audiences at its performances for almost four hundred years. While scholars may assure us it is an outstanding example of Elizabethan tragedy written in blank verse, Shakespeare's play about the quest for power in the Scottish Middle Ages is—first and foremost—vigorously entertaining.

William Hazlitt (1778–1830), one of the most outspoken critics in the Romantic era, recorded his thoughts about Shakespeare and other dramatists in essay form. Initially unsuccessful as a writer, Hazlitt was surprised and delighted when, soon after taking a job as a reporter for a London newspaper in 1812, he developed a faithful readership. Five years later, he was able to publish his essays as a book, *Characters of Shakespeare's Plays*. The following is an excerpt from the essay "Macbeth."

"The poet's eye in a fine
frenzy rolling
Doth glance from heaven to
earth, from earth to heaven;
And as imagination bodies forth
The forms of things
unknown, the poet's pen
Turns them to shape, and
gives to airy nothing
A local habitation and a name."
(from *A Midsummer Night's Dream*)

LADY MACBETH. Give him tending;
He brings great news. [*Exit* MESSENGER.]
The raven himself is hoarse
That croaks the fatal entrance of Duncan
Under my battlements. Come, you spirits
That tend on mortal[8] thoughts, unsex me here,
And fill me, from the crown to the toe, top-full
Of direst cruelty! Make thick my blood,
Stop up th' access and passage to remorse[9]
That no compunctious visitings of nature[10]
Shake my fell[11] purpose, nor keep peace between
Th' effect[12] and it! Come to my woman's breasts,
And take my milk for gall,[13] you murd'ring ministers,[14]
Wherever in your sightless[15] substances
You wait on[16] nature's mischief! Come, thick night,
And pall[17] thee in the dunnest[18] smoke of hell,
That my keen knife see not the wound it makes,
Nor heaven peep through the blanket of the dark,
To cry "Hold, hold!" ❺

[*Enter* MACBETH.]

Great Glamis! Worthy Cawdor!
Greater than both, by the all-hail hereafter!
Thy letters have transported me beyond
This ignorant[19] present, and I feel now
The future in the instant.[20]

MACBETH. My dearest love,
Duncan comes here tonight.

LADY MACBETH. And when goes hence?

MACBETH. Tomorrow, as he purposes.

LADY MACBETH. O, never
Shall sun that morrow see!
Your face, my Thane, is as a book where men
May read strange matters. To beguile the time,[21]
Look like the time; bear welcome in your eye,
Your hand, your tongue: look like th' innocent flower,
But be the serpent under 't. He that's coming
Must be provided for: and you shall put
This night's great business into my dispatch;[22]
Which shall to all our nights and days to come
Give solely sovereign sway and masterdom.

MACBETH. We will speak further.

LADY MACBETH. Only look up clear.[23]
To alter favor ever is to fear.[24] ❻

8. **mortal:** Deadly.
9. **remorse:** Compassion.
10. **compunctious . . . nature:** Natural feelings of pity.
11. **fell:** Savage.
12. **effect:** Fulfillment.
13. **milk for gall:** Kindness in exchange for bitterness.
14. **ministers:** Agents.
15. **sightless:** Invisible.
16. **wait on:** Assist.
17. **pall:** Enshroud.
18. **dunnest:** Darkest.
19. **ignorant:** Unknowing.
20. **instant:** Present.
21. **beguile the time:** Deceive the people tonight.
22. **dispatch:** Management.
23. **look up clear:** Appear innocent.
24. **To alter . . . fear:** To show a disturbed face will arouse suspicion.

◆ Build Vocabulary

sovereign (säv´ rən) *adj.*: Supreme in power, rank, or authority

◆ Critical Thinking

❺ Compare and Contrast Have students compare Lady Macbeth's response to the witches' predictions to Macbeth's. *Lady Macbeth immediately commits herself to take whatever bloody steps necessary to secure the crown. She openly invokes evil spirits to assist her in her purpose. Macbeth, on the other hand, entertains the thought, but seems reluctant to give voice to his secret, inner thoughts.*

◆ Critical Thinking

❻ Compare and Contrast Have students compare these lines to the king's statement in lines 11–12 of Scene iv: "There's no art / To find the mind's construction in the face . . ." *Students should note that the innocent appearance of Cawdor deceived the king, but ended in his capture and execution. Now Lady Macbeth is advising Macbeth to follow that example—to appear innocent to deceive others.*

Macbeth and Lear, Othello and Hamlet, are usually reckoned Shakespeare's four principal tragedies. Lear stands first for the profound intensity of the passion: Macbeth for the wildness of the imagination and the rapidity of the action; Othello for the progressive interest and powerful alternations of feeling; Hamlet for the refined development of thought and sentiment. If the force of genius shown in each of these works is astonishing, their variety is not less so. They are like different creations of the same mind, not one of which has the slightest reference to the rest. This distinctness and originality is indeed the necessary consequence of truth and nature. Shakespeare's genius alone appeared to possess the resources of nature. He is "your only tragedy maker." His plays have the force of things upon the mind. What he represents is brought home to the bosom as a part of our experience, implanted in the memory as if we had known the places, persons, and things of which he treats.

Macbeth is like a record of a preternatural and tragical event. It has the rugged severity of an old chronicle with all that the imagination of the poet can engraft upon traditional belief. The castle of Macbeth, round which "the air smells wooingly" and where "the temple-haunting martlet builds," has a real subsistence in the mind; the Weird Sisters meet us in person on "the blasted heath"; the "air-drawn dagger" moves slowly before our eyes; the "gracious Duncan," the "blood-boltered Banquo" stand before us; all that passed through the mind of Macbeth passes, without the loss of [the tiniest particle], through ours. All that could actually take place, and all that is only possible to be conceived, what was said and what was done, the workings of passion, the spells of magic, are brought before us with the same absolute truth and vividness.

◆ Literary Focus

❶ **Elizabethan Drama** What two reasons might Shakespeare have had for this extended description of Macbeth's castle? *The dialogue reveals the physical aspects of the castle and setting, which were not visually re-created in the Elizabethan theater; the description also lends irony to the play, because Macbeth's castle is described in the warmest of terms, although the readers know that it is a place of deception and treachery.*

◆ Critical Thinking

❷ **Connect** In what way is Lady Macbeth's dialogue reminiscent of the witches' dialogue? *Lady Macbeth's phrases "twice done" and "done double" sound like the witches' spells.*

Leave all the rest to me. [*Exit.*]

Scene vi. *Before* MACBETH'S *castle.*

[*Hautboys.*[1] *Torches. Enter* KING DUNCAN, MALCOLM, DONALBAIN, BANQUO, LENNOX, MACDUFF, ROSS, ANGUS, *and* ATTENDANTS.]

KING. This castle hath a pleasant seat;[2] the air
Nimbly and sweetly recommends itself
Unto our gentle[3] senses.

BANQUO. This guest of summer,
The temple-haunting martlet,[4] does approve[5]
By his loved mansionry[6] that the heaven's breath
Smells wooingly here. No jutty,[7] frieze,
Buttress, nor coign of vantage,[8] but this bird
Hath made his pendent bed and procreant cradle.[9]
Where they most breed and haunt,[10] I have observed
The air is delicate. ❶

[*Enter* LADY MACBETH.]

KING. See, see, our honored hostess!
The love that follows us sometime is our trouble,
Which still we thank as love. Herein I teach you
How you shall bid God 'ield us for your pains
And thank us for your trouble.[11]

LADY MACBETH. All our service
In every point twice done, and then done double, ❷
Were poor and single business[12] to contend
Against those honors deep and broad wherewith
Your Majesty loads our house: for those of old,
And the late dignities heaped up to them,
We rest your hermits.[13]

KING. Where's the Thane of Cawdor?
We coursed[14] him at the heels, and had a purpose
To be his purveyor:[15] but he rides well,
And his great love, sharp as his spur, hath holp[16] him
To his home before us. Fair and noble hostess,
We are your guest tonight.

LADY MACBETH. Your servants ever
Have theirs, themselves, and what is theirs, in compt,[17]
To make their audit at your Highness' pleasure,
Still[18] to return your own.

KING. Give me your hand.
Conduct me to mine host: we love him highly,

1. **Hautboys:** Oboes announcing the arrival of royalty.
2. **seat:** Location.
3. **gentle:** Soothed.
4. **temple-haunting martlet:** Martin, a bird that usually nests in churches. In Shakespeare's time, *martin* was a slang term for a person who is easily deceived.
5. **approve:** Show.
6. **mansionry:** Nests.
7. **jutty:** Projection.
8. **coign of vantage:** Advantageous corner.
9. **procreant** (prō krē ənt) **cradle:** Nest where the young are hatched.
10. **haunt:** Visit.
11. **The love . . . trouble:** Though my visit inconveniences you, you should ask God to reward me for coming, because it was my love for you that prompted my visit.
12. **single business:** Feeble service.
13. **rest your hermits:** Remain your dependents bound to pray for you. Hermits were often paid to pray for another person's soul.
14. **coursed:** Chased.
15. **purveyor:** Advance supply officer.
16. **holp:** Helped.
17. **compt:** Trust.
18. **Still:** Always.

Beyond the Classroom

Career Connection

Commercial Photography and Art

Movie theaters, retail stores, and other industries use photographs and graphics to project a positive picture of the services and the products they offer. The poster on page 287 attempts to convince viewers to buy a ticket to see the movie *Macbeth.* A good commercial photographer or artist must be able to analyze the product or service to identify the elements with greatest appeal for potential customers. Then he or she must be able to portray those elements in a way that convinces the viewer to buy the product or service.

Have interested students choose a scene in Act I they think would be most likely to make someone want to see *Macbeth.* Have them sketch a graphic and create an advertisement they could place in a newspaper.

Community Connection

Encourage students to visit the advertising department of a local newspaper or an advertising agency. Have them observe how an advertisement is put together. Specifically, have them investigate how a graphic is selected. Are certain "stock" graphics or pictures available? Do some advertisers supply their own graphics or photographs?

Have students collect newspaper advertisements for movies showing in the community. Discuss which advertisements have the most compelling graphics. Ask which movies they would like to see as a result of the advertisements.

Highlights from the film production of MACBETH

ORSON WELLES as Macbeth
JEANETTE NOLAN as Lady Macbeth
DAN O'HERLIHY as Macduff
RODDY McDOWALL as Malcolm
EDGAR BARRIER as Banquo

▲ **Critical Viewing** How does this poster capture the suspense created in Act I of *Macbeth*? **[Connect]** ❸

▶**Critical Viewing**◀

❸ **Connect** The sinister shadows reflect the treachery that is hatched in the first act. The eyes of Macbeth reflect a sense of shock at the horrible nature of the crime. Lady Macbeth's posture and facial expression suggest cold, almost mechanical determination.

Humanities: Art

Poster for Orson Welles's film of *Macbeth*.

Orson Welles, famous for *Citizen Kane* and *War of the Worlds,* adapted Shakespeare's *Macbeth* for the screen and then directed and starred in the production. This 1948 version also featured Jeanette Nolan and Roddy McDowall. The production is notable for its papier-mâché sets and brooding atmosphere.

The shadowy poster for the Welles's 1948 version of *Macbeth* emphasizes the darkness of the play's content. Orson Welles's face, made up as Macbeth at various points during the drama, conveys to viewers that the play is about a tortured individual.

Use these questions for discussion:

1. What emotion is expressed by each of the expressions on Welles's face in this poster? *Possible answers include cold-blooded determination, fear, hate, helplessness, and resignation.*
2. Do you find that the poster captures the essence of *The Tragedy of Macbeth?* *Possible responses: Yes, the various expressions of Macbeth show that it is ultimately a human tragedy; no, the poster focuses too much on the Macbeth character and not enough on the others.*

◆ Literature and Your Life

❶ Ask students if they have ever used the argument Macbeth uses in lines 1–2 with themselves or others when faced with a difficult situation. *Students may say they have felt this way when facing an unpleasant task or when having to confront a friend.*

◆ Critical Thinking

❷ **Analyze** Direct students to identify the arguments against murdering Duncan. *Arguments against murdering Duncan include: What Macbeth does to Duncan will likely happen to him; Duncan's a guest in Macbeth's house; Duncan is so beloved that people will seek retribution.*

And shall continue our graces towards him.
By your leave, hostess. [*Exit.*]

Scene vii. MACBETH'S *castle.*
[*Hautboys. Torches. Enter a* SEWER,[1] *and diverse* SERVANTS *with dishes and service over the stage. Then enter* MACBETH.]

MACBETH. If it were done[2] when 'tis done, then 'twere well ❶
It were done quickly. If th' assassination
Could trammel up the consequence, and catch,
With his surcease, success;[3] that but this blow
Might be the be-all and the end-all—here,
But here, upon this bank and shoal of time,
We'd jump the life to come.[4] But in these cases
We still have judgment here; that we but teach
Bloody instructions, which, being taught, return
To plague th' inventor: this even-handed[5] justice
Commends[6] th' ingredients of our poisoned chalice[7]
To our own lips. He's here in double trust:
First, as I am his kinsman and his subject,
Strong both against the deed; then, as his host,
Who should against his murderer shut the door,
Not bear the knife myself. Besides, this Duncan
Hath borne his faculties[8] so meek, hath been ❷
So clear[9] in his great office, that his virtues
Will plead like angels trumpet-tongued against
The deep damnation of his taking-off;
And pity, like a naked newborn babe,
Striding the blast, or heaven's cherubin[10] horsed
Upon the sightless couriers[11] of the air,
Shall blow the horrid deed in every eye,
That tears shall drown the wind. I have no spur
To prick the sides of my intent, but only
Vaulting ambition, which o'erleaps itself
And falls on th' other—

[*Enter* LADY MACBETH.]
How now! What news?

LADY MACBETH. He has almost supped. Why have you left the chamber?

MACBETH. Hath he asked for me?

LADY MACBETH. Know you not he has?

MACBETH. We will proceed no further in this business:
He hath honored me of late, and I have bought[12]
Golden opinions from all sorts of people,

1. **sewer:** Chief butler.
2. **done:** Over and done with.
3. **If . . . success:** If the assassination could be done successfully and without consequence.
4. **We'd . . . come:** I would risk life in the world to come.
5. **even-handed:** Impartial.
6. **commends:** Offers.
7. **chalice:** Cup.
8. **faculties:** Powers.
9. **clear:** Blameless.
10. **cherubin:** Angels.
11. **sightless couriers:** Unseen messengers (the wind).
12. **bought:** Acquired.

Which would be worn now in their newest gloss,
Not cast aside so soon.

LADY MACBETH. Was the hope drunk
Wherein you dressed yourself? Hath it slept since?
And wakes it now, to look so green and pale
At what it did so freely? From this time
Such I account thy love. Art thou afeard
To be the same in thine own act and valor
As thou art in desire? Wouldst thou have that
Which thou esteem'st the ornament of life,[13]
And live a coward in thine own esteem,
Letting "I dare not" wait upon[14] "I would,"
Like the poor cat i' th' adage?[15]

MACBETH. Prithee, peace!
I dare do all that may become a man;
Who dares do more is none.

LADY MACBETH. What beast was 't then
That made you break[16] this enterprise to me?
When you durst do it, then you were a man;
And to be more than what you were, you would

13. ornament of life: The crown.
14. wait upon: Follow.
15. poor . . . adage: From an old proverb about a cat who wants to eat fish but is afraid of getting its paws wet.
16. break: Reveal.

▲ Critical Viewing What sort of person would be worthy of wearing a crown such as this one? **[Generalize]** 5

◆ Critical Thinking

3 Analyze According to Lady Macbeth, what constitutes manliness? *Lady Macbeth equates manliness with strength of mind and body. Lady Macbeth feels that the more a man does, the more manly he becomes.*

◆ Critical Thinking

4 Interpret What arguments does Lady Macbeth use to convince Macbeth to carry out the murder? *Lady Macbeth asks him if his hopes have all died out. She implies that her love is directly linked to his ambitions. She also accuses him of being cowardly.*

▶Critical Viewing◀

5 Generalize Possible response: Someone honorable, trustworthy, and noble in spirit would be worthy of wearing this crown.

◆ *Literature and Your Life*

❶ The thought of a mother dashing out the brains of her nursing child is shocking. Shakespeare uses this image to convey the depth of Lady Macbeth's ambition.

◆ Critical Thinking

❷ **Analyze** What is Lady Macbeth's plan? What does it reveal about her character? *Lady Macbeth plans to get the king's servants drunk so they pass out and are unable to guard his bedchamber. Then Macbeth and Lady Macbeth will use the guards' daggers to murder Duncan. The guards are to be blamed for the crime. These coldblooded preparations reveal Lady Macbeth's ruthlessness and hunger for power.*

◆ Critical Thinking

❸ **Criticize** Call students' attention to the couplet that concludes Act I. Ask: Is this an effective way to conclude Act I? *Responses may include: Yes, because it reveals Macbeth's evil intentions; no, because it gives away the plot events to come.*

Looking at Literature Videodisc In this segment, Professor Ian Frederick Moulton, Shakespeare expert, discusses how Shakespeare borrowed from historical sources when writing his plays, "enhancing" the facts to suit his purposes. Play Chapter Four of this videodisc to spark a class discussion of which events and characters in Act I of *Macbeth* were based on historical fact.

Chapter 4

Be so much more the man. Nor time nor place
Did then adhere,[17] and yet you would make both.
They have made themselves, and that their[18] fitness now
Does unmake you. I have given suck, and know
How tender 'tis to love the babe that milks me:
I would, while it was smiling in my face,
Have plucked my nipple from his boneless gums,
And dashed the brains out, had I so sworn as you
Have done to this.

MACBETH. If we should fail?

LADY MACBETH. We fail?
But[19] screw your courage to the sticking-place[20]
And we'll not fail. When Duncan is asleep—
Whereto the rather shall his day's hard journey
Soundly invite him—his two chamberlains
Will I with wine and wassail[21] so convince,[22]
That memory, the warder of the brain,
Shall be a fume, and the receipt of reason
A limbeck only:[23] when in swinish sleep
Their drenchèd natures lies as in a death,
What cannot you and I perform upon
Th' unguarded Duncan, what not put upon
His spongy[24] officers, who shall bear the guilt
Of our great quell?[25]

MACBETH. Bring forth men-children only;
For thy undaunted mettle[26] should compose
Nothing but males. Will it not be received,
When we have marked with blood those sleepy two
Of his own chamber, and used their very daggers,
That they have done 't?

LADY MACBETH. Who dares receive it other,[27]
As we shall make our griefs and clamor roar
Upon his death?

MACBETH. I am settled, and bend up
Each corporal agent to this terrible feat.
Away, and mock the time[28] with fairest show:
False face must hide what the false heart doth know.
[*Exit.*]

17. **Did then adhere:** Was then suitable (for the assassination).
18. **that their:** Their very.

◆ *Literature and Your Life*

❶ What is shocking about the ambition Lady Macbeth expresses in ll. 54–59?

19. **But:** Only.
20. **sticking-place:** The notch that holds the bowstring of a taut crossbow.
21. **wassail:** Carousing.
22. **convince:** Overpower.
23. **That . . . only:** That memory, the guardian of the brain, will be confused by the fumes of the drink, and the reason become like a still, distilling confused thoughts.
24. **spongy:** Sodden.
25. **quell:** Murder.
26. **mettle:** Spirit.
27. **other:** Otherwise.
28. **mock the time:** Mislead the world.

Speaking and Listening Mini-Lesson

Oral Interpretation

This mini-lesson supports the Speaking and Listening activity in the Idea Bank, on p. 292.

Introduce the Concept Unlike acting, which employs costumes and movement to convey meaning, oral interpretation requires the performer to convey the meaning of the lines through voice alone. Through the use of pauses, inflection, pacing, and similar techniques, the performer conveys the meaning and emotion of the lines. You might refer students to the elements of vocal delivery in the Speaking and Listening Handbook, page 1200.

Develop Background Students should begin by paraphrasing Macbeth's speech sentence by sentence (not line by line). Doing so will clarify their understanding of the passage, an essential first step for oral interpretation. Students can then annotate a copy of the speech, noting where sentences begin and end, which words should be emphasized, and so on.

Applying the Information Have students practice reading the speech aloud, working with a partner or alone with the aid of a tape recorder. Then have students deliver the oral interpretation to the class.

Assess the Outcome Students may use the Peer Assessment form for Oral Interpretation, p. 120, in ***Alternative Assessment.***

Beyond Literature

History Connection

The Real Macbeth There is not much similarity between the real Macbeth, a *moarmaer* or (subking) of Moray, a region that was annexed to Scotland, and Shakespeare's Macbeth. It is true, as Shakespeare wrote, that Macbeth became king of Scotland by killing King Duncan, who was a relative by marriage and whom he had served as a general. However, Macbeth's claim to the throne was quite legitimate due to the ancient Scottish custom of tanistry. According to this system, kingships were not passed from father to son. Instead the ablest, oldest male in an extended royal family was chosen by a family council, or chose himself by declaring war on his competitors. That's what the real Macbeth did. He declared war on King Duncan and killed him fairly in battle.

Macbeth ruled for seventeen years (from 1040 to 1057), and contemporary accounts describe it as a prosperous period. Things were even peaceful enough for him to take a trip to Rome in 1050. Four years later, however, he was invaded by a Northumbrian force led by Duncan's son Malcolm Canmore and, in 1057, was killed by Canmore.

Hardly any of Shakespeare's play, *Macbeth*, is historically accurate. If you were writing a fictional account of Macbeth, or another real person, how closely would you want to stick to the facts? Explain.

Guide for Responding

◆ Literature and Your Life

Reader's Response Do you find the developments in Macbeth's character believable? Why or why not?

Thematic Focus Which scene do you think would be most effective on stage? Why?

Role Play Imagine that Macbeth and Lady Macbeth continue to discuss whether or not to kill Duncan. With a partner, role-play their discussions.

☑ Check Your Comprehension

1. What do we learn about Macbeth's battlefield deeds and the activities of the Thane of Cawdor?
2. What reward does Macbeth receive from the king?
3. What do the three witches predict for Macbeth and Banquo?
4. (a) How does Lady Macbeth first learn of the witches' predictions? (b) What in Macbeth's personality does she fear will hold him back?
5. (a) What action does Lady Macbeth plan to take during the king's visit? (b) How does she intend to accomplish it?

◆ Critical Thinking

INTERPRET

1. Both the witches and Macbeth make statements about "foul and fair." (a) What are two possible meanings for the witches' words? (b) What does Macbeth mean by his remark? **[Interpret]**
2. Compare and contrast Banquo's and Macbeth's reactions to the witches. **[Compare and Contrast]**
3. Why is Macbeth indecisive about killing the king? **[Analyze Cause and Effect]**
4. How does Lady Macbeth's understanding of her husband's character help her to convince him that the murder plot should be carried out? **[Analyze]**

APPLY

5. How should Macbeth have answered Lady Macbeth when, speaking of the planned murder, she said, "What beast was't then / That made you break this enterprise to me?" **[Apply]**

EXTEND

6. Identify someone in history who is similar to a character in *Macbeth*. Explain your choice. **[Social Studies Link]**

Reinforce and Extend

Answers

◆ Literature and Your Life

Reader's Response Suggested responses: Yes, Macbeth's character is believable because he didn't immediately fall into evil; no, Macbeth's character is not believable because a hero wouldn't succumb to evil so quickly.

Thematic Focus Students may suggest that Scene iii could be most effectively staged, since special effects could be used to highlight the supernatural elements.

☑ Check Your Comprehension

1. Macbeth has led his troops bravely and with great determination in King Duncan's service; the Thane of Cawdor has been found to have traitorously conspired with Duncan's enemies.
2. As a reward, Macbeth is named Thane of Cawdor by the king.
3. The three witches predict that Macbeth will become Thane of Cawdor and King. They predict that Banquo will have kings among his descendants.
4. (a) Lady Macbeth reads her husband's letter to her describing his encounter with the witches. (b) She fears that his nature, filled with the "milk of human kindness," may hold him back.
5. (a) Lady Macbeth plans to murder Duncan in his bed. (b) She will lay the blame on Duncan's servants, whom she will make drunk and smear with Duncan's blood as they sleep.

◆ Critical Thinking

1. (a) The entire play turns on the ways in which fair things are linked with or turn into things foul. The fair Lady Macbeth shows greater evil (foulness) than her warrior husband, Macbeth. The fair promise of a crown is fulfilled, but only through foul treachery and death. (b) Macbeth appears to be referring to the awful weather and the great victory.
2. Ambition surges through Macbeth, filling his mind with the possibilities of wearing the crown. Banquo wonders if the instruments of darkness aren't tempting them with promises only to bring them harm in the end. Macbeth is uncritical, taking the witches' words as true; Banquo is skeptical, questioning their motives.
3. Macbeth's ambition struggles with his sense of decency and logic. The additional crime of harming a guest enjoying one's hospitality makes the contemplated crime even more troublesome. Macbeth is also aware that Malcolm must be dealt with afterwards, and that a great cry will follow the death of this kind and good man.
4. She knows that, by questioning his manhood when he hesitates, she will spur him on.
5. Students may say that he should have replied that, whatever beast moved him then, the beast of logic and decency now hold him back.
6. Students may suggest that Julius Caesar is similar to Macbeth.

Answers

◆ Reading Strategy

1. (a) Act I, Scene i, takes place during a storm in an open place. (b) Lady Macbeth is alone in a part of Macbeth's castle at Inverness as she reads a letter aloud.
2. (a) at once (b) a Scots title of nobility (c) a term of courtesy between fellow noblemen

◆ Literary Focus

1. An apt set for I, vi, would include a castle exterior populated with birds (the "temple-haunting martlet"), with flowers in evidence to account for the pleasant air.
2. They suggest that patches of fog and cloud obscure and then let in the light.
3. Lines 48–58 of I, ii, let us know that the Norwegian invaders, assisted by the Thane of Cawdor, have been defeated by Macbeth.

◆ Grammar and Style

1. linking/linking (is/is); 2. linking/action (am/cry); 3. action (Speak)

◆ Build Vocabulary

Using Words About Power
Power: sovereign, king, sergeant, victory, thane, crown, prince
Political loyalty: honor, valor, worthy, trust, service, noble
Political betrayal: assassination, traitor, rebels, treasons, execution

Using the Word Bank
1. (c) cowardice; 2. (a) loyalty; 3. (b) submissive; 4. (c) peasant; 5. (a) insignificant

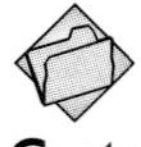

Idea Bank

Customizing for
Learning Modalities
Following are suggestions for matching Idea Bank topics with your students' learning modalities:
Verbal/Linguistic: 1, 2, 3
Musical/Rhythmic: 3
Intrapersonal: 3

Customizing for
Performance Levels
Following are suggestions for matching Idea Bank topics with your students' ability levels:
Less Advanced Students: 1
Average Students: 3
More Advanced Students: 2

Guide for Responding (continued)

◆ Reading Strategy

Use Text Aids

Notes and stage directions help you to understand the action in *Macbeth.* For example, the directions at the beginning of I, ii, help you imagine the scene as the king and his followers encounter a bleeding captain. The side note tells you that a trumpet is sounding offstage.

1. Use the stage directions and side notes to describe the action in these scenes.
a. I, i **b.** Beginning of I, v

2. Use the side notes to explain the following terms:
a. anon **b.** Thane **c.** cousins

◆ Literary Focus

Elizabethan Drama

In **Elizabethan drama,** words did extra work. As in modern dramas, the characters' dialogue provided information on the story behind the play. However, words also created the illusion that elaborate sets and fancy lighting do in modern drama. For example, the dialogue between Banquo and the king helps the audience "see" Macbeth's castle: "This castle hath a pleasant seat . . . (I, vi, 1 – 10).

1. Use this dialogue to describe a set that would work for I, vi.
2. What "lighting effects" do the witches' words in I, i, 10– 11 suggest? Explain.
3. What important background information do you learn from the speech in I, ii, 48–58?

◆ Grammar and Style

Action Verbs and Linking Verbs

Shakespeare uses **action verbs** to depict physical or mental actions that heighten the drama. He uses **linking verbs**—like *seem* and forms of the verb *to be*—to connect nouns and pronouns with vivid modifiers.

Practice Identify each verb in the following sentences from *Macbeth* as an action or a linking verb.
1. Fair is foul, and foul is fair. (I, i, 10)
2. But I am faint; my gashes cry for help. (I, ii, 42)
3. Speak then to me . . . (I, iii, 60)

◆ Build Vocabulary

Using Words About Power

Shakespeare uses words relating to the themes of power, political loyalty, and political betrayal. Write these three themes in your notebook. Then, under each, list words from the play that relate to that theme. Use these three examples to begin your lists: Power—*sovereign, king;* political loyalty—*honor;* political betrayal—*assassination.*

Using the Word Bank

On your paper, write the letter of the word that is the antonym (opposite in meaning) of the first word.
1. valor: (a) courage, (b) bravery, (c) cowardice
2. treason: (a) loyalty, (b) betrayal, (c) treachery
3. imperial: (a) royal, (b) submissive, (c) powerful
4. liege: (a) authority, (b) king, (c) peasant
5. sovereign: (a) insignificant, (b) supreme, (c) solid

Idea Bank

Writing

1. Speech of Welcome Write the speech of welcome that Macbeth might have addressed to Duncan as Duncan entered Macbeth's castle. You can use prose or you can imitate Shakespeare's blank verse.

2. Comparison and Contrast Compare and contrast Macbeth and Lady Macbeth. Support your points with references to at least two passages from Act I. Consider such traits as courage, imagination, and ruthlessness.

Speaking and Listening

3. Oral Interpretation Reread Macbeth's speech in I, vii, 1 –28. Practice reciting it, allowing the meaning of the passage to guide you, not the line endings. Decide where to quicken or slow your pace, and choose the words you want to emphasize. When you finish rehearsing, read the speech aloud for the class. **[Performing Arts Link]**

✓ ASSESSMENT OPTIONS

Formal Assessment, Selection Test, pp. 65–67, and Assessment Resources Software. The selection test is designed so that it can be easily customized to the ability levels of your students.
Alternative Assessment, p. 12, includes options for less advanced students, more advance students, visual and spatial learners, and auditory learners.

PORTFOLIO ASSESSMENT
Use the following rubrics and assessment guidelines in the *Alternative Assessment* booklet to assess student writing and speaking:
Speech of Welcome: Self-Assessment: Speech, p. 118
Comparison and Contrast: Comparison/Contrast Rubric, p. 104
Oral Interpretation: Peer Assessment: Oral Interpretation, p. 120

Guide for Interpreting, Act II

◆ Review and Anticipate

In Act I, we learn that Macbeth has distinguished himself in battle. Returning from the battlefield, he and Banquo meet three witches. These "weird sisters" predict that Macbeth will not only be rewarded by King Duncan but that he will become king himself. However, the witches also greet Banquo as a father of kings. Motivated by the witches' prophecy, Macbeth considers killing Duncan. The assassination becomes more likely when the king decides to visit Macbeth's castle. Lady Macbeth, on hearing about the witches' predictions and the king's visit, resolves that she and her husband will kill Duncan. When Macbeth hesitates, she urges him on.

As Act II begins, Macbeth and Lady Macbeth are about to commit this evil deed.

◆ Literary Focus

Blank Verse

Blank verse—unrhymed iambic pentameter—was invented during the English Renaissance to reflect natural speech rhythms. An ***iamb*** is a metrical foot consisting of an unstressed syllable followed by a stressed syllable, and the term ***pentameter*** means that there are five such feet to the line. *Macbeth* is written mainly in blank verse:

Me thought I heard a voice cry, "Sleep no more" (II, ii, 34)

(Unstressed syllables are represented by ˘ and stressed syllables by ´.) Unvaried blank verse would soon grow dull, however. That's why Shakespeare introduces variations, like a trochaic foot (´ ˘) at the beginning of a line: "List'ning their fear . . . (II, ii, 28–29). As you hear the "melody" of Shakespeare's dialogue, listen for the rhythm too: a drumbeat iambic, with variations.

◆ Grammar and Style

Commonly Confused Words: *Lie* and *Lay*

Shakespeare correctly uses two easily confused words, *lie* and *lay*.

Lie (past: *lay*; past participle: *lain*) means "lie down or on":

"A heavy summons *lies* like lead upon me . . ." (II, i, 6)

Lay (past and past participle: *laid*) means "to place":

"I *laid* their daggers ready. . . ." (II, ii, 11)

◆ Reading Strategy

Read Verse for Meaning

When you first learn about blank verse, you may find yourself beating out the rhythm of each line and stopping at the ends of lines. However, to **read blank verse for meaning**, you should focus on sentences and not lines.

To make sense of Shakespeare's sentences, you must follow them past the line endings. If you don't follow this sentence to the next line, you don't learn what the owl does. "It was the owl that shriek'd, the fatal bellman / Which gives the stern'st good-night . . ." (II, ii, 3–4).

◆ Build Vocabulary

Word Roots: *-voc-*

The word *equivocate* in Act II has the root *-voc-*, which means "voice." To equivocate is to speak in two equal "voices" so that two meanings can be given to what you say. Equivocation is a way of deceiving others without technically lying.

Word Bank

Before you read, preview this list of words from Act II of *Macbeth*.

augment
palpable
stealthy
multitudinous
equivocate
predominance

Prepare and Engage

Objectives

1. To read, comprehend, interpret, and respond to an Elizabethan drama
2. To relate an Elizabethan drama to personal experience
3. To read verse for meaning
4. To identify and interpret blank verse
5. To build vocabulary in context and learn the word root *-voc-*
6. To use correctly the commonly confused words *lie* and *lay*
7. To respond to Act II of *Macbeth* through writing and projects

Skills Instruction

Vocabulary: Word Roots: *-voc-*

Grammar Commonly Confused Words: Lie and Lay

Reading Strategy: Read Verse for Meaning

Literary Focus: Blank Verse

Critical Viewing: Deduce; Interpret

Portfolio Opportunities

Writing: Detective's Journal; Response to Criticism

Project: Costume Design

Interest Grabber Review the plan Macbeth and Lady Macbeth have made for the "perfect crime." Students should recall that the plan calls for Lady Macbeth to provide wine to the king's attendants to make them drunk, thereby leaving the king unguarded. Macbeth is then to kill the king with the attendants' daggers, and smear them with the king's blood. Ask students if this plan seems sound and whether there are any flaws in the plan. Ask them to anticipate how Duncan's sons, especially Malcolm, might react and how Macbeth and Lady Macbeth might deal with them. Also have them consider the attendants. What might their reaction be, and how will Macbeth deal with them?

Have students turn to page 304 and note that the painting depicts Macbeth meeting Lady Macbeth after committing the murder. Ask what they might anticipate in this act based on this painting.

Prentice Hall Literature Program Resources

REINFORCE / RETEACH / EXTEND

Selection Support Pages
Build Vocabulary: Word Roots: *-voc-*, p. 63
Grammar and Style: Commonly Confused Words: *Lie* and *Lay*, p. 64
Reading Strategy: Read Verse for Meaning, p. 65
Literary Focus: Blank Verse, p. 66

Strategies for Diverse Student Needs
Complete a Sequence Chain, p. 13

Beyond Literature Career Connection: Military Careers, p. 13

Formal Assessment Selection Test, pp. 68–70; Assessment Resources Software

Alternative Assessment, p. 13

Listening to Literature Audiocassettes
The Tragedy of Macbeth, Act II

Develop Understanding

One-Minute Insight

In this act, thoughts become deeds. It appears that Macbeth and Lady Macbeth have committed the perfect crime. In fact, it may have been carried out more successfully than they had hoped—the attendants are slain and therefore unable to defend themselves, and Duncan's sons flee, thereby casting suspicion on themselves. However, in Act II the plot is unraveling and the hints of tragedy begin to appear. One of the play's major themes—beware of excessive ambition—begins to be developed as Macbeth becomes tortured by guilt and begins to see visions. Throughout Act II, a supernatural foreboding of evil hangs in the air as chaos begins.

Customize for
More Advanced Students
Shakespeare uses a number of techniques to suggest divine disapproval of the murder: Lady Macbeth hears an owl scream; Macbeth is unable to utter "Amen"; Lennox reports an "unruly night" in which chimneys were blown down. Have these students record examples of such instances as they read Act II.

◆ Critical Thinking

❶ **Infer** Ask students how Shakespeare uses the opening dialogue to inform the audience of the time of the action. *Banquo asks Fleance how the night is going. Fleance expresses his belief that it is past midnight.*

◆ Grammar and Style

❷ **Lie and Lay** Ask: Why is *lies* the correct word to use here? *Lies is correct here because the sentence calls for the meaning "to lie down or on."*

◆ Critical Thinking

❸ **Make a Judgment** How does the king's gift of a diamond to Lady Macbeth heighten the impact of his impending death? *This gift shows the generosity of the king and therefore makes his undeserved death more pitiful.*

Act II

Scene i. *Inverness. Court of* MACBETH'S *castle.*
[*Enter* BANQUO, *and* FLEANCE, *with a torch before him.*]

BANQUO. How goes the night, boy?

FLEANCE. The moon is down; I have not heard the clock.

BANQUO. And she goes down at twelve.

FLEANCE. I take't, 'tis later, sir. ❶

BANQUO. Hold, take my sword. There's husbandry[1] in heaven.
Their candles are all out. Take thee that[2] too.
A heavy summons[3] lies like lead upon me,
And yet I would not sleep. Merciful powers, ❷
Restrain in me the cursèd thoughts that nature
Gives way to in repose!

[*Enter* MACBETH, *and a* SERVANT *with a torch.*]
Give me my sword!
Who's there?

MACBETH. A friend.

BANQUO. What, sir, not yet at rest? The King's a-bed:
He hath been in unusual pleasure, and
Sent forth great largess to your offices:[4]
This diamond he greets your wife withal,
By the name of most kind hostess; and shut up[5] ❸
In measureless content.

MACBETH. Being unprepared,
Our will became the servant to defect,
Which else should free have wrought.[6]

BANQUO. All's well.
I dreamt last night of the three weird sisters:
To you they have showed some truth.

MACBETH. I think not of them.
Yet, when we can entreat an hour to serve,
We would spend it in some words upon that business,
If you would grant the time.

1. **husbandry:** Thrift.
2. **that:** Probably his sword belt.
3. **summons:** Weariness.
4. **largess . . . offices:** Gifts to your servants' quarters.
5. **shut up:** Retired.
6. **Being . . . wrought:** Because we did not have enough time to prepare, we were unable to entertain as lavishly as we wanted to.

◆ Build Vocabulary

augment (ôg ment′) *v.*: To make greater; enlarge

palpable (pal′ pə bəl) *adj.*: Capable of being touched or felt

stealthy (stel′ thē) *adj.*: Sly; furtive

Block Scheduling Strategies

Consider these suggestions to take advantage of extended class time:

- Model the Reading Strategy on page 293. After students read Act II, have them answer the Reading Strategy questions on page 308.
- Before students read Act II, ask the class to predict what will happen. Write their predictions on the board. After they read Act II, have them review and discuss their predictions.
- Introduce the Literary Focus on page 293. You also may wish to use the Literary Focus page in ***Selection Support,*** p. 66. Have students answer the Literary Focus questions on page 308 after they have read Act II.
- Ask volunteers to read the porter's speech to the class (Scene iii, p. 299). Then discuss with the class how this speech differs from most of the others in the drama.
- Have students work individually or in small groups to complete the Costume Design Project, p. 308.

BANQUO. At your kind'st leisure.

MACBETH. If you shall cleave to my consent, when 'tis,[7]
It shall make honor for you.

BANQUO. So[8] I lose none
In seeking to augment it, but still keep
My bosom franchised[9] and allegiance clear,
I shall be counseled.

MACBETH. Good repose the while! ❹

BANQUO. Thanks, sir. The like to you!

[*Exit* BANQUO *with* FLEANCE.]

MACBETH. Go bid thy mistress, when my drink is ready,
She strike upon the bell. Get thee to bed.
[*Exit* SERVANT.]
Is this a dagger which I see before me,
The handle toward my hand? Come, let me clutch thee.
I have thee not, and yet I see thee still.
Art thou not, fatal vision, sensible[10]
To feeling as to sight, or art thou but
A dagger of the mind, a false creation,
Proceeding from the heat-oppressèd brain?
I see thee yet, in form as palpable
As this which now I draw.
Thou marshal'st[11] me the way that I was going;
And such an instrument I was to use.
Mine eyes are made the fools o' th' other senses,
Or else worth all the rest. I see thee still;
And on thy blade and dudgeon[12] gouts[13] of blood,
Which was not so before. There's no such thing. ❻
It is the bloody business which informs[14]
Thus to mine eyes. Now o'er the one half-world
Nature seems dead, and wicked dreams abuse[15]
The curtained sleep; witchcraft celebrates
Pale Hecate's offerings;[16] and withered murder,
Alarumed by his sentinel, the wolf,
Whose howl's his watch, thus with his stealthy pace,
With Tarquin's[17] ravishing strides, towards his design
Moves like a ghost. Thou sure and firm-set earth,
Hear not my steps, which way they walk, for fear
Thy very stones prate of my whereabout,
And take the present horror from the time,
Which now suits with it.[18] Whiles I threat, he lives:
Words to the heat of deeds too cold breath gives.
[*A bell rings.*]

7. cleave . . . 'tis: Join my cause when the time comes.

8. So: Provided that.

9. bosom franchised: Heart free (from guilt).

❺ ◆ Reading Strategy
How many sentences are in lines 35–39?

10. sensible: Able to be felt.

11. marshal'st: Leads.

12. dudgeon: Wooden hilt.

13. gouts: Large drops.

14. informs: Takes shape.

15. abuse: Deceive.

16. Hecate's (hek´ə tēz) **offerings:** Offerings to Hecate, the Greek goddess of witchcraft.

17. Tarquin's: Of Tarquin, a Roman tyrant.

18. take . . . it: Remove the horrible silence which suits this moment.

◆ Literary Focus

❹ **Blank Verse** Point out that the five iambic feet in this line fall within the speeches of two characters. Have students mark off the iambic feet and stress syllables in this line. *I shall | be coun | seled. Good | repose | the while!*

◆ Reading Strategy

❺ **Reading Verse for Meaning** *There are two sentences in lines 35–39.*

◆ Critical Thinking

❻ **Analyze** Have students locate the point at which Macbeth ceases to hallucinate and proceeds with his plan. *Line 47, when he says "There's no such thing," is the point at which Macbeth stops hallucinating.*

Preparing for Standardized Tests

Reading and Vocabulary Developing an awareness of common Latin roots like *-voc-* will help students unlock the meaning of unfamiliar words on standardized vocabulary tests. For example, the *-voc-* root appears in words such as *vocation, evocative, irrevocable,* and *vouch.* The Build Vocabulary lesson on page 63 in ***Selection Support,*** provides practice in recognizing this root.

Grammar and Language The troublesome words *lie* and *lay* appear frequently on tests of English usage. Review the principal parts, pointing out that the past of *lie (lay)* is the same as the present *lay.* This common spelling is part of the confusion between the words. Most test items that address this issue will ask students to choose the correct form of *lie* or *lay* for a particular sentence.

After I ran the race, I (laid, lay) down for a few minutes. *lay*

The book had (lain, laid) on the wet ground for days before anyone noticed it. *lain*

Don't (lie, lay) your clothes on that chair. *lay*

The Grammar and Style lesson for Act II focuses on these commonly confused words. For additional practice, give students the Grammar and Style page in ***Selection Support,*** p. 64.

◆ Grammar and Style

❶ ***Lie* and *Lay*** Have students explain why *laid* is correct in line 11. *Laid, meaning "placed," is the past tense of lay. The sentence requires the meaning of "placed" or "set down."*

◆ Critical Thinking

❷ **Analyze** What new element of Lady Macbeth's character is revealed in these lines? *Prior to this, Lady Macbeth has shown a cold, inhuman attitude toward the murder. Here, for the first time, she reveals an understanding of the human face of murder.*

◆ Reading Strategy

❸ **Read Verse for Meaning** What mood or atmosphere does this series of short lines create? Is Macbeth talking to Lady Macbeth or does he seem detached from his surroundings? *These lines suggest an atmosphere of tension, as though the characters are jumping at the sound of each other's voice. Macbeth seems only vaguely aware of Lady Macbeth's words. He seems out of touch with his surroundings.*

I go, and it is done: the bell invites me.
Hear it not, Duncan, for it is a knell
That summons thee to heaven, or to hell. [*Exit.*]

Scene ii. *Macbeth's castle.*
[*Enter* LADY MACBETH.]

LADY MACBETH. That which hath made them drunk hath made me bold;
What hath quenched them hath given me fire. Hark! Peace!
It was the owl that shrieked, the fatal bellman,
Which gives the stern'st good-night.[1] He is about it.
The doors are open, and the surfeited grooms[2]
Do mock their charge with snores. I have drugged their possets,[3]
That death and nature do contend about them,
Whether they live or die.

MACBETH. [*Within*] Who's there? What, ho?

LADY MACBETH. Alack, I am afraid they have awaked
And 'tis not done! Th' attempt and not the deed
Confounds[4] us. Hark! I laid their daggers ready; ❶
He could not miss 'em. Had he not resembled
My father as he slept, I had done 't. ❷

[*Enter* MACBETH.]

My husband! ❸

MACBETH. I have done the deed. Didst thou not hear a noise?

LADY MACBETH. I heard the owl scream and the crickets cry.
Did not you speak?

MACBETH. When?

LADY MACBETH. Now.

MACBETH. As I descended?

LADY MACBETH. Ay.

MACBETH. Hark!
Who lies i' th' second chamber?

LADY MACBETH. Donalbain.

1. **bellman . . . goodnight:** It was customary for a bell to be rung at midnight outside a condemned person's cell on the night before an execution.
2. **surfeited grooms:** Overfed servants.
3. **possets:** Warm bedtime drinks.

4. **Confounds:** Ruins.

Ellen Terry as Lady Macbeth, John Singer Sargent, Tate Gallery, on Loan to National Portrait Gallery, London

▶Critical Viewing◀

❹ **Deduce** The actress's posture and regal bearing indicate that she would have spoken these lines with confidence and strength.

◆ Literary Focus

❺ **Blank Verse** This line is in iambic pentameter. Each foot consists of a unstressed syllable followed by a stressed syllable.

A fool | ish thought, | to say | a sor | ry sight.

❹ ▶ **Critical Viewing** This is an artist's rendering of nineteenth-century actress Ellen Terry playing Lady Macbeth. Judging by the picture, how do you think Terry would have spoken lines 1–2 in II, ii? **[Deduce]**

❸

MACBETH. This is a sorry[5] sight.

LADY MACBETH. A foolish thought, to say a sorry sight.

MACBETH. There's one did laugh in 's sleep, and one cried "Murder!"
That they did wake each other. I stood and heard them.
But they did say their prayers, and addressed them
Again to sleep.

5. **sorry:** Miserable.

❺ ◆ **Literary Focus** What is the pattern of accented and unaccented syllables in line 21?

Humanities: Art

Ellen Terry as Lady Macbeth, 1889, by John Singer Sargent.

Sargent (1856–1925) was born in Italy of American parents. He began his training as a painter at the Paris studio of Carolus-Duran. He eventually settled in London and became one of the most sought-after portrait painters of his day.

Ellen Terry was a brilliant actress and one of the most socially prominent people of the time. Her pose is theatrical and impressive. The drapery of the costume is painted in many tones and textures to convey the richness of nobility. The crown was added for dramatic effect. The painting reveals more of the actress than of the character she represents.

Use these questions for discussion:

1. Which period is most apparent in this painting: eleventh-century Scotland, Elizabethan England, or late nineteenth-century England? *Except for the crown, which is a relic of an earlier time, Sargent is reflecting the fashion of 1889.*
2. Sargent was best known as a portrait painter. How is this reflected in this painting? How might Henry Fuseli, whose paintings appear on pages 273 and 304, have rendered this scene? *The painting is static, realistic, and somewhat posed. Fuseli has a more dynamic quality and is less concerned with realism than with evoking emotions from those who view his work.*

◆ Critical Thinking

❶ Infer Ask students what significance they draw from the fact that Macbeth is unable to respond to the blessing with "Amen." *Macbeth's inability to engage in the prayer suggests that he feels a strong sense of guilt and divine disapproval of his act.*

◆ Critical Thinking

❷ Analyze Have students analyze lines 34–38 and list at least three qualities that Macbeth ascribes to sleep. Ask what Macbeth means when he says he has murdered sleep. *Sleep causes one to forget cares and worries, soothes and rests the aching body, cures the troubled mind, and provides the primary source of strength for life. By murdering sleep, Macbeth has lost these vital gifts bestowed by sleep.*

◆ Critical Thinking

❸ Compare and Contrast Ask: How does Macbeth's reaction to the blood on his hands differ from Lady Macbeth's reaction to this same blood? *Lady Macbeth sees the blood as evidence that must be removed from her hands and smeared on the grooms. Macbeth sees the blood as a symbol of his crime and the overwhelming guilt he is unable to escape.*

LADY MACBETH. There are two[6] lodged together.

MACBETH. One cried "God bless us!" and "Amen" the other,
As they had seen me with these hangman's hands:
List'ning their fear, I could not say "Amen,"
When they did say "God bless us!"

LADY MACBETH. Consider it not so deeply.

MACBETH. But wherefore could not I pronounce "Amen"?
I had most need of blessing, and "Amen"
Stuck in my throat.

LADY MACBETH. These deeds must not be thought
After these ways; so, it will make us mad.

MACBETH. Methought I heard a voice cry "Sleep no more!
Macbeth does murder sleep"—the innocent sleep,
Sleep that knits up the raveled sleave[7] of care,
The death of each day's life, sore labor's bath,
Balm of hurt minds, great nature's second course,[8]
Chief nourisher in life's feast—

LADY MACBETH. What do you mean?

MACBETH. Still it cried "Sleep no more!" to all the house:
"Glamis hath murdered sleep, and therefore Cawdor
Shall sleep no more: Macbeth shall sleep no more."

LADY MACBETH. Who was it that thus cried? Why, worthy Thane,
You do unbend[9] your noble strength, to think
So brainsickly of things. Go get some water,
And wash this filthy witness[10] from your hand.
Why did you bring these daggers from the place?
They must lie there: go carry them, and smear
The sleepy grooms with blood.

MACBETH. I'll go no more.
I am afraid to think what I have done;
Look on 't again I dare not.

LADY MACBETH. Infirm of purpose!
Give me the daggers. The sleeping and the dead
Are but as pictures. 'Tis the eye of childhood
That fears a painted devil. If he do bleed,
I'll gild[11] the faces of the grooms withal,
For it must seem their guilt. [*Exit. Knock within.*]

6. **two:** Malcolm and Donalbain, Duncan's sons.

7. **knits . . . sleave:** Straightens out the tangled threads.

8. **second course:** Main course; sleep.

9. **unbend:** Relax.

10. **witness:** Evidence.

11. **gild:** Paint.

◆ Build Vocabulary

multitudinous: (mul′ tə to͞od′ 'n əs) *adj.*: Existing in great numbers

equivocate: (ē kwiv′ə kāt) *v.*: To use terms that have two or more meanings to mislead purposely or deceive

MACBETH. Whence is that knocking?
How is 't with me, when every noise appalls me?
What hands are here? Ha! They pluck out mine eyes!
Will all great Neptune's ocean wash this blood
Clean from my hand? No; this my hand will rather
The multitudinous seas incarnadine,[12]
Making the green one red. ❸

[*Enter* LADY MACBETH.]

LADY MACBETH. My hands are of your color, but I shame
To wear a heart so white. [*Knock.*] I hear a knocking
At the south entry. Retire we to our chamber.
A little water clears us of this deed:
How easy is it then! Your constancy
Hath left you unattended.[13] [*Knock.*] Hark! more knocking.
Get on your nightgown, lest occasion call us
And show us to be watchers.[14] Be not lost
So poorly in your thoughts.

MACBETH. To know my deed, 'twere best not know myself. [*Knock.*]
Wake Duncan with thy knocking! I would thou couldst!
[*Exit.*]

Scene iii. *Macbeth's castle.*
[*Enter a* PORTER.[1] *Knocking within.*] ❺

PORTER. Here's a knocking indeed! If a man were porter of hell gate, he should have old[2] turning the key. [*Knock.*] Knock, knock, knock! Who's there, i' th' name of Beelzebub?[3] Here's a farmer, that hanged himself on th' expectation of plenty.[4] Come in time! Have napkins enow[5] about you; here you'll sweat for 't. [*Knock*] Knock, knock! Who's there, in th' other devil's name? Faith, here's an equivocator, that could swear in both the scales against either scale;[6] who committed treason enough for God's sake, yet could not equivocate to heaven. O, come in, equivocator. [*Knock.*] Knock, knock, knock! Who's there? Faith, here's an English tailor come hither for stealing out of a French hose:[7] come in, tailor. Here you may roast your goose.[8] [*Knock.*] Knock, knock; never at quiet! What are you? But this place is too cold for hell. I'll devil-porter it no further. I had thought to have let in some of all professions that go the primrose way to th' everlasting bonfire. [*Knock.*] Anon, anon! [*Opens an entrance.*] I pray you, remember the porter.

12. incarnadine (in kär′ nə din): Redden.

◆ *Literature and Your Life*

❹ What does Macbeth realize about his ambition that Lady Macbeth does not?

13. Your constancy . . . unattended: Your firmness of purpose has left you.
14. watchers: Up late.

1. porter: Doorkeeper.

2. should have old: Would have plenty of.
3. Beelzebub (bē el′ zə bub): The chief devil.
4. A farmer . . . plenty: A farmer who hoarded grain, hoping that the prices would come up as a result of a bad harvest.
5. enow: Enough.
6. an equivocator . . . scale: A liar who could make two contradictory statements and swear that both were true.
7. stealing . . . hose: Stealing some cloth from the hose while making them.
8. goose: Pressing iron.

Customize for
More Advanced Students
Have these students reread and catalog the repeated imagery involving death and sleep in Scene ii. Challenge them to generalize about Shakespeare's use of this imagery. *Duncan is murdered in his sleep, and the drunk, sleeping grooms are framed for the murder. Macbeth hears a voice saying he has murdered sleep. Macbeth wishes that the knocking would "wake" Duncan. As Lady Macbeth seems to summarize the images when she says, "The sleeping and the dead / Are but as pictures."*

Customize for
Visual/Spatial Learners
Have students visualize the action taking place in Scene iii as they read. Encourage them to refer to the diagram of the Globe on page 265 to help them mentally create the action of the play onstage.

◆ *Literature and Your Life*

❹ Lady Macbeth does not seem to realize that Macbeth's ambition is not as great as hers. Macbeth seems to recognize that his deeds were monstrous; Lady Macbeth does not.

◆ Critical Thinking

❺ **Compare and Contrast** Ask: How does the mood at the beginning of Scene iii compare with the mood at the close of Scene ii? What do you think was Shakespeare's purpose for such a shift? *The mood shifts drastically from one of great tension to one of light-hearted humor; this scene offers some relief from the tension. An audience cannot sustain tension indefinitely.*

Cross-Curricular Connection: Psychology

Psychologists have devoted considerable research to the subject of guilt and its effect on an individual who has committed a crime. Certain patterns of behavior have been noted in research and have been used to identify suspects and to further our understanding of human behavior.

The effect of profound guilt on individuals is also an important theme in literature. One of the best known examples is Hawthorne's *The Scarlet Letter,* which explores the effects of concealed guilt and confessed guilt. Shakespeare's *Macbeth* is, to a large degree, also a study of the effects of guilt. In Act II the guilt Macbeth feels after he murders Duncan is manifest in several ways: He is unable to answer a blessing with "Amen," and he thinks he hears a voice saying "Sleep no more!" The effects of guilt are manifested even more dramatically in later acts.

Have students discuss what Macbeth's reaction suggests about his personality. Expand the discussion to Lady Macbeth as the class studies her subsequent actions. Have interested students do some research into the psychology of guilt and report to the class.

Enrichment Beginning with his appearance in this scene, Macduff plays an important role in the drama. Some scholars believe his absence in earlier scenes bolsters the argument that parts of the play are missing.

Enrichment

❶ The Porter's Scene Following is an excerpt from Thomas De Quincey's (1785–1859) famous essay "On the Knocking at the Gate in *Macbeth*":

> From my boyish days I had always felt a great perplexity on one point in *Macbeth*. It was this: The knocking at the gate which succeeds to the murder of Duncan produced to my feelings an effect for which I never could account. The effect was that it reflected back upon the murderer a peculiar awfulness and a depth of solemnity; yet, however obstinately I endeavored with my understanding to comprehend this, for many years I never could see *why* it should produce such an effect.
>
> . . . All action in any direction is best expounded, measured, and made apprehensible, by reaction. Now apply this to the case in *Macbeth*. Here, as I have said, the retiring of the human heart and the entrance of the fiendish heart was to be expressed and made sensible. Another world has stepped in; and the murderers are taken out of the region of human things, human purposes, human desires. . . . The murderers and the murder must be insulated—cut off by an immeasurable gulf from the ordinary tide and succession of human affairs. . . . Hence it is that, when the deed is done, when the work of darkness is perfect, then the world of darkness passes away like a pageantry in the clouds: the knocking at the gate is heard, and it makes known audibly that the reaction has commenced; the human has made its reflux upon the fiendish; the pulses of life are beginning to beat again; and the re-establishment of the goings-on of the world in which we live first makes us profoundly sensible of the awful [episode] that had suspended them.

[*Enter* MACDUFF *and* LENNOX.]

MACDUFF. Was it so late, friend, ere you went to bed,
That you do lie so late?

PORTER. Faith, sir, we were carousing till the second cock:[9] and drink, sir, is a great provoker of three things.

MACDUFF. What three things does drink especially provoke?

PORTER. Marry, sir, nose-painting, sleep, and urine. Lechery, sir, it provokes and unprovokes; it provokes the desire, but it takes away the performance: therefore much drink may be said to be an equivocator with lechery: it makes him and it mars him; it sets him on and it takes him off; it persuades him and disheartens him; makes him stand to and not stand to; in conclusion equivocates him in a sleep, and giving him the lie, leaves him.

MACDUFF. I believe drink gave thee the lie[10] last night.

PORTER. That it did, sir, i' the very throat on me: but I requited him for his lie, and, I think, being too strong for him, though he took up my legs sometime, yet I made a shift to cast[11] him.

MACDUFF. Is thy master stirring?

[*Enter* MACBETH.]

Our knocking has awaked him; here he comes.

LENNOX. Good morrow, noble sir.

MACBETH. Good morrow, both.

MACDUFF. Is the king stirring, worthy Thane?

MACBETH. Not yet.

MACDUFF. He did command me to call timely[12] on him:
I have almost slipped the hour.

9. second cock: 3:00 A.M.

A Critic's Response
❶ "Hence it is, that when the deed is done . . . the knocking at the gate is heard . . . and the re-establishment of the goings-on of the world in which we live, first makes us profoundly sensible of the awful [episode] that had suspended them."
—Thomas De Quincey

10. gave thee the lie: Laid you out.

11. cast: Vomit.

12. timely: Early.

MACBETH. I'll bring you to him.

MACDUFF. I know this is a joyful trouble to you;
But yet 'tis one.

MACBETH. The labor we delight in physics pain.[13]
This is the door.

MACDUFF. I'll make so bold to call,
For 'tis my limited service.[14] [*Exit* MACDUFF.]

LENNOX. Goes the king hence today?

MACBETH. He does: he did appoint so.

LENNOX. The night has been unruly. Where we lay,
Our chimneys were blown down, and, as they say,
Lamentings heard i' th' air, strange screams of death,
And prophesying with accents terrible
Of dire combustion[15] and confused events
New hatched to th' woeful time: the obscure bird[16]
Clamored the livelong night. Some say, the earth
Was feverous and did shake. ❸

MACBETH. 'Twas a rough night. ❹

LENNOX. My young remembrance cannot parallel
A fellow to it.

[*Enter* MACDUFF.]

MACDUFF. O horror, horror, horror! Tongue nor heart
Cannot conceive nor name thee.

MACBETH AND LENNOX. What's the matter?

MACDUFF. Confusion[17] now hath made his masterpiece.
Most sacrilegious murder hath broke ope
The Lord's anointed temple,[18] and stole thence
The life o' th' building.

MACBETH. What is 't you say? The life?

13. labor . . . pain: Labor that we enjoy cures discomfort.

14. limited service: Assigned duty.

❷ ◆ **Reading Strategy**
Read lines 55–60, aloud. How many sentences are there?

15. combustion: Confusion.

16. obscure bird: Bird of darkness, the owl.

17. Confusion: Destruction.

18. The Lord's anointed temple: The King's body.

◆ Reading Strategy

❷ Reading Verse for Meaning There are three sentences in this speech.

Enrichment

❸ Elizabethans' World View The Elizabethans believed that the universe extended in a great chain of being from God down to the lowliest creature. Every item in this chain had its proper place, reflecting a universal order. Harmony in heaven mirrored harmony in the natural world, the political state, and the family. When this order was disrupted, the whole structure of the universe was at risk.

Elizabethan spectators were probably not surprised, therefore, when the killing of Duncan leads to disturbances in nature. As Shakespeare wrote in *Troilus and Cressida* (I.iii. 109–110): "Take but degree [established rank] away, untune that string, / And hark, what discord follows!"

◆ Critical Thinking

❹ Speculate Call attention to the understatement in this line. Ask students to speculate on how an audience might react to Macbeth's remark. *An audience might be briefly amused by this understatement since murdering a king and the near madness it spawned was certainly more than just "rough."*

Cultural Connection

Only the Bible has been translated into more languages than Shakespeare's works. In addition to appearing in every language of Western Europe, Shakespeare has been translated into twenty-eight of the languages spoken in the former Soviet Union.

In addition to translations, Shakespeare's plays have been adapted to other art forms. In Italy, composer Guiseppe Verdi turned three of Shakespeare's plays into operas: *Macbeth, Otello* (Othello), and *Falstaff* (based on *The Merry Wives of Windsor*). Japanese film director Akira Kurosawa turned *Macbeth* into a film called *Throne of Blood.* His story is set in medieval Japan and the Scottish king was changed to a samurai lord.

Have interested students listen to parts of Verdi's opera *Macbeth* and discuss how Verdi captures the mood of the play.

◆ Critical Thinking

❶ **Connect** Ask students to recall the events of the night of the murder. Why are Macduff's remarks ironic in light of what took place the night before? *Far from being inappropriate for a "gentle lady," the bloody murder of Duncan affected Lady Macbeth far less than it affected Macbeth, the man involved in the plot.*

◆ Reading Strategy

❷ **Read Verse for Meaning** Have students read these lines for meaning and paraphrase them. *Paraphrases may resemble this one: Before this terrible event, my life had meaning and value. Now there is nothing of value left in the world.*

LENNOX. Mean you his Majesty?

MACDUFF. Approach the chamber, and destroy your sight
With a new Gorgon:[19] do not bid me speak;
See, and then speak yourselves. Awake, awake!
[*Exit* MACBETH *and* LENNOX.]
Ring the alarum bell. Murder and Treason!
Banquo and Donalbain! Malcolm! Awake!
Shake off this downy sleep, death's counterfeit,
And look on death itself! Up, up, and see
The great doom's image![20] Malcolm! Banquo!
As from your graves rise up, and walk like sprites,[21]
To countenance[22] this horror. Ring the bell.

[*Bell rings. Enter* LADY MACBETH.]

LADY MACBETH. What's the business,
That such a hideous trumpet calls to parley[23]
The sleepers of the house? Speak, speak!

MACDUFF. O gentle lady,
'Tis not for you to hear what I can speak:
The repetition, in a woman's ear,
Would murder as it fell. ❶

[*Enter* BANQUO.]

O Banquo, Banquo!
Our royal master's murdered.

LADY MACBETH. Woe, alas!
What, in our house?

BANQUO. Too cruel anywhere.
Dear Duff, I prithee, contradict thyself,
And say it is not so.

[*Enter* MACBETH, LENNOX, *and* ROSS.]

MACBETH. Had I but died an hour before this chance,
I had lived a blessèd time; for from this instant
There's nothing serious in mortality:[24]
All is but toys.[25] Renown and grace is dead,
The wine of life is drawn, and the mere lees[26]
Is left this vault[27] to brag of. ❷

[*Enter* MALCOLM *and* DONALBAIN.]

19. **Gorgon:** Medusa, a mythological monster whose appearance was so ghastly that those who looked at it turned to stone.

20. **great doom's image:** Likeness of Judgment Day.
21. **sprites:** Spirits.
22. **countenance:** Be in keeping with.

23. **parley:** War conference.

24. **serious in mortality:** Worthwhile in mortal life.
25. **toys:** Trifles.
26. **lees:** Dregs.
27. **vault:** World.

Beyond the Classroom

Career Connection

Detective In Shakespeare's time, little was known of blood types, fingerprints, and similar modern evidence-gathering methods. As seen in Act II, conclusions about the manner in which a crime was committed and the guilt or innocence of a suspect were made largely on the basis of appearances and unsubstantiated theories.

Today crime scenes are preserved and investigated in depth. Samples of blood and prints are collected. Weapons are scientifically examined, and appropriate people questioned. Ask students if modern detective work and scientific investigation might have immediately revealed the real murderer of Duncan. Have interested students describe how a professional investigator might have handled the crime scene today. Have them make a list of samples to be taken and the analysis that would be performed. Have them prepare a list of questions for those in the castle the night of the murder and for the person who discovered the body.

DONALBAIN. What is amiss?

MACBETH. You are, and do not know 't.
The spring, the head, the fountain of your blood
Is stopped; the very source of it is stopped.

MACDUFF. Your royal father's murdered.

MALCOLM. O, by whom?

LENNOX. Those of his chamber, as it seemed, had done 't:
Their hands and faces were all badged[28] with blood;
So were their daggers, which unwiped we found
Upon their pillows. They stared, and were distracted.
No man's life was to be trusted with them.

MACBETH. O, yet I do repent me of my fury, 
That I did kill them.

MACDUFF. Wherefore did you so?

MACBETH. Who can be wise, amazed, temp'rate and furious,
Loyal and neutral, in a moment? No man.
The expedition[29] of my violent love
Outrun the pauser, reason. Here lay Duncan,
His silver skin laced with his golden blood,
And his gashed stabs looked like a breach in nature
For ruin's wasteful entrance: there, the murderers,
Steeped in the colors of their trade, their daggers
Unmannerly breeched with gore.[30] Who could refrain,
That had a heart to love, and in that heart
Courage to make 's love known?

LADY MACBETH. Help me hence, ho!

MACDUFF. Look to the lady.

MALCOLM. [*Aside to* DONALBAIN] Why do we hold our tongues,
That most may claim this argument for ours?[31]

DONALBAIN. [*Aside to* MALCOLM] What should be spoken here,
Where our fate, hid in an auger-hole,[32]
May rush, and seize us? Let's away:
Our tears are not yet brewed.

MALCOLM. [*Aside to* DONALBAIN] Nor our strong sorrow
Upon the foot of motion.[33]

◆ Literary Focus
3 Write out lines 99–100 of blank verse and mark syllables as unstressed and stressed. Where is there a pause in line 100? How does it reinforce the meaning?

28. **badged:** Marked.

29. **expedition:** Haste.

30. **breeched with gore:** Covered with blood.

31. **That most . . . ours:** Who are the most concerned with this topic.

32. **auger-hole:** Tiny hole, an unsuspected place because of its size.

33. **Our tears . . . motion:** We have not yet had time for tears nor to turn our sorrow into action.

◆ Literary Focus

3 Blank Verse The | spring | the | head | the | foun- | tain | of | your | blood | Is | stopped | the | ver | y | source | of | it | is | *stopped;* The pause in line 100 occurs after the first *stopped.* By reiterating and intensifying the word, the meaning is driven home more effectively.

◆ Literature and Your Life

4 Macbeth's murder of the innocent grooms is reported almost casually in comparison to the report of his murder of Duncan. Ask students if they think it is human nature to lose one's sense of guilt over committing a crime when it is done a second or third time.

Customize for
Less Proficient Readers

5 Have students turn these questions into statements and summarize the reasons Macbeth gives for killing the grooms. *No one can be calm and rational at such moment. No one who so loved the king and had the courage to demonstrate that love could stop himself from murdering the grooms. Macbeth says he loved the king so much that his emotions got the better of him.*

◆ Critical Thinking

6 Interpret Ask students if they think Lady Macbeth has actually fainted or she is merely pretending to faint to deflect any suspicion (line 119). *A case can be made for either position. However, most students will probably think that Lady Macbeth has shown herself to be a treacherous, plotting villain, and her actions mimic the falsehood of Macbeth's reasons for murdering the grooms.*

7 Clarification Contrary to their sequential occurrence in the script, the fainting of Lady Macbeth and the dialogue between Malcolm and Donalbain take place simultaneously. The commotion caused by Lady Macbeth serves to make the private nature of the aside more plausible.

◆ Critical Thinking

❶ **Analyze** Ask students what is significant about Banquo's words. *Banquo's words suggest that he feels that things are not as simple as they seem and warrant further investigation. This is the first hint that the initial explanation of Duncan's murder may not be satisfactory and the road to the final tragedy is about to begin.*

▶Critical Viewing◀

❷ **Interpret** Lady Macbeth's face and body suggest a determined and aggressive personality. She seems to dominate the more shrinking, frightened rendering of her husband.

BANQUO. Look to the lady.
[LADY MACBETH *is carried out.*]
And when we have our naked frailties hid,[34]
That suffer in exposure, let us meet
And question[35] this most bloody piece of work,
To know it further. Fears and scruples[36] shake us. ❶
In the great hand of God I stand, and thence
Against the undivulged pretense[37] I fight
Of treasonous malice.

MACDUFF. And so do I.

ALL. So all.

34. when . . . hid: When we have put on our clothes.
35. question: Investigate.
36. scruples: Doubts.
37. undivulged pretense: Hidden purpose.

Lady Macbeth Seizing the Daggers, Henry Fuseli, The Tate Gallery, London

▲ **Critical Viewing** This painting depicts the moment when Macbeth comes from murdering Duncan (II, ii, 14). However, it also captures the nature of the relationship between Macbeth and Lady Macbeth in the first part of the play. What do their facial expressions and body language suggest about that relationship? **[Interpret]** 

Humanities: Art

Lady Macbeth Seizing the Daggers, 1812, by Henry Fuseli.

This painting by Henry Fuseli (1741–1825) depicts the scene immediately after the murder of Duncan. It shows the horror Macbeth feels for what he has done and the unshaken control Lady Macbeth has over him. Like most of Fuseli's work, it has a surrealist, nightmarish quality that reflects the disordered minds of the characters. He created this painting from a sketch he made in 1760 after seeing David Garrick and Mrs. Pritchard in a performance of *Macbeth.*

Use these questions for discussion:

1. How does the lack of color contribute to the mood of this scene? *The lack of color creates a dream-like scene, as if the characters were from another world.*
2. How does the artist's depiction of these two characters compare with your conception of them? *Some students will be surprised by the cowardly, submissive appearance of Macbeth. Lady Macbeth's aggressive posture and determined look may be more in keeping with students' mental picture of the character.*

MACBETH. Let's briefly[38] put on manly readiness,
And meet i' th' hall together.

ALL. Well contented.
[*Exit all but* MALCOLM *and* DONALBAIN.]

MALCOLM. What will you do? Let's not consort with them.
To show an unfelt sorrow is an office[39]
Which the false man does easy. I'll to England.

DONALBAIN. To Ireland, I; our separated fortune
Shall keep us both the safer. Where we are
There's daggers in men's smiles; the near in blood,
The nearer bloody.[40]

MALCOLM. This murderous shaft that's shot
Hath not yet lighted,[41] and our safest way
Is to avoid the aim. Therefore to horse;
And let us not be dainty of leave-taking,
But shift away. There's warrant [42] in that theft
Which steals itself[43] when there's no mercy left.
[*Exit.*]

Scene iv. *Outside Macbeth's castle.*
[*Enter* ROSS *with an* OLD MAN.]

OLD MAN. Threescore and ten I can remember well:
Within the volume of which time I have seen
Hours dreadful and things strange, but this sore[1] night
Hath trifled former knowings.

ROSS. Ha, good father,
Thou seest the heavens, as troubled with man's act,
Threatens his bloody stage. By th' clock 'tis day,
And yet dark night strangles the traveling lamp:[2]
Is 't night's predominance, or the day's shame,
That darkness does the face of earth entomb,
When living light should kiss it?

OLD MAN. 'Tis unnatural,
Even like the deed that's done. On Tuesday last
A falcon, tow'ring in her pride of place,[3]
Was by a mousing owl hawked at and killed.

38. **briefly:** Quickly.

◆ **Reading Strategy**
❸ How do the brief sentences in lines 136–138 reinforce the meaning?

39. **office:** Function.

40. **the near . . . bloody:** The closer we are in blood relationship to Duncan, the greater our chance of being murdered.
41. **lighted:** Reached its target.
42. **warrant:** Justification.
43. **that theft . . . itself:** Stealing away.

1. **sore:** Grievous.

2. **traveling lamp:** The sun.

3. **tow'ring . . . place:** Soaring at its summit.

◆ **Build Vocabulary**
predominance (pri däm´ ə nəns) *n.*: Superiority

◆ Reading Strategy

❸ **Read Verse for Meaning** The brief sentences in these lines lend a sense of urgency to the conversation and to the actions that follow.

Comprehension Check ☑

❹ Ask: (a) What reasons do Malcolm and Donalbain give for fleeing? (b) Why do they separate? (c) How do their actions further suggest that the simple explanation that the drunken grooms killed Duncan is not easily accepted? *(a) They feel that as heirs to the throne their lives are now in danger. (b) They separate because they feel it is safer to be apart. (c) If Duncan's murder was the random act of the grooms, Malcolm and Donalbain would not be in danger.*

❺ **Clarification** Here, the old man is referring to the rumor that Duncan's sons were responsible for his murder.

◆ Literary Focus

❶ **Blank Verse** The line begins with two stressed syllables: Thóse | thát | Măc | béth | hăs | sláin.

◆ Reading Strategy

❷ **Read Verse for Meaning** Ask students: What important information is given in these lines? *Macduff has concluded that the grooms killed Duncan and that they were bribed to do so by Donalbain and Malcolm, who have fled. Macbeth has been named king and will be crowned in Scone.*

ROSS. And Duncan's horses—a thing most strange
and certain—
Beauteous and swift, the minions of their race,
Turned wild in nature, broke their stalls, flung out,
Contending 'gainst obedience, as they would make
War with mankind.

OLD MAN. 'Tis said they eat[4] each other.

ROSS. They did so, to th' amazement of mine eyes,
That looked upon 't.

[*Enter* MACDUFF.]

Here comes the good Macduff.
How goes the world, sir, now?

MACDUFF. Why, see you not?

ROSS. Is 't known who did this more than bloody deed?

MACDUFF. Those that Macbeth hath slain.

ROSS. Alas, the day!
What good could they pretend?[5]

MACDUFF. They were suborned:[6]
Malcolm and Donalbain, the king's two sons,
Are stol'n away and fled, which puts upon them
Suspicion of the deed.

ROSS. 'Gainst nature still.
Thriftless ambition, that will ravin up[7]
Thine own life's means! Then 'tis most like
The sovereignty will fall upon Macbeth.

MACDUFF. He is already named, and gone to Scone[8]
To be invested.

ROSS. Where is Duncan's body?

MACDUFF. Carried to Colmekill,
The sacred storehouse of his predecessors
And guardian of their bones.

A Critic's Response

"This world, which is at once without and within Macbeth, can be most easily described as 'strange.' The word, like the witches, is always somewhere doing its work."

—**Mark Van Doren**

4. **eat:** Ate.

◆ Literary Focus

❶ What rhythmic variation in the blank verse do you find at the beginning of line 23?

5. **pretend:** Hope for.

6. **suborned:** Bribed.

7. **ravin up:** Devour greedily.

8. **Scone** (skōōn): Where Scottish kings were crowned.

Enrichment

Shakespeare's Diction From time to time, schools of writers have insisted on using certain types of words rather than others. One fashion is to prefer the honest, bare-bones words derived from Anglo-Saxon, while another favors the sophistication of Latin-derived terminology. Great writers, however, have always been alive to the full range of English diction, playing rare words against those that are more mundane.

Shakespeare is especially notable for the range and contrast of his word choice, or diction. Take for example, Macbeth's speech as he waits for Lady Macbeth to falsify the evidence at the scene of the murder (II.ii.59–62):

> Will all great Neptune's ocean wash this blood / Clean from my hand? No; this my hand will rather / The multitudinous seas incarnadine, / Making the green one red.

The words *multitudinous* and *incarnadine* are Latin derivatives. The size and sonority of the words seem to suggest the vastness of Macbeth's guilt.

Quickly and adeptly, however, Shakespeare contrasts these impressive but somewhat hollow terms with simple words derived from Old English: *green* and *red.* This sudden shift of direction brings the sea-swollen rhetoric back to earth. The abruptness of the change emphasizes the finality of the situation. The fact of Duncan's death and Macbeth's guilt is stated in plain English.

ROSS. Will you to Scone?

MACDUFF. No, cousin, I'll to Fife.[9]

ROSS. Well, I will thither.

MACDUFF. Well, may you see things well done there. Adieu,
Lest our old robes sit easier than our new!

ROSS. Farewell, father.

OLD MAN. God's benison[10] go with you, and with those
That would make good of bad, and friends of foes!
[*Exit.*]

9. **Fife:** Where Macduff's castle is located.

10. **benison:** Blessing.

Guide for Responding

◆ Literature and Your Life

Reader's Response Who do you think bears the greatest responsibility for the murder of King Duncan—Macbeth or Lady Macbeth? Explain.

Thematic Focus What conflicts will Macbeth experience as the play continues?

☑ Check Your Comprehension

1. Briefly summarize how Macbeth and Lady Macbeth conspire to murder Duncan.
2. What does the drunken porter imagine he is doing?
3. How is the murder discovered?
4. (a) What action does Macbeth take against the grooms? (b) Why do Malcolm and Donalbain leave the castle?
5. (a) Who does Macduff say has killed Duncan? (b) Why do Malcolm and Donalbain fall under suspicion, according to Macduff?

◆ Critical Thinking

INTERPRET

1. Compare and contrast Macbeth's reaction to the murder with Lady Macbeth's. **[Compare and Contrast]**
2. (a) Why do you think critics consider the porter's speech comic relief? (b) How do the porter's comments on the people arriving at "hell gate" mirror Macbeth's dilemma? **[Interpret]**
3. What causes Lady Macbeth to faint? **[Infer]**
4. Why does Ross have doubts about accepting the grooms as murderers? **[Draw Conclusions]**

APPLY

5. In his soliloquy in Scene i, Macbeth speaks of "vaulting ambition." (a) How can "vaulting ambition" result in great success? (b) How can it result in destruction? **[Speculate]**

EXTEND

6. Could an assassination like this happen in our times? Why or why not? **[Social Studies Link]**

Reinforce and Extend

Answers

◆ Literature and Your Life

Reader's Response Students may argue that Macbeth bears the most responsibility because he actually stabbed Duncan; other students may say Lady Macbeth is the one who persuaded Macbeth to commit the crime.

Thematic Focus Students may suggest that Macbeth will face conflicts with his conscience, with Duncan's sons, if they return, with Macduff, with Banquo, and possibly with his wife.

☑ Check Your Comprehension

1. Macbeth and Lady Macbeth plan to stab Duncan while he sleeps, then plant evidence on the sleeping servants whom they have made drunk for this purpose. Lady Macbeth cannot bring herself to stab the King, though. She takes charge of the daggers and the planning after Macbeth has killed Duncan.
2. The porter imagines that he stands at the gates of hell observing the entrants, whom he describes as they pass.
3. Macduff enters the King's chamber to find him slaughtered.
4. (a) Macbeth rushes in and kills the blood-smeared grooms. (b) Malcolm and Donalbain flee for fear that their lives are in jeopardy, too, since presumably they stand between the killer and the throne.
5. (a) Macduff says that the grooms have killed the king. (b) Since Malcolm and Donalbain have fled, Macduff suspects that they ordered the grooms to kill the king.

◆ Critical Thinking

1. Macbeth is immediately swept up in feelings of guilt. Lady Macbeth, on the other hand, immediately and coolly takes charge of things.
2. (a) The porter's speech is ludicrous: his doddering complaints and fantasies contrast with the urgency of the knocking, and conclude, for all his delay, with a plea for a tip. The speech comes just as the main action reaches a point of high tension. (b) The imagined characters entering hell are all liars and cheats who thought they could get away with their misdeeds. Macbeth must also act as if he can "get away" with murder.
3. Plausible responses: She faints under the stress of the moment; she pretends to faint in order to demonstrate her shock over Duncan's death; she faints to stop Macbeth from talking too much about the murders, so he will have less opportunity to slip up.
4. Ross wonders what the grooms have to gain by killing the king.
5. (a) Only an ambition that is pursued for its own sake can lead to great results. (b) Vaulting ambition entails great risks of loss, precisely because it will stake everything merely on the desire it represents.
6. Possible responses: No; leaders are too well guarded for this to happen; yes, many world leaders have been assassinated.

Answers

◆ **Reading Strategy**

1. There are two sentences in this passage.
2. Possible answer: I will go and commit the murder. Don't listen to it, Duncan, for it signals your death.

◆ **Literary Focus**

1. Will all great Neptune's ocean wash this blood / Clean from my hand? No; this my hand will rather / The multitudinous seas incarnadine, / Making the green one red.
2. Line 60 begins with a trochee; the word *multitudinous* breaks out of iambic rhythm and begins with an anapest; line 62 begins with a trochee.

◆ **Grammar and Style**

1. lying 2. lie, lay 3. lie

◆ **Build Vocabulary**

Using the Root *-voc-*

1. one who uses the voice as an instrument
2. using the voice to call out
3. spoken prayer

Using the Word Bank

1. (b) reduce
2. (a) imperceptible
3. (c) open
4. (a) scarce
5. (b) declare
6. (c) inferiority

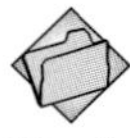

Idea Bank

Customizing for
Learning Modalities

Following are suggestions for matching Idea Bank topics with your students' learning modalities:

Verbal/Linguistic: 2
Visual/Spatial: 3
Interpersonal: 1

Customizing for
Performance Levels

Following are suggestions for matching Idea Bank topics with your students' ability levels:

Less Advanced Students: 3
Average Students: 1
More Advanced Students: 2

Guide for Responding (continued)

◆ Reading Strategy

READ VERSE FOR MEANING

Read Shakespeare's verse for meaning by following the sentences past the line endings. In reading II, i, 62–64, for example, do not stop at line 63.

1. How many sentences are there in this passage?
2. Express the meaning of these sentences in your own words.

◆ Literary Focus

BLANK VERSE

Most of the lines in Shakespeare's plays are in **blank verse**—unrhymed iambic pentameter. Each line has ten syllables, with stress falling on every other syllable:

I have thee not, and yet I see thee still (II, i, 35)

To vary this rhythm, Shakespeare introduces pauses in lines, ends lines with unstressed syllables, and substitutes trochees (stress, unstressed) and anapests (unstressed, unstressed, stressed) for iambs. Here are some examples:

- Trochee (´˘) begins a line:
  It is the bloody business which informs (II, i, 48)
- Anapest (˘˘´)replaces an iamb in final foot:
  Macbeth does murder sleep—the innocent sleep

1. Mark stressed and unstressed syllables in II, ii, 59–62.
2. Identify three metrical variations in these lines.

◆ Grammar and Style

COMMONLY CONFUSED WORDS: *LIE* AND *LAY*

Don't confuse *lie* with *lay*. *Lie* means "to lie down or on" and *lay* means "to place."

Practice In your notebook, write each of these sentences using *lie* or *lay* correctly.

1. Macbeth kills Duncan as the king is __?__ in bed.
2. Lady Macbeth thought the daggers should __?__ beside King Duncan, so she went to __?__ them there.
3. Before the knocking started, Lady Macbeth intended to __?__ down and pretend to have been asleep.

◆ Build Vocabulary

USING THE ROOT *-voc-*

Use the meaning of the root *-voc-* ("voice or calling") to define each of the italicized words.

1. The *vocalist* stood near the piano.
2. The young woman was *vocal* about the rights to which she was entitled.
3. The minister spoke the *invocation* at the beginning of the dinner.

USING THE WORD BANK

In your notebook, write the letter of the word that is an antonym (opposite in meaning) to the first word.

1. augment: (a) add, (b) reduce, (c) move
2. palpable: (a) imperceptible, (b) impolite, (c) obvious
3. stealthy: (a) reputable, (b) sneaky, (c) open
4. multitudinous: (a) scarce, (b) agitated, (c) ample
5. equivocate: (a) falsify, (b) declare, (c) ruin
6. predominance: (a) equality, (b) superiority, (c) inferiority

Idea Bank

Writing

1. Detective's Journal As a medieval detective, keep a journal of the clues you find at the scene of Duncan's murder. Record each person's version of what happened.

2. Response to Criticism G. B. Harrison argues that Macbeth "is controlled by an overpowering imagination which makes him see not only . . . the results of an action . . . but also its essential meaning." Agree or disagree with this statement, citing specific passages from Act II.

Project

3. Costume Design Using the pictures that accompany the play and your own imagination as guides, design costumes for Macbeth, Lady Macbeth, and Duncan. **[Art Link]**

✓ ASSESSMENT OPTIONS

Formal Assessment, Selection Test, pp. 68–70, and Assessment Resources Software. The selection test is designed so that it can be easily customized to the ability levels of your students. ***Alternative Assessment,*** p. 13, includes options for less advanced students, more advance students, visual and spatial learners, and auditory learners.

PORTFOLIO ASSESSMENT

Use the following rubrics in the ***Alternative Assessment*** booklet to assess student writing:
Detective's Journal: Scoring Rubric: Description, p. 98
Response to Criticism: Scoring Rubric: Critical Review, p. 112

Guide for Interpreting, Act III

OBJECTIVES

1. To read, comprehend, interpret, and respond to an Elizabethan drama
2. To relate an Elizabethan drama to personal experience
3. To read between the lines to deepen comprehension
4. To identify conflict
5. To build vocabulary in context and learn the prefix *mal-*
6. To understand and apply subject and verb agreement
7. To respond to Act III of *Macbeth* through writing and speaking and listening

SKILLS INSTRUCTION

Vocabulary: Prefixes: *mal-*
Grammar: Subject and Verb Agreement
Reading Strategy: Read Between the Lines
Literary Focus: Conflict
Speaking and Listening: Performance (teacher edition)
Critical Viewing: Connect; Interpret

PORTFOLIO OPPORTUNITIES

Writing: Diary Entry; Critical Note
Speaking and Listening: Performance

◆ Review and Anticipate

In Act II, Lady Macbeth drugs those who are guarding Duncan, enabling Macbeth to kill the king. Macbeth then kills the guards too so that he can more easily blame them for this murder. Duncan's sons, Malcolm and Donalbain, flee. They are afraid that they will be murdered by a kinsman eager to claim the throne. Because they run away, some people suspect them of killing their own father. As the act closes, it seems that Macbeth will be named king.

Act III begins with Macbeth on the throne, as the witches had predicted. All is going well for him—or is it? There's still Banquo to think of, whom the witches hailed as "Lesser than Macbeth, and greater."

◆ Literary Focus

Conflict

Conflict—the struggle between two forces—is what creates drama. This struggle can be an **external conflict** between two characters or groups, or it can be an **internal conflict** within a character. The **climax** of a play is the point at which the internal and external conflicts are greatest. Usually the action rises to the climax—the moment of highest tension—and then falls as the conflicts are resolved.

In *Macbeth,* Act III, the rising action leads the new king to a state dinner and the sight of a guest—who should not be there!

◆ Grammar and Style

Subject and Verb Agreement

In Shakespeare's writing, verbs agree with subjects in number (singular or plural). Notice that the verbs change form to agree with a singular or a plural subject.

Singular: After life's fitful fever *he sleeps* well.

Plural: Our *fears* in Banquo / *Stick* deep . . .

◆ Reading Strategy

Read Between the Lines

When you read a play or any work of literature, you read it line by line to follow the action. However, you can also **read between the lines** by considering what the lines suggest and by connecting earlier passages with later ones. Reading line by line tells you *what* happens, but reading between the lines tells you *why* it happens.

In *Macbeth,* Act III, read between the lines by asking yourself why Macbeth is so concerned with Banquo's afternoon plans: "Is't far you ride?" Macbeth asks his friend.

◆ Build Vocabulary

Prefixes: *mal-*

Act III contains the word *malevolence.* The prefix *mal-*, meaning "bad," contributes to the definition of this word, which means "bad will toward others; evil influence."

Word Bank

Before you read, preview this list of words from Act III of *Macbeth.*

indissoluble
dauntless
jocund
infirmity
malevolence

Write the following famous line spoken by Macbeth on the chalkboard: "To be thus [king] is nothing, but to be safely thus" (III, i, 48). Ask students: What might Macbeth mean by this statement? Students should realize that Macbeth has achieved his desire—to become king—but he is still not happy. Have students discuss possible ways in which Macbeth might try to ensure the safety of his position. Who might pose a threat to his position? Ask them to consider what Lady Macbeth might mean when she says "Nought's had, all's spent,/Where our desire is got without content" (III, ii, 6–7). Based on these quotations, have students predict the course of action in Act III.

Prentice Hall Literature Program Resources

Selection Support Pages
Build Vocabulary: Prefixes: *mal-*, p. 67
Grammar and Style: Subject and Verb Agreement, p. 68
Reading Strategy: Read Between the Lines, p. 69
Literary Focus: Conflict, p. 70

Strategies for Diverse Student Needs
Visualize the Scene, p. 14

Beyond Literature Art Connection: Design a Playbill, p. 14

Formal Assessment Selection Test, pp. 71–73; Assessment Resources Software

Alternative Assessment, p. 14

Listening to Literature Audiocassettes
The Tragedy of Macbeth, Act III

One-Minute Insight Act III marks a turning point in the action. Up until now, things have gone very much the way Macbeth had planned. However, his sense of insecurity leads him to fear Banquo and his offspring. When his plan to murder Banquo and his son is only partially successful, a series of events is set in motion, leading to Macbeth's downfall.

Customize for *Less Proficient Readers*

Review the reading strategy introduced with Act II. Remind these students to pay special attention to punctuation as they read Act III, as many sentences in poetry do not end at the end of a line. Students may find it helpful to read one scene aloud with a partner, pausing briefly at the end of each complete sentence. Have the students summarize each scene after reading it aloud.

Customize for *More Advanced Students*

Ask these students to pay careful attention to Macbeth's dialogue in Act III. Have them point out instances where his dialogue seems to take a more poetic turn—where he begins to use vivid imagery, metaphors, and other poetic devices. (See Scene ii, lines 46–56, for an example.) Ask students to determine when Macbeth's tone becomes more poetic and to what effect.

◆ Reading Strategy

❶ Read Between the Lines Ask students to consider Banquo's speech and to discuss what threat Banquo poses to Macbeth. Why might Banquo have kept the information he learned from the witches to himself? *Banquo may have hoped to use the information to his advantage and gain power over Macbeth. Macbeth knows that Banquo's children will inherit the throne. Banquo may be afraid to share his knowledge because he doesn't want to implicate himself in Duncan's murder.*

◆ Critical Thinking

❷ Speculate Ask students: Why might Macbeth be curious about where Banquo is going? *Macbeth may be planning to keep a close eye on Banquo because he, too, knows of the witches' prophecies.*

ACT III

***Scene i.** Forres. The palace.*

[*Enter* BANQUO.]

BANQUO. Thou hast it now: King, Cawdor, Glamis, all,
As the weird women promised, and I fear
Thou play'dst most foully for 't. Yet it was said
It should not stand[1] in thy posterity,
But that myself should be the root and father
Of many kings. If there come truth from them—
As upon thee, Macbeth, their speeches shine—
Why, by the verities on thee made good,
May they not be my oracles as well
And set me up in hope? But hush, no more! ❶

[*Sennet*[2] *sounded. Enter* MACBETH *as King,* LADY MACBETH, LENNOX, ROSS, LORDS, *and* ATTENDANTS.]

MACBETH. Here's our chief guest.

LADY MACBETH. If he had been forgotten,
It had been as a gap in our great feast,
And all-thing[3] unbecoming.

MACBETH. Tonight we hold a solemn[4] supper, sir,
And I'll request your presence.

BANQUO. Let your Highness
Command upon me, to the which my duties
Are with a most indissoluble tie
For ever knit.

MACBETH. Ride you this afternoon?

BANQUO. Ay, my good lord.

MACBETH. We should have else desired your good advice
(Which still hath been both grave and prosperous[5])
In this day's council; but we'll take tomorrow.
Is't far you ride? ❷

BANQUO. As far, my lord, as will fill up the time
'Twixt this and supper. Go not my horse the better,[6]
I must become a borrower of the night
For a dark hour or twain.

1. **stand:** Continue.

2. **Sennet:** Trumpet call.

3. **all-thing:** Altogether.

4. **solemn:** Ceremonious.

5. **grave and prosperous:** Weighty and profitable.

6. **Go not . . . better:** Unless my horse goes faster than I expect.

◆ Build Vocabulary

indissoluble (in′di säl′ yo͞o bəl) *adj.*: Not able to be dissolved or undone

dauntless (dônt′ lis) *adj.*: Fearless; cannot be intimidated

Block Scheduling Strategies

Consider these suggestions to take advantage of extended class time.

- Use the Interest Grabber suggestions to provide an anticipatory set for Act III.
- Review with students the concept of conflict, presented in the Literary Focus on page 309. Have them consider Act III in terms of conflict. After they have read Act III, have them answer the Literary Focus questions on page 326.
- Play Macbeth's soliloquy in Scene i, beginning with "Our fears in Banquo" on the **Listening to Literature Audiocassettes** to generate interest in what Macbeth will do.
- To clarify what's happening in the banquet scene, cast students as Macbeth, Lady Macbeth and Banquo's ghost and have them read the scene as the class follows along.
- When students have finished reading Act III, have them answer the Critical Thinking questions on page 325.

MACBETH. Fail not our feast.

BANQUO. My lord, I will not.

MACBETH. We hear our bloody cousins are bestowed
In England and in Ireland, not confessing
Their cruel parricide, filling their hearers
With strange invention.[7] But of that tomorrow,
When therewithal we shall have cause of state
Craving us jointly.[8] Hie you to horse. Adieu,
Till you return at night. Goes Fleance with you?

BANQUO. Ay, my good lord: our time does call upon 's.

MACBETH. I wish your horses swift and sure of foot,
And so I do commend you to their backs.
Farewell. [*Exit* BANQUO.]
Let every man be master of his time
Till seven at night. To make society
The sweeter welcome, we will keep ourself
Till suppertime alone. While[9] then, God be with you!

[*Exit* LORDS *and all but* MACBETH *and a* SERVANT.]

Sirrah,[10] a word with you: attend those men
Our pleasure?

ATTENDANT. They are, my lord, without the palace gate.

MACBETH. Bring them before us. [*Exit* SERVANT.]
To be thus[11] is nothing, but[12] to be safely thus—
Our fears in Banquo stick deep,
And in his royalty of nature reigns that
Which would be feared. 'Tis much he dares;
And, to[13] that dauntless temper of his mind,
He hath a wisdom that doth guide his valor
To act in safety. There is none but he
Whose being I do fear: and under him
My genius is rebuked,[14] as it is said
Mark Antony's was by Caesar. He chid[15] the sisters,
When first they put the name of King upon me,
And bade them speak to him; then prophetlike
They hailed him father to a line of kings.
Upon my head they placed a fruitless crown
And put a barren scepter in my gripe,[16]
Thence to be wrenched with an unlineal hand,
No son of mine succeeding. If 't be so,
For Banquo's issue have I filed[17] my mind;
For them the gracious Duncan have I murdered;
Put rancors in the vessel of my peace

7. **invention:** Lies.
8. **cause . . . jointly:** Matters of state demanding our joint attention.
9. **While:** Until.
10. **Sirrah:** Common address to an inferior.
11. **thus:** King.
12. **but:** Unless.
13. **to:** Added to.
14. **genius is rebuked:** Guardian spirit is cowed.
15. **chid:** Scolded.
16. **gripe:** Grip.
17. **filed:** Defiled.

Customize for
More Advanced Students
Explain or review the concept of irony. Then direct more advance students to write down instances of irony they find in Act III. Then ask them to evaluate the use of irony through Act III and its impact on the drama.

◆ Critical Thinking

❸ **Interpret** Ask: Who are the "bloody cousins" referred to by Macbeth? *Duncan's sons are the "bloody cousins," because they are rumored to have plotted their father's murder.*

◆ Critical Thinking

❹ **Analyze** Have students divide this soliloquy into two parts and explain the division. *The first part (lines 49–57) reveals that Macbeth fears Banquo; the second part (lines 57–72) reveals Macbeth's resentment of the witches' prophecy concerning Banquo.*

◆ Critical Thinking

1 Infer Ask students: What can you infer from lines 75–84 that Macbeth told the murderers about Banquo? Why might he have told them this? *He probably told them Banquo was responsible for their misery. He did so to give them a reason to murder Banquo.*

◆ Reading Strategy

2 Reading Between the Lines The murderer means that they, as men, would not let such outrage go unpunished. This view about manhood matches Lady Macbeth's, stated in Act I, Scene vii, lines 49–54.

Only for them, and mine eternal jewel[18]
Given to the common enemy of man,[19]
To make them kings, the seeds of Banquo kings!
Rather than so, come, fate, into the list,
And champion me to th' utterance![20] Who's there?

[*Enter* SERVANT *and* TWO MURDERERS.]

Now go to the door, and stay there till we call.

[*Exit* SERVANT.]

Was it not yesterday we spoke together?

MURDERERS. It was, so please your Highness.

MACBETH. Well then, now
Have you considered of my speeches? Know
That it was he in the times past, which held you
So under fortune,[21] which you thought had been
Our innocent self: this I made good to you
In our last conference; passed in probation[22] with you,
How you were born in hand,[23] how crossed, the instruments,
Who wrought with them, and all things else that might
To half a soul[24] and to a notion[25] crazed
Say "Thus did Banquo."

FIRST MURDERER. You made it known to us.

MACBETH. I did so; and went further, which is now
Our point of second meeting. Do you find
Your patience so predominant in your nature,
That you can let this go? Are you so gospeled,[26]
To pray for this good man and for his issue,
Whose heavy hand hath bowed you to the grave
And beggared yours for ever?

FIRST MURDERER. We are men, my liege.

MACBETH. Ay, in the catalogue ye go for[27] men;
As hounds and greyhounds, mongrels, spaniels, curs,
Shoughs, water-rugs[28] and demi-wolves, are clept[29]
All by the name of dogs: the valued file[30]
Distinguishes the swift, the slow, the subtle,
The housekeeper, the hunter, every one
According to the gift which bounteous nature
Hath in him closed,[31] whereby he does receive
Particular addition,[32] from the bill
That writes them all alike: and so of men.
Now if you have a station in the file,[33]
Not i' th' worst rank of manhood, say 't,

18. eternal jewel: Soul.
19. common . . . man: The Devil.
20. champion me to th' utterance: Fight against me to the death.
21. held . . . fortune: Kept you from good fortune.
22. passed in probation: Reviewed the proofs.
23. born in hand: Deceived.
24. half a soul: Halfwit.
25. notion: Mind.

◆ Reading Strategy 2 What does the first murderer mean in line 91 when he answers Macbeth "We are men"?

26. gospeled: Ready to forgive.
27. go for: Pass as.
28. Shoughs (shuks), **water-rugs:** Shaggy dogs, long-haired dogs.
29. clept: Called.
30. valued file: Classification by valuable traits.
31. closed: Enclosed.
32. addition: Distinction (to set it apart from other dogs).
33. file: Ranks.

Preparing for Standardized Tests

Reading and Vocabulary The ability to read between the lines is similar to "drawing inferences" and is often assessed in tests of reading comprehension and critical reading. For additional practice, see the Reading Strategy page in ***Selection Support,*** p. 69.

Learning the meaning of prefixes will help students decode unfamiliar words appearing in analogy questions such as the following:

BENEVOLENCE : MALEVOLENCE : : GENEROUS : *(B) miserly*
(A) kind
(B) miserly
(C) hopeful
(D) magnanimous

For additional practice with the prefix *mal-*, use the Build Vocabulary page, p. 67, in ***Selection Support.***

Grammar and Language The concept of subject and verb agreement is a very important one in tests of usage. On standardized tests students may be asked to choose the verb that agrees with the subject, as in the following example:

The gentleman, a friend to many, (were, was) a great conversationalist. *was*

For additional practice, use the Grammar and Style page on Subject and Verb Agreement, p. 68, in ***Selection Support.***

And I will put that business in your bosoms
Whose execution takes your enemy off,
Grapples you to the heart and love of us,
Who wear our health but sickly in his life,[34]
Which in his death were perfect.

SECOND MURDERER. I am one, my liege,
Whom the vile blows and buffets of the world
Hath so incensed that I am reckless what
I do to spite the world.

FIRST MURDERER. And I another
So weary with disasters, tugged with fortune,
That I would set[35] my life on any chance,
To mend it or be rid on 't.

MACBETH. Both of you
Know Banquo was your enemy.

BOTH MURDERERS. True, my lord.

MACBETH. So is he mine, and in such bloody distance[36]
That every minute of his being thrusts
Against my near'st of life:[37] and though I could
With barefaced power sweep him from my sight
And bid my will avouch[38] it, yet I must not,
For certain friends that are both his and mine,
Whose loves I may not drop, but wail his fall[39]
Who I myself struck down: and thence it is
That I to your assistance do make love,
Masking the business from the common eye
For sundry weighty reasons.

SECOND MURDERER. We shall, my lord,
Perform what you command us.

FIRST MURDERER. Though our lives—

MACBETH. Your spirits shine through you. Within this hour at most
I will advise you where to plant yourselves,
Acquaint you with the perfect spy o' th' time,
The moment on 't;[40] for 't must be done tonight,
And something[41] from the palace; always thought[42]
That I require a clearness:[43] and with him—
To leave no rubs[44] nor botches in the work—
Fleance his son, that keeps him company,
Whose absence is no less material to me

34. **wear . . . life:** Are sick as long as he lives.

35. **set:** Risk.

36. **distance:** Disagreement.

37. **near'st of life:** Most vital parts.

38. **avouch:** Justify.

39. **wail his fall:** (I must) bewail his death.

40. **the perfect . . . on't:** Exact information of the exact time.
41. **something:** Some distance.
42. **thought:** Remembered.
43. **clearness:** Freedom from suspicion.
44. **rubs:** Flaws.

◆ Critical Thinking

❸ Draw Conclusions Ask students why Macbeth is so successful at convincing the murderers of Banquo's blame, despite his lack of evidence. *The murderers say they've had terrible lives and that Banquo has caused their misery. They may be vulnerable to Macbeth's suggestions because they are looking for someone to blame for their misery or because they are desperate to find a better life.*

◆ Reading Strategy

❹ Read Between the Lines Ask students: Do you believe the reasons Macbeth gives for not killing Banquo himself? What reasons might he really have for not wanting to kill Banquo himself? *Macbeth's reasoning seems invalid considering his role in Duncan's murder and his pretense of mourning for him. He may feel that now he is king, he can have someone else perform his murderous deeds. He may not have wanted to feel guilty for Banquo's murder, or he may not have wanted to risk being caught.*

◆ Critical Thinking

❶ **Analyze** Point out that in this passage, Macbeth refers to Fleance almost as an afterthought. Ask: How important to Macbeth is Fleance's death? *Killing Banquo would be of no use to Macbeth unless he also kills his son. The witches' prophecy stated that Banquo would father kings.*

◆ *Literature and Your Life*

❷ Lady Macbeth has realized that her dishonest, corrupt actions have given her power without stability and happiness. Her evil actions have cost her more than she's gained.

◆ Critical Thinking

❸ **Interpret** Ask: (a) What is Macbeth suggesting might be better than the terrible dreams that torment him nightly? (b) Who is "sleeping" more soundly than he? *(a) Macbeth is suggesting that he might be better off dead than tortured with his sleepless nights. (b) Duncan is "sleeping" more soundly than Macbeth.*

Than is his father's, must embrace the fate
Of that dark hour. Resolve yourselves apart:[45] ❶
I'll come to you anon.

MURDERERS. We are resolved, my lord.

MACBETH I'll call upon you straight.[46] Abide within.
It is concluded: Banquo, thy soul's flight,
If it find heaven, must find it out tonight. [*Exit.*]

Scene ii. *The palace.*
[*Enter* MACBETH'S LADY *and a* SERVANT.]

LADY MACBETH. Is Banquo gone from court?

SERVANT. Ay, madam, but returns again tonight.

LADY MACBETH. Say to the King, I would attend his leisure
For a few words.

SERVANT. Madam, I will. [*Exit.*]

LADY MACBETH. Nought's had, all's spent,
Where our desire is got without content:
'Tis safer to be that which we destroy
Than by destruction dwell in doubtful joy.

[*Enter* MACBETH.]

How now, my lord! Why do you keep alone,
Of sorriest fancies your companions making,
Using those thoughts which should indeed have died
With them they think on? Things without all remedy
Should be without regard: what's done is done.

MACBETH. We have scotched[1] the snake, not killed it:
She'll close[2] and be herself, whilst our poor malice
Remains in danger of her former tooth.[3]
But let the frame of things disjoint,[4] both the worlds[5] suffer,
Ere we will eat our meal in fear, and sleep
In the affliction of these terrible dreams
That shake us nightly: better be with the dead,
Whom we, to gain our peace, have sent to peace,
Than on the torture of the mind to lie
In restless ecstasy.[6] Duncan is in his grave;
After life's fitful fever he sleeps well.
Treason has done his worst: nor steel, nor poison,
Malice domestic, foreign levy,[7] nothing,
Can touch him further. ❸

45. **Resolve yourselves apart:** Make your own decision.

46. **straight:** Immediately.

◆ *Literature and Your Life*

❷ What has Lady Macbeth realized about her actions?

1. **scotched:** Wounded.
2. **close:** Heal.
3. **in . . . tooth:** In as much danger as before.
4. **frame of things disjoint:** Universe collapse.
5. **both the worlds:** Heaven and earth.
6. **ecstasy:** Frenzy.
7. **Malice . . . levy:** Civil and foreign war.

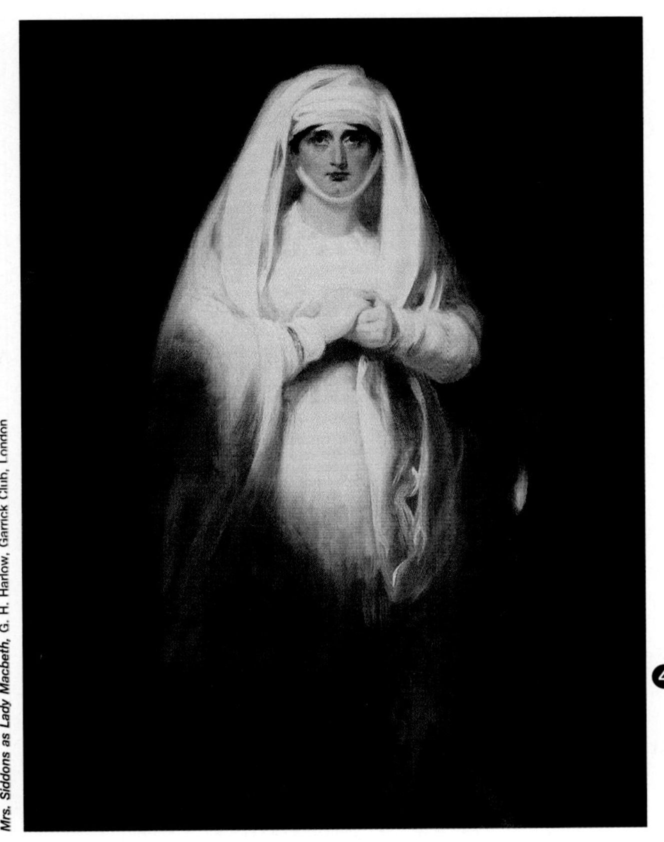

Mrs. Siddons as Lady Macbeth, G. H. Harlow, Garrick Club, London

◀ **Critical Viewing** This artist depicted actress Sarah Siddons (1755–1831) playing Lady Macbeth. How does Mrs. Siddons's body language suggest the same inner conflict as do lines 4–7 in Act III, ii? **[Connect]** ❹

LADY MACBETH. Come on.
Gentle my lord, sleek o'er your rugged looks;
Be bright and jovial among your guests tonight.

MACBETH. So shall I, love; and so, I pray, be you:
Let your remembrance apply to Banquo;
Present him eminence,[8] both with eye and tongue:
Unsafe the while, that we must lave[9]
Our honors in these flattering streams
And make our faces vizards[10] to our hearts,
Disguising what they are. ❺

LADY MACBETH. You must leave this.

MACBETH. O, full of scorpions is my mind, dear wife!
Thou know'st that Banquo, and his Fleance, lives. ❻

LADY MACBETH. But in them nature's copy's not eterne.[11]

8. **Present him eminence:** Honor him.
9. **Unsafe . . . lave:** We are unsafe as long as we have to wash.
10. **vizards** (viz´ ərdz): Masks.
11. **nature's . . . eterne:** Nature's lease is not eternal.

▶**Critical Viewing**◀

❹ **Connect** Students should see that by clasping her hands and looking somber, Mrs. Siddons's body language suggests the insecurity and unhappiness that Lady Macbeth describes in lines 4–7.

◆ Critical Thinking

❺ **Interpret** In assuring Lady Macbeth that he will strike the proper mood at the party, what does Macbeth reveal about himself and his relationship with his wife? *Macbeth reveals that he, like his wife, is cunning and has a black heart, and that he is prepared to present a false front to the guests.*

◆ Grammar and Style

❻ **Subject and Verb Agreement** Ask student to explain why the singular verbs *is* and *lives* are correct in lines 36 and 37. What are the subjects with which they agree? *Line 36: The subject is "mind" not "scorpions"; in regular subject-verb-object order, the sentence would read: "My mind is full of scorpions!" Line 37: the verb "lives" agrees with the subject "Banquo." The phrase "and his Fleance," ringed with commas, is not part of the subject.*

Humanities: Art

Mrs. Siddons as Lady Macbeth
by G. H. Harlow.

The actress depicted in this painting is Sarah Siddons (1755–1831), one of the greatest English actresses of her time. She came from a family of traveling actors and began acting as a child. She played the part of Lady Macbeth early in her career and performed the role at London's Drury Lane theater for the first time in 1785, terrifying audiences with her vivid portrayal of the famous character.

Use these questions for discussion:

1. How does Harlow portray Sarah Siddons as Lady Macbeth? *Harlow has chosen to portray Lady Macbeth in a timid posture. She is surrounded by darkness. She looks more fearful and demure than sinister. Her white robe gives her an angelic, or perhaps ghostly, appearance. The shadows in the painting produce an eerie, surreal mood.*
2. Ask students how this portrait of Lady Macbeth compares with the ones on pages 297 and 304. *Most students will say that this portrait portrays Lady Macbeth as quieter, meeker, and more dainty than the other portraits in which she's depicted as larger than life, vibrant, and wild.*

◆ Critical Thinking

❶ **Speculate** Ask students: Why might Macbeth have chosen to keep his plans for Banquo's murder from Lady Macbeth? *He may feel that she would give him away at the banquet that night. He may not trust anyone at this point. Perhaps he wants to impress her by carrying out this act without urging from her.*

❷ **Clarification** Tell students that the identity of the third murderer has been the subject of debate among scholars for centuries. The mysterious third murderer may be Macbeth himself, an emissary of the witches, or a messenger from Macbeth. He may also be a plot device to indicate Macbeth's mistrust of the two murderers, as well as his mistrust in general.

MACBETH. There's comfort yet; they are assailable.
Then be thou jocund. Ere the bat hath flown
His cloistered flight, ere to black Hecate's summons
The shard-borne[12] beetle with his drowsy hums
Hath rung night's yawning peal, there shall be done
A deed of dreadful note.

LADY MACBETH. What 's to be done?

MACBETH. Be innocent of the knowledge, dearest chuck,[13]
Till thou applaud the deed. Come, seeling[14] night,
Scarf up[15] the tender eye of pitiful day,
And with thy bloody and invisible hand
Cancel and tear to pieces that great bond[16]
Which keeps me pale! Light thickens, and the crow
Makes wing to th' rooky[17] wood. ❶
Good things of day begin to droop and drowse,
Whiles night's black agents to their preys do rouse.
Thou marvel'st at my words: but hold thee still;
Things bad begun make strong themselves by ill:
So, prithee, go with me. [*Exit.*]

12. **shard-borne:** Borne on scaly wings.
13. **chuck:** Term of endearment.
14. **seeling:** Eye-closing. Falconers sometimes sewed a hawk's eyes closed in order to train it.
15. **Scarf up:** Blindfold.
16. **great bond:** Between Banquo and fate.
17. **rooky:** Full of rooks, or crows.

Scene iii. *Near the palace.*
[*Enter* THREE MURDERERS.]

FIRST MURDERER. But who did bid thee join with us?

THIRD MURDERER. Macbeth. ❷

SECOND MURDERER. He needs not our mistrust; since he delivers
Our offices[1] and what we have to do
To the direction just.[2]

FIRST MURDERER. Then stand with us.
The west yet glimmers with some streaks of day.
Now spurs the lated traveler apace
To gain the timely inn, and near approaches
The subject of our watch.

THIRD MURDERER. Hark! I hear horses.

BANQUO. [*Within*] Give us a light there, ho!

SECOND MURDERER. Then 'tis he. The rest
That are within the note of expectation[3]
Already are i' th' court.

1. **offices:** Duties.
2. **direction just:** Exact detail.
3. **within . . . expectations:** On the list of expected guests.

Cross-Curricular Connection: Art

Shakespeare's plays have provided inspiration to many artists over the centuries. Such artists as William Blake, Henry Fuseli, and George Cattermole have attempted to draw the character of *Macbeth.* They each used the same literature as a source of inspiration, but their depictions of the literature are very different. Each of these artists used his or her own interpretation of the play, plus the influences of his or her own time, to illustrate the characters.

Encourage interested students to follow the example of artists like Blake and Fuseli and choose a setting, character, or event in Macbeth to capture artistically.

FIRST MURDERER. His horses go about.[4]

THIRD MURDERER. Almost a mile: but he does usually—
So all men do—from hence to th' palace gate
Make it their walk.

[*Enter* BANQUO *and* FLEANCE, *with a torch.*]

SECOND MURDERER. A light, a light!

THIRD MURDERER. 'Tis he.

FIRST MURDERER. Stand to 't

BANQUO. It will be rain tonight.

FIRST MURDERER. Let it come down.

[*They set upon* BANQUO.]

BANQUO. O, treachery! Fly, good Fleance, fly, fly, fly! (4)
[*Exit* FLEANCE.]
Thou mayst revenge. O slave! [*Dies.*]

THIRD MURDERER. Who did strike out the light?

FIRST MURDERER. Was't not the way?[5] (5)

THIRD MURDERER. There's but one down; the son is fled.

SECOND MURDERER. We have lost best half of our affair. (6)

FIRST MURDERER. Well, let 's away and say how much is done. [*Exit.*]

4. **His . . . about:** His horses have been taken to the stable.

◆ **Literary Focus**
(3) Why does Fleance's escape create an external conflict for Macbeth?

5. **way:** Thing to do.

Scene iv. *The palace.*
[*Banquet prepared. Enter* MACBETH, LADY MACBETH, ROSS, LENNOX, LORDS, *and* ATTENDANTS.]

MACBETH. You know your own degrees;[1] sit down:
At first and last, the hearty welcome.

1. **degrees:** Ranks. At state banquets guests were seated according to rank.

◆ Build Vocabulary

jocund (jäk′ ənd) *adj.*: Cheerful; jovial

◆ Literary Focus

(3) Conflict Macbeth had hoped to change the course of fate by killing both Banquo and Banquo's only son, Fleance. As long as Fleance lives, the witches' prophecy about Banquo's sons can come true and MacBeth's throne is threatened.

◆ Literary Focus

(4) Conflict Tell students that many scholars believe the exact climax of the play occurs with the stage direction "Exit Fleance." Ask: Why is Fleance's escape important to the drama? *The escape is important because it means that Macbeth still has a force or enemy to reckon with and that the witches' prophecy about Banquo's heirs can come true. It is the first time that one of Macbeth's plots has gone wrong. It also means that someone has lived to tell of attempted murder, leading people to conclude that Duncan may not have been murdered by the grooms.*

◆ Critical Thinking

(5) Criticize In the melee, Fleance escapes. Ask: Does this event seem likely, considering the odds and Fleance's youth and inexperience? *Most students will say that Fleance's escape may be unlikely; some students will point out that perhaps the mysterious third murderer was actually on Banquo's side and therefore helped Fleance escape. Perhaps the third murderer extinguished the light, assisting Fleance's escape.*

◆ Reading Strategy

(6) Read Between the Lines To show students the importance of connecting previous passages, point out to them the oddity of the second murderer's statement in line 21. Point out that Macbeth never told the murderers that killing Fleance was more important than killing Banquo. Ask them to consider why Shakespeare might have included this line. *Possible response: To show that the murderers knew more than they let on; to highlight the fact that Fleance's escape is important to the plot.*

1 Clarification Macbeth would have had this conversation with the murderers as an aside, at the side of the stage, so that the other guests would not have heard it.

◆ Literary Focus

2 Conflict Although some scholars argue that the climax occurs when Fleance actually escapes, others believe that the climax of the play, the point at which the internal and external conflicts are greatest, occurs here, when Macbeth learns of Fleance's escape. Ask: With which group of scholars do you side? Why? *Possible responses: The climax is the actual escape, because it is the audience's knowledge that builds their suspense; Macbeth's knowledge of the escape is the climax, because at that point, his character faces a crisis point.*

3 Clarification *Worm* held a broader meaning in Shakespeare's time, often referring to a snake.

LORDS. Thanks to your Majesty.

MACBETH. Ourself will mingle with society[2]
And play the humble host.
Our hostess keeps her state,[3] but in best time
We will require[4] her welcome.

LADY MACBETH. Pronounce it for me, sir, to all our friends,
For my heart speaks they are welcome.

[*Enter* FIRST MURDERER.]

MACBETH. See, they encounter thee with their hearts' thanks.
Both sides are even: here I'll sit i' th' midst:
Be large in mirth; anon we'll drink a measure[5]
The table round. [*Goes to* MURDERER] There's blood upon thy face. **1**

MURDERER. 'Tis Banquo's then.

MACBETH. 'Tis better thee without than he within.[6]
Is he dispatched?

MURDERER. My lord, his throat is cut; that I did for him.

MACBETH. Thou art the best o' th' cutthroats.
Yet he's good that did the like for Fleance;
If thou didst it, thou art the nonpareil.[7]

MURDERER. Most royal sir, Fleance is 'scaped. **2**

MACBETH. [*Aside*] Then comes my fit again: I had else been perfect,
Whole as the marble, founded as the rock,
As broad and general as the casing[8] air:
But now I am cabined, cribbed, confined, bound in
To saucy[9] doubts and fears.—But Banquo's safe?

MURDERER. Ay, my good lord: safe in a ditch he bides,
With twenty trenchèd[10] gashes on his head,
The least a death to nature.[11]

MACBETH. Thanks for that.
[*Aside*] There the grown serpent lies; the worm that's fled
Hath nature that in time will venom breed,
No teeth for th' present. Get thee gone. Tomorrow
We'll hear ourselves[12] again. **3** [*Exit* MURDERER.]

2. **society:** Company.
3. **keeps her state:** Remains seated on her throne.
4. **require:** Request.
5. **measure:** Toast.
6. **thee . . . within:** You outside than he inside.
7. **nonpareil:** Without equal.
8. **as . . . casing:** As unrestrained as the surrounding.
9. **saucy:** Insolent.
10. **trenchèd:** Trenchlike.
11. **nature:** Natural life.
12. **hear ourselves:** Talk it over.

Cultural Connection

When Shakespeare included ghosts in his plays, he knew that many people in the audience believed in restless spirits who returned to earth. In Western folklore, ghosts are normally feared. Some people in Western culture believe that the ghosts of murdered people, and people treated unjustly in life, appear on earth to seek retribution.

Other cultures have a different view of ghosts. Some groups of Native Americans and Pacific Islanders, for instance, believe that ghosts return to earth for both good and evil purposes; ghosts are not considered as fearful as they often are in Western culture. In fact, some members of these cultures perform ceremonies to call forth the ghosts and ask for their help in earthly matters.

LADY MACBETH. My royal lord,
You do not give the cheer.[13] The feast is sold
That is not often vouched, while 'tis a-making,
'Tis given with welcome.[14] To feed were best at home;
From thence, the sauce to meat is ceremony;[15]
Meeting were bare without it.

[*Enter the* GHOST OF BANQUO *and sits in* MACBETH'S *place.*] ❹

MACBETH. Sweet remembrancer!
Now good digestion wait on appetite,
And health on both!

LENNOX. May't please your Highness sit.

MACBETH. Here had we now our country's honor roofed,[16]
Were the graced person of our Banquo present—
Who may I rather challenge for unkindness
Than pity for mischance![17]

ROSS. His absence, sir,
Lays blame upon his promise. Please 't your Highness
To grace us with your royal company?

MACBETH. The table's full.

LENNOX. Here is a place reserved, sir.

MACBETH. Where?

LENNOX. Here, my good lord. What is 't that moves your Highness?

MACBETH. Which of you have done this?

LORDS. What, my good lord?

MACBETH. Thou canst not say I did it. Never shake
Thy gory locks at me.

ROSS. Gentlemen, rise, his Highness is not well.

LADY MACBETH. Sit, worthy friends. My lord is often thus,
And hath been from his youth. Pray you, keep seat.
The fit is momentary; upon a thought[18]
He will again be well. If much you note him,
You shall offend him and extend his passion.[19]
Feed, and regard him not.—Are you a man?

13. give the cheer: Make the guests feel welcome.

14. The feast . . . welcome: The feast at which the host fails to make the guests feel welcome while the food is being prepared is no more than a bought dinner.

15. From . . . ceremony: Ceremony adds a pleasant flavor to the food.

16. our . . . roofed: The most honorable men in the country under one roof.

17. Who . . . mischance: Whom I hope I may reproach for being absent due to discourtesy rather than pity because he has had an accident.

❺ **◆ Reading Strategy**
How might you connect Macbeth's agitation with his knowledge that Fleance has escaped?

An Actor's Response
"I cannot accept the idea . . . that in the banquet scene the ghost of Banquo, which appears to Macbeth, is seen at the same time by his wife . . . Lady Macbeth is no ghost-seer."
—**Fanny Kemble**

18. upon a thought: In a moment.

19. passion: Suffering.

Customize for
Visual/Spatial Learners
Have these students study Macbeth's reaction to Banquo's ghost and then describe what the ghost may have looked like. They may also want to describe or demonstrate Macbeth's expression as he encounters the ghost at the banquet. This event might be effectively staged as a tableau by several students.

❹ **Enrichment** In modern productions of *Macbeth,* the banquet seat usually remains empty, indicating that the ghost, which can only be seen by Macbeth, is a figment of Macbeth's imagination. Note, though, that the stage directions call for the entrance of the ghost. In Elizabethan times, the ghost would have appeared through a trapdoor in the back of the stage.

◆ Reading Strategy

❺ **Read Between the Lines** It is after learning of Fleance's escape that Macbeth sees the ghost. Macbeth is concerned about the power the witches predicted for Fleance, and he is upset that his murder plot was not executed as planned.

Enrichment

Ghosts and Witches at the Globe

The arrival of Banquo's ghost at the banquet might prompt curiosity about how Elizabethan theater companies managed the entrances and exits of supernatural beings. Remind students that the outer stage of the Globe thrust forward into the ground-floor audience (see page 265). Actors standing at the edge of this stage could therefore play to a surrounding crowd. Behind the outer stage was an area called the rear stage, open to the audience but enclosed by a rigid wall in the back and cloth hangings on the sides.

The trapdoor (trap) in the floor of the rear stage was the means by which Banquo's ghost made an entrance. Since the trap operated silently, there was no need for accompanying music to disguise the creaking of ropes. It also had the advantage of being not completely visible to the audience. This trap was therefore ideal for the stealthy, unannounced appearance of a spirit. In addition to serving as the entrance for Banquo's ghost, the trap also served as the means by which Caesar's ghost in *Julius Caesar* appeared.

As for the appearance of the three witches, they rose through a trap door in the floor of the outer stage. This trap, with a platform raised by rope and pulley, was frequently required to lift such prodigious items as a "King . . . riding upon a Lyon or dragon." The witches, being supernatural creatures, probably appeared with a racket of thunder and lightning, trumpeting, and falling chains. Not only did this commotion convey a proper feeling of terror, but it disguised the less bloodcurdling noise of the trap's straining ropes.

◆ Literary Focus

❶ **Conflict** The ghost appears when Macbeth mentions Banquo, indicating that he is probably feeling guilty about Banquo's death. Macbeth's shock at the sight of the ghost reveals his agitation—both about the actions he's taken and the course of future events.

◆ Critical Thinking

❷ **Analyze** What does Macbeth's discussion with Lady Macbeth in lines 76–84 indicate about his view of murder? Does he seem concerned with the immorality of murder, or with something else? *Macbeth has a rather callous attitude toward murder. His discussion indicates that he is more concerned about the possibility of seeing ghosts than about the immorality of murder.*

◆ Critical Thinking

❸ **Draw Conclusions** Ask: What causes the ghost to reappear at the banquet? *Macbeth is telling yet another lie and showing a false face to his guests, so the ghost of Banquo reappears to throw him into confusion and reveal his guilt.*

MACBETH. Ay, and a bold one, that dare look on that
Which might appall the devil.

LADY MACBETH. O proper stuff!
This is the very painting of your fear.
This is the air-drawn dagger which, you said,
Led you to Duncan. O, these flaws[20] and starts,
Impostors to true fear, would well become
A woman's story at a winter's fire,
Authorized[21] by her grandam. Shame itself!
Why do you make such faces? When all's done,
You look but on a stool.

MACBETH. Prithee, see there!
Behold! Look! Lo! How say you? ❶
Why, what care I? If thou canst nod, speak too.
If charnel houses[22] and our graves must send
Those that we bury back, our monuments
Shall be the maws of kites.[23] [*Exit* GHOST.]

LADY MACBETH. What, quite unmanned in folly?

MACBETH. If I stand here, I saw him.

LADY MACBETH. Fie, for shame!

MACBETH. Blood hath been shed ere now, i' th' olden time,
Ere humane statute purged the gentle weal;[24] ❷
Ay, and since too, murders have been performed
Too terrible for the ear. The times has been
That, when the brains were out, the man would die,
And there an end; but now they rise again,
With twenty mortal murders on their crowns,[25]
And push us from our stools. This is more strange
Than such a murder is.

LADY MACBETH. My worthy lord,
Your noble friends do lack you.

MACBETH. I do forget.
Do not muse at me, my most worthy friends;
I have a strange infirmity, which is nothing
To those that know me. Come, love and health to all!
Then I'll sit down. Give me some wine, fill full.

[*Enter* GHOST.]

I drink to th' general joy o' th' whole table, ❸
And to our dear friend Banquo, whom we miss;

20. flaws: Gusts of wind; outbursts of emotion.

21. Authorized: Vouched for.

◆ **Literary Focus** ❶ How does the incident with Banquo's ghost convey Macbeth's inner conflict?

22. charnel houses: Vaults containing human bones dug up in making new graves.

23. our . . . kites: Our tombs shall be the bellies of birds of prey.

24. Ere . . . weal: Before humane laws civilized the state and made it gentle.

25. mortal . . . crowns: Deadly wounds on their heads.

◆ Build Vocabulary

infirmity (in fur´ mə tē) *n.*: Physical or mental defect; illness

Scene from Macbeth, Cattermole, The Folger Shakespeare Library, Washington, D.C.

▲ **Critical Viewing** In what ways does the artist's use of light and shadow suggest the conflict in III, iv? **[Interpret]** ❹

Would he were here! To all and him we thirst,[26] ❸
And all to all.

LORDS. Our duties, and the pledge.

MACBETH. Avaunt![27] and quit my sight! Let the earth hide thee!
Thy bones are marrowless, thy blood is cold;
Thou hast no speculation[28] in those eyes
Which thou dost glare with.

LADY MACBETH. Think of this, good peers,
But as a thing of custom, 'tis no other.
Only it spoils the pleasure of the time. ❺

MACBETH. What man dare, I dare.
Approach thou like the rugged Russian bear,
The armed rhinoceros, or th' Hyrcan[29] tiger;
Take any shape but that,[30] and my firm nerves
Shall never tremble. Or be alive again,
And dare me to the desert[31] with thy sword.
If trembling I inhabit[32] then, protest me

26. **thirst:** Drink.

27. **Avaunt:** Be gone!

28. **speculation:** Sight.

29. **Hyrcan** (hər′ kən): From Hyrcania, a province of the ancient Persian and Macedonian empires south of the Caspian Sea.
30. **that:** Banquo's shape.
31. **desert:** Place where neither of us could escape.
32. **inhabit:** Remain indoors.

▶Critical Viewing◀

❹ **Interpret** Possible response: The artist's use of shadow may symbolize Macbeth's emotional state: He attempts to stay in the light, acting the jovial host, but the shadows, Banquo's ghost, and Macbeth's guilty conscience keep intruding.

◆ *Literature and Your Life*

❺ Ask students: How might you react if your dinner host acted as Macbeth does here? *Students will probably say they would be concerned or afraid that the host was hallucinating or unwell.*

Humanities: Art

Scene from Macbeth by George Cattermole.

George Cattermole (1800–1868) was born in Norfolk, England. Trained as an architectural draftsman, he later turned his focus from the history of buildings and cathedrals to the romantic characters of history. He is best known for his watercolors and for his illustrations of romantic figures, such as the characters of Sir Walter Scott's novels. Cattermole illustrated a number of literary works, always paying careful attention to such details as the costumes the characters wore.

Use the following question for discussion:

Does Macbeth's body language suggest anything about his state of mind? What might the bright light in the center of the picture represent? *Macbeth is depicted as a large, intimidating man, but his body language suggests that he is fearful and taken aback. The bright light in the center of the picture may represent Macbeth's fear that the truth about his plot will surface.*

◆ Critical Thinking

❶ **Analyze** Ask: What might be the significance of the other guests' inability to see the ghost? *Macbeth is alone in his suffering; he alone plotted Banquo's murder.*

◆ Critical Thinking

❷ **Interpret** Ask: Why is Lady Macbeth covering up for Macbeth? Do you think that she sees the ghost, too? *Lady Macbeth is fearful that, in his mental state of unrest and disturbance, Macbeth will reveal his guilty deed, implicating her as well. Most students will probably say that Macbeth alone sees the ghost, but some students, like some scholars, may say that Lady Macbeth, being as guilty as Macbeth, also sees the ghost.*

❸ **Clarification** "What is the night?" means "What time is it?"

The baby of a girl. Hence, horrible shadow!
Unreal mock'ry, hence! [*Exit* GHOST.]
Why, so: being gone,
I am a man again. Pray you, sit still.

LADY MACBETH. You have displaced the mirth, broke the
good meeting,
With most admired[33] disorder.

MACBETH. Can such things be,
And overcome us[34] like a summer's cloud,
Without our special wonder? You make me strange
Even to the disposition that I owe,[35]
When now I think you can behold such sights,
And keep the natural ruby of your cheeks,
When mine is blanched with fear.

ROSS. What sights, my lord? ❶

LADY MACBETH. I pray you, speak not: He grows worse and worse;
Question enrages him: at once, good night.
Stand not upon the order of your going,[36]
But go at once.

LENNOX. Good night; and better health
Attend his Majesty!

LADY MACBETH. A kind good night to all! ❷

[*Exit* LORDS.]

MACBETH. It will have blood, they say: blood will have blood.
Stones have been known to move and trees to speak;
Augures and understood relations[37] have
By maggot-pies and choughs[38] and rooks brought forth
The secret'st man of blood.[39] What is the night?

LADY MACBETH. Almost at odds[40] with morning, which is which. ❸

MACBETH. How say'st thou, that Macduff denies his person
At our great bidding?

LADY MACBETH. Did you send to him, sir?

MACBETH. I hear it by the way, but I will send:
There's not a one of them but in his house
I keep a servant fee'd.[41] I will tomorrow,

33. **admired:** Amazing.

34. **overcome us:** Come over us.

35. **disposition . . . owe:** My own nature.

36. **Stand . . . going:** Do not wait to depart in order of rank.

37. **Augures and understood relations:** Omens and the relationship between the omens and what they represent.

38. **maggot-pies and choughs** (chufs): Magpies and crows.

39. **man of blood:** Murderer.

40. **at odds:** Disputing.

41. **fee'd:** Paid to spy.

And betimes[42] I will, to the weird sisters:
More shall they speak, for now I am bent[43] to know
By the worst means the worst. For mine own good
All causes shall give way. I am in blood
Stepped in so far that, should I wade no more,
Returning were as tedious as go o'er.
Strange things I have in head that will to hand,
Which must be acted ere they may be scanned.[44]

LADY MACBETH. You lack the season of all natures,[45] sleep.

MACBETH. Come, we'll to sleep. My strange and self-abuse[46]
Is the initiate fear that wants hard use.[47]
We are yet but young in deed. [*Exit.*]

Scene v. *A witches' haunt.*
[*Thunder. Enter the* THREE WITCHES, *meeting* HECATE.]

FIRST WITCH. Why, how now, Hecate! you look angerly.

HECATE. Have I not reason, beldams[1] as you are,
Saucy and overbold? How did you dare
To trade and traffic with Macbeth
In riddles and affairs of death;
And I, the mistress of your charms,
The close contriver[2] of all harms,
Was never called to bear my part,
Or show the glory of our art?
And, which is worse, all you have done
Hath been but for a wayward son,
Spiteful and wrathful; who, as others do,
Loves for his own ends, not for you.
But make amends now: get you gone,
And at the pit of Acheron[3]
Meet me i' th' morning: thither he
Will come to know his destiny.
Your vessels and your spells provide,
Your charms and everything beside.
I am for th' air; this night I'll spend
Unto a dismal and a fatal end:
Great business must be wrought ere noon.
Upon the corner of the moon
There hangs a vap'rous drop profound;
I'll catch it ere it come to ground:
And that distilled by magic sleights[4]
Shall raise such artificial sprites[5]
As by the strength of their illusion
Shall draw him on to his confusion.[6]
He shall spurn fate, scorn death, and bear
His hopes 'bove wisdom, grace, and fear:

42. **betimes:** Quickly.
43. **bent:** Determined.

◆ **Literary Focus** ❹
How do lines 137–139 mark a turning point in Macbeth's inner conflict?

44. **scanned:** Examined.
45. **season . . . natures:** Preservative of all living creatures.
46. **My . . . self-abuse:** My strange delusion.
47. **initiate . . . use:** Beginner's fear that will harden with experience.

1. **beldams:** Hags.
2. **close contriver:** Secret inventor.
3. **Acheron** (ak´ ər än´): Hell; in Greek mythology the river of Hades.
4. **sleights:** Devices.
5. **artificial sprites:** Spirits created by magic.
6. **confusion:** Ruin.

◆ Literary Focus

❹ **Conflict** Macbeth realizes he cannot turn back. He makes a decision to continue his murderous plot.

❺ **Enrichment** This scene is almost unanimously considered to have been written by someone other than Shakespeare. Because Elizabethan audiences thoroughly enjoyed the witches, it is thought that playwright Thomas Middleton wrote and interjected this scene, which contributes nothing to the action of the play.

Customize for ***Musical/Rhythmic Learners***
Have these students perform the scene at the witches' haunt, setting the dialogue to music. If students are hesitant to perform a solo, Hecate's lines may be sung by a chorus.

Beyond the Classroom

Career Connection

Movie/Theater Critic Even in Shakespeare's time, dramas were criticized by audience and professionals alike. Most professional drama critics today research the history of a play, if it's a revival, as well as review the careers of the director and actors taking part before they critique a production. Some critics devise their own rating system to provide a quick reference for readers or viewers who want to decide whether or not to see a performance.

Have interested students read the movie or theater reviews from two different newspapers or magazines and watch a review on television. Have them discuss the rating system the reviewers used and whether or not the reviewers' opinions seemed logical. Ask students if the reviewers seemed knowledgeable about the actors and their past performances.

Community Connection

Encourage students to arrange a visit with a local newspaper critic or to write to a favorite, nationally-known critic. Have them ask the reviewer what research he or she does and what kind of rating system he or she uses. They may also want to ask if the reviewer has different standards for different genres, and, if so, what those standards are.

Have students attend a local production of a play or rent a movie version. Ask them to write a review, using as a guide the information they learned from the critic they questioned.

◆ Reading Strategy

❶ **Read Between the Lines** Lennox is really indicating his doubts about Macbeth's sincerity and his suspicion about Macbeth's role in the murders of Duncan and Banquo. He uses verbal irony when he speaks of how Duncan's death "did grieve Macbeth."

◆ Critical Thinking

❷ **Connect** Ask: What does this line tell you about the lords' feelings about Macbeth? *They think that Macbeth is a tyrant.*

◆ Critical Thinking

❸ **Interpret** Ask students: Where has Macduff gone? Why? *He's gone to England to meet King Edward and ask for his help in dethroning Macbeth.*

And you all know security[7]
Is mortals' chiefest enemy.

[*Music and a song.*]

Hark! I am called; my little spirit, see,
Sits in a foggy cloud and stays for me. [*Exit.*]

[*Sing within,* "Come away, come away," *etc.*]

FIRST WITCH. Come, let's make haste; she'll soon be back
again. [*Exit.*]

Scene vi. *The palace.*
[*Enter* LENNOX *and another* LORD.]

LENNOX. My former speeches have but hit[1] your thoughts,
Which can interpret farther.[2] Only I say
Things have been strangely borne.[3] The gracious Duncan
Was pitied of Macbeth: marry, he was dead.
And the right-valiant Banquo walked too late;
Whom, you may say, if 't please you, Fleance killed,
For Fleance fled. Men must not walk too late.
Who cannot want the thought,[4] how monstrous
It was for Malcolm and for Donalbain
To kill their gracious father? Damnèd fact![5]
How it did grieve Macbeth! Did he not straight,
In pious rage, the two delinquents tear,
That were the slaves of drink and thralls[6] of sleep?
Was not that nobly done? Ay, and wisely too;
For 'twould have angered any heart alive
To hear the men deny 't. So that I say
He has borne all things well: and I do think
That, had he Duncan's sons under his key—
As, an 't[7] please heaven, he shall not—they should find
What 'twere to kill a father. So should Fleance.
But, peace! for from broad[8] words, and 'cause he failed
His presence at the tyrant's feast, I hear,
Macduff lives in disgrace. Sir, can you tell
Where he bestows himself? ❷

LORD. The son of Duncan,
From whom this tyrant holds the due of birth,[9]
Lives in the English court, and is received
Of the most pious Edward[10] with such grace
That the malevolence of fortune nothing
Takes from his high respect.[11] Thither Macduff
Is gone to pray the holy King, upon his aid[12]
To wake Northumberland and warlike Siward;[13] ❸
That by the help of these, with Him above
To ratify the work, we may again
Give to our tables meat, sleep to our nights,

7. **security:** Overconfidence.

1. **hit:** Coincided with.
2. **Which . . . farther:** From which you can draw your own conclusions.
3. **borne:** Managed.
4. **cannot . . . thought:** Can fail to think.
5. **fact:** Deed.
6. **thralls:** Slaves.

❶ ◆ **Reading Strategy** In lines 1–24, what is Lennox really saying?

7. **an 't:** If it.
8. **broad:** Unguarded.
9. **due of birth:** Birthright; claim to the throne.
10. **Edward:** Edward the Confessor, king of England 1042–1066.
11. **with . . . respect:** Does not diminish the high respect he is given.
12. **upon his aid:** To aid Malcolm.
13. **To . . . Siward:** To call to arms the commander of the English forces, the Earl of Northumberland, and his son Siward.

Speaking and Listening Mini-Lesson

Performance

This mini-lesson supports the Speaking and Listening activity in the Idea Bank on page 326.

Introduce the Concept For this performance, students should use vocal expression and movement to convey the meaning of the scene. Have students list the characters involved in the scene and decide who will play each role.

Develop Background Students should read over the scene individually and note any passages they find confusing. As a group, they should discuss the meaning of these confusing passages as well as the important themes and ideas conveyed in the scene. Using this information, the group should decide on the tone and setting of the scene and the motivation of each character. They can then use clues from the text to plan the actual staging of the scene.

Applying the Information Have the students practice their scenes, using props or costumes to complement their performance.

Assess the Outcome Once students have rehearsed have them perform the banquet scene for the class. You might have students use the Peer Assessment sheet for a Dramatic Performance, page 121 in ***Alternative Assessment.***

Free from our feasts and banquets bloody knives,
Do faithful homage and receive free honors:[14]
All which we pine for now. And this report
Hath so exasperate the King that he
Prepares for some attempt of war.

LENNOX. Sent he to Macduff?

LORD. He did: and with an absolute "Sir, not I,"
The cloudy[15] messenger turns me his back,
And hums, as who should say "You'll rue the time
That clogs[16] me with this answer." ❹

LENNOX. And that well might
Advise him to a caution, t' hold what distance
His wisdom can provide. Some holy angel
Fly to the court of England and unfold
His message ere he come, that a swift blessing
May soon return to this our suffering country
Under a hand accursed!

LORD. I'll send my prayers with him.

[*Exit.*]

14. **free honors:** Honors given to freemen.

15. **cloudy:** Disturbed.

16. **clogs:** Burdens.

◆ Build Vocabulary

malevolence (mə lev´ ə ləns) *n.*: Ill will; spitefulness

Guide for Responding

◆ Literature and Your Life

Reader's Response Did you find the banquet scene frightening, funny, or something else? Explain.

Thematic Focus Macbeth is making Scotland into an evil place. Who will lead the forces of good in a campaign against him?

☑ Check Your Comprehension

1. In III, i, what does Banquo say about the witches' prophecies?
2. What does Macbeth plan to do to Banquo and Fleance?
3. How does Macbeth's plot against Banquo and Fleance go wrong?
4. Briefly summarize what happens at the banquet.
5. What does the final scene reveal about the opposition to Macbeth?

◆ Critical Thinking

INTERPRET

1. Compare and contrast Macbeth's feelings about murdering Duncan with his feelings about murdering Banquo. **[Compare and Contrast]**
2. What is similar about Macbeth's arguments for murder in III, i, 92–108, and Lady Macbeth's arguments for murder in I, vii, 47–51? **[Connect]**
3. How has the relationship between Macbeth and Lady Macbeth changed? **[Analyze]**
4. Support the idea that Macbeth will not be satisfied with Banquo's death, but will go further into evil. **[Support]**

EVALUATE

5. Is the banquet scene an effective piece of dramatic action? Why or why not? **[Make a Judgment]**

APPLY

6. What does this act suggest about the effects of evil on an evil-doer? **[Generalize]**

❹ **Clarification** Tell students that this line translates as "You'll be sorry!"

Reinforce and Extend

Answers

◆ Literature and Your Life

Reader's Response Possible responses: Students might find a kind of grim humor in the banquet scene or sense that the appearance of Banquo's ghost confronts and personifies Macbeth's guilty conscience.

Thematic Focus Students should realize that Macduff has gone to England to seek the aid of King Edward in an effort to dethrone Macbeth and free Scotland from his tyranny.

☑ Check Your Comprehension

1. Because the prophecies have come true for Macbeth, Banquo wonders if they will come true for himself as well, making him the father of a line of kings.
2. Macbeth plans to have assassins kill Banquo and Fleance.
3. Banquo is killed, but Fleance escapes.
4. When Macbeth makes a pretentious fuss about Banquo's absence, and gives a false toast in his honor, Banquo's ghost appears twice, completely unnerving Macbeth.
5. The final scene reveals that the lords suspect Macbeth to be a tyrant.

◆ Critical Thinking

1. Leading up to the murder of Duncan, Macbeth's natural decency is consumed by his raw ambition, which is inflamed by his wife's greed. In contrast, Macbeth coldly plans the death of Banquo because he fears the witches' predictions and now seems capable of doing anything to prevent them from coming true.
2. Macbeth implies that they are less than men if they choose to let the fabricated wrongs of Banquo go unpunished. Lady Macbeth's earlier implications are similar, scorning her husband's sense of decency as making him seem less than a man.
3. Obsessed, Macbeth has drawn into himself, no longer consulting with Lady Macbeth about his plans for Banquo and Fleance. His letter to her earlier in the play suggests that, prior to this, he had shared his thoughts with her.
4. Macbeth says that he is so deep in blood now that there is no turning back, implying that future sacrifices will be made to protect their bloody gains.
5. Most students will respond that the banquet scene is very effective in its use of irony and suspense, and in the dramatic way it reveals Macbeth's guilt to the court. On the negative side, they might point out that it is unacceptable for Lady Macbeth also to see the ghost.
6. Sample response: Evil feeds on a person's character until it consumes and changes the person utterly, and in the end nothing is gained but misfortune.

◆ Reading Strategy

1. Manhood is defined as a kind of daring fearlessness and malevolent use of power that lets nothing stand in the way of one's desires.
2. Possible answers: Macbeth is obsessed about getting the bloody deed done, so he sends a third murderer to check on the other two; the witches send the third murderer to give fate extra help by bungling the job and causing Fleance to escape.

◆ Literary Focus

1. The witches predicted that Banquo would become the father of a line of kings.
2. Macbeth becomes consumed by jealousy because the witches prophesied that Banquo's heirs would be kings. After the murder, however, Banquo continues to torment Macbeth.
3. Macbeth acts disturbed and distraught as he sees Banquo's ghost.
4. Macbeth resolves to go visit the witches.

◆ Build Vocabulary

Using the Prefix *mal-*
1. poorly adjusted; 2. illness; 3. dissatisfied

◆ Grammar and Style

1. is; 2. is; 3. does; 4. begins; 5. supports

Idea Bank

Customizing for *Learning Modalities*

Following are suggestions for matching Idea Bank topics with your students' learning modalities:

Verbal/Linguistic: 2
Bodily/Kinesthetic: 3
Intrapersonal: 1

Customizing for *Performance Levels*

Following are suggestions for matching Idea Bank topics with your students' ability levels:

Less Advanced Students: 1
Average Students: 3
More Advanced Students: 2

Guide for Responding *(continued)*

◆ Reading Strategy

Read Between the Lines

By **reading between the lines**—linking earlier and later passages and finding suggested meanings—you can enrich your understanding of the play. For example, you can figure out that one theme of the play is manhood. Macbeth tells the murderers that they aren't real men if they don't dare to kill Banquo. Later, when Macbeth is startled by Banquo's ghost, he asserts that he's as much of a man as anyone: "What man dares, I dare."

1. Use these and other passages to define manhood, according to Macbeth and Lady Macbeth.
2. By reading between the lines, figure out what the presence of the third murderer suggests about Macbeth.

◆ Literary Focus

Conflict

The **conflicts** in Act III include an external struggle between Macbeth and Banquo and a struggle within Macbeth as he faces the ghost of Banquo.

1. Why does Macbeth view Banquo as his opponent?
2. In what way does Macbeth fail to resolve his conflict with Banquo?
3. How is Macbeth's behavior at the dinner an outward sign of an inner conflict?
4. How does Macbeth resolve his inner conflict, at least temporarily?

◆ Build Vocabulary

Using the Prefix *mal-*

Knowing that the prefix *mal-* means "bad, ill, or poorly," define these words.

1. maladjusted **2.** malady **3.** malcontent

Using the Word Bank

In your notebook, write a brief profile of Macbeth using all the words in the Word Bank.

◆ Grammar and Style

Subject and Verb Agreement

Use the **verb form that agrees with its subject in number**. Do not be misled by other words that come between the subject and the verb.

Practice Write these sentences in your notebook, choosing the singular or plural form of the verb.

1. Macbeth, of all the Scottish kings, (is, are) most evil.
2. Scotland, country of stark contrasts, (is, are) the setting of *Macbeth.*
3. Malcolm, despite his worries, (does, do) what must be done.
4. Lady Macbeth, expressing some concerns, (begin, begins) to doubt what she has done.
5. Not everyone in this country of ghosts (support, supports) Macbeth.

Idea Bank

Writing

1. **Diary Entry** As a lord returning from Macbeth's feast, write a diary entry about the strange events you have just witnessed.
2. **Critical Note** Some critics have argued that the third murderer is Macbeth himself. Write a brief critical note agreeing or disagreeing with this theory. Support your argument with specific passages.

Speaking and Listening

3. **Performance** With a group of classmates, perform the banquet scene (iv) for the class. Use stage directions and clues from the dialogue—for example, "Sit, worthy friends"—to map out the action in this scene. Also, remember to follow sentences, not line endings, in reading speeches. **[Performing Arts Link]**

✓ ASSESSMENT OPTIONS

Formal Assessment, Selection Test, pp. 71–73, and Assessment Resources Software. The selection test is designed so that it can be easily customized to the ability levels of your students. ***Alternative Assessment,*** p. 14, includes options for less advanced students, more advanced students, visual and spatial learners, and auditory learners.

PORTFOLIO ASSESSMENT
Use the following rubrics in the ***Alternative Assessment*** booklet to assess student writing:
Diary Entry: Fictional Narrative Rubric, p. 96
Critical Note: Literary Analysis/Interpretation Rubric, p. 113

Guide for Interpreting, Act IV

◆ Review and Anticipate

Macbeth hires murderers to kill Banquo and Banquo's son, Fleance. The murderers botch the job, killing Banquo but letting Fleance escape. Then, at a state dinner, Macbeth is shocked to see the ghost of Banquo sitting in the king's chair. Macbeth decides to visit the witches again, determined to know "the worst." At the end of Act III, we learn that Malcolm is in England, preparing to invade Scotland, and that Macduff has gone to join him.

Act IV will be a turning point in the play. Macbeth seeks help from the witches to secure his power. The forces of good, however, are beginning to gather against him.

◆ Literary Focus

IMAGERY

Imagery is the language that writers use to re-create sensory experiences. It is what helps you see, hear, feel, smell, and taste, rather than just read words or listen to them spoken. In Elizabethan theater, imagery was especially important because there was no lighting or elaborate scenery to "paint" a scene for the audience. Words alone had to do the work.

Shakespeare was a master of imagery, packing sense experiences into every line: "Though bladed corn be lodged and trees blown down." Notice how this line appeals to the senses of touch and sight.

In addition, Shakespeare creates patterns of images that run through a whole play. In *Macbeth*, for instance, images relating to blood, ill-fitting clothes, and babies are just three of the patterns he uses to create a mood and enhance the play's meaning.

◆ Grammar and Style

POSSESSIVE FORMS: SINGULAR AND PLURAL

Most singular nouns form the **possessive** by adding an apostrophe and *s*. Plural nouns ending in *s* form the possessive by adding an apostrophe, and plural nouns not ending in *s* add an apostrophe and *s*.

Shakespeare uses both singular and plural possessives in this act:

Singular:	adder's	traitor's	baboon's
Plural:	witches'	warders'	men's

◆ Reading Strategy

USE YOUR SENSES

You will enjoy a literary work more if you use your senses to experience the imagery it contains.

In reading this passage from Act IV, for example, understand it with your mind but also experience it with your senses of sight, touch, and hearing:

> Though you untie the winds and let them fight / Against the churches; though the yesty waves / Confound and swallow navigation up / Though bladed corn be lodged and trees blown down; / Though castles topple on their warders' heads . . .

◆ Build Vocabulary

WORD ROOTS: *-cred-*

The word credulous in Act IV, has the root -cred-, which means "belief." To be credulous is "to believe something too readily."

WORD BANK

Before you read, preview this list of words from Act IV of *Macbeth*.

pernicious
judicious
sundry
intemperance
avarice
credulous

Prepare and Engage

OBJECTIVES

1. To read, comprehend, and interpret Elizabethan drama
2. To relate an Elizabethan drama to personal experience
3. To use one's senses to enhance a reading experience
4. To identify imagery
5. To build vocabulary in context and learn the word root *-cred-*
6. To form possessive nouns, both singular and plural, correctly
7. To respond to Act IV of *Macbeth* through writing, speaking and listening

SKILLS INSTRUCTION

Vocabulary: Word Roots: *-cred-*
Grammar: Possessive Forms: Singular and Plural
Reading Strategy: Use Your Senses
Literary Focus: Imagery
Speaking and Listening: Role Play (teacher edition)
Critical Viewing: Evaluate, Interpret

PORTFOLIO OPPORTUNITIES

Writing: Malcolm Wants You! (flyer), Plot Analysis
Writing Mini-Lesson: Macbeth: The Film Version?
Speaking and Listening: Role Play

Call students' attention to lines 123–124 in Scene i of Act IV: ". . . the blood-bolted Banquo smiles upon me." Point out that *Macbeth* contains so much blood it has been cause for comment. The critic Mark Van Doren claimed, "Never in a play has there been so much of this substance, and never has it been so sickening. . . . It is so real that we see, feel, and smell it on everything. And it sticks." Ask students to recall the images of blood they have encountered so far in the play and to say if they agree with Van Doren's statement. Ask them to think about Shakespeare's reason(s) for making this drama so bloody.

Customize for
Visual/Spatial Learners
Shakespeare leaves a lot to the imagination as far as the physical interaction between characters goes. Have these students choose one scene from this act and diagram how they would have the characters move on the stage.

REINFORCE / RETEACH / EXTEND

Selection Support Pages
Build Vocabulary: Word Roots: *-cred-*, p. 71
Grammar and Style: Possessive Forms: Singular and Plural, p. 72
Reading Strategy: Use Your Senses, p. 73
Literary Focus: Imagery, p. 74
Strategies for Diverse Student Needs, p. 15

Beyond Literature Cross-Curricular Connection: Marketing Interview, p. 15
Formal Assessment Selection Test, pp. 74–76; Assessment Resources Software
Alternative Assessment, p. 15
Listening to Literature Audiocassettes *The Tragedy of Macbeth,* Act IV

Develop Understanding

One-Minute Insight

In Act IV, Macbeth's decline is in full swing. He see apparitions, who make seemingly contradictory predictions, and Macbeth, grown desperate to secure his throne, interprets the apparitions' words in the most favorable way. Forces begin to gather against Macbeth, and his situation becomes more desperate.

Customize for *Verbal/Linguistic Learners*

Embedded in Shakespeare's language are many universal truths. Point these students towards lines 23–24 in Scene iii: "Though all things foul would wear the brows of grace,/Yet grace must look so." Ask the students to explain how these lines are true, then ask them to find other such truths embedded in the text.

Customize for *More Advanced Students*

❶ Point out to students that the number three keeps cropping up. Ask: Where else have students seen the number three in the play? Have students investigate further and watch for more occurrences as they read. *The number three is a "magical" number commonly found in fairy tales and myths. There are three witches and three apparitions. The witches often repeat words and phrases three times as in "Hail! Hail! Hail!" in Act I. In Scene i of Act IV, the number three is given special emphasis in lines 1 and 2.*

◆ Critical Thinking

❷ **Infer** The third witch's attendant, Harpier, cries out that " 'tis time." Ask: What is it time for? *Students may say it's time to cast the final spell upon Macbeth.*

◆ Reading Strategy

❸ **Use Your Senses** Tell students to use their senses to imagine the brew that is being concocted. Suggest that they see it, smell it, taste it, and feel it. Then ask them to describe the concoction. *Students' descriptions should include the appearance of the brew, including its color and the ingredients floating in it; its smell; its consistency; and the sound of it bubbling.*

Act IV

Scene i. *A witches' haunt.*
[*Thunder. Enter the* THREE WITCHES.]

FIRST WITCH. Thrice the brinded[1] cat hath mewed. ❶

SECOND WITCH. Thrice and once the hedge-pig[2] whined.

THIRD WITCH. Harpier[3] cries. 'Tis time, 'tis time. ❷

FIRST WITCH. Round about the caldron go:
In the poisoned entrails throw.
Toad, that under cold stone
Days and nights has thirty-one
Swelt'red venom sleeping got,[4]
Boil thou first i' th' charmèd pot.

ALL. Double, double, toil and trouble;
Fire burn and caldron bubble.

SECOND WITCH. Fillet of a fenny snake,
In the caldron boil and bake;
Eye of newt and toe of frog,
Wool of bat and tongue of dog,
Adder's fork[5] and blindworm's[6] sting,
Lizard's leg and howlet's[7] wing,
For a charm of pow'rful trouble,
Like a hell-broth boil and bubble.

ALL. Double, double, toil and trouble;
Fire burn and caldron bubble.

THIRD WITCH. Scale of dragon, tooth of wolf, ❸
Witch's mummy, maw and gulf[8]
Of the ravined[9] salt-sea shark,
Root of hemlock digged i' th' dark,
Liver of blaspheming Jew,
Gall of goat, and slips of yew
Slivered in the moon's eclipse,
Nose of Turk and Tartar's lips,[10]
Finger of birth-strangled babe
Ditch-delivered by a drab,
Make the gruel thick and slab:[11]
Add thereto a tiger's chaudron,[12]
For th' ingredience of our caldron.

1. **brinded:** Striped.
2. **hedge-pig:** Hedgehog.
3. **Harpier:** One of the spirits attending the witches.
4. **Swelt'red . . . got:** Venom sweated out while sleeping.
5. **fork:** Forked tongue.
6. **blindworm's:** Small, limbless lizards.
7. **howlet's:** Small owl's.
8. **maw and gulf:** Stomach and gullet.
9. **ravined:** Ravenous.
10. **blaspheming Jew . . . Tartar's lips:** For many in Shakespeare's audience, the words "Jew," "Turk," and "Tartar" evoked stereotypical enemies of Christianity.
11. **slab:** Sticky.
12. **chaudron** (shō′ drən): Entrails.

Block Scheduling Strategies

Consider these suggestions to take advantage of extended class time.

- Introduce imagery using the Literary Focus on page 327 and review with the class imagery they've already encountered in *Macbeth*. You may also use the Literary Focus page in ***Selection Support,*** p. 74. After students have read Act IV, have them answer the Literary Focus questions on page 346.
- Play Act IV, Scene i from the **Listening to Literature Audiocassettes** after students have read the scene. Hold a class discussion about the mood the scene sets for the rest of the act.
- Have students answer the Reader's Response, Thematic Focus, and Critical Thinking questions on page 345.
- Let interested students work on the "Malcolm Wants You!" flyer described in the Idea Bank on page 346. Post the finished flyers in the classroom.
- Let volunteers perform one of the scenes from Act IV for the class.

Poster for Macbeth, His Majesty's Theater, 1911, Edmund Dulac

▲ **Critical Viewing** Has this artist captured the spirit of the witches as it is portrayed in IV, i? Explain. **[Evaluate]** ❹

▶Critical Viewing◀

❹ **Evaluate** Students might say that the gloomy colors and the ragged appearance of the witches do seem appropriate. They also might say the artist has successfully depicted the witches' brew as a powerful, supernatural force that is capable of bringing forth the apparitions.

Humanities: Art

Poster for Macbeth by Edmund Dulac.

Edmund Dulac (1882–1953) was born in France and settled in England in 1904. He is most widely known as a book illustrator of fairy tales and legends, but he also was a caricaturist and a portrait painter. He did a lot of work for the British stage, such as this poster for *Macbeth*. In 1953, he was commissioned to produce a stamp commemorating the coronation of Queen Elizabeth II.

Use these questions for discussion:

1. Why is it ironic that Macbeth should be standing above the witches with his arms crossed as he is? *Despite the fact that Macbeth is commanding with the three witches, he is actually at their mercy.*
2. How does this depiction of the witches compare with the one on pages 273? *Students may say that the picture on page 273 shows three old women who look strange and gnarled, but the picture on page 329 depicts the witches as more obviously demonic or evil.*

❶ Clarification The entrance of Hecate, the ancient Greek goddess of night and witchcraft, has little to do with the action of the play and is considered to be an addition to the play by someone other than Shakespeare.

◆ Reading Strategy

❷ Use Your Senses *Possible response: The scene is probably very dark and remote, with a clear sky full of stars. You can smell the witches' foul brew. Macbeth is disheveled at this point from neglect, and the witches swoon and roll their eyes dramatically.*

◆ Literary Focus

❸ Imagery Have students analyze the imagery in this speech and explain its effect. *The images are all of destruction and mayhem. The images reinforce the idea that something has gone terribly wrong in Macbeth's life and world.*

ALL. Double, double, toil and trouble;
Fire burn and caldron bubble.

SECOND WITCH. Cool it with a baboon's blood,
Then the charm is firm and good.

[*Enter* HECATE *and the other* THREE WITCHES.]

HECATE. O, well done! I commend your pains; ❶
And every one shall share i' th' gains:
And now about the caldron sing,
Like elves and fairies in a ring,
Enchanting all that you put in.

[*Music and a song:* "Black Spirits," *etc. Exit* HECATE *and the other* THREE WITCHES.]

SECOND WITCH. By the pricking of my thumbs,
Something wicked this way comes:
Open, locks,
Whoever knocks!

[*Enter* MACBETH.]

MACBETH. How now, you secret, black, and midnight hags!
What is 't you do?

ALL. A deed without a name.

MACBETH. I conjure you, by that which you profess,
Howe'er you come to know it, answer me:
Though you untie the winds and let them fight
Against the churches; though the yesty[13] waves
Confound[14] and swallow navigation up;
Though bladed corn be lodged[15] and trees blown down; ❸
Though castles topple on their warders' heads;
Though palaces and pyramids do slope[16]
Their heads to their foundations; though the treasure
Of nature's germens[17] tumble all together,
Even till destruction sicken, answer me
To what I ask you.

FIRST WITCH. Speak.

SECOND WITCH. Demand.

A Critic's Response
"The feeling of fear, horror, and pain is increased by the constant and recurring images of blood . . ."
—Carolyn F. E. Spurgeon

❷ **◆ Reading Strategy**
Use your senses to imagine this scene from another world that Shakespeare depicts in IV, i.

13. yesty: Foamy.
14. Confound: Destroy.
15. lodged: Beaten down.
16. slope: Bend.

17. nature's germens: Seeds of all life.

THIRD WITCH. We'll answer.

FIRST WITCH. Say, if th' hadst rather hear it from our mouths,
Or from our masters?

MACBETH. Call 'em, let me see 'em.

FIRST WITCH. Pour in sow's blood, that hath eaten
Her nine farrow;[18] grease that's sweaten
From the murderer's gibbet[19] throw
Into the flame.

ALL. Come, high or low,
Thyself and office[20] deftly show!

[*Thunder.* FIRST APPARITION: *an Armed Head.*[21]]

MACBETH. Tell me, thou unknown power—

FIRST WITCH. He knows thy thought:
Hear his speech, but say thou nought.

FIRST APPARITION. Macbeth! Macbeth! Macbeth! Beware Macduff! ❹
Beware the Thane of Fife. Dismiss me: enough.
[*He descends.*]

MACBETH. Whate'er thou art, for thy good caution thanks:
Thou hast harped[22] my fear aright. But one word more—

FIRST WITCH. He will not be commanded. Here's another,
More potent than the first.

[*Thunder.* SECOND APPARITION: *a Bloody Child.*[23]]

SECOND APPARITION. Macbeth! Macbeth! Macbeth!

MACBETH. Had I three ears, I'd hear thee.

SECOND APPARITION. Be bloody, bold, and resolute! Laugh to scorn
The pow'r of man, for none of woman born ❺
Shall harm Macbeth. [*Descends.*]

MACBETH. Then live, Macduff: what need I fear of thee?
But yet I'll make assurance double sure,
And take a bond of fate.[24] Thou shalt not live;

18. **farrow:** Young pigs.

19. **gibbet** (jib′ it): Gallows.

20. **office:** Function.

21. **an Armed Head:** Symbol of Macduff.

22. **harped:** Hit upon.

23. **a Bloody Child:** Symbol of Macduff at birth.

24. **take . . . fate:** Get a guarantee from fate (by killing Macduff).

◆ Critical Thinking

❹ **Analyze** Ask students: Why might the apparition speak Macbeth's name three times? *Throughout the play, the number three has been given special emphasis. The witches in Act I hail Macbeth three times. Macbeth heard three prophecies during his first encounter with the witches; during this encounter, he meets their "masters," three apparitions, who will deliver three more prophecies.*

Comprehension Check ☑

❺ Ask: What is the second apparition's warning? How does Macbeth misconstrue it? *The second apparition says that "none of woman born" shall harm Macbeth. Macbeth immediately assumes that the second prophecy negates the first prophecy, which is "beware Macduff."*

Preparing for Standardized Tests

Reading and Vocabulary Recognizing and interpreting imagery is an important literary skill that is tested in Critical Reading items on standardized tests. Students may also be required to apply this skill in essay portions of tests. For further practice, have students do the Literary Focus page on Imagery in ***Selection Support***, p. 74.

Grammar and Language Understanding the difference between singular and plural possessives is essential to tests of English usage and in writing and revision items on tests.

The Grammar and Style lesson for this selection addresses the formation of possessives, singular and plural. For additional practice, use the Grammar and Style page on Possessive Forms, p. 72, in ***Selection Support.***

Enrichment Shakespeare often incorporates stage directions into his dialogue. The rising of the apparition that Macbeth refers to in line 87 was probably achieved with a trap door. Similarly, point students to line 106, where the cauldron is sinking.

Comprehension Check ☑

❶ Ask: What is the third prophecy? *Macbeth will never be defeated until Birnam Wood comes to Dunsinane, Macbeth's castle.*

◆ Critical Thinking

❷ **Draw Conclusions** Ask: Why won't the spirits reveal Banquo's destiny? *Possible response: They want Macbeth to continue on his disastrous course.*

◆ Literary Focus

❸ **Imagery** The second apparition is covered in blood, and blood has been a recurring image in the play. Also pervading the play are references to manhood and the ruthlessness associated with being a man. Having two apparitions with the appearance of children may symbolize lost innocence.

❹ **Clarification** Hautboys (hō´ boiz) are wooden, pipelike wind instruments. They would be used here to signal the appearance of the kings.

That I may tell pale-hearted fear it lies,
And sleep in spite of thunder.

[*Thunder.* THIRD APPARITION: *a Child Crowned, with a tree in his hand.*[25]]

What is this,
That rises like the issue of a king,
And wears upon his baby-brow the round
And top of sovereignty?[26]

ALL. Listen, but speak not to 't.

THIRD APPARITION. Be lion-mettled, proud, and take no care
Who chafes, who frets, or where conspirers are:
Macbeth shall never vanquished be until
Great Birnam Wood to high Dunsinane Hill
Shall come against him. [*Descends.*] ❶

MACBETH. That will never be.
Who can impress[27] the forest, bid the tree
Unfix his earth-bound root? Sweet bodements,[28] good!
Rebellious dead, rise never, till the Wood
Of Birnam rise, and our high-placed Macbeth
Shall live the lease of nature,[29] pay his breath
To time and mortal custom.[30] Yet my heart
Throbs to know one thing. Tell me, if your art
Can tell so much: shall Banquo's issue ever
Reign in this kingdom?

ALL. Seek to know no more. ❷

MACBETH. I will be satisfied. Deny me this,
And an eternal curse fall on you! Let me know.
Why sinks that caldron? And what noise is this?

[*Hautboys.*] ❹

FIRST WITCH. Show!

SECOND WITCH. Show!

THIRD WITCH. Show!

ALL. Show his eyes, and grieve his heart;
Come like shadows, so depart!

[*A show of eight* KINGS *and* BANQUO, *last* KING *with a glass*[31] *in his hand.*] ❺

25. **a Child . . . hand:** Symbol of Malcolm.

26. **top of sovereignty:** Crown.

27. **impress:** Force into service.

28. **bodements:** Prophecies.

29. **lease of nature:** Natural lifespan.

30. **mortal custom:** Natural death.

31. **glass:** Mirror.

❸ **◆ Literary Focus** How do the apparitions that Macbeth sees at IV, i, 68, 75, and 86 connect with the patterns of imagery in the play?

MACBETH. Thou art too like the spirit of Banquo. Down!
Thy crown does sear mine eyelids. And thy hair,
Thou other gold-bound brow, is like the first.
A third is like the former. Filthy hags!
Why do you show me this? A fourth! Start, eyes!
What, will the line stretch out to th' crack of doom?
Another yet! A seventh! I'll see no more. ❺
And yet the eighth appears, who bears a glass
Which shows me many more: and some I see
That twofold balls and treble scepters[32] carry:
Horrible sight! Now I see 'tis true;
For the blood-boltered[33] Banquo smiles upon me,
And points at them for his.[34] What, is this so?

FIRST WITCH. Ay, sir, all this is so. But why
Stands Macbeth thus amazedly?
Come, sisters, cheer we up his sprites,
And show the best of our delights:
I'll charm the air to give a sound,
While you perform your antic round,[35]
That this great king may kindly say
Our duties did his welcome pay.

[*Music.* THE WITCHES *dance, and vanish.*]

MACBETH. Where are they? Gone? Let this pernicious hour
Stand aye accursèd in the calendar!
Come in, without there!

[*Enter* LENNOX.]

LENNOX. What's your Grace's will?

MACBETH. Saw you the weird sisters?

LENNOX. No, my lord.

MACBETH. Came they not by you?

LENNOX. No indeed, my lord.

MACBETH. Infected be the air whereon they ride,
And damned all those that trust them! I did hear
The galloping of horse. Who was 't came by?

LENNOX. 'Tis two or three, my lord, that bring you word
Macduff is fled to England.

❻ ◆ **Literary Focus**
What does Macbeth learn from the images of the kings?

32. twofold . . . scepters: Coronation emblems and insignia of the kingdoms of England. Scotland, and Ireland, united in 1603 when James VI of Scotland became James I of England.
33. blood-boltered: With his hair matted with blood.
34. his: His descendants.
35. antic round: Grotesque circular dance.

◆ Build Vocabulary

pernicious (pər nish′ əs) *adj.*: Fatal; deadly

◆ Critical Thinking

❺ **Analyze** Ask students: What does Macbeth learn from the appearance of the kings and Banquo? What should he learn about the prophecies but does not? *Macbeth sees that Banquo, indeed, has a line of kings behind him. Macbeth should realize that he should not take the prophecies literally; they may have subtle or hidden meanings.*

◆ Literary Focus

❻ **Imagery** Macbeth learns that Banquo's descendants are still a threat to his throne, although two of the apparitions seemed to suggest he had nothing to worry about.

Cultural Connection

When Macbeth murdered Duncan, he broke two tenets of his society: He killed his king, and at the same time, he killed a guest under his roof.

According to the rules of hospitality in most cultures, guests are to be treated with a deliberate respect and kindness. In ancient Greek culture, Zeus was the god of hospitality, and people treated all guests well, lavishing them with gifts, lest they discover that the poor traveler they had treated badly was actually Zeus in disguise, testing them. Even today, in many areas of Latin America, Africa, and Asia, any traveler, whether an acquaintance or a complete stranger, can expect to receive the warmest welcome. "My house is your house" is taken literally in many cultures.

Have students from different cultural backgrounds explain the rules of hospitality in their cultures.

◆ Critical Thinking

❶ Compare and Contrast Have students compare Macbeth's attitude toward murdering Macduff and his family with his attitude about murdering King Duncan. *Students should point out that Macbeth has lost all semblance of humanity and is coldbloodedly planning the execution of an entire family.*

◆ Literature and Your Life

❷ Macbeth interprets the prophecies in the way that is most favorable to him. The murders he is planning are worse because they are crimes against people who pose no threat to him. There is no good reason these people should be eliminated.

◆ Literary Focus

❸ Imagery Point out the bird imagery used by Lady Macduff. Ask students how this imagery both highlights her noble intentions and yet suggests she will be powerless against the murderers. *By comparing herself with a wren, an enemy to the owl, she is suggesting that in a fight, she'll bravely protect her children but will ultimately be defeated.*

MACBETH. Fled to England?

LENNOX. Ay, my good lord.

MACBETH. [*Aside*] Time, thou anticipat'st[36] my dread exploits.
The flighty purpose never is o'ertook
Unless the deed go with it.[37] From this moment
The very firstlings of my heart[38] shall be
The firstlings of my hand. And even now,
To crown my thoughts with acts be it thought and done:
The castle of Macduff I will surprise; ❶
Seize upon Fife; give to th' edge o' th' sword
His wife, his babes, and all unfortunate souls
That trace[39] him in his line. No boasting like a fool;
This deed I'll do before this purpose cool:
But no more sights!—Where are these gentlemen?
Come, bring me where they are.
[*Exit.*]

36. **anticipat'st:** Foretold.
37. **The flighty . . . it:** The fleeting plan is never fulfilled unless it is carried out at once.
38. **firstlings . . . heart:** First thoughts, impulses.
39. **trace:** Succeed.

Scene ii. *Macduff's castle.*
[*Enter* MACDUFF'S WIFE, *her* SON, *and* ROSS.]

> **◆ Literature and Your Life**
> ❷ How does Macbeth blindly interpret what the witches show him in IV, i? How are the murders he is planning worse than the others?

LADY MACDUFF. What had he done, to make him fly the land?

ROSS. You must have patience, madam.

LADY MACDUFF. He had none:
His flight was madness. When our actions do not,
Our fears do make us traitors.

ROSS. You know not
Whether it was his wisdom or his fear.

LADY MACDUFF. Wisdom! To leave his wife, to leave his babes,
His mansion and his titles,[1] in a place
From whence himself does fly? He loves us not;
He wants the natural touch:[2] for the poor wren,
The most diminutive of birds, will fight, ❸
Her young ones in her nest, against the owl.
All is the fear and nothing is the love;
As little is the wisdom, where the flight
So runs against all reason.

ROSS. My dearest coz,[3]
I pray you, school[4] yourself. But, for your husband, ❹
He is noble, wise, judicious, and best knows

1. **titles:** Possessions.
2. **wants . . . touch:** Lacks natural affection.
3. **coz:** Cousin.
4. **school:** Control.

The fits o' th' seasons,[5] I dare not speak much further:
But cruel are the times, when we are traitors
And do not know ourselves;[6] when we hold rumor
From what we fear,[7] yet know not what we fear,
But float upon a wild and violent sea
Each way and move. I take my leave of you.
Shall not be long but I'll be here again.
Things at the worst will cease, or else climb upward
To what they were before. My pretty cousin,
Blessing upon you!

4

LADY MACDUFF. Fathered he is, and yet he's fatherless.

ROSS. I am so much a fool, should I stay longer,
It would be my disgrace and your discomfort.[8]
I take my leave at once. [*Exit* ROSS.]

LADY MACDUFF. Sirrah, your father's dead;
And what will you do now? How will you live?

SON. As birds do, mother.

LADY MACDUFF. What, with worms and flies?

SON. With what I get, I mean; and so do they.

LADY MACDUFF. Poor bird! thou'dst never fear the net nor lime,[9]
The pitfall nor the gin.[10]

SON. Why should I, mother? Poor birds they are not set for.
My father is not dead, for all your saying.

LADY MACDUFF. Yes, he is dead: how wilt thou do for a father?

SON. Nay, how will you do for a husband?

LADY MACDUFF. Why, I can buy me twenty at any market.

SON. Then you'll buy 'em to sell[11] again.

LADY MACDUFF. Thou speak'st with all thy wit, and yet i' faith,
With wit enough for thee.[12]

SON. Was my father a traitor, mother?

5. fits o' th' season: Disorders of the time.
6. when . . . ourselves: When we are treated as traitors but do not know of any treason.
7. when . . . fear: Believe rumors based on our fears.
8. It . . . discomfort: I would disgrace myself and embarrass you by weeping.

5 ◆ **Literary Focus** What does the imagery in IV, ii, 34–35, suggest about what might happen?

9. lime: Birdlime, a sticky substance smeared on branches to catch birds.
10. gin: Trap.
11. sell: Betray.
12. for thee: For a child.

◆ **Build Vocabulary**
judicious (jo͞o dish′ əs) *adj.*: Showing good judgment

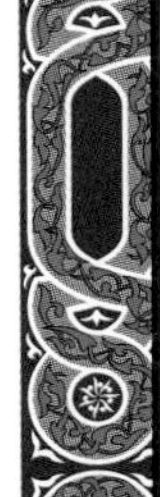

◆ Critical Thinking

4 Infer Ask: Why is Ross so hesitant to speak plainly to his cousin? *Ross may be fearful for his own life. He seem uncomfortable with the idea of being a traitor and does not seem to trust those around him.*

◆ Literary Focus

5 Imagery These images suggest that Lady Macduff and her son will be trapped by the murderers.

Beyond the Classroom

Career Connection

Public Relations/"Spin Control" One piece of evidence scholars used to determine that *Macbeth* was presented to King James I is that the surviving version of the play is much shorter than the one originally presented at the Globe. Shakespeare adapted the play for the court performance and that adaptation has become the standard version. Shakespeare was mindful of his audience (the King), and was careful to highlight the good qualities of James I's ancestors (Banquo and sons) and to emphasize the role of the witches (to pander to the king's fascination with witches).

Shakespeare, in effect, rewrote history, depicting as a martyr Banquo, who was purportedly a traitorous scoundrel who assisted Macbeth in the murder of Duncan. In modern times, "spin control" experts in public relations do much the same sort of activity, casting the dubious actions of companies and politicians in a more positive light.

Hold a discussion in which students identify instances of "spin control" regarding national figures or corporations. (Examples may include environmental disasters or a television star's clothing line being sewn by underage, underpaid laborers.) Then have students assume the role of a spin control analyst working for Macbeth and offer suggestions for showing him in a more positive light.

◆ Critical Thinking

❶ Analyze Unlikely characters are often clever and wise in Shakespeare's plays. Ask students why it is significant that Macduff's son makes this observation about liars and swearers, when just eight lines earlier he had to ask what a traitor was. *Suggested response: Shakespeare seems to be juxtaposing childlike innocence with a more mature, unadulterated truth. Shakespeare may be implying that children are wiser that the adults around them.*

◆ Critical Thinking

❷ Speculate Ask: Who sent this messenger? Why did Shakespeare include this brief warning in the form of a messenger? *Students may speculate that the messenger was sent by no one; the messenger serves as a plot device to heighten the suspense of the drama.*

LADY MACDUFF. Ay, that he was.

SON. What is a traitor?

LADY MACDUFF. Why, one that swears and lies.[13]

SON. And be all traitors that do so?

LADY MACDUFF. Every one that does so is a traitor, and must be hanged.

SON. And must they all be hanged that swear and lie?

LADY MACDUFF. Every one.

SON. Who must hang them?

LADY MACDUFF. Why, the honest men.

SON. Then the liars and swearers are fools; for there are liars and swearers enow[14] to beat the honest men and hang up them. ❶

LADY MACDUFF. Now, God help thee, poor monkey! But how wilt thou do for a father?

SON. If he were dead, you'd weep for him. If you would not, it were a good sign that I should quickly have a new father.

LADY MACDUFF. Poor prattler, how thou talk'st!

[*Enter a* MESSENGER.]

MESSENGER. Bless you, fair dame! I am not to you known,
Though in your state of honor I am perfect.[15]
I doubt[16] some danger does approach you nearly:
If you will take a homely[17] man's advice,
Be not found here; hence, with your little ones.
To fright you thus, methinks I am too savage;
To do worse to you were fell[18] cruelty,
Which is too nigh your person. Heaven preserve you!
I dare abide no longer. [*Exit* MESSENGER.] ❷

LADY MACDUFF. Whither should I fly?
I have done no harm. But I remember now
I am in this earthly world, where to do harm ❸

13. **swears and lies:** Takes an oath and breaks it.

14. **enow:** Enough.

15. **in . . . perfect:** I am fully informed of your honorable rank.

16. **doubt:** Fear.

17. **homely:** Simple.

18. **fell:** Fierce.

Is often laudable, to do good sometime
Accounted dangerous folly. Why then, alas,
Do I put up that womanly defense,
To say I have done no harm?—What are these faces? ❸

[*Enter* MURDERERS.]

MURDERER. Where is your husband?

LADY MACDUFF. I hope, in no place so unsanctified
Where such as thou mayst find him.

MURDERER. He's a traitor.

SON. Thou li'st, thou shag-eared[19] villain!

19. **shag-eared:** Hairy-eared.

▲ Critical Viewing This engraving shows the murderers menacing Macduff's family. In what way does the artist capture the defiance reflected in IV, ii, 81? **[Interpret]** 

◆ Critical Thinking

❸ **Compare and Contrast** How do Lady Macduff's ideas about herself compare with Lady Macbeth's? *Whereas Lady Macbeth viewed herself as manlike and strong, Lady Macduff views herself as helpless and "womanly."*

▶Critical Viewing◀

❹ **Interpret** As the murderers approach, Lady Macduff's son appears defiant and protective. The expression on Lady Macduff's face is also stern and adversarial.

Humanities: Art

Wood Engraving After Sir John Gilbert. This is a wood engraving made from a drawing by Sir John Gilbert. He created this drawing of Lady Macduff and the murderers for Mackey's *Shakespeare,* an illustrated book in a series that won Gilbert great acclaim as an illustrator. The ease with which the figures are drawn highlights the superior sketching ability that Gilbert achieved through continual practice. This drawing is balanced in terms of motion and placement of the characters, yet it contains a deadly tension.

Use these questions for discussion:

1. Judging from this engraving, how did Sir John Gilbert envision the murderers in Act IV, Scene iii of *Macbeth? Gilbert imagined the murders as large, brutish men against whom Macduff's family would not have a chance.*
2. Does Lady Macduff's protective action seem appropriate given her earlier description of herself as a "wren"? *Students may find Lady Macduff's protective stance and fierce expression appropriate because when a child is threatened with actual danger, a mother's protective instincts take over.*

◆ Critical Thinking

1 Compare and Contrast Ask: How do Malcolm's and Macduff's attitudes differ? *Malcolm is showing a sentimental, emotional side; Macduff is displaying no weakness and remains warrior-like.*

◆ Critical Thinking

2 Analyze Ask: In what ways is Malcolm's comment in line 14 ironic? *Malcolm states that Macduff has yet to suffer personal loss at the hands of Macbeth. However, unbeknown to both of them, Macduff's entire family has just been murdered at the order of Macbeth.*

◆ Critical Thinking

3 Analyze Ask: What evidence in this passage displays Malcolm's wisdom? *Malcolm shows that, although he is young, he is aware of his present danger. He recognizes that Macduff has the power and wherewithal to betray him.*

MURDERER. What, you egg!
[*Stabbing him.*]
Young fry[20] of treachery!

SON. He has killed me, mother:
Run away, I pray you! [*Dies.*]

[*Exit* LADY MACDUFF *crying "Murder!" followed by* MURDERERS.]

Scene iii. *England. Before the King's palace.*
[*Enter* MALCOLM *and* MACDUFF.]

MALCOLM. Let us seek out some desolate shade, and there
Weep our sad bosoms empty.

MACDUFF. Let us rather
Hold fast the mortal[1] sword, and like good men
Bestride our down-fall'n birthdom.[2] Each new morn
New widows howl, new orphans cry, new sorrows
Strike heaven on the face, that it resounds
As if it felt with Scotland and yelled out
Like syllable of dolor.[3]

MALCOLM. What I believe, I'll wail;
What know, believe; and what I can redress,
As I shall find the time to friend,[4] I will.
What you have spoke, it may be so perchance.
This tyrant, whose sole[5] name blisters our tongues,
Was once thought honest:[6] you have loved him well;
He hath not touched you yet. I am young; but something
You may deserve of him through me;[7] and wisdom[8]
To offer up a weak, poor, innocent lamb
T' appease an angry god.

MACDUFF. I am not treacherous.

MALCOLM. But Macbeth is.
A good and virtuous nature may recoil
In an imperial charge.[9] But I shall crave your pardon;
That which you are, my thoughts cannot transpose:[10]
Angels are bright still, though the brightest[11] fell:
Though all things foul would wear[12] the brows of grace,
Yet grace must still look so.[13]

MACDUFF. I have lost my hopes.

20. **fry:** Offspring.

1. **mortal:** Deadly.
2. **Bestride . . . birthdom:** Protectively stand over our native land.
3. **Like . . . dolor:** Similar cry of anguish.
4. **to friend:** Be friendly.
5. **sole:** Very.
6. **honest:** Good.
7. **deserve . . . me:** Earn by betraying me to Macbeth.
8. **wisdom:** It is wise.
9. **recoil . . . charge:** Give way to a royal command.
10. **transpose:** Transform.
11. **the brightest:** Lucifer.
12. **would wear:** Desire to wear.
13. **so:** Like itself.

MALCOLM. Perchance even there where I did find my doubts.
Why in that rawness[14] left you wife and child,
Those precious motives, those strong knots of love,
Without leave-taking? I pray you,
Let not my jealousies[15] be your dishonors.
But mine own safeties.[16] You may be rightly just
Whatever I shall think.

MACDUFF. Bleed, bleed, poor country:
Great tyranny, lay thou thy basis sure,
For goodness dare not check thee: wear thou thy wrongs:
The title is affeered.[17] Fare thee well, lord:
I would not be the villain that thou think'st
For the whole space that's in the tyrant's grasp ❹
And the rich East to boot.

MALCOLM. Be not offended:
I speak not as in absolute fear of you.
I think our country sinks beneath the yoke;
It weeps, it bleeds, and each new day a gash
Is added to her wounds. I think withal
There would be hands uplifted in my right;[18]
And here from gracious England[19] have I offer
Of goodly thousands: but, for all this,
When I shall tread upon the tyrant's head,
Or wear it on my sword, yet my poor country
Shall have more vices than it had before,
More suffer, and more sundry ways than ever,
By him that shall succeed.

MACDUFF. What should he be? ❻

MALCOLM. It is myself I mean, in whom I know
All the particulars of vice so grafted[20]
That, when they shall be opened,[21] black Macbeth
Will seem as pure as snow, and the poor state
Esteem him as a lamb, being compared
With my confineless harms.[22]

MACDUFF. Not in the legions
Of horrid hell can come a devil more damned
In evils to top Macbeth.

MALCOLM. I grant him bloody,
Luxurious,[23] avaricious, false, deceitful,
Sudden,[24] malicious, smacking of every sin
That has a name: but there's no bottom, none,
In my voluptuousness: your wives, your daughters,
Your matrons and your maids, could not fill up

14. **rawness:** Unprotected state or condition.
15. **jealousies:** Suspicions.
16. **safeties:** Protections.
17. **affeered:** Legally confirmed.

❺ **◆ Literary Focus**
Why are the images Malcolm uses to describe Scotland in lines 39–42 more effective than simply stating that the country is in trouble and getting worse?

18. **in my right:** On behalf of my claim.
19. **England:** King of England.
20. **grafted:** Implanted.
21. **opened:** In bloom.
22. **confineless harms:** Unbounded evils.
23. **luxurious:** Lecherous.
24. **Sudden:** Violent.

◆ Build Vocabulary
sundry (sun′ drē) *adj.*: Various; miscellaneous

◆ Grammar and Style
❹ **Possessive Forms** Ask students which apostrophe in this passage indicates a possessive. Is it singular or plural? *Tyrant's is the possessive, and it is singular.*

◆ Literary Focus
❺ **Imagery** Speaking of Scotland in human terms, as being wounded and bloody, gives the passage more impact and immediacy.

◆ Critical Thinking
❻ **Infer** Ask: What's happening here? What is Malcolm's purpose in describing his own vices? *Malcolm is explaining why Scotland will be even more steeped in evil if he becomes king. Students may say that Malcolm is testing Macduff to see if he will remain loyal to him.*

Cross-Curricular Connection: History
The Tragedy of Macbeth was probably performed for King James I and his brother-in-law during the summer of 1606. Scholars believe that Shakespeare wanted to flatter the king, so although the play is rooted in historical fact, Shakespeare did exercise poetic license. For instance, the actual, historical Banquo was an ancestor of King James, so Shakespeare depicted him in his play as being nobler than he in fact was. (Refer students to Act IV, Scene i, lines 112–124, in which Shakespeare depicts Banquo's lineage as being an endless line of descendants to the throne.) In real life, Banquo was a rebel who assisted Macbeth in the assassination of Duncan.

Have interested students go to the library and find Raphael Holinshed's *Chronicles,* which Shakespeare used as the historical source for *Macbeth.* Ask them to report additional information to the class.

◆ Critical Thinking

❶ **Analyze** Do Malcolm's claims about himself seem believable? *No. If these things were really true of him, he probably wouldn't be telling anyone about them. The truly immoral person would be secretive like Macbeth.*

◆ Critical Thinking

❷ **Interpret** Ask: How does Macduff compare this failing with Malcolm's first? How does he reply to Malcolm's confession? *Macduff considers Malcolm's avarice to be more serious than his first failing. Macduff says that Scotland can afford to satisfy Malcolm's greediness.*

◆ Literary Focus

❸ **Imagery** Both images are of milk, something sweet and nourishing, being turned into something evil. Both images reflect the nature of this tragedy, where something good has turned to something bad.

The cistern of my lust, and my desire
All continent impediments[25] would o'erbear,
That did oppose my will. Better Macbeth
Than such an one to reign.

MACDUFF. Boundless intemperance
In nature[26] is a tyranny; it hath been
Th' untimely emptying of the happy throne,
And fall of many kings. But fear not yet
To take upon you what is yours: you may
Convey[27] your pleasures in a spacious plenty,
And yet seem cold, the time you may so hoodwink.
We have willing dames enough. There cannot be
That vulture in you, to devour so many
As will to greatness dedicate themselves,
Finding it so inclined.

MALCOLM. With this there grows
In my most ill-composed affection[28] such
A stanchless[29] avarice that, were I King,
I should cut off the nobles for their lands,
Desire his jewels and this other's house:
And my more-having would be as a sauce
To make me hunger more, that I should forge
Quarrels unjust against the good and loyal,
Destroying them for wealth. ❶

MACDUFF. This avarice
Sticks deeper, grows with more pernicious root
Than summer-seeming[30] lust, and it hath been
The sword of[31] our slain kings. Yet do not fear. ❷
Scotland hath foisons[32] to fill up your will
Of your mere own.[33] All these are portable,[34]
With other graces weighed.

MALCOLM. But I have none: the king-becoming graces,
As justice, verity, temp'rance, stableness,
Bounty, perseverance, mercy, lowliness,
Devotion, patience, courage, fortitude,
I have no relish of them, but abound
In the division of each several crime,[35]
Acting it many ways. Nay, had I pow'r, I should
Pour the sweet milk of concord into hell,
Uproar the universal peace, confound[36]
All unity on earth.

MACDUFF. O Scotland, Scotland!

25. continent impediments: Restraints.

26. nature: Man's nature.

27. Convey: Secretly manage.

28. affection: Character.

29. stanchless: Never-ending.

30. summer-seeming: Summerlike.

31. of: That killed.

32. foisons (foiˊ zənz): Plenty.

33. mere own: Own property.

34. portable: Bearable.

35. division . . . crime: Variations of each kind of crime.

36. confound: Destroy.

❸ **◆ Literary Focus**
How does the image in IV, iii, 98, echo those in I, v, 47–48?

MALCOLM. If such a one be fit to govern, speak:
I am as I have spoken.

MACDUFF. Fit to govern!
No, not to live. O nation miserable!
With an untitled[37] tyrant bloody-sceptered,
When shalt thou see thy wholesome days again,
Since that the truest issue of thy throne[38]
By his own interdiction[39] stands accursed,
And does blaspheme his breed?[40] Thy royal father ❹
Was a most sainted king: the queen that bore thee,
Oft'ner upon her knees than on her feet,
Died[41] every day she lived. Fare thee well!
These evils thou repeat'st upon thyself
Hath banished me from Scotland. O my breast,
Thy hope ends here!

MALCOLM. Macduff, this noble passion,
Child of integrity, hath from my soul
Wiped the black scruples, reconciled my thoughts
To thy good truth and honor. Devilish Macbeth
By many of these trains[42] hath sought to win me
Into his power; and modest wisdom[43] plucks me
From over-credulous haste: but God above
Deal between thee and me! For even now
I put myself to thy direction, and
Unspeak mine own detraction,[44] here abjure
The taints and blames I laid upon myself,
For[45] strangers to my nature. I am yet ❺
Unknown to woman, never was forsworn,
Scarcely have coveted what was mine own,
At no time broke my faith, would not betray
The devil to his fellow, and delight
No less in truth than life. My first false speaking
Was this upon myself. What I am truly,
Is thine and my poor country's to command:
Whither indeed, before thy here-approach,
Old Siward, with ten thousand warlike men,
Already at a point,[46] was setting forth.
Now we'll together, and the chance of goodness
Be like our warranted quarrel![47] Why are you silent?

MACDUFF. Such welcome and unwelcome things at once
'Tis hard to reconcile.

[*Enter a* DOCTOR.]

MALCOLM. Well, more anon. Comes the King forth, I pray you?

37. untitled: Having no right to the throne.

38. truest . . . throne: Child of the true king.

39. interdiction: Exclusion.

40. blaspheme his breed: Slander his ancestry.

41. Died: Prepared for heaven.

42. trains: Enticements.

43. modest wisdom: Prudence.

44. detraction: Slander.

45. For: As.

46. at a point: Prepared.

47. the chance . . . quarrel: May our chance of success equal the justice of our cause.

◆ Build Vocabulary

intemperance (in tem´ pər əns) *n.*: Lack of restraint

avarice (av´ ər is) *n.*: Greed

credulous (krej´ oo ləs) *adj.*: Tending to believe too readily

◆ Critical Thinking

❹ Analyze Ask: Was this the reaction Malcolm was hoping for? Explain. *Yes, in this speech, Macduff reveals his love for the slain Duncan and his intention to leave his beloved Scotland rather than serve someone so evil as Malcolm has made himself out to be.*

◆ Critical Thinking

❺ Interpret Ask: What is happening in this passage? What good news does Malcolm give Macduff? *In this passage, Malcolm reveals that he has been testing Macduff's loyalty. The good news is that Siward is approaching with a large army, and victory is close.*

Speaking and Listening Mini-Lesson

Role Play

This mini-lesson supports the Speaking and Listening activity in the Idea Bank on page 346.

Introduce the Concept Point out to students that role-playing requires them to get "inside" a character and act as the character would in a given situation.

Develop Background Have students prepare to role-play by reading and rereading the lines of both the character they will play and the character with whom they will be conversing.

Apply the Information Let students practice the role-playing interview. Have them take turns practicing, so those who are watching can offer constructive criticism. When finished practicing, the pairs of students can role-play for the class, one pair at a time.

Assess the Outcome Evaluate students based on the realistic relationship of their interviews to the plot of *Macbeth,* the effectiveness of the dialogue, and the quality of their characterizations.

❶ **Enrichment** This brief scene with the doctor is a digression, presumably written to compliment James I. Edward the Confessor supposedly had the power to cure the disease scrofula with his saintly touch. This power and the kings' use of it to cure their subjects appeared to come to an end with James I, who was reluctant to continue the practice until persuaded by his ministers. These lines praise King James's decision.

◆ Reading Strategy

❷ **Use Your Senses** Ross's description appeals mostly to the senses of sight and sound, but the flower also appeals to the sense of smell. This description gives the impression of a chaotic country, helpless and numb to its own suffering.

DOCTOR. Ay, sir. There are a crew of wretched souls
That stay[48] his cure: their malady convinces
The great assay of art;[49] but at his touch,
Such sanctity hath heaven given his hand,
They presently amend.[50]

MALCOLM. I thank you, doctor.
[*Exit* DOCTOR.]

MACDUFF. What's the disease he means?

MALCOLM. 'Tis called the evil:[51] ❶
A most miraculous work in this good King,
Which often since my here-remain in England
I have seen him do. How he solicits heaven,
Himself best knows: but strangely-visited people,
All swoll'n and ulcerous, pitiful to the eye,
The mere[52] despair of surgery, he cures,
Hanging a golden stamp[53] about their necks,
Put on with holy prayers: and 'tis spoken,
To the succeeding royalty he leaves
The healing benediction. With this strange virtue
He hath a heavenly gift of prophecy,
And sundry blessings hang about his throne
That speak him full of grace.

[*Enter* ROSS.]

MACDUFF. See, who comes here?

MALCOLM. My countryman; but yet I know him not.

MACDUFF. My ever gentle[54] cousin, welcome hither.

MALCOLM. I know him now: good God, betimes[55] remove
The means that makes us strangers!

ROSS. Sir, amen.

MACDUFF. Stands Scotland where it did?

ROSS. Alas, poor country!
Almost afraid to know itself! It cannot
Be called our mother but our grave, where nothing[56]
But who knows nothing is once seen to smile;
Where sighs and groans, and shrieks that rent the air,
Are made, not marked, where violent sorrow seems

48. stay: Wait for.
49. convinces . . . art: Defies the efforts of medical science.
50. presently amend: Immediately recover.
51. evil: Scrofula (skräf' yə lə), Skin disease called "the king's evil" because it was believed that it could be cured by the king's touch.
52. mere: Utter.
53. stamp: Coin.
54. gentle: Noble.
55. betimes: Quickly.

❷ **◆ Reading Strategy** To which senses does Ross's description of Scotland in lines 164–174 appeal? How does the description help you envision the state of Scotland?

56. nothing: No one.

Enrichment

Fate Versus Free Will Scholars have long debated whether Macbeth's tragedy results from the inexorable pressures of fate or from his own free choice of evil. This debate tends to focus on the role of the witches. The great Shakespearean scholar George Lyman Kittredge argued that these weird sisters were not just run-of-the-mill crones but arbiters of human destiny. He identified them with the Norns, Scandinavian goddesses of fate:

> The Norns were goddesses who shaped beforehand the life of every man. Sometimes they came in the night and stood by the cradle of the new-born child, uttering their decrees. . . . Sometimes they were met in wild places at unexpected moments. . . . They were great powers of destiny. . . . they not only foresaw the future, but decreed it.

If the Witches do in fact determine Macbeth's fate, then he has no power of choice and is lost from the instant he sets eyes upon them. In this view, he is merely a plaything of fate.

Irving Ribner, among others, argued against this position. He felt that Shakespeare was writing from a Christian rather than a pagan perspective. While Christians acknowledge the reality of evil, in the person of the devil, they believe that God gave humans the power to choose evil or good. Though he is presented with temptation to do wrong, Macbeth chooses his own course. An argument for Macbeth's free will is that Banquo, subject to the same or similar temptation, remains virtuous.

A modern ecstasy.[57] The dead man's knell
Is there scarce asked for who,[58] and good men's lives
Expire before the flowers in their caps,
Dying or ere they sicken. ❸

MACDUFF. O, relation
Too nice,[59] and yet too true!

MALCOLM. What's the newest grief?

ROSS. That of an hour's age doth hiss the speaker;[60]
Each minute teems[61] a new one.

MACDUFF. How does my wife?

ROSS. Why, well.

MACDUFF. And all my children? ❹

ROSS. Well too.

MACDUFF. The tyrant has not battered at their peace?

ROSS. No; they were well at peace when I did leave 'em.

MACDUFF. Be not a niggard of your speech: how goes 't?

ROSS. When I came hither to transport the tidings,
Which I have heavily borne, there ran a rumor
Of many worthy fellows that were out; [62]
Which was to my belief witnessed[63] the rather,
For that I saw the tyrant's power[64] afoot.
Now is the time of help. Your eye in Scotland
Would create soldiers, make our women fight,
To doff[65] their dire distresses. ❺

MALCOLM. Be 't their comfort
We are coming thither. Gracious England hath
Lent us good Siward and ten thousand men;
An older and a better soldier none
That Christendom gives out.

ROSS. Would I could answer
This comfort with the like! But I have words
That would be howled out in the desert air,
Where hearing should not latch[66] them.

57. modern ecstasy: Ordinary emotion.
58. The dead . . . who: People can no longer keep track of Macbeth's victims.
59. nice: Exact.
60. That . . . speaker: Report of the grief of an hour ago is hissed as stale news.
61. teems: Gives birth to.
62. out: In rebellion.
63. witnessed: Confirmed.
64. power: Army.
65. doff: Put off.
66. latch: Catch.

◆ Grammar and Style

❸ **Possessive Forms:** Ask students to explain the difference between *man's* and *men's* in this passage. *Man's refers to a single person's death knell; men's refers to the lives of more than one man.*

◆ Literature and Your Life

❹ Ross hesitates to tell Macduff the unpleasant truth about his wife and son. Ask students if they have ever been in a situation where they hesitated before delivering an unpleasant message. *Students may say they hesitated to tell their parents they had broken something, or they may say they had a hard time breaking up with a girlfriend or boyfriend.*

◆ Critical Thinking

❺ **Interpret** Ask: What opinion of Malcolm does Ross have? Explain. *Ross believes that Malcolm's presence in Scotland would inspire more people to take up his cause and defeat Macbeth.*

◆ Critical Thinking

❶ **Deduce** Ask: Whom is Malcolm addressing? What is his advice? *Malcolm is addressing Macduff; he tells him not to hold in his grief, but to release his sorrows.*

◆ Critical Thinking

❷ **Interpret** Ask: What does Macduff mean by "He has no children"? How is this comment ironic in light of Malcolm's comment in Act III, Scene iii, line 13? *Macduff implies that Malcolm cannot possibly fathom the depth of Macduff's despair because Malcolm has no children. This statement is ironic because in the earlier scene, Malcolm states that Macduff could not possibly feel the same hatred for Macbeth because Macduff had not been personally attacked by him.*

◆ Literary Focus

❸ **Imagery** Point out to students that Shakespeare follows up on the bird imagery introduced in Act IV Scene ii with these images of the hell-kite and the chickens. Ask students to consider why Shakespeare might have chosen images of birds as opposed to flies or other creatures that can be trapped. *Shakespeare might have chosen birds because birds are usually looked upon by humans as being naturally free. He also might have chosen birds because birds navigate the winds in the way that humans navigate the more figurative winds of fate.*

MACDUFF. What concern they?
The general cause or is it a fee-grief[67]
Due to some single breast?

ROSS. No mind that's honest
But in it shares some woe, though the main part
Pertains to you alone.

MACDUFF. If it be mine,
Keep it not from me, quickly let me have it.

ROSS. Let not your ears despise my tongue for ever,
Which shall possess them with the heaviest sound
That ever yet they heard.

MACDUFF. Humh! I guess at it.

ROSS. Your castle is surprised; your wife and babes
Savagely slaughtered. To relate the manner,
Were, on the quarry[68] of these murdered deer,
To add the death of you.

MALCOLM. Merciful heaven!
What, man! Ne'er pull your hat upon your brows;
Give sorrow words. The grief that does not speak
Whispers the o'er-fraught heart[69] and bids it break. ❶

MACDUFF. My children too?

ROSS. Wife, children, servants, all
That could be found.

MACDUFF. And I must be from thence!
My wife killed too?

ROSS. I have said.

MALCOLM. Be comforted.
Let's make us med'cines of our great revenge,
To cure this deadly grief.

MACDUFF. He has no children. All my pretty ones? ❷
Did you say all? O hell-kite![70] All?
What, all my pretty chickens and their dam ❸
At one fell swoop?

67. **fee-grief:** Personal grief.

68. **quarry:** Heap of game slain in a hunt.

69. **o'er-fraught:** Overburdened.

70. **hell-kite:** Hellish bird of prey.

MALCOLM. Dispute it[71] like a man.

MACDUFF. I shall do so;
But I must also feel it as a man.
I cannot but remember such things were,
That were most precious to me. Did heaven look on,
And would not take their part? Sinful Macduff,
They were all struck for thee! Naught[72] that I am,
Not for their own demerits but for mine
Fell slaughter on their souls. Heaven rest them now! ❹

MALCOLM. Be this the whetstone of your sword. Let grief
Convert to anger; blunt not the heart, enrage it.

MACDUFF. O, I could play the woman with mine eyes,
And braggart with my tongue! But, gentle heavens,
Cut short all intermission; front to front[73]
Bring thou this fiend of Scotland and myself;
Within my sword's length set him. If he 'scape,
Heaven forgive him too!

MALCOLM. This time goes manly.
Come, go we to the King. Our power is ready;
Our lack is nothing but our leave.[74] Macbeth
Is ripe for shaking, and the pow'rs above
Put on their instruments.[75] Receive what cheer you may.
The night is long that never finds the day. [*Exit.*]

71. **Dispute it:** Counter your grief.

72. **Naught:** Wicked.

73. **front to front:** Face to face.

74. **Our . . . leave:** We need only to take our leave.

75. **Put . . . instruments:** Urge us onward as their agents.

◆ Critical Thinking

❹ **Interpret** Ask: Whom does Macduff blame? Why? *Macduff blames himself because his actions caused Macbeth to seek retaliation, and he was not at home to defend his family.*

Reinforce and Extend

Answers

◆ Literature and Your Life

Reader's Response Suggested responses: Yes, Macduff was to blame. He could have secured his castle with guards and warned his family of potential danger, or taken his family with him to England. No, Macduff was blameless. He couldn't have foreseen the extent of Macbeth's wrath.

Thematic Focus England has an immense army at its disposal to support Malcolm's claim to Scotland's throne.

☑ Check Your Comprehension

1. (a) The first apparition tells Macbeth to beware of Macduff. (b) The second apparition says that none of woman born shall harm Macbeth. (c) The third apparition tells Macbeth that he'll not be vanquished until Birnam Wood comes to Dunsinane.
2. They are all slaughtered by Macbeth and his men.
3. Malcolm tests Macduff by claiming to be worse than Macbeth.
4. Macduff says he cannot support Malcolm in his quest to rule Scotland if he is indeed worse than Macbeth.
5. Ross tells Malcolm that England has provided ten thousand soldiers to fight against Macbeth. Then he sadly tells Macduff about the murder of his family and entire household.

Guide for Responding

◆ Literature and Your Life

Reader's Response Do you blame Macduff for abandoning his family? Why or why not?

Thematic Focus In what way does the English monarch influence events in Scotland?

☑ Check Your Comprehension

1. Briefly summarize what each of the three apparitions tells Macbeth and what the final vision shows him.
2. What happens to Macduff's family?
3. How does Malcolm test Macduff?
4. What convinces Malcolm that Macduff is trustworthy?
5. What news does Ross bring from Scotland?

◆ Critical Thinking

INTERPRET

1. Why does Macbeth accept the predictions made by the second and third apparitions? **[Analyze]**
2. What does the murder of Macduff's family suggest about Macbeth's state of mind? **[Draw Conclusions]**
3. What does the dialogue in IV, iii, reveal about Malcolm's character? **[Analyze]**
4. How would you characterize Macduff based on his reaction to the murder of his wife and son? **[Interpret]**

APPLY

5. In staging Macbeth, some producers eliminate IV, ii. Indicate why they might make this cut, and state your reaction to it. **[Speculate]**

◆ Critical Thinking

1. Because the witches' prophecies made earlier came true, Macbeth assumes these predictions are accurate, too. Rather than wonder if they are told in some riddle form, he quickly assumes he is safe until he dies of old age.
2. Macbeth has degenerated into total madness and murderous insanity. He has become an insatiable, monstrous fiend.
3. Malcolm is a cautious man, testing Macduff, but he is no fool and shows the glimmerings of being a great leader. He reacts to Macduff's sorrow with a righteous anger to convert Macduff's grief to rage and thus avenge his family's death.
4. Macduff reacts as a deeply loving man who cannot take in the enormity of his entire family's death. He responds to Malcolm, who chides him to control his grief, with "But I must also feel it as a man."
5. This scene is the murder of Macduff's family, so some producers might feel it is too violent. Some students might agree, but others would respond that cutting this scene would lessen the emotional impact of the play.

Answers

◆ Reading Strategy

1. Shakespeare appeals largely to the sense of hearing: sighs, groans, shrieks, and sounds of anguish.
2. Scotland is a country torn by violence, death, and sorrow.

◆ Literary Focus

1. (a) Macbeth intends to murder Macduff's family so that his entire lineage will be wiped out.
   (b) Babies represent future generations, and thus the future.
2. (a) Scene iii, lines 140–146 and Scene iii, lines 170–174 contain imagery of sickness and disease.
   (b) Macbeth is the disease, and Malcolm is the cure.

◆ Grammar and Style

1. the Macbeths'; 2. Fleance's; 3. the witches'; 4. the women's; 5. Ross's; 6. Lennox's

◆ Build Vocabulary

Using the Word Root *-cred-*

incredible: not credible, unbelievable; *credulous:* easily convinced; *incredulous:* not easily convinced; *credible:* believable; *credulity:* a tendency to believe too readily

Using the Word Bank

1. Macbeth's influence is *pernicious;* he is evil and destructive.
2. Malcolm is the most *judicious;* he is cautious and wise.
3. *Sundry* items include eye of newt, toe of frog, wool of bat and so on.
4. Yes, *intemperance* caused Macbeth's downfall. He showed a total lack of restraint and excessive behavior.
5. Ambition can become a kind of *avarice* when it crosses the line into greed.
6. Malcolm, although young, doesn't believe anyone too readily.

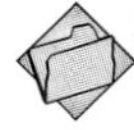

Idea Bank

Customizing for
Learning Modalities

Following are suggestions for matching Idea Bank topics with your students' learning modalities:

Verbal/Linguistic: 3
Visual/ Spatial: 2
Interpersonal: 3

Guide for Responding *(continued)*

◆ Reading Strategy

Use Your Senses

By **using your senses** as you read *Macbeth,* you experience the play more powerfully. For example, the descriptions of the cauldron in IV, i, address the senses of sight, sound, and touch. Many of these images are repellent, but they reveal in a powerful way the evil that Macbeth has chosen.

1. To which senses does Shakespeare appeal in Ross's description of Scotland (IV, iii, 164–173)?
2. Briefly describe the overall impression of Scotland that these images convey.

◆ Literary Focus

Imagery

The varied sensory descriptions in Shakespeare's **imagery** not only add liveliness to the play, but also contribute to its meaning. In Act IV, i, for example, the second and third apparitions are babies, "a Bloody Child" and a child "who wears upon his baby-brow the round / And top of sovereignty." These images reflect Macbeth's concern about who will inherit the throne.

1. (a) How does Macbeth's final speech in this scene indicate that he's making war on babies? (b) In what way is a war against babies a war against the future itself?
2. (a) Find two passages in Act IV with images of sickness. (b) Explain how these images relate to the conflict between Macbeth and Malcolm.

◆ Grammar and Style

Possessive Forms

Most singular nouns and plural nouns not ending in *s* form the **possessive** by adding an apostrophe and *s.* Plural nouns ending in *s* just add an apostrophe. Do not use an apostrophe to make a word plural.

Practice Write possessives for the following nouns:

1. the Macbeths **3.** the witches **5.** Ross
2. Fleance **4.** the women **6.** Lennox

◆ Build Vocabulary

Using the Word Root *-cred-*

The root *-cred-* means "belief." Use these word parts to build five *-cred-* words:

in- *-ulous* *-ible* *-ulity*

Write the meanings of these words. Verify your definitions by referring to a dictionary.

Using the Word Bank

In your notebook, answer each question.

1. Whose influence in this play is the most *pernicious?* Why?
2. Which character do you think is most *judicious?* Why?
3. If you were staging IV, i, what *sundry* items might you have lying around the witches' haunt?
4. Does *intemperance,* rather than ambition, cause Macbeth's downfall? Explain.
5. Is ambition a kind of *avarice?* Why or why not?
6. How would you refute someone claiming that Malcolm is too *credulous* to rule Scotland?

Idea Bank

Writing

1. **Malcolm Wants You!** As a consultant to Malcolm, write a flyer he could use to recruit soldiers. The flyer should motivate young working-class Englishmen to join the army that will be invading Scotland. **[Social Studies Link]**

2. **Plot Analysis** Often the fourth act in a five-act Shakespearean drama discloses a crucial shift, or turning point, in the play's action. Explain why this is or is not the case in *Macbeth.* Refer to specific passages in Act IV of the play to support your analysis.

Speaking and Listening

3. **Role Play** With a small group, role-play an interview between Malcolm's staff and a young Englishman who wants to join their cause. Have the staff test the young man's motivation and abilities. **[Performing Arts Link]**

Customizing for
Performance Levels

Following are suggestions for matching Idea Bank topics with your students' ability levels:

Less Advanced Students: 1
Average Students: 3
More Advanced Students: 2

✓ ASSESSMENT OPTIONS

Formal Assessment, Selection Test, pp. 74–76, and Assessment Resources Software. The selection test is designed so that it can be easily customized to the ability levels of your students.

Alternative Assessment, p. 15, includes options for less advanced students, more advanced students, visual and spatial learners, and auditory learners.

PORTFOLIO ASSESSMENT

Use the following rubrics and assessment guidelines in the Alternative Assessment booklet to assess student writing:
Speech of Welcome: Self-Assessment: Speech, p. 118
Comparison and Contrast: Comparison/Contrast Rubric, p. 104

Guide for Interpreting, Act V

◆ Review and Anticipate

In Act IV, Macbeth learns from the witches that he must "Beware Macduff" but that he need not fear any man "of woman born." He also learns that he will never be vanquished until the forest itself marches against him. However, he sees a vision indicating that Banquo will indeed father a long line of kings.

Armed with his new knowledge, Macbeth orders the murder of Macduff's wife and son. Macduff himself is in England to join forces with Malcolm and is overcome when he hears the news. Nevertheless, he and Malcolm will lead an army against Macbeth.

Act V will determine the outcome as Macbeth, grown reckless in evil, battles against Malcolm and his men.

◆ Literary Focus

SHAKESPEAREAN TRAGEDY

In **Shakespearean tragedy**, the central character is a person of high rank and personal quality. Through some fatal weakness—a **tragic flaw**—this person is enmeshed in events that lead to his or her downfall. As the audience views the destruction of this character, its members experience a mixture of pity, fear, and awe that lifts them out of their everyday lives.

At the beginning of this play, the hero, Macbeth, is pictured as courageous and loyal. By the end of the play, his ambition has driven him to commit a series of horrendous acts. Shakespeare, however, adds nobility to Macbeth's destruction by giving him a reckless bravery in Act V—even when everything is lost. This courage in the face of impossible odds reminds us of the man's stature and increases the awe that his downfall inspires.

◆ Grammar and Style

PRONOUNS AND ANTECEDENTS

Like other writers, Shakespeare uses **pronouns** to avoid the monotony of repeating names. The word or group of words to which a pronoun refers is its **antecedent**. Pronouns and their antecedents must agree in gender and number.

The English pow'r is near, led on by Malcolm,
His uncle Siward and the good Macduff.

The pronoun *His* agrees with its antecedent, *Malcolm*, in gender (masculine) and number (singular).

◆ Reading Strategy

INFER BELIEFS OF THE PERIOD

Great plays are timeless, but they are also historical documents. As products of a certain era, they reflect the **beliefs** and assumptions of those who lived during that period. You can **infer** those beliefs by looking carefully at the ideas the characters express and comparing them to modern ideas on the same subject.

In *Macbeth V, i,* for example, you have the opportunity to watch a doctor in action. Listen carefully to what he says about a case of mental disturbance, and compare his ideas with those that a modern psychologist might express.

◆ Build Vocabulary

WORD ROOTS: *-turb-*

As you read Act V, you will encounter the word *perturbation*. The root of this word, *-turb-*, means "to disturb." To experience perturbation is "to experience a great disturbance."

WORD BANK

Before you read, preview this list of words from Act V of *Macbeth*.

perturbation
pristine
clamorous
harbingers

Prepare and Engage

OBJECTIVES

1. To read, interpret, and respond to an Elizabethan drama
2. To relate an Elizabethan drama to personal experience
3. To deepen comprehension by inferring from the literature beliefs of the period
4. To identify elements of Shakespearean tragedy
5. To build vocabulary in context and learn the root word *-turb-*
6. To recognize the antecedents of pronouns
7. To write an analysis of a play using precise details
8. To respond to *Macbeth* through writing, speaking and listening, and projects

SKILLS INSTRUCTION

Vocabulary: Word Roots: *-turb-*
Grammar: Pronouns and Antecedents
Reading Strategy: Infer Beliefs of the Period
Literary Focus: Shakespearean Tragedy
Writing: Precise Details
Speaking and Listening: Battlefield Report (teacher edition)
Critical Viewing: Infer

PORTFOLIO OPPORTUNITIES

Writing: Independence Day (proclamation); Dear Diary; Response to Criticism
Writing Mini-Lesson: Macbeth: The Film Version?
Speaking and Listening: Performance; Battlefield Report
Projects: Set Design; Macbeth, the Opera

Interest Grabber Review the last three predictions made by the apparitions in Act IV.

- Macbeth should beware Macduff.
- No man born of woman shall ever harm Macbeth.
- Macbeth will never be vanquished until Birnam Wood come to Dunsinane.

Solicit ideas from the class about how these predictions may or may not come true. Also ask students to predict what will become of Lady Macbeth.

Prentice Hall Literature Program Resources

REINFORCE / RETEACH / EXTEND

Selection Support Pages
Build Vocabulary: Word Roots: *-turb-*, p. 75
Grammar and Style: Pronouns and Antecedents, p. 76
Reading Strategy: Infer Beliefs of the Period, p. 77
Literary Focus: Shakespearean Tragedy, p. 78

Strategies for Diverse Student Needs, p. 16

Beyond Literature
Community Connection: Qualities of Leadership, p. 16

Formal Assessment Selection Test, p. 77–79; Assessment Resources Software

Alternative Assessment, p. 16

Listening to Literature Audiocassettes
The Tragedy of Macbeth, Act V

Develop Understanding

One-Minute Insight

This act shows with great poignancy the final effects of Macbeth's actions on himself, his wife, and the kingdom of Scotland. As the act begins, Macbeth has fortified himself behind the stone walls of Dunsinane, armed with the prophecy of the apparitions. Lady Macbeth had suffered a mental and emotional breakdown. As the army of angry Scots who are determined to overthrow Macbeth approaches, Lady Macbeth kills herself. What's left of Macbeth's former glory will not allow him to die without a fight.

The final speech by Malcolm is meant to lift the mood of the audience. However, this play's main message is a dark one: Even the noblest and most heroic humans can fall into the depths of depravity and ruin.

Enrichment Point out to students that most of this scene is in prose. Explain to them that class differences were apparent through spoken language and that servants spoke in a more simple, plain language than did their superiors. Some scholars also note that Shakespeare might have used prose here as a temporary relief from the intensity of the scene.

◆ Reading Strategy

❶ Infer Beliefs of the Period Draw students' attention to the gentlewoman's hesitation to report, without a witness to back her up, what she has heard Lady Macbeth confess in her sleep. Ask: What sort of protection might the woman have had under the justice system of the time? *Because of her hesitancy to speak without a witness, chances are the woman would have had little or no chance of being believed by others. This may be because she was of a lower social status or because women in general needed male corroboration to be taken seriously.*

◆ Grammar and Style

❷ Pronouns and Antecedents Ask students: What is the antecedent for the pronoun *their*? *Eyes in line 25 is the antecedent for the pronoun* their.

Act V

Scene i. *Dunsinane. In the castle.*
[*Enter a* DOCTOR OF PHYSIC *and a* WAITING-GENTLEWOMAN.]

DOCTOR. I have two nights watched with you, but can perceive no truth in your report. When was it she last walked?

GENTLEWOMAN. Since his Majesty went into the field.[1] I have seen her rise from her bed, throw her nightgown upon her, unlock her closet,[2] take forth paper, fold it, write upon 't, read it, afterwards seal it, and again return to bed; yet all this while in a most fast sleep.

DOCTOR. A great perturbation in nature, to receive at once the benefit of sleep and do the effects of watching![3] In this slumb'ry agitation, besides her walking, and other actual performances, what, at any time, have you heard her say?

GENTLEWOMAN. That, sir, which I will not report after her.

DOCTOR. You may to me, and 'tis most meet[4] you should.

GENTLEWOMAN. Neither to you nor anyone, having no witness to confirm my speech. ❶

[*Enter* LADY MACBETH, *with a taper.*]

Lo you, here she comes! This is her very guise,[5] and, upon my life, fast asleep! Observe her; stand close.[6]

DOCTOR. How came she by that light?

GENTLEWOMAN. Why, it stood by her. She has light by her continually. 'Tis her command.

DOCTOR. You see, her eyes are open.

GENTLEWOMAN. Ay, but their sense[7] are shut. ❷

DOCTOR. What is it she does now? Look, how she rubs her hands.

GENTLEWOMAN. It is an accustomed action with her,

1. **field:** Battlefield.
2. **closet:** Chest.
3. **effects of watching:** Deeds of one awake.
4. **meet:** Suitable.
5. **guise:** Custom.
6. **close:** Hidden.
7. **sense:** Powers of sight.

◆ Build Vocabulary

perturbation (pur´ tər bā´ shən) *n.*: Disturbance

Block Scheduling Strategies

Consider these suggestions to take advantage of extended class time.

- Introduce students to Shakespearean Tragedy in the Literary Focus on page 347. As they read the selection, have them respond to the Literary Focus notes within the text and answer Literary Focus questions on page 362.
- Play Scenes vi, vii, and viii of Act V from the **Listening to Literature Audiocassettes** and encourage students to visualize the battlefield action taking place.
- Have students respond to the question in Thematic Focus on page 361. Then hold a class discussion about the theme of Macbeth.
- Have small groups of students discuss the Critical Thinking questions on page 362.
- Allow students to choose and complete one of the projects in the Idea Bank on page 363.

Lady Macbeth Sleepwalking, Henry Fuseli, Louvre, Paris

▲ **Critical Viewing** What can you infer about Lady Macbeth's state of mind from her facial expressions and gestures? **[Infer]** ❸

▶Critical Viewing◀

❸ **Infer** Students might point out that the fearful expression of Lady Macbeth's eyes and slightly opened mouth reveal a mind plagued with terrifying thoughts. The sweeping gesture of her left arm suggests she is pushing something back, as if in resistance to the visions of horror her sleeping mind cannot escape. Students might mention how tightly she seems to be grasping the torch, as a form of light and comfort, to help her fight off her fears.

Customize for *English Language Learners*

Point out to these students that Shakespeare often employs sentence inversion, which is rarely heard in modern spoken English. For example in line 12 of Scene ii, Caithness says, "Great Dunsinane he strongly fortifies." In modern English the sentence becomes "He strongly fortifies Great Dunsinane." Encourage them to identify the main subjects and verbs in difficult passages.

Enrichment Explain to students that the ritual of washing one's hands to try to remove guilt has a long history. Perhaps the most famous example occurs in the Bible when Pontius Pilate, Roman governor of Judea, washes his hands in public before releasing Jesus to the crowd. Pilate, who found no harm in the religious leader, sought to absolve himself of any part of his death. Today, when people say "I wash my hands of the matter," it means they want nothing more to do with the situation and take no further responsibility.

Humanities: Art

Lady Macbeth Sleepwalking by Henry Fuseli.

After moving to London in 1764, Henry Fuseli saw many of Shakespeare's plays. These plays inspired him to explore the shadowy realm of dream-worlds. It is no wonder this powerful scene of sleepwalking inspired him to capture, in pen and gray-wash, the nightmarish vision of a tormented Lady Macbeth succumbing to her fears. The painting was probably completed in 1775–1776. It is 30.7 cm x 43.2 cm and hangs in the British Museum in London.

Use these questions for discussion:

1. How well does this painting capture the feel of the sleepwalking scene? How does your own mental image of the scene compare with the one in the painting? *Students may say that the painting captures the agitation suffered by Lady Macbeth. Students may say that this painting differs from their own mental image, because Lady Macbeth seems stronger and more vibrant than the character they pictured.*
2. In what ways do the colors used in the painting capture the mood of the sleepwalking scene? *The yellow color of Lady Macbeth's gown and her vivid red hair make her the focal point of the painting. The shadowy dark colors used in the background emphasize that this is a nightmarish scene.*

◆ Critical Thinking

❶ **Interpret** Ask students to point out the irony of Lady Macbeth's words here. Also ask them to speculate on the causes of Lady Macbeth's mental state as they are revealed through this speech. *Students should refer to her advice to her husband when she told him to wash the blood from his hands. They should point out that she is weighted down by her husband's fear, because in order to fight it, she must mask her own. Her own hidden fears and guilt contribute to her unstable mental state.*

◆ Critical Thinking

❷ **Analyze** Ask: What do these statements indicate about Lady Macbeth's state of mind? *Lady Macbeth may be missing her former life as wife of Thane of Fife (Macbeth's title at the start of the play). She seems to be feeling deserted by her husband as he's gone forward in his evil deeds.*

◆ Literary Focus

❸ **Shakespearean Tragedy** Ask: In what ways is Lady Macbeth a tragic figure? *Lady Macbeth is tragic because although she showed no compunction at performing evil deeds early in the play, it seems that her consciousness has caught up with her and that she is suffering and alone.*

to seem thus washing her hands: I have known her continue in this a quarter of an hour.

LADY MACBETH. Yet here's a spot.

DOCTOR. Hark! She speaks. I will set down what comes from her, to satisfy[8] my remembrance the more strongly.

LADY MACBETH. Out, damned spot! Out, I say! One: two: why, then 'tis time to do 't. Hell is murky. Fie, my lord, fie! A soldier, and afeard? What need we fear who knows it, when none can call our pow'r to accompt?[9] Yet who would have thought the old man to have had so much blood in him? ❶

DOCTOR. Do you mark that?

LADY MACBETH. The Thane of Fife had a wife. Where is she now? What, will these hands ne'er be clean? No more o' that, my lord, no more o' that! You mar all with this starting. ❷

DOCTOR. Go to, go to! You have known what you should not.

GENTLEWOMAN. She has spoke what she should not, I am sure of that. Heaven knows what she has known.

LADY MACBETH. Here's the smell of the blood still. All the perfumes of Arabia will not sweeten this little hand. Oh, oh, oh! ❸

DOCTOR. What a sigh is there! The heart is sorely charged.[10]

GENTLEWOMAN. I would not have such a heart in my bosom for the dignity[11] of the whole body.

DOCTOR. Well, well, well—

GENTLEWOMAN. Pray God it be, sir.

DOCTOR. This disease is beyond my practice. Yet I have known those which have walked in their sleep who have died holily in their beds.

LADY MACBETH. Wash your hands; put on your nightgown; look not so pale! I tell you yet again, Banquo's

8. **satisfy:** Support.

9. **to accompt:** Into account.

10. **charged:** Burdened.

11. **dignity:** Worth.

An Actor's Response

"[Macbeth] . . . has been continually pouring out his miseries to his wife. His heart has therefore been eased, from time to time, by unloading its weight of woe; while she, on the contrary, has perseveringly endured in silence the uttermost anguish of a wounded spirit."

—Sarah Siddons

Preparing for Standardized Tests

Reading and Vocabulary The reading skill of inferring beliefs of the period will help students on standardized tests. Making inferences is a key skill that is tested in both reading comprehension and critical reading portions of tests. For further practice, give students the Reading Strategy page on Inferring Beliefs of the period, p. 77, in ***Selection Support.***

Grammar and Language Understanding the relationship between pronouns and antecedents will help students in tests of English usage and in those portions of standardized tests in which they are to revise text passages. Students need to know the relationship between a pronoun and its antecedent in order to be able to make pronouns agree and to avoid vague and ambiguous references. For more practice, use the Grammar and Style page on Pronouns and Antecedents, p. 76, in ***Selection Support.***

buried. He cannot come out on 's[12] grave. ❹

DOCTOR. Even so?

LADY MACBETH. To bed, to bed! There's knocking at
the gate. Come, come, come, come, give me your hand!
What's done cannot be undone. To bed, to bed, to bed! ❺
[*Exit* LADY MACBETH.]

DOCTOR. Will she go now to bed?

GENTLEWOMAN. Directly.

DOCTOR. Foul whisp'rings are abroad. Unnatural deeds
Do breed unnatural troubles. Infected minds
To their deaf pillows will discharge their secrets.
More needs she the divine than the physician.
God, God forgive us all! Look after her;
Remove from her the means of all annoyance,[13]
And still keep eyes upon her. So good night.
My mind she has mated[14] and amazed my sight:
I think, but dare not speak.

GENTLEWOMAN. Good night, good doctor.
[*Exit.*]

12. **on 's:** Of his.

❻ ◆ **Reading Strategy** What can you infer about medicine and disease during this time from the doctor's words in V, i, 72–80?

13. **annoyance:** Injury.

14. **mated:** Baffled.

Scene ii. *The country near Dunsinane.*
[*Drum and colors. Enter* MENTEITH, CAITHNESS, ANGUS, LENNOX, SOLDIERS.]

MENTEITH. The English pow'r[1] is near, led on by Malcolm,
His uncle Siward and the good Macduff.
Revenges burn in them; for their dear causes
Would to the bleeding and the grim alarm
Excite the mortified man.[2]

ANGUS. Near Birnam Wood
Shall we well meet them; that way are they coming.

CAITHNESS. Who knows if Donalbain be with his brother?

LENNOX. For certain, sir, he is not. I have a file[3]
Of all the gentry: there is Siward's son,
And many unrough[4] youths that even now
Protest[5] their first of manhood.

MENTEITH. What does the tyrant?

1. **pow'r:** Army.

2. **Would . . . man:** Would incite a dead man to join the bloody, grim call to arms.

3. **file:** List.

4. **unrough:** Beardless.

5. **Protest:** Assert.

◆ Critical Thinking

❹ **Analyze** Point out to students that scholars disagree about whether or not Lady Macbeth sees Banquo's ghost at the banquet or if Macbeth alone sees it. Ask: What does this line indicate to you? *Students may say that Lady Macbeth says this because she thinks Macbeth was hallucinating when he saw Banquo's ghost; other students may say this line is inconclusive because Lady Macbeth may be trying to shield and bolster Macbeth.*

◆ Critical Thinking

❺ **Connect** Ask: To what previous event might Lady Macbeth be referring in this passage? *Lady Macbeth seems to be recalling the night when Duncan was murdered. The knocking at the gate (II, iii) occurred when the porter was slow to answer Macduff's hails.*

◆ Reading Strategy

❻ **Infer Beliefs of the Period** Students should note that the doctor recognizes that Lady Macbeth's illness stems not from physical suffering, but from emotional suffering. The medicine of the time was unable to treat psychiatric illnesses that can be treated today. Realizing the depth of her emotional suffering, he admits that while he is unable to help her, perhaps God could. Students should remark that the doctor's willingness to call on divine aid represents a blending of religion and medicine that was characteristic of the time.

Customize for *Less Proficient Readers*

This scene sets the stage for the battle that follows. Help these readers follow the plot by looking for key words in this passage. At what point does the reader know which side the Scottish men are on? Direct them to line 3 for clues to the direction of the plot. *Key words include: Macduff . . . Revenges burn . . . for their . . . causes; Readers know which side the Scottish men are on when they begin talking of revenge.*

Cross-Curricular Connection: History

As the play closes, Duncan's son Malcolm takes the throne of Scotland. In reality, Malcolm does become king in 1057, seventeen years after Duncan's death. He reigned as Malcolm III Canmore for thirty-five years.

Malcolm had been protected during exile by Edward the Confessor and was later able to return the favor to England. After England was defeated in the Battle of Hastings in 1066 by William of Normandy, the grandchildren of Edmund Ironside, half-brother to Edward the Confessor, fled in exile to Scotland to be protected by Malcolm. The names of the grandchildren were Edgar and Margaret. Malcolm and Margaret eventually married.

After the brief reign of Malcolm's brother, Donalbain, three of Malcolm and Margaret's sons ruled in succession. It was from the last of these sons, David I, that all future kings of Scotland, including the Stuarts, descended. Queen Elizabeth II is the twenty-eighth generation of this line.

Have one or more students draw a chart of the line of succession of Scottish Kings, highlighting the names included in the play *Macbeth*.

◆ Literary Focus

❶ Shakespearean Tragedy Students who agree Macbeth is mad should support their answers by pointing out that the theme of evil runs throughout the play, and that Macbeth has become evil and cannot redeem himself. His lack of restraint or human caring at this point might indicate madness. Those who say he is not mad might state that he was led on to perform evil deeds by outside forces, but is suffering for them now. They might mention that it is a weakness of character, not madness, that drives his actions.

◆ Critical Thinking

❷ Analyze Have students explain the clothes imagery in Angus's speech. What is he saying about Macbeth's character? *He is saying that Macbeth, with his flawed character, is not a great enough person to fulfill the role of king. He points out that what Macbeth did, in an attempt at power and glory, is now common knowledge and reveals him to be a weak, despicable character, not an honorable one.*

◆ Critical Thinking

❸ Analyze Remind students that this is Macbeth's first appearance since his conversation with the witches. Tell them to note the change in his demeanor, referring to specific lines and phrases. *He seems more determined, perhaps even overly confident, as though trying to cover up deeper doubts. He repeats the prophesy to himself, as reassurance.*

CAITHNESS. Great Dunsinane he strongly fortifies.
Some say he's mad; others, that lesser hate him,
Do call it valiant fury: but, for certain,
He cannot buckle his distempered cause
Within the belt of rule.[6]

ANGUS. Now does he feel
His secret murders sticking on his hands;
Now minutely revolts upbraid his faith-breach.[7]
Those he commands move only in command,
Nothing in love. Now does he feel his title
Hang loose about him, like a giant's robe ❷
Upon a dwarfish thief.

MENTEITH. Who then shall blame
His pestered[8] senses to recoil and start,
When all that is within him does condemn
Itself for being there?

CAITHNESS. Well, march we on,
To give obedience where 'tis truly owed.
Meet we the med'cine of the sickly weal,[9]
And with him pour we, in our country's purge,
Each drop of us.[10]

LENNOX. Or so much as it needs
To dew the sovereign flower and drown the weeds.[11]
Make we our march towards Birnam.
[*Exit, marching.*]

Scene iii. *Dunsinane. In the castle.*
[*Enter* MACBETH, DOCTOR, *and* ATTENDANTS.]

MACBETH. Bring me no more reports; let them fly all![1]
Till Birnam Wood remove to Dunsinane
I cannot taint[2] with fear. What's the boy Malcolm?
Was he not born of woman? The spirits that know
All mortal consequences[3] have pronounced me thus:
"Fear not, Macbeth; no man that's born of woman
Shall e'er have power upon thee." Then fly, false thanes,
And mingle with the English epicures.[4]
The mind I sway[5] by and the heart I bear
Shall never sag with doubt nor shake with fear. ❸

[*Enter* SERVANT.]

◆ Literary Focus ❶ Do you agree with those that Caithness quotes—Is Macbeth "mad"? Why or why not?

6. **rule:** Self-control.

7. **minutely . . . faith-breach:** Every minute revolts rebuke his disloyalty.

8. **pestered:** Tormented.

9. **Med'cine . . . weal:** Malcolm and his supporters are "the medicine" that will heal "the sickly" commonwealth.

10. **Each . . . us:** Every last drop of our blood.

11. **dew . . . weeds:** Water the royal flower (Malcolm) and drown the weeds (Macbeth).

1. **let . . . all:** Let them all desert me!

2. **taint:** Become infected.

3. **mortal consequences:** Future human events.

4. **epicures:** Gluttons.

5. **sway:** Move.

The devil damn thee black, thou cream-faced loon.[6]
Where got'st thou that goose look?

SERVANT. There is ten thousand—

MACBETH. Geese, villain?

SERVANT. Soldiers, sir.

MACBETH. Go prick thy face and over-red thy fear.
Thou lily-livered boy. What soldiers, patch?[7]
Death of thy soul! Those linen[8] cheeks of thine
Are counselors to fear. What soldiers, whey-face?

SERVANT. The English force, so please you.

MACBETH. Take thy face hence. [*Exit* SERVANT.]
Seyton!—I am sick at heart. ❹
When I behold—Seyton, I say!—This push[9]
Will cheer me ever, or disseat[10] me now.
I have lived long enough. My way of life
Is fall'n into the sear,[11] the yellow leaf,
And that which should accompany old age,
As honor, love, obedience, troops of friends,
I must not look to have; but, in their stead,
Curses not loud but deep, mouth-honor, breath, ❺
Which the poor heart would fain deny, and dare not.
Seyton!

[*Enter* SEYTON.]

SEYTON. What's your gracious pleasure?

MACBETH. What news more?

SEYTON. All is confirmed, my lord, which was reported.

MACBETH. I'll fight, till from my bones my flesh be hacked.
Give me my armor.

SEYTON. 'Tis not needed yet.

❼

MACBETH. I'll put it on.
Send out moe[12] horses, skirr[13] the country round.
Hang those that talk of fear. Give me mine armor.
How does your patient, doctor?

6. **loon:** Fool.

7. **patch:** Fool.
8. **linen:** Pale as linen.

9. **push:** Effort.
10. **disseat:** Unthrone.
11. **the sear:** Withered state.

❻ **◆ Literary Focus** Does this passage, lines 20–28, evoke sympathy for Macbeth? Explain.

12. **moe:** More.
13. **skirr:** Scour.

❹ **Clarification** Seyton, Macbeth's attendant, is offstage. Macbeth is calling to him here.

❺ **Clarification** For *mouth-honor,* read "lip service."

◆ Literary Focus

❻ **Shakespearean Tragedy**
Shakespeare seems to be trying to evoke sympathy for Macbeth at this point. As the possibility of death approaches, Macbeth experiences a moment of truth when the consequences of his actions become clear to him. He knows that life could bring no joy to him now and, in weariness, makes his peace with the thought of dying. If students do not think this speech evokes pity, they might point out the fact that Macbeth here seems to be concerned for only himself.

◆ Critical Thinking

❼ **Analyze** Ask: What does it indicate about Macbeth's state of mind that he will don his armor before it is needed? *Since eleventh-century armor was heavy and cumbersome, it indicates that Macbeth is not showing good judgment and may be panicking.*

Cultural Connection

Shakespeare's play *Macbeth* reflects the cultural realities of the time period. The play includes historical and cultural references about the blending of Scottish and English influences. Similarly, modern drama reflects the cultural atmosphere of our time. Modern American drama in particular reveals the rich blending of cultures in this country. Playwrights such as August Wilson, Tennessee Williams, and Lorraine Hansberry have all written plays drawn from different regional, ethnic, and gender perspectives.

Have students identify the names of several plays and playwrights from cultural viewpoints that they are interested in. They could then use a keyword search on the Internet (Asian theater, Kabuki, for example) to help them locate playwrights' names and play titles.

◆ Grammar and Style

❶ Pronouns and Antecedents Have students identify the antecedent of the pronoun *she* in line 38. *The antecedent is "your patient" (line 37)—Lady Macbeth.*

◆ Reading Strategy

❷ Infer Beliefs of the Period Yes; a modern psychologist would probably, like the doctor, state that Lady Macbeth's malady is the result of mental anguish, not physical illness.

◆ Critical Thinking

❸ Analyze Ask students to describe Macbeth's mental state as he gives this speech. *Students will probably say that Macbeth is becoming unhinged; his speech borders on the hysterical, and he shows increasing impatience and irrationality in dealing with Seyton and the armor.*

◆ Critical Thinking

❹ Speculate Ask: What effect might these lines have had on the audience? *Depending on their delivery, they could reinforce the grimness of the situation or they could be played for laughs, giving the audience a much-needed break from the mounting tension.*

DOCTOR. Not so sick, my lord,
As she is troubled with thick-coming fancies
That keep her from her rest. ❶

MACBETH. Cure her of that.
Canst thou not minister to a mind diseased,
Pluck from the memory a rooted sorrow,
Raze out[14] the written troubles of the brain,
And with some sweet oblivious antidote
Cleanse the stuffed bosom of that perilous stuff
Which weighs upon the heart?

DOCTOR. Therein the patient
Must minister to himself.

MACBETH. Throw physic[15] to the dogs, I'll none of it.
Come, put mine armor on. Give me my staff.
Seyton, send out.—Doctor, the thanes fly from me.—
Come, sir, dispatch. If thou couldst, doctor, cast
The water[16] of my land, find her disease
And purge it to a sound and pristine health,
I would applaud thee to the very echo,
That should applaud again.—Pull 't off,[17] I say.—
What rhubarb, senna, or what purgative drug,
Would scour these English hence? Hear'st thou of them? ❸

DOCTOR. Ay, my good lord; your royal preparation
Makes us hear something.

MACBETH. Bring it[18] after me.
I will not be afraid of death and bane[19]
Till Birnam Forest come to Dunsinane.

DOCTOR. [*Aside*] Were I from Dunsinane away and clear,
Profit again should hardly draw me here. [*Exit.*] ❹

Scene iv. *Country near Birnam Wood.*
[*Drum and colors. Enter* MALCOLM, SIWARD, MACDUFF, SIWARD'S SON, MENTEITH, CAITHNESS, ANGUS, *and* SOLDIERS, *marching.*]

MALCOLM. Cousins, I hope the days are near at hand
That chambers will be safe.[1]

MENTEITH. We doubt it nothing.

SIWARD. What wood is this before us?

14. **Raze out:** Erase.

> ◆ **Reading Strategy** ❷
> Would a modern psychologist answer as the doctor does in V, iii, 45–46?

15. **physic:** Medicine.

16. **cast the water** Diagnose the illness.

17. **Pull 't off:** Pull off a piece of armor which has been put on incorrectly in Macbeth's haste.

18. **it:** His armor.

19. **bane:** Destruction.

1. **That . . . safe:** That people will be safe in their own homes.

◆ Build Vocabulary

pristine (pris tēn´) *adj.*: Original; unspoiled

Beyond the Classroom

Career Connection

Funding for Careers in Art Shakespeare wrote at a time when patronage, or support of the arts by wealthy individuals, was imperative. Without it, there would have been no money to build theaters or to stage performances. In order to court that patronage, a playwright often found it necessary to flatter the patron in some way or, at least, to avoid offending the patron. As a result, many of Shakespeare's plays reflect the officially accepted attitudes of the time so that he could ensure continued support for his theater company. Today, various forms of funding for artists are available. College scholarships, national and local grants, and corporate funding exist to help support the arts.

Have students who are considering careers in art to research the various forms of funding available to them. Tell them to begin taking note of the requirements for the various forms of funding.

MENTEITH. The Wood of Birnam.

MALCOLM. Let every soldier hew him down a bough
And bear 't before him. Thereby shall we shadow[2]
The numbers of our host, and make discovery[3]
Err in report of us.

SOLDIERS. It shall be done.

SIWARD. We learn no other but the confident tyrant
Keeps still in Dunsinane, and will endure
Our setting down before 't.[4]

MALCOLM. 'Tis his main hope,
For where there is advantage to be given
Both more and less[5] have given him the revolt,
And none serve with him but constrained things
Whose hearts are absent too.

MACDUFF. Let our just censures
Attend the true event,[6] and put we on
Industrious soldiership.

SIWARD. The time approaches,
That will with due decision make us know
What we shall say we have and what we owe.[7]
Thoughts speculative their unsure hopes relate,
But certain issue strokes must arbitrate:[8]
Towards which advance the war.[9] [*Exit, marching.*]

2. **shadow:** Conceal.
3. **discovery:** Those who see us.
4. **setting down before 't:** Laying seige to it.
5. **more and less:** People of high and low rank.
6. **our . . . event:** True judgment awaits the actual outcome.
7. **owe:** Own.
8. **strokes . . . arbitrate:** Fighting must decide.
9. **war:** Army.

Scene v. *Dunsinane. Within the castle.*
[*Enter* MACBETH, SEYTON, *and* SOLDIERS, *with drum and colors.*]

MACBETH. Hang out our banners on the outward walls.
The cry is still "They come!" Our castle's strength
Will laugh a siege to scorn. Here let them lie
Till famine and the ague[1] eat them up.
Were they not forced[2] with those that should be ours,
We might have met them dareful,[3] beard to beard,
And beat them backward home.
[*A cry within of women.*]
What is that noise?

❻

SEYTON. It is the cry of women, my good lord. [*Exit.*]

MACBETH. I have almost forgot the taste of fears:

1. **ague:** Fever.
2. **forced:** Reinforced.
3. **dareful:** Boldly.

◆ Critical Thinking

❺ **Speculate** Have students explain the rationale behind the strategy suggested by Malcolm in lines 4–7. Ask students: Based on the final prophecy, what effect do you think this strategy will have on Macbeth? *They will carry large tree limbs in front of them in order to hide their true numbers and appear to be a larger force than they really are. Students should speculate that the soldiers carrying boughs might look to Macbeth like the forest marching against him. At that point, he should begin to fear that he has once again been misled by the prophecy.*

❻ **Enrichment** While some readers might interpret Macbeth's attitude here as pure bravado, he did have some reasons to believe Dunsinane might withstand attack. In those times, such battles were just as hard on the attackers as on the attacked. Poor hygiene and exposure to the elements often seriously diminished the ranks of the besiegers. In addition, history shows that normally hostile groups joined together in battle, such as the English and Scottish, sometimes fell to fighting among themselves.

◆ Literary Focus

❶ Shakespearean Tragedy Students who agree with the statement should remark that this speech directly follows Macbeth's discovery of his wife's death. At this point, all that he has lost becomes clear to him. The glory he sought, the false hopes he counted on, and the wife he drew strength from have all left him now. Students who disagree might point out that the story itself is significant in that it might serve as a lesson and a warning for those who encounter it.

◆ Critical Thinking

❷ Interpret Have students describe Macbeth's reaction to the messenger's news. What does his reaction imply about his emotional stability? *Macbeth is beside himself with fury. He states that he'll hang the messenger if he is lying. His reaction reveals that he is on the edge of desperation and sheer panic.*

The time has been, my senses would have cooled
To hear a night-shriek, and my fell[4] of hair
Would at a dismal treatise[5] rouse and stir
As life were in 't. I have supped full with horrors.
Direness, familiar to my slaughterous thoughts,
Cannot once start[6] me.

[*Enter* SEYTON.]

Wherefore was that cry?

SEYTON. The queen, my lord, is dead.

MACBETH. She should[7] have died hereafter;
There would have been a time for such a word.[8]
Tomorrow, and tomorrow, and tomorrow
Creeps in this petty pace from day to day,
To the last syllable of recorded time;
And all our yesterdays have lighted fools
The way to dusty death. Out, out, brief candle!
Life's but a walking shadow, a poor player
That struts and frets his hour upon the stage
And then is heard no more. It is a tale
Told by an idiot, full of sound and fury
Signifying nothing.

[*Enter a* MESSENGER.]

Thou com'st to use thy tongue; thy story quickly!

MESSENGER. Gracious my lord,
I should report that which I say I saw,
But know not how to do 't.

MACBETH. Well, say, sir.

MESSENGER. As I did stand my watch upon the hill,
I looked toward Birnam, and anon, methought,
The wood began to move.

MACBETH. Liar and slave!

MESSENGER. Let me endure your wrath, if 't be not so.
Within this three mile may you see it coming;
I say a moving grove.

MACBETH. If thou speak'st false,

4. fell: Scalp.
5. treatise: Story.
6. start: Startle.
7. should: Inevitably would.
8. word: Message.

◆ Literary Focus
❶ This speech, lines 17-28, is a powerful expression of life's futility. Is Macbeth's story really "a tale/ Told by an idiot, full of sound and fury,/ Signifying nothing"? Why or why not?

❷

Speaking and Listening Mini-Lesson

Battlefield Report

This mini-lesson supports the Speaking and Listening activity on page 363.

Introduce the Concept Discuss with students the types of war reporting they've seen on network or cable news. Have them identify the elements that make a story immediate and exciting.

Develop Background Tell students that it has been only recently that war reports have been instantaneous news, with the war events actually occurring while the world watches the live broadcast. Have students form groups and work together to report the news "live" from Dunsinane.

- Tell students to decide on their roles for the broadcast—who's covering each event and conducting battlefield interviews.
- Have students review the battlefield events in Act V and take notes.
- Then students should decide whom they plan to interview.

Apply the Information Tell students to use notes to create the live broadcast of the battle of Dunsinane. Remind students that they should look at the "camera" and to speak slowly and clearly.

Assess the Outcome Have classmates evaluate the effectiveness of their peers' reports, based on content, clarity, interest, and originality.

Upon the next tree shalt thou hang alive,
Till famine cling[9] thee. If thy speech be sooth,[10]
I care not if thou dost for me as much.
I pull in resolution, and begin
To doubt th' equivocation of the fiend ❸
That lies like truth: "Fear not, till Birnam Wood
Do come to Dunsinane!" And now a wood
Comes toward Dunsinane. Arm, arm, and out!
If this which he avouches[11] does appear,
There is nor flying hence nor tarrying here.
I 'gin to be aweary of the sun,
And wish th' estate o' th' world were now undone.
Ring the alarum bell! Blow wind, come wrack!
At least we'll die with harness[12] on our back. [*Exit.*]

Scene vi. *Dunsinane. Before the castle.*
[*Drum and colors. Enter* MALCOLM, SIWARD, MACDUFF, *and their army, with boughs.*]

MALCOLM. Now near enough. Your leavy[1] screens throw down,
And show like those you are. You, worthy uncle,
Shall, with my cousin, your right noble son,
Lead our first battle.[2] Worthy Macduff and we
Shall take upon 's what else remains to do,
According to our order.[3]

SIWARD. Fare you well.
Do we find the tyrant's power[4] tonight,
Let us be beaten, if we cannot fight.

MACDUFF. Make all our trumpets speak; give them all breath.
Those clamorous harbingers of blood and death.
[*Exit. Alarums continued.*]

Scene vii. *Another part of the field.*
[*Enter* MACBETH.]

MACBETH. They have tied me to a stake; I cannot fly,
But bearlike I must fight the course.[1] What's he
That was not born of woman? Such a one
Am I to fear, or none.

[*Enter* YOUNG SIWARD.]

YOUNG SIWARD. What is thy name?

9. cling: Wither.
10. sooth: Truth.

11. avouches: Asserts.

12. harness: Armor.

1. leavy: Leafy.

2. battle: Battalion.

3. order: Plan.

4. power: Forces.

1. bearlike . . . course: Like a bear chained to a stake being attacked by dogs, I must fight until the end.

◆ Build Vocabulary

clamorous (klam´ ər əs) *adj.*: Noisy
harbingers (här´ bin jərs) *n.*: Forerunners

❸ **Clarification** *Equivocation* here refers to the ambiguous language of the prophecy.

❹ **Clarification** Point out that the action in these final three scenes (vi, vii, viii) is continuous, focusing in turn on different groups of soldiers and different parts of the battlefield. Encourage visual/spatial learners to diagram the scene of battle as they read.

◆ Literature and Your Life

❺ Point out to students that although everything is against Macbeth, his soldiers' resolve drives him to fight on until the end. Ask them what stories of perseverance they rely on when it seems that everything is against them. *Students should share stories with the theme of "never give up," based either on personal experience or on stories that are meaningful to them.*

◆ Literary Focus

❶ Shakespearean Tragedy Students who say Macbeth is showing bravery should note the fact that Shakespeare has left him some of the admirable traits he had in the beginning in order to evoke pity in the audience. Students who say he is simply overconfident should explain that he is overcompensating for the fact that he already knows the truth: he was misled by the prophecies, and there is really no hope left for him.

◆ Critical Thinking

❷ Make a Judgment Ask: Is it surprising that Macbeth so easily defeats young Siward? Why or why not? *Some students will say it's not surprising because Macbeth was once, after all, a great warrior; some students may say it is surprising because Macbeth is so mentally unhinged that it's a wonder he can see straight.*

❸ Clarification *Kerns* were hired Irish foot soldiers.

◆ Critical Thinking

❹ Interpret Ask: According to Siward, who's winning the battle at this point? *Malcolm's forces appear to be winning, but Malcolm cautions that they should not take victory for granted.*

MACBETH. Thou'lt be afraid to hear it.

YOUNG SIWARD. No; though thou call'st thyself a hotter name
Than any is in hell.

MACBETH. My name's Macbeth.

YOUNG SIWARD. The devil himself could not pronounce a title
More hateful to mine ear.

MACBETH. No, nor more fearful.

YOUNG SIWARD. Thou liest, abhorrèd tyrant; with my sword
I'll prove the lie thou speak'st.
[*Fight, and* YOUNG SIWARD *slain.*]

MACBETH. Thou wast born of woman.
But swords I smile at, weapons laugh to scorn,
Brandished by man that's of a woman born. [*Exit.*]

[*Alarums. Enter* MACDUFF.]

MACDUFF. That way the noise is. Tyrant, show thy face!
If thou be'st slain and with no stroke of mine,
My wife and children's ghosts will haunt me still.
I cannot strike at wretched kerns, whose arms ❸
Are hired to bear their staves.[2] Either thou, Macbeth,
Or else my sword, with an unbattered edge,
I sheathe again undeeded.[3] There thou shouldst be;
By this great clatter, one of greatest note
Seems bruited.[4] Let me find him, Fortune!
And more I beg not. [*Exit. Alarums.*]

[*Enter* MALCOLM *and* SIWARD.]

SIWARD. This way, my lord. The castle's gently rend'red:[5]
The tyrant's people on both sides do fight;
The noble thanes do bravely in the war;
The day almost itself professes yours,
And little is to do.

MALCOLM. We have met with foes
That strike beside us.[6]

SIWARD. Enter, sir, the castle.
[*Exit. Alarum.*]

◆ Literary Focus
❶ In V, vii, does Macbeth show signs of bravery or is he just overconfident because of what the witches said? Explain.

2. staves: Spears.

3. undeeded: Unused.

4. bruited: Reported.

5. gently rend'red: Easily surrendered.

6. strike . . . us: Deliberately miss us.

Scene viii. *Another part of the field.*
[*Enter* MACBETH.]

MACBETH. Why should I play the Roman fool, and die
On mine own sword?[1] Whiles I see lives,[2] the gashes
Do better upon them.

[*Enter* MACDUFF.]

MACDUFF. Turn, hell-hound, turn!

MACBETH. Of all men else I have avoided thee. ❺
But get thee back! My soul is too much charged
With blood of thine already.

MACDUFF. I have no words:
My voice is in my sword, thou bloodier villain
Than terms[3] can give thee out!
[*Fight. Alarum.*]

MACBETH. Thou losest labor:
As easy mayst thou the intrenchant[4] air
With thy keen sword impress[5] as make me bleed:
Let fall thy blade on vulnerable crests;
I bear a charmèd life, which must not yield
To one of woman born.

MACDUFF. Despair thy charm, ❻
And let the angel[6] whom thou still hast served
Tell thee, Macduff was from his mother's womb
Untimely ripped.[7]

MACBETH. Accursèd be that tongue that tells me so,
For it hath cowed my better part of man![8]
And be these juggling fiends no more believed,
That palter[9] with us in a double sense;
That keep the word of promise to our ear, ❼
And break it to our hope. I'll not fight with thee.

MACDUFF. Then yield thee, coward,
And live to be the show and gaze o' th' time:[10]
We'll have thee, as our rarer monsters[11] are,
Painted upon a pole,[12] and underwrit,
"Here may you see the tyrant."

MACBETH. I will not yield,
To kiss the ground before young Malcolm's feet,

1. **play . . . sword:** Die like Brutus or Cassius, who killed themselves with their own swords in the moment of defeat.
2. **While . . . lives:** So long as I see living men.
3. **terms . . . out:** Words can describe you.
4. **intrenchant:** Incapable of being cut.
5. **impress:** Make a dent in.
6. **angel:** Fallen angel; fiend.
7. **his . . . ripped:** Macduff's mother died before giving birth to him.
8. **better. . . man:** Courage.
9. **palter:** Juggle.
10. **gaze o' th' time:** Spectacle of the age.
11. **monsters:** Freaks.
12. **Painted . . . pole:** Pictured on a banner stuck on a pole by a showman's booth.

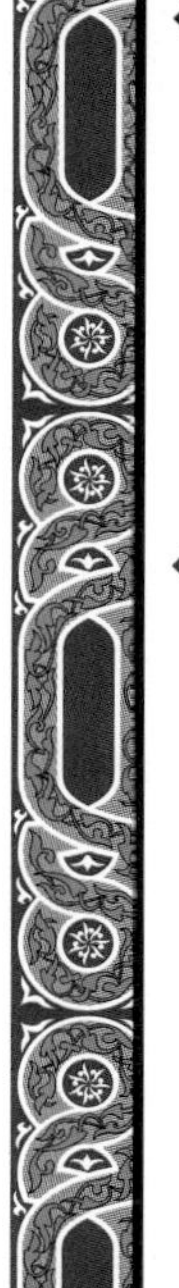

◆ Critical Thinking

❺ **Interpret** Ask students why Macbeth has avoided Macduff during the battle and whether his reason reflects that he has any feelings about what he did. *Macbeth has avoided Macduff because he killed his wife and children. Students should state whether they think he is motivated by guilt over his actions or fear of Macduff's rage.*

◆ Critical Thinking

❻ **Interpret** Ask students to describe the significance of this exchange. *Macbeth's last hope—that no one born of woman shall harm him—is destroyed here. He realizes that he's misread the prophecies and is doomed.*

◆ Literary Focus

❼ **Shakespearean Tragedy** Ask students what Macbeth is finally admitting in lines 19–21. How do these lines increase the tragic feel of this scene? *Macbeth is admitting that it is time to stop clinging to the prophecies for hope. He realizes that the final prophecy did not mean that no man could cause him harm. These lines cause the audience to realize that Macbeth was to some extent led by outside forces. He appears for the moment to be a victim of fate.*

Enrichment

Sword-play on the Elizabethan Stage Macbeth ends with a flurry of sword-play. In furious succession, the villainous king stabs young Siward and then is outdueled by the virtuous Macduff. As seasoned viewers of Hollywood stunt performers, we may wonder just how realistically these battle scenes were staged for an Elizabethan audience.

Actually, Londoners of Shakespeare's time were connoisseurs of the art of fencing. They would have been just as disappointed to see a half-hearted duel as a modern movie audience would be to see someone fall six feet instead of from a skyscraper.

Some Elizabethan actors became so skillful at fencing that they won awards for it. Richard Tarleton, for example, a theater star of the 1580's, was made Master of Fence. As the highest degree offered by fencing schools, this designation was something like today's black belt in karate.

Elizabethan audiences, however, wanted blood as well as skill. As a result, Elizabethan actors would wear bladders of animal blood, such as a sheep's, which would burst open the instant he was "stabbed." The chances are that Elizabethan theatergoers watched Macbeth die after a dazzling exhibit of sword-play and a copious spilling of blood.

❶ **Clarification** Wounds in the back would have suggested a cowardly death during flight. His wounds in front tell the story that he died bravely.

◆ Reading Strategy

❷ **Infer Beliefs of the Period** Siward comments that no matter how many sons he had, he would wish them no better death than that of young Siward. Ask students what this statement reveals about ideals of honor in Shakespeare's time. *Students should infer that to die fighting for a good cause was one of the highest honors a young man could attain.*

◆ Critical Thinking

❸ **Interpret** What is the "newer comfort" to which Siward refers? *The "newer comfort" is Macbeth's head, which is being carried onstage by Macduff.*

And to be baited with the rabble's curse.
Though Birnam Wood be come to Dunsinane,
And thou opposed, being of no woman born,
Yet I will try the last. Before my body
I throw my warlike shield. Lay on, Macduff;
And damned be him that first cries "Hold, enough!"
[*Exit, fighting. Alarums.*]

[*Re-enter fighting, and* MACBETH *slain. Exit* MACDUFF, *with* MACBETH. *Retreat and flourish.*[13] *Enter, with drum and colors,* MALCOLM, SIWARD, ROSS, THANES, *and* SOLDIERS.]

MALCOLM. I would the friends we miss were safe arrived.

SIWARD. Some must go off;[14] and yet, by these I see,
So great a day as this is cheaply bought.

MALCOLM. Macduff is missing, and your noble son.

ROSS. Your son, my lord, has paid a soldier's debt:
He only lived but till he was a man;
The which no sooner had his prowess confirmed
In the unshrinking station[15] where he fought,
But like a man he died.

SIWARD. Then he is dead?

ROSS. Ay, and brought off the field. Your cause of sorrow
Must not be measured by his worth, for then
It hath no end.

SIWARD. Had he his hurts before? ❶

ROSS. Ay, on the front.

SIWARD. Why then, God's soldier be he! ❷
Had I as many sons as I have hairs,
I would not wish them to a fairer death:
And so his knell is knolled.

MALCOLM. He's worth more sorrow,
And that I'll spend for him.

SIWARD. He's worth no more:
They say he parted well and paid his score:
And so God be with him! Here comes newer comfort. ❸

13. **Retreat and flourish:** Trumpet call to withdraw and fanfare.

14. **go off:** Die.

15. **unshrinking station:** Place where he stood firmly.

A Critic's Response
". . . the movement throughout is the most rapid of all Shakespeare's plays."
—Samuel Taylor Coleridge

[*Enter* MACDUFF, *with* MACBETH'S *head.*]

MACDUFF. Hail, King! for so thou art: behold, where stands
Th' usurper's cursèd head. The time is free.[16]
I see thee compassed with thy kingdom's pearl,[17]
That speak my salutation in their minds,
Whose voices I desire aloud with mine:
Hail, King of Scotland!

ALL. Hail, King of Scotland!

[*Flourish.*]

MALCOLM. We shall not spend a large expense of time
Before we reckon with your several loves,[18]
And make us even with you.[19] My thanes and kinsmen,
Henceforth be earls, the first that ever Scotland
In such an honor named. What's more to do,
Which would be planted newly with the time[20]—
As calling home our exiled friends abroad
That fled the snares of watchful tyranny,
Producing forth the cruel ministers
Of this dead butcher and his fiendlike queen,
Who, as 'tis thought, by self and violent hands
Took off her life—this, and what needful else
That calls upon us, by the grace of Grace
We will perform in measure, time, and place:[21]
So thanks to all at once and to each one,
Whom we invite to see us crowned at Scone.

[*Flourish. Exit all.*]

4

16. The . . . free: Our country is liberated.
17. compassed . . . pearl: Surrounded by the noblest people in the kingdom.

18. reckon . . . loves: Reward each of you for your devotion.
19. make . . . you: Pay what we owe you.
20. What's . . . time: What remains to be done at the beginning of this new age.

21. in measure . . . place: Fittingly at the appropriate time and place.

Guide for Responding

◆ Literature and Your Life

Reader's Response Does the ending of the play satisfy you? Why or why not?

Thematic Focus Why do you think this drama continues to appeal to audiences after nearly four hundred years?

Director's Memo Jot down some camera shots and special effects to enhance the final battle scene in a film version of *Macbeth.*

☑ Check Your Comprehension

1. To what three previous events in the play does Lady Macbeth refer in her sleepwalking?
2. What happens to Lady Macbeth before the final battle?
3. What does Macbeth learn in V, v, that makes him doubt the apparitions' prophecies?
4. (a) In V, viii, why does Macbeth tell Macduff he doesn't wish to fight him? (b) What does Macduff tell Macbeth concerning the apparitions' second prophecy?
5. (a) What is Macbeth's fate in the battle? (b) At the end of the play, who is to be crowned king of Scotland?

◆ Critical Thinking

4 Draw Conclusions Ask students what they think is the main message of Malcolm's speech. *Malcolm is bestowing an English title of nobility on his Scottish nobles as a symbolic act. He is repaying England for protecting him while he was in exile.*

◆ Critical Thinking

Analyze Give students this definition of tragedy: a type of drama in which the major character undergoes a morally significant struggle that ends disastrously. Point out that, according to Aristotle in the *Poetics,* the purpose of tragedy is to arouse the emotions of pity and fear in the audience and thus to produce a catharsis of these emotions. Ask student to describe ways in which Macbeth fits the tragic mold. *Macbeth begins as a hero, who is loyal to the king and a worthy friend. Once he is presented as thus, however, he undergoes a fundamental change, succumbing to a lust for power and, in the process, losing every shred of humanity and decency he once had.*

Reinforce and Extend

Answers

◆ Literature and Your Life

Reader's Response Students might respond that they enjoyed how the witches' predictions came true in clever, surprising ways; and that they cheered Macduff when he exacted his revenge. Others might respond that Malcolm's closing speech was rather anticlimatic.

Thematic Focus Students may cite action-packed plot; strong characterizations; universal themes; and, beautiful, memorable language as reasons for the play's appeal.

Beyond the Selection

FURTHER READING

Other Tragedies by Shakespeare

The Tragedy of Julius Caesar
Romeo and Juliet
Hamlet, Prince of Denmark

Other Famous Tragedies

Oedipus the King, by Sophocles
The Tragical History of the Life and Death of Dr. Faustus, by Christopher Marlowe
Death of a Salesman, by Arthur Miller

☑ Check Your Comprehension

1. During her sleepwalking, Lady Macbeth refers to the murders of Duncan, Banquo, and Macduff's family.
2. Lady Macbeth kills herself.
3. Macbeth learns that Birnam Wood seems to be moving towards Dunsinane.
4. (a) Macbeth does not wish to fight Macduff because he has already killed the entire family. (b) Macduff tells Macbeth that he was taken from his mother's womb upon her death, and strictly speaking, was not "born."
5. (a) Macbeth is killed by Macduff. (b) Malcolm is crowned king of Scotland.

Guide for Responding (continued)

◆ Critical Thinking

Interpret

1. (a) What causes Lady Macbeth to sleepwalk? (b) How have Macbeth and Lady Macbeth reversed roles by the end of the play? **[Infer]**

2. Judging by the way Macbeth behaves in V, iii and v, describe his state of mind. **[Interpret]**

3. On learning of his wife's death, why does Macbeth say, "She should have died hereafter"? **[Interpret]**

4. What admirable traits does Macbeth show at the end? **[Draw Conclusions]**

Evaluate

5. Would this play be as effective if Macbeth's temptations came from within and not from the witches? Explain. **[Make a Judgment]**

Extend

6. How would the recently foiled Guy Fawkes plot have influenced the way Shakespeare's audience viewed *Macbeth* (p. 270)? **[Social Studies Link]**

◆ Reading Strategy

Infer Beliefs of the Period

You can **infer** early seventeenth-century **beliefs** about sleepwalking and mental disturbances by reading what the doctor says in V, i and iii.

1. Find two speeches by the doctor suggesting that he doesn't feel qualified to treat mental illness.

2. (a) What line indicates that the doctor knows the cause of Lady Macbeth's disturbance? (b) To whose care would he refer her? Why?

◆ Grammar and Style

Pronoun and Antecedents

Pronouns must agree in gender, number, and person with their **antecedents**—the words to which they refer.

Practice Identify the antecedents of the italicized pronouns, and explain the ways in which the pronouns and their antecedents agree.

1. Who knows if Donalbain be with *his* brother?

2. Make all our trumpets speak, give *them* all breath.

3. What does the tyrant? / Great Dunsinane *he* strongly fortifies.

◆ Literary Focus

Shakespearean Tragedy

The last act of this **Shakespearean tragedy** depicts the downfall of Macbeth, the tragic hero. The road to Dunsinane and destruction begins for him in Act I, when he first meets the three witches. In response to their "supernatural soliciting," he is tempted to murder Duncan. His **tragic flaw**—a weakness in his nature—makes it possible for him to have these evil thoughts and then to turn them into evil deeds.

1. (a) In your own words, what is Macbeth's tragic flaw? (b) How does Banquo's response to the witches emphasize that flaw?

2. What role does Lady Macbeth play in Macbeth's choice of evil?

3. Once Macbeth kills Duncan, can he turn back? Why or why not?

4. Find three passages that show how the intensity of Macbeth's imagination adds to the tragedy. Support your choices.

5. Explain how the positive qualities that Macbeth demonstrates in V add to the sense of tragedy.

◆ Build Vocabulary

Using the Word Root *-turb-*

Knowing that the root *-turb-* means "to disturb," define the italicized words.

1. The pilot said that they would encounter some *turbulence.*

2. The eleventh century must have been a *turbulent* time in Scotland.

3. Elizabethans believed that a *perturbation* in the heavens meant disorder in society too.

Using the Word Bank

Fill in each blank space with a word from the Word Bank, using each word only once.

The movement of Birnam Wood was a strange development. The first ___?___, rustling trees that approached Dunsinane were ___?___ of the army. Farmers who saw the ___?___ wood suddenly begin to move confessed to feeling a ___?___ in their hearts.

Answers

◆ Critical Thinking

1. (a) Lady Macbeth is haunted by Duncan's death. (b) At first, Macbeth is aghast at the thought of murder, yet at the end he resorts to wiping out entire families; Lady Macbeth initiated the idea of killing Duncan, yet in the end she cannot live with the guilt.
2. Macbeth's mind is frenzied and fearless, and he believes that nothing can harm him.
3. This line suggests that, had she not died then, she surely would have been killed in battle.
4. Macbeth chooses to die fighting like a soldier. He would not kill himself, nor give up in defeat.
5. Sample response: The witches make the plot much more suspenseful and interesting, and contribute to the play's atmosphere of predictable doom.
6. Sample answer: The near-miss act of terrorism would have angered Shakespeare's audience, making them relish Macduff's revenge on Macbeth all the more.

◆ Reading Strategy

1. In V, i, line 60, the doctor states, "This disease is beyond my practice." In V, iii, lines 45–46, the doctor rebukes Macbeth's charge that he heal a diseased mind, but replies, "Therein the patient must minister to himself."
2. (a) In V, i, lines 72–74, the doctor reflects that "Unnatural deeds do breed unnatural troubles." (b) In V, i, lines 75–76, the doctor exclaims, "More needs she the divine than the physician."

◆ Literary Focus

1. (a) Suggested response: Ruthless, uncontrolled ambition might be considered Macbeth's flaw. (b) Banquo's suspicion of the witches emphasizes Macbeth's pathetic readiness to believe the witches' predictions.
2. Lady Macbeth serves as a catalyst, fueling his ambition.
3. Sample response: Once the first evil deed is done, Macbeth continues to kill all who might stand in his way.
4. Sample answers: In I, vii, Macbeth fantasizes about killing Duncan, but decides he cannot as his kinsman, subject, and host. In II, ii, after killing Duncan, Macbeth's guilty conscience frightens him so that he dares not think about what he has done. In III, iv, Macbeth's visions of the ghost of Banquo betray his inner turmoil.
5. If Macbeth were always evil, there would be no real tragedy. But when an honorable person falls it emphasizes the vulnerability of all humans.

◆ Build Vocabulary

Using the Word Root - *turb-*

1. *turbulence:* irregular, disruptive air motion; 2. *turbulent:* time marked by turmoil; 3. *perturbation;* planetary disturbance

Using the Word Bank

clamorous; harbingers; pristine; perturbation

◆ Grammar and Style

1. *his*: Donalbain; 2. *them*: trumpets; 3. *he*: tyrant

For additional instruction and practice, use the lesson in the Language Lab CD-ROM on Pronouns and Antecedents and practice page 64 in the *Writer's Solution Grammar Practice Book.*

Build Your Portfolio

Idea Bank

Writing

1. Independence Day Write a proclamation for King Malcolm establishing a yearly celebration on the day of Macbeth's downfall. Indicate the purpose of the day and how it will be celebrated.

2. Dear Diary As Lady Macbeth, write a series of diary entries that reveal your deteriorating relationship with your husband. Date the first entry sometime after the murder of Duncan.

3. Response to Criticism A. C. Bradley wrote about *Macbeth*: "Darkness, we may even say blackness, broods over this tragedy. . . . all the scenes which at once recur to memory take place either at night or in some dark spot." Agree or disagree with this statement, supporting your points with specific references to the play.

Speaking and Listening

4. Performance With a group of classmates, perform a scene from *Macbeth*. In rehearsing, focus on conveying the meaning and emotion of the dialogue. **[Performing Arts Link]**

5. Battlefield Report With a group, cover the battle described in Act V for television. Combining blow-by-blow descriptions with battlefield interviews, perform your coverage for the class. **[Media Link; Social Studies Link]**

Projects

6. Set Design With a partner, choose a scene from *Macbeth* and design a set that captures its mood. **[Art Link]**

7. Macbeth, the Opera Find a recording of Verdi's opera based on *Macbeth*. Play a portion of it for the class, explaining how Verdi adapted Shakespeare's drama. **[Music Link]**

Writing Mini-lesson

Macbeth: The Film Version?

Before directors decide whether to film a play, they might ask someone to analyze its screen potential. Write such an analysis of *Macbeth*. Considering elements like dialogue, setting, characters, and theme, advise the director whether to go ahead with filming the production. To make your analysis convincing, refer to precise details in the play.

Writing Skills Focus: Precise Details

Whether you write an analysis of a play or a play itself, use **precise details** to support arguments or depict characters. For example, to convince the director that special effects could play a role in the film, you can quote specific passages that invite such effects:

Is this a dagger which I see before me,
The handle toward my hand? Come, let me clutch thee! (II, i, 33–34)

Then, having quoted the precise passage, you can describe how it might be filmed.

Even before you start to write, find precise details that will help you make your case.

Prewriting Identify elements of the play that will or won't work in a film; a universal theme is a plus but hard-to-understand dialogue might be a minus. Jot down precise details from the play that illustrate these elements.

Drafting Refer to your notes as you write. Be sure to support each point you make with details or quotations from the play.

Revising Ask yourself whether you've helped the director envision the wonderful or disastrous film that the play could become. If not, use precise details to describe a scene from the potential movie. For example, you might want to show how the murder of Banquo or the final battle could make good action scenes.

ASSESSMENT OPTIONS

Formal Assessment, Selection Test, pp. 77–79, and Assessment Resources Software. The selection test is designed so that it can be easily customized to the ability levels of your students. ***Alternative Assessment,*** p. 16, includes options for less advanced students, more advanced students, visual and spatial learners, and verbal/linguistic learners.

PORTFOLIO ASSESSMENT

Use the following rubrics and assessment guidelines in the ***Alternative Assessment*** booklet to assess student writing and speaking:
Independence Day (proclamation): Description Rubric, p. 98
Dear Diary: Fictional Narrative Rubric, p. 96
Response to Criticism: Literary Analysis/Interpretation Rubric, p. 113
Writing Mini-Lesson: Literary Analysis/Interpretation Rubric, p. 113

Idea Bank

Customizing for *Learning Modalities*

Following are suggestions for matching Idea Bank topics with your students' learning modalities:
- Verbal/Linguistic: 1, 2, 3
- Musical/Rhythmic: 4, 7
- Bodily/Kinesthetic: 4, 5
- Visual/Spatial: 6
- Interpersonal: 5

Customizing for *Performance Levels*

Following are suggestions for matching Idea Bank topics with your students' ability levels:
- Less Advanced Students: 4, 6
- Average Students: 1, 2, 5
- More Advanced Students: 3, 7

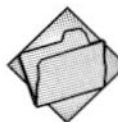

Writing Mini-Lesson

Refer students to the Writing Handbook, page 1189, for instruction on the writing process, and page 1193 for further information on responding to literature.

Writing and Language Transparencies As they write "Macbeth: The Film Version?"—their analysis of the play—encourage students to use the Story Map on page 126 to keep track of the play's details.

Writer's Solution

Writing Lab CD-ROM

Direct students to complete the tutorial on Response to Literature. Follow these steps:

1. Complete the Audience and Purpose Profiles.
2. Answer questions on the Self-Interview to generate your responses to the drama.
3. Create a draft on the computer.
4. Use the Revision Checker for Vague Language to ensure that the details are precise.

Sourcebook

Have students refer to Chapter 7, Response to Literature (pp. 196–229), for additional support. The chapter gives in-depth instruction on gathering details.

Prepare and Engage

OBJECTIVES

1. To read, comprehend, and interpret a scene from a Greek tragedy
2. To explore the literary connection between a Greek tragedy and a Shakespearean tragedy
3. To respond to a Greek tragedy through writing, speaking and listening, and a project

PORTFOLIO OPPORTUNITIES

Writing: Greece's Most Wanted; Journal of a King; The Tragic Flaw
Speaking and Listening: Performance
Project: Greek Mask

More About the Author
Sophocles is one of three great Greek writers of tragedy. Of the other two, Aeschylus preceded him, and Euripides followed him. Of Sophocles' seven surviving plays, the best known are *Electra, Antigone, Ajax, Trachinian Women,* and *Philoctetes*.

Little is known of Sophocles' life. He was born in Colonus, a town not far from Athens, and apparently came from a well-to-do family. He was active in government affairs, serving as a general on at least one occasion.

Sophocles was recognized as a master of tragedy in his own time, as evidenced by the twenty-four first–prize awards he received in the drama competitions. However, *Oedipus the King,* generally considered his greatest play today, was awarded only second prize.

Pose the following situation to the class: Suppose that fortune-teller who has never been wrong tells you that you are fated to murder your father. What do you do? *Students will devise different ways of making sure that the prophecy doesn't come true.* Explain that in the play they are about to read, a young man leaves home and journeys far away because of a prophecy that he will murder his father and marry his mother. What he doesn't know is that he is adopted; his attempt to thwart the prophecy in fact sets events in motion.

CONNECTIONS TO WORLD LITERATURE

from Oedipus the King

Sophocles

Literary Connection

Shakespeare did not invent tragedy, although he wrote a number of great tragedies, including *Macbeth*. The honor of creating this literary form, and of creating drama itself, goes to the ancient Greeks. Drama and tragedy may have evolved from the religious festivals honoring the Greek god Dionysius, who exercised power over the grape harvest and the production of wine.

What Makes a Tragedy?

In this section, you will read an excerpt from *Oedipus the King*, an ancient Greek tragedy by Sophocles. Like Macbeth, Oedipus is high-born and comes to grief through his own choices. The destruction of a noble character is an essential ingredient of tragedy—whether Greek or Elizabethan.

The element of choice in tragedy is not so clear-cut, however. Macbeth obviously makes an evil choice or is coaxed into one by his wife. Oedipus, however, seems less evil than unaware. His own choices and acts lead him to destruction, but he isn't fully conscious of what he is doing. He may be overproud (the Greeks called this haughty spirit *hubris*), but he doesn't traffic with evil as Macbeth does.

The Mystery of Tragedy

The meaning of choice in tragedy brings us to an unsolvable mystery—one that may be related to the origins of tragedy in religion. The mystery of tragedy is that it presents two contradictory ideas: The central character is free to choose, and yet he or she also seems fated to be destroyed. When viewed rationally, these two possibilities could not exist at the same time. By uniting these opposite ideas, however, tragedy forces us to go beyond reason. In that realm beyond reason, we encounter the emotions of pity, fear, and awe that make us tremble.

SOPHOCLES
(496–406 B.C.)

Sophocles' life corresponded with the splendid rise and tragic fall of fifth-century B.C. Athens. As a young man, he performed in a public celebration of Athens's great naval victory over the Persians at Salamis. He died only two years before Athens surrendered to Sparta in the Peloponnesian War.

His life also coincided with the rise and fall of the Golden Age of Greek tragedy. His career as a dramatist began in 468 B.C., when he entered an annual theatrical competition and defeated the established and brilliant playwright Aeschylus. Over the next 62 years, Sophocles wrote more than 120 plays, twenty-four of which won first prize. Unfortunately, only seven of Sophocles' plays have survived, one of them being *Oedipus the King*.

Sophocles was an innovative dramatist who made many significant contributions to Greek tragedy. For example, Sophocles expanded the use of stage machinery and sets. He was the first to use the *mechane*, a crane that lowered the gods "miraculously" onto the stage at the end of the play.

Prentice Hall Literature Program Resources

REINFORCE / RETEACH / EXTEND

Selection Support Pages
Build Vocabulary, p. 79
Thematic and Literary Connections, p. 80

Formal Assessment, Selection Test, pp. 80–81; Assessment Resources Software

Resource Pro CD-ROM
from *Oedipus the King*—includes all resource material and customizable lesson plan

Listening to Literature Audiocassettes
from *Oedipus the King*

from Oedipus THE KING

Sophocles

Translated by David Grene

CHARACTERS

Oedipus, King of Thebes	**First Messenger**
Jocasta, His Wife	**Second Messenger**
Creon, His Brother-in-Law	**A Herdsman**
Teiresias, an Old Blind Prophet	**A Chorus of Old Men of Thebes**
A Priest	

It had been prophesied that the son of Jocasta and Laius would kill his father and marry his mother. When their son Oedipus was born, the infant was to be left to die of exposure, but the servant given the task pitied him. He was eventually given to Merope, wife of King Polybus. In a search for the truth about his identity, Oedipus learns of the prophecy and flees from his adoptive parents. During his journey, he gets in a conflict with a charioteer who purposely runs over Oedipus' foot, and the man in the chariot strikes Oedipus in the head. Furious, Oedipus kills both men; one of the men was his real father, King Laius. When he arrives at Thebes, he rescues the city from the Sphinx and marries Queen Jocasta, widow of Laius and his mother. At the beginning of the play, Oedipus' city is suffering from a blight, which he has caused by fulfilling the prophecy. At this point Oedipus is still unaware of what he has done.

PART I

[***Scene:*** *In front of the palace of Oedipus at Thebes. To the right of the stage near the altar stands the priest with a crowd of children. Oedipus emerges from the central door.*]

OEDIPUS. Children, young sons and daughters of old Cadmus,[1]
why do you sit here with your suppliant crowns?[2]
The town is heavy with a mingled burden
❶ of sounds and smells, of groans and hymns and incense;
I did not think it fit that I should hear
of this from messengers but came myself,—
I Oedipus whom all men call the Great.

[*He turns to the* PRIEST.]

You're old and they are young; come, speak for them.
What do you fear or want, that you sit here

1. **Cadmus** (kad′ məs): Mythical founder and first king of Thebes, a city in central Greece where the play takes place.
2. **suppliant** (sup′ lē ənt) **crowns:** Wreaths worn by people who ask favors of the gods.

One-Minute Insight

This play addresses the apparent contradiction between human free will and the foreknowledge of the gods. Unlike Macbeth, Oedipus seems to be the victim of fate rather than his own evil deeds. However, some critics argue that the hero's decision to frustrate the will of the gods is the evil choice that leads to tragedy. This view preserves a measure of free will for man within the broader context of all-powerful, all-knowing gods. Like the opening scenes of *Macbeth*, this scene supplies background information and sets the inevitable tragedy in motion. In vowing to find the "pollution" in Thebes, Oedipus ultimately vows to expose himself as an incestuous murderer. His pride, self-confidence, and determination come across dramatically in this opening scene.

◆ Literary Connection

Tragedy Have students discuss why, despite the audience's knowledge of its outcome, tragedy has endured as one of the most popular dramatic forms for two thousand years. *According to Aristotle, tragedy arouses pity for the hero and fear for our own well-being. By experiencing these emotions, we cleanse ourselves of these feelings. This process is called catharsis.*

◆ Critical Thinking

❶ Compare and Contrast What similarities and differences can be found in the openings of *Macbeth* and *Oedipus the King*? *Thebes is described as burdened with sounds, groans, and incense; the witches refer to the "foul and filthy air." Macbeth is called great for his bravery in battle; Oedipus calls himself great.*

Customize for *Less Proficient Readers*
Remind students to read sentences according to punctuation and to ignore line breaks.

Customize for *More Advanced Students*
The first eighty-six lines consist of lengthy statements by Oedipus and the Priest. Have these students study these lines carefully and rewrite them into a dialogue made up of shorter statements.

Enrichment

The Greek theater was a large amphitheater that lacked the intimacy of Shakespeare's Globe. Consequently, the dialogue often takes on the qualities of a speech rather than a personal conversation. These opening statements serve as good examples. In addition, some scholars believe that the masks that all actors wore were, at least in part, devices to amplify the actors' voices so they could be heard by people in the last row. Like the Globe, the stage lacked lighting and scenery, therefore the opening dialogue served to inform the audience about the time, place, and circumstances of the characters.

Literary Connection

Tragedy Both *Macbeth* and *Oedipus the King* concern the hero's reaction to a prophecy. Macbeth ruthlessly pursues a course of action leading to what he feels is the fulfillment of a prophecy. Oedipus, on the other hand, attempts to escape the dire prediction. In both cases the prophecies come tragically true. However, the difference lies in the involvement of the gods. The witches, though "otherworldly," are not all-knowing gods. It is Macbeth's ambition that moves the tragedy forward. The prophecy regarding Oedipus comes from the gods and in fact has already come to pass when the play opens. Oedipus' foolish attempt to thwart the will of the gods only leads him to fulfill their will. All that is left for him is the unmasking of his past sins.

Literary Connection

❶ **Tragedy** An alternate title for this play, *Oedipus Tyrannos*, highlights the events that brought Oedipus to rule Thebes and which also cause his downfall. *Tyrannos* is the word from which *tyrant* comes, and in ancient Greece it eventually came to have the negative connotation we associate with it. Originally, however, it was simply the title given to a ruler who came to the throne through his merit, not in the course of hereditary succession. Have students think about the irony of the title: Oedipus is thought to be a tyrannos, someone who earned the throne—in Oedipus' case, by answering the riddle of the sphinx and thus saving Thebes from that monster. However, Oedipus is in fact the legitimate heir of Laius.

◆ Critical Thinking

❷ **Analyze** Ask students to analyze how Thebes is described in these lines. *The city is compared to a storm-battered ship.* Have students extend the analogy by describing the role Oedipus plays on the ship of state. *Students may say that Oedipus is to Thebes as a captain or pilot is to a ship.*

suppliant? Indeed I'm willing to give all
that you may need; I would be very hard
should I not pity suppliants like these.

PRIEST. O ruler of my country, Oedipus, ❶
you see our company around the altar;
you see our ages; some of us, like these,
who cannot yet fly far, and some of us
heavy with age; these children are the chosen
among the young, and I the priest of Zeus.
Within the market place sit others crowned
with suppliant garlands,[3] at the double shrine
of Pallas[4] and the temple where Ismenus
gives oracles by fire.[5] King, you yourself
have seen our city reeling like a wreck
already; it can scarcely lift its prow
out of the depths, out of the bloody surf. ❷
A blight is on the fruitful plants of the earth,
a blight is on the cattle in the fields,
a blight is on our women that no children
are born to them; a God that carries fire, ❸
a deadly pestilence,[6] is on our town,
strikes us and spares not, and the house of Cadmus
is emptied of its people while black Death
grows rich in groaning and in lamentation.[7]
We have not come as suppliants to this altar
because we thought of you as of a God,
but rather judging you the first of men
in all the chances of this life and when
we mortals have to do with more than man.
You came and by your coming saved our city,
freed us from tribute which we paid of old
to the Sphinx,[8] cruel singer. This you did
in virtue of no knowledge we could give you,
in virtue of no teaching; it was God
that aided you, men say, and you are held
with God's assistance to have saved our lives. ❹
Now Oedipus, Greatest in all men's eyes,
here falling at your feet we all entreat you,
find us some strength for rescue.
Perhaps you'll hear a wise word from some God
perhaps you will learn something from a man
(for I have seen that for the skilled of practice
the outcome of their counsels live the most).
Noblest of men, go, and raise up our city,
go,—and give heed. For now this land of ours
calls you its savior since you saved it once.
So, let us never speak about your reign
as of a time when first our feet were set
secure on high, but later fell to ruin.
Raise up our city, save it and raise it up.
Once you have brought us luck with happy omen;

3. **suppliant garlands** *n.*: Branches wound in wool, that were placed on the altar and left there until the suppliant's request was granted.

4. **double shrine of Pallas:** Two temples of Athena.

5. **temple where Ismenus gives oracles by fire:** Temple of Apollo, located by Ismenus, the Theban river, where the priests studied patterns in the ashes of sacrificial victims to foretell the future.

6. **pestilence** (pes´ tə ləns) *n.*: Fatal, contagious disease of epidemic proportions.

7. **lamentation** (lam ən tā´ shən) *n.*: Act of expressing deep sorrow and grief.

8. **Sphinx** (sfinks) *n.*: Winged female monster who ate Theban men who could not answer her riddle: "What is it that walks on four legs at dawn, two legs at midday, and three legs in the evening, and has only one voice, when it walks on most feet, it is weakest?" Creon, appointed ruler of Thebes, offered the kingdom and the hand of his sister, Jocasta, to anyone who could answer the riddle. Oedipus saved Thebes by answering correctly, "Man, who crawls in infancy, walks upright in his prime, and leans on a cane in old age." Outraged, the Sphinx destroyed herself, and Oedipus became King of Thebes.

Enrichment

In lines 80–81, Oedipus mentions sending Creon to consult Apollo's "Pythian temple." This is a reference to the famous oracle at Delphi. The oracle was believed to provide answers to questions and problems and to forecast the future. In ancient times there was a crack in the Earth there that released vapors. A priestess sat over the vapor and went into a trance and made strange sounds. The priests interpreted the sounds to arrive at the revelations of Apollo. Often their pronouncements were ambiguous.

▲ **Critical Viewing** ❺ In what ways is this costume appropriate for Oedipus? **[Evaluate]**

be no less now in fortune.
If you will rule this land, as now you rule it,
better to rule it full of men than empty.
For neither tower nor ship is anything
when empty, and none live in it together.

OEDIPUS. I pity you, children. You have come full of longing,
but I have known the story before you told it
only too well. I know you are all sick,
yet there is not one of you, sick though you are,
that is as sick as I myself.
Your several sorrows each have single scope
and touch but one of you. My spirit groans
for city and myself and you at once.
You have not roused me like a man from sleep;
know that I have given many tears to this,
gone many ways wandering in thought,
but as I thought I found only one remedy
and that I took. I sent Menoeceus' son
Creon, Jocasta's brother, to Apollo,
to his Pythian temple,[9]
that he might learn there by what act or word
I could save this city. As I count the days,
it vexes me what ails him; he is gone
far longer than he needed for the journey.
But when he comes, then, may I prove a villain,
if I shall not do all the God commands.

PRIEST. Thanks for your gracious words. Your servants here
signal that Creon is this moment coming.

9. **Pythian** (pith´ ē ən) **temple:** Shrine of Apollo at Delphi, below Mount Parnassus in central Greece.

◆ Critical Thinking

❸ **Connect** Point out that in many ancient cultures, the prosperity of the land was believed to be directly linked to the righteousness and health of the ruler. How is this belief reflected in this passage? *Because Oedipus has committed the gravest of sins by murdering his father and marrying his mother, his land and people suffer.*

Literary Connection

❹ **Tragedy** The Priest expresses the belief that God gave Oedipus the knowledge to solve the riddle of the Sphinx and save the city. Unlike the audience, however, the Priest is ignorant of the prophecy that Oedipus will murder his father and marry his mother. How does this knowledge affect the audience's understanding of these lines? *The audience will see that the gods had a more important motive for giving Oedipus the power to solve the riddle. By doing so, Oedipus became king of Thebes and fulfilled the prophecy by marrying his mother.*

▶Critical Viewing◀

❺ **Evaluate** The rich robes and crown are appropriate for a king.

Speaking and Listening Mini-Lesson

Performance

This mini-lesson supports the Speaking and Listening activity in the Idea Bank, p. 371.

Introduce the Concept In this activity, students will work in groups of three to present this scene from *Oedipus the King*. (If necessary, some groups may contain four members and divide up the Priest's lines.)

Develop Background As a class, generate a list of the elements of a good dramatic performance. Students may suggest and elaborate on elements like the following:

- Actors speak with feeling, using their voices to express the meaning of the words.
- Actors use gestures and facial expressions to clarify and emphasize what they say.
- Actors move purposefully and coordinate their actions on stage.

Explain that students should keep these ideas in mind as they prepare their performances.

Apply the Information You may allow students to use their scripts on stage but caution them to avoid burying their faces in the scripts during their performance. When students have rehearsed sufficiently, have them give their performances for the class.

Assess the Outcome Have students evaluate one another's performances using the list generated in Develop Background. You may also want students to use the Peer Assessment: Dramatic Performance page in ***Alternative Assessment,*** p. 121.

Customize for
Less Proficient Readers

❶ Have students explain how Oedipus' reaction helps them understand Creon's statement. *Oedipus reacts with concern and uncertainty.* Then have them paraphrase lines 96–97. *Creon indicates that the news he brings may be difficult to take, but if it proves to be a cure for the ills of Thebes, it will be good news.*

◆ Critical Thinking

❷ **Draw Conclusions** Ask students: How might the story have changed if Oedipus had decided to hear the news from Delphi in private? *Had Oedipus heard the god's command to find the murderer of Laius, he might have been able to call off the search when it began to lead to him.*

▶Critical Viewing◀

❸ **Speculate** Students may say that the followers' submissive, almost worshipping posture indicates the high regard in which Oedipus is held as king and savior of Thebes.

OEDIPUS. His face is bright. O holy Lord Apollo,
grant that his news too may be bright for us and bring us safety.

PRIEST. It is happy news,
I think, for else his head would not be crowned
with sprigs of fruitful laurel.[10]

OEDIPUS. We will know soon,
he's within hail. Lord Creon, my good brother,
what is the word you bring us from the God?

[CREON *enters.*]

CREON. A good word,—for things hard to bear themselves
if in the final issue all is well I count complete good fortune.

❶

OEDIPUS. What do you mean?
What you have said so far
leaves me uncertain whether to trust or fear.

CREON. If you will hear my news before these others
I am ready to speak, or else to go within.

❷

OEDIPUS. Speak it to all;
the grief I bear, I bear it more for these
than for my own heart.

CREON. I will tell you, then, what I heard from the God.
King Phoebus[11] in plain words commanded us
to drive out a pollution from our land,
pollution grown ingrained within the land;
drive it out, said the God, not cherish it, till it's past cure.

❸

OEDIPUS. What is the rite
of purification? How shall it be done?

10. sprigs of fruitful laurel: Laurel symbolized triumph; a crown of laurel signified good news.

11. King Phoebes (fē′ bəs): Apollo, god of sun.

▼ **Critical Viewing** Examine the pose of these two followers of Oedipus. What does their pose indicate about their feelings toward Oedipus? **[Speculate]**

CREON. By banishing a man, or expiation[12]
of blood by blood, since it is murder guilt
which holds our city in this destroying storm.

OEDIPUS. Who is this man whose fate the God pronounces?

CREON. My Lord, before you piloted[13] the state
we had a king called Laius.

OEDIPUS. I know of him by hearsay.[14] I have not seen him.

CREON. The God commanded clearly: let some one
punish with force this dead man's murderers.

OEDIPUS. Where are they in the world? Where would a trace
of this old crime be found? It would be hard to guess where.

CREON. The clue is in this land;
that which is sought is found;
the unheeded thing escapes:
so said the God.

OEDIPUS. Was it at home,
or in the country that death came upon him,
or in another country traveling?

CREON. He went, he said himself, upon an embassy,[15]
but never returned when he set out from home.

❹

OEDIPUS. Was there no messenger, no fellow traveller
who knew what happened? Such a one might tell
something of use.

CREON. They were all killed save one. He fled in terror
and he could tell us nothing in clear terms
of what he knew, nothing, but one thing only.

OEDIPUS. What was it?
If we could even find a slim beginning
in which to hope, we might discover much.

CREON. This man said that the robbers they encountered
were many and the hands that did the murder
were many; it was no man's single power.

OEDIPUS. How could a robber dare a deed like this
were he not helped with money from the city,
money and treachery?[16]

CREON. That indeed was thought.
But Laius was dead and in our trouble
there was none to help.

12. **expiation** (eks´ pē ā shən) *n.*: Act of making amends for wrongdoing.

13. **piloted** (pī´ lət əd) *v.*: Led or guided through difficulty.

14. **hearsay** (hir´ sā´) *n.*: Rumor; gossip.

15. **embassy** (em´ bə sē) *n.*: Important mission or errand.

16. **treachery** (trech´ ər ē) *n.*: Disloyalty or treason.

◆ Critical Thinking

❹ **Infer** What can students infer about Oedipus' character from the numerous questions he asks of Creon? *Oedipus appears determined to find the truth about the murder of Laius.*

Customize for More Advanced Students

Explain that Sophocles wrote *Oedipus the King* when war-torn Athens had just been ravaged by a severe plague that devastated the city, killing its people and undermining faith in the laws and religious customs of the commonwealth. In his *History of the Peloponnesian War,* the historian Thucydides, himself a surviving plague victim, describes the horrible conditions within the city. He writes that lawlessness increased, noting, "Those who saw all [good and bad] perishing alike concluded that the worship or neglect of the gods made no difference." Challenge students to explain how these conditions may have shaped Sophocles' play. *Students may speculate that the Athenians could readily identify with the sickness described in lines 29–33, having recently experienced an epidemic. The play's emphasis on fate and the will of the gods may have been crafted to counteract people's loss of faith in the gods and in human law.*

Literary Connection

Tragedy For hundreds of years, literary critics have searched for Oedipus' "tragic flaw," and debated whether he deserved his horrible fate. However, there is little agreement about whether the tragic events are best attributed to a character flaw or simply to fate.

One way to look at the play is that what was destined to happen would have happened anyway, one way or another; it happened the way it did because Oedipus was who he was. For the ancient Greeks, fate could be visualized as a weaving: The parameters are fixed, as are some elements of the final cloth; some variation is possible, but it will not change the size of the cloth. What this play reveals is that because they are human, all mortals have limited vision; they do not have all they need to see clearly what the target should be, and so they miss the mark, as a hunter's arrow might miss its target. The Greek work for "missing the mark" is *hamartia,* often translated as "tragic flaw." *Hamartia* can have ethical overtones, but it retains its basic meaning as well. According to Aristotle in the *Poetics,* being who you are, and in the culture or situation that constrains you, prevents you from sorting out all the information at hand, so you "miss the mark."

Customize for *Verbal/Linguistic Learners*

❶ Have these students compare these lines by Oedipus to any of similar length by Macbeth. Ask them to compare Macbeth's blank verse with Oedipus' stately prose. Have them decide which they prefer and the reasons for their choice. *Some students may prefer the prose of Oedipus because it is more natural and realistic. Other may prefer the poetic power of the blank verse.*

Customize for *Musical/Rhythmic Learners*

Students may enjoy hearing some humorous musical responses to *Oedipus the King*. These include "Oedipus Rex" by Tom Lehrer and *Oedipus Tex* by Peter Schickele as P.D.Q. Bach. Because the underlying premise of *Oedipus the King* is highly sensitive, we suggest that you preview these works before recommending them to students.

Reinforce and Extend

Answers

◆ Literature and Your Life

Reader's Response Most students will say that Oedipus is a good king, because he is concerned about his people and eager to do everything he can to lift the curse from his land.

Thematic Focus Key problems include that Oedipus has unwittingly fulfilled the prophecy: he has murdered his father and married his mother. This has brought down the anger of the gods; the crops and cattle are sick, women are not having children, and a disease is killing people.

☑ Check Your Comprehension

1. There is a blight on the crops, cattle, and women, and a "deadly pestilence" has struck the city.
2. He sends Creon to the oracle to find out what the problem is and how to fix it.
3. Creon is Jocasta's brother, and thus Oedipus' brother-in-law. His mission was to obtain information from Apollo's oracle.
4. He brings back word that the people of Thebes must "drive out a pollution" from the land. This "pollution" is the murderer of the old king, Laius.

CONNECTIONS TO WORLD LITERATURE

OEDIPUS. What trouble was so great to hinder you
inquiring out the murder of your king?

CREON. The riddling Sphinx induced[17] us to neglect
mysterious crimes and rather seek solution
of troubles at our feet.

OEDIPUS. I will bring this to light again. King Phoebus
fittingly took this care about the dead,
and you too fittingly.
And justly you will see in me an ally,
a champion of my country and the God.
For when I drive pollution from the land
I will not serve a distant friend's advantage,
but act in my own interest. Whoever
he was that killed the king may readily
wish to dispatch me with his murderous hand;
so helping the dead king I help myself.
Come, children, take your suppliant boughs and go;
up from the altars now. Call the assembly
and let it meet upon the understanding
that I'll do everything. God will decide
whether we prosper or remain in sorrow. ❶

PRIEST. Rise, children—it was this we came to seek,
which of himself the king now offers us.
May Phoebus who gave us the oracle
come to our rescue and stay the plague.

[*Exeunt all but the* CHORUS.]

17. **induced** (in dōōst′) *v.*: Persuaded; caused.

Guide for Responding

◆ Literature and Your Life

Reader's Response Do you think Oedipus is a good king? Why or why not?

Thematic Focus What key problems does Sophocles introduce at the start of the drama?

☑ Check Your Comprehension

1. From what is the city of Thebes suffering?
2. How does Oedipus respond to the pleas of his people?
3. Who is Creon, and what was his mission?
4. What news does Creon bring back?

Beyond the Selection

FURTHER READING

Works About Oedipus and His Children

Mythology, Edith Hamilton; *Oedipus Coloneus,* Sophocles; *Antigone,* Sophocles; *Antigone,* Jean Anouilh

Other Tragedies

Electra, Sophocles; *Mourning Becomes Electra,* Eugene O'Neill; *The Flies,* Jean-Paul Sartre

We suggest that you preview these works before recommending them to students.

INTERNET

You and your students may find additional information about Sophocles on the Internet.

For the text of all three plays in the Oedipus trilogy, go to **gopher://gopher.vt.edu:10010/02/142/4**

You may also find related information about Greek tragedy on the Internet. We *strongly recommend* that you preview the sites before you send students to them.

◆ Critical Thinking

INTERPRET

1. Is there any evidence of Oedipus' *hubris*—excessive pride—in this scene? **[Infer]**

2. Oedipus has two main interests in locating Laius' murderer. One is to lift the plague from Thebes. (a)What is Oedipus' second reason for wanting to bring the murderer to justice? (b) What is strange about this reason? **[Interpret]**

3. What is ironic—contradictory or surprising—about the priest's appeal to Oedipus as savior of Thebes? **[Analyze]**

APPLY

4. What does this excerpt from *Oedipus the King* suggest about the religious beliefs of the ancient Greeks? **[Generalize]**

EXTEND

5. Compare and contrast the characters of Oedipus and Macbeth as they first appear in their respective plays. **[Literary Link]**

Literary Connection

DRAMA

Two thousand years separate Greek tragedy from Shakespearean tragedy. Despite this gap in time and differences between ancient Greece and Elizabethan England, some elements of tragedy remain constant: a central character who through a tragic flaw and the action of fate is led to destruction.

1. What is the earliest evidence of Macbeth's tragic flaw?

2. In this scene from Oedipus, is there any evidence as yet of the central character's tragic flaw? Explain.

3. Compare the role of the witches in Act I of *Macbeth* with that of Apollo in this scene from *Oedipus the King.*

Idea Bank

Writing

1. Greece's Most Wanted Write the script for an episode of a crime-fighting television show that reenacts the murder of Laius and offers a reward for further information.

2. Journal of a King As Oedipus, write a journal entry that chronicles the events of the day. Describe your reactions to events and include a plan of action for saving Thebes.

3. The Tragic Flaw Both Oedipus and Macbeth are brave and honorable men, yet something makes the good men evil. Analyze the use of the tragic flaw in presenting both men's characters. Who do you think is more evil? Should both men be brought to justice? Are their circumstances different?

Speaking and Listening

4. Performance With a small group, act out this scene from *Oedipus the King.* As you rehearse, decide on the emotion or emotions that each character should convey in a speech. Also, remember to avoid pausing at line endings unless there is a comma or end mark. **[Performing Arts Link]**

Project

5. Greek Mask Research Greek masks. From your findings, choose a design that you would like to imitate. Then, using cardboard, papier-mâché, or some other suitable material, create a mask like those worn by actors in ancient Greece. **[Art Link]**

Answers

◆ Critical Thinking

1. Students might point to line 7, in which Oedipus identifies himself as "whom all men call the great."
2. (a) The murderer might also want to kill Oedipus. (b) Although he does not know it, Oedipus is the murderer.
3. It is ironic because Oedipus is the reason the gods have set the plague on Thebes.
4. Fate is unavoidable; although gods have to be obeyed, they do not make it easy for mortals to do so; incest is the worst of sins; killing a stranger is permissible, but killing a parent invokes the wrath of the gods.
5. They both appear as brave and honorable men. Macbeth is a victorious general, and Oedipus is a king. Both are confronted by a puzzling situation: the witches hail Macbeth as Thane of Cawdor and as a future king; Oedipus' future was predicted by the oracle.

Literary Connection

1. Suggested response: Macbeth's excessive ambition is first seen when Ross and Angus tell him he has been made Thane of Cawdor. His aside, "The greatest is behind," and his remark to Banquo about Banquo's children being kings, indicate that he hopes the witches' prophecy comes true.
2. Suggested response: If Oedipus' tragic flaw is *hubris,* then this flaw is seen in his speech to the crowd.
3. The witches and Apollo both give the critical piece of information that sets the events of the tragedy in motion.

✓ ASSESSMENT OPTIONS

Formal Assessment, Selection Test, pp. 80–81, and Assessment Resources Software. The selection test is designed so that it can be easily customized to the performance levels of your students.

PORTFOLIO ASSESSMENT

Use the following rubrics in the ***Alternative Assessment*** booklet to assess student writing:

Greece's Most Wanted: Summary Rubric, p. 99

Journal of a King: Problem-Solution Rubric, p. 102

The Tragic Flaw: Comparison/Contrast Rubric, p. 104

Idea Bank

Customizing for
Performance Levels

Following are suggestions for matching the Idea Bank topics with your students' performance levels:

- Less Advanced Students: 1, 5
- Average Students: 2, 4
- More Advanced Students: 3

Customizing for
Learning Modalities

Following are suggestions for matching Idea Bank topics with your students' learning modalities:

- Visual/Spatial: 5
- Bodily/Kinesthetic: 4
- Intrapersonal: 2
- Interpersonal: 4
- Verbal/Linguistic: 1, 2, 3, 4

Prepare and Engage

Establish Writing Guidelines
Review the following key characteristics of a drama:

- Most dramas are narrative in nature; they should tell a story.
- Character and plot are revealed through dialogue.
- Because dramas are intended to be performed, they include stage directions.

You may want to distribute the Scoring Rubric for Drama (p. 110 in ***Alternative Assessment***). Review with students the criteria on which their dramas will be evaluated. To customize this rubric for this assignment, add the criteria on page 374.

Make students aware of the additional help available in the Writing Handbook. Refer them to page 1189 for instruction on the writing process and page 1192 for further information on drama.

Writing and Language Transparencies You may use Writing Process Model 4: Dramatic Scene (pp. 25–34) to provide a model and to review the writing process.

Review the model on this page and the Writing Skills Focus points that are addressed in the annotations.

Writer's Solution

Writers at Work Videodisc
Introduce students to professional poet and playwright Derek Walcott by playing the videodisc segment. Ask students to note what motivates him to write. Then ask students to think about topics that might motivate them to write and how they might use these topics for their dramas.

Play frames 9291 to 19694

Writing Stage Directions
Explain to students that the performance of a drama may differ greatly from their understanding of it from a reading. For example, many plays are accompanied by music, dialogue may be sung, and settings may vary according to the decisions of the director—Macbeth might have a discussion with Macduff while playing a round of golf—and special effects. Remind students that plays are open to interpretation. When they write stage directions, they should write precise instructions unless they want the staging to be open to interpretation by the director.

Writing Lab CD-ROM
Allow students the option of writing their dramas on the computer. Have them work in the tutorial on Creative Writing. They should follow these steps:

1. Review the audio-annotated model on drama.
2. Use the Character, Conflict, and Setting wheel to come up with possible topics for their dramas.
3. Review the interactive tips on using dialogue in a drama.
4. Use the Story Line Diagram to organize details of the play.
5. Draft their dramas.
6. Use the Evaluation Checklist for Monologues, Soliloquies, Plays, or Video Scripts.

Sourcebook
For additional instruction on writing a drama, refer students to Chapter 6 on Creative Writing, pp. 166–195.

Drama

Writing Process Workshop

The Tragicall Hiſtorie of the Life and Death of Doctor Fauſtus.

With new Additions.

Written by Ch. Mar.

Printed at London for *Iohn Wright*, and are to be ſold at his ſhop without Newgate. 1631.

Although Shakespeare wrote *The Tragedy of Macbeth* about four hundred years ago, the elements that contributed to its success are still used by dramatists today. Write a drama in which you tell a story through your characters' dialogue and action.

The following skills will help you write a dramatic piece.

Writing Skills Focus

- **Complete a storyline diagram** to build a plot that hinges on a conflict and that has a logical sequence of events.
- **Develop characters** that are interesting and believable. Identify their traits and flaws, and have their actions and motives make sense within the play.
- **Write realistic dialogue** that fits each character's personality and background.
- **Use precise details** in stage directions to describe the settings in which the drama takes place. (See p. 363.)

Model From Literature

from *The Tragical Life and Death of Doctor Faustus*, by Christopher Marlowe

[Enter MEPHOSTOPHILIS.] ①
MEPHOSTOPHILIS. Now, Faustus, what wouldst thou have me do?
FAUSTUS. I charge thee wait upon me whilst I live,
To do whatever Faustus shall command, ②
Be it to make the moon drop from her sphere,
Or the ocean to overwhelm the world. ③
MEPHOSTOPHILIS. I am a servant to great Lucifer,
And may not follow thee without his leave.
No more than he commands must we perform.
FAUSTUS. Did he not charge thee to appear to me?
MEPHOSTOPHILIS. No, I came hither of my own accord. ④

① Precise details in stage directions reveal such things as entrances, exits, actors' gestures, and sound effects.

② Marlowe's dialogue is written in blank verse, which closely approximates the rhythms of everyday speech.

③ This passage of dialogue reveals Faustus's thirst for power.

④ The last two lines of dialogue develop the plot: We learn that Mephostophilis came to Faustus of his own free will.

Prewriting

Choose a Subject for Your Drama You may want to base your play on a story you've read, or you could continue in dramatic form a story that already exists. Other options are to write a drama about a historical event, an event you've experienced or witnessed, or a totally imaginary incident.

Create a Story-Line Diagram Since a play tells a story, it should have a plot, or sequence of events, that develops around a conflict. Create a story-line diagram like this one in which you plan the exposition, rising action, climax, falling action, and resolution.

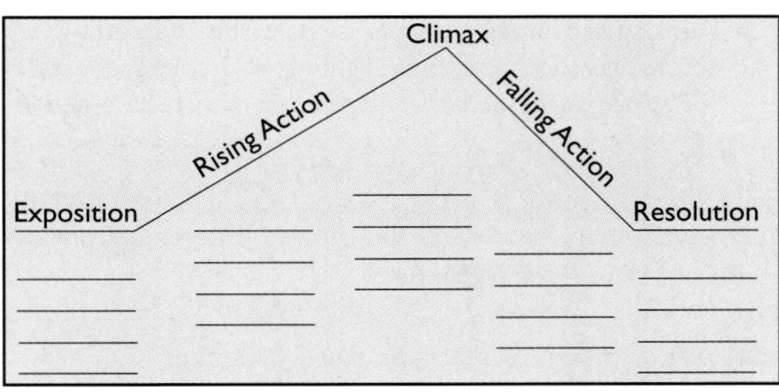

Jot Down Precise Details The setting, character descriptions, and notes about costumes, lighting, and sound effects all contribute to the effectiveness of a drama. Jot down some precise details about each of these aspects before you begin drafting.

Develop Interesting Characters Create a Character Trait chart in which you list characters' traits, habits, attitudes, and levels of intelligence. You might also jot down ideas about how each character might speak.

Drafting

Refer to Your Story-Line Diagram Review the plot events in your story-line diagram before you begin drafting. You may elect to write a scene involving the climax first, then write the surrounding scenes.

Let the Characters Take Over Put yourself in the place of each character, and, as you draft your drama, let the voice of each character "take over." Let each character's personality come through the words he or she speaks.

Use Precise Details Include concise stage directions that tell actors how to deliver their lines, what props to use, and what gestures to make. You may also include precise details about costumes, sets, lighting, and sound effects.

Applying Language Skills: Informal English

Informal English is the language of everyday speech. When creating realistic dialogue, writers often use slang, contractions, and sentence fragments to mimic real speech.

Formal Language:
Hello, Mary! What are you doing this afternoon?

Informal Language:
Hey Mary! What's up?

Practice Label the following sentences formal or informal English.

1. Today, I present to you my farewell to politics.
2. Mary, Queen of Scots and her sister Elizabeth I couldn't stand each other.
3. Henry, as your friend, listen to my advice. I would never steer you wrong.
4. Thomas, the choice is yours. Either support me or meet your death.

Writer's Solution Connection
Language Lab

For help in using precise words and details, complete the lesson on Writing with Nouns and Verbs in the Writing Style section.

Applying Language Skills

Informal Language Explain to students that although informal language comes naturally in speech, it does not always do so when they are writing. Remind students that it is important to make dialogue realistic by making it informal.

Answers

1. Formal; 2. Informal
3. Informal; 4. Formal

Develop Student Writing

Prewriting

To help students choose a subject for their dramas, place Art Transparency 18 (p. 75), *The Reflection in the Store Window Glass* by Yuan Lee, on an overhead projector. Ask students to describe the different scenes that are reflected in the store window. List their ideas on the chalkboard. Then suggest that students choose either one of those scenes to dramatize or write a drama on what is seen from inside the shop from the store owner's point of view.

Customize for
Intrapersonal Learners

Students who work better alone rather than with others may create a character description for each character, in which they describe this character's physical appearance, intelligence, emotions and so on. They may also list characters' favorite and least favorite foods, movies, seasons, colors, and so on. Have them include things that make the characters happy, sad, or angry. Students should refer to this sheet as they develop the plot for their dramas. Understanding how characters will react is crucial to creating a story line.

Tell students how to use the Story Line Diagram on this page. Explain each part of the diagram: the exposition provides the background necessary to understand the play; the rising action includes the events that lead to a confrontation; the climax is the turning point of the play; the falling action consists of the repercussions of the climax; and in the resolution, the conflict is resolved.

Writer's Solution

Writing Lab CD-ROM

Some students may prefer to complete their Story Line Diagram on the computer in the Creative Writing tutorial.

Drafting

As students draft their dramas, remind them to refer to their Story Line Diagrams and incorporate the events and details into their dramas. Also review the tips on this page on letting characters' voices take over and on incorporating precise details.

Revising

As students revise their dramas, have them use the revising checklist on this page. In addition, have students review their papers according to the criteria in the Scoring Rubric for Drama, p. 110.

Writer's Solution

Writing Lab CD-ROM
Students may use the self-evaluation checklist for drama in the Creative Writing tutorial to evaluate conflict, dialogue, setting, and stage directions. You may also have students review the interactive tips for improving a drama.

Publishing

In addition to the suggestions on this page, encourage students to turn their dramas into video scripts. By adding camera directions and scenery suggestions, they can prepare their dramas for videotaping. Ask them to share their videos with the class.

Reinforce and Extend

To reinforce and extend students' understanding of the key characteristics of dramas, suggest that students attend a school performance or rent a videotape of a dramatic performance. Students should first read the play, and then evaluate how the key characteristics of a drama were transferred to the stage.

Applying Language Skills
Formatting Drama Review with students the guidelines for script formatting on this page. Have students apply them to their drafts and then review each other's papers for accuracy. Writers should then revise as necessary for correct format.

APPLYING LANGUAGE SKILLS: Formatting Drama

Although there is no single way to format a script the following tips will help you determine a style and follow it consistently.

(*Lights up.* RONALD *is revealed in the center of a sparsely furnished room.*) (1)

RONALD (2) Whew. It's a hot one. (3)

General Guidelines

1. Stage directions are usually italicized and appear in parentheses or brackets.
2. Dialogue is preceded by the character's name in boldfaced capital letters. A period or colon may separate it from the dialogue.
3. Following a character's name are lines of dialogue. These are the words that are actually spoken onstage.

Writing Application Review your draft and standardize the format of the script.

Writer's Solution Connection
Writing Lab
For guidance, see the Proofreading Checklist for Dramas in the Revising and Editing section of the Creative Writing tutorial.

Revising

Use a Checklist Use the writing skills listed on page 372 as a checklist to evaluate and revise your dramatic piece.

- Does one plot event follow logically from another?
  Review the events and rearrange those that are out of order.
- Does the dialogue develop interesting characters and further the action of the play?
  Reexamine your notes on each character and reveal his or her traits through dialogue. Cut out dialogue that isn't realistic, or that is unimportant to the action of the play.
- Have I used precise details to describe the setting, actors' gestures, costume, lighting, and sound effects?
  Replace vague or misleading details with precise details.

REVISION MODEL

(QUEEN ELIZABETH I *seated on the throne. She is surrounded by various writers of her court:* SIR WALTER RALEIGH, EDMUND SPENSER, and SIR PHILIP SIDNEY. *There is confusion, and voices are raised.* ①)

QUEEN. (*in a raised, aristocratic voice*) Silence!

SIR WALTER. ~~I'm sorry,~~ A thousand pardons, ② Your Majesty.

QUEEN Silence! ~~You will all be invited to the festival, but~~ ③ only one of you is to go to the festival and wear my favor. By tomorrow, submit your best verse to me, and I'll choose the victor then.

① These precise details were added to deepen the readers' understanding of the events.

② The phrase "I'm sorry" was changed to one more realistic for this era, situation, and character.

③ The writer changed the dialogue to add suspense to the plot.

Publishing

- **Internet** Post your writing on a message board for theater enthusiasts.
- **Drama Club** Have a local drama group act out your play.
- **School Literary Magazine** Publish your dramatic work for your peers to critique. Ask them to submit alternative endings to your play.
- **Classroom** With classmates playing roles, conduct a reading of your play.

ASSESSMENT		4	3	2	1
PORTFOLIO ASSESSMENT Use the Scoring Rubric for Drama in ***Alternative Assessment*** (p. 110) to assess students' writing. Add these criteria to customize the rubric to this assignment.	**Realistic Dialogue**	The dialogue of the characters in the play is completely realistic.	Most of the dialogue of the characters is realistic.	The dialogue of the characters is frequently forced and rarely realistic.	The dialogue of the characters is not realistic.
	Stage Directions and Settings	The writer consistently uses precise details to create clear and thorough stage directions and settings.	The writer uses precise details, but gives insufficient detail in stage directions and settings.	The stage directions and settings are unclear and insufficient.	The writer does not include stage directions and settings.

Real-World Reading Skills Workshop

Following Test Directions

Strategies for Success

Just as an actor in a performance of *Macbeth* needs to follow the director's instructions, you need to follow written directions when taking a test. In both cases, the directions are the key to a good performance.

Read the Directions In order to be a successful test taker, use the following strategies when reading directions:

- Don't Rush. Take the time to read directions all the way through. Just reading *Choose the letter of the word that is the best . . .* doesn't tell you what to do. Don't make assumptions; just because your teacher always asks you to find the antonym of a word does not mean she will do so this time.
- Take advantage of examples. Many tests provide sample questions. Work back and forth between directions and examples, noting how each part of the example relates to the corresponding part of the directions. If an answer is given, try to figure out why it's correct.
- Ask questions. If you don't understand the directions, ask your teacher or the test facilitator for help.

Apply the Strategies

Read the SAT directions presented on this page. Then answer the following questions to make sure you understand the directions correctly.

1. Which words are the original words and phrases, and which are the A–E answer choices?
2. Which phrase tells you what analogies are?
3. How could you figure out what the symbols : and :: mean? What do they mean?
4. Why is *C* the correct answer?

Here are other tests that require you to carefully follow directions:
- *Driver's license test*
- *Employment tests*
- *College achievement tests*

The analogies questions present two words or phrases that are related in some way. Determine which A-through-E answer choice below has a relationship similar to the original words or phrases.
Example: BOOK: AUTHOR::
(A) poem: novel
(B) parent: child
(C) statue: sculptor
(D) law: judge
(E) word: writer

Introduce the Strategy

Students probably already have experience with standardized tests. Remind them of the importance of good test-taking strategies, such as carefully reading directions, which can help them to raise their scores. Have students review the key points on this page about following test directions.

Apply the Strategy

1. *Book* and *author* are the original words, the A–E choices are *poem:novel; parent:child; stature:sculptor; law:judge* and *word:writer.*
2. Analogies are defined in the first line as "words or phrases that are related in some way."
3. By using the direction line "Determine which A-through-E answer choice below has a relationship similar to the original words or phrases," you can assume that the colon means "is to" and the double colon means "as," indicating a relationship to the example.
4. *C* is the correct answer because it shows the relationship of a product to its creator. A statue is a product of a sculptor as a book is the product of an author.

Beyond the Classroom

Workplace Skills

Following Directions Explain to students that although following directions may seem to be a simple task, it often is not. One can misinterpret directions—either written or oral—and follow procedures incorrectly. Encourage students to make a habit of using the following tactics when following directions:

1. If directions are given orally, take notes. Don't assume you will remember everything.
2. Review the directions with the person who supplied them.
3. After you have completed the task, review the directions to make sure you have followed them correctly.

Emphasize to students that when they start out in a career, they will be following the directions of supervisors and completing tasks assigned. In order to advance, employees must prove that they can follow directions carefully to accomplish tasks efficiently.

Introduce the Strategy

Explain to students that reprocessing information is something people do on a daily basis. when communicating, most people unconsciously determine what information is important and what is unimportant—or safely left unsaid. When information is unsifted, main points are hard to identify because they are buried within the mass of irrelevant data. In order to be a good information provider, students need to think about what they are going to tell others. Tell students to read the following strategies on oral retelling. Ask them if they already use some of the strategies. If so, do they think they are successful?

Customize for
Verbal/Linguistic Learners
For those learners who are not necessarily good communicators, the task of providing information may be difficult. Have these students write out all the details of the information they would like to pass on. Then have them apply the strategies on this page to what they have written. They should use these strategies as guidelines for determining what information is important enough to convey to someone else.

Apply the Strategy

Role-playing will help students hone their communication skills. Ask peers to give honest, yet tactful, feedback on their peers' retellings.

Speaking and Listening Workshop: Oral Retelling

What you tell others is often a *re*telling, whether you're repeating a joke you heard from your best friend or describing the latest twist of events on your favorite soap opera. Sometimes, it's not a story but information that you need to pass on. Perhaps your friend missed soccer practice and wants to know what happened. By keeping in mind a few rules of retelling, you'll be a better storyteller and information passer.

Grabbing and Keeping Your Audience's Attention To grab your audience's attention when retelling a story, use the following strategies:

- ▶ Decide on your purpose for telling the story before you start. Do you want your listener to laugh? Be inspired? Feel sympathy?
- ▶ Briefly go over your story in your head before you start and plan to build toward some kind of climax.

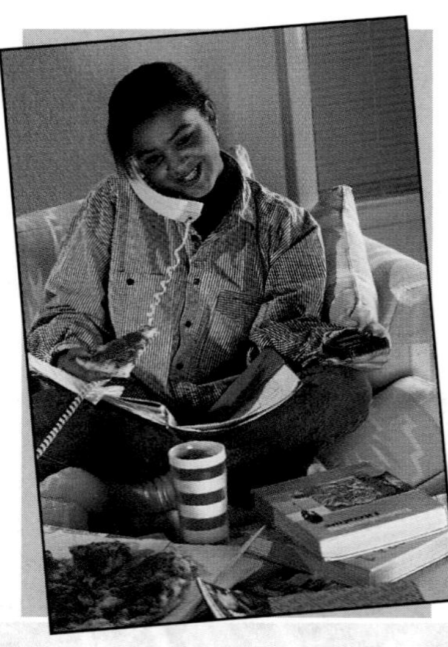

When conveying information, use the following strategies to keep your audience's attention:

- ▶ Organize the facts you want to convey around a few main topics. Make sure all the topics are relevant and eliminate any unnecessary information.
- ▶ Hit the high points. Ground your listener in the *who, where,* and *when* before you get to the *what.* Avoid digressions, side events that come to your mind but lead you away from the main point.

Tips for Retelling a Story

- *Decide on your purpose.*
- *Structure a story to build to a climax.*

Conveying Information

- *Don't tell more than is needed.*
- *Put essential information first.*

Apply the Strategies

Role-play these situations with a partner:

1. Pretend your partner missed yesterday's English class. In five minutes or less, tell him or her what happened. Does your partner agree that you covered the important points?
2. Recall a story you especially enjoyed or a television show or movie that stirred your feelings. Then retell the story or plot so that your listener shares your feelings.
3. Exaggerate the bad habits of a dull storyteller or a boring information giver to produce a humorous effect.

Beyond the Classroom

Workplace Skills

Conveying Information Conveying information is one key to a successful working environment. Due to people's hectic schedules, information sometimes does not get passed on to people who need it to do their jobs well. Students should be aware that lack of information can slow up a project and waste time, often resulting in work that must be redone. Let students know that they should convey important information to others in a timely way.

Extended Reading Opportunities

The following works reflect the exploration of the arts, foreign lands, and the human condition that occurred during the English Renaissance.

Suggested Titles

Hamlet
William Shakespeare

One of Shakespeare's greatest tragedies, *Hamlet* is the tale of a young man forced to confront and question all he formerly believed as true. As the play begins, Prince Hamlet is mourning the death of his father, the King of Denmark. In addition, he must accept the new marriage of his mother to the king's brother, who now rules Denmark. As Hamlet struggles with these changes, the ghost of the dead king appears to him; the king tells Hamlet that he was poisoned by his brother and urges Hamlet to avenge his murder.

The Tempest
William Shakespeare

This drama is a tale of magic, mystery, and love that takes place on what at first appears to be a deserted island. Prospero, the rightful Duke of Milan, his daughter Miranda, the spirit Ariel, and the man-monster Caliban inhabit the island. Through his magic and the aid of Ariel, Prospero is able to lure a boat to the island that contains his brother Antonio, who dispossessed him of his throne. Prospero works his magic to arrive at a wonderful marriage for his daughter and the prince of Naples and to reclaim his rightful title.

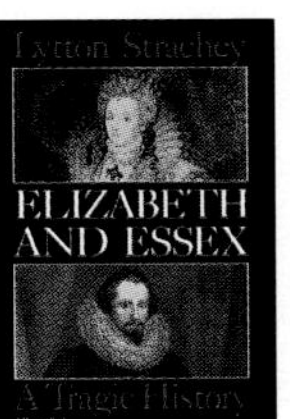

Elizabeth and Essex
Lytton Strachey

She was the Queen of England and 53 years old. He was a young courtier of 20. For thirteen years he remained her favorite. Then he disobeyed orders, setting into motion the events that led to his tragic end. Innovative biographer Lytton Strachey wrote nonfiction as absorbing as any novel. In this classic account of Queen Elizabeth and Robert Devereaux, Earl of Essex, the world of the Tudor Queen and her courtiers comes vividly to life.

Other Possibilities

Edmund Spenser	*The Faerie Queene*
Thomas Stoppard	*Rosencrantz and Guildenstern are Dead*

Planning Students' Extended Reading

The works listed on this page capture the glory and adventure of the Renaissance period. The following information may help you choose which works to assign.

Customize for *Varying Student Needs and Interests*

- *The Tragedy of Hamlet, Prince of Denmark* includes difficult language and concepts and would work best with advanced students. You might provide students with focus points or summaries for each act to prepare them for reading.
- Although *The Tempest* includes difficult language, it is one of Shakespeare's lighter plays and would be enjoyed by students of all ability levels and interests.
- *Elizabeth and Essex* may interest those students who prefer to read prose.

Sensitive Issues If you choose to teach either *Hamlet* or *The Tempest*, you should be aware that they contain some issues that you might find sensitive in your classroom.

Hamlet is considered Shakespeare's most famous tragedy. You may wish to use caution in teaching it since it involves murder, inappropriate relationships, a teenager grappling with the loss of a father and the new marriage of his mother, and suicide. *The Tempest*, a much lighter work, includes an allusion to an attempted rape and many instances of magic.

Literature Study Guides
Literature study guides are available for both Shakespeare plays. These guides include section summaries, discussion questions, and activities.

Resources for Teaching Novels, Plays and Literature Collections
This resource contains graphic organizers, teaching strategies, and transparencies that will be invaluable in teaching any of these three works.

Customize for *Special Needs*

For your special-needs students, you may want to consider using Globe Fearon's Adapted Classics series version of *Hamlet*.

Planning Instruction and Assessment

Unit Objectives

1. To read selections from seventeenth and eighteenth century English literature
2. To apply a variety of reading strategies, particularly strategies for constructing meaning, appropriate for reading these selections
3. To recognize literary elements used in these selections
4. To build vocabulary in context.
5. To learn elements of grammar, usage, and style
6. To write in a variety of modes and about situations based on the selections
7. To develop speaking and listening skills, by completing proposed activities

Meeting the Objectives

With each selection, you will find instructional material and portfolio opportunities through which students can meet these objectives. Further, you will find additional practice pages for reading strategies, literary elements, vocabulary, and grammar in the ***Selection Support*** booklet in the Teaching Resources box.

Setting Goals Work with your students at the beginning of the unit to set goals for unit outcomes. Plan what skills and concepts you wish students to acquire. You may individualize these according to students' performance levels or learning modalities.

Portfolios You may have students keep portfolios of their work or of their work in progress. The activities and prompts on the Build Your Portfolio page of each selection provide opportunities for students to apply the concepts presented with the selection.

King Charles I After the Battle of Naseby, *(June 14, 1645)*

Humanities: Art

King Charles I After the Battle of Naseby (June 14, 1645).

This painting portrays one of the closing events in the turbulent reign of King Charles I. After Charles battled with Parliament and ruled without Parliament, his insistence on the divine right of kings prompted a civil war. Charles's army lost several important battles, and the king finally surrendered to the army of Scotland in 1646. Put into Parliament's custody, Charles escaped, was recaptured, and was executed as a traitor in 1649.

Ask students to identify the king, who is on horseback with his sword raised. Encourage them to imagine the situation: A Scottish soldier, who is probably not a nobleman, gives orders to the king himself, a ruler who had claimed that his authority over other humans was God-given.

Have your students link the art to the focus of Unit 3, "A Turbulent Time," by answering the following questions:

1. Does King Charles seem to behave like a defeated man, being taken prisoner? Explain. *Most students will answer that the king looks more defiant than defeated, because he remains on horseback in full regalia with his sword raised.*
2. What is the soldier is pointing at? *He may be pointing to show the king where they are going, or perhaps he is showing the king that the battle has gone against him.*

A Turbulent Time (1625–1798)

Methinks I see in my mind a noble . . . nation rousing herself like a strong man after sleep, and shaking her invincible locks.

—John Milton, from *Areopagitica*

Assessing Student Progress

The following tools are available to measure the degree to which students meet the unit objectives:

Informal Assessment

The questions in the Guide for Responding sections are a first level of response to the concepts and skills presented with the selection. Students' responses are a brief informal measure of their grasp of the material. Their responses on this level can indicate where further instruction and practice are needed. You may then follow up with the practice pages in the ***Selection Support*** booklet.

You will find literature and reading guides in the ***Alternative Assessment*** booklet, which you may give students on an individual basis for informal assessment of their performance.

Formal Assessment

In the ***Formal Assessment*** booklet, you will find selection tests and part tests.

Selection Tests The selection tests measure comprehension and skills acquisition for each selection or group of selections.

Part Tests Each part test, which calls on students to read a passage of literature they have not previously seen, applies the unit skills on a broader level. The Critical Reading section measures Unit Objectives 1, 2, and 3. The Vocabulary and Grammar section measures Objectives 4 and 5. The Essay section measures Objectives 1 and 6. Both the Critical Reading and Vocabulary and Grammar sections use formats similar to those found on many standardized tests, including the SAT.

Assessment Options

Portfolios As you review individual pieces or the collected work in students' portfolios, you will find assessment sheets available in the portfolio section of the ***Alternative Assessment*** booklet.

Scoring Rubrics You will find scoring rubrics for writing modes in the ***Alternative Assessment*** booklet. You can apply these to Writing Mini-Lessons and to Writing Process Workshop lessons.

Speaking and Listening The ***Alternative Assessment*** booklet contains assessment sheets for speaking and listening activities.

Learning Modalities The ***Alternative Assessment*** booklet contains activities that appeal to different learning styles. You may use these also as an alternative assessment of students' growth.

Using the Timeline

The Timeline can serve a number of instructional purposes, as follows:

Getting an Overview Use the Timeline to help students get a quick overview of themes and events of the period. This approach will benefit all students but may be especially helpful for visually oriented students, English language learners, and those less proficient in reading. (For strategies in using the Timeline as an overview, see the bottom of this page.)

Thinking Critically Questions are provided on the facing page. Use these questions to have students review the events, discuss their significance, and examine the *so what* behind the *what happened.*

Connecting to Selections Have students refer to the Timeline when reading individual selections. By consulting the Timeline regularly, they will gain a better sense of the period's chronology. In addition, they will appreciate what was occurring in the world that gave rise to these works of literature.

Projects Students can use the Timeline as a launching pad for projects like these:

- **The Beginnings of Modernity** Have students look for events in the Timeline that helped make the world look more as it does today. Ask them to create a customized timeline charting the beginnings of the modern world, adding dates of related events and themes as they read new selections.
- **Report on a Painting** Have students scan the Timeline for a painting title that interests them, research the work and its significance, then report on their findings to the class.

Timeline

1625–1798

1625 | 1640 | 1655

British Events

- **1627** Sir Francis Bacon's *The New Atlantis* is published. ▼
- **1628** William Harvey explains blood circulation.
- **1633 John Donne's** *Songs and Sonnets* published.
- **1633** George Herbert's *The Temple* published.
- **1635** Public mail service established.
- **1637 John Milton** publishes *Lycidas.*
- **1640** Charles I summons Long Parliament.
- **1642** English Civil War begins.
- **1646 John Suckling** publishes *Fragmenta Aurea.*
- **1647** George Fox founds Society of Friends (Quakers).

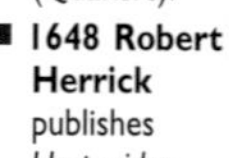

- **1648 Robert Herrick** publishes *Hesperides.*
- **1649** Charles I beheaded. ▲
- **1649** Puritans close theaters.
- **1649 Richard Lovelace** publishes *Lucasta.*
- **1649** Oliver Cromwell becomes Lord Protector.
- **c. 1650** Early newspaper ads appear.
- **c. 1650** Full-bottomed wigs come into fashion. ▶

- **1658** Oliver Cromwell dies.
- **1658** Puritan government collapses.
- **1660** Monarchy restored.
- **1660** Theaters reopened.
- **1660 Samuel Pepys** begins *Diary.*
- **1662** Royal Society chartered.
- **1663** Drury Lane Theater opens. ▲
- **1666** Great Fire of London.
- **1666** First cheddar cheese produced.
- **1667 John Milton's** *Paradise Lost* published. ▼
- **1668** John Dryden publishes *An Essay of Dramatic Poesy.*
- **1670** Covent Garden Market opens.

World Events

- **c. 1600** Japan: Kabuki theater developed. ▲
- **1614** North America: Dutch found New Amsterdam. ▼
- **1630** North America: William Bradford begins writing *Of Plymouth Plantation.*

- **1630** Boston founded by John Winthrop.
- **1635** Japan: All Europeans expelled.
- **1636** North America: Rhode Island founded by Roger Williams.
- **1640** India: English settlement established at Madras.
- **1640** North America: *Bay Psalm Book* published in Massachusetts.
- **1642** Holland: Rembrandt paints *Night Watch.*
- **1643** France: Louis XIV becomes king.
- **1644** China: Ming Dynasty ends. ▶
- **1650** North America: Anne Bradstreet's collection of poems *The Tenth Muse Lately Sprung Up in America* published.
- **1651** North America: William Bradford finishes *Of Plymouth Plantation.*
- **1661** Holland: Rembrandt paints *The Syndics.*

- **1662** France: Louis XIV begins building palace at Versailles. ▲
- **1664** North America: Britain seizes New Netherlands.
- **1664** France: Molière's *Tartuffe* first produced.
- **1666** Italy: Stradivari labels first violin.

Getting an Overview of the Period

Introduction To give students an overview of the period, indicate the span of dates in the upper left-hand corner. How much time is covered in this unit? *A period of 173 years is covered.* Next, point out that the Timeline is divided into specifically British Events (on top) and World Events (on bottom). Have them practice scanning the Timeline across, looking both at the British Events and the World Events. Finally, point out that the events in the Timeline often represent beginnings, turning points, and endings. *The restoration of the monarchy in 1660 is an example.*

Key Events Have students chart important political events. *In 1642, the Civil War begins; in 1649, the king is executed.* Then have them find evidence of cultural trends running parallel to these political developments. *In 1649, the year of the king's execution, the theaters are closed; they reopen when monarchy is restored, in 1660. In 1688, the Glorious Revolution occurs; in 1702, daily newspapers appear.* Ask students to formulate questions about possible relationships among political events and cultural trends. Using their own questions, ask them to speculate about changes in British society.

1680 | 1710 | 1755 | 1798

British Events

- **1685** James II becomes king.
- **1687** Sir Isaac Newton publishes his *Principia*.
- **1688** Glorious Revolution.
- **1688** Bill of Rights becomes law.
- **1690** John Locke publishes his *Two Treatises of Government*. ▼
- **1702** First daily newspaper begins publication.
- **1707** Great Britain created by Act of Union.
- **1709** First Copyright Act.
- **1709** First literary magazine, *The Tatler*, begins publication.
- **1712 Alexander Pope** publishes *The Rape of the Lock*.
- **1714** George I becomes king.
- **1719** First organized cricket match takes place. ▼
- **1719 Daniel Defoe** publishes *Robinson Crusoe*.
- **1726 Jonathan Swift** publishes *Gulliver's Travels*.
- **1735** William Hogarth paints *The Rake's Progress*.
- **1745** Last Jacobite rebellion in Scotland.
- **1749** Henry Fielding publishes *Tom Jones*.
- **1751 Thomas Gray** publishes "Elegy in a Country Churchyard."

- **1755 Samuel Johnson** publishes *Dictionary of the English Language*.
- **1756** Britain enters Seven Years' War.
- **1766** Oliver Goldsmith publishes *The Vicar of Wakefield*.
- **1775** Actress Sarah Siddons debuts at Drury Lane Theater. ▼
- **1786 Robert Burns** publishes *Poems Chiefly in Scottish Dialect*.
- **1791 James Boswell** publishes *The Life of Samuel Johnson*.
- **1793** England goes to war with France.
- **1798** Admiral Nelson defeats the French off Alexandria, Egypt.

World Events

- **1680** Dodo becomes extinct.
- **1680** China: All ports open to foreign trade. ▲
- **1682** North America: La Salle claims Louisiana for France.
- **1690** India: Calcutta founded by British.
- **1703** Russia: Peter the Great begins building St. Petersburg.

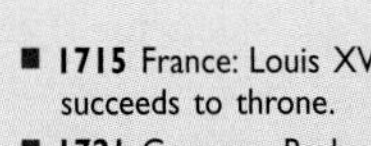

- **1715** France: Louis XV succeeds to throne.
- **1721** Germany: Bach composes *Brandenburg Concertos*. ▶
- **1727** Brazil: First coffee planted.
- **1728** Pacific: Bering explores Alaskan waters.
- **1740** Prussia: Frederick the Great succeeds to the throne.
- **1748** France: Montesquieu publishes *The Spirit of the Laws*.
- **1752** North America: Benjamin Franklin invents lightning rod.

- **1759** Canada: British troops capture Quebec.
- **1773** North America: Boston Tea Party. ▲
- **1775** North America: American Revolution begins.
- **1784** France: First school for the blind established.
- **1789** France: Revolution begins with storming of the Bastille.

▶Critical Viewing◀

1. (a) What elements do the Kabuki theater (c. 1600) and Charles I's beheading (1649) share? (b) What connection does this suggest between politics and theater? **[Speculate]** *(a) Both are witnessed by an audience. (b) Possible connection: Political events as well as theatrical events engage the interest of audiences.*
2. In a theater designed like the Drury Lane (1663), the spectators are part of the show. Explain how this is the case. **[Support]** *People sitting in the boxes can see into the boxes across the way as well as into the audience below.*
3. What does the difference between the shape of the Versailles palace (1661) and that of a cathedral suggest about the values each represents? **[Interpret]** *The inverted V-shapes of a cathedral's spires direct the eye up, towards God; Versailles's low horizontals and receding perspectives suggest a world of uniform space ordered by human power.*
4. Given what you can learn from the image, compare cricket (1719) with baseball. **[Compare and Contrast]** *Cricket, like baseball, appears to pit an individual using a bat against a "field." Like baseball, cricket probably has umpires (the figure in black in the upper left).*

◆ Critical Thinking

1. (a) Name two scientific achievements in this period. (b) What do these achievements suggest about the kind of observations made by scientists of the period? **[Hypothesize]** *(a) possible answers: Harvey explained the circulation of blood in 1628; Fahrenheit built a thermometer in Holland in 1709. (b) Their observations were probably "hands-on." Also, scientists were just beginning to discover things that we take for granted today.*
2. (a) What dramatic change marked English political life between 1649 and 1660? (b) What later world events might this period have influenced? Explain. **[Speculate]** *(a) During this time, England was not ruled by a monarch. (b) The American Revolution, begun in 1775, may have owed some inspiration to the prior English experience of government without a king.*
3. (a) What trend in publishing characterizes this period? (b) What does this trend suggest about society of the time? **[Hypothesize]** *(a) Newspapers and magazines were popular (see c. 1650, 1702, 1709). (b) Possible answers: More people at this time could read; people took an active interest in the general affairs of the day.*
4. (a) Name two events before 1710 showing Britain's expanding power. (b) What connection might there be between these events and events after 1750? **[Connect]** *(a) Madras (1640), New Netherlands (1664), and Calcutta (1691) became British territories. (b) British colonial expansion led to rivalry with other European nations, reflected in the Seven Years' War (1756) and its taking of Quebec (1763).*
5. (a) Name two items suggesting the chaos and unrest that mark this period. (b) What do these items indicate about the direction in which government was moving? **[Speculate]** *(a) Possible answers: England fought a civil war (1642); the king was beheaded (1649); the Puritan government collapsed (1658); London was ravaged by fire (1666); the Glorious Revolution took place (1688). (b) After going through a period of instability characterized by the conflicts of Charles I with Parliament, government became more centralized—with Cromwell and then Charles II. However, Parliament also seemed to be asserting its power and limiting that of the monarch.*

Develop Understanding

Customize for
Less Proficient Readers
Explain to these students that, during this time, people were shaken up by major changes in their lives and basic beliefs. Ask students to look for two of these major changes as they read.

Customize for
English Language Learners
Have these students look over A Graphic Look at the Period, and, for each of three pictures, create a question they would like answered. Ask them to see if they can find answers to their questions in The Story of the Times.

Customize for
Intrapersonal Learners
Students with an intrapersonal orientation will benefit by discussing the consequences of historical events for people's self-image. For example, you can ask how people saw themselves after the earth ceased to be thought of as the center of the universe, or during the period when they were no longer the subjects of a king.

Customize for
More Advanced Students
Challenge more advanced students to use A Graphic Look at the Period and The Story of the Times to examine how changes in institutions, symbols, ideas, and work through this period changed the ties that bound people together in society.

Answers to

A GRAPHIC LOOK

Analyze Primary Sources (a) The fact that the sun is at the center of the solar system, the representation of day and night as dependent on the Earth's orientation, and the mapping of the elliptical orbits of the planets all reflect a scientific view of the universe. (b) The face on the sun, the familiar zodiacal signs, and the mottos and symbolic human figures around the border reinforce a human-centric picture of the universe.

Interpret (a) Charles's execution is rendered in a crude, blocky, but literal way. (b) A more realistic picture might excite more disgust or sympathy with suffering—reactions that might make the viewer more sympathetic to the king's cause.

A GRAPHIC LOOK AT THE PERIOD

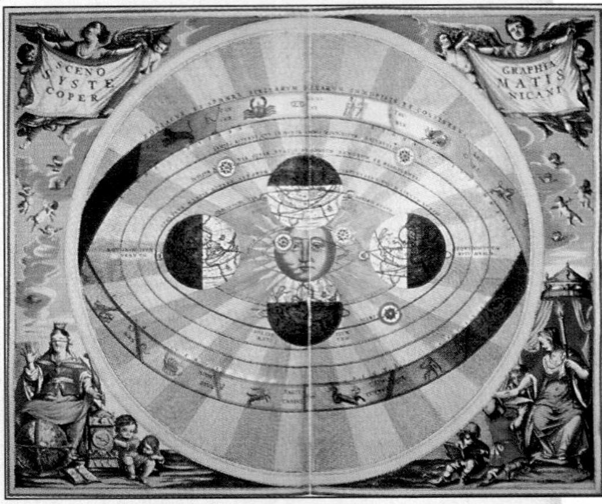

▲ **Analyze Primary Sources** By the seventeeth century the sun-centered solar system of Copernicus had gained greater acceptance. (a) What features of this Copernican map of the solar system reflect a scientific view of the universe? (b) What features tend to reinforce a reassuring "human-centric" perspective?

▲ **Interpret** (a) Describe the style in which Charles's execution is rendered in this picture. (b) How would the mood of the picture and your sense of the event be different if the picture were more realistic?

The Story of the Times
(1625–1798)

Historical Background

In 1649, the English shocked the world by beheading their king and abolishing the monarchy. Even in the decades before civil war tore England apart, revolutions in science and religion had unsettled people's world view. The new astronomy had exiled the Earth from the center of the universe to the vastness of infinite space: new religious creeds had brought down the traditions of centuries. John Donne wrote with his new found insecurity: "Tis all in pieces, all coherence gone." By the 1700's, though, a monarch was back on the throne, and a new, competitive society had sprung up, with a looser social structure and greater freedom in religion and politics.

Charles I and Parliament Charles I, crowned in 1625, clashed with Parliament frequently over a basic question: money. Charles needed money for his wars; Parliament refused to fund them. The king then extorted loans from his wealthy subjects and pressed the poor into service as soldiers and sailors. Parliament tried to prevent such abuses of power; Charles eventually dissolved Parliament, and would not call it into session for the next eleven years.

Charles I also turned up the flame under a simmering religious controversy. He insisted that clergymen "conform," or observe all the ceremonies of the Anglican Church. Puritans—Calvinists who wished to purify the Church of its Catholic traditions—were enraged by some of these requirements.

Radical Puritans believed that each group of worshipers, moved by the members' divinely granted consciences, had the right to choose its own minister—an idea dangerously close to democracy. For these and other ideas "dissenters" were persecuted and tortured as criminals.

Humanities: Music

Music Before and After the Civil War.

Born in 1592, John Jenkins was already a respected instrumentalist, composer, and teacher at the court of Charles I when Oliver Cromwell came to power. Like other court musicians, he left the turmoil of London for the countryside, where he taught. When the monarchy was restored in 1660, he was reappointed to the "King's Musicke."

The greater portion of Jenkins's output consists of compositions for small groups of string instruments called "consorts of viols." His works mark a transition from many-voiced consorts to a form resembling the trio sonata with its fewer voices.

Play the "Seven Fancies in Three Parts" on the **Listening to Music** Audio CD. Then ask students the following questions:

1. What musical elements reflect the turbulent political climate of the time? *The minor key makes it somber; dissonances create tension; the three voices almost compete with each other.*
2. This piece uses fewer instruments than earlier music. What can you infer from this fact about changing tastes? *Tastes may have moved towards music that was more introspective.*

The Civil War Charles's problems grew worse after he was forced to fight Scottish rebels outraged by his insistence on religious conformity. Desperate for money, he summoned a hostile Parliament, which passed wave upon wave of reforms. Angered when Charles tried to outmaneuver the reformers, Parliament condemned him as a tyrant in 1642. Civil war broke out. In 1645, Parliament's forces, led by Oliver Cromwell, defeated a royalist army and captured Charles. Radical Puritans, who by then dominated Parliament, tried the king and convicted him of treason. Charles I was beheaded on January 30, 1649.

Cromwell led the new government, called the English Commonwealth. Facing discontent at home and wars abroad, he dissolved Parliament in 1653 and named himself Lord Protector. Until his death in 1658, he ruled as a virtual dictator.

Civil war had not led to the free society for which many who fought against the king had hoped. Their idealistic hopes, coupled with economic hardships, led to social unrest. The Commonwealth also fueled popular discontent by outlawing gambling, horse racing, newspapers, fancy clothes, public dancing, and theater.

The Restoration By the time of Cromwell's death, England had had enough of taxation, violence, and disorder. In 1658, Parliament offered the crown to the exiled son of Charles I, who became Charles II in 1660. The monarchy was restored.

In sharp contrast to the drab Puritan leaders, Charles II's court copied the plush fashions of Paris. An avid patron of the arts and sciences, Charles invited Italian composers and Dutch painters to live and work in London. In 1662, he chartered the Royal Society, devoted to the study of natural science.

A Glorious Revolution Religious differences resurfaced with Charles II's successor, James II, a devout Catholic. Parliament eventually invited Mary, the Protestant daughter of James II, to rule England jointly with her husband, William of Orange. Rather than fight, James escaped to France. The people of England hailed the event as the "Glorious Revolution of 1688" since not a drop of blood had been shed.

In 1689, William and Mary agreed to respect a Bill of Rights passed by Parliament. The Bill guar-

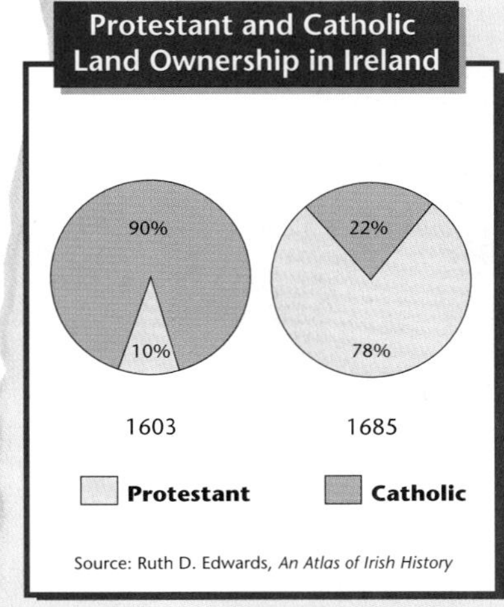

▲ **Read a Chart** The religious differences that drove the Civil War also festered in Ireland, where English and Scottish Protestants took over Irish Catholic lands. Judging from the chart, what was the rate at which the native Irish were losing land to others?

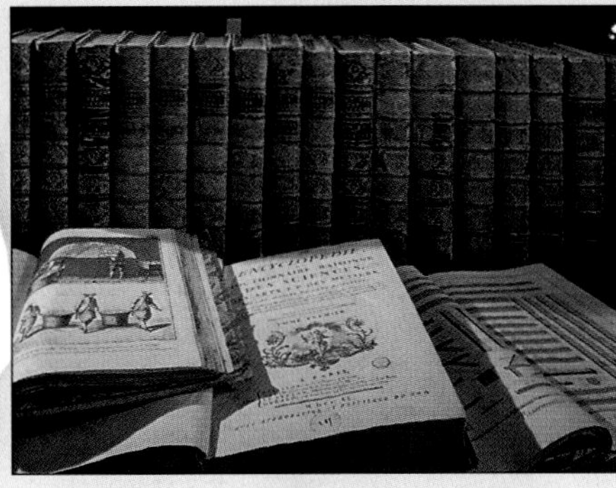

▲ **Speculate** The *Encyclopedia* produced by the French writer Diderot (1772) aimed to be a compendium of all knowledge. Its emphasis on what could be known by reason, unassisted by faith, angered some religious thinkers. What sort of eighteenth-century reader would have referred to Diderot's massive work on human knowledge?

Cross-Curricular Connection: Social Studies

The Bill of Rights and John Locke The 1688 Bill of Rights restated the traditional rights of English citizens, such as trial by jury. It abolished cruel or unusual punishment. It also affirmed the principle of *habeas corpus*—that no one could be jailed without being charged with a specific crime. Later, the Toleration Act of 1689 granted limited toleration to Protestant dissenters.

William and Mary accepted the Bill of Rights as part of the bargain by which Parliament granted them the throne. This historic event—a bargain between ruler and subjects—inspired some of the political thought of John Locke (1632–1704). True sovereignty, he argued, lies with the people. Legitimate government depends on the people's consent.

1. What connection is there between the English and American Bill of Rights? *The American document, influenced by the British, covers each of the rights listed above.*
2. What influential American document may have been influenced by Locke's ideas? *The Declaration of Independence emphasizes Locke's idea that governement depends on consent.*

Answers to

A GRAPHIC LOOK

Read a Chart The native Irish share of land dropped about 75% (from a 90% share to a 22% share) over 82 years—a decline of .9% per year.

Speculate Students may identify a reader with some education and money (to purchase the work), but perhaps in a profession not directly linked to Church or State, who might have a skeptical attitude towards established authority.

Connections to the Literature

- Students will get the flavor of the period's mood of uncertainty when they read Donne's "Meditation 17," p. 393. His "A Valediction: Forbidding Mourning," p. 398, shows how fragments of old, increasingly disputed cosmologies could be put to use to construct a new faith in personal love.
- As students read the excerpt from Milton's *Paradise Lost*, p. 434, they may think of how Milton answered the deep disruptions of the Civil War with an ambitious, poetic retelling of humanity's beginnings.
- Students will better understand the dilemmas faced by those who fought in the Civil War when they read Richard Lovelace's poems, beginning on page 448.
- For a mock-ingenuous look back at England's bloody seventeenth-century religious disputes—and a devastating indictment of human folly—have students read Jonathan Swift's "A Voyage to Lilliput," p. 476.

More About the Glorious Revolution When Charles II's brother James II inherited the throne of England in 1685, he made no secret of his Catholic faith. Riding roughshod over Parliamentary laws that he did not like, he appointed a number of Catholics to high offices. Parliament resented his lack of respect for their power. Fears spread among the people that James II, like Bloody Mary before him, would restore the Catholic Church to England.

Rather than risk returning to the kingless days of Cromwell's rule, Parliamentary leaders took an innovative step. It asked James's Protestant daughter, Mary, and her husband, William III of Orange, to become rulers of England.

Historical Background

Comprehension Check

1. Over what did Parliament and King Charles I clash? *Parliament and the king clashed over money—Parliament refused to give him any for his wars.*
2. Describe Charles I's policies regarding religion. *The king insisted that all clergyman use all of the ceremonies of the Church of England and persecuted religious dissenters, such as the Puritans.*
3. (a) What actions did Parliament finally take against Charles I? (b) Who led England after him? *(a) Parliament named him traitor, raised an army against him, captured him, and, eventually, executed him. (b) Oliver Cromwell led England after Charles I.*
4. How was monarchy restored to England? *Parliament invited Charles's son, Charles II, back to rule.*
5. What did Parliament do during the Glorious Revolution? *Parliament asked William and Mary to rule in place of James II, and to accept a Bill of Rights.*
6. Name two changes after the 1660's that contributed to Britain's wealth. *Agriculture became more efficient; industry developed more efficient ways of spinning and weaving cloth.*

Critical Thinking

1. What political consequences did some Puritan ideas have? **[Infer]** *Some believed that groups of worshippers, guided by their inner light, were competent to pick their own ministers. This challenged the idea that the Church (led by the king) had special authority over worshippers; it also resembled democracy.*
2. (a) Into what classes could Britain be divided at the beginning of the period? (b) What political trends demonstrate the rise of new classes after the Glorious Revolution? **[Analyze]** *(a) The king's quarrels with Parliament show a society divided between royalty, the wealthy, and the poor. (b) Political parties formed in Parliament, one representing a new merchant class, different from traditional aristocrats.*
3. How did greater efficiency in agriculture contribute to an industrial revolution? **[Analyze Cause and Effect]** *More efficient agriculture made more food available, which helped the population grow; laborers moved to growing towns, supplying a workforce for the new factories.*

▲ **Infer** At the beginning of this era, the majority of people farmed the land. Judging from the painting, what was the role of women in farming during this period?

◀ **Draw Conclusions** After the mid-1700's, many people left farms and traveled to cities. What conclusion can you draw from this engraving about the conditions that met workers who came to the cities?

anteed Parliament the right to approve all taxes and forbade a king from suspending the law. England thus attained a limited, or constitutional, monarchy. In ensuing decades, two political factions crystallized in Parliament: the conservative, aristocratic Tories and the Whigs, drawn largely from Britain's growing merchant class. A cabinet of ministers drawn from Parliament, and eventually unified under the leadership of a prime minister, began to rule the country.

An Agricultural Revolution In 1660, the vast majority of the British people were farmers who rented their fields from a landlord or cultivated a patch of common land. By the late 1600's, new farm tools made it possible for farmers to plant and harvest a much bigger crop. Landlords began to fence in the land they had once rented out, hiring laborers to work the land for them. Bigger, more efficient estates replaced the small holdings of earlier times.

By the mid-1700's, British farms were producing much more food. With more food available, the population of the small island surged upward. Since fewer farmhands were needed, many people left the countryside. In the growing towns, they became the factory hands who ran the machines of the early Industrial Revolution.

The Industrial Age British inventions after 1750 made the spinning and weaving of cloth much more efficient. The steam engine was perfected and adapted to run a power loom. Factories were built to produce vast quantities of cotton cloth. Merchants sold the goods all over the world, adding more gold to the nation's coffers. As late as the 1790's, a majority of British people still earned their living as farmers. Yet the economic revolution of the 1700's increased Britain's wealth enormously.

The Enlightenment The scientific revolution that made industry possible stemmed from a larger development in thought known as the Enlightenment. Enlightenment thinkers in all fields believed that, through reason and observation of nature, human beings can discover the order underlying all things. In 1687, Sir Isaac Newton published one of the touchstone works of the Enlightenment, a monumental study of gravity and the movement of the planets.

Cross-Curricular Connection: Social Studies

The Early Industrial Revolution Emphasize for students that the Industrial Revolution began with agriculture. In the 1700's, new technologies increased food production. Jethro Tull, for instance, invented a seed drill, a plow with a hopper that deposited seeds in straight lines. Seeds were no longer scattered and lost.

The next advance was the discovery of steam power, much more efficient than wind or water power. In a steam engine, water is heated by burning fuel, such as coal; the resulting steam enters an enclosed cylinder, where it pushes against a piston. James Watt's clever 1769 design improved fuel-efficiency by three-fourths.

Ask students the following questions:

1. Speculate about the relationship of people to their tools in the days before "progress." *Possible answers: Tools may have been treasured as gifts from fate, rather than judged as human inventions.*
2. What invention do you depend on most? Explain. *Possible answer: the electric dynamo, which powers many other inventions on which we depend.*

By 1750, Britain was rapidly industrializing and the theories of the Enlightenment were eclipsed. Mills and factories belched smoke into the country air. Men, women, and children toiled at machines for twelve and fourteen hours a day. Poor people crowded into the towns and cities, unable to find regular work and barely able to survive. By the late 1700's, "progress" seemed to mean misery for millions. Writers and intellectuals began to lose faith in the ability of human reason to solve every problem.

Literature of the Period

The Schools of Jonson and Donne In his writing Ben Jonson (1572–1637) strove for the perfection and harmony he found in his beloved classical authors, turning away from the ornate style of Elizabethan times to create his own modern, strong voice. He wrote poems, plays, and masques (court entertainments). His critical opinion exercised a powerful influence on other poets of the time. Among the best-known "Sons of Ben" were Robert Herrick (1591–1674), Sir John Suckling (1609–1642), and Richard Lovelace (1618–1657).

John Donne (1572–1631) pioneered a new witty, cerebral style known as metaphysical poetry. Metaphysical poetry is characterized by the use of the intellect in the service of the imagination, drawing on science, philosophy, and legend for images. His poems are frequently structured like ingenious, subtle arguments. The most notable followers of John Donne were George Herbert (1593–1633) and Andrew Marvell (1621–1678). Herbert's best poems are the religious lyrics collected in *The Temple.* Marvell's best lyrics blend the metaphysical brilliance of Donne and the classical finish of Jonson.

The Puritan Writers Like Ben Jonson, John Milton (1608–1674) was a learned disciple of the Greek and Latin authors. He was also a profound Calvinist. In his later life, Milton set about composing an epic on Christian themes—a poetic act on an audacious scale. *Paradise Lost,* published in 1667, reflects Milton's humanistic love of poetry and his Puritan devotion to God.

John Bunyan (1628–1688) had little education beyond reading the Bible. A tinker by trade,

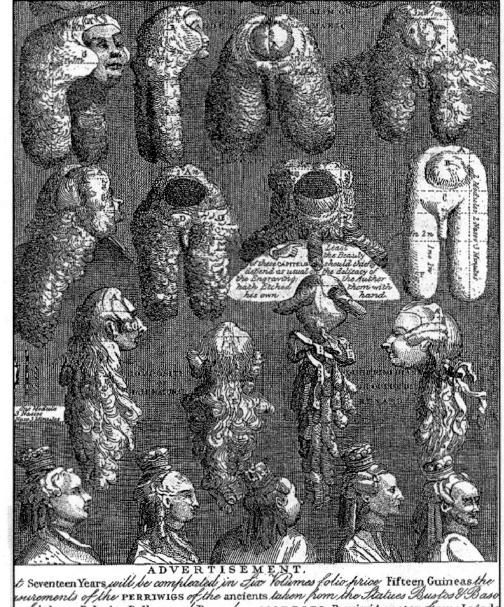

▲ **Speculate** After the Restoration in 1660, stark Puritan dress was replaced by new fashions. Middle-class men began wearing the wig that King Louis XVI of France had first popularized. What inconveniences might the wearers of wigs such as those in the picture suffer? Explain.

▲ **Speculate** By the end of the eighteenth century, England's middle classes had begun to come into their own. Newspapers sprang up to keep them informed; coffee houses like the one in the painting offered a place to read, meet, and socialize. Judging from this scene, what place do you suppose paintings had in the lives of middle-class people?

Answers to A Graphic Look

(from page 384)
Infer Women had an equal share of at least some physical labor on a farm.

Draw Conclusions Judging from the engraving, squalor, hunger, and possibly crime or homelessness, awaited new arrivals in the city.

(from page 385)
Speculate Wearers of wigs might suffer discomfort such as sweating and itching (the wigs appear to be made of thick material); some seem back-heavy, and would perhaps fall off if the wearer were to run.

Speculate Students may say that paintings served to decorate the homes of middle-class people.

Connections to the Literature

- Students can better gauge the plight of small farmers in England's agricultural revolution—and the steps some took to improve their situation—when they have read the excerpt from Caryl Churchill's *Light Shining in Buckinghamshire,* p. 453.
- Samuel Pepys's *Diary,* p. 462, and Defoe's *A Journal of the Plague Year,* p. 468, can introduce students to seventeenth- and eighteenth-century England from the "inside."

More About Ben Jonson

Jonson took seriously the role of the poet. He believed, in fact, that no other profession could compare to it. Poets, he wrote, encourage "young men to all good disciplines, inflame grown men to all great virtues, [and] keep old men in their best and supreme state." A person could not be "the good poet without first being a good man," he asserted. Jonson lived up to this moral duty in several ways: by giving good advice in some poems; by honoring worthy men and women in others; and, in his plays, by satirizing corruption and immorality.

Cross-Curricular Connection: Social Studies

Technology and Society Emphasize for students that efficiency in agriculture and industry had deep social consequences. In the 1700's, rich landowners pushed ahead with enclosure, by which they took over and fenced off the common land formerly shared by peasant villagers. Enclosures enabled them to consolidate small strips of farmland into more efficient fields.

As millions of acres were enclosed, farm output rose. Profits also rose because large fields needed fewer people to work them. Small farmers were forced off their land because they could not compete with large landholders. The jobless or landless farmworkers who migrated to towns and cities formed the growing labor force crucial to the success of the factories of the future.

Ask students the following questions:

1. What values besides "efficiency" can determine the way in which society uses wealth? *Possible answers: Society might emphasize meeting people's needs, or promoting community.*
2. Do the benefits of industry outweigh its costs? Explain. *Discussion may weigh freedom from drudgery against pollution and alienation.*

More About the Early Novel

Daniel Defoe was not the only novelist of the day. Later in the eighteenth century, Samuel Richardson's *Pamela* and *Clarissa,* Fanny Burney's *Evelina,* Henry Fielding's *Tom Jones* and *Joseph Andrews,* and Laurence Sterne's *Tristram Shandy* all appeared. These novels do not simply represent the first struggles of a form being born. On the contrary, they are classics in their own right and continue to influence novelists today. For example, the quirky, self-conscious play with storytelling conventions that marks *Tristram Shandy* is evident also in the work of novelists like John Barth and Thomas Pynchon.

Answers to A GRAPHIC LOOK

(from page 386)

Draw Conclusions The light rays look like a kind of ghostly substance, suggesting the mystery and otherworldliness of science.

Read a Chart Both Locke and Hobbes believe that government arises from people's original surrender of their full liberty. Locke emphasizes government's duty to protect that limited liberty. Hobbes emphasizes the danger of individuals acting without constraint, and views government as a necessarily oppressive force.

(from page 387)

Draw Conclusions The fathers of the bride and groom look as if they are involved in a business deal. The father with his hand on his breast looks as if he is making a self-consciously dramatic point.

Speculate They inspire feelings of peace and a longing for solitude.

◀ **Draw Conclusions** Alexander Pope's couplet attests to popular appreciation of Sir Isaac Newton's achievements: "Nature and Nature's laws lay hid in night: /God said, Let Newton be! and all was light." The artist depicts light rays in a distinctive manner. What ideas do they suggest about the spirit of science?

Bunyan, like many others of the day, wandered from town to town in rural England, preaching wherever people would listen. After the restoration of Charles II, Bunyan was imprisoned, and it was there that he wrote *The Pilgrim's Progress.* The allegory tells the story of a man who flees sin to lead a holy life.

Literature of the Age of Reason Enlightenment writers discovered the qualities they admired most—harmony, restraint, and clarity—among the writers of ancient Greece and Rome, such as Homer, Virgil, and Horace. Neoclassical writers—English writers who imitated the styles of classical writers—often referred to the myths, gods, and heroes of ancient times. They favored generalities rather than the viewpoint of the individual, had a fondness for satires poking fun at society's follies, and often expressed their thoughts in aphorisms—short, quotable sentences—such as "The proper study of mankind is man."

From 1660 to 1700, a period known as the Restoration, John Dryden (1631–1700) dominated literature. Named poet laureate, England's official poet, by Charles II, he wrote celebratory poems, which hailed the achievements of humanity; plays; and satirical poems. His essays about drama and his other prose compositions represent the first modern prose.

Restoration Theater The Restoration was also noted for its plays, especially comedies. When Charles II became king, he reopened the London theaters. The Restoration theaters, fancier and more costly than those of Shakespeare's time, did a thriving business.

The Age of Pope and Swift The poetry of Alexander Pope (1688–1744), written in the early 1700's, is a shining example of neoclassical style, exhibiting wit, elegance, and moderation. All these qualities show forth in his most famous work, *The Rape of the Lock,* a satire on the war between the sexes. Pope also had enormous influence as a critic.

European Political Thinkers

Thinker	Major Ideas	Quotation
Thomas Hobbes *Leviathan* (1651) 	People are driven by selfishness and greed. To avoid chaos, they give up their freedom to a government that will ensure order. Such a government must be strong and able to suppress rebellion.	The condition of man [in the state of nature] . . . is a condition of war of everyone against everyone.
John Locke *Two Treatises of Government* (1690)	People have a natural right to life, liberty, and property. Rulers have a responsibility to protect those rights. People have the right to change a government that fails to do so.	Men being . . . by nature all free, equal, and independent, no one can be put out of this estate and subjected to the political power of another without his own consent.
Baron de Montesquieu *The Spirit of the Laws* (1748)	The powers of government should be separated into executive, legislative, and judicial branches, to prevent any one group from gaining too much power.	In order to have . . . liberty, it is necessary that government be set up so that one man need not be afraid of another.

▲ **Read a Chart** Compare Locke's and Hobbes's notions of what drives human society.

Humanities: Art

The Paintings of Hogarth.

William Hogarth (1697–1764) was one of the first English-born artists to gain recognition abroad. Committed to a realistic, popular, satirical art, he compared his paintings to a stage on which the characters silently acted their parts. His idea of beauty was "a composed intricacy of form" that "leads the eye a kind of chase"—a justification for the humorous exaggeration and dynamic quality of his paintings and engravings. Many of Hogarth's works enjoy an easy familiarity with the tumult of ordinary life. Often, they have morals, and a few take the form of full-blown narratives. The eight paintings that make up "A Rake's Progress," for instance, tell the tale of a young man who falls prey to the temptations and follies of the world. To a large extent, this naturalism of Hogarth's put him at odds with the neoclassical ideals of his day, though he shared a taste for satire with Dryden, Pope, and Swift.

Ask students to describe narrative visual art they know (e.g., comic strips). Then have a group find and present reproductions of two Hogarth paintings and explain their details for the class.

Jonathan Swift (1667–1745), a close friend of Pope's, was a scornful critic of the rising merchant class, whom he viewed as shameless money grubbers. In his great satires, *Gulliver's Travels* and *A Modest Proposal*, he presents human nature as deeply flawed, suggesting that moral progress must begin from a recognition of our intellectual and moral limitations.

The first English novel, *Robinson Crusoe* by Daniel Defoe (1660–1731), appeared in this period. This new form of fiction would, in the 1800's, become the favorite reading matter of the growing middle classes. England's first literary periodicals, *The Tatler and The Spectator*, also appeared in the early 1700's. Written by Joseph Addison (1672–1719) and Richard Steele (1672–1729), these one-page papers included crisply written reflective essays and news addressed to the middle classes.

The Age of Johnson Samuel Johnson (1709–1784) dominated his age not only by his writings but also by his conversation and acquaintanceships. A brilliant and inexhaustible talker, he was friendly with most of the writers, painters, and actors of his time. His wise advice helped nurture the careers of many younger talents. *The Dictionary of the English Language*, published in 1755, is his most important work. It is the first dictionary that could be considered a standard and authoritative reference work on English.

The Eclipse of the Enlightenment By 1750, Britain was launched on a course of rapid industrialization. Mills and factories began to belch smoke into the air of new towns. Inside, men, women, and children toiled at machines for over twelve hours a day. Every year more poor people crowded into the towns and cities, unable to find regular work and barely able to survive. By the late 1700's, the "progress" celebrated by Enlightenment thinkers seemed to be bringing misery to millions.

As they lost faith in the power of human reason, writers turned away from the standards of neoclassicism. Writing in the language of everyday life, writers such as Thomas Gray charged their poems with new emotion. The Age of Reason was coming to an end. Emerging new voices would make the 1800's a new literary age.

▲ **Draw Conclusions** In William Hogarth's *Signing the Marriage Contract*, one of a series of six paintings poking fun at British marriage customs, the fathers of the groom and the bride (both seated), and two lawyers discuss the bride's dowry—the property that she will give her new husband. Using the details of their dress, posture, and expression, draw conclusions about the characters' attitudes and Hogarth's opinion of them.

▲ **Speculate** Richard Wilson's (1714–1782) landscape paintings influenced the work of nineteenth-century Romantic painters such as John Constable and J.W.M. Turner. What feelings do the lighting and the view inspire in you?

Literature of the Period

Check Your Comprehension

1. Name two influential authors of the early seventeenth century. *Ben Jonson and John Donne were the early seventeenth century's key authors.*
2. What two influences combined in John Milton's poetry? *Milton combined a humanist's appreciation of the Greek and Latin classics with a Calvinist's devotion to God.*
3. Name two literary genres that came into prominence after the Restoration of Charles II. *The popularity of the drama burgeoned when Charles reopened the theaters. The first novel, Robinson Crusoe, and the first essayistic periodicals appeared later in the period.*
4. (a) Define neoclassical style. (b) Name two exponents of this style. *(a) Neoclassical writers modeled their style after classical writers, emphasizing harmony, restraint, and clarity. (b) John Dryden and Alexander Pope are two important practitioners of this style.*
5. What new class of reader began to influence literature in the eighteenth century? *The growing middle classes were the audience for the novels and periodical essays of the day.*
6. Aside from his writing, how did Samuel Johnson contribute to literature? *Johnson befriended and encouraged young talents.*

Critical Thinking

1. What innovations did early seventeenth-century poets introduce? **[Infer]** *They gave poetry a new, mature voice and exploited new sources of imagery.*
2. (a) Contrast Milton's use of poetry of the past with the neoclassicists' use. (b) Relate your contrast to the times in which each lived. **[Compare and Contrast]** *(a) Milton used an old poetic form (the epic) to give grandeur to* Paradise Lost*—he was trying to equal the past. The neoclassicists took the past as a source of standards for taste and sense.*
3. The Restoration enjoyed satire—literature that pokes fun at people's ways. Speculate about a society that nurtures satire. (a) Is it large or small? (b) Are roles rigidly defined, or is there social mobility? Explain. **[Speculate]** *(a) It is probably large, with more institutions to satirize. (b) It may be rigid and pretentious because those qualities suggest more targets for satirists.*

Activities

1. **Graphic Organization of Events** Give students the Comparison and Contrast organizer, p. 115, in ***Writing and Language Transparencies.*** Have them use the form to compare the Civil War of the 1640's with the Glorious Revolution of 1688.
2. **Role Play** Have students choose a person mentioned in The Story of the Times. Then, speaking as that person, they can comment on a contemporary issue that would interest him or her. For example, Oliver Cromwell might have a great deal to say about censorship and Charles I might comment on the troubles of today's royal family.
3. **Fathers and Sons** Have students write an entry from Charles II's journal in which he reflects on his father's policies, virtues, shortcomings, and eventual fate. They should explore the ways in which exile and his father's fate have shaped Charles II's outlook.
4. **Connections to the Literature** Challenge students to find a passage in a selection that reflects an insight, description, narrative, or idea from The Story of the Times. Have them read the passage aloud to the class and explain how it relates to The Story of the Times. Students giving the presentation should then be prepared to answer questions about the passage.

Develop Understanding

◆ Critical Thinking

1. Speculate about the state of spelling in English in the days before dictionaries. **[Speculate]** *Possible answers: There may have been more than one way to spell a word; people may have improvised spellings more.*
2. Why might Johnson's illustrative quotations have been valuable to historians of the language? **[Hypothesize]** *By gathering together earlier usages, Johnson allowed later readers to chart changes in the meaning of words.*

▶Critical Viewing◀

1. What three items found in modern dictionaries are missing from the entries in this depiction of a page of Johnson's dictionary? **[Interpret Layout]** *The part of speech, pronunciation, and derivation of each word are missing.*
2. Judging from this mock-up of a page from the *Dictionary*, how reliable is Johnson's capitalization? **[Analyze]** *It is not faultless: Tory, a proper noun, is capitalized, while Whig, another proper noun, is not.*

Answers to Activities

1. Johnson's opinionated definitions contrast sharply with the neutral definitions we expect from contemporary dictionaries. His solemn definition of *Tory*, and abbreviated definition of *whig* shows him to be a Tory.
2. Encourage students to be opinionated and biased, as Johnson is.
3. Have students look for definitions that are clearly influenced by Johnson's opinions and prejudices or that reflect ideas that seem unusual to us today.

The Changing English Language

NO HARMLESS DRUDGE, HE

by Richard Lederer

On April 15, 1755, Dr. Samuel Johnson—blind in one eye, impoverished, and incompletely educated—produced the first modern *Dictionary of the English Language*. "Languages are the pedigrees of nations," he proclaimed, and, in compiling his wordbook, Johnson conferred a pedigree on the English-speaking nations. In garnering the rich, exuberant vocabulary of eighteenth-century England, the *Dictionary of the English Language* marks a turning point in the history of our tongue.

dedication. A servile address to a patron
excise. A hateful tax levied upon commodities, and adjudged not by the common judges of property, but wretches hired by those to whom excise is paid.
gambler. (A cant word, I suppose, for game, or gamster.) A knave whose practice it is to invite the unwary to game and cheat them.
opera. An exotic and irrational entertainment.
parasite. One that frequents rich tables, and earns his welcome by flattery.
patron. One who supports with insolence, and is paid with flattery.
pensioner. A slave of state hired by a stipend to obey his master. In England it is generally understood to mean pay given to a state hireling for treason to his country.
Tory. One who adheres to the ancient constitution of the state, and the apostolical hierarchy of the church of England, opposed to a whig.
whig. The name of a faction.

Johnson's Firsts

Johnson set himself the task of making a different kind of dictionary, one of the first that would include all the words in the English language, not just the difficult ones. In addition, he would show how to divide words into syllables and where words came from. He would establish a consistent system of defining words and draw from his own gigantic learning to provide, for the first time in any dictionary, illustrative quotations from famous writers. Johnson's lexicon, like its modern descendants, is a report on the way writers actually used the English language.

Underfunded and working almost alone in a Fleet Street garret room, Johnson defined some 43,000 words and illuminated their meanings with more than 114,000 supporting quotations drawn from every area of literature. Laboring for almost nine years, he captured the majesty of the English language and gave it a dignity that was long overdue.

Johnson defined a lexicographer as "a writer of dictionaries, a harmless drudge that busies himself in tracing the original and detailing the signification of words." However, he was obviously far more than a harmless drudge, and his two-volume dictionary was by far the most comprehensive and readable that had appeared. The reputation of the *Dictionary of the English Language* was so great that it dominated the field until the turn of this century.

Activities

1. How do these definitions (above) differ from those you would find in current dictionaries? For example, what can you tell about Johnson's political loyalties from his definition of Tory and Whig?
2. Reviewing Johnson's definitions, (above) write three definitions in his style.
3. Secure a copy from your school or local library of *Johnson's Dictionary: A Modern Selection*, edited by E. L. McAdam, Jr., and George Milne (Pantheon Books). Browse through it and report any interesting and unusual definitions to the class.

Humanities: Literature

Dictionaries and Their Makers.

Explain to students that, while we take dictionaries very much for granted, Johnson's dictionary actually had a great deal of influence in shaping the language we use today.

Early dictionary makers made, for instance, some useful decisions that have become laws for English users since: after Johnson, for instance, *flower* always means a growing thing, *flour* an ingredient of bread. The American Noah Webster (1758–1843) was famous for his attempt to standardize spelling. For better or worse, his insistence in a 1788 spelling guide that *tough* was better spelled *tuf* and *group* spelled *groop* never caught on. His support, though, of *theater* instead of *theatre* and *aluminum* instead of *aluminium* (among others) helped establish the differences between American and British spelling.

Ask students the following questions:

1. Why is uniform spelling a good idea? *Possible answers: It prevents miscommunication.*
2. Should dictionaries include all the words currently in use, or should it exclude some? *Possible answers: For brevity, it should exclude words that may become quickly outdated.*

PART 1 The War Against Time

A Musical Garden Party (detail)
Metropolitan Museum of Art

One-Minute Planning Guide

The selections in this section present the great writers of seventeenth-century England. The section opens with four works by John Donne, "Meditation 17," "Song," "A Valediction: Forbidding Mourning," and "Holy Sonnet 10," works that capture the essence of the metaphysical writings that characterized his era and that captivated the twentieth century as well. Three pieces by Ben Jonson make up the next grouping: "On My First Son," "To Celia," and "Still to Be Neat." Three love poems with the theme of *carpe diem* follow in the next grouping, "To His Coy Mistress" by Andrew Marvell, "To the Virgins, to Make Much of Time" by Robert Herrick, and "Song" by Sir John Suckling. The Connections to World Literature presents two modern thematically-connected folk songs, "Freeze Tag" by Suzanne Vega and "New Beginning" by Tracy Chapman.

Customize for
Varying Student Needs

When assigning the selections in this part to your students, keep in mind the following factors:

"Meditation 17"
- Contains difficult language that will require rereading by most students.

"On My First Son"
- Treats the subject of the death of a young child, which may be a sensitive issue for some students.

"To His Coy Mistress"
- Contains references that should be treated sensitively.

"To the Virgins, to Make Much of Time"
- Ideal for musical/rhythmic learners.

Humanities: Art

A Musical Garden Party (detail).

This work celebrates the momentary triumph of order over time and mortality. The well-ordered garden suggests the attempt of seventeenth-century people to recreate Eden (the angel hovering in the background is actually part of a Garden of Eden scene). Yet the triumph of order is momentary, for the visual allusion to the Garden of Eden reminds the viewer of Adam and Eve's fall.

Have students link the art to the focus of Part 1, "The War Against Time," by answering the following questions:

1. Create a story around the artwork: Who are the people shown here, why are the ladies performing for the gentleman, and how do they all feel about one another?
   Sample answer: The ladies have offered to entertain the gentleman; whichever one of them plays better shall sit next to him at dinner that night. Each lady thinks she is winning the contest. The gentleman is enjoying the attention.
2. Describe the mood of this scene, and tell what elements help create this mood.
   Most students will probably feel that the scene projects a joyous, positive mood. The mood is created by the smiles on the faces of all the figures—including the dog, as well as the well-ordered garden and lovely manor in the background.

Prepare and Engage

OBJECTIVES

1. To read, comprehend, and interpret poems and a meditation
2. To relate the literature to personal experience
3. To read for success using strategies for constructing meaning
4. To identify the characteristics of metaphysical poetry
5. To build vocabulary in context and learn the prefix *inter-*
6. To use active and passive voice effectively
7. To write a unified speech
8. To respond to the literature through writing, speaking and listening, and projects

SKILLS INSTRUCTION

Vocabulary: Prefixes: *inter-*

Grammar: Active and Passive Voice

Reading for Success: Strategies for Constructing Meaning

Literary Focus: Metaphysical Poetry

Writing: Unity

Speaking and Listening: Oral Interpretation (teacher edition)

Critical Viewing: Deduce; Compare and Contrast; Connect

PORTFOLIO OPPORTUNITIES

Writing: Journal Entry; The Lady's Turn; Critical Response

Writing Mini-Lesson: Speech

Speaking and Listening: Oral Interpretation; Presentation of a Conceit

Projects: Sculpture of a Conceit; Map of the Universe

More About the Author
Although John Donne is known for his poetry, his poetry was published only after his death, although manuscripts of his work circulated during his lifetime. He did publish mainly religious tracts before his ordination and became an extremely popular preacher. His meditations and sermons were widely read and discussed.

Donne's popularity took a two-century hiatus. Interest in Donne and his work was rekindled early in the twentieth century, mainly as the result of a 1921 essay by poet T. S. Eliot, "The Metaphysical Poets."

Guide for Interpreting

John Donne *(1572(?)–1631)*

Donne's life and poetry seem to fall neatly into two, contradictory parts. Wild young "Jack" Donne wrote clever love poems read by sophisticated aristocrats. In later life, sober Dr. John Donne, Dean of St. Paul's and England's most popular preacher, published widely read meditations and sermons.

Contradiction and conflict were the stuff of Donne's life; they are also at the heart of his poetic style.

As Jack or as John, in his writings Donne excelled at dramatizing—and wittily resolving—the contradictions of life.

Religious Conflict Donne, a distant relative of Sir Thomas More, was raised Catholic. In Queen Elizabeth's England, Catholics faced prejudice and restrictive laws. Though Donne studied law, he never obtained his degree, probably because of religious issues. Later, he abandoned Catholicism and joined the official church of England, the Anglican Church. To this day, scholars debate whether Donne experienced a genuine conversion or made a shrewd move to try to gain advancement in court society.

A Secret Marriage A highly educated young man, Donne served as private secretary to one of the Queen's highest-ranking officials. Bright, clever, and charming, he secretly wed Anne More, his employer's niece, in 1602. Donne's marriage ruined his chances for social advancement.

The devoted couple lived for sixteen years plagued by poverty and illness, during which Donne managed to write widely read, influential poetry. He finally attained a secure position in 1615 when, at King James's insistence, he entered the clergy, becoming first a royal chaplain and then, in 1621, dean of St. Paul's Cathedral in London, where he served until his death.

A Modern Individual John Donne's reputation has changed over time. He was very popular during his own lifetime, but his writings soon went out of favor. At the beginning of the twentieth century, interest in Donne's poetry was rekindled. Perhaps this is because the conflicts Donne faced have a distinctively modern flavor. His family's faith and his secret marriage pitted the private man against the demands of the world. Society was no longer ready with clear answers to the question, Where do I fit in? Donne, in his contradictory life and complex poetry, had to invent answers on his own.

◆ Background for Understanding

History: Donne and the System of Patronage

There were no bestsellers, movie deals, or syndicated columns in Donne's time. Before the eighteenth century, a writer trying to make a living had to attract the patronage—money and other support—of a well-born person. In return, the writer might write on subjects chosen by or pleasing to the patron. The young Donne did not publish his poems (most were printed only after his death). Instead, they circulated among a select literary audience, which included patrons like the Countess of Bedford.

After Donne was dismissed from his position with Sir Thomas Egerton as a result of his secret marriage, he and his family depended in part on patrons for financial support. Eventually, Donne gained the patronage of Sir Robert Drury by writing an elegy on his fourteen-year-old daughter, who had died in December 1610.

Prentice Hall Literature Program Resources

REINFORCE / RETEACH / EXTEND

Selection Support Pages
Build Vocabulary: Prefixes: *inter-*, p. 81
Grammar and Style: Active and Passive Voice, p. 82
Reading for Success: Strategies for Constructing Meaning, pp. 83–84
Literary Focus: Metaphysical Poetry, p. 85

Strategies for Diverse Student Needs, p. 17

Beyond Literature, p. 17

Formal Assessment Selection Test, pp. 86–88; Assessment Resources Software

Alternative Assessment, p. 17

Writing and Language Transparencies
Daily Language Practice, Week 13, p. 148; Writing Process Model 5: Persuasive Essay, pp. 37–43

Resource Pro CD-ROM Includes all resource material and customizable lesson plan.

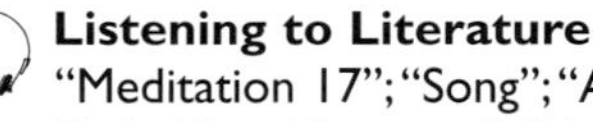

Listening to Literature Audiocassettes "Meditation 17"; "Song"; "A Valediction: Forbidding Mourning"; "Holy Sonnet 10"

Looking at Literature Videodisc John Donne, Chapter 5

MODEL SELECTION

Works of John Donne

◆ Literature and Your Life

Connect Your Experience

When night falls in a strange and lonely place, solitary travelers become uneasy. By calling up a cheerful memory, repeating a parent's advice, or even by whistling a tune, many can keep their spirits up despite the night.

Donne is perhaps our greatest whistler in the dark. His poems confront the uncertainties of parting and death. Nimble-witted, he improvises extravagantly to fill the silence, inventing fresh answers to old doubts. Perhaps he shows, too, that the imagination is the only source of certainties.

Journal Writing Describe two ways in which people use their imagination to keep up their courage.

Thematic Focus: The War Against Time

As you read, notice how Donne uses wit to turn the tables on separation and death, two of time's destructive effects.

◆ Build Vocabulary

Prefixes: *inter-*

In "Meditation 17," Donne writes of the bell that, having rung, "intermits." The prefix *inter-* means "between," "among," or "with each other," and *intermit* means "to put between," or "to pause."

Word Bank

As you read, preview this list of words from the selections.

contention
piety
intermit
covetousness
profanation
laity
trepidation
breach

◆ Grammar and Style

Active and Passive Voice

A verb expressing an action performed by the subject of a sentence is in the **active voice.** To express an action received by the subject, the verb is in the **passive voice,** which uses a form of *to be* with a past participle. In the following passage, Donne uses both active and passive voice:

Active Voice: God *employs* several translators;

Passive Voice: . . . some pieces *are translated* by age, . . .

◆ Literary Focus

Metaphysical Poetry

Metaphysical poetry is characterized by the use of metaphysical conceits and of paradoxes. Metaphysical conceits are extended comparisons that link objects or ideas not commonly associated, often mixing abstract ideas and emotional matters. A paradox is an image or description that appears to contradict itself but that reveals a truth. Metaphysical poetry is also known for carrying the rhythms of conversational English into verse.

Donne's detailed comparison of two lovers to the two legs of a drawing compass in "A Valediction: Forbidding Mourning" is a metaphysical conceit. Donne uses paradox in "Holy Sonnet 10" when he writes "Death, thou shalt die." (How can the power of death die?) Whatever the conceits and paradoxes he expresses, Donne voices them in a forceful, conversational English that makes a poem into a dramatic speech.

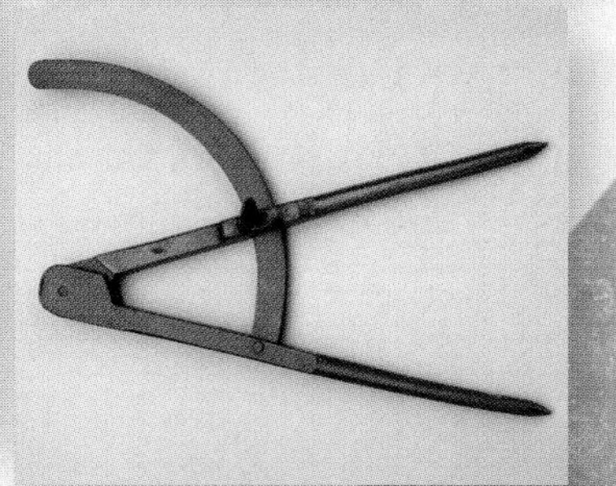

Preparing for Standardized Tests

Reading and Vocabulary Vocabulary development helps students improve performance on the verbal portion of standardized tests. The Build Vocabulary lesson focuses on learning word meaning through the use of the prefix *inter-*. Students can apply this skill on vocabulary portions of tests on questions such as the following.

Which of the following phrases explains the meaning of *interstate?* (C)
(A) in the middle of a state
(B) around a state
(C) between states

For additional practice, use the Build Vocabulary page in ***Selection Support,*** p. 81.

Grammar and Language Tests such as the SAT II often require a student to improve sentences by choosing an active verb instead of a passive verb.

The Grammar and Style lesson for this selection focuses on this topic. For additional practice, use the Grammar and Style page on Active and Passive Voice, p. 82, in ***Selection Support.***

Ask students to think of people they know with a dramatic flair. Perhaps there is a student who would qualify for the title "Most Dramatic" in their school yearbook. Without naming students, have students consider the qualities they would use to describe that person—for example, lively, outspoken, personable. Tell students that John Donne was such a person, but that he also had a quiet, meditative aspect to his personality. Suggest as they read his poetry that students look for these two sides to Donne's personality—the dramatic and the meditative—along with any other surprising facets they may note.

Customize for
More Advanced Students
Point out to students that much of Donne's work includes intellectual arguments. In "Meditation 17," for example, he tries to prove that suffering on earth is rewarded in an afterlife. Encourage students as they read to imagine each work as part of a verbal sparring match with imaginary foes; have them think about the point Donne is making and what arguments he marshals as support for his argument.

Customize for
English Language Learners
Have students form pairs and take turns reading each work aloud. Encourage them to work together to create an oral reading that emphasizes meaning.

Customize for
Logical/Mathematical Learners
These students may enjoy Donne's work more if they see his arguments as battles of wits. Students can take turns using Donne's words to "convince" classmates of the points the poet was trying to make. For instance, a student might begin by citing the claim that all the church's actions belong to all. When others disagree, the student might repeat Donne's conceit about no man as an island.

Reading for Success

The Reading for Success page in each unit presents a set of problem-solving procedures to help readers understand authors' words and ideas on multiple levels. Good readers develop a bank of strategies from which they can draw as needed.

Unit 3 introduces strategies for constructing meaning. Students examine a writer's ideas in light of what they already know. They hypothesize, make inferences, draw conclusions, interpret, and use their knowledge of the historical time period in order to construct meaning.

These strategies for constructing meaning are modeled with "Meditation 17." Each green box shows an example of the thinking process involved in applying one of these strategies.

How to Use the Reading for Success Page

- Introduce the strategies for constructing meaning, presenting each as a problem-solving procedure. Be sure students understand what each strategy involves and under what circumstances to apply it.
- Before students read the selection, have them preview it, looking at the annotations in the green boxes that model the strategies.
- To reinforce these strategies after students have read "Meditation 17," have students do the Reading for Success pages in ***Selection Support,*** pp. 83–84. These pages give students an opportunity to read a selection and practice strategies for constructing meaning by writing their own annotations.

Reading for Success

Strategies for Constructing Meaning

As soon as you begin reading a work of literature, you are already constructing meaning. Is it a poem or a piece of nonfiction? Why did the author write it? What ideas are at work in it? What does it mean to you? As you read, you naturally ask and answer such questions to understand what you are reading. Here are a few strategies to help you sharpen these skills:

Recognize the speaker's voice and purpose.
The words of a literary work do not always directly represent the thoughts of the author. A work's speaker is often a special voice used by the author. The speaker can even be a fictional character, with motives that color what he or she says. Ask yourself about the speaker's motives for speaking, and identify the situation that gives rise to the speech.

Hypothesize.
As you read, ask yourself who the speaker is and what situation he or she is in. Test the possible answers you come up with as you read further.

Make inferences.
Writers don't always tell you everything directly, but they often provide details from which you can infer their message. You need to "read between the lines" to uncover the ideas writers suggest but don't spell out.

Draw conclusions.
A conclusion is a general statement about a work that is supported by details in the text. A series of inferences can lead you to a conclusion. Drawing conclusions about a text helps you to understand the work as a whole and recognize its purpose.

Interpret the text.
Explain to yourself the meaning or the significance of what the author is saying. Figure out the author's perspective on the subject or on life.

Use your knowledge of the historical time period.
The political climate and the intellectual trends of a specific time period are reflected in the writing that comes out of it. Apply the information from the introduction to this unit as you read the selections.

As you read "Meditation 17," look at the notes along the sides. These notes demonstrate how to apply these strategies to a work of literature.

Reading Strategies: Support and Reinforcement

Appropriate Reading Strategies Students are given a reading strategy to apply in reading each selection. Most of the strategies in this unit help them to construct meaning from the text. In other selections a strategy is suggested that is appropriate to the selection.

Reading Prompts To encourage application of the given reading strategy, there are occasional prompts, within green boxes, at appropriate and significant points.

In addition, there are red boxes prompting application of the Literary Focus concept and maroon boxes prompting students to connect with their lives.

Using the Boxed Annotations and Prompts
The material in the green, red, and maroon boxes along the sides of selections is intended to help students apply the literary element and the reading strategy and to make a connection with their lives.

You may use the boxed material in several ways:

- Have students pause when they come to a box and respond to its prompt before they continue reading.
- Urge students to read through the selection ignoring the boxes. After they have read the selection completely, they may go back and review the selection, responding to the prompts.

Meditation 17

MODEL

John Donne

◀ Critical Viewing The bells in this tower would ring on the occasion of someone's death, as Donne notes. On what other occasions might they ring? **[Deduce]** ❷

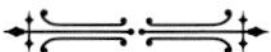

Nunc lento sonitu dicunt, Morieris.
(Now, this bell tolling softly for another,
says to me, Thou must die.)

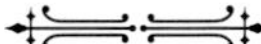

Perchance he for whom this bell tolls may be so ill as that he knows not it tolls for him; and perchance I ❸ may think myself so much better than I am as that they who are about me and see my state may have caused it to toll for me, and I know not that. The church is catholic,[1] universal, so are all her actions; all that she does ❹ belongs to all. When she baptizes a child, that action concerns me; for that child is thereby connected to that head

1. **catholic:** Applying to humanity generally.

Develop Understanding

One-Minute Insight In "Meditation 17," the author faces his own mortality when he listens to a bell toll for someone else's death. Donne used memorable comparisons or "conceits" to express the idea that all people are connected to each other and to God.

◆ Reading for Success

❶ **Recognize the Speaker's Purpose** Ask students: For what purpose is a meditation written? Have students read to identify Donne's purpose. *A meditation is designed to express someone's thoughts and make others think about the same topic. The title word "meditation" expresses this idea.*

▶Critical Viewing◀

❷ **Deduce** Students may suggest other major life events, such as marriage, the birth of a child, or a religious holiday.

❸ **Enrichment** When Ernest Hemingway used a phrase from this work as the title for his novel *For Whom the Bell Tolls* and included some of the text inside the book, he sparked so much interest that publishers rushed to reissue "Meditation 17." The concept that "No man is an island" was used to stir interest in a war half a world away.

◆ Critical Thinking

❹ **Contrast** Ask students how this idea of the church being universal differs from modern views. *People today recognize that there are a number of different churches and different religions.*

Block Scheduling Strategies

Consider these suggestions to take advantage of extended class time:

- Introduce the Strategies for Constructing Meaning on page 392 and have students work in pairs to respond to the prompts in boxes as they read. For more practice on the strategies, use the Reading for Success pages in ***Selection Support,*** pp. 83–84.
- Use the Daily Language Practice for Week 13. You may put the transparency on an overhead and have students write the passages correctly, or you may dictate the sentences and have students write them.
- Encourage students to listen to the audiocassette recording of one or more of the selections. Groups can discuss the insights they gained into the logical arguments of the works from hearing them read aloud in addition to reading them.
- Students can form groups to work on the Oral Interpretation or the Map of the Universe as described in the Idea Bank (p. 403).

Cultural Connection

Donne writes of a bell tolling at death. People throughout the world have different customs that are associated with death. For example, some cultures bury their dead quickly; others have long public viewings. Some people grieve silently; other cultures make noise to scare away spirits. In some countries, black is associated with death. In other countries, white is. Invite students to investigate the customs of other cultures.

◆ Critical Thinking

❶ **Analyze** Ask students to analyze the conceit—the extended comparison—in which mankind is compared to a book or volume. *Mankind is the volume; God is the author; each individual is a chapter; death is not destruction of that chapter but a kind of translation. Sickness, war, and justice are translators, and all show God's work. That library is everyone's final end.*

◆ Grammar and Style

❷ **Active and Passive Voice** Have students identify the effect of the shift from active to passive voice. *The passive construction "[I] who am brought so near the door by this sickness" indicates how powerless he was over sickness.*

◆ Build Vocabulary

❸ **The Prefix *inter-*** Point out that the word *intermit* contains the prefix *inter-*, meaning "between." It is related to the more familiar word *intermission*. Ask how *intermit* and *intermission* are alike. *Both words describe a pause. One is a verb and the other is a noun.*

◆ Reading for Success

❹ **Interpret** Focus attention on the statement "Never send to know for whom the bell tolls; it tolls for thee." Ask students what other situations this might refer to besides the literal one of hearing a tolling bell. *Students might say that one person's trouble touches everyone or that we should all recognize our common humanity.*

◆ Literary Focus

❺ **Metaphysical Poetry** Briefly review the distinctive elements of metaphysical poetry with students and ask them to identify examples that appear in this passage. *Students should identify the conceits, the emphasis on the spiritual life as opposed to the physical, and the conversational tone.*

Knowing the **historical context** enables you to appreciate how influential the Christian church was in Donne's time.

which is my head too, and ingrafted into that body[2] whereof I am a member. And when she buries a man, that action concerns me: all mankind is of one author and is one volume; when one man dies, one chapter is not torn out of the book, but translated[3] into a better language; and every chapter must be so translated. God employs several translators; some pieces are translated by age, some by sickness, some by war, some by justice; but God's hand is in every translation, and his hand shall bind up all our scattered leaves again for that library where every book shall lie open to one another. ❶ As therefore the bell that rings to a sermon calls not upon the preacher only, but upon the congregation to come, so this bell calls us all; but how much more me, who am brought so near the door by this sickness. ❷ There was a <u>contention</u> as far as a suit[4] (in which both <u>piety</u> and dignity, religion and estimation,[5] were mingled) which of the religious orders should ring to prayers first in the morning; and it was determined that they should ring first that rose earliest. If we understand aright the dignity of this bell that tolls for our evening prayer, we would be glad to make it ours by rising early, in that application, that it might be ours as well as his whose indeed it is. The bell doth toll for him that thinks it doth; and though it <u>intermit</u> again, yet from that minute that that occasion wrought upon him, he is united to God. ❸ Who casts not up his eye to the sun when it rises? but who takes off his eye from a comet when that breaks out? Who bends not his ear to any bell which upon any occasion rings? but who can remove it from that bell which is passing a piece of himself out of this world? No man is an island, entire of itself; every man is a piece of the continent, a part of the main.[6] If a clod be washed away by the sea, Europe is the less, as well as if a promontory were, as well as if a manor of thy friend's or of thine own were. ❹ Any man's death diminishes me because I am involved in mankind, and therefore never send to know for whom the bell tolls; it tolls for thee. Neither can we call this a begging of misery or a borrowing of misery, as though we were not miserable enough of ourselves but must fetch in more from the next house, in taking upon us the misery of our neighbors. Truly it were an excusable <u>covetousness</u> if we did; for affliction is a ❺

When Donne writes that the bell tolls for "him that thinks it doth" you might **interpret** his meaning this way: The anticipation of one's own death is itself a spiritual step towards death and union with God.

Donne's purpose in using rhetorical questions is to achieve the agreement and engage the passions of his audience.

2. **head . . . body:** The Church is both a head (a spiritual leader) and a body (a group of the faithful).
3. **translated:** Carried across on a spiritual level from one sphere to another.
4. **suit:** Lawsuit.
5. **estimation:** Self-esteem.
6. **main:** Mainland.

Cross-Curricular Connection: Art

Death and the afterlife is a common theme in Donne's work, as well as in the work of other writers and artists. Personifications of death and visions of the afterlife are depicted on gravestones, in paintings, and in illustrations. Death has been portrayed as a skull, an angel, a grim reaper, and a mythological figure; the afterlife may be filled with clouds or with fire, depending on whose view is shown.

Have students search folk and fine art to find depictions of death or the afterlife. Encourage them to look at the art of many cultures, since people of different times and places may have different views of this universal part of life.

From Donne's explanation of how we can learn from another's suffering, you can **draw the conclusion** that Donne places such importance on the awareness of death because it helps detach us from this world, causing us to turn to God for security.

treasure, and scarce any man hath enough of it. No man hath affliction enough that is not matured and ripened by it, and made fit for God by that affliction. If a man carry treasure in bullion, or in a wedge of gold, and have none coined into current money, his treasure will not defray him as he travels. ❺ Tribulation is treasure in the nature of it, but it is not current money in the use of it, except we get nearer and nearer our home, heaven, by it. ❻ Another man may be sick too, and sick to death, and this affliction may lie in his bowels as gold in a mine and be of no use to him; but this bell that tells me of his affliction digs out and applies that gold to me, if by this consideration of another's danger, I take mine own into contemplation and so secure myself by making my recourse to my God, who is our only security.

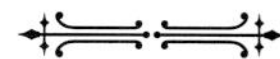

◆ Build Vocabulary

contention (kən ten´shən) *n.*: Dispute; argument

piety (pī´ ə tē) *n.*: Devotion or loyalty

intermit (in´ tər mit´) *v.*: Stop for a time

covetousness (kuv´ət əs ness) *n.*: Greediness

Guide for Responding

◆ Literature and Your Life

Reader's Response Is suffering ever a good thing for people? Explain why you agree or disagree with Donne's idea that "affliction is a treasure."

Thematic Focus According to Donne, how does knowing that the bell tolls for you help you conquer time and suffering?

☑ Check Your Comprehension

1. On what occasions does the bell toll?
2. Why might someone not realize that the bell tolls for him or her?
3. According to Donne, what happens when a person dies?
4. Donne uses several conceits—extended comparisons—in "Meditation 17." In one conceit, he compares people to chapters in a book. Describe two other conceits he uses.

◆ Critical Thinking

INTERPRET

1. Why does Donne say the tolling bell applies to him as well as to others? **[Analyze]**
2. What does Donne mean by "No man is an island entire of itself; every man is a piece of the continent"? **[Interpret]**
3. (a)What is the difference between treasure, such as gold, and "current money"? (b) In Donne's metaphor, when does the "treasure" of affliction turn into "current money"? **[Analyze]**
4. Why does Donne say that contemplation of the tolling bell brings one closer to God? **[Interpret]**

APPLY

5. During World War II, Donne's phrase "No man is an island" was widely used as a slogan to justify Britain's joining the fight against Nazi Germany. How does this use of the phrase compare with Donne's intended meaning? **[Synthesize]**

Beyond the Classroom

Career Connection

Law The speaker in Donne's work argues points much as a lawyer in a courtroom might. Logical arguments are used to defend and uphold a particular point of view.

Have interested students gather information about different careers in law, including paralegal positions.

Community Connection

Funerary Art and Epitaphs Many older cities and towns contain old cemeteries that have a variety of funerary art, such as gravestone carvings, monuments, or elaborate crypts. Many show stylized symbols that had specific meanings. For instance, a winged skull, a death's head, was supposed to stand for the soul's flight from the body. In addition, many cemeteries contain epitaphs, or inscriptions that relate either to death or to the person who died. Some are religious, others witty, and still others poignant. Encourage students to explore the art and epitaphs in an older cemetery, and have them share their findings with the class.

◆ Reading for Success

❻ **Draw Conclusions** Ask students to draw conclusions about why Donne refers to heaven as "our home." *He assumes that everyone will be united with God after death.*

Reinforce and Extend

Answers

◆ Literature and Your Life

Reader's Response Most students may recoil at the idea, but others may observe how they or others have grown as a result of overcoming hardships.

Thematic Focus It helps you to know that you are not alone and to empathize with another's suffering.

☑ Check Your Comprehension

1. The bell tolls for a person's death, calls people to a sermon, and announces a baptism.
2. Someone might be too ill to realize it tolls for him or her; some may think they are too young to die.
3. When people die, they get "translated into a better language"—carried across on a spiritual level from one sphere to another.
4. Examples of other conceits: Heaven is compared to a library, and affliction to treasure.

◆ Critical Thinking

1. We all share the same common fate; the death of one person affects another.
2. We are all connected—no one is isolated or so alone that he or she doesn't need other human beings, or is not affected by them.
3. (a) "Treasure" is all one's assets; "current money" is cash in hand. (b) The "treasure of affliction" turns into "current money" when we wisely use our hardships to grow and transcend them, moving closer to heaven by doing so.
4. The tolling bell reminds one of one's own mortality and the necessity of assuring one's salvation.
5. Britain applied Donne's meaning by considering that what Nazi Germany was doing to the rest of Europe was affecting it as well.

Develop Understanding

One-Minute Insight This poem expresses what it feels like to be separated from the person one loves. Donne's argument is artfully presented through a conceit that compares a temporary absence to the permanent absence of death. The speaker compares his love to the constancy of the sun and asserts that a love that overcomes absence in life will triumph over absence by being ever together in death.

◆ Critical Thinking

❶ **Compare and Contrast** To what does the poet compare himself in the second stanza, and why? How does he say he is different? *He compares himself to the sun, because it too leaves and returns. He says it has neither desire nor sense to motivate it and yet it returns; so, too, will he, as he has greater motivation and less distance to travel.*

◆ Literary Focus

❷ **Metaphysical Poetry** Ask students how this stanza reflects the metaphysical poets' interest in large philosophical questions. *The speaker here makes a general statement about good and bad fortune; the first can not add another hour to life; the second can overtake us if we allow it to.*

◆ Literary Focus

❸ **Metaphysical Poetry** Ask students what paradox is contained in this stanza. Point out that a paradox, because it is puzzling and seems contradictory, emphasizes a point by drawing readers' attention to it. *The paradox is "unkindly kind." The paradox also contains a pun, wordplay on the double meaning of* kind, *meaning "loving" and also meaning "related," as in* kindred.

Customize for
Musical/Rhythmic Learners
Help students appreciate the music of the words as well as the content by pointing out the *ababcddc* rhyme scheme.

Song

John Donne

Sweetest love, I do not go,
For weariness of thee,
Nor in hope the world can show
A fitter love for me;
But since that I
Must die at last, 'tis best
To use[1] myself in jest,
Thus by feigned[2] deaths to die.

> You can **infer** from the speaker's comparison of his departure to death that his parting from his beloved is a fearful, painful event.

Yesternight the sun went hence,
And yet is here today;
He hath no desire nor sense,
Nor half so short a way; ❶
Then fear not me,
But believe that I shall make
Speedier journeys, since I take
More wings and spurs than he.

O how feeble is man's power,
That if good fortune fall,
Cannot add another hour,
Nor a lost hour recall! ❷
But come bad chance,
And we join to it our strength,
And we teach it art and length,
Itself o'er us to advance.

When thou sigh'st, thou sigh'st not wind,
But sigh'st my soul away;
When thou weep'st, unkindly kind, ❸
My life's blood doth decay.
It cannot be
That thou lovest me as thou say'st,
If in thine my life thou waste,
That art the best of me.

> You can **hypothesize** from the poem's very first line that the speaker is about to depart from his beloved. Her reactions to his departure, described in lines 25–32, confirm that hypothesis.

1. **use**: Condition.
2. **feigned** (fānd) *v.*: Imagined.

Humanities: Art

Fair Is My Love by Edwin A. Abbey.

Although Abbey (1852–1911) was an American painter, muralist, and illustrator, he lived in England. He was an excellent draftsman, which is especially evident in his pen-and-ink drawings. He later began working in oils, and created this painting after 1890. The picture shows a castle garden, and its historical accuracy shows Abbey's love of the British Middle Ages.

Use these questions to stimulate discussion:

1. How does the painter show the man's feelings for the woman? *The man's feelings are apparent in his expression; in the detailed depiction of the woman; and in the light that shines on her like a spotlight.*
2. Do you think this piece of art is a good or poor choice for an illustration of this poem? Why? *Some students may find it too romantic and not cerebral enough; others may think it is a good choice because it shows such strong emotion.*

Fair Is My Love, Edwin A. Abbey
The Harris Museum and Art Gallery, Preston

◀ **Critical Viewing** How does the relationship of the man and woman in this painting compare with the relationship described in the poem? **[Compare and Contrast]** ❹

Let not thy divining heart
  Forethink me any ill,
Destiny may take thy part,
  And may thy fears fulfill; ❺
    But think that we
Are but turned aside to sleep.
They who one another keep
  Alive, ne'r parted be.

Guide for Responding

◆ Literature and Your Life

Reader's Response Do you agree with the speaker when, in lines 17–24, he says we contribute to our own misfortunes? Why or why not?

Thematic Focus What assessment of time's power does Donne give in lines 17–20?

☑ Check Your Comprehension

1. What does the speaker say is his reason for leaving his beloved?
2. What does the speaker say happens when "bad chance" comes (lines 21–24)?
3. What does the speaker say may happen if his beloved worries about him (lines 33–36)?
4. How does the speaker suggest that his beloved view their parting (lines 37–40)?

◆ Critical Thinking

INTERPRET

1. To what remark of the speaker's beloved could this poem be a response? **[Infer]**
2. To what is the sun compared in stanza 2? **[Interpret]**
3. (a) Of what is the speaker trying to convince his beloved? (b) How would you outline the speaker's argument? **[Analyze]**
4. Why might the speaker have chosen to present his ideas in the form of an argument? **[Draw Conclusions]**

APPLY

5. The speaker in this poem uses exaggeration as a means of persuasion. Do you think that exaggerating in order to win an argument is a valid technique? Explain. **[Generalize]**

▶Critical Viewing◀

❹ Compare and Contrast Students might comment on the fact that the man seems deeply attached to the woman. His attention is focused on her; he seems to be thinking about her; she seems the bright spot in his world.

◆ Reading for Success

❺ Why does the speaker not want his beloved to think bad thoughts? What does this suggest about his views on good and bad fortune? *He is afraid that destiny will fulfill her fears. It suggests that bad thoughts create bad luck.*

Customize for
English Language Learners
Point out to students that each stanza discusses a single topic. Help students understanding by briefly summarizing what each stanza is about. For instance, point out that the second stanza compares the speaker to the sun.

Reinforce and Extend

Answers

◆ Literature and Your Life

Reader's Response Some students may believe that bad luck just happens; others will recall misfortunes that resulted from mistakes or bad choices.

Thematic Focus Man is powerless to affect time; time is all powerful and marches on, regardless of what happens in life.

☑ Check Your Comprehension

1. He says that his departure is a preparation for their ultimate separation in death.
2. By our own actions, we make bad things worse.
3. The speaker believes that fate may listen to her fears, and he may indeed become ill and die.
4. He suggests she think of their parting as being "turned aside to sleep."

◆ Critical Thinking

1. Sample remarks: How could you leave me if you loved me? You must no longer care for me.
2. As the sun disappears and returns predictably each day, so too will the speaker journey and return.
3. (a) He asks her not to grieve over their separation. (b) First he denies that he would ever leave her because he tired of her, or found a better love. Then he exaggerates a worse separation, a rehearsal for his eventual death. He reminds her that like the sun, he will inevitably return. Tenderly, he scolds her not to make it worse by crying, and he begs her not to think ill of him less she tempt fate and he truly die. She should think of them as merely turned aside in sleep, since remembering their devoted love keeps them ever together.
4. He needs to soothe her fears about separation and to persuade her not to be sad.
5. Sample response: Although exaggeration can undermine credibility, it can also make arguments more vivid, persuasive, and powerful.

Develop Understanding

One-Minute Insight This is considered to be one of Donne's best love poems. Its numerous references to the science of the day, its intellectual tone, its paradoxes, and its conceit at the end—the comparison involving the compass—make it a showcase for the elements that define metaphysical poetry.

◆ Critical Thinking

❶ **Synthesize** Ask how the first two stanzas are related to each other. *The first describes a situation, and the second urges the listener to act the same way.*

❷ **Clarification** "Moving of th' earth" is an earthquake.

◆ Literary Focus

❸ **Metaphysical Poetry** Ask students how the poet connects the science of his day with his emotions. *He contrasts himself and his beloved to "dull sublunary lovers," whose love is earthly and based on the senses. He compares his love to the great movement of the planets in their orbits ("trepidation of the spheres") and to the science of metallurgy, which "refined" ores into pure metals.*

◆ Build Vocabulary

❹ **Prefixes: *inter-*** Ask students what *assurèd* means (sure, confident) and what *inter-* means (between). Ask how the prefix helps them understand the unfamiliar word *inter-assurèd. The word describes a confidence between two people.*

◆ Literary Focus

❺ **Metaphysical Poetry** Ask students to identify the seeming paradox and explain what it means. *Two souls which are one sounds contradictory, but it emphasizes their unity.*

A Valediction:[1] Forbidding Mourning

John Donne

❶
As virtuous men pass mildly away,
And whisper to their souls to go,
Whilst some of their sad friends do say
The breath goes now, and some say, No;

So let us melt, and make no noise,
No tear-floods, nor sigh-tempests move,
'Twere profanation of our joys
To tell the laity our love.

❷
Moving of th'earth brings harms and fears,
Men reckon what it did and meant;
❸
But trepidation of the spheres,[2]
Though greater far, is innocent.

Dull sublunary[3] lovers' love
(Whose soul is sense) cannot admit
Absence, because it doth remove
Those things which elemented it.[4]

But we by a love, so much refined,
That our selves know not what it is,
❹
Inter-assurèd of the mind,[5]
Care less, eyes, lips, and hands to miss.

❺
Our two souls therefore, which are one,
Though I must go, endure not yet
A breach, but an expansion,
Like gold to airy thinness beat.

1. **valediction:** Farewell speech.

2. **trepidation of the spheres:** Movements of the stars and planets that are inconsistent with a perfect circular orbit.

3. **sublunary** (sub´ lo͞o nər´ ē): Referring to the region below the moon, considered in early astronomy the domain of changeable and perishable things.

4. **Those things . . . elemented it:** The basic materials or parts of their love.

5. **Inter-assurèd of the mind:** Mutually confident of each other's thoughts.

Speaking and Listening Mini-Lesson

Oral Interpretation

This mini-lesson supports the Speaking and Listening activity in the Idea Bank on page 403.

Introduce the Concept Explain that an oral interpretation is a reading that uses speaking techniques to express the emotion and mood of a piece of writing.

Develop Background Have students pair with partners and choose the poem or writing they wish to present. They should consider the following in preparing for their readings:

- What is the mood or tone of the work?
- What points does the poet emphasize?
- At what points would it be appropriate, to pause or raise or lower one's voice?

Apply the Information Students should practice their reading with their partners before presenting their interpretations to the class.

Assess the Outcome Students can use the Peer Assessment: Oral Interpretation page in ***Alternative Assessment,*** p. 120, to evaluate the presentations.

6 If they be two, they are two so
As stiff twin compasses[6] are two;
Thy soul the fixed foot, makes no show
To move, but doth, if th'other do.

And though it in the center sit,
Yet when the other far doth roam,
It leans, and hearkens after it,
And grows erect, as that comes home.

7 Such wilt thou be to me, who must
Like th'other foot, obliquely[7] run;
Thy firmness makes my circle just,[8]
And makes me end where I begun.

6. **twin compasses:** The two legs of a drawing compass.

7. **obliquely:** At an angle; not straight.

8. **just:** True; perfect.

◆ Build Vocabulary

profanation (präf´ ə nā´ shən) *n.*: Action showing disrespect for something sacred

laity (lā´ ət ē) *n.*: Those not initiated into the priesthood or other profession

trepidation (trep´ ə dā´ shən) *n.*: Trembling

breach (brēch) *n.*: Breaking open; the opening created by a break

8 ▶ **Critical Viewing** The mapmaker in the painting holds a compass like the one to which Donne refers in the poem. Using the painted compass as a clue, describe the picture "painted" by Donne's metaphysical conceit. **[Connect]**

A Geographer, Johannes Vermeer

◆ Reading for Success

6 Hypothesize Point out that Donne's comparison of two lovers' souls to the two legs of a compass is famous. Ask students why Donne uses a compass as the basis of a comparison in this stanza. *Students' responses may include the following: it is unexpected; it is apt; it is long; it joins the scientific and the spiritual worlds.*

◆ Literary Focus

7 Metaphysical Poetry Ask students to identify elements of metaphysical poetry in the last three verses. *Answers may include the conceit comparing a connection between souls to the movement of a compass; the interest in science; the seeming paradox in the last line.*

▶Critical Viewing◀

8 Connect Students should mention that the compass has two points, or feet; the woman's soul is compared to the foot that does not move, although it leans when the other foot moves. If it holds a fixed position, it causes the other foot to describe a complete circle and wind up at its starting point.

Customize for *Visual/Spatial Learners*

Encourage these students to demonstrate the operation of a drawing compass, pointing out the separate actions of each of the "legs."

Humanities: Art

A Geographer by Johannes Vermeer.

Today Johannes Vermeer (1632–1675) is considered one of the great Dutch painters, on a par with Rembrandt. Vermeer, however, painted only a few pictures, perhaps 35 or 36 in all. Most of these show a single figure, often a woman, inside a room containing an open door or window. The light streams through this opening, illuminating its subject. Vermeer's real fame came centuries after his death, when artists and critics alike focused on his mastery in rendering light and shade. This skill is particularly apparent in this picture.

You may wish to use these questions for discussion:

1. What signs of the geographer's trade are apparent in this painting? *The geographer would use the globe, the open map, the compass.*
2. Why do you think the painter illuminated some parts of the picture and left others in shade? *The lighting is realistic; it focuses attention on certain objects.*
3. How does the theme of this painting relate to the poem? *It shows a man of science, a person who measures and reasons, using a compass; the speaker of the poem is also learned and uses a compass in his trade.*

One-Minute Insight This is one of the best-known poems about death and how it was viewed by Donne and his contemporaries. Donne addresses Death directly, as if Death were a personal adversary whom the speaker no longer fears. Donne explains why he does not fear Death, and his argument is relatively easy to follow. It may help students understand the logical playfulness that Donne and other metaphysical poets enjoyed.

Looking at Literature Videodisc Introduce the poem by playing Chapter 5 of the videodisc. Students will see an actor portraying John Donne's friend reading "Holy Sonnet 10."

Chapter 5

Customize for
More Advanced Students
Explain that writer John Gunther used the opening words from this sonnet as the title to a book he wrote about the death of his son. Ask students why a parent who lost a child might find this poem comforting. *The poem suggests an eternal life after death; it also suggests that someone who died did not lose a battle.*

◆ Reading for Success

❶ Recognize the Speaker's Purpose Ask students what the speaker's purpose is in the first two lines of the poem. *His purpose is to show how powerless Death is.*

◆ Reading for Success

❷ Interpret the Text What does the speaker mean in lines 9–10? *Death is a slave because it is the tool of other forces, rather than a free agent.*

◆ Literary Focus

❸ Metaphysical Poetry Ask students what elements of metaphysical poetry they can identify in these lines. *Students can identify the intellectual argument; the interest in the life of the spirit; the extended metaphor, or conceit of Death as a person; the paradox of Death dying.*

Holy Sonnet 10

John Donne

❶ Death be not proud, though some have called thee
Mighty and dreadful, for thou art not so;
For those whom thou think'st thou dost overthrow,
Die not, poor death, nor yet canst thou kill me.
From rest and sleep, which but thy pictures[1] be,
Much pleasure; then from thee much more must flow,
And soonest our best men with thee do go,
Rest of their bones, and soul's delivery[2]
❷ Thou art slave to fate, chance, kings, and desperate men,
And dost with poison, war, and sickness dwell,
❸ And poppy,[3] or charms can make us sleep as well
And better than thy stroke; why swell'st[4] thou then?
One short sleep past, we wake eternally,
And death shall be no more; Death, thou shalt die.

1. **pictures:** Images.
2. **And . . . delivery:** Our best men go with you to rest their bones and find freedom for their souls.
3. **poppy:** Opium.
4. **swell'st:** Swell with pride.

Humanities: Art

Sir Thomas Astor at the Deathbed of His Wife by John Souch.

John Souch was a British portrait painter who did most of his work between 1617 and 1636. This, one of his few remaining portraits, was probably commissioned by Thomas Aston, high sheriff of Cheshire, as a memorial to his first wife, Magdalene.

Use the following questions for discussion:

1. In what ways does this painting reflect the ideas of the sonnet? *It shows that death is not final; memory can overcome it; it reflects the idea that death lives with sickness.*
2. Why is the wife, Magdalene, shown twice, do you think? *It shows her in her life as well as in her death; perhaps it indicates the continuum between life and death.*
3. What can you infer about the man from this picture? *Answers may include the following: His clothes show he is wealthy and in mourning; his hand on the skull shows that he has accepted death.*

Sir Thomas Aston at the Deathbed of His Wife
John Souch, Manchester City Art Galleries

◀ Critical Viewing The painting shows Lady Aston both when she is alive and when she is dead. Compare the relation between death and life implied by the painting with that developed in "Holy Sonnet 10." **[Compare and Contrast]** ❹

Guide for Responding

◆ Literature and Your Life

Reader's Response If you were the woman addressed by the speaker in "Valediction," how persuasive would you find his reassurances? Explain.

Thematic Focus From these two poems, what do you think were Donne's views on mortality—humans' time on earth?

☑ Check Your Comprehension

1. In what manner does the poem's speaker in "Valediction" suggest that he and his beloved should part?
2. In what way does the speaker's relationship with his lover differ from relationships of other couples?
3. Whom or what is the speaker addressing in "Holy Sonnet 10"?
4. In what sense does the speaker in "Holy Sonnet 10" claim that death shall be no more?

◆ Critical Thinking

INTERPRET

1. Why might the speaker of "Valediction" be unwilling to announce their love to the general population (lines 7–8)? **[Infer]**
2. In the final stanza, the speaker in "Valediction" compares himself to the moveable foot of a compass and his love to the fixed foot. What might this comparison indicate about their relationship? **[Draw Conclusions]**
3. In "Holy Sonnet 10," how are lines 3–4 reinforced by lines 13–14? **[Analyze]**
4. (a) What does the statement "Death, thou shalt die" mean? (b) What makes it paradoxical? **[Interpret]**

EVALUATE

5. How reassuring is the compass conceit in the "Valediction"? To what extent do you think it merely conceals the pain of parting? **[Criticize]**

Beyond the Selection

FURTHER READING

Books of Donne's Works
John Donne's Poetry: An Annotated Text with Critical Essays, A. L. Clements, ed.
Poems, John Donne, ed. by H.J.C. Grierson

Works About Donne
John Donne, Frank J. Warnke
"The Metaphysical Poets" in *Selected Essays,* T. S. Eliot

We suggest that you preview these works before recommending them to students.

INTERNET

You and your students may find additional information about John Donne on the Internet at the following site. Please be aware, however, that sites may have changed from the time we published this information.

For poems by Donne and a brief biographical sketch, go to **http://absolute-sway.com/pfp/donne.html**

We *strongly recommend* that you preview the site before you send students to it.

▶Critical Viewing◀

❹ Compare and Contrast Students might mention that both show a form of life everlasting. The picture shows Lady Astor as being alive in memory.

◆ Critical Thinking

Analyze Explain that the speaker personifies death in this poem, meaning that death is given human qualities and treated as if it were a person. Have students give examples from the poem. Then ask what that personification adds to the poem. *The speaker addresses Death directly, as if it were a person, and suggests that it not feel pride or pleasure. Personification makes death seem less powerful. It also makes the argument seem more personcl and immediate.*

Reinforce and Extend

Answers

◆ Literature and Your Life

Reader's Response Sample response: She would be persuaded by the description of a love so deeply felt that their souls were one.

Thematic Focus Sample response: Mortal life is not as important as the afterlife.

☑ Check Your Comprehension

1. He suggests they should part "mildly."
2. Suggested response: Their love is more "refined and spiritual, and thus transcends physical separation."
3. The speaker is addressing Death.
4. Death shall be no more when people die, for they shall have eternal life.

◆ Critical Thinking

1. It would show a disrespect for something special and sacred.
2. It shows that he relies on his beloved; his life revolves around her.
3. The last two lines explain that those who have died have really gone on to eternal life.
4. (a) Death will no longer have power or meaning. (b) Only Death has the power to kill.
5. Some students may say that the image is comforting; it does not conceal the pain of parting, but it does provide reassurance that the separation is only temporary.

Answers

◆ Reading for Success

1. (a) The speaker is a very devout Christian in his beliefs about eternal life. In "Song" and "Valediction," he speaks to his true love on the occasion of a separation, either through a journey or deadly illness. In "Holy Sonnet 10" the speaker addresses Death at an occasion where Death seems triumphant. (b) In "Song" and "Valedicton," he intends to reassure his beloved that they will never be apart. In "Holy Sonnet 10," he points out that Death does not win in the end.
2. Students may say that the speaker in "Song" and "Valediction" has a deep and loving relationship with the person he is addressing. In "Holy Sonnet," the speaker has an adversarial relationship with Death.

◆ Literary Focus

1. (a) In "Meditation 17," a library is a conceit for heaven; in "Holy Sonnet 10," a proud person is a conceit for death; in "Song," a separation by a journey is a conceit for separation in death. (b) Since people were compared to chapters in a book, another conceit, it is only fitting that they eventually end up in a library. Death, the proud person, is defeated by his own acts. Separation by a journey works to describe the worse separation of death.
2. (a) Examples of paradox: In "Song" his beloved is described as being "unkindly kind;" in "A Valediction" he says their two souls are one. (b) She is kind because she cares for him and mourns his departure, but her grieving distresses and distracts him. Their two souls are fused into an expanded soul, so they will never be alone.
3. (a) A compass is drastically unlike a relationship between two people. (b) Johnson is lacking imagination, because the compass is a beautiful image for depicting love as a endless circle.

Guide for Responding *(continued)*

◆ Reading for Success

Strategies for Constructing Meaning

A Donne lyric is often like a speech from a little drama. You can better understand the poem by figuring out what is going on in the "play."

1. What can you infer about the speaker in this poem? (a) Who is he, to whom is he speaking, and what is the occasion? (b) What is his purpose in speaking?
2. What conclusions can you draw about the relationship between the speaker and the person he is addressing?

◆ Literary Focus

Metaphysical Poetry

Metaphysical poetry challenges your intellect through paradoxes (contradictory statements) and conceits (unusual comparisons).

Donne's "A Valediction: Forbidding Mourning" contains a famous conceit. Donne compares two lovers who are temporarily parting to the two feet of a compass. The comparison is strange but it is also strangely accurate. Picture a compass with the point fixed and the extension, with the pencil, circling around it. The "fixed foot" of the compass, as it leans, does seem to "hearken" after the moving one, just as the speaker's love will yearn after him when he is gone.

1. (a) Give one example of a metaphysical conceit from each of the following: "Meditation 17," "Holy Sonnet 10," and "Song." (b) For each conceit, explain how, despite the differences between the things being compared, the comparison "works."
2. (a) Give one example of a paradox from each of the following: "Song" and "A Valediction: Forbidding Mourning." (b) In each case, explain the sense behind the apparent contradiction.
3. The eighteenth-century writer Samuel Johnson complained that in metaphysical poetry, "The most heterogeneous [different] ideas are yoked by violence together." (a) Explain how Johnson's criticism applies to the conceit of the compass in "A Valediction: Forbidding Mourning." (b) What, if anything, is Johnson missing?

◆ Build Vocabulary

Using the Prefix *inter-*

Knowing that the prefix *inter-* means "among," "between," or "with each other," define these words in your notebook:

1. intermingle **2.** intertwine **3.** interact **4.** interwoven **5.** interrupt

Using the Word Bank

Choose the lettered word or words closest in meaning to the first word:

1. contention: a) gathering, b) campsite, c) dispute
2. piety: a) devotion, b) partiality, c) roundness
3. intermit: a) interfere, b) pause, c) deny
4. covetousness: a) greed, b) agreement, c) sloth
5. profanation: a) violation, b) arson, c) prediction
6. laity: a) the uninitiated, b) those who stand, c) professionals
7. trepidation: a) hunger, b) fear, c) calm
8. breach: a) birth, b) pants, c) break

◆ Grammar and Style

Active and Passive Voice

In the **active voice,** the verb expresses an action performed by the subject. In the **passive voice,** which uses a form of *to be* with the past participle, the subject receives the action of the verb.

Practice In your notebook, rewrite the following sentences in the active voice.

1. Their love is expanded by separation.
2. His soul is sighed away by her sighs.
3. His life's blood is weakened by her weeping.
4. It has been said that Death is mighty.
5. Life is not conquered by death.

Writing Application The passive voice tends to hide who did what to whom. That's why it is often used in press releases. As a public relations consultant for John Donne, write a statement about his recent dismissal from the service of Sir Thomas Egerton. Use five examples of the passive voice to disguise exactly what happened. For example, you might begin, "It was agreed that . . ." (Check Donne's biography on p. 390 for details.)

◆ Build Vocabulary

Using the Prefix *inter-*

1. *intermingle:* to mix together
2. *intertwine:* to interlace
3. *interact:* to act on one another
4. *interwoven:* to weave together
5. *interrupt:* to break in upon

Using the Word Bank

1. c 2. a 3. b 4. a 5. a
6. a 7. b 8. c

◆ Grammar and Style

1. Separation expanded their love.
2. Her sighs sighed away his soul.
3. Her weeping weakened his life's blood.
4. Someone has said that Death is mighty.
5. Death does not conquer life.

Writer's Solution

For additional instruction and practice use the page on Voice, in the *Writer's Solution Grammar Practice Book, p. 56.*

Build Your Portfolio

Idea Bank

Writing

1. Journal Entry When parting, some draw out their good-byes. Others may say as little as possible. Write a journal entry exploring the best way to say good-bye.

2. The Lady's Turn Write a poem in which the speaker's beloved in "Song" or "Valediction" answers his attempts to reassure her.

3. Critical Response The modern poet T. S. Eliot celebrated Donne as one of the best (and last) poets to integrate mind and heart: "A thought to Donne was an experience; it modified his sensibility [feeling and perception]." Evaluate Eliot's idea, using examples from Donne's work.

Speaking and Listening

4. Oral Interpretation With a partner, rehearse reading two of Donne's poems. Practice reading the poems as dramatic speeches and perform your reading for the class. **[Performing Arts Link]**

5. Presentation of a Conceit Analyze the movements of a common device, like a blender. Diagram a comparison of the device with human relations or feelings, and present your diagrammed conceit to the class. **[Art Link]**

Projects

6. Sculpture of a Conceit Make a sculpture of a metaphysical conceit by yoking together two things that seem to be different but really do belong together in some way. **[Art Link]**

7. Map of the Universe Create an annotated map that illustrates Donne's "trepidations of the spheres." **[Art Link; Science Link]**

Writing Mini-Lesson

Speech

Many of Donne's poems are like little speeches for specific occasions. Graduation from school can be a very important occasion and is usually marked by speeches. Write a speech that you would like to give (or to hear) at your graduation ceremony. Use the following skill to give your speech unity.

Writing Skills Focus: Unity

A good speech, like most writing, has an introduction with a strong statement of the theme, a body, and a conclusion. Each part of an effective speech—one that can move or please an audience—is connected to the others in clear ways. Such a speech has **unity.**

To keep your speech unified, make sure that

- the introduction clearly introduces a main theme.
- the ideas in the body relate to the main theme.
- the conclusion sums up the development of the main theme in the body.

Prewriting Jot down memories from your school career and your hopes for the future. Draw on the connections between memories and hopes to identify your main theme.

Drafting Introduce your theme using humor or a story. Develop the theme in the body of the speech, supporting your ideas with examples. Use only those examples that relate to your theme. Leave out other details. Then write a conclusion summing up your insights.

Revising Verify that your introduction states your theme, that each paragraph in the body supports the theme, and that sentences within each paragraph support the topic sentence. Finally, be sure that your conclusion sums up your development of the main theme.

ASSESSMENT OPTIONS

Formal Assessment, Selection Test, pp. 86–88, and Assessment Resources Software. The selection test is designed so that it can be easily customized to the performance levels of your students.

Alternative Assessment, p. 17, includes options for less advanced students, more advanced students, visual/spatial learners and verbal/linguistic learners.

PORTFOLIO ASSESSMENT

Use the following rubrics in the ***Alternative Assessment*** booklet to assess student writing:
Journal Entry: Expression Rubric, p. 95
The Lady's Turn: Poetry Rubric, p. 109
Critical Response: Evaluation/Review Rubric, p. 105
Writing Mini-Lesson: Persuasion Rubric, p. 106

Idea Bank

Customizing for Performance Levels

Following are suggestions for matching Idea Bank topics with your students' performance levels:

Less Advanced Students: 1, 6
Average Students: 2, 4, 7
More Advanced Students: 3, 5

Customizing for Learning Modalities

Following are suggestions for matching Idea Bank topics with your students' learning modalities:

Verbal/Linguistic: 1, 2, 3, 4, 5
Bodily/Kinesthetic: 6
Visual/Spatial: 7

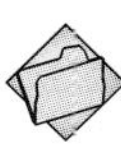

Writing Mini-Lesson

Refer students to the Writing Handbook, page 1189, for instruction on the writing process, and page 1192 for further information on persuasion. Point out to students that most speeches employ persuasive techniques to convey their message to an audience.

Writing and Language Transparencies Use the Writing Process Model 5: Persuasive Essay, pp. 37–43, to model the writing and revising of a persuasive essay.

Writing Lab CD-ROM

Have students complete the tutorial on Persuasion. Follow these steps:

1. Students may use the Issues Wheel to spark writing ideas.
2. Suggest they use the Outliner to organize their speeches.
3. Have students draft on computer.
4. Use the tips on presenting a speech.

Allow approximately 90 minutes of class time to complete these steps.

Sourcebook

Have students use Chapter 4, Persuasion (pp. 96–129), for additional support. The chapter includes a workplace writing model of a persuasive essay (p. 102).

Prepare and Engage

OBJECTIVES

1. To read, comprehend, and interpret poems
2. To relate poems to personal experience
3. To hypothesize about the speaker and situation to improve comprehension
4. To recognize epigrams
5. To build vocabulary in context and recognize common archaic words
6. To develop skill in the placement of the word *only*
7. To write a letter to a school newspaper
8. To respond to poems through writing, speaking and listening, and projects

SKILLS INSTRUCTION

Vocabulary: Archaic Words
Grammar: The Placement of *Only*
Reading Strategy: Hypothesize
Literary Focus: Epigrams
Writing: Elaboration
Speaking and Listening: Fashion Debate (teacher edition)
Critical Viewing: Compare and Contrast

PORTFOLIO OPPORTUNITIES

Writing: T-shirt Saying; Fashion Essay; Literary Analysis
Writing Mini-Lesson: Persuasive Letter
Speaking and Listening: Love Song; Fashion Debate
Projects: Songs of Ben; Biographical Report

More About the Author
Jonson's poor-orphan-makes-good story is so dramatic that he could have been a fictitious character. From modest beginnings, through a life filled with fights, jail, and personal excesses, he rose to a genuine celebrity, with money, fame, and prestige. However, when Charles I came to power, Jonson's life began to go downhill. Jonson lost his position in court to a rival; he suffered a paralyzing stroke; and an audience hissed one of his later plays. When Jonson asked the King for space in Westminster Abbey for a grave, the monarch gave him so little—one square foot—that the writer had to be buried in an upright position.

Guide for Interpreting

Ben Jonson *(1572(?)–1637)*

Not only did Ben Jonson's life have mythic proportions, but his physique did too. He was a large man with boundless energy and enormous courage. Coming from a working-class background, Ben Jonson became a friend as well as chief rival of Shakespeare and Donne.

From bricklayer to poet laureate, Ben Jonson's life story is a true "rags to riches" tale.

Brilliant in his poetry and dangerous in a duel, a classical scholar and a veteran soldier, an astute critic and a brassy talker, Jonson's colorful, sometimes violent, career culminated with his being recognized as the most influential judge of literature, setting literary taste for a generation of poets.

A Poet at War Adopted in infancy, Jonson worked for his stepfather, a bricklayer, while attending the equivalent of high school under a private tutor. Too poor to study at a university, Jonson joined the army and fought in the wars for Dutch independence from Spain. A large, energetic man, Jonson at one point met an enemy champion in single combat before the massed armies of Holland and Spain. Jonson won.

Scandal and Success After returning to England, Jonson went on the stage as an actor. Despite his turbulent life—jailed for his part in a "slanderous" play, almost hanged for killing a fellow actor in a duel, and even suspected of plotting against the king—Jonson became a major dramatist. William Shakespeare acted in his first play, and noted acting companies performed his later plays.

Jonson was so successful that he was granted a handsome pension by King James I and treated as if he were poet laureate of England. Over the years he wrote masques—elaborate entertainments—for the royal court, where he was a favorite writer. He was also extremely influential, functioning as a virtual dictator over the literary efforts of the day.

A Lasting Influence Jonson's influence on writers is still felt today, and his plays, such as *Volpone* and *The Alchemist,* continue to be produced. What Jonson said of Shakespeare can be said of Jonson as well: "He was not of an age, but for all time."

◆ Background for Understanding

LITERATURE: THE SONS OF BEN

Historic accounts help us picture Jonson at the Mermaid Tavern, surrounded by admirers and engaged in duels of wit with Shakespeare. The best of the young court writers, including Robert Herrick and Sir John Suckling, flocked about Jonson, calling themselves the "Sons of Ben" or "Tribe of Ben."

Jonson's emphasis on graceful, balanced expression in verse shaped their work, offering an alternative to Donne's "rough" lines. Critic Douglas Bush writes, "Jonson demanded, and unceasingly strove for, the ageless classical virtues of clarity, unity, symmetry, and proportion." Jonson was the first English poet with a "school"; he was also the first to insist that poetry was in itself an important vocation. Shakespeare, who did not publish his plays, regarded himself as a working dramatist, a tradesman in words. Jonson, however, risked controversy by publishing his verse in the form of a "Collected Works"—a format previously reserved for theological or historical works.

As you read, note the examples of superb craftsmanship that inspired so many other poets to admire and imitate Jonson.

Prentice Hall Literature Program Resources

REINFORCE / RETEACH / EXTEND

Selection Support Pages
Build Vocabulary: Archaic Words, p. 86
Grammar and Style: The Placement of *Only,* p. 87
Reading Strategy: Hypothesize, p. 88
Literary Focus: Epigrams, p. 89

Strategies for Diverse Student Needs, p. 18

Beyond Literature
Cross-Curricular Connection: Social Studies, p. 18

Formal Assessment Selection Test, pp. 89–91; Assessment Resources Software

Alternative Assessment, p. 18

Resource Pro CD-ROM
Includes all resource material and customizable lesson plan.

Writing and Language Transparencies
Writing Process Model 5: pp. 37–43

Listening to Literature Audiocassettes
"On My First Son"; "Song: To Celia"; "Still to Be Neat"

On My First Son ◆ Song: To Celia ◆ Still to Be Neat ◆

◆ Literature and Your Life

Connect Your Experience

Memorable sayings are all around you—inscribed in rings and on mugs, emblazoned on T-shirts and bumper stickers, and printed on plaques and posters.

Ben Jonson probably would have understood this desire to preserve witty and profound sayings. He wanted his poems to contain truths that could be engraved in metal or carved in stone.

Journal Writing Jot down your favorite sayings, slogans, or words to live by.

Thematic Focus: The War Against Time

One way to win the war against time is to create an image or make an observation that will hold true for all time. As you read these poems, think about how Jonson's unique and profound observations remain timeless.

◆ Build Vocabulary

Archaic Words

Ben Jonson's poetry contains **archaic words**—words that are no longer in general use. Because these words appear frequently in classic English literature, it is useful to become familiar with them.

Pairs of Archaic and Modern Words: wast-was; wert-were; hast-have; hath-has; dost-do; doth-does; thou-you; thy-your; thine-yours

Before reading the poems, become familiar with these words.

◆ Grammar and Style

The Placement of *Only*

In crafting the line, "Drink to me only with thine eyes," Jonson carefully **placed the modifier *only*** to ensure that the meaning of the line was clear. For clarity, modifiers such as *only* should always be placed as close as possible to the words that they modify.

Example: Drink only to me with thine eyes (Gaze upon the speaker and upon no one else.)

Example: Only drink to me with thine eyes (Only gaze at the speaker, do nothing else.)

◆ Literary Focus

Epigrams

An **epigram** is a short poem in which brevity, clarity, and permanence are emphasized. (*Epigram* is derived from the Greek word meaning "inscription," words preserved on a monument.)

Jonson sometimes uses statements that seem to go against common sense in order to give his work the little "twist" that makes it memorable. One such statement is "Drink to me only with thine eyes." How could the woman drink to the poet with her eyes but not with her mouth? The answer is, she can give him a loving look.

◆ Reading Strategy

Hypothesize

As you read, you can **hypothesize**—make informed guesses—based on the information that is given. Reading further, you encounter more information that either proves or disproves your hypothesis.

For example, when you read Jonson's line, "Farewell, thou child of my right hand," you might guess that the speaker is a father. When you reach the line, "here doth lie Ben Jonson his best piece of poetry," you realize that the speaker is also the poet.

Preparing for Standardized Tests

Vocabulary Some standardized tests require students to complete analogies, as in the following example:

Thou : You :: Thine : ______ *(A)*
(A) your
(B) thy
(C) their

Recognizing the modern equivalents of archaic words helps students understand them in context and identify their meanings. For additional practice, use the Build Vocabulary page in ***Selection Support,*** p. 86.

Reading Many standardized tests present students with a reading passage and ask questions about the content. The Reading Strategy for this selection, hypothesize, helps students to interact with the text and thereby improve their comprehension. For more practice, use the Reading Strategy page in ***Selection Support,*** p. 88

Ask students what makes them remember a line of poetry or a quotation from a speech. Ask them to cite a few memorable quotations and explain why they are memorable. Then tell them that Ben Jonson's writing was designed to produce quotable lines and phrases.

Customize for
Less Proficient Readers
The short, memorable lines in these poems offer these students an opportunity to memorize passages or whole poems. Memorization allows people to share poetry with others and to appreciate it deeply themselves. Encourage students to choose one of the poems to memorize.

Customize for
More Advanced Students
Encourage students to compare and contrast these poems with those of John Donne, as well as with other poems on similar themes. For example, you might want to suggest "To an Athlete Dying Young" by A. E. Housman or "To Drink" by Jane Hirshfield.

Customize for
Musical/Rhythmic Learners
Many students enjoy listening to music and do not connect it with written poetry. "Song: To Celia" has been reworked as a folk song called "Drink to Me Only With Thine Eyes." Encourage students to find and listen to a recording of it.

Customize for
English Language Learners
Although some of the archaic language will be addressed during class, students may also have trouble with some of the less familiar words that are still in current use, such as *lament, henceforth, withered,* and *presumed.* To help these students, you may wish to paraphrase each poem briefly.

Develop Understanding

One-Minute Insight Whereas Donne's work argues that death does not matter because it leads to eternal life, Jonson's poem "On My First Son" shows that death sorely wounds those grieving people left behind. Jonson developed "Song: To Celia" from some prose pieces written by a third-century Greek writer, Philostratus. Like other Greek and Roman lyrics, it exhibits a sense of balance, proportion, simplicity, and conciseness.

◆ Build Vocabulary

❶ **Archaic Words** Ask students to "translate" the words *thou, thee, thou wert, thee,* and *thy* in the first four lines. *They translate as "you," "you," "you were," "you," and "your."*

❷ **Clarification** During the Renaissance, the words *like* and *love* were used interchangeably.

◆ Literary Focus

❸ **Epigrams** Ask students what makes the last line so memorable. *It seems paradoxical; it is snappy and alliterative.*

◆ Grammar and Style

❹ **The Placement of *Only*** Have students explain what the first line means and suggest alternatives that are eliminated by the placement of *only*. *It means use only your eyes to drink to me, and not your lips or hands or any other part.*

◆ Reading Strategy

❺ **Hypothesize** Ask students if they think Celia feels the same way about the speaker as he feels about her. Ask for evidence from the poem. *Some students will think she does not, since she returns the wreath.*

On My First Son

Ben Jonson

❶
Farewell, thou child of my right hand,[1] and joy;
    My sin was too much hope of thee, loved boy,
Seven years thou wert lent to me, and I thee pay,
    Exacted by thy fate, on the just[2] day.
O, could I lose all father,[3] now. For why
    Will man lament the state he should envy?
To have so soon scaped world's, and flesh's rage,
    And, if no other misery, yet age?
Rest in soft peace, and, asked, say here doth lie
    Ben Jonson his best piece of poetry.
❷ For whose sake, henceforth, all his vows be such,
    As what he loves may never like too much.
❸

1. **child. . . hand:** Literal translation of the Hebrew name Benjamin. Jonson's son was born in 1596 and died in 1603.
2. **just:** Exact.
3. **lose. . . father:** Give up all thoughts of being a father.

Block Scheduling Strategies

Consider these suggestions to take advantage of extended class time:

- Have students work on the journal writing activity in Literature and Your Life (p. 405).
- Introduce the Literary Focus, Epigrams, on page 405. After students read the selection, assign the questions on page 410. Students may then complete the Literary Focus page in ***Selection Support,*** p. 89.
- Students can form teams to prepare for the debate in the Speaking and Listening activity on page 411.
- Students may work together on the Love Song, as described in the Speaking and Listening activities in the Idea Bank (p. 411).
- Have students research Jonson's life for the Biographical Report in the Idea Bank (p. 411).
- Students can work on their Persuasive Letter for the Writing Mini-Lesson (p. 411). A panel of student reviewers can decide which letters to submit to the newspaper.

Drink to me only with thine eyes,
And I will pledge with mine:
Or leave a kiss but in the cup,
And I'll not look for wine.
The thirst that from the soul doth rise, ❹
Doth ask a drink divine:
But might I of Jove's[1] nectar sup,
I would not change for thine.

I sent thee late[2] a rosy wreath,
Not so much honoring thee,
As giving it a hope, that there
It could not withered be. ❺
But thou thereon did'st only breathe,
And sent'st it back to me;
Since when it grows and smells, I swear,
Not of itself, but thee.

1. **Jove's:** Jupiter's. In Roman mythology, Jupiter is the ruler of the gods.
2. **late:** Recently.

Guide for Responding

◆ Literature and Your Life

Reader's Response Do you think the speaker in "On My First Son" is wise in not wanting to love anything so strongly again? Explain.

Thematic Focus What attitude toward time and loss is suggested by lines 3–4 of "On My First Son"?

☑ Check Your Comprehension

1. In line 5 of "On My First Son," how does the speaker wish he could respond to his son's death?
2. To what does "Ben Jonson his best piece of poetry" refer?
3. What vow does the speaker make as part of his son's epitaph?
4. (a) In lines 5–8 of "Song: To Celia," what does the speaker say the soul requires? (b) What does he choose to fill this need?
5. (a) Why does the speaker send a wreath to Celia? (b) What happens to the wreath?

◆ Critical Thinking

INTERPRET

1. How would you explain the "sin" the speaker of "On My First Son" attributes to himself in line 2? **[Interpret]**
2. Why does the speaker say in lines 6–8 that an early death is enviable? **[Infer]**
3. In line 5 of "Song: To Celia," what is "the thirst that from the soul doth rise"? **[Interpret]**
4. (a) What do the images of love in the poem—eyes, drinks, and the wreath—have in common? (b) What does this suggest about love? **[Draw Conclusions]**

EVALUATE

5. In "On My First Son," is Jonson's way of presenting the speaker's grief effective? Why or why not? **[Criticize]**
6. (a) How much do you know about the speaker of "Song: To Celia" or his beloved? (b) How would more information affect your appreciation of his poem? **[Make a Judgment]**

Reinforce and Extend

Answers

◆ Literature and Your Life

Reader's Response Most students will sympathize with the speaker's grief, but may think him unwise for not wanting to love so strongly again.

Thematic Focus Seven years of joy will take the rest of one's life to pay.

☑ Check Your Comprehension

1. He wishes he could forget what it is like to be a father.
2. His best piece of poetry is the brief life of his young son.
3. He vows never again to love anything so strongly.
4. (a) The soul asks for a divine drink. (b) Even if the speaker could have the drink of the gods, he would prefer the love of Celia.
5. (a) He sends the wreath in hope that in Celia's presence it will never die. (b) Celia sends it back to the speaker, but it acquires Celia's scent.

◆ Critical Thinking

1. The sin is loving his son too much.
2. The youthful dead have escaped the pain of this world, and the decay and the misery of old age.
3. The soul has a thirst for love.
4. (a) Eyes, drinks, and the wreath all appeal to and heighten the senses. (b) Love is felt through all the senses.
5. Jonson speaks directly to his son in a powerful farewell, making it immediate and intensely heartfelt.
6. (a) We only know that this is an attraction—the flirting, first stages of a relationship. (b) If we knew more about the people involved, it would add more interest. On the other hand, the poem expresses a universal feeling of being newly attracted to someone.

Cross-Curricular Connection: Science

Courting rituals are not confined to humans; many birds, animals, and insects follow them as well. Often, the rituals may involve displays of health, beauty, or ability. They may also involve gifts. Some of the more interesting courting customs are those displayed by bower birds, salamanders, eagles, hornbills, fighting fish, anglerfish, and peacocks.

Have students work in pairs and choose one of the animals listed above or some other animal that interests them. Have them research the animal's courting rituals and prepare a brief description. Then have them compare their findings with those of their classmates and hold a discussion about the purpose of such activities.

Develop Understanding

One-Minute Insight

This poem comes from the first act of *Epicoene; or, The Silent Woman,* a comedy written in 1609. This helps explain the poem's lighthearted tone. The speaker expresses his admiration for the natural style of beauty, feeling that powders and perfumes cover up a lack of sweetness and soundness. Students who imagine this poem as part of a modern musical comedy can appreciate how timeless Jonson's ideas are.

Customize for
Bodily/Kinesthetic Learners
Invite students to tap out the rhythm of this poem, which is quick and bouncy. This may help students appreciate its tone.

Customize for
Less Proficient Readers
Students will be able to enjoy this poem with little help. You may wish to point out that *sound* here means "without flaw."

◆ Literary Focus

❶ **Epigrams** Ask students which lines or phrases they find most memorable. *Some students may suggest the first or last line of either stanza.*

◆ Build Vocabulary

❷ **Archaic Words** Ask students what the word *mine* means in this context. Point out that the usage of a word can change over time. *It means* my.

Still to Be Neat

Ben Jonson

Still[1] to be neat, still to be dressed,
As you were going to a feast;
Still to be powdered, still perfumed;
Lady, it is to be presumed,
Though art's hid causes[2] are not found,
All is not sweet, all is not sound. ❶

Give me a look, give me a face,
That makes simplicity a grace;
Robes loosely flowing, hair as free;
Such sweet neglect more taketh me
Than all th'adulteries[3] of art,
❷ They strike mine eyes, but not my heart.

1. **still:** Always.
2. **causes:** Reasons.
3. **adulteries:** Adulterations; corruptions.

Guide for Responding

◆ *Literature and Your Life*

Reader's Response Do you agree with the speaker about the attractiveness of a "spontaneous" look? Why or why not?

Thematic Focus In what ways do beauty regimes and fashion wage a war against time?

Fashion Discussion With a group of classmates, discuss whether modern fashion emphasizes the simple or the artificial.

☑ Check Your Comprehension

1. Does the speaker approve of the woman's fashion sense?
2. What sort of look does the speaker prefer?

◆ Critical Thinking

INTERPRET

1. What hidden causes might the speaker have in mind in line 6? **[Interpret]**
2. (a) How does Jonson use the repetition of words and word patterns in the first stanza to support his meaning? (b) How does Jonson adapt this structure in the second stanza? **[Analyze]**

APPLY

3. What trends in modern advertising can you connect with the attitude expressed in Jonson's poem? **[Relate]**

Speaking and Listening Mini-Lesson

Debate
This mini-lesson supports the Speaking and Listening activity in the Idea Bank on p. 411.

Introduce the Concept Explain that a debate is a contest of wits, in which each side tries to find overwhelming evidence to support a particular point of view. Explain that political candidates often debate an issue. The object is not only to convince voters, but also to show their expertise, intelligence, and preparation.

Develop Background Before students begin, discuss the steps that lead to success in a debate.

- Prepare, by brainstorming for reasons that support their point of view.
- Find facts, details, and statistics to support the viewpoints.
- Anticipate the other team's arguments and be prepared to refute them.
- Listen carefully to the other side's arguments before responding.

Apply the Information Students should now debate a position that is assigned them. Remind them to begin by preparing an opening statement that clearly sets forth their position.

Assess the Outcome Ask students to vote on which side offered the greatest number of reasons and the most convincing reasons. Use the Peer Assessment: Speaker/Speech page in ***Alternative Assessment,*** p. 119.

The Interrupted Sleep, François Boucher, The Metropolitan Museum of Art

▲ Critical Viewing Compare what the painting suggests about the attractiveness of artifice and disarray with the speaker's opinion in the poem. [Compare and Contrast] ❸

Beyond Literature

History Connection

Ben Jonson and Renaissance Warfare

War was all too common in sixteenth- and seventeenth-century Europe, and Ben Jonson was not the only poet of the time with military as well as literary talents. The one story that survives of his battlefield adventures—his triumph over an enemy soldier in single combat—suggests that warfare was still governed by the laws of chivalry. However, by Jonson's time, the knights of the Middle Ages had been replaced by soldiers-for-hire and other professionals.

Victory increasingly depended on foot-soldiers. The knight's lance had met its match in the pike, a spear long enough to give a foot-soldier the advantage over a horseman. A knight's armor was also vulnerable to the long-bows wielded by trained archers, to the cross-bows given to less experienced recruits, and to the latest innovation of violence, the musket.

The Spanish style of fighting dominated the battlefield. Disciplined columns of pikemen with musket-men at the corners would advance against the enemy. War in Jonson's time was less and less a matter of honor and skill, and more and more a question of discipline and sheer firepower. While Jonson the man was understandably proud of his wartime exploits, Jonson the poet devoted his pen to more peaceful subjects.

From the fact that Jonson's poetry was rarely preoccupied with battle, what conclusions can you draw about his attitude toward his own military exploits?

Reinforce and Extend

Answers

◆ ***Literature and Your Life***

Reader's Response Sample response: There is something very appealing about a look that is fresh and not artificial, as long as it is not sloppy.

Thematic Focus Fear of aging creates big business for the fashion and cosmetics industry. Fashion is designed for the younger, slimmer figure, and cosmetics add moisture and hide wrinkles.

Check Your Comprehension

1. He is quite annoyed at her contrived or artificial prettiness.
2. He much prefers natural beauty.

◆ Critical Thinking

1. The speaker suspects a repellent odor and flawed skin are beneath the perfume and powder.
2. (a) The repetition of "still to be" indicates his displeasure at finding her always overly made up. (b) The repetition of "give me" is softer and modulates into examples of the simplicity he prefers.
3. Perfume, cosmetics, and fashion ads all spotlight natural beauty and the spontaneous look as being desirable. This is somewhat ironic, as cosmetics are examples of the artifice Jonson deplores.

Customize for
Visual/Spatial Learners
Invite students to find advertisements or pictures of women who fit both types described in this poem.

►Critical Viewing◄

❸ Compare and Contrast
Students may suggest that the disarray of sleep is attractive; or, they may think that the sloppiness is not attractive.

Humanities: Art

The Interrupted Sleep by François Boucher.

The legacy of François Boucher (1703–1770) includes some of the finest examples of Louis XV rococo art. Teacher of Fragonard, a favorite of Madame Pompadour, he was dubbed "first painter" of the King of France. Boucher's style includes excellent draftsmanship, fine brushwork, and an eye for drama and decoration. His work, which included portraits, religious works, and stylish genre paintings, was designed to delight viewers. As a result, critics sometimes claimed that his work was merely pretty. However, his art reflected the tastes of his time, and his talent has come to be appreciated.

Use the following questions for discussion:

1. How does this picture show a love of nature? *It has a beautiful natural setting.*
2. Do you think this is a good choice to illustrate this poem? Why or why not? *Some students may think it is a good choice, because it illustrates a woman who is dressed as if going to a feast. Others may argue that her disarray is not particularly attractive.*

◆ Reading Strategy

1. Lines 1–4 establish that this is a young child who died and was very much beloved.
2. No, they only underscore the torment of loss and grief.
3. His grief for his son is inconsolable and hurts too deeply.

◆ Grammar and Style

1. Drink *only* to me with thine eyes.
2. Drink to me with *only* thine eyes.
3. Drink to me *only* with thine eyes.
4. *Only* they strike mine eyes.
5. They strike *only* mine eyes.

Writing Application
Sample response: Ben Jonson was not *only* brilliant in poetry, but dangerous in a duel. Once he was the *only* champion to meet an enemy in single combat before the armies of Holland and Spain; he won.

◆ Literary Focus

1. Two additional examples of parallelism are: "Still to be powdered, still perfumed"; and "All is not sweet, all is not sound."
2. *Neglect* would mean "sloppy" except for *sweet*, which changes its meaning to "natural."
3. It is succinct and memorable.
4. Even though he swears never to love so much again, he will never stop loving his son.
5. (a) Yes; they express a father's love and grief and thus are a moving tribute. (b) They are brief and memorable.

◆ Build Vocabulary

For if I thought my judgment were of years/I should commit *you* surely with *your* peers/And tell, how far *you did* our Lyly outshine,/Or sporting Kyd, or Marlowe's mighty line./And though *you had little* Latin, and less Greek,/From *that* to honor *you*, I would not seek/For names; but call forth thund'ring Aeschylus. . . .

Writer's Solution

For additional instruction and practice, use the lesson in the **Language Lab CD-ROM** on Sentence Errors and the page on Misplaced and Dangling Modifiers, p. 45, in the *Writer's Solution Grammar Practice Book.*

Guide for Responding (continued)

◆ Reading Strategy

Hypothesize

As you read Ben Jonson's poems, you **hypothesized** by forming and testing ideas about the situation and the speaker.

Reenact this process for "On My First Son" by answering these questions.

1. Using only lines 1–4, make a hypothesis about the situation and the speaker's relationship with his son.
2. Do lines 5–8 require you to modify your hypothesis about the speaker's feelings for his son? Why or why not?
3. Basing your answer on lines 11–12, what final hypothesis can you make about the speaker's feelings for his son?

◆ Grammar and Style

The Placement of *Only*

As you can see in the first line of "Song: To Celia," it's important to **place the modifier *only*** as close as possible to the word that it modifies. When *only* is misplaced, it can confuse or mislead the reader.

Practice In your notebook, add the word *only* to the following sentences to reflect the meaning indicated in parentheses.

1. Drink to me with thine eyes. (just to me, no one else)
2. Drink to me with thine eyes. (use your eyes, no one else's)
3. Drink to me with thine eyes. (drink to me using just your eyes)
4. They strike mine eyes. (they, and no others)
5. They strike mine eyes. (only my eyes, not my heart)

Writing Application Write a paragraph about Ben Jonson, using biographical information from page 404. In your paragraph, use the modifier *only* at least twice.

◆ Literary Focus

Epigrams

Jonson's poems are **epigrams** because they are brief and witty, expressing truths in a memorable fashion. In "Still to Be Neat," for example, Jonson uses parallel phrases ("Still to be neat, still to be dressed") that are elegant and easy to remember. In addition, phrases like "sweet neglect" grab your attention and linger in your mind because they seem to be contradictory. Yet when you puzzle them out, they contain a hidden truth.

1. Find two additional examples of parallelism in the first stanza of "Still to Be Neat."
2. Explain how the phrase "sweet neglect" appears to violate common sense but really doesn't.
3. What gives the first stanza of "Song: To Celia" an epigrammatic quality?
4. Identify and explain the paradoxical sentiment expressed in the final line of "On My First Son."
5. (a) Would "On My First Son" be suitable for putting on the subject's gravestone? Explain. (b) Why do some epigrams make good epitaphs?

◆ Build Vocabulary

Using Archaic Words

Use your knowledge of **archaic words** to "translate" the following passage from Jonson's "To the Memory of My Beloved Master, William Shakespeare" into modern English. Remember that *hast* and *hath* are present tenses of *have, dost* and *doth* are present tenses of *do,* and *wast* and *wert* are past tenses of *be. Thy* and *thine* indicate possession, and *thou* and *thee* are subjective and objective pronouns.

For, if I thought my judgment were of years,
I should commit thee surely with thy peers,
And tell, how far thou didst our Lyly outshine,
Or sporting Kyd, or Marlowe's mighty line.
And though thou hadst small Latin, and less Greek,
From thence to honor thee, I would not seek
For names; but call forth thund'ring Aeschylus . . .

Beyond the Selection

FURTHER READING

Other Works by Ben Jonson
Volpone, or the Fox
Bartholomew Fair

Works About Ben Jonson
Ben Jonson: A Life, D. Riggs
Ben Jonson: His Life and Work, R. Miles

We suggest that you preview these works before recommending them to students.

INTERNET

You and your students may find additional information about Ben Jonson on the Internet. We suggest the following sites. Please be aware, however, that sites may have changed from the time we published this information.

For more on Jonson go to **http://history.hanover.edu/early/literatu.htm** or visit **http:// library.utoronto.ca/www/utel/rp/authors/jonson.html**

We *strongly recommend* that you preview the sites before you send students to them.

Build Your Portfolio

Idea Bank

Writing

1. **T-shirt Saying** These days, epigrammatic statements are found on T-shirts as well as on monuments. Jot down two or three brief, insightful statements that would be worthy of capturing on a T-shirt.

2. **Fashion Essay** In "Still to Be Neat" Jonson reveals his views on fashion. What would Jonson have to say about fashion in today's world? Capture his views in a brief essay.

3. **Literary Analysis** Reread "On My First Son" carefully. Analyze the poem's structure, rhyme scheme, and imagery, and evaluate how these elements help convey heart-wrenching emotion.

Speaking and Listening

4. **Love Song** With a group, write a modern version of "Song: To Celia," set it to music, and perform it for your class. **[Music Link; Performing Arts Link]**

5. **Fashion Debate** Organize a classroom debate about the value of "natural" styles (grunge, afros) versus artificial styles (punk, permed hair). Hold your debate in front of your class. **[Social Studies Link]**

Projects

6. **Sons of Ben** Obtain pictures of the writers who called themselves the "Sons of Ben." Then draw a scene depicting all the writers sitting together, discussing their art. **[Art Link]**

7. **Biographical Report** Research and write a biographical report on Jonson's colorful life and career. Using several sources, reconstruct his personality as well as the events of his life. **[Social Studies Link]**

Writing Mini-Lesson

Persuasive Letter

In "Still to Be Neat," Jonson delivers strong opinions about artificial styles that have gotten out of hand. Write a letter to your school newspaper in which you reveal your opinions on a similar subject.

As Jonson does in his poem, use elaboration to support your opinions.

Writing Skills Focus: Elaboration to Support an Argument

An argument—in a courtroom, in a newspaper column, or in a professional journal—will not be persuasive unless the writer uses **elaboration** to support it. Elaboration in support of an argument may include:

- Evidence in the form of facts, statistics, experiences, and quotations
- Answers to counterarguments
- Freshly and succinctly stated ideas

Prewriting Jot down your opinions about contemporary fashion. Also jot down some counterarguments. Find statistics, quotations, or other evidence that supports your argument and undercuts the counterargument. You may also take a poll and use the results as statistical evidence to support your argument.

Drafting Begin your letter with the date and the salutation "To the Editor." Weave together your argument using the evidence you collected. Include evidence intended to destroy the counterargument. Close the letter with your name and signature.

Revising Make sure you have followed the proper format for a letter. Use elaboration to strengthen arguments that you haven't supported. Also, reword any phrases or ideas that sound stale, and delete examples of wordiness. Proofread your letter carefully before sending it to the editor of your school newspaper.

✓ ASSESSMENT OPTIONS

Formal Assessment, Selection Test, pp. 89–91, and Assessment Resources Software. The selection test is designed so that it can be easily customized to the performance levels of your students.

Alternative Assessment, p. 18, includes options for less advanced students, more advanced students, verbal/linguistic learners, musical/rhythmic learners, and visual/spatial learners.

PORTFOLIO ASSESSMENT

Use the following rubrics in the ***Alternative Assessment*** booklet to assess student writing:
T-shirt Saying: Expression Rubric, p. 95
Fashion Essay: Evaluation/Review Rubric, p. 105
Literary Analysis: Literary Analysis/Interpretation Rubric, p. 113
Writing Mini-Lesson: Persuasion Rubric, p. 106

Idea Bank

Customizing for *Performance Levels*

Following are suggestions for matching Idea Bank topics with your students' performance levels:

Less Advanced Students: 1, 6
Average Students: 2, 4, 7
More Advanced Students: 3, 5

Customizing for *Learning Modalities*

Following are suggestions for matching Idea Bank topics with your students' learning modalities:

Visual/Spatial: 1, 2, 6
Verbal/Linguistic: 3, 4, 5, 7

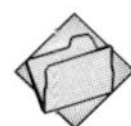

Writing Mini-Lesson

Refer students to the Writing Handbook, page 1189, for instruction on the writing process, and page 1192 for further information on persuasion.

Writing and Language Transparencies Use the Writing Process Model 5: Persuasive Essay, pp. 37–43, to guide students through the Writing Mini-Lesson.

Writer's Solution

Writing Lab CD-ROM

Have students complete the tutorial on Persuasion. Follow these steps:

1. Have students use the Self-interview to help them focus their ideas.
2. Suggest that they use the Pros and Cons Chart to organize and evaluate arguments.
3. Students should draft on computer.
4. Students can use the Proofreading Checklist to help them correct their drafts.

Allow approximately 100 minutes of class time to complete these steps.

Sourcebook

Have students use Chapter 4, Persuasion (pp. 96–129), for additional support. The chapter includes a workplace writing model of a position paper (p. 103).

Prepare and Engage

OBJECTIVES

1. To read, comprehend, and interpret seventeenth-century poems
2. To relate seventeenth-century poetry to personal experience
3. To infer speakers' attitudes
4. To recognize the *carpe diem* theme
5. To build vocabulary in context and learn forms of *prime*
6. To use irregular forms of adjectives correctly
7. To write a witty poem using a persuasive tone
8. To respond to seventeenth-century poetry through writing, speaking and listening, and projects

SKILLS INSTRUCTION

Vocabulary:
Related Words: Forms of *Prime*

Grammar:
Irregular Forms of Adjectives

Literary Focus:
Carpe Diem Theme

Writing:
Persuasive Tone

Reading Strategy:
Infer Speakers' Attitudes

Speaking and Listening:
Phone Conversation (teacher edition)

Critical Viewing:
Infer

PORTFOLIO OPPORTUNITIES

Writing: Persuasive Essay; Advice Column; Comparison and Contrast

Writing Mini-Lesson: Write a Witty Poem

Speaking and Listening: Phone Conversation; Oral Interpretation

Projects: Wedding Plan; Song

More About the Authors

During his life, **Andrew Marvell** was mainly known as a politician. Fiercely independent, he refused both favors and money from King Charles II and then went on to write political pamphlets and satires attacking what he saw as problems of the monarchy.

Robert Herrick was a clergyman and a "Son of Ben," a follower of Ben Jonson. This influence is reflected in Herrick's light touch and restrained manner.

Sir John Suckling was a bit of a playboy. Born into a wealthy family, he lost much of his wealth through gambling.

Guide for Interpreting

Andrew Marvell (1621–1678)

Marvell showed an extraordinary ability to adjust to the realities of his turbulent time. Although he was the son of a Puritan minister and frowned on the abuses of the monarch, he enjoyed close friendships with supporters of Charles I in the king's dispute with the largely Puritan Parliament.

Several years later, however, he worked for Lord Fairfax, the commanding general of the antiroyalist Parliamentary army. Still later, Marvell tutored the ward of Oliver Cromwell, leader of the Puritan rebellion and ruler of England. Obviously capable, Marvell gained the attention and sponsorship of the great English poet John Milton. Eventually he served as Milton's assistant.

In 1659, after Cromwell's death and shortly before Charles II was restored, Marvell was elected the Member of Parliament from Hull. He served in that position until his death, almost twenty years later.

Robert Herrick (1591–1674)

Born into a family of London goldsmiths, Herrick went to Cambridge when he was twenty-two and graduated at the age of twenty-nine. After graduation, he served as a military chaplain and was assigned to a parish in rural England. Here he performed his churchly duties and wrote religious verse and musical love poems.

Though not politically active, Herrick was evicted from his parish by the Puritans and allowed back only with the Restoration of Charles II. While barred from his church, Herrick returned to his native and much-loved London and published his poetry—his religious verse in *Noble Numbers* and his other poems in *Hesperides*, an ancient Greek name for a garden at the edge of the world.

Published during a turbulent time, Herrick's light verses were ignored by his contemporaries; however, these verses are highly regarded today.

Sir John Suckling (1609–1642)

In some ways, Sir John Suckling lived a life more romantic than those of Marvell and Herrick. A privileged young courtier, Suckling inherited his vast estates when he was only eighteen, and he later served as a gentleman in the privy chamber of Charles I. Praised as the cleverest of conversationalists, Suckling was said to be able to compose a poem at a moment's notice. He incorporated some of his best lyrics, including the poem "Song," into plays that he lavishly produced at his own expense.

Suckling's military exploits proved less successful than his poems, however. The cavalry troop he raised and lavishly uniformed for the king was defeated in Scotland, and Suckling was mocked for caring more about his men's uniforms than about their military performance. After joining a failed Cavalier plot to rescue a royal minister from prison, he fled to France, where he died in despair at the age of thirty-three.

◆ Background for Understanding

LANGUAGE: WORD PLAY AND WIT

By the seventeenth century, English had become a fluid combination of Anglo-Saxon, Gaelic, Latin, and French. As such, English was far more than a language of basic communication. Through it, one could express philosophical ideas, convey abstract theories, and create humorous word play.

Shakespeare excelled in brilliant word-play, sometimes losing himself in a labyrinth of puns. Following Shakespeare's lead, seventeenth-century poets took up the witty "*sword*play" of humor.

As you read these poems, look for examples of witty word play: puns, putdowns, and clowning.

Prentice Hall Literature Program Resources

REINFORCE / RETEACH / EXTEND

Selection Support Pages
Build Vocabulary: Forms of *Prime,* p. 90
Grammar and Style: Irregular Forms of Adjectives, p. 91
Reading Strategy: Infer Speakers' Attitudes, p. 92
Literary Focus: *Carpe Diem* Theme, p. 93

Strategies for Diverse Student Needs, p. 19

Beyond Literature, p. 19

Formal Assessment Selection Test, pp. 92–94; Assessment Resources Software

Alternative Assessment, p. 19

Writing and Language Transparencies
Daily Language Practice, Week 14, p. 149

Resource Pro CD-ROM
Includes all resource material and customizable lesson plan

Listening to Literature Audiocassettes
"To His Coy Mistress"; "To the Virgins, to Make Much of Time"; "Song"

◆ To His Coy Mistress ◆ To the Virgins, to Make Much of Time ◆ Song

◆ Literature and Your Life

Connect Your Experience

It's easy for students to feel that, with studying for tests and preparing for graduation, life is one, big, totally booked schedule. If there's no time anymore for enjoyment, maybe it's time to add enjoyment to the schedule.

That's exactly the message that these poets convey as they urge you to hurry up and—have fun!

Journal Writing Note some things you enjoy doing—like having a long talk with a friend—but haven't had time for lately.

Thematic Focus: The War Against Time

These poems were written during a troubled era of English history. Look for evidence of that trouble in the urgency with which these writers plead for fun and happiness.

◆ Build Vocabulary

Related Words: Forms of *Prime*

When Herrick refers to a person's "prime," he means both the first and the most important years. (The word comes from a Latin word meaning "first in importance" or "first in time.") Similarly, the noun *primer* refers to "a first or earliest textbook," and the adjective *primary* can mean "most important" or "earliest."

Word Bank

Before you read, preview this list of words from the poems.

coyness
amorous
languish
prime
wan

◆ Grammar and Style

Irregular Forms of Adjectives

Herrick's poem contains adjectives whose comparative and superlative forms are **irregular**—they do not add *-er* or *-est* and are not preceded by *more* or *most.* Following are common examples:

Positive Form	Comparative	Superlative
good	better	best
bad	worse	worst

This line from the poem contains the superlative form of the adjective *good:* "That age is *best* which is the first . . ."

◆ Literary Focus

***Carpe Diem* Theme**

The imperative "Gather ye rosebuds while ye may" from Robert Herrick's "To the Virgins" best expresses the ***carpe diem* theme** (kär´ pē dē´ em). This theme—*carpe diem* is Latin for "seize the day"—permeates world literature and has come to mean "Time is fleeting, so enjoy life."

In reading these poets, look for the playful imperatives that are a sign of this theme: "Let us . . . tear our pleasures" (Marvell); "use your time . . ." (Herrick); "Quit, quit, for shame . . ." (Suckling).

◆ Reading Strategy

Infer Speakers' Attitudes

A poem's **speaker**, who may or may not be the poet, usually expresses a certain **attitude** toward the subject or toward the person he or she is addressing. You can infer this attitude, and better understand the poem, by focusing on the words, images, and rhythms the speaker uses.

In "Song," for example, words like "Nothing" and "The devil" signal the speaker's impatience with his friend's love-sickness:

If of herself she will not love,/Nothing can make her:/The devil take her!

Notice, too, how the clipped rhythms of the last two lines suggest the speaker's exasperation with the whole business.

Ask students which statement below best reflects modern attitudes of young people.

- Life is short. Do it now.
- Look before you leap.

Briefly discuss different reasons that might be behind the two opposing pieces of advice. Then point out that the "Do it now" school of thought actually goes back many centuries. An ancient Roman poet, Virgil, first said, "Time flies." One of his contemporaries coined the phrase "Seize the day, put no trust in tomorrow." The writers whom they will read next also subscribed to this idea.

Customize for
Less Proficient Readers

Encourage students to read each poem through entirely. Some students may be stopped by a reference or word they do not understand. Explain that they should read a poem entirely to see its main ideas and then reread it to put the words and references in context.

Customize for
More Advanced Students

These students will probably delight in the cleverness of the argument and the lightheartedness of the tone in each poem. Encourage them to focus on the persuasive techniques that each speaker used.

Customize for
English Language Learners

Students will benefit from hearing these poems read aloud, since they are all musical and contain mainly simple words.

Customize for
Interpersonal Learners

Encourage students to imagine two people involved in each poem: a speaker, and a particular person that the speaker is addressing. Encourage students to see each poem as a dialogue in which only one person is currently speaking. They can imagine what the other person either said or might say.

Preparing for Standardized Tests

Reading and Vocabulary Many reading comprehension tests require students to read a passage and then infer the attitude expressed toward its subject. For example, students might read a poem such as Marvell's and then be asked this question:

Which statement most closely expresses the speaker's belief? *(D)*
(A) Vegetable loves grow vast.
(B) The grave's the best place for love.
(C) Coyness is a virtue.
(D) We should enjoy ourselves now.

For additional practice, use the Reading Strategy page in ***Selection Support,*** p. 92.

Grammar and Language Portions of some standardized tests require students to use correct forms of irregular adjectives, as in the following:

Tara is (better, more better) than I at math.
better

The Grammar and Style lesson for this selection focuses on this topic. For additional practice, use the Grammar and Style page in ***Selection Support,*** p. 91.

Develop Understanding

One-Minute Insight Marvell's work has been called "the most major minor verse in English," and this poem in particular shows why so many readers enjoy it. Rich in sensory images and flattery, "To His Coy Mistress" is designed to appeal to feelings as well as to intellect. Its exaggerated emotion and its persuasive tone are humorous to readers who recognize the speaker's goal: to get his sweetheart to return his love.

Cultural Connection

The *carpe diem* theme is not confined to this culture. It can be found among the writings of different cultures and different times. For example, in 24 B.C., the Egyptian Ptahhotpe wrote, "The wasting of time is an abomination to the spirit." The Persian poet Omar Khayyam noted the passage of time in *The Rubáiyát.* There he wrote, "The Moving Finger Writes; and having writ,/Moves on."

Invite students to explore the concept of time in other cultures. Encourage students to look for quotations about time or attitudes about it, which might be expressed in a culture's literature, religion, or philosophy.

◆ Literary Focus

❶ ***Carpe Diem* Theme** Ask students how these lines express the theme of *carpe diem*. *The speaker urges the lady to sport now, while they are still in their youthful prime.*

◆ Grammar and Style

❷ **Irregular Forms of Adjectives** Ask students why the poet uses *more slow* instead of *slower. It fits the meter and rhyme.*

◆ Reading Strategy

❸ **Infer Speakers' Attitudes** Ask students what the speaker's feelings for the woman are. *Students may say that the fierce images suggest passion and playfulness.*

To His Coy Mistress

Andrew Marvell

❶ Had we but world enough, and time,
This coyness lady were no crime.
We would sit down, and think which way
To walk, and pass our long love's day.
Thou by the Indian Ganges' side
Should'st rubies find; I by the tide
Of Humber[1] would complain. I would
Love you ten years before the Flood,
And you should if you please refuse
Till the conversion of the Jews.[2]
❷ My vegetable love should grow
Vaster than empires, and more slow;
An hundred years should go to praise
Thine eyes, and on thy forehead gaze;
Two hundred to adore each breast,
But thirty thousand to the rest;
An age at least to every part,
And the last age should show your heart.
For, lady, you deserve this state,[3]
Nor would I love at lower rate.
  But at my back I always hear
Time's wingèd chariot hurrying near:
And yonder all before us lie
Deserts of vast eternity.
Thy beauty shall no more be found,
Nor, in thy marble vault, shall sound
My echoing songs; then worms shall try
That long-preserved virginity,
And your quaint honor turn to dust,
And into ashes all my lust:
The grave's a fine and private place,
But none I think do there embrace.

1. **Humber:** River flowing through Hull, Marvell's home town.

2. **conversion of the Jews:** According to Christian tradition, the Jews were to be converted immediately before the Last Judgment.

3. **state:** Dignity.

Block Scheduling Strategies

If you have extended class time, consider these suggestions:

- Introduce the Literary Focus on page 413. Have students make notes on the theme as they read the poems and then answer the questions on page 418. For more practice, have them use the Literary Focus page in ***Selection Support,*** p. 93.
- Use the Daily Language Practice for Week 14 in ***Writing and Language Transparencies***, p. 149, and ***Daily Language Practice,*** p. 32.
- Play the audiocassette recording of the poems and have students listen for inflection and expression in the poems as they read along.
- Students may form groups to discuss ideas they might include in the Persuasive Essay described in the Idea Bank on page 419.
- Have students work on the Advice Column described in the Idea Bank (p. 419).
- Assign the Writing Mini-Lesson (p. 419). Before students begin, have them identify clever lines or phrases that they enjoyed in the poems.

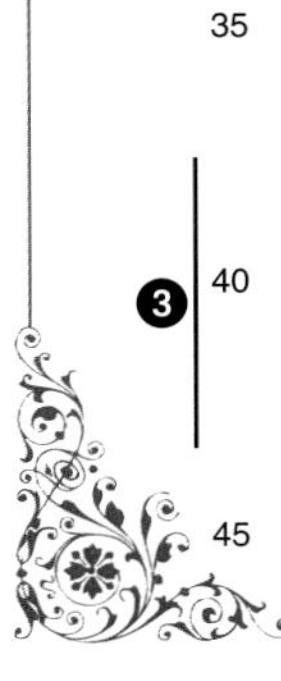

Now therefore, while the youthful hew
Sits on thy skin like morning dew,
And while thy willing soul transpires[4]
At every pore with instant fires,
Now let us sport us while we may,
And now, like amorous birds of prey,
Rather at once our time devour
3 Than languish in his slow-chapped[5] power.
Let us roll all our strength, and all
Our sweetness, up into one ball,
And tear our pleasures with rough strife
Thorough[6] the iron gates of life:
Thus, though we cannot make our sun
Stand still, yet we will make him run.

4. transpires: Breathes out.

5. slow-chapped: Slow-jawed.

6. thorough: Through.

◆ Build Vocabulary

coyness (koiˊ nis) *n.*: Reluctance to make a commitment

amorous (amˊ ə res) *adj.*: Full of love

languish (laŋˊ gwish) *v.*: To become weak; droop

Guide for Responding

◆ Literature and Your Life

Reader's Response What is your impression of the speaker in this poem? How would you respond to him?

Thematic Response Explain how the message of Marvell's poem is suited to the turbulent time in which it was written.

☑ Check Your Comprehension

1. Under what conditions would the lady's coyness not be a crime?
2. What would the speaker do if time weren't an issue?
3. Why is the speaker anxious?
4. What does the speaker conclude that he and his coy mistress should do?

◆ Critical Thinking

INTERPRET

1. How would you define the speaker's attitude toward time? **[Interpret]**
2. Point to the word pictures and to the comparisons that convey the slow or rapid passage of time. **[Analyze]**
3. Explain the role that each of the poem's sections (lines 1–20, 21–32, and 33–46) plays in the poem's "argument." **[Draw Conclusions]**

EXTEND

4. Using *x* and *y* as you would in an algebraic equation, express the basic logic behind the speaker's argument. (Hint: If *x* were true, then . . .) **[Math Link]**

Reinforce and Extend

Answers

◆ Literature and Your Life

Reader's Response The speaker is impatient and persistent. Students might advise him to cool down.

Thematic Focus Marvell wrote this during England's civil war. Times of war create the sense that life is short and must be lived to the fullest, now.

☑ Check Your Comprehension

1. If the lovers had all of time and space in which to live and love, then her coyness would not matter.
2. They could walk and talk of love for ages.
3. He fears they shall soon die without having loved each other.
4. They should seize the moment and enjoy each other now.

◆ Critical Thinking

1. He sees time as limited.
2. Examples of slow include great biblical ages—"ten years before the Flood" to until the Last Judgment; a slow-growing vegetable love; a hundred years, two hundred, thirty thousand years pass until she shows her heart. Examples of rapid are: "winged chariot hurrying," "instant fires," "make him run."
3. The first section describes the hypothetical situation of having an eternity in which to love. The second section reminds the coy mistress that they are mortals with a limited time on earth, and if she waits too long she may be in her grave. The third section describes how they should seize the day and enjoy each other now while they are still young.
4. If *x* equals *life is too short and therefore we may die tomorrow,* then *y* equals *we should seize the day and enjoy each other while we can today.*

Speaking and Listening Mini-Lesson

Phone Conversation

This mini-lesson supports the first Speaking and Listening activity in the Idea Bank on page 419.

Introduce the Concept Explain that in this activity, students will simulate a phone conversation between a lovesick person and a close friend.

Develop Background Have students discuss how people behave when they have a hopeless crush on someone. What can friends do or say to remedy the situation? After students pair up for the activity, have them consider the following:

- What are the main ideas in "Song"? How would you express these ideas?
- Which character—the lovesick person or the advising friend—calls the other and why?
- How would the lovesick person describe the situation? How would the friend?

Apply the Information Have students rehearse and present their scenes to the class.

Assess the Outcome Have students assess their peers' performances according to originality and creativity.

Develop Understanding

One-Minute Insight Robert Herrick has been called a happy poet, and his cheer is evidenced in this, his most famous poem. Many students may have heard the first line without knowing that it came from a poem. While Marvell seems to delight in the mischief of painting a word picture showing the dust and worms associated with death, Herrick focuses more on life—on the rosebuds and the glorious lamp of the sun. Herrick was one of the Cavalier poets, English lyricists who were supporters of Charles I during the Civil Wars. These poets affected a lighthearted attitude toward life and even toward serious matters, such as war or honor.

◆ Critical Thinking

❶ **Evaluate** Why are rosebuds a good choice for a poem about how fleeting time is? *They are beautiful; they do not last long.*

◆ Critical Thinking

❷ **Hypothesize** This poem has been set to music numerous times. Ask students why it might be such a perennial favorite. *It has a catchy rhythm; it has a popular theme; it is simple to understand.*

◆ Grammar and Style

❸ **Irregular Forms of Adjectives** Have students identify the irregular adjectives in the third stanza and tell their positive forms. *The irregular adjectives are* best *and* worse, worst*; their positive forms are* good *and* bad.

◆ Critical Thinking

❹ **Interpret** What reasons does the speaker give for the advice he offers in this stanza? *Time is moving on; the best times are in youth; if you wait until you are past your prime, you may never marry.*

►Critical Viewing◄

❺ **Infer** Their youth and the carefree activity they are engaged in can both vanish quickly. They are gathering flowers, which can fade.

To the Virgins, to Make Much of Time

Robert Herrick

Three Ladies Adorning a Term of Hymen, Sir Joshua Reynolds
The Tate Gallery, London

◄ **Critical Viewing** In what ways do the women in this painting, created more than a century after Herrick's poem was written, express the *carpe diem* theme? **[Infer]** ❺

❶
Gather ye rosebuds while ye may,
 Old time is still a-flying;
And this same flower that smiles today
 Tomorrow will be dying.

❷
The glorious lamp of heaven, the sun,
 The higher he's a-getting,
The sooner will his race be run,
 And nearer he's to setting.

❸
That age is best which is the first,
 When youth and blood are warmer:
But being spent, the worse, and worst
 Times still succeed the former.

❹
Then be not coy, but use your time,
 And, while ye may, go marry;
For, having lost but once your prime,
 You may forever tarry.[1]

1. **tarry** (tar´ ē) *v.*: Delay.

◆ Build Vocabulary

prime (prīm) *n.*: Best stage of time

Humanities: Art

Three Ladies Adorning a Term of Hymen by Sir Joshua Reynolds.

The young women in this painting were the daughters of a London gentleman who commissioned it almost a century after "To the Virgins" was written. It is more of a "conversation piece" than a true portrait. It shows the women adorning a *term*, or Roman boundary marker. The *term* is in the shape of Hymen, the god of marriage.

Joshua Reynolds (1723–1792) often painted portraits of the British upper class. Reynolds helped form and was the first president of the Royal Academy.

Use these questions for discussion:

1. Why would people in the 1700's want classical themes in their pictures? *Perhaps this was the style of the day; perhaps they admired the ancients; they thought this added class to a modern portrait.*
2. Do you think this is a good illustration for this poem? Why or why not? *Many students will think it is, since it shows young women and flowers.*

Song

Sir John Suckling

Why so pale and wan, fond lover? 
Prithee, why so pale?
Will, when looking well can't move her,
Looking ill prevail?
Prithee, why so pale?

Why so dull and mute, young sinner?
Prithee, why so mute?
Will, when speaking well can't win her,
Saying nothing do't?
Prithee, why so mute?

Quit, quit, for shame; this will not move,
This cannot take her.
If of herself she will not love, ❼
Nothing can make her:
The devil take her!

◆ Build Vocabulary

wan (wän) *adj.*: Sickly pale; faint or weak

Guide for Responding

◆ Literature and Your Life

Reader's Response What experiences, past, present, or future, do these poems call to mind?

Thematic Focus Why might finding love become more important in times of war and uncertainty?

Group Activity In a small group, identify songs you know that express the *carpe diem* theme.

Journal Writing Describe a situation in which you might give advice to a friend similar to the advice given by the speaker of "Song."

☑ Check Your Comprehension

1. What advice does the speaker in Herrick's poem give the young women in lines 1–4?
2. What warning does this speaker issue in lines 13–16?
3. In "Song," whom is the speaker addressing?
4. How is the lover described in the first stanza of "Song"? In the second stanza?
5. What advice does the speaker in "Song" give in the final stanza?

Develop Understanding

One-Minute Insight Although this is a poem about love, the topic is treated rather facetiously. The poem is decidedly unromantic. Suckling takes a humorous, mocking tone that may draw attention away from the poem's careful construction. It has a traditional form of three separate stanzas with a repeating rhyme scheme. The first two containing teasing questions, while the third provides advice.

◆ Literature and Your Life

❻ Discuss with students how people usually look and act when they are in love with someone who does not love them.

◆ Critical Thinking

❼ **Hypothesize** Have students consider reasons why someone would have the attitude that the speaker has. *Answers may include the following: Perhaps he was unlucky in love; perhaps he is cynical by nature; perhaps he is looking with a logical eye only.*

Reinforce and Extend

Answers

◆ Literature and Your Life

Reader's Response These poems recall experiences with love.

Thematic Focus In times of war and uncertainty, there's danger that life may be cut short before people have a chance to live full lives.

☑ Check Your Comprehension

1. He advises them to enjoy the rosebuds—the joys of youth—because the days of our youth are short.
2. If they don't marry now, maybe they never will.
3. In "Song" the speaker is addressing a rejected lover.
4. The lover is described in the first stanza of "Song" as looking pale and ill, and in the second stanza, as silent.
5. He advises his friend to stop moping. If she can't love him for himself, then there's nothing he can do to make her love him, so forget her.

Beyond the Selection

FURTHER READING

Other Works by These Poets

"To His Coy Mistress" and Other Poems, Andrew Marvell

Selected Poems, Robert Herrick

Poems, Plays and Other Remains of Sir John Suckling, Sir John Suckling

We suggest that you preview these works before recommending them to students.

INTERNET

You and your students may find additional information about the poets on the Internet. We suggest the following sites. Please be aware, however, that sites may have changed from the time we published this information.

For a page on these writers go to **http://history.hanover.edu/early/literatu.htm**

For more on Marvell and Herrick, go to **http://www.unomaha.edu/~wwwengl/17thcentury/styles.html**

We *strongly recommend* that you preview the sites before you send students to them.

Answers

◆ Critical Thinking

1. He uses the images of rosebuds and dying flowers to convey the idea that life is short.
2. He believes that youth is better than old age.
3. The lover's appearance and behavior is in reaction to his being rejected in love.
4. The speaker's attitude is that moping over a lost love is a waste of time.
5. It's told not from the viewpoint of the rejected lover, but from that of a concerned friend. Thus, the tone doesn't sigh and dream on, but splashes the cold water of reality on the subject.

◆ Reading Strategy

1. (a) Three vivid verbs used are: *sport, devour,* and *tear*. (b) The speaker's attitude is to seize life and love right now.
2. The speaker moves from a questioning mode to an impatiently demanding mode in the last stanza.
3. Sample response: In "To the Virgins" and "To His Coy Mistress," the speakers have the same *carpe diem* attitude.

◆ Literary Focus

1. The *carpe diem* lines in "To the Virgins" are: "Gather ye rosebuds while ye may, / Old time is still a-flying"; and in "To His Coy Mistress," they are: "Now let us sport us while we may" and "at once our time devour."
2. Students might say that they find "To the Virgins" more persuasive because it is shorter and to the point. Others may say that "To His Coy Mistress" is more effective because of its logical argument.
3. It addresses the lovelorn to move on, and not waste time on someone who doesn't care.

◆ Build Vocabulary

1. major; 2. best, most vigorous condition; 3. chief; 4. main; 5. first textbooks

Using the Word Bank

1. false; 2. false; 3. true; 4. true; 5. false

Guide for Responding *(continued)*

◆ Critical Thinking

INTERPRET

1. How does Herrick use images in lines 1–4 to convey the idea of passing time? **[Interpret]**
2. What attitude toward age does the speaker in Herrick's poem reveal in lines 9–12? **[Analyze]**
3. In "Song," what has caused the lover's pale, wan appearance and dull, mute behavior? **[Infer]**
4. What attitude toward love does the third stanza of "Song" reflect? **[Draw Conclusions]**

EXTEND

5. How does "Song" differ from other poems about unrequited, unreturned, love? **[Literary Link]**

◆ Reading Strategy

INFER SPEAKERS' ATTITUDES

To **infer the speaker's attitude** toward the subject of the poem or the person being addressed, make educated guesses based on imagery, word choice, and rhythm. For example, the ridiculous images in lines 1–20 of "To His Coy Mistress" suggest that the speaker is humorously exaggerating his lover's delay.

1. (a) Find three vivid verbs that convey the speaker's attitude toward love in lines 37–46 of "To His Coy Mistress." (b) Explain this attitude.
2. Explain where and in what way the speaker's attitude in Suckling's "Song" undergoes a change.
3. Choose two of these poems and compare the speakers' attitudes toward love.

◆ Literary Focus

***CARPE DIEM* THEME**

"To His Coy Mistress" and "To the Virgins, to Make Much of Time" are probably the best-known English poems expressing the ***carpe diem*** **theme**, which urges people to enjoy life while they can.

1. Which line or lines in each poem most memorably express the *carpe diem* theme? Explain.
2. Of the two poems, which do you find more persuasive in its *carpe diem* message? Why?
3. Suckling's "Song" has a different take on this theme. Explain how it conforms with yet deviates from the traditional meaning of the theme.

◆ Build Vocabulary

USING RELATED FORMS OF *PRIME*

Knowing that the root of *prime* means "first in importance" or "first in time," define the underlined forms of the word in these sentences.

1. The Democrats will hold a <u>primary</u> election.
2. Marvell wrote the poem while still in his <u>prime</u>.
3. Who is the <u>prime</u> minister of Great Britain?
4. Every television star wants a <u>prime</u>-time show.
5. In earlier years, schoolchildren used <u>primers</u>.

USING THE WORD BANK

In your notebook, indicate whether each statement is true or false.

1. When a person turns purple with rage, his or her cheeks are quite <u>wan</u>.
2. *The <u>Prime</u> of Miss Jean Brodie* is probably about a woman on her deathbed.
3. A plant without water may <u>languish</u>.
4. An <u>amorous</u> couple will probably hug and kiss.
5. A person's <u>coyness</u> indicates that he or she is one-hundred percent committed.

◆ Grammar and Style

IRREGULAR FORMS OF ADJECTIVES

By using a few common **irregular forms of adjectives**, the speaker in Herrick's poem demonstrates a knowing assurance. Irregular comparative and superlative forms of adjectives do not end in *-er* or *-est* and are not preceded by *more* or *most.*

Practice Identify the comparative or superlative form of each irregular adjective.

> That age is best which is the first / When youth and blood are warmer; / But being spent, the worse, and worst / Times still succeed the former.

Writing Application In your notebook, correct errors in irregular forms of adjectives.

1. Herrick's speaker feels that the most best time to marry is in one's prime.
2. He says that old age is worser than youth.
3. In "Song" the speaker suggests that the bestest thing to do is to find someone else.
4. All three poems imply that one of the baddest things you can do is to waste time.

◆ Grammar and Style

best: superlative
warmer: comparative
worse: comparative
worst: superlative
former: comparative

Writing Application

1. Herrick's speaker feels that the *best* time to marry is in one's prime.
2. He says that old age is *worse* than youth.
3. In "Song," the speaker suggests that the *best* thing to do is to find someone else.
4. All three poems imply that one of the *worst* things you can do is to waste time.

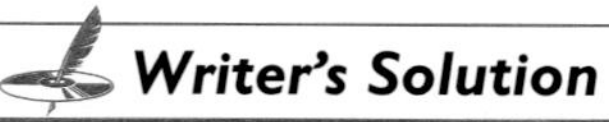

Writer's Solution

For additional instruction and practice, use the pages on Degrees of Comparison, pp. 68–69, in the *Writer's Solution Grammar Practice Book.*

Build Your Portfolio

Idea Bank

Writing

1. Persuasive Essay Write a brief persuasive essay for your school yearbook, convincing readers to "seize the day."

2. Advice Column Rewrite one of these poems as an advice columnist's letter. Change the language as appropriate, but continue to express the poem's basic ideas.

3. Comparison and Contrast Compare and contrast "Song" with "To the Virgins" or "To His Coy Mistress." Citing specific examples from the poems, discuss theme, rhythm, imagery, and speakers' attitudes.

Speaking and Listening

4. Phone Conversation Using modern language, express the ideas of "Song" in a simulated phone conversation that you perform in class with another student. **[Performing Arts Link]**

5. Oral Interpretation Perform one of these poems for the class, capturing the speaker's attitude in your tone of voice. Follow sentences, not lines, as you read. **[Performing Arts Link]**

Projects

6. Wedding Plan Plan a wedding for the lovers from one of these poems. Be sure the theme of the wedding is in keeping with the poem's message as you provide for the clothing, the ceremony, the wedding feast, and the entertainment. **[Social Studies Link]**

7. Song Set one of the poems to music that you compose or to an existing tune that suits it. Perform your song version on audiocassette, or on videotape. **[Music Link]**

Writing Mini-Lesson

Witty Poem

The speakers in these poems display cleverness and wit as they attempt to persuade their listeners to "seize the day." Write a poem in which you use humor and word play to make a point or to win an argument.

Use the following skill to make your poem persuasive as well as witty.

Writing Skills Focus: Persuasive Tone

Create a **persuasive tone** by doing the following:

- Sounding confident about your arguments.
- Using words that create a sense of urgency about the action you recommend.
- Choosing details and creating images that will capture the imagination of your audience.

Marvell uses all these techniques in this passage from "To His Coy Mistress":

But at my back I always hear
Time's winged chariot hurrying near:
And yonder all before us lie
Deserts of vast eternity.

Prewriting Identify the speaker of your poem and its audience, and decide on the type of humor that will work with this audience. List some key words that will add urgency to your argument.

Drafting Keep the dramatic situation in mind as you draft. If you "discover" appealing words and images as you write, see where they will take you. Go with the flow rather than trying to control it.

Revising Read your draft as if you were the person the speaker is trying to convince. If the speaker doesn't win you over, delete words like *maybe* and *perhaps,* and replace neutral terms with those that convey a sense of urgency—for example, use *hurrying* not *moving.*

✓ ASSESSMENT OPTIONS

Formal Assessment, Selection Test, pp. 92–94, and Assessment Resources Software. The selection test is designed so that it can be easily customized to the performance levels of your students.

Alternative Assessment, p. 19, includes options for less advanced students, more advanced students, verbal/linguistic learners, bodily/kinesthetic learners, and interpersonal learners.

PORTFOLIO ASSESSMENT

Use the following rubrics in the ***Alternative Assessment*** booklet to assess student writing:
Persuasive Essay: Persuasion Rubric, p. 106
Advice Column: How-to/Process Explanation Rubric, p. 101
Comparison and Contrast: Comparison/Contrast Rubric, p. 104
Writing Mini-Lesson: Poetry Rubric, p. 109

Idea Bank

Customizing for
Performance Levels

Following are suggestions for matching Idea Bank topics with your students' performance levels:

Less Advanced Students: 1, 5, 7
Average Students: 2, 4, 7
More Advanced Students: 3, 6

Customizing for
Learning Modalities

Following are suggestions for matching Idea Bank topics with your students' learning modalities:

Verbal/Linguistic: 1, 2, 3, 4, 5
Bodily/Kinesthetic: 4, 5
Logical/Mathematical: 6
Musical/Rhythmic: 7

Writing Mini-Lesson

Refer students to the Writing Handbook, page 1189, for instruction on the writing process, and page 1192 for further information on creative writing.

Writer's Solution

Writers at Work Videodisc

Have students view the videodisc segment (Ch. 6) featuring Derek Walcott to hear him discuss writing poems. Have students discuss how they can use his techniques in writing their poems.

Play frames 11452 to 13004

Writing Lab CD-ROM

Have students complete the tutorial on Creative Writing. Follow these steps:

1. Use the Audio-annotated Literary Models for poetry and the Word Bins for poetry.
2. Have students draft on computer.
3. Students can use the Peer Evaluation Checklist for Poetry to revise their drafts.
4. Use the Audio-annotated Writing Models for punctuating creative writing.

Allow approximately 60 minutes of class time to complete these steps.

Sourcebook

Have students use Chapter 6, Creative Writing (pp. 167–195), for additional support. The chapter includes an annotated student model of a poem (p. 191).

Prepare and Engage

OBJECTIVES

1. To read, comprehend, and interpret song lyrics
2. To explore thematic connections between contemporary song lyrics and seventeenth-century poems
3. To respond to the song lyrics through writing, speaking and listening, and a project

PORTFOLIO OPPORTUNITIES

Writing: Time Log; Song; Editorial for Teenagers

Speaking and Listening: Talk-Show Host

Project: Time Experiment

More About the Authors

These songs are the products of two of the best-known female folk-song writers. **Suzanne Vega** attended a performing arts high school and then went on to college, where she was a literature major. Her 1987 song, "Luka," about an abused child, jumped to the top of the record charts. A meeting with two people who were starting a music promotion helped Vega land a recording contract; her first album was an international hit.

Tracy Chapman, who grew up in a music-loving family, became interested in folk-rock music in high school. A college classmate, whose father was in the music business, heard Chapman perform and recommended her to his father, who helped her get a recording contract. Her first album won critical reviews, but only modest attention until Chapman performed at a tribute to Nelson Mandela. (South African freedom is only one of the social and political causes that Chapman supports. For instance, she has also sung in benefits for Amnesty International.) The performance for Mandela was so widely hailed that sales of her album skyrocketed. She wound up winning four Grammys, including Best New Artist.

CONNECTIONS TO WORLD LITERATURE

Freeze Tag
Suzanne Vega

New Beginning
Tracy Chapman

Thematic Connection

THE WAR AGAINST TIME

The poets in this section wrote during one of the most turbulent periods of English history, the years leading up to and including the Civil War. Religious persecution and political strife created a new awareness of the limited time one has on earth. Against this backdrop of conflict, poets like Marvell and Herrick remind us that time is fleeting and advise us to seize each moment and fill it with pleasure. The elusiveness of time, central to the works of these seventeenth-century poets, is still a popular theme in today's literature, movies, and songs.

SONGS THAT REFLECT ON TIME

The lyrics of popular songwriters Suzanne Vega and Tracy Chapman also reflect anxieties about time. Vega's "Freeze Tag" presents a moment frozen in time due to inaction. The song speaks of how indecision can prevent us from making the best of what we have. The central message of the song echoes the *carpe diem* ("seize the day") theme of Marvell and Herrick. Chapman's "New Beginning" describes a world in turmoil. Her socially conscious lyrics encourage people to stop time, erase the past, and re-create the world.

"SEIZE THE DAY"

The fast pace of today's world often robs us of the opportunity to make the most of our time. The advice given by the seventeenth-century poets to "seize the day" and make the most of life is still valid today.

SUZANNE VEGA

(1959–) Songwriter Suzanne Vega grew up in New York's Spanish Harlem. She began writing music by age fourteen and was performing in coffeehouses by the time she was sixteen. Her simple folk style and relevant themes appeal to a diverse audience. Vega won nominations for the Grammy Awards for record of the year, song of the year, and best female pop performance in 1987.

TRACY CHAPMAN

(1964–) Tracy Chapman grew up in a working-class neighborhood in Cleveland, Ohio. At an early age, she taught herself to play guitar and began to write music. Chapman's love of music and knowledge motivated her to seek the best education possible. After attaining a scholarship to a prestigious prep school, she observed that her wealthy classmates were often ignorant of the harshness of poverty. Chapman uses her music to combat that ignorance and raise social awareness of issues from spirituality to racism.

Connections to World Literature

The elegant, romantic lyrics of seventeenth-century poets may be unfamiliar to teens today, but lyrics like those of Vega and Chapman will not be. Comparing the two types of work helps readers recognize that techniques from different centuries may be different, but the themes are timeless.

Prentice Hall Literature Program Resources

REINFORCE / RETEACH / EXTEND

Selection Support Pages
Build Vocabulary, p. 94
Thematic Connection, p. 95

Formal Assessment Selection Test, pp. 95–96; Assessment Resources Software

We go to the playground
in the wintertime
the sun is fading fast
upon the slides into the past
upon the swings of indecision
in the winter time

in the dimming diamonds
scattering in the park
in the tickling
and the trembling
of freeze tag
in the dark

We play that we're actors
on a movie screen
I will be Dietrich
❶ and you can be Dean

you stand
with your hand
in your pocket
and lean against the wall
You will be Bogart
and I will be
Bacall

And we can only say yes now
to the sky, to the street, to the night

Slow fade now to black
Play me one more game
of chivalry
you and me
do you see
where I've been hiding
in this hide-and-seek?

We go to the playground
in the wintertime
the sun is fading fast
upon the slides into the past
upon the swings of indecision
in the wintertime
wintertime
wintertime

We can only say yes now,
to the sky, to the street, to the night
We can only say yes now
to the sky, to the street, to the night

Develop Understanding

This poem focuses on a relationship between a contemporary urban couple. Although these people are in a modern setting, the indecision and uncertainty that they experience is universal.

❶ **Clarification** You may need to explain to students that freeze tag is a game in which one person chases another. A person who is caught must freeze, or stand still. You should also mention that Dietrich and Bacall were two famous film actresses, Marlene Dietrich and Lauren Bacall. Dean and Bogart were well-known actors, James Dean and Humphry Bogart. Bogart and Bacall were in several films together and later married.

Thematic Connection

The War Against Time Ask students to identify references to passing time that appear in this song. *These include "The sun is fading fast," "we can only say yes now," "play me one more game."*

Customize for
Musical/Rhythmic Learners
Encourage students to try to find recorded copies of this song to listen to, and to try to sing it themselves. Hearing it and singing it will help them appreciate the song's rhythm and repetition.

◆ Critical Thinking

Analyze Ask students to identify the following poetic elements in this song: repetition; rhyme; alliteration; sensory details. *These include the repetition of words and lines, including the first; rhymes include "fast/past," "park/dark," "stand/hand"; alliteration includes "fading fast," "dimming diamonds," "tickling/trembling"; sensory details include the fading sun; the dimming diamonds; and the tickling and trembling.*

One-Minute Insight This is a love song not to an individual, but to the world at large. Like Sir John Suckling's "Song," this one, too, has a distinct attitude. However, unlike his, which is light and mocking, Chapman's speaker is determined and serious. Her speaker's notion of "Seize the day" does not translate into merely finding a mate; instead, she wants listeners to reshape their attitudes and redefine their world.

◆ Critical Thinking

❶ **Compare and Contrast** The seventeenth-century English poets were writing during a time of political and social conflict. In what ways is the world that Chapman writes about similar? *Students may mention that there is political strife today between different parties, or between rich and poor, or between developing countries and the industrial nations; they may point to social problems.*

◆ Critical Thinking

❷ **Hypothesize** The writer was born in the early 1960's and grew up during the 70's and 80's. What pain, suffering, and separation might she have been writing about? *Students may think she is writing about civil rights issues, racial or class problems; the generation gap; or any other current problems.*

Themetic Connection

Songs That Reflect on Time Ask students if they think Chapman's poem is basically optimistic or pessimistic and why. *Some students will find it pessimistic because it lists problems; others, though, will think it is optimistic because the writer thinks we can start over, or because of the title, "New Beginning."*

◆ Literature and Your Life

Chapman talks about creating new symbols, signs, and language to define the world. Ask students what symbols, signs, and language they think define the present world. *Students might suggest symbols of wealth, such as money; signs of power, such as fame or position. The language that defines today's world might be what is heard on the news; in the street; or in the media, including the output of the music industry.*

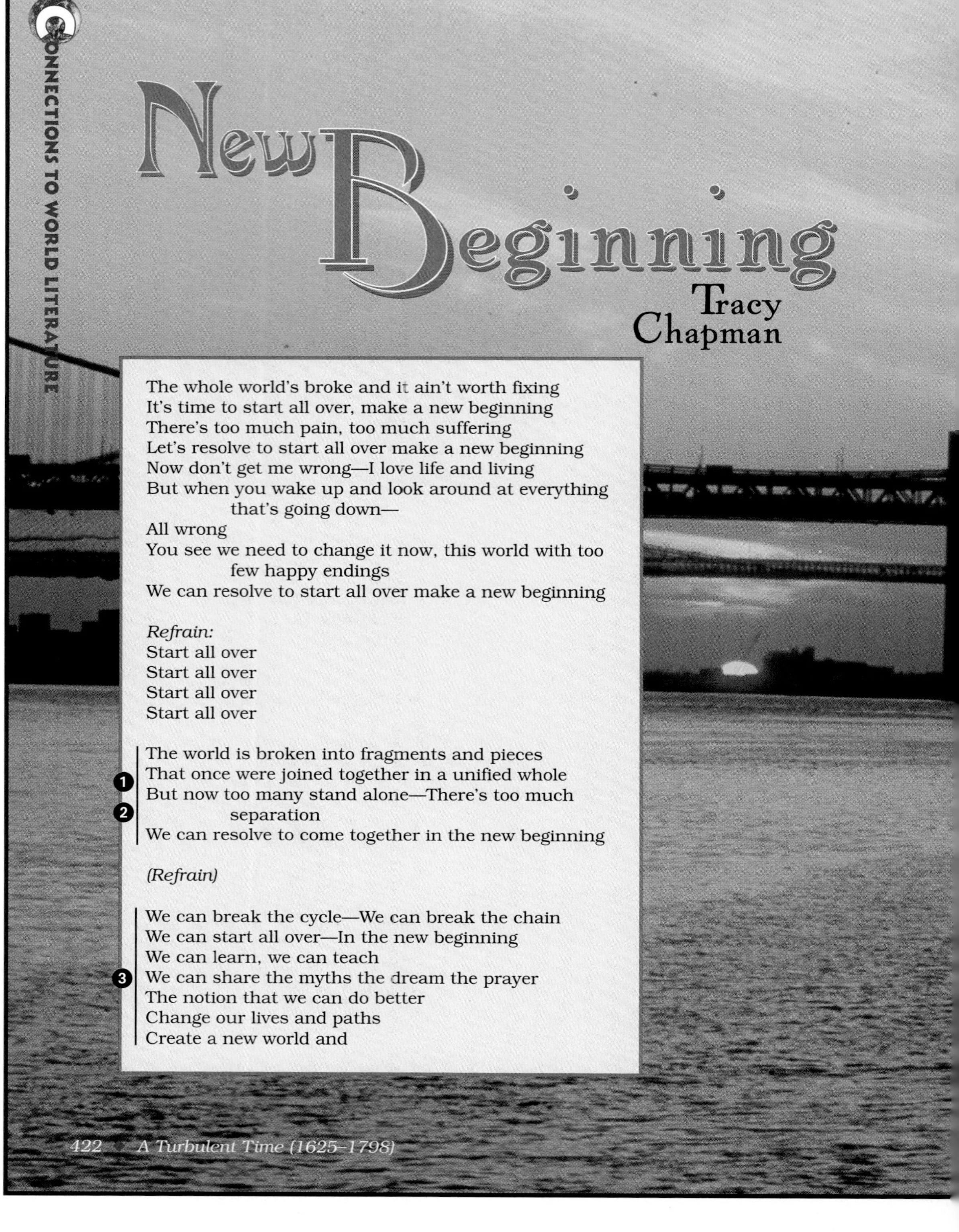

New Beginning

Tracy Chapman

The whole world's broke and it ain't worth fixing
It's time to start all over, make a new beginning
There's too much pain, too much suffering
Let's resolve to start all over make a new beginning
Now don't get me wrong—I love life and living
But when you wake up and look around at everything
 that's going down—
All wrong
You see we need to change it now, this world with too
 few happy endings
We can resolve to start all over make a new beginning

Refrain:
Start all over
Start all over
Start all over
Start all over

The world is broken into fragments and pieces
❶ That once were joined together in a unified whole
But now too many stand alone—There's too much
❷ separation
We can resolve to come together in the new beginning

(Refrain)

We can break the cycle—We can break the chain
We can start all over—In the new beginning
We can learn, we can teach
❸ We can share the myths the dream the prayer
The notion that we can do better
Change our lives and paths
Create a new world and

(Refrain)

The whole world's broke and it ain't worth fixing
It's time to start all over, make a new beginning
There's too much fighting, too little understanding
It's time to stop and start all over
Make a new beginning ❸

(Refrain)

We need to make new symbols
Make new signs
Make a new language
With these we'll define the world

(Refrain)

Guide for Responding

◆ Literature and Your Life

Reader's Response Do you believe we can control time by freezing a moment or starting all over again? Explain.

Thematic Focus In what ways do these songs tell us to "seize the day"?

Advertisement As the owner of a futuristic time-travel company, create an advertisement that invites people to use your time-travel machine. Include the *carpe diem* theme in your message.

☑ Check Your Comprehension

1. (a) What is the setting for "Freeze Tag"? (b) What words and images does Vega use to describe the setting?
2. What games do the characters in "Freeze Tag" play?
3. In Chapman's "New Beginning" what are some of the problems the songwriter identifies?
4. What does Chapman suggest should be done about these problems?

◆ Critical Thinking

INTERPRET

1. How do the images in Vega's song explain the title "Freeze Tag"? **[Connect]**
2. Speculate about the type of situation Vega may be writing in her song. **[Speculate]**
3. Explain what Chapman means by "We can break the cycle." In what ways is this method of dealing with time effective? **[Interpret]**

EVALUATE

4. (a) Compare and contrast Vega's and Chapman's attitudes toward time. (b) Which treatment do you find more effective? Why? **[Evaluate]**

APPLY

5. Chapman speaks about making "new symbols" and a "new language." Suggest what such a language might be like. **[Speculate]**

EXTEND

6. How do these modern treatments of time compare to those in seventeenth-century poems? **[Literature Link]**

Customize for
Verbal/Linguistic Learners
Have students discuss why Chapman, a college-educated songwriter, would include slang, such as "ain't" and "everything that's going down." *Her songs are written for a contemporary audience made up of educated and uneducated people; she is speaking directly and informally.*

◆ Critical Thinking

❸ **Analyze** Have students note what words and phrases are repeated at the beginning of the song, in the middle, and at the end. What is the effect of this repetition? *At the beginning, the repetition of "too much" and "too few" focuses on negative things: "pain" and "suffering," "few happy endings." In the middle, the words we can are repeated; at the end, the word new is repeated. The effect is that the song becomes progressively more positive.*

Reinforce and Extend

Answers

◆ Literature and Your Life

Reader's Response Students may say that sharing memories with old friends is a way of freezing a moment, or starting a new job or relationship is a way of starting over again.

Thematic Focus They tell us to seize the day by stopping, starting over, and by saying yes, now.

☑ Check Your Comprehension

1. (a) A playground in winter is the setting for "Freeze Tag." (b) She uses images of slides, swings, snow-covered park, and playing games.
2. The characters play hide and seek and freeze tag, and pretend they are romantic film stars.
3. She pictures a world with too much pain and suffering, too much fragmentation and separation.
4. She suggests that we resolve to start all over and make a new beginning, to make new symbols, new signs, and a new language to redefine the world.

◆ Critical Thinking

1. She describes wintry scenes in a park playground as a backdrop to playing games.
2. Vega may be describing those times in our lives when we are undecided about the unknown future, and feel more comfortable in the past; how we pretend to be someone other than we are to get by; but when we freeze the moment and focus on the now, we can move on.
3. We can only make changes when we recognize patterns of behavior and then break them. It is a way of seizing the day.
4. Suggested Response: (a) Vega focuses on the moment, since worrying about the past only leads to indecision. Chapman wants to stop and start all over. (b) Chapman is more ambitious: she wants to change the whole world; Vega is just focusing on herself and a friend, which is a more feasible arena for change.
5. Chapman's new language might use more words of love, understanding, respect, and connection, and would include listening, caring, and helping one another.
6. The songs also deal with the *carpe diem* theme.

Answers
Thematic Connection

1. Students may agree with the idea of not being able to control anything but today and making the best possible use of the moment, rather than worrying about yesterday or tomorrow; or with the idea that time is fleeting so enjoy life. Sample excerpts: "Thus, though we cannot make our sun/ Stand still, yet we will make him run"; "Gather ye rosebuds while ye may,/Old time is still a-flying"; "We can only say yes now,/to the sky, to the street, to the night"; "It's time to stop and start all over/Make a new beginning."
2. Poems and songs in their carefully chosen brevity, strong rhythms, and repetition create powerful images that strike the heart and reflect life so we can see ourselves more clearly.
3. Suggest that the students choose phrases that convey the theme of *carpe diem.*

Idea Bank
Customizing for
Performance Levels
Following are suggestions for matching Idea Bank topics with your students' performance levels:
Less Advanced Students: 1, 4
Average Students: 2, 5
More Advanced Students: 3

Customizing for
Learning Modalities
Following are suggestions for matching Idea Bank topics with your students' learning modalities:
Logical/Mathematical: 1
Musical/Rhythmic: 2
Verbal/Linguistic: 3, 4
Visual/Spatial: 5

Thematic Connection

The War Against Time

The lyrics of songwriters Suzanne Vega and Tracy Chapman, like the poems of this section, express the elusiveness of time. They show how time flows by almost too quickly to be seized, captures us in a frozen moment, or needs the blessing of a new start.

1. What attitudes toward time expressed by these writers do you share? Why? Support your answer with specific passages from the poems or songs.
2. How can the words of songs and poems help people experience life more deeply?
3. Write a refrain—a repeated phrase—for your own song about time. If you like, borrow words from any of the poems or songs you have read.

Idea Bank

Writing

1. **Time Log** Create a time journal in which you log how you spend all of your time for one week. Did you waste time? Do you feel you used it wisely? Conclude your journal with a brief passage evaluating your use of time.
2. **Song** Write a song expressing your ideas about the value of time. Include a refrain, a repeated phrase or verse placed between stanzas, that sums up your central idea about time. You may want to set your song to the tune of a popular song or write your own music.
3. **Editorial for Teenagers** As a senior, write an editorial for the yearbook in which you provide advice for younger students on making the most of their high school years.

Speaking and Listening

4. **Talk-Show Host** As a talk-show host, prepare interview questions that will help your guests elaborate on how they manage their time. Ask several classmates to act as guests and then conduct your "show" for your class. **[Performing Arts Link]**

Project

5. **Time Experiment** Do an experiment to compare subjective impressions of time with actual clock time. Have classmates focus on a pleasant memory with their eyes closed. Stop them after three minutes and then ask them how much time they *think* has passed. After performing the experiment with several classmates, write your conclusions and share them with the class. **[Science Link]**

✓ ASSESSMENT OPTIONS

Formal Assessment, Selection Test, pp. 95–96, and Assessment Resources Software. The selection test is designed so that it can be easily customized to the performance levels of your students.

PORTFOLIO ASSESSMENT
Use the following rubrics in the ***Alternative Assessment*** booklet to assess student writing:
Time Log: Evaluation/Review Rubric, p. 105
Song: Poetry Rubric, p. 109
Editorial for Teenagers: How-to/Process Explanation Rubric, p. 101

Writing Process Workshop

Editorial

In many seventeenth-century poems, the speaker tries to persuade his audience to believe or do something. Those who write or broadcast editorials today have the same task. Their messages may not be rhymed, but the destination of their words is still the heart and mind of the reader or listener.

Write a radio, television, or newspaper editorial, taking a clear position on a current issue. In the brief space or time allowed to you, defend your opinion with statistics, examples, reasons, or other details.

These skills, introduced in the Writing Mini-Lessons, will help you write an effective editorial.

Writing Skills Focus

- ▶ Create **unity** by relating your argument and supporting details to the main topic. (See p. 403.)
- ▶ **Elaborate to support your argument** by providing reasons, facts, and examples. (See p. 411.)
- ▶ Set a **persuasive tone** by using language that expresses confidence, carries positive associations, and dramatizes your argument. (See p. 419.)

Workplace Writing Model

from an editorial in *The Oakland* (Michigan) *Press*

A generation ago our parents could earn a good living without a college education. Well-paying jobs were open to high school graduates. . . . Now, high tech manufacturing processes demand ① sophisticated abilities at all levels of employment ② . . . where do we hone these abilities? ③ In college . . . while a year or two of college may do for entry-level jobs, advancement and career development often depend on a four-year degree—at least. . . .

① A forceful word, *demand*, dramatizes the author's argument.

② The author elaborates on the argument by demonstrating how a change in jobs has caused a change in conditions.

③ The author's question helps to unify the editorial by leading back to the central topic—college education—that was introduced at first.

Prepare and Engage

Establish Writing Guidelines

Introduce students to the following key elements of an editorial before beginning this lesson:

- An editorial is a form of persuasive writing, taking a clear position on an issue.
- The introduction grabs the reader's attention and states the writer's position on the issue.
- The body of the editorial supports the position with statistics, examples, and logical reasons.
- Conciseness—sticking to the essentials—is key.

Review with students the criteria in the Scoring Rubric for a persuasive piece in ***Alternative Assessment,*** p.109. See the suggestions on page 427 for additional points for customizing the rubric to this workshop.

Refer students to the Writing Handbook, page 1189, for instruction in the writing process, and to page 1192 for further information on persuasive writing.

Writer's Solution

Writing Lab CD-ROM

Have students work in the tutorial for Persuasive Writing. They should follow these steps:

1. Review the annotated model of an editorial in the About Persuasion section.
2. Use the Issues Wheel for topic ideas under Choosing a Topic.
3. For help identifying their audience, examine the examples of audiences for editorials under Considering Audience and Purpose.
4. Use a Pros and Cons Chart under Gathering Evidence to strengthen their arguments.
5. Draft their editorial on the computer, referring to the instruction on faulty logic and unreasonable appeals under Drafting.
6. Use the Language Variety Checker in the Revising and Editing section.

Sourcebook

For additional help with writing an editorial, students can review the chapter on Persuasion, pages 96–129.

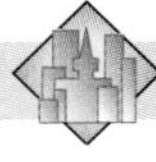

Beyond the Classroom

Career Connection

Lobbyist Lobbyists—people representing political movements, businesses, and public interest groups—work to influence editorial writers, voters, and legislators. They often write press releases, advertisements, even letters mailed to people's homes, that resemble editorials. To compose such persuasive pieces, lobbyists research the evidence supporting their position, conducting public opinion surveys, for instance, or examining studies on the subject. An environmental lobbyist, for example, might conduct a telephone poll concerning proposed construction in town. He or she might also examine the studies on file with the town regarding the environmental impact of the project. Using the results of the poll and details from the study, the lobbyist may prepare a pamphlet, general letter, or press release to persuade people whether the project should be pursued or not.

Tell students that lobbyists' persuasive efforts can address different audiences, from voters to Congresspersons. Each is carefully gauged to a specific audience.

Develop Student Writing

Prewriting

Have students break into groups and discuss issues that have recently appeared in the news. Each group should select a topic and work out a brief list of arguments on either side. You may wish to make copies of the Argument Organizer in the ***Writing and Language Transparencies,*** p. 103, and distribute them for students' use. Explain to students that, whichever side of an issue they take, knowing both sides will help them construct an effective persuasive piece.

Customize for
English Language Learners
These students may not yet have developed an appreciation of the nuances of English vocabulary. After they have made lists of persuasive words, pair each of these students with a peer who has a good grasp of English vocabulary. Have the peer review the student's list and suggest more forceful (or more tactful) synonyms for words that seem too neutral (or too strong). Students may use the Branching Organizer, page 96 in ***Writing and Language Transparencies,*** to organize these words and their suggested replacements into groups, according to their positive or negative connotations.

Writing Lab CD-ROM
Have students use the Persuasive Word Bin to come up with forceful words for effective arguments.

Drafting

Point out to students that effective editorials are often organized around a single image, statistic, analogy, or story that crystallizes the writer's perspective and draws the reader in. Once they have a basic grasp of the arguments on either side of an issue, they should select such a focal point, introduce it in their introduction, follow it through in the body, and return to it in the conclusion.

Applying Language Skills

Avoiding Logical Fallacies
Explain to students that, by examining their guiding assumptions, they can eliminate logical fallacies. For instance, the writer who asserts that "it is essential to be stylish because it is important to be fashionably dressed" may assume that dressing well commands the respect of others. By making this assumption explicit, the writer can avoid the circular reasoning of the example sentence.

Fixing Misplaced Modifiers
Explain to students that, in the brief space allotted to editorials, a lot of information may get packed into each sentence, making the placement of modifying clauses and phrases especially important. Have student review their papers, revising to correct any instances of misplaced modifiers.

Answer
For most people, designing a garden. . . . Nearly all gardeners will benefit. . . . Some plants, such as dahlias, cannot survive.

For additional practice in developing coherent arguments, have students complete the ***Language Lab CD-ROM*** lesson on Unity and Coherence in Paragraphs and the worksheet on Avoiding Proble in Logic, page 111 in the *Write Solution Grammar Practice Book.*

For additional help with mi placed modifiers, have student complete the **Language Lab ROM** lesson on Misplaced Modifiers as well as the practi on page 45 in the *Writer's Solu Grammar Practice Book.*

Applying Language Skills: Avoiding Logical Fallacies

Following are some common types of faulty logic and ways to correct them:

- **Circular reasoning:** You expect readers to assume that the conclusion is true in order to prove it.
  Example: It is essential to be stylish because it is important to be fashionably dressed.
- **Faulty generalization:** You make a sweeping statement based on little or no evidence.
  Example: Studies prove that Americans dislike cereal.
- **Either/or arguments:** You allow for only two possibilities.
  Example: Either I get the lead role, or I might as well forget about an acting career.

Writing Application Check your paper for examples of faulty logic. Then delete or revise them.

Writer's Solution Connection
Writing Lab
For help with the Pro-and-Con chart, review the Organizing Evidence section of the Persuasion tutorial.

Prewriting

Choose a Topic The next time you watch the news, look for a current issue on which you can take a stand. Develop a Pro-and-Con chart to consider the arguments for and against your opinion. This chart will help you determine whether there are enough arguments to make the topic worthy of an editorial.

Topic: The "V" Chip

Pros	Cons
Helps working parents control what TV children watch	Results in more government regulations
	Increases cost to consumers

Consider the following topic ideas for your editorial:

Topic Ideas

- Enacting mandatory sentencing laws
- Supporting or attacking a particular politician
- Repealing mandatory school attendance
- Raising the minimum wage

List Words that Will Set a Persuasive Tone List commonly used persuasive words. Next to each, put a more urgent or dramatic synonym that will help you set a persuasive tone in your draft. For example, use *imperative* instead of *important* or *sluggish* instead of *slow.*

Drafting

Maintain Unity by Orienting Yourself As you write be alert to where you are in your editorial—introduction, body, or conclusion—and write appropriately. For example, use the conclusion to restate or summarize arguments. Include words or phrases from the introduction, without mechanically repeating your points, to give readers or listeners a sense of unity.

Support Your Arguments For every argument you make, include supporting facts, statistics, examples, or quotations. Refer to your Prewriting chart to identify these details.

Revising

Consult a Peer Reviewer Get specific suggestions for strengthening your argument from someone who is neutral towards it or opposes it.

Use a Revision Checklist Ask yourself questions based on the writing skills focus:

- Have I created unity by relating each argument to the central topic?
- Have I supported each point with details that relate to it?
- Have I used vivid words that convey confidence and dramatize my argument?

Add Visuals While reviewing your editorial, note places where a chart or graph will support your argument. Revise your editorial to introduce and incorporate such effective visual support.

Revision Model

Because the prom is the ~~most fun~~ crowning ① event of the year, the seniors deserve a live band. The absence of the live band makes our prom merely a dance with a disc jockey. ~~As we all know, our school is closing next year.~~ Having live music will give us an experience to reminisce over at reunions. ② We must fight to preserve the live band tradition at our Senior Prom. ③

① The writer replaces a weak phrase with a vivid word to enhance the persuasive tone.

② The writer eliminates an irrelevant statement and adds a strong supporting detail.

③ This sentence helps unify the paragraph by restating the main topic.

Publishing

- **Internet** Send your editorial to a friend or chat group concerned about the topic.
- **Local Newspaper** Send your editorial to a local newspaper for publication on the op ed or letters page.
- **Videotape** Record your editorial on videotape, using charts, props, and other visual aids to enhance your presentation. Then play your tape for the class.

Applying Language Skills: Fixing Misplaced Modifiers

A misplaced modifier can cause writing to be unclear and ineffective. Place modifiers as close as possible to the words they modify.

Example:

Misplaced Modifier:

The rose, who finds it too demanding, is avoided by many weekend gardeners.

The gardeners not the rose find the flower too demanding. The modifier should be placed after gardeners.

Practice Correct any misplaced modifiers in the following passage.

Designing a garden begins with an inspection of the site where the garden will be located for most people. All gardeners will nearly benefit from taking the time to determine the uses to which the garden will be put. Some plants cannot survive the winters in areas where the temperatures drop below freezing, such as dahlias.

Writer's Solution Connection
Language Lab

For more help identifying and fixing misplaced modifiers, see the lesson on misplaced modifiers on the Language Lab CD-ROM.

Revising

Students may work together in pairs to revise their work. As they review their partner's papers, they should follow the suggestions on this page. In addition, have students refer to the Writing Skills Focus on page 425 to check that the drafts they are reviewing incorporate the suggestions there.

Writers at Work Videodisc
Play the videodisc section in which Cary Bricker discusses her approach to revising and editing.

Play frames 39870 to 40926

Writing Lab CD-ROM
Have students use the audio-annotated models to learn how a draft can be revised to incorporate more supporting details.

Reinforce and Extend

Reflect on the Form of Writing After students have completed their papers, ask them to discuss what they have learned from this writing experience about the nature of editorials. Did they find that they had more to say than the requirements of "punchy" writing would let them include, or did they find that they were scraping to find support? As they learned more, were they less happy about taking a strong, black-and-white position on the subject?

Extension Have students recast their editorials as a letter to the editor of a school or local paper. Students can first share their letters with the class, then revise them if necessary and mail them in.

✓ Assessment

PORTFOLIO ASSESSMENT		4	3	2	1
Use the Scoring Rubric for a persuasive piece in ***Alternative Assessment,*** p. 109, and add the following criteria to customize the rubric to this assignment.	**Elaboration for Support**	The editorial provides ample supporting reasons, facts, examples, and statistics, each clearly related to the main argument.	The editorial provides some supporting reasons, facts, examples, and statistics; most details are clearly related to the main argument.	The supporting reasons, facts, examples, and statistics are either insufficient or are not clearly linked to the main argument.	The editorial presents little support for its position.
	Setting a Persuasive Tone	The writer's language carries strong associations and helps dramatize the argument.	The writer's language carries strong associations and dramatizes some parts of the argument.	The writer occasionally uses effective, energized language.	The writer's language fails to carry persuasive force.

Introduce the Strategy

Explain to students that, from mail campaigns to infomercials, attempts to persuade them are often packaged as "information." Grasping the author's purpose is essential for understanding such pieces, just as it is crucial to understanding a work of literature or history. Grasping an author's purpose is also necessary before one can form one's own opinion on a subject or make a real decision about accepting the author's statements and viewpoint.

Customize for
Interpersonal Learners
Ask these students to imagine what the phrase "You're really great at math" means when said

1. by a math teacher.
2. by a younger brother asking for help on his homework.
3. by a manager at the store where you work who has just assigned you to cash register duty for the second shift in a row.
4. by a parent who has just asked you to do the grocery shopping for the week.
5. by a person of the opposite sex when a school dance is coming up.

Emphasize that, as these examples show, a statement of "fact" can take on different meanings, depending on the utterer's purpose.

Apply the Strategy

Answers

Suggested responses:

1. The author's purpose is not only to provide information but to make judgments about the injustices done to these young idealists.
2. The words *victim, sacrificed, innocence, idealism, vulnerability,* and *loyalty* all suggest that the four young people suffered unfairly. The words and phrases *ambitious, quest after power, cruelty, greed, indifference,* and *turned against them* all suggest that the adults concerned are wicked and selfish.
3. The book may not be the best source for a complete, factual picture of Lady Jane Grey's life. It is clearly dedicated to painting her as a young martyr, and may play down facts that would detract from that picture.

Judging a Writer's Purpose
Real-World Reading Skills Workshop

Strategies for Success

Understanding and judging a writer's purpose will help you respond more appropriately to your reading. For example, a novelist may simply want to entertain you but may also want to get across a message about society. A magazine writer may want to inform you about an interesting subject but may also want to persuade you to think or act in a certain way. Whatever you're reading, whether it's a textbook, a novel, or a manual, be alert to the author's purpose so that you can take it into account.

Your Purpose and the Writer's Align your purpose for reading with the writer's purpose for writing. This idea is so obvious that most of the time you don't even have to think about it. You wouldn't read an instruction to discover an exotic new fictional world. Sometimes, however, this process of alignment does take thought. For example, if you usually read nonfiction designed to convey information, you should remind yourself not to approach a novel *primarily* as a source of facts. The main purpose of fiction is to create an imaginary world. As a reader of fiction, you should savor the details of that world in order to enter into it.

Unstated Purposes Writers don't always state their purposes clearly. A challenge you have as a reader is to discover a writer's unstated purpose. Often you can identify a hidden purpose by noticing what a writer includes or omits. For example, a biographer wishing to convey a positive image of a subject may leave out certain controversial details. Also, writers' attitudes are often clues to their purpose. These attitudes are evident in the connotations of words. For example, if a writer describes a Hollywood awards program as gaudy, she probably doesn't approve of it and doesn't want you to either.

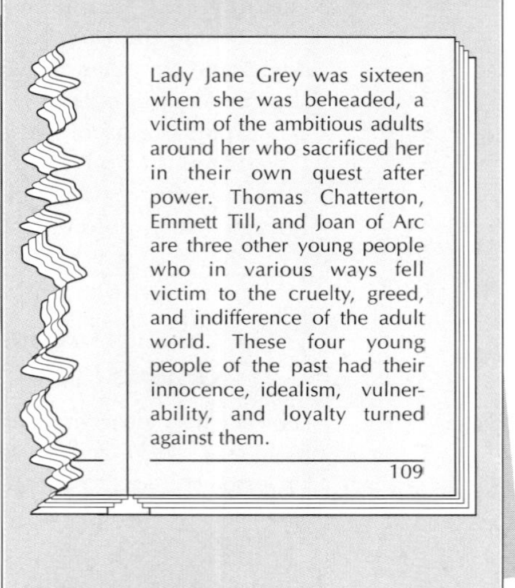
Lady Jane Grey was sixteen when she was beheaded, a victim of the ambitious adults around her who sacrificed her in their own quest after power. Thomas Chatterton, Emmett Till, and Joan of Arc are three other young people who in various ways fell victim to the cruelty, greed, and indifference of the adult world. These four young people of the past had their innocence, idealism, vulnerability, and loyalty turned against them.

109

Apply the Strategies

Imagine you are writing a history report on Lady Jane Grey. As you read the section of *Brief Lives* shown on this page, determine the author's purpose and the suitability of the source.

1. Is the author's purpose solely to provide information about Lady Jane Grey? Why or why not?
2. Which words, if any, reveal an unstated purpose? Explain.
3. Would you use this book as a source? Why or why not?

Here are other forms of writing that challenge you to judge a writer's purpose:
- *Political columns*
- *Advertisements*
- *College catalogs*

Cross-Curricular Connection: Social Studies

Historians analyze accounts of events—histories, letters, public records, and pamphlets—from various times. In order to get a balanced view of "what happened," they must evaluate the sources of information and the purpose for which it may have been recorded.

In earlier periods of history, the idea of authorship was less well-established than in modern times. People copying over manuscripts might easily combine accounts of an event from different sources. In the nineteenth century, some scholars focused on the critical study of ancient documents to determine their source—comparing different versions of a manuscript, as well as the various styles that might be found within the same document. By determining who was speaking, they hoped to get a better idea of how much to credit the information related.

Ask students the following question:

1. Is it necessary that one obtain news only from an unbiased source? Explain. *(b) Students may respond that sources may be balanced against each other, if one knows the bias of each.*

PART 2 A Nation Divided

Whitehall, January 30th, 1649, (Execution of Charles I)
Ernest Crofts, Forbes Magazine

In 1651, Thomas Hobbes asserted that without laws, "the life of man" is "solitary, poor, nasty, brutish, and short." This philosopher wasn't merely spinning ideas. The English had just beheaded their king after a bloody civil war between Calvinist Puritans and Cavalier supporters of the monarchy. That war still echoes in the contrast between the mighty words of Milton, "God's poet," and the verbal flourishes of the Cavalier Lovelace.

Humanities: Art

Whitehall, January 30, 1649 (Execution of Charles I), by Ernest Crofts.

This painting depicts the moment before King Charles I was beheaded for treason in 1649. The execution took place on a scaffolding built outside the banqueting hall of Whitehall. The king, who stands at the far left, faced his death bravely, insisting that he was a "martyr for the people." The man next to Charles is probably a clergyman, praying with the king. The executioner, hooded and dressed in red, stands among the soldiers on the right end. Charles was the only English king to be tried and executed as an act of government.

Have students link the art to the theme of Part 2, "A Nation Divided," with this question:

Why do you think the artist has chosen to present a "long shot" that includes the crowd, rather than a close-up of the king? *The artist seems to want to focus on the historic, rather than the personal, aspects of the execution, thereby suggesting the event's significance for the nation.*

One-Minute Planning Guide

The selections in this section highlight the conflicts that existed in seventeenth-century England. "Sonnet VII" and "Sonnet XIX" deal with problems of a personal nature, whereas the excerpt from Paradise Lost, inspired perhaps by events of the English Civil War, deals with the epic conflict between God and Satan. "*Eve's Apology in Defense of Women*" addresses the long-standing conflict between men and women. "To Lucasta, on Going to the Wars," speaks both to the battles for the control of England and to the conflict between a soldier and a woman who does not want him to leave. "To Althea, from Prison," touches on the conflict between Cavaliers and Puritans. The excerpt from *Light Shining in Buckinghamshire* depicts the conflict between the Diggers and government forces in the aftermath of the English Civil War.

Customize for *Varying Student Needs*

When assigning the selections in this part, keep in mind these factors:

"Sonnet VII"
- Archaic language may be difficult for English language learners
- Most students will relate to the idea of wanting to have accomplished more

"Sonnet XIX"
- Inverted sentences may be difficult for English language learners

from *Paradise Lost*
- Long poem (271 lines)
- Vivid details will appeal to verbal/linguistic and visual/spatial learners.

from *Eve's Apology in Defense of Women*
- Rhyme and meter will appeal to musical/rhythmic learners

"To Lucasta, on Going to the Wars"
- Very short poem
- Inverted sentences may prove challenging for less proficient readers

"To Althea, from Prison"
- Archaic language may be difficult for English language learners

from *Light Shining in Buckinghamshire*
- Short drama (1 page)
- Dramatic presentation brings words from historical accounts to life

Prepare and Engage

OBJECTIVES

1. To read, comprehend, and interpret Milton's poetry
2. To relate poetry to personal experience
3. To break down sentences to facilitate comprehension
4. To recognize the distinguishing characteristics of Italian sonnets and epic poetry
5. To build vocabulary in context and learn the word root *-lum-*
6. To use *who* and *whom* correctly
7. To retell a story, using a consistent point of view
8. To respond to poetry through writing, speaking and listening, and projects

SKILLS INSTRUCTION

Vocabulary:
Word Roots: *-lum-*

Grammar:
Correct Use of *Who* and *Whom*

Reading Strategy:
Break Down Sentences

Literary Focus:
The Italian Sonnet; Epic Poetry

Writing:
Consistent Point of View

Critical Viewing:
Speculate; Evaluate; Interpret

PORTFOLIO OPPORTUNITIES

Writing: Description of a Place; Poem; Response to Criticism

Writing Mini-Lesson: Retelling a Story

Speaking and Listening: Dramatic Readings; Reading *Paradise Lost*

Projects: Illustration for *Paradise Lost;* Blindness and Creativity

More About the Author
John Milton was not an easygoing man. An austere Puritan, he was also ambitious and proud. His wife, Mary Powell, left him after only a few weeks of marriage. His wife eventually returned, but she and their children were not treated well. Despite Milton's problems, both physical and political, he retained a measure of arrogance. At one point, James II suggested that Milton's blindness might be divine retribution for his supporting the execution of Charles I. Milton's retort was succinct and persuasive: "If your Highness thinks that misfortunes are the indexes of the wrath of heaven, what must you think of your father's tragical end? I have only lost my eyes—he lost his head."

Guide for Interpreting

John Milton *(1608–1674)*

Never lacking self-confidence, Milton clearly and loudly voiced his opinions on the political, religious, and moral issues of his time. He spent the major part of his life studying literature and writing political pamphlets, but the few poems he managed to complete, especially the epic *Paradise Lost,* firmly establish him along with Chaucer and Shakespeare as one of the greatest English poets ever to live.

A Privileged Childhood

Milton was born in London to a middle-class family and grew up in a highly cultured environment. His father, a notary and money-lender, was a composer of considerable ability. Milton's father was also deeply religious and devoted to the Protestant cause. Milton, educated at first by tutors, started his formal education in the equivalent of high school before the age of thirteen. There he mastered Greek, Latin, and Hebrew as well as several modern European languages.

God's Poet After Milton entered Cambridge University, he decided to prepare himself for a career as a great poet in the service of God. From this point until the English Civil War broke out, he devoted himself to a life of study. After earning his degrees from Cambridge, he withdrew to his father's house for nearly six years, reading everything that was written in the ancient and modern languages that he knew. During this time he wrote one of his best-known poems, "Lycidas." That work, together with poems he had written during his college career, would have earned him lasting fame as a major poet, even if he had never written *Paradise Lost.*

A Man of Ideals Following his studies, Milton went to Europe for a two-year "Grand Tour." While he was away, Parliament rebelled against King Charles I. Learning of the revolt, Milton cut short his trip and returned to England. He began writing political pamphlets during the English Revolution and the Civil War that followed. As a result of his brilliant writings, Oliver Cromwell, the new head of England, made Milton Secretary for Foreign Tongues. This position required him to translate documents into Latin and to defend the government against royalist attacks.

Milton was imprisoned when the monarchy was restored. His friend, the poet Andrew Marvell, may have been instrumental in gaining his release. Having lost most of his property, Milton withdrew into his blindness and poverty to write *Paradise Lost*, the greatest epic of the English language.

◆ Background for Understanding

HISTORY: MILTON'S EPIC RESPONSE TO CONFLICT

Paradise Lost was written as the dust was settling after years of war and turmoil. From 1642 to 1660, England went from being a monarchy (Charles I) to a commonwealth (Oliver Cromwell) to a protectorate (Lord Protector Cromwell) to a restored monarchy (Charles II). No matter which side of the civil war you were on or how you regarded Cromwell and his politics, at some point during this two-decade period, you experienced both defeat and triumph.

Perhaps Milton wrote *Paradise Lost* because he sensed that the nation needed an anchor, a work of literature that would once again help define and unite a culture. In his epic, Milton seems to have the nation's strife in mind as he offers a poetic explanation for God's allowing suffering and unhappiness in the world. He also seems to have recent conflicts in mind when he describes the fierce "civil war" in heaven between God and Lucifer!

Prentice Hall Literature Program Resources

REINFORCE / RETEACH / EXTEND

Selection Support Pages
Build Vocabulary: Word Roots: *-lum-*, p. 96
Grammar and Style: Use of *Who* and *Whom,* p. 97
Reading Strategy: Break Down Sentences, p. 98
Literary Focus: The Italian Sonnet; Epic Poetry, p. 99

Strategies for Diverse Students Needs, p. 20

Beyond Literature Community Connection: Equal Access for the Blind, p. 20

Formal Assessment Selection Test, pp. 100–102; Assessment Resources Software

Alternative Assessment, p. 20

Writing and Language Transparencies
Daily Language Practice, Week 15, p. 150

Resource Pro CD-ROM
Poetry of John Milton—includes all resource material and customizable lesson plan

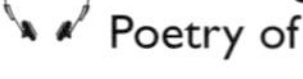

Listening to Literature Audiocassettes
Poetry of John Milton

Literature CD-ROM
How to Read and Understand Poetry, Feature 5: Milton's *Paradise Lost*

◆ Poetry of John Milton ◆

◆ Literature and Your Life

CONNECT YOUR EXPERIENCE

Throughout life you will reach milestones that mark the stages of your growth. In the sonnets that follow, you can trace two milestones in Milton's life: his twenty-fourth birthday and—a sadder event—the onset of his blindness.

Journal Writing Jot down three positive goals that you hope to achieve in the next five years.

THEMATIC FOCUS: A NATION DIVIDED

What specific evidence of the conflict between Royalists and Puritans do you see in the excerpt from *Paradise Lost?*

◆ Literary Focus

THE ITALIAN SONNET; EPIC POETRY

The **Italian sonnet** is a fourteen-line lyric poem divided into an octave of eight lines and a sestet of six. The octave, which rhymes *abbaabba,* presents a problem, and the sestet, whose rhyme scheme can vary, offers a response. In Milton's Italian sonnets, the sestet flows easily and naturally from the octave.

The **epic** is a long narrative poem written in a lofty style. It tells the story of a cultural hero and reflects the values of the society in which it was produced. However, it also deals with universal themes, like the struggle between good and evil.

In *Paradise Lost,* Milton follows classical epic traditions by beginning in the middle of the story and by calling on the muse for aid. However, he also says he will justify "the ways of God to men."

◆ Reading Strategy

BREAK DOWN SENTENCES

When you encounter complex sentences like those in *Paradise Lost,* **break them down** to find the main clause, which can stand by itself, and supporting clauses, which can't. In this passage from *Paradise Lost,* the main clause is underlined.

> Of man's first disobedience and the fruit/Of that forbidden tree, whose mortal taste/Brought death into the world, and all our woe,/With loss of Eden, till one greater Man/Restore us, and regain the blissful seat,/Sing Heavenly Muse . . .

To clarify the sentence, place the main clause at the beginning.

◆ Build Vocabulary

WORD ROOTS: *-lum-*

As you read *Paradise Lost* you'll find the word *illumine,* which means "to light up." The root of this word, *-lum-,* is from a Latin word meaning "light" or "lamp."

semblance
illumine
transgress
guile
obdurate
tempestuous
transcendent
suppliant
ignominy

WORD BANK

Before you read, preview this list of words from the poems.

◆ Grammar and Style

CORRECT USE OF *WHO* AND *WHOM*

Milton uses both ***who*** and ***whom*** in these poems. He uses *who* as the subject of a verb and *whom* as the object of a verb or preposition.

Subjective case
who best/Bear his mild yoke . . .

Objective case
if he whom mutual league/ . . . /
Joined with me. . .

In the first example, *who* is the subject of the verb *bear,* and in the second example, *whom* is the object of the verb *joined.*

Interest Grabber Ask students to consider this question: In a hundred years, what would you like to be remembered for?

Invite answers and encourage discussion. Then point out that many people have a desire to leave a mark on the world. John Milton was no exception. Near the end of his life, poor, blind, and politically out of favor, he retired from public view to write, hoping, he said, to "leave something to aftertimes as they should not willingly let die." The result was *Paradise Lost,* which many critics have called the greatest epic ever written in English.

Customize for
Less Proficient Readers
Students may find Milton's long sentences hard to read at first. Help them read the sonnets by first paraphrasing each and then reading it aloud. Then have students read it independently. Break *Paradise Lost* into smaller assignments. Have students read a certain number of lines at a time, first providing them with a brief summary of what happens.

Customize for
More Advanced Students
Students may obtain a better understanding of line 3 in "Sonnet XIX" by reading the parable of the talents, Matthew 25:14–30. To provide background for *Paradise Lost* and "Eve's Apology in Defense of Women" (p. 446) you may wish to have students read Genesis 1:26–3:24.

Customize for
English Language Learners
You may wish to define or provide simpler synonyms for unfamiliar or archaic words such as the following: *hasting, doth, Taskmaster, ere, therewith,* and so on.

Customize for
Visual/Spatial Learners
Encourage students to look at how various artists have envisioned Milton's world. For example, the nineteenth-century French illustrator and engraver Gustave Doré illustrated *Paradise Lost,* as did writer and artist William Blake.

Preparing for Standardized Tests

Reading and Vocabulary Vocabulary development helps students improve performance on the verbal portion of standardized tests. The Build Vocabulary lesson focuses on the word root *-lum-.* Students can apply word roots when faced with unfamiliar words on tests. For example:

ILLUMINATE : LAMP *(B)*
(A) think : understand
(B) sharpen : whetstone
(C) manuscript : book
(D) extinguish : fire

For practice with the word root *-lum-,* use the Build Vocabulary exercise on page 442 and the practice page in ***Selection Support,*** p. 96.

Grammar and Language Standardized tests often require a student to identify errors in sentences and then correct them. Such questions may require students to know the correct usage of *who* and *whom.*

The Grammar and Style lesson for this selection focuses on the correct use of *who* and *whom.* For additional practice, use the Grammar and Style page in ***Selection Support,*** p. 97.

Develop Understanding

One-Minute Insight Readers who know Milton as a literary giant may be surprised to discover that he was not always sure of himself, his abilities, or his future. While Milton expresses his faith in Sonnet VII, he also voices his dissatisfaction.

◆ Critical Thinking

❶ **Infer** Point out that Milton had already published two major poems. From the concerns he voices here, what does he think of them? *They do not represent any great accomplishment.*

◆ Critical Thinking

❷ **Draw Conclusions** Milton refers to God as "the great Taskmaster." What does this suggest about his view of God? *God expects people to accomplish goals.*

Reinforce and Extend

Answers

◆ *Literature and Your Life*

Reader's Response Students should define what people should have accomplished at different ages.

Thematic Focus Milton wishes he had accomplished more, but tries to accept the fact that achievements will come in time.

☑ Check Your Comprehension

1. He is reflecting upon his twenty-third birthday.
2. He looks like an adult, but feels young and unaccomplished.
3. He puts his trust in God.

◆ Critical Thinking

1. (a) Milton's concern is that at this stage in his life, he has not more worthy work to show. (b) "Late spring" means the last stages of his youth.
2. They counsel patience and trust in God.
3. Students may say that he handles it realistically.
4. Other poems that show alarm about the passage of time are "To the Virgins" (p. 416) and "To His Coy Mistress" (p. 414).

Sonnet VII ("How soon hath Time")

John Milton

❶
How soon hath Time, the subtle thief of youth,
Stolen on his wing my three and twentieth year!
My hasting days fly on with full career,[1]
But my late spring no bud or blossom showeth.
Perhaps my semblance might deceive[2] the truth,
That I to manhood am arrived so near,
And inward ripeness doth much less appear,
That some more timely-happy spirits[3] endueth.[4]
Yet be it less or more, or soon or slow,
It shall be still[5] in strictest measure even
To that same lot,[6] however mean or high,
Toward which Time leads me, and the will of Heaven;
All is, if I have grace to use it so,
❷ As ever in my great Taskmaster's eye.

1. **career:** Speed.
2. **deceive:** Prove false.
3. **timely-happy spirits:** Others who seem to be more accomplished poets at the age of twenty-three.
4. **endueth:** Endoweth.
5. **still:** Always.
6. **lot:** Fate.

◆ Build Vocabulary
semblance (sem´ bləns) *n.*: Appearance; image

Guide for Responding

◆ *Literature and Your Life*

Reader's Response Do you usually judge people by how much they've accomplished by a certain age? Why or why not?

Thematic Focus Explain how this poem reveals Milton's unrest and dissatisfaction.

☑ Check Your Comprehension

1. What occasion causes Milton to express these thoughts?
2. What is the contrast between Milton's outward appearance and his inward sense of himself?
3. To what does Milton trust himself and his life in lines 9–14?

◆ Critical Thinking

INTERPRET

1. (a) Overall, what are Milton's concerns in the first eight lines? (b) What does he mean by his "late spring"? **[Infer]**
2. How do the last six lines answer the concern expressed in the first eight? **[Draw Conclusions]**

EVALUATE

3. Does Milton deal well with the process of growing older? Explain. **[Evaluate]**

EXTEND

4. What other poems have you read that express alarm about the passage of time? **[Literature Link]**

Block Scheduling Strategies

Consider these suggestions to take advantage of extended class time:

- Use the Literary Focus on page 431 as a starting point in the discussion of the Italian sonnet and epic poetry. You may want to show students other examples of Italian sonnets, such as "On First Looking into Chapman's Homer," p. 684, or epic poems such as *Beowulf,* p. 40, the *Iliad,* p. 67, and *Sir Gawain and the Green Knight,* p. 142.
- Introduce Milton's poetry with the **Literature CD-ROM**. Feature 5 *How to Read and Understand Poetry* includes a reading from *Paradise Lost,* and feature 8 defines metrical feet in the context of poems by Milton.
- Before or after they read the selection, have students perform the Amanuensis activity in ***Alternative Assessment,*** p. 20.
- Have students work on the Dramatic Readings activity in the Idea Bank, p. 443. This activity is supported by a Speaking and Listening Mini-Lesson on p. 439.

Sonnet XIX

("When I consider how my light is spent")

John Milton

When I consider how my light is spent
Ere half my days, in this dark world and wide,
And that one talent[1] which is death to hide,
Lodged with me useless, though my soul more bent
To serve therewith my Maker, and present
My true account, lest he returning chide;
"Doth God exact day labor, light denied?"
I fondly[2] ask; but Patience to prevent
That murmur, soon replies, "God doth not need
❸ Either man's work or his own gifts; who best
Bear his mild yoke, they serve him best. His state
Is kingly. Thousands[3] at his bidding speed
And post[4] o'er land and ocean without rest:
They also serve who only stand and wait."

1. **talent:** Allusion to the parable of the talents (Matthew 25: 14–30).
2. **fondly:** Foolishly.
3. **thousands:** Thousands of angels.
4. **post:** Travel.

▲ Critical Viewing How does Milton's pose in this portrait reflect the theme of the poem? **[Speculate]** 

Guide for Responding

◆ *Literature and Your Life*

Reader's Response Milton is facing the physical challenge of blindness. What is a challenge that you have successfully met?

Thematic Focus What words indicate that Milton feels he still has a mission to perform?

☑ Check Your Comprehension

1. According to the poem, at what point in the speaker's life did his eyesight fail?
2. When the speaker thinks about serving God, he voices a complaint. What is this complaint?
3. What qualities does the second speaker attribute to God?
4. What image of God and his angels does the speaker paint in the last three lines?

◆ Critical Thinking

INTERPRET

1. Why do you think Milton feels that blindness has made his "talent . . . / . . . useless . . ."? **[Infer]**
2. What is the meaning of the question, "Doth God exact day labor, light denied?" **[Interpret]**
3. The sestet in this poem is the answer to the question in line 7. Explain that answer, paying special attention to line 14. **[Interpret]**

EVALUATE

4. Does Milton's use of dialogue make the sonnet more effective? Why or why not? **[Criticize]**

APPLY

5. Do you think this poem could inspire someone today who is facing a physical challenge? Explain. **[Hypothesize]**

Humanities: Art

John Milton, 1878, by Mihaly von Munkacsy.

This oil painting shows Milton as an old, blind man dressed in Puritan garb. The Puritans showed their lack of interest in fashionable whimsy by deliberately choosing to dress in unfashionable, plain clothes. Men and women alike wore dark colors, plain collars and cuffs, and none of the fancy trimmings that distinguished the trendy folk. Because the men wore their hair cut short, they were called "Roundheads," which distinguished them from the Cavaliers, who wore elaborate curls.

Use these questions for discussion:

1. How do simple clothes make a statement about what is important to a spiritual or religious person? *They show that the person is not interested in worldly appearance.*
2. Do you think that this portrait is a good or poor choice to illustrate this poem? Why? *Many students will think it a good choice, because it shows the poet's blindness.*

Develop Understanding

One-Minute Insight In this poem, Milton muses on his blindness, which he thought that he had caused by his voracious reading. Although he bemoans his loss of sight, he recognizes that he has to accept it as God's will.

◆ Grammar and Style

❸ Correct Use of *Who* and *Whom* Ask students why the word *who* is used in line 10, instead of *whom*. *It is the subject of the clause.*

▶Critical Viewing◀

❹ Speculate Students may point out that the poet looks downcast or blind in this picture.

◆ Literary Focus

The Italian Sonnet Ask students to describe the mood of the octave and sestet. *The mood of the octave is somber; the mood of the sestet is more accepting and hopeful.*

Reinforce and Extend

Answers

◆ *Literature and Your Life*

Reader's Response Possible responses include winning a place on a sports team or overcoming shyness in group situations.

Thematic Focus Milton indicates he has a mission in lines 3–6.

☑ Check Your Comprehension

1. He became blind at midlife.
2. He feels useless.
3. The second speaker says God is accepting, wise, and merciful.
4. The image is that God and his thousands of angels are busily attending to everyone.

◆ Critical Thinking

1. Sample response: He would not be able to write, or study his work, or read other material.
2. How does God expect him to work when he is blind?
3. God does not demand work, only faith, devotion, and acceptance.
4. Suggested response: It dramatizes first speaker's conflicting feelings.
5. This poem might inspire someone to accept a physical challenge.

Develop Understanding

One-Minute Insight In these opening lines to *Paradise Lost,* Milton tells of Satan's rebellion against God, and describes how the fallen archangel and his followers, defeated, are cast into a fiery pit. In creating a Satan that is unrepentant, proud, and in his own way heroic, Milton makes a powerful statement about the alluring nature of evil. It would be easy to avoid evil if it were completely repugnant; evil that has admirable qualities is far more insidious and dangerous.

Customize for
Less Proficient Readers
Milton's words are far easier to understand when they are read aloud, since his long sentences, with clause added to clause, have somewhat the rhythm of speech. Encourage students to say the words to themselves while they read, instead of just moving their eyes along the lines.

Literature CD-ROM
Use the CD-ROM *How to Read and Understand Poetry,* Feature 8, to help students appreciate the relationship of content to form in poetry.

❶ **Clarification** "That shepherd" is Moses. The sequence of events that led to Moses being given the Ten Commandments and the books of the Law at Mount Sinai began when Moses, looking for a lost sheep, encountered a burning bush and heard the word of God (Exodus 3:1–6).

John Milton

from Paradise Lost

Of man's first disobedience, and the fruit
Of that forbidden tree, whose mortal[1] taste
Brought death into the world, and all our woe,
With loss of Eden, till one greater Man[2]
Restore us, and regain the blissful seat,
Sing Heavenly Muse,[3] that on the secret top
Of Oreb, or of Sinai,[4] didst inspire
❶ That shepherd, who first taught the chosen seed,
In the beginning how the Heavens and Earth
Rose out of Chaos: or if Sion hill[5]
Delight thee more, and Siloa's brook[6] that flowed
Fast[7] by the oracle of God, I thence
Invoke thy aid to my adventurous song,
That with no middle flight intends to soar

1. **mortal:** Deadly.
2. **one . . . Man:** Christ.
3. **Heavenly Muse:** Urania, the muse of astronomy and sacred poetry in Greek mythology. Here, Milton associates Urania with the holy spirit that inspired Moses ("That shepherd") to receive and interpret the word of God for the Jews ("the chosen seed"). To convey the message of God to his people, Moses wrote the first five books of the Bible, including Genesis. Genesis is the book on which *Paradise Lost* is based.
4. **Oreb** (ôr´ eb) **. . . Sinai** (sī´ nī): Alternate names for the mountain where God communicated the laws to Moses.
5. **Sion** (sī´ ən) **hill:** Hill near Jerusalem on which the temple ("the oracle of God") stood.
6. **Siloa's** (sī lō´ əz) **brook:** Stream near Sion hill.
7. **fast:** Close.

Cultural Connection

Views of Paradise Curiously, the description of paradise differs little among various cultures. Throughout the ages, it is seen as a beautiful garden free from violence or pain.

An early account of paradise appears on tablets produced by the Sumer tribe in southern Mesopotamia around the year 5000 B.C. The plain of Babylon, called "Edinn," is described as an innocent, clean, and sun-filled land, where gods are forever young, healthy, and amiable. At the command of the water god Enki, the sun god Utu brings water to paradise and creates a lush garden bursting with fruit.

In Greek mythology, paradise is the garden of the Hesperides, the home of the daughters of Atlas, the evening star. Assisted by a dragon, the inhabitants guard the tree that gives the golden apples.

In African tales, paradise is a beautiful garden with ample food and leisure. There is no death or disease. Humans live in harmony with animals, able to understand their language. To the Buddhists, India will become paradise when the next Buddha, called *Maitreya,* appears. Evil will vanish and people will be strong and healthy. The earth will effortlessly yield an abundance of rice. Calm, broad rivers will nourish a wonderful variety of fruits and flowers.

Above the Aonian mount,[8] while it pursues
Things unattempted yet in prose or rhyme.
And chiefly thou O Spirit,[9] that dost prefer
Before all temples the upright heart and pure,
Instruct me, for thou know'st; thou from the first
Wast present, and with mighty wings outspread
Dovelike sat'st brooding on the vast abyss
And mad'st it pregnant: what in me is dark
Illumine, what is low raise and support;
That to the height of this great argument[10]
I may assert Eternal Providence,
And justify the ways of God to men.
Say first, for Heaven hides nothing from thy view
Nor the deep tract of Hell, say first what cause
Moved our grand[11] parents in that happy state,
Favored of Heaven so highly, to fall off
From their Creator, and transgress his will
For[12] one restraint,[13] lords of the world besides?[14]
Who first seduced them to that foul revolt?
The infernal Serpent; he it was, whose guile
Stirred up with envy and revenge, deceived
The mother of mankind, what time his pride
Had cast him out from Heaven, with all his host
Of rebel angels, by whose aid aspiring
To set himself in glory above his peers,
He trusted to have equaled the Most High,
If he opposed; and with ambitious aim
Against the throne and monarchy of God
Raised impious war in Heaven and battle proud
With vain attempt. Him the Almighty Power
Hurled headlong flaming from the ethereal sky
With hideous ruin and combustion down
To bottomless perdition, there to dwell
In adamantine[15] chains and penal fire,
Who durst defy the Omnipotent to arms.
Nine times the space that measures day and night
To mortal men, he with his horrid crew
Lay vanquished, rolling in the fiery gulf,
Confounded though immortal. But his doom
Reserved him to more wrath; for now the thought
Both of lost happiness and lasting pain
Torments him; round he throws his baleful eyes
That witnessed[16] huge affliction and dismay,
Mixed with obdurate pride and steadfast hate.
At once as far as angels' ken,[17] he views

8. Aonian (ā ō´ nē ən) **Mount:** Mount Helicon in Greek mythology, home of the Muses. Milton is drawing a comparison between the epic he is now presenting and the epics written by the classical poets, Homer and Virgil.

9. Spirit: The Holy Spirit, the voice that provided inspiration for the Hebrew prophets.

10. argument: Theme.

11. grand: First in importance and in time.

12. For: Because of.

13. one restraint: That Adam and Eve should not eat of the fruit of the tree of knowledge.

14. besides: In every other respect.

15. adamantine (ad´ ə man´ tēn) *adj.*: Unbreakable.

16. witnessed: Gave evidence of.

17. ken: Can see.

◆ **Reading Strategy**

5 On a sheet of paper reorder the words of line 34 to make the meaning clearer.

◆ Build Vocabulary

illumine (i lo͞o´ mən) *v.*: Light up

transgress (trans gres´) *v.*: Violate a law or command

guile (gīl) *n.*: Artful trickery; cunning

obdurate (äb´ door it) *adj.*: Stubborn; unyielding

◆ Critical Thinking

2 Analyze Have students identify the speaker's purpose. *In line 26, the speaker says that he will justify the ways of God to men.* Then ask students why this purpose is particularly significant, given the work's historical context. *Students may recall from the Background for Understanding on page 430 that Paradise Lost was written during the aftermath of the English Civil War, which caused much human suffering. Paradise Lost can be seen as both an explanation for the suffering that occurs in the world and also a way of giving that suffering meaning.*

Comprehension Check ☑

3 Ask students: Where does the actual story begin? *It begins after line 26.* Where do you learn who the characters will be? *The characters are introduced in lines 29 through 34.* Who are they? *They are "our grand parents" (Adam and Eve), "their Creator" (God), and "the infernal Serpent" (Satan).*

◆ Literary Focus

4 Epic Poetry Students will find Milton's syntax complex. Point out that he was deliberately writing in what was known as the "high style"—a dignified style that used sentence forms modeled on Latin grammar. Ask why this is appropriate for an epic. *An epic is supposed to be lofty.*

◆ Reading Strategy

5 Break Down Sentences One way to reorder the words is as follows: *It was the infernal Serpent whose guile . . .*

Customize for *Visual/Spatial Learners*

6 Have students read lines 45–56 and identify phrases that create visual images. *Such phrases include "Hurled headlong flaming from the ethereal sky"; "he with his horrid crew/Lay vanquished, rolling in the fiery gulf"; "round he throws his baleful eyes."*

Cross-Curricular Connection: Social Studies

The Search for Paradise People have long searched the four corners of the globe for paradise. The Guarani Indians of South America provide perhaps the best recorded instance of an actual quest. For more than 400 years, the tribe has conducted numerous voyages to find what they call the "land without evil."

Christopher Columbus claimed that the freshwater tides he found in the Gulf of Paria between Trinidad and the coast of South America originated in the four rivers that flow out of Eden. He took as proof the area's sweet climate, fragrant flowers, and lush vegetation.

Spanish explorer Ponce de León, who sailed on Columbus's second voyage to America, conducted several expeditions in search of an imaginary paradise called Bimini, said to be the site of the legendary Fountain of Youth. He explored the area of the Bahamas, discovered several islands, and eventually landed in Florida, believing he had found Bimini, and claimed the land for Spain.

Have interested students collect stories of other quests for paradise throughout history.

◆ Critical Thinking

❶ **Apply** Ask students to visualize the place where Satan and his crew were thrown. If it were a film set, what would they see? *Students may say they envision swirling darkness, flames, and a lake of sulfur glowing red with heat.*

Customize for *More Advanced Students*

❷ Have interested students use a dictionary or other resource to look up the meanings of the names *Satan* and *Beelzebub*. Why are these names appropriate? *Satan comes from a Hebrew word meaning "adversary," which is appropriate for a former angel that rebelled against God.* Beelzebub *also comes from the Hebrew and means "god of flies"—a distasteful name suitable for a fallen angel.*

Students might be interested to learn that *Lucifer*, which means "light-bearer" in Greek, is, according to Christian theology, Satan's name when he was the Angel of Light, before he rebelled against God. Have students evaluate the appropriateness of Satan's punishment given this information. *Students will probably find it appropriate that the former angel of light is punished by being cast into darkness.*

◆ Grammar and Style

❸ **Correct Use of *Who* and *Whom*** Ask students why Milton uses the objective form in line 81. *Whom is the object of the preposition* to.

The dismal situation waste and wild:
A dungeon horrible, on all sides round,
As one great furnace flamed, yet from those flames
No light, but rather darkness visible
Served only to discover sights of woe,
Regions of sorrow, doleful shades, where peace
And rest can never dwell, hope never comes
❶ That comes to all; but torture without end
Still urges,[18] and a fiery deluge, fed
With ever-burning sulfur unconsumed:
Such place eternal justice had prepared
For these rebellious, here their prison ordained
In utter darkness, and their portion set
As far removed from God and light of Heaven
As from the center thrice to the utmost pole.[19]
O how unlike the place from whence they fell!
There the companions of his fall, o'erwhelmed
With floods and whirlwinds of tempestuous fire,
He soon discerns, and weltering by his side
One next himself in power, and next in crime,
❷ Long after known in Palestine, and named
❸ Beelzebub.[20] To whom the archenemy,
And thence in Heaven called Satan, with bold words
Breaking the horrid silence thus began:
"If thou beest he; but O how fallen! how changed
From him, who in the happy realms of light
Clothed with transcendent brightness didst outshine
Myriads though bright: if he whom mutual league,
❹ United thoughts and counsels, equal hope
And hazard in the glorious enterprise,
Joined with me once, now misery hath joined
In equal ruin: into what pit thou seest
From what height fallen, so much the stronger proved
He with his thunder:[21] and till then who knew
The force of those dire arms? Yet not for those,
Nor what the potent Victor in his rage
Can else inflict, do I repent or change,
Though changed in outward luster, that fixed mind
And high disdain, from sense of injured merit,
That with the Mightiest raised me to contend,
And to the fierce contention brought along
Innumerable force of spirits armed
That durst dislike his reign, and me preferring,
❺ His utmost power with adverse power opposed
In dubious battle on the plains of Heaven,
And shook his throne. What though the field be lost?
All is not lost; the unconquerable will,
And study[22] of revenge, immortal hate,
And courage never to submit or yield:
And what is else not to be overcome?
That glory never shall his wrath or might
Extort from me. To bow and sue for grace

18. **urges:** Afflicts.

19. **center . . . pole:** Three times the distance from the center of the universe (Earth) to the outermost sphere of the universe.

20. **Beelzebub** (bē el′ zə bub′): Traditionally, the chief devil, or Satan. In this poem, Satan's chief lieutenant among the fallen angels.

21. **He . . . thunder:** God.

22. **study:** Pursuit.

◆ Literary Focus
Is Satan a typical epic character?

Cultural Connection

Angels Milton's poem had a profound influence on the way Christians viewed angels. The term "angel" comes from the Greek word *angelos*, which means messenger. However, angels are not unique to the related religions of Judaism, Christianity, and Islam. Many cultures have benevolent or mischievous spirits that act as messengers between humans and a deity.

Encourage students to look for similarities and differences among cultures in regard to angels. They may also be interested in finding how the Christian view of angels has changed over time. *Angels were not always thought of as looking like humans with a single pair of bird wings, and the notion of the souls of the dead becoming angels appears to have arisen quite recently, during Victorian times.*

Besides having them research written information, have students look at depictions of angels in illustrations and other works of art.

Paradise Lost, 1688, From the British Library

◀ Critical Viewing Is this illustration an accurate visual representation of Milton's text? Explain. [Evaluate] ❼

◆ **Build Vocabulary**

tempestuous (tem pes´ choo wəs) *adj.*: Turbulent; violently stormy

transcendent (tran sen´ dənt) *adj.*: Surpassing; exceeding beyond all limits

◆ Critical Thinking

❹ **Compare and Contrast** Have students compare what Beelzebub was like before to what is he like now. *He was once clothed in light; now he is lying in the dark pit with Satan.*

◆ Critical Thinking

❺ **Generalize** Have students consider how Milton shows the power and stubbornness of evil. What does this suggest about his view of evil in general? *Despite being tossed out of Heaven, Satan says that all is not lost. Hate never gives up. This suggests that Milton feels that evil is a constant force in life, and that battling it will be a constant struggle.*

◆ Literary Focus

❻ **Epic Poetry** Students may say that Satan is a typical epic character in his grandiose words and in his determination to persevere with his plans.

▶Critical Viewing◀

❼ **Evaluate** Students might comment on the lack of flames or a furnace or darkness. There are no whirlwinds of tempestuous fire, for instance. However, the mood is similar.

Humanities: Art

Paradise Lost, 1688, by Jacob Tonson.

Jacob Tonson (1656–1736), a London printer and the secretary of a local literature club, the Kit-Cat Club, bought the rights to publish *Paradise Lost.* It turned out to be a highly profitable endeavor. He then produced this engraving as an illustration for a large-sized 1688 edition of the work. The engraving reflects the art style that was then current, the baroque style, which features fantastic, elaborate, and highly decorative images. The images are designed to be dramatic and to engage the viewer with their energy. Like *Paradise Lost,* the image is grotesque and nightmarish.

Use these questions for discussion:

1. Do you think the style is in keeping with Milton's literary style? Why? *Most students will think it is, since Milton includes many specific details.*
2. Which details of the picture are most striking to you? Why? *Students may mention the figure of Satan, the writhing snakes, the black hole, or some other detail.*

◆ Reading Strategy

1 Break Down Sentences Have students break down this complex sentence. What is revealed in the main clause? *The main clause reveals what Satan intends to do: to "wage by force or guile eternal war" against God.*

Comprehension Check ☑

2 Ask students who is speaking in lines 128–155. *Beelzebub is speaking.*

◆ Critical Thinking

3 Analyze Have students summarize Beelzebub's words and identify his main point. *Beelzebub's main point is that God is so powerful that it would be useless to continue fighting. Students' summaries should include the following details: Beezelbub regrets the rebellion that has brought the fallen angels as low as they can go; he believes God is almighty; he wonders if they have been left their strength and spirit in order to make them suffer or, alternatively, to serve God in Hell.*

◆ Reading Strategy

4 Break Down Sentences
Possible response: *"Although we are eternal and feel that our strength is undiminished, what is the point of undergoing eternal punishment?" Students may assert that Milton chose the word order for the sound.*

◆ Literature and Your Life

Ask students why two individuals in trouble might discuss what to do next. How does this relate to times in their own lives when they might confer about different courses of action? *People might confer when they are lost or unsure of what to do.*

With suppliant knee, and deify his power
Who from the terror of this arm so late
Doubted[23] his empire, that were low indeed,
That were an ignominy and shame beneath
This downfall; since by fate the strength of gods
And this empyreal[24] substance cannot fail,
Since through experience of this great event,
In arms not worse, in foresight much advanced,
1 We may with more successful hope resolve
To wage by force or guile eternal war
Irreconcilable, to our grand Foe,
Who now triumphs, and in the excess of joy
Sole reigning holds the tyranny of Heaven."
So spake the apostate angel, though in pain,
Vaunting aloud, but racked with deep despair;
2 And him thus answered soon his bold compeer.[25]
"O prince, O chief of many thronèd Powers,
That led the embattled Seraphim[26] to war
Under thy conduct, and in dreadful deeds
Fearless, endangered Heaven's perpetual King,
And put to proof his high supremacy,
Whether upheld by strength, or chance, or fate!
Too well I see and rue the dire event[27]
That with sad overthrow and foul defeat
Hath lost us Heaven, and all this mighty host
In horrible destruction laid thus low,
As far as gods and heavenly essences
Can perish: for the mind and spirit remains
Invincible, and vigor soon returns,
Though all our glory extinct, and happy state
Here swallowed up in endless misery.
But what if he our conqueror (whom I now
3 Of force[28] believe almighty, since no less
Than such could have o'erpowered such force as ours)
Have left us this our spirit and strength entire
Strongly to suffer and support our pains,
That we may so suffice[29] his vengeful ire,
Or do him mightier service as his thralls
By right of war, whate'er his business be
Here in the heart of Hell to work in fire,
Or do his errands in the gloomy deep?
What can it then avail though yet we feel
Strength undiminished, or eternal being
To undergo eternal punishment?"
Whereto with speedy words the Archfiend replied:
"Fallen cherub, to be weak is miserable,
Doing or suffering:[30] but of this be sure,
To do aught[31] good never will be our task,
5 But ever to do ill our sole delight,
As being the contrary to his high will
Whom we resist. If then his providence
Out of our evil seek to bring forth good,

23. **Doubted:** Feared for.

24. **empyreal** (em pir´ ē əl) **substance:** The indestructible substance of which Heaven, or the empyrean, is composed.

25. **compeer:** Comrade, equal.

26. **Seraphim** (ser´ ə fim): The highest order of angels.

27. **event:** Outcome.

28. **Of force:** Necessarily.

29. **suffice:** Satisfy.

◆ Reading Strategy
4 Rewrite lines 153–155, reordering the words. Why do you think Milton used the word order he did?

30. **doing or suffering:** Whether one is active or passive.

31. **aught:** Anything.

Beyond the Classroom

Career Connection

Gardener, Landscape Architect The word *paradise* comes from the old Persian word *pairidaeza,* which meant a walled garden or other pleasing enclosure. Milton's Garden of Eden is an enclosed area on the top level of a steep hill whose sides are covered with rows of shrubs. His account owes much to the traditional seventeenth-century European gardens, private estates and parks cleverly planted in geometrical patterns and stocked for the sport of their wealthy owners.

Throughout history, people have enjoyed gardens. Gardening is a field which offers opportunities for both unskilled and skilled workers. Unskilled workers are those who mainly do the planting and the maintenance work in public, corporate, and private gardens. The skilled work includes horticulture and landscape architecture.

Have interested students investigate the aptitudes, abilities, and education needed for careers in this field. Ask them to identify schools in the city or state that can provide the necessary education.

Our labor must be to pervert that end,
And out of good still[32] to find means of evil;
(5) Which oft times may succeed, so as perhaps
Shall grieve him, if I fail not,[33] and disturb
His inmost counsels from their destined aim.
But see the angry Victor[34] hath recalled
His ministers of vengeance and pursuit
Back to the gates of Heaven: the sulfurous hail
Shot after us in storm, o'erblown hath laid
The fiery surge, that from the precipice
Of Heaven received us falling, and the thunder,
(6) Winged with red lightning and impetuous rage,
Perhaps hath spent his shafts, and ceases now
To bellow through the vast and boundless deep.
Let us not slip[35] the occasion, whether scorn,
Or satiate[36] fury yield it from our Foe.
Seest thou yon dreary plain, forlorn and wild,
The seat of desolation, void of light,
Save what the glimmering of these livid flames
Casts pale and dreadful? Thither let us tend
From off the tossing of these fiery waves,
There rest, if any rest can harbor there,
And reassembling our afflicted powers,[37]
Consult how we may henceforth most offend
Our Enemy, our own loss how repair,
How overcome this dire calamity,
What reinforcement we may gain from hope,
If not what resolution from despair."
Thus Satan talking to his nearest mate,
(8) With head uplift above the wave, and eyes
That sparkling blazed; his other parts besides
Prone on the flood, extended long and large,
Lay floating many a rood,[38] in bulk as huge
As whom the fables name of monstrous size,
Titanian, or Earthborn, that warred on Jove,
Briareos or Typhon,[39] whom the den
By ancient Tarsus[40] held, or that sea beast
Leviathan,[41] which God of all his works
Created hugest that swim the ocean stream:
Him haply slumbering on the Norway foam
The pilot of some small night-foundered skiff,
Deeming some island, oft, as seamen tell,
With fixed anchor in his scaly rind
Moors by his side under the lee, while night
Invests[42] the sea, and wished morn delays:
So stretched out huge in length the Archfiend lay

32. still: Always.

33. if . . . not: Unless I am mistaken.

34. angry Victor: God.

35. slip: Fail to take advantage of.

36. satiate: (sā´ shē it´) Satisfied.

◆ *Literature and Your Life*

(7) Satan and Beelzebub disagree about what to do now that they have been cast from Heaven. (lines 128–191) With whose point of view do you agree?

37. afflicted powers: Overthrown armies.

38. rood: Old unit of measure equal to seven or eight yards.

39. Titanian (tī tā´ nē ən) **. . . Earthborn . . . Briareos** (brī ar´ ē əs) **. . . Typhon** (tī´ fən): In classical mythology, both the Titans, led by Briareos, who had a hundred hands, and the Giants (Earthborn), led by Typhon, a hundred-headed serpent monster, fought with Jove. As punishment for their rebellion, both Briareos and Typhon were thrown into the underworld.

40. Tarsus (tär´ səs): Capital of Cilicia (sə lish´ ə). Typhon is said to have lived in Cilicia near Tarsus.

41. Leviathan (lə vī´ ə thən): Great sea monster.

42. Invests: Covers.

◆ Build Vocabulary

suppliant (sup´ lē ənt) *adj.*: Beseeching prayerfully; imploring

ignominy (ig´ nə min´ ē) *n.*: Humiliation; dishonor; disgrace

Customize for *Less Proficient Readers*

(5) Draw attention to lines 157–165, since they sum up Satan's goals. Help students reorder the words and paraphrase their meaning. *Students' paraphrases may resemble the following: "To be weak is miserable, whether you accept it or fight it. We will do what we can to thwart God. If he means to get good out of our evil, we will prevent it. We will sometimes succeed in preventing what he wants, which will upset him."*

◆ Critical Thinking

(6) **Analyze** Have students identify the sensory details included in lines 170–176 and tell what senses they involve. *Students may identify the following details: sulfurous hail—smell and touch; fiery—touch; falling—touch; thunder—sound; red lightning—sight; bellow through the vast and boundless deep—sound, sight.*

◆ *Literature and Your Life*

(7) Students who support Satan's point of view might like to know that several critics, including writer William Blake, mentioned that Milton seemed to admire Satan. Certainly Milton portrayed Satan as having an indomitable will.

◆ Critical Thinking

(8) **Infer** Have students explain why Satan's eyes sparkled. *He was excited; he was filled with emotion. This kindles the hellfire within him.*

◆ Critical Thinking

Compare and Contrast Ask students to think of the scariest film characters they know. How do they compare with the villains here? *Answers will differ depending on the characters that students name.*

Speaking and Listening Mini-Lesson

Dramatic Reading

This mini-lesson supports the Dramatic Reading activity in the Idea Bank on page 443.

Introduce the Concept Explain that a dramatic reading is a theatrical presentation, in which the reader tries to showcase the author's style, as well as illuminate the personalities of characters. Students should select the sonnet that most appeals to them.

Develop Background Before students read, you may wish to focus their attention on the following issues:

- A reader's voice, movements, posture, and expression should reflect the content.
- The voice should be expressive. It should rise and fall instead of being monotonous.
- The words should be clear. The reader should not read too quickly or too softly.
- The volume, pitch, and pauses should emphasize the important ideas.

Apply the Information Students should rehearse their readings. You might encourage them to mark their scripts to indicate emphasis or pauses.

Assess the Outcome Ask the audience to critique each reader by noting at least one element that was presented well or poorly. You may wish to distribute the Peer Assessment: Oral Interpretation page, which is found in ***Alternative Assessment,*** p. 120.

▶Critical Viewing◀

❶ **Interpret** Students might say that the angel looks angry, or that he's blowing a horn as if to summon others into battle. Also, this angel has horns and sharp wings. Students may recognize this figure as one of the fallen angels from the illustration on page 437.

◆Critical Thinking

❷ **Infer** What is suggested by line 213? *It suggests that Heaven allows Satan to do evil; he could not even move his head if heaven did not permit it.*

Comprehension Check ☑

❸ What will the result of Satan's malice be? *It will bring forth infinite goodness, grace and mercy shown to people seduced by Satan; it will bring confusion, wrath, and vengeance to him.*

Customize for *Less Proficient Readers*

❹ Draw attention to this passage and ask what Satan ("the lost Archangel") means. Help students understand that he is saying good-bye to the place where joy dwells forever, and saying hello to the horrors of hell.

Customize for *More Advanced Students*

❺ Ask students to read lines 255–256 and explain what they suggest about human labels of what is pleasant, unpleasant, good, or bad. How might this apply to the blind poet? *The speaker suggests that the mind can make a Heaven out of Hell and vice versa. This suggests that human interpretation of events can change depending on how people look at them. Milton's blindness may not be a curse but a blessing; the horrors of the English Civil War may also be a blessing in disguise.*

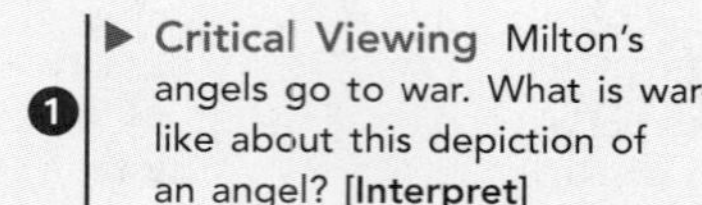

❶ ▶ **Critical Viewing** Milton's angels go to war. What is war-like about this depiction of an angel? **[Interpret]**

Paradise Lost, 1688, (detail) John Milton British Library

❷ Chained on the burning lake, nor ever thence
Had risen or heaved his head, but that the will
And high permission of all-ruling Heaven
Left him at large to his own dark designs,
That with reiterated crimes he might
Heap on himself damnation, while he sought
❸ Evil to others, and enraged might see
How all his malice served but to bring forth
Infinite goodness, grace and mercy shown
On man by him seduced, but on himself
Treble confusion, wrath and vengeance poured.
Forthwith upright he rears from off the pool
His mighty stature; on each hand the flames
Driven backward, slope their pointing spires, and rolled
In billows leave in the midst a horrid vale.
Then with expanded wings he steers his flight
Aloft, incumbent[43] on the dusky air
That felt unusual weight, till on dry land
He lights, if it were land that ever burned
With solid, as the lake with liquid fire;
And such appeared in hue, as when the force
Of subterranean wind transports a hill
Torn from Pelorus, or the shattered side
Of thundering Etna,[44] whose combustible
And fueled entrails thence conceiving fire,
Sublimed[45] with mineral fury, aid the winds,
And leave a singèd bottom all involved[46]
With stench and smoke: such resting found the sole
Of unblessed feet. Him followed his next mate,
Both glorying to have scaped the Stygian[47] flood
As gods, and by their own recovered strength,
Not by the sufferance[48] of supernal[49] power.
"Is this the region, this the soil, the clime,"
Said then the lost Archangel, "this the seat
That we must change[50] for Heaven, this mournful gloom
❹ For that celestial light? Be it so, since he
Who now is sovereign can dispose and bid
What shall be right: farthest from him is best,
Whom reason hath equaled, force hath made supreme
Above his equals. Farewell happy fields,

43. **incumbent:** Lying.

44. **Pelorus** (pə lôr′ əs) **. . . Etna:** Volcanic mountains in Sicily.

45. **Sublimed:** Vaporized.

46. **involved:** Enveloped.

47. **Stygian** (stij′ ē ən): Of the river Styx, which, in Greek mythology, encircled Hades, (hā′ dēz′): the home of the dead.

48. **sufferance:** Permission.

49. **supernal:** (sə purn′ əl): Heavenly.

50. **change:** Exchange.

Beyond the Selection

FURTHER READING

Other Works by Milton

Samson Agonistes
Comus: A Masque

Works About Milton and His Works

Dore's *Illustrations for "Paradise Lost"*
John Milton, Annabel Patterson
John Milton: A Short Study of His Life and Works, William Peterfield

We suggest that you preview these works before recommending them to students.

INTERNET

You and your students may find additional information about John Milton on the Internet. We suggest the following sites. Please be aware, however, that sites may have changed from the time we published this information.

For a list of books and articles on Milton, with links to other Milton sites, go to **http://www.richmond.edu/~creamer/ mweb.html**

For the Online Milton Quarterly, a journal about the poet's life and work, go to **http://voyager.cns.ohiou.edu/~somalley/milton.html**

We *strongly recommend* that you preview the sites before you send students to them.

Where joy forever dwells. Hail horrors! Hail
Infernal world! and thou, profoundest Hell
❹ Receive thy new possessor, one who brings
A mind not to be changed by place or time.
The mind is its own place, and in itself
❺ Can make a Heaven of Hell, a Hell of Heaven.
What matter where, if I be still the same,
And what I should be, all but less than he
Whom thunder hath made greater? Here at least
We shall be free; the Almighty hath not built
Here for his envy, will not drive us hence:
Here we may reign secure, and in my choice
To reign is worth ambition though in Hell:
❼ Better to reign in Hell than serve in Heaven.
But wherefore[51] let we then our faithful friends,
The associates and copartners of our loss
Lie thus astonished[52] on the oblivious[53] pool,
And call them not to share with us their part
In this unhappy mansion, or once more
With rallied arms to try what may be yet
Regained in Heaven, or what more lost in Hell?"

❻ ◆ Literary Focus
Is there anything heroic about Satan's speech? Explain.

51. **wherefore:** Why.

52. **astonished:** Stunned.

53. **oblivious:** Causing forgetfulness.

Guide for Responding

◆ *Literature and Your Life*

Reader's Response What in Milton's description of Hell do you find the most vivid? Explain.

Thematic Focus How does the war in heaven, as described by Satan, mirror events that had recently occurred in England?

☑ Check Your Comprehension

1. Summarize the story of Adam and Eve, as Milton tells it in lines 29–36.
2. Lines 36–53 tell of another, earlier fall from grace. Who fell that earlier time and what caused the fall?
3. Lines 59–74 describe Hell. What are its main features?
4. (a) When Satan and Beelzebub have a conversation, what does Satan vow to do? (b) What is Beelzebub's advice?
5. To what creatures is Satan compared in lines 193–209?

◆ Critical Thinking

1. What effect does Milton create in lines 1–26 by mixing Hebrew allusions and references to classical mythology? **[Interpret]**
2. How is the Fall of Adam and Eve paralleled by the Fall of Satan and his cohorts? **[Connect]**
3. In lines 242–270, identify words and phrases that show Satan's despair and those that demonstrate his resolve. **[Analyze]**
4. Is Satan petty, mean, grand, self-pitying, stubborn, heroic, weak, rebellious, or some combination of these? Support your answer with specific references. **[Draw Conclusions]**

EVALUATE

5. Will Satan's efforts ever bring him satisfaction? Explain. **[Make a Judgment]**
6. In your opinion, how well has Milton "justified the ways of God to men"? Explain. **[Assess]**

◆ Literary Focus

❻ **Epic Poetry** Students may say that Satan's determination to make the best of what he has, his desire for freedom at all costs, and his perseverance in continuing to fight are heroic.

◆ Critical Thinking

❼ **Interpret** Have students explain the meaning of line 264. *It is better to be the leader even in an awful situation than it is to be led, even in the best situation.*

Reinforce and Extend

Answers

◆ *Literature and Your Life*

Reader's Response You may suggest that students compare and contrast Milton's description of Hell with other portrayals they have read or seen.

Thematic Focus England had recently experienced a civil war.

☑ Check Your Comprehension

1. Milton writes that Satan deceived Eve out of revenge on God for casting him out of heaven.
2. Satan himself fell earlier. Satan fell because he challenged God's sovereign rule.
3. Milton's hell is dark, eternally burning, and filled with tortured souls who have no hope of relief.
4. (a) Satan vows to continue the war. (b) Beelzebub's advice is to accept the fact that God is almighty and therefore cannot be overthrown.
5. Satan is compared to the Titans and to the Leviathan.

◆ Critical Thinking

1. Milton's choice of references places the poem on a grand scale because the poem seems to encompass all Western cultures.
2. Adam and Eve, like Satan, question God's sovereignty. God punished Satan by exiling him from heaven, and he punished Adam and Eve by exiling them from Eden. Both had been God's favorites.
3. In despair, Satan calls Hell "this mournful gloom," and he exclaims, "Hail horrors! Hail / Infernal world!" He shows his resolve "not to be changed by place or time." Satan decides "Here we may reign secure, and in my choice / To reign is worth ambition though in Hell: / Better to reign in Hell than serve in Heaven."
4. Satan is certainly rebellious and stubborn—Beelzebub speaks of Satan's "Fixed mind," in line 97—but he is also courageous in refusing to be conquered.
5. Sample response: If Satan can indeed "make a Heaven of Hell," then perhaps he can be satisfied.
6. Suggested response: Lines 211–221 reasonably explain why God allows evil in the world.

Answers

◆ Literary Focus

Italian Sonnet

1. In "Sonnet XIX," Milton changes the pattern with the use of run-on rhymes. He also shifts the tone of the sestet from anxiety to assurance by having a second speaker reply to the first speaker in the octave.
2. (a) In "Sonnet VII" the sestet has a more regular, end-stopping rhyme pattern. (b) It gives a strong feeling of resolution.

Epic Poetry

1. Satan's great mental anguish is the humiliation of being cast out of heaven.
2. (a) The statement suggests that Heaven and Hell, or good and evil, are merely states of mind. (b) Satan is trying to delude himself into preferring Hell, to pretend to be satisfied with what he is being forced to take.
3. (a) He may yet rally arms to regain heaven. (b) They create a powerful anticipation of a potential sequel.

◆ Reading Strategy

1. (a) The main clause is "Doth God exact day labor, light denied?" It expresses this idea: How does God expect him to work and thus serve God when he is blind? (b) All the lines before are supporting clauses: For half of his life, he has developed a talent to serve God that he can not use in the dark.
2. (a) In lines 27–32, the main clause is: "Say first." (b) Milton means to first describe the happy state Adam and Eve lived in, how they were so favored to be as lords of the world, with their only restraint being not to eat the fruit from the tree of knowledge.
3. (a) The main clause is: "He with his horrid crew / Lay vanquished, . . ." (b) The position suggests that it was a fierce battle, but Satan was losing.

◆ Build Vocabulary

Using the Word Root *-lum-*

1. b 2. a 3. c

Using the Word Bank

1. f 2. i 3. e 4. g 5. c 6. b 7. a 8. d 9. h

Guide for Responding *(continued)*

◆ Literary Focus

Italian Sonnet

In his **Italian sonnets,** Milton is famous for closely linking the first eight lines—the octave, rhymed *abbaabba*—and the following six lines—the sestet. In Sonnet VII for example, the sestet answers a concern about his achievements that he voices in the octave.

1. In which sonnet does Milton slightly break the pattern of octave and sestet to link the problem and solution even more closely? Explain.
2. (a) Which sonnet has the more regular pattern of rhymes in the sestet? (b) What effect does this regular pattern have on the "solution" or "answer" in the sestet?

Epic Poetry

Epic poems express cultural values and universal themes. A timeless theme in *Paradise Lost* is the conflict between good and evil. In expressing this theme, however, Milton had a problem. God, champion of the good, is all-powerful, according to Christian doctrine. The battle between God and Satan is therefore no contest. However, Milton dramatizes the conflict by giving you glimpses into the mind of Satan.

1. What causes Satan the greatest anguish? Why?
2. (a) What does Satan mean by saying, "The mind . . . / Can make a Heaven of Hell, a Hell of Heaven"? (b) How does this remark reflect his own inner conflict?
3. (a) What plans does Satan have for the future? (b) How do these plans create suspense?

◆ Grammar and Style

Correct Use of *Who* and *Whom*

Who is used as the subject of a verb, and *whom* can be the object of a verb or preposition.

Practice In your notebook, write *who* or *whom.*

1. With ___?___ did the Serpent quarrel?
2. ___?___ lay chained on the burning lake?
3. To ___?___ did Eve offer the apple?
4. The pair was condemned to eternal punishment by ___?___
5. ___?___ did Adam and Eve blame for their suffering?

◆ Reading Strategy

Break Down Sentences

Because Milton's sentences tend to be complicated, it helps to **break them down** into the clause expressing the main idea and the supporting clauses. Often you'll find that Milton places the main clause in the middle or at the end of a sentence for a special effect. By holding back the main clause of the epic's first sentence—"Sing Heavenly Muse"—Milton piles up supporting clauses that impress readers with the weightiness of his theme.

1. In Sonnet XIX ("When I consider . . ."), lines 1–8 are a single sentence. (a) Identify the main clause and the idea it expresses. (b) Identify the supporting clauses and the ideas they express.
2. (a) Find the main clause in the sentence in lines 27–32 of *Paradise Lost.* (b) Restate the sentence in a paraphrase that makes its meaning clear.
3. Read lines 50–53 of *Paradise Lost.* (a) Find the main clause of this sentence. (b) How does the position of this clause in the sentence suggest the position of Satan and his men in "the fiery gulf"?

◆ Build Vocabulary

Using the Word Root *-lum-*

Knowing that the word root *-lum-* means "light" or "lamp," match each numbered *-lum-* word with its lettered definition.

1. luminary	a. shining
2. luminous	b. person who enlightens mankind
3. illumine	c. to light up

Using the Word Bank

In your notebook, match each word with its synonym.

1. transcendent	a. appearance
2. ignominy	b. stubborn
3. tempestuous	c. sin
4. suppliant	d. trickery
5. transgress	e. stormy
6. obdurate	f. beyond
7. semblance	g. begging
8. guile	h. light
9. illumine	i. disgrace

◆ Grammar and Style

1. whom; 2. Who; 3. whom; 4. whom; 5. Whom

For additional instruction and practice, use the page on Using *Who* and *Whom* Correctly in the *Writer's Solution Grammar Practice Book,* p. 60.

Build Your Portfolio

Idea Bank

Writing

1. Description of a Place Milton's description of Hell in *Paradise Lost* has captured the imagination of many readers. In your own words, describe the strange world into which Satan has fallen.

2. Poem Take stock of your life up to this point, and write a poem about a milestone you've reached. If you wish, write your poem using the Italian sonnet form.

3. Response to Criticism Douglas Bush writes of *Paradise Lost*, "Its characterization of Satan is one of the supreme achievements of world literature." Support or refute this view in an essay.

Speaking and Listening

4. Dramatic Readings With a small group, take turns reading Milton's sonnets as if they were dramatic monologues. Remember to follow sentences past line endings, stopping only where punctuation indicates a pause. **[Performing Arts Link]**

5. Reading *Paradise Lost* In a small group, take turns reading *Paradise Lost*, pausing after long or involved sentences to paraphrase them.

Projects

6. Illustration for *Paradise Lost* Translate one of Milton's vivid word pictures into a drawing or painting. **[Art Link]**

7. Blindness and Creativity Milton's blindness did not deter him from creating his masterpiece, *Paradise Lost*. Research a well-known, creative person who is blind, like Stevie Wonder, and prepare a report on his or her life. Present your report to the class. **[Career Link]**

Writing Mini-Lesson

Retelling a Story

In *Paradise Lost*, Milton vividly retells the story of Satan's fall from Heaven. Choose a well-known story that you can retell. Keep the same plot, but add a few new details to give the story your signature. Whatever twist you give to the story, be consistent in the point of view from which you retell it.

Writing Skills Focus: Consistent Point of View

There are a few different points of view from which to tell a story. Whichever one you choose, keep a **consistent point of view** so that readers do not become confused. Milton, for example, writes from an omniscient point of view that enables him to tell you the thoughts of any character: "So spake the apostate angel, though in pain, /Vaunting aloud, but racked with deep despair."

You can also use the first-person point of view, allowing a character to tell the story. Another choice is the third-person limited point of view, in which someone outside the events tells the story and knows only the thoughts of a single character.

Prewriting Decide on the point of view you will use in your retelling. A first-person narrator, who refers to himself or herself as "I," will give your story a greater sense of immediacy. However, an omniscient narrator will be able to give readers a sense of everyone's thoughts.

Drafting As you draft your retellings, keep your point of view in mind. Don't have an omniscient narrator say "I" or don't assume that a third-person limited narrator knows the thoughts of several characters.

Revising Review your retelling critically, making sure that the characters and plot events are true to the original. Also have several classmates read your retelling and double-check that the point of view from which the story is told is consistent.

Idea Bank

Customizing for *Performance Levels*

Following are suggestions for matching Idea Bank topics with your students' performance levels:

Less Advanced Students: 1, 5, 6
Average Students: 2, 4
More Advanced Students: 3, 7

Customizing for *Learning Modalities*

Following are suggestions for matching Idea Bank topics with your students' learning modalities:

Visual/Spatial: 6
Intrapersonal: 2
Interpersonal: 5
Verbal/Linguistic: 1, 2, 3, 4, 5
Musical/Rhythmic: 4

Writing Mini-Lesson

Refer students to the Writing Handbook, page 1189, for instructions on the writing process, and page 1191 for further information on narration.

Writer's Solution

Writing Lab CD-ROM

Have students complete the tutorial on Narration. Follow these steps:

1. Fill out a Purpose Profile to focus on intended purpose.
2. View the interactive sample of a narrative written from different points of view.
3. Draft on the computer, using the sensory word bin to enliven descriptions.
4. Use the Revision Checkers to find ways to improve the narrative.

Sourcebook

Have students use Chapter 2, Narration (pp. 31–62), for additional support. The chapter includes in-depth instruction on developing a point of view (p. 49) and organizing a narrative (pp. 51–52).

✓ ASSESSMENT OPTIONS

Formal Assessment, Selection Test, pp. 99–101, and Assessment Resources Software. The selection test is designed so that it can be easily customized to the performance levels of your students.

Alternative Assessment, p. 20, includes options for less advanced students, more advanced students, verbal/linguistic learners, musical/rhythmic learners, intrapersonal learners, and visual/spatial learners.

PORTFOLIO ASSESSMENT

Use the following rubrics in the ***Alternative Assessment*** booklet to assess student writing:

Description of a Place: Description Rubric, p. 98
Poem: Poetry Rubric, p. 109
Response to Criticism: Literary Analysis/ Interpretation Rubric, p. 113
Writing Mini-Lesson: Fictional Narrative Rubric, p. 96

Prepare and Engage

OBJECTIVES

1. To read, comprehend, and interpret three seventeenth-century poems
2. To relate poems to personal experience
3. To use historical context to understand ideas in the literature of an era
4. To recognize elements of tradition and reform in literature
5. To build vocabulary in context and learn terms with *breach*
6. To recognize and use correlative conjunctions
7. To enliven a college application essay with dramatic effects
8. To respond to poems through writing, speaking and listening, and projects

SKILLS INSTRUCTION

Vocabulary: Terms with *Breach*

Grammar: Correlative Conjunctions

Reading Strategy: Use Historical Context

Literary Focus: Tradition and Reform

Writing: Using Dramatic Effects

Critical Viewing: Connect; Compare and Contrast

PORTFOLIO OPPORTUNITIES

Writing: Editorial; Declaration of Parliament; Response to Criticism

Writing Mini-Lesson: College Application

Speaking and Listening: Ballad; Role Play

Projects: Poster; Civil War

More About the Authors

These two writers both had the courage of their convictions.

Amelia Lanier's ideas were considered quite radical, since she argued against not only male privilege, but also class privilege. Lanier, fearless in her personal life, had an ongoing legal battle with her landlord, an attorney, because she refused to pay her entire rent. Instead, she deducted the repairs from her payment. Although the landlord had her arrested, she was not contrite and continued to battle him.

Richard Lovelace, one of the Cavalier poets and a "son of Ben," went to jail for his beliefs. Although Lovelace wrote a comedy, painted well, and was an accomplished musician, he is mainly remembered for the two poems included here.

Guide for Interpreting

Amelia Lanier *(1569–1645)*

Amelia Lanier saw the need for women's rights three hundred years before any Western woman had even won the right to vote. She was a writer who saw beyond her times and dared to question the unfair treatment of women.

From Court Life to Working Woman Throughout her life, Lanier had ties to the royal court, where her father, Baptista Bassano, was musician to Queen Elizabeth I. Lanier's husband, Alphonso, and her son, Nicholas, were also court musicians. Despite her court connections, however, Lanier and her husband were not wealthy. When her husband died in 1613, Lanier opened a school outside London in order to make a living.

A Radical Work In 1611, Lanier published a volume of poetry called *Salve Deus Rex Judaeorum* (Hail, God, King of the Jews) in which she questioned class privilege and called for women's social and religious equality with men. Today she is considered a visionary feminist who spoke out when few realized the need to do so.

Richard Lovelace *(1618–1657)*

Born to an extremely wealthy family, Richard Lovelace was the handsome favorite of Charles I and a firm supporter of those traditional values that the king symbolized.

Looks and Talent A rumor from the time has it that Lovelace was so handsome that the king and queen ordered that he be granted a master's degree before he completed his studies at Oxford! Lovelace was, however, also talented. While at Oxford he wrote a play, painted pictures, and played several instruments.

An Exciting Life Lovelace was chosen by the Royalists to demand of Parliament the restoration of the king's authority. He was immediately arrested. After his release from prison, he rejoined Charles's forces and spent most of his fortune equipping the king's army. Upon Charles's defeat in 1645, Lovelace went to France and fought against Holland. Returning to England years later, Lovelace was again imprisoned by the Puritans. No one knows for certain how his life ended, but it is believed that he died in discouragement and poverty.

◆ Background for Understanding

HISTORY: AFTERMATH OF THE CIVIL WAR

During the reign of Charles I, tensions between Catholics and Puritans rose to a dangerous level. To make matters worse, wars against Spain and France had led to a money shortage, and the king was pressuring the nobles for money and forcing commoners to fight in England's armies.

Charles I's handling of his increasingly turbulent country eventually cost him his life. He was beheaded by anti-Royalists, and England became a Commonwealth. However, during the years of the Commonwealth, Oliver Cromwell enforced order with an iron hand and new tensions arose. The sternest and most radical Puritans controlled the country, and they had little tolerance for Royalists, Catholics, or more moderate Puritans.

Richard Lovelace, a Royalist, was imprisoned twice during these turbulent years. During his incarceration, he wrote some of his finest poetry, including "To Althea, from Prison" and "To Lucasta, on Going to the Wars."

Prentice Hall Literature Program Resources

REINFORCE / RETEACH / EXTEND

Selection Support Pages
Build Vocabulary: Terms with *Breach* p. 100
Grammar and Style: Correlative Conjunctions, p. 101
Reading Strategy: Use Historical Context, p. 102
Literary Focus: Tradition and Reform, p. 103

Strategies for Diverse Student Needs, p. 21

Beyond Literature Cross-Curricular Connection: Social Studies, p. 21

Formal Assessment Selection Test, pp. 102–104; Assessment Resources Software

Alternative Assessment, p. 21

Writing and Language Transparencies Writing Process Model 1, pp. 5–11

Resource Pro CD-ROM from *Eve's Apology in Defense of Women,* "To Lucasta, on Going to the Wars," "To Althea, from Prison"—includes all resource material and customizable lesson plan

Listening to Literature Audiocassettes from *Eve's Apology in Defense of Women,* "To Lucasta, on Going to the Wars," "To Althea, from Prison"

from Eve's Apology in Defense of Women
To Lucasta, on Going to the Wars ◆ To Althea, from Prison

◆ Literature and Your Life

Connect Your Experience

Throughout history, people dissatisfied with our country's laws and values have campaigned for various causes—equal rights, environmental protection, and campaign reforms, to name a few. Sometimes their efforts have won the support of the majority, but in other cases their efforts have failed because the opposing forces were too strong.

Lanier was like some of today's campaigners for reform. Lovelace, however, was a passionate supporter of things-as-they-are at a time when things were changing.

Journal Writing Jot down some "reforms" that you'd like to see made in your community or in the country as a whole.

Thematic Focus: A Nation Divided

Why do you think that strongly clashing points of view emerge during certain periods of history?

◆ Literary Focus

Tradition and Reform

Tradition and reform go hand in hand. Few reformers propose ideas that come out of thin air. Even when their proposals are radical, reformers base them on traditional ideas and beliefs familiar to everyone in the culture.

For example, Lanier bases her ideas on a reinterpretation of the Bible. She reinterprets the story of Adam and Eve to give Adam more responsibility for the Fall.

◆ Build Vocabulary

Terms with *Breach*

In the excerpt from "Eve's Apology," you will encounter the word *breach,* meaning "breaking." This word appears in many phrases, especially those related to the law. An example is *breach of the peace,* which means "creating a public disturbance."

Word Bank

Before you read, preview this list of words from the selections.

breach
discretion
inconstancy

◆ Reading Strategy

Use Historical Context

As you read a work, place it in a **historical context** by asking whether its ideas and assumptions are typical of its era. Also ask how its ideas, whether typical or not, are a response to events of the period.

Before reading these authors, for instance, remind yourself of the turbulent events to which they were responding. (You'll find historical information in the Introduction on p. 382 and in the biographies and Background on p. 444.) Then look for evidence of the conflicts and beliefs of the time in the works themselves. Such evidence might take the form of direct statements or images.

◆ Grammar and Style

Correlative Conjunctions

Lanier and Lovelace use **correlative conjunctions,** paired coordinating conjunctions that connect two equal words or groups of words. Such conjunctions enable them to express ideas briefly and clearly, as in this example:

> For he was Lord and King of all the earth,
> Before poor Eve had *either* life *or* breath. (Lanier, "Eve's Apology")

Correlative conjunctions are especially useful in poems, where space is tight and every word must count.

Preparing for Standardized Tests

Reading and Vocabulary The reading strategy for this selection, Use Historical Context, will help students improve their performance on reading-comprehension items on standardized tests. It will also help them on achievement tests in history and science, which often present historical documents or analyses and ask students questions about them.

Grammar and Language Standardized tests may require that students choose the best revision of a passage. Making the correct decision may hinge on knowing the use and meaning of correlative conjunctions, as in the following:

Amelia Lanier was a poet. Amelia Lanier was also a visionary feminist. *(C)*
(A) Amelia Lanier was either a poet or a visionary feminist.
(B) Amelia Lanier was a poet and a visionary feminist.
(C) Amelia Lanier was not only a poet but also a visionary feminist.

For practice on Correlative Conjunctions, use the Grammar and Style exercises on page 450 and the practice page in ***Selection Support,*** p. 101.

Write the sentence "The pen is mightier than the sword." on the chalkboard. Ask students what it means. Discuss examples, including editorials, pamphlets, and other works that have changed public sentiment.

Explain that the poets featured in this grouping were people who disagreed with each other in matters of politics but were united in their belief that people should be outspoken supporters of ideas, even if those ideas were unpopular.

Customize for
Less Proficient Readers
You may wish to play the recording of the poems on the **Listening to Literature Audiocassettes** and have students read along in the text. Stop the recording at strategic points, such as the end of every stanza or two, and ask questions to check comprehension.

Customize for
More Advanced Students
Most major historians date the start of feminism or women's studies from Mary Wollstonecraft, author of *Vindication of the Rights of Women,* even though she lived almost two centuries after Amelia Lanier. Invite students to research Lanier to determine whether she deserves the honor now reserved for Wollstonecraft.

Customize for
English Language Learners
Provide the background students will need to understand these poems. For Lanier's work, explain that an apology can be a defense as well as a statement of regret. Then provide a brief summary of the story of Adam and Eve. For Lovelace's work, emphasize the main idea of each poem.

Customize for
Musical/Rhythmic Learners
Encourage students to pay attention to the different rhythm each poet used. Lanier's iambic pentameter has a more serious feeling than Lovelace's shorter, song-like lines.

Develop Understanding

One-Minute Insight Lanier would have made a wonderful lawyer. The book from which this passage is taken argues that women should have full equality with men both socially and in religion. Men, she argues, were responsible for Christ's crucifixion and far more sinful than women; also, men are more responsible for the banishment from Eden as well. Such ideas were considered quite radical in Lanier's day, and some people might find them so today. Her work bears testament to the fact that not everyone was happy with the *status quo* of the time—clearly, some railed against the social structures as others fought the political ones.

▶Critical Viewing◀

❶ **Connect** Students may say that the subject's portrayal supports the argument. Eve appears ready to share the fruit, but does not appear to be coercing Adam into eating the fruit or knowingly luring him into temptation.

Comprehension Check ☑

❷ Ask students: To whom does the word *her* in line 2 refer? *It refers to Eve.*

◆Critical Thinking

❸ **Evaluate** Have students summarize the speaker's arguments in the first stanza. *Adam was created first and was stronger than Eve, so he was more to blame than she was.* Ask students to explain whether they think this argument is reasonable, and why. *Some students may say that the argument makes sense. Other students may think that Eve is still not excused for eating the fruit in the first place.*

from *Eve's Apology in Defense of Women*

Amelia Lanier

Dorothy Seton—A Daughter of Eve
1903, James McNeil Whistler, University of Glasgow, Scotland

◀ **Critical Viewing** In this poem, Lanier argues that Eve has been judged too harshly. Does the way in which the artist portrays his subject, called "A daughter of Eve," support Lanier's arguments? Why or why not? **[Connect]** ❶

But surely Adam cannot be excused;
Her fault though great, yet he was most to blame.
What weakness offered, strength might have refused; ❷
Being lord of all, the greater was his shame;
Although the serpent's craft had her abused, ❸
God's holy word ought all his actions frame;
   For he was lord and king of all the earth,
   Before poor Eve had either life or breath,

Who being framed by God's eternal hand
The perfectest man that ever breathed on earth,
And from God's mouth received that strait command,

Block Scheduling Strategies

Consider these suggestions to take advantage of extended class time:

- Introduce the Reading Strategy, Use Historical Context on page 445. After students have read the poems, have them answer the Reading Strategy questions on page 450 and complete the Reading Strategy page in ***Selection Support*** (p. 102).
- Play the recordings of the poems that are found on the **Listening to Literature Audiocassettes.**
- Direct students to work individually or in pairs to answer the Check Your Comprehension and Critical Thinking questions (pp. 447, 449).
- Allow students to work on a writing activity of their choice in the Idea Bank (p. 451).
- Students may work on the writing Mini-Lesson (p. 451). As a prewriting activity, students may wish to discuss ideas for their essay with a writing partner. You may want to allow students to adjust the topic so that it matches that of an actual college-application essay that they need to write.

The breach whereof he knew was present death;
Yea, having power to rule both sea and land,
Yet with one apple won to lose that breath
    Which God had breathéd in his beauteous face,
    Bringing us all in danger and disgrace;

And then to lay the fault on patience's back,
That we (poor women) must endure it all;
We know right well he did discretion lack,
Being not persuaded thereunto at all.
If Eve did err, it was for knowledge sake;
The fruit being fair persuaded him to fall.
    No subtle serpent's falsehood did betray him;
    If he would eat it, who had power to stay him?

Not Eve, whose fault was only too much love,
Which made her give this present to her dear,
That what she tasted he likewise might prove,
Whereby his knowledge might become more clear;
He never sought her weakness to reprove
With those sharp words which he of God did hear;
    Yet men will boast of knowledge, which he took
    From Eve's fair hand, as from a learned book.

◆ **Build Vocabulary**

breach (brēch) *n.*: Breaking or being broken; failure to observe terms

discretion (di skresh′ ən) *n.*: Freedom or authority to make decisions and choices

Guide for Responding

◆ Literature and Your Life

Reader's Response Is Lanier's argument convincing? Why or why not?

Thematic Focus Lanier's poem appeared in 1611, while King James I was experiencing increasing conflicts with the Puritans. How do you think it was received by the public when it was published?

☑ Check Your Comprehension

1. Whom does Lanier blame more for the Fall, Adam or Eve? Why?
2. According to Lanier, why did Eve taste of the tree of knowledge?
3. According to Lanier, what was Eve's real fault?

◆ Critical Thinking

INTERPRET

1. (a)What can you infer about Eve's character from this poem? (b)What can you infer about Adam's character? **[Infer]**
2. To whom does Lanier give most of the responsibility for what happened in the Garden of Eden? Why has she done this? **[Draw Conclusions]**
3. According to this poem, in what way do men apply a double standard to the story of Adam and Eve? **[Interpret]**

EVALUATE

4. Does this poem place women in a good light in terms of today's standards? Explain. **[Evaluate]**

Humanities: Art

Dorothy Seton—A Daughter of Eve, 1903, by James McNeil Whistler.

The portrait that this artist is best known for is that of his mother. Most people call that painting *Whistler's Mother,* although its actual title is *Arrangement in Grey and Black.*

Whistler (1834–1903) was American born. He liked to draw so much that he often fell behind in his other subjects in school. He was dismissed from West Point after failing a chemistry test, and later worked as a draftsman for the Coast Survey. He learned etching, a skill that he practiced throughout his life. At the age of 22, he went to Europe to study art. In France, he was influenced by the Impressionists, and his paintings reflect this influence.

Use these questions for discussion:

1. Why would this portrait be subtitled "A Daughter of Eve"? *Possible responses: The subject is holding an apple; the subject is a woman.*
2. What is the advantage of having the background and the subject's clothing indistinct? *The portrait could show any time or setting; it seems more universal.*

◆ Reading Strategy

4 Use Historical Context Ask students to infer from the poem the common attitude at the time toward the actions of Adam and Eve. *Eve was blamed for the fall, and Adam was seen as the victim.* How might this belief have affected people's attitudes toward women in general? *People may have perceived women as weak and the source of humanity's troubles.*

◆ Literary Focus

Tradition and Reform Ask students how the poet uses details from the traditional story to strengthen her position. *She turns Adam's characteristics into reasons why he was more at fault. For example, he was stronger, he was perfect. Therefore, he should have been the one to say no.*

Reinforce and Extend

Answers

◆ Literature and Your Life

Reader's Response Students may respond that Lanier's argument is convincing; she gives realistic insight into Eve's character and makes Adam responsible for his own actions.

Thematic Focus The Puritans were very strict in their interpretation of the Bible; they would not have favored Lanier's poem.

☑ Check Your Comprehension

1. Lanier blames Adam more for the Fall. He was strong, the lord of all, and hadn't been tempted by the serpent, so he could have refused.
2. She was tempted into tasting the fruit by the deceitful serpent.
3. Eve's only fault was wanting to give Adam a precious gift.

◆ Critical Thinking

1. (a) Eve is loving and kind, not evil. (b) Adam tends to blame others for his own wrong choices, and then boasts about what he got.
2. Lanier gives most of the responsibility to Adam in order to balance the perception that women are the cause of men's woes.
3. Men blame Eve for being banished from the Garden of Eden, but boast about the knowledge they gained from Eve's hand.
4. Students may say that Lanier's portrayal of Eve as weak would be objectionable by today's standards.

Develop Understanding

One-Minute Insight Like that of other Cavalier poets, Richard Lovelace's work reflects an upper-class attitude that focuses on such courtly themes as love, honor, and loyalty. In "To Lucasta," the speaker explains to his love that she should be glad that he is going off to war; he could not love her so much if he did not value honor so highly.

▶Critical Viewing◀

❶ **Compare and Contrast**
Suggested response: The knight appears to be leaving in a more subdued, regretful spirit than the speaker of the poem.

◆ Critical Thinking

❷ **Interpret** Ask students: What is the significance of the terms *nunnery* and *chaste?* *Possible answers: They suggest that Lucasta is innocent and protected; they may also suggest that the speaker feels cloistered when he is with her.*

Customize for
More Advanced Students
Have students compare and contrast this poem with John Donne's "Song," which is also an argument designed to convince a beloved to accept a leave-taking.

To Lucasta, on Going to the Wars

Richard Lovelace

Going to the Battle, Edward Burne-Jones, Fitzwilliam Museum, Cambridge

❶ ▲ **Critical Viewing** Like the speaker in "To Lucasta," the knight in the background is going to war. Do the knight and the poem's speaker seem to be leaving in the same spirit? Explain. **[Compare and Contrast]**

❷ Tell me not, Sweet, I am unkind,
That from the nunnery
Of thy chaste breast, and quiet mind,
To war and arms I fly.

True, a new mistress now I chase,
The first foe in the field;
And with a stronger faith embrace
A sword, a horse, a shield.

Yet this inconstancy is such,
As you too shall adore;
I could not love thee, Dear, so much,
Loved I not honor more.

◆ Build Vocabulary

inconstancy (in kän´ stən sē) *n.*: Fickleness; changeableness

Humanities: Art

Going to the Battle, 1858, by Edward Burne-Jones.

Sir Edward Burne-Jones (1833–1898) called his paintings "romantic dreams," and they were. He loved to include images from mythology, legends, and medieval times in his work. He was acquainted with many of the artists of his time, including William Morris and Dante Gabriel Rossetti, to whom he was briefly apprenticed.

During the nineteenth century, Burne-Jones was an important figure in the English Arts and Crafts Movement. His elegant designs influenced members of the Art Nouveau movement, especially Aubrey Beardsley.

Use these questions for discussion:

1. In what way is this painting stylized? *The patterns, the drapery, and the poses are stylized.*
2. What aspects of the poem are reflected in the drawing? *Aspects of the poem reflected in the drawing include the man leaving for war, the women staying behind, and the romantic tone of the piece.*

To Althea, from Prison

Richard Lovelace

When love with unconfined wings
  Hovers within my gates,
And my divine Althea brings
  To whisper at the grates;
When I lie tangled in her hair
  And fettered to her eye,
The gods[1] that wanton[2] in the air
  Know no such liberty.

❸ ❹

When flowing cups run swiftly round,
  With no allaying Thames,[3]
Our careless heads with roses bound,
  Our hearts with loyal flames;
When thirsty grief in wine we steep,
  When healths[4] and drafts[5] go free,
Fishes that tipple in the deep,
  Know no such liberty.

When, like committed linnets,[6] I
  With shriller throat shall sing
The sweetness, mercy, majesty,
  And glories of my King;
When I shall voice aloud how good
  He is, how great should be,
    Enlarged[7] winds that curl the flood,
    Know no such liberty.

❸ ❹

Stone walls do not a prison make,
  Nor iron bars a cage;
Minds innocent and quiet take
  That for an hermitage;
If I have freedom in my love,
  And in my soul am free,
Angels alone that soar above,
  Enjoy such liberty.

1. **gods:** The word *gods* is replaced by *birds* in some versions of this poem.
2. **wanton:** Play.
3. **cups . . . Thames** (temz): Wine that has not been diluted by water (from the river Thames).
4. **healths:** Toasts.
5. **drafts:** Drinks.
6. **committed linnets:** Caged finches.
7. **enlarged:** Released.

Guide for Responding

◆ Literature and Your Life

Reader's Response Were you persuaded by Lovelace's arguments in these poems? Why or why not?

Thematic Focus In times of crisis we are likely to interpret traumatic events in ways that keep us hopeful. How do these poems serve such a purpose?

Definition of Honor Lovelace was concerned with honor above all. Write your own definition of *honor* and give examples of honorable behavior.

☑ Check Your Comprehension

1. What do lines 1–4 of "To Lucasta" indicate that the poet is doing?
2. According to lines 9–12 of "To Lucasta," why will the abandoned lady "adore" the speaker's "inconstancy"?
3. In "To Althea," what are three things the poet does in prison?
4. Why does the poet say in lines 25–32 of "To Althea" that he is really "free"?

Beyond the Selection

FURTHER READING

Other Works by the Authors

The Poems of Aemilia Lanyer: Salve Deus Rex Judaeorum, Susanne Woods, editor

Renaissance Woman: The Plays of Elizabeth Cary, the Poems of Aemilia Lanyer, Diane Purkiss, editor

The Poems of Richard Lovelace, Richard Lovelace

Lucasta, 1649, Richard Lovelace

We suggest that you preview these works before recommending them to students.

INTERNET

You and your students may find additional information about the poets on the Internet.

A biography of Lanier is located at **http://www.uarizona.edu/~kari/lanbio.htm**

For selected works by Lovelace, go to **http://library.utoronto.ca/www/ utel/rp/authors/lovelace.html**

We *strongly recommend* that you preview the sites before you send students to them.

One-Minute Insight

"To Althea, from Prison" explores the nature of freedom—that freedom of thought is true freedom, not an absence of walls around the body. This poem is also a political poem that states the poet's Royalist sentiments explicitly in the third stanza.

Customize for
Less Proficient Readers
Point out to students that each stanza of "To Althea" is one separate sentence about a particular kind of pleasure. Tell them to first read the stanza through, and then reread it looking for the main idea.

◆ Critical Thinking

❸ **Analyze** Have students analyze the movement in the poem from specific to general. *The first stanza is about love of one woman; the second about love of friends; the third about love of King, and therefore country; the fourth is about freedom in general.*

◆ Critical Thinking

❹ **Interpret** Ask students if they think this poem is primarily a love poem or an expression of support for the King. Have them give reasons for their answers. *It could be a love poem, since it begins and ends with verses about love; however, it could be political because the writer is content to be in jail and sing the praises of the King.*

Reinforce and Extend

Answers

◆ Literature and Your Life

Reader's Response Have the class discuss how they would feel if they received such arguments.

Thematic Focus These poems help serve to keep alive the hope of being reunited.

☑ Check Your Comprehension

1. The speaker is setting up an excuse for leaving her.
2. She will love his pursuit of honor.
3. He dreams about Althea, toasts his friendships, and sings the praises of his king.
4. When he has freedom in his love and loyalties, his soul is free and cannot be caged by iron bars.

Answers

◆ Critical Thinking

1. Lucasta is Lovelace's true love; he is trying to convince her to accept his leaving her to go to war.
2. The "stronger faith" is his duty and honor to serve his king loyally in battle.
3. Prisons cannot bar from one's heart the freedom to love, to have friendships, and to be loyal to one's king.
4. Lovelace refers to "The sweetness, mercy, majesty, / And glories of my King."

◆ Reading Strategy

1. The Puritans had come into power, and thus the Royalists became political prisoners.
2. In defiance of his imprisonment, Lovelace glorifies his king in the third stanza.
3. (a) Women in seventeenth-century English society did not have rights equal to those of men, which men justified by their pious belief in the primal sin of Eve (and thus all women). (b) It gives a deeper understanding. This is not just a clever poem, but an argument to improve the status of women.

◆ Literary Focus

1. (a) The characters and plot are the same. (b) She explains Eve's motives for giving the fruit to Adam, and points out why Adam should have known better.
2. It provides a common point of reference.

◆ Build Vocabulary

1. A *breach of promise* is the breaking of a promise.
2. A *breach of the peace* is a violation of the peace.

Using the Word Bank

1. a 2. a 3. c

◆ Grammar and Style

Practice

1. Lanier put neither woman nor man before God.
2. Whether Lovelace was in prison or spending time with friends, he was able to feel free.
3. Both Lanier and Lovelace had strong opinions about politics.
4. Either you agree with Lovelace, or you agree with Lanier.
5. Lovelace was not only a poet but also a soldier.

Guide for Responding (continued)

◆ Critical Thinking

Interpret

1. What is Lovelace's relationship to Lucasta, and what is the purpose of his speech to her in "To Lucasta"? **[Hypothesize]**
2. What is the "stronger faith" Lovelace refers to in line 7 of "To Lucasta"? **[Interpret]**
3. Summarize Lovelace's conception of freedom in "To Althea." **[Interpret]**

Extend

4. What attitudes expressed in these poems mark Lovelace as a Royalist? **[Social Studies Link]**

◆ Reading Strategy

Use Historical Context

In reading about the **historical context** of Lovelace's poems, you learned that the poet came from the upper classes and was a favorite of Charles I at a time when the Royalist supporters of the king were in conflict with the Puritans. This information helps you appreciate that Lovelace's poem "To Althea, from Prison" is as much a political poem as it is a love poem.

1. Given the historical context, why do you think Lovelace was writing his poem from prison?
2. Which stanza of "To Althea" is a defiant expression of the poet's politics? Explain.
3. (a) What have you learned about the role of women in seventeenth-century English society? (b) How does that information add to your understanding of Lanier's poem "Eve's Apology"?

◆ Literary Focus

Tradition and Reform

Amelia Lanier was a radical in her day, but she drew on the widely known **tradition** of Biblical stories and beliefs to support her ideas.

1. Read the story of Adam and Eve in Genesis. (a) What elements of the story remain the same in her poem? (b)How does Lanier reinterpret the story in order to make her point?
2. How does Lanier's use of a Bible story make it easier for her to communicate with readers, even if they disagree with her arguments?

◆ Build Vocabulary

Using Terms with Breach

Use your knowledge of the word *breach* to define each of the italicized terms:

1. The woman sued her fiancé for a *breach of promise*.
2. The policewoman arrested the girls for a *breach of the peace*.

Using the Word Bank

In your notebook write the lettered word closest in meaning to the first word.

1. discretion: (a) prudence, (b) falseness, (c) speed
2. inconstancy: (a) faithlessness, (b) doubt, (c) anger
3. breach: (a) promise, (b) help, (c) violation

◆ Grammar and Style

Correlative Conjunctions

These writers use **correlative conjunctions**, pairs of conjunctions that link two words or groups of words both elegantly and economically. The words *both . . . and* in the previous sentence are correlative conjunctions. Other examples are *neither . . . nor, either . . . or, not so . . . as,* and *not only . . . but also.*

Practice In your notebook, copy these sentences and underline the correlative conjunctions in each.

1. Lanier put neither woman nor man before God.
2. Whether Lovelace was in prison or spending time with friends, he was able to feel free.
3. Both Lanier and Lovelace had strong opinions about politics.
4. Either you agree with Lovelace, or you agree with Lanier.
5. Lovelace was not only a poet but also a soldier.

Writing Application Use correlative conjunctions to combine these sentences.

1. Lanier believed that men had to take some of the responsibility for sin. She believed that women had to take some of the responsibility for sin.
2. Richard Lovelace wasn't only fighting for the King. He was fighting for honor.
3. Lanier was traditional in her poem. Lanier was radical in her poem.

Writing Application

Sample responses:

1. Lanier believed that both women and men had to take some of the responsibility for sin.
2. Richard Lovelace was fighting not only for the King, but also for honor.
3. Either Lanier was traditional in her poem, or she was radical.

Writer's Solution

For additional instruction and practice, use the lesson in the **Writing Lab CD-ROM** on Varying Sentence Structure and the page on Conjunctions in the *Writer's Solution Grammar Practice Book*, p. 13.

Build Your Portfolio

Idea Bank

Writing

1. **Editorial** Lanier's defense of women was, in a sense, an editorial. With your school or local newspaper in mind, write your own editorial about a current issue.

2. **Declaration of Parliament** As a member of the English Parliament, respond to the demands of Lovelace to reinstate absolute power to the King. **[Social Studies Link]**

3. **Response to Criticism** The critic Douglas Bush says that in Lovelace's best poems, he displays the Royalist values of "beauty, love, and loyal honor." Agree or disagree with this observation, citing specific passages from the poems.

Speaking and Listening

4. **Ballad** For several centuries people have written ballads designed to express points of view about social issues or current events. Write a simple rhymed song about a cause you want to support, and perform it for the class. **[Music Link]**

5. **Role Play** With a partner, perform a scene in which Lovelace departs from Lucasta to go to the wars. Have him express the sentiments he voices in "To Lucasta," and have her respond. **[Performing Arts Link]**

Projects

6. **Poster** As a seventeenth-century artist, design a poster that promotes the political beliefs of Lovelace or Lanier. **[Art Link]**

7. **Civil War** Research and report on the English Civil War of the seventeenth century. **[Social Studies Link]**

Writing Mini-Lesson

College Application

To capture their readers' interest and emphasize important points, these writers make bold and dramatic statements. They also link their ideas to traditions with which their audience is familiar. Use both these devices in writing a college application essay on how you would change the world. These tips will help you turn a ho-hum essay into a dramatic one.

Writing Skills Focus: Using Dramatic Effects

Speeches, poems, editorials, and many types of essays use dramatic effects to engage readers. For example, Amelia Lanier begins with a startlingly new take on an time-honored story:

Model From the Poem

But surely Adam cannot be excused;
Her fault though great, yet he was most to
 blame.
What weakness offered, strength might have
 refused;
Being Lord of all, the greater was his shame; . . .

This beginning must have startled readers, but it probably kept them reading as well.

Prewriting Think of a traditional idea or saying that you can slant in a surprising way. For example, if you want log-rolling included in the Olympics, you might say, "log-rolling is as American as apple pie, but it's also a sport that the whole world can enjoy."

Drafting Dramatize your subject with an unusual comparison. If you are proposing ways to change schools, for example, you might compare schools to something unusual, like circuses. However, be sure you can show that the comparison makes sense.

Revising Have classmates read your essay. In passages where their interest flags, try using an unusual comparison or a surprising take on a familiar saying.

✓ ASSESSMENT OPTIONS

Formal Assessment, Selection Test, pp. 102–104, and Assessment Resources Software. The selection test is designed so that it can be easily customized to the performance levels of your students.
Alternative Assessment, p. 21, includes options for less advanced students, more advanced students, interpersonal learners, verbal/linguistic learners, bodily/kinesthetic learners, intrapersonal learners, and visual/spatial learners.

PORTFOLIO ASSESSMENT
Use the following rubrics in the ***Alternative Assessment*** booklet to assess student writing:
Editorial: Critical Review Rubric, p. 112
Declaration of Parliament: Evaluation/Review Rubric, p. 105
Response to Criticism: Literary Analysis/Interpretation Rubric, p. 113
Writing Mini-Lesson: Expression Rubric, p. 95

Idea Bank

Customizing for *Performance Levels*
Following are suggestions for matching Idea Bank topics with your students' performance levels:
Less Advanced Students: 1, 6
Average Students: 2, 5, 7
More Advanced Students: 3, 4

Customize for *Learning Modalities*
Following are suggestions for matching Idea Bank topics with your students' learning modalities:
Visual/Spatial: 6
Interpersonal: 5
Verbal/Linguistic: 1, 2, 3, 4, 5, 7
Musical/Rhythmic: 4

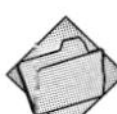

Writing Mini-Lesson

Refer students to the Writing Handbook, page 1189, for instructions on the writing process, and page 1191 for further information on exposition.

Writing and Language Transparencies To review the steps of the writing process for an essay, use Writing Process Model 1: Reflective Essay, pp. 5–11.

Writer's Solution

Writing Lab CD-ROM
Have students complete the tutorial on Exposition. Follow these steps:
1. Fill out the Audience and Purpose profiles to aid in identifying the audience and purpose for a college essay.
2. View the audio-annotated writing models on writing an introduction.
3. Draft on the computer.
4. Use the interactive instruction on promoting a purpose to get inspirations for revision.

Allow approximately 70 minutes of class time to complete these steps.

Sourcebook
Have students use Chapter 3, Exposition (pp. 63–95), for additional support. The chapter includes in-depth instruction on considering audience and purpose (pp. 78–79), organizing details (pp. 82–84), and writing the introduction, body, and conclusion of an exposition (pp. 85–86).

Prepare and Engage

OBJECTIVES

1. To read, comprehend, and interpret a scene from a play
2. To connect a play to the theme of "A Nation Divided"
3. To respond to a play through writing, speaking and listening, and projects

PORTFOLIO OPPORTUNITIES

Writing: Newspaper Article; Press Release; Retelling
Speaking and Listening: Panel Discussion
Project: Collage

More About the Author
Playwright Caryl Churchill was a young adult during the turbulent 1960's. Much of her work shows a socialist viewpoint, as well as an opposition to various abuses of power. Her work is often distinguished by its fresh language and dramatic innovations. Two of Churchill's plays, *Cloud Nine* and *Top Girls,* have won Obie awards, which are given to plays that are produced off-Broadway. These were about gender politics. Later plays have dealt with the financial excesses of the 1980's and the horrors of the Romanian revolution.

Ask students: What are the most important social issues today? Have students clarify and support their responses. Then explain that in the seventeenth century, as today, one of the biggest social issues was poverty. *Light Shining in Buckinghamshire* deals with one faction whose actions were designed to call attention to the plight of the poor and the need for land reform.

CONNECTIONS TO TODAY'S WORLD

from Light Shining in Buckinghamshire

Caryl Churchill

Thematic Connection

A Nation Divided

The writers in this section comment upon the political, social, and religious issues that divided England before, during, and after the Civil War. Milton's *Paradise Lost* includes passages that criticize the monarchy and express his religious values and beliefs. Lanier calls the public's attention to the unfair treatment of women, and Lovelace defiantly asserts his support for Charles I even from prison.

Amid all this conflict, splinter groups like the Diggers were formed to call attention to the plight of the oppressed. The Diggers believed that the English Civil Wars had been fought against the king and the great landowners. Now that Charles I had been executed, they demanded that land be made available for the very poor to cultivate and live on.

Injustice Today

Caryl Churchill's play *Light Shining in Buckinghamshire* is about the plight of the Diggers in the seventeenth century. She uses their plight to draw attention to oppression that continued after the Civil War. In this scene, Gerrard Winstanley, a founder of the Diggers, proclaims the group's right to freedom. Churchill uses the scene to expose the injustices suffered by the group and leaves a vivid impression of the hardships endured by the poor during the turbulent seventeenth century. Churchill wants to demonstrate how the inequities in seventeenth-century society resemble the injustices of our own time.

CARYL CHURCHILL

(1938–)

English dramatist and scriptwriter Caryl Churchill is one of the most successful female playwrights in British theater. Churchill's plays are known for their treatment of controversial issues, for their innovative use of casting and characters, and for their groundbreaking dramatic structure.

Among Churchill's most famous plays are *Cloud Nine* (1978), *Top Girls* (1980–82), and *Serious Money* (1987). In addition to stage plays, Churchill has also written several television and radio plays.

Customize for
Less Proficient Readers
Help students by explaining the main purpose of various sections. For instance, the first speech tells how the Diggers formed. The second explains their philosophy. The numbered actors list the sufferings that the Diggers endured.

Customize for
Verbal/Linguistic Learners
Since this is a short piece, you might want to suggest that seven students line up in front of the class. As each character speaks, a student can step forward and read the lines. Then the student can step back while another comes forward.

Prentice Hall Literature Program Resources

REINFORCE / RETEACH / EXTEND

Selection Support Pages
Build Vocabulary, p. 104
Thematic and Literary Connections, p. 105

Formal Assessment, Selection Test, pp. 106–107; Assessment Resources Software

Resource Pro CD-ROM
from Light Shining in Buckinghamshire—*includes all* resource material and customizable lesson plan

Listening to Literature Audiocassettes
from *Light Shining in Buckinghamshire*

from Light Shining in Buckinghamshire

Caryl Churchill

CONNECTIONS TO TODAY'S WORLD

ACT TWO DIGGERS

ONE OF THE ACTORS [*announces*]: Information of Henry Sanders, Walton-upon-Thames, April the sixteenth, sixteen hundred and forty-nine.

One Everard, Gerrard Winstanley, and three more, all living at Cobham, came to St. George's Hill in Surrey and began to dig, and sowed the ground with parsnips and carrots and beans. By Friday last they were increased in number to twenty or thirty. They invite all to come in and help them, and promise them meat, drink and clothes.

WINSTANLEY [*announces*]: The true Levellers' standard advanced, sixteen hundred and forty-nine:

A declaration to the powers of England and to all the powers of the world, showing the cause why the common people of England have begun to dig up, manure and sow corn upon George Hill in Surrey. Take notice that England is not a free people till the poor that have no land have a free allowance to dig and labor the
❶ commons. It is the sword that brought in property and holds it up, and everyone
❷ upon recovery of the conquest ought to return into freedom again, or what benefit have the common people got by the victory over the king?

All men have stood for freedom; and now the common enemy has gone you are all like men in a mist, seeking for freedom, and know not where it is: and those of the richer sort of you that see it are afraid to own it. For freedom is the man that will turn the world upside down, therefore no wonder he hath enemies.

True freedom lies where a man receives
❸ his nourishment and that is in the use of the earth. A man had better have no body than have no food for it. True freedom lies in the true enjoyment of the earth. True religion and undefiled is to let every one quietly have earth to manure. There can be no universal liberty till this universal community be established. ❸

1ST ACTOR [*announces*]: A Bill of Account of the most remarkable sufferings that the Diggers have met with since they began to dig the commons for the poor on George Hill in Surrey.

2ND ACTOR: We were fetched by above a hundred people who took away our spades, and some of them we never had again and taken to prison at Walton.

3RD ACTOR: The dragonly enemy pulled down a house we had built and cut our spades to pieces.

4TH ACTOR: One of us had his head sore wounded, and a boy beaten. Some of us were beaten by the gentlemen, the sherriff looking on, and afterwards five were taken to White Lion prison and kept there about five weeks.

5TH ACTOR: We had all our corn spoilt, for the enemy was so mad that they tumbled the earth up and down and would suffer no corn to grow.

6TH ACTOR: Next day two soldiers and two or three men sent by the parson pulled down another house and turned an old man and his wife out of doors to lie in the field on a cold night.

1ST ACTOR: It is understood the General gave his consent that the soldiers should come to help beat off the Diggers, and it is true the soldiers came with the gentle- ❹
men and caused others to pull down our houses; but I think the soldiers were sorry to see what was done.

Clarification In this context, *corn,* mentioned by the 5th Actor, refers to any kind of seed or grain, not just maize.

◆ Critical Thinking

❹ **Hypothesize** Ask students: Why might the soldiers have sympathized with the Diggers? *Sample responses: Because the soldiers are not rich, they can identify with the Diggers; the soldiers felt bad about pulling down people's homes; the soldiers thought that the Diggers were being treated too harshly. Other answers are possible.*

Develop Understanding

This excerpt sums up the ideas of and some of the reaction to the Diggers, a seventeenth-century group that believed that the landless poor should be allowed to farm the commons. They got their name from their practice of digging to plant crops. They were harshly treated by the authorities as a result of their actions. You may want to point out to students that during the 1960's, a California group who shared many of this group's ideas also called itself the Diggers. As part of a counter-culture experiment, the group distributed free food, some through a free store.

Customize for *English Language Learners*

❶ Students may be unfamiliar with the use of *common* as a noun. Explain that a common is a tract of open land that is owned and used by all the inhabitants in a place. In many towns in England and New England, a common is a large, centrally located park often used for public gatherings.

Thematic Connection

❷ **A Nation Divided** Direct students' attention to this passage. Ask them to identify the ways in which England is a nation divided. *England is divided politically between the defeated Cavaliers and the victorious Puritans. It is also divided socially between property-owners and the poor.*

◆ *Literature and Your Life*

❸ Have students summarize the Diggers' view on the nature of freedom. *The Diggers believed that true freedom comes from being able to cultivate land of one's own.* Encourage students to discuss their own ideas about freedom and to contrast their views with those of the Diggers. *As products of a technologically advanced age, students are unlikely to associate agriculture with freedom. However, they will sympathize with the broader idea that freedom involves the right to be able to make a living.*

Reinforce and Extend

Answers

◆ *Literature and Your Life*

Reader's Response Students may observe that the Diggers did not have a legal right to the land, but they may have had a moral right.

Thematic Focus The poor are more likely to live in urban areas and to receive assistance from the government. However, they still face danger (although from crime rather than soldiers), hopelessness, and a sense of disenfranchisement.

☑ Check Your Comprehension

1. The Diggers had built houses and planted corn.
2. The sheriff and soldiers tore down their houses, broke up their spades, spoiled their corn, beat up several of them, took many to prison, and left an old man and his wife to lie in the cold all night.

◆ Critical Thinking

Interpret

1. Freedom disturbs the *status quo,* and therefore is not welcomed by everyone.
2. The Diggers believed that unless there was freedom for the poorest man to support himself, there is no freedom for all.
3. Winstanley's ideas of freedom are basic to the survival of the common people to support themselves.

Thematic Connection

1. (a) Milton raises a problem with freedom: it might *not* be better to reign in Hell than to serve in Heaven. Lanier's poem suggests that men and women should be equals, or at least that women should not be subjugated by men because of the story of Eve. Lovelace's poem expresses the need for freedom to voice political loyalties. Churchill's play deals with the freedom to own land and be able to support oneself. (b) Students should point out ways in which their notions of freedom compare to the authors'.
2. Suggested responses: The countries should create a constitution that supports human rights; the government must act to help the poor and preserve the rights of all; there must be checks and balances in the political system.

Guide for Responding

◆ *Literature and Your Life*

Reader's Response Were the Diggers entitled to freely cultivate the land of England? Explain.

Thematic Focus How have the problems of England's poor changed since the seventeenth century?

☑ Check Your Comprehension

1. What were people doing at St. George's Hill?
2. What injustices were suffered by the Diggers?

◆ Critical Thinking

INTERPRET

1. What is meant by "For freedom is the man that will turn the world upside down, therefore no wonder he hath enemies"? **[Interpret]**
2. How does this support the belief of the Diggers that all people are entitled to the land? **[Support]**
3. Compare and contrast Winstanley's ideas of freedom with those of the common people. **[Compare and Contrast]**

Thematic Connection

A NATION DIVIDED

The authors of the selections in this section have opposing viewpoints. For example, while Milton supported the Commonwealth, Royalists like Lovelace supported the monarchy. In countries that treasure freedom, people still have opposing views on many different issues. Although these viewpoints may not divide the nation, they often upset communities and greatly change people's relationships and outlook.

1. (a) How do the authors in this section treat the subject of equality and freedom? (b) Compare and contrast your definition of freedom with the definitions given or suggested by these authors.
2. The former colonies of England, such as India, Trinidad, West Indies, and Jamaica, now find themselves free from England's rule. What do you think a country should do in re-establishing itself as a "free" country?

Idea Bank

Writing

1. **Newspaper Article** As a seventeenth century reporter, write a brief newspaper article based on the scene from *Light Shining in Buckinghamshire.*
2. **Press Release** As a politician, prepare a press release that addresses the issues involving the Diggers that are depicted in Churchill's play. The release should be an attempt to calm temperaments not incite more trouble.
3. **Retelling** Rewrite this scene so it is based on a current-day controversial issue. Define the viewpoint of your characters, and use dialogue to reveal any injustices suffered.

Speaking and Listening

4. **Panel Discussion** Create a panel of historical freedom fighters. Each member should research the person he or she is to portray. Have your classmates ask each panel member questions that pertain to his or her historical struggles. **[Social Studies Link]**

Project

5. **Collage** Create a collage that illustrates your own personal definition of freedom. You may choose poems or songs that also present your ideas on freedom to accompany the collage. **[Art Link]**

Idea Bank

Customizing for *Performance Levels*

Following are suggestions for matching Idea Bank topics with your students' performance levels:
Less Advanced Students: 1, 5; Average Students: 2, 4; More Advanced Students: 3

Customizing for *Learning Modalities*

Following are suggestions for matching Idea Bank topics with your students' learning modalities:
Visual/Spatial: 5; Verbal/Linguistic: 1, 2, 3, 4

☑ ASSESSMENT OPTIONS

Formal Assessment, Selection Test, pp. 105–106, and Assessment Resources Software. The selection test is designed so that it can be easily customized to the performance levels of your students.

PORTFOLIO ASSESSMENT

Use the following rubrics in the ***Alternative Assessment*** booklet to assess student writing:
Newspaper Article: Summary Rubric, p. 99
Press Release: Persuasion Rubric, p. 106
Retelling: Drama Rubric, p. 110

Writing Process Workshop

Autobiographical Incident

The writers in this section express feelings, thoughts, and insights about their personal experiences. Invite readers to learn more about you by writing an autobiographical incident—a real-life story of something you experienced.

When writing an **autobiographical incident**, tell your story using the first-person point of view and refer to yourself using the pronouns *I* and *me*. The following skills will help you write about an autobiographical incident:

Writing Skills Focus

- ▶ **Maintain a consistent point of view** by presenting events from one perspective. Being consistent will help readers follow the events in your incident. (See p. 443.)
- ▶ **Use dramatic effects,** such as startling facts or unusual perspectives, to capture your audience's attention and emphasize important points. (See p. 451.)
- ▶ A **personal tone** will help you express feelings, thoughts, and insights about your experiences.

These skills are evident in the passage from Fanny Burney's *Diary,* which is excerpted below. In the excerpt, Burney relates an autobiographical incident, in which the author observed Dr. Samuel Johnson, who wrote *A Dictionary of the English Language,* reacting violently to criticism of his writings.

Fanny Burney (1752–1840)

Model From Literature

from *The Diary of Fanny Burney*

I ① was quite frightened to hear my own name mentioned in a debate which began so seriously; but Dr. Johnson made not this any answer: he repeated his attack and his challenge, and a violent disputation ensued, in which this great but mortal man did, to own the truth, appear unreasonably furious and grossly severe ②. I never saw him so before, and I heartily hope I never shall again ③.

① Burney consistently uses the pronoun *I* to indicate the first-person viewpoint from which the story is told.

② This vivid description of Johnson's temper emphasizes the dramatic effect of the situation.

③ By revealing her innermost feelings, Burney gives this incident a personal tone.

Humanities: Art

Self-Portraits An autobiographical incident is a kind of self-portrait. Explain to students that, since the Renaissance, many painters have painted pictures of themselves. The self-portraits of Rembrandt and Van Gogh, for instance, are among their most famous pieces of work. The increase in self-portraiture reflects the changing status of arts and artists.

In the Middle Ages, artists worked as anonymous craftsmen who created to glorify God. By the end of the Renaissance, the status of the artist and the subject-matter of art was changing. Artists such as Michaelangelo achieved a new status as visionaries.

At about this same time, paintings celebrated the lives of the middle class. Self-portraiture reflected both art's turn to life in this world for its subject matter, and perhaps to new ideas of the importance of the artist as well.

Ask students to speculate about how a self-portrait might present a special challenge to an artist. *Suggested response: Vanity can make it difficult for people to see themselves as they are.*

Prepare and Engage

Establish Writing Guidelines
Introduce students to the following key elements of an autobiographical incident before beginning this lesson:

- An autobiographical incident tells a story about an experience of the author's, one which sheds light on an important aspect of the writer's life.
- By expressing reactions to events as well as reporting events dramatically the writer creates a personal tone that works to keep the reader interested in the narrative.

Review with students the criteria in the Scoring Rubric for a personal narrative in ***Alternative Assessment,*** p. 97. See the suggestions on page 457 for additional criteria to customize the rubric to this workshop.

Refer students to the Writing Handbook, p. 1189, for instruction in the writing process, and to page 1191 for further information on narration.

Writer's Solution

Writers at Work Videodisc
To let students share the insights of an accomplished narrative writer, play the videodisc segment featuring James Berry. Then ask students: What elements of narrative does Berry emphasize?

Play frames 11464 to 21147

Writing Lab CD-ROM
Have students who wish to write their narrative on the computer work in the tutorial for Narration. They should follow these steps:

1. Review the annotated model of an autobiographical incident and the evaluation guidelines in the About Narration section.
2. Use the Chain of Events organizer under Developing Narrative Elements for help organizing the events of their incident.
3. Draft their editorial on computer, referring to the audio-annotated writing models for different examples of narrative organization.
4. Use the interactive writing models on dialogue and setting under Revising and Editing.

Sourcebook
For additional help with writing an editorial, students can review Chapter 2, Narration, pages 30–61.

Develop Student Writing

Prewriting

To help students choose a topic, ask them to imagine that they are talking to a friend they have not seen since kindergarten. What defining events or periods will they feel they simply must tell their old friend about?

Drafting

Invite students to experiment with a few different starting points for their narrative. An intriguing description of a character, situation, or setting; an enigmatic bit of dialogue; or a strong thematic statement can all make effective starting points.

Writer's Solution

Writers at Work Videodisc

Play the videodisc sections in which James Berry discusses developing narrative elements. Ask students the following questions: How does it help Berry to "hear" characters' voices in his head? How would this approach work for an autobiographical incident?

Play frames 15185 to 17838

Connect to Literature Students will find an amusing example of an autobiographical incident in the excerpt from James Boswell's *Life of Johnson*, p. 510. Ask them to pay special attention to the way in which Boswell conveys his admiration for Johnson indirectly, through incident and word choice, rather than through direct statements.

Writer's Solution

Writing Lab CD-ROM

Have students consult the audio-annotated models for examples of narratives that begin with a character, a setting, a situation, or an action.

Applying Language Skills

Agreement With Indefinite Pronouns Explain to students that indefinite pronouns are small but crucial tools for formulating generalizations; used improperly, they will distract the reader from the point being made.

Applying Language Skills: Agreement With Indefinite Pronouns

Because indefinite pronouns vary in number, they can cause problems in agreement.

Always Singular:

another, either, neither, other, anybody, no one, everyone, anything, each, someone, everybody

Always Plural:

both, few, many, several

Can be Singular or Plural:

all, some, any, most, none, enough, more, plenty

Practice Complete the following sentences with the correct verb.

1. All the athletes (is/are) varsity.
2. Few of these people (has/have) acrophobia.
3. Each of the actors (was/were) talented.

Writing Application Check your paper for possible errors in agreement.

Writer's Solution Connection Writing Lab

For help in organizing your writing, review the audio-annotated writing models of types of organization in the Drafting section of the Narration tutorial.

Prewriting

Choose a Topic If you keep a diary, look through it to find a writing idea. If you do not keep a diary, recall humorous, unexpected, interesting, or strange situations in which you've found yourself. Consider the following topics for your autobiographical incident:

Topic Ideas

- Your most recent birthday
- A lesson learned
- A time of hardship

Create a Personal Tone Jot down some details about the incident that uniquely reveal your personal thoughts and insights. For example, take notes about what you saw, heard, thought, and felt during the incident you're describing.

Plan Dramatic Effects Identify the high point of your autobiographical incident. Then jot down interesting comparisons, vivid images, or startling details that spring to mind when you relive it.

Drafting

Maintain a Consistent Point of View As you draft, maintain a consistent perspective. Keep in mind that you, as the narrator, are participating in the action. Refer only to incidents as you see, feel, hear, or participate in them.

Create a Personal Tone Review the notes you took during prewriting, and create a personal tone as you draft. Avoid clichés and neutral observations, and let your unique standpoint shine through. To do this, use personal pronouns such as *I, me, my, mine,* and include dialogue where appropriate. Also give information that makes the story uniquely yours.

> **Neutral Tone:** Aunt Sophia opened the door and let me in.
>
> **Personal Tone:** My dearest Auntie Sophie greeted me with an excited "Hiya!"

Build Dramatic Effects As you write your autobiographical incident, use dramatic effects to lead up to, and describe, the high point of your story.

> **No Dramatic Effects:** I scored the winning touchdown.
>
> **Dramatic Effects:** As the audience roared, I sprinted past the goal posts, scoring the winning touchdown!

Practice

1. All the athletes *are* varsity.
2. Few of these people *have* acrophobia.
3. Each of the actors *was* talented.

Writer's Solution

Have students who need additional help with indefinite pronouns and subject-verb agreement complete the **Language Lab CD-ROM** lesson on Special Problems in Agreement in the Subject-Verb Agreement Unit. Students may also complete the worksheet on page 63 in the *Writer's Solution Grammar Practice Book.*

Applying Language Skills

Appositive Phrases

Explain to students that appositive phrases are especially effective for providing readers with context without interrupting the narrative flow.

Answers

1. Jackie and Philippa, Jackie's best friend, sang together.
2. The house, an architectural marvel, was built in the last century.
3. We saw Tough Jackets, the nation's best-selling rock band.
4. Our guests, Eric and Trudy, left early.

Revising

Look Critically at What You Have Written Ask yourself, "If this wasn't my own story, would I find it interesting?" Be sure you have included details that create a personal tone and capture your readers' attention.

Ask a Peer Reviewer Ask a peer to read your autobiographical incident and mark places where the point of view was inconsistent or events were confusing. Then revise your incident so it flows smoothly.

Revision Model

Seeing pictures of the ocean reminds me of a family vacation my family took when I was eleven years old. ~~They~~ ① We went during the summer; ② , during a sweltering, record-breaking summer right after Independence Day. We spent several days sitting on the beach and splashing in the surprisingly cool ocean. ~~We walked down the boardwalk for ice cream every night.~~ ③ Indulging our passion for ice cream, we went each evening to Coneheads, an ice cream parlor on the boardwalk.

① The writer changed *they* to *we* to maintain a consistent point of view.

② The writer added this detail to create a dramatic effect.

③ The writer revised an impersonal sentence to give it a more personal tone.

Publishing

- **Home** Compile a scrapbook focusing on a specific time in your life. Start with your autobiographical incident, and include pictures and other memorabilia.
- **School** Organize a storytelling festival at your school. Select a theme, for example: *Taking the Driver's Exam*. Have several classmates relate their own experience. Videotape the festival.
- **Classroom Collection** Collect and bind together autobiographical incidents of your classmates. You may sort them according to theme, time period, or another organizational method.

Applying Language Skills: Appositive Phrases

An appositive phrase is a noun or pronoun with modifiers that is placed next to a noun or pronoun to add information or detail.

Examples:
Virginia Trask, my mother's aunt, voted in every national election from 1921 to 1994.

Practice Identify the appositive phrase in each sentence.

1. Jackie and Philippa, Jackie's best friend, sang together.
2. The house, an architectural marvel, was built in the last century.
3. We saw Tough Jackets, the nation's best-selling rock band.
4. Our guests, Eric and Trudy, left early.

Writing Application Check your autobiographical incident for places where appositive phrases may provide more information.

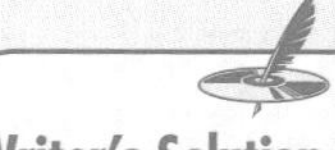

Writer's Solution Connection Writing Lab

For help in making your writing more interesting, review the Sensory Details Word Bins in the Revising and Editing section of the Narration tutorial.

Revising

Peer review can be particularly important when the subject of a narrative is the writer's own experience. As an alternative to peer review, have students put aside their drafts for a few days, then reread them quickly, noting places where they must call on their memories to understand their own words. Ask them to revise such sections for clarity.

Customize for ***Bodily/Kinesthetic Learners***
Suggest to these learners that they review the physical sensations and movements their story involves. To recover these details, they might even act out parts of the story in exaggerated pantomime.

Writing Lab CD-ROM
Ask peer reviewers to use the Peer Evaluation Checklist in the Revising and Editing section.

Writing and Language Transparencies Walk students through Writing Process Model 3, Personal Narrative, pp. 17–23.

Publishing

Students may not be as ready to share an autobiographical incident as they might be to share other kinds of writing. Suggest that students use their autobiographical incident as the first entry in a private journal.

Reinforce and Extend

Reflect on Style and Substance
Ask students to discuss the relation between substance and style in the autobiographical incidents they have written and (if applicable) reviewed. What approaches would they suggest to next year's students?

ASSESSMENT		4	3	2	1
PORTFOLIO ASSESSMENT Use the Scoring Rubric for a personal narrative in ***Alternative Assessment***, p. 97, and add the following criteria to customize it to this assignment.	**Dramatic Effects**	The writer uses dramatic effects to sustain the reader's interest.	The writer uses some dramatic effects to sustain the reader's interest.	The writer occasionally uses dramatic effects to sustain the reader's interest.	The writer does not use dramatic effects, or those used are not integrated with the rest of the piece.
	Creating a Personal Tone	The writer tells the story in a distinctive voice, "centered" in the narrator's situation and character.	The narrative voice is lively and descriptions are vivid.	Some of the descriptions are vivid, and some of the dialogue is convincing.	The writer does not incorporate any personal touches to help the audience see the work as a whole.

Introduce the Strategy

Ask students to name their favorite courtroom drama or police procedural in movies or on television. Have them reconstruct a typical scene in which opposing lawyers give their summations to the jury. If the defendant is a young, pretty mother, what words will her own lawyer use to describe her? What qualities will the opposing lawyer try to attribute to her? Lawyers use description strategically, because they know that the way in which a person or event is *described* can have a big effect on how the person or event is *judged.*

Customize for
Bodily/Kinesthetic Learners
Invite these students to read the model editorial out loud. After they read it once, coach them in the use of gestures, facial expressions, and a tone of voice suited to the words. Encourage them to focus on words and phrases they can act out or underscore with gesture, such as *knuckling under, revealing,* and *sudden.* Then have them read the passage again, putting the expressive resources of their body to work.

Apply the Strategy

Answers

1. (a) The topic at issue is a school district's plans to condemn property. (b) The writer favors one viewpoint. (c) The writer favors-the homeowners.
2. (a) Homeowners affected by the plan are presented favorably. (b) The phrases "knuckling under" and "sudden measure" implies that the plan is being promoted in an unfair way. The writer depicts homeowners as innocent victims, wronged by not being given a chance to be heard.
3. Sample answer: After consulting with the state legislature, the school board announced that it plans to expand school facilities, in part through the appropriation of some private property. A few of the affected property owners have been heard to complain, but the proposal, part of a $25 million school bond issue, has the support of a number of farsighted state legislators.

Recognizing Bias in Articles
Real-World Reading Skills Workshop

Strategies for Success

We tend to think that newspaper and magazine articles report the facts. However, writers may word facts to create a bias in favor of one point of view. Certain signs can help you recognize bias.

Identify Different Points of View Many subjects, especially controversial ones, can be approached from different angles. Decide whether the subject of the article is one about which people hold different opinions. Check to see if one side seems to be favored more than the others.

Look for Biases in Characterization A writer may present one group of people as more normal or acceptable, in hopes that you'll identify with their point of view. Look for descriptions that portray people on one side of an issue more sympathetically than people on the other side.

Look for Loaded Language Look for words or phrases that spark an emotional response, such as "horrible conditions" or "as innocent as a child," especially when such charged words replace objective evidence.

Here are other forms of writing that often call for recognizing bias:
- Campaign literature
- Editorials
- Textbooks

Apply the Strategies

Use your reading skills to detect bias in this article.

NEWS CHRONICLE
NEWS CHRONICLES Section II February 19, 1984

SCHOOL BOARD CONDEMNS HOUSES

Knuckling under to a few misguided state legislators, the school board revealed that it plans to condemn private property and homes worth $10 million for expansion of school facilities. One homeowner affected by this sudden measure declared, "We never had a chance to state our case." The condemnation would be part of a $25 million school bond issue going before voters this November.

1. (a) What is the topic at issue? (b) Does the writer favor one point of view? (c) Which one?
2. (a) Which group of people does the writer present more favorably? (b) Which words or images contribute to this impression? Explain.
3. Rewrite this paragraph, keeping the same facts, but introducing a bias in the opposite direction.

Beyond the Classroom

Career Connection

Lawyers Explain to students that the American legal system is adversarial—each case is presented before the court by two opposing sides, each of which calls and examines witnesses. In Europe, by contrast, a judge may have sole responsibility for questioning witnesses at a trial. Although in America lawyers are forbidden to conceal evidence, encourage perjury, or abet crimes, they are expected to be—and paid to be—biased.

To do their job effectively, lawyers often use charged language when questioning witnesses and when making statements at the opening and conclusion of a trial. Through such language, a lawyer creates a clear, believable picture of the people and events in a case, one favorable to the side he or she represents.

Part 3 *The Ties That Bind*

Illustration From *Gulliver's Travels*

One-Minute Planning Guide

The selections in this section all reveal or comment on the ties that bind together a family, community, or nation. Samuel Pepys's *Diary* provides a firsthand glimpse of how citizens of London pulled together as they dealt with two terrible disasters that struck in the mid-1600's: the bubonic plague and the Great Fire.

Although Defoe's *A Journal of the Plague Year* is a work of fiction, it contains profound and heartbreaking insights into the effects the bubonic plague had on families and communities.

Jonathan Swift, too, through his satiric *Gulliver's Travels,* reveals how, for better or worse, religious and national identities and affiliations inform the actions and thoughts of congregations and citizenry.

Customize for Varying Student Needs

When assigning the selections in this part, keep in mind these factors:

Pepys's *Diary*
- Diary entries; short excerpts
- Pepys's shorthand and vocabulary may be challenging for less proficient readers
- Real-life account of plague and fire may be highly interesting to students

Defoe's *A Journal of the Plague Year*
- Gruesome descriptions may offend some readers and be highly interesting to others
- Short prose piece

Swift's *Gulliver's Travels*
- Students may already be familiar with the character Gulliver
- Medium-length prose work
- Historical set-up may be necessary prior to reading

Humanities: Art

Illustration From *Gulliver's Travels*.

Explain to students that this illustration depicts Lemuel Gulliver of *Gulliver's Travels* in Lilliput. He is surrounded by people of small stature and is tethered to the ground with ropes and stakes.

Point out to students that the theme of this section, "The Ties That Bind," has several levels of meaning. Have your students link the art to this theme by answering the following questions:

1. In what ways is Gulliver literally bound? In what other ways might he be bound? *Sample responses: Gulliver is literally bound by the cords or ropes tethering him to the ground. He may be figuratively bound in that he could probably escape from his situation but not from himself. He could be bound by a code of honor or vow of silence.*
2. What ideas does the image of a large man bound by many small people suggest to you? *Sample answer: It suggests the idea of a tyrant being brought down by the united force of (or ties among) less powerful people.*

Prepare and Engage

OBJECTIVES

1. To interpret and respond to writings about historical events
2. To relate writings about historical events to personal experience
3. To use details to draw conclusions
4. To identify the characteristics of diaries and journals
5. To build vocabulary in context and learn the prefix *dis-*
6. To identify gerunds and the ways in which they're used
7. To write a diary entry using accurate details
8. To respond to writings about historical events through writing, speaking and listening, and projects

SKILLS INSTRUCTION

Vocabulary: Prefixes: *dis-*
Grammar: Gerunds
Reading Strategy: Draw Conclusions
Literary Focus: Diary or Journal
Writing: Accuracy
Speaking and Listening: Town Crier (teacher edition)
Critical Viewing: Connect; Infer; Make a Judgment

PORTFOLIO OPPORTUNITIES

Writing: Poster; News Report; Response to Criticism
Writing Mini-Lesson: Diary Entry
Speaking and Listening: Town Crier; Oral Report
Projects: Map; Timeline of Plagues

More About the Authors

Samuel Pepys was described as a "very worthy, industrious, and curious person." His diary touched not only on the major events of his day, but on the day-to-day details that, three hundred years later, still fascinate readers.

Daniel Defoe was also a keen chronicler of his day. Between 1704 and 1713, he put out a periodical called *The Review,* which was a forerunner of modern newspapers. Defoe was a literary groundbreaker. Besides being credited with shaping the modern realistic novel, he was the first writer of ghost stories in modern English literature.

Guide for Interpreting

Samuel Pepys (1633–1703)

Samuel Pepys (pēps) is an unusual literary celebrity. Not only does his fame rest on a single work but that work was never intended for publication! The work in question is Pepys's diary, which he wrote in shorthand and in his own private code. Undeciphered until the nineteenth century, the Diary provides a fascinating glimpse of London from 1660 to 1669, when Pepys's failing eyesight forced him to abandon the project.

An Ideal Observer Pepys was in a good position to report on the era. The son of a London tailor, he attended Cambridge University and after graduation became the secretary of his influential cousin, the Earl of Sandwich. In 1660, the year the monarchy was restored, he got his first government post as a clerk for the navy. From there, his rise to fame and fortune was rapid, though not always smooth. Twice his political connections made him a prisoner in the Tower of London, once on charges of treason. Despite these setbacks, Pepys earned a lasting reputation as a man of intelligence and a keen observer.

Daniel Defoe (1660–1731)

"A false, shuffling, prevaricating rascal"— that was how fellow author Joseph Addison described Daniel Defoe. In many ways, Addison was not far wrong. Constantly in debt, Defoe often engaged in shady business deals and declared bankruptcy in 1692, owing a small fortune to his creditors. He was also a sometime government spy and propagandist who even upgraded his own name, originally Foe, by adding an aristocratic De.

An Innovative Novelist Despite all these flaws, we remember Defoe for an important literary achievement. He practically invented the modern realistic novel. He did so with a handful of works published around his sixtieth birthday: *Robinson Crusoe* (1719), his almost documentary narrative of a man marooned on a desert island; *Moll Flanders* (1722), a satirical tale of a lowborn woman seeking respectability; and *A Journal of the Plague Year* (1722), his fictional journal of the great plague that devastated England in 1664–1665, "the plague year."

◆ Background for Understanding

HISTORY: TWIN DISASTERS

In the 1660's, following years of upheaval and a short period of peace, London was struck by twin disasters. The first of these was a plague that began in 1664 and by the next year killed nearly 70,000 Londoners—in a population of about 460,000.

A usually fatal infectious disease, bubonic plague is spread by fleas from an infected host, such as the black rat. Then, in 1666, just as the city was beginning to recover, the Great Fire of London broke out, destroying more than 13,000 buildings.

Like the plague, the Great Fire of London also had a devastating effect on London.

You will read about these disasters in two unusual literary works, a novel about the plague that is written in journal form, and an actual diary that contains an account of the plague and the Great Fire of London.

The Great Fire of London, 1666

Prentice Hall Literature Program Resources

REINFORCE / RETEACH / EXTEND

Selection Support Pages
Build Vocabulary: Prefixes: *dis-*, p. 106
Grammar and Style: Gerunds, p. 107
Reading Strategy: Draw Conclusions, p. 108
Literary Focus: Diary or Journal, p. 109

Strategies for Diverse Student Needs, p. 22

Beyond Literature
Science Connection: Epidemics, p. 22

Formal Assessment Selection Test, pp. 101–103; Assessment Resources Software

Alternative Assessment, p. 22

Writing and Language Transparencies
Daily Language Practice, Weeks 17 and 18, pp. 152 and 153

Resource Pro CD-ROM
Includes all resource material and customizable lesson plan

Listening to Literature Audiocassettes
from *The Diary* and *A Journal of the Plague Year*

Looking at Literature Videodisc
Chapter 6: Modern-Day Plagues

◆ from The Diary ◆ from A Journal of the Plague Year

◆ Literature and Your Life

CONNECT YOUR EXPERIENCE

Despite the best efforts of scientists and doctors, disasters and diseases still threaten us. Although, on average, we may live longer than our ancestors, we're not yet germproof or fireproof. As you read this diary and journal, you will become familiar with two disasters that threatened seventeenth-century England, the bubonic plague and the Great Fire of London.

Journal Writing Jot down in your journal any unfortunate events that you've experienced or seen reported on television.

THEMATIC FOCUS: THE TIES THAT BIND

Although misfortunes strike at human relationships, they may strengthen emotional ties. As you read, look for evidence of compassion on the part of Pepys and the narrator of Defoe's *Journal.*

◆ Literary Focus

DIARY OR JOURNAL

A **diary** or **journal** is a daily account of a writer's experiences and reactions. The words *diary* and *journal* are from the Latin (*dies*) and French (*jour*) words for "day" respectively. Most diaries or journals record the small details of a life, but diaries that become literature provide insights into important historical events or periods.

Pepys's *Diary* describes not only his personal life but also historical events that he witnessed, like the bubonic plague and the Great Fire of London. Defoe's *Journal of the Plague Year* is actually a well-researched novel posing as a journal to make it seem more realistic.

◆ Grammar and Style

GERUNDS

In Pepys's *Diary* and Defoe's *Journal,* you'll find many examples of **gerunds,** verb forms that end in *-ing* and function as nouns. Gerunds can be preceded by articles, as nouns are.

> Church being done, my Lord Bruncker, Sir J. Minnes, and I up to the vestry . . . in order to the *doing* something for the *keeping* of the plague from *growing.*

As you read, note the different ways gerunds are used.

◆ Reading Strategy

DRAW CONCLUSIONS

You can learn more about a person or a period by using given details to **draw conclusions.** As you read, keep a chart of details from the selections and conclusions that you draw from them.

The Diary	Conclusions
"I had appointed a boat to attend me. . . ."	Pepys was probably fairly rich since he could hire his own boat.

◆ Build Vocabulary

PREFIXES: *dis-*

In *A Journal of the Plague Year* you'll see the word *distemper*, a term for an infectious disease. Its prefix *dis-,* which means "apart," combines with *temper,* meaning "balance," to suggest the imbalance of the disease.

WORD BANK

Before you read, preview this list of words from the selections.

apprehensions
abated
lamentable
combustible
malicious
discoursing
distemper
importuning
prodigious

Ask students to name disaster movies they have seen or know about. Point out that disaster movies have large audiences partly because they provide safety for the audience while showing them dangerous and exciting events. With the exception of science fiction films, most disaster movies are based on events that could or did actually happen, such as shipwrecks or volcanic eruptions. The two selections in this group are the disaster stories of their time. Based on two real and awful events—the deadly plague of 1665 and the great London fire that followed a year later—these selections provide unforgettable images of the horror that real people faced.

Customize for
More Advanced Students
Have students focus on the level of detail that each writer includes—one of the reasons that these two works have maintained their popularity. Suggest that students make a mental note of each time a writer answers one of the questions journalists are trained to ask: who? what? when? where? and why?

Customize for
Intrapersonal Learners
Suggest that students imagine how they would have reacted had they lived during the plague or fire. Remind them that medicine was helpless in the face of the plague, and that firefighting techniques were almost nonexistent. As they read, encourage these learners to use their insights about the human condition to understand the experiences of Pepys and the narrator of *A Journal of the Plague Year.*

Preparing for Standardized Tests

Reading and Vocabulary Many tests of reading comprehension ask students to draw conclusions based on material in a passage. For example,

> Lady Batten's cart arrived at about four A.M. Into it Pepys was able to toss his money, his silver, and his "best things" before clambering in himself, still dressed in his nightgown.

The author seems to suggest that: *(C)*

(A) the cart was small.
(B) Pepys was lazy.
(C) Pepys was in a hurry.
(D) the nightgown was warm.

The Reading Strategy focuses on the skill of drawing conclusions. For additional practice, use the Reading Strategy page in ***Selection Support,*** p. 108.

Grammar and Language Because tests of English usage may require students to identify parts of speech, knowledge that gerunds serve as nouns will help them. The Grammar and Style lesson for this selection focuses on gerunds. For additional practice, use the Grammar and Style page on Gerunds, p. 107, in ***Selection Support***.

Develop Understanding

One-Minute Insight Samuel Pepys wrote his diary in code, confident that it would not be read by prying eyes. The diary has remained popular because it shows an extraordinarily honest and detailed picture of one person's real life, as well as the historical events that he witnessed or of which he was a part. Just as people today ask their parents and grandparents about the historical events they witnessed, so do readers who want to learn about seventeenth-century London turn to the pages of Pepys's diary.

◆ Literary Focus

1 Diary or Journal The detailed list of names, as well as the parenthetical aside, are two reasons for this diary's popularity. Ask students what they reveal that a more formal history might not. *The names are not particularly famous and might not be included in a formal history; the titles that are part of the names, Lord and Sir, reveal that Pepys kept company with men of rank. The parenthetical comment reveals a specific cause that explains the behavior of the people.*

◆ Reading Strategy

2 Draw Conclusions Ask: What can you conclude from the fact that the child was stripped of its clothes? *People feared that the clothes might spread the plague.*

◆ Reading Strategy

3 Draw Conclusions Pepys was happy that his money and silverware were all safe. From this, ask students what they can conclude about his feelings about his survival. *Pepys must have felt he would survive the plague, because otherwise the possessions would have been of no use to him.*

4 Clarification Point out that, in the first paragraph of the Sept. 14 entry, the phrases "For the first" and "Then, on the other side" refer to the phrase "content on one hand and melancholy on an other."

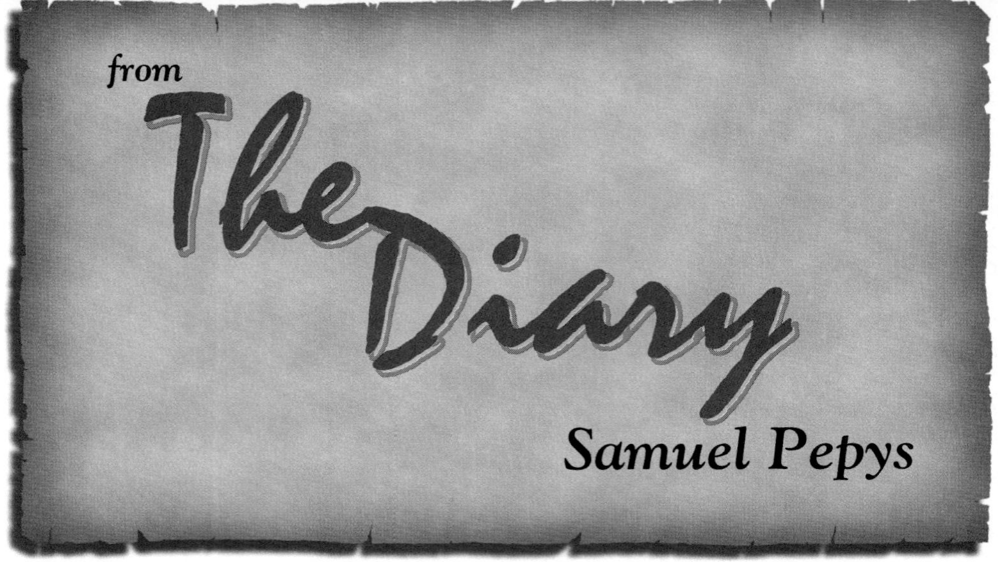

The Plague

Sept. 3, 1665. (Lord's Day.) Church being done, my Lord Bruncker, Sir J. Minnes, and I up to the vestry[1] at the desire of the Justices of the Peace, Sir Theo. Biddulph and Sir W. Boreman and Alderman Hooker, in order to the
1 doing something for the keeping of the plague from growing; but Lord! to consider the madness of the people of the town, who will (because they are forbid) come in crowds along with the dead corps[2] to see them buried; but we agreed on some orders for the prevention thereof.[3] Among other stories, one was very passionate, methought of a complaint brought against a man in the town for taking a child from London from an infected house. Alderman Hooker told us it was the child of a very able citizen in Gracious Street, a saddler,[4] who had buried all the rest of his children of the plague,
2 and himself and wife now being shut up and in despair of escaping, did desire only to save the life of this little child; and so prevailed to have it received stark-naked into the arms of a friend, who brought it (having put it into new fresh clothes) to Greenwich; where upon hearing the story, we did agree it should be permitted to be received and kept in the town. 2
Thence with my Lord Bruncker to Captain Cocke's, where we mighty merry and supped, and very late I by water to Woolwich, in great apprehensions of an ague . . . .

Sept. 14, 1665. When I come home I spent some thoughts upon the occurrences of this day, giving matter for as much content on one hand and melancholy on another, as any day in all my life. For the first; the finding of my money and plate,[5] and all safe at London, and speeding in my business of money this day. The hearing of this good news to such excess, 3
after so great a despair of my Lord's doing anything this year; adding to that, the decrease of 4
500 and more, which is the first decrease we have yet had in the sickness since it begun: and great hopes that the next week it will be greater. Then, on the other side, my finding that though the bill[6] in general is abated, yet the city within the walls is increased, and likely to continue so, and is close to our house there. My meeting dead corpses of the plague, carried to be buried close to me at noonday through the city in Fanchurch Street. To see a person

1. **vestry** (ves´ trē) *n.*: Church meeting-room.
2. **corps:** Corpses.
3. **but we . . . thereof:** Funeral processions were forbidden in London during the plague. However, the law was often ignored.
4. **saddler** *n.*: Person who makes, sells, and repairs saddles.
5. **plate:** Valuable serving dishes and flatware.
6. **bill:** Weekly list of burials.

Block Scheduling Strategies

Consider these suggestions to take advantage of extended class time:

- Introduce students to gerunds using the Grammar and Style lesson on page 461. Use the Grammar and Style notes in the teacher edition to help students identify gerunds in text. Then have students do the Grammar and Style exercise on page 472.
- Use Daily Language Practice for Weeks 17 and 18. You may either dictate the passages to students and have them write the passges correctly, or place the transparency on an overhead and have students correct the passages.
- Use the Background for Understanding on page 460 to introduce students to the "twin disasters" that hit London in the mid-1660's.
- Have students create a special news report on either the Great Fire or the plague. Assign the News Report in the Idea Bank on page 473. Then direct students to work together to assemble a newpaper using their individual articles.

5 **▶ Critical Viewing** What line from Pepys's account of the fire would be an appropriate caption for this painting? Why? **[Connect]**

The Great Fire of London, 1666

sick of the sores, carried close by me by Grace church in a hackney coach.[7] My finding the Angell Tavern at the lower end of Tower Hill, shut up, and more than that, the alehouse at the Tower Stairs, and more than that, the person was then dying of the plague when I was
6 last there, a little while ago, at night, to write a short letter there, and I overheard the mistress of the house sadly saying to her husband somebody was very ill, but did not think it was of the plague. To hear that poor Payne, my waiter, hath buried a child, and is dying himself. To hear that a laborer I sent but the other day to Dagenhams, to know how they did there, is dead of the plague; and that one of my own watermen, that carried me daily, fell sick as soon as he had landed me on Friday morning last, when I had been all night upon the water (and I believe he did get his infection that day at Brainford), and is now dead of the plague. To hear that Captain Lambert and Cuttle are killed in the taking these ships; and that Mr. Sidney Montague is sick of a desperate fever at my Lady Carteret's, at Scott's Hall. To hear that Mr. Lewes hath another daughter sick. And, lastly, that both my servants, W. Hewer and Tom Edwards, have lost their fathers, both in St. Sepulcher's parish, of the plague this week, do put me into great apprehensions of melancholy, and with good reason. But I put off the thoughts of sadness as much as I can, and the rather to keep my wife in good heart and family also. After supper (having eat nothing all this day) upon a fine tench[8] of Mr. Shelden's taking, we to bed.

7 **◆ Literary Focus** What abbreviated language in this passage is evidence of Pepys's own personal shorthand?

The Fire of London

Sept. 2, 1666. (Lord's day.) Some of our maids sitting up late last night to get things ready against our feast today, Jane called us
up about three in the morning, to tell us of a 8
great fire they saw in the city. So I rose and slipped on my night-gown, and went to her window, and thought it to be on the back side of Mark Lane at the farthest; but, being unused to such fires as followed, I thought it far enough off; and so went to bed again and to sleep. About seven rose again to dress myself, and there looked out at the window, and saw the fire not so much as it was and farther off.

7. **hackney coach:** Carriage for hire.

8. **tench** *n.*: Type of fish.

◆ Build Vocabulary

apprehensions (ap′ rē hen′ shəns) *n.*: Fears; concerns

abated (ə bāt′ id) *v.*: Lessened

▶Critical Viewing◀

5 **Connect** Students may select different lines, but most will probably choose "Jane called us up about three in the morning, to tell us of a great fire they saw in the city" or "And there I did see the houses at that end of the bridge all on fire, and an infinite great fire on this and the other side of the bridge."

Comprehension Check ☑

6 What kinds of events is Pepys listing here? *Pepys is listing the melancholy events that he referred to earlier in this entry.*

◆ Literary Focus

7 **Diary or Journal** Pepys's use of incomplete sentences throughout this passage indicates that he was writing in his own personal shorthand.

◆ Reading Strategy

8 **Draw Conclusions** Since there were no telephones in Pepys's time, how might someone "call up" at three in the morning? *Pepys means that someone would actually call up the stairs or send a messenger.*

Humanities: Art

The Great Fire of London, 1666.

This painting of the disaster, which hangs in the Museum of London, England, is by an unknown artist. Students who are accustomed to seeing photographs and televised accounts of disasters need to realize that during the time of Pepys, only artists could make a visual record of news events. Just as courtroom artists today work quickly to capture court scenes, so did artists of the past capture events as they happened.

Use these questions for discussion:

1. If such a fire took place today, how would the events be recorded and shared? *Students might mention that photographs and television video would record events. The results would be shared through newpapers, television reports, and on the Internet.*
2. Was this artist an eyewitness to the fire? Explain. *Students may hold different opinions, but they should support their opinions by referring to details from the picture.*

Customize for
Visual/Spatial Learners

Help students follow the narrative by locating as many landmarks as they can on the map of London at the time of the fire, on page 466.

▶Critical Viewing◀

❶ **Infer** Most students will conclude that Pepys did not mean to share his writing, because he used obscure symbols, or code, instead of any recognizable alphabet.

◆ Critical Thinking

❷ **Infer** Ask students why the fire might have started in a bakery in that century. What would cause the fire to spread? *The ovens were heated by actual fires; fires were easily spread because the buildings were constructed of timber, were built close together, and had no sprinker systems or fire extinguishers.*

◆ Reading Strategy

❸ **Draw Conclusions** Ask students what conclusions they might draw from the description that Pepys includes about the pigeons. Have them give their reasons. *Pepys probably likes pigeons, since he refers to them as "poor pigeons."*

◆ Critical Thinking

❹ **Analyze** Point out that Pepys includes more clues that explain why this fire spread so quickly. Have students identify at least two possible causes. *Students might mention high winds, the drought, or the combustibility of the building materials.*

---

❶ ▶ **Critical Viewing** Judging from this facsimile of Pepys's *Diary*, do you think Pepys meant to share his writing with the world? Why or why not? **[Infer]**

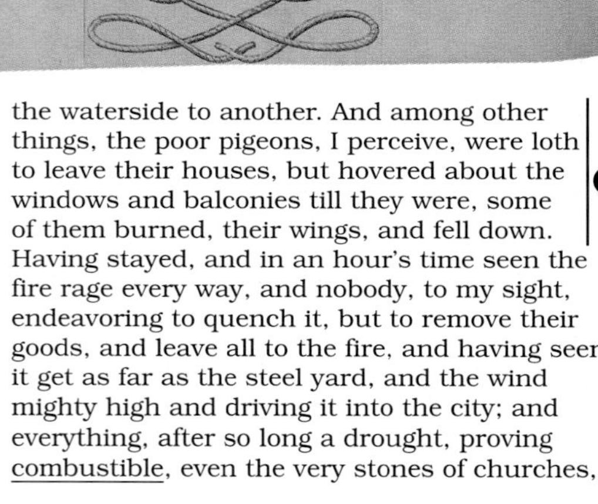

So to my closet to set things to rights after yesterday's cleaning. By and by Jane comes and tells me that she hears that above 300 houses have been burned down tonight by the fire we saw, and that it is now burning down all Fish Street, by London Bridge. So I made myself ready presently, and walked to the Tower,[9] and there got up upon one of the high places, Sir J. Robinson's little son going up with me; and there I did see the houses at that end of the bridge all on fire, and an infinite great fire on this and the other side the end of the bridge; which, among other people, did trouble me for poor little Michell and our Sarah on the bridge. ❷ So down, with my heart full of trouble, to the Lieutenant of the Tower, who tells me that it begun this morning in the King's baker's house in Pudding Lane, and that it hath burned St. Magnus's Church and most part of Fish Street already. So I down to the waterside, and there got a boat and through bridge, and there saw a <u>lamentable</u> fire. Poor Michell's house, as far as the Old Swan, already burned that way, and the fire running farther, that in a very little time it got as far as the steel yard, while I was there. Everybody endeavoring to remove their goods, and flinging into the river or bringing them into lighters that lay off; poor people staying in their houses as long as till the very fire touched them, and then running into boats, or clambering from one pair of stairs by the waterside to another. And among other things, the poor pigeons, I perceive, were loth to leave their houses, but hovered about the windows and balconies till they were, some of them burned, their wings, and fell down. ❸ Having stayed, and in an hour's time seen the fire rage every way, and nobody, to my sight, endeavoring to quench it, but to remove their goods, and leave all to the fire, and having seen it get as far as the steel yard, and the wind mighty high and driving it into the city; and everything, after so long a drought, proving <u>combustible</u>, even the very stones of churches, ❹

9. **Tower:** Tower of London.

Humanities: Art

Last Page of Samuel Pepys's Diary 31 May 1669.

Pepys wrote this diary using a particular system of shorthand devised by Thomas Shelton. However, since some passages contained very sensitive details, Pepys added additional safeguards to these, using a cipher that he had created as well as foreign words. He succeeded in keeping the contents secret until 1822, when the diary was finally decoded. However, certain parts were omitted from publication until 1983, more than 300 years after Pepys wrote them. Pepys was not the first writer to encode his private thoughts. Julius Caesar, for example, wrote in a sort of shorthand, and Leonardo da Vinci used mirror writing, written backwards from right to left, in his journals.

Use these questions for discussion:

1. What kinds of details would a person such as Pepys want to keep private? *Details might include those that would show the writer in a bad light as well as personal details and private opinions.*
2. What value does a diary such as this one have for the person who keeps it? *It helps the person remember events; writing it may help the person see events in a new light.*

and among other things the poor steeple by which pretty Mrs.—lives, and whereof my old schoolfellow Elborough is parson, taken fire in the very top, and there burned till it fell down. I to Whitehall (with a gentleman with me who desired to go off from the Tower, to see the fire, in my boat), and there up to the King's closet in the chapel, where people come about me, and I did give them an account dismayed them all, and word was carried in to the King. So I was called for, and did tell the King and Duke of York what I saw, and that unless his Majesty did command houses to be pulled down nothing could stop the fire. They seemed much
5 troubled, and the King commanded me to go to my Lord Mayor from him, and command him to spare no houses, but to pull down before the fire every way. The Duke of York bid me tell him that if he would have any more soldiers he shall; and so did my Lord Arlington afterwards, as a great secret. Here meeting with Captain Cocke, I in his coach, which he lent me, and Creed with me to Paul's,[10] and there walked along Watling Street, as well as I could, every creature coming away loaden with goods to save, and here and there sick people carried away in beds. Extraordinary good goods carried in carts and on backs. At last met my Lord Mayor in Canning Street, like a man spent,
6 with a handkerchief about his neck. To the King's message he cried, like a fainting woman, "Lord! what can I do? I am spent: people will not obey me. I have been pulling down houses; but the fire overtakes us faster than we can do it." That he needed no more soldiers; and that, for himself, he must go and refresh himself, having been up all night. So he left me, and I him, and walked home, seeing people all al-
7 most distracted, and no manner of means used to quench the fire. The houses, too, so very thick thereabouts, and full of matter for burning, as pitch and tar, in Thames Street; and warehouses of oil, and wines, and brandy, and other things. Here I saw Mr. Isaake Houblon, the handsome man, prettily dressed and dirty, at his door at Dowgate, receiving some of his brothers' things, whose houses were on fire; and, as he says, have been removed twice already; and he doubts (as it soon proved) that they must be in a little time removed from his house also, which was a sad consideration. And to see the churches all filling with goods by people who themselves should have been quietly there at this time. By this time it was about twelve o'clock; and so home. Soon as dined, and walked through the city, the streets full of nothing but people and horses and carts loaden with goods, ready to run over one another, and removing goods from one burned house to another. They now removing out of Canning Street (which received goods in the morning) into Lumbard Street, and farther; and among others I now saw my little goldsmith, Stokes, receiving some friend's goods, whose house itself was burned the day after. 8 I to Paul's Wharf, where I had appointed a boat to attend me, and took in Mr. Carcasse and his brother, whom I met in the street, and carried them below and above bridge to and again to see the fire, which was now got farther, both below and above, and no likelihood of stopping it. Met with the King and Duke of York in their barge, and with them to Queen-hithe, and there called Sir Richard Browne to them. Their order was only to pull down houses apace, and so below bridge at the waterside; but little was or could be done, the fire coming upon them so fast. Good hopes there was of stopping it at the Three Cranes above, and at Buttolph's Wharf below bridge, if care be used; but the wind carries it into the city, so as we know not by the waterside what it do there. River full of lighters and boats taking in goods, and good goods swimming in the water, and only I observed that hardly one lighter or boat in three that had the goods of a house in, but there was a pair of virginals[11] in it. Having seen as much as I could now, I away to Whitehall by appointment, and there walked to St. James's Park,

◆ *Literature and Your Life*

In what ways is Pepys's account similar to an account you may have heard on television or radio news or read in the newspaper? 9

10. Paul's: St. Paul's Cathedral.

11. virginals *n.*: Small, legless harpsichords.

◆ Build Vocabulary

lamentable (lam´ ən tə bəl) *adj.*: Distressing

combustible (kəm bus´ tə bəl) *adj.*: Capable of igniting and burning; flammable

◆ Reading Strategy

5 Draw Conclusions Ask students what they can conclude about Pepys' position in society. *Since the King and Duke of York sent for him, Pepys must be a trusted court figure and have an important role in society.*

◆ Literary Focus

6 Diary or Journal Have students identify details that are so small or so personal that they would be unlikely to be in anything other than a diary or journal. *Students might mention the Mayor's handkerchief, or his words, or the fact that Pepys compared his reaction to that of a fainting woman.*

◆ Build Vocabulary

7 Prefixes: *dis-* Point out that the word *distracted* contains the prefix *dis-*, meaning "apart." The word *distracted* actually means to draw or pull apart. Ask students what is drawn apart when someone is distracted. *The person's attention is pulled away.*

◆ Reading Strategy

8 Draw Conclusions Ask students what conclusion they can draw from the detail that goods were moved into houses and then later had to be moved again. *The fire kept spreading to houses that were first assumed to be safe.*

◆ *Literature and Your Life*

9 Students might point out that the details of the spreading disaster, including the place names and names of people involved, are similar to those on newscasts, as are the frequent updates or the human-interest stories.

Cross-Curricular Connection: Social Studies

Point out to students that the Great Fire of London is only one of history's major fires. Others include the burning of Rome in A.D. 64, the Great Chicago Fire of 1871, the Boston fire of 1872, and the giant California brush fires of 1991. Many accounts of these fires are mixtures of fact, legend, and outright fiction.

Have students choose one fire to research. (Lists of famous fires can be found in most almanacs.) Ask them to find out the amount of damage done, the loss to life, the cause if known, and what changes, if any, were taken afterwards to prevent future fires. Have students share their findings and create a chart showing what they have learned.

Customize for
Verbal/Linguistic Leaners
Have students picture the scene that Pepys describes. Have them explain what kinds of sounds they might expect to hear. *Possible response: Students might expect to hear the crackle of flames, the shouts of people, and the crash of burning buildings.*

▶Critical Viewing◀

❶ **Make a Judgment** Most students will say that the map enhances Pepys's description because it shows the huge area of devastation caused by the fire.

◆Critical Thinking

❷ **Interpret** Ask students what "firedrops" might be. *The term may mean "drops of fire that fall from the sky."*

◆Critical Thinking

❸ **Infer** Ask why Pepys thought his money and metal boxes would be safe in his cellar and why he might have included such details in a diary. *The valuables would be safe because they were below ground and therefore protected; reasons for including such details might include proving later that those things were his, or the inclusion of these details may indicate that Pepys' was worried about losing his wealth.*

◆Literature and Your Life

❹ Discuss with students what they might do with their valuables if faced with a spreading fire such as the one that Pepys describes.

❶ ▶ **Critical Viewing** This map of London includes an inset depicting the area destroyed by the Great Fire. Does this image enhance Pepys's eyewitness description? Explain. **[Make a Judgment]**

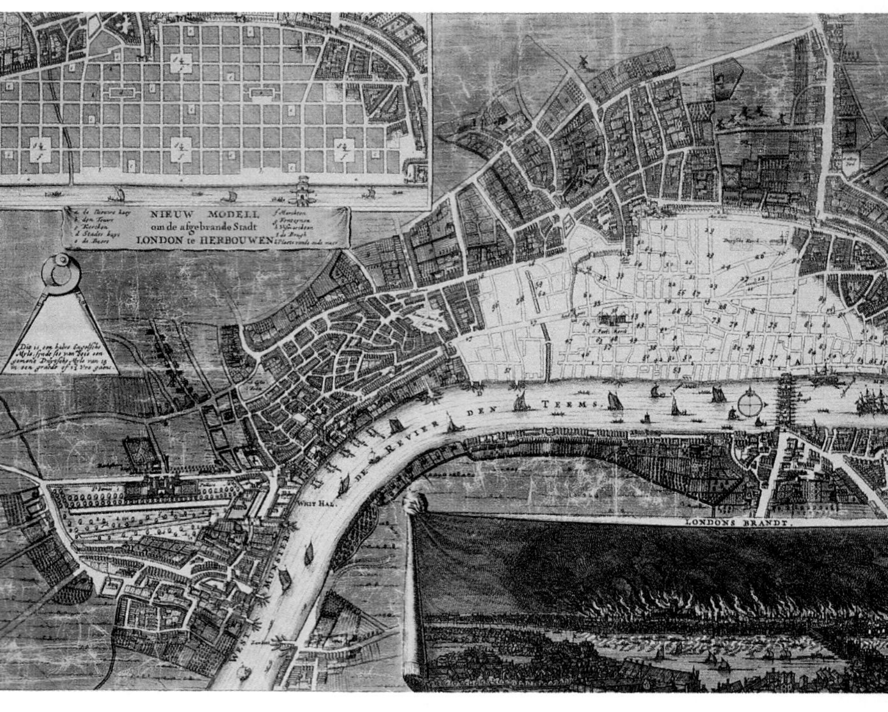

and there met my wife and Creed and Wood and his wife, and walked to my boat; and there upon the water again, and to the fire up and down, it still increasing, and the wind great. So near the fire as we could for smoke; and all over the Thames, with one's face in the wind, you were almost burned with a shower of fire-
❷ drops. This is very true; so as houses were burned by these drops and flakes of fire, three or four, nay, five or six houses, one from another. When we could endure no more upon the water, we to a little alehouse on the Bankside, over against the Three Cranes, and there stayed till it was dark almost, and saw the fire grow; and, as it grew darker, appeared more and more, and in corners and upon steeples, and between churches and houses, as far as we could see up the hill of the city, in a most horrid malicious bloody flame, not like the fine flame of an ordinary fire. Barbary and her husband away before us. We stayed till, it being darkish, we saw the fire as only one entire arch of fire from this to the other side the bridge, and in a bow up the hill for an arch of above a mile long: it made me weep to see it. The churches, houses, and all on fire and flaming at once; and a horrid noise the flames made, and the cracking of houses at their ruin. So home with a sad heart, and there find everybody discoursing and lamenting the fire; and poor Tom Hater come with some of his few goods saved out of his house, which is burned upon Fish Street Hill. I invited him to lie at my house, and did receive his goods, but was deceived in his lying there, the news coming every moment of the growth of the fire; so as we were ❸
forced to begin to pack up our own goods, and prepare for their removal; and did by moonshine (it being brave dry, and moonshine, and warm weather) carry much of my goods into the garden, and Mr. Hater and I did remove my money and iron chests into my cellar, as thinking that the safest place. And got my bags of

◆ Build Vocabulary

malicious (mə lish´ əs) *adj.*: Deliberately harmful; destructive

discoursing (dis kôrs´ iŋ) *v.*: Talking about; discussing

Humanities: Art

The Great Fire, 1666, by Marcus Willemsz Doornik.

This map is a good example of the cartographer's, or mapmaker's, art, which saw many changes during the seventeenth century. New developments in astronomy, which helps determine longitude, and an interest in exploration helped to create more accurate maps. Maps, such as the one illustrated here, were usually engraved, with each color requiring a different engraved plate. Maps such as this one are considered by many to be works of art as well as utilitarian objects.

Use these questions for discussion:

1. This map shows the area of London that was devastated by the Great Fire. What other information can you get from this map? *Students might mention London's general layout, major thoroughfares, location of landmarks, and the course of the river Thames.*
2. Do you consider this map more effective in practical terms or as a work of art? Explain. *Some students will say that practically, it shows clearly and effectively the aftermath of the Great Fire. Other students will say that the map is more a work of art because one cannot use it to navigate through the city.*

The Great Fire, 1666, Marcus Willemsz Doornik, Guildhall Library, Corporation of London

gold into my office, ready to carry away, and my chief papers of accounts also there, and my tallies into a box by themselves. So great was our fear, as Sir W. Batten hath carts come out of the country to fetch away his goods this night. We did put Mr. Haters, poor man, to bed a little; but he got but very little rest, so much noise being in my house, taking down of goods. 4

3rd. About four o'clock in the morning, my Lady Batten sent me a cart to carry away all my money, and plate, and best things, to Sir W. Rider's at Bednall Green. Which I did, riding myself in my nightgown in the cart; and, Lord! to see how the streets and the highways are crowded with people running and riding, 5 and getting of carts at any rate to fetch away things. I find Sir W. Rider tired with being called up all night, and receiving things from several friends. 6 His house full of goods, and much of Sir W. Batten's and Sir W. Pen's. I am eased at my heart to have my treasure so well secured. Then home, with much ado to find a way, nor any sleep all this night to me nor my poor wife.

> ◆ **Reading Strategy** What conclusions can you draw about Pepys from the last two sentences?

Guide for Responding

◆ Literature and Your Life

Reader's Response Does Pepys's *Diary* make the plague and fire seem real to you? Why or why not?

Thematic Focus What does the excerpt reveal about Pepys's ties to family, friends, and colleagues?

Letter Write a letter to Samuel Pepys in which you express your appreciation for his diary and explain how it has affected you.

☑ Check Your Comprehension

1. According to the entry for September 3, 1665, what happened to the saddler's family?
2. When does Pepys first learn of the Great Fire?
3. (a) What does Pepys recommend to the King and the Duke of York? (b) What is the reply?
4. Summarize Pepys's actions on Sept. 3, 1666.

◆ Critical Thinking

INTERPRET

1. What does the entry for September 3, 1665, reveal about Pepys? Explain. **[Infer]**
2. (a) What seems to be Pepys's attitude toward business? (b) What seems to be his attitude toward pleasure? **[Infer]**
3. From the evidence of these diary entries, how would you describe Pepys's character and personality? **[Draw Conclusions]**

APPLY

4. (a) In Pepys's London, which do you think was a greater disaster—the plague in 1665 or the Great Fire in 1666? Explain. (b) What disasters in modern times do you think compare with these unfortunate events? **[Relate]**

◆ Reading Strategy

5 Draw Conclusions Most students will conclude that Pepys was very concerned about his "treasure" because he rode through the streets of London in his nightgown in the middle of the night to ensure its safety.

◆ Grammar and Style

6 Gerunds Ask students to identify the gerunds in the prepositional phrase "with being called up all night, and receiving things from several friends." *The gerunds are* "being" *and* "receiving."

Reinforce and Extend

Answers

◆ Literature and Your Life

Reader's Response Sample responses: Yes; the details and first-person commentary vividly bring to life the plague and fire. No; the language is too old-fashioned to effectively bring to life the fire and plague for a modern audience.

Thematic Focus Pepys seems to be very caring and considerate of his family, friends, and colleagues.

☑ Check Your Comprehension

1. A saddler and his wife, who had lost all but one of their children to the plague and feared for their own lives, asked a friend to take the sole surviving child to safety. Pepys and his peers agreed that the child should be allowed to stay where it had been taken.
2. Pepys first learns of the fire at three o'clock in the morning of September 2, 1666.
3. (a) Pepys recommends that houses be torn down to stop the advance of the fire. (b) The King tells Pepys to command the mayor to tear down houses in the fire's path.
4. At four o'clock in the morning, Pepys used a borrowed cart to take his valuables to a friend's house that was safe from the fire. Then he found his way home, but got no sleep.

◆ Critical Thinking

1. The entry for September 3, 1665, reveals that Pepys is a compassionate man. He bent the rules and allowed a saddler, who had lost most of his family to the plague, to send his only remaining child to Greenwich for safety.
2. (a) Pepys seems to take his occupation seriously; he does what he can to help control the plague, and reports to the King results of the fire he has seen firsthand. (b) Pepys seems to enjoy dining and socializing with friends. In the entry of Sept. 3, 1665, he stays out late with Lord Bruncker and Captain Cocke.
3. Pepys was a friendly, curious, religious, and compassionate man, who was apparently well-liked and respected.
4. (a) Sample responses: The greater disaster was probably the fire, which not only destroyed lives but property as well; the plague was the greater disaster because it took a much larger toll on human lives. (b) Sample response: The Great Earthquake and Fire of San Francisco in 1906 resulted in many deaths and much damage.

Develop Understanding

One-Minute Insight Daniel Defoe combined his journalism skills with his creative energy, and developed an unusual hybrid: a fictional narrative in the form of a journal. Although this "true history," was narrated by a fictional inhabitant of London identified only as H. F., the book contained a great deal of historical accuracy. Defoe, who was born just four years before the plague epidemic, perhaps had vague memories of it personally. Certainly he had access to people who remembered it vividly, as well as to official documents. Defoe's groundbreaking work of fiction set English literature on a new path.

Customize for
Intrapersonal Learners
Remind students that neither Defoe nor his fictional narrator witnessed the events of the plague year: the events were researched by Defoe and then woven into the fictional narrative. As students read, encourage them to identify the elements of the narrator's character that ring true to life.

Customize for
More Advanced Students
Have students consider the advantages and disadvantages of using the first-person point of view. Advantages include a sense of immediacy and reality. Disadvantages include a limited viewpoint from which the events are retold. Encourage students to note, also, the types of details in this journal that they would not expect to find in a modern-day news report.

▶Critical Viewing◀

❶ **Infer** The streets seem deserted because the plague killed much of the population, and those that were still alive probably were hesitant to venture out into the germ-infested streets. Judging from the characters in the picture, their grim job of picking up dead bodies had become mundane and commonplace.

from
A Journal of the Plague Year
Daniel Defoe

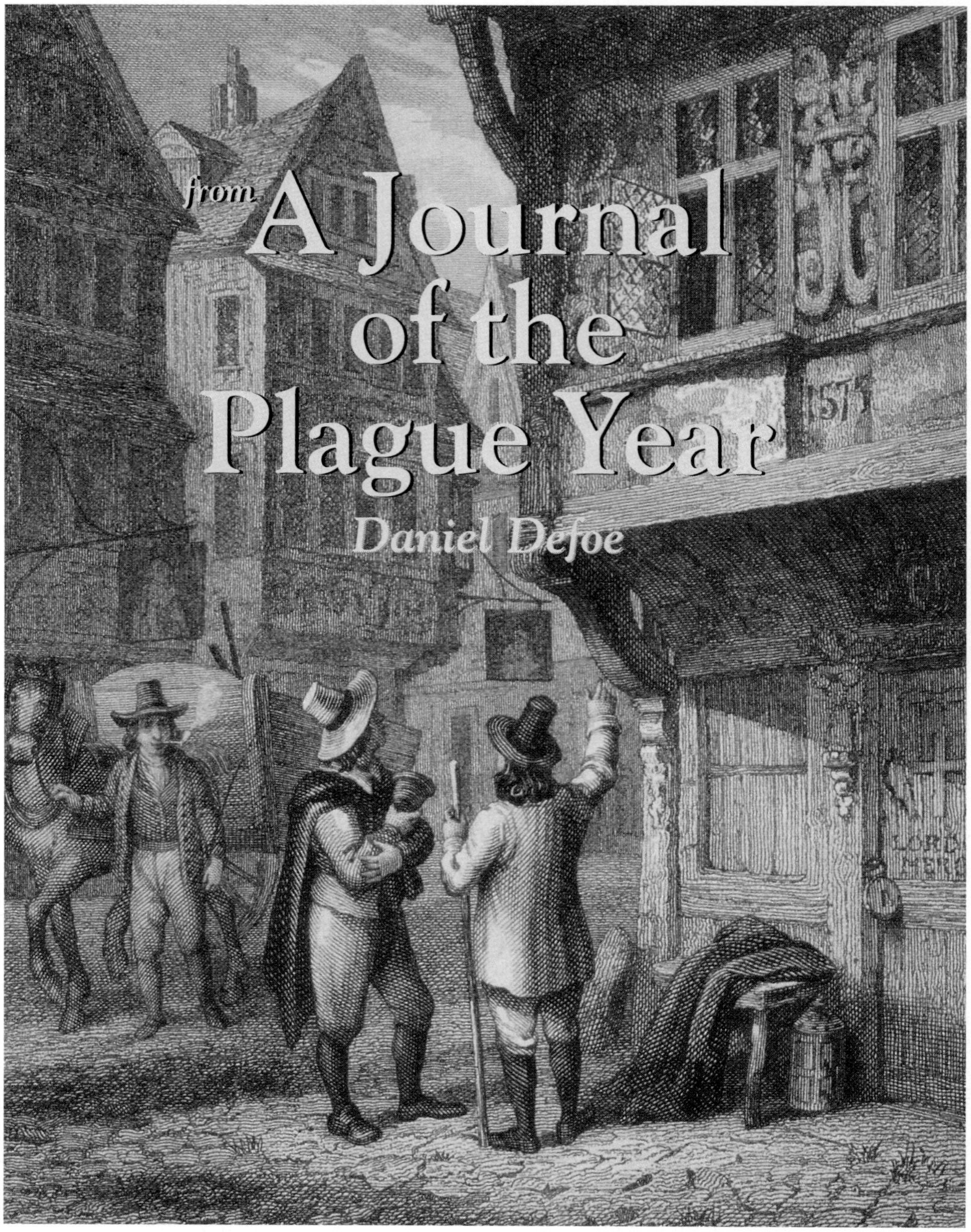

The Dead Cart, The British Library

❶ ▶ Critical Viewing The cart in this picture is carrrying the bodies of people killed by the plague. What can you infer about the plague's impact on daily life from the number of people on the street and from the gestures of the men in conversation? **[Infer]**

Humanities: Art

The Dead Cart.

This wood engraving, by an unknown artist, was created for an early edition of Defoe's *A Journal of the Plague Year,* first published in 1722. Wood engraving was one of the earliest means of reproducing illustrations in a printed book. It differs from metal engraving in that it is a relief process, the printed parts stand out from the background, whereas metal engraving is an intaglio process, where the printed parts are cut into the background.

Use these questions for discussion:

1. What was the purpose of the dead cart? *The dead cart was used to carry away dead bodies for burial.*
2. What seems to be the artist's attitude toward the subject? What suggests this? *The attitude seems to be matter-of-fact; the cart is shown in the context of everyday life.*

The face of London was now indeed strangely altered, I mean the whole mass of buildings, city, liberties, suburbs, Westminster, Southwark, and altogether; for as to the particular part called the city, or within the walls, that was not yet much infected. But in the whole the face of things, I say, was much altered; sorrow and sadness sat upon every face; and though some parts were not yet overwhelmed, yet all looked deeply concerned; and as we saw it apparently coming on, so everyone looked on himself and his family as in the utmost danger. Were it possible to represent those times exactly to those that did not see them, and give the reader due ideas of the horror that everywhere presented itself, it must make just impressions upon their minds and fill them with surprise. London might well be said to be all in tears; the mourners did not go
2 about the streets indeed, for nobody put on black or made a formal dress of mourning for their nearest friends; but the voice of mourning was truly heard in the streets. The shrieks of women and children at the windows and doors of their houses, where their dearest relations were perhaps dying, or just dead, were so frequent to be heard as we passed the streets, that it was enough to pierce the stoutest heart in the world to hear them. Tears and lamentations were seen almost in every house, especially in the first part of the visitation; for toward the latter end men's hearts were hard-
3 ened, and death was so always before their eyes, that they did not so much concern themselves for the loss of their friends, expecting that themselves should be summoned the next hour . . . .

I went all the first part of the time freely about the streets, though not so freely as to run myself into apparent danger, except when they dug the great pit in the churchyard of our parish of Aldgate. A terrible pit it was, and I could not resist my curiosity to go and see it. As near as I may judge, it was about forty feet in length, and about fifteen or sixteen feet broad, and, at the time I first looked at it, about nine feet deep; but it was said they dug it near twenty feet deep afterwards in one part of it, till they could go no deeper for the water; for they had, it seems, dug several large pits before this. For though the plague was long a-coming to our parish, yet, when it did come, there was no parish in or about London where it raged with such violence as in the two parishes of Aldgate and Whitechapel.

4 **◆ Literary Focus**
What details in this paragraph show that the narrator is giving a personal account of what he saw?

I saw they had dug several pits in another ground, when the distemper began to spread in our parish, and especially when the dead carts began to go about, which was not, in our parish, till the beginning of August. Into these pits they had put perhaps fifty or sixty bodies each; then they made larger holes, wherein they buried all that the cart brought in a week, which, by the middle to the end of August, came to from 200 to 400 a week; and they could not well dig them larger, because of the order of the magistrates confining them to leave no bodies within six feet of the surface; and the water coming on at about seventeen or eighteen feet, they could not well, I say, put more in one pit. But now, at the beginning of September, the plague raging in a dreadful manner, and the number of burials in our parish increasing to more than was ever buried 5
in any parish about London of no larger extent, they ordered this dreadful gulf to be dug, for such it was rather than a pit.

They had supposed this pit would have supplied them for a month or more when they dug it, and some blamed the churchwardens for suffering[1] such a frightful thing, telling them they were making preparations to bury the whole parish, and the like; but time made it appear the churchwardens knew the condition of the parish better than they did, for the pit being finished the 4th of September, I think, they began to bury in it the 6th, and by the 20th, which was just two weeks, they had thrown into it 1114 bodies, when they were obliged to fill it up, the bodies being then come to lie within six feet of the surface. I doubt not

1. **suffering:** Allowing.

◆ Build Vocabulary
distemper (dis tem´ pər) *n.*: Infectious disease such as the plague

◆ Reading Strategy

2 Draw Conclusions Ask students why the mourners did not put on formal mourning clothes. *Too many people were dying; the mourners were themselves ill or fearful of becoming ill; society was in too much disarray to bother with such a formality.*

◆ Critical Thinking

3 Generalize Ask students if they think that the reaction of hardening one's heart against human misery is common during great tragedies. Have them give reasons for their opinions. *Some students may feel that hardening one's heart is inevitable and a way to survive; others may think that truly caring people would never shut off their feelings.*

◆ Literary Focus

4 Diary or Journal Students may mention use of the pronouns *I* and *my* when referring to himself, the detail about his curiosity, the nonscientific observations in phrases such as "As near as I may judge."

◆ Grammar and Style

5 Gerunds Ask students to locate the gerund in this sentence. *The gerund is the word beginning.*

Customize for
Logical/Mathematical Learners
Have students use the figures on this page to estimate how many people died from the plague in a one-month period.

Beyond the Classroom

Career Connection
Public Health Official The plague, such as that described in these accounts, has had numerous outbreaks that have been recorded since 430 B.C. However, the cause of the disease was not discovered until 1894. Until researchers realized that the bacterium traveled from fleas to rats to people, scientists were unable to halt these horrible pandemics that periodically killed millions.

Have interested students find out how people determine the cause of major outbreaks, and what kinds of doctors and researchers are involved. Students who are familiar with disaster movies such as *Outbreak* may be interested to learn how much of the story is fiction and how much is fact.

Community Connection
Firefighting The firefighters in Pepys's London had to rely on bucket brigades and other now-archaic firefighting techniques. Although most towns in the Western world have a fire department, students may be unaware of modern firefighting techniques and of the training that firefighters receive.

In addition to quelling blazes, most firefighters are also skilled in dealing with hazardous materials, giving emergency medical care, and working with builders and contractors to ensure that homes, offices, and other buildings are designed to meet fire safety standards.

◆ Reading Strategy

❶ Draw Conclusions The narrator said that he was curious, and like many people, he was probably both attracted to and repelled by the horror of the scene.

◆ Grammar and Style

❷ Gerunds Have students identify the gerund in this passage and tell what it means in this context. *The gerund is running. It means "taking on or exposing oneself to" something.*

◆ Critical Thinking

❸ Evaluate Have students identify the sensory details in this paragraph and discuss whether such a scene could be effectively captured on film. *Details include the lights, the bell, the muffled figure in the cloak moving his hands, the groans, and the sighs. This scene contains enough interesting details to be effectively captured on film.*

Looking at Literature Videodiscs As follow-up, play Chapter 6: Modern-Day Plagues. Hold a discussion in which students draw parallels between the bubonic plague and modern-day plagues and illnesses.

Chapter 6

but there may be some ancient persons alive in the parish who can justify the fact of this, and are able to show even in what place of the churchyard the pit lay better than I can. The mark of it also was many years to be seen in the churchyard on the surface, lying in length parallel with the passage which goes by the west wall of the churchyard out of Houndsditch, and turns east again into Whitechapel, coming out near the Three Nuns' Inn.

It was about the 10th of September that my curiosity led, or rather drove, me to go and see this pit again, when there had been near 400 people buried in it; and I was not content to see it in the daytime, as I had done before, for then there would have been nothing to have been seen but the loose earth; for all the bodies that were thrown in were immediately covered with earth by those they called the buriers, which at other times were called bearers; but I resolved to go in the night and see some of them thrown in. ❶

> **◆ Reading Strategy** From the information in this paragraph, what do you conclude about the narrator's motives?

There was a strict order to prevent people coming to those pits, and that was only to prevent infection. But after some time that order was more necessary, for people that were infected and near their end, and delirious also, would run to those pits, wrapped in blankets or rugs, and throw themselves in, and, as they said, bury themselves. I cannot say that the officers suffered any willingly to lie there; but I have heard that in a great pit in Finsbury, in the parish of Cripplegate, it lying open then to the fields, for it was not then walled about, [some] came and threw themselves in, and expired there, before they threw any earth upon them; and that when they came to bury others, and found them there, they were quite dead, though not cold.

This may serve a little to describe the dreadful condition of that day, though it is impossible to say anything that is able to give a true idea of it to those who did not see it, other than this, that it was indeed very, very, very dreadful, and such as no tongue can express.

I got admittance into the churchyard by being acquainted with the sexton who attended, who, though he did not refuse me at all, yet earnestly persuaded me not to go, telling me very seriously, for he was a good, religious, and sensible man, that it was indeed their business and duty to venture, and to run all hazards, and that in it they might hope to be preserved; but that I had no apparent call to it but my own curiosity, which, he said, he believed I would not pretend was sufficient to justify my running that hazard. ❷ I told him I had been pressed in my mind to go, and that perhaps it might be an instructing sight, that might not be without its uses. "Nay," says the good man, "if you will venture upon that score, name of God go in; for, depend upon it, 't will be a sermon to you, it may be, the best that ever you heard in your life. 'T is a speaking sight," says he, "and has a voice with it, and a loud one, to call us all to repentance"; and with that he opened the door and said, "Go, if you will."

His discourse had shocked my resolution a little, and I stood wavering for a good while, but just at that interval I saw two links[2] come over from the end of the Minories, and heard the bellman, and then appeared a dead cart, as they called it, coming over the streets; so I could no longer resist my desire of seeing it, and went in. There was nobody, as I could perceive at first, in the churchyard, or going into it, but the buriers and the fellow that drove the cart, or rather led the horse and cart; but when ❸ they came up to the pit they saw a man go to and again,[3] muffled up in a brown cloak, and making motions with his hands under his cloak, as if he was in a great agony, and the buriers immediately gathered about him, supposing he was one of those poor delirious or desperate creatures that used to pretend, as I have said, to bury themselves. He said nothing as he walked about, but two or three times groaned very deeply and loud, and sighed as he would break his heart.

When the buriers came up to him they soon found he was neither a person infected and desperate, as I have observed above, or a person distempered in mind, but one oppressed with a dreadful weight of grief indeed, having his wife and several of his children all in the cart that was just come in with him, and he followed in an agony and excess of sorrow. He mourned heartily, as it was easy to see, but

2. **links:** Torches.
3. **to and again:** To and fro.

Speaking and Listening Mini-Lesson

Town Crier

This mini-lesson supports the Speaking and Listening activity in the Idea Bank on page 473.

Introduce the Concept Explain to students that one way of broadcasting news reports in seventeenth-century London was through town criers, who literally called out newsworthy events of the day. To be effective, town criers had to summarize important stories loudly and clearly for the listeners.

Develop Background Direct students to choose an event from Pepy's *Diary* or Defoe's *Journal* to announce as "town crier." If time permits, encourage interested students to perform additional research and come up with an "original" bit of news to announce. As they prepare their reports, remind students to do the following:

- Summarize the news story, without leaving out important information.
- Create notecards on which are printed the facts in the news report.
- Practice speaking loudly and clearly.

Apply the Information When students have prepared their reports, have them act as "town crier." Remind them, if necessary, that brevity and clarity are important aspects of being an effective town crier.

Assess the Outcome Assess students' efforts based on the following criteria: content, interest of story, ability to be heard loudly and clearly.

with a kind of masculine grief that could not give itself vent by tears; and calmly defying the buriers to let him alone, said he would only see the bodies thrown in and go away, so they left importuning him. But no sooner was the cart turned round and the bodies shot into the pit promiscuously,[4] which was a surprise to him, for he at least expected they would have been decently laid in, though indeed he was afterwards convinced that was impracticable; I say, no sooner did he see the sight but he cried out aloud, unable to contain himself. I could not hear what he said, but he went backward two or three steps and fell down in a swoon. The buriers ran to him and took him up, and in a little while he came to himself, and they led him away to the Pie Tavern over against the end of Houndsditch, where, it seems, the man was known, and where they took care of him. He looked into the pit again as he went away, but the buriers had covered the bodies so immediately with throwing in earth, that though there was light enough, for there were lanterns, and candles in them, placed all night round the sides of the pit, upon heaps of earth, seven or eight, or perhaps more, yet nothing could be seen.

This was a mournful scene indeed, and affected me almost as much as the rest; but the other was awful and full of terror. The cart had in it sixteen or seventeen bodies: some were wrapped up in linen sheets, some in rags, some little other than naked, or so loose that what covering they had fell from them in the shooting out of the cart, and they fell quite naked among the rest; but the matter was not much to them, or the indecency much to anyone else, seeing they were all dead, and were to be huddled together into the common grave of mankind, as we may call it, for here was no difference made, but poor and rich went together; there was no other way of burials, neither was it possible there should, for coffins were not to be had for the prodigious numbers that fell in such a calamity as this. ❹

4. **promiscuously:** Without care or thought.

◆ **Build Vocabulary**

importuning (im′ pôr to͞on′ iŋ) *v.*: Pleading

prodigious (prō̆ dij′ əs) *adj.*: Enormous; huge

Guide for Responding

◆ Literature and Your Life

Reader's Response Which passages in *A Journal of the Plague Year* seem especially vivid to you? Why?

Thematic Focus What does the selection reveal about family and community feelings during a time of crisis?

☑ Check Your Comprehension

1. What was the purpose of the great pit dug in Aldgate?
2. (a) What prompts the narrator to visit the pit? (b) Why does he go at night?
3. Summarize the incident concerning the man in the brown cloak.

◆ Critical Thinking

INTERPRET

1. Why do you think the narrator describes the pit in such a specific way? **[Infer]**
2. What does the sexton mean when he says that visiting the pit will "be a sermon" to the narrator? **[Interpret]**
3. Judging by the tone of this excerpt and the narrator's actions, what kind of person do you think the narrator is? **[Classify]**

EVALUATE

4. What is your opinion of the narrator's decision to visit the pit? Why? **[Make a Judgment]**

Beyond the Selection

FURTHER READING

More Works by the Authors

The Diary of Samuel Pepys, Volumes 1–11, Samuel Pepys; *A Journal of the Plague Year,* Daniel Defoe; *The Life and Adventures of Robinson Crusoe,* Daniel Defoe

Works About the Authors

Samuel Pepys and the World He Lived In, P. Wheatley

Daniel Defoe: His Life, Paula R. Backscheider

We suggest that you preview these works before recommending them to students.

INTERNET

You and your students may find additional information about the authors on the Internet at the following site.

For more information on Daniel Defoe go to **http://www.incompetech.com/Helpdesk/Authors/defoe**

We *strongly recommend* that you preview the sites before you send students to them.

◆ Reading Strategy

❹ **Draw Conclusions** Ask students why this final scene affected the narrator so much. *The narrator was filled with terror because the bodies were treated so inhumanely and with so little ceremony.*

Reinforce and Extend

Answers

◆ Literature and Your Life

Reader's Response Students should provide reasons for choosing particular passages.

Thematic Focus The selection reveals that people became somewhat numbed and disoriented by the disaster.

☑ Check Your Comprehension

1. The pit served as a communal grave for plague victims.
2. (a) Curiosity prompts the visitor to visit the pit. (b) By day the bodies had already been covered with dirt. He wanted to see the bodies thrown into the pit.
3. The man in the brown cloak was mourning the deaths of his wife and several of his children, and had come to see his family buried. When he saw their bodies being dumped into the pit with hundreds of others, he cried out in anguish and fainted. When he revived, the buriers took him to a tavern where he was looked after by friends.

◆ Critical Thinking

1. The narrator is trying to convey the horrible realities of the plague.
2. The sexton warns the narrator that he will be reminded of his own mortality and will be moved to repent his sins.
3. The narrator is a curious person, who wants to see things for himself. Although he recounts the events dispassionately as a news reporter might do, the details evoke compassion in the readers.
4. Possible responses: The narrator's decision to visit the pit is understandable because it was provoked by curiosity; the narrator's decision to visit the pit is not a wise one, because he was exposing himself to infection and possibly hindering the burial process.

Guide for Responding (continued)

◆ Reading Strategy

Draw Conclusions

Reading a diary such as Pepys's, you can **draw conclusions** about its author's personality, attitude, or situation. In the case of a fictional journal like Defoe's, your conclusions will apply to the fictional narrator. For example, when Defoe's narrator says "I went all the first part of the time freely about the streets, though not so freely as to run myself into apparent danger . . ." you can conclude that the narrator is bold, but not reckless.

1. What does the entry dated Sept. 14, 1665, in Pepys's *Diary* reveal about his position in society? Support your conclusion with details.

2. (a) Which narrator—Pepys or Defoe's fictional narrator—seemed more observant to you? (b) On what details do you base your conclusion?

◆ Build Vocabulary

Using the Prefix *dis-*

Knowing that the prefix *dis-* can mean "apart," "not," or "do the opposite of" define the following words.

1. disease **3.** disable **5.** dishonest

2. dismiss **4.** disobey

Using the Word Bank

In your notebook, write the word from the Word Bank that best completes each sentence.

1. London's wooden buildings were highly __?__.

2. The flames of the fire seemed __?__ as if they wanted to devour all in their path.

3. People trying to escape the flames began __?__ boatmen to take them aboard.

4. The fire did a ___ amount of damage.

5. When the fire at last __?__, 13,000 buildings had been destroyed.

6. Worried people were __?__ about raising money to rebuild their homes.

7. For years afterward, many Londoners had __?__ that another fire would destroy the city.

8. Others just wished to forget the __?__ episode.

◆ Literary Focus

Diary or Journal

As day-to-day accounts of writers' personal experiences and reactions, **diaries** and **journals** offer fresh and immediate descriptions of people, places, and events. The descriptions are often so engaging because the author was on the scene and refers to himself or herself as "I." This personal pronoun gives you a personal stake in events.

In reading Pepys's entry of Sept. 2, 1666, for example, you experience both daily concerns (planning a feast) and historic events (a catastrophic fire) through Pepys's "I." With Pepys as guide and companion, you get a firsthand look at the ordinary and extraordinary events of London life.

1. (a) Find a passage in *The Diary* that conveys the flavor and freshness of real life. (b) Explain what makes the passage so immediate.

2. In what ways does Defoe's novel, *A Journal of the Plague Year,* resemble a real journal?

3. How do the accounts by Pepys and Defoe differ from typical news reports of a disaster?

◆ Grammar and Style

Gerunds

Both Pepys and Defoe extend the range of nouns in their writing by using **gerunds,** verbs with an *-ing* ending that serve as nouns.

Because gerunds end in *-ing*, it is easy to mistake them for present participles, verbs with *-ing* endings. Keep in mind that gerunds serve as nouns, while present participles function as verbs or as adjectives modifying nouns and pronouns.

Practice In your notebook, identify the gerund in the sentence, or write *none* if there is no gerund.

1. The plague was a time for deep mourning.

2. Human suffering was all around.

3. Wailing people were fleeing London.

4. The ranks of the dead and dying were swelling every day.

5. Still shuddering from the tragedy, the city had barely finished burying its dead when the Great Fire broke out.

Answers

◆ Reading Strategy

1. The entry on Sept. 14, 1665, reveals that Pepys is a wealthy man with servants, waiter, and his own watermen; he is an official of the high court, in touch with the King ("my Lord") on business matters.
2. (a) Possible responses: Defoe's narration is focused on one event and contains more detail; Pepys's is more observant because he names many specific people and the many specific situations he encounters. (b) Have students cite the details to support their choice.

◆ Build Vocabulary

Using the Prefix *dis-*

1. *disease:* not well, sickness
2. *dismiss:* to send away; or apart
3. *disable:* to make unable
4. *disobey:* not obey
5. *dishonest:* not honest

Using the Word Bank

1. London's wooden buildings were highly *combustible*.
2. The flames of the fire seemed *malicious* as if they wanted to devour all in their path.
3. People trying to escape the flames began *importuning* boatmen to take them aboard.
4. The fire did a *prodigious* amount of damage.
5. When the fire at last *abated,* 13,000 buildings had been destroyed.
6. Worried people were *discoursing* about raising money to rebuild their homes.
7. For years afterward, many Londoners had *apprehensions* that another fire would destroy the city.
8. Others just wished to forget the *lamentable* episode.

◆ Literary Focus

1. (a) Possible response: The entry of Sept 3 is fresh and true to life. (b) The details about being awakened, riding through London in his pajamas, and spending a sleepless night reinforce the freshness and reality of Pepys's experience.
2. Defoe uses dates, references to daytime or nighttime, and creates scenarios that seem true-to-life.
3. Defoe includes religious connotations and morbid detail; Pepys crowds his accounts with lesser details, anecdotes involving personal acquaintances, and personal opinions.

◆ Grammar and Style

1. *mourning;* 2. *suffering;* 3. none; 4. *dying;* 5. none

Writer's Solution

For additional practice identifying gerunds, use the Types of Nouns lesson in the **Language Lab CD-ROM** and the practice page on Gerunds and Gerund Phrases in the *Writer's Solution Grammar Practice Book*, p. 30.

Build Your Portfolio

Idea Bank

Writing

1. Poster Sometimes, simple precautions can help prevent fires and illnesses. Create a warning poster about fire safety or disease prevention.

2. News Report Write an article about the plague or fire as it might have been reported in an English newspaper of the day. Incorporate factual information from the selections.

3. Response to Criticism Brian Fitzgerald says of Defoe, "He used literature to express his views on social and other questions and only secondarily as a craftsman and artist." Use the excerpt from Defoe's *A Journal of the Plague Year* to refute or support Fitzgerald's comment.

Speaking and Listening

4. Town Crier Many seventeenth-century Londoners got their news orally from a town crier, who called it out. As a town crier, call out news and warnings at the time of the plague or fire. **[Performing Arts Link]**

5. Oral Report Using library resources, learn the causes and history of bubonic plague. Present your findings in an oral report. **[Science Link; Social Studies Link]**

Projects

6. Map With a partner, research and create a map of the London area at the time of the plague and fire. Include major streets and landmarks mentioned in the selections. **[Social Studies Link]**

7. Timeline of Plagues Europe experienced several devasting epidemics of plague. Construct a timeline showing when those epidemics struck, how long they lasted, and the casualties they caused. **[Social Studies Link; Science Link]**

Writing Mini-Lesson

Diary Entry

Samuel Pepys captured what life was like for an upper-class Londoner living in an extraordinary time. Like Samuel Pepys, bring to life in a diary entry an incident you witnessed today. It might be an event of significance to your area or simply something important to you. A diary entry should be descriptive, honest, and accurate.

Writing Skills Focus: Accuracy

In all types of writing, it is important to be precise and **accurate**. Since diaries are kept to capture fleeting events and impressions, the more accurate diary entries are the more fully you can relive your experiences later on.

Here are some tips to ensure accuracy:
- Choose vivid and precise words to describe the people or events you see.
- Include correct names, dates, times, and locations, when appropriate.
- Truthfully record your observations and reactions. Your ideas and feelings *count.*

The following strategies will help you maintain accuracy as you write your diary entry.

Prewriting Jot down the event you plan to describe. Also list the people you saw, the time of day it occurred, and the main impression you wish to convey.

Drafting Put yourself back in the moment and capture on paper the event as it really happened. When you are uncertain about a name or fact, put a question mark beside it.

Revising Reread your diary entry, and verify names or facts about which you were uncertain. Make sure that you've described the event from your personal point of view. Date the diary entry if you have not already done so.

Idea Bank

Customizing for *Performance Levels*

Following are suggestions for matching Idea Bank topics with your students' ability levels:

Less Advanced Students: 1, 4
Average Students: 2, 6, 7
More Advanced Students: 3, 5

Customizing for *Learning Modalities*

Following are suggestions for matching Idea Bank topics with your students' learning modalities:

Visual/Spatial: 1, 6, 7
Bodily/Kinesthetic: 4
Verbal/Linguistic: 2, 3, 5
Interpersonal: 6

Writing Mini-Lesson

Refer students to the Writing Handbook, page 1189, for instruction on the writing process, and page 1191 for further information on description.

Writer's Solution

Writing Lab CD-ROM

Direct students to complete the tutorial on Description. Follow these steps:

1. Answer questions on the Self-Interview to generate ideas for the diary entry.
2. Use the Word Bins to choose sensory details.
3. Create a draft on the computer.
4. Complete interactive instruction on eliminating unnecessary words and phrases

Sourcebook

Have students complete Chapter 1: Description, pp. 1–29, for additional support.

✓ ASSESSMENT OPTIONS

Formal Assessment, Selection Test, pp. 111–113, and Assessment Resources Software. The selection test is designed so that it can be easily customized to the ability levels of your students.
Alternative Assessment, p. 22, includes options for less advanced students, more advanced students, visual/spatial learners, and interpersonal, verbal/linguistic learners.

PORTFOLIO ASSESSMENT

Use the following rubrics in the ***Alternative Assessment*** booklet to assess student writing:
Poster: How-to/Process Explanation Rubric, p. 101
News Report: Description Rubric, p. 98
Response to Criticism: Literary Analysis/Interpretation Rubric, p. 113
Writing Mini-Lesson: Expression Rubric, p. 95

Prepare and Engage

OBJECTIVES

1. To read, interpret, and respond to selections from a satirical novel
2. To relate the ideas in the selections to personal experience
3. To interpret satire
4. To identify characteristics of satire
5. To build vocabulary in context and learn the word root *-jec-*
6. To use *between* and *among* correctly
7. To write a satirical essay, taking into account its appropriateness for its medium
8. To respond to selections from *Gulliver's Travels* through writing, speaking and listening, and projects

SKILLS INSTRUCTION

Vocabulary
Word Roots: *-jec-*

Grammar:
Correct Use of *Between* and *Among*

Reading Strategy:
Interpret

Writing:
Appropriateness of Medium

Literary Focus:
Satire

Speaking and Listening:
Readers Theater (teacher edition)

Critical Viewing:
Infer; Assess; Compare and Contrast

PORTFOLIO OPPORTUNITIES

Writing: Imaginary Language; Spy's Report; News Story

Writing Mini-Lesson: Satirical Essay

Speaking and Listening: Film Conference; Readers Theater

Projects: A New Adventure; Gunpowder Report

More About the Author
In a letter written in 1725 to his friend Alexander Pope, Jonathan Swift declared that his chief goal in writing was to "vex the world rather than divert it." Because of the popularity of Swift's writing, there is a temptation to overlook an important part of Swift's personality. It is with this in mind that scholar A. L. Rowse notes the following: "One side of Swift's mind is hardly at all noticed—the scholarly side. He was extraordinarily widely read, and one must place the emphasis on the width of his intellectual interests. We know that at Moor Park he laid in a stock of reading sufficient to last a lifetime."

Guide for Interpreting

Jonathan Swift *(1667–1745)*

While Swift was writing *Gulliver's Travels*, he had already started to suffer from the inner ear disease that eventually disabled him. "I always expect tomorrow to be worse," he wrote in a letter, "but I enjoy today as well as I can." The result of the author's determination to keep up his spirits was that rarest of books: a literary masterpiece that is loved by children and adults alike.

Finding His Way Swift was born in Dublin, Ireland, to English parents. His father died before he was born. With the assistance of relatives, he received a good education and then obtained an appointment in the household of Sir William Temple, a wealthy kinsman who lived on an estate in Surrey, England. Swift hoped for a career in politics, but receiving no support from Sir William, however, he decided on a career in the church. After Temple's death in 1699, he was given a small parish near London.

The satirical writing Swift had done while in the Temple household was out of character for a clergyman, but its brilliance was widely acknowledged when it appeared as two separate books in 1704. Published anonymously, *A Tale of a Tub* satirizes excesses in religion and learning, while *The Battle of the Books* describes a comic encounter between ancient and modern literature.

Ambition and Achievement In Swift's day, religion was interwoven with politics. A staunch Anglican, Swift changed his allegiance in 1710 from the Whig party to the Tory party favored by Queen Anne. He benefited immediately from the switch. As the leading party writer for the government, he wrote many pamphlets and wielded considerable political influence.

The Story Behind the Novel The concept of writing a series of imaginary journeys probably originated in 1714 at the meetings of the Scriblerus Club, a group of Swift's literary friends. Apparently, the group assigned this project to Swift because they knew he enjoyed reading travel books. When *Gulliver's Travels* was published in 1726, it was an instant triumph: ten thousand copies were sold in the first three weeks.

Later Years Embittered by his failure to be named a bishop, Swift served for more than thirty years as dean of St. Patrick's Cathedral in Dublin. He continued to write satires, including *Drapier's Letters* (1724) and *A Modest Proposal* (1729).

Swift's death in 1745 deprived the world of a generous and learned man who despised the fanaticism, selfishness, and pride of people in general but admired individual human beings.

◆ Background for Understanding

HISTORY: SWIFT'S TARGETS FOR SATIRE

Swift's lifetime was a turbulent era in England due to religious strife and the struggles of political factions. These conflicts inspired Swift to ridicule in satire those whose intolerance and pride overcome their reason.

Swift satirizes the conflicts between the established Anglican Church and Roman Catholicism in "A Voyage to Lillliput," where the followers of each denomination are portrayed as Little-Endians and Big-Endians, respectively. Swift also ridicules the wars between officially Protestant England and heavily Catholic France, under the guise of conflict between Lilliput and Blefuscu.

In "A Voyage to Brobdingnag," Swift attacks the political institutions of England, though he can see some "half erased" value in their foundations. He suggests that the politicians leading the country are guilty of "ignorance, idleness, and vice."

Prentice Hall Literature Program Resources

REINFORCE / RETEACH / EXTEND

Selection Support Pages
Build Vocabulary: Word Roots: *-jec-*, p. 110
Grammar and Style: Correct Use of *Between* and *Among*, p. 111
Reading Strategy: Interpret, p. 112
Literary Focus: Satire, p. 113

Strategies for Diverse Student Needs, p. 23

Beyond Literature Cross Cultural Connection: Social Studies, p. 23

Formal Assessment Selection Test, pp. 114–116; Assessment Resources Software

Alternative Assessment, p. 23

Writing and Language Transparencies
Daily Language Practice, Week 19, p. 154
Writing Process Model 5: pp. 37–44

Resource Pro CD-ROM from *Gulliver's Travels* —includes all resource material and customizable lesson plan

Listening to Literature Audiocassettes from *Gulliver's Travels*

from Gulliver's Travels

◆ Literature and Your Life

CONNECT YOUR EXPERIENCE

Have you ever caught sight of your reflection without realizing that it was you? Funhouses use distorted mirrors to create this effect.

Literature has its own funhouse mirror—the satire, which exposes human weaknesses. By stretching and shrinking our image, satire gives us a new perspective on ourselves, just as Gulliver discovers on his visits with the tiny Lilliputians and giant Brobdingnagians.

Journal Writing List examples of modern-day satire. Then jot down two reasons why people enjoy satirical humor.

THEMATIC FOCUS: THE TIES THAT BIND

Swift aimed his satire at the conflicts of his age. What is his opinion of the bonds that connect people in society?

◆ Literary Focus

SATIRE

Satire is writing that uses wit and humor to expose and ridicule human vice and folly. Satire can be light and good-humored, or it can be bitter and unsparing. It can take the form of a story, a novel, or a song.

This type of writing may have grown from ancient harvest celebrations, where the entertainment included mocking wisecracks. Roman poets developed satire still further, using it as a way to get people to recognize their faults.

Gulliver's Travels extends this tradition by using realistic details to create a vivid fantasy world. He uses this world to mirror and criticize the follies of his time.

◆ Grammar and Style

CORRECT USE OF *BETWEEN* AND *AMONG*

Swift correctly uses the prepositions *between* and *among*. He uses *between* when referring to two items: "a bloody war hath been carried on *between* the two empires. . . ."

He uses *among* when referring to more than two items: "I kept *among* other little necessaries a pair of spectacles in a private pocket. . . ."

As you read the story, look for other examples of Swift's use of these prepositions in their proper places.

◆ Reading Strategy

INTERPRET

Satirists don't always state their opinions or name their targets directly. **Interpreting** clues to determine who is the object of the satire and why is part of the fun of reading satire.

For example, Swift's reference in "A Voyage to Lilliput" to "schism in religion" and to an (imaginary) sacred book help you interpret the Lilliputian wars as a satire on religious conflict. The fact that the fuss is about which end of the egg to break—not a very meaningful question—is an indication of Swift's opinion on the importance of some of the religious differences of the time.

◆ Build Vocabulary

WORD ROOTS: *-jec-*

In this selection, you will find the words *conjecture* and *project*. Both contain the root *-jec-*, which means "throw." To *conjecture* is to guess by "throwing" facts or inferences together. A *project* is literally a "throw forward"—"a plan or scheme for the future."

WORD BANK

Before you read, preview this list of words from the selection.

conjecture
expostulate
schism
expedient
habituate
odious

List the following on the chalkboard and ask students to make connections among the entries. (Students should recognize that all of these mock or satirize something.)

- Doonesbury
- Saturday Night Live skits
- Weird Al Yankovic songs

Explain to the class that during the time Jonathan Swift wrote, openly mocking or criticizing religious and political leaders was too dangerous, so he opted to write a satire in which he camouflaged, exaggerated, and then skewered the objects of his scorn. If a religious figure or member of the king's court were to have recognized himself in the story, it would have been as good as saying "If the shoe fits, wear it!"

Customize for
Verbal/Linguistic Learners

Written almost three hundred years ago, *Gulliver's Travels* contains language no longer in use. For example, at one point, Gulliver refers to the "glasses of his spectacles." Instruct these students as they read to create a glossary of terminology that has passed out of use.

Preparing for Standardized Tests

Reading and Vocabulary In reading comprehension portions of standardized tests and in some essay questions, students will be required to interpret a passage of literature. The lesson on interpreting will enable them to look beyond the printed word to arrive at a deeper meaning. For more practice with interpreting, use the Reading Strategy: Interpret in ***Selection Support,*** p. 112.

Grammar and Language Portions of some standardized tests require students to identify sentence errors such as the misuse of *between* and *among*. Following is an example:

Following a dispute (A) between several warring factions (B) the king decided to exile (C) the three rebel leaders (D). *(B)*

The Grammar and Style lesson for this selection will help students recognize that *B* should read "among several warring factions."

Develop Understanding

One-Minute Insight Swift sends Gulliver to Lilliput to do a job he probably could never have done so well at home: make fun of the religious conflicts of his day. By exposing the conflict between the Big-Endians and Little-Endians over which end of the egg to break, Swift, through Gulliver, comments with wry wit on the religious and political absurdities over which people do serious battle.

In "A Voyage to Brobdingnag," Swift satirizes English attitudes and modern warfare. To do so, he sends Gulliver to Brobdingnag, a place in which the people are twelve times as tall as Gulliver. There, Gulliver is treated almost as a pet by the royal family, who express their amazement and horror at his tales of life in his native land.

❶ **Clarification** Explain that "we" are the Lilliputians, who resemble the English, and that Blefuscu, which resembles France, is Lilliput's enemy and is threatening to invade. The Principal Secretary of Private Affairs is speaking here; he continues to speak until the first full paragraph on page 478.

◆ Literary Focus

❷ **Satire** Ask students why they think Swift suggests such a ridiculous and petty difference as the cause of a war. *Swift may be suggesting that all wars are, at root, absurd, or he may be saying people ought to be more accepting about differences in habits or preferences.*

from GULLIVER'S TRAVELS

Jonathan Swift

In Gulliver's Travels, *Swift exposes the corruption and defects in England's political, social, and economic institutions. The work centers on the four imaginary voyages of Lemuel Gulliver, the narrator, a well-educated but unimaginative ship's surgeon. Each of these voyages takes Gulliver to a different remarkable and bizarre world. During his stays in these imaginary lands, Gulliver is led toward realizations about the flawed nature of the society from which he had come, and he returns to England filled with disillusionment.*

from A VOYAGE TO LILLIPUT

After being shipwrecked, Gulliver swims to shore and drifts off to sleep. When he awakens, he finds that he has been tied down by the Lilliputians (lil′ ə pyōō′ shənz), *a race of people who are only six inches tall. Though he is held captive and his sword and pistols are taken from him, Gulliver gradually begins to win the Lilliputians' favor because of his mild disposition, and he is eventually granted his freedom. Through Gulliver's exposure to Lilliputian politics and court life, the reader becomes increasingly aware of the remarkable similarities between the English and Lilliputian affairs of state. The following excerpt begins during a discussion between the Lilliputian Principal Secretary of Private Affairs and Gulliver concerning the affairs of the Lilliputian empire.*

We are threatened with an invasion from the island of Blefuscu,[1] which is the other great empire of the universe, almost as large and powerful as this of his Majesty. For as to what we have heard you affirm, that there are other kingdoms and states in the world, inhabited by human creatures as large as yourself, our philosophers are in much doubt, and would rather conjecture that you dropped from the moon, or one of the stars; because it is certain, that an hundred mortals of your bulk would, in a short time, destroy all the fruits and cattle of his Majesty's dominions. Besides, our histories of six thousand moons make no mention of any other regions, than the two great empires of Lilliput and Blefuscu. Which two mighty powers have, as I was going to tell you, been engaged in a most obstinate war for six and thirty moons past. It began upon the following occasion. It is allowed on all hands, that the primitive way of breaking eggs before we eat them, was upon the larger end; but his present Majesty's grandfather, while he was a boy, going to eat an egg, and breaking it according to the ancient practice, happened to cut one of his fingers. Where-

1. **Blefuscu:** Represents France.

Block Scheduling Strategies

Consider these suggestions to take advantage of extended class time:

- Read and discuss with students the Background for Understanding on page 474 so that students will be able to recognize the institutions or people being satirized in the selection. Encourage students to read the footnoted information in the selection to clarify events and the people being satirized.
- Introduce students to the concept of satire presented in Literary Focus on page 475. As they read the selection, have them answer the Literary Focus questions boxed within the text. Then have them answer the Literary Focus questions on page 484.
- Display on an overhead the Daily Language Practice for Week 19. Have students write the passages correctly. Alternatively, you may prefer to dictate the passages for students to write correctly.
- Have pairs or groups work together on a project of their choice from the Idea Bank on page 485.
- Direct students to write a satirical essay as described in the Writing Mini-Lesson on page 485. When students' essays are completed, they may bind the essays together to create a satiric magazine.

◀ Critical Viewing Judging from this picture, what situation does Gulliver find himself in? [Infer] ❸ ❹

upon the Emperor, his father, published an edict, commanding all his subjects, upon great penalties, to break the smaller end of their
❷ eggs. The people so highly resented this law that our histories tell us there have been six rebellions raised on that account; wherein one emperor lost his life, and another his crown.[2] These civil commotions were constantly fomented by the monarchs of Blefuscu; and when they were quelled, the exiles always fled for refuge to that empire. It is computed that eleven thousand persons have,
at several times, suffered ❺
death rather than submit to break their eggs at the smaller end. Many hundred large volumes have been published upon this controversy; but the books of the Big-Endians have been long forbidden, and the whole party rendered incapable by law of holding employments.[3] During the course of these troubles, the emperors of Blefuscu did frequently expostulate by their ambassadors, accusing us of making a schism in religion, by offending against a fundamental doctrine of our great prophet Lustrog, in the fifty-fourth chapter of the *Brundecral* (which is their Alcoran).[4] This, however, is thought to be a mere strain upon the text, for the words are these: That all true believers shall break their eggs at the convenient end; and which is the convenient end, seems, in my humble opinion, to be left to every man's conscience, or at least in the power of the chief magistrate[5] to determine. Now the Big-Endian ↓

2. It is allowed . . . crown: Here, Swift satirizes the dispute in England between the Catholics (Big-Endians) and Protestants (Little-Endians). King Henry VIII who "broke" with the Catholic church, King Charles I, who "lost his life," and King James, who lost his "crown," are each referred to in the passage.

3. the whole party . . . employments: The Test Act (1673) prevented Catholics from holding office.

4. Alcoran: Koran, the sacred book of the Moslems.

5. chief magistrate: Ruler.

◆ Build Vocabulary

conjecture (kən jek′ chər) *v.*: Guess

expostulate (ik späs′ chə lāt′) *v.*: Reason earnestly with

schism (siz′ əm) *n.*: Division into groups or factions

▶Critical Viewing◀

❸ **Infer** Gulliver has been captured. The people who have captured him are tiny, yet their number is so great that they have been able to tie him down. Although they have used plenty of rope, it is unlikely that such small people will be able to keep Gulliver trussed.

Customize for *Visual/Spatial Learners*

❹ Ask students to make inferences from the expression on Gulliver's face about his attitude toward the situation in which he finds himself. *The expression of his eyes seems to suggest patient acceptance. It might also be logically read as wide-eyed wonder.*

◆ Reading Strategy

❺ **Interpret** Ask students to determine whether the loss of life and other suffering is to be blamed on the rulers, the people, or both. *Suggested response: The absurd edict began with the Emperor, and he may be blamed for beginning the tragedy, but the people themselves seemed almost eager to participate in it.*

Humanities: Art

Illustration from a nineteenth-century edition of *Gulliver's Travels*.

This illustration shows a large, wide-eyed, and somewhat cherubic looking Gulliver in the typical English dress of his day. Pink-cheeked and serene, Gulliver seems undisturbed by the extraordinary situation in which he finds himself—tied down to a vast plain, and surrounded by endless regiments of Lilliputians.

Use these questions for discussion:

1. Why do you think the artist shows Gulliver looking so relaxed? *Students may say that Gulliver is not worried about these little people. He may realize that the cords cannot hold him. Perhaps Gulliver is amused by what he sees. Perhaps Gulliver looks so relaxed because he is actually in a state of shock.*
2. Why are there so many Lilliputians in this picture? Why are they arranged in regiments, or what seem to be military groupings? *The number of Lilliputians makes it clear that Gulliver has found himself among an entire race of people who are just six inches tall. The Lilliputians may be shown in "formations" to make them appear just as organized and serious as "big" people: they are an organized, legitimate society, capable of doing the things full-size people do.*

◆ Grammar and Style

❶ Correct Use of *Between* and *Among* Ask students to explain why *between* is used in this sentence. *The relationship signaled by the preposition is between only two things, not three or more.*

◆ Literature and Your Life

❷ Ask students to explain the ways in which their responses would be the same as or different from Gulliver's if they found themselves in the same situation. *Students may say that Gulliver really has no choice except to offer to defend the Emperor, although he need not pledge his very life.*

◆ Reading Strategy

❸ Interpret Suggested response: A narrow channel, the English Channel, separates England and France.

▶Critical Viewing◀

❹ Assess Possible response: The artist has effectively conveyed Gulliver's patience. The expression on Gulliver's face is serene and even slightly amused. Gulliver's posture shows him bent to the task, working hard to achieve what is in the best interests of the Lilliputians.

❶ exiles have found so much credit in the Emperor of Blefuscu's court, and so much private assistance and encouragement from their party here at home, that a bloody war hath been carried on between the two empires for six and thirty moons with various success; during which time we have lost forty capital ships, and a much greater number of smaller vessels, together with thirty thousand of our best seamen and soldiers; and the damage received by the enemy is reckoned to be somewhat greater than ours. However, they have now equipped a numerous fleet, and are just preparing to make a descent upon us; and his Imperial Majesty, placing great confidence in your valor and strength, hath commanded me to lay this account of his affairs before you.

❷ I desired the Secretary to present my humble duty to the Emperor, and to let him know, that I thought it would not become me, who was a foreigner, to interfere with parties; but I was ready, with the hazard of my life, to defend his person and state against all invaders.

The empire of Blefuscu is an island situated to the north-northeast side of Lilliput, from whence it is parted only by a channel of eight hundred yards wide. I had not yet seen it, and upon this notice of an intended invasion, I avoided appearing on that side of the coast, for fear of being discovered by some of the enemy's ships, who had received no intelligence of me, all intercourse between the two empires having been strictly forbidden during the war, upon pain of death, and an embargo laid by our Emperor upon all vessels whatsoever. I communicated to his Majesty a project I had formed of seizing the enemy's whole fleet; which, as our scouts assured us, lay at anchor in the harbor ready to sail with the first fair wind. I consulted the most experienced seamen upon the depth of the channel, which they had often plumbed, who told me, that in the middle at high water it was seventy *glumgluffs* deep (which is about six feet of European measure), and the rest of it fifty *glumgluffs* at most. I

❸ **◆ Reading Strategy** How might the mention of a narrow channel suggest England and France?

▼ Critical Viewing How well has the artist conveyed Gulliver's extreme patience when dealing with the Lilliputians? **[Assess]** ❹

A Voyage to Lilliput, Illustration from a nineteenth-century edition of *Gulliver's Travels*

Humanities: Art

A Voyage to Lilliput: Illustration from a nineteenth-century edition of *Gulliver's Travels*.

Here Gulliver indulgently helps the Lilliputians and averts violence by stealing the fleet of their enemies, the Blefuscudians. In the illustration, Gulliver seems intent only on his task, while the Lilliputians cheer their new hero and celebrate such an easy victory over their enemy.

Use these questions for discussion:

1. Why are the Lilliputians pictured in full military dress? *Suggested response: The Lilliputians could not be sure how Gulliver's efforts would turn out. They are ready for attack by the Blefuscudians.*
2. Why doesn't Gulliver smile and wave in light of the fact that the crowd is delighted by his efforts on their behalf? *Suggested responses: Gulliver has done what he felt needed to be done. He actually has no personal stake in the outcome, and he has no reason to feel particularly proud: what he accomplished was accomplished primarily because he was simply bigger than his opponents.*

walked to the northeast coast over against Blefuscu, where, lying down behind a hillock, I took out my small pocket perspective-glass, and viewed the enemy's fleet at anchor, consisting of about fifty men of war, and a great number of transports. I then came back to my house and gave order (for which I had a warrant) for a great quantity of the strongest cable and bars of iron. The cable was about as thick as packthread, and the bars of the length and size of a knitting-needle. I trebled the cable to make it stronger, and for the same reason I twisted three of the iron bars together, bending the extremities into a hook. Having thus fixed fifty hooks to as many cables, I went back to the northeast coast and, putting off my coat, shoes, and stockings, walked into the sea in my leathern jerkin, about half an hour before high water. I waded with what haste I could, and swam in the middle about thirty yards until I felt ground; I arrived at the fleet in less than half an hour. The enemy was so frightened when they saw me, that they leaped out of their ships, and swam to shore, where there could not be fewer than thirty thousand souls. I then took my tackling, and, fastening a hook to the hole at the prow of each, I tied all the
5 cords together at the end. While I was thus employed, the enemy discharged several thousand arrows, many of which struck in my hands and face and, besides the excessive smart, gave me much disturbance in my work. My greatest apprehension was for my eyes, which I should have infallibly lost, if I had not suddenly thought of an expedient. I kept among other little necessaries a pair of spectacles in a private pocket, which, as I observed before, had escaped the Emperor's searchers. These I took out and fastened as strongly as I could upon my nose and thus armed went on boldly with my work in spite of the enemy's arrows, many of which struck against the glasses of my spectacles, but without any other effect further than a little to discompose them. I had now fastened all the hooks and, taking the knot in my hand, began to pull, but not a ship would stir, for they were all too fast held by their anchors, so that the boldest part of my enterprise remained. I therefore let go the cord, and, leaving the hooks fixed to the ships, I resolutely cut with my knife the cables that fastened the anchors, receiving above two hundred shots in my face and hands; then I took up the knotted end of the cables to which my hooks were tied and, with great ease, drew fifty of the enemy's 5
largest men-of-war after me.

The Blefuscudians, who had not the least imagination of what I intended, were at first confounded with astonishment. They had seen me cut the cables and thought my design was only to let the ships run adrift or fall foul on each other; but when they perceived the whole fleet, moving in order, and saw me pulling at the end, they set up such a scream of grief and despair that it is almost impossible to describe or conceive. When I had got out of danger, I stopped a while to pick out the arrows that stuck in my hands and face, and rubbed on some of the same ointment that was given me at my first arrival, as I have formerly mentioned. I then took off my spectacles, and, waiting about an hour until the tide was a little fallen, I waded through the middle with my cargo and arrived safe at the royal port of Lilliput.

The Emperor and his whole court stood on the shore expecting the issue of this great adventure. They saw the ships move forward in a large half-moon but could not discern me, who was up to my breast in water. When I advanced to the middle of the channel, they were yet more in pain, because I was under water to my neck. The Emperor concluded me to be drowned, and that the enemy's fleet was approaching in a hostile manner; but he was soon eased of his fears; for, the channel growing shallower every step I made, I came in a short time within hearing, and holding up the end of the cable by which the fleet was fastened, I cried in a loud voice, Long live the most puissant[6] Emperor of Lilliput! This great prince received me at my landing with all possible encomiums and created me a *Nardac* 6
upon the spot, which is the highest title of honor among them.

His Majesty desired I would take some other opportunity of bringing all the rest of his enemy's ships into his ports. And so unmea-

6. **puissant** (pyōō´ i sənt): Powerful.

◆ Build Vocabulary

expedient (ik spē´ dē ənt) *n.*: Device used in an emergency

Customize for *English Language Learners*

To help students with the dense description on this page, explain how the illustration on page 478 helps sum up what happens. You might point out that Gulliver is wading in water that is almost up to his waist, that he has stripped down to his vest, that he is wearing spectacles to protect his eyes from the arrows, that cables are attached to the ships by hooks, and that the waiting Lilliputians welcome Gulliver's return.

Customize for *Visual/Spatial Learners*

The passage telling of Gulliver's actions is full of descriptive detail. Encourage visual/spatial learners to use the details to map out Gulliver's movements described in this section of the story.

◆ Literary Focus

5 Satire Ask students: Is this passage more indicative of satire or plain narrative? Explain. *This passage does not contain elements of satire; instead it is a straightforward descriptive passage that furthers the plot of the story.*

◆ Grammar and Style

6 Correct Use of *Between* and *Among* Ask students to explain why *among* is used in this sentence. *The relationship signaled by the preposition is among more than two persons.*

Beyond the Classroom

Workplace Skill

Problem Solving In this story, Gulliver confronts problems he has never encountered before, but he solves them in a step-by-step fashion using a combination of prior knowledge, mathematical skill, scientific principles, and logic. Have students identify the types of problem-solving skills Gulliver is using in each of these actions: (a) using his perspective-glass *(he is assessing the situation, gathering knowledge, using tools);* (b) giving the order for a great quantity of cable and bars of iron *(he is gathering materials);* (c) tripling the cable and twisting the iron *(he is using knowledge of scientific principles and mathematics to increase the strength of his tools);* (d) fastening a hook to the prow of each boat *(he is using prior knowledge about the need for a something strong enough to hold the weight and stand up to the force of his pulling).*

Customize for
Interpersonal Learners
To explore character and to understand the satire better, invite students to create personality profiles for both Gulliver and the king. These might include straightforward "facts" such as occupation and personality traits, as well as creative ideas like last book read, favorite hobby, and favorite quotation.

◆ Critical Thinking

❶ **Interpret** Ask students why, given Gulliver's aid, Gulliver refuses to help the Lilliputians take over Blefuscu. *Gulliver does not believe that such an action is right. He did not help the Lilliputians in order to further their political ends but to end the threat of invasion and resulting loss of life.*

◆ Grammar and Style

❷ **Correct Use of *Between* and *Among*** Ask students to explain why *between* is used in this sentence. *The relationship signaled by the preposition is between only two things, even though one of those two things, the junta, clearly consists of many people. Nevertheless, because the junta acts as one unit, it is regarded as one thing.*

◆ Critical Thinking

❸ **Compare and Contrast** Ask students to name the similarities and differences between Gulliver's situation in Lilliput and his situation in Brobdingnag. *In Lilliput, Gulliver was captured; in Brobdingnag he has been sold; in Lilliput, Gulliver was among short people; in Brobdingnag he is among giants; in Lilliput, Gulliver took action; in Brobdingnag, he is called upon to explain.*

◆ Literary Focus

❹ **Satire** References to the King and Queen, Whig and Tory, and "the scourge of France" point specifically to England. A more general mockery can be found in references to trade, wars by sea and land, schisms in religion, and political parties.

surable is the ambition of princes, that he seemed to think of nothing less than reducing the whole empire of Blefuscu into a province and governing it by a viceroy; of destroying the Big-Endian exiles and compelling that people to break the smaller end of their eggs, by
❶ which he would remain sole monarch of the whole world. But I endeavored to divert him from this design by many arguments drawn from the topics of policy as well as justice, and I plainly protested that I would never be an instrument of bringing a free and brave people into slavery. And when the matter was debated in council, the wisest part of the ministry were of my opinion.

This open bold declaration of mine was so opposite to the schemes and politics of his Imperial Majesty that he could never forgive me; he mentioned it in a very artful manner at council, where I was told that some of the wisest appeared, at least, by their silence, to be of my opinion; but others, who were my secret enemies, could not forbear some expressions, which by a sidewind reflected on me. And from this time began an intrigue between his
❷ Majesty and a junta of ministers maliciously bent against me, which broke out in less than two months and had like to have ended in my utter destruction. Of so little weight are the greatest services to princes when put into the balance with a refusal to gratify their passions.

from A Voyage to Brobdingnag

Gulliver's second voyage leads him to Brobdingnag (bräb΄ diŋ nag΄), *an island located near Alaska that is inhabited by giants twelve*
❸ *times as tall as Gulliver. After being sold to the Queen of Brobdingnag, Gulliver describes the English social and political institutions to the King, who reacts to his description with contempt and disgust.*

It is the custom that every Wednesday (which, as I have before observed, was their Sabbath) the King and Queen, with the royal issue of both sexes, dine together in the apartment of his Majesty, to whom I was now become a favorite; and at these times my little chair and table were placed at his left hand before one of the saltcellars. This prince took a pleasure in conversing with me, inquiring into the manners, religion, laws, government, and learning of Europe, wherein I gave him the best account I was able. His apprehension was so clear, and his judgment so exact, that he made very wise reflections and observations upon all I said. But I confess, that after I had been a little too copious in talking of my own beloved country, of our trade, and wars by sea and land, of our schisms in religion, and parties in the state, the prejudices of his education prevailed so far, that he could not forbear taking me up in his right hand, and stroking me gently with the other, after an hearty fit of laughing, asked me whether I were a Whig or a Tory.[7] Then turning to his first minister, who waited behind him with a white staff, near as tall as the mainmast of the *Royal Sovereign*,[8] he observed how contemptible a thing was human grandeur, which could be mimicked by such diminutive insects as I. And yet, said he, I dare engage, those creatures have their titles and distinctions of honor, they contrive little nests and burrows, that they call houses and cities; they make a figure in dress and equipage;[9] they love, they fight, they dispute, they cheat, they betray. And thus he continued on, while my color came and went several times, with indignation to hear our noble country, the mistress of arts and arms, the scourge of France, the arbitress of Europe, the seat of virtue, piety, honor and truth, the pride and envy of the world, so contemptuously treated. . . .

◆ Literary Focus ❹
What details in this paragraph show Swift's satire to be directed against English affairs? Which details suggest a more general mockery of humanity?

He laughed at my odd kind of arithmetic (as he was pleased to call it) in reckoning the numbers of our people by a computation drawn from the several sects among us in religion and politics. He said he knew no reason why those who entertain opinions prejudicial to the public should be obliged to change or should not be obliged to conceal them. And, as it was tyranny in any government to require

7. **Whig . . . Tory:** British political parties.
8. ***Royal Sovereign*:** One of the largest ships in the British Navy.
9. **equipage** (ek΄ wi pij΄): Horses and carriages.

Cross-Curricular Connection: Social Studies

Britain and France At the beginning of the eighteenth century, France was the most populous and powerful state in the world, and Britain was its enemy. When the Tory party came into power in 1710 in Britain (and Swift became a Tory at that time), Britain eventually made peace with France.

Religious Discrimination In the early 1700's, there were some Britons who did not have the right to vote, but even they had rights to petition, to a trial by jury, and to freedom from arbitrary arrest. To have full political privileges, a person had to be a member of the Anglican church. Swift was himself a clergyman and spirited supporter of the Anglican church in Ireland. Have interested students find out more about the place and times in which he lived.

5 ▶ **Critical Viewing** Compare the relationship between Gulliver and the King of Brobdingnag as portrayed by the artist with that portrayed in the text. **[Compare and Contrast]**

the first, so it was weakness not to enforce the second; for, a man may be allowed to keep poisons in his closets, but not to vend them about as cordials.

He observed, that among the diversions of our nobility and gentry[10] I had mentioned gaming.[11] He desired to know at what age this entertainment was usually taken up, and when it was laid down. How much of their time it employed; whether it ever went so high as to affect their fortunes. Whether
6 mean vicious people by their dexterity in that art might not arrive at great riches, and sometimes keep our very nobles in dependence, as well as habituate them to vile companions, wholly take them from the improvement of their minds, and force them, by the losses they received, to learn and practice that infamous dexterity upon others.

A Voyage to Brobdingnag, Illustration from a nineteenth-century edition of *Gulliver's Travels*

He was perfectly astonished with the historical account I gave him of our affairs during the last century, protesting it was only an
7 heap of conspiracies, rebellions, murders, massacres, revolutions, banishments, the very worst effects that avarice, faction, hypocrisy, perfidiousness, cruelty, rage, madness, hatred, envy, lust, malice, and ambition could produce. 7

His Majesty in another audience was at the pains to recapitulate the sum of all I had spoken; compared the questions he made with the answers I had given; then taking me into his hands, and stroking me gently, delivered himself in these words, which I shall never forget, nor the manner he spoke them in. "My little

10. **gentry:** The class of landowning people ranking just below the nobility.
11. **gaming:** Gambling.

◆ **Build Vocabulary**

habituate (hə bich′ o͞o āt′) *v.*: Make used to

▶ **Critical Viewing** ◀

5 **Compare and Contrast** In the text, Gulliver sits at a small table at the king's left hand, in front of one of the saltcellars. In this illustration, he sits, with no table or saltcellar in sight, at the king's right hand. In the text, the king is described at first as making very wise reflections on what Gulliver had to say. The artist has captured the look of wise conjecture in this illustration, which shows the king in an attitude of concentrated attention and thoughtfulness.

◆ Literary Focus

6 **Satire** Ask students to explain the ways in which Swift satirizes gambling. *Gambling is being criticized indirectly and humorously. The king's progression of questions suggests that vicious people use the practice to take advantage of others; that foolish people become dependent on gambling and choose that occupation over others that might improve their minds.*

Customize for
More Advanced Students

7 Challenge advanced students to name one or more events from American history during the last century that could make our own nation's affairs seem like a "heap of conspiracies, rebellions, murders, massacres," and so on. *Students may mention such events as the assassination of President Kennedy, Watergate, Contragate, and the bombing of the World Trade Center.*

Humanities: Art

A Voyage to Brobdingnag: Illustration from a nineteenth-century edition of *Gulliver's Travels.*

In this illustration, a king who is dressed like a European king of Swift's day, carefully listens as Gulliver talks. Like a European king, he wears a golden and jeweled crown, and his dress bespeaks splendor. Gulliver, with one hand behind his chair and the other reaching forward in a gesture of explanation, seems perfectly at ease in the royal presence.

Use these questions for discussion:

1. What does the look on the king's face convey? *Suggested responses: The king is sadly amused by what he hears. He may feel compassion for Gulliver, who appears to come from such an ignoble world. Some students may interpret the look on the king's face as a sign of reluctance to believe what he is hearing.*
2. Gulliver's pose is relaxed. Why do you think the artist chose to represent him in such a relaxed manner? *Suggested responses: The artist seems to suggest that the king is listening without undue censure; he is creating an atmosphere in which it is easy for Gulliver to say whatever comes to mind. Also, as is seen in the novel, Gulliver is unaware of the impact of his stories on the king; what seems normal and civilized to Gulliver seems barbaric to the king.*

❶ **Clarification** Explain that the king may be referring here to the lofty ideals of the Magna Carta, the basis of English constitutional rights, as well as, perhaps, to the Petition of Right (1628) and the Bill of Rights (1689), both of which upheld English rights and liberties.

◆ *Literature and Your Life*

❷ Ask students: If you were in the same situation, would you feel as Gulliver did? Explain. *Possible answer: It would be difficult to hear one's country mocked so openly. Many people in Gulliver's situation would omit this part of the story.*

◆ Literary Focus

❸ **Satire** (a) The king does not seem to suffer from narrowness of thinking, because he listens with great concentration and thoughtfulness. Also he does not condemn Gulliver, even though Gulliver represents the people whom he describes. The king also makes intelligent observations and asks thoughtful questions, such as those he makes and asks about gaming. (b) Gulliver seems to be rationalizing here, as perhaps England rationalizes its behavior. He is blaming the king's reaction on the king rather than on the information Gulliver himself is conveying.

❹ **Enrichment** Point out that the use of gunpowder was considered a great advance in military history and a means of saving lives since less brutal forms of hand-to-hand combat could thereby be avoided.

◆ Literary Focus

❺ **Satire** Ask students how Gulliver's description of gunpowder and the king's reaction help Swift satirize modern warfare. *Gulliver's brutal description of the destructive and lethal effects of gunpowder and warfare echoes Swift's ideas about it. The king's horrified reaction and Swift's seem to be one and the same.*

friend Grildrig, you have made a most admirable panegyric upon your country. You have clearly proved that ignorance, idleness, and vice are the proper ingredients for qualifying a legislator. That laws are best explained, interpreted, and applied by those whose interest and abilities lie in perverting, confounding, and eluding them. ❶ I observe among you some lines of an institution, which in its original might have been tolerable, but these half erased, and the rest wholly blurred and blotted by corruptions. It doth not appear from all you have said how any one perfection is required toward the procurement of any one station among you, much less that men are ennobled on account of their virtue, that priests are advanced for their piety or learning, soldiers for their conduct or valor, judges for their integrity, senators for the love of their country, or counselors for their wisdom. As for yourself," continued the King, "who have spent the greatest part of your life in traveling, I am well disposed to hope you may hitherto have escaped many vices of your country. But, by what I have gathered from your own relation, and the answers I have with much pains wringed and extorted from you, I cannot but conclude the bulk of your natives to be the most pernicious race of little odious vermin that nature ever suffered to crawl upon the surface of the earth."

❷ Nothing but an extreme love of truth could have hindered me from concealing this part of my story. It was in vain to discover my resentments, which were always turned into ridicule; and I was forced to rest with patience while my noble and most beloved country was so injuriously treated. I am heartily sorry as any of my readers can possibly be that such an occasion was given, but this prince happened to be so curious and inquisitive upon every particular that it could not consist either with gratitude or good manners to refuse giving him what satisfaction I was able. Yet thus much I may be allowed to say in my own vindication that I artfully eluded many of his questions and gave to every point a more favorable turn by many degrees than the strictness of truth would allow. For I have always borne that laudable partiality to my own country, which Dionysius Halicarnassensis[12] with so much justice recommends to an historian. I would hide the frailties and deformities of my political mother and place her virtues and beauties in the most advantageous light. This was my sincere endeavor in those many discourses I had with that mighty monarch, although it unfortunately failed of success.

But great allowances should be given to a king who lives wholly secluded from the rest of the world, and must therefore be altogether unacquainted with the manners and customs that most prevail in other nations: the want of which knowledge will ever produce many prejudices, and a certain narrowness of thinking, from which we and the politer countries of Europe are wholly exempted. And it would be hard indeed, if so remote a prince's notions of virtue and vice were to be offered as a standard for all mankind. ❸

> **◆ Literary Focus**
> (a) What clues in the preceding paragraphs suggest that the king does not suffer from "narrowness of thinking"? (b) Given these clues, what can you infer about Gulliver's attitude in this paragraph?

To confirm what I have now said, and further to show the miserable effects of a confined education, I shall here insert a passage which will hardly obtain belief. In hopes to ingratiate myself farther into his Majesty's favor, I told him of an invention discovered between three and four hundred years ago, to make a certain powder, into an heap of which the smallest spark of fire falling, would kindle the whole in a moment, although it were as big as a mountain, and make it all fly up in the air together, with a noise and agitation greater than thunder. ❹ That a proper quantity of this powder rammed into an hollow tube of brass or iron, according to its bigness, would drive a ball of iron or lead with such violence and speed as nothing was able to sustain its force. That the largest balls, thus discharged, would not only destroy whole ranks of an army at once, but batter the strongest

◆ Build Vocabulary

odious (ō′ dē əs) *adj.*: Hateful; disgusting

12. **Dionysius** (dī′ ə nish′ əs) **Halicarnassensis** (hal′ ə kär na sen′ sis): Greek writer who lived in Rome and attempted to persuade the Greeks to submit to their Roman conquerors.

Speaking and Listening Mini-Lesson

Readers Theater

This mini-lesson supports the Speaking and Listening activity in the Idea Bank on page 485.

Introduce the Concept Explain that in readers theater a group of readers work together to re-create a work of literature or a portion of a literary work in a dramatic way without action or props. The readers use only vocal inflection to capture emotion or drama.

Develop Background Tell students to take parts, and plan and practice their performance. They may mark directions for loudness, softness, pauses, gestures, and other movements on photocopies of the text.

Apply the Information After students have rehearsed, have them perform their scenes for the class with the goal of bringing to life the characters from the selection.

Assess the Outcome Have the audience assess the performance in terms of adherence to the original selection, clarity and effectiveness of the dialogue, and energy level of the participants.

walls to the ground, sink down ships, with a thousand men in each, to the bottom of the sea; and when linked together by a chain, would cut through masts and rigging, divide hundreds of bodies in the middle, and lay all waste before them. That we often put this powder into large hollow balls of iron, and discharged them by an engine into some city we were besieging, which would rip up the pavement, tear the houses to pieces, burst and throw splinters on every side, dashing out
5 the brains of all who came near. That I knew the ingredients very well, which were cheap, and common; I understood the manner of compounding them, and could direct his workmen how to make those tubes of a size proportionable to all other things in his Majesty's kingdom, and the largest need not be above two hundred foot long; twenty or thirty of which tubes, charged with the proper quantity of powder and balls, would batter down the walls of the strongest town in his dominions in a few hours, or destroy the whole metropolis, if ever it should pretend to dispute his absolute commands. This I humbly offered to his Majesty as a small tribute of acknowledgment in return of so many marks that I had received of his royal favor and protection.

The King was struck with horror at the description I had given of those terrible engines and the proposal I had made. He was amazed how so impotent and groveling an insect as I 5
(these were his expressions) could entertain such inhuman ideas, and in so familiar a manner as to appear wholly unmoved at all the scenes of blood and desolation which I had painted as the common effects of those destructive machines; whereof he said some evil genius, enemy to mankind, must have been the first contriver. As for himself, he protested that although few things delighted him so much as new discoveries in art or in nature, yet he would rather lose half his kingdom than be privy to such a secret, which he commanded me, as I valued my life, never to mention any more.

Guide for Responding

◆ Literature and Your Life

Reader's Response Explain why you would or would not like to travel with Gulliver.

Thematic Focus What might Swift find to satirize in today's society?

Gulliver on TV If you were to adapt these tales for television, would you target adults or children? Explain.

☑ Check Your Comprehension

1. Describe the conflict between Lilliput and Blefuscu over the breaking of eggs.
2. How does Gulliver aid the King of Lilliput?
3. What are the consequences of Gulliver's refusal to destroy the King of Lilliput's enemies?
4. How does the King of Brobdingnag view English history of the preceding hundred years?
5. What is the King of Brobdingnag's reaction to Gulliver's proposal that he use gunpowder?

◆ Critical Thinking

INTERPRET

1. What does Swift's attitude seem to be toward the dispute between English Catholics and Protestants? Explain your answer. **[Infer]**
2. Swift gives a realistic account of how Gulliver captures the Blefuscudian fleet. Explain how this episode adds to or detracts from his satirical points. **[Analyze]**
3. (a) How is Gulliver's perspective on the Lilliputians different from his perspective on the Brobdingnagians? (b) How is the Brobdingnagians' view of Gulliver similar to Gulliver's view of the Lilliputians? **[Compare and Contrast]**
4. Find a passage suggesting that Swift thinks there is hope for human beings. **[Support]**

EVALUATE

5. In this excerpt, Gulliver visits one tiny race and one huge one. (a) Why does Swift use this device? (b) Explain how effective it is. **[Assess]**

Beyond the Selection

FURTHER READING

Other Works by Jonathan Swift

"A Tale of a Tub"

"The Battle of the Books"

"A Modest Proposal"

"The Spider and the Bee"

More Works on Politics and Government

"The Morals of the Prince," Nicolò Machiavelli

"The Rabbits Who Caused All the Trouble," James Thurber

INTERNET

You and your students may find additional information about Jonathan Swift on the Internet at the following site. Please be aware, however, that sites may have changed from the time we published this information.

For a *Gulliver's Travels* home page including text, sources, images, and dates, go to **http://www.jaffebros.com/lee/gulliver**

You may also find related information on Swift and satire on the Internet. We *strongly recommend* that you preview the sites before you send students to them.

Reinforce and Extend

Answers

◆ Literature and Your Life

Reader's Response Possible responses: Traveling with Gulliver would be interesting and adventure-filled; traveling with Gulliver would be too dangerous to enjoy.

Thematic Focus Swift might satirize the same types of things: religious conflicts, warfare, and political figures.

☑ Check Your Comprehension

1. When the Emperor of the Lilliputians ordered his subjects to break the small end of their eggs, the Blefuscudians supported the Lilliputian rebels who wished to continue breaking their eggs at the large end.
2. Gulliver aids the King of Lilliput by seizing the fleet of his enemy's (the Blesfuscudians') ships.
3. The King never forgave Gulliver and conspired to get rid of him.
4. The King of Brobdingnag views English history as a "heap of conspiracies, rebellions, murders [and] massacres. . . ."
5. The King is struck with horror at such inhuman ideas.

◆ Critical Thinking

1. Swift seems to think that the dispute between the Catholics and Protestants is as silly as the dispute over the proper way to break an egg.
2. The realistic detail serves to create a vivid fantasy world that enhances Swift's satiric points.
3. (a) Gulliver sees the Lilliputians as silly and uncivilized; he sees the Brobdingnagians as naïve and unrealistic. (b) The Brobdingnagians' view of Gulliver is similar to Gulliver's view of the Lilliputians.
4. The final paragraph subtly conveys Swift's hopes for humanity. The King of the Brobdingnagians is so civilized and humane that readers can hope that others will learn from him.
5. (a) Swift uses the device to symbolize humanity: smaller people are less humane and more cruel in nature, whereas larger people are more civilized and greater in tolerance and humanity. (b) The device is effective. Swift makes his point on several levels, literal as well as philosophical.

Answers

◆ Reading Strategy

1. (a) Although the character Gulliver states that the King of Brobdingnag is narrow-minded, Swift probably does not think so: the qualities he gives the King are human and civilized. (b) It shows that Swift believes that mankind, through Gulliver, has yet a few things to learn, that we are not as "big" as we think we are.
2. Swift is referring to the continual conflict and intolerance between Catholics and Protestants. Students may cite: religious martyrs such as Thomas More and Thomas à Beckett; Queen Elizabeth I's persecution of Catholics and the execution of Mary, Queen of Scots.

◆ Build Vocabulary

Using the Word Root *-jec-*

1. *projection:* something that is thrown forward
2. *eject:* to throw out
3. *trajectory:* the path of something thrown
4. *inject:* to throw in
5. *reject:* to throw back

Using the Word Bank

1. c 2. f 3. a 4. b 5. e 6. d

◆ Literary Focus

1. Swift satirizes the religious disputes by likening the point of dispute to an argument over which end of an egg it is proper to break.
2. (a) ". . . taking me up in his right hand, and stroking me gently with the other, ..." (b) This difference graphically illustrates that the King is the larger person in deed as well as size.
3. Comparisons should show that Gulliver's perceptions of the Lilliputians as silly and barbaric is mirrored in the King of Brobdingnag's perceptions of Gulliver and his people as silly and barbaric. The characterization of the King of Brobdingnag leaves the reader with a sense that there is hope for humanity.

Guide for Responding *(continued)*

◆ Reading Strategy

Interpret

To appreciate satire, readers must **interpret** authors' attitudes and their references to historical facts. For example, before the King of Brobdingnag asks Gulliver which political party he belongs to, he laughs and picks Gulliver up. His laughter, and the fact that he treats Gulliver like a pet or child, are clues to Swift's meaning. You can interpret them as a reflection of how small and insignificant human politics can appear.

1. Before telling how the King of Brobdingnag reacts to the idea of gunpowder, Gulliver requests the reader to make "great allowances" for the King of Brobdingnag's "narrowness of thinking." (a) Does Swift think the King is narrow-minded? Explain. (b) Show how Gulliver's inability to see the King's point of view makes the satire more effective.

2. To what actual historical facts does Swift refer when he says that thousands have "suffered death rather than submit to break their eggs at the smaller end"?

◆ Build Vocabulary

Using the Word Root *-jec-*

Knowing that the word root *jec-* means "throw," write definitions for the following words.

1. projection
2. eject
3. trajectory
4. inject
5. reject

Using the Word Bank

For each word in Column A, write on your paper the letter of the term in Column B whose meaning is its opposite.

1. conjecture	**a.** fusion
2. expostulate	**b.** unworkable device
3. schism	**c.** certainty
4. expedient	**d.** pleasant
5. habituate	**e.** surprise
6. odious	**f.** demand

◆ Literary Focus

Satire

Satire uses wit, humor, and sharp contrasts to expose human vice and folly. One such contrast in *Gulliver's Travels* is Gulliver's pride in gunpowder and the king's horror at its uses. The contrast creates effective satire—Swift lets us look at gunpowder through the eyes of the "ignorant" king, forcing us to see the evil of what we might otherwise accept unquestioningly.

1. Describe the method Swift uses to satirize disputes between Catholics and Protestants.

2. (a) Find a passage that emphasizes the difference in size between Gulliver and the King of Brobdingnag. (b) Explain how the difference helps Swift make a satirical point.

3. Compare Gulliver's perceptions of Lilliput with the King of Brobdingnag's perceptions of Gulliver and the English. Which picture leaves you with more hope for humanity? Why?

◆ Grammar and Style

Correct Use of *Between* and *Among*

Use **between** when referring to only two items or groups of items. Use **among** when referring to more than two items.

Practice In your notebook, fill in each blank with the correct preposition: *between* or *among*.

1. I learned about the war ___?___ Lilliput and Blefuscu from the Principal Secretary of the Lilliputians.
2. A channel eight hundred yards wide lies ___?___ the two countries.
3. ___?___ the Lilliputians, a Big-Endian faction refused to accept the emperor's edict.
4. Wednesday is the Sabbath ___?___ the Brobdingnagians.
5. The difference in size ___?___ Gulliver and the Lilliputians was remarkable.
6. The king noticed gambling was ___?___ the upper-class pastimes mentioned by Gulliver.
7. The Lilliputians did not agree ___?___ themselves whether Gulliver should destroy Blefuscu.

◆ Grammar and Style

1. I learned about the war *between* Lilliput and Blefuscu from the Principal Secretary of the Lilliputians.
2. A channel eight hundred yards wide lies *between* the two countries.
3. *Among* the Lilliputians, a Big-Endian faction refused to accept the emperor's edict.
4. Wednesday is the Sabbath *among* the Brobdingnagians.
5. The difference in size *between* Gulliver and the Lilliputians was remarkable.
6. The king noticed gambling was *among* the upper-class pastimes mentioned by Gulliver.
7. The Lilliputians did not agree *among* themselves whether Gulliver should destroy Blefuscu.

Build Your Portfolio

Idea Bank

Writing

1. **Imaginary Language** Invent five imaginary words like the ones used in Lilliput that would be useful in Brobdingnag. Then write a dictionary entry for each, giving the pronunciation, part of speech, and meaning.

2. **Spy's Report** A (small) spy for Brobdingnag is among us! Write the letter such a spy might send the King, emphasizing features of today's world that would surprise or horrify His Majesty.

3. **News Story** Write a news article for Lilliputian readers, reporting on Gulliver's achievements against the Blefuscudians and summarizing the reactions of the Emperor and his ministers. **[Media Link]**

Speaking and Listening

4. **Film Conference** With a small group, plan the special effects for a filmed version of *Gulliver's Travels*. Discuss where in the story you will use them and how you will carry them out. **[Media Link]**

5. **Reader's Theater** With a small group, design and present a reader's theater production of either selection, converting Swift's reported dialogue into direct speech. **[Performing Arts Link]**

Projects

6. **A New Adventure** Write and illustrate a story in which Gulliver visits another land. Decide on its inhabitants, and focus your satire on one aspect of human folly. **[Social Studies Link]**

7. **Gunpowder Report** Write a research report on how the invention of gunpowder changed the rules of war. Include reactions of people of the time to its invention. **[Social Studies Link]**

Writing Mini-Lesson

Satirical Essay

In his novel, Swift uses outlandish settings and situations to ridicule human vices and follies. You can write a satirical essay that describes, exaggerates, and mocks a foolish behavior or trend in today's world. Also, you can design your essay for print, radio, or television, whichever medium will help you reach the audience you want.

Writing Skills Focus: Appropriateness for Medium

In writing your satire, take into account the **medium** in which it will appear. Because people can reread a newspaper essay, you can use longer sentences than you could for a radio or television piece. Radio and television require punchier writing. For television, you will probably also want to come up with a visual or visuals that will accompany the reading of the essay.

Prewriting Target your satire. Choose a particular behavior, trend, or attitude to attack. Then consider how you can exaggerate or describe it to make it seem even more foolish. Sometimes an unusual point of view—like that of a visiting Brobdingnagian—can give you a satiric "angle" on your subject. Also, decide whether your essay will appear in a newspaper or on the radio or television.

Drafting Write a punchy lead to capture readers' or listeners' attention. For example, ask a provocative question or tell an anecdote that illustrates the foolishness of what you are mocking. For the electronic media, be briefer than you would be in print. If you're writing for television, think of a dramatic picture or film clip to help you make your point.

Revising Have classmates read your print essay or respond to a "broadcast" of your radio or television piece. Ask them to suggest ways of using the medium to better advantage—for example, including more vivid imagery in a print or radio essay.

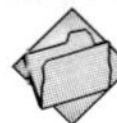

Idea Bank

Customizing for *Performance Levels*

Following are suggestions for matching Idea Bank topics with your students' ability levels:

Less Advanced Students: 1, 2, 5
Average Students: 3, 4, 6
More Advanced Students: 7

Customizing for *Learning Modalities*

Following are suggestions for matching Idea Bank topics with your students' learning modalities:

Visual/Spatial: 4, 6
Verbal/Linguistic: 1, 2, 3, 4, 7
Interpersonal: 4, 5
Intrapersonal: 2

Writing Mini-Lesson

Refer students to the Writing Handbook, page 1189, for instruction on the writing process, and page 1192 for further information on writing a satirical essay, a type of persuasion.

Writing and Language Transparencies To provide guidance in writing and revising a persuasive or satirical essay, use Writing Process Model 5: Persuasive Essay, pages 37–43.

Writer's Solution

Writing Lab CD-ROM

Direct students to complete the tutorial on Persuasion to help them write their satirical essays. Follow these steps:

1. Complete the interactive instruction on identifying an audience.
2. Listen to audio-annotated example of how to organize details.
3. Create a draft on the computer.
4. See tips for peer revision.

Sourcebook

Have students refer to Chapter 4: Persuasion, pp. 96–129, for additional support.

✓ ASSESSMENT OPTIONS

Formal Assessment, Selection Test, pp. 114–116, and Assessment Resources Software. The selection test is designed so that it can be easily customized to the performance levels of your students.

Alternative Assessment, p. 23, includes options for less advanced students, more advanced students, visual/spatial learners, verbal/linguistic learners, and interpersonal learners.

PORTFOLIO ASSESSMENT

Use the following rubrics in the ***Alternative Assessment*** booklet to assess student writing:

Imaginary Language: Definition/Classification Rubric, p. 100
Spy's Report: Description Rubric, p. 98
News Story: Summary Rubric, p. 99
Writing Mini-Lesson: Persuasion Rubric, p. 106

Prepare and Engage

OBJECTIVES

1. To read, comprehend, and interpret selections from a mock epic and an essay in poetic form
2. To relate the literature to personal experience
3. To understand author's purpose
4. To identify characteristics of a mock epic
5. To build vocabulary in context and learn related words about society
6. To recognize inverted word order
7. To imitate an author's style, maintaining a consistent style
8. To respond to the mock epic and poem through writing, speaking and listening, and projects

SKILLS INSTRUCTION

Vocabulary: Related Words: Words About Society
Grammar: Inverted Word Order
Reading Strategy: Author's Purpose
Literary Focus: Mock Epic
Writing: Maintain a Consistent Style
Speaking and Listening: Reading and Pantomime (teacher edition)
Critical Viewing: Speculate; Analyze; Evaluate

PORTFOLIO OPPORTUNITIES

Writing: Paraphrase; Reply; Comparison and Contrast
Writing Mini-Lesson: Imitation of an Author's Style
Speaking and Listening: Reading and Pantomime; Graduation Speech
Projects: High Society in Pope's Day; Classical Glossary

More About the Author
Alexander Pope made a fortune by writing poetry. In an age when patrons usually made political demands on the writers they supported, Pope stayed remarkably independent for his times. With characteristic wit and rhyme, Pope expressed his freedom this way: "Thanks to Homer, I live and thrive/Indebted to no Prince or Peer alive." This quotation, which praises learning, may not seem to come from the man who first said, "A little learning is a dangerous thing." What Pope meant by that famous remark was that a lot of learning is much better than just a little learning.

Guide for Interpreting

Alexander Pope *(1688–1744)*

Despite a crippling childhood disease and persistent ill health, Alexander Pope triumphantly achieved his boyhood ambition of becoming a great poet. By the time he was twenty-four, he had captured the attention of the leading literary figures of England with *An Essay on Criticism* and *The Rape of the Lock.* A brilliant satirist in verse, Pope gave his name to the literary era (the Age of Pope and Swift) in which he lived and wrote.

A Struggle for Position Born into the Roman Catholic family of a London linen merchant, Pope had to struggle for a position or place in society. After the expulsion of King James II, English Catholics could not legally vote, hold office, attend a university, or live within ten miles of London. To comply with the rule of residency, his family moved to Binfield, a rural setting where Pope spent his formative years writing poetry, studying the classics, and becoming broadly self-educated. Pope's physical problems were as severe as his religious ones. Deformed by tuberculosis of the spine, Pope stood only about four and a half feet tall. He also suffered from nervousness and excruciating headaches. In 1718 Pope moved to an estate at Twickenham (twit′ nəm), a village on the Thames, where he lived until his death.

A Satiric Circle Although Pope, "the Wasp of Twickenham," is more often remembered for his quarrels than for his cordiality, he became friends, and remained so for life, with members of a Tory group that included Jonathan Swift, John Gay, and Lord Bolingbroke. Pope instigated the formation of the Scriblerus Club, whose purpose was to ridicule what its members regarded as "false tastes in learning." The club's satiric emphasis probably inspired Swift's *Gulliver's Travels* and Pope's *The Dunciad*—an attack on his literary enemies.

A Turn to Philosophy In the 1730's Pope's writing became increasingly philosophical. He embarked on a massive work concerning morality and government, but completed only *An Essay on Man* and *Moral Essays*. Nevertheless, the entire body of his work is sufficient for critics today to accord him exceptionally high praise. The twentieth-century poet Edith Sitwell calls Pope "perhaps the most flawless artist our race has yet produced."

◆ Background for Understanding

LITERATURE: THE STORY BEHIND THE POEM

Pope's mock-epic *The Rape of the Lock*, a tale about the theft of a lock of hair, is based on a real incident. Two families, the Petres and the Fermors, became involved in a dispute when Robert Petre flirtatiously cut a lock of hair from the head of beautiful Arabella Fermor.

Pope wrote about this incident, in the hopes that a humorous poem would bring the families together. The result was an early two-part version of the five-part poem we know as *The Rape of the Lock*. In the longer version, published two years later, he added among other things the passage on the parlor game, which is presented here.

A silly feud therefore inspired Pope's affectionate mockery of high society and its displays. Those displays were so elaborate that a gentleman would not venture out without wearing a freshly powdered wig and a gilt, diamond-hilted sword. He would probably be scented with flower water, and would have been groomed with tweezers and brushes. Be ready for such pretense, and Pope's mockery of it, as you read a poem inspired by a petty theft.

Prentice Hall Literature Program Resources

REINFORCE / RETEACH / EXTEND

Selection Support Pages
Build Vocabulary: Words About Society, p. 114
Grammar and Style: Inverted Word Order, p. 115
Reading Strategy: Author's Purpose, p. 116
Literary Focus: Mock Epic, p. 117

Strategies for Diverse Student Needs, p. 24

Beyond Literature Community Connection: Government Support of the Arts, p. 24

Formal Assessment Selection Test, pp. 117–119; Assessment Resources Software

Alternative Assessment, p. 24

Resource Pro CD-ROM from *The Rape of the Lock;* from *An Essay on Man*—includes all resource material and customizable lesson plan

Listening to Literature Audiocassettes from *The Rape of the Lock;* from *An Essay on Man*

Literature CD-ROM Feature 8, *How to Read and Understand Poetry*

◆ Literature and Your Life

Connect Your Experience

When you attend the prom, your attire, mode of transportation, and pre- and post-prom activities are determined by certain "unwritten rules." Whether you care about such "rules" or not, violating them can cause some people to disapprove of you.

In upper-class English society of Pope's time, the "unwritten" rules were so elaborate, and the pretension so great, that Pope made fun of them in *The Rape of the Lock*.

Journal Writing Jot down social customs associated with your prom. Which are worthwhile and which are absurd?

Thematic Focus: The Ties That Bind

How does Pope's mockery of false values call attention to the true values that bind society together?

◆ Literary Focus

Mock Epic

A **mock epic** is a long, humorous narrative poem that treats a trivial subject in the grand, elevated style of a true epic such as the *Odyssey* or *Paradise Lost*. It applies to petty matters the standard elements of an epic: descriptions of heroic actions and the participation of gods and goddesses in human affairs.

In *The Rape of the Lock*, Pope applies the mighty style of Homer and Milton to the theft of a lock of hair. He describes a high society parlor game, for instance, with terms more appropriate for a bloody battle: "And particolored troops, a shining train, Draw forth to combat on the velvet plain."

◆ Grammar and Style

Inverted Word Order

In *The Rape of the Lock*, Pope uses **inverted word order**, a change in the normal English word order of subject-verb-complement. He does this to achieve regular rhythm, emphasize key words, and place strong rhyme words at the end of a line.

Normal Order: The hungry judges (s) soon sign (v) the sentence (c).

Inverted Order: The hungry judges (s) soon the sentence (c) sign (v).

◆ Reading Strategy

Author's Purpose

Understanding an **author's purpose**, the reason for writing, gives you insight into a work of literature. Knowing the author's intention, you can understand why he or she includes certain details or descriptions.

For example, Pope's exaggerated descriptions of a parlor game called *omber* can be puzzling: "Belinda now, whom thirst of fame invites,/Burns to encounter two adventurous knights,/ At *ombre* singly to decide their doom." When you know that Pope's purpose was to make fun of petty social pursuits, the heroic language becomes understandable.

◆ Build Vocabulary

Related Words: Words About Society

In a poem mocking high society and its pursuits, it isn't surprising that Pope uses words relating to social classes and attitudes, such as *plebeian*, which refers to common people, and *haughty*, which means "proud" or "arrogant."

Word Bank

Before you read, preview this list of words from the poems.

obliquely
plebeian
destitute
assignations
stoic
disabused

Ask students to imagine that someone stole the lace from someone else's sneaker during gym class. Now tell them that their job is to write 794 rhyming lines about that event! With the class, brainstorm for a list of things they might include to lead up to the event and to tell about its consequences. For example, students might construct an elaborate story about revenge, love, or spite; they might also, along the way, expose cliques or other social groups in the school, as well as comment on school fads and fashions. Once students have developed a list of ideas, explain that they can read to find out how Pope used a similarly trivial event to generate 794 rhyming lines.

Customize for
Less Proficient Readers

These students might benefit from keeping a reading log as they read. Encourage them to list specific parts of the poem that are difficult to envision, parts that seem confusing, or parts that surprise them. Have them point out line numbers, and jot responses to them. When they have finished reading, have them compare their reading log with a partner's and discuss interpretations of the troublesome passages.

Customize for
More Advanced Students

There are plenty of scenes and actions to imagine as "The Rape of the Lock" unfolds. Invite students to choose one sequence, or series of lines, such as the card game, to dramatize. Encourage them to be as fanciful and imaginative in the creation of nearly animate playing cards—or anything else in the poem that they wish.

Customize for
English Language Learners

Have these students gather in small discussion groups to read the title, the introductory text, and first page together. Have them list vocabulary and references that are puzzling. Collect these phrases and have students explain them in class discussion or in small groups.

Preparing for Standardized Tests

Reading and Vocabulary Practice in determining an author's purpose will help students perform well on the verbal portions of standardized tests, especially on reading comprehension questions. Have students answer the Reading Strategy questions on page 500. For additional practice, use the Reading Strategy page on Author's Purpose in ***Selection Support,*** p.116.

Grammar and Language Some standardized tests may include items with inverted word order. It is important for students to understand that inverted word order, though unexpected, does not necessarily constitute an error. Sometimes inverted word order can make it difficult to determine subject and verb agreement, in which case it is often useful to restate the sentence in normal word order.

The Grammar and Style lesson for this selection focuses on this topic. For additional practice, use the Grammar and Style page on Inverted Word Order, p. 115, in ***Selection Support.***

Develop Understanding

One-Minute Insight At Hampton Court, amid the "heroes and nymphs," life is pure and petty amusement. There are games of cards; there are tea and coffee; there are gossip and fashion; and there is even—at least in the scene described here—the game of cutting a lock of hair as a kind of prize from the head of a beautiful woman. Pope treats this situation as if it were a scene from an epic battle.

Literature CD-ROM To help students explore the relationship between the content of *The Rape of the Lock* and its poetic form, use Feature 8 of the CD-ROM entitled *How to Read and Understand Poetry.* Among the topics students may explore are rhythm, rhyme, and alliteration. There is also coverage of iambic pentameter, the meter of Pope's heroic couplets.

Customize for
Less Proficient Readers
❶ A great deal of important information is compressed in the introductory text. Be sure to emphasize that Belinda is the main character, and that the baron is determined to cut her hair. (You might explain the meaning of the multiple-meaning word *lock* as a ringlet of hair.) Also be sure students understand that there are spirits present in the poem as there would be on epic battlefields, such as those in the *Iliad.*

◆ Grammar and Style

❷ **Inverted Word Order** Read aloud the first four lines of the poem with students not only to make the meaning clear but also to point out the characteristically inverted word order of so many of this mock epic's lines. Have students find the subject of the sentence. *The subject is* structure.

◆ Literary Focus

❸ **Mock Epic** Explain that part of the mock epic is a humorous imitation of everyday life in which trivial things are made great. Note here how the Queen is mentioned in the same couplet with a trivial description of a charming Indian screen.

from
The Rape of the Lock
Alexander Pope

❶ *The Rape of the Lock, a mock epic, or a humorous poem written in the style of and recalling situations from the famous epic poems of Homer, Virgil, and Milton, is based on an actual incident. Filled with allusions to the great literary works of the past, the poem is a poignant appraisal of the social manners and human behavior of the time.*

The first of the poem's five cantos opens with a formal statement of theme and an invocation to the Muse for poetic inspiration. Then Belinda, the poem's heroine, receives a warning from the sylph Ariel that a dreadful event will take place in her immediate future. In Canto II, during a boat ride on the Thames, an adventurous baron admires Belinda's hair and is determined to cut two bright locks from her head and keep them as a prize. Aware of the baron's desires, Ariel urges the spirits to protect Belinda.

Canto III

❷ Close by those meads, forever crowned with flowers,
Where Thames with pride surveys his rising towers,
There stands a structure of majestic frame,[1]
Which from the neighboring Hampton takes its name.
Here Britain's statesmen oft the fall foredoom
Of foreign tyrants, and of nymphs at home;
Here thou, great Anna![2] whom three realms obey,
Dost sometimes counsel take—and sometimes tea.
Hither the heroes and the nymphs resort,
To taste awhile the pleasures of a court;
In various talk th' instructive hours they passed,
Who gave the ball, or paid the visit last;
❸ One speaks the glory of the British Queen,
And one describes a charming Indian screen;
❹ A third interprets motions, looks, and eyes;
At every word a reputation dies.

1. **structure . . . frame:** Hampton Court, a royal palace near London.
2. **Anna:** Queen Anne, who ruled England, Ireland, and Scotland from 1702 through 1714.

Block Scheduling Strategies

Consider these suggestions to take advantage of extended class time:

- Before students read *The Rape of the Lock,* have them read both Background for Understanding (p. 486) and the History Connection (p. 492). Have them use this information in combination with the illustrations (pp. 489, 491, and 493) to make predictions about both the content and style of the poem.
- Read and discuss the Literature and Your Life feature (p. 487). You may wish to brainstorm for ideas as a class before students write in their journals.
- Have students listen to all or part of the selections on audiocassette. For *The Rape of the Lock,* you might suggest stopping points at which small groups can summarize what they heard, discuss it, and confirm what they understand of the plot so far.
- Provide class time for planning and working on the Projects (p. 501).

Snuff, or the fan,[3] supply each pause of chat,
With singing, laughing, ogling, and all that.
Meanwhile, declining from the noon of day,
The sun obliquely shoots his burning ray;
The hungry judges soon the sentence sign,
And wretches hang that jurymen may dine; ❺
The merchant from th' Exchange[4] returns in peace,
And the long labors of the toilet[5] cease.

The Barge, 1895–96 Aubrey Beardsley

◀ **Critical Viewing** Has the artist approached the drawing of Belinda sincerely or mockingly? Explain. **[Speculate]** ❻

Belinda now, whom thirst of fame invites,
Burns to encounter two adventurous knights,
At omber[6] singly to decide their doom;
And swells her breast with conquests yet to come.
Straight the three bands prepare in arms to join,
Each band the number of the sacred nine.[7]
Soon as she spreads her hand, th' aerial guard
Descend, and sit on each important card:
First Ariel perched upon a Matadore,[8] ❼

3. **snuff . . . fan:** At the time, gentlemen commonly took snuff and ladies usually carried a fan.
4. **Exchange:** London financial center where merchants, bankers, and brokers conducted business.
5. **toilet:** Dressing tables.
6. **omber:** Popular card game.
7. **sacred nine:** Reference to the nine Muses of Greek mythology.
8. **Matadore:** Powerful card that could take a trick.

◆ Build Vocabulary

obliquely (ə blēkˊ lē) *adv.*: At a slant; indirect

◆ Reading Strategy

❹ **Author's Purpose** Ask students how lines 15–16 reveal the author's purpose. *Pope is clearly satirizing the gossip that takes place at Hampton Court; from this it is possible to infer that one of his purposes is to poke fun at high society.*

◆ Critical Thinking

❺ **Interpret** Ask students to interpret lines 21–22. *Jurymen, or those deciding the fate of someone convicted of a crime, quickly deliver a verdict of guilty so that their deliberation won't postpone their dinner.*

▶Critical Viewing◀

❻ **Speculate** Considering that the intention of the poet is to mock, the artist has followed suit. He can be said to have accurately recreated Belinda's flamboyant hairstyle, with its enormous height and top-feather, and her costume, with its ornate decoration, including an oversized fan.

❼ **Clarification** Point out that Belinda is embarking on a game of omber, a three-handed card game played in the seventeenth and eighteenth centuries and in parts of the Spanish-speaking world even today.

Customize for *Logical/Mathematical Learners*

These students may research the game of omber and demonstrate how it is played to the class. They might also comment on why Pope chose to incorporate this game in his mock epic.

Customize for *Musical/Rhythmic Learners*

Encourage musical/rhythmic learners to find, tap out, and demonstrate for the class an appropriate beat to which most of this poem can be read.

Humanities: Art

The Barge, 1895–96, by Aubrey Beardsley.

The British illustrator Aubrey Beardsley (1872–1898) achieved in his six productive years a strange and wonderful style. His only formal art training was one year of lessons at the Westminster School of Art in London. His lifelong illness, tuberculosis, did not leave him the strength to explore any form of artistic expression other than the pen-and-ink drawing for which he is remembered. He received his first illustration commission by chance through a bookseller he frequented. This commission led to many others and to fame as an illustrator. His career ended abruptly with his death at the age of twenty-six.

In executing this drawing, Beardsley introduced a technique of using dots to give texture and variety to his usually severe lines.

Use these questions for discussion:

1. What deductions can you make about the people with whom Belinda interacts? *She moves among the rich and privileged. These people may be quite stiff and formal. On the other hand, they may be so bored as to take risks when speaking or acting. They may also be just as silly as their clothing.*
2. How would you describe the detail in this illustration? *There is a huge amount of detail, which, to the modern eye, seems overdone. Nevertheless, this elaborate detailing accurately reproduces the style of the rich of the period.*

❶ **Clarification** Assure students that they do not need to follow every play of the card game to understand what is happening. Instead, help them see that Belinda begins the game in fine form, playing her trump cards and taking four tricks. Aided by the nymphs, she seems to be the hands-down winner.

◆ Build Vocabulary

❷ **Words About Society** Point out the word *plebeian.* Tell students that this word means "one of the common people." Ask students why this word would be grouped with other words related to society. *Society is thought of as having levels; plebeians would be at one of the lowest levels of a society.*

◆ Literary Focus

❸ **Mock Epic** First, the mock epic takes a trivial subject—a mere card game—and treats it on a grand scale. Second, it makes playing the card game seem as if it were a heroic act. Also, not in these lines, but in others, fairy-like creatures intervene on the part of the human participants.

❹ **Clarification** The Baron trumps Belinda's king of clubs with his queen of spades.

◆ Grammar and Style

❺ **Inverted Word Order** Call attention to the word order in line 75. Here the subject, *baron,* is at the beginning of the sentence, as would be expected, but the direct object, *diamonds,* precedes the verb *pours.* Ask students why Pope may have decided to cast the sentence in this unexpected fashion. *Through this choice, Pope achieves regular rhythm and rhyme:* apace *rhymes with* face.

Then each, according to the rank they bore;
For sylphs, yet mindful of their ancient race,
Are, as when women, wondrous fond of place.
Behold, four kings in majestry revered,
With hoary whiskers and a forky beard;
And four fair queens whose hands sustain a flower,
Th' expressive emblem of their softer power;
Four knaves in garbs succinct,[9] a trusty band,
Caps on their heads, and halberts[10] in their hand;
And particolored troops, a shining train,
Draw forth to combat on the velvet plain.
The skilful nymph reviews her force with care:
Let spades be trumps! she said, and trumps they were.
Now move to war her sable Matadores,
In show like leaders of the swarthy Moors.
Spadillio[11] first, unconquerable Lord!
Led off two captive trumps, and swept the board.
As many more Manillio[12] forced to yield,
And marched a victor from the verdant field.[13]
Him Basto[14] followed, but his fate more hard
❶ Gained but one trump and one plebeian card.
❷ With his broad saber next, a chief in years,
The hoary majesty of spades appears,
Puts forth one manly leg, to sight revealed,
The rest, his many-colored robe concealed.
The rebel knave, who dares his prince engage,
Proves the just victim of his royal rage.
Even mighty Pam,[15] that kings and queens o'erthrew
And mowed down armies in the fights of loo,
Sad chance of war! now destitute of aid,
Falls undistinguished by the victor spade!
Thus far both armies to Belinda yield;
Now to the baron fate inclines the field.
His warlike Amazon her host invades,
Th' imperial consort of the crown of spades.
The club's black tyrant first her victim died,
❹ Spite of his haughty mien, and barbarous pride.
What boots[16] the regal circle on his head,
His giant limbs, in state unwieldy spread;
That long behind he trails his pompous robe,
And, of all monarchs, only grasps the globe?
❺ The baron now his diamonds pours apace;
Th' embroidered king who shows but half his face,
And his refulgent queen, with powers combined

◆ Literary Focus
What elements of the mock epic does Pope employ by comparing the card game to a battle in lines 60–75? ❸

9. **succinct** (sək siŋkt′): Belted.
10. **halberts:** Long-handled weapons.
11. **Spadillio:** Ace of spades.
12. **Manillio:** Two of spades.
13. **Verdant field:** The card table, covered with a green cloth.
14. **Basto:** Ace of clubs.
15. **Pam:** Knave of clubs, the highest card in the game called "loo."
16. **what boots:** Of what benefit is.

Speaking and Listening Mini-Lesson

Reading and Pantomime

This mini-lesson supports the Speaking and Listening activity on page 501.

Introduce the Concept Tell students that their job in this project is to bring "The Rape of the Lock" to life by dramatic reading, which is reading with feeling, and pantomime, which is using actions and gestures as a means of expression.

Develop Background Individuals or small groups should select the passages for which each will be responsible. Groups can discuss ways to present given passages; individuals may try out ideas on each other as they decide their approach. Remind everyone that this poem is highly stylized and their actions and manner of speaking may be the same: brash, flamboyant, lively, and overdone.

Apply the Information After allowing time for developing their passages and practicing them, have students perform. Students will be taking turns being performers and being members of the audience; remind them that each of these roles has its responsibilities.

Assess the Outcome Students may be assessed on both how well they used their voices and how well they used movement and gesture to convey meaning. You may wish to weigh the use of the voice more heavily. Those who deliver their lines in a spirit that most nearly approaches that of the poem should receive the highest ratings.

Of broken troops an easy conquest find.
Clubs, diamonds, hearts, in wild disorder seen,
With throngs promiscuous strew the level green.
Thus when dispersed a routed army runs,
Of Asia's troops, and Afric's sable sons,
    With like confusion different nations fly,
Of various habit, and of various dye,
The pierced battalions disunited fall,
In heaps on heaps; one fate o'erwhelms them all.
    The knave of diamonds tries his wily arts,
And wins (oh shameful chance!) the queen of hearts. ❻
At this, the blood the virgin's cheek forsook,

The Rape of the Lock, 1895–96, Aubrey Beardsley

◀ **Critical Viewing** In this poem, Pope glorifies a trivial event. In what manner does this artist do the same? Explain. **[Analyze]** ❼

A livid paleness spreads o'er all her look;
She sees, and trembles at th' approaching ill,
Just in the jaws of ruin, and codille.[17] ❽
And now (as oft in some distempered state)
On one nice trick depends the general fate.
An ace of hearts steps forth; the king unseen
Lurked in her hand, and mourned his captive queen. ❾
He springs to vengeance with an eager pace,
And falls like thunder on the prostrate ace.
The nymph exulting fills with shouts the sky;

◆ Build Vocabulary

plebeian (pli bē´ ən) *adj.*: Common; ordinary

destitute (des´ tə to͞ot) *adj.*: Lacking

17. **codille:** Term meaning the defeat of a hand of cards.

Customize for
Bodily/Kinesthetic Learners
Have groups of students work together to interpret the card game and then to act it out. In places where students are not clear about the rules of omber, they may improvise. Nevertheless, their reenactment should show that at first Belinda seems to be winning (with the help of the nymphs who declare spades trumps), but then the baron takes over, taking Belinda's queen of hearts with his knave of diamonds.

Customize for
Musical/Rhythmic Learners
Challenge groups of students to imagine that this poem is to be performed on the radio or recorded on audiocassette. Invite students to choose, describe, or create appropriate background music for this scene.

❻ **Clarification** The baron takes Belinda's queen of hearts with his jack of diamonds, since she cannot follow suit.

▶Critical Viewing◀

❼ **Analyze** Although the artist devotes an illustration to cutting the hair, this event is not at the center of the portrait. Instead, details that tell the viewer more about the scene in which the act takes place are given more importance. These include a view of the ornate drawing room with its screens, brocaded drapes, and elegant furnishings; a view of the grounds; and highly detailed visual descriptions of some of the others present at the event. Just as the actual cutting of the hair occupies only a few lines in the poem, it occupies only a minor part of the illustration.

◆ *Literature and Your Life*

❽ Ask students whether Belinda's reaction to the likelihood of losing the card game seems believable to them. *Some students may say that she overreacts. Others may say that sometimes people react more strongly to little things like card games or other games than they should or than seems logical.*

❾ **Clarification** The baron plays his ace of hearts. Since hearts are not trump, though, this card is worth less than the king of hearts, which Belinda plays. She wins the game by taking the fifth trick.

Humanities: Art

The Rape of the Lock, 1895–96, by Aubrey Beardsley.

The drawing entitled *The Rape of the Lock* is one of the nine produced by Aubrey Beardsley for an 1896 edition of this poem. The satiric nature of the poem appealed to Beardsley's sense of the burlesque. He depicts the incident of the cutting of the hair with a mocking humor comparable to Pope's. The artist's appreciation of the poet's wit and humor adds an extra element to these drawings.

Use these questions for discussion:

1. Who might the central figure in the foreground be? *It is possible that this is Ariel, a male spirit who intercedes on behalf of Belinda. Although he is dressed like others in the drawing room, he is half their size, and he has an entirely different kind of expression on his face.*
2. Why do you think the illustrator does not show Belinda's face? *Belinda does not know what is happening. What is important in this illustration is both the act of cutting and the milieu in which the cutting takes place; both of these the artist captures.*

Customize for
Verbal/Linguistic Learners
Part of the power of the poem comes from the vivid verbs used, for the most part, in the active voice. Invite verbal/linguistic students to find some of these verbs and to comment on their variety, as well as their ability to convey precise actions.

◆ Critical Thinking

❶ **Interpret** Ask students what Pope means by lines 101–104. *Belinda was too soon dejected by the thought of losing at cards: she actually won. Belinda is also too soon "elate," or happy: she will "lose" later when the baron cuts her lock.*

❷ **Clarification** Note that the scene is changing slightly here. Although the characters are in the same room, coffee is now being served. The vapors from the coffee seem to have quite an effect on the baron: they cause him to devise a new plan to cut the lock.

◆ Literary Focus

❸ **Mock Epic** Have students find one characteristic of a mock epic in this passage. *The trivial is made grand; for example, a woman handing a man a pair of scissors is compared with a lady handing a knight his spear. Also "a thousand sprites" become involved in the action to protect Belinda's curl.*

The walls, the woods, and long canals reply.
 Oh thoughtless mortals! ever blind to fate,
Too soon dejected, and too soon elate.
❶ Sudden, these honors shall be snatched away,
And cursed forever this victorious day.
 For lo! the board with cups and spoons is
 crowned,
The berries crackle, and the mill turns round;[18]
On shining altars of Japan[19] they raise
The silver lamp; the fiery spirits blaze;
From silver spouts the grateful liquors glide,
While China's earth[20] receives the smoking tide.
At once they gratify their scent and taste,
❷ And frequent cups prolong the rich repast.
Straight hover round the fair her airy band;
Some, as she sipped, the fuming liquor fanned,
Some o'er her lap their careful plumes displayed,
Trembling, and conscious of the rich brocade.
Coffee (which makes the politician wise,
And see through all things with his half-shut eyes)
Sent up in vapors to the baron's brain
New stratagems, the radiant lock to gain.
Ah cease, rash youth! desist ere 'tis too late,
Fear the just gods, and think of Scylla's fate![21]
Changed to a bird, and sent to flit in air,
She dearly pays for Nisus' injured hair!
 But when to mischief mortals bend their will,
How soon they find fit instruments of ill!
Just then, Clarissa drew with tempting grace
A two-edged weapon from her shining case:
So ladies in romance assist their knight,
Present the spear, and arm him for the fight.
He takes the gift with reverence, and extends
❸ The little engine[22] on his fingers' ends;
This just behind Belinda's neck he spread,
As o'er the fragrant steams she bends her head.
Swift to the lock a thousand sprites repair,
A thousand wings, by turns, blow back the hair;
And thrice they twitched the diamond in her ear;
Thrice she looked back, and thrice the foe drew
 near.
Just in that instant, anxious Ariel sought
The close recesses of the virgin's thought;
As on the nosegay in her breast reclined,
He watched th' ideas rising in her mind,

18. **the berries . . . round:** Coffee beans are ground in a hand mill at the table.
19. **altars of Japan:** Small imported lacquer tables.
20. **China's earth:** Earthenware cups imported from China.
21. **Scylla's** (sil´ əz) **fate:** Scylla, the daughter of King Nisus, was turned into a sea bird because she cut off the lock of her father's hair on which his safety depended and sent it to his enemy.
22. **engine:** Instrument.

Beyond Literature

History Connection:

Eighteenth-Century Fashions

The obsession with fashion satirized by Alexander Pope was a genuine phenomenon of the upper classes in the 1700's. The world's first fashion magazine dates from 1785, and although it was French, fashion had become an international affair. Queen Marie Antoinette's hairdresser, Leonard, had stunned the world when he rolled her hair over pads of horse hair, then added accessories such as gauze and feathers to create elegant "hair statues" sometimes as high as four feet. His masterpiece, celebrating a French naval victory, transformed waves of hair into a raging sea battering the sides of a French frigate in full sail.

At war with France in fashion as well as on the battlefield, the English quickly responded to Leonard. English hairdressers decorated fashionable heads with horsedrawn carriages, zoos with miniature lions and tigers and, if accounts can be believed, a lit stove complete with pots and pans.

For the most part, men of the period showed considerably less imagination when it came to hair. There were exceptions, however. Chief among them was the Macaroni Club, a group of young men who wore bizarrely shaped wigs in order to annoy their more conservative elders. (The club is memorialized in the line from "Yankee Doodle Dandy": "Put a feather in his cap, and called it Macaroni.")

Do you think attitudes about fashion are different now from those in the eighteenth century? Explain.

Beyond the Classroom

Career Connection

Interior Decorating In eighteenth-century Europe, decorative items from the Orient, such as porcelain and lacquerware, were in vogue. Such items did not replace characteristic English items, but were often used in combination with them. In this section of the poem, silver lamps sit on small, Japanese lacquer tables, and drinks are served in Chinese cups.

Today's interior designs often combine furnishings, designs, and objects from different parts of the world to create a single interior setting. Have interested students gather illustrations of interiors that combine objects from different periods and places and tell what they do and do not find pleasing about them. Then invite students to design an interior space of their own.

Community Connection

Local Historic Homes Local historic homes may be famous for the people who lived in them or for the events that occurred in them, but no matter from what their fame issues, their furnishings are often of enormous interest to visitors. Students may be encouraged to visit a local historic home open to the public and to identify the objects in it that were used for tea time or entertaining. Have students explain what insights these objects provide about the lives of the occupants and the times in which they lived.

The Battle of the Beaux and Belles
Aubrey Beardsley

▲ **Critical Viewing** In what ways is the elaborate decorative style of the drawing similar to the language of the poem? **[Evaluate]** ❹

Customize for
Visual/Spatial Learners
Have these students interpret the event that is depicted in the painting. *Although the baron's hand does not show the scissors or the lock of hair, Belinda's anger indicates that the lock has been cut.*

▶Critical Viewing◀

❹ **Evaluate** If students say Pope has similarly "decorative" or ornate prose, urge them to select an example of it from the text, and then restate it in a simpler, less "decorative" fashion. For example, the "elaborate" lines, "He takes the gift with reverence, and extends/The little engine on his fingers' end;/This just behind Belinda's neck he spread . . ." might be restated plainly and simply as "He thankfully accepted the scissors, opening them behind Belinda's neck. . . ."

Humanities: Art

The Battle of the Beaux and the Belles, 1895–1896, by Aubrey Beardsley.

This drawing is one of the nine pen-and-ink drawings by Beardsley for the 1896 edition of Alexander Pope's poem, *The Rape of the Lock.* This rococo scene is executed with the skill and mocking wit for which Beardsley is noted. The abundance of ruffles and flounces and the extravagance of embroidery and pattern serve to emphasize the silliness of the situation depicted. Beardsley's satiric style appropriately illustrates this social parody by Pope.

Use the following question for discussion:

Do you feel that the elaborate decorative style of the drawing is similar to the language of the poem? Explain. *Students should observe that the characters, while caricatured and exaggerated, are attractive and engaging, much like the characters whom Pope playfully mocks in his poem.*

◆ Critical Thinking

❶ **Interpret** Ask students what these lines suggest about Belinda's feelings for the baron. *She is fond of him; she may wish to give him a lock of her hair.*

◆ Reading Strategy

❷ **Author's Purpose** Students may say that because Pope is turning a trivial event into the subject of an epic, he makes it far more dramatic and important than it really is.

Comprehension Check ☑

❸ Ask: Who is speaking? What is being referred to? *The baron is speaking. He is the "victor" because he has just cut the lock, "the glorious prize."*

Customize for *Less Proficient Readers*

Remind students to pause frequently during their reading to monitor their own comprehension. Students might ask themselves whether they have understood what just happened, as well as whether they need to slow down or go back and reread.

Customize for *English Language Learners*

Ask these readers to be sure they have understood Canto IV before moving on to Canto V. You might suggest they summarize what they have read, share their summaries with classmates, and work with others to fill in any gaps in their understanding.

Sudden he viewed, in spite of all her art,
An earthly lover lurking at her heart.[23]
❶ Amazed, confused, he found his power expired,
Resigned to fate, and with a sigh retired.
The peer now spreads the glittering forfex[24] wide,
T' enclose the lock; now joins it, to divide.
Even then, before the fatal engine closed,
A wretched sylph too fondly interposed;
Fate urged the shears, and cut the sylph in twain,
(But airy substance soon unites again).
The meeting points the sacred hair dissever
From the fair head, forever, and forever!
Then flashed the living lightning from her eyes,
And screams of horror rend th' affrighted skies.
Not louder shrieks to pitying heaven are cast,
When husbands, or when lap dogs breathe their last;
Or when rich China vessels fallen from high,
In glittering dust, and painted fragments lie!
"Let wreaths of triumph now my temples twine,"
❸ The victor cried, "the glorious prize is mine!"
While fish in streams, or birds delight in air,
Or in a coach and six the British Fair,
As long as *Atalantis*[25] shall be read,
Or the small pillow grace a lady's bed,
While visits shall be paid on solemn days,
When numerous wax lights in bright order blaze,
While nymphs take treats, or assignations give,
So long my honor, name, and praise shall live!
What time would spare, from steel receives its date,[26]
And monuments, like men, submit to fate!
Steel could the labor of the gods destroy,
And strike to dust th' imperial towers of Troy;
Steel could the works of mortal pride confound,
And hew triumphal arches to the ground.
What wonder then, fair nymph! thy hairs should feel,
The conquering force of unresisted steel?

◆ Reading Strategy Why does the author describe the scene in lines 145-160 in such an elevated manner? 

from Canto V

In Canto IV, after Umbriel, "a dusky, melancholy sprite," empties a bag filled with "the force of female lungs, sighs, sobs, and passions, and the war of tongues" onto Belinda's head, the lady erupts over the loss of her lock. Then she "bids her beau," Sir Plume, to "demand the precious hairs," but Plume is unable to persuade the baron to return the hair.

---

23. **earthly lover . . . heart:** If in her heart Belinda wants the baron to succeed, they cannot protect her.
24. **forfex:** Scissors.
25. ***Atalantis:*** Popular book of scandalous gossip.
26. **receives its date:** Is destroyed.

Cultural Connection

Hair Explain that people have been concerned about the hair on their head since the dawn of time. Hairpins dating from 8000 B.C. have been recovered by archaeologists. The ancient Egyptians shaved their heads for relief from the heat and covered their baldness with elaborate wigs. Wealthy Greek men powdered their hair with gold dust. Early Germanic people dyed their hair orange, blue, or green.

Have students compare what people have done with their hair in earlier times and other cultures with the way people wear their hair in our society today. What are the similarities and differences?

In the beginning of Canto V, Clarissa, a level-headed nymph, tries to bring an end to the commotion, but rather than being greeted with applause, her speech is followed by a battle cry. ❹

"To arms, to arms!" the fierce virago[27] cries,
And swift as lightning to the combat flies.
All side in parties, and begin th' attack;
Fans clap, silks rustle, and tough whalebones crack;
Heroes' and heroines' shouts confusedly rise,
And bass and treble voices strike the skies.
No common weapons in their hands are found,
Like gods they fight, nor dread a mortal wound.
So when bold Homer makes the gods engage,
And heavenly breasts with human passions rage;
'Gainst Pallas, Mars, Latona, Hermes[28] arms;
And all Olympus[29] rings with loud alarms:
Jove's[30] thunder roars, heaven trembles all around,
Blue Neptune[31] storms, the bellowing deeps resound;
Earth shakes her nodding towers, the ground gives way,
And the pale ghosts start at the flash of day!
Triumphant Umbriel on a sconce's height[32]
Clapped his glad wings, and sat to view the fight;
Propped on their bodkin spears,[33] the sprites survey
The growing combat, or assist the fray.
While through the press enraged Thalestris[34] flies,
And scatters death around from both her eyes,
A beau and witling[35] perished in the throng,
One died in metaphor, and one in song. ❻
"O cruel nymph! a living death I bear,"
Cried Dapperwit, and sunk beside his chair.
A mournful glance Sir Fopling[36] upwards cast,
"Those eyes are made so killing"—was his last.
Thus on Maeander's[37] flowery margin lies

◆ **Literary Focus**
In what ways does the preparation for battle in lines 1–20 fit the mock heroic? ❺

27. **virago** (vi rā′ gō): Scolding woman.
28. **Pallas . . . Hermes:** Gods who directed the Trojan War. Pallas and Hermes supported the Greeks, while Mars and Latona sided with the Trojans.
29. **Olympus:** Mountain which was supposed to be the home of the gods.
30. **Jove's:** Referring to Jupiter, the ruler of the Gods in Roman mythology: identified with Zeus in Greek mythology.
31. **Neptune:** Roman god of the sea; identified with Poseidon in Greek mythology.
32. **sconce's height:** Candleholder attached to the wall.
33. **bodkin spears:** Large needles.
34. **Thalestris** (thə lēs′ tris): An Amazon (a race of female warriors supposed to have lived in Scythia) who played a role in the medieval tales of Alexander the Great.
35. **witling:** Person who fancies himself or herself a wit.
36. **Dapperwit, Sir Fopling:** Names of amusing characters in comedies of the time.
37. **Maeander's:** Referring to a river in Asia.

◆ **Build Vocabulary**
assignations (as′ ig nā′ shənz) *n.*: Appointments to meet

❹ **Clarification** Be sure that students understand that there is a gap in the action here; this is a selection from Canto V, where the battle continues.

◆ Literary Focus

❺ **Mock Epic** The preparation for battle elevates a trivial event to heroic status. The scene is also compared to the raging of the gods on Olympus.

◆ Build Vocabulary

❻ **Words About Society** Explain that the word *beau* means "boyfriend," but it may also refer to a certain kind of dressed-up, fancy man who gives exaggerated attention to his appearance. The plural of this word, which is French, is *beaux.* You might also explain that the feminine counterpart of *beau* is *belle,* which may be an "attractive woman," or, more commonly, "a woman whose charm and beauty make her stand out in a crowd."

Customize for
Bodily/Kinesthetic Learners
Suggest that the battle between the belles and beaux makes an excellent choice for dramatic re-enactment.

Enrichment

In *An Essay on Criticism* (1711), Pope discussed the role of wit in literature and memorably defined "True Wit" as "Nature to advantage dress'd/What oft was thought but ne'er so well express'd." This impressive poetic essay, written by a young man of twenty-two, appeared at a crucial time in literary history. Earlier, the term *wit* had been associated with poetic inspiration and the highly imaginative conceits of metaphysical poets like Donne. More recently, however, Dryden had defined wit as "a propriety of thoughts and words," stressing decorum over scintillation.

"True Wit," for Pope, related more to the balance of the whole work than to the sputtering fireworks in particular lines or images. Similarly, "What oft was thought . . ." referred not to platitudes but to widely applicable truths.

Pope believed that the works of ancient authors like Homer were superlative embodiments of "True Wit." These works had stood the test of time because they spoke to all of humanity. As Pope wrote, "To copy nature is to copy them." That he did not mean slavish imitation, however, is evident from his own writing. He had immersed himself in the ancients and yet had produced, in his biographer Maynard Mack's words, "a fully contemporary 'conversational' idiom, pithy, pointed, witty, and smart. . . ."

Customize for
Bodily/Kinesthetic Learners
Invite students to act out the lively exchange of words and actions between Belinda and the baron. Encourage students to use props to represent the bodkin and the snuff.

◆ Literary Focus

❶ **Mock Epic** Point out that Jove, or Jupiter, holds the scales of justice, which are used to decide which cause "weighs more" or has greater worth: the men's wits or the lock of hair. For a while, the scale moves from side to side, as if it's a close call. Ask students how this action illustrates the mock epic. *The scales of justice decide epic battles and great causes; here they are applied to the weight of a lock of hair.*

◆ Critical Thinking

❷ **Analyze** Have students describe the actions of the battle in this passage. *Belinda throws snuff into the baron's nose and draws a needle to threaten him with.*

◆ Literature and Your Life

❸ Students may respond that even when there is no particular "in" look in hair, there are some definitely "out" looks, such as the styles conveyed in the illustrations here. Students may also describe current hair fashions that mark someone as "in the know" or part of a certain social group.

Comprehension Check ☑

❹ What has happened to the lock? *It has disappeared.*

Th' expiring swan, and as he sings he dies.
When bold Sir Plume had drawn Clarissa down,
Chloe[38] stepped in, and killed him with a frown;
She smiled to see the doughty hero slain,
But, at her smile, the beau revived again.
Now Jove suspends his golden scales in air, ❶
Weighs the men's wits against the lady's hair;
The doubtful beam long nods from side to side;
At length the wits mount up, the hairs subside.
See, fierce Belinda on the baron flies,
With more than usual lightning in her eyes;
Nor feared the chief th' unequal fight to try,
Who sought no more than on his foe to die.
But this bold lord with manly strength endued, ❷
She with one finger and a thumb subdued:
Just where the breath of life his nostrils drew,
A charge of snuff the wily virgin threw;
The gnomes direct, to every atom just,
The pungent grains of titillating dust.
Sudden with starting tears each eye o'erflows,
And the high dome re-echoes to his nose.
"Now meet thy fate," incensed Belinda cried,
And drew a deadly bodkin[39] from her side . . .
"Boast not my fall," he cried, "insulting foe!
Thou by some other shalt be laid as low.
Nor think, to die dejects my lofty mind;
All that I dread is leaving you behind!
Rather than so, ah let me still survive,
And burn in Cupid's flames—but burn alive."
"Restore the lock!" she cries; and all around
"Restore the lock!" the vaulted roofs rebound.
Not fierce Othello in so loud a strain
Roared for the handkerchief that caused his pain.[40]
But see how oft ambitious aims are crossed,
And chiefs contend till all the prize is lost!
The lock, obtained with guilt, and kept with pain, ❹
In every place is sought, but sought in vain.
With such a prize no mortal must be blessed,
So Heaven decrees! with Heaven who can contest?
Some thought it mounted to the lunar sphere,
Since all things lost on earth are treasured there.
There heroes' wits are kept in ponderous vases,
And beaux' in snuffboxes and tweezer cases.
There broken vows and deathbed alms are found,

◆ Literature and Your Life ❸
Hair has always been an important aspect of fashion. In what ways is it an important part of today's fashions?

38. **Chloe** (klō′ ē): Heroine of the ancient Greek pastoral romance, *Daphnis and Chloe*.
39. **bodkin:** Ornamental pin shaped like a dagger.
40. **not . . . pain:** In Shakespeare's *Othello*, the hero is convinced that his wife is being unfaithful to him when she cannot find the handkerchief that he had given her. Actually, the handkerchief had been taken by the villain, Iago, who uses it as part of his evil plot.

Cross-Curricular Connection: Science

The type of scale Jove would probably have been using to weigh men's wits against the lock of hair is a balance scale. The principles of a balance scale can be understood by thinking about levers and fulcrums. Usually when a balance scale is used, the object to be weighed, called the load, is placed on one side of the scale, which is balanced in the center by a pivot (fulcrum). Traditionally, weights make up the effort: the number of weights needed to achieve balance measures the load.

Balance scales used today are based on a design pioneered only about fifty years before Pope published *The Rape of the Lock.* In 1669, the French mathematician Roberval devised a scale that used the principle of levers to support the weight of the pans holding objects to be weighed. This enabled people to place a weight or object anywhere on a pan and still obtain an accurate measure.

Have students draw their concept of such a scale, identifying the lever or levers, fulcrum, effort, and load.

And lovers' hearts with ends of riband bound . . .
But trust the Muse—she saw it upward rise,
Though marked by none but quick, poetic eyes . . .
A sudden star, it shot through liquid[41] air
And drew behind a radiant trail of hair . . .[42]
Then cease, bright Nymph! to mourn thy ravished hair, ❺
Which adds new glory to the shining sphere!
Not all the tresses that fair head can boast,
Shall draw such envy as the lock you lost.
For, after all the murders of your eye,[43]
When, after millions slain, yourself shall die;
When those fair suns shall set, as set they must,
And all those tresses shall be laid in dust,
This lock, the Muse shall consecrate to fame, ❻
And midst the stars inscribe Belinda's name.

41. **liquid:** Clear.
42. **trail of hair:** The word *comet* comes from a Greek word meaning long-haired.
43. **murders . . . eye:** Lovers struck down by her glances.

Guide for Responding

◆ Literature and Your Life

Reader's Response Do you think Pope effectively satirizes his subject? Explain.

Thematic Focus Is there any evidence in the poem of the true values that should bind a people together? Explain.

Group Discussion What social conventions would Pope have written about if he were writing now? As a group, come up with a few possible subjects and the ways he may have satirized them.

☑ Check Your Comprehension

1. (a) In what activity is Belinda engaged during the first half of Canto III? (b) What is the outcome?
2. (a) What is the "two-edged weapon" that Clarissa gives the baron? (b) How many times does the baron fail to get the lock of hair?
3. (a) How does Belinda respond when the baron manages to get the lock of hair? (b) How does the baron react?
4. What has happened to the lock of hair at the end of Canto V?

◆ Critical Thinking

INTERPRET

1. Why do you think Pope precedes the trivial episodes in Canto III with such a grisly image as "wretches hang that jurymen may dine"? **[Analyze]**
2. What similarity is there between Pope's description of the omber game and his description of the events following the theft of the lock? **[Compare and Contrast]**
3. Lines 79–88 in Canto V are "elegant spoofing," according to one critic. Yet, in a sense, Pope made the poem's extravagant claim come true. How did he do it? **[Interpret]**

APPLY

4. Pope based *The Rape of the Lock* on an actual incident. What incident in the news today might provide the basis for a similar mock epic? **[Apply]**

EXTEND

5. (a) How would you compare *The Rape of the Lock* with Swift's *Gulliver's Travels*? (b) How are they similar in their treatment of social manners? How do they differ? **[Literature Link]**

◆ Literary Focus

❺ **Mock Epic** Ask students to explain why this is or is not a fitting ending for this mock epic. *Students may say it is a perfect ending, with the hair going up to Heaven, or the "lunar sphere," as if it were something grand instead of just a lock of hair. The petty little lock is elevated and made sublime —even consecrated to fame.*

◆ Reading Strategy

❻ **Author's Purpose** Ask students to evaluate how well the ending fulfills the author's purpose. *Students might like the idea that Belinda's name will be inscribed in the stars: she is, after all, little more than a witless victim of an absurd prank. Interestingly enough however, the lock was, indeed, consecrated to fame: Pope and his poem will forever be remembered.*

Reinforce and Extend

Answers

◆ Literature and Your Life

Reader's Response Students should observe that Pope mocks the manners of his characters but doesn't deflate them. He is not criticizing them as strongly as a satirist would.

Thematic Focus Students should decide whether the tone and intent of the poem is to address serious values or to ridicule absurd social pretensions.

☑ Check Your Comprehension

1. (a) Belinda is engaged in a social "hour," which includes a card game. (b) Belinda beats the baron at omber, a card game.
2. (a) Clarissa gives the baron a pair of scissors. (b) The baron fails three times to get a lock of Belinda's hair.
3. (a) Belinda screams with horror. (b) The baron cries out in glee.
4. In the end the lock flies heavenward, changing into a star in the heavens that bears Belinda's name.

◆ Critical Thinking

1. Such biting satire is quite typical of Pope.
2. Both are described as military conflicts elevated to epic scope by the use of numerous allusions.
3. By immortalizing Belinda in his poem, Pope made good on his extravagant claim.
4. Some students may suggest an incident involving mobbing celebrities for bits of clothing or other memorabilia.
5. (a) *The Rape of the Lock* is lighter in spirit than *Gulliver's Travels* (b) They both point out the vanity, pride, and folly of mankind. Swift differs in tone from Pope because he is satirizing more serious faults, while Pope is poking affectionate fun at the pretensions of high society.

Develop Understanding

One-Minute Insight Pope's heroic couplets are the perfect vehicle to balance the contrary attributes of mankind. The passage asks: What is man? Its answer is: Man is a creature in the middle—more than a beast, less than a god, unsure about whether to trust his mind or body more. Both the glory and jest of the world, man is, above all, a riddle.

Customize for
Less Proficient Readers
Have pairs of students work together to find examples of the opposites in the poem that could describe a middle state. Then ask pairs to summarize their findings.

◆ Background for Understanding

❶ Explain that it was Sophocles who first said, "Know thyself." Pope gives the same advice, but overall his purpose is more to comment on man's condition than to dispense advice.

◆ Critical Thinking

❷ **Interpret** Ask: What do these lines say about human beings? *Thought and passion, or mind and body, seem to work against each other. Man can abuse himself or hurt himself; he can also, with his mind, free himself from false notions.*

◆ Literature and Your Life

❸ Ask students whether they think Pope has done a good job of summing up the nature of man. *Students may say that this excerpt from Pope's poem encompasses both man's most noble impulses, such as helping others or loving, and man's worst impulses, such as making war or murdering.*

from An Essay on Man

Alexander Pope

An Essay on Man is an examination of human nature, society, and morals. In the following passage, Pope cautions against intellectual pride by vividly describing the uncertain "middle state" in which humans have been placed.

❶ Know then thyself, presume not God to scan;
The proper study of mankind is man.
Placed on this isthmus of a middle state,
A being darkly wise, and rudely great:
With too much knowledge for the skeptic side,
With too much weakness for the stoic's pride,
He hangs between; in doubt to act, or rest;
In doubt to deem himself a god, or beast;
In doubt his mind or body to prefer;
Born but to die, and reasoning but to err;
❷ Alike in ignorance, his reason such,
Whether he thinks too little, or too much:
Chaos of thought and passion, all confused;
Still by himself abused, or disabused;
Created half to rise, and half to fall;
Great lord of all things, yet a prey to all;
❸ Sole judge of truth, in endless error hurled:
The glory, jest, and riddle of the world!

◆ Build Vocabulary

stoic (stō´ ik) *n.*: Person indifferent to joy, grief, pleasure, or pain

disabused (dis´ ə byo͞ozd´) *adj.*: Freed from false ideas

Humanities: Art

The Thinker, 1888, by Auguste René Rodin.

Refused admittance to the art school of his choice, Rodin became the foremost sculptor of the nineteenth and early twentieth centuries. Working in bronze and marble, Rodin created two general styles of sculptures. One style, for which he is more well known, reflects a painstaking concern for surface modeling and is characterized by a deliberate roughness of form. The second produces delicate forms with highly polished surfaces. *The Thinker,* cast in bronze, is executed in Rodin's more characteristic style.

Use these questions for discussion:

1. Rodin's *Thinker* has a very muscular body, powerful hands and feet, and a low brow. Is this your idea of a thinker? Explain. *Students should note that more noble embodiments of thinking are possible. This may well be a thinker who is part beast. Students may be interested to know that the first bronze cast of this piece was put in front of the Pantheon. When it was unveiled, the speaker at the event thought it must represent work, so the figure became a sort of monument to labor.*
2. In your opinion, is this sculpture a good choice for illustrating this selection? *Possible response: Yes, this thinker occupies a middle state, with his extremely physical body. The head, or workings of the mind, of this thinker do not seem to be elevating him.*

Guide for Responding

◆ Literature and Your Life

Reader's Response How does your understanding of human nature compare with Pope's? Explain.

Thematic Focus Judging by Pope's description of human nature, do you think he believed that people needed rules to restrain them? Explain.

☑ Check Your Comprehension

1. What does Pope say should be the object of man's study?
2. According to Pope, what prevents man from being a skeptic or a stoic?

◆ Critical Thinking

INTERPRET

1. Pope writes that man stands on an "isthmus of a middle state." In a single word, what is (a) at one end of the isthmus? (b) at the other end? **[Analyze]**
2. What do you think Pope means by the line "In doubt his mind or body to prefer"? **[Interpret]**
3. Is Pope's view of human nature original? Why or why not? **[Make a Judgment]**

APPLY

4. Most writers today reject the idea that literature should present an obvious moral. Pope believed that poetry has a didactic, or instructional, role to play. What do you think? **[Generalize]**

Beyond the Selection

FURTHER READING

Other Works by Alexander Pope
"Eloisa to Abelard"
"Windsor Forest"

Other Works on the Nature of Man
"A Dog's Eye View of Man," James Thurber
The Tragedy of Macbeth, William Shakespeare

We suggest that you preview these works before recommending them to students.

INTERNET

You and your students may find additional information about Alexander Pope on the Internet. We suggest the following site.

For recent articles about *The Rape of the Lock,* go to **http://www-unix.oit.umass.edu/~sconstan/offlineref.html**

We *strongly recommend* that you preview the site before you send students to it.

▶Critical Viewing◀

Analyze Ask students: Do you think this sculpture, *The Thinker* by Rodin, shows man more as beast, more as god, or somewhere in a middle state? *Students may say that this is more than beast; this is a man thinking. It is also less than a god: the man is in a hunched, contemplative position that does not seem to communicate great power or authority. Rather, this man seems to be in a middle state. Perhaps this man is even contemplating the nature of man.*

Reinforce and Extend

Answers

◆ Literature and Your Life

Reader's Response Students may say they have observed the "battle of the sexes" at work in their own social situations.

Thematic Focus In Pope's time people believed in a rational order of things and in their willingness to subordinate their emotions to the intellect. Laws or rules would help provide control.

☑ Check Your Comprehension

1. The proper study of mankind, according to Pope, is man.
2. Too much knowledge keeps a person from becoming a skeptic; and too much weakness keeps a person from becoming a stoic.

◆ Critical Thinking

1. (a) At one end of the isthmus is the skeptic (or beast); (b) on the other is the stoic (or god).
2. The line suggests that people have trouble deciding whether to be ruled by their minds or by their passions.
3. Pope's view of human nature as being susceptible to its own intellectual pride is not original. There are examples in earlier works, such as the Bible and in mythology.
4. Students may observe that there are lessons to be learned in most stories, even if no specific moral is included.

Answers

◆ Reading Strategy

1. These lines hearken to a Greek Chorus bemoaning the fate of mortals. The rhyme of "fate" and "elate" underscores the humor in the lines.
2. The pouring of coffee takes on heroic proportions in the descriptions of tables as "altars of Japan" and coffee cups as "China's earth."
3. Pope uses the description of the "two-edged" weapon to compare handing the baron a pair of scissors with arming a knight for combat.
4. The use of such fantastic characters enables Pope to give mythic proportions to simple actions.
5. Pope compares a fight to the death to the loss of the lock of hair.

◆ Build Vocabulary

Using Words About Society

1. The king would be haughty to the baron, because the baron is lower.
2. The baron would be haughty to the plebeian, because the plebeian is a lowly commoner.
3. The lady would be haughty, since the baron is acting like a lowly commoner.

Using the Word Bank

1. h 2. f 3. g 4. c 5. b
6. d 7. a 8. e

◆ Literary Focus

1. (a) In lines 60–75, Pope likens the card game to a heroic battle. In lines 125–132, he describes the pair of scissors as if they were a knight's weapon. (b) In the card game, each card played represents a military force of kings and queens on a battlefield. The scissors, which are meant to snip a small ringlet of hair, are compared to the lance with which a knight will kill an opponent in battle.
2. (a) Ariel, Clarissa, Umbriel, Chloe, and Jove are five of the deities and muses mentioned. (b) These add to the epic exaggeration and thus comic effects of the poem.

Guide for Responding *(continued)*

◆ Reading Strategy

Author's Purpose

Once you know that the **author's purpose** in *The Rape of the Lock* is to poke affectionate fun at the pretensions of high society, many details in the poem become more understandable. Explain how each of these lines or devices accomplishes Pope's purpose:

1. "Oh thoughtless mortals ever blind to fate,
Too soon dejected, and too soon elate."
(Canto III, lines 101–102)

2. Heroic description of the pouring of coffee (Canto III, lines 105–110)

3. Elaborate description of a pair of scissors (Canto III, lines 125–132)

4. Use of fantastic characters like Ariel, sprites, and sylphs (Canto III, lines 135–154)

5. "But see how often ambitious aims are crossed,
And chiefs contend till all the prize is lost!"
(Canto V, lines 63–64)

◆ Build Vocabulary

Using Related Words About Society

Knowing Pope's words about society and social attitudes, tell who would be *haughty* in the following encounters and why:

1. a baron and a king
2. a baron and a plebeian person
3. a baron acting in a plebeian way and a lady

Using the Word Bank

In your notebook, write down the letter of the word or phrase in Column B that is closest in meaning to the word in Column A.

Column A	Column B
1. plebeian	**a.** lacking
2. obliquely	**b.** arrogant
3. assignations	**c.** impassive person
4. stoic	**d.** cease
5. haughty	**e.** undeceived
6. desist	**f.** indirectly
7. destitute	**g.** meetings
8. disabused	**h.** common

◆ Literary Focus

Mock Epic

Pope's **mock epic** is a humorous narrative poem that treats a petty incident—the theft of a lock of hair—in the grand manner of epics like the *Odyssey*. That grand manner includes descriptions of heroic deeds, references to mythology, and supernatural beings who help or hinder human actions.

Notice how in Canto III, lines 105–115, for example, Pope describes the pouring of coffee as if it were a sacred, heroic ritual. He also refers to the supernatural "airy band" who "hover round" Belinda. These supernatural creatures help her not to achieve heroic deeds but to drink a cup of coffee!

As you can see, the contrast between the grand manner of description and the trivial activities described produces a humorous contrast.

1. (a) Find two trivial incidents in *The Rape of the Lock* that Pope presents in a heroic manner. (b) Show how in each case the description humorously contrasts with the action.

2. (a) What are some of the mythical creatures, including deities and muses, mentioned in the poem? Find at least five. (b) Would the poem be less humorous without them? Why or why not?

◆ Grammar and Style

Inverted Word Order

To achieve a certain rhythm or to emphasize ideas, Pope uses **inverted word order**—a change in the normal English word order of subject-verb-complement.

Practice After labeling the subject, verb, and complement in each of these lines, rewrite the lines in normal English word order.

1. Here Britain's statesmen oft the fall foredoom. . . . (III, 5)

2. His warlike Amazon her host invades. . . . (III, 67)

3. The baron now his diamonds pours apace. . . . (III, 75)

◆ Grammar and Style

1. Here Britain's statesmen *(subj.)* oft foredoom *(verb)* the fall *(complement)* . . .
2. His warlike Amazon *(subject)* invades *(verb)* her host *(complement)* . . .
3. The baron *(subject)* now pours *(verb)* apace his diamonds *(complement)* . . .

Writer's Solution

For additional instruction and practice use the page on Subjects in Different Kinds of Order, page 19 in the *Writer's Solution Grammar Practice Book*.

Build Your Portfolio

Idea Bank

Writing

1. **Paraphrase** Review the main points of the passage from *An Essay on Man.* Then write a prose version of the selection, expressing Pope's ideas in your own words.

2. **Reply** As one of the characters in *The Rape of the Lock*, write a letter to Pope letting him know how you feel about his portrayal of you.

3. **Comparison and Contrast** *An Essay on Man* and *The Rape of the Lock* are works that differ widely in purpose and attitude. Write a comparison-and-contrast paper pointing out differences and similarities, if any, between the two works.

Speaking and Listening

4. **Reading and Pantomime** Present a dramatic reading of *The Rape of the Lock*. Assign passages to readers and have actors pantomime the actions being described. **[Performing Arts Link]**

5. **Graduation Speech** Present your ideas on humankind in a speech to be given at your high school graduation. If you like, quote words and phrases from Pope's *An Essay on Man.* **[Performing Arts Link]**

Projects

6. **High Society in Pope's Day** Using books like Maynard Mack's biography of Pope, do further research on the high society that Pope makes fun of in *The Rape of the Lock*. Present your findings in a written report. **[Social Studies Link]**

7. **Classical Glossary** List terms from ancient Greek and Roman literature and mythology in *The Rape of the Lock*. Use encyclopedias, dictionaries, and other reference sources to help you define the terms listed. **[Literature Link]**

Writing Mini-Lesson

Imitating an Author's Style

In *The Rape of the Lock*, Pope's use of rhyming couplets and his serious treatment of silly matters contribute to a distinctive style. Choose an author—Pope or someone else—whose style is unmistakable, and write an imitation of it.

These hints will help you keep the author's style in focus as you imitate it.

Writing Skills Focus: Maintain Consistent Style

Whether you write an imitation of an author's style or a piece of your own, it's important to maintain a consistent style:

- Use the same level of formal or informal language throughout
- Be consistent in your use of imagery, meter, or inverted word order
- Keep the same attitude toward your subject and the same mood.

You can deal with these style issues at every stage of the writing process.

Prewriting Choose the author you will imitate and carefully analyze his or her style. Consider such factors as average sentence length, word choice and vocabulary level, literary devices, and attitude toward the subject.

Drafting Approach the drafting like an acting assignment. After studying the author's stylistic mannerisms and rereading a passage from his or her work, write as if you were the author. It may help you keep samples of the author's writing at hand for easy reference.

Revising Read your draft critically, and look for places where you slipped into your own style. Rewrite them by taking on an attitude typical of your author or using a literary device that he or she uses.

Idea Bank

Customizing for *Performance Levels*

Following are suggestions for matching Idea Bank topics with your students' performance levels:

Less Advanced Students: 1, 4, 6
Average Students: 2, 4, 6
More Advanced Students: 3, 5, 7

Customizing for *Learning Modalities*

Following are suggestions for matching Idea Bank topics with your students' learning modalities:

Verbal/Linguistic: 1, 2, 3, 5, 6, 7
Bodily/Kinesthetic: 4

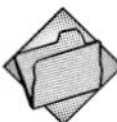

Writing Mini-Lesson

Refer students to the Writing Handbook, page 1189, for instruction on the writing process, and page 1192 for further information on creative writing.

Writer's Solution

Sourcebook

Have students use Chapter 6, Creative Writing (pp. 167–195), for additional support. The chapter includes an annotated student model from literature of an imitation of an author's style (p. 174).

ASSESSMENT OPTIONS

Formal Assessment, Selection Test, pp. 107–109, and Assessment Resources Software. The selection test is designed so that it can be easily customized to the performance levels of your students.

Alternative Assessment, p. 24, includes options for less advanced students, more advanced students, visual/spatial learners, interpersonal learners, bodily/kinesthetic learners, verbal/linguistic learners, and intrapersonal learners.

PORTFOLIO ASSESSMENT

Use the following rubrics in the ***Alternative Assessment*** booklet to assess student writing:
Paraphrase: Summary Rubric, p. 99
Reply: Fictional Narrative Rubric, p. 96
Comparison and Contrast: Comparison/Contrast Rubric, p. 104
Writing Mini-Lesson: Fictional Narrative Rubric, p. 96, or Poetry Rubric, p. 109

Prepare and Engage

OBJECTIVES

1. To read, comprehend, and interpret selections from a dictionary and a biography
2. To relate the selections to personal experience
3. To set a purpose for reading
4. To identify characteristics of dictionaries and biographies
5. To build vocabulary in context and learn the word root *-dict-*
6. To develop skill in using commas with parenthetical expressions
7. To write a dictionary of new words
8. To respond to the dictionary and biography through writing, speaking and listening, and projects

SKILLS INSTRUCTION

Vocabulary: Word Roots: *-dict-*
Grammar: Commas with Parenthetical Expressions
Reading Strategy: Set a Purpose
Literary Focus: Dictionary; Biography
Writing: Keeping to a Format
Speaking and Listening: Interpretation of Attitudes (teacher edition)
Critical Viewing: Infer; Interpret

PORTFOLIO OPPORTUNITIES

Writing: Book Ad; Revised Preface; Response to Criticism
Writing Mini-Lesson: Dictionary of New Words
Speaking and Listening: Reenactment; Interpretation of Attitudes
Projects: First-Person Biography; The School of Johnson

More About the Authors

Success came late for **Samuel Johnson.** He was finally freed from worries about money in 1762, when he was awarded an annual pension of 300 pounds. Late in life, Johnson received honorary degrees from Oxford and from Trinity College, Dublin, granting him the title "Dr."

Ironically, more is known about his biographer, **James Boswell,** than is known about Johnson himself. Stifled during his own lifetime by biting criticism, Boswell has taken his rightful place as one of the best English writers of his time.

Guide for Interpreting

Samuel Johnson *(1709–1784)*

With his fine mind and dazzling conversation, Johnson was at the center of a circle that included most of Britain's leading artists and intellectuals. So great was his influence on English literature that the second half of the eighteenth century is often called the Age of Johnson.

A Life of Hardship Samuel Johnson overcame severe physical and economic hardships to become one of England's most outstanding figures. The son of a bookseller in Lichfield, England, Johnson suffered a series of childhood illnesses that left him weak and disfigured. Bright enough to read Shakespeare at the age of eight, he was too poor to attend the schools of the aristocracy and instead pursued his education largely by reading books in his father's shop. Even when he was able to enter Oxford in 1728, lack of funds forced him to leave early.

A Great Work In 1737 Johnson moved to London to try to earn his living as a writer; a decade later he began work on his *Dictionary of the English Language.* This landmark effort took eight years to complete—eight difficult years in which Johnson lost his wife and continued to be dogged by poverty. When at last the dictionary was published, however, it ensured Johnson's place in literary history.

James Boswell *(1740–1795)*

Not until the twentieth century did James Boswell take his place as perhaps the greatest biographer in English letters. Best known for his biography of Samuel Johnson, Boswell wrote with vigor, training his eye on both the picturesque and the grotesque.

Celebrity Chaser The son of a prominent and demanding Scottish judge, James Boswell was made to study law when he would have preferred literature. Riddled with insecurities, he became something of a celebrity chaser, introducing himself to famous figures like the French philosophers Voltaire and Rousseau. In Samuel Johnson he found not only a friendly celebrity but also the father figure he apparently sought. Deciding to become Johnson's biographer, he devoted thirty years to compiling detailed records of Johnson's life.

A Brilliant Biographer Though Boswell's *Life of Samuel Johnson* (1791) was a popular book, for decades its subject far outshone its author, and Boswell was viewed much as a ghost writer is today. In recent years it has been affirmed that Boswell had a genius of his own, which is evident from studying the trove of his personal papers discovered in the twentieth century. His powers of listening, observation, and recall enabled him to bring the subject of a biography to life as no one had done before.

◆ Background for Understanding

CULTURE: SYSTEMATIZING KNOWLEDGE

Eighteenth-century thinkers seemed to sense that a "summit of knowledge" had been reached, and they set down in writing scientific, philosophical, and historical facts and ideas.

Among the intellectual "mountaineers" were Samuel Johnson and James Boswell, whose dictionary and biography, respectively, set the standard for nonfiction works of their type. The eighteenth century also saw the birth of the first Encyclopedia Britannica (1768–1771), and Adam Smith's *Wealth of Nations* (1776), which revolutionized economics.

As you read the following selections, notice how Boswell is "setting down" Samuel Johnson even as Johnson "sets down" the English language!

Prentice Hall Literature Program Resources

REINFORCE / RETEACH / EXTEND

Selection Support Pages
Build Vocabulary: Word Roots *-dict-*, p. 118
Grammar and Style: Commas With Parenthetical Expressions, p. 119
Reading Strategy: Set a Purpose, p. 120
Literary Focus: Dictionary, p. 121

Strategies for Diverse Student Needs, p. 25

Beyond Literature Career Connection: Documentary Filmmaker, p. 25

Formal Assessment Selection Test, pp. 120–122; Assessment Resources Software

Alternative Assessment, p. 25

Resource Pro CD-ROM from "The Preface to *A Dictionary of the English Language,*" from *A Dictionary of the English Language,* from *The Life of Samuel Johnson*—includes all resource material and customizable lesson plan

Listening to Literature Audiocassettes from "The Preface" to *A Dictionary of the English Language,* from *A Dictionary of the English Language,* from *The Life of Samuel Johnson*

from The Preface to A Dictionary of the English Language ◆ *from* A Dictionary of the English Language ◆ *from* The Life of Samuel Johnson

◆ Literature and Your Life

Connect Your Experience

Think about some of the new words that have entered your vocabulary recently that describe things as varied as fashion trends and scientific discoveries. Johnson's *Dictionary* was one man's heroic attempt to master a changing language by setting down all the English words in existence and defining them!

Journal Writing Jot down three slang words that have entered your language within the past year.

Thematic Focus: The Ties That Bind

How do Johnson's *Dictionary* and Boswell's biography strengthen social bonds by sharing language and experience?

◆ Literary Focus

Dictionary; Biography

A **dictionary** lists and defines words and usually provides information about their pronunciation, history, and usage. The achievement of Samuel Johnson, who created the first standard dictionary, is remarkable. Not only did he think up the idea of such a dictionary, but he executed it so well that its format is still used today!

A **biography** presents the life story of someone other than the writer. A good biography presents an accurate and complete picture of the subject against the backdrop of the times in which he or she lived. Some biographies are written by people who've never met the subject. Others, like Boswell's *Life of Samuel Johnson*, are written after intense, personal interviews with the subject.

◆ Grammar and Style

Commas With Parenthetical Expressions

In *The Life of Samuel Johnson*, you'll encounter several **parenthetical expressions**, which interrupt the main part of a sentence to comment on it or to give additional information. Boswell sets these expressions off with commas, to avoid confusion.

> The character of Samuel Johnson has, *I trust*, been so developed in the course of this work . . .
>
> Man is, *in general*, made up of contradictory qualities . . .

◆ Reading Strategy

Set a Purpose

Set a purpose before you read to identify the type of information for which you're looking. By giving yourself a goal, you'll get something specific from your reading and avoid being overwhelmed by facts.

For example, you might read Johnson's *Preface* to learn about Johnson's writing style, about the process of creating a dictionary, about Johnson's attitudes, or some combination of these. Once you've decided on your purpose, set up a KWL chart showing what you Know of the subject, what you Want to know, and what you Learn from your reading. Then fill in the chart as you read.

K	W	L

◆ Build Vocabulary

Word Roots: *-dict-*

In this unit, you'll read a portion of the earliest standard dictionary of English. *Dictionary,* a listing of words, contains the root *-dict-*, from the Latin for "to say."

Word Bank

Before you read, preview these words.

recompense
caprices
adulterations
propagators
risible
abasement
credulity
malignity
pernicious
inculcated

What does it take to write a dictionary? You can give students the tiniest taste of the difficulty and complexity of the task by asking them to work in pairs to write an entry for just one word. Suggest a multiple-meaning word such as *try* or *wonder* for their effort. Ask students to include just some of the things modern dictionaries include: pronunciation, meanings for different parts of speech, idioms, guidance on usage or usage labels, as well as, perhaps, see references or synonyms. When students are finished, invite them to look up the word in a classroom dictionary and see how well they did. Students might then estimate how long they spent writing their entry, add to it the time they might spend to revise it or to make it publishable, and then multiply that time by the number of entries in a college dictionary, which is roughly 100,000 to 160,000 words.

Customize for
Less Proficient Readers

Because the sentences in both the Preface and Boswell's *The Life of Samuel Johnson* are long and complex, and because some of the words and usages are archaic, less proficient readers might benefit from listening to the audiocassette recording as they follow along in their text.

Listening to Literature Audiocassettes

Customize for
More Advanced Students

Encourage word lovers to read both Johnson and Boswell for insights into the English language. Have them record their ideas about how the meanings of some words have changed and how language continues to change today.

Customize for
English Language Learners

Have these students pause after reading the long sentences in these selections and break the sentences down into meaningful parts.

Preparing for Standardized Tests

Reading and Vocabulary When students take standardized tests, they may apply their knowledge of the word root *-dict-* to understand unfamiliar words such as *indictment,* and *dictatorial,* that appear in reading comprehension passages, vocabulary items, and analogy items. For example:

FORESEE: PREDICT : *(B)*
(A) contradict: agree (B) echo: reverberate
(C) distance: ratio (D) economize: waste

For additional practice, use the Build Vocabulary page in ***Selection Support,*** p. 118.

Grammar and Language Standardized tests may test knowledge of punctuation. Students may be asked to recognize as an error the absence of commas with parenthetical expressions: *(B)*

The United States (A) remains as ever a (B) culturally (C) diverse nation of immigrants. (D) no error (E)

The Grammar and Style lesson for this selection focuses on this topic. For additional practice, use page 119, on Commas with Parenthetical Expressions, in ***Selection Support.***

►Critical Viewing◄

❶ Infer The title page gives a great deal of information. It explains that many of the words are accompanied by examples of their use, and that these examples come from "the best writers." It says that information on both the history of the language and on grammar are contained in the dictionary. It says that the work consists of two volumes. Because of its claims, in addition to the quotation from Horace, the reader can infer that this is a scholarly work based on research.

Enrichment Boswell had this to say about Johnson's monumental project: "The world contemplated with wonder [a work] achieved by one man, while other countries had thought such undertakings fit only for whole academies." To produce his *Dictionary*, Johnson labored alone for seven years. By way of comparison, to complete the authoritative *Dictionary* of the French Academy required the labors of forty scholars for forty years.

A

DICTIONARY

OF THE

ENGLISH LANGUAGE:

IN WHICH

The WORDS are deduced from their ORIGINALS,

AND

ILLUSTRATED in their DIFFERENT SIGNIFICATIONS

BY

EXAMPLES from the beſt WRITERS.

TO WHICH ARE PREFIXED,

A HISTORY of the LANGUAGE,

AND

AN ENGLISH GRAMMAR.

BY SAMUEL JOHNSON, A. M.

IN TWO VOLUMES

VOL. I.

Cum tabulis animum cenſoris ſumet honeſti:
Audebit quæcunque parum ſplendoris habebunt,
Et ſine pondere erunt, et honore indigna ferentur.
Verba movere loco; quamvis invita recedant,
Et verſentur adhuc intra penetralia Veſtæ:
Obſcurata diu populo bonus eruet, atque
Proferet in lucem ſpecioſa vocabula rerum,
Quæ priſcis memorata Catonibus atque Cethegis,
Nunc ſitus informis premit et deſerta vetuſtas. HOR.

LONDON,

Printed by W. STRAHAN,

For J. and P. KNAPTON; T. and T. LONGMAN; C. HITCH and L. HAWES;
A. MILLAR; and R. and J. DODSLEY.

MDCCLV.

◄ **Critical Viewing** What does this title page of Johnson's *Dictionary* tell you about the contents? **[Infer]**

Humanities: Art

Title Page of Dr. Samuel Johnson's A Dictionary of the English Language, **1755.**

This page tells a bit about the history of printing conventions. Students may notice that almost the entire page is set in capital letters, as if the title page were a matter of the utmost importance. Also, by modern standards, the page is very labored: phrases such as "in which the words are deduced from their originals, and illustrated in their different significations" would not be on a modern title page. The Latin quotation also would no doubt appear on a different page. Finally, the date would most likely appear in Arabic, not Roman, numerals.

Use these questions for discussion:

1. Do you think Johnson would have been proud of this title page? *It is quite likely he would have. Not only does it tell readers that a dictionary lies within these covers, but it also proclaims the presence of a history of the language and an English grammar.*
2. Why do you think Samuel Johnson's name appears in relatively small letters? *Johnson gained fame through his dictionary; he was not famous before its publication. As a nobody, his name is buried in a fairly insignificant place on the page. Furthermore, it is possible that conventions of the day called more attention to the titles of works than to their authors.*

from

The Preface to A Dictionary of the English Language

❷

SAMUEL JOHNSON

❸ It is the fate of those who toil at the lower employments of life, to be rather driven by the fear of evil, than attracted by the prospect of good; to be exposed to censure, without hope of praise; to be disgraced by miscarriage, or punished for neglect, where success would have been without applause, and diligence without reward.

Among these unhappy mortals is the writer of dictionaries; whom mankind have considered, not as the pupil, but the slave of science, the pioneer of literature, doomed only to remove rubbish and clear obstructions from the paths through which learning and genius press forward to conquest and glory, without bestowing a smile on the humble drudge that facilitates their progress. Every other author may aspire to praise; the lexicographer can only hope to escape reproach, and even this negative recompense has been yet granted to very few.

❹ I have, notwithstanding this discouragement, attempted a dictionary of the English language, which, while it was employed in the cultivation of every species of literature, has itself been hitherto neglected; suffered to spread under the direction of chance, into wild exuberance; resigned to the tyranny of time and fashion: and exposed to the corruptions of ignorance and caprices of innovation.

When I took the first survey of my undertaking, I found our speech copious without order and energetic without rule: wherever I turned my view, there was perplexity to be disentangled and confusion to be regulated; choice was to be made out of boundless variety, without any established principle of selection; adulterations were to be detected, ❺ without a settled test of purity; and modes of expression to be rejected or received, without the suffrages of any writers of classical reputation or acknowledged authority.

Having therefore no assistance but from general grammar, I applied myself to the perusal of our writers; and noting whatever

◆ Build Vocabulary

recompense (rek′əm pens′) *n.*: Reward; payment

caprices (kə prē sis′) *n.*: Whims

adulterations (ə dul′tər ā′ shənz) *n.*: Impurities; added ingredients that are improper or inferior

Develop Understanding

One-Minute Insight Writing a dictionary is a huge and nearly impossible undertaking, and the writer is bound to get at least some parts of it wrong. No matter what he left out or mistook, however, Johnson is proud of his accomplishment. Besides, no dictionary is ever perfect.

◆ Background for Understanding

❷ Explain to students that one reason why it was so difficult for Johnson to write the dictionary is that England has never had an Academy, as France does, where scholars work together to determine standards of correctness. Because no one had ever "made the rules" for English, Johnson faced the Herculean task of not only recording every word in the language, but deciding which of its usages were "correct."

◆ Reading Strategy

❸ **Set a Purpose** Ask students what purpose they might set for reading this preface. *Students might read to find out why Johnson decided to write the dictionary; what methods he may have used; what decisions he faced; and who or what helped him to make those decisions.*

◆ Grammar and Style

❹ **Commas With Parenthetical Expressions** Point out the commas that surround the expression "notwithstanding this discouragement." Explain that this expression interrupts the main idea and provides additional information. Also note that the sentence would most likely be difficult or confusing for the reader if the commas were not used correctly.

Customize for
Less Proficient Readers

❺ Paragraph-length sentences like this one may pose difficulties for less proficient readers. Suggest that they think of the information as a list. This list presents some of the many problems Johnson knew he faced at the outset of his task. Suggest that students use their own paper to number or bullet these problems, or that they restate them one by one.

Block Scheduling Strategies

Consider these suggestions to take advantage of extended class time:

- Read the Background for Understanding note (p. 502) as a class. Relate the information about Johnson and Boswell to what students have already learned about Swift and Pope.
- Use Daily Language Practice for Week 21, based on Johnson, in ***Writing and Language Transparencies,*** p. 156.
- As a class, set a purpose for reading the Preface or one of the other selections in this grouping. Complete the KWL chart in the Reading Strategy (p. 503).
- Provide class time for students to complete one of the writing activities suggested in the Idea Bank (p. 517).
- Help students start on the Writing Mini-Lesson (p. 517) by brainstorming a list of recently coined words, ranging perhaps, from *broast* to *laptop* to include in their dictionaries. You might also work as a class to develop a consistent style for the entries.

◆ Literary Focus

❶ **Dictionary** Because Johnson was creating the first dictionary, he had almost no one else's work on which to build, as lexicographers do today. (Actually, he did have glosses; these were books of specialized terms, but no one before Johnson had also sought to define common words.) Also, today, lexicographers gather cite slips from experts in every field. Their work is facilitated by advances in communication and technology. (Of course, the rapid change in our language has also been encouraged by the same things!)

◆ Background for Understanding

❷ Explain that the most important job in writing dictionaries today is gathering information about recorded uses of words. Dictionary editors often contact experts in various fields to gather these examples. Then the editors pore over the information, make generalizations about meanings and senses of a word, and write the definitions for those words.

◆ Literature and Your Life

❸ Ask students to whom they might dedicate a work of such consequence and import as a dictionary. *They might dedicate it to their country, to their family, or to future generations.*

◆ Reading Strategy

❹ **Set a Purpose** Johnson is proud of his accomplishment. Even though he apologizes for "much" that may have been omitted, he asserts that "much likewise [was] performed." Johnson is also proud that he did this job on his own—without a rich patron, the help of the learned, or under the shelter of a university job.

Customize for
English Language Learners
Consider providing familiar synonyms for difficult words in difficult passages. Among the many words and synonyms you might write on the board or distribute on a handout are *endeavored—tried; blunders—mistakes; diligence—effort; folly—foolishness.*

◆ Literary Focus
❶ How was Johnson's task in creating his dictionary different from that of lexicographers today?

might be of use to ascertain or illustrate any word or phrase, accumulated in time the materials of a dictionary, which, by degrees, I reduced to method, establishing to myself, in the progress of the work, such rules as experience and analogy suggested to me; experience, which practice and observation were continually increasing; and analogy, which, though in some other words obscure, was evident in others . . . ❷

❸ In hope of giving longevity to that which its own nature forbids to be immortal, I have devoted this book, the labor of years, to the honor of my country, that we may no longer yield the palm of philology, without a contest to the nations of the continent. The chief glory of every people arises from its authors. Whether I shall add anything by my own writings to the reputation of English literature, must be left to time. Much of my life has been lost under the pressures of disease; much has been trifled away; and much has always been spent in provision for the day that was passing over me; but I shall not think my employment useless or ignoble, if by my assistance foreign nations and distant ages gain access to the propagators of knowledge, and understand the teachers of truth; if my labors afford light to the repositories of science, and add celebrity to Bacon, to Hooker, to Milton, and to Boyle.[1]

When I am animated by this wish, I look with pleasure on my book, however defective, and deliver it to the world with the spirit of a man that has endeavored well. That it will immediately become popular, I have not promised to myself. A few wild blunders, and risible absurdities, from which no work of such multiplicity was ever free, may for a time furnish folly with laughter, and harden ignorance into contempt; but useful diligence will at last prevail, and there never can be wanting some who distinguish desert; who will consider that no dictionary of a living tongue ever can be perfect, since, while it is hastening to publication, some words are budding, and some falling away; that a whole life cannot be spent upon syntax and etymology, and that even a whole life would not be sufficient; that he, whose design includes whatever language can express, must often speak of what he does not understand; that a writer will sometimes be hurried by eagerness to the end, and sometimes faint with weariness under a task which Scaliger[2] compares to the labors of the anvil and the mine; that what is obvious is not always known, and what is known is not always present; that sudden fits of inadvertency will surprise vigilance, slight avocations[3] will seduce attention, and casual eclipses of the mind will darken learning; and that the writer shall often in vain trace his memory at the moment of need, for that which yesterday he knew with intuitive readiness, and which will come uncalled into his thoughts tomorrow.

In this work, when it shall be found that much is omitted, let it not be forgotten that much likewise is performed; and though no book was ever spared out of tenderness to the author, and the world is little solicitous to know whence proceed the faults of that which it condemns; yet it may gratify curiosity to inform it, that the *English Dictionary* was written with little assistance of the learned, and without any patronage of the great; not in the soft obscurities of retirement, or under the shelter of academic bowers, but amidst inconvenience and distraction, in sickness and in sorrow. It may repress the triumph of malignant criticism to observe that if our language is not here fully displayed, I have only failed

◆ Reading Strategy
❹ If your purpose were to find out more about Samuel Johnson's feelings about creating his dictionary, what information in the final paragraphs would be helpful?

1. **Bacon . . . Boyle:** Writers quoted by Johnson in the *Dictionary*.

2. **Scaliger:** Joseph Justus Scaliger (1540–1609), a scholar who suggested that criminals should be condemned to writing dictionaries.

3. **avocation:** Something that calls one away or distracts one from something.

Cultural Connection

Dictionaries and Academies In Johnson's day, in countries other than England, preserving language was the task of an academy (named after the grove of Academe, in which the ancient Greek philosopher Plato taught).

After Plato's time, academies were established to consolidate and purify the language of a nation. These academies set out clear rules of usage. One of the earliest of them, the Accademia della Crusca, was founded during the Renaissance to preserve and purify the Italian language.

In 1635, Cardinal Richelieu established the Académie Française to ensure correct usage of the French language. Similar academies were launched in Spain, Sweden, Switzerland, and the Netherlands. Today there are also academies for Hebrew and Arabic.

None of these academies, however, has been able to prevent the change of any language. Most modern dictionaries and grammar handbooks, therefore, are less concerned with dictating standards than with recording current usage.

5 in an attempt which no human powers have hitherto completed. If the lexicons of ancient tongues, now immutably fixed and comprised in a few volumes, be yet, after the toil of successive ages, inadequate and delusive; if the aggregated knowledge and cooperating diligence of the Italian academicians did not secure them from the censure of Beni;[4] if the
6 embodied critics of France, when fifty years had been spent upon their work, were obliged to change its economy[5] and give their second edition another form, I may surely be contented without the praise of perfection, which, if I could obtain, in this gloom of solitude, what would it avail me? I have protracted my work till most of those whom I wished to please have sunk into the grave,[6] and success and miscarriage are empty sounds: I therefore dismiss it with frigid tranquility, having little to fear or hope from censure or from praise. 7

4. **Beni:** Paolo Beni severely criticized the first Italian dictionary.
5. **economy:** Organization.
6. **sunk . . . grave:** Johnson's wife had died three years earlier.

◆ Build Vocabulary

propagators (präp′ə gāt′ərz) *n.*: Those who cause something to happen or to spread

risible (riz′ə bəl) *adj.*: Prompting laughter

Guide for Responding

◆ Literature and Your Life

Reader's Response Based on this preface, what do you expect the body of Johnson's dictionary to be like? Why?

Thematic Focus Would you guess that Johnson's ties to literature and reading were important to him? Explain.

Dictionary How-To Describe the step-by-step process that you might use if you had to create the first English language dictionary.

☑ Check Your Comprehension

1. Among what class of workers does Johnson place writers of dictionaries?
2. (a) What was English lacking when Johnson "took the first survey"? (b) What gave him his only assistance in compiling his dictionary?
3. Why, according to the preface, can "no dictionary of the living tongue ever be perfect"?

◆ Critical Thinking

INTERPRET

1. What is Johnson's chief reason for undertaking the creation of a dictionary? **[Interpret]**
2. Do you think Johnson is hopeful or pessimistic (or perhaps both) about the fate of his dictionary? Explain.

EVALUATE

3. Johnson devotes his dictionary to the "honor of my country." In what ways, if any, do you think his dictionary honors England? **[Assess]**

APPLY

4. What opinion do you think Johnson would have of today's unabridged dictionaries? **[Hypothesize]**

EXTEND

5. How have computers changed the task of making dictionaries? **[Science Link]**

5 Clarification Explain that Johnson is pointing out that it is difficult to write a dictionary even for a language that is not spoken anymore, such as Latin—imagine how much harder it is to write a dictionary for a language, such as English, that is constantly changing.

Comprehension Check ☑

6 Ask students what the reaction was to the French dictionary, which, according to Johnson, had taken fifty years to write. *It was found wanting. The second edition required a complete reorganization.*

◆ Critical Thinking

7 Draw Conclusions What does Johnson expect the public reaction to his dictionary to be? *He expects it will be mixed. He knows errors will be found; he also knows no one has ever written a perfect dictionary.*

Customize for *Intrapersonal Learners*

Ask intrapersonal learners to record their thoughts and feelings about Johnson's preface. When Johnson says he has "little to fear or hope from censure or from praise," do they believe him? Why or why not?

Reinforce and Extend

Answers

◆ Literature and Your Life

Reader's Response Students might respond that Johnson's dictionary is opinionated, learned, and even drily witty.

Thematic Focus Yes, Johnson quotes numerous writers and compares himself to many writers of dictionaries in his preface.

☑ Check Your Comprehension

1. Writers of dictionaries are among those "who toil at the lower employments of life;" their labors are like those of miners and blacksmiths.
2. (a) Among other things, Johnson found English to be lacking in order and in rules. (b) General grammar was his only assistance.
3. Any living tongue is constantly changing—adding words, dropping words, changing meanings, and so on.

◆ Critical Thinking

1. Johnson wrote the *Dictionary* to help codify English—that is, put some order into the language.
2. Johnson expresses confidence that, eventually, the "useful diligence" of his labor will be discerned by some. At the same time, his claim to "frigid tranquility" after seven year's work and his wife's death may ring true to some readers.
3. Johnson's dictionary honored England by quoting great English writers, and by bringing together a standard for the language.
4. Johnson would most likely have a low opinion of today's dictionary writers, who look upon themselves as reporters of the language rather than as arbiters of good taste and correctness; at the same time, the magnitude of their efforts outstrip his own seven-year effort.
5. Computers have simplified the organization of information, the storage of information, and the changing or updating of information.

Develop Understanding

One-Minute Insight Like a sampler of needlework stitches, this page shows but a few of the entries in Johnson's two-volume dictionary. These entries demonstrate not only some of the difficulties Johnson faced in writing but also how much our language has changed since his times.

Customize for
Visual/Spatial Learners
Today's college dictionaries have illustrations in the margins that help define some words. Which of these words would students choose to illustrate? What would they show? Invite students to describe or carry out their choices.

◆ Background for Understanding

❶ Point out the spelling of the word *athletick*. Explain that words have changed in many ways since Johnson's day: spelling is one example of this change. Here the sound of /k/ is spelled the same way it is spelled at the end of *lick* and *kick;* this spelling may also remind students of the verbal *picnicking*. As they read, students will also see how much meaning has also changed for some words.

◆ Literature and Your Life

❷ Ask students which of these definitions they find most amusing or memorable and why. *Buffleheaded may be a good choice since the word seems like a great insult, but one that we no longer use.*

◆ Critical Thinking

❸ **Compare and Contrast** Invite students to choose a single entry, such as *electricity,* and compare and contrast an entry in a modern dictionary for this word with the entry found here. Then ask students to give a reason for the contrast. *Our understanding of electricity has advanced considerably since Johnson's day.*

from

A Dictionary of the English Language

SAMUEL JOHNSON

❶ **athle´ tick.** Strong of body; vigorous; lusty; robust.

Science distinguishes a man of honor
from one of those *athletick* brutes,
whom undeservedly we call heroes.
Dryden.

bang. A blow; a thump; a stroke: a low word.

I am a bachelor. That's to say, they are
fools that marry; you'll bear me a *bang*
for that. Shakespeare, *Julius Caesar.*

to ba´rbecue. A term used in the West Indies for dressing a hog whole; which, being split to the backbone, is laid flat upon a large gridiron, raised about two foot above a charcoal fire, with which it is surrounded.

❷ Oldfield, with more than harpy throat
endu'd,
Cries, send me, gods, a whole hog *barbecu'd.* Pope.

bu´ffleheaded. A man with a large head, like a buffalo; dull; stupid; foolish.

cream. The unctuous or oily part of milk, which, when it is cold, floats on the top, and is changed by the agitation of the churn into butter; the flower of milk.

electri´city. A property in some bodies, whereby, when rubbed so as to grow warm, they draw little bits of paper, or such like substances, to them. Quincy.

Such was the account given a few years ago of electricity; but the industry of the present age, first excited by the experiments of Gray, has discovered in electricity a multitude of philosophical wonders. Bodies electrified by a sphere of glass, turned nimbly round, not only emit flame, but may be fitted with such a quantity of the electrical vapor as, if discharged at once upon a human body, would endanger life. The force of this vapor has hitherto appeared instantaneous, persons at both ends of a long chain seeming to be struck at once. The philosophers are now endeavoring to intercept the strokes of lightning. ❸

to fu´rnace. To throw out as sparks from a furnace. A bad word.

He *furnaces*
The thick sighs from him. Shakespeare's *Cymbeline.*

gang. A number herding together; a troop; a company; a tribe; a herd. It is seldom used but in contempt or abhorrence.

Cross-Curricular Connection: Science

Johnson's definition of *electricity* reflects some understanding of static electricity and the beginning of an understanding of current electricity, which is produced by electrons flowing in a current. In order to make the electrons move, an energy source is needed. This energy may come from heat, light, pressure, or a chemical reaction. It is not entirely clear what the source of energy is in Johnson's example, but the fact that it produces a surge of current is clear. Johnson also seems to understand that electricity is conducted and may flow in a circuit. Students might research how strokes of lightning were first intercepted, and how they are intercepted, and deflected, today.

ha´tchet-face. An ugly face; such, I suppose, as might be hewn out of a block by a hatchet.

> An ape his own dear image will embrace;
> An ugly beau adores a *hatchet-face.*
> Dryden.

❹ **lifegua´rd.** The guard of a king's person.

mo´dern. In Shakespeare, vulgar; mean; common.

> We have our philosophical persons to make *modern* and familiar things supernatural and causeless. Shakespeare.

pa´tron. One who countenances, supports or protects. Commonly a wretch who supports with insolence, and is paid with flattery.

pi´ckle. Condition; state. A word of contempt and ridicule.

> How cam'st though in this *pickle*?
> Shakespeare.

plu´mper. Something worn in the mouth to swell out the cheeks.

> She dex'trously her *plumpers* draws,
> That serve to fill her hollow jaws. *Swift's Miscellanies.*

shill-I-shall-I. A corrupt reduplication of *shall I?* The question of a man hesitating. To stand *shill-I-shall-I,* is to continue hesitating and procrastinating.

> I am somewhat dainty in making a resolution, because when I make it, I keep it; I don't stand shill-I-shall-I then; if I say't, I'll do't. Congreve's *Way of the World.*

to sneeze. To emit wind audibly by the nose. ❻

wi´llow. A tree worn by forlorn lovers.

to wipe. To cheat; to defraud.

> The next bordering lords commonly encroach one upon another, as one is stronger, or lie still in wait to *wipe* them out of their lands. Spenser, *On Ireland.*

you´ngster, you´nker. A young person. In contempt.

youth. The part of life succeeding to childhood and adolescence; the time from fourteen to twenty-eight.

◆ Literary Focus
In addition to definitions, what information does Johnson supply about entry words? ❺

Guide for Responding

◆ Literature and Your Life

Reader's Response Do you find Johnson's definitions fair? funny? prejudiced? Explain.

Thematic Focus Johnson cites examples from great works of literature in some of his dictionary entries. How do these works serve to bridge centuries and cultures?

Paraphrase Rewrite one of the dictionary entries in your own words.

☑ Check Your Comprehension

1. What is Johnson's definition of *modern?*
2. According to Johnson, what is "a tree worn by forlorn lovers"?
3. What years does Johnson assign to youth?

◆ Critical Thinking

INTERPRET

1. How does Johnson indicate that a word is a verb? **[Infer]**
2. Which definitions are most like those in a modern dictionary? Explain. **[Compare and Contrast]**
3. Why do you think the word *electricity* receives such a long definition? **[Speculate]**
4. (a) Which definitions are the most revealing about Johnson's character and situation? (b) What are some of the things they reveal? **[Analyze]**

EVALUATE

5. Do you find Johnson's definitions more or less useful than those in modern dictionaries? Explain. **[Assess]**

Cultural Connection

The First Dictionaries The earliest preserved dictionary is an Akkadian word list from central Mesopotamia. It dates from approximately 600 B.C. Greek philosophers were developing the first Western-style dictionaries at approximately the same time. Pamphilus of Alexandria is credited with the creation of a lengthy Greek dictionary in the first century; after that, the Greeks seemed to have created many dictionaries—and many revisions of their dictionaries. Students might do research to find out about the first American dictionary, created by Noah Webster in 1828.

◆ Critical Thinking

❹ **Speculate** Ask: How does the definition of *lifeguard* reflect Johnson's own life and times? *It is likely there was no such thing as a lifeguard at swimming spots then.*

◆ Literary Focus

❺ **Dictionary** Point out that in many instances Johnson supplies an example of how a great writer used the word. He also gives nuances, as when he notes that *youngster* is generally used in "contempt."

◆ Critical Thinking

❻ **Speculate** Ask: Why might this definition of *sneeze* have been the best one Johnson could come up with at the time? *It is likely that no one yet understood the causes of a sneeze.*

Reinforce and Extend

Answers

◆ Literature and Your Life

Reader's Response Johnson's definitions have a prejudicial flair that is often funny, particularly in the quotations or explanations.

Thematic Focus These works use words in memorable ways, which may yet be different from current usage.

☑ Check Your Comprehension

1. The word *modern* means "vulgar," "mean," or "common."
2. The tree is a willow.
3. *Youth* is the ages from fourteen years to twenty-eight.

◆ Critical Thinking

1. Johnson indicates verbs by using the word *to.*
2. The definitions most like those in a modern dictionary are those that do not include comments or quotes from literature.
3. The entry explains something new and unfamiliar in Johnson's day.
4. (a) In the definitions of *athletick* and *patron,* (b) Johnson reveals that he is a man of letters, not athletics, and values his independence in his work.
5. Possible answers: Johnson's definitions are more entertaining, but less economical and useful than those in modern dictionaries.

Develop Understanding

One-Minute Insight For Boswell, as indeed for modern biographers, telling the story of a man's life did not mean painting the prettiest possible picture. In this forthright look at Johnson, the overall impression is positive, but negative qualities like impatience and prejudice also make their way into the portrait.

Customize for ***Bodily/Kinesthetic Learners*** Students may enjoy assuming the persona of Boswell as he chats with the listener about Johnson. Invite students to choose part of his biography to retell aloud in character. Encourage students to dress as Boswell might dress and assume a posture he might assume. Students should also develop appropriate gestures and movements to accompany the passage they select.

◆ Critical Thinking

1 Analyze Ask students to tell what they learn about Boswell in this opening paragraph. *In 1763 Boswell was twenty-two; he was already writing; he already knew a great deal about Johnson. Boswell had come to regard Johnson the way some people regard sports and movie celebrities today.*

◆ Literary Focus

2 Biography Point out that it is unusual to tell a biography in the first person; usually the third person is used. Most times, very little or nothing is revealed about the author, who is, after all, not the subject of the work.

◆ Reading Strategy

3 Set a Purpose As students read, they might set one of the following purposes, or a purpose they decide on their own: to determine ways in which this biography differs from modern biographies; to find out as much about Johnson as they can; to find out as much about Boswell as they can; to learn about the time period.

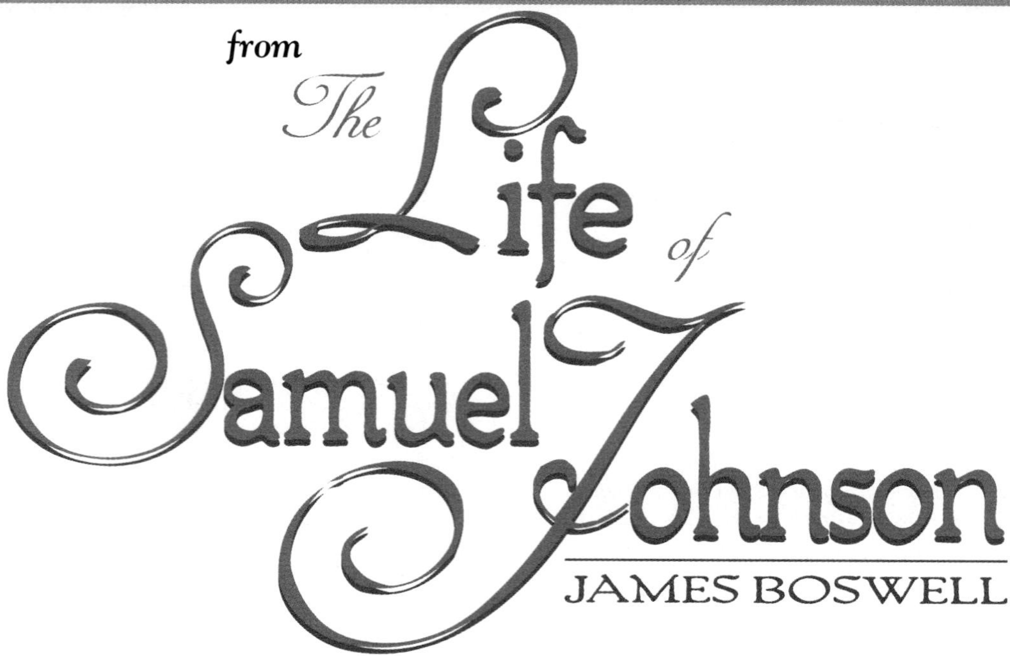

from The Life of Samuel Johnson

JAMES BOSWELL

Boswell Meets Johnson 1763

This is to me a memorable year; for in it I had the happiness to obtain the acquaintance of that extraordinary man whose memoirs I am
1 now writing; an acquaintance which I shall ever esteem as one of the most fortunate circum-
2 stances in my life. Though then but two-and-twenty, I had for several years read his works with delight and instruction, and had the highest reverence for their author, which had grown up in my fancy into a kind of mysterious veneration, by figuring to myself a state of solemn elevated abstraction, in which I supposed him to live in the immense metropolis of London ....

3 Mr. Thomas Davies[1] the actor, who then kept a bookseller's shop in Russel Street, Covent Garden, told me that Johnson was very much his friend, and came frequently to his house, where he more than once invited me to meet him; but by some unlucky accident or other he was prevented from coming to us.

At last, on Monday the 16th day of May, when I was sitting in Mr. Davies's back parlor, after having drunk tea with him and Mrs. Davies, Johnson unexpectedly came into the shop; and Mr. Davies having perceived him through the glass door in the room in which we were sitting, advancing towards us—he announced his aweful[2] approach to me, somewhat in the manner of an actor in the part of Horatio, when he addresses Hamlet on the appearance of his father's ghost, "Look, my Lord, it comes,"[3] I found that I had a very perfect idea of Johnson's figure, from the portrait of him painted by Sir Joshua Reynolds[4] soon after he had published his *Dictionary*, in the attitude

1. **Thomas Davies:** English bookseller and unsuccessful actor (1712–1785).

2. **aweful:** Awe-inspiring.
3. **Horatio ". . . it comes":** From Shakespeare's *Hamlet* (Act I, Scene iv).
4. **Sir Joshua Reynolds:** Celebrated portrait painter at the time (1723–1792).

of sitting in his easy chair in deep meditation, which was the first picture his friend did for him, which Sir Joshua very kindly presented to me, and from which an engraving has been made for this work. Mr. Davies mentioned my name, and respectfully introduced me to him. I was much agitated; and recollecting his prejudice against the Scotch, of which I had heard much, I said to Davies, "Don't tell where I come from." "From Scotland," cried Davies roguishly. "Mr. Johnson," said I, "I do indeed come from Scotland, but I cannot help it." I am willing to flatter myself that I meant this as light pleasantry to sooth and conciliate him, and not as an humiliating abasement at the expense of my country. But however that might be, this speech was somewhat unlucky; for with that quickness of wit for which he was so remarkable, he seized the expression "come from Scotland," which I used in the sense of being of that country; and, as if I had said that I had come away from it, or left, retorted, "That, Sir, I find, is what a very great many of your countrymen cannot help." This stroke stunned me a good deal; and when we had sat down, I felt myself not a little embarrassed, and apprehensive of what might come next. He then addressed himself to Davies: "What do you think of Garrick?[5] He has refused me an order for the play for Miss Williams, because he knows the house will be full, and that an order would be worth three shillings." Eager to take any opening to get into conversation with him, I ventured to say, "O, Sir, I cannot think Mr. Garrick would grudge such a trifle to you." "Sir," said he, with a stern look, "I have known David Garrick longer than you have done: and I know no right you have to talk to me on the subject." Perhaps I deserved this check; for it was rather presumptuous in me, an entire stranger, to express any doubt of the justice of his animadversion upon his old acquaintance and pupil. I now felt myself much mortified, and began to think that the hope which I had long indulged of obtaining his acquaintance ❹

5. **Garrick:** David Garrick (1717–1779), a famous actor who had been educated by Johnson. Garrick was also one of the managing partners of the Drury Lane Theater in London.

was blasted. And, in truth, had not my ardor been uncommonly strong, and my resolution uncommonly persevering, so rough a reception might have deterred me forever from making any further attempts. Fortunately, however, I remained upon the field not wholly discomfited; and was soon rewarded by hearing some of his conversation, of which I preserved the following short minute,[6] without marking the questions and observations by which it was produced.

◆ Reading Strategy
If your purpose in reading were to find out more about eighteenth-century English theater, on which details in this paragraph would you focus? ❺

"People," he remarked, "may be taken in once, who imagine that an author is greater in private life than other men. Uncommon parts require uncommon opportunities for their exertion."

"In barbarous society, superiority of parts is of real consequence. Great strength or great wisdom is of much value to an individual. But in more polished times there are people to do everything for money; and then there are a number of other superiorities, such as those of birth and fortune, and rank, that dissipate men's attention, and leave no extraordinary share of respect for personal and intellectual superiority. This is wisely ordered by Providence, to preserve some equality among mankind." ❻

"Sir, this book (*The Elements of Criticism*,[7] which he had taken up) is a pretty essay, and deserves to be held in some estimation, though much of it is chimerical." ❼

Speaking of one[8] who with more than ordinary boldness attacked public measures and the royal family, he said, "I think he is safe

6. **minute:** Note.
7. ***Elements of Criticism*:** One of the works of Scottish philosophical writer Henry Home (1696–1782).
8. **one:** John Wilkes (1727–1797), an English political agitator.

◆ Build Vocabulary
abasement (ə bās′mənt) *n.*: Condition of being put down or humbled

◆ Critical Thinking

❹ **Draw Conclusions** The reader has already seen several aspects of Johnson's personality. So far, is the picture of Johnson a flattering one? Why or why not? *No, for the most part, it is not flattering. Johnson is prejudiced against the Scottish, and while he is quick-witted, he is also quick to criticize or shut down someone who offers an opinion contrary to his own.*

◆ Reading Strategy

❺ **Set a Purpose** To learn more about eighteenth-century theater, students would need to pay attention to the details about the actor David Garrick.

Customize for *More Advanced Students*

❻ Invite more advanced students to explain the meaning of these words. Then ask them to comment on what they tell the reader about Johnson, as well as why Boswell included them.

◆ Literature and Your Life

❼ Ask students how they might feel if they were present at this historic meeting at this moment. *Some students might say that they would feel rather out of it or confused by the topics; others might say that they would enjoy being in the presence of great minds at work.*

Beyond the Classroom

Career Connection

Journalism In this selection, Boswell acts much like a modern journalist. He awaits the opportunity to interview his subject; he asks leading questions; he observes carefully; and, it would seem, he reveals all he has learned. Johnson said that he disliked most of the biography of his day because it "endeavour[ed] to hide the man [in order to] produce a hero." Instead, his ideal was to diminish the distance between the reader and the subject. Ask students to find examples of ways in which modern writers do this in newspaper and magazine articles and interviews.

Workplace Skill

Interpersonal Relations Boswell demonstrates that he can stay with his subject, and his goal, even when the subject proves difficult. Ask students to discuss the types of interpersonal skills Boswell displays and to explain when and why these skills are needed in the workplace.

Customize for
English Language Learners
Have pairs of students work together to identify the speaker. Explain that even though new paragraphs begin and end here, the speaker does not necessarily change. Students may also be reminded that while Boswell does insert himself into the biography, his purpose here is to reveal the workings of Johnson's mind.

◆ Literary Focus

❶ **Biography** Boswell has, in fact, supported his statement. Johnson seems very quick witted and extremely articulate. He shows that he is informed about matters of his day. He uses a Latin term in conversation; he is witty about both the matter of ducking and the butcher; and he produces a pun on the spot about "outrunning [a] character" and the character catching up.

◆ Critical Thinking

❷ **Infer** Ask students: What does the inclusion of this detail reveal about Boswell? *Students may observe that he wants to be liked and is willing to endure pain to gain acceptance.*

◆ Critical Thinking

❸ **Make Judgments** Ask: Do you think this physical description of Johnson is objective? Why or why not? *It appears to be quite objective. Johnson wasn't, evidently, very pleasing to look at, and Boswell doesn't hesitate to tell the reader so. In addition, he tells the reader that Johnson walked strangely and cut a rather ludicrous figure on his horse when he rode. Because it is clear that Boswell keenly admired Johnson, the reader can infer that these details are here simply because they are part of the portrait of the man.*

◆ Build Vocabulary

❹ **Word Roots: *-dict-*** Point out the word *contradictory.* Explain that the prefix *contra-* means "against," and the ending letters *-ory* constitute an adjective-making suffix. Ask students to put this information together with their knowledge of the word root *-dict-* to come up with a definition of *contradictory.* *It is an adjective meaning "opposite"; something contradictory is "against," or opposite what has already been said or shown.*

from the law, but he is an abusive scoundrel; and instead of applying to my Lord Chief Justice to punish him, I would send half a dozen footmen and have him well ducked."[9]

"The notion of liberty amuses the people of England, and helps to keep off the *taedium vitae.*[10] When a butcher tells you that his heart bleeds for his country, he has, in fact, no uneasy feeling."

"Sheridan[11] will not succeed at Bath with his oratory. Ridicule has gone down before him, and, I doubt,[12] Derrick[13] is his enemy."

"Derrick may do very well, as long as he can outrun his character; but the moment his character gets up with him, it is all over."

It is, however, but just to record, that some years afterwards, when I reminded him of this sarcasm, he said, "Well, but Derrick has now got a character that he need not run away from."

I was highly pleased with the extraordinary vigor of his conversation, and regretted that I was drawn away from it by an engagement at another place. I had, for a part of the evening, been left alone with him, and had ventured to make an observation now and then, which he received very civilly; so that I was satisfied that though there was a roughness in his manner, there was no ill nature in his disposition. Davies followed me to the door, and when I complained to him a little of the hard blows which the great man had given me he kindly took upon him to console me by saying, "Don't be uneasy. I can see he likes you very well." ❷

> **◆ Literary Focus** ❶
> Do you think Boswell has sufficiently supported his statement about the "extraordinary vigor" of Johnson's conversation? Why or why not?

Johnson's Character

The character of Samuel Johnson has, I trust, been so developed in the course of this work, that they who have honored it with a perusal, may be considered as well acquainted with him. As, however, it may be expected that I should collect into one view the capital and distinguishing features of this extraordinary man, I shall endeavor to acquit myself of that part of my biographical undertaking, however difficult it may be to do that which many of my readers will do better for themselves.

His figure was large and well formed, and his countenance of the cast of an ancient statue; yet his appearance was rendered strange and somewhat uncouth by convulsive cramps, by the scars of that distemper[14] which it was once imagined the royal touch could cure,[15] and by a slovenly mode of dress. He had the use only of one eye; yet so much does mind govern and even supply the deficiency of organs, that his visual perceptions, as far as they extended, were uncommonly quick and accurate. So morbid was his temperament, that he never knew the natural joy of a free and vigorous use of his limbs: when he walked, it was like the struggling gait of one in fetters; when he rode, he had no command or direction of his horse, but was carried as if in a balloon. That with his constitution and habits of life he should have lived seventy-five years, is a proof that an inherent *vivida vis*[16] is a powerful preservative of the human frame. ❸

Man is, in general, made up of contradictory qualities; and these will ever show themselves in strange succession, where a consistency in ❹ appearance at least, if not in reality, has not been attained by long habits of philosophical discipline. In proportion to the native vigor of the mind, the contradictory qualities will be the more prominent, and more difficult to be adjusted; and, therefore, we are not to wonder that Johnson exhibited an eminent example of this remark which I have made upon human nature. At different times, he seemed ❺

9. **ducked:** Tied to a chair at the end of a plank and plunged into water.
10. ***taedium vitae*** (tī´ dē əm vē´ tī): Boredom.
11. **Sheridan:** Thomas Sheridan (1719–1788), an Irish actor and author. At the time, Sheridan was reading lectures at the Oratory at Bath.
12. **doubt:** Fear.
13. **Derrick:** The Master of Ceremonies of the Oratory at Bath.
14. **distemper:** Scrofula, a type of tuberculosis that causes swelling and scarring of the neck.
15. **royal touch . . . cure:** It was at one time believed that the touch of an English monarch had the power to heal. As a child Johnson was taken to Queen Anne to receive her touch in the hope that it would cure him.
16. ***vivida vis:*** Lively force.

Cultural Connection

Biographies The first biographies were probably elaborate inscriptions on the tombs of ancient rulers of Assyria and Babylonia. The accuracy of these glorious accounts is dubious. Plutarch's classic *Lives of the Greeks* contained the first biographies that sought objectivity. The insights and intimacy of Boswell's famous biography of Johnson influenced many later writers. Only since the nineteenth century, however, have biographers in general striven to give a complete picture of their subjects, showing both favorable and unfavorable aspects of their character. Students might identify one such modern biography and explain to the class why it is relatively objective.

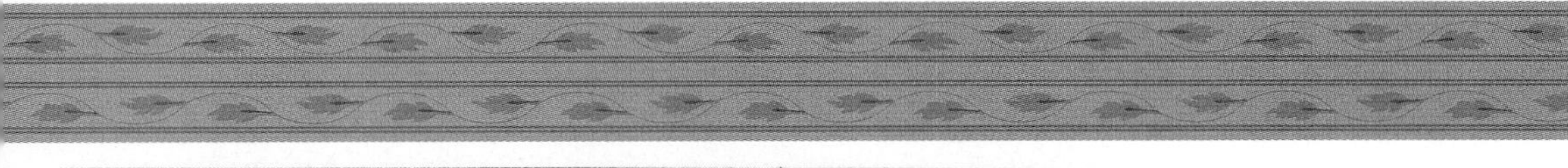

Johnson and Boswell, The Trustees of the British Museum

◀ **Critical Viewing** This engraving shows the ghost of Samuel Johnson haunting Boswell. What does this suggest about the relationship between Johnson and Boswell? **[Interpret]** 7

5 a different man, in some respects; not, however, in any great or essential article, upon which he had fully employed his mind, and settled certain principles of duty, but only in his manners and in the display of argument and fancy in his talk. 6 He was prone to superstition, but not to credulity. Though his imagination might incline him to a belief of the marvelous and the mysterious, his vigorous reason examined the evidence with jealousy.[17] He was a sincere and zealous Christian, of high Church of England and monarchical principles, which he would not tamely suffer to be questioned; and had, perhaps, at an early period, narrowed his mind somewhat too much, both as to religion and politics. His being impressed with the danger of extreme latitude in either, though he was of a

17. **jealousy:** Suspicion.

◆ Build Vocabulary

credulity (krə do͞o′ lə tē) *n.*: Tendency to believe too readily

Customize for ***Musical/Rhythmic Learners***
Encourage students to think of different types of music that might be played as the soundtrack for a documentary portrayal of the life of Johnson. For example, students might suggest music that could be played while Johnson is shown riding his horse, at work on his dictionary, or deep in conversation with Boswell.

5 **Clarification** Explain that even though Johnson could be unpredictable or changeable in some regards, in matters that were deeply intellectual or moral, and which he had considered well, he did not change his mind.

Comprehension Check ☑
6 Ask: Was Johnson superstitious, or wasn't he? *He appears to have enjoyed repeating, and perhaps acting on certain superstitions, as many people might flirt with the idea that the number thirteen is unlucky without committing themselves to it.*

▶Critical Viewing◀
7 **Interpret** This image may suggest that Boswell can never really get Johnson out of his mind. This may be because of the profound impression Johnson made on Boswell. It may also suggest that Boswell's own reputation rests on his acquaintance with Johnson.

Humanities: Art

Johnson and Boswell, engraving.

This engraving of the ghost of Samuel Johnson haunting his biographer, Boswell, appeared in the 1803 edition of the play *The Way of the World* by William Congreve. A caption below the art reads "Thou art a Retailer of Phrases/And dost deal in Remnants of Remnants/Like a Maker of Pincushions." William Congreve (1620–1729) was known to Boswell and Johnson, who admired him greatly.

Use these questions for discussion:

1. What do you think the caption means? By whom is it spoken, Johnson or Boswell? *Johnson is addressing Boswell. He is suggesting that Boswell sells, or retails, phrases, mere bits and pieces of larger ideas. His works are like pincushions, that is, they are made out of scraps—the leftover memories of Boswell's conversations with Johnson.*
2. Boswell admits in his biography that he himself was a silly fop next to the stern and stately Johnson. Does this comparison come across in the illustration? Explain. *The difference between the two in the illustration is not as enormous as in Boswell's statement. In the illustration, Boswell seems like the lesser person, if only by virtue of being seated and looking subservient. Johnson imperiously greets Boswell, while Boswell seems more tentative as he grasps a pincushion in one hand and awkwardly greets Johnson with the other.*

◆ Critical Thinking

1 Analyze What negative aspects of Johnson's character are contained in this description? *Several negative aspects are expressed, including Johnson's prejudices, his sternness, his tendency to be easily offended, his irritability, his moodiness, and his ability to say nasty things even about his friends.*

◆ *Literature and Your Life*

2 Ask students whether, based on Boswell's description, they would have wanted to be acquainted with Samuel Johnson. *Students who say yes should mention positive qualities mentioned by Boswell, such as Johnson's benevolence and wit; those who say no should mention negative qualities, such as Johnson's prejudices.*

◆ Grammar and Style

3 Commas With Parenthetical Expressions Ask students to find the parenthetical expression in this passage. *The expression is "in that respect."* Note the use of commas; ask students why they are needed. *They are needed to set off information that interrupts the main part of the sentence.*

◆ Literary Focus

4 Biography Tell students that a critic once said that Boswell's *Life of Samuel Johnson* was an accidental masterpiece, produced by a fool who happened to have a perfect subject. Ask students whether they think a biographer can be a fool who needs only a great subject to write well. *A great subject helps, of course, but a good biographer must have many skills, including the ability to gather information, interpret it accurately, and present it in an interesting fashion. Not any "fool" can do this.*

◆ Critical Thinking

5 Make Judgments Does everything Boswell has said prior to this point justify the conclusion he draws here? *In general, it does. Although Boswell has presented many negative aspects of his subject, throughout the biography, he has constantly returned to Johnson's overwhelmingly positive qualities.*

very independent spirit, occasioned his appearing somewhat unfavorable to the prevalence of that noble freedom of sentiment which is the best possession of man. Nor can it be denied, that he had many prejudices; which, however, frequently suggested many of his pointed sayings that rather show a playfulness of fancy than any settled malignity. He was steady and inflexible in maintaining the obligations of religion and morality; both from a regard for the order of society, and from a veneration for the Great Source of all order; correct, nay, stern in his taste; hard to please, and easily offended; impetuous and irritable in his temper, but of a most humane and benevolent heart, which showed itself not only in a most liberal charity, as far as his circumstances would allow, but in a thousand instances of active benevolence. He was afflicted with a bodily disease, which made him often restless and fretful; and with a con-
1 stitutional melancholy, the clouds of which darkened the brightness of his fancy, and gave
2 a gloomy cast to his whole course of thinking: we, therefore, ought not to wonder at his sallies of impatience and passion at any time; especially when provoked by obtrusive ignorance, or presuming petulance; and allowance must be made for his uttering hasty and satirical sallies even against his best friends. And, surely, when it is considered, that, "amidst sickness and sorrow," he exerted his faculties in so many works for the benefit of mankind, and particularly that he achieved the great and admirable Dictionary of our language, we must be astonished at his resolution. The solemn text, "of him to whom much is given, much will be required," seems to have been ever present to his mind, in a rigorous sense, and to have made him dissatisfied with his labors and acts of goodness, however comparatively great; so that the unavoidable consciousness of his su-
3 periority was, in that respect, a cause of disquiet. He suffered so much from this, and from the gloom which perpetually haunted him and made solitude frightful, that it may be said of him, "If in this life only he had hope, he was of all men most miserable."[18] He loved praise, when it was brought to him; but was too proud to seek for it. He was somewhat susceptible of flattery. As he was general and unconfined in his studies, he cannot be considered as master of any one particular science; but he had accumulated a vast and various collection of learning and knowledge, which was so arranged in his mind, as to be ever in readiness to be brought forth. But his superiority over other learned men consisted chiefly in what may be called the art of thinking, the art of using his mind; a certain continual power of seizing the useful substance of all that he knew and exhibiting it in a clear and forcible manner; so that knowledge, which we often see to be no better than lumber[19] in men of dull understanding, was, in him, true, evident, and actual wisdom. His moral precepts are practical; for they are drawn from an intimate acquaintance with human nature. His maxims carry conviction; for they are founded on the basis of common sense, and a very attentive and minute survey of real life. His mind was so full of imagery, that he might have been perpetually a poet; yet it is remarkable, that, however rich his prose is in this respect, his poetical pieces, in general, have not much of that splendor, but
are rather distinguished by strong sentiment 4
and acute observation, conveyed in harmonious and energetic verse, particularly in heroic couplets. Though usually grave, and even aweful, in his deportment, he possessed uncommon and peculiar powers of wit and humor; he frequently indulged himself in colloquial pleasantry; and the heartiest merriment was often enjoyed in his company; with this great advantage, that as it was entirely free from any poisonous tincture of vice or impiety, it was salutary to those who shared in it. He had accustomed himself to such accuracy in his common conversation, that he at all times expressed his thoughts with great force, and an elegant choice of language, the effect of which was aided by his having a loud voice, and a slow deliberate utterance. In him were united a most logical head with a most fertile imagination, which gave him an extraordinary advantage

18. **"If . . . miserable":** From I Corinthians 15:19.

19. **lumber:** Rubbish.

Speaking and Listening Mini-Lesson

Interpretation of Attitudes

This mini-lesson supports the Speaking and Listening activity in the Idea Bank on page 517.

Introduce the Concept Tell students that the purpose of this activity is first to make inferences about the attitudes conveyed in each definition and then to convey those attitudes through speech.

Develop Background Discuss some of the definitions with students and ask them where in the definition they sense Johnson's attitudes. For example, is there a sense of wonder or certainty in the definition of *electricity?* Have students work in pairs to discern attitudes.

Apply the Information Once students have determined attitudes, have them work on volume, pacing, and pitch while reading to bring those attitudes to life.

Assess the Outcome Have members of the audience evaluate the accuracy and the effectiveness of the presentation. Use the Peer Assessment: Oral Interpretation page in ***Alternative Assessment,*** p. 120.

in arguing: for he could reason close or wide, as he saw best for the moment. Exulting in his intellectual strength and dexterity, he could, when he pleased, be the greatest sophist[20] that ever contended in the lists of declamation; and, from a spirit of contradiction and a delight in showing his powers, he would often maintain the wrong side with equal warmth and ingenuity; so that, when there was an audience, his real opinions could seldom be gathered from his talk; though when he was in company with a single friend, he would discuss a subject with genuine fairness: but he was too conscientious to make error permanent and pernicious, by deliberately writing it; and, in all his numerous works, he earnestly inculcated what appeared to him to be the truth; his piety being constant, and the ruling principle of all his conduct.

Such was Samuel Johnson, a man whose talents, acquirements, and virtues, were so extraordinary, that the more his character is considered the more he will be regarded by the present age, and by posterity, with admiration and reverence. 5

20. **sophist** (säf′ ist) *n.*: One who makes misleading arguments.

◆ Build Vocabulary

malignity (mə lig′ nə tē) *n.*: Strong desire to harm others

pernicious (pər nish′ əs) *adj.*: Causing serious injury; deadly

inculcated (in kul′ kāt id) *v.*: Impressed upon the mind by frequent repetition

Guide for Responding

◆ Literature and Your Life

Reader's Response Based on this selection, do you think you would have liked Samuel Johnson? Why or why not?

Thematic Focus What ties seemed to bind Boswell to Johnson and Johnson to his admirers?

Personality Profile Capture the personality of someone you admire in a brief paragraph.

☑ Check Your Comprehension

1. Why was 1763 such a memorable year for Boswell?
2. How did Boswell meet Johnson?
3. What aspects of Johnson's appearance prompt Boswell to describe him as "strange and somewhat uncouth"?
4. According to the selection, what was Johnson's position on (a) superstition? (b) religion? (c) praise? (d) flattery?

◆ Critical Thinking

INTERPRET

1. What are Samuel Johnson's chief qualities? **[Connect]**
2. What details of Johnson's personality explain (a) his sarcastic remark about Scotland? (b) his desire to claim a free theater ticket for a friend? (c) his harsh reply to Boswell's comment on Garrick? **[Connect]**
3. What do you learn about Boswell himself from this selection? Explain. **[Infer]**

EVALUATE

4. Do you think Boswell paints a fairly objective portrait of Johnson? Why or why not? **[Assess]**

APPLY

5. What similarities and differences do you detect between the lifestyles and habits of eighteenth-century celebrities and those in our own age? **[Relate]**

Beyond the Selection

FURTHER READING

Other Works by the Authors

Rasselas, Samuel Johnson

"Letter to Lord Chesterfield," Samuel Johnson

The Lives of the Poets, Samuel Johnson

An Account of Corsica, James Boswell

Other Notable Biographies of Authors

Mr. Clemens and Mark Twain, Justin Kaplan

Papa Hemingway, A. E. Hotchner

We suggest that you preview these works before recommending them to students.

INTERNET

You and your students may find information about Johnson at the following sites. The site may have changed since we published this information.

To visit the Samuel Johnson Birthplace Museum, go to **http://www.lichfield.gov.uk/sjmuseum**

Preview the site before you send students to it..

Reinforce and Extend

Answers

◆ Literature and Your Life

Reader's Response Many students would be interested to know someone with such strength of character and intellect.

Thematic Focus Johnson's literary works and his evident character and talent bound Boswell to Johnson and Johnson to his admirers.

☑ Check Your Comprehension

1. In 1763 Boswell met Johnson in person.
2. Boswell met Johnson by accident when Johnson unexpectedly came into a shop Boswell was visiting.
3. As a result of illness, Johnson's body cramped convulsively and was scarred; one eye was useless; he walked with a struggling gait. Johnson's clothes were slovenly.
4. (a) Johnson was superstitious, but not gullible. (b) He met his religious duties. (c) He loved praise, but would not seek it. (d) He was somewhat susceptible to flattery, but despised flatterers.

◆ Critical Thinking

1. Johnson had a wonderful wit, a benevolent heart, a vast amount of learning, common sense, and high morals.
2. (a) The quick wit and irritable humor explain his sarcastic remark. (b) He was charitable and actively benevolent. (c) He was impatient when provoked by ignorance.
3. Sample response: Boswell felt inferior to Johnson. His admiration for Johnson is almost slavish.
4. Since Boswell so admired Johnson, his descriptions are likely to be more subjective than objective. However, he does mention Johnson's negative qualities.
5. Example: Most celebrities of any century, like Johnson, enjoy commanding the attention of others. Today's celebrities run the risk, though, of being mobbed by their admirers.

Answers

◆ Reading Strategy

1. (a) Johnson shows a quick and ready wit in the joke on "come from Scotland," and an impatience with ignorant fawning by giving Boswell a stern look and sharp remark. (b) Boswell's inferiority complex and eagerness at meeting his favorite celebrity is making him nervous and bumbling, causing him to utter stupid and thoughtless remarks.
2. Some details, such as Boswell's remark that he "cannot help" coming from Scotland, will appear in both lists, but from different perspectives.

◆ Literary Focus

Dictionary

1. The first sentence of Johnson's definition might appear in a modern dictionary, though it is a little vague; the pointedly prejudicial remarks that follow would not.
2. A dictionary helps to create a standard of usage, and to build knowledge.

Biography

1. Facts include: Johnson rebuked Boswell for foolishness; Johnson had scars and suffered cramps; Johnson attempted to supply a friend with theater tickets. Opinions include: Boswell deserved the rebuke; Johnson looked "strange"; Johnson was generous.
2. While the facts are revealing, Boswell's haste in apologizing for Johnson speaks much of Johnson's strong effect on others.

◆ Build Vocabulary

Using the Word Root *-dict-*

1. *dictate:* to speak words to be written down
2. *dictator:* one whose word is law
3. *predict:* to foretell

Using the Word Bank

1. caprices
2. malignity
3. adulterations
4. credulity
5. propagators
6. pernicious
7. recompense
8. risible
9. abasement

◆ Grammar and Style

1. Boswell, *I have heard,* was a young man when he first met Johnson.
2. Johnson, *on the other hand,* was much older.
3. Many in Johnson's circle were contemptuous of Boswell, *by the way.*
4. *Sad to say,* the poet Thomas Gray made scathing remarks about Boswell.
5. Johnson, *in contrast,* was kind to Boswell.

Writer's Solution

For additional instruction and practice, use the lesson in the **Writing Lab CD-ROM** on Commas and the page on Commas That Set Off Added Elements, p. 83, in the *Writer's Solution Grammar Practice Book.*

Guide for Responding (continued)

◆ Reading Strategy

Set a Purpose

By reading with a **purpose** in mind, you're able to locate and absorb the information you need. For example, if your purpose in reading Johnson's *Dictionary* was to learn how to pronounce a word, you'd turn immediately to the pronunciation respellings. If your purpose was to verify a word's meaning, you'd skim the listing of definitions until you found what you were looking for.

1. Read the second and third paragraphs of the excerpt from *The Life of Samuel Johnson* with these two purposes: (a) to learn about Johnson's sense of humor and (b) to learn more about Boswell's character. Then list the details that suit each purpose.
2. Explain the differences between the lists you made for the questions above.

◆ Literary Focus

Dictionary

Like **dictionaries** today, Johnson's *Dictionary* lists words alphabetically and includes definitions, pronunciations, word histories, and parts of speech. It is unusual in that Johnson allowed his personal attitudes about the entries to color the definitions!

1. How is the listing for *patron* in Johnson's *Dictionary* similar to and different from one in a modern dictionary?
2. What is the value, if any, of a dictionary?

Biography

Boswell's **biography** of Johnson is an account of the life of a writer written by a close personal friend. Besides offering factual information like names, dates, and conversations, Boswell weaves in his personal opinions and observations, as when he says that a comment of Johnson's "stunned him." This combination of fact and opinion gives this literary portrait an especially personal feeling.

1. Reread the section titled "Johnson's Character." Find three examples of facts and three examples of opinions.
2. Which do you find more revealing about the character of Johnson, Boswell's facts or his opinions? Why?

◆ Build Vocabulary

Using the Word Root *-dict-*

Words that contain the root *-dict-* convey the idea of something said or spoken. For example, *diction* refers to the words people choose to say things, and a *dictionary* is a book that provides information about spoken words. Explain how these words convey the idea of saying or speaking.

1. dictate **2.** dictator **3.** predict

Using the Word Bank

Complete these sentences with the words from the Word Bank. Use each word only once.

1. One of Boswell's __?__ led to his meeting Johnson.
2. Johnson expressed joking disaffection for the Scots, but he felt no __?__ toward them.
3. Because of misuses and __?__ of the English language, Johnson created a dictionary.
4. Johnson took advantage of Boswell's __?__ .
5. __?__ of badly spoken English annoyed Johnson.
6. A __?__ illness left Johnson's face disfigured.
7. Johnson received little monetary __?__ for his *Dictionary*.
8. Although Boswell's celebrity-chasing was __?__ , he was an excellent biographer.
9. Boswell's __?__ resulted from Johnson's scolding him.

◆ Grammar and Style

Commas With Parenthetical Expressions

Boswell gives his biography the flavor of speech by setting off in **parenthetical expressions** his comments on the main ideas. He uses commas to separate these opinions and observations.

Practice Identify each parenthetical expression, and add commas where necessary.

1. Boswell I have heard was a young man when he first met Johnson.
2. Johnson on the other hand was much older.
3. Many in Johnson's circle were contemptuous of Boswell by the way.
4. Sad to say the poet Thomas Gray made scathing remarks about Boswell.
5. Johnson in contrast was kind to Boswell.

Build Your Portfolio

Idea Bank

Writing

1. **Book Ad** Write an ad that the publishers of Johnson's *Dictionary* or Boswell's biography might have used to lure readers. You might also use quotations from the work that will generate interest in the book.

2. **Revised Preface** Rewrite Johnson's preface for a modern audience. Express the same ideas, but use vocabulary suited for modern readers.

3. **Response to Criticism** Edmund Wilson writes: "Boswell, in spite of his great respect . . . could not help making Johnson a character in an eighteenth-century comedy . . ." Using examples from the text, explain what Wilson means.

Speaking and Listening

4. **Reenactment** Working with another student, reenact the meeting between Johnson and Boswell, as Boswell describes it. **[Performing Arts Link]**

5. **Interpretation of Attitudes** Read aloud Johnson's dictionary definitions, using your voice to express the different attitudes Johnson's definitions convey. **[Performing Arts Link]**

Projects

6. **First-Person Biography** Like James Boswell, create a biography of someone you know well. Include anecdotes, pictures, and quotations. **[Social Studies Link]**

7. **The School of Johnson** Create a diagram showing the writers on whom Samuel Johnson had a direct influence. If possible, include pictures or drawings of each writer along with a list of his or her major works. **[Art Link]**

Writing Mini-Lesson

Dictionary of New Words

Samuel Johnson created a dictionary of English that was so thorough and well thought out that it set the standard for years to come. Like Johnson, create a dictionary of your own. In it, define words that have recently entered the language. As you compile your dictionary, decide on a format and maintain it throughout.

Writing Skills Focus: Keeping to a Format

To be clear and well organized, informational writing should maintain a **consistent format.** Dictionaries, in particular, should be formatted consistently from entry to entry. Follow these rules:

- List entries alphabetically.
- Use capitalization, punctuation, boldface, italics, and underscoring consistently.
- List the elements of each entry—pronunciation, part of speech, definitions, word history—in the same order from entry to entry.

The following strategies will help you keep to your format at every stage of the writing process.

Prewriting List the words that you plan to define. Work out each word's pronunciation, spelling, part of speech, and definition. Also jot down context sentences or examples, if you like.

Drafting Alphabetize the entries and decide on the order in which to present the elements of the entries. Copy out the words and definitions, along with all the examples and illustrations you plan to include.

Revising Check spellings, pronunciation guides, and definitions for accuracy. Check the format for consistency, making sure the entries are listed in alphabetical order and that the elements within each entry are arranged in the same order.

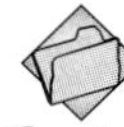

Idea Bank

Customizing for *Performance Levels*

Following are suggestions for matching Idea Bank topics with your students' performance levels:

Less Advanced Students: 1, 4, 6
Average Students: 2, 4, 5, 7
More Advanced Students: 3, 6

Customizing for *Learning Modalities*

Following are suggestions for matching Idea Bank topics with your students' learning modalities:

Verbal/Linguistic: 1, 2, 3, 6
Bodily/Kinesthetic: 4, 5
Visual/Spatial: 7

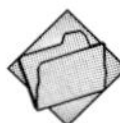

Writing Mini-Lesson

Refer students to the Writing Handbook, page 1189, for instruction on the writing process, and page 1192 for further information on research writing.

Writer's Solution

Writing Lab CD-ROM

Have students complete the tutorial on Research Writing following these steps:

1. Use the Idea Wheel to get ideas for words to include in their dictionary.
2. Use the interactive instruction on using on-line services as an aid to research.
3. Draft entries on computer.
4. Use the tips on checking for accuracy to help fact-check their work.

Allow approximately 90 minutes of class time to complete these steps.

Sourcebook

Have students use Chapter 5, Research Writing (pp. 130–165), for additional support.

✓ ASSESSMENT OPTIONS

Formal Assessment, Selection Test, pp. 120–121, and Assessment Resources Software. The selection test is designed so that it can be easily customized to the performance levels of your students.

Alternative Assessment, p. 25, includes options for less advanced students, more advanced students, visual/spatial learners, interpersonal learners, verbal/linguistic learners, and intrapersonal learners.

PORTFOLIO ASSESSMENT

Use the following rubrics in the ***Alternative Assessment*** booklet to assess student writing:
Book Ad: Persuasion Rubric, p. 106
Revised Preface: Persuasion Rubric, p. 106
Response to Criticism: Evaluation/Review Rubric, p. 105
Writing Mini-Lesson: Definition/Classification Rubric, p. 100

Prepare and Engage

OBJECTIVES

1. To read, comprehend, and interpret preromantic poetry
2. To relate the ideas in the poems to personal experience
3. To paraphrase poems
4. To identify characteristics of preromantic poetry
5. To build vocabulary in context and learn the prefix *circum-*
6. To develop skill in using pronoun-antecedent agreement
7. To write a reflective essay
8. To respond to preromantic poetry through writing, speaking and listening, and projects

SKILLS INSTRUCTION

Vocabulary: Prefixes: *circum-*

Grammar: Pronoun-Antecedent Agreement

Reading Strategy: Paraphrase

Literary Focus: Preromantic Poetry

Writing: Elaboration to Make Writing Personal

Speaking and Listening: Eulogy (teacher edition)

Critical Viewing: Deduce; Analyze

PORTFOLIO OPPORTUNITIES

Writing: Diary Entry; Epitaphs; Response to Criticism

Writing Mini-Lesson: Reflective Essay

Speaking and Listening: Choral Reading; Eulogy

Projects: Nighttime Walk; Brain Study

More About the Author

Thomas Gray's scant output was more a result of his perfectionism than it was of any lack of ideas. Had he lived in an era more compatible with the romantic yearnings of his soul, he might, as the poet Matthew Arnold suggested, have been capable of greater things. As it is, his reputation rests entirely on three major poems and three or four short lyrics.

The lesser-known **Anne Finch, Countess of Winchilsea,** commented on her own relative anonymity when she wrote, "Women are education's and not nature's fools." Finch's choice to publish her own poems was indeed a bold one for her day.

Guide for Interpreting

Thomas Gray (1716–1771)

Life's uncertainty was something that Thomas Gray understood all too well. The only one of twelve Gray children to survive infancy, he himself barely made it out of boyhood. Remarkably, he managed to withstand the primitive medical treatment for his childhood convulsions. Lavishing her affections on this one surviving son, Gray's mother, a London shopkeeper, saved up her pennies to pay for his schooling at prestigious Eton and Cambridge.

A Quiet Life After making the Grand Tour of Europe with his friend Horace Walpole, Gray lived with his mother and aunts in the village of Stoke Poges, whose church and graveyard probably inspired his best-known poem, "Elegy Written in a Country Churchyard." After age thirty, Gray returned to Cambridge and busied himself with private studies of classical literature and Celtic and Norse mythology. Never in the best of health, he died of an extremely painful attack of gout. Though his literary output was rather small, he is today remembered as one of England's finest poets.

Anne Finch, Countess of Winchilsea (1661–1720)

Anne Kingsmill Finch, Countess of Winchilsea, lived in an era in which women intellectuals were looked on with scornful amusement. Even her friend Alexander Pope poked fun of her as the character Phoebe Clinket in the play *Three Hours After Marriage.* Despite this mockery, Finch pursued her interest in poetry, publishing a volume of verse in 1713 and leaving behind additional manuscripts at her death.

A Poet and Countess Anne Kingsmill met her husband, Heneage Finch, when he was serving as a royal attendant and she was a maid of honor to the wife of the Duke of York, later James II. The Finches' fortunes soured when James II was driven from power in 1688, but after a period of poverty, Heneage inherited from a distant cousin the title Earl of Winchilsea and a lovely estate at Eastwell in rural Kent. It was here that Anne Finch wrote most of her poems, many of which applaud the rural pleasures of Eastwell.

◆ Background for Understanding

LITERATURE: DAYLIGHT OF REASON, NIGHTTIME OF FEELING

In the eighteenth century, many writers placed a high value on reason, clarity, and logic, qualities that they found in ancient Greek and Roman poetry. In a sense, these are "daylight" qualities, associated with the brightness of sunlight. Alexander Pope compared Sir Isaac Newton, the greatest scientist of the age, to the sun itself: "God said, Let Newton be! And there was light."

Pope's own bright couplets, Johnson's all-explaining dictionary, Addison's popular essays—these works communicate in the light of day. They address readers not as isolated individuals but as members of society and fellow reasoners. They are witty, brisk, and businesslike.

By contrast, Gray's "Elegy Written in a Country Churchyard" and Anne Finch's "A Nocturnal Reverie" are set in twilight or nighttime. The authors present themselves as isolated, feeling individuals, reaching out to others like themselves. These works represent the "nighttime" side of eighteenth-century literature. In stressing what other works neglect—emotion, the worth of the individual—they anticipate the artistic movement we call Romanticism.

Prentice Hall Literature Program Resources

REINFORCE / RETEACH / EXTEND

Selection Support Pages
Build Vocabulary: Prefixes: *circum-*, p. 122
Grammar and Style: Pronoun-Antecedent Agreement, p. 123
Reading Strategy: Paraphrase, p. 124
Literary Focus: Preromantic Poetry, p. 125

Strategies for Diverse Student Needs, p. 26

Beyond Literature Cultural Connection: Cultural Recognition of Death, p. 26

Formal Assessment Selection Test, pp. 123–125; Assessment Resources Software

Alternative Assessment, p. 26

Writing and Language Transparencies
Writing Process Model 1: Reflective Essay, pp. 5–11

Resource Pro CD-ROM "Elegy . . ."; ". . . Reverie"

Listening to Literature Audiocassettes "Elegy . . ."; ". . . Reverie"

Literature CD-ROM *How to Read and Understand Poetry*

Elegy Written in a Country Churchyard
◆ A Nocturnal Reverie ◆

◆ Literature and Your Life

Connect Your Experience

What situations prompt your thoughts to turn inward? Sometimes nighttime walks bring on such thoughts; sometimes, simply being alone makes people introspective.

In the poems that follow, the speakers share their innermost thoughts and personal feelings during solitary evening walks.

Journal Writing Briefly describe a place or a situation that prompted you to think more deeply about life.

Thematic Focus: The Ties That Bind

How do these poems suggest that even our quiet thoughts when alone can join us with other people?

◆ Literary Focus

Pre-Romantic Poetry

Pre-Romantic poetry has the polish of formal eighteenth-century poetry, but it also anticipates the Romantic emphasis on mystery, emotion, and individual expression.

In simple terms, the difference between poetry like Pope's and pre-Romantic poetry is the difference between the head and the heart. Pope's brilliant lines—"The proper study of mankind is man"—speak to your mind. However, Gray's lonely musings stir your emotions: "... all the air a solemn stillness holds."

Even the types of poems that Gray and Finch write are linked to emotion and mystery. Gray's poem is an **elegy**, a solemn work that mourns someone's death or reflects on a serious theme. Finch's is a **reverie**, which is a fanciful, dreamlike poem.

◆ Grammar and Style

Pronoun-Antecedent Agreement

In the poems that follow, you'll find several examples of **pronouns** and **antecedents**, the words to which pronouns refer. A pronoun must agree with its antecedent in gender and number, as in these examples from Gray's "Elegy":

Examples: The *plowman* homeward plods *his* weary way . . .
No *children* run to lisp *their* sire's return . . .

◆ Reading Strategy

Paraphrase

To ensure understanding, **paraphrase** passages by identifying key ideas and expressing them in your own words. Paraphrasing poetry is an especially useful strategy for unlocking the meaning of lines that contain difficult words or sentence structures.

Use a chart like the following when paraphrasing difficult lines in poetry.

Original	Paraphrase
Now fades the glimmering landscape on the sight . . .	Nightfall is making it difficult to see the landscape.

◆ Build Vocabulary

Prefixes: *circum-*

From *circus*, Latin for "circle," comes the prefix *circum-*, which means "around." When combined with the root *scribe*, as in the word *circumscribed*, it creates a word meaning "limit the activity of" or "draw a line around."

Word Bank

Before you read, preview this list of words from the poems.

penury
circumscribed
ingenuous
ignoble
nocturnal
temperate
venerable
forage

Preparing for Standardized Tests

Reading and Vocabulary Paraphrasing will help students comprehend and correctly answer questions about reading comprehension passages that appear on standardized tests. Students should complete the lesson on paraphrasing and also the Reading Strategy page in ***Selection Support***, p. 124. Knowing the prefix *circum-* will help students with vocabulary items, such as analogies and sentence completions, on standardized tests. For additional practice, use the Build Vocabulary page in ***Selection Support,*** p. 122.

Grammar and Language Portions of some standardized tests require students to correct an error in the agreement of pronouns and antecedents, as in the following.

Everyone on the boys' golf team has their own clubs. *(C)*

(A) has their own clubs. (C) has his own clubs.
(B) have their own clubs. (D) have his own clubs.

For additional practice, use the page on Pronoun-Antecedent Agreement, p. 123, in ***Selection Support.***

Ask students: What are the best times and places for reflection? Poll students to determine where and at what time of day they are most likely to reflect on topics such as the following:

- the meaning of life
- destiny or fate in life
- relationships
- death

Tell students that the elegy by Thomas Gray is a reflection about subjects such as these. Have them look for clues that indicate the time and place of the reflection and to discuss the appropriateness to the subject of the poem.

Customize for
Less Proficient Readers
Because the rhythm may drive the reading for these students, have them pause at the end of each stanza and summarize the meaning expressed in the lines. Have them list unfamiliar words and possible definitions, based on context clues.

Customize for
More Advanced Students
Invite more advanced students to focus not only on meaning and the characteristics of preromantic poetry, but also on sound devices, such as alliteration, assonance, and consonance. Students might prepare a report on the use of these devices in one or both of the poems.

Customize for
English Language Learners
Encourage these students to paraphrase as they read and to ask questions about unfamiliar words. Depending on the proficiency of the English language learner, you may wish to encourage native speakers to read parts of the poems aloud, so that English language learners can hear the rhythm of the lines.

Customize for
Musical/Rhythmic Learners
Both poems can be described as musical: their rhythm is predictable and even; they maintain a steady beat. Ask students to decide which type of music would best capture the mood and message of both these poems.

Develop Understanding

One-Minute Insight This famous poem uses the melancholy setting of a graveyard at twilight to meditate on the lives of the ordinary people interred there. In soulful song, Gray laments not one particular death, but the obscurity into which death may plunge all of us.

Literature CD-ROM Use CD-ROM *How to Read and Understand Poetry* to introduce students to reading poetry. You may wish to use Feature 6 to provide a comparison to Tennyson's *In Memoriam,* perhaps the most famous elegy in the English language. For a discussion of iambic pentameter, the meter of both Gray's elegy and Finch's reverie, use Feature 8.

◆ Reading Strategy

❶ Paraphrase Have students write paraphrases of the first stanza. When they have finished, ask them to check their paraphrases to be sure they include the time of day and the setting. *The speaker hears the curfew bell that calls workers home at sunset; he waits alone in the gathering darkness.*

❷ Clarification Explain that the speaker's focus on the graveyard and its inhabitants begins at line 13. You might mention that the turf is said to "heave" where the earth is mounded upward as a result of burial, and *moldering* means "decaying."

◆ Grammar and Style

❸ Pronoun-Antecedent Agreement Point out the word *Each,* which is a pronoun. Then point out the word *his,* which is the antecedent of the pronoun. Explain that these words agree: both are singular.

Elegy Written in a Country Churchyard

Thomas Gray

❶ The curfew tolls the knell of parting day,
The lowing herd winds slowly o'er the lea,[1]
The plowman homeward plods his weary way,
And leaves the world to darkness and to me.

Now fades the glimmering landscape on the sight,
And all the air a solemn stillness holds,
Save where the beetle wheels his droning flight,
And drowsy tinklings lull the distant folds;

Save that from yonder ivy-mantled tower,
The moping owl does to the moon complain
Of such as, wandering near her secret bower,
Molest her ancient solitary reign.

❷ Beneath those rugged elms, that yew tree's shade,
Where heaves the turf in many a moldering heap,
❸ Each in his narrow cell forever laid,
The rude[2] forefathers of the hamlet sleep.

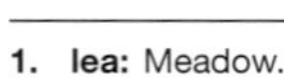

1. **lea:** Meadow.
2. **rude:** Uneducated.

Block Scheduling Strategies

Consider these suggestions to take advantage of extended class time:

- Students can do the journal writing activity in Literature and Your Life (p. 519) and share their responses with a classmate before reading. Then lead students in a discussion of the Thematic Focus, "The Ties that Bind."
- Have students listen to the selections on audiocassette. Suggest that students comment on the emotional quality of the poems as they listen.
- Work as a class to practice using the paraphrase chart in Reading Strategy (p. 519) before students read on their own.
- Use the Literary Focus questions on Preromantic Poetry (p. 530) as a springboard for class discussion of the poems.
- Let students answer the Critical Thinking questions (p. 529) orally in discussion groups.
- Provide time for peer conferences during the drafting and revising stages of the Writing Mini-Lesson (p. 531).

▲ **Critical Viewing** The churchyard in this photograph looks untended and forgotten. How does the photograph reflect the meaning of Gray's poem? **[Deduce]** ❹

►Critical Viewing◄

❹ **Deduce** Students may say that the photograph reflects the loneliness reflected in the first stanzas of Gray's poem. As time goes by, and as fewer and fewer people tend to the graveyard or even visit it, the dead become even more anonymous.

Customize for
Visual/Spatial Learners

Invite visual/spatial learners to name everything they can see in their mind's eye as they read these stanzas. Ask these students to compare the graveyard in this photograph to the one described in the first four stanzas of the poem. *Students should note the absence of the passing herds of cattle, the owl;, the "ivy mantled tower," the "rugged elms," and the yew tree mentioned in the poem.*

Humanities: Art

British Isles, Church with Tombstones by Lenore Weber.

This photograph evokes a strong sense of the passage of time. As the roiling clouds suggest the ever-changing yet cyclical patterns in weather, so the graveyard suggests the eternal cycles of life and death. The photograph effectively contrasts the drama and movement of the sky, or life, with the stillness of the earth—and death.

Use these questions for discussion:

1. How do the clouds in this photograph help create a mood and express a theme similar to the mood and theme expressed by the poem? *Students may say that the clouds suggest a storm to come, just as the poet describes death, which will come to everyone. The clouds in this photograph are both ominous and beautiful, just as the elegy is both sad and beautiful.*
2. What deductions might you make about this churchyard and its occupants? *Sample answer: The church is old and crumbling; moss has begun to grow on it. The tombstones are weathered; their epitaphs are most likely erased by time. The surrounding community, and those buried in the churchyard, is probably poor and obscure.*

Customize for
Less Proficient Readers
Call attention to the many words that are explained in the footnotes. In addition, you may wish to list the following words and their synonyms or short definitions on the chalkboard: clarion—*a trumpetlike sound;* rouse—*to wake up from sleep;* hearth—*fireplace;* furrow—*trench in the earth made by a plow;* annals—*records of events;* celestial—*heavenly.*

◆ Literary Focus

1 Preromantic Poetry These lines are characteristic of preromantic poetry in that they are quite emotional. Ask students to explain why these lines stir the emotions of readers. *The lines evoke the simple joys of life—people sitting by a fireplace, children running to a father or sitting on his knee; the repeated tasks of daily living that bring forth the crops—that the dead no longer share.*

Comprehension Check ☑

2 Gray refers to poor people who lived simple lives. Is he saying that their lives, or deaths, were any less significant than those of the rich and ambitious? *No. The homely ways of the poor and their obscure destiny are not to be mocked.*

◆ Critical Thinking

3 Extend This line is often quoted. Why do you think it is so famous? *It says that no matter what you pursue in life, your destiny is the same as everyone else's: the grave. This line may be famous because it is so beautifully expressed, because it is true, and because it causes people to reflect on their own mortality.*

◆ Reading Strategy

4 Paraphrase Have students paraphrase this stanza, identifying the implied references. *Sample paraphrase: Perhaps among the people interred here is a potential ruler ("the rod of empire might have swayed") or an unrealized poet or musician ("waked . . . the living lyre."*

The breezy call of incense-breathing morn,
  The swallow twittering from the straw-built shed,
The cock's shrill clarion, or the echoing horn,[3]
  No more shall rouse them from their lowly bed.

For them no more the blazing hearth shall burn,
  Or busy housewife ply her evening care;
No children run to lisp their sire's return,
  Or climb his knees the envied kiss to share.

1 Oft did the harvest to their sickle yield,
  Their furrow oft the stubborn glebe[4] has broke;
How jocund[5] did they drive their team afield!
  How bowed the woods beneath their sturdy stroke!

Let not Ambition mock their useful toil,
2 Their homely joys, and destiny obscure;
Nor Grandeur hear with a disdainful smile
  The short and simple annals of the poor.

The boast of heraldry,[6] the pomp of power,
  And all that beauty, all that wealth e'er gave,
Awaits alike the inevitable hour.
3 The paths of glory lead but to the grave.

Nor you, ye proud, impute to these the fault,
  If memory o'er their tomb no trophies[7] raise,
Where through the long-drawn aisle and fretted vault[8]
  The pealing anthem swells the note of praise.

Can storied urn,[9] or animated[10] bust,
  Back to its mansion call the fleeting breath?
Can honor's voice provoke[11] the silent dust,
  Or Flattery soothe the dull cold ear of Death?

Perhaps in this neglected spot is laid
4 Some heart once pregnant with celestial fire;
Hands, that the rod of empire might have swayed,
  Or waked to ecstasy the living lyre.

---

3. **horn:** Hunter's horn.
4. **glebe:** Soil.
5. **jocund:** Cheerful.
6. **heraldry:** Noble descent.
7. **trophies:** Symbolic figures or pictures depicting the achievements of the dead man.
8. **fretted vault:** Church ceiling decorated with intersecting lines.
9. **storied urn:** Funeral urn with an epitaph inscribed on it.
10. **animated:** Lifelike.
11. **provoke:** Call forth.

Cultural Connection

Gravestones Students might be interested to know that gravestones are among the earliest examples of sculpture in the United States, dating back to colonial times. New England gravestones are decorated with elaborate symbolic figures and objects. For example, a skeleton represents death and is often shown snuffing out the candle of life; grapes represent eternal life. Epitaphs written on gravestones are often equally memorable, and even humorous, such as this one: "Here lies as silent as clay Miss Arabella Young/Who on the 21st of May began to hold her tongue."

Have students research gravestones in different cultures and historical periods. How do they reflect different attitudes toward death?

But Knowledge to their eyes her ample page
Rich with the spoils of time did ne'er unroll; ❺
Chill Penury repressed their noble rage,
And froze the genial current of the soul.

Full many a gem of purest ray serene
The dark unfathomed caves of ocean bear: ❻
Full many a flower is born to blush unseen,
And waste its sweetness on the desert air.

Some village Hampden,[12] that, with dauntless breast,
The little tyrant of his fields withstood,
Some mute inglorious Milton[13] here may rest,
Some Cromwell[14] guiltless of his country's blood.

The applause of listening senates to command,
The threats of pain and ruin to despise,
To scatter plenty o'er a smiling land,
And read their history in a nation's eyes,

Their lot forbade: nor circumscribed alone
Their growing virtues, but their crimes confined ❼
Forbade to wade through slaughter to a throne,
And shut the gates of mercy on mankind,

The struggling pangs of conscious truth to hide,
To quench the blushes of ingenuous shame,
Or heap the shrine of Luxury and Pride
With incense kindled at the Muse's flame.

Far from the madding[15] crowd's ignoble strife,
Their sober wishes never learned to stray; ❽
Along the cool sequestered vale of life
They kept the noiseless tenor[16] of their way.

Yet even these bones from insult to protect
Some frail memorial still erected nigh,
With uncouth rhymes and shapeless sculpture decked,[17]
Implores the passing tribute of a sigh.

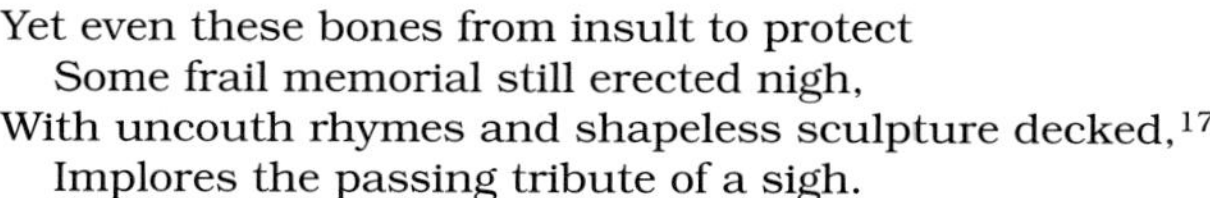

12. **Hampden:** John Hampden (1594–1643), an English statesman who defied King Charles I by resisting the king's efforts to revive an obsolete tax without the authority of Parliament.
13. **Milton:** English poet, John Milton (1608–1674).
14. **Cromwell:** Oliver Cromwell (1599–1658), English revolutionary leader and Lord Protector of the Commonwealth from 1653 to 1658.
15. **madding:** Frenzied.
16. **tenor:** General tendency or course.
17. **Some . . . decked:** Contrasts with "the storied urn[s] or animated bust[s]" (line 41) inside the church.

◆ Build Vocabulary

penury (pen′ yo͞o rē) *n.*: Poverty

circumscribed (sur′ kəm skrībd) *v.*: Limited; confined

ingenuous (in jen′ yo͞o əs) *adj.*: Naive; simple

ignoble (ig nō′ bəl) *adj.*: Not noble; common

❺ **Clarification** Have students note the inverted word order in the first two lines. Point out that normal word order would be: "But Knowledge never unrolled her ample page, rich with the spoils of time, to their eyes." Encourage students to restate the lines in normal word order and then tell what they mean. *The lines mean that the potential leaders and artists buried there were uneducated.*

◆ Literary Focus

❻ **Preromantic Poetry** Have students point out the emotional quality of these lines that goes beyond the factual. *On the factual level, beautiful gems and sweet flowers are hidden away in underwater caves and deserts; the emotional poignancy arises from the thought of such beauties wasted, unappreciated by anyone.*

◆ Build Vocabulary

❼ **Prefixes: *circum-*** Call attention to the word *circumscribed*. Note that the root *-scribe-* means "to write." Ask students to combine their knowledge of the prefix *circum-* with this information to define *circumscribed.* Circumscribed*—"written around"—means "having definite borders" or "limited."*

Customize for *Verbal/Linguistic Learners*

❽ Ask these students to explain what Gray means by "far from the madding crowd" in this stanza. Then challenge them to identify the author who later used this phrase as a title for a novel and to explain why he did so. *It means "away from hectic crowds of people"; Thomas Hardy used it as the title for his novel,* Far from the Madding Crowd. *Hardy's novel focuses on life in the barren, isolated landscape of rural England.*

◆ Literary Focus

❶ **Preromantic Poetry** Ask students to point out the characteristics of preromantic poetry in these lines. *These lines express the human need to be cared about and remembered. The combination of formal rhythm and structure with such deeply emotional content is characteristic of preromantic poetry.*

❷ **Clarification** Point out the shift that occurs here. The conclusion of the poem is Gray's meditation on his own fate after death.

◆ Critical Thinking

❸ **Interpret** Ask: Does Gray think he will be remembered in a positive way? *He will be remembered for doing what other humans have done: making his way through the world, sometimes in joy, sometimes in sorrow.*

Customize for
Bodily/Kinesthetic Learners
Challenge groups of learners to dramatically recreate any part of this poem they wish. One option might be for one member of the group to read it dramatically while other members pantomime the emotions and actions that it suggests.

Their name, their years, spelt by the unlettered Muse,[18]
   The place of fame and elegy supply:
And many a holy text around she strews,
   That teach the rustic moralist to die.

For who, to dumb Forgetfulness a prey,
   This pleasing anxious being e'er resigned,
Left the warm precincts of the cheerful day,
   Nor cast one longing lingering look behind?

❶

On some fond breast the parting soul relies,
   Some pious drops[19] the closing eye requires;
Even from the tomb the voice of Nature cries,
   Even in our ashes live their wonted fires.

For thee,[20] who, mindful of the unhonored dead,
   Dost in these lines their artless tale relate;
If chance, by lonely contemplation led,
❷
   Some kindred spirit shall enquire thy fate,

Haply[21] some hoary-headed[22] swain may say,
   "Oft have we seen him at the peep of dawn
Brushing with hasty steps the dews away,
   To meet the sun upon the upland lawn.

"There at the foot of yonder nodding beech,
   That wreathes its old fantastic roots so high,
His listless length at noontide would he stretch,
   And pore upon the brook that babbles by.

"Hard by yon wood, now smiling as in scorn,
   Muttering his wayward fancies he would rove;
Now drooping, woeful wan, like one forlorn,
❸
   Or crazed with care, or crossed in hopeless love.

"One morn I missed him on the customed hill,
   Along the heath, and near his favorite tree;
Another came; nor yet beside the rill,[23]
   Nor up the lawn, nor at the wood was he;

"The next, with dirges due in sad array
   Slow through the churchway path we saw him borne.
Approach and read (for thou canst read) the lay
   Graved on the stone beneath yon aged thorn."[24]

18. **the unlettered Muse:** Uneducated gravestone carver.
19. **drops:** Tears.
20. **thee:** Gray himself.
21. **haply:** Perhaps.
22. **hoary-headed:** White-haired.
23. **rill:** Brook.
24. **thorn:** Hawthorn tree.

Cross-Curricular Connection: History

Funerals reflect social significance and may symbolize the values of a society. For example, the rituals surrounding the burials of Egyptian kings were a testimony to their authority, which even carried over into the land of the dead. Entombing the pharaohs in huge and everlasting pyramids was a symbol of their lasting authority.

Invite students to research the funeral and burial of an important figure from ancient or modern history. How did his or her ceremony and/or burial reflect the values of the culture and the significance of this leader in it?

The Epitaph

Here rests his head upon the lap of Earth
A youth, to Fortune and to Fame unknown.
Fair Science[25] *frowned not on his humble birth,* 
And melancholy marked him for her own.

Large was his bounty, and his soul sincere,
Heaven did a recompense as largely send:
He gave to misery (all he had) a tear,
He gained from Heaven ('twas all he wished) a friend.

No farther seek his merits to disclose,
Or draw his frailties from their dread abode
(There they alike in trembling hope repose),
The bosom of his Father and his God.

25. **Science:** Learning.

Guide for Responding

◆ Literature and Your Life

Reader's Response Did you share the speaker's sense of loss? Why or why not?

Thematic Focus What does the poem suggest about the ties that bind all human beings, regardless of status in society?

Added Stanza Continue Gray's elegy by writing a stanza praising an everyday person who was unappreciated in life. Your person could be modern and actual or from the past and fictional.

☑ Check Your Comprehension

1. At what time of day does the speaker find himself in the country churchyard?
2. (a) Who are the forefathers referred to by the speaker? (b) Of what will those forefathers no longer partake, according to lines 21–25?
3. In lines 57–60, what does the speaker say about the lives these people *might* have led?
4. To whom is "The Epitaph" in the last three stanzas dedicated?

◆ Critical Thinking

INTERPRET

1. (a) What is meant by "the inevitable hour" in line 35? (b) by "its mansion" in line 42? **[Interpret]**
2. To what is Gray comparing the "gem" and the "flower" in lines 53–56? **[Interpret]**
3. How would you explore the sentiment in lines 77–92? **[Interpret]**
4. Does the speaker come to accept his loss by the end of the poem? Explain your answer. **[Draw Conclusions]**

EVALUATE

5. Gray's "Elegy" is often quoted. Which lines do you find the most memorable? Why? **[Assess]**

EXTEND

6. Thomas Hardy wrote a famous novel called *Far from the Madding Crowd*, whose title comes from line 73 of Gray's poem. What sort of life would you guess this book celebrates? Explain. **[Literature Link]**

◆ Grammar and Style

❹ Pronoun-Antecedent Agreement Point out the word *youth*. Ask students to identify whether it is singular or plural. *It is singular.* Then ask students to identify the singular antecedent that agrees with youth. *The pronoun is* his. Students might then be challenged to identify the pronouns in the next two lines and their antecedents. *Pronouns* his *and* him *refer to* youth; *the pronoun* her *refers to* Science.

Customize for
Interpersonal Learners
Small groups might discuss whether graveyards and memorials help the living come to terms with the deaths of others as well as with their own future deaths.

Reinforce and Extend

Answers

◆ Literature and Your Life

Reader's Response Students may reflect upon what they hope to accomplish before they die.

Thematic Focus Death is common to all, and so connects all people, regardless of their social status.

☑ Check Your Comprehension

1. The speaker finds himself in the country churchyard at twilight.
2. (a) The forefathers are the uneducated poor who have died. (b) They will no longer enjoy domestic warmth or labor in the fields.
3. These people, under other circumstances, might have been great leaders—in literature and in politics, for example.
4. "The Epitaph" is dedicated to a youth, probably the poet himself.

◆ Critical Thinking

1. (a) The "inevitable hour" is the moment of death. (b) Its mansion is the living body.
2. Gray is comparing the gem and the flower to the potential that may be hidden and unused in an obscure person's life.
3. Even humble people long to be remembered after death.
4. The poet accepts his loss, believing that these dead repose in heaven.
5. Students may cite "The paths of glory lead but to the grave" or the stanza in lines 53–56.
6. *Far from the Madding Crowd* celebrates simple, country living.

Beyond the Classroom

Career Connection

Landscape Architecture Landscape architecture is both a science and an art. Landscape architects design the grounds for large homes, developments, civic centers, memorial parks, and many other sites. Although earliest notions of landscape architecture were limited to gardening, today's landscape architect considers not only the decorative elements and the plantings but aspects of civil engineering including drainage and grading.

Community Connection

Historic Burial Ground Cemeteries tell stories about individuals and their time. Small groups of students may visit a local, historic cemetery and make notes on the inscriptions, epitaphs, and gravestone designs they find there. Students may then make inferences about the historical period during which they were composed by thinking about the concerns and values they express.

Develop Understanding

One-Minute Insight In this meditative poem, poet Anne Finch reflects how in the softness of twilight, the sounds and sights of nature reveal their beauty. The poem celebrates the restorative power of this twilight world, where the mind may roam freely, unfettered by the confusion of the day.

Customize for ***Less Proficient Readers***
Have pairs of students work together to create a two-column chart as they read. In the first column, have them list some of the many things the speaker observes at twilight. In the second column, have students decide what the speaker's attitude is toward each of them.

◆ Literary Focus

❶ **Preromantic Poetry** Call attention to these first four lines. Have students note their regular rhyme and rhythm. Have them also note that Finch uses names from classical mythology. These characteristics help classify the lines as formal. Ask students: What characterizes these lines as preromantic? *The first strains of emotion creep into the poem with only and lonely, providing the reader with the Romantic sense of mystery and emotion.*

◆ Critical Thinking

❷ **Draw Conclusions** What mood does Finch create in the opening lines of her poem? *The mood is calm. There is some sense of mystery. Overall, however, the images are positive and pleasing.*

◆ Reading Strategy

❸ **Paraphrase** Remind students to paraphrase to help them determine the meaning of lines that elude them on first reading. How might they paraphrase these lines? *Sample paraphrase: "The foxglove turns a paler color, although its red stands out in the thicket; and here and there glow-worms reveal little bits of beauty, whose time has come to shine, in the fine twilight."*

A Nocturnal Reverie

Anne Finch,
Countess of Winchilsea

In such a night, when every louder wind
Is to its distant cavern safe confined;
❶ And only gentle Zephyr[1] fans his wings,
And lonely Philomel,[2] still waking, sings;
Or from some tree, famed for the owl's delight,
She, hollowing clear, directs the wanderer right:
In such a night, when passing clouds give place,
Or thinly veil the heavens' mysterious face;
When in some river, overhung with green,
❷ The waving moon and trembling leaves are seen;
When freshened grass now bears itself upright,
And makes cool banks to pleasing rest invite,
Whence springs the woodbind, and the bramble-rose,
And where the sleepy cowslip sheltered grows;
Whilst now a paler hue the foxglove takes,
❸ Yet checkers still with red the dusky brakes:[3]
When scattered glow-worms, but in twilight fine,
Show trivial beauties watch their hour to shine;

1. **Zephyr** (zef´ ər): West Wind; a breeze.
2. **Philomel** (fil´ ə mel´): Nightingale from mythology.
3. **brakes:** Overgrown areas; thickets.

Speaking and Listening Mini-Lesson

Eulogy
This mini-lesson supports the Speaking and Listening activity in the Idea Bank on page 531.

Introduce the Concept The goal of this mini-lesson is to deliver a eulogy, which is a formal speech praising a person who has recently died.

Develop Background The first step is to select a famous person to eulogize. As students make their choices, remind them that eulogies are positive, and they should pick accordingly.

Apply the Information Give students time to draft their eulogy, to exchange it with a peer reader and review each other's work, and to practice delivering it aloud. Students should evaluate whether their eulogy will hold their audience's interest.

Assess the Outcome Assess the eulogy using these criteria, which students should be aware of ahead of time: 1. The eulogy praises its subject; 2. it uses concrete examples; 3. it is organized in a logical fashion; and 4. it is delivered effectively and maintains the interest of the listeners.

Whilst Salisbury[4] stands the test of every light,
In perfect charms, and perfect virtue bright: ❹
When odors, which declined repelling day,
Through temperate air uninterrupted stray;
When darkened groves their softest shadows wear,
And falling waters we distinctly hear;
When through the gloom more venerable shows ❺
Some ancient fabric,[5] awful in repose,
While sunburnt hills their swarthy looks conceal, ❻
And swelling haycocks thicken up the vale:
When the loosed horse now, as his pasture leads,
Comes slowly grazing through the adjoining meads,[6]

---

4. Salisbury: This may refer to a Lady Salisbury, daughter of a friend, not to the town of Salisbury.
5. ancient fabric: Edifice or large, imposing building.
6. meads: Archaic term for "meadows."

◆ Build Vocabulary

nocturnal (näk tur´ nəl): *adj.*: Occurring at night

temperate (tem´ pər it) *adj.*: Mild

venerable (ven´ ər ə bəl) *adj.*: Commanding respect by virtue of age, character, or social rank

❹ **Clarification** Explain that this line suggests that Salisbury is no "trivial" beauty: she "glows" in all light, unlike glow-worms, which must wait until twilight.

◆ *Literature and Your Life*

❺ The speaker glories in the twilight, in which sounds, sights, and smells are different and more evocative. Ask students whether they like twilight as well and to explain why. *Some students may agree that twilight changes everything to make it more poetic, beautiful, or mysterious. Others may think twilight a bit frightening. Some may say that a love of twilight depends on where the speaker is and how familiar or safe he or she feels in those surroundings.*

◆ Critical Thinking

❻ **Analyze** Ask students to study these lines and then to describe their structure. *These lines are made up of rhyming couplets in iambic pentameter. Like others in the poem, they read like a list: "When this . . . ; when that . . .; while this. . . ."*

Customize for
Verbal/Linguistic Learners
This poem contains many vivid verbs as well as many participles used as adjectives. Invite students to identify and discuss their favorites.

▶Critical Viewing◀

❶ **Analyze** The house in the picture is bathed in light that is too dark for day, too bright for night, just as the poem is set in twilight. In this painting, this eerie half-light is made a bit more eerie or mysterious by the predominance of the color blue. Yet both the poem and the painting ultimately create an impression that is more pleasing and positive than mysterious and frightening.

Comprehension Check ☑

❷ Ask whether the horse's approach frightens the speaker. *At first, the shadow thrown by the horse is frightening, but when the speaker realizes the horse is just eating, she is no longer afraid.*

◆Grammar and Style

❸ **Pronoun-Antecedent Agreement** Have students identify the pronoun in this line; its number; and its antecedent. *The pronoun their refers to the antecedent creatures; they are plural in number.*

◆Literary Focus

❹ **Preromantic Poetry** Explain that in its celebration of nature, this poem anticipates the poetry of the Romantic movement. Point out the "sedate content" the spirit feels in nature; also point out that in such a setting the mind seeks something "high." Such thoughts anticipate Wordsworth and other Romantics.

Cottage and Pond, Moonlight, Thomas Gainsborough, Victoria and Albert Museum, London

❶ ▲ **Critical Viewing** What visual elements in this picture help create a mood like that of the poem? **[Analyze]**

Whose stealing pace, and lengthened shade we fear,
❷ Till torn-up forage in his teeth we hear:
When nibbling sheep at large pursue their food,
And unmolested kine[7] rechew the cud;
When curlews cry beneath the village walls,
And to her straggling brood the partridge calls;
❸ Their shortlived jubilee the creatures keep,
Which but endures, whilst tyrant man does sleep;
❹ When a sedate content the spirit feels,
And no fierce light disturbs, whilst it reveals;
But silent musings urge the mind to seek
Something, too high for syllables to speak;

7. **kine:** Archaic plural of "cow"; cattle.

Humanities: Art

Cottage and Pond, Moonlight by Thomas Gainsborough.

A master of both the landscape painting and the portrait, Gainsborough created more than five hundred paintings during his lifetime. He was very much influenced by the French painter Watteau, as well as by the seventeenth-century Dutch landscape painters. Successful during his lifetime, Gainsborough became the favorite of the British aristocracy and grew wealthy from his commissions.

Faint, melancholic lighting is a feature of many of Gainsborough's paintings. His typical landscape subjects include rough, broken country and forest scenes.

Use these questions for discussion:

1. Do you find the location pictured here inviting? Explain. *Students may find in this location an escape from civilization, or they may think it too remote or even eerie. While the presence of a human figure in the doorway may not dispel a sense of loneliness, it does make the landscape less eerie.*
2. If you were to write a nocturnal reverie about this scene, what details might you include? *Students might focus on the pond, with its plant and animal life, and the sounds of the animals and the water. The clouds seem to be in motion and may suggest the sounds of breezes.*

Till the free soul to a composedness charmed,
Finding the elements of rage disarmed, ❺
O'er all below a solemn quiet grown,
Joys in the inferior world, and thinks it like her own: ❻
In such a night let me abroad remain,
Till morning breaks, and all's confused again;
Our cares, our toils, our clamors are renewed,
Or pleasures, seldom reached, again pursued.

◆ **Build Vocabulary**

forage (fôr′ ij) *n.*: Food for farm animals, especially any food found by grazing outdoors

Guide for Responding

◆ Literature and Your Life

Reader's Response Could you share the speaker's mood? Why or why not?

Thematic Focus What does the poem suggest about the ties that bind nature together and the ties that bind us to nature?

Nocturnal Reverie List some of the details that you would put in your own "nocturnal reverie."

☑ Check Your Comprehension

1. (a) Describe the setting of the poem. (b) List specific images from the poem that support your description of the setting.
2. Where does the speaker want to remain on such a night?
3. According to the speaker, what happens when morning breaks again?

◆ Critical Thinking

INTERPRET

1. What is the mood of the poem? **[Classify]**
2. According to lines 9–12, is the night fresh, dull, or chaotic? Explain. **[Analyze]**
3. This poem is one sentence containing many thoughts. How does the poem's structure affect its meaning? **[Interpret]**

APPLY

4. If the speaker were taking a nocturnal walk in modern times, would her observations be the same? Explain. **[Hypothesize]**

EXTEND

5. In Act V, Scene i, of *The Merchant of Venice* by William Shakespeare, the lovers Lorenzo and Jessica speak of famous lovers, using the phrase "in such a night" seven times. Why do you think Finch opened her poem with the phrase made famous in this scene? **[Literature Link]**

Beyond the Selection

FURTHER READING

More Works by the Authors

"Ode on a Distant Prospect of Eton College,"
"Hymn to Adversity," Thomas Gray
"On Myself," "The Petition for an Absolute Retreat," Anne Finch, Countess of Winchilsea

Other Elegies

"Lycidas," John Milton
In Memoriam, Alfred, Lord Tennyson

We suggest that you preview these works before recommending them to students.

INTERNET

You and your students may find additional information about Thomas Gray and Ann Finch on the following Internet sites. (Note: sites may have changed from the time of publication.)

For selected poetry and criticism of Gray and Finch, go to **http://library.utoronto/ca/www/utel/rp/authors/gray.html** and **http://library.utoronto/ca/www/utel/rp/authors/finch.html**

We *strongly recommend* that you preview the sites before you send students to them.

◆ Literature and Your Life

❺ Ask students to name settings that have provided them with similar moments of inner peace. *Students may recall sitting by a waterfall or looking out over a canyon.*

❻ **Clarification** Explain that the "inferior world" is the world of nature. In Platonic thought, nature is merely a changing copy of eternal ideas (principles).

Reinforce and Extend

Answers

◆ Literature and Your Life

Reader's Response Students can relate to the contrast between a time of solemn calm and the hectic confusion of daytime activities.

Thematic Focus Nature is united by a calm in which everything has its place; people are bound to nature by the peace contemplating it brings.

☑ Check Your Comprehension

1. (a) The setting is a quiet twilight in the country. (b) The foxglove takes "a paler hue" (line 15); the "darkened groves their softest shadows wear" (line 23).
2. The speaker wishes to remain outside in the nocturnal countryside.
3. When morning breaks, confusion returns as people resume their cares and pursuits.

◆ Critical Thinking

1. The mood is of quiet, reflective enjoyment of nature.
2. According to Finch, the night is fresh, with gentle breezes and rippling waters.
3. By accumulating rich details while holding off a conclusion, the poem itself imitates the lulling effect of a rambling twilight walk.
4. It may be difficult to find such a rich rural setting untouched by urban development.
5. Finch uses the associations of the phrase to help set the mood of intense, dreamlike emotion.

◆ Reading Strategy

1. (a) Beautiful gems are hidden in the depths of the ocean's darkness unseen, and many beautiful flowers bloom unseen in the desert. (b) Gray is comparing the gem and the flower to the unknown lives that go unnoticed in the world at large.
2. When it is so peaceful, the speaker wishes to remain outside all night.

◆ Build Vocabulary

1. *circumnavigating:* to sailor or fly around
2. *circumvented:* went around
3. *circumlocutions:* indirect phrases
4. *Circumspect:* Thinking carefully around all possibilities
5. *circumference:* distance around the outside of a circle

Using the Word Bank

1. penury, wealth: *antonyms*
2. ingenuous, sophisticated: *antonyms*
3. ignoble, lowly: *synonyms*
4. nocturnal, daytime: *antonyms*
5. temperate, moderate: *synonyms*
6. venerable, respected: *synonyms*
7. forage, fodder: *synonyms*

◆ Literary Focus

1. In these concluding lines, Finch contrasts her peaceful reverie with a jarring return to the clamor of human endeavors.
2. (a) Both poets imply that value and dignity lie in the simple beauties of life, not in ambitious pursuits. (b) It deals with the common people and things and the mysteries of life; it emphasizes emotions rather than reason.
3. Nighttime represents emotion, and daytime represents reason.

◆ Grammar and Style

1. Everything had *its* beauty.
2. The nightingale or the owl sang *its* song.
3. Correct.
4. The woodbine and the bramble-rose wafted *their* scent into the nighttime air.
5. Each of the farm animals had *its* habits.

Guide for Responding *(continued)*

◆ Reading Strategy

Paraphrase

Paraphrasing, or restating in your own words a writer's key ideas, helps you understand and enjoy literature. Once you've paraphrased an author's words, you are better able to understand the author's message. Here, for example, is a paraphrase of two lines from Gray's "Elegy":

Original: Let not Ambition mock their useful toil, / Their homely joys, and destiny obscure . . .

Paraphrase: Those who are ambitious shouldn't make fun of their useful work, simple pleasures, and unknown lives.

1. (a) Paraphrase lines 53–56 of Thomas Gray's "Elegy." (b) What key ideas do these lines express?

2. Lines 47–50 of "A Nocturnal Reverie" reveal the speaker's wishes. Express these wishes in your own words.

◆ Build Vocabulary

Using the Prefix *circum-*

Explain how the prefix *circum-*, which means "around" or "surrounding," contributes to the meaning of the italicized words.

1. Magellan is known for *circumnavigating* the globe.

2. She *circumvented* the rules by sneaking into line.

3. When people don't want to say something outright, they use *circumlocutions.*

4. *Circumspect,* he always thought before acting.

5. Have you learned how to measure a circle's radius and *circumference?*

Using the Word Bank

Copy these word pairs into your notebook and indicate whether they are synonyms or antonyms.

1. penury, wealth
2. ingenuous, sophisticated
3. ignoble, lowly
4. nocturnal, daytime
5. temperate, moderate
6. venerable, respected
7. forage, fodder

◆ Literary Focus

Pre-Romantic Poetry

Poems like Gray's "Elegy" and Finch's "Reverie" are **pre-Romantic** in their emphasis on the worth of the common person, the mystery of life, and the importance of emotions. The **elegy** that Gray writes, for example, mourns for an ordinary person, rather than for a well-known figure: "A youth, to Fortune and to Fame unknown." This "youth" is mysterious for the very fact that he is unknown, and the poem expresses sadness concerning his fate.

Finch's dreamlike **reverie** shares the quiet of Gray's poem, a quiet in which deep thought flows into feeling.

1. Explain how lines 39–50 of Finch's "A Nocturnal Reverie" stress mystery and emotion rather than achievement and intellectual striving.

2. (a) What is similar about Gray's concern for the unknown dead of a village graveyard and Finch's loving attention to humble "creatures"? (b) What is pre-Romantic about this type of subject?

3. Both poets choose a nighttime setting. How is this choice itself a reflection of pre-Romantic ideals?

◆ Grammar and Style

Pronoun-Antecedent Agreement

Pronouns agree with their **antecedents,** the words to which they refer, in number and gender. When an antecedent is a compound linked by *and*, the number is plural. If a compound is linked by *or*, the number may be singular.

Practice Copy these sentences and correct errors in pronoun-antecedent agreement. If a sentence is correct as is, write *correct.*

1. Everything in the woods had their beauties.
2. The nightingale or the owl sang their song.
3. Some of the flowers opened their petals.
4. The woodbine and the bramble-rose wafted its scent into the nighttime air.
5. Each of the farm animals had their habits.

Writer's Solution

For additional instruction and practice use the lesson in the **Writing Lab CD-ROM** on Nouns and Pronouns and the pages on Pronoun and Antecedent Agreement, pp. 64–65 in the *Writer's Solution Grammar Practice Book.*

Build Your Portfolio

Idea Bank

Writing

1. Diary Entry Imagine that you are the speaker of Gray's "Elegy" or Finch's "Reverie." Write a diary entry describing the experience behind your poem.

2. Epitaphs Drawing on biographical information as well as on the poems, write epitaphs for the graves of Gray and Finch. Each epitaph should say something important about the writer.

3. Response to Criticism Dr. Johnson wrote of Gray's elegy, "The Churchyard abounds with images which find a mirror in every mind, and with sentiments to which every bosom returns an echo." Agree or disagree with this statement, citing specific references from the poem.

Speaking and Listening

4. Choral Reading Working in a group, prepare and perform a choral reading of either poem. **[Performing Arts Link]**

5. Eulogy Gray's elegy praises the forgotten dead. Choose a hero of the past, real or fictional, to praise in a eulogy. Recite your eulogy to the class. **[Performing Arts Link]**

Projects

6. Nighttime Walk The thoughts of the speakers in Gray's and Finch's poems are inspired by the nighttime. Design a park that would allow people to take safe nighttime walks. **[Social Studies Link]**

7. Brain Study Use science magazines to research brain waves and their effects on dreams and daydreams. Present your findings to the class, explaining the scientific basis for Finch's reverie. **[Science Link]**

Writing Mini-Lesson

Reflective Essay

In both Gray's "Elegy" and Finch's "Reverie," a particular time and place inspire a reflective journey. Take a journey of your own by writing a reflective essay. In it, re-create a special time and place, together with your personal response to the setting.

These tips will help you give your essay a distinctive, personal flavor.

Writing Skills Focus: Elaboration to Make Writing Personal

Some types of writing are more powerful if they express the personal thoughts and feelings of the writer. In a reflective essay, for example, a writer reveals a personal experience and his or her reactions to it.

Here are some ways to reveal yourself in an essay:

- Base the essay on a setting that inspired you.
- Describe the time and place vividly, just as you experienced it.
- Trace any changes in your thoughts and feelings that may have taken place over time.

Prewriting Begin to gather details that will effectively convey your reflective journey. You may want to use a two-column chart to list details describing the source of inspiration (col. 1) and the thoughts and feelings inspired in you (col. 2).

Drafting As you draft, refer to the details you've gathered in order to relive your original experience. If you remember additional thoughts and feelings inspired by that experience, add them to your essay.

Revising Have a friend read your essay and ask if he or she senses your personality in it. If a passage seems distant and purely descriptive, add your thoughts and feelings about what you're describing. Also, be sure that you've noted any changes in your thoughts and feelings that have been inspired by the original experience.

✓ ASSESSMENT OPTIONS

Formal Assessment, Selection Test, pp. 123–125, and Assessment Resources Software. The selection test is designed so that it can be easily customized to the performance levels of your students.

Alternative Assessment, p. 26, includes options for less advanced students, more advanced students, visual/spatial learners, verbal/linguistic learners, and musical/rhythmic learners.

PORTFOLIO ASSESSMENT

Use the following rubrics in the ***Alternative Assessment*** booklet to assess student writing:

Diary Entry: Description Rubric, p. 98

Epitaphs: Research Report/Paper, p. 107

Response to Criticism: Evaluation/Review Rubric, p. 105

Writing Mini-Lesson: Description Rubric, p. 98

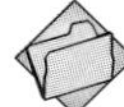

Idea Bank

Customizing for ***Performance Levels***

Following are suggestions for matching Idea Bank topics with your students' performance levels:

Less Advanced Students: 1, 4, 6
Average Students: 2, 4, 7
More Advanced Students: 3, 5

Customizing for ***Learning Modalities***

Following are suggestions for matching Idea Bank topics with your students' learning modalities:

Verbal/Linguistic: 1, 2, 3, 4, 5
Visual/Spatial: 7
Logical/Mathematical: 7

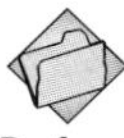

Writing Mini-Lesson

Refer students to the Writing Handbook, page 1189, for instruction on the writing process, and page 1191 for more about description.

Writing and Language Transparencies Use Writing Process Model 1: Reflective Essay, pp. 5–11 to guide students in writing and revising a reflective essay.

Writers at Work Videodisc

Have students view the videodisc segment (Ch. 1) featuring Guy Garcia for tips on making descriptive writing memorable. Have students discuss how they can apply Garcia's.

Play frames 335 to 10062

Writing Lab CD-ROM

Have students complete the tutorial on Description. Follow these steps:

1. Use the Word Bins of sensory details and places to get started.
2. The Chain of Events tool can help in gathering and organizing information for students' essays.
3. Students can draft on computer.
4. Have students use the audio-annotated examples of figurative language to improve their reflective essays.

Allow approximately 120 minutes to complete these steps.

Sourcebook

Have students use Chapter 1, Description (pp. 1–29), for additional support. The chapter includes a model reflective essay (p. 8).

Prepare and Engage

OBJECTIVES

1. To read, comprehend, and interpret statements of belief
2. To relate statements of belief to personal experience
3. To connect statements of belief to works of literature that have served to bring people together
4. To write moral lessons
5. To respond to statements of belief through writing, speaking and listening, and projects

PORTFOLIO OPPORTUNITIES

Writing: Yearbook Entry; Analects for Today; Imaginary Correspondence
Speaking and Listening: Ask Confucius
Project: Charter or Constitution

More About the Authors

One of the most important thinkers in Chinese history, **Confucius** did not write down his ideas. Instead, they were recorded and handed down by his disciples. Placing great emphasis on the power of setting a good example, Confucius himself acted as a ruler briefly during the politically turbulent times in which he lived. When he was 50, he was appointed a magistrate; the next year he became a minister of crime. He introduced reforms and crime nearly disappeared.

A midwife at the birth of American politics, **Thomas Jefferson** is known for countless achievements; he asked that his tombstone list only *The Declaration of Independence,* the establishment of the University of Virginia, and a law separating church and state.

CONNECTIONS TO WORLD LITERATURE

from The Analects
Confucius

from The Declaration of Independence
Thomas Jefferson

Cultural Connection

THE TIES THAT BIND

The pieces in this section and the ones you are about to read illustrate the shared experiences and beliefs that bind people together. You have had such experiences in your own school. As you study and participate in activities with others, you begin to feel like a member of a community.

A country is obviously larger than a school. However, the citizens of a country can face challenges and threats that bring them together. The two disasters documented by Pepys and Defoe, a fire and a plague, were national tragedies. Yet the English experienced them as communal misfortunes.

In a more positive way, Johnson's *Dictionary* also contributed to a national identity. With its publication, the English language became touchable and portable. It moved from the breath and tongue to the page. Now people could carry around and study the words that united them as a nation.

Like Johnson's *Dictionary,* the collected sayings of the Chinese philosopher Confucius, *The Analects,* and Thomas Jefferson's *Declaration of Independence* serve to link people together. *The Analects* states the beliefs of Confucianism, which was for centuries the dominant political, ethical, and social philosophy of China. Jefferson's *Declaration* delineates the bond that united Americans in their struggle to become a nation.

CONFUCIUS (551–479 B.C.)

Confucius was a Chinese philosopher and reformer who lived during a time of conflict and corruption. In this dark period of Chinese history, he wandered the land and instructed any young men who appeared to have a talent for learning. In all his teachings, Confucius emphasized the importance of right conduct. He taught his students to be morally and spiritually superior men.

As compiled in *The Analects,* Confucian beliefs have deeply influenced the Chinese way of life. These beliefs were the official state doctrine of China until the overthrow of the imperial system in 1911. Even under communism, Confucian thinking still exerts a strong, underground influence.

THOMAS JEFFERSON (1743–1826)

Thomas Jefferson was an American revolutionary leader, political philosopher, author of *The Declaration of Independence,* and third President of the United States. In 1774, Jefferson wrote *Summary View of the Rights of British America,* in which he argued that the connection between the colonies and the crown was voluntary and that England therefore had no power over American communities. The eloquence and power of this document made Jefferson the obvious choice as writer of the *Declaration.* Jefferson succeeded in his assignment beyond anyone's dreams, giving voice to the American goal of independence and liberty.

Thematic Connection

The *Analects* show how a ruler works together with the people to create the ideal state. *The Declaration of Independence* argues that government is founded on the consent of the people. Both interpret the ties binding a people to a government.

Genre Connection

Statements of belief, such as the *Analects* and *The Declaration of Independence*, are nonfiction; they are usually also persuasive, using both logic and appeals to emotion to support their premises.

Prentice Hall Literature Program Resources

REINFORCE / RETEACH / EXTEND

Selection Support Pages
Build Vocabulary: p. 126
Cultural Connection, p. 127

Formal Assessment Selection Test, pp. 126–127; Assessment Resources Software

Resource Pro CD-ROM
from the *Analects;* from *The Declaration of Independence*

Listening to Literature Audiocassettes from the *Analects;* from *The Declaration of Independence*

from The Analects ❷

Confucius

Translated by Arthur Waley

The Master said, He who rules by moral force is like the pole-star, which remains in its place while all the lesser stars do homage[1] to it. ❸

The Master said, Govern the people by regulations, keep order among them by chastisements,[2] and they will flee from you, and lose all self-respect. Govern them by moral force, keep order among them by ritual, and they will keep their self-respect and come to you of their own accord.

1. **homage** (häm′ ij) *n.*: Anything given or done to show honor or respect.
2. **chastisements** (chas tiz′ mənts) *n*: Acts of scolding or condemning.

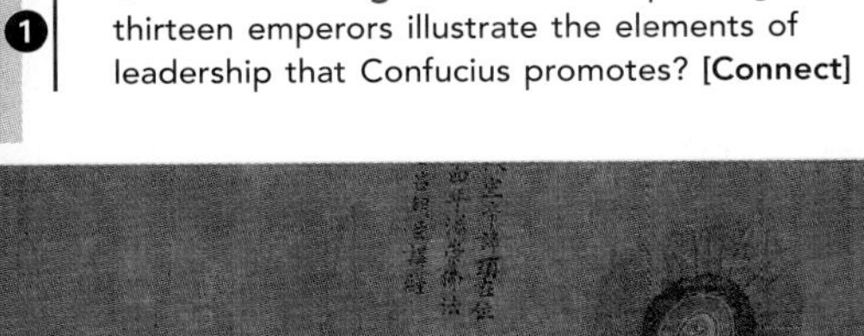

❶ ▼ **Critical Viewing** How does this painting of thirteen emperors illustrate the elements of leadership that Confucius promotes? **[Connect]**

The Thirteen Emperors, Yan Liben, Museum of Fine Arts, Boston

Develop Understanding

One-Minute Insight What is proper and right for a leader? According to Confucius, the leader should act as a model to his subjects and command the respect of the common people. Being elected is not necessary; nor is ruling by threats or punishment. The honorable ruler governs not by physical force but by moral force.

►Critical Viewing◄

❶ **Connect** The emperors shown in this detail may be said to be acting properly, in a dignified fashion that sets an example for their subjects. All seem to embody self-respect.

Customize for *Less Proficient Readers*

Explain that "the Master" and Master K'ung refer to Confucius. Explain that this is a conversation between Confucius and his disciples. You might also assist students in placing quotation marks around the words of each speaker so that they know when each speaker's words begin and end.

❷ **Clarification** Explain that the teachings of Confucius were not a religion but principles of conduct. The *Analects* are a collection of writings (*analects* means "selected written passages") explaining Confucius' moral and political philosophy.

◆Critical Thinking

❸ **Interpret** Ask students to speculate about what Confucius means by "moral force." *Sample answer: He means the opposite of governing by regulations (laws) or chastisements (punishments). Governing by "moral force" means leading by setting an example of virtue.*

Humanities: Art

The Thirteen Emperors (detail), second half of the seventh century, handscroll by Yen Li-pen.

Tell students that this is just a detail from the painting of thirteen emperors; not all of the thirteen are shown here. Of the figures presented, the emperors are obviously the more well-dressed: they include the largest of all the people shown, the seated emperor, and the two emperors at the far right. The others are attendants: note how their footwear, their pants, and their activities identify them.

This handscroll, which was created during the Tang dynasty, portrays emperors stretching back to the Han dynasty. It was created for ethical instruction of the imperial family: this purpose is a Confucian one.

Use these questions for discussion:

1. How would you describe the posture of these emperors? *The figures are upright and dignified. The posture seems to convey dignity; it may even convey "moral force."*
2. This painting was created to instruct. What do you think it teaches? *It teaches history. It shows various emperors from various dynasties. It also teaches a sense of interconnectedness: all thirteen emperors, whose history spans hundreds of years, go forth together in one procession. Finally, it teaches values: the emperors are the great and good rulers, who go forth in dignity, who enact ritual, who inspire and lead.*

◆ *Literature and Your Life*

❶ Ask students whether these words strike them as wise or as obvious, and why. *Students may say that while it is easy to criticize narrow-mindedness and insincerity, people may need reminders of the value of their opposites. Also, Confucius' idea that a healthy society is one in which formal ritual and people's internal sentiments are harmonized is a striking alternative to today's individualism and cynicism.*

Customize for
Visual/Spatial Learners
Invite students to find or create images that express the importance of the ruler in relation to those ruled.

◆ Background for Understanding

❷ Explain that this reference to "the Way" is a reference to Taoism. Laotzu, who originated the Taoist philosophy, was active during the sixth century B.C. Confucius was born in 551 B.C.; he became influential after Taoism had begun to take hold in China.

◆ Critical Thinking

❸ **Compare and Contrast** How is Confucius' idea of the ruler's relationship to the people different from modern American ideas? *Suggested answer: In modern times people don't regard rulers as paragons, nor do they regard the ruled as "small people" who are like grass. In a democracy, rulers are held accountable to the people: The rulers must bend, not the ruled.*

Customize for
Intrapersonal Learners
Intrapersonal learners may be encouraged to record their thoughts about this conversation in their journals.

❶ The Master said, High office filled by men of narrow views, ritual performed without reverence,[3] the forms of mourning observed without grief—these are things I cannot bear to see!

Chi K'ang-tzu asked Master K'ung ❷ about government, saying, Suppose I were to slay those who have not the Way in order to help on those who have the Way, what would you think ❸ of it? Master K'ung replied saying, You are there to rule, not to slay. If you desire what is good, the people will at once be good. The essence of the gentleman is that of wind; the essence of small people is that of grass. And when a wind passes over the grass, it cannot choose but bend.

Tzu-kung asked about government. The Master said, sufficient food, sufficient weapons, and the confidence of the common people. Tzu-kung said, Suppose you had no choice but to dispense with one of these three, which would you forgo? The Master said, Weapons. Tzu-kung said, Suppose you were forced to dispense with one of the two that were left, which would you forgo? The Master said, Food. For from of old death has been the lot of all men; but a people that no longer trusts its rulers is lost indeed.

Master Yu said, Those who in private life behave well towards their parents and elder brothers, in public life seldom show a disposition to resist the authority of their superiors. And as for such men starting a revolution, no instance of it has ever occurred. It is upon the trunk that a gentleman works. When that is firmly set up, the Way grows. And surely proper behavior towards parents and elder brothers is the trunk of Goodness?

3. **reverence** (rev´ ər əns) *n.*: Feeling or attitude of deep respect, love, and awe.

Cross-Curricular Connection: Social Studies

Explain to students that Confucius' ideas of order emerged from a time of disorder and upheaval. Though he often speaks as one who wants to restore traditions, Confucius himself became a source of a new tradition in the centuries after his death.

During the Zhou dynasty in China (1111–825 B.C.) the old feudal regions, each ruled from a walled city, grew into big states. While the old feudal nobility kept power through family ties and traditional loyalties, the rulers of the new big states governed through administrative bureaucracies, staffed by bright young men, like Confucius himself, who might travel far to find a post. Peasant farmers, formerly tied to the land, came to own their own plots. Traditional ways of life were eroding as individuals came to depend more and more on their own efforts for success. War became more frequent during this time as rulers struggled for power.

Peace finally came. Over 300 years after Confucius' birth, the Han emperors, ruling a united China, made Confucianism the basis of their government. Texts associated with Confucius, including the *Analects,* became the core curriculum around which education and the country's civil service exams were based. Confucianism remained central to Chinese culture until 1912, when the Chinese Revolution put an end to the rule of China's Emperors.

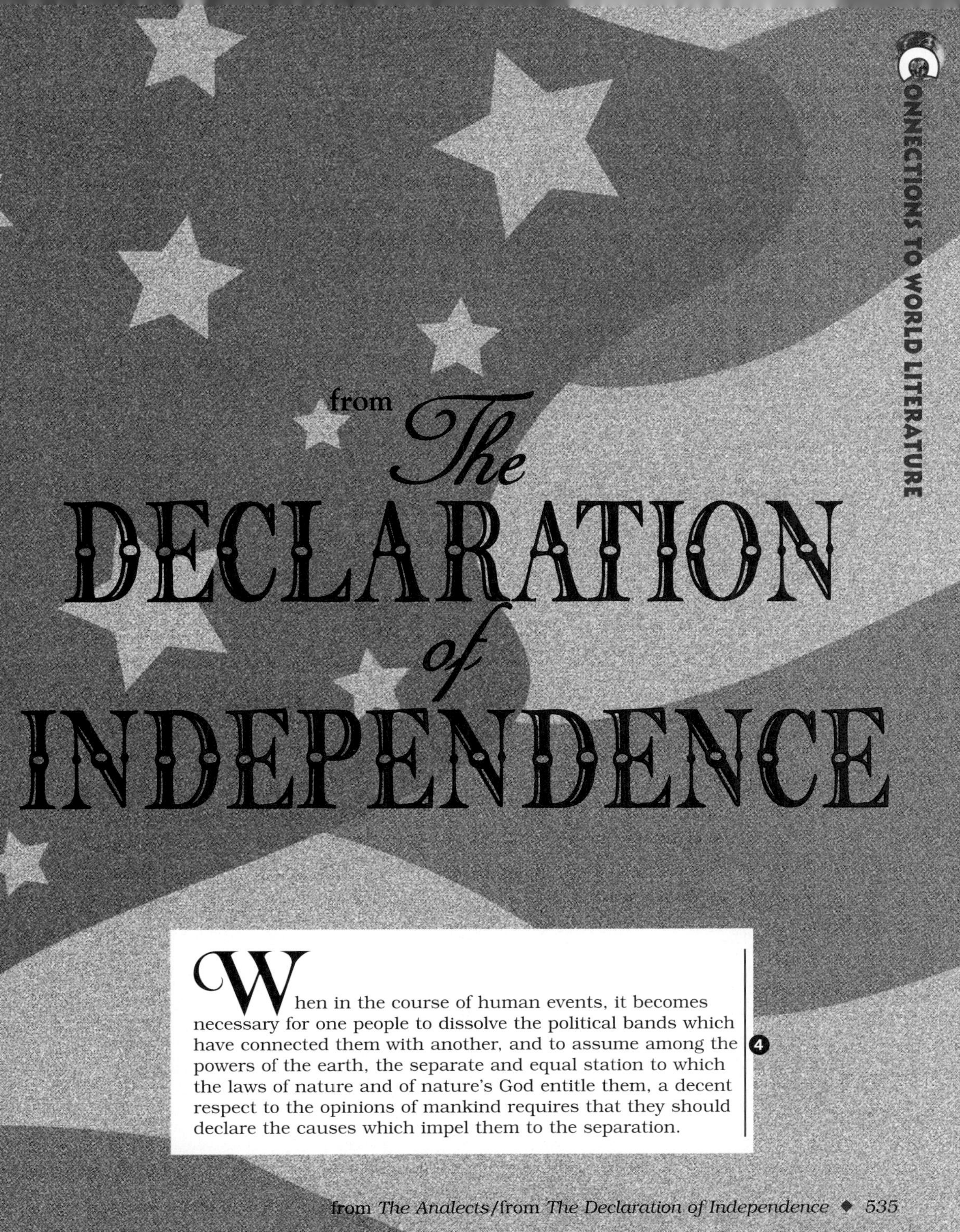

from *The* DECLARATION *of* INDEPENDENCE

When in the course of human events, it becomes necessary for one people to dissolve the political bands which have connected them with another, and to assume among the powers of the earth, the separate and equal station to which the laws of nature and of nature's God entitle them, a decent respect to the opinions of mankind requires that they should declare the causes which impel them to the separation. 4

One-Minute Insight Do the people of the colonies have the right to declare independence? Yes, says Jefferson in this brief excerpt from the beginning of *The Declaration of Independence*. Nevertheless, they must state their reasons; furthermore, those reasons must be serious ones. He goes on to explain that the colonies have such reasons; it is both their right and their duty to throw off abusive, tyrannical British rule.

Customize for
English Language Learners
Long sentences make *The Declaration of Independence* challenging reading for most readers. To help English language learners, encourage them to use marks of punctuation as a guide to meaning. For example, the comma in the first sentence signals that the long dependent, explanatory clause is ending and the main idea is coming up. In the second sentence (beginning on page 537), the colon signals that a list is coming up, and each item in the list is separated by a semicolon.

◆ Critical Thinking

4 **Make Inferences** What forces does Jefferson say are on the side of the American people and give them the right to declare their independence? *Jefferson says the laws of nature and of nature's god "entitle" the people to assume their powers and dissolve their political bands.*

Comprehension Check ☑

❶ According to Jefferson, when do people have the right to alter or abolish a form of government? *People have the right to do so when government becomes destructive of, or interferes with, the rights Jefferson has named.*

◆ Critical Thinking

❷ **Analyze** Jefferson uses extremely harsh words to present the actions of the crown. Why does he do so? *He is attempting to justify a desperate, arguably criminal act of rebellion.*

►Critical Viewing◄

❸ **Evaluate** Students may say that Jefferson appears to be serious and even struck by his own importance, as a leader needs to be. They may also think they see compassion in his eyes, which is a good quality for a leader.

Customize for
Musical/Rhythmic Learners

The Declaration of Independence is full of balance and parallelism. Invite students to identify musical sentences by finding examples of balanced and parallel phrases and clauses. Have them suggest ways such balance and parallelism have been expressed in music. (If you wish, make the entire *declaration* available for this purpose. A great deal of parallelism exists in the outlining of King George III's "abuses," and one of the most famous of all parallel constructions ends the *Declaration:* "our lives, our fortunes, and our sacred Honor.")

CONNECTIONS TO WORLD LITERATURE

Thomas Jefferson, Gilbert Stuart, National Portrait Gallery, Smithsonian Institution

Humanities: Art

Thomas Jefferson by Gilbert Stuart.

Gilbert Stuart was the leading American portrait painter of his day. He painted nearly one thousand portraits, which brought him lasting fame; of these, he is most famous for his paintings of George Washington. He also painted the portraits of Presidents John Adams, James Madison, and Thomas Jefferson.

In this portrait, the rich tones Stuart used to create Jefferson's flesh, combined with expressive brushwork, contrast with the simple background and the dark dignity of the subject's clothing. The result is a quiet yet expressive portrait of a great man, whose power may be seen in the expression of his eyes, the set of his mouth, and his dignified, upright posture.

Use these questions for discussion:

1. Does this painting suggest that its subject is a great man? Why or why not? *The clothing suggests high social stature for the time period. The simplicity of the composition itself suggests dignity: Here is Jefferson, it seems to say; that is enough.*
2. If you had been the painter, what would you have done differently? *Students might, for example, have shown Jefferson at work on* The Declaration of Independence *or in discussion with the Founding Fathers. They might have placed him in front of his home at Monticello or in the front of the University of Virginia.*

We hold these truths to be self-evident: that all men are created equal; that they are endowed by their Creator with certain unalienable[1] rights; that among these are life, liberty and the pursuit of happiness; that to secure these rights, governments are instituted among men, deriving their just powers from the consent of the governed; that whenever any form of government becomes destructive of these ends, it is the right of the people to alter or to abolish it, and to institute new government, laying its foundation on such principles and organizing its powers in such form, as to them shall seem most likely to effect their safety and happiness. Prudence, indeed, will dictate that governments long established should not be changed for light and transient causes; and accordingly all experience hath shown, that mankind are more disposed to suffer while evils are sufferable than to right themselves by abolishing the forms to which they are accustomed. But when a long train of abuses and usurpations,[2] pursuing invariably the same object, evinces a design to reduce them under absolute despotism,[3] it is their right, it is their duty, to throw off such government, and to provide new guards for their future security. Such has been the patient sufferance of these colonies; and such is now the necessity which constrains them to alter their former systems of government. The history of the present king of Great Britain is a history of repeated injuries and usurpations, all having in direct object the establishment of an absolute tyranny over these states.

1. **unalienable** (ən āl´ yən ə bəl) *adj.*: That which may not be taken away or transferred.
2. **usurpations** (yo͞o´ zər pā´ shənz) *n.*: Unlawful or violent seizure of a throne.
3. **despotism** (des´ pət iz´ əm) *n.*: Methods or acts of a tyrant.

◀ **Critical Viewing** How does Gilbert Stuart's rendering of Jefferson reveal some of the attributes that made Jefferson a great leader? **[Evaluate]**

CONNECTIONS TO WORLD LITERATURE

Guide for Responding

◆ Literature and Your Life

Reader's Response Would you define yourself as a Confucian or a Jeffersonian? Explain.

Thematic Focus Could Jefferson have been a Confucian? Why or why not? Would Confucius have endorsed the American Revolution, as justified by Jefferson? Explain.

☑ Check Your Comprehension

1. How does Confucius suggest that people be governed?
2. (a) According to Confucius, what are the three most important aspects of government? (b) Which of these is the most crucial?
3. What reason does Jefferson give for writing the Declaration?
4. What are the unalienable rights that Jefferson mentions?

Reinforce and Extend

Answers

◆ Literature and Your Life

Reader's Response Students may resist categorizing themselves in either "camp," preferring to draw the best from each: the strong belief in moral force from Confucius and the strong belief in justice from Jefferson.

Thematic Focus Sample responses: Jefferson would have agreed that those governing must have the trust and respect of the common people. Because England had lost the trust of Americans, Confucius would not have been surprised at the Americans' desire for independence, yet he may have believed that Americans were not raised properly by their families, since among gentlemen there was no need to resist authority.

☑ Check Your Comprehension

1. Confucius suggests that people be governed by regulations, moral force, and by rituals of reverence.
2. (a) According to Confucius, the three most important aspects of government are: sufficient food, sufficient weapons, and the confidence of the common people. (b) The confidence of the common people is the most crucial.
3. A "decent respect" for the world's opinion compels him to state the reasons behind the Revolution.
4. The unalienable rights are: life, liberty, and the pursuit of happiness.

Beyond the Selection

FURTHER READING

More Works by the Authors

The Dragon Book, E. D. Edwards, ed.
The Portable Thomas Jefferson, Merrill D. Peterson, ed.
The Family Letters of Thomas Jefferson, Edwin Morris Betts and James Adam Bear, Jr., eds.

Works About the Authors

The Heart of Confucius, Archie J. Bahm
Confucianism, Chai, Ch'u, and Winberg
Thomas Jefferson, William K. Bottoroff

Answers

◆ Critical Thinking

1. For Confucius, proper behavior within the family was the cornerstone of good government.
2. Jefferson states that there are "the laws of nature and of nature's God."
3. Both Confucius and Jefferson believed that effective government helps guide a people, and that it can only rule with the consent of the common people. Jefferson trusted the common people to overthrow a bad government; Confucius trusted that rebellion would not be necessary if people raised their families properly.
4. By invoking high principles and the colonists' patient suffering, and by writing in long, serious sentences, Jefferson makes revolution seem like the only reasonable, dignified course.
5. Confucius would say that if rules have moral force behind them they need not be written. If they are not backed by moral force, they are ineffective even if written down.

Thematic Connection

1. (a) Students may cite technological events such as the successful operation of the Hubbel Space Telescope, and the cooperative venture on the Mir Space Station. Disasters such as the World Trade Center and Oklahoma City bombings have also brought Americans together. (b) Pepys and Defoe described disasters of fire and disease that affected people more directly than most events in America do.
2. (a) Examples include: School anthems before an athletic competition rouse school and team spirit; military marches boast a nation's strength and boost its confidence to combat the enemy. (b) Students may cite "The Star-Spangled Banner"and "We Shall Overcome."

◆ Critical Thinking

INTERPRET

1. For Confucius, what is the relationship between behavior in a family and behavior in a nation? **[Interpret]**
2. Does Jefferson imply that there is a law above the laws that nations make? Explain. **[Infer]**
3. Compare and contrast effective and ineffective leadership as described by Confucius and Jefferson. **[Compare and Contrast]**

EVALUATE

4. How well does the language of *The Declaration* motivate people to unite in opposition to England? **[Assess]**

EXTEND

5. Judging by this passage from *The Analects*, what would Confucius say about the "unwritten rules" of athletic competitions? **[Physical Education Link]**

Thematic Connection

THE TIES THAT BIND

Pepys and Defoe write as witnesses to tragedies that brought a nation together in grief. Samuel Johnson, Confucius, and Jefferson all used words to bring people together—Johnson as a compiler of words that everyone spoke; Confucius as the speaker of words that almost everyone followed; and Jefferson as the shaper of words that moved people's hearts.

1. (a) In the past few years, what national triumphs or tragedies have brought Americans together? Explain. (b) Are these events similar to the ones that Pepys and Defoe describe? Why or why not?
2. (a) How can the words of songs lift and unite an audience or a people? (b) Name some songs that serve this purpose.

Idea Bank

Writing

1. **Yearbook Entry** In a brief paragraph that will accompany your yearbook photo, describe the experiences that have united you and your schoolmates.
2. **Analects for Today** Write three brief passages in the style of *The Analects* that teach moral lessons by using current-day situations.
3. **Imaginary Correspondence** Suppose that Samuel Johnson and Thomas Jefferson could have written to each other about American independence. Create a letter for each of them. **[Social Studies Link]**

Speaking and Listening

4. **Ask Confucius** With a group, do a call-in radio show called "Ask Confucius." Have people call in daily problems for Confucius to solve—callers can even be historical figures like Pepys or Jefferson. Be sure that the person playing Confucius answers in the spirit of *The Analects*. **[Media Link; Performing Arts Link]**

Project

5. **Charter or Constitution** Write a charter or constitution setting up a new organization, whether a study group or an athletic team. Be sure you specify the ties that bind the members together. **[Social Studies Link]**

Idea Bank

Customizing for
Performance Levels

Following are suggestions for matching Idea Bank topics with your students' performance levels:

Less Advanced Students: 1, 4
Average Students: 2, 4, 5
More Advanced Students: 3, 5

Customizing for
Learning Modalities

Following are suggestions for matching Idea Bank topics with your students' learning modalities:

Verbal/Linguistic: 1, 2, 3, 4, 5
Interpersonal: 4
Intrapersonal: 3

ASSESSMENT OPTIONS

Formal Assessment, pp. 126–127

PORTFOLIO ASSESSMENT

Use the following rubrics in the ***Alternative Assessment*** booklet to assess student writing:
Yearbook Entry: Narrative Based on Personal Experience Rubric, p. 97
Analects for Today: Problem-Solution Rubric, p. 102
Imaginary Correspondence: Persuasion Rubric, p. 106

Writing Process Workshop

Multimedia Presentation

The writers in this section present their ideas through one medium: written text. If you want to present ideas and information in a lively and engaging way, do a multimedia presentation. A multimedia presentation supplies information through a variety of media: slide shows, videos, audio recordings, graphs, charts, and fine art, as well as written materials.

Whether written or oral, your presentation is built on solid research and supported with a variety of media. The following skills, introduced in this section's Writing Mini-Lessons, will help make your multimedia presentation effective.

A
DICTIONARY
OF THE
ENGLISH LANGUAGE:
IN WHICH
The WORDS are deduced from their ORIGINALS,
AND
ILLUSTRATED in their DIFFERENT SIGNIFICATIONS
BY
EXAMPLES from the beſt WRITERS.
TO WHICH ARE PREFIXED,
A HISTORY of the LANGUAGE,
AND
AN ENGLISH GRAMMAR.
BY SAMUEL JOHNSON, A.M.
IN TWO VOLUMES
VOL. I.

HOR.

LONDON,
Printed by W. STRAHAN,
For J. and P. KNAPTON; T. and T. LONGMAN; C. HITCH and L. HAWES;
A. MILLAR; and R. and J. DODSLEY.
MDCCLV.

Writing Skills Focus

- ▶ **Accuracy** in a factual report creates a strong and effective presentation. It gives the viewer confidence in the conclusions you draw from your research. (See p. 473.)
- ▶ **Choosing sources that are appropriate for the medium** will allow you to create an effective presentation. (See p. 485.)
- ▶ **Elaborating to add a personal dimension** enables the viewer to make the connection between the media and the written or spoken part of your presentation. (See p. 531.)

Writing Model

A Multimedia Presentation of Samuel Johnson's *Dictionary*

Samuel Johnson's *Dictionary of the English Language* was published in 1755 and provided the first record of the English language. ①
The following are examples from his *Dictionary:*

pátron: One who countenances, supports or protects. Commonly a wretch who supports with insolence, and is paid with flattery. ②

As shown in this image of a current-day patron, a patron is still someone who supports but is not necessarily a "wretch." ③

① By providing the exact year of publication, the writer shows that the presentation includes accurate, factual details.

② The writer uses appropriate sources, such as Johnson's *Dictionary*.

③ By explaining why she includes the photo, the writer adds a personal dimension.

Beyond the Classroom

Career Connection

Media Editor Magazines, CD-ROMs, and film documentaries all present information in two or more media. Explain to students that photo editors and other media professionals are responsible for researching, acquiring, and even commissioning visual material.

A magazine editor who is working on an article on endangered animals might hire a photo editor to assemble pictures, charts, and maps to complement the article. After reading drafts of the article and noting points that will lend themselves well to illustration, the photo editor will begin to research what images various sources have to offer. If the editor notes a group of statistics in the article, he or she may hire a graphic artist to create a graph representing these facts. To capture a special subject, the editor might even organize a photo shoot in a wild animal preserve. Part of a photo editor's job is to ensure that the credit information required by each source appears with the piece.

Prepare and Engage

Establish Writing Guidelines
Introduce students to the following key elements of a multimedia presentation before beginning this lesson:

- A multimedia presentation provides information through a variety of media (forms of communication).
- A multimedia presentation may take the form of an oral presentation with audiovisual aids, or it may be displayed on a computer.
- Multimedia presentations must document and, where appropriate, cite their sources of information.
- Multimedia presentations require a thoughtful integration of media.

Review with students the criteria in the Scoring Rubric for a multimedia report in ***Alternative Assessment***, p. 108. See the suggestions on page 541 for additional criteria for customizing the rubric.

Refer students to the Writing Handbook, page 1189, for instruction in the writing process, and to page 1192 for further information on research writing.

Writer's Solution

Writers at Work Videodisc
To expose students to one of the many fields involving research, show them the videodisc segment featuring sports broadcaster Peter Ginsburg. Then ask students: How could they apply Ginsburg's suggestions to creating multimedia presentations?

Play frames 3 to 7599

Writing Lab CD-ROM
Have students who wish to draft on the computer work in the tutorial for Research Writing. They should follow these steps:

1. Review the annotated model of a multimedia presentation in the About Research section.
2. Under Organizing Information, use the Timeline to help storyboard their own presentation.
3. Draft their presentation on-line, referring to the instruction on citing and crediting sources.

Sourcebook
For additional help with multimedia presentations, students can review the chapter on Research Writing, pp. 130–165.

Develop Student Writing

Prewriting

Before they draft, students should create an outline under the general heads of which they group images, sound clips, as well as points to cover. You will find an Outline Organizer on pages 123–125 of the ***Writing and Language Transparencies***. If their final project will take the form of a computer presentation that allows users to visit different "areas," students might benefit from the Branching Organizer, page 95 of the ***Writing and Language Transparencies***.

Customize for
Visual/Spatial Learners

Invite these learners to imagine that each subtopic in their presentation is a room in a museum. As they draft, they should ask themselves, What objects—images, sounds, video clips—would I want to find in each room? What rooms should be close to each other?

Writing Lab CD-ROM

As they prepare to make an outline, students may benefit from the audio-annotated instruction under Organizing Information comparing different organizational strategies.

Drafting

Explain to students that elaboration to provide a personal dimension should help to unify the piece as well as create interest. For instance, the author can explain how he or she first became interested in the topic, then show how he or she responded to each new piece of information in light of this original motivation. In a presentation on her family history, for instance, the author might explain that the birth of a sibling inspired her research. She might then frame a story about a pioneer ancestor by noting how proud she will be one day to tell the story to her new sibling.

Customize for
Interpersonal Learners

Ask these students to sketch bits of a letter to a friend about the subject they have selected and about their discoveries as they research and assemble their project. They should then review the "letter" to get ideas about a possible unifying, personal viewpoint.

Applying Language Skills: Using Documentation

Through the following methods of documentation, you give credit to the sources used in your presentation.

Parenthetical Documentation: Include the source information in parentheses immediately after quoted passages.

Footnotes: Place a number at the end of the cited passage. Place the same number at the bottom of the page followed by source information. A subsequent citation from a book would include the note number, author's last name, and page number.

Endnotes: Place a number at the end of each cited passage. Create a separate page at the end for all of your source notes.

Writing Application Review your paper for quoted material or another person's ideas and make sure you have used appropriate documentation.

Writer's Solution Connection
Writing Lab

For more help in formatting citations, see the Drafting section in the Writing Lab tutorial on Research Writing.

Prewriting

Choose a Topic Do you have a strong interest in the literature or culture of another country? A unique hobby or skill? A high-tech profession? One of these interests may lead you to an idea for a multimedia presentation. You can also choose one of the topic ideas listed here.

Topic Ideas

- Poking fun at eighteenth-century high society
- Famous baseball players and statistics
- Great musicians
- Dictionary of British writers

Find Appropriate Print Sources Use an encyclopedia as a springboard for finding other sources; do not base your research on encyclopedia entries. Look for nonfiction books, CD-ROMs, and magazine or newspaper articles. The Internet is a great source of information, but sites may not be appropriate for a factual report if they are based on the creator's views. Evaluate them carefully before incorporating information from them in your report.

Find Media Sources Choose media carefully. Just because a piece of media may be related to your topic and purpose does not mean that it will reinforce the points you want to make. Look for pieces that directly support your topic and purpose. If audio, video, slideshows, illustrations, charts, or graphs require too much explanation, then they should not be included.

Drafting

Elaborate to Add a Personal Dimension As you put your multimedia presentation together, include details that make your presentation personal. Letting readers know your purpose can provide a personal element.

Document Accurately As you incorporate quotations and media into your report, make sure that you document them correctly in the written version of your report. Follow your teacher's requirements for footnotes or parenthetical documentation. Also make sure you copy all quotations exactly as they appear in the original text. If you only present orally, complete a Works Cited page that lists all your sources.

Writer's Solution

Writing Lab CD-ROM

Have students consult the instruction under Drafting on creating a strong introduction.

Writers at Work Videodisc

Play the videodisc segment in which Peter Ginsburg talks about writing his first draft. Ask students the following question: What considerations does Ginsburg keep in mind when he's writing?

Play frames 4970 to 5708

Applying Language Skills

Using Documentation Explain that while styles of documentation may vary, its purpose remains the same: to attribute ideas and facts to their original sources; to give the reader a sense of the sources drawn on (of their age, for instance); and to enable readers to consult the sources themselves.

Language Lab Have students who are quoting directly from sources complete the **Language Lab** lessons on Problems with Capitalization and on Semicolons, Colons, and Quotation Marks in the Punctuation unit. Students may also complete the worksheet on Quotation Marks and Underlining, page 87 in the *Writer's Solution Grammar Practice Book*.

Revising

Use the following checklist to help you evaluate and revise your presentation.

- ▶ Have I used elaboration to add a personal dimension?
  Look for places where adding personal details or explanation will clarify why you used certain information or media.
- ▶ Are my facts and citations accurate?
  Double-check dates, quotations, and page numbers to make sure your information is accurate. Look for statements that are not definitive, or use terms such as probably and I assume. Revise statements in which you draw conclusions but present them as fact.
- ▶ Did I use sources appropriate for the medium?
  Present your work to a peer and ask him or her to evaluate whether your presentation of media and fact are appropriate for a multimedia presentation based on research. If anything seems inappropriate, eliminate it.

Revision Model

Multimedia Report on Samuel Johnson's *Dictionary*

Although Johnson's *Dictionary* made him ~~really famous~~ ① a well-known writer it did not make him financially secure. ~~(Show cover of The Rambler.)~~ ② (Show picture of *The Dictionary*) ③ Who would have thought that this modest-looking *Dictionary* would be such a great contribution to literature.

① Changing *really famous*, which implies that Johnson received world-wide fame for his publication, to *a well-known writer*, which implies he was popular only among a certain group of people, is more accurate.
② Showing a picture of *The Rambler* is inappropriate because it is not directly related to the *Dictionary*.
③ This final detail adds a personal dimension to the piece.

Publishing

- ▶ **Internet** Publish your work on a site devoted to your topic.
- ▶ **Presentation to the Public** Show your multimedia presentation to an organization where your topic would be of particular interest. For example, if it's on basketball, present it to the high school basketball team.

Applying Language Skills: Incorporating Media

When preparing your multimedia presentation, work your media smoothly into your presentation. Include statements of introduction or explanations of inclusion.

For example:
When touring the homes of the literary figures of England, I saw Charles Dickens's home. As you can see from the photo, he worked in a comfortable setting.

Practice Rewrite the following paragraph, adding introductory statements for the media being presented.

Samuel Johnson was born September 18, 1709 in Lichfield, England. He was a scholar, but not an ideal student. Johnson did much of his learning on his own from books at his parents' home. He is best known for his creation of *A Dictionary of the English Language.*

Writer's Solution Connection
Writing Lab

For more help in incorporating media into your presentation, see instruction on creating maps, charts, and graphs in the Drafting section of the tutorial on Research Writing.

Revising

Students who are working on oral presentations should form small groups and rehearse by presenting to each other. Those who are preparing computer presentations may work in pairs to review each other's work. Reviewers should check that the drafts they are reviewing incorporate the suggestions in the Writing Skills Focus on page 539.

Writing Lab CD-ROM
Have students use the audio-annotated model of a revised bibliography to learn what revisions to their documentation may be necessary.

Publishing

Consider asking a CD replication house to put the class's computer-based multimedia work on a CD-ROM.

Reinforce and Extend

Reflect on Form and Content
After students have viewed each other's work, ask them to discuss what they have learned about multimedia. What kind of material became clearer or more engaging through multimedia? What kind of material did not?

Applying Language Skills

Sample Answer
Samuel Johnson was born September 18, 1709, in Lichtfield, England—a far cry from the big city, as this nineteenth-century drawing of the town makes plain. He was a scholar, but not an ideal student. Johnson did much of his learning on his own from books at his parent's home, perhaps studying late into the night in the room shown. He is best known for his creation of *A Dictionary of the English Language*, some definitions from which you can hear being read.

ASSESSMENT		4	3	2	1
PORTFOLIO ASSESSMENT Use the rubric on Description in ***Alternative Assessment*** (p. 11) to assess students' writing. Add these criteria to customize the rubric to this assignment.	**Accuracy and Precision**	The facts are adequately documented and stated with precision, as are connections between them.	The facts are adequately documented. For the most part, they are expressed with the appropriate degree of precision.	The facts are adequately documented.	In many cases, the presentation does not adequately document the facts. The facts are expressed in a vague, imprecise manner.
	Elaborating to Add Interest	The writer weaves personal touches throughout, integrating the work.	The writer weaves personal touches throughout most of the presentation.	The writer occasionally incorporates personal touches in the presentation.	The writer either does not incorporate any personal touches or uses them inappropriately.

Introduce the Strategy

Invite students to think of the last time they consulted the user's manual to an appliance or tool. At what point did their frustrations peak—when reading the step-by-step instructions, or when looking over a diagram? Chances are they found the graphic display of information a much easier route to mastery. Even using visual aids, though, requires some skill.

Customize for
Visual/Spatial Learners
Encourage these students to envision charts and graphs in terms of movement and effort. They might envision an historical chart such as the one on this page as a kind of race. With this imaginative framework in mind, the student can then begin to interpret the information by asking questions such as, Who is pushing ahead in the race for largest city in the year A.D. 2000?

Apply the Strategy

Answers

Suggested response:

1. The chart provides estimates of the population of the world's largest cities from ancient times to the year A.D. 2000.
2. The largest city in 1350 B.C. was Thebes. In 1925, it was New York. In 1985, it was Tokyo.
3. Constantinople, New York, Mexico City, Tokyo, and São Paulo each appear more than once.
4. Changes in urban population may have occurred because of wars and plagues (which would have decreased populations) or because of shifts in the center of economic power (people would be attracted to thriving cities).

Reading Visual Information

Real-World Reading Skills Workshop

Strategies for Success

A graph on your math final, a population chart in a history text, a weather map in the newspaper or on television—visual information is everywhere. Just as you need to be able to read and interpret the written word, you will need to read and interpret visual information as well.

Get an Overview Determine the purpose of the visual. What is it trying to show? Identify the elements that are being shown or measured, and restate the information in your own words.

Practice Reading Ask yourself questions about the information. For example, when looking at statistics about attendance at a state university ask yourself questions like, *How many people attended the university in 1987? How many people applied to the school in 1997?* Asking and answering questions will help you get the information you need.

Find Relationships Link items of information by identifying relationships between them. For example, is one piece of information the cause or effect of another? Also, draw conclusions about why the information was presented in this manner.

✓ *Here are other forms of writing that often call for reading visual information:*

- ▶ Weather reports
- ▶ Newspaper articles
- ▶ Reference books
- ▶ How-to articles and books

Apply the Strategies

Imagine you are researching the patterns of world population growth. Using this chart on population growth, answer the questions that follow.

Population of the World's Largest Urban Areas
(in thousands)

1350 B.C.		1000 A.D.		1600 A.D.	
Thebes, Egypt	100	Cordova, Spain	450	Peking, China	706
Memphis, Egypt	74	Constantinople, Turkey	450	Constantinople, Turkey	700
Babylon, Iraq	54	Kaifeng, China	400	Agra, India	500
Chengchow, China	40	Sian, China	300	Cairo, Egypt	400
Khattushas, Turkey	40	Kyoto, Japan	200	Osaka, Japan	400
1925 A.D.		**1985 A.D.**		**2000 A.D.**	
New York, US	7,774	Tokyo, Japan	19,000	Mexico City, Mexico	24,400
London, England	7,742	Mexico City, Mexico	16,700	São Paulo, Brazil	23.600
Tokyo, Japan	5,300	New York, US	15,600	Tokyo, Japan	21,300
Paris, France	4,800	São Paulo, Brazil	15,500	Calcutta, India	16,900
Berlin, Germany	4,013	Shanghai, China	12,100	Greater Bombay, India	16,400

All figures are estimates.

Source: Statistical Abstract of the United States.

1. What information does this chart provide?
2. What was the largest urban city in 1350 B.C.? In 1925? In 1985?
3. What cities appear more than once? Are there any relationships among the locations of largely populated cities in any given time period?
4. Draw conclusions about why changes in urban population may have occurred.

Cross-Curricular Connection: Social Studies

Information and Society Charts such as this one were made possible in part by the invention of the mechanical printing press. Printing allows the storage and wide dissemination of vast amounts of information, which can then be easily accessed and summarized by authors of charts. Such developments enable new kinds of knowledge, even new kinds of politics: with the accumulation of such statistics, scientists can study world population trends, and politicians can then conceptualize and debate the "population explosion." The way information is packaged can have a great effect on society itself.

Ask students the following questions:

1. By what means do you receive most of your information about the world? *Students may respond with "television," "the Internet," or "books and newspapers."*
2. What characteristics of this medium might influence society? Explain. *Students may reflect on the fact that television, for instance, is a medium of fleeting images and words: it emphasizes information and images with an immediate impact. Scandal and violence are natural subjects for it. The representation of scandal and violence arguably diminishes respect for public figures and for human life generally.*

Invite more advanced students to explore the work of Marshall McLuhan or others on the social effects of information technology, then report back to the class.

PART 4

Focus on Literary Forms: The Essay

Girl Writing by Lamplight
William Henry Hunt, The Mass Gallery, London

The titles of the new eighteenth-century periodicals—*The Rambler, The Spectator, The Tatler*—expressed the fun of getting out into the world, looking, listening, and telling. In the pages of these periodicals, the informal essay was also getting around. Like a friendly companion and guide, it was whispering into the public's ear, advising it what to think and telling it that it *was* a public!

One-Minute Planning Guide

The selections in this section focus on the informal essay, a form that came into being in periodicals of the eighteenth century. "On Spring" expresses the views of the erudite Samuel Johnson about that season and about the way he thought people should spend their spare time. The excerpt from Joseph Addison's "On the Aims of *The Spectator*," provides not only a mission statement for the newspaper, but also a satirical look at English society. The contemporary essay "Homeless" provides Anna Quindlen's views on a contemporary social issue, and shows how Johnson and Addison's journalistic legacy continues.

Customize for *Varying Student Needs*

When assigning the selections in this part, keep in mind these factors:

"On Spring"
- Short essay (3 pages)
- High-level vocabulary may prove challenging to less proficient readers and to English language learners
- Long, complex sentences may be difficult for English language learners

from "The Aims of *The Spectator*"
- Short essay (2 pages)
- Satirical tone will appeal to many students
- Long sentences may be difficult for English language learners

"Homeless"
- Short essay (2 pages)
- Most students will be able to relate readily to the topic

Humanities: Art

Girl Writing by Lamplight, by William Henry Hunt.

William Henry Hunt (1790–1864) ensured his later reputation with his experiments in watercolor. At first, he used watercolors as a wash or stain to fill in color between drawn lines. Interest in narrative paintings was growing in the eighteenth century, and Hunt began to portray solitary figures, whose activity suggests a surrounding story, as the figure in this watercolor. (He often chose more humorous subjects, as well, such as a boy sneaking a cigar.)

To better depict such interior scenes, though, and to concentrate on effects of light, Hunt combined watercolors with "body"—a mixture of watercolor with an opaque white paint. Later watercolorists followed in Hunt's experimental path.

Use the following questions for discussion:

1. How does the painter dramatize the interior life of his subject? *The portrait and other objects on the desk suggest the girl's interests. The fact that we cannot read what the girl is absorbed in writing, that her face is in shadow, and that, if she looks up, she will see a picture of which we can see only the back, suggest interior thoughts.*
2. How does the position of the lamp give the painting depth? *The lamp stands between the objects at the edge of the table and the girl behind, creating a transition into the painting's depth.*

Prepare and Engage

OBJECTIVES

1. To read, comprehend, interpret, and respond to two essays
2. To relate essays to personal experience
3. To make inferences about writers' underlying attitudes
4. To recognize the distinguishing characteristics of essays
5. To build vocabulary in context and learn the word root *-spec-*
6. To identify and use adjective clauses
7. To write an essay on human behavior using precise details
8. To respond to essays through writing, speaking and listening, and projects

SKILLS INSTRUCTION

Vocabulary: Word Roots: *-spec-*
Grammar: Adjective Clauses
Reading Strategy: Make Inferences
Literary Focus: Essay
Writing: Precise Details
Speaking and Listening: Satiric Monologue (teacher edition)
Critical Viewing: Interpret; Relate

PORTFOLIO OPPORTUNITIES

Writing: Advertisement; Seasonal Essay; Letter to the Editor
Speaking and Listening: Monologue; Satiric Monologue
Projects: Satirical Cartoons; Press Wars

More About the Authors

A recurring theme in most of **Samuel Johnson's** work is "wishful thinking": he believes people see things as they hope for them to be instead of as they are; he says people fill their minds with imaginings of better times to avoid the realities of the present moment. A prolific writer, Johnson slowed his pace when he finally received his pension in 1762, explaining that no one but a "blockhead" would write for any other reason but to make a living.

Joseph Addison, along with his partner Richard Steele, was clear to readers about his magazine's moral mission: to improve its readers. Decidedly agreeable and even charming in his essays, Addison could be both cold and calculating in real life.

Guide for Interpreting

Samuel Johnson *(1709–1784)*

Writing was never a promising way of making a living, but Samuel Johnson was determined to try. After a few unsuccessful projects, Johnson finally decided to move to London in 1737.

He got a break in the big city.

Success When he arrived, he bombarded *The Gentleman's Magazine*—the most successful magazine of the day—with his ideas and became an influential contributor. From 1750 to 1752, Johnson published his own magazine, *The Rambler*, twice a week. The essays and moral tales in the journal became popular after they were reprinted in book form.

Classics and Commerce Johnson's style is meticulously balanced, yet much of his work was done to meet the needs of the moment. Even the classic essays in *Lives of the Poets* were written for the market—a publisher, facing tough competition, commissioned them to dress up a new edition of English poetry. (For more on Johnson's life and his *Dictionary*, see p. 502.)

Joseph Addison *(1672–1719)*

In 1709, Joseph Addison, an Oxford-educated government official, eagerly read an article in *The Tatler,* an entertaining new literary magazine that had become all the rage in the coffeehouses of London. The article was signed "Isaac Bickerstaff," but Addison immediately recognized the style of Sir Richard Steele, an old college friend.

A Lifetime Partnership After Addison began submitting articles, notes, and suggestions to *The Tatler*, the two formed a lifetime partnership. Addison and Steele became the most celebrated journalists in England. Their essays in Steele's papers, *The Tatler* and *The Spectator,* earned them a permanent place in English literature.

A Stellar Career Addison's rapid rise as a journalist was one more step in a prospering literary career. Now, Addison's literary works, such as *The Campaign*, are remembered only by specialists. However, almost every magazine you can buy today uses the informal, popular style that he invented.

◆ Background for Understanding

CULTURE: NEWSPAPERS AND MAGAZINES

The first daily newspapers began appearing in England in 1702, the result of increased literacy, more efficient printing, and the fact that some people had more money to spend. The growing middle class was clamoring for information about the world. They also wanted a cheap source of written entertainment. Newspapers provided both.

As the market for words grew more sophisticated, magazines began to come into their own in the mid-1700's. The first periodical to take the name *magazine* (meaning "a storehouse") was *The Gentleman's Magazine,* founded in 1731. Originally, it reprinted selected articles from other journals. With Johnson's help, it expanded to include original writing, including criticism and poetry.

Johnson's, Addison's, and Steele's magazines helped create a new popular taste for sophisticated writing about books, ideas, and fashions. They popularized the brief, informal essay, which discussed issues in a relaxed, conversational manner. This tradition continues—*The New Yorker, The Atlantic,* and *Harper's* are, in spirit, the great-grandchildren of *The Tatler.*

Prentice Hall Literature Program Resources

REINFORCE / RETEACH / EXTEND

Selection Support Pages
Build Vocabulary: Word Roots: *-spec-*, p. 128
Grammar and Style: Adjective Clauses, p. 129
Reading Strategy: Make Inferences, p. 130
Literary Focus: Essay, p. 131

Strategies for Diverse Student Needs, p. 27

Beyond Literature
Career Connection: Periodical Writer, p. 27

Formal Assessment Selection Test, pp. 132–134; Assessment Resources Software

Alternative Assessment, p. 27

Writing and Language Transparencies
Writing Process Model 1: Reflective Essay, pp. 5–11

Resource Pro CD-ROM
"On Spring," from "The Aims of *The Spectator*"

Listening to Literature Audiocassettes
"On Spring," from "The Aims of *The Spectator*"

Art Transparencies
Transparency 12, p. 51; Transparency 14, p. 59; Transparency 17, p. 71

◆ On Spring ◆
from The Aims of the Spectator

◆ Literature and Your Life

Connect Your Experience

Kids bubble over with questions about what's out there and how it all fits together. As you grow older, you begin to ask questions about yourself: Who am I? What's important to me? These are not questions about facts but about your viewpoint and values.

Essays are a way of asking this kind of question. When Johnson writes on spring, he does not just give you facts. Using humor and argument, he lets you watch his mind work out a view of the world.

Journal Writing Compare some questions you asked as a kid with an important question you have about life now.

Thematic Focus: A Nation Divided

How do these essays show that, with turbulent times behind them, eighteenth-century authors could address life playfully?

◆ Reading Strategy

Make Inferences

To appreciate a writer's attitudes, you need to **make inferences**—reach logical conclusions about what the writer leaves unstated.

In the second paragraph of "On Spring," Johnson describes how, even after disappointments, we still find things to anticipate "with equal eagerness." Johnson implies that we do not learn from our setbacks. Because he seems easygoing about this fact, you can infer that his attitude toward this human weakness is one of mild amusement.

◆ Literary Focus

Essay

An **essay** is a short prose piece that explores a topic, as if the author were letting you overhear his or her thoughts. The word *essay* means an "attempt" or "a test" and was first applied to writing by Montaigne (1533–1592), a Frenchman whose essays questioned life without always finding answers. Although he wrote on many subjects, he said that his aim was always to learn about himself.

Johnson's and Addison's essays are each in their own way "tests"—experiments to discover the connections the mind can make as it reviews experience. In reading them, be aware of the observations they contain *and* of the mind that is doing the observing.

◆ Build Vocabulary

Word Roots: *-spec-*

Johnson calls his essay a speculation, meaning "reflections on a subject"—what the mind can "see," beyond what is there. *-Spec-*, the root in *speculation*, is from a Latin word meaning "to look."

Word Bank

Before you read, preview this list of words from the selections.

procured
divert
speculation
transient
affluence
contentious
trifles
embellishments

◆ Grammar and Style

Adjective Clauses

Both Johnson and Addison use **adjective clauses** —subordinate clauses beginning with the relative pronouns *who, whom, which, that,* and *whose*. These clauses qualify or describe nouns or pronouns that precede them, as in this example from Addison's essay:

. . . the mind *that lies fallow but a single day*

Interest Grabber As a homework assignment, ask students to bring in a copy of their favorite magazine. Stand the magazines on the chalk holder. Have students discuss why they like their magazines. Then explain today's magazine articles owe their informative, informal, fun style to the work of the authors in this selection.

Customize for
Less Proficient Readers
Have these students skim each essay from beginning to end. Then direct them to read it carefully and identify the main idea for each paragraph. Work with students individually or in a group to confirm that they can identify the main idea.

Customize for
More Advanced Students
Enlist the assistance of more advanced students to work as peer tutors with students who are having difficulty with the essays.

Customize for
English Language Learners
As needed, provide English language learners with simpler synonyms for the words in these essays.

Customize for
Visual/Spatial Learners
Have students bring some of the images in each of these essays to life by describing or drawing what they envision as, for example, Johnson describes "the variegated verdure of field and woods" and Addison describes "the blanks of society."

Preparing for Standardized Tests

Reading and Vocabulary The Build Vocabulary lesson focuses on the word root *-spec-*. Students may encounter words ranging from *inspection* to *circumspect* in reading-comprehension passages and sentence-completion items on standardized tests. Their ability to recognize a word root may help them understand the whole word. For additional practice, use the Build Vocabulary page in ***Selection Support,*** p. 128.

Grammar and Language Some standardized tests include questions that ask students to choose the best way to revise a passage. Usually, this passage is found within a larger paragraph. In some cases, the question may test students' ability to recognize adjective clauses. The following is an example:

Which is the best way to revise and combine the following sentences?
My aunt gave me the book. About the journalist. Name of Joseph Addison. *(B)*

(A) [As it is now.]
(B) The book that my aunt gave me was about the journalist Joseph Addison.
(C) My aunt gave me the book. About the journalist Joseph Addison.

The Grammar and Style lesson for this selection focuses on adjective clauses. For additional practice, use the Grammar and Style page in ***Selection Support,*** p. 129.

Develop Understanding

One-Minute Insight This essay is more than just a tribute to the beauty of spring; it is also a reflection on how people can adjust their attitudes and appreciate their surroundings in order to lead happier, more fulfilling lives.

◆ Literary Focus

❶ **Essay** Note that Johnson starts out right away with one of his central ideas. You might paraphrase it for students in this way: "Everyone is just unhappy enough with the present moment to look ahead to the future as a better time." Explain that the essay will explore this idea and use it to lead to other thoughts about spring and about life.

◆ Reading Strategy

❷ **Make Inferences** Ask students to make an inference to determine in which three parts of the year this person's hopes were in "full bloom" and in which part they were "never wholly blasted." *His hopes were in full bloom during winter, summer, and autumn; they were never wholly blasted in spring, even if hoped-for changes did not arrive.*

◆ Grammar and Style

❸ **Adjective Clauses** Point out the clause "whom it can be no shame to resemble." Call attention to the relative pronoun *whom* with which it begins. Ask students which word this clause modifies. *It modifies the word many.* Explain that *many* functions as a noun in this sentence, and that this clause is, therefore, an adjective clause.

On Spring

Samuel Johnson

Tuesday, April 3, 1750

Et nunc omnis ager, nunc omnis parturit arbos,
Nunc frondent silvae, nunc formosissimus annus.

Now ev'ry field, now ev'ry tree is green;
Now genial nature's fairest face is seen.

Virgil, *Eclogues III*, v. 56; Translator, Elphinston

❶ Every man is sufficiently discontented with some circumstances of his present state, to suffer his imagination to range more or less in quest of future happiness, and to fix upon some point of time, in which, by the removal of the inconvenience which now perplexes him, or acquisition of the advantage which he at present wants, he shall find the condition of his life very much improved.

When this time, which is too often expected with great impatience, at last arrives, it generally comes without the blessing for which it was desired; but we solace ourselves with some new prospect,[1] and press forward again with equal eagerness.

It is lucky for a man, in whom this temper prevails, when he turns his hopes upon things wholly out of his own power; since he forbears then to precipitate his affairs,[2] for the sake of the great event that is to complete his felicity, and waits for the blissful hour, with less neglect of the measures necessary to be taken in the mean time.

I have long known a person of this temper, who indulged his dream of happiness with less hurt to himself than such chimerical[3] wishes commonly produce, and adjusted his scheme with such address, that his hopes were in full bloom three parts of the year, and in the other part never wholly blasted. ❷ Many, perhaps, would be desirous of learning by what means he procured to himself such a cheap and lasting satisfaction. It was gained by a constant practice of referring the removal of all his uneasiness to the coming of the next spring; if his health was impaired, the spring would restore it; if what he wanted was at a high price, it would fall in value in the spring.

The spring, indeed, did often come without any of these effects, but he was always certain that the next would be more propitious; nor was ever convinced that the present spring would fail him before the middle of summer; for he always talked of the spring as coming till it was past, and when it was once past, everyone agreed with him that it was coming.

By long converse with this man, I am, perhaps, brought to feel immoderate pleasure in the contemplation of this delightful season; but I have the satisfaction of finding many, whom it can be no shame to resemble, infected with the same enthusiasm; ❸ for there is, I believe, scarce any poet of eminence, who has not left some

---

1. **solace ourselves with some new prospect:** Comfort ourselves with something new to look forward to.
2. **forbears then to precipitate his affairs:** Refrains from rushing his affairs.
3. **chimerical:** Unrealistic; fantastic.

Block Scheduling Strategies

Consider these suggestions to take advantage of extended class time:

- Introduce the concept of the essay, using the Literary Focus (p. 545) as a starting point. Reinforce the concept with the Literary Focus page in ***Selection Support,*** p. 131.
- In addition to the Build Vocabulary terms, go over any another terms that you think may be difficult for your students. Consider having students, particularly English language learners and less proficient readers, prepare a glossary before reading the essays.
- After students have read Addison's essay describing the purpose of *The Spectator,* they can apply its ideas of journalism to modern media through a round-table discussion, as described on page 27 in ***Alternative Assessment.***
- Enhance the Seasonal Essay writing activity in the Idea Bank (p. 553) by showing artwork to illustrate the seasons of summer, autumn, and winter. You may wish to display on the overhead projector Art Transparencies 12 (*Summer* by John Atkinson Grimshaw), 17 (*Wheat Field with Cypresses* by Vincent Van Gogh), and 14 (*Frosty Morning* by J.M.W. Turner), which are found on pages 51, 71, and 59 in ***Art Transparencies,*** respectively.

testimony of his fondness for the flowers, the zephyrs, and the warblers of the spring. Nor has the most luxuriant imagination been able to describe the serenity and happiness of the golden age,[4] otherwise than by giving a perpetual spring, as the highest reward of uncorrupted innocence.

4 ◆ **Literary Focus** Johnson tests the value of his own pleasure in spring. What tests does he use?

There is, indeed, something inexpressibly pleasing, in the annual renovation of the world, and the new display of the treasures of nature. The cold and darkness of winter, with the naked deformity of every object on which we turn our eyes, make us rejoice at the succeeding season, as well for what we have escaped, as for what we may enjoy; and every budding flower, which a warm situation brings early to our view, is considered by us as a messenger to notify the approach of more joyous days.

The spring affords to a mind, so free from the disturbance of cares or passions as to be vacant to calm amusements, almost every thing that our present state makes us capable of enjoying. The variegated verdure[5] of the fields and woods, the succession of grateful odors, the voice of pleasure pouring out its notes on every side, with the gladness apparently conceived by every animal, from the growth of his food, and the clemency of the weather, throw over the whole earth an air of gaiety, significantly expressed by the smile of nature.

Yet there are men to whom these scenes are able to give no delight, and who hurry away from all the varieties of rural beauty, to lose their hours, and divert their thoughts by cards, or assemblies, a tavern dinner, or the prattle of the day. 5

It may be laid down as a position which will seldom deceive, that when a man cannot bear his own company there is something wrong. He must fly from himself, either because he feels a tediousness in life from the equipoise[6] of an empty mind, which, having no tendency to one motion more than another but as it is impelled by some external power, must always have

4. **golden age:** In mythology, the time in the past when the world was free from suffering and evil.
5. **variegated verdure:** Varied greenery, striped or spotted with different colors.

6. **equipoise:** Balanced state.

◆ **Build Vocabulary**

procured (prō kyoord′) *v.*: Obtained; found

divert (də vurt′) *v.*: Amuse; entertain; distract

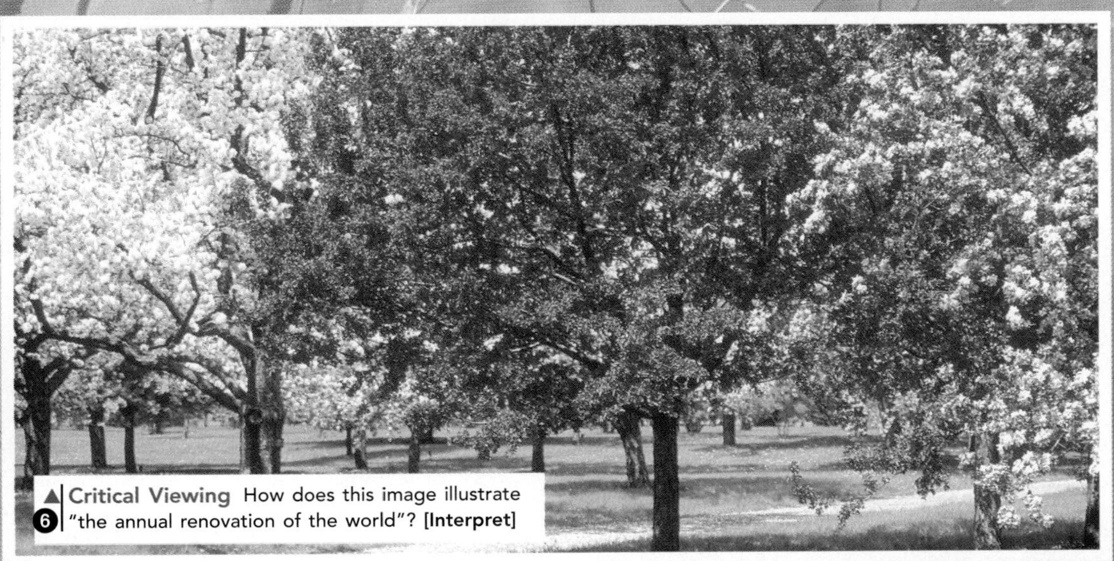

▲ **Critical Viewing** How does this image illustrate "the annual renovation of the world"? **[Interpret]** 6

Customize for
English Language Learners

Encourage English language learners to read "On Spring" slowly and to go back and reread. Reassure them that native speakers may well have to do the same thing to grasp this essay fully, because the sentences are longer, more complicated, and more flowery than those of modern English. You may wish to suggest the option of listening to the essay in whole or in part on the **Listening to Literature Audiocassettes.**

◆ Literary Focus

4 **Essay** Johnson finds that the best poets have all stated their fondness for spring and used spring as an image for humanity's Golden Age. Johnson's "test" of his feelings is the authority of literature.

◆ Reading Strategy

5 **Make Inferences** What can students infer about Johnson's attitudes toward the activities mentioned in the paragraph? *Suggested response: Johnson does not approve of socializing for the sake of socializing; he believes that people should take advantage of opportunities to enjoy nature or think quietly.* What modern activities might Johnson disapprove of for similar reasons? *Students may suggest that Johnson would look unfavorably on activities that cut a person off from nature or from being alone to think. Such activities might include hanging out at a mall, playing video games, or watching television.*

▶Critical Viewing◀

6 **Interpret** Each year the world is "renovated," or redone, or renewed, when spring comes. In the photograph, this renovation takes the form of new leaves and blossoms on trees.

Humanities: Photography

Buds on trees are among the time-honored heralds of spring. Here a grove of trees practically shimmers in the full light of midday. The day is perfect; the setting unspoiled.

Use these questions for discussion:

1. How does this photograph help to express "the variegated verdure" of spring? *The trees in new leaf exhibit an array of greenery; the modulations in the color green suggest variety, or variegated greenness.*
2. What do you find most inviting about the setting pictured here? *Students may respond to the color, the light, the suggestion of perfect weather and fresh air, the lack of any other human presence, the regularity of the plantings, and the possible freshness of the smells.*

Comprehension Check ☑

❶ Have students summarize these two paragraphs in their own words. *Student responses may contain the following points: Diversions are appropriate for those who are troubled, since they are already unable to enjoy contemplation. People who engage in diversions to keep themselves from worrying would be better off finding ways of preventing what they fear. Johnson means his advice for those who fail to engage in contemplation of nature not because they are grieving, ill, or worried, but because they apparently do not know how.*

◆ Critical Thinking

❷ **Interpret** Ask students to explain the metaphor "to whom the volume of nature is thrown open, without affording them pleasure or instruction, because they never learned to read the characters." *This metaphor compares nature to a book. Those who cannot enjoy nature are like those who cannot enjoy a book because they cannot read.*

◆ Literary Focus

❸ **Essay** Johnson has just made the point that people need to be open to new experiences—they need to be able to "take a walk" mentally and emotionally; they need to be able to find something new in their surroundings. Ask how Johnson explores this topic in this paragraph. *He mentions that some animals will change color when they change place; likewise, people ought to be able to readily change their thoughts, or look at things in new ways, as they move in new surroundings.*

▶Critical Viewing◀

❹ **Relate** The flowers are open, as people must be open to the experience of spring and to the experience of life. For Johnson, the flowers might also constitute one of the "productions of nature" in which people can find "an inexhaustible stock of materials upon which [to] employ [themselves.]"

recourse to foreign objects; or he must be afraid of the intrusion of some unpleasing ideas, and, perhaps, is struggling to escape from the remembrance of a loss, the fear of a calamity, or some other thought of greater horror.

Those whom sorrow incapacitates to enjoy the pleasures of contemplation, may properly apply to such diversions, provided they are innocent, as lay strong hold on the attention; and those, whom fear of any future affliction chains down to misery, must endeavor to obviate the
❶ danger.

❷ My considerations shall, on this occasion, be turned on such as are burthensome to themselves merely because they want subjects for reflection, and to whom the volume of nature is thrown open, without affording them pleasure or instruction, because they never learned to read the characters.[7]

A French author has advanced this seeming paradox, that *very few men know how to take a walk*; and, indeed, it is true, that few know how to take a walk with a prospect of any other pleasure, than the same company would have afforded them at home.

❸ There are animals that borrow their color from the neighboring body, and, consequently, vary their hue as they happen to change their place. In like manner it ought to be the endeavor of every man to derive his reflections from the objects about him; for it is to no purpose that he alters his position, if his attention ❸
continues fixed to the same point. The mind should be kept open to the access of every new idea, and so far disengaged[8] from the predominance of particular thoughts, as easily to accommodate itself to occasional entertainment.

A man that has formed this habit of turning every new object to his entertainment, finds in the productions of nature an inexhaustible stock of materials upon which he can employ himself, without any temptations to envy or malevolence; faults, perhaps, seldom totally avoided by those, whose judgment is much exercised upon the works of art. He has always a certain prospect of discovering new reasons for adoring the sovereign author of the universe, and probable hopes of making some discovery

7. **the characters:** Nature's signs.

8. **disengaged:** Free.

▼ **Critical Viewing** Relate the qualities of the flowers in the photograph to Johnson's description of spring. **[Relate]** ❹

Humanities: Photography

This photograph captures one of the quintessential spring flowers, the crocus, in full and beautiful bloom. The bright colors and satiny texture of the flowers form a pleasing contrast with the rough gray bark of the fallen log.

Use these questions for discussion:

1. Johnson might advise you to look at these crocuses as a form of "entertainment." What would he suggest you do with them? *Possible answer: Johnson would suggest that the onlooker study them and, perhaps, conduct experiments with them. The entertainment would consist of learning what one could from them.*
2. What would Johnson say about a person who could behold a sight like this one in nature and pass by it unmoved or unaffected? *Johnson might regard that person as guilty of wasting time, of wasting the possibility of spring, and of wasting his or her life. Such a person would have a "blighted spring," and the only thing that could follow such a spring is a "barren year."*

◆ **Reading Strategy**
What inference can you make about Johnson's attitude toward experimental science?

5 of benefit to others, or of profit to himself. There is no doubt but many vegetables and animals have qualities that might be of great use, to the knowledge of which there is not required much force of penetration, or fatigue of study, but only frequent experiments, and close attention. What is said by the chemists of their darling mercury, is, perhaps, true of everybody through the whole creation, that if a thousand lives should be spent upon it, all its properties would not be found out.

Mankind must necessarily be diversified by various tastes, since life affords and requires such multiplicity of employments, and a nation of naturalists is neither to be hoped, or desired; but it is surely not improper to point out a fresh amusement to those who languish in health, and repine in plenty, for want of some source of diversion that may be less easily exhausted, and to inform the multitudes of both sexes, who are burthened with every new day, that there are many shows which they have not seen.

He that enlarges his curiosity after the works of nature, demonstrably multiplies the inlets to happiness; and, therefore, the younger part of my readers, to whom I dedicate this vernal[9] speculation, must excuse me for calling upon them, to make use at once of the spring of the year, and the spring of life; to acquire, while their minds may be yet impressed with new images, a love of innocent pleasures, and an ardor for useful knowledge; and to remember, that a blighted spring makes a barren year, and that the vernal flowers, however beautiful and gay, are only intended by nature as preparatives to autumnal fruits.

9. **vernal:** Concerning spring

◆ **Build Vocabulary**

speculation (spek´ yo͞o lā´ shən) *n.*: Train of thought on a subject, especially one using hypotheses or guesses

Guide for Responding

◆ Literature and Your Life

Reader's Response What is your reaction to the coming of spring? How in tune is it with Johnson's feelings about the season?

Thematic Focus How does Johnson's idea of time compare with those of Donne or Marvell?

☑ Check Your Comprehension

1. According to Johnson, how do people take their minds off their present unhappiness?
2. What does the man who always fixes his thoughts on the coming spring do when spring turns out to be a disappointment?
3. According to Johnson, who is not heartened by the coming of spring?
4. What does Johnson think about science as a hobby?
5. What does nature offer the man who pays attention to the objects around him?

◆ Critical Thinking

INTERPRET

1. What is Johnson's opinion of people who are afraid to be alone with themselves? **[Interpret]**
2. What is the difference between Johnson's idea of happiness and the idea of those who are always looking forward to something? **[Compare and Contrast]**
3. Does Johnson claim that the person who is open to the wonders of nature will be a moral person? Explain your answer. **[Analyze]**
4. This essay is itself like a wandering walk. (a) List three of the points made along the way. (b) For each, show how it connects (or does not connect) to the others. **[Draw Conclusions]**

APPLY

5. Are you in the "spring of your life"? Explain. **[Relate]**

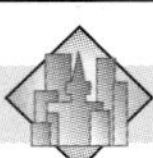

Beyond the Classroom

Career Connection

Botany and Conservation For the "budding" naturalist, many careers beckon. Students may consider careers in botany and in environmental science. Some may specialize to become park rangers; advocates for conservation groups; researchers for hospitals, health-care companies, and pharmaceutical corporations; or environmental lawyers.

Community Connection

Public Land Ask students to find out about conservation and recreation land in your community. Students might list sites, note their acreage and distinguishing features, and describe their intended use, such as active or passive recreation. Students might also visit such sites and record the types of animal and plant life they observe there.

◆ Reading Strategy

5 Make Inferences Johnson is a great fan of experimental science. He believes that through frequent experiments and close attention people can find peace and a renewed appreciation of God and nature, as well as learning useful or profitable things.

Reinforce and Extend

Answers

◆ **Literature and Your Life**

Reader's Response Students may find that they enjoy spring, and that their feelings about the season are in tune with Johnson's.

Thematic Focus For Donne and Marvell, time means loss and must be overcome, through passion, love or faith. For Johnson, our expectations determine the effect of time on us: playful contemplation of nature can free us from time.

☑ **Check Your Comprehension**

1. They console themselves with some new prospect.
2. He fixes his thoughts on the upcoming spring.
3. Those who prefer to socialize indoors do not relish spring.
4. It provides both entertainment and beneficial discoveries.
5. Nature offers entertainment; gives reasons for praising God; and promotes hope.

◆ **Critical Thinking**

1. The person either has "an empty mind" or is afraid of thinking about something unpleasant.
2. Johnson sees happiness as a habit of mind in the present, not as a possible future result.
3. Yes; according to Johnson, natural wonders can be studied "without any temptation to envy" and provide new reasons for "adoring" God.
4. (a) Themes include (1) the paradox of expectations, (2) the beauties of spring, and (3) the benefits of science. (b) Johnson links 1 and 2 by the anecdote about his spring-loving friend. 1 and 3 are linked by the contrasting ideas of happiness they involve.
5. Students may say that they are because they are young and full of potential.

Thrilled with the success of his paper, Addison sets out to tell his readers what his "aims" are. In an agreeable, witty voice, Addison promises to uplift his faithful readers by treating them to useful ideas and by instilling in them sound and useful sentiments.

◆ Build Vocabulary

❶ **The Word Root *-spec-*** Point out the word *spectator.* Ask students to relate the meaning of *spectator* to the meaning of the word root *-spec-.* *The root -spec- means "to look." A spectator is one who looks at or watches, especially at a sporting match.*

◆ Literary Focus

❷ **Essay** Explain that Addison's focus is more narrow than Johnson's: he sets out to tell the aims, or goals, of *The Spectator.* Yet, in doing so, he also explores an attitude towards life and the characteristics of his audience.

◆ Critical Thinking

❸ **Interpret** According to this statement, what does Addison intend to do for his readers? *He plans to make knowledge more easily accessible to them.*

◆ Reading Strategy

❹ **Make Inferences** Addison pokes gentle fun at some of his "good brothers and allies." He calls them lazy onlookers who cannot or do not form their own opinions. He thinks his paper will be good for them; he thinks it will give them something useful and productive to do. At the same time, he and his paper are not above them, since Addison calls himself a spectator.

from The Aims *of the* Spectator

❶ *The Spectator, No. 10,*
Monday, March 12, 1711

It is with much satisfaction that I hear this great city inquiring day by day after these my papers, and receiving my morning lectures with a becoming seriousness and attention. My publisher tells me that there are already three thousand of them distributed every day. So that if I allow twenty readers to every paper, which I look upon as a modest computation, I may reckon about three-score thousand[1] disciples in London and Westminster, who I hope will take care to distinguish themselves from the thoughtless herd of their ignorant and unattentive brethren. Since I have raised to myself so ❷ great an audience, I shall spare no pains to make their instruction agreeable, and their diversion useful. For which reasons I shall endeavor to enliven morality with wit, and to temper wit with morality, that my readers may, if possible, both ways find their account in the speculation of the day. And to the end that their virtue and discretion may not be short, transient, intermitting[2] starts of thought, I have resolved to refresh their memories from day to day, till I have recovered them out of that desperate state of vice and folly into which the age is fallen. The mind that lies fallow[3] but a single day sprouts up in follies that are only to be killed by a constant and assiduous culture. It was said of Socrates[4] that he brought philosophy down from heaven, to inhabit among men; and I shall be ambitious to have it said of me that I have brought philosophy ❸ out of closets and libraries, schools and colleges, to dwell in clubs and assemblies, at tea tables and in coffeehouses.

I would therefore in a very particular manner recommend these my speculations to all well-regulated families that set apart an hour in every morning for tea and bread and butter; and would earnestly advise them for their good to order this paper to be punctually served up, and to be looked upon as part of the tea equipage. . . .

In the next place, I would recommend this paper to the daily perusal of those gentlemen whom I cannot but consider as my good brothers and allies, I mean the fraternity of spectators, who live in the world without having anything to do in it; and either by the affluence of their fortunes or laziness of their dispositions have no other business with the rest of mankind but to look upon them. Under this class of men are comprehended all contemplative tradesmen, titular physicians, fellows of the Royal Society, Templars[5] that are not given to be contentious, and statesmen that are out of business; in short, everyone that considers the world as a theater, and desires to form a right judgment of those who are the actors on it.

> ◆ **Reading Strategy** From what Addison says about his "good brothers and allies," what inferences can you make about his attitude toward his paper and his readers? ❹

There is another set of men that I must likewise lay a claim to, whom I have lately called the blanks of society, as being altogether unfurnished with ideas, till the business and conversation of the day has supplied them. I have often considered these poor souls with an eye of great commiseration, when I have heard them asking the first man they have met with, whether there was any news stirring? and by that means gathering together materials for thinking. These needy persons do not know what to talk of till about twelve o'clock in the morning; for by that time they are pretty good judges of the weather, know which way the wind sits, and whether the Dutch mail[6] be come in. As they lie at the mercy of the first man they meet, and are grave or impertinent all the day long, according to the notions which they have imbibed in the morning, I would earnestly entreat them not to stir out of their chambers till they have read this paper, and do promise them that I will daily instil into them such sound and wholesome sentiments as shall have a good effect on their conversation for the ensuing twelve hours.

1. **three-score thousand:** Sixty thousand.
2. **intermitting:** Pausing at times; not constant.
3. **fallow:** Unused; unproductive.
4. **Socrates:** Ancient Greek philosopher (470?–399 B.C.), immortalized as a character in Plato's dialogues, who cross-examined ancient Athenians about their lives and values.
5. **titular physicians, fellows of the Royal Society, Templars:** Physicians in title only; members of a group dedicated to scientific research; lawyers or law students with offices in the Inner or Middle Temple.
6. **Dutch mail:** Mail from Europe bearing news of the war.

Speaking and Listening Mini-Lesson

Satiric Monologue
This mini-lesson supports the Speaking and Listening activity in the Idea Bank on p. 553.

Introduce the Concept A monologue is a dramatic speech for one person. A satiric monologue incorporates satire, which is humor mixed with criticism. Tell students that their monologues must be satiric and address the topic of "blanks."

Develop Background You might brainstorm with the class for a list of current-day "blanks." (Students might think of couch potatoes, people who never vote, or trendy people.)

Apply the Information Students may wish to work with a partner or small group. Each student may then practice before the group or partner, then critique the work of others. After students have rehearsed sufficiently, have them perform their monologues for the class.

Assess the Outcome You may wish to assess both how well students perform the monologue as well as how actively and politely they listen to the monologues performed by others. Work with the class to develop assessment criteria for both categories. For performing, criteria might include creating and sustaining interest and speaking loudly and clearly. For listening, criteria might include reacting appropriately and maintaining appropriate posture.

But there are none to whom this paper will be more useful than to the female world. I have often thought there has not been sufficient pains taken in finding out proper employments and diversions for the fair ones. Their amusements seem contrived for them, rather as they are women, than as they are reasonable creatures; and are more adapted to the sex than to the species. The toilet is their great sense of business, and the right adjusting of their hair the principal employment of their lives. The sorting of a suit of ribbons is reckoned a very good morning's work; and if they make an excursion to a mercer's or a toyshop,[7] so great a fatigue makes them unfit for anything else all the day after. Their more serious occupations are sewing and embroidery, and their greatest drudgery the preparation of jellies and sweetmeats. This, I say, is the state of ordinary women; though I know there are multitudes of those of a more elevated life and conversation, that move in an exalted sphere of knowledge and virtue, that join all the beauties of the mind to the ornaments of dress, and inspire a kind of awe and respect, as well as love, into their male beholders. I hope to increase the number of these by publishing this daily paper, which I shall always endeavor to make an innocent if not an improving entertainment, and by that means at least divert the minds of my female readers from greater trifles. At the same time, as I would fain give some finishing touches to those which are already the most beautiful pieces in human nature, I shall endeavor to point all those imperfections that are the blemishes, as well as those virtues which are the embellishments, of the sex.

7. **suit of ribbons . . . mercer's or a toyshop:** A suit of ribbons was a set of matching ribbons; a mercer's store sold fabrics, ribbons, and so on; a toyshop sold small items of little value.

◆ Build Vocabulary

speculation (spek´ yoo lā´ shən) *n.*: Train of thought on a subject, especially one using hypotheses or guesses

transient (tran´ shənt) *adj.*: Temporary; passing

affluence (af´ loo əns) *n.*: Abundant wealth

contentious (kən ten´ shus) *adj.*: Quarrelsome

trifles (trī´ fəlz) *n.*: Things of little value or importance; trivial matters

embellishments (em bel´ ish məntz) *n.*: Decorative touches; ornamentation

Guide for Responding

◆ Literature and Your Life

Reader's Response Did you identify with any of the readers to whom Addison is recommending *The Spectator?* Why or why not?

Thematic Focus What kinds of things would Addison change about English society?

☑ Check Your Comprehension

1. What reason does Addison give for making the instruction of his readers agreeable?
2. What does Addison think of the age in which he is living?
3. How does Addison define a "spectator"?
4. Aside from spectators, to what two groups of people does Addison recommend his paper?

◆ Critical Thinking

INTERPRET

1. Addison felt that *The Spectator* would set a high standard for the common reader. What proof of this attitude can you find in this selection? **[Support]**
2. Addison uses a sympathetic tone to discuss the "blanks of society." Do you believe his tone, or is he being funny? Explain your answer. **[Analyze]**
3. Explain Addison's attitude toward women. **[Interpret]**
4. What is Addison's attitude toward his own aims and towards his audience? Explain, using three examples. **[Draw Conclusions]**

EVALUATE

5. What's your opinion of Addison's introduction of his paper to the public? Will people want to read it? **[Assess]**

Reinforce and Extend

Answers

◆ Literature and Your Life

Reader's Response No one wants to be thought an empty-headed spectator, but students may see themselves in this role when watching television.

Thematic Focus Suggested response: Addison would want people to be concerned about and to discuss the real issues of the day, and to be less uninvolved, uninformed, or frivolous.

☑ Check Your Comprehension

1. Suggested response: He realizes he cannot maintain his large readership and infuse wit and morality into society unless he makes his instruction agreeable.
2. He thinks it is in a "desperate state of vice and folly."
3. Spectators live in the world without doing anything in it, either because they are wealthy and do not have to or because they are lazy.
4. He recommends it to "the blanks" and to females.

◆ Critical Thinking

1. Addison states that he hopes his readers will "take care to distinguish themselves from the thoughtless herd," and that he will increase the population of women "that move in an exalted sphere of knowledge and virtue."
2. Addison is getting a good laugh out of describing aggravating people whom everyone despises, people who cannot think for themselves.
3. Addison does not have a very favorable view of women, because he believes most only think of trivial matters. Yet he faults the amusements society has contrived for them, not women themselves.
4. Addison humorously exaggerates both his aims and the baseness of his audience. Examples include comparing himself to a coffee-house Socrates; acknowledging that his readers have nothing better to do; recommending a place for his paper at the breakfast table.
5. Possible response: The introduction is interesting and different. It would thus inspire people to read the paper.

Beyond the Selection

FURTHER READING

More Essays by Johnson, Addison and Steele

Rambler Nos. 31, 60: "On Idleness," "Biography"; "Thoughts in Westminster Abbey," "On the Scale of Being," "Country Manners"

More Famous Essays

"Advice to Youth," Mark Twain

"A Modest Proposal," Jonathan Swift

Preview these works before recommending them to students.

INTERNET

You and your students may find additional information about Samuel Johnson at the following Internet site. (Note: sites may have changed since publication.)

For Johnson, go to **http://www.english.upenn.edu/~jlynch/Johnson/index.html**

We *strongly recommend* that you preview the site before you send students to it.

Reinforce and Extend

Answers

◆ Reading Strategy

1. Johnson is making fun of the man who is always looking forward to next spring.
2. Johnson is contemptuous of men who do not delight in the scenes of spring.
3. Johnson is most earnest about the delights of refreshing thought with new objects.
4. Addison pokes fun at his readers, yet appeals to their sense of humor.
5. Addison's description of his age is overblown, yet probably not far from the truth of what some people of the day believed.

◆ Literary Focus

1. Possible responses: (a), (b) Johnson refers to "us" repeatedly when describing the joys of spring; this serves to draw the audience into an inclusive agreement. Johnson also speaks about "my considerations" as if he were speaking solely to the reader.
2. (a) Johnson turns from hopes for the future to happiness by discussing a friend who hopes for spring, then moving to the subject of spring. (b) The transition is not like a step in a logical argument; it is a digression that somehow, by the end of the essay, returns us to the opening subject.
3. (a) Addison belies his humorous attitude in the very beginning when he calls his readers "disciples," and likens himself to Socrates. (b) Addison identifies himself with his "good brothers and allies . . . the fraternity of spectators," and indeed has named his paper *The Spectator*. Yet by poking fun at society, he sets himself outside it, just like Socrates and the spectators.

Guide for Responding (continued)

◆ Reading Strategy

Make Inferences

You can **make inferences** from what writers state directly to figure out their underlying attitudes. For example, when Addison compares himself to the legendary Greek thinker Socrates, common sense tells you that he intends the comparison as an exaggeration. You can infer that Addison is gently poking fun at his own aims.

Make inferences about the author's attitude toward his subject in the following passages:

1. Johnson's description of the man who is always looking forward to spring
2. Johnson's description of men who do not delight in the scenes of spring
3. Johnson's description of the man who makes all new objects his entertainment
4. Addison's descriptions of his readers
5. Addison's description of his age as "a desperate state of vice and folly"

◆ Build Vocabulary

Using the Word Root *-spec-*

Now that you know that the word root *-spec-* means "to look," write definitions for these words:

1. inspection
2. respect
3. spectacle
4. aspect
5. spectacular

Using the Word Bank

On your paper write the letter of the word whose meaning is the closest to that of the first word.

1. embellishment: (a) food, (b) decoration, (c) remark
2. divert: (a) distract, (b) horrify, (c) inform
3. trifles: (a) trivia, (b) wonders, (c) dangers
4. contentious: (a) mild, (b) argumentative, (c) proud
5. procured: (a) obtained, (b) killed, (c) borrowed
6. affluence: (a) speed, (b) poverty, (c) wealth
7. transient: (a) powerful, (b) passing, (c) near
8. speculation: (a) reflection, (b) fear, (c) belief

◆ Literary Focus

Essay

Essays are informal discussions of a topic in which writers test out ideas and attitudes. You can sense this informality when Johnson tells you, "I have long known a person of this temper . . ." and proceeds to make gentle fun of his friend. You feel that he is chatting with you.

1. (a) Give two other examples from Johnson's essay showing an informal, personal tone. (b) Explain your choices.
2. (a) Where does Johnson's discussion turn from hopes for the future to happiness? (b) Is this transition "logical"? Explain.
3. (a) Give two examples of Addison's not-so-serious attitude toward himself or his readers. (b) Does Addison identify himself with a particular group, or does his attitude set him above the society he observes? Explain.

◆ Grammar and Style

Adjective Clauses

Adjective clauses provide further information about nouns and pronouns. You can use them to combine ideas in a single sentence.

Adjective clauses are clauses beginning with the relative pronouns *who, whom, which, that,* and *whose*. These clauses describe nouns or pronouns that precede them.

Practice On your paper, identify the adjective clauses in these sentences:

1. When this time, which is too often expected with great impatience, at last arrives. . . .
2. Every budding flower, which a warm situation brings early to our view, is considered by us as a messenger. . . .
3. I . . . recommend these my speculations to all well-regulated families that set apart an hour in every morning for tea and bread and butter. . . .
4. . . . they . . . are grave or impertinent all the day long, according to the notions which they have imbibed in the morning. . . .
5. . . . I allow twenty readers to every paper, which I look upon as a modest computation. . . .

◆ Build Vocabulary

1. inspection: careful examination; 2. respect: high regard; 3. spectacle: something to look at; 4. aspect: view; 5. spectacular: elaborately showy

Using the Word Bank

1. b 2. a 3. a 4. b 5. a 6. c 7. b 8. a

◆ Grammar and Style

1. which is too often expected with great impatience; 2. which a warm situation brings early to our view; 3. that set apart an hour in every morning for tea and bread and butter; 4. which they have imbibed in the morning; 5. which I look upon as a modest computation

For additional instruction and practice use the page on Adjective Clauses in the *Writer's Solution Grammar Practice Book*, p. 31.

Build Your Portfolio

Idea Bank

Writing

1. **Advertisement** Using the information from Addison's essay, make up an advertisement to promote the sale of *The Spectator*.

2. **Seasonal Essay** Write an informal essay on a season besides spring. Just as Johnson moves from the subject of spring to that of happiness and nature, tie your essay to larger themes.

3. **Letter to the Editor** Choose an article from a newspaper or magazine that interests you. Write a response to it and mail it to the editor.

Speaking and Listening

4. **Monologue** Practice reading aloud part of an essay to capture its tone—sarcastic, generous, or serious. Read your selection to the class. **[Performing Arts Link]**

5. **Satiric Monologue** Who are the "blanks" of today's society? Write and perform a brief monologue in which you poke fun at a contemporary "blank"—the surfer, perhaps, or the slacker. **[Performing Arts Link]**

Projects

6. **Satirical Cartoons** Magazines entertain their readers or express their opinions with cartoons. Create your own cartoons that comment on issues or trends, then display them in class. **[Art Link]**

7. **Press Wars** Magazines often compete with each other for readers. Divide into teams to produce two or more magazines about events and trends in school during the last couple of months. **[Career Link]**

Writing Mini-Lesson

Essay on Human Behavior

These essays offer sharp insights into human behavior and character. Write an essay about an aspect of human behavior that interests you. For example, you might describe the behavior of people at the beach. To convey your subject and your attitude toward it, choose precise details.

Writing Skills Focus: Precise Details

Your essay on human behavior will seem vital and relevant if you are able to furnish vivid, **precise details**—as Addison does when he describes the lounging lifestyle of some women:

Model From the Essay

The sorting of a suit of ribbons is reckoned a very good morning's work; and if they make an excursion to a mercer's or a toyshop, so great a fatigue makes them unfit for anything else all the day after.

By using precise details like these, you can create a perspective on your subject.

Prewriting Before you write, jot down precise impressions of your subject, including sensory details and adjectives describing attitudes.

Drafting Develop your notes as you draft. Focus your essay on a single scene or on several examples of a specific type of behavior. Choose specific details that highlight your attitude toward your subject.

Revising Ask a classmate to look over your draft and sum up the behavior you describe. Discuss where you could clarify your descriptions. Check your spelling, grammar, and punctuation. Finally, consider using adjective clauses to link your precise details to the nouns they concern. (For more on adjective clauses, see pp. 545 and 552.)

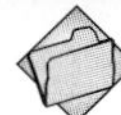

Idea Bank

Customizing for
Performance Levels

Following are suggestions for matching Idea Bank topics with your students' performance levels:

Less Advanced Students: 1, 4
Average Students: 2, 5, 6
More Advanced Students: 3, 7

Customizing for
Learning Modalities

Following are suggestions for matching Idea Bank topics with your students' learning modalities:

Visual/Spatial: 6
Interpersonal: 7
Verbal/Linguistic: 1, 2, 3, 4, 5, 6, 7

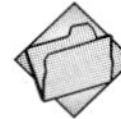

Writing Mini-Lesson

Refer students to the Writing Handbook, page 1189, for instruction on the writing process, and page 1191 for further information on exposition.

Art Transparencies

Display Art Transparency 12, John Atkinson Grimshaw's *Summer,* p. 51 in ***Art Transparencies,*** on the overhead projector. As an alternative to the Writing Mini-Lesson, you might want to assign Learning Option 4, p. 54 in ***Art Transparencies,*** which also focuses on precise details. This transparency may also be used to support the Seasonal Essay in the Idea Bank.

Writer's Solution

Writing Lab CD-ROM

Have students complete the tutorial on Exposition. Follow these steps:

1. Use the audio-annotated examples of different kinds of details.
2. View the interactive instruction on gathering details.
3. Draft on computer.
4. To help identify areas for revision, use the revision checker for unity and coherence.

Allow approximately 60 minutes of class time to complete these steps.

Sourcebook

Have students use Chapter 3, Exposition (pp. 62–95) for additional support. The chapter includes in-depth instruction on gathering details (pp. 80–81) and varying sentence structure (p. 92).

✓ ASSESSMENT OPTIONS

Formal Assessment, Selection Test, pp. 132–134, and Assessment Resources Software. The selection test is designed so that it can be easily customized to the performance levels of your students.
Alternative Assessment, p. 27, includes options for less advanced students, more advanced students, musical/rhythmic learners, interpersonal learners, and visual/spatial learners.

PORTFOLIO ASSESSMENT

Use the following rubrics in the ***Alternative Assessment*** booklet to assess student writing:
Advertisement: Persuasion Rubric, p. 106
Seasonal Essay: Description Rubric, p. 98
Letter to the Editor: Response to Literature Rubric, p. 111
Writing Mini-Lesson: Description Rubric, p. 98

Prepare and Engage

OBJECTIVES

1. To read, comprehend, and interpret a contemporary essay
2. To connect a modern essay to the essays of Johnson and Addison
3. To respond to the essay through writing, speaking and listening, and projects

PORTFOLIO OPPORTUNITIES

Writing: Public Service Advertisement; Newspaper Column; Response to Criticism
Speaking and Listening: Reporter's Interview
Project: Newsletter

More About the Author
After receiving the Pulitzer Prize, Quindlen told a *New York Times* reporter that she regarded her output as a journalist as akin to "having a conversation with a person . . . I can't see." Because Quindlen's following grew quite large and faithful, it seems her audience was hearing her part of the "conversation" and responding in their own way by continuing to read this fresh, different voice on the opinion pages of the newspaper. Instead of providing stuffy political analysis, Quindlen spoke concretely, sensitively, and caringly on the topics that concerned her most: families, child care, and homelessness.

Have students share their impressions of the homeless people they have observed. Encourage students to discuss how to solve the problem of homelessness in the United States. Explain that the essay that they are about to read deals with homelessness.

Customize for ***Logical/Mathematical Learners***
Invite these students to collect data about homelessness in the United States and present their findings in graphical form.

CONNECTIONS TO WORLD LITERATURE

Homeless

Anna Quindlen

Literary Connection

The Essay

The French writer Montaigne (män tān´) invented the **essay** in the sixteenth century as a brief prose work for exploring ideas, and the word *essay* itself means "an attempt or trial." In other words, you don't have to get things *right* in an essay. You just have to get them down, honestly following your thoughts wherever they lead.

In the eighteenth century—with works like Johnson's "On Spring" and Addison's "Aims of the Spectator"—the essay found a new home. It took up residence in the pages of the periodicals created by men like Addison and Steele. From those pages, it became a means of entertaining and informing a wider readership.

Anna Quindlen's column "Homeless" is a direct descendant of these periodical essays. It also appeared in a "periodical," although one with a slightly larger circulation than Steele's *Tatler: The New York Times*. Quindlen's column may be briefer and more politically oriented than those earlier essays but, like them, it speaks directly with readers about their world. Quindlen's whole effort is to make readers see with fresh eyes what is everywhere around them in the city—not "the homeless," but people without homes.

ANNA QUINDLEN
(1953–)

Anna Quindlen is currently a best-selling novelist. However, she first won recognition as a columnist for the *New York Times*. She provided a fresh voice in the editorial pages of that paper, addressing controversial issues like homelessness in a sensitive and caring manner. Her commentary won her the highest award in journalism, the Pulitzer Prize.

Thematic Connection

Even as Johnson's essay looks for tranquility amid shifting expectations of the future, and Addison contemplates a society that creates "empty" lives, Anna Quindlen's "Homeless" looks at a source of both inner and outer turbulence created by society in our own times.

Prentice Hall Literature Program Resources

REINFORCE / RETEACH / EXTEND

Selection Support Pages
Build Vocabulary, p. 132
Literary Connection, p. 133

Formal Assessment Selection Test, pp. 135–136; Assessment Resources Software

Resource Pro CD-ROM
"Homeless"—includes all resource material and customizable lesson plan

Listening to Literature Audiocassettes
"Homeless"

HOMELESS

ANNA QUINDLEN

CONNECTIONS TO WORLD LITERATURE

Her name was Ann, and we met in the Port Authority Bus Terminal[1] several Januarys ago. I was doing a story on homeless people. She said I was wasting my time talking to her; she was just passing ❶ through, although she'd been passing through for more than two weeks. To prove to me that this was true, she rummaged through a tote bag and a manila envelope and finally unfolded a sheet of typing paper and brought out her photographs.

They were not pictures of family, or friends, or even a dog or cat, its eyes brown-red in the flashbulb's light. They were pictures of a house. It was like a thousand houses in a hundred towns, not suburb, not city, but somewhere in between, with aluminum siding and a chain-link fence, a narrow driveway running up to a one-car garage and a patch of backyard. The house was yellow. I looked on the back for a date ❷ or a name, but neither was there. There was no need for discussion. I knew what she was trying to tell me, for it was something I had often felt. She was not adrift, alone, anonymous, although her bags and her raincoat with the grime shadowing its creases had made me believe she was. She had a house, or at least once upon a time had had one. Inside were curtains, a couch, a stove, potholders. You are where you live. She was somebody.

1. **Port Authority Bus Terminal:** Bus terminal located in New York City.

I've never been very good at looking at the big picture, taking the global view, and I've always been a person with an overactive sense of place, the legacy of an Irish grandfather. So it is natural that the thing that seems most wrong with the world to me right now is that there are so many people with no homes. I'm not simply talking about shelter from the elements, or three square meals a day or a mailing address to which the welfare people can send the check—although I know that all these are important for survival. I'm talking about a home, about precisely those kinds of feelings that have wound up in cross-stitch and French knots on samplers over the years.

Home is where the heart is. There's no place like it. I love my home with a ferocity totally out of proportion to its appearance or location. I love dumb things about it: the hot-water heater, the plastic rack you drain dishes in, the roof over my head, which occasionally leaks. And yet it is precisely those ❸ dumb things that make it what it is—a place of certainty, stability, predictability, privacy, for me and for my family. It is where I live. What more can you say about a place than that? That is everything.

Yet it is something that we have been edging away from gradually during my lifetime and the lifetimes of my parents and grandparents. There was a time when where you lived often was where you worked and where you grew the food you ate and even where you were buried. When that era passed,

Literary Connection

The Essay Call attention to the characteristics of Quindlen's essay. Note her use of the first-person singular *I* and the first-person plural *we*. Also note the essay's conversational tone and its images and metaphors from everyday life. Finally, point out how personal the author is: not only does she seem to "chat" with the reader, but she even goes so far as to bring up details about her own home.

Essays remain a vehicle for chatting with an audience. Sometimes these essays appear in newspapers, often under the headings of regular columns that, weekly or daily, draw the same readers. The voice of the columnist, who may be wise, shrewd, caring, or witty, calls out to readers in some way. In Quindlen's voice, readers have heard openness, emotion, inner searching, and even secret desires. A voice of the baby-boom generation, Quindlen is a modern-day Addison with a following that cuts more widely across class lines.

Develop Understanding

One-Minute Insight Quindlen makes the point that the term *homeless* is nothing but an adjective. When we use it, we ignore the nouns: the people who are homeless and the homes or the sense of home for which they yearn.

Customize for
Intrapersonal Learners
Invite intrapersonal learners to record their thoughts and feelings about the essay paragraph by paragraph. If you wish, provide these examples: In paragraph one, students might put themselves in Quindlen's shoes and imagine what it would be like to interview such people in such a place; in paragraph two, students might think about how they might respond to Ann's appearance as well as to her action of showing the photograph.

◆ Critical Thinking

❶ **Assess** Ask students whether they think Quindlen was wasting time by talking to Ann. How do they know? *No, Quindlen was not wasting her time. This is clear because she opens the essay with a mention of this encounter; clearly it was important; clearly it affected her.*

◆ Critical Thinking

❷ **Analyze** Ask students: How does Quindlen transform the homeless person she meets into a real person, a person without a home? *She recounts the story of the photograph. She shows that the woman has, or once had, a real place to live.*

Literary Connection

❸ **The Essay** Ask: How does this particular paragraph help the reader understand the problem of homelessness? *It mentions the concrete everyday objects that everyone uses and depends on; it associates them with certainty and stability; it elevates them in importance, showing how even little things like a dish drainer give a person a sense of place. By emphasizing what homeless people are missing, the paragraph helps the reader empathize with them.*

▶Critical Viewing◀

❶ **Infer** Her clothing is worn and dingy, assembled for warmth and ease rather than style. She is using a shopping cart to carry her belongings, probably all she owns. Her white plastic bag may contain cans to sell to a recycler.

◆ Literary Focus

❷ **The Essay** Some essays are more factual, some more emotional. Which aspect is emphasized in this paragraph? *The paragraph does not use facts, figures, or logical explanations. Rather it emphasizes emotions—a sense of loss and a feeling of connection.*

◆ Critical Thinking

❸ **Evaluate** Do students find these reasons for avoiding shelters convincing? *Students may find the fears listed reasonable, but wonder if pride of "ownership" can justify the discomfort of a doorway.*

◆ Critical Thinking

❹ **Make a Judgment** Have students decide whether making the distinction between *homeless* and *homeless people* can help solve problems. *Possible answers: Yes, because the problem must be solved in human terms; no, it takes more than new words to solve difficult problems.*

Reinforce and Extend

Answers

◆ Literature and Your Life

Reader's Response Students may respond that learning personal information about a homeless person makes it harder to dismiss homeless people as "a problem."

Thematic Focus It is a symptom of a fractured, disconnected, and ailing society.

Check Your Comprehension

1. (a) Ann is homeless, wears a grimy raincoat and carries a tote bag. (b) They meet in a bus terminal; Ann says she is "passing through," but remains for weeks.
2. Home used to be where families worked, lived, and were buried. Now it is often temporary real estate.
3. According to Quindlen, most people "walk around it."

CONNECTIONS TO WORLD LITERATURE

where you lived at least was where your parents had lived and where you would live with your children when you became enfeebled. Then, suddenly, where you lived was where you lived for three years, until you could move on to something else and something else again.

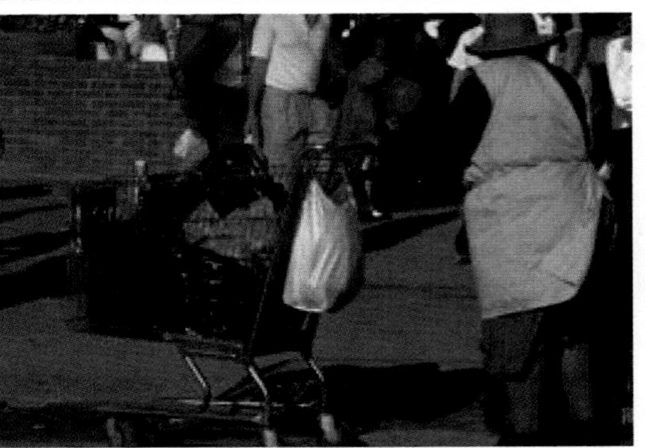

❶ ▲ **Critical Viewing** What details in this photograph show the conditions of this woman's situation? **[Infer]**

❷ And so we have come to something else again, to children who do not understand what it means to go to their rooms because they have never had a room, to men and women whose fantasy is a wall they can paint a color of their own choosing, to old people reduced to sitting on molded plastic chairs, their skin blue-white in the lights of a bus station, who pull pictures of houses out of their bags. Homes have stopped being homes. Now they are real estate.

❸ People find it curious that those without homes would rather sleep sitting up on benches or huddled in doorways than go to shelters. Certainly some prefer to do so because they are emotionally ill, because they have been locked in before and they are [darned] if they will be locked in again. Others are afraid of the violence and trouble they may find there. But some seem to want something that is not available in shelters, and they will not compromise, not for a cot, or oatmeal, or a shower with special soap that kills the bugs. "One room," a woman with a baby who was sleeping on her sister's floor, once told me, "painted blue." That was the crux of it; not size or location, but pride of ownership. Painted blue.

This is a difficult problem, and some wise and compassionate people are working hard at it. But in the main I think we work around it, just as we walk around it when it is lying on the sidewalk or sitting in the bus terminal—the problem, that is. It has been customary to take people's pain and lessen our own participation in it by turning it into an issue, not a collection of human beings. We turn an adjective into a noun: the poor, not poor people; the homeless, not Ann or the man who lives in the box or the woman who sleeps on the subway grate.

❹ Sometimes I think we would be better off if we forgot about the broad strokes and concentrated on the details. Here is a woman without a bureau. There is a man with no mirror, no wall to hang it on. They are not the homeless. They are people who have no homes. No drawer that holds the spoons. No window to look out upon the world. My [word]. That is everything.

Guide for Responding

◆ Literature and Your Life

Reader's Response In what ways did this essay change how you think about homeless people?

Thematic Focus How is the problem of homelessness a threat to society as a whole?

Check Your Comprehension

1. (a) Describe Ann. (b) Where does the author meet her, and what is Ann doing there?
2. Summarize Quindlen's description of how the definition of a home has changed.
3. According to Quindlen, how do most people deal with homelessness?

Beyond the Selection

FURTHER READING

Nonfiction by Anna Quindlen

Living Out Loud

Thinking Out Loud: On the Personal, the Political, the Public, and the Private

Poems for Life: Famous People Select Their Favorite Poem and Say Why It Inspires Them

We suggest that you preview these works before recommending them to students.

INTERNET

You and your students may find additional information about homelessness on the Internet. We suggest the following sites. Please be aware, however, that sites may have changed from the time we published this information.

The National Coalition for the Homeless site is at **http://nch.ari.net**

54 Ways You Can Help the Homeless, an electronic book, is found at **http://earthsystems.org/ways/**

We *strongly recommend* that you preview the sites before you send students to them.

◆ Critical Thinking

INTERPRET

1. What did Ann always carry with her at all times? Why is this possession so important to her? **[Interpret]**
2. Explain what Quindlen means when she says "Homes have stopped being homes. Now they are real estate." **[Interpret]**
3. (a) Why does Quindlen make a distinction between *the homeless* and *homeless people*?
   (b) What is the purpose of her essay? **[Draw Conclusions]**

EVALUATE

4. Is Quindlen's essay effective in getting you to see the homeless as real people? Why or why not? **[Criticize]**

APPLY

5. What do you think individuals and communities should do to help homeless people? **[Resolve]**

Connections to World Literature

THE ESSAY

The essay was invented as a means of exploring thoughts and feelings in a personal way. Whether the writer is Samuel Johnson or Anna Quindlen, you are always aware of the writer's presence. Writers use their personality on the page—and this is especially true in periodical and newspaper essays—to get you to see the social or political world in a fresh way.

1. Give two examples of Quindlen's use of an informal, personal tone. Explain your choices.
2. In what ways does Quindlen guide you to experiences you may not be able or willing to have on your own?
3. Compare and contrast Quindlen's essay with Johnson's or Addison's. Focus on differences of style—sentence and paragraph length, for example—and on differences in themes or concerns.
4. Will the essay find a new home and new life on the Internet? Why or why not?

Idea Bank

Writing

1. **Public Service Advertisement** Design a public service advertisement—for print, radio, television, or the Internet—in which you urge people to help the homeless.
2. **Newspaper Column** Select a social issue about which you have strong opinions. Express your ideas in a newspaper column like Quindlen's.
3. **Response to Criticism** After receiving the Pulitzer Prize for Commentary, Anna Quindlen remarked, "I think of a column as having a conversation with a person it just so happens I can't see." In an essay, discuss whether Quindlen's essay seems like such a "conversation."

Speaking and Listening

4. **Reporter's Interview** Reenact Quindlen's interview with Ann. Take your cues from what Quindlen says in her column, and add dialogue as necessary. **[Social Studies Link]**

Project

5. **Newsletter** Have your classmates write informal essays on a variety of subjects or on one particular theme. Then combine them into a newsletter that you distribute in your school. **[Social Studies Link]**

Answers

◆ Critical Thinking

1. She carried a photograph of the house she used to live in. It stands for her identity and self-worth.
2. She means that real estate is the mere basics: a shelter from the elements and a mailing address; whereas, a home comes with warmth, pride, and privacy.
3. (a) *Homeless* names an issue, "not a collection of human beings."
   (b) She gives us the details that enable us to see "the homeless" as people.
4. Quindlen's essay hits home with real details.
5. Answers may range from job programs to private acts of charity to public housing programs.

Connections to World Literature

1. Quindlen writes with a personal tone: ". . . I've always been a person with an overactive sense of place. . . ." She is informal in structure, using incomplete sentences as if they were thoughts strung together: "No drawer that holds the spoons. No window to look out upon the world."
2. Quindlen skillfully guides us *not* by describing homelessness, but by exploring what makes a home and so enabling us to feel what it would be like to lose a home.
3. Johnson's sentences are lengthy, balanced, and ornate; Addison's less so. Quindlen's are varied; many are short and punchy. Johnson speaks for all people; Addison writes from outside society, for society of a definite time; Quindlen speaks as a member of a particular society at a particular time.
4. Yes; magazines already exist on the Internet. Essays gain new life through the use of hypertext.

✓ ASSESSMENT OPTIONS

Formal Assessment, pp. 135–136.

PORTFOLIO ASSESSMENT

Use the following rubrics in the ***Alternative Assessment*** booklet to assess student writing:
Public Service Advertisement: Persuasion Rubric, p. 106
Newspaper Column: Persuasion Rubric, p. 106
Response to Criticism: Literary Analysis/Interpretation Rubric, p. 113

Customizing for
Learning Modalities
Following are suggestions for matching Idea Bank topics with your students' learning modalities:
Visual/Spatial: 1
Interpersonal: 5
Verbal/Linguistic: 1, 2, 3, 4, 5

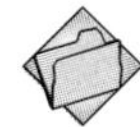

Idea Bank

Customizing for
Performance Levels
Following are suggestions for matching Idea Bank topics with your students' performance levels:
Less Advanced Students: 1
Average Students: 2, 5
More Advanced Students: 3, 4

Prepare and Engage

Establish Writing Guidelines
Introduce students to the following key elements of a reflective essay before beginning this lesson:

- In a reflective essay, a writer describes an experience that has helped shape his or her life in some way.
- The essay gives vivid details of the experience and also conveys the writer's emotional responses to it.
- The writer often reflects on the new significance the experience has acquired with the passage of time.

Review with students the criteria in the Scoring Rubric for a descriptive piece in ***Alternative Assessment***, page 98. See on page 560 for criteria you can add to the rubric to customize it for this workshop.

Refer students to the Writing Handbook, page 1189, for instruction in the writing process, and to page 1191 for more on description.

Writer's Solution

Writers at Work Videodisc
Play the videodisc segment featuring travel writer Guy Garcia for some insights into effective description. Then ask students: How does Garcia approach the task of describing for others what he has experienced first-hand? How might his comments apply to the composition of a reflective essay?

Play frames 335 to 10062

Writing Lab CD-ROM
Have students who wish to write their reflective essay on the computer work in the Description tutorial. They should follow these steps:

1. Use the Self-Interview Activity for topic ideas under Choosing a Topic.
2. Answer questions about their topic to help narrow it under Narrowing Your Topic.
3. Use the Notecards under Gathering Details to accumulate and organize material.
4. Draft their essay on-line, referring to the model under Drafting for tips on using figurative language.

Sourcebook
For additional help with writing an editorial, students can review Chapter 1, Description, pages 1–29.

Reflective Essay

Writing Process Workshop

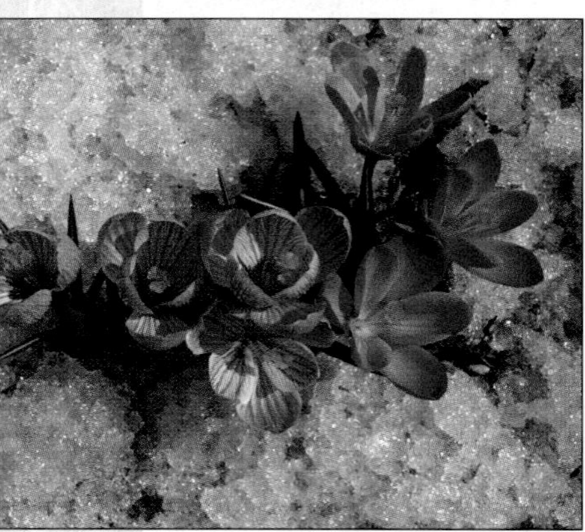

In Samuel Johnson's reflective essay "On Spring," he shares his thoughts about the nature of happiness and relates an anecdote about a friend of his. Write a reflective essay in which you describe an important personal event, experience, or observation. Bring your essay to life by providing vivid and precise details that convey your insights and emotional responses.

The following skills will help you write an effective reflective essay.

Writing Skills Focus

- **Keep a consistent point of view.** Write from the first-person point of view as you share your thoughts and emotional responses.
- **Set the mood** for readers by using colors, sounds, and other sensory details to capture an emotion.
- **Use precise details** to create pictures and capture sensations that convey the richness of your experience. (To learn more about this skill, see p. 553.)

Samuel Johnson used all these skills in his essay, "On Spring."

Model From Literature

from "On Spring" by Samuel Johnson

There is, indeed, something inexpressibly pleasing in the annual renovation of the world, and the new display of the treasures of nature. ① The cold and darkness of winter, with the naked deformity of every object on which we turn our eyes, make us rejoice at the succeeding season, as well for what we have escaped, as for what we may enjoy; and every budding flower, which a warm situation brings early to our view, is considered by us ② as a messenger to notify the approach of more joyous days. ③

① *Johnson establishes a mood of joy through his word choice.*

② *Johnson writes from a first-person plural point of view, using the pronouns us, we, and our.*

③ *Here, the first flower of spring is compared to a messenger bearing good news. Precise comparisons like this bring essays to life for readers.*

Enrichment

The Essay in History Explain to students that the reflective essay is a relatively late literary form. Before the 1500's, people did not publicly explore the details of their experiences except in a religious context. Montaigne's essays, published in 1595, were a breakthrough. Through his question, *Que sais-je?* ("What do I know?"), Montaigne put himself—his curiosity, his doubts, his feelings—at the center of his writing, albeit in a skeptical vein. Beginning in the late 1700's, Romantic writers such as William Hazlitt, Charles Lamb, and Thomas De Quincey also used the form as a tool of self-discovery or self-definition.

The reflective essay helped invent the modern idea of the individual—the person considered independently of social roles, defined by his or her experiences and sentiments. In our own time, we can perhaps see a strange outgrowth of this idea in talk shows that invite guests to reveal the grotesque or unhappy aspects of their personal lives.

Prewriting

Choose a Topic Since reflective essays revolve around personal experience, you may find a topic by recalling holidays, neighborhood adventures, schooltime experiences, or outings with friends. You can also use one of the topic ideas listed here.

Topic Ideas

- Your first day of high school
- A favorite place
- A memorable family celebration
- A remarkable friend

Develop a List of "Mood" Details Colors, sounds, and other sensory details will create a mood for your writing. To set the tone for your reflective writing, begin with a list of sensory details that support the mood you want to create.

Take Notes as You Recall the Experience Cast your thoughts back to the experience you're writing about. Jot down precise details that capture the events and your emotional response to them.

Drafting

Use a Consistent Point of View Use the first-person point of view as you draft your reflective essay. To make the experience immediate and interesting, give your personal reactions to these events, people, or circumstances.

Create a Mood Through Word Choice Establish a mood as you draft by using details that create a mood or atmosphere. Use comparisons, images, or words that have positive or negative associations to help you create a mood.

Use Precise Details Choose vivid verbs, precise nouns, and accurate comparisons to share with readers your personal experience.

▶ Neutral Mood
I saw that she was happy with my news.

▶ Mood of Happiness
Her face lit up like a ray of sunshine when I gave her the news.

Applying Language Skills: Using Vivid Verbs

Use vivid verbs to bring your essay to life. A vivid verb describes a precise action and needs no modifier.

Weak Verb With Modifiers:
Louise walked slowly and painfully around the track.

Vivid Verb:
Louise limped around the track.

Practice Write the following sentences in your notebook, replacing the underlined words with one precise verb.

1. The children at the playground shrilly yelled.
2. The band slowly ended the last song.
3. In Italy, we drove slowly through the wine country.
4. The students in the cafeteria quickly ate the ice cream.

Writing Application When drafting your essay, don't spend too much time thinking up vivid verbs. Mark the place and continue writing. When your draft is finished, use a thesaurus to help you find vivid verbs.

Writer's Solution Connection Writing Lab

For tips on organizing, see the Writing Models in the Organizing Details section of the tutorial on Description.

Develop Student Writing

Prewriting

Students may find topics by looking through any journals, scrapbooks, yearbooks, or photo albums that they keep, or by browsing through their music collection and playing songs they have not heard for a while. You may wish to distribute copies of the Branching organizer in the ***Writing and Language Transparencies,*** pages 95–97, which students may find useful for keeping track of chains of associations.

Customize for *Interpersonal Learners*
Pair these students and ask them to chat about interesting events in their lives. Each should then ask the other which of the topics he or she mentioned sounds most interesting.

Customize for *Visual/Spatial Learners*
Ask these students to take an imaginary walk through a building or place from their past. As they pass through each room or area in their mind's eye, they should jot down important details, both of the surroundings and of associated thoughts and feelings.

Drafting

Suggest to students that they work up an imaginary character, one who would be an ideal reader for their reflective essay. The person might be much older than they are (someone with varied experiences of their own) or much younger (someone who may learn from the essay). Encourage students to keep this imaginary reader in mind as their audience: this exercise will help them keep a consistent point of view and mood.

Applying Language Skills

Using Vivid Verbs Explain to students that much of the force of a reflective essay depends on the reader's feeling that he or she is "there," involved in the events being recounted or the thoughts being worked through. Vivid verbs let the action speak for itself, drawing the reader into the scene.

Answers

1. The children at the playground screeched.
2. The band wound down the last song
3. In Italy, we rambled through the wine country.
4. The students in the cafeteria wolfed down the ice cream.

Writer's Solution

For additional practice in using vivid verbs, have students complete the **Language Lab** lesson on Writing with Nouns and Verbs, in the Writing Style unit.

Revising

Students may work together in pairs to revise their work. As they review their partners' papers, they should follow the suggestions on this page. In addition, have students check that the drafts they are reviewing incorporate the suggestions in the Writing Skills Focus on page 558.

Writer's Solution

Writers at Work Videodisc

Play the videodisc section in which Guy Garcia discusses his approach to revision and editing. Ask students the following questions: What does Garcia believe an outside editor contributes to the revision process?

Play frames 8629 to 10062

Writing Lab CD-ROM

Have peer reviewers use the Peer Evaluation Checklist under Revising and Editing to help them give drafts a thorough review.

Reinforce and Extend

Reflect on Reflection

After students have completed their papers, ask them to discuss what they learned about reflective writing from this process. Did they feel that the process of putting experience into words on a page helped them better understand the past?

Extension Have students, individually or in collaboration with an artistically talented fellow-student, produce illustrations to accompany the student's reflective essay in an anthology.

Applying Language Skills

Answers

1. good; 2. badly; 3. these; 4. this

Applying Language Skills: Using Troublesome Modifiers Correctly

These commonly used modifiers are often used incorrectly.

1. good/well: Use *good* as an adjective, *well* as an adverb.
2. bad/badly: Use *bad* after linking verbs such as *feel*, *look*, and *seem*. Use *badly* as an adverb.
3. this (these)/that (those): Use *this* to distinguish the thing that is nearer in comparison.

Practice Rewrite each sentence, choosing the correct term.

1. That birthday cake looks (good, well).
2. They were (bad, badly) injured in the skiing accident.
3. (These, Those) students in this room went to Washington.
4. The summer session is only for students who earned a C or a D in (this, that) class.

Writer's Solution Connection
Language Lab

For help in using Modifiers, see the lesson on Problems with Modifiers in the Modifiers unit.

Revising

Read Your Reflective Essay Aloud Make an audiotape of your reflective essay. Listen and ask yourself the following questions:

- ▶ What language and details should I add or change to give my reflective essay a mood?
- ▶ What examples of elaboration can I add to give my writing a more personal feel?
- ▶ Does my reflective essay have a consistent point of view?

Proofread Read your paper beginning with the last paragraph searching for grammatical and spelling errors.

Revision Model

① The students stared at me as I entered the classroom.
~~The students studied the new kid.~~ Red with embarrassment,
② The clock on the wall seemed to be abnormally loud as the students silently pronounced a judgment on me.
I felt myself shrinking within my stiff new school uniform.
③ saying in his thin reedy voice, "Meet Jim Harte, who has recently moved here from Scranton."
Mr. Kelso broke the silence by ~~introducing me~~.

① This sentence was changed to make the first-person point of view more consistent.
② To enhance the mood of the essay, this detail about the sound of the clock was added.
③ Using precise details—sharing the teacher's exact words—gives the essay a more personal appeal.

Publishing

- ▶ **Classroom** Read your essay aloud to a small group of students.
- ▶ **School Magazine** Submit your reflective essay to your school literary magazine.
- ▶ **Writing Contest** Ask your teacher or librarian for information on student writing contests.
- ▶ **Anthology** Collect and organize the essays written by your class into a single volume. Consider organizing essays according to mood or time period.

ASSESSMENT		4	3	2	1
PORTFOLIO ASSESSMENT Use the rubric on Description in ***Alternative Assessment*** (p. 98) to assess students' writing. Add these criteria to customize the rubric to this assignment.	**Setting a Mood**	The essay maintains a consistent mood through ample details describing setting and emotion.	Most details contribute to the mood of the piece.	It is not always clear what mood details are intended to create.	The essay provides few descriptive details. No overall mood is indicated.
	Use of Precise Details	Descriptive details and figurative language create a strong picture of events and feelings.	Vivid verbs and precise nouns convey details sharply.	For the most part, the writer uses vivid verbs and precise nouns.	The writer's language is neutral or flat; it fails to present details vividly.

Real-World Reading Skills Workshop

Reading to Enrich Your Life

Strategies for Success

Imagine being able to participate in a challenging mountain climb, an expedition to the North Pole, or a sailing trip around the world. Although these adventures may seem beyond reach, you can experience them vicariously by reading articles, essays, and books.

Enlarge Your Experience For the space of time it takes to read an article, you can become someone else. You can identify with the writer and live vicariously, partaking of experience as though you were seeing and doing right along with the writer.

Relate Your Experience to Others' Perhaps your experience compares in some way to the author's. In that case, you can have a dialogue as you might with a friend. If you have never experienced anything similar, you may want to dream that you will, or be glad that you never will!

Gain Understanding By reading about someone else's experiences, you can begin to understand his or her viewpoint. Understanding other people's perspectives will help you become more tolerant and accepting. It may also inspire you to reach out to others in new ways.

Apply the Strategies

Reading through a college newsletter, you come across a student's description of how she spent spring break. Read about the student's trip to Ireland (in the left column). Answer the following questions to show how you might use the piece to enrich your life.

1. What experiences have you had that are similar to the one the writer describes?
2. Does this article inspire you to travel? Why or why not?
3. Does this article give you any new understanding of other people? Explain.

TRIP TO IRELAND

I traveled to Ireland during spring break this year. I had saved a great deal of money by working, so I thought I deserved to take a trip to Ireland to celebrate St. Patrick's Day. This trip opened my eyes in many ways. For example, I discovered that the Irish, like people in Savannah, Georgia, dye the water green. Also, I discovered that being an American, I was treated almost as a celebrity and was even asked to join the parade. I had never been in a foreign country where I felt so much at home.

Here are other forms of writing that can enrich your life:

- Novels
- Short stories
- Memoirs
- Humorous essays

Introduce the Strategy

Invite students to consider a cranky baby, squalling because it is hungry or needs its diaper changed. Consumed by its immediate needs, the baby knows nothing of the future or past.

People stop being babies when they learn to see beyond the present, and project themselves into a future self, realizing that "tomorrow things can be different for me." Suggest to students that this habit involves almost as great a stretch of the imagination as the ability to lose oneself in a fictional character.

The uncanny ability to be someone else, then, is actually important to being who one is. It helps one envision a future; it also helps one to re-envision the present and its burdens, so one doesn't have to just sit there squalling about them. Suggest to students that, by reading fiction and identifying with characters different from themselves, they are actually developing a talent for addressing reality.

Customize for
Musical/Rhythmic Learners
Suggest to these students that understanding someone else's viewpoint is something like appreciating a particular melody or rhythmic pattern. Ask these students to think of a character from their recent reading. What kind of music or rhythm would they associate with this character? Why?

Apply the Strategy

Answers

Suggested responses:

1. Students may respond that they have also traveled on spring break; worked hard to save money; or had a travel experience that changed their perspective.
2. Students may respond that the article encourages them to travel by making them curious about the customs of others, or that it discourages them since it suggests that life is pretty much the same everywhere.
3. Students may reply that the excerpt made them think how the familiar can seem foreign (an ordinary American becomes a celebrity in Ireland) and the foreign familiar (the Irish themselves dye the water green on St. Patrick's Day).

Enrichment

Art Transparencies Explain to students that painters often suggest their subjects' viewpoint on life, as well as their external appearance. Place Art Transparencies 12 and 13, *Summer* by John Atkinson Grimshaw and *Standing Spinner* by John François Millet, in ***Art Transparencies,*** pp. 51 and 53, on an overhead projector.

Ask students the following questions. List their ideas on the board in two columns, one for each painting. Elicit and indicate connections between descriptive details and interpretations.

1. Describe the different environments of the two paintings. *Grimshaw's setting is middle-class, over-filled with decorations; Millet's is a peasant's work area, bare of any but essential details.*
2. (a) Contrast the attitudes of the main figures towards their environment. (b) Explain which details express this attitude. *(a) Grimshaw's lady is looking away from where she is, as if she wishes to escape her environment. Millet's peasant looks deeper into the painting's interior, as if she wants to remain lost in her environment. (b) Grimshaw's woman's face stands out as a welcome relief from the rich patterns; we wonder what natural sights she sees; Millet's peasant, half in shadow, her face expressionless, seems an extension of the spinning wheel.*

Introduce the Strategy

From spreadsheets to multimedia demos, the integration of word and image is a defining feature of today's business world. In less "high tech" settings, a diagram on a chalkboard can help a speaker make a point effectively. Tell students that the skills they acquire coordinating their oral presentation with visual displays is a vital skill in a number of careers.

Activity Have a school staff person who is familiar with the school's audiovisual equipment conduct a few small, hands-on seminars for students. Each student should each get a chance to practice using each different kind of equipment. They should make it their goal to determine which equipment is best suited for their presentation.

Customize for
Bodily/Kinesthetic Learners
Encourage these students to lend their expertise to the class by examining the other students' drafted setups for their presentations. Where are the controls for each piece of equipment to be used? How easy will it be for the presenter to reach them at various points in the presentation? What are the best locations for monitors for the audience? Bodily/kinesthetic learners should be able to assist other students in devising workable setups for presentations.

Apply the Strategy

Answers

1. Students should consider what means they will use to project the map; whether they should mark spots of interest on the map prior to the presentation; and how they will coordinate the use of the map with other visuals.
2. Students should consider how to avoid redundant images. Students should also consider including "before and after" shots, as well as photos of participants in the project, a map of the trail, and information on its history.
3. Students should consider the style of these drawings (how stylized or how detailed), their size, the means used to display them, and how to coordinate them with any role-playing.

Speaking and Listening Workshop

Oral Presentation with Visuals

Strategies for Success

Visuals like maps, videotapes, overhead projections, and charts can make a speech or other oral presentation more effective. If you don't have sophisticated visual displays and equipment, drawing or writing on a board or pad as you talk can help convey key ideas. These visuals may include maps, videotapes, overhead projections, graphs, charts, or notes you write on a board or drawing pad as you talk.

Good Planning Pays Off You may have sat through presentations where the speaker has fumbled with a VCR that wasn't hooked up correctly or has displayed maps showing the wrong country. Planning and practice can help you avoid these mishaps and smoothly combine what you say and what you show.

Tips for Giving an Oral Presentation With Visuals

Follow these strategies to use visuals effectively:

- Only include visuals that illustrate your points. Otherwise, they will distract from your presentation.
- Be sure that any equipment such as the VCR, if you are using one, is in working order. If you will need to dim the lights, have a partner work with you. Be sure that you agree on signals and timing.
- Rehearse your presentation several times. If possible, have a dress rehearsal in front of someone who can critique your presentation.
- In general, make your point orally first, then show the visual to illustrate it. Gesture toward the visual as you explain the key points.

Apply the Strategies

With a partner, take turns role-playing one of these situations. Work out an integrated verbal and visual presentation that will inform your audience in an entertaining way. Have your partner critique your presentation when you are done.

1. You're an exchange student just back from six months in another country. Use a map of the city where you lived to talk about places you saw.
2. You're a member of a hiking club involved in a trail reclamation project. Use photographs of overgrown areas of the trail to demonstrate the work that needs to be done.
3. You're a camp counselor teaching a class in life-saving techniques. Use drawings to teach the Heimlich Maneuver to your campers.

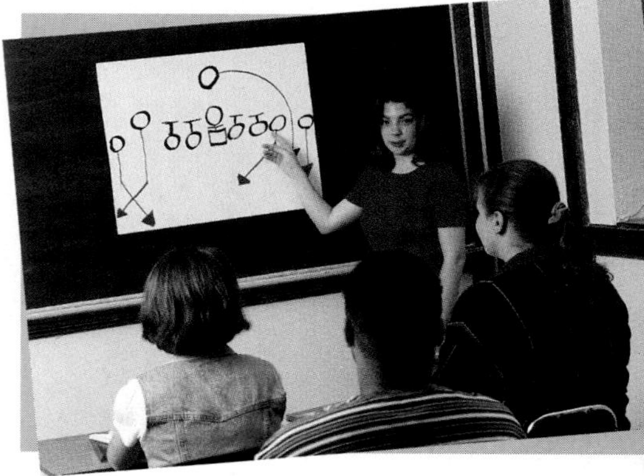

Beyond the Classroom

Career Connection

Sales Representative The computer revolution has enabled more people than ever to incorporate visuals into their presentations. From overhead transparencies to multimedia demos, teachers and businesspeople of all sorts must design and sometimes even produce visual aids. Sales representatives, for instance, may use CD-ROMs with a laptop computer hooked up to a video monitor. When they talk to clients about a new facility, procedure, or product, they can quickly call up graphs, charts, or pictures underscoring its virtues. The sales reprentative must be familiar with the use of the laptop computer, though, to ensure that he or she does not become entangled in technical difficulties and lose the client's interest.

Extended Reading Opportunities

These novels of adventure, satire, and comedy depict different aspects of life during the seventeenth and eighteenth centuries.

Suggested Titles

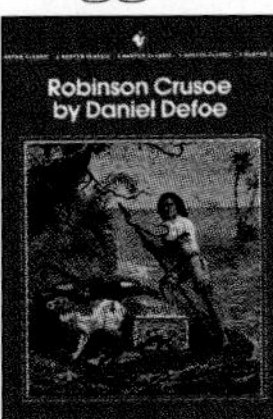

Robinson Crusoe
Daniel Defoe

Defoe's *Robinson Crusoe* marked the beginning of the modern English novel. It is, however, a novel populated mostly by a single character. In 1659, Crusoe is shipwrecked on an island off the coast of South America and begins a twenty-eight-year stay on the island. Although specific history is not alluded to, Crusoe is very much a product of his time—he grew up during England's Civil War and its restoration. Crusoe's attempts to create a decent society and improve his own moral character echo England's struggles to restore itself after the political turmoil of the Civil War.

Gulliver's Travels
Jonathan Swift

Swift's *Gulliver's Travels* is a children's story, a fantasy, a parody of travel books, and a sophisticated satire of English politics all in one. This masterpiece describes four voyages of Lemuel Gulliver, a ship's physician, to exotic lands. Gulliver begins in Lilliput, where the inhabitants are one-twelfth the size of human beings. By the story's end, the playful elements have yielded to a bitter indictment of humankind's corruption of reason. Swift's unique combination of allegory—using settings, objects, or characters to stand for ideas and qualities beyond themselves—has made his work appeal to all audiences.

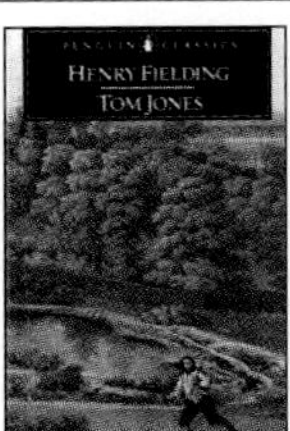

Tom Jones
Henry Fielding

During this turbulent period of history, many writers of this time were disgusted by the selfishness of the upper classes. Fielding's *Tom Jones* paints a vivid picture of eighteenth-century class struggles. Tom Jones, a poor foundling, is raised in the household of the wealthy and benevolent Squire Allworthy. When young Tom quarrels with a rival over Sophia Western, a neighbor, Tom is thrown out of the house. His wanderings on the road to London become the main strand of the comic novel. All is set right at the end of the tale, though, when Tom's true identity comes to light.

Other Possibilities

Tristram Shandy	Laurence Sterne
The Life of Johnson	James Boswell
Evelina	Fanny Burney

Resources for Teaching Novels, Plays, and Literature Collections This resource contains graphic organizers, teaching strategies, and transparencies that will be invaluable in teaching any of these novels.

Planning Students' Extended Reading

The following works extend students' understanding of the kind of social concerns stirred up in the turbulent time of seventeenth- and eighteenth-century England. The following information will help you decide which works to assign.

Customize for *Varying Student Needs and Interests*

This information will give you a better idea of which works would best suit your students' needs and interests.

- *Robinson Crusoe* and *Tom Jones* are high-interest novels that will appeal to most students. Both depict an individual on his own, struggling to survive independently of the support of others—a theme that may readily appeal to adolescents. The style of both is archaic, though; the sentences can be unwieldy. It would be helpful to prepare some focus questions for students before they read.
- The fantastic and adventuresome qualities of *Gulliver's Travels* ensure that it will interest young readers. To help sustain extended reading, ask students to research the targets of Swift's satire and to come up with plausible contemporary parallels.

Sensitive Issues Both *Gulliver's Travels* and *Tom Jones* contain issues and references that you may find sensitive in your classroom. While the religious quarrels that fuel some of Swift's savagery have receded in importance, his occasional indictments of the lusty life of the times—including references to gambling and prostitution—may encourage you to recommend *Gulliver's Travels* with caution.

Fieldings' Tom Jones is a free-living, amorous young man. His weakness for romance clearly stems from a joy in life; still, the sexual element is strongly suggested. The social status of illegitimate children is central to the plot of the book.

Planning Instruction and Assessment

Unit Objectives

1. To read selections from the Romantic period in English literature
2. To apply a variety of reading strategies, particularly interactive reading strategies, appropriate for reading these selections
3. To recognize literary elements used in these selections
4. To build vocabulary in context
5. To learn elements of grammar, usage, and style
6. To write in a variety of modes and about situations based on the selections
7. To develop speaking and listening skills, by completing proposed activities

Meeting the Objectives

With each selection, you will find instructional material and portfolio opportunities through which students can meet these objectives. Further, you will find additional practice pages for reading strategies, literary elements, vocabulary, and grammar in the ***Selection Support*** booklet in the Teaching Resources box.

Setting Goals Work with your students at the beginning of the unit to set goals for unit outcomes. Plan what skills and concepts you wish students to acquire. You may individualize these according to students' performance levels or learning modalities.

Portfolios You may have students keep portfolios of their work or of their work in progress. The activities and prompts on the Build Your Portfolio page of each selection provide opportunities for students to apply the concepts presented with the selection.

Two Men Observing the Moon, Caspar David Friedrich, Staatl, Kunstsammlungen, Neue Meister, Dresden, Germany

Humanities: Art

Two Men Observing the Moon by Caspar David Friedrich.

The German painter Caspar David Friedrich (1774–1840) is one of the most emotionally expressive painters of the Romantic period. He studied art in Copenhagen and then settled in Dresden near the turn of the 19th century. Friedrich's work took its dark tone from the harsh Baltic coast and Hartz Mountains. His haunting landscapes embody "the sublime," celebrated by Romanticism—nature as an awe-inspiring, powerful force that confounds human understanding.

Call students' attention to such details in the painting as the nearly uprooted tree; the burning moon, which turns the world an infernal shade of copper; and the two men, whose comradely pose seems at odds with the harsh, ungiving landscape. To help students link the art to the focus of Unit 4, "Rebels and Dreamers," ask these questions:

1. Friedrich looked for symbols in nature—objects that point to a meaning. Suggest possible symbolic meanings for one of the painting's details. Sample answers: *The partly uprooted tree might symbolize mortality; the burning moon, the imagination.*
2. Literature of the period often focuses on dreams and the imagination. What elements of this painting strike you as dreamlike? *The coppery mist and burning moon are dreamlike, as is the tree's eerie attitude.*

Rebels and Dreamers (1798–1832)

Come forth into the light of things,
Let Nature be your teacher.

—William Wordsworth
from "The Tables Turned"

Assessing Student Progress

The following tools are available to measure the degree to which students meet the unit objectives:

Informal Assessment

The questions in the Guide for Responding sections are a first level of response to the concepts and skills presented with the selection. Students' responses are a brief informal measure of their grasp of the material. Their responses on this level can indicate where further instruction and practice are needed. You may then follow up with the practice pages in the ***Selection Support*** booklet.

You will find literature and reading guides in the ***Alternative Assessment*** booklet, which you may give students on an individual basis for informal assessment of their performance.

Formal Assessment

In the ***Formal Assessment*** booklet, you will find selection tests and part tests.

Selection Tests The selection tests measure comprehension and skills acquisition for each selection or group of selections.

Part Test Each part test, which calls on students to read a passage of literature they have not previously seen, applies the unit skills on a broader level. The Critical Reading section measures Unit Objectives 1, 2, and 3. The Vocabulary and Grammar section measures Objectives 4 and 5. The Essay section measures Objectives 1 and 6. Both the Critical Reading and Vocabulary and Grammar sections use formats similar to those found on many standardized tests, including the SAT.

Alternative Assessment

Portfolios As you review individual pieces or the collected work in students' portfolios, you will find assessment sheets available in the portfolio section of the ***Alternative Assessment*** booklet.

Scoring Rubrics You will find scoring rubrics for writing modes in the ***Alternative Assessment*** booklet. You can apply these to Writing Mini-Lessons and to Writing Process Workshop lessons.

Speaking and Listening The ***Alternative Assessment*** booklet contains assessment sheets for speaking and listening activities.

Learning Modalities The ***Alternative Assessment*** booklet contains activities that appeal to different learning styles. You may use these, too, as an alternative assessment of students' growth.

Using the Timeline

The Timeline can serve a number of instructional purposes, as follows:

Getting an Overview Use the timeline to help students get a quick overview of themes and events of the period. This approach will benefit all students but may be especially helpful for visually oriented students, English language learners, and those less proficient in reading. (For strategies in using the Timeline as an overview, see the bottom of this page.)

Thinking Critically Questions are provided on the facing page. Use these questions to have students review the events, discuss their significance, and examine the *so what* behind the *what happened.*

Connecting to Selections Have students refer back to the Timeline when reading individual selections. By consulting the Timeline regularly, they will gain a better sense of the period's chronology. In addition, they will appreciate what was occurring in the world that gave rise to these works of literature.

Projects Students can use the Timeline as a launching pad for projects like these:

- **Relate Literature to History** As students read material in this unit, have them record allusions or facts linked to events on the Timeline. In a notebook, they should list any events they can find on the Timeline that are connected in some way to each item in their notes. At the end of the class's time with this unit, have the class compile the notes of individual students and construct a "Literature in History" Timeline.
- **Report on Scientific Advance** Have students scan the Timeline for an invention, scientific experiment, or other advance in knowledge that interests them, research the advance and its significance, and then report on their findings to the class.

Timeline

1798–1832

1798 | 1804 | 1810

British Events

- **1798 William Wordsworth** and **Samuel Taylor Coleridge** publish *Lyrical Ballads.*
- **1798** Wolfe Tone Rebellion in Ireland.
- **1801** Act of Union creates United Kingdom of Great Britain and Ireland.
- **1801** Union Jack becomes official flag. ▼

- **1802** J.M.W. Turner's *Calais Pier* exhibited in London.
- **1803** Henry Shrapnel invents exploding shell.
- **1805** Battle of Trafalgar. ▼
- **1807** Thomas Moore writes *Irish Melodies.*

- **1811** King George III declared permanently insane.
- **1812 Byron** publishes *Childe Harold's Pilgrimage.*
- **1813 Jane Austen** publishes *Pride and Prejudice.* ▶
- **1814** George Stephenson constructs first successful steam locomotive. ▼
- **1814** Walter Scott publishes *Waverley.*
- **1815** John MacAdam constructs roads of crushed stone.

World Events

- **1799** France: Napoleon becomes head of revolutionary government. ▶
- **1799** Egypt: Rosetta Stone, key to deciphering hieroglyphics, discovered.
- **1800** Italy: Volta builds first electric battery.
- **1800** Spain: Goya paints *The Two Majas.*
- **1802** Haiti: Toussaint L'Ouverture leads rebellion against French rule. ▶
- **1803** United States: Louisiana Territory purchased from France.

- **1804** Germany: Beethoven composes *Symphony No. 3.*
- **1804** France: Napoleon crowns himself emperor.
- **1805** Eastern Europe: Napoleon defeats allies at Austerlitz.
- **1807** United States: Fulton's steamboat navigates Hudson River. ▲
- **1808** Italy: Excavation of Pompeii begins.
- **1808** Germany: Goethe publishes *Faust,* Part I.
- **1809** United States: Washington Irving writes "Rip Van Winkle."
- **1810** South America: Simón Bolivar leads rebellions against Spanish rule.
- **1812** Russia: Napoleon loses hundreds of thousands of troops in retreat from Moscow.
- **1812** United States: War with Britain declared.
- **1813** Mexico: Independence declared.
- **1814** France: Napoleon abdicates and is exiled to Elba.
- **1815** France: Napoleon returns for "Hundred Days."
- **1815** Belgium: Napoleon defeated at Waterloo.

Getting an Overview of the Period

Introduction To give students an overview of the period, indicate the span of dates in the upper left-hand corner. How much time is covered in this unit? *A period of 34 years is covered.* Next, point out that the Timeline is divided into specifically British Events (on top) and World Events (on bottom). Have them practice scanning the Timeline across, looking both at the British Events and the World Events. Finally, point out that the events in the Timeline often represent beginnings, turning points, and endings. *The 1801 Act of Union is an example of both an ending and a beginning.*

Key Events Have students chart important technological developments. *In 1815, John MacAdam constructs roads of crushed stone.* Then have them note evidence of new social trends. *In 1832, the First Reform Act gave more people the right to vote.* Ask students to formulate a theme linking the scientific and social trends they have identified. *Suggested answer: people's common needs and rights were being addressed.* Elicit plausible generalizations about the changing character of British life. *Sample answer: progress in both politics and technology was taking hold.*

1816	1822	1828	1832

British Events

- **1817** William Hazlitt writes *Characters of Shakespeare's Plays.*
- **1818 Mary Wollstonecraft Shelley** publishes *Frankenstein or the Modern Prometheus.* ▶
- **1819** Peterloo Massacre in Manchester.
- **1819 Percy Bysshe Shelley** writes "Ode to the West Wind"
- **1820 John Keats** publishes "Ode on a Grecian Urn."
- **1821** *Manchester Guardian* begins publication.
- **1821** John Constable paints *The Hay-Wain*
- **1825** Horse-drawn buses begin operating in London.
- **1825** John Nash completes rebuilding of Buckingham Palace.
- **1827** System for purifying London water installed.
- **1829** Catholic Emancipation Act passed.
- **1829** Robert Peel establishes Metropolitan Police in London.
- **1830** Liverpool-Manchester railway opens. ▼

- **1831** Michael Faraday demonstrates electromagnetic induction. ▼
- **1832** First Reform Act extends voting rights.

World Events

- **1817** United States: William Cullen Bryant publishes "Thanatopsis."
- **1818** First steamship crosses Atlantic.
- **1819** France: René Läennec invents stethescope. ▶
- **1821** Greece: War with Turkey begins.
- **1821** Germany: Heinrich Heine publishes *Poems.*

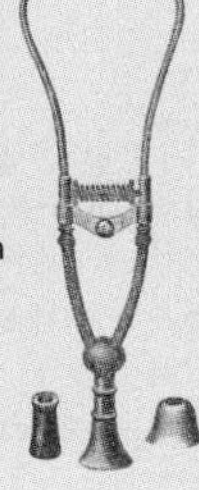

- **1822** Russia: Aleksandr Pushkin publishes *Eugene Onegin.*
- **1823** United States: Monroe Doctrine closes Americas to further Euro pean colonization.
- **1825** Russia: Bolshoi Ballet founded. ▶
- **1826** Germany: Mendelssohn composes *Overture to A Midsummer Night's Dream.*
- **1826** United States: James Fenimore Cooper publishes *The Last of the Mohicans.*
- **1830** France: Stendhal publishes *The Red and the Black.*
- **1831** United States: Edgar Allan Poe publishes *Poems.*
- **1831** France: Victor Hugo publishes *The Hunchback of Notre Dame.*

◆ Critical Thinking

1. (a) Name two technological improvements in this period. (b) What do these improvements suggest about the state of life before this time? **[Hypothesize]** *(a) Answers include: MacAdam constructed roads of crushed stone (1815); a water purification system was installed in London (1827). (b) These changes suggest that such public matters as transportation and sanitation were primitive, and may not have been systematically supervised.*
2. (a) Name two changes in English political life after 1817. (b) What do these changes suggest about the nature of government? Explain. **[Speculate]** *(a) The Catholic Emancipation Act was passed (1829) and the First Reform Act extended voting rights (1832). (b) These changes suggest that government was growing more democratic and secular.*
3. (a) What nation's affairs dominated the European scene prior to 1816? (b) Speculate about how these events may have affected Britain. **[Speculate]** *(a) French affairs (specifically, the rise of Napoleon) dominated Europe. (b) France can obstruct Britain's most direct route to Europe, the English Channel. Turmoil in France, and hostility toward Britain, would hinder British trade.*
4. (a) What general trends are evident in the United States in this period? (b) Speculate about relations with Britain during this time, citing events to support your conclusions. **[Connect]** *(a) The United States was expanding and had grown sufficiently powerful to close off the region to Europeans (the Louisiana Territory was purchased in 1803; the Monroe Doctrine was formulated in 1823); it has an active literary life, with publications by Irving (1809) and others. (b) Relations were poor; the two countries fought in 1812, and the Monroe Doctrine warned Britain off the Americas.*
5. (a) Name three events suggesting that Britain suffered from popular unrest in the years after 1816. (b) Speculate about the issues that sparked this unrest. **[Speculate]** *(a) A "massacre" occured in 1819; a police force was established in 1829; and the First Reform Act extended voting rights in 1832. (b) Answers include: commoners may have been agitating for political rights; laborers, for fair pay and better conditions.*

▶Critical Viewing◀

1. From what period of Napoleon's career does this portrait (1799) appear to be taken? Support your answer with details. **[Speculate]** *Napoleon's youth, the simplicity of his dress, and the map suggest the young war hero, pre-dating the Emperor (1804) and the defeated exile (1814).*
2. (a) Describe the artist's depiction of the ship's sails in the painting of the Battle of Trafalgar (1805). (b) What does the attention paid to the sails suggest about the artist's focus? **[Interpret]** *(a) The ship's sails are atmospheric, tinted like the sky and billowing like clouds. (b) The attention suggests that the artist is at least as concerned with the poetic treatment of the image as with celebrating the event.*
3. What does the dress of the men manning an early steam engine (1814) suggest about their occupation? **[Speculate]** *Their top hats and collars suggest that they are perhaps the designers of the engine, not men employed to run it regularly.*
4. What does this book cover suggest about *Frankenstein*'s popularity (1818)? Explain. **[Infer]** *The cover is modern and done in a "mass-market" style, suggesting that the novel was popular long after it was written.*

Develop Understanding

Customize for
Less Proficient Readers
Explain to these students that their own ideas of "equal rights" owe a lot to this period. Similarly, an awareness of the beauty of a nature unspoiled by human hands, is an idea created during this time. Ask students to look for signs of the growth of these new ideas as they read.

Customize for
English Language Learners
Inform these students that this period is called "the Romantic Age." Ask them to define the word *romantic,* using the dictionary if necessary. Then have them add to their definition by reading the Story of the Times.

Customize for
More Advanced Students
The scholar Isaiah Berlin said that "The Romantics made a greater difference to us than anything else since the Renaissance. . . . Before the Romantics came along there was only one answer to any question . . . . The Romantics were the first to say that the answer was not built into the universe." Challenge more advanced students to find evidence in A Graphic Look at the Period and The Story of the Times for or against Berlin's contention.

Answers to
A GRAPHIC LOOK

Interpret By implying that their new state repeated classical models, the revolutionaries gave it greater legitimacy.

Speculate The massed crowd of figures at the bottom of the painting, who have perhaps spilled out of a beached ship, and the turmoil of the sails suggest chaos.

A GRAPHIC LOOK AT THE PERIOD

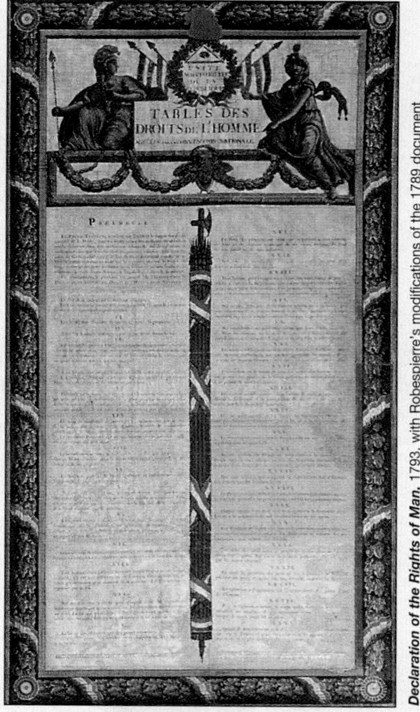

Declaration of the Rights of Man, 1793, with Robespierre's modifications of the 1789 document

▲ **Interpret** Featured in this presentation of the French Revolution's Declaration of the Rights of Man is a *fasces* (a bundle of rods surrounding an ax)—an ancient Roman symbol of the government's power. Explain why the revolutionaries included classical references in this document.

The Battle of Trafalgar, October 21, 1805, J.M.W. Turner, The Granger Collection, Ltd.

▲ **Speculate** The British fleet under Lord Nelson defeated Napoleon's fleet at the Battle of Trafalgar, off Spain. Using the details in this painting, describe the experience of participating in a sea battle.

The Story of the Times

(1798–1832)

Historical Background

After nearly a century of progress in science and industry, the faith of poets in reason had been eroded. Where eighteenth-century poets had celebrated the power of human understanding—their most bitter satire could say no more than, "humanity is unreasonable"—Wordsworth marked the end of the century with the warning "Our meddling intellect/Misshapes the beauteous forms of things—/We murder to dissect."

In the ensuing period, which was named the Romantic Age by historians during the late 1800's, nearly all the attitudes and tendencies of eighteenth-century classicism and rationalism were redefined or changed dramatically. To understand how these changes occurred, it is necessary to examine not only the impact of events in Britain, but also the effects of the social and political upheaval that began taking place in other parts of the world.

Revolution and Reaction Some of the defining events for British thought and politics at the end of the eighteenth century took place, not in England, but in France. The French Revolution began on July 14, 1789, when a group of French citizens stormed the Bastille, a Paris prison for political prisoners. The revolutionaries placed limits on the powers of King Louis XVI, established a new government, and approved a document called the Declaration of the Rights of Man, affirming the principles of "liberty, equality, and fraternity." France became a constitutional monarchy.

In England, the ruling class felt threatened by the events in France, which seemed to strike at the roots of social order. Most intellectuals, including the most important and influential writers of the Romantic Age, such as William Wordsworth, enthusiastically supported the revolution and the democratic ideals on which it was grounded.

Cross-Curricular Connection: Social Studies

Exporting the French Revolution
Explain to students that the French Revolution quickly became an international force. In the 1789 *Declaration of the Rights of Man,* the French revolutionaries stated their basic principles. All men had by nature a right to liberty, property, and security. All were declared equal before the law—the privileges of aristocrats were suspended. In 1793, the revolutionaries added a clause stating that liberty was a human cause, not just a French one, and that every king ruled by usurping the people's liberty—kings were criminals against all humanity.

As Napoleon's troops swept through Europe, he reformed the governments of the conquered countries, replacing the remains of feudal society with an order based on wealth, merit, and equality, creating modern-style administrative bureaucracies, and redefining national boundaries to resemble today's. Some Europeans welcomed him as a liberator.

Ask students to speculate what Europe might be like today if Napoleon had not been so successful at war. *Answers include: kings might still rule; people might not have basic rights.*

The Reign of Terror As royalists, moderates, and radicals jockeyed for power, the French Revolution became more and more chaotic. In 1792, France declared war on Austria, touching off an invasion by Austrian and Prussian troops. Fuming with patriotic indignation, a radical group called the Jacobins gained control of the French legislative assembly, abolished the monarchy, and declared the nation a republic. Mobs attacked and killed many prisoners—including former aristocrats and priests—in the bloody "September massacres."

Within weeks the revolutionaries had tried and convicted Louis XVI on a charge of treason, then sent him to the guillotine early in 1793. The Jacobins, under the leadership of Maximilien Robespierre, then began what is called the Reign of Terror. Over the next year, they sent some 17,000 royalists, moderates, and even radicals—including finally Robespierre himself—to the guillotine.

At the same time, France's new "citizen army" was making war across Europe in the name of liberty. In 1793, France declared war on Britain. Thus began a series of wars that would drag on for twenty-two years, ending only when Britain and its allies defeated Napoleon in 1815. Lord Nelson, who broke the French navy at the Battle of Trafalgar, and the Duke of Wellington, who led the British forces in the final showdown with Napoleon, were two of Britain's great military heroes from the time.

British Reaction The September massacres and the Reign of Terror were so shocking that even Britons who had sympathized with the French Revolution now turned against it. Conservative Britons demanded a crackdown on reformers, whom they denounced as dangerous Jacobins. Adding to British alarm was the success of France's new "citizen army," which expelled the Austrian and Russian invaders and then set out to "liberate" other European nations from despotic rule. British leaders did not want France or any other nation to win dominance on the European continent. In 1793, France took the initiative by declaring war on Britain. Thus began a series of

Napoleon's French Campaign of 1814, Jean Louis Ernest Meissonier
The Granger Collection, Ltd.

▲ **Compare and Contrast** In the years of turmoil following the Revolution, Napoleon rose to lead France to victory. By 1807, France ruled Europe as far east as Russia. Contrast Napoleon with the other figures in the painting.

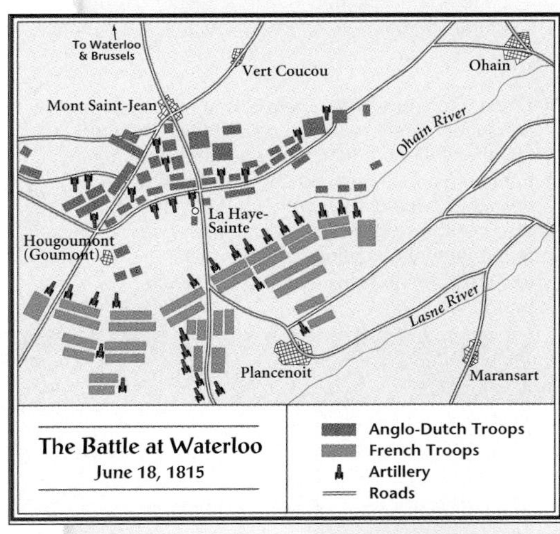

▲ **Read a Map** A crucial moment in the Battle of Waterloo came when one of Napoleon's officers, Marshall Ney, captured the farmhouse of La Haye-Sainte. (a) Describe the location of this farmhouse in relation to the British troops. (b) Why would its capture by the French give them an advantage?

Answers to

A GRAPHIC LOOK

Compare and Contrast Napoleon rides, solitary, at the head of the column, while the other figures ride abreast. Napoleon's horse is white, those of the other riders are darker. Napoleon's figure is the largest one in the composition.

Read a Map (a) The farmhouse is near the British lines at their center. It guards a road along which the British might advance towards the French. (b) The French could use the farmhouse to defend the road, effectively dividing the British forces.

More about Nelson and Wellington

Explain to students that Arthur Wellesley, Duke of Wellington (1769–1852), and Horatio Nelson, Lord Nelson (1758–1805), were among the greatest heroes of their time.

Nelson cut his teeth in naval service during the American Revolution. When he destroyed a French squadron at the mouth of the Nile in 1798, he became a celebrity. He was adored by the British people, but his love for Lady Hamilton soon plunged him into scandal. He guaranteed his place in British history when, at the Battle of Trafalgar, he crippled the combined French and Spanish fleet, thereby averting an invasion of Britain. Wounded during that battle, he held onto life until he heard that fifteen enemy ships had been captured. His last words were, "Now I am satisfied. Thank God I have done my duty."

Wellington led a small force to victory in the Peninsular Wars. By 1814, he had pushed the French out of Portugal and Spain. When Napoleon was defeated once and for all at Waterloo, it was Wellington who led the British forces. Wellington's military prowess made him one of the most respected men in Europe.

Cross-Curricular Connection: Social Studies

Political Thought: Burke and Bentham

Explain to students that Edmund Burke's *Reflections on the French Revolution* (1790) is an important statement of conservative ideas. Burke (1729–97) opposed the revolutionaries' assumption that society could not be judged by abstract principles such as "reason" and "liberty." Governments, Burke thought, are not created, but grow, and so evolve ways to meet people's needs. A nation's traditions, however "irrational," represent a kind of inherited wisdom. Burke had supported the rebellious American colonists—who had their own tradition of liberty—on similar grounds.

In strong contrast to Burke, Jeremy Bentham (1748–1832) argued that actions, including the laws passed by government, should be judged by the standard of "utility" alone—that is, by their usefulness in satisfying people's interests. Ultimately, the basic human interest was pleasure. A rational government was one which created the greatest pleasure for the greatest number. Bentham's principles, known as Utilitarianism, influenced numerous reformist politicians and thinkers, including the philosopher John Stuart Mill.

Ask students whether Burke's or Bentham's ideas apply better to today's society. *Answers include: as Bentham would have wished, political discussion in the United States is often framed as an analysis of interests.* Invite advanced students to find out more about these ideas, then sketch a response from each thinker to a contemporary issue.

Develop Understanding

Historical Background

Comprehension Check

1. Name two developments in France during the period affecting Britain. *The French Revolution led to fear in Britain of social unrest; France declared war on Britain in 1793.*
2. How did British intellectuals respond to the first stages of the French Revolution? *Many supported the Revolution's democratic ideals.*
3. (a) What direction did the French Revolution take after its first stages? (b) How did the British respond to this new development? *(a) A radical group called the Jacobins began a Reign of Terror in which they guillotined their opponents. (b) British conservatives used the Terror to justify suppressing dissent; even former sympathizers turned against the French.*
4. (a) What new troubles came to Britain as a result of the Industrial Revolution? (b) What was the government's initial response? *(a) Workers agitated for better working conditions, higher pay, and shorter hours. (b) The government helped suppress the workers' movement.*
5. What reforms did Parliament eventually bring about? *Parliament legalized labor unions, restored the rights of Catholics, and extended the vote to middle-class males.*

Critical Thinking

1. For those who thought society had corrupted natural human goodness, the French Revolution was compelling. Explain why. **[Interpret]** *The Revolution looked like an attempt to re-make society "from the ground up," returning to fundamental values.*
2. (a) How did the French Revolution affect the British movement for reform? (b) Explain how this result might have led to a new passion in the arts. **[Support]** *(a) Conservatives used the French Terror to justify suppressing reformers. (b) Arguably, people turned to art as an outlet for the idealism thwarted in politics.*
3. Middle-class reformers often allied themselves with working class radicals. Explain how such alliances led the government to give the middle-classes the vote. **[Hypothesize]** *The government hoped to end their support of more radical reforms.*

Tea Time, David Emil

▲ **Interpret** By the early 1800's, tea was truly a national drink, popular with all classes.
a) Does the painting represent a formal tea, or a "tea break"? (b) What techniques does the artist use to emphasize how relaxing the act of drinking tea can be?

▼ **Draw Conclusions** Early cotton mills employed mostly women and children. The first factories were not thoroughly automatized. Factory workers retained some self-directedness and pride in their craft. (a) What does the dress of the workers in this picture suggest about factory conditions of the time?
(b) Describe the tasks that you see being performed.

Power Loom, Anonymous, 18th Century

wars that would drag on for twenty-two years, creating fear and rigidity, and squelching all hope of reform within British society. The Tory government led by William Pitt (the Younger) outlawed all talk of parliamentary reform outside the halls of Parliament, banned public meetings, and suspended certain basic rights.

Liberal-minded Britons had no political outlet for their hopes and dreams. Many turned to literature and art instead.

Coping With Society's Problems Throughout the long wars with France, Britain's government kept a tight lid on domestic dissent. It ignored the problems caused by the Industrial Revolution—overcrowded factory towns, unpleasant and unsafe working conditions in the factories, and long working hours and low pay. The working class grew steadily larger and more restless. In the factory towns of northern England, workers protested the loss of jobs to new machinery in the violent Luddite Riots (1811–1813). Some attempted to organize in unions.

Britain's government claimed to be following a hands-off policy, but in fact it sided openly with factory owners against workers, even helping to crush the workers' attempts to form unions. In Manchester, mounted soldiers charged a peaceful mass meeting of cotton workers and killed several of them in what came to be known as the Peterloo Massacre (1819). To many, it seemed that British society was splitting into two angry camps—the working classes, who demanded reform, and the ruling classes, who resisted fiercely.

A new generation of Tories emerged in the 1820's, and a trickle of reforms began. A law was passed in 1824 permitting Britain's first labor unions to organize, and in 1829 the Catholic Emancipation Act restored economic and religious freedoms to Roman Catholics.

The trickle grew into a stream following a Whig victory in the election of 1830. The Reform Bill of 1832 brought sweeping changes to British political life. By extending voting rights to the small but important middle class (males only), this law threatened the traditional dominance of land-owning aristocrats in Parliament. Moreover, in 1833 Parlia-

Cross-Curricular Connection: Science

The Technology of Travel

The railroad, which had its beginnings in the early nineteenth century, was to change the face of the nation. Businessses could ship materials and products more quickly, more reliably, and in greater quantities than ever before. Better transportation encouraged industry to grow even faster. By the middle of the century, extensive, fast travel was available even to the poor—Parliament decreed that certain trains take passengers for only a penny per mile.

Horse drawn rail-cars were first used in coal mines. The first steam-powered locomotive, built in 1804, ran at five miles per hour. By the 1850's, trains would average speeds around 20 miles per hour—quadruple their original speed.

Ask students to speculate about how life might have changed for the average Briton when passenger service began on trains. *Student may answer that families spread out more, or that it became easier to maintain relations over a distance.*

ment passed the first law governing factory safety. In that same year, it also abolished slavery.

Literature of the Period

The Beginnings of Romanticism The British Romantic writers responded to the climate of their times. Their new interest in the trials and dreams of common people and their desire for radical change developed out of the democratic idealism that characterized the early part of the French Revolution. Their deep attachment to nature and to a pure, simple past was a response to the misery and ugliness born of industrialization. For the Romantics, the faith in science and reason, so characteristic of eighteenth-century thought and literature, no longer applied in a world of tyranny and factories.

Many of the ideas that influenced the British Romantics, though, originally arose on continental Europe well before the turn of the century. Swiss-born writer Jean-Jacques Rousseau (1712–1778), a leading philosopher of eighteenth-century France, saw society as a force that, through history, deformed and imprisoned an originally free human nature. "Man is born free," he wrote, "and everywhere he is in chains." His ideas influenced both American and French revolutionaries.

A group of late-eighteenth-century writers and artists living in German-speaking Europe began incorporating Rousseau's ideas into poetry, fiction, and drama. The most famous of this group, Johann Wolfgang von Goethe (1749–1832) found a primitive simplicity much in keeping with Rousseau's ideas and values in the German literature of the Middle Ages, works filled with myth, adventure and passion, not unlike the Anglo-Saxon *Beowulf.* The Romantic movement takes its name from this interest in medieval romances. Goethe's own works show a new attention to feelings and express an ideal of self-fulfillment and growth through experience.

The Romantic Age in British Poetry In music, Romanticism produced such brilliant European

▲ **Relate** With roughly one million inhabitants, London in 1800 was the biggest city in the West and probably in the world. (a) Name three details that the scene in the picture shares with a modern city. (b) Name three characteristics of a modern city that do not appear in the picture.

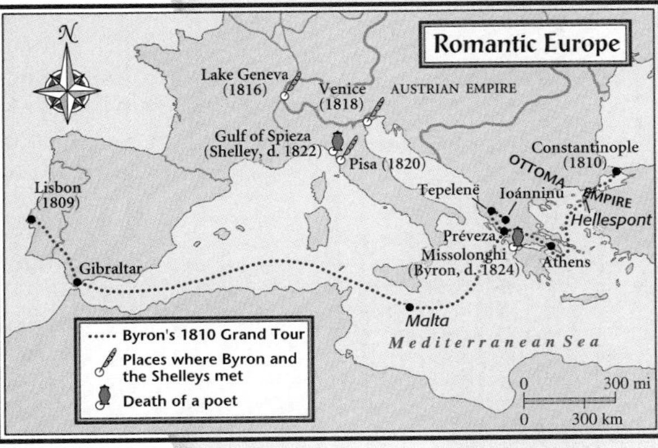

▲ **Read a Map** When peace with France came in 1815, the British discovered a passion for travel. At least one celebrity had already paved the way: Lord Byron went on an extensive tour of Europe in 1809. (a) How many years passed between Byron's Grand Tour of Europe and his move to Pisa? (b) Where in Europe and when did Shelley and Byron die?

Answers to A Graphic Look

(from page 570)

Interpret (a) The painting shows a "tea break;" the woman and child have perhaps paused in the middle of arranging flowers. (b) The chaos in the foreground of the painting contrasts strongly with the relaxed face of the tea-drinker and the clean white table cloth next to her.

Draw Conclusions (a) The dress of the woman in the foreground suggests that concerns of safety and efficiency did not define life in the factory; her long skirts might become entangled in a machine or slow down her movements. The man's open collar suggests informality. (b) The man is performing some duty of oversight; the woman may be fixing the machine; others appear to be weaving.

(from page 571)

Relate (a) Like a modern city, the London pictured has congested traffic, numerous pedestrians, street lights (rear left), and large buildings. (b)There are no traffic signals, automobiles, or skyscrapers; the distinction between sidewalk and street does not seem clear; no form of public transportation is evident.

Read a Map (a) About 11 years passed between Byron's Grand Tour and his meeting with the Shelleys in Pisa (1810; 1820). (b) Shelley died in the Gulf of Spieza, off Italy, in 1822; Byron died in Missolonghi, in Greece, in 1824.

Connections to the Literature

- For an early, sympathetic view of the human cost of the Industrial Revolution, refer students to Blake's "The Chimney Sweeper," p. 600.
- Though Wordsworth and Coleridge became more conservative, their poetic heirs continued the tradition of Romantic radicalism. Refer students to Shelley's "Men of England," page 708.
- For a sympathetic view of the rioting Luddites—from an aristocrat, no less, and one whose district they had terrorized—refer students to Byron's "Speech to Parliament: In Defense of the Lower Classes," page 706. (Byron's speech as a young man did not go unremembered; at his funeral, thousands of working-class people lined the streets to honor him.)

Humanities: Music

Romanticism influenced music throughout Europe for several decades. Although Felix Mendelssohn (1780–1847) was born and lived most of his life in Germany, he traveled to England no fewer than ten times. In 1829, travels in Scotland inspired his Scottish Symphony.

As a child, Mendelssohn read Shakespeare's plays, and at age seventeen he composed an overture to *A Midsummer Night's Dream*. Seventeen years later, he wrote incidental music (music played between and during scenes) for the play. These compositions are crowning examples of program music—music with narrative or descriptive content. The "Scherzo," played prior to Act II, introduces the characters of the fairy world.

Inform students that Romantic music was often meant to suggest a mood and setting. Play Mendelssohn's "Scherzo" on the ***Listening to Music*** Audio CD. Ask students to describe the feelings and images the music evokes. *Students' answers should reflect the sprightly yet mysterious quality of the piece.*

More About the Romantic Essayists Both Thomas de Quincey and William Hazlitt were early admirers of William Wordsworth and Coleridge. The young de Quincey was so impressed by the *Lyrical Ballads* that he moved to the Lake District to be near Wordsworth. *Recollections of the Lake Poets* records his friendship with and eventual estrangement from Wordsworth and Coleridge. Hazlitt also wrote a memoir of the early Romantics, entitled *My First Acquaintance with the Poets.*

Connection to the Literature Students will find a letter by Jane Austen regarding the manners of the day on page 716. They will also find an excerpt from a contemporary adaptation of one of her novels to the screen on page 725.

Answers to

A GRAPHIC LOOK

(from page 572)

Draw Conclusions The smokestack suggests that air quality began to change; the heaped tools in the foreground suggest disruptions caused by new construction. (b) A horse-drawn carriage suggests that other forms of transportation were not replaced immediately; the trees in the background and small wooden buildings suggest that rural areas were still widespread.

Compare and Contrast The wheels on top suggest that the Engine worked on mechanical, not microelectronic, principles; the "interface" does not conceal the inner workings or make its functions more easily intelligible to people; it appears freestanding, and is probably bigger than a desktop.

(from page 573)

Interpret (a) Dark dominates the painting; light breaks through the sky in the center and illuminates the ship below. (b) The interaction of light and dark might suggest that life erupts briefly amid surrounding, dark uncertainties.

Interpret (a) Sample answer: Constable may have wanted to create a mood of grandeur and tumult, suggesting freedom. (b) The clouds have a restless, shapeless look, as if they have been blown up by a storm.

The Train between Stockton and Darlington, Great Britain, September 27, 1827

▲ **Draw Conclusions** In 1825, the Stockton and Darlington Railway became the first to carry passengers as well as freight. Sixteen years later, 1,300 miles of railroad track covered Britain. (a) What details in the picture suggest changes the railroad made in British life and the British landscape? (b) What details suggest ways in which life stayed the same?

▲ **Compare and Contrast** In 1812, well before the invention of the microprocessor, the English inventor Charles Babbage thought up the idea of a "Difference Engine"—a machine that would compute tables of logarithms and other mathematical values. Name three differences between the Difference Engine depicted here and one of today's computers.

composers as Germany's Ludwig van Beethoven (1770–1827) and Austria's Franz Schubert (1797–1828). In painting, it influenced the intensely personal and warmly spontaneous rural landscapes of Britain's John Constable (1776–1837) and J. M. W. Turner (1775–1851). However, it is for literature, and especially for poetry, that Britain's Romantic Age is most famous. William Wordsworth provided an early statement of the goals of Romantic poetry in his preface to *Lyrical Ballads* (1798), his early collaboration with his friend Samuel Taylor Coleridge. The preface defined poetry as "the spontaneous overflow of powerful feelings" and explained that poetry "takes its origin from emotion recollected in tranquility." An emphasis on the emotions, then, was central to the new Romantic poetry.

Equally important was subject matter. The new poetry dealt with "incidents and situations from common life" over which the poet throws "a certain coloring of imagination, whereby ordinary things should be presented . . . in an unusual way."

Finally, Wordsworth's preface spoke about incorporating human passions with "the beautiful and permanent forms of nature." An emphasis on nature would become another important characteristic of British Romantic verse.

The Romantic view of nature was quite different from that of most eighteenth-century literature. Nature was not a force to be tamed and analyzed scientifically; rather, it was a wild, free force that could inspire poets to instinctive spiritual understanding.

Wordsworth and Coleridge blazed the way for a new generation of British Romantic poets—the so-called "second generation" of poets, which included George Gordon, Lord Byron; Percy Bysshe Shelley; and John Keats. These younger poets rebelled even more strongly than Wordsworth and Coleridge against the British conservatism of the time. All three died abroad after tragically short lives, and their viewpoints were those of disillusioned outsiders.

The Romantic Age in British Prose British readers of the Romantic Age could find brilliant literary criticism and topical essays in a variety of new periodicals. *The London Magazine,* although it appeared only from 1820 to 1829, attracted major

Cross-Curricular Connection: Social Studies

J. M. W. Turner's *Frosty Morning*

The Romantic movement in literature found echoes in the other arts. The landscapes of J. M. W. Turner (1775–1851) shared the Romantics' new attention to and respect for nature. Turner was noted for his depictions of scenes at sea as well as landscapes. His emphasis on the effects of light, at the expense of objects, suggest, perhaps, a perception of the spirit in nature comparable to Wordsworth's—"A presence that disturbs me with the joy / Of elevated thoughts . . . / Whose dwelling is the light of setting suns . . ."

Show students Turner's *Frosty Morning*, on page 59 of the Art Transparencies. Point out that Turner's composition suggests a strong contrast between a human viewpoint and a higher one. Ask the following questions:

1. What decisions about composition does Turner make that suggest such a contrast? *The people are placed within the dark, lower portion of the painting, screened off from the sky.*
2. Describe the trees' role in the composition. *The trees join sky and earth, but also break into and emphasize the emptiness of the sky.*

contributions from the three greatest essayists of the era: Charles Lamb (1775–1834), William Hazlitt (1778–1830), and Thomas De Quincey (1785–1859). Lamb, in particular, transformed the informal essay of the eighteenth century into a more personal, more introspective Romantic composition.

Unlike the Romantic poets, the novelists of the Romantic Age did not make a sharp break with the past. The Gothic novel first appeared in the middle of the eighteenth century. It featured a number of standard ingredients, including brave heroes and heroines, threatening scoundrels, vast eerie castles, and ghosts. The Romantic fascination with mystery and the supernatural made such novels quite popular during the Romantic Age. One of the most successful was *Frankenstein, or the Modern Prometheus* (1818), written by Shelley's wife, Mary Wollstonecraft Shelley (1797–1851).

The Romantic novel of manners carried on in the tradition of earlier writers by turning a satirical eye on British customs. The most highly regarded writer of novels of manners was Jane Austen (1775–1817), whose works include *Sense and Sensibility* (1811) and *Pride and Prejudice* (1813). Her incisive portrayals of character are more reflective of the classical sensibility of the eighteenth century than the Romantic notions of the new age.

Historical romances—imaginative works of fiction built around a real person or historical event—had appeared long before the Romantic Age, but they attained their peak of popularity in the work of Sir Walter Scott (1771–1832). Passionately devoted to his native Scotland, Scott wrote about the days of knights and chivalry.

The close of Britain's Romantic Age is usually set in 1832, the year of the passage of the First Reform Bill. However, the ideas of Romanticism remained a strong influence on many writers from following generations. In fact, even today we can detect elements of Romanticism in many major works of contemporary fiction and poetry as well as in television dramas, movies, and popular songs.

Calais Pier: An English Packet Arriving, J. M. W. Turner

▲ **Interpret** The Romantic movement in literature found echoes in the other arts. The landscapes of J. M. W. Turner (1775–1851) shared the Romantics' new attention to and respect for nature. (a) Describe the relation between light and dark in the painting. (b) What does the interaction of light and dark in the painting suggest about the nature of life?

Sketch for Hadleigh Castle, John Constable

▲ **Interpret** Another painter linked with the Romantics is John Constable (1776–1837). (a) What mood do you think Constable wanted to create with this scene? (b) How do the clouds add to this mood?

Literature of the Period

Check Your Comprehension

1. What views about nature and science did the Romantics reject? *The Romantics rejected the eighteenth-century view that nature was to be understood and mastered; they had lost faith in science's power to improve life.*
2. Name two figures that influenced British Romantics, and their nationalities. *Rousseau, a Swiss-born Frenchman, and Goethe, a German, influenced the British Romantics.*
3. (a) Name two poets prominent in the early Romantic movement in England. (b) What role did they think feeling had in poetry? *(a) William Wordsworth and Samuel Taylor Coleridge were two prominent early Romantics. (b) According to Wordsworth, poetry was the result of feeling—its "spontaneous overflow."*
4. What form of prose flourished and was transformed during the period? (b) Where did readers encounter works in this form? *(a) The essay flourished and was transformed. (b) Readers encountered essays in periodicals.*
5. Name two important genres of novels from the period. *Answers include: Gothic novels, novels of manners, and historical romances.*

Critical Thinking

1. Wordsworth notes that poets have an "ability of conjuring up" passions in themselves. How does this idea qualify his definition of poetry as a "spontaneous overflow of powerful feelings"? **[Analyze]** *If poets can conjure up the feelings that overflow into their poems, they are free from the requirements of sincerity that the word spontaneous suggests.*
2. Some Romantic poets rejected traditional "poetical" language, turning instead to common speech. Speculate about the reason for this choice of style. **[Speculate]** *Suggested answer: The Romantics chose a common style and communicated their feelings clearly, rather than distancing the reader with artificial language.*
3. Describe a contemporary trend that hearkens back to Romantic ideas. Explain the connection. *Answers include the environmental movement (for its valuing of "innocent" nature); and the "me generation" (for its emphasis on expressing feelings.)*

1. **Graphic Organization of Events** Give students the Context Chart, p. 131, in ***Writing and Language Transparencies***. Have them use the form to chart the context in which Wordsworth and Coleridge's *Lyrical Ballads* appeared.
2. **Society on Trial** Divide students into a defense and a prosecution. The prosecution should search periodicals for evidence supporting Rousseau's idea that society prevents human beings from fulfilling their potential. The defense should look for counter-evidence. Each side should present its case, the class can vote on a verdict.
3. **Reflective Essay** Have students write a reflective essay on what it might have felt like to live through the Reign of Terror. Encourage them to compare the experience to events of the twentieth century with which they are familiar.
4. **Connections to the Literature** Challenge students to find a passage in a selection that reflects an insight, description, narrative, or idea from The Story of the Times. Have them read the passage aloud to the class and explain how it relates to The Story of the Times. Students giving the presentation should then be prepared to answer questions about the passage.

Develop Understanding

◆ Critical Thinking

1. (a) Give an example of an English word that you have heard that "sounds" foreign. (b) At what point in its history does a borrowed word stop sounding foreign? (c) What sort of extra significance can "foreign-sounding" words have that familiar words do not? **[Speculate]** *(a) Students may name foreign phrases that have been adopted into English, such as* déjà vu. *They may also name new slang words. (b) Sample answer: when people, their friends, and associates use the word frequently enough (c) "Foreign-sounding" words can signify class, or pretension to it; they can suggest mystery.*
2. Name another way besides borrowing in which languages adjust to new ideas and things. **[Analyze]** *Answers include: new words are formed by combining two or more old words; adjectives and nouns are formed from the name of the person associated with an idea or invention.*

▶Critical Viewing◀

1. (a) Name two kinds of things that predominate among the things named in the chart. (b) Explain why nouns naming such things are common among the words English borrows from other languages. **[Hypothesize]** *Answers include: foods and animals. (b) Suggested answers: Because of differences in wildlife and plants around the world, these items were not found in England or in Europe, and so English speakers adopted the local names.*
2. (a) What populated continents do not appear in the chart? (b) What does this absence indicate about England's relations with those continents at this time? **[Infer]** *(a) Europe and North and South America do not appear. (b) England was not then colonizing them.*

Answers to Activities

1. Students' searches may turn up more borrowed than native words. Many of these words will have Latin origins.
2. Students may find that there is a greater preponderance of native English words in the passage they analyze.

The Changing English Language

THE ROMANTIC AGE

by Richard Lederer

The Sun Never Set on the British Empire

During the Romantic Age, Britannia ruled the waves and English ruled much of the land. Great Britain's smashing conquests in the Napoleonic Wars at the beginning of the nineteenth century—culminating in Nelson's famous victory at Trafalgar in 1805—established an undisputed naval supremacy. This, in turn, gave Great Britain control over most of the world's commerce. As British ships traveled throughout the world, they left the language of the mother country in their wake but also came home from foreign ports laden with cargoes of words from other languages freighted with new meanings for English speakers.

The following are words that became part of the English language as a result of England's great economic expansion.

Country	Borrowed Words
India	*bandanna, bungalow, calico, cashmere, china, cot, curry, juggernaut, jungle, loot, nirvana, polo, punch* (beverage), *thug*, and *verandah*
Asia	*gingham, indigo, mango*, and *typhoon*
New Zealand	*kiwi*
Australia	*boomerang* and *kangaroo*
Africa	*banana, boorish, chimpanzee, gorilla, gumbo*, and *zebra*

Words, Words, Words

The biggest and fattest unabridged English dictionaries hold more than 600,000 words, compared to German in second place with 185,000 words, and then Russian and French at 130,000 and 100,000. One reason we have accumulated the world's largest and most varied vocabulary is that English continues to be the most hospitable and democratic language that has ever existed, unique in the number and variety of its borrowed words. Although Anglo-Saxon is the foundation of the English language, more than seventy percent of our words have been imported from other lands, ancient and modern, far and near. No wonder Ralph Waldo Emerson waxed ecstatic about "English speech, the sea which receives tributaries from every region under heaven" and Dorothy Thompson, employing a more prosaic metaphor, referred to "that glorious and imperial mongrel, the English language."

Activities

1. Open your dictionary at random and examine the etymology of the words listed at the top of fifteen pages. Record the earliest source for each word. Words noted as *AS* or *OE* are native; the rest are borrowed. What is the ratio of native versus borrowed words? Among the borrowed words, what percentage are derived from Latin? from Greek? from French? from other languages? Compare your results with those of your classmates and discuss the implications.
2. Now choose a passage from a newspaper or magazine. Analyze the first thirty words of that passage in the manner described above. Do you notice a different ratio of native to borrowed words? Discuss your conclusions regarding random dictionary entries versus the words in actual sentences.

Cross-Curricular Connection: Social Studies

The American Influence

Explain to students that English also picked up a good number of words through the earlier British colonial experience in North America. Pilgrims and other early settlers picked up words such as squash, moose, and racccoon from the Native Americans they met. Sometimes, they named the new plants and animals they saw by combining old words in a descriptive fashion: eggplant and bullfrog are two such results. As time went on, isolation from England ensured that Americans would talk their own language.

Ask students to reconstruct how new words enter their own vocabulary. *Students may respond that they pick up words that their friends use.*

PART 1 *Fantasy and Reality*

Hummingbird Hunters, 1884, James Farrington Gookins, Shelden Swope Art Museum, Terre Haute, Indiana

One-Minute Planning Guide

The selections that follow may be described as wild imaginings or as glimpses of real life. This strange truth stems from the fact that the writings all straddle fantasy and reality, making the works almost unclassifiable. Mary Shelley's Introduction to Frankenstein, for example, is the author's true account of how she came to write the popular novel. Imbedded in the account, however, are the author's remembrances of her fantastic dreams and visions that she claims inspired the tale of horror.

The poems of Robert Burns and Joanna Baillie also combine fantasy and reality. Although the settings and circumstances in Burns's "To a Mouse" and "To a Louse" are realistic, the speakers imbue a mouse and a louse with human characteristics and motivations. Baillie's "Woo'd and Married and A'" contains equal doses of clear-eyed realism, voiced by the bride's parents, and romantic fancy, as expressed by the poor but lovestruck groom.

William Blake's poems, as well as his personal beliefs and philosophies, are strange but compelling combinations of reality and fancy. For example, Blake's "The Lamb" and "The Tyger" treat the beasts as if they were the embodiments of good and evil. In "The Chimney Sweeper" and "Infant Sorrow," Blake paints realistic, sad pictures of life then endows the poems with his ideas of sin and salvation.

Finally, Edgar Allan Poe's "The Oval Portrait" explores the fragile, sometimes indistinguishable line between reality and fantasy.

Customizing for *Varying Student Needs*

When assigning the selections in this part, keep in mind these factors:

Introduction to *Frankenstein*

- Short, real-life account
- High-interest story of how Frankenstein came to be written

Poems of Robert Burns and Joanna Baillie

- Scots dialect may prove difficult to read and understand
- Students may find subject matter amusing

Poems of William Blake

- Short, easy to read poems
- Familiarity with Christianity important in understanding his poems

Humanities: Art

Hummingbird Hunters by James Farrington Gookins.

In this richly colored and intricately detailed painting, tiny people hunt for hummingbirds among flower buds in a lavish garden setting. Apart from their miniature size, the artist portrays the people in a realistic fashion, with true to life features and gestures. The flowers, too, contain exquisite, realistic detail. The painting presents an interesting and unusual blend of realistic and fantastic elements.

Use these questions for discussion:

1. If you could choose one word to describe this painting, what word would you choose? *Sample responses include: lush, flowery, pixielike, vibrant, and interesting.*
2. Is this painting more realistic or more fantastic? Explain. *Suggested responses: The painting is more fantastic because, taken as a whole, it depicts a fantasy setting; the painting is more realistic because the manner in which the setting and characters are painted is realistic.*

Prepare and Engage

OBJECTIVES

1. To read, interpret, and respond to an author's introduction to a gothic novel
2. To relate an author's experience to personal experience
3. To use interactive reading strategies to deepen the reading experience
4. To identify elements of gothic literature
5. To build vocabulary in context and learn the related words *phantasm* and *fantasy*
6. To identify past participial phrases
7. To write a comparison-and-contrast essay that is organized logically and effectively
8. To respond to the author's introduction through writing, speaking and listening, and projects

SKILLS INSTRUCTION

Vocabulary: Related Words *phantasm* and *fantasy*

Grammar: Past Participial Phrases

Reading Strategy: Interactive Reading Strategies

Literary Focus: The Gothic Tradition

Writing: Organization

Speaking and Listening: Radio Narration (teacher edition)

PORTFOLIO OPPORTUNITIES

Writing: Journal Entry; Physical Description; Gothic Tale

Writing Mini-Lesson: Comparison-and-Contrast Essay

Speaking and Listening: Radio Narration; Movie Review

Projects: Set Design; Scientific Research

More About the Author
Mary Wollstonecraft Shelley was the only daughter of the philosopher William Godwin and Mary Wollstonecraft, an early feminist. She eloped to France with poet Percy Bysshe Shelley in July of 1814, a few months after meeting him. They were married two years later. After her husband's death in 1822, she devoted herself to promoting his writings. She published a number of his poems and edited all of his work, providing important notes to them. Besides *Frankenstein,* Mary Wollstonecraft Shelley wrote several other novels. Her 1826 novel, *The Last Man,* tells of the future destruction of the human race through a plague. Many consider it to be her finest work.

Guide for Interpreting

Mary Wollstonecraft Shelley

(1797–1851)

Perhaps you've sat around on a rainy day with your friends exchanging thrilling "tales of terror." The classic Gothic novel *Frankenstein* was born in a similar way. One day in 1816 Mary Shelley and her husband (the poet Percy Bysshe Shelley), the poet Lord Byron, and another friend challenged one another to write ghost stories.

***The product of a challenge, Mary Shelley's horrific tale of the creation of a monster eventually became the full-length classic horror novel,* Frankenstein.**

Since its publication in 1818, *Frankenstein* has thrilled countless readers and has been interpreted and reinterpreted by generations of filmmakers.

Literary and Political Legacy Literature and politics were in Mary Shelley's blood: her mother, Mary Wollstonecraft Godwin (who died at Mary's birth), wrote one of the first feminist books ever published, *A Vindication of the Rights of Woman* (1792). Her father, William Godwin, was an author and political philosopher. Amid this atmosphere of literary and political consciousness, Mary Godwin met her future husband, Percy Bysshe Shelley, a radically-minded young poet who had become William Godwin's admirer after reading his book *Political Justice.* Mary Godwin and Percy Bysshe Shelley fell in love and later married.

A Career of Her Own Married to one of the most famous poets of the nineteenth century, Mary Shelley had an active literary career of her own. After *Frankenstein,* she produced five more novels: *Valperga* (1823) and *The Fortunes of Perkin Warbeck* (1830), which are historical works; the autobiographical *Lodore* (1835); *Falkner* (1837), a complicated mystery tale; and *The Last Man* (1826). *Frankenstein* was the first of many works to explore the potential dangers of technology used for the wrong purposes—still an important theme today.

◆ Background for Understanding

LITERATURE: SHELLEY, FRANKENSTEIN, AND THE PROMETHEUS MYTH

During the Romantic era, when Mary Shelley wrote *Frankenstein,* the Greek mythological figure Prometheus was drawing renewed attention. Prometheus was one of the Titans—a race of giants; later myths say that Prometheus created man. He was the subject of part of a trilogy by the classic Greek writer Aeschylus, *Prometheus Bound,* and later of a lyric drama by Percy Shelley, *Prometheus Unbound.* Society's interest in this Titan was not far from Mary Shelley's mind when she wrote *Frankenstein*, about a doctor who attempts to create a man. In fact, the complete title of her famous work is *Frankenstein, or the Modern Prometheus.*

Journal Writing Jot down the title and plot of another myth or story you know that explains the origin of humans.

Prentice Hall Literature Program Resources

REINFORCE / RETEACH / EXTEND

Selection Support Pages
Build Vocabulary: Related Words: *Phantasm* and *Fantasy,* p. 134
Grammar and Style: Past Participial Phrases, p. 135
Reading for Success: Interactive Strategies, pp. 136–137
Literary Focus: The Gothic Tradition, p. 138

Strategies for Diverse Student Needs
Identify the Sequence of Events, p. 28

Beyond Literature
Cross-Curricular Connection: Science, p. 28

Formal Assessment Selection Test, pp. 140–142; and Assessment Resources Software

Alternative Assessment, p. 28

Writing and Language Transparencies
Comparison-and-Contrast Essay, pp. 85–92

Resource Pro CD-ROM
From the Introduction to *Frankenstein*

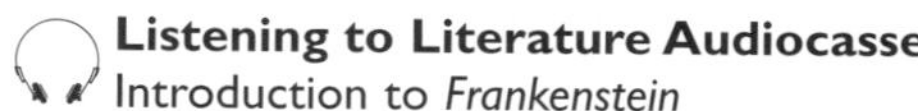

Listening to Literature Audiocassettes
Introduction to *Frankenstein*

MODEL SELECTION

Introduction to *Frankenstein*

◆ Literature and Your Life

CONNECT YOUR EXPERIENCE

Looking back on your achievements during your high school years, you'll probably discover that you were greatly influenced by encouragement from or competition with your friends. Similarly, Mary Shelley's greatest accomplishment, the novel *Frankenstein,* was the result of a competition among friends. Just nineteen at the time, Shelley created a book that inspired dozens of movies—some of which you've probably seen. You may not realize, however, that Frankenstein is not the name of the soulless man-monster who eventually destroys his creator. Frankenstein is the creator himself—the infamous Dr. Frankenstein.

THEMATIC FOCUS: FANTASY AND REALITY

At the movies today, we're more likely to see space aliens than monsters (composites of animals and humans). Why are the fantastic creatures we envision now different from those envisioned in Shelley's time?

◆ Literary Focus

THE GOTHIC TRADITION

Mary Shelley's *Frankenstein* is a classic example of **gothic literature,** a form of literature in which the reader passes from the reasoned order of the everyday world into the dark and dreadful world of the supernatural. Gothic literature emerged in the eighteenth century as part of Romanticism, a movement that rejected the Age of Reason's claim that everything could be explained scientifically.

Gothic literature is characteristically set in castles, monasteries with underground passages, dark towers, and torture chambers—all featuring the Gothic architectural style of the period.

◆ Build Vocabulary

RELATED WORDS: *PHANTASM* AND *FANTASY*

Shelley uses the word *phantasm,* meaning "supernatural form or shape; figment of the imagination," to describe the monster she creates. The word is related to one with which you're probably quite familiar: *fantasy.*

WORD BANK

Preview the words on this list before you read the selection.

appendage
ungenial
acceded
platitude
phantasm
incitement

◆ Grammar and Style

PAST PARTICIPIAL PHRASES

Shelley frequently uses **past participial phrases,** which include a past participle—the past tense of a verb, usually ending in *-ed,* that functions as an adjective—and its modifiers and complements. The entire phrase functions as an adjective.

> . . . he would hope that, *left to itself,* the slight spark of light . . .

In this example, the participial phrase beginning with the irregular past participle *left* modifies the noun *spark.*

Interest Grabber Elicit from the class examples of "urban myths," alien abductions, or ghost stories about which they remember hearing or reading (Alligators in the sewer, Man abducted for his kidneys, Alien landings in Roswell, New Mexico and so on). Then inform students that two young literary rebels, Percy Bysshe Shelley and Lord Byron, along with nineteen-year-old Mary Shelley, and Byron's friend, Polidori, indulged in the very same sort of brainstorming activity while vacationing in Italy. The result of the session was Mary Shelley's masterpiece, *Frankenstein,* which to this day rates as one of the best examples of science-fiction horror ever written.

Customize for
Less Proficient Readers

Be certain that these students are familiar with the broad outline of the Frankenstein story. Explain that in the introduction they are about to read, the author explains how she got the idea for the story. Have students list several questions they would like answered. *Questions may include: Where was she when she got the idea? Did it come all at once or gradually?* As they read the selection, have students write down any answers they find.

Customize for
More Advanced Students

Write the following quotation from the selection on the chalkboard: "Frightful must it be, for supremely frightful would be the effect of any human endeavor to mock the stupendous mechanism of the Creator of the world." Point out that in 1816 the possibilities for creating human life were less certain than they are today. Have these students identify some modern "human endeavors" which might "mock the stupendous mechanism of the Creator." *Possibilities include: invitro fertilization, genetic engineering, and the cloning of animals.*

Preparing for Standardized Tests

Reading and Vocabulary The interactive reading strategies will help students successfully complete many portions of standardized tests. The skills of questioning and predicting will help students in critical reading sections of tests. Using prior knowledge of the historical time period helps students make inferences which will be useful in reading comprehension questions. For more practice with interactive reading strategies, give students the Reading for Success pages in ***Selection Support,*** pp. 136–137.

Grammar and Language Students' ability to recognize past participial phrases and their function may be a focus in tests of English usage. The Grammar and Style lesson for this selection focuses on this topic. For additional practice, use the Grammar and Style page on Past Participial Phrases in ***Selection Support,*** p. 135.

Reading for Success

The Reading for Success page in each unit presents a set of problem-solving procedures to help readers understand authors' words and ideas on multiple levels. Good readers develop a bank of strategies from which they can draw as needed. Unit 4 introduces strategies for interactive reading. These strategies give readers an approach for understanding the text on many levels: using prior knowledge, questioning, predicting, clarifying details and information, using historical knowledge, and responding to the work.

These strategies for interactive reading are modeled with Mary Shelley's Introduction to *Frankenstein.* Each green box shows an example of the thinking process involved in applying one of these strategies.

How to Use the Reading for Success Page

- Introduce the strategies for interactive reading, presenting each as a problem-solving procedure. Be sure students understand what each strategy involves and under what circumstances to apply it.
- Before students read the selection, have them preview the annotations in the green boxes that model the strategies.
- To reinforce these strategies after students have read the selection, have them complete the Reading for Success pages in ***Selection Support***, pp. 136–137. These pages give students an opportunity to read a selection and practice interactive reading strategies by writing their own annotations.

Reading for Success

Interactive Reading Strategies

When you read critically, you're interacting with a literary work. You're using your inner voice to probe, recall bits of your own experience, and question. Use these strategies for interactive reading:

Use prior knowledge.

Special facts or incidents that you remember can help you connect with a given literary work. For example, if you know from Jewish folklore that a golem is an artificially created human being, you'll have a point of reference for Frankenstein's monster. As you read, trust your memory; it can annotate a literary work with useful references.

Question.

One role of your critical "voice" is to ask questions. In works of nonfiction, such as the "Introduction to *Frankenstein,*" it's important to ask: What evidence supports these statements? What point of view influenced the author to draw this conclusion (or form this opinion)?

Predict.

Making predictions about what will happen in a literary work keeps you involved in your reading. Base your predictions on clues that the writer provides, along with what you learn about the characters and the pattern in which the work is organized. As you read, check your predictions, and revise them as necessary.

Clarify details and information.

When you're unclear about a detail in a selection, try rephrasing the detail to yourself. Review what you've read, or read ahead to see if you can find the information you need. In some cases, the information may not be included in the text, and you may want to look up the information later.

Use your knowledge of the historical time period.

If you know that one distinguishing feature of the period was the growth in scientific thought, you'll be better prepared to understand the "Introduction to *Frankenstein*." Using your knowledge of historical periods helps you connect a literary work to the society that gave birth to it.

Respond to the work.

Even solitary reflection on a literary work is a way of interacting with it. You may finish "Introduction to *Frankenstein,*" and two days later an event in your own life will call forth an aspect of the work. Remain open to the ideas in a literary work, and you'll see them echoed in the world around you.

As you read Mary Shelley's "Introduction to *Frankenstein,*" look at the notes along the sides. These notes demonstrate how to apply these strategies to a work of literature.

Reading Strategies: Support and Reinforcement

Appropriate Reading Strategies Students are given a reading strategy to apply in reading each selection. In other selections, a strategy is suggested that is appropriate to the selection.

Reading Prompts To encourage application of the given reading strategy, there are occasional prompts, within green boxes, at appropriate and significant points.

In addition, there are red boxes prompting application of the Literary Focus concept and maroon boxes prompting students to connect with their lives.

Using the Boxed Annotations and Prompts

The material in the green, red, and maroon boxes along the sides of selections is intended to help students apply the literary element and the reading strategy and to make a connection with their lives.

You may use the boxed material in several ways:

- Have students pause when they come to a box and respond to its prompt before they continue reading.
- Urge students to read through the selection, ignoring the boxes. After they have read the selection completely, they may go back and review the selection, responding to the prompts.

Introduction to

FRANKENSTEIN

MARY WOLLSTONECRAFT SHELLEY

In this introduction to the third edition of Frankenstein, *published in 1831, Mary Shelley recalls the circumstances that led her to write the novel during the summer of 1816.*

The Publishers of the Standard Novels, in selecting *Frankenstein* for one of their series, expressed a wish that I should furnish them with some account of the origin of the story. I am the more willing to comply, because I shall thus give a general answer to the question, so very frequently asked me: "How I, then a young girl, came to think of, and to dilate upon, so very hideous an idea?" It is true that I am very averse to bringing myself forward in print; but as my account will only appear as an appendage to a former production, and as it will be confined to such topics as have connection with my authorship alone, I can scarcely accuse myself of a personal intrusion. . . .

❶ Using your **knowledge** of the Romantic period and the expectations of women at that time will help you understand the shock people felt about a young lady creating such a hideous tale.

In the summer of 1816, we[1] visited Switzerland, and became the neighbors of Lord Byron. At first we spent our pleasant hours on the lake or wandering on its shores; and Lord Byron, who was writing the third canto of *Childe Harold*, was the only one among us who put his thoughts upon paper. These, as he brought them successively to us, clothed in all the light and harmony of poetry, seemed to stamp as divine the glories of heaven and earth, whose influences we partook with him.

But it proved a wet, ungenial summer, and incessant rain often confined us for days to the house. Some volumes of ghost stories, translated from the German into French,[2] fell ❷ into our hands. There was "The History of the Inconstant Lover,"[3] who, when he thought to clasp the bride to whom he had pledged his vows, found himself in the arms of the pale ghost of her whom he had deserted. There was the tale of the sinful founder of his race,[4]

1. **we:** Mary Shelley, her husband Percy Bysshe Shelley, and their two children.

2. **volumes . . . French:** *Fantasmagoriana,* or *Collected Stories of Apparitions of Specters, Ghosts, Phantoms, Etc.,* published anonymously in 1812.
3. **"The History . . . Lover":** The true name of the story is "The Dead Fiancée."
4. **the tale . . . race:** "Family Portraits."

◆ Build Vocabulary

appendage (ə pen´ dij) *n.*: Something added on

ungenial (un jēn´ yəl) *adj.*: Unfriendly; characterized by bad weather

One-Minute Insight The nature and source of a writer's inspiration has always been the subject of wonder and speculation. In this Introduction to *Frankenstein,* students should gain a rare insight into the process. This highly personal account provides not only a narrative of the events that led to the idea of this story but also a glimpse of the author's emotional reaction to the idea before it took shape in words.

◆ Critical Thinking

❶ **Speculate** Ask students: Why do you suppose Shelley does not like the idea of bringing herself "forward in print?" *Many authors prefer to let their work speak for itself. By commenting on the creative process or "meaning" of the work, Shelley may feel that she is unfairly coming between the reader and the selection.*

◆ Grammar and Style

❷ **Past Participial Phrases** Have students locate the past participial phrase and explain what it modifies. *The past participial phrase is "translated from the German into French." It modifies "volumes of ghost stories."*

Block Scheduling Strategies

Consider these suggestions to take advantage of extended class time:

- Have students complete the journal writing activity in Background for Understanding on page 576 and share their titles and plots in small groups.
- Have students form groups to discuss the question posed in Thematic Focus: Fantasy and Reality in Literature and Your Life on page 577. Have a recorder in each group report the conclusions of the group.
- Introduce and model the Interactive Reading Strategies on page 578. Direct students to read the prompt boxes that model the strategies within the selection. Have students answer the Reading for Success questions on page 584.
- Have students answer Critical Thinking questions, 1 through 5 on page 583. Then as a class, discuss the question posed in number 6.
- Initiate a class discussion of the students' ideas about *Frankenstein* when they read Mary Shelley's Introduction. Then have students complete the Writing Mini-Lesson on page 585.

◆ Literature and Your Life

❶ In these lines, Shelley recalls two stories she read while in Switzerland fifteen years earlier, yet, she says, they are "as fresh in my mind as if I had read them yesterday." Have students recall stories that made a strong impression on them.

◆ Critical Thinking

❷ **Draw Conclusions** Why might Shelley refer to Polidori as "poor"? *Suggested response: Polidori alone of the group was not a writer, and his attempts at writing a ghost story were pathetic.*

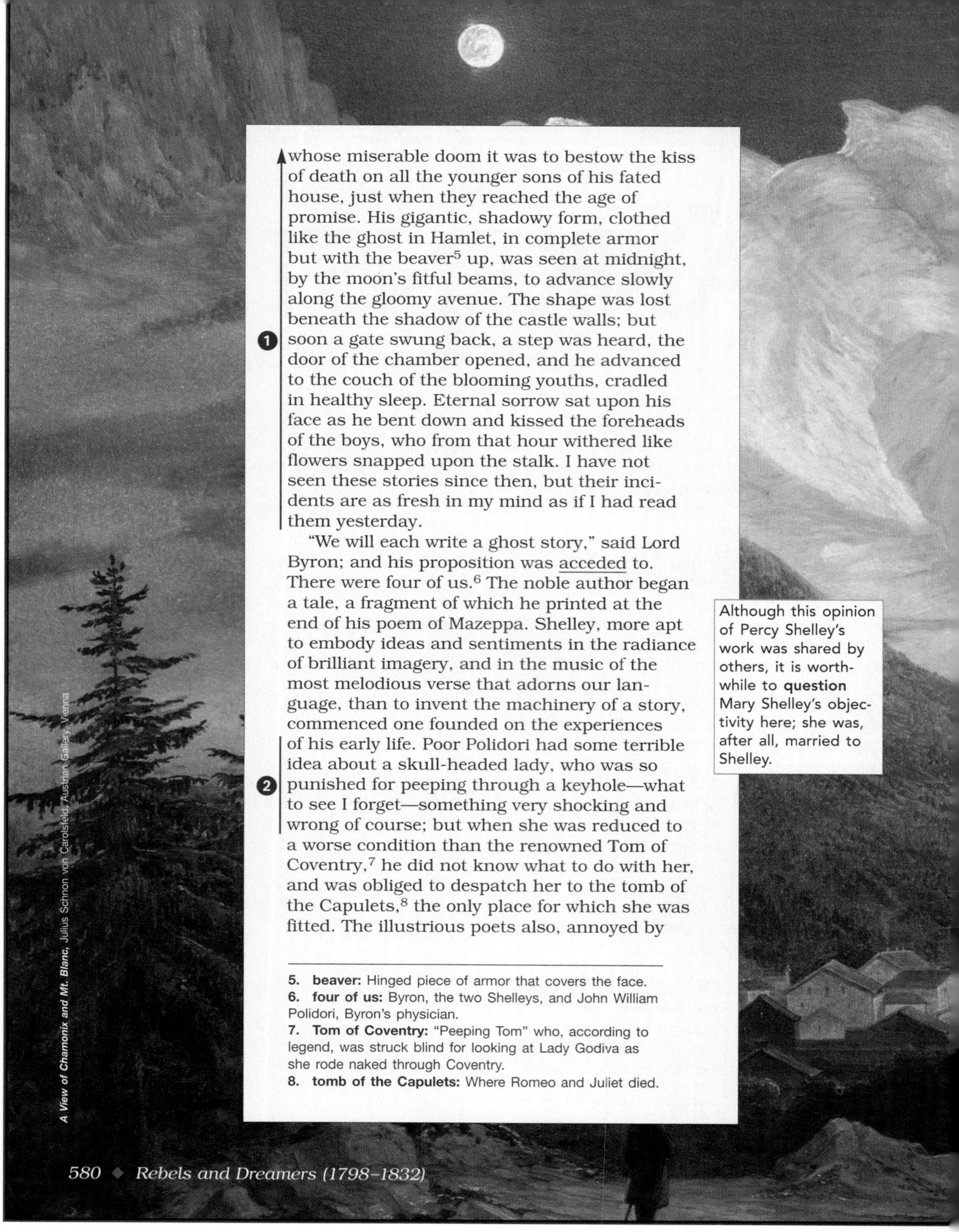

❶ whose miserable doom it was to bestow the kiss of death on all the younger sons of his fated house, just when they reached the age of promise. His gigantic, shadowy form, clothed like the ghost in Hamlet, in complete armor but with the beaver[5] up, was seen at midnight, by the moon's fitful beams, to advance slowly along the gloomy avenue. The shape was lost beneath the shadow of the castle walls; but soon a gate swung back, a step was heard, the door of the chamber opened, and he advanced to the couch of the blooming youths, cradled in healthy sleep. Eternal sorrow sat upon his face as he bent down and kissed the foreheads of the boys, who from that hour withered like flowers snapped upon the stalk. I have not seen these stories since then, but their incidents are as fresh in my mind as if I had read them yesterday.

"We will each write a ghost story," said Lord Byron; and his proposition was acceded to. There were four of us.[6] The noble author began a tale, a fragment of which he printed at the end of his poem of Mazeppa. Shelley, more apt to embody ideas and sentiments in the radiance of brilliant imagery, and in the music of the most melodious verse that adorns our language, than to invent the machinery of a story, commenced one founded on the experiences of his early life. ❷ Poor Polidori had some terrible idea about a skull-headed lady, who was so punished for peeping through a keyhole—what to see I forget—something very shocking and wrong of course; but when she was reduced to a worse condition than the renowned Tom of Coventry,[7] he did not know what to do with her, and was obliged to despatch her to the tomb of the Capulets,[8] the only place for which she was fitted. The illustrious poets also, annoyed by

Although this opinion of Percy Shelley's work was shared by others, it is worthwhile to **question** Mary Shelley's objectivity here; she was, after all, married to Shelley.

5. **beaver:** Hinged piece of armor that covers the face.
6. **four of us:** Byron, the two Shelleys, and John William Polidori, Byron's physician.
7. **Tom of Coventry:** "Peeping Tom" who, according to legend, was struck blind for looking at Lady Godiva as she rode naked through Coventry.
8. **tomb of the Capulets:** Where Romeo and Juliet died.

A View of Chamonix and Mt. Blanc, Julius Schnorr von Carolsfeld, Austrian Gallery, Vienna

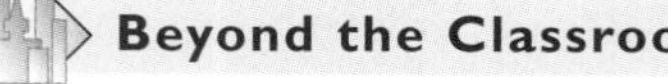

Beyond the Classroom

Career Connection

Architecture Gothic literature like *Frankenstein* gets its name from the architectural style of the castles and monasteries that were so often the setting for these stories. This architectural style flourished in Western Europe from the twelfth to the sixteenth century. It is distinguished by its pointed arches, stained-glass windows, slender spires, detailed ornamentation, and a generally vertical appearance that suggested heavenly aspirations.

Have interested students research the elements of gothic architecture and find photographs or illustrations of good examples.

Community Connection

Local Features Gothic architecture, though not as popular as it was in the medieval period, is also used in some modern buildings, reflecting a link with past traditions. Gothic-style architecture is most often used in churches and universities. However, particular elements inspired by gothic architecture, such as stained glass windows or pointed arches, can be found in other modern structures.

Have students identify examples of gothic architecture in your area or region.

◆ **Build Vocabulary**

acceded (ak sēd′ id) *v.*: Yielded to; agreed upon

Humanities

A View of Chamonix and Mt. Blanc by Julius Schnon von Carolsfeld.

Julius Schnon von Carolsfeld (1794-1872) was a German Nazarene painter. The Nazarenes were a group of Viennese artists who sought a return to the art of the Middle Ages. In their efforts to achieve the proper atmosphere, they occupied an abandoned monastery in Rome and worked as artist-monks. Their art was romantic, sentimental, and realistic.

The academically trained Julius von Carolsfeld often expressed this Nazarene form of Romanticism in landscape painting. *A View of Chamonix and Mt. Blanc* was painted in 1824. Beautifully detailed, it is a moonlit view of a famous glacier-covered mountain and a small village in the French Alps. As is common in German Romanticism, the painting has a weird or mysterious feeling to it, perhaps because of the extreme realism. This weirdness is the very quality that makes this an appropriate illustration for the environment in which Mary Shelley wrote the horror classic *Frankenstein*.

Use the following questions for discussion:

1. How would you describe the setting of this painting? *Suggested response: The landcape shows the setting to be bleak and austere. The colors give the painting a bleak but romantic atmosphere.*
2. What relationship does the artist of this painting suggest between people and nature? *The human figure and the houses in the valley seem almost insignificant beside the mountains and trees, suggesting that human beings are simply part of a much larger natural universe.*

Cross-Curricular Connection: Science and Ethics

Mary Shelley describes the Dr. Frankenstein of her vision as the "pale student of unhallowed arts" because his experiments "mock" the Creator. Modern science and medicine has also experimented with certain life and death issues that have caused some to question the moral propriety of such work. So called "test tube babies," cloning, and genetic experiments have provoked heated discussion of science and ethics. Have students discuss some of the latest medical and scientific experiments that parallel those of the fictional Dr. Frankenstein in 1816. Interested students can research the position taken by various professional associations on the ethics of such experiments.

◆ Literature and Your Life

❶ In this passage, Shelley describes the difficulty of coming up with a story. Have students recall a time when they were required to write something, but drew a complete blank. *Students may recall a time in school when they were given a hard-to-meet deadline or were given complete freedom to choose a topic.*

❷ **Enrichment** In 1831 electricity was in its infancy. Few understood exactly what it was and what it might be capable of doing. Street lights, for example, which are so commonplace today, were still more than fifty years away from becoming a reality. Students can use this knowledge to better comprehend the speculation about galvinism as a means of creating life.

❸ **Clarification** From midnight to one o'clock A.M. is sometimes referred to as "the witching hour."

◆ Build Vocabulary

❹ **Related Words: *Phantasm* and *Fantasy*** The word *phantom* comes from the same Greek root as *phantasm* and *fantasy*. Ask: What element of meaning do these three words share? *All three words have to do with something seen or sensed, but having no physical reality.*

Comprehension Check ☑

❺ Have students list or graph the chain of events that led to the sudden "I have found it!" *(1) Reading ghost stories leads to the suggestion that everyone write a ghost story. (2) The conversation about Dr. Darwin causes Shelley to imagine the human experiment. (3) She has a terrifying dream about such an experiment. (4) Upon waking, it occurs to her that the vision that frightened her would also frighten others.*

the platitude of prose, speedily relinquished their uncongenial task.

I busied myself to *think of a story*—a story to rival those which had excited us to this task. One which would speak to the mysterious fears of our nature and awaken thrilling horror—one to make the reader dread to look round, to curdle the blood, and quicken the beatings of the heart. If I did not accomplish these things, my ghost story would be unworthy of its name. I thought and pondered—vainly. I felt that blank incapability of invention which is the greatest misery of authorship, when dull Nothing replies to our anxious invocations. *Have you thought of a story?* I was asked each morning, and each morning I was forced to reply with a mortifying negative. . . . ❶

> You might **predict** from this statement that if Shelley succeeded in her task of writing a horror story, she would do so splendidly.

Many and long were the conversations between Lord Byron and Shelley, to which I was a devout but nearly silent listener. During one of these, various philosophical doctrines were discussed, and among others the nature of the principle of life and whether there was any probability of its ever being discovered and communicated. They talked of the experiments of Dr. Darwin[9] (I speak not of what the Doctor really did or said that he did, but, as more to my purpose, of what was then spoken of as having been done by him), who preserved a piece of vermicelli in a glass case till by some extraordinary means it began to move with voluntary motion. Not thus, after all, would life be given. Perhaps a corpse would be reanimated: galvanism[10] had given token of such things. Perhaps the component parts of a creature might be manufactured, brought together, and endued with vital warmth. ❷

> If you want to know more about reanimation, jot down a note to look up and **clarify** the concept later.

Night waned upon this talk, and even the witching hour had gone by, before we retired ❸ to rest. When I placed my head on my pillow, I did not sleep, nor could I be said to think. My imagination, unbidden, possessed and guided me, gifting the successive images that arose in my mind with a vividness far beyond the usual bounds of reverie. I saw—with shut eyes but acute mental vision—I saw the pale student of unhallowed arts kneeling beside the thing he had put together. I saw the hideous phantasm ❹ of a man stretched out, and then, on the working of some powerful engine, show signs of life and stir with an uneasy, half vital motion. Frightful must it be, for supremely frightful would be the effect of any human endeavor to mock the stupendous mechanism of the Creator of the world. His success would terrify the artist; he would rush away from his odious handiwork, horror-stricken. He would hope that, left to itself, the slight spark of life which he had communicated would fade; that this thing, which had received such imperfect animation, would subside into dead matter; and he might sleep in the belief that the silence of the grave would quench forever the transient existence of the hideous corpse which he had looked upon as the cradle of life. He sleeps; but he is awakened; he opens his eyes; behold the horrid thing stands at his bedside, opening his curtains, and looking on him with yellow, watery, but speculative eyes.

I opened mine in terror. The idea so possessed my mind, that a thrill of fear ran through me, and I wished to exchange the ghastly image of my fancy for the realities around. I see them still: the very room, the dark parquet,[11] the closed shutters, with the moonlight struggling through, and the sense I had that the glassy lake and white high Alps were beyond. I could not so easily get rid of my

9. **Dr. Darwin:** Erasmus Darwin (1731–1802), physician, natural scientist, and poet.

10. **galvanism:** Use of electric current to induce twitching in dead muscles.

11. **parquet** (pär kā′): Flooring made of wooden pieces arranged in a pattern.

Speaking and Listening Mini-Lesson

This mini-lesson supports the Radio Narration activity on page 585.

Introduce the Concept Initiate a discussion about radio plays and the advantages and limitation of that medium. Students should observe that, unlike staged dramas, radio dramas unfold through dialogue, sound effects, and narration, leaving it up to the listeners to imagine the rest. Radio drama actors can play several parts by simply changing their vocal inflection.

Develop Background Students should follow these clearly defined steps:

- Decide on a horror story or an episode from a horror story that can be presented in 10 to 15 minutes.
- Prepare the script through improvisation or by transcribing details from the original story into a script form.
- Cast the speaking parts and assign production roles such as director.
- Finally, add appropriate background music and sound effects.

Apply the Information Students should rehearse and refine their radio dramas, striving to create a coherent, suspenseful story. You may elect to have students record their dramas and play the audiotapes to the class.

Assess the Outcome Have students evaluate the radio dramas according to clarity, interest, suspense, and creativity.

hideous phantom: still it haunted me. I must try to think of something else. I recurred to my ghost story—my tiresome unlucky ghost story! O! if I could only contrive one which would frighten my reader as I myself had been frightened that night!

Swift as light and as cheering was the idea
5 that broke in upon me. "I have found it! What terrified me will terrify others, and I need only describe the specter which had haunted my midnight pillow." On the morrow I announced that I had *thought of a story*. I began that day with the words, *It was on a dreary night of November*, making only a transcript of the grim terrors of my waking dream.

At first I thought but of a few pages—of a short tale—but Shelley urged me to develop the idea at greater length. I certainly did not owe the suggestion of one incident, nor scarcely of one train of feeling, to my husband, and yet but for his incitement, it would never have taken the form in which it was presented to the world. From this declaration I must except the preface. As far as I can recollect, it was entirely written by him.

And now, once again, I bid my hideous progeny go forth and prosper. I have an affection for it, for it was the offspring of happy days, when death and grief were but words, which found no true echo in my heart. Its several pages speak of many a walk, many a drive, and many a conversation, when I was not alone; and my companion was one who, in this world, I shall never see more. But this is for myself: my readers have nothing to do with these associations.

◆ Build Vocabulary

platitude (plat´ ə to͞od´) *n.*: Statement lacking originality

phantasm (fan´ taz'm) *n.*: Supernatural form or shape; ghost; figment of the mind

incitement (in sīt´ mənt) *n.*: Cause to perform; encouragement

Guide for Responding

◆ Literature and Your Life

Reader's Response Did you find Shelley's account interesting? Why or why not?

Thematic Focus Why do you think horror stories appeal to people?

☑ Check Your Comprehension

1. What is Shelley referring to when she says, "I have not seen these stories since then, but their incidents are as fresh in my mind . . . "?
2. Why did the "illustrious poets . . . relinquish their ungenial task"?
3. What provided the author with her inspiration for *Frankenstein?*
4. What did Shelley think she needed to do in order to write a successful ghost story?

◆ Critical Thinking

INTERPRET

1. Find the passage that supports Shelley's implication that her husband would fail at the ghost story assignment. Explain. **[Interpret]**
2. What effect does Mary Shelley's inability to think of a story have on her? **[Analyze]**
3. What do you think Shelley's attitude is toward Darwin's experiments? Explain. **[Draw Conclusions]**

APPLY

4. What does the "Introduction to *Frankenstein*" suggest about how writers get ideas? **[Generalize]**
5. What does this selection reveal to you about the relationship between Mary Shelley and her husband? **[Synthesize]**

EXTEND

6. What kinds of scientific experimentation today are comparable to Darwin's in the eighteenth century? Explain. **[Science Link]**

Beyond the Selection

FURTHER READING

Other Works by the Author

Valperga and Lodore; Falkner; The Last Man

Works About the Author

The Woman Who Created Frankenstein: A Portrait of Mary Shelley, Janet Harris

Child of Light: A Reassessment of Mary Wollstonecraft Shelley, Muriel Spark

We suggest that you preview these works before recommending them to students.

INTERNET

You and your students may find additional information about Mary Shelley on the Internet. We suggest the following site. Please be aware, however, that sites may have changed from the time we published this information. For information about Shelley's life and works go to **http://www.accd.edu/sac/english/bailey/mshelley.htm**

You may also find related information on *Frankenstein* on the Internet. We *strongly recommend* that you preview the sites before you send students to them.

Reinforce and Extend

Answers

◆ Literature and Your Life

Reader's Response Students may find Shelley's restless night and dream interesting because they may have experienced similar unrest after hearing a late-night tale.

Thematic Focus Sample response: People enjoy the adrenalin rush that accompanies fear.

☑ Check Your Comprehension

1. She is referring to the ghost stories she, her husband, and Lord Byron read one summer in Italy.
2. The poets were more accustomed to the music and imagery of poetry, not fictional narratives.
3. The talk of Dr. Darwin's experiments with inanimate substances caused her to imagine the terrifying image of a reanimated man.
4. Shelley felt that she needed only to make her readers become as frightened as she was the night she saw the "hideous phantasm."

◆ Critical Thinking

1. In the second paragraph of page 580, Shelley states her husband is more attuned to the music and imagery of poetry than to the machinery of a story.
2. Shelley is embarrassed and frustrated. She answers with a "mortifying negative" when asked if she has thought of a story.
3. She seems to think that Dr. Darwin's experiments are valid as far as they go. It is the extension of these experiments to human subjects she finds horrible.
4. It suggests that ideas grow from association and expansion of other ideas.
5. Mary Shelley has a great admiration for her husband's talents, even crediting him for *Frankenstein's* success. She also seems to be aware of his limitations, as evidenced by her frank assessment of his failure to write a ghost story.
6. Numerous genetic and DNA experiments are allowing science to manipulate life as never before. Cloning and genetic engineering are just a few examples.

Develop Understanding

Answers

◆ Reading for Success

Interactive Reading Strategies

1. (a) Answers may include: How successful were the first two editions of *Frankenstein?* How long did it take Mary Shelley to convert her mental image into a novel? (b) Knowing about the first two editions would clarify the publisher's desire to have Shelley write an Introduction to the third edition. Knowing how long it took Shelley to write *Frankenstein* will clarify whether or not she was able to finish it before her husband died.
2. Knowing the time and circumstances of Percy Bysshe Shelley's death will clarify the nature of the death, grief, and loneliness Mary Shelley describes.

◆ Literary Focus

The Gothic Tradition

1. Elements of Gothic tradition include: the supernatural elements of ghosts; the mysterious kiss of death; and the castle setting with its shadows and armor.
2. Because *Frankenstein* deals with science run amok, resulting in the creation of a beast or monster who inspires terrror, it is considered a Gothic tale.
3. Suggested response: *Frankenstein* probably addresses the question of the proper limitations of science in human life and whether certain areas of "learning" are best left alone.
4. Students may observe that science or science fiction figures prominently in both Gothic and modern tales of horror. Most modern horror stories probably contain fewer references to the morality or ethics of the story's protagonist.

◆ Grammar and Style

1. Participial phrase: clothed in all the light and harmony of poetry; modifies *them;* pronoun
2. Participial phrase: translated from the German into French; modifies *stories;* noun
3. Participial phrase: clothed like the ghost in *Hamlet;* modifies *form;* noun
4. Participial phrase: cradled in healthy sleep; modifies *youths;* noun
5. Participial phrase: annoyed by the platitude of prose; modifies *poets;* noun

For additional practice use the practice page on Participles and Participial Phrases, p. 29 in the *Writer's Solution Grammar Practice Book.*

◆ Build Vocabulary

Using Related Words

1. A *phantom* is a ghostly apparition with no physical form.
2. A *phantasmagoric* is an adjective describing a series of fantastic images that appear in an irrational sequence as in a dream.

Both come from the Greek word *phantos,* meaning visible.

Using the Word Bank

1. c; addition
2. b; mean
3. c; agreed
4. b; cliché
5. b; illusion
6. c; motivation

Guide for Responding (continued)

◆ Reading for Success

INTERACTIVE READING STRATEGIES

Review the reading strategies and the notes showing how to read interactively. Then apply them to answer the following:

1. (a) Give an example of a detail from the selection you'd like clarified. (b) In what specific ways will this clarification help you to understand "Introduction to *Frankenstein*"?
2. Explain how knowing that Percy Shelley died of drowning before the age of thirty will help you understand the last paragraph of the "Introduction to *Frankenstein*."

◆ Grammar and Style

PAST PARTICIPIAL PHRASES

Participial phrases are groups of words that serve as adjectives; the entire phrase modifies a noun or pronoun. "Introduction to *Frankenstein*" has several participial phrases that include past participles, verb forms ending in *-ed.*

Practice In the following passages, past participial phrases modify nouns and pronouns, including relative pronouns. Write each passage in your notebook. Underline the participial phrase, circle the word it modifies, and, after each item, identify the part of speech of the modified word.

1. ... as he brought them successively to us, clothed in all the light and harmony of poetry, seemed....
2. Some volumes of ghost stories, translated from the German into French, fell into....
3. His gigantic shadowy form, clothed like the ghost in *Hamlet,* in complete armor ... was seen....
4. ... and he advanced to the couch of the blooming youths, cradled in healthy sleep.
5. The illustrious poets also, annoyed by the platitude of prose, speedily relinquished their uncongenial task.

Writing Application Write a paragraph or two summarizing the key details in this selection. Include at least two past participial phrases.

◆ Literary Focus

THE GOTHIC TRADITION

The **Gothic novel** was a late-eighteenth-century revival of the tale of terror, which has its roots in antiquity. Gothic novels and stories are often set in sinister medieval times, with Gothic architecture as their backdrop. Mixing everyday events with supernatural ones, as Shelley does in *Frankenstein,* is another important trademark of Gothic tales.

1. What characteristics of Gothic literature do the ghost stories described in the third paragraph of the introduction share? Explain.
2. Explain why Mary Shelley's idea for *Frankenstein* fits within the defining parameters of the Gothic tradition.
3. Based on your reading of the introduction, what most likely is the theme of *Frankenstein?*
4. Compare and contrast the ingredients of Gothic tales that you learn about here with those used in current-day horror movies and books.

◆ Build Vocabulary

USING RELATED WORDS

Knowing that the word *phantasm* means "supernatural form or shape," define the following terms. If necessary, use a dictionary to help you.

1. phantom **2.** phantasmagoric

How do these words relate to the word *fantasy?*

USING THE WORD BANK

In your notebook, write the letter of the word that is closest in meaning to the first word.

1. appendage: (a) accessory, (b) part, (c) addition
2. ungenial: (a) friendly, (b) mean, (c) unhappy
3. acceded: (a) defied, (b) broken, (c) agreed
4. platitude: (a) innovation, (b) cliché, (c) statement
5. phantasm: (a) reality, (b) illusion, (c) creation
6. incitement: (a) deterrent, (b) apparition, (c) motivation

Build Your Portfolio

Idea Bank

Writing

1. **Journal Entry** In a journal entry, explain why "Introduction to *Frankenstein*" does or does not inspire you to read the novel.

2. **Physical Description** What would a monster created by Dr. Frankenstein look like today? Write a page-long description, using sensory images and precise details.

3. **Gothic Tale** Write a Gothic tale (at least two pages long) in which the familiar becomes sinister. Include shocking events and details that will horrify your audience. You might use horror movies you've seen to help you come up with ideas.

Speaking and Listening

4. **Radio Narration** Only a few decades ago, large audiences listened eagerly to tales of horror presented on radio. Think of a horror story you know, and re-create it as a radio drama. **[Performing Arts Link; Media Link]**

5. **Movie Review** View a movie based on *Frankenstein*. Then present a television-style review of the movie to the class. If possible, show segments to support your points. **[Media Link]**

Projects

6. **Set Design** Research Gothic architecture and create a set for a movie or play in the tradition of Gothic horror stories. The play or movie can be based on a story with which you're familiar, or it can be one you make up. **[Art Link; Social Studies Link]**

7. **Scientific Research** Biogenesis is the doctrine that living organisms develop only from other living organisms. Research biogenesis, and present your findings to the class. **[Science Link]**

Writing Mini-Lesson

Comparison-and-Contrast Essay

Before reading Shelley's introduction, you probably knew about *Frankenstein* even though you might not have had direct exposure to the story. Write an essay in which you compare and contrast the impressions you had of *Frankenstein* before you read Shelley's "Introduction" with your impressions after reading it. Follow this tip as you develop and draft your essay:

Writing Skills Focus: Organization

A piece of writing should be **organized** in a way that fits the form and purpose of the writing. For example, when you write a comparison-and-contrast essay, you'll want to organize your details by points of comparison. You can either present all the similarities in one section and present the differences in another section or you can focus each paragraph on an aspect of your subject and point out both similarities and differences.

Prewriting To help gather details, use a chart like this one. In one column, list what you thought before you read Shelley's "Introduction." In the other column, list what you thought after reading it.

Before Reading	After Reading

Drafting Using the information in your chart, draft your comparison. Use terms that emphasize comparing and contrasting, such as *similar to* and *contrary to*, to show the relationships among ideas.

Revising Give your paper to a writing partner for feedback on whether your comparisons are clear and well organized.

✓ ASSESSMENT OPTIONS

Formal Assessment, Selection Test, pp. 140–142, and Assessment Resources Software. The selection test is designed so that it can be easily customized to the ability levels of your students. ***Alternative Assessment***, p. 28, includes options for less advanced students, more advanced students, visual/spatial learners, interpersonal learners, and intrapersonal learners.

PORTFOLIO ASSESSMENT

Use the following rubrics in the ***Alternative Assessment*** booklet to assess student writing:
Journal Entry: Expression Rubric, p. 95
Physical Description: Description Rubric, p. 98
Gothic Tale: Fictional Narrative Rubric, p. 96
Writing Mini-Lesson: Comparison-and-Contrast Rubric, p. 104

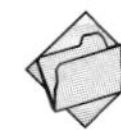

Idea Bank
Customizing for
Learning Modalities

Following are suggestions for matching Idea Bank topics with your students' learning modalities:

Visual/Spatial: 2, 6
Verbal/Linguistic: 3, 4, 5
Interpersonal: 7
Intrapersonal: 1

Customizing for
Performance Levels

Following are suggestions for matching Idea Bank topics with your students' ability levels:

Less Advanced Students: 1, 2
Average Students: 3, 5, 6
More Advanced Students: 4, 7

Writing Mini-lesson

Refer students to the Writing Handbook, page 1189, for instruction on the writing process, and page 1191 for further information on exposition.

Writing and Language Transparencies Use the Writing Process Model 10: Comparison-and-Contrast Essay, pp. 85–92, to help students understand the process of writing and revising. You may also use the Comparison-and-Contrast Chart, p. 115, to assist students as they organize the details for their essays.

Writing Lab CD-ROM

Direct students to complete the tutorial on Exposition. Follow these steps:

1. Play a video from *Star Trek* to see an example of comparison and contrast.
2. Look at the audio-annotated models for comparison-and-contrast organization.
3. Create a draft on the computer.
4. Use a Revision Checker for Unity and Coherence.

Sourcebook

Have students complete Chapter 3: Exposition, pp. 62–95, for additional support as they write their comparison-and-contrast essays.

Guide for Interpreting

OBJECTIVES

1. To interpret and respond to poetry
2. To relate poetry to personal experience
3. To translate dialect
4. To recognize use and effect of dialect
5. To build vocabulary in context and learn words related to clothing
6. To recognize and use interjections
7. To write a scene with dialogue that has a clear beginning, middle, and end
8. To respond to poetry through writing, speaking and listening, and projects

SKILLS INSTRUCTION

Vocabulary: Words Related to Clothing

Grammar: Interjections

Reading Strategy: Translate Dialect

Literary Focus: Dialect

Writing: Clear Beginning, Middle, and End

Speaking and Listening Lecture (teacher edition)

Critical Viewing: Connect; Compare and Contrast

PORTFOLIO OPPORTUNITIES

Writing: Advice to the Newlyweds; Comparison and Contrast; Response to Criticism

Writing Mini-Lesson: Scene With Dialogue

Speaking and Listening: Oral Interpretation; Lecture

Projects: Comic Strip; Multimedia Presentation

More About the Authors

Because **Robert Burns** was a stern critic of the Calvinist religion, the family of Jean Armour forbade him to marry her, so he turned his affections instead to Mary Campbell, whom he calls "Highland Mary" in his poems. After Mary died, Burns reconciled with the family of Jean Armour and married her in 1788. Burns died of rheumatic fever on July 21, 1796, the same day his wife gave birth to their youngest son.

Joanna Baillie's reputation rests on her plays, which won critical acclaim in a era when serious drama was in decline. Long forgotten, her work has been recently rediscovered by critics. A memorial to Joanna Baille in Larnarkshire, Scotland, is inscribed with a celebratory verse by Sir Walter Scott.

Robert Burns *(1759–1796)*

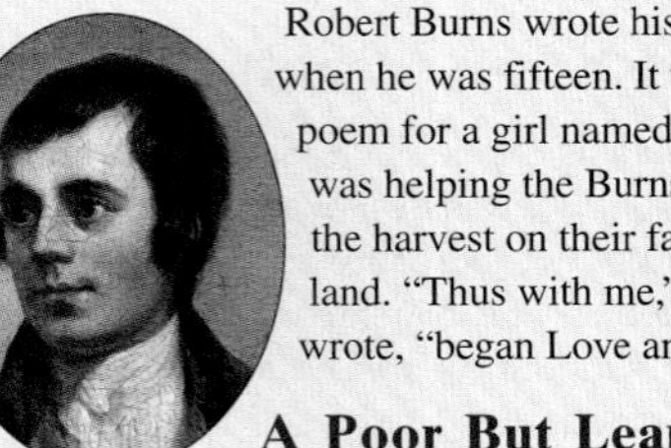

Robert Burns wrote his first verse when he was fifteen. It was a love poem for a girl named Nellie, who was helping the Burns family with the harvest on their farm in Scotland. "Thus with me," Burns later wrote, "began Love and Poesy."

A Poor But Learned Life Burns was born at Alloway, in Ayrshire. Although his family's poverty prevented him from receiving a formal education, with his father's encouragement he read widely, studying the Bible, Shakespeare, and Alexander Pope on his own. His mother, though herself illiterate, instilled in him a love of Scottish folk songs, legends, and proverbs.

Literary Triumph In 1786, Burns published his first collection of poems through a small local press. Although the collection, which included "To a Mouse," was successful, Burns didn't come to the attention of the general public until the following year, when *Poems, Chiefly in the Scottish Dialect* was published at Edinburgh. He was invited to the Scottish capital, where he was swept into the social scene and hailed as the "heaven-taught plowman."

A Lasting Contribution Although Burns died prematurely in his thirties, having suffered for years from a weak heart, his brief career resulted in a lasting contribution to literature. Burns's poems are among the most natural and spontaneous ever produced in the English language. Written for the most part in dialect, they are characterized by innocence, simplicity, and honesty. Though some of the poet's work had its origins in folk tunes, "it is not," as James Douglas writes, "easy to tell where the vernacular ends and the personal magic begins."

Joanna Baillie *(1762–1851)*

When Joanna Baillie (bā´ lē) achieved literary fame in 1800 with the publication of a volume of plays, Sir Walter Scott hailed her as "the immortal Joanna." Born in Lanarkshire, Scotland, Baillie moved to London in her early twenties, and spent the rest of her life there.

A Successful Dramatist Baillie is best-known for her plays, including *De Montfort* (1800) and *The Family Legend* (1810). However, she was also a successful poet and essayist who foreshadowed the Romantics by arguing that poetry should focus on naturalness in language and subject matter. Like Robert Burns, she wrote poems in the dialect of her homeland, many of them on nature and rustic manners.

◆ Background for Understanding

CULTURE: ROBERT BURNS'S USE OF LANGUAGE

Before Robert Burns published his poetry, works of literature were almost always modeled on the classics in which structure, grammar, and vocabulary were polished and complex.

Robert Burns ignored these conventions and boldly put poetry in the hands of the people, writing in their language, Scottish dialect, and using them as subject matter. This use of regional dialect had several effects: It flouted the idea that poems should deal with heroic topics and be written in heroic language, and it celebrated Scottish rural life. Writing in regional language also made the poetry accessible to the ordinary Scottish citizen, not just to scholars.

Prentice Hall Literature Program Resources

REINFORCE / RETEACH / EXTEND

Selection Support Pages
Build Vocabulary: Words Related to Clothing, p. 139
Grammar and Style: Interjections, p. 140
Reading Strategy: Translate Dialect, p. 141
Literary Focus: Dialect, p. 142

Strategies for Diverse Student Needs
Paraphrase, p. 29

Beyond Literature
Cross-Curricular Connection: Social Studies, p. 29

Daily Language Practice, Week 22, p. 48

Formal Assessment Selection Text, pp. 143–145; Assessment Resource Software

Alternative Assessment, p. 29

Writing and Language Transparencies
Dramatic Scene, pp. 25–35

Resource Pro CD-ROM "To a Mouse," "To a Louse," "Woo'd and Married and A'"

Listening to Literature Audiocassettes "To a Mouse," "To a Louse," "Woo'd and Married and A'"

To a Mouse ◆ To a Louse ◆ Woo'd and Married and A' ◆

◆ Literature and Your Life

Connect Your Experience

Your manner of speaking may reveal where you were brought up, your interests, or your education level. As you read the following poems, written in Scottish dialect, think about what the language of the speakers reveals about them.

Journal Writing Jot down in your journal three or four words or phrases that you often use in everyday speech. What, if anything, do they reveal about you?

Thematic Focus: Fantasy and Reality

If language can reveal a person's background, what does the theme of fantasy and reality in Burns's and Baillie's poems reveal about the poets and their culture?

◆ Literary Focus

Dialect

Dialect is the language, and particularly the speech habits, of a particular social class, region, or group. A dialect may vary from the standard form of a language in grammar, in pronunciation, and in the use of certain expressions.

In literature, dialect helps establish character, mood, and setting. The use of dialect can also give warmth and familiarity to a piece of literature. As you read, think about the ways in which use of dialect enhances the poems' meaning and effect.

◆ Reading Strategy

Translate Dialect

The poems in this section are written in Scottish dialect. As you read, **translate dialect** using these strategies.

1. Read footnotes to get definitions of dialect words.
2. Guess the meanings of other words by using the context. (*Cow'rin'* and *tim'rous* help you deduce that *wee* means "small".)
3. Speak words aloud and listen for similarities to standard English words. (Thou need *na* start *awa sae* hasty)
4. Look for similarities between the dialect words and standard English words. (*beastie* = *beast)*
5. Pay attention to apostrophes, which signal that a letter has been omitted. (*an'* = *and*; *lea'e* = *leave*)

◆ Build Vocabulary

Words Related to Clothing

Both poets help you picture settings and people by using a number of words related to clothing, such as *bonnet* (a woman's hat) and *bodice* (the upper part of a woman's dress). As you read, look for other examples of words related to clothing.

Word Bank

Before you read, preview this list of words from the poems.

dominion
impudence
winsome
discretion
inconstantly

◆ Grammar and Style

Interjections

The speakers in these poems vividly convey feelings by the use of **interjections**, words or phrases used to express emotion. A comma separates a mild interjection from the rest of the sentence, and an exclamation mark follows a stronger interjection. Look at these examples from the poems you're about to read.

O, what a panic's in thy breastie!

But, *och!* I backward cast my e'e

Preparing for Standardized Tests

Reading and Vocabulary The development of students' vocabulary will help them to improve performance on verbal sections of standardized tests such as reading comprehension, analogies, and other vocabulary items. For example, students may be expected to complete an analogy exercise such as this one:

COCKPIT : AIRPLANE: *(C)*
(A) teen : adult
(B) boxer : dog
(C) bodice : dress
(D) hand : foot

The Build Vocabulary lesson focuses on learning words related to clothing and on five more general terms. For additional practice, use the Build Vocabulary page in ***Selection Support***, p. 139.

Inform students that before Robert Burns and Joanna Baillie, only complex, classic language was considered to be appropriate for poetry. Burns and Baillie were rebels of their time, writing their poetry in the Scottish dialect—in the language of the people. Much like rap stars of today, who write their songs in the vernacular of urban youth, Burns and Baille used the vernacular of the Scots people in their poetry.

Customize for
Less Proficient Readers
To help less proficient readers with this dialect, have them first review the notes that define the unfamiliar words, then have them read each selection as they listen to a recording of it.

Customize for
More Advanced Students
Burns uses an unusual rhythm and rhyme scheme. Using a photocopy of the poem, have these students mark the metric feet and indicate the rhyme scheme using the standard AB notations. Have them note differences in pronunciation from modern English. For example, *thieve* rhymes with *live*. You might also have them research the etymology of interesting words.

Customize for
English Language Learners
To help these students cope with the dialect, have them paraphrase each stanza as they read the poems. They may do this in two steps: First, translate the stanza into standard English. Then rephrase the lines in shorter form.

Customize for
Musical/Rhythmic Learners
Instruct musical/rhythmic learners to read these poems aloud, noting the effect the poems' rhythms have on their meanings.

Develop Understanding

One-Minute Insight The unexpected encounter with a field mouse, whose home he has inadvertently destroyed with his plow, prompts the sympathetic speaker to apologize to the mouse. However, in the final two stanzas, the speaker uses the incident to generalize on the similarities between the mouse's situation and that of human beings. Just as the mouse's plans for a winter home have come to nothing, so do the humans' plans come undone.

◆ Critical Thinking

❶ **Infer** Ask students: Judging from what Burns says to the mouse, how did the mouse react to having her nest plowed up? *The mouse apparently scurried off and is now hiding for fear of being pursued.*

◆ Background for Understanding

❷ Burns is commonly regarded as a forerunner of the Romantic movement in art and literature. Largely a reaction to the earlier emphasis on the mind and intellect, the romantic movement favored the emotions as a guide. Unlike the previous age in which nature was something to be conquered, romantics see themselves as part of nature and consider meddling with the natural state of things a violation of natural law. Hence, Burns apologizes for man's intrusion with the plow into Nature's (note the capital *N*) "social union."

◆ Literary Focus

❸ **Dialect** Ask students to identify those words of dialect in this passage that vary from standard English in (a) usage and (b) pronunciation. *Words that vary in terms of usage include* thou, brattle, whyles, maun, daimen icker, thrave, foggage, *and* snell. *Words that vary from standard English pronunciation include* wa's *(walls),* win's *(winds),* naething *(nothing),* an' *(and), and* ensuin' *(ensuing).*

To a Mouse

On Turning Her up in Her Nest with the Plow, November, 1785

Robert Burns

❶ Wee, sleekit,[1] cow'rin', tim'rous beastie,
O, what a panic's in thy breastie!
Thou need na start awa sae hasty,
Wi' bickering brattle![2]
I wad be laith[3] to rin an' chase thee
Wi' murd'ring pattle![4]

❷ I'm truly sorry man's <u>dominion</u>
Has broken Nature's social union,
An' justifies that ill opinion,
Which makes thee startle,
At me, thy poor, earth-born companion,
An' fellow-mortal!

I doubt na, whyles,[5] but thou may thieve;
What then? poor beastie, thou maun[6] live!
A daimen icker in a thrave[7]
'S a sma' request:
I'll get a blessin' wi' the lave,[8]
And never miss't!

❸ Thy wee bit housie, too, in ruin!
Its silly wa's[9] the win's are strewin'!
An' naething, now, to big[10] a new ane,
O' foggage[11] green!
An' bleak December's winds ensuin',
Baith snell[12] an' keen!

Thou saw the fields laid bare and waste,
An' weary winter comin' fast,

1. **sleekit:** Sleek.
2. **Wi' . . . brattle:** With a quick pattering sound.
3. **wad be laith:** Would be loath.
4. **pattle:** Paddle for cleaning a plow.
5. **whyles:** At times.
6. **maun:** Must.
7. **A . . . thrave:** An occasional ear of grain in a bundle.
8. **lave:** Rest.
9. **silly wa's:** Feeble walls.
10. **big:** Build.
11. **foggage:** Rough grass.
12. **snell:** Sharp.

Block Scheduling Strategies

Consider these suggestions to take advantage of extended class time:

- Have students complete the journal activity in Literature and Your Life on page 587. Then have groups of students assemble a list of commonly used words or phrases.
- Introduce the Reading Strategy to students on page 587. Model for them how to translate a line of dialect from one of Robert Burns's poems. When students have finished reading, have them answer the Reading Strategy questions on page 594.
- Before reading the poems, have students preview the vocabulary words on page 587. When students have finished the poems, have them answer the Build Vocabulary questions on page 594.
- Play for students a poem by Burns on the **Listening to Literature Audiocassettes**. Then hold a discussion with students about whether or not listening to Burns's poem aids their comprehension.
- Have students complete individually or with a group one of the activities described in the Idea Bank on page 595.

An' cozie here, beneath the blast,
Thou thought to dwell,
Till crash! the cruel coulter[13] past
Out through thy cell.

4 That wee bit heap o' leaves an' stibble,
Has cost thee mony a weary nibble!
Now thou's turned out, for a' thy trouble,
But[14] house or hald,[15]
To thole[16] the winter's sleety dribble,
An' cranreuch[17] cauld!

But, Mousie, thou art no thy lane,[18]
In proving foresight may be vain:
5 The best laid schemes o' mice an' men
Gang aft a-gley,[19]
An' lea'e us nought but grief an' pain,
For promised joy.

Still thou art blest, compared wi' me!
The present only toucheth thee:
But, och! I backward cast my e'e
On prospects drear!
An' forward, though I canna see,
I guess an' fear!

13. **coulter:** Plow blade.

14. **But:** Without.
15. **hald:** Property.
16. **thole:** Withstand.
17. **cranreuch** (krən´ rəkh): Frost.
18. **no thy lane:** Not alone.

19. **Gang aft a-gley:** Go often awry.

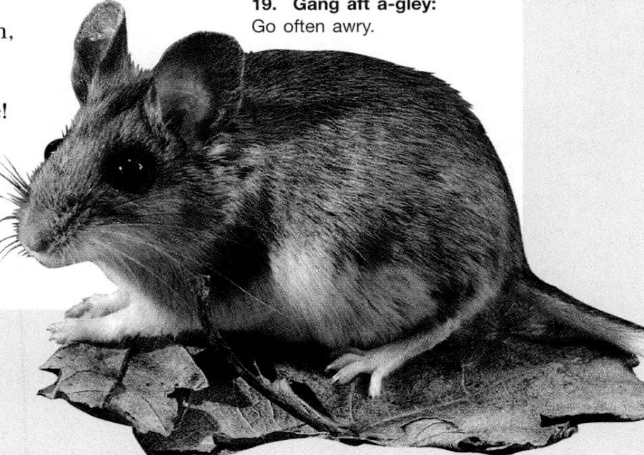

◆ **Build Vocabulary**

dominion (də min´ yən) *n.*: Rule; authority

Guide for Responding

◆ Literature and Your Life

Reader's Response How would you have reacted to the plight of the mouse? Explain.

Thematic Focus Burns uses fantasy to imagine how the mouse must have felt. How does the speaker balance fantasy with reality in this poem?

☑ Check Your Comprehension

1. For what reason does the speaker apologize to the mouse?
2. Why does the speaker say that, compared with him, the mouse is blessed?

◆ Critical Thinking

INTERPRET

1. What does the sentiment in lines 13–14 suggest about the speaker's own social code? **[Infer]**
2. (a) What famous line in the poem carries the poem's theme about human life? (b) How would you state this theme in your own words? **[Synthesize]**

APPLY

3. What value do you place on foresight? Explain your answer. **[Evaluate]**

Speaking and Listening Mini-Lesson

Lecture

This mini-lesson supports the Speaking and Listening activity in the Idea Bank on page 595.

Introduce the Concept Explain to students that an academic lecture is a type of oral presentation that is meant to enlighten and educate. An effective lecture captures the interest of the audience and presents information clearly.

Develop Background Tell students to decide on which aspects of Burns's life and poetry they want to focus, then to research and take notes on the information they find. Once information has been gathered, have students organize it, create or locate any visual aids they'd like to use and practice their presentations, focusing on delivering their information in a lively, and interesting manner.

Apply the Information After rehearsing, students should be ready to present lectures to the class. You may want to provide a lecture podium, chair, chalkboard, for each "lecturer" to use.

Assess the Outcome Have students evaluate the lectures of their peers according to clarity, interest, and content.

◆ Literature and Your Life

4 Have students paraphrase this stanza. Then ask if they can recall a time when their hard work was abruptly snuffed out through an accident of some kind. *Students may recall losing a homework assignment on which they spent hours.*

◆ Reading Strategy

5 **Translate Dialect** Have students translate these lines of dialect into standard English. *The best plans of mice and men often go wrong and leave us grief and pain instead of the joy expected.*

◆ Critical Thinking

Analyze Ask students: How do stanzas seven and eight differ from the first six stanzas? *The last two stanzas relate the small incident described in the first six to a general statement about humanity*

Reinforce and Extend

Answers

◆ Literature and Your Life

Reader's Response Some students may say they would feel compassion, whereas other's may say they would be unmoved .

Thematic Focus Students should note that while Burns imagines how the mouse had planned her winter home, his description of the situation and the mouse's panic are realistic.

☑ Check Your Comprehension

1. The speaker has plowed up home.
2. The mouse cannot remember past disappointments and anticipate future grief.

◆ Critical Thinking

1. The speaker can forgive theft for survival. This suggests a code that puts mercy above property.
2. (a) "The best laid schemes o' mice an' men/ Gang aft a-gley . . ." (b) The best plans often go wrong.
3. Students may value foresight as part of freedom, though it leads to more anxiety.

To a LOUSE

On Seeing One on a Lady's Bonnet at Church

Robert Burns

The Bow, Talbot Hughes, Warrington Museum and Art Gallery, Great Britain

(1) ▲ **Critical Viewing** Does this lady's pose and costume link her to the lady in the poem? Explain. **[Connect]**

(2) Ha! whare ye gaun, ye crowlin' ferlie![1]
Your impudence protects you sairly:[2]
I canna say but ye strunt[3] rarely,
Owre gauze and lace;
Though faith! I fear ye dine but sparely
On sic a place.

Ye ugly, creepin', blastit wonner,[4]
Detested, shunned by saunt an' sinner,
How dare ye set your fit[5] upon her,
Sae fine a lady?
Gae somewhere else, and seek your dinner
On some poor body.

(3) Swith![6] in some beggar's haffet[7] squattle;[8]
There ye may creep, and sprawl, and sprattle[9]
Wi' ither kindred, jumping cattle,
In shoals and nations:
Whare horn nor bane[10] ne'er dare unsettle
Your thick plantations.

Now haud[11] ye there, ye're out o' sight,
Below the fatt'rels,[12] snug an' tight;
Na, faith ye yet![13] ye'll no be right
Till ye've got on it,
The vera tapmost, tow'ring height
O' Miss's bonnet.

1. **crowlin' ferlie:** Crawling wonder.
2. **sairly:** Sorely.
3. **strunt:** Strut.
4. **blastit wonner:** Blasted wonder.
5. **fit:** Foot.
6. **swith:** Swift.
7. **haffet:** Locks.
8. **squattle:** Sprawl.
9. **sprattle:** Struggle.
10. **horn nor bane:** Comb made of horn or bone.
11. **haud:** Hold.
12. **fatt'rels:** Ribbon ends.
13. **Na faith ye yet!:** Confound you!

Develop Understanding

One-Minute Insight In "To a Louse," Burns sees a louse (the singular form of lice) on the bonnet of a well-dressed lady and uses the incident to satirize pretentious behavior. The louse's presence has made the lady's fine clothes and adornments seem silly. Burns enlarges on this situation in the final stanza by saying all of us could be saved from foolish behavior and an inflated sense of our worth if only we could see how we look to others.

▶Critical Viewing◀

(1) **Infer** Yes, the posture and the dainty manner in which the lady ties her bow suggest a degree of self-importance, even conceit, in her personality. Her costume, with its frills and bows, also seems similar to the costume worn by the woman in the poem.

◆ Grammar and Style

(2) **Interjections** Call attention to the exclamation mark that sets off the interjection from the rest of the sentence. Discuss the effect Burns achieves by beginning the poem this way. *The interjection startles the reader and reflects the surprise of the speaker in seeing the louse.*

◆ Reading Strategy

(3) **Translate Dialect** This stanza contains many examples of dialect. Have students use the footnotes and context to interpret the dialect. Then have them paraphrase the stanza. *Suggested paraphrase: Quick, go crawl on some beggar. There you will be among others of your kind, and you will not be bothered.*

◆ Critical Thinking

(4) **Analyze** Ask students: What literary convention is Burns using here to give humor to the poem? *Burns is using a combination of exaggeration (description of the louse and of the speaker's threats) and personification (speaking to the louse as if it had human qualities). This stanza also has the feel of a mock epic, such as Pope's* The Rape of the Lock *and Chaucer's "The Nun's Priest's Tale."*

Humanities: Art

The Bow (detail), by Talbot Hughes

This painting depicts a fashionable woman who is tying a bow around her neck. Point out to students that the woman is elaborately costumed and made up according to the dictates of fashion of the times.

Use these questions for discussion:

1. How well does the subject of this painting fit the description of the lady in "To a Louse"? *Like the lady in the poem, the lady in the painting wears delicate lace, ribbons, a bonnet, and possibly gauze. However, the bonnet lacks the balloon shape of a Lunardi.*
2. Burns's poem suggests there is a difference between how we see ourselves and how others see us. Judging from the woman's expression, how do you think she sees herself? How might others see her? *She appears to make an effort to appear well groomed and seems quite satisfied with the results. Other people might see her as filled with vanity and a false sense of superiority.*

My sooth! right bauld ye set your nose out,
As plump and gray as onie grozet;[14]
O for some rank, mercurial rozet,[15]
Or fell,[16] red smeddum,[17]
I'd gie you sic a hearty dose o't,
Wad dress your droddum![18]

I wad na been surprised to spy
You on an auld wife's flannen toy;[19]
Or aiblins some bit duddie boy,[20]
On's wyliecoat;[21]
But Miss's fine Lunardi![22] fie,
How daur ye do't?

O, Jenny, dinna toss your head,
An' set your beauties a' abread![23]
Ye little ken what cursèd speed
The blastie's[24] makin'!
Thae[25] winks and finger-ends, I dread,
Are notice takin'!

O wad some Pow'r the giftie gie us
To see oursels as ithers see us!
It wad frae monie a blunder free us
And foolish notion:
What airs in dress an' gait wad lea'e us,
And ev'n devotion!

14. **onie grozet** (gräz´ it): Any gooseberry.
15. **rozet** (räz´ it): Rosin.
16. **fell:** Sharp.
17. **smeddum:** Powder.
18. **Wad . . . droddum:** Would put an end to you.
19. **flannen toy:** Flannel cap.
20. **Or . . . boy:** Or perhaps on some little ragged boy.
21. **wyliecoat** (wī´ lē kōt´): Undershirt.
22. **Lunardi:** Balloon-shaped bonnet, named for Vincenzo Lunardi, a balloonist of the late 1700's.
23. **abread:** Abroad.
24. **blastie's:** Creature's.
25. **Thae:** Those.

◆ **Build Vocabulary**

impudence (im´ pyoo dəns) *n.*: Lack of shame; rudeness

Guide for Responding

◆ Literature and Your Life

Reader's Response What do you think of a louse (singular of lice) as a subject for a poem?

Thematic Focus What elements of fantasy does this poem contain? What elements of reality?

Sketchbook Draw a picture of the louse as you see it in your mind's eye.

☑ Check Your Comprehension

1. (a) What is the louse doing? (b) What does the speaker command it to do instead?

2. (a) Whom does the speaker address in the seventh stanza? (b) Against what does he warn her?

◆ Critical Thinking

INTERPRET

1. (a) What is the louse's crime? (b) What does the speaker have in common with those he seems to associate with the louse? **[Analyze]**

2. (a) What conclusions can you draw about Jenny's character? (b) What evidence supports these conclusions? **[Draw Conclusions]**

EVALUATE

3. In "To a Louse," Burns pokes fun at vanity in society. Do you agree with his standpoint? Explain. **[Make a Judgment]**

Beyond the Classroom

Career Connection

Public Health Officer Because lice can transmit a variety of diseases, they are a community concern. Unlike private health efforts, which are concerned with the health of individuals, public health officers direct their efforts toward the health of a community. Combating an infestation of lice, for example, might involve a combination of several community resources: education, sanitation, and political action, as well as medical resources. A public health officer attempts to bring together such experts to protect the health of a community. Have interested students write to your local seat of government to learn more about the skills and education necessary for a career in public health.

◆ Build Vocabulary

❺ Words Related to Clothing Ask students: What words for clothing are used in this first stanza? *Flannen toy, wyliecoat, and Lunardi are all terms referring to clothing.*

◆ Critical Thinking

❻ Evaluate Ask students: What "blunder" and "foolish notion" might we be freed from if we could see ourselves as others see us? *Most students will say that we would be freed from personal vanity if we could see ourselves as others do.*

Reinforce and Extend

Answers

◆ Literature and Your Life

Reader's Response Most students will say that a poem about a louse would have to be humorous and cynical.

Thematic Focus The poem's elements of fancy include scolding the louse as if it were human. Elements of reality include a true-to-life description of the woman and her fashionable clothing.

☑ Check Your Comprehension

1. (a) The louse is crawling on a well-dressed lady's lace and bonnet. (b) The speaker tells the impudent louse to go crawl on some poor beggar.
2. (a) The speaker addresses Jenny, the lady on whom the louse is crawling. (b) He warns her not to toss her head or move.

◆ Critical Thinking

1. (a) The louse is guilty of trespassing on the clothes of a refined lady. The speaker identifies with the common man.
2. (a) Jenny is apparently a fashion-conscious and highly respected member of the community. (b) The speaker calls her a "fine lady." Her bows, lace, and bonnet suggest she is careful about her dress.
3. Most students will feel that society is full of pretensions and vanity.

Develop Understanding

One-Minute Insight

"Woo'd and Married and A'" offers interesting points of view about the nature of true love and marital happiness. The poem begins with the bride sorrowing over her lack of finery and possessions and the prospect of marrying someone who has no more wealth than she. The bride's parents chastise the bride, declaring that she is fortunate to find anyone to marry her at all, given her poverty. The bridegroom's point of view is sweet and nonmaterialistic. He believes that love is all the wealth he and his bride will need for happiness.

▶Critical Viewing◀

❶ Compare and Contrast The village setting depicted in the painting seems to parallel the humble surroundings suggested indirectly in the poem. The dress of the groom and those following him appear to be finer than one would expect in the scene described in the poem. The poem mentions the bride's dress has a blue bodice, which is not the case in the portrait.

◆ Critical Thinking

❷ Analyze Ask students: What prompts this question? What does it suggest about the attitude toward women and marriage? *The question is prompted by the bride's tears for having no wealth of her own and because the man she's marrying has no wealth either. It suggests that a woman's value depends on her being well married.*

◆ *Literature and Your Life*

❸ Ask students to recall a situation in which an adult made a similar comment to them. *Students will doubtless be able to recall situations when they were told how easy they have it now compared to former times. Adults tend to recall having less money, more hardships, and a longer walk to school than today's youth.*

◆ Reading Strategy

❹ Translate Dialect Have students translate the father's words in these lines. *He compares his young daughter's marriage to taking a young horse from the pasture before it is ready.*

Woo'd and Married and A'

Joanna Baillie

▲ **Critical Viewing** ❶ Compare and contrast the setting and costumes in this painting with the scene described in Joanna Baillie's poem. **[Compare and Contrast]**

The bride she is winsome and bonny,
  Her hair it is snooded[1] sae sleek,
And faithfu' and kind is her Johnny,
  Yet fast fa' the tears on her cheek.
New pearlins[2] are cause of her sorrow,
  New pearlins and plenishing[3] too;
The bride that has a' to borrow
  Has e'en right mickle[4] ado.
    Woo'd and married and a'!
    Woo'd and married and a'!
❷ Is na' she very weel aff
    To be woo'd and married at a'?

❸ Her mither then hastily spak,
  "The Lassie is glaikit[5] wi' pride;
In my pouch I had never a plack[6]
  On the day when I was a bride.
E'en tak to your wheel and be clever,
  And draw out your thread in the sun;
The gear[7] that is gifted it never
  Will last like the gear that is won.
    Woo'd and married and a'!
    Wi' havins and toucher[8] sae sma'!
  I think ye are very weel aff
    To be woo'd and married at a'."

❹ "Toot, toot," quo' her gray-headed faither,
  "She's less o' a bride than a bairn,[9]
She's ta'en like a cout[10] frae the heather,
  Wi' sense and discretion to learn.
Half husband, I trow, and half daddy,
  As humor inconstantly leans,
The chiel maun be patient and steady[11]

1. **snooded:** Bound up with a ribbon.
2. **pearlins:** Lace trimmings.
3. **plenishing:** Furnishings.
4. **mickle:** Much.
5. **glaikit:** Foolish.
6. **plack:** Farthing; a small coin equal to one fourth of a penny.
7. **gear:** Wealth or goods.
8. **havins and toucher:** Possessions and dowry.
9. **bairn:** Child.
10. **cout:** Colt.
11. **The chiel maun . . . steady:** The man must be patient and steady.

Humanities: Art

The Village Wedding by Sir Luke Fildes.

Sir Luke Fildes (1843–1927) began his career as a magazine illustrator in London. He illustrated Dickens's last novel, *Edwin Drood,* before turning to painting in the 1870's. His paintings are judged to be part of the social realism movement, which seeks to depict the unadorned beauty of contemporary life while criticizing the evils of poverty and immortality.

Fildes's works were very popular and were often made available as engravings. He earned a knighthood in 1906.

Use these questions for discussion:

1. If this painting depicted some event described in the poem, which moment would you think it represents? Why? *Most students will say the painting captures the last stanza of the poem where it says the bride blushed, smiled, and looked down bashfully.*
2. Judging from the expressions of the people in the painting, was this wedding solemn or festive? *Students may point out that the bride and groom seem serious and solemn, whereas the surrounding guests seem more happy and animated.*

The Village Wedding, (detail) Sir Luke Fildes, Christopher Wood Gallery, London

(5) That yokes wi' a mate in her teens.
A kerchief sae douce[12] and sae neat
O'er her locks that the wind used to blaw!
I'm baith like to laugh and to greet[13]
When I think of her married at a'!"

Then out spak the wily bridegroom,
Weel waled[14] were his wordies, I ween,
"I'm rich, though my coffer be toom,[15]
Wi' the blinks o' your bonny blue e'en.[16]
I'm prouder o' thee by my side,
Though thy ruffles or ribbons be few,
Than if Kate o' the Croft were my bride
(6) Wi' purfles[17] and pearlins enow.
Dear and dearest of ony!
Ye're woo'd and buikit[18] and a'!
And do ye think scorn o' your Johnny,
And grieve to be married at a'?"

She turn'd, and she blush'd, and she smiled,
And she looked sae bashfully down;
The pride o' her heart was beguiled,
And she played wi' the sleeves o' her gown.
(7) She twirled the tag o' her lace,
And she nipped her boddice sae blue,
Syne blinkit sae sweet in his face,
And aff like a maukin[19] she flew.
Woo'd and married and a'!
Wi' Johnny to roose[20] her and a'!
She thinks hersel very weel aff
To be woo'd and married at a'!

12. **douce:** Respectable.
13. **greet:** Weep.
14. **waled:** Chosen.
15. **toom:** Empty.
16. **e'en:** Eyes.
17. **purfles:** Embroidered trimmings.
18. **buikit:** "Booked"; entered as married in the official registry.
19. **maukin:** Hare.
20. **roose:** Praise.

◆ Build Vocabulary

winsome (win´ səm) *adj.*: Having a charming, attractive appearance or manner

discretion (di skresh´ ən) *n.*: Good judgment; prudence

inconstantly (in kän´ stənt lē) *adv.*: Changeably; in a fickle way

Guide for Responding

◆ Literature and Your Life

Reader's Response What advice might you offer the bride before her wedding? Explain.

Thematic Focus The characters all combine fantasy and reality in different ways. Which character is your favorite, and why?

☑ Check Your Comprehension

1. Why is the bride unhappy at the beginning of the poem?
2. Which speaker succeeds in changing the bride's outlook?

◆ Critical Thinking

INTERPRET

1. How would you describe the personality of the bridegroom? Support your answer with evidence from the fourth stanza. **[Support]**
2. Judging from the final stanza, do you think the marriage will be a happy one? Explain. **[Draw Conclusions]**

APPLY

3. If the bridegroom had remained silent, what do you think the outcome would have been? Explain. **[Hypothesize]**

◆ Critical Thinking

(5) Interpret What does the father's use of the word *yokes* in line 32 suggest about his attitude toward marriage? *Yoking is the process of joining two beasts of burden within a heavy collar so they can work together. The father's choice of words implies that he sees marriage as a chore or task.*

◆ Reading Strategy

(6) Translate Dialect Have students use context to determine the meaning of *enow* in line 44. *Enow is an archaic form of* enough.

◆ Critical Thinking

(7) Speculate The bridegroom's question is never directly answered by his bride. Ask students: Judging from the actions of the bride described in the last stanza, how would she answer this question? *Most students will say that the bride's actions point to her answer, which would be "no."*

Reinforce and Extend

Answers

◆ Literature and Your Life

Reader's Response Sample response: Be happy with what you've got.

Thematic Focus Students' favorites may be the bride, because her concerns seem practical; the mother, because of her good advice; or the bridegroom, who appears to genuinely love the bride.

☑ Check Your Comprehension

1. The bride is sad because she does not have fine clothes or furnishings.
2. The bridegroom's words change the bride's outlook.

◆ Critical Thinking

1. The bridegroom values love over material things as reflected in his saying that he is rich in spite of his empty "coffer."
2. Most students will say that the marriage has a good chance for success since it is based on love and a positive attitude.
3. Had the bridegroom remained silent, the outcome may have been different. The bride's "cold feet" may have caused her to call off the wedding.

Beyond the Selection

FURTHER READING

More Works by the Authors

Poems and Songs, Robert Burns
The Glenriddell Manuscripts, Robert Burns
Poems 1790 (Revolution and Romanticism, 1789–1834), Joanna Baillie

Works About the Authors

The Real Robert Burns, J. L. Hughes
The Life and Work of Joanna Baillie, Margaret Sprague Carhart

We suggest that you preview these works before recommending them to students.

INTERNET

You and your students may find additional information about the authors on the Internet. We suggest the following sites. Please be aware, however, that sites may have changed from the time we published this information.

For information about Robert Burns go to **http://www.sc.edu/library/scotlit/l-rb.html**

For information about Joanna Baillie go to **http://www2.uwindsor.ca/~white1h/index.htm**

We *strongly recommend* that you preview the sites before you send students to them.

Answers

◆ Literary Focus

1. (a) The speaker's language suggests that he was familiar with the daily life of everyday people and not educated in university as people in more affluent circumstances might have been. (b) The dialect of "Woo'd and Married and A'" emphasizes the humble circumstances of the people described in the poem.
2. (a) Examples include *cow'rin'* (line 1), *strewin'* (line 20), and *comin'* (line 26). (b) Examples include *ane* for "one" (line 21), *mony* for "many" (line 32), and *aft* for "oft" (line 40).
3. Suggested response: The character of the poem would be different with the loss of dialect. The dialect gives the poetry warmth and makes the characters seem true-to-life.

◆ Reading Strategy

1. Sample translation: Stanza One of "To a Mouse": Poor little, scared thing! You're terrified of me! You don't need to run away from me. I would never chase you with my plow.
2. Dialect words and their translations include: lea'e = leave; sae = so; an' = and; na = not

◆ Build Vocabulary

Using Words Related to Clothing

1. A *wyliecoat* is an undershirt. While the term is rarely used today, undershirts are still worn.
2. A *kerchief* is a square cloth worn as a head covering. It is rarely seen today.
3. A *bodice*, the upper part of a dress, is still a common term today.
4. A *Lunardi* is a balloon-shaped bonnet. It is not worn in modern times.
5. A *gown*, a long, loose garment, is still common today.

Using the Word Bank

1. b; rule
2. a; rudeness
3. c; attractive
4. b; good judgment
5. a; changeably

Guide for Responding (continued)

◆ Literary Focus

DIALECT

Dialect, the speech habits and patterns of a specific group, class, or region, contributes to the character, tone, and setting of a literary work. Robert Burns and Joanna Baillie were two of the first poets to write using the Scottish dialect of English, incorporating its own unique grammar, pronunciation, and vocabulary. By doing so, they invested their poems with a warmth and familiarity that was lacking in poems of classical style.

1. (a) What does the use of dialect in the poems by Burns suggest about the speaker's social station? (b) What does dialect contribute to the setting of Joanna Baillie's "Woo'd and Married and A' "?
2. Like standard language, dialects of a language follow patterns. Find at least two examples in "To a Mouse" of the following pronunciation rules for Scottish English: (a) Final consonants are dropped. (b) The letter *o* is replaced by either *ae* or *a*.
3. How would the effect of these poems have been different if they had been written in standard English?

◆ Reading Strategy

TRANSLATE DIALECT

The regional dialect in which these poems were written may seem very foreign to non-Scots readers. **Translating dialect** allows you to understand the meaning and appreciate the unique flavor of poems such as these. Strategies such as using context clues, looking for similarities in spelling and sound, and reading footnotes help in the translation process. For example, using these strategies, you may translate the line "Wee, sleekit, cow'rin', tim'rous beastie" as "small, sleek, crouching, timid beast."

1. Choose one stanza from a Burns or Baillie poem and translate the stanza into standard English.
2. List words in dialect that appear in both poems and their equivalents in standard English.

◆ Build Vocabulary

USING WORDS RELATED TO CLOTHING

"To a Louse" and "Woo'd and Married and A' " contain several references to clothing and accessories, some of which are familiar to modern readers, some of which are not. For example, *bonnet* is still in use today, but *fatt'rels*, ribbon ends, is not. Explain the meaning of each word below, and tell whether it is still in use today.

1. wyliecoat
2. kerchief
3. boddice (bodice)
4. Lunardi
5. gown

USING THE WORD BANK

In your notebook, write the letter of the term that is the best synonym of the first word.

1. dominion: (a) ability, (b) rule, (c) pride
2. impudence: (a) rudeness, (b) shyness, (c) test
3. winsome: (a) competitive, (b) bold, (c) attractive
4. discretion: (a) disappointment, (b) good judgment, (c) gratitude
5. inconstantly: (a) changeably, (b) emptily, (c) sadly

◆ Grammar and Style

INTERJECTIONS

The speakers in "To a Mouse" and "To a Louse" use **interjections**, words or phrases expressing emotion, that give the poems a conversational feel. A comma separates a mild interjection from the rest of the sentence. An exclamation mark follows a stronger interjection.

Practice Identify the interjection in each line and punctuate the sentence correctly on your paper.

1. But och I backward cast my e'e
2. What then poor beastie thou maun live!
3. My sooth right bauld yet set your nose out,
4. O Jenny dinna toss your head,
5. Though faith I fear ye dine but sparely

Writing Application Write a short paragraph about a funny incident. In it, use at least two interjections, punctuated correctly.

◆ Grammar and Style

1. But, och! I backward cast my e'e.
2. What then? Poor beastie, thou maun live!
3. My sooth! Right bauld ye set your nose out,
4. O, Jenny, dinna toss your head,
5. Though faith! I fear ye dine but sparely.

Build Your Portfolio

Idea Bank

Writing

1. Advice to the Newlyweds Write a brief letter to the couple in "Woo'd and Married and A'," giving them advice on married life.

2. Comparison and Contrast Reread "To a Mouse" and "To a Louse." Write a short paper, comparing and contrasting the poems' messages and tones.

3. Response to Criticism William Hazlitt wrote, "Life is the art of being well deceived." How do you think Burns would respond to this statement? Write an essay in which you present your views. Support your points with details from the poems.

Speaking and Listening

4. Oral Interpretation With a partner, choose one of these poems and practice reading it aloud. When you are comfortable with the poem, read it aloud to the class. **[Performing Arts Link]**

5. Lecture Give an academic lecture on the life and poetry of Robert Burns. Research and write up your lecture in note form, then present your lecture to the class.

Projects

6. Comic Strip Using the situation in "To a Mouse" as a springboard, create a comic strip in which the mouse has a dialogue with the human who has disturbed its nest. **[Art Link]**

7. Multimedia Presentation Although united with England since 1707, Scots have always been proud of their distinctive land, history, language, and culture. Assemble a multimedia presentation about Scotland that includes photographs, recordings, and maps. **[Social Studies Link]**

Writing Mini-Lesson

Scene With Dialogue

Although perfectly understandable to a native of Scotland, poems in Scottish dialect, like the ones in this section, are difficult for others to understand. Write a scene with dialogue between two people who are having a communication problem due to specialized language, slang, or dialect. At the end of your dialogue, add a glossary in which you list and define all the specialized or unfamiliar words or phrases.

Writing Skills Focus: Clear Beginning, Middle, and End

Although organizational structures vary from work to work, all types of literature contain a basic structure: **a beginning, middle,** and **end.**

As you write your scene with dialogue, create a beginning, in which the audience meets the characters; a middle, in which the conflict or problem develops; and an end, in which the scene is concluded and loose ends tied up.

Use the following strategies as you write your scene.

Prewriting Before you begin to write, plan how the scene will begin, proceed, and end. Think up two characters, and list and define at least five jargon terms that one character will speak in dialogue. Later, these terms will become glossary entries.

Drafting Draft your scene, showing how the characters meet, what happens as they speak, and how the meeting ends. Use the list of slang or jargon words in the dialogue of one character, and create a glossary defining those terms.

Revising With a partner, read your scene through. Be sure that your scene has a clear beginning, middle, and end. Check the glossary of slang or jargon terms for errors in definition and mistakes in spelling.

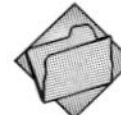

Idea Bank

Customizing for
Performance Levels

Following are suggestions for matching Idea Bank topics with your students' ability levels:

Less Advanced Students: 1, 4, 6
Average Students: 2, 7
More Advanced Students: 3, 5

Customizing for
Learning Modalities

Following are suggestions for matching Idea Bank topics with your students' learning modalities:

Visual/Spatial: 5, 6
Verbal/Linguistic: 2, 3, 4
Interpersonal: 1
Musical/Rhythmic: 4

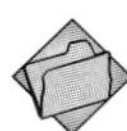

Writing Mini-Lesson

Refer students to the Writing Handbook, page 1189, for instruction on the writing process, and page 1192 for further information on writing a dramatic scene.

Writer's Solution

Writing Lab CD-ROM

Direct students to complete the tutorial on Creative Writing. Follow these steps:

1. Spin the Characters, Conflict, and Setting Wheel to spark ideas for the dramatic scene.
2. Use the interactive tips for dialogue in drama.
3. Create a draft on the computer.
4. Look at the audio-annotated writing models for help strengthening a dramatic scene.

Sourcebook

Have students complete Chapter 6, Creative Writing, pp. 167–196, for additional support.

✓ ASSESSMENT OPTIONS

Formal Assessment, Selection Test, pp. 143–145, and Assessment Resources Software. The selection test is designed so that it can be easily customized to the ability levels of your students.

Alternative Assessment, p. 29, includes options for less advanced students, more advanced students, verbal/linguistic learners, musical/rhythmic learners, and interpersonal learners.

PORTFOLIO ASSESSMENT

Use the following rubrics in the ***Alternative Assessment*** booklet to assess student writing:

Advice to the Newlyweds: Expression Rubric, p. 95
Comparison and Contrast: Comparison/Contrast Rubric, p. 104
Response to Criticism: Literary Analysis/Interpretation Rubric, p. 113
Writing Mini-lesson: Drama Rubric, p. 110

Prepare and Engage

OBJECTIVES

1. To interpret and respond to poems of William Blake
2. To relate the poems to personal experience
3. To use visuals as a key to meaning
4. To identify and analyze symbols
5. To build vocabulary in context and learn the word root *-spir-*
6. To distinguish between and use correctly the words *rise* and *raise*
7. To write a comparative analysis, using placement for emphasis
8. To respond to Blake's poems through writing, speaking and listening, and projects

SKILLS INSTRUCTION

Vocabulary:
Word Roots: *-spir-*

Grammar:
Commonly Confused Words: *Rise* and *Raise*

Reading Strategy:
Use Visuals as a Key to Meaning

Literary Focus:
Symbols

Writing:
Placement for Emphasis

Speaking and Listening:
Blake Reading (teacher edition)

Critical Viewing:
Infer, Compare and Contrast

PORTFOLIO OPPORTUNITIES

Writing: Journal Entry; Research Report; Response to Criticism

Speaking and Listening: Blake Reading; Setting Blake to Music

Projects: Advertisement; Illuminated Poem

More About the Author
William Blake's belief in a union of opposites is reflected in his famous "Doctrine of Contraries": "Without Contraries," he wrote, "there is no progression. Attraction and repulsion, reason and energy, love and hate, are necessary to human existence." Likewise, Blake's poetry can be said to operate on two levels: one of them symbolic, the other literal. Both levels, however, address a single purpose—the renewal of the human spirit.

Guide for Interpreting

William Blake *(1757–1827)*

"I must create a system or be enslaved by another man's." So spoke William Blake, an artist and poet whose work defied all the conventions of the time.

Blake was a truly original thinker, claiming to find his inspiration from mystical visions.

Blake's visions began early, when, at the age of four, he suddenly began to scream because he thought he saw God at his window. Four years later, while working in the fields, Blake said he saw a tree filled with angels. Blake's parents, who were followers of the mystical teachings of Emanuel Swedenborg, a Swedish philosopher, inventor, and spiritualist, believed that their son had a "gift of vision" and did all they could to nurture this gift.

Finding His Way Blake's father was a poor Londoner, with a small hosiery shop. He did not send his son to school, choosing instead to educate him at home. By the age of twelve, the boy was already highly educated and wrote some of the simple, eloquent poems that became part of a collection entitled *Poetical Sketches* (1783). Because he also showed artistic talent, Blake became an engraver's apprentice and then went on to study at the Royal Academy.

Formal study did not last long, however. Rebelling against all the artistic conventions of the Academy, Blake left and set up his own print shop. He was to live most of his life eking out a poor living as an engraver, barely making enough to support his writing and his artistic pursuits.

Innocence and Experience When Blake was thirty-two, he published *Songs of Innocence*, a series of poems expressing deep spiritual and philosophical insights that he illustrated himself. Five years later, having grown disillusioned and no longer believing in the possibility of easy human perfection, he wrote *Songs of Experience*, which explored the darker side of life. Taken together, these two collections seem to be saying that true purity and innocence is impossible without experience and that all opposites depend upon each other to exist.

An Unrecognized Genius Unfortunately, Blake's talent was never recognized by his peers or by the public during his lifetime. Yet, while living only slightly above the poverty level, Blake spent his seventy years in constant creative activity. Many years after his death, his work finally achieved recognition and Blake came to be regarded as one of the most important poets of his time.

◆ Background for Understanding

HUMANITIES: BLAKE AS AN ARTIST

Blake illustrated his poems with striking, integrated designs. These illustrations seemed to swirl through the words and become part of their meaning. No one fully understands Blake's method of creating illustrated pages. It is thought that he drew words and pictures on a copper plate, using a liquid that could not be eaten away by acid. Then he applied acid that would eat away the areas of uncovered copper. The raised surfaces that were left could be inked. Finally, he hand-colored the page using water colors. Blake claimed that many of the images he drew as illustrations were likenesses of his inner visions. They had a childlike feeling and were very different from the strict classical styles of the time.

Journal Writing Note the expression on the tiger's face on p. 599. Why do you think Blake made the face look the way it does?

Prentice Hall Literature Program Resources

REINFORCE / RETEACH / EXTEND

Selection Support Pages
Build Vocabulary: Word Roots: *-spir-*, p. 143
Grammar and Style: Commonly Confused Words: *Rise* and *Raise*, p. 144
Reading Strategy: Use Visuals as a Key to Meaning, p. 145
Literary Focus: Symbols, p. 146

Strategies for Diverse Student Needs
Ask and Answer Questions, p. 30

Beyond Literature
Humanities Connection: Fine Art, p. 30

Formal Assessment Selection Test, pp. 146–148; Assessment Resources Software

Alternative Assessment, p. 30

Writing and Language Transparencies
Interpreting a Work of Literature, pp. 45–55
Comparison-and-Contrast Chart, p. 115

Resource Pro CD-ROM—includes all resource material and customizable lesson plan

Listening to Literature Audiocassettes
Poetry of William Blake

The Lamb ◆ The Tyger
The Chimney Sweeper ◆ Infant Sorrow

◆ Literature and Your Life

Connect Your Experience

When childhood beliefs, such as the existence of the tooth fairy, are proved untrue, the former believer can become mistrustful or even sad. However, the learning experience may lead to a deeper understanding of how the world works. In "The Tyger," William Blake re-explores from a more mature stance a subject he explored in an earlier poem, "The Lamb."

Thematic Focus: Fantasy and Reality

The eighteenth century into which Blake was born valued reason and classical forms. Blake, on the other hand, valued imagination, intuition, and spirituality. As you read, notice how Blake invests ordinary subjects, such as a lamb and tiger, with elements of fantasy.

◆ Reading Strategy

Use Visuals as a Key to Meaning

When you read any literature that is accompanied by illustrations, you can **use the visuals as a key to meaning** by looking closely at the details of the illustrations and thinking about how they support or add to the author's words. For example, illustrations accompanying a novel might help you picture the characters or fill in details about the characters' personalities.

William Blake intended his illustrations to help convey the underlying meaning of his poems. Look at Blake's illustrations. What do they add to the details in the poems?

◆ Grammar and Style

Commonly Confused Words: *Rise* and *Raise*

In "The Chimney Sweeper," you'll encounter the verb *rise,* which means "to get up." It is sometimes confused with the verb *raise,* which means "to lift or elevate." Notice how these two words are used in the following examples:

Present: They *rise* upon clouds, and sport in the wind.
Past: And so Tom awoke and we *rose* in the dark.
Past Participle: We had *risen* together yesterday.
Present: I *raise* my hand when I'm ready.
Past: They *raised* the flag on the pole.
Past Participle: We had *raised* a strong family.

◆ Literary Focus

Symbols

Throughout literature, you'll encounter **symbols,** which are words, images, or ideas that stand for something else. Often, a symbol is something tangible, or solid, that stands for and helps readers to understand something intangible, like an emotion. Look at this line from "The Chimney Sweeper."

> And wash in a river, and
> shine in the Sun.

This line contains two actions that are religious symbols. To wash in the river symbolizes baptism, in which one is cleansed of sin; to "shine in the Sun" is to bask in the glory of God.

As you read, look for other symbols and analyze their meaning.

◆ Build Vocabulary

Word Roots: *-spir-*

In "The Tyger," you'll encounter the word *aspire,* meaning "to yearn or seek after." *Aspire* contains the root *-spir-,* meaning "breath" or "life." When you aspire to something, you live to reach it.

Word Bank

Before you read, preview this list of words from the poems.

vales
symmetry
aspire

Write the word pairs good/evil; right/wrong; and heaven/hell on the chalkboard. Introduce the class to William Blake's extreme and unusual belief that pure opposites such as those listed above were necessary in order for the world to function. Blake's belief in this philosophy was so total that it informed his life as well as his poetry. Have students identify the opposition in the poems as they read.

Customize for
Less Proficient Readers

Encourage these students to read the poem several times. Explain that rarely does a poem's meaning reveal itself to anyone on a first reading. Assure students that only through rereading and thinking about the words, images, and other aspects of the poem can any reader begin to understand a poem.

Customize for
More Advanced Students

Invite more advanced students to find clues in these poems that reveal Blake's religious and philosophical beliefs.

Customize for
Visual/Spatial Learners

Have visual/spatial learners preview the art that accompanies these poems. Invite students to predict what the poems may be about. After they read, have students compare their predictions about the poem's content with their understanding of the poems.

Preparing for Standardized Tests

Reading and Vocabulary A large vocabulary and knowledge of word roots will help students meet with success on the vocabulary, analogy, and reading comprehension portions of standardized tests. For additional practice, use the Build Vocabulary page in ***Selection Support***, p. 143.

Grammar and Language Sentence and paragraph improvement sections on standardized tests may include items that test the correct use of the commonly confused words *rise* and *raise*. In the following example, students are asked to find the error in the underlined passages.

The women's job (A) was to rise (B) the flag each morning (C) at sunrise. *(B)*
(A) The women's job
(B) was to rise
(C) each morning

The Grammar and Style lesson for this selection focuses on this topic. For additional practice, use the Grammar and Style page on Commonly Confused Words: *Rise* and *Raise*, p. 144, in ***Selection Support.***

Develop Understanding

One-Minute Insight In this light, bright-sounding poem, a child talks to a little lamb, and both emerge as symbols of innocence.

◆ Literary Focus

❶ **Symbols** Ask students to identify and interpret the main symbol in this stanza. *The lamb is the main symbol; it stands for goodness and innocence.*

❷ **Clarification** Explain to students that Christ is referred to as "the lamb of God" and sometimes as "the lamb of God who takes away the sins of the world." Jesus was described as "the Lamb" in the Bible, both in John 1:29 and Revelation 5:11.

◆ Reading Strategy

❸ **Use Visuals as a Key to Meaning** Direct students' attention to the visual accompanying "The Lamb." Ask them the ways in which the picture serves as a key to meaning. *The child is in the midst of the sheep but not threatened by them. The child seems to need no protection from anything. The setting is calm and idyllic.*

▶Critical Viewing◀

❹ **Infer** Nature appears innocent, harmonious, and unthreatening.

Reinforce and Extend

Answers

◆ *Literature and Your Life*

Reader's Response Students may say that their response would not be so childlike.

☑ Check Your Comprehension

1. The speaker asks whether the lamb knows its creator.
2. The speaker is a child of the creator.

◆ Critical Thinking

1. The lamb is soft and tender.
2. The creator is meek and mild.
3. Answers include: springtime images in a simpler, colorful, relaxed style.

The Lamb

WILLIAM BLAKE

Little Lamb who made thee
Dost thou know who made thee
Gave thee life & bid thee feed.
By the stream & o'er the mead;
❶ Gave thee clothing of delight,
Softest clothing wooly bright;
Gave thee such a tender voice,
Making all the vales rejoice!
Little Lamb who made thee
Dost thou know who made thee

Little Lamb I'll tell thee,
Little Lamb I'll tell thee!
He is called by thy name,
For he calls himself a Lamb:
❷ He is meek & he is mild,
He became a little child:
I a child & thou a lamb,
We are called by his name.
Little Lamb God bless thee.
Little Lamb God bless thee.

◆ Build Vocabulary

vales (vālz) *n.*: Hollows or depressions in the ground

symmetry (sim′ə trē) *n.*: Beauty resulting from balance of forms

aspire (ə spīr′) *v.*: Rise high, yearn or seek after

From a manuscript of "The Lamb" by William Blake, Lessing J. Rosenwald Collection, Library of Congress, Washington, D.C. ❸

▲ **Critical Viewing** What view of nature is expressed by the style of Blake's drawing? **[Infer]** ❹

Guide for Responding

◆ *Literature and Your Life*

Reader's Response Is your response to the lamb similar to Blake's response?

☑ Check Your Comprehension

1. What questions does the speaker ask in the first stanza of "The Lamb"?
2. Who is the speaker in this poem?

◆ Critical Thinking

INTERPRET

1. How would you sum up the characteristics of the lamb? **[Interpret]**
2. What are the characteristics of the creator of the lamb? **[Draw Conclusions]**

APPLY

3. What kind of images would you use to represent the words? **[Modify]**

Block Scheduling Strategies

Consider these suggestions to take advantage of extended class time:

- Present the Background for Understanding on page 596 to students before they read Blake's poems. Have them complete the Journal Writing activity and share their responses with the class.
- Introduce the Literary Focus on Symbols, p. 597, then ask students to name symbols that are contained in popular songs. When students have finished reading, have them answer the Literary Focus questions on page 602.
- Have student read the Historical Connection note on page 602 before they read Blake's poems.
- To help students with the Writing Mini-Lesson, p. 603, photocopy the Comparison-and-Contrast Outline Master on page 116 and distribute to students. Ask volunteers to present their essays to the class.

The Tyger

William Blake

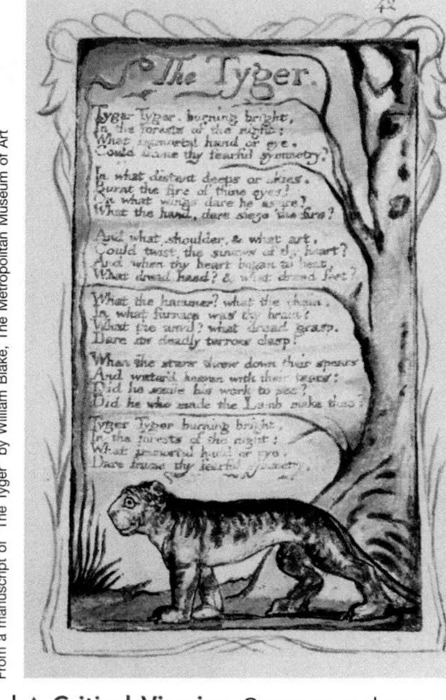

From a manuscript of "The Tyger" by William Blake, The Metropolitan Museum of Art

Tyger Tyger, burning bright,
In the forests of the night;
What immortal hand or eye,
Could frame thy fearful symmetry?

In what distant deeps or skies
Burnt the fire of thine eyes!
On what wings dare he aspire?
What the hand, dare seize the fire?

And what shoulder, & what art,
Could twist the sinews of thy heart?
And when thy heart began to beat,
What dread hand? & what dread feet?

What the hammer? what the chain,
In what furnace was thy brain?
What the anvil? what dread grasp,
Dare its deadly terrors clasp? ❻

When the stars threw down their spears
And water'd heaven with their tears: ❼
Did he smile his work to see?
Did he who made the Lamb make thee? ❽

Tyger, Tyger burning bright,
In the forests of the night:
What immortal hand or eye,
Dare frame thy fearful symmetry?

❺ ▲ **Critical Viewing** Compare and contrast the tiger's expression with the poem's image of the animal. **[Compare and Contrast]**

Guide for Responding

◆ Literature and Your Life

Reader's Response How does this poem set you thinking about life's mysteries? Explain.

☑ Check Your Comprehension

1. What question is asked in the first stanza of "The Tyger"?
2. Is this question ever answered?

◆ Critical Thinking

INTERPRET

1. What kind of creature does Blake portray the tiger to be? **[Interpret]**
2. Explain lines 15 and 16. **[Infer]**

EVALUATE

3. Do "The Lamb" and "The Tyger" cover the extremes of the human spirit effectively? **[Assess]**

Humanities: Art

The Lamb by William Blake.

A boy converses with a sheep. He stands outside the simple hut of a shepherd, with a thatched roof and open window. The vines and leaves that encircle the poem and illustrations seem to create an Eden-like frame for the action.

Use this question for discussion:

Why do you think the boy is shown with his arms outstretched? *He may be offering something to the lamb; perhaps he is instructing the lamb or explaining something to it.*

The Tyger, by William Blake.

This engraving shows a tiger that is a strong-looking animal, with muscular haunches and a stance that seems ready for pouncing. His eye appears to "burn bright" with an intense yellow light.

Use this question for discussion:

What effect do the tree branches have on the layout of the poem? *The branches seem to divide the poem into stanzas or pairs of stanzas. The tree is an otherworldly color. A suggestion of flame seems to outline part of it; its branches have no leaves.*

This poem opposes "The lamb." The voice is now harsh, incessantly questioning; the vocabulary is more adult as darkness replaces light, night replaces day, and experience replaces innocence.

▶Critical Viewing◀

❺ **Compare and Contrast** The tiger's expression in the illustration—perhaps a mischievous smile—seems far less threatening than its image in the poem.

◆ Literary Focus

❻ **Symbols** Ask how the words *twist, hammer, chain, furnace,* and *anvil* suggest the tiger's place of origin. *These words seem to suggest that the tiger is "forged" in hell. Hell is often depicted as a giant furnace or pit of fire.*

◆ Critical Thinking

❼ **Interpret** Ask: What figure of speech is used in these lines? To what do the lines refer? *The lines give human qualities to stars (personification). They may refer to Lucifer's rebellion against heaven.*

❽ **Analyze** Ask students; What question is Blake really asking? *Blake is asking the tiger if he is a product of God or the devil. Blake may be questioning the nature of evil and God's plan.*

Reinforce and Extend

Answers

Reader's Response The poem prompts questions about the nature of good and evil.

☑ Check Your Comprehension

1. The question is "Who made the tiger?"
2. The question is not answered.

◆ Critical Thinking

1. Blake's tiger is vibrant, strong, and dangerous.
2. Lines 15 and 16 ask what tool or worker could have shaped the tiger.
3. Sample response: Yes, the poems effectively symbolize the extremes of innocence and appetite.

One-Minute Insight

Blake's intense religious beliefs pervade this short poem about the miseries suffered by child laborers. The speaker of this poem, Tom Dacre, is a young child who is sold as a child and forced to work as a chimney sweep, toiling long hours in a dangerous profession. One night a bright angel visits the speaker and tells him that if he's good, he'll go to heaven and never feel misery again.

◆ Background for Understanding

Explain that small children once did the work of sweeping chimneys because they could actually climb into the chimneys and scrape them clean. Enclosed in a tiny space, children were often terrified by such work.

❶ **Clarification** Explain that the words "cry weep weep weep weep" are presented in some printings of this poem as "cry 'weep! 'weep! 'weep! 'weep!" so as to suggest *weep* as a shortened form of *sweep*. By repeatedly crying "weep" or "sweep," children advertised their services. The omission of the *s* was probably meant to suggest childlike lisping.

◆ Literary Focus

❷ **Symbols** Have student locate symbols in these two stanzas and explain their meanings. *Blake uses Tom's hair—curly like a lamb's and white—to symbolize innocence. The soot and "coffins of black" symbolize the children's miseries and impending death.*

◆ Grammar and Style

❸ **Commonly Confused Words: *Rise* and *Raise*** Point out the use of the word *rise* in line 18 and the use of the word *rose* in line 21. Ask students to tell what each word means. *Rise and rose are the present and past tenses of the verb rise.*

▶Critical Viewing◀

❹ **Infer** Yes, Blake's portrayal appears to be similar to this artist's rendering: The working conditions appear to be bad, the girls appear to be wearing ragged clothing and some have no shoes, the interior space is unwelcoming and dark.

The Chimney Sweeper

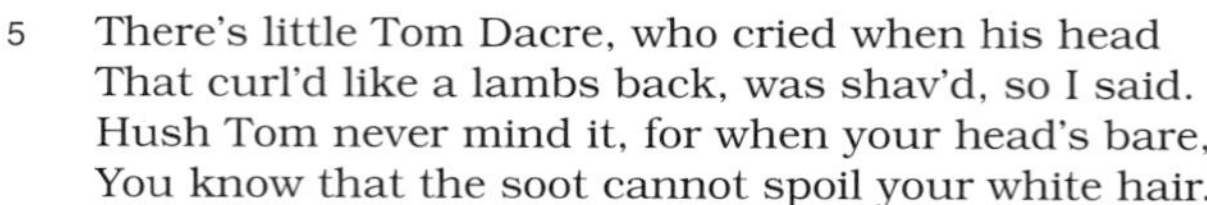

William Blake

▲ **Critical Viewing** Does Blake portray children's working conditions in nineteenth-century England as this artist does? Explain. **[Compare and Contrast]** ❹

When my mother died I was very young,
And my father sold me while yet my tongue,
❶ Could scarcely cry weep weep weep weep.
So your chimneys I sweep & in soot I sleep.

There's little Tom Dacre, who cried when his head
That curl'd like a lambs back, was shav'd, so I said.
Hush Tom never mind it, for when your head's bare,
You know that the soot cannot spoil your white hair.

❷

And so he was quiet, & that very night,
As Tom was a sleeping he had such a sight,
That thousands of sweepers Dick, Joe, Ned & Jack
Were all of them lock'd up in coffins of black

And by came an Angel who had a bright key,
And he open'd the coffins & set them all free.
Then down a green plain leaping laughing they run
And wash in a river and shine in the Sun.

Then naked & white, all their bags left behind,
They rise upon clouds, and sport in the wind.
And the Angel told Tom if he'd be a good boy,
❸ He'd have God for his father & never want joy.

And so Tom awoke and we rose in the dark
And got with our bags & our brushes to work.
Tho' the morning was cold, Tom was happy & warm,
So if all do their duty, they need not fear harm.

Humanities: Art

Paying Children for Their Labor in the Brick Yards, 1871.

In this wood engraving, children line up single file in front of an adult who looks very large by comparison. He seems to be doling out the children's wages. The children approach humbly, and probably very slowly, for two girls near the front of the line have sat down in order to endure the waiting. The children make very little for their labor; otherwise, they might be able to purchase less ragged clothes and some shoes.

Use these questions for discussion:

1. In what ways are these children similar to the chimney sweepers? *They are doing jobs they do not want to do; they are exploited. Yet they "do their duty." Maybe, like Tom, they have been afraid.*
2. What do you think these children say to the man who pays them? What do you think they might wish to say that they don't say? *The children probably say "thank you." They may wish to say that they are cold, hungry, scared, or tired, but they probably don't say that.*

Paying Children for Their Labor in the Brick Yards, wood engraving, English 1871
The Granger Collection Ltd.

Infant Sorrow

WILLIAM BLAKE

My mother groand![1] my father wept.
Into the dangerous world I leapt,
Helpless, naked, piping loud;
Like a fiend hid in a cloud. 5

Struggling in my father's hands,
Striving against my swaddling bands; 6
Bound and weary, I thought best
To sulk upon my mother's breast. 7

1. **groand:** groaned; an example of Blake's often eccentric spelling.

Guide for Responding

◆ Literature and Your Life

Reader's Response Which poem's portrayal of life do you agree with more? Why?

Thematic Focus Do these poems come closer to "fantasy" or "reality"? Explain.

☑ Check Your Comprehension

1. How does the child in the first stanza of "The Chimney Sweeper" become a chimney sweep?
2. What is the dream that gives the chimney sweeper hope to go on?
3. In "Infant Sorrow," what are the reactions of the parents to the birth of the child?
4. How does the child react upon first being born, and how does this reaction change?

◆ Critical Thinking

INTERPRET

1. What social commentary do you find in "The Chimney Sweeper"? **[Interpret]**
2. In "Infant Sorrow," aside from tight "swaddling bands," in what larger sense is the speaker "bound"? **[Interpret]**
3. What conclusions about Blake's ideas on the meaning of life can you draw from these poems? **[Draw Conclusions]**

EVALUATE

4. How do these poems inspire readers to rethink assumptions about life and death? **[Assess]**

Beyond the Selection

FURTHER READING

Other Songs of Innocence
"Infant Joy"; "Laughing Song"; "A Cradle Song"; "Nurse's Song"

Other Songs of Experience
"The Fly"; "A Poison Tree"; "London"; "The Human Abstract"; "A Cradle Song"

We suggest that you read these selections before recommending them to your students.

INTERNET

The Internet provides opportunities for students to learn more about Blake. Please be aware that sites may have changed from the time we published this information.

For an on-line conference dedicated to the life and work of Blake, go to **http://www.albion.com/blake/**

For more on Blake's life and works, go to **http://www.aa.net/~urizen/blake.html**

We *strongly recommend* that you preview the sites before you send students to them.

One-Minute Insight Like "The Tyger," this is a song of experience. Turning the stereotype of the joy of new life on its head, this poem presents a newborn that is not received with joy by its parents; furthermore, the infant struggles, fights, and sulks.

◆ Critical Thinking

5 Interpret Ask: What does Blake mean by this simile? *Blake implies that a child is just a monster or fiend in the making; that the innocence is temporary.*

6 Clarification Explain that swaddling is wrapping a newborn tightly, usually in a blanket. This practice continues today, because it is thought that the newborn wants to experience the kind of tightness it experienced in the womb.

◆ Critical Thinking

7 Analyze What attitude about life and birth do these lines convey? *Birth and life are not joyous or a cause for optimism; instead, they are a reason to "sulk" or to be negatively or moodily silent.*

Reinforce and Extend

Answers

◆ Literature and Your Life

Reader's Response Students may agree with the optimistic message of "The Chimney Sweeper"; some students may agree with the cynical portrayal of life in "Infant Sorrow."

Thematic Focus Most students will say that these poems are closer to reality than to fantasy because the subject matter—abuse of young children and the nature of sin—is so serious.

☑ Check Your Comprehension

1. The child's mother died and his father sold him.
2. The dream is of happiness in heaven with God.
3. The mother groaned and the father wept.
4. At first the child struggled, then the child sulked.

(Answers continue on page 602.)

◆ Critical Thinking

1. The poem condemns the maltreatment of the young children who are forced to work in dangerous conditions.
2. The speaker is bound by the human condition—full of misery and unhappiness.
3. Blake may have felt that life was full of struggle and misery.
4. Students may be inspired to challenge Blake's acceptance of earthly sorrow in "The Chimney Sweeper." "Infant Sorrow" may prompt students to rethink ideas the qualities a newborn baby has or is soon to develop.

Answers

◆ Literary Focus

1. Answers may include innocence, childhood, and Christ.
2. Taken together, the fire images might suggest hell.
3. Sample answer: It helps the reader understand the notion that the child is not innocent at birth.

◆ Grammar and Style

Practice

1. rise
2. raises
3. rises

Writing Application

The chimney sweepers *rose* early. They *raised* their brooms to their shoulders and went out to the street. It was still early, and the sun had not *risen*.

◆ Reading Strategy

1. The mood is calm and peaceful. The poem captures the voice of an innocent child in a calm setting free from worry or interruption.
2. The tiger in the illustration does not seem as vicious as the one in the poem; its coloration and strange humanlike expression, however, do suggest evil.

◆ Build Vocabulary

Using the Word Root *-spir-*

1. *Respiration* means the process of breathing.
2. *Expire* means to die, or to breathe one's last.
3. *Inspire* means to breathe life into; to create enthusiasm in someone.
4. *Spirit* means a lively show of enthusiasm.

Using the Word Bank

1. They traveled through *vales* and over hills.
2. The *symmetry* of the animal's body made it look graceful and powerful.
3. The student *aspired* to attend a top college.

Guide for Responding (continued)

◆ Literary Focus

Symbols

Blake's poems are filled with **symbols**—words, images, or ideas that have an underlying meaning. In "The Chimney Sweeper," for example, Tom Dacre's hair, which was like a "lamb's back," symbolizes, or represents, youthful innocence. When it is shaved, it is a symbolic loss of his innocence and youth.

1. What two things does the lamb symbolize?

2. In "The Tyger," there are several images that pertain to fire: "burning bright," "fire of thine eyes," "seize the fire." Taken together, what might these images symbolize?

3. "Infant Sorrow" contains allusions to the Christian belief that as a result of Adam and Eve's sin, life is painful and full of struggles. How does this knowledge deepen your understanding of the work?

◆ Grammar and Style

Commonly Confused Words: *Rise* and *Raise*

The verbs *rise* and *raise* are often confused. The forms of the verb *rise,* which means "to get up," are *rise, rose,* and *risen.* The forms of the verb *raise,* which means "to lift or elevate," are *raise, raised,* and *raised.*

Practice On your paper, write the present tense of each of the verbs used in these sentences.

1. Most mornings I rose early.

2. Hearing a sound, the bird raised its head.

3. Ever since the sun came out, the mist has risen from the lake.

Writing Application In your notebook, rewrite these sentences, correcting each improperly used verb form.

The chimney sweepers raised early. They rose their brooms to their shoulders and went out to the street. It was still early, and the sun had not raised.

◆ Reading Strategy

Use Visuals as a Key to Meaning

Look at the illustrations accompanying "The Lamb" and "The Tyger," and consider how or whether they add to the poems' meanings.

1. How would you describe the mood of the illustration accompanying "The Lamb"? How does it relate to the poem's mood?

2. How does the tiger in Blake's illustration compare to the tiger described in the poem?

◆ Build Vocabulary

Using the Word Root *-spir-*

The following words contain the root *-spir-*, which means "breath" or "life." Define each word, incorporating the meaning of the root into your definition.

1. respiration **2.** expire **3.** inspire **4.** spirit

Using the Word Bank

Use words from the Word Bank to replace italicized words in the following sentences.

1. They traveled through *valleys* and over hills.

2. The *balanced forms* of the animal's body made it look graceful and powerful.

3. The student *desired* to attend a top college.

Beyond Literature

History Connection

Blake and His Time It would be an error to think of Blake as a poet and painter lost in his own visions and oblivious to the key events of his time. Scholars like David Erdman have pointed out that Blake was aware of, and responded to, all the major historical events of his era. These include the French Revolution and the American Revolution. Erdman even compares "the fire in which the tiger is forged" ("The Tyger") to "the fires" of conflict flaring up around the world during "the first year of the French Republic."

Is there any other evidence in these poems that Blake responded to the issues of his time? Explain.

Build Your Portfolio

Idea Bank

Writing

1. **Journal Entry** Write a journal entry about the wonders of childhood. Discuss the kinds of innocence that you value and hope will never be lost.

2. **Research Report** Blake's poem "The Chimney Sweeper" deals with a serious problem of the time—child labor. Do research on child labor in the nineteenth century and prepare a written report. **[Social Studies Link]**

3. **Response to Criticism** Northrop Frye has written of Blake's poetry: "Much of Blake's poetry is for the common reader, and will not mislead him. The lyrics speak for themselves . . ." Write a short paper agreeing or disagreeing with this statement. Support your argument with details from the poems.

Speaking and Listening

4. **Blake Reading** Hold a poetry reading in which you and classmates read aloud several of Blake's poems. **[Performing Arts Link]**

5. **Setting Blake to Music** Several composers and song writers have set Blake's simple poems to music. Choose one or two of his shorter poems and do the same. **[Performing Arts Link]**

Projects

6. **Advertisement** Even as far back as Blake's time, advertisers used symbols to lend a certain aura or to build associations with their products. Choose a product and create an advertisement for it centered on a single symbol. **[Career Link]**

7. **Illuminated Poem** Like Blake, write a poem and create an illustration that captures its meaning. As an alternative, you may want to create an illustration for one of Blake's poems. **[Art Link]**

Writing Mini-Lesson

Comparative Analysis

"The Lamb," which is from *Songs of Innocence* and "The Tyger," which is from *Songs of Experience*, explore the same subject from different points of view. Write a comparative analysis in which you explore the similarities and differences between the two poems and analyze how the view presented in each poem relates to the period of Blake's life in which it was written. Keep in mind the following tip as you develop your essay.

Writing Skills Focus: Placement for Emphasis

Emphasize your main point by placing a clear, concise statement of your thesis both at the beginning and at the end of your essay. By starting with your thesis statement, you'll make your point clear to readers from the beginning. By ending with a restatement of your thesis, you'll leave a lasting impression on your readers' minds.

Prewriting Start by reviewing the information about Blake and his work in the Guide for Interpreting on page 596. Then review the two poems. Use a Venn diagram like this one to record similarities and differences in the views the two poems present. Jot down details and passages from the poems that illustrate the views presented.

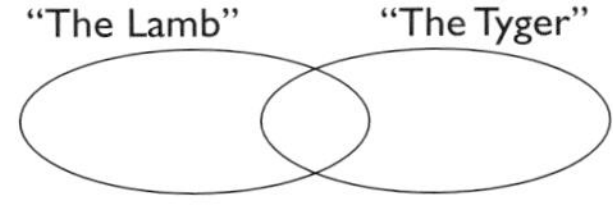

Drafting After stating your thesis in your opening paragraph, present evidence to back up your position. Cite passages and details from both poems.

Revising Carefully review your essay. Check to see that you've organized your ideas in a way that makes sense and that you've thoroughly supported your thesis.

✓ ASSESSMENT OPTIONS

Formal Assessment, Selection Test, pp. 146–148, and Assessment Resources Software. The selection test is designed so that it can be easily customized to the ability levels of your students. ***Alternative Assessment,*** p. 30, includes options for less advanced students, more advanced students, visual/spatial learners, verbal/linguistic learners, bodily/kinesthetic learners, and interpersonal learners.

PORTFOLIO ASSESSMENT

Use the following rubrics in the ***Alternative Assessment*** booklet to assess student writing:
Journal Entry: Expression Rubric, p. 95
Research Report: Research Report/Paper Rubric, p. 107
Response to Criticism: Literary Analysis/Interpretation Rubric, p. 113
Writing Mini-Lesson: Comparison/Contrast Rubric, p. 104

Idea Bank

Customizing for *Performance Levels*

Following are suggestions for matching Idea Bank topics with your students' ability levels:
- Less Advanced Students: 1, 4
- Average Students: 2, 5, 6
- More Advanced Students: 3, 7

Customizing for *Learning Modalities*

Following are suggestions for matching Idea Bank topics with your students' learning modalities:
- Musical/Rhythmic; 4, 5
- Visual/Spatial: 6, 7
- Verbal/Linguistic: 2, 3
- Intrapersonal: 1

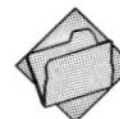

Writing Mini-Lesson

Refer students to the Writing Handbook, page 1189, for instruction on the writing process, and page 1193 for further information on response to literature.

Writing and Language Transparencies Display Writing Process Model 6: Interpreting a Work of Literature, pp. 45–55, to assist students in writing their own response. You may also display the Comparison-and-Contrast Chart, p. 115, for students to copy and use as they gather details.

Writer's Solution

Writers at Work Videodisc

Chapter 7: Play the video segment in which poet Eavan Boland discusses responding to literature.

Play frames 21571 to 31063

Writing Lab CD-ROM

Direct students to complete the tutorial on Response to Literature. Follow these steps:
1. Use an interactive Literary Elements Chart to gather details.
2. Have student use a Venn Diagram to gather and organize similarities and differences.
3. Create a draft on the computer.
4. Use a Transitions Checker to make sure ideas are clearly introduced and linked.

Sourcebook

Have students complete Chapter 7: Response to Literature, pp. 196–228, for additional support.

Prepare and Engage

OBJECTIVES

1. To read and interpret a short story
2. To relate a short story to personal experience
3. To learn vocabulary in context
4. To connect a short story to the theme of fantasy and reality
5. To respond to a short story through writing, speaking and listening, and projects

PORTFOLIO OPPORTUNITIES

Writing: Description of a Gothic Setting; Literary Analysis; Response to Criticism
Speaking and Listening: Dramatic Recitation
Project: Poe on Film

More About the Author
Although Edgar Allan Poe is one of the most beloved American authors of all time, when he was writing his stories and poetry, they were not well received. He was so ignored by his own generation that when, twenty-six years after his death, a stone monument was finally erected over his grave, the only American writer to attend the ceremony was Walt Whitman.

Thematic Focus

Poe often took a realistic setting and "haunted it," endowing it with spirits of the past, with characters weighed down by deep secrets and missions, and with supernatural effects. He sometimes also blurred the line between reality and fantasy as characters or a plot slowly but inexorably crossed over the borders of reality or, as in "The Oval Portrait," the borders of life itself.

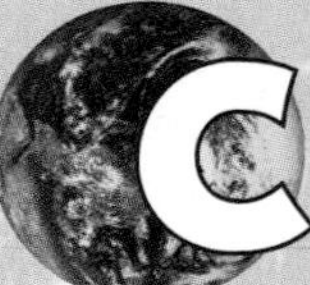

CONNECTIONS TO WORLD LITERATURE

The Oval Portrait

Edgar Allan Poe

Thematic Connection

FANTASY AND REALITY

Although the Romantic movement led the writers in this section to focus on the realities of the common man, it also inspired them to explore more fantastic realms. For example, William Blake wrote visionary poetry like "The Tyger," in which he seems to travel to the ends of the universe seeking answers to his questions: "In what distant deep skies/Burnt the fire of thine eyes!" Mary Shelley goes on an even stranger journey in her novel *Frankenstein,* in which she shows what goes wrong when a scientist attempts to create life itself.

Her novel has its roots in the Gothic tradition, which combined supernatural events with historical settings. The popularity of Gothic stories like *Frankenstein* reached beyond England into other cultures and countries. American writer Edgar Allan Poe, for example, is considered a master of Gothic writing.

THE MASTER OF HORROR

In stories like "The Oval Portrait," Poe begins with what seems to be realistic description. However, he soon crosses the border between reality and fantasy so that you become disoriented and subject to feelings of anxiety and fear.

THE LURE OF THE UNKNOWN

Stories and movies that echo the Gothic tradition of mystery and the supernatural are still popular today. A great part of their fascination lies in their plausibility. This fine line between fantasy and reality keeps us in suspense and wondering, "Could this have really happened?" As you read "The Oval Portrait," try to identify where the author crosses from reality to fantasy.

EDGAR ALLAN POE
(1809–1849)

Poe's real-life troubles must have inspired his dark imaginings. An orphan before he was three years old, he was taken in by the Allans, a prosperous family in Richmond, Virginia. However, Poe quarreled with his foster father, John Allan, and was disowned. When Poe was expelled by the University of Virginia, he enrolled at West Point, where he was court-martialed while still a cadet.

Poe's writing career was a mixture of literary success and financial failure. He won recognition as a poet, critic, and short story writer while earning a meager living as a magazine editor in Richmond, Philadelphia, and New York. His earnings were hardly enough to support his young wife, Virginia Clemm, and his mother-in-law.

Virginia's early death from tuberculosis was a blow from which Poe never recovered. He himself died two years afterward.

Ask students to name tales of the supernatural with which they are familiar. (*Carrie,* by Stephen King; "The Monkey's Paw," by W. W. Jacobs; and "The Tell-Tale Heart," by Edgar Allan Poe may come to mind.) Then ask students why these stories remain so popular. Lead them to realize that, because these stories are based in reality with real settings and characters, the supernatural or fantastic occurrences are all the more thrilling.

Inform students that the story they are about to read was written by Edgar Allan Poe, a master of blurring the lines between the actual and the fantastic.

Prentice Hall Literature Program Resources

REINFORCE / RETEACH / EXTEND

Selection Support Pages
Build Vocabulary, p. 147
Thematic Connection, p. 148

Formal Assessment Selection Test, pp. 146–148; Assessment Resources Software

Resource Pro CD-ROM
"The Oval Portrait"—includes all resource material and customizable lesson plan

Listening to Literature Audiocassettes
"The Oval Portrait"

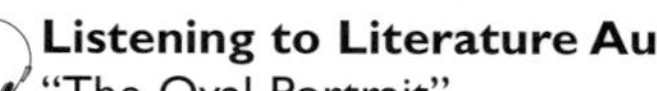

CONNECTIONS TO WORLD LITERATURE

The Oval Portrait

EDGAR ALLAN POE

The chateau into which my valet had ventured to make forcible entrance, rather than permit me, in my desperately wounded condition, to pass a night in the open air,
❶ was one of those piles of commingled gloom and grandeur which have so long frowned among the Apennines,[1] not less in fact than in the fancy of Mrs. Radcliffe.[2] To all appearance it had been temporarily and very lately abandoned. We established ourselves in one of the smallest and least sumptuously furnished apartments. It lay in a remote turret of the building. Its decorations were rich, yet tattered and antique. Its walls were hung with tapestry and bedecked with manifold and multiform armorial trophies, together with an unusually great number of very spirited modern paintings in frames of rich golden arabesque.[3] In these paintings, which depended from the walls not only in their main surfaces, but in very many nooks which the bizarre architecture of the chateau rendered necessary—in these paintings my incipient delirium, perhaps, had caused me to ❷
take deep interest; so that I bade Pedro to close the heavy shutters of the room—since it was already night—to light the tongues[4] of a tall candelabrum which stood by the head of my bed—and to throw open far and wide the fringed curtains of black velvet which enveloped the bed itself. I wished all this done that I might resign myself, if not to sleep, at least alternately to the contemplation of these

❸ ▲ **Critical Viewing** Does this portrait, like the one in the story, capture "Life" itself? Explain. **[Connect]**

Elizabeth Beale Bordley, Gilbert Stuart, Courtesy of the Museum of American Art of the Pennsylvania Academy of the Fine Arts, Philadelphia, Bequest of Elizabeth Mifflin

1. **Appennines** (ap´ ə ninz): Mountain range located in Italy.
2. **Mrs. Radcliffe:** Ann Radcliffe (1764–1823), English novelist.
3. **arabesque** (ar´ ə besk´): Complex and elaborate design.
4. **tongues** (tuŋz): Candles.

One-Minute Insight

An obsessed painter transforms life into art, with each brush stroke breathing life into the portrait, yet killing its model. As the narrator discovers the painting and reveals the story behind it, Poe shifts the borders between reality and fantasy, art and life.

Customize for *Less Proficient Readers*

To help less proficient readers understand this story, with its complex sentence structure and unusual or archaic vocabulary, have them listen to the **Listening to Literature Audiocassettes,** "The Oval Portrait," as they follow along in their books.

Comprehension Check ☑

❶ Ask: Who's speaking and what's happening? *The narrator is unnamed, but he reveals that he is wounded and that his servant had to force his or her way into a gloomy and forbidding chateau so the narrator could avoid spending the night out-of-doors.*

◆ Critical Thinking

❷ **Analyze** Remind students that Gothic tales usually combine historic settings with supernatural events. Ask students to find clues within this passage that hint at the story's Gothic underpinnings. *Clues include the "nooks" and "bizarre architecture" of a chateau filled with paintings contained in ornate frames. The narrator mentions that he is close to delirium, and he has become intrigued with the pictures that hung upon the walls.*

►Critical Viewing◄

❸ **Connect** Suggested responses: Yes, the woman in the portrait appears lifelike because of her natural pose and the gentle colors that mimic reality; no, the woman seems too "posed" and two-dimensional to be lifelike.

Humanities: Art

Elizabeth Beale Bordley, by Gilbert Stuart.

Gilbert Stuart (1755–1828) was an American portrait painter. He spent much of his early career in London, England, where he was influenced by such master portraitists as Joshua Reynolds and Thomas Gainsborough.

He eventually moved back to the United States in 1792 and painted luminaries such as George Washington. In fact, Stuart painted Washington several times, but perhaps his most famous portrait of him is the *Athenaeum Portrait,* which hangs in the Boston Museum of Fine Arts.

Use these questions for discussion:

1. What kind of personality do you think the woman in the portrait has? Explain. *She seems to have a serious personality. Her direct gaze and calm expression, coupled with her plain dress, seem to suggest that she is quiet and thoughtful.*
2. Does the woman's face show life, death, or death in life? *Suggested answer: Because the woman seems tired and solemn, it seems to show life that is diminishing, or death in life.*

◆ Critical Thinking

1 Speculate Ask: Why might the narrator have reacted as he did? *Students may suggest that the narrator was unnerved by his first impression of the painting; the narrator may have senses that something mystical or unnatural was associated with the portrait.*

Thematic Connection

2 Fantasy and Reality Ask students: In what way is the portrait itself a blend of fantasy and reality? *The portrait is of a real woman, painted in a lifelike manner, but the figure "melts" into the background in the vignette style, lending it an ethereal or ghostlike quality.*

Comprehension Check ☑

3 What had occurred to the narrator in "his fancy"? *He had mistaken the head for that of a living person.*

◆ Critical Thinking

4 Analyze Ask students to explain the way in which this story shifts here. *This passage begins another story, as the narrator reads about the life of the woman in the portrait.*

◆ Critical Thinking

5 Interpret Ask students to identify the ways in which the two characters—the narrator of the story and the portrait painter—are similar or parallel. *The painter of the portrait is losing all perspective and getting wilder and wilder. He resembles the narrator of the story, who is also in a turret, obsessed by art.*

◆ Critical Thinking

6 Infer Ask students whether or not the artist realized that he was killing his wife as he painted her. *It appears that he knew it on a subconscious level, but he would not let himself acknowledge or admit it. The italicized word would seems to make this point.*

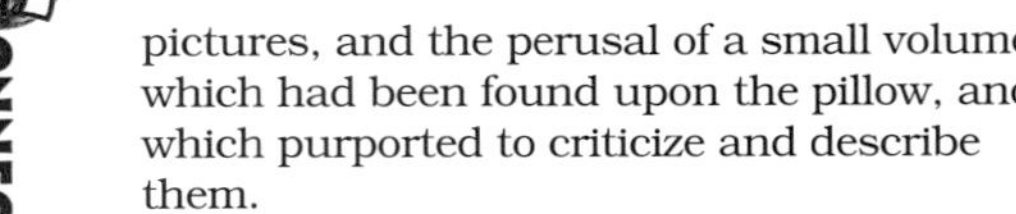

CONNECTIONS TO WORLD LITERATURE

pictures, and the perusal of a small volume which had been found upon the pillow, and which purported to criticize and describe them.

Long—long I read—and devoutly, devotedly I gazed. Rapidly and gloriously the hours flew by, and the deep midnight came. The position of the candelabrum displeased me, and outreaching my hand with difficulty, rather than disturb my slumbering valet, I placed it so as to throw its rays more fully upon the book.

But the action produced an effect altogether unanticipated. The rays of the numerous candles (for there were many) now fell within a niche of the room which had hitherto been thrown into deep shade by one of the bed-posts. I thus saw in vivid light a picture all unnoticed before. It was the portrait of a young girl just ripening into womanhood. I
1 glanced at the painting hurriedly, and then closed my eyes. Why I did this was not at first apparent even to my own perception. But while my lids remained thus shut, I ran over in mind my reason for so shutting them. It was an impulsive movement to gain time for thought—to make sure that my vision had not deceived me—to calm and subdue my fancy for a more sober and more certain gaze. In a very few moments I again looked fixedly at the painting.

That I now saw aright I could not and would not doubt; for the first flashing of the candles upon that canvas had seemed to dissipate the dreamy stupor which was stealing over my senses, and to startle me at once into waking life.

The portrait, I have already said, was that of a young girl. It was a mere head and shoulders, done in what is technically termed a *vignette*[5] manner; much in the style of the
2 favorite heads of Sully.[6] The arms, the bosom and even the ends of the radiant hair, melted imperceptibly into the vague yet deep shadow which formed the background of the whole. The frame was oval, richly gilded and filigreed in *Moresque*.[7] As a thing of art nothing could be more admirable than the painting itself. But it could have been neither the execution of the work, nor the immortal beauty of the countenance, which had so suddenly and so vehemently moved me. Least of all, could it have been that my fancy, shaken from
its half slumber, had mistaken the head for 3
that of a living person. I saw at once that the peculiarities of the design, of the *vignetting*, and of the frame, must have instantly dispelled such idea—must have prevented even its momentary entertainment. Thinking earnestly upon these points, I remained, for an hour perhaps, half sitting, half reclining, with my vision riveted upon the portrait. At length, satisfied with the true secret of its effect, I fell back within the bed. I had found the spell of the picture in an absolute *life-likeliness* of expression, which at first startled, finally confounded, subdued and appalled me. With deep and reverent awe I replaced the candelabrum in its former position. The cause of my deep agitation being thus shut from view, I sought eagerly the volume which discussed the paintings and their histories. Turning to the number which designated the oval portrait, I there read the vague and quaint words which follow:

'She was a maiden of rarest beauty, and 4
not more lovely than full of glee. And evil was the hour when she saw, and loved, and wedded the painter. He, passionate, studious, austere, and having already a bride in his Art; she a maiden of rarest beauty, and not more lovely than full of glee: all light and smiles, and frolicksome as the young fawn: loving and cherishing all things: hating only the Art which was her rival: dreading only the pallet and brushes and other untoward instruments which deprived her of the countenance of her lover. It was thus a terrible thing for this lady to hear the painter speak of his desire to portray even his young bride. But she was humble and obedient, and sat meekly for many weeks in the dark high turret-chamber where the light dripped upon the pale canvas only from overhead. But he, the painter, took glory in his work, which

5. ***vignette*** (vin yet′) *n.*: Picture or photograph with no definite border.
6. **Sully:** Thomas Sully (1783–1872), American painter born in England.

7. ***Moresque*** (mô resk′): Decoration characterized by intricate tracery and bright colors.

went on from hour to hour and from day to day. And he was a passionate, and wild and moody man, who became lost in reveries; so
5 that he *would* not see that the light which fell so ghastlily in that lone turret withered the health and the spirits of his bride, who pined visibly to all but him. Yet she smiled on and still on, uncomplainingly, because she saw that the painter, (who had high renown,) took a fervid and burning pleasure in his task, and wrought day and night to depict her who so loved him, yet who grew daily more dispirited and weak. And in sooth[8] some who beheld the portrait spoke of its resemblance in low words, as of a mighty marvel, and a proof not less of the power of the painter than of his deep love for her whom he depicted so surpassingly well. But at length, as the labor drew nearer to its conclusion, there were admitted none into the turret; for the painter had grown wild with the ardor of his work, and turned his eyes from the canvas rarely, even to regard the countenance of his wife. And he *would* not see that the tints which
he spread upon the canvas were drawn from 6
the cheeks of her who sat beside him. And when many weeks had passed, and but little remained to do, save one brush upon the mouth and one tint upon the eye, the spirit of the lady again flickered up as the flame within the socket of the lamp. And then the brush was given, and then the tint was placed; and, for one moment, the painter stood entranced before the work which he had wrought; but in the next, while he yet gazed, he grew tremulous and very pallid, and aghast, and crying with a loud voice, "This is indeed *Life* itself!" turned suddenly to regard his beloved:—*She was dead!'*

8. **sooth** (sōōth): Truth; fact.

Guide for Responding

◆ Literature and Your Life

Reader's Response Were you surprised by the ending of this story? Why or why not?

Thematic Focus In what way did the artist who painted the portrait go too far?

Alternate Ending Working with a partner, make up a different ending for this story.

☑ Check Your Comprehension

1. Why does the narrator's valet break into the chateau?
2. Briefly describe the chateau's appearance.
3. (a) What is the narrator's first reaction to the portrait of the young girl? (b) What causes this reaction?
4. What is the relationship between the subject of the painting and the artist?
5. What happens to the subject when the artist finally finishes the painting?

◆ Critical Thinking

INTERPRET

1. (a) In what way does "The Oval Portrait" contain two stories? (b) How does the first story serve as an introduction to the second? **[Analyze]**
2. What is surprising about the artist's remark in the final sentence? **[Interpret]**
3. This story was originally called "Life in Death." Do you prefer this title to "The Oval Portrait"? Explain. **[Support]**
4. What statement is Poe making about the relationship between reality and fantasy, life and art? **[Draw Conclusions]**

APPLY

5. Jacques Barzun has written, "Art distills sensation and embodies it with enhanced meaning in memorable form—or else it is not art." How do Barzun's words relate to the painting in the story and to the story itself? **[Apply]**

Beyond the Selection

FURTHER READING

Other Works by the Author

"The Masque of the Red Death"
"The Black Cat"
Eight Tales of Terror
"The Tell-Tale Heart" and Other Writings

INTERNET

You and your students may find additional information about the author on the Internet at the following site:

For more information about Poe and links to other sites, go to Peter Forrest's House of Usher Web site at **http://www.comnet.ca/~forrest/index.html**

We *strongly recommend* that you preview the sites before you send students to them.

Reinforce and Extend

Answers

◆ Literature and Your Life

Reader's Response Some students may say they were not surprised because of the narrator's earlier intuition that the painting was somehow alive; some students may say that they were surprised because the cause of the wife's death is so unusual and supernatural.

Thematic Focus The artist went too far by exchanging the life of his wife for the perfection of his art.

☑ Check Your Comprehension

1. The narrator's valet breaks into the chalet because the narrator is wounded and the valet doesn't want him to pass the night in the open air.
2. The chateau is large and grand, but it looks recently abandoned and gloomy.
3. (a) The narrator impulsively closes his eyes. (b) Yes. He needs time to think about what he just saw.
4. The subject and the artist are husband and wife.
5. The subject of the painting dies because the painter has "painted the life out of her."

◆ Critical Thinking

1. (a) The first story is about the narrator coming to the chateau and being transfixed by the painting. The second story is about the subject of the portrait and the artist who painted it. (b) The first story establishes the lifelike nature of the painting; the second story explains why this is so.
2. The artist exclaims that the portrait is "life itself" while his wife lies there dead.
3. Some students will prefer "Life in Death" because it sounds more strange and eerie; some students will prefer "The Oval Portrait" because it doesn't give away the theme of the story in advance.
4. Poe seems to suggest that both fantasy and reality and life and art can overlap or be confused.
5. Barzun means that for art to be truly "art," it should have a heightened reality or "enhanced meaning" that renders it memorable.

Thematic Connection

1. Sample response: Mary Shelley's work is most rooted in reality because the characters and settings are most true-to-life. Even the animation of Frankenstein's monster is based on scientific principles.
2. Suggested reponse: No, Blake's tiger is not as lifelife as the oval portrait. The tiger's expression is too similar to that of a smirking human to be realistic.
3. Students' responses should identify specific similarities and differences between the stories.

Idea Bank

Customizing for
Performance Levels

Following are suggestions for matching Idea Bank topics with your students' ability levels:

Less Advanced Students: 1, 4
Average Students: 2, 5
More Advanced Students: 3

Customizing for
Learning Modalities

Following are suggestions for matching Idea Bank topics with your students' learning modalities:

Musical/Rhythmic: 4
Verbal/Linguistic: 1, 2, 3
Interpersonal: 5

Thematic Connections

FANTASY AND REALITY

The writers of the Romantic period deal with the realities of existence as well as the possibilities of the imagination. Poe, like Mary Shelley and William Blake, begins from realistic experiences and then moves into realms of imagination. In blurring the line between reality and fantasy, these writers open the reader's mind to a world of possibilities.

1. (a) Of Poe's, Mary Shelley's, or Blake's works, which selection is most rooted in reality? Explain. (b) Which is the most fantastic? Why?
2. Is Blake's depiction of a tiger lifelike in the same way Poe's oval portrait is? Give reasons for your answer.
3. Choose a modern tale of horror and explain how it is similar to or different from Poe's.

Idea Bank

Writing

1. **Description of a Gothic Setting** Write a description of a setting for a modern Gothic tale like Poe's.
2. **Literary Analysis** Write an analysis of Poe's story in which you identify the point or points at which reality crosses into fantasy.
3. **Response to Criticism** G. R. Thompson has suggested that "The Oval Portrait" can be read as "the dream of a man delirious from pain and lack of sleep." Write an essay in which you agree or disagree with this statement.

Speaking and Listening

4. **Dramatic Recitation** Perform a dramatic reading of "The Oval Portrait." Emphasize the story's drama by using your voice expressively and pausing at key points. **[Performing Arts link]**

Project

5. **Poe on Film** Several of Poe's works or combinations of them have been made into films. View one of these films and report on it to the class. Evaluate the camera work, the mood, and the balance between fantasy and reality. **[Media Link]**

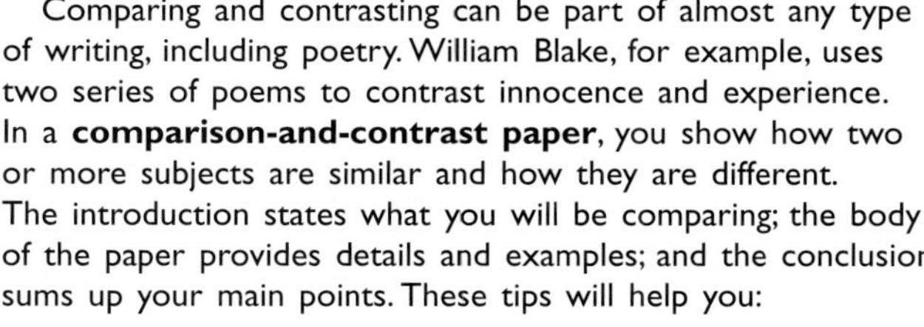

Writing Process Workshop

Comparison-and-Contrast Paper

Comparing and contrasting can be part of almost any type of writing, including poetry. William Blake, for example, uses two series of poems to contrast innocence and experience. In a **comparison-and-contrast paper**, you show how two or more subjects are similar and how they are different. The introduction states what you will be comparing; the body of the paper provides details and examples; and the conclusion sums up your main points. These tips will help you:

Two Farmers, Kasimir Malevich

Writing Skills Focus

- ▶ To make your comparison-and-contrast paper easy to follow, **choose an organizational strategy**. (See p. 585.)
- ▶ Provide a clear **beginning, middle and end** for your paper. (See p. 595.)
- ▶ **Place your ideas for emphasis** by putting key points at the beginning or the end. (See p. 603.)

Model From Literature

Excerpt from *An Essay of Dramatic Poesy* by John Dryden

Those who accuse [Shakespeare] to have wanted [lacked] ① learning give him the greater commendation: he was naturally learned; he needed not the spectacles of books to read nature;. . . . He is many times flat, insipid; his comic wit degenerating into clenches [clichés], ② his serious swelling into bombast. But he is always great when some great occasion is presented to him.

As for Jonson, ... I think him the most learned and judicious writer. . . . One cannot say he wanted wit, but rather that he was frugal of it. . . . If there was any fault in his language, 'twas that he weaved it too closely and laboriously . . . . If I would compare him with Shakespeare, I must acknowledge him the more correct poet, but Shakespeare the greater wit. . . . I admire him, but I love Shakespeare. ③

① Dryden used subject-by-subject organization, discussing first Shakespeare, then Jonson.

② Dryden's audience was familiar with the works of Jonson and Shakespeare and comfortable with this style of language.

③ The placement of this statement gives it emphasis and impact.

Cross-Curricular Connection: Math

Remind students that mathematics explains similarities and differences in numerical fashion. Simple subtraction points out differences; fractions show relationships; ratios show comparisons. A mathematical formula can describe how the length of a building compares to its width.

You might have a group of students use a mathematical formula as the basis for a comparison-and-contrast essay and then use comparison-and-contrast principles to share their results with the class.

Prepare and Engage

Establish Writing Guidelines
Review the following key characteristics of a comparison-and-contrast paper:

- A comparison-and-contrast paper shows the similarities and differences in two or more subjects.
- It uses subject-by-subject or point-by-point organization.
- The introduction names the subjects compared; the body gives details and examples; the conclusion summarizes.

Before students begin, you may share with them the Scoring Rubric for Comparison/Contrast (p. 104 in ***Alternative Assessment***) so that students see the criteria by which they will be evaluated. Suggestions on page 611 customize the rubric to this workshop.

Writing and Language Transparencies You may wish to use Writing Process Model 10, Comparison-and-Contrast Essay (p. 91) to show the process of writing and revising a comparison-and-contrast essay.

Connect to Literature You may wish to refer students to George Orwell's "Shooting an Elephant" in Unit 6, p. 938. Discuss how Orwell compares what is expected of him with what he wants to do.

Writer's Solution

Sourcebook
To help students see the methods of organizing a comparison-and-contrast paper, have them study the models on page 84 in Chapter 3, Exposition.

Writing Lab CD-ROM
If students have access to computers, have them work in the Exposition tutorial to complete all or part of their literary analysis. Follow these steps:

1. Students can find topic ideas using the Comparison-and-Contrast Wheel.
2. Have students use a Venn Diagram to focus their topics.
3. Have students use the audio-annotated models for comparison-and-contrast organization.
4. Have students use the Revision Checker for transition words to refine their work.

Develop Student Writing

Prewriting

You may want to have students use a Comparison-and-Contrast Organizer (***Writing and Language Transparencies,*** p. 116) to help organize their thoughts.

Customize for
Visual Learners
To help these students organize, have them list details for their comparisons and draw boxes around details for one subject and circles around details for the other. They can manipulate the circles and boxes to form a subject-by-subject or point-by-point organizational picture.

Writer's Solution

Writing Lab CD-ROM
In the Gathering Details section, students can view a video clip from *Star Trek: The Next Generation* to see an example of comparison and contrast.

Drafting

Remind students that details should be arranged by order of importance, usually with the most important last and the second most important first.

Writers at Work Videodisc
Play the videodisc segment on Exposition (Ch. 3) to let students hear film critic Anne Billson discuss how she adjusts content, vocabulary, and writing style for different kinds of audiences.

Play frames 26184 to 27200

Play frames 29740 to 30502

Applying Language Skills

Using Comparative and Superlative Modifiers Remind students that Comparison-and-Contrast Essays rely on modifiers to show the degree of comparison. Thus, confusing comparative and superlative modifiers can change the essay's message.

Answers

1. sadder
2. more
3. scariest

Applying Language Skills: Using Comparative and Superlative Modifiers

Most modifiers have a comparative form for comparing two items and a superlative form for comparing more than two items. Almost all one-syllable modifiers and some two-syllable modifiers use *-er* to form the comparative and *-est* to form the superlative. For most modifiers that are two syllables and longer, use *more* to form the comparative and *most* to form the superlative.

Practice Choose the correct modifier in these sentences.

1. Emmett Kelly had a (sadder, saddest) face than the average clown did.
2. Of Hurricane Paula and Hurricane Fran, Paula was the (more, most) recent storm.
3. Mary Shelley's *Frankenstein* is the (more scary, scariest) book ever written.

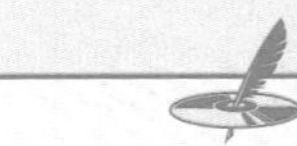
Writer's Solution Connection Writing Lab

For help narrowing your topic, review the Venn Diagram in the Narrowing Your Topic section of the tutorial on Exposition.

Prewriting

Choose a Topic If you need a topic for a comparison-and-contrast paper, consider using one listed below. Whatever your topic, be sure that there are enough similarities and differences between the subjects to make the examination worthwhile.

Know Your Audience Gauge what your readers know about your subject, as well as their level of interest in it. As you gather details, keep your readers in mind, choosing details that will help them understand your topic and hold their interest.

Topic Ideas

- U.S. Congress and British Parliament
- Nuclear fission and nuclear fusion
- Scots dialect and British English
- The novel *Frankenstein* and a movie version

Organize Details As you gather details, sort them into categories or groups: subject by subject or point by point.

Topic: Spiders and Insects	
Subject by Subject	Point by Point
A. Spiders	A. Body
a. 2 part body	a. Spiders: 2 part
b. 8 legs	b. Insects: 3 part

Drafting

Use Placement for Emphasis As you draft, place your details for the greatest impact. For example, if you have an intriguing fact that will interest your readers, you may present it in the introduction to whet their interest in reading further.

Consider Your Audience Keep your readers in mind as you draft your paper. Use a style of language and degree of formality that will appeal to them. Compare these examples:

- ▶ **Audience: School Children** Mars is the fourth planet from the sun. It is most like the Earth in climate, but its surface features—mountains, valleys, rocky soil—would make it almost impossible for humans to live there.
- ▶ **Audience: Scientists** Although Martian atmospheric conditions are close to Earth's, its topography alone would make it virtually impossible to colonize.

Writer's Solution

For additional instruction and practice, use the **Language Lab CD-ROM** lessons on Using Modifiers and Forms of Comparison. You may also use the practice pages on Degrees of Comparison, pp. 68–69, in the *Writer's Solution Grammar Practice Book.*

Revising

Use a Checklist Use the following questions, or develop your own, as you read your draft:

1. Could my writing be made more suitable for my readers?
2. How can I improve the organization to clarify comparison-and-contrast relationships?
3. Are any important or interesting details lost because of where they're placed?

REVISION MODEL

The Carolina wren is small, only about 5 inches at maturity. Its distinctive call, "TEA-kettle, TEA-kettle" ~~as opposed to the *chug-chug-chug* of the Cactus wren~~ ① can be heard throughout the southeastern United States at all times of the year. ② Habitats for this wren ~~Places the Carolina wren lives include~~ include dense thickets in ravines and woodlands. Nesting spots include tree stumps, stone walls, and even mailboxes. ③ ¶ The larger cousin to the Carolina wren is the Cactus wren, measuring up to 8 inches. . . .

① This statement is confusing and out of place in the subject-by-subject organization used in this paper.

② More sophisticated language reflects the high level of the audience.

③ A new paragraph should begin here. This will help emphasize the differences between the two wrens.

Publishing

- **Multimedia Presentation** Use a page layout program to format your work and to add media.
- **Literary Magazine** Send your paper to a publication devoted to your subject.
- **On-line Publishing** Find a site or bulletin board that is appropriate for your topic. Post your paper there.

APPLYING LANGUAGE SKILLS: Using Past Participial Phrases

A past participial phrase contains a past participle of a verb and any modifiers that go with it. The entire phrase acts as an adjective and should be placed close to the word it modifies.

Examples:

Held together with only a bit of glue, the equipment was unsafe for the climb.

The pianist, prepared from weeks of practice, gave an outstanding recital.

Practice Identify each past participial phrase and the word it modifies.

1. Supported by several million dollars, the Governor was ready for the race.
2. Buried under tons of lava, the treasures of Pompeii were preserved forever.
3. I was eager to read Poe's short story, "The Oval Portrait," reputed to be very mysterious.

Writer's Solution Connection
Language Lab

For help in avoiding the use of double comparisons, see the Problems with Modifiers lesson.

Revising

After discussing the Revision Model, you may want also to use the Revision Overlay for the Writing Process Model 10: Comparison-and-Contrast Essay (***Writing and Language Transparencies,*** p. 89) to further model the revising process.

Publishing

Discuss with students the effectiveness of comparison-and-contrast topics in letters to the editor. They may wish to consider this means of publication.

Applying Language Skills

Using Past Participial Phrases
Point out to students how past participial phrases add maturity to sentence structure and sentence variety.

Answers

1. *Supported by several million dollars* modifies *Governor*.
2. *Buried under tons of lava* modifies *treasures*.
3. *Reputed to be very mysterious* modifies *"The Oval Portrait."*

For additional support, use the practice page on Verbals and Verbal Phrases, p. 29, in the *Writer's Solution Grammar Practice Book*.

Reinforce and Extend

Applying Knowledge After students have completed their papers, ask them to discuss how comparison and contrast is used in the workplace, including advertising, sales, insurance policies, computer technology, and so on.

ASSESSMENT		4	3	2	1
PORTFOLIO ASSESSMENT Use the rubric for Comparison/Contrast (p. 104 in ***Alternative Assessment***) to assess students' writing. Add these criteria to customize the rubric to this assignment.	**Placement for Emphasis**	All important ideas are placed for emphasis at the beginning or end of the essay.	Some important ideas are placed for emphasis.	One important idea is placed for emphasis.	Important ideas are buried.
	Sentence Variety	Sentence structures include several past participial phrases placed in a variety of locations within sentences.	Sentence structures include several past participial phrases.	Sentence structures include one or two past participial phrases.	Sentence structures include no past participial phrases.

Introduce the Strategy

Ask students to name sources they might read to find specific information at school, at home, or at work. Ask them how the information is usually organized in each. Ask how they can use scanning in each.

Customize for
Visual/Spatial Learners
Ask these students to use examples of visuals (like advertisements, cartoons, comic books) to see how scanning strategies apply. Then have them transfer the strategies to written text.

Apply the Strategy

Have students scan the Help Wanted postings focusing only on the phrases "part-time" and "students." Ask them to note, without looking at other details, which ads they should read further. Then have students read to find only ads that meet the specific requirements.

Answers
Students may respond along these lines:

1. Capital letters name categories; thus those specifying *college grads* and *full-time* are eliminated.
2. Words like *landscaper* eliminate ads; words like *will train, experience necessary*, and *general clerical* identify possibilities.
3. Ads for apartment cleaners, mother's helpers, and office assistant fit the bill; experience or training is appropriate or the applicant can be trained.

Reading to Find Specific Information

Real-World Reading Skills Workshop

Strategies for Success

You're looking in an encyclopedia or in the want ads for a specific item. Somewhere on that page of densely packed type, you'll probably find the information you need. If you know how to use a technique called *scanning*, you'll be able to locate that information in a few seconds.

Scanning When you scan, you move your eyes rapidly back and forth over the page looking for elements of organization or for key words. This type of focused search enables you to save time by disregarding information you don't need.

Scan for Organization Quickly scan to discover whether information is arranged alphabetically, chronologically, or by some other method, so you can limit the rest of your search to the section that covers what you need. Look for headings, titles, and subtitles. Does the information you're looking for come under any of these heads?

HELP WANTED

FULL-TIME JOBS
Apartment Cleaners
Earn $20 an hour.
Easy work. Will train.
Call xxx-xxxx

STUDENTS WANTED
Landscaper's Assistant
Mow Lawns, tend gardens, three afternoons a week.
References needed.
Call xxx-xxxx

Place your ad here
Call xxx-xxxx

STUDENTS WANTED
Landscaper's Assistant
Mow Lawns, tend gardens, three afternoons a week.
References needed.
Call xxx-xxxx

MOTHER'S HELPER
Care for two children.
Three to six o'clock, Mon - Fri.
Experience Necessary.
Call xxx-xxxx

PART-TIME JOBS
Receptionist and Office Assistant. Great communication skills.
General clerical.
Physically fit and very bright. Part-and full-time position available.
Call xxx-xxxx

COLLEGE GRADS
Part-time Accountant
Work for small business.
Choose your own hours.
Call xxx-xxxx

MOTHER'S HELPER
Care for two children.
Three to six o'clock, Mon - Fri.
Experience Necessary.
Call xxx-xxxx

FULL-TIME JOBS
Apartment Cleaners
Earn $20 an hour.
Easy work. Will train.
Call xxx-xxxx

Place your ad here
Call xxx-xxxx

Think of Key Words What words will identify the material for which you're looking? If you're scanning the classifieds in hopes of buying a used bicycle, then *bike* may be a key word for you. Look for it as you scan blocks of text.

If you can't seem to find what you need, consider looking for a different key word. For example, if you have been looking only for the word *bike*, consider scanning for the more formal word *bicycle*. As you become familiar with reference sources, you'll develop a feel for the types of key words that work for each source.

Apply the Strategies

Scan the Help Wanted postings on this page to find a part-time job after school. Imagine that you've taken some clerical courses and know how to type. You've also done some babysitting. However, you're allergic to pollen and would prefer a job indoors.

1. Scan the words in capital letters. What do they signify? Which can you eliminate right away?
2. Scan the words under the heads. Which key words eliminate the ads or identify them as possibilities?
3. Which job openings seem to fit the bill? Why?

Here are the other kinds of items in which you read to find specific information:

- Phone book
- Reading-comprehension tests
- Classified ads

Cross-Curricular Connection: Science

Studying a science text means absorbing many details. To precede careful reading by scanning, however, establishes an overall picture so that details fit into place. For instance, by scanning chapter subheadings, visuals, and end-of-chapter questions, a reader grasps the general chapter contents. Careful reading, instead of overwhelming, thus provides supporting details to the existing general idea. Have students bring in science texts to practice scanning strategies.

PART 2

Focus on Literary Forms: Lyric Poetry

The Wanderer over the Sea of Clouds, Caspar David Friedrich, Kunsthalle, Hamburg

Lyric poems express a writer's thoughts and feelings. The ancient Greeks, who set this type of poem to lyre music, gave the lyric its name. Romantic poets of the nineteenth century devoted themselves to lyric poetry, "singing" about nature and society's injustices. Today, songwriters are still influenced by the Romantic lyric as they bare their souls to driving rock rhythms.

One-Minute Planning Guide

The selections in this section present a sampling of lyric poetry, with an emphasis on the English Romantic poets Wordsworth, Coleridge, Byron, Shelley, and Keats. In their works, these poets examine humanity's relationship with nature, explore realms of the imagination and of feeling, and contemplate the notions of freedom, beauty, truth, reality, fame, and justice.

Customize for *Varying Student Needs*

When assigning the selections in this part, keep in mind these factors:

Poetry of William Wordsworth
- Less proficient readers and English language learners will need assistance with complicated and inverted sentences

Poetry of Samuel Taylor Coleridge
- Archaic and poetic words may be difficult for English language learners
- "The Rime of the Ancient Mariner" is a very long poem (625 lines)

Poetry of George Gordon, Lord Byron
- Students will enjoy the satiric humor of "Don Juan," especially when Byron pokes fun at the lofty long-windedness of the other Romantic poets
- Especially appealing to musical/rhythmic learners

Poetry of Percy Bysshe Shelley
- Political undercurrents will appeal to most teens
- Less proficient readers may require guidance in reading the odes in sentences.

Poetry of John Keats
- Sonnets are short and relatively easy to read
- Imagery in odes will appeal to visual/spatial learners

"The Lorelei"
- Story-like lyric is easy to read and understand

Haiku
- Very short, understandable poems

Humanities: Art

The Wanderer, 1818, by Caspar David Friedrich.

This dramatic oil-on-canvas painting of a man standing alone to ponder a fog-covered landscape is emblematic of the Romantic writer contemplating his or her relationship with nature.

Although Caspar David Friedrich was German-born, he studied at the Royal Academy in Copenhagen, Denmark. Many of his paintings, like *The Wanderer*, were landscapes or seascapes capturing human isolation and suggesting people's ultimate impotence against nature's overwhelming force.

Use these questions for discussion:

1. What elements of the painting suggest the Romantics' several views of nature? *The light and beauty of the landscape suggest the Romantics' optimistic views about nature while the dark jagged rocks suggest the Romantics' sense of nature's dangerous powers.*
2. How does the central figure's posture reflect Romantic attitudes toward nature and society? *The central figure has his back to the viewer—the world—and faces or embraces nature, much as the Romantics turned from society and toward nature.*

Prepare and Engage

OBJECTIVES

1. To read, comprehend, and interpret poetry
2. To relate poetry to personal experience
3. To use literary context to improve comprehension
4. To identify Romanticism and the lyric
5. To build vocabulary in context and learn words related to *anatomize*
6. To develop skill in using present participial phrases
7. To write a public service announcement, adapting the message to the medium
8. To respond to the poetry through writing, speaking and listening, and projects

SKILLS INSTRUCTION

Vocabulary: Related Words: Forms of Anatomize

Grammar: Present Participial Phrases

Reading Strategy: Use Literary Context

Literary Focus: Romanticism and the Lyric

Writing: Adapting the Message to the Medium

Speaking and Listening: Debate (teacher edition)

Critical Viewing: Infer; Compare and Contrast; Make a Judgment

PORTFOLIO OPPORTUNITIES

Writing: Literary Analysis; Travel Brochure; Response to Criticism

Writing Mini-Lesson: Public Service Announcement

Speaking and Listening: Debate; Ask the Poet

Projects: Ecology and Romanticism; History of Gardening

More About the Author
William Wordsworth believed that poetry should be "a spontaneous overflow of emotion." He gravitated toward nature and common people from a conviction that in these settings emotions are more accessible. According to Wordsworth, people who live and work closely with nature are attuned to its simple but powerful emotions and speak a language derived from that close connection rather than one influenced by "social vanity."

Guide for Interpreting

William Wordsworth

(1770–1850)

One of England's greatest poets, William Wordsworth was a visionary who grew more conservative as his work became accepted. Today he is known as the pioneer of the Romantic movement, which took literature in a dramatic new direction.

The Lake District Born in the beautiful Lake District of England, Wordsworth spent his youth roaming the countryside. In later years, too, he found peace and reassurance in the gentle hills and serene lakes of this district. It is this region of northwestern England that is the cradle of the Romantic movement.

Revolution and Love By the time Wordsworth was a young teenager, both his parents had died. However, his education was provided for, and in 1787, he entered Cambridge University. After graduating from Cambridge, he traveled through Europe, spending considerable time in France. There he embraced the ideals of the newly born French Revolution, ideals that stressed social justice and individual rights. He also found time to fall in love with a young woman named Annette Vallon.

Disillusionment and Crisis Wordsworth's involvement with the revolution and with Annette Vallon ended abruptly in 1793 when England declared war on France, and Wordsworth had to return home. As the French Revolution became increasingly violent, Wordsworth lapsed into a depression. Two people who saw him through this crisis were his beloved sister Dorothy and fellow poet Samuel Taylor Coleridge.

Revolution in Art It is as if Wordsworth translated his revolutionary hopes from politics to literature. With Coleridge, he composed a collection of poems called *Lyrical Ballads* (1798). These poems were revolutionary in their use of the language of ordinary people rather than specialized "poetic" words. Also, these "ballads" showed how the lives and experiences of ordinary people, when properly viewed, were really *extra*ordinary. In both language and subject matter, these poems broke sharply with the past.

Poetry and Autobiography Critics agree that Wordsworth's greatest work is his autobiography in poetry, *The Prelude*. Wordsworth completed an early version of this poem in 1799. By 1805, he had expanded the poem considerably. As he wrote to a friend, *The Prelude* told the story of "the growth of my own mind." It is not always factually accurate but in its combination of —in Stephen Gill's words— "satire and narrative, description and meditation, the visionary and the deliberately banal," it was unique. Wordsworth grew more conservative in his politics as his revolutionary poetry gained acceptance. However, as time went on, his place as the father of English Romanticism was assured.

◆ Background for Understanding

HISTORY: WORDSWORTH, THE FRENCH REVOLUTION, AND ROMANTICISM

When Wordsworth traveled to France in 1790, the French Revolution was under way. On July 14, 1789, a Parisian mob had stormed the Bastille prison. Wordsworth was caught up in the revolutionary fervor and saw "France standing on the top of golden hours." In 1791, when he returned to France, the country was more chaotic, and hopes for peaceful social reform seemed unrealistic. The declared war between England and France (1793) and the violent turn taken by the French Revolution (1793–1794) dashed Wordsworth's hopes.

The crisis he experienced when his political hopes failed led Wordsworth to his revolution in literature: Romanticism. This movement embodied the same faith in ordinary people that had inspired his politics.

Prentice Hall Literature Program Resources

REINFORCE / RETEACH / EXTEND

Selection Support Pages
Build Vocabulary: Related Words: Forms of *Anatomize,* p. 149
Grammar and Style: Present Participial Phrases, p. 150
Reading Strategy: Use Literary Context, p. 151
Literary Focus: Romanticism, p. 152

Strategies for Diverse Student Needs, p. 31

Beyond Literature
Cross-Curricular Connection: Social Studies
Rural to Urban Shift of Population, p. 31

Formal Assessment Selection Test, pp. 154–156; Assessment Resources Software

Alternative Assessment, p. 31

Writing and Language Transparencies
Writing Process Model 5: Persuasive Essay, pp. 37–44

Resource Pro CD-ROM
Poetry of William Wordsworth—includes all resource material and customizable lesson plan

Listening to Literature Audiocassettes
Poetry of William Wordsworth

Poetry of William Wordsworth

◆ Literature and Your Life

Connect Your Experience

Most people would list rock music and the ecology movement as products of twentieth-century America. Actually, both these cultural developments are the intellectual "grandchildren" of Romanticism, which began about two hundred years ago.

William Wordsworth's poems may not sound like rock music, but his ideas can still be found in our music and our politics.

Journal Writing Jot down your thoughts about freedom and nature, and then compare them to Wordsworth's.

Thematic Focus: Fantasy and Reality

Notice how Wordsworth considers the growth of his own mind an important element of reality.

◆ Literary Focus

Romanticism and the Lyric

Romanticism was a late-eighteenth-century literary movement that reacted against the Neoclassical style of the previous generation. The Neoclassicists favored rationalism, wit, and outward elegance. The Romantics wrote not from the head but from the heart and often used **lyric poems** to express personal emotions.

English Romanticism began with a great-hearted poet, William Wordsworth. Calling himself a "worshipper of Nature," he saw behind the things of nature a "motion and a spirit" that "rolls through all things." These words come from the lyric "Tintern Abbey," but you can sense this same depth of feeling in everything he wrote.

◆ Reading Strategy

Use Literary Context

Literary context refers to the whole climate of practices and assumptions that influence a writer. Sometimes that climate changes, as when the artificial verse of Neoclassicism yielded to the sincere poetry of Romanticism.

Wordsworth is one of those rare writers who actually brings about a change in literary context. You will understand him better if you realize that the qualities you find in his work—sincerity, spontaneity, a deep feeling for nature—were revolutionary at the time.

◆ Build Vocabulary

Related Words: Forms of *Anatomize*

Although the noun *anatomy* and the related verb and adjective *anatomize* and *anatomical* pertain to "the study of the structure of animals or plants," they can also be applied to society. In *The Prelude*, for example, Wordsworth tries to *anatomize* society; that is, he tries "to study or dissect" it.

Word Bank

Before you read, preview this list of words from the poems.

recompense
roused
presumption
anatomize
confounded
sordid
stagnant

◆ Grammar and Style

Present Participial Phrases

Wordsworth's long, easily flowing sentences contain many **present participial phrases**—phrases containing a present participle with its modifiers and complements. Such phrases function as adjectives. In the following example from "The World Is Too Much with Us," the present participial phrase modifies the pronoun "I":

So might I, standing on this
pleasant lea.

Preparing for Standardized Tests

Reading and Vocabulary Students may encounter analogy or sentence completion items on the verbal portions of standardized tests. Recognizing words related to other familiar words will enable students to grasp intended meanings in verbal items. The Build Vocabulary lesson focuses on learning words related to *anatomize*. Students can apply this skill to recognizing and deciphering such words when they appear on standardized tests. For additional practice, use the Build Vocabulary page in ***Selection Support***, p. 149.

Grammar and Language Test items on some standardized tests require students to demonstrate effective use of modifying structures. The Grammar and Style lesson for this selection focuses on present participial phrases, providing students with practice in recognizing and using these modifiers effectively. For additional practice, use the Grammar and Style page on Present Participial Phrases, p. 150, in ***Selection Support***.

To prepare students for Wordsworth's emotional link to nature, take a nature walk with students, either physically or with pictures or slides, through a beautiful natural setting. Charge students with noting both sensory images and emotional responses. Discuss how the emotions evoked by nature could inspire social or political views. Lead students to understand that the poetry of William Wordsworth is noted for its focus on nature.

Customize for
Less Proficient Readers

Less proficient readers may have difficulty with the poetic diction and syntax in these works. Encourage students to use punctuation clues to identify Wordsworth's sentences and then to paraphrase these to clarify meaning.

Customize for
More Advanced Students

To facilitate students' appreciation of Wordsworth's style, have them compare his word choices with synonyms that he might have chosen. Then have them identify the specific emotion or attitude that is conveyed by the words selected by Wordsworth.

Customize for
English Language Learners

To help language learners cope with Wordsworth's historical word usages, review footnoted words such as *suffer* and *faint*. Then discuss their contemporary meanings and clarify their historical meanings.

Customize for
Musical/Rhythmic Learners

For greater appreciation of the poetry, have musical/rhythmic learners follow the text of the poems as they listen to them on **Listening to Literature Audiocassettes.** How do the emotions of the poetry come across to the ear?

Listening to Literature Audiocassettes

Develop Understanding

One-Minute Insight This poem perfectly illustrates Wordsworth's belief in nature as a healer and teacher. In it, he speaks to his much-loved sister Dorothy, describing and hoping to share his profound joy in returning to Tintern Abbey after a five-year absence. Through Dorothy's pleasure, still molded by the openness of her youth (she was five years his junior), Wordsworth recaptures the powerful link to nature his own maturity has diminished.

◆ Literature and Your Life

❶ Have students compare the speaker's experience to one they may have had in a visit to a special place after an absence of several years. *Students may say that certain sights and sounds associated with the place suddenly rushed back into their memory, as they did for Wordsworth.*

❷ **Clarification** Copses (line 14) are thickets of small trees.

◆ Literary Focus

❸ **Romanticism** Some students will conclude that Wordsworth's sensory observations are consistent with Romanticism's celebration of nature and of human emotion; others may observe that the hermit by his fire is almost a comic stereotype of the Romantic view.

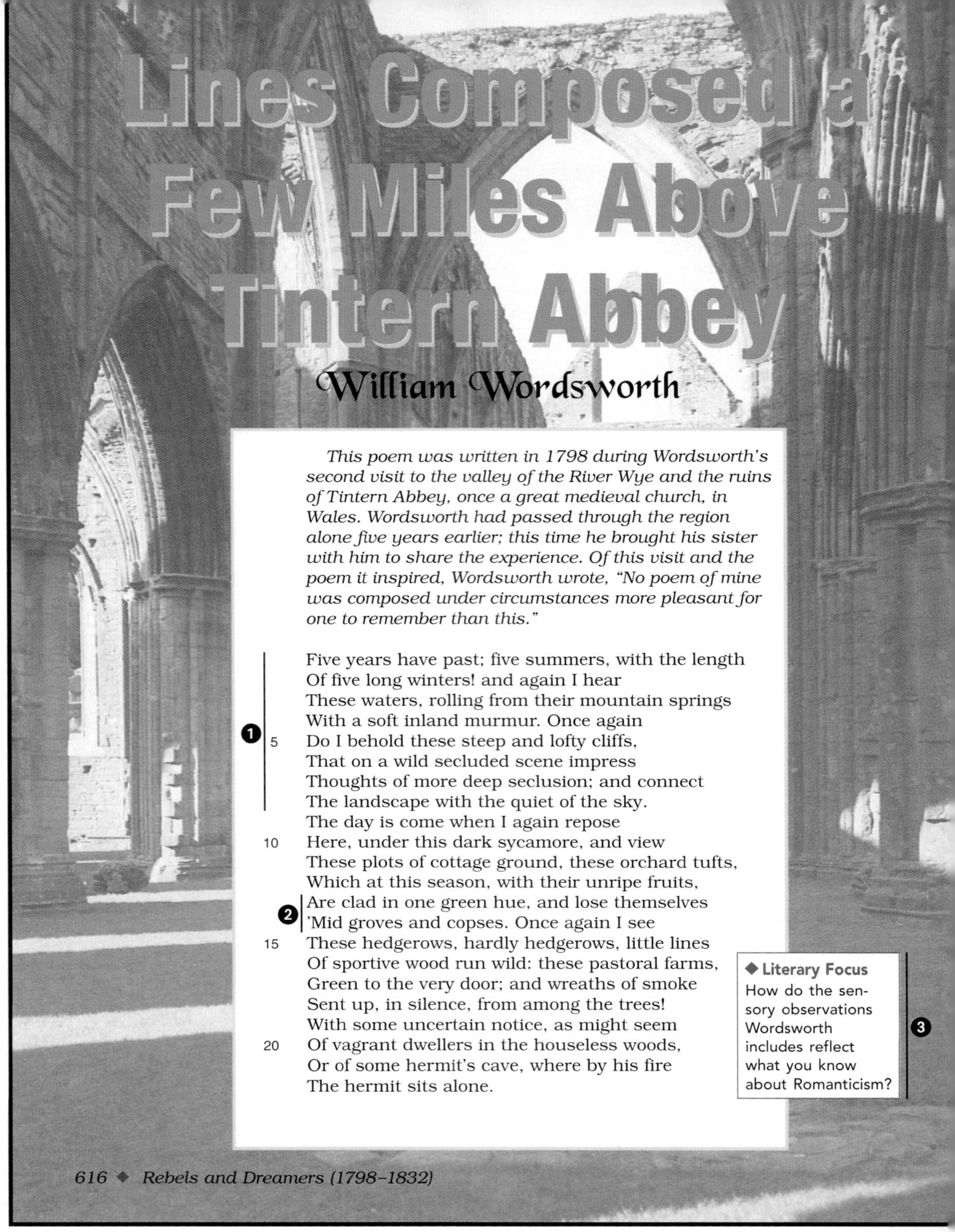

Lines Composed a Few Miles Above Tintern Abbey

William Wordsworth

This poem was written in 1798 during Wordsworth's second visit to the valley of the River Wye and the ruins of Tintern Abbey, once a great medieval church, in Wales. Wordsworth had passed through the region alone five years earlier; this time he brought his sister with him to share the experience. Of this visit and the poem it inspired, Wordsworth wrote, "No poem of mine was composed under circumstances more pleasant for one to remember than this."

❶
Five years have past; five summers, with the length
Of five long winters! and again I hear
These waters, rolling from their mountain springs
With a soft inland murmur. Once again
Do I behold these steep and lofty cliffs,
That on a wild secluded scene impress
Thoughts of more deep seclusion; and connect
The landscape with the quiet of the sky.
The day is come when I again repose
Here, under this dark sycamore, and view
These plots of cottage ground, these orchard tufts,
Which at this season, with their unripe fruits,
Are clad in one green hue, and lose themselves
❷ 'Mid groves and copses. Once again I see
These hedgerows, hardly hedgerows, little lines
Of sportive wood run wild: these pastoral farms,
Green to the very door; and wreaths of smoke
Sent up, in silence, from among the trees!
With some uncertain notice, as might seem
Of vagrant dwellers in the houseless woods,
Or of some hermit's cave, where by his fire
The hermit sits alone.

◆ Literary Focus How do the sensory observations Wordsworth includes reflect what you know about Romanticism? ❸

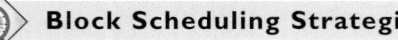

Block Scheduling Strategies

Consider these suggestions to take advantage of extended class time:

- Use the Daily Language Practice for Week 24, based on Wordsworth's ideas. Use an overhead to project the transparency in ***Writing and Language Transparencies,*** p. 159, or dictate the examples from ***Daily Language Practice,*** p. 52.
- Invite students to share their journal descriptions from Literature and Your Life (p. 615) and discuss their responses to the social commentary.
- Students can brainstorm to list additional words related to *anatomize* before completing the Build Vocabulary page in ***Selection Support,*** p. 149
- Have students research Romanticism and William Wordsworth on the Internet. Ask students how the information adds to their understanding of the poem.
- Students can work in groups to complete the History of Gardening project (p. 627). Suggest that they begin by brainstorming for appropriate research avenues. Invite groups to display their completed visual histories in a class exhibit.
- Before students begin the Writing Mini-Lesson (p. 627), hold a class discussion of meaningful and effective public service messages.

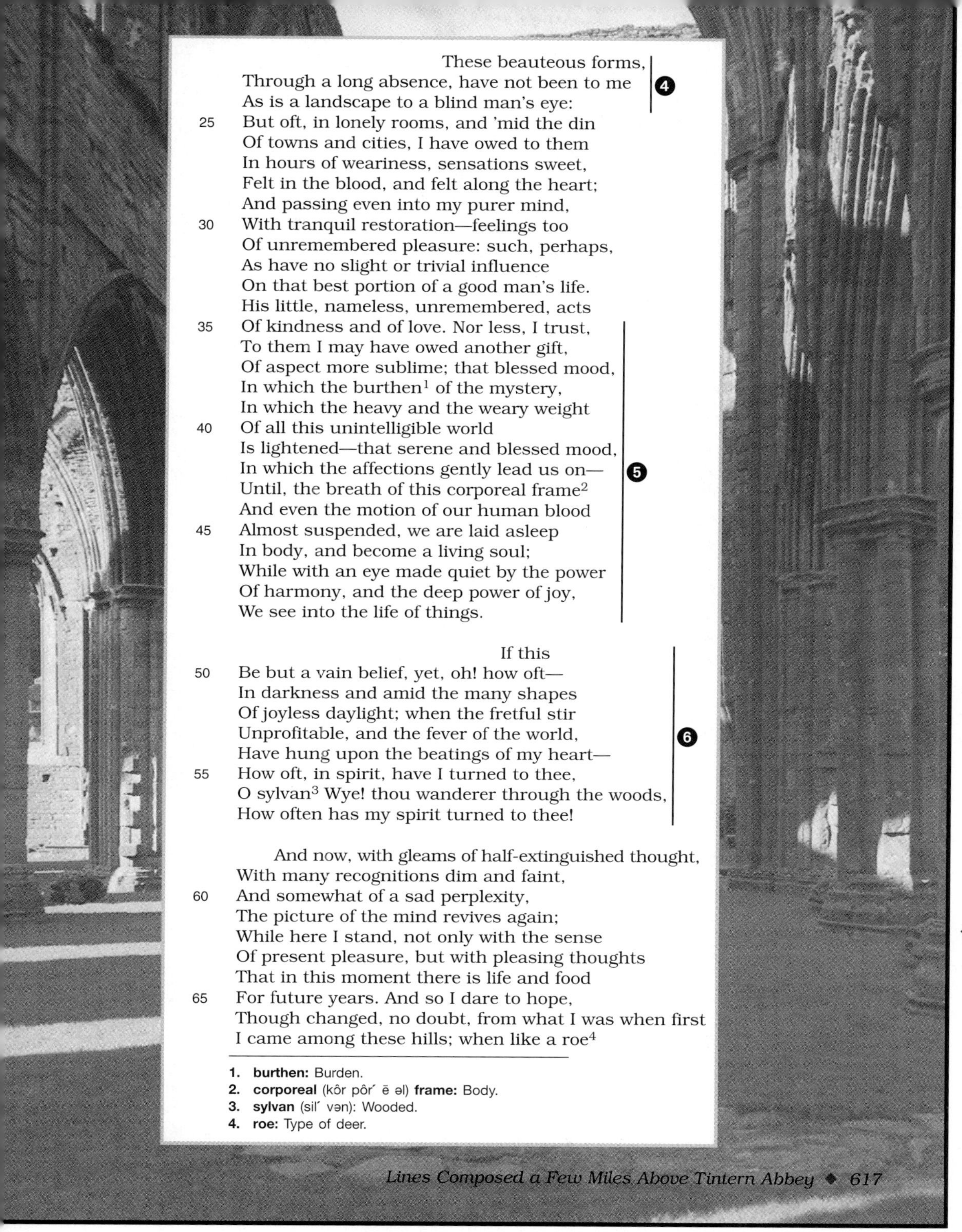

These beauteous forms,
Through a long absence, have not been to me
As is a landscape to a blind man's eye: ❹
But oft, in lonely rooms, and 'mid the din
Of towns and cities, I have owed to them
In hours of weariness, sensations sweet,
Felt in the blood, and felt along the heart;
And passing even into my purer mind,
With tranquil restoration—feelings too
Of unremembered pleasure: such, perhaps,
As have no slight or trivial influence
On that best portion of a good man's life.
His little, nameless, unremembered, acts
Of kindness and of love. Nor less, I trust,
To them I may have owed another gift,
Of aspect more sublime; that blessed mood,
In which the burthen[1] of the mystery,
In which the heavy and the weary weight
Of all this unintelligible world
Is lightened—that serene and blessed mood,
In which the affections gently lead us on— ❺
Until, the breath of this corporeal frame[2]
And even the motion of our human blood
Almost suspended, we are laid asleep
In body, and become a living soul;
While with an eye made quiet by the power
Of harmony, and the deep power of joy,
We see into the life of things.

If this
Be but a vain belief, yet, oh! how oft—
In darkness and amid the many shapes
Of joyless daylight; when the fretful stir
Unprofitable, and the fever of the world,
Have hung upon the beatings of my heart— ❻
How oft, in spirit, have I turned to thee,
O sylvan[3] Wye! thou wanderer through the woods,
How often has my spirit turned to thee!

And now, with gleams of half-extinguished thought,
With many recognitions dim and faint,
And somewhat of a sad perplexity,
The picture of the mind revives again;
While here I stand, not only with the sense
Of present pleasure, but with pleasing thoughts
That in this moment there is life and food
For future years. And so I dare to hope,
Though changed, no doubt, from what I was when first
I came among these hills; when like a roe[4]

1. **burthen:** Burden.
2. **corporeal** (kôr pôr´ ē əl) **frame:** Body.
3. **sylvan** (sil´ vən): Wooded.
4. **roe:** Type of deer.

Cultural Connection

A person's view of nature is strongly influenced by his or her culture. Native American cultures, for example, recognize humans' dependence on nature and strive to maintain a harmonious relationship with it.

Traditional Eastern cultures also seek to integrate human existence gracefully with nature. For example, Japanese architecture is always conceived in relation to surrounding landscape and changing seasons. Asian methods of agriculture, such as the rice paddy, strive to adapt farming to the terrain at hand as simply as possible. Western cultures, on the other hand, demonstrate in their technology, architecture, and agriculture a view of nature as a challenging force that must be defended against for safety or harnessed to serve human goals.

Provide, or have students research, books that compare the two cultural approaches to nature. Then organize a panel discussion entitled "Viewing Nature: East versus West."

Customize for
Less Proficient Readers
Note with students that the poem's structure reflects its content—Wordsworth introduced new ideas at the close of each section (lines 22, 49, 58, 111). Urge students to summarize the main idea of each section before continuing.

Customize for
Visual/Spatial Learners
These learners can appreciate the highly visual images of the poem best by illustrating the poem or viewing visuals of the Abbey and its surroundings. Refer them first to the painting on page 618, which depicts the Abbey's interior.

◆ Critical Thinking

❹ **Evaluate** Ask students: Why is this simile effective? *Wordsworth contrasts the clear, appreciative vision of his memory to the lack of sight of a blind man.*

◆ Reading Strategy

❺ **Use Literary Context** Remind students that the Romantics often looked to nature for meaning. Ask students what these lines suggest nature can offer. *Nature offers emotional sustenance, healing, a lighter view of the world, and insights into the meaning of life.*

◆ Literary Focus

❻ **Romanticism** Point out to students the words *heart* and *spirit* in these lines. Explain that such words are consistent with the Romantic poet's quest to explore his or her innermost feelings. Ask students to explain Wordsworth's exclamation in these lines. *Wordsworth describes the sorrows he has felt in the urban world and recalls how he has fled, mentally, to the healing powers of nature.*

▶Critical Viewing◀

❶ **Infer** It shows the Abbey as a ruin, which offers only glimpses of its medieval past, leaving the balance a mystery for the viewer to fantasize about.

❷ **Clarification** Point out that a cataract is a waterfall.

◆Critical Thinking

❸ **Interpret** Ask students: How does Wordsworth feel about the changes maturity has brought to his attitudes about nature? *He accepts the changes as natural and feels he has gained wisdom to replace the raw joy lost to maturity.*

Customize for
Verbal/Linguistic Learners
Encourage these students to enjoy Wordsworth's choice of words, using dictionaries and other sources to learn word histories and multiple meanings of selected examples, such as *mourn, murmur,* and *recompense.*

Customize for
More Advanced Students
Point out that this poem is written in blank verse—lines of unrhymed iambic pentameter, five metrical feet to each line. Challenge students to compare Wordsworth's use of this verse form—often used with serious, even stately works—to that of Shakespeare's in *Macbeth* (p. 272).

▶ **Critical Viewing** Romantic writers liked to immerse themselves in fantasies about the ❶ mysterious past. How is this painting appropriate to such an attitude? **[Infer]**

Tintern Abbey, J. M. W. Turner, British Museum

I bounded o'er the mountains, by the sides
Of the deep rivers, and the lonely streams,
Wherever nature led: more like a man
Flying from something that he dreads, than one
Who sought the thing he loved. For nature then
(The coarser pleasures of my boyish days,
And their glad animal movements all gone by)
To me was all in all—I cannot paint
What then I was. The sounding cataract
❷ Haunted me like a passion: the tall rock,
The mountain, and the deep and gloomy wood,
Their colors and their forms, were then to me
An appetite; a feeling and a love,
That had no need of a remoter charm,
By thought supplied, nor any interest
Unborrowed from the eye. That time is past,
And all its aching joys are now no more,
❸ And all its dizzy raptures. Not for this
Faint[5] I, nor mourn nor murmur; other gifts
Have followed; for such loss, I would believe,

5. **faint:** Lose heart.

Humanities: Art

Tintern Abbey, watercolor, by Joseph Mallord William Turner.

This painting illustrates Tintern Abbey, perhaps as Wordsworth had viewed it. He and Turner were contemporaries, both born in the latter part of the eighteenth century and dying in the mid-nineteenth century.

J.M.W. Turner (1775–1851) is known as a premier British landscape painter. He began exhibiting his work at the early age of fifteen, later studying at the Royal Academy and with an architectural draftsman. Turner then made a walking tour of England, painting watercolors of regional scenes. *Tintern Abbey* was painted on one of these tours and reflects his experience with architectural drafting.

Use these questions for discussion:

1. How does Turner's view of the Abbey reflect Wordsworth's emotions in visiting it? *The trees growing from within the building, the small group chatting, and the light suggest Wordsworth's reverence for nature and his awe in its presence.*
2. Why might the Abbey appeal to both Turner and Wordsworth? *It is a striking visual image that links the human past with nature. The openness to sky and light may also have attracted them.*

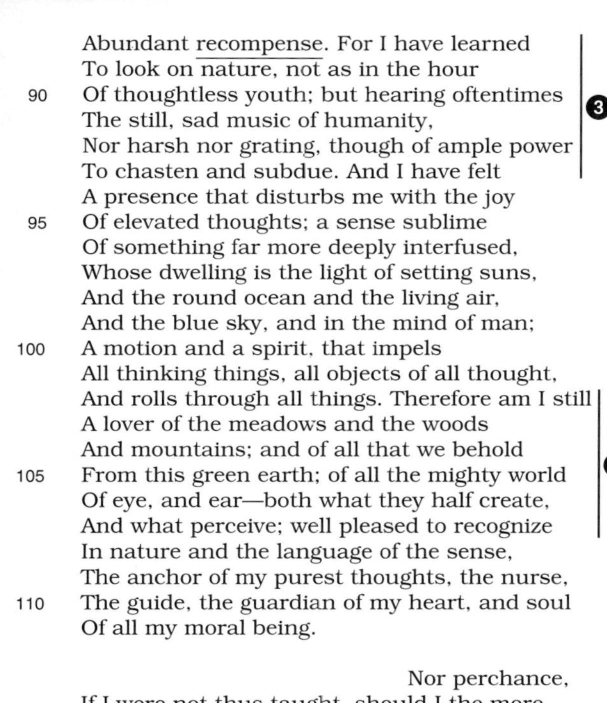

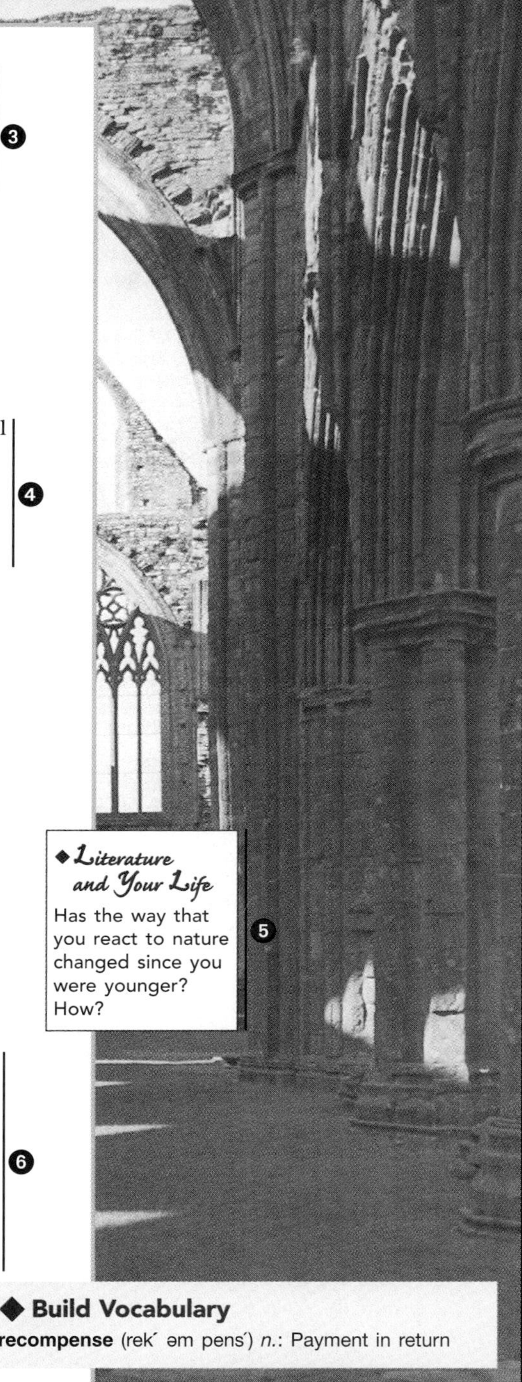

Abundant recompense. For I have learned
To look on nature, not as in the hour
Of thoughtless youth; but hearing oftentimes ❸
The still, sad music of humanity,
Nor harsh nor grating, though of ample power
To chasten and subdue. And I have felt
A presence that disturbs me with the joy
Of elevated thoughts; a sense sublime
Of something far more deeply interfused,
Whose dwelling is the light of setting suns,
And the round ocean and the living air,
And the blue sky, and in the mind of man;
A motion and a spirit, that impels
All thinking things, all objects of all thought,
And rolls through all things. Therefore am I still
A lover of the meadows and the woods
And mountains; and of all that we behold
From this green earth; of all the mighty world ❹
Of eye, and ear—both what they half create,
And what perceive; well pleased to recognize
In nature and the language of the sense,
The anchor of my purest thoughts, the nurse,
The guide, the guardian of my heart, and soul
Of all my moral being.

Nor perchance,
If I were not thus taught, should I the more
Suffer[6] my genial spirits[7] to decay;
For thou art with me here upon the banks
Of this fair river; thou my dearest Friend,[8]
My dear, dear Friend, and in thy voice I catch
The language of my former heart, and read
My former pleasures in the shooting lights
Of thy wild eyes. Oh! yet a little while
May I behold in thee what I was once,
My dear, dear Sister! and this prayer I make
Knowing that Nature never did betray
The heart that loved her; 'tis her privilege,
Through all the years of this our life, to lead
From joy to joy; for she can so inform
The mind that is within us, so impress
With quietness and beauty, and so feed
With lofty thoughts, that neither evil tongues,
Rash judgments, nor the sneers of selfish men, ❻
Nor greetings where no kindness is, nor all
The dreary intercourse of daily life,
Shall e'er prevail against us, or disturb
Our cheerful faith, that all which we behold

6. **suffer:** Allow.
7. **genial spirits:** Creative powers.
8. **Friend:** His sister Dorothy.

◆ ***Literature and Your Life***

Has the way that you react to nature changed since you were younger? How? ❺

◆ **Build Vocabulary**

recompense (rek´ əm pens´) *n.*: Payment in return

Customize for
Less Proficient Readers
Explain to these students that lines 109–111 contain metaphors that compare nature to an anchor, a nurse, a guide, a guardian and the speaker's soul.

Customize for
English Language Learners
Explain to these students that Wordsworth uses poetic language uncommon in everyday English, for example, *thou* and *thee,* meaning "you," and *'tis,* meaning "it is." Model for students how to use context to define these words.

◆ Critical Thinking

❹ **Interpret** Have students explain what Wordsworth implies about the role of his senses in appreciating nature. *Students should note that the eye and ear both "perceive" and "create" this appreciation. He implies that an individual's perception in part also creates nature's majesty.*

◆ *Literature and Your Life*

❺ Most students will say that their reactions to nature have changed as they grew older, perhaps becoming more intellectual, more protective, less careless.

◆ Literary Focus

❻ **Romanticism** Ask students: How are the views expressed in these lines consistent with the Romantic literary movement? *Students should recognize the criticism of civilization, especially of what Wordsworth saw as the negative and uncaring aspects of commerce and daily life: "evil tongues, rash judgment, . . . selfish men," "greetings where no kindness is."*

Beyond the Classroom

Career Connection

Psychology In "Lines Composed a Few Miles Above Tintern Abbey," Wordsworth compares his more mature response to the experience with his younger sister's primitive delight.

Psychologists study the progression of human development, from infancy through adulthood and old age, to understand how human responses and behavior change. Have interested students read about developmental features common to those in their twenties (Wordsworth was twenty-eight years old at the time he wrote the poem, while his sister was twenty-three). After students share these features with the class, ask them to discuss in what ways Wordsworth and his sister are typical young adults.

Community Connection

Natural Features Point out that the poem "Tintern Abbey" celebrates nature and its restorative powers. Have students share knowledge of the natural features in your community, especially those set aside for community enjoyment. Urge students to survey the community and create an inventory of such natural spaces, ranging from parks to nature preserves to landscaped playgrounds. Discuss why preserving natural places might be especially important in today's world.

❶ **Clarification** Point out that Wordsworth is addressing his sister and beginning the prayer he introduced in lines 119–123.

Customize for
More Advanced Students
Review with students the background information about the Romantic literary movement and its adherents. Then challenge them to explain how Wordsworth's attitudes can be seen as a form of religion.

Reinforce and Extend

Answers

◆ ***Literature and Your Life***

Reader's Response Students may report the emotional sensation of recognition, followed by a flood of memories.

Thematic Focus Wordsworth's mind has learned to perceive things beyond the everyday, as when he says: "For I have learned/To look on nature . . . hearing oftentimes/The still, sad music of humanity" (lines 88–91).

1. It has been five years.
2. The poet realizes he has matured and become more subdued.
3. (a) He hopes to reinforce his love of nature. (b) He hopes she will gain the deeper devotion to nature that he now feels.

◆ Critical Thinking

1. (a) The time of year is summer. (b) We learn this from lines 10–14.
2. The gift is the ability nature has to ease our burdened minds.
3. During the first trip, the poet experienced nature with the boundless energy of youth. During the second trip, the poet feels a profound connection to nature within his heart, soul and moral being.
4. Suggested responses: Yes; he describes his feelings fully in lines 111–159. No; he uses ornate language that is difficult to understand.
5. The Romantic attitude toward cities must be one of abhorrence: "lonely rooms . . . 'mid the din/Of towns and cities."

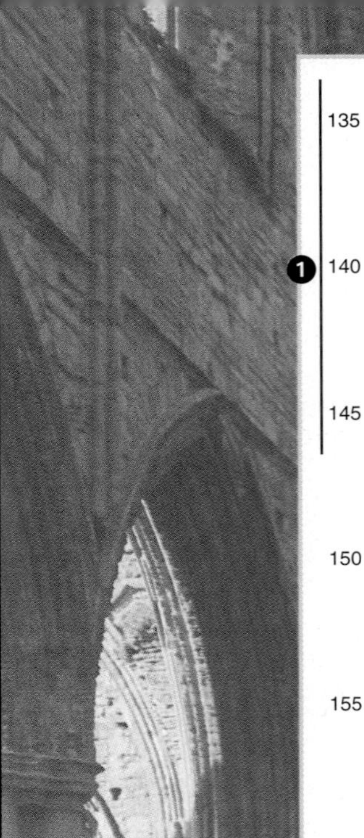

Is full of blessings. Therefore let the moon
Shine on thee in thy solitary walk;
And let the misty mountain winds be free
To blow against thee: and, in after years,
When these wild ecstasies shall be matured
Into a sober pleasure; when thy mind
❶ Shall be a mansion for all lovely forms,
Thy memory be as a dwelling place
For all sweet sound and harmonies; oh! then,
If solitude, or fear, or pain, or grief,
Should be thy portion, with what healing thoughts
Of tender joy wilt thou remember me,
And these my exhortations! Nor, perchance—
If I should be where I no more can hear
Thy voice, nor catch from thy wild eyes these gleams
Of past existence—wilt thou then forget
That on the banks of this delightful stream
We stood together; and that I, so long
A worshipper of Nature, hither came
Unwearied in that service: rather say
With warmer love—oh! with far deeper zeal
Of holier love. Nor wilt thou then forget,
That after many wanderings, many years
Of absence, these steep woods and lofty cliffs,
And this green pastoral landscape, were to me
More dear, both for themselves and for thy sake!

Guide for Responding

◆ *Literature and Your Life*

Reader's Response When have you returned to a special place after an absence? What was your reaction?

Thematic Focus What does Wordsworth say about the growth of his mind that makes it seem as real as the things he sees around him?

☑ Check Your Comprehension

1. How long has it been since the poet visited Tintern Abbey?
2. How have the poet's memories of his first visit to the Wye Valley affected him?
3. (a) Apart from his pleasure in the moment, what does the poet hope to gain from his second visit? (b) What does he hope his sister will gain?

◆ Critical Thinking

INTERPRET

1. (a) At what time of year does the poet make his second visit to the area near Tintern Abbey? (b) Find evidence in the poem that supports your answer. **[Support]**
2. In line 36 of the poem, the poet mentions "another gift" that his contact with this rural scene has bestowed upon him. Briefly describe this gift. **[Interpret]**
3. Compare and contrast the differences in the poet's behavior and thoughts during each trip. **[Compare and Contrast]**

EVALUATE

4. Does Wordsworth succeed in expressing his feelings toward his sister? Explain. **[Evaluate]**

APPLY

5. What can you infer from this poem about the Romantic attitude toward cities? **[Generalize]**

Humanities: Music

The Romantic movement was not confined to literature, as the J.M.W. Turner painting on page 618 demonstrates. Music was also deeply affected by Romantic ideals, reverberating with new emotional significance. Composers such as Ludwig van Beethoven, Robert Schumann (and his wife, pianist Clara Schumann), and Felix Mendelssohn created works ranging from symphonies to chamber music to *lieder* (popular songs).

Like Wordsworth's poetry, Romantic music often reflected social commentary. For example, Beethoven's Symphony No. 3 was written in response to Napoleon Bonaparte's dramatic efforts to popularize France. When Bonaparte made himself Emperor, rather than populist leader, an angry and disappointed Beethoven changed the symphony's name (it had been entitled *Great Symphony for Napoleon Bonaparte*).

Play some Romantic music for students and discuss how its qualities reflect the ideals and views of the Romantic movement.

from **The Prelude**

William Wordsworth

O pleasant exercise of hope and joy!
For mighty were the auxiliars which then stood
Upon our side, us who were strong in love! ❷
Bliss was it in that dawn to be alive,
But to be young was very Heaven! O times,
In which the meager, stale, forbidding ways
Of custom, law, and statute, took at once
The attraction of a country in romance!
When Reason seemed the most to assert her rights
When most intent on making of herself
A prime enchantress—to assist the work,
Which then was going forward in her name!
Not favored spots alone, but the whole Earth,
The beauty wore of promise—that which sets
(As at some moments might not be unfelt
Among the bowers of Paradise itself)
The budding rose above the rose full blown.
What temper at the prospect did not wake
To happiness unthought of? The inert
Were roused, and lively natures rapt away!
They who had fed their childhood upon dreams,
The play-fellows of fancy, who had made
All powers of swiftness, subtlety, and strength
Their ministers,—who in lordly wise had stirred
Among the grandest objects of the sense,
And dealt with whatsoever they found there
As if they had within some lurking right
To wield it;—they, too, who of gentle mood
Had watched all gentle motions, and to these
Had fitted their own thoughts, schemers more mild,
And in the region of their peaceful selves;—
Now was it that *both* found, the meek and lofty
Did both find helpers to their hearts' desire,
And stuff at hand, plastic as they could wish,—
Were called upon to exercise their skill,
Not in Utopia,—subterranean fields,— ❸
Or some secreted island, Heaven knows where!
But in the very world, which is the world
Of all of us,—the place where, in the end,
We find our happiness, or not at all!

. . .

But now, become oppressors in their turn,
Frenchmen had changed a war of self-defense
For one of conquest, losing sight of all
Which they had struggled for: now mounted up,
Openly in the eye of earth and heaven,
The scale of liberty. I read her doom,

◆ **Build Vocabulary**

roused (rouzd) *v.*: Stirred up; risen from cover

Develop Understanding

"The Prelude" is Wordsworth's lament over the failure of the French Revolution to bring real social change and to elevate human behavior. Through Wordsworth's voice, the poem describes the corruption and betrayal of France's revolutionary ideals and the poet's struggle to understand how the atrocities committed in the name of Revolution could have happened. By his efforts to honor all his allegiances and his despair at failing to do so, Wordsworth acknowledges the complexity of achieving social change.

Customize for
More Advanced Students
Explain that this excerpt from "The Prelude" is a small fraction of the full text. In fourteen sections and containing more than 8,000 lines, "The Prelude" is a huge literary undertaking. Even Book X (XI in the final version), from which this excerpt comes, contains additional text. Have these students read more of the complete work and then share their insights with the class.

❷ **Clarification** "Our side" refers to Wordsworth and others who embraced the Revolution as a means of effecting social change. Point out that Wordsworth wrote this poem when the French Revolution had deteriorated into a reign of terror under Robespierre (1794) and a dictatorship under Napoleon (1799).

◆ Literary Focus

❸ **Romanticism and the Lyric**
Have students identify the sentiment expressed in these lines that fits the Romantic philosophy. *In lines 38–40, Wordsworth expresses the Romantic belief that the real world—not a mystical, mythical, or magical land—is where one finds true happiness.*

Cross-Curricular Connection: Social Studies

French Revolution Begun with the hope of reapportioning power from the royal family and nobles to a more populist system, the French Revolution descended several times into mob riots. During one such riot—the September Massacres of 1792—hundreds of royal prisoners were killed. Shortly after this, the King was executed and a reign of terror began under extremist Maximilien Robespierre. These events form the backdrop to this portion of "The Prelude."

Have students discuss how the atmosphere of revolution would have enhanced Wordsworth's Romantic views.

◆ Build Vocabulary

❶ Related Words: *Anatomize* Have students confirm their understanding of *anatomize*. Then ask them to paraphrase these lines using a word related to *anatomize*. *Sample paraphrase: I used my greatest abilities and worked hard to analyze the anatomy of society.*

◆ Literary Focus

❷ Romanticism and the Lyric Point out the poet's call to "Friend" as part of his Romantic role in broadcasting society's ills to his readers.

◆ Critical Thinking

❸ Interpret Ask students: What choice is Wordsworth here regretting? *Students should recognize that the poet regrets his former belief in reasoning over emotion, in society over nature.*

▶Critical Viewing◀

❹ Compare and Contrast Students should note that the painting depicts the human violence, suffering, and carnage that resulted from the revolution whereas this portion of "The Prelude" reveals the philosophical torment that resulted from the failure of the revolutionaries to live up to their ideals.

With anger vexed, with disappointment sore,
But not dismayed, nor taking to the shame
Of a false prophet. While resentment rose
Striving to hide, what nought could heal, the wounds
Of mortified presumption, I adhered
More firmly to old tenets, and, to prove
Their temper, strained them more; and thus, in heat
Of contest, did opinions every day
Grow into consequence, till round my mind
They clung, as if they were its life, nay more,
The very being of the immortal soul.

. . . .

I summoned my best skill, and toiled, intent
❶ To anatomize the frame of social life,
Yea, the whole body of society
Searched to its heart. Share with me, Friend! the wish
That some dramatic tale, endued with shapes
❷ Livelier, and flinging out less guarded words
Than suit the work we fashion, might set forth
What then I learned, or think I learned, of truth,
And the errors into which I fell, betrayed
By present objects, and by reasonings false
From their beginnings, inasmuch as drawn
❸ Out of a heart that had been turned aside
From Nature's way by outward accidents,
And which are thus confounded, more and more
Misguided, and misguiding. So I fared,
Dragging all precepts, judgments, maxims, creeds,
Like culprits to the bar; calling the mind,

Storming of the Bastille, 14 July 1789, , Anonymous, Chateau, Versailles, France

❹ ▶ **Critical Viewing** Compare and contrast the view of the French Revolution presented in this poem to the one portrayed in this picture. **[Compare and Contrast]**

Humanities: Art

Storming of the Bastille, 14 July 1789, Anonymous.

This painting illustrates an important event in the French Revolution. Perhaps the anonymous artist feared for his or her life in recording this chaotic moment in French history. On July 14, 1789, an angry mob protesting actions by King Louis XVI tried to seize control of the long-hated Bastille prison. A symbol of royalty's absolute power, the Bastille had imprisoned many held without trial or cause. *The Storming of the Bastille, 14 July 1789,* vividly captures both the glory and the failure of the Revolution.

Use these questions for discussion.

1. How might Wordsworth respond to the scene depicted in the painting? *He might have responded with enthusiasm for the change it hoped to bring but with disappointment at the aftermath.*
2. How does the painting add to the poem's impact? *It explains some of the context and creates a visual image of revolutionary fervor.*

▶ Critical Viewing
5 This painting depicts the execution of the King during the French Revolution. Compare the mood the artist has created with the mood Wordsworth expresses in lines 4–17. **[Connect]**

Execution of King Louis XVI on January 21, 1793, Musée de la Ville de Paris, Musée Carnavalet, Paris, France

◆ **Build Vocabulary**

presumption (prē zump´ shən) *n.*: Audacity, tending to assume certain things

anatomize (ə nat´ ə mīz´) *v.*: To dissect in order to examine structure

confounded (kən fo͝ond´ id) *adj.*: Confused; bewildered

Suspiciously, to establish in plain day
Her titles and her honors; now believing,
Now disbelieving; endlessly perplexed
With impulse, motive, right and wrong, the ground
Of obligation, what the rule and whence
The sanction; till, demanding formal *proof*,
And seeking it in every thing, I lost
All feeling of conviction, and, in fine,
Sick, wearied out with contrarieties,
Yielded up moral questions in despair.

Guide for Responding

◆ Literature and Your Life

Reader's Response What emotions come through most clearly in this excerpt? Explain.

Thematic Focus According to this poem, in what way does society repeat its mistakes?

☑ Check Your Comprehension

1. How does the poet describe his first reaction to the French Revolution?
2. According to the poet, in what important way did the French change?

◆ Critical Thinking

INTERPRET

1. (a) What turn of events causes an inner conflict in Wordsworth? (b) Describe this conflict. (c) Is it resolved? Explain. **[Interpret]**
2. Would it be accurate to describe this episode in Wordsworth's life as one of soul-searching? Why or why not? **[Draw Conclusions]**

EVALUATE

3. How well does Wordsworth convey his initial joy at the French Revolution? Explain. **[Criticize]**

Humanities: Art

Execution of King Louis XVI on January 21, 1793, Unknown painter of the Danish School.

This painting illustrates the execution of France's King Louis XVI, which took place several years into the French Revolution, and to which Wordsworth may be referring in *The Prelude*.

Many Danish painters studied at the Royal Danish Academy of Fine Arts, opened in 1754. A painting such as *The Execution of King Louis XVI* would no doubt have shocked viewers of the late eighteenth century for whom the execution of a monarch was an earthshaking event. Still, its orderly lines and organized soldiers may have offered the hope of reason amidst chaos.

Use these questions for discussion:

1. Which lines of Wordsworth's poem may allude to the event depicted in this painting? *"But now, become oppressors in their turn,/Frenchman had changed a war of self-defense/For one of conquest."*
2. How does the painting convey Wordsworth's mood at the end of this excerpt? *The sky's looming storm is reminiscent of the poet's emotional tumult and ultimate despair in the excerpt's closing lines.*

▶Critical Viewing◀

5 **Connect** There appears a chilling order in the scene of execution, but it is not an order that Wordsworth looked forward to in his poem.

◆ Reading Strategy

6 **Use Literary Context** Ask students to infer the Romantic sensibility indicated in this passage. *Students should note that Wordsworth has plumbed the depths of despair in these lines.*

Reinforce and Extend

Answers

◆ Literature and Your Life

Reader's Response The poem reflects a torturous journey from initial hope and joy to the ultimate feelings of betrayal and despair.

Thematic Focus Society repeats its mistakes by making presumptions, using false reasoning, and by not searching its heart for truth.

☑ Check Your Comprehension

1. His first reaction is one of hope and joy.
2. The French became the oppressors in their turn and "changed a war of self-defense / For one of conquest, losing sight of all / Which they had struggled for . . ."

◆ Critical Thinking

1. (a) When the French became their own worst oppressors, Wordsworth had to search his conscience for his support of them. (b) He tried hard to justify their behavior, but was confronted with "reasonings false / From their beginnings." (c) He lost all feeling of conviction, "wearied out with contrarieties."
2. Yes; Wordsworth confronted the depths of his despair.
3. Possible response: Wordsworth conveys his initial joy very effectively. He gives vivid descriptions of his emotions and creates interesting metaphors to more fully reveal his emotional state and philosophical ideas.

Develop Understanding

One-Minute Insight These sonnets convey something of the conflict Wordsworth experienced about the natural and human world around him. In "The World Is Too Much with Us," Wordsworth expresses his dismay over growing materialism amidst the French Revolution. "London, 1802," written just a short time later, turns instead to Wordsworth's growing acceptance of the flawed aspects of life and people. Together, these sonnets demonstrate how rapidly emotions can swing and how experiences, such as observing the French Revolution, can lead to maturity and greater understanding of life's complexity.

◆ Background for Understanding

Both these poems are sonnets, fourteen-line poems in iambic pentameter, in which each line contains five accented and five unaccented syllables. Sonnets usually follow recognizable rhyme schemes, as here: *abba, bccb, dedede*. Tell students that Petrarch and Shakespeare used characteristic rhyme schemes in their sonnets; Wordsworth has followed the Petrarchan model in these.

◆ Literary Focus

❶ **Romanticism** Ask students: How are the ideas Wordsworth presents consistent with Romanticism? *The speaker laments that the "getting and spending" of the world interferes with the direct experience of nature that heals and restores humankind.*

◆ Critical Thinking

❷ **Interpret** Ask students: With what does the speaker feel we are out of tune? *The speaker feels we are out of tune with nature.*

►Critical Viewing◄

❸ **Make a Judgment** Some students will say that the moon does move us emotionally; others will say that the moon's constancy dulls its ability to move us emotionally.

▲ **Critical Viewing** Do you agree with Wordsworth that the moonlit sea, such as the one pictured here, "moves us not"? Explain. **[Make a Judgment]** ❸

The World Is Too Much with Us

William Wordsworth

The world is too much with us; late and soon,
Getting and spending, we lay waste our powers: ❶
Little we see in Nature that is ours;
We have given our hearts away, a sordid boon![1]
This Sea that bares her bosom to the moon;
The winds that will be howling at all hours,
And are upgathered now like sleeping flowers;
For this, for everything, we are out of tune; ❷
It moves us not.—Great God! I'd rather be
A Pagan suckled in a creed outworn;
So might I, standing on this pleasant lea,[2]
Have glimpses that would make me less forlorn;
Have sight of Proteus[3] rising from the sea;
Or hear old Triton[4] blow his wreathèd horn.

1. **boon:** Favor.
2. **lea:** Meadow.
3. **Proteus** (prō´ tē əs): In Greek mythology, a sea god who could change his appearance at will.
4. **Triton:** In Greek mythology, a sea god with the head and upper body of a man and the tail of a fish.

◆ Build Vocabulary

sordid (sôr´ did) *adj.*: Unclean, dirty

Speaking and Listening Mini-Lesson

Debate

This mini-lesson supports the Speaking and Listening activity in the Idea Bank on page 627.

Introduce the Concept Remind students that a debate is a formal argument about the pros and cons of a subject: in this case, about whether people put too much emphasis on acquiring material goods. Have them form teams, one presenting the "pro," the other the "con" side of the topic.

Develop Background Have students keep the following in mind: Arguments should be clearly structured and logical; they should be supported by facts; they should be presented politely, without excessive emotion.

Apply the Information Once teams have outlined their arguments and completed their research, they can present the debate. Assign a moderator and set time guidelines for arguments, rebuttals, and responses.

Assess the Outcome After the debate, have students discuss which arguments were more effective and vote for the winning team.

London, 1802

William Wordsworth

Milton![1] thou should'st be living at this hour: ❹
England hath need of thee: she is a fen[2]
Of stagnant waters: altar, sword, and pen,
Fireside, the heroic wealth of hall and bower,
Have forfeited their ancient English dower 
Of inward happiness. We are selfish men;
Oh! raise us up, return to us again;
And give us manners, virtue, freedom, power.
Thy soul was like a Star, and dwelt apart:
Thou hadst a voice whose sound was like the sea:
Pure as the naked heavens, majestic, free,
So didst thou travel on life's common way,
In cheerful godliness; and yet thy heart
The lowliest duties on herself did lay.

1. **Milton:** Seventeenth-century English poet John Milton.
2. **fen** (fen) *n.*: Area of low, flat, marshy land.

◆ Build Vocabulary

stagnant (stag′ nənt) *adj.*: Motionless, stale

Guide for Responding

◆ Literature and Your Life

Reader's Response When have you felt that "the world is too much with us"?

Thematic Focus How are these poems similar in describing the realities of Wordsworth's time?

☑ Check Your Comprehension

1. In "The World Is Too Much with Us," what activities cause people to give up their "powers"?
2. Why does England "need" the person Wordsworth addresses in "London, 1802"?

◆ Critical Thinking

INTERPRET

1. (a) In "The World Is Too Much with Us," what does Wordsworth mean by "The World"? (b) Why is he so "forlorn"? **[Interpret]**
2. What does Wordsworth feel England is lacking in "London, 1802"? **[Interpret]**
3. Do both of these poems address the same problem? Explain. **[Compare and Contrast]**

APPLY

4. Does Wordsworth's criticism of England also apply to modern America? Explain. **[Relate]**

Beyond the Selection

FURTHER READING

Other Works by William Wordsworth

The Excursion; The Borderers; The River Duddon

Other Works With the Theme of Social Protest

"Apostrophe to Man," Edna St. Vincent Millay
"The Mask of Anarchy," Percy Bysshe Shelley
"Peace Walk," William Stafford

We suggest that you preview these works before recommending them to students.

INTERNET

You and your students may find additional information about Wordsworth and Romanticism on the Internet at the following sites.

To visit the Wordsworth Trust, go to **http://www.dovecott.demon.co.uk/**

To follow links to articles about Wordsworth's life and work, visit **http://lummi.stanford.edu/class/engl9/WWW/wordsworth.html**

We *strongly recommend* that you preview the sites before you send students to them.

◆ Reading Strategy

❹ **Use Literary Context** The Romantics were often interested in faraway times, recalling the better world they thought once existed. Point out that here Wordsworth treats John Milton, a poet from the previous century (see pages 432–433), as a mentor whose wisdom might save England.

❺ **Clarification** Help less proficient readers understand that Wordsworth is listing parts of English society by naming their symbols: "altar" for the church and religion; "sword" for the military; "pen" for the literary, and so on.

Customize for
More Advanced Students
Help students appreciate the changes in Wordsworth's attitudes during the course of his life. Have them compare and contrast the views about daily life expressed in "London, 1802" with those of "Lines Composed a Few Miles Above Tintern Abbey."

Reinforce and Extend

Answers

◆ Literature and Your Life

Reader's Response Students may describe feeling overwhelmed by the false values of commercialism.

Thematic Focus The poems focus on the need to turn away from the false values of materialism—a reality in Wordsworth's time.

☑ Check Your Comprehension

1. People waste their powers by "getting and spending."
2. England has become a nation of selfish men and needs Milton's moral strength to guide them.

◆ Critical Thinking

1. (a) "The World" means everyday material concerns. (b) He feels cut off from the restorative powers of nature.
2. England is lacking generosity, manners, virtue, and strength.
3. Both deplore society's lack of virtue, and advise looking for guidance in historical sources of wisdom: in the classical gods of nature and in Milton's writings.
4. Yes, Wordsworth's criticism of England may also apply to modern America, a capitalist society.

◆ Reading Strategy

Sample responses:

1. It cannot be fathomed how one can find devout love in a waterfall and gloomy wood, when one could instead worship at the glorious ancient temples of Greece.
2. What glorious works of art and fashion can nature produce? We lay waste to our time and minds by remaining so reposed and idle in nature.

◆ Grammar and Style

1. *Calling for social change and praising nature,* today's world is still full of Romantics.
2. Sometimes I stand on the shore, *wishing I could travel to distant lands.*

◆ Literary Focus

Sample responses:

1. Wordsworth's deep feeling for nature is revealed in these lines: ". . . And I have felt / A presence that disturbs me with the joy / Of elevated thoughts, a sense sublime / Of something far more deeply interfused, /. . . A motion and a spirit, that impels / All thinking things, all objects of all thought, / And rolls through all things." ("Tintern Abbey," lines 93–102) Wordsworth's concern for his personal development is found in these lines: "I bounded o'er the mountains . . . / more like a man / Flying from something that he dreads, than one / Who sought the thing he loved." ("Tintern Abbey," lines 68–72)
2. In the first passage, Wordsworth revels in a profound devotion to the interconnection of all living things. The second passage illustrates how Wordsworth respected the dignity of ordinary people and their language.

◆ Build Vocabulary

1. A detailed analysis of melancholy
2. A guide to the structure of the human body
3. The life of Claude Levi-Strauss, a person who analyzes societies in great detail

Using the Word Bank

1. e 2. c 3. g 4. d 5. b 6. a 7. f

Guide for Responding *(continued)*

◆ Reading Strategy

Use Literary Context

The **literary context** of a work is the climate of literary opinions and practices in which it was written. Most writers follow the assumptions and practices of the time in which they write. A few, like Wordsworth, challenge these assumptions and change the literary context for writers who come after them.

Suppose you are a Neoclassical writer, a sociable city-dweller committed to writing verse that is polished, witty, and rational. Now you are reading the work of this poet from the Lake District, William Wordsworth. Tell how you might react to each of these passages:

1. . . . The sounding cataract
Haunted me like a passion; the tall rock,
The mountain, and the deep and gloomy wood,
Their colors and their forms, were then to me
An appetite; a feeling and a love . . .
("Tintern Abbey," lines 76–80)

2. The world is too much with us; late and soon,
Getting and spending, we lay waste our powers:
Little we see in Nature that is ours;
We have given our hearts away, a sordid boon!
("The World Is Too Much with Us," lines 1–4)

◆ Grammar and Style

Present Participial Phrases

Present participial phrases consist of a verb form ending in *-ing* and its complements and modifiers. The entire phrase functions as an adjective. Wordsworth, who writes in long, flowing sentences, uses such phrases to add information about nouns and pronouns.

Writing Application In your notebook, combine the following sentences using present participial phrases.

1. Today's world is still full of Romantics. They call for social change and praise nature.

2. Sometimes I stand on the shore. I wish I could travel to distant lands.

◆ Literary Focus

Romanticism and the Lyric

Wordsworth was one of the inventors of English Romanticism. For him, **Romanticism** arose from several personal passions: his deep feeling for nature, in which he saw a "spirit" that united all things; his sense of the dignity and importance of ordinary people and their language, especially in a rural setting; and his concern with his own personal development. This last concern was not a selfish one. Wordsworth viewed his own changing perceptions with amazement, as if they were a natural phenomenon, and in **lyric poems** he offers them to readers as an aid in their own development.

1. Find a passage from the poems to illustrate two of these Wordsworthian passions.

2. For each passage you find, explain how it illustrates an aspect of Wordsworth's Romanticism.

◆ Build Vocabulary

Using Forms of *Anatomize*

Use your knowledge of the related forms of *anatomize* to explain the meanings of these book titles:

1. *An Anatomy of Melancholy*

2. *Anatomical Guide to the Human Body*

3. *The Life of Claude Lévi-Strauss, Anatomist of Societies*

Using the Word Bank

In your notebook, write the letter of the word or phrase in Column B that is closest in meaning to each word in Column A.

Column A	Column B
1. roused	**a.** audacity
2. sordid	**b.** dissect
3. stagnant	**c.** shameful
4. confounded	**d.** perplexed
5. anatomize	**e.** stirred
6. presumption	**f.** reward
7. recompense	**g.** stale

Writer's Solution

For additional instruction and practice use the lesson in the **Language Lab CD-ROM** on Sentence Errors and the page on Verbals and Verbal Phrases, p. 29, in the *Writer's Solution Grammar Practice Book.*

Build Your Portfolio

Idea Bank

Writing

1. Literary Analysis Review the beginnings of Wordsworth's two sonnets, "The World Is Too Much with Us" and "London, 1802." Then explain how he immediately captures readers' interest.

2. Romantic Travel Brochure As Wordsworth, write a travel brochure for a scenic natural area. Describe the sights as he might describe them.

3. Response to Criticism Thomas Wolfe defined the true Romantic feeling as "not the desire to escape life, but to prevent life from escaping you." In an essay, explain whether or not Wordsworth exhibits this "feeling."

Speaking and Listening

4. Debate With a group of classmates, debate the point that Wordsworth makes in "The World Is Too Much with Us": that people put too much emphasis on acquiring material goods. **[Social Studies Link]**

5. Ask the Poet Create a call-in radio program with Wordsworth as the guest. Have one student pose as Wordsworth while others call in questions about Romanticism. **[Media Link]**

Projects

6. Ecology and Romanticism Read material published by an ecological group. Then using what you know about Romanticism, look for any Romantic influences in the group's statements. **[Science Link; Social Studies Link]**

7. History of Gardening Compare the different approaches to gardening taken by Neoclassicists and Romanticists. Present your findings, using the photos and illustrations from a history of gardening to make your points. **[Art Link]**

Writing Mini-Lesson

Public Service Announcement

In "The World Is Too Much with Us," Wordsworth warns readers that pursuing material possessions may cost them their souls. Turn his message into an effective public-service advertisement for print, radio, or television. Using words alone or a combination of words and images, convince your audience to find more time for family, friends, and personal interests. Adapt your message to the requirements of the medium you choose.

Writing Focus: Adapting the Message to the Medium

Whether you write for print, radio, or television, you must consider the best way to **adapt your message to the medium** in which it will appear. Knowing the different requirements of these media will help you achieve this goal. In print, for example, you may be able to use longer sentences than you could in other media. Briefer, punchier statements work better for radio and television. Also, because television is a visual medium, it requires a coordination between words and images.

Prewriting Note contrasts that will help you get your message across—for example, the contrast between a mindless rush to acquire goods and a mindful attitude of concern for others. Then come up with phrases and images that convey these contrasts. Also, think about the medium you will use and whether it requires you to create images.

Drafting Know whether you're writing a print ad, a radio spot, or a television commercial. Grab the attention of your audience with a powerful image and supporting words (television), image-creating phrases (radio), or words and design (print).

Revising To evaluate the suitability of your message for the medium, do a rough layout of words and design (print), read your script aloud (radio), or create a storyboard of words and images (television).

✓ ASSESSMENT OPTIONS

Formal Assessment, Selection Test, pp. 154–156, and Assessment Resources Software. The selection test is designed so that it can be easily customized to the performance levels of your students. ***Alternative Assessment,*** p. 31, includes options for less advanced students, more advanced students, visual/spatial learners, musical/rhythmic learners, and verbal/linguistic learners.

PORTFOLIO ASSESSMENT
Use the following rubrics in the ***Alternative Assessment*** booklet to assess student writing:
Literary Analysis: Response to Literature Rubric, p. 111
Romantic Travel Brochure: Description Rubric, p. 98
Response to Criticism: Evaluation/Review Rubric, p. 105
Writing Mini-Lesson: Persuasion Rubric, p. 106

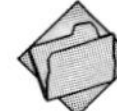

Idea Bank

Customizing for
Performance Levels
Following are suggestions for matching Idea Bank topics with your students' performance levels:
Less Advanced Students: 1, 4, 7
Average Students: 2, 4, 6
More Advanced Students: 3, 5

Customizing for
Learning Modalities
Following are suggestions for matching Idea Bank topics with your students' learning modalities:
Verbal/Linguistic: 1, 3, 4, 5, 6
Visual/Spatial: 2, 7
Interpersonal: 4, 5

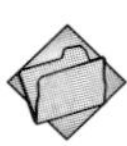

Writing Mini-Lesson

Refer students to the Writing Handbook, page 1189, for instruction on the writing process, and page 1192 for further information on persuasion.

Writing and Language Transparencies Use the Writing Process Model 5: Persuasive Essay, pp. 37–43, to guide students through the process of writing persuasively.

Writer's Solution

Writing Lab CD-ROM
Have students complete the tutorial on Persuasion. Follow these steps:

1. Refer students to the Pros and Cons Chart.
2. Have students complete an Audience Profile.
3. Suggest that students use the Notecards Activity to organize their public service announcements.
4. Have students draft on computer.
5. Suggest they consult the tips for sending a position paper to an official to help them publish their announcements.

Allow approximately 120 minutes of class time to complete these steps.

Sourcebook
Have students use Chapter 4, Persuasion (pp. 96–129), for additional support. The chapter includes a group project on a public service announcement (p. 110).

Prepare and Engage

OBJECTIVES

1. To read, comprehend, and interpret two poems
2. To relate poems to personal experience
3. To recognize poetic effects to improve appreciation of poetry
4. To identify poetic sound devices
5. To build vocabulary in context and learn the word root *-journ-*
6. To recognize inverted word order and convert it to standard word order
7. To write a poem with sound effects, creating dramatic effects through sound
8. To respond to the poems through writing, speaking and listening, and projects

SKILLS INSTRUCTION

Vocabulary: Word Roots: *-journ-*

Grammar: Inverted Word Order

Reading Strategy: Poetic Effects

Literary Focus: Poetic Sound Devices

Writing: Dramatic Effects Through Sound

Speaking and Listening: Panel Discussion (teacher edition)

Critical Viewing: Infer; Speculate; Hypothesize; Support; Connect; Predict; Compare and Contrast

PORTFOLIO OPPORTUNITIES

Writing: Utopia; Response to the Poem; Response to the Poet

Writing Mini-Lesson: Poem With Sound Effects

Speaking and Listening: Dramatic Reading; Panel Discussion

Projects: Research Project; Illustrated Journey

More About the Author
In his mid twenties, Coleridge considered becoming a Unitarian minister, although he feared limiting his creative freedom. William Hazlitt, a famed literary critic, who wrote the following description of Coleridge's trial sermon, given on January 14, 1798:

> . . . when he came to the two last words, which he pronounced loud, deep, and distinct, it seemed to me . . . as if the sounds had echoed from the bottom of the human heart, and as if that prayer might have floated in solemn silence through the universe.

Guide for Interpreting

Samuel Taylor Coleridge

(1772–1834)

The poetry of Samuel Taylor Coleridge stands at the place where real life slips into dreams, where facts are reborn as fantasies. More than any other Romantic poet, he dared to journey inward—into the world of the imagination. However, in many ways, the imaginary life that fed his poetry was an escape from some very serious problems, including poor health and self-doubt.

Early Fantasies Coleridge was born in Ottery St. Mary on the Devon coast of England, the last of ten children, only four of whom survived. At an early age, he developed the habit of retreating into a world of books and fantasy. When he was nine, his father died, and Coleridge was sent to school in London. There, he became a riveting public speaker, who held his audience's attention with his originality and intelligence.

At Cambridge University, Coleridge's hunger for new ideas led him into radical politics. He became friends with an idealistic poet named Robert Southey. Together, they planned to form a settlement in Pennsylvania based on their utopian political ideas. The plan collapsed, however, when Southey's aunt refused to fund their project.

A Literary Breakthrough In 1795, Coleridge and his wife, Sara Fricker, moved to Somerset, where he became friends with poet William Wordsworth. In 1798, the two turned out *Lyrical Ballads*, a joint collection of their work. The four poems that make up Coleridge's contribution to the volume deal with spiritual matters and include his masterpiece, "The Rime of the Ancient Mariner." The collection of poems slowly gained critical attention and caused a revolution in poetic style and thought, firmly establishing the movement known as Romanticism.

Failing Health Coleridge's fame grew, but his marriage, his health, and his friendship with Wordsworth all crumbled. He suffered increasingly from asthma and rheumatism and began to rely heavily on painkillers. He moved to Germany, and despite his downward spiral, he kept writing on many subjects, and lectured on Shakespeare and Milton.

A Romantic Legacy Perhaps Coleridge's greatest legacy is the insight he affords readers on the role of imagination in literature. His belief that literature is a magical blend of thought and emotion is at the very heart of his great works, in which the unreal is often made to seem real.

◆ Background for Understanding

LITERATURE: COLERIDGE'S DREAMSCAPES

Coleridge used dreams as inspiration for many of his great poems. For example, Coleridge claimed to have dreamed his poem "Kubla Khan" line for line, after falling asleep while reading a passage from a work about the founder of the great Mongol dynasty. Upon awakening, he transcribed the lines as fast as he could. When interrupted by a visitor, however, the lines in his head disappeared, never to be remembered. As a result, he was unable to complete the poem.

Coleridge's "The Rime of the Ancient Mariner" was based on a dream reported by his friend John Cruikshank. Starting with the dream as raw material, Coleridge and William Wordsworth began to elaborate upon it. Wordsworth suggested that the act that would drive the entire poem was a crime committed at sea. Using this material and his own peculiar imagination, Coleridge wrote "The Rime of the Ancient Mariner," which has chilled and enthralled audiences to this day.

Prentice Hall Literature Program Resources

REINFORCE / RETEACH / EXTEND

Selection Support Pages
Build Vocabulary: Word Roots: *-journ-*, p. 153
Grammar and Style: Inverted Word Order, p. 154
Reading Strategy: Poetic Effects, p. 155
Literary Focus: Poetic Sound Devices, p. 156

Strategies for Diverse Student Needs, p. 32

Beyond Literature p. 32

Formal Assessment, Selection Test, pp. 157–159; Assessment Resources Software

Alternative Assessment, p. 32

Writing and Language Transparencies
Daily Language Practice, Week 25, p. 160

Art Transparency 8, page 35

Resource Pro CD-ROM
"Ancient Mariner," "Kubla Khan"—includes all resource material and customizable lesson plan

Listening to Literature Audiocassettes
"Ancient Mariner," "Kubla Khan"

Literature CD-ROM *How to Read and Understand Poetry,* Features 5, 7, 9

◆ Literature and Your Life

CONNECT YOUR EXPERIENCE

In your dreams or in childhood fantasies, you may have sailed the oceans, ventured deep into space, or journeyed back in time. Like those vivid dreams, these poems will sweep you away into imaginary worlds and stretch the boundaries of your experience.

Journal Writing Examine how dreams can be a positive incentive for real-life actions.

THEMATIC FOCUS: FANTASY AND REALITY

Coleridge relied upon fantasy and dreams as a creative tool. As you read his poems, look for elements of fantasy.

◆ Literary Focus

POETIC SOUND DEVICES

Romantic poetry like Coleridge's achieves some of its emotional effect and beauty through **poetic sound devices**. Chief among these is **alliteration**, the repetition of a consonant sound at the beginnings of words. **Consonance**, another sound device, is the repetition of similar final consonant sounds in stressed syllables with dissimilar vowel sounds, and **assonance** is the repetition of a vowel sound in stressed syllables with dissimilar consonant sounds. **Internal rhyme**, in which rhymes occur within a poetic line, can make a line of poetry more compelling and memorable.

Alliteration: The fair breeze blew, the white foam flew,

Consonance: a frightful fiend / Doth close behind . . .

Assonance: The western wave was all aflame.

Internal Rhyme: With heavy thump, a lifeless lump. . .

◆ Build Vocabulary

WORD ROOTS: *-journ-*

In the prose sidenotes accompanying "The Rime of the Ancient Mariner," Coleridge uses the verb *sojourn,* which means "to visit for a short while." This word contains the root *-journ-,* which is derived from French and Latin words meaning "day." How does the root contribute to the meaning of the word *sojourn?*

WORD BANK

Before you read, preview this list of words from the poems.

averred
sojourn
expiated
reverence
sinuous
tumult

◆ Reading Strategy

POETIC EFFECTS

Recognizing **poetic effects**, such as sound devices, will help you to appreciate poetry. For example, the internal rhyme in the following lines emphasizes the quickness and abruptness of the actions. The assonance in *loud* and *southward* stresses a sound that seems to howl with the wind:

The ship drove fast, loud roared the blast, / And southward aye we fled.

Keep track of poetic effects in a chart such as this one:

Sound Device	Image	Reference

◆ Grammar and Style

INVERTED WORD ORDER

Inverted word order is a change in the normal English word order of subject-verb-complement. In his poems, Coleridge often inverts word order to achieve a particular rhythm, rhyme scheme, or poetic sound effect.

Inverted Order: . . . what evil looks / Had I from old and young!

Standard Order: I had evil looks from old and young!

Play a clip from a well-known movie in which strange events turn out to be the products of a dream, such as *The Wizard of Oz* or *Alice in Wonderland.* Ask volunteers to describe what happens in the movie. Elicit the idea that the strange events turn out to be a dream. Discuss how the distinction between reality and the fantastic can be blurred in dreams, taking care to protect students' privacy. Tell students that both of the poems that they are about to read were inspired by dreams.

Customize for
Less Proficient Readers

Urge students to jot down thoughts, questions, and responses in a reader response log, citing specific page or line numbers for reference.

Customize for
More Advanced Students

Distribute photocopies of the poems or download copies from the Internet. Have students work individually to analyze the rhyme and meter of the poems, using standard scansion marks and notation. Then have them form small groups to discuss their observations.

Customize for
English Language Learners

Assist students with words that are unfamiliar to them. In "The Rime of the Ancient Mariner," students may need help with archaic verb forms, such as *meeteth, detaineth, stoppeth, may'st, quoth, hath,* and *spake.* Poetic and uncommon words in "Kubla Khan" include *girdled, chaffy, mazy,* and *thrice.*

Customize for
Musical/Rhythmic Learners

After students read the Reading Strategy and Literary Focus lessons, have them listen to part or all of the poems on the **Listening to Literature Audiocassettes.** Encourage them to respond actively to the emotional impact of Coleridge's sound devices.

Preparing for Standardized Tests

Reading and Vocabulary Knowledge of word roots enables students to decipher unfamiliar words encountered in test-taking situations. Thus, familiarity with word roots can help students improve their scores on vocabulary and reading-comprehension items on standardized tests. The Build Vocabulary lesson focuses on the word root *-journ-.* For additional practice, use the Build Vocabulary page in ***Selection Support***, p. 153.

Grammar and Language To be successful test-takers, students must be comfortable with many styles and formats. Whether developing essays or analyzing content-linked text, familiarity with inverted word order leads to versatile writing and accurate comprehension. The Grammar and Style lesson for this selection focuses on inverted word order. For additional practice, use the Grammar and Style exercises on page 654 and the practice page in ***Selection Support***, p. 154.

Develop Understanding

One-Minute Insight This poem vividly illustrates the torments guilt can create and the horror of complete isolation from society. The central character, the Ancient Mariner, recounts the tale of his crime against life—the killing of an albatross—and the physical and emotional punishments his action sets in motion. The Mariner's struggle to redeem himself and escape his isolation captures the interdependence of humanity and nature, the necessity for respectful order and mercy amongst all living creatures, and the healing power of love.

◆ Background for Understanding

❶ **Literature** This poem, along with the works of Coleridge's contemporary, Sir Walter Scott, is often cited as an example of archaism, or the use of a style of an earlier period. Archaism reflects a longing for an earlier time that is seen as being more natural or noble. Have students point out ways in which this passage shows archaism. *Students may cite the use of "argument" to mean "summary;" archaic words such as* thence *and* befell, *and the spelling of* "Ancyent Marinere." You may want to point out that Coleridge captures the sound of archaic English, but does not duplicate it exactly. For example, *thence* actually means "from there"; the phrase *from thence* is redundant.

❷ **Enrichment** When "The Rime of the Ancient Mariner" was first published in *Lyrical Ballads* in 1798, it did not include the margin notes. Coleridge added the marginal notes when the poem was reprinted in 1817 in *Sibylline Leaves;* this revised version has become the "official" version of Coleridge's masterpiece.

Customize for *Less Proficient Readers*

❸ Remind students to use Coleridge's margin notes, printed in italics, to help them understand what is happening.

The RIME of the ANCIENT MARINER

SAMUEL TAYLOR COLERIDGE

Argument

❶ How a Ship having passed the Line[1] was driven by storms to the cold Country towards the South Pole: and how from thence she made her course to the tropical Latitude of the Great Pacific Ocean; and of the strange things that befell: and in what manner the Ancyent Marinere came back to his own Country.

Part I

❷ ❸ *An ancient Mariner meeteth three Gallants bidden to a wedding feast and detaineth one.*

It is an ancient Mariner,
And he stoppeth one of three.
"By thy long gray beard and glittering eye,
❹ ❺ Now wherefore stopp'st thou me?

"The Bridegroom's doors are opened wide,
And I am next of kin;
The guests are met, the feast is set:
May'st hear the merry din."

The Wedding Guest is spellbound by the eye of the old seafaring man and constrained to hear his tale.

He holds him with his skinny hand,
"There was a ship," quoth he.
"Hold off! unhand me, graybeard loon!"
Eftsoons[2] his hand dropped he.

❻ **◆ Reading Strategy** Can you find any internal rhymes and assonance in lines 5–8?

❼ He holds him with his glittering eye—
The Wedding Guest stood still,
And listens like a three years' child:
The Mariner hath his will.

The Wedding Guest sat on a stone:
He cannot choose but hear;
And thus spake on that ancient man,
The bright-eyed Mariner.

1. **Line:** Equator.
2. **eftsoons:** Immediately.

Block Scheduling Strategies

Consider these suggestions to take advantage of extended class time:

- After students have completed the Journal Writing in Literature and Your Life (p. 629), have them complete the Cross-Curricular Connection: Science page on the psychology of dreams in ***Beyond Literature*** (p. 32).
- Introduce poetic sound effects in Literary Focus on page 629. Then encourage students to fill out a Reading Strategy chart (p. 629) as they read the poems. Have students answer the Literary Focus and Reading Strategy questions on page 654.
- Invite students to perform their dramatic readings from "The Rime of the Ancient Mariner," as described in the Idea Bank (p. 655). Initiate class discussion of the performances and the passages.
- Have students begin the Writing Mini-Lesson (p. 655) by sharing favorite sound devices from Coleridge's poetry.

The Mariner tells how the ship sailed southward with a good wind and fair weather till it reached the Line.

"The ship was cheered, the harbor cleared,
Merrily did we drop
Below the kirk,[3] below the hill,
Below the lighthouse top.

"The Sun came up upon the left,
Out of the sea came he!
And he shone bright, and on the right
Went down into the sea.

"Higher and higher every day,
Till over the mast at noon[4]—"
The Wedding Guest here beat his breast,
For he heard the loud bassoon.

The Wedding Guest heareth the bridal music; but the Mariner continueth his tale.

The bride hath paced into the hall.
Red as a rose is she;
Nodding their heads before her goes
The merry minstrelsy.

The Wedding Guest he beat his breast,
Yet he cannot choose but hear;
And thus spake on that ancient man
The bright-eyed Mariner. ❽

The ship driven by a storm toward the South Pole.

"And now the Storm blast came, and he
Was tyrannous and strong:
He struck with his o'ertaking wings,
And chased us south along.

"With sloping masts and dipping prow,
As who pursued with yell and blow
Still treads the shadow of his foe,
And forward bends his head,
The ship drove fast, loud roared the blast,
And southward aye[5] we fled.

"And now there came both mist and snow.
And it grew wondrous cold;
And ice, mast-high, came floating by,
As green as emerald.

The land of ice, and of fearful sounds, where no living thing was to be seen.

"And through the drifts the snowy clifts[6]
Did send a dismal sheen;
Nor shapes of men nor beasts we ken[7]—
The ice was all between.

3. **kirk:** Church.
4. **over . . . noon:** The ship has reached the equator.
5. **aye:** Ever.
6. **clifts:** Icebergs.
7. **ken:** Knew.

◆ Grammar and Style

❹ **Inverted Word Order** Point out to students the inverted word order in line 4. Discuss how the inversion enables Coleridge to rhyme line 4 with line 2.

❺ **Clarification** Point out that *wherefore* means "why."

◆ Reading Strategy

❻ **Poetic Effects** The internal rhymes are *Bride*[groom]/*wide* and *met/set*. There is assonance in *next/guests/met/set*.

❼ **Clarification** His "glittering eye" suggests that the Mariner is a hypnotist or mesmerist, like the vampire Geraldine in "Christabel," another long poem by Coleridge.

◆ Literature and Your Life

❽ Direct students' attention to the Wedding Guest's fascination with the tale he is hearing. When have students been so gripped by an interest that they were unable to focus elsewhere? *Students may mention recent efforts to reach a particular athletic goal; stories they have read, viewed, or heard; or emotional involvements they found riveting.*

Customize for *Less Proficient Readers*

Make sure students realize that the text in lines 31–40 is not part of the Mariner's tale. Urge students to watch for opening and closing quotation marks, which signal interruptions.

Cross-Curricular Connection: Social Studies

The Antarctic Region begins at 60° south latitude. Within this area is ice-filled water, enormous ice shelves, and the continent of Antarctica. The massive ice formations continually break up into huge icebergs. These have proven a deadly danger to ships, as have the frigid temperatures, turbulent prevailing west winds, and the crossing currents of the Pacific, Atlantic, and Indian oceans. Still, in the early 1800's, those who hunted seals for their fur forged their way in wooden hulled ships through the Antarctic (or Southern) ocean to finally reach the continent itself.

Have students discuss the impact such extreme climate conditions might have on sailors.

◆ Background for Understanding

Literature Coleridge uses archaic verb forms to create the sound of a medieval or Renaissance ballad. The suffix *-eth* forms the archaic third-person singular present indicative form of a verb.

Customize for *English Language Learners*

To help students manage Coleridge's antiquated word endings, especially in the marginalia, point out that *-eth* can be replaced with *-s*. For example, *proveth* means "proves."

❶ **Enrichment** Tell students that Coleridge's friend, poet William Wordsworth, contributed the idea of the albatross.

◆ Critical Thinking

❷ **Infer** Ask students: Why do you think the sailors are so happy to see the Albatross? *Students should recognize that the sailors might be afraid in such forbidding and isolated territory. The Albatross reassures them of some life around them and becomes an omen for their survival.*

Comprehension Check ☑

❸ What significant event happens at the end of Part I? *The Mariner shoots the Albatross.*

◆ Reading Strategy

❹ **Poetic Effects** Alliteration, assonance, and internal rhyme tend to add emphasis and slow down lines of poetry. These sound devices make the stanza portentous and contribute to the fatal feeling of the Mariner's action.

Customize for *More Advanced Students*

Point out the repetition in lines 72–74 and lines 88–90. Discuss how the second version echoes the first version and emphasizes the change that has occurred.

"The ice was here, the ice was there,
The ice was all around;
It cracked and growled, and roared and howled,
Like noises in a swound![8]

Till a great sea bird, called the Albatross, came through the snowfog, and was received with great joy and hospitality.

"At length did cross an Albatross, ❶
Thorough[9] the fog it came;
As if it had been a Christian soul, ❷
We hailed it in God's name.

"It ate the food it ne'er had eat,[10]
And round and round it flew.
The ice did split with a thunder-fit;
The helmsman steered us through!

And lo! the Albatross proveth a bird of good omen, and followeth the ship as it returned northward through fog and floating ice.

"And a good south wind sprung up behind;
The Albatross did follow,
And every day, for food or play,
Came to the mariner's hollo!

"In mist or cloud, on mast or shroud,[11]
It perched for vespers[12] nine;
Whiles all the night, through fog-smoke white,
Glimmered the white Moonshine."

The ancient Mariner inhospitably killeth the pious bird of good omen.

"God save thee, ancient Mariner!
From the fiends, that plague thee thus!—
Why look'st thou so?"[13] "With my crossbow
I shot the Albatross." ❸

Part II

"The Sun now rose upon the right:[14]
Out of the sea came he,
Still hid in mist, and on the left
Went down into the sea.

❹ **◆ Reading Strategy** How does the use of alliteration, assonance, and internal rhyme in lines 91–94 give a fatal feeling to the Mariner's curse?

"And the good south wind still blew behind,
But no sweet bird did follow,
Nor any day for food or play
Came to the mariners' hollo!

His shipmates cry out against the ancient Mariner for killing the bird of good luck.

"And I had done a hellish thing,
And it would work 'em woe:
For all averred, I had killed the bird
That made the breeze to blow.

◆ Build Vocabulary

averred (ə vʉrd') *v.*: Stated to be true

8. **swound:** Swoon.
9. **thorough:** Through.
10. **eat** (et): Old form of *eaten.*
11. **shroud** *n.*: Ropes stretching from the ship's side to the masthead.
12. **vespers:** Evenings.
13. **God . . . so:** Spoken by the Wedding Guest.
14. **The Sun . . . right:** The ship is now headed north.

Cross-Curricular Connection: Science

Several different albatross species can be found in the colder regions near Antarctica: the Royal albatross (wingspan 10.5 feet); the Sooty albatross (wingspan 7 feet); and the Wandering albatross (wingspan 11 feet). All share the ability to glide, sometimes for hours, if there is sufficient wind. In calm, size forces albatross to rest frequently, on land or the water surface.

Albatross breed on shore islands, bearing only one chick at a time. Young albatross mature very slowly, taking nearly a year to learn to fly and 5 to 10 years to become independent navigators.

Explain that albatross often follow ships and feed on scraps of food and carrion. Discuss why this huge bird might have come to signify bad luck, inclement weather, and death for sailors.

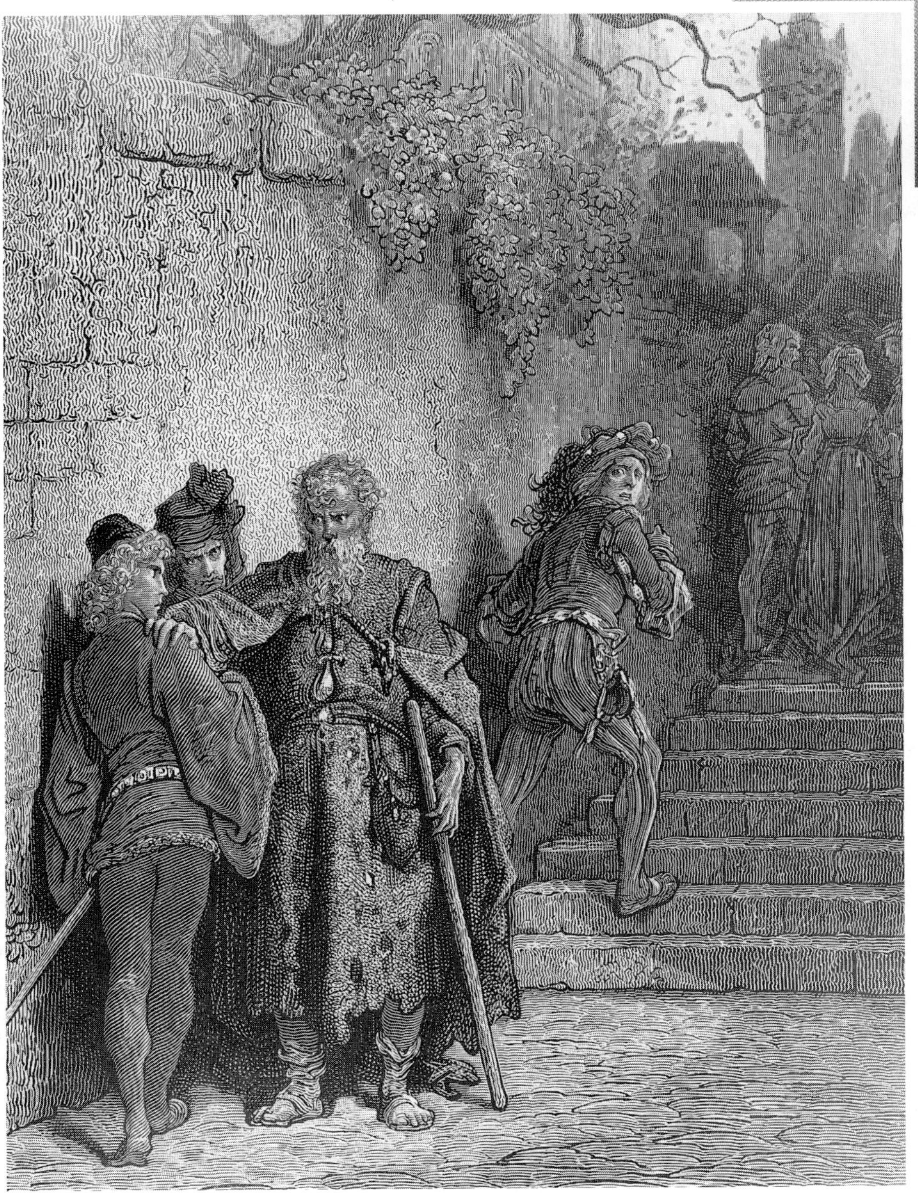

Engraving by Gustave Doré for "The Rime of the Ancient Mariner" by Samuel Taylor Coleridge

▲ **Critical Viewing** From the expression on the wedding guest's face (figure on far left), what can you infer about his reaction to the Ancient Mariner? **[Infer]** ❺

▶Critical Viewing◀

❺ **Infer** Students may say that the Wedding Guest is surprised, a bit annoyed, and reluctant to talk with the Mariner.

Customize for
Visual/Spatial Learners
To help students visualize the action thus far, urge them to overlay tracing paper on a map of the South Pacific and Antarctic regions. Using data from the first 95 lines of the poem, have students draw the ship's path.

Customize for
Less Proficient Readers
To ensure the comprehension of less proficient readers, have these students summarize the events of Part I. *Summaries should include: The Mariner accosts a Wedding Guest, gripping his attention with the story of a long-ago ship voyage. That ship is blown southward to Antarctic regions by a terrible storm. Greeted by an albatross, the sailors take hope but the Mariner destroys that hope by shooting the albatross.*

Customize for
More Advanced Students
Instruct students to copy lines 83–86 on a piece of paper, mark the stressed and unstressed syllables, and make note of the end rhymes. What is the structure of a typical stanza in this poem? *A typical stanza consists of four iambic lines, with four beats in the first and third lines and three beats in the second and fourth lines. The second and fourth lines are rhymed.* Explain that this form is called a ballad stanza, because it is often used in ballads, songs that tell a story.

Humanities: Art

Engraving for "The Rime of the Ancient Mariner," 1875, by Gustave Doré.

This engraving illustrates the stanzas of the poem, in which the Mariner accosts the Wedding Guest. Like the other engravings shown with the poem, this engraving was created specifically to accompany Coleridge's poem.

French illustrator Gustave Doré was born in 1832 and began his career as a cartoonist and caricaturist in Paris. A self-taught artist, Doré refined his technique through independent study of engraving at the National Library in Paris. Doré's skillful figure drawing and composition are evident in this drawing.

Use these questions for discussion:

1. What lines in the poem are reflected in the engraving's portrayal of the Mariner's eyes? *This image suggests lines 3 and 13.*
2. What does the engraving suggest about the attitudes of other wedding guests? *They appear to be repulsed by the Mariner or afraid of him; they are rushing to be away or staring with distaste.*

Enrichment This poem was the opening selection in Wordsworth's and Coleridge's famous *Lyrical Ballads* (1798). Later, Wordsworth expressed doubt about placing the poem first, thinking it would put readers off with its mystical and supernatural feeling. Wordsworth's own "Tintern Abbey," p. 616, was the final poem in the collection.

Customize for
Bodily/Kinesthetic Learners

These students will better appreciate the impact of the Mariner's actions if they compare the kinetic imagery in Part I with that of lines 95–130. Ask them to show with movement how the ship and sea move differently after the shooting. *Student motions should reflect how the ship moves swiftly, then is becalmed.*

◆ Literary Focus

❶ Poetic Sound Devices Have students identify the use of internal rhyme and alliteration in these lines. *The internal rhymes are* red/head, averred/bird, they/slay, blew/flew, *and* first/burst. *The repeated initial* f *sound in lines 103–105 is an example of alliteration.*

◆ Critical Thinking

❷ Connect Ask students to describe the immediate natural consequences of the Mariner's actions. *Students may cite the lack of wind, the hot and red sun, or the lack of rain.*

Ah wretch! said they, the bird to slay,
That made the breeze to blow!

But when the fog cleared off, they justify the same, and thus make themselves accomplices in the crime.

"Nor dim nor red, like God's own head,
The glorious Sun uprist;[15]
Then all averred, I had killed the bird
That brought the fog and mist.
'Twas right, said they, such birds to slay,
That bring the fog and mist. ❶

The fair breeze continues; the ship enters the Pacific Ocean, and sails northward, even till it reaches the Line.

"The fair breeze blew, the white foam flew,
The furrow[16] followed free;
We were the first that ever burst
Into that silent sea.

The ship hath been suddenly becalmed.

"Down dropped the breeze, the sails dropped down,
'Twas sad as sad could be;
And we did speak only to break
The silence of the sea!

"All in a hot and copper sky,
The bloody Sun, at noon,
Right up above the mast did stand,
No bigger than the Moon.

"Day after day, day after day,
We stuck, nor breath nor motion;
As idle as a painted ship
Upon a painted ocean.

❷

And the Albatross begins to be avenged.

"Water, water, everywhere,
And all the boards did shrink;
Water, water, everywhere,
Nor any drop to drink.

"The very deep did rot: O Christ!
That ever this should be!
Yea, slimy things did crawl with legs
Upon the slimy sea.

"About, about, in reel and rout[17]
The death fires[18] danced at night;
The water, like a witch's oils,
Burned green, and blue and white.

15. **uprist:** Arose.
16. **furrow:** Ship's wake.
17. **rout:** Disorderly crowd.
18. **death fires:** St. Elmo's fire, a visible electrical discharge from a ship's mast, believed by sailors to be an omen of disaster.

Cultural Connection

Birds

Throughout history, birds were believed to be divine messengers through which people could foretell the future. This idea is preserved in the words *augury* and *auspice,* which originally mean "bird talk" and "bird view," respectively. Before undertaking any action of consequence, some ancient peoples would observe the birds, looking for an omen. This practice still occurs in some areas of Southeast Asia and the Western Pacific.

Particular birds often mean different things in different cultures. For example, the dove was a messenger of war to the Japanese, but it is an emblem of peace in the West. The owl meant death to the ancient Egyptians but wisdom to the ancient Greeks.

Have students research the symbolic meaning of a specific bird—such as an owl, crow, falcon, eagle, crane, or vulture—to the people of a present-day or ancient culture.

Engraving by Gustave Doré for "The Rime of the Ancient Mariner" by Samuel Taylor Coleridge

▲ **Critical Viewing** Locate the arrow in this picture. Speculate how the artist's capturing it in flight adds to the drama of the situation depicted. **[Speculate]** ❸

Cross-Curricular Connection

Science Many of the strange phenomena that the ship's crew observes after the death of the albatross have a perfectly rational scientific explanation. Challenge students to find out more about swarming polychaete worms, St. Elmo's fire, and bioluminescent plankton. Have them relate their findings to the class and describe in detail what the Mariner would have seen.

Customize for *Visual/Spatial Learners*

Discuss with these students the vivid and colorful sensory images of the poem. Invite them to create color illustrations of the changes in nature that occurred after the death of the albatross.

Enrichment In planning the *Lyrical Ballads,* Coleridge and Wordsworth agreed to divide up their efforts. Wordsworth would focus on giving the "charm of novelty to things of every day," hoping to inspire readers to new perspectives on the world. Coleridge would direct his efforts towards describing supernatural, "or at least romantic," characters in order to explore the limits of imagination.

▶Critical Viewing◀

❸ **Speculate** Students may say that capturing the arrow in flight causes viewers to wonder if it will strike the bird. This may cause them to read on for the answer, thereby becoming engaged in the visual and written story.

Humanities: Art

Engraving for "The Rime of the Ancient Mariner," 1875, by Gustave Doré.

This illustration depicts the albatross's shooting, capturing the instant just prior to the arrow's strike.

Doré, who was born in Strasbourg, France, near the German border, moved to Paris in 1847. He was commissioned in 1848 to create weekly lithograph caricatures for a French humor magazine. It was his woodcut illustrations for the work of well-known writers such as Honoré de Balzac and François Rabelais that firmly established Doré's fame.

Use these questions for discussion:

1. What elements in the engraving capture the setting of the poem? *Elements that capture the setting include the icicles dripping from mast and lines; the drifting ice in the water and the grayish sky all suggest the cold and barren setting.*
2. What effect does the pictured moment have on the ship's crew? *First they call the Mariner "wretch," believing him to have cursed the ship, then they praise him for saving the ship from fog and mist.*

▶Critical Viewing◀

❶ **Hypothesize** Students may say they would assume the ship was sinking or otherwise in distress because its passengers are clearly suffering.

◆ Critical Thinking

❷ **Analyze** Direct students' attention to the sailors' punishment described in lines 135–138. Ask them to explain why it was so terrible. *Students should note that thirst, when surrounded by endless but undrinkable water, is a cruel punishment. In addition, the inability to talk leaves the sailors further isolated in their misery.*

◆ Literary Focus

❸ **Poetic Sound Devices** Have students note the internal rhyme in line 141: *"cross"* and *"Albatross:"* You might also point out that Coleridge inverts the word order in line 142 in order to achieve the rhythm of this internal rhyme.

Customize for *English Language Learners*

Have these students refer to any notes they have made while reading, and to their regular paraphrasing in order to summarize the events of Part II. Invite them to share and verify their summaries. *Summaries should include: The ship turns north; the crew at first criticizes then praises the Mariner for shooting the Albatross; the ship is becalmed and the sailors suffer from heat, and drought, and torment. Finally, the Albatross is hung around the Mariner's neck as a reminder of his evil deed.*

Engraving by Gustave Doré for "The Rime of the Ancient Mariner" by Samuel Taylor Coleridge

❶ ▶ **Critical Viewing** If you had seen this illustration before reading the poem, how would you have interpreted it? **[Hypothesize]**

A Spirit had followed them; one of the invisible inhabitants of this planet, neither departed souls nor angels. They are very numerous, and there is no climate or element without one or more.

"And some in dreams assurèd were
Of the Spirit that plagued us so;
Nine fathom deep he had followed us
From the land of mist and snow.

❷ "And every tongue, through utter drought,
Was withered at the root;
We could not speak, no more than if
We had been choked with soot.

The shipmates, in their sore distress, would fain throw the whole guilt on the ancient Mariner: in sign whereof they hang the dead sea bird round his neck.

❸ "Ah! well a-day! what evil looks
Had I from old and young!
Instead of the cross, the Albatross
About my neck was hung.

Part III

The ancient Mariner beholdeth a sign in the element afar off.

"There passed a weary time. Each throat
Was parched, and glazed each eye.
A weary time! a weary time!
How glazed each weary eye,
When looking westward, I beheld
A something in the sky.

Humanities: Art

Engraving for "The Rime of the Ancient Mariner," 1875, by Gustave Doré.

This illustration depicts the sailors' hopelessness and suffering while stranded at sea.

Though Doré also worked in painting and sculpture, particularly after 1870, he was never as successful in these arts as he was with book illustrating. Apparently quite obsessed with Coleridge's poem, he created in this series of illustrations some of his most eerie and disturbing images. Although the illustrated volume of Coleridge's poem was not a commercial success, it is considered an artistic triumph for Gustave Doré.

Use these questions for discussion:

1. What details in the engraving convey the peril of the ship? *Students may cite the sailors' agonized expressions, the calm seas around the ship, and the sailors' desperate efforts to see into the distance and perhaps signal the faraway ship.*
2. What mood does this illustration evoke? *The mood is despairing and hopeless.*

"At first it seemed a little speck,
And then it seemed a mist;
It moved and moved, and took at last
A certain shape, I wist.[19]

"A speck, a mist, a shape, I wist!
And still it neared and neared:
As if it dodged a water sprite,
It plunged and tacked and veered.

At its nearer approach, it seemeth him to be a ship; and at a dear ransom he freeth his speech from the bonds of thirst.

"With throats unslaked, with black lips baked,
We could nor laugh nor wail;
Through utter drought all dumb we stood!
I bit my arm, I sucked the blood,
And cried, A sail! a sail! ❹

A flash of joy;

"With throats unslaked, with black lips baked,
Agape they heard me call:
Gramercy![20] for joy did grin,
And all at once their breath drew in,
As they were drinking all.

And horror follows. For can it be a ship that comes onward without wind or tide?

"See! see! (I cried) she tacks no more!
Hither to work us weal;[21]
Without a breeze, without a tide,
She steadies with upright keel!

❺ **◆ Reading Strategy**
Lines 167–170 use the repetition of vowel sounds as well as the repetition of whole words. What effect do you think this achieves?

"The western wave was all aflame.
The day was well nigh done!
Almost upon the western wave
Rested the broad bright Sun;
When that strange shape drove suddenly
Betwixt us and the Sun.

It seemeth him but the skeleton of a ship.

"And straight the Sun was flecked with bars,
(Heaven's Mother send us grace!)
As if through a dungeon grate he peered
With broad and burning face.

And its ribs are seen as bars on the face of the setting Sun.

"Alas! (thought I, and my heart beat loud)
How fast she nears and nears!
Are those *her* sails that glance in the Sun,
Like restless gossameres?[22]

The Specter Woman and her Death- mate, and no other on board the skele- ton ship.

"Are those *her* ribs through which the Sun
Did peer, as through a grate?
And is that Woman all her crew?
Is that a Death? and are there two?
Is Death that woman's mate?

19. **wist:** Knew.
20. **Gramercy** (grə mur′ sē): Great thanks.
21. **work us weal:** Assist us.
22. **gossameres:** Floating cobwebs.

Literature CD-ROM "The Rime of the Ancient Mariner" is featured in *How to Read and Understand Poetry.* Feature 7 uses the poem to illustrate the form of poetry, and Feature 9 uses it to demonstrate alliteration.

Customize for
Musical/Rhythmic Learners
These learners will enjoy the highly rhythmic flow of the poem. Encourage student pairs to take turns reading aloud and listening to Part III. Have pairs share favorite stanzas and sound devices.

◆ Literature and Your Life

❹ Discuss with students the Mariner's extraordinary response to seeing the distant ship. Have students share stories about people who have taken drastic action or experienced sudden physical ability when faced with a crisis. *Students may draw their anecdotes from personal experience or from stories they have heard or read. They may mention moments of danger when their senses became fully alert or when they overcame an aversion, such as to heights, in order to reach a goal.*

◆ Reading Strategy

❺ **Poetic Effects** Students may say that the sound and repetition emphasizes the dreamlike quality of the stanza text, almost like a chant.

Cross-Curricular Connection: Science/Social Studies

Following the killing of the Albatross, the sailors suffer dehydration when their water supply runs out. Their suffering is true to life, since water is a necessary requirement for physical performance, as well as for life itself. Human beings can survive without food for longer than they can without water. The normal adult male requires two to three liters of water each day to replace that lost through perspiration and excretion. Without this replacement water, dehydration begins, performance diminishes and serious health dangers soon develop.

People throughout the world are dependent on having supplies of fresh water to live a healthy life. Have interested students examine the impact that drought, pollution, or warfare has had on the water supply of a particular region or nation. Then have students propose solutions for fixing the problems and ensuring that the world's population is never deprived of fresh drinking water.

Customize for
Less Proficient Readers
Remind students to read Coleridge's margin notes. Often these explain or elaborate on the verse text, enabling students to build clear meaning.

◆ Critical Thinking

❶ **Evaluate** Ask students: Do you think the term "Nightmare Life-in-Death" is appropriate for the specter who gambled for the souls of the crew? *Yes, because some of her features signify life (red lips) while others symbolize death (overly white skin); no, her description is too colorful to be a "Nightmare Life-in-Death."*

◆ Critical Thinking

❷ **Assess** Have students copy line 194—"Who thicks man's blood with cold"—on a separate sheet of paper and mark the stresses in the line. *The second, third, fourth, and sixth syllables are stressed.* Point out that in a regular iambic line, the third syllable would not be stressed. Ask students to discuss how the extra stress affects the line. *The extra stress (spondaic substitution) slows down the line, giving the impression of blood freezing in one's veins.*

❸ **Clarification** Life-in-Death won the life of the Mariner, who will live on and suffer, condemned to a sort of living death.

◆ Literature and Your Life

❹ Students may say that they have had nightmares in which, like the Mariner, they watched helplessly as their fate was determined by others' actions.

◆ Grammar and Style

❺ **Inverted Word Order** Ask students to restate line 220 in standard word order and to explain Coleridge's purpose in the inversion. *Possible restatement: "The souls flew from their bodies." The inversion places the verb fly at the end of the phrase in order to rhyme lines 220 and 223.*

Like vessel, like crew! Death and Life-in-Death have diced for the ship's crew, and she (the latter) winneth the ancient Mariner.

"*Her* lips were red, *her* looks were free,
Her locks were yellow as gold;
Her skin was as white as leprosy,
The Nightmare Life-in-Death was she, ❶
Who thicks man's blood with cold. ❷

"The naked hulk alongside came,
And the twain were casting dice;
'The game is done! I've won! I've won!'
Quoth she, and whistles thrice.

No twilight within the courts of the Sun.

"The Sun's rim dips; the stars rush out:
At one stride comes the dark;
With far-heard whisper, o'er the sea,
Off shot the specter bark.

At the rising of the Moon,

"We listened and looked sideways up!
Fear at my heart, as at a cup,
My lifeblood seemed to sip!
The stars were dim, and thick the night,
The steersman's face by his lamp gleamed white;
From the sails the dew did drip—
Till clomb[23] above the eastern bar
The hornèd[24] Moon, with one bright star
Within the nether tip.

One after another,

"One after one, by the star-dogged Moon,[25]
Too quick for groan or sigh,
Each turned his face with a ghastly pang,
And cursed me with his eye.

His shipmates drop down dead.

"Four times fifty living men,
(And I heard nor sigh nor groan)
With heavy thump, a lifeless lump,
They dropped down one by one.

❸ *But Life-in-Death begins her work on the ancient Mariner.*

"The souls did from their bodies fly— ❺
They fled to bliss or woe!
And every soul, it passed me by,
Like the whizz of my crossbow!"

❹ **◆ Literature and Your Life**
Does the dice game in lines 195–198 remind you of a nightmare? Have you ever had a similar nightmare?

23. **clomb:** Climbed.
24. **hornèd:** Crescent.
25. **star-dogged Moon:** Omen of impending evil to sailors.

Beyond the Classroom

Workplace Skills

Individual Responsibility In this epic, the action—shooting the albatross—of one sailor causes the entire crew to suffer. This type of cause-and-effect relationship holds true in the modern-day world in which workers (such as rescue squad employees, construction workers, and aviation employees) are in a position to endanger their coworkers' and clients' safety. In some instances, workers may even be responsible for coworkers' and clients' lives. Invite students to discuss the behaviors and attitudes they think responsible workers should display in these situations. Ask students whether they think workers should receive training in how to cope with the responsibility for another person's safety.

Part IV

The Wedding Guest feareth that a Spirit is talking to him;

"I fear thee, ancient Mariner!
I fear thy skinny hand!
And thou art long, and lank, and brown,
As is the ribbed sea sand. ❻

"I fear thee and thy glittering eye,
And thy skinny hand, so brown."

But the ancient Mariner assureth him of his bodily life, and proceedeth to relate his horrible penance.

"Fear not, fear not, thou Wedding Guest!
This body dropped not down.

"Alone, alone, all, all alone,
Alone on a wide wide sea!
And never a saint took pity on ❼
My soul in agony.

He despiseth the creatures of the calm,

"The many men, so beautiful!
And they all dead did lie:
And a thousand thousand slimy things
Lived on; and so did I.

And envieth that they should live, and so many lie dead.

"I looked upon the rotting sea,
And drew my eyes away;
I looked upon the rotting deck,
And there the dead men lay.

❽ **◆ Reading Strategy** What creates the strong emotional effect in lines 236–239?

"I looked to heaven, and tried to pray;
But or[26] ever a prayer had gushed,
A wicked whisper came, and made
My heart as dry as dust.

"I closed my lids, and kept them close,
And the balls like pulses beat;
For the sky and the sea and the sea and the sky
Lay like a load on my weary eye,
And the dead were at my feet.

But the curse liveth for him in the eye of the dead men.

"The cold sweat melted from their limbs,
Nor rot nor reek did they;
The look with which they looked on me ❾
Had never passed away.

"An orphan's curse would drag to hell
A spirit from on high;
But oh! more horrible than that
Is the curse in a dead man's eye!
Seven days, seven nights, I saw that curse,
And yet I could not die.

---

26. or: Before.

Beyond the Classroom

Career Connection

Merchant Marine The Mariner never reveals the original purpose of his crew's journey, though it was almost certainly commercial in nature. Today, ships manned by merchant marines carry freight all around the world. Sailors may be out at sea for several weeks or months at a time, then in port for a similar period. Some travel the same route over and over during the year, becoming familiar with the sea and ports along the way. Have interested students learn about commercial shipping that takes place in a port city of their choosing. (The Port Authority of that city is a good starting point for research.) Urge students to focus on the experiences of merchant sailors and to compare this lifestyle with that of the Ancient Mariner.

Customize for
Verbal/Linguistic Learners

Have students summarize the events of Part III. Ask them to choose specific words or phrases from the stanzas to create an abbreviated linguistic summary. *Summaries might include the following words and phrases:* parched; glazed; I beheld; a certain shape; cried, A sail! A sail!; strange shape; Death; Nightmare Life-Death; casting dice; I've won; comes the dark; my lifeblood seemed to sip; cursed me with his eye; dropped down one by one; every soul, it passed me by.

❻ **Clarification** Point out that the Wedding Guest has once again interrupted the Mariner; lines 224–229 are spoken by the Guest.

◆ Critical Thinking

❼ **Analyze** Have students analyze the effect of the repetition, alliteration, and assonance in these lines. *Repetition adds emphasis, and the alliteration and assonance a haunting, mournful sound, like a howl of despair.* How might the Mariner's situation symbolize his spiritual condition? *He had cut himself off from nature and its life-giving properties, as shown by his shooting of the Albatross. His physical isolation with the death of his companions is a reflection of his spiritual isolation.*

◆ Reading Strategy

❽ **Poetic Effects** Students should note the repetition of words and whole lines. These emphasize the Mariner's horror and the nightmare scene he is witnessing.

◆ Literature and Your Life

❾ Direct students' attention to the Mariner's inability to free his mind of the crew's final cursing look. What experiences have students had when they could not get a sensory image—whether of sight, sound, smell, taste, or touch—out of their mind? *Students will mention songs they could not forget, scents that bring back certain memories, times that they couldn't get an image or a phrase out of their minds.*

Customize for
English Language Learners
To ensure that students are keeping pace with Coleridge's poetic diction and syntax, ask them to summarize Section IV. *Summaries should include: The Wedding Guest interrupts in fear, but the Mariner continues his story. The Mariner drifts all alone on the sea in physical and spiritual agony, tormented by the dead faces of his crewmates. When the moon arises, he gains new perspective on the world, the sea snakes become beautiful, he feels love, and the Albatross falls from his neck.*

Customize for
Less Proficient Readers
❶ Clarify for these students some of the poetic anomalies Coleridge uses to complete his rhymes. For example, in line 270, the word "alway" rather than "always" is used to rhyme with "lay." Urge students to build meaning from context when faced with similar unfamiliar or modified words.

◆ Critical Thinking
❷ **Interpret** Ask students: How does the Mariner's attitude change in these stanzas? *Students should note that the Mariner begins to see the snakes as beautiful examples of living nature; he begins to feel love.*

◆ Critical Thinking
❸ **Connect** Ask students: What is the relationship between the Mariner's attitude toward the water snakes and the Albatross falling from his neck? *When he admires and feels love for the water snakes, he reconnects himself to nature and the forces of life, so the dead Albatross, the symbol of his rejection of nature, falls from him.* What does this reveal about his spiritual condition? *He has taken the first step toward his redemption.*

◆ Literary Focus
❹ **Poetic Sound Devices**
Students should note that the repeated *d* in "dank," "drunken," and "dreams" creates alliteration.

In his loneliness and fixedness he yearneth towards the journeying Moon, and the stars that still sojourn, yet still move onward; and everywhere the blue sky belongs to them, and is their appointed rest, and their native country and their own natural homes, which they enter unannounced, as lords that are certainly expected and yet there is a silent joy at their arrival.

"The moving Moon went up the sky,
And nowhere did abide:
Softly she was going up,
And a star or two beside—

"Her beams bemocked the sultry main,[27]
Like April hoarfrost spread;
But where the ship's huge shadow lay,
The charmèd water burned alway ❶
A still and awful red.

By the light of the Moon he beholdeth God's creatures of the great calm.

"Beyond the shadow of the ship,
I watched the water snakes:
They moved in tracks of shining white,
And when they reared, the elfish light
Fell off in in hoary flakes.

"Within the shadow of the ship
I watched their rich attire:
Blue, glossy green, and velvet black,
They coiled and swam; and every track ❷
Was a flash of golden fire.

Their beauty and their happiness.

"O happy living things! no tongue
Their beauty might declare:
A spring of love gushed from my heart,
And I blessed them unaware;

He blesseth them in his heart.

Sure my kind saint took pity on me,
And I blessed them unaware.

The spell begins to break.

"The selfsame moment I could pray;
And from my neck so free
The Albatross fell off, and sank ❸
Like lead into the sea.

Part V
"Oh sleep! it is a gentle thing,
Beloved from pole to pole!
To Mary Queen the praise be given!
She sent the gentle sleep from Heaven,
That slid into my soul.

By grace of the holy Mother, the ancient Mariner is refreshed with rain.

"The silly[28] buckets on the deck,
That had so long remained,
I dreamed that they were filled with dew;
And when I awoke, it rained.

"My lips were wet, my throat was cold,
My garments all were dank;
Sure I had drunken in my dreams,
And still my body drank.

❹ **◆ Literary Focus**
What repeated consonant sound in lines 303–304 above creates alliteration?

27. main: Open sea.
28. silly: Empty.

Cultural Connection

Dreams
When the Mariner dreams the buckets are filled with water, it rains upon his awakening. In some cultures, this would be seen as an expected result of a dream. For example, in ancient Greece gods might visit a dreaming person to predict or order specific future actions. In another view, the Eskimo of Hudson Bay believe the dreamer's soul has actually left his or her body; it is therefore forbidden to awaken those who sleep. Psychoanalyst Sigmund Freud's more recent perspective on dreams suggest that they reflect elements of the waking experience that are too painful or difficult to address except during sleep.

Have students share their own views about the function and impact of dreams. How might the Mariner's dreamlike state affect his thought processes?

"I moved, and could not feel my limbs:
I was so light—almost
I thought that I had died in sleep,
And was a blessèd ghost.

He heareth sounds and seeth strange sights and commotions in the sky and the element.

"And soon I heard a roaring wind:
It did not come anear;
But with its sound it shook the sails,
That were so thin and sere.[29]

"The upper air burst into life!
And a hundred fire flags sheen,[30]
To and fro they were hurried about!
And to and fro, and in and out,
The wan stars danced between.

"And the coming wind did roar more loud,
And the sails did sigh like sedge;[31]
And the rain poured down from one black cloud;
The Moon was at its edge.

"The thick black cloud was cleft, and still
The Moon was at its side:
Like waters shot from some high crag,
The lightning fell with never a jag,
A river steep and wide.

The bodies of the ship's crew are inspired[32] and the ship moves on;

"The loud wind never reached the ship,
Yet now the ship moved on!
Beneath the lightning and the Moon
The dead men gave a groan.

"They groaned, they stirred, they all uprose,
Nor spake, nor moved their eyes;
It had been strange, even in a dream,
To have seen those dead men rise.

"The helmsman steered, the ship moved on: 5
Yet never a breeze up-blew;
The mariners all 'gan work the ropes,
Where they were wont[33] to do;
They raised their limbs like lifeless tools—
We were a ghastly crew.

"The body of my brother's son
Stood by me, knee to knee;
The body and I pulled at one rope,
But he said nought to me."

6 ◆ ***Literature and Your Life***

How does the image of the body of the speaker's brother's son make you feel?

◆ **Build Vocabulary**

sojourn (sō´ jʉrn) *v.*: Stay for a while

29. sere: Dried up.
30. fire flags sheen: The aurora australis, or southern lights, shone.
31. sedge *n.*: Rushlike plant that grows in wet soil.
32. inspired: Inspirited.
33. wont: Accustomed.

Customize for
Visual/Spatial Learners
To help these learners appreciate the commotion and tumult of this scene (lines 310–340), challenge them to draft a set layout. Encourage them to use the sensory language in the text as a starting point and strive to reflect the turbulent mood in the visual elements of the scene.

◆ Critical Thinking

5 **Compare and Contrast** Ask students: What has happened to the crew members since the change in the Mariner's attitude occurs? *Students should recognize that the crew has begun to work the ship again, performing the tasks of living men though they are not actually alive.*

◆ *Literature and Your Life*

6 Students may say the image in lines 341–342 makes them feel queasy—a dead body behaving like a living person. Other students may say they feel uplifted by the idea that the Mariner's redemption has the power to reanimate the crew.

Cross-Curricular Connection: Science

The Southern Lights, or Aurora Australis, that the Mariner sees can be observed around 70° south latitude. At about 70° north latitude, a similar phenomenon called the Northern Lights, or Aurora Borealis, can be observed. Both displays of light may take many shapes, from arcs or bands to fan-shaped coronas. They originate in the upper atmosphere when auroral electrons and protons collide at high-speed with atoms, causing the atoms to glow. Because these auroral particles are linked to solar activity, changes in the sun's behavior can increase the frequency and intensity of the light displays.

Ask any students who have viewed the Northern or Southern Lights to describe the experience. Otherwise, show students photographs of these extraordinary lights. Have students discuss how such a phenomenon might contribute to an atmosphere of wonder.

Customize for
Bodily/Kinesthetic Learners
To guide students' understanding of the crews' posture, offer them access through these benchmarks: a crowded bus or train, an audience leaving a concert or sports activity, queues of people waiting to reach a service desk. Discuss how in crowds, individuals lose some of the animation that makes them special and alive. Here, though the crew has become animate again, they lack the individuality that would make them truly human.

Enrichment According to the writings of William Wordsworth, he contributed to "The Rime of the Ancient Mariner" the idea that the ship would be navigated homeward by the dead crew. He worked with Coleridge in plotting out the general outline of the poem while the two were on a walking tour.

Clarification Point out to students that Doré's engraving shows the albatross still around the Mariner's neck, although in the text it falls off before the ship's crew is reanimated.

▶Critical Viewing◀

❶ **Support** Students may say that the heaped bodies and vacant expressions, along with the Mariner's despairing posture and countenance, contribute to the mood of hopelessness.

Engraving by Gustave Doré for "The Rime of the Ancient Mariner" by Samuel Taylor Coleridge

❶ ▶ **Critical Viewing** What details support the mood of hopelessness in this illustration? **[Support]**

Humanities: Art

Engraving for "The Rime of the Ancient Mariner," 1875, by Gustave Doré.

This engraving depicts the dead crew navigating the ship as the Mariner looks on in despair. Doré has reordered the poem's events to present the Mariner still carrying the Albatross. Although the poem emphasizes the positive aspects of this bizarre scene, the artist has chosen to emphasize the nightmarish aspects.

As photographic expertise grew in the 1860's, Frenchman Gustave Doré began to use sketches as his original illustrations, transferring these to the wood block photographically rather than by cutting. Doré often created fantastic, dreamlike images. Critics feel these have been most successful in black-and-white mediums such as this engraving. It presents an unforgettable, eerie vision of the cursed ship sailed by animated spirits.

Use these questions for discussion:

1. Why might the engraver have chosen to reorganize the events for this image?
Possible responses: The artist thought the image would be more interesting and memorable if he emphasized the horrific aspects of the scene; the artist, like the Wedding Guest, found the thought of a zombie crew frightening even if "a troop of spirits blessed" inhabited the dead bodies.
2. What elements of the engraving reflect Coleridge's description of the situation?
As in Coleridge's descriptions, the spirit crew members' postures show them to be working hard while their faces reflect death.

But not by the souls of the men, nor by demons of earth or middle air, but by a blessed troop of angelic spirits, sent down by the invocation of the guardian saint.

"I fear thee, ancient Mariner!"
"Be calm, thou Wedding Guest!
'Twas not those souls that fled in pain, ❷
Which to their corses[34] came again,
But a troop of spirits blessed:

"For when it dawned—they dropped their arms,
And clustered round the mast;
Sweet sounds rose slowly through their mouths,
And from their bodies passed.

"Around, around, flew each sweet sound,
Then darted to the Sun;
Slowly the sounds came back again,
Now mixed, now one by one.

"Sometimes a-dropping from the sky
I heard the skylark sing;
Sometimes all little birds that are,
How they seemed to fill the sea and air
With their sweet jargoning![35] ❸

"And now 'twas like all instruments,
Now like a lonely flute;
And now it is an angel's song,
That makes the heavens be mute.

"It ceased; yet still the sails made on
A pleasant noise till noon,
A noise like of a hidden brook ❹
In the leafy month of June,
That to the sleeping woods all night
Singeth a quiet tune.

"Till noon we quietly sailed on,
Yet never a breeze did breathe;
Slowly and smoothly went the ship,
Moved onward from beneath.

The lonesome Spirit from the South Pole carries on the ship as far as the Line, in obedience to the angelic troop, but still requireth vengeance.

"Under the keel nine fathom deep, ❺
From the land of mist and snow,
The spirit slid; and it was he
That made the ship to go.
The sails at noon left off their tune,
And the ship stood still also.

34. corses: Corpses.
35. jargoning: Singing.

Customize for
Less Proficient Readers

❷ Ask students who is speaking in line 345. Clarify as necessary that this line contains an interruption by the Wedding Guest. Point out that the text is addressed to the Mariner and thus is likely to be spoken by another character.

◆ Reading Strategy

❸ **Poetic Effects** Invite students to locate repetition of whole words or phrases. Discuss the impact of the repetition. *Students should note the repetition of "Sometimes" in lines 358 and 360; "And now" in lines 363 and 365. The repetition gives the stanza a musical quality.*

◆ Grammar and Style

❹ **Inverted Word Order** Ask students to locate the inverted word order in this stanza and to restate the inverted phrase in standard word order. Discuss how the restated order would change the stanza's poetic impact. *Restatements might read: "[A noise]... that singeth a quiet tune to the sleeping woods all night." Students may say the reordering would disrupt both the rhyme and rhythm of the stanza.*

❺ **Clarification** Explain that a fathom is equal to six feet; therefore, water "nine fathom deep" is water that is fifty-four feet deep.

Cross-Curricular Connection: Math

The Pacific Ocean covers more than a third of the earth's surface, about 70,000,000 square miles in area. It has an average depth of 12,925 feet, though at its deepest point, the Challenger Deep of the Marianas Trench, the Pacific is 36,198 feet deep. At its longest point, the Pacific is about 9,000 miles, while at its widest, it is about 11,000 miles.

Using the formula for converting feet to fathoms, (1 fathom = 6 ft) have students calculate the average and greatest Pacific depths in fathoms. *The average depth is 2,154 fathoms; the greatest depth is 6,033 fathoms.* Then have them estimate approximately how long the Mariner's journey—from the Equator to the Antarctic Circle and back again—would take. Using speeds based on current shipping or on the sail power of an earlier time. *The Antarctic circle is at 66° 34'S, and a degree of latitude is approximately 69 statute miles. In the 1800's a sailing ship took approximately four weeks to sail from Liverpool to New York, a distance of approximately 3,320 miles. If a sailing ship traveled 118 miles in a day, a trip from the equator to the Antarctic circle and back would take about 78 days.*

Customize for
English Language Learners

❶ Explain that *'gan stir* (line 385) means "began to stir," and that *swound* means "swoon" or "faint."

◆ Literary Focus

❷ **Poetic Sound Devices** Prompt students to locate and identify the internal rhyme in this stanza. *"With his bow he laid full low" is the line containing internal rhyme, with the rhyming words underlined.*

◆ Critical Thinking

❸ **Interpret** Ask students: What fate remains in store for the Mariner? *Students should note that the Mariner still faces more penance; his redemption is not complete.*

Comprehension Check ☑

Have students summarize the events in Part V. *Summaries should include: The Mariner is revived by rain. A celestial storm signals supernatural events as the dead crew is animated and begins to sail the ship. Positive natural omens surround the ship, and it progresses until two spirits arrive to discuss the Mariner's fate. They decide that he must repent further under the guidance of the Polar Spirit.*

Customize for
Less Proficient Readers

Less proficient readers may be confused by the change in speakers at the beginning of part VI. Explain that the First Voice and Second Voice belong to other characters. Explain that according to the marginal notes, the Mariner is in a trance; therefore these may be voices within a dream. Alternatively, he may be "in tune" with the spirit world.

"The Sun, right up above the mast,
Had fixed her to the ocean:
But in a minute she 'gan stir,
With a short uneasy motion—
Backwards and forwards half her length
❶ With a short uneasy motion.

"Then like a pawing horse let go,
She made a sudden bound:
It flung the blood into my head,
And I fell down in a swound.

The Polar Spirit's fellow demons, the invisible inhabitants of the element, take part in his wrong; and two of them relate, one to the other, that penance long and heavy for the ancient Mariner hath been accorded to the Polar Spirit, who returneth southward.

"How long in that same fit I lay,
I have not to declare;
But ere my living life returned,
I heard and in my soul discerned
Two voices in the air.

"'Is it he?' quoth one, 'Is this the man?
By him who died on cross,
❷ With his cruel bow he laid full low
The harmless Albatross.

"'The spirit who bideth by himself
In the land of mist and snow,
He loved the bird that loved the man
Who shot him with his bow.'

"The other was a softer voice,
As soft as honeydew:
❸ Quoth he, 'The man hath penance done,
And penance more will do.'

Part VI

FIRST VOICE

"'But tell me, tell me! speak again,
Thy soft response renewing—
What makes that ship drive on so fast?
What is the ocean doing?'

SECOND VOICE

"'Still as a slave before his lord,
The ocean hath no blast;
His great bright eye most silently
Up to the Moon is cast—

"'If he may know which way to go;
For she guides him smooth or grim.
See, brother, see! how graciously
She looketh down on him.'

The Mariner hath been cast into a trance; for the angelic power causeth the vessel to drive northward faster than human life could endure.

FIRST VOICE

"'But why drives on that ship so fast,
Without or wave or wind?'

SECOND VOICE

"'The air is cut away before,
And closes from behind.

"'Fly, brother, fly! more high, more high! ❹
Or we shall be belated;
For slow and slow that ship will go, ❺
When the Mariner's trance is abated.'

The super-natural motion is retarded; the Mariner awakes, and his penance begins anew.

"I woke, and we were sailing on
As in a gentle weather:
'Twas night, calm night, the moon was high; ❻
The dead men stood together.

"All stood together on the deck,
For a charnel dungeon[36] litter;
All fixed on me their stony eyes,
That in the Moon did glitter.

"The pang, the curse, with which they died,
Had never passed away;
I could not draw my eyes from theirs,
Nor turn them up to pray.

The curse is finally expiated.

"And now this spell was snapped; once more
I viewed the ocean green,
And looked far forth, yet little saw
Of what had else been seen—

"Like one, that on a lonesome road
Doth walk in fear and dread,
And having once turned round walks on,
And turns no more his head;
Because he knows, a frightful fiend
Doth close behind him tread.

"But soon there breathed a wind on me,
Nor sound nor motion made:
Its path was not upon the sea,
In ripple or in shade.

"It raised my hair, it fanned my cheek
Like a meadow-gale of spring— ❼
It mingled strangely with my fears,
Yet it felt like a welcoming.

◆ Build Vocabulary

expiated (ěk′ spē āt′ əd) *v.*: Forgiven; absolved

36. **charnel dungeon:** Vault where corpses or bones are deposited.

Clarification To help students understand what is going on in lines 395–430, have three volunteers read the lines aloud. Assign to the volunteers the roles of Ancient Mariner (Narrator), First Voice, and Second Voice. Then guide them in reading their individual roles.

◆ Reading Strategy

❹ **Poetic Effects** Have students discuss how sound devices clarify meaning in this stanza. *Students may say the internal rhymes in line 428 drag it out, so that, like the ship it describes, it becomes slower.*

Customize for
English Language Learners

❺ Tell students that *belated* means "delayed" or "late" and that *abated* means "ended."

◆ Critical Thinking

❻ **Analyze** Instruct students to copy lines 432–433 on a separate sheet of paper and mark the stressed syllables. *The second, third, fourth, and sixth (and eighth, in line 432) syllables are stressed.* How does the pattern of stresses affect the mood of the lines? *Suggested response: It slows down the lines and adds emphasis. In line 432, it helps to create a sense of slow serenity. In line 433, it creates a sense of shocking contrast with the peaceful image in line 432 and a mood of grim finality.*

◆ Critical Thinking

❼ **Connect** Point out to students the simile in lines 456–457. Ask them why the reference to a meadow is especially significant. *Students should recognize that the reference to a meadow (land) suggests that safety and rescue may be near at hand for the Mariner.*

Speaking and Listening Mini-Lesson

Panel Discussion

This mini-lesson supports the Speaking and Listening Mini-Lesson on page 655.

Introduce the Concept Discuss how sharing points of view, knowledge, and expertise can lead to a creative development of ideas. Explain that in a panel discussion, a group of experts discusses an issue in front of an audience. At the end of the discussion, the panel usually receives questions and comments from the audience.

Develop Background Have students consider the following tips for their panel discussion:

- Individuals involved in group discussion should offer carefully reasoned arguments.
- Information presented to the panel should be well documented and clearly explained.
- Organizing the discussion around specific topic ideas is a useful structure.

Apply the Information Provide an appropriate time limit on each group, such as eight minutes for the discussion and two minutes for questions from the audience. Remind all students to be respectful speakers and listeners.

Assess the Outcome Have students evaluate each panel's discussion: Were a range of ideas exchanged? Did panelists listen carefully to one another and respond thoughtfully? Did individual panelists participate fully?

▶Critical Viewing◀

❶ **Connect** Students may say that this illustration more accurately depicts events very early in the poem, when the ship is storm-tossed. In Part V, though the ship sails swiftly, the sailing is "smooth." The image is not being portrayed from the Mariner's view but rather from above.

◆ Reading Strategy

❷ **Poetic Effects** Ask students to identify the alliteration in this stanza. *Alliteration appears with the repeated initial s sound in* swiftly, sailed, softly, *and* sweetly. *It also occurs with repeated b sounds in blew and breeze.* What is the effect of the alliteration? *It creates a sense of softness and of a whispering wind.*

Customize for
English Language Learners

❸ Define unfamiliar words to aid student comprehension. *Kirk* means "church;" *countree* means "country;" *o'er* is a poetic contraction of "over;" *alway* means "always." A *harbor bar* is a sandbar or breakwater across the mouth of a harbor. The bar breaks the impact of waves, so the water in a harbor is relatively calm.

◆ Critical Thinking

Support Prompt students to explain the Mariner's return journey. Ask them to cite evidence to support a conclusion of either a normal or supernatural sailing. *Students should conclude that the sailing is miraculous, at least in part. The ship travels so fast that the Mariner needs to be entranced to survive it. Also, the breeze in line 463 blows only on the Mariner.*

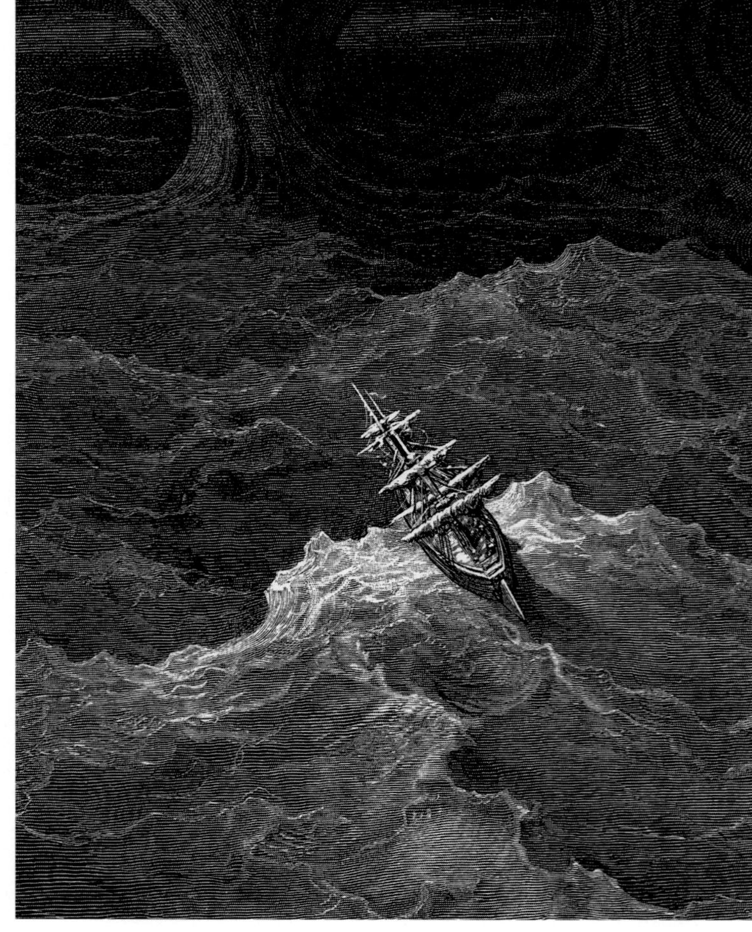

Engraving by Gustave Doré for "The Rime of the Ancient Mariner" by Samuel Taylor Coleridge

◀ **Critical Viewing** How closely can you connect this illustration to the events in the poem? Is the image being portrayed from the Ancient Mariner's point of view? Why or why not? **[Connect]** ❶

"Swiftly, swiftly flew the ship,
Yet she sailed softly too:
Sweetly, sweetly blew the breeze—
On me alone it blew. ❷

And the ancient Mariner beholdeth his native country.

"Oh! dream of joy! is this indeed
The lighthouse top I see?
Is this the hill? is this the kirk?
Is this mine own countree? ❸

Humanities: Art

Engraving for "The Rime of the Ancient Mariner," 1875, by Gustave Doré.

This illustration, while one of the series created for Coleridge's poem, does not exactly depict events in Part VI. Rather it evokes the ship's isolation throughout the poem.

The French engraver, Gustave Doré, shared the exuberance of Romantic lyric poets and illustrated many other Romantic works. In addition, Doré is credited with developing a technique called the illustration chronicle. In these generally chronological sequences of illustrations, an apparently unrelated grouping of images or visual effects was scattered, almost collage-like.

Use these questions for discussion:

1. How does the light in the illustration relate to the Mariner's description of events? *The light is only on the boat, just as the wind blows only on the Mariner and his ship.*
2. What element of the composition reflects the Mariner's spiritual experience? *The boat is isolated amidst a sea of dark and turbulent water; the Mariner is spiritually isolated amidst the dark and turbulent experiences of death and despair.*

"We drifted o'er the harbor bar,
And I with sobs did pray— ❸
O let me be awake, my God!
Or let me sleep alway.

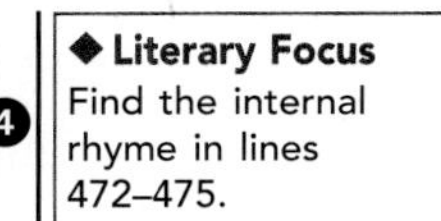
◆ **Literary Focus**
❹ Find the internal rhyme in lines 472–475.

"The harbor bay was clear as glass,
So smoothly it was strewn![37]
And on the bay the moonlight lay,
And the shadow of the Moon.

"The rock shone bright, the kirk no less,
That stands above the rock;
The moonlight steeped in silentness
The steady weathercock.

The angelic spirits leave the dead bodies,

"And the bay was white with silent light,
Till rising from the same, ❺
Full many shapes, that shadows were,
In crimson colors came.

And appear in their own forms of light.

"A little distance from the prow
Those crimson shadows were;
I turned my eyes upon the deck—
Oh, Christ! what saw I there!

"Each corse lay flat, lifeless and flat,
And, by the holy rood![38]
A man all light, a seraph[39] man, ❻
On every corse there stood.

"This seraph band, each waved his hand:
It was a heavenly sight!
They stood as signals to the land,
Each one a lovely light;

"This seraph band, each waved his hand,
No voice did they impart—
No voice; but oh! the silence sank ❼
Like music on my heart.

"But soon I heard the dash of oars,
I heard the Pilot's cheer;
My head was turned perforce away
And I saw a boat appear.

"The Pilot and the Pilot's boy,
I heard them coming fast:
Dear Lord in Heaven! it was a joy
The dead men could not blast.

---

37. **strewn:** Spread.
38. **rood:** Cross.
39. **seraph:** Angel.

◆ Literary Focus

❹ **Poetic Effects** The internal rhyme, *bay/lay,* is in line 474.

◆ Grammar and Style

❺ **Inverted Word Order** Challenge students to reorganize these lines into standard word order. *Possible reorganization: The bay was white with silent light until many crimson shadows rose from it.*

❻ **Clarification** Explain that *corse* in lines 488 and 491 is a version of *corpse.*

◆ Literature and Your Life

❼ Point out the simile here comparing silence and music. Ask students to recall moments when they experienced silence as not so silent. *Students may mention times when silence felt ominous or soothing, when its mood seemed to lend it sound.*

Enrichment

In his introduction to *Twentieth Century Interpretations of "The Rime of the Ancient Mariner,"* James D. Boulger discusses the imaginative, other-worldly qualities of the Mariner's voyage:

> In the world of Imagination in which the voyage takes place four aspects are noticeable, as evidence that the world of the poem is quite different from the land world—
>
> 1. the "Dream" quality of the voyage and all its events, with the participation of reality, living and nonliving in one organic whole, and the unending series of shifts between subjects and objects, sights and sounds, in the phenomena of the perceived world;
> 2. a special kind of logic, or "non-logic" if you will, in the main events and symbols of the poem;
> 3. a machinery of "spirits" of various orders not found in the ordinary world;
> 4. a special definition of appearance and reality, substance and surface, developed in the descriptions of objects, especially the sea, during the voyage.
>
> Taken together, this special world contributes to define the nature of the major parable (Fall, redemption, scepticism, spiritual will, and Faith) not merely by [decree] and statement, but as the total poetic logic of the poem.

Customize for
Interpersonal Learners
Working in pairs, prompt these learners to summarize Part VI for their partners. Encourage pairs to discuss and clarify any discrepancies between the two summaries, referring to the text as needed. *Summaries should include: The Mariner is entranced by angelic power while his boat is sped miraculously northward to home; sensing spirits around him, he feels reassured by the wind; joy at seeing his home mixes with horror over the now lifeless corpses all around him; the harbor Pilot, with a Hermit on board, approaches the Mariner's ship, which is lit by angels; the Mariner wishes for absolution from the holy Hermit.*

◆ Critical Thinking

❶ **Interpret** Ask students what the Mariner wishes for in these lines. *The Mariner wishes for forgiveness of his crime; he hopes the Hermit can absolve him of sin.*

◆ Literary Focus

❷ **Poetic Sound Devices**
Challenge students to locate examples of internal rhyme, alliteration, and consonance in this stanza. *The internal rhyme good/wood occurs in line 514. An example of alliteration is the s sound at the beginning of slopes, sea, and sweet. An example of consonance is the s sound at the end of this, lives, slopes, voice, loves, and mariners.*

Customize for
Less Proficient Readers
❸ Urge students to read carefully for signals that characters other than the Mariner are speaking. Quotation marks and introductory remarks such as "the Hermit said" are useful signposts.

Customize for
English Language Learners
❹ Terms in this passage may be unfamiliar to English language learners. *Cheer* means "hail" or "call." *Sere* means "dried up." *Aught* means "anything." *Perchance* means "maybe." *Lag*, in this context, means "clog" or "slow down."

"I saw a third—I heard his voice:
It is the Hermit good!
He singeth loud his godly hymns ❶
That he makes in the wood.
He'll shrieve[40] my soul, he'll wash away
The Albatross's blood.

Part VII

The Hermit of the Wood,

"This Hermit good lives in that wood
Which slopes down to the sea.
How loudly his sweet voice he rears! ❷
He loves to talk with mariners
That come from a far countree.

"He kneels at morn, and noon, and eve—
He hath a cushion plump:
It is the moss that wholly hides
The rotted old oak-stump.

"The skiff boat neared; I heard them talk.
'Why, this is strange, I trow![41]
Where are those lights so many and fair,
That signal made but now?' ❸

Approacheth the ship with wonder.

"'Strange, by my faith!' the Hermit said—
'And they answered not our cheer!
The planks looked warped! and see those sails,
How thin they are and sere!
I never saw aught like to them, ❹
Unless perchance it were

"'Brown skeletons of leaves that lag
My forest brook along;
When the ivy tod[42] is heavy with snow,
And the owlet whoops to the wolf below,
That eats the she-wolf's young.'

"'Dear Lord! it hath a fiendish look'
(The Pilot made reply)
'I am a-feared'—'Push on, push on!'
Said the Hermit cheerily.

"The boat came closer to the ship,
But I nor spake nor stirred;
The boat came close beneath the ship,
And straight[43] a sound was heard.

---

40. **shrieve** (shrēv): Absolve from sin.
41. **trow:** Believe.
42. **tod:** Bush.
43. **straight:** Immediately.

Beyond the Classroom

Career Connection

Philosopher The Hermit who appears late in the Mariner's story has achieved wisdom and holiness through time spent contemplating ideas rather than interacting with others. Such a thinker might also be called a philosopher. Philosophy is the "love or pursuit of wisdom" and can trace its history to ancient Greek culture. Have interested students learn about the five branches of philosophy: metaphysics; logic; epistemology; ethics; and aesthetics. Then discuss as a class how the role of the philosopher—or thinker—is valued in our contemporary society.

Community Connection

Institutions for Thought In this poem, the Hermit uses his wisdom to pass judgment on the Mariner. Today, communities assign the task of evaluating behavior to many different institutions. Research institutions, or think-tanks, review ethics and policies; religious orders reflect on humanity's relationship with the divine; and, universities study the meaning of human behavior. Invite students to identify and evaluate the power of the institutions in your community charged with the analysis of ideas or policies.

Engraving by Gustave Doré for "The Rime of the Ancient Mariner" by Samuel Taylor Coleridge

❺ ▶ **Critical Viewing** In what way does this illustration help you predict how the albatross will first be treated by the sailors? **[Predict]**

The ship suddenly sinketh.

"Under the water it rumbled on,
Still louder and more dread;
It reached the ship, it split the bay;
The ship went down like lead.

The ancient Mariner is saved in the Pilot's boat.

"Stunned by that loud and dreadful sound,
Which sky and ocean smote,
Like one that hath been seven days drowned
My body lay afloat;
But swift as dreams, myself I found
Within the Pilot's boat.

"Upon the whirl, where sank the ship, ❻
The boat spun round and round;
And all was still, save that the hill
Was telling of the sound. ❼

"I moved my lips—the Pilot shrieked
And fell down in a fit; ❽
The holy Hermit raised his eyes,
And prayed where he did sit.

▶Critical Viewing◀

❺ **Predict** The illustration shows the bundled-up sailors grinning at the bird in a friendly manner and trying to entice it with bits of food. From this, students could have predicted that the bird would be regarded with favor at first.

◆ Reading Strategy

❻ **Poetic Effects** Ask students to identify the internal rhyme in these lines. *The internal rhyme located in line 558 is still/hill.* Discuss how the rhyme adds momentum to the already accelerating content.

Comprehension Check ☑

❼ What does Coleridge mean by "the hill/ Was telling of the sound"? *It means that the sound of the ship sinking echoed off the hill.*

◆ Literature and Your Life

❽ Discuss with students the two reactions displayed here to a frightening sight: shrieking and praying. How have students responded when faced with a startling stimulus? *Students may say that they too pray or that they react physically with sweaty palms or racing heart, or that they proactively engage with the stimulus.*

Humanities: Art

Engraving for "The Rime of the Ancient Mariner," 1875, by Gustave Doré.

Between 1855 and 1865, Doré focused heavily on illustrating literary texts. These woodcuts accompanied such well-known works as Dante's *Inferno* and Cervantes' *Don Quixote*. Doré's efforts to illustrate an 1865 edition of the Bible were hugely ambitious and are today considered among his most highly successful. In this engraving, Doré's evocative portrayal of the sailors clustering together to gawk at the enormous Albatross adds a extra dimension of meaning to Coleridge's words.

Use these questions for discussion:

1. What lines in the poem might have inspired this engraving? *Lines 63–65 may have inspired it.*
2. How does the engraving convey the sailors' attitude? *Their foolish grins, amazed expressions, and arms stretched out to offer food indicate the sailors' feelings.*

Customize for
More Advanced Students

In *Specimens of the Table Talk of Samuel Taylor Coleridge,* Henry Nelson Coleridge recounts the following anecdote told by his uncle about "The Rime of the Ancient Mariner": "Mrs. Barbauld once told me that she admired the Ancient Mariner very much, but there were two faults in it,—it was improbable and had no moral. As for the probability, I owned that that might admit some question; but as to the want of a moral, I told her that in my judgment the poem had too much. . . ."

Ask students to reflect on this as they read the poem's closing lines. Do they agree with Mrs. Barbauld or the poet? Why?

◆ Critical Thinking

❶ **Connect** Ask students why the Mariner must tell his tale. *It is a continuing punishment for killing the Albatross.* Challenge students to identify where this outcome was foreshadowed. *It is foreshadowed by the words of the second voice at the end of Part V: "'The man hath penance done,/ And penance more will do.'"*

◆ Literature and Your Life

❷ Discuss the Mariner's feelings in these lines, noting how he treasures human company. Ask students to describe what companionship means to them and to mention any experiences that have influenced their feelings about human company. *Students may comment that their friends and companions are important in their lives just now; they may mention absences or life changes that enhanced their attachment to the companionship of friends and family.*

◆ Critical Thinking

❸ **Apply** Ask students: How might this advice be especially useful for today's world? *Students should recognize that universal love of the world's creatures would lessen political and ethnic strife as well as environmental damage.*

Art Transparency

Place Art Transparency 8, *Dialogue of Two Poets Disguised as Birds,* by Alfred Castañeda, on an overhead and ask the class to note the ways in which its combination of realistic and fantastic elements mirrors Coleridge's treatment of those elements in "The Rime of the Ancient Mariner."

"I took the oars; the Pilot's boy,
Who now doth crazy go,
Laughed loud and long, and all the while
His eyes went to and fro.
'Ha! ha!' quoth he, 'full plain I see,
The Devil knows how to row.'

"And now, all in my own countree,
I stood on the firm land!
The Hermit stepped forth from the boat,
And scarcely he could stand.

The ancient Mariner earnestly entreateth the Hermit to shrieve him; and the penance of life falls on him.

"'O shrieve me, shrieve me, holy man!'
The Hermit crossed his brow.[44]
'Say, quick,' quoth he, 'I bid thee say—
What manner of man art thou?'

"Forthwith this frame of mine was wrenched
With a woeful agony,
Which forced me to begin my tale;
And then it left me free.

And ever and anon through out his future life an agony constraineth him to travel from land to land;

"Since then, at an uncertain hour,
That agony returns;
And till my ghastly tale is told,
This heart within me burns. ❶

"I pass, like night, from land to land;
I have strange power of speech;
That moment that his face I see,
I know the man that must hear me:
To him my tale I teach.

"What loud uproar bursts from that door!
The wedding guests are there;
But in the garden bower the bride
And bridemaids singing are;
And hark the little vesper bell,
Which biddeth me to prayer!

"O Wedding Guest! this soul hath been
Alone on a wide wide sea:
So lonely 'twas, that God himself
Scarce seemed there to be. ❷

"O sweeter than the marriage feast,
'Tis sweeter far to me,
To walk together to the kirk
With a goodly company!—

44. **crossed his brow:** Made the sign of the cross on his forehead.

Beyond the Selection

FURTHER READING

Other Works by Coleridge

"Christabel"; *Biographia Literaria; Remorse; Aids to Reflection*

Other Works About Redemption

"God's Grandeur," Gerard Manley Hopkins; "Redemption," Herbert of Cherbury (Edward Herbert); *Paradise Regained,* John Milton

We suggest that you preview these works before recommending them to students.

INTERNET

You and your students may find additional information about Samuel Taylor Coleridge at the following sites.

The Coleridge homepage is at **http://www.cc.gatech.edu/home/idris/Poetry/Coleridge.htm**

To read critical essays about Coleridge, visit **http://andromeda.ociw.edu/LITERATURE/Coleridge.html**

We *strongly recommend* that you preview the sites before you send students to them.

And to teach, by his own example, love and reverence to all things that God made and loveth.

"To walk together to the kirk,
And all together pray,
While each to his great Father bends,
Old men, and babes, and loving friends
And youths and maidens gay!

"Farewell, farewell! but this I tell
To thee, thou Wedding Guest!
He prayeth well, who loveth well
Both man and bird and beast. ❸

"He prayeth best, who loveth best
All things both great and small:
For the dear God who loveth us,
He made and loveth all." ❹

The Mariner, whose eye is bright,
Whose beard with age is hoar,
Is gone; and now the Wedding Guest
Turned from the bridegroom's door.

He went like one that hath been stunned
And is of sense forlorn;
A sadder and a wiser man,
He rose the morrow morn.

◆ **Build Vocabulary**

reverence (rēv´ ər əns) *n.*: Respect

Guide for Responding

◆ Literature and Your Life

Reader's Response What was your reaction to the Ancient Mariner's story? Explain.

Thematic Focus In what ways is this poem a blend of the real and the fantastic?

Sentence the Mariner What kind of punishment would you mete out to the Mariner? Explain.

☑ Check Your Comprehension

1. What "hellish thing" does the Mariner do, and how do the other sailors react to it?
2. What happens to the Mariner's shipmates soon after the appearance of the Specter Woman and her Death-mate in Part III?
3. What does the Mariner hope the hermit will do for him?
4. What is the Mariner's lifelong penance?

◆ Critical Thinking

INTERPRET

1. Why do you think Coleridge chose a wedding as the destination of the Mariner's listener? **[Interpret]**
2. What do you think the Albatross symbolizes? Find evidence to support your answer. **[Interpret]**
3. As soon as the Mariner feels love, the albatross falls off his neck. Why do you think this happens? **[Infer]**
4. In what ways might the journey of the Mariner be seen as spiritual as well as actual? **[Analyze]**

EVALUATE

5. Coleridge includes both realistic and supernatural descriptions. Why do you think he includes both kinds in this poem? **[Evaluate]**

◆ Critical Thinking

❹ **Draw Conclusions** Point out to students that these lines reveal the theme, or moral, or the tale. Ask them to restate that moral, using lines from the poem for support. *Students should recognize that the tale's moral is to love all things, both great and small. Support from the text should include the turning point, when the Mariner's love for the sea snakes begins his redemption.*

Comprehension Check ☑

Have students summarize Part VII. *Summaries should include: The Pilot boat and Mariner's ship converge. When the Pilot and Hermit see the Mariner and his surroundings, the Pilot collapses and the Hermit prays. The Mariner requests absolution from the Hermit. The Mariner is compelled to tell his tale. The Mariner rejoins human company with greater appreciation for it and with a new value for love of all things.*

◆ Literature and Your Life

Discuss with students the suffering the Mariner must endure to gain new wisdom and appreciation of life. Do students feel suffering is necessary to such insights? *Some students will say suffering enhances people's ability to appreciate life while others will say it is an unnecessary prompt.*

Customize for
Less Proficient Readers

Urge less proficient readers to read the poem several times. Suggest that they keep a reader's response log for notes or clarifying data. Direct them to read a final time solely for emotional impact.

Reinforce and Extend

Answers

◆ Literature and Your Life

Reader's Response Most students will find it disturbing or fantastic.

Thematic Focus The poem combines realistic descriptions and characters with supernatural events.

☑ Check Your Comprehension

1. The Mariner shoots the Albatross with a crossbow. At first the sailors were angry. Then they praised the Mariner.
2. The Mariner's shipmates drop dead.
3. The Mariner hopes the Hermit will absolve him of his sin.
4. He has to wander the earth telling his tale and teaching love for all things both great and small.

◆ Critical Thinking

1. The lighthearted festivities of a wedding contrast with the events of the story.
2. Possible responses: The Albatross is a symbol of guilt for the way man treats nature; it symbolizes nature and how in nature everything is connected, including humans.
3. It means his guilt is forgiven.
4. The Mariner's journey symbolizes one's spiritual passage through life—from innocence to sin to grace and penitence.
5. Suggested response: Including the realistic makes the story more credible; including the supernatural makes it more dramatic and memorable.

Develop Understanding

One-Minute Insight This poem captures the Romantic love of nature and interest in the exotic, the faraway, and the strange. The speaker imagines the sumptuous pleasure dome of Kubla Khan. By portraying that fantasy so vividly, the speaker demonstrates the extraordinary power of the imagination.

Enrichment This poem was inspired by a passage about Kubla Khan, the founder of the Mongol dynasty in China in the thirteenth century, in Samuel Purchas's *Purchas His Pilgrimage (1613):* "Here the Khan Kubla commanded a palace to be built, and a stately garden thereunto. And thus ten miles of fertile ground were inclosed with a wall." Coleridge claims to have fallen asleep while reading this passage due to the effects of medication he was taking for an illness at the time (1797). Three hours later, he awoke from a dream, finding his mind was filled with two to three hundred lines of poetry, which were an elaboration of the description he had read immediately before drifting off to sleep. Coleridge immediately began to write down the lines that filled his head, but when he was interrupted by a visitor, he forgot the lines that he had not yet transcribed. As a result, he was unable to complete the poem.

►Critical Viewing◄

❶ Compare and Contrast
Similarities include encircling walls, a garden, an elaborate building with domes, and a river (the stylized arcs at the bottom of the box). Differences may include the scale of the palace, ice caves, and romantic chasm.

Customize for
English Language Learners
❷ Point out that in this context, *pants* means "heavy breaths," not "trousers."

Kubla Khan

Samuel Taylor Coleridge

Box and Cover, Ming Dynasty, first half of 16th century, The Seattle Art Museum

▲ **Critical Viewing**
Coleridge's images of the pleasure dome seem based partly on what he knew about ancient Chinese culture. ❶ How do they compare with the details on this sixteenth-century box cover?
[Compare and Contrast]

In Xanadu[1] did Kubla Khan
A stately pleasure dome decree:
Where Alph,[2] the sacred river, ran
Through caverns measureless to man
Down to a sunless sea.
So twice five miles of fertile ground
With walls and towers were girdled round;
And there were gardens bright with sinuous rills,[3]
Where blossomed many an incense-bearing tree;
And here were forests ancient as the hills,
Enfolding sunny spots of greenery.

But oh! that deep romantic chasm which slanted
Down the green hill athwart[4] a cedarn cover![5]
A savage place! as holy and enchanted
As e'er beneath a waning moon was haunted
By woman wailing for her demon lover!
And from this chasm, with ceaseless turmoil seething,
❷ As if this earth in fast thick pants were breathing.
A mighty fountain momently was forced;
Amid whose swift half-intermitted burst
Huge fragments vaulted like rebounding hail,
Or chaffy grain beneath the thresher's flail;

---

1. **Xanadu** (zan′ ə do͞o): Indefinite area in China.
2. **Alph:** Probably derived from the Greek river Alpheus, the waters of which, it was believed in Greek mythology, joined with a stream to form a fountain in Sicily.
3. **rills:** Brooks.
4. **athwart:** Across.
5. **cedarn cover:** Covering of cedar trees.

Humanities: Art

Box and Cover, first half of 16th century.

This lacquer box cover shows a Chinese palace or large estate much like the one Coleridge describes in his poem.

In sixteenth-century China, Ming artisans responded creatively to the demands of an increasingly wealthy—and consumer-oriented—merchant class. A box such as this one was typical of the precise and delicate workmanship prized by wealthy clients. Its picture is pieced together from minute slivers and petals of mother-of-pearl, shaped in myriad ways to represent buildings, natural elements, and figures. Additional details, such as the elaborate designs on the clothing, are made from individual pieces.

Use these questions for discussion:

1. How might the poem's Kubla Khan feel about this box and cover? *He'd probably want it for his palace.*
2. What elements of the box and cover reflect the sumptuousness of the poem's descriptions? *The bright and glittering mother-of-pearl, and the elaborate level of detail both reflect the luxuriousness of Coleridge's palace.*

And 'mid these dancing rocks at once and ever
It flung up momently the sacred river.
❸ Five miles meandering with a mazy motion
Through wood and dale the sacred river ran,
Then reached the caverns measureless to man,
And sank in tumult to a lifeless ocean:
And 'mid this tumult Kubla heard from far
Ancestral voices prophesying war!
The shadow of the dome of pleasure
Floated midway on the waves;
Where was heard the mingled measure
From the fountain and the caves.
It was a miracle of rare device.[6]
A sunny pleasure dome with caves of ice!

A damsel with a dulcimer[7]
In a vision once I saw:
It was an Abyssinian[8] maid,
And on her dulcimer she played,
Singing of Mount Abora.[9]
Could I revive within me
Her symphony and song,
To such a deep delight 'twould win me,
That with music loud and long,
I would build that dome in air,
That sunny dome! those caves of ice!
❹ And all who heard should see them there,
And all should cry, Beware! Beware!
His flashing eyes, his floating hair!
Weave a circle round him thrice,
And close your eyes with holy dread,
For he on honeydew hath fed,
And drunk the milk of Paradise.

---

6. **device:** Design.
7. **dulcimer:** (dul´ sə mər) *n.*; Musical instrument with metal strings which produce sounds when struck by two small hammers.
8. **Abyssinian** (ab ə sin´ ē ən): Ethiopian.
9. **Mount Abora:** Probably Mount Amara in Abyssinia.

◆ Build Vocabulary

sinuous (sin´ yo͞o əs) *adj.*: Bending, winding, or curving in and out

tumult (to͞o´ mult´) *n.*: Noisy commotion

Guide for Responding

◆ Literature and Your Life

Reader's Response Were you drawn to the description of Kubla Khan's pleasure dome? Did it remind you of any place you know?

Thematic Focus Do you think the world of this poem was an escape from the real world for Coleridge? How does Xanadu resemble a fantasy?

☑ Check Your Comprehension

1. What was the size of the palatial estate ordered to be built by Kubla Khan?
2. What did Kubla Khan hear over the noise made by the river emptying into the ocean?
3. According to the last stanza, what did the speaker once see in a vision?

◆ Critical Thinking

INTERPRET

1. Using your own words, explain what the speaker says would happen to him and "all who heard" if he were able to revive his vision. **[Interpret]**
2. Kubla Khan's pleasure dome seems both like a paradise on earth and like something sinister. Which elements make it beautiful? What is sinister about it? **[Analyze]**
3. What statement do you think Coleridge is making about the power of the imagination? **[Draw Conclusions]**

EVALUATE

4. Do you feel that Coleridge's imagination and "music" combine to make his vision real to the reader? Support your answer. **[Criticize]**

Literature CD-ROM Encourage students to view Feature 5 in *How to Read and Understand Poetry.* This feature uses "Kubla Khan" as an example in a discussion of how poets show us things we haven't noticed or help us to better understand thoughts and feelings.

◆ Reading Strategy

❸ **Poetic Effects** Ask students to identify the alliteration in this line. Discuss how it works with the rhythm of the line to imitate the motion of the river. *The alliteration includes the initial m sounds: Five miles meandering with a mazy motion.*

◆ Literature and Your Life

❹ Discuss how this poem presents the power of imagination. Ask students whether they feel more affected by their imagination and emotions or by their reason. Which influence do they feel is more appropriate? *Students will be divided among those who feel more influenced by emotion and those who find reason more compelling. Most will likely say that a balance of influences is most appropriate.*

Reinforce and Extend

Answers

◆ Literature and Your Life

Reader's Response Students may be reminded of gardens, museums, theme parks, or resorts.

Thematic Focus Coleridge uses his imagination to create a kind of surreal reality with singing damsels, ancestral voices, and sunny domes with caves of ice.

☑ Check Your Comprehension

1. The grounds of the pleasure dome were "twice five miles" in size.
2. Kubla Khan heard "Ancestral voices prophesying war!"
3. The speaker once saw a damsel singing and playing a dulcimer.

(Critical Thinking answers appear on page 654.)

Cross-Curricular Connection: Social Studies

Kubla Khan's grandfather, Genghis Khan, began the Mongols' road to conquest by uniting his own people. He then conquered China and parts of Europe in the early thirteenth century. The Mongols raised the status of merchants in China and encouraged trade with the outside world by patroling the trade route known as the Silk Road. It was the Silk Road that brought Venetian merchant Marco Polo to China later in the thirteenth century. A special relationship arose between the ruler Kubla Khan and the merchant, who joined Khan's civil service for some twenty years.

Have students read passages from Polo's *Travels of Marco Polo* and compare these descriptions of Kubla Khan's empire with those of Samuel Taylor Coleridge.

Answers

◆ Critical Thinking

1. They would cry "beware" and form a circle around him three times and close their eyes in fear.
2. Beautiful elements include "gardens bright with sinuous rills," incense-bearing trees in blossom, and "sunny spots of greenery." Sinister elements include "a sunless sea," "a waning moon," "woman wailing for her demon lover," and "lifeless ocean."
3. Suggested response: The imagination is all-powerful in creating its own reality.
4. Students may say that Coleridge's vividly imagined details and "music" created by sound devices make his vision seem real. Others may say the imagery is too strange to seem "real."

◆ Literary Focus

1. The initial *h* sounds are the alliteration in lines 9-12: "He holds him with his skinny hand, . . ."
2. He uses consonance and internal rhyme.
3. The long *i* sound creates assonance: "Whiles all the night . . . white . . ."
4. Assonance is the sound device used: "But oh! that deep romantic chasm which slanted."
5. They make the last few lines of "Kubla Khan" more musical and hypnotic, enhancing the description of the wild-eyed visionary.

◆ Reading Strategy

1. Suggested response: Coleridge uses the many *s* sounds to give the scene a mood of stillness and serenity. Most students will say that the use of sound devices helps Coleridge set a mood.
2. Coleridge uses alliteration, consonance, and assonance to create memorable images, hypnotic rhythms, and a mood of fantasy.

◆ Grammar and Style

1. That moment that I see his face.
2. She is red as a rose.
3. At length, an Albatross did cross. . .
4. Nodding their heads, the merry minstrelsy goes before her.
5. Whiles all the night . . . the white moonshine glimmered.

Guide for Responding *(continued)*

◆ Literary Focus

Poetic Sound Devices

Coleridge skillfully uses **poetic sound devices** such as alliteration, consonance, assonance, and internal rhyme within his poetry. These sound devices, in addition to pleasing the ear, create vivid imagery, help to establish mood, and make the poetic lines interesting and memorable.

1. Find an example of alliteration in lines 9–12 of "The Rime of the Ancient Mariner."
2. What two sound devices does Coleridge use in the line: "It cracked and growled and roared and howled"?
3. Which words in this line create assonance? "Whiles all the night through fog-smoke white . . ."
4. What sound device is evident in this line from "Kubla Khan": "But oh! that deep romantic chasm which slanted"?
5. In what way do the sound devices in lines 45–54 enhance the mood and meaning of what is being described?

◆ Reading Strategy

Poetic Effects

In these poems by Coleridge, **poetic effects** are created by sound devices such as alliteration, consonance, assonance, and rhyme. These sound devices please the ear, reinforce meaning, and create mood. In lines 41–44 of "The Rime of the Ancient Mariner," for example, the use of alliteration and consonance enables you almost to hear the hissing of the sea foam as the ship is tossed about.

1. Reread lines 472–483 of "The Rime of the Ancient Mariner." State the feeling you think Coleridge was trying to establish. Tell whether, in your opinion, his use of sound devices helps, and give your reasons.
2. What sound devices does Coleridge use in the first stanza of "Kubla Khan"? Explain how the sound devices enhance the poem's mood, imagery, and appeal or "catchiness."

◆ Grammar and Style

Inverted Word Order

When poets create certain rhymes, rhythms, or word pictures, they sometimes **invert word order**, or change the normal English word order of subject-verb-complement. For example, to rhyme *drowned* and *found,* Coleridge inverted the standard word order "I found myself."

Like one that hath been seven days *drowned*
My body lay afloat
But swift as dreams, myself I *found*

Practice In your notebook, rewrite these lines in standard word order.

1. That moment that his face I see.
2. Red as a rose is she.
3. At length did cross an Albatross . . .
4. Nodding their heads before her goes/ The merry minstrelsy.
5. Whiles all the night . . ./Glimmered the white Moonshine.

Writing Application Write poetic lines in which you invert normal word order. You may find it helpful to begin with standard word order, then invert subject, verb, and object to achieve rhyme or rhythm.

◆ Build Vocabulary

Using the Word Root *-journ-*

The word root *-journ-* means "day." Explain how the root contributes to the meaning of each of these words. If necessary, use a dictionary.

1. journey **2.** adjourn **3.** journalism

Using the Word Bank

Write the word or phrase whose meaning is most opposite to that of the first word.

1. sinuous: (a) narrow, (b) straight, (c) dark
2. expiated: (a) sold, (b) atoned, (c) sinned
3. averred: (a) denied, (b) claimed, (c) wished
4. reverence: (a) respect, (b) contempt, (c) hope
5. tumult: (a) peace, (b) pleasure, (c) wealth
6. sojourn: (a) leave, (b) visit, (c) rest

◆ Build Vocabulary

Using the Word Root *-journ-*

1. *journey:* day's trip
2. *adjourn:* to close for the day
3. *journalism:* the news of the day

Using the Word Bank

1. b 2. c 3. a 4. b
5. a 6. a

Writer's Solution

For additional instruction and practice, use the lesson on Special Problems in Agreement in the **Language Lab CD-ROM** and the page on Inverted Patterns in the *Writer's Solution Grammar Practice Book,* p. 23.

Build Your Portfolio

Idea Bank

Writing

1. Utopia Coleridge was deeply interested in forming a Utopian, or perfect, community. Write a short paper describing what a Utopia of your own might be like.

2. Response to the Poem Write a short paper explaining why you would or would not want to visit Xanadu.

3. Response to the Poet Coleridge wrote that poetry should arouse "the sympathy of the reader by a faithful adherence to the truth of nature" while "giving the interest of novelty by modifying colors of the imagination." Write an essay in which you explain whether he has done that in "The Rime of the Ancient Mariner."

Speaking and Listening

4. Dramatic Reading With a group of classmates, present a dramatic reading of a section of "The Rime of the Ancient Mariner." Assign parts and rehearse your reading, striving to evoke the atmosphere in the poem. **[Performing Arts Link]**

5. Panel Discussion With a small group of classmates, hold a panel discussion on what you think people can learn from their dreams. **[Science Link]**

Projects

6. Research Project Wordsworth and Coleridge were successful poetic collaborators. Research portraits, letters, and other primary sources that give information about their friendship and writing. Present your findings to the class. **[Literature Link]**

7. Illustrated Journey Create a poster-sized collage that illustrates the Ancient Mariner's journey. Represent major events from the story realistically or symbolically. **[Art Link]**

Writing Mini-Lesson

Poem With Sound Effects

Coleridge and many other poets use sound devices to add music and beauty to their poems. Write a poem describing an imaginary world like the one in "Kubla Khan." In your poem, use a variety of sound devices such as rhyme, alliteration, assonance, and consonance.

Writing Skills Focus: Dramatic Effects Through Sound

Use **sound devices** to help establish the mood of your poem and to create a dramatic effect that will engage your readers. For example, notice how the sound devices in this stanza from "The Rime of the Ancient Mariner" reinforce the actions that Coleridge is describing and draw the reader into these actions.

Model From Literature

"The ice was here, the ice was there, / The ice was all around; / It cracked and growled, and roared and howled, / Like noises in a swound!"

Use the following strategies as you draft your poem.

Prewriting Use your imagination to come up with a fantastic setting that you can bring to life in your poem. Jot down details that capture how this setting looks, sounds, smells, and feels. Brainstorm for rhyming words, alliterative phrases, and other effective sound devices to use in creating your setting.

Drafting Using the details you've gathered, draft your poem. Then use a variety of sound devices to reinforce meaning and draw readers into the world you're describing.

Revising Read your poem aloud, first to yourself and then to some classmates. To strengthen it, add sound devices or improve upon the ones you've already created.

✓ ASSESSMENT OPTIONS

Formal Assessment, Selection Test, pp. 157–159, and Assessment Resources Software. The selection test is designed so that it can be easily customized to the performance levels of your students. ***Alternative Assessment,*** p. 32, includes options for less advanced students, more advanced students, visual/spatial learners, verbal/linguistic learners, and intrapersonal learners.

PORTFOLIO ASSESSMENT
Use the following rubrics in the ***Alternative Assessment*** booklet to assess student writing:
Utopia: Description Rubric, p. 98
Response to the Poem: Cause-Effect Rubric, p. 103
Response to the Poet: Critical Review Rubric, p. 112
Writing Mini-Lesson: Poetry Rubric, p. 109

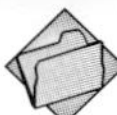

Idea Bank

Customizing for *Performance Levels*
Following are suggestions for matching Idea Bank topics with your students' performance levels:
- Less Advanced Students: 1, 5
- Average Students: 2, 4, 7
- More Advanced Students: 3, 6

Customizing for *Learning Modalities*
Following are suggestions for matching Idea Bank topics with your students' learning modalities:
- Visual/Spatial: 7
- Interpersonal: 4, 5
- Verbal/Linguistic: 1, 2, 3, 4, 5
- Musical/Rhythmic: 4

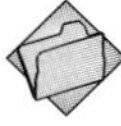

Writing Mini-Lesson

Refer students to the Writing Handbook, page 1189, for instruction on the writing process, and page 1192 for further information on creative writing.

Writers at Work Videodisc
Have students view the videodisc segment (Ch. 6) featuring Nobel laureate Derek Walcott to hear his thoughts on writing poetry. Have students discuss the importance of sound in poetry.

Play frames 9291 to 19694

Writing Lab CD-ROM
Have students complete the tutorial on Creative Writing. Follow these steps:
1. Examine the examples of sound devices in the audio-annotated Literary Models for poetry.
2. Use the audio examples of poetry for assistance and inspiration.
3. Create a draft on the computer.
4. Use the Proofreading Checklist for Poetry and Drama.

Sourcebook
Have students use Chapter 6, Creative Writing (pp. 167–195) for additional support. The chapter includes an annotated student model of a poem (p. 191).

Prepare and Engage

OBJECTIVES

1. To read, comprehend, and interpret poetry
2. To relate poetry to personal experience
3. To question to improve reading comprehension
4. To recognize figurative language
5. To build vocabulary in context and learn the suffix *-ous*
6. To develop skill in subject and verb agreement
7. To write a dramatic monologue, using realistic speech
8. To respond to the poems through writing, speaking and listening, and projects

SKILLS INSTRUCTION

Vocabulary: Suffixes: -ous
Grammar: Subject and Verb Agreement
Reading Strategy: Question
Literary Focus: Figurative Language
Writing: Realistic Speech
Speaking and Listening: Eulogy (teacher edition)
Critical Viewing: Analyze; Assess

PORTFOLIO OPPORTUNITIES

Writing: Health Regimen; Ocean's Response; Response to Criticism
Writing Mini-Lesson: Dramatic Monologue
Speaking and Listening: Oral Reading; Eulogy
Projects: Portrait; Music

More About the Author
George Gordon, Lord Byron, was born with a clubfoot, an affliction that shaped both his early years and his developing character. As a boy, he remained at home with a nurse for a tutor and was regarded as a sensitive child. As a young man, though his clubfoot was minimized by a brace, the abnormality contrasted with Byron's handsomeness and candid emotional verse to enhance his romantic reputation.

Guide for Interpreting

George Gordon, Lord Byron *(1788–1824)*

As famous for the life he led as for the things he wrote, George Gordon, Lord Byron, came from a long line of handsome but irresponsible aristocrats. Byron lived life in the "fast lane," and was looked on with disapproval by his contemporaries.

From Rags to Riches Byron was born in London, poor, but a member of the aristocracy. His father, a handsome ladies' man, died when Byron was just three years old. At the age of ten, while living in Aberdeen with his mother, Byron inherited his great-uncle's title, Baron, along with an estate at Newstead. Byron lived there until he was seventeen, when he left home to attend Trinity College at Cambridge.

A Zest for Life While at Cambridge Byron made lots of friends, played lots of sports, and spent lots of money. He even kept a pet bear. He also published a volume of verse, *Hours of Idleness* (1807), that received harsh criticism in Scotland's *Edinburgh Review.* In response he wrote his first major work, the satirical poem *English Bards and Scotch Reviewers* (1809), in which he pokes fun at the magazine that gave him a terrible review.

On graduating, Byron traveled to out-of-the-way corners of Europe and the Middle East. When he came home he brought with him two sections of a book-length poem entitled *Childe Harold's Pilgrimage,* which depicted a young hero not unlike himself—moody, reckless, sensitive, and adventuresome. The work was very well received, and Byron became very popular.

"I awoke one morning and found myself famous," Byron observed.

For a time Byron was the darling of London society. Hostesses vied to lure him to parties; women flocked to his side. But his lifestyle soon brought scandal, and in 1816 he left England, never to return.

Italy and Tragedy Eventually Byron settled in Italy, and worked on his masterful mock epic, *Don Juan* (pronounced jo͞o′ en). While there, however, tragedy struck: one of Byron's daughters died, and his good friend, the poet Percy Bysshe Shelley, drowned in a sailing accident in rough seas.

A Budding Revolutionary A champion of liberty, in 1823 Byron joined a group of revolutionaries seeking to free Greece from Turkish rule. Tragically, Byron died of a rheumatic fever soon after, while training troops to fight for Greek independence. To this day he is revered in Greece as a national hero.

◆ Background for Understanding

LITERATURE: THE BYRONIC HERO

Lord Byron was a true celebrity, a public figure of literary genius who in turn thrilled and scandalized his contemporaries. "Mad, bad, and dangerous to know"—that was Lady Caroline Lamb's famous description of Lord Byron.

Though Byron actually could be quite charming and friendly, his readers insisted on associating him with the dark, brooding hero, passionate about causes, whom he so often described. Such a figure—a staple of Romanticism—is known as the Byronic hero.

Because of this persona, or adopted personality, readers throughout the nineteenth century saw Byron as the quintessential Romantic poet.

Prentice Hall Literature Program Resources

REINFORCE / RETEACH / EXTEND

Selection Support Pages
Build Vocabulary: Suffixes: *-ous,* p. 157
Grammar and Style: Subject and Verb Agreement, p. 158
Reading Strategy: Question, p. 159
Literary Focus: Figurative Language, p. 160

Strategies for Diverse Student Needs, p. 33

Beyond Literature, p. 33

Formal Assessment Selection Test, pp. 160–162; Assessment Resources Software

Alternative Assessment, p. 33

Writing and Language Transparencies
Writing Process Model 4: Dramatic Scene, pp. 25–35

Resource Pro CD-ROM
"She Walks in Beauty"; "Apostrophe to the Ocean"; from *Don Juan*—includes all resource material and customizable lesson plan

Listening to Literature Audiocassettes
"She Walks in Beauty"; "Apostrophe to the Ocean"; from *Don Juan*

◆ She Walks in Beauty ◆ Apostrophe to the Ocean ◆ *from* Don Juan

◆ Literature and Your Life

Connect Your Experience

Many musicians, writers, and other creative people are known for their artistic temperament and rebellious tendencies. Two centuries ago, Lord Byron, a creative and romantic person, exhibited the same kind of restless and rebellious nature.

Thematic Focus: The Reaction to Society's Ills

Byron flouted social convention and dreamed of liberating oppressed people. As you read, determine to which of society's ills Byron is reacting.

Journal Writing In your journal, describe a modern writer or celebrity who is also a social activist.

◆ Literary Focus

Figurative Language

Poetry usually contains **figurative language**, language not meant to be taken literally. The most common figures of speech are **simile,** which makes a direct comparison using the word *like* or *as*; **metaphor,** which implies a comparison between two apparently unlike things; and **personification,** in which human qualities are attributed to nonhuman subjects. The following lines, addressed to the ocean, contain these three types of figurative language.

> These are thy toys, and, as the snowy flake, / They melt into thy yeast of waves, . . .

◆ Grammar and Style

Subject and Verb Agreement

Even in creative writing like Byron's poetry, it's important for the **verb to agree with its subject** in number. Don't be misled when other words intervene between the subject and the verb:

> The *monsters* of the deep *are* made.

Also be careful when the subject comes after the verb, as in this sentence:

> There *is* a *pleasure* in the pathless woods.

◆ Reading Strategy

Question

Questioning as you read leads to a better comprehension of literature. Begin with *Who? What? Where? When?* and *Why?* questions. For example:

> She walks in beauty, like the night / Of cloudless climes and starry skies; / And all that's best of dark and bright / Meet in her aspect and her eyes . . .

From these lines, you might ask: Who is *she*? What is her relationship with the speaker? To what does the speaker compare her? Why is she special?

Use this questioning strategy as you read Byron's poems.

◆ Build Vocabulary

Suffixes: *-ous*

In line 29 of *Don Juan*, the speaker uses the phrase "credulous hope of mutual minds." The suffix of the word *credulous*, *-ous*, means "full of," and its root *-cred-* means "belief." Therefore, *credulous* means "full of belief" or "too willing to believe."

Word Bank

Before you read, preview this list of words from the poems.

arbiter
tempests
torrid
fathomless
retort
insensible
credulous
copious
avarice

Call students' attention to the information on the Byronic hero in Background for Understanding on page 656. Have students cite examples from cartoon and film of the stereotypical Romantic hero. Discuss with students the positive and negative aspects of this type of character—for example, colorful, vivacious, charismatic and dashing, but also brooding, moody, impatient, and melancholic. Have students look for clues to Byron's personality as they read his poems.

Customize for
Less Proficient Readers
To help less proficient readers understand Byron's use of figurative language, review the Literary Focus definition (p. 657) and model how to interpret similes, metaphors, and personification.

Customize for
More Advanced Students
Paraphrasing can enable more advanced students to fully appreciate Byron's range and skill with figurative language. Urge students to compare their paraphrases with Byron's original wording.

Customize for
English Language Learners
Poetic diction and syntax often create difficulties for language learners. To help them navigate Byron's poems, suggest they pay close attention to structure. By noting where lines and stanzas begin and end, and how they are punctuated, students may gain understanding of text meaning.

Customize for
Musical/Rhythmic Learners
Encourage these students to read the poems with an ear to their rhythms. Urge them to listen for sound repetitions. How do these musical/ rhythmic qualities contribute to the mood and meaning of the work?

Preparing for Standardized Tests

Reading and Vocabulary Interacting with text will improve students' scores on reading comprehension passages of standardized tests. The Reading Strategy for this selection, Question, instructs students to apply this strategy as they read. For additional practice, use the Reading Strategy page in ***Selection Support***, p. 159.

Grammar and Language Some standardized tests ask students to identify and correct errors in grammar and usage. A commonly presented question involves knowledge of subject-verb agreement, as in the following:

> Neither Laura nor her paintings (is, are) going to win the award. *is*

The Grammar and Style lesson for this selection focuses on subject and verb agreement. For additional practice, use the Grammar and Style page on Subject and Verb Agreement, p. 158, in ***Selection Support.***

Develop Understanding

One-Minute Insight This sonnet vividly describes womanly beauty, capturing its essential power and linking it to nature's universal images. The poem reflects the speaker's wonder at such beauty. Byron catalogs the woman's physical charms and spiritual depth to demonstrate the intense impact the stunning woman's beauty had on him.

◆ Literary Focus

❶ **Figurative Language** Tell students that the simile in the opening lines is famous. Ask them to identify the two things being compared and explain why the comparison is appropriate and striking. *Lady Horton is being compared to a cloudless night sky filled with stars. The image is appropriate because she is wearing a black gown with spangles. The image is striking because it's original and vivid.*

◆ Critical Thinking

❷ **Analyze** Ask students: Does Byron emphasize the physical or spiritual aspect of the lady? *Students may say that he emphasizes her physical beauty by spending more lines on it or that he emphasizes her spiritual beauty by closing the poem discussing it.*

Cultural Note The poem was published in Byron's *Hebrew Melodies,* which was written to be set to adaptations of traditional Jewish tunes. If possible, play a recording of such music for students. How would a musical accompaniment affect the poem's power?

She Walks in Beauty

George Gordon, Lord Byron

This poem, written to be set to music, was inspired by Byron's first meeting with Lady Wilmot Horton, his cousin by marriage, who wore a black mourning gown with spangles.

She walks in beauty, like the night
   Of cloudless climes and starry skies;
❶ And all that's best of dark and bright
   Meet in her aspect and her eyes:
Thus mellowed to that tender light
   Which heaven to gaudy day denies.

One shade the more, one ray the less,
   Had half impaired the nameless grace
Which waves in every raven tress,
   Or softly lightens o'er her face;
Where thoughts serenely sweet express
   How pure, how dear their dwelling place.

And on that cheek, and o'er that brow,
   So soft, so calm, yet eloquent,
❷ The smiles that win, the tints that glow,
   But tell of days in goodness spent,
A mind at peace with all below,
   A heart whose love is innocent!

Block Scheduling Strategies

Consider these strategies to take advantage of extended class time.

- Introduce ideas about Romanticism with the ***Daily Language Practice*** activities for Week 32, p. 50, in Daily Language Practice.
- Suggest that students share and compare the descriptions of social activists created in Literature and Your Life (p. 657).
- Students may work in groups to review the Grammar and Style and Build Vocabulary concepts and complete the activities on pages 657 and 666.
- Have student pairs prompt each other in answering the Guide for Responding questions (pp. 659, 662, and 665).
- Students can complete the Media Connection: Film Proposal activity in ***Beyond Literature,*** p. 33.
- Have students complete the Eulogy activity (p. 667), which is supported by the Speaking and Listening Mini-Lesson (p. 664).
- To help students begin the Writing Mini-Lesson (p. 667), play the audiocassettes of dramatic monologues such as those of Robert Browning, or have students read from scripts of contemporary dramatic monologues. Invite students to identify speech they find realistic.

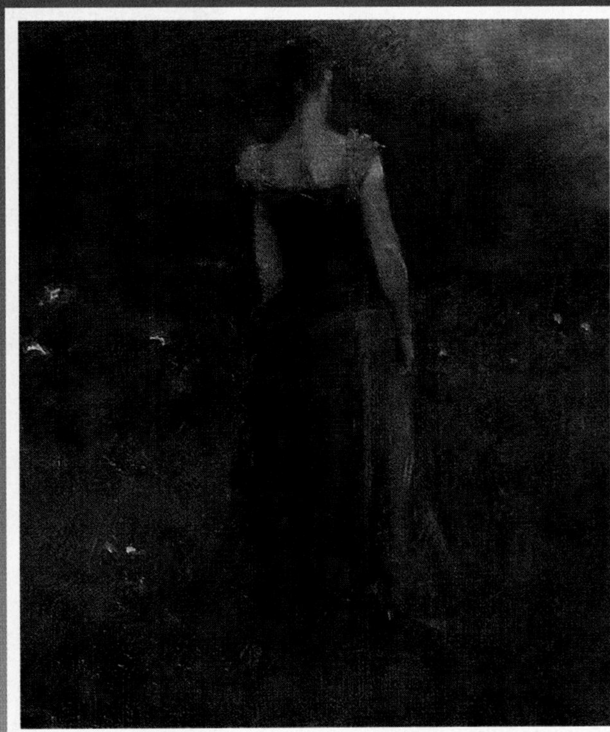

In The Garden, (detail) Thomas Wilmer Dewing, National Museum of American Art, Washington, D.C.

◀ **Critical Viewing** How does the rendering of this woman suggest that, like Byron's cousin, she is intriguing? **[Analyze]** ❸

Guide for Responding

Reader's Response Do you think the speaker idealizes the subject of this poem? Explain.

Thematic Response How does the poem's speaker remove the woman he describes from all of society's ills?

Sensory Switch This poem is full of visual imagery of dark and light. Rewrite the poem in your journal, describing the woman's beauty in terms of sound, scent, and touch.

☑ Check Your Comprehension

1. To what does the speaker compare the lady's beauty?
2. What does the speaker say about the lady's mind and heart?

◆ Critical Thinking

INTERPRET

1. What might "that tender light" in line 5 be? **[Interpret]**
2. What does the speaker suggest that the woman's appearance reveals about her character? **[Connect]**
3. Does Byron's picture emphasize the spiritual or physical aspect of the lady? Explain. **[Draw Conclusions]**

EVALUATE

4. Do you agree that goodness is part of beauty? Explain. **[Evaluate]**

APPLY

5. Do you think people today put too much emphasis on physical beauty? Explain. **[Relate]**

Humanities: Art

In the Garden, detail, 1892–94, by Thomas Wilmer Dewing.

This painting (also known as *Spring Moonlight*) illustrates a beautiful young woman—one of three in the full painting—like the one described in Byron's sonnet.

Artist Thomas Wilmer Dewing was born in New England, where his early interest in art extended to both drawing and music. He studied at the Boston Art Club and later at Académie Julian in Paris, developing a particular knowledge of anatomical drawing. On his return to America, Dewing also taught young artists at the Art Students League.

Use these questions for discussion:

1. What elements in the painting suggest Byron's notions of a link between nature and a woman's beauty? *The woman's standing at the center of glorious nature emphasizes the connection between her beauty and nature.*
2. How is the woman in the painting different from the woman described in the poem? *The woman in the painting seems to have auburn rather than "raven" hair. Her dress does not appear to be spangled.*

▶Critical Viewing◀

❸ **Analyze** She is beautifully dressed and has a graceful appearance. Her mystery is enhanced because her back is turned from the viewer.

Customize for *English Language Learners*

Language learners may be confused by some of Byron's poetic liberties, for example, rhyming "brow" with "glow" and "below" or inverting word orders. Suggest that students rearrange words and take approximate rhymes into account to aid their comprehension.

Reinforce and Extend

Answers

◆ Literature and Your Life

Reader's Response Some students will say that the last three lines exaggerate the purity of Lady Horton; others will point our that such people do, in fact, exist.

Thematic Focus The speaker describes the woman's attributes of perfection: "The smiles that win, the tints that glow, / But tell of days in goodness spent. . . . "

☑ Check Your Comprehension

1. The speaker compares the lady's beauty to a cloudless, starry night.
2. "A mind at peace with all below, / A heart whose love is innocent!"

◆ Critical Thinking

1. "Tender light" may refer to the glow in the woman's eyes.
2. Her appearance suggests a character imbued with radiant purity and innocent love.
3. Byron first emphasizes the physical and then the spiritual.
4. Possible responses: Yes, goodness invests a person with beauty. No, many vain people are handsome or beautiful. A mean and nasty demeanor can distort one's physical features.
5. Sample responses: Yes, the media emphasizes the importance of physical beauty. No, brains and personality get you further than physical beauty.

Develop Understanding

One-Minute Insight This poem expresses Byron's admiration and awe for the ocean. He describes its effect on him: the comfort it offers, the excitement it inspires, the humility its power elicits. Using historical references to great kingdoms, Byron also points out the ocean's continuity and its disregard for human political concerns. With his highly vivid account of the ocean's magic, Byron illustrates once again nature's extraordinary impact and durability.

◆ Background for Understanding

❶ Explain to students that an apostrophe is a literary device by which the speaker addresses an absent person, place, or thing as if he, she, or it were present.

◆ Reading Strategy

❷ **Question** In discussion, help students formulate and answer the questions: *Who* is the speaker talking to? *What* power does the speaker ascribe to the ocean? *He is addressing the ocean; it has the power to destroy ships and kill men.*

❸ **Clarification** Point out that "His" refers to people, or mankind, while "thy" and "thou" refer to the ocean.

◆ Literary Focus

❹ **Figurative Language** Point out the personification in line 23, in which the speaker talks of the ocean's "bosom," as if it were human.

►Critical Viewing◄

❺ **Assess** Students may say yes, citing the bowed figure on shore, the crashing waves, and the broken ship in the waves as evidence of its "roar."

from

Childe Harold's Pilgrimage

❶ Apostrophe to the Ocean

George Gordon, Lord Byron

There is a pleasure in the pathless woods,
There is a rapture on the lonely shore,
There is society, where none intrudes,
By the deep sea, and music in its roar;
I love not man the less, but nature more,
From these our interviews, in which I steal
From all I may be, or have been before,
To mingle with the universe, and feel
What I can ne'er express, yet cannot all conceal.

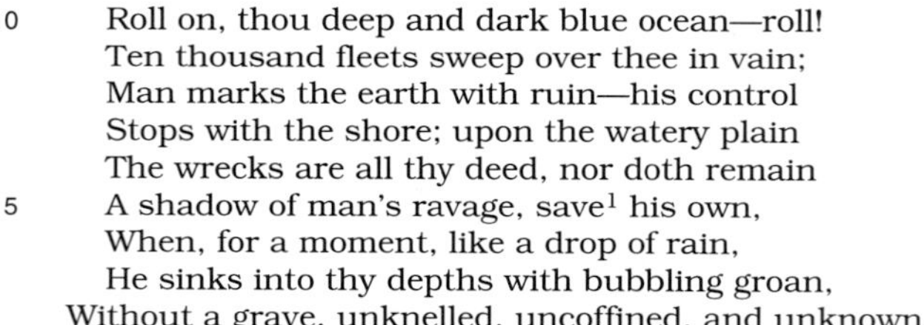

❷
Roll on, thou deep and dark blue ocean—roll!
Ten thousand fleets sweep over thee in vain;
Man marks the earth with ruin—his control
Stops with the shore; upon the watery plain
The wrecks are all thy deed, nor doth remain
A shadow of man's ravage, save[1] his own,
When, for a moment, like a drop of rain,
He sinks into thy depths with bubbling groan,
Without a grave, unknelled, uncoffined, and unknown.

❸
His steps are not upon thy paths—thy fields
Are not a spoil for him—thou dost arise
And shake him from thee; the vile strength he wields
❹ For earth's destruction thou dost all despise,
Spurning him from thy bosom to the skies,

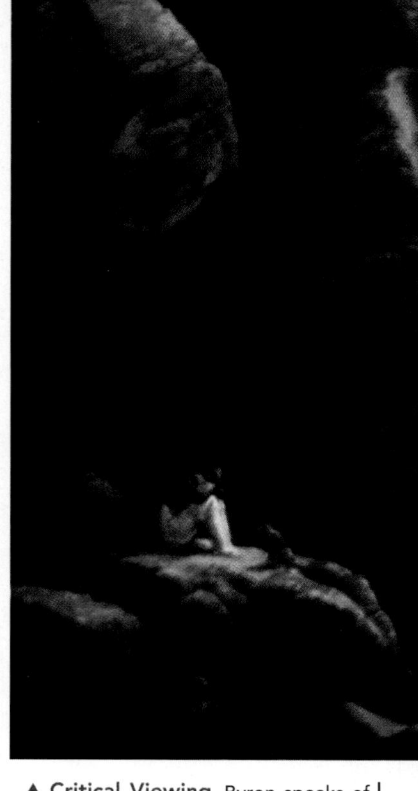

▲ **Critical Viewing** Byron speaks of the sea with "music in its roar." Does this artist succeed in visually communicating the sound of the ocean? **[Assess]** ❺

1. **save:** Except.

◆ Build Vocabulary

arbiter (är′ bət ər) *n.*: Judge; umpire

Cultural Connection

Before space exploration was possible, the sea represented the most vast and mysterious place of exploration. Sea gods, sea myths, and sea sagas in various cultures date back as far as recorded history. For example, the Roman god Neptune (Poseidon to the Greeks) was believed responsible for ocean weather. Centuries later, seventeenth-century maps showed a magical and bountiful island, Atlantis, which appears to have mysteriously disappeared. Other sea sagas describe enormous fire-breathing sea monsters.

Have students research a coastal or island culture, such as that of Haiti or the Ainu of northern Japan to learn about indigenous religious beliefs and myths concerning the sea. How do these beliefs compare to those of Byron, and why is the ocean's lure and appeal so universal?

Shipwreck, J.C.C. Dahl, Munich Neue Pinakothek/Kavaler

And send'st him, shivering in thy playful spray
And howling, to his gods, where haply[2] lies
His petty hope in some near port or bay,
And dashest him again to earth—there let him lay.[3]

The armaments which thunderstrike the walls
Of rock-built cities, bidding nations quake,
And monarchs tremble in their capitals,
The oak leviathans,[4] whose huge ribs make
Their clay creator[5] the vain title take
Of lord of thee, and arbiter of war—
These are thy toys, and, as the snowy flake,
6 They melt into thy yeast of waves, which mar
Alike the Armada's[6] pride or spoils of Trafalgar.[7]

Thy shores are empires, changed in all save thee—
Assyria, Greece, Rome, Carthage, what are they?
Thy waters washed them power while they were free,
And many a tyrant since; their shores obey
The stranger, slave, or savage: their decay
Has dried up realms to deserts—not so thou,

2. **haply:** Perhaps.
3. **lay:** A note on Byron's proof suggests that he intentionally made this grammatical error for the sake of the rhyme.
4. **leviathans** (lə vī′ ə thənz): Monstrous sea creatures, described in the Old Testament. Here the word means giant ships.
5. **clay creator:** Human beings.
6. **Armada's:** Refers to the Spanish Armada, defeated by the English in 1588.
7. **Trafalgar:** Battle in 1805 during which the French and Spanish fleets were defeated by the British fleet led by Lord Nelson.

◆ Reading Strategy

6 Question Suggest that students at this point question *when* the sea's power has exerted itself. *Students should recognize that Byron's many references to historical events emphasize the continuity of the sea's power, implying that the sea always has been and always will be more powerful than people.*

Customize for
Visual/Spatial Learners
Urge these students to access the poem's meaning through its visual imagery. As you read the poem aloud, have students mentally picture the images described. How does the exercise enhance students' comprehension and enjoyment of the poem?

Customize for
More Advanced Students
Explain that in the great English sea victories Byron mentions (over the Spanish Armada and at Trafalgar), nature played a role as storms destroyed enemy ships. Challenge students to use their understanding of background information to interpret Byron's message in stanza #4.

Humanities: Art

Shipwreck by Johan Christian Clausen Dahl.

This painting, like Byron's poem in lines 13–18, depicts a sinking ship.

Painter J.C.C. Dahl, a Norwegian, was interested in the naturalist approach to art—not merely mimicking nature but conveying a deeper meaning. Dahl studied and pursued his art as he traveled throughout Europe, carefully observing nature and capturing its fierce elemental forces. In The Shipwreck, Dahl imbues the scene with a sense of immediacy and drama.

Use these questions for discussion:

1. How might the artist's feelings about the ocean compare with those expressed by Byron in his poem? *Byron admires the ocean whereas Dahl seems more awestruck. Both recognize the ocean's power.*
2. What effect might the scene depicted have had on Byron? *He might have viewed it as confirmation of the ocean's obvious power to subdue people. He might even have reveled in that power.*

◆ Literary Focus

❶ **Figurative Language** Ask students to identify and explain the figurative language in these lines. *Byron personifies time and the ocean. Line 46 contains a metaphor comparing the ocean to a mirror.*

◆ Grammar and Style

❷ **Subject and Verb Agreement** Ask students to explain why the verb in "they to me were a delight:" is plural. *The plural subject they requires a plural verb.*

◆ Literary Focus

❸ **Figurative Language** Ask students: What is the metaphor implied in the last line? With what other images does it fit? *The word mane implies a comparison between the ocean and a wild animal. This fits with the image of the ocean rising up and shaking off a swimmer (lines 20–21).*

Reinforce and Extend

Answers

◆ *Literature and Your Life*

Reader's Response Students may cite images such as that of Byron as a boy, floating like a bubble on an ocean wave.

Thematic Focus He may refer to manmade structures such as buildings.

☑ Check Your Comprehension

1. He loves nature more than man.
2. The speaker addresses the ocean.
3. The ocean sinks warships, and sea monsters obey.
4. The memories are of joy, delight, and a pleasing fear.

◆ Critical Thinking

1. No matter how important the fleets of warships are, they cannot control the ocean itself.
2. The speaker admires the ocean's unchangeable and enduring quality.
3. Sample response: The ocean reflects the glory of the heavens, both peaceful and tempestuous.
4. He admires the ocean more.
5. The longer last line creates a crest on the stanza's "wave."
6. Sample response: Despite scientific advances, the ocean remains as wild and powerful as ever.

Unchangeable, save to thy wild waves' play.
Time writes no wrinkle on thine azure brow;
Such as creation's dawn beheld, thou rollest now.

❶ Thou glorious mirror, where the Almighty's form
Glasses[8] itself in tempests: in all time,
Calm or convulsed—in breeze, or gale, or storm,
Icing the pole, or in the torrid clime
Dark-heaving—boundless, endless, and sublime;
The image of eternity, the throne
Of the Invisible; even from out thy slime
The monsters of the deep are made: each zone
Obeys thee; thou goest forth, dread, fathomless, alone.

And I have loved thee, ocean! and my joy
Of youthful sports was on thy breast to be
Borne, like thy bubbles, onward; from a boy
❷ I wantoned with thy breakers—they to me
Were a delight: and if the freshening sea
Made them a terror—'twas a pleasing fear,
❸ For I was as it were a child of thee,
And trusted to thy billows far and near,
And laid my hand upon thy mane—as I do here.

8. **Glasses:** Mirrors.

◆ Build Vocabulary

tempests (tem′ pists) *n.*: Storms

torrid (tôr′ id) *adj.*: Very hot; scorching

fathomless (fath′ əm lis) *adj.*: Too deep to be measured or understood

Guide for Responding

◆ *Literature and Your Life*

Reader's Response What images from the poem linger in your mind? What thoughts and feelings do you associate with the ocean?

Thematic Focus What do you think the speaker means when he says "Man marks the earth with ruin"?

Journal Writing Write your own apostrophe, in verse or prose, directly addressing something in nature that evokes a strong reaction in you.

☑ Check Your Comprehension

1. What is the speaker's attitude toward nature?
2. An apostrophe is a figure of speech in which a speaker directly addresses an absent person or a personified quality or idea. Whom or what is the speaker addressing from stanza 2 on?
3. How does the ocean treat such things as warships and sea monsters?
4. What are the speaker's childhood memories of the ocean?

◆ Critical Thinking

INTERPRET

1. In line 11, the speaker describes the movement of ships over the ocean as "in vain." What might he mean by this? **[Interpret]**
2. What quality of the ocean does the speaker admire in the fifth stanza? **[Infer]**
3. When referring to the ocean as a "glorious mirror" in line 46, what does the speaker mean? **[Analyze]**
4. Whom does the speaker admire more—human beings or the ocean? **[Draw Conclusions]**

EVALUATE

5. The poem uses the Spenserian stanza, a nine-line stanza rhymed *ababbcbcc,* in which the ninth line is iambic hexameter (six beats to a line). What effect do the longer, last lines give the poem? **[Assess]**

EXTEND

6. Is the sea still as mysterious and powerful today as it was in Byron's day? Explain. **[Science Link]**

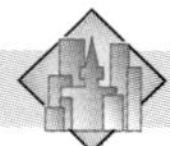

Beyond the Classroom

Career Connection

Engineering In this poem, Byron describes as vain human efforts to conquer the sea. Using maritime engineering, however, humans have harnessed and guided the sea to some extent.

Beginning in the eleventh century, the Dutch have used engineering and steady effort to reclaim 3,000 square miles of land, much of which lies below sea level.

Have students interested in maritime engineering research how engineering has changed people's feelings about the ocean and its power.

Community Connection

Water Pollution Byron says "Man marks the earth with ruin—his control /Stops with the shore." Point out that today, some oceans and other natural water bodies have become polluted. Challenge students to survey community for evidence of water pollution. Urge them as well to learn about regulations protecting regional waters. Have students discuss ways in which water pollution harms the community and propose additional regulations, if needed, to increase protection of the region's waters.

from

Don Juan

Lord Byron, shaking the dust of England from his shoes, from "The Poet's Corner" pub. by William Heinemann, 1904 (engraving by Max Beerbohm) Central Saint Martins College of Art and Design

George Gordon, Lord Byron

Though it is unfinished, Don Juan *is generally regarded as Byron's finest work. A mock epic described by Shelley as "something wholly new and relative to the age," it satirizes the political and social problems of Byron's time.*

Traditionally Don Juan, the poem's hero, had been portrayed as a wicked and immoral character driven solely by his obsession with beautiful women. In Byron's work Don Juan is depicted as an innocent young man whose physical beauty, charm, and spirit prove to be extremely alluring to ladies. As a result, he finds himself in many difficult situations.

Many people feel that Don Juan *would not be a great poem without the periodic pauses in the story during which the narrator drifts away from the subject. In these digressions the narrator comments on the issues of the time and on life in general. In this excerpt the narrator sets aside the adventures of his hero to reflect on old age and death.*

But now at thirty years my hair is gray
 (I wonder what it will be like at forty?
I thought of a peruke[1] the other day)—
 My heart is not much greener; and in short, I
Have squandered my whole summer while 'twas May,
 And feel no more the spirit to retort; I
Have spent my life, both interest and principal,
And deem not, what I deemed, my soul invincible.

No more—no more—Oh! never more on me
 The freshness of the heart can fall like dew,
Which out of all the lovely things we see
 Extracts emotions beautiful and new,
Hived in our bosoms like the bag o' the bee:
 Think'st thou the honey with those objects grew?
Alas! 'twas not in them, but in thy power
To double even the sweetness of a flower.

1. **peruke** (pə rōōk′): Wig.

◆ Build Vocabulary

retort (ri tôrt′) *v.*: Respond with a clever answer or wisecrack

Develop Understanding

One-Minute Insight This excerpt from the comic epic poem recounts the speaker's thoughts on ambition, aging, and death. The narrator, or speaker, at thirty years of age, finds himself exhausted, rather disappointed in himself, and somewhat disillusioned by the world around him. He feels that since his chance for romantic passion is past and ambition is a vain idol, he will dispense advice, based on his experience: be grateful things didn't turn out worse, read your Bible, and watch out for pickpockets! In expressing his poetic philosophy, the speaker takes humorous jabs at contemporary poets Southey and Wordsworth, the first of whom he considers unreadable and the latter incomprehensible.

Customize for ***Visual/Spatial Learners***
Point out the word *greener* in line 4. Ask students to describe the stage of life they associate with green. What colors might they associate with other stages of life, for example, death? *Green is associated with youth because it is linked to natural growth; students may say they associate black with death.*

◆ Critical Thinking

4 Analyze Ask students to identify the narrator's mood in the first stanza. *Don Juan's mood seems to be wry and somewhat rueful as he reveals that he has misspent his youth.*

◆ Literary Focus

5 Figurative Language Point out the metaphor in line 5 and the simile in line 13. Discuss the comparison in each. *The metaphor compares a person's life to the seasons of the year, with May as the spring or youth and summer as adulthood. The simile compares the "ability of the heart" to extract emotion from experience as the bee extracts nectar from a flower.*

Cultural Connection

The character of Don Juan is legendary and has appeared in written and musical works from several cultures over many centuries. One early version, the play *The Deceiver of Seville,* was written by Spanish author Tirso de Molina in 1634. French playwright Molière dramatized Don Juan's life in his 1665 *Don Juan.* The great eighteenth-century Austrian musical composer Wolfgang Amadeus Mozart wrote an opera called *Don Giovanni* about the legendary rake. Long after Byron wrote his poem, fellow Englishman Bernard Shaw featured Don Juan in his play *Man and Superman* (1903).

Have students discuss why this character—the aristocratic womanizer—has been so universally appealing. Based on this excerpt, why do they think Byron chose Don Juan as his hero? *Students may say that the Don Juan character is one who chose to live life to the fullest, a quality the speaker admires.*

◆ Reading Strategy

❶ Question Here students might ask themselves, To whom is the speaker addressing his words? Help them recognize that the narrator is addressing his own heart.

◆ Critical Thinking

❷ Compare and Contrast Ask students: How do lines 21–24 relate to Wordsworth's memorable lines 83–91 in "Tintern Abbey" (pp. 618–619)? *Students may note that Byron is playfully mocking Wordsworth's notion of exchanging wisdom for the rash passions of youth.*

◆ Critical Thinking

❸ Analyze Point out the rhyming couplet. Have students explain its effect. *Students should note the humor in the sight rhyme of "vice" and "avarice."*

◆ Critical Thinking

❹ Interpret Ask students: How did the narrator manage to lose his ambition? *He lost it by pursuing pleasure too much and experiencing too much sorrow.*

◆ Build Vocabulary

❺ Suffixes: *-ous* Point out that the coined word *burglariously* in line 54 contains the suffix *-ous*. Combined with their knowledge of the suffix *-ly* meaning "in a particular manner," have students use the meanings of the base word *burglar* and the suffix *-ous* ("full of") to define the word. *The word means "full of a burglar's manner."*

Lord Byron, shaking the dust of England from his shoes, from "The Poet's Corner" pub. by William Heinemann, 1904 (engraving by Max Beerbohm) Central Saint Martins College of Art and Design

No more—no more—Oh! never more, my heart,
   Canst thou be my sole world, my universe!
Once all in all, but now a thing apart,
❶ Thou canst not be my blessing or my curse:
The illusion's gone forever, and thou art
❷ Insensible, I trust, but none the worse,
And in thy stead I've got a deal of judgment,
Though heaven knows how it ever found a lodgment.

My days of love are over; me no more
   The charms of maid, wife, and still less of widow
Can make the fool of which they made before—
   In short, I must not lead the life I did do;
The credulous hope of mutual minds is o'er,
   The copious use of claret is forbid too,
So for a good old-gentlemanly vice,
❸ I think I must take up with avarice.

Ambition was my idol, which was broken
   Before the shrines of Sorrow and of Pleasure;
And the two last have left me many a token
   O'er which reflection may be made at leisure:
Now, like Friar Bacon's brazen head, I've spoken,
   "Time is, Time was, Time's past,"[2] a chymic[3] treasure
Is glittering youth, which I have spent betimes—
My heart in passion, and my head on rhymes.

❹ What is the end of fame? 'tis but to fill
   A certain portion of uncertain paper:
Some liken it to climbing up a hill,
   Whose summit, like all hills, is lost in vapor;
For this men write, speak, preach, and heroes kill,
   And bards burn what they call their "midnight taper,"
To have, when the original is dust,
A name, a wretched picture, and worse bust.

What are the hopes of man? Old Egypt's King
   Cheops erected the first pyramid
And largest, thinking it was just the thing
   To keep his memory whole, and mummy hid:
But somebody or other rummaging
❺ Burglariously broke his coffin's lid:
Let not a monument give you or me hopes,
Since not a pinch of dust remains of Cheops.

But I, being fond of true philosophy,
   Say very often to myself, "Alas!
All things that have been born were born to die,
   And flesh (which Death mows down to hay) is grass;
You've passed your youth not so unpleasantly,
   And if you had it o'er again—'twould pass—
So thank your stars that matters are no worse,
And read your Bible, sir, and mind your purse."

2. **Friar Bacon . . . Time's past:** In Robert Greene's comedy *Friar Bacon and Friar Burgandy* (1594), these words are spoken by a bronze bust, made by Friar Bacon.
3. **chymic** (kim´ ik): Alchemic: counterfeit.

Speaking and Listening Mini-Lesson

Eulogy

This mini-lesson supports the Speaking and Listening activity in the Idea Bank on p. 667.

Introduce the Concept Invite students to share their experiences with eulogies, especially those they found particularly effective. Discuss how such a speech can portray a person's essential characteristics. Point out that Don Juan is an extremely dynamic personality whose absence would be very noticeable.

Develop Background Before students draft their eulogy, review and discuss some descriptive strategies:

- Choose a few notable characteristics to eulogize.
- Include anecdotes to enable listeners to imagine the subject's presence.
- Spark listeners' emotional response with humor, if possible.

Apply the Information Encourage students to organize their eulogy as they would any essay: begin with an introduction; give main points and supporting details in the body; end with a memorable conclusion. Remind students to speak forcefully but formally.

Assess the Outcome Evaluate the eulogies for organization, characterization, and use of detail. Then ask students which eulogy they think comes closest to what Byron would have written about the passing of his hero.

But for the present, gentle reader! and
  Still gentler purchaser! the bard—that's I—
Must, with permission, shake you by the hand,
  And so your humble servant, and good-bye!
We meet again, if we should understand
  Each other; and if not, I shall not try
Your patience further than by this short sample—
'Twere well if others followed my example.

"Go, little book, from this my solitude!
  I cast thee on the waters—go thy ways!
And if, as I believe, thy vein be good,
  The world will find thee after many days."[4]
When Southey's read, and Wordsworth understood,
  I can't help putting in my claim to praise—
The four first rhymes are Southey's, every line:
For God's sake, reader! take them not for mine!

4. **Go . . . days:** Lines from the last stanza of Robert Southey's (1774–1843) *Epilogue to The Lay of the Laureate.*

◆ Build Vocabulary

insensible (in sen′sə bəl) *adj.*: Unable to feel or sense anything; numb

credulous (krej′ o͞o ləs) *adj.*: Willing to believe; naive

copious (kō′ pē əs) *adj.*: Abundant; plentiful

avarice (av′ə ris) *n.*: Greed

Guide for Responding

◆ Literature and Your Life

Reader's Response Did you find the narrator amusing? Why or why not?

Thematic Response In examining his life, the narrator states that his illusions are gone forever. Explain what he means by this statement.

Cast *Don Juan* With a small group, come up with casting suggestions for *Don Juan.*

☑ Check Your Comprehension

1. (a) What is the narrator's age? (b) In what condition does he find himself?
2. (a) What, according to lines 17 and 18, has been the narrator's "sole world" and "universe"? (b) According to the fourth stanza, with what "old gentlemanly vice" will he replace it?
3. What is the narrator's attitude toward death?

◆ Critical Thinking

INTERPRET

1. In the fifth stanza, the narrator notes that "glittering youth" is "chymic," or counterfeit treasure. What do you think he means by this? **[Interpret]**
2. What point does stanza 7 make about fame? **[Infer]**
3. What might the narrator mean when he says, in stanza 8, "flesh is grass"? **[Interpret]**
4. In line 72, whom is the narrator poking fun at? **[Infer]**

EVALUATE

5. Do you share the narrator's attitude toward ambition? Why or why not? **[Make a Judgment]**

APPLY

6. What modern figures might be labeled Byronic? Why? **[Relate]**

Beyond the Selection

FURTHER READING

Other Works by George Gordon, Lord Byron
Hours of Idleness; The Corsair; English Bards and Scotch Reviewers

Other Works About the Passage of Time
"Sonnet 130," William Shakespeare; "The Last Chantey," Rudyard Kipling; "How Soon Hath Time," John Milton

We suggest that you preview these works before recommending them to students.

INTERNET

You and your students may find additional information about Lord Byron at the following sites.

The Byron home page is at **http://www.geocities.com/Athens/Acropolis/8916/byron.html**

To read selected Byron letters and quotations, visit **http://csm.astate.edu/~engphil/gallery/byron.html**

We *strongly recommend* that you preview the sites before you send students to them.

Customize for
Less Proficient Readers
Remind these students that Byron, like other Romantic poets, uses the more formal (and flowery) terms *thee* and *thy,* as well as contractions such as *'Twere.* Help students clarify this specialized vocabulary to ensure their comprehension.

Reinforce and Extend

Answers

◆ Literature and Your Life

Reader's Response Possible responses: The narrator is amusing in his attitude and honesty; the narrator is not amusing because he should take himself more seriously.

Thematic Focus He has reached a point where he believes he sees life clearly, not through the passionate illusions of youth.

☑ Check Your Comprehension

1. (a) The narrator is thirty years old. (b) He thinks himself as being old too soon.
2. (a) His heart—his passion—has been his whole world—his universe. (b) He will take up avarice.
3. The narrator's attitude toward death is that it is inevitable.

◆ Critical Thinking

1. Youth is "false treasure" because it soon tarnishes and cracks as age sets in.
2. Fame does not last, nor is it substantial.
3. Death is often pictured as the Grim Reaper with his scythe, cutting the grass of life. Flesh, like grass, will be cut down in death.
4. He is poking fun at Wordsworth's *The Prelude, or Life of the Poet.* He is also poking fun at himself for being long-winded.
5. Some students may feel that personal ambition is an important motivator in their lives. Some may say that ambition is unimportant.
6. Possible modern Byronic figures include Daniel Day-Lewis and U2's Bono.

Answers

◆ Literary Focus

1. (a) The figurative language is a metaphor, an implied comparison between life and the seasons of spring and summer. (b) It implies he used up his years of maturity by living so fully in his youth.
2. (a) The simile is "like a drop of rain." (b) The comparison suggests that humans are insignificant compared to the ocean. It also suggests that humans and the ocean are made up of the same element—water.
3. Sample response: The figurative language gives the ocean a vivid and powerful presence.
4. (a) metaphor; (b) simile

◆ Build Vocabulary

1. *glorious:* full of glory
2. *marvelous:* full of marvel
3. *porous:* possessing pores
4. *plenteous:* plentiful

Using the Word Bank

1. a 2. c 3. b 4. a
5. a 6. c 7. c

◆ Reading Strategy

1. (a) Sample response: Some students may have asked, "What is Byron like?" "What does he believe in?" (b) They would find him passionate, observant, wise, and theatrical, with a keen sense for all kinds of beauty.
2. Some students may respond that questioning made their reading process more meaningful because they read with specific purposes in mind.

◆ Grammar and Style

1. The joys of the narrator of *Don Juan* have shrunk.
2. There are many gray hairs on his head.
3. The charms of romance no longer seem possible.
4. The fame of writers escapes him.
5. Over the waters goes his book of verse.

Writing Application

The works of Byron *reflect* his romantic attitudes. Each of his poems *illustrates* his talent for writing. His audience of enthusiastic readers also admires him for his deep sympathy for the downtrodden.

Guide for Responding *(continued)*

◆ Literary Focus

Figurative Language

Figurative language—not to be taken literally—makes descriptions vivid and abstract ideas concrete. For example, when Byron says "She walks in beauty like the night / Of cloudless climes and starry skies," he is using a simile that provides a concrete image of the woman's beauty.

1. In *Don Juan,* the speaker says he "squandered [his] whole summer while 'twas May." (a) What type of figurative language is in this line? (b) What meaning does the comparison convey?

2. (a) Identify the simile in the second stanza of "Apostrophe to the Ocean." (b) What does the comparison suggest about the drowning man?

3. Throughout "Apostrophe to the Ocean," the speaker addresses the ocean and personifies it. What effect does this use of figurative language have on the poem as a whole?

4. Identify the types of figurative language in the following lines: (a) "Thou glorious mirror, where the Almighty's form/Glasses itself..." (b) "The freshness of the heart can fall like dew..."

◆ Build Vocabulary

Using the Suffix *-ous*

Knowing that the suffix *-ous,* as in *credulous,* means "full of" or "possessing," define the following words.

1. glorious **3.** porous
2. marvelous **4.** plenteous

Using the Word Bank

In your notebook, write the letter of the word that is most nearly the opposite in meaning to the first word.

1. arbiter: (a) plaintiff, (b) jury, (c) award
2. torrid: (a) angry, (b) obedient, (c) freezing
3. fathomless: (a) deep, (b) measurable, (c) dry
4. retort: (a) ask, (b) a dessert, (c) rescue
5. insensible: (a) sensitive, (b) nonsensical, (c) furious
6. copious: (a) anxious, (b) typed, (c) scarce
7. avarice: (a) earthbound, (b) sin, (c) generosity

◆ Reading Strategy

Question

If you **question** as you read, you'll better understand the details and the larger meaning of a work. For instance, after reading the introduction to "She Walks in Beauty" and the poem itself, you might ask and answer these questions:

- *Question*: Who is *she*? *Answer*: Lady Wilmot Horton
- *Question*: What is her relationship to the speaker or poet? *Answer*: Byron's cousin by marriage
- *Question*: What does she look like? *Answer*: beautiful; serene; dressed in black with spangles
- *Question*: To what does the speaker compare her? *Answer*: the night; the stars

1. (a) What questions did you ask prior to reading Byron's poems? (b) What answers did you find?

2. Did questioning make your reading process more active or focused? Explain.

◆ Grammar and Style

Subject and Verb Agreement

In all types of writing, from reports to poetry, **verbs must agree in number** with their subjects. Following are examples from poems of Lord Byron.

Singular: There *is* a *rapture* on the lonely shore.
Plural: My *days* of love *are* over.

Practice In your notebook, write the form of the verb that agrees with the subject.

1. The joys of the narrator of *Don Juan* (has, have) shrunk.
2. There (is, are) many gray hairs on his head.
3. The charms of romance no longer (seems, seem) possible.
4. The fame of writers (escapes, escape) him.
5. Over the waters (goes, go) his book of verse.

Writing Application Rewrite this paragraph, correcting errors in agreement.

The works of Byron reflects his romantic attitudes. Each of his poems illustrate his talent for writing. His audience of enthusiastic readers also admires him for his deep sympathy for the downtrodden.

Writer's Solution

For additional instruction and practice, use the lesson in the **Language Lab CD-ROM** on Special Problems with Agreement and the pages on Subject and Verb Agreement, pages 61–63, in the *Writer's Solution Grammar Practice Book.*

Build Your Portfolio

Idea Bank

Writing

1. **Health Regimen** At the age of thirty, Don Juan seems washed up. Create a health regimen detailing the life-style changes he should make to revive himself, including information on exercise and diet.

2. **Ocean's Response** Write a brief poem in which the ocean responds to the musing of the speaker in "Apostrophe to the Ocean."

3. **Response to Criticism** "For all its bursts of cynicism, savagery, and melancholy, there is a fundamental good humor in *Don Juan*," wrote literary scholar Helen Gardner. React to her comment in a critical essay.

Speaking and Listening

4. **Oral Reading** Read aloud "Apostrophe to the Ocean," recording your performance on audio-cassette or videotape. Include background music and sounds. **[Performing Arts Link]**

5. **Eulogy** Write a eulogy, or farewell speech, to mourn the passing of Don Juan. Use details from the poem in your speech to make its subject vivid and interesting. Deliver the eulogy to the class. **[Performing Arts Link]**

Projects

6. **Portrait** Bring one of Byron's poems to life visually. You can create a seascape based on "Apostrophe to the Ocean," a portrait of the woman in "She Walks in Beauty," or a sketch of the narrator of *Don Juan*. **[Art Link]**

7. **Music** "She Walks in Beauty" was originally intended to be set to music. Do as Byron intended, and write music to accompany the poem. Then perform your song for classmates. **[Music Link; Performing Arts Link]**

Writing Mini-Lesson

Dramatic Monologue

The speaker in *Don Juan* reveals his innermost thoughts and emotions through poetry, just as dramatic characters reveal their thoughts and emotions through a **monologue**. Write a monologue—a dramatic speech—for a modern Byronic hero. Make it sound authentic by using realistic speech.

Writing Skills Focus: Realistic Speech

Realistic dialogue appears in many types of creative writing, from television scripts to dramatic poems. To make your modern-day character come alive, use speech that captures the flavor of contemporary life. Your monologue might even include sentence fragments and slang where appropriate.

Too formal and poetic: I have squandered my whole summer while 'twas May.

More realistic and contemporary: I burned my candle at both ends when I was young, and now I'm paying for it.

Prewriting Jot down things a Byronic hero like Childe Harold or Don Juan would have to say today. Identify both the central message and attitude that your hero would express. Then list words and phrases that convey the message and the attitude.

Drafting Take on the persona of your Byronic speaker and begin drafting the monologue. As you draft, use words and an attitude that are appropriate for your character.

Revising Review your word choice to make sure your monologue is as realistic as possible. Also check to be sure your writing is free from grammar, spelling, and other errors. (Sentence fragments are acceptable.) Check especially that your verbs agree with their subjects. For more on subject and verb agreement, see pp. 657 and 666.

✓ ASSESSMENT OPTIONS

Formal Assessment, Selection Test, pp. 160–162, and Assessment Resources Software. The selection test is designed so that it can be easily customized to the performance levels of your students.
Alternative Assessment, p. 33, includes options for less advanced students, more advanced students, visual/spatial learners, interpersonal learners, and intrapersonal learners.

PORTFOLIO ASSESSMENT
Use the following rubrics in the ***Alternative Assessment*** booklet to assess student writing:
Health Regimen: How-to Process Explanation Rubric, p. 101
Ocean's Response: Poetry Rubric, p. 109
Response to Criticism: Evaluation/Review Rubric, p. 105
Writing Mini-Lesson: Fictional Narrative Rubric, p. 96

Idea Bank

Customizing for *Performance Levels*
Following are suggestions for matching Idea Bank topics with your students' performance levels:
Less Advanced Students: 1, 4, 7
Average Students: 2, 4, 6
More Advanced Students: 3, 5

Customizing for *Learning Modalities*
Following are suggestions for matching Idea Bank topics with your students' learning modalities:
Verbal/Linguistic: 1, 2, 3, 4, 5
Visual/Spatial: 6
Musical/Rhythmic: 4, 7

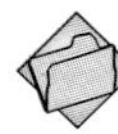

Writing Mini-Lesson

Refer students to the Writing Handbook, page 1189, for instruction on the writing process, and page 1191 for further information on narration.

Writing and Language Transparencies Use the Writing Process Model 4: Dramatic Scene, pp. 25–35, to guide students through the process of writing a drama.

Writer's Solution

Writers at Work Videodisc
Have students view the videodisc segment (Ch. 2) featuring James Berry to see how he develops narrative elements in his writing. Have students discuss how they can apply his ideas to writing their dramatic monologues.

Play frames 15185 to 17838

Writing Lab CD-ROM
Have students complete the tutorial on Narration. Follow these steps:
1. Use the interactive instruction on using dialogue to develop character.
2. Find descriptive words in the Character Traits Word Bin.
3. Draft the monologue on the computer.
4. Use the revision tips to improve their dramatic monologues.

Allow approximately 90 minutes of class time to complete these steps.

Sourcebook
Have students use Chapter 2, Narration (pp. 30–61), for additional support.

Prepare and Engage

OBJECTIVES

1. To read, comprehend, and interpret three poems
2. To relate poems to personal experience
3. To respond to imagery to enrich the reading experience
4. To recognize and interpret imagery in poetry
5. To build vocabulary in context and learn the word root *-puls-*
6. To correctly identify and use the subjunctive mood
7. To write a research report, incorporating necessary background
8. To respond to the poems through writing, speaking and listening, and projects

SKILLS INSTRUCTION

Vocabulary: Word Roots: *-puls-*
Grammar: Subjunctive Mood
Reading Strategy: Respond to Imagery
Literary Focus: Imagery
Writing: Necessary Background
Speaking and Listening: Weather Report (teacher edition)
Critical Viewing: Compare and Contrast; Evaluate; Connect

PORTFOLIO OPPORTUNITIES

Writing: Direct Address; Comparison and Contrast; Response to Criticism
Writing Mini-Lesson: Research Report
Speaking and Listening: Role Play; Weather Report
Projects: Observation Journal; Art Presentation

More About the Author
Percy Bysshe Shelley believed that a poet's task was to combine existing images or ideas in new ways, to create "by combination and representation" prompts to human "emotion and thought." Despite what is now celebrated as his poetic talent, Shelley was not appreciated for his poetry during his lifetime.

Guide for Interpreting

Percy Bysshe Shelley

(1792–1822)

A poet of rare gifts, Percy Bysshe (bish) Shelley was also a self-appointed reformer who believed that humankind was capable of attaining a nearly perfect society.

A Loner and Rebel Born into the British upper class, Shelley was raised on a country estate in Sussex. He attended the finest schools, including the prestigious boarding school Eton, but spent most of his time wandering the countryside and performing private scientific experiments. At Oxford University, he published the radical tract *The Necessity of Atheism*. As a result of this incident, he was expelled and became estranged from his father.

Love and Tragedy Instead of going home, Shelley headed for London. There he met Harriet Westbrook, an unhappy schoolgirl who persuaded him to elope. Their marriage was a failure, and the two eventually separated. Continuing his travels in radical intellectual circles, Shelley fell in love with Mary Wollstonecraft Godwin, daughter of the radical philosopher William Godwin and the late Mary Wollstonecraft. After Harriet's tragic death in 1816, Shelley and Mary Godwin married.

A Poet and Outcast The radical politics, the elopement and separation, the tract about atheism—all helped make Shelley an outcast from his homeland. He and Mary settled in Italy, where he became close friends with Lord Byron, another famous exile. In fact, it was during a storytelling session with Shelley, Byron, and another friend that Mary Shelley was inspired to begin work on her famous novel *Frankenstein*.

Italy was a place of inspiration for Shelley as well. There he wrote many of his finest works, including "Ode to the West Wind," "To a Skylark," and his verse drama *Prometheus Unbound* (1820). This drama predicts that someday humanity will be free of tyranny.

An Early Death Shelley never lived to see his dreams for humanity come true. He was only thirty when he died in a boating accident. Grief-stricken, Lord Byron eulogized his friend as "without exception the best and least selfish man I ever knew."

◆ Background for Understanding

HUMANITIES: NATURE IN ROMANTIC POETRY AND ART

Romanticism influenced not just literature but all the arts. Reacting to this new movement, the visual arts became more personal. Perhaps the most important sign of Romanticism in painting was a new interest in the world of nature. As the eighteenth century ended, British art turned increasingly from portraits to landscapes, which blossomed in the hands of two of England's finest artists, J. M. W. Turner (1775–1851) and John Constable (1776–1837).

Turner's Subjective Landscapes Working in both water colors and oils, Turner produced highly subjective landscapes and seascapes that pioneered the use of light and color to capture atmosphere.

Getting Nature Right John Constable is often called the father of modern landscape painting. Not only did he express strong feelings in his work, but he also stressed the need to get nature right. Like Shelley, Constable loved science, and the accuracy of his cloud studies testifies to that love.

Journal Writing Observe the paintings by Constable on pp. 673 and 676. Jot down your impressions or any thoughts they evoke in you.

Prentice Hall Literature Program Resources

REINFORCE / RETEACH / EXTEND

Selection Support Pages
Build Vocabulary: Word Roots: *-puls-*, p. 161
Grammar and Style: Subjunctive Mood, p. 162
Reading Strategy: Respond to Imagery, p. 163
Literary Focus: Imagery, p. 164

Strategies for Diverse Student Needs, p. 34

Beyond Literature
Career Connection: Meterology, p. 34

Formal Assessment, Selection Test, pp. 163–165; Assessment Resources Software

Alternative Assessment, p. 34

Writing and Language Transparencies
Writing Process Model 7: Research Report, pp. 57–70; Outline, p. 123

Resource Pro CD-ROM
"Ozymandias," "Ode to the West Wind," "To a Skylark"—includes all resource material and customizable lesson plan

Listening to Literature Audiocassettes
"Ozymandias," "Ode to the West Wind," "To a Skylark"

◆ Literature and Your Life

Connect Your Experience

It could be a pet you've raised, a flower you've planted, or a tree you've learned to notice—once you develop a special interest in an animal or plant, it takes on an identity. It isn't just an *it* anymore, but a living being with which you have a relationship.

No wonder romantic authors like Shelley wrote poems in which they addressed natural forces and beings. In two of the poems that follow, Shelley "speaks" to the west wind and to a skylark.

Thematic Focus: The Reaction to Society's Ills

In what ways are Shelley's poems about nature also poems about society and its problems? How can the west wind and the skylark help us to live better?

◆ Build Vocabulary

Word Roots: *-puls-*

Romantic poetry, especially Shelley's, often portrays movement. It's not surprising, therefore, to encounter the word *impulse* in "Ode to the West Wind." The root of this word is *-puls-,* which means "push or drive" and appears in many words that express motion of one kind or another.

Word Bank

Before you read, preview this list of words from the poems.

visage
verge
sepulcher
impulse
blithe
profuse
vernal
satiety

◆ Grammar and Style

Subjunctive Mood

Shelley uses verbs in the **subjunctive mood**, which expresses a wish or a condition contrary to fact. The subjunctive form of the verb *be* is *were* (it does not matter whether the subject is singular or plural):

If I *were* (not *was*) a swift cloud to fly with thee . . .

If we *were* things born / Not to shed a tear. . .

◆ Literary Focus

Imagery

Imagery is the descriptive language that poets and other writers use to re-create sensory experience. Poets often create patterns of images that support the theme of a poem. By recognizing and interpreting these patterns, you can understand the poem's meaning.

Notice, for example, how wind images—which appeal to the senses of sight, sound, and touch—appear throughout "Ode to the West Wind." Think about how your sensory experience of the wind, through imagery, helps you understand Shelley's prophetic message in the poem.

◆ Reading Strategy

Respond to Imagery

You will enrich your reading of a poem by **responding to imagery**—experiencing a poem through your senses. Often it's possible to enjoy a poem this way before you fully understand it with your mind.

Before approaching "Ozymandias" as a puzzle to be figured out, respond to its visual imagery as if it were a scene in a music video. Picture the strange and marvelous sight that the "traveler" describes:

Two vast and trunkless legs of stone / Stand in the desert.

Interest Grabber Take a moment at the beginning of class to greet the birds and trees outside the classroom windows. If you have no access to the natural world outside, find a visual or photographic representation of a bird or other animal to greet. Once students' interest is piqued, explain to them that you've been addressing the natural and physical world around you. Inform students that Romantic poets such as Percy Bysshe Shelley revered nature and abhorred artifice. Point out that in the following poems by Shelley, he reveals his scorn for manmade monuments like the sphinx, personifies the wind, and speaks to a skylark.

Customize for
Less Proficient Readers
Review the Reading Strategy with less proficient readers and encourage them to employ it as you read the poems aloud.

Customize for
More Advanced Students
Tell these students that Shelley has been called the perfect Romantic poet. As they read, challenge students to find evidence to support or refute this statement.

Customize for
English Language Learners
Language learners may stumble over Shelley's diction and poetic structure. Pair these students with more advanced poetry readers to analyze and paraphrase difficult passages.

Preparing for Standardized Tests

Reading and Vocabulary An expanded vocabulary base and a knowledge of word roots will enable students to improve their performance on standardized tests. The Build Vocabulary lesson focuses on learning word meaning through familiarity with the word root *-puls-*. Students can use word roots to decipher unfamiliar words encountered in content-area or verbal-reasoning test items. For additional practice, use the Build Vocabulary exercises on page 680 and the practice page in ***Selection Support***, p. 161.

Grammar and Language Standardized tests may require that students understand the use of the subjunctive mood. For example, students may be asked to choose the best version of the following sentence:

I wouldn't do it if I <u>was</u> you. *(D)*
(A) was
(B) be
(C) are
(D) were

The Grammar and Style lesson for this selection addresses the subjunctive mood. Students can practice the use of the subjunctive mood by answering the questons in the Guide for Responding, p. 680, and completing the Grammar and Style page in ***Selection Support***, p. 162.

Develop Understanding

One-Minute Insight This poem both celebrates and satirizes human achievement. In the poem, a traveler describes the ruins of an ancient statue. On its base is an arrogant inscription: "Look on my works, ye Mighty, and despair!" However, what is left of the statue stands in an empty desert; the works of Ozymandias have crumbled under the onslaught of time and nature.

Customize for
Verbal/Linguistic Learners
Point out to these students how the poem's structure reinforces its meaning. The first eight lines describe the statue while the final six lines emphasize the irony in its wrecked condition. Encourage students to study the structure and the rhyme sequence for additional clues to meaning.

Customize for
English Language Learners
❶ Remind students that a single word can have different meanings. Ask what the word *trunk* means to them. *Students may say it refers to luggage, an elephant's nose, or the stem of a tree.* Explain that in this context, the word *trunk* mean "torso" or "body." The suffix *-less* means "without." Ask students: What does the statue look like? *It consists only of the legs; the rest of the statue is missing.*

❷ **Clarification** In this context, the word *beside* means "else."

◆ Critical Thinking

❸ **Analyze** Ask students what effect the alliterative phrases "boundless and bare" and "lone and level" have on the poem. *Suggested response: They emphasize the emptiness of the setting and provide a sense of finality or closure.*

▶Critical Viewing◀

❹ **Compare and Contrast** The statue in the photograph is similar because it is large, made of stone, weathered, and on a flat plain. It is different because it has a trunk, its head is still attached, and it is surrounded by grasslands.

OZYMANDIAS[1]

PERCY BYSSHE SHELLEY

I met a traveler from an antique land
❶ Who said: Two vast and trunkless legs of stone
Stand in the desert. Near them, on the sand,
Half sunk, a shattered visage lies, whose frown,
And wrinkled lip, and sneer of cold command,
Tell that its sculptor well those passions read
Which yet survive, stamped on these lifeless things,
The hand that mocked them and the heart that fed:
And on the pedestal these words appear:
"My name is Ozymandias, king of kings:
Look on my works, ye Mighty, and despair!"
❷ Nothing beside remains. Round the decay
❸ Of that colossal wreck, boundless and bare,
The lone and level sands stretch far away.

1. **Ozymandias** (ōz´ i män´ dē əs): The Greek name for Ramses II, the king referred to in the poem, a pharaoh who ruled Egypt during the thirteenth century B.C. and built many great palaces and statues. One statue was inscribed with the words: "I am Ozymandias, king of kings, if anyone wishes to know what I am and where I lie, let him surpass me in some of my exploits."

▶ **Critical Viewing** How is this Egyptian statue like and unlike the one in the poem? **[Compare and Contrast]** ❹

◆ **Build Vocabulary**
visage (viz´ ij) *n.*: Person's face or facial expression

Guide for Responding

◆ Literature and Your Life

Reader's Response Do you think that the message of this poem is pertinent to today's world? Explain.

Thematic Focus How does Shelley use Ozymandias to comment on political power?

☑ Check Your Comprehension

1. Whom does the speaker meet?
2. What sight does this person describe?

◆ Critical Thinking

INTERPRET

1. Think of the words on the pedestal. (a) Why is it ironic that the statue crumbled? (b) Why is it ironic that it is surrounded by desert? **[Interpret]**
2. What is the theme of the poem? **[Interpret]**

APPLY

3. (a) What is your definition of *power?* (b) What is your definition of *pride?* (c) In what way do the two complement each other? **[Define]**

Block Scheduling Strategies

Consider these strategies to take advantage of extended class time.

- Students may discuss their journal writing from Background for Understanding (p. 668).
- After reading the poems, have students work in pairs or small groups to complete the questions about imagery (p. 680). For reinforcement, assign the Reading Strategy and Literary Focus pages, pp. 163 and 164, in ***Selection Support***.
- Instruct pairs of students to quiz each other on the Word Bank, using the exercise on page 680.
- After students complete the Career Connection page on meterology, p. 34, in ***Beyond Literature,*** invite volunteers to present their results to the class.
- Students may brainstorm for research avenues for either the Research Project or Art Presentation (p. 681).
- Use Writing Model 7: Research Report, pp. 57–70, in ***Writing and Language Transparencies,*** to support the Writing Mini-Lesson (p. 681).

Customize for
More Advanced Students
Urge these students to read the poem "Ozymandias Revisited" by Morris Bishop and compare it with Shelley's sonnet.

Enrichment Ozymandias, or Ramses II, ruled Egypt from 1292 to 1225 B.C. He is known for his extensive building program, and was responsible for having the largest statue in Egypt built. He is often identified as the pharaoh who oppressed the Israelites in a chapter of Exodus in the Bible.

Reinforce and Extend

Answers

◆ Literature and Your Life

Reader's Response Yes, it puts accomplishments, pride, and power in perspective; no, it is rare to find people creating such self-glorifying monuments in today's world.

Thematic Focus Through the example of the colossus, Shelley shows how political power eventually crumbles with time.

☑ Check Your Comprehension

1. The speaker meets a traveler from an ancient land.
2. He describes the crumbling remains of a statue commemorating the Egyptian pharaoh Ozymandias.

◆ Critical Thinking

1. (a) It is ironic because Ozymandias, whose proud words appear on the pedestal, obviously expected his works to last forever; the crumbling statue undermines the expectations of the once great ruler. (b) The great civilization once commanded by the ruler has long since disappeared, leaving the crumbling statue in the middle of a vast desert.
2. Possible responses: "Pride goeth before a fall," "Don't take yourself too seriously," and "Time wins in the end."
3. Sample responses: (a) Power is authority. (b) Pride is a person's sense of self-worth. (c) Possible response: When one achieves power, one's sense of pride increases.

Humanities: Art

The Colossus of Memnon.

According to legend, this gigantic statue emitted a musical noise at sunrise. Like the enormous statue of Ozymandias in the poem, this statue was built to represent the power and divine kingship of an Egyptian pharaoh.

The colossus of Memnon is located in Thebes, which sits on the banks of the Nile River. From about 4,000 years ago to about 2,700 years ago, Thebes was the capital city for many Egyptian pharoahs. Today, the city houses many examples of splendid royal monuments and tombs.

Use these questions for discussion:

1. How can this statue help you appreciate the imagery of Shelley's poem? *This statue visually conveys the physical aspects of a decaying monument.*
2. How might Shelley's poem be different had this statue been its inspiration? *It might be less ironic because this statue has no inscription and has survived in a somewhat more intact state.*

Develop Understanding

One-Minute Insight The speaker of this poem describes the elemental force of the West Wind as it drives dead leaves, stirs up the ocean, destroys plants, and heralds winter's arrival. Awed by the wind's natural strength, Shelley celebrates that power and in so doing, also rejoices in the knowledge that each aspect of decay will lead ultimately to the renewal of spring.

Customize for
English Language Learners
Students may have difficulty with poetic or archaic words in this poem, such as *chariotest, azure, o'er,* and *art.* Provide students with simpler substitutes for such terms. (For example, "drives," "blue," "over," and "are.")

◆ Literary Focus

❶ **Imagery** Urge students to visualize Shelley's description, to see the many-colored autumn leaves. Encourage them to imagine how the leaves look, "driven, like ghosts from an enchanter fleeing."

◆ Reading Strategy

❷ **Respond to Imagery** Have students identify the main images in these two stanzas. Ask students to describe how the images make them feel. *Suggested response: Lines 7–8, which convey an image of death, make students feel solemn; lines 9–10, which convey an image of a trumpeter, like a bugler blowing reveille, make students feel excited; lines 11–12, which compare blossoms clustered on trees to flocks of sheep, make students feel cheerful.*

Ode to the West Wind

PERCY BYSSHE SHELLEY

Shelley composed this poem in the woods near Florence, Italy. He described the day of its composition as one "when that tempestuous wind, whose temperature is at once mild and animating, was collecting the vapors which pour down the autumnal rains."

I

O wild West Wind, thou breath of Autumn's being,
Thou, from whose unseen presence the leaves dead
Are driven, like ghosts from an enchanter fleeing,

❶ Yellow, and black, and pale, and hectic red,
Pestilence-stricken multitudes: O thou,
Who chariotest to their dark and wintry bed

The wingèd seeds, where they lie cold and low,
Each like a corpse within its grave, until
Thine azure sister of the Spring[1] shall blow

❷ Her clarion[2] o'er the dreaming earth, and fill
(Driving sweet buds like flocks to feed in air)
With loving hues and odors plain and hill:

Wild Spirit, which art moving everywhere;
Destroyer and preserver; hear, oh, hear!

1. **sister of the Spring:** South wind.
2. **clarion** *n.*: Trumpet producing clear, sharp, shrill tones.

Cross-Curricular Connection: Science

Shelley's poem addresses the West Wind, or wind blowing from the west. That wind usually brings new weather because of the Earth's rotation from west to east. At the same time, cold air from the poles moves toward the equator while warm air moves from the equator outward to the poles. Thus, as the North Pole gets colder with winter's approach, more frigid air reaches the earth's middle regions. That air is carried on the prevailing west wind around the globe to bring autumn. Come spring, the Earth's equatorial regions warm up from proximity to the sun, and warm air is circulated by the winds to bring spring.

Locate, or have students locate, a Beaufort Scale with which to rate the wind. Direct students to observe and rate the wind twice a day for several days. How do their observations compare with Shelley's?

Cirrus Cloud Study, John Constable, Victoria and Albert Museum Trustees

▲ **Critical Viewing** Would you say that Constable captured the spirit of Shelley's west wind? Why or why not? **[Evaluate]** ❸

II

Thou on whose stream, 'mid the steep sky's commotion,
Loose clouds like earth's decaying leaves are shed,
Shook from the tangled boughs of Heaven and Ocean,

Angels[3] of rain and lightning: there are spread
On the blue surface of thine aery surge, ❹
Like the bright hair uplifted from the head

Of some fierce Maenad,[4] even from the dim verge
Of the horizon to the zenith's height,
The locks of the approaching storm. Thou dirge

Of the dying year, to which this closing night
Will be the dome of a vast sepulcher,
Vaulted with all thy congregated might

Of vapors, from whose solid atmosphere
Black rain, and fire, and hail will burst: oh, hear!

3. **angels:** Messengers.
4. **Maenad** (mē´ nad): A priestess of Bacchus, the Greek and Roman god of wine and revelry.

◆ Build Vocabulary

verge (vʉrj) *n.*: Edge; rim
sepulcher (sep´ əl kər) *n.*: Tomb

◆ Background for Understanding

Humanities Point out that this ode, as well as "To a Skylark" on page 676, is in the form of an apostrophe—an address to an inanimate object. In such a form, poets often use personification to give human characteristics to inanimate objects. In this poem, Shelley uses both, addressing the wind directly ("O wild West Wind") and personifying it ("thou breath").

Customize for ***Less Proficient Readers***
Remind students to read poems in sentences and to ignore line breaks and stanza breaks when reading for basic meaning. Point out how the ideas and images in the poem flow from one line to the next and from stanza to the next.

Customize for ***Visual/Spatial Learners***
Prompt these students to look at the painting on page 673. Discuss how the painting relates to the poem's imagery. What might a painting created to illustrate this poem look like? *Paintings might depict colorful fall leaves or seeds being blown, a stormy night, or a turbulent ocean.*

►Critical Viewing◄

❸ **Evaluate** Some students may say he did because he shows the wind's movement and power. Other students may say he didn't because he doesn't show the wind's effects on people or the landscape.

◆ Literary Focus

❹ **Imagery** Here Shelley describes the wind's "aery surge," eliciting visual and auditory sensory images with both "aery" and "surge." Point out that the word "surge" also suggests the wind's power.

Humanities: Art

Cirrus Cloud Study, 1822, by John Constable.

This painting depicts a wind-driven mass of clouds, similar to what Shelley might have seen on the day he wrote "Ode to the West Wind."

John Constable (1776–1837) is known as one of his native England's most notable landscape painters. Unlike his artistic contemporaries, Constable used fresh, vibrant color. A lover of the outdoors, Constable was a close observer of nature and of the effects light, weather, and season had upon the landscape. Constable saw the sky, as depicted in *Cirrus Cloud Study,* as an important landscape and worked to paint it realistically and effectively.

Use these questions for discussion:

1. How do Constable's feelings about the wind compare with Shelley's? *Both appear to admire its grace and power; whereas Constable used light colors and an airy treatment in his depiction, Shelley used darker imagery to portray the wind.*
2. Which of Shelley's images are reflected in the painting? *Examples include: "breath of Autumn's being," "Wild Spirit," "loose clouds . . . are shed."*

◆ Literary Focus

❶ **Imagery** Invite students to identify sensory imagery in these lines. To what senses do the images appeal? What mood do they suggest? *Students should identify "blue" and "crystalline" as visual imagery. Both suggest a cool, crisp mood that holds some optimism.*

◆ Reading Strategy

❷ **Respond to Imagery** Ask students to describe the scene Shelley outlines here. How might a video shot of this scene unfold? *In this passage, the Atlantic Ocean is described as roiling and trembling as the West Wind approaches. Shots might begin as a long shot of the ocean beginning to churn, moving down through the water's turbulence to focus on the reactions of undersea plant and animal life.*

◆ Grammar and Style

❸ **Subjunctive Mood** Have students explain the use of the subjunctive mood in these stanzas. *The phrase "If I were" is in the subjunctive mood. It expresses Shelley's wishful thinking by expressing a condition contrary to fact —he is not a leaf, cloud, wave or boy, although he might wish to be these things.*

Customize for
Less Proficient Readers
Point out to these students that the final two sections of the poem will differ from the first three. To ready students for the poem's ending, ask them to identify the main points of the first three sections. *Main points include: the west wind carries decaying leaves, the west wind brings stormy weather, the west wind churns up the ocean waters.*

III

Thou who didst waken from his summer dreams
❶ The blue Mediterranean, where he lay,
Lulled by the coil of his crystalline streams,

Beside a pumice[5] aisle in Baiae's bay,[6]
And saw in sleep old palaces and towers
Quivering within the wave's intenser day,

All overgrown with azure moss and flowers
So sweet, the sense faints picturing them! Thou
For whose path the Atlantic's level powers

Cleave themselves into chasms, while far below
The sea-blooms and the oozy woods which wear
❷ The sapless foliage of the ocean, know

Thy voice, and suddenly grow gray with fear,
And tremble and despoil themselves: oh, hear!

IV

If I were a dead leaf thou mightest bear;
If I were a swift cloud to fly with thee;
A wave to pant beneath thy power, and share
❸
The impulse of thy strength, only less free
Than thou, O uncontrollable! If even
I were as in my boyhood, and could be

The comrade of thy wanderings over Heaven,
As then, when to outstrip thy skyey speed
Scarce seemed a vision; I would ne'er have striven

As thus with thee in prayer in my sore need.
Oh, lift me as a wave, a leaf, a cloud!
I fall upon the thorns of life! I bleed!

A heavy weight of hours has chained and bowed
One too like thee: tameless, and swift, and proud.

5. **pumice** (pum′ is) *n.:* Volcanic rock.
6. **Baiae's** (bā′ yēz) **bay:** Ancient Roman resort near Naples.

Beyond the Classroom

Career Connection
Career Counselors Point out that Shelley's poem personifies the West Wind, characterizing it as elemental, dynamic, and aggressive. Have the class think of people they know who share these qualities. Then brainstorm for a list of types of careers that these people would be well-suited for. You may also create a list of careers that would be inappropriate for such dynamic personalities to pursue.

Career Connection
Ocean Diver As the poem describes, wind and resulting ocean currents affect life deep beneath the ocean surface. Many scientists study ocean life with the help of data gathered by ocean divers. After learning to safely use diving equipment and how to manage the effects of diving on the human body, ocean divers can gain an intimate view of undersea life. Encourage interested students to brainstorm for different possible uses for the information resulting from these dives.

V

Make me thy lyre,[7] even as the forest is:
What if my leaves are falling like its own!
The tumult of thy mighty harmonies
Will take from both a deep, autumnal tone,
Sweet though in sadness. Be thou, Spirit fierce,
My spirit! Be thou me, impetuous one! ❹

Drive my dead thought over the universe
Like withered leaves to quicken a new birth!
And, by the incantation of this verse,

Scatter, as from an extinguished hearth
Ashes and sparks, my words among mankind!
Be through my lips to unawakened earth

The trumpet of a prophecy! O Wind,
If Winter comes, can Spring be far behind?

7. **lyre:** Aeolian (ē ō′ lē ən) lute, or wind harp, a stringed instrument which produces musical sounds when the wind passes over it.

◆ Build Vocabulary

impulse (im′ puls′) *n.*: Driving force forward

Guide for Responding

◆ Literature and Your Life

Reader's Response What natural force or creature would you choose to express the ideas of renewal and freedom?

Thematic Focus Could the poem's message be interpreted politically? Explain.

☑ Check Your Comprehension

1. What season does the poem associate with the west wind?
2. What does the wind do to (a) the leaves and seeds, (b) the clouds, and (c) the ocean?
3. What does the speaker ask of the wind in section V of the poem?

◆ Critical Thinking

INTERPRET

1. In what sense is the wind both a "destroyer and preserver"? **[Interpret]**
2. (a) How, according to section IV, has the speaker changed? (b) What caused the change? **[Infer]**
3. What is the "new birth" the speaker wants to bring about? **[Infer]**
4. (a) What is the meaning of the famous last line? (b) How does this line tie the poem together? **[Draw Conclusions]**

EVALUATE

5. Is the poem successful in conveying a sense of breathless excitement? Explain. **[Evaluate]**

APPLY

6. How are the last five lines of the poem related to Shelley's lifelong mission? **[Generalize]**

Speaking and Listening Mini-Lesson

Weather Report

This mini-lesson supports the Speaking and Listening activity in the Idea Bank on page 681.

Introduce the Concept Ask students to describe a typical weather report and the information it provides.

Develop Background Encourage students to consider the following suggestions before beginning their weather reports.

- Weather reports should identify the location and severity of expected weather conditions.
- Possible dangers, travel or environmental concerns should be included where appropriate.
- Weather reports should present clear and concise information in everyday language.

Apply the Information Have students list all the weather details in the poem and organize these details into a lively weather report, complete with charts and maps.

Assess the Outcome Evaluate each weather report for clarity, accuracy, and creativity. With students, rate each report's success.

◆ Literature and Your Life

❹ Point out that the speaker sees himself in the bittersweet autumn wind. With what season do students identify themselves? *Students may see themselves as the spring, growing and encouraging others to grow. Many answers are possible.*

Reinforce and Extend

Answers

◆ Literature and Your Life

Reader's Response Possible response: Butterflies are often seen as symbols of freedom and renewal.

Thematic Focus Yes; the poem could be seen as supporting individual liberty and free speech.

☑ Check Your Comprehension

1. It is associated with autumn.
2. (a) The leaves and seeds are driven and blown. (b) The wind loosens and spreads out the clouds. (c) The wind forms waves on the ocean.
3. The speaker asks the wind to scatter his thoughts and words among "mankind."

◆ Critical Thinking

1. It brings winter, which destroys plant life, but it also distributes seeds that sprout in the spring.
2. (a) In section IV the speaker wishes to share the wind's power and freedom. (b) The speaker has experienced the thorns, or pains, of life.
3. He speaks of a new age of freedom for all people.
4. Suggested response: (a) Even the bleakest situations are followed by times of renewal and hope. (b) It sums up the poem's theme of hope for a new beginning.
5. Suggested response: Yes; the poem's short stanzas, numerous exclamation points, and breezy rhythms and rhymes give it a breathless excitement.
6. Suggested response: Shelley believed strongly in personal freedom for all people. In this poem he uses the wind to represent freedom and to "scatter" his beliefs to all corners of the earth.

Develop Understanding

One-Minute Insight This poem honors nature's glorious songs and aspires to its pure joy. Addressed to a bird, the poem captures the skylark's spiraling flight and describes its soaring music, whether in the fading evening or earliest dawn. The skylark, whose joy is contrasted to humans' more limited emotional experience, cannot be restricted in its song and thus becomes a symbol of the freedom Shelley so fervently believed in.

Customize for
More Advanced Students
Direct students to other poems with birds as the subject, including Keats's "Ode to a Nightingale," p. 686, and Thomas Hardy's "The Darkling Thrush," p. 850. Challenge students to compare and contrast the three poets' approaches to a common subject.

Enrichment Critics divide Shelley's "To a Skylark" into three main sections. The first part (lines 1–30) describes the bird's flight while also defining the skylark as a symbol of something broader. In the second part (lines 31–60), Shelley tries to define his symbol by comparing the bird with various things from humans to insects. Finally, in the third part (lines 61–105) Shelley accepts that the symbol may be undefinable but is nonetheless a powerful creative inspiration.

▶Critical Viewing◀

1 Connect Any passages within lines 6–20 could be illustrated by this painting.

Cloud Study, 1821, John Constable, Yale Center for British Art

To a Skylark

PERCY BYSSHE SHELLEY

1 ▲ **Critical Viewing** Which lines from Shelley's poem does this painting by Constable best illustrate? **[Connect]**

Humanities: Art

Cloud Study, 1821, by John Constable.

This painting shows several birds—similar to those in the poem—in high flight against a cloudy sky.

Englishman and painter John Constable studied at the Royal Academy. He departed from his training in artificial painting techniques to create landscapes with truth and originality, for example by painting outdoors rather than in a studio.

Cloud Study was one of a series of small oil sketches through which Constable studied the effects of weather, time of day, and season on the sky.

Use these questions for discussion:

1. How is the painting's mood similar to that of the poem? *Both evoke wonder at nature's wonders—the poem at the skylark's song and the painting at the birds' soaring flight.*
2. What emotions might this painting evoke for Shelley? *He would likely feel wonder and envy at the birds' seemingly limitless flight.*

Hail to thee, blithe spirit!
Bird thou never wert,
That from heaven, or near it,
Pourest thy full heart
In profuse strains of unpremeditated art.

Higher still and higher,
From the earth thou springest
Like a cloud of fire;
The blue deep thou wingest,
And singing still dost soar, and soaring ever singest.

In the golden lightning
Of the sunken sun,
O'er which clouds are brightening,
Thou dost float and run;
Like an unbodied joy whose race is just begun.

The pale purple even[1]
Melts around thy flight;
Like a star of heaven,
In the broad daylight
Thou art unseen, but yet I hear thy shrill delight,

Keen as are the arrows
Of that silver sphere,[2]
Whose intense lamp narrows
In the white dawn clear,
Until we hardly see—we feel that it is there.

All the earth and air
With thy voice is loud,
As, when night is bare,
From one lonely cloud
The moon rains out her beams, and Heaven is overflowed.

What thou art we know not;
What is most like thee?
From rainbow clouds there flow not
Drops so bright to see,
As from thy presence showers a rain of melody.

Like a poet hidden
In the light of thought,
Singing hymns unbidden,
Till the world is wrought
To sympathy with hopes and fears it heeded not:

Like a highborn maiden
In a palace tower,
Soothing her love-laden
Soul in secret hour
With music sweet as love, which overflows her bower:

◆ Build Vocabulary

blithe (blīth) *adj.*: Cheerful

profuse (prō fyo͞os´) *adj.*: Abundant; pouring out

1. **even:** Evening.
2. **silver sphere:** Morning star.

Customize for
Less Proficient Readers

Direct students' attention to the opening lines in which Shelley says the skylark is not a bird. Explain that these lines hint that Shelley views the bird as a symbol. Encourage less proficient readers to read on for Shelley's explanation of that symbol.

◆ Reading Strategy

❷ Respond to Imagery Ask students to close their eyes and listen to the sounds these lines present. Read the lines to them, or play the recording on the **Listening to Literature Audiocassettes.** Then have students describe a musical score that would serve as appropriate accompaniment to these lines. Would the music be loud or soft? Constant or intermittent? *Students may say that the music should be constant and loud though not unpleasant.*

◆ Literary Focus

❸ Imagery Explain that Shelley uses imagery to link the comparisons he makes in these stanzas. Invite students to identify the common imagery and to relate it to Shelley's message. *Students should note the sound imagery in both stanzas: "singing hymns unbidden," and "With music sweet as love." Shelley incorporates these images to highlight the power of music.*

Cross-Curricular Connection: Science

Though all birds create sound, there are about 4,000 bird species that are considered songbirds because of the beauty of their music. Though often quite ordinary in appearance, the male bird (usually the most noticable singer) uses his song, like the bright plumes of some other birds, as both a mating tool and a defensive warning to enemies. Songs vary from species to species. For example, the song thrush's music is cheerful and uplifting whereas the male robin's warning call is often described as sad. Birdwatchers learn to recognize birds' songs and record their melodies using accepted symbols.

Have students listen at dawn and dusk to the bird sounds in your area. Invite them to describe the music they hear.

◆ Critical Thinking

❶ **Compare and Contrast** Ask students: In what ways is the skylark similar to a rose? *Both are beautiful, both send their message on the wind and both present their beauty because it is in their nature, rather than to achieve any goal.*

◆ Literary Focus

❷ **Imagery** Point out to students how Shelley uses sound and sight images here to reinforce his view of the skylark's musical perfection. Language such as "vernal showers" and "twinkling grass" creates images of spring's freshness—of its purity and hope—to describe the skylark's song.

◆ Literature and Your Life

❸ Discuss with students the questions in this stanza. Elicit the idea that all these questions can be encompassed in the query: What is the skylark's inspiration? Then ask students to describe their own creative inspirations. *Students may mention natural beauty, strong political or social views, or sensory stimuli such as music.*

Like a glowworm golden
  In a dell of dew,
Scattering unbeholden
  Its aerial hue
Among the flowers and grass, which screen it from the view!

Like a rose embowered
  In its own green leaves,
❶ By warm winds deflowered,[3]
  Till the scent it gives
Makes faint with too much sweet those heavy-wingèd thieves.[4]

Sound of vernal showers
  On the twinkling grass,
❷ Rain-awakened flowers,
  All that ever was
Joyous, and clear, and fresh, thy music doth surpass:

Teach us, sprite or bird,
  What sweet thoughts are thine:
I have never heard
  Praise of love or wine
That panted forth a flood of rapture so divine.

Chorus Hymeneal,[5]
  Or triumphal chant,
Matched with thine would be all
  But an empty vaunt,
A thing wherein we feel there is some hidden want.

What objects are the fountains[6]
  Of thy happy strain?
❸ What fields, or waves, or mountains?
  What shapes of sky or plain?
What love of thine own kind? what ignorance of pain?

With thy clear keen joyance
  Languor cannot be;
Shadow of annoyance
  Never came near thee;
Thou lovest—but ne'er knew love's sad satiety.

Waking or asleep,
  Thou of death must deem[7]
Things more true and deep
  Than we mortals dream,
Or how could thy notes flow in such a crystal stream?

3. **deflowered:** Fully open.
4. **thieves:** The "warm winds."
5. **Chorus Hymeneal** (hī´ mə nē´ əl): Marriage song, named after Hymen, the Greek god of marriage.
6. **fountains:** Sources, inspiration.
7. **deem:** Know.

◆ Build Vocabulary

vernal (vûrn´ əl) *adj.*: Relating to spring

satiety (sə tī´ ə tē) *n.*: State of being filled to excess

Cross-Curricular Connection: Science

Many birds of North America migrate southward for the winter. Most of them spend the winter months in Central America, the Caribbean, or northern South America. While some winter habitats have been endangered by destruction of rainforests, perhaps contributing to the endangerment of species such as the imperial parrot, feeding and studying birds has also become a popular pastime in some southern migration destinations. Many hotels keep feeding stations near public areas for their guests' viewing pleasure. Different foods, usually sweet in taste, are used as incentives. Species such as bananaquits, motmots, and warblers flock to these feeding stations while some birds will even feed from dining patrons' tables, if allowed.

Have students learn the migration habits of the skylark, including its winter and summer habitats, and plot these on an annotated map.

We look before and after,
And pine for what is not;
Our sincerest laughter
With some pain is fraught;
Our sweetest songs are those that tell of saddest thought.

Yet if[8] we could scorn
Hate, and pride, and fear;
If we were things born
Not to shed a tear,
I know not how thy joy we ever should come near. ❹

Better than all measures
Of delightful sound,
Better than all treasures
That in books are found,
Thy skill to poet were,[9] thou scorner of the ground!

Teach me half the gladness
That thy brain must know,
Such harmonious madness
From my lips would flow,
The world should listen then, as I am listening now.

---

8. **if:** Even if.
9. **were:** Would be.

Guide for Responding

◆ Literature and Your Life

Reader's Response Do you think that the pure joy of the skylark, as Shelley describes it, is possible for human beings? Why or why not?

Thematic Focus Does the last stanza of the poem hold out a promise for curing society's ills? Explain.

Joyful Birds List some other birds that, like Shelley's skylark, convey feelings of joy and delight.

☑ Check Your Comprehension

1. What does the speaker say the skylark pours from its heart?
2. To what four things does Shelley compare the lark in lines 36–55?
3. In the end, what does the speaker ask the bird to teach him?

◆ Critical Thinking

INTERPRET

1. Why do you think the poet avoids a precise physical description of the bird, calling it a "blithe spirit" and "an unbodied joy"? **[Infer]**
2. How is the skylark different from the poet and from other humans? **[Compare and Contrast]**
3. What changes could the skylark help the poet make in his own life and in the lives of others? **[Draw Conclusions]**

EVALUATE

4. Is the long line at the end of each stanza an effective device? Why or why not? **[Criticize]**

APPLY

5. Do you agree with the speaker's views of humanity in lines 76–95? Explain. **[Generalize]**

Beyond the Selection

FURTHER READING

Other Works by Shelley
Prometheus Unbound; Epipsychidion; Hellas

Other Works About Nature, Inspiration, and Freedom
"The Song of Nature," Ralph Waldo Emerson
"Liberty," Archibald Macleish
"Inspiration," Henry David Thoreau

We suggest that you preview these works before recommending them to students.

INTERNET

You and your students may find additional information about Percy Bysshe Shelley at the following sites.

The Shelley home page is at **http://www.geocities.com/Athens/Acropolis/8916/shelly.html**

To read the newsletter of the Keats-Shelley Association of America, visit **http://www.luc.edu/publications/keats-shelley/ksjweb.htm**

We *strongly recommend* that you preview the sites before you send students to them.

◆ Grammar and Style

❹ **Subjunctive Mood** Point out the subjunctive mood used in this sentence to lament the human state. Ask students what condition contrary to fact the speaker recognizes. *The speaker notes the essential sadness of the human condition. By using the subjunctive mood, he stresses that in fact we are things born to shed a tear.*

Customize for *Intrapersonal Learners*

Discuss with these learners the emotions evoked by Shelley's poem, the passions and inspirations the poet ascribed to the skylark and its song. As they reread the poem, ask students whether they think humans can hope to experience the joy of the skylark.

Reinforce and Extend

Answers

◆ Literature and Your Life

Reader's Response No, people are aware of the pain and suffering in the world; yes, at times humans do experience pure joy.

Thematic Focus Possible responses: Yes, by learning gladness from the nightingale, the speaker would be able to teach it to others; no, gladness is a result, but not a cure.

☑ Check Your Comprehension

1. The skylark pours its song from its heart.
2. He compares it to a poet, a high-born maiden, a glowworm, and a rose.
3. The speaker asks the bird to teach him how to enjoy life.

◆ Critical Thinking

1. The poet wants to convey a more symbolic meaning.
2. It has not experienced the pains that mortals must endure.
3. The skylark could help the poet learn to enjoy life, and thus inspired, the poet could teach others.
4. Possible response: The longer lines effectively sum up the main point of each stanza.
5. Suggested response: Yes; people are subject to discontentment, and happiness is always tempered by pain or sorrow.

Reinforce and Extend

Answers

◆ Reading Strategy

1. (a) They are like close-up camera shots. (b) It is a panoramic shot of the barren desert.
2. Suggested response: (a) Two vivid camera shots include a close-up of maple seeds on the ground, perhaps on a grave, and a panoramic shot of the hills with "loving hues." (b) Two noises might be howling wind and scuttling leaves or pouring rain and crackling thunder.

◆ Build Vocabulary

Using the Word Root *-puls-*

1. *expulsion:* forcing out
2. *impulse:* a sudden force
3. *compulsion:* driving force
4. *pulse:* vibration
5. *pulsating:* throbbing

Using the Word Bank

1. e 2. g 3. a 4. f 5. b
6. d 7. c

◆ Literary Focus

1. (a) Examples of sound images are: "clarion," "rain of melody," "singing hymns." (b) The imperfections of human joy is suggested by pained laughter.
2. (a) Examples of sight, sound, and touch are: "pestilence-stricken multitudes," "Thou dirge," and "thorns of life." (b) The sensory images evoked by the wind indicate the "aliveness" of the speaker, thus supporting Shelley's message of renewal.

◆ Grammar and Style

1. Correct
2. He wishes he were more like the bird.
3. He thinks that if he were a skylark, he would not know pain.
4. "If I were you," he was saying, "I would know true gladness."
5. Correct

Writer's Solution

For additional instruction and practice, use the page on the Subjunctive Mood in the *Writer's Solution Grammar Practice Book,* p. 55.

Guide for Responding *(continued)*

◆ Reading Strategy

Respond to Imagery

By **responding to imagery,** you can experience Shelley's poems with your senses, and you can enter a world as vivid as that of a music video. "Ozymandias," for example, begins with a long shot that reveals "Two vast and trunkless legs of stone" standing in a desert. Then the camera zooms down for a closeup: "a shattered visage lies" next to the legs.

1. (a) Describe lines 4–5 and 9–11 of "Ozymandias" in terms of camera shots. (b) What is the long shot that ends the poem?

2. (a) Describe two vivid camera shots suggested by the visual imagery of "Ode to the West Wind." (b) Now describe two noises, suggested by the imagery, that could be used for the sound track of a "West Wind" video.

◆ Build Vocabulary

Using the Word Root *-puls-*

Show how the word root *-puls-,* meaning "push or drive," contributes to the definition of each italicized word.

1. Shelley's *expulsion* from Oxford University disappointed his father.

2. This poet often acted on *impulse,* without thinking things through.

3. He rebelled against all forms of *compulsion* and tyranny.

4. The only drum to which Shelley marched was the beating of his own *pulse.*

5. Shelley did not think of nature as dead matter but as a *pulsating* force.

Using the Word Bank

On a separate sheet, write the lettered word from Column B that is opposite in meaning to the numbered word in Column A.

Column A	Column B
1. visage	**a.** careworn
2. vernal	**b.** scarce
3. blithe	**c.** hunger
4. sepulcher	**d.** center
5. profuse	**e.** back
6. verge	**f.** cradle
7. satiety	**g.** wintry

◆ Literary Focus

Imagery

Shelley uses **imagery**—sensory language—that gives you clues to the meaning of his poems. You can interpret these clues by relating one image to another and seeing the patterns they make.

In "Ode to a Skylark," for example, you probably noticed that many images relate to sound: "singing still dost soar," "shrill delight," "music sweet as love," and others. You can figure out that Shelley uses these sound images to suggest the mysterious "unbodied joy" of a bird he can hear but not see.

1. (a) Find another sound image that Shelley uses to suggest the bird's perfect delight. (b) What sound image in lines 86–90 suggests the imperfectness of human joy?

2. (a) In "Ode to the West Wind," find images of sight, sound, and touch that indicate the wind's power. (b) How does this sensory experience of the wind support Shelley's message of renewal?

◆ Grammar and Style

Subjunctive Mood

Romantic poets like Shelley, who were disappointed with things as they were, often used the subjunctive mood. In their hands, this grammatical tool became a means of expressing their hopes for a more just society and a more harmonious world.

The **subjunctive mood** expresses a wish or a condition contrary to fact. The subjunctive form of the verb *be* is *were.*

Practice Rewrite the following sentences in your notebook, correcting the verbs that require the subjunctive mood. If a sentence is correct as is, write *correct.*

1. The speaker was addressing the skylark.

2. He wishes he was more like the bird.

3. He thinks that if he was a skylark, he would not know pain.

4. "If I was like you," he was saying, "I would know true gladness."

5. He said he was sure that the skylark was happy.

Build Your Portfolio

Idea Bank

Writing

1. Direct Address Write a poem or a paragraph that directly addresses something in nature, such as the west wind or a skylark. Focus on the thoughts and feelings it inspires.

2. Comparison and Contrast "Ozymandias" is about a tyrant, and "Ode to the West Wind" predicts a new birth of freedom. Compare and contrast the political themes in these two poems.

3. Response to Criticism In "A Defense of Poetry," Shelley writes, "Poets are the unacknowledged legislators of the world." Use passages from these poems to illustrate what he means.

Speaking and Listening

4. Role Play With a partner, role-play the incident in which the speaker of "Ozymandias" meets the traveler and hears about the Egyptian king or the incident in which Ozymandias posed for the sculptor centuries ago. **[Performing Arts Link]**

5. Weather Report Give a series of radio or television weather reports that capture the same conditions as those described in "Ode to the West Wind." **[Science Link; Media Link]**

Projects

6. Observation Journal Both Shelley and the artist John Constable were very interested in the science of weather. Write a journal in which you record your observations of the weather. **[Science Link]**

7. Art Presentation Research the landscape paintings of John Constable. Present your findings to the class, showing reproductions and pointing out similarities between Constable and the romantic poets. **[Art Link]**

Writing Mini-Lesson

Research Report

Shelley's poems suggest many topics that it would be fun to study further. Choose such a topic—anything from the real-life Ozymandias, Ramses II, to ideas about weather that Shelley used in "Ode to the West Wind"—and write a research paper on it. Whichever topic you select, provide readers with the background they'll need to understand it.

Writing Skills Focus: Necessary Background

Many different types of writing—from video scripts to research papers—require you to provide **necessary background** for readers. If you choose to write about scientific concepts that influenced Shelley, readers may want you to answer questions like these:

- What scientific concepts influenced Shelley?
- How did scientists of the time develop these concepts?
- In what ways do these concepts differ from ours?
- What evidence is there that Shelley knew about these ideas and used them in his poems?

Prewriting Choose a topic related to Shelley's poetry, and begin to ask yourself questions about it. These questions will help point you toward the background information that readers will need. As you research these questions in biographies of Shelley and in books and articles about him, use note cards to record key details and ideas.

Drafting Begin by formulating a working thesis that will guide your writing and that you can modify as you draft your paper. Refer to your note cards as you write so that you can introduce facts and examples to support your arguments.

Revising Ask several classmates to read your paper and suggest where you could provide more information. Then evaluate their suggestions, giving special consideration to points on which they agree.

✓ ASSESSMENT OPTIONS

Formal Assessment, Selection Test, pp. 163–165, and Assessment Resources Software. The selection test is designed so that it can be easily customized to the performance levels of your students.

Alternative Assessment, p. 34, includes options for less advanced students, more advanced students, bodily/kinesthetic learners, musical/rhythmic learners, and visual/spatial learners.

PORTFOLIO ASSESSMENT

Use the following rubrics in the ***Alternative Assessment*** booklet to assess student writing:
Direct Address: Expression Rubric, p. 95; Poetry Rubric, p. 109
Comparison and Contrast: Comparison/Contrast Rubric, p. 104
Response to Criticism: Literary Analysis/Interpretation Rubric, p. 113
Writing Mini-Lesson: Research Report/Paper Rubric, p. 107

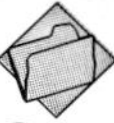

Idea Bank

Customizing for *Performance Levels*

Following are suggestions for matching Idea Bank topics with your students' performance levels:

Less Advanced Students: 1, 6
Average Students: 2, 4, 5
More Advanced Students: 3, 7

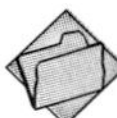

Customizing for *Learning Modalities*

Following are suggestions for matching Idea Bank topics with your students' learning modalities:

Visual/Spatial: 7
Bodily/Kinesthetic: 4
Interpersonal: 4
Verbal/Linguistic: 1, 2, 3, 4, 5, 6

Writing Mini-Lesson

Refer students to the Writing Handbook, page 1189, for instruction on the writing process, and page 1192 for information on research writing.

Writing and Language Transparencies Guide students through the process of writing a research report by using Writing Model 7: Research Report, pp. 57–70.

Writer's at Work Videodisc

Have students view the videodisc segment (Ch. 5) featuring sportswriter Peter Ginsburg to see how he adjusts his writing depending on his audience's background.

Play frames 7602 to 8059

Writing Lab CD-ROM

Have students complete the tutorial on Research Writing.

1. Fill out an Audience Profile.
2. Use the audio-annotated instructions on using library resources.
3. View the interactive instruction on note-taking.
4. Create a draft on the computer.
5. Use the revision checkers for coherence, transitions, and passive voice.

Sourcebook

Have students use Chapter 5, Research Writing (pp. 131–165), for additional support. The chapter includes an annotated student model of research paper (pp. 159–160).

Prepare and Engage

OBJECTIVES

1. To read, comprehend, and interpret poetry
2. To relate poetry to personal experience
3. To paraphrase to facilitate comprehension
4. To identify features of an ode
5. To build vocabulary in context and learn the suffix *-age*
6. To recognize words of direct address and understand their impact on tone
7. To write a description of a moment in time, using precise details
8. To respond to the poems through writing, speaking and listening, and projects

SKILLS INSTRUCTION

Vocabulary: Suffixes: *-age*
Grammar: Direct Address
Reading Strategy: Paraphrase
Literary Focus: Ode
Writing: Precise Details
Speaking and Listening: Oral Report (teacher edition)
Critical Viewing: Predict; Infer; Compare and Contrast; Speculate

PORTFOLIO OPPORTUNITIES

Writing: Prose Tribute; Irregular Ode; Response to Criticism
Writing Mini-Lesson: Description of a Moment in Time
Speaking and Listening: Informal Retelling; Oral Report
Projects: Museum Catalog; Science Display

More About the Author
Despite Keats's boyhood inclination towards worthy causes, his poetry is nearly devoid of the social and political commentary favored by his fellow Romantics Byron, Wordsworth, and Shelley. Rather, it displays the enthusiastic intensity of youth, with a focus on sensual and emotional experiences, and an interest in symbolism.

Guide for Interpreting

John Keats *(1795–1821)*

Every now and then, someone comes along who leaves a lasting imprint on the world in a life that is tragically cut short. John Keats was one of those people. Although he lived just twenty-five years, Keats left an indelible mark on the world of literature.

A Defender of Worthy Causes Unlike his contemporaries Byron and Shelley, John Keats was not a well-born aristocrat. Instead, he was born in London of working-class parents. As a child, he earned attention for his striking good looks and his restless spirit. Keats developed a reputation for fighting, not as a bully but as a defender of worthy causes. It was not until he became friends with the schoolmaster's son that Keats became interested in poetry and reading.

From Medicine to Poetry In 1815, Keats began studying medicine at a London hospital and earned a pharmacist's license before abandoning medicine for poetry. In 1818, he published his first major work, *Endymion,* a long poem that critics panned, in part because of Keats's association with the radical writer and publisher, Leigh Hunt. Despite the negative reviews, Keats did not swerve from his new career.

A Year of Sorrow and Joy The year 1818 was significant to Keats in other ways. He lost his brother Tom to tuberculosis, but he also met the light of his life, Fanny Brawne, to whom he became engaged. A year later he wrote many of the poems for which he is famous, including "The Eve of St. Agnes" and his odes. The engagement and burst of creativity might have been the prelude to a happy, productive life, but Keats's own health soon deteriorated.

An Early Death Recognizing that he suffered from the same illness as his brother, he moved to Italy in the hopes that the warmer climate would reverse the disease. Sadly, those hopes proved false, and, in 1821, his own battle with tuberculosis also ended in death. Keats wrote his own epitaph, which stresses the brevity of his life: "Here lies one whose name was writ in water."

A Legacy of Beauty Despite his early death and the fact that the most important of his works were composed in the space of two years, John Keats remains one of the major influences of English poetry. Known as a pure artist, Keats saw the appreciation of beauty as an end in itself and made the pursuit of beauty the goal of his poetry. As Keats himself so eloquently put it, "Beauty is truth, truth beauty."

◆ Background for Understanding

History: The Influence of Ancient Greece on Keats's Poetry

Romantic poets such as Byron, Shelley, and Keats admired the culture of ancient Greece, deriving inspiration from its art and literature. Keats, in particular, was inspired by its art, and this admiration is reflected in his poetry.

Keats's friend Charles Cowden Clarke introduced him to Elizabethan poet George Chapman's translation of Homer's ancient Greek epics. They spent an evening reading the translations, and early the next morning Keats produced his famous sonnet "On First Looking into Chapman's Homer."

Keats often associated his ideas about beauty with Greek antiquities. This tendency is exhibited in his poem "Ode on a Grecian Urn," which was inspired by an urn such as this one.

The Orchard Vase (Column Krater), Side A: Gathering Apples, The Metropolitan Museum of Art

Journal Writing Describe some paintings, sculptures, or buildings you've admired.

Prentice Hall Literature Program Resources

REINFORCE / RETEACH / EXTEND

Selection Support Pages
Build Vocabulary: Suffixes: *-age,* p. 165
Grammar and Style: Direct Address, p. 166
Reading Strategy: Paraphrase, p. 167
Literary Focus: Ode, p. 168

Strategies for Diverse Student Needs, p. 35

Beyond Literature Humanities Connection: Greek Art, p. 35

Formal Assessment Selection Test, pp. 166–168; Assessment Resources Software

Alternative Assessment, p. 35

Writing and Language Transparencies
Descriptive and Observational Writing, pp. 13–17; Daily Language Practice, Week 26, p. 161

Art Transparencies 9, 10, and 15

Resource Pro CD-ROM Poetry of John Keats—includes all resource material and customizable lesson plan

Listening to Literature Audiocassettes "Chapman's Homer," "When I Have Fears," "Ode to a Nightingale," "Ode on a Grecian Urn"

Poetry of John Keats

◆ Literature and Your Life

Connect Your Experience

Think about all the experiences in your life that have made strong impressions on you. If you could freeze just one moment, what would it be, and why? In many of Keats's poems, such as the ones presented here, the poet explores fleeting moments in time.

Thematic Focus: Fantasy and Reality

During flights of fancy it's sometimes possible to arrive at a truth that otherwise eludes you. For example, during a daydream, you may come to a realization about yourself. As you read, notice how flights of fancy lead the speakers of the poems to realizations of truths.

◆ Literary Focus

Ode

An **ode** is a lyric poem on a single, usually serious subject. Often it honors someone or something that the speaker addresses directly. The **Pindaric ode** (after the ancient Greek poet Pindar) was originally meant to be performed by a chorus of people onstage; it has three types of stanzas. In contrast, Rome's homostrophic or **Horatian odes** contain only one type of stanza, which is repeated throughout the poem. A third type of ode, the **irregular ode**, contains no set pattern.

Keats created ten-line stanzas of iambic pentameter (lines containing ten beats with a pattern of weak-strong) for his odes. The rhyme scheme of the stanzas varied from poem to poem. As you read Keats's odes, focus on their content as well as their form.

◆ Reading Strategy

Paraphrase

You'll come to a greater understanding of virtually any literary work if you **paraphrase**, or restate the text in your own words. Since poems use unusual language and word order, paraphrasing is especially helpful. For example:

Original: Forlorn! The very word is like a bell / To toll me back from thee to my sole self!

Paraphrase: The word *forlorn* is like a bell bringing me to my senses.

◆ Build Vocabulary

Suffixes: *-age*

In "Ode to a Nightingale," the speaker says "O, for a draft of vintage!" *Vintage* contains the suffix *-age*, which means "state or quality of, amount of, cost of, place of, or collection of." Combined with the root *-vint-*, meaning "wine," the word *vintage* means "wine collected at a certain time."

Word Bank

Before you read, preview this list of words from the poems.

ken
surmise
gleaned
teeming
vintage
requiem

◆ Grammar and Style

Direct Address

Throughout Keats's poetry you'll find terms of **direct address**, in which a person or thing is addressed by name or by a descriptive phrase. Commas set off terms of direct address. For example:

Bold lover, never, never
canst thou kiss . . .

And, *little town*, thy streets
forevermore will silent be . . .

Thou wast not born for
death, *immortal Bird!*

Notice how Keats's use of direct address gives his poems an intimate, personal tone.

Interest Grabber Invite students to bring in recordings of favorite songs that they believe define truth and beauty. Play selected recordings. Discuss how contemporary views of truth and beauty compare with those of a nineteenth-century poet.

Customize for
Less Proficient Readers
Less proficient readers may lack the historical knowledge base to understand Keats's many allusions. Have these students review footnoted references before reading.

Customize for
More Advanced Students
Keats's many allusions to historical events and characters offer more advanced students a starting point to expand both their knowledge base and their appreciation of Keats's work. Invite students to learn more about these historical references before rereading the poems.

Customize for
English Language Learners
Encourage language learners to use Keats's poetic structure as a guide. Urge them to read sentences as they are punctuated, rather than pausing at line breaks. Also, suggest that students recognize that stanzas usually contain related ideas.

Customize for
Interpersonal Learners
Review with these students the lesson on Direct Address (p. 683). Suggest that students read each poem as if it addressed them. How does it make them feel? What thoughts does it evoke?

Preparing for Standardized Tests

Reading and Vocabulary On some standardized tests, students may be asked to read subject-linked material and answer both comprehension and vocabulary questions about it. Expanded vocabulary will facilitate more successful responses. The Build Vocabulary lesson focuses on learning word meaning through the use of the suffix *-age*. Students can apply this skill to understanding text stimulus material, selecting correct vocabulary answers, or identifying accurate content responses. For additional practice, use the Build Vocabulary page in ***Selection Support,*** p. 165.

Grammar and Language Knowledge of direct address and how to punctuate it may be tested on standardized tests in exercises such as the following:

"Because of your outstanding achievements Kadisha, the PTA is naming you Student of the Year." *(D)*

(A) achievements Kadisha, the
(B) achievements, Kadisha the
(C) achievements Kadisha the
(D) achievements, Kadisha, the

The Grammar and Style lesson for this selection focuses on direct address. For additional practice, use the Grammar and Style page in ***Selection Support,*** p. 166.

Develop Understanding

One-Minute Insight

"On First Looking into Chapman's Homer" celebrates Chapman's translation of Homer's work, which gives Keats illuminating new insights into the literature. The octave, with its formal diction and archaic words, suggests the dignified antiquity of classical poetry. The sestet, in contrast, uses simple language to convey the immediacy and excitement of discovery.

Clarification The Greek poet Homer is believed to have authored the epic poems the *Iliad* and the *Odyssey,* which recount events of the Trojan War and the travels of heroic Odysseus.

▶Critical Viewing◀

❶ **Predict** Students may predict that the book deals with wars and warriors in ancient times.

◆ Reading Strategy

❷ **Paraphrase** Tell students to reverse the order of "never" and "I" before restating this text in their own words. *Sample paraphrase: I'd heard a lot about Homer's works, but didn't appreciate their magnificence until I read Chapman's translation.*

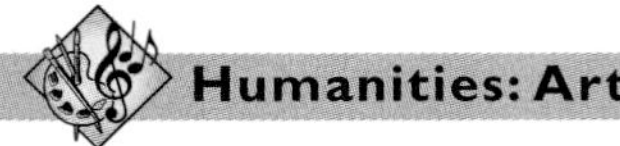

Humanities: Art

Frontispiece for Homer's Iliad and Odyssey, 1612, by William Hole.

This engraving depicts the frontispiece, or page opposite the title page, of the book that inspired Keats's sonnet.

Englishman William Hole is best known for his sheet music engravings, authors' portraits, and title pages such as the one shown here. Classical allusions are the main component to the engraving, with a laurel—crowned Homer as the central image.

Use this question for discussion: What elements of this engraving reflect Keats's approach to Homer? *The formal composition is reminiscent of Keats's dignified language.*

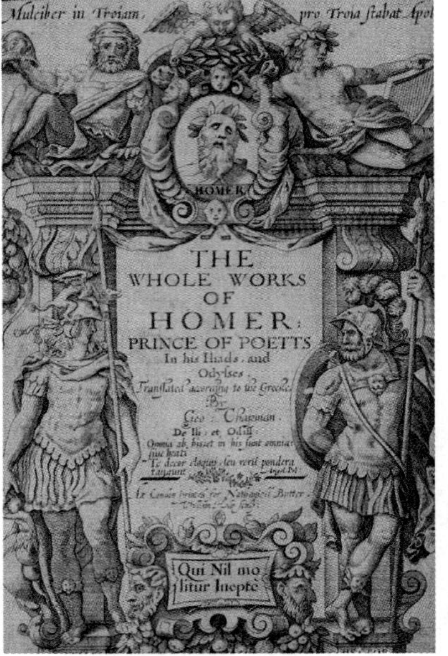

Frontispiece, Homer's Iliad and Odyssey, 1612, William Hole, The British Library

▲ **Critical Viewing** ❶ From the design of the engraving, what would you predict about the content of the book? **[Predict]**

On First Looking into Chapman's HOMER

John Keats

When Keats was twenty-one, his former teacher, Charles Cowden Clarke, introduced him to a translation of Homer by Elizabethan poet George Chapman. The two men spent the evening reading this book, and early the next morning Keats presented this sonnet to Clarke.

Much have I traveled in the realms of gold,
    And many goodly states and kingdoms seen;
    Round many western islands have I been
Which bards in fealty to Apollo[1] hold.
Oft of one wide expanse had I been told
    That deep-browed Homer ruled as his demesne;[2] ❷
    Yet did I never breathe its pure serene[3]
Till I heard Chapman speak out loud and bold:
Then felt I like some watcher of the skies
    When a new planet swims into his ken;
Or like stout Cortez[4] when with eagle eyes
    He stared at the Pacific—and all his men
Looked at each other with a wild surmise—
    Silent, upon a peak in Darien.[5]

1. **Apollo:** In Greek and Roman mythology, the god of music, poetry, and medicine.
2. **demesne** (di mān´): Realm.
3. **serene:** Clear air.
4. **Cortez:** Here, Keats was mistaken. The Pacific was discovered in 1513 by Balboa, not Cortez.
5. **Darien** (der´ ē ən): The Isthmus of Panama.

◆ Build Vocabulary

ken (ken) *n.*: Range of sight or knowledge

surmise (sər mīz´) *n.*: Guess; assumption

Block Scheduling Strategies

Consider these strategies to take advantage of extended class time.

- Introduce the Grammar and Style focus, Direct Address (p. 683). Reinforce this skill with the exercises in the Guide for Responding (p. 692) and the practice pages in ***Selection Support,*** p. 166.
- After reading the poems, student groups may share their responses to the Literature and Your Life questions (pp. 685, 689, and 691).
- Direct students to brainstorm for research avenues for the Museum Catalog project (p. 693).
- Prepare for the Writing Mini-Lesson (p. 693) by having students share ideas about special moments in time. You might invite students to offer one or two examples of effective precise details from Keats's poems.
- Students may prepare, practice, and present their oral reports about the Elgin Marbles. This activity, described in the Idea Bank (p. 693), is supported by a Speaking and Writing Mini-Lesson on page 688 of this teacher edition.

When I Have Fears That I May Cease to Be

John Keats

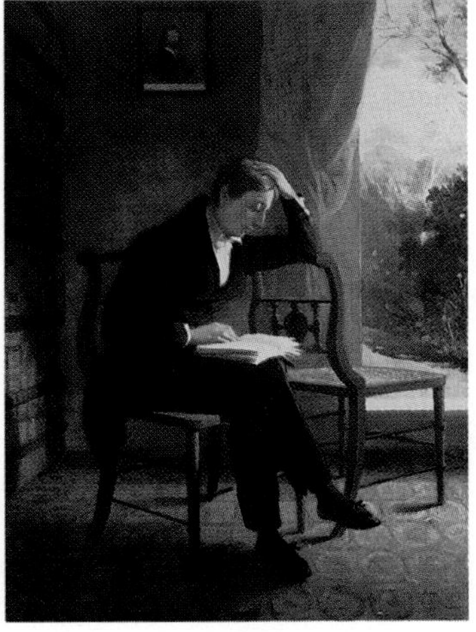

John Keats, 1821, Joseph Severn, By courtesy of the National Portrait Gallery, London

When I have fears that I may cease to be
    Before my pen has gleaned my teeming brain, ❹
Before high-piled books, in charactery,[1]
    Hold like rich garners[2] the full ripened grain;
When I behold, upon the night's starred face,
    Huge cloudy symbols of a high romance,
And think that I may never live to trace
    Their shadows, with the magic hand of chance;[3]
And when I feel, fair creature of an hour,
    That I shall never look upon thee more,
Never have relish in the fairy power
    Of unreflecting love—then on the shore
Of the wide world I stand alone, and think
Till love and fame to nothingness do sink. ❺

1. **charactery:** Written or printed letters of the alphabet.
2. **garners:** Storehouses for grain.
3. **chance:** Inspiration.

❸ ▲ Critical Viewing From this rendering of Keats, how would you characterize him? **[Infer]**

◆ Build Vocabulary

gleaned (glēnd) *v.*: Picked or gathered, as one does with fruit or crops

teeming (tēm′ iŋ) *adj.*: Filled to overflowing

Guide for Responding

◆ Literature and Your Life

Reader's Response Do you find the speakers' observations in these poems believable or moving?

Thematic Response Would you describe these poems as fantastic, realistic, or both? Explain.

☑ Check Your Comprehension

1. To what two things does the speaker in "Chapman's Homer" liken himself after reading it?
2. Of what is the speaker in "When I Have Fears" fearful?
3. How does the speaker resolve his fears?

◆ Critical Thinking

INTERPRET

1. What feelings about Chapman's Homer do the similes in lines 9–14 convey? **[Connect]**
2. What is meant by "cloudy symbols of a high romance" in "When I Have Fears"? **[Interpret]**
3. What does the speaker mean by "unreflecting love" in line 12? **[Interpret]**

APPLY

4. Can books change people's lives, as is suggested in "Chapman's Homer"? Explain. **[Generalize]**
5. What does "When I Have Fears" suggest about Keats's views on death? **[Apply]**

Humanities: Art

John Keats, 1821, by Joseph Severn.

This painting portrays poet John Keats in a moment of sadness and perhaps doubt.

Joseph Severn, in whose arms John Keats died in 1821, was born and raised in England. After apprenticing to an engraver and studying with the Royal Academy, Severn risked his connection to the Academy to travel to Italy with the ailing Keats. He created this painting after Keats's death, basing it on a moment observed just after the writing of "Ode to a Nightingale," and using memory and masks made of Keats's face both before and after death.

Use these questions for discussion:

1. What elements of the painting suggest a mood appropriate to "When I Have Fears"? *Keats's despondent expression and posture, and the dark and somber colors of the carpet and walls create an atmosphere of sadness and doubt.*
2. How does the painting's composition reflect the themes of the poem? *As in the poem, Keats is shown isolated with his thoughts while the bright world beckons from outside.*

The speaker expresses fears that he will not live to fulfill his potential. This lyric is particularly poignant because Keats died less than three years after he wrote it.

▶Critical Viewing◀

❸ **Infer** Students may say that Keats is serious, contemplative, moody.

Comprehension Check ☑

❹ Have students explain the simile in this stanza. Do they find it appropriate? *The writing of poems is like the harvesting of grain. Students may agree or disagree with the implication that poetry "grows," rather than being created.*

◆ Critical Thinking

❺ **Interpret** Ask: What conclusion does the speaker reach in the final two lines? *Possible response: The vastness of the universe makes the speaker realize that love and fame are ultimately unimportant.*

Reinforce and Extend

Answers

◆ Literature and Your Life

Reader's Response Most students will relate to the elation of discovery and the fear of early death.

Thematic Focus The poems address life realities, but contain fantastic images.

☑ Check Your Comprehension

1. He likens himself to an astronomer who discovers a new planet, and to the explorer who first saw the Pacific Ocean.
2. He fears dying before he's reached his goals.
3. He thinks, until personal love and fame seem unimportant.

◆ Critical Thinking

1. They convey excitement and wonder.
2. The speaker may mean nighttime clouds that suggest stories.
3. He means love accepted by another.
4. Yes, books can have great impact by changing the way people think.
5. Possible answer: Keats doesn't welcome death, but he accepts it.

Develop Understanding

One-Minute Insight This poem captures what Keats termed "negative capability"—the capacity of a poet to negate himself or herself and enter fully into his or her subject so as to represent it with an especially rich and vibrant objectivity. In this case, the speaker subsumes himself into the joyous nightingale, and so transcends the pain of the mortal world.

◆ Literary Focus

❶ **Ode** The pattern of rhyme and meter in this poem is typical of what is sometimes referred to as an English ode. Have students analyze this stanza to determine the form of the English ode. *An English ode consists of ten-line stanzas in iambic pentameter with the rhyme scheme ababcdecde.* Challenge students to explain why this form has been described as a fusion of the English and Italian sonnets. *The first part of the stanza is structured like the quatrain in an English (Shakespearean) sonnet, and the second part is structured like the sestet of an Italian (Petrarchan) sonnet.*

◆ Critical Thinking

❷ **Classify** Have students identify how the images in stanza 2 appeal to the different senses. *Possible response: Lines 16–18, and 20, appeal to the sense of sight; line 14 appeals to the sense of hearing; line 13 appeals to the sense of taste; and lines 12, 14, 15, and 20 appeal to the sense of touch.*

Customize for
Less Proficient Readers
Encourage these students to engage their senses in Keats's vivid imagery as a way of accessing the poem. Urge them to read first for a sensory experience, second for meaning and comprehension.

Ode to a Nightingale

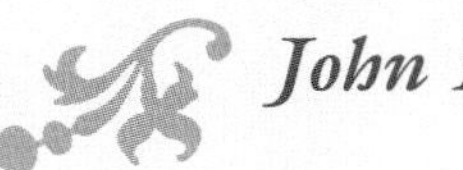

John Keats

Keats composed the following ode in 1819, while living in Hampstead with his friend Charles Brown. Brown wrote the following description about how the ode was composed: "In the spring of 1819 a nightingale had built her nest near my house. Keats felt a tranquil and continued joy in her song; and one morning he took his chair from the breakfast table to the grass plot under the plum tree, where he sat for two or three hours. When he came into the house, I perceived he had some scraps of paper in his hand, and these he was quietly thrusting behind the books. On inquiry, I found those scraps, four or five in number, contained his poetic feeling on the song of our nightingale."

I

❶
My heart aches, and drowsy numbness pains
　My sense, as though of hemlock[1] I had drunk,
Or emptied some dull opiate to the drains
　One minute past, and Lethe-wards[2] had sunk:
'Tis not through envy of thy happy lot,
　But being too happy in thine happiness,—
　　That thou, light-wingèd Dryad[3] of the trees,
　　　In some melodious plot
　Of beechen green, and shadows numberless,
　　Singest of summer in full-throated ease.

II

❷
O, for a draft[4] of vintage! that hath been
　Cooled a long age in the deep-delvèd earth,
Tasting of Flora[5] and the country green,
　Dance, and Provençal[6] song, and sunburnt mirth!

1. **hemlock:** Poisonous herb.
2. **Lethe-wards:** Toward Lethe, the river of forgetfulness in Hades, the underworld, in classical mythology.
3. **Dryad** (drī´ əd): In classical mythology, a wood nymph.
4. **draft:** Drink.
5. **Flora:** In classical mythology, the goddess of flowers, or the flowers themselves.
6. **Provençal** (prō´ vən säl´): Pertaining to Provence, a region in southern France, renowned in the late Middle Ages for its troubadours, who composed and sang love songs.

◆ Build Vocabulary

vintage (vin´ tij) *n.*: Wine of fine quality

Cultural Connection

Birds in Song and Story
Like poets, musicians and storytellers have long been inspired by the beautiful calls of songbirds. In many cultures, bird flight and birdsong are associated with freedom from material concerns. In Japanese haiku, the nightingale is a symbol invoking spring. Some well-known examples of tunes, poems, and folk tales involving songbirds include: Charlie "Bird" Parker's "Ornithology," Hans Christian Andersen's "The Emperor's Nightingale," Yeats's "Sailing to Byzantium," Wilde's "The Nightingale and the Rose," Stevens's "Thirteen Ways of Looking at a Blackbird," and Frost's "Never Again Would Birds' Song Be the Same." If possible, read or play some of these musical and literary works for students. Discuss reasons why poets and musicians in particular would find bird calls inspiring.

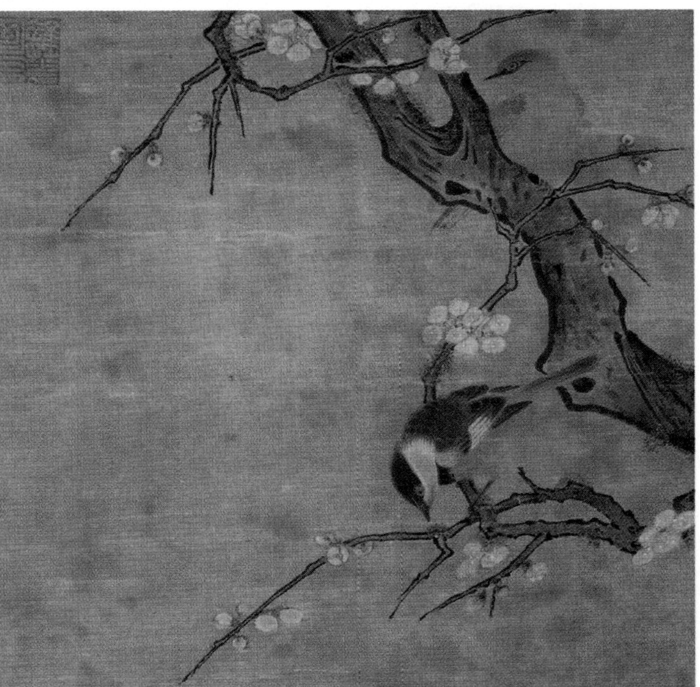

Small Bird on a Flowering Plum Branch
Attributed to Ma Lin, The Gotoh Museum

▲ Critical Viewing ❸
Compare the mood of this painting with that of stanza III. **[Compare and Contrast]**

❷

O for a beaker full of the warm South,
Full of the true, the blushful Hippocrene,[7]
With beaded bubbles winking at the brim,
And purple-stained mouth;
That I might drink, and leave the world unseen,
And with thee fade away into the forest dim:

III

Fade far away, dissolve, and quite forget
What thou among the leaves hast never known,
The weariness, the fever, and the fret
Here, where men sit and hear each other groan;
Where palsy shakes a few, sad, last gray hairs,
Where youth grows pale, and specter-thin, and dies;[8]
Where but to think is to be full of sorrow
And leaden-eyed despairs,
Where Beauty cannot keep her lustrous eyes,
Or new Love pine at them beyond tomorrow.

---

7. **Hippocrene** (hip′ ə krēn′): In classical mythology, the fountain of the Muses on Mt. Helicon. From this fountain flowed the waters of inspiration.
8. **youth . . . dies:** Keats is referring to his brother, Tom, who had died from tuberculosis the previous winter.

►Critical Viewing◄

❸ Compare and Contrast
Students may say that the painting conveys a sense of serenity and timeless beauty that contrasts sharply with the suffering and lack of time described in stanza III.

Humanities: Art

Small Bird on a Flowering Plum Branch, attributed to Ma Lin, twelfth or thirteenth century.

This painting on silk depicts a bird similar to the poem's nightingale. Like Keats's nightingale, the bird is perched upon a plum tree branch.

Ma Lin was a landscape painter of China's Sung Dynasty. The bird and flower were a favored Sung motif. The serenity of the scene suggests the freedom from earthly concerns for which the speaker longs in "Ode to a Nightingale."

Use these questions for discussion.

1. What elements of beauty would Keats admire in this painting? *He might admire the simple composition of the bird and tree, the delicacy of the blossoms, and the contrast of blank background with subject.*
2. How might Keats view the bird's beauty as an affirmation of his poetry? *If the beautiful bird can exist in a chaotic world, then so can the beauty of poetry.*

Beyond the Classroom

Career Connection

Historian/Classicist Many of Keats's poems contain allusions to historical events or people, particularly but not exclusively those from classical times. Like Keats, historians today use their knowledge of earlier cultures to understand current events. Have interested students contact history or classics departments at local colleges, universities, or libraries to learn more about becoming a historian or classicist.

Community Connection

For John Keats, the nightingale was a strong poetic inspiration. Ask students what they think inspires artists in your community. Encourage students to learn about artistic expression around them, visiting galleries or museums, joining poetry or literary reading groups, attending public theater, and experiencing street art. Urge students to consider all forms of art and to speak with artists if possible. As a class, compare the inspirations of today's artists with the things that inspired John Keats.

◆ Reading Strategy

❶ **Paraphrase** Have students paraphrase this passage. *Sample paraphrase: Fly away nightingale! I'll fly to you using the magic of my poetry, not on Bacchins' leopard-driven chariot.*

❷ **Enrichment** Novelists and songwriters sometimes obtain the titles of their works by borrowing a line from a poem. F. Scott Fitzgerald entitled one of his novels *Tender is the Night.* This phrase is also the title of a song by Jackson Browne. Fantasy writer Dave Duncan produced a series of books with titles taken from stanza vii of Keats's poem: *Magic Casement, Fairylands Forlorn, Perilous Seas,* and *Emperor and Clown.*

Customize for *Verbal/Linguistic Learners*

❸ Stanza V is justly acclaimed as a beautifully lyrical evocation of the scents and sounds of an early summer woodland evening. Challenge students to write a similarly short but vivid description of the scents, sounds, and other non-visual details of the setting of their choice. Alternatively, you may want to have students use their imaginations to describe the nonvisual elements of the settings in one or more of the following ***Art Transparencies:*** 9 (*Big Catch,* by Carleton Murrel, p. 39), 10 (*African Jazz Series #5,* by Michael Cummings), and 15 (*Piccadilly Circus,* by Charles Ginner, p. 63).

◆ Critical Thinking

❹ **Interpret** Ask students: If the poet should die, what would happen to the nightingale's song? *Students may say that it would continue unabated, though the poet would no longer hear it.*

IV

❶ Away! away! for I will fly to thee,
Not charioted by Bacchus[9] and his pards,
But on the viewless[10] wings of Poesy,[11]
Though the dull brain perplexes and retards:
❷ Already with thee! tender is the night,
And haply[12] the Queen-Moon is on her throne,
Clustered around by all her starry Fays;[13]
But here there is no light,
Save what from heaven is with the breezes blown
Through verdurous[14] glooms and winding mossy ways.

V

❸ I cannot see what flowers are at my feet,
Nor what soft incense hangs upon the boughs,
But, in embalmed[15] darkness, guess each sweet
Wherewith the seasonable month endows
The grass, the thicket, and the fruit-tree wild;
White hawthorn, and the pastoral eglantine;[16]
Fast fading violets covered up in leaves;
And mid-May's eldest child,
The coming musk-rose, full of dewy wine,
The murmurous haunt of flies on summer eves.

VI

Darkling[17] I listen; and, for many a time
I have been half in love with easeful Death,
Called him soft names in many a mused[18] rhyme,
To take into the air my quiet breath;
❹ Now more than ever seems it rich to die,
To cease upon the midnight with no pain,
While thou art pouring forth thy soul abroad
In such an ecstasy!
Still wouldst thou sing, and I have ears in vain—
To thy high requiem become a sod.

---

9. **Bacchus** (bak´ əs): In classical mythology, the god of wine, who was often represented in a chariot drawn by leopards ("pards").
10. **viewless:** Invisible.
11. **Poesy:** Poetic fancy.
12. **haply:** Perhaps.
13. **Fays:** Fairies.
14. **verdurous:** Green-foliaged.
15. **embalmed:** Perfumed.
16. **eglantine** (eg´ lən tīn´): Sweetbrier or honeysuckle.
17. **Darkling:** In the dark.
18. **mused:** Meditated.

◆ Build Vocabulary

requiem (rek´ wē əm) *n.*: Musical composition honoring the dead

Speaking and Listening Mini-Lesson

Oral Report

This mini-lesson supports the Speaking and Listening activity in the Idea Bank (p. 693).

Introduce the Concept Explain to students that the oral reports they will be presenting combine the elements of an informative speech and a research report.

Develop Background Have students discuss these tips.

For an informative speech:

- Speak slowly, clearly, and with feeling.
- Start with an overview of your talk.
- Cover points in a clear, organized manner.
- Provide clear transitions.
- In your conclusion, include a summary of your main points.

For a research report:

- Use a variety of sources.
- Organize details logically.
- Support main ideas with details.
- Use charts, illustrations, and diagrams to clarify your ideas.

Apply the Information Have students work in groups to gather information, organize their materials, and divide the parts of their presentation among the members of the group. After they rehearse, have them give their report to the class.

Assess the Outcome Have students assess their peers' performance based on the criteria in Develop Background.

VII

Thou wast not born for death, immortal Bird! ❺
No hungry generations tread thee down;
The voice I hear this passing night was heard
In ancient days by emperor and clown:
Perhaps the selfsame song that found a path
Through the sad heart of Ruth,[19] when, sick for home,
She stood in tears amid the alien corn;
The same that ofttimes hath
Charmed magic casements, opening on the foam
Of perilous seas, in fairylands forlorn. ❻

VIII

Forlorn! the very word is like a bell
To toll me back from thee to my sole self!
Adieu! the fancy cannot cheat so well
As she is famed[20] to do, deceiving elf.
Adieu! adieu! thy plaintive anthem[21] fades
Past the near meadows, over the still stream,
Up the hillside; and now 'tis buried deep
In the next valley-glades:
Was it a vision, or a waking dream?
Fled is that music:—Do I wake or sleep?

19. **Ruth:** In the Bible (Ruth 2:1–23), a widow who left her home and went to Judah to work in the corn (wheat) fields.
20. **famed:** Reported.
21. **anthem:** Hymn.

Guide for Responding

◆ *Literature and Your Life*

Reader's Response Have you ever experienced a mood similar to the speaker's while you were in natural surroundings? Explain.

Thematic Response Is the nightingale real or a figment of the poet's imagination? Explain.

☑ Check Your Comprehension

1. What wish does the speaker express in lines 19–20 and again in lines 31–35?
2. For what was the nightingale not born, according to line 61?
3. (a) What does hearing the word *forlorn* do to the speaker? (b) With what question does he conclude the poem?

◆ Critical Thinking

INTERPRET

1. What causes the speaker's emotional state in stanza I? **[Infer]**
2. (a) What differences between the speaker's world and the bird's are described in stanza IV? (b) What is meant in line 38 by "here there is no light"? **[Interpret]**
3. (a) What does the speaker find tempting in stanza VI? (b) In what ways does the poem shift focus in stanza VII? **[Interpret]**

APPLY

4. This poem ends with a question. What is its relevance, both to the poem and to the spirit of the Romantic movement? **[Apply]**

◆ Grammar and Style

❺ Direct Address Point out the words of direct address in this line, "immortal Bird." Ask students how the direct address affects the tone of the poem. *Students should note that it reestablished the personal, almost conversational tone of the poem by reminding readers that a specific bird is being addressed.*

◆ Reading Strategy

❻ Paraphrase Ask students: How would you paraphrase the poet's thoughts in these lines? *Paraphrases should include the idea that beauty, such as in the nightingale's song, is permanent and changeless.*

Reinforce and Extend

Answers

◆ *Literature and Your Life*

Reader's Response Yes, dusk in the park inspires a similar mood; no, natural surroundings fail to inspire such a mood.

Thematic Focus Students may say that although the poem is inspired by a real nightingale, the bird in the poem may be symbolic or part of a dream.

☑ Check Your Comprehension

1. He wishes to leave the world behind and join the nightingale.
2. It was not born for death.
3. (a) The word *forlorn* brings the poet out of his reverie. (b) Once the nightingale's song is over, he questions whether he is awake or asleep.

◆ Critical Thinking

1. The nightingale's song causes the speaker's emotional state.
2. (a) The real world is one in which the brain is perplexed and dull; the nightingale's world is one of permanent, dreamlike joy. (b) He means that Earth is dull and devoid of "light."
3. (a) The speaker finds the idea of death tempting. (b) It focuses on the nightingale's song through time, instead of at the moment; it deals with the idea of permanence.
4. Suggested response: For both the poem and the Romantic movement, the speaker's poetic vision is a kind of an awakening to an intenser life and higher reality; a return to ordinary life is, by contrast, a kind of sleep.

Develop Understanding

One-Minute Insight In this poem, Keats comes to an understanding about the nature of truth and beauty as he gazes upon an ancient Greek urn. The scenes depicted on the urn, frozen in time, eternally beautiful and unchanging, symbolize that the urn's beauty embodies the eternity of truth.

Customize for
More Advanced Students
❶ Have students write line 2 on a separate sheet of paper and mark the stressed and unstressed syllables. *The second, fourth, sixth, ninth and tenth syllables are stressed.* Have students discuss what is unusual about this line. *Although there are five stresses in the line, they do not follow the pattern of pure iambic pentameter.* Explain that the poet has substituted a pyrrhic foot of two unstressed syllables and a spondee (spondaic foot) of two stressed syllables for the expected iambic feet (unstressed-stressed). Encourage students to speculate on the effect created by such metrical variations. *A pyrrhic foot speeds up the line; a spondee slows down the line and adds emphasis. Metrical variations in general make poetry more interesting and lively.* You may want to mention that Keats often used terminal spondees in his work.

◆ Critical Thinking

❷ **Draw Conclusions** Ask students: What conclusions can you draw from the opening stanza? *Possible responses: The urn has on it pictures of people or gods; Keats does not know the story behind the urn's creation or its picture, but admires it.*

◆ Literature and Your Life

❸ Guide students in relating lines 11–14 to their own experience. *Students may describe times when the way they imagined something was far superior to the real thing. For example, they may have imagined more terrifying monsters when reading a horror story than were produced for the movie version of the book.*

Ode on a Grecian Urn

John Keats

I

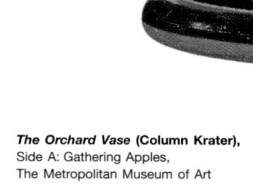

Thou still unravished bride of quietness
❶ Thou foster child of silence and slow time,
Sylvan[1] historian, who canst thus express
A flowery tale more sweetly than our rhyme:
What leaf-fringed legend haunts about thy shape
Of deities or mortals, or of both,
❷ In Tempe[2] or the dales of Arcady?[3]
What men or gods are these? What maidens loath?[4]
What mad pursuit? What struggle to escape?
What pipes and timbrels?[5] What wild ecstasy?

II

Heard melodies are sweet, but those unheard
Are sweeter; therefore, ye soft pipes, play on;
❸ Not to the sensual[6] ear, but, more endeared,
Pipe to the spirit ditties of no tone:
Fair youth, beneath the trees, thou canst not leave
Thy song, nor ever can those trees be bare;
Bold Lover, never, never canst thou kiss,
Though winning near the goal—yet, do not grieve;
She cannot fade, though thou hast not thy bliss,
Forever wilt thou love, and she be fair!

III

Ah, happy, happy boughs! that cannot shed
Your leaves, nor ever bid the Spring adieu;
And, happy melodist, unwearied,
Forever piping songs forever new;
More happy love! more happy, happy love!
Forever warm and still to be enjoyed,
Forever panting, and forever young;
All breathing human passion far above,
That leaves a heart high-sorrowful and cloyed,
A burning forehead, and a parching tongue.

***The Orchard Vase* (Column Krater),**
Side A: Gathering Apples,
The Metropolitan Museum of Art

1. **Sylvan:** Rustic, representing the woods or forest.
2. **Tempe** (tem′ pē): Beautiful valley in Greece that has become a symbol of supreme rural beauty.
3. **Arcady** (är′ kə dē): Region in Greece that has come to represent supreme pastoral contentment.
4. **loath:** Unwilling.
5. **timbrels:** Tambourines.
6. **sensual:** Involving the physical sense of hearing.

Humanities: Artifact

The Orchard Vase (Column Krater), Side A: Women Gathering Apples, ancient Greek artifact, c. 525 B.C.

This vase depicts scenes from ancient Greek life that may be similar to those that inspired Keats to write his poem.

Painted vessels such as this one were usually created for utilitarian purposes. Nonetheless, they often contained highly individual drawings that show scenes from mythology, legend, and everyday life. The figures and decoration depicted here reflect the red-figure style and its interest in three-dimensional space, realistic features, and natural details.

Use these questions for discussion:

1. How might Keats feel about the apples depicted on this vase? *He might admire their eternal beauty and ripeness.*
2. How does the existence of this vase support the feelings Keats expresses in his poem? *Its survival over so many years symbolizes the enduring quality of beauty and therefore, of truth.*

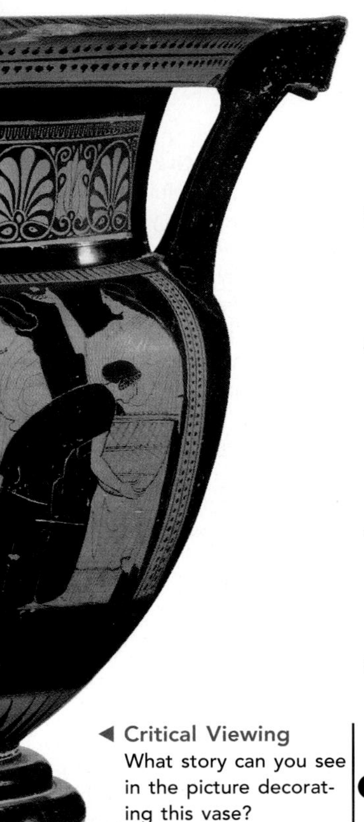

IV

Who are these coming to the sacrifice?
To what green altar, O mysterious priest,
Lead'st thou that heifer lowing at the skies,
And all her silken flanks with garlands dressed?
What little town by river or seashore,
Or mountain-built with peaceful citadel,
Is emptied of this folk, this pious morn?
And, little town, thy streets forevermore
Will silent be; and not a soul to tell
Why thou art desolate, can e'er return.

V

O Attic[7] shape! Fair attitude! with brede[8]
Of marble men and maidens overwrought,[9]
With forest branches and the trodden weed;
Thou, silent form, dost tease us out of thought
As doth eternity: Cold[10] Pastoral!
When old age shall this generation waste,
Thou shalt remain, in midst of other woe
Than ours, a friend to man, to whom thou say'st,
"Beauty is truth, truth beauty,"—that is all
Ye know on earth, and all ye need to know.

◀ Critical Viewing
What story can you see in the picture decorating this vase? **[Speculate]**

7. **Attic:** Attica was the region of Greece in which Athens was located; a region characterized by grace and simplicity.
8. **brede:** Interwoven pattern.
9. **overwrought:** All over.
10. **Cold:** Unchanging.

Guide for Responding

◆ *Literature and Your Life*

Reader's Response For Keats, great art embodies the ideas of unchanging beauty, love, and truth. What values do you place on art?

Thematic Response To what reality, or realization, does the speaker arrive at the end of this poem?

☑ Check Your Comprehension

1. Whom or what does this poem address in stanza II? in stanza III?
2. Summarize the two scenes that the urn depicts.
3. What message does the urn convey in line 49?

◆ Critical Thinking

INTERPRET

1. How can the urn tell its "flowery tale more sweetly than our rhyme"? **[Analyze]**
2. What does the speaker feel the leaves, the melodist, and the lovers on the urn all have in common? **[Infer]**
3. (a) Why might the lover in stanza II grieve? (b) Why does the speaker advise him not to grieve? **[Interpret]**

EVALUATE

4. What do you think of the urn's message in line 49? Support your answer. **[Assess]**

Beyond the Selection

FURTHER READING

Other Works by John Keats
Endymion; Hyperion; "The Eve of St. Agnes"

Other Poems About Truth and Beauty
"The History of Truth," Wystan Hugh Auden
"The Wayfarer," Stephen Crane
"Go, Lovely Rose!" Edmund Waller

We suggest that you preview these works before recommending them to students.

INTERNET

You may find additional information about John Keats at the following sites. Please be aware that sites may have changed since we published this information.

For a biography and selected criticism of Keats's work, visit **http://portico.bl.uk/exhibitions/keats/overview.html**

To read Keats's letters, visit **http://www.wfu.edu/~nowvibp4/keats.htm**

We *strongly recommend* that you preview the sites before you send students to them.

▶Critical Viewing◀

❹ **Speculate** Students should come up with stories that have something to do with women in ancient costume who are picking apples.

Customize for
English Language Learners
These students will likely need assistance to successfully navigate the ode's language. Go over the poem line by line, helping students paraphrase each sentence.

Reinforce and Extend

Answers

◆ *Literature and Your Life*

Reader's Response Students may agree with Keats. They may also value art because it makes people think or respond, or because it expresses the ideas and feelings of the artist.

Thematic Focus He realizes that "Beauty is truth, truth beauty."

☑ **Check Your Comprehension**

1. In stanza II the poem addresses the "fair youth" who is pursuing his love. In stanza III the poem addresses the trees and a musician.
2. The scenes on the urn depict a youth pursuing his lover against a background of trees and piping musicians, and a ritual sacrificing of an animal to the gods.
3. Line 49 conveys that beauty conveys essential truth, and truth in itself is beauty.

◆ **Critical Thinking**

1. It tells its tale through pictures whose beauty the poet feels he cannot emulate in words.
2. They are all happy.
3. (a) The youth in stanza II might grieve because he cannot catch and kiss his love. (b) The youth should not grieve because his love is eternal and the maid always fair and young.
4. Some students may agree with this axiom; other students may point out that truth can be ugly and beauty deceptive.

Reinforce and Extend

Answers

◆ Reading Strategy

Students' paraphrases may be similar to the following:

1. Then I felt like an astronomer who discovers a new planet.
2. Nightingale, you are not meant to die. The passage of time does not wear you down. Your voice, heard in ancient times by king and fool, comforted the homesick Ruth, a widow from the Bible, and opened the windows of the imagination.
3. I've traveled often and at one time visited Greece, Homer's homeland.
4. When I fear that I shall never see you again and never enjoy the power of love, then I think about the enormity of the world and realize that personal love and fame are of little importance in the grand scheme of things.

Paraphrasing should aid students' understanding.

◆ Build Vocabulary

Using the Suffix *-age*

1. *wattage:* amount of watts
2. *shortage:* deficiency in amount
3. *patronage:* quality of being a patron
4. *leverage:* action of a lever
5. *storage:* state of storing
6. *wastage:* amount of waste

Using the Word Bank

1. requiem
2. gleaned
3. surmise
4. ken
5. teeming
6. vintage

◆ Literary Focus

1. (a) Keats's odes honor a nightingale and a Grecian urn. (b) Yes; he is passionate about classical and natural beauty.
2. Keats's odes are Horatian, because they consist entirely of ten-line stanzas that follow a regular rhyme pattern: an *abab* quatrain and a *cdecde, cdeced,* or *cdedce* sestet.

◆ Grammar and Style

1. light-winged Dryad of the trees
2. happy, happy boughs
3. O mysterious priest

Guide for Responding *(continued)*

◆ Reading Strategy

PARAPHRASE

When you **paraphrase**, restating an author's ideas in your own words, it helps you understand complex or poetic language such as you'll find in Keats's poetry. For example, the line "When I have fears that I may cease to be" is poetically elegant, but its meaning may elude readers. When paraphrased, the line's meaning becomes more evident: "When I'm scared that I'll die." Paraphrase the following:

1. "Then felt I like some watcher of the skies / When a new planet swims into his ken"
2. Stanza VII of "Ode to a Nightingale"
3. First seven lines of "On First Looking into Chapman's Homer"
4. Lines 10–14 of "When I Have Fears That I May Cease to Be"

How did paraphrasing these passages aid your understanding?

◆ Build Vocabulary

USING THE SUFFIX *-age*

Knowing that the suffix *-age,* as in *vintage,* means "state or quality of, cost of , place of, or collection of," define the following words.

1. wattage	**2.** shortage	**3.** patronage
4. leverage	**5.** storage	**6.** wastage

USING THE WORD BANK

Complete these sentences with the best word from the Word Bank. Write the words in your notebook, and use each word only once.

1. At the funeral, the organist played a ___?___.
2. At harvest time, all the farmer's children ___?___ grain from the reaped fields.
3. Despite the evidence, nothing could sway his initial ___?___.
4. There are many mysteries beyond our ___?___.
5. The bird's breast was ___?___ with song.
6. The wine collector carefully labeled and stored each ___?___.

◆ Literary Focus

ODE

Two of Keats's poems, "Ode on a Grecian Urn" and "Ode to a Nightingale," are powerful **odes**—lyric poems that focus on a single, usually serious subject, often honoring that subject and addressing it directly. There are three basic types of odes. The **Pindaric ode** contains three different types of stanzas, and the **Horatian ode** contains one type of stanza that is repeated. A third type of ode, the **irregular ode**, follows no pattern.

1. (a) What do Keats's two odes honor? (b) Would you say he treats his subjects seriously? Why or why not?
2. Classify Keats's two odes as regular or Pindaric, Horatian, or irregular. Explain.

◆ Grammar and Style

DIRECT ADDRESS

Terms of **direct address**, in which a person or thing is addressed by name or by a phrase, appear frequently in Keats's poetry, investing the poems with an intimate tone. Commas are used to set off terms of direct address from the rest of a clause or sentence. In the following example, note how the inclusion of a term of direct address personalizes the poem, giving it immediacy and warmth.

And when I feel, *fair creature of an hour,*
That I shall never look upon thee more,

Practice In your notebook, identify the words of direct address within each passage.

1. "That thou, light-winged Dryad of the trees, / In some melodious plot . . ."
2. "Ah, happy, happy boughs! that cannot shed / Your leaves . . ."
3. "To what green altar, O mysterious priest, / Lead'st thou . . ."

Writing Application Rewrite this paragraph in your notebook, inserting two terms of direct address and punctuating them correctly.

I wandered through Athens thinking of you. Your memory burns bright in my mind. All others fade to nothingness when you're near. Please stay true.

Students' rewrites may be similar to the following:

I wandered through Athens thinking of you, Ellen. Your memory, my love, burns bright in my mind. Darling, all others fade to nothingness when you're near.

Writer's Solution

For additional instruction and practice, use the lesson on Punctuation in the **Writing Lab CD-ROM** and the page on Commas in the *Writer's Solution Grammar Practice Book,* p. 83.

Build Your Portfolio

Idea Bank

Writing

1. **Prose Tribute** Write a prose tribute to the nightingale or the Grecian urn. Express ideas and attitudes similar to those of Keats, but in less lofty, more informal language.

2. **Irregular Ode** Write an irregular ode, or ode with no fixed stanza pattern, that pays tribute to someone or something you admire.

3. **Response to Criticism** Scholar Douglas Bush writes of Keats: "The romantic elements in him remained . . . central, sane, normal—in everything but their intensity—and did not run into transcendental . . . excesses. . . ." Write an essay in which you use passages from Keats's poetry to support this statement.

Speaking and Listening

4. **Informal Retelling** Perform for the class an informal retelling of either "When I Have Fears" or "Chapman's Homer" in contemporary English. **[Performing Arts Link]**

5. **Oral Report** Some of Keats's poems were inspired by the Elgin Marbles in the British Museum. Give an oral report on these works of art, which sparked much controversy. **[Science Link]**

Projects

6. **Museum Catalog** Working in a small group, create a catalog of ancient Greek pieces found in the British Museum or another museum housing Greek antiquities. You might obtain your information from books or tourist pamphlets. **[Art Link]**

7. **Science Display** Research the nightingale's call, appearance, habits, and habitat. Present your findings in a display that includes photos or other illustrations. **[Science Link]**

Writing Mini-Lesson

Description of a Moment in Time

In many of his poems, Keats explores significant moments in his life, such as discovering the magic of Homer through Chapman's words, or finding the essence of beauty while gazing at a Grecian urn. Write a description that captures an important moment in your life. Use precise details to convey a main impression of the moment you're re-creating.

Writing Skills Focus: Precise Details

Your description will be more effective if you choose **precise details** to create a main impression. Precise details include these features:

- Vivid verbs and precise nouns
- Interesting and apt comparisons

Model From Literature

Then felt I like some watcher of the skies
When a new planet swims into his ken;

In these two lines, Keats creates a strong impression of the moment of discovery. The precise details include a comparison of the poet to an astronomer and the vivid verb *swims*.

Prewriting Determine the main impression you wish to convey. Then gather precise details that will help you convey this impression.

Drafting Weave together the precise details you've gathered in an order your readers can follow. For example, if you are describing a scene, you might use a spatial order—for example, presenting details from left to right.

Revising Be sure your details convey a strong, single impression and make clear the significance of the moment you've tried to capture. Delete details that detract from the impression you're making and add details that will more clearly convey the significance of the moment.

✓ ASSESSMENT OPTIONS

Formal Assessment, Selection Test, pp. 166–168, and Assessment Resources Software. The selection test is designed so that it can be easily customized to the performance levels of your students. ***Alternative Assessment***, p. 35, includes options for less advanced students, more advanced students, visual/spatial learners, musical/rhythmic learners, and verbal/linguistic learners.

PORTFOLIO ASSESSMENT
Use the following rubrics in the ***Alternative Assessment*** booklet to assess student writing:
Prose Tribute: Expression Rubric, p. 95
Irregular Ode: Poetry Rubric, p. 109
Response to Criticism: Literary Analysis/Interpretation Rubric, p. 113
Writing Mini-Lesson: Description Rubric, p. 98

Idea Bank

Customizing for *Performance Levels*
Following are suggestions for matching Idea Bank topics with your students' performance levels:
Less Advanced Students: 1, 4
Average Students: 2, 5, 7
More Advanced Students: 3, 6

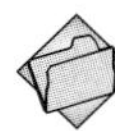

Customizing for *Learning Modalities*
Following are suggestions for matching Idea Bank topics with your students' learning modalities:
Visual/Spatial: 6, 7
Verbal/Linguistic: 1, 2, 3, 4, 5
Interpersonal: 6

Writing Mini-Lesson

Refer students to the Writing Handbook, page 1189, for instruction on the writing process, and page 1191 for further information on description.

Writer's Solution

Writers at Work Videodisc
Have students view the videodisc segment (Ch. 1) featuring travel writer Guy Garcia to see how he uses description to convey the experience of being in a new place. Have students discuss how vivid, detailed descriptions help people share their experiences with others.

Play frames 335 to 10062

Writing Lab CD-ROM
Have students complete the tutorial on Description. Follow these steps:

1. View the interactive examples of sensory details.
2. Draft on the computer, using the word bins of sensory details, places, character traits, and modifiers to create a vivid picture of a moment in time.
3. Use the revision checker for vague adjectives.

Allow approximately 80 minutes of class time to complete these steps.

Sourcebook
Have students use Chapter 1, Description (pp. 1–29), for additional support. The chapter includes in-depth instruction on using sensory details (pp. 18–19) and creating a main impression (p. 19), and using modifiers (p. 27).

Prepare and Engage

OBJECTIVES

1. To read, comprehend, and interpret lyric poetry
2. To explore literary connections between world lyric poetry and the selections in Part 2
3. To respond to the poems through writing, speaking and listening, and a project

PORTFOLIO OPPORTUNITIES

Writing: Japanese "Lorelei"; Personality Profile; Response to Criticism

Speaking and Listening: Music and Poetry

Project: Personalities of Poets

More About the Authors

Heinrich Heine became known around the world through the musical adaptations of Schumann and Schubert. Collected in *The Book of Songs,* these poems largely arise from Heine's despair after an unhappy love experience.

Matsuo Basho spent his early adult years as a samurai warrior in the service of a feudal lord. When his lord died, Basho returned with renewed focus to his longtime interest in poetry. Basho's studies of Zen philosophy, with his rejection of popular trivialized poetry, were strong influences on his haiku.

Yosa Buson left behind a life of wealth and comfort to pursue his many artistic talents. His haiku reflect his knowledge of Chinese and Japanese classics, as well as the influence of the much-admired Basho.

Kobayashi Issa studied haiku with Chikua Nirokuan in what is Tokyo. Then, like Basho and Buson, he traveled extensively. His first collection of poems, *Travel Gleanings,* was published after these travels.

Interest Grabber Write the following questions on the chalkboard: 1) What do you find irresistible? 2) What inspires you? Have students jot their answers on a slip of paper and submit it anonymously. Read some or all of the slips, censoring as necessary and discuss class results. Then tell students that for centuries, poets around the world have addressed questions like these.

CONNECTIONS TO WORLD LITERATURE

The Lorelei
Heinrich Heine

Haiku
Matsuo Bashō Yosa Buson Kobayashi Issa

Literary Connection

Lyric Poetry

In ancient Greece, lyric poetry was verse recited or sung to the accompaniment of the stringed instrument called the lyre. Today, lyric poems provide their own verbal "music" as they express the personal thoughts and emotions of the poet.

The Romantic Lyric Poem

Although lyric poems have been written for thousands of years, the Romantic era put its special stamp on the lyric. The preference of Romantic poets for brief, expressive poems isn't surprising, given their commitment to personal emotion. Wordsworth and Coleridge, writing in the Preface to *Lyrical Ballads* (1800), defined poetry itself as "the spontaneous overflow of powerful feelings."

A second generation of poets—Shelley, Byron, and Keats—contributed their own melodies and perspectives to the Romantic lyric. In "Ode to the West Wind," Shelley gives a political meaning to images from nature as the wind heralds a new era in history. Byron expresses awe at nature's power, and disdain for human pride, in his lyrical "Apostrophe to the Ocean" from *Childe Harold's Pilgrimage.* This poet's brooding pose as a mysterious, despairing hero, at home in nature and scornful of society, influenced Romantic poetry throughout Europe.

Lyric Poetry Around the World

One European contemporary of Byron's was the German poet Heinrich Heine (hīn′rih hī nə). This talented lyric poet gave the time-honored subject of love a bittersweet flavor in his work, as you will see in "The Lorelei." His lyrics weren't written for music, as ancient Greek verse was, but they were later set to music by such famous composers as Robert Schumann and Franz Schubert.

Writing earlier than the English Romantics, Japanese poets like Bashō (ba′ shō), Buson (bo͞o′ sän), and Issa (ē′ sä′) anticipated the Romantics' love of nature. These writers conveyed suggestive images in the miniature poetic form of the haiku, which consists of three lines of five, seven, and five syllables each. Precise and simple, haiku always contain a reference to a particular season.

HEINRICH HEINE (1797–1856)

The German poet Heinrich Heine was a brilliant love poet and a gifted satirist and political writer whose fierce attacks on repression made him a controversial figure.

MATSUO BASHŌ (1644–1694)

Matsuo Bashō traveled widely through Japan, recording his observations and insights in poems and travel diaries.

YOSA BUSON (1716–1783)

Yosa Buson presents a romantic view of the Japanese landscape, vividly capturing the wonder and mystery of nature.

KOBAYASHI ISSA (1763–1827)

The poetry of Kobayashi Issa captures the essence of daily life in Japan, as experienced by common people, and conveys his compassion for the less fortunate.

Prentice Hall Literature Program Resources

REINFORCE / RETEACH / EXTEND

Selection Support Pages
Build Vocabulary, p. 169
Thematic and Literary Connections, p. 170

Formal Assessment Selection Test, pp. 169–170; Assessment Resources Software

Resource Pro CD-ROM
"The Lorelei," Haiku—includes all resource material and customizable lesson plan

Listening to Literature Audiocassettes
"The Lorelei," Haiku

The Lorelei

Heinrich Heine

Translated by

Aaron Kramer

I cannot explain the sadness
That's fallen on my breast.
An old, old fable haunts me,
And will not let me rest.

The air grows cool in the twilight,
And softly the Rhine[1] flows on;
The peak of a mountain sparkles
Beneath the setting sun.

More lovely than a vision,
A girl sits high up there;
Her golden jewelry glistens,
She combs her golden hair.

With a comb of gold she combs it,
And sings an evensong;
The wonderful melody reaches
A boat, as it sails along.

The boatman hears, with an anguish
More wild than was ever known;
He's blind to the rocks around him;
His eyes are for her alone.

—At last the waves devoured
The boat, and the boatman's cry;
And this she did with her singing,
The golden Lorelei.

1. **Rhine** (rīn): River in western Europe.

Develop Understanding

One-Minute Insight Like so many Romantic lyric works, "The Lorelei" captures passion and pain while also linking beauty to nature. The speaker recounts his sorrow over the fable of Lorelei, whose beauty and glorious song cause boatmen to fall so madly in love with her that they are blinded to the dangers around them. His reason overwhelmed by love, a boatman caught by the Lorelei's spell is doomed to drown.

Customize for *Visual/Spatial Learners*
Encourage these learners to capitalize on the vivid imagery in this poem for greater understanding. Urge them to engage their senses to see the girl's "golden jewelry glisten" as she "combs her golden hair."

Literary Connection

❶ **Lyric Poetry** Point out to students the speaker's emphasis on his uncontrollable emotions, a common feature in Romantic lyric poetry. Then ask students to name additional evidence of the genre in the first two stanzas. *Students should note the detailed description of nature, linking the speaker with that surrounding.*

◆ Critical Thinking

❷ **Interpret** Ask students: In what way are the boatman's feelings ironic? *Students may note that love is usually thought of as a pleasant emotion, thus the boatman's "anguish" over hearing a song of such beauty is ironic.*

Speaking and Listening Mini-Lesson

Music and Poetry

This mini-lesson supports the Speaking and Listening activity in the Idea Bank (p. 698).

Introduce the Concept Play some excerpts from contemporary songs that clearly show how lyrics and music work together to convey a message. Possibilities include Simon and Garfunkel's "Bridge Over Troubled Water," which uses hymn-like music to convey a message of comfort and reassurance.

Develop Background Explain to students that they will be working in small groups to find out how some nineteenth-century composers created music to support Heine's poetry.

Apply the Information Each group is responsible for locating a song, bringing in a recording, introducing and summarizing the song, and making a list of key points to bring up during the discussion. You may want to have groups prepare a handout or overhead transparency of the lyrics of their song.

Assess the Outcome Consider the following questions when evaluating each group's work:

- Did students provide information about the composer and when the music was composed?
- Did they provide a clear, concise, and accurate summary of what the song was about?
- Did they make logical, insightful points about the way the music supported the words?

Develop Understanding

One-Minute Insight Freezing a single moment in time, these haiku can be linked to Romantic lyric poetry by their emphasis on nature and emotion. Whether describing the connection between people and the clouds, noting a child's toy made wet by the rain, or offering a snapshot of a frog contemplating the distant horizon, these haiku demonstrate nature's constant presence in our lives.

Clarification Make sure students understand that each of the "stanzas" shown on these pages represents a separate haiku, though they may be linked together by subject.

Customize for *Less Proficient Readers*
Explain to these students that haiku is necessarily abbreviated in its language. Model how to analyze a haiku for its implied meanings—noting the connotative impact of words, hearing the sound rhythms, mentally replacing dashes with additional content.

◆ Critical Thinking

❶ **Analyze** Ask students: How would you characterize Bashō's attitude in his fifth and sixth haiku? *Students may say that the poet sees the human world as interrupting nature.*

▶Critical Viewing◀

❷ **Interpret** Students may say that the painting shows the coming of spring in the new growth on trees and hills.

Literary Connection

❸ **Lyric Poetry** The last line of a haiku often presents a flash of insight into nature or the speaker. Ask students: What startling insights do these two haiku present? *Suggested response: The first haiku captures the chill of revulsion the speaker feels when he hears a rat scampering through a cupboard. The second haiku reveals what a person can infer about individuals and society through observation—in this case, the speaker sees the straw cape of a poor peasant and the umbrella of a wealthier person.*

CONNECTIONS TO WORLD LITERATURE

HAIKU

Bashō

Translated by
Harold G. Henderson (first 3)
and Geoffrey Bownas (last 3)

The sun's way:
Hollyhocks turn toward it
Through all the rain of May.

Poverty's child—
He starts to grind the rice,
And gazes at the moon.

Clouds come from time to time—
And bring to men a chance to rest
From looking at the moon.

The cuckoo—
Its call stretching
Over the water.

❶ Seven sights were veiled
In mist—then I heard
Mii Temple's bell.[1]

Summer grasses—
All that remains
Of soldiers' visions.

1. **Mii** (mē´ ē´) **Temple's bell:** The bell at Mii Temple is known for its extremely beautiful sound. The temple is located near Otsu, a city in southern Japan.

❷ ▶ **Critical Viewing** How does this painting reflect the changing of seasons in the first haiku? **[Interpret]**

Crows Taking Flight Through Spring Haze, (1782–1846) Hanging scroll, Edo period, dated 1841: Toyama Kinenkan Okada, Foundation Toyama Memorial Museum

HAIKU

Yosa Buson

Translated by
Geoffrey Bownas

Scampering over saucers—
The sound of a rat.
Cold, cold. ❸

Spring rain:
Telling a tale as they go,
Straw cape, umbrella.

Spring rain:
In our sedan
Your soft whispers.

Spring rain:
A man lives here—
Smoke through the wall.

Spring rain:
Soaking on the roof
A child's rag ball.

Fuji[1] alone
Left unburied
By young green leaves.

1. **Fuji** (fo͞o´ jē): Mount Fuji is the highest peak in Japan (12,388 ft).

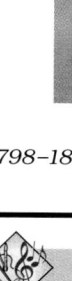

Humanities: Art

Crows Taking Flight Through Spring Haze, 1841, by Toyama Kinenkan Okada.

This hanging scroll depicts a spring landscape, capturing a moment in nature in much the same way as a haiku. In Japanese art, as in haiku, what is not shown or only hinted at is often as important as what is shown.

Japanese painter Toyama Kinenkan Okada was born in 1782 and is associated with the Edo period of Japanese art. This 250 year period of peace in Japan was centered in the city of Edo, now Tokyo. This hanging scroll dates from late in the Edo period, which ended in 1867.

Use these questions for discussion:

1. Which of Issa's haiku could describe this painting? *The third and sixth haiku both include distant views of a hilly landscape.*
2. Why might the mood of this painting be appropriate to haiku? *The delicately drawn landscape conveys a mood of simple serenity which is similar to the finely tuned language of haiku.*

HAIKU

Kobayashi Issa

Translated by

Geoffrey Bownas

❹ Melting snow:
And on the village
Fall the children.

Beautiful, seen through holes
Made in a paper screen:
The Milky Way.

Far-off mountain peaks
Reflected in its eyes:
The dragonfly.

❺ A world of dew:
Yet within the dewdrops—
Quarrels.

Viewing the cherry-blossom:
Even as they walk,
Grumbling.

With bland serenity
Gazing at the far hills:
A tiny frog.

Guide for Responding

CONNECTIONS TO WORLD LITERATURE

◆ Literature and Your Life

Reader's Response Did you prefer the short, direct form of haiku or the longer lyric poem "The Lorelei"? Explain.

Thematic Focus Which poem best combines fantasy with reality? Why?

Lyric Subjects List experiences from your own life that might make suitable subjects for a lyric poem. Jot down some details and images you might use in a poem about these subjects.

☑ Check Your Comprehension

1. Describe the woman who entrances the boatman in "The Lorelei."
2. Name three images from nature captured in the poems of Bashō.
3. What season dominates Buson's haiku?
4. Which two haiku by Issa combine far things with near ones?

◆ Critical Thinking

INTERPRET

1. According to German legend, the Lorelei was a sea nymph whose singing on a rock in the Rhine River lured sailors to shipwrecks. (a) What impression of the Lorelei does Heine convey in his poem? (b) Which images contribute to this impression? **[Infer]**
2. Buson establishes the setting in the first line of each of his haiku. How does the setting shape your impression of the image in the final lines of each of these poems? **[Analyze]**
3. Do any of these haiku reflect the bittersweet attitude of Heine's "The Lorelei"? Explain. **[Compare and Contrast]**

EVALUATE

4. Which poet is most effective at conveying images of nature? Why? **[Make a Judgment]**

◆ Critical Thinking

❹ **Infer** Ask students: What double meaning can you infer from Issa's first haiku? *Students may note that both the snow and the children "fall" upon the city.*

Literary Connection

❺ **Lyric Poetry** Ask students: How does this haiku reflect the values of Romantic lyric poetry? *Students should note that the haiku acknowledges the emotions beyond nature and the tumult of human life.*

Reinforce and Extend

Answers

◆ Literature and Your Life

Reader's Response Some students will prefer the detail and plot of a longer lyric poem. Other students will prefer the "sound bite" terseness and precision of a haiku.

Thematic Focus Students may find that "The Lorelei," with its imaginative and realistic details, best combines fantasy and reality.

☑ Check Your Comprehension

1. She is golden-haired and young, wears sparkling gold jewelry, and is combing her hair.
2. Possible response: Images from nature include hollyhocks, clouds, and a cuckoo's song.
3. Spring figures prominently in the featured haiku.
4. The second, third, and sixth haiku combine far things with near ones.

◆ Critical Thinking

1. (a) The Lorelei is beautiful and irresistible. (b) She is "more lovely than a vision," sings "a wonderful melody," and the boatman has "eyes for her alone."
2. Each setting arouses certain associations. These associations carry over to the images that follow.
3. Students may say that the sixth haiku by Bashō is also bittersweet. Other answers are possible.
4. Some students may say that Issa excels at conveying small, exquisite, easily overlooked images of nature. Other students may favor one of the other poets.

Beyond the Selection

FURTHER READING

Other Works by the Authors

Travel Sketches, Heine; *Homage to Hokuju Rosen,* Buson; *The Narrow Road the Deep North,* Bashō; *Travel Gleanings,* Issa

Other Works About Nature

"Lady Moon," Christina Rossetti; "A Description of Morning," Jonathan Swift; "Mushrooms," Sylvia Plath

We suggest that you preview these works before recommending them to students.

INTERNET

You and your students may find additional information about the poets at the following sites.

For information and discussion of Buson and Bashō, visit **http://www.snet.org/edu/qvsd/mim/mim.proj.jap.frog.html**

For biographical data and other information about Issa, visit **http://www.threeweb.ad.jp/logos/ainet.issa2.html**

We *strongly recommend* that you preview the sites before you send students to them.

Answers
Literary Connection

1. Suggested response: Love may cloud a person's reason and blind him or her to potential problems or dangers.
2. Possible response: Issa has the best sense of humor, because some of his haiku poke fun at lofty attitudes. For example, the serene dewdrops contain (or reflect) quarrels, people quarrel while engaged in the supposedly uplifting experience of viewing cherry blossoms, and the individual engaged in the profound task of contemplating mountains is a frog.
3. Keep in mind that songs that seem profound to one person may seem superficial to another. Evaluate student responses based on how well they provide evidence to support their case, not on their choice of song.

Idea Bank

Customizing for
Performance Levels

Following are suggestions for matching Idea Bank topics with your students' performance levels:

Less Advanced Students: 1
Average Students: 2, 4
More Advanced Students: 3, 5

Customizing for
Learning Modalities

Following are suggestions for matching Idea Bank topics with your students' learning modalities:

Interpersonal: 4, 5
Verbal/Linguistic: 1, 2, 3, 4, 5,
Musical/Rhythmic: 4

Literary Connection

Lyric Poetry

Today, we expect lyric poetry to express a writer's deepest personal feelings, and that expectation is based on the practice of the British Romantic poets. Heine, a European poet influenced by Romanticism, also reveals personal emotion in his work. However, the Japanese haiku, which predate Romanticism and come from a non-European culture, express emotion more indirectly. At first, all the haiku seem to come from the same cookie-cutter. The more you compare them, however, the more you will see the feeling and personality hidden between the lines.

1. What conflict about love does Heine disclose in "The Lorelei"?
2. Which of the haiku writers reveals the best sense of humor? Use specific passages to prove your case.
3. (a) Choose a modern song that, like a Romantic lyric, expresses the writer's deepest emotions. (b) Cite passages from the song to explain what those emotions are.

Idea Bank

Writing

1. Japanese "Lorelei" Rewrite Heine's "The Lorelei" as a haiku without losing the essence of the poem.

2. Personality Profile Write a profile of one of these poets based on the thoughts and feelings he expresses in his work. Imagine that this profile will appear on the back cover of his book.

3. Response to Criticism Robert Hass has written:

> The spirit of haiku required that the language be kept plain. . . . It also demanded accurate and original images, drawn mostly from common life.

In an essay, verify or contradict this observation by citing passages from the work of Bashō, Buson, or Issa.

Speaking and Listening

4. Music and Poetry Robert Schumann and Franz Schubert set Heine's poems to music. Bring in a recording of one such setting and play it for the class. Then lead a discussion in which students analyze how words and music support each other. **[Music Link]**

Project

5. Personalities of Poets Research the life of Heinrich Heine or one of the haiku poets, and present your findings to the class. For information on the Japanese poets, look at books like *The Essential Haiku* by Robert Hass. **[Literature Link]**

✓ ASSESSMENT OPTIONS

Formal Assessment, Selection Test, pp. 169–170, and Assessment Resources Software. The selection test is designed so that it can be easily customized to the performance levels of your students.

PORTFOLIO ASSESSMENT
Use the following rubrics in the ***Alternative Assessment*** booklet to assess student writing:
Japanese "Lorelei": Poetry Rubric, p. 109
Personality Profile: Description Rubric, p. 98
Response to Criticism: Literary Analysis/Interpretation Rubric, p. 113

Writing Process Workshop

Video Script

Wordsworth, Coleridge, Byron, Shelley, and Keats—the poets of the Romantic Age—pioneered a new kind of lyric poetry to express their observations, thoughts, and feelings. In our time, many people use film or video as new ways to express observations and ideas. Join them by writing a **video script**—a drama written for video production. A video script is different from a play, since, in addition to dialogue and stage directions, it includes detailed camera directions.

Use the following skills to help you write a video script.

Writing Skills Focus

- ▶ Your script should contain **details appropriate to the medium.** Such details include lighting directions, camera angles, and dialogue. (See p. 627.)
- ▶ **Dramatic sound effects** will add excitement and energy to your script. (See p. 655.)
- ▶ **Realistic speech** will lend authenticity to your work. The style of language and word choice should suit your setting and characters. (See p. 667.)
- ▶ Your script should **convey one main impression** by carefully focusing on one main topic or character. The details of setting, lighting, costumes, and sound effects should contribute to the one impression. (See p. 693.)

The following video script is adapted from Jane Austen's *Sense and Sensibility.*

Model From Literature

from *The Sense and Sensibility Screenplay and Diaries*
by Emma Thompson

2. INT. NORLAND PARK. MR. DASHWOOD'S BEDROOM. NIGHT.
In the dim light shed by candles we see a bed in which a MAN (MR. DASHWOOD, 52) *lies—his skin waxy, his breathing labored.* ① *Around him two silhouettes move and murmur, their clothing susurrating* ② *in the deathly hush.* DOCTORS. A WOMAN (MRS. DASHWOOD, 50) *sits by his side, holding his hand, her eyes never leaving his face.* ③

MR. DASHWOOD (*urgent*)
Is John not yet arrived? ④

① This description gives the main impression of a deathwatch.

② The use of sound adds tension and creates drama.

③ Extensive use of visual and auditory details makes this story appropriate for film or video.

④ The formality and word choice in this line of dialogue is realistic for an English gentleman of the 1800's.

Extension

Explain to students that a video script has all the elements of literature as well as those of the visual arts. Thus, color, line, balance, and movement combine with character, setting, and plot. Dialogue, action, music, and other sound effects convey literary elements. For instance, the script writer can convey tone and mood through characters' words, tone of voice, and nonverbal cues; through setting, including color and lighting; through camera angles; and through sound effects, especially music. Ask students to view a short video clip to analyze how it combines literary and visual arts.

Prepare and Engage

Establish Writing Guidelines
Review the following key characteristics of a video script:

- A video script conveys one main impression about an observation or idea.
- It includes dialogue, stage directions, lighting directions, and camera angles.
- It relies on realistic speech for authenticity.

Before students begin, share with them the Scoring Rubric for Drama (p. 110 in ***Alternative Assessment***) so that students see the criteria by which they will be evaluated. Suggestions on page 701 customize the rubric to this workshop.

Writing and Language Transparencies Use Writing Process Model 4: Dramatic Scene (pp. 25–35) to provide a model of the writing and revising process.

Connect to Literature Refer students to the excerpt from Emma Thompson's "*Sense and Sensibility* Screenplay and Diaries" (p. 725). Have students look at the differences between the format for a screenplay and that for a drama.

Writer's Solution

Writers at Work Videodisc
To introduce students to the key elements of drama and to let them hear poet and playwright Derek Walcott discuss what motivates him to write poetry and drama, play the following.

Play frames 9291 to 19694

Writing Lab CD-ROM
Have students work in the Creative Writing tutorial as they write their video scripts. Follow these steps:

1. Students can review the audio-annotated video script model.
2. Have them review the Inspirations for a video script topic.
3. Suggest students use a Story Line Diagram to plot the video script.
4. Listen to Eavan Boland discuss revising drama.

Sourcebook
Students can find additional support in Creative Writing (Ch. 6), pp. 166–195.

Develop Student Writing

Prewriting

You may want to have students use a Story Map graphic organizer (***Writing and Language Transparencies,*** p. 127) to help organize their thoughts.

Customize for
More Advanced Students
To challenge these students, ask them to incorporate symbolism into their video scripts. Suggest that they consider a visual or audio symbol that enhances the main idea of the video script.

Writer's Solution

Writing Lab CD-ROM
The Gathering Details section of the Creative Writing tutorial includes Interactive Tips on using dialogue in drama. Ask students to note how the dialogue creates memorable characters.

Drafting

Remind students that all details—light, sound, dialogue, setting, camera angle—should work in unity to convey a single impression.

Applying Language Skills

Special Problems with Agreement Remind students that subject-verb agreement affects video scripts just as it does any other mode of writing.

Answers
Two hours . . . *are.* Inside, grunts and groans *fill.* . . . Large machines *creak.* . . . Cheers *are* heard. . . . Still, crowds *stand.* . . .

Writer's Solution

For additional instruction and practice, use the practice pages on Subject and Verb Agreement, pp. 61–65, in the *Writer's Solution Grammar Practice Book.*

Applying Language Skills: Special Problems With Agreement

As you write dialogue or voice-over narration for your video script, avoid making errors in subject-verb agreement.

A verb should agree with its subject in number. If you are unsure about whether certain nouns, like *data,* are singular or plural, look them up in a dictionary.

Practice Rewrite the following paragraph, selecting the correct form of the verb from the choices given.

Two hours a day here (is, are) more than most people can endure. Inside, grunts and groans (fill, fills) the air. Large machines (creak, creaks) as devoted athletes build strength. Cheers (is, are) heard infrequently. Still, crowds (stand, stands) in line to join health clubs.

Writer's Solution Connection
Language Lab

For more help with agreement, see the Agreement in Number and Special Problems in Agreement lessons in the Subject-Verb unit.

Prewriting

Choose a Topic To find a topic for your video script, look at an art book, visit a museum, or simply take a walk and observe the people and places you see. Following are more topic ideas.

Topic Ideas

- A chapter from a favorite novel
- An episode for a television series

Selection-Related Topic Ideas

- A biography of Lord Byron
- A dramatization of Coleridge's and Wordsworth's friendship and parting of the ways
- A tour of Grecian art and antiques

Select Appropriate Details Select details that will bring your topic to life through visuals and sounds. Jot down sound effects and settings that you would like to capture on film. Also note camera angles, lighting effects, and other special effects that will enhance your video.

Organize the Action If you're telling a story, whether fictional or true, create a plot diagram listing events in order. Show how conflict arises, builds, and reaches a resolution. If your video script is more experimental in nature, plan the order of your camera shots and sound effects.

Drafting

Establish a Main Impression As you draft your video script, focus on creating a main impression—a dominant atmosphere or mood. Use lighting, sound, costumes, setting, and dialogue to create this mood.

Create Effects Through Sound and Voice Sounds alone can establish a setting. For example, the chirping of crickets may indicate to an audience that a scene takes place on a summer night in the country. As you draft your video script, include notes about sound effects.

Use Realistic Speech Have your characters use a level of formality and word choice that is right for the time and place. You wouldn't have an early nineteenth-century aristocrat like Lord Byron speak like a twentieth-century gangster.

Revising

Turn the Script into a Mental Video Ask friends to read your video script aloud while you listen. View the video in your mind, noting where you can change details to support your main impression, revise dialogue to make it realistic, and add sound or camera effects to enhance drama or suspense. Jot down your ideas so that you can use them later as you revise the script.

Revision Model

a video script based on
Percy Bysshe Shelley's "Ozymandias"

(Exterior. Temple Ruins. Mid Afternoon. Camera shows ①
The traveler, an old man whose features are shrouded in a black cape.)

NARRATOR (speaks slowly, almost reverently.) ②

I met a traveler from an antique land

Who said:
(camera pans up the monument.) ③

TRAVELER (solemn)

"Two vast and trunkless legs of stone

Stand in the Desert. Near them on the sand . . ."

① Adding details of setting and a camera direction makes the script more appropriate for this medium.

② Speech directions like these help create a main impression.

③ A timely camera direction helps coordinate words and images.

Publishing

- **Storyboards** Illustrate each scene as you envision it would be filmed. Display these "storyboards" for classmates.
- **Reading** Cast the roles in your video script and hold a reading. If you like, invite your classmates to watch.
- **Rough Footage** Film your video script using a home video recorder. Show your footage to a group of friends.

Applying Language Skills: Formatting Scripts

Video scripts contain many types of information. To avoid confusion, establish and adhere to a standard format in scripts.

In the following example, notice how the character names, technical directions, dialogue, and directions for actors have been formatted.

[Exterior. Lake in morning sunlight. Camera shows WORDSWORTH and COLERIDGE strolling along path]

NARRATOR: It's morning in Somerset, 1797, and Wordsworth and Coleridge are discussing ideas for poetry.

WORDSWORTH: *(with excitement)* Samuel! You've got to listen to this dream of my friend John!

Writing Application Write dialogue first, then go back and add technical and stage directions as necessary.

Writer's Solution Connection
Writing Lab

For help with camera and stage directions, see the Writing Models for Drama in the Drafting section of the tutorial on Creative Writing.

Revising

You may want to use the Revision Overlay for the Writing Process Model 4: Dramatic Scene (***Writing and Language Transparencies,*** p. 31) to model the revising process further.

Publishing

Some students may want to publish the video script as a hypermedia program, scanning in storyboards and inputting audio dialogue and sound effects and sharing with the class.

Applying Language Skills

Formatting Scripts Discuss with students the formatting details: brackets, parentheses, characters' names in all capital letters, bold type, and colons.

Answers

Students should review their scripts for the use of brackets, parentheses, capital letters, bold type, and colons.

Writer's Solution

Sourcebook

Chapter 6, Creative Writing shows a model video script (p. 173). Ask students to note how the formatting details differ from the model here. Remind them that formatting consistency is as important as form.

Reinforce and Extend

Applying Knowledge

View a two-minute video segment, perhaps from the *Writer's Solution* videodisc. As a group, have students attempt to re-create the video script. Begin with the dialogue. Then note other scripting details. Ask students how this activity affects how they now view a film.

ASSESSMENT		4	3	2	1
PORTFOLIO ASSESSMENT Use the rubric on Drama (p. 110 in ***Alternative Assessment***) to assess students' writing. Add these criteria to customize the rubric to this assignment.	**Lighting and Camera Directions**	The script includes complete camera directions that support the main impression.	It includes some camera directions that support the main impression.	It includes few camera directions that support the main impression.	It includes no camera directions that support the main impression.
	Sound and Voice	The script includes ample sounds to support the main impression.	It includes some sounds to support the main impression.	It includes few sounds to support the main impression.	It includes no sounds to support the main impression.

Introduce the Strategy

Ask students to name the visual cues they notice when they thumb through a book, magazine, or newspaper. Ask them to discuss in what reading materials they are likely to find visuals (photographs, drawings, diagrams, maps, charts, captions, callouts, bulleted lists, and boxed information) and how these items usually relate to the text.

Customize for
English Language Learners
Have these students study examples of magazine and newspaper articles. Discuss with them how visual cues can help them understand the text by defining words and illustrating ideas.

Apply the Strategy

Have students study the layout of the textbook pages, noting first, without reading the words, the main parts of the two pages. Call attention to bold type, bulleted items, headings (both centered and run-in), indented parts, boxed information, and illustrations. Then ask students to answer the questions.

Answers
Possible responses:
1. Summary questions appear in the bulleted list.
2. The boxed information to the right of the art gives details.
3. On the left page, the words within the colored quotation marks are probably quotations from someone who lived in the time period.

Using Visual Cues

Real-World Reading Skills Workshop

Strategies for Success

Graphic designers employ many devices to organize information on a page. Use these visual cues to focus your attention, you will better understand what you read.

Design Elements Visuals—photographs, drawings, diagrams, charts—sum up information. It's often worth studying them because they reinforce the main points. Notice the treatments of type—its style, size, or position—signal importance or transitions.

Captions and Callouts Captions tell you about a visual. If there is more than one visual on a page, the captions may be grouped. Look for clues like arrows or phrases like *above left* to match a caption to its visual. Callouts—labels connected to a visual by lines—explain the separate parts of a visual. Just follow the lines to learn more about each part.

Displayed Summaries Often in textbooks a summary of the main ideas appears at the beginning or end of a section. You may want to scan this boxed or bulleted list first to get a sense of the whole section.

Boxed Information Sometimes information is set off by itself and boxed. Boxed information presents related information without interrupting the flow of the main text. If you are in a hurry and only need to know the key ideas, focus on the main text. Then go back and read the boxed information.

Apply the Strategy

You can often pick up information from visual cues. See how much you can learn from the layout of the textbook pages reproduced here, even without reading the words.

1. Where might you find a brief summary of the topics covered in this section?
2. Where can you find out about the artwork on the lower left? Why?
3. Where would you look for a quotation from somebody who lived during the time period covered in this section?

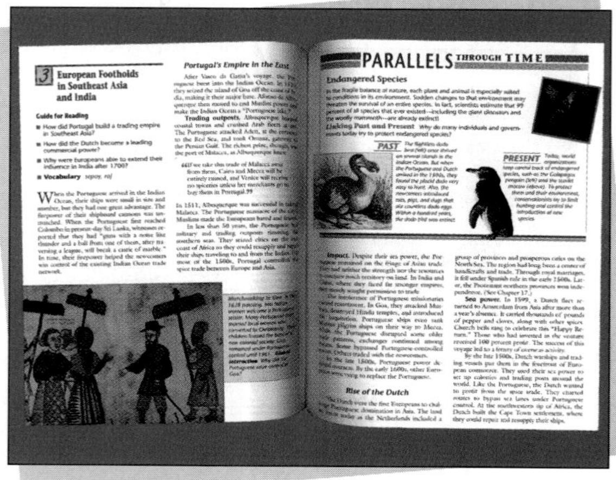
3 European Footholds in Southeast Asia and India

Portugal's Empire in the East

PARALLELS THROUGH TIME

Endangered Species

PAST

PRESENT

Rise of the Dutch

Here are other forms of writing in which you should observe visual cues:

- Advertisements
- Magazine spreads
- Web pages

Cross-Curricular Connection: Science

To convey critical information, science books include detailed visuals, including charts, diagrams, and photographs. These visuals often provide information that would be unwieldy or nearly impossible to convey concisely in text. Have students bring in sample pages from science textbooks to analyze visual cues and the information they convey.

PART 3 The Reaction to Society's Ills

Forging the Anchor, 1831, William James Muller, City of Bristol Museum and Art Gallery

The Industrial Revolution, while increasing the national wealth, also created sharper divisions between rich and poor, ruling aristocrats and disenfranchised workers. Poets and historians knew better than politicians that England could not continue as a divided nation. Writers took the lead in the battle for reform.

One-Minute Planning Guide

The selections in this section highlight the societal problems that arose during the Industrial Revolution. Byron, Shelley, and Macauley address the need for better treatment of the working class and for political reform. Austen and Wollstonecraft comment on the foibles and unfairness in society, particularly in regards to the status of women. The excerpt from Thompson's screenplay for *Sense and Sensibility* provides a modern perspective on the early nineteenth century.

Customizing for *Varying Student Needs*

When assigning the selections in this part, keep in mind these factors:

"In Defense of the Lower Classes"
- Sophisticated vocabulary may prove difficult

"A Song: Men of England"
- This short poem is easy to read and comprehend

"On the Passing of the Reform Bill"
- Short letter

"On Making an Agreeable Marriage"
- Long sentences may be difficult for less proficient readers
- Engaging, chatty, informal letter

from *A Vindication of the Rights of Women*
- Timeless appeal for fairness and gender equity touches on issues of concern to students
- Complicated sentences may be difficult for English language learners

from *The Sense and Sensibility Screenplay and Diaries*
- High-interest connection to contemporary film

Humanities: Art

Forging the Anchor, 1831, by William James Muller.

Although William James Muller was primarily a landscape painter, here he has dramatically re-created two of the arduous steps in the process of making a ship's anchor. At left a fire blazes and figures who appear entirely too close to it to be either safe or comfortable wield mallets in order to shape the iron that is being forged. At right, a large number of muscular men pull in unison, like a large human machine, in order to lift and move the weight of the iron that is suspended from a hook. The setting is dark and cavernous.

Use these questions for discussion:

1. Why do you think there is a huge chain in the foreground? *The huge chain in the foreground may be symbolic of the men's enslavement to harsh labor.*
2. What would be different in a photograph taken today of a factory in which ships' anchors are made? *There would probably be no open fire. People doing the work would wear safety clothes, shoes, and glasses. Jobs such as lifting an anchor would be done using heavy equipment, driven by an operator. The iron or, today, steel would be forged by machine.*

Prepare and Engage

Guide for Interpreting

OBJECTIVES

1. To interpret and respond to political commentary
2. To relate political commentaries to personal experience
3. To set a purpose for reading
4. To identify characteristics of political commentary
5. To build vocabulary in context and learn the word roots *-deci-* or *-deca-*
6. To identify and correctly use correlative conjunctions
7. To write a news article on a political issue, using elaboration to give information
8. To respond to the selections through writing, speaking and listening, and projects

SKILLS INSTRUCTION

Vocabulary: Word Roots: *-deci-* or *-deca-*
Grammar: Correlative Conjunctions
Reading Strategy: Set a Purpose for Reading
Literary Focus: Political Commentary
Writing: Elaboration to Give Information Political Speech
Speaking and Listening: Panel Discussion (teacher edition)
Critical Viewing: Support; Interpret

PORTFOLIO OPPORTUNITIES

Writing: Casting Memo; Letter to the Editor; Response to Criticism
Speaking and Listening: Political Speech; Panel Discussion
Projects: Political Cartoon; Song

More About the Authors

Just as **George Gordon, Lord Byron** could express himself vehemently in his poetry, so too could he engage himself in a political cause with ardor and passion.

Percy Bysshe Shelley believed that the bettering of social institutions could only come about by stirring the heart in each individual.

Thomas Babington Macaulay, the son of a well-known anti-slavery agitator, entered the House of Commons in 1830 and made his mark there with his speech on the Reform Bill. His accomplishments include reconstructing the educational system and drawing up a criminal code for India.

George Gordon, Lord Byron

(1788–1824)

Though less of a firebrand than his friend Shelley, Lord Byron was in his day a far more prominent supporter of radical reform and political liberty. In Britain, he made his first speech in the House of Lords defending workers who sabotaged factory equipment that had caused them to lose their jobs. (You can read a portion of that speech in the following pages.) Overseas he was closely associated with the Italian freedom fighters known as the Carbonari and lost his life in the cause of independence for Greece. (For more on Byron, see p. 656.)

Percy Bysshe Shelley

(1792–1822)

Of the major romantic poets, Percy Bysshe Shelley was probably the most politically radical. Some of his poems are rallying cries encouraging the British working class to rebel. In 1820 Shelley wanted to publish a collection of these poems, including "A Song: 'Men of England.'" He asked a friend if he knew of "any bookseller who would like to publish a little volume of popular songs wholly political & destined to awaken & direct the imagination of the reformers." (For more on Shelley, see p. 668.)

Thomas Babington Macaulay

(1800–1859)

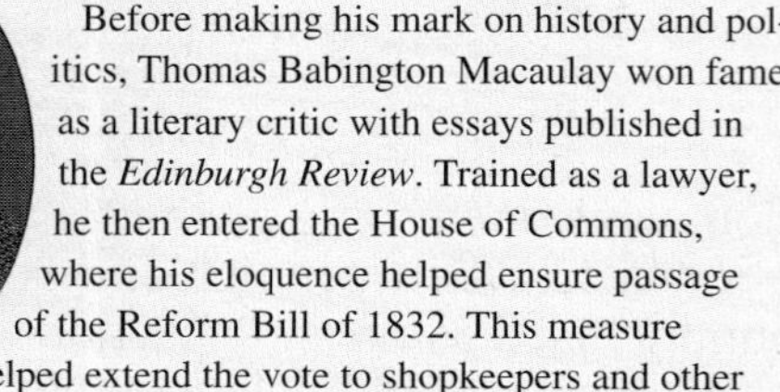

Before making his mark on history and politics, Thomas Babington Macaulay won fame as a literary critic with essays published in the *Edinburgh Review*. Trained as a lawyer, he then entered the House of Commons, where his eloquence helped ensure passage of the Reform Bill of 1832. This measure helped extend the vote to shopkeepers and other middle-class men. When his party was out of power, Macaulay devoted himself to his writing, producing among other things a famous history of seventeenth-century England.

◆ Background for Understanding

HISTORY: REFORM IN BRITAIN

From the outbreak of the French Revolution in 1789 until Napoleon's defeat at the Battle of Waterloo in 1815, Britain focused on foreign affairs at the expense of much-needed domestic reform. In fact, those demanding reform were often branded as French-inspired revolutionaries. Even after Waterloo, reform was delayed by a dangerous cycle of protests and government crackdowns. These protests, sometimes violent, were caused by postwar depression, high unemployment, and an 1815 Corn Law protecting landowners' high grain prices.

In the Luddite riots from 1811 to 1817, unemployed workers in the industrial north, claiming as their leader the mythical working-class hero General (or King) Ludd, wrecked factory equipment that they felt had taken their jobs. In the "Peterloo Massacre" of 1819, mockingly named after Waterloo, local officials ordered the cavalry to charge a crowd assembled in St. Peter's Field, Manchester, to hear reformer Henry Hunt.

Not until the 1820's did the reform movement begin to see some successes. In 1823, Tory politician Sir Robert Peel reformed Britain's harsh penal code. In 1828 and 1829, Parliament passed laws giving political rights to non-Anglicans. Finally, the Whig party came to power and, in 1832, passed the Reform Bill, extending the vote and ending many unfair election practices.

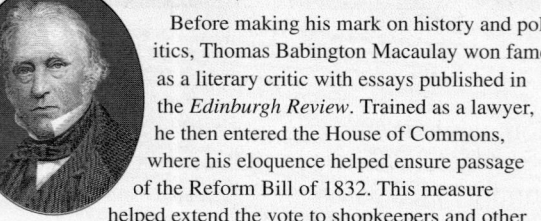

Prentice Hall Literature Program Resources

REINFORCE / RETEACH / EXTEND

Selection Support Pages
Build Vocabulary: Word Roots, p. 171
Grammar and Style: Conjunctions, p. 172
Reading Strategy: Set a Purpose for Reading, p. 173
Literary Focus: Political Commentary, p. 174

Strategies for Diverse Student Needs, p. 36

Beyond Literature, p. 36

Formal Assessment Selection Test, pp. 175–177; Assessment Resources Software

Alternative Assessment, p. 36

Writing and Language Transparencies
Argument Organizer, p. 103

Resource Pro CD-ROM
Includes all resource material and customizable lesson plan

Listening to Literature Audiocassettes *"Speech to Parliament: In Defense of the Lower Classes,"* "A Song: 'Men of England,'" *"On the Passing of the Reform Bill"*

Looking at Literature Videodisc Chapter 7: "A Song: 'Men of England'"

Speech to Parliament: In Defense of the Lower Classes ◆ A Song: "Men of England" ◆ On the Passing of the Reform Bill

◆ Literature and Your Life

CONNECT YOUR EXPERIENCE

The struggle for greater justice in society is evident today in protest marches, editorials, and civil-rights laws that are meant to right wrongs. Shelley, Byron, and Macaulay also worked to make nineteenth-century England a more just society.

Journal Writing Write a bumper sticker or a T-shirt slogan for a cause in which you believe.

THEMATIC FOCUS: THE REACTION TO SOCIETY'S ILLS

As you read the three selections, consider which author would probably be the most effective in remedying society's ills.

◆ Literary Focus

POLITICAL COMMENTARY

Political commentary is speech or writing that provides opinions on political issues. Today, a great deal of political commentary appears on electronic media. In the nineteenth century, such commentary appeared in print or was passed on by word of mouth.

These selections demonstrate three different forms of political commentary in early-nineteenth-century England. Shelley's poem is meant as a rallying cry for working-class people and reformers. Byron's speech is a defense, in Parliament, of textile workers who had destroyed their looms out of desperation. Macaulay's letter is a private communication on a major political event in which he played a role—the passage of the Reform Bill of 1832.

◆ Reading Strategy

SET A PURPOSE FOR READING

You'll often get more from your reading if you **set a purpose** and then read to fulfill it. You might read political commentary from another era to find out more about the writers, to learn about the issues that prompted them to write, or to compare those issues with problems that we face today.

In reading Byron's defense of impoverished workers, for example, your purpose might be to compare the issue of job losses because of technological advances in Byron's time and today.

◆ Build Vocabulary

WORD ROOTS: *-deci-* OR *-deca-*

The word *decimation,* from Byron's speech, contains the Latin root *-deci-* (or *-deca-*), meaning "ten." *Decimation* originally referred to punishment for mutiny in the Roman army—killing every tenth person. Today it means "any large-scale killing or destruction."

WORD BANK

Before you read, preview this list of words from the selections.

impediments
decimation
efficacious
emancipate
balm
inauspicious

◆ Grammar and Style

CORRELATIVE CONJUNCTIONS

Macaulay and Byron use **correlative conjunctions**, conjunctions that work in pairs to link grammatically equal words or groups of words:

It is clear that the Reform Bill must pass, *either* in this *or* in another Parliament. (Macaulay)

Correlative conjunctions include *either . . . or; not only . . . but (also); both . . . and;* and *neither . . . nor.*

Write the names of rock musicians on the chalkboard who are active politically. Such a list might include Sting, Peter Gabriel, and Tracy Chapman. Introduce the subject of politically active artists such as these, and ask students to add to the list. Whenever possible, ask them to describe the cause for which each musician fights.

Then tell students that Byron and Shelley were like rock musicians of their time in that they were considered "wild" and "liberal," and they championed the underdog in political causes.

Customize for
More Advanced Students

Suggest that more advanced students look at each of the three works and assess them to determine their most or least politically effective words or phrases. For example, students might determine when Byron is reaching his audience and when he is not; with which words Shelley is most likely to stir the hearts of workingmen; and when Macaulay is most interesting, most direct, and most exciting in his description of political events.

Customize for
Less Proficient Readers

Build additional background for these students by discussing with them the political events in England that sparked these political commentaries. Then, before reading, ask these readers to imagine that they are among the members of the lower classes and to discuss some of the thoughts and feelings they would have about Parliament and what was happening in England at the time.

Preparing for Standardized Tests

Reading and Vocabulary Setting a purpose for reading may help students identify main and supporting ideas in reading comprehension passages on standardized tests. By previewing the questions in critical reading portions of tests, students will read passages with a purpose: to find the answers to the question posed, as in the following example:

When a proposal is made to emancipate or relieve, you hesitate, you deliberate for years, you temporize and tamper with the minds of men; but a deathbill must be passed offhand, without a thought of the consequences.

In this speech, the speaker's tone is best described as *(C)*

(A) apologetic and nervous.
(B) subdued and sorrowful.
(C) angry and ironic.
(D) enthusiastic and joyful.

For additional practice, use the Reading Strategy page in ***Selection Support,*** p. 173.

Grammar and Language Some portions of standardized tests and other tests of English usage require students to identify sentence errors, such as the misuse of correlative conjunctions.

The Grammar and Style lesson for this selection focuses on this topic. For additional practice, use the Grammar and Style page on Correlative Conjunctions, p. 172, in ***Selection Support.***

Speech to Parliament: In Defense of the Lower Classes

George Gordon, Lord Byron

"As a person in some degree connected with the suffering county, though a stranger not
1 only to this House in general but to almost every individual whose attention I presume to solicit, I must claim some portion of your Lordships' indulgence, . . .

"When we are told that these men are leagued together, not only for the destruction of their own comfort, but of their very means of subsistence, can we forget that it is the bitter policy, the destructive warfare, of the last eigh-
2 teen years which has destroyed their comfort, your comfort, all men's comfort—that policy which, originating with 'great statesmen now no more,' has survived the dead to become a curse on the living, unto the third and fourth generation! These men never destroyed their looms till they were become useless—worse than useless; till they were become actual impediments to their exertions in obtaining their daily bread.

Can you then wonder that in times like these, when bankruptcy, convicted fraud, and imputed felony are found in a station not far beneath that of your Lordships, the lowest, though once most useful, portion of the people should forget their duty in their distresses, and become only less guilty than one of their representatives? But while the exalted[1] offender can find means to baffle the law, new capital punishments must be devised, new snares of death must be spread for the wretched mechanic who is famished[2] into guilt. These men were willing to dig, but the spade was in other hands: they were not ashamed to beg, but there was none to relieve them. Their own means of subsistence were cut off; all other employments preoccupied; and their excesses, however to be deplored or condemned, can hardly be the subject of surprise.

> ◆ **Literary Focus**
> What political com-
> ments about the 3
> upper classes does Byron imply here?

"I have traversed the seat of war in the Peninsula;[3] I have been in some of the most oppressed provinces of Turkey; but never, under the most despotic of infidel[4] governments, did I behold such squalid wretchedness as I have seen since my return, in the very heart of a Christian country. And what are your remedies? After months of inaction, and months of action worse than inactivity, at length comes forth the grand specific, the never-failing nostrum of all state physicians from the days of Draco[5] to the present time. After feeling the pulse and shaking the head over the patient, prescribing the usual course of warm water and bleeding[6]—the warm water of your mawkish police, and the lancets of your military—these convulsions must terminate in death, the sure consummation of the prescriptions of all political Sangrados.[7] Setting aside the palpable injustice and the certain inefficiency of the bill,
are there not capital punishments sufficient on 4
your statutes? Is there not blood enough upon

1. **exalted:** Well-born; of high rank.
2. **famished:** Forced by hunger.
3. **the Peninsula:** Iberian Peninsula (Spain and Portugal).
4. **infidel** (in´ fə del) *n.*: Non-Christian.
5. **Draco** (drā´ kō): Ancient Greek politician famous for his very severe code of laws.
6. **bleeding:** In Byron's day, doctors often bled patients as a remedy for fever, convulsions, and so on.
7. **Sangrados:** Doctors who bled patients.

Develop Understanding

One-Minute Insight Byron seems to hold no insult back as he asks Parliament to reconsider the "death-bill" it is evidently about to enact in order to punish workers who have wrecked their own looms. Through a passionate series of comparisons and questions, he calls on Parliament to reconsider what it is planning to do.

◆ Background for Understanding

History Explain to students that the time period is the beginning of England's industrial revolution. Between 1760 and 1830, the production of cotton textiles in England increased twelvefold: this was due in large part to new inventions that mechanized the spinning and weaving of imported cotton. As this transition began, people who had spent their lives doing farming or working as artisans left old ways of life to become factory workers. But as one technology quickly replaced the last, their jobs were threatened. Furthermore, the French revolutionary government declared war on England in February 1793. The result was twenty-two years of war. Among the effects on the economy were rapid inflation and rates of pay that lagged far behind prices.

1 Clarification Lord Byron is referring to the House of Lords, a governing body consisting of the nobility. Byron automatically became a member when he inherited his title.

◆ Grammar and Style

2 Correlative Conjunctions Ask students to identify the correlative conjunctions in this sentence. Then have them name the grammatical structures this pair of conjunctions joins. *The correlative conjunctions are* not only *and* but; *they join prepositional phrases.*

◆ Literary Focus

3 Political Commentary Byron states that the law deals unequally with the citizenry: the upper classes —unlike the lower classes—can find ways to "baffle the law," or elude punishment.

Block Scheduling Strategies

Consider these suggestions to take advantage of extended class time:

- Direct students to read the information in the Background for Understanding on page 704. Encourage students to read the footnotes, which accompany these selections to get more information on the times. You may also have students read the Technology feature on page 712 before they read Byron's Speech to Parliament.
- Introduce the Literary Focus on political commentary, p. 705, before students read the selections. When they have finished reading, have them answer the Reading Strategy questions on page 712.
- Allow students to plan or develop responses to activities in the Idea Bank on page 713.
- Introduce the Writing Mini-Lesson on page 713. Then display, on an overhead projector, the Argument Organizer from the ***Writing and Language Transparencies,*** p. 103. Have students copy it and use it to list details for their reports.

your penal code, that more must be poured forth to ascend to heaven and testify against you? How will you carry this bill into effect? Can you commit a whole country to their own prisons? Will you erect a gibbet[8] in every field, and hang up men like scarecrows? Or will you proceed (as you must, to bring this measure into effect) by decimation; place the country under martial law; depopulate and lay waste all around you, and restore Sherwood Forest as an acceptable gift to the crown in its former
4 condition of a royal chase, and an asylum for outlaws?[9] Are these the remedies for a starving and desperate populace? Will the famished wretch who has braved your bayonets be appalled by your gibbets? When death is a relief, and the only relief it appears that you will afford him, will he be dragooned[10] into tranquillity? Will that which could not be effected by your grenadiers,[11] be accomplished by your executioners? If you proceed by the forms of law, where is your evidence? Those who refused to impeach their accomplices when transportation[12] only was the punishment will hardly be tempted to witness against them when death is the penalty.

With all due deference to the noble lords opposite, I think a little investigation, some previous inquiry, would induce even them to change their purpose. That most favorite state measure, so marvelously efficacious in many and recent instances, *temporizing*, would not be without its advantage in this. When a proposal is made to emancipate or relieve, you hesitate, you deliberate for years, you temporize and tamper with the minds of men; but a deathbill must be passed offhand, without a thought of the consequences."

8. **gibbet** (jib´ it): Device used for a hanging a person.
9. **Sherwood Forest . . . outlaws:** Sherwood Forest, near Nottingham, was famous as the refuge of Robin Hood and his band of outlaws.
10. **dragooned** (drə go͞ond´): Compelled by violence, especially as exerted by military troops.
11. **grenadiers** (gren´ ə dirz´): Members of Britain's royal infantry.
12. **transportation:** Practice of sending people convicted of crimes to overseas penal colonies.

◆ Build Vocabulary

impediments (im ped´ ə mənts) *n.*: Hindrances; obstructions

decimation (des´ ə mā´ shun) *n.*: Destruction or killing of one in ten, or of any large group

efficacious (ef´ i kā´ shəs) *adj.*: Producing the desired result; effective

emancipate (ē man´ sə pāt) *v.*: To free from slavery or oppression

Guide for Responding

◆ Literature and Your Life

Reader's Response Did you find this speech persuasive? Why or why not?

Thematic Response Do you think this speech made legislators more willing to remedy society's ills? Explain.

Group Activity Assume the roles of the nobility that Byron is addressing and discuss his ideas.

☑ Check Your Comprehension

1. (a) According to Byron, why did the men wreck the looms? (b) How do they contrast with upper-class lawbreakers?
2. What does Byron predict will happen if those who destroy machinery are executed?

◆ Critical Thinking

INTERPRET

1. How would you describe Byron's attitude in the opening paragraph? **[Infer]**
2. In the third paragraph, what is Byron comparing to a doctor's patient? **[Analyze]**
3. To what extent is this address an appeal to emotion and to what extent is it an appeal to reason? Explain. **[Draw Conclusions]**

EVALUATE

4. Note an example of exaggeration in the speech and evaluate its effectiveness. **[Evaluate]**

EXTEND

5. Are there any laws today whose punishments you consider too strong or too weak? Explain. **[Social Studies Link]**

Cross-Curricular Connection: Social Studies

The British Parliament is the model on which the United States Congress is, in large part, based. Technically, the Parliament today consists of the Crown, the House of Lords, and the House of Commons, but the main part is the House of Commons, whose 651 members are elected from equal-size districts.

Have students find out more about the present-day Parliament. Then ask them to create a two-column chart comparing and contrasting it with the United States Congress.

◆ Critical Thinking

4 Speculate Ask why Byron chose to use a series of questions here instead of statements. *Suggested answer: This strategy increases the effectiveness of his emotional appeal; it seems to suggest that the audience, Parliament, cannot answer these questions, just as it cannot justify its actions in punishing the lower classes.*

Reinforce and Extend

Answers

◆ Literature and Your Life

Reader's Response Yes, because Byron points out that the lower classes are judged unfairly; no, Byron does nothing more than point an accusing finger at people like himself.

Thematic Focus Sample responses: Yes, Byron's points would have made legislators feel uncomfortable and willing to change; no, the nobility would be too entrenched in privilege to take notice of or care about unfair treatment of the lower classes.

☑ Check Your Comprehension

1. (a) Byron says the looms were wrecked because they had become useless. (b) They commit less serious offenses, but are punished more severely.
2. Byron predicts that if the workers are executed, the lower classes will rise up and challenge the nobility.

◆ Critical Thinking

1. Byron's attitude is polite.
2. Byron compares the wretched state of the lower classes to that of a doctor's patient.
3. The address is an emotional appeal because it employs passionate persuasive language and compelling comparisons; it is an appeal to reason in that it uses factual evidence and reasoning to support Byron's opinions.
4. "Will you erect a gibbet in every field, and hang up men like scarecrows?" is an example of exaggeration. It is effective because Byron makes the point that the men who destroyed their looms are just one segment of the lower classes who are desperate.
5. Students may say that punishment for tax evaders are too stringent.

One-Minute Insight

Shelley's song uses a series of simple questions, with implied but grim answers, followed by a series of commands, to incite the men of England to revolution. In line after line, Shelley counsels the workers to stop giving more power and wealth to the powerful and rich because it results in less power and comfort for the powerless and poor.

This poem demonstrates how a poet's skill can be employed to effect social change.

Looking at Literature Videodisc Play Chapter 7: "A Song: 'Men of England'" to introduce students to England's Industrial Revolution before they read the poem.

Chapter 7

Customize for ***Musical/Rhythmic Learners***
Many folk songs embody sentiments similar to the ones found in this song. Invite students to set this song to music and play it for the class.

◆ Literary Focus

❶ Political Commentary Have students identify the details in this stanza that make comment on the political situation of the time. *The "men of England" are distinguished from the "lords" for whom they work. Shelley refers to the nobility as "tyrants."*

◆ Critical Thinking

❷ Interpret Ask: Who are the "stingless drones" to which Shelley refers? Why does Shelley choose this comparison? *The "stingless drones" are members of the nobility. The comparison implies that the workers and worker bees are the productive members of the "hive" or society and that the nobility or drones (male bees who do nothing but reproduce) do nothing.*

◆ Critical Thinking

❸ Analyze Ask: In what way does this stanza employ persuasive techniques? *Shelley uses parallelism of phrases and repetition to make his points memorable and persuasive in this stanza.*

Percy Bysshe Shelley

A Song: "Men of England"

❶ Men of England, wherefore[1] plough
For the lords who lay ye low?
Wherefore weave with toil and care
The rich robes your tyrants wear?

Wherefore feed and clothe and save
From the cradle to the grave
Those ungrateful drones[2] who would
Drain your sweat—nay, drink your blood?

Wherefore, Bees of England, forge
Many a weapon, chain, and scourge,[3]
❷ That these stingless drones may spoil
The forced produce of your toil?

Have ye leisure, comfort, calm,
Shelter, food, love's gentle balm?
Or what is it ye buy so dear
With your pain and with your fear?

❸ The seed ye sow, another reaps;
The wealth ye find, another keeps;
The robes ye weave, another wears;
The arms ye forge, another bears.

Sow seed—but let no tyrant reap:
Find wealth—let no impostor heap:
Weave robes—let not the idle wear:
Forge arms—in your defense to bear.

Shrink to your cellars, holes, and cells—
In halls ye deck another dwells.
Why shake the chains ye wrought? Ye see
The steel ye tempered[4] glance on ye.

With plough and spade and hoe and loom
Trace your grave and build your tomb
And weave your winding-sheet[5]—till fair
England be your Sepulchre.

1. **wherefore:** For what purpose? Why?

2. **drones:** Male bees who perform no work and whose only function is to mate with the Queen Bee.

3. **scourge** (skurj): Whip used to inflict punishment.

4. **tempered:** Made hard by alternately heating and cooling.

5. **winding-sheet** (wīn′diŋ shēt): Sheet for wrapping a corpse; shroud.

◆ Build Vocabulary
balm *n.*: Anything healing or soothing

Speaking and Listening Mini-Lesson

Panel Discussion
This mini-lesson supports the Speaking and Listening activity in the Idea Bank on page 713.

Introduce the Concept Explain to students that panel discussions are informal discussions about a issue in which several experts participate.

Apply the Information Have students form groups of four, with one person taking the part of moderator, who will ask questions and steer the discussion, and the others taking the parts of Byron, Shelley, and Macaulay. Each person should prepare a list of opinion, viewpoints, and ideas that suit their role. The moderator should prepare a list of questions relating to the Reform Bill. Have students familiarize themselves with their roles before beginning the panel discussion.

Let students hold their panel discussions with the rest of the class as audience. Arrange the chairs in a semicircle so the panel participants and moderator can interact with one another and the audience.

Assess the Outcome When the panel discussion is over, have the audience assess the performance according to content, clarity, and liveliness.

The Workshops at the Gobelins, 1840, Jean-Charles Develly, Musée Carnavalet, Paris

◀ Critical Viewing In what ways is this painting an appropriate accompaniment to Shelley's song for working men? **[Support]** ❹

Guide for Responding

◆ Literature and Your Life

Reader's Response How do you think the men of England reacted to this poem?

Thematic Response What advice does the speaker give to "the men of England" about responding to society's ills?

Group Activity Identify contemporary song-writers whose songs convey a message similar to that of Shelley's poem.

☑ Check Your Comprehension

1. What questions does the speaker ask of his audience?
2. What does the speaker ask his audience to do?

◆ Critical Thinking

INTERPRET

1. Sum up all the speaker's questions in a single ironic question to the men of England. **[Connect]**
2. Explain in your own words the comparison of workers to bees. **[Analyze]**
3. Is this a poem that advocates reform or revolution? Support your answer with specific passages from the poem. **[Draw Conclusions]**

EVALUATE

4. Would this poem make a good anthem for radical groups? Why or why not? **[Assess]**

EXTEND

5. Which is more radical, Byron's speech or Shelley's poem? Explain. **[Literature Link]**

Humanities: Art

The Workshops at the Gobelins, 1840, by Jean-Charles Develly.

This scene shows workers in a factory, a typical occupation of the "lower classes" in England at the time of the Industrial Revolution. The factory setting is austere and unwelcoming, with workers lined up performing their separate tasks from early in the morning until late at night. In dark, uninviting rooms, with high ceilings, workers toil at looms and spinning wheels, producing textiles by, apparently, no other light than the natural light that comes from very few windows.

Use these questions for discussion:

1. What do you think you would hear if you were in this setting? *There would be a constant racket of the looms. This sound might echo in the cavernous, wooden space.*
2. What do you think it was like to work in this factory? *Working conditions were probably harsh in this factory. There probably wasn't enough light and or heat. Because the tasks were repetitive, workers' backs and wrists probably ached, and they may have gotten headaches from the deafening roar and echo of the looms.*

▶Critical Viewing◀

❹ **Support** The workers shown in this painting seem to be almost like parts of a machine—interchangeable and devoid of individuality or humanity. Shelley's song is appropriate because the workers seem to be in need of self-esteem and pride.

Reinforce and Extend

Answers

◆ Literature and Your Life

Reader's Response Suggested response: The men of England probably were glad to use this song as a rallying cry because the song depicts the workers in a positive light.

Thematic Focus The speaker advises the men of England to revolt —to stop being complaisant and to challenge the unfairness of the laws.

☑ Check Your Comprehension

1. The speaker asks many questions, including: Why do you work so hard to make the rich richer? Why do you feed and clothe the rich, who remain ungrateful for your efforts? What are you gaining for all your efforts?
2. The speaker wants his audience to rise up and challenge the unfairness of the laws, which favor the rich.

◆ Critical Thinking

1. Sample summation: Are you going to continue to work yourself into the grave for the benefit of your rich, lazy lord?
2. Like the society of a beehive, the workers resembles the worker bees who toil all day long for the benefit of the queen bee. The drones of the hive, who resemble the nobility, have no responsibility except to mate with the queen, and thus reproduce.
3. This poem seems to advocate revolution because it exhorts the workers to confront their lords for whom they work.
4. Most students will say that this poem would make a good anthem because it is passionate, memorable, and timeless in its sympathy for downtrodden workers.
5. Most students will say that Shelley's poem is more radical, because it encourages rebellion.

With what seems like the whole future of England riding on the vote to pass the Reform Bill, the moments of tallying are tense indeed. Thomas Babington Macaulay recounts them vividly here—and with all the pleasure of the victor.

This personal letter to a friend reveals an insider's view on the working of government during an exciting time in England's history.

◆ Background for Understanding

History Explain that the Reform Bill was the biggest political issue in England in 1831 and 1832. When it became law in 1832, the Reform Bill resulted in a redistribution of seats in Parliament, which gave more power and voice to the growing industrial cities. It also extended the right to vote to all middle-class men and some artisans. This meant that the electorate increased by an incredible fifty percent in both England and Wales; it grew by even more than that in Ireland and Scotland. By extending the vote to more and more "common" people, the measure weakened the power of both the monarch and the House of Lords. In short, it was a giant step toward greater democracy.

◆ Reading Strategy

❶ Set a Purpose for Reading Students may want to learn what the Reform Bill sought to change, who supported it and who opposed it, and why it was of special importance to Macaulay.

▶Critical Viewing◀

❷ Interpret The tree being chopped down is called the "rotten borough system," which represents the way in which seats in Parliament were formerly distributed. Nesting, or sitting pretty, in the tree are ducks, which no doubt represent those who have seats in Parliament. Those chopping down the tree (most of whom are dressed in rough clothing of commoners) are the reformers, those holding the tree up (most of whom are dressed in fine clothing of aristocracy) are against reform.

On the Passing of the Reform Bill

Thomas Babington Macaulay

Caricature showing those for and against the 1832 Reform Bill, British Museum

◀ Critical Viewing How does this cartoon interpret the struggle over the reform bill that Macaulay describes? **[Interpret]** 

Dear Ellis,

I have little news for you, except what you will learn from the papers as well as from me. It is clear that the Reform Bill must pass, either in this or in another Parliament. The majority of one does not appear to me, as it does to you, by any means inauspicious. We should perhaps have had a better plea for a dissolution[1] if the majority had been the other way. But surely a dissolution under such circumstances would have been a most alarming thing. If there should be a dissolution now there will not be that ferocity in the public mind which there would have been if the House of Commons had refused to entertain the Bill at all.—I confess that, till we had a majority, I was half inclined to tremble at the storm which we had raised. At present I think that we are absolutely certain of victory, and of victory without commotion.

> ◆ Reading Strategy ❶
> What would you like to learn about the Reform Bill from this letter?

Such a scene as the division of last Tuesday I never saw, and never expect to see again. If I should live fifty years the impression of it will be as fresh and sharp in my mind as if it had just taken place. It was like seeing Caesar stabbed in the Senate House,[2] or seeing Oliver taking the mace from the table,[3] a sight to be seen only once and never to be forgotten. The crowd overflowed the House in every part. When the strangers were cleared out and the doors locked we had six hundred and eight members present, more by fifty five than ever were at a division before. The Ayes and Noes were like two vollies of cannon from opposite sides of a field of battle. When the opposition went out into the lobby,—an operation by the by which took up twenty minutes or more,—we spread ourselves over the benches on both sides of the House. For there were many of us who had not been able to find a seat during the evening. When the doors were shut we began to speculate on our numbers. Every body was desponding. 'We have lost it. We are only two hundred and eighty at most. I do not think we are two hundred and fifty. They are three hundred. Alderman Thompson has counted them. He says they are two hundred and ninety-nine.' This was the talk on our benches. I wonder that men who have been long in parliament do not acquire a better coup d'œil[4] for numbers. The House when only the Ayes were in it looked to me a very fair house,—much fuller than it generally is even on debates of considerable interest. I had no hope however of three hundred. As the tellers[5] passed along our lowest row on the left hand side the interest was insupportable,—two hundred and ninety-one:—two hundred and ninety-two:—we were all standing up and stretching forward, telling with the tellers. At three hundred there was a short

1. **dissolution** (dis´ ə lo͞o´ shən): Dismissal of Parliament in order to hold a new election of members of the House of Commons.

2. **Caesar** (sē´zər) **stabbed in the Senate House:** Emperor Julius Caesar, assassinated in the legislative council of ancient Rome.
3. **Oliver taking the mace from the table:** Puritan leader Oliver Cromwell overriding Parliamentary authority by demanding removal of the mace, traditional symbol of the Speaker's authority in the House of Commons.
4. **coup d'œil** (ko͞o dē´ y´): Glance.
5. **tellers:** Those appointed to count votes.

 **Humanities: Art**

Caricature showing those for and against the 1832 Reform Bill.

This cartoon shows large numbers of people engaged in the struggle for reform, which has reached the intensity of a pitched battle. The tree representing the existing "rotten borough system" is being upheld and supported by some, and hatcheted by others. The contest is being observed by those who stand to benefit from it: the middle-class men and artisans of England, Scotland, Ireland, and Wales.

Use these questions for discussion:

1. Why do you think so many people are shown in this cartoon? *Sample answer: The Reform Bill affected huge segments of the population of England, Scotland, Wales, and Ireland. A broad range of people had strong feelings about it.*
2. Judging from this illustration, who seems to be winning? Explain. *Those who want to chop down the tree, or overturn the "rotten borough system," are greater in number, and they are also armed. In fact, they were the victors.*

cry of joy, at three hundred and two another—suppressed however in a moment. For we did not yet know what the hostile force might be. We knew however that we could not be severely beaten. The doors were thrown open and in they came. Each of them as he entered brought some different report of their numbers. It must have been impossible, as you may conceive, in the lobby, crowded as they must have been, to form any exact estimate. First we heard that they were three hundred and three—then the number rose to three hundred and ten, then went down to three hundred and seven. Alexander Baring told me that he had counted and that they were three hundred and four. We were all breathless with anxiety, when Charles Wood who stood near the door jumped on a bench
3 and cried out, 'They are only three hundred and one.' We set up a shout that you might have heard to Charing Cross[6]—waving our hats—stamping against the floor and clapping our hands. The tellers scarcely got through the crowd:—for the house was thronged up to the table, and all the floor was fluctuating with heads like the pit of a theatre. But you might have heard a pin drop as Duncannon read the numbers. Then again the shouts broke out—and many of us shed tears—I could scarcely refrain. And the jaw of Peel[7] fell; and the face of Twiss[8] was as the face of a damned soul; and Herries[9] looked like Judas taking his neck-cloth off for the last operation. We shook hands and clapped each other on the back, and went out laughing, crying, and huzzaing into the lobby. And no sooner were the outer doors opened than another shout answered that within the house. All the passages and the stairs into the waiting rooms were thronged by people who had waited till four in the morning to know the issue. We passed through a narrow lane between two thick masses of them; and all the way down they were shouting and waving their hats; till we got into the open air. I called a cabriolet—and the first thing the driver asked was, 'Is the Bill carried?'—'Yes, by one.' 'Thank God for it, Sir.' And away I rode to Grey's Inn—and so ended a scene which will probably never be equalled till the reformed Parliament wants reforming; and that I hope will not be till the days of our grandchildren—till that truly orthodox and apostolical person Dr Francis Ellis[10] is an archbishop of eighty.

6. **Charing Cross:** London neighborhood some distance from the Houses of Parliament.

7. **Peel:** Sir Robert Peel (1788–1850), a leading member of the Tory party, which opposed the bill.
8. **Twiss:** Horace Twiss, another Tory who opposed the bill.
9. **Herries:** J. C. Herries, another Tory who opposed the bill.
10. **Francis Ellis:** Six-year-old son of Thomas Ellis.

◆ Build Vocabulary

inauspicious (in´ ô spish´əs) *adj.*: Not promising a good outcome; unfavorable

Guide for Responding

◆ Literature and Your Life

Reader's Response Were you swept up in the excitement of Macaulay's account? Explain.

Thematic Response To what extent is Macaulay a rebel, a dreamer, a reformer, or a combination of these? Why?

☑ Check Your Comprehension

1. (a) What does Macaulay's friend Ellis find inauspicious? (b) What is Macaulay's argument against Ellis's view?
2. Summarize the events leading up to the passage of the Reform Bill of 1832.

◆ Critical Thinking

INTERPRET

1. In what ways does Macaulay add suspense to his account? **[Analyze]**
2. Give three details that help you picture the events that Macaulay describes. **[Distinguish]**
3. How does Macaulay's final statement convey the importance of the occasion? **[Draw Conclusions]**

EVALUATE

4. Does Macaulay convey the spirit of these historic events as well as the simple facts? Why or why not? **[Assess]**

Beyond the Selection

FURTHER READING

More Works by the Authors

"When a Man Hath No Freedom to Fight for at Home," Lord Byron
"England in 1819," Percy Bysshe Shelley
The History of England, Thomas Babington Macaulay

We suggest you read these selections before recommending them to students.

INTERNET

Students may learn more about the authors on the Internet. Please be aware, however, that sites may have changed from the time we published this information.

For information about Shelley, go to **http://www.luc.edu/publications/keats-shelley/ksaa.htm**

We *strongly recommend* that you preview the sites before you send students to them.

Comprehension Check ☑

❸ Ask students to explain why this detail is important. *This detail is important because it means the opposition (those against the Reform Bill) have failed to come up with enough votes to prevent the bill's passage.*

Reinforce and Extend

Answers

◆ Literature and Your Life

Reader's Response Yes, Macaulay's account is exciting and engrossing; no, it's hard to be swept up by a story that took place so long ago.

Thematic Focus Possible response: Macaulay seems to be a rebel and reformer politically and a dreamer in his predictions for the future.

☑ Check Your Comprehension

1. (a) Ellis thinks that those for reform having a majority of only one in the House of Commons is inauspicious. (b) Macaulay disagrees, saying that if they had been in the minority, the House might have been dismissed to hold new elections, and their cause might founder in the meantime.
2. First the members of the House convened. Those against the Reform went into the lobby while those for the passage stayed and were counted as "Aye" votes. Then those against the bill filed in, being counted as they entered. The number of members for passage of the bill was larger, so they won.

◆ Critical Thinking

1. By detailing the counting of the members and votes, Macaulay built suspense at the outcome.
2. By describing the scene as reminiscent of Caesar being stabbed at the Senate, the crowd as "overflowing" and Herries looking like Judas, Macaulay helps readers picture the events.
3. Macaulay's final statement reveals his joy and satisfaction at the reform laws that should hold true for many years.
4. Yes, Macaulay's account conveys more than facts: it conveys the anticipation, excitement, and elation of having been a part of the passage of the Reform Bill.

Answers

◆ Build Vocabulary

Using the Word Root *-deci-* or *-deca-*

1. d; decade
2. a; decimals
3. e; decathlon
4. c; decahedron
5. b; deciliter

Using the Word Bank

Both Byron and Shelley saw the practices of the English upper class as *impediments* to their efforts to *emancipate* people and transform them into *efficacious* individuals. These poets thought of poetry not as a *balm,* but as a force that would *decimate* outmoded ideas. In their minds, the most *inauspicious* political sign was the reluctance of the upper classes to yield any power.

◆ Grammar and Style

Sample answers:

1. Neither Byron nor Macaulay wrote "A Song: 'Men of England.'"
2. Not only Byron but also Shelley supported workers' rights.
3. Just as Shelley compares English workers to bees, so too he compares England to the workers' tomb.
4. Either the Tories would win the crucial vote, or the Whigs would win it.
5. Both the Whigs and Macaulay celebrate the passage of the bill.

Writer's Solution

For additional instruction and practice, use the page on Conjunctions in the *Writer's Solution Grammar Practice Book,* p. 13.

◆ Literary Focus

1. Answers may include: Macaulay's goal is to relate events surrounding the actual vote on the Reform Bill; his audience is a friend named Ellis; and his attitude is one of celebration. For both, Byron and Shelley, the goal is to persuade; they have a focused, serious attitude. Byron's audience is the assembled members of Parliament; Shelley's audience is the working men of England.
2. Sample answer: Macaulay's letter is the least formal and most personal; the speech is the most formal and least personal; Shelley's song is somewhat formal and impersonal.
3. Students may say Shelley's song is most effective, because it is memorable and inspirational.

◆ Reading Strategy

1. The ending of the speech reveals his purpose most clearly and effectively.
2. Sample answer: Students might focus on information about the looms becoming "useless," the information about the workers being willing to dig or beg, and the information about being "famished into guilt."
3. Sample answer: (a) Paragraph two of Macaulay's letter is interesting and enjoyable to read. (b) If the reader's purpose is to learn about the voting process, the details in this paragraph reveal how votes were counted; if the reader's purpose is to learn about Macaulay's political sympathies, the details reveal his ardent support for the passage of the Reform Bill.

Guide for Responding (continued)

◆ Build Vocabulary

Using the Word Root *-deci-* or *-deca-*

Match the lettered word with the root *-deci-* or *-deca-* in Column B with its definition in Column A.

Column A	Column B
1. ten years	**a.** decimals
2. fractions in tenths	**b.** deciliter
3. contest with ten events	**c.** decahedron
4. ten-sided figure	**d.** decade
5. tenth of a liter	**e.** decathlon

Using the Word Bank

Replace each italicized word with a synonym from the Word Bank.

Both Byron and Shelley saw the practices of the English upper class as *hindrances* to their efforts to *free* people and transform them into *effective* individuals. These poets thought of poetry not as a *salve,* but as a force that would *slaughter* outmoded ideas. In their minds, the most *unfavorable* political sign was the reluctance of the upper classes to yield any power.

◆ Grammar and Style

Correlative Conjunctions

Correlative conjunctions work in pairs to link grammatically equal words or groups of words.

Practice Use the following correlative conjunctions to combine each pair of sentences into a single sentence. Make any other changes needed.

not only . . . but (also) — neither . . . nor — both . . . and — just as . . . so (too) — either . . . or

1. a. Byron did not write "A Song: 'Men of England.'"
b. Macaulay did not write "A Song: 'Men of England.'"

2. a. Byron supported workers' rights.
b. Shelley supported workers' rights.

3. a. Shelley compares English workers to bees.
b. He compares England to the workers' tomb.

4. a. The Tories would win the crucial vote.
b. The Whigs would win the crucial vote.

5. a. The Whigs celebrate the passage of the bill.
b. Macaulay celebrates the passage of the bill.

◆ Literary Focus

Political Commentary

These works of **political commentary** agree on the need for greater justice in early-nineteenth-century England, but each writer has a different goal, audience, and attitude.

1. Compare and contrast Macaulay's goal, audience, and attitude to those of Shelley or Byron.
2. How do the forms these writers use (poem, speech, letter) influence (a) the formality of their language? (b) the inclusion of personal details?
3. Which of these pieces do you think was probably most effective in achieving its goal? Why?

◆ Reading Strategy

Set a Purpose for Reading

When you set a purpose for reading—determining beforehand what you want to learn—you can read a work more effectively and efficiently.

1. Which passages of Byron's speech reveal his purpose for making the speech?
2. Find three passages on which you could focus if you wanted to learn about workers' grievances.
3. (a) Find a paragraph or stanza you like in one of the other pieces. (b) Show how reading it with two different purposes helps you uncover different facts and ideas.

Beyond Literature

Technology Connection

The Luddites Between 1811 and 1816, bands of stocking weavers destroyed the new, more efficient weaving frames that had put tens of thousands of skilled workers out of work. The rebellious weavers said they were acting on the authority of "King Ludd," "General Ludd," or "Captain Ludd"—hence their name, the Luddites. The original Ned Ludd was a legendary character who, in a fit of madness, destroyed several weaving frames. Do you see any parallel between the increasing reliance on computers in business today and the problems of the Luddites?

Build Your Portfolio

Idea Bank

Writing

1. Casting Memo Reread the biographies of Byron on pp. 656 and 704. Then choose an actor to play him in a movie, and write a memo to the director explaining your choice.

2. Letter to the Editor Imagine you are living in England during the early 1800's. Write a letter to the editor of a London newspaper, expressing your opinion of Byron's speech or Shelley's poem.

3. Response to Criticism Harold Bloom says, "Ideologically Shelley is of the permanent Left . . . he is nothing short of an extremist, and knew it." Using evidence from "A Song: 'Men of England,'" support or refute this statement.

Speaking and Listening

4. Political Speech Rehearse and give Byron's speech as he might have given it. Use your voice, pitch, tone, and volume to deliver your speech emphatically. **[Performing Arts Link]**

5. Panel Discussion What might Byron, Shelley, and Macaulay have said to each other in a panel discussion of the issues they address in these selections? Working with a group, role-play such discussion for a television appearance. **[Social Studies Link]**

Projects

6. Political Cartoon Research a controversial issue from history, like the Luddite riots, the 1815 Corn Law, or the Peterloo Massacre. Then create a political cartoon expressing an opinion on it. **[Social Studies Link; Visual Arts Link]**

7. Song Working alone or with a partner, set Shelley's poem to music. Then perform it live, on audiotape, or on videotape. **[Music Link]**

Writing Mini-Lesson

News Article on a Political Issue

The authors of these selections were deeply involved with the political issues of their time. Imagine that you are a news reporter, and write a news article about a political issue of today.

The following pointers will help you decide what details to include.

Writing Skills Focus: Elaboration to Give Information

In writing articles, you will have to **elaborate to give information.** In writing a news article, answer the questions *who, what, where, when, why,* and *how* to generate the information you need. Here's how you might answer those questions if you were writing a news article about Byron's speech.

- *who*—Lord Byron, poet and Whig
- *what*—speech against frame-breaking bill to make destroying factory machinery a capital offense
- *where*—House of Lords
- *when*—February 27, 1812
- *why*—sympathy for lower classes based on his own sense of being an outsider
- *how*—by appealing to both reason and emotion

Prewriting After choosing a political event or issue to write about, jot down answers to the questions listed above. Include as much detail as you know in response to each question.

Drafting Use a pyramid structure in which the most important information comes first. Add further elaborating details as you develop your article. Make sure to present both sides of the issue and to support general statements with specific details.

Revising Have a classmate read your news article and find the answers to the questions. If he or she cannot easily do so, provide any missing information. Carefully proofread your work for errors in grammar, punctuation, and spelling.

✓ ASSESSMENT OPTIONS

Formal Assessment, Selection Test, pp. 175–177, and Assessment Resources Software. The selection test is designed so that it can be easily customized to the ability levels of your students. ***Alternative Assessment,*** p. 36, includes options for less advanced students, more advanced students, visual/spatial learners, and verbal/linguistic learners.

PORTFOLIO ASSESSMENT
Use the following rubrics in the ***Alternative Assessment*** booklet to assess student writing:
Casting Memo: Description Rubric, p. 98
Letter to the Editor: Business Letter/Memo Rubric, p. 114
Response to Criticism: Response to Literature Rubric, p. 111
Writing Mini-Lesson: Summary Rubric, p. 99

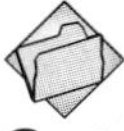

Idea Bank

Customizing for *Learning Modalities*
Following are suggestions for matching Idea Bank topics with your students' learning modalities:
Visual/Spatial: 6
Musical/Rhythmic: 4, 7
Verbal/Linguistic: 3, 5
Interpersonal: 2
Intrapersonal: 1

Customizing for *Performance Levels*
Following are suggestions for matching Idea Bank topics with your students' ability levels:
Less Advanced Students: 1, 2, 4
Average Students: 5, 6, 7
More Advanced Students: 3

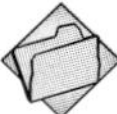

Writing Mini-Lesson

Refer students to the Writing Handbook, page 1189, for instruction on the writing process, and page 1191 for further information on expository writing.

Writing and Language Transparencies For help gathering details for a news article, display the Argument Organizer, p. 103, on the overhead and have students copy it.

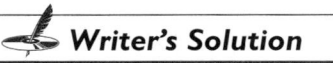

Writing Lab CD-ROM
Direct students to complete the tutorial on Exposition to help them write their satirical essays. Follow these steps:

1. Complete the Audience and Purpose Profile.
2. Use interactive instruction on making observations, poll-taking, and getting expert advice.
3. Create a draft on the computer.
4. Use a Proofreading Checklist.

Sourcebook
Have students refer to Chapter 3: Exposition, pp. 62–95, for additional support.

Prepare and Engage

OBJECTIVES

1. To interpret and respond to social commentary
2. To relate the ideas in the selections to personal experience
3. To determine the writer's purpose
4. To identify characteristics of social commentary
5. To build vocabulary in context and learn the word root *-fort-*
6. To correctly use commas in a series
7. To write a letter to an author, using appropriate language for a purpose
8. To respond to social commentary through writing, speaking and listening, and projects

SKILLS INSTRUCTION

Vocabulary
Word Roots: *-fort-*
Grammar:
Commas in a Series
Reading Strategy:
Determine the Writer's Purpose
Literary Focus:
Social Commentary
Writing:
Appropriate Language for a Purpose
Speaking and Listening:
Persuasive Speech (teacher edition)
Critical Viewing:
Evaluate

PORTFOLIO OPPORTUNITIES

Writing: Letter; Comparison and Contrast; Response to Criticism
Speaking and Listening: Conversation; Persuasive Speech
Projects: Portrait; Timeline of Women's Rights

More About the Authors

Henry Austen, who wrote the first published biographical sketch of his sister, **Jane Austen,** asserted that: "Every thing came finished from her pen, for on all subjects she had ideas as clear as her expressions were well chosen. It is not hazarding too much to say that she never dispatched a note or letter unworthy of publication."

Unlike the modest and ever socially and politically correct Austen, **Mary Wollstonecraft** lived a life associated with scandal. As a result, for about one hundred years after Wollstonecraft broke ground with her pioneering work in women's rights, most Victorian writers would not even mention her name.

Guide for Interpreting

Jane Austen *(1775–1817)*

Modest about her own genius, Jane Austen lived a quiet life, one devoted to her family. Never married, she nonetheless explored ideas about love, beauty, and marriage in her novels.

A Reserved Life Jane Austen was born in Steventon, Hampshire, England, the daughter of a clergyman. The seventh of eight children, Jane was educated at home by her father. In her teens Austen began writing parodies and skits primarily to amuse her family.

An Anonymous Novelist Austen's keen sense of awareness and observation helped her to become a successful novelist who captured the absurdities and injustices of society of the time. Like most women writers in her day, Austen published her work anonymously.

After her identity became known, she was honored by the Prince Regent a few years before her death. Her novel *Emma* is dedicated to him.

Hollywood Tributes Jane Austen's sharp satirical eye and brilliant use of dialogue have made her enormously popular in our own day. For example, Hollywood has "discovered" Austen and many of her works have been made into feature films, television films, and mini-series.

Mary Wollstonecraft *(1759–1797)*

Mary Wollstonecraft is recognized as one of the first major feminists. Despite growing up in poverty, Mary Wollstonecraft was given an education, and after a brief fiasco as a lady's companion, she, her sisters, and a friend established a girls' school near London. In 1787, she wrote *Thoughts on the Education of Daughters*, criticizing the poor education given to most females of her day.

A Voice for Women In 1790, when Edmund Burke attacked the French Revolution, Wollstonecraft defended it in *A Vindication of the Rights of Men.* Two years later she produced *A Vindication of the Rights of Woman,* a landmark work on women's rights. After a brief stay in Paris in which she witnessed the revolution, Wollstonecraft returned home and wed radical thinker William Godwin. A year later she died giving birth to their daughter Mary, who later became the author of *Frankenstein.*

◆ Background for Understanding

CULTURE: THE ROLE OF WOMEN

British women in the early nineteenth century had few economic or legal rights. In most cases a woman's property was legally her father's until she married, after which the property became her husband's. If a woman never wed, her property often remained in the hands of male relatives.

Abused women had little protection under the law, and divorces were almost impossible to obtain. Jobs, too, were limited: Whereas lower-class women might work as household help or in factories, more "genteel" females had to live on the charity of relatives, find posts as governesses or perhaps teach at a girls' school.

Women's education focused mainly on "ladylike" accomplishments such as embroidery, singing, and playing a musical instrument. Women who showed an interest in things beyond marriage and the home were generally regarded as unfeminine.

Prentice Hall Literature Program Resources

REINFORCE / RETEACH / EXTEND

Selection Support Pages
Build Vocabulary: Word Roots: *-fort-*, p. 175
Grammar and Style: Commas in a Series, p. 176
Reading Strategy: Determine the Writer's Purpose, p. 177
Literary Focus: Social Commentary, p. 178

Strategies for Diverse Student Needs, p. 37

Beyond Literature, p. 37

Formal Assessment Selection Test, pp. 178–180; Assessment Resources Software

Alternative Assessment, p. 37

Writing and Language Transparencies
Argument Organizer, p. 103

Resource Pro CD-ROM
Includes all resource material and customizable lesson plan

Listening to Literature Audiocassettes
"On Making an Agreeable Marriage" and from *A Vindication of the Rights of Woman*

Looking at Literature Videodisc Chapter 8: "On Making an Agreeable Marriage"

◆ On Making an Agreeable Marriage ◆
from A Vindication of the Rights of Woman

◆ *Literature and Your Life*

Connect Your Experience

Gender sometimes unfairly influences people's judgment of a person. Think about an assumption you've made about someone based on his or her gender, only to be proved wrong. Notice what these selections reveal about bias and gender roles in nineteenth-century England.

Journal Writing Jot down three assumptions someone might make about you because of your gender. Then write three facts that disprove those assumptions.

Thematic Focus: The Reaction to Society's Ills

As you read the following, think about how ideas about marriage and the role of women might be classified as "society's ills."

◆ Build Vocabulary

Word Roots: *-fort-*

From the Latin word *fortis*, which means "strong," comes the English root *-fort-*, which means "strength." The word *fortitude*, used by Mary Wollstonecraft in *Vindication*, means "strength of mind that allows one to endure pain or misfortune courageously."

Word Bank

Before you read, preview the words on this list from the selections.

scruple
amiable
vindication
solicitude
fastidious
specious
fortitude
preponderates
gravity

◆ Reading Strategy

Determine the Writer's Purpose

When reading any work of literature, it's important to **determine the writer's purpose**. Knowing what the writer wants to accomplish enables you to read with the appropriate attitude. These techniques help you determine a writer's purpose.

- Look for clues in the work's title and opening paragraph.
- Identify the writer's tone, or attitude, toward the subject, and observe how it affects your opinion of the topic.
- Consider why the writer chose to include particular details and examples.

◆ Literary Focus

Social Commentary

Social commentary is writing or speech that offers insights about society and its customs. Some social commentary is unconscious, reflecting social attitudes of its period without intentionally discussing them. Other social commentary is purposefully written to criticize society or record its customs.

As you read Jane Austen's letter and the passage from Mary Wollstonecraft's *A Vindication of the Rights of Woman,* use a chart like this to record social commentary that is conscious or unconscious.

Conscious	Unconscious

◆ Grammar and Style

Commas in a Series

Austen and Wollstonecraft use **commas in a series**; they separate the items in a list with commas. Although it is common to include a comma before the conjunction, it is also acceptable to omit the final comma.

Example: His situation in life, family, friends, & above all his Character—

Interest Grabber With the class, speculate on the rights women did or did not have at the end of the eighteenth and beginning of the nineteenth centuries in England. Make a three-column chart with the headings Careers, Education, and Marriage. List all conjectures.

Then tell students that the selections that follow were written by two remarkable women, Jane Austen and Mary Wollstonecraft. Austen, in her novels, subtly and slyly comments upon the unfair way women are treated socially and legally. In this personal letter, Austen's ideas about love and marriage are revealed to her niece. In *A Vindication*, Wollstonecraft, however, boldly states her views on the rights women should enjoy.

Customize for
Verbal/Linguistic Learners

Invite verbal/linguistic learners to focus attention on how these social commentaries differ in style and language from commentaries they might read today. Students might comment on, for example, the length and tone of Austen's letter, as well as the sentence structure, word choice, and even the use of such conventions as the ampersand. Students might also comment on how Wollstonecraft's use of metaphors and figurative language is different from any use that readers might encounter today.

Preparing for Standardized Tests

Reading and Vocabulary Determining the writer's purpose will help students interpret and correctly answer questions about literary passages that appear on standardized tests. For example, this type of exercise may appear on a standardized test:

Read the following passage and identify the author's probable purpose.

The education of women has of late been more attended to than formerly; yet they are still reckoned a frivolous sex, and ridiculed or pitied by the writers who endeavor by satire or instruction to improve them. It is acknowledged that they spend many of the first years of their lives in acquiring a smattering of accomplishments; meanwhile strength of body and mind are sacrificed to libertine notions of beauty, to the desire of establishing themselves—the only way women can rise in the world—by marriage. *(D)*

(A) To encourage women to marry
(B) To excuse the behavior of women
(C) To highlight the importance of beauty for women
(D) To demand equal education for men and women
(E) To explain why women are inferior students

For additional practice, use the Reading Strategy page in ***Selection Support,*** p. 177.

Develop Understanding

One-Minute Insight Responding in a letter to her niece Fanny Knight, who has recently expressed doubts to Austen about her suitor, Austen not only advises her niece, but comments neatly on what makes a desirable marriage in Austen's social class in the early 1800's.

Looking at Literature Videodisc Play Chapter 8: "On Making an Agreeable Marriage," before students read the selection. Elicit students' ideas concerning marriages and the customs that relate to matrimonial ceremonies.

Chapter 8

Customize for Less Proficient Readers
Encourage less proficient readers to paraphrase long, complicated sentences, reread to clarify ideas, and adjust their reading rate to fully understand and appreciate this letter.

1 Clarification Point out to students that the unusual punctuation and capitalization have been reproduced from the original letter Jane Austen wrote. This type of writing style, full of italics, various punctuation marks, and nonstandardized capitalization, was usual during the early 1800's.

On Making an Agreeable Marriage

Jane Austen

To Fanny Knight[1]
Friday 18–Sunday 20 November 1814
Chawton Nov: 18.—Friday

1 I feel quite as doubtful as you could be my dearest Fanny as to *when* my Letter may be finished, for I can command very little quiet time at present, but yet I must begin, for I know you will be glad to hear as soon as possible, & I really am impatient myself to be writing something on so very interesting a subject, though I have no hope of writing anything to the purpose.—I shall do very little more I dare say than say over again, what you have said before.—I was certainly a good deal surprised *at first*—as I had no suspicion of any change in your feelings, and I have no scruple in saying that you cannot be in Love. My dear Fanny, I am ready to laugh at the idea—and yet it is no laughing matter to have had you so mistaken as to your own feelings—And with all my heart I wish I had cautioned you on that point when first you spoke to me;—but tho' I did not think you then so *much*

1. **Fanny Knight:** Fanny Austen Knight was the daughter of Austen's brother Edward, who had been made the heir of wealthy cousins on the understanding that he would adopt their surname, *Knight*. The practice was not unusual in Austen's day.

◆ **Build Vocabulary**
scruple (skroo͞ʹ pəl) *n.*: Hesitation caused by one's conscience or principles; uneasy feeling; qualm

Block Scheduling Strategies

Consider these suggestions to take advantage of extended class time:

- Before reading the selections, have students read the Background for Understanding on page 714. Then hold a class discussion on how things have changed since the 1800's.
- Have students do the journal writing activity in Literature and Your Life on page 715. Students can share their responses with a classmate before reading.
- Introduce the Literary Focus on social commentary on page 715. Encourage students to copy the chart and fill it in as they read the selections.
- When students have finished reading, have them answer the Literary Focus questions on page 722.
- When students have finished reading the selections, play the **Listening to Literature Audiocassettes** recordings for them. Discuss with the class whether or not listening to the selections make the writer's purpose more evident.
- Provide class time for students to answer the Critical Thinking questions on pages 719 and 721.

Marriage à la Mode: The Marriage Contract, 1743, William Hogarth, National Gallery of Art, London

▲ **Critical Viewing:** In what ways does Hogarth's satirical depiction of the signing of a wedding contract echo attitudes toward marriage that are present in Austen's letter? **[Evaluate]** ❷

▶**Critical Viewing**◀

❷ **Evaluate** Hogarth seems to present the signing of the contract as something of an ordeal. Many people are involved, most of whom look either very intent on or worn out by the process. Hogarth seems to be suggesting that the event is a combination of a social affair and a business transaction. This attitude echoes Austen in that both concern themselves with the social conventions and monetary considerations surrounding marriage.

◆ Literature and Your Life

Point out that the criteria for making a good marriage vary from culture to culture. In television shows, movies, romance novels, and works of literature such as *Romeo and Juliet*, passionate, romantic love is generally regarded as the only appropriate reason for a couple to marry. From Austen's letter and the Hogarth painting, it is clear that while love was considered to be of critical importance during the early nineteenth century, there were other considerations in selecting a spouse, such as the person's situation in life, family, and character. In cultures where arranged marriages are the norm, romantic love is considered to be irrelevant to whether two people should marry. Encourage students to discuss their thoughts about love and marriage. What do they think about prenuptial agreements, dowries, arranged marriages, and other matrimonial practices? Have volunteers share their opinions about desirable characteristics in a prospective spouse.

Humanities: Art

Marriage à la Mode: The Marriage Contract, 1743, by William Hogarth.

Explain to students that *à la mode* means "according to the fashion." This painting shows a part of the marriage process according to the social conventions of the time in which it was painted.

This painting, which is the first in a series of six that Hogarth painted, shows the beginning of the marriage: the contract. At the left of the picture sit the bride- and groom-to-be. Notice that the groom is so busy looking at himself in the mirror that he doesn't notice the lawyer flirting with his bride-to-be (who plays with her engagement ring as if it were a toy). At the table, the two fathers work out the financial details of the arrangement.

Use these questions for discussion:

1. Would you describe the scene in the painting as one of social or business activity? Why? *The prospective groom and bride seem to be enjoying themselves, although not with each other. The fathers seem to be discussing serious business matters.*
2. Among the many things the painting shows is a slight difference in social stature between the bride and groom. In fact, the bride's father is a merchant, while the groom's father is an earl. How is this difference shown in the painting? *It is shown primarily through dress: the earl and his son are dressed far more elegantly than the merchant. It is also shown through posture: the earl and his son have the posture of the self-assured rich.*

◆ Critical Thinking

❶ Compare and Contrast Inform students that when Fanny Knight first spoke with Austen about her feelings, the two women had different ideas about just how much in love Fanny was. Ask students to compare and contrast those opinions. *Fanny thought herself very much in love, whereas Austen thought Fanny not so much in love as she had thought herself to be, but sufficiently in love to be happy.*

◆ Reading Strategy

❷ Determine the Writer's Purpose Possible response: Although she knows that her own opinions about her niece's situation fluctuate, Austen's purpose is to council and reassure her niece.

◆ Critical Thinking

❸ Draw Conclusions Point out to students that Austen is, in many ways, just beginning to make her opinion known here. Ask students why she has spent so much time "warming up" and why, even at this point, she does not come right out and say something like, "I think you should marry Mr J. P." *Possible response: A matter like this one is delicate. Austen wants to show regard for her niece's feelings. On the other hand, she wants to say what she thinks is in her niece's best interests. By being indirect, she softens her message.*

◆ Literary Focus

❹ Social Commentary These lines suggest that once a woman has encouraged a suitor, the situation is serious and has gone quite far. In Austen's times, such encouragement was not to be given lightly, nor backed away from without just cause.

Comprehension Check ☑

❺ Ask: According to Austen, how likely is it that Fanny will find a better suitor? *It is very unlikely. Such a chance is, perhaps, "one in a Thousand."*

❻ Clarification Explain that Austen is being playful, or mildly ironic, here as she tells her niece not to worry about a man who is more likely to live up to Christian principles than other men.

---

❶ in love as you thought yourself, I did consider you as being attached in a degree—quite sufficiently for happiness, as I had no doubt it would increase with opportunity.—And from the time of our being in London together, I thought you really very much in love.—But you certainly are not at all—there is no concealing it.—What strange creatures we are!—It seems as if your being secure of him (as you say yourself) had made you Indifferent.—There was a little disgust I suspect, at the Races—& I do not wonder at it. His expressions then would not do for one who had rather more Acuteness, Penetration & Taste, than Love, which was your case. And yet, after all, I *am* surprised that the change in your feelings should be so great.—He is, just what he ever was, only more evidently & uniformly devoted to *you.* This is all the difference.—How shall we account for it?—My dearest Fanny, I am writing what will not be of the smallest use to you. I am feeling differently every moment, & shall not be able to suggest a single thing that can assist your Mind.—I could lament in one sentence & laugh in the next, but as to Opinion or Counsel I am sure none will [be *omitted*] extracted worth having from this Letter.—I read yours through the very even[2] I received it—getting away by myself—I could not bear to leave off, when I had once begun.—I was full of curiosity & concern. Luckily Your Aunt C. dined at the other house, therefore I had not to maneuver away from *her;*—& as to anybody else, I do not care.—Poor dear Mr J. P![3]—Oh! dear Fanny, Your mistake has been one that thousands of women fall into. He was the *first* young Man who attached himself to you. That was the charm, & most powerful it is.—Among the multitudes however that make the same mistake with Yourself, there can be few indeed who ❸ have so little reason to regret it;—*his* Character & *his* attachment leave you nothing to be ashamed of.—Upon the whole, what is to be done? You certainly *have* encouraged him to such a point as to make him feel almost secure of you—you have no inclination for any other person —His situation in life, family, friends, & above all his Character—his uncommonly amiable mind, strict principles, just notions, good habits—*all* that *you* know so well how to value, *All* that really is of the first importance—everything of this nature pleads his cause most strongly.—You have no doubt of his having superior Abilities—he has proved it at the University—he is I dare say such a Scholar as your agreeable, idle Brothers would ill bear a comparison with.—Oh! my dear Fanny, the more I write about him, the warmer my feelings become, the more strongly I feel the sterling worth of such a young Man & the desirableness of your growing in love with him again. I recommend this most thoroughly.—There *are* such beings in the World perhaps, one in a Thousand, as the Creature You & I should think perfection, where Grace & Spirit are united to Worth, where the Manners are equal to the Heart & Understanding, but such a person may not come in your way, or if he does, he may not be the eldest son of a Man of Fortune,[4] the Brother of your particular friend, & belonging to your own County.—Think of all this Fanny. ❺ Mr J. P.- has advantages which do not often meet in one person. His only fault indeed seems Modesty. If he were less modest, he would be more agreeable, speak louder & look Impudenter;—and is not it a fine Character, of which Modesty is the only defect?—I have no doubt that he will get more lively & more like yourselves as he is more with you;—he will catch your ways if he belongs to you. And as to there being any objection from his *Goodness,* from the danger of his becoming even Evangelical,[5] I cannot admit *that.* I am by no means convinced that we ought not all to be Evangelicals, & am at least persuaded that they who are so from Reason & Feeling, must be happiest & safest.—Do not be frightened from the connection by your Brothers having most wit. Wisdom is better than Wit, & in the long run ❻

> **◆ Reading Strategy** ❷
> Why, if she believes that she has "no hope of writing anything to the purpose," do you think Austen writes anyway?

> **◆ Literary Focus** ❹
> What do these details reveal about the criteria for judging a suitor in Austen's day?

2. **even:** Evening.
3. **Mr J. P.:** Fanny's suitor.
4. **eldest son of a Man of Fortune:** In Austen's day, the bulk of a British family's lands and wealth usually passed to the eldest son.
5. **Evangelical:** Of or relating to a group of earnest Church of England members active in social reform movements at the time of the letter.

Cultural Connection

The Institution of Marriage While marriage is still regulated by varying laws all over the world, social and cultural regulations often prove equally strong or stronger than civil law. Endogamy, for example, which is a social concept, limits marriage to members of one's own tribe or section of a tribe, to one's own religion, or to one's own social class.

In Austen's day and among members of her class, endogamy was a key regulatory factor. The families concerned often controlled the marriage, negotiating the dowry, the living arrangements, and other crucial matters related to the union and future lives of the couple involved. The courtship period was characterized by the exchange of visits, which were chaperoned.

Invite students to research a marriage ceremony or ritual that is different from that of their own culture or religion. For example, students might find out how a Hindu ceremony differs from the kind of ceremony in which their own parents or other relatives participated, or they might compare and contrast a typical Jewish wedding with a typical Islamic one.

6 will certainly have the laugh on her side; & don't be frightened by the idea of his acting more strictly up to the precepts of the New Testament than others.—And now, my dear Fanny, having written so much on one side of the question, I shall turn round & entreat you not to commit yourself farther, & not to think of accepting him unless you really do like him. Anything is to be preferred or endured rather than marrying without Affection; and if his deficiencies of Manner &c &c[6] strike you more than all his good qualities, if you continue to think strongly of them, give him up at once.—

7 Things are now in such a state, that you must resolve upon one or the other, either to allow him to go on as he has done, or whenever you are together behave with a coldness which may convince him that he has been deceiving himself.—I have no doubt of his suffering a good deal for a time, a great deal, when he feels that he must give you up;—but it is no creed of mine, as you must be well aware, that such sort of Disappointments kill anybody.—Your sending the Music was an admirable device,[7] it made everything easy, & I do not know how I could have accounted for the parcel otherwise; for tho' your dear Papa most conscientiously hunted about till he found me alone in the Din^g-parlor,[8] Your Aunt C. had seen that he *had* a parcel to deliver.—As it was however, I do not think anything was suspected.—We have heard nothing fresh from Anna. I trust she is very comfortable in her new home. Her Letters have been very sensible & satisfactory, with no *parade* of happiness, which I liked them the better for.—I have often known young married Women write in a way I did not like, in that respect.

You will be glad to hear that the first Edit: of M.P.[9] is all sold.—Your Uncle Henry is rather wanting me to come to Town, to settle about a 2^d Edit:—but as I could not very conveniently leave home now, I have written him my Will & pleasure, & unless he still urges it, shall not go.—I am very greedy & want to make the most of it;—but as you are much above caring about money, I shall not plague you with any particulars.—The pleasures of Vanity are more within your comprehension, & you will enter into mine, at receiving the *praise* which every now & then comes to me, through some channel or other.—

6. **&c &c:** Et cetera (the & symbol, called an ampersand, stands for et, Latin for "and").
7. **device:** Trick; ruse; ploy.

8. **Din^g-parlor:** Dining room.
9. **M.P.:** Austen's novel *Mansfield Park*.

◆ Build Vocabulary

amiable (ā′ mē ə bəl) *adj.*: Friendly; agreeable

Guide for Responding

◆ Literature and Your Life

Reader's Response How would you have reacted to this letter if you were Fanny? Explain.

Thematic Response Do you think Austen viewed marriage as one of society's ills? Explain.

☑ Check Your Comprehension

1. What is the "very interesting" subject of this letter?
2. (a) What virtues in Mr. J. P. does Austen ask Fanny to consider? (b) What does Austen think about marrying without affection?

◆ Critical Thinking

INTERPRET

1. What prompts Austen to write "What strange creatures we are"? **[Interpret]**
2. According to Austen, what good points about Mr. J. P. recommend him as a suitor? **[Support]**
3. What does Austen mean when she says that "Wisdom is better than Wit"? **[Interpret]**

EVALUATE

4. Based on this letter, would you say Austen is a good judge of human nature? Why or why not? **[Make a Judgment]**

◆ Literary Focus

7 Social Commentary Ask: What does this passage reveal about behavior of love and courtship in Austen's time? *In Austen's era, marriage need not be based on love. There was little frank communication between the engaged couple.*

Reinforce and Extend

Answers

◆ Literature and Your Life

Reader's Response Sample response: Fanny may have been more confused than ever.

Thematic Focus No, although Austen implies that true love rarely enters into marriage.

☑ Check Your Comprehension

1. Love and marriage are the "very interesting" subject.
2. (a) Austen asks Fanny to consider Mr J. P.'s amiable mind, strict principles, just notions, and good habits. (b) Marrying without affection is not to be endured.

◆ Critical Thinking

1. Austen is commenting on the fact that people have the ability to fall in and out of love.
2. Mr J. P.'s amiable mind, strict principles, just notions, good habits recommend him as a suitor.
3. Austen implies that wit is superficial and wisdom is more desirable.
4. Sample response: Yes, Austen's observations of human nature are insightful.

Speaking and Listening Mini-Lesson

Persuasive Speech

This mini-lesson supports the Speaking and Listening activity in the Idea Bank on page 723.

Introduce the Concept Explain to students that a persuasive speech is a formal speech in which the speaker tries to persuade an audience to think or act in a certain way. Persuasive speeches rely not only on the information to make a point but also on the presenter's tone, pacing, and, perhaps, rhythm.

Develop Background Students should first select a segment of Wollstonecraft's essay (pp. 720–721) to deliver as a speech. Instruct students to change the wording in any way that will make the speech clear and persuasive to their listeners. Caution them that while they may change every word, they must preserve Wollstonecraft's meaning.

Apply the Information Have students practice delivering their speeches, varying their pace, intonation, and emphases to the best effect. Place a podium at the front of the classroom and have students present their speeches to the class.

Assess the Outcome Assess the speeches based on these criteria, which students should be aware of ahead of time: the point of the speech is clear to listeners; the message is consistent with Wollstonecraft's meaning; the speaker uses an effective tone and persuasive word choice; and the speech is delivered effectively and maintains the interest of the listeners.

Develop Understanding

One-Minute Insight Wollstonecraft sadly reflects on the fact that women's poor educational opportunities coupled with society's expectations about feminine beauty have rendered women silly and vain. In what begins as a sad voice and gradually becomes a more strident one, Wollstonecraft attacks this degradation of women.

◆ Reading Strategy

❶ **Determine the Writer's Purpose** Ask students which part of this opening passage seems as if it might state Wollstonecraft's purpose. *Her assertions that "neglected education" is the source of misery and that women's minds "are not in a healthy state" suggest that her purpose is to explain this sad state of affairs and propose solutions.*

◆ Literary Focus

❷ **Social Commentary** Wollstonecraft says that education is a "false system" in which men do not consider women as "human creatures." Women are, as a result, taught to be "alluring."

◆ Grammar and Style

❸ **Commas in a Series** Ask students to find the commas in a series in this passage. *The list of items separated by commas is: "they dress, they paint, and nickname God's creatures."*

◆ Reading Strategy

❹ **Determine the Writer's Purpose** The author wants women to become more "masculine and respectable" and to "engage in the nobler passions that open and enlarge the soul."

◆ Literature and Your Life

❺ Ask students to name examples from the media in which women are degraded by "mistaken notions of female excellence." *Students may cite advertisements, especially for beauty products, or television shows that feature pretty, brainless female characters.*

from A Vindication of the Rights of Woman

Mary Wollstonecraft

After considering the historic page,[1] and viewing the living world with anxious solicitude, the most melancholy emotions of sorrowful indignation have depressed my spirits, and I have sighed when obliged to confess that either Nature has made a great difference between man and man,[2] or that the civilization which has hitherto taken place in the world has been very partial. I have turned over various books written on the subject of education, and patiently observed the conduct of parents and the management of schools; but what has been the result?—a profound conviction that the neglected education of my fellow ❶ creatures is the grand source of the misery I deplore, and that women, in particular, are rendered weak and wretched by a variety of concurring causes, originating from one hasty conclusion. The conduct and manners of women, in fact, evidently prove that their minds are not in a healthy state; for, like the flowers which are planted in too rich a soil, strength and usefulness are sacrificed to beauty; and the flaunting leaves, after having pleased a fastidious eye, fade, disregarded on the stalk, long before the season when they ought to have arrived at maturity. One cause of this barren blooming I attribute to a false system of education, gathered from the books written on this subject by men who, considering females rather as women than human creatures, have been more anxious to make them alluring . . . than affectionate wives and rational mothers; and the understanding of the sex has been so bubbled by this specious homage, that the civilized women of the present century, with a few exceptions, are only anxious to inspire love, when they ought to cherish a nobler ambition, and by their abilities and virtues exact respect. . . .

❷ **◆ Literary Focus** What observations about the education of females in her society does the author make?

The education of women has of late been more attended to than formerly; yet they are still reckoned a frivolous sex, and ridiculed or pitied by the writers who endeavor by satire or instruction to improve them. It is acknowledged that they spend many of the first years of their lives in acquiring a smattering of accomplishments; meanwhile strength of body and mind are sacrificed to libertine[3] notions of beauty, to the desire of establishing themselves—the only way women can rise in the world—by marriage. And this desire making mere animals of them, when they marry they act as such children may be expected to act—they dress, they paint, and nickname God's creatures. . . . Can they be ❸ expected to govern a family with judgment, or take care of the poor babes whom they bring into the world?

If, then, it can be fairly deduced from the present conduct of the sex, from the prevalent fondness for pleasure which takes place of ambition and those nobler passions that open and enlarge the soul, that the instruction which women have hitherto received has only tended,

1. **the historic page:** The page of history.
2. **man and man:** Used here in the generic sense to mean human being and human being.
3. **libertine:** Wasteful.

◆ Build Vocabulary

vindication (vin´ də kā´ shən) *n.*: Act of providing justification or support for

solicitude (sə lis´ ə to͞od) *n.*: Care; concern

fastidious (fas tid´ ē əs) *adj.*: Difficult to please

specious (spē´ shəs) *adj.*: Deceptively attractive; seeming valid but actually illogical or untrue

Beyond the Classroom

Workplace Skills

Women and the Top Jobs Although women have made great strides in the workplace, they remain underrepresented in the top jobs. As of 1997, women headed only four of the major American corporations and less than five percent held the highest positions, such as chief executive officer, in Fortune 500 companies.

Ask interested students to learn more about women in the workplace. They might do this by researching a local company or they might gather statistics from government documents on the Web that detail changes in women's salaries and rates of pay relative to men over the last decade.

Community Connection

Interview a Working Woman Ask students to interview a woman who holds a position formerly reserved for men. Students may find out what she does, how she achieved her position, problems she encountered along the way, and problems she confronts now.

with the constitution of civil society, to render them insignificant objects of desire—mere propagators of fools!—if it can be proved that in aiming to accomplish them, without cultivating their understandings, they are taken out of their sphere of duties, and made ridiculous and useless when the short-lived bloom of beauty is over, I presume that *rational* men will excuse me for endeavoring to persuade them to become more masculine and respectable.

> ◆ **Reading Strategy**
> 4 What basic advice does the author want women to accept?

Indeed the word masculine is only a bugbear;[4] there is little reason to fear that women will acquire too much courage or fortitude, for their apparent inferiority with respect to bodily strength must render them in some degree dependent on men in the various relations of life; but why should it be increased by prejudices that give a sex to virtue, and confound simple truths with sensual reveries?

5 Women are, in fact, so much degraded by mistaken notions of female excellence, that I do not mean to add a paradox when I assert that this artificial weakness produces a propensity to tyrannize, and gives birth to cunning, the natural opponent of strength, which leads them to play off those contemptible infantine[5] airs that undermine esteem even whilst they excite desire. Let me become more chaste and modest, and if women do not grow wiser in the same ratio it will be clear that they have weaker understandings. It seems scarcely necessary to say that I now speak of the sex in general. Many individuals have more sense than their male relatives; and, as nothing preponderates where there is a constant struggle for an equilibrium without it has[6] naturally more gravity, some women govern their husbands without degrading themselves, because intellect will always govern.

4. **bugbear:** Frightening imaginary creature, especially one that frightens children.
5. **infantine:** Infantile; childish.
6. **without it has:** Without having.

◆ Build Vocabulary

fortitude (fôrt′ ə to͞od) *n.*: Strength of mind that allows one to endure courageously

preponderates (prē pän′ də rāts′) *v.*: Becomes larger or heavier than something else

gravity (grav′ i tē) *n.*: Seriousness

Guide for Responding

◆ Literature and Your Life

Reader's Response Do you agree that, for a woman, respect may be more important than admiration? Why or why not?

Thematic Focus Which specific social ills does this selection address?

Group Activity In a small group, discuss whether or not Wollstonecraft's observations about women still apply today.

☑ Check Your Comprehension

1. What does Wollstonecraft say is the direct cause of the difference between men and women of the time?
2. What, according to Wollstonecraft, is the result of women being poorly educated?

◆ Critical Thinking

INTERPRET

1. Judging from the first paragraph, what is the author's attitude toward the subject? **[Analyze]**
2. What does Wollstonecraft mean by the phrase "barren blooming" in the first paragraph? **[Interpret]**
3. According to Wollstonecraft, what role do "notions of beauty" play in most women's lives? **[Infer]**
4. Wollstonecraft, in paragraph three, says "I presume that *rational* men will excuse me . . ." Why do you think she emphasized *rational*? **[Infer]**

EVALUATE

5. Which elements of Wollstonecraft's argument do you find effective? Which elements are not? Explain. **[Assess]**

APPLY

6. Do you think there is still inequality in male-female education? Cite examples to support your opinion. **[Relate]**

Reinforce and Extend

Answers

◆ Literature and Your Life

Reader's Response Yes, with respect comes admiration, but admiration does not necessarily bring with it respect; no, admiration is just as important as respect.

Thematic Focus This selection addresses the unfair educational opportunities afforded men and women.

☑ Check Your Comprehension

1. Wollstonecraft says the main difference between men and women is quality of education.
2. Because women are poorly educated, they spend too much time and effort becoming objects of beauty, becoming shallow and simple in the process.

◆ Critical Thinking

1. The author seems sad and depressed.
2. "Barren blooming" refers to women's being disregarded after the fading of their youthful beauty.
3. "Notions of beauty" cause women to abandon the improvement of their physical and mental strength.
4. Wollstonecraft implies that those who disagree are irrational.
5. Possible response: Wollstonecraft's argument is effective in that she gives many examples of how women's behavior is an outgrowth of their education. The argument could be made even more effective if she had been more scientific or specific in her examples.
6. Yes, males still dominate classrooms and are called on more often than female students; no, males and females receive equal educational opportunities.

Beyond the Selection

FURTHER READING

Other Works by Jane Austen
Pride and Prejudice; Sense and Sensibility

Other Social Commentaries by and About Women
"Ain't I a Woman?," Sojourner Truth; *On the Equality of the Sexes,* Judith Sargent Murray
"I Want a Wife," Judy Syfers

We suggest you read these works before recommending them to students.

INTERNET

For information on Mary Wollstonecraft, go to **http://www.inform/umd.edu/RC/rc.html**

For a Jane Austen information page, go to **http://www.pemberly.com/janeinfo/janeinfo.html**

Please be aware, however, that sites may have changed since we published this information. We *strongly recommend* that you preview the sites before you send students to them.

Answers

◆ Literary Focus

1. Possible answer: It is a commentary on society because it suggests that a good match in marriage should not be based solely on love but on other more important societal concerns, including the suitor's character, his "Abilities," and his economic standing (i.e., whether he is the eldest son of a "Man of Fortune").
2. Possible answer: Yes, it was meant to be a commentary that points out a social injustice.
3. Possible answer: Wollstonecraft's work is a more effective social commentary because it is direct and to the point. Her opinions are stated openly, and her language is highly persuasive.

◆ Grammar and Style

1. *Pride and Prejudice* is filled with grace, wit, and satire.
2. Characters include Jane, Elizabeth, Mary, Kitty, and Lydia Bennet.
3. Their amusements include balls, visits, and letter writing.
4. The Bennets meet Mr. Darcy, Mr. Bingley, and two of Mr. Bingley's sisters at a ball.
5. Jane falls ill at the Bingley's home, is put to bed, and is visited by Elizabeth.

◆ Build Vocabulary

Using the Root *-fort-*

1. A *fortress* is a stronghold, a place that is built to protect those within against attack.
2. *Comfort* can be the act of giving strength to another.
3. To *fortify* means to strengthen; for example, to fortify milk is to add vitamins that make it more nutritious.
4. One's *forte* is one's particular strength or talent, such as mental multiplication or jump shots.

Using the Word Bank

1. antonyms
2. synonyms
3. synonyms
4. antonyms
5. antonyms
6. antonyms
7. synonyms
8. antonyms
9. antonyms

Guide for Responding *(continued)*

◆ Literary Focus

Social Commentary

Social commentaries, such as Austen's letter and Wollstonecraft's *Vindication,* offer insights into the customs and values of the time in which they were written. Some social commentary is unconscious, reflecting social attitudes of its period without intentionally discussing them. Other social commentary is intentionally written to criticize society or record its customs. To answer the following questions, use the chart you created while reading.

1. In what ways is Jane Austen's "On Making an Agreeable Marriage" a commentary on society?
2. Do you think *A Vindication of the Rights of Woman* was meant to be a social commentary? Why or why not?
3. Which of the two works do you find more effective as a social commentary? Why?

◆ Grammar and Style

Commas in a Series

Writers use commas in a series to separate items for clarity. The usual practice is to include a comma before the conjunction, but it is also acceptable to omit the final comma.

Practice Copy the following sentences into your notebook and punctuate them with serial commas.

1. *Pride and Prejudice* is filled with grace wit and satire.
2. Characters include Jane Elizabeth Mary Kitty and Lydia Bennet.
3. Their amusements include balls visits and letter writing.
4. The Bennets meet Mr. Darcy Mr. Bingley and two of Mr. Bingley's sisters at a ball.
5. Jane falls ill at the Bingleys' home is put to bed and is visited by Elizabeth.

Writing Application Write a paragraph in response to Wollstonecraft's *Vindication*. In it, list reasons you agree or disagree with her ideas. Use serial commas to separate the reasons you list.

◆ Build Vocabulary

Using the Root *-fort-*

The root *-fort-* means "strong." Explain how its meaning is conveyed in the following words.

1. fortress **2.** comfort **3.** fortify **4.** forte

Using the Word Bank

Indicate in your notebook whether the word pairs are synonyms or antonyms.

1. preponderates, dwindles
2. specious, false
3. vindication, justification
4. amiable, hostile
5. gravity, frivolity
6. solicitude, thoughtlessness
7. scruple, qualm
8. fastidious, sloppy
9. fortitude, weakness

◆ Reading Strategy

Determine the Writer's Purpose

Once you determine the **writer's purpose**—the writer's goal—by observing clues as you read, you'll read more effectively. In *Vindication,* Wollstonecraft's sad tone helps her achieve her purpose, which is to persuade. "After . . . viewing the living world with anxious solicitude, the most melancholy emotions of sorrowful indignation have depressed my spirits . . ."

Identifying a writer's purpose is not an exact science. Different readers may identify different purposes in the same material, and sometimes, a writer may have more than one purpose in a piece of writing.

1. (a) Identify Austen's main purpose in writing "On Making an Agreeable Marriage." What clues point you toward this purpose? (b) Might Austen have had any other purpose in writing to her niece? Explain.
2. (a) Mary Wollstonecraft's purpose in *Vindication* is to persuade. By what means did she convey this purpose? (b) Were you persuaded by her argument? Explain.
3. In what ways does identifying a writer's purpose focus your reading?

◆ Reading Strategy

1. (a) Austen's purpose is to help her niece make up her mind about whether or not to marry her suitor. (b) Austen may have had another purpose, such as to instruct her niece on the ways of love and marriage.
2. (a) Wollstonecraft's persuasive purpose is conveyed by her title—a vindication is a justification—and by her strongly asserted ideas about women. She uses such emotionally charged words as *indignation, wretched,* and *false*. (b) Yes, her argument is well stated and supported with examples; no, her argument is too general and lacks specific data and proof.
3. Possible answer: Determining the writer's purpose helps the reader identify the main points and observe the ways in which they are developed or supported.

Build Your Portfolio

Idea Bank

Writing

1. Letter Write Fanny Knight's response to her Aunt Jane. Present her thoughts and feelings.

2. Comparison and Contrast Did Wollstonecraft and Austen have similar views about the role of women in society? Write a brief essay in which you compare and contrast their views.

3. Response to Criticism Author Virginia Woolf once spoke of "the high-handed and hot-blooded manner" in which Mary Wollstonecraft "cut her way to the quick of life." Write a response to this quotation, using excerpts from the work to support your ideas.

Speaking and Listening

4. Conversation In Austen's day, conversations between people separated by distance took place by letter. Update this "conversation" by role-playing a phone call between Jane Austen and her niece Fanny. **[Performing Arts Link]**

5. Persuasive Speech Deliver a portion of Wollstonecraft's *Vindication* to the class as a persuasive speech. Change the wording as necessary to fit an oral presentation. **[Performing Arts Link]**

Projects

6. Portrait Create a portrait of Fanny Knight's suitor, Mr. J. P., based on the details provided in Austen's letter. **[Art Link]**

7. Timeline of Women's Rights Research important dates in the history of English women and create a timeline for display. For example, note when women won the right to hold property and when they won the right to vote. **[Art Link; Social Studies Link]**

Writing Mini-Lesson

Letter to an Author

Write a letter to Jane Austen or Mary Wollstonecraft in which you express your agreement or disagreement with the ideas she presents in the corresponding selection. For example, you might agree with Austen's views on love and marriage yet disagree with her interference in her niece's life. To be convincing, use language that will help you achieve your purpose.

Writing Skills Focus: Appropriate Language for a Purpose

In writing a letter expressing an opinion, you'll want to be as persuasive as possible. To do this, choose words that will help you to achieve your goal. In the following passage, Wollstonecraft uses strong words to help her accomplish her purpose, to persuade:

Model From the Selection

. . . a *profound conviction* that the *neglected* education of my fellow-creatures is the *grand* source of the *misery* I *deplore* . . .

Prewriting Decide to which author you will respond. Jot down your reactions to the work and the author's opinions. Find specific passages within the work with which you agree or disagree.

Drafting State your opinion and then support it with details. As you do so, carefully choose words that express your feelings.

Revising Add details, if necessary, to give your argument more weight. Review your word choice to determine if your words accomplish your purpose. Change words as necessary to get the effect you want. Be sure that you have used the correct format for a business letter, and check to see that your writing is free from grammar, spelling, and punctuation errors.

✓ ASSESSMENT OPTIONS

Formal Assessment, Selection Test, pp. 178–180, and Assessment Resources Software. The selection test is designed so that it can be easily customized to the ability levels of your students. ***Alternative Assessment,*** p. 37, includes options for less advanced students, more advanced students, visual and spatial learners, and auditory learners.

PORTFOLIO ASSESSMENT

Use the following rubrics in the ***Alternative Assessment*** booklet to assess student writing:
Letter: Expression Rubric, p. 95
Comparison and Contrast: Comparison/Contrast Rubric, p. 104
Response to Criticism: Response to Literature Rubric, p. 111
Writing Mini-Lesson: Business Letter, Memo Rubric, p. 114

Idea Bank

Customizing for
Learning Modalities

Following are suggestions for matching Idea Bank topics with your students' learning modalities:
- Visual/Spatial: 6, 7
- Musical/Rhythmic: 5
- Verbal/Linguistic: 1, 2, 3
- Interpersonal: 4, 5

Customizing for
Performance Levels

Following are suggestions for matching Idea Bank topics with your students' ability levels:
- Less Advanced Students: 1, 6
- Average Students: 2, 4, 5
- More Advanced Students: 3, 5, 7

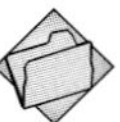

Writing Mini-Lesson

Refer students to the Writing Handbook, page 1189, for instruction on the writing process, and page 1193 for further information on response to literature.

Writing and Language Transparencies Display the Argument Organizer, p. 103, on an overhead projector for students to copy. Encourage them to use a chart as they collect and organize details for their letters.

Writer's Solution

Writing Lab CD-ROM

Direct students to complete the tutorial on Response to Literature to help them write their letters to an author. Follow these steps:
1. Complete the Audience and Purpose Profile.
2. Use interactive tips on using excerpts and quotations.
3. Create a draft on the computer.
4. Use a Transition Words Checker to be sure ideas are clearly and smoothly connected.

Sourcebook

Have students refer to Chapter 7: Exposition, pp. 196–229, for additional support.

Prepare and Engage

OBJECTIVES

1. To read, comprehend, and interpret a contemporary screenplay
2. To relate the screenplay to personal experience
3. To connect a modern screenplay to the theme of reaction to society's ills
4. To respond to the screenplay through writing, speaking and listening, and a project

PORTFOLIO OPPORTUNITIES

Writing: Letter to the President; Prediction; Social Criticism
Speaking and Listening: Interview
Project: Historical Account

Connections to World Literature

The theme of social injustice is timeless, even if the emphasis may change from one era to another. The selections in this grouping focus on economic, social, and political inequalities that have been issues since the onset of the industrial revolution. Jane Austen's *Sense and Sensibility* recently adapted into a successful film, touches on social and economic inequalities that are still relevant today.

More About the Author
Winning an Academy Award for the first screenplay she ever wrote was quite a coup for Thompson. Of course she didn't only write the screenplay: she also played the role of Elinor Dashwood.

Thematic Focus Society's ills are often reflected in the choices, or lack of choices, available to individuals. Sometimes choice is circumscribed by class, sometimes by economic conditions, sometimes by gender, and sometimes by other factors.

Genre Focus Call attention to the characteristics of this screenplay. It is written like a drama script, except it contains additional information about the use of the camera.

CONNECTIONS TO TODAY'S WORLD

from The *Sense and Sensibility* Screenplay and Diaries

Emma Thompson

Thematic Connection

THE REACTION TO SOCIETY'S ILLS

The pieces in this section serve as political and social commentary on the problems of early-nineteenth-century England. Shelley urges workers to fight for fair treatment, Byron defends the common worker from the tyranny of aristocrats, and Macaulay joyfully describes the passage of an important reform measure. In the field of women's rights, Wollstonecraft powerfully states the need for reform. Austen, in her private correspondence, offers not a political program but a playful commentary on social conditions.

SOCIAL AWARENESS TODAY

Contemporary writers also use their work to make people aware of social injustice. In her screenplay for the movie version of Jane Austen's *Sense and Sensibility,* Emma Thompson deals with issues relevant to both Austen's time and ours. These issues concern differences in the opportunities available to men and women, and to people of various backgrounds.

Thompson skillfully explores these issues in what appears to be an innocent conversation between two friends. Notice how Thompson uses the directions in italics to explain the emotional atmosphere in which this revealing discussion takes place.

As you read, note the CAM abbreviation that indicates camera direction. EXT stands for exterior or outside shot, and the numbers indicate the scene or shot.

EMMA THOMPSON
(1959–)

London-born Emma Thompson is one of England's most talented and successful actors. She studied literature at Cambridge, originally planning on becoming a writer. She then pursued a career in stand-up comedy and gained notoriety in a television comedy series in which she starred with her mother and sister. Thompson went on to achieve success in films; she has received an Academy Award for her performance in *Howard's End* and two other nominations for performances in *The Remains of the Day* and *In the Name of the Father.* Her writing career began with her script for an adaptation of Jane Austen's *Sense and Sensibility,* for which she won an Academy Award.

Prentice Hall Literature Program Resources

REINFORCE / RETEACH / EXTEND

Selection Support Pages
Build Vocabulary: Language of Social Awareness, p. 179
Thematic Focus: Contemporary Social Reformers, p. 180

Formal Assessment Selection Test, pp. 181–182; Assessment Resources Software

Resource Pro CD-ROM
from the screenplay of *Sense and Sensibility*—includes all resource material and customizable lesson plan

Listening to Literature Audiocassettes
from the screenplay of *Sense and Sensibility*

from Sense and Sensibility

Jane Austen, dramatized by Emma Thompson

CONNECTIONS TO TODAY'S WORLD

After the recent death of Mr. Dashwood, his daughters Elinor, Marianne, and Margaret are trying to overcome their grief. Mr. Dashwood's eldest son and his wife, Fanny, have taken possession of the family home. Edward Ferrars, Fanny's brother, makes a great effort to comfort Margaret, the youngest, and in doing so begins to win the love of the eldest daughter, Elinor.

27 INT. NORLAND PARK. VELVET ROOM. ANOTHER DAY. EDWARD *comes into the doorway and sees* ELINOR *who is listening to* MARIANNE *playing a concerto.* ELINOR *stands in a graceful, rather sad attitude, her back to us. Suddenly she senses* EDWARD *behind her and turns. He is about to turn away, embarrassed to have been caught admiring her, when he sees she has been weeping. Hastily she tries to dry her eyes. He comes forward and offers her a handkerchief, which she takes with a grateful smile. We notice his monogram in the corner:* ECF.

ELINOR *(apologetic)*
That was my father's favorite.

EDWARD *nods kindly.*

ELINOR
❶ Thank you so much for your help with Margaret, Mr. Ferrars. She is a changed girl since your arrival.

EDWARD
Not at all. I enjoy her company.

ELINOR
Has she shown you her tree-house?

EDWARD
Not yet. Would you do me the honor, Miss Dashwood? It is very fine out.

ELINOR
With pleasure.

They start to walk out of shot, still talking. ❷

ELINOR
Margaret has always wanted to travel.

EDWARD
I know. She is heading an expedition to China shortly. I am to go as her servant but only on the understanding that I will be very badly treated.

Develop Understanding

One-Minute Insight In this excerpt from the screenplay for Jane Austen's novel, It wasn't just the women of Austen's day who had their futures decided for them. Here the viewer sees both a man and woman lament their lack of choices.

Customize for Bodily/Kinesthetic Learners
Invite these students to bring the screenplay to life by acting it out, using whatever simple costume items or props they might gather to enhance the sense of character, action, or setting.

Customize for Less Proficient Readers
Explain that this selection is a conversation between Miss Elinor Dashwood and Mr. Edward Ferrars. Invite two readers to take those parts. Explain that Margaret, who is referred to in the conversation, is Elinor's younger sister, and that Mrs. Dashwood and Fanny, who watch Elinor and Edward, are, respectively, Elinor's mother and Edward's sister. Encourage readers to stop reading and ask questions whenever they are unsure about what is happening or what is being discussed.

◆ Background for Understanding

❶ Explain that a woman and man in Austen's day who were acquainted but not related by marriage or by being members of the same immediate family would have addressed each other as Miss and Mr. Thus, Edward Ferrars' relationship to the Dashwoods is close, a decided level of formality exists in the way in which Elinor and Edward address each other.

Customize for English Language Learners
❷ English language learners may stumble on this transition not only because the camera directions may be unexpected but also because of the multiple-meaning of the word *shot*. Explain that this is a camera shot or picture; the actors are moving into a new scene—presumably they are walking out of the house to stroll the grounds.

Customize for
Less Proficient Readers

❶ Explain that Edward is being slightly ironic and humorous here. He is saying that Margaret, who is presumably a young child (she is still building or hanging out in tree-houses) fancies taking him to China as her servant. The "bad" treatment he refers to is likely Margaret's (imagined) ordering him around to do every little thing she requires.

◆ Critical Thinking

❷ **Connect** Ask: In what ways might the reaction of these two women be regarded as social commentary? *These two women watch Elinor and Edward interact closely. Mrs. Dashwood approves, as the relationship could provide Elinor a future; Fanny disapproves, as the relationship would cut into her own fortunes.*

❸ **Clarification** Point out that walking arm in arm does not suggest intimacy. In Austen's day, any gentleman would have been expected to offer his arm to a lady while walking with her. This convention reflected the common social assumption that women needed help while doing anything as physical and challenging as walking outdoors.

◆ *Literature and Your Life*

❹ Ask: Edward's mother seems to want to tell him what to do, even though Edward appears to be a grown man who can decide for himself. Do you think this problem of parents trying to make their adult children's decisions is still common in our own times? *Students may reasonably say that the problem still exists, though perhaps to a lesser extent or degree.*

▶Critical Viewing◀

❺ **Interpret** The looks on the actors' faces suggest that the conversation is a serious one. Both appear to be thoughtful, although in this particular still it seems as if Edward is posing the difficult questions and Elinor is merely contemplating them.

❶ **ELINOR**
What will your duties be?

EDWARD
Sword-fighting, administering rum and swabbing.

ELINOR
Ah.

❷ ❸ *CAM tilts up to find* MRS. DASHWOOD *on the middle landing of the staircase, smiling down at them.* CAM *tilts up yet further to find* FANNY *on the landing above, watching* EDWARD *and* ELINOR *with a face like a prune.*
28 EXT. NORLAND PARK. GARDENS. DAY.
EDWARD *and* ELINOR *are still talking as they walk arm in arm in the late-afternoon sun.*

❹ **EDWARD**
All I want—all I have ever wanted—is the quiet of a private life but my mother is determined to see me distinguished.

Humanities: Movie Still

Movie Still from *Sense and Sensibility*.
This still shows just a single moment in the conversation between Elinor and Edward. You might point out that the still provides background information. Note the pastoral setting, with its grazing farm animals, and the kinds of clothing in which the actors are dressed.

Use these questions for discussion:

1. How does this movie still reveal the social conventions of the day? *One can surmise from the formality of dress that life itself was more formal. Riding sidesaddle, as Elinor does here, was probably proper for ladies.*
2. In what ways does this still seem to suggest that there is some sympathy between Edward and Elinor? *Suggested answer: They are riding close together and slowly; they seem to be discussing something serious or taking what each other has to say quite seriously.*

CONNECTIONS TO TODAY'S WORLD

ELINOR
As?

EDWARD
She hardly knows. Any fine figure will suit—a great orator, a leading politician, even a barrister would serve, but only on the condition that I drive my own barouche[1] and dine in the first circles. 6

His tone is light but there is an under-lying bitterness to it. 7

ELINOR
And what do you wish for?

EDWARD
I always preferred the church, but that is not smart enough for my mother—she prefers the army, but that is a great deal too smart for me. 8

ELINOR
Would you stay in London?

EDWARD
I hate London. No peace. A country living is my ideal—a small parish where I might do some good, keep chickens and give short sermons. 9

30 EXT. FIELDS NEAR NORLAND. DAY. EDWARD *and* ELINOR *are on horseback. The atmosphere is intimate, the quality of the conversation rooted now in their affections.* 10

ELINOR
You talk of feeling idle and useless—imagine how that is compounded when one has no choice and no hope whatsoever of any occupation.

1. **barouche** (bə ro͞osh′) *n.*: Four-wheeled carriage with a collapsible hood and two seats on each side.

5 ▲ **Critical Viewing** What can you tell from this movie still about the type of conversation Edward and Elinor are having? **[Interpret]**

◆ Critical Thinking

6 **Generalize** Ask students to sum up what Edward's mother seems to want for him. *She wants him to be a socially successful person, with the kind of career and possessions that suggest he has "made it."*

Customize for
Musical/Rhythmic Learners

7 Explain that this direction goes with the dialogue that precedes it. Ask students to read the dialogue with a light tone that captures "under-lying bitterness."

◆ Background for Understanding

8 Explain that in Austen's day a career in the military, presumably as a high ranking officer, had much greater status, or was more "smart," than a career as a clergyman.

◆ Literature and Your Life

9 This dialogue reveals Edward's personality. Ask students whether Edward appeals to them as a person at this moment. *Students are likely to say yes: he seems sweetly humorous, polite, and kind throughout the dialogue. Here, where he says he would give short sermons, he seems to say that he would be sensitive as a clergyman and not harangue or bore his congregation.*

10 **Clarification** Note that this text indicates a change in scene. Students who are reading carefully will notice that the camera direction 30 EXT appears here, but the previous shot, 29, has not been included. This may indicate that scene 28 was cut out of the final film.

Customize for
English Language Learners
❶ The word *piracy* is pivotal here, yet it may well be unfamiliar to English language learners. Write the words *pirate* and *piracy* on the board, and connect them visually. Put familiar words with the same relationship, like *literate* and *literacy*, on the board next to them, and make the same connection to show the relationship.

Customize for
English Language Learners
❷ Explain that the word *swabbing*, as used by a sailor, appears in the phrase "swabbing the decks," or cleaning the floor surfaces of a ship.

Reinforce and Extend

Answers

◆ ***Literature and Your Life***

Reader's Response Students may say they feel sympathy for both characters because they seem like nice people whose choices are limited.

Thematic Focus They reflect expectations about what men and women are allowed to do.

Check Your Comprehension

1. (a) Edward's mother wants him to be some kind of leader. (b) Edward wants to be a pastor.
2. (a) Their situations are the same because others are in control of what they will become. (b) Elinor cannot earn her fortune as Edward can.

◆ Critical Thinking

1. The social rules that limit women's choices also limit men, although to a lesser degree.
2. (a) Few occupations were open to women. (b) For some women, marriage to a wealthy man was the only way to ensure financial security.
3. This excerpt shows that the rules of society limited everyone's choices, but especially those of women.
4. Screenplays may communicate not only the world as it is or was but the author's attitude toward it. Here, the screenplay captures Austen's awareness of societal injustice.

EDWARD *nods and smiles at the irony of it.*

EDWARD
Our circumstances are therefore precisely the same.

ELINOR
Except that you will inherit your fortune.

He looks at her slightly shocked but enjoying her boldness.

ELINOR (*cont.*)
We cannot even earn ours.

EDWARD
Perhaps Margaret is right.

ELINOR
Right?

EDWARD
Piracy is our only option. 

They ride on in silence for a moment.

EDWARD (*cont.*)
What *is* swabbing exactly? ❷

Guide for Responding

◆ ***Literature and Your Life***

Reader's Response Do you feel sorry for either Edward or Elinor? Explain.

Thematic Connection What problems in society do the problems of Edward and Elinor reflect?

Journal Writing What problem in current-day society would you change? How would you go about achieving this goal?

Check Your Comprehension

1. (a) What does Edward's mother want him to do? (b) What does Edward want to do?
2. (a) Why does Edward believe his and Elinor's situations are the same? (b) What is the major difference that Elinor points out?

◆ Critical Thinking

INTERPRET

1. Edward's mother seems to have set ideas about what he should do with his life. How might this be a reflection of the restrictions placed on women at this time? **[Infer]**
2. In response to Edward's comment about their similarities, Elinor replies, "Except that you will inherit your fortune. We cannot even earn ours." (a) What does Elinor mean by this? (b) How does her comment relate to the issues of the day? **[Interpret]**
3. How does this excerpt from the screenplay reflect the attitudes of Austen's letter and Wollstonecraft's essay? Explain. **[Compare and Contrast]**

EXTEND

4. In what ways can a screenplay be effective in making people socially aware? **[Media Link]**

Beyond the Selection

FURTHER READING

Other Novels in Film
Sense and Sensibility, Jane Austen
Pride and Prejudice, Jane Austen
Emma, Jane Austen

We suggest that you preview these works before recommending them to students.

INTERNET

You and your students may find additional information about Jane Austen on the Internet at the following site. Please be aware, however, that the site may have changed from the time we published this information.

For information about Jane Austen, see **http://www.pemberley.com/janeinfo/janebblg.html**

We *strongly recommend* that you preview the site before you send students to it.

Thematic Connection

The Reaction to Society's Ills

The writers in this section react to the oppressive roles that society defines for women and those belonging to certain social classes. For example, in the screenplay of *Sense and Sensibility,* Elinor and Edward are limited by their gender and social class. Even in a democratic society, barriers still exist based on social class, gender, and race.

1. What limitations in requesting reform might Shelley and Byron have experienced as a result of being men and belonging to upper-class society?
2. Which selections in this section convey themes of injustice that are still relevant today?
3. What successes has society had in improving social conditions for all people?

Idea Bank

Writing

1. **Letter to the President** If there was one social issue that you believed needed more attention, what would it be? Write a letter to the President in which you describe the issue and offer solutions for it.
2. **Prediction** Looking back on the problems of the early part of the nineteenth century, you can probably see that many have been solved. Write a list of predictions that describe how some social problems that exist now may be solved in the future.
3. **Social Criticism** Write a scene from a play in which you use the dialogue and action to make people socially aware.

Speaking and Listening

4. **Interview** Interview someone from an older generation or different culture. Ask the person how societal norms and expectations shaped his or her life decisions, such as career or marriage. Ask what he or she might have done differently given today's opportunities. Ask permission to publish the interview in your school paper. **[Social Studies Link]**

Project

5. **Historical Account** Research a moment in history that especially interests you. Then write a first-person account of the event as if you were present. Share your account with your classmates. **[Social Studies Link]**

Answers
Thematic Connection

1. They would be largely unaware of the problems of the poor or even those of women in their own social strata of society.
2. Sample response: Shelley's "A Song: 'Men of England'" addresses the problem of technology displacing workers, still of great concern in today's highly technological society. Austen and Wollstonecraft address issues of women's rights; the existence of such groups as National Organization for Women as well as the controversy over issues such as the Equal Rights Amendment and equal pay for women in the marketplace indicates that these issues are far from resolved.
3. Sample responses: Some students may cite social welfare programs that help people through difficult times; others may mention laws banning workplace discrimination.

Idea Bank
Customizing for
Performance Levels

Following are suggestions for matching Idea Bank topics with your students' performance levels:

Less Advanced Students: 1, 4,
Average Students: 2, 4
More Advanced Students: 3, 5

Customizing for
Learning Modalities

Following are suggestions for matching Idea Bank topics with your students' learning modalities:

Verbal/Linguistic: 1, 2, 3, 4, 5
Interpersonal: 4

✓ ASSESSMENT OPTIONS

Formal Assessment, Selection Test, pp. 181–182, and Assessment Resources Software. The selection test is designed so that it can be easily customized to the performance levels of your students.

PORTFOLIO ASSESSMENT
Use the following rubrics in the ***Alternative Assessment*** booklet to assess student writing:
Letter to the President: Persuasion Rubric, p. 106
Prediction: Problem-Solution Rubric, p. 102
Social Criticism: Drama Rubric, p. 110

Prepare and Engage

Establish Writing Guidelines
Review the following key characteristics of a job portfolio:

- A job portfolio sells an applicant's qualifications to a potential employer.
- It includes a cover letter which briefly introduces the applicant.
- It includes a résumé which gives a brief summary of work experience, educational history, and special skills.

Before students begin, you may want to share with them the Scoring Rubric for Résumé and Cover Letter (page 115 in ***Alternative Assessment***) so that students see the criteria by which they will be evaluated. Suggestions on page 732 customize the rubric to this workshop.

Writer's Solution

Sourcebook
Ask students to study the model résumé and cover letter in Chapter 8, Practical and Technical Writing (pp. 234–235). Use the teacher's edition marginal notes to guide discussion.

Writing Lab CD-ROM
If students have access to computers, have them work in the tutorial on Practical and Technical Writing to complete all or part of their résumés and cover letters. Follow these steps:

1. Students can use the audio-annotated model in Gathering Details to identify key details to include in a resume.
2. Have students use the résumé model in Organizing Details to organize effectively.
3. Have them use the letter shell in the Drafting section to draft a cover letter.
4. The Technical Word Bins can help students refine their job portfolios.

Other portions of the Practical and Technical Writing tutorial will help students prepare other parts of the job portfolio.

Job Portfolio Writing Process Workshop

In the commentaries in this section the writers "sell" their ideas by supporting them with factual details. If these writers were selling their qualifications to a potential employer, they would use the same basic strategies. Promote yourself by creating a job portfolio that includes a cover letter and résumé. In your cover letter, briefly introduce yourself. In your résumé, give a brief summary of your work experience, educational history, and special skills.

Use the following skills as you develop a job portfolio.

Writing Skills Focus

- **Elaborate to give information.** Give prospective employers details about your education, skills, talents, and participation in clubs and organizations. (See p. 713.)
- **Use appropriate language for your purpose.** Persuade a prospective employer to hire you by using language that is clear, confident, enthusiastic, and correct. (See p. 723.)
- **Structure your résumé and letter** according to standard formats.

Writing Model: Cover Letter

Anna Turpin
874 Farley Road
Cornwells Heights, PA 19020
June 3, 2000 ①

Ms. Leslie Throckmorton
Village Bookery
Clinton, NY 13323

Dear Ms. Throckmorton: ②

I'm interested in obtaining a sales position at your bookstore. ③ This fall I'll be attending Hartsdale College, where I plan to study literature. I feel that my deep interest in literature would work to our mutual advantage.

Enclosed please find my résumé.

Sincerely, ④

Anna Turpin

① Your name, address, and the date appear at the top. The name and address of your potential employer should appear next.

② This standard greeting followed by a colon opens the letter.

③ It's advisable to state your objective at the outset.

④ The cover letter should end with a closing such as this one.

Beyond the Classroom

Workplace Skills

Job Portfolio A job portfolio includes more than a cover letter and résumé. It should include samples of work appropriate to the job sought. For instance, someone seeking a job in sales should include a video of a sales presentation. Someone applying for a clerical position might include examples of detailed, formatted documents and an audio tape of a telephone conversation. Virtually every job portfolio must include evidence of familiarity with technology. The evidence may be in the form of print, computer disk, video or audio tape, hypermedia program, photographs, or other visuals. Ask the class to brainstorm for a list of possible components in a job portfolio.

WRITING MODEL: RÉSUMÉ

Anna Turpin
874 Farley Road
Cornwells Heights, PA 19020
(215) 649-0086 ①

EMPLOYMENT: ②

Summer 1999 to Fall 1999: ③ Cornwells Public Library
Job Title: Assistant to Librarian
Responsibilities: Read stories to children; helped at check-out desk ④
Summer 1998 to Fall 1998: Mindy's Ice Cream
Job Title: Counter clerk
Responsibilities: Filled orders; operated cash register

EDUCATION:

June 2000: Graduated from Cornwells High

SKILLS AND ABILITIES: Driver's license; Scuba certified

① This information should appear prominently.
② Details should appear under headings like this one.
③ List work experience in reverse chronological order.
④ Entries should be brief, yet clear. Omit the pronoun "I."

Prewriting

Choose a Topic and Select Details To find a position for which you'd like to apply, look through the want ads in your local newspaper. After choosing a position, plan your cover letter and résumé. Jot down relevant details from your employment history, school activities, and education that might help you win the job.

Drafting

Be Sure Your Language Is Appropriate Your purpose is to persuade someone to offer you a job. To do this, use clear and specific details, an enthusiastic and confident tone, and language that is formal and sincere. For example, change "I'd get a kick out of working for you" to "I'm eager to work for you."

Use a Consistent Résumé Format In writing your résumé, keep to a consistent format. For example, use words with capital letters to head each section, use bold typeface for words such as *job title* and *responsibilities*, and underline dates.

Use Proper Format for a Cover Letter Use the standard business-letter format that you see in the model on the previous page.

APPLYING LANGUAGE SKILLS: Using Positive Language

Emphasize your skills with words and phrases that have positive, rather than neutral or negative, associations. Following are some examples:

Neutral Examples:

This is an interesting book.

I learned AutoCAD last summer.

Positive Examples:

This is an incomparable book.

My internship gave me first-rate experience with AutoCAD.

Practice Rewrite the following sentences, using positive language.

1. I would like this job.
2. Your firm has a decent reputation.
3. Having had four years of experience as a day-care aide, I would make a satisfactory teacher.
4. I trained some of my co-workers.

Writer's Solution Connection Language Lab

For more help organizing your cover letter, see the lessons on Unity and Coherence in Paragraphs and Composition.

Develop Student Writing

Prewriting

If students have access to the Internet, they can find numerous positions for which they may develop a job portfolio.

Customize for *Kinesthetic Learners*

The job portfolio offers these students ample opportunities for filming and taping performances like speeches or sales presentations. Encourage them to seek positions which let them tout their kinesthetic skills.

Writer's Solution

Writing Lab CD-ROM

In the Organizing Details section, have students study the interactive examples of organizing technical writing with numbered or bulleted lists, charts, maps or diagrams, or headings to highlight sections of a resume or letter.

Drafting

As they write, encourage students to use standard English, strong connotative language, and mature sentence structure.

Applying Language Skills

Using Positive Language

Remind students that the résumé and cover letter are sales tools. As such they must be truthful, but word choice can make the truth more forceful.

Answers

Possible responses:

1. This job fits my training and experience perfectly.
2. Your firm is highly respected.
3. . . . I would make an excellent teacher.
4. I have trained all ten employees new to our team.

Writer's Solution

Students may find additional help with writing style in the **Language Lab CD-ROM** unit "Writing Style."

Revising

Have students work with a three-member editorial board to revise their résumés and cover letters. One board member should respond to the format, another to the organization, and another to the language.

Writer's Solution

In the Revising and Editing section of the Practical and Technical Writing tutorial, the audio-annotated student model of a first draft and revised draft of a résumé will show students why and how changes were made.

Publishing

Remind students that while e-mail and faxes make up an integral part of the business world, résumés and cover letters must still arrive on quality paper in superb form.

Applying Language Skills

Using Concise Language
Successful use of concise language depends on the understanding of connotation as well as denotation. Suggest that students explore possible word choices with a thesaurus and a good dictionary.

Answers

Possible student responses:
Job Title: Assistant to the Principal
Job Responsibilities: hall monitor during and between classes

Reinforce and Extend

Review the Writing Process
After students have completed their job portfolios, suggest they solicit successful résumés and cover letters from adults in the community. Ask students to analyze how these résumés and cover letters compare with their own.

Applying Language Skills: Using Concise Language

Because space on a résumé is limited, it's important to be brief and concise in describing your job qualifications and work history.

Wordy:

Overseer of the collection of garbage

Typed letters; filed letters

Concise:

Sanitation Chief

Clerical duties

Practice Rewrite this portion of a résumé, making the language as brief and concise as possible.

Job Title: Administrative helper of principal

Job Responsibilities: standing in the hallways of a busy school, making sure that traffic flows smoothly and that no one is cutting class

Writing Application Review your résumé and cover letter, and delete instances of wordiness.

Writer's Solution Connection
Writing Lab
For more help in revising, see the interactive Self-Evaluation checklists in the Revising and Editing section of the Practical and Technical Writing tutorial.

Revising

Revision Checklist As you review your cover letter and résumé, ask yourself the following:

1. Have I included all relevant work experience, education, and activities?
2. Have I conveyed confidence and enthusiasm through positive language?
3. Is the format of the résumé and cover letter proper and consistent?

Revision Model

Julia Rose
143 Summer Walk Avenue
Boca Raton, FL 33268
November 17, 1999

Mr. James Evans
2000 Bayview Parkway
Tampa, FL 35987

Dear Mr. Evans, ① :

I am interested in a ~~job in your office.~~ ② summer internship at your law firm. As valedictorian of my class, I have a strong academic background. ③ I volunteer for legal aid two hours a week. My goal is to pursue a career in law. . . .

① The comma was replaced with a colon, which is standard in business letters

② The writer replaces a vague statement with specific, positive information.

③ This sentence adds relevant information about the job seeker's experience and enthusiasm for the profession.

Publishing

- **Personal Portfolio** Add your job portfolio to your collection of other writing you've kept over the years.
- **Job Fair** Hold a job fair with other interested classmates. Invite prospective employers to meet your classmates and discuss career options with them. Ask them also to review your job portfolio.
- **Real-life Job Applications** Send your completed portfolio to potential employers.

✓ ASSESSMENT		4	3	2	1
PORTFOLIO ASSESSMENT Use the rubric on Résumé and Cover Letter in ***Alternative Assessment,*** p. 115, to assess students' writing. Add these criteria to customize the rubric to this assignment.	**Positive Language**	The writer consistently uses positive, enthusiastic language.	The writer uses mostly positive, enthusiastic language.	The writer uses some positive, enthusiastic language.	The writer uses almost no positive, enthusiastic language.
	Concise Language	The writer consistently uses concise language.	The writer uses concise language most of the time.	The writer sometimes uses concise language.	The writer rarely uses concise language.

Real-World Reading Skills Workshop

Evaluating Perspective in Historical Accounts

Strategies for Success

Modern historians attempt to be as objective as possible. However, historical accounts can contain bias of one sort or another. Documents from a particular historical era can also reflect the beliefs of the writer. As a reader of history, therefore, you should be alert for possible biases and have a method for evaluating them.

Know the Period The more you know about a period, the better you can judge whether an account is biased. When you read authors from a different era, be sensitive to their language. If you suspect that they are using familiar words in an unfamiliar way, consult the *Oxford English Dictionary*. This reference work shows how the meaning of words has changed over time.

Address to the Soldiers.

GENTLEMEN,

YOU are about to embark for *America*, to compel your Fellow Subjects there to submit to POPERY and SLAVERY.

It is the Glory of the British Soldier, that he is the *Defender*, not the *Destroyer*, of the Civil and Religious Rights of the People. The *English* Soldiery are immortalized in History, for their Attachment to the Religion and Liberties of their Country...You will be called upon to imbrue your Hands in the Blood of your Fellow Subjects in *America*, because they will not admit to be Slaves, and are alarmed at the Establishment of Popery and Arbitrary Power in one Half of their County.

Whether you will draw those Swords which have defended them against their Enemies, to butcher them into a Resignation of their Rights, which they hold as the Sons of *Englishmen*, is in your breasts. That you will not stain the Laurels you have gained from *France*, by dipping them in Civil Blood, is every good Man's Hope.

—I am, GENTLEMEN,

your sincere Well-wisher,

AN OLD SOLDIER.

Know the Writer Another way to evaluate bias is to know as much as possible about the writer. If the author is a modern historian, what beliefs does he or she hold that might influence the account? If the author lived during the period you are studying, what was his or her stake in the conflicts of the time? Even anonymous authors can divulge bias through strong emotional language. It's also important whether the writing was meant for public or private consumption. What people write in a diary may be more candid than what they write for publication.

Apply the Strategy

In writing a paper on the American Revolution, you come across the "Address to Soldiers" shown on this page, first published in a British newspaper in 1775. Evaluate its possible bias by answering these questions.

1. What background do you need to know to make sense of this letter?
2. Who are the soldiers being addressed?
3. What can you infer about the writer's political position?
4. What is the writer trying to achieve?
5. What makes you suspect that the writer is not completely objective?

Here are other forms of writing in which you should evaluate perspective in historical accounts:

- Letters
- Diary entries
- Newspapers and journals
- Broadsides and pamphlets

Introduce the Strategy

Point out to students that understanding how to evaluate perspective in historical accounts will help them understand how to analyze today's news accounts and political rhetoric. You might have the class compile a list of situations in which such an understanding will be helpful.

Customize for
English Language Learners
These students may need help identifying emotionally laden words that establish bias. As they read the soldier's letter, have them work with native speakers to identify such words.

Apply the Strategy

Have students read carefully the "Address to the Soldiers." You may ask students to work in five groups, each responding to one question. Next, form new groups with one member from each of the original five. This jigsaw approach makes each student a discussion leader in response to one question.

Answers

Student responses may include these points:

1. Readers must understand the English reaction to the American Revolution and France's support of the revolution.
2. They are British soldiers.
3. The writer supports the Crown.
4. The writer encourages his fellow British soldiers to maintain their country's honor.
5. His references to *defender, not destroyer,* his comments about Americans who will *not admit to be slaves,* and other phrases show his bias.

Introduce the Strategy

Explain to students that by being prepared for an interview, they gain an advantage over competitors. Help students understand the importance of learning about the organization or company for which they want to work and planning what they should say as well as ask during the interview.

Apply the Strategy

Remind students that the interview is the final opportunity to promote themselves as best candidate for the job. You may want to ask students to tape record their responses to the questions and then listen to them from the point of view of an interviewer. Ask how they think the interviewer would respond. Have them revise until they (and their classmates) anticipate a positive interviewer's reaction.

Speaking and Listening Workshop

Handling a Job Interview

Suppose you're looking for a job. You've polished your résumé, written letters, and talked to people who might know of available work. Now you've received that long-awaited letter or phone call summoning you to an interview. Of course, you're nervous. However, if you're well prepared, you'll be able to make a good impression.

Before the Interview Preparation is the key to a successful interview. Ask around and consult reference books to learn all you can about the organization or company for which you want to work. Plan what you will say. Also, think about questions your interviewer might ask about your work experience, skills, strengths and weaknesses, and reasons for seeking the job. Write down the answers and practice saying them to a friend. Then, using your research, jot down questions for which *you* would like answers. Bring these questions to the interview. Asking questions will show your interest in the job and demonstrate your knowledge of the organization.

At the Interview Dress formally unless told otherwise. On entering the room, introduce yourself briefly, smile, and make eye contact. Maintain eye contact during the interview, and sit up straight with your hands in your lap. Be prepared to begin with some small talk. Speak politely, correctly, and clearly enough to be heard. If you are asked an unexpected question, don't let it throw you. Relax and give yourself time to think.

Tips for Handling a Job Interview

To make a good impression in the interview, apply these strategies:

- **Prepare answers in advance to questions you may be asked.**
- **Role-play the interview with a friend.**
- **Be calm, alert, and courteous during the interview itself.**

Apply the Strategies

You have an interview scheduled for a summer job that relates to your major career interest. Decide what the job will be: park-maintenance worker? retail clerk? newspaper intern?

1. List your experiences and skills that apply to the job you want.
2. Decide how you would answer each of these questions:
   - Tell me about yourself.
   - Why do you want to work for us?
   - What qualifications do you have?
   - What kind of career do you want?
   - What do you know about us?
3. Role-play a job interview with a partner. Take turns being interviewer and interviewee.

Beyond the Classroom

Workplace Skills

Body Language in the Interview Education, training, and experience amount to nothing if a potential employee gives a poor interview. Good grooming, appropriate dress, and posture give instantaneous nonverbal cues to the interviewer. Simple body language, like giving a firm handshake and looking the interviewer in the eye, can make or break an interview in the first sixty seconds. A positive and cheerful attitude, courteous behavior, and proper speech convey nonverbal cues and add to the interview's success. These nonverbal parts of an interview, either for a job, a scholarship, or admission to college, are as important as oral responses to questions.

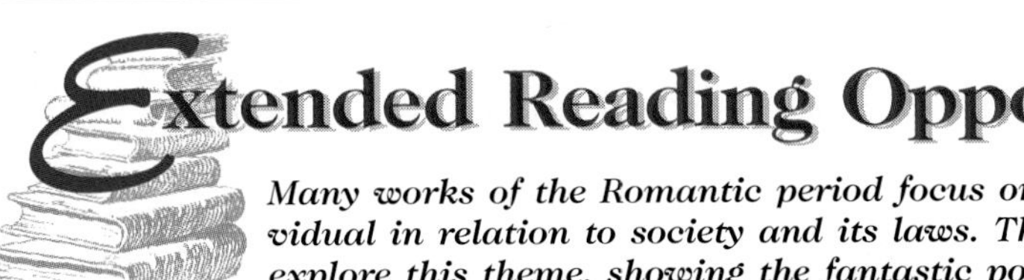

Extended Reading Opportunities

Many works of the Romantic period focus on the individual in relation to society and its laws. These novels explore this theme, showing the fantastic possibilities of science or the comic realities of social constraints.

Suggested Titles

Frankenstein
Mary Shelley

Mary Shelley's suspenseful tale of horror warns of the misuse of human intelligence. A young student attempts to do what no person has ever done before: create life. Using electricity, he is able to animate a monster fashioned out of corpses from graveyards and dissecting rooms. This creature is surprisingly sensitive. However, when his efforts to approach humans arouse only horror, he blames his creator for giving him a life of pain and suffering. The monster then turns evil, and Dr. Frankenstein must pay a terrible price for his experiments.

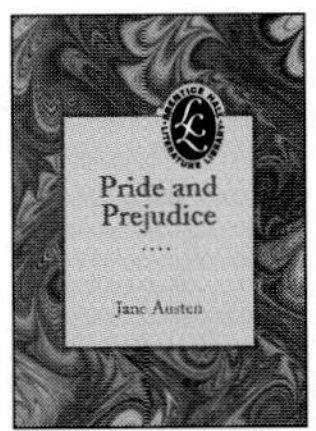

Pride and Prejudice
Jane Austen

With her usual comic flair and common sense, Austen explores the relentless pressure on women to succeed in the marriage market. Mrs. Bennet, all too aware of this market's demands, shamelessly pursues marriage for each of her daughters. Although one of those daughters, Elizabeth, is socially inferior to the charming Fitzwilliam Darcy, he loses his heart to her all the same. This victory of romance shows that feelings are at least as important as the shrewd calculations of amateur matchmakers. Austen's common sense prevails over pounds and shillings.

Emma
Jane Austen

Austen has great fun with her busybody heroine Emma Woodhouse. Emma has appointed herself matchmaker for her whole community, meddling in just about everyone's affairs. Though her friend Mr. Knightly cautions her against the reckless pursuit of marital bliss for others, she learns the folly of her ways only through bitter experience. Also, it is almost too late when she realizes that her frantic activity has led her to ignore her own happiness and the person best suited to guarantee it: the same Mr. Knightly who has been scolding her.

Other Possibilities

British

The Castle of Otranto	Horace Walpole
The Prelude	William Wordsworth
Ivanhoe	Sir Walter Scott

Literature Study Guides
A literature study guide is available for *Pride and Prejudice*. This guide includes summaries, discussion questions, and activities.

Resources for Teaching Novels, Plays, and Literature Collections In addition to graphic organizers, teaching strategies, and transparencies, this booklet includes a formal test for *Pride and Prejudice*.

Customize for ***Special Needs***
To meet the needs of your special needs students, you may want to consider the adapted version of *Frankenstein* from Globe Fearon's Pacemaker Classics series.

Planning Students' Extended Reading

The novels listed on this page explore the focus of the Romantic period—the individual and his or her place in society. These works move from the scrutiny and mockery of social conventions to serious warnings about the abuse of scientific power.

Customize for ***Students of Varying Needs and Interests***
When assigning these novels, keep in mind the following factors:

- *Frankenstein* may especially interest students who like science and may plan to pursue a medical career. Since most people have preconceived ideas about the novel, which has been the basis of so many movies, it is a good idea to give students background on the name of the novel. Make students aware that *Frankenstein* is the name of the doctor who created the monster, not the monster.
- Students reading *Pride and Prejudice* or *Emma* may benefit from background about social class and the positions of women in society during the Romantic period.

Sensitive Issues

- Although Mary Shelley's intention in writing *Frankenstein* was to stress the limits of human power and warn that scientific creation of life is not for mortals, the issue may still be sensitive for some students. Prepare students for dealing with this issue by explaining that the novel criticizes the abuse of science and suggests that humans are not fit to create life in any unnatural way.
- Both *Pride and Prejudice* and *Emma* are delightful books that most students will enjoy, but issues of social standing and women's role in society may stir some sensitive discussion. Prepare students for these issues by stressing how much has changed in society's structure and women's place in it since the time the novels were written.

Planning Instruction and Assessment

Unit Objectives

1. To read selections from the Victorian period in English literature
2. To apply a variety of reading strategies, particularly interactive reading strategies, appropriate for reading these selections
3. To recognize literary elements used in these selections
4. To build vocabulary in context
5. To learn elements of grammar, usage, and style
6. To write in a variety of modes and about situations based on the selections
7. To develop speaking and listening skills by completing proposed activities

Meeting the Objectives

With each selection, you will find instructional material and portfolio opportunities through which students can meet these objectives. Further, you will find additional practice pages for reading strategies, literary elements, vocabulary, and grammar in the ***Selection Support*** booklet in the Teaching Resources box.

Setting Goals Work with your students at the beginning of the unit to set goals for unit outcomes. Plan what skills and concepts you wish students to acquire. You may individualize these according to students' performance levels or learning modalities.

Portfolios You may have students keep portfolios of their work or of their work in progress. The activities and prompts on the Build Your Portfolio page of each selection provide opportunities for students to apply the concepts presented with the selection.

The Railway Station, 1862, William Powell Frith, Royal Holloway and Bedford New College, Surrey

Humanities: Art

The Railway Station, 1862, by William Powell Frith.

A prominent English painter, Frith (1819–1909) was best known for depicting scenes of nineteenth-century English life, usually involving large crowds. He first became successful in his early twenties. His most famous works are detailed records of the world around him; however, his later paintings, from the 1880's, tend to make moral comments about Victorian society.

Have your students link *The Railway Station,* one of Frith's most famous paintings, to the focus of Unit 5, Progress and Decline, by answering the following questions:

1. Does the painting present society in a negative or positive light? Support your answer with details from the painting. *The numerous expressions of affection and the air of bustling activity contribute to a positive view. The oppressive crowdedness of the station and the scene on the right, in which someone is apparently being arrested, contribute to a negative view.*
2. Contrast this portrait of a busy train station in 1862 with the scene you would see in such a place today. Would the contemporary scene represent progress or decline over the one painted in 1862? *On the grounds that crowds today are larger and urban public spaces are often dirtier and more chaotic, students may point to a decline.*

UNIT 5

Progress and Decline (1833–1901)

In order that people may be happy in their work, these three things are needed: They must be fit for it. They must not do too much of it. And they must have a sense of success in it.

—John Ruskin, from *Pre-Raphaelitism*

Assessing Student Progress

The following tools are available to measure the degree to which students meet the unit objectives:

Informal Assessment

The questions on the Guide for Responding sections are a first level of response to the concepts and skills presented with the selection. Students' responses are a brief informal measure of their grasp of the material. Their responses on this level can indicate where further instruction and practice are needed. You may then follow up with the practice pages in the ***Selection Support*** booklet.

You will find literature and reading guides in the ***Alternative Assessment*** booklet, which you may give students on an individual basis for informal assessment of their performance.

Formal Assessment

In the ***Formal Assessment*** booklet, you will find selection tests and part tests.

Selection Tests The selection tests measure comprehension and skills acquisition for each selection or group of selections.

Part Tests Each part test, which calls on students to read a passage of literature they have not previously seen, applies the unit skills on a broader level. The Critical Reading section measures Unit Objectives 1, 2, and 3. The Vocabulary and Grammar section measures Objectives 4 and 5. The Essay section measures Objectives 1 and 6. Both the Critical Reading and Vocabulary and Grammar sections use formats similar to those found on many standardized tests, including the SAT.

Alternative Assessment

Portfolios As you review individual pieces or the collected work in students' portfolios, you may use assessment sheets available in the portfolio section of the ***Alternative Assessment*** booklet.

Scoring Rubrics You will find scoring rubrics for writing modes in the ***Alternative Assessment*** booklet. You can apply these to Writing Mini-Lessons and to Writing Process Workshop lessons.

Speaking and Listening The ***Alternative Assessment*** booklet contains assessment sheets for speaking and listening activities.

Learning Modalities The ***Alternative Assessment*** booklet contains activities that appeal to different learning styles. You may use these too as an alternative assessment of students' growth.

Using the Timeline

The Timeline can serve a number of instructional purposes, as follows:

Getting an Overview Use the Timeline to help students get a quick overview of themes and events of the period. This approach will benefit all students but may be especially helpful for visually oriented students, English language learners, and those less proficient in reading. (For strategies in using the Timeline as an overview, see the bottom of this page.)

Thinking Critically Questions are provided on the facing page. Use these questions to have students review the events, discuss their significance, and examine the *so what* behind the *what happened*.

Connecting to Selections Have students refer to the Timeline when reading individual selections. By consulting the Timeline regularly, they will gain a better sense of the period's chronology. In addition, they will appreciate what was occurring in the world that gave rise to these works of literature.

Projects Students can use the Timeline as a launching pad for projects like these:

- **Charting Responses to Change** As students read material in this unit, have them look for responses to technological and social change in literature. Using this Timeline as a framework, have them add the date of each response and the date of any specific change or development involved. (Encourage students to "stretch" to find connections: students might include, for instance, the loom in Tennyson's "The Lady of Shalott," p. 754, as harkening back to pre-industrial technology.)
- **Report on a Scientist or Reformer** Have students scan the Timeline for an invention or scientific advance, or for a reform in society, research the people behind the advance or reform, then report on their findings to the class. Did the people concerned have any interesting literary or political connections?

Timeline

1833–1901

1833 | 1845 | 1855

British Events

- **1833** Slavery abolished in British empire.
- **1837** Victoria becomes queen. ▼
- **1837 Charles Dickens** writes *Oliver Twist.*
- **1837** Thomas Carlyle publishes *The French Revolution.*
- **1840** Michael Faraday experiments with electric currents.
- **1843 William Wordsworth** becomes poet laureate.
- **1844** George Williams founds YMCA.
- **1845** Irish Potato Famine begins. ▼
- **1847** Factory Act passed.
- **1847 Charlotte Brontë** publishes *Jane Eyre.*
- **1847 Emily Brontë** publishes *Wuthering Heights.*
- **1848** Women begin attending University of London.
- **1850 Elizabeth Barrett Browning** publishes *Sonnets from the Portuguese.*
- **1854** Britain enters Crimean War.

- **1859** Charles Darwin publishes *On the Origin of Species.*
- **1860** Florence Nightingale founds school for nurses. ▼

- **1863** Construction of London Underground begins.
- **1868** Robert Browning publishes *The Ring and the Book.*

World Events

- **1836** United States: Ralph Waldo Emerson publishes *Nature.*
- **1841** South Pacific: New Zealand becomes a British colony.
- **1842** Asia: Hong Kong becomes a British Colony.
- **1842** France: Honoré de Balzac publishes *The Human Comedy.*
- **1844** United States: Samuel F. B. Morse patents telegraph. ▶

- **1848** France: Revolution establishes new republic under Louis Napoleon.
- **1848** Belgium: Marx and Engels publish the *Communist Manifesto.*
- **1850** France: Life insurance introduced.
- **1850** Germany: Wagner's opera *Lohengrin* first performed.
- **1851** Australia: Gold discovered in New South Wales.
- **1853** Eastern Europe: Crimean War begins.
- **1854** Japan: Trade with West reopened.
- **1854** United States: Henry David Thoreau publishes *Walden.* ▲
- **1856** France: Gustave Flaubert publishes *Madame Bovary.*
- **1857** India: Sepoy Mutiny against British.
- **1858** India: Political power of East India Company abolished.
- **1861** United States: Civil War begins. ▶

Getting an Overview of the Period

Introduction To help students get an overview of the period, have them determine the amount of time covered. (Use the dates in the upper left-hand corner.) *A period of 68 years is covered.* Next, point out that the Timeline is divided into specifically British Events (on top) and World Events (on bottom). Have them practice scanning the Timeline across, looking both at the British Events and the World Events.Point out that the events charted often indicate larger trends. *The construction of the Underground (1863) and establishment of a fire department show a new attention to public services.*

Key Events Have students note events that may indicate the investment of new energy in social reform. *Slavery was abolished (1833); a Factory Act was passed (1847); debtor's prisons were abolished (1869); the Salvation Army was established (1878).* Have students find evidence of Britain's growing role in the world. *New Zealand (1841) and Hong Kong became colonies (1842); the British fought a mutiny in India (1832); and there were wars in Africa (1879, 1882).* Then ask students to speculate about the size and strength of British government. *The government was probably large and powerful.*

1865	1875	1885	1901

British Events

- **1865** London Fire Department established.
- **1865** Lewis Carroll publishes *Alice's Adventures in Wonderland.* ▼
- **1869** Debtors' prisons abolished.

- **1878** Salvation Army established.
- **1880** Joseph Swan installs first electric lighting. ▶
- **1883** Robert Louis Stevenson publishes *Treasure Island.*
- **1884** First edition of *Oxford English Dictionary* published.

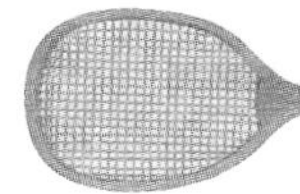

- **1887** First Sherlock Holmes tale published.
- **1888** English Lawn Tennis Association founded at Wimbledon. ▼

- **1888** Jack the Ripper stalks London's East End.
- **1891** **Thomas Hardy** publishes *Tess of the d'Urbervilles.*
- **1892** **Rudyard Kipling** publishes *Barrack-room Ballads.*
- **1895** Oscar Wilde publishes *The Importance of Being Earnest.*
- **1896** **A.E. Housman** publishes *A Shropshire Lad.*
- **1901** Queen Victoria dies.

World Events

- **1865** Russia: **Leo Tolstoy** publishes *War and Peace.*
- **1865** Austria: Gregor Mendel proposes laws of heredity. ▼
- **1866** Europe: Seven Weeks' War leads to unification of modern Germany.
- **1869** Egypt: Suez Canal completed.
- **1873** France: Jules Verne publishes *Around the World in Eighty Days.*

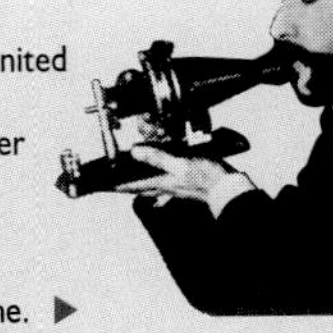

- **1876** United States: Alexander Graham Bell patents telephone. ▶
- **1877** United States: Thomas Edison patents phonograph.
- **1879** South Africa: Zulu War against British.
- **1880** Russia: Feodor Dostoevsky publishes *The Brothers Karamazov.*
- **1882** Egypt: Britain conquers nation.
- **1884** United States: Mark Twain publishes *The Adventures of Huckleberry Finn.*

- **1894** Asia: Sino-Japanese War begins.
- **1896** Greece: First modern Olympics held.
- **1897** Russia: Anton Chekhov publishes *Uncle Vanya.*
- **1898** China: Boxer Rebellion against foreign influence.
- **1898** France: Marie and Pierre Curie discover radium. ▶

▶Critical Viewing◀

1. From the picture (1845), what conclusions can you draw about agriculture in Ireland? **[Draw Conclusions]** *For some Irish, farming was small-scale and primitive, without draft animals or machinery.*
2. What qualities does the picture of Florence Nightingale (1860) convey? Support your answer with details. **[Interpret]** *Her solitary, perhaps nighttime vigil (she holds a candle) over the sick suggests dedication; the slope of her shoulders convey care and humility rather than strength. The viewer is meant to be impressed with her watchful mercy.*
3. (a) Judging from the illustration, who were *Alice in Wonderland*'s intended readers? (b) What does this suggest about the reading public of the time? **[Draw Conclusions]** *(a) Its readers included children, judging from the whimsical characters, but also perhaps adults, judging from the sophisticated drawing style. (b) They read for pleasure; parents bought books for their children.*
4. Name two improvements that have been made to the telephone (1876) since Bell's time. **[Compare and Contrast]** *Answers include: The speaker can be held against the ear, for convenience and privacy; two free hands are no longer required to hold or operate a phone.*

◆ Critical Thinking

1. (a) Name two technological improvements of the period. (b) What do these improvements suggest about the use to which science was being put? **[Generalize]** *(a) Answers include: Construction on the London Underground began (1863); the first electric lighting was installed (1880). (b) Science was being used to create convenience and comfort.*
2. (a) Name two events suggesting a new interest in public-spirited or charitable activities. (b) What do these events suggest about the middle class's values? **[Speculate]** *(a) The YMCA was founded (1844); the Salvation Army was established (1878). (b) The middle class thought it had an obligation to help others to improve themselves; self-improvement was probably valued.*
3. (a) What evidence can you find of women's changing status before 1855? (b) What does this development suggest about their economic role before this time? **[Infer]** *(a) Women were admitted into University of London (1848). (b) They probably didn't make much money since they lacked a college education.*
4. (a) Name a British development after 1865 that "made the day longer." (b) Speculate on what Britons used for this purpose previously. (c) Why does this development represent an improvement? **[Speculate]** *(a) Electric lighting was first installed in 1880. (b) People may have used gas, kerosene, or oil lamps. (c) Electric light is constant; it does not flicker or diminish in intensity as fuel burns down, unlike lamps and candles.*
5. (a) Name a nation that, like Britain, made technological progress at this time. Explain. (b) Speculate about how progress in the West affected other areas of the world. **[Speculate]** *(a) Answers include: the United States, where the telephone (1876) and phonograph (1877) were invented. (b) Progress required raw material, which led to colonization of other areas of the world.*

Develop Understanding

Customize for
Less Proficient Readers
Explain to these students that, during this period, some thought that society had become a monster grown out of control. To others, society looked like a wise, helpful magician that could solve any problem. Ask these students to keep a chart with two columns as they read The Story of the Times. They should jot down details that add to the "monster" view in one column, and details that add to the "magician" view in the other.

Customize for
English Language Learners
Inform these students that this period is called "The Age of Industry." Explain to them that industry involves making things in factories. Ask them to review, first the Graphic Look at the Period, then The Story of the Times, looking for words or phrases that might have to do with industry. They should list these words, then confirm their meanings in a dictionary.

Customize for
More Advanced Students
Challenge these students by asking them to study the Graphic Look at the Period and The Story of the Times for events and trends—new modes of travel, new scientific theories, new forms of work—that would affect how people perceived or thought of time. What idea might Victorians have had of the future?

To get students thinking, suggest contrasting ideas of time. For instance, agricultural peoples might think of time as a circle, in which the seasons repeat each year. The Middle Ages thought of the "past" (biblical and Roman) as a source of knowledge and truth, not just "another" period in history.

Answers to
A Graphic Look

Infer (a) Some of the medallions that circle Victoria's head probably refer to Britain's oversea conquests: one shows an elephant; another the Southern Cross, which appears on the flag of New Zealand. They are "ornaments" to her authority. (b) Victorians probably thought that progress had a clear aim (conquering nature) and moral justification.

A Graphic Look at the Period

The Story of the Times

(1833–1901)

Plate Presented by the Ladies of Derby to Queen Victoria on Her 1887 Golden Jubilee

▲ **Infer** This plate honors Queen Victoria. (a) What signs can you find in it of the pride the British took in their overseas Empire? (b) The motto around the rim of the plate refers to humanity's "great and sacred mission" to discover the laws of nature in order to "conquer nature." What inferences can you make about the Victorian faith in progress?

Historical Background

Living in the Victorian Age During Queen Victoria's sixty-four–year reign, from 1837 to 1901, Britain's booming economy and rapid expansion encouraged great optimism. Factory towns grew into large cities as Britain became the world leader in manufacturing. Banks, retail shops, and other businesses expanded. These changes in turn spurred the growth of two important classes—an industrial working class and a modern middle class, able to live a better life because of the low cost and large variety of mass-produced factory goods.

Economic and military power—especially naval power—helped Britain to acquire new colonies in far-flung parts of the globe. Echoing the ringing confidence of the Victorian Age, Robert Browning exclaimed of morning in spring, "God's in his heaven—/All's right with the world!"

A Reforming Age All was not really "right with the world" of industrial England, though. Writers exposed a dark underside of a manufacturing economy—brutal factory conditions and stinking slums. Nonetheless, Victorian reformers had great faith that their hard work could indeed make all right in the future. Goaded by reformers and radicals of many sorts, Victorian leaders did indeed take steps to expand democracy and better the lot of the poor.

Two key issues—trade policy and electoral reform—dominated domestic politics during the first half of the Victorian era. The trade controversy centered on the Corn Laws, which had long slapped high tariffs on "corn" (grain). These laws discouraged food imports and helped British landlords and farmers keep food prices high, which angered the poorer classes. Popular organizations

Cross-Curricular Connection: Social Studies

Victorian Social Ideas Explain to students that there were three kinds of Victorian political and economic theories dealing with the changes of the industrial age. *Laissez-faire theory:* This theory holds that government should avoid meddling in the affairs of business (the French term means "let be"). Left alone, the theory goes, industry will use the most efficient techniques and reach the highest possible level of prosperity. *Reformist liberalism:* Those who held this theory believed that rapid change brings special problems requiring action. They argued that government intervention and regulation were sometimes necessary to protect the rights of the weak against the strong. *Socialism:* Some thinkers and activists favored a more far-reaching policy, ending private ownership of major industries and substituting public ownership, with sweeping government measures to promote equality and help the poor.

Ask students to name figures from American history who might be associated with each of these positions. *Answers include: Ronald Reagan, laissez-faire; Lyndon Johnson, reformist liberalism; Eugene Debbs, socialism.*

sprang up to fight the Corn Laws. Reform came in 1846 when Parliament, confronting a massive famine in Ireland, sought to increase the food supply by suspending the Corn Laws. Over the following decade, it established a policy of free trade beneficial to rising British industries.

The other burning issue of the day involved strengthening democracy. In 1838, a working-class group drew up a "People's Charter" demanding, among other things, universal suffrage for all males, not just the wealthy and middle-class. Renewed demands for electoral change led to the Second Reform Bill of 1867. The Bill doubled the electorate by granting voting rights to tenant farmers and to better-paid male workers. In 1885, Britain established almost complete male suffrage.

Reform affected many areas. Women were allowed to attend universities. Parliament passed laws to reduce the working day for women and children, to establish a system of free grammar schools, and to legalize trade unions. It voted to provide public sanitation and to regulate factories and housing. Agitation continued, however, for further reform.

The Imperialist Urge Britons who supported a policy of imperialism could cite a long list of arguments: Colonies would provide raw materials and markets for British industry; they would offer a home for British settlers; Britain had no choice—if it didn't seize a territory, one of its European rivals would. Many Victorians tended to believe that Western civilization—commonly perceived as white, Christian, and progressive—was superior to all other cultures. This attitude led many Victorians to look condescendingly on non-Westerners as people in need of assistance. While such an attitude seems outrageous by today's standards, many people of the time sincerely believed it.

The Crimean War The Victorian years were generally peaceful. Britain fought only one major European war—the Crimean War (1853–1856), so called because it took place on the Crimean peninsula in southern Russia. Britain, France, and Turkey teamed up to thwart Russian expansion, but the battles were largely inconclusive. Today we remember the war mainly for the brave but disastrous charge of Britain's light brigade. This was commemorated in a famous

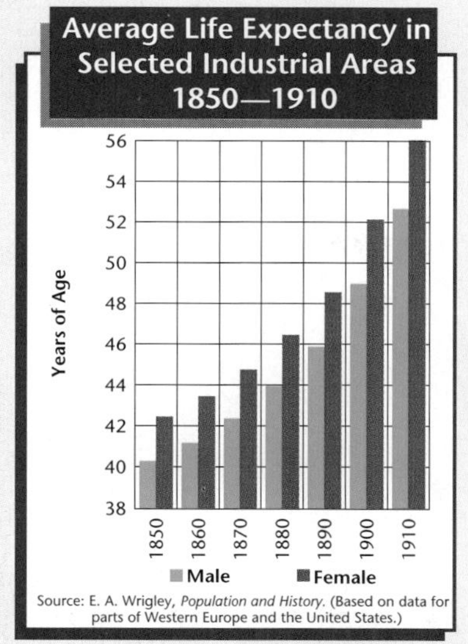

▲ **Read a Chart** (a) What was the difference between a man's average life expectancy in 1850 and 1890? (b) During which decade did women's life expectancy increase the most?

▲ **Speculate** The Crystal Palace, built for a trade show in 1851, was made of iron rods and glass; it became a symbol of the idea of progress. (a) Name two reasons why the Palace would have been built out of glass. (b) Why does the use of glass as a building material suggest progress or the future?

Cross-Curricular Connection: Science

Victorian Social Ideas Technological advances abounded throughout the industrializing world in this period. Steel was invented in 1856, replacing iron as a major material. By the 1890's, dynamos (electric generators) powered factories. The Age of Iron and Steam was over; the Age of Steel and Electricity had begun.

Progress was not confined to industry. Paved streets; gas, then electric lighting; improved sewer systems: these were among the changes that transformed the cities of the day. Chemists produced hundreds of new products, from aspirin to new soaps to margarine to dynamite. Anesthesia was introduced in surgery. Joseph Lister, an English surgeon, discovered the importance of antiseptics in preventing infection. He was the first to insist that surgeons wash their hands. In 1870, Pasteur linked disease to germs.

Ask students to explain how people's views of the world may have changed during this time of progress. *Students may emphasize that human beings appeared to dominate the world; they may also point out that people became less comfortable with chance and mortality.*

Answers to A Graphic Look

Read a Chart (a) The difference in life expectancy is roughly six years. (b) Women's average life expectancy increased most (by four years) during the decade from 1900 to 1910.

Speculate (a) Glass would have let in natural light to illuminate the interior; glass would appear to be a "modern" material. (b) Answers include: Its transparency and fragility contrast greatly with traditional materials of stone and wood.

Connection to the Literature

- For an example of Victorian optimism, see Sydney Smith's memoir, "Progress in Personal Comfort," p. 805.
- Direct students to the excerpt from Dickens's *Hard Times*, p. 822, for an example of the reforming instinct at work.
- For one response to Victorian colonialism, have students read Kipling's "Recessional," p. 794.

More About the Chartists Called the Chartists after the document (charter) in which they made their demands, working class protesters in the 1830's asked for the vote for all males; frequent Parliamentary elections; payment of representatives and waiver of the property requirement for candidates (at the time, only the rich could afford or qualify to serve); secret voting (to prevent the intimidation of voters); and electoral districts of equal population (to make every person's vote count equally). Poorly led, the movement seemed to fail in its own day. Most of its points were adopted after 1860, however.

More About the Crystal Palace The Crystal Palace housed the Great Exhibition of 1851, organized by Prince Albert. Fourteen thousand exhibitors proudly put on view their nations' contributions to technology and agriculture. The total floor area of the Crystal Palace was perhaps 23 acres; the display tables stretched for eight miles. The offerings were varied: false teeth, chewing tobacco, the Colt pistol, articles made of rubber, and McCormick's reaper were all displayed. Over three months, from May 1 to October 11, 1851, more than 6,000,000 visitors browsed through the exhibition.

Historical Background

Comprehension Check

1. Name two consequences of the Industrial Revolution in Britain. *Answers include: Factory towns grew into major cities; banks and other business expanded; a modern working class and middle class grew; cheap mass-produced goods improved life; Britain acquired more colonies.*
2. (a) Name two key concerns of Victorian reformers. (b) Whom did reformers seek to help through these reforms? *(a) Their concerns included repealing the Corn Laws and giving the right to vote to more people. (b) They sought to help the poor and, by opening free trade, industry.*
3. (a) Name one reason Victorians gave for establishing colonies overseas. (b) Name one colony Britain acquired during this period. *(a) Answers include: to acquire raw material; to give settlers a home; to stop the expansion of other countries; to "improve" the natives. (b) Answers include: Hong Kong; Kenya; Uganda; Nigeria; Rhodesia; and South Africa.*
4. Name two issues that concerned Victorian thinkers. *Issues of concern included the material benefits versus the human suffering caused by the Industrial Revolution, and the religious implications of new scientific theories.*

Critical Thinking

1. (a) Explain how landowners benefited from the Corn Laws. (b) Name two groups who probably opposed these laws. **[Analyze]** *(a) Through high taxes on imports, these laws enabled British landowners to keep the price of their grain high. (b) The poor and the factory-owners probably opposed them.*
2. What do Tennyson's lines on the charge of the light brigade suggest about Victorian attitudes towards authority and war? **[Interpret]** *The lines suggest that unquestioning obedience to authority was deemed good for its own sake and that people focused on the nobility of dutiful death rather than the irrationality of war.*
3. Speculate on the type of people who served as administrators in British colonies. **[Speculate]** *Answers include: They would probably be male and middle-class, with few opportunities for advancement at home.*

▼ **Make a Judgment** The children in this print are laborers in a brickyard, paying for their lodgings. Do you believe that it is fundamentally cruel to employ children for work, or do you think there may be circumstances in which it is acceptable? Explain.

Children Paying Innkeeper

Suffragist medal with portrait of Pankhurst

▲ **Speculate** Though a woman sat on the British throne, her female subjects were not entitled to vote in national elections. Suffragists such as Emmeline Pankhurst (1858–1928), shown in the medallion, lobbied to gain the vote for women. On what occasions might someone have worn this medal?

poem by Alfred, Lord Tennyson, some lines of which follow:

Theirs not to make reply,
Theirs not to reason why,
Theirs but to do and die.

Britain as a World Power Though the Liberals (formerly the Whigs) advocated limits to British rule, the Empire continued to grow. Britain acquired Hong Kong from China in 1842. After a rebellion in 1857 by sepoys (Indian troops under British command), Britain shouldered aside the British East India Company and took direct control of India.

In the last three decades of Victoria's rule Britain expanded its influence in Africa. It gained control of the new Suez Canal in Egypt and acquired such territories as Kenya, Uganda, Nigeria, and Rhodesia (Zimbabwe). Britain also consolidated its control over what is now South Africa, defeating Dutch settlers there in the Boer War of 1899–1902.

Victorian Thought Victorian thinkers often disagreed on the crucial issues of their times but they shared a deep confidence in humanity's ability to better itself. The changes brought about by the Industrial Revolution stirred conflicting feelings among Victorian thinkers. On the one hand, they admired the material benefits industrialization had brought. On the other, they deplored the brutality of factory life and of industrial slums. Much debate concerned whether business should be allowed free rein or whether, for the welfare of people, the government should take a strong role in the economy.

The Victorians grappled with the religious and philosophical as well as the social implications of modern life. The theory of evolution proposed by Charles Darwin (1809–1882) in *On the Origin of Species* (1859), for instance, stirred bitter controversy. Darwin believed that a process he called "natural selection" explained how different forms of life evolved from previous forms. His account is quite different from the Creation story found in the Bible. Some Victorian thinkers took Darwin's theory as a direct challenge to Biblical truth and traditional religious faith. Some accepted both Darwin and religion, striving to reconcile scientific and religious insights.

Cross-Curricular Connection: Social Studies

Middle-Class Life By mid-century, the modern middle class had evolved its own way of life. The nuclear family lived in a large house or apartment. Even a small middle-class household was expected to have at least a cook and a maid. A strict code of etiquette dictated how to dress for every occasion, when to write letters, and how long to mourn relatives who had died. Parents strictly supervised their children, who were expected to be "seen but not heard."

When choosing a wife or husband, middle-class people considered economic reasons and their parents' wishes, yet the idea of "falling in love" was growing increasingly acceptable. Most middle-class husbands went to work in an office or a shop, and aspired to make enough to keep their wives at home. Women spent their days raising children, directing the servants, and doing charitable work. Books, magazines, and songs celebrated the cult of domesticity that idealized women and the home.

Ask students to explain how middle-class life is different today. *Students may note that more women work outside the home; that more attention is paid to children; and that "falling in love" is highly valued.*

Literature of the Period

Romanticism and Realism Romanticism continued to influence Victorian writers, but it had by now become part of mainstream culture. When Victorian writers confronted the rapid technological and social change amidst which they lived, the Realist literary movement was born. Realist literature focused on ordinary people facing the day-to-day problems of life, an emphasis that reflected the trend toward democracy and the growing middle-class audience for literature.

Naturalism A related movement, known as Naturalism, sought to put the spirit of scientific observation to literary use. Naturalists crammed their novels with details—the sour smells of poverty, the harsh sounds of factory life—often with the aim of promoting social reform. They directly contradicted the Romantic idea that nature mirrored human feelings and portrayed nature instead as harsh and indifferent to the human suffering it caused.

The Anti-Realists Rather than embracing "real" life as the Realists did, two groups of artists attempted to refine art. The poets and painters of the Pre-Raphaelite Brotherhood (formed about 1848) rejected the ugliness of industrial life. They turned for inspiration to the spiritual intensity of medieval Italian art—art before the time of the painter Raphael (1483–1520). Toward the end of the Victorian Age, aesthetes like the writer Oscar Wilde (1854–1900) turned away from the everyday world and sought to create "art for art's sake"—works whose sole reason for being was their perfection or beauty.

Victorian Poetry The Victorian Age produced a large and diverse body of poetry. The most popular poet of the era—Alfred, Lord Tennyson (1809–1892)—was influenced by earlier Romantic poets. His verse displays a keen sense of the music of language. By contrast, Robert Browning's (1812–1889) dramatic monologues—long speeches in which a character reveals his or her inward thoughts—explore human personality in all its un-Romantic details. Browning's wife, Elizabeth Barrett (1806–1861), was the more famous poet at the time of their marriage. Today she is remembered mostly for the beautiful love poems she wrote her husband.

"The Old Rotten Tree," jug, 1832

▲ **Relate** Not the least effect of the Industrial Revolution was the widespread availability of cheap, mass-produced goods, such as Staffordshire chinaware. The jug bears a cartoon criticizing corrupt electoral policies. (a) On what household items do cartoons appear today? (b) Are they generally political?

Bayswater Omnibus, G. W. Joy

▲ **Speculate** Originally French, the first horse-drawn omnibuses came to London in 1829.How do you suppose the development of public spaces such as the inside of a bus may have influenced later fashion? Explain.

Answers to A Graphic Look

(from page 742)

Make a Judgment Students may respond that making children work is always cruel, either because children do not have the endurance or attention-span that a day's work requires, or because, by being deprived of education and play, they are being deprived of a richer adult life. Others may respond that, as long as they are treated well, children can benefit from the discipline of work and the sense that they are being useful.

Speculate Answers include: The medallion might have been worn on marches or at mass meetings, when shows of solidarity, rank, and seriousness of purpose are important.

(from page 743)

Relate (a) Answers include: Cartoons often appear on coffee mugs and lunchboxes (but rarely on dining ware such as pitchers and plates). (b) Coffee-mug cartoons can be political, but these generally reflect only a neutral, non-partisan cynicism.

Speculate The women's skirts and their hats, as well as the gentleman's top-hat, all take up a lot of space. Crowded spaces such as this bus would encourage more practical, less showy wear. Additionally, as men and women became used to mingling in such close physical quarters, ideas of what was "modest" and what wasn't may have changed.

Connections to the Literature

- For a poem that may be read as a comment on the transition from Romanticism to Realism, turn to "The Lady of Shalott," p. 754.

Humanities: Music

"When I Was a Lad," from *H.M.S. Pinafore,* by Gilbert and Sullivan.

Some Victorian attitudes and beliefs were so patriotic and extreme that they were criticized, mocked, and parodied. W. S. Gilbert and Arthur Sullivan, who collaborated on thirteen comic operas, often parodied English life—showing it at its most absurd.

"When I Was a Lad," sung by a character named The Rt. Hon. Sir Joseph Porter, KCB (First Lord of the Admiralty), is an account of an unusual rise to high office, parodying the kind of success-through-hard-work story that Victorians loved. It is a "patter song," combining words and melody to create a "pitter-patter" effect.

Play students "When I Was a Lad" on the **Listening to Music** Audio CD: *The British Tradition.* Ask them to raise their hands when they first hear the "patter" effect.

Then ask the following questions:

1. What is being satirized in this song? Explain. *The song satirizes a bureaucrat's model of success.*
2. Would the song be as successful without the patter effect? *Students may answer that the effect adds humor; it gives the words a "chatty" effect.*

Connections to the Literature

- Students will find Arnold's definitive statement of Victorian despair, "Dover Beach," on page 792. Examples of Hardy's and Housman's naturalism appear beginning on pages 850 and 860, respectively.
- Far from the liquid elegance of Tennyson's poetry, Kipling's verse marches with common soldiers and other builders of empire, as students will find beginning on page 794.
- Excerpts from the novels of Charles Dickens and of Charlotte Brontë appear beginning on pages 822 and 828, respectively.

Answers to

A GRAPHIC LOOK

Speculate Without lighting, people would probably not be out in such numbers, both because of the difficulties of finding one's way and the possible danger of attack.

Infer The phone doesn't have an obvious, intuitive means (such as a dial or touch-tone pad) to dial a long string of numbers. Large numbers of telephone users require long telephone numbers to distinguish one user from another in a systematic way. It is therefore likely that this phone was designed when the phone system was limited, and when few people used phones.

(from page 745)

Connect The simplicity of the figure's face, the simple, relaxed lines of her pose and of the drapery of her robe, all suggest a clear, straightforward idea of study, grace, and repose. There are no complicating "psychological" ambiguities or tensions in her expression or manner; the painter does not use any special effects to show off his technique. In this sense, the communication of feeling is simple and direct.

Assess Some students may respond that, because of the variety of shapes and the dynamic, flowing line, the pattern keeps the eye busy—there is too much going on. Others may respond that because the graceful flow of the lines saves the pattern from harsh contrast and abrupt transitions, it is restful.

Edwardian London, 1901, Eugene Joseph McSwiney

▲ **Speculate** Public gas lighting was one of the innovations of Victorian England. Without this lighting, would so many people be on the street? Explain.

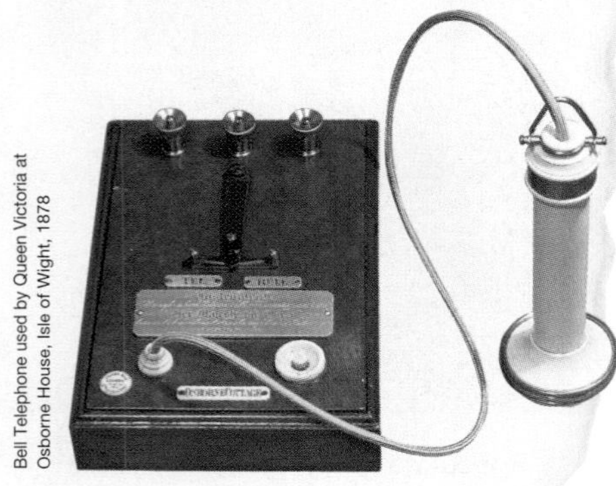

Bell Telephone used by Queen Victoria at Osborne House, Isle of Wight, 1878

▲ **Infer** What does the absence of a rotary dial or touch-tone pad suggest about the extent of the telephone system—and the number of people using telephones—in 1878? Explain.

Matthew Arnold (1822–1888) was probably the first Victorian poet to focus on "the bewildering confusion" of the industrial age—the loss of individuals' close ties to nature and with each other. Arnold was a forerunner of the more pessimistic Naturalist writers, such as Thomas Hardy (1840–1928) and A. E. Housman (1859–1936), for whom life's disappointments and the erosion of rural society were frequent subjects.

The poetry of Rudyard Kipling (1865–1936) spoke to the expansive spirit of the age, ranging across the breadth of the Empire with action-packed narratives like "Gunga Din" and poems written in the colorful speech of working-class soldiers in *Barrack-room Ballads.*

While Tennyson's and Kipling's well-known lyrics turned up occasionally as popular songs, Gerard Manley Hopkins (1844–1889) remained unpublished during his own century. His innovative rhythms and Romantic-inspired religious verse would later inspire twentieth-century poets.

Victorian Drama Playhouses in the Victorian Age were few in number and hemmed in by government restrictions. Only toward the end of the century did the theater begin to show some sparkle, with serious dramas like Sir Arthur Wing Pinero's *The Second Mrs. Tanqueray* (1893) and satirical ones like Oscar Wilde's *The Importance of Being Earnest* (1895).

Victorian Fiction Members of the new middle class were avid readers, and they loved novels—especially novels that reflected the main social issues of the day. Responding to the demand, weekly and monthly magazines published novels chapter by chapter, in serial form.

Emily Brontë's (1818–1848) classic *Wuthering Heights* (1847) tells the tale of the doomed passion of Catherine Earnshaw and Heathcliff, one of English fiction's outstanding Romantic heroes. Her sister Charlotte (1816–1855) wrote *Jane Eyre* (1847), a novel recounting the adventures of a governess who falls in love with her mysterious employer, Mr. Rochester.

The Realist elements of *Jane Eyre* probably owe much to the influence of Charles Dickens (1812–1870), who surpassed all other Victorian novelists in popularity. Dickens filled his novels with poignant, realistic details that dramatized

Humanities: Art

The Birth of Photography By the 1840's, a new art form, photography, was emerging. Louis Daguerre in France and William Fox Talbot in England had improved on earlier technologies to produce successful photographs. At first, many photos were stiff-posed portraits of middle-class families or prominent people. Other photographs reflected Romantic fascination with faraway places.

In time, photographers used the camera to expose slum conditions and other social ills. Photographs provided shocking evidence to prod governments toward reform.

Photography even posed a challenge to painters. Why try for realism, some artists asked, when a camera could do the same thing better? By the 1870's, instead of attempting to reproduce reality "photographically," the French painters called the Impressionists were seeking to capture fleeting impressions of the world.

Ask students to judge whether photographs are direct presentations of reality, or whether they can evoke mystery.

the problems of a grimy industrial England. To his eye for injustice he married a marvelous sense of humor. His novels abound in deliciously eccentric characters, whose every peculiarity of speech and gesture affirms how individual people are.

Other, less sentimental Victorian Realists included William Makepeace Thackeray (1811–1863), Anthony Trollope (1815–1882), Elizabeth Gaskell (1810–1865), and Samuel Butler (1835–1902). George Meredith produced careful psychological studies of his characters in novels such as *The Egoist* (1879). Mary Ann Evans, writing as George Eliot (1819–1880), examined social issues and personal relationships in novels such as *Adam Bede* (1859).

As the century drew to a close, British novelists such as Thomas Hardy leaned more and more to Naturalism. Late Victorian readers shied away from Naturalism's dark outlook, though, preferring instead the adventure stories of writers like Robert Louis Stevenson (1850–1894) and Rudyard Kipling or the Sherlock Holmes mysteries of Sir Arthur Conan Doyle (1859–1930).

Nonfiction Prose All the great Victorian thinkers produced influential prose works. Matthew Arnold, for example, attacked the British class system in *Culture and Anarchy* (1869), his most famous work of social criticism. Other influential works included *Modern Painters* (1843) by John Ruskin (1819–1900), *On Liberty* (1859) by John Stuart Mill (1806–1873), *The Idea of a University Defined* (1873) by John Henry Newman (1801–1890), and *Studies in the History of the Renaissance* (1873) by Walter Pater (1839–1894). Greatest of the Victorian historians were Thomas Carlyle (1795–1881) and Thomas Babington Macaulay (1800–1859).

All in all, the Victorian Age produced a diverse body of literature—entertaining, scholarly, humorous, profound. Because the era is so close to our own times—and because in it we see the beginnings of our own problems, many of them still unresolved, Victorian literature has a special relevance to readers today. In addition, the Victorian writers were brilliant storytellers, and we read their works not only for literary appreciation and historical understanding but for pure reading pleasure.

Princess Sabra ou la Fille de Roi, 1865-66
Sir Edward Burne-Jones

▲ **Connect** In 1848, a group of young painters, led by Dante Gabriel Rosetti, formed the Pre-Raphaelite Brotherhood. They sought to recapture the direct, sincere communication of feeling they found in medieval art. Which elements in this painting seem to achieve that goal?

Granville, Wallpaper, Designed by John Henry Dearle (1860-1932) for Morris and Company, 1896

▲ **Assess** William Morris, a close associate of the Pre-Raphaelites and, like them, a lover of medieval art, single-handedly revolutionized Victorian decorative taste. How successful do you think this pattern, designed for his company, would be on wallpaper? Is it too "busy" or does it soothe the eye? Explain.

Literature of the Period

Check Your Comprehension

1. What defined the Realist literary movement? *The Realists chose as their subject matter the struggles of ordinary people with everyday problems.*
2. What defined the Naturalist literary movement? *The Naturalists attended to the details of life with almost scientific precision; they depicted nature as indifferent to human suffering.*
3. Name a group or writer who turned away from "realistic" depictions of life. *The Pre-Raphaelites, the Aesthetes, and Oscar Wilde all turned away from Realism.*
4. (a) Name a Victorian poet influenced by the Romantics. (b) Name one influenced by Realism. (c) Name one influenced by Naturalism. *(a) Answers include: Tennyson; Hopkins. (b) Answers include: Browning; Kipling. (c) Answers include: Arnold; Housman; Hardy.*
5. (a) What developing genre of writing was especially popular during this period? (b) To what new audience did it appeal? *(a) The novel was especially popular. (b) Novels appealed to the new middle class.*

◆ Critical Thinking

1. (a) What kind of subject matter did Realists depict? (b) Show how the rise of Realism is connected to two social changes during this period. **[Connect]** *(a) Realism depicted the lives of ordinary people. (b) Realism reflected the concern of reformers with the lower classes, and the growth of a middle-class readership, whose lives it documented.*
2. (a) What elements of life did the Naturalists focus on? (b) Is their approach more "realistic" or "natural" than other approaches to literature? Explain. **[Make a Judgment]** *(a) Naturalists focused on the "grit" of modern life and on the indifference of nature to human suffering. (b) Answers include: Yes, because it resembles a practical attitude often called "being realistic"; no, because this approach involves the imagination and selection of details as much as any other.*
3. (a) How did readers react to the pessimism of serious late Victorian novels? (b) Name a similar modern trend. **[Relate]** *(a) Readers turned to escapist fiction instead. (b) Answers include: the split between "highbrow" and "lowbrow" culture, such as between art films and Hollywood movies.*

Activities

1. **Graphic Organization of Events** Have students use the Problem/Solution Organizer, page 107 in ***Writing and Language Transparencies,*** to chart a problem faced by Victorians and the competing solutions they offered. Students can offer their own "Decision" on the best solution.
2. **Society on Trial** Victorian reformers often tried to pick up the messes left behind by growing industry. Others, such as Herbert Spencer, argued that society was best left to develop on its own. Divide students into the Spencerians and the Reformers, and have them debate government's role in times of economic change.
3. **Social Comment** Have students envision a scene in a poor family's apartment in a London slum. Ask them to write two paragraphs describing this scene, one in a Romantic, the other in a Naturalist style.
4. **Connections to the Literature** Challenge students to find a passage in a selection that reflects an insight, description, narrative, or idea from The Story of the Times. Have them read the passage aloud to the class and explain how it relates to The Story of the Times. Students giving the presentation should then be prepared to answer questions about the passage.

Develop Understanding

◆ Critical Thinking

1. Having grown in numbers and power, the middle class began to "discover" itself during this period, defining itself apart from the nobility and the poor (into whose ranks a middle class person might slip). (a) Do Lady Gough's rules suggest a secure or insecure attitude about how one comes across in public? (b) What connection can you make between the desire of the middle class to establish its own identity and these new standards for proper speech? **[Speculate]** *(a) These standards show an insecurity about how one appears in public. (b) These standards may have emerged as the middle class's way of claiming moral superiority (justifying its success) and of distinguishing itself from the poor.*
2. (a) Speculate on whether all middle-class Victorians took standards like Lady Gough's seriously. Explain your answer. (b) Speculate on what kind of opposing reaction such standards may have led to. **[Speculate]** *(a) Answers include: Some of her rules seem ludicrous, and people may have grown impatient with them. (b) Answers include: Some people may have intentionally acted to shock others.*

Critical Viewing

1. (a) What attitude towards the human body is suggested by the use of euphemisms for pregnancy? (b) How does the woman's clothing in the picture also express that attitude? **[Interpret]** *(a) The use of such euphemisms suggest a discomfort in publicly acknowledging the body. (b) The woman's clothing covers all of her except face, feet, and hands. The shawl and draping of the dress conceal her outline.*

Answers to Activities

1. Students supporting Juliet should show that the important things about a person or thing remain unchanged by what they are called; students rebutting her might point to names that categorize and link people will make good examples: family names, for instance, "create" ties to other people.
2. Answers may include: *Administrative assistant* has replaced *secretary; consultant* often replaces *free lance adviser.*

The Changing English Language

THE VICTORIAN AGE

by Richard Lederer

Euphemisms: The Fig Leaves of Language

Prudishness reached its golden age in the straitlaced Victorian era. Take the widely read *Lady Gough's Book of Etiquette.* Among Lady Gough's social pronouncements was that under no circumstances should books written by male authors be placed on shelves next to books written by "authoresses." Married writers, however, such as Robert and Elizabeth Barrett Browning, could be shelved together without impropriety.

So delicate were Victorian sensibilities that members of polite society would blush at the mention of anything physical. Instead of being *pregnant,* women were *in a delicate condition, in a family way,* or *expectant.* Women did not give birth; they experienced a *blessed event.* Their children were not born; rather, they were *brought by the stork,* or *came into the world.*

Such words and expressions are called *euphemisms* (from two Greek roots that mean "pleasant speech," "words of good omen"). A euphemism is a mild, indirect word or phrase used in place of one that is more direct or that may have an unpleasant connotation for some people. Using a euphemism is "calling a spade a heart" . . . or "telling it like it isn't."

Children were not born but rather brought by the stork.

In the Victorian Age, prudery extended even to animals and things. *Bull* was considered an indecent word, and the proper substitute was *he cow, male cow,* or (gasp!) *gentleman cow.* Victorian standards were so exacting that Victorians couldn't refer to something as vulgar as legs. They had to call them *limbs,* even when talking about the legs on a chicken or a piano. Instead of asking for a leg of chicken, they would ask for dark meat, and they went so far as to cover up piano legs with little skirts!

Activities

1. Shakespeare's Juliet sighs, "What's in a name? A rose by any other name would smell as sweet." Would it? Write an essay in which you defend or rebut Juliet's opinion of the relationship between words and things.
2. Many occupations have taken on glorified, euphemistic titles. Nowadays, a garbage collector is called a sanitation engineer and a dogcatcher an animal control warden. Collect other examples and share them with classmates.

Cross-Curricular Connection: Social Studies

Domestic Sentiment The euphemism is one way of "idealizing" life. The Victorians are also remembered for an extreme sentimentalization of the middle-class domestic scene. In paintings, songs, novels, and those famous samplers bearing the words "Home Sweet Home," motherhood, marriage, and domestic duty were glorified.

Home, though, was a "haven in a heartless world." The middle-class husband battled his way through the cruel, indifferent war zone of business, then took shelter in the warm household ordered and filled with love by his dutiful spouse.

Ask students whether this ideal of the home has changed. *Students may respond that many modern women aspire to careers other than homemaker, but that middle-class people still think of their homes as islands of private satisfaction sheltered from a cold, impersonal public world.*

PART 1 *Relationships*

Faustine, 1904
Maxwell Armfield, Museé d'Orsay, Paris, France

Humanities: Art

Faustine, 1904, by Maxwell Armfield.

This colorful painting is typical of the works of the Pre-Raphaelite movement, which idealized the vivid coloration and detail of High Renaissance art. In addition, the influence of the aesthetic Art Nouveau movement can be seen in the artist's fascination with pattern—in the border of the painting, the rug, the teapot, and the woman's gown.

Have students link the art to the focus of Part 1, "Relationships," by answering the following questions:

1. What do you think is going on between the couple in this painting, and what elements of the painting lead you to this idea? *Sample answer: The man is calling on the woman, indicated by his hat on the sofa. Their relative positions suggest that he loves her, while she is indifferent to him or is playing hard to get.*
2. Choose one of the two figures in this painting and write the thoughts he or she might be having at this moment. *Sample answer: He says he loves me, but I worry that he will not love me for long. I must not show him how much I love him.*

One-Minute Planning Guide

The selections in this part are poems by Alfred, Lord Tennyson, and Robert and Elizabeth Barrett Browning that explore the theme, "Relationships." The section opens with excerpts from Tennyson's tribute to his friend, Arthur Hallam: "In Memoriam, A.H.H." Another exploration of a relationship between death and love is found in "The Lady of Shalott," a lyric narrative of a romantic heroine who chooses love and finds death. Tennyson's famous dramatic monologue, "Ulysses," provides contrasts to Browning's "My Last Duchess," and "Life in a Love," evoking multiple variations on relationships of love and life. Elizabeth Barrett Browning's famous love poem "Sonnet 43" epitomizes a loving relationship between a woman and her husband.

Customize for *Varying Student Needs*

When assigning the selections in this part to your students, keep in mind the following factors:

from "In Memoriam, A.H.H."
- Treats the sensitive subject of grieving for the death of a close friend who dies young

"The Lady of Shalott"
- Contains an excellent study for musical/rhythmic learners of music in poetry

"Ulysses"
- A memorable example of a dramatic monologue

from *The Princess:* "Tears, Idle Tears"
- Tennyson's poetry evokes a lament for things past that will never be recovered.

"My Last Duchess"
- This dramatic monologue provides a psychological study of a destructive relationship.

"Life in a Love"
- Students can compare the speaker in this dramatic monologue to the repellent speaker in "My Last Duchess."

"Love Among the Ruins"
- Contains challenging descriptions from which students can identify the setting and situation of the poem

Sonnet 43
- Students can respond to one of the most famous love poems of all time.

Prepare and Engage

OBJECTIVES

1. To read, comprehend, and interpret poems
2. To relate poems to personal experience
3. To use strategies for reading critically to read for success
4. To identify the speaker in poetry
5. To build vocabulary in context and learn related medieval words
6. To identify and use parallel structure
7. To write an essay of tribute using a clear explanation of cause and effect
8. To respond to poems through writing, speaking and listening, and projects

SKILLS INSTRUCTION

Vocabulary:
Related Words: Medieval Words

Grammar:
Parallel Structure

Reading for Success:
Strategies for Reading Critically

Literary Focus:
The Speaker in Poetry

Writing:
Clear Explanation of Cause and Effect

Speaking and Listening:
Camelot Late-Night News (teacher edition)

Critical Viewing:
Evaluate; Interpret; Compare and Contrast; Apply

PORTFOLIO OPPORTUNITIES

Writing: Song; Literary Analysis; Critical Response
Writing Mini-Lesson: Essay of Tribute
Speaking and Listening: Oral Interpretation; Camelot Late-Night News
Projects: Set Design; Tennyson on Tape

More About the Author
By the mid-1800's, when Alfred, Lord Tennyson, was writing much of his poetry, the Industrial Revolution had had a tremendous effect on life in England. Tennyson was fascinated by the technological advances of the time, such as electricity and the gasoline engine, but he also clearly saw the negative effects of industrialization—filthy slums and choking pollution. In reaction, many of his best-known poems focus on the past—either his own past, or a historical or literary past.

Guide for Interpreting

Alfred, Lord Tennyson
(1809–1892)

You may think of Tennyson—or any male Victorian poet—as a bearded old man whose picture you see in a book. Think again. Here's the author Carlyle's description of the tall and handsome (if moody) young Tennyson: "One of the finest looking men in the world. A great shock of rough dusty-dark hair; bright-laughing hazel eyes . . . of sallow-brown complexion, almost Indian-looking." This is the young Alfred who in middle age became the most famous and celebrated poet of Victorian England: Alfred, Lord Tennyson.

An Unhappy Childhood Tennyson was born in the rural town of Somersby in Lincolnshire, the fourth of twelve children. He was a sensitive boy who, even before he could read, was charmed by the magical words "far, far away." His father, a clergyman, had a large library and personally supervised Tennyson's early education. He even predicted that his son would be "the greatest Poet of the Time." However, this well-educated clergyman was also extremely bitter, enraged at being disinherited by his own father. His anger poisoned the atmosphere of the Tennyson household, and as a teenager, Alfred was probably eager to escape to Cambridge University.

The Power of Friendship At first, Tennyson was disappointed by Cambridge. He wrote about his studies: "None but dry-headed, calculating, angular little gentlemen can take much delight in them." Then he met the young man who became his closest friend, Arthur Henry Hallam. They were often together, and Hallam intended to marry Tennyson's sister Emily.

Tragedy In 1833, however, Hallam died suddenly while traveling. Grief-stricken, Tennyson considered questions of death, religious faith, and immortality in a series of short poems that eventually became an elegy for his friend, "In Memoriam, A.H.H." (1850). The elegy so impressed Prince Albert that he encouraged Queen Victoria to appoint Tennyson the Poet Laureate of England when Wordsworth died in 1850. In 1884, the Queen made Tennyson a baron, the first English writer to be so titled.

Land, Literature, Long Life When royalties from "In Memoriam, A.H.H." began to flow in, Tennyson was able to buy the "acre" of land he'd always longed for, a farm on the Isle of Wight. There he and his wife Emily Sellwood raised two children. Tennyson remained alert to the end of his life, publishing poems when he was past eighty.

◆ Background for Understanding

LITERATURE: TENNYSON'S SOURCES OF INSPIRATION

The boy who was charmed by the words "far, far away" became a poet whose mind traveled far to find sources of inspiration: ancient Greece and medieval Italy and England.

In "Ulysses" (Latin for *Odysseus*) Tennyson continues the story of the *Odyssey*, describing life on the isle of Ithaca following the Greek hero's return home. To do this, Tennyson built upon hints about the final vogage found in the original epic by the ancient Greek poet Homer. Tennyson also drew upon Dante's *Inferno,* in which the hero Odysseus describes the final voyage home in his own words.

In the tragic "Lady of Shalott," Tennyson uses as his source Arthurian legend—medieval tales that describe the deeds of King Arthur and his knights of the Round Table.

Knowing Tennyson's sources, you can take a greater interest in his poetic "relay race."

Prentice Hall Literature Program Resources

REINFORCE / RETEACH / EXTEND

Selection Support Pages
Build Vocabulary: Related Words: Medieval Words, p. 181
Grammar and Style: Parallel Structure, p. 182
Reading for Success: Strategies for Reading Critically, p. 183–184
Literary Focus: The Speaker in Poetry, p. 185

Strategies for Diverse Student Needs, p. 38

Beyond Literature, p. 38

Formal Assessment Selection Test, pp. 186–188; Assessment Resources Software

Alternative Assessment, p. 38

Writing and Language Transparencies
Cause-and-Effect Organizer, pp. 119–121

Resource Pro CD-ROM
from "In Memoriam"; "Shalott"; "Ulysses"; from *The Princess*

Listening to Literature Audiocassettes
from "In Memoriam"; "Shalott"; "Ulysses"; from *The Princess*

from In Memoriam, A.H.H. ◆ The Lady of Shalott ◆ Ulysses ◆ Tears, Idle Tears

MODEL SELECTION

◆ *Literature and Your Life*

Connect Your Experience

You write a song praising the virtues of someone special in your life. You lay a wreath of dried flowers at a relative's grave. These are two of many ways to pay tribute—to mark your respect or affection for someone.

Tennyson's poem "In Memoriam, A.H.H." is a personal tribute to a beloved friend who died too young. His poems "The Lady of Shalott" and "Ulysses" are literary tributes to the timeless works that inspired them: medieval romances, Homer's *Odyssey*, and Dante's *Inferno*.

Thematic Focus: Relationships

As you read "In Memoriam," notice how Tennyson's tribute to his friend transforms an ordinary person into a hero.

Journal Writing Describe some ways in which you honor your own friends and relatives.

◆ Build Vocabulary

Related Words: Medieval Words

Tennyson uses medieval words such as *churls,* meaning "farmers or peasants," to add atmosphere to his poems. In the poem "The Lady of Shalott," his choice of a medieval word helps create setting and atmosphere.

Word Bank

Before you read, preview this list of words from the poems.

diffusive
churls
waning
furrows

◆ Grammar and Style

Parallel Structure

Tennyson uses **parallel structure**—similar grammatical form for similar ideas—to give rhythm and unity to his poems and to emphasize underlying meanings.

In lines 11–12 of "In Memoriam," for example, he uses three parallel infinitive phrases to lend his grief a haunting rhythm and to stress the importance of giving in to grief:

Ah, sweeter *to be drunk with loss,*
To dance with death, to beat the ground . . .

◆ Literary Focus

The Speaker in Poetry

The **speaker** in a poem—the person who "says" its words—is not necessarily the poet. It can also be a fictional character. If the speaker is fictional, however, the chances are that his or her situation relates to that of the poet. By knowing the identity of the speaker and the conflicts he or she faces, you can better understand the poet's purpose and meaning.

Tennyson himself is the speaker of "In Memoriam, A.H.H.," a tribute to his friend Arthur Hallam. In these excerpts from the poem, be aware of the passages in which Tennyson faces, and tries to make meaning of, his friend's early death.

In "The Lady of Shalott" and "Ulysses," however, Tennyson wears the mask of fictional characters: a woman hiding from life in medieval England and an aging Greek hero, respectively. Think about the conflicts that these characters face and why Tennyson might find these conflicts especially meaningful. Consider, for example, how the medieval lady, weaving her "magic web" on a "silent isle," is like an artist or poet.

Interest Grabber Ask students to think of tributes to famous people they have heard in music or poetry. For example, some may mention Elton John's song "Candle in the Wind," originally written as tribute to Marilyn Monroe and reworked as a tribute to Diana, Princess of Wales. Tell students that poet Alfred, Lord Tennyson, became famous for the tribute he wrote in memory of a friend who died young—at the age of twenty-two. As they read Tennyson's tribute and other of his poems, have them consider what quality of Tennyson's poetry makes it so memorable.

Customize for *Less Proficient Readers*
In order to aid their comprehension, less proficient students may benefit from listening to the recording of the poems on the **Listening to Literature Audiocassettes.**

Customize for *More Advanced Students*
These students may wish to judge Tennyson's work for themselves, both poem by poem and as a whole. Encourage them to find reasons and examples to support their judgments.

Customize for *English Language Learners*
English language learners may have trouble with the formal language and sentence structures in the poems. Have them paraphrase important sections of each poem, restating some of the more difficult sections of the poems in their own words. Direct them especially to lines 29–44 of "In Memoriam" and lines 62–70 of "Ulysses." For "The Lady of Shalott," have them retell the main events of the story.

Customize for *Musical/Rhythmic Learners*
Tell students that a musical elegy is called a *requiem.* Have them listen to excerpts from the requiems by Verdi, Berlioz, or Fauré. Draw their attention to the slow tempo and the mournful, melancholy mood.

Preparing for Standardized Tests

Grammar and Language Identifying and using parallel structure is a skill that is often tested in the grammar/composition section of tests such as the SAT II. Students might be asked to correct sentences such as the following:

The volunteer group helped at the playground, visited shut-ins, and they planted a neighborhood garden. *(C)*
(A) and they planted a neighborhood garden
(B) and planting a neighborhood garden.
(C) and planted a neighborhood garden.

For additional practice, students can complete Grammar and Style: Parallel Structure in ***Selection Support***, p. 182.

Reading and Vocabulary The Critical Reading section of the SAT may ask students to read a passage and choose the reasons or examples the author gives to support his or her assumptions. One of the Reading for Success skills for this selection, Evaluate Author's Points or Statements, will help prepare students to read with the purpose of evaluating assumptions. For additional practice, have students complete the Reading for Success pages in ***Selection Support,*** pp. 183–184.

Reading for Success

The Reading for Success page in each unit presents a set of problem-solving procedures to help readers understand authors' words and ideas on multiple levels. Good readers develop a bank of strategies from which they can draw as needed.

Unit 5 introduces strategies for reading critically. It is important for students to develop their comprehension to a level on which they can apply higher-level critical thinking skills. These strategies for reading critically give readers an approach for attacking text on a level beyond literal comprehension, where they can make inferences, recognize emotive language, evaluate a writer's statements, and judge a writer's work.

These strategies for reading critically are modeled with the excerpt from "In Memoriam, A.H.H." Each green box shows an example of the thinking process involved in applying one of these strategies.

How to Use the Reading for Success Page

- Introduce the strategies for reading critically, presenting each as a problem-solving procedure. Be sure students understand what each strategy involves and under what circumstances to apply it.
- Before students read the poem, have them preview it, looking at the annotations in the green boxes that model the strategies.
- To reinforce these strategies after students have read the excerpt from "In Memoriam, A.H.H.," have them do the Reading for Success pages in ***Selection Support***, pp. 183–184. These pages give students an opportunity to read a selection and practice strategies for literal comprehension by writing their own annotations.

Reading for Success

Strategies for Reading Critically

Reading critically requires you to examine and evaluate an author's ideas, whether the ideas are presented in prose or poetry. When you read critically, you identify the writer's purpose and you examine the ideas the writer includes (or doesn't include) in support of that purpose. Then you form a judgment about the validity of the work.

These strategies will help you read critically.

Make inferences.

Writers don't always say everything they mean. Often they only suggest ideas, which you must infer from the details and evidence they provide. For example, knowing that Tennyson's best friend died, you can infer that Tennyson wrote "In Memoriam, A.H.H." from a deep personal grief.

Recognize an author's purpose or bias.

- An author's purpose influences what he or she includes and how he or she chooses to present material. When you recognize an author's purpose, you can examine his or her ideas in light of that purpose.
- Be alert also for an author's *bias*, a preference for one person, thing, or idea above another.

Distinguish between emotive and neutral language.

Emotive language—"Let love clasp Grief lest both be drowned"—excites emotion. Neutral language—"On either side the river lie / long fields of barley and of rye"—is without color or emotion. Writers use emotive language to engage your feelings; neutral language describes a situation more objectively.

Evaluate the writer's points or statements.

To evaluate a writer's assertions, weigh the evidence the writer brings to bear on a subject. Consider whether the examples, reasons, or illustrations used to support points are sound and effective.

Consider the historical and biographical context.

In evaluating a writer's work, think about the prevailing social attitudes of the time and place in which a writer lived.

Judge the writer's work.

Apply your critical judgment to the work as a whole. As you look at a work in its totality, consider questions like these: Do the statements or points follow logically? Is the writer's evidence appropriate and relevant? Are the characters and situations true to life?

As you read "In Memoriam, A.H.H.," look at the side notes. These notes demonstrate how to apply these strategies to your reading.

Reading Strategies: Support and Reinforcement

Appropriate Reading Strategies Students are given a reading strategy to apply in reading each selection. For example, students may be asked to determine whether a passage used emotive or neutral language in a highly emotive piece. In other selections a strategy is suggested that is appropriate to that selection.

Reading Prompts To encourage application of the given reading strategy, there are occasional prompts, within green boxes, at appropriate and significant points.

In addition, there are red boxes prompting application of the Literary Focus concept and maroon boxes prompting students to connect with their lives.

Using the Boxed Annotations and Prompts The material in the green, red, and maroon boxes along the sides of selections is intended to help students apply the literary element and the reading strategy and to make a connection with their lives.

You may use the boxed material in these ways:

- Have students pause when they come to a box and respond to its prompt before they continue reading.
- Urge students to read through the selection, ignoring the boxes. After they have read the selection completely, they may go back and review the selection, responding to the prompts.

MODEL

from

In Memoriam, A. H. H.

Alfred, Lord Tennyson

The Stages of Life, Caspar David Friedrich, Museum der Bildenden Kunst, Leipzig

▲ Critical Viewing In what ways does this painting reflect ideas expressed in Tennyson's poem? **[Evaluate]** 

1

I held it truth, with him who sings
  To one clear harp in divers[1] tones,
  That men may rise on stepping stones
Of their dead selves to higher things.

1. **divers** (dī′ vərz) *adj.*: Varied; having many parts.

Develop Understanding

One-Minute Insight

"In Memoriam, A.H.H.," an elegy, or poem that mourns the death of an individual, was written as a tribute to Tennyson's closest friend, Arthur Henry Hallam, who died at the age of twenty-two. It took Tennyson seventeen years to complete "In Memoriam," which, in its entirety, consists of 133 separate sections. It is a diary in poetry of Tennyson's emotional journey as he struggled to overcome despair, doubt, and anger over his friend's death.

◆ Reading for Success

❶ **Recognize Author's Purpose or Bias** Ask students what they think these lines reveal about the poet's reason for writing. *Sample answer: He wants to express his thoughts (bias) that once he had faith in God ("him who sings") and immortality ("men may rise . . . to higher things"), but now he has doubts.*

▶Critical Viewing◀

❷ **Evaluate** Suggested response: The people onshore watching the ships at sea may symbolize the idea that friends move away, passing out of life into death. The three ages represented—youth, maturity, and old age—emphasize the fact that Tennyson's young friend never lived to experience old age.

Block Scheduling Strategies

Consider these suggestions to take advantage of extended class time:

- Encourage students to discuss in groups what they know about the Arthurian legends of "The Lady of Shalott" and Ulysses' journeys, treated in "Ulysses," as introduced in Background for Understanding on page 748.
- Students may work in groups to complete the Critical Thinking questions on pages 753, 758, and 763.
- Students may work with musically talented classmates to compose and record music for the songs they write for the Writing section of the Idea Bank on page 765.
- Students may enjoy working with partners to complete the Writing Mini-Lesson on page 765. Before they start, have pairs discuss whom they would praise in their tribute and why.
- Have students work in groups to complete the Reading for Success questions on page 764 and the Reading for Success pages in ***Selection Support,*** pp. 183–184.

Comprehension Check ☑

❶ Be sure students understand the meaning of these lines. *The poet believes in joining love and grief in order to avoid melancholy, or depression ("darkness"). It is better to give oneself up to grief ("dance with death") than to be scorned for having nothing left ("all he was is overworn").*

◆ Reading for Success

❷ **Evaluate the Writer's Points or Statements** Point out the poet's assertion that it is "sweeter to . . . dance with death." What leads the poet to be able to make this statement? *Suggested response: The poet has had a recent "dance" with death when his friend died, and as a result he feels he must express his grief to the fullest ("sweeter to be drunk with loss").*

◆ Reading for Success

❸ **Make Inferences** Ask students what the word *chrysalis* implies about Hallam. *Sample answer: The word refers to a butterfly's cocoon; it implies that Hallam did not have a chance to mature before he died.*

◆ Critical Thinking

❹ **Analyze** Ask students what emotion the poet expresses in this stanza. *The poet is angry and wants revenge on Death.*

But who shall so forecast the years
And find in loss a gain to match?
Or reach a hand through time to catch
The far-off interest of tears?

Let Love clasp Grief lest both be drowned,
Let darkness keep her raven gloss.
Ah, sweeter to be drunk with loss,
❶ To dance with death, to beat the ground,

❷ Than that the victor Hours should scorn
The long result of love, and boast,
"Behold the man that loved and lost,
But all he was is overworn."

The poet clearly establishes that his **purpose** in writing is to express grief.

7

Dark house, by which once more I stand
Here in the long unlovely street,
Doors, where my heart was used to beat
So quickly, waiting for a hand,

A hand that can be clasped no more—
Behold me, for I cannot sleep,
And like a guilty thing I creep
At earliest morning to the door.

He is not here; but far away
The noise of life begins again,
And ghastly through the drizzling rain
On the bald street breaks the blank day.

From what you've read so far, you can **infer** that this is the house where the speaker's friend had lived.

82

I wage not any feud with Death
For changes wrought on form and face;
No lower life that earth's embrace
May breed with him, can fright my faith.

Eternal process moving on,
From state to state the spirit walks;
❸ And these are but the shattered stalks,
Or ruined chrysalis of one.

Nor blame I Death, because he bare
The use of virtue out of earth;
I know transplanted human worth
Will bloom to profit, otherwhere.

For this alone on Death I wreak
The wrath that garners in my heart;
❹ He put our lives so far apart
We cannot hear each other speak.

This use of **emotive language**—words and phrases meant to excite the emotions—helps you to feel the depth of the speaker's grief.

Humanities: Art

The Stages of Life, 1835, by Caspar David Friedrich.

Friedrich (1774–1840) is considered the most important of the German Romantic painters. His landscapes are often haunting and lonely, juxtaposing humans and relentless nature.

The painting *The Stages of Life* (p. 751) shows Friedrich himself with his family. It was painted shortly after he suffered a stroke, and the central figure, the artist (with the cane), is staring out to sea. The large ship is Friedrich's ship of life, and approaching night (sunset) in the painting symbolizes the artist's death.

Use these questions to help move discussion along:

1. How does the artist use light and darkness to suggest the stages of life? *The day is ending, suggesting that as night is part of day, so death is part of life.*
2. Why are the people in darkness? *The artist might be suggesting a moral or spiritual darkness suffered by humans.*
3. How does the use of dark and light in the painting reflect the changes the poet goes through in "In Memoriam"? *The poet moves through despair into hope, just as the artist looks from a dark foreground into the light of the background.*

130

Thy voice is on the rolling air;
5 I hear thee where the waters run;
Thou standest in the rising sun,
And in the setting thou art fair.

What art thou then? I cannot guess;
But though I seem in star and flower
To feel thee some diffusive power,
I do not therefore love thee less.

My love involves the love before;
My love is vaster passion now;
6 Though mixed with God and Nature thou,
I seem to love thee more and more.

Far off thou art, but ever nigh;
I have thee still, and I rejoice;
7 I prosper, circled with thy voice;
I shall not lose thee though I die.

> To judge this poem, **question** whether this conclusion is powerful and convincing, and if so, why.

◆ Build Vocabulary

diffusive (di fyo͞o′siv) *adj.*: Spread out

Guide for Responding

◆ Literature and Your Life

Reader's Response Were you moved by Tennyson's lament for his friend? Why or why not?

Thematic Focus What does Tennyson reveal about his friendship by writing such a tribute?

☑ Check Your Comprehension

1. In Part 1, what truth does the speaker say he once held but now doubts?
2. Where is the speaker standing in Part 7?
3. In Part 82, what is the one reason the speaker gives for being angry with Death?
4. In Part 130, what does the speaker say has happened to his love for his friend?

◆ Critical Thinking

INTERPRET

1. (a) In what way is the poet's friend lost forever? (b) What part of his friend will live forever? **[Interpret]**
2. Explain the paradox in line 57: "Far off thou art, but ever nigh." **[Interpret]**
3. How does a comparison of the first two parts with the last two show that the poet's feelings have changed? **[Draw Conclusions]**

EVALUATE

4. How would you assess the speaker's adjustment to the death of his friend? **[Assess]**

APPLY

5. Judging from Tennyson's poem, what are the qualities of a good elegy? **[Define]**

◆ Critical Thinking

5 Interpret Ask students to explain why the poet sees his friend in nature. *Suggested response: Natural settings spark remembrances of him, and they also reflect the beauty that he felt his friend possessed.*

◆ Reading for Success

6 Distinguish Between Emotive and Neutral Language Have students determine whether the language in this stanza is neutral or emotive. Encourage them to give examples. *Suggested answer: The language is emotive; the poet uses words such as* passion, love, *and* God.

◆ Critical Thinking

7 Interpret Ask students what the poet is feeling in these lines, and why. *Suggested response: He is joyful because he realizes that he hasn't really lost his friend; the friend will be with him even beyond death.*

Reinforce and Extend

Answers

◆ Literature and Your Life

Reader's Response Sample responses: Yes, the poem's use of imagery was touching; no, the poem is too full of grand imagery to be genuinely affecting.

Thematic Focus The speaker reveals the profound depth of his feelings for his friend.

☑ Check Your Comprehension

1. The speaker had thought men could elevate themselves beyond emotions like grief. Later, he sees that grief must be embraced to appreciate the extent of a loss and the value of the departed.
2. The speaker stands by the house where his friend had lived.
3. The speaker is angry with Death for robbing him of his friend's conversation.
4. The speaker's love has grown, because his friend's memory is invoked all the time, by nature and the events of daily life.

◆ Critical Thinking

1. (a) The speaker will never know the pleasure of direct contact with his friend, like conversation or a friendly embrace. (b) The speaker's memories will keep his friend alive in his mind.
2. Although the friend is dead and his voice and physical presence are gone, the speaker feels close to his spirit at all times.
3. In the first parts, the speaker is tormented by unbearable grief; in the last two, his sense of loss is softened by awareness of the memories he carries with him.
4. There is a progression from agonizing grief and resentment to serene acceptance, and the speaker's sense that he is spiritually richer for fond recollections of his late friend.
5. A good elegy gives readers a sense of the speaker's feelings toward the person mourned, and an awareness of how the speaker views that person, both in life and in death.

Develop Understanding

One-Minute Insight "The Lady of Shalott" is a poem based in Arthurian legend, but it is also about the position of the creative artist in society. The central character, the Lady of Shalott, has lived under a curse barring her from looking at or experiencing the real world—under pain of death. The Lady is locked in her tower away from the vital movements of society, seeing life only through a mirror and rendering it unmoving on her tapestry. In the same way, Tennyson is suggesting that many artists are locked away from life, looking at it secondhand and not experiencing it for themselves.

◆ Reading for Success

❶ **Make Inferences** Ask students to determine what this description of her island implies about the Lady of Shalott. *Sample answer: Her castle is gray and silent, implying that she is isolated and that her life in some way lacks color.*

◆ Literary Focus

❷ **The Speaker in Poetry** Ask students why the speaker asks these questions. *He is pointing out that though life moves past her island, the Lady cannot see it firsthand, and she has not been seen by anybody.*

Enrichment

Arthurian Legends Explain to students that many writers have treated the legends of King Arthur and his knights of the Round Table. Tennyson himself wrote a long poem called *The Idylls of the King,* which is about Arthur's life and death. Sir Thomas Malory wrote a collection of prose romances, *Le Morte d'Arthur,* based on Arthurian legends, printed in 1485. Other well-known treatments include *Sir Gawain and the Green Knight,* a poem written in the fourteenth century, *A Connecticut Yankee in King Arthur's Court,* written by Mark Twain in 1889, and *The Once and Future King,* published in 1958 by T. H. White.

The Lady of Shalott

Alfred, Lord Tennyson

Part I

On either side the river lie
Long fields of barley and of rye,
That clothe the wold[1] and meet the sky;
And though the field the road runs by
To many-towered Camelot,[2]
And up and down the people go,
Gazing where the lilies blow[3]
Round an island there below,
The island of Shalott.

Willows whiten, aspens quiver,
Little breezes dusk and shiver
Through the wave that runs forever
By the island in the river
Flowing down to Camelot.
❶ Four gray walls, and four gray towers,
Overlook a space of flowers,
And the silent isle imbowers
The Lady of Shalott.

❷ By the margin, willow-veiled,
Slide the heavy barges trailed
By slow horses; and unhailed
The shallop[4] flitteth silken-sailed
Skimming down to Camelot:
But who hath seen her wave her hand?
Or at the casement seen her stand?
Or is she known in all the land,
The Lady of Shalott?

Only reapers, reaping early
In among the bearded barley,
Hear a song that echoes cheerly,
From the river winding clearly,
Down to towered Camelot:
And by the moon the reaper weary,
Piling sheaves in uplands airy,
Listening, whispers, " 'Tis the fairy
Lady of Shalott."

1. **wold:** Rolling plains.
2. **Camelot:** Legendary English town where King Arthur had his court and Round Table.
3. **blow:** Bloom.
4. **shallop:** Light, open boat.

◆ Build Vocabulary

churls (chʉrlz) *n.:* Farm laborers; peasants

Cross-Curricular Connection: Social Studies

Tennyson and Evolution Although Charles Darwin's great treatise on evolution, *The Origin of Species,* was not published until 1859, after Tennyson published "In Memoriam," the idea of evolution was in the air for decades before. A geologist named Charles Lyell put forth a theory stating that changes in the surface of the earth are caused by processes still in operation, an idea that Darwin built upon.

Tennyson was familiar with Lyell's writings, and was probably also aware of the work of Jean Baptiste Lamarck, a naturalist who proposed a theory of evolution in the early 1800's. Lamarck suggested that all life forms have arisen from a process of gradual change, a theory that Darwin also held. However, Lamarck's theory of acquired characteristics, which held that new traits develop as a result of environmental demands and are then transmitted to offspring, was later rejected.

These ideas about evolution clashed with the religious beliefs of the time, causing doubt and fear for many people. Discuss with students how this clash might have affected Tennyson and how it might show up in "In Memoriam."

The Lady of Shalott, John Waterhouse, The Tate Gallery, London

▲ **Critical Viewing** What symbols of the fate of the Lady of Shalott are in this painting? Explain why they are significant. **[Interpret]** ❺

Part II

There she weaves by night and day
A magic web with colors gay.
She has heard a whisper say,
A curse is on her if she stay
To look down to Camelot.
❸ She knows not what the curse may be,
And so she weaveth steadily,
And little other care hath she,
The Lady of Shalott.

And moving through a mirror[5] clear
That hangs before her all the year,
Shadows of the world appear.
There she sees the highway near
❹ Winding down to Camelot:
There the river eddy whirls,
And there the surly village churls,
And the red cloaks of market girls,
Pass onward from Shalott.

Sometimes a troop of damsels glad,
An abbot on an ambling pad,[6]
Sometimes a curly shepherd lad,

5. **mirror:** Weavers placed mirrors in front of their looms, so that they could view the progress of their work.

6. **pad:** Easy-paced horse.

◆ Background for Understanding

❸ Be sure students know that the Lady has been put under a curse that forbids her to look at the real world.

Comprehension Check ☑

❹ Why does the poet have the Lady look at life through a mirror? What is the effect on her? *Suggested response: She avoids the curse by looking at life in this way. As a result, life to her is static and unreal. It removes her from the vigor and vitality of the highway, river, and village that she gazes upon.*

▶Critical Viewing◀

❺ **Interpret** The chain in the Lady's hand may represent her bondage to fate; the flickering candle suggests the flickering flame of her life.

Humanities: Art

The Lady of Shalott by John Waterhouse.

John William Waterhouse (1849–1917) studied and exhibited at the Royal Academy in London. He is considered to be both a Classical and a pre-Raphaelite painter of mainly romantic and poetic subjects. Much of his work was inspired by the poetry of Tennyson and Keats.

This painting, beautifully detailed and executed, was done in iridescent colors that lend a supernatural feel to it. Note the Lady's grief-stricken expression, which registers her resignation to her fate.

Some additional points for class discussion include the following.

1. How true to the details of the poem do you feel the artist kept? *Sample answer: Details are very true to the poem: The Lady in the painting is dressed in white, afloat on a boat that resembles the boat in the poem. She appears beautiful, mysterious, and very much alone.*
2. In what way does the mood of the painting effectively mirror that of the poem? *Suggested response: The painting is dark and sadly romantic, as is the poem's overall mood.*

◆ Build Vocabulary

❶ Related Words: Medieval Words Ask students what the word "page" meant in medieval times. *A page was a young man who attended a noble or who was being trained for knighthood.*

❷ Clarification Horses that drew a hearse at a funeral wore long black plumes.

◆ Literary Focus

❸ The Speaker in Poetry Ask students why they think the poet chose to have the Lady speak at this point in the poem. *Sample answer: She is beginning to awaken to her isolation; her response to seeing the lovers makes clear her longing for love. The previous lines describe the images in which she is absorbed; the poem breaks into direct speech at the point where she breaks away from the mirror.*

◆ Background for Understanding

❹ In Arthurian legend, Lancelot, or Launcelot, was the most famous of the knights of the Round Table. He was first introduced in a French romance by the 12th century writer Chrétien de Troyes. Lancelot joins the Round Table later in the story, and as in Tennyson's poem, his arrival on the scene creates disorder. He is noble and virtuous, and so very attractive. Many legends blame the dissolution of the Round Table of Lancelot's love for Arthur's queen, Guinevere.

◆ Critical Thinking

❺ Make Judgments Ask students how the Lady must feel about Sir Lancelot. What does he represent to her? *Suggested response: She sees Lancelot as the embodiment of knightly beauty, bravery, and chivalry. He represents the life and the love she has missed by staying in her tower.*

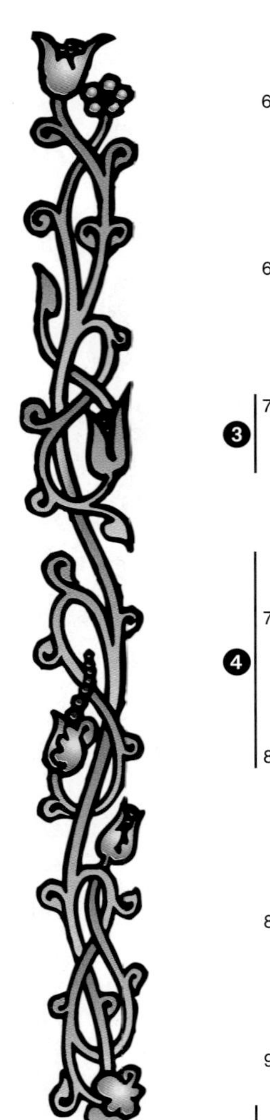

❶ Or long-haired page in crimson clad,
   Goes by to towered Camelot;
And sometimes through the mirror blue
The knights come riding two and two:
She hath no loyal knight and true,
   The Lady of Shalott.

But in her web she still delights
To weave the mirror's magic sights,
For often through the silent nights
❷ A funeral, with plumes and lights
   And music, went to Camelot:
Or when the moon was overhead,
Came two young lovers lately wed;
❸ "I am half sick of shadows," said
   The Lady of Shalott.

Part III

A bow-shot from her bower eaves,
He rode between the barley sheaves,
The sun came dazzling through the leaves,
And flamed upon the brazen greaves[7]
❹   Of bold Sir Lancelot.
A red-cross knight[8] forever kneeled
To a lady in his shield,
That sparkled on the yellow field,
   Beside remote Shalott.

The gemmy[9] bridle glittered free,
Like to some branch of stars we see
Hung in the golden Galaxy.[10]
The bridle bells rang merrily
   As he rode down to Camelot:
And from his blazoned baldric[11] slung
A mighty silver bugle hung,
And as he rode his armor rung,
   Beside remote Shalott.

All in the blue unclouded weather
Thick-jeweled shone the saddle leather,
The helmet and the helmet feather
Burned like one burning flame together,
   As he rode down to Camelot.
As often through the purple night,
Below the starry clusters bright,
❺ Some bearded meteor, trailing light,
   Moves over still Shalott.

His broad clear brow in sunlight glowed;
On burnish'd hooves his war horse trode;
From underneath his helmet flowed
His coal-black curls as on he rode,

7. **greaves:** Armor that protects the legs below the kneecaps.
8. **red-cross knight:** Refers to the Redcrosse Knight from *The Faerie Queene* by Edmund Spenser. In Spenser's work, the knight represents St. George, the patron saint of England, in addition to being a symbol of holiness.
9. **gemmy:** Jeweled.
10. **Galaxy:** The Milky Way.
11. **blazoned baldric:** Decorated sash worn diagonally across the chest.

As he rode down to Camelot.
From the bank and from the river
He flashed into the crystal mirror,
"Tirra lirra," by the river
Sang Sir Lancelot.

She left the web, she left the loom,
6 She made three paces through the room,
She saw the waterlily bloom,
She saw the helmet and the plume,
She looked down to Camelot.
Out flew the web and floated wide;
The mirror cracked from side to side;
7 "The curse is come upon me," cried
The Lady of Shalott.

Part IV

In the stormy east wind straining,
The pale yellow woods were waning,
The broad stream in his banks complaining,
Heavily the low sky raining
Over towered Camelot;
Down she came and found a boat
Beneath a willow left afloat,
And round about the prow she wrote
The Lady of Shalott.

And down the river's dim expanse
Like some bold seër in a trance,
8 Seeing all his own mischance—
With a glassy countenance
Did she look to Camelot.
And at the closing of the day
She loosed the chain, and down she lay;
The broad stream bore her far away,
The Lady of Shalott.

Lying, robed in snowy white
That loosely flew to left and right—
The leaves upon her falling light—
Through the noises of the night
She floated down to Camelot:
And as the boathead wound along
The willowy hills and fields among,
They heard her singing her last song,
The Lady of Shalott.

Heard a carol, mournful, holy,
Chanted loudly, chanted lowly,
Till her blood was frozen slowly,
And her eyes were darkened wholly,

◆ Build Vocabulary

waning (wān′ iŋ) *v.*: Gradually becoming dimmer

Customize for More Advanced Students

This poem is written in rhyme and meter in stanzas of nine lines. The end-words rhyme in the following pattern: *a a a a b c c c b*. The meter is generally trochaic tetrameter (four feet)—except for the last line in each stanza which is iambic trimeter (three feet). Explain that "qués tiŏn" is a trochaic word with the stressed syllable coming first, followed by an unstressed one. (The word "tŏ dáy" is iambic.) Write these lines on the board to show students how the stresses and feet work for trochaic trimeter:

Foúr grăy / wálls ănd / foúr grăy / tówĕrs,/
Óvĕr / lóok ă / spáce ŏf / flówĕrs./

This stanza scheme is a variation on a medieval stanza called the *tail-rhyme stanza* because of the short line (or tail), at the end of the stanza.

◆ Grammar and Style

6 Parallel Structure Have students determine the effect of the parallel structure of the lines in this stanza. *Sample answer: The lines all start with "she" and a verb, indicating that the Lady is beginning to move against the constraints of her life within her room.*

◆ Reading for Success

7 Make Inferences Ask students what the cracking of the mirror represents. *Suggested response: It represents the ending of the Lady's old way of life and the beginning of the "curse"—her ability to see and experience life and the passage of time.*

◆ Critical Thinking

8 Interpret Ask students what the river represents for the Lady. *Sample answer: The river represents the movement of life, and by floating upon it she has become "alive."*

Speaking and Listening Mini-Lesson

Camelot Late-Night News

This mini-lesson supports the Speaking and Listening activity in the Idea Bank on page 765.

Introduce the Concept Discuss with students what kind of information is given in news spots on the nightly news. Have them decide what information they, as newscasters, would like to give to their viewers.

Develop Information Encourage students to work in groups. One student can act as the reporter, and with the group can plan questions to ask Lancelot, King Arthur, and the citizens of Camelot. One student in each group can take the role of each interview subject.

Apply the Information Groups can present their news story to the class, including on-the-spot interviews. Encourage the reporter to answer the news questions *who, what, where, when,* and *why.*

Assess the Outcome Have the class assess each news report, judging the accuracy and thoroughness of the information given and the believability of the interviews.

◆ Reading for Success

❶ **Make Inferences** Why does the Lady of Shalott have to die when she moves out of her tower? *Sample answer: She has defied fate by ignoring the curse.*

◆ Reading for Success

❷ **Judge the Writer's Work** Have students use what they have learned about "The Lady of Shalott" to evaluate the poem. Encourage them to offer reasons for their opinions. *Sample answer: The poem was moving and evocative. Tennyson's description of the Lady as isolated and alone, her sudden awakening to life, and her subsequent death create a tragic vision of the transience, or fleeting quality, of human life.*

Reinforce and Extend

Answers

◆ *Literature and Your Life*

Reader's Response Sample responses: She was wise to attempt an escape from the tower, because she had no real "life" there; she was unwise, because she knew that she'd die if she left the tower.

Thematic Focus Students might say this is the price the artist pays—sacrificing life for the sake of art.

☑ Check Your Comprehension

1. The Lady spends her time weaving, avoiding the real world.
2. The lady glimpses "shadows of the world"—reflections—in a mirror.
3. She abandons her weaving, and sees Lancelot directly.
4. Drawn by her fascination, she sails to Camelot, but the power of the emotions she had never felt before is so strong that she dies.

◆ Critical Thinking

1. Sample response: The curse is the power of experiencing life fully.
2. Although she can safely view life through the mirror of art, the pull of real experience makes the pale copy of art pall by comparison.
3. (a) The author wants to provide a vivid image of Lancelot as he would have appeared to the Lady at first sight. (b) The Lady's sheltered existence is suddenly shattered by the force of her feelings for Lancelot.
4. Students might speculate about a romance between Lancelot and the Lady of Shalott.

Turned to towered Camelot.
For ere she reached upon the tide
The first house by the waterside,
❶ Singing in her song she died,
The Lady of Shalott.

Under tower and balcony,
By garden wall and gallery,
A gleaming shape she floated by,
Dead-pale between the houses high,
Silent into Camelot.
Out upon the wharfs they came,
Knight and burgher, lord and dame,
And round the prow they read her name,
The Lady of Shalott.

Who is this? and what is here?
And in the lighted palace near
Died the sound of royal cheer;
And they crossed themselves for fear,
❷ All the knights at Camelot:
But Lancelot mused a little space;
He said, "She has a lovely face;
God in his mercy lend her grace,
The Lady of Shalott."

Guide for Responding

◆ *Literature and Your Life*

Reader's Response Do you think the Lady was wise or unwise in deciding to sail for Camelot? Explain.

Thematic Focus Why do you think the Lady of Shallot has decided to live on an island, cut off from all relationships?

Letter As the Lady, write a letter to Lancelot explaining why you plan to come to Camelot.

☑ Check Your Comprehension

1. What does the Lady spend all her time doing, and why?
2. Where does the Lady glimpse "shadows of the world"?
3. What does the Lady do after seeing Sir Lancelot in the mirror?
4. What happens to her as a result of the action she takes?

◆ Critical Thinking

INTERPRET

1. In line 42 the speaker says the Lady "knows not what the curse may be." Explain the curse in your own words. **[Infer]**
2. Critics have seen this poem as a commentary on the plight of the artist. Keeping this interpretation in mind, what do you think is meant by the Lady's complaint in lines 71–72? **[Interpret]**
3. (a) Why do you think the author devotes so much space to his description of Sir Lancelot? (b) How does this description relate to the Lady's action and to the overall meaning of the poem? **[Draw Conclusions]**

APPLY

4. What do you think might have happened if the Lady had actually met Sir Lancelot? Why? **[Apply]**

Ulysses

Alfred, Lord Tennyson

In this poem Tennyson extends the story of Ulysses (yoo lis′ ēz), *the hero of the* Odyssey, *beyond the narrative in Homer's epic. Here we learn that he has grown restless in the years since returning to his home in Ithaca. Although he had been away for twenty long years—ten fighting in the Trojan War and another ten making the long and adventure-filled voyage back—Ulysses finds that he is contemplating making another, final journey.*

It little profits that an idle king,
By this still hearth, among these barren crags,
❸ Matched with an aged wife, I mete and dole[1]
Unequal[2] laws unto a savage race,
That hoard, and sleep, and feed, and know not me.
❹ I cannot rest from travel; I will drink
Life to the lees.[3] All times I have enjoyed
Greatly, have suffered greatly, both with those
That loved me, and alone; on shore, and when
Through scudding drifts the rainy Hyades[4]
Vexed the dim sea. I am become a name;
For always roaming with a hungry heart
Much have I seen and known—cities of men
And manners, climates, councils, governments,
❺ Myself not least, but honored of them all—
And drunk delight of battle with my peers,
Far on the ringing plains of windy Troy.
I am a part of all that I have met;
Yet all experience is an arch wherethrough

1. **mete and dole:** Measure and give out.
2. **unequal:** Unfair.
3. **lees:** Sediment.
4. **Hyades** (hī′ ə dēz′): Group of stars whose rising was assumed to be followed by rain.

Develop Understanding

One-Minute Insight "Ulysses" is based on the story of the Greek king who fought at Troy for one decade and then wandered the seas for another. The poem takes place after Ulysses' return home to Ithaca, as he is facing old age. It raises a central question about the speaker, Ulysses himself: Did Tennyson intend him to be a heroic figure, eternally questing and fighting death, or is the poet's portrayal ironic—is Ulysses a selfish, self-justifying character who longs to cast off boredom and indulge himself by fleeing a clinging wife and unpleasant kingship?

◆ Reading for Success

❸ **Make Inferences** Ask students what they can infer about Ulysses' feelings about his life from the first five lines. *Sample answer: He is unhappy with his idleness, his position, and his subjects.*

◆ Literary Focus

❹ **The Speaker in Poetry** Have students determine who the speaker is in this poem. *It is Ulysses, himself.* Then invite students to discuss what Ulysses' desire to "drink life to the lees" reveals about his character. *Sample answer: He is discontented with inaction and longs for the most extreme experiences; he likes to "live on the edge."*

◆ Reading for Success

❺ **Make Inferences** Ask students what they can infer about Ulysses' feelings about his previous adventures. *Suggested response: He is proud of his travels to faraway places where he was honored for his actions in the Trojan War.*

Enrichment

Ulysses in Dante's *Inferno* Explain to students that in Dante's epic poem *The Inferno,* Dante as the speaker journeys through the various levels of Hell, viewing the torments of figures from history and literature. In the eighth *bolgia,* or ditch, of the eighth circle of Hell, Dante finds the Evil Counselors, those who abused the gifts of God for their own purposes. There he hears Ulysses speak, describing his final voyage and death. After traveling past Morocco and Spain, Ulysses urged his men to sail southwest through the Straits of Gibraltar, considered by the Greeks to be the western limit of the world. They sighted a high peak, which Dante intends to be the Mountain of Purgatory. As they cheered at the sight, the boat was struck by a squall, which sunk the vessel and drowned all aboard.

▶Critical Viewing◀

❶ **Compare and Contrast** In the portrait, Ulysses looks both noble and tragic. He is longing for home, while in the poem he longs for adventure. He looks every inch a king with his crown and scepter.

◆ Reading for Success

❷ **Make Inferences** Ask students why Ulysses feels discontented with his life. *Sample answer: He feels it is dull, that he has become useless, and that he no longer "shines"—that is, he can no longer achieve fame as an adventurer.*

Ulysses Mourning for Home, Staatliche Museen zu Berlin

❶ ▲ **Critical Viewing** What qualities of Ulysses revealed in the poem are depicted in this rendering? **[Compare and Contrast]**

❷
Gleams that untraveled world, whose margin fades
Forever and forever when I move.
How dull it is to pause, to make an end,
To rust unburnished, not to shine in use!
As though to breathe were life. Life piled on life
Were all too little, and of one to me
Little remains; but every hour is saved
From that eternal silence, something more,
A bringer of new things; and vile it were
For some three suns to store and hoard myself,

Humanities: Art

Ulysses Mourning for Home, Carved Gem of Light Brown Sardonyx, Roman, 3rd to 2nd Century B.C.

This gem is a cameo carved in sardonyx, a semiprecious gemstone prized for its varicolored bands of light and dark stone. Ornamental cameos such as this made their appearance in Roman jewelry craft about the third century B.C. They were used as personal ornaments, set in gold rings, brooches, and pendants, and worn by both Roman men and women.

Emperors, gods, and heroes were the subjects for this cameo art. In this gem, Ulysses in a dejected pose gazes at the empty sea.

You might ask students these questions.

1. What feelings or moods are suggested by the face and attitude of Ulysses in the gem? *He is despondent and lonely. His far-off gaze reveals his longing for home.*
2. Might the Ulysses of the poem have felt this way earlier in his life, when he was traveling the seas? *Sample answers: Yes, he is portrayed as a dissatisfied man, always longing for that which he cannot have; no, Ulysses reveled in his youth, enjoying his adventures.*

And this gray spirit yearning in desire
❸ To follow knowledge like a sinking star,
Beyond the utmost bound of human thought.
  This is my son, mine own Telemachus,
To whom I leave the scepter and the isle[5]
Well-loved of me, discerning to fulfill
This labor, by slow prudence to make mild
A rugged people, and through soft degrees
Subdue them to the useful and the good.
Most blameless is he, centered in the sphere
Of common duties, decent not to fail
In offices of tenderness, and pay
Meet[6] adoration to my household gods,
When I am gone. He works his work, I mine.
  There lies the port; the vessel puffs her sail;
There gloom the dark broad seas. My mariners,
Souls that have toiled and wrought, and thought with
  me—
That ever with a frolic welcome took
The thunder and the sunshine, and opposed
Free hearts, free foreheads—you and I are old;
Old age hath yet his honor and his toil;
❹ Death closes all; but something ere the end,
Some work of noble note, may yet be done,
Not unbecoming men that strove with Gods.
The lights begin to twinkle from the rocks;
The long day wanes; the slow moon climbs; the deep
Moans round with many voices. Come, my friends,
'Tis not too late to seek a newer world.
Push off, and sitting well in order smite
The sounding furrows; for my purpose holds
To sail beyond the sunset, and the baths
Of all the western stars, until I die.
It may be that the gulfs will wash us down;
It may be we shall touch the Happy Isles,[7]
And see the great Achilles,[8] whom we knew.
Though much is taken, much abides; and though
We are not now that strength which in old days
❺ Moved earth and heaven, that which we are, we are—
One equal temper of heroic hearts,
❻ Made weak by time and fate, but strong in will
To strive, to seek, to find, and not to yield.

5. **isle:** Ithaca, an island off the coast of Greece.

6. **meet:** Appropriate.

7. **Happy Isles:** Elysium, or the Islands of the Blessed: in classical mythology, the place heroes went after death.

8. **Achilles** (ə kil′ ēz′): Greek hero of the Trojan War.

◆ Build Vocabulary

furrows (fur′ ōz) *n.*: Narrow grooves made in the ground by a plow

◆ Reading for Success

❸ **Make Inferences** Have students determine what it is Ulysses longs for. *Sample answer: He longs to learn more about life by journeying to unknown places.*

◆ Critical Thinking

❹ **Analyze** Ask students why Ulysses is not satisfied with the prospect of aging in Ithaca. *Suggested response: He "strove with Gods" and feels that he still has noble work to do before he faces death.*

◆ Reading for Success

❺ **Evaluate the Writer's Points or Statements** Ask students if they think that Ulysses' longing to journey on is heroic or if he is merely justifying his own desire to desert his responsibilities. *Sample answer: Though he may be self-deceiving, his desire to "strive . . . and not to yield" to his fate and his death are heroic in nature.*

◆ Grammar and Style

❻ **Parallel Structure** Note the parallel structure in the last line of the poem. Ask students what grammatical structure is repeated and why. *There are four infinitives in this line. They underscore Ulysses' restlessness for adventure and his desire to fight old age and death.*

Beyond the Classroom

Career Connection

Life on the Sea Point out to students that Ulysses is first and foremost a sailor and explorer. Discuss with them modern career opportunities that are linked with the sea. Students may mention the navy, the merchant marines, oceanography, careers involving cruise ships, and fishing. Interested students can look into one of these careers and find out what background and skills are required and what seafarers do in their work. Discuss with them whether Ulysses, as he is portrayed in the poem, would be suited for any present-day seafaring careers.

"Tears, Idle Tears" treats a theme common in Tennyson's works: the transience, or fleeting quality, of life and the nearness of death. Tennyson said about this poem: "This song came to me on the yellowing autumn-tide at Tintern Abbey, full for me of its bygone memories. It is the sense of abiding in the transient." The poem focuses on regret for that which passes and cannot truly be possessed—love and the happy times of the past.

Customize for
Musical/Rhythmic Students
Students who respond well to music might enjoy hearing one of the renditions of this poem as it was set to music. If you can find a recording of the song, play it for the students.

▶Critical Viewing◀

1 Apply The muted, yet vibrant colors suggest passionate emotions dulled by time.

◆Reading for Success

2 Consider the Historical and Biographical Context Ask students what event in Tennyson's life he might have been thinking of when he wrote these lines. *Suggested response: He might have been considering the death of Arthur Hallam, his close friend who died as a young man, when speaking of "the days that are no more."*

◆Grammar and Style

3 Parallel Structure Have students determine how the poet uses parallel structure in this stanza to draw a comparison. *The sentences that begin "Fresh as the first beam" and "Sad as the last" are in parallel structure (as is line 30 "Dear as remembered kisses . . . ."). All start with adjectives that begin a comparison. The comparisons describe the memory of times past, reinforcing the idea of "death in life."*

◆Reading for Success

4 Judge the Writer's Work Ask students if they believe Tennyson to be a pessimist. Have them support their opinions. *Though he mourns the passing of time, love, and friendship, he still values those things, calling them "dear" and "sweet." He is filled with regret, not pessimism.*

Beach at Heist (Belgium), 1892, Georges Lemmen, Musée d'Orsay, Paris, France

▲ **Critical Viewing** How does this painting evoke the feelings of sadness and longing for the past that "Tears, Idle Tears" expresses? **[Apply]** 1

from
The Princess
Alfred, Lord Tennyson

The Princess *(1847) is a long narrative poem that contains a number of songs. Some of these songs, including the one that follows, are considered to be among the finest of Tennyson's lyrics.*

Tears, Idle Tears

Tears, idle tears, I know not what they mean,
Tears from the depth of some divine despair
Rise in the heart, and gather to the eyes,
In looking on the happy autumn fields,
And thinking of the days that are no more. 2

762 ◆ Progress and Decline (1833–1901)

Humanities: Art

Beach at Heist, 1892, by Georges Lemmen.

Georges Lemmen (1865–1916) was a Belgian painter whose early works featured portraits rendered in the pointillist style—innumerable tiny dots that together create a picture. Much of his art focuses on the effects of industry and the plight of the working class in society.

A neo-Impressionist, Lemmen appropriated the styles of French Impressionists, whose paintings were intended to create an impression of a scene rather than a literal rendering.

Use these questions for discussion:

1. How does the pointillist technique in the painting work to create an impression of the scene? *The dots blend together, blurring lines of distinction and creating a hazy, somewhat unfocused impression of sea, sand, and sky.*
2. In what way do the lone boat and lowering clouds at sunset reflect the theme of "Tears, Idle Tears"? *The boat evokes a feeling of loneliness, and the dying day reflects the death in life of which Tennyson speaks.*

Fresh as the first beam glittering on a sail,
That brings our friends up from the underworld,
Sad as the last which reddens over one
That sinks with all we love below the verge;
So sad, so fresh, the days that are no more. ❸

Ah, sad and strange as in dark summer dawns
The earliest pipe of half-awakened birds
To dying ears, when unto dying eyes
The casement slowly grows a glimmering square;
So sad, so strange, the days that are no more.

Dear as remembered kisses after death,
And sweet as those by hopeless fancy feigned
On lips that are for others; deep as love,
Deep as first love, and wild with all regret;
O Death in Life, the days that are no more. ❹

Guide for Responding

◆ Literature and Your Life

Reader's Response Which of these poems seems more hopeful to you? Why?

Thematic Focus Compare and contrast Ulysses' relationship to the past with that of the speaker in "Tears, Idle Tears."

Group Discussion In a small group, discuss how these poems might have been different if the speaker of "Ulysses" had been the speaker of "Tears, Idle Tears" and vice versa.

☑ Check Your Comprehension

1. (a) How does Ulysses describe his current situation? (b) What past experiences does he mention?
2. What work is Ulysses leaving to his son?
3. According to lines 58–61, what is Ulysses' purpose?
4. According to the first stanza of "Tears, Idle Tears," what causes the tears to rise?
5. What three comparisons in "Tears, Idle Tears" describe "the days that are no more"?

◆ Critical Thinking

INTERPRET

1. How does Ulysses' current situation contrast with his previous experiences? **[Compare and Contrast]**
2. (a) What is Ulysses' attitude toward his experiences and accomplishments? (b) What are his feelings about aging? (c) What is his attitude toward life in general? **[Draw Conclusions]**
3. (a) What is the refrain—repeated line or phrase—in "Tears, Idle Tears"? (b) What feeling do you think Tennyson wanted it to evoke in readers? **[Interpret]**

APPLY

4. In what way is the nostalgia expressed in "Tears, Idle Tears" a bittersweet emotion? **[Synthesize]**

EXTEND

5. In Dante's *Inferno*, Ulysses explains how he and his crew drowned soon after setting forth. Does knowing that the voyage will end in disaster lead you to question Ulysses' judgment? Why or why not? **[Literature Link]**

Beyond the Selection

FURTHER READING

Other Works by Alfred, Lord Tennyson

The Idylls of the King
"The Charge of the Light Brigade"
"Crossing the Bar"

Other Works About The Hero's Journey

The Odyssey, Homer
Beowulf
Sir Gawain and the Green Knight

We suggest that you preview these works before recommending them to students.

INTERNET

For more information about Tennyson, we suggest the following site: **http://www.stg.brown.edu/projects/...w/victorian/tennyson/tennybio.html**

Please be aware, however, that sites may have changed since this information was published. We *strongly recommend* that you preview sites before you send students to them.

Reinforce and Extend

Answers

◆ Literature and Your Life

Reader's Response Most students will feel the upbeat conclusion of "Ulysses" makes it more optimistic than the other poems.

Thematic Focus Students should note that Ulysses' memory of the past is of glory, whereas in "Tears, Idle Tears" the speaker's memory is of sad times.

☑ Check Your Comprehension

1. (a) Ulysses leads a dull life without adventure or risk. (b) He mentions his many voyages and adventures.
2. Ulysses expects Telemachus to civilize his subjects.
3. Ulysses' aim is to continue seeking challenges until he dies.
4. The tears come from despair, caused by looking back at happy times that are gone forever.
5. The days are (1) fresh as the first gleam of sunrise and sad as the last ray of sunset; (2) strange as the first peep of birds at sunrise heard by dying ears and sad as fading light seen through a window by dying eyes; and (3) deep as love and dear as kisses recalled after a loved one's death.

◆ Critical Thinking

1. Ulysses' situation offers no challenges or risks, unlike his adventure-filled life of the past.
2. (a) He has fond memories of past adventures and looks back with pride. (b) He sees aging as a process that robs him of his cherished way of life. (c) He sees life as empty unless it offers excitement or discoveries.
3. (a) The repeated refrain is "the days that are no more." (b) Tennyson wanted to evoke the sense of loss and nostalgia for past joys that cannot be brought back.
4. The poet uses contrasting adjectives to stress the bittersweet emotions of nostalgia: sad and fresh, sad and strange, dear and deep.
5. Sample responses: Yes, Ulysses should have used more common sense before risking his life and his crew's. No, his judgment was sound; the drownings could not have been avoided.

Answers

Strategies for Reading Critically

1. The language in these lines from "In Memoriam" is primarily emotive. Such words and phrases as "ghastly," "bald street," and "blank day" convey the speaker's feelings of melancholy and gloom.
2. The speaker in "In Memoriam" is expressing his belief in the immortality of the soul ("Eternal process moving on / From state to state"). The bodies left behind are "but the shattered stalks."
3. (a) Tennyson means this description in the emotional sense. He sees the beauty of his friend in the rising and setting of the sun. (b) Possible response: Yes, Tennyson probably reveals an emotional truth in the line.
4. Suggested response: The change in Tennyson's feeling over time from despair to joy reflects a true sense of personal grief. The transitory, or fleeting, quality of life and the hope of eternal life for the soul are timeless concerns.

◆ Build Vocabulary

Using Medieval Words

1. A *knight* is a mounted soldier from a noble family who is sworn to gallant, chivalrous acts.
2. *Reapers* (line 28) are people who cut barley stalks or other grain.
3. A *baldric* (line 87) is an ornamental belt worn diagonally across the chest.
4. A *plume* (lines 67 and 112) is a long, large ornamental feather which might be worn by a horse drawing a coffin or by a knight on his helmet.
5. A *burgher* (line 160) is a well-to-do member of the middle class.
6. *Mischance* (line 129) is bad luck.

Using the Word Bank

Long ridges—furrows
Farm laborers—churls
Spreading—diffusive
Growing dim—waning

Guide for Responding (continued)

◆ Reading for Success

Strategies for Reading Critically

The skill of critical reading is useful, whether you're reading poetry, legal documents, or science-fiction. Review the strategies for reading critically on page 750 and apply them to answer the following questions.

1. Are lines 25–28 of "In Memoriam" examples of emotive or neutral language? Explain.
2. Reread lines 33–36 of "In Memoriam." What can you infer from these lines about the speaker's beliefs? Explain.
3. Evaluate what Tennyson says in line 47 of the poem: "Thou standest in the rising sun." (a) Does he mean this statement in an objective or in an emotional sense? (b) Do you think it is true in the sense that he means it? Explain.
4. Do you think "In Memoriam" conveys Tennyson's personal grief and expresses timeless concerns? Why or why not?

◆ Build Vocabulary

Using Medieval Words

Words such as *churls* in Tennyson's "The Lady of Shalott" contribute to the poem's medieval atmosphere. Using the context of "The Lady of Shalott," define the following words.

1. knight **2.** reapers **3.** baldric **4.** plume **5.** burgher **6.** mischance

Using the Word Bank

In your notebook, write the Work Bank word that is closest in meaning to each underlined word or phrase.

From the old dirt road leading to the medieval village, the long ridges made by the plows were clearly visible. Off in the distance, you could hear the farm laborers on their long journey home after a hard day's work. The spreading scent of newly turned earth pervaded the air as the moon was growing dim.

◆ Literary Focus

The Speaker in Poetry

The **speakers** in these poems may be Tennyson himself or a character he creates. Even when he puts on the mask of a character, however, Tennyson may be expressing conflicts that relate to his own situation or experiences.

One speaker, the Lady of Shalott, must choose between a secret existence in which she weaves a "magic web" and the life of action that passes by her window. This poem could mirror Tennyson's own conflict about hiding from or facing life.

1. Tennyson wrote "In Memoriam" in direct response to Arthur Hallam's death. How does the speaker's conflict in this poem reflect one that Tennyson might have been feeling?
2. What is similar about the choices made by the speakers in "Ulysses" and "The Lady of Shalott"?

◆ Grammar and Style

Parallel Structure

Tennyson, whose verse is so musical, uses the equal grammatical forms of **parallel structure** to achieve balanced rhythms and memorable phrases. The forms he uses include, among others, single words, phrases beginning with infinitives (*to* + a verb), phrases beginning with prepositions like *from,* and clauses with subjects, verbs, and objects.

Practice On your paper, identify the examples of parallel structure in these passages from Tennyson's poems. Then tell whether they involve single words, infinitive phrases, prepositional phrases, or clauses.

1. "How dull it is to pause, to make an end, / To rest unburnished, not to shine in use!"
2. "My love involves the love before; / My love is vaster passion now . . ."
3. "One equal temper of heroic hearts, / Made weak by time and fate, but strong in will / To strive, to seek, to find, and not to yield."
4. "So sad, so fresh, the days that are no more."
5. "From the bank and from the river . . ."

Writing Application Write an additional stanza for any of Tennyson's poems. Use at least one example of parallel structure.

764 ◆ Progress and Decline (1833–1901)

◆ Literary Focus

1. The speaker's conflict in this poem mirrors the process of grieving that Tennyson experienced as a result of the death of Hallam.
2. Both speakers choose to experience life to the fullest even if the result is death.

◆ Grammar and Style

1. Infinitive phrases: "to pause, to make. . . . / To rest"
2. Clauses: "My love involves. . . . / My love is. . . ."
3. Infinitives: "To strive, to seek, to find, . . . to yield."
4. Adjective phrases: "So sad, so fresh"
5. Prepositional phrases: "From the bank . . . from the river"

Writer's Solution

For additional instruction and practice, use the lessons on Developing Mature Style and Strengthening Sentences in the **Language Lab CD-ROM,** and the page on Faulty Parallelism, p. 46, in the *Writer's Solution Grammar Practice Book.*

Build Your Portfolio

Idea Bank

Writing

1. Song "Tears, Idle Tears" meditates upon the past. Write a song expressing your ideas about the past. Include a strong refrain (a verse recurring at intervals).

2. Literary Analysis Write a literary analysis in which you draw conclusions about the speaker of "In Memoriam." Explain how the poem reveals the speaker's beliefs and disposition.

3. Critical Response Christopher Ricks says of the last line in "Ulysses": "Does not the last line poignantly convey a sense that 'Tis far too late to seek a newer world'?" Do you agree with this critic's reading of the line? Why or why not?

Speaking and Listening

4. Oral Interpretation Practice reading "Ulysses" aloud, varying your tone of voice to capture the discontent and final determination of the speaker. Then perform the poem for your class. **[Performing Arts Link]**

5. Camelot Late-Night News As the anchor for this news show, report on the discovery of the Lady of Shalott's body. In spot interviews, get reactions from Lancelot, King Arthur, and an ordinary citizen of Camelot. **[Media Link]**

Projects

6. Set Design Sketch a set for a play based on "The Lady of Shalott." Include her room, with the loom and mirror. **[Art Link; Performing Arts Link]**

7. Tennyson on Tape Tennyson may have been the first major English poet to be recorded. Ask a librarian to help you find that recording and play it for the class. Find material to explain how the recording was made. **[Media Link]**

Writing Mini-Lesson

Essay of Tribute

"In Memoriam" pays tribute to Arthur Hallam, who died too young. You can write your own tribute —an essay expressing praise and gratitude—for a living person who has contributed to your school this year. Write this essay as a piece to be included in your school's yearbook.

Writing Skills Focus: Clear Explanation of Cause and Effect

In a yearbook tribute, it's important to give clear **explanations of cause and effect**. For example, you might show step by step how the qualities or actions of your subject (causes) helped create a desirable outcome for the school (effect).

Prewriting To help you focus on your subject's accomplishments, fill in a cause-and-effect chart like this one:

Cause	Effect
1. poor math scores in middle school	After D. tutored five students, all scored in upper 85 percentile
2.	

Drafting In your draft, piece together the causes and effects that illustrate your subject's special qualities. Include transitional words that signal a relationship between thoses causes and effects, such as *therefore, because, as a result, consequently,* and *due to.*

Revising Read your tribute aloud to a friend and ask if it expresses gratitude or esteem. Also ask if your friend understands exactly what the subject did to earn this tribute. If not, clarify how the subject's actions led to his or her position of respect or esteem.

✓ ASSESSMENT OPTIONS

Formal Assessment Selection Test, pp. 186–188, and Assessment Resources Software. The selection test is designed so that it can be easily customized to the performance levels of your students.

Alternative Assessment, p. 38, includes options for less advanced students, more advanced students, visual/spatial learners, verbal/linguistic learners, and bodily/kinesthetic learners.

PORTFOLIO ASSESSMENT

Use the following rubrics in the ***Alternative Assessment*** booklet to assess student writing:
Song: Poetry Rubric, p. 109
Literary Analysis: Literary Analysis/Interpretation Rubric, p. 113
Critical Response: Response to Lit. Rubric, p. 111
Writing Mini-Lesson: Cause-Effect Rubric, p. 103

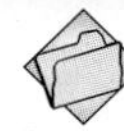

Idea Bank

Customizing for *Performance Levels*

Following are suggestions for matching Idea Bank topics with your students' performance levels:

Less Advanced Students: 1, 5, 7
Average Students: 2, 5, 6
More Advanced Students: 3, 4

Customizing for *Learning Modalities*

Following are suggestions for matching Idea Bank topics with your students' learning modalities:

Verbal/Linguistic: 1, 2, 3, 4, 5, 7
Interpersonal: 5
Visual/Spatial: 6

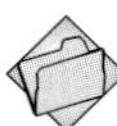

Writing Mini-Lesson

Refer students to the Writing Process Handbook, page 1189, for instruction on the writing process, and page 1191 for further information on exposition.

Writing and Language Transparencies Use the Cause–and–Effect Organizer, pp. 119–121, to help students plan their essays of tribute.

Writer's Solution

Writing Lab CD-ROM

Have students complete the tutorial on Exposition. Follow these steps:

1. Use the interactive instruction for narrowing a topic to solve problems when writing a problem-and-solution essay.
2. The Cluster Diagram can help identify areas in which to gather details.
3. Students should draft on the computer.
4. Use the Revision Checker for unity and coherence in revising.

Allow approximately 120 minutes of class time to complete these steps.

Sourcebook

Have students use Chapter 3, Exposition (pp. 62–95), for additional support. The chapter includes a model from literature of a Cause–and–Effect Essay (p. 67).

Prepare and Engage

OBJECTIVES

1. To read, comprehend, and interpret poems
2. To relate poems to personal experience
3. To make inferences about the speaker of a poem
4. To recognize elements of dramatic monologues
5. To build vocabulary in context and learn the suffix *-ence*
6. To use *like* and *as* correctly
7. To write a written recommendation, using cause-and-effect transitions
8. To respond to the poem through writing, speaking and listening, and projects

SKILLS INSTRUCTION

Vocabulary: Suffixes: *-ence*

Grammar: The Use of *Like* and *As*

Reading Strategy: Make Inferences About the Speaker

Literary Focus: Dramatic Monologue

Writing: Cause-and-Effect Transitions

Speaking and Listening: Oral Interpretation (teacher edition)

Critical Viewing: Infer; Support; Assess

PORTFOLIO OPPORTUNITIES

Writing: Profile; Messenger's Report; Response to Criticism

Writing Mini-Lesson: Written Recommendation

Speaking and Listening: Oral Interpretation; Fateful Meeting

Projects: The Brownings in the Media; The Brownings in Italy

More About the Authors

Robert Browning had a special fascination for the Renaissance and an extensive knowledge of Italian art, music, and history. Two of his best-known dramatic monologues are about Renaissance painters: Fra Lippo Lippi and Andrea del Sarto.

Elizabeth Barrett Browning's ill health resulted from an injury to her spine when she was only fifteen years old. Her condition worsened after the shock of losing one of her brothers in a drowning accident.

Guide for Interpreting

Robert Browning (1812–1889)

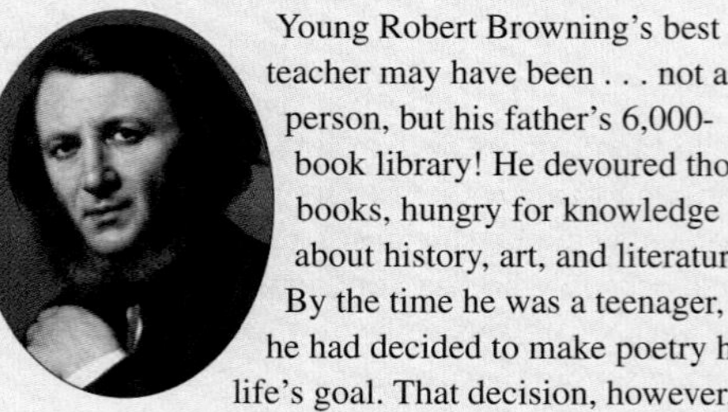

Young Robert Browning's best teacher may have been . . . not a person, but his father's 6,000-book library! He devoured those books, hungry for knowledge about history, art, and literature. By the time he was a teenager, he had decided to make poetry his life's goal. That decision, however, did not ensure immediate success. His first book, the long poem *Pauline*, modeled after Shelley's work, sold no copies!

Like *Pauline*, his other early volumes of poetry attracted little public notice, and his literary reputation was eclipsed by that of his wife, the poet Elizabeth Barrett Browning. However, the 1869 publication of *The Ring and the Book* marked a turning point in Browning's career. A long poem that tells the story of a murder in dramatic monologues (speeches by characters), *The Ring and the Book* achieved wide recognition for its author. It led readers to see how much Browning had given to nineteenth-century poetry: a more down-to-earth, less "poetic" language and the dramatic monologue itself, a form ideally suited to reveal character.

Today Browning ranks with Tennyson as one of the greatest Victorian poets. His shorter dramatic monologues, such as "My Last Duchess," remain favorites of many readers.

Elizabeth Barrett Browning (1806–1861)

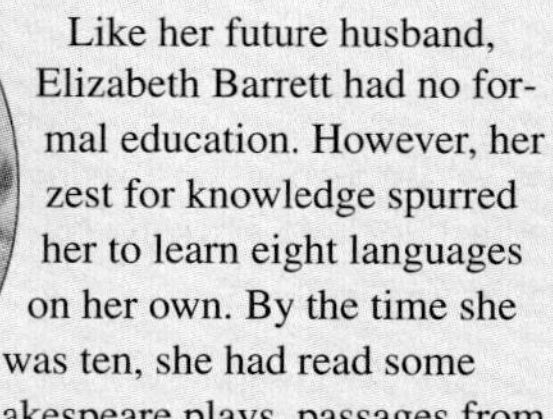

Like her future husband, Elizabeth Barrett had no formal education. However, her zest for knowledge spurred her to learn eight languages on her own. By the time she was ten, she had read some Shakespeare plays, passages from *Paradise Lost*, and the histories of England, Greece, and Rome. She began writing poetry as a child, and by the time she reached adulthood she had published four popular volumes of verse.

Elizabeth Barrett's frail health made her something of a recluse, yet she met and fell in love with Robert Browning. After a secret romance, she eloped with him to Florence, Italy, in 1846. They had a son, whom they nicknamed Pen, and the family lived in a happy Italian exile until Elizabeth Barrett's death in 1861.

It's hard for us to believe today, when Robert Browning's reputation is so high, that his wife was the better-known poet during her lifetime. Her love story in verse, *Aurora Leigh* (1857), was so popular that the income from it helped support the Brownings. Also popular was her *Sonnets from the Portuguese*, a sequence of forty-four love poems written to her husband. Sonnet 43, which comes from this collection, has appeared in countless anthologies.

◆ Background for Understanding

LITERATURE: THE BROWNING LEGEND

When Elizabeth Barrett met Robert Browning in 1845, she was a well-known poet of thirty-nine. However, she was extremely isolated due to her frail health and possessive father. She saw only family members and a few close friends.

One of those friends arranged for Elizabeth to meet Robert Browning, a great admirer of Barrett's poems. That meeting marks the beginning of one of the most famous courtships in literature. The two poets fell deeply in love, but Elizabeth's father disapproved, and they had to conduct a secret courtship, exchanging love letters every day. In September 1846, they were secretly wed.

A week after their marriage, they moved to Italy, where many of their poems are set. Mr. Barrett disinherited his daughter and never forgave her for having made the romantic match that has since become legendary.

Prentice Hall Literature Program Resources

REINFORCE / RETEACH / EXTEND

Selection Support Pages
Build Vocabulary: Suffixes: *-ence*, p. 186
Grammar and Style: The Use of *Like* and *As*, p. 187
Reading Strategy: Make Inferences About the Speaker, p. 188
Literary Focus: Dramatic Monologue, p. 189

Strategies for Diverse Student Needs, p. 39

Beyond Literature, p. 39

Formal Assessment Selection Test, pp. 189–191; Assessment Resources Software

Alternative Assessment, p. 39

Writing and Language Transparencies
Status Report, pp. 81–85

Resource Pro CD-ROM
Includes all resource material and customizable lesson plan for all selections

Listening to Literature Audiocassettes
"My Last Duchess"; "Life in a Love"; "Love Among the Ruins"; "Sonnet 43"

Looking at Literature Videodisc
Marriage Customs Around the World

My Last Duchess ◆ Love Among the Ruins
Life in a Love ◆ Sonnet 43

◆ Literature and Your Life

Connect Your Experience

How do people find true love? Maybe you think that finding the right person takes work and patience. Perhaps you believe that two people are meant for each other. Robert Browning and Elizabeth Barrett Browning felt that they had been destined to meet. They not only wrote about true love—in poems like "Love Among the Ruins," "Life in a Love," and Sonnet 43—but they lived it!

Thematic Focus: Relationships

What do the Brownings say or suggest about the importance of love between two people?

Journal Writing Jot down the title of your favorite poem, story, or movie dealing with romantic love. Then briefly explain why you like it so much.

◆ Literary Focus

Dramatic Monologue

Both Shakespeare and Chaucer gave us versions of the form we call the **dramatic monologue**, in which a single character delivers a speech. However, Browning perfected the form and made it his own. In his hands, and at its best, it contains these elements: a speaker who reveals his or her soul, knowingly or not; and a silent listener who interacts with the speaker.

"My Last Duchess," contains both these elements. Notice how Browning turns the page into a little stage, allowing the Duke to reveal his soul in apparently casual remarks to a silent listener.

◆ Reading Strategy

Make Inferences About the Speaker

You make **inferences**, educated guesses, about people who speak to you every day. Similarly, in a poem you can infer a speaker's thoughts or feelings from his or her words and actions. Often, as in life, words and actions carry a double message. They reveal something that the speaker doesn't even realize.

Look carefully behind the words of the speakers in these poems. What, for example, do the comments of the Duke in "My Last Duchess" reveal about his relationship with his first wife?

◆ Build Vocabulary

Suffixes: *-ence*

The suffix *-ence* means "quality, or state of being." When you add *-ence* to an adjective, you create a noun suggesting a state of being. The adjective *munificent* from "My Last Duchess," for example, means "very generous." By dropping the final *-ent* and adding *-ence*, you create the noun *munificence*, meaning "the state of being very generous."

Word Bank

Before you read, preview this list of words from the poems.

countenance
officious
munificence
dowry
eludes
vestige
sublime
minions

◆ Grammar and Style

The Use of *Like* and *As*

The Brownings frequently use the words *like* and *as* to make comparisons. These words, however, are not interchangeable. *Like*, meaning "similar to," is used to compare nouns or pronouns. It is the preposition in a prepositional phrase. *As*, a subordinating conjunction, is used to compare actions. It introduces a clause with a noun and verb.

Strangers *like* you . . .

I love thee freely, *as* men strive for Right.

Interest Grabber To motivate students to read the love poems in this section, have them brainstorm to list the qualities that they would look for in a loved one. Ask them as a class to rank the qualities. Then make a list of the five most important qualities and keep them to compare and contrast with the qualities they find in these poems.

Customize for
Less Proficient Readers

To help these students interact with these poems, model a reading of the long dramatic monologue "My Last Duchess," pausing often to paraphrase and clarify what is going on and what points the speaker is trying to make about his first wife. Each time you stop, ask students how their opinion of the speaker is changing as he reveals more about himself.

Customize for
More Advanced Students

These students may enjoy the project ideas on page 779, which involve reading biographies and viewing movies about the Brownings. They may also enjoy reading aloud or memorizing shorter poems by the famous couple.

Customize for
English Language Learners

These students will find Brownings' language difficult to follow. When reading "My Last Duchess," have them focus on lines 21–34, in which the speaker expresses his main difficulty with his first wife: She was too easily pleased by other people—especially men—and didn't seem to appreciate her husband's "gift" of his title.

Customize for
Intrapersonal Learners

Encourage these students to "read between the lines" of the dramatic monologues and make inferences about the speakers. As they read, encourage them to imagine that the speaker is talking directly to them and to look for clues as to what the speaker is really like as a person.

Preparing for Standardized Tests

Reading and Vocabulary Making inferences about speakers and other literary characters is a skill that is tested in the reading comprehension section of standardized tests. Students may apply the strategy by completing the Reading Strategy page in ***Selection Support***, p. 188.

Grammar and Language The grammar lesson for this section focuses on correct use of the words *like* and *as*. Students might encounter this usage issue on the Writing Skills section of standardized tests, in which they must identify sentence errors. For example, they might be asked to choose the best revision for the underlined part of a sentence:

She ran swiftly and gracefully, like a deer escapes from its enemies. *(C)*

(A) like a deer escaping from its enemies.
(B) like a deer escapes from it's enemies.
(C) as a deer escapes from its enemies.

The Grammar and Style lesson will help students understand the incorrect usage of *like* in the example. For more practice, use the Grammar and Style page in ***Selection Support***, p. 187.

Develop Understanding

One-Minute Insight In "My Last Duchess," Browning skillfully uses the dramatic monologue to provide a brilliant portrait of a jealous, possessive, arrogant man who gave orders to kill his first wife ("I gave commands; Then all smiles stopped together.") because she displeased him. The Duke describes at length his dead wife's supposed faults (she appeared to like other men as well as she liked him: "she liked whate'er / She looked on, and her looks went everywhere"). As the Duke talks, he reveals to the reader—and to his unheard listener in the poem—his chilling character flaws.

Comprehension Check ☑

❶ Ask students to tell in their own words what is happening in these first four lines. *The Duke is speaking and pointing to a painted portrait of his first wife. He says the painter, Frà Pandolf, worked hard for a day to make her look so lifelike.*

◆ Grammar and Style

❷ **The Use of *Like* and *As*** Ask students why the word *like* is used in the phrase "strangers like you." *The preposition* like *is used to compare the noun* strangers *and the pronoun* you.

◆ Grammar and Style

❸ **The Use of *Like* and *As*** Ask students why the word *as*, rather than *like*, is used in the comparison in line 11. *The subordinating conjunction* as *introduces the clause "they would ask me."*

My Last Duchess

Robert Browning

▶ **Critical Viewing** What do you think is the artist's attitude toward the subject of this painting? How does it compare with the Duke's attitude toward his "Last Duchess"? **[Infer]**

This poem, set in the sixteenth century in a castle in northern Italy, is based on events from the life of the Duke of Ferrara, an Italian nobleman, whose first wife died after only three years of marriage. Following his wife's death, the Duke began making arrangements to remarry. In Browning's poem, the Duke is showing a painting of his first wife to an agent who represents the father of the woman he hopes to marry.

❶ That's my last Duchess painted on the wall,
Looking as if she were alive. I call
That piece a wonder, now: Frà Pandolf's[1] hands
Worked busily a day, and there she stands.
Will't please you sit and look at her? I said
❷ "Frà Pandolf" by design, for never read
Strangers like you that pictured countenance,
The depth and passion of its earnest glance,
But to myself they turned (since none puts by
The curtain I have drawn for you, but I)
❸ And seemed as they would ask me, if they durst,[2]
How such a glance came there; so, not the first
Are you to turn and ask thus. Sir, 'twas not

1. **Frà Pandolf's:** Work of Brother Pandolf, an imaginary painter.
2. **durst:** Dared.

Block Scheduling Strategies

- Before students read the poems in this section, screen one of the film versions of the play *The Barretts of Wimpole Street*, described on page 777. The play includes a scene in which the playwright imagines the first meeting of the famous couple. Students can use this scene to inspire their own role-plays for the Speaking and Listening activity in the Idea Bank on page 779.
- Introduce the class to the elements of a dramatic monologue in Literary Focus on page 767. Then have students answer the Literary Focus questions on page 778.
- Have students listen to the audiocassette recording of each poem as they read. Suggest that they listen for clues to the relationship between Robert Browning and his wife Elizabeth Barrett Browning.
- Teach the Reading Strategy, p. 767, to students before they read. For extra practice have students complete Reading Strategy: Make Inferences About the Speaker and Grammar and Style: The Use of *Like* and *As* in ***Selection Support***, pp. 187 and 188.

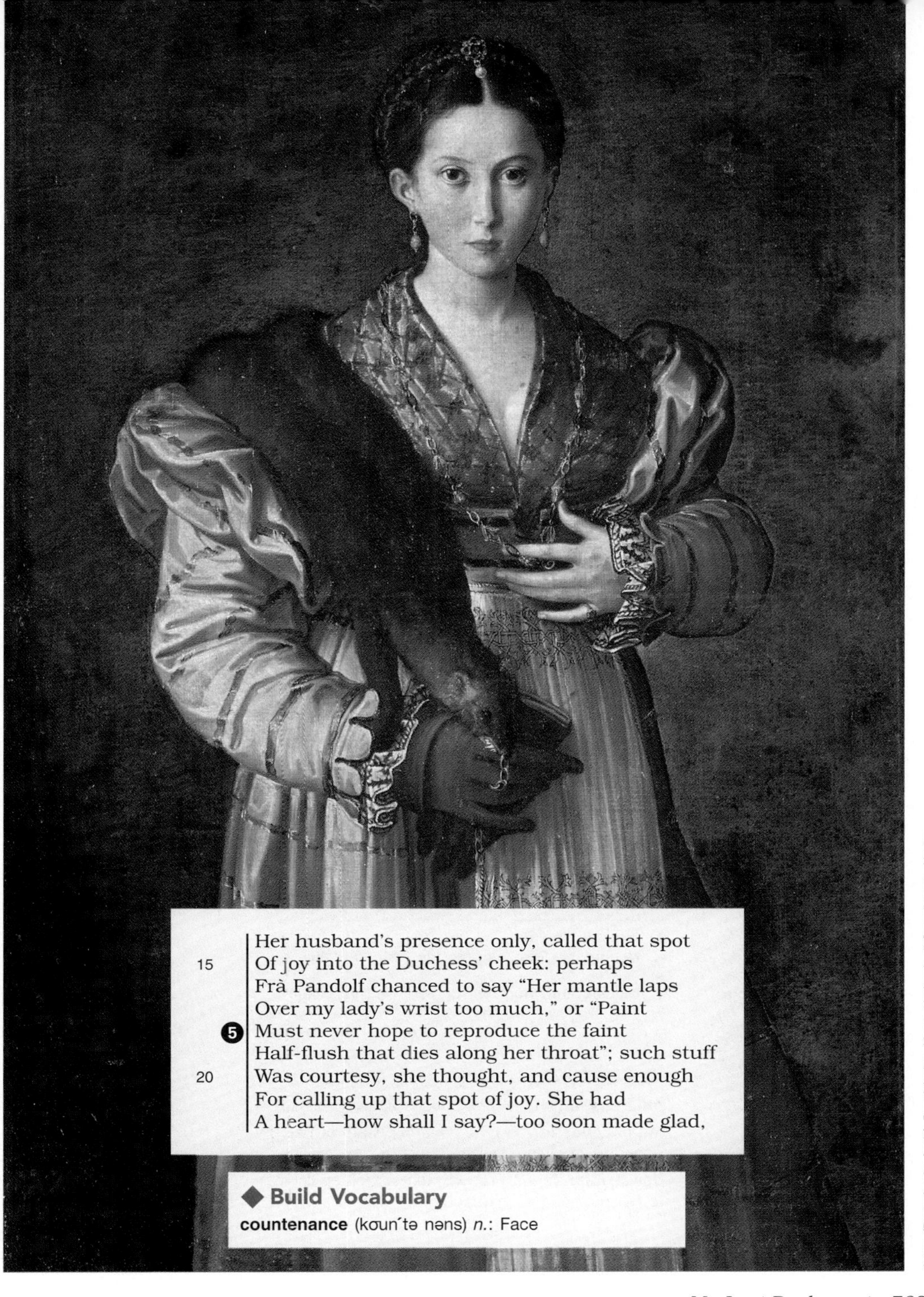

Her husband's presence only, called that spot
Of joy into the Duchess' cheek: perhaps
Frà Pandolf chanced to say "Her mantle laps
Over my lady's wrist too much," or "Paint
❺ Must never hope to reproduce the faint
Half-flush that dies along her throat"; such stuff
Was courtesy, she thought, and cause enough
For calling up that spot of joy. She had
A heart—how shall I say?—too soon made glad,

◆ **Build Vocabulary**

countenance (koun′tə nəns) *n.*: Face

Antea (Portrait of a Lady), Parmigianino, Museo Nazionale di Capodimonte, Naples

▶Critical Viewing◀

❹ **Infer** Help students appreciate the following points: *The artist's attitude is respectful and admiring but also cold and unsentimental. The Duke's attitude toward his "last Duchess" could be described as cold and reserved on the outside but passionately jealous on the inside.*

◆ Reading Strategy

❺ **Make Inferences About the Speaker** Ask students what clues they can find in this passage that the Duke is a jealous man. *Suggested response: In lines 14–15, he seems angry that men other than he could bring "a spot of joy" into his wife's cheek. In line 22 he says she had "A heart—how shall I say—too soon made glad" by people and things other than himself.*

Customize for
Visual/Spatial Learners
Encourage these students to infer character traits of the woman in the portrait and to compare them to the Duchess in the poem.

Humanities: Art

Antea (Portrait of a Lady) by Parmigianino.

In this painting, also called *La Bella*, Parmigianino's expert draftsmanship is apparent. The lady's wealth and refinement are obvious through the artist's depiction of her rich clothing and graceful posture. The artist has sacrificed emphasis on her femininity in favor of portraying elegance.

Parmigianino (1503–1540) was the last true northern Italian High Renaissance painter. He painted with mannered, or formal, realism.

Use these questions for discussion:

1. How would you describe the subject's posture and facial expression? *She is formally posed and appears to be in a serious mood.*
2. How well do you think this painting matches the one of the Duke's "last Duchess" described in the poem? *Students may say the portrait's sad and vulnerable expression matches that of the murdered Duchess.*

◆ Critical Thinking

❶ **Make Inferences** Ask students which actions of the Duchess displeased the Duke. *Suggested answer: The Duke was displeased by her appreciation of things. She was as equally pleased by the sunset, a bough of cherries, or a white mule as she was by the Duke's attention.*

◆ Grammar and Style

❷ **Use of *Like* and *As*** Ask students why the words *as if* are used here. *As if is a subordinate conjunction that introduces the clause "she ranked. . . ." Like is never used to introduce a clause.*

◆ Reading Strategy

❸ **Make Inferences About the Speaker** Ask students what inferences they can make about the speaker, based on his use of the phrase "disgusts me" and the claim "I choose/Never to stoop." *Suggested response: The speaker is a man who judges other people harshly and is too proud to discuss his grievances openly with people who hurt or offend him.*

◆ Critical Thinking

❹ **Interpret** Ask students what they think the Duke means when he says, "I gave commands; Then all smiles stopped together." *Sample answer: The implication seems to be that the Duke had the Duchess put to death.*

◆ Critical Thinking

❺ **Draw Conclusions** Ask students why someone like the Duke might enjoy seeing an image of a wild creature "tamed" and "cast in bronze." *Suggested response: Judging by his attitude toward his first wife, the Duke likes being in control of the people and circumstances in his life. Things that are "tamed" and "cast in bronze" have no will of their own and are totally under control.*

Too easily impressed; she liked whate'er
She looked on, and her looks went everywhere.
Sir, 'twas all one! My favor at her breast,
The dropping of the daylight in the West,
❶ The bough of cherries some officious fool
Broke in the orchard for her, the white mule
She rode with round the terrace—all and each
Would draw from her alike the approving speech,
Or blush, at least. She thanked men—good! but
thanked
Somehow—I know not how—as if she ranked
❷ My gift of a nine-hundred-years-old name
With anybody's gift. Who'd stoop to blame
This sort of trifling? Even had you skill
In speech—(which I have not)—to make your will
Quite clear to such an one, and say, "Just this
Or that in you disgusts me; here you miss,
❸ Or there exceed the mark"—and if she let
Herself be lessoned so, nor plainly set
Her wits to yours, forsooth,[3] and made excuse,
—E'en then would be some stooping; and I choose
Never to stoop. Oh sir, she smiled, no doubt,
Whene'er I passed her; but who passed without
Much the same smile? This grew; I gave commands;
❹ Then all smiles stopped together. There she stands
As if alive. Will 't please you rise? We'll meet
The company below, then. I repeat,
The Count your master's known munificence
Is ample warrant that no one just pretense
Of mine for dowry will be disallowed;
Though his fair daughter's self, as I avowed
At starting, is my object. Nay, we'll go
❺ Together down, sir! Notice Neptune,[4] though,
Taming a sea horse, thought a rarity,
Which Claus of Innsbruck[5] cast in bronze for me!

3. **forsooth:** In truth.
4. **Neptune:** In Roman mythology, the god of the sea.
5. **Claus of Innsbruck:** Imaginary Austrian sculptor.

◆ Build Vocabulary

officious (ə fish´ əs) *adj.*: Overly eager to please

munificence (myo͞o nif´ə səns) *n.*: State of being very generous in giving; lavish

dowry (dou´ rē) *n.*: Property that a woman brings to her husband at marriage

Cross-Curricular Connection: Social Studies

This poem is set in the sixteenth century in northern Italy. At this time, the Italian Renaissance brought emphasis on individualism and enjoyment of this world. Gentlemen such as the speaker of "My Last Duchess" sought to develop a well-rounded personality, with a wide range of knowledge and interests. This social ideal was clearly presented in *Book of the Courtier*, written by Baldassare Castiglione. He wrote that a gentleman must not only be nobly born, but also have an understanding of the arts and all types of learning. He must be graceful, charming, and well-mannered.

The Renaissance was also a time of rapid social change, in which powerful men challenged all authority. Such men could demonstrate both a delicate appreciation of the arts and extreme cruelty in their personal lives.

Ask students how well the speaker of "My Last Duchess" represents the qualities of a Renaissance aristocrat.

Life in a Love

Robert Browning

Escape me?
  Never—
6 Beloved!
While I am I, and you are you,
7 So long as the world contains us both,
Me the loving and you the loth,
While the one eludes, must the other pursue.
My life is a fault at last, I fear:
It seems too much like a fate, indeed!
Though I do my best I shall scarce succeed.
But what if I fail of my purpose here?
It is but to keep the nerves at strain,
To dry one's eyes and laugh at a fall,
And, baffled, get up and begin again,—
So the chase takes up one's life, that's all.
While, look but once from your farthest bound
At me so deep in the dust and dark,
No sooner the old hope goes to ground
Than a new one, straight to the self-same mark,
I shape me—
Ever
Removed!

◆ Build Vocabulary

eludes (ē lo͞odz′) *v.*: Avoids or escapes

Guide for Responding

◆ Literature and Your Life

Reader's Response In what ways are these poems alike? How do they differ?

Thematic Focus What ideas about romantic relationships do the speakers in these two poems have?

Songwriting With a small group, discuss changes you could make to either of these poems so that it would work as a contemporary rock song.

☑ Check Your Comprehension

1. In "My Last Duchess" what are the speaker and his companion looking at?
2. What was the Duke's "gift" to his wife?
3. What does the Duke say in his final remark to the agent?
4. What does the speaker of "Life in a Love" do as his beloved eludes him?

◆ Critical Thinking

INTERPRET

1. In "My Last Duchess," what initial question do you think the speaker's companion asked him? **[Infer]**
2. (a) What has happened to the last Duchess? (b) Where in the poem is this revealed? **[Interpret]**
3. What does the final remark in "My Last Duchess" reveal about the speaker and his attitudes toward marriage and life? **[Draw Conclusions]**
4. To what does the speaker of "Life in a Love" refer when he mentions "the chase" that "takes up one's life"? **[Infer]**

EVALUATE

5. If you had to choose one of these speakers as a spouse or a friend, which one would you prefer? **[Make a Judgment]**

Develop Understanding

One-Minute Insight In this dramatic monologue, the male speaker describes his persistence in pursuing a reluctant woman. Students' attitude toward this speaker may vary widely. Some may be charmed and amused by his persistence, while others may find it sad or scary.

◆ Literary Focus

6 Dramatic Monologue Ask students to describe the dramatic conflict described here by the speaker. *Suggested response: The speaker is passionately attracted to the woman he is addressing, but she resists his advances. The more she resists, the harder he tries to win her over.*

7 Clarification "Loth" is a variant of the adjective "loath," used here as a noun meaning "an unwilling or reluctant person."

Reinforce and Extend

Answers

◆ Literature and Your Life

Reader's Response Both poems are dramatic monologues in which a lover talks about his beloved. In "My Last Duchess" the speaker is unloving and controlling; in "Life in a Love" the speaker is loving and controlling.

Thematic Focus The Duke wants to possess and control the speaker in "Life in a Love" and considers the pursuit of his beloved to be the goal of his life.

☑ Check Your Comprehension

1. They are looking at a portrait of the speaker's late first wife.
2. His gift was his "900-year-old name"—a tie to a noble house.
3. He draws the agent's attention to a sculpture of Neptune taming a sea horse.
4. He keeps pursuing his goal and looking for a sign of encouragement.

◆ Critical Thinking

1. The speaker's companion must have asked about the subject of a portrait that had caught his eye.
2. (a) The last Duchess has died. (b) It is revealed in line 45— "Then all smiles stopped together."
3. The speaker has the same attitude toward the sculpture, the portrait, and the duchess—pride of possession. He equates love with ownership.
4. The speaker refers to the quest for the return of unrequited love.
5. Most students would prefer the speaker in "Life in a Love," as he doesn't indicate that he would dispose of his beloved if she displeased him.

Develop Understanding

One-Minute Insight In this poem, the speaker (a shepherd) describes the private joys of the rural retreat, among the ruins of an old city, that he shares with his beloved. He contrasts the pastoral scene with the public monuments, chariot race track, and battles that existed on the same site in ancient times when it was a great city and capital of an empire. The speaker expresses sadness over the lives wasted in the empty pursuit of imperial glory and greed ("folly, noise, and sin"), asserting that "love is best" and endures, whereas other pursuits crumble in ruin.

▶Critical Viewing◀

❶ **Support** The phrase "quiet-colored" from line 1 of the poem could be used to describe the painting.

❷ **Clarification** The word *tinkle* adds an auditory detail to this vividly described scene. The sound is made by bells on the collars of the sheep.

Comprehension Check ☑

❸ Have students describe the setting of this monologue and tell how the setting has changed over the years. *The poem is set at twilight in a rural pasture. To the west is the site of a once-great ancient city, which is now in ruins.*

Italian Ruins, John Claude Nattes, Victoria and Albert Museum

❶ ▲ **Critical Viewing** Which phrase in the first line of Browning's poem could describe this painting? Explain. **[Support]**

Love Among the Ruins

Robert Browning

Where the quiet-colored end of evening smiles,
    Miles and miles
On the solitary pastures where our sheep
    Half asleep
❷ Tinkle homeward through the twilight, stray or stop
    As they crop—
❸ Was the site once of a city great and gay
    (So they say),
Of our country's very capital, its prince
    Ages since
Held his court in, gathered councils, wielding far
    Peace or war.

Humanities: Art

Italian Ruins by John Claude Nattes.

This undated watercolor was probably painted in the years between 1781 and 1784. It is done in the style Nattes preferred, sepia details tinted with color. The ruined temple or building rises out of an Italian urban scene. A tree grows in the center, showing the degree of decay to which the ruin has succumbed. The descriptive scene has a romantic air and a poetic charm.

The English watercolor artist John Claude Nattes (1765–1822) was born of Irish parents. His work is among that of the early English topographical painters—descriptive painters of towns, parishes, ruins, tracts of land, estates, and buildings. He published books describing Scotland, England, France, and Italy, which he illustrated with his watercolor paintings.

Use these questions for discussion:

1. How well does this picture of ancient ruins reflect the spirit of Browning's poem? *Suggested response: The painting illustrates the quiet colors and ruin that Browning describes.*
2. Why might ruins like these inspire poetry? *Suggested response: Because ruins are remains of bygone civilizations, they prompt viewers to reflect on the nature of time and mortality, inspiring poetry.*

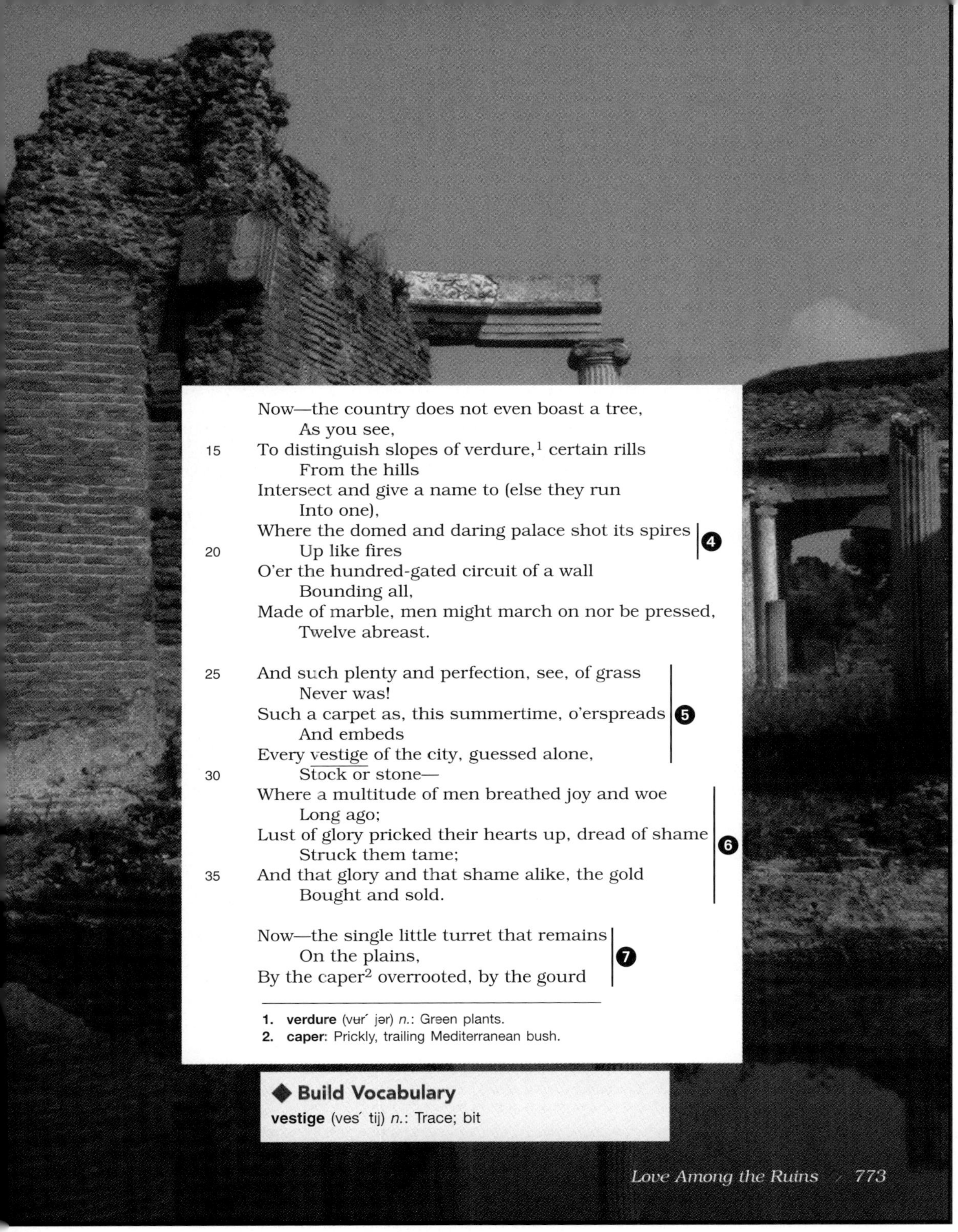

Now—the country does not even boast a tree,
As you see,
To distinguish slopes of verdure,[1] certain rills
From the hills
Intersect and give a name to (else they run
Into one),
Where the domed and daring palace shot its spires ❹
Up like fires
O'er the hundred-gated circuit of a wall
Bounding all,
Made of marble, men might march on nor be pressed,
Twelve abreast.

And such plenty and perfection, see, of grass
Never was!
Such a carpet as, this summertime, o'erspreads ❺
And embeds
Every vestige of the city, guessed alone,
Stock or stone—
Where a multitude of men breathed joy and woe
Long ago;
Lust of glory pricked their hearts up, dread of shame ❻
Struck them tame;
And that glory and that shame alike, the gold
Bought and sold.

Now—the single little turret that remains
On the plains, ❼
By the caper[2] overrooted, by the gourd

1. **verdure** (vʉr′ jər) *n.*: Green plants.
2. **caper**: Prickly, trailing Mediterranean bush.

◆ **Build Vocabulary**
vestige (ves′ tij) *n.*: Trace; bit

◆ Grammar and Style

❹ **The Use of *Like* and *As*** Ask students why the word *like* is used in this comparison. *The preposition* like *is used to compare two nouns—*spires *and* fires.

◆ Reading Strategy

❺ **Make Inferences About the Speaker** Ask students what the words *plenty* and *perfection* in line 25 suggest about the speaker's feelings toward the current state of the land. *Suggested response: These descriptive words reveal the speaker's love for the land as it is now and his preference for the glories of nature over the glories of past empires.*

◆ Reading Strategy

❻ **Make Inferences About the Speaker** Ask students what feelings the speaker seems to have about the past civilization he describes. *Sample answer: His description of the empire seems to express contempt and sadness for lives wasted in the empty pursuit of glory and gold.*

◆ Critical Thinking

❼ **Analyze** Ask students what word in stanza four is used to bring the reader dramatically back to the present. *Suggested answer: The speaker opens the stanza with the word "Now" to bring readers back to the present.*

Beyond the Classroom

Career Connection

Archaeology Archaeology is the study of ancient ruins and other artifacts in order to gain evidence about what past civilizations were like. Archaeologists reconstruct the past by excavating artifacts and then analyzing, dating, and comparing them to other finds. Today, archaeologists use aerial photography to help them locate promising sites for excavation.

Have students research the latest techniques used for excavating, interpreting, and dating archaeological finds and sites.

Community Connection

Local History Have students visit a local historical society or museum to find out how historians have reconstructed or documented the history of your community.

◆ Critical Thinking

❶ **Analyze** Ask students how the lines of the poem vary in length. Then ask how the rhyme scheme affects the meaning of the poem. *The shortness of every other line, along with the end rhymes of each pair of lines gives the poem a singsong quality, trivializing the grandeur of the ruined empire.*

◆ Critical Thinking

❷ **Analyze** Ask students: Who looks out of the tower now and who used to look out of the tower in ancient times? What opposing ideas about life do the king and the girl represent? *The speaker's love looks out of the tower now, waiting for him. In ancient times a king looked out of the tower at his kingdom. The king represents political power, the girl, present love.*

◆ Critical Thinking

❸ **Interpret** What happened to the temples and colonnades that used to top the mountains? What do they represent? *The temples and colonnades have all fallen into ruin. They are examples of how works of pride perish, while love prevails.*

Enrichment

Architecture and Engineering in Ancient Rome The unnamed civilization in the poem resembles ancient Rome, famous for its magnificent temples, statues, monuments, forums, palaces, and public baths. Roman engineers planned wide, straight streets and great aqueducts to bring water into cities. Even private homes were carefully designed and built with painstaking precision. The ruins of the ancient city of Pompeii, preserved in volcanic ash, demonstrate the relative luxury of public and private architecture in the time of the Roman Empire, a standard that would not be reached again for several centuries.

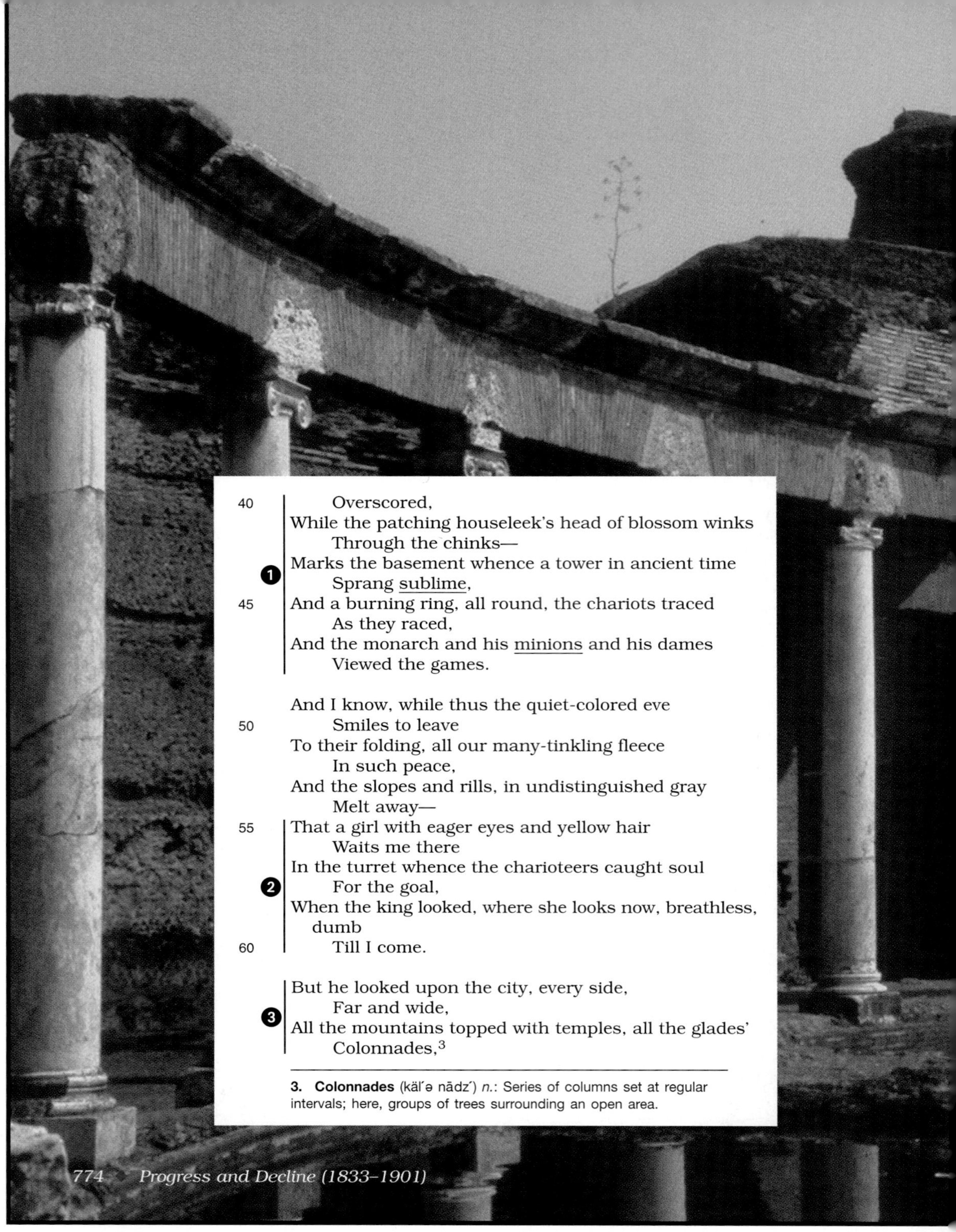

        Overscored,
While the patching houseleek's head of blossom winks
        Through the chinks—
❶ Marks the basement whence a tower in ancient time
        Sprang sublime,
And a burning ring, all round, the chariots traced
        As they raced,
And the monarch and his minions and his dames
        Viewed the games.

And I know, while thus the quiet-colored eve
        Smiles to leave
To their folding, all our many-tinkling fleece
        In such peace,
And the slopes and rills, in undistinguished gray
        Melt away—
That a girl with eager eyes and yellow hair
        Waits me there
❷ In the turret whence the charioteers caught soul
        For the goal,
When the king looked, where she looks now, breathless, dumb
        Till I come.

But he looked upon the city, every side,
        Far and wide,
❸ All the mountains topped with temples, all the glades'
        Colonnades,[3]

3. **Colonnades** (käl′ə nādz′) *n.*: Series of columns set at regular intervals; here, groups of trees surrounding an open area.

Speaking and Listening Mini-Lesson

Oral Interpretation
This mini-lesson supports the Speaking and Listening activity in the Idea Bank on page 779.

Introduce the Concept Explain that a dramatic monologue is like one side of an overheard conversation. An oral interpretation of the monologue must convey the personality and changing emotions of the speaker and the presence of an unheard listener.

Develop Information When preparing an oral interpretation, students should be alert to punctuation such as dashes or parentheses that indicate a pause or a sudden change in tone.

Have students work in pairs. One should be the speaker and the other the director. First have them mark up a copy of the poem, indicating places where the speaker should pause, change his tone, or use facial expressions or gestures.

Apply the Information Have the speaker practice the performance while the director makes notes for improvement. Then have students present their monologues in small groups.

Assess the Outcome Have students use the Peer Assessment: Oral Interpretation page in ***Alternative Assessment*** (p. 120) to evaluate each other's performances based on how well each expresses the personality and changing emotions of the speaker.

All the causeys,[4] bridges, aqueducts—and then,
    All the men!
When I do come, she will speak not, she will stand,
    Either hand
❹ On my shoulder, give her eyes the first embrace
    Of my face,
Ere we rush, ere we extinguish sight and speech
    Each on each.

In one year they sent a million fighters forth
    South and North,
And they built their gods a brazen pillar[5] high
    As the sky,
Yet reserved a thousand chariots in full force—
    Gold, of course.
Oh heart! oh blood that freezes, blood that burns!
    Earth's returns
❺ For whole centuries of folly, noise and sin!
    Shut them in,
With their triumphs and their glories and the rest!
    Love is best.

4. **causeys:** Causeways or raised roads.
5. **brazen pillar:** Built from the brass of captured chariots.

◆ Build Vocabulary

sublime (sə blīm′) *adj.*: Inspiring admiration through greatness or beauty

minions (min′ yənz) *n.*: Attendants or agents

Guide for Responding

◆ Literature and Your Life

Reader's Response Do you agree with the speaker's conclusion that present love is worth more than past glories? Explain.

Thematic Focus Would you rather read about a romance or a conflict between empires? Why?

Sketch Briefly sketch a view of the ruins described by the speaker.

☑ Check Your Comprehension

1. What once stood where the speaker's sheep now head homeward?
2. Compare and contrast the way the city once looked with the way it looks now.
3. Who waits in the old turret for the speaker?

◆ Critical Thinking

INTERPRET

1. Explain the speaker's feelings toward the civilization he describes. **[Interpret]**
2. (a) In what way is the whole poem based on a contrast between past and present? (b) How do the alternating long and short lines help emphasize this contrast? **[Analyze]**
3. In your own words, express the conclusion at which the poem arrives. **[Draw Conclusions]**

EVALUATE

4. Is "Love Among the Ruins" a good title for this poem? Explain your answer. **[Assess]**

EXTEND

5. Compare the message of this poem with that of Shelley's "Ozymandias" on p. 670. **[Literature Link]**

◆ Reading Strategy

❹ Make Inferences About the Speaker Ask students how the speaker seems to feel about the girl waiting for him in the tower.
Suggested answer: He is passionately in love with her and is anticipating their reunion.

◆ Critical Thinking

❺ Analyze Ask students what phrase in this stanza sums up the speaker's view of the ancient civilization he describes in the poem.
Sample answer: The phrase "whole centuries of folly, noise and sin!" sums up his attitude.

Reinforce and Extend

Answers

◆ Literature and Your Life

Reader's Response Possible responses: Yes, finding love is the most important thing a person can do; no, past glories allow us to learn about history and enrich our lives.

Thematic Focus Students should support their preferences with an explanation.

☑ Check Your Comprehension

1. A great city once stood there.
2. The city was full of imposing buildings and home to many people; the only remaining structure is a turret, surrounded by meadows and brooks.
3. The speaker's beloved waits for him.

◆ Critical Thinking

1. Although the speaker acknowledges the glories of the past, he has an ironic attitude toward those long-dead people and their "lust for glory."
2. (a) The poem shifts between images of the epic past and intimate images of a simple, appealing present. (b) The rhythm, with its unevenly matched couplets, undercuts the grandeur of the heroic pictures of the past, but supports the modest images of the present.
3. Sample response: Even the most ambitious expressions of human vanity eventually crumble, but love endures.
4. Possible responses: Yes, the title is interesting and hints at romance; no, the title should emphasize the eternity of love, not ancient ruins.
5. Both poems share the viewpoint that it's futile to build monuments in a quest for immortality.

Develop Understanding

One-Minute Insight In order to describe her deep and abiding love for her husband, Elizabeth Barrett Browning proposes the question "How do I love thee?" and then provides eight answers, all beginning with the words "I love thee." Browning's famous sonnet is a personal, intimate statement that has also become a universal tribute to love, admired by generations of readers.

Customize for
Less Proficient Readers
Have these students keep a list of the ways in which Browning loves her husband. Students should paraphrase their answers.

◆ Background for Understanding

❶ This sonnet was part of a cycle presented by the poet to her husband in 1847. The poems were so private that it was only after much persuasion that she agreed to let her husband publish them under the title *Sonnets from the Portuguese*, which suggested that the poems were translations, not her intimate expressions.

◆ Grammar and Style

❷ **The Use of *Like* and *As*** Ask students why the word *as*, rather than *like*, is used in the comparisons in lines 7 and 8. *In both sentences the word* as *introduces a clause: "as men strive for Right" and "as they turn from Praise."* Like *should not be used to introduce a clause.*

◆ Reading Strategy

❸ **Make Inferences About the Speaker** Ask students to describe how seriously the speaker takes her love. *Suggested answer: To her, it is the most important thing in her life.*

▶Critical Viewing◀

❹ **Assess** Some students may say that the clasped hands convey the same tenderness, commitment, and enduring nature as the love described in the poem. Others may say that clasped hands suggest friendship more than deep, passionate love.

◀ **Critical Viewing** Does this image capture for you the depth of love des cribed in the poem? Explain. **[Assess]** ❹

How do I love thee? Let me count the ways.
❶ I love thee to the depth and breadth and height
My soul can reach, when feeling out of sight
For the ends of Being and ideal Grace.
I love thee to the level of every day's
Most quiet need, by sun and candlelight.
❷ I love thee freely, as men strive for Right;
I love thee purely, as they turn from Praise.
I love thee with the passion put to use
In my old griefs, and with my childhood's faith.
I love thee with a love I seemed to lose
With my lost saints—I love thee with the breath,
❸ Smiles, tears, of all my life!—and, if God choose,
I shall but love thee better after death.

Looking at Literature Videodisc To spark discussion of the famous love poem by Elizabeth Barrett Browning, play Chapter 8 of the videodisc, Marriage Customs Around the World.

Chapter 8

Beyond Literature

Media Connection

The Barretts of Wimpole Street

The romance between Robert Browning and Elizabeth Barrett Browning was brought to the stage by English playwright Rudolph Bessier in 1930. The next year *The Barretts of Wimpole Street* opened on Broadway, starring Katherine Cornell, considered by many to be the greatest actress of American theater. The play ran for a year, toured all over the United States and Elizabeth Barrett Browning became Cornell's most popular role. In 1934, though, Katherine Cornell turned down an offer to play the role in an MGM movie production. The part of Elizabeth went to Norma Shearer, and it catapulted her from mere popularity to icon status. The success of the 1934 film version helped its director, Sidney Franklin, become a producer. When he made a return to directing in 1957, his first project was a remake of *The Barretts of Wimpole Street*, starring Jennifer Jones. Do you think that a new version of the story of the romance between Robert Browning and Elizabeth Barrett Browning would be as popular today as it was previously? Explain.

Guide for Responding

◆ Literature and Your Life

Reader's Response Do you find the speaker's description of the depth of her love effective or moving? Explain.

Thematic Focus How would you describe the speaker's relationship with her love?

☑ Check Your Comprehension

1. In Sonnet 43, what question does the speaker ask?
2. Briefly summarize the speaker's answers to her own questions.

◆ Critical Thinking

INTERPRET

1. What does the speaker of Sonnet 43 mean in lines 9–10 by the words "...with the passion put to use / In my old griefs..."? **[Interpret]**
2. Describe the kind of love expressed by the speaker in Sonnet 43. **[Draw Conclusions]**

APPLY

3. Give two ways in which you might complete the line "I love thee...." **[Apply]**
4. Cite a popular song that praises love, and compare its language, attitude, and images to those of Sonnet 43. **[Relate]**

Beyond the Selection

FURTHER READING

Other Poems by the Brownings

"If Thou Must Love Me, Let It Be for Naught," Elizabeth Barrett Browning
"Andrea del Sarto," Robert Browning
"Ah, Love, But a Day," Robert Browning

Other Poems on the Theme of Relationships

"somewhere i have never traveled," E. E. Cummings
Sonnet 24, William Shakespeare

We suggest that you preview these works before recommending them to students.

INTERNET

Students can read biographies of the Brownings as well as read and listen to several of their poems, at the following Web site: **www.pbs.org/wnet.ihas.poet/browning.html.**

Please be aware, however, that sites may have changed since this information was published. We *strongly recommend* that you preview sites before you send students to them.

Reinforce and Extend

Beyond Literature

Media Connection If you have difficulty locating videos of the film versions of *The Barretts of Wimpole Street*, you can find in many libraries either the book on which the movie is based or the Caedmon record album of important scenes from the play.

Answers

◆ Literature and Your Life

Reader's Response Students' responses should note the scope of the comparisons the poet uses to describe the extent of her love.

Thematic Focus The speaker expresses an enduring, all-encompassing passion for her beloved.

☑ Check Your Comprehension

1. The speaker asks: In how many ways do I love you?
2. Sample response: She loves her beloved to the limit of which her soul is capable when reaching for its ultimate limits; her love is always sufficient to the demands of each particular day; she loves with all the passion she has ever been capable of feeling.

◆ Critical Thinking

1. The speaker is as passionate in her present love as she was in her youthful passions.
2. The speaker describes love that exceeds human limitations; it is strong enough to survive even the speaker's death.
3. Students should provide images that suggest different aspects of love, such as its intensity or its duration.
4. Students should cite songs that express various aspects of romantic love.

Answers

◆ Reading Strategy

1. In "My Last Duchess," the Duke wants to indicate how valuable his collections are, as well as possibly to send a message to his prospective wife, telling her how she will be expected to behave.
2. (a) In "Love Among the Ruins," the shepherd expresses sadness for the lives lost in the pursuit of glory and contempt for the pride and greed of the "monarch and his minions" of long ago. (b) He expresses joy and eagerness to join his beloved.
3. In "Love in a Life," we can infer that the speaker is very persistent in his pursuit of the object of his attentions.

◆ Build Vocabulary

Using the Suffix *-ence*

1. innocence: the state of being innocent or pure
2. prominence: the quality of standing out
3. permanence: the state of being permanent or enduring

Using the Word Bank

1. officious; 2. countenance; 3. minions; 4. munificence; 5. sublime; 6. vestige; 7. eludes; 8. dowry

◆ Literary Focus

1. (a) In "My Last Duchess," the Duke reveals that he did not like the fact that his first wife seemed to like everyone equally well—as well as she liked him. (b) He ordered her to be killed. (c) The next Duchess will have to please the Duke or she, too, will be disposed of.
2. (a) In "Love Among the Ruins," the dramatic situation is a meeting between lovers among the ruins of an ancient city. (b) The conflict is between the ideas of enduring love and that of fleeting power and glory.
3. In "Life in a Love," the speaker is a man talking to the woman he is courting. The conflict arises because the woman does not want this man's attentions.

◆ Grammar and Style

1. like; 2. as; 3. as; 4. like

Guide for Responding *(continued)*

◆ Reading Strategy

Make Inferences About the Speaker

Although Browning does not directly describe the speakers in these poems, by examining their speech and actions, you were probably able to make **inferences** that enabled you to know them. When the speaker of "My Last Duchess" says, "She had /a heart—how shall I say?—too soon made glad," he's telling you that his wife was too easily pleased by any act of kindness. Yet he's also revealing that he is an extremely proud and bitterly jealous man.

1. Why does the Duke in "My Last Duchess" show the Count's agent the portrait of his dead wife?
2. In "Love Among the Ruins," what can you infer about the speaker's attitude (a) toward the ruined civilization? (b) toward the woman he is going to meet?
3. What inferences can you make about the speaker in "Life in a Love" from lines 18–20?

◆ Build Vocabulary

Using the Suffix *-ence*

Knowing that the suffix *-ence* means "quality, or state of being," add *-ence* to the following adjectives to make nouns. Write the definition for each noun.

1. innocent **2.** prominent **3.** permanent

Using the Word Bank

On your paper, write the correct word from the Word Bank to complete each sentence.

1. In "My Last Duchess," the Duke calls those who gave his wife things __?__ and too helpful.
2. The former Duchess's __?__ in the portrait reveals her earnestness.
3. The Duke probably expects his __?__ to bow when he passes.
4. At the end of the poem, he suggests that the Count's __?__ will result in a generous dowry.
5. The empire recalled in "Love Among the Ruins" was grand and __?__.
6. A turret is the only __?__ of the empire the speaker describes in "Love Among the Ruins."
7. In "Life in a Love" one person __?__ another.
8. If the woman hadn't had a __?__, the Duke would not have married her.

◆ Literary Focus

Dramatic Monologue

Reading a **dramatic monologue** by Browning is like going to a mini-play: In a speech (sometimes to a silent listener), a character indicates a setting and a dramatic conflict. More important, this character reveals his or her inmost feelings, sometimes without knowing it.

In "My Last Duchess," the setting is the private gallery of a Duke living in sixteenth-century Italy. He is speaking to a messenger from the Count whose daughter he wants to marry.

1. (a) What conflict relating to his first wife does the Duke reveal? (b) How did he solve that conflict? (c) What will his next marriage be like, assuming the negotiation is successful?
2. (a) What is the dramatic situation in "Love Among the Ruins"? (b) Is the conflict in the poem between two people or between two different ideas about life? Explain.
3. What are the setting and conflict in "Life in a Love"?

◆ Grammar and Style

The Use of *Like* and *As*

In making comparisons, do not confuse ***like,*** a preposition used to compare nouns and pronouns, with ***as,*** a conjunction used to compare actions.

Practice Write these sentences in your journal, replacing the blanks with the correct word, *like* or *as*. Remember that *as* can introduce a clause in which the verb is implied or understood.

1. No interpretation of Robert Browning's *The Ring and the Book* is exactly __?__ another.
2. The Duke depicted his last duchess __?__ he chose.
3. When Robert Browning and Elizabeth Barrett were married, his poems were not as famous __?__ hers.
4. Do you think Elizabeth Barrett Browning's sonnets are __?__ contemporary love songs?

Writing Application Write a paragraph comparing Sonnet 43 to "Life in a Love." Use *like* and *as* at least once each.

Build Your Portfolio

Idea Bank

Writing

1. Profile Write a profile of any speaker in the four poems. Use the speaker's words to speculate on various aspects of his or her personality.

2. Messenger's Report As the agent who listens to the Duke in "My Last Duchess," report on your meeting to the Count. Tell simply and clearly what the Duke wants.

3. Response to Criticism Philip Langbaum says, "Most successful dramatic monologues deal with speakers who are in some way reprehensible" (deserving of blame). Agree or disagree with him, using evidence from the poems in this group.

Speaking and Listening

4. Oral Interpretation Perform one of Browning's dramatic monologues for the class. Vary the tone of your voice and the words you emphasize to capture the speaker's personality. **[Performing Arts Link]**

5. Fateful Meeting With a partner, role-play the first meeting of Robert Browning and Elizabeth Barrett. Remember that she is an invalid and he is an enthusiastic, but perhaps nervous, young poet. **[Performing Arts Link]**

Projects

6. The Brownings in the Media View movies that depict the Brownings, like *The Barretts of Wimpole Street.* Then report to the class on the way in which these films portray the famous couple. **[Media Link]**

7. The Brownings in Italy Using biographies of the Brownings, research their life in Italy. Present your results to the class, indicating on a map exactly where they lived. **[Social Studies Link]**

Writing Mini-Lesson

Written Recommendation

Imagine that you are the count's agent. After having just heard the Duke's account of his relationship with his previous wife, what recommendation would you present to the father of the woman the Duke hopes to marry? State your opinion in a formal written recommendation to present to the father upon your return from visiting the Duke. Keep the following tip in mind as you develop your paper.

Writing Skills Focus: Cause-and-Effect Transitions

As you build your argument, use **transitions to show cause-and-effect relationships.** Following are just a few of the transitions you'll want to consider: *the reason for, as a result, because, therefore,* and *consequently*.

Prewriting Start by reviewing the poem and noting what it reveals about the Duke's personality and his relationship with his first wife. Review these details and decide on your position regarding the proposed marriage.

Drafting Start with a paragraph in which you present your position clearly and succinctly. Then follow with a series of paragraphs in which you explain the reasons for your recommendation. Use details from the poem to back up your argument. Wherever appropriate use cause-and-effect transitions to show how your details fit together.

Revising Have a classmate assume the role of the woman's father and read your recommendation. Have you presented your case clearly? Have you backed up your argument? Have you written in a respectful tone? Use your classmate's answers to these questions to help you revise.

✓ ASSESSMENT OPTIONS

Formal Assessment, Selection Test, pp. 189–191, and Assessment Resources Software. The selection test is designed so that it can be easily customized to the performance levels of your students. ***Alternative Assessment,*** p. 39, includes options for less advanced students, more advanced students, bodily/kinesthetic learners, interpersonal learners, visual/spatial learners, verbal/linguistic learners, musical/rhythmic learners, and intrapersonal learners.

PORTFOLIO ASSESSMENT

Use the following rubrics in the ***Alternative Assessment*** booklet to assess student writing:
Profile: Description Rubric, p. 98
Messenger's Report: Business Letter/Memo Rubric, p. 114
Response to Criticism: Response to Literature Rubric, p. 111
Writing Mini-Lesson: Cause-Effect Rubric, p. 103

Idea Bank

Customizing for *Performance Levels*

Following are suggestions for matching Idea Bank topics with your students' performance levels:

Less Advanced Students: 1, 4, 7
Average Students: 2, 5, 6
More Advanced Students: 3, 7

Customizing for *Learning Modalities*

Following are suggestions for matching Idea Bank topics with your students' learning modalities:

Verbal/Linguistic: 1, 2, 3, 4, 5, 7
Bodily/Kinesthetic: 5
Visual/Spatial: 6

Writing Mini-Lesson

Refer students to the Writing Process Handbook, page 1189, for instruction on the writing process, and page 1193 for further information on practical and technical writing.

Writing and Language Transparencies Use the Writing Process Model 9: Technical Writing: Status Report, pp. 81–85, to guide students through the process of writing a business report.

Writer's Solution

Writers at Work Videodisc

Have students view the videodisc segment on Practical and Technical Writing (Ch. 8), featuring Jeff Christian, to see how he organizes his ideas. Have students discuss how they can apply his techniques to writing their written recommendations.

Play frames 37727 to 39423

Writing Lab CD-ROM

Have students complete the tutorial on Practical and Technical Writing. Follow these steps:

1. Suggest that students use the Cluster Diagram tool to help them subdivide topics.
2. Have them complete the Audience Profile.
3. Students may use the Memorandum Shell as they draft.
4. Have students use the Proofreading Checklist.

Sourcebook

Have students use Chapter 8, Practical and Technical Writing (pp. 230–264), for additional support.

Prepare and Engage

OBJECTIVES

1. To read, comprehend, and interpret poems
2. To relate poems to personal experience
3. To connect poems to the theme of love
4. To respond to poems through writing, speaking and listening, and a project

PORTFOLIO OPPORTUNITIES

Writing: Invitation; Literary Analysis; Response to Criticism
Speaking and Listening: Love Songs
Project: Poetry Reading

Have students close their eyes and imagine a romantic setting where two people might fall in love. Then ask them to open their eyes and write a quick description of the place they imagined. As they read the two poems in this section, have them compare their vision of a romantic setting with the ones described in the poems.

More About the Poets

Sappho grew up in an aristocratic family, married a rich man, and became a mother. Many of her poems were written for wedding celebrations or women's festivals. Her poems describe a woman's life from girlhood to marriage.

In his poetry, **Charles Baudelaire** explored the warring impulses of the self. He showed how his own mind was torn between idealism and despair, tenderness and cruelty, the spirit and the body. His bold psychological analysis makes him one of the first truly modern poets.

CONNECTIONS TO WORLD LITERATURE

You Know the Place: Then
Sappho

Invitation to the Voyage
Charles Baudelaire

Cultural Connection

RELATIONSHIPS

Most of the poems in this section arise from and describe close relationships between friends or lovers. For example, Alfred, Lord Tennyson's "In Memoriam" expresses grief at the death of his good friend Arthur Henry Hallam. Elizabeth Barrett Browning counts up the uncountable ways she loves her husband in a poem that could sum up every lover's devotion.

The poems of the ancient Greek poet Sappho (saf′ ō) and the nineteenth-century French poet Charles Baudelaire (shärl bōd ler′) also express wholehearted devotion to a loved one. For Sappho, the loved one is Aphrodite herself, the Greek goddess of love. For Baudelaire, the beloved is a mortal woman whom he addresses endearingly as "child" and "sister."

INVITATIONS TO LOVE

Both Sappho and Baudelaire write their poems in the form of invitations. Sappho urges Aphrodite to come from Crete and take up residence on the poet's own island. She wants Aphrodite to accept her devotions and bless her loves. Baudelaire paints for his beloved the image of a magical world of "Richness, quietness, and pleasure" where they can "live together" at peace.

You, too, can accept the invitations these poets offer and journey to distant lands of love.

SAPPHO
(c. 610 B.C.–570 B.C.)

Sappho was an ancient Greek lyricist whose works were known for a personal expression of love and loss. Sappho was one of the first poets to write in the first person rather than from the viewpoint of gods and muses. Although Sappho wrote nearly five hundred poems, only a small fraction of these survive, either intact or in fragments.

CHARLES BAUDELAIRE
(1821–1867)

Known as much for his unconventional life style as his poetry, Baudelaire was one of the most startling and innovative poets of the nineteenth century. Attempting to break away from the Romantic tradition, Baudelaire created poems that are objective rather than sentimental and celebrate the city and the artificial rather than nature. Yet his work still exhibits many of the imaginative and mystical qualities associated with Romanticism.

Prentice Hall Literature Program Resources

REINFORCE / RETEACH / EXTEND

Selection Support Pages
Build Vocabulary: The Language of Relationships, p. 190
Cultural Connection: Relationships, p. 191

Formal Assessment Selection Test, pp. 192–193; Assessment Resources Software

Resource Pro CD-ROM
"You Know the Place: Then"; "Invitation to the Voyage"—includes all resource material and customizable lesson plan

Listening to Literature Audiocassettes
"You Know the Place: Then"; "Invitation to the Voyage"

Sappho, L. Alma Tadema, The Walters Art Gallery, Baltimore, Maryland

CONNECTIONS TO WORLD LITERATURE

▲ Critical Viewing This poem describes a place of beauty and peace. What details in this picture reflect the place described in the poem? [Connect] ❶

You Know the Place: Then

Sappho

Translated by Mary Barnard

You know the place: then ❷

Leave Crete and come to us
waiting where the grove is
pleasantest, by precincts

sacred to you; incense
smokes on the altar, cold
streams murmur through the

apple branches, a young
rose thicket shades the ground
and quivering leaves pour ❸

down deep sleep; in meadows
where horses have grown sleek
among spring flowers, dill

scents the air. Queen! Cyprian![1]
Fill our gold cups with love ❹
stirred into clear nectar

1. **Cyprian** (si′ prē ən) *n.*: Name Sappho uses to address the goddess Aphrodite.

Develop Understanding

One-Minute Insight In this lyric, the speaker (Sappho) addresses the goddess of love, Aphrodite, and invites her to bring her spirit of love to the enticing setting that Sappho has prepared for her.

▶Critical Viewing◀

❶ **Connect** Students will note that although many of the details in the painting differ from those in the poem—the trees are olive, not apple; the music is from a lyre rather than from the murmur of cold streams; the flowers are garlands on the women's heads rather than in meadows filled with grazing horses—the general atmosphere of peace and contentment is the same.

◆ Background for Understanding

❷ Remind students that the "You" addressed by the speaker in the first line of the poem is Aphrodite, the Greek goddess of love. The cult of Aphrodite was centered on the islands of Crete and Cyprus. That is why the speaker asks the goddess to "Leave Crete" in line 2 and why she refers to her later as "Cyprian" in line 14.

Ask students why the speaker is inviting Aphrodite to come to the place described in the poem. *Sample answer: The speaker wants to be in love, so she is inviting the goddess who inspires love to visit.*

◆ Critical Thinking

❸ **Compare and Contrast** Have students describe the place where Sappho thinks love will flourish. Then have them compare this place to the romantic setting they imagined for the Interest Grabber activity on page 780. *Sappho describes a place of great natural beauty: streams, roses, rustling leaves, meadows, horses, and the scent of dill. Students' own imagined romantic settings will vary.*

❹ **Clarification** Remind students that in Greek mythology, nectar was the life-giving drink of the gods and so it is particularly appropriate as an offering for Aphrodite.

Humanities: Art

Sappho by Lawrence Alma Tadema.

This piece of art illustrates the artist's vision of the setting in ancient Greece in which Sappho created her poetry.

Sir Lawrence Alma Tadema (1836–1912) was born in the Netherlands and immigrated to England in 1869. After a visit to the ruins of ancient Pompeii, Alma Tadema focused his art on depicting everyday life in ancient Greece and Rome. He is noted for his accurate depiction of archaeological detail.

Use this question for discussion:

If you could, would you enjoy traveling back in time and attending a performance such as the one shown here? Why or why not? *Some students may prefer listening to music on CD or audiocassette; others may appreciate the beautiful outdoor concert arena.*

Develop Understanding

One-Minute Insight In this famous lyrical poem, the speaker (Baudelaire) invites his love to escape to an idealized, dreamlike, "sumptuous" world of "Richness, quietness, and pleasure." There, he believes, love can flourish in a "kind land" and a "glowing chamber."

Customize for
More Advanced Students
These students may enjoy the Poetry Reading activity in the Idea Bank on page 784. Encourage them to find and compare different translations of the same poem. Students fluent in French may even enjoy reading part of "Invitation to the Voyage" aloud to the class in the original French.

◆ Critical Thinking

1 Analyze Ask students what "mystery" in nature and in his beloved are linked in the speaker's mind. *The image of the sunset glimmering through clouds is a mystery of nature that is linked in the speaker's mind with the image of his beloved's eyes shining at him through her tears.*

◆ Critical Thinking

2 Infer Ask students why the speaker might have used the words *sumptuous* and *disheveled* to describe the weather of his ideal place. *He sees nature as "sumptuous," or magnificent, like his love, and "disheveled," as a woman who has been crying may appear.*

◆ Critical Thinking

3 Compare and Contrast Have students note important details of Baudelaire's ideal room for love. Then have them compare Baudelaire's vision of a romantic place with their own vision from the Interest Grabber activity. *Details of the place include a glowing chamber with antique, glowing furniture; rare, amber-fragrant flowers; gold ceilings, and mirrors; and tapestry-hung walls.*

▶Critical Viewing◀

4 Interpret They might be sailing to a sunset-bathed town of "Richness, quietness, and pleasure."

CONNECTIONS TO WORLD LITERATURE

Invitation to the Voyage

Charles Baudelaire
Translated by Richard Wilbur

Marine. Marcel Mouillot, Galleria d'arte Moderna, Nancy

▲ **Critical Viewing** Where, according to the speaker in this poem, might these "drowsy ships" be sailing? **[Interpret]** 4

My child, my sister, dream
How sweet all things would seem
Were we in that kind land to live together
And there love slow and long,
There love and die among
Those scenes that image you, that sumptuous[1]
weather.
1 Drowned suns that glimmer there
Through cloud-disheveled[2] air
2 Move me with such a mystery as appears
Within those other skies
Of your treacherous eyes
When I behold them shining through their tears.

There, there is nothing else but grace and
measure,
Richness, quietness, and pleasure.

Furniture that wears
The luster of the years
Softly would glow within our glowing chamber,
Flowers of rarest bloom
3 Proffering their perfume
Mixed with the vague fragrances of amber;
Gold ceilings would there be,
Mirrors deep as the sea,

1. **sumptuous** (sump´ cho͞o əs) *adj.*: Magnificent or splendid.
2. **disheveled** (di shev´ əld) *adj.*: Disarranged and untidy.

Humanities: Art

Marine by Marcel Mouillot.

Although the sails of the boats and ships in this painting appear puffed with wind, the darkness of the scene and the smoothness of the water make the boats themselves seem static and unreal, like a dream scene.

Use the following questions for discussion:

1. In what ways is the mood of the painting similar to the mood of the poem? *Both suggest slowness, quietness, and peacefulness. Both create a feeling of unreality.*
2. Which lines of the poem might the painting illustrate? *Students should suggest lines 30 ("See, Sheltered from the swells") through 34 ("Hither through all the waters of the earth").*
3. What makes the ships in the painting like "Those drowsy ships that dream of sailing forth"? *The darkness of the painting and the smoothness of the water make the ships look "drowsy," as though they may only "dream of setting forth."*

The walls all in an Eastern splendor hung—
Nothing but should address
The soul's loneliness,
Speaking her sweet and secret native tongue. ❸

There, there is nothing else but grace and measure,
Richness, quietness, and pleasure.

See, sheltered from the swells
There in the still canals
Those drowsy ships that dream of sailing forth;
It is to satisfy
Your least desire, they ply
Hither through all the waters of the earth. ❺
The sun at close of day
Clothes the fields of hay,
Then the canals, at last the town entire
In hyacinth and gold:
Slowly the land is rolled
Sleepward under a sea of gentle fire.

There, there is nothing else but grace and measure,
Richness, quietness, and pleasure.

Guide for Responding

◆ Literature and Your Life

Reader's Response Are the invitations issued by these poets persuasive? Why or why not?

Thematic Focus Could either of these poems have been written in today's world? Explain.

Journal Writing Briefly describe an ideal place to which you'd like to journey.

☑ Check Your Comprehension

1. What two requests does the speaker of "You Know the Place: Then" make of Aphrodite?
2. For what is the speaker of "You Know the Place: Then" waiting?
3. How does Baudelaire describe the "kind land"?

◆ Critical Thinking

INTERPRET

1. How does Sappho present love as being imposed by external forces? **[Infer]**
2. What impression of love does Baudelaire convey by linking it to the notion of escaping to an ideal, dreamlike world? **[Infer]**
3. How does Baudelaire suggest a sense of longing for the place he describes? **[Interpret]**
4. Compare and contrast the places in which Sappho and Baudelaire believe they will find love. **[Compare and Contrast]**

EVALUATE

5. Do you find the world that Baudelaire describes an ideal place to pursue a love relationship? **[Make a Judgment]**

Beyond the Selection

FURTHER READING

Other Works by Baudelaire
"Man and the Sea"; "The Albatross";
"The Ruined Garden"

Other Works About Relationships
"The Passionate Shepherd to His Love," Christopher Marlowe
"To His Coy Mistress," Andrew Marvell
"Annabel Lee," Edgar Allan Poe

We suggest that you preview these works before recommending them to students.

INTERNET

Students can read English translations of Baudelaire's poetry at the following Web site: **http://www.depotbbs.com/minstrel/CB1.htm** They can read and listen to Baudelaire's poetry in the original French at **http://www.webnet.fr/poesie**

Please be aware, however, that sites may have changed since this information was published. We *strongly recommend* that you preview sites before you send students to them.

◆ Critical Thinking

❺ **Interpret** Have students find details in this stanza that suggest the speaker is longing for peace and quiet in his life. *Suggested response: Details that suggest this longing include "sheltered" (line 29), "still canals" (line 30), "sleepward" (line 40), and his description of the land at sunset as "a sea of gentle fire" (line 40).*

Reinforce and Extend

Answers

◆ Literature and Your Life

Reader's Response Most students will respond positively to images of apple branches, rose thickets, meadows with horses, sunsets, and richly-furnished chambers.

Thematic Focus Students should note that most of the images are timeless, whereas the language style dates the poems to an earlier era.

☑ Check Your Comprehension

1. She requests that Aphrodite leave Crete and come to the speaker's home, and that she fill their gold cups with love.
2. She awaits the coming of love, in the form of the goddess Aphrodite.
3. He describes it as peaceful, quiet, beautiful, and sumptuous.

◆ Critical Thinking

1. She uses sensory images linked to the forces of nature: the scent of dill, the sight of horses in meadows, the sound of murmuring streams.
2. He suggests that the realm of love is a world apart from everyday life.
3. He repeats the refrain at the end of each stanza, reinforcing the desire for "grace and measure, / Richness, quietness, and pleasure."
4. Sappho's setting is made up of images drawn from reality, though carefully arranged. Baudelaire's images belong to a world of dream and fantasy.
5. Possible responses: Yes, Baudelaire describes an ideal place to fall in love; no, the setting is too dreamy, lacking energy and vibrancy.

Answers
Cultural Connection

1. Students could restate the invitations as follows:

   Sappho: "Come on over to our grove by the meadow this afternoon. Bring some nectar and we'll provide the gold cups."

   Baudelaire: "Come on over to my open house. The sunset's great from my antique-furnished rooms so come in time to enjoy it."
2. Browning's poem is about the depths of romantic love. Baudelaire's is about an ideal setting in which to fall in love.
3. (a) Students can cite a "golden oldie" such as "Come, Go With Me" or list numerous contemporary examples. (b) Like the poets, songwriters rely on images and rhythm to make their invitations attractive.

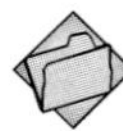

Idea Bank

Customizing for *Performance Levels*

Following are suggestions for matching Idea Bank topics with your students' performance levels:

Less Advanced Students: 1, 4,
Average Students: 2, 5
More Advanced Students: 3, 5

Customizing for *Learning Modalities*

Following are suggestions for matching Idea Bank topics with your students' learning modalities:

Verbal/Linguistic: 1, 2, 3, 4, 5
Musical/Rhythmic: 4, 5

Cultural Connection

Relationships

Like Tennyson and the Brownings, Sappho and Baudelaire capture the essence of a relationship in the rhythms and imagery of their poetry. For these two poets, the love that inspires their work becomes inseparable from the magical place where their love will be fulfilled. That place, in turn, becomes an enticement to the god or person they are inviting.

1. Show how both Sappho and Baudelaire use the same techniques in their poetic invitations that you would use to invite a friend on a date.
2. Compare and contrast the relationship Elizabeth Barrett Browning describes in Sonnet 43 with the one Baudelaire describes in the poem "Invitation to the Voyage."
3. (a) Identify a contemporary song that, like the poems of Sappho and Baudelaire, is also an invitation to love. (b) What devices does the songwriter use to make the invitation seem attractive?

Idea Bank

Writing

1. Invitation Use poetry or prose to invite a friend on a date or to a special occasion.

2. Literary Analysis Choose one of the poems in this section, and analyze its use of imagery. Show how the images in the poem contribute to its meaning.

3. Response to Criticism Geoffrey Brereton writes that "Baudelaire's choice of words and images... gave his verse its original force and has now raised him ... to the status of 'classic.'" Use passages from "Invitation to the Voyage" to analyze Baudelaire's "words and images." Then support or refute this critic's claim.

Speaking and Listening

4. Love Songs Choose a contemporary love song and compare and contrast it to one of the poems in this section. Play the song for your class and then present your comparison in an oral report. **[Music Link; Performing Arts Link]**

Projects

5. Poetry Reading Find other translations of the work of Sappho and Baudelaire, and read them aloud to your class. If possible, find recordings of the same poems in their original language as well, so that your classmates can have the sounds of the original poems in their ears. **[Performing Arts Link]**

✓ ASSESSMENT OPTIONS

Formal Assessment, Selection Test, pp. 192–193, and Assessment Resources Software. The selection test is designed so that it can be easily customized to the performance levels of your students.

PORTFOLIO ASSESSMENT

Use the following rubrics in the ***Alternative Assessment*** booklet to assess student writing:
Invitation: Expression Rubric, p. 95
Literary Analysis: Literary Analysis/Interpretation Rubric, p. 113
Response to Criticism: Evaluation/Review Rubric, p. 105

Writing Process Workshop

Cause-and-Effect Essay

Life is an ongoing series of cause-and-effect relationships—we respond to actions and cause others to happen. In a cause-and-effect essay, you examine such relationships in greater detail. You focus on the results of a particular event or situation (effects) or the factors giving rise to a particular event or situation (causes). You can also analyze causes and effects of events in the past, present, or future. Even the poets in this section, although they're not writing essays, speculate about the causes of past events. Browning, for example, writes of the emotions that motivated an ancient people: ". . . dread of shame/Struck them tame . . ."

Use the following skills as you prepare your cause-and-effect essay:

Writing Skills Focus

- Organize your details to **show connections among causes and effects.** (See p. 765.)
- **Use cause-and-effect transitions** such as *because, since, then, as a result,* to indicate relationships. (See p. 779.)
- **Give specific examples** of causes and effects.

In the following passage, two writers explore cause-and-effect relationships between animals and their habitats.

Model From Literature

from *Last Chance to See* by Douglas Adams and Mark Carwardine

① An island, on the other hand, is small. There are far fewer species, and the competition for survival has never reached anything like the pitch that it does on the mainland. Species are only as tough as they need to be. . . . This is why you find on Madagascar, for instance, species like the lemurs that were overwhelmed eons ago on the mainland. ② Islands are fragile time capsules.

So what happens on Mauritius, or indeed any island, is that when the endemic vegetation or animals are destroyed for any reason, the exotic forms leap into the breach ③.

① The writers use these two paragraphs to examine the effects of island life on the survival of species.

② The reference to lemurs is a specific example of the effect of less competition.

③ The transition *when* links cause (destruction of endemic species) to effect (exotic forms take over).

Prepare and Engage

Establish Writing Guidelines
Review the following key characteristics of a cause-and-effect essay:

- A cause-and-effect essay examines the results or causes of a particular event or situation.
- It often analyzes past events or speculates about future ones.
- Details should be organized using transitions to show connections among causes and effects.
- Specific details are included to explain causes and effects fully.

Distribute the Scoring Rubric for Cause-Effect (p. 103 in ***Alternative Assessment***) to familiarize students with the criteria on which they will be evaluated. See the additional suggestions on page 787 to customize the rubric to this lesson.

Refer students to the Writing Handbook, p. 1189 for an overview of the writing process. For more about cause-and-effect essays, refer students to page 1191.

Art Transparencies To introduce cause-and-effect relationships, place Art Transparency 20, *Troops Resting* by Christopher R.W. Nevinson (page 83 in ***Art Transparencies***), on an overhead projector. Ask students to list reasons the soldiers might be exhausted. Also have them list other effects that might result from the causes they have listed. As a summation of this exercise, discuss how life is a series of cause-and-effect relationships.

Have students read the Model From Literature on this page. Point out numbered annotations that reinforce the writing guidelines and Writing Skills Focus.

Writing Lab CD-ROM
Students may work on the computer following these steps in the Exposition tutorial:

1. Review the model of a cause-and-effect essay.
2. Organize details using the Chain of Events.
3. Use the proofreading checklist.

Sourcebook
Students can find additional instruction on writing a cause-and-effect essay in Chapter 3, (pp. 62–95).

Cross-Curricular Connection: Science

Explain to students that analyzing causes and effects is the backbone of scientific research. Tell students that professional scientists—and science students—keep experiment journals, in which they record each step of an experiment, the conditions of the experiment, or the causes, and the results of the experiments, or the effects. By analyzing the causes and effects of their experiments, scientists often make discoveries about the behavior of animals and functions of the human body, and find cures for diseases.

Develop Student Writing

Prewriting
Suggest that students review the topic ideas on this page. You may also want to use Art Transparency 20, *Troops Resting* by Christopher R.W. Nevinson (page 83 in ***Art Transparencies***), to spark writing ideas about war, soldiers, and the conditions under which men and women function during war time.

Customize for
Visual/Spatial Learners
These students will benefit from visually charting details for their cause-and-effect essay. Point out the chart on this page. Then have students either draw, use pictures from magazines, or label examples of details and the way events lead from one to another. This activity will help students organize details to show clear connections among causes and effects.

Writing and Language Transparencies Have students use the Cause-and-Effect Organizer (p. 120) to organize details for their essays.

Writing Lab CD-ROM
It is important that students establish their audience and purpose before writing their essays. Students can receive guidance by viewing tips from writer Anne Billson on considering one's audience and choosing language and content. Students should also complete the Audience and Purpose Profiles.

Drafting
Explain to students that the drafting process is an opportunity to get their ideas on paper. Caution students against spending a great deal of time proofreading at this stage; they can do so at the revising stage.

Applying Language Skills
Revising Stringy Sentences
When revising their papers, students may find that they have strung sentences together. Have them complete the following practice and writing application to help them identify and correct such sentences.

Applying Language Skills: Revising Stringy Sentences

Stringy sentences result when a writer runs together a long series of clauses connected by conjunctions. Avoid stringy sentences as you draft your cause-and-effect essay.

Practice Rewrite the following stringy sentence. Make it into a series of related sentences in a paragraph.

Most infants have little control over their bodies at first, and then they develop from the head down and from the torso out, and as a result, they generally will have control of their heads and necks before their bodies and of their arms and legs before their fingers and hands, so that it takes several months for a baby to move its fingers or toes voluntarily.

Writing Application As you write scientific cause-and-effect essays, consider creating bulleted lists of details to avoid stringy sentences.

Writer's Solution Connection Writing Lab

For help in narrowing your topic, see the activities in the Narrowing Your Topic section of the tutorial on Exposition.

Prewriting

Choose a Topic To find a topic, think about cause-and-effect relationships that you discussed in a history or science class. You might also use the topic ideas below:

Topic Ideas
- Causes and effects of "brown tide"
- An unexpected effect of an action

Selection-Related Topic Ideas
- Events and situations that led to Tennyson's writing of "In Memoriam—"
- Real-life inspirations for the poetry of the Brownings

Limit Your Topic If you limit your focus to a few causes and effects, you'll be able to write a clearer and more thoughtful explanation. For example, to cover a topic like "The Causes of World War II" would require a whole book. You'll probably have more success with a narrower topic, like "The Events That Brought Churchill to Power."

Create a Cause-and-Effect Chain or Cluster Diagram Gather details for your cause and effect essay, and list them in a chain like the one below. If there is more than one effect per cause, you may want to use a cluster diagram.

Drafting

Create a Logical Organization If the organization of your paper is clear, readers will readily understand the links between causes and effects. Within each paragraph, you might want to examine just one cause-and-effect relationship.

Use Cause-and-Effect Transitions Use transitions to help clarify the links between causes and effects. Following are examples of commonly used cause-and-effect transitions: *following, after, because, since, as a result,* and *then.*

Answers
Suggested response: Most infants have little control over their bodies at first; they develop from the head down and from the torso out. As a result, they generally will have control of their heads and necks before their bodies and of their arms and legs before their fingers and hands. It takes several months for a baby to move its fingers or toes voluntarily.

For more practice have students complete the lesson on Strengthening Sentences on the **Language Lab CD-ROM.** In addition, have students complete page 104 on Improving Sentences in the *Writer's Solution Grammar Practice Book.*

Revising

Add Transitions Where Necessary Mark transitions as you proofread to avoid repeating the same words. Check to see that each transition provides a clear link between your ideas.

Revision Checklist As you revise, answer the following questions:

1. Does my essay's organization make cause-and-effect relationships clear?
2. What transitions might I add or revise to strengthen the relationships between ideas?
3. Have I included examples of specific causes and effects?

Revision Model

from *A Retirement Speech*

① I am often asked, "Why specialize in cancer?" and I am reminded of a quotation by Robert Henri in *The Art of the Spirit*: "No knowledge is so easily found as when it is needed."

~~I am a cancer specialist.~~

② My decision to specialize in oncology was made the day my own cancer was diagnosed.

~~I chose to pursue a career in medicine.~~ For me medicine was not only the obvious, but the only choice. ③ As a result I was able to apply not only my intellect, but my heart to my studies, and later to my patients.

① By rewriting the opening sentence, the author makes it clear that the essay will focus on a cause-and-effect relationship.

② The author replaces a general sentence with a specific detail to clarify a causal relationship.

③ The author adds a transition to link his illness with his success as a student and as a physician.

Publishing

- **Internet** Post your essay on an appropriate site or bulletin board.
- **Science Magazine** Collect scientific cause-and-effect essays from your classmates and publish them in a science magazine.
- **Oral Presentation** Have a group of classmates read their essays aloud for an audience. Then invite questions from the audience about the topics.

Applying Language Skills: Using Precise Language

Cause-and-effect essays are more effective when you use precise language to describe events and situations. These techniques will help you make your language precise.

- To make nouns and verbs more exact, narrow their focus as much as possible.

General: food
Specific: broccoli

- Use specific nouns or verbs.

General: pull it through the hole
Specific: thread

- Use specific adjectives.

Vague: The result will be a nice sweater.
Specific: The result will be a bright blue angora sweater.

Practice Rewrite these sentences, making the italicized words more precise.

1. The Spaniards brought *animals* to America.
2. That runner *moves* down the track very fast.

Writer's Solution Connection
Language Lab

For help in writing unified and coherent paragraphs, work through the Topic Sentence and Support lesson and the Unity in Paragraphs lesson.

Revising

Review the Writing Skills Focus and the guidelines for a cause-and-effect essay. Use the Cause-and-Effect Organizer (page 119 in ***Writing and Language Transparencies***) to model methods of organization.

Writers at Work Videodisc
Share with students film critic Anne Billson's views on editing and revising. Then ask students: How does Billson approach revising?

Play frames 30616 to 31352

Reinforce and Extend

Review the Writing Guidelines
Review the characteristics of a cause-and-effect essay, and encourage students to evaluate their own papers using these criteria.

Applying Language Skills

Using Precise Language
Encourage them to replace vague language with precise and specific language.

Practice

1. The Spaniards brought *horses* to America.
2. That runner *sprints* down the track very fast.

For additional practice, have students complete page 99 in the *Writer's Solution Grammar Practice Book* on Using Words Effectively or the **Language Lab CD-ROM** lesson on Writing with Nouns and Verbs.

ASSESSMENT		4	3	2	1
PORTFOLIO ASSESSMENT Use the Cause-Effect Rubric in ***Alternative Assessment*** (p. 103) to assess students' writing. Add these criteria to customize the rubric to this assignment.	**Transitions to Indicate Cause and Effect**	The writer effectively uses transitions that indicate cause-and-effect relationships.	The writer uses cause-and-effect transitions, but needs more for clarification.	The cause-and-effect relationships among details needs to be made clear with transitions.	The writer does not use any transitions to indicate cause-and-effect relationships.
	Specific Examples	The writer uses sufficient and appropriate specific examples that strengthen the cause-and-effect relationship of the essay.	The writer uses some specific examples but needs more to reinforce the cause-and-effect relationship of the essay.	The writer's examples are not specific and do not always strengthen the cause-and-effect relationship.	The writer does not use any specific examples.

Introduce the Strategy

Students may have experience finding the main idea in textbooks and other information for their social studies and science classes. These texts are not usually written with the sharp headlines, eye-catching visuals, and punchy language that characterize magazine and newspaper articles but also obscure the main idea. The following strategies will help students transfer prior skills and acquire new skills in identifying main ideas in articles.

Customize for *Non-Visual/Spatial Learners*

Have these students write a brief summary of each illustration in the sample article on this page. Then have them identify common points in each summary. After reading the sample article and looking at their list of common themes, students will be better able to determine the article's main idea.

Apply the Strategy

Have students scan the sample article on time management and jot down their ideas based on appearance. Then have students read the article and answer the questions.

Answers

1. The main idea of the opening section is implied.
2. Students can infer that the main idea is that P3 will make them more relaxed.
3. The cartoon supports the main idea of the excerpt by showing a man, before P3, who looks rushed, and a man, after P3, who looks calm and relaxed.
4. The second section of this article suggests that in order to manage your time better, you need to prioritize.

Identify Main Ideas in an Article — Real-World Reading Skills Workshop

Strategies for Success

Journalists use sharp headlines, punchy language, and eye-catching visuals to communicate their ideas. At times, all that style can make the substance hard to find. Looking for main ideas as you read can help you filter through the attention-grabbers to find the core of an article.

Look for Stated Main Ideas Some writers state their ideas directly. You'll often find important ideas stated in the introduction or conclusion of an article. Be aware of generalizations or inferences drawn by the author—these often summarize a main idea.

Read for Implied Ideas Not all main ideas are stated directly. Writers often require active reading by presenting a variety of information and allowing the reader to draw conclusions. To identify implied main ideas, pause after you read each section and ask yourself these questions:

- What was that section about?
- Why did the writer include these details?
- How can I state the main idea of this section in one sentence?

Analyze Visuals The photographs, charts, graphs, or illustrations that accompany an article can offer valuable clues about the article's main ideas. After reading an article, go back and review the graphic elements, including the headline typography. Your evaluation will help you identify the main idea.

You will also find it helpful to identify main ideas in these types of material:
- Newspaper articles
- Political brochures and leaflets
- Transcripts of speeches

Apply the Strategies

Look at this article about time management. Then answer the questions that follow.

1. Is the main idea of the opening section stated or implied?
2. What is the main idea of the opening?
3. How does the cartoon support the main idea of this excerpt?
4. What main idea does the second section of the article suggest?

Take Time For P3

Before 3

After 3

"There aren't enough hours in a day!"
"Don't talk to me—I've got no time."
"If time is money, I'm BROKE."

Sound familiar? You probably face difficult deadlines all the time. Need some help organizing your time? P3 to the rescue! This simple strategy can help you get a grip on your time.

So what's P3? Three easy steps to successful time management: Prioritize, Plan, and Proceed.

Prioritize The first thing you need to do is set some priorities. Make a list of everything you need to do and then rank the tasks from most to least important. To prioritize realistically, you'll need to consider your personal goals as well as your responsibilities.

Beyond the Classroom

Career Connection

Graphic Artist A graphic artist is responsible for the layout of articles, such as the one shown on this page, that appear in books, magazines, and advertisements. They come up with designs that complement text and include attention-getting graphics that hook readers. Graphic artists may be responsible for choosing art and designs, or they may work from ideas given by writers.

PART 2

The Empire and Its Discontents

Miniature photographic portraits commemorative 1897
Jubilee Victoria (adult and child) Alexandra and George V

In one sense, the Victorian Age was a time of optimism and progress. Abroad, the British Empire was expanding. At home, new goods and gadgets were improving the quality of life. Yet beneath the blare of self-congratulation, the poet Matthew Arnold heard "an eternal note of sadness." One troubling foreign policy issue, Irish independence, was all too close to home. Also, those foreigners in their own country, Britain's urban poor, were not sharing in the general prosperity.

One-Minute Planning Guide

The selections in this section reveal the opposing faces of the Victorian Era. "Progress in Comfort" shows the joyful face of progress. The poems "Dover Beach," "Recessional," "The Widow at Windsor," and the journalistic essay "Condition of Ireland" reveal the uncertainty and social problems that existed at the height of the British Empire. The speech "Opening Statement for the Inaugural Session of the Forum for Peace and Reconciliation," touches on one troubling legacy of the Empire—a divided Ireland.

Customize for
Varying Student Needs

When assigning the selections in this part, keep in mind these factors:

"Dover Beach"
- Evocative lyric poem
- Less proficient readers may need guidance in reading in sentences.

"Recessional"
- Historical context will make the poem's meaning more apparent.

"The Widow at Windsor"
- Students may have difficulty with the Cockney dialect in which this poem is written.

"Condition of Ireland"
- High-level vocabulary and sentence structure may prove daunting to less proficient readers.

"Progress in Personal Comfort"
- Entertaining look at technological advances

"Opening Statement …"
- Provides insight into current and ongoing events

Humanities: Art

Miniature Photographic Portraits, 1897.

These photographic miniatures commemorate the sixtieth anniversary of Queen Victoria's reign. The portraits on the top are of Queen Victoria at the age of 78 (top left) and as a child (top right). Victoria became queen in 1837, at the age of eighteen, and ruled for more than sixty-three years. The portrait on the bottom right is Victoria's grandson, George Frederick, who became King George V in 1910; he is the grandfather of Queen Elizabeth II. The remaining portrait is of Princess Alexandra. A Danish princess, Alexandra had married Victoria's oldest son, Albert Edward, who became King Edward VII when Victoria died in 1901.

Ask students the following:

1. What attitude toward monarchs do these photographs suggest? *They suggest distant respect; the framing ribbons and flowers suggest reverence.*
2. How do you think the English people's attitude toward their royal family has changed in the past century? What factors have contributed to this change? *Most students will say that the English people feel less respect for the royal family, both because of the behavior of its individual members and because the media publicize details of the family's personal life that would have been kept private a century ago.*

Prepare and Engage

OBJECTIVES

1. To read, comprehend, and interpret poems
2. To relate poems to personal experience
3. To draw conclusions, to make connections
4. To recognize the relationship between mood and theme
5. To build vocabulary in context and learn the word root *-domi-*
6. To identify and use present tense verbs
7. To write a speech, using statistics as a form of support
8. To respond to the poems through writing, speaking and listening, and projects

SKILLS INSTRUCTION

Vocabulary: Word Roots: *-domi-*
Grammar: Present Tense
Reading Strategy: Draw Conclusions
Literary Focus: Mood as a Key to Theme
Writing: Statistics as a Form of Support
Speaking and Listening: Oral Interpretation (teacher edition)
Critical Viewing: Support; Relate; Criticize

PORTFOLIO OPPORTUNITIES

Writing: Letter to the Editor; Proposal; Literary Analysis
Writing Mini-Lesson: World Responsibility Speech
Speaking and Listening: Address to England; Oral Interpretation
Projects: Film Review; Tour of a Castle

More About the Authors

The poems of **Matthew Arnold** are sometimes considered "dark," because they deal with people's alienation from nature and from one another. Perhaps surprisingly, then, upon the publication of his first volume of poetry, his sister stated that the book was "almost like a new introduction to him. . . . I felt there was so much more of . . . practical questioning in Matt's book than I was prepared for. . . ."

Rudyard Kipling supported the colonial expansion of the British, opposed giving the vote to women, and favored a military draft. Because of these views, he lost and was never able to regain his early popularity. Today, however, Kipling's works are once more anthologized, and most critics agree that his works have literary merit.

Guide for Interpreting

Matthew Arnold (1822–1888)

Matthew Arnold's poetry deals with themes of isolation and alienation that are as relevant today as they were in the nineteenth century. In fact, the American novelist Norman Mailer used a modified quotation from Arnold's "Dover Beach" for the title of his book about a major Vietnam War protest, *Armies of the Night*.

A Social Conscience While attending Oxford University, Arnold developed the social conscience that was to guide his career as a public servant, poet, and literary critic. In 1851, he accepted the post of Inspector of Schools. In this job he did much to improve education in Great Britain. All the while, he remained a poet at heart, though his first two books, published in 1849 and 1852, met with little success.

Literary Achievement Arnold's literary fortunes changed in 1853 with the publication of *Poems,* which included a long preface that established the author as a major critic. *New Poems*, published in 1867, contained Arnold's celebrated "Dover Beach." After completing this collection, Arnold believed that he had expressed everything he had to say in poetry. From that point on he wrote literary criticism, like the essays in *Culture and Anarchy* (1869). There, he argues that literature should train us to open our minds to what is true and valuable in life.

Rudyard Kipling (1865–1936)

Rudyard Kipling's works are known for their celebration of the British Empire, yet they also warn of the costs and responsibilities of world dominion. While praising the benefits of imperialism, he emphasizes the responsibility of the British to bring their "civilized" ways to other parts of the world.

Early Success Kipling was born to British parents in India, one of Britain's largest colonies. At the age of five, he was placed in a foster home in England, due to the belief that British children should be educated in England. However, he returned to India in 1882 to work as a journalist. During the next seven years, he published a number of witty poems and stories, and by the time he visited London in 1890, he was a celebrity.

Kipling's Achievements Kipling is known as a Victorian author because he produced his best work before the death of Queen Victoria in 1901. In its great variety, that work includes children's classics—*The Jungle Book* (1895), *Second Jungle Book* (1896), *Captains Courageous* (1897), and *Kim* (1901) in addition to well-known poems like "Recessional," and his autobiography, *The Best of Me.* For many years Kipling was the most popular English poet and in 1907 he became the first English writer to be awarded the Nobel Prize for Literature.

◆ Background for Understanding

HISTORY: ARNOLD, KIPLING, AND IMPERIALISM

In 1857, Britain took direct control of all India, and in the 1880's and 1890's, seized the African colonies of Kenya and the Sudan. Even as the Empire expanded, however, writers expressed doubts about life in the world's most powerful nation.

In "Dover Beach," for example, Matthew Arnold laments the decline of religious faith and depicts the world as a place where "ignorant armies clash by night."

Even Kipling, who supported British imperialism, uses "Recessional" to warn against the perils of pride. Written for the sixtieth anniversary of Queen Victoria's reign, the poem was a warning to those who boasted of Britain's world domination.

Prentice Hall Literature Program Resources

REINFORCE / RETEACH / EXTEND

Selection Support Pages
Build Vocabulary: Word Roots: *-domi-*, p. 192
Grammar and Style: Present Tense, p. 193
Reading Strategy: Draw Conclusions, p. 194
Literary Focus: Mood as a Key to Theme, p. 195

Strategies for Diverse Student Needs, p. 40

Beyond Literature
Cross-Curricular Connection: Science, p. 40

Formal Assessment Selection Test, pp. 197–199; Assessment Resources Software

Alternative Assessment, p. 40

Writing and Language Transparencies
Persuasive Essay, pp. 37–43

Resource Pro CD-RM
"Dover Beach," "Recessional," "The Widow at Windsor"—includes all resource material and customizable lesson plan

Listening to Literature Audiocassettes
"Dover Beach," "Recessional," "The Widow at Windsor"

Dover Beach ◆ Recessional ◆ The Widow at Windsor ◆

◆ Literature and Your Life

Connect Your Experience

The photo of Earth taken from the moon shows a blue jewel of a planet, alone in the darkness of outer space, giving us a Big Picture of where we stand in the universe.

About a century before space travel, poets took flights of inspiration through Inner Space, allowing them to see another kind of Big Picture, a vision of things as a whole. Works like "Dover Beach" and "Recessional" convey this vision.

Journal Writing Briefly list some major trends that will influence life on this planet in the next century.

Thematic Focus: The Empire and Its Discontents

What are some problems that Arnold and Kipling see when they view things as a whole?

◆ Build Vocabulary

Word Roots: *-domi-*

In "Recessional," Kipling uses the word *dominion* when referring to the power of the British empire. This word contains the word root *-domi-*, which means "lord" or "master." To have *dominion* means "to be master of, to rule."

Word Bank

Before you read, preview this list of words from the poems.

tranquil
cadence
turbid
dominion
contrite

◆ Literary Focus

Mood as a Key to Theme

Poems contain emotional thoughts and thoughtful emotions. With thought and emotion so closely linked in a poem, the **mood** or feeling it calls up in you is bound to be related to its central idea or **theme**. By reading a poem with your feelings—responding to emotionally charged words and images—you'll gradually find your way to its ideas.

In "Dover Beach," the crash of waves brings "The eternal note of sadness in." This mood of sadness leads you to the poem's theme, which concerns a world that has "neither joy, nor love, nor light."

◆ Reading Strategy

Draw Conclusions

By **drawing conclusions** about what you read—making generalizations based on evidence—you can link elements that at first seem unrelated.

In "The Widow at Windsor," for example, it may not be clear at first why a "widow" has a "gold crown" and "ships on the foam." However, when you see the reference to "Missis Victorier's sons," you can conclude that the widow is Queen Victoria herself. Using this information, you can draw further conclusions about who the speaker is and why the poem is written in dialect.

Read the other poems in the same way, drawing conclusions about the connections between details.

◆ Grammar and Style

Present Tense

In "Dover Beach," Matthew Arnold uses **present tense** verbs like *lies* and *gleams* to convey both the immediacy of an experience and the truth revealed by that experience:

Experience: ". . . the light / *Gleams* and *is* gone . . ."

Truth: "And we *are* here as on a darkling plain / Swept with confused alarms of struggle and flight, / Where ignorant armies *clash* by night."

Interest Grabber

Write on the chalkboard: "Our country, right or wrong." Have students discuss the meaning of the phrase. Ask students if they believe this is an appropriate attitude. Encourage students to think about the phrase as they read the poems that follow and consider whether Matthew Arnold and Rudyard Kipling would agree or disagree with the statement.

Customize for
Less Proficient Readers
Have students follow along in their texts as they listen to the poems on the **Listening to Literature Audiocassettes.** Then have students work in pairs, taking turns reading each poem aloud and taking notes on the feelings each poem evokes. Finally, students should compare their notes.

Customize for
More Advanced Students
After students have read each poem, have them reread and write down the mood and rhyme scheme of each. Have them determine how the rhyme affects both the mood and basic meaning of the poem.

Customize for
English Language Learners
Use gestures, pictures, and simplified vocabulary to help students understand what the poems are about. If your students have a basic command of English, you might focus on teaching the nuances of different terms such as *gleam* and *glimmer.*

Customize for
Interpersonal Learners
Have these students work in small groups. Assign an entire poem or a stanza to a group member. That student should become an expert on that poem or stanza and teach it to the rest of the group.

Preparing for Standardized Tests

Reading and Vocabulary The verbal reasoning portion of the SAT contains sentence completion questions that hinge on a student's using context clues to choose the words that make sense in the sentence.

Knowledge of word roots can help students discern the meaning of unfamiliar words. For example, students might be given an item such as the following:

The ______ reason for his failure is his inability to ______ his time. *(D)*

(A) secondary, facilitate
(B) preeminent, serialize
(C) temporary, utilize
(D) predominant, organize
(E) comprehensive, languish

The Build Vocabulary lesson for this selection focuses on the word root *-domi-*. After students have learned the meaning of the root and completed the activities on page 798, have a volunteer choose the correct answer for the sample exercise. For additional practice, use the Build Vocabulary page, in ***Selection Support,*** p. 192.

Develop Understanding

One-Minute Insight Looking out a window from the white chalk cliffs of Dover over to France, the speaker describes a lovely moonlit scene over a tranquil bay. Then a note of sadness creeps in as he bemoans the loss of certainty, faith, and peace in the world. The speaker holds the late Victorian view that the world was changing as a result of Darwin's theory, the Industrial Revolution, and British imperialism.

❶ **Enrichment** Because Matthew Arnold and his wife stopped at Dover on their wedding journey, most critics assume that Arnold wrote "Dover Beach" with his wife in mind.

◆ Critical Thinking

❷ **Interpret** The speaker states that "the cliffs of England stand, / Glimmering and vast." Ask students with what they associate the word "cliffs." *Most students will associate the word* cliffs *with something tall, strong, immovable, and dangerous.*

◆ Literary Focus

❸ **Mood as a Key to Theme** Imagery is one device that poets use to establish mood. Ask students if the mood seems positive or negative in lines 9–10. Explain. *Suggested response: The mood seems more negative because the words "grating roar" evoke an unpleasant sound and the words "draw back and fling" evoke a negative image of forcefulness.*

▶Critical Viewing◀

❹ **Support** Sample answer: Yes, the photograph captures the "eternal note of sadness" because the scene looks deserted, the color of the sea is dark, and the cliffs look black. The sun appears to be setting, which implies an ending and adds to the feeling of sadness.

Dover Beach

Matthew Arnold

❶ The sea is calm tonight.
The tide is full, the moon lies fair
Upon the straits:[1] on the French coast the light
❷ Gleams and is gone; the cliffs of England stand,
Glimmering and vast, out in the tranquil bay.
Come to the window, sweet is the night air!
Only, from the long line of spray

❸ Where the sea meets the moon-blanched land,
Listen! you hear the grating roar
Of pebbles which the waves draw back, and fling,
At their return, up the high strand,[2]
Begin, and cease, and then again begin,
With tremulous cadence slow, and bring
The eternal note of sadness in.

▼ Critical Viewing Does this photograph capture the "eternal note of sadness" Arnold describes? Explain. [Support] ❹

1. **straits:** Straits of Dover, between England and France.
2. **strand:** Shore.

Block Scheduling Strategies

Consider these suggestions to take advantage of extended class time.

- Have students complete the journal writing activity (p. 791) and discuss their responses as a class.
- Introduce the Literary Focus and have students discuss the link between mood and theme based on their observations of movies, songs, and literature. After students read the poems, have them answer the Literary Focus questions on page 798. For further practice, assign the Literary Focus page in ***Selection Support,*** p. 195.
- Direct students to work on the Grammar and Style activity on page 798. For further practice, have them complete the Grammar and Style page, p. 193, in ***Selection Support.***
- After students have read each poem, have them answer the Check Your Comprehension and Critical Thinking questions (pp. 793, 795, 797).
- Students may conduct a debate about imperialism, as suggested in ***Alternative Assessment,*** p. 40.

Sophocles[3] long ago
Heard it on the Aegean,[4] and it brought
Into his mind the turbid ebb and flow
Of human misery; we
Find also in the sound a thought,
Hearing it by this distant northern sea. (5)

The Sea of Faith
Was once, too, at the full, and round earth's shore (6)
Lay like the folds of a bright girdle furled.
But now I only hear
Its melancholy, long, withdrawing roar,
Retreating, to the breath
Of the night wind, down the vast edges drear
And naked shingles[5] of the world.

Ah, love, let us be true
To one another! for the world, which seems
To lie before us like a land of dreams,
So various, so beautiful, so new,
Hath really neither joy, nor love, nor light,
Nor certitude, nor peace, nor help for pain;
And we are here as on a darkling[6] plain
Swept with confused alarms of struggle and flight,
Where ignorant armies clash by night.

3. **Sophocles** (säf´ ə klēz´): Greek tragic dramatist (496?-406 B.C.).
4. **Aegean** (ē jē´ ən): Arm of the Mediterranean Sea between Greece and Turkey.
5. **shingles** *n.*: Beaches covered with large, coarse, water-worn gravel.
6. **darkling** *adj.*: In the dark.

◆ Build Vocabulary

tranquil (tran´kwil) *adj.*: Calm; serene; peaceful

cadence (kād´ əns) *n.*: Measured movement

turbid (tur´ bid) *adj.*: Confused; perplexed

Guide for Responding

◆ Literature and Your Life

Reader's Response Do you agree with the speaker's view of the world? Why or why not?

Thematic Focus How does the final image of the poem challenge the Victorian idea of progress?

☑ Check Your Comprehension

1. What does the speaker see from his window?
2. Who else does the speaker say "long ago" heard the "tremulous cadence slow"?
3. What does the speaker urge his beloved to do?
4. What sad reality does the speaker describe for his companion in lines 30-34?

◆ Critical Thinking

INTERPRET

1. A symbol is a thing, person, or place that stands for something beyond itself. Explain the symbolism of the "cliffs of England" (line 4) and "night" (line 37). **[Interpret]**
2. State the message of lines 35-37 in your own words. **[Draw Conclusions]**

EVALUATE

3. To what extent does Arnold's plea to "be true / To one another" in lines 29-30 provide a satisfactory answer to the problem "Of human misery"? **[Make a Judgment]**

Speaking and Listening Mini-Lesson

Oral Interpretation

This mini-lesson supports the Speaking and Listening activity in the Idea Bank on page 799.

Introduce the Concept Explain that an oral interpretation is an oral reading of a work of literature in which the reader conveys his or her understanding of the work through the way he or she speaks the words. In this activity, students will convey the tone of "Dover Beach."

Develop Background For oral interpretation to be effective, the reader must know the work well, both on a literal and on an emotional level.

Students should read over "Dover Beach," making notes as to how to read each line, which words to emphasize, and when to lower or raise their voices.

Apply the Information Encourage students to use a tape recorder to practice their presentation. Then have each student do their oral interpretation for the class.

Assess the Outcome Have the listeners evaluate the presentations on the basis of feeling, emphasis, modulation, and tone.

◆ Grammar and Style

(5) **Present Tense** Ask in what way the use of the present tense verb "find" in line 19 emphasizes the immediate truth of the experience. *It implies that the truth has not changed over all the centuries.*

(6) **Clarification** The "Sea of Faith" refers to religious faith, which Darwin's theory of evolution had badly shaken. Arnold, along with many other Victorians, felt that a choice had to be made between science and religion.

Reinforce and Extend

Answers

◆ Literature and Your Life

Reader's Response Students' responses should show a grasp of the speaker's pessimistic view of the world.

Thematic Focus The final image suggests that the human race is still "in the dark" rather than approaching enlightenment.

☑ Check Your Comprehension

1. He sees the sea and the moon.
2. The speaker says Sophocles "Heard it on the Aegean . . ."
3. The speaker urges that he and his beloved "be true/To one another . . ."
4. The speaker says the world is not as wonderful as it seems; there is no joy, certainty, or peace.

◆ Critical Thinking

1. The "cliffs of England" stand for England itself—something seemingly fixed, immutable, and solid. "Night" symbolizes a world in which nothing is fixed, immutable, and solid.
2. Possible response: The world is confusing, uncertain, dangerous, and frightening.
3. The speaker implies that faith and goodness in a personal relationship between two people can help alleviate "human misery."

Develop Understanding

One-Minute Insight As a recessional signals the end of a religious service, this poem heralds the end of the British Empire. Although Rudyard Kipling was a staunch supporter of British imperialism, he recognized the dangers of complacency and overblown pride.

▶Critical Viewing◀

❶ **Relate** Students may point out that, like a modern parade, this parade is held on a main street in the center of town, and people view it from any available space—the side of the road, windows, balconies, and rooftops.

❷ **Clarification** Here the word "awful" means "awe-inspiring."

◆Critical Thinking

❸ **Infer** Have students draw upon their knowledge of biomes from science class. What does this phrase say about the extent of the Empire? *It extends from subpolar forests characterized by pines to tropical regions where palms are the dominant trees.*

◆Critical Thinking

❹ **Interpret** Ask students what Kipling means by "Lest we forget." *Suggested response: Kipling is warning the people of England not to take their preeminent status for granted. By using "we" at such a public celebration, Kipling seems to imply that he means everyone—from Queen Victoria down to the lowliest laborer.*

Recessional[1]

Rudyard Kipling

Queen Victoria's Diamond Jubilee procession in London in 1897

❶ ▶ **Critical Viewing** Although the parade shown here took place in 1897, what elements are common to parades of today? **[Relate]**

In 1897 a national celebration called the "Diamond Jubilee" was held in honor of the sixtieth anniversary of Queen Victoria's reign. The occasion prompted a great deal of boasting about the strength and greatness of the empire. Kipling responded to the celebration by writing this poem, reminding the people of England that the British empire might not last forever.

God of our fathers, known of old—
    Lord of our far-flung battle-line—
❷ Beneath whose awful Hand we hold
    ❸ Dominion over palm and pine—
Lord God of Hosts, be with us yet
Lest we forget—lest we forget!

The tumult and the shouting dies—
    The Captains and the Kings depart—
Still stands Thine ancient Sacrifice,
    An humble and a contrite heart.[2]
Lord God of Hosts, be with us yet,
❹ Lest we forget—lest we forget!

1. **Recessional** *n.*: Hymn sung at the end of a religious service.
2. **An . . . heart:** Allusion to the Bible (Psalms 51:17): "The sacrifices of God are a broken spirit: a broken and contrite heart, O God, thou wilt not despise."

Beyond the Classroom

Career Connection

Events Coordinator "Recessional" was written for the national celebration of Queen Victoria's Diamond Jubilee. One can only imagine the amount of planning that went into staging the event. If a similar event were held today, an events coordinator would be hired to oversee the proceedings. Ask students what they know about events coordinators. You might share the following information and suggest that interested students find out more by contacting an events coordinator.

- Events coordinators have outgoing personalities and enjoy meeting people.
- They have a "can do" attitude and thrive on challenges.
- They understand the "big picture."
- They know how to hire (and fire) people.
- They have outstanding organizational skills or delegate the work to those who do.
- Events coordinators often have degrees in Public Relations or Marketing.

Far-called, our navies melt away—
    On dune and headland sinks the fire[3]—
Lo, all our pomp of yesterday
    Is one with Nineveh[4] and Tyre![5]
Judge of the Nations, spare us yet,
Lest we forget—lest we forget!

If, drunk with sight of power, we loose
    Wild tongues that have not Thee in awe—
Such boasting as the Gentiles use
    Or lesser breeds without the Law—[6]
Lord God of Hosts, be with us yet,
Lest we forget—lest we forget!

For heathen heart that puts her trust
    In reeking tube[7] and iron shard[8]—
All valiant dust that builds on dust,
    And guarding calls not Thee to guard—
For frantic boast and foolish word,
Thy mercy on Thy People, Lord!

---

3. **On . . . fire:** Bonfires were lit on high ground all over Britain as part of the opening ceremonies of the Jubilee celebration.
4. **Nineveh** (nin´ ə və): Ancient capital of the Assyrian Empire, the ruins of which were discovered buried in desert sands in the 1850's.
5. **Tyre** (tīr): Once a great port and the center of ancient Phoenician culture, now a small town in Lebanon.
6. **Such boasting . . . Law:** Allusion to the Bible (Romans 2:14): "For when the Gentiles, which have not the law, do by nature the things contained in the law, these, having not the law, are a law unto themselves."
7. **tube:** Barrel of a gun.
8. **shard:** Fragment of a bombshell.

◆ Build Vocabulary

dominion (də min´yen) *n.*: Place of rule; home territory

contrite (kən trīt´) *adj.*: Willing to repent or atone

Guide for Responding

◆ Literature and Your Life

Reader's Response Do you think this poem is relevant to contemporary society? Explain.

Thematic Focus What warning does Kipling give in this poem?

☑ Check Your Comprehension

1. To whom is this poem addressed?
2. In lines 15–16, what does the speaker suggest happens to "our pomp of yesterday"?
3. What does the speaker beg for in the last line?

◆ Critical Thinking

INTERPRET

1. To whom is this poem really addressed? **[Interpret]**
2. What qualities and actions does the poem condemn? Support your answer. **[Infer]**
3. (a) What double meaning is contained in the poem's title? (b) How is this ambiguity appropriate to the overall mood? **[Interpret]**
4. What is the poem's theme? **[Draw Conclusions]**

APPLY

5. Does anyone today issue warnings similar to Kipling's? Explain. **[Relate]**

◆ Grammar and Style

❺ **Present Tense** Have students identify the present tense verbs in lines 13–16 and explain how the use of present tense affects the message. *The present tense verbs are "melt," "sinks," and "is." By using present tense, Kipling forces the reader to consider that these things could happen to the British Empire and, in fact, could even be starting to happen that very day.*

◆ Critical Thinking

❻ **Evaluate** Kipling does not end the last stanza with the same last line that he has used throughout. Ask students if this change makes the poem more effective or less effective. *Sample answer: The poem is more effective with this final line because it removes the emphasis from "we" and puts the emphasis on God.*

Reinforce and Extend

Answers

◆ Literature and Your Life

Reader's Response Students may say that the message is timeless; modern empires such as the Soviet Union have crumbled, and the United States should not assume that it will always dominate world politics.

Thematic Focus Kipling warns that the British Empire may not last forever.

☑ Check Your Comprehension

1. The poem is addressed to God.
2. The speaker suggests that, like empires of old, the British Empire, too, will crumble.
3. The speaker begs for the mercy and forgiveness of God.

Enrichment

Remind students that an allusion is a reference to a well-known person, place, event, literary work, or work of art.

In "Recessional," Rudyard Kipling alludes to the ancient cities of Ninevah and Tyre (lines 15–16). No longer glorious, these cities were once the capitals of mighty empires. Kipling's allusion, therefore, reminds Britons that their Empire may decline as all previous empires have. Encourage students to find other allusions in the poems of Kipling and Arnold and explain the references.

◆ Critical Thinking

1. The poem is really addressed to the people of England.
2. The poem condemns pride and lust for power; it condemns lack of humility before God. Students may cite lines 10, 15–16, 19–20, 25–26, and 29.
3. (a) The poem is in the form of a recessional hymn and speaks of the receding power of the British Empire. (b) This ambiguity is appropriate because the poem itself directly addresses God, yet is really meant as a warning to the British people.
4. The theme of the poem is the importance of humility and faith in God over pride and faith in any temporal entity.
5. Students may cite warnings about global warming, pollution, poverty, financial markets, and other issues that are presented by conservation groups, United Nations committees, aritists, economists, and so on.

Develop Understanding

One-Minute Insight During the sixty-three-year reign of Queen Victoria, Great Britain reached the height of its power. By the last decade of the nineteenth century, however, cracks in the strength of the British Empire were beginning to show. In "The Widow at Windsor," the speaker is a common soldier who reminds Britons that one country's domination always comes at a price.

❶ **Clarification** Remind students that the speaker in this poem is a common soldier who speaks in Cockney dialect. The initial "h" is omitted from words along with the final "f" in "of," the "d" in "and," and the "g" in "morning."

❷ **Clarification** "[H]er nick on the cavalry 'orses" refers to the V.R.I. mark that shows that the horses belong to the queen. The letters stand for Victoria, Regina Imperatrix, "Victoria, Queen and Empress."

◆ Literary Focus

❸ **Mood as a Key to Theme**
Have students analyze the mood created in these lines. *The mood is cheerful on the surface, but there is an undercurrent of bitterness; when taken literally, lines 11–14 seem to be a toast to the queen. However, the repetition of "poor beggars" in line 15 is ironic and angry.* What does the mood reveal about the theme of the poem? *The mood shows that the theme is not a happy one and will probably deal with the reasons the soldiers are bitter.*

▶Critical Viewing◀

❹ **Criticize** Suggested response: *The photographs capture the relationship well. Queen Victoria, dressed in black mourning clothes, looks larger than life. She appears to be looking down at all the soldiers, who are referred to as her sons in the poem.*

The Widow at Windsor

Rudyard Kipling

❶ 'Ave you 'eard o' the Widow at Windsor
With a hairy gold crown on 'er 'ead?
She 'as ships on the foam—she 'as millions at 'ome,
An' she pays us poor beggars in red.
(Ow, poor beggars in red!)
❷ There's 'er nick on the cavalry 'orses,
There's 'er mark on the medical stores—
An' 'er troops you'll find with a fair wind be'ind
That takes us to various wars.
(Poor beggars!—barbarious wars!)
Then 'ere's to the Widow at Windsor,
An' 'ere's to the stores an' the guns,
❸ The men an' the 'orses what makes up the forces
O' Missis Victorier's sons.
(Poor beggars! Victorier's sons!)

Walk wide o' the Widow at Windsor,
For 'alf o' Creation she owns:
We'ave bought 'er the same with the sword an' the flame,
An' we've salted it down with our bones.

❹ ◀ **Critical Viewing** How well do these two visuals capture the familial relationship between Queen Victoria and her soldiers? **[Criticize]**

BRITISH INFANTRY IN BARRACKS, AT GALLIPOLI.

Cross-Curricular Connection: Social Studies

A great deal of progress had been made during the reign of Queen Victoria. Yet, much greater change was still to come. Discuss references to concepts or objects in the poem that have gone through a great deal of change or that seem outdated today. Discussion topics might include some of the following:

- The monarchy in Britain has undergone tremendous change over the past one hundred years. Once the rulers of the country, the monarchy today are mere figureheads.
- The reference to the cavalry, the swords, and the men's horses seems almost quaint, as modern warfare retired horses and most hand-to-hand combat.

Interested students might make a timeline that documents the chronology of some of the changes.

(Poor beggars!—it's blue with our bones!)
Hands off o' the sons o' the widow,
Hands off o' the goods in 'er shop.
For the kings must come down an' the emperors frown
When the Widow at Windsor says "Stop!"
(Poor beggars!—we're sent to say "Stop!")
Then 'ere's to the Lodge o' the Widow,
From the Pole to the Tropics it runs—
To the Lodge that we tile with the rank an' the file, ❺
An' open in form with the guns.
(Poor beggars!—it's always they guns!)

We 'ave 'eard o' the Widow at Windsor,
It's safest to leave 'er alone:
For 'er sentries we stand by the sea an' the land
Wherever the bugles are blown.
(Poor beggars!—an' don't we get blown!)
Take 'old o' the Wings o' the Mornin', ❻
An' flop round the earth till you're dead;
But you won't get away from the tune that they play
To the bloomin' old rag over'ead.
(Poor beggars!—it's 'ot over'ead!)
Then 'ere's to the sons o' the Widow,
Wherever, 'owever they roam.
'Ere's all they desire, an' if they require
A speedy return to their 'ome.
(Poor beggars!—they'll never see 'ome!)

Guide for Responding

◆ Literature and Your Life

Reader's Response What images, ideas, or lines in this poem do you find most striking? Explain.

Thematic Focus Does the speaker reveal any problems in the British empire? Why or why not?

☑ Check Your Comprehension

1. (a) Who is the Widow at Windsor? (b) According to line 17, what does she own?
2. (a) Who is the poem's speaker? (b) What does he do for the Widow at Windsor?
3. According to the last line of the poem, what fate lies in store for the soldiers?

◆ Critical Thinking

INTERPRET

1. What is surprising about the speaker's description of Queen Victoria as the Widow of Windsor? **[Infer]**
2. Would you describe the speaker's tone as disloyal or disrespectful? Explain. **[Analyze]**
3. Why does Kipling describe the empire from the perspective of a common soldier? **[Draw Conclusions]**

EVALUATE

4. Is Kipling's use of a cockney accent an effective way to convey that the speaker is a common man? Explain. **[Evaluate]**

Beyond the Selection

FURTHER READING

Other Works by Matthew Arnold
"To Marguerite—Continued"
"Growing Old"

Other Works by Rudyard Kipling
"Tommy"; "The Song of the Sons"; "The Song of the Cities"; "England's Answer"

We suggest that you preview these works before recommending them to students.

INTERNET

You can find additional information about Matthew Arnold and Rudyard Kipling on the Internet at the following sites.

For information about Matthew Arnold, go to **http://www.library.utoronto.ca/www/utel/RP/authors/arnold.html**

For more about Rudyard Kipling, visit **http://www.kipling.org.uk/rudyard.htm**

We *strongly recommend* that you preview sites before you send students to them.

◆ Grammar and Style

❺ Present Tense Have students identify the present tense verbs in these verses. *The present tense verbs are* is *("'ere's"),* runs, tile, *and* open. Ask how the present tense verbs affect the meaning. *The present tense verbs emphasize that the acts of the British Empire are current and ongoing.*

❻ Clarification The "Wings o' the Mornin'" is an allusion to Psalm 139: "If I take the wings of the morning, / And dwell in the uttermost parts of the sea; / Even there shall thy hand lead me . . ." Kipling may be suggesting that it is just as impossible for the soldier to get away from Queen Victoria and her policies.

Reinforce and Extend

Answers

◆ Literature and Your Life

Reader's Response Sample response: The "bloomin' old rag over'ead" is a striking image, revealing the speaker's negative attitude toward the British flag.

Thematic Focus Yes, the lives of the poor people are sacrificed to the greatness of the Queen and the Empire.

☑ Check Your Comprehension

1. (a) She is Queen Victoria. (b) She owns much of the world.
2. (a) He is a soldier. (b) He risks his life in battle to expand and defend the Empire.
3. They will die far from home.

◆ Critical Thinking

1. Suggested response: It is both fondly familiar and disrespectful.
2. Suggested response: The tone is disrespectful, but not necessarily disloyal. The speaker resents that soldiers are sent off to die to preserve the Queen's power, but also seems to take pride in that power.
3. Students may say that this makes the reader aware of the unsung heroes that make the Empire possible.
4. Most students will say that Kipling's use of dialect provides a constant reminder that the speaker is a common man.

Reinforce and Extend

Answers

◆ Reading Strategy

1. In "Dover Beach," the setting of nighttime symbolizes the darkness in the world caused by loss of faith, confusion, and ignorance.
2. (a) The first four stanzas end with the same line. (b) It suggests his message is important and bears repeating.
3. (a) The phrases "the sons o' the widow" and "poor beggars" are repeated. Both phrases refer to the common soldiers in Queen Victoria's army. (b) The message is that it is the common soldiers who bear the burden of fighting and dying in the wars that maintain the British Empire.

◆ Build Vocabulary

1. Domineering: acting like a lord or master; 2. Predominant: having power, authority, or mastery over another; 3. Domain: a field of influence, or mastery; 4. Dominion: a territory ruled over (mastered) by another country; 5. Domination: rule or mastery

1. c 2. e 3. d 4. a 5. b

◆ Literary Focus

1. By scolding the Queen, Kipling hints at her behavior's being like a spoiled child's.
2. (a) The rhythm gives the poem a seemingly lighthearted feeling. (b) These words invest the poem with a more serious message. (c) The imagery creates a harsh comparison that is critical of the queen.
3. The theme is "Maintaining an empire is a deadly serious game." Kipling reminds the reader of the hardships suffered by the common soldiers and of the responsibilities for keeping up the British Empire.

◆ Grammar and Style

Practice

1. is; 2. hear; 3. dies; 4. depart; 5. stands

Writing Application

1. The winning of empires requires great sacrifices.
2. For me, the ebb and flow of the tide represents the cycle of human life.

Guide for Responding *(continued)*

◆ Reading Strategy

Draw Conclusions

Drawing conclusions about what you read is a process by which you link different parts of a text to create meaningful patterns. For example, you may notice that "Dover Beach" is set at night and that the words *tonight* or *night* appear several times. In fact, the last word of the poem is *night.* You might conclude from this pattern that night, and what is associated with it, is important to the mood and theme of the poem.

1. What does the imagery of night contribute to the meaning and mood of "Dover Beach"?
2. (a) In "Recessional," what pattern do you notice with regard to the ends of the stanzas? (b) What does this pattern suggest about Kipling's message in the poem?
3. (a) Identify repeated words and phrases in "The Widow at Windsor." (b) Basing your answer on these repetitions, what conclusions can you draw about the poem's message?

◆ Build Vocabulary

Using the Word Root *-domi-*

Use your knowledge of the word root *-domi-* to explain the meaning of each underlined word:

1. a domineering person
2. the predominant reason for doing something
3. a domain of knowledge
4. the dominion a country has over its territory
5. domination of one nation by another

Using the Word Bank

On your paper, match the words in Column A with the words in Column B that are most nearly opposite in meaning to them.

Column A	Column B
1. tranquil	**(a)** clear
2. cadence	**(b)** unrepentant
3. dominion	**(c)** agitated
4. turbid	**(d)** powerlessness
5. contrite	**(e)** noise

◆ Literary Focus

Mood as a Key to Theme

In poetry, feeling and thought are so closely linked that **mood is a key to theme.** If you respond to elements that create mood—imagery, rhythm, and word associations—your feelings will lead you to a poem's meaning.

1. Explain how the mood of solemn scolding is related to the message about empire that Kipling wants to convey.
2. In "The Widow at Windsor," show how these elements contribute to the mood: (a) a rollicking rhythm, (b) emotionally charged words like *sword, flame,* and *bones,* and (c) imagery that compares an empire to a widow's possessions and shop.
3. Basing your answer on the mood of "The Widow at Windsor," explain which of these sentences best describes the poem's theme: (a) Maintaining an empire is ridiculous. (b) Maintaining an empire is a deadly serious game.

◆ Grammar and Style

Present Tense

The **present tense** of a verb expresses an action or state of being that is occurring now. However, both Arnold and Kipling know that the present tense is also effective in expressing a timeless truth.

Practice On your paper, identify the present-tense verb in each of these passages from the poems.

1. The sea is calm tonight.
2. Listen! You hear the grating roar / Of pebbles . . .
3. The tumult and the shouting dies . . .
4. The Captains and the Kings depart . . .
5. Still stands Thine ancient Sacrifice . . .

Writing Application In your notebook, make each statement into a timeless truth by using a present-tense verb. If necessary, add or delete words.

1. The winning of empires required great sacrifices.
2. For me, the ebb and flow of the tide represented the cycle of human life.

Writer's Solution

For additional instruction and practice, use the lesson on Correct and Effective Use of Verbs in the **Language Lab CD-ROM** and the pages on The Correct Uses of Tenses in the *Writer's Solution Grammar Practice Book*, pp. 53–54.

Build Your Portfolio

Idea Bank

Writing

1. **Letter to the Editor** As a Victorian, write a letter to the editor of a newspaper expressing your feelings about the queen and the empire.

2. **Proposal** As an advisor to Queen Victoria, write a proposal for celebrating the sixtieth anniversary of her reign. Include details on location, speakers, and appropriate music.

3. **Literary Analysis** Write a brief analysis of Arnold's poetic devices—varied line length and irregular rhythm—and how they relate to the overall theme of "Dover Beach."

Speaking and Listening

4. **Address to England** Create and present an address that Queen Victoria may have given to her empire on the day of her Diamond Jubilee. **[Performing Arts Link]**

5. **Oral Interpretation** Give a reading of "Dover Beach" in which you capture the poem's melancholy tone. Also, emphasize key words to convey Arnold's meaning. **[Performing Arts Link]**

Projects

6. **Film Review** View one of the films based on Kipling's works, such as *Kim, Captains Courageous,* and *The Jungle Book*. Read the work as well so you can evaluate the film adaptation of it. Then present your analysis to the class. **[Media Link]**

7. **Tour of a Castle** Windsor Castle has long been the chief residence of British monarchs. It also houses much of the royal art collection. Research the history and architecture of Windsor. Then present your findings to the class in an oral report. **[Art Link; Social Studies Link]**

Writing Mini-Lesson

World Responsibility Speech

In "Recessional," Kipling warns his fellow Britons against an unthinking pride. You, too, can issue a warning. As a presidential advisor, write a television speech for the president that deals with an urgent global issue, like safeguarding human rights or protecting the environment. Have the president use statistics to support key points.

Writing Skills Focus: Statistics as a Form of Support

When you write a persuasive speech, you may want to include **statistics**, numerical data, as evidence or support for your position. The responsible use of statistics adds an objective, authoritative note to a report or speech. Here are a few points to keep in mind when using statistics:

- Be sure your numbers come from reliable sources.
- Use statistics that can serve as a basis for generalization and don't just represent a small number of cases.
- Present statistics in a form that your audience can easily understand, like a chart, table, or graph.

Prewriting After choosing a topic, research statistics that will support your position. To find data on human rights, for example, you can check publications of Amnesty International and Human Rights Watch.

Drafting As you draft, incorporate statistics, examples, and reasons to support your position. However, avoid turning your audience off by bombarding them with numbers.

Revising Read the speech to a friend who isn't good with numbers, and see whether he or she "gets" your point. If not, eliminate statistics that are confusing or include additional explanations.

✓ ASSESSMENT OPTIONS

Formal Assessment, Selection Test, pp. 197–199, and Assessment Resources Software. The selection test is designed so that it can be easily customized to the performance levels of your students. ***Alternative Assessment***, p. 40, includes options for less advanced students, more advanced students, visual/spatial learners, logical/mathematical learners, and interpersonal learners.

PORTFOLIO ASSESSMENT
Use the following rubrics in the ***Alternative Assessment*** booklet to assess student writing:
Letter to the Editor: Expression Rubric, p. 95
Proposal: Description Rubric, p. 98
Literary Analysis: Literary Analysis/Interpretation Rubric, p. 113
Writing Mini-Lesson: Persuasion Rubric, p. 106

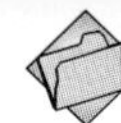

Idea Bank

Customizing for
Performance Levels
Following are suggestions for matching Idea Bank topics with your students' performance levels:
Less Advanced Students: 1, 5
Average Students: 2, 4, 7
More Advanced Students: 3, 6

Customizing for
Learning Modalities
Following are suggestions for matching Idea Bank topics with your students' learning modalities:
Visual/Spatial: 6, 7
Intrapersonal: 1
Verbal/Linguistic: 1, 2, 3, 4, 5, 7
Musical/Rhythmic: 2, 3

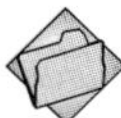

Writing Mini-Lesson

Refer students to the Writing Handbook, page 1189, for instruction on the writing process, and page 1192 for information on persuasion.

Writing and Language Transparencies Point out that a persuasive speech can be thought of as a persuasive essay that is given orally. Use the transparencies for Writing Process Model 5, Persuasive Essay, pp. 37–44, to demonstrate revising their world responsibility speeches.

Writer's Solution

Writing Lab CD-ROM
Have students complete the tutorial on Persuasion. Follow these steps:

1. Use the interactive instruction on choosing persuasive strategies.
2. View the interactive instruction on identifying different types of evidence.
3. While drafting on the computer, refer to the persuasive Word Bin.
4. Use the Revision Checker for Language Variety to find overused words that should be replaced.

Sourcebook
Have students use Chapter 4, Persuasion (pp. 97–129), for additional support. The chapter includes instruction on considering purpose (p. 113) and researching and evaluating evidence (pp. 114–115).

Prepare and Engage

OBJECTIVES

1. To read, comprehend, and interpret two Victorian newspaper articles
2. To relate the articles to personal experience
3. To distinguish emotive and informative language
4. To identify a journalistic essay and its purpose
5. To build vocabulary in context and learn about words derived from the four humors
6. To identify and use coordinating conjunctions
7. To write an evaluation of technology, using supporting details
8. To respond to the articles through writing, speaking and listening, and projects

SKILLS INSTRUCTION

Vocabulary: The Humors
Grammar: Coordinating Conjunctions
Reading Strategy: Distinguish Emotive and Informative Language
Literary Focus: Journalistic Essay
Writing: Supporting Details
Speaking and Listening: Comic Monologue (teacher edition)
Critical Viewing: Compare and Contrast; Analyze; Relate

PORTFOLIO OPPORTUNITIES

Writing: Compare Opinions; Fictional Memoir; Journalistic Essay
Writing Mini-Lesson: Written Evaluation
Speaking and Listening: Comic Monologue; Television Editorial
Projects: History of the Newspaper; Contemporary Famine

More About the Author
Sydney Smith (1771–1845) was born in England and educated at Winchester and New College, Oxford. He was a talented preacher and a humane man who spoke out against injustices. In 1802, he helped found *The Edinburgh Review* and was a frequent contributor of articles. Known for his witty conversation, Smith also displayed his wit in essays and letters. This essay, "Progress in Personal Comfort," was written approximately a year before he died.

Guide for Interpreting

Newspapers and Progress

The British empire in the nineteenth century measured itself with a yardstick called *progress.* People wondered whether things were better in the present than they had been in the past or whether present trends would lead to a more reasonable future. These two articles from Victorian newspapers give two very different answers to these questions—one a cry of outrage, the other an exclamation of pride.

A Picture of the World The idea of progress was perhaps born with the modern newspaper. To even ask whether progress has been made, the mind must view the world as a collection of measurable facts—the number of people fed, of miles traveled, of diseases cured. By bringing together news from near and far, Victorian newspapers assemble an image of such a world. The reader cannot directly influence or experience this larger, public world but is nevertheless called on as its witness, critic, even judge. This is the world of progress—a world that belongs to no one but which is everyone's business, a world that can be judged in terms of efficiency, fairness, and common sense.

Ideals of Reform The Victorians who measured the world with these values often found it wanting. The "Condition of Ireland," an essay from a Victorian newspaper, criticizes England's policies towards the Irish Famine—policies built on the most up-to-date economic ideas. Progress in economic theory meant disaster in Ireland. The article judges this disaster, though, in terms that are themselves part of the ideal of progress—efficiency and the reasonable use of resources.

The "Conveniences" We Share Other Victorians used the yardstick of progress with more cheering results. Sydney Smith's nineteenth-century letter to the editor takes a rosy view of the progress in personal comfort—the innovations, some large, some small, that seem to have come out of nowhere but which ended up feeling indispensable: street-lighting, railways, umbrellas. Like the statistics in the *London News* editorial, Smith's conveniences belong to an anonymous, common world—the world of newspaper ads, say.

Both gloomy doomsayers and cheerleaders for progress judge the common world imagined by the newspaper. From the trivia of daily life to weighty political questions, the two newspaper articles span the extremes of this vast, new world.

◆ Background for Understanding

SCIENCE: PROGRESS AND POTATOES

At the center of the scenes of suffering and despair painted by the essay "Condition of Ireland" is the lowly Irish potato. The potato was the product of progress—of the improved navigational technology used by early European explorers to reach the New World. In the sixteenth century, Spanish explorers brought potatoes back to Europe from Peru.

By the mid-nineteenth century, the potato had become woven into the fabric of Irish life—one-third of the Irish ate potatoes almost exclusively. When disease ruined the potato crop of 1845, the Irish began to starve. More than a million people died of starvation and disease from 1846 to 1851. More than a million and a half emigrated, many to the United States.

The British government's disastrous attempts to deal with the famine were based on accepted economic theory, which favored large, efficient farms that hired wage-laborers and sold crops for trade. To promote such farms, the British government took land away from poor small farmers and heavily taxed Irish landowners to pay for aid to those starving in their own districts. In a sense, the British government acted in the name of progress—its measures were designed to promote general economic health, rather than merely to alleviate suffering.

Prentice Hall Literature Program Resources

REINFORCE / RETEACH / EXTEND

Selection Support Pages
Build Vocabulary: The Humors, p. 196
Grammar and Style: Coordinating Conjunctions, p. 197
Reading Strategy: Distinguish Emotive and Informative Language, p. 198
Literary Focus: Journalistic Essay, p. 199

Strategies for Diverse Student Needs, p. 41

Beyond Literature
Career: Information Management, p. 41

Formal Assessment, Selection Test, pp. 200–202; Assessment Resources Software

Alternative Assessment, p. 41

Writing and Language Transparencies
Daily Language Practice, Week 27, p. 162

Resource Pro CD-ROM
Includes all resource materials and customizable lesson plan for the selections

Listening to Literature Audiocassettes
"Condition of Ireland," "Progress in Personal Comfort"

◆ Condition of Ireland ◆
Progress in Personal Comfort

◆ Literature and Your Life

Connect Your Experience

Do you remember life before personal computers and fax machines? In your lifetime, you may already have witnessed progress.

In the nineteenth century, a flood of technological changes began to alter daily life. As you read Sydney Smith's "Progress in Personal Comfort," you may chuckle over the "improvements" he finds exciting. As you read the *News* article, though, you may shake your head when you consider how much suffering the world still contains.

Journal Writing Jot down a few of the ways in which the world has progressed since you were a kid.

Thematic Focus: The Empire and Its Discontents

To what discontents did progress give rise? What satisfactions did it create?

◆ Literary Focus

Journalistic Essay

Journalistic essays are short prose pieces providing perspectives on current events or trends. These essays confront a world larger than any one individual's experience. Unlike essayists who explore the world to learn about themselves, journalistic essayists build unified stories out of the day's jumble of news. Their pieces may be written in the voice of an all-knowing witness, as in the *London News* editorial. They may also use the voice of an isolated individual, as in Mr. Smith's letter. Essay topics range from the weighty, the *News*'s protest against injustice, to the trivial, Smith's celebration of comfort.

◆ Reading Strategy

Distinguish Emotive and Informative Language

The first sentence of the *London News* article mixes **emotive** and **informative language**. Emotive language uses words, phrases, and examples for emotional effect. Informative language conveys facts. To identify emotional language, look for words that express the author's attitude. For instance, the emotional adjectives "ignorant and vicious" in the first sentence of "Condition of Ireland" tell us about the writer's feelings, not about the Poor-Laws.

◆ Build Vocabulary

The Humors

The *London News* article uses the word *melancholy,* meaning "sad," to describe the plight of the Irish. The word originally meant "black bile," one of the four humors, or liquids, that people from ancient Greece to the Renaissance believed governed human health and personality. We still use words from this theory, such as *choleric* (from the humor *choler*), meaning ill-tempered, to describe people.

Word Bank

Before you read, preview this list of words from the selections.

requisites
sanction
exonerate
melancholy
indolence
depredation

◆ Grammar and Style

Coordinating Conjunctions

A **coordinating conjunction** links two sentence parts of the same grammatical kind. There are seven coordinating conjunctions: *and, but, or, nor, yet, so,* and *for.*

They were little used,
and very dear.

As you read, recognize the writers' use of coordinating conjunctions to connect similar parts of speech or grammatical units.

Interest Grabber Bring to class a facsimile of a newspaper article reporting a famous historical event (the sinking of the *Titanic,* the assassination of President Kennedy, the 1929 stock market crash). Discuss the informative and emotive language found in the article. Alternatively, you may bring in a recent copy of your local daily newspaper. Compare and contrast the informational facts found on the news pages with the opinions expressed in the editorials and letters to the editor.

Customize for
More Advanced Students
Have students take notes as they read the selections. Then challenge them to use these notes to write a poem or poems that capture the essence, meaning, and mood of the journalistic essays.

Customize for
English Language Learners
Students may need assistance with the long sentences and higher-level vocabulary in these selections. Assist students in finding simpler synonyms for words like *hesitation, ignorant,* and *calamity,* and in breaking down long or complicated sentences.

Customize for
Intrapersonal Learners
Have students divide a sheet of paper into two columns. The first column should be headed "Taking Notes"; the second, "Making Meaning." Encourage students to take notes in the first column and to comment on these notes in the second column.

Preparing for Standardized Tests

Reading and Vocabulary Standardized achievement tests in the content areas often include questions based on lengthy passages or on excerpts from historical documents. The questions may be designed to test critical thinking skills in addition to reading comprehension. Students will improve their performance by being able to distinguish between emotive and informative language. For additional practice, use the Reading Strategy page in ***Selection Support,*** p. 198.

Grammar and Language The Grammar and Style activity focuses on recognizing and using coordinating conjunctions. Knowing the kind of connection between things or ideas that each conjunction represents will help students on the writing-skills sections of standardized tests. For example, students may be given a sentence with a portion underlined. They must determine what, if any, correction that portion of the sentence needs, as in the following:

I like poetry and prefer short stories. *(C)*
(A) poetry and prefer
(B) poetry, or I prefer
(C) poetry but prefer
(D) poetry and I also prefer
(E) poetry, so I prefer

The Grammar and Style lesson for this selection focuses on Coordinating Conjunctions. For additional practice, assign the Grammar and Style page, p. 197, in ***Selection Support.***

Develop Understanding

One-Minute Insight This journalistic essay from the *Illustrated London News* of the mid 1800's points out the injustices being done to the Irish people as a result of rigid adherence to economic policies. The author argues that these policies do not make sense during a natural disaster—in this case, when potato blight has destroyed most of the food supply.

▶Critical Viewing◀

❶ Compare and Contrast Students may say that the picture aptly illustrates the starvation of the Irish people as described in the article. One difference between the picture and the article, however, is that the picture focuses on a mother and child, whereas the article focuses on the men who were put out of work and could not grow or afford food for their families.

◆Reading Strategy

❷ Distinguish Emotive and Informative Language Draw attention to this passage: "The destruction of the potato for one season, though a great calamity, would not have doomed them." Ask students if this passage is largely an example of emotive or informative language. Why? *Sample answer: It is an example of emotive language because it expresses the author's feelings and is meant to sway the readers with phrases such as "great calamity" and "doomed them."* Then ask students to rewrite the passage, using less emotive language. *Sample rewrite: Although the loss of the potato crop for one season was a setback, the Irish people could have overcome it.*

CONDITION OF IRELAND: Illustrations of the New Poor-Law

The Illustrated London News, December 15, 1849

Woman Begging at Clonakilty, James Mahony, The Illustrated London News, 1847

During the Great Famine, progressive economic theories clashed with the realities of starvation. Guided by new ideas of economic health, British policy toward the poor changed in the early nineteenth century. To promote year-round employment and larger, more productive farms, the new Poor-Laws made unemployment as unattractive as possible. Rather than giving hand-outs to workers suffering from low wages and periodic unemployment, the new laws emphasized confining the poor in oppressive workhouses.

Whatever the merits of the theory, it could not accommodate a catastrophe of the magnitude of the Great Famine. Irish landowners were frequently bankrupted by the requirement that they pay for all aid in their district (some theorists believed that high taxes would encourage them to make their farms more productive, hire more workers, and so end poverty). The Irish Poor-Laws required that any Irishman farming a quarter acre or less give up his land before he could receive government aid—in effect, forbidding the poor from trying to grow their own food. In the meantime, export wheat continued to be shipped out of the country while millions starved or emigrated.

The following article was one of a series in which The Illustrated London News *presented, in words and pictures, the plight of the Irish.*

❶ **▲ Critical Viewing** Compare the portrayal of the Irish in this picture with the portrayal of the Irish in the article. **[Compare and Contrast]**

The present condition of the Irish, we have no hesitation in saying, has been mainly brought on by ignorant and vicious legislation. The destruction of the potato for one season, though a great calamity, would not have doomed them, fed as they were by the taxes of the state and the ❷

Block Scheduling Strategies

Consider these suggestions to take advantage of extended class time.

- Direct students to complete the journal activity in Literature and Your Life (p. 801). Have students to share their responses in a class discussion.
- Introduce the Reading Strategy, Distinguish Emotive and Informative Language. Instruct students to jot down in their notebooks examples of emotive language as they read the articles. For additional practice, assign the Reading Strategy page in ***Selection Support,*** p. 198.
- After students have read "Progress in Personal Comfort," have them complete the Literature and Your Life activities (p. 807). Discuss the relationship between progress and expectations.
- Each of the Literary Focus questions (p. 808) can be used for discussion. You might have the class form three groups and each group prepare an answer to one of the questions before coming together as a class.
- Students may work on the writing activity of their choice (p. 809).
- Allow students to present their Comic Monologue or Television Editorial to the class. These activities are described in the Idea Bank (p. 809). The Comic Monologue is supported by a Speaking and Listening Mini-Lesson on page 805 of this teacher edition.

charity of the world, to immediate decay; but a
❸ false theory, assuming the name of political economy,[1] with which it has no more to do than with the slaughter of the Hungarians by General Haynau,[2] led the landlords and the legislature to believe that it was a favorable opportunity for changing the occupation of the land and the cultivation of the soil from potatoes to corn.[3] When more food, more cultivation, more employment, were the requisites for maintaining the Irish in existence, the Legislature and the landlords went about introducing a species of cultivation that could only be successful by requiring fewer hands, and turning potato gardens, that nourished the maximum of human beings, into pasture grounds for bullocks,[4] that nourished only the minimum. The Poor-Law, said to be for the relief of the people and the means of their salvation, was the instrument of their destruction. In their terrible distress, from that temporary calamity with which they were visited, they were to have no relief unless they gave up their holdings.[5] That law, too, laid down a form for evicting the people, and thus gave the sanction and encouragement of legislation to exterminate them. Calmly and quietly, but very ignorantly—though we cheerfully exonerate the parties from any malevolence; they only committed a great mistake, a terrible blunder, which in legislation is worse than a crime—but calmly and quietly from Westminster
❺ itself, which is the center of civilization, did the decree go forth which has made the temporary but terrible visitation[6] of a potato rot the means of exterminating, through the slow process of disease and houseless starvation, nearly the half of the Irish.

❹ **◆ Literary Focus**
Does the "we" in this sentence participate in Westminster's decisions or in the suffering of the Irish, or neither? What is the role of "we" in a journalistic essay?

The land is still there, in all its natural beauty and fertility. The sparkling Shannon, teeming with fish, still flows by their doors, and might bear to them, as the Hudson and Thames bear to the people of New York and of London, fleets of ships laden with wealth. The low grounds or *Corcasses* of Clare are celebrated for their productiveness. The country abounds in limestone: coal, iron, and lead have been found. It has an area of 827,994 acres, 372,237 of which are uncultivated, or occupied by woods or water. It is estimated that there are 296,000 acres of unoccupied land; and that of these 160,000 are capable of cultivation and improvement. Why are they not cultivated and improved, as the wilds of America are cultivated and improved by the brethren of the Irish? Why are these starving people not allowed and encouraged to plant their potato-gardens on the wastes? ❻ Why are they not married to the unoccupied soil, as a humane politician proposes to provide for the starving needlewomen of the metropolis by marrying them to the *Currency Lads* of New South Wales?[7] A more important question cannot be asked. There is about Kilrush, and in Clare, and throughout Ireland, the doubly melancholy spectacle of a strong man asking for work as the means of getting food; ❼ and of the fertile earth wooing his labors, in order to yield up to him its rich but latent[8] stores: yet it lies idle and unfruitful. Why is not this doubly melan-

1. **political economy:** Theory of economics and society.
2. **General Haynau:** Julius Jacob; an Austrian general notorious for the brutality with which he suppressed uprisings by the Hungarians and other peoples who revolted against the Austrian empire in the 1840's. When Haynau visited London in 1850, he was attacked by outraged mobs.
3. **corn:** (Brit.) Grain.
4. **bullocks:** Oxen.
5. **The Poor-Law . . . gave up their holdings:** The Poor-Law determined how aid was to be given to the poor. During the famine, farmers with small farms ("holdings") were required to give them up before they would be given aid.
6. **visitation:** Divine punishment or reward.
7. **needlewomen . . . New South Wales:** Probably referring to a scheme encouraging emigration to Australia. The "New Currency Lads" are native-born Australians.
8. **latent:** Potential; not yet actual.

◆ Build Vocabulary

requisites (rek′wə zits) *n.*: Things necessary for a given purpose

sanction (saŋk′ shən) *n.*: Authorized approval or permission

exonerate (eg zän′ ər āt′) *v.*: Free from a charge of guilt; declare or prove blameless

melancholy (mel′ ən käl′ ē) *adj.*: Sad and depressed

◆ Critical Thinking

❸ **Make a Judgment** The writer uses the term "false theory." Ask students if they, too, think that the government theory was false. Explain. *Sample response: Yes; In attempting to maximize profits, exports, or overall benefits, the government failed to take into account the adverse effects on the poor.*

◆ Literary Focus

❹ **Journalistic Essay** Possible response: The "we" does not actually participate in Westminster's decisions or in the suffering of the Irish; the "we" in a journalistic essay is an all-knowing witness to the events of the times.

❺ **Clarification** "Westminster" refers to the Houses of Parliament (in the borough of Westminster, London), where the laws are passed.

◆ Critical Thinking

❻ **Infer** Point out that the article lists a series of questions. Ask students if they think the writer intends for the reader to answer the questions. Why or why not? *No; The questions are rhetorical, and are intended to make the reader think.*

◆ Critical Thinking

❼ **Evaluate** The article refers to a "doubly melancholy spectacle." Ask students what the author proposes as a solution. *The solution is to let the people use the land to grow food. This provides jobs and puts the fallow land to good use.* What do students think of this solution? *Some students will think it a good solution. Others may express reservations, citing concerns about the owners' rights to the land and whether creating jobs in subsistence farming benefits the economy in the long run.*

Beyond the Classroom

Career Connection

Farming Since people cannot live without food, one would think that there are many career opportunities in farming, but that is not the case. Because of the increased industrialization of farms, fewer farmers are needed. By contrast, in the mid-nineteenth century, most Americans lived on farms. Each farm produced enough food for four people. Currently, less than three percent of the population lives on farms, yet these farms often produce a surplus of food. Discuss with students some of the problems a farmer of today faces, such as pest control, unusual weather patterns, and crop surpluses.

Community Connection

Local Growers Although not farmers, many people enjoy growing some of their own food. Ask students if they or their families have tried to grow fruits or vegetables. Encourage students to share their own experiences. Then discuss what kind of crops can be grown in your area. For example, are there any varieties of fruit trees commonly found in people's yards? Do people grow their own tomatoes or other vegetables? Are there any community gardens? Are there any farms, small or large, in the area? If so, what do they grow? If students were to operate a farm, what kind of crop would they choose to raise?

◆ Reading Strategy

❶ Distinguish Emotive and Informative Language Since scientific facts are objective, they lend authority to the proposal. The analogy makes the reader feel that putting a man and the land together is a scientific, natural solution.

◆ Grammar and Style

❷ Coordinating Conjunctions Have students identify the conjunction and the parts of speech or grammatical unit that it connects. *"But" connects two independent clauses.*

Reinforce and Extend

Answers

◆ Literature and Your Life

Reader's Response Students should use examples from the text to support their answsers.

Thematic Focus Students may say that the government should have done more to help the Irish people.

☑ Check Your Comprehension

1. They are starving.
2. The condition was caused by economic policies that worsened the effects of the potato famine.
3. Ireland has fertile lands, the Shannon river, and natural resources such as coal, iron, and lead.
4. It is to allow the people to cultivate small farms and make use of their natural resources.

◆ Critical Thinking

1. Economic aid from the state and charities could have averted the crisis.
2. Britain's objectives were to change the basis of Ireland's economy from small independently-owned farms to large, efficient farms that hired wage-laborers and sold crops for trade.
3. Students may say that questions make readers think and capture their attention better than statements.
4. Students may say that a first-person narration makes an account of suffering more real and personal. Others may find that a third-person article is less distracting because it omits personal issues and focuses on facts.

> ◆ Reading Strategy
> What, if any, is the emotional effect of the scientific analogy in this paragraph?

❶ choly spectacle destroyed by their union, and converted into life and happiness, as oxygen and hydrogen, each in itself destructive, become, when united as water, the pabulum[9] of existence? We shall fully consider that question before we quit the subject, but we shall now only say that the whole of this land, cultivated and uncultivated, is owned by a few proprietors—that many of them are absentees[10] ❷—that almost all are in embarrassed circumstances—and that, from ignorance, or false theory, or indolence, they prefer seeing the land covered with such misery as we have described, to either bringing the land under cultivation themselves, or allowing the people to cultivate it. Their greatest ambition, apparently, is to get rid of the people.

9. **pabulum:** Nourishing substance.
10. **absentees:** Many landowners who rented to small Irish farmers lived in England and were thought to lack sufficient motivation to make the best use of their lands.

◆ Build Vocabulary

indolence (in′ də lens) *n.*: Idleness; laziness

Beyond Literature

History Connection

The Potato Famine The Irish potato famine that *The Illustrated London News* blamed on "ignorant and vicious legislation" killed at least one million people—one eighth of Ireland's population—and forced another 1.5 million to emigrate. Trouble began in 1845 when a potato peeling carrying a wind-borne fungus washed up on the Isle of Wight and spread through the potato crop. Starvation was initially averted by the Tory government of Sir Robert Peel, which bought 100,000 pounds of corn in America, then subsidized Ireland's purchase of it. In the fall of 1846, though, the new Whig government of John Russell cut direct aid. Making matters worse, an unusually cold winter in 1846 worsened the effects of the fungus. By 1847, the worst year of the famine, the hills of the Irish countryside were littered with corpses. It wasn't until 1853 that conditions started to return to normal.

What is a government's responsibility in the face of natural disasters? Explain.

Guide for Responding

◆ Literature and Your Life

Reader's Response Does this article move you to feel outrage on behalf of the Irish, or does it leave you cold? Explain why.

Thematic Focus What responsibility should the British government have taken for Ireland during the famine?

☑ Check Your Comprehension

1. What is the "current condition" of the Irish?
2. According to the article, what is mainly responsible for this condition?
3. What kind of wealth does Ireland have?
4. According to the article, what is the obvious solution to Ireland's difficulties?

◆ Critical Thinking

INTERPRET

1. What measures, according to the article, would have kept the famine from becoming a crisis? **[Interpret]**
2. What were the objectives, according to the article, of Britain's response to the famine? **[Infer]**
3. The article poses a solution in a series of questions. Why is this more effective than making a simple statement? **[Analyze]**

EXTEND

4. Think of a firsthand memoir of suffering you have read, such as *Anne Frank: Diary of a Young Girl.* Which did you find more affecting, this editorial or the first-person account? Explain. **[Literature Link]**

Cross-Curricular Connection: Science

"Condition of Ireland" focuses on the problems that were caused by the failure of the potato crop. But what do students actually know about potatoes? Elicit or share the following facts:

- The part of the potato plant that we eat is the tuber, which is actually a type of specialized stem, not a root. Each potato plant produces from three to twenty tubers.
- The potato plant seen above the ground has leafy stems and purple, pink, or white flowers. The flowers grow small green seedballs, which contain a few hundred yellow seeds.
- Potatoes contain trace, harmless amounts of solanine, a poison also found in deadly nightshade. With improper storage, however, the solanine content in a potato can increase to dangerous levels.
- Potatoes are grown from small, whole tubers and segments called seed pieces. Both are referred to as seed potatoes.

Have interested students research more information about potatoes including their uses.

Progress in Personal Comfort

Sydney Smith

MODERN LOCOMOTIVE.

▲ **Critical Viewing** Describe what features (shapes, lines) give this "modern locomotive"—and this drawing—an "old-fashioned" look. How might such a locomotive appear through the eyes of Mr. Smith? **[Analyze]** 3

It is of some importance at what period a man is born. A young man, alive at this period, hardly knows to what improvements of human life he has been introduced; and I would bring before his notice the following eighteen changes which have taken place in England since I first began to breathe in it the breath of life—a period amounting now to nearly seventy-three years.

Gas[1] was unknown: I groped about the streets of London in all but the utter darkness of a twinkling oil lamp, under the protection of watchmen in their grand climacteric,[2] and exposed to every species of depredation and insult.

◆ **Reading Strategy** Name two facts presented in this paragraph. Then find two phrases that add emotional effect. 4

◆ Build Vocabulary

depredation (dep´ rə dā´ shən) *n.*: Act or instance of robbing, plundering or laying waste

1. **gas:** Coal gas, piped under the streets of London and used in street lamps after 1814.
2. **climacteric:** Old age; a period of great change associated in some theories with the age of 63.

Develop Understanding

One-Minute Insight In this article from the mid-nineteenth century, Sydney Smith reflects on the scientific and technological advances that have taken place, noting that he can name at least eighteen improvements that have occurred in his lifetime. Important changes for the nineteenth century were gas street lamps, the steam boat, railroads, savings banks, and the postal service.

Customize for *Less Proficient Readers*
As they read, have students keep a list of the eighteen improvements Smith lists as having happened during his lifetime. Then have them mark those that they feel are significant.

▶Critical Viewing◀

3 **Analyze** Students may say that his locomotive appears old-fashioned because modern trains are streamlined and have no smokestacks. Smith would probably have been quite impressed with the modernity of this locomotive.

◆ Reading Strategy

4 **Distinguish Emotive and Informative Language** Sample response: Two facts are that gas was unknown and light came from an oil lamp. Some phrases that add emotional effect are "I groped about," "the utter darkness," and "exposed to every species of depredation and insult."

Speaking and Listening Mini-Lesson

Comic Monologue

This mini-lesson supports the Speaking and Listening activity in the Idea Bank on page 809.

Introduce the Concept Explain that a comic monologue is a humorous speech delivered by one person. Usually, the monologue is presented in a conversational manner.

Develop Background Students should draw on their experiences with computers and other high-tech but fallible "conveniences" to prepare the material for their monologue. Suggest that they jot down all mishaps, even if they do not seem humorous at first glance. Then students should consider if some of these incidents can be presented in a humorous light.

Apply the Information Students should jot down notes on what they want to say and then practice delivering their monologues. Remind them that timing and speaking clearly will help them convey the humor of the situation. After students have rehearsed sufficiently, have them present their comic monologues to the class.

Assess the Outcome Have each student complete Self Assessment: Speech page in ***Alternative Assessment,*** p. 118. Their peers can evaluate their speeches on the basis of comic content, timing, organization, and speaking clearly.

◆ Critical Thinking

❶ **Analyze** Smith makes a point of telling about how long his various travels took. Ask students what the reader needs to know in order to be impressed by this information. *The reader needs to know the distance from Taunton to Bath (about 60 miles) and from Taunton to London (about 180 miles).* Then ask if it is likely that Smith's readers were knowledgeable about these distances. Why or why not? *Suggested response: Yes, it is likely that Smith's readers knew the distances because Smith was writing for a local newspaper.*

◆ Literary Focus

❷ **Journalistic Essay** Suggested response: The omissions make it seem as if progress happened very quickly; otherwise, the reader would become bogged down in details, and progress would seem very slow.

▶Critical Viewing◀

❸ **Relate** Sample answer: *This advertisement appeals to family values because the man is shown with his wife. In addition, the importance of looking good is also implicit in the ad. Advertising a particular brand of umbrella did not seem silly because it was a new product, whereas today umbrellas are so common that no one pays any attention to them.*

❹ **Clarification** *Very dear* means "quite expensive."

MY WIFE AND I BOTH
ARE DRY WITH OUR
140
UMBRELLA
AND ITS
HERCULES FRAME.
For Sale Everywhere.

◀ **Critical Viewing** To what values does this advertisement appeal? Why was the idea of advertising a particular brand of umbrella not silly in Mr. Smith's day, though it seems so in our own? **[Relate]** ❸

❶ I have been nine hours in sailing from Dover to Calais before the invention of steam. It took me nine hours to go from Taunton to Bath, before the invention of railroads, and I now go in six hours from Taunton to London! In going from Taunton to Bath, I suffered between 10,000 and 12,000 severe contusions,[3] before stone-breaking Macadam[4] was born.

❷ **◆ Literary Focus** Smith does not tell us the history behind the design and implementation of wooden pavements (or gas-lighting, or steam power). What picture of progress do such omissions help create?

I paid £15 in a single year for repairs of carriage-springs on the pavement of London; and I now glide without noise or fracture, on wooden pavements.

I can walk, by the assistance of the police, from one end of London to the other, without molestation; or, if tired, get into a cheap and active cab, instead of those cottages on wheels, which the hackney coaches[5] were at the beginning of my life.

I had no umbrella! They were little used, and very dear. There were no waterproof hats, and ❹ *my* hat has often been reduced by rains into its primitive pulp.

I could not keep my smallclothes in their proper place, for braces were unknown.[6] If I had the gout, there was no colchicum. If I was bilious, there was no calomel. If I was attacked by ague, there was no quinine.[7] There were filthy coffee houses instead of elegant clubs. Game could not be bought. Quarrels about uncommuted tithes[8] were endless. The corruption

3. **contusions:** Bruises.
4. **Macadam:** Road-surfacing made of small stones bound with adhesive.
5. **cheap and active cab . . . hackney coaches:** Hackney coaches were used, four-wheeled carriages for hire. The faster two-wheeled hansom cabs appeared in London in the 1830's.
6. **smallclothes . . . braces:** There were no suspenders to support his trousers.
7. **If I had the gout . . . there was no quinine:** Gout, bilious conditions, and ague are afflictions. Colchicum, calomel, and quinine are remedies.
8. **uncommuted tithes:** Taxes paid to the Church in the form of produce, "commuted" (changed to) an equivalent payment in money in 1840.

Cross-Curricular Connection: Social Studies

Sydney Smith mentions how his life has changed since the invention of the railroad. At one time railroads were important not only for carrying people but also for transporting goods. Although trains are used mostly for freight in the United States today, commuter trains are important in many areas. Passenger train lines like AMTRAK, however, are not profitable even with governmental subsidies.

Ask students how many of them have ever taken a long trip, perhaps overnight, on a train? Discuss the advantages and disadvantages of taking trips by train.

In Europe, trains are used more for travel than in the United States. Why do students think such a difference exists? Ask: "Should travel by train be encouraged in the United States?"

Have interested students find out more about the trains in England and other European countries and compare their systems with our own.

of Parliament, before Reform, infamous.[9] There were no banks to receive the savings of the poor. The Poor Laws were gradually sapping the vitals of the country; and whatever miseries I suffered, I had no post to whisk my complaints for a single penny[10] to the remotest corners of the empire; and yet, in spite of all these privations, I lived on quietly, and am now ashamed that I was not more discontented, and utterly surprised that all these changes and inventions did not occur two centuries ago.

I forgot to add, that as the basket of stage coaches, in which luggage was then carried, had no springs, your clothes were rubbed all to pieces. . . .

5 ◆ *Literature and Your Life*
What "comforts" do you consider vital to your life? Do you know where they came from or why they spread?

9. **The corruption of Parliament . . . infamous:** Before the reforms of the 1800's, the House of Commons was dominated by a few corrupt, wealthy landowners.

10. **I had no post . . . single penny:** Penny postage, in the form of an adhesive stamp, was first introduced in England in 1840.

Guide for Responding

◆ *Literature and Your Life*

Reader's Response Name one kind of change seen by Mr. Smith in his own lifetime that you found impressive. Name one that did not impress you. Explain.

Thematic Focus How important is the kind of progress that Mr. Smith describes? Explain.

Brainstorm for Progress In a group, come up with a list of areas in which you think the modern world most needs to make progress.

☑ Check Your Comprehension

1. Over what period of time did the changes Smith reports take place?
2. What two improvements in public safety were noted in the article?
3. According to Smith, what two improvements in public transportation have occurred?
4. How does Smith view his own acceptance of life before it was "improved"?

◆ Critical Thinking

INTERPRET

1. How would the "young man" whom Smith addresses view the improvements he describes? **[Speculate]**
2. Judging from the details Smith reports, how "uncomfortable" was life before "improvements" were made? Explain. **[Infer]**
3. Give a definition of "personal comfort" that might cover all of the improvements Smith lists. **[Draw Conclusions]**

EVALUATE

4. Smith does not consider the possibility that people in the future might find *his* world fairly uncomfortable. Does his pride in his own time strike you as naïve? Explain. **[Make a Judgment]**

EXTEND

5. Smith's essay reflects a wider modern experience—the present is quickly outdated. Discuss a development in entertainment, sports, or fashion that demonstrates this trend. **[Social Studies Link]**

Beyond the Selection

FURTHER READING

Other Works by Sydney Smith
The Letters of Peter Plymley

Other Works About Progress and the Poor
Midnight is a Place, Joan Aiken; *The Coldest Winter,* Elizabeth Lutzier; *Mary Reilly,* Valerie Martin; *The Mechanical Age: The Industrial Revolution in England,* Celia Bland

We suggest that you preview these works before recommending them to students.

INTERNET

You can find additional information about Sydney Smith on the Internet at the following site.

For more quotations of Sydney Smith, go to **http://www.columbia.edu/acis/bartleby/bartlett/330.html**

You may also find information about Victorian England and the Irish Potato Famine on the Internet. We *strongly recommend* that you preview the sites before you send students to them.

◆ *Literature and Your Life*

5 Based on their experiences and values, students are apt to mention comforts such as personal computers, the Internet, cable television, VCRs, microwave ovens, and cellular telephones.

Reinforce and Extend

Answers

◆ *Literature and Your Life*

Reader's Response Students may be most impressed by his being able to walk throughout the city without fear of crime; they may not be impressed by the speed of the railroad trains.

Thematic Focus Most students will recognize that the progress described led to a better quality of life for most people.

☑ Check Your Comprehension

1. They took place from his birth in the late eighteenth century to nearly seventy-three years later.
2. The streets are now lighted; the police force is more efficient.
3. Two improvements in public transportation were Macadam roads and "cheap and active" cabs.
4. He views his acceptance of his former life with embarrassment.

◆ Critical Thinking

1. He probably took these improvements for granted.
2. Students may mention discomforts such as unlit streets, slower and less comfortable transportation, more crime, no umbrellas, no suspenders, no medication for various ailments, "filthy coffee houses," and no postal service.
3. Sample definition: *Personal comfort* involves living in sanitary and safe conditions, with access to conveniences such as umbrellas, a postal service, and clean restaurants.
4. In light of present technology, students may find Smith naive in taking such pride in improvements that in retrospect seem trivial and absurd.
5. Sample response: The phonograph was supplemented by the 8-track, and both have been replaced by compact disks.

Answers

◆ Reading Strategy

Possible responses:

1. Emotive language: "exposed to every species of depredation"
   Informative language: "twinkling oil lamp"
2. Emotive language: "whatever miseries I suffered"
   Informative language: "for a single penny"
3. Emotive language: "Why are these starving people not allowed and encouraged to plant their potato-gardens on the wastes?"
   Informative language: "It has an area of 827,994 acres, 372,237 of which are uncultivated"
4. Emotive language: "Why is not this doubly melancholy spectacle destroyed by their union"
   Informative language: "as oxygen and hydrogen, each in itself destructive, become, when united as water, the pabulum of existence"

◆ Build Vocabulary

Using the Humors

1. cheerful; 2. bad-tempered; 3. sluggish

Using the Word Bank

1. e 2. b 3. f 4. d 5. c 6. a

◆ Literary Focus

Possible responses:

1. In the last paragraph, the writer acts as judge and condemns the absentee proprietors who own most of the land and whose "greatest ambition, apparently, is to get rid of the people."
2. By "personal comfort," Sydney Smith means those innovations that directly affect his daily physical and financial well-being. The personal affairs he mentions are travel, clothing, medicines, and money. Concerns he left out include the broader problems facing people living in the mid-1800's, such as industrialization, loss of faith in religion, and imperialism and its effects.
3. Smith appears to judge the quality of someone else's life by what he currently experiences himself. He seems to forget that "comfort" is relative, and that it's possible to do without and be happy.

Guide for Responding *(continued)*

◆ Reading Strategy

DISTINGUISH EMOTIVE AND INFORMATIVE LANGUAGE

To form a reasonable opinion when you read, you must distinguish between **emotive language** (words that attempt to influence your feelings) and **informative language** (words that give you facts). Even language that sounds informative may be emotive. For instance, Sydney Smith's statement that "I suffered between 10,000 and 12,000 severe contusions," uses numbers for emotive effect (it is unlikely that he counted each bruise).

In the passages cited below, identify one example each of emotive language and informative language:

1. Smith's description of life before gas
2. his description of the benefits of the penny post
3. the description in the *London News* of Ireland's natural resources
4. the sentence in the *London News* comparing Ireland's situation to hydrogen and oxygen

◆ Build Vocabulary

USING THE HUMORS

The word *melancholy,* used by the *London News,* comes from a word for black bile, a humor believed to make a person sad. Other modern words originate from the theory that humors control people's emotions and characters. In your notebook, write a definition for each "humor" word italicized below:

1. Despite the setbacks, she remained *sanguine.*
2. Some people are sunny through the day; is he always this *bilious* first thing in the morning?
3. Yelling "fire" just might get him going, but he's a pretty *phlegmatic* fellow.

USING THE WORD BANK

Match each Word Bank word in Column A with its antonym, or opposite, in Column B.

Column A	Column B
1. requisites	a. construction
2. sanction	b. disapprove
3. exonerate	c. industry
4. melancholy	d. joy
5. indolence	e. luxuries
6. depredation	f. convict

◆ Literary Focus

JOURNALISTIC ESSAY

Journalistic essays are short prose pieces on current events or trends. Their authors focus their attention on what would concern "anyone," rarely reflecting on themselves. For instance, when the *London News* essayist writes, "we cheerfully exonerate the parties from any malevolence; they only committed a great mistake," he does not write as someone involved in the action he describes but as a witness and judge.

1. Find another passage in which the *London News* writer shows his relation to his subject. What relations are they?
2. What does Sydney Smith mean by "personal comfort"? What other kinds of concerns might he be leaving out of his memoir?
3. Sydney Smith is "ashamed" that he did not miss modern conveniences before they were invented. According to what standards would he judge the quality of someone's life? Explain.

◆ Grammar and Style

COORDINATING CONJUNCTIONS

Each **coordinating conjunction** names a different kind of connection between things or ideas. A coordinating conjunction links two sentence parts of the same grammatical kind.

> **The coordinating conjunctions are** *and, but, yet, so, for, or, nor*

Practice In your notebook, fill in the blank with a suitable coordinating conjunction from the list above:

1. He could not keep his smallclothes in their proper place, __?__ braces were unknown.
2. He now glides without noise __?__ fracture, on wooden pavements.
3. Calmly and quietly, __?__ very ignorantly, did the decree go forth, according to the *Times.*
4. In those days, he could walk without being bothered, __?__ he could take a cab.
5. The *News* thought that their greatest ambition was to get rid of the people, __?__ they would not allow the people to cultivate the land.

◆ Grammar and Style

1. for; 2. nor, or; 3. but, yet, and; 4. or, and; 5. so

Writer's Solution

For additional instruction and practice, use the page on Conjunctions in the *Writer's Solution Grammar Practice Book,* p. 13.

Build Your Portfolio

Idea Bank

Writing

1. Compare Opinions Find editorials in two different newspapers commenting on the same event in the news. Compare the opinions that are presented.

2. Fictional Memoir Write a memoir in which Sydney Smith explains how his life would have been changed if progress had occurred earlier—what crime might have been prevented, or love saved, if only there had been a train to Taunton.

3. Journalistic Essay Write a journalistic essay on an event in the news. Research the facts, then connect the facts with a dramatic theme—for instance, success, courage, or neglect. **[Career Link]**

Speaking and Listening

4. Comic Monologue Computers are more convenient than typewriters—until they crash. Present a comic monologue about how inconvenient "conveniences" can be. **[Performing Arts Link]**

5. Television Editorial Present a television opinion-piece set in the future, looking back at today. Comment on how daily life in the future has changed from the present and why the change represents progress. **[Media Link]**

Projects

6. History of the Newspaper Write a research paper on the rise of the *London News* or another English newspaper. **[Social Studies Link]**

7. Contemporary Famine Find a magazine article documenting starvation. Compare this situation with the Great Famine described in the *London News* article. **[Social Studies Link]**

Writing Mini-Lesson

Written Evaluation

In "Progress in Personal Comfort," Sydney Smith makes no bones about it—technology leads to a better life. Sometimes, though, technology that seems "reasonable," a faster or safer means to an end, has unintended bad results. Write an evaluation of a recent piece of technology in which you show whether it makes life better or not. To support your evaluation, present evidence.

Writing Skills Focus: Supporting Details

An evaluation, like other nonfiction pieces that present a point of view, must back up its conclusions with **supporting details**. Here are a few different kinds of evidence:

- eyewitness accounts
- logical analysis (examining statements for contradictions or self-consistency)
- scientific experiment
- statistics
- expert opinion
- examples
- analogies

Prewriting Browse through newspapers and magazines to find a technological innovation to evaluate. Look for precise, factual details that will support your opinions.

Drafting Discuss each aspect of your subject, giving evidence for each of your conclusions. Do not merely present your evidence. Show how it supports your conclusions, using transition words such as *therefore, because*, and *by comparison*.

Revising Reread your paper carefully to make sure that you clearly link your evidence to your conclusions. If links are weak, add sentences that explain the connection or transition words like the ones above to connect your ideas.

✓ ASSESSMENT OPTIONS

Formal Assessment, Selection Test, pp. 200–202, and Assessment Resources Software. The selection test is designed so that it can be easily customized to the performance levels of your students.
Alternative Assessment, p. 41, includes options for less advanced students, more advanced students, verbal/linguistic learners, interpersonal learners, and visual/spatial learners.

PORTFOLIO ASSESSMENT
Use the following rubrics in the ***Alternative Assessment*** booklet to assess student writing:
Compare Opinions: Comparison/Contrast Rubric, p. 104
Fictional Memoir: Fictional Narrative Rubric, p. 96
Journalistic Essay: Description Rubric, p. 98
Writing Mini-Lesson: Evaluation/Review Rubric, p. 105

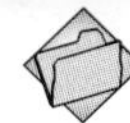

Idea Bank

Customizing for *Performance Levels*
Following are suggestions for matching Idea Bank topics with your students' performance levels:
Less Advanced Students: 1, 4
Average Students: 2, 5, 6
More Advanced Students: 3, 7

Customizing for *Learning Modalities*
Following are suggestions for matching Idea Bank topics with your students' learning modalities:
Verbal/Linguistic: 1, 2, 3, 4, 5, 6, 7
Interpersonal: 4, 5

Refer students to the Writing Handbook, page 1189, for instruction on the writing process, and page 1191 for further information on exposition.

Writing Lab CD-ROM
Have students complete the tutorial on Exposition. Follow these steps:

1. Complete the audience and purpose profiles.
2. View the interactive annotated instruction on using specific, concrete details.
3. Draft on the computer, using the Transitions Word Bin as needed.
4. Use the Revision Checker for Unity and Coherence to aid in revision.

Allow approximately 80 minutes of class time to complete these steps.

Sourcebook
Have students use Chapter 3, Exposition (pp. 63–95) for additional support. The chapter includes a model of a consumer report similar to the evaluation students are writing (p. 66), tips on gathering details (pp. 80–81), and in-depth instruction on organizing details (pp. 82–84).

Prepare and Engage

OBJECTIVES

1. To read, comprehend, and interpret a contemporary speech
2. To explore the thematic connection between nineteenth-century works and a contemporary speech
3. To respond to a contemporary speech through writing, speaking and listening, and a project

PORTFOLIO OPPORTUNITIES

Writing: Reporter's Questions; Personal Profile; Guidelines for Conflict Resolution
Speaking and Listening: Press Conference
Project: Teens Caught up in Conflicts

Have students imagine that they live in a deeply divided community like Northern Ireland. Ask students: What can you do to help heal your community? What problems will you face, and how will you address them? After students have discussed their answers, explain that the author of this speech, like the people she is addressing, must answer these questions.

Progress is the word that best exemplifies the Victorian period and, of course, even greater progress has been made during the twentieth century. One area, however, in which progress has been lacking is in the relationship between Irish Protestants and Catholics. Just as the Poor Laws of the nineteenth century victimized the Irish people, so too do the people of Northern Ireland today find themselves victims of violence in a country divided in two. Judge Catherine McGuinness hopes that people can put aside their differences and attain progress toward achieving a lasting peace in Ireland.

CONNECTIONS TO TODAY'S WORLD

Opening Statement for the Inaugural Session of the Forum for Peace and Reconciliation

Judge Catherine McGuinness

Thematic Connection

THE EMPIRE AND ITS DISCONTENTS

During the Victorian period, Great Britain saw rapid advances in science and technology and exercised great imperial power. The writers in this section focus on the positive and negative aspects of empire. Sydney Smith, for example, notes the progress in personal comfort that made life easier, at least for the privileged. In sharp contrast, the article from *The Illustrated London News* reveals the harsh treatment of the Irish by the British during the potato famine. Arnold and Kipling are not as specific in their criticisms of the empire. Arnold conveys a general sense of sadness and alienation, while Kipling offers a solemn warning against imperial pride and overconfidence.

DISCONTENTS THAT SURVIVE AN EMPIRE

In "Recessional," Kipling cautions against believing that the empire will last forever. History has proved him right. Countries once under England's rule, like India, are now independent. Southern Ireland is also a free nation. Yet Britain still retains control of Northern Ireland, where Protestants loyal to Britain battle with Catholics who want a united Ireland. In this last surviving corner of British imperial rule, the discontents have outlived the empire.

Many people of goodwill, like Judge Catherine McGuinness, are trying to solve these remaining discontents. This selection is a speech by Judge McGuinness to the Forum for Peace and Reconciliation (1995), which attempted to bring together Protestants and Catholics in Northern Ireland.

In her opening address to this group, McGuinness shares her hopes that the past can be overcome and peace established.

JUDGE CATHERINE MCGUINNESS (1934–)

Judge Catherine McGuinness is the Chairperson of the Forum for Peace and Reconciliation and Judge of the High Court of Ireland. McGuinness, of British and Irish ancestry, spent her childhood in Belfast and adult years in Dublin. Her strong Protestant background and fierce pride in her Irish citizenship provide her with a unique perspective on the conflict in Northern Ireland. Active in Irish politics, she has dedicated her career to seeking a lasting peace and improved quality of life for all of Ireland's citizens.

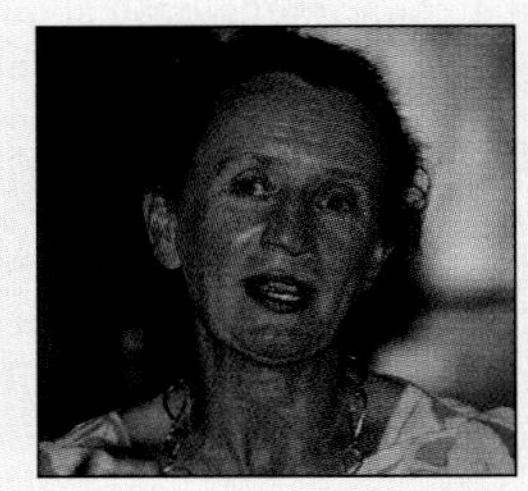

Prentice Hall Literature Program Resources

REINFORCE / RETEACH / EXTEND

Selection Support Pages
Build Vocabulary, p. 200
Thematic Connection, p. 201

Formal Assessment Selection Test, pp. 203–204; Assessment Resources Software

Resource Pro CD-ROM
"Opening Statement . . ."

Listening to Literature Audiocassettes
"Opening Statement . . ."

CONNECTIONS TO TODAY'S WORLD

Opening Statement *for the* Inaugural Session *of the* Forum *for* Peace *and* Reconciliation

Judge Catherine McGuinness

I am happy to welcome all who are here today in Dublin Castle, participants in the Forum, observers and distinguished guests.

The Forum for Peace and Reconciliation has been established by the Government in Accordance with the intentions expressed in the Joint Declaration, to consult on, and examine, ways in which lasting peace, stability and reconciliation can be established by agreement among all the people of Ireland, and on the steps required to remove barriers of distrust, on the basis of promoting respect for the equal rights and validity of both traditions and identities. In accordance with its terms of reference it will also explore ways in which new approaches can be developed to serve economic interests common to both parts of Ireland.

It will be a fundamental principle of the Forum that all differences [in] relation to the exercise of the right to self-determination of the people of Ireland, and to all other matters, will be resolved exclusively [by] peaceful and democratic means. The purpose of the Forum will be to provide an opportunity to both major traditions, as well as to others, to assist in identifying and clarifying issues which could most contribute to creating a new era of trust and cooperation. Participation in the Forum will be entirely without prejudice to the position on constitutional issues held by any Party.

❶ It is clear that major negotiations regarding Ireland's future, North and South, are now taking place and will continue to take place elsewhere. This Forum is a consultative and advisory body, which I hope will create a background of mutual understanding against which those other negotiations may more readily move forward. ❶

The Forum is inclusive in its nature; already it contains members from all of the island of Ireland. I very much hope that in the future other Parties and other individuals will feel able to join in our deliberations. The forum does not represent a threat to any section of the people of Ireland. As I have already said, participation in it is entirely without prejudice to the position on constitutional issues held by any Party. The only entry test is a commitment to "peaceful and democratic means."

This Forum is about people rather than about territory. It is about people's right to live peacefully on this island "which we love and for whose welfare we pray," as that courageous Presbyterian minister, James Armour of Ballymoney, once said. All who live in Ireland must be made [to] feel that their right to be here is unquestioned and that they and their traditions are valued, whether they arrived here a few years ago or whether their ancestors came here four thousand years or four hundred years ago. ❷ People's rights and freedoms should not be affected by their religion, by their political or social outlook, by their economic standing, by their race, or by the country of origin of their ancestors. "Ireland, as distinct from her people, is nothing to me" said James Connolly, in a ringing denunciation of mindless so-called patriotism. James Connolly, who established Ireland's first republican and socialist party, ❸ and who was executed following the 1916 Ris-

Customize for
Less Proficient Readers
Have students make a *KWL* chart before they begin reading. Have the group brainstorm for what they know about the conflict in Ireland and jot down notes in the *K* column. Then have them write what they want to find out in the *W* column. As they read, have them write what they learn in the *L* column.

Comprehension Check ☑

❶ What kind of authority does the Forum have? *The Forum has no real authority, but it is a consultative and advisory board.*

Thematic Connection

❷ The Empire and Its Discontents James Connolly (1868–1916) was an Irish Labour leader and rebel. He joined the British Army at fourteen, but deserted to marry. In 1896, he founded the Irish Socialist Republican party. He was an organizer of a massive transport strike in Ireland in 1913. Connolly was seriously wounded in the Easter rebellion of 1916, after which he was arrested and executed.

◆ Critical Thinking

❸ Infer "Our country, right or wrong" is a motto that some people live by. Ask students if they think Connolly would have agreed or disagreed with this statement. Explain. *Connolly would probably disagree because his statement indicates that the people are more important to him than the country. He appears to believe that sometimes a country's actions are not in the best interest of its people.* Then ask what the author would think of this statement. *Catherine McGuiness would also disagree, because she quotes Connolly and James Armour, both of whom appear to put people above political concerns.*

Speaking and Listening Mini-Lesson

Press Conference
This mini-lesson supports the Speaking and Listening activity in the Idea Bank on page 814.

Introduce the Concept Explain that a press conference is an event in which reporters get information from a politician, celebrity, or spokesperson about a course of action or a current event. In this activity, one student will act out the part of Judge McGuinness while several other students will take the roles of reporters.

Develop Information The reporters should plan their questions, using the standard queries: *who, what, why, where,* and *how.* "Judge McGuinness" should consider her stand on issues that are likely to arise.

Apply the Information The press conference should begin with brief remarks by Judge McGuinness. Then she should open the floor to questions from the reporters, answering each question that is posed. McGuinness and the reporters should speak clearly and politely.

Assess the Outcome Have students evaluate the press conference on the basis of relevance of questions, completeness of answers, tone, and clarity.

▶Critical Viewing◀

❶ **Deduce** Students may cite the conservative attire, the microphones, the reading lamp, the notes, and the attentive, serious expressions of the people in the background.

◆Critical Thinking

❷ **Draw Conclusions** McGuinness points out that the people of Ireland come from many different backgrounds. Ask students why she mentions this fact. *Suggested response: She wants people to realize that there is not one kind of "correct" or "model" Irish person. There are many people of varied backgrounds, all of whom make up the country.*

Comprehension Check ☑

❸ What is McGuinness's background? *She is a Protestant, born in Belfast, Northern Ireland, but she has lived all her adult life in Dublin in the Republic of Ireland.*

Judge Catherine McGuinness at podium, Forum for Peace and Reconciliation, Dublin Castle, October 28, 1994

▲ ❶ Critical Viewing What elements in this photograph point to the solemnity of the occasion? **[Deduce]**

ing, was born in Scotland of Ulster parents, and first arrived in Ireland as a British soldier in the Royal Scots Regiment.

❷ The people of this country have many origins; these strands are woven together to make us what we are. My own personal background is, perhaps, an illustration. My great great grandfather, William Ellis, was twice Lord Mayor of York in England in 1799 and 1807. My great grandfather arrived in this country as a soldier in the 93rd Sutherland Highlanders regiment in 1803. He married a Clare woman whose mother's name was Morony. Their son settled in Spanish Point in County Clare, my own father's place of origin. My mother, whose family had both Irish and Scottish ancestors, came from Tullamore in County Offaly. My parents spent virtually all their adult life in Dunmurry, near Belfast. I was born into the Belfast Protestant community, a "Child of the Rectory," and spent my childhood there. I in my turn have spent my adult life in Dublin. My love for Ulster is deep-rooted and my Protestant background is strong, but I am nonetheless proud to be a citizen of Ireland. ❸

To say that this country faces many problems is to understate the position. In each jurisdiction the level of unemployment and under-employment is far too high; some of those in paid work or working in the home are exploited. There is poverty and deprivation in Dublin and in Belfast, in Leitrim and in Tyrone. Poverty and hardship dominate the lives of far too many people in Ireland, Protestant and Catholic, whether their government is in

Beyond the Classroom

Career Connection

Careers in Law Catherine McGuinness is a judge, an officer of the government who presides over a court of law. In both Great Britain and the United States, the judges of high courts are referred to as justices.

United States federal judges are appointed for life. In Great Britain judges serve until their retirements. Judges very often come from the ranks of lawyers, who generally attend a four-year college and then a two-year law school. Good verbal skills are necessary for anyone considering a career in law.

Have interested students research careers in law, such as paralegal, legal secretary, bailiff, attorney, clerk, law professor, court reporter, and judge. Students may also be interested in finding out about various legal specialities, such as environmental law, taxation, or family law.

Dublin or in London. Of this we must not lose sight; it is part and parcel of the Irish situation and cannot be ignored. The economic aspects of the work of this Forum are vitally important.

We cannot pretend that the armed conflict of the past twenty five years did not happen; nor can we say that it left no legacy. We mourn all those who died; we think of all who were wounded, some of whom will suffer from their injuries all their lives; we grieve for bereaved and broken families; we are conscious of homes where there are empty chairs; we know that all wars are cruel, bloody, harsh and merciless. We rejoice at the ending of violence. We salute all those who have worked for peace and who ultimately brought about the silence of the guns. Some of those are now members of this Forum; others are unsung, and wish to remain so; they each have earned the thanks and respect of us all.

This Forum is described as a Forum for Peace and Reconciliation. I would almost rather reverse the wording of the title and call it a forum for reconciliation and peace. At present we have a cessation of violence and the continuing peace process, but reconciliation is truly a prerequisite for a real and lasting peace. If we are to be reconciled we must be able to admit the errors and mistakes of the past; we must be able to express regret for past wrongs. Yet each of us must be able to retain pride and confidence in our history and in our traditions. Reconciliation can grow where there is both honesty and confidence, and where the old fears of each other are put behind us. ❹

Unionist, socialist, republican, nationalist, liberal, conservative, feminist and all other views have legitimate rights and should be heard. There is no political test here; there is no censorship; there is openness. No party or group or tradition has a monopoly of wisdom. We hope to help banish hatred, incitement to hatred and intolerance from the politics of Ireland, and to lead through reconciliation to a true and lasting peace. ❺

CONNECTIONS TO TODAY'S WORLD

Guide for Responding

◆ Literature and Your Life

Reader's Response Do you find this an inspiring speech? Explain.

Thematic Focus How does this speech reveal discontents that have continued from Victorian times and even earlier?

Journal Writing In your journal, note some of the elements needed to make a conference like this one successful.

☑ Check Your Comprehension

1. What does McGuinness see as the job of the Forum for Peace and Reconciliation?
2. What are some of the problems faced by the Irish people?
3. According to McGuinness, what is the key to achieving lasting peace?

◆ Critical Thinking

INTERPRET

1. (a) Explain the significance of James Connolly's statement that "Ireland, as distinct from her people, is nothing to me." (b) Why is it relevant in the context of this speech? **[Connect]**
2. (a) Why does McGuinness spend so much time discussing her ancestry? (b) How does this add to the significance of her speech? **[Analyze]**
3. What would you say is the overall aim of this forum? **[Draw Conclusions]**

EVALUATE

4. Does the tone of the speech add to or detract from its effectiveness? **[Criticize]**

EXTEND

5. What trouble spot in the world today would benefit from a forum like this one? Explain. **[Social Studies Link]**

Beyond the Selection

FURTHER READING

Other Works About Ireland

Trinity, Leon Uris
"Easter 1916," William Butler Yeats
Belfast Diary, John Conray
Children of 'the Troubles,' Laurel Holliday (editor)
A New Ireland: Politics, Peace, and Reconciliation, John Hume, et al

We suggest that you preview these works before recommending them to students.

INTERNET

You can find additional information about Ireland on the Internet at the following sites.

To see historic and contemporary articles on Ireland, go to **http://www.theatlantic.com/unbound/flashbks/ireland/irintro.htm**

For a multimedia data base of resources on Northern Ireland, visit **http://cain.ulst.ac.uk/**

We *strongly recommend* that you preview the sites before you send students to them.

◆ Critical Thinking

❹ **Analyze** Invite students to describe the tone of this passage. *The tone is positive, thoughtful, and serious.*

◆ Critical Thinking

❺ **Evaluate** Ask students if they think this last paragraph is an effective way to end the speech. Explain. *Suggested response: Yes, this is an effective end because it calls together all the Irish people.*

Reinforce and Extend

Answers

◆ Literature and Your Life

Reader's Response Most students will find the speech inspiring because it eloquently urges all factions to work toward reconciliation and peace.

Thematic Focus The speech mentions James Connolly who founded the Irish Socialist Republican party in 1896; it mentions the importance of admiting the errors of the past and expressing regret for past wrongs.

☑ Check Your Comprehension

1. She sees the job of the Forum as threefold: to discover ways in which peace can be established; to agree on the steps required to establish trust and respect between factions; and to explore ways to improve Ireland's economy.
2. Students may mention unemployment, poverty, and armed conflict.
3. The key is establishing mutual trust and cooperation among conflicting factions.

◆ Critical Thinking

1. (a) Connolly meant that true patriotism requires a comittment to all the people of Ireland, not just one group. (b) Many people in Ireland still put the rights of one group over those of another.
2. (a) She wants to stress that the people of Ireland are of many origins. (b) The story of her ancestry emphasizes similarities among different groups over their differences.
3. The aim is to help create a new era of trust and cooperation.
4. Students may say that the serious tone adds to its effectiveness.
5. Chronic trouble spots include the Middle East, eastern Turkey, northern India, and northern Spain.

Thematic Connection

1. Major issues dividing Ireland are "barriers of distrust" and "the armed conflict of the past twenty-five years." Students may notice that McGuinness emphasizes the challenges ahead, such as poverty and unemployment, the struggle against which may unify people, and glosses over the divisive issues: "Protestant and Catholic . . . government in Dublin or in London."
2. The issues are not explicitly addressed, although "Recessional" and "The Widow at Windsor" allude to the military force needed to keep people in the empire against their will. The issues of poverty and injustice toward the poor are addressed in "The Widow at Windsor" and "Conditions of Ireland."
3. Students may say that this advice might help to ease conflicts between racial groups and between recent immigrants and established families. Following McGuinness's advice might eliminate the counterproductive posturing that occurs when groups feel that they have been left out.
4. Possible responses: Empires are formed by subjugating other peoples, which leads to deep-seated resentments; because the power in imperial rule is centralized, lands under imperial rule may not obtain any experience in governing, which leads to trouble when imperial rule is suddenly lifted; empires suppress religious or ethnic conflict, but do nothing to solve these conflicts, so they flare up again when the empire decays.

Idea Bank

Customizing for
Performance Levels

Following are suggestions for matching Idea Bank topics with your students' performance levels:

Less Advanced Students: 1
Average Students: 2, 4
More Advanced Students: 3, 5

Customizing for
Learning Modalities

Following are suggestions for matching Idea Bank topics with your students' learning modalities:

Visual/Spatial: 5
Logical/Mathematic: 3
Interpersonal: 1, 3, 4
Verbal/Linguistic: 1, 2, 3, 4, 5

Thematic Connection

The Empire and Its Discontents

When you read Arnold's "Dover Beach" and Kipling's "Recessional," you may think of them as part of a vanished historical era. The British Empire, which they comment on indirectly or directly, ceased to exist after World War II. However, conflict between Protestants and Catholics in Northern Ireland still continues, an unwelcome legacy of empire.

Judge McGuinness attempts to deal with this legacy in her speech to a Northern Ireland peace conference. She urges the participants in the conference to put aside their differences and recognize the rights of all those living in Ireland. This step, she hopes, will create an atmosphere in which the different parties can resolve conflicts peacefully.

1. According to McGuinness's speech, what are the major issues dividing Northern Ireland?
2. Are these issues discussed in any of the other works in this section? Explain.
3. McGuinness states that "Each of us must be able to retain pride and confidence in our history and traditions." What conflicts in the United States could be resolved more easily if people followed this advice?
4. Why does the establishment and decay of empires create problems that last for hundreds of years?

Idea Bank

Writing

1. **Reporter's Questions** As a reporter covering the Forum for Peace and Reconciliation, formulate three or four questions you can ask Judge McGuinness about her speech.
2. **Personal Profile** Judge McGuinness discusses her own heritage as a way of illustrating the varied backgrounds of the participants. Profile your own background to show why you are the right person to do a job or solve a problem.
3. **Guidelines for Conflict Resolution** Establish common-sense procedures for any group trying to resolve conflicts. Then arrange these procedures in their order of importance.

Speaking and Listening

4. **Press Conference** With several classmates, role-play a press conference at which reporters question Judge McGuinness about the Forum for Peace and Reconciliation. **[Social Studies Link; Media Link]**

Project

5. **Teens Caught up in Conflicts** Teens around the world have had to live with conflicts in their homelands. Research teenagers' views on these conflicts and their ways of coping with them. Then give a multimedia presentation on your findings, using films, recordings, and photographs. **[Social Studies Link]**

ASSESSMENT OPTIONS

Formal Assessment, Selection Test, pp. 203–204, and Assessment Resources Software. The selection test is designed so that it can be easily customized to the performance levels of your students.

PORTFOLIO ASSESSMENT

Use the following rubrics in the ***Alternative Assessment*** booklet to assess student writing:
Reporter's Questions: Evaluation/Review Rubric, p. 105
Personal Profile: Problem-Solution Rubric, p. 102
Guidelines for Conflict Resolution: How-to/Process Explanation Rubric, p. 101

Writing Process Workshop

Statistical Report

During Victorian times, statistics became an increasingly important way of recording and evaluating dramatic advances in technology and equally dramatic changes in society. Write a statistical report about a social, historical, or scientific issue that can be understood through numbers. In a statistical report you use numerical data to support a thesis statement concerning the issue you have chosen. Interpret and draw conclusions from your data in order to persuade readers of your thesis. Consider including tables, charts, and graphs as an effective way of displaying your statistics in easy-to-read form.

Use the following skills to research and write a statistical report:

Writing Skills Focus

- ▶ **Build a thesis based on statistical information.** (See p. 799.)
- ▶ **Support statistical data with details,** such as expert opinions, experiment results, eyewitness accounts, and analogies. (See p. 809.)
- ▶ **Accuracy** in your data is critical to drawing valid conclusions.

Model From Literature

from *A Review of Southey's Colloquies*
by Thomas Babington Macaulay

. . . the amount of parochial relief required by the laborers . . . is almost exactly in inverse proportion to the degree in which the manufacturing system has been introduced into those counties. ① The returns for the years ending in March, 1825, and in March, 1828, are now before us. In the former year we find the poor rate highest in Sussex, about twenty shillings to every inhabitant. . . . and when we come to Lancashire, ② we find it at four shillings, one-fifth of what it is in Sussex. ③

① The author states a thesis: The need for relief varies inversely with the presence of manufacturing.

② The author provides details on where (Sussex and Lancashire) and when (years ending March, 1825, and March, 1828).

③ Macaulay's thesis is supported by the data.

Prepare and Engage

Establish Writing Guidelines
Before beginning this lesson, review with students the following key characteristics of a statistical report:

- In a statistical report, writers use numerical data to build a thesis.
- The writer not only reports numerical data but interprets and draws conclusions from it.
- Credit source materials and include a bibliography.

To provide students with an overview of the writing process, refer them to the Writing Handbook, pages 1189–1193.

Prepare students for writing by explaining that a statistical report is a type of research writing. Distribute copies of the Scoring Rubric for Research Writing (p.107 in ***Alternative Assessment***) and review criteria on which students will be evaluated.

After reviewing the criteria for research writing, reinforce the Writing Skills Focus and the model of a statistical report on this page.

Writer's Solution

Writing Lab CD-ROM
If students have access to computers, have them work in the Research Writing tutorial to complete their statistical reports. They should follow these steps:

1. Review the audio-annotated model of a statistical report.
2. Narrow their topic using a topic web.
3. Review the audio-annotated instruction on taking notes from maps, charts, and graphs.
4. Draft their papers on the computer.
5. Review tips on accuracy that will help them use statistics correctly.

Sourcebook
Students can find additional help, such as models, graphic organizers, and tips for writing a statistical report, in Chapter 5 on Research Writing (pp. 130–165).

Cross-Curricular Connection: Social Studies

Statistics Indicating Trends Explain to students that sociologists—people who study society—use statistics to draw conclusions about people's needs and behavior, and society's organization. For example, population growth in certain parts of the country may indicate the movement of companies to these areas, therefore bringing more jobs, larger school systems, and a better quality of life.

Have students conduct a statistical analysis of themselves, giving information such as height, hair and eye color, birth date, education level, income level, and so on. When finished, students should "draw conclusions" about themselves based on the statistics they gathered.

Develop Student Writing

Prewriting

Ask students to share their own experiences interpreting statistical information. For example, students may have been faced with statistical information when they were researching colleges. Ask students to share their methods of interpretation and how they used the information. Make a list on the chalkboard of students' strategies for interpreting statistics. Suggest that they refer to these strategies when gathering and interpreting information for their statistical reports.

Refer students to the topic ideas listed on this page. Also encourage them to pursue a topic that interests them, such as a hobby or a curiosity about their town, a vacation place, and so on.

Customize for
Non-Logical/Mathematical Learners

Students who are not comfortable with mathematical or logical reasoning may have difficulty interpreting statistics. Suggest that these students create a graph or chart that illustrates the importance or insignificance of the statistical information. Transferring numerical information to a visual will enable students to decipher it better. Having a visual for reference will also help students when they incorporate statistics into their reports.

Writing Lab CD-ROM

When writing a research paper, one of the most important aspects of prewriting is gathering information. Instruction on using library resources, on-line services, and using maps, charts and graphs will help students gather information for their statistical reports.

Drafting

Explain to students that it is more important to get their ideas on paper than to perfect grammar and style at this point. Statistics should be incorporated at this stage, but advise students to concentrate on the smooth introduction of statistics during the revision stage. Also refer students to the Applying Language Skills section on this page for tips on incorporating statistics.

APPLYING LANGUAGE SKILLS: Introducing Statistical Information

Introducing data is much like introducing quotations. Just as you wouldn't introduce a quotation without explaining who said it, you should explain to readers the source of the numerical data you are presenting. You can introduce your data in a variety of ways. Notice the following examples: They also identify for readers the source of, or method for, obtaining the information.

- According to *The Times*, "Seventeen percent . . ."
- A thorough analysis of census figures indicates that infant mortality has steadily decreased . . .
- Students polled by the newspaper staff gave the following responses:

Writing Application As you introduce your data, be sure to note clearly the source or collection method.

Writer's Solution Connection
Writing Lab

For guidelines on making inferences and drawing conclusions, review the writing tips in the Drafting section of the tutorial on Research Writing.

Prewriting

Choose a Topic In selecting a topic, you may want to consider numbers that are important in your life—for example, what you spend or earn or data on an exercise routine. You can also choose from among these topics.

Topic Ideas

- The cost of a trip to London
- Success of movies based on novels
- Hurricanes of the Atlantic

Selection-Related Topic Ideas

- Analysis of Queen Victoria's popularity
- Importance of potato crop to Ireland's economy in the mid-nineteenth century

Gather Data Identify the sources that would be most helpful for numerical data, tables, charts, and graphs. The following chart will help guide you in locating appropriate sources:

Topic:	Resources:
Rainfall in Edinburgh	atlas, travel guide, almanacs
British economy, before and after repeal of the Corn Laws	history text, encyclopedia, nonfiction books
Herb gardening for profit	vertical files, nonfiction books

Formulate a Working Thesis Use the preliminary data you collect to formulate a working thesis—the point you are going to prove—that will guide further research. Then revise your working thesis as you find data.

Check Your Data Review the data you've collected for accuracy and completeness. Avoid drawing conclusions based on insufficient or incomplete data.

Drafting

Write a Thesis Statement After reviewing all your data, revise your working thesis into a formal thesis statement.

Begin Where it Feels Comfortable Once you formulate your thesis, you may find that it's easier to start at the end and work backward. The order in which you write is not important, as long as you end up with an introduction that states your thesis, a body that supports it, and a conclusion that restates it.

Reinforce and Extend

Applying Language Skills

Introducing Statistical Information In an effort to include as much statistical information as possible in their reports, students may not provide introductions or incorporate numerical information smoothly. The statistical information then loses its effect as support for the thesis. Have students review the examples and complete the writing application before they revise their papers.

Revising

Use a Revision Checklist Use the following questions, based on this lesson's focus points, to help you revise your statistical analysis:

1. Do all the statistics in my report support my thesis?
2. Have I clearly explained my data by answering relevant *who, what, where, when,* and *how* questions?
3. Are my statistics complete, accurate, and clearly presented?

Revision Model

A Statistical Report on the Reading Habits of High School Students

What are seniors reading? At Lake Shore High School, the word is MYSTERY. ① A whopping 58% ~~Over half~~ of the students surveyed ② Surveys asking students to identify the genre of the most recent book they had read revealed that reported having read a mystery within the past month. 137 of the ③ 229 ~~237~~ students surveyed were reading mysteries: everything from Arthur Conan Doyle to Patricia Cornwell. Other categories were reported as follows: *10% identified biography, 12% historical fiction, and 20% science fiction.*

① A statistic supporting the thesis replaces a vague detail.

② The author adds details that explain how the survey was conducted.

③ This statistic was not accurate, so it was revised.

Proofread Proofread your report, eliminating errors in grammar, punctuation, capitalization, and spelling. Also, proofread your statistics to make sure they are accurate.

Publishing

- **Illustrations** Use a computer program to illustrate and add media to your report.
- **Presentation** Invite an interested audience to a presentation of your statistical report. Add charts and graphs to support your presentation.
- **Internet** Publish your paper on an electronic bulletin board.

Applying Language Skills: Interpreting Statistics

In your statistical analyses, don't stretch the facts to prove a particular point. Avoid sweeping generalizations based on small samples.

Misleading:
Ninety percent of poets prefer rhyming verse.

Accurate:
Of the ten poets surveyed, nine preferred rhyming verse.

Whether you conduct your own research or draw on others', describe for readers the data collection methods and the sample sizes. This information will allow readers to determine whether or not the data support your generalizations.

Writing Application When reporting data in percentage form, be sure to explain situations in which numbers may not add up to exactly 100%.

Writer's Solution Connection
Language Lab

To help you review your report for subject-verb agreement, see the lesson on Agreement in Number.

Revising

You may want to have students work with peer reviewers to revise their reports. Have peer reviewers follow the revision checklist and instruct them to offer concrete suggestions for improvement.

Writing Lab CD-ROM
Have students review the audio-annotated instruction on detecting logical fallacies in the Research Writing tutorial.

Writers at Work Videodisc
Show students the segment of the videodisc in which Peter Ginsburg discusses his process of revising. Then ask: Would you use the same revision methods? Why or why not?

Play frames 8795 to 9265

Publishing

Encourage students to write up their conclusions and submit them to the school newspaper or town paper. Then they should leave copies of their papers at the school and local libraries for anyone interested in reading them in their entirety.

Reinforce and Extend

Applying Language Skills

Interpreting Statistics Explain to students that a study is only credible if it details all relevant variables, such as the number of people involved, their locations, and their ages. Have students make sure they have all statistical information represented correctly.

ASSESSMENT		4	3	2	1
PORTFOLIO ASSESSMENT Use the rubric on Research Writing in ***Alternative Assessment*** (p.107) to assess students' writing. Add these criteria to customize the rubric to this assignment.	**Crediting Sources**	The writer credits direct quotations, summarized information, and ideas that are not his or her own.	Most of the direct quotations, summarized information, and ideas are credited, which raises questions about plagiarism.	Most of the information in the paper is not credited creating problems with plagiarism.	Information is not credited and therefore appears to be plagiarized.
	Supporting Details	The writer includes statistical details that directly support the thesis.	The writer supports most information with statistical details. Some details do not directly support the thesis.	The writer infrequently uses statistical details to support the thesis.	The writer does not use statistical details to support the thesis.

Introduce the Strategy

Students may not be aware that information is available to help them make informed buying decisions. Explain that consumer reports offer product information in which various brands are compared and rated. This type of information will help students make informed purchases.

Ask students to share buying experiences in which they had to make informed decisions. List different ways in which students prepared themselves for making the right purchase or choosing a specific brand. Then compare their findings to the strategies on this page.

Customize for *English Language Learners*

These learners may not recognize the jargon that often accompanies consumer reports. They should make lists of terms with which they are unfamiliar and then work with a partner to help them decipher the terms.

Apply the Strategy

Answers

Suggested responses:

1. It offers the option of riding on pavement and trails instead of having to use two separate bikes.
2. The highest rated bike is not necessarily the best buy. The second-highest rated bike costs considerably less at $229, and its rating is almost equivalent to the highest rated bike.
3. Of the four brands, Zip 875 with ratings of excellent and very good at $229 and Al Touring with ratings of good and very good at $175, appear to be the best buys. Both bicycles are in the same price range with good ratings. The best bike is considerably more expensive, and the other bike has the lowest rating.

Reading Consumer Reports

Real-World Reading Skills Workshop

Strategies for Success

In making purchasing decisions, rely on consumer reports by reputable writers and agencies. Learning how to read such reports may save you a great deal of money.

Compare Specific Brands Before reading an article, do some preparation. Keeping in mind that consumer reports compare commonly available brands, visit several stores and survey the products in which you are interested. Write down model numbers and names so that you can recognize them in the article. Also, reach some preliminary conclusions that you can test against the report findings.

Study Ratings Products are often rated in a chart or in pictures. Read the key to such visuals to familiarize yourself with abbreviations used. Then look for a highly-rated product that suits your specific needs. Remember to interpret ratings from your own point of view: The brand rated highest in several categories may not be the best one for your needs.

Look for General Product Information Most consumer articles also give general buying advice. These tips are important because you may not find the brands you want in the article, but you can still apply the advice. Look for summaries that offer buying guidelines.

Apply the Strategy

You're thinking about buying a new bicycle. Before you make the purchase, you're using the report on this page, "Hybrid Bicycles," to gather information.

1. Why might you consider buying a hybrid bicycle?
2. Do you think the highest-rated bicycle is the best buy? Explain.
3. If you decide to buy a hybrid, which of the four brands are you most likely to consider? Why?

Here are some sources you can use to help you make informed buying decisions:

- consumer magazines and newsletters
- pamphlets produced by government or nonprofit organizations
- Internet sites sponsored by consumers

Hybrid Bicycles

Not long ago, bicyclists had two basic choices: buy a road bike suited for long-distance rides on pavement or a mountain bike suited for rough, off-road riding. Now a new class of bicycle, the hybrid, has become increasingly popular. The hybrid bicycle has medium-thickness tires that resist puncture. They ride comfortably on pavement and light trails. For many riders, they offer a perfect compromise.

Brand	Score	Price	Braking	Comfort	Colors	Comments
AJ Touring	***	$175	G	VG	pearlized blue or aqua	Wider tires than most other hybrids.
Stealth 2	**	$250	G	F	silver	Handlebars difficult to adjust.
X-way III	*****	$469	E	E	black, red, copper	Gel seat; high-quality reflectors.
Zip 875	****	$229	E	VG	purple	Water-bottle not included.

Scale: E (Excellent), VG (Very Good), G (Good), F (Fair), P (Poor)

Beyond the Classroom

Community Connection

Consumer Advocacy The research of products like those that appear in consumer reports have resulted in helping to ensure the rights of the consumer. Often products can be dangerous or faulty, and services can be misleading. Consumer advocates and support groups use the objective information in the reports to fight for safety standards and fairness in business and advertising. The Better Business Bureau gives people the opportunity to file grievances against companies, and consumer advocates work hard to expose companies, products, and services that may be harmful or take advantage of the public.

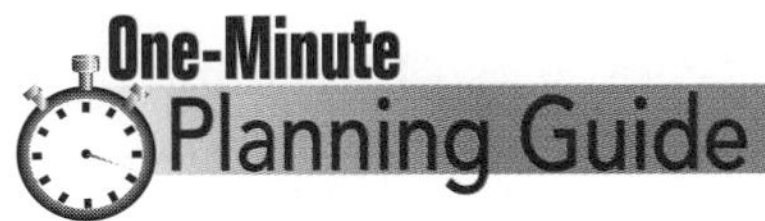

The selections in this section reveal how nineteenth-century novelists expressed their views about society and its problems in their works of fiction. In *Hard Times,* Dickens shows how the education system stifled individuality and imagination. The unfairness and meager living conditions in Jane Eyre's school reflect Brontë's opinions about educational institutions for poor girls. In *War and Peace,* Tolstoy criticizes the way society uses appearance rather than substance to form its opinions of people.

Customize for
Varying Student Needs

When assigning the selections in this part, keep in mind these factors:

from *Hard Times*

- The names of the characters, which often reflect their personalities, will appeal to most students' senses of humor
- Students will respond to the basic conflict between conformity and individuality

from *Jane Eyre*

- English language learners and less proficient readers may have difficulty with archaic vocabulary
- Students can relate the characters' conversation to their own experiences of "deep" conversations with friends

from *War and Peace*

- Russian names may intimidate students
- English language learners may need help with vocabulary

Part 3 Focus on Literary Forms: *The Novel*

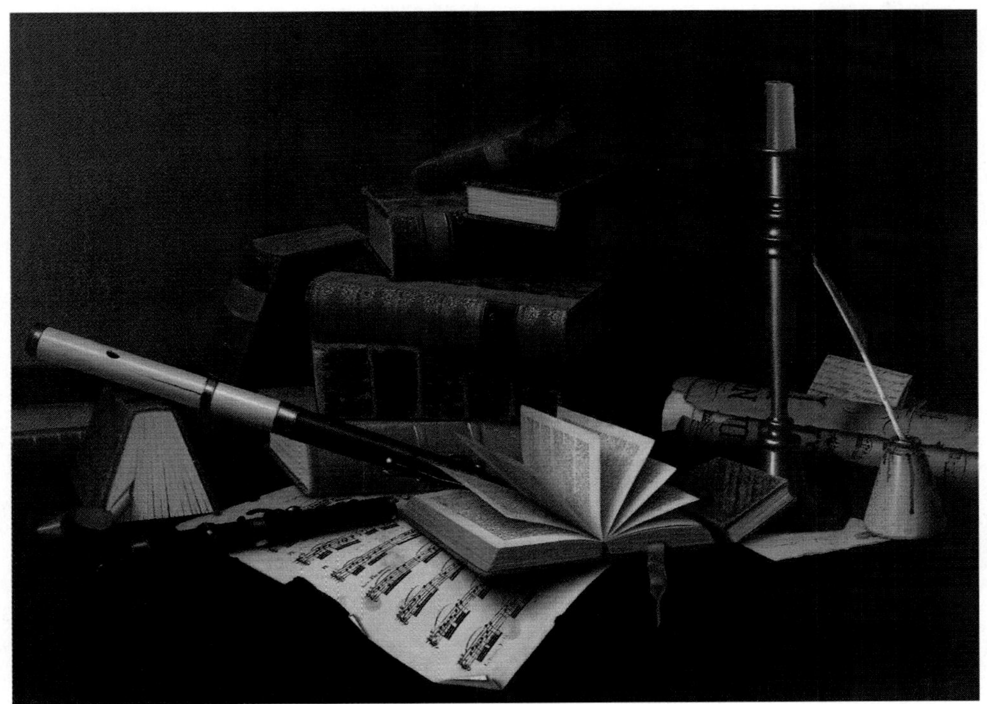

Music and Literature, 1878
William M. Harnett, Albright-Knox Art Gallery Buffalo, New York

In an era before mass media, the new middle class looked to the novel for entertainment, ideas, and a fictional world they could share and discuss. Dickens, the premier British novelist, pioneered the publication of novels in magazines, episode by episode. In this way, the hungry public got its big fictions in bite-size tidbits. Britain still has its bestsellers today, but they have to compete with television and the movies.

Humanities: Art

Music and Literature, 1878, by William M. Harnett.

William Michael Harnett (1848–1892) was born in Ireland but came to the United States as a child, growing up in Philadelphia and studying art at the Pennsylvania Academy of Fine Arts. He spent much of his professional life in Europe, where he painted his best-known work. Harnett had a few favorite subjects—firearms, books, and musical instruments—and created a number of still-life paintings of these subjects.

Encourage students to examine the painting's lovingly-rendered details carefully: Ask if anyone can identify the musical instruments (they are probably flutes or piccolos). Call attention to the stamped yellow envelope under the inkwell at right and the handwritten letter near it.

Have your students link the art to the focus of Part 3, "The Novel," by answering the following question:

1. What do you think is the painter's attitude toward "music and literature," and how can you tell from the painting? *Most students will probably feel that Harnett loved music and literature—from the way he has reproduced the books, sheet music, and musical instruments here, as well as from the information that he frequently painted such subjects.*

Prepare and Engage

OBJECTIVES

1. To read, comprehend, and interpret excerpts from two novels
2. To relate novels to personal experience
3. To recognize the writer's purpose for creating a novel
4. To identify social criticism in a novel
5. To build vocabulary in context and learn the word root *-mono-*
6. To punctuate dialogue correctly
7. To write an observation of a person using an incident to reveal character
8. To respond to novels through writing, speaking and listening, and projects

SKILLS INSTRUCTION

Vocabulary: Word Roots: *-mono-*

Grammar: Punctuation of Dialogue

Reading Strategy: Recognize the Writer's Purpose

Literary Focus: The Novel and Social Criticism

Writing: Using an Incident to Reveal Character

Speaking and Listening: Dialogue (teacher edition)

Critical Viewing: Speculate; Connect; Evaluate

PORTFOLIO OPPORTUNITIES

Writing: Diary Entry; Comparison and Contrast; Response to Criticism

Writing Mini-Lesson: Observation of a Person

Speaking and Listening: Oral Presentation; Dialogue

Projects: Caricature; Exploring Historical Background

Guide for Interpreting

Charles Dickens *(1812–1870)*

No writer since Shakespeare has occupied as important a place in popular culture as Charles Dickens. His novels have held a special appeal for scholars and the public alike and have been dramatized time and again in plays and films.

A Childhood of Hardship Born in Portsmouth on England's southern coast, Dickens had a generally unhappy childhood. His father was sent to debtor's prison, and the boy was sent to a "prison" of his own—a factory in which he worked long hours pasting labels. Such experiences, dramatizing the ills of the newly industrialized society, were to figure prominently in Dickens's novels.

The Birth of a Writer After becoming a court stenographer at the age of seventeen, Dickens became a court reporter. At twenty-one, he began to apply his keen powers of observation in humorous literary sketches of everyday life in London. A collection of these, *Sketches by Boz* (1836), earned him a small following, which he built up considerably with his first novel, *The Pickwick Papers,* published in 1837. Next came such favorites as *Oliver Twist* (1838) and *Nicholas Nickleby* (1839).

A Serious Novelist A turn toward more serious planning and characterization of greater psychological depth are evident in *Dombey and Son* (1848) and *David Copperfield* (1850). These novels emphasize social criticism, as do later masterpieces like *Bleak House* (1853) and *Hard Times* (1854).

Charlotte Brontë *(1816–1855)*

Charlotte Brontë came from one of the most famous literary families ever. Educated at home, siblings Charlotte, Emily, Anne, and Branwell had a rich fantasy life that nurtured their artistic development.

Early Failure, Then Success In 1846 the three sisters published a volume of poems under the pseudonyms Currer, Ellis, and Acton Bell, but the book found little success. Charlotte's first novel, *The Professor,* failed to find a publisher, but she persevered, and when *Jane Eyre* was published in 1847 it became very popular.

Personal Struggle The final years of Charlotte Brontë's life were clouded by tragedy. Her brother died in 1848, and Emily and Anne died soon after. Despite her loneliness, Charlotte found the strength to complete the novels *Shirley* (1849) and *Villette* (1853). She married Arthur Bell Nicholls, her father's curate, a few months before she died.

◆ Background for Understanding

HISTORY: DICKENS AND UTILITARIANISM

Much as Spock in *Star Trek* irritates the crew of the *Enterprise* with his coldly logical view of life, Jeremy Bentham (1748–1831) irritated Dickens with a philosophy called Utilitarianism. Bentham used statistics and logic to bring about useful (which is the meaning of *utilitarian*) changes in law and government. He believed, however, that humans are selfish and that this selfishness is a positive trait.

Dickens felt that Utilitarianism did away with the qualities of sympathy and imagination. In *Hard Times,* Thomas Gradgrind is a relentless utilitarian, and Dickens uses him to show that this philosophy is deadening and destructive. The novel begins with Gradgrind's humorless praise of "Facts."

More About the Authors

One reason for **Charles Dickens's** power as a social critic was his popularity. His novels first appeared, not in book form, but serialized in magazines. Each new installment was eagerly awaited by devoted readers everywhere. There are accounts of horsemen galloping from village to village, with the tidings of newly issued chapters.

Jane Eyre draws on **Charlotte Brontë's** own experiences. She herself went to a boarding school she detested and later became a governess. Her portrayal of Jane as a strong, independent woman shocked many of her readers.

Prentice Hall Literature Program Resources

REINFORCE /RETEACH / EXTEND

Selection Support Pages
Build Vocabulary: Word Roots: *-mono-*, p. 202
Build Grammar Skills: Punctuation of Dialogue, p. 203
Reading Strategy: Writer's Purpose, p. 204
Literary Focus: Novel and Social Criticism, p. 205

Strategies for Diverse Student Needs, p. 42

Beyond Literature
Humanities Connection: Utilitarian Philosophy, p. 42

Formal Assessment Selection Test, p. 208–210; Assessment Resources Software

Alternative Assessment, p. 42

Writing and Language Transparencies
Descriptive and Observational Writing, pp. 13–16
Daily Language Practice, Week 28, p. 60

Resource Pro CD-ROM
from *Hard Times*, from *Jane Eyre*—includes all resource material and customizable lesson plan

Listening to Literature Audiocassettes
from *Hard Times*, from *Jane Eyre*

Looking at Literature Videodisc
Hard Times

◆ Literature and Your Life

Connect Your Experience

Your image of a crusader may come from the movies: a dynamic but downtrodden figure who stands up to corrupt officials.

Many nineteenth-century crusaders were novelists like Dickens and Brontë, armed only with their pens. By writing about characters who experience social injustices, they won the sympathy of their readers for the disadvantaged and misunderstood.

Journal Writing Jot down some possible subjects for a crusading novelist of today.

Thematic Focus: Relationships

How do the educational institutions depicted by these novelists prove harmful to human relationships?

◆ Literary Focus

The Novel and Social Criticism

A **novel** is a long work of fiction, which usually has a complex plot, major and minor characters, a significant theme, and several settings. The novel became popular during the nineteenth century, a period of disturbing social and economic change. It isn't surprising, therefore, that many novelists of the time include **social criticism** in their works, calling attention to society's injustices.

In this passage from *Hard Times,* for example, Dickens strongly condemns the mind-numbing system of education inflicted on the poor. Similarly, Brontë devotes an episode from *Jane Eyre* to painting a terrifying picture of a boarding school for poor girls.

◆ Reading Strategy

Recognize the Writer's Purpose

A **writer's purpose** for creating a novel might be to redress a wrong, to satirize an institution, to amuse readers, or a combination of these. You can find clues to a writer's purpose in details like the writer's ideas, the outcome of events, the writer's attitudes toward characters, and the writer's choice of character names.

In *Hard Times*, for example, Dickens names a teacher M'Choakumchild, indicating his disgust with certain educational ideas and methods. These clues suggest that Dickens's purpose is to satirize the educational system of Victorian England.

◆ Build Vocabulary

Word Roots: *-mono-*

In *Hard Times,* Dickens describes a schoolroom as *monotonous*. The Greek word root *-mono-*, which means "single" or "alone," contributes to the meaning of *monotonous*: "having a single 'tone' and therefore dull and unvarying." A *monotonous* room is boring in its sameness.

Word Bank

Before you read, preview this list of words from the novels.

monotonous
obstinate
adversary
indignant
approbation
obscure
comprised
sundry

◆ Grammar and Style

Punctuation of Dialogue

Whenever dialogue appears in literature, the speaker's words are enclosed in quotation marks to distinguish them from the surrounding text.

In the following passage from *Hard Times,* the words spoken by Gradgrind appear in quotation marks.

> "Girl number twenty," said Mr. Gradgrind, squarely pointing with his square forefinger, "I don't know that girl. Who is that girl?"

Preparing for Standardized Tests

Reading and Vocabulary Students will improve their performance on the reading-comprehension portions of standardized tests, particularly content-area achievement tests, when they recognize the writer's purpose and keep it in mind as they evaluate a piece of writing. Students can practice identifying the writer's purpose and examining its implications by doing the Reading Strategy exercises on page 834 and completing the practice page in ***Selection Support***, p. 204.

Grammar and Style On standardized tests, correcting a sentence may require students to punctuate dialogue:

> "You have three choices," she explained: study hall, clubs, or early dismissal."

This incorrectly puncutated sentence would then be followed by several possible revisions. Help students choose the correct answer for this and other similar questions by having them complete the Grammar and Style page in ***Selection Support***, p. 203.

Tell students that their school will be the site for filming a new television series on teenagers. Have them brainstorm to create an episode for the pilot show and to cast the main characters. Remind them that they can use the show to call viewers' attention to flaws in the educational system. After they have sketched out an episode and selected actors, tell them that some nineteenth-century novels were as popular as television series are today. Novelists like Dickens and Brontë used their works to call attention to society's ills.

Customize for
Less Proficient Readers
Less proficient readers may have trouble with vocabulary in this selection. Have them list problem words, like *farrier, peremptorily, galvanizing, pugilist, pianoforte, disconsolate*, and *meed*, and find definitions—by themselves—in dictionaries, if possible.

Customize for
More Advanced Students
Advanced readers might compare the attitudes of the authors in this selection. They can discuss how Dickens might have treated Brontë's characters and situations, and how Brontë might have written about the school portrayed by Dickens.

Customize for
English Language Learners
Students learning English may be confused by the archaic language in the excerpt from *Hard Times*. Go over it with them, explaining that words like *thy, thou, dost*, and *wilt* reflect the fact that the familiar form of the second person was once common in English, as it is now in many languages.

Customize for
Interpersonal Learners
Interpersonal learners might find it interesting to imagine themselves at school with either Cecilia Jupe or Jane Eyre. Encourage them, as they read, to jot down advice they might give to either of those two to help them get on with their lives.

Develop Understanding

One-Minute Insight In this episode from the beginning of *Hard Times,* Thomas Gradgrind questions children in his model school. Then he turns the proceedings over to the schoolmaster M'Choakumchild. Dickens uses the occasion to satirize the deadening utilitarian philosophy of these "educators," with its devotion to facts at the expense of living knowledge. A student named Sissy Jupe, for example, is the daughter of a man who makes his living from horses. However, her inability to define a horse according to the dictionary is regarded as a deficiency. Dickens uses names—Gradgrind speaks volumes— as well as descriptions and dialogue to score more satiric points.

◆ Background for Understanding

❶ **History** Ask students how the schoolroom reflects the precepts of Utilitarianism that the speaker is extolling and Dickens is criticizing. Students may point out that the room has no ornament whatever or any feature unnecessary for its purpose. It is, in fact, "utilitarian."

◆ Critical Thinking

❷ **Make Judgments** Invite students to suggest a relationship between Dickens's description of the speaker and the speaker's message. *Student responses can reflect the utter lack of warmth or softness in the speaker. His geometrical angularity underscores his rigidity of character and viewpoint.*

◆ Critical Thinking

❸ **Draw Conclusions** Invite students to suggest reasons for the way in which Dickens introduces the students in this passage. *Students should note that the students are not described as people but as things—reflecting the way in which the adults present apparently view them.*

from Hard Times

Charles Dickens

Chapter 1
The One Thing Needful

"Now, what I want is, Facts. Teach these boys and girls nothing but Facts. Facts alone are wanted in life. Plant nothing else, and root out everything else. You can only form the minds of reasoning animals upon Facts: nothing else will ever be of any service to them. This is the principle on which I bring up my own children, and this is the principle on which I bring up these children. Stick to Facts, sir!"

The scene was a plain, bare, monotonous
❶ vault of a schoolroom, and the speaker's
square forefinger emphasized his observations by underscoring every sentence with a line on the schoolmaster's sleeve. The emphasis was helped by the speaker's square wall of a forehead, which had his eyebrows for its base, while his eyes found commodious cellarage in two dark caves, overshadowed by the wall. The
❷ emphasis was helped by the speaker's mouth,
which was wide, thin, and hard set. The emphasis was helped by the speaker's voice, which was inflexible, dry, and dictatorial. The emphasis was helped by the speaker's hair, which bristled on the skirts of his bald head, a plantation of firs to keep the wind from its shining surface, all covered with knobs, like the crust of a plum pie, as if the head had scarcely warehouse-room for the hard facts
stored inside. The speaker's obstinate carriage, ❷
square coat, square legs, square shoulders—nay, his very neckcloth, trained to take him by the throat with an unaccommodating grasp, like a stubborn fact, as it was—all helped the emphasis.

"In this life, we want nothing but Facts, sir; nothing but Facts!"

The speaker, and the schoolmaster, and the third grown person present, all backed a little, and swept with their eyes the inclined plane of
little vessels, then and there arranged in order, ❸
ready to have imperial gallons of facts poured into them until they were full to the brim.

Chapter 2
Murdering the Innocents

Thomas Gradgrind, sir. A man of realities. A man of fact and calculations. A man who proceeds upon the principle that two and two are four, and nothing over, and who is not to be
talked into allowing for anything over. Thomas ❹
Gradgrind, sir—peremptorily Thomas—Thomas Gradgrind. With a rule and a pair of scales, and the multiplication table always in his pocket, sir, ready to weigh and measure any parcel of

◆ Build Vocabulary

monotonous (mə nät′ ən əs) *adj.*: Having little or no variation or variety

obstinate (äb′ stə nət) *adj.*: Stubborn; dogged; mulish

Block Scheduling Strategies

Consider these suggestions to take advantage of extended class time:

- Use the Background for Understanding note (p. 820) to help students grasp the meaning and implications of Utilitarianism. After students have read the excerpts from *Hard Times* and *Jane Eyre,* have them complete the page on Utilitarianism in ***Beyond Literature,*** p. 42.
- To introduce Charles Dickens and give students an opportunity to practice their grammar skills, use the Daily Language Practice, Week 28, in ***Writing and Language Transparencies,*** p. 60. Display the transparency on the overhead and instruct students to write their corrected versions of the sentences in their notebooks.
- After they have read the excerpts from the novels, allow students to work in small groups to answer the Literature and Your Life, Check Your Comprehension, and Critical Thinking questions (pp. 827, 833).

London School for Orphan Boys, Wood engraving, 1870

5 ▲ **Critical Viewing** Judging from the details in this engraving, what was school like in London of the 1870s? **[Speculate]**

human nature, and tell you exactly what it comes to. It is a mere question of figures, a case of simple arithmetic. You might hope to get some other nonsensical belief into the head of George Gradgrind, or Augustus Gradgrind, or John Gradgrind, or Joseph Gradgrind (all suppositious, non-existent persons), but into the head of Thomas Gradgrind—no, sir!

4 In such terms Mr. Gradgrind always mentally introduced himself, whether to his private circle of acquaintance, or to the public in general. In such terms, no doubt, substituting the words "boys and girls," for "sir," Thomas Gradgrind now presented Thomas Gradgrind to the little pitchers before him, who were to be filled so full of facts.

Indeed, as he eagerly sparkled at them from the cellarage before mentioned, he seemed a kind of cannon loaded to the muzzle with facts, and prepared to blow them clean out of the regions of childhood at one discharge. He seemed a galvanizing apparatus, too, charged with a grim mechanical substitute for the tender young imaginations that were to be stormed away.

"Girl number twenty," said Mr. Gradgrind, squarely pointing with his square forefinger, "I don't know that girl. Who is that girl?"

◆ **Literary Focus**
What outlook is Dickens criticizing by having Gradgrind use a number to call on Sissy Jupe? 6

"Sissy Jupe, sir," explained number twenty, blushing, standing up, and curtseying.

"Sissy is not a name," said Mr. Gradgrind. "Don't call yourself Sissy. Call yourself Cecilia."

"It's father as calls me Sissy, sir," returned the young girl in a trembling voice, and with another curtsey.

"Then he has no business to do it," said Mr. Gradgrind. "Tell him he mustn't. Cecilia Jupe. Let me see. What is your father?"

"He belongs to the horse-riding, if you please, sir."

◆ Critical Thinking

4 Infer Ask students why Dickens adopts the writing style he has chosen for this passage. *The author is demonstrating the way Gradgrind thinks and speaks.* What do they believe it conveys? *Gradgrind is self-assured, no-nonsense, mathematical, closed-minded, mechanical. He appears to regard students as passive, practically inanimate objects.*

▶Critical Viewing◀

5 Speculate Students may observe that there are two adult instructors, the class contains boys only, there are no desks, and a student appears to be leading the rest of the class in a reading lesson. Students may conclude from this that classes were single-gender with a confusing mix of simultaneous activities, that taking notes was not encouraged or not allowed, and that students received little individualized attention.

◆ Literary Focus

6 The Novel and Social Criticism Students may recognize that using numbers rather than names to refer to people is a way to dehumanize them and strip away their individuality.

Looking at Literature Videodisc

For background on the excerpt from *Hard Times,* play Chapter 9 of the videodisc. This segment provides a brief overview of some of the uses and misuses of education througout history. Discuss the purpose of education in the United States today.

Chapter 9

Humanities: Art

London School for Orphan Boys, 1870.

This illustration, which shows a classroom in an orphanage, was created through the technique of wood engraving, which involves incising designs into a block of wood. This block is then inked and pressed onto paper, leaving a black-and-white image. It is an exacting art that requires strength and precision. The details in this engraving display a wide variety of textures and shading.

Use these questions for discussion.

1. Does the absence of color in this black-and-white picture enhance the mood of the excerpt it illustrates? Explain. *Suggested answer: The absence of color underscores the colorlessness and coldness of the schoolroom portrayed in the excerpt.*
2. Would the teachers and students shown in the engraving meet with the approval of Gradgrind? Why or why not? *Gradgrind might well find the school shown to be sufficiently like a factory to meet with his approval. The teacher in the foreground, however, has a look which Gradgrind might find unacceptably caring and relaxed.*

◆ Critical Thinking

❶ **Criticize** Have students analyze the exchange between Sissy and Mr. Gradgrind. Ask students what they think of Mr. Gradgrind's conclusion that Sissy does not know any facts about horses. *Suggested response: Mr. Gradgrind jumped to conclusions about the cause for Sissy's alarm. He assumed that she was upset because she could not define what a horse was. In reality, however, she was too flustered by his forceful, condemning manner that she did not know how to respond to his question.*

◆ Reading Strategy

❷ **Recognize the Writer's Purpose** Ask students why they think the writer chose to describe Bitzer in the way he did. *Students should note that Dickens deprives Bitzer of all color, especially in contrast to Sissy Jupe. Bitzer's pallor and coldness make him a perfect prototype of the citizen of the new industrial world that Gradgrind wishes to create.*

▶Critical Viewing◀

❸ **Connect** Students should realize that this wallpaper, with its horses and floral motif, would be abhorrent to Mr. Gradgrind, because horses are not found on walls, nor will flowers grow on interior walls, at any rate.

Customize for *Visual/Spatial Learners*

Students may enjoy creating their own illustration of Gradgrind's classroom. They might draw or paint the scene or create a collage out of magazine pictures of people, rooms, sunbeams, horses or other appropriate subjects.

Humanities: Art

Victorian Decoration

Dickens could exaggerate to make a point, but sometimes he did not have to go far beyond reality to create a ridiculous image. In 1852, a Department of Practical Arts was established in Britain to study designs of textiles and other consumer products. Henry Cole, the General Superintendent, decried the use of representational portrayals of inappropriate subjects. One of his attacks, in fact, was aimed specifically at wallpaper showing representations of horses and at carpets with floral designs, thereby giving Dickens an obvious target for his sarcastic pen.

Some critics, though, feel that Dickens may have been unfair. The Department argued against the more vulgar stylistic excesses in which Victorians sometimes indulged. They would cram their homes with furnishings and decorative pieces of all sorts in a confusion of dark wood, lacquer, gilt, and mother-of-pearl. Velvet and lace fabrics covered all available surfaces; glass miniatures, shells, porcelain statuettes, bronze sculptures, Berlin-work pillows, and a profusion of other knickknacks were scattered everywhere. The walls were covered with elaborately patterned wallpaper and hung with huge paintings in heavy, gilded frames. Perhaps the urge to show some restraint may not have been so ill-advised.

Mr. Gradgrind frowned, and waved off the objectionable calling with his hand.

"We don't want to know anything about that, here. You mustn't tell us about that, here. Your father breaks horses, don't he?"

"If you please, sir, when they can get any to break, they do break horses in the ring, sir."

"You mustn't tell us about the ring, here. Very well, then. Describe your father as a horsebreaker. He doctors sick horses, I dare say?"

"Oh yes, sir."

"Very well, then. He is a veterinary surgeon, a farrier and horsebreaker. Give me your definition of a horse."

(Sissy Jupe thrown into the greatest alarm by this demand.)

1 "Girl number twenty unable to define a horse!" said Mr. Gradgrind, for the general behoof of all the little pitchers. "Girl number twenty possessed of no facts, in reference to one of the commonest of animals! Some boy's definition of a horse. Bitzer, yours."

The square finger, moving here and there, lighted suddenly on Bitzer, perhaps because he chanced to sit in the same ray of sunlight which, darting in at one of the bare windows of the intensely whitewashed room, irradiated Sissy. For, the boys and girls sat on the face of the inclined plane in two compact bodies, divided up the center by a narrow interval; and Sissy, being at the corner of a row on the sunny side, came in for the beginning of a sunbeam, of which Bitzer, being at the corner of a row on the other side, a few rows in advance, caught the end. But, whereas the girl was so dark-eyed and dark-haired, that she seemed to receive a deeper and more lustrous color from the sun when it shone upon her, the boy was so light-eyed and light-haired that the self-same rays appeared to draw out of him what little color he
2 ever possessed. His cold eyes would hardly have been eyes, but for the short ends of lashes which, by bringing them into immediate contrast with something paler than themselves, expressed their form. His short-cropped hair might have been a mere continuation of the sandy freckles on his forehead and face. His skin was so unwholesomely deficient in the natural tinge, that he looked as though, if he were 2 cut, he would bleed white.

"Bitzer," said Thomas Gradgrind. "Your definition of a horse."

"Quadruped. Graminivorous. Forty teeth, namely twenty-four grinders, four eye-teeth, and twelve incisive. Sheds coat in the spring; in marshy countries, sheds hoofs, too. 4 Hoofs hard, but requiring to be shod with iron. Age known by marks in mouth." Thus (and much more) Bitzer.

"Now girl number twenty," said Mr. Gradgrind. "You know what a horse is."

She curtseyed again, and would have blushed deeper, if she could have blushed deeper than she had blushed all this time. Bitzer, after rapidly blinking at Thomas Gradgrind with both eyes at once, and so catching the light upon his quivering ends of lashes that they looked like the antennae of busy insects, put his knuckles to his freckled forehead, and sat down again.

The third gentleman now stepped forth. A mighty man at cutting and drying, he was; a government officer; in his way (and in most other people's too), a professed pugilist; always in training, always with a system to force down the general throat like a bolus,[1] always to be heard of at the bar of his little Public-office, ready to fight all England. To continue in fistic phraseology, he had a genius for coming up to the scratch, wherever and whatever it was, and proving himself an ugly customer. He would go in and damage any subject whatever with his 5 right, follow up with his left, stop, exchange, counter, bore his opponent (he always fought All England[2]) to the ropes, and fall upon him neatly. He was certain to knock the wind out of common sense, and render that unlucky adversary deaf to the call of time. And he had it in charge 6 from high authority to bring about the great public-office Millennium, when Commissioners should reign upon earth.

1. **bolus:** Small, round mass, often of chewed food.
2. **fought All England:** Fought according to the official rules of boxing.

3 ◀ **Critical Viewing** According to the selection, what would Mr. Gradgrind think of this wallpaper design? **[Connect]**

◆ Build Vocabulary

adversary (ad′vər ser′ē) *n.*: Opponent; enemy

Customize for
English Language Learners

4 Explain unfamiliar terms in Bitzer's definition of a horse. For example, a quadruped is an animal with four legs; *graminivorous* means "grain-eating;" *grinders* are "molars;" *eye-teeth* are "canine teeth," and *incisive* [teeth] are "incisors."

5 **Clarification** Explain that in this passage Dickens describes the government official as if he were a boxer. Elicit from or tell the class that *pugilist* means "boxer," *fistic* means "having to do with boxing or fisticuffs," *the ropes* refers to the fence around a boxing ring, and the *call of time* refers to a boxing referee counting off seconds to a downed boxer—if the boxer is "down for the count," his opponent wins. Point out that Dickens uses phrases from the sports journalism of his day to enhance the image he is creating. *Coming up to the scratch* means "making a good show of oneself under pressure," and *ugly* means "fierce and vicious."

◆ Literary Focus

6 **The Novel and Social Criticism** Ask students what aspect of society Dickens is criticizing here. *Lead students to the understanding that Dickens is criticizing the sort of person who believes that bureaucracy is not just a means to an end, but an end in itself. Such individuals were becoming powerful in Dickens's day and have been targets for social critics ever since.*

◆ Reading Strategy

1 Recognize the Writer's Purpose Suggested response: Dickens's purpose is to poke fun at the attitude that there is one, and only one, proper way to do things. Dickens shows the ridiculousness of such an attitude by taking it to an extreme—in this case, Gradgrind's insistence that walls cannot be painted, only papered.

◆ Literary Focus

2 The Novel and Social Criticism Ask students what aspect of education Dickens is criticizing in this passage. *Students may say that he is criticizing the insistence of the educational system on eliminating imagination —"fancy"—from education.*

◆ Critical Thinking

3 Analyze Character Ask students to summarize what kind of person the speaker is on the basis of this passage. *Students should be aware that the speaker is high-handed and has a low opinion in the ability of people in general to run or organize their lives. His idea of the world of the future is one in which all decisions, important or trivial, would be made by a small group of individuals very much like himself.*

"Very well," said this gentleman, briskly smiling, and folding his arms. "That's a horse. Now, let me ask you girls and boys, Would you paper a room with representations of horses?"

After a pause, one half of the children cried in chorus, "Yes, sir!" Upon which the other half, seeing in the gentleman's face that Yes was wrong, cried out in chorus, "No, sir!"—as the custom is, in these examinations.

"Of course, No. Why wouldn't you?"

A pause. One corpulent slow boy, with a wheezy manner of breathing, ventured the answer, Because he wouldn't paper a room at all, but would paint it.

1 **◆ Reading Strategy** What does Gradgrind's insistence hint about Dicken's purpose in this scene?

"You *must* paper it," said Thomas Gradgrind, "whether you like it or not. Don't tell *us* you wouldn't paper it. What do you mean, boy?"

"I'll explain to you, then," said the gentleman, after another and a dismal pause, "why you wouldn't paper a room with representations of horses. Do you ever see horses walking up and down the sides of rooms in reality—in fact? Do you?"

"Yes, sir!" from one half. "No, sir!" from the other.

"Of course no," said the gentleman, with an indignant look at the wrong half. "Why, then, you are not to see anywhere, what you don't see in fact; you are not to have anywhere, what you don't have in fact. What is called Taste, is only another name for Fact."

Thomas Gradgrind nodded his approbation.

"This is a new principle, a discovery, a great discovery," said the gentleman. "Now, I'll try you again. Suppose you were going to carpet a room. Would you use a carpet having a representation of flowers upon it?"

There being a general conviction by this time that "No, sir!" was always the right answer to this gentleman, the chorus of No was very strong. Only a few feeble stragglers said Yes; among them Sissy Jupe.

"Girl number twenty," said the gentleman, smiling in the calm strength of knowledge.

Sissy blushed, and stood up.

"So you would carpet your room—or your husband's room, if you were a grown woman, and had a husband—with representations of flowers, would you," said the gentleman. "Why would you?"

"If you please, sir, I am very fond of flowers," returned the girl.

"And is that why you would put tables and chairs upon them, and have people walking over them with heavy boots?"

"It wouldn't hurt them, sir. They wouldn't crush and wither if you please, sir. They would be the pictures of what was very pretty and pleasant, and I would fancy—"

"Ay, ay, ay! but you mustn't fancy," cried the gentleman, quite elated by coming so happily to his point. "That's it! You are never to fancy."

"You are not, Cecilia Jupe," Thomas Gradgrind solemnly repeated, "to do anything of that 2
kind."

"Fact, fact, fact!" said the gentleman. And "Fact, fact, fact!" repeated Thomas Gradgrind.

"You are to be in all things regulated and governed," said the gentleman, "by fact. We hope to have, before long, a board of fact, composed of commissioners of fact, who will force the people to be a people of fact, and of nothing but fact. You must discard the word Fancy altogether. You have nothing to do with it. You are not to have, in any object of use or ornament, what would be a contradiction in fact. You don't walk upon flowers in fact; you cannot be allowed to walk upon flowers in carpets. You 3
don't find that foreign birds and butterflies come and perch upon your crockery. You never meet with quadrupeds going up and down walls; you must not have quadrupeds represented upon walls. You must use," said the gentleman, "for all these purposes, combinations and modifications (in primary colors) of mathematical figures which are susceptible of proof and demonstration. This is the new discovery. This is fact. This is taste."

The girl curtseyed, and sat down. She was very young, and she looked as if she were frightened by the matter of fact prospect the world afforded.

◆ Build Vocabulary

indignant (in dig´nənt) *adj.*: Be displeased about

approbation (ap´rə bā´shən) *n.*: Official approval, sanction or commendation

Speaking and Listening Mini-Lesson

Dialogue

This mini-lesson supports the Speaking and Listening activity in the Idea Bank on page 835.

Introduce the Concept Remind students that a dialogue is a conversation between two people. This dialogue will feature the characters Sissy Jupe and Bitzer from the novel *Hard Times*. Explain that students will work in pairs to write and perform a dialogue for the rest of the class.

Develop Information Students should look back over the scene with Mr. Gradgrind and notice the way Sissy and Bitzer behave. Keeping their characters in mind, students can develop a dialogue about the events of the day. While students write, they should try to bear in mind the speech styles of the characters.

Apply the Information After they have written a satisfactory dialogue, students can perform their dialogues for the class. If possible, the presentations might be audiotaped or videotaped.

Assess the Outcome Classmates can assess the dialogues by judging whether the characterizations of Sissy and Bitzer are consistent with the way they are portrayed in the novel and by completing the Peer Assessment: Dramatic Performance page in ***Alternative Assessment,*** p. 121.

"Now, if Mr. M'Choakumchild," said the gentleman, "will proceed to give his first lesson here, Mr. Gradgrind, I shall be happy, at your request, to observe his mode of procedure."

Mr. Gradgrind was much obliged. "Mr. M'Choakumchild, we only wait for you."

So, Mr. M'Choakumchild began in his best manner. He and some one hundred and forty other schoolmasters, had been lately turned at the same time, in the same factory, on the same principles, like so many pianoforte legs. He had been put through an immense variety of paces, and had answered volumes of head-
4 breaking questions. Orthography, etymology, syntax, and prosody, biography, astronomy, geography, and general cosmography, the sciences of compound proportion, algebra, land-surveying and leveling, vocal music, and drawing from models, were all at the ends of his ten chilled fingers. He had worked his stony way into Her Majesty's most Honorable Privy
5 Council's Schedule B, and had taken the bloom off the higher branches of mathematics and physical science, French, German, Latin, and Greek. He knew all about all the Water Sheds of all the world (whatever they are), and all the histories of all the peoples, and all the names of all the rivers and mountains, and all the productions, manners, and customs of all the countries, and all their boundaries and bearings on the two-and-thirty points of the compass. Ah, rather overdone, M'Choakumchild. If he had only learnt a little less, how infinitely better he might have taught much more!

He went to work in this preparatory lesson, not unlike Morgiana in the Forty Thieves:[3] looking into all the vessels ranged before him, one
after another, to see what they contained. Say, 6
good M'Choakumchild. When from thy boiling
store, thou shalt fill each jar brim full by and 7
by, dost thou think that thou wilt always kill outright the robber Fancy lurking within— or sometimes only maim him and distort him!

3. **Morgiana in the Forty Thieves:** In the tale "Ali Baba and the Forty Thieves," Ali Baba's clever servant, Morgiana, saves him from the thieves.

Guide for Responding

◆ Literature and Your Life

Reader's Response How did you feel about Mr. Thomas Gradgrind, Mr. M'Choakumchild, and their theory of education?

Thematic Focus What kind of people will students like Bitzer grow up to be? Explain.

Summary of a School Day With a small group, briefly summarize what the students in this school might study on a typical day.

☑ Check Your Comprehension

1. What does Thomas Gradgrind believe to be the key to all learning?
2. Summarize the exchange between Gradgrind and Sissy Jupe.
3. How does Bitzer define a horse?
4. According to the government officer, what are the students never to do?

◆ Critical Thinking

INTERPRET

1. (a) Who are the "little pitchers" referred to at the beginning of Chapter 2? (b)Why is this an appropriate image? **[Interpret]**
2. What does Bitzer's definition of a horse reveal about his character? **[Connect]**
3. In his description of Gradgrind, Dickens compares him to "a kind of cannon." How is this simile appropriate? **[Analyze]**
4. What conclusion does Dickens want the reader to draw about the three adults in the schoolroom? Explain. **[Draw Conclusions]**

APPLY

5. Dickens hints at some important elements of education that are neglected by Gradgrind and his colleagues. Do modern schools address these elements? Explain. **[Apply]**

◆ Literary Focus

4 The Novel and Social Criticism Have students state the point that Dickens makes about teachers. *Students may see that he faults the mechanical training they receive. He implies that mastery of "facts" is not sufficient to produce a good teacher.*

5 Clarification In 1846, a government syllabus, Schedule B, listed what teacher candidates had to learn to be certified.

◆ Reading Strategy

6 Recognize the Writer's Purpose Ask students why they think the writer changes his prose style here. *He uses the style of fantastical tales to put the question in a ridiculously elaborate and formal way.*

Comprehension Check ☑

7 Check that students understand the allusion by asking them how Morgiana killed the forty thieves. *Morgiana discovered the thieves hiding in oil-storage jars and then poured boiling oil into each of the jars.*

Reinforce and Extend

Answers

◆ Literature and Your Life

Reader's Response Students will probably express a dislike of the three men's theory of education.

Thematic Focus Students may predict that Bitzer is going to grow up into a boring, robotlike know-it-all with no personality.

☑ Check Your Comprehension

1. He sees "facts" as the important element in learning.
2. Gradgrind tells her she cannot use a nickname, distorts the facts about her father's job to make it more proper, asks her what a horse is, and announces to the class that she does not know any facts about horses when she is too flustered to reply immediately.
3. Bitzer gives a formal dictionary definition in short, unrelated phrases.
4. Students are never to fancy.

◆ Critical Thinking

1. (a)"Little pitchers" are students. (b) They are passive vessels to be filled with facts.
2. Bitzer has no imagination or language skills. He merely parrots memorized data.
3. Gradgrind explodes at children, leaving them helpless to question or disagree.
4. All the adults are tyrants, with no tolerance for disagreement or matters they consider trivial.
5. Some neglected elements are creativity, reasoning, and freedom to examine issues. Modern schools are generally concerned with teaching critical thinking and emphasizing concepts rather than facts.

Develop Understanding

One-Minute Insight In this episode from Charlotte Brontë's *Jane Eyre,* Jane is at a boarding school named Lowood. Jane describes the harsh physical conditions, the lack of sufficient food for the girls, and the cruel way in which one of the teachers treats a girl named Helen Burns. Later, Jane has the opportunity to speak with Helen in private and is surprised by Helen's meek acceptance of the wrongs done to her. Brontë may not editorialize quite the way Dickens does, but many of her descriptions and dialogues represent criticisms of the conditions suffered by disadvantaged girls like Jane and Helen.

◆ Literary Focus

❶ The Novel and Social Criticism Ask students why they think that Brontë chose to open this chapter in this fashion. *Suggested response: This opening establishes the setting and shows the cruelty of the conditions at the school.* Tell students that this description is key to understanding events that occur later in the chapter.

❷ Clarification Explain that "animadversion" means negative criticism or comment. The word is little used today.

◆ Reading Strategy

❸ Recognize the Writer's Purpose Have students explain the effect of the type of criticisms made by the teacher in this passage. *Students may say that all the criticisms relate to personal appearance, making the issue of outward appearance of primary importance to this teacher.*

Chapter 6

The next day commenced as before, getting up and dressing by rushlight; but this morning we were obliged to dispense with the ceremony of washing: the water in the pitchers was frozen. A change had taken place in the weather the preceding evening, and a keen northeast wind, whistling through the crevices of our bedroom windows all night long,
❶ had made us shiver in our beds, and turned the contents of the ewers to ice.

Before the long hour and a half of prayers and Bible reading was over, I felt ready to perish with cold. Breakfast time came at last, and this morning the porridge was not burnt; the quality was eatable, the quantity small; how small my portion seemed! I wished it had been doubled.

In the course of the day I was enrolled a member of the fourth class, and regular tasks and occupations were assigned to me: hitherto, I had only been a spectator of the proceedings at Lowood, I was now to become an actor therein. At first, being little accustomed to learn by heart, the lessons appeared to me both long and difficult: the frequent change from task to task, too, bewildered me; and I was glad, when, about three o'clock in the afternoon, Miss Smith put into my hands a border of muslin two yards long, together with needle, thimble, etc., and sent me to sit in a quiet corner of the school room, with directions to hem the same. At that hour most of the others were sewing likewise; but one class still stood round Miss Scatcherd's chair reading, and as all was quiet, the subject of their lessons could be heard, together with the manner in which each girl acquitted herself, and the animadversions or commendations of Miss ❷
Scatcherd on the performance. It was English history; among the readers, I observed my acquaintance of the verandah; at the commencement of the lesson, her place had been at the top of the class, but for some error of pronunciation or some inattention to stops, she was suddenly sent to the very bottom. Even in that obscure position, Miss Scatcherd continued to make her an object of constant notice: she was continually addressing to her such phrases as the following:—

"Burns" (such it seems was her name: the girls here, were all called by their surnames, as boys are elsewhere), "Burns, you are standing on the side of your shoe, turn your toes out im- ❸
mediately." "Burns, you poke your chin most unpleasantly, draw it in." "Burns, I insist on your holding your head up: I will not have you before me in that attitude," etc. etc.

A chapter having been read through twice, the books were closed and the girls examined. The lesson had comprised part of the reign of

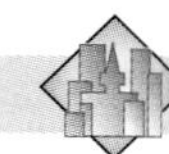

Beyond the Classroom

Community Connection

Local Schools Lowood school is modeled after the Cowan Bridge School, which Charlotte Brontë actually attended. That school was opened in 1824, with the purpose of educating the daughters of poor clergy. She may have exaggerated some of the bad points of the real school in creating Lowood, but she did encounter some harsh policies at Cowan.

Encourage students to find out about the different public and private schools in their area. Are there any single-gender schools, as Jane's was? Are there any boarding schools?

Have students discuss the pros and cons of boarding schools and how they differ from the school Charlotte Brontë describes. Encourage them to offer opinions, also, about the advantages and disadvantages they see in single-gender versus coeducational schools.

Charles I, and there were sundry questions about tonnage and poundage, and ship-money, which most of them appeared unable to answer; still, every little difficulty was solved instantly when it reached Burns: her memory seemed to have retained the substance of the whole lesson, and she was ready with answers on every point. I kept expecting that Miss Scatcherd would praise her attention; but, instead of that, she suddenly cried out:—

"You dirty, disagreeable girl! you have never cleaned your nails this morning!"

> ◆ **Reading Strategy**
> 4 What does Miss Scatcherd's reaction suggest about the writer's purpose in this scene?

Burns made no answer: I wondered at her silence.

"Why," thought I, "does she not explain that she could neither clean her nails nor wash her face, as the water was frozen?"

My attention was now called off by Miss Smith, desiring me to hold a skein of thread: while she was winding it, she talked to me from time to time, asking whether I had ever been at school before, whether I could mark, stitch, knit, etc.; till she dismissed me, I could not pursue my observations on Miss Scatcherd's movements. When I returned to my seat, that lady was just delivering an order, of which I did not catch the import; but Burns immediately left the class, and going into the small inner room where the books were kept, returned in half a minute, carrying in her hand a bundle of twigs tied together at one end. This ominous tool she presented to Miss Scatcherd with a re-
5 spectful courtesy; then she quietly, and without being told, unloosed her pinafore, and the teacher instantly and sharply inflicted on her neck a dozen strokes with the bunch of twigs. Not a tear rose to Burns's eye; and, while I paused from my sewing, because my fingers quivered at this spectacle with a sentiment of 5
unavailing and impotent anger, not a feature of her pensive face altered its ordinary expression.

"Hardened girl!" exclaimed Miss Scatcherd, "nothing can correct you of your slatternly 6
habits: carry the rod away."

Burns obeyed: I looked at her narrowly as she emerged from the book closet; she was just putting back her handkerchief into her pocket, and the trace of a tear glistened on her thin cheek.

The play-hour in the evening I thought the pleasantest fraction of the day at Lowood: the bit of bread, the draught of coffee swallowed at five o'clock had revived vitality, if it had not satisfied hunger; the long restraint of the day was slackened; the school room felt warmer than in the morning: its fires being allowed to burn a little more brightly to supply, in some measure, the place of candles, not yet introduced; the ruddy gloaming,[1] the licensed uproar, the confusion of many voices gave one a welcome sense of liberty.

On the evening of the day on which I had seen Miss Scatcherd flog her pupil, Burns, I wandered as usual among the forms and tables and laughing groups without a companion, yet not feeling lonely: when I passed the windows, I now and then lifted a blind and looked out; it snowed fast, a drift was already forming against the lower panes; putting my ear close to the window, I could distinguish from the gleeful tumult within, the disconsolate moan of the wind outside.

Probably, if I had lately left a good home and kind parents, this would have been the hour when I should most keenly have regretted the separation: that wind would then have saddened my heart; this obscure chaos would 7
have disturbed my peace: as it was I derived from both a strange excitement, and reckless and feverish, I wished the wind to howl more

◆ Build Vocabulary

obscure (əb skyoor′) *adj.*: Not easily understood, vague or undefined

comprised (kəm prīz′ d) *v.*: Consisted of; to include, contain

sundry (sun′drē) *adj.*: Various, miscellaneous

1. **ruddy gloaming:** Glowing twilight; the sunset.

◆ Reading Strategy

4 Recognize the Writer's Purpose Students may say that Miss Scatcherd is harsh and appears determined to find fault with Burns. Moreover, Miss Scatcherd's only concern is for personal appearance; she takes no notice of Burns's superior grasp of the subject being taught. This suggests that education for girls at that time emphasized superficial values over real education.

◆ Critical Thinking

5 Analyze Ask students what they think Helen Burns's reaction to her whipping reveals about her character. *Students may reach any of several possible conclusions: Burns may be too timid or passive to complain when ill-treated; she may be accustomed to this treatment and recognize that it is futile to complain; she may be refusing to give Miss Scatcherd the satisfaction of knowing that she has hurt her; or she may have believed that it is more Christian to forgive those who injure her.*

6 Clarification Explain that *slatternly* means "slovenly" or "untidy." The word *slattern,* meaning "an unkempt or slovenly woman," seldom occurs in modern usage.

◆ Critical Thinking

7 Infer Have students discuss how they think Jane's orphanhood has affected her. *Students may point out that, as an orphan, Jane has had to leave less behind than girls from families, and therefore, finds a certain attraction in gloomy scenes that might, in more fortunate girls, lead to sad thoughts of past pleasures.*

Cross-Curricular Connection: Social Studies

Explain that universal education was less widespread in the Victorian era, when the idea was in the process of becoming accepted. Though many children received schooling, there was a wide range of quality, depending on children's social standing and gender.

Poor children, if they went to school, went to "ragged schools" that gave food, clothing, and a minimal education. For working- and lower-middle-class sons and daughters, there were elementary schools, often run by religious groups. Such schools might have one room, where children from age 3 to 12 were taught. Middle- and upper-class orphans were often sent to boarding schools early; otherwise, boarding schools were for girls and boys in their teens. Wealthy families hired tutors and governesses to teach children until they could go to boarding schools. For girls, education was usually confined to domestic skills.

In 1880, a nationwide education act gave local authorities the power to require school attendance to age 13.

◆ Grammar and Style

1 Punctuation of Dialogue Direct students' attention to the conversation between Jane Eyre and Helen Burns. Ask questions like the following to check students' understanding of the conventions for punctuating dialogue: Why are there single quotation marks around *Rasselas?* *Single quotation marks are used to denote a title or quotation within a direct quotation.* In the next paragraph, why is the word *yes* enclosed in quotation marks while the words *she said* are not? *Yes is a direct quotation and thus is enclosed in quotation marks. The words she said serve to identify the speaker, but are not spoken by either of the characters, so they are not enclosed in quotation marks.*

◆ *Literature and Your Life*

2 Brontë is pointing out that it is unfair that poor young women must endure harsh treatment and petty cruelty to obtain an education.

◆ Reading Strategy

3 Recognize the Writer's Purpose Ask students: What do you think is Brontë's purpose in writing this description of Jane's school? *In addition to revealing Jane's background and character, Brontë's description criticizes the cruelty and hypocrisy in the schools of her day.* How do Helen's words help Brontë support her purpose? *Helen's patient, forgiving attitude sharply contrasts with Miss Scatcherd's petty cruelty. Although the school day starts off with a "long hour and a half of prayers and Bible reading," the religious ideals of charity and mercy do not extend to daily life at the school; the despised, mistreated Helen embodies the religious ideals more than the school's instructors.*

wildly, the gloom to deepen to darkness, and the confusion to rise to clamor.

Jumping over forms, and creeping under tables, I made my way to one of the fire-places: there, kneeling by the high wire fender, I found Burns, absorbed, silent, abstracted from all round her by the companionship of a book, which she read by the dim glare of the embers.

"Is it still 'Rasselas'?"[2] I asked, coming behind her.

"Yes," she said, "and I have just finished it."

And in five minutes more she shut it up. I
1 was glad of this.

"Now," thought I, "I can perhaps get her to talk." I sat down by her on the floor.

"What is your name besides Burns?"

"Helen."

"Do you come a long way from here?"

"I come from a place further north; quite on the borders of Scotland."

"Will you ever go back?"

"I hope so; but nobody can be sure of the future."

"You must wish to leave Lowood?"

"No: why should I? I was sent to Lowood to get an education; and it would be of no use going away until I have attained that object."

> ◆ *Literature and Your Life*
>
> 2 What is the main point of Brontë's social criticism in the following paragraphs?

"But that teacher, Miss Scatcherd, is so cruel to you?"

"Cruel? Not at all! She is severe: she dislikes my faults."

"And if I were in your place I should dislike her: I should resist her; if she struck me with that rod, I should get it from her hand; I should break it under her nose."

"Probably you would do nothing of the sort: but if you did, Mr. Brocklehurst would expel you from the school; that would be a great grief
3 to your relations. It is far better to endure patiently a smart which nobody feels but yourself, than to commit a hasty action whose evil consequences will extend to all connected with
you— and, besides, the Bible bids us return 3
good for evil."

"But then it seems disgraceful to be flogged, and to be sent to stand in the middle of a room full of people; and you are such a great girl: I am far younger than you, and I could not bear it."

"Yet it would be your duty to bear it, if you 4
could not avoid it: it is weak and silly to say you *cannot bear* what it is your fate to be required to bear."

I heard her with wonder: I could not comprehend this doctrine of endurance; and still less could I understand or sympathize with the forbearance she expressed for her chastiser. Still I felt that Helen Burns considered things by a light invisible to my eyes. I suspected she might be right and I wrong; but I would not ponder the matter deeply: like Felix,[3] I put it off to a more convenient season.

"You say you have faults, Helen: what are they? To me you seem very good."

"Then learn from me, not to judge by appearances: I am, as Miss Scatcherd said, slatternly; I seldom put, and never keep, things in order; I am careless; I forget rules; I read when I should
learn my lessons; I have no method; and some- 5
times I say, like you, I cannot *bear* to be subjected to systematic arrangements. This is all very provoking to Miss Scatcherd, who is naturally neat, punctual, and particular."

"And cross and cruel," I added; but Helen Burns would not admit my addition: she kept silence.

"Is Miss Temple as severe to you as Miss 6
Scatcherd?"

At the utterance of Miss Temple's name, a soft smile flitted over her grave face.

"Miss Temple is full of goodness; it pains her to be severe to anyone, even the worst in the school: she sees my errors, and tells me of them gently; and, if I do anything worthy of
praise, she gives me my meed liberally. One 7
strong proof of my wretchedly defective nature

2. **Rasselas:** *The History of Rasselas, Prince of Abyssinia*, a moralizing novel by Samuel Johnson.

3. **Felix:** In the Bible, governor of Judea who released Paul from prison and deferred his trial until a more "convenient season" (Acts 24:25).

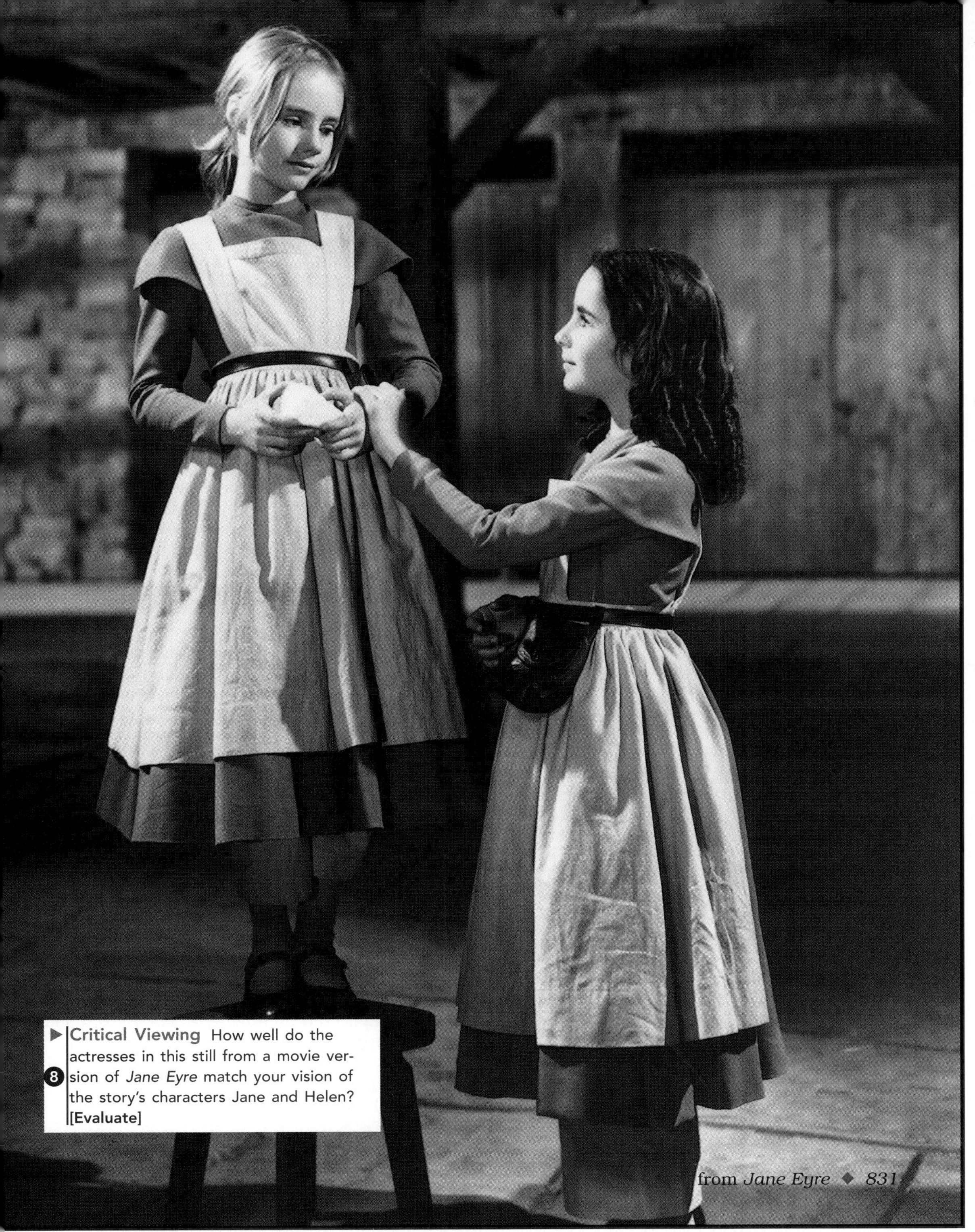

▶ Critical Viewing How well do the actresses in this still from a movie version of *Jane Eyre* match your vision of the story's characters Jane and Helen? **[Evaluate]** 8

Humanities: Media

Filmmakers have found *Jane Eyre* to be an inspirational story. Charlotte Brontë's novel is the basis for four silent movies (*Jane Eyre*, 1914, which ran about 40 minutes; *The Castle of Thornfield*, 1915; *Woman and Wife*, 1918; and *Jane Eyre*, 1921), three sound era movies (1934, 1944, and 1996) and at least three made-for-television versions (including a mini-series in 1983).

The movie still shown on this page is from the film released in 1944 in which a young Elizabeth Taylor (on the right) played Helen.

The most recent film adaptation, from 1996, was directed by Franco Zeffirelli. The BBC filmed the most recent television version in 1997, with Samantha Morton in the title role.

◆ Critical Thinking

4 Make Judgments Ask students who they think is stronger: Helen, for bearing what fate requires, or Jane, for fighting her fate. Have them explain their answers. *Students might find Jane the stronger of the two for refusing to bow, not only to the power of the adult over the child, but to social pressures that urged submission. They might, however, see a kind of strength in Helen as well—the strength to absorb punishment without letting it make her bitter and angry.*

◆ Reading Strategy

5 Recognize the Writer's Purpose Have students determine why the writer chose to include this statement by Helen. *Students may see this as a means to show how the system convinces children that blame for such a situation belongs to them, for their unworthiness, rather than to the adult, regardless of the adult's actions.*

◆ Reading Strategy

6 Recognize the Writer's Purpose Direct students' attention to the names that Brontë gives to the two teachers: the petty and cruel Miss Scatcherd and the patient and fair Miss Temple. What is the author's purpose in giving these names to her characters? *The names reveal the characters of the two teachers. The name Scatcherd suggests the words* scratch, hard, *and* herd*—appropriate words for a mean teacher who demands conformity. The name* Temple *suggests holiness and goodness, traits suitable for an idealized teacher.*

Customize for *Less Proficient Readers*

7 Encourage students to determine the meaning of *meed* from context clues. *Meed is an archaic word that means "a deserved reward."*

▶Critical Viewing◀

8 Evaluate Students may say that the actresses *match* their vision of Helen and Jane; the two girls appear to be close friends.

Customize for
Less Proficient Readers
Assist students in using context clues to determine the meaning of *expostulations* (line 1, column 1). Ask students to identify the purpose of Miss Temple's expostulations. *They are meant to cure Helen of her faults.* What sort of methods are used to cure people of their faults? *Students may suggest corporal punishment, scolding, nagging, well-reasoned arguments, behavioral modification training, and so on.* Given the time period and Miss Temple's character, what method would she use to cure Helen's faults? *She would use gentle reproofs or reason with Helen to show her why what she was doing was wrong.* What does *expostulations* mean? *It means "reasons, objections, or complaints meant to alter another person's behavior."*

◆ Reading Strategy

❶ Recognize the Writer's Purpose Ask students why the writer had Helen reflect on Charles the First. *Students may observe, first, that Helen shows an active and analytical mind. Her statement indicates a great respect on her part for authority (in contrast to Jane's attitude). Students may also note a parallel between Helen's musings on good intentions and bad actions, which might fit a school like hers as well as King Charles.*

◆ Critical Thinking

❷ Make Judgments Ask students if they agree with Jane's statement, and have them explain their reasons for agreeing or disagreeing. *Students may find themselves in agreement or disagreement with Jane, for reasons like the following: If we do not resist the cruel actions of others, we shall continue to be victims; or, it is more virtuous to turn the other cheek and teach kindness through kind actions.*

❸ Clarification Mrs. Reed is Jane's aunt, who resents having responsibility for the orphaned Jane and is cruel to her.

is that even her expostulations, so mild, so rational, have not influence to cure me of my faults; and even her praise, though I value it most highly, cannot stimulate me to continued care and foresight."

"That is curious," said I: "it is so easy to be careful."

"For *you* I have no doubt it is. I observed you in your class this morning, and saw you were closely attentive: your thoughts never seemed to wander while Miss Miller explained the lesson and questioned you. Now, mine continually rove away: when I should be listening to Miss Scatcherd, and collecting all she says with assiduity,[4] often I lose the very sound of her voice; I fall into a sort of dream. Sometimes I think I am in Northumberland, and that the noises I hear round me are the bubbling of a little brook which runs through Deepden, near our house;— then, when it comes to my turn to reply, I have to be wakened; and, having heard nothing of what was read for listening to the visionary brook, I have no answer ready."

"Yet how well you replied this afternoon."

"It was mere chance: the subject on which we had been reading had interested me. This afternoon, instead of dreaming of Deepden, I was wondering how a man who wished to do right could act so unjustly and unwisely as Charles the First sometimes did; and I thought what a pity it was that, with his integrity and conscientiousness, he could see no farther
❶ than the prerogatives of the crown. If he had but been able to look to a distance, and see how what they call the spirit of the age was tending! Still, I like Charles— I respect him— I pity him, poor murdered king! Yes, his enemies were the worst: they shed blood they had no right to shed. How dared they kill him!"

Helen was talking to herself now: she had forgotten I could not very well understand her— that I was ignorant, or nearly so, of the subject she discussed. I recalled her to my level.

"And when Miss Temple teaches you, do your thoughts wander then?"

"No, certainly, not often; because Miss Temple has generally something to say which is newer to me than my own reflections: her language is singularly agreeable to me, and the information she communicates is often just what I wished to gain."

"Well, then, with Miss Temple you are good?"

"Yes, in a passive way: I make no effort; I follow as inclination guides me. There is no merit in such goodness."

"A great deal: you are good to those who are good to you. It is all I ever desire to be. If people were always kind and obedient to those who are cruel and unjust, the wicked people would have it all their own way: they would never feel afraid, and so they would never alter, but would grow worse and worse. When we are struck at without a reason, we should strike back again very hard; I am sure we should—so hard as to teach the person who struck us never to do it again."

"You will change your mind, I hope, when you grow older: as yet you are but a little untaught girl." ❷

"But I feel this, Helen: I must dislike those who, whatever I do to please them, persist in disliking me; I must resist those who punish me unjustly. It is as natural as that I should love those who show me affection, or submit to punishment when I feel it is deserved."

". . . Love your enemies; bless them that curse you; do good to them that hate you and despitefully use you."

"Then I should love Mrs. Reed, which I cannot do; I should bless her son John, which is impossible." ❸

In her turn, Helen Burns asked me to explain; and I proceeded forthwith to pour out, in my way, the tale of my sufferings and resentments. Bitter and truculent when excited, I spoke as I felt, without reserve or softening.

Helen heard me patiently to the end: I expected she would then make a remark, but she said nothing.

"Well," I asked impatiently, "is not Mrs. Reed a hard-hearted, bad woman?"

"She has been unkind to you, no doubt; because, you see, she dislikes your cast of char-

4. **assiduity** (as′ə dyōō′ə tē) *n.*: Constant care and attention; diligence.

Cross-Curricular Connection: Social Studies

Jane and Helen's conversation reveals religious attitudes in Victorian England, and provides particular insight into Charlotte Brontë's religious beliefs. The Brontës belonged to the Church of England and subscribed to the tenets of what was called the *low church.*

The *high church* stresses the importance of maintaining ongoing traditions, especially in forms of worship. High church buildings tend to be more ornate and embellished, and their services are generally more elaborate and full of established ritual. In contrast, *low church* adherents care less about ritual and tradition, and believe in expressing themselves through good works, with a greater emphasis on the personal aspects of religion. They also refer to themselves as *evangelicals.* The character of Helen in this excerpt may be considered an exemplar of low church virtue.

acter, as Miss Scatcherd does mine: but how minutely you remember all she has done and said to you! What a singularly deep impression her injustice seems to have made on your heart! No ill usage so brands its record on my feelings. Would you not be happier if you tried to forget her severity, together with the passionate emotions it excited? Life appears to me too short to be spent in nursing animosity or registering wrongs. We are, and must be, one and all, burdened with faults in this world: but the time will soon come when, I trust, we shall put them off in putting off our corruptible bodies; when debasement and sin will fall from us with this cumbrous frame of flesh, and only
4 the spark of the spirit will remain,—the impalpable principle of life and thought, pure as when it left the Creator to inspire the creature: whence[5] it came it will return; perhaps again to be communicated to some being higher than man—perhaps to pass through gradations of glory, from the pale human soul to brighten to the seraph![6] Surely it will never, on the contrary, be suffered to degenerate from man to fiend? No; I cannot believe that: I hold another creed; which no one ever taught me, and which I seldom mention; but in which I delight, and to which I cling: for it extends hope to all: it makes Eternity a rest—a mighty home, not a terror and abyss. Besides, with this creed, I can so clearly distinguish between the criminal and his crime; 4 I can so sincerely forgive the first while I abhor the last: with this creed revenge never worries my heart, degradation never too deeply disgusts me, injustice never crushes me too low: I live in calm, looking to the end."

Helen's head, always drooping, sank a little lower as she finished this sentence. I saw by her look she wished no longer to talk to me, but rather to converse with her own thoughts. She was not allowed much time for meditation: a monitor, a great rough girl, presently came up, exclaiming in a strong Cumberland accent—

"Helen Burns, if you don't go and put your drawer in order, and fold up your work this minute, I'll tell Miss Scatcherd to come and look at it!"

Helen sighed as her reverie fled, and getting up, obeyed the monitor without reply as without delay.

5. **whence:** Place from which.
6. **seraph:** Angel of the highest order.

Guide for Responding

◆ Literature and Your Life

Reader's Response Do you relate more to Helen's or to Jane's attitude toward life? Explain.

Thematic Focus How does the relationship between Jane and Helen bring to light differences in philosophies of life?

☑ Check Your Comprehension

1. (a) For what offense does Miss Scatcherd punish Helen Burns? (b) What is the punishment?
2. Why does Helen Burns admire Miss Temple?
3. When Jane confesses her dislike of the Reed family, what advice does Helen give her?

◆ Critical Thinking

INTERPRET

1. When punished, why does Helen make every effort to hold back tears? **[Infer]**
2. Why might Jane wish "the wind to howl more wildly, the gloom to deepen to darkness"? **[Infer]**
3. Compare and contrast Jane's and Helen's views on how to treat those who mistreat them. **[Compare and Contrast]**

EVALUATE

4. Is this episode from *Jane Eyre* effective in criticizing schools like Lowood? Why or why not? **[Evaluate]**

◆ Literary Focus

4 The Novel and Social Criticism Ask students if they think Brontë subscribes to Helen's views on how to react to the cruelty of others. Ask them to explain their reasoning. *Students may say that the author might see passive acceptance of injustice as wrong if social reform is to take place. They may, however, feel that a gentle nature might win over one's enemies.*

Reinforce and Extend

Answers

◆ Literature and Your Life

Reader's Response Most students will identify more with the feisty Jane; a few may identify more with the philosophical Helen.

Thematic Focus Although the two have very different philosophies, their friendship allows them to explore their attitudes and ideas.

☑ Check Your Comprehension

1. (a) She punishes Helen for untidiness. (b) She beats Helen with a bundle of twigs.
2. Helen admires Miss Temple for her gentleness and goodness.
3. She urges Jane to love her enemies and return good for evil.

◆ Critical Thinking

1. Helen would think crying self-indulgent; she feels she must bear ill treatment without complaint.
2. Jane is angry and finds storms and darkness a good background for her emotions.
3. Jane feels that she "must resist those who punish [her] unjustly." Helen says that people should love their enemies and return good for evil.
4. Students may say that the episode clearly illustrates the harsh conditions at schools like Lowood.

Beyond the Selection

FURTHER READING

Other Works by the Authors
Oliver Twist, Charles Dickens
Bleak House, Charles Dickens
Shirley, Charlotte Brontë

Other Works With the Theme of Institutions and Relationships
The Mill on the Floss, George Eliot
A Little Princess, Frances Hodges Burnett

We suggest that you preview these works before recommending them to students.

INTERNET

For information about Dickens, go to **http://www.liunet.edu/cwis/csp/palmer/lis512/digitallibraries/dickens**

To learn more about Charlotte and the other Brontës, visit **http://members.tripod.com/JeanneAnn/Brontësis.html**

Please be aware, however, that sites may have changed since this information was published. We *strongly recommend* that you preview sites before you send students to them.

Reinforce and Extend

Answers

◆ Reading Strategy

Students' answers may resemble the following.

1. The name Gradgrind suggests that the character grinds away at the spirits and imaginations of the students who eventually graduate from the school in *Hard Times*.
2. The description of Lowood in *Jane Eyre* reveals that it is a place that chills and starves both the body and the spirit.
3. The dialogue between Sissy Jupe and the nameless bureaucrat shows that Dickens does not think highly of bureaucrats or unimaginative thinking.
4. Helen Burns's decision not to explain that her unwashed hands are the result of the water in the sewers freezing reveals her patient, resigned character and Miss Scatcherd's unreasonableness.

◆ Literary Focus

1. Suggested responses: (a) It shows that they have very different outlooks on life. (b) It reveals that the school is harsh and unreasonable.
2. Suggested responses: (a) The details about the physical appearance of the characters and the way they speak make the setting vivid. (b) These details show how the schools stifle creativity.

◆ Build Vocabulary

Using the Word Root *-mono-*

1. monopoly: the single company that sells a particular product; 2. monorail: a train that travels on a single rail; 3. monarch: the single person who rules a country; 4. monologue: a speech spoken by one character alone; 5. monocle: a device to enhance vision that consists of one lens.

Using the Word Bank

1. b 2. b 3. b 4. b 5. b
6. a 7. c 8. c

Guide for Responding (continued)

◆ Reading Strategy

Recognize the Writer's Purpose

Writers can reveal their **purpose**, their reason for writing a book, in several ways. Often their attitudes toward characters, events, and ideas are a clue to their purpose. In the excerpt from *Hard Times*, notice how Dickens's attitude toward M'Choakumchild comes out in this description of his education:

> He and some one hundred and forty other schoolmasters, had been lately turned at the same time, in the same factory, on the same principles, like so many pianoforte legs.

Dickens obviously thinks that this man is less than fully human, the mechanical product of a mechanical process. This attitude, in turn, suggests that one of Dickens's purposes in writing may have been to attack a coldly logical approach to education.

Using either the excerpt from *Hard Times* or the excerpt from *Jane Eyre*, show how each of the following elements is a clue to the author's attitude and purpose.

1. the name of a place or character
2. the description of a place or character
3. dialogue
4. an event or incident

◆ Build Vocabulary

Using the Word Root *-mono-*

Use your knowledge of the word root *-mono-* ("single" or "alone") to define these words:

1. monopoly **3.** monarch **5.** monocle
2. monorail **4.** monologue

Using the Word Bank

In your notebook, write the letter of the word that is opposite in meaning to the first word.

1. monotonous: (a) lengthy, (b) varied, (c) loud
2. obstinate: (a) still, (b) cooperative, (c) taciturn
3. adversary: (a) turncoat, (b) friend, (c) enemy
4. indignant: (a) worthy, (b) pleased, (c) wrathful
5. approbation: (a) freedom, (b) disapproval, (c) sin
6. obscure: (a) prominent, (b) sad, (c) realistic
7. comprised: (a) counted, (b) agreed, (c) excluded
8. sundry: (a) mixed, (b) tedious, (c) homogeneous

◆ Literary Focus

The Novel and Social Criticism

The **novels** of Dickens and Brontë are fictional worlds, with invented plots, characters, and settings. However, these fictional worlds mirrored nineteenth-century English society. In this way, made-up characters or places gave authors the chance to comment on real types of people and social institutions. This use of fiction to comment on fact is called **social criticism**.

For example, in *Jane Eyre,* Lowood is a fictional version of real institutions designed for young women without title or money. Jane's relationships at Lowood give Brontë the opportunity to criticize this type of institution.

1. (a) What does the relationship between Jane and Helen in *Jane Eyre* reveal about their characters? (b) What does it also reveal about the school?
2. (a) In *Hard Times,* what details make the setting vivid? (b) How do these details contribute to Dickens's social criticism?

◆ Grammar and Style

Punctuation of Dialogue

Following are rules for using other punctuation with quotation marks as you **punctuate dialogue:**

- Commas and periods fall within the close-quotation marks.
- Question marks and exclamation marks fall within the close-quotation marks when they end quotations, and outside them when they belong to a sentence that includes a quotation.

Example: "Sissy Jupe, give me the Facts!"

Practice Copy these passages in your notebook, correctly punctuating the dialogue.

1. Sissy is not a name, said Mr. Gradgrind.
2. Girl number twenty unable to define a horse! said Mr. Gradgrind . . .
3. Bitzer, said Thomas Gradgrind. Your definition of a horse.
4. Well, I asked impatiently, is not Mrs. Reed a hard-hearted, bad woman?
5. Well, then, with Miss Temple you are good?

◆ Grammar and Style

1. "Sissy is not a name," said Mr. Gradgrind.
2. "Girl number twenty unable to define a horse!" said Mr. Gradgrind.
3. "Bitzer," said Thomas Gradgrind. "Your definition of a horse."
4. "Well," I asked impatiently, "is not Mrs. Reed a hard-hearted, bad woman?"
5. "Well, then, with Miss Temple you are good?"

For additional instruction and practice, use the lesson on Quotation Marks in the **Language Lab CD-ROM** and the pages on Quotation Marks for Direct Quotations, p. 86, and Other Punctuation Marks with Quotation Marks, p. 87, in the *Writer's Solution Grammar Practice Book*.

Build Your Portfolio

Idea Bank

Writing

1. Diary Entry Write a diary entry from the point of view of Helen Burns in *Jane Eyre*. In your diary, record story events as well as Helen's own feelings and reactions to those events.

2. Comparison and Contrast Write a paper in which you compare and contrast the characters of Jane and Helen in *Jane Eyre*. Also, speculate as to what further adventures Jane will have.

3. Response to Criticism George Bernard Shaw wrote that, in *Hard Times*, Dickens "casts off, and casts off for ever, all restraint on his wild sense of humor." Is there evidence for this assertion in the section of the novel you have read? Explain.

Speaking and Listening

4. Oral Presentation View the film version of *Jane Eyre* starring Orson Welles as Rochester. Then present a critical film review to your class, explaining your recommendation. **[Media Link]**

5. Dialogue Imagine that, after school on the day of Mr. Gradgrind's visit, Sissy Jupe and Bitzer talk over what has happened. Keeping in mind Dickens's descriptions of these characters, role-play their dialogue with a partner. **[Performing Arts Link]**

Projects

6. Caricature A caricature is an exaggerated portrayal intended to make a person seem comic or ridiculous. Draw a caricature of one of the characters in *Hard Times*. **[Art Link]**

7. Exploring Historical Background Find out more about the educational system in Victorian times, and reveal your results in a report. **[Social Studies Link]**

Writing Mini-Lesson

Observation of a Person

Both Dickens and Brontë used their powers of observation to create memorable characters. Follow their lead and observe people with a novelist's eye. Then write a vivid observation of a person you have watched. To make this person come alive for readers, show him or her in action.

Writing Skills Focus: Using an Incident to Reveal Character

When you write an observation of a person, you can show his or her character by describing a revealing **incident.** Dickens isn't writing an observation in *Hard Times*, but he does use an incident to characterize Gradgrind at the start of the book—the brief conversation with Sissy Jupe. Gradgrind addresses Sissy as "Girl number twenty" and tells her that Sissy is not a name. The incident shows how cold and unfeeling he is.

Prewriting Before you write a formal observation, jot down notes about the person you have observed. Your notes might include such information as age, gender, physical appearance, clothing, style of speaking, gestures, beliefs, and values. Then identify a revealing incident that vividly shows this person's character.

Drafting As you narrate an incident, remember to tell events in chronological order. Also, bring the incident you describe to life by using dialogue, precise details, and even a few striking figures of speech, like metaphors or similes.

Revising Delete any descriptions that don't reveal your subject's character. Also, glance back at your notes to see whether you have left out any revealing details that you can weave back in. If your observation seems too ordinary, write it from an unusual vantage point—for example, looking at your subject in a car's rear-view mirror.

✓ ASSESSMENT OPTIONS

Formal Assessment, Selection Test, pp. 208–210, and Assessment Resources Software. The selection test is designed so that it can be easily customized to the performance levels of your students.

Alternative Assessment, p. 42, includes options for less advanced students, more advanced students, verbal/linguistic learners, visual/spatial learners, and bodily/kinesthetic learners.

PORTFOLIO ASSESSMENT

Use the following rubrics in the ***Alternative Assessment*** booklet to assess student writing:
Diary Entry: Fictional Narrative Rubric, p. 96
Comparison and Contrast: Comparison/Contrast Rubric, p. 104
Response to Criticism: Literary Analysis/Interpretation Rubric, p. 113
Writing Mini-Lesson: Description Rubric, p. 98

Idea Bank

Customizing for *Performance Levels*

Following are suggestions for matching Idea Bank topics with your students' performance levels:

- Less Advanced Students: 1, 6
- Average Students: 2, 4, 5
- More Advanced Students: 3, 7

Customizing for *Learning Modalities*

Following are suggestions for matching Idea Bank topics with your students' learning modalities:

- Visual/Spatial: 4, 6
- Intrapersonal: 1
- Interpersonal: 5
- Verbal/Linguistic: 1, 2, 3, 4, 5, 7

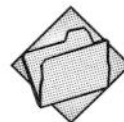

Writing Mini-Lesson

Refer students to the Writing Handbook, page 1189, for instruction on the writing process, and page 1191 for further information on description.

Writer's Solution

Writers at Work Videodisc

Have students view the videodisc segment (Ch. 1) featuring travel writer Guy Garcia to hear his ideas bout descriptive writing.

Play frames 335 to 10062

Writing Lab CD-ROM

Have students complete the tutorial on Description. Follow these steps:

1. Use the Chain of Events tool to organize the incident chronologically.
2. While drafting on the computer, use the word bins for sensory details, place, character traits, and modifiers.
3. Obtain tips for revision by viewing the interactive instruction on eliminating unnecessary words.

Allow approximately 60 minutes of class time to complete these steps.

Sourcebook

Have students use Chapter 1, Description (pp. 1–29), for additional support. The chapter includes a model from literature of a character profile (p. 7), instruction on organizing a description (pp. 19–20), and tips on revision and peer evaluation (p. 21).

Prepare and Engage

OBJECTIVES

1. To read, comprehend, and interpret an excerpt from a nineteenth-century Russian novel
2. To explore literary connections between a Russian novel and the selections in Part 3
3. To respond to the novel through writing, speaking and listening, and projects

PORTFOLIO OPPORTUNITIES

Writing: Character Description; Scene from Everyday Life; Essay on Leadership
Speaking and Listening: Music as the Messenger
Project: Novel Study

Pose the following situation: Suppose you felt that someone was being judged unfairly. Perhaps he or she was being blamed for something she or he didn't do, or people were harshly criticizing his or her actions without understanding the real situation. What would you do to right this wrong? After students have discussed their ideas, explain that in this excerpt from *War and Peace,* Tolstoy defends a general whose actions are being judged unfairly.

Customize for
More Advanced Students
Challenge students to find out more about Napoleon's military campaigns, especially in Russia. Have students report their findings to the class.

More About the Author
As Tolstoy aged, the contempt he showed for the force of public opinion (seen in this selection) grew greater. He eventually attacked *all* forces that sought to mold and channel the individual will, especially the government and established church. He renounced his wealth, dressed like a peasant, and worked in his fields. He even denounced his own great works—including *War and Peace.*

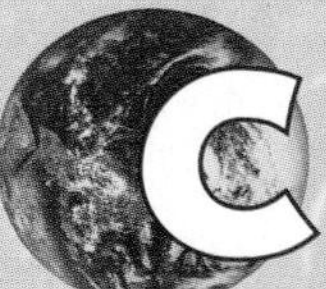

CONNECTIONS TO WORLD LITERATURE

from War and Peace

Leo Tolstoy

Literary Connection

THE NOVEL

Charles Dickens's *Hard Times* and Charlotte Brontë's *Jane Eyre* are representative of the growing popularity of the novel during the nineteenth century. A novel is a long work of fiction with a complicated plot, many major and minor characters, a significant theme, and various settings. In the nineteenth century, The Realists made daily life a subject of literature and explored the scope of human experience in the novel. Their approach and the growing literacy rate made novels appealing to a large group of people. For the same reasons, the novel was also popular in France, the United States, and Russia.

THE RUSSIAN NOVEL

Russian novelist Leo Tolstoy was considered the greatest of the nineteenth-century Russian writers. In 1869, *War and Peace,* his masterful historical novel about Napoleon's invasion of Russia in 1812, was published. In this novel Tolstoy weaves together numerous plots and settings and includes more than 1,000 characters. The novel was immediately recognized as a masterpiece for its graphic depiction of war, insights into Russian life, and exploration into the meaning of life.

In the following excerpt from *War and Peace,* Tolstoy defends Kutuzov, a military general, when his tactics are criticized. Tolstoy presents the general as noble and true to himself—not as a man who is simply out for fame. As you read, note the ways in which Tolstoy brings Kutuzov to life as a character.

LEO TOLSTOY

(1828–1910)

Leo Tolstoy was a nineteenth-century Russian writer as well known for his radical life style and personal beliefs as for his writing. After briefly attending law school, Tolstoy joined the army in 1851. While serving as an artillery officer, he spent most of his free time writing, and in 1852 he published his first novel, *A History of My Childhood.*

He married Sonya Bers at age thirty-four. She was so supportive of his literary career that she would recopy Tolstoy's manuscripts to make them legible for his publisher. *War and Peace* (1869), and *Anna Karenina* (1876), a portrait of the lives of the Russian upper classes, were among the most popular of Tolstoy's works.

Prentice Hall Literature Program Resources

REINFORCE / RETEACH / EXTEND
Selection Support Pages
Build Vocabulary, p. 206
Literary Connections, p. 207

Formal Assessment Selection Test, pp. 211–212; Assessment Resources Software

Resource Pro CD-ROM
from *War and Peace*—includes all resource material and customizable lesson plan

Listening to Literature Audiocassettes
from *War and Peace*

from WAR and Peace

Leo Tolstoy

Chapter V

In 1812 and 1813[1] Kutuzov[2] was openly accused of blunders. The Tsar[3] was dissatisfied with him. And in a recent history inspired by promptings from the highest quarters, Kutuzov is spoken of as a designing, intriguing schemer, who was panic-stricken at the name of Napoleon, and guilty through his blunders at Krasnoe and Berezina of robbing the Russian army of the glory of complete victory over the French. Such is the lot of men not recognized by Russian intelligence as "great men," *grands hommes*; such is the destiny of those rare and always solitary men who divining the will of
❶ Providence submit their personal will to it. The hatred and contempt of the crowd is the punishment of such men for their comprehension of higher laws.

Strange and terrible to say, Napoleon, the most insignificant tool of history, who never even in exile displayed one trait of human dignity, is the subject of the admiration and enthusiasm of the Russian historians; in their
❷ eyes he is a *grand homme*.

Kutuzov, the man who from the beginning to the end of his command in 1812, from Borodino to Vilna, was never in one word or deed false to himself, presents an example exceptional in history of self-sacrifice and recognition in the present of the relative value of events in the future. Kutuzov is conceived of by historians as a nondescript, pitiful sort of creature, and whenever they speak of him in the year 1812, they seem a little ashamed of him.

And yet it is difficult to conceive of an historical character whose energy could be more invariably directed to the same unchanging aim. It is difficult to imagine an aim more noble and more in harmony with the will of a whole people. ❷
Still more difficult would it be to find an example in history where the aim of any historical personage has been so completely attained as the aim towards which all Kutuzov's efforts were devoted in 1812.

Kutuzov never talked of "forty centuries looking down from the Pyramids," of the sacrifices he was making for the fatherland, of what he meant to do or had done. He did not as a rule talk about himself, played no sort of part, always seemed the plainest and most ordinary man, and said the plainest and most ordinary things. He wrote letters to his daughters and to Madame de Staël,[4] read novels, liked the company of pretty women, made jokes with the generals, the officers, and the soldiers, and never contradicted the people, who tried to prove anything to him. When Count Rastoptchin galloped up to him at Yautsky bridge, and reproached him personally with being responsible for the loss of Moscow, and said: "Didn't you promise not to abandon

1. **In 1812 and 1813:** In June 1812, Napoleon and his troops invaded Russia. The French retreat from Russia began in October 1812.
2. **Kutuzov:** Mikhail Illarionovich Kutuzov (1745–1813); commander in chief of all Russian forces during Napoleon's invasion.
3. **Tsar:** Czar Alexander I, emperor of Russia, 1801–1825.
4. **Madame de Staël:** Anne-Louise-Germaine de Staël (1766–1817) French-Swiss woman of letters; regarded as personal enemy of Napoleon and banished from Paris.

Cross-Curricular Connection: Social Studies

In 1799, Napoleon Bonaparte emerged from the chaos of the French Revolution to seize dictatorial power. Regarded as a great military strategist, he conquered much of Europe. By 1810, he controlled Austria, Prussia, Denmark, and parts of Italy, and ruled the Netherlands and Spain.

In 1812, however, Czar Alexander I of Russia opened trade with England, France's great enemy. Napoleon attacked Russia with an army of 600,000, triple the size of Russia's army. France won some bloody battles and eventually burned Moscow. However, as winter approached, Napoleon saw that he lacked proper supplies and retreated. During the long retreat, the French suffered terrible losses from bitter cold and starvation; much of Napoleon's force was destroyed. This enabled allied forces of Russia, Prussia, Great Britain, Sweden, and Austria to defeat Napoleon and force his abdication.

Though Napoleon tried to return to power, he was defeated in the Battle of Waterloo (1815), and died in exile.

Develop Understanding

One-Minute Insight One of the main themes of *War and Peace* is "There is no greatness where there is no simplicity, goodness, and truth." For Tolstoy, the man who led the Russian forces during Napoleon's invasion of Russia, Kutuzov, embodies those qualities. In praising Kutuzov, Tolstoy criticizes Russian society, which Tolstoy feels is too swayed by popular opinion to understand "higher laws" or to appreciate a true hero.

Customize for Less Proficient Readers

Go over the names of people and places before students begin reading. Stress that they should not "skip over" names as they read. If students still find the Russian names too difficult to manage, have them prepare a glossary that gives the name in the excerpt, such as *Kutuzov* and a simpler substitute, such as "General K."

Customize for English Language Learners

Have students look over the excerpt and make a list of the words they do not know. Then help students define or find simpler substitutes for the unfamiliar words. Students can then use this annotated list while reading the excerpt.

Customize for Visual/Spatial Learners

Have students prepare a map that shows the places mentioned: Krasnoe, Berezina, Borodino, Vilna, Moscow, Tarutino, Vyazma, and Austerlitz.

Literary Connection

❶ **The Novel** Ask students to indicate what aspect of society Tolstoy is criticizing here. *Tolstoy deplores the fact that mass opinion cannot respect or take into account the superior vision of the truly exceptional individual.*

◆ Critical Thinking

❷ **Compare and Contrast** Ask students how Kutuzov and Napoleon differ, according to the writer. *Tolstoy regards Napoleon as a boastful, unworthy man, given an aura of greatness by historians; he sees Kutuzov as a man who did his duty, but has been unfairly portrayed by the same historians as a failure.*

◆ Critical Thinking

❶ **Draw Conclusions** Ask students what they think Tolstoy means when he says that Kutuzov believed that "the thoughts and words that serve its expression are never the motive force of man." *Underlying convictions and beliefs motivate a person, and in a worthy person, those convictions remain constant.* Then ask students if they agree with Tolstoy's assessment. *Students may agree, but might question whether this was the reason that the general said things that didn't make sense.*

◆ Critical Thinking

❷ **Infer** Have students explain what these quotes of Kutuzov reveal about his character. *Students may say that while some public figures tailor their public statements to serve their reputations and justify themselves to the world, Kutuzov does not do so. He has a unique grasp of the overall picture and bases his statements on his awareness of Russia's situation.*

►Critical Viewing◄

❸ **Compare and Contrast** Students may say that Kutuzov appears confident and capable in this portrait, which is consistent with the story. The portrait, however, does not show his conflict with those who valued appearance over substance or his determination to be true to his ideals.

◆ Critical Thinking

❹ **Analyze** Ask students what Kutuzov's willingness to stand up to the Tsar's displeasure reveals about him. *It shows that Kutuzov is willing to stand by his principles, even when to do so jeopardized his career and even his life. This incident also provides evidence that Kutuzov is not the scheming courtier he is accused of being.*

◆ Critical Thinking

❺ **Infer** By describing Kutuzov's goals, Tolstoy calls into question the goals of those considered *"grands hommes."* How might the goals of a *grand homme* differ from Kutuzov's? *Students may say that a so-called grand homme would be concerned primarily with gaining glory and avoiding blame, and would have little concern about minimizing the "sufferings of the people and the soldiers."*

CONNECTIONS TO WORLD LITERATURE

Moscow without a battle?" Kutuzov answered: "And I am not abandoning Moscow without a battle," although Moscow was in fact already abandoned. When Araktcheev came to him from the Tsar to say that Yermolov was to be appointed to the command of the artillery, Kutuzov said: "Yes, I was just saying so myself," though he had said just the opposite a moment before. What had he, the one man who grasped at the time all the vast issues of events, to do in the midst of that dull-witted crowd? What did he care whether Count Rastoptchin put down the disasters of the capital to him or to himself? Still less could he be concerned by the question which man was appointed to the command of the artillery.

This old man, who through experience of life had reached the conviction that the thoughts and words that serve as its expression are never the motive force of men, ❶ frequently uttered words, which were quite meaningless—the first words that occurred to his mind.

But heedless as he was of his words, he never once throughout all his career uttered a single word which was inconsistent with the sole aim for the attainment of which he was working all through the war. With obvious unwillingness, with bitter conviction that he would not be understood, he more than once, under the most difficult circumstances, gave expression to his real thought. His first differed from all about him after the battle of Borodino,[5] which he alone persisted in calling a victory, and this view he continued to assert ❷ verbally and in reports and to his dying day. He alone said that *the loss of Moscow is not the loss of Russia.* In answer to the overtures for peace, his reply to Lauriston was: *There can be no peace, for such is the people's will.* He alone during the retreat of the French said that *all our maneuvers are unnecessary; that everything is being done of itself better than we could desire; that we must give the enemy a "golden bridge"; that the battles of Tarutino, of Vyazma, and of Krasnoe, were none of them necessary; that we must keep some men to reach the frontier with; that he wouldn't give one Russian for ten Frenchmen.* And he, this intriguing courtier, as we are told, who lied to Araktcheev to propitiate[6] the Tsar, he alone dared to face the Tsar's displeasure by telling him at Vilna that *to carry the war beyond the* ❹

Portrait of Koutouzov, Prince of Smolensk, George Dawe, Hermitage, St. Petersburg, Russia

▲ **Critical Viewing** Compare and contrast this rendering of Kutuzov with the description of him in the story. **[Compare and Contrast]** ❸

5. **battle of Borodino:** Kutuzov was pressured into fighting this battle against his better judgment. Although the outcome was inconclusive, Kutuzov lost half his troops.

6. **propitiate** (prō pish´ ē āt´) *v.*: To cause to become favorably inclined.

Humanities: Art

Portrait of Kutuzov, Prince of Smolensk (detail), by George Dawe.

George Dawe (1781–1829), born in England, lived for years at the Russian imperial court in Petersburg, where he painted portraits of many prominent men, including Tsar Alexander I. This portrait shows General Kutuzov in a traditional formal pose.

Have students list and discuss elements of the portrait that are included because they are traditional in such pictures, and those that may reveal something of this individual. Invite them to explain ways in which the portrait resembles or differs from how they thought Kutuzov would look. *Students might include the following as traditional: the medals, the hand holding the cape, the formal stance, the pointing hand, the stylized setting with weapons in the foreground. Students may see self-confidence in the stance and expression. The pointing hand and Kutuzov's being placed on a high elevation might be taken as signs of Kutuzov's vision and grasp of the broad strategic picture.*

CONNECTIONS TO WORLD LITERATURE

4 *frontier would be mischievous and useless.*

But words alone would be no proof that he grasped the significance of events at the time. His actions—all without the slightest deviation—were directed toward the one threefold aim: first, to concentrate all his forces to strike
5 a blow at the French; secondly, to defeat them; and thirdly, to drive them out of Russia, alleviating as far as was possible the sufferings of the people and the soldiers in doing so.

He, the lingerer Kutuzov, whose motto was always "Time and Patience," the sworn opponent of precipitate action, he fought the battle of Borodino, and made all his preparations for it with unwonted solemnity. Before the battle of Austerlitz he foretold that it would be lost, but at Borodino, in spite of the conviction of the generals that the battle was a defeat, in spite of the fact, unprecedented in history, of his army being forced to retreat after the victory, he alone declared in opposition to all that it was a victory, and persisted in that opinion to his dying day. He was alone during the whole latter part of the campaign in insisting that there was no need of fighting now, that it was a mistake to cross the Russian frontier and to begin a new war. It is easy enough now that all the events with their consequences lie before us to grasp their significance, if only we refrain from attributing to the multitude the aims that only existed in the brains of some dozen or so of men.

But how came that old man, alone in opposition to the opinion of all, to gauge so truly the importance of events from the national standard, so that he never once was false to the best interests of his country?

The source of this extraordinary intuition into the significance of contemporary events lay in the purity and fervor of patriotic feeling in his heart.

It was their recognition of this feeling in him that led the people in such a strange manner to pick him out, an old man out of favor, as the chosen leader of the national war, against the will of the Tsar. And this feeling alone it was to which he owed his exalted position, and there he exerted all his powers as commander-in-chief not to kill and maim men, but to save them and have mercy on them. 6

This simple, modest, and therefore truly great figure, could not be cast into the false mold of the European hero, the supposed leader of men, that history has invented.

To the flunky no man can be great, because the flunky has his own flunky conception of greatness.

Guide for Responding

◆ Literature and Your Life

Reader's Response What is your opinion of Kutuzov? Explain.

Thematic Focus How does this excerpt show the gloom and glory of being a public figure?

Trait List Make a list of the character traits that Kutuzov possesses based upon Tolstoy's description of him.

☑ Check Your Comprehension

1. Was Kutuzov more popular with the Russian people or with the Russian military?
2. (a) What were Kutuzov's achievements? (b) What did others point out as his failings?
3. What was Kutuzov's threefold aim in the war with France?

◆ Critical Thinking

INTERPRET

1. What does Tolstoy mean when he states that Kutuzov "could not be cast into the false mold of the European hero . . ."? **[Interpret]**
2. What evidence is given that Kutuzov was "never once false to the interests of his country"? **[Support]**
3. (a) Compare and contrast the two opposing views of Kutuzov. (b) With which view do you agree? Explain. **[Compare and Contrast]**
4. Explain the meaning of the following statement in relation to Kutuzov: "To the flunky no man can be great, because the flunky has his own flunky conception of greatness." **[Interpret]**

EVALUATE

5. How does Tolstoy's attitude toward Kutuzov affect your opinion of the general? **[Evaluate]**

Beyond the Selection

FURTHER READING

Other Works by Leo Tolstoy

Anna Karenina
Sevastapol Stories
"The Death of Ivan Ilyich"

A Work About Leo Tolstoy

Tolstoy by Henri Troyat

We suggest that you preview these works before recommending them to students.

INTERNET

You and your students may find additional information about Tolstoy's life and works on the Internet. We suggest the following site. Please be aware, however, that the site may have changed since this information was published.

For more about Tolstoy, go to **http://www.funet.fi/pub/culture/russian/books/Tolstoy/Tolstoy.html**

We *strongly recommend* that you preview site before you send students to it.

◆ Literary Focus

6 The Novel Ask students what element of Russia's social structure Tolstoy would see as the purest and most sincere, and why. *Students should see that the common people alone, to Tolstoy, were pure enough to value Kutuzov's greatness.*

Reinforce and Extend

Answers

◆ Literature and Your Life

Reader's Response Most students will admire Kutuzov. A few students will question whether Tolstoy correctly interprets Kutuzov's actions.

Thematic Focus Students may say that gloom might arise from unfair treatment by history, and glory from a sense of doing one's duty.

Trait List Listed traits could include selflessness, loyalty, patriotism, concern for common people, and clarity of vision.

☑ Check Your Comprehension

1. He was more popular with the Russian people.
2. (a) He succeeded in defeating the French without needless slaughter. (b) They said he was not aggressive enough; his military blunders prevented complete victory over the French.
3. He wanted to strike a blow at France, to defeat them, and force them out of Russia while minimizing the suffering of the Russian people and soldiers.

◆ Critical Thinking

1. He lacked outward greatness and gave no thought to making a good impression.
2. Kutuzov was true to his principles, even against strong opposition; his plans worked, and he saved many lives.
3. (a) Some called him weak and small-minded; Tolstoy saw him as selfless and Russia's savior. (b) Students should support their views with evidence from the selection and from their own knowledge.
4. Mean-spirited people can't recognize Kutuzov's greatness because they can't imagine it.
5. Suggested response: Tolstoy's admiration makes a reader more likely to approve of Kutuzov.

Answers
Literary Connection

1. Based on the excerpts, students may conclude that characterization predominates.
2. Brontë tends to use indirect characterization, Dickens uses a mixture of indirect and direct characterization, and Tolstoy tends to use direct characterization. Some students may prefer Tolstoy because he makes it clear what the reader should think of Kutuzov. Other students may prefer Brontë, because requiring readers to draw their own conclusions about the characters is more meaningful.
3. Criteria that students may use to evaluate a novel when they are deciding whether to read it may include the following: author's reputation; experience with other works by the author; interesting setting; appealing characters; attractive cover art; intriguing blurb; thickness of the book; and recommendations from friends, teachers, book reviews, and so on.

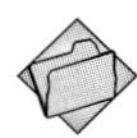

Idea Bank

Customizing for
Performance Levels

Following are suggestions for matching Idea Bank topics with your students' performance levels:

Less Advanced Students: 1
Average Students: 2, 4
More Advanced Students: 3, 5

Customizing for
Learning Modalities

Following are suggestions for matching Idea Bank topics with your students' learning modalities:

Verbal/Linguistic: 1, 2, 3, 5
Musical/Rhythmic: 4

Literary Connection

The Novel

"The art of novels," wrote Thackeray, "*is* to represent nature: to convey as strongly as possible the sentiment of reality." The nineteenth century saw the flowering of the novel, not only in England but all across Europe. Novels explored all aspects of human life and experience. Tolstoy's picture of Russian life in *War and Peace*, set against a background of Napoleon's invasion, is one of the great novels of world literature. In its great length and complexity, it explores sociological, psychological, historical, and political issues. The popularity of novels as a vehicle for exploring human thought and interaction continues to this day.

1. What literary elements—plot, setting, characterization—predominate in the works of Dickens, Brontë, and Tolstoy? Explain.
2. Compare and contrast the methods by which Dickens, Brontë, and Tolstoy develop their main characters. Which author do you think is the most effective? Explain.
3. What criteria do you use to evaluate a novel? Explain how your criteria affect your decision to read a novel.

Idea Bank

Writing

1. **Character Description** Make a list of character traits of Kutuzov. Then write a character description in which you include your own opinions of the general.
2. **Scene from Everyday Life** Novels sometimes explore the details of everyday life. Write a one-page description of a scene from everyday life that might be part of a novel. Your scene should develop an interaction between two or more characters and may be a part of a larger plot.
3. **Essay on Leadership** Tolstoy presents Kutuzov as a significant military leader. Write a brief essay in which you describe the qualities you believe modern leaders need in order to address the world's problems effectively. **[Social Studies Link]**

Speaking and Listening

4. **Music as the Messenger** Much Russian music and literature from the nineteenth century focused on the many military battles in Russian history. Find musical pieces from the period that depict themes of battle. Present the musical compositions to your class with an explanation of how they depict war and peace. **[Music Link]**

Project

5. **Novel Study** Choose a favorite novelist and study his or her technique. Read one or more novels by this author, then write an analysis of the author's literary style and themes. Analyze the use of character, setting, and plot, and give your opinion on whether the author employs them successfully. **[Literature Link]**

✓ ASSESSMENT OPTIONS

Formal Assessment, Selection Test, pp. 211–212, and Assessment Resources Software. The selection test is designed so that it can be easily customized to the performance levels of your students.

PORTFOLIO ASSESSMENT

Use the following rubrics in the ***Alternative Assessment*** booklet to assess student writing:
Character Description: Description Rubric, p. 98
Scene from Everyday Life: Description Rubric, p. 98
Essay on Leadership: Description/Classification Rubric, p. 100

Writing Process Workshop

Character Sketch

Oliver Twist and Fagin, Miss Havisham and Pip—these characters sprang to life under the pen of Charles Dickens. Dickens was a master at characterization, using a character's words, physical appearance, actions, and thoughts to bring him or her to life.

Taking your cue from Dickens, write a character sketch describing a real person you know, a famous figure, or a fictional character. Make readers feel they have actually met the subject by describing his or her physical appearance and personality. Also, provide insights into the subject's behavior and motivation. If appropriate, include other people's responses to the subject and directly quote remarks made to, about, or by the subject. These tips will help you:

Writing Skills Focus

- ▶ **Relate an incident** that offers background information on and insight into the subject. (See p. 835.)
- ▶ **Use precise language** to give readers details about the subject's physical and mental traits.
- ▶ **Set a personal tone** by using intimate, familiar descriptions that help readers feel that they have met the subject.

Charles Dickens's famous character Ebenezer Scrooge, portrayed here, would make an excellent subject for a character sketch.

Model From Literature

from *A Description of Bruce Chatwin* by Paul Theroux

When I think of Bruce Chatwin, who was my friend, ① I am always reminded of a particular night, a dinner at the royal Geographical Society, hearing him speak animatedly about various high mountains he had climbed. . . . ②

He spoke in his usual way, very rapidly and insistently, stuttering and interrupting and laughing. . . . ③ This talking was the most striking thing about him, yet there were so many other aspects of him that made an immediate impression. He was handsome; he had piercing eyes; he was very quick—full of nervous gestures, a rapid walker . . . ④

① The author sets a personal tone by identifying his relationship with the subject.

② Theroux describes an incident that gives background information on Chatwin's lifestyle, and insight into his personality.

③ With a dramatic, "rapid-fire" series of words, Theroux "shows" the reader Chatwin's style of speech.

④ The author gives a precise description of Chatwin's physical appearance.

Beyond the Classroom

Workplace Skills Connection

Presenting Your Personality Explain to students that when they are applying for jobs they are, in effect, presenting character sketches of themselves through their cover letters and résumés. These character sketches, or character profiles, must be professional and factual. Suggest that students include a line on their résumé for hobbies and interests as well as one for unusual experiences that might reveal characteristics such as courage, honesty, and dependability. In their cover letters, students should refer to an experience that reveals character traits appropriate for the job for which they are applying.

Prepare and Engage

Establish Writing Guidelines
Review with students the following key characteristics of a character sketch.

- A character sketch describes the physical appearance and personality of a real person or fictional character.
- It can provide insights into the subject's motivation and behavior.
- A good character sketch makes readers feel that they have met the subject.
- Character sketches may include other people's responses to the subject and direct quotations by or about the subject.

To help students recognize the key characteristics of a character sketch, ask students to examine the illustration of Ebenezer Scrooge on this page. From the picture and their knowledge of Scrooge, have the class come up with key personality traits, physical descriptions, quotations about or by Scrooge, and a description of his actions that reveals personality.

Review the Writing Skills Focus with students and point out examples in the Model From Literature that appears on this page.

You may want to distribute the Scoring Rubric for Description (p. 98 in ***Alternative Assessment***) so that students are aware of the criteria on which they will be evaluated. To customize the rubric, see suggestions on page 843.

Writer's Solution

Writing Lab CD-ROM
If students have access to computers, have them complete their papers using the tutorial for Descriptive Writing. Have them follow these steps:

1. Review the audio-annotated model of a character sketch.
2. Gather details using the Word Bin of Character Traits.
3. Review an audio-annotated student model of a first draft.
4. Use self-evaluation and proofreading checklists.

Develop Student Writing

Prewriting

Refer students to the topic ideas on this page. If students are uninterested in these topics, suggest that they choose a person for their character sketch who interests them and whom they also admire.

Art Transparencies Place Art Transparency 12, *Summer* by John Atkinson Grimshaw (page 51 in ***Art Transparencies***) on the overhead projector. Suggest the subject of this painting as a possible topic for students' character sketches. Have students examine the details of the painting for clues to the lady's personality.

Customize for
Bodily/Kinesthetic Learners
Suggest that after they gather some information, these students role-play with a partner an interview between their subject and an interviewer. They should then decide what the subject's answers indicate about him or her.

Suggest that students complete the character chart suggested on this page before beginning their character sketches. In addition to gathering information, they can use this chart to organize information.

Writing Lab CD-ROM
To help students gather precise details for their character sketches, have them review the interactive examples of sensory details and figurative language in the Description tutorial.

Drafting

As students draft, tell them to try to create a personal tone. Refer them to the instruction on this page that gives examples of word choice that creates a personal tone. For more examples of different tones, have students complete pages 99 and 100 of the *Writer's Solution Grammar Practice Book* on Using Words Effectively.

APPLYING LANGUAGE SKILLS: Using Figurative Language

Spice up your character sketch with figurative language. Here are some tips:

- Use a simile to compare your subject's appearance to that of someone or something else.
- Use a metaphor to describe a person's emotional state.
- Exaggerate a person's behavior or personality with hyperbole.
- Avoid clichés.

Simile: His gestures, sudden and angular, were like those of a marionette.

Metaphor: Jim set off to work, a walking time bomb.

Hyperbole: Her smile outshone the spotlight.

Cliché: . . . as strong as an ox

Writing Application Use figurative language, but use it sparingly so readers don't lose sight of the real person or situation.

Writer's Solution Connection
Writing Lab

To learn more about tone, see the audio-annotated models in the Drafting section of the tutorial on Description.

Prewriting

Choose a Topic Choose a person you find interesting to be the subject of your character sketch. If you prefer, choose a character from fiction, or create a character of your own. If you need help choosing a subject, use one of the following ideas.

Topic Ideas

- An older person whom you admire
- Joan of Arc
- An interesting extraterrestrial

Selection-Related Topic Ideas

- Charlotte Brontë
- Jeremy Bentham
- A Dickensian hero

Develop the Character Create a chart in which you list various details of your subject's physical appearance and personality, and refer to this chart as you draft your sketch. Here's an example:

Appearance: 5'10"; brunette, neatly dressed
Habits: chewing gum, pointing toes
Hopes: to be a dancer
Talents: dancing, crocheting, gymnastics

Identify a Revealing Incident Select an incident that will give your readers insight into your subject's thoughts and feelings. Sometimes it's more effective to reveal personality through action rather than describing it directly.

Drafting

Use Descriptive Words Help readers "see" your subject by writing clear and precise descriptions. Instead of describing a teen as being tall and thin, use words like *lanky*, *rangy*, or *gangly*.

Create a Personal Tone As you draft your character sketch, use words and phrases that give readers a sense of "knowing" your subject. Notice how the word choice in the second example below conveys a personal tone.

- ▶ **Neutral Tone:** *She was a kind, loving woman.*
- ▶ **Personal Tone:** *Her warm, cinnamon-colored eyes hugged you even before she reached out with soft, round arms.*

Applying Language Skills

Using Figurative Language To help create a precise picture of their character, students may want to make vivid comparisons using figurative language. Have students review the guidelines in this section and then review their papers for places where figurative language may enhance their description. For additional practice with figurative language, have students complete page 102 in the *Writer's Solution Grammar Practice Book*.

Revising

Clarify Vague Descriptions Reread your draft and replace vague, imprecise words with ones that create a stronger impression of your subject.

Draft: He was full because he ate too much.

Revision: He felt stuffed to bursting because he ate dozens of the spicy and delicious empanadas.

Use a Revision Checklist Answer the following questions as you revise your character sketch.

1. Does the incident described provide background about the subject and offer insight into his or her personality?
2. Do the physical descriptions create a clear and accurate picture of the subject?
3. Will the tone make readers feel as if they have actually met the subject?

Revision Model

① my bouncing, bubbly niece, a bundle of energy who embraces each day as if it were an adventure more exciting than a walk in space.

② At thirty-three pounds, and three feet, three inches tall,

She is ~~a happy child~~. ~~She loves to throw tea parties.~~

③ was determined that I would attend a gala tea party in the nursery.

① The writer replaced this bland description with a warmer, more personal one.

② The writer added a concise physical description to help readers picture the child.

③ By describing a specific event, the writer revealed his niece's personality.

Publishing

- **Contest** Submit your character sketch to an appropriate writing contest.
- **Anthology** Collect character sketches from your classmates and bind them together. Organize them according to three categories: Fictional Characters, Historical Figures, and Actual People.

Applying Language Skills: Dangling Modifiers

Avoid dangling modifiers, words or phrases that do not modify other elements of the sentence. Often dangling modifiers create ridiculous images:

Dangling Modifier

Laughing heartily, tears rolled down Joshua's cheeks.

Revised Sentence

Joshua laughed so heartily that tears rolled down his cheeks.

Practice Identify and correct the dangling modifiers in these sentences. If necessary, add words or change the word order.

1. Skating down the ramp, his new wheel fell off.
2. To understand the man's character, examination of his life is our first task.
3. Watching her perform, the quickness of her hands astonished me.

Writing Application In proofreading, review your sketch to make sure you haven't used any dangling modifiers.

Writer's Solution Connection Language Lab

For help in revising your sketch, see the Strengthening Sentences lesson in the Writing Style section.

Revising

Have students work in pairs reading their character sketches to each other. After one student reads, the other should provide a summary of the character the reader described. This summary should be used to help evaluate whether a character sketch was effective by showing that the reader understood the main impression the writer was trying to convey about the character.

Writing Lab CD-ROM

To help students revise their papers, have them use the revision checkers for vague adjectives, sentence openers, and repeated language. After they identify instances of weaknesses, students can revise their papers by adding precise language, varying sentence openers, and eliminating repeated language.

Reinforce and Extend

To reinforce and extend students' understanding of character, have them prepare skits and monologues to dramatize the character in their sketch.

Applying Language Skills

Dangling Modifiers Have students complete the Practice and then revise any dangling modifiers in their papers.

Answers

Suggested responses:

1. His new wheel fell off his skate as he skated down the ramp.
2. To understand the man's character, we must first examine his life.
3. Watching her perform, I was astonished by the quickness of her hands.

ASSESSMENT		4	3	2	1
PORTFOLIO ASSESSMENT Use the rubric on Description in ***Alternative Assessment*** (p.98) to assess students' writing. Add these criteria to customize the rubric to this assignment.	**Precise Language**	The writer consistently uses precise language to create a vivid character sketch.	The writer uses precise language but needs to include more.	The character sketch includes some but far too few instances of precise language.	The writer does not use precise language.
	Personal Tone	The writer establishes and maintains a personal tone.	The writer establishes a personal tone but does not always maintain it.	The character sketch includes some instances of personal tone but is mostly impersonal.	The paper does not have a personal tone.

Introduce the Strategy

During the school years, students develop an expertise for absorbing information in short blocks of text. They have not had as many opportunities for sustained involvement in longer works. The following strategies will help them with longer works.

Customize for
Less Proficient Readers
These students may have difficulty absorbing and keeping track of large amounts of information. In addition to the strategies listed on this page, have students create a diagram that shows the chain of events described in the piece as well as list the significance of any characters introduced. For nonfiction, have students create a summary at the end of each section.

Apply the Strategy

Suggested response:

1. The novel is organized into parts and chapters, indicated by *Part I* at the top of the page and *One* above the block of text.
2. The epigraph suggests that the characters in this novel are going to be made aware of new and surprising things.
3. Adrana's actions are going to be central to the story.

Reading Novels and Other Extended Works

Real-World Reading Skills Workshop

Strategies for Success

The experience of reading an extended work, like a novel or a biography, is different from that of reading a short story, an article, or a poem. To meet the different demands of a longer work, you need to adapt your reading strategies.

Get an Overview Often it helps to get an overview of a work before you become lost in the details. For a novel, look at the parts or chapters into which the book is divided. Note whether they have titles that hint at the plot or are preceded by epigraphs, brief quotations from other works that suggest themes and meanings. When previewing nonfiction, you may also want to scan maps, photographs, and other visuals.

Part I

The Awakening

"There are more things in heaven and earth, Horatio, Than are dreamt of in your philosophy."
William Shakespeare
Hamlet, Act I, Scene V

One

When the workday tone sounded, Adrana did not stop working. The men and women on her squad pulled the protective hoods over their work stations and lined up quietly at the monitor station. One by one they placed their palm on the cold metal platform and one by one they were registered in the system.

As the last worker boarded the employee rail-link, a message appeared on Adrana's screen: "Your shift has been completed. Please report to the monitor station to conclude." Adrana tried not to look nervous. She knew that the video cameras scanned the room and heat sensors would pick up fluctuations in her body temperature. As calmly as possible, she pressed the secret key sequence that Chanda taught her yesterday. A new message appeared "System override. Press Return to continue."

Adrana pressed Return.

Pace Yourself Reading a long work is a little like running a long-distance race. If you try to sprint through the book, you may get winded. Pace yourself, allowing a reasonable amount of time to read each chapter or section.

Pause to Reflect Chapter and section breaks offer you an opportunity to pause and think about what you have just read. Taking time out to reflect on your reading will help you understand a book's main themes or ideas. Ask yourself questions like these: What was that chapter about? What happened or what were the main ideas? Where will the story or the discussion go next? Jot down predictions or questions.

Reread Going back to reread an important scene or explanation is an excellent way to reinforce your understanding. Facts or details you learn at the end of a book may help you better understand other sections when you reread them.

Apply the Strategy

The opening pages of a novel contain a great deal of information. Read the first pages from this novel and answer the questions.

1. What can you determine about the organization of this novel?
2. What does the epigraph suggest about the novel's theme?
3. What prediction might you make about Adrana's role in the novel?

Here are some other extended works which you can read strategically :

- multi-part magazine articles
- instruction manuals and textbooks
- research reports

Beyond the Classroom

Workplace Skills Connection

Reading Business Reports Explain to students that in their careers they may have to read lengthy business reports, which include jargon and statistics that may not always be easy to follow. The reports may also include research results from which they must make informed decisions. Explain to them that using the strategies on this page will help them find the main point of the report and also help them discern information that is relevant to their business.

PART 4 Gloom and Glory

Past and Present (no. 2)
Augustus Leopold Egg, Tate Gallery, London

One-Minute Planning Guide

The selections in this part all deal with the theme of gloom and glory. Emily Brontë's "Remembrance" and Thomas Hardy's "Ah, Are You Digging on My Grave?" comment on death and love, and Hardy's "The Darkling Thrush" explores how hope can exist even in the midst of loneliness and despair.

In Gerard Manley Hopkins's poem "God's Grandeur" the speaker marvels at the presence of God in nature. In Hopkins's "Spring and Fall," the speaker conjectures that a young girl's sorrow is caused by her sense of mortality. A. E. Housman, too, examines subjects of gloom and glory in his poetry. The speaker in "To an Athlete Dying Young" tells how a young runner has died at the peak of his talent. Yet in the same poem, the speaker suggests that the runner died in his glory. Housman's "When I Was One-and-Twenty" also examines the theme of gloom and glory, but in a much lighter vein.

In Arthur Rimbaud's "Eternity," the speaker anticipates the glories of Eternity.

Customizing for *Varying Student Needs*

When assigning the selections in this part, keep in mind these factors:

"Remembrance"
- Short, easy-to-read poem on the nature of love and life

"The Darkling Thrush"
- Exploration of despair and hope, written in anticipation of the twentieth century

"Ah, Are You Digging on My Grave?"
- Darkly humorous poem

"God's Grandeur"
- Many references to Christianity

"Spring and Fall: To a Young Child"
- Short poem reflecting on the mortality of humans

"To an Athlete Dying Young"
- Message about achievement that students will understand

"When I Was One-and-Twenty"
- Humorous, self-mocking poem about youth and wisdom

Humanities: Art

Past and Present (no. 2) by Augustus Leopold Egg.

Augustus Leopold Egg (1816–1863) was both a painter and an actor. A friend of Charles Dickens, he performed in Dickens's acting company. He also painted "genre paintings," which referred to works of novelists such as William Thackeray and Sir Walter Scott.

Have your students link this art to the theme of Part 4, "Gloom and Glory," by answering the following questions:

1. Describe the atmosphere in this painting, and point out elements that contribute most to its atmosphere. *Most students will say that the painting has a melancholy atmosphere, created by the weeping child, the darkness of the room, the haunting moon, and the ashen cityscape.*
2. Suggest a situation that would account for what you see in the painting. The situation should include elements of both "gloom" and "glory." *Sample answer: The poor young mother tries to comfort her child, who cries because a friend has died; the woman gazes at the moon and recalls her dreams of being a great writer.*

Prepare and Engage

OBJECTIVES

1. To read and interpret three poems
2. To relate three poems to personal experience
3. To read stanzas as units of meaning
4. To identify stanza structure and irony
5. To build vocabulary in context and learn the word root *-terr(a)-*
6. To correctly choose pronoun case following *than* or *as*
7. To write a remembrance using elaboration to make writing personal
8. To respond to the poems through writing, speaking and listening, and projects

SKILLS INSTRUCTION

Vocabulary: Word Roots: *-terr(a)-*
Grammar: Pronoun Case Following *Than* or *As*
Reading Strategy: Read Stanzas as Units of Meaning
Literary Focus: Stanza Structure and Irony
Writing: Elaboration to Make Writing Personal
Speaking and Listening: Dramatic Reading (teacher edition)
Critical Viewing: Analyze; Speculate

PORTFOLIO OPPORTUNITIES

Writing: Remembrance; Comparison and Contrast; Critical Essay
Writing Mini-Lesson: Remembrance
Speaking and Listening: Dramatic Reading; Role-Play
Projects: Biography; Timeline of the Century

More About the Authors

Emily Brontë and her sisters, Charlotte and Anne, wrote their first books under male pseudonyms, hoping that their work would be taken more seriously if it was attributed to male authors. Emily Brontë's novel *Wuthering Heights*, for example, was published under the pseudonym Ellis Bell.

Thomas Hardy was actually trained as an architect and worked in that field until the early 1870's, when he gave up architecture to become a full-time writer.

Guide for Interpreting

Emily Brontë (1818–1848)

Although some literary critics attacked her for the violent passions of her writing, Emily Brontë's dark romanticism now is regarded as the focus of her genius.

A Writer's Beginnings Emily Brontë was born in Yorkshire, a barren wasteland in the north of England dominated by fog, hedges, and scruffy grasses. As a child, Emily and her sisters, Charlotte and Anne, created fantasy stories about a magical kingdom, using their wooden soldiers as characters. They wrote their stories in tiny handwriting in dozens of little notebooks.

Recognition and Fame As adults, the three sisters first wrote poetry. Then each began work on a novel. Emily's ever-popular novel, *Wuthering Heights,* was published in 1847. It tells the story of a tragic love affair played out against the turbulent and mysterious landscape of the moors. A year after *Wuthering Heights* was published, Emily suffered her own tragedy: She caught cold at her brother's funeral, and a short time later, she died.

Thomas Hardy (1840–1928)

Thomas Hardy, known as "the last of the great Victorians," was born in Dorset, a region of southwest England, on which he based his fictional setting of Wessex.

The Novelist Fascinated by the fates of his neighbors in his native Dorset, Hardy used his writing to elaborate his own pessimistic view of life. His tragic novels, which include *Far from the Madding Crowd* (1874), *Tess of the D'Urbervilles* (1891), and *Jude the Obscure* (1895), all sought to show what happens when human beings rebel against their circumstances. Using vivid imagery to describe the changing seasons, weather, and landscape of his region, Hardy matched it to the psychological states of his characters.

The Poet The bleakness of his fiction was disturbing to readers, and the response to *Jude the Obscure* was so hostile that Hardy abandoned fiction and turned to writing poetry. He earned immense public acclaim with *The Dynasts*, an epic verse drama about the Napoleonic Wars. With each book of verse he produced, Hardy's reputation as a poet grew.

A Poetic Legacy Hardy's poetry marks a transition from the Victorian Age to the Modernist movement of the twentieth century. In his use of strict meter and stanza structure, Hardy was unmistakably Victorian, but his "nonpoetic" language and odd rhymes, coupled with a fatalistic outlook, inspired numerous twentieth-century writers.

◆ Background for Understanding

LITERATURE: BRONTË'S ROMANTICISM; HARDY'S NATURALISM

Victorian poets wrote in many voices and styles. Some writers like Emily Brontë are classified as Romantic because they explore and celebrate the human soul, nature's wildness, and the powers of the imagination. Thomas Hardy, however, embraced Naturalism, which focused on the victimization of ordinary people by social and natural forces.

The poems that follow call to mind both Romanticism and Naturalism. For example, although Brontë lived before the start of Naturalism, her poem contains an attitude that is more usual in Naturalist poets, and Hardy's poems contain instances of Romanticism, Brontë's specialty.

Prentice Hall Literature Program Resources

REINFORCE / RETEACH / EXTEND

Selection Support Pages
Build Vocabulary: Word Roots: *-terr(a)-*, p. 208
Grammar and Style: Pronoun Case, p. 209
Reading Strategy: Read Stanzas, p. 210
Literary Focus: Stanza Structure and Irony, p. 211

Strategies for Diverse Student Needs, p. 43

Beyond Literature
Cross-Curricular Connection: Science, p. 43

Formal Assessment Selection Test, pp. 216–218; Assessment Resources Software

Alternative Assessment, p. 43

Writing and Language Transparencies
Art Transparency 14, Writing Process Model 1

Resource Pro CD-ROM
"Remembrance," "The Darkling Thrush," "Ah, Are You Digging on My Grave?"—includes all resource material and customizable lesson plan

Listening to Literature Audiocassettes
"Remembrance," "The Darkling Thrush," "Ah, Are You Digging on My Grave?"

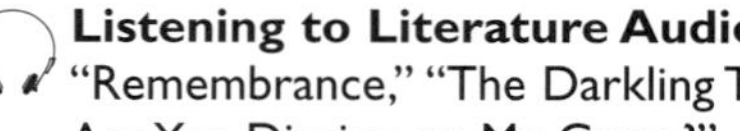

Remembrance ◆ The Darkling Thrush "Ah, Are You Digging on My Grave?"

◆ Literature and Your Life

As time passes, we all experience losses of some kind: loss of youth, love, friendship. Human responses to loss can vary widely, from anger to intense sorrow. Think about a time in which you and a friend reacted differently to a loss of some kind.

Brontë's "Remembrance" and Hardy's "Ah, Are You Digging . . . ?" both deal with loss through death, but in very different ways.

Thematic Focus: Gloom and Glory

As you read these poems by Brontë and Hardy, look for ways in which they express a gloomy outlook on life.

◆ Literary Focus

Stanza Structure and Irony

Many poets use elements of both predictability and surprise in their works. For example, **stanza structure** helps poets to establish expectations for their poems, whereas **irony** allows them to upset those expectations to amuse or surprise. A stanza usually consists of a certain number of lines arranged in a recurring pattern, rhythmic structure, and rhyme. Irony, on the other hand, is a deliberate contradiction between expectation and reality.

One interesting feature of the following poems is that they contain a consistent stanza structure, but the attitude toward their subjects changes, which ultimately creates irony. For example, the wildly dark, romantic mood in "Remembrance" is contradicted by the speaker's final resolution and outlook.

◆ Grammar and Style

Pronoun Case Following *Than* or *As*

In actual speech as well as in poetry, you find incomplete constructions, instances in which words are omitted because they are understood. When a **pronoun** occurs in an incomplete construction, especially following the words *than* or *as*, its **case** is what it would be if the construction were complete.

The following example contains an incomplete construction with the pronoun *I* following the word *as*. The word in brackets is the unspoken word that completes the sentence.

And every spirit upon earth / Seemed fervorless as *I* [was]

◆ Reading Strategy

Read Stanzas as Units of Meaning

Stanzas in poetry are not arbitrary chunks of poetry. Stanzas usually convey **a unit of meaning** or a main idea, as paragraphs do in prose. Some stanzas contain no complete sentences and serve instead to create a mood or single idea. Other stanzas may contain several complex ideas that together convey a larger idea or theme. By observing how the meaning of a poem's stanzas progress or build, you build an understanding of the poem as a whole.

As you read, look for the main idea, image, or thought within each stanza.

Journal Writing Jot down the main idea of each stanza as you read.

◆ Build Vocabulary

Word Roots: *-terr(a)-*

In "The Darkling Thrush," the word *terrestrial,* meaning "of the earth," contains the word root *terr(a)-*, which is derived from the Latin word for "land."

Word Bank

Before you read, preview this list of words from the poems.

languish
rapturous
gaunt
terrestrial

To spark interest in this group of poems, display Art Transparency 14: *Frosty Morning*, on an overhead projector. Elicit from students whether the painting conveys a hopeful mood or a sad one, or some combination of these emotions. Tell students that the poems that follow are an unusual blend of hope and despair. Encourage students to identify each speaker's outlook as they read the poems.

Customize for
English Language Learners

These students may be puzzled by the oxymorons "rapturous pain" and "divinest anguish" in the last stanza of "Remembrance." Explain that these are paradoxical—purposely contradictory—expressions, and ask students to describe any similar expressions from their first languages.

Customize for
Intrapersonal Learners

These students are skillful in observing and analyzing their own thoughts, feelings, and moods. Encourage them to recognize the speakers' responses to loss and to express those responses in writing, artwork, song, or dance.

Preparing for Standardized Tests

Reading and Vocabulary Understanding that stanzas are units of meaning will help students as they interpret poetry in Critical Reading portions of standardized tests. For more practice, use the Reading Strategy page on Reading Stanzas as Units of Meaning, p. 210, in ***Selection Support***.

Grammar and Language The Grammar and Style lesson for this selection gives students instruction and practice in choosing the correct pronoun case following incomplete constructions that use the words *than* or *as*. Students can apply this skill when they are asked to identify sentence errors. Following is an example:

Identify the error in the following sentence.
Despite the acclaim his latest novel received, no one could be more humble than him. *(D)*
(A) later
(B) nobody
(C) humbler
(D) he
(E) no error

For additional practice, use the Grammar and Style page on Pronoun Cases Following *Than* or *As* in ***Selection Support***, p. 209.

Develop Understanding

One-Minute Insight The speaker in Emily Brontë's poem addresses her only love, a man who died fifteen years earlier. She asks him to forgive her for not indulging in "Memory's rapturous pain." To do so would not allow her to live in a world that is admittedly "empty" without his presence.

The speaker of this poem expresses an interesting blend of pragmatic and romantic thought. She is pragmatic in that she recognizes that her life is one to be lived and cherished, even without the "aid of joy." The speaker, however, while denying that love is necessary for existence, in doing so achingly expresses her passionate longing for her long-dead lover.

◆ Literary Focus

❶ Stanza Structure and Irony Have students use the first stanza to analyze the poem's stanza structure. Ask how many lines are in each stanza and what the rhyme scheme is for each. *There are four lines in each stanza. The rhyme scheme is abab.*

◆ Reading Strategy

❷ Read Stanzas as Units of Meaning Ask students what mood is conveyed in the first stanza and what details help convey that mood. *The first stanza creates a gloomy mood. Details that convey the mood include "Cold," "deep snow piled above thee," "dreary grave," "Severed," and "Time's all-wearing wave."*

▶Critical Viewing◀

❸ Analyze Suggested response: Like the speaker in the poem, the woman in the painting looks sad and reflective, as she smells a rose and looks as if she were thinking of someone or something far away or far in the past.

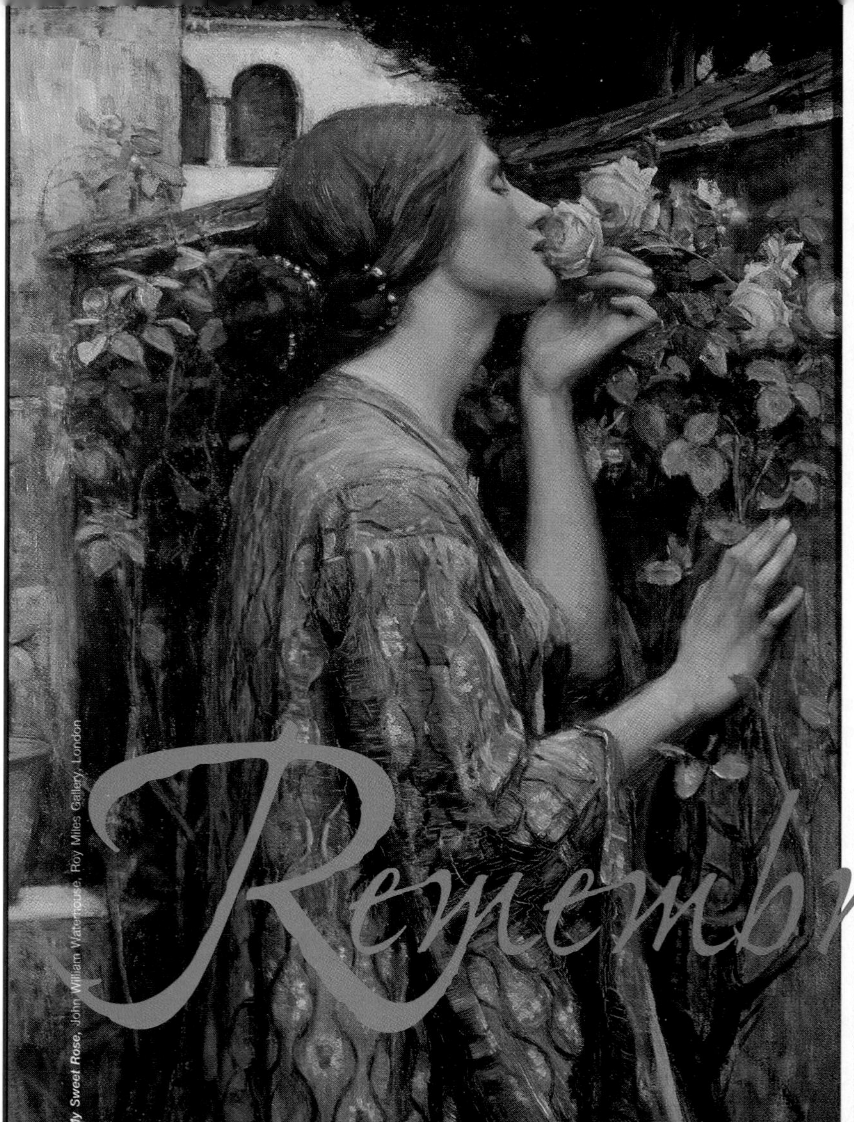

My Sweet Rose, John William Waterhouse. Roy Miles Gallery, London

◀ **Critical Viewing** In what ways might the woman in this painting represent the poem's speaker? **[Analyze]** ❸

Remembrance

Emily Brontë

❶ Cold in the earth, and the deep snow piled above thee!
Far, far removed, cold in the dreary grave!
Have I forgot, my Only Love, to love thee,
❷ Severed at last by Time's all-wearing wave?

Now, when alone, do my thoughts no longer hover
Over the mountains, on that northern shore;
Resting their wings where heath and fern-leaves cover
Thy noble heart for ever, ever more?

Block Scheduling Strategies

Consider these suggestions to take advantage of extended class time:

- Introduce the Reading Strategy. Discuss the information about reading stanzas as units of meaning on page 847. Encourage students to jot down main ideas as they read, as suggested in the Journal Writing activity on page 847.
- Use the Literary Focus on page 847 as the basis of a class discussion on stanza structure and irony. Have students work individually or in pairs after reading the poems to answer the Literary Focus questions on page 854. Follow up with the Literary Focus page in ***Selection Support***, p. 211.
- Have students explore scientist Charles Darwin's influence on Thomas Hardy and on the Victorians in ***Beyond Literature,*** p. 43.
- Assign students the Writing Mini-Lesson on page 855. Before they begin, display and model Writing Process 1: Reflective Essay, pp. 5–12, in the ***Writing and Language Transparencies*** booklet.

Cold in the earth, and fifteen wild Decembers
From those brown hills have melted into spring—
Faithful indeed is the spirit that remembers
After such years of change and suffering!

Sweet Love of youth, forgive if I forget thee
While the World's tide is bearing me along:
Other desires and other hopes beset me,
Hopes which obscure but cannot do thee wrong. ❹

No later light has lightened up my heaven,
No second morn has ever shone for me:
All my life's bliss from thy dear life was given— ❺
All my life's bliss is in the grave with thee.

But when the days of golden dreams had perished
And even Despair was powerless to destroy,
Then did I learn how existence could be cherished,
Strengthened and fed without the aid of joy;

Then did I check the tears of useless passion,
Weaned my young soul from yearning after thine;
Sternly denied its burning wish to hasten
Down to that tomb already more than mine!

And even yet, I dare not let it languish,
Dare not indulge in Memory's rapturous pain;
Once drinking deep of that divinest anguish, ❻
How could I seek the empty world again?

◆ **Build Vocabulary**

languish (laŋ´gwish) *v.*: Become weak; depressed

rapturous (rap´chər us) *adj.*: Ecstatic

Guide for Responding

◆ Literature and Your Life

Reader's Response Do you approve of the speaker's plan to forget her love and loss? Explain.

Thematic Focus In what ways is the speaker's outlook a gloomy one?

☑ Check Your Comprehension

1. Where and when is the poem set?
2. How long ago did the speaker's love die?
3. What does the speaker plan to do? Why is she planning this action?

◆ Critical Thinking

INTERPRET

1. Why has the speaker decided to forget her love? **[Infer]**
2. What does the speaker mean by "no later light has lightened up my heaven"? **[Interpret]**
3. Why is the speaker afraid to give in to her old feelings? **[Draw Conclusions]**
4. What do you consider the basic conflict of the speaker of this poem? **[Draw Conclusions]**

APPLY

5. What might an existence fed "without . . . joy" be like? **[Relate]**

Humanities: Art

My Sweet Rose by John William Waterhouse.

John William Waterhouse (1847–1917) was an English painter who studied at the Royal Academy in London. He is considered to be both a Classical and Pre-Raphaelite painter of mainly romantic and poetic subjects. Much of his work was inspired by the work of poets.

This painting depicts a woman savoring a rose's sweet perfume, perhaps remembering a "sweet love of youth."

Use this question for discussion.

What is your interpretation of the painting's title: "My Sweet Rose"? *Some students may say that the rose represents the beloved of the woman shown in the painting. Others may say that the title refers to the woman herself—that is, the painting depicts the artist's beloved.*

◆ Critical Thinking

❹ **Speculate** Ask: What might the speaker mean by "Other desires and other hopes"? *The speaker may be referring to concerns related to family or work.*

◆ Reading Strategy

❺ **Read Stanzas as Units of Meaning** Have students summarize the main idea of this stanza. *The speaker says that since her first love died, she has not reexperienced love.*

◆ Critical Thinking

❻ **Interpret** Ask students how a painful memory might be "rapturous." *Remembering a lost love, though painful, keeps that love alive in some way.*

Reinforce and Extend

Answers

◆ Literature and Your Life

Reader's Response Some students may say that they approve. Others may feel that the speaker should not ever forget her love.

Thematic Focus Students may cite the speaker's preoccupation with the past and her assumption that she will never experience love or joy again.

☑ Check Your Comprehension

1. The poem is set during the winter; the speaker reveals that she is "Over the mountains" from where her love is buried.
2. The speaker's love died fifteen years ago.
3. The speaker plans to "forget" her lost love. Otherwise, she would be too sad.

◆ Critical Thinking

1. The speaker has decided that she must become part of the world of the living.
2. The speaker has not fallen in love with anyone else.
3. She is afraid that her old feelings will take over and prevent her from proceeding with her life.
4. Suggested answer: The basic conflict is between living in a joyless present and giving oneself up to painful memories of a joyous past.
5. Such an existence might be peaceful and rewarding, but without excitement or emotional ups and downs.

Develop Understanding

One-Minute Insight Hardy's bleak reflections—and tentative expression of hope—on the eve of the twentieth century are especially poignant as we begin the twenty-first century and look back on both the tragedies and progress of the past century.

◆ Literary Focus

❶ Stanza Structure and Irony Have students use the first stanza to identify the structure of the poem's stanzas: number of lines per stanza, rhyme scheme, and rhythm. *Each stanza has eight lines; the rhyme scheme is ababcdcd. Lines of iambic tetrameter alternate with lines of iambic trimeter.*

◆ Reading Strategy

❷ Read Stanzas as Units of Meaning Ask students to identify the meaning or main idea of this stanza. *Possible response: The speaker is alone in a bleak, twilight setting.*

◆ Critical Thinking

❸ Classify Have students find images of death in this stanza and tell what feeling the images create. *Images of death include "The Century's corpse," "crypt," "death lament" and "spirit." They create a feeling of gloom and despair.*

The Darkling[1] Thrush

Thomas Hardy

I leant upon a coppice gate[2]
　　When Frost was specter-gray,
And Winter's dregs made desolate
❶ 　　The weakening eye of day.
The tangled bine-stems[3] scored the sky
❷ 　　Like strings of broken lyres,
And all mankind that haunted nigh
　　Had sought their household fires.

The land's sharp features seemed to be
　　The Century's corpse[4] outleant,
❸ His crypt the cloudy canopy,
　　The wind his death-lament.
The ancient pulse of germ[5] and birth

1. **darkling** *adj.*: In the dark.
2. **coppice** (kop′ is) **gate:** Gate leading to a thicket, or small wood.
3. **bine-stems:** Twining stems.
4. **Century's corpse:** This poem was written on December 31, 1900, the last day of the nineteenth century.
5. **germ:** Seed or bud.

Cross-Curricular Connection: Social Studies

At the approach of the twentieth century, the world was already beginning a period of rapid social and technological change. In 1900, the electrocardiograph was invented, Max Planck formulated the quantum theory of physics, and Sigmund Freud published *The Interpretation of Dreams*, launching a new understanding of human psychology and motivation. In the following year, 1901, Marconi tested radio transmissions between England and Newfoundland, and Queen Victoria died. By 1903 Orville Wright had made his first flight in a self-propelled airplane, and Edwin S. Porter had directed one of the world's first movies, *The Great Train Robbery*. The modern world as we know it was approaching rapidly.

Have students discuss what differing reactions writers, scientists, and ordinary citizens might have to a period of rapid social and technological change.

Was shrunken hard and dry,
And every spirit upon earth
Seemed fervorless as I. 

At once a voice arose among
The bleak twigs overhead
In a full-hearted evensong
Of joy illimited;
An aged thrush, frail, gaunt, and small, ❹
In blast-beruffled plume,
Had chosen thus to fling his soul
Upon the growing gloom.

So little cause for carolings
Of such ecstatic sound
Was written on terrestrial things
Afar or nigh around,
That I could think there trembled through ❺
His happy good-night air
Some blessed Hope, whereof he knew
And I was unaware.

◆ Build Vocabulary

gaunt (gônt) *adj.*: Very thin and angular

terrestrial (tə res′ trē əl) *adj.*: Relating to the earth

◀ Critical Viewing Why might Hardy have chosen a thrush like the one pictured to symbolize hope? **[Speculate]** 

Guide for Responding

◆ Literature and Your Life

Reader's Response Does the ending of this poem surprise you? Why or why not?

Thematic Focus In what ways is this poem gloomy? Does it convey any hope for the future? Explain.

Setting Capture the scene described in the poem by drawing or painting it.

☑ Check Your Comprehension

1. In what season and time of year is "The Darkling Thrush" set?
2. What does the speaker suddenly hear in the third stanza?
3. Of what is the speaker unaware?

◆ Critical Thinking

INTERPRET

1. (a) What mood does the poet establish in the first two stanzas of "The Darkling Thrush"? (b) How does the mood change in the last two stanzas? **[Classify]**
2. To what are the land's "sharp features" compared? Why is this comparison appropriate for the time and place of the poem? **[Analyze]**
3. (a) Why do you think the poet characterizes the thrush as he does in lines 21–22? (b) What might the thrush symbolize? **[Interpret]**

EXTEND

4. Hardy wrote this poem on the eve of the twentieth century. Was his pessimistic outlook about the future justified? **[Social Studies Link]**

Cross-Curricular Connection: Science

Although people today remain charmed and delighted by the singing of birds, we now know that birdsong is related to hormonal secretions and is primarily a means for male birds to claim their territory and attract a mate. Some birds have more complex and variable songs than others. Among these are some varieties of thrushes, such as the mockingbird, which can mimic the songs of other birds and produce more than a hundred individual sounds.

Have students discuss whether having an increased scientific knowledge about natural phenomena such as birdsong adds to or detracts from their sense of nature's mystery and romance.

◆ Literary Focus

❹ **Stanza Structure and Irony**
Ask students how this stanza marks a turning point in the poem. *The joyful singing of the weak, old thrush begins to lift the gloom of the preceding stanzas.*

◆ Literary Focus

❺ **Stanza Structure and Irony**
Ask students which word in this last stanza contradicts the spirit of the rest of the poem. *The word "Hope" is in ironic contrast to the despairing tone of the rest of the poem.*

▶Critical Viewing◀

❻ **Speculate** The thrush seems small and vulnerable to the cold. It must deal with a harsh climate, but it keeps singing anyway.

Reinforce and Extend

Answers

◆ Literature and Your Life

Reader's Response Students may be surprised by the hopeful note.

Thematic Focus It paints a bleak picture of the setting. It conveys hope through the image of the thrush and its song.

☑ Check Your Comprehension

1. It is wintertime, toward the close of the day and year.
2. The speaker hears a thrush singing.
3. The speaker is unaware of the cause for hope.

◆ Critical Thinking

1. (a) The mood is one of gloom. (b) An image of hope appears.
2. The land's "sharp features" are compared to "The Century's corpse." The comparison is appropriate because the poem is set in a desolate place at the end of a winter's day and of a century.
3. (a) The characterization of the thrush as gaunt creates a sense of irony because the bird is full of hope. (b) The bird might symbolize the indomitability of the human spirit.
4. Yes, the world wars show that Hardy's pessimism was justified; no, the twentieth century has seen the advent of remarkable advances.

Develop Understanding

One-Minute Insight In Hardy's bitterly humorous and ironic poem, a dead woman keeps asking who is digging on her grave—assuming that someone who once loved or hated her still has feelings for her. An unidentified voice answers her questions. The voice is finally revealed to be that of her dog. The woman is relieved to find that her dog still remembers her, but—in the poem's final irony—the dog claims he was just burying a bone and had forgotten his mistress was buried there.

❶ **Clarification** Tell students that *rue* is the name of a wildflower with yellow petals and bitter-tasting leaves that were once used to make medicine. The plant became a symbol of sorrow and mourning, and the word *rue* means "regret or sorrow."

◆ Literary Focus

❷ **Stanza Structure and Irony** Using the punctuation clues, ask students to identify how many speakers are in this poem and to describe the structure of this stanza. *There are two speakers—a dead woman and an unidentified voice. The first voice is the woman's, the second is the unidentified speaker's. The rhyme scheme is abcccb.*

◆ Literary Focus

❸ **Stanza Structure and Irony** Ask students how repeated questions and answers create suspense and irony. *They create suspense because each question intensifies our curiosity about who the digger is. They create irony because the speaker suspects the digger is either someone who loves her or someone who hates her, when, in fact, all the important people in her life have already forgotten her.*

"Ah, Are You Digging on My Grave?"

Thomas Hardy

"Ah, are you digging on my grave
My loved one?—planting rue?" ❶
—"No: yesterday he went to wed
One of the brightest wealth has bred. ❷
'It cannot hurt her now,' he said,
'That I should not be true.'"

"Then who is digging on my grave?
My nearest dearest kin?"
—"Ah, no: they sit and think, 'What use!
What good will planting flowers produce?
No tendance of her mound can loose
Her spirit from Death's gin.'"[1]

"But some one digs upon my grave?
My enemy?—prodding sly?"
—"Nay: when she heard you had passed the Gate ❸
That shuts on all flesh soon or late,
She thought you no more worth her hate,
And cares not where you lie."

"Then, who is digging on my grave?
Say—since I have not guessed!"

1. **gin** *n.*: Trap.

Speaking and Listening Mini-Lesson

Dramatic Reading

This mini-lesson supports the Speaking and Listening activity in the Idea Bank, p. 855.

Introduce the Concept Explain that in a dramatic reading, people assume the roles of the characters in the literary work, speaking the dialogue attributed to the characters. Unlike a play, a dramatic reading does not involve costumes, sets, or staging. Instead, the actors convey through voice tone, emphasis, and inflection the meaning of the work.

Develop Background Tell students that because a poem has no stage directions, it is up to the performers themselves to decide how the characters should say their lines. Have students copy out by hand or photocopy the poem "Ah, Are You Digging on My Grave?" Have student pairs (or quartets, if they wish to have students read the parts of the woman's love and family) rehearse their dramatic readings, marking up their copies of the poem to assist them in their performance.

Apply the Information Have students perform their dramatic readings for the class. To enhance the mood, you may wish to draw the window blinds.

Assess the Outcome Have students discuss the effectiveness of the performances, basing their evaluations on how well the group interprets and presents the poem. Also, they can use in their evaluations the Peer Assessment: Oral Interpretation, p. 120, in the ***Alternative Assessment*** booklet.

—"O it is I, my mistress dear,
Your little dog, who still lives near,
And much I hope my movements here ❹
Have not disturbed your rest?"

"Ah, yes! *You* dig upon my grave . . .
Why flashed it not on me
That one true heart was left behind!
What feeling do we ever find
To equal among human kind
A dog's fidelity!"
❺
"Mistress, I dug upon your grave
To bury a bone, in case
I should be hungry near this spot
When passing on my daily trot.
I am sorry, but I quite forgot
It was your resting-place."

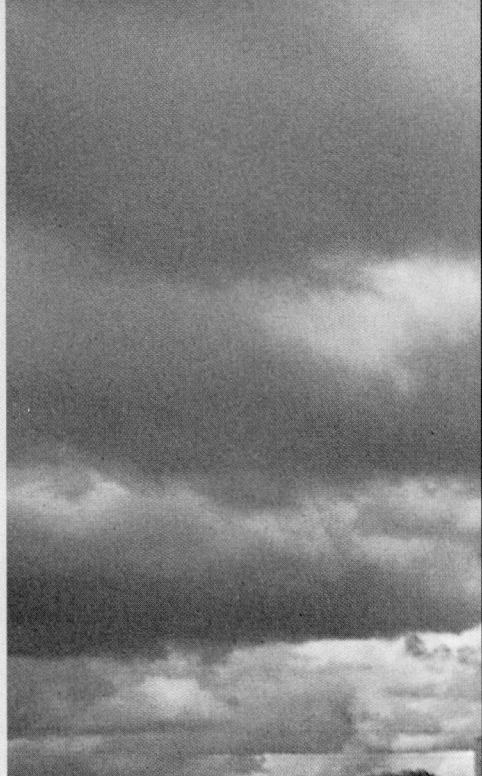

Guide for Responding

◆ Literature and Your Life

Reader's Response Do you feel sorry for the speaker in this poem? Why or why not?

Thematic Focus Is this poem gloomy or humorous or both? Explain.

Diary Write a diary entry that the speaker might have written while alive. Use clues from the poem about the people in the speaker's life to help you.

☑ Check Your Comprehension

1. (a) In the first stanza, who does the speaker suspect is digging on her grave? (b) In the second stanza? (c) In the third stanza?

2. (a) Who is actually digging on the speaker's grave? (b) What reason does the digger give for disturbing the grave?

◆ Critical Thinking

INTERPRET

1. (a) At what point do you begin to suspect the identity of the voice responding to the woman's questions? (b) What effect does Hardy achieve by withholding this information? **[Analyze]**

2. What mood does Hardy create by having a dead person speak? (b) How does this mood change once the digger is identified? **[Interpret]**

3. What point about human vanity and self-esteem is Hardy making in this poem? **[Draw Conclusions]**

EVALUATE

4. Do you find the message of this poem overly pessimistic? Explain. **[Assess]**

Beyond the Selection

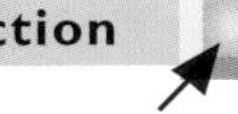

FURTHER READING

Other Poems by Emily Brontë

"Wild Nights"

"Last Lines"

Other Poems by Thomas Hardy

"The Man He Killed"

"The Reminder"

We suggest that you preview these works before recommending them to students.

INTERNET

For information on Emily Brontë, go to **http://members.tripod.com/~JeanneAnn/brontesis. html**

For information about Victorian authors, go to **http://www.stg.brown.edu/projects/hypertext/landow/victorian** and **http://humanitas.ucsb.edu/shuttle/engvict.html**

Please be aware that sites may have changed since this information was published. We *strongly recommend* that you preview sites before you send students to them.

◆ Critical Thinking

❹ Interpret Ask students what Hardy intended by this dramatic disclosure. *Students may note that Hardy intended this dark humor as an ironic comment on human vanity.*

◆ Literary Focus

❺ Stanza Form and Irony Have students explain how the structure of the last two stanzas upsets the expectations of the reader. *The final two stanzas break the question-and-answer pattern the reader has come to expect.*

Reinforce and Extend

Answers

◆ Literature and Your Life

Reader's Response Yes, the woman is pitiable and deserving of remembrance; no, the woman must not have been too lovable.

Thematic Focus Students may say that it is both—the notion of being forgotten after death is gloomy, but the way in which Hardy pokes fun at human vanity is humorous.

☑ Check Your Comprehension

1. (a) The speaker believes it is her widower who is digging. (b) The speaker believes it is her relatives. (c) The speaker believes it is her enemy.
2. (a) The digger is the speaker's dog. (b) The dog was burying a bone and forgot that this was its mistress's grave.

◆ Critical Thinking

1. (a) Students may say that they first begin to suspect the identity of the voice in the third stanza. (b) By withholding information, Hardy builds suspense and creates humor.
2. (a) Hardy creates a mock-melancholic mood by having a dead person as a speaker. (b) Any pretense of mourning has been cast aside.
3. We are never as important as we think we are.
4. Some students may argue yes, citing that people often are honored after death. Others may say that the poem's pessimism is offset by its humor.

Answers

◆ Literary Focus

1. (a) Each stanza is a quatrain—a stanza of four lines; the rhyme scheme is *abab.* (b) Suggested response: The last stanza creates a sense of irony as the speaker admits her potential weakness—to "indulge in Memory's rapturous pain"—after declaring her resolve to put her past behind her.
2. (a) The consistent form of the first four stanzas helps the reader understand that there are two speakers. The pattern also sets up expectations in the reader. (b) The pattern changes in the fifth stanza, in which the woman expresses her thoughts about why her little dog is digging upon her grave, and in the sixth, in which the dog replies and reveals the real—and unexpected—reason.

◆ Build Vocabulary

Using the Word Root *-terr(a)-*

1. *Terrain* means a tract of land or Earth.
2. *Terrestrial* means earthly, or related to the Earth.
3. *Subterranean* means beneath the Earth's surface.

Using the Word Bank

Although Brontë's hero, Heathcliff, is a terrestrial being, he has an almost supernatural aura. When parted from his beloved Cathy, he becomes gaunt and he languishes in ill health. After his reunion with Cathy, Heathcliff is rapturous.

◆ Reading Strategy

Read Stanza as Units of Meaning

1. (a) The speaker, addressing her lover's grave, asks if it is possible that she has forgotten their love, now that so much time has passed. (b) The speaker says that in order to live, she dare not remember her love.
2. Details such as "Frost was specter-gray," "Winter's dregs," "weakening eye of day," "tangled bine-stems," and "broken lyres" work together to convey a cold, gray, desolate setting and a bleak, hopeless mood.
3. Stanzas 1–3 introduce the idea that those who might be expected to remember the woman who died have in fact forgotten her. Stanzas 4–6 reveal that even the woman's hope that her little dog remembers her is in vain.

Guide for Responding *(continued)*

◆ Literary Focus

Stanza Forms and Irony

Each of these poems has a different type of **stanza form**, containing a set number of lines, rhythmic pattern, and rhyme scheme. However, each poem contains only one type of stanza, which sets up expectations in the reader and helps to give the poem balance. When this balance is upset by the introduction of a surprising idea or outcome, it creates an interesting contradiction or **irony**.

For example, in "The Darkling Thrush" the stanzas are octets and each line contains eight alternating weak-strong beats. The singsong quality of the stanzas combined with the bleak descriptions and gloomy outlook of the speaker creates an interesting contrast, making the poem memorable.

1. (a) Describe the type of stanza—number of lines, type of meter, if any, and rhyme scheme—used in "Remembrance." (b) Explain how the surprising thoughts of the speaker in "Remembrance" help to create a sense of irony.
2. (a) Explain how the consistent stanza form in "Ah, Are You Digging on My Grave?" helps you understand the poem's meaning. (b) In which stanza does the pattern change? How does this change create irony?

◆ Build Vocabulary

Using the Word Root *-terr(a)-*

Now that you are aware that the word root *-terr(a)-* is derived from a Latin word for "land," explain how these words relate to the meaning of the root.

1. terrain **2.** terrestrial **3.** subterranean

Using the Word Bank

Replace the underlined word or phrase with the correct word from the Word Bank. You will need to use an alternate form of one of the Word Bank words.

Although Brontë's hero, Heathcliff, is an earthly being, he has an almost supernatural aura. When parted from his beloved Cathy, he becomes very thin and he weakens in ill health. After his reunion with Cathy, Heathcliff is extremely happy.

◆ Reading Strategy

Read Stanzas as Units of Meaning

Once you discover **units of meaning** within stanzas of poems such as these, you'll be able to see the poem as a whole. For example, string together the main idea of each stanza and see if there's a progression of thoughts, sequence of events, or building argument within the poem.

1. (a) What is the overall meaning of the first stanza of "Remembrance"? (b) Given the title "Remembrance," what surprising attitude toward memory does the poem's speaker express in line 30?
2. Stanza one of "The Darkling Thrush" serves to create a setting and mood. Find details within the stanza that work together to do this.
3. Review the stanzas in "Ah, Are You Digging on My Grave?" Explain how the main ideas within the stanzas build to create a darkly humorous story.

◆ Grammar and Style

Pronoun Case Following *Than* or *As*

Sentences sometimes contain incomplete constructions, which contain omitted words whose meaning is understood. Incomplete constructions occur in real speech and in dialogue in poetry and prose. In an incomplete construction introduced by the words *than* or *as*, it's especially important to choose the correct **pronoun case** to complete the construction (*I, me, he, him, she, her, they, them*). To do this, mentally complete the sentence and it will become clear which pronoun to use.

Practice In your notebook, write the correct pronoun for each incomplete construction.

1. Charlotte Brontë was as talented as (she, her).
2. Brontë's *Jane Eyre* pleased me more than (he, him).
3. The bird had more hope than (he, him).
4. The dog was as forgetful as (I, me).
5. No group wrote more poetry than (they, them).

Writing Application Write a comparison involving two people or a person and a thing. Whenever you end a sentence with a pronoun that follows *than* or *as*, mentally complete the sentence to be sure you've chosen the correct pronoun.

◆ Grammar and Style

Pronoun Case Following *Than* or *As*

Practice

1. she; 2. him; 3. he; 4. I; 5. they

For additional instruction and practice, use the lesson in the **Language Lab CD-ROM** on Pronoun Case.

Build Your Portfolio

Idea Bank

Writing

1. **Remembrance** Write a remembrance of something past, like a winning football season, a friendship, or a summer long ago.

2. **Comparison and Contrast** Write an essay in which you compare and contrast Brontë's and Hardy's views of the passing of loved ones.

3. **Critical Essay** Hardy once said, "A sense of the truth of poetry, of its supreme place in literature, had awakened itself in me." Write an essay in which you agree or disagree with the idea that poetry has a "supreme place in literature." Use these poems to support your argument.

Speaking and Listening

4. **Dramatic Reading** Cast the parts of "Ah, Are You Digging on My Grave?" Then perform the poem for the class. **[Performing Arts Link]**

5. **Role-Play** The speaker of "Remembrance" is eager to embrace a world without love or pain. With a friend, role-play a scene in which a counselor gives advice to the speaker. **[Performing Arts Link]**

Projects

6. **Biography** Emily, Charlotte, and Anne Brontë were part of a remarkable family of writers. Learn more about the Brontës, and write a brief biography of their lives and accomplishments. **[Literature Link]**

7. **Timeline of the Century** In "The Darkling Thrush" Hardy tells of a bird's song of hope on the brink of the twentieth century. Show Hardy what has indeed happened this century by creating a timeline of significant events. **[Social Studies Link]**

Writing Mini-Lesson

Remembrance

Brontë's "Remembrance" is a sensitive, extremely personal memorial to a deceased love. Write your own memorial or remembrance of someone or something that is now absent from your life. For example, your remembrance could be about a favorite glove that got lost, a childhood pet, or a film star who passed away. An effective remembrance should convey the writer's personal views and attitudes about the subject.

Writing Skills Focus: Elaboration to Make Writing Personal

Put your own personal stamp on your writing to make it more believable and interesting. To do this, give specific details that reveal your responses to people, places, things, and ideas. Including candid details about your subject will draw your readers into your remembrance.

Prewriting Jot down those physical descriptions, remarks, or incidents that will help you bring the subject of your remembrance to life. Include details that reveal your personal ideas about the subject. Plan how you will fit these details together into a complete portrait.

Drafting Since you want to take your reader with you as you journey back in time, begin your draft with an interesting detail, quotation, or incident. Then weave together the details to create a full picture of the person, place, thing, or event you're describing.

Revising Ask some classmates to read your remembrance and respond to the following: Is the remembrance interesting? Does the writing contain enough personal details? Are any crucial details missing? Incorporate your classmates' suggestions into your final draft and proofread carefully.

Idea Bank

Customizing for
Learning Modalities
Following are suggestions for matching Idea Bank topics with your students' learning modalities:
Visual/Spatial: 7
Verbal/Linguistic: 1, 2, 3, 6
Musical/Rhythmic: 4
Interpersonal: 4, 5

Customizing for
Performance Levels
Following are suggestions for matching Idea Bank topics with your students' performance levels:
Less Advanced Students: 1, 4
Average Students: 2, 5, 7
More Advanced Students: 3, 6

Writing Mini-Lesson

Refer students to the Writing Process Handbook, page 1189, for instruction on the writing process, and page 1191 for further information on description.

Writing and Language Transparencies Use the Writing Process Model 1: Reflective Essay, pp. 5–12, to introduce students to the process of writing and editing a reflective essay such as a remembrance.

Writing Lab CD-ROM
Have students complete the tutorial on Description. Follow these steps:
1. Use the Sunburst Diagram to spark ideas for a remembrance.
2. Look at interactive examples of sensory details that will bring their remembrance to life.
3. Create a draft on the computer.
4. Use the Revision Checker for Vague Adjectives.

Sourcebook
Have students use Chapter 1, Description, pp. 1–27, for additional support. The chapter includes an annotated student model of a reflective essay.

✓ ASSESSMENT OPTIONS

Formal Assessment, Selection Test, pp. 216–218, and Assessment Resources Software. The selection test is designed so that it can be easily customized to the performance levels of your students.
Alternative Assessment, p. 43, includes options for students of varying learning modalities.

PORTFOLIO ASSESSMENT
Use the following rubrics in the ***Alternative Assessment*** booklet to assess student writing:
Remembrance: Description Rubric, p. 98
Comparison and Contrast: Comparison/Contrast Rubric, p. 104
Critical Essay: Literary Analysis Rubric, p. 113
Writing Mini-Lesson: Description Rubric, p. 98

Prepare and Engage

OBJECTIVES

1. To read and interpret four poems
2. To relate four poems to personal experience
3. To apply biography to gain insight into an author's work
4. To identify rhythm and meter
5. To build vocabulary in context and learn coined words
6. To use capitalization correctly with compass points
7. To write a literary analysis, presenting a thesis
8. To respond to the poems through writing, speaking and listening, and projects

SKILLS INSTRUCTION

Vocabulary: Coined Words
Grammar: Capitalization: Compass Points
Reading Strategy: Apply Biography
Literary Focus: Rhythm and Meter
Writing: Presenting a Thesis
Speaking and Listening: Newspaper Interview (teacher edition)
Critical Viewing: Apply

PORTFOLIO OPPORTUNITIES

Writing: Tribute; Comparative Analysis; Response to Criticism
Writing Mini-Lesson: Literary Analysis
Speaking and Listening: Victorian Poetry Contest; Newspaper Interview
Projects: Biographical Report; Multimedia Presentation

More About the Authors
Throughout his life, **Gerard Manley Hopkins** kept detailed journals and notebooks in which he recorded his love of nature.
A. E. Housman's *A Shropshire Lad* centers on rural life, but he wrote the poems in London, where he lived from 1886 to 1905.

Guide for Interpreting

Gerard Manley Hopkins (1844–1889)

The most innovative poet of the Victorian period, Hopkins did not publish a collection of his work during his lifetime. It was not until 1918 that a generation of poets could read, and be influenced by, his startling poetry.

Fearless Youth This quietly rebellious poet was born just outside of London, the oldest of eight children in a prosperous middle-class family. While in grammar school, he began to write poetry and also showed artistic talent. Although physically slight, he was fearless and would perch at the top of a tree for hours, swaying in the wind and observing the landscape.

A Life of Devotion After entering Oxford University, Hopkins decided to become a Catholic priest in the Jesuit order. His parents, who were devout Anglican Protestants, were dismayed. The discipline of Hopkins's religious vocation was sometimes at odds with his writing of verse. However, he found in the fourteenth-century theologian Duns Scotus a verification of his own ideas about the individuality of all things, from a pebble to a leaf to a person. Hopkins called this precious individuality *inscape*, and he tried to capture it in highly original poems like "God's Grandeur" and "Spring and Fall."

Meanwhile, he worked tirelessly among the poor, dying of typhoid fever a month before his forty-fifth birthday.

A. E. Housman (1859–1936)

A man of solitary habits and harsh self-discipline, Housman was also capable of creating delicately crafted poems, full of gentle regret.

Challenges of Youth He grew up in Worcestershire, a region northwest of London. His childhood came to an end on his twelfth birthday, when his mother died. Later, at Oxford University, his despair over unrequited love darkened his life still further. Perhaps because of this double grief, his poetry has bitter undertones.

Upon leaving Oxford, Housman went to work in the Patent Office. Determined to prove himself in the classics, he studied Greek and Latin at night and wrote scholarly articles. In 1892, his hard work paid off when he won a position as professor of Latin at University College in London.

Literary Success Though Housman spent most of his life engaged in teaching and scholarly pursuits, he is most remembered for three slender volumes of poetry that are as romantic and melancholy as any ever written. His first and most famous collection of verse, *A Shropshire Lad* (1896), has as its fictitious narrator a homesick farm boy living in the city.

Housman's image is that of an emotionless intellectual, but his poems display deep feelings. He himself maintained that a good poem should affect readers like a shiver down the spine or a punch in the stomach.

◆ Background for Understanding

LITERATURE: GERARD MANLEY HOPKINS, FROM OBSCURITY TO FAME

It is a surprising fact that when Gerard Manley Hopkins died, none of his obituaries mentioned that he was a poet! Only a few close friends knew that he was the author of highly original poems.

Chief among these friends was Oxford classmate Robert Bridges who was later to become the British Poet Laureate. Bridges was interested in the subject of rhythm in poetry and took an interest in Hopkins's experiments with sprung rhythm.

It was through Bridges's efforts that the first collection of Hopkins's poetry was published in 1918. Today Robert Bridges is little known, but his once-obscure friend Gerard Manley Hopkins is a famous Victorian poet!

Prentice Hall Literature Program Resources

REINFORCE / RETEACH / EXTEND

Selection Support Pages
Build Vocabulary: Coined Words, p. 212
Grammar and Style: Capitalization: Compass Points, p. 213
Reading Strategy: Apply Biography, p. 214
Literary Focus: Rhythm and Meter, p. 215

Strategies for Diverse Student Needs, p. 44

Beyond Literature Cross-Curricular Connection: Social Studies, p. 44

Formal Assessment Selection Test, pp. 219–221; Assessment Resources Software

Alternative Assessment, p. 44

Writing and Language Transparencies
Writing Process Model 6: Interpreting a Work of Literature, pp. 45–55
Analysis Map, p. 111

Resource Pro CD-ROM
"God's Grandeur," "Spring and Fall . . .," "To an Athlete . . .," "When I Was One-and-Twenty"—includes all resource material and customizable lesson plan

Listening to Literature Audiocassettes "God's Grandeur," "Spring and Fall . . .," "To an Athlete . . .," "When I Was One-and-Twenty"

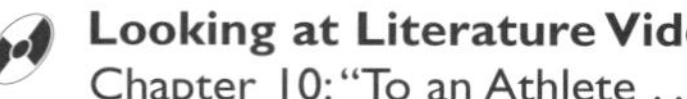

Looking at Literature Videodisc
Chapter 10: "To an Athlete . . ."

Writers at Work Videodisc
Chapter 7: Eavan Boland

God's Grandeur ◆ Spring and Fall: To a Young Child
To an Athlete Dying Young ◆ When I Was One-and-Twenty

◆ Literature and Your Life

Connect Your Experience

As you enter each new period of your life, your views change. Certainly the games you played as a small child might bore you now, just as the fears you had then may seem petty today. In several of these poems, Hopkins and Housman examine how the passing of time colors emotions and changes priorities.

Journal Writing Briefly explain how your understanding of a word like *work* has deepened as you have grown.

Thematic Focus: Gloom and Glory

How do these poets express, sometimes in the same poem, the pain and triumph of living and growing?

◆ Literary Focus

Rhythm and Meter

Rhythm refers to the flow and movement of words in a poem, and poetry without a regular rhythm is called **free verse**. However, before the twentieth century, most poets wrote **metrical verse**, with set patterns of stressed and unstressed syllables.

The unit of metrical poetry is the **foot**, a combination of stressed and unstressed syllables. Common feet in English are the **iamb** (ī′am)—unstressed, stressed (˘ ′)—and the **trochee** (trō′ kē)—stressed, unstressed (′ ˘). Number of feet per line is indicated by terms like **trimeter**, **tetrameter**, and **pentameter**—three, four, and five feet per line, respectively. Iambic tetrameter would be verse with four iambic feet per line.

Housman uses such regular meters as iambic and trochaic tetrameter. Hopkins, however, anticipates twentieth-century, free-verse poets by trying to develop rhythms more natural to speech. One experiment is **counterpoint rhythm** ("God's Grandeur"), in which two opposing rhythms appear together. Two trochaic feet, for example, can pop up in the middle of an iambic line:

> Thĕ wórld ĭs chárged wĭth thĕ grándeŭr ŏf Gód.

Another, more famous, Hopkins experiment is **sprung rhythm** ("Spring and Fall"), in which all feet begin with a stressed syllable and contain a varying number of unstressed syllables. In sprung rhythm, Hopkins often joins lines to form a rhythmic unit and marks stressed syllables with accents:

> Márgarét, áre you gríeving…

◆ Reading Strategy

Apply Biography

You can often get more from your reading by applying what you know about an author's life to his or her work.

Reread the authors' biographies on p. 856 to find evidence of Housman's self-restraint and bitterness, and Hopkins's religious beliefs and love of nature.

◆ Build Vocabulary

Coined Words

Gerard Manley Hopkins sometimes combines old words to make new ones. In "Spring and Fall," Hopkins coins the words *wanwood* and *leafmeal,* which mean "pale trees" and "ground-up, mealy leaves," respectively.

Word Bank

Preview these words before you read.

grandeur
blight
rue

◆ Grammar and Style

Capitalization: Compass Points

In "God's Grandeur," words referring to specific regions are capitalized. Words that merely indicate direction are not: "last lights off the black *West went* . . . /. . . morning . . . *eastward*, springs—"

Interest Grabber

To build students' awareness of rhythm and meter, bring in a recording of rap music and encourage them to analyze the pattern of beats in the music. Inform them that Gerard Manley Hopkins was a pioneer in inventing poetic rhythms, much as rap revolutionized the music industry with its compelling and insistent rhythms.

Customize for *English Language Learners*

English language learners may be confused by the coined words used by Hopkins. Explain how words can be combined to form new words in English, giving recent examples such as *software* and *laptop*.

Customize for *Musical/Rhythmic Learners*

These students will be most attuned to the rhythms and meter of the poems. Encourage them to meet in small groups and read the poems aloud, focusing on the rhythm and other sound effects used by the poets, and perhaps adding sound effects or music of their own. These students may also enjoy participating in the Victorian Poetry Contest idea in the Idea Bank on page 863.

Preparing for Standardized Tests

Reading and Vocabulary Students taking the Advanced Placement test in English will benefit from the Literary Focus: Rhythm and Meter and from the Reading Strategy: Apply Biography, both on page 857. Understanding that there is often a link between a writer's life and his or her works will help students to analyze and criticize literature thoughtfully. The Reading Strategy, page 214 in ***Selection Support***, focuses on relating biographical information on the author to his or her works.

Grammar and Language The grammar lesson for this selection focuses on when to capitalize the compass points *north, south, east,* and *west.* Students might encounter this issue when questions on standardized tests ask them to correct grammatical errors. You can reinforce this skill by using the Grammar and Style page on Capitalization: Compass Points, on page 213 of ***Selection Support***.

Develop Understanding

One-Minute Insight Hopkins's devotional stance toward nature is similar to that of the Romantic poets, although Hopkins's poetry has a stronger religious theme. In "God's Grandeur," Hopkins marvels at how the glory of God shines out through all of nature, even though most people no longer see it clearly because they have corrupted nature or insulated themselves against it. In "Spring and Fall," Hopkins reflects on how a young girl is intuitively responding to a sense of her own mortality as she mourns the falling leaves in autumn. As she grows up, she may lament her mortality more knowingly but not more truly than she does now.

◆ Critical Thinking

❶ **Analyze** Ask student with what force of nature the verb *charge* is usually associated. Then ask them what effect the word has as used here. *The word charged is usually associated with electricity. By using the word here, Hopkins invests God with an electrical, dynamic presence.*

❷ **Clarification** Tell students that in Christian theology the Holy Ghost, or Holy Spirit, is believed to be one aspect of God. The other two are the Father (or Creator) and the Son (or Redeemer). The Holy Ghost is often symbolized as a dove, and that is why Hopkins uses bird imagery to describe its presence in the world.

◆ Reading Strategy

❸ **Apply Biography** Have students reread Hopkins's biography on page 856. Then ask what two lifelong passions of his are linked in this stanza. *He links his love of nature with his religious feelings, connecting "the dearest freshness deep down things" in nature with his religious belief in the presence of the Holy Ghost.*

▶Critical Viewing◀

❹ **Apply** The painting reflects Hopkins's ideas because it focuses on small details of nature in an intense way. The painting reveals the "freshness" of natural glory in the world, a freshness that is never "spent," despite the intrusions of humanity.

God's Grandeur

Gerard Manley Hopkins

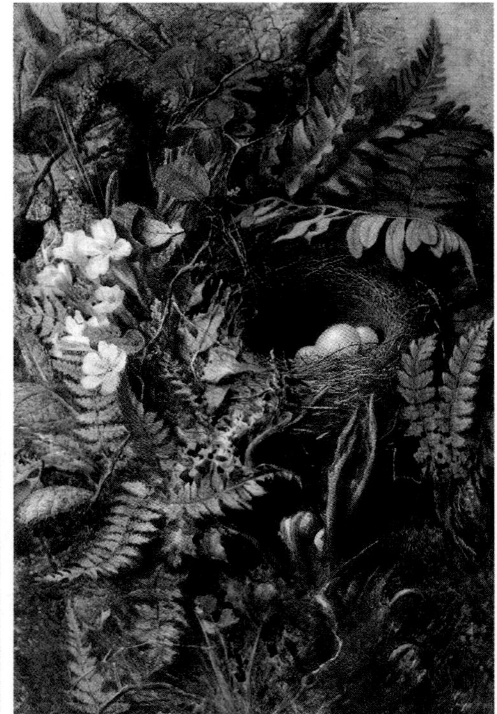

Bird's Nest, Ros. W. Jenkins, Warrington Museum and Art Gallery

◀ **Critical Viewing** How does this painting reflect Hopkins's ideas in "God's Grandeur"? **[Apply]**

❶ The world is charged with the grandeur of God.
It will flame out, like shining from shook foil;[1]
It gathers to a greatness, like the ooze of oil
Crushed.[2] Why do men then now not reck his rod?[3]
Generations have trod, have trod, have trod;
And all is seared with trade; bleared, smeared with toil;
And wears man's smudge and shares man's smell: the soil
Is bare now, nor can foot feel, being shod.

And for all this, nature is never spent;
There lives the dearest freshness deep down things;
❷ And though the last lights off the black West went
Oh, morning, at the brown brink eastward, springs—
❸ Because the Holy Ghost over the bent
World broods with warm breast and with ah! bright wings.

1. **foil** *n.*: Tinsel.
2. **crushed:** Squeezed from olives.
3. **reck his rod:** Heed God's authority.

Block Scheduling Strategies

Consider the following suggestions to take advantage of extended class time:

- Introduce the concept of rhythm and meter in Literary Focus on page 857. Then direct students to work in pairs or small groups to tap out the rhythm and analyze the meter of one or more of the poems. When they have finished reading, have them answer the Literary Focus questions on page 862.
- Review the examples of coined words in context in the poems. Then have students answer the Build Vocabulary questions on page 862 and complete the Build Vocabulary page in ***Selection Support***, p. 212.
- When students have finished reading the Hopkins poems, play the recorded version for them on **Listening to Literature Audiocassettes.** Then hold a discussion about whether or not the poems' rhythms were enhanced when they were read aloud.
- Have students work individually to complete an activity from the Idea Bank on page 863.

Spring and Fall: To a Young Child

Gerard Manley Hopkins

Márgarét, áre you grieving
Over Goldengrove unleaving?
Leáves, like the things of man, you
With your fresh thoughts care for, can you?
Áh! ás the heart grows older
It will come to such sights colder
By and by, nor spare a sigh
Though worlds of wanwood[1] leafmeal[2] lie;
And yet you will weep and know why.
Now no matter, child, the name:
❺ Sórrow's springs áre the same.
Nor mouth had, no nor mind, expressed
What heart heard of, ghost[3] guessed:
❻ It is the blight man was born for,
It is Margaret you mourn for.

1. **wanwood** (wän´ wood): Pale wood.
2. **leafmeal:** Ground-up decomposed leaves.
3. **ghost:** Spirit.

◆ Build Vocabulary

grandeur (grän´ jər) *n.*: Splendor, magnificence

blight (blīt) *n.*: Condition of withering

Guide for Responding

◆ Literature and Your Life

Reader's Response In which of these two poems do you find the more meaningful sentiment? Explain.

Thematic Focus What aspects of life, according to these poems, seem to make Hopkins feel gloomy?

☑ Check Your Comprehension

1. According to lines 5–8 of "God's Grandeur," what has humanity done to God's grandeur?
2. What has been the effect on the nature of humankind's behavior? Explain.
3. (a) To what is the Holy Ghost compared in lines 13-14? (b) What verb describes its action?
4. What is making Margaret unhappy in "Spring and Fall"?
5. According to the speaker, in what way will Margaret change as she grows older?

◆ Critical Thinking

INTERPRET

1. What opposition is present in lines 1–8 of "God's Grandeur"? **[Analyze]**
2. How does Hopkins resolve that opposition? **[Draw Conclusions]**
3. Explain how the speaker in "Spring and Fall" suggests Margaret will outgrow and not outgrow this sadness. **[Interpret]**
4. In what way is this a poem about death? **[Support]**
5. What lesson does the speaker offer to Margaret in this poem? **[Draw Conclusions]**

EVALUATE

6. Would you consider Hopkins's general outlook in "God's Grandeur" optimistic or pessimistic? Explain. **[Classify]**
7. Is the lesson in "Spring and Fall" a good one for a child to learn? Why or why not? **[Criticize]**

◆ Critical Thinking

❺ **Analyze** Ask: What meanings can you attach to the word *springs*? *It can mean a season, a flow of water or a mechanism.*

◆ Critical Thinking

❻ **Interpret** Ask students what is the "blight" of man? *Mortality is the blight of man.*

Reinforce and Extend

Answers

◆ Literature and Your Life

Reader's Response Students should support answers with details.

Thematic Focus Hopkins may be saddened by human "treading" on nature and by mortality.

☑ Check Your Comprehension

1. People have tainted nature with trade and toil.
2. In spite of humanity's incursions, "nature is never spent."
3. (a) The Holy Ghost is compared to a bird. (b) It "broods" over the world.
4. She is unhappy because the leaves are falling off the trees.
5. As she grows older, Margaret will mourn for her own mortality.

◆ Critical Thinking

1. Lines 1–8 present an opposition between God's grandeur in nature and the power of humans to obscure it.
2. He asserts that no matter what people do, they can never obliterate God's grandeur in nature.
3. Margaret will always be sad, but as she grows older, she will be sad for herself.
4. The seasonal death of leaves and plants in fall is a reminder of human mortality.
5. The speaker teaches Margaret that death is a part of the human condition.
6. Most students will say that the poem is optimistic because the Holy Ghost is present, tending to nature.
7. Students should support their answers.

Humanities: Art

Bird's Nest by Ros. W. Jenkins.

This depiction of a bird's nest filled with eggs resting on a forest floor is typical of the kind of artwork that Victorians were delighted to hang in their homes. Influenced by the Pre-Raphaelite Movement, Jenkins uses intense detail to create an image true to nature.

Ros. W. Jenkins was a British watercolorist of the Victorian era. Inspired by fellow British painter William Henry Hunt, Jenkins builds up layers of color and then creates detail by stippling (applying dots of color) and crosshatching (using a grid of intersecting lines to create texture).

Use these questions for discussion:

1. How does this artist seem to regard nature? *He seems delighted by the smallest details of natural life and wants to record them as closely as possible so that other people can share them.*
2. Which passage in "God's Grandeur" most closely matches the content of this painting? *The closest match is in lines 13 and 14: "Because the Holy Ghost over the bent / World broods with warm breast and with ah! bright wings."*

One-Minute Insight In two of his most famous poems, "To an Athlete Dying Young" and "When I was One-and-Twenty," A. E. Housman reflects on the fleeting glories of youth and the inevitable disillusionment that comes with age and experience. However, he gives the theme of disillusionment an ironic, humorous twist by having a young man voice it in a world-weary tone ("When I was One-and-Twenty").

Looking at Literature Videodisc Play Chapter 10: "To an Athlete Dying Young" for students before they read the selections to introduce the topic of trials and hardships of athletes.

Chapter 10

◆ Literary Focus

1 Rhythm and Meter Ask students how the rhythm of line 3 varies from that of lines 1, 2, and 4. *Each line has four stressed syllables. Lines 1, 2, and 4 are iambic because each foot has one unstressed syllable followed by one stressed syllable. Line 3, however, is trochaic: Each of the first three feet has one stressed syllable followed by one unstressed syllable.*

◆ Critical Thinking

2 Interpret Have students use the title of the poem as a clue to help them interpret what is now being carried "Shoulder-high" and what "stiller town" the runner is now being carried to. *The runner's dead body is now being carried in a coffin. He is being brought to the "stiller town" of the cemetery.*

3 Clarification This is an inverted sentence; its subject is "the strengthless dead."

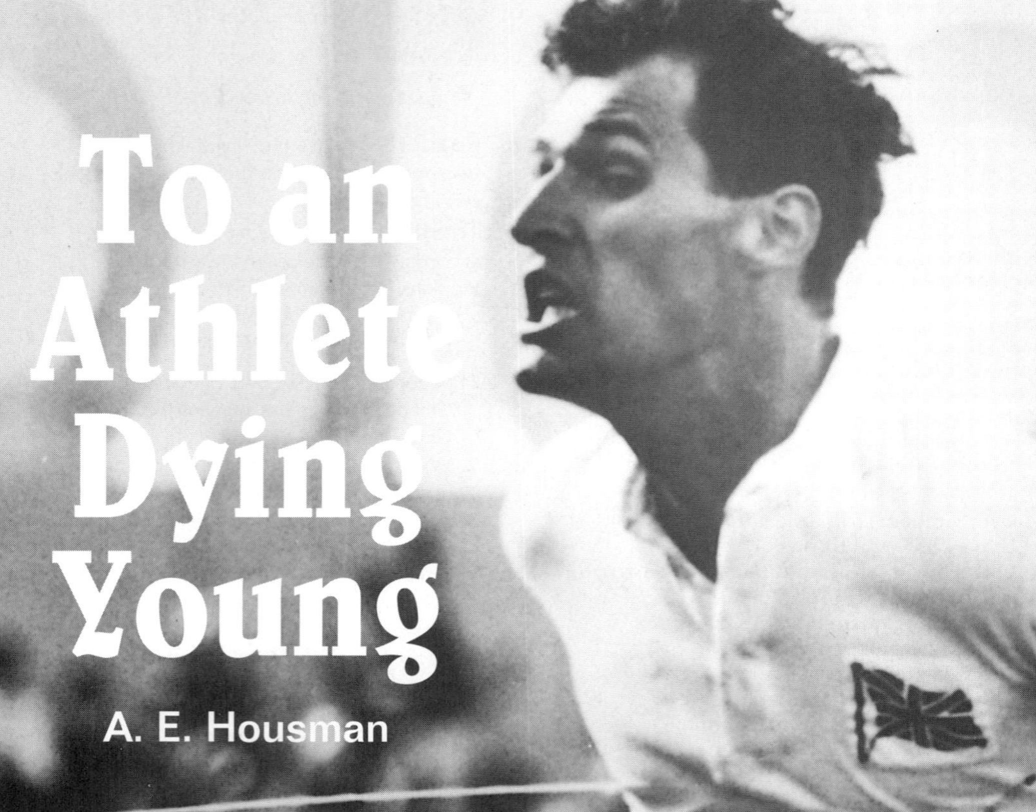

To an Athlete Dying Young

A. E. Housman

(1) The time you won your town the race
We chaired you through the marketplace;
Man and boy stood cheering by,
And home we brought you shoulder-high.

(2) Today, the road all runners come,
Shoulder-high we bring you home,
And set you at your threshold down,
Townsman of a stiller town.

Smart lad, to slip betimes away
From fields where glory does not stay
And early though the laurel[1] grows
It withers quicker than the rose.

Eyes the shady night has shut
Cannot see the record cut,
And silence sounds no worse than cheers
After earth has stopped the ears:

Now you will not swell the rout
Of lads that wore their honors out,
Runners whom renown outran
And the name died before the man.

So set, before its echoes fade,
The fleet foot on the sill of shade,
And hold to the low lintel up
The still-defended challenge cup.

(3) And round that early-laureled head
Will flock to gaze the strengthless dead,
And find unwithered on its curls
The garland briefer than a girl's.

1. **laurel:** Symbol of victory.

Speaking and Listening Mini-Lesson

Newspaper Interview

This mini-lesson supports the Speaking and Listening activity in the Idea Bank on page 863.

Introduce the Concept The interviewer should ask specific, clear, engaging questions. The person being interviewed should use listening skills to understand what is being asked and speaking skills to convey clearly his or her answers and attitudes.

Develop Background Present the following information:

- The interviewer may ask questions that he or she personally already knows the answers to, but that readers do not.
- A newspaper interviewer may ask the subject to clarify answers for the average reader.
- The subject's replies will convey not only answers, but his or her attitude and other clues to his or her personality.

Apply the Information Have pairs of students conduct their interview sessions in front of the class, as if the interview were taking place on a television show.

Assess the Outcome When interviews are concluded, have the class assess the effectiveness of the interview based on the content, originality, and quality of the questions asked and the responses given.

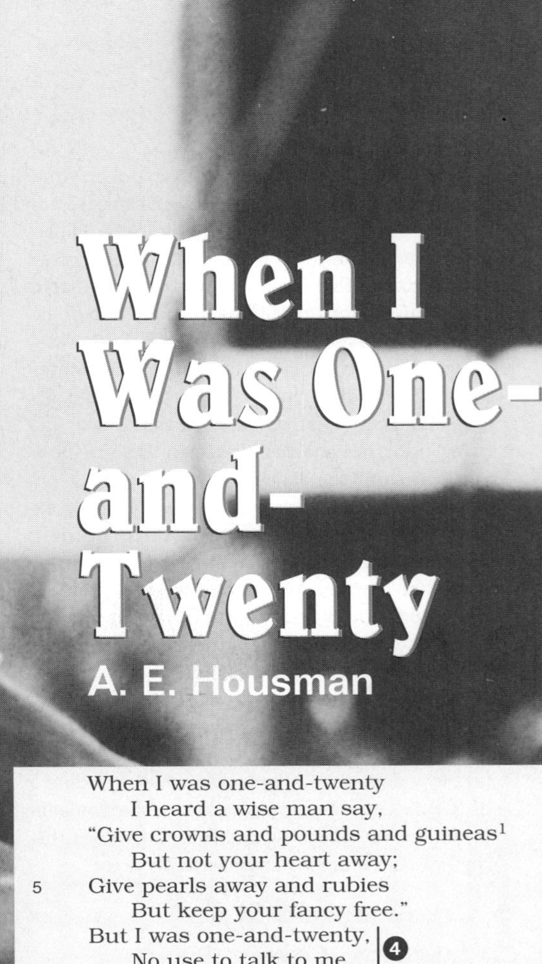

When I Was One-and-Twenty

A. E. Housman

When I was one-and-twenty
I heard a wise man say,
"Give crowns and pounds and guineas[1]
But not your heart away;
Give pearls away and rubies
But keep your fancy free."
But I was one-and-twenty, ❹
No use to talk to me.

When I was one-and-twenty
I heard him say again,
"The heart out of the bosom
Was never given in vain;
'Tis paid with sighs a plenty ❺
And sold for endless rue."
And I am two-and-twenty,
And oh, 'tis true, 'tis true.

1. **crowns . . . guineas:** Denominations of money.

◆ Build Vocabulary

rue (ro͞o) *n.*: Sorrow

Guide for Responding

◆ Literature and Your Life

Reader's Response If you were the young athlete Housman is addressing and could respond from beyond the grave, what would you say to the poet?

Thematic Focus Which of these two poems is the more gloomy? Why?

☑ Check Your Comprehension

1. In "To an Athlete Dying Young," in what sport did the athlete excel?
2. How did the townspeople show their admiration for the athlete?
3. In "When I Was One-and-Twenty," what advice did the speaker receive and how did he react?
4. (a) What is the second piece of advice the speaker receives?

◆ Critical Thinking

INTERPRET

1. (a) What visual image appears in each of the first two stanzas of "To an Athlete"? (b) How is the meaning of the image different in the second stanza? **[Interpret]**
2. (a) Summarize the speaker's comments in lines 9–20 of "To an Athlete." (b) What is meant by "the name died before the man"? **[Interpret]**
3. Does Housman believe completely that the young athlete was "smart" to die? Explain. **[Draw Conclusions]**
4. What clues are there in "When I Was One-and-Twenty" that Housman is mocking his speaker? **[Interpret]**

APPLY

5. Suppose you were to take a different position on the death of the young athlete. How would you modify the poem? **[Modify]**

EXTEND

6. Compare and contrast the attitude toward youth in both these poems.

◆ Literature and Your Life

❹ Ask students if they have ever received advice that they ignored and didn't appreciate until it was too late.

◆ Reading Strategy

❺ **Apply Biography** Ask students what event in Housman's life may have inspired "When I Was One-and-Twenty." *The poem may have been inspired by Housman's sadness over unrequited love.*

Reinforce and Extend

Answers

◆ Literature and Your Life

Reader's Response Students should respond to points made in the poem.

Thematic Focus "To an Athlete Dying Young" may seem gloomier, since it reacts to death.

☑ Check Your Comprehension

1. The athlete excelled at running.
2. After his victory, they carried the athlete home on their shoulders.
3. He was told not to fall in love. He ignored the advice.
4. The speaker was told he would pay with sighs for falling in love.

◆ Critical Thinking

1. (a) The visual image of the athlete being carried "shoulder high" appears. (b) The meaning is different in the second stanza because now the athlete is dead.
2. (a) The athlete was smart to die at the peak of his glory so that he will not join the ranks of those who outlived their honors. (b) It means outliving one's fame.
3. Suggested response: No, Housman does not believe the runner was "smart" to die. He is merely trying to console himself.
4. The line "And I am two-and-twenty" shows that the speaker takes his new wisdom a bit too seriously.
5. Students might say that instead of focusing on the losses the athlete was spared by dying young, they might have focused on what further glory he might have achieved.
6. Both comment on the fleeting quality of youth. "To an Athlete," however, mourns a death, while "One-And-Twenty" humorously comments on the folly of youth.

Beyond the Selection

FURTHER READING

Other Poems by Gerard Manley Hopkins

"Pied Beauty"
"The Windhover"

Other Poems by A. E. Housman

"Loveliest of Trees"
"Reveille"

We suggest that you preview these works before recommending them to students.

INTERNET

For more information on Gerard Manley Hopkins, go to **http://www.creighton.edu/~dcallon/gmhpage.html**

For poems by both Housman and Hopkins, go to **http://english.cla.umn.edu/CourseWeb.1017/Poetry Wall**

Please be aware that sites may have changed since this information was published. We *strongly recommend* that you preview sites before you send students to them.

Answers

◆ Reading Strategy

1. Sample answer: (a) The phrase "dearest freshness deep down things" reflects Hopkins's belief that nature's freshness is not only beautiful but also enduring. (b) By inventing and using the word *leafmeal*, Hopkins calls attention to the mealy collective texture of the leaves, a unique quality.
2. Sample answer: (a) Housman was melancholy, disciplined, and inventive. (b) His melancholy is reflected in the overall theme of "To an Athlete Dying Young"; his discipline is reflected in his well-crafted verse; his inventiveness is revealed by the surprise ending—that is, the last two lines—of "When I was One-and-Twenty."

◆ Build Vocabulary

Using Coined Words

Sample answer: At the *summerend* a few *chillmorns* remind us that the *snow-lawns* of winter can't be far away.

Using the Word Bank

1. blight; 2. rue; 3. grandeur

◆ Literary Focus

1. (a) The meter is iambic trimeter. (The last foot in line 1 has an extra unstressed syllable; this is known as a feminine ending.) (b) The predictable, slightly singsong quality of the meter makes the speaker seem a bit silly.
2. (a) Possible answer: The initial two trochees capture the heaviness of the generations treading, while the three iambs and the repeated words "have trod, have trod, have trod" capture the mechanical quality of the treading. (b) The bunching of stressed syllables at the beginning of the line emphasizes the point that certain sorrows are inevitable and universal. The stress on the word *are* is strongly emphatic.

◆ Grammar and Style

Capitalization: Compass Points

1. northwest
2. southwest
3. northwest
4. West
5. west

Guide for Responding (continued)

◆ Reading Strategy

Apply Biography

Knowing about these poets' lives can give you greater insight into their work. Hopkins's biography, for example, suggests that he was deeply religious, loved nature, and looked for the uniqueness in things, their *inscape*. The first two lines of "God's Grandeur" reflect his religious nature—he senses the magnificence of God everywhere in the world. They also suggest his eye for the uniqueness of "shook foil" and the way in which it shines out.

1. (a) Find an image or phrase in "God's Grandeur" that reflects Hopkins's love of nature and explain your choice. (b) In "Spring and Fall," how does the coined word *leafmeal* show Hopkins's eye for the uniqueness of fallen leaves?

2. (a) List three traits or qualities of Housman suggested by his biography. (b) Explain how each of these is reflected in a specific word, phrase, or idea from a poem.

◆ Build Vocabulary

Using Coined Words

Hopkins combines *wan*, meaning "pale," and *wood* to make a new word, *wanwood*, that describes pale-looking trees in autumn. He also coins *leafmeal* to describe dead leaves ground into a kind of meal.

Imitate Hopkins and replace each italicized phrase in the following sentence with a new, understandable combination-word:

At the *end of summer* a few *chilly mornings* remind us that the *snow-covered lawns* of winter can't be far away.

Using the Word Bank

In your notebook write the word bank word that best matches the meaning of the underlined word or phrase.

1. The apple tree looks withered due to a ravaging disease.

2. Leave your sadness behind and begin rejoicing.

3. My eyes were dazzled by the magnificence of the blooming field of flowers.

◆ Literary Focus

Rhythm and Meter

As you read the work of these two poets, you probably sensed the **rhythmic** flow of stressed and unstressed syllables. Hopkins and Housman differ sharply, however, in their approach to **meter**, the regular pattern of stressed and unstressed syllables.

Housman is more traditional, although he does use variations in meter. In lines 1–8 of "To an Athlete," for example, he varies the iambic tetrameter with three lines of trochaic tetrameter (lines 3, 6, and 8). The trochee (stressed, unstressed) is a "slower" foot and enables Housman to show how death "slows up" the runner.

Hopkins reinforces his meanings with daring experiments like the two opposing **counterpoint rhythms** in line 5 of "God's Grandeur": The first two feet are trochaic and the last three iambic. Still more daring is the **sprung rhythm** of "Spring and Fall," with stresses that pile up like fallen leaves (as in line 11, where a single stress can be a foot).

1. (a) Identify the meter in the first two lines of "One-and-Twenty." (b) In what way does the meter make the speaker seem a bit silly?

2. (a) How does the counterpoint rhythm in line 5 of "God's Grandeur" reinforce the line's meaning? (b) In line 11 of "Spring and Fall," how does the rhythm help Hopkins emphasize his point?

◆ Grammar and Style

Capitalization: Compass Points

Compass points referring to places are capitalized, but those indicating direction are not.

Practice On your paper, choose a capital or lower-case letter for each compass point.

1. Housman's Shropshire is located n/Northwest of London.

2. The Shropshire lad would have traveled s/Southeast to get to London.

3. Hopkins traveled n/Northwest from London to attend Oxford University.

4. Worcestershire, Housman's birthplace, is in the w/West of England, near the Severn river.

5. Ireland, where Hopkins served as a priest, is an island w/West of England.

Build Your Portfolio

Idea Bank

Writing

1. **Tribute** Hopkins writes a poetic tribute to an athlete who died young. Write a tribute in prose to a professional athlete who is still living.

2. **Comparative Analysis** Write a comparative analysis of the work of Hopkins and Housman. Consider such elements as meter, attitude of the poets toward their subjects, and theme.

3. **Response to Criticism** W. H. Gardner writes, "Of all poets who have revered Shakespeare, Hopkins has learnt most from the master's skill in utilizing the full resources of the English language." Agree or disagree, citing specific passages.

Speaking and Listening

4. **Victorian Poetry Contest** Have a Hopkins team and a Housman team alternate in giving readings of their poet's work. Measure audience reaction to the readings and declare a winner. **[Performing Arts Link]**

5. **Newspaper Interview** With a partner, role-play a newspaper interview with Robert Bridges in 1918, just after he has published Hopkins's work. Remember that few readers will have heard of Hopkins. **[Media Link]**

Projects

6. **Biographical Report** Read a biography of one of these poets, such as Robert Bernard Martin's *Gerard Manley Hopkins: A Very Private Life*, and report on it to the class.

7. **Multimedia Presentation** Both of these poets attended Oxford University. Use readings, photographs, film clips, and artifacts to give a presentation on Oxford today. **[Social Studies Link]**

Writing Mini-Lesson

Literary Analysis

Choose one of the four poems in this group. Then write an essay in which you analyze the poem's theme, or central message. Explain how the various elements of the poem—the images, the speaker, the tone, the main character, and so on—work together to convey the theme. Keep the following tip in mind as you develop your analysis.

Writing Skills Focus: Presenting a Thesis

Like many other types of writing, a literary analysis should be built around a thesis—a main point or general conclusion about the topic. All of the details presented should support the thesis. In a literary analysis the most effective support for a thesis usually consists of passages and details from the work.

Prewriting Start by reviewing the poem you've chosen. Read it over several times, considering the following questions: What is the poem about? Who is the poem's speaker? What is the speaker's attitude toward the subject? Which images stand out? Why? Use your answers to these questions to help you reach a conclusion about the poem's theme.

Drafting Start with an introduction in which you state your thesis in a sentence or two. Follow with a series of paragraphs in which you develop and support your thesis. Each of your body paragraphs should focus on a single subpoint of your thesis. In each paragraph cite details and passages from the poem for support. End your paper with a conclusion in which you restate your thesis.

Revising As you revise, look for places where you can add support for your thesis. In addition, eliminate any sections of your paper that do not directly relate to your thesis.

✓ ASSESSMENT OPTIONS

Formal Assessment, Selection Test, pp. 219–221, and Assessment Resources Software. The selection test is designed so that it can be easily customized to the performance levels of your students. ***Alternative Assessment,*** p. 44, includes options for less advanced students, more advanced students, musical/rhythmic learners, verbal/linguistic learners, and visual/spatial learners.

PORTFOLIO ASSESSMENT

Use the following rubrics in the ***Alternative Assessment*** booklet to assess student writing:
Tribute: Expression Rubric, p. 95
Comparative Analysis: Comparison/Contrast Rubric, p. 104
Response to Criticism: Literary Analysis/ Interpretation Rubric, p. 113
Writing Mini-Lesson: Literary Analysis/ Interpretation Rubric, p. 113

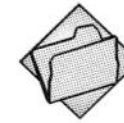

Idea Bank

Customizing for *Learning Modalities*

Following are suggestions for matching Idea Bank topics with your students' learning modalities:

Visual/Spatial: 7
Verbal/Linguistic: 1, 2, 3, 6
Interpersonal: 5
Musical/Rhythmic: 4

Customizing for *Performance Levels*

Following are suggestions for matching Idea Bank topics with your students' performance levels:

Less Advanced Students: 1, 4
Average Students: 2, 5, 7
More Advanced Students: 3, 6

Writing Mini-Lesson

Refer students to the Writing Process Handbook, page 1189, for instruction on the writing process, and page 1193 for further information on response to literature.

Writing and Language Transparencies Use the Writing Process Model 6: Interpreting a Work of Literature, pp. 45–56, to model the process of writing a literary analysis. You may want to copy and distribute the Analysis Map, p. 112.

Writers at Work Videodisc

Have students view the videodisc segment on Responding to Literature, Chapter 7, featuring poet Eavan Boland, to see how she typically responds to literature.

Play frames 21571 to 31063

Writing Lab CD-ROM

Have students use the tutorial on Response to Literature, following these steps:

1. View interactive tips for responding to different aspects of literature.
2. Create a draft on the computer.
3. Look at an audio-annotated student model for tips on revision.

Sourcebook

Have students use Chapter 7, Response to Literature, pp. 196–229, for additional support.

Prepare and Engage

OBJECTIVES

1. To read and interpret a poem
2. To explore the thematic connections between poems of different cultures
3. To respond to "Eternity" through writing, speaking and listening, and projects

PORTFOLIO OPPORTUNITIES

Writing: Perfect Place; Dictionary of Abstract Words; Response to Criticism
Speaking and Listening: Ask the Poet
Projects: Past Glory; Multimedia Presentation

More About the Author
Arthur Rimbaud grew up in a poor household and was raised by his mother after his father abandoned the family when Rimbaud was only six years old. Rimbaud was a quiet, industrious student until, at the age of fifteen, he rebelled and ran away to Paris. He became a defining contributor to the French Symbolist movement in poetry. The Symbolists—forerunners of the surrealists—tried to express the mysteriousness of human consciousness, using their own esoteric metaphors and symbols.

Customize for
Logical/Mathematical Learners
Have these students explain the mathematical concept of *infinity* to the class. Ask them to compare the concept of *infinity* to that of *eternity*—both as most people understand the word *eternity* and as Rimbaud envisions it.

Have students recall depictions of eternity in movies, advertisements, and literary works. What images from the temporal (changing) world have been used to depict that which never changes (eternity)? Tell students that, in the poem that follows, Rimbaud does not put forward a simple image of eternity. Instead, he uses complex images, abstract ideas, and suggestive words to indicate a complex truth. In this way, he sets the reader's mind in motion.

CONNECTIONS TO WORLD LITERATURE

Eternity
Arthur Rimbaud

Thematic Connection

GLOOM AND GLORY

The Victorian period marks a time of great progress for the British Empire. It also marks the beginning of its decline. The poems in this section reflect the passing of glory as part of a cyclical process of growth and decline. For example, in Gerard Manley Hopkins's poem "Spring and Fall: To a Young Child" he provides a contrast between birth and the decay that follows later in life. Thomas Hardy and A. E. Housman reinforce the contrast by juxtaposing the glory of life with the gloom of death. In "Ah, Are You Digging on My Grave?" Hardy offers the disturbing truth that we are never as important as we think we are. The poets examine their place in life and its cycles. While celebrating life, the poets also warn of assuming too much importance, for all must come to an end, just as the empire came to an end.

ETERNITY

While the poets in this section concentrate on the cycles of life, Arthur Rimbaud (ram bō′) focuses on the possibility of eternal life. Like other Victorian writers, he romanticizes a mundane concept and adds an air of mystery to its presentation. His poem "Eternity" contrasts the reality of life and the anguish of the ordinary with the freedom that a glimpse of eternity provides him. As you read "Eternity," note what is temporary and what is truly eternal.

ARTHUR RIMBAUD
(1854–1891)

A poet of rare genius, French native Arthur Rimbaud first earned recognition for his poetry at age eight and was published when he was only fifteen. He stopped writing poetry at the age of nineteen and embarked on a life of adventure that has inspired scores of writers, musicians, and artists during the last one hundred years. Rimbaud spent the remainder of his life traveling throughout Africa and the Middle East. By the time of his death, his poetry had begun to influence other writers. His bohemian lifestyle became a model for such vagabond writers, musicians, and artists as Jack Kerouac and Bob Dylan.

Prentice Hall Literature Program Resources

REINFORCE / RETEACH / EXTEND

Selection Support Pages
Build Vocabulary, p. 216
Thematic Connection: Gloom and Glory, p. 217

Formal Assessment Selection Test, pp. 222–223

Resource Pro CD-ROM
"Eternity"—includes all resource material and customizable lesson plan

Listening to Literature Audiocassettes
"Eternity"

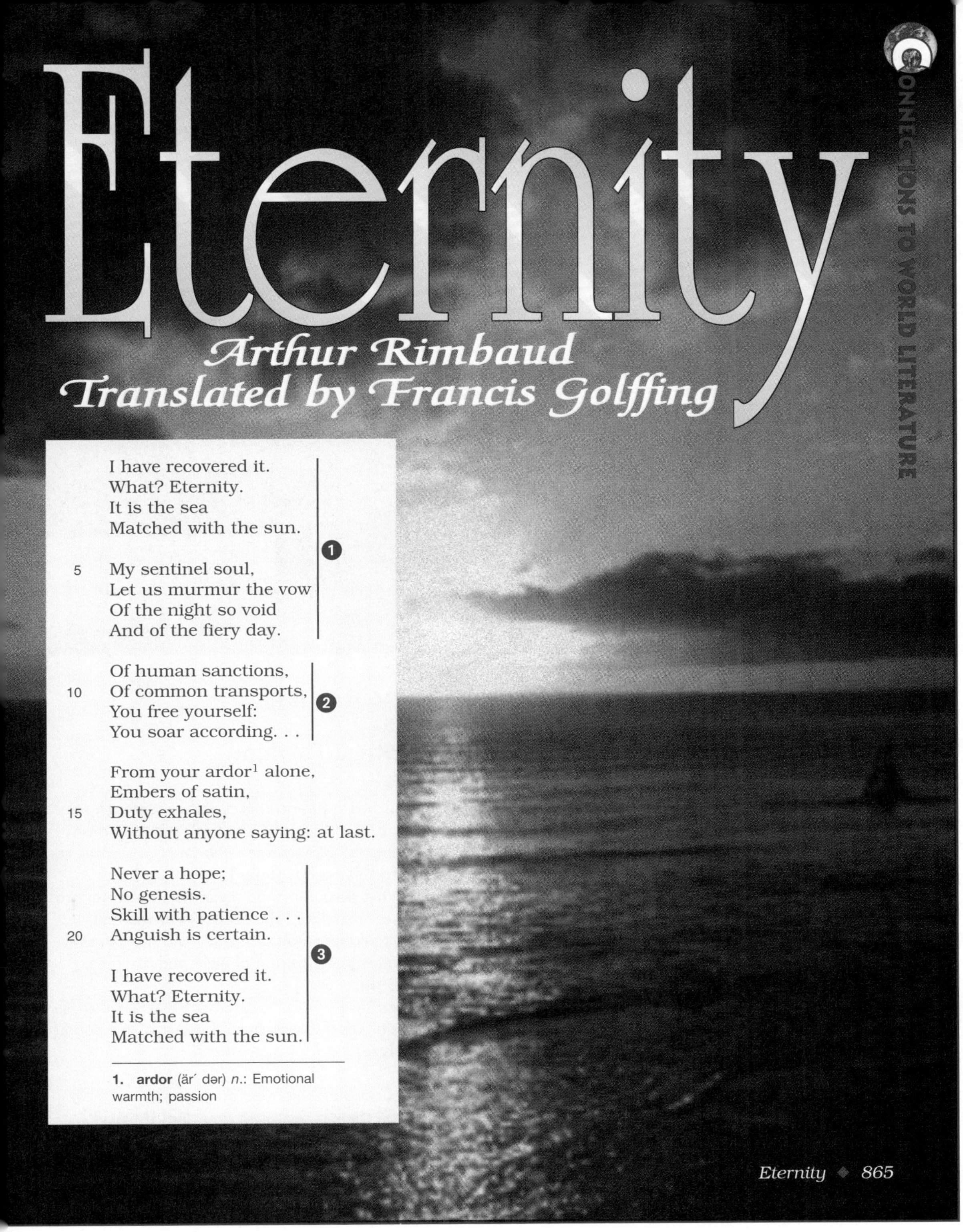

Eternity

Arthur Rimbaud
Translated by Francis Golffing

I have recovered it.
What? Eternity.
It is the sea
Matched with the sun. ❶

My sentinel soul,
Let us murmur the vow
Of the night so void
And of the fiery day.

Of human sanctions,
Of common transports, ❷
You free yourself:
You soar according. . .

From your ardor[1] alone,
Embers of satin,
Duty exhales,
Without anyone saying: at last.

Never a hope;
No genesis.
Skill with patience . . .
Anguish is certain. ❸

I have recovered it.
What? Eternity.
It is the sea
Matched with the sun.

1. **ardor** (är′ dər) *n.*: Emotional warmth; passion

Develop Understanding

This poem describes the speaker's quest to escape the normal bounds of consciousness and, by rubbing images and abstract ideas together, offers a vision of eternity.

◆ Critical Thinking

❶ **Classify** Ask students to identify images of light and darkness in the first two stanzas. Then ask how the images relate to Rimbaud's image of eternity. *Images of light and dark in the first stanza are the sun and the sea. Images of light and dark in the second stanza are the night and the "fiery day." Taken together, these opposites form the totality of experience. The images of light stand for a vision of eternity (seen by a "soaring" soul), those of dark for despair. Rimbaud realizes that both are moments of an eternal cycle.*

Critical Reading

❷ **Apply** Tell students that Rimbaud was very interested in mysticism and religion. Ask how these interests are reflected in the poem. *Suggested response: Eternity is a religious concept, as is the soul. Mysticism involves ways of releasing the soul from the mundane concerns of everyday life, just as this stanza describes how the soul frees itself from "human sanctions" and "common transports" so that it may "soar."*

◆ Critical Thinking

❸ **Connect** Ask students to identify the details in stanzas five and six that convey gloom and glory. *In stanza five, the details are gloomy—no hope, no genesis, anguish is certain. Stanza six points to glory, as the speaker says he has "recovered" eternity and describes it as "the sea matched with the sun."*

Enrichment

Taoism Rimbaud's concept of eternity as the union of the dark sea and the bright sun is related to Taoist ideas of the yin and the yang. According to this ancient Chinese religion, which is related to Buddhism, the ultimate source of eternal truth is based on a union of opposites: the yin and the yang. Yin represents the dark, passive, "feminine" aspects of life, while yang symbolizes the light, active, "masculine" aspects. Only by combining the two aspects could a person follow the true path, or Tao, to the ultimate source of truth. The poetic, mystical ideas of Taoism have been a source of inspiration to poets, both in the ancient world and in modern times.

Reinforce and Extend

Answers

◆ Literature and Your Life

Reader's Response Students may say that the following images come to mind as they read the poem: the sea; sunsets; the horizon; dark, lonely nights; the beach on a sunny day; the soul soaring like an eagle.

Thematic Connection Some students may say the poem is optimistic because the speaker has found the vision of eternity he has been seeking. Others may say that the speaker's need to escape from "human sanctions" offers a pessimistic view of everyday life. Others may note that the poem is optimistic, since it indicates that both finding and losing eternity (hope and despair) are part of the eternal cycle.

Check Your Comprehension

1. He suggests that escape from "human sanctions" and "common transports" is necessary to acquire eternity.
2. He uses the images of "the sea/Matched with the sun," "the night so void," and "the fiery day" to spark thoughts of immortality.

◆ Critical Thinking

1. In the first and last stanzas, Rimbaud describes his image of eternity: "the sea/Matched with the sun." By clearly envisioning eternity, the speaker has "recovered it." The repetition of the first lines in the last stanza suggests, however, that eternity will be lost (and recovered) yet again.
2. (a) Sample answers: Rimbaud may mean that the sea reflects the sun; that, at sunset, the sea appears to swallow up the sun; or that the sun gives light, while the water does not give light but reflects it, absorbs it, or lets it pass through. (b) Both pairs of images juxtapose light and dark aspects of nature to form a complete image of what is.
3. The statement in line 20 emphasizes the fact that the soul's effort to free itself from the mundane is a constant struggle and source of anguish. The struggle is itself eternal.
4. Accept any reasonable responses that students can relate to their own experiences.

▲ **Critical Viewing** How does the "sea / Matched with the sun" suggest eternity? **[Interpret]**

Guide for Responding

◆ Literature and Your Life

Reader's Response What images come to mind as you read this poem? Explain.

Thematic Connection In your opinion, is this an optimistic or pessimistic poem? Why?

Journal Writing In your journal, list ways a person is immortalized, for example through fame, writing, painting, etc.

☑ Check Your Comprehension

1. What does the poet suggest is required to acquire eternity?
2. What images of nature does the poet use to engage the reader in thinking about immortality?

◆ Critical Thinking

INTERPRET

1. In this poem Rimbaud expresses the desire to escape from "human sanctions" and "common transports." How do the first and last stanzas relate to this desire? **[Infer]**
2. (a) What does Rimbaud mean when he refers to the sea "matching" the sun? (b) How is Rimbaud's juxtaposition of the sea and the sun similar to his juxtaposition of night and day (lines 7–8)? **[Interpret]**
3. How does Rimbaud's statement that "anguish is certain" (line 20) relate to the rest of the poem? **[Analyze]**

APPLY

4. What does eternity represent to you and how do you think it relates to your life? **[Relate]**

Beyond the Selection

FURTHER READING

Other Works by Rimbaud

"Illuminations"
"The Golden Age"
"Ordinary Nocturne"

Other Poems of Gloom and Glory

"Eternity," Robert Herrick
"The Sea," John Keats
"Dover Beach," Matthew Arnold

We suggest that you preview these works before recommending them to students.

INTERNET

More information about Rimbaud and his poetry is available at the following Internet sites. (Note: sites may have changed since this information was published.)

For a biography and related links, go to **http://www.levity.com/corduroy.rimbaud.htm**

To listen to Rimbaud's poetry in the original French, go to **http://www.webnet.fr/poesie**

We *strongly recommend* that you preview sites before you send students to them.

Thematic Connection

Gloom and Glory

Some of the writers of this period explored the dichotomy—two contradictory parts—of life as we experience it. Birth and death, present and eternal, man and nature, gloom and glory are common themes in the literature as these writers observe the cycles of life and its passing.

1. Compare and contrast the various ways the writers in this section and Rimbaud treat the cycles of life in their poetry.
2. Which poet's view of the gloom and glory of life do you think is most realistic? Explain why.
3. Without opposing emotions, such as happiness and sadness, we would not truly be able to experience either emotion because we wouldn't have a basis for comparison. Do you agree or disagree with this statement? Explain.

Idea Bank

Writing

1. **Perfect Place** In "Eternity," Rimbaud describes an ideal place where he could escape from anguish and the duties of ordinary life. What place provides you with the same feelings? Write a description of a perfect place to spend time.

2. **Dictionary of Abstract Words** Rimbaud uses a number of abstract words, words that express qualities that exist apart from any particular object. However, he links most of these words to concrete images. Make a list of abstract words in his poem. Then define them using concrete images in the poem.

3. **Response to Criticism** Some readers do not understand Rimbaud's poetry but are moved by his struggle to express an inner truth entirely his own. One critic states the point this way:

> To those who read poetry for the sake of its accomplished beauty there is little promise in his outpourings, though dictated by a most genuine, impatient need to vent the burning truth within. —L. Cazamian

Write an essay in which you either agree or disagree that the poems are lacking in "accomplished beauty."

Speaking and Listening

4. **Ask the Poet** Choose one of the poets in this section or Rimbaud to be the guest on a radio interview program. Have one student play the part of the poet, one the interviewer, and three others as callers. The callers' questions can range from the style and theme of the poetry to the poet's opinion on modern issues. **[Media Link]**

Projects

5. **Past Glory** Choose a subject, such as sports, or theater, and research amazing people in that field. Find a lesser-known person, who once enjoyed fame and is now forgotten. Write a paper explaining the person's fame, disappearance from the news, and your opinion on why he or she did not achieve lasting fame.

6. **Multimedia Presentation** Using pictures, video, and drawings, prepare a visual description of a perfect place to spend time. Then present your multimedia report to your class. If you described the place in writing according to writing activity 1 on this page, you can combine your multimedia presentation with your writing.

Thematic Connection

Gloom and Glory

1. In their comparisons, students might make the following points: Hardy suggests that we cannot "get out of" the cycle of hope and despair; both Hopkins and Housman suggest that it is possible to find wisdom about life's cycles, and so to escape them in some sense (Hopkins approaches this topic seriously in "Spring and Fall," while Housman approaches it with gentle humor in "When I Was One-and-Twenty"); Rimbaud in "Eternity" reaches beyond the other poets' views of the cycles of life; the dichotomies that he explores—the sun and sea, night and day, light and dark—ultimately merge to produce his transcendent vision, in which both hope and despair have a place.
2. Possible response: "To an Athlete Dying Young" is the most realistic because it depicts an actual tragic occurrence; "Eternity" is realistic because it accepts both the achievement and the loss of transcendent vision.
3. Many students will agree with the statement, citing the happiness that comes with relief from a burden and the unhappiness that comes when a hope is disappointed. Some students, however, may point out that humans do not need to experience an emotion to understand it.

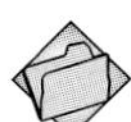

Idea Bank

Customizing for *Learning Modalities*

Following are suggestions to match Idea Bank topics with your students' learning modalities:

- Visual/Spatial: 6
- Verbal/Linguistic: 2, 3, 5
- Interpersonal: 4
- Intrapersonal: 1

Customizing for *Performance Levels*

Following are suggestions for matching Idea Bank topics with your students' ability levels:

- Less Advanced Students: 1, 6
- Average Students: 2, 4, 5
- More Advanced Students: 3

✓ ASSESSMENT OPTIONS

Formal Assessment, Selection Test, pp. 222–223, and Assessment Resources Software

PORTFOLIO ASSESSMENT

Use the following rubrics in the ***Alternative Assessment*** booklet to assess student writing.

Perfect Place: Description Rubric, p. 98

Dictionary of Abstract Words: Definition/Classification Rubric, p. 100

Response to Criticism: Literary Analysis, p. 113

Prepare and Engage

Establish Writing Guidelines
To prepare students for this writing lesson, review the following key characteristics of a parody.

- A parody imitates the style of another work in a mocking or humorous way.
- A parody usually applies the style of a serious work to an inappropriate subject.
- The writer's attitudes and response to a work are revealed through the parody.

Review with students the rubric on page 870 so that they are aware of the criteria on which their parodies will be evaluated.

Refer students to the Model From Literature on this page and the original work that it parodies, showing how it exemplifies the key characteristics of a parody. Additional help with the writing process is available in the Writing Handbook on page 1189. For further clarification of a parody, refer students to page 1193.

Writer's Solution

Writers at Work Videodisc
Show students the videodisc segment in which Eavan Boland discusses how she responds to literature. Then ask students: In what ways is a parody a response to literature?

Play frames 21571 to 31063

Writing Lab CD-ROM
Some students may benefit from writing their parodies on the computer. Have these students work in the Response to Literature tutorial and follow these steps:

1. Review the audio-annotated model of a parody.
2. Decide on a purpose using the audio-annotated writing model for considering purpose and reviewing the interactive tips.
3. Draft the parody on computer.
4. Use a self-evaluation checklist.

Sourcebook
Students can find topic ideas, graphic organizers, and tips on drafting and revising in Chapter 7, Response to Literature, pp. 196–229.

Parody

Writing Process Workshop

Home-Thoughts, from Abroad
Robert Browning

Oh, to be in England
Now that April's there,
and whoever wakes in England
sees, some morning, unaware,
That the lowest boughs and the brushwood sheaf
Round the elm-tree bole are in tiny leaf
While the chaffinch sings on the orchard bough
In England —now!

The Victorian poets in this unit wrote strongly and memorably about serious subjects, making their works a target for parody. A parody imitates the style of another work in a satirical or humorous way. Often, a parody applies the style of a serious work to an inappropriate subject. For example, if a serious poem is about a graceful seagull, the parody might feature an ungainly chicken. Choose a serious poem, preferably one with a highly recognizable style or structure, and write a parody of it. As a general strategy, you may want to refocus the poem on a trivial or absurd subject.

The following writing skills will be useful as you write a parody.

Writing Skills Focus

- ▶ **Elaborate to make writing personal.** Identify the point you want to make in your parody and choose details that will help you convey that message. (See p. 855.)
- ▶ **Present a "thesis"** by revealing your attitude toward the subject. (See p. 863.)
- ▶ **Identify and imitate** the structure and style that make the original work unique and memorable; use your words to create a humorous or satirical imitation.

The following stanza parodies the first stanza of Robert Browning's "Home Thoughts, From Abroad":

Model From Literature

Original: "Home Thoughts, From Abroad"
Parody: "That English Weather"

"Oh! To be in England (1)
Now that April's there,
And whoever wakes in England
Sees, some morning" in despair,
There's a horrible fog i' the heart
o' town, (2)
And the greasy pavement is damp
and brown;
While the rain-drop falls from the
laden bough, (3)
In England—now!

(1) The author of the parody begins by quoting the original work.

(2) The author creates a main impression with a sarcastic tone.

(3) Such details contrast with those in the original work and convey the writer's personal views of England.

Humanities: Performing Arts

Parodies in the Other Arts Explain to students that parody is not confined to literature. Just when singer Michael Jackson's song "Beat It" had saturated the radiowaves, a musician by the name of Weird Al Yankovic released his response, entitled "Eat It." The rock band Led Zeppelin perhaps got more than its fair share of airtime with the song "Stairway to Heaven," a fact that moved another group of musicians to set the lyrics of a television comedy *(Gilligan's Island)* to Led Zeppelin's music. Even television turns out to have a sense of humor about itself: Certain television shows—from Ernie Kovacs' innovative program of the 1950's to *Saturday Night Live* in the 1970's and *The David Letterman Show* in the 1980's—abound in parodies of typical television fare (sitcoms, commercials, and news programs).

The possibility of parody is open wherever creative work establishes a characteristic form. Every form creates expectations in an audience. That master of subversion, the parodist, can then play with an audience's expectations by calling on the established form (rhyme scheme, beat, drawing style), then doing the unexpected.

Prewriting

Choose a Topic Look through your literature textbook or an anthology to find a work you'd like to parody. If you're having trouble finding a work, use one of these ideas.

Topic Ideas

- Hamlet's famous soliloquy, "To be or not to be"
- One of Stephen King's short stories
- Any popular rock song

Selection-Related Topic Ideas

- "Remembrance" by Emily Brontë
- "Ulysses" by Alfred Lord Tennyson
- "The Darkling Thrush" by Thomas Hardy

Evaluate the Author's Style Read the original poem several times, asking and answering questions like these:

- ▶ **Formality** Does the writer use sophisticated vocabulary or simple words? A serious tone or a familiar one? What key words will convey the flavor of the author's language?
- ▶ **Poetic Devices and Dramatic Effects** What types of simile, metaphor, or other figures of speech characterize the writer's style? What rhythms and rhymes will tell readers that you are imitating this writer?

Gather Personal Details Gather details that will help you give your own twist to the writer's subject matter. In the model on the previous page, for instance, the parodist adds details about England's *bad* weather to poke fun at the original poem.

Drafting

Present a Humorous "Thesis" Keep clearly in mind the "thesis" or main impression you want to create. To convey that impression, use a consistent tone, like the sarcasm in the parody of the Browning poem. Also, be sure that the imagery and details you use contribute to the main impression.

Work With the Original A successful parody continually reminds readers of the original work while poking fun at it. To make sure your parody stays in touch with the original, keep a copy of that work in front of you as you write, and refer to it frequently.

Applying Language Skills: Imitate Sentence Types

In imitating a writer's style, you may want to identify and mimic the types of sentences that he or she uses most often. Following are examples of different types of sentences, as used by a variety of authors:

Declarative:
"The world is charged with the grandeur of God." (Hopkins)

Imperative:
"Come live with me, and be my love." (Marlowe)

Inverted:
"Death be not proud. . . " (Donne)

Exclamatory:
"Judge of the Nations, spare us yet, / Lest we forget–lest we forget!" (Kipling)

Interrogative:
"Ah, are you digging on my grave / My loved one?" (Hardy)

Writing Application Identify and imitate the types of sentences that appear most often in the work you are parodying.

Writer's Solution Connection
Language Lab

For help in identifying and imitating a writer's style, see the lessons in the Writing Style unit of the Language Lab.

Prewriting

Refer students to the topic ideas on this page. You may want to assign a selection-related topic as a means of evaluating students' understanding of the literature.

Customize for
English Language Learners
These learners may have difficulty identifying and imitating an author's style and structure. Have these learners identify the tone and central message of the piece. Using the same basic form as the original—short story, essay, poem—they can parody its tone and theme.

Writing Lab CD-ROM
Students should review the Literary Elements Chart in the Response to Literature tutorial to help them identify the elements of the work they are going to parody. This interactive chart shows types of literary works and elements.

Review with students the tips on the student page on evaluating an author's style. Also have them complete the Applying Language Skills section on imitating sentence types.

Drafting

Have students apply the two points in the drafting section on this page. Suggest to students that they memorize the poem they are parodying.

Applying Language Skills

Imitate Sentence Types Before they begin their parodies, have students review the list of sentence types. Then have them complete the Writing Application.

For more help with sentence types, have students complete the Varying Sentence Structure lesson on the **Language Lab CD-ROM**. For further practice, have students complete pages 18 and 19 on sentence types in the *Writer's Solution Grammar Practice Book*.

Revising

Review with students the description of the key characteristics of a parody and the Writing Skills Focus on page 868. Then review with them the Revision Model. Finally, have students use the Revision Checklist to evaluate their work.

Writer's Solution

Writing Lab CD-ROM
Have students use the Revision Checker for Vague Language in the Response to Literature tutorial.

Publishing

Hold a poetry reading in which students share their parodies. Students can work in pairs to read originals, then their parodies.

Reinforce and Extend

Connect to Literature Have students find parodies of a famous literary work. A good starting place is *Parodies from Chaucer to Beerbohm—and After*. Have students write a response to a parodist from the author of the original.

Applying Language Skills

Avoid Redundancy Explain to students that, in creating vivid descriptions, they should avoid overdescription or redundancy. Have students review the examples on this page and then complete the Writing Application.

For additional help avoiding redundancy, have students complete the lesson on Eliminating Unnecessary Words on the **Language Lab CD-ROM.** For further practice, students should complete page 101 on Using Words Concisely in the *Writer's Solution Grammar Practice Book*.

Applying Language Skills: Avoid Redundancy

Eliminate instances of redundancy, the unnecessary use of words that don't contribute to the meaning. Redundancy makes all types of writing heavy and dull.

Examples of Redundant Phrases:
free gift; past history; completely finished; end result; advance warning

First Draft:
When in August the rain showers fall down . . .

Revision:
When in August it rains . . .

Writing Application Eliminate instances of redundancy in your parody, unless they are meant to be comic.

Writer's Solution Connection Writing Lab

For help in revising, see the Self-Evaluation Checklist in the Revising and Editing section of the Response to Literature tutorial.

Revising

Read Aloud Have a classmate or group of classmates listen as you read the original work and your parody aloud. Ask them whether the parody is similar enough to the original to be recognizable. Also find out whether or not you've succeeded in creating a humorous main impression.

Revision Checklist Use this checklist to evaluate and revise your parody:

- ▶ What details might you add or revise to strengthen the main impression and create humor?
- ▶ Would additional details or a stronger tone make the parody reflect your ideas more clearly?

Revision Model

The Eagle: A Fragment by Alfred, Lord Tennyson

He clasps the crag with crooked hands;
Close to the sun in lonely lands,
Ringed with the azure world, he stands. . . .

Parody: The Corporate Raider

He clasps the pen with ~~big~~ (1) greedy hands,
Close to ~~the sun on landscaped grounds,~~ (2) acquiring corporate lands
~~He stands flush with the bottom line~~ (3) Flush with the bottom line, he stands

① A weak word is replaced by an adjective that creates a stronger main impression.
② This line was revised to fit the rhyme scheme and rhythm of the original work.
③ The writer inverted the sentence order to imitate the inverted order in the original.

Publishing

- ▶ **Bulletin-Board Anthology** Collect your classmates' parodies, and post them on a bulletin board along with the original works. You may also want to include humorous illustrations.
- ▶ **School Paper** Send your parody, along with the original work, to the school newspaper.

☑ ASSESSMENT		4	3	2	1
PORTFOLIO ASSESSMENT Use this rubric to evaluate students' parodies.	**Imitating Structure and Style**	The writer precisely imitates the structure and the style of the original to create an effective parody.	The writer adequately imitates the structure and style of the original.	The writer loosely follows the structure and style of the original.	The writer does not imitate the structure or style of the original.
	Conveying a Main Impression	The writer successfully conveys a main impression in the parody.	The main impression is sometimes unclear.	The main impression or purpose is unclear and confusing.	The writer does not convey a main impression.

Real-World Reading Skills Workshop

Adjust Reading Rate

Strategies for Success

How fast do you read? The answer should depend on what you're reading. Learning to adjust your reading rate will help you get the most out of what you read, whether it's a comic novel, an age-old ballad, or a science textbook.

How to Adjust Your Reading Rate You should adjust your reading rate according to what and why you are reading. If you want to give a poem, a novel, or a textbook careful consideration, read slowly. Take time to pause and reflect as well as to go back and reread. If you want an overview of a magazine article, read through it quickly and focus on its main ideas, as reflected in topic sentences.

Population Trends: Urbanization

During the nineteenth century, the population of Britain increased dramatically, owing to a variety of factors. The rising fertility patterns established in the eighteenth century continued, due in part to marriages at a younger age. Surprisingly, death rates remained the same or even increased, as large numbers of people faced hazardous conditions as they moved into urban areas.

England and Wales: Population 1801 to 1901

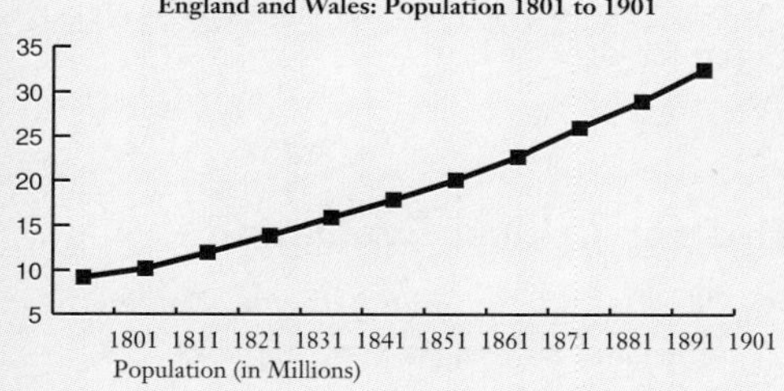

Indeed, urbanization, the movement of populations into large cities, was the dominant migratory trend during this period. This trend began during the eighteenth century, but continued aggressively as industrial manufacturing drew people to cities throughout the nineteenth century. In 1700, about sixteen percent of the English population lived in urban regions: by 1800 this percentage increased to twenty-seven. By 1900, almost eighty percent of the population was urbanized.

Living in Cities The rapid increase in urban populations led to difficult living conditions in most English cities. Overcrowded urban areas offered poor sanitation, paving, and water supply. As conditions worsened, wealthier families moved to outer regions, leaving cities with less financial support for necessary improvements.

Slow Down for Details You can also adjust your reading rate while reading different parts of one work. You may need to slow down if you come to a section containing many specific details or visuals like charts, graphs, and tables. You may want to read more quickly if you come to a section that isn't closely related to your interest or to your reading goal.

Scan to Plan When reading nonfiction, you may find it helpful to scan the article or book first, looking for sections or chapters that you will want to study closely. You might even mark these sections with bookmarks or stick-on notes. When you go back and start reading, you'll remember to slow down when you see your reminders.

Apply the Strategy

Imagine that you're using the English history text book in which the page at the left appears. Answer these questions about how you might adjust your reading rate.

1. Describe a purpose for reading that would require only a quick scan of the details on this page.
2. What elements on this page would help you quickly grasp the key ideas? Explain.
3. Describe a purpose for reading that would require a careful study of the text on this page.
4. If you looked at this page quickly, what information might you miss? Why?

✔ *Here are some other situations in which you may need to adjust your reading rate:*

- ▶ poetry excerpted in criticism
- ▶ statistics reported in news reports
- ▶ descriptive images used in letters

Introduce the Strategy

Whether students go to college or straight to work, they will be confronted with large amounts of information to absorb and little time to do it. By learning the strategies on this page for adjusting their reading rate, they will benefit directly.

Customize for ***Logical/Mathematical Learners***

These learners may benefit from creating a logical plan for determining when to adjust reading rate and exactly how to do it. Have students review the strategies on this page and then devise a set of steps that they can follow when tackling different types of literature.

Apply the Strategy

1. Determining whether the population in England and Wales grew during the years 1801 to 1901 would require only a quick scan of the page.
2. The chart on this page and the headings would help a reader quickly grasp the main ideas.
3. Learning the reasons for the population increase in England and Wales after 1801 would require a careful study of the text.
4. If you looked at this page quickly, you might miss the following information: the reasons why people were moving to cities; the fact that an increase in marriages at a younger age and rising fertility rates were also responsible for the rise in population. These details are not included in the headings or chart on the page, so they can only be found by careful reading.

Beyond the Classroom

Workplace Skill

Efficiency Explain to students that doing a very close examination of documents is not always an efficient way to work. Often the key ideas of workplace documents can be absorbed from headings, charts, and a quick scan of the material. A worker who takes the time to examine such documents too closely may be kept from other important aspects of his or her job. This results in inefficiency, which can hold up the progress of a project. Tell students that it is important that they learn to discern what types of information in their work situations need close attention and what types can be scanned.

Introduce the Strategy

Students are often unaware that bias may occur in news reports. Explain to them that although news programs report facts, the facts that are presented and the way they are presented can influence viewers' interpretations of them. Have students use the strategies on this page for evaluating news reports.

Customize for
Non-Bodily/ Non-Kinesthetic Learners
These learners may not feel comfortable role-playing the situations on this page. As an alternative assignment, have students watch two news programs and read one news article reporting the same incident. Have students compare the ways the incident is presented in each. Finally, have students write an objective news report based on the information they have gathered.

Apply the Strategy

Have students work in groups to present their news reports. You may want to have groups hand in a written version of their news reports. Have students watching each group identify bias in the news presentations given by their peers.

Speaking and Listening Workshop

Critically Evaluating a News Report

Listening to a news report is not a passive activity. You need to listen with a critical ear, ready to challenge sweeping generalizations, cloudy assertions, or bold misstatements.

What Choices Did They Make? Begin your critical evaluation by thinking about the choices broadcasters made when presenting a story. Ask yourself the following questions:

- What did they include? What did they leave out?
- Were both sides of a controversial issue given equal air time?
- Did the choice of images influence your interpretation of the event? If so, how?

How Else Can You Tell the Same Story? One of the best ways to evaluate a newscast is to compare it with another report about the same topic. Listen for words that reflect hidden bias. For example, notice how the following reports present the same information in a very different manner.

Yesterday, the mayor succumbed to pressure from local environmentalists and issued a sharp statement against industrial water pollution.

After months of delaying, the mayor finally launched a campaign to decrease the deadly pollution flooding our city's water.

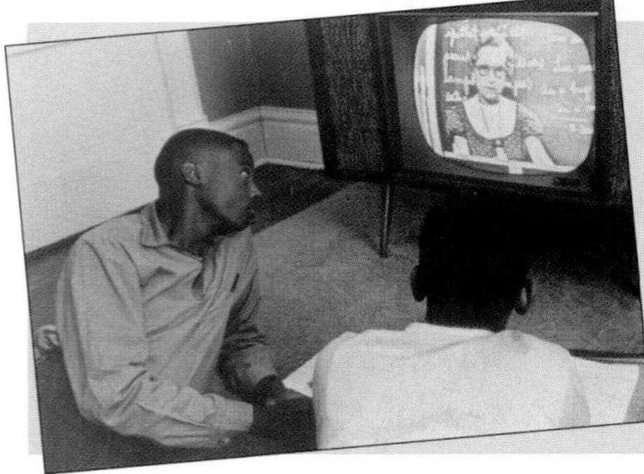

Apply the Strategies

Role-play these news presentations in your classroom. Practice critical evaluation strategies while you listen to or view the news reports.

1. A radio announcer presents a summary of a recent school event, such as a charity carnival or science fair. Listen for loaded words in the report.
2. Two television reporters interview a candidate for a position in your local government, such as mayor or city council member. Watch and listen for signs of bias.

Tips for Critical Evaluation

These strategies can help you evaluate television and radio news reports.

- Pay attention to negative or positive connotations that can slant a story.
- On television broadcasts, pay attention to the speaker's body language.
- Listen for sources. Unattributed details may not be based on facts.
- Think of questions that remain unanswered. Jot them down and listen for answers in other broadcasts.

Cross-Curricular Connection: Social Studies

Elections Students will soon be able to vote and should be aware of bias that occurs in media coverage of elections. The way a candidate is presented by the media and the amount of media coverage a candidate receives can influence a voter's decision. Have students research all the facts about candidates in an impending election. Suggest that students call political parties if they need more information about candidates. They should then use the strategies on this page to examine all presentations of information about candidates. Then ask them to assemble all of the information they have gathered and make a decision on whom to support.

Extended Reading Opportunities

Full-length works of the nineteenth century explore a range of conflicts. These works feature an outsider's desperate love, a woman's attempt to achieve her ambitions, and a spoof on Victorian social conventions.

Suggested Titles

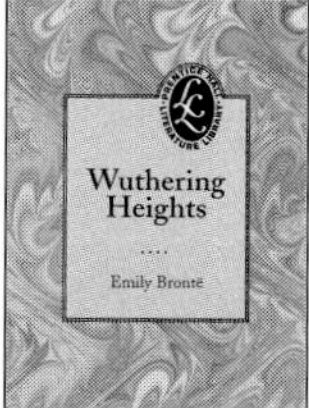

Wuthering Heights
Emily Brontë

The setting of *Wuthering Heights* is the wild and windy moors of northern Yorkshire. Central to the story is the romantic and brooding Heathcliff, a gypsy adopted into a family and mistreated by his foster-brother. The story revolves around Heathcliff's thwarted love for Catherine and his revenge on those who mistreated him. By the end of the tale, however, Heathcliff's passion is spent, and happiness becomes possible for two of the younger members of the family, who are able to make a new beginning.

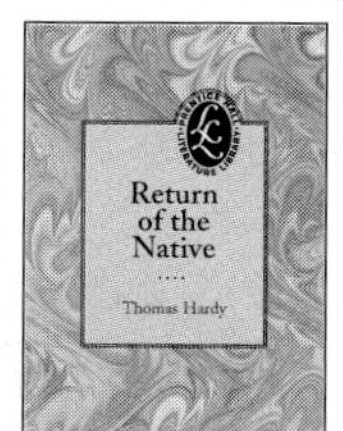

The Return of the Native
Thomas Hardy

Conflicts occur when a young woman, Eustacia Vye, tries to escape the constrictions of her life in Egdon, a sprawling wasteland. The "native" of Hardy's tale is Clym Yeobright, who returns to rural Egdon Heath from Paris in order to open a school. Clym falls in love with Eustacia; she marries him with the hope that he will help her escape. When he fails to do so, she turns to Damon Wildeve, an old flame. He attempts to save her but cannot. Eustacia is a woman who breaks the rules and cannot survive in a world that will not accept her.

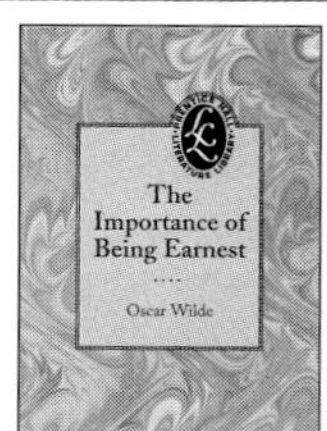

The Importance of Being Earnest
Oscar Wilde

Mocking the social conventions of the Victorian period, *The Importance of Being Earnest* is one of the wittiest comedies ever written. Jack Worthing invents a mischievous younger brother named Ernest to allow him to adventure in London. Algernon Moncrieff appears at Jack's home assuming the identity of Ernest Worthing to meet Jack's attractive ward, Cecily Cardew. Both men have told their romantic interests that their names are Ernest because the women want to marry men named Ernest!

Other Possibilities

Jane Eyre	Charlotte Brontë
Hard Times	Charles Dickens
The Mill on the Floss	George Eliot

Planning Students' Extended Reading

The works listed on this page cover the conflicts of the Victorian period, presenting individuals struggling with social constraints of class and gender.

Customize for Varying Student Needs and Interests

When assigning these works, keep the following in mind:

- *Wuthering Heights* is a novel that all students will enjoy. To help students understand the novel, review its setting on the wild and windy moors of northern Yorkshire, England, and explain that the setting mirrors the personality of Heathcliff, the main character.
- To understand *The Return of the Native*, students should keep in mind that the Industrial Revolution resulted in the disappearance of traditional ways of life in such places as Egdon Heath, the setting of the novel. A newly emerging middle class, represented by characters such as Eustacia Vye, was beginning to upset the static social structure.
- In *The Importance of Being Earnest*, Wilde mocks the upper class and its idleness. To understand the play's central conflict, students should know that, even though the emerging middle class of the day was growing powerful, anyone who had earned his or her wealth instead of inheriting it was not accepted by the upper classes.

Customize for Special Needs

To meet the needs of your special needs students, you may want to consider using the adapted version of *Wuthering Heights* from Globe Fearon's Pacemaker Classics series.

Literature Study Guides

Literature study guides are available for all three suggested titles. These guides include section summaries, discussion questions, and activities.

Sensitive Issues

- While reading *Wuthering Heights*, some students may be upset that adoption is shown to upset a happy family. Point out that Heathcliff represents a force of passion and wildness outside the order of the family—the novel is not intended as a realistic portrayal of adoption, but as a revelation of the disorder and self-assertion lurking under the orderly surface of Victorian society.
- Some students may be disturbed by the negative picture that is painted of marriage in *The Return of the Native*, though Hardy does represent marriage as an institution that carries both respect and responsibility.

Resources for Teaching Novels, Plays, and Literature Collections

This booklet contains graphic organizers, teaching strategies, and transparencies that will be invaluable in teaching any of these novels.

Planning Instruction and Assessment

Unit Objectives

1. To read selections from English literature of the twentieth century
2. To apply a variety of reading strategies, particularly strategies for reading fiction, appropriate for reading these selections
3. To recognize literary elements used in these selections
4. To build vocabulary in context
5. To learn elements of grammar, usage, and style
6. To write in a variety of modes and about situations based on the selections
7. To develop speaking and listening skills, by completing proposed activities

Meeting the Objectives

With each selection, you will find instructional material and portfolio opportunities through which students can meet these objectives. Further, you will find additional practice pages for reading strategies, literary elements, vocabulary, and grammar in the ***Selection Support*** booklet in the Teaching Resources box.

Setting Goals Work with your students at the beginning of the unit to set goals for unit outcomes. Plan what skills and concepts you wish students to acquire. You may individualize these according to students' performance levels or learning modalities.

Portfolios You may have students keep portfolios of their work or of their work in progress. The activities and prompts on the Build Your Portfolio page of each selection provide opportunities for students to apply the concepts presented with the selection.

The City Rises, 1911, (tempera on card), Umberto Boccioni, Jesi Collection, Milan

Humanities: Art

The City Rises, 1911, by Umberto Boccioni.

The Italian painter and sculptor Umberto Boccioni (1882–1916) became a leading light of Futurism, an early twentieth-century literary and artistic movement that rejoiced in technology and sought to incorporate it into art. In 1910 he and other artists produced the "Technical Manifesto of the Futurist Painters," proclaiming that contemporary art should wed itself to the driving spirits of modern technology: violence, power, and speed.

The City Rises is regarded as Boccioni's Futuristic masterpiece. Have your students link the art to the focus of Unit 6, "A Time of Rapid Change," by answering the following questions:

1. What ideas about the growth of a modern city does this painting communicate, and what elements convey these ideas? *The swirling figures and driving brushstrokes suggest that the city is constantly moving and changing—almost too quickly for humans to take in. The dominating reds suggest that the city is born out of violence against nature.*
2. What might this turbulent, non-representational cityscape suggest about literature from the twentieth century? *The art and literature of the twentieth century is turbulent and seeks the meaning of modern experience in forces that cannot be pictured directly.*

A Time of Rapid Change (1901–Present)

We are living at one of the great turning points of history. . . . Yesterday, we split the atom. We assaulted that colossal citadel of power, the tiny unit of the substance of the universe. And because of this, the great dream and the great nightmare of centuries of human thought have taken flesh and walk beside us all, day and night.

—Doris Lessing, from "The Small, Personal Voice"

Assessing Student Progress

The following tools are available to measure the degree to which students meet the unit objectives:

Informal Assessment

The questions in the Guide for Responding sections are a first level of response to the concepts and skills presented with the selection. Students' responses are a brief informal measure of their grasp of the material. Their responses on this level can indicate where further instruction and practice are needed. You may then follow up with the practice pages in the ***Selection Support*** booklet.

You will find literature and reading guides in the ***Alternative Assessment*** booklet, which you may give students on an individual basis for informal assessment of their performance.

Formal Assessment

In the ***Formal Assessment*** booklet, you will find selection tests and part tests.

Selection Tests The selection tests measure comprehension and skills acquisition for each selection or group of selections.

Part Tests Each part test, which calls on students to read a passage of literature they have not previously seen, applies the unit skills on a broader level. The Critical Reading section measures Unit Objectives 1, 2, and 3. The Vocabulary and Grammar section measures Objectives 4 and 5. The Essay section measures Objectives 1 and 6. Both the Critical Reading and Vocabulary and Grammar sections use formats similar to those found on many standardized tests, including the SAT.

Alternative Assessment

Portfolios As you review individual pieces or the collected work in students' portfolios, you will find assessment sheets available in the portfolio section of the ***Alternative Assessment*** booklet.

Scoring Rubrics You will find scoring rubrics for writing modes in the ***Alternative Assessment*** booklet. You can apply these to Writing Mini-Lessons and to Writing Process Workshop lessons.

Speaking and Listening The ***Alternative Assessment*** booklet contains assessment sheets for speaking and listening activities.

Learning Modalities The ***Alternative Assessment*** booklet contains activities that appeal to different learning styles. You may use these too as an alternative assessment of students' growth.

Using the Timeline

The Timeline can serve a number of instructional purposes, as follows:

Getting an Overview Use the Timeline to help students get a quick overview of themes and events of the period. This approach will benefit all students but may be especially helpful for visually oriented students, English language learners, and those less proficient in reading. (For strategies in using the Timeline as an overview, see the bottom of this page.)

Thinking Critically Questions are provided on the facing page. Use these questions to have students review the events, discuss their significance, and examine the *so what* behind the *what happened.*

Connecting to Selections Have students refer back to the Timeline when reading individual selections. By consulting the Timeline regularly, they will gain a better sense of the period's chronology. In addition, they will appreciate what was occurring in the world that gave rise to these works of literature.

Projects Students can use the Timeline as a launching pad for projects like these:

- **Building Context** For each selection students read in this unit, have them check the Timeline for possible background events. To what events is a poet or fiction writer responding directly? Does the writer's experiments with form have anything to do with major, contemporary upheavals in life and perception? To what events does the writer *not* seem to respond? Students can develop Cluster Diagrams in which each selection is surrounded by relevant events.
- **Report on a Movement or Trend** Have students scan the Timeline for political movement or social trend, research the people behind it, then report on their findings to the class. What role, if any, did literary figures play in this movement or trend?

Timeline

1901–Present

1901 | 1920 | 1945

British Events

- **1901** Edward VII becomes king.
- **1902 Joseph Conrad** publishes *Heart of Darkness.*
- **1903** Emmeline Pankhurst founds women's suffrage organization.
- **1910** George V becomes king.
- **1913 D. H. Lawrence** publishes *Sons and Lovers.*
- **1914** Britain enters World War I. ▶
- **1918** Married women over thirty achieve right to vote.

- **1922** Irish Free State formed.
- **1922 T. S. Eliot** publishes *The Waste Land.*
- **1922 James Joyce** publishes *Ulysses.*
- **1924** First British airline begins regular operations.
- **1930 W. H. Auden** publishes *Poems.*
- **1936** First BBC television broadcast.
- **1939** Britain enters World War II. ▼
- **1940 Winston Churchill** becomes prime minister.

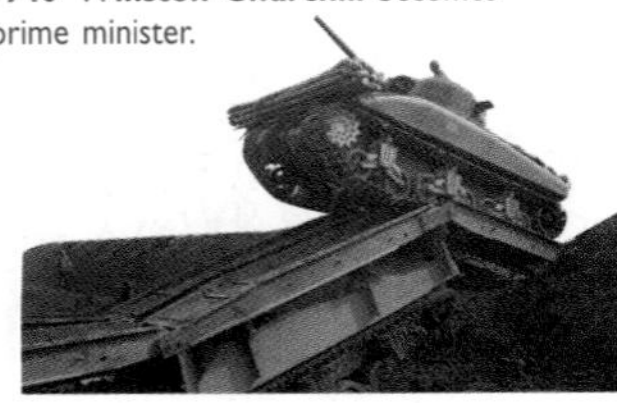

- **1945 George Orwell** publishes *Animal Farm.*
- **1947** Coal mines nationalized.
- **1947** India and Pakistan gain independence.
- **1949** Irish Free State becomes Republic of Ireland. ▶
- **1952** Elizabeth II becomes queen.
- **1954** William Golding publishes *Lord of the Flies.*
- **1954** Roger Bannister breaks four-minute mile. ▶

World Events

- **1901** Germany: Thomas Mann publishes *Buddenbrooks.*
- **1903** Orville and Wilbur Wright build first successful airplane.
- **1904** Asia: Russo-Japanese War begins.
- **1905** Germany: Albert Einstein proposes theory of relativity. ▶
- **1917** Austria: Sigmund Freud publishes *Introduction to Psychoanalysis.*
- **1917** Russia: Czar overthrown; Bolsheviks seize power.
- **1920** India: **Mohandas Gandhi** leads nonviolent protests.
- **1925** Czechoslovakia: Franz Kafka publishes *The Trial.*
- **1927** United States: Charles Lindbergh flies solo to Paris. ▲
- **1936** Spain: Civil War begins.
- **1939** Europe: Hitler invades Poland; World War II begins.
- **1941** United States: Japan bombs Pearl Harbor; United States enters World War II.
- **1945** Japan: World War II ends as Japan surrenders. ▲
- **1947** Middle East: Palestine partitioned.
- **1948** Middle East: Israel established.
- **1949** China: Mao Zedong establishes People's Republic.
- **1954** United States: Jonas Salk begins polio inoculations.
- **1955** United States: Martin Luther King, Jr., leads civil rights bus boycott.
- **1957** Russia: Sputnik I, first spaceship launched.

Getting an Overview of the Period

Introduction To help students get an overview of the period, have them determine how far back the Timeline starts (use the date in the upper left-hand corner). *The Timeline begins in 1901.* Next, point out that the Timeline is divided into specifically British Events (on top) and World Events (on bottom). Have them practice scanning the Timeline across, looking both at the British Events and the World Events. Point out that global events often involve Britain. *Hitler's aggression (1939) leads to Britain's entry into World War II (1939); Gandhi's protests (1920) lead to Indian independence from Britain (1947).*

Key Events Have students note world events that had an impact on Britain. *Answers include: Britain fought in World War I (1914), World War II (1939), and the Persian Gulf War (1991); the Maastricht Treaty was signed (1991).* Have students note British events indicating Britain's changing place in the world. *Britain pioneered commercial aviation (1924) and television (1936); Britain gave up colonies (1947); Britain suffered economically (1980).* Then ask students to generalize about Britain's position in the world today. *Britain is no longer a world empire, but is still prominent in world affairs.*

1960	1975	1990	PRESENT

British Events

- **1962 Doris Lessing** publishes *The Golden Notebook*.
- **1965** Miniskirt becomes fashionable.
- **1967** The Beatles release *Sgt. Pepper's Lonely Hearts Club Band*.
- **1972** Britain imposes direct rule on Northern Ireland.

- **1975** North Sea oil production begins. ▶
- **1977** John Fowles publishes *Daniel Martin*.
- **1979** Margaret Thatcher becomes first woman prime minister. ▼

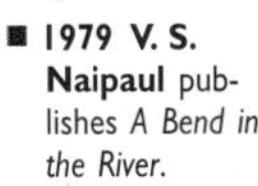

- **1979 V. S. Naipaul** publishes *A Bend in the River*.
- **1980** Britain suffers worst recession since 1930's.
- **1982** British troops force Argentinians from Falkland Islands.
- **1985** Thatcher breaks coal miners' strike.
- **1985** Hillsborough Agreement gives Republic of Ireland voice in governing Northern Ireland.
- **1989** Parliament privatizes national electric and water companies.
- **1991 Nadine Gordimer** wins Nobel Prize for Literature.
- **1991** Great Britain participates in Persian Gulf War.
- **1992** Scandal-mongering about the royal family reaches new heights.
- **1994** Cease-fire agreed to between factions in Northern Ireland.
- **1997 Tony Blair** elected Prime Minister.
- **1997** Scotland and Wales gain right to form separate parliaments.

World Events

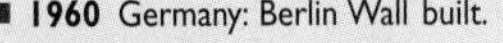

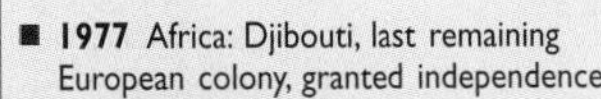

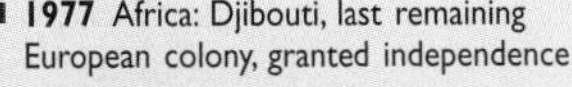

- **1960** Germany: Berlin Wall built.
- **1963** United States: President John F. Kennedy assassinated.
- **1964** Vietnam: American troops join fighting.
- **1966** India: Indira Gandhi becomes prime minister.
- **1967** Colombia: Gabriel García Márquez publishes *One Hundred Years of Solitude*.
- **1969** United States: Apollo 11 lands on moon. ▲
- **1977** Africa: Djibouti, last remaining European colony, granted independence.
- **1979** Iran: Ayatollah Khomeini overthrows Shah.
- **1980** United States: Ronald Reagan elected president.
- **1985** Ethiopia: warfare and drought result in great famine.
- **1989** Germany: Berlin Wall torn down; reunification of East and West Germany follows. ▼

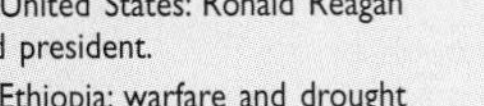

- **1991** Eastern Europe: Soviet Union dissolved.
- **1991** Yugoslavia: Civil war breaks out.
- **1991** Europe: Maastricht Treaty providing for a common European currency signed.
- **1991** Middle East: Iraq defeated by United Nations forces in Persian Gulf War.
- **1993** Middle East: Israel and the PLO sign peace agreement.
- **1994** South Africa: Nelson Mandela elected president.
- **1997** China: Hong Kong returns from British to Chinese rule.

▶Critical Viewing◀

1. Contrast the spirit of war suggested by the recruiting poster (1914) with that suggested by the tank (1939)? **[Compare and Contrast]** *The poster suggests that war is a matter of community effort, of individuals "pitching in"; the tank suggests anonymous, wide-scale destruction.*
2. What idea of modern scientists does the photograph of Einstein (1905) suggest? **[Interpret]** *The photograph suggests that scientists are slightly dishevelled, and so presumably absent-minded and consumed by their work, absorbed in arcane formulae such as the one on the blackboard.*
3. (a) Describe the expressions of the sailors who have just heard that the war has ended (1945). (b) What feelings—pride, accomplishment, relief—do you imagine dominate? Explain. *(a) They appear ecstatically happy. (b) Answers include: Relief from personal uncertainty would be the most immediate, and so dominant, feeling.*
4. (a) What does the presence of the man on the moon (1969) suggest about progress? (b) What might the fact that we cannot see his face suggest about the price of progress? **[Interpret]** *(a) Human beings can transcend their physical environment through technology. (b) The price of progress may be dehumanization.*

◆Critical Thinking

1. (a) Name two signs of social change before 1960. (b) Note the larger implications of each change. **[Deduce]** *(a) Answers include: women get the vote (1918) and coal mines are nationalized (1947). (b) By obtaining the vote, women paved the way to assuming more power and independence, changing the structure of the family. By nationalizing coal, the British could better regulate the economy, protecting the lower classes, though perhaps discouraging entrepreneurism.*
2. (a) Name two signs of social change after 1960. (b) Note the larger implications of each change. **[Deduce]** *(a) The miniskirt becomes fashionable (1965); national utilities companies are privatized (1989); the royal family is subject to scandals (1992). (b) The rise of the miniskirt suggests that women are exploring new roles; the privatization of national companies suggests that government is less involved in regulating the economy; the royal scandals indicate an erosion of the symbols binding society together.*
3. (a) What evidence can you find of Britain's declining power during this period? (b) What role might Britain have in world affairs today? **[Speculate]** *(a) India and Pakistan gain independence (1947); part of Ireland becomes independent (1949); Hong Kong is given back to China (1997). (b) While no longer a "superpower," Britain may still be a key player in international affairs.*
4. The twentieth century is the "Age of the Masses"—a time of mass political movements, mass entertainment, and so on. (a) Find three events that support this description of the period. (b) Explain how one idea of "the masses" leads to movements for social justice, while another leads to mass entertainment. **[Support]** *(a) Answers include: women's struggle for the vote (1903, 1918); workers' revolution in Russia (1917); Gandhi's protests in India (1920); television develops (1936); coal mines nationalized (1947); workers' revolution in China (1949); miniskirt fad (1965); tabloid coverage of royal scandals (1992). (b) In movements for social justice, masses means "people without social privileges." For the purposes of mass entertainment, masses means "the average person," or even "the complacent side of all people."*

Develop Understanding

Customize for
Less Proficient Readers
Explain to these students that, during this period, huge wars swept the planet. Instruct them to scan the subheads in The Story of the Times: Historical Background and the pictures in the Graphic Look at the Period. For each subhead and picture, have them write down whether it concerns war or peacetime, or whether they cannot be sure. Then have them read the sections and captions, filling in their notes with the name of the war or of an important peacetime event that each section or caption concerns.

Customize for
English Language Learners
Give these students the following words and phrases: *armistice, fad, Iron Curtain, mod,* and *cease-fire.* Have them write down the meaning of each from the dictionary. They should then scan The Story of the Times for each word or phrase. Based on what they learn in the paragraph where the word or phrase appears, they should add an original sentence using the word to their dictionary definition.

Customize for
More Advanced Students
Challenge these students to trace the themes of memory and recognition through A Graphic Look at the Period and The Story of the Times. What events involve a "forgetting" of the past? What events should be remembered as a warning to the future? What trends attempt to create the utterly new—that which is not remembered or recognized, but which shocks at first (and afterwards is often forgotten)? When these students have grouped and commented on events, ask them to generalize about the importance of memory and forgetting for a healthy society.

A Graphic Look at the Period

P-1860
A Wolseley Six-Horsepower Two-Seater, 1904

▲ **Deduce** The spread of mass-produced automobiles eventually allowed the middle-classes to enjoy opportunities for travel. Judging from details of its appearance, what kind of driving—pleasure, work, or family-related—was this 1904 car designed for?

▲ **Draw Conclusions** Gas masks such as this one were a standard part of a soldier's equipment during World War I, when the widespread use of mustard gas turned the very air hostile. Knowing that chemical warfare has since been banned, what conclusions can you draw about the effects of mustard gas?

The Story of the Times

(1901–Present)

Historical Background

The twentieth century dawned bright with promise. Progress in science and technology was helping to make life easier and the world more comprehensible. Yet while steady advances in communications and transportation drew the world closer together, the scourge of modern war soon wrenched it apart. The First World War (1914–1918) killed more than 8 million people, the Second World War (1939–1945), some 45 million more. British military and political power declined after the Second World War, yet British literary and artistic life remained vibrant. Disillusionment, though widespread, was accompanied by vigorous inventiveness.

The Edwardian Age The rigid class distinctions and moral certainties of Victorian times lingered on into the Edwardian Age (1901–1914), named for Victoria's successor, Edward VII. From the widespread use of electricity to the women's movement for the vote, rapid changes doomed the genteel life of the early twentieth century. By the time King George V came to the British throne in 1910, the nineteenth-century way of life was fading into memory.

The First World War In 1914, long-standing tensions among the nations of Europe exploded, ignited by the assassination of Austria-Hungary's Archduke Francis Ferdinand. When Germany invaded neutral Belgium, Britain joined with France to stem the tide of aggression.

The people of Great Britain went to war optimistically, expecting an easy victory. Soon, however, they recoiled with horror as the realities of poison gas, massive artillery barrages, and the terrible futility of trench warfare became evident.

In 1917, in the midst of war, revolution broke out in Russia, resulting in the overthrow of the czar and the establishment of the world's first communist state, the Soviet Union. By the time the Armistice was signed on November 11,

Answers to A Graphic Look

Deduce Judging from its sporty look, limited seating, and lack of a roof, this car was designed for individual pleasure, not family or work.

Draw Conclusions Mustard gas was not only a deadly way of slaughtering the unprotected in masses; it made people suffer cruelly.

Humanities: Art

Troops Resting by Christopher R. W. Nevinson.

British Painter Christopher R. W. Nevinson (1889–1946) studied art in France, where he met the Italian Futurists. Nevinson was greatly influenced by these artists and became one of the first British Futurist painters. The art produced by this group glorified modern machinery and the beauty of speed. During World War I, Nevinson served in France as an Official War Artist.

Show the students Nevinson's *Troops Resting,* on page 83 of the ***Art Transparencies.*** Note that its strong diagonals and the reduction of men to geometric shapes are typical of the Futurist style. Then ask the following questions:

1. What mood does Nevinson create through color? *The ashen shade of the faces and the blue of the helmet suggest fatigue and cold.*
2. (a) Is Nevinson using Futurist techniques for Futurist reasons? *No; rather than celebrating technology, he shows human suffering.* (b) Why does it make sense that Futurism ended after World War I? *It was hard to remain enthusiastic about technology after the war had demonstrated its destructive power.*

1918, other empires and monarchies had also been swept away, including imperial Germany and the Austro-Hungarian Empire. An uneasy peace, its harsh terms spelled out in the Treaty of Versailles, followed.

Between the Wars The disillusioned youth of postwar Europe were known as a "lost generation." Some young people masked their lack of purpose by the pursuit of pleasure—fast cars, wild jazz, giddy fads. Not all was disenchantment or frivolity, of course. Married British women over thirty won the right to vote in 1918.

The future, however, was being determined by political developments in Europe, exhausted and desperate after the Great War. Adolf Hitler began to aggressively expand Germany's borders. Only when Germany invaded Poland on September 1, 1939, did Britain admit that Hitler could not be stopped without violent intervention.

The Second World War World War II was even more destructive than World War I. Hitler's "final solution" to the "Jewish problem" brought death to 6 million Jews. The German invasion of Russia in 1941 killed soldiers and civilians by the millions. Fighting raged from Europe to North Africa, from the mountains of Burma and China to the Hawaiian Islands. Massive bombing raids turned London, Dresden, and Tokyo into infernos.

The darkest days for Britain came in 1940, when France had fallen and Britain alone bore the brunt of German air attacks. Inspired by Prime Minister Winston Churchill, and joined in 1941 by two powerful allies, the United States and the Soviet Union, Britain fought on.

Finally, in August of 1945, American atomic bombs blasted two Japanese cities, Hiroshima and Nagasaki, into cinder and ash, bringing the war to a brutal and abrupt end. The war's death toll by then had mounted to at least four times that of the First World War.

The End of an Empire The British Empire came undone after the Second World War. In addition to its domestic problems, like food shortages and cities lying in ruins, Britain began to lose its possessions and colonies. Part of Ireland had already won independence in 1921. In Asia and Africa, nationalist leaders challenged colonial rule and gained freedom. Ethnic, racial, and

Flapper Dancing the Charleston

▲ **Speculate** The flapper—a woman who cut her hair short, wore dresses without waists, and otherwise did as she pleased—appeared in the 1920's in Britain as well as in America. Why might this woman's clothing and the dance she is performing have shocked ladies of her mother's generation?

Scenes from the Blitz: Londoners Sheltering in Underground Station

▲ **Infer** During "the Blitz," which lasted from September, 1940, to May, 1941, German planes dropped bombs on London almost every night. Name two reasons why people would have taken shelter in subways during air raids.

Answers to A Graphic Look

Speculate The woman's clothing shows off her arms from wrist to shoulder, and her legs above the knee. The dance looks "wild" or "disorderly," suggesting unregulated passion—and also risking further exposure of her limbs.

Infer Subways are underground, and therefore better protected than the street against the flying debris created by a bomb. They also provide an efficient shelter-system: Their entrances are easily identified, and are designed to let large numbers of people enter at once; they are located throughout a city, convenient to the places where people gather for business or pleasure.

Connection to Literature

- To give students a sense of life in the trenches of the First World War, and of the effect of war's barbarity on refined sensibilities, have them read the War Poets, Brooke, Sassoon, and Owen, beginning on page 960.
- The sufferings of war were widespread during the first half of the twentieth century. W. H. Auden provides a thought-provoking meditation on the place of suffering in art and the world in "Musée des Beaux Arts," p. 928.
- For a taste of early twentieth-century "quiet despair," students should walk through the brown city smogs with T. S. Eliot in the "Preludes," p. 910.
- Like a ghost returned from the grave, the Second World War repeated the traumas of the First—as if nothing had been learned in the meantime. Elizabeth Bowen mirrors the "haunting" of the twentieth century by war in her tale of a woman haunted by her past, "The Demon Lover," p. 889.

Cross-Curricular Connection: Science

The Atomic Age In 1938, scientists split the atom. By firing a neutron (a subatomic particle identified by British physicist James Chadwick in 1932) at a uranium atom, they produced enormous amounts of energy. A worldwide vision of horror and hope, of world destruction or of miraculous, plentiful power, was unleashed.

The two atomic bombs dropped by the United States on the Japanese cities of Hiroshima and Nagasaki in 1945 used this process, known as nuclear fission. The later hydrogen bomb used a process called nuclear fusion.

Merely by existing, these deadly weapons have military value. Nations possessing nuclear weapons are thought unlikely to risk direct war with each other, for fear of the destruction that would result. Scientists postulate that a major nuclear war would kill half a billion people initially. Four billion more would die later, though, as the intense heat from the bombs set off fires, blocking the sun with smoke and causing a "nuclear winter."

Ask students how the world may have looked to Britons in the shadow of the Bomb. *Answers include: People lived with feelings of powerlessness and fear.*

Historical Background

Comprehension Check

1. Name two worldwide, traumatic events affecting Britain in this period. *Britain fought in both World Wars.*
2. What effect did World War I have on British attitudes? *People were disillusioned and eager for frivolity.*
3. What new power emerged at the end of World War I? *The Soviet Union emerged in 1917.*
4. In what distinctive way did Britain suffer during World War II? *Britain faced German airpower alone until new allies joined the war.*
5. Name two ways in which Britain's international influence declined after World War II. *Its colonies achieved independence; the superpowers overshadowed Britain in Europe.*
6. After World War II, the British created a modern welfare state. What happened to this system in the 1980's? *Britain's welfare state was partially dismantled by Margaret Thatcher.*

Critical Thinking

1. (a) How did the British attitude change through World War I? (b) How might this shift have affected the literature of the time? **[Analyze]** *(a) The British began the war confidently; grim reality disillusioned them. (b) Literature shifted from flag-waving to attempts to show the reality of war.*
2. How might Britain's experience in World War II explain the sudden rise to power of the Labour Party after the war? **[Connect]** *The people turned to leaders who offered domestic reform to ensure that peace would be comfortable for all.*
3. What links Britain's industrial failure to its artistic success in the 1960's? **[Speculate]** *Answers include: People turned to the arts when kept from using their energy in industry.*

Answers to

A Graphic Look

Assess The painting shows workers voting; it emphasizes the democratic, representative nature of unions.

Compare and Contrast In one, government acts as a benevolent assistant to the people; in the other, as a perhaps repressive force for order. In both cases, government intervenes in people's lives at points of crisis.

English Coal-Miners Decide to Strike

▲ **Assess** The power of labor increased during the twentieth century. Unions had become legal in 1871. Their leaders helped form a political party, the Labor Party, in 1900. By 1914, unions were roughly four million members strong. What aspect of the worker's movement does the artist focus on in this painting?

Unemployed Men Inquiring for Work at an Employment Bureau; A Protesting Hunger Striker Is Hauled Off by Police During the Great Depression

▲ **Compare and Contrast** Though early reforms had instituted measures such as the labor exchange for job-seekers shown in the photo, workers such as the hunger marcher (see inset) continued to agitate for changes. Contrast the roles of the government in people's lives as shown by these two photographs.

border conflicts, however, led to bloodshed in many of the newly independent former colonies. On the Continent, British power declined sharply, and an "iron curtain" divided Eastern and Western Europe. The United States and the Soviet Union now dominated the world between them.

By the 1960's Britons had apparently put many of their troubles behind them. From rock music to "mod" clothing, Britain influenced fashion around the world. However, basic industries—textiles, steelmaking, shipbuilding—that had been vital to Britain were no longer competing successfully. Factories were forced to close their gates.

British society was also changing rapidly in a number of ways. Immigrants from Britain's former colonies, working-class people, and women were seizing opportunities from which they had formerly been excluded.

Contemporary Britain Margaret Thatcher, a member of the Conservative party, and the first woman prime minister, came to power in 1979 and dismantled much of the government's role in the economy. Prosperity resulted for some, but many Britons did not benefit from "Thatcherism." She resigned her office in 1990 to be replaced by her own handpicked Conservative party successor, John Major. In 1997, however, Major was defeated by Tony Blair, the Labor candidate.

Many problems and challenges remain as Britain adjusts to a rapidly changing world. Its participation in the European Economic Community—a trading bloc of some 300 million people—should be a benefit, but is still in its early stages. Intervals of cease-fire in Northern Ireland are interrupted by episodes of violence as negotiations continue. Wales and Scotland voted in 1997 to set up their own parliaments, and the nation ponders the monarchy's role in the twenty-first century.

Tradition has always been strong in Great Britain. As in previous times of trial, Britons can turn to the past as a source of pride and comfort while moving forward into the swirl and bustle of contemporary life.

Cross-Curricular Connection: Social Studies

The Cold War During World War II, the Soviet Union and the nations of the West, including Britain, had cooperated to defeat Nazi Germany. By 1945, however, the wartime alliance was crumbling. Conflicting ideologies and mutual distrust soon led to the conflict known as the Cold War. (Part of this distrust was created in 1918 when, in response to the Russian Revolution, the United States and Britain sent troops into Russia.) The Cold War was a state of tension and hostility among nations without armed conflict between the major rivals.

By 1946, the Cold War was under way. By that time, Josef Stalin (1879–1953), the Soviet leader, had succeeded in installing pro-Soviet communist governments throughout Eastern Europe, creating a buffer zone against Germany. Soon, the United States and its allies were engaged in an arms race with the Soviet Union, each side stockpiling greater quantities of increasingly destructive weapons.

Ask students to explain how the world is different today. *Answers include: The Soviet Union has dissolved; Eastern Europe has changed its economic policies; some progress has been made limiting arms.*

Literature of the Period

Modernism and Poetry Modernism has been perhaps the most important artistic movement of the twentieth century, committed to creating new forms and styles. Many Modernists used images as symbols, leading to indirect, evocative work. They often presented experiences in fragments, rather than as a coherent whole.

Modernism lent itself to charting a world fragmented by war and increasingly removed from traditional sources of meaning. In his later poetry, William Butler Yeats (1865–1939) adopts the direct, more colloquial diction of Modernism, using images in powerful, symbolic ways and exploring troubling questions of modern life.

A few first-rate British poets died in the Great War, including Rupert Brooke (1887–1915) and Wilfred Owen (1893–1918). Others, such as Siegfried Sassoon (1886–1967), survived. Preeminent among the postwar poets was T. S. Eliot (1888–1965), whose poem "The Love Song of J. Alfred Prufrock" reflects the despair of the "lost generation."

The Auden Generation In the 1930's and 1940's, poets such as W. H. Auden (1907–1973), Louis MacNeice (1907–1963), and Stephen Spender (1909–1995) showed an increasing concern with political and social issues, though they did not abandon subtle symbolism and imagery. By contrast, Romanticism flared into wild brilliance in the poetry of Dylan Thomas (1914–1953).

The Movement During the 1950's and 1960's, British poets of "the Movement," such as Philip Larkin (1922–1985), Donald Davie (born 1922), and Thom Gunn (born 1929), tried to capture everyday experiences in common, yet tightly wrought, language.

Contemporary Poets Noteworthy British poets of recent years, such as Ted Hughes (born 1930), Peter Redgrove (born 1932), and the Irish-born Seamus Heaney (born 1939) have a visionary intensity. Two remarkable poets have appeared from former British colonies in the West Indies: James Berry (born 1925), a Jamaican, and Nobel Prize-winner Derek Walcott (born 1930), from the island of St. Lucia.

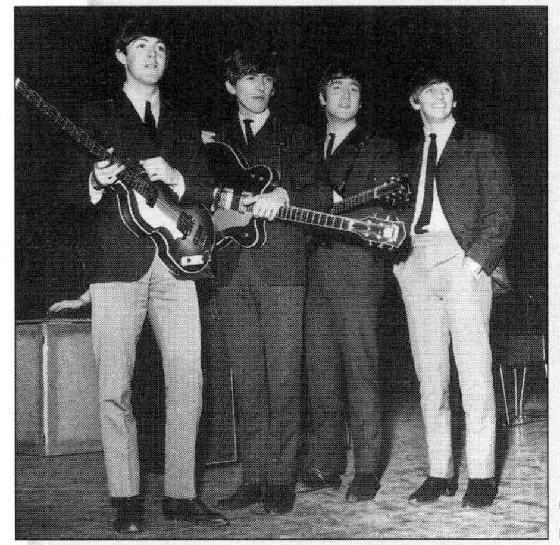

The Beatles

▲ **Compare and Contrast** The Beatles exploded as an international success in 1964. Compare this image of the Beatles with the image presented by a contemporary band you know.

A Model Wearing a Cheetah Print Miniskirt.

▲ **Speculate** During the 1960's, London's Carnaby Street set the pace for world fashion. Hemlines soared and plummeted with amazing speed. Fashion kept stepping into the future, and shock and outrage often followed. What kind of "statement" does the model's outfit in the photograph make?

Compare and Contrast Though their hair and clothing was challenging at the time, the Beatles here look mild-mannered and respectable in their jackets and ties. Males in contemporary bands tend to have long hair, no hair, dyed hair, or emphatically styled hair. Ties and jackets are rarely worn, perhaps only for irony. Contemporary bands tend to project images of anger, lunacy, intense boredom, or artistic abstraction—not the willingness to hold a pose for fans and photographers (obediently smiling and looking off at some distant point) shown by the Beatles. By posing, the Beatles allow others to transform them into icons; modern bands aggressively convert themselves into icons through hair, clothing, and lifestyle.

Speculate The model's outfit asks for attention; it creates its wearer as a spectacle, someone to be looked at. The leopard print suggests the savage or primitive; it may already suggest, in the 1960's, what it comes to mean in the 1980's—an ironic assertion of the desire for the exotic, found in what is artificial and mass-produced.

Connections to the Literature

- For a look at the new shape of British politics after Thatcher, direct students to Tony Blair's essay, "The Rights We Enjoy, the Duties We Owe," on page 1023.

Humanities: Art

"Memory," from *Cats*, Andrew Lloyd Weber.

The musical *Cats* had as its inspiration T. S. Eliot's *Old Possum's Book of Practical Cats*. Eliot's widow, Valerie Eliot, encouraged Andrew Lloyd Webber to develop these poems into a full-scale musical with director Trevor Nunn. *Cats* opened on Broadway in 1982 and enjoyed huge success.

The plot is rather simple: A number of cats who live in a garbage dump attend the "Jellicle Ball." On stage, the personalities and dreams of the cats take on near mythic proportions. The song "Memory" is sung by Grizabella, the Glamour Cat, who is given a second chance at life.

Play students "Memory" on the **Listening to Literature Audiocassettes.** Then ask the following questions:

1. How does the fact that the character singing is a cat affect your experience of the song? *Answers include: The song is less "sentimental" than if it were spoken by a person.*
2. Why do you think contemporary adult audiences find the characters in *Cats* so compelling? *Answers include: Animal characters "get by" people's sophistication and so let people experience strong emotion.*

Connections to Literature
Answers to
A GRAPHIC LOOK

Speculate Possible answers include: The United States was the leading economic success in the twentieth century; it rescued Europe during and after World War II. Because it figures as a "fantasy" land in the imagination of Europeans (the land of opportunity, the victorious ally), its own fantasies have a special resonance.

Generalize (a) Ticket prices are presumably strictly regulated on a nationalized airline. Schedules are presumably arranged, not for maximum profit, but to best serve the public. (b) Privately owned airlines will presumably compete to offer the best service and most comfort to attract more passengers. Competition will also drive ticket prices down.

Interpret (a) Each photograph shows a different part of the same scene, or the same part from a slightly different angle or at a slightly different time. They overlap, but not seamlessly: Photographs of the man's head and of the woman's head are separated from each other, suggesting that the two are sitting side by side, but we see both of them in a few poses, and there are roughly two, displaced images of each pose or aspect. (b) The "breaking up" insists that still images cannot capture time, or it attempts to introduce the passage of time into the still image. (c) The relation of subject and technique is a pun: each photograph is like a filled-in square in a crossword puzzle; read the photos in relation to each other and, like the letters in a crossword, they make sense in two directions (time and space).

Speculate (a) If London has skyscrapers, it will also have heavy traffic, public transportation, zones in which businesses are concentrated, and zones which are primarily residential. (b) London probably still retains evidence of the past, in the form of old buildings and street patterns at the center of the city that are not "rational" (laid out in a grid or other pattern for efficiency). One would expect to find some buildings reflecting the past power of the monarchy and of the established Church.

The Cool Hearth

▲ **Speculate** British inventors pioneered television technology, yet from commercials to "Dallas," the United States contributed much of what is uniquely characteristic of the content of television. Why do you think this is so?

Airplane

▲ **Generalize** In 1952, the British de Haviland Comet—the world's first large commercial jet—began carrying passengers. British airlines at the time were owned by the government; they did not become private corporations until 1987. (a) Name two advantages of a nationalized airline. (b) Name two advantages of privately owned airlines, such as the United States has.

Twentieth-Century Drama George Bernard Shaw (1856–1950) dominated late Victorian, Edwardian, and early modern drama. His witty, socially conscious plays manage to evoke laughter while examining social issues. Influenced by the Irish Literary Revival, John Millington Synge (1871–1909) vividly captures Irish rural life in plays like *The Playboy of the Western World* (1907). In the depression years of the 1930's, Noel Coward (1899–1973) won attention with a series of smartly sophisticated dramas and musicals.

Angry Young Men and Absurdists In the 1950's and 1960's, a group of dramatists known as Britain's "angry young men," which included John Osborne, used realistic techniques in plays attacking the injustices of Britain's class system. A second strain of contemporary British drama, the theater of the absurd, uses disconnected dialogue and action to depict life itself as a pointless series of misfortunes. Dublin-born Samuel Beckett (1906–1989), author of *Waiting for Godot* (1952), pioneered this form, which has also influenced Harold Pinter (born 1930) and Tom Stoppard (born 1930).

Twentieth-Century Fiction The Edwardian Age produced a number of brilliant writers of realist and naturalist fiction. Joseph Conrad, one of the pioneers of psychological realism, examines the individual's struggle with the self in tales such as *Lord Jim* (1900) and *Heart of Darkness* (1902). D. H. Lawrence (1885–1930) unleashes a savage hatred of conventional British manners and morals in novels like *Sons and Lovers* (1913). E. M. Forster opposes the hypocrisies of society in a gentler fashion in novels such as *A Passage to India* (1924).

Perhaps the greatest pioneer of Modernist fiction was the Irish writer James Joyce (1882–1941). Joyce revolutionized the form and structure of both the short story and the novel. His brilliant novel *Ulysses* (1922), contains a great variety of innovative techniques—including stream of consciousness, symbolism, and disjointed typography. Another innovative Modernist novelist is Virginia Woolf (1882–1941), best known for stream-of-consciousness novels like *To the Lighthouse* (1927).

Political and social issues gained increasing attention among novelists in the 1930's and

Cross-Curricular Connection: Social Studies

The Welfare State World War II left Britain physically battered and economically drained. In 1945, voters put the Labour party in power. The war had helped change old attitudes towards the working class. A Labour official noted that if a working-class boy "can save us in a Spitfire [a warplane], the same brain can be turned to produce a new world."

In that new world, government nationalized major industries and expanded social welfare benefits such as unemployment insurance and old-age pensions. The government built housing for the poor and opened new state-funded universities. A national health service extended free, low-cost medical care to all citizens. Other programs gave aid to the poor and created an economic cushion to help people through hard times. To pay for all these benefits, taxes rose a great deal.

Ask students to contrast the values of the welfare state with current American values. *Answers include: The welfare state assumes that society as a whole has an obligation to the poor and the sick; by contrast, many in the United States emphasize fiscally responsible government and the virtue of work.*

1940's, when a new group of novelists emerged. Aldous Huxley's (1894–1963) *Brave New World* (1932) and George Orwell's (1903–1950) *1984* (1949) paint frightening pictures of the future based on the present. Two of Britain's most popular novelists are Graham Greene (1904–1991), author of novels such as *The Power and the Glory* (1940), and P. G. Wodehouse (1881–1975), a brilliant humorist. Among more recent British novelists are William Golding (1911–1993), Anthony Burgess (1917–1993), Kingsley Amis (1922–1995), John Fowles (born 1926), and Alan Sillitoe (born 1928).

In literature, as in other aspects of British life, women have been highly visible and productive in the latter half of the twentieth century. Irish-born Iris Murdoch (born 1919) is known for her intricate novels exploring human relationships, among them *The Message to the Planet* (1990). Doris Lessing (born 1919) grew up in Rhodesia (now Zimbabwe) and gained fame for a series of novels set in Africa, including *The Four-Gated City* (1969). Nobel Prize–winner Nadine Gordimer (born 1923) writes novels and short stories that examine the moral and political dilemmas of racially divided South Africa, where she lives.

From Former Colonies In recent years, a number of talented writers from what used to be the far-flung British Empire have added to the richness of English literature. Among these are Frank Sargeson (1903–1982) of New Zealand; Patrick White (1912–1990), the Nobel Prize-winner from Australia; Wilson Harris (born 1921) of Guyana; Chinua Achebe (born 1930) and Nobel Prize-winner Wole Soyinka (born 1934), both of Nigeria. A writer from the island of Trinidad, V. S. Naipaul (born 1932), has achieved success with both fiction and nonfiction. The award-winning novel *In a Free State* (1971) is one of his finest works.

These ex-colonial writers are busy making classics for a new age. Borrowing a famous line from Shakespeare's *The Tempest*, we can say that they are transforming English literature "into something rich and strange."

The Crossword Puzzle
David Hockney

▲ **Speculate** British-born David Hockney's paintings and art works are groundbreaking and influential. (a) How does Hockney's use of photographs in this piece "break up" images? (b) What does this "breaking up" suggest about the relation between still images and time? (c) Why did he match this technique with a crossword puzzle as his subject?

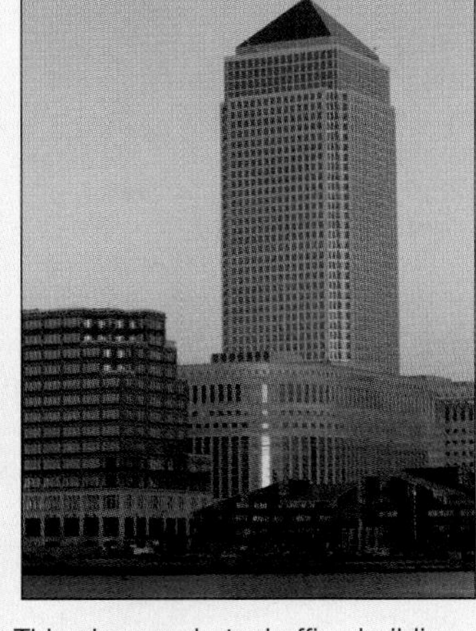

Canada Tower, London,Corbis

▲ **Speculate** This glass-and-steel office building has left its mark on the skyline of contemporary London. (a) What characteristics would you expect London to share with other major cities? (b) What characteristics would you expect to be particular to London?

Literature of the Period

Check Your Comprehension

1. Name two features characterizing Modernist literature. *Answers include: Modernists use symbolic images; they present experience in fragmentary form; and they use colloquial language.*
2. Name two focuses of British poetry after Modernism, and name a poet associated with each. *Answers include: political and social issues (W.H. Auden); a rekindled Romanticism (Dylan Thomas); everyday experience (Philip Larkin).*
3. What part of Great Britain was associated with a renewal of the drama? *Ireland was central in the renewal of the drama.*
4. (a) What kind of plays did the Angry Young Men write? (b) What kind of plays did the absurdists write? *(a) They wrote realistic attacks on social injustice. (b) They wrote plays depicting life's pointlessness, filled with disconnected dialogue and action.*
5. How did the novel evolve in this time? *Novelists such as Joyce and Woolf began to use innovative techniques such as stream-of-consciousness.*

Critical Thinking

1. The Modernists show reality in fragments of images and speech. Name two modern realities that have a fragmentary quality. **[Make a Connection]** *Answers include: Train rides show us glimpses of places passing; advertisements excerpt tiny moments of people's lives.*
2. Modern writers have experimented with the basics of storytelling, often making their work difficult for audiences. (a) Why might these artists reject ordinary storytelling? (b) Explain whether their experimentation is or is not justified. **[Make a Judgment]** *(a) Answers include: Old forms of storytelling may seem dishonest about the complexity or meaninglessness of modern experience. (b) Answers include: They are justified in showing the truth as they see it; they are not justified in shutting out an audience.*
3. Important writers have emerged from Britain's former colonies. What special issues might they face in their work? **[Hypothesize]** *Answers include: the English tradition is not entirely "theirs"—they may have spoken another language at home, or have suffered from the same colonization that brought that tradition to them.*

Activities

1. **Graphic Organization of Events** Have students use the Cause and Effect Diagram, pages 119–120 in ***Writing and Language Transparencies,*** to chart the causes and effects of a major twentieth-century event.
2. **Moderated Discussion** Has the world run out of control? Have students organize a television round-table with a moderator, in which the "guests" represent major twentieth-century events (such as World War I or women's suffrage), each played by a student. The guests should discuss what they show about humanity's mastery of its own destiny.
3. **Reflective Essay** Some would say that events and ideas in the contemporary world are too complex to be easily grasped. Have students write an essay reflecting on this complexity and discussing how it affects their view of themselves.
4. **Connections to the Literature** Challenge students to find a passage in a selection that reflects an insight, description, narrative, or idea from The Story of the Times. Have them read the passage aloud to the class, explain how it relates to The Story of the Times, then answer questions about the passage.

Develop Understanding

◆ Critical Thinking

1. a) Name a television program produced in Britain that shows on American television. (b) Is the dialogue difficult to follow? Explain where difficulties arise. **[Analyze]** *(a) Answers will vary. Students may name* Masterpiece Theater, The Benny Hill Show, *or* The Young Ones. *(b) Students may note that accent and cultural references present as much of a problem for understanding as differing word usage, but that the universal humor or drama of these shows makes understanding easy.*
2. Are there splits in the language of the United States that are similar to the split between British and American English? Explain. **[Speculate]** *There are distinctive differences in usage between the American Southeast, the Northeast, and Midwest (e.g., in the varying uses of* stoop *and* porch*).*
3. (a) How is the split between British and American English changing? (b) Is this development good or bad? Explain. **[Make a Judgment]** *(a) The degree of similarity between the two is increasing. (b) Greater similarity will make communication between the two countries easier. Greater similarity suggests the prospect of a boring world in which everything is the same from one place to the next.*

▶Critical Viewing◀

1. Find a British word in the chart for which you would easily guess the American equivalent. *Answers include:* hair grip *for* bobby pin.
2. Do the differing usages charted have to do with a few specialized areas of life? Explain. *No; they range from the calendar to food.*

Answers to Activities

1. Other examples include: *bonnet* (British for *hood), boot* (for *trunk), tracks* (for *treads), gearbox* (for *transmission), windscreen* (for *windshield), silencer* (for *muffler), wing* (for *fender).*
2. *Biscuit* means *cookie; braces, suspenders; chemist, drugstore; chips, French fries; crisp, potato chip; lift, elevator; plaster, bandaid; pudding, sausage; spectacles, glasses; tin, can; torch, flashlight.*

The Changing English Language

BRITSPEAK, A TO ZED

by Richard Lederer

At the end of World War II, Winston Churchill tells us, the Allied leaders nearly came to blows over a single word during their negotiations when some diplomats suggested that it was time to "table" an important motion. For the British, *table* meant that the motion should be put on the table for discussion. For the Americans it meant just the opposite—that it should be put on the shelf and dismissed from discussion.

This confusion serves to illustrate the truth of George Bernard Shaw's pronouncement that "England and America are two countries divided by a common language." Or, as Oscar Wilde put it, "We have really everything in common with America nowadays, except, of course, language." Wilde made this comment when he heard that audiences in New York weren't queuing up to see his plays. Instead, they were waiting in line.

British	American
gangway	aisle
hair grip	bobby pin
ironmonger	hardware store
serviette	napkin
fortnight	two weeks
zed	the letter Z [pronounced-zē]
prawn	shrimp

Separated by the Same Language

Many of the most beguiling misunderstandings can arise where identical words have different meanings in the two cultures and lingoes. When an American exclaims, "I'm mad about my flat," he is upset about his tire. When a Brit exclaims, "I'm mad about my flat," she is not bemoaning the "puncture" of her "tyre"; she is delighted with her apartment. When a Brit points out that you have "a ladder in your hose," the situation is not as bizarre as you might at first think. Quite simply, you have a run in your stocking.

Our buses are their coaches. When a hotel in the British Isles posts a large sign proclaiming, "No football coaches allowed," the message is not directed at the Don Shulas and Joe Paternos of the world. *No football coaches allowed* means "No soccer buses permitted."

With the increasing influence of film, radio, television, and international travel, the two main streams of the English language are rapidly converging like the streets of a circus (British for "traffic circle"). Nonetheless, there are scores of words, phrases, and spellings about which Brits and Yanks still don't agree.

Activities

1. If you choose to rent an automobile in the UK, with it will come a whole new vocabulary. Be sure to fill it with petrol, not gas. Investigate other differences between the words that Brits and Americans have for vehicles and roadways.
2. Define these words in American English first, then British English: biscuit, braces, chemist, chips, crisp, lift, plaster, pudding, spectacles, tin, torch.

Cross-Curricular Connection: Social Studies

Other Englishes The divisions in English do not stop with the distance between Britain and the United States. Various regions of Britain still have their own distinctive accents, vocabulary, and idiom, as do regions of the United States. Additionally, English, like other languages, has developed numerous vernaculars and slangs—words and expressions that are used by people practicing the same profession or leading similar lifestyles. These pockets of new vocabulary can shift and fade over time. Some words may become fashionable with a group wider than the one that introduced them. Some may even become part of the larger, "official" English language.

Have students discuss the social conditions for the development of dialects and slangs. *Students may reflect on the fact that geographic isolation or social exclusion help foster linguistic invention.*

PART 1 *Waking From the Dream*

The Children Enter the Palace of Luxury
Frederick Cayley Robinson, The Fine Art Society, London

Humanities: Art

The Children Enter the Palace of Luxury.

This painting shows two children outside a classical archway beneath the night sky, gazing intently on what lies within.

British painter, mural decorator, and book illustrator Frederick Cayley Robinson studied art at the Royal Academy and at Paris's Académie Julian. *The Children Enter the Palace of Luxury* probably appeared as an illustration in Maurice Maeterlinck's play *The Bluebird,* which expressed his belief in a reality deeper than ordinary, waking life.

Use these questions for discussion:

1. In what way does the painting resemble a scene from a dream? **[Analyze]** *There are few specific details characterizing the place; those presented (the statue, the stars) are striking.*
2. (a) What is the difference between a person dreaming and a person remembering a dream? (b) In what way is becoming an adult like awakening from a dream? **[Interpret]** *(a) The person remembering distinguishes dreams and reality, the dreamer does not. (b) An adult distinguishes a time when he or she saw things differently (childhood).*

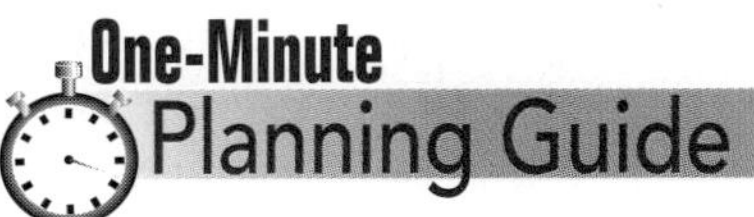

One-Minute Planning Guide

The selections in this section present the great writers of the twentieth century confronting disillusionment—and the renewal of perception to which dillusionment sometimes leads. In "The Demon Lover" the return of a ghostly past shatters a woman's illusion of normal life. Yeats charts the dreams of love, age, and art, as well as the nightmare of history. Disenchantment with modern life finds its own voice in T. S. Eliot's poems. While Auden, MacNeice, and Spender question the task of poetry, Orwell tells of adventure and political disillusionment.

Customize for
Varying Student Needs

When assigning selections in this part, keep in mind the following factors:

"The Demon Lover"
- Introduce less proficient readers to the setting and situation; they can enjoy the story as a simple ghost tale.

"Shooting an Elephant"
- Orwell's direct style and dramatic situation will keep readers' interest.

Amichai, Akhmatova, Dao
- Though the language is clear and simple, less proficient readers should paraphrase to grasp the theme.

Yeats, Auden, Eliot, MacNeice, Spender
- Their work is highly allusive, marked by compressed expression and abstract ideas. For the most difficult poems, readers should work as a group, proposing and testing interpretations. Of particular note are the following:

"The Wild Swans at Coole"
- Less proficient readers and musical/rhythmic learners can appreciate the poem's language and images.

"The Hollow Men"
- After an introduction to Eliot's ideas of modern life and his stylistic tactics, readers will find the poem's message relevant.

"In Memory of W. B. Yeats"
- Prepare students by discussing what poetry should do for its readers and the relation of poets' lives to their work.

Prepare and Engage

OBJECTIVES

1. To read, comprehend, and interpret a short story
2. To relate a story to personal experience
3. To employ strategies for reading and interpreting fiction
4. To identify the features of a ghost story
5. To build vocabulary in context and learn the word root *-loc-*
6. To develop skill in using participial phrases as sentence beginnings
7. To write a sequel with a clear and logical organization
8. To respond to the story through writing, speaking and listening, and projects.

SKILLS INSTRUCTION

Vocabulary: Word Roots: *-loc-*
Grammar: Sentence Beginnings: Participial Phrases
Reading for Success: Strategies for Reading and Interpreting Fiction
Literary Focus: The Ghost Story
Writing: Clear and Logical Organization
Speaking and Listening: Dramatic Retelling (teacher edition)
Critical Viewing: Compare and Contrast

PORTFOLIO OPPORTUNITIES

Writing: Journal Entry; Critical Evaluation; Response to Criticism
Writing Mini-Lesson: Sequel
Speaking and Listening: Dramatic Retelling; Ballad
Projects: Portrait of the Demon Lover; Blitz Report

More About the Author

After the war, Bowen published her literary criticism and book reviews in journals such as the *Tatler* and wrote scripts for the British Broadcasting Corporation. In 1948, she received the prestigious C.B.E. (Commander, Order of the British Empire). During the 1950's she spent a great deal of time in the United States, writing and lecturing. The death of her husband in 1952 preceded her return to Ireland.

While her later works grew away from the psychological realism influenced by Henry James, Bowen's works are consistently concerned with sensitive characters who don't fit into the world they inhabit.

Guide for Interpreting

Elizabeth Bowen *(1899–1973)*

The fiction of Elizabeth Bowen is distinguished by her subtle observation of landscape, by her innovative and believable use of the supernatural, and by her haunting portrayal of England during one of the darkest eras of the country's history.

A Troubled Childhood Though she was born in comfortable circumstances—her parents were well-off, and she grew up on their country estate in County Cork, Ireland—Elizabeth Bowen's early life was marked by losses. Her father had a breakdown when she was seven years old and was confined to an institution. She and her mother moved to England, where her mother died of cancer when Elizabeth was thirteen.

Her family preferred to avoid or deny strong emotion. Bowen later said that she and her mother waged a "campaign of not noticing" her father's absence. Later, she was not allowed to attend her mother's funeral.

As an adult, Bowen was to write about the helplessness of the heart to understand itself or others in the absence of love.

In her characters' insecure lives, one can still trace the marks left by Bowen's own early abandonment.

Her Ambition to Write After her mother's death, Bowen lived with her relatives, then attended boarding school until she was seventeen, when she moved to London. Her one ambition was to write, and her family's money was enough to support her as she wrote her first short stories.

A Writer's Life Her first collection of short stories, published in 1923, received little attention. Through the 1930's, while living with her husband in Oxford, she perfected her craft, publishing regularly. During the war Bowen observed England's hardships keenly and with compassion. The brutal realities of the conflict were incorporated into some of her best stories. In 1938, she completed one of her best-known works, *The Death of the Heart*, a novel about the disillusionment of an innocent, teenage girl, taken in by uncaring relatives after her mother's death.

After the war, Bowen widened her literary activities to include literary criticism and book reviews. After 1952, Bowen returned to Ireland and wrote novels that exhibit a symbolic, poetic style.

Bowen defined the novel as the "non-poetic statement of poetic truth." Through her deceptively simple style, her explorations of human relationships, guided by the hardship she had undergone, she achieved this goal.

◆ Background for Understanding

HISTORY: BOWEN IN LONDON DURING THE BLITZ

Elizabeth Bowen lived in London during the Second World War, serving as an air-raid warden. War was a daily fact in 1940's London. After decisive victories in Europe, the Germans began a steady bombardment of Britain, with London as a focus. During "the Blitz," which lasted from September 1940 to May 1941, German planes dropped bombs on London almost every night. Warning sirens and blackouts were common; whole communities were evacuated periodically, leaving street after street of deserted buildings. Yet, amid the bombing, people continued to live in the city. The eeriness of Bowen's story stems from her experience of a time when war's unthinkable horrors had become all too "ordinary."

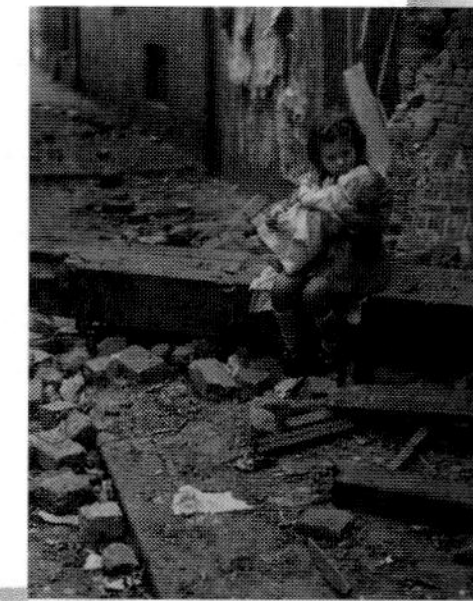

Prentice Hall Literature Program Resources

REINFORCE / RETEACH / EXTEND

Selection Support Pages
Build Vocabulary: Word Roots: *-loc-* , p. 218
Grammar and Style: Sentence Beginnings: Participial Phrases, p. 219
Reading for Success: Strategies for Reading and Interpreting Fiction, pp. 220–221
Literary Focus: The Ghost Story, p. 222

Strategies for Diverse Student Needs, p. 45

Beyond Literature Social Studies Connection: Ghosts in Other Cultures, p. 45

Formal Assessment Selection Test, pp. 227–229; Assessment Resources Software

Alternative Assessment, p. 45

Writing and Language Transparencies Story Map, pp. 127–130

Resource Pro CD-ROM "The Demon Lover"—includes all resource material and customizable lesson plan

Listening to Literature Audiocassettes "The Demon Lover"

MODEL SELECTION

The Demon Lover

◆ Literature and Your Life

CONNECT YOUR EXPERIENCE

Becoming a "ghost" is easy; it's just a trick of time and place. Walk by your old elementary school . . . linger in your old home after the movers have come and emptied all the rooms. All becoming a ghost takes is a sideways step out of familiar routines into the past. When you are in a place where you no longer have a place, it is easy to feel like a ghost—or to meet one.

Elizabeth Bowen has a sharp sense of these tricks of time and place. In "The Demon Lover," Mrs. Drover returns like a ghost to her own shut-up house, only to find that it is, perhaps, haunted.

Journal Writing Describe a once-familiar place that made you feel like a "ghost."

THEMATIC FOCUS: WAKING FROM THE DREAM

As you read the story, notice how the dreamlike atmosphere that occurs during war makes everything seem out of place.

◆ Literary Focus

THE GHOST STORY

A **ghost story** is a tale that leaves you wondering whether there's a supernatural force at work. Some ghost stories allow either a supernatural or a natural explanation of the events they recount. By causing the mind to hesitate between these alternatives, a ghost story blurs the line between the familiar and the unfamiliar.

Elizabeth Bowen, for instance, makes us wonder whether the "ghost" in "The Demon Lover" is actually Mrs. Drover's dead fiancé or a hallucination, based on her unresolved feelings about him.

◆ Build Vocabulary

WORD ROOTS: *-loc-*

Before her marriage, Bowen writes, Kathleen experiences "a complete dislocation from everything." *Dislocation*—built on the root *-loc-*, meaning "place"— refers to the condition of being out of place.

WORD BANK

Before you read, preview this list of words from the story.

spectral
dislocation
arboreal
circumscribed
aperture

◆ Grammar and Style

SENTENCE BEGINNINGS: PARTICIPIAL PHRASES

To add variety to her writing, Bowen begins some sentences with participial phrases. A **participle** is a verb form, usually ending in *-ed* or *-ing*, that is used as an adjective. A **participial phrase** is a participle, together with its modifiers and complements.

Shifting some parcels under her arm, she slowly forced round her latchkey . . .

A participial phrase can often be placed at the beginning of a sentence, as long as it is near the word it modifies. For example, *Shifting some parcels under her arm* appears next to the pronoun *she*, which it modifies.

Notice how Bowen adds a rhythm to her writing by occasionally beginning a sentence with a participial phrase. The sentence seems to start "in the middle" of an action or event that is already under way—an effect that helps draw the reader in.

Interest Grabber Have students imagine they are living in London during the Blitz (the place and time of this story). Bombs are dropping on the city every night. Sirens pierce the air as fire engines and ambulances rush to burning buildings. Have students describe daily life under these conditions. How would they shop? Go to school? See friends? Take shelter from bombs? They can then better appreciate the eerie atmosphere of the story—especially its scanty references to the violence that was all around.

Customize for
Less Proficient Readers

Some of Elizabeth Bowen's long sentences or list-like descriptions may prove confusing for less proficient readers. Encourage these students to read slowly, translating the complicated sentences into a simple list of events and actions.

Customize for
More Advanced Students

Urge students to focus on Bowen's masterful ability to create a particular mood. Challenge students to identify descriptive and sensory language that contributes to the mood.

Customize for
English Language Learners

For these students, try annotating the margins of a copy of the story with simple descriptions of the actions and events. Then have them follow along as they listen to the story on audiotape.

Customize for
Bodily/Kinesthetic Learners

Ask these students to act out Mrs. Drover's physical movements as the story progresses. Have them speculate about how her changing movements create and convey the story's mood.

Preparing for Standardized Tests

Reading and Vocabulary Test preparers recommend that students expand their knowledge of word roots and other vocabulary elements to increase success on standardized tests. Such skill enables test-takers to decipher unfamiliar words, whether in vocabulary items, verbal reasoning sections, or reading comprehension passages. The Build Vocabulary lesson for this selection focuses on learning word meaning through the use of the root *-loc-*. For additional practice, use the Build Vocabulary page in ***Selection Support,*** p. 218.

Grammar and Language Many test situations require students to write essays or other prose material. Developing a fluid writing style that includes varied sentence beginnings will enhance students' success in these situations. The Grammar and Style lesson for this selection focuses on using participial phrases as sentence beginnings. As students gain expertise with this skill, their writing will become more immediate and engaging to test reviewers. For additional practice, use the Grammar and Style page on Sentence Beginnings: Participial Phrases, p. 219, in ***Selection Support.***

The Reading for Success page in each unit presents a set of problem-solving procedures to help readers understand authors' words and ideas on multiple levels. Good readers develop a bank of strategies from which they can draw as needed.

Unit 6 introduces strategies for reading and interpreting fiction. These strategies give readers an approach for understanding an author's intent and for deriving their own meaning from fiction.

These strategies for reading and interpreting fiction are modeled with "The Demon Lover." Each box outlined in green shows an example of the thinking process involved in applying one of these strategies.

How to Use the Reading for Success Page

- Introduce the strategies for reading and interpreting fiction, presenting each as a problem-solving procedure. Be sure students understand what each strategy involves and under what circumstances to apply it.
- Before students read the story, have them preview it, looking at the annotations in the boxes outlined in green that model the strategies.
- To reinforce these strategies after students have read "The Demon Lover," have students do the Reading for Success exercises in ***Selection Support,*** pp. 200–221. These pages give students an opportunity to read a selection and practice strategies for reading and interpreting fiction by writing their own annotations.

Reading for Success

Strategies for Reading and Interpreting Fiction

When reading fiction, turn your mind into a kind of theater, in which the mind is the stage, the actors, and the director all at the same time. Use this theater to find the relationship between the details the author presents and the meaning of the piece. Here are a few strategies to help you find that meaning.

Identify with a character or the situation.

Short stories can take you through all kinds of experiences. When you identify with a situation, you live it with the character: You share the character's feelings and perceptions of the events. In this way you may relate to experiences from your own life—or to experiences that you may never actually have had firsthand.

Read between the lines.

By implying meanings without stating them directly, writers offer us a world in which the mind can stretch itself, finding connections wherever it looks. As you read, look for significant word choices, patterns of events, and other clues to understand what a writer is saying between the lines.

Question and challenge the text.

A story will reveal its secrets only if you pursue them. Question as you read: What is happening? Why did he say that? You may not always find an answer right away, but pieces of the story will start to collect around your questions, and a larger picture will take shape. Then challenge the story: Are the characters and situations true? Do you accept the author's view of the world?

Draw conclusions about what you read.

Once you have understood and thought about the events and characters in a story, make judgments about the author's message–the overall picture the author is painting.

Respond to the story.

An important step in understanding a text is identifying your own reaction. Are you puzzled, thrilled, or scared? You may then judge whether your response was intended by the author, and how he or she evoked it. Even the most sophisticated critical responses must start with these reactions.

As you read "The Demon Lover," notice the notes along the side. The notes demonstrate how to apply these strategies to your reading.

Reading Strategies: Support and Reinforcement

Appropriate Reading Strategies Students are given a reading strategy to apply in reading each selection. Each strategy provides a way for students to gain insight into the selection. If the selection is fiction, an appropriate strategy reinforces the Reading for Success instruction.

Reading Prompts To encourage application of the given reading strategy, there are occasional prompts, within green boxes, at appropriate and significant points.

In addition, there are red boxes prompting application of the Literary Focus concept and maroon boxes prompting students to connect with their lives.

Using the Boxed Annotations and Prompts

The material in the green, red, and maroon boxes along the sides of selections is intended to help students apply the literary element and the reading strategy and to make a connection with their lives.

You may use the boxed material in several ways:

- Have students pause when they come to a box and respond to its prompt before they continue reading.
- Urge students to read through the selection ignoring the boxes. After they have read the selection completely, they may go back and review the selection, responding to the prompts.

MODEL

ELIZABETH BOWEN

Toward the end of her day in London Mrs. Drover went round to her shut-up house to look for several things she wanted to take away.
1 Some belonged to herself, some to her family, who were by now used to their country life. It was late August; it had been a steamy, showery day: at the moment the trees down the pavement glittered in an escape of humid yellow afternoon sun. Against the next batch of clouds, already piling up ink-dark, broken chimneys and parapets stood out. In her once familiar street, as in any unused channel, an unfamiliar queerness had silted up; a cat wove itself in and out of railings, but no human eye watched Mrs. Drover's return. Shifting some parcels under her arm, she slowly forced round her latchkey in an unwilling lock, then gave the door, which had warped, a push with her knee. Dead air came out to meet her as she went in.

The staircase window having been boarded up, no light came down into the hall. But one
2 door, she could just see, stood ajar, so she went quickly through into the room and unshuttered the big window in there. Now the prosaic woman, looking about her, was more perplexed than she knew by everything that she saw, by traces of her long former habit of life—the yellow smoke stain up the white marble mantelpiece, the ring left by a vase on the top of the escritoire,[1] the bruise in the wallpaper where, on the door being thrown open widely, the china handle had always hit the wall. The piano, having gone away to be stored, had left what looked like claw marks on its part of the parquet.[2] Though not much dust had seeped in, each object wore a film of another kind; and, the only ventilation being the chimney, the whole drawing room smelled of the cold hearth. Mrs. Drover put down her parcels on the escritoire and left the room to proceed upstairs; the things she wanted were in a bedroom chest.

> **Read between the lines** to detect the pattern that Bowen sets up in this passage. Stains, rings,
> bruises, and claw 3
> marks—all repeat the image of a trace—a mark left by a thing now absent.

She had been anxious to see how the house was—the part-time caretaker she shared with some neighbors was away this week on his holiday, known to be not yet back. At the best of times he did not look in often, and she was never sure that she trusted him. There were some cracks in the structure, left by the last bombing, on which she was anxious to keep an eye. Not that one could do anything—

A shaft of refracted daylight now lay across the hall. She stopped dead and stared at the hall table—on this lay a letter addressed to her.

She thought first—then the caretaker *must* be back. All the same, who, seeing the house shuttered, would have dropped a letter in at the box? It was not a circular, it was not a bill. And the post office redirected, to the address in the country, everything for her that came through the post. The caretaker (even if he *were* back) did not know she was due in ↓

1. **escritoire** (es′ krə twär′) *n.*: A writing desk or table.

2. **parquet** (pär kā′) *n.*: Flooring of inlaid woodwork in geometric forms.

Develop Understanding

This chilling ghost story poses the question: Are there supernatural elements at work here, or is the inexplicable a product of the human imagination? When the story's main character, Mrs. Drover, returns to her deserted London home during a pause in World War II bombing, she discovers a letter that appears to be from a long-ago, and presumably dead, fiancé, calling for an assignation on that very day. Her responses to the letter demonstrate the vulnerability of the human psyche, especially during wartime. They also leave readers wondering: Is there really a ghost or is Mrs. Drover hallucinating? Even more profoundly, the story suggests a larger social meaning: A world that can go to war a second time is perhaps, like Mrs. Drover, in love with a demon.

◆ Literary Focus

1 The Ghost Story Point out to students that Bowen does not explain the Drovers' absence from their London home. Why might the writer choose to leave this information a mystery? *Students should note that omitting this information helps set up the mysterious and eerie mood of the story and invites readers to question the situation from the very beginning.*

◆ Literature and Your Life

2 Discuss with students Mrs. Drover's situation, that of entering an empty house she once lived in. What feelings have students experienced returning to their homes after a long absence? *Students may respond that they felt strange, as if they were haunting a once-familiar place.*

◆ Reading for Success

3 Read Between the Lines Have students look for other examples of this type of image as they read.

Block Scheduling Strategies

Consider these suggestions to take advantage of extended class time:

- Review and model each of the Reading for Success strategies before students begin reading.
- Invite students to read aloud and discuss their Literature and Your Life (p. 887) journal entries.
- Introduce the concept of the ghost story in the Literary Focus on page 887. Have students complete and discuss the Literary Focus questions on page 894 and the Literary Focus page on The Ghost Story, p. 222, in ***Selection Support.***
- Use the Cross-Curricular Connection page on Ghosts in Other Cultures, p. 45 in ***Beyond Literature,*** to help students understand what is universal about ghost stories.
- Prepare students for the Dramatic Retelling activity (p. 895), using the Speaking and Listening Mini-Lesson on page 891.
- Have students begin the Writing Mini-Lesson (p. 895) by exchanging plot outlines with a partner. Urge pairs to discuss the organization Bowen uses as they review their own choices.

Develop Understanding

◆ Critical Thinking

❶ **Interpret** What clues are there that something odd has happened or is about to happen? *Bowen hints at inexplicable aspects of the letter's arrival with clues such as the caretaker's absence and the lack of a stamp on the letter.*

◆ Reading for Success

❷ **Respond to the Story** Ask students to respond to the opening sentences of the second paragraph. What is the effect of these sentences on the reader? *Students may feel suspense after the description of Mrs. Drover's lips and the fear that it implies. Some may feel a twinge of dread, sensing malignity or even the supernatural in the hint that the letter's arrival has been timed to coincide with her arrival at the house.*

❸ **Clarification** *Jumper* is a British word for a pullover sweater.

◆ Reading for Success

❹ **Question the Text** The fact that her lips go white, that she drops the letter, and that she must consult the mirror to see if it registers the extent of the change she feels, all paint a clear picture of Mrs. Draper's fear and surprise. The persistence of her fear or wonder is attested to by her continued glances back at the letter.

◆ Reading for Success

❺ **Read Between the Lines** Ask students to recall previous images of traces. *Answers include: a smoke stain, a bruise in the wallpaper.* Then ask what these traces have in common with the mark left on Kathleen's palm. *All are marks, even literally indentations, left behind by an object.* Ask students in what sense a ghost is like such marks. *Students should reflect that a ghost is something "left behind" by a dead person, just as these marks are left behind by absent objects. (Consider drawing a diagram to illustrate the trace-like qualities of a ghost.)*

❶ London today—her call here had been planned to be a surprise—so his negligence in the manner of this letter, leaving it to wait in the dusk and the dust, annoyed her. Annoyed, she picked up the letter, which bore no stamp. But it cannot be important, or they would know . . . She took the letter rapidly upstairs with her, without a stop to look at the writing till she reached what had been her bedroom, where she let in light. The room looked over the garden and other gardens: the sun had gone in; as the clouds sharpened and lowered, the trees and rank lawns seemed already to smoke with dark. Her reluctance to look again at the letter came from the fact that she felt intruded upon—and by someone contemptuous of her ways. However, in the tenseness preceding the fall of rain she read it: it was a few lines.

DEAR KATHLEEN,

You will not have forgotten that today is our anniversary, and the day we said. The years have gone by at once slowly and fast. In view of the fact that nothing has changed, I shall rely upon you to keep your promise. I was sorry to see you leave London, but was satisfied that you would be back in time. You may expect me, therefore, at the hour arranged.

Until then . . . K.

❷ As you read about the letter and Mrs. Drover's reaction to it, **note your own response.** Is it fear, curiosity, dread, or suspense?

Mrs. Drover looked for the date: it was today's. She dropped the letter onto the bedsprings, then picked it up to see the writing again—her lips, beneath the remains of lipstick, beginning to go white. She felt so much the change in her own face that she went to the mirror, polished a clear patch in it and looked at once urgently and stealthily in. She was confronted by a woman of forty-four, with eyes starting out under a hatbrim that had been rather carelessly pulled down. She had not put on any more powder since she left the shop where she ate her solitary tea. The pearls her husband had given her on their marriage hung loose round ❸ her now rather thinner throat, slipping into the V of the pink wool jumper her sister knitted last autumn as they sat round the fire. Mrs. Drover's most normal expression was one of controlled worry, but of assent. Since the birth of the third of her little boys, attended by a quite serious illness, she had had an intermittent muscular flicker to the left of her mouth, but in spite of this she could always sustain a manner that was at once energetic and calm.

Turning from her own face as precipitately as she had gone to meet it, she went to the chest where the things were, unlocked it, threw up the lid and knelt to search. But as rain began to come crashing down she could not keep from looking over her shoulder at the stripped bed on which the letter lay. Behind the blanket of rain the clock of the church that still stood struck six—with rapidly heightening apprehension she counted each of the slow strokes. "The hour arranged . . . My God," she said, "*What* hour? How should I . . . ? After twenty-five years. . . ."

Question the text to learn from the descriptive details how Mrs. Drover reacts to the letter. ❹

The young girl talking to the soldier in the garden had not ever completely seen his face. It was dark; they were saying goodbye under a tree. Now and then—for it felt, from not seeing him at this intense moment, as though she had never seen him at all—she verified his presence for these few moments longer by putting out a hand, which he each time pressed, without very much kindness, and painfully, on to one of the breast buttons of his uniform. That cut of the button on the palm of her hand was, principally, what she was to carry away. This was so near the end of a leave from France that she could only wish him already gone. It was August 1916. Being not kissed, being drawn away from and looked at intimidated Kathleen till she imagined spectral glitters in the place of his eyes. Turning away and looking back up the lawn she saw, through branches of trees, the drawing-room window alight; she caught a breath for the moment when she could go running back there into the safe arms of her mother and sister, and cry: "What shall I do, what shall I do? He has gone."

Read between the lines to tie together the mark left in Kathleen's palm—a trace of her fiancé's button—with the earlier images of "traces." A ghost is itself a kind of trace—the present mark of a person now absent. ❺

Cross-Curricular Connection: Social Studies

World War I began in 1914, sparked by the assassination of Austro-Hungarian Archduke Francis Ferdinand. At first, Germany advanced quickly through Belgium and France. After a certain point, the war became primarily defensive. Soldiers from England and France dug themselves into a maze of trenches to fight off German attack. Three horrible and disillusioning years followed, in which neither side gained much ground but both sides suffered great losses. This was warfare of a type Europeans had never seen before—poison gas, mud, and a shockingly high number of casualties. Among the millions of war dead, a generation of young Englishmen was decimated.

Have students discuss how the memory of World War I horrors might contribute to Mrs. Drover's state of mind. *Anticipating similar horrors in this war, she may be "on edge." At the same time, not having gotten over the previous war's horrors, she may be more vulnerable in the current crisis.*

Hearing her catch her breath, her fiancé said, without feeling: "Cold?"

"You're going away such a long way."

"Not so far as you think."

"I don't understand?"

"You don't have to," he said. "You will. You know what we said."

"But that was—suppose you—I mean, suppose."

"I shall be with you," he said, "sooner or later. You won't forget that. You need do nothing but wait."

6 **Read between the lines** to understand this strange scene. The fiancé has neither left, nor is he truly, warmly present; Kathleen is ready to miss him, but feels frozen while he lingers. He is already a "ghost"—a trace of her past to which she cannot say goodbye.

Only a little more than a minute later she was free to run up the silent lawn. Looking in through the window at her mother and sister, who did not for the moment perceive her, she already felt that unnatural promise drive down between her and the rest of all humankind. No other way of having given herself could have made her feel so apart, lost and foresworn. She could not have plighted a more sinister troth.

Kathleen behaved well when, some months later, her fiancé was reported missing, presumed killed. Her family not only supported her but were able to praise her courage without stint because they could not regret, as a husband for her, the man they knew almost nothing about. They hoped she would, in a year or two, console herself—and had it been only a question of consolation things might have gone much straighter ahead. But her trouble, behind just a little grief, was a complete dislocation from everything. She did not reject other lovers, for these failed to appear: for
7 years she failed to attract men—and with the approach of her thirties she became natural enough to share her family's anxiousness on this score. She began to put herself out, to wonder; and at thirty-two she was very greatly relieved to find herself being courted by William Drover. She married him, and the two of them settled down in this quiet, arboreal part of Kensington; in this house the years piled up, her children were born and they all lived till they were driven out by the bombs of the next war. Her movements as Mrs. Drover were circumscribed, and she dismissed any idea that they were still watched. 7

When Bowen tells you that Kathleen "dismissed" any idea that her movements "were still watched," **read between the lines** to learn that, before she was married, she felt as if she were being watched. 8

As things were—dead or living the letter writer sent her only a threat. Unable, for some minutes, to go on kneeling with her back exposed to the empty room, Mrs. Drover rose from the chest to sit on an upright chair whose back was firmly against the wall. The desuetude[3] of her former bedroom, her married London home's whole air of being a cracked cup from which memory, with its reassuring power, had either evaporated or leaked away, made a crisis—and at just this crisis the letter writer had, knowledgeably, struck. The hollowness of the house this evening canceled years on years of voices, habits and steps. Through the shut windows she only heard rain fall on the roofs around. To rally herself, she said she was in a mood—and, for two or three seconds shutting her eyes, told herself that she imagined the letter. But she opened them—there it lay on the bed.

From this passage, you might **draw conclusions** about how fragile Bowen thinks our identity becomes when we are stripped of our habits and when familiar surroundings become foreign. 9

On the supernatural side of the letter's entrance she was not permitting her mind to dwell. Who, in London, knew she meant to call at the house today? Evidently, however, this had been known. The caretaker, *had* he come back, had had no cause to expect her: he would have taken the letter in his pocket, to forward it, at his own time, through the post. There was no other sign that the caretaker had been in—but, if not? Letters dropped in at doors of deserted

◆ Build Vocabulary

spectral (spek´ trəl) *adj.*: Ghostly

dislocation (dis´ lō kā´ shən) *n.*: Condition of being out of place; the event of becoming out of place

arboreal (är bôr´ ē əl) *adj.*: Of, near, or among trees

circumscribed (sʉr´ kəm skrīb'd') *adj.*: Limited; having a definite boundary

3. **desuetude** (des´ wi to͞od') *adj.*: Condition of not being used any more.

Customize for
Less Proficient Readers
Clarify the jumps in time taking place in the story. Mrs. Drover's flashback begins, "The young girl . . ." (p. 890). Explain that the leap from present to past occurs quickly while the transition back to the present is gradual. Have students list events in their proper order.

◆ Reading for Success

6 Read Between the Lines Have students find words in the passage describing the leave-taking that suggest the fiancé is ghostlike or threatening. *His eyes have a "spectral" glitter, and Kathleen is so disturbed by him that she thinks of the "arms of her mother and sister" as "safe."*

◆ Literary Focus

7 The Ghost Story Ask students how they explain young Kathleen's failure to attract suitors. In what way does this information contribute to the uneasy, mysterious mood of the story? *Students may say that Kathleen was depressed and therefore withdrawn. Her inability to attract men could also suggest that her fiancé had a ghostly hold over her. Both the psychological and the supernatural explanation are plausible, adding to the reader's uncertainty.*

◆ Reading for Success

8 Read Between the Lines You might want to follow up the prompt by asking students *who* might be doing the watching? *Most students will respond that she probably felt watched by her fiancé, who had promised that he would "be with" her.*

◆ Reading for Success

9 Draw Conclusions Help students find specific words that suggest the fragility. *Examples are "cracked," "leaked," "crisis," and "hollowness."*

Speaking and Listening Mini-Lesson

Dramatic Retelling

This mini-lesson supports the Speaking and Listening activity on page 895.

Introduce the Concept Have students share examples of favorite ghost stories from books, films, or storytelling sessions. Discuss what makes these so effective, reviewing both content and presentation. Point out that "The Demon Lover" has no violence or bloodshed in it, yet it is very frightening.

Develop Background Before students present their retellings, encourage them to review and discuss the following dramatic strategies:

- In retelling a story, it is probably more effective to focus on character and situation rather than on setting.
- Tone of voice and gesture can lend dramatic effect to retellings.

Apply the Information Have students work together to create a versatile backdrop for the retellings, perhaps draped black cloth behind a single chair. Allow them to rehearse their stories and plan effective changes in tone and appropriate gestures. Point out that overacting may undercut the suspense they want to create. Have them present their retellings to the class.

Assess the Outcome Have students find examples of good retelling techniques in as many of the performances as possible. Then ask students how these stories compared with "The Demon Lover."

◆ Critical Thinking

❶ **Connect** Ask students: How does Mrs. Drover's practicality work against her here? How does it contribute to the story's sense of fated disaster? *Students should note that Mrs. Drover's practicality keeps her from fleeing the house instantly and perhaps escaping whatever fate awaits her. Her determination to carry on contributes to the growing certainty that something sinister lies ahead.*

◆ Reading for Success

❷ **Identify with a Character** Students may say that they flee without thinking when truly afraid; some may say that they try to gather their thoughts and resist the panic.

▶Critical Viewing◀

❸ **Compare and Contrast** Students may say that some objects in the story, the letter, for example, are definitely threatening. The objects in the engraving may seem similarly threatening to students, either because they are partly in shadow or because the light mysteriously suggests that the chair itself is watching through the doorway.

◆ Critical Thinking

❹ **Connect** Encourage students to recognize the link between young Kathleen's inability to see her fiancé's face during the leave-taking and the mature Mrs. Drover's inability to recall that face. This link suggests that there is, and perhaps always was, a disturbing blankness about the fiancé. More sophisticated students may be encouraged to recognize that the mature Mrs. Drover has somehow built her practical personality around the refusal to look her demon "in the face." Rather than face a traumatic memory, she will lose her mind.

◆ Reading for Success

❺ **Identify with a Character** Have students describe a time when something startled them.

houses do not fly or walk to tables in halls. They do not sit on the dust of empty tables with the air of certainty that they will be found. There is needed some human hand—but nobody but the caretaker had a key. Under circumstances she did not care to consider, a house can be entered without a key. It was possible that she was not alone now. She might be being waited for, downstairs. Waited for—until when? Until "the hour arranged." At least that was not six o'clock; six has struck.

She rose from the chair and went over and locked the door.

❶ The thing was, to get out. To fly? No, not that: she had to catch her train. As a woman whose utter dependability was the keystone of her family life she was not willing to return to the country, to her husband, her little boys and her sister, without the objects she had come up to fetch. Resuming work at the chest she set about making up a number of parcels in a rapid, fumbling-decisive way. These, with her shopping parcels, would be too much to carry; these meant a taxi—at the thought of the taxi her heart went up and her normal breathing resumed. I will ring up the taxi now; the taxi cannot come too soon; I shall hear the taxi out there running its engine, till I walk calmly down to it through the hall. I'll ring up—But no: the telephone is cut off . . . She tugged at a knot she had tied wrong.

❷ It is not hard to **identify with a character** like Mrs. Drover in this situation. When you are caught up in a panic, do you just run as fast as you can, or do you try to calm your mind and stick to your plans?

The idea of flight . . . He was never kind to me, not really. I don't remember him kind at all. Mother said he never considered me. He was set on me, that was what it was—not love. Not love, not meaning a person well. What did he do, to make me promise like that? I can't remember—But she found that she could.

She remembered with such dreadful acuteness that the twenty-five years since then dissolved like smoke and she instinctively looked for the weal[4] left by the button on the palm of her hand. She remembered not only all that he said and did but the complete suspension of *her* existence during that August week. I was not

4. **weal** *n.*: Raised mark, line, or ridge on the skin caused by an injury.

Ox House, Shaftsbury, 1932, John R. Biggs

▲ **Critical Viewing** Compare the suggestion of "life" this engraving gives to material objects with the role of objects in the story. Are they a threat, a consolation, or indifferent? **[Compare and Contrast]** ❸

myself—they all told me so at the time. She remembered—but with one white burning blank as where acid has dropped on a photograph: *under no conditions* could she remember his face. ❹

So wherever he may be waiting, I shall not know him. You have no time to run from a face you do not expect.

The thing was to get to the taxi before any clock struck what could be the hour. She would slip down the street and round the side of the square to where the square gave on the main road. She would return in the taxi, safe, to her own door, and bring the driver into the house with her to pick up the parcels from room to room. The idea of the taxi driver made her decisive, bold; she unlocked her door, went to the top of the staircase and listened down.

She heard nothing—but while she was hearing nothing the *passé*[5] air of the staircase was disturbed by a draft that traveled up to her face. It emanated from the basement: down there a door or window was being opened by someone who

Mrs. Drover feels a draft from the basement—a door or window has opened. **Identify with** her feelings at this moment. ❺

5. **passé** (pa sā´) *adj.*: Stale.

◆ Build Vocabulary

aperture (ap´ ər chər´) *n.*: Opening

Humanities: Art

Ox House, Shaftsbury (wood engraving), 1932, by John R. Biggs.

This scene offers a partial glimpse from one room into another. Like Mrs. Drover or the ghost in the story, the viewer might be either hesitantly or stealthily moving through a home.

John R. Biggs created this black-and-white wood block print. Once a flourishing means of reproducing pictorial images, wood block printing was by 1932 less common. The process—lines are incised into wooden blocks, which are then inked and pressed onto paper—enabled Biggs to create a striking but hauntingly quiet scene.

Use these questions for discussion:

1. If this were a room in Mrs. Drover's house, what might happen next? *Allow students to speculate freely. Some may say that the ghost might be hiding in the room beyond or that Mrs. Drover might walk fearfully but with determination into the room beyond to complete her tasks.*
2. What elements in the engraving evoke the mysterious mood of the story? *The contrast of darkness and light lends an eerie feeling of a mysterious presence.*

chose this moment to leave the house.

The rain had stopped; the pavements steamily shone as Mrs. Drover let herself out by inches from her own front door into the empty street. The unoccupied houses opposite continued to meet her look with their damaged stare. Making toward the thoroughfare and the taxi, she tried not to keep looking behind. Indeed, the silence was so intense—one of those creeks of London silence exaggerated this summer by the damage of war—that no tread could have gained on hers unheard. Where her street debouched on the square where people went on living, she grew conscious of, and checked, her unnatural pace. Across the open end of the square two buses impassively passed each other; women, a perambulator,[6] cyclists, a man wheeling a barrow signalized, once again, the ordinary flow of life. At the square's most populous corner should be—and was—the short taxi rank. This evening, only one taxi—but this, although it presented its blank rump, appeared already to be alertly waiting for her. Indeed, without looking round the driver started his engine as she panted up from behind and put her hand on the door. As she did so, the clock struck seven. The taxi faced the main road. To make the trip back to her house it would have to turn—she had settled back on the seat and the taxi *had* turned before she, surprised by its knowing movement, recollected that she had not "said where." She leaned forward to scratch at the glass panel that divided the driver's head from her own.

The driver braked to what was almost a stop, turned round and slid the glass panel back. The jolt of this flung Mrs. Drover forward till her face was almost into the glass. Through the aperture driver and passenger, not six inches between them, remained for an eternity eye to eye. Mrs. Drover's mouth hung open for some seconds before she could issue her first scream. After that she continued to scream freely and to beat with her gloved hands on the glass all round as the taxi, accelerating without mercy, made off with her into the hinterland of deserted streets.

> The end of the story might have you on the edge of your seat, or it may lead you to **challenge the text.** Does this scene spoil the story's effect by directly introducing the supernatural? ❻

6. **perambulator** *n.*: Baby carriage.

Guide for Responding

◆ *Literature and Your Life*

Reader's Response How effective was the ending of the story? Explain.

Thematic Focus In what sense has the war turned ordinary life into an illusion for Mrs. Drover?

☑ Check Your Comprehension

1. Why is Mrs. Drover's house empty?

2. (a) Who has written the letter Mrs. Drover discovers? (b) Why is she so upset by it?

3. Under what circumstances did she last meet the writer of the letter? What effect did their relationship have on her?

4. (a) How does Mrs. Drover plan to escape from the house? (b) Explain whether she succeeds.

◆ Critical Thinking

INTERPRET

1. (a) Identify three points where Mrs. Drover feels that she is being watched. (b) Describe what each adds to the story. **[Infer]**

2. (a) How does the author describe Mrs. Drover's reaction to the letter? (b) What feelings does this description prompt in you? **[Analyze]**

3. Contrast the young Kathleen with Mrs. Drover. **[Compare and Contrast]**

4. What does Mrs. Drover's fate suggest about the importance of habit and the familiar in human life? **[Draw Conclusions]**

APPLY

5. Name a place that is ripe for "haunting." Explain what it shares with wartime London. **[Relate]**

◆ Reading for Success

❻ **Challenge the Text** To answer, have students scan the final page, first explaining every occurrence naturally and then supernaturally.

Reinforce and Extend

Answers

◆ *Literature and Your Life*

Reader's Response Have students support their point with details.

Thematic Focus By forcing her to abandon daily routines, the war has canceled her ordinary life. At the same time, her breakdown demonstrates that her "ordinary" self was just an illusion waiting to dissolve.

☑ Check Your Comprehension

1. The war forced her and her family to leave.
2. (a) The letter appears to be from her former fiancé. (b) He's probably dead, and she can't figure out how the letter got there.
3. Mrs. Drover last met the letter writer as he left to fight in World War I. She didn't become involved with other men for years after her fiancé was reported missing.
4. (a) She hopes to get a taxi to take her away. (b) She fails because the driver appears to be her fiancé.

◆ Critical Thinking

1. (a) She feels watched after the disappearance of her fiancé, after noticing the letter, when she is searching through the chest, and when she feels a draft from the staircase. (b) Each heightens the story's tension.
2. (a) She is annoyed, puzzled, and worried at first; then she becomes upset. (b) Students may respond with sympathy, puzzlement, annoyance, or a combination of these.
3. Kathleen is impressionable and somewhat passive. As the older Mrs. Drover, she seems businesslike and practical.
4. Her fate suggests that, without familiar routines, human beings are extremely vulnerable.
5. Students' places should share the abandoned feeling of wartime London.

Beyond the Selection

FURTHER READING

Other Works by Elizabeth Bowen

The Hotel
The Heat of the Day
The Last September

Other Works Involving the Supernatural

A Stranger Here, Thelma Hatch Wyss
Historic Haunted America, M. Norman/B. Scott
Come Like Shadows, Welwyn Wilton Katz

We suggest that you preview these works before recommending them to students.

INTERNET

You and your students may find additional information about Elizabeth Bowen on the Internet. We suggest the following site. Please be aware, however, that sites may have changed since we published this information.

For critical responses to Bowen's work, visit **http://www.nadn.navy.mil/EnglishDept/ILV/bowen.htm**

You may also find information about ghost stories on the Internet. We *strongly recommend* that you preview all sites before you send students to them.

Answers

◆ Build Vocabulary

Using the Word Root *-loc-*

1. getting from one place to another
2. a specific and defined place
3. move from one place to another

Using the Word Bank

1. correct; 2. incorrect; 3. incorrect; 4. correct; 5. incorrect

◆ Reading for Success

1. Feelings of discomfort and tension are appropriate to the atmosphere of disuse and decay.
2. (a) Mrs. Drover is practical, prosaic, and determined. She is also greatly upset by her current situation. (b) Accept all answers that are supported by details from the story. Some students may find her sympathetic because she is so clearly frightened by the situation. Her stubbornness about completing tasks may somewhat reduce that sympathy, or it may seem courageous.
3. (a) Students may have expected her to be chased by a ghost or a living letter writer, or to escape from a strictly imaginary enemy. (b) Students may find the ending surprising in its ambiguity and suddenness but not in its sinister tone, which has been foreshadowed.
4. Students may answer that she believes the war has damaged people's ability to cope with emotional issues.

◆ Literary Focus

1. Students may respond that Mrs. Drover encounters the "ghost" through the mysterious letter and her sense of another presence in the house. She then tries to outsmart the ghost by leaving the house, only to find him in the taxi.
2. (a) These details could indicate he's not a normal person: She never sees his face; he never kisses her; she imagines spectral glitters instead of eyes; he says he'll always be with her. (b) These details make the parting seem psychologically realistic: She wishes the scene over because it is painful; she feels intimidated by the lack of intimacy; he, perhaps terrified of the war to which he is returning, has perhaps coerced a commitment from her to assuage his fears of dying.
3. (a) Possible answers include: When Mrs. Drover returns to her abandoned street at the beginning of the story, the street seems strange as a result of wartime disuse. After her fiancé is reported missing, she feels not only normal "grief" but "a . . . dislocation from everything." This strange reaction may result from the pressures of the war and her emotional unreadiness for a relationship with this man. Students may find other examples. (b) The passages suggest that Bowen views life as quite fragile, open to frightening influences.

◆ Grammar and Style

1. Boarded up by the owner, the staircase window let no light come into the hall.
2. Suddenly halting her conversation, the young girl ran from the soldier.
3. Stored for many months, the piano had left what looked like claw marks on the parquet.
4. Left by the last bombing, the cracks in the structure ran vertically down the side of the building.
5. Entering the lighted room, the soldier pulled his hat down to cover his face.

For additional instruction and practice, use the **Language Lab CD-ROM** lesson on Writing Style: Varying Sentence Structure.

Guide for Responding (continued)

◆ Build Vocabulary

Using the Word Root *-loc-*

Apply your knowledge that the word root *-loc-* means "place." Write the following sentences, filling in the blanks with a phrase that makes clear the meaning of the italicized word:

1. An animal's method of *locomotion* is its way of ___?___ .
2. The anesthetic is a *local* one; it affects only ___?___ .
3. His company is *relocating*; will they pay for him to ___?___ ?

Using the Word Bank

For each of the sentences below, write "correct" if the italicized word is used correctly. If the word is not used correctly, write "incorrect."

1. I was relieved when I reached out and touched, instead of a *spectral* presence, solid flesh and bone.
2. Given the pollution in the world's waterways, I am surprised that more *arboreal* species are not endangered.
3. Take whatever you wish; my generosity is strictly *circumscribed*.
4. The letter fit through the door's *aperture*.
5. The doctor has caused a permanent *dislocation* of your shoulder; you should feel fine in a day or so.

◆ Reading for Success

Strategies for Reading and Interpreting Fiction

Reading a short story like "The Demon Lover" is like staging a play in your mind. Your "performance" of the story will be more powerful, the more fully you explore the text and the wider the conclusions you draw about the author's message.

1. What was your response to the atmosphere Bowen creates at the beginning of the story?
2. (a) Describe Mrs. Drover's character. (b) Do you find her sympathetic? Explain why or why not.
3. (a) What did you expect would happen after Mrs. Drover left the house? (b) Were you surprised by the story's ending? Explain.
4. What conclusions can you draw from the story about Bowen's view of the damage done by war?

◆ Literary Focus

The Ghost Story

Ghost stories—tales in which the supernatural may be at work—often create a feeling of dread. This feeling arises from the appearance of the inexplicable or nameless in the midst of the ordinary. A good ghost story may also prevent you from deciding between a natural or a supernatural explanation of events.

1. Describe Mrs. Drover's conflict with the ghost.
2. (a) In the passage describing Mrs. Drover's last meeting with her soldier-lover, name two details suggesting there are supernatural influences at work. Explain your choice. (b) Name two details that make the parting seem psychologically realistic, and not supernatural. Explain your choice.
3. Find two passages in the story that contrast the familiar with what is "outside" the familiar. (a) In these passages, what allows the strange to "leak into" the familiar? (b) What do these passages suggest about Bowen's view of the fragility of life?

◆ Grammar and Style

Sentence Beginnings: Participial Phrases

Bowen often begins sentences with **participial phrases**, a participle and all its modifiers and complements, to create variety. For clarity, she places the participial phrase next to the word it modifies.

Writing Application In your notebook, rewrite each of the following sentences so it begins with a participial phrase.

1. The staircase window, boarded up by the owner, let no light come into the hall.
2. The young girl, suddenly halting her conversation, ran from the soldier.
3. The piano, stored for many months, had left what looked like claw marks on the parquet.
4. The cracks in the structure, left by the last bombing, ran vertically down the side of the building.
5. The soldier, entering the lighted room, pulled his hat down to cover his face.

Build Your Portfolio

Idea Bank

Writing

1. **Journal Entry** Write a brief summary of a "ghost" story or movie that you found really scary. Explain which parts you found scariest, and examine what they had in common.

2. **Critical Evaluation** Write a critical review of a movie you have seen or a book you have read dealing with "ghostly" events. Spell out what makes such movies or books enjoyable, then discuss how well the one you are reviewing fits your criteria.

3. **Response to Criticism** "The fantastic," writes critic Tzvetan Todorov, "lasts only as long as a certain hesitation" between supernatural and natural explanations of events. Write an essay showing how Bowen produces this hesitation. **[Literature Link]**

Speaking and Listening

4. **Dramatic Retelling** Choose a ghost tale that you find especially effective. Dim the lights, and give a dramatic reading of this story for your class. **[Performing Arts Link]**

5. **Ballad** The title of Bowen's story comes from a ballad. Find a copy of this or another ballad about a lover and perform it for your class. **[Music Link; Performing Arts Link]**

Projects

6. **Portrait of the Demon Lover** In a drawing or painting, depict the demon lover, emphasizing the fact that he does not "belong" to this world. **[Visual Arts Link; Social Studies Link]**

7. **Blitz Report** Do library research about the London Blitz during World War II. What was life like for the people who stayed in London? **[Social Studies Link]**

Writing Mini-Lesson

Sequel

In a sense, "The Demon Lover" ends perfectly, yet the story leaves all sorts of loose ends. Write a sequel to "The Demon Lover," answering the question What happened next? An effective sequel weaves parts of the original story in with new events, filling the reader in about what happened in the original without simply retelling it. To ensure that your sequel is connected with the original, use a clear and logical organization.

Writing Skills Focus: Clear and Logical Organization

A sequel, like other kinds of fiction, must weave together past and present. To ensure your readers get a full picture of events, order information in your story using a **clear and logical organization**.

In "The Demon Lover," Bowen waits until Mrs. Drover looks in the mirror to tell us what Mrs. Drover looks like. Bowen's organization is clear—she does not clutter up her descriptions of place and action by telling us what Mrs. Drover looks like. It is also logical. Bowen tells the story from Mrs. Drover's point of view, so the best place to describe Mrs. Drover is when she is looking at herself.

Prewriting To get ideas for your sequel, jot down questions that "The Demon Lover" leaves unanswered. Then outline the events of your story. Note the parts of your story where readers will need to know what happened in Bowen's story in order to understand what is happening in yours.

Drafting As you draft, make sure that you order events in a clear and reasonable way. Choose logical places to give your reader the information about what happened in the original.

Revising Reread your story as if you had never read it. Look for points where only prior knowledge of Bowen's story can help you understand what is happening. Add necessary information.

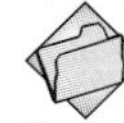

Idea Bank

Customizing for *Learning Modalities*
Following are suggestions for matching Idea Bank topics with your students' learning modalities:
- Intrapersonal: 1, 3
- Interpersonal: 4, 5
- Bodily/Kinesthetic: 5
- Verbal/Linguistic: 1, 2, 3, 7
- Visual/Spatial: 6

Customizing for *Performance Levels*
Following are suggestions for matching Idea Bank topics with your students' ability levels:
- Less Advanced Students: 1, 5
- Average Students: 2, 4, 6
- More Advanced Students: 3, 7

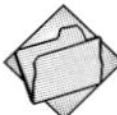

Writing Mini-Lesson

Refer students to the Writing Process Handbook, page 1189, for instruction on the writing process, and page 1191 for further information on narration.

Writing and Language Transparencies Have students use the Story Map Organizer, pp. 127–130, to plan their sequel to Bowen's story

Writing Lab CD-ROM
Have students write their sequels using the tutorial on Narration. Follow these steps:
1. Have students use the Chain of Events organizer to plot their sequel.
2. Have students draft on computer.
3. Use the sentence opener checker to aid revision.

Sourcebook
Have students use Chapter 2, Narration (pp. 31–61), for additional support. The chapter includes a discussion on Ending Your Narrative, p. 52.

✓ ASSESSMENT OPTIONS

Formal Assessment, Selection Test, pp. 227–229, and Assessment Resources Software. The selection test is designed so that it can be easily customized to the performance levels of your students.

Alternative Assessment, p. 45, includes options for less advanced and more advanced students, and for verbal/linguistic learners, interpersonal learners, and visual/spatial learners.

PORTFOLIO ASSESSMENT
Use the following rubrics in the ***Alternative Assessment*** booklet to assess student writing:
Journal Entry: Summary Rubric, p. 99
Critical Evaluation: Evaluation/Review Rubric, p. 105
Response to Criticism: Literary Analysis Rubric, p. 113
Writing Mini-Lesson: Fiction Rubric, p. 96

Prepare and Engage

OBJECTIVES

1. To read, comprehend, and interpret poetry
2. To relate poetry to personal experience
3. To apply literary background
4. To analyze symbolism
5. To build vocabulary in context and learn the word root *-ques-*
6. To develop skill in using noun clauses
7. To write a prediction for the millennium, appropriate to the knowledge level of readers
8. To respond to the poetry through writing, speaking and listening, and projects

SKILLS INSTRUCTION

Vocabulary:
Word Roots: *-ques-*

Grammar:
Noun Clauses

Reading Strategy:
Apply Literary Background

Literary Focus:
Symbolism

Writing:
Knowledge Level of Readers

Speaking and Listening:
Irish Poetry (teacher edition)

Critical Viewing:
Classify; Infer; Interpret

PORTFOLIO OPPORTUNITIES

Writing: Description; Essay; Response to Criticism

Writing Mini-Lesson: Prediction Essay

Speaking and Listening: Irish Poetry; Music and Swans

Projects: Yeats Timeline; Byzantium

More About the Author
In his *Memoirs* (New York: Macmillan, 1973), p. 40, Yeats introduces his early love, Maud Gonne, in this way: "I was twenty-three years old when the troubling of my life began. . . . I had never thought to see in a living woman so great beauty. It belonged to famous pictures, to poetry, to some legendary past. A complexion like the blossom of apples, and yet face and body had the beauty of lineaments which Blake calls the highest beauty because it changes least from youth to age, and a stature so great that she seemed of a divine race." Yeats never did marry Maud Gonne—he even proposed to her daughter when she refused him—but he made from "the troubling of his life" a great deal of fine poetry.

Guide for Interpreting

William Butler Yeats
(1865–1939)

As the changes of the twentieth century swept away tradition, this poet delved into his nation's mythological past. William Butler Yeats was born in Dublin, Ireland, but his heart lay westward, in the Irish county of Sligo. Here he spent his childhood vacations with his grandparents. It was in the shadow of Sligo's barren mountains that he immersed himself in the magical mythology and legends of Ireland. This experience led to a lifelong enthusiasm for the roots of Irish culture.

Philosophical Influences After three years of studying painting in Dublin, Yeats moved to London to pursue a literary career. He became friends with the poet Arthur Symons, who awakened his interest in the symbolic poetry of William Blake and the French Symbolists. Yeats's early poems show the Symbolist influence as well as that of the Pre-Raphaelites, a group of painters and writers who strove for a medieval simplicity and beauty. Symbolism, Pre-Raphaelism, and Irish myth combined in Yeats's first important collection, *The Wanderings of Oisin,* published in 1889.

Political and Personal Influences In the 1890's, Yeats led the Irish Literary Revival, helping to establish the Irish Literary Society in London and the Irish National Literary Society in Dublin. He also became involved in politics and was a fierce supporter of the movement for Irish independence from England. Perhaps some of this political activity was spurred by Yeats's love for a beautiful Irish actress and revolutionary named Maud Gonne. This attraction lasted his entire life, but it was never reciprocated. To his sorrow—after many refusals of his proposals—she chose a soldier, and Yeats, many years later, married another woman.

From Poetry to Plays to Poetry As the century turned, Yeats became interested in drama. He joined his friend Lady Augusta Gregory in founding the Irish National Theatre Society. He began writing plays, among them *The Shadowy Waters* (1900) and *Deirdre* (1907). When Yeats returned to poetry, it was with a new voice, subtler and more powerful than the one he had used before. The poems in *The Tower* (1928) show Yeats at the height of his abilities.

Ireland's Hero In 1922, Yeats was appointed a senator of the new Irish Free State, and on his seventieth birthday he was hailed by his nation as the greatest living Irishman. He kept writing poems until a day or two before his death in France. One of his last poems contains his famous epitaph: "Cast a cold eye / On life, on death. / Horseman, pass by!"

◆ Background for Understanding

CULTURE: YEATS'S IDEAS ABOUT CIVILIZATION AND CULTURE

In 1925, Yeats published *A Vision,* a serious prose work that explained the mythology, symbolism, and philosophy that he strove to express in his poetry. Yeats believed that history occurs in two-thousand-year cycles, during which a particular civilization passes through the states of birth, growth, and decay. It then gives way to a new civilization that is the direct opposite of it. He thought that twentieth-century society was undergoing the final stages of decay. The birth of Christ had brought about a similar transition two thousand years ago, and Yeats believed that the society of the early twentieth century was in a state of decay that would lead to another sort of rebirth. These ideas appear vividly in the pageant of images in the poem "The Second Coming."

Prentice Hall Literature Program Resources

REINFORCE / RETEACH / EXTEND

Selection Support Pages
Build Vocabulary: Word Roots: *-ques-,* p. 223
Grammar and Style: Noun Clauses, p. 224
Reading Strategy: Apply Literary Background, p. 225
Literary Focus: Symbolism, p. 226

Strategies for Diverse Student Needs, p. 46

Beyond Literature
Humanities Connection: Philosophy: Spiritual Eclecticism, p. 46

Formal Assessment Selection Test, pp. 230–232; Assessment Resources Software

Alternative Assessment, p. 46

Writing and Language Transparencies
Daily Language Practice: Week 31, p. 166

Resource Pro CD-ROM
Poetry of William Butler Yeats—includes all resource material and customizable lesson plan

Listening to Literature Audiocassettes
Poetry of William Butler Yeats

Poetry of William Butler Yeats

Write this description on the chalkboard and have students begin to improvise a horror movie based on it: "Somewhere in sands of the desert is a shape with lion body and the head of a man. The creature, its gaze blank and pitiless, is just beginning to move." After students have launched into their "movies," tell them that the image comes from Yeats's poem "The Second Coming" and invite them to compare their scenarios with his.

◆ Literature and Your Life

Connect Your Experience

What transitions do you experience in life? New Year's Eves? Birthdays? Yeats believed that major civilizations occurred in cycles of two-thousand years. He viewed the twentieth century as a transition from one cycle into another.

Journal Writing List a few important dates in your journal and describe how they relate to your life.

Thematic Focus: Waking From the Dream

As you read, notice the poetic dreams—and the historical nightmares—that Yeats describes.

◆ Build Vocabulary

Word Roots: *-ques-*

The root *-ques-* derives from a word meaning "seek." The word *conquest* refers to "a seeking for something by force."

Word Bank

Preview this list of words from the poems before you read.

clamorous
conquest
anarchy
conviction
paltry
artifice

◆ Literary Focus

Symbolism

In literature, a **symbol** is a word, character, object, or action that stands for something beyond itself. The swans in "The Wild Swans at Coole," for example, may symbolize eternal, unchanging life, which the aging speaker knows is denied to him.

The use of symbols allows writers to achieve intensity and complexity in their work. Yeats embraced symbolism in his early poems, abandoned it for a while, then returned to it with enthusiasm, inventing an elaborate symbolic system of his own. In his best poems, the symbols do not require expertise in his system, but only the practiced eye of a careful reader.

◆ Reading Strategy

Apply Literary Background

No poem is written in a vacuum. Poems are often inspired by a person, a landscape, an experience, or a memory. A writer's knowledge of literature may also become part of a poem and take the form of allusions or references, to other works. As you read, apply your knowledge of **literary background**—including information about a writer's philosophical beliefs, reading, and personal history—to help you understand as you read.

For example, knowing that Yeats was an admirer of Thoreau may lead you to recognize that "The Lake Isle of Innisfree" was inspired by Yeats's appreciation of *Walden Pond*.

◆ Grammar and Style

Noun Clauses

In his poetry, Yeats often uses **noun clauses** to connect one image or complex thought to another. A noun clause is a subordinate clause that functions as a noun. It is used in a sentence in the same way a noun can be used. For example, it might be used as subject, direct object, or object of a preposition.

Noun Clause as Direct Object: Fish, flesh, or fowl, commend all summer long/*Whatever is begotten, born, and dies.*

Noun Clause as Object of a Preposition: To sing . . . / Of *what is past, or passing, or to come.*

Customize for *Less Proficient Readers*

Poetry communicates viscerally when it is heard. Play for these students the readings of Yeats's poems on the **Listening to Literature Audiocassettes.** Then have them identify the feelings that the poetry stirs in them.

Customize for *More Advanced Students*

These students may wish to focus on Yeats's symbolism. Urge them to read in pairs, identifying and discussing some of the poems' symbols: lake isle, swans, Byzantium. Remind students to support their interpretations with details from the poems.

Customize for *English Language Learners*

Help these students understand the poems by making up a situation that might have given rise to the poem. For "The Lake Isle of Innisfree," for example, have students picture a young man from the country who is confused and overwhelmed by city life. Ask students to elaborate on the situation you give them. Then have them read the poem as a response to the situation.

Customize for *Visual/Spatial Learners*

Invite these learners to use the illustrations on pages 898, 901, 902, and 905, as well as Yeats's highly vivid sensory language, to "see" the poems' images.

Preparing for Standardized Tests

Reading and Vocabulary As students prepare for standardized tests, they will review a great deal of written material. The ability to decipher unfamiliar words improves comprehension of review material while accelerating the reading process. The Build Vocabulary lesson for this selection focuses on learning word meaning through the use of the word root *-ques-*. Students can apply this skill to both review and test reading. For additional practice, use the Build Vocabulary page in ***Selection Support,*** p. 223.

Grammar and Language On some standardized tests, students may be asked to complete sentences with text of appropriate content and correct grammatical structure. The ability to recognize and correctly incorporate noun clauses will improve students' performance with items of this type. The Grammar and Style lesson for this selection focuses on the correct use of noun clauses. For additional practice, refer students to the Grammar and Style page on Noun Clauses, p. 224, in ***Selection Support.***

Develop Understanding

One-Minute Insight All five poems are attempts to overcome the disappointments of mortal life. The first two poems, "When You Are Old" and "The Lake Isle of Innisfree," offer softer-edged, more "poetic" strategies to solve this problem. In the first poem, the speaker takes gentle revenge on the lover who spurned him by imagining her regret in old age. In the second poem, he imagines a Walden-like retreat to which he can flee from "the pavements gray."

◆ Reading Strategy

1 Apply Literary Background Remind students of Yeats's long, but unrequited, love for Maud Gonne. Have them find evidence of this love in lines 1–8. *Yeats seems to be talking about Maud, who was loved by "many." Yeats could be saying he's the "one man" who loved her truly.*

▶Critical Viewing◀

2 Classify Students may note that the soft light and the woman's serene expression are sweet; her isolation, however, may suggest bitterness.

◆ Reading Strategy

3 Apply Literary Background Ask students to review their knowledge of Yeats's childhood (see p. 896). Then point out that his early years in, and continuing affection for, Sligo's countryside is revealed in these lines. Yeats wrote in his *Autobiography,* "I had still the ambition, formed in Sligo in my teens, of living in imitation of Thoreau on Innisfree, a little island in Lough Gill . . ."

◆ Literary Focus

4 Symbolism Ask students what Innisfree might symbolize for Yeats. *Possible answers include: a peaceful retreat from society or the busy city, or a place where the poet can create while communing with nature.*

When You Are Old

William Butler Yeats

1

When you are old and gray and full of sleep,
And nodding by the fire, take down this book,
And slowly read, and dream of the soft look
Your eyes had once, and of their shadows deep;

How many loved your moments of glad grace,
And loved your beauty with love false or true,
But one man loved the pilgrim soul in you,
And loved the sorrows of your changing face;

And bending down beside the glowing bars,
Murmur, a little sadly, how Love fled
And paced upon the mountains overhead
And hid his face amid a crowd of stars.

Her Signal, Norman Garstin, The Royal Cornwall Museum, Truro

2 ▶ **Critical Viewing** The mood in "When You Are Old" is gentle and bittersweet. What elements in this painting mirror that mood? **[Classify]**

Humanities: Art

Her Signal (detail), c. 1892, by Norman Garstin.

This painting depicts an old woman reading a book, just as in Yeats's poem.

Irishman Norman Garstin was both a painter and writer. He studied art in Antwerp, Paris, and finally in Venice, where he was influenced by a group of painters later known as the Newlyn school. Later in life, Garstin taught and wrote about art, sharing his broad artistic experience and knowledge with both students and readers. *Her Signal* was one of the many portraits or large anecdotal scenes Garstin produced primarily for financial motives.

Use these questions for discussion:

1. If this is the woman the poet describes, what is going through her mind? *She might be thinking with regret of how much the poet loved her.*
2. How are the painter's and poet's attitudes toward old age similar? *Both see it as a time of quiet and reflection, when strong emotions are distant.*

The Lake Isle *of* Innisfree

William Butler Yeats

I will arise and go now, and go to Innisfree,
And a small cabin build there, of clay and wattles[1] made:
Nine bean-rows will I have there, a hive for the honeybee,
And live alone in the bee-loud glade.

❸ And I shall have some peace there, for peace comes dropping slow,
Dropping from the veils of the morning to where the cricket sings;
There midnight's all a glimmer, and noon a purple glow,
And evening full of the linnet's wings.[2]

I will arise and go now, for always night and day
❹ I hear lake water lapping with low sounds by the shore:
While I stand on the roadway, or on the pavements gray,
I hear it in the deep heart's core.

1. **wattles:** Stakes interwoven with twigs or branches.

2. **linnet's wings:** Wings of a European singing bird.

Guide for Responding

◆ Literature and Your Life

Reader's Response With which poem's speaker do you identify more? Explain.

Thematic Focus What outer forces might inspire a poet to long for the dreamlike serenity of these poems?

Sketch Draw the lake isle of Innisfree, using clues in the poem to guide you.

☑ Check Your Comprehension

1. In "When You Are Old," what does the speaker ask the reader to do?
2. (a) In "The Lake Isle of Innisfree," what does the speaker want most to find at Innisfree? (b) How will each of the four times of day he mentions contribute to his goal?

◆ Critical Thinking

INTERPRET

1. Who is the "one man" in the second stanza of "When Your Are Old"? Explain. **[Interpret]**
2. What does the phrase "pilgrim soul" in "When You Are Old" suggest about the person being addressed? **[Infer]**
3. In "Innisfree," does the speaker intend to leave for Innisfree immediately? Explain. **[Deduce]**
4. What does Innisfree offer that the speaker does not find where he is now? **[Infer]**
5. How do these poems suggest that devotion to art makes up for disappointments? **[Support]**

APPLY

6. Name a contemporary song that deals with the desire to leave for another place. Compare this place to Innisfree. **[Relate]**

Reinforce and Extend

Answers

◆ Literature and Your Life

Reader's Response Some will identify with the rejected lover; some will feel affinity with the lover of nature and quiet.

Thematic Focus The need to make money, the fast pace of city life, and the pressures of responsibility might inspire a poet to long for escape.

☑ Check Your Comprehension

1. He asks her to read this book and dream about herself as a young woman.
2. (a) The speaker desires peace. (b) Morning (mist and cricket song), noon ("a purple glow"), evening (flocks of linnets), and midnight ("all a glimmer") will contribute to his feeling of peace.

◆ Critical Thinking

1. The man is probably the speaker, Yeats himself. The description fits Yeats's own unrequited love for Maud Gonne.
2. The phrase suggests that the woman is a wanderer or seeker.
3. Possible responses: The speaker seems to be expressing a dream of an ideal type of existence rather than an intent to leave immediately. He dwells more on visualizing the ideal than on a plan for departure. By repeating "I will arise and go now," he shows that the words do not state an immediate intention.
4. The peaceful retreat contrasts with the speaker's city life.
5. Both poems show the speaker finding fulfillment in art—his book and imagined revenge in "When You Are Old" and his imagined ideal place in "The Lake Isle of Innisfree."
6. Students will suggest currently popular songs. They should draw plausible links between the named place and Innisfree.

Block Scheduling Strategies

Consider these suggestions to take advantage of extended class time:

- Have students listen to the poems on the **Listening to Literature Audiocassette.** Discuss how the reader's rhythm and tone reflect the poems' themes and moods.
- Introduce the concept of symbolism in the Literary Focus on page 897. After reading the poems, have students work together to answer the Literary Focus questions (p. 906). They may also complete the Literary Focus: Symbolism page in ***Selection Support,*** p. 226.
- As a class, discuss and answer the Critical Thinking questions (pp. 899, 901, 903, 905).
- Use ***Daily Language Practice*** for Week 31.
- Have students exchange research ideas for their chosen Project (p. 907).
- Direct students to do the Writing Mini-Lesson (p. 907). They may begin with an exchange of ideas about the next millennium, comparing their ideas with those Yeats expresses in "The Second Coming."

Develop Understanding

One-Minute Insight "The Wild Swans at Coole," "The Second Coming," and "Sailing to Byzantium" are tougher, more impersonal solutions to the problem of mortality. They represent attempts to imagine a pattern of existence beyond the individual—the immortality of art or nature, or the great cycles of history.

◆ Reading Strategy

1 Apply Literary Background This poem is set in Coole Park, the estate of Lady Gregory. She was Yeats's patron as well as his collaborator in establishing the Irish National Theatre Society. Yeats spent a great deal of time at Coole Park, a large estate with ponds for swans, forest paths, and orchards. Judging by the poem, what did Coole Park mean to Yeats? *It was a place where he could meditate on changes in his life.*

◆ Critical Thinking

2 Infer Ask students: What has changed for the speaker over the nineteen years of watching the swans? *Students should recognize that the poet has aged and no longer experiences "passion or conquest"; he laments the losses that aging brings, losses to which the swans seem immune.*

◆ Literature and Your Life

3 What bird or other feature of the wild seems "Mysterious, beautiful" to students? *Students should support whatever answers they give.*

▶Critical Viewing◀

4 Infer Students may respond that the curve of the swans' backs and the bend in their necks give them a mysteriously balanced beauty.

The Wild Swans at Coole

William Butler Yeats

The trees are in their autumn beauty,
The woodland paths are dry,
Under the October twilight the water
Mirrors a still sky;
Upon the brimming water among the stones
Are nine-and-fifty swans.

The nineteenth autumn has come upon me
Since I first made my count;
I saw, before I had well finished,
All suddenly mount
And scatter wheeling in great broken rings
Upon their clamorous wings.

I have looked upon those brilliant creatures,
And now my heart is sore.
All's changed since I, hearing at twilight,
The first time on this shore,
The bell-beat of their wings above my head,
Trod with a lighter tread.

Unwearied still, lover by lover,
They paddle in the cold
Companionable streams or climb the air;
Their hearts have not grown old;
Passion or conquest, wander where they will,
Attend upon them still.

But now they drift on the still water,
Mysterious, beautiful;
Among what rushes will they build,
By what lake's edge or pool
Delight men's eyes when I awake some day
To find they have flown away?

▶ **Critical Viewing** Why might a poet like Yeats describe swans such as these as "mysterious" and "beautiful"? **[Infer]**

◆ Build Vocabulary

clamorous (klam′ ər əs) *adj.*: Loud and confused; noisy

conquest (kän′ kwest′) *n.*: The winning of another's affection or favor

Speaking and Listening Mini-Lesson

Irish Poetry

This mini-lesson supports the Speaking and Listening activity on page 907.

Introduce the Concept Play readings of Yeats's poems on the **Listening to Literature Audiocassette.** Have students analyze the readings by focusing on pace, volume, and emphasis. Point out that readers pause after sentences rather than arbitrarily stopping after each line.

Develop Background Assist students in finding works by poets like Yeats, J. M. Synge, George Russell ("A. E."), and James Stephens. Have students follow these guidelines:

- Choose poems to which you have a strong personal response.
- Know the meaning and pronunciation of all the words in the poem, and understand the poem's mood and theme.
- Rehearse the poem and mark up a photocopy of it to indicate pauses and stresses.

Apply the Information Have students briefly introduce their chosen poet to listeners; then have them present their readings.

Assess the Outcome Have students evaluate the presentations using two main categories: emotional power and technical ability. You may have students use the Peer Assessment page for Oral Interpretation, p. 120, in ***Alternative Assessment.***

Guide for Responding

◆ Literature and Your Life

Reader's Response In what ways do beautiful, wild animals remind you, as the swans remind the speaker, of the mysteries of human life?

Thematic Focus How is the speaker's realization that time is passing like an awakening?

☑ Check Your Comprehension

1. For how many years has the speaker been coming to Coole and counting the swans?
2. What is different in the speaker's state since he first heard the "bell-beat" of swans' wings?
3. What may the speaker awaken to find one day?

◆ Critical Thinking

INTERPRET

1. For what thematic purpose does the speaker emphasize the setting in the first two stanzas? **[Interpret]**
2. (a) What is the speaker doing in the second stanza when the swans take flight? (b) How does their sudden flight affect him? **[Infer]**
3. According to stanza three, why is the speaker unhappy? **[Interpret]**
4. What might the swans symbolize to the speaker? **[Draw Conclusions]**

APPLY

5. Why does great beauty sometimes arouse a sense of sadness and loss? **[Speculate]**

Cross-Curricular Connection: Science

A Scientist's View of Swans There are seven or eight different species of swans, but all share some of the characteristics Yeats describes. Though some swans weigh as much as 50 pounds, they are graceful in flight, with their long, outstretched necks and steady wingstrokes.

Swans mate for life, producing about six babies (called *cygnets*) each breeding season. The cygnets are gray or brown; most gradually become white, but a few species have other colorations. Although the male swan, or *cob*, will defend his family against outsiders, these families do merge with others to migrate in a large group. Flying at high altitudes, in either diagonal or V-formations, swans travel southward in fall or northward in spring.

Have students observe swans, either in your community, at a zoo, or in books. Ask students to compare and contrast a scientist's view of swans with Yeats's. *Scientists compile observations to describe and explain swans as a fact of nature. Yeats's impressions, while based on careful observation, help him transform the swan into a powerful fusion of meaning, emotion, and image.*

Reinforce and Extend

Customize for
English Language Learners
Encourage language learners to use signal words such as *since, before,* and *will* to track past, present, and future in Yeats's poem. Then have them list the poem's events in chronological order.

Customize for
More Advanced Students
Encourage students to extend the poem's meaning by analyzing the depiction of swans in other cultures. Direct them to architectural decorations, book illustrations, fairy tales, fiction, and poetry as possible sources.

Answers

◆ Literature and Your Life

Reader's Response Students may respond that certain animals suggest possibilities of strength or skill that are mysteriously closed to humans; they also may seem to embody these qualities in a timeless way.

Thematic Focus The speaker seems to awaken from his "sleep"—his obliviousness to time's passing—to recognize how much he has changed.

☑ Check Your Comprehension

1. He has been counting the swans at Coole for nineteen years.
2. He is older and perhaps sadder and more tired.
3. He may awaken one day to find the swans have flown away.

◆ Critical Thinking

1. The speaker emphasizes autumn, generally symbolic of old age and of approaching death.
2. (a) He is counting them. (b) He feels sad and contrasts this moment with earlier moments spent watching the swans.
3. He is unhappy because he has grown older and more tired.
4. The swans represent eternal youth and enduring love and passion. When the speaker dies, he will awaken to find them gone.
5. Knowing that a beautiful thing will not last is sad. Students may also reflect that beauty affirms the value and the perishability of things at the same time.

Develop Understanding

◆ Background for Understanding

Yeats wrote this poem in January 1919, just after World War I came to a close and just as a war in Ireland was breaking out between the English forces and Irish patriots. The "blood-dimmed tide" of the poem is therefore an image of the violence that seemed to be filling the world.

Customize for
Less Proficient Readers
To help these students understand the symbolism in this poem, explain the historical background and write on the chalkboard the phrase "Things fall apart." Have these students come up with their own images and symbols to convey this idea. Then have them compare these symbols to Yeats's.

Customize for
More Advanced Readers
Have these students respond to critic Richard Ellmann's appraisal of this poem: ". . . an awareness of [Yeats's mythological] system was more useful for writing than it is for reading the poem. . . . It is more necessary that we be familiar with the ancient, traditional myth of a second coming . . . than that we understand [Yeats's system]."

The Second Coming

WILLIAM BUTLER YEATS

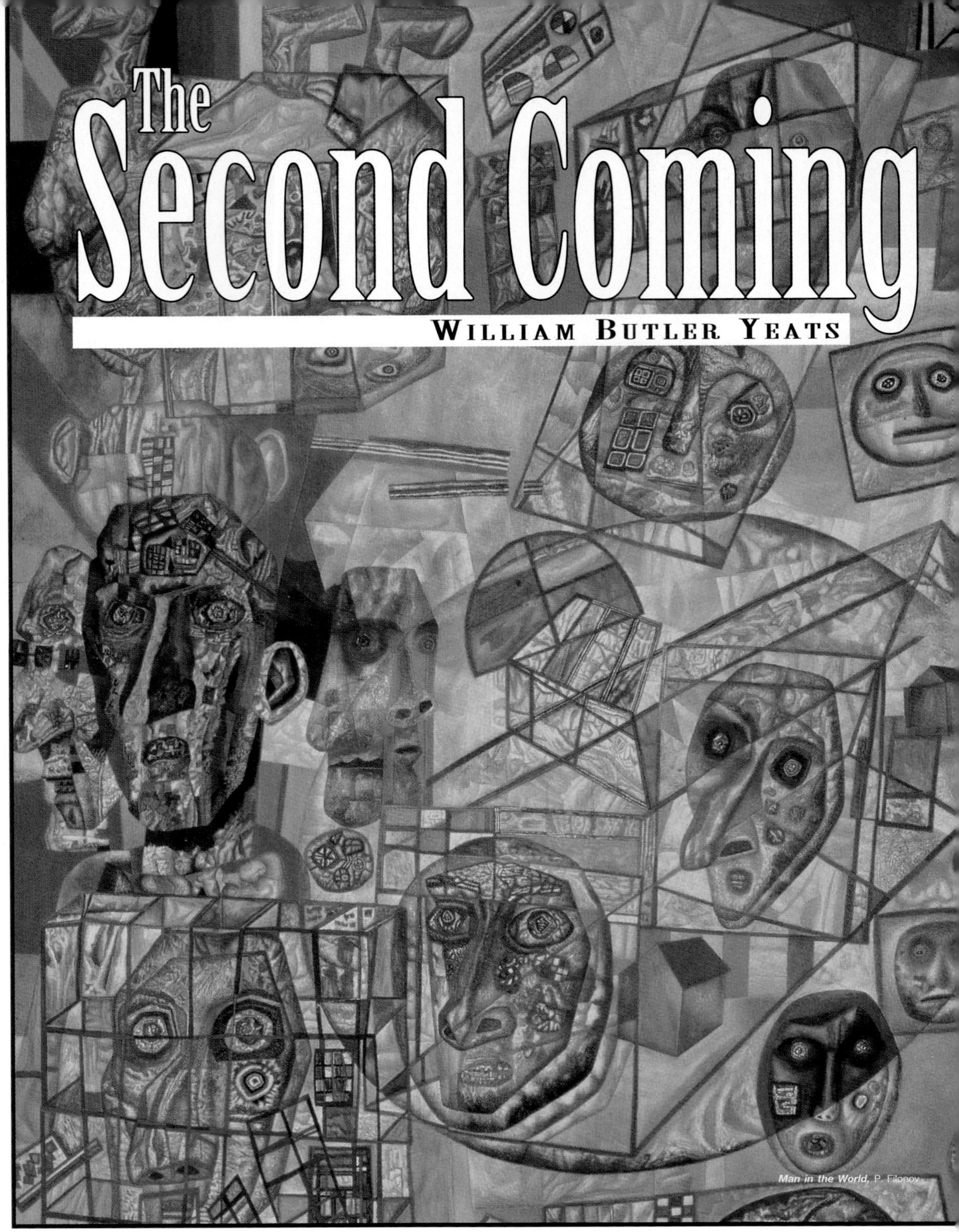

Man in the World, P. Filonov

Humanities: Art

Man in the World (oil on canvas), 1925, by Pavel Nikolaevic Filonov.

This painting illustrates the artist's view of the modern world, just as the poem describes Yeats's view.

Russian painter Pavel Filonov was trained at St. Petersburg's Academy of Fine Arts and by painter Lev Dmitriev-Kavkazsky. Filonov developed his own theory of painting, called Analytical Painting, which sought to capture "life as a whole," rather than merely representing form and color. His work is finely detailed and, in the case of *Man in the World,* highly colorful.

Use these questions for discussion:

1. How does this painting evoke the anarchy discussed in the poem? *The abstract composition, distorted faces and shapes, contrasting colors, all suggest lack of order.*
2. What elements of the painting convey Yeats's sense of anxiety about the state of civilization? *The masklike, distressed faces, often placed inside boxes, suggest that people are frightened and feel trapped by an inevitable disaster.*

Yeats believed that history occurs in two-thousand-year cycles. The birth of Christ ended one cycle and began another, and now a similar transition was about to occur.

❶ Turning and turning in the widening gyre
The falcon cannot hear the falconer;
Things fall apart; the center cannot hold;
Mere anarchy is loosed upon the world,
The blood-dimmed tide is loosed, and everywhere
The ceremony of innocence is drowned;
The best lack all conviction, while the worst
Are full of passionate intensity.[1]

Surely some revelation is at hand;
Surely the Second Coming is at hand.
The Second Coming! Hardly are those words out
When a vast image out of Spiritus Mundi[2]
Troubles my sight: somewhere in sands of the desert
A shape with lion body and the head of a man,[3]
A gaze blank and pitiless as the sun,
Is moving its slow thighs, while all about it
Reel shadows of the indignant desert birds.
The darkness drops again; but now I know
That twenty centuries[4] of stony sleep
Were vexed to nightmare by a rocking cradle,[5]
And what rough beast, its hour come round at last,
Slouches towards Bethlehem to be born?

1. **Mere . . . intensity:** Refers to the Russian Revolution of 1917.
2. ***Spiritus Mundi*** (spir´ i təs mōōn´dē): Universal Spirit or Soul, in which the memories of the entire human race are forever preserved.
3. **A . . . man:** Sphinx.
4. **twenty centuries:** Historical cycle preceding the birth of Christ.
5. **rocking cradle:** Cradle of Jesus Christ.

◆ Build Vocabulary

anarchy (an´ ər kē) *n.*: Absence of government; confusion, disorder, and violence

conviction (kən´ vik´ shən) *n.*: Belief in something meaningful, such as a creed

Guide for Responding

◆ Literature and Your Life

Reader's Response Do you agree that in the modern world "things fall apart"?

Thematic Focus Explain how the first stanza can be said to represent "waking from a dream."

☑ Check Your Comprehension

1. Why does the falcon not return to the falconer, as it ordinarily would?
2. In the first stanza of "The Second Coming," what is happening to innocence?
3. What does the speaker believe is at hand?
4. (a) In stanza two, of "The Second Coming," what has begun to stir in the desert? (b) What is about to be born?

◆ Critical Thinking

INTERPRET

1. What imagery is used in lines 5–6 of "The Second Coming"? **[Analyze]**
2. When did the "twenty centuries of stony sleep" (line 19) occur? **[Interpret]**
3. (a) What would you expect to appear at the Second Coming? (b) How does that differ from what the speaker suggests will appear? **[Draw Conclusions]**

EXTEND

4. Chinua Achebe titled his novel *Things Fall Apart,* using the phrase from line 3 of "The Second Coming." What might the book be about, based on its title? **[Literature Link]**

Beyond the Selection

FURTHER READING

Other Works by William Butler Yeats

The Autobiography of William Butler Yeats; The Shadowy Waters; The Tower

Other Works About Change and the Power of Dreams

"Mutability," Percy Bysshe Shelley
"Dreams," Langston Hughes
"I dwell in Possibility . . . ," Emily Dickinson

We suggest that you preview these works before recommending them to students.

INTERNET

You and your students may find additional information about William Butler Yeats on the following Internet site. (Note: Sites may have changed since publication.)

For a history of Yeats and the Irish Literary Renaissance, visit **http://www.lm.com/~Kaydee/Irish.html**

You may also find related information about Yeats and the Irish literary renaissance on the Internet. We *strongly recommend* that you preview sites before you send students to them.

❶ **Enrichment** Students will not fully appreciate this opening image, and its symbolism, unless they understand something about falconry. This sport involved the use of trained falcons to hunt small birds and animals. After killing the prey, but otherwise leaving it untouched, falcons return to the trainer's wrist. (They cannot be trained to retrieve prey.) Falconry was practiced by the ancient Chinese and was popular among the nobility in Europe during the Middle Ages and the Renaissance. In Yeats's poem, the falcon, flying in wider and wider circles, "cannot hear the falconer" and is therefore out of control.

Reinforce and Extend

Answers

◆ Literature and Your Life

Reader's Response Students should support their answers with examples, anecdotes, or statistics.

Thematic Focus Students may say that the stanza depicts harsh realities of modern life as the end of the dream of order.

☑ Check Your Comprehension

1. It cannot hear its master.
2. Anarchy has been "loosed upon the world," drowning the rituals that return us to, or perhaps guide us out of, innocence.
3. The speaker believes that "some revelation is at hand."
4. (a) A beast dormant for twenty centuries has begun to stir. (b) A "rough beast" is about to be born.

◆ Critical Thinking

1. The imagery is of the sea, of a rising, bloody tide.
2. Some students, following the footnote, will say that this period preceded the birth of Christ. Others may argue, following the dramatic logic of the poem, that this period follows the birth of Christ.
3. (a) Responses will be consistent with students' beliefs. (b) Students should point out differences between their expectations and Yeats's vision.
4. The book might be about the ways in which a society falls apart, perhaps after a revolution.

Develop Understanding

◆ Critical Thinking

❶ **Interpret** Ask students: To what "country" is Yeats referring? *Yeats means the world of nature and time, not a specific country.*

◆ Literary Focus

❷ **Symbolism** Point out to students the symbolism explained in Footnote 1. Then read to students Yeats's own description (from *A Vision*) of what Byzantium symbolized for him: "I think that if I could be given a month of antiquity and leave to spend it where I chose, I would spend it in Byzantium [Istanbul, Turkey, today] . . . I think that in early Byzantium, maybe never before or since in recorded history, religious, aesthetic, and practical life were one, that architects and artificers . . . spoke to the multitude in gold and silver."

◆ Literature and Your Life

❸ Byzantium is Yeats's ideal place from the past. Encourage students to use their prior reading and prior knowledge to envision a place and time in the past that would appeal to them. *Have students elaborate on the sights and sounds of their ideal place.*

◆ Critical Thinking

❹ **Interpret** (a) How does the speaker picture the relation between his "heart" and his body? (b) What does he ask to happen to his heart? (c) What might the heart symbolize? *(a) Though his heart is "fastened" to his body, it is of a different nature, but it does not know this. (b) The speaker asks that his heart be destroyed or burned away. (c) The heart is perhaps all of the speaker's desires insofar as they are directed at fleshly, changing things. The heart combines the visionary abilities of the soul with the limitations of the body, and so is "sick."*

◆ Literary Focus

❺ **Symbolism** Ask students what the golden bird might symbolize for Yeats. Discuss the paradoxical nature of the symbol. *Students should recognize that the bird symbolizes the artist who has, through his work, transcended the natural world. However, the bird sings about that very world. With help, students should grasp this paradox.*

Sailing to Byzantium

William Butler Yeats

I
❶
That is no country for old men. The young
In one another's arms, birds in the trees
—Those dying generations—at their song,
The salmon-falls, the mackerel-crowded seas,
Fish, flesh, or fowl, commend all summer long
Whatever is begotten, born, and dies.
Caught in that sensual music all neglect
Monuments of unaging intellect.

II
An aged man is but a paltry thing,
A tattered coat upon a stick, unless
Soul clap its hands and sing, and louder sing
For every tatter in its mortal dress,
Nor is there singing school but studying
Monuments of its own magnificence;
❷❸
And therefore I have sailed the seas and come
To the holy city of Byzantium.[1]

III
O sages standing in God's holy fire
As in the gold mosaic of a wall,[2]
Come from the holy fire, perne in a gyre,[3]
And be the singing-masters of my soul.
❹
Consume my heart away; sick with desire
And fastened to a dying animal
It knows not what it is; and gather me
Into the artifice of eternity.

IV
❺
Once out of nature I shall never take
My bodily form from any natural thing,
But such a form as Grecian goldsmiths make
Of hammered gold and gold enameling
To keep a drowsy Emperor awake;
Or set upon a golden bough to sing[4]
To lords and ladies of Byzantium
Of what is past, or passing, or to come.

1. **Byzantium** (bi zan´ shē əm): Ancient capital of the Eastern Roman (or Byzantine) Empire and the seat of the Greek Orthodox Church; today, Istanbul, Turkey. For Yeats, it symbolized the world of art as opposed to the world of time and nature.
2. **sages . . . wall:** Wise old men and saints portrayed in gold mosaic on the walls of Byzantine churches.
3. **perne . . . gyre:** Spin in a spiraling motion.
4. **To . . . sing:** Yeats wrote, "I have read somewhere that in the Emperor's palace at Byzantium was a tree made of gold and silver, and artificial birds that sang."

◆ Build Vocabulary

paltry (pôl´ trē) *adj.*: Practically worthless; insignificant

artifice (ärt´ə fis) *n.*: Skill or ingenuity

Cross-Curricular Connection: Social Studies

The Real Byzantium As a center of art, architecture, and religion, the Byzantine empire flourished for over a thousand years, well into the late Middle Ages. The city of Byzantium (later named Constantinople, then Istanbul) was its center. This empire and its rich cultural life rose in the East as the Roman Empire was declining. For poets, historians, and chroniclers of art in the West, Byzantium held a certain exoticism and mystery. This reputation was exploited by Western writers, especially in the nineteenth century, and came to be called orientalism, a poetic stereotyping of the Middle East and Far East.

Have students, especially those with knowledge of Middle Eastern cultures, evaluate the realism of Yeats's poetic portrayal.

Ravenna: City and Port of Classis, Mosaic, late 6th century, from Basilica of St. Apollinare Nuovo

▲ **Critical Viewing** In what way do the colors and textures of this mosaic convey the idea that the ships have arrived at a wondrous place? **[Interpret]** 

Guide for Responding

◆ *Literature and Your Life*

Reader's Response Do you think it is possible to escape the effects of time? Explain.

Thematic Focus In your view, which is a "dream," Byzantium or the world of begetting? Explain.

☑ Check Your Comprehension

1. (a) What do the people and things of the country referred to in the first stanza "commend"? (b) What do they neglect?
2. What does the speaker ask of the sages in the third stanza?

◆ Critical Thinking

INTERPRET

1. How does Byzantium contrast with the country described in the first two stanzas? **[Compare and Contrast]**
2. (a) What do stanzas 3 and 4 reveal abut the speaker's attitude toward aging and death? (b) How does he hope to immortalize himself? **[Interpret]**
3. What does this poem suggest about the motives of artists and the purpose of art? **[Draw Conclusions]**

▶Critical Viewing◀

❻ Interpret The glowing earth-colors and the tops of buildings seen over the wall convey a sense of magical luxury.

Reinforce and Extend

Customize for
More Advanced Students
Challenge these students to analyze the poem orally for the class. Invite them to include Yeats's symbolism in the discussion.

Answers

◆ *Literature and Your Life*

Reader's Response Some students may respond that, physically, time is irreversible. Others may reflect on experiences—listening to a special song, falling in love, reliving a childhood memory—that seem to "stop" or stand outside of time.

Thematic Focus Answers include: Byzantium is a dream, since time and death are real; the world of begetting is a dream, since it passes away.

☑ **Check Your Comprehension**

1. (a) They commend "Whatever is begotten, born, and dies." (b) They "neglect/Monuments of unaging intellect."
2. He asks them to move in a spiral, teach him to sing, consume his heart, and gather him "Into the artifice of eternity."

◆ **Critical Thinking**

1. Byzantium is an eternal, artificial city, not subject to the processes of mortality.
2. (a) He wants to escape age and death. (b) He wants to immortalize himself by transcending nature and creating art.
3. The poem suggests that artists want to somehow escape age and death through their art. Paradoxically, however, as an artificial, golden bird, the artist will sing about mortality.

Humanities: Art

Ravenna: City and Port of Classis, early sixth century mosaic.

This mosaic illustrates the city of Ravenna and its nearby port of Classis, both in what is now Italy.

Ravenna was an important city during both the latter years of the Western Roman Empire and the Byzantine effort to recapture Italy from the Goths. This mosaic—and the basilica of St. Apollinare Nuovo in which it resides—was created during the reign of Ostrogothic Emperor Theodoric (493–526). Theodoric's palace appears at the far right of the picture. The mosaic is one of the earliest in the West to reflect the features of Byzantine art—for example, the gold background and the continuous path around the church walls.

Use these questions for discussion:

1. What language from the poem could be used to describe this mosaic? *Apt phrases include: "holy city of Byzantium" and "gold mosaic of a wall."*
2. What elements of the mosaic suggest the comparison Yeats makes between the worlds of art and nature? *The port (left) could stand for the world of nature, while the intricate palace (right) can stand for the world of art.*

Answers

◆ Literary Focus

Symbolism

1. (a) Yeats uses a shape with lion body and the head of a man—the Sphinx—to symbolize the twenty centuries. (b) Suggested response: Describing the Sphinx is more visually evocative than merely naming it.
2. Suggested response: This image symbolizes the loss of innocence in the modern world. (b) The indignant desert birds could represent those individuals aware of—and alarmed by—a change in the status quo.
3. Suggested responses: (a) "Monuments" symbolize works of art. (b) The gold mosaic and the golden bird are both used to symbolize perfection.

◆ Build Vocabulary

Using the Word Root *-ques-*

1. A search
2. An examination before a jury; the goal of an inquest is to seek information.
3. A stated wish for something; the goal of a request is to communicate the search for something.
4. A stated desire to learn information; a question seeks information.

Using the Word Bank

1. c 2. a 3. c 4. b 5. c 6. a

◆ Reading Strategy

1. Suggested responses: (a) His lifelong unrequited love for Maud Gonne. (b) One would be reading this poem in a volume of verse, so one can infer that the speaker is the author of "this book."
2. Suggested responses: (a) It enables readers to recognize "anarchy" as a reference to World War I or the Russian Revolution. (b) He describes the twenty centuries since Christ's birth as one cycle of civilization and suggests that another cycle of 2,000 years is about to begin.
3. Suggested responses: (a) Knowing Yeats is older helps to clarify the poem's concern with passing time. (b) Yeats refers to the mosaics of Byzantium, which were created by teams of artists, working together rather than for personal glory or gain.

Guide for Responding *(continued)*

◆ Literary Focus

Symbolism

Symbolism, the use of words, images, characters, to stand for something else, is found throughout many of Yeats's poems. The skillful use of symbolism gives literature complexity and allows the writer to show readers ways in which aspects of humanity and the world interrelate.

For example, in "The Second Coming," the falcon flying in circles represents, or symbolizes, something. To interpret the symbol, it helps to understand Yeats's theory about "gyres" or cycles, but the information is not necessary for understanding.

1. Yeats does not only write about twenty centuries of stony sleep, he also symbolizes them. (a) What symbol does he use? (b) Why do you think he presents it through a description of its features rather than by naming it directly?
2. (a) What symbolism, if any, do you find in line 6 of "The Second Coming"? (b) What might the "indignant desert birds" in line 17 represent?
3. (a) In "Sailing to Byzantium" Yeats refers to monuments, once in line 8 and again in line 14. What might the word *monument* symbolize? (b) Find two examples in this poem of Yeats using Byzantine art to symbolize perfection.

◆ Build Vocabulary

Using the Word Root *-ques-*

Knowing that the word root *-ques-* means "to seek," write a definition for each word, showing how the root affects its meaning:

1. quest **3.** request
2. inquest **4.** question

Using the Word Bank

On your paper, write the letter of the word whose meaning is closest to that of the first word.

1. clamorous: (a) angry, (b) peaceful, (c) loud
2. conviction: (a) belief, (b) system, (c) violence
3. artifice: (a) greed, (b) beauty, (c) ingenuity
4. paltry: (a) magnificent, (b) trivial, (c) lying
5. anarchy: (a) peace, (b) cold, (c) disorder
6. conquest: (a) victory, (b) failure, (c) riches

◆ Reading Strategy

Apply Literary Background

Apply your knowledge of **literary background** as you read to help you to identify a poem's speaker, who's being addressed, references or allusions within the poem, a speaker's attitude, and other important information.

1. (a) What event in Yeats's life might have inspired him to write "When You Are Old?" (b) In line 2, the speaker advises the person being addressed to "take down this book." How might that advice furnish a clue to the speaker's identity?
2. (a) How does knowing the time period of "The Second Coming" help you to understand what's being referred to in stanza one? (b) In what ways do Yeats's ideas about cycles of civilization find their way into lines 18–22?
3. (a) How does knowing the age of Yeats at the time "Sailing to Byzantium" was written help you to understand its theme? (b) In what ways does Yeats's admiration for the "impersonal" qualities of Byzantine art find its way into this poem?

◆ Grammar and Style

Noun Clauses

Noun clauses, subordinate clauses that function as nouns, help writers to vary sentence length and tie ideas together. Noun clauses can be used as the subject, direct object, or object of a preposition.

Practice Identify the noun clause and its function in each of the following passages.

1. Dropping from the veils of the morning to where the cricket sings . . .
2. It knows not what it is . . .
3. [D]ream . . . how many loved your moments of peace . . .

Writing Application Write a sentence using the given clause in the function indicated.

1. What the Irish National Movement sought . . . (subject)
2. . . . that the twentieth century was witnessing the decay of civilization. (direct object)

◆ Grammar and Style

Practice

1. where the cricket sings; object of a preposition
2. what it is; direct object
3. how many loved your moments of peace; direct object

Writing Application

1. What the Irish National Monument sought was to raise people's awareness.
2. Yeats believed that the twentieth century was witnessing the decay of civilization.

Build Your Portfolio

Idea Bank

Writing

1. Description Yeats admired Byzantium, which is modern-day Istanbul. Write a brief description of a city or culture you admire, and explain why.

2. Essay Does the late twentieth century really signal the end of an era? Write an essay, using examples to support your opinion.

3. Response to Criticism Scholar Reuben A. Brower wrote that Yeats succeeded "by letting his dreamlike symbols materialize to express and connect conflict he could never resolve outside his poetry." This suggests that Yeats had no solutions for world problems. Write an essay in which you agree or disagree with this view.

Speaking and Listening

4. Irish Poetry Yeats led the Irish literary revival of the late nineteenth and early twentieth centuries. Research some Irish poets who were inspired by this rebirth and perform some of their poems for the class. **[Performing Arts Link]**

5. Music and Swans Yeats's fascination with swans was shared by many artists, including a number of composers. Play Tchaikovsky's *Swan Lake* and Saint-Saens's *Carnival of the Animals* for the class and explain how swans inspired these artists. **[Music Link]**

Projects

6. Yeats Timeline Create a bulletin board display of Yeats's life, unified by a timeline, with visuals representing some of the key events of his life. **[Social Studies Link]**

7. Byzantium Research and present a visual display showing Byzantium's treasures. **[Social Studies Link]**

Writing Mini-Lesson

Prediction Essay

Yeats believed that the twentieth century would witness the end of one civilization (its 2000-year span being up) and the twenty-first century would witness the birth of a new one. What will the twenty-first century, our new millennium, be like? Write an essay detailing your predictions. Before you begin, think about who will read your prediction.

Writing Skills Focus: Knowledge Level of Readers

Good writers always keep their **audience**, or readers, in mind as they write, choosing details that will interest them and that suit their knowledge of the subject. For example, if you were writing your prediction for very young readers, you'd use a different style and include different information than you would if you wrote this essay for your peers.

Yeats's "The Second Coming," for example, is appropriate for an audience that is familiar with Christianity, mythology, and the idea of the Second Coming of Christ.

Prewriting Before you write, jot down a list of ideas you have about the upcoming or newly begun millennium. Decide on your likely audience, and choose details that will grab their interest and suit their level of understanding.

Drafting Choose a format or organizational style and begin drafting. As you write, keep your audience in mind. Thoroughly explain any references or ideas with which they may not be familiar.

Revising Revise your prediction, adjusting your word choice where necessary to suit your audience. Then review your writing for style and consider combining some of your shorter sentences using noun clauses.

To learn more about **noun clauses** and how writers use them, see p. 897.

✓ ASSESSMENT OPTIONS

Formal Assessment, Selection Test, pp. 230–232, and Assessment Resources Software. The selection test is designed so that it can be easily customized to the performance levels of your students.

Alternative Assessment, p. 46, includes options for less advanced students, more advanced students, musical/rhythmic learners, bodily/kinesthetic learners, verbal/linguistic learners, and visual/spatial learners.

PORTFOLIO ASSESSMENT

Use the following rubrics in the ***Alternative Assessment*** booklet to assess student writing:
Description: Description Rubric, p. 98
Essay: General Rubric, p. 94
Response to Criticism: Critical Review Rubric, p. 112
Writing Mini-Lesson: Description Rubric, p. 98

Writer's Solution

For additional instruction and practice, use page 33, on noun clauses, in the *Writer's Solution Grammar Practice Book.*

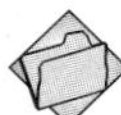

Idea Bank

Customizing for *Performance Levels*

Following are suggestions for matching Idea Bank topics with your students' performance levels:
Less Advanced Students: 1, 6
Average Students: 2, 7
More Advanced Students: 3, 4

Customizing for *Learning Modalities*

Following are suggestions for matching Idea Bank topics with your students' learning modalities:
Visual/Spatial: 6, 7
Musical/Rhythmic: 5

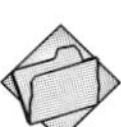

Writing Mini-Lesson

Refer students to the Writing Handbook, page 1189, for instruction on the writing process, and page 1191 for further information on description.

Writer's Solution

Writing Lab CD-ROM

Students might write their predictive essays using the tutorial on Description. Follow these steps:

1. Have students use the segment on Considering Audience and Purpose to determine the knowledge level of their audience. They may then develop an Audience Profile and follow the interactive tips on audience expectations.
2. Students may draft their essays on the computer.
3. Suggest that students use the Self-Evaluation Checklist and the Revision Checkers as they revise their essay.

Sourcebook

Have students use Chapter 1, Description (pp. 1–29), for additional support.

Prepare and Engage

OBJECTIVES

1. To read, comprehend, and interpret poetry
2. To relate poetry to personal experience
3. To interpret text to facilitate comprehension
4. To explore features of modernism
5. To build vocabulary in context and learn the word root *-fract-*
6. To develop skill in using adjectival modifiers
7. To write a music video treatment, using a variety of sources
8. To respond to poetry through writing, speaking and listening, and projects

SKILLS INSTRUCTION

Vocabulary:
Word Roots: *-fract-*

Grammar:
Adjectival Modifiers

Reading Strategy:
Interpret

Literary Focus:
Modernism

Writing:
Variety of Sources

Speaking and Listening:
Debate (teacher edition)

Critical Viewing:
Modify; Classify; Interpret; Evaluate

PORTFOLIO OPPORTUNITIES

Writing: Analysis of an Image; Critical Evaluation; Response to Criticism

Writing Mini-Lesson: Music Video Treatment

Speaking and Listening: Choral Reading; Debate

Projects: Imagism; Modern Dance

More About the Author

The range of historical and literary allusions in T.S. Eliot's work derives in part from the breadth of his education. Eliot's father, a businessman, encouraged his son to pursue education to the farthest reaches and placed no practical pressures on him. Eliot thus studied widely and deeply, for example, discussing philosophy at the Sorbonne in Paris and learning Sanskrit at Harvard University. Eliot's erudition enabled him to excel as an editor and critic as well as poet.

Guide for Interpreting

T. S. Eliot *(1888–1965)*

T. S. Eliot was the most famous English poet of his time. He also was the most influential. His style and his ideas influenced not only poets, but also critics, fiction writers, playwrights, and thinkers in many fields besides literature. From the 1920's on, he was the leader of what is called the Modernist movement. With fellow poet Ezra Pound, he rejected the outdated Romantic tradition. Together they transformed English poetry, making it more responsive to the nervous energy of a new era.

Crossing the Atlantic Eliot had ties to both the United States and Great Britain. Born Thomas Stearns Eliot in St. Louis, Missouri, he was educated at Harvard. However, he also studied at Oxford University in England and at the Sorbonne in Paris. The outbreak of World War I found Eliot in England, where he remained throughout most of his adult life, eventually becoming a British citizen.

Early Work Eliot's earliest work, owing to its unconventional style, was greeted with less than universal acclaim, although the poet Ezra Pound was a vocal supporter from the beginning. Pound saw, as many did not, that Eliot spoke in an authentic new voice and offered an original, if bleak, vision. From *Prufrock and Other Observations* (1917) through *The Waste Land* (1922) and "The Hollow Men" (1925), Eliot portrayed the fragmented, despairing modern world. In part, Eliot may have been responding to the events surrounding World War I. However, work like "Preludes" and "The Love Song of J. Alfred Prufrock" predated the war.

A Spiritual Rebirth Gradually, religion provided hope and led him in 1927 to join the Church of England. His faith shaped the writing of "Journey of the Magi" (1927), "Ash Wednesday" (1930), and the *Four Quartets* (1943), completed during World War II.

As he grew older, Eliot turned his attention to poetic drama and criticism. Although *Murder in the Cathedral* (1935) and *The Cocktail Party* (1950) are often performed, none of his plays have gained the critical admiration accorded his poetry. As a literary critic, Eliot had a profound influence on his contemporaries. His *Notes Towards the Definition of Culture* appeared in 1948, the year in which he received the Nobel Prize for Literature.

Poet's Corner On the second anniversary of Eliot's death (1967), a memorial was unveiled in Poet's Corner, Westminster Abbey. The descendant of Andrew Eliot, who had journeyed to America in the 1700's, was now home.

◆ Background for Understanding

LITERATURE: ELIOT'S ALLUSIONS

In his work, Eliot often uses allusions—indirect references to well-known people, places, or events from the past, or to works of literature. "Journey of the Magi," for instance, is a dramatic monologue spoken by one of the three "wise men" who visited the infant Jesus. In the poem, the speaker uses the conversational language of today to describe historic events. In this way, the spiritual agony of a man who lived long ago becomes vividly present.

In a different vein, Eliot's allusions at the beginning of "The Hollow Men" help him contrast the past and the present. "A penny for the Old Guy" is a traditional cry of children on Guy Fawkes Day. Fawkes (1570–1606) was executed for attempting to blow up the king and Parliament in 1605. He was one of the "lost/ Violent souls" (lines 15–16) of the past who contrast with "the hollow men" of the modern world.

Prentice Hall Literature Program Resources

REINFORCE / RETEACH / EXTEND

Selection Support Pages
Build Vocabulary: Word Roots: *-fract-*, p. 227
Grammar and Style: Adjectival Modifiers, p. 228
Reading Strategy: Interpret, p. 229
Literary Focus: Modernism, p. 230

Strategies for Diverse Students Needs, p. 47

Beyond Literature Music Connection: Modernist Compositions, p. 47

Formal Assessment Selection Test, pp. 233–235; Assessment Resources Software

Alternative Assessment, p. 47

Writing and Language Transparencies
Daily Language Practice: Week 34. p. 169

Resource Pro CD-ROM
"Preludes," "Magi," "Hollow Men"

Listening to Literature Audiocassette
"Preludes," "Magi," "Hollow Men"

Looking at Literature Videodisc
"Preludes," "Magi," "Hollow Men"

◆ Literature and Your Life

Connect Your Experience

Suppose you want to make a short video to go with a song performed by a rock band. You try to remember mixed-up images from a dream so you can use them for your script—but putting them together so they make sense turns out to be hard work!

The use of quick-changing, dreamlike images is a technique modern poets invented long before movie special effects and MTV, as you'll see in T. S. Eliot's poems.

Journal Writing Write down the images you can recall from a music video. What links these images together?

Thematic Focus: Waking From the Dream

How did Eliot's use of dreamlike images help readers awaken to the realities of twentieth-century life?

◆ Literary Focus

Modernism

Modernism in art began with the rejection of Realism. Modernists felt that democracy and industrialism had created a depressing, fragmented world. Rather than creating realistic pictures of this world, they treated it as mere raw material, to be made beautiful by art. Poetry would work on this "material" with its own suggestive language, full of images, musical and indirect.

In the "Preludes," for example, Eliot hints at his meanings through images like this one: "The showers beat/On broken blinds . . ." Such images indirectly express his vision of a sad, ugly, modern world that results from a loss of spiritual life.

◆ Reading Strategy

Interpret

Because it often suggests themes rather than stating them directly, modernist literature makes greater demands on readers. It asks you to **interpret** meanings by linking different passages in a work and drawing conclusions from the patterns you find.

To interpret "The Hollow Men," you might consider the connotations of the words Eliot uses to describe these men—words like "hollow," "stuffed," "dried," and "broken." Ask yourself what the words suggest about the life these men are leading.

◆ Build Vocabulary

Word Roots: *-fract-*

In "Journey of the Magi," Eliot describes camels as *refractory,* meaning "stubborn" or "hard to control." The root *-fract-* means "to break." A refractory animal is one that "breaks away" from the direction in which you want it to go.

Word Bank

Before you read, preview this list of words from the poems.

galled
refractory
dispensation
supplication
tumid

◆ Grammar and Style

Adjectival Modifiers

Different types of structures act as adjectives. Among the structures that Eliot uses as **adjectival modifiers** are the following:

Prepositional phrase:

The burnt-out ends *of smoky days*

The prepositional phrase *of smoky days* modifies *ends.*

Participial phrase:

Headpiece *filled with straw*

The participial phrase *filled with straw* modifies *headpiece.*

Adjective clause:

. . . hands *that are raising dingy shades*

The adjective clause *that are raising dingy shades* modifies *hands.*

Preparing for Standardized Tests

Reading and Vocabulary Many students will encounter tests as part of employment or military service applications. Specific advance preparation for such tests may be difficult but enhanced vocabulary will ensure greater readiness for all reading and vocabulary tasks. The Build Vocabulary lesson for this selection focuses on learning word meaning through the use of the word root *-fract-*. Students can apply this skill to verbal items on standardized tests. For additional practice, use the Build Vocabulary page in ***Selection Support,*** p. 227.

Grammar and Language A mature writing style includes the ability to use a variety of modifying structures. Students may apply their knowledge of these structures in essay portions of tests. The Grammar and Style lesson for this selection focuses on this topic. For additional practice, use the Grammar and Style page on Adjectival Modifiers, p. 228, in ***Selection Support.***

Interest Grabber People who punch the clock, day in and day out, and wonder what they do it for . . . People who can't encounter something new or different without asking, "I don't know, what do *you* think?" . . . For Eliot, this kind of uncertainty and despair characterizes life in modern times. Point out to students that Eliot's diagnosis of modern ills might be confirmed by the number of "answers" available today. Have students bring in examples from advertising, books, films, or their own lives, of modern responses to despair. Discuss what these alternatives—psychiatry, crystals, yoga, exercise, 12-Step Programs, religious reawakening, health foods, etc.—have in common and how they seek to ameliorate some of the despair in modern life.

Customize for ***Less Proficient Readers***
Less proficient readers may have difficulty interpreting Eliot's suggested themes. Pair these students with accomplished poetry readers to analyze and paraphrase difficult passages.

Customize for ***More Advanced Students***
Encourage more advanced students to pay close attention to Eliot's poetic structure. Have students rewrite passages in sentence form and then compare the sentences to Eliot's version. What role does structure play in the expression of ideas?

Customize for ***English Language Learners***
English language learners may struggle with the poems' subtle allusions and implied themes. Urge students to carefully read the Guide for Interpreting and margin notes. Have student groups discuss the influences of the social, political, economic, and literary context on Eliot's poetry.

Customize for ***Visual/Spatial Learners***
Have these students scan the images on pages 915 and 916. What mood do these images convey? Urge students to read the poetry for language supporting or modifying this mood.

Develop Understanding

One-Minute Insight

This poem presents a bleak and despairing vision of the world—a world in which suffering, grime, and dreariness are the main features. Yet Eliot may not just have been reveling in despair: He may have seen it as a necessary "prelude" to spiritual awakening. Each segment, or prelude, describes a different urban scene: a cold, smoky winter evening in a run-down neighborhood; the morning routine of facing yet another hopeless day; a dream-filled night spent in misery. In Prelude IV, though, a new note is sounded—that of something "infinitely gentle/ Infinitely suffering."

◆ Literary Focus

❶ **Modernism** Here, Eliot uses images such as "stale," "trampled," "muddy," "masquerades," and "dingy" to convey his view of a faded and soiled world. Ask students how the stanza's final line emphasizes Eliot's view. *After creating an image of despair, Eliot stresses it by multiplying it a thousandfold.*

◆ Critical Thinking

❷ **Infer** Ask students: What does Eliot's description indicate about his opinion of the human spiritual condition? *Students should infer from "sordid images" and a "soul constituted" (rather than inspired) that Eliot has a dim view of the human spiritual condition. He assumes people have sordid thoughts and a damaged soul.*

◆ Literature and Your Life

❸ Point out that Eliot assumes people's dreams reflect their spiritual poverty. What do students dream of, while asleep or in their daydreams? Urge students to respond in a journal for privacy if they wish. *Those students willing to answer may say that they dream of important emotional connections; of anxieties about the future of their lives and the world; or of confusion about expectations and roles.*

Preludes

T. S. ELIOT

I

The winter evening settles down
With smell of steaks[1] in passageways.
Six o'clock.
The burnt-out ends of smoky days.
And now a gusty shower wraps
The grimy scraps
Of withered leaves about your feet
And newspapers from vacant lots;
The showers beat
On broken blinds and chimney-pots,
And at the corner of the street
A lonely cab-horse steams and stamps.
And then the lighting of the lamps.

II

The morning comes to consciousness
Of faint stale smells of beer
From the sawdust-trampled street
With all its muddy feet that press
To early coffee-stands.
❶ With the other masquerades
That time resumes,
One thinks of all the hands
That are raising dingy shades
In a thousand furnished rooms.

III

You tossed a blanket from the bed,
You lay upon your back, and waited;
You dozed, and watched the night revealing
❷ The thousand sordid images
Of which your soul was constituted;
They flickered against the ceiling.
And when all the world came back
And the light crept up between the shutters
And you heard the sparrows in the gutters,
❸ You had such a vision of the street
As the street hardly understands;

1. **steaks:** In 1910, when this poem was composed, steaks were inexpensive and were commonly eaten by members of the lower class.

Block Scheduling Strategies

Consider these suggestions to take advantage of extended class time:

- Discuss the Literary Focus concept of Modernism as background for Eliot's poems. You may provide the Literary Focus page from ***Selection Support,*** p. 230, as additional background. After students have read the poems, have them answer the Literary Focus questions on page 920.
- Use ***Daily Language Practice*** for Week 34. You may place the transparency on an overhead projector and have students write the sentences correctly.
- Allow students to work on a writing activity of their choice from the Idea Bank on page 921.
- Have students hold the debate suggested in the Idea Bank on page 921. Use the Mini-Lesson on page 914 to develop this activity.

Bolton, 1938, William Coldstream, The National Gallery of Canada, Ottawa

Sitting along the bed's edge, where
You curled the papers from your hair,
Or clasped the yellow soles of feet
In the palms of both soiled hands.

IV

His soul stretched tight across the skies
That fade behind a city block,
Or trampled by insistent feet
At four and five and six o'clock;
And short square fingers stuffing pipes,
And evening newspapers, and eyes
Assured of certain certainties,
The conscience of a blackened street
Impatient to assume the world.

I am moved by fancies that are curled
Around these images, and cling:
The notion of some infinitely gentle
Infinitely suffering thing.

Wipe your hands across your mouth, and laugh;
The worlds revolve like ancient women
Gathering fuel in vacant lots.

▲ **Critical Viewing** This painting captures visually the bleak outlook of the speaker in Eliot's poem. In what ways would you modify this painting if you wanted it to evoke a cheerful atmosphere? **[Modify]** 5

◆ Grammar and Style

4 Adjectival Modifiers Prompt students to identify the adjectival modifiers in these lines. What word does it modify and what is its grammatical structure? *The adjectival modifiers include: "that fade behind a city block," which modifies "skies" and is an adjective clause; "stretched tight across the skies," which modifies "soul" and is a participial phrase; and "trampled by insistent feet," which also modifies "soul" and is a participial phrase.*

▶Critical Viewing◀

5 Modify Students may say that they would lighten the painting, clarify the edges of buildings, add some color and/or natural elements, and remove some smoke and fog in order to create a more cheerful atmosphere.

Customize for *Less Proficient Readers*

Help these students access Eliot's poem by directing them to focus on his mood, rather than on literal meaning. Explain that, like a musical prelude to a longer work, each of these preludes establishes a mood. Give students some signposts to that mood by pointing out words such as "withered," "soiled," and "vacant."

Customize for *More Advanced Students*

Tell these students that about the time Eliot was writing these poems in the United States, Ezra Pound was helping to create the Imagist movement in England. That movement generally favored briefer poems, concrete descriptions, deletion of unnecessary words, and the use of free verse rather than traditional meters. Challenge more advanced students to evaluate "Preludes" using these Imagist criteria.

Humanities: Art

Bolton, 1938, by Sir William Coldstream.

This painting illustrates a mill and factory worker's dwellings in England's industrialized North: a setting that might easily form the backdrop for "The Preludes."

British artist Sir William Coldstream studied at London's Slade School of Art. After working in film for a few years, Coldstream renewed his commitment to painting. In his painting and his teaching, Coldstream stressed the idea that images should speak directly to the viewing public by drawing upon the simple beauty of the commonplace.

Use these questions for discussion:

1. What elements of this painting are described in Eliot's poem? *The wintry light, smoky days, and empty streets are all described in the poem.*
2. How is the mood of this painting different than that of the poem? *The painting has a somewhat nostalgic and romantic mood, while Eliot's poem is brutally realistic.*

This poem offers a brief respite from Eliot's despairing view of modern life in the form of spiritual faith—instead, he offers a view of despair in *ancient* times. The speaker, one of the three biblical wise men who honor the baby Jesus, recounts the practical challenges and physical discomforts of the long journey to Bethlehem. By affiliating those discomforts and the harsh realities of the Birth with the religious awakening of Christianity, the speaker acknowledges the difficulties of spiritual growth and change.

❶ **Clarification** Explain that in this usage, the word *regretted* means "longed for" or "missed."

Comprehension Check ☑

❷ The speaker says that "this" is all folly. What is "this"? *Students should grasp that the speaker is referring to the long, hard journey and its premise of viewing the birth of a savior.*

◆ Critical Thinking

❸ **Interpret** Ask students: Why do others, and perhaps the wise men themselves, think that "this was all folly"? *Students should note that the Magi had little besides hope and a sign to support their belief, so it was easy to believe that there was no point to the difficult journey.*

◆ Reading Strategy

❹ **Interpret** Ask students: How does Eliot's repetition here support his theme that spiritual reawakening is difficult? *Students should note that the repetition serves to emphasize the lines that follow in which the trauma of rebirth is described.*

In this poem, the speaker, one of the three wise men who traveled to Bethlehem to pay homage to the baby Jesus, reflects upon the meaning of the journey.

"A cold coming we had of it,
Just the worst time of the year
For a journey, and such a long journey:
The ways deep and the weather sharp,
The very dead of winter."[1]
And the camels galled, sore-footed, refractory,
Lying down in the melting snow.
❶ There were times we regretted
The summer palaces on slopes, the terraces,
And the silken girls bringing sherbet.
Then the camel men cursing and grumbling
And running away, and wanting their liquor and women,
And the night-fires going out, and the lack of shelters,
And the cities hostile and the towns unfriendly
And the villages dirty and charging high prices:
A hard time we had of it.
At the end we preferred to travel all night,
Sleeping in snatches,
❷ With the voices singing in our ears, saying
❸ That this was all folly.

Then at dawn we came down to a temperate valley,
Wet, below the snow line, smelling of vegetation;
With a running stream and a water-mill beating the darkness,
And three trees on the low sky,
And an old white horse galloped away in the meadow.
Then we came to a tavern with vine-leaves over the lintel,
Six hands at an open door dicing for pieces of silver,
And feet kicking the empty wine-skins.
But there was no information, and so we continued
And arrived at evening, not a moment too soon
Finding the place; it was (you may say) satisfactory.

1. **"A . . . winter":** Adapted from a part of a sermon delivered by 17th-century Bishop Lancelot Andrews: "A cold coming they had of it at this time of year, just the worst time of the year to take a journey, and specially a long journey in. The ways deep, the weather sharp, the days short, the sun farthest off . . . the very dead of winter."

◆ Build Vocabulary

galled (gôld) *adj.*: Injured or made sore by rubbing or chafing

refractory (ri frakʹ tər ē) *adj.*: Hard to manage; stubborn

dispensation (disʹ pən sāʹ shən) *n.*: Religious system or belief

Cultural Connection

In many Christian cultures, the Magi who visited the baby Jesus on his twelfth day of life are nearly as honored as Jesus himself. The commemoration of their visit, called Epiphany, is celebrated on January 6 with feasting, bright lights, religious services, and gift-giving. In Cataluña, in eastern Spain, children spend the day banging on drums and blowing tin whistles to make sure the gift-bearing kings don't pass their town over. Throughout the Spanish-speaking world, *El Dia de los Reyes,* "The Day of the Kings," is celebrated with a parade in which stand-ins for the three kings ride camels through the streets. In the United States, such a parade can be seen in New York City's Hispanic communities.

Tell students that people of many religions undertake pilgrimages. Have students share knowledge of such journeys gleaned from their own experience and encyclopedia research. What common features exist amongst the many pilgrimages discussed?

All this was a long time ago, I remember,
❹ And I would do it again, but set down
This set down
This: were we led all that way for
Birth or Death? There was a Birth, certainly,
We had evidence and no doubt. I had seen birth and death,
But had thought they were different; this Birth was
Hard and bitter agony for us, like Death, our death.
We returned to our places, these Kingdoms,
But no longer at ease here, in the old dispensation,
❺ With an alien people clutching their gods.
I should be glad of another death.

▲ **Critical Viewing** This poem gives gritty realism to the story of the three wise men. In what ways is this photograph realistic? In what ways does it evoke a time and place of wonder? **[Classify]** ❻

Guide for Responding

◆ *Literature and Your Life*

Reader's Response Does Eliot make beauty from ugliness in these poems? Explain.

Thematic Focus In what sense are the speakers in these poems awakened from a dream?

☑ Check Your Comprehension

1. In Prelude I, what is (a) the time of year, and (b) the time of day?
2. In Prelude II, what is taking place "in a thousand furnished rooms"?
3. Describe four problems encountered by the speaker in "Journey of the Magi."

◆ Critical Thinking

INTERPRET

1. What cycle of time do you find in the movement from Prelude I to Prelude IV? **[Connect]**
2. What is the "infinitely gentle/Infinitely suffering thing" (lines 50–51) in "Preludes"? Explain. **[Interpret]**
3. Consider the Magi's own religious traditions in "Journey." (a) Why is "this Birth . . . like Death" for them? (b) Why is the speaker "no longer at ease" (line 41) back home? **[Draw Conclusions]**

EVALUATE

4. Which is more convincing to you, Eliot's expression of despair in "Preludes" or his expression of faith in "Journey of the Magi"? Why? **[Assess]**

◆ Literary Focus

❺ **Modernism** Ask students: How do the closing lines reinforce the themes of Modernism? *Because of his new spiritual insights, the speaker feels out of place, homeless in his own land, just as modern people are portrayed by the Modernists. At the same time, Eliot offers the hope that in this despair (this Death), there is hope.*

▶Critical Viewing◀

❻ **Classify** The photograph is realistic in showing the barrenness around travelers crossing the desert. It evokes wonder through the absence of modern civilization, the glory of nature in the colorful sky, and the contrast of dark against light.

Reinforce and Extend

Customize for
Visual/Spatial Learners
To help these students visualize the Magi's journey, have them create an illustrated map.

Answers

◆ *Literature and Your Life*

Reader's Response Students may point to Eliot's highly evocative language and imagery to say that he does create beauty. Others may say that Eliot's vision, especially in "The Preludes," is so bleak that no beauty of language will temper it.

Thematic Focus Students may note that the poems begin in mid-thought, like a person awakening from a dream. The speakers are awakening from illusions of certainty and complacency.

☑ Check Your Comprehension

1. (a), (b) The setting is a winter evening.
2. Dingy windows are being raised; people are awakening.
3. Suggested responses: The Magi encounter cold temperature; irritable camels; irresponsible camel drivers; lack of shelter and fires; hostile cities; unfriendly towns; dirty villages; high prices.

◆ Critical Thinking

1. The cycle is evening to day to evening again with little change or variety.
2. Suggested response: Eliot refers to the human spirit.
3. (a) The birth of a new spiritual consciousness requires the death of the Magi's existing religious ideas. (b) They feel alienated from the old forms of worship.
4. Some students will say despairing views are always more convincing because they are grounded in real-life details, while faith is based on belief rather than facts. Others will say they found Eliot's faith more convincing because it seems to matter so to him.

Develop Understanding

One-Minute Insight Perhaps the bleakest of the Eliot poems presented here, "The Hollow Men" describes a world in which people have no faith, no courage, no spirit, and no awareness. Spoken by the hollow men themselves, the poem is a self-portrait of the typical modern person. The hollow men contrast poorly with men of purpose, even men of evil purpose. They are sightless and directionless. Finally, in mourning the hollow men's lack of faith, the poem comments that without prayer, people will be unable to transcend the realities of modern life.

Customize for
Musical/Rhythmic Learners
Have students listen to the audiotape of this poem. Encourage them to note the differences in tone from one portion of the poem to another.

Customize for
More Advanced Students
Point out the many footnoted allusions to more advanced students. Challenge them to explain these more fully, reading from or about the referenced texts if they wish.

◆ Background for Understanding

In addition to the social and political changes of the modern post-World War I experience, Eliot had faced personal despair in caring for his deeply troubled first wife Vivien Haigh-Wood. Haigh-Wood was ultimately unable to function in the world and spent her latter years in a psychiatric hospital.

The Hollow Men

T. S. ELIOT

Speaking and Listening Mini-Lesson

Debate
This mini-lesson supports the Speaking and Listening activity in the Idea Bank on page 921.

Introduce the Concept Refer students to the entry on debate, page 1201 in the Speaking and Listening Handbook.

Develop Background Before students begin their debate, urge them to incorporate the following strategies:

- Choose one side of the proposition to debate. Focus first on an emotional response, then try to support it intellectually.
- Use research and discussion to identify supporting reasons, facts, and examples.
- Structure arguments in a logical manner, beginning or ending with the most effective points.

Apply the Information Assign a moderator, or act as moderator yourself, and organize the debate in an argument-rebuttal sequence. Remind students to be courteous listeners and to argue their points without resorting to emotional appeals or inappropriate language.

Assess the Outcome Evaluate the debate based on the preparedness of the teams, the strength of the arguments, and the presentation. Have all students vote for a winning team. Discuss which arguments were most convincing and why.

Mistah Kurtz[1]*—he dead.*

A penny for the Old Guy[2]

I

We are the hollow men
We are the stuffed men
Leaning together
Headpiece filled with straw. Alas!
❶ Our dried voices, when
We whisper together
Are quiet and meaningless
As wind in dry grass
Or rats' feet over broken glass
In our dry cellar

Shape without form, shade without color,
Paralyzed force, gesture without motion;

Those who have crossed
With direct eyes, to death's other Kingdom[3]
Remember us—if at all—not as lost
Violent souls, but only
As the hollow men
The stuffed men.

1. **Mistah Kurtz:** Character in Joseph Conrad's *Heart of Darkness* who hopes to improve the lives of native Africans, but finds that, instead, he is corrupted by his power over them.
2. **A . . . Guy:** Traditional cry used by children on Guy Fawkes Day (November 5), celebrating the execution of a famous English traitor of the same name. The "Old Guy" refers to stuffed dummies representing Fawkes.
3. **Those . . . kingdom:** Allusion to Dante's *Paradiso*, in which those "with direct eyes" are blessed by God in Heaven.

▼ **Critical Viewing** In what way does this photograph convey "shape without form, shade without color" (line 11)? **[Interpret]** ❷

Cross-Curricular Connection: Art

Modernism had a dramatic impact on the visual arts. The invention of the camera in the mid-1800's had already begun to free painters of their task as recorders of reality. Now, like Modernist poets, they rejected the idea that their work must be representational. Artists such as Paul Cézanne focused on the shapes in a painting rather than the actual objects being depicted. Pablo Picasso pursued this idea even further, developing a modern approach called cubism. Cubist paintings use geometric shapes and exaggerated features to present all sides of an object.

Have students scan art books containing modern paintings and sculpture or visit a modern art exhibit at an on-line gallery or museum. Discuss how modern works of art reflect the goals and tone of T.S. Eliot's poetry.

Enrichment Though Eliot's poetry, filled with complex literary and historical allusions, makes him seem inaccessible and even intimidating, friends suggest he was not like that on a personal level. Poet Dylan Thomas, for example, was struggling financially. After asking countless successful friends and colleagues for help, Thomas dared to approach Eliot, who willingly and generously responded with financial support and perhaps professional sponsorship.

Customize for *Less Proficient Readers*

To help less proficient readers navigate this difficult poem, suggest contemporary images of "hollow men": couch potatoes, slackers. Urge these students to identify the poem's speakers. As students read on, direct them to continually analyze the speakers' attitudes.

◆ Reading Strategy

❶ **Interpret** Here, Eliot uses a collection of auditory and tactile images —"hollow," "filled with straw," "dried," "wind in dry grass," "rats' feet over broken glass"—to suggest the emotional vacuum of the hollow men.

▶Critical Viewing◀

❷ **Interpret** Students may say that the photograph suggests human shapes without enough detail to determine their identity—their form. It is primarily a contrast of visual shading, rather than specific colors.

Customize for
More Advanced Readers
"The Hollow Men" shares some characteristics with Eliot's most famous poem, *The Waste Land*. That lengthy poem of 433 lines reflects the physical and spiritual fragmentation and decay of modern urban life. Ask more advanced students to read part or all of *The Waste Land* and share their comments with the class.

Customize for
Verbal/Linguistic Learners
Help these learners appreciate Eliot's linguistic choices. Point out the lack of punctuation, for example, in the first stanza of Section III. Discuss how omitting punctuation enables the poetic structure—formless—to mirror and emphasize the poetic content—hollow men.

▶Critical Viewing◀

❶ **Evaluate** Students may say that this shadow depicts the figure's hesitation, thus successfully conveying the idea that the Shadow—fear—falls between the idea and the reality, the motion and the act.

◆ Critical Thinking

❷ **Infer** Ask students: Whose eyes are the speakers afraid of meeting? *Students may say the speakers are afraid of meeting the eyes of the blessed, those whose lives are not hollow because they are shaped by faith.*

◀ **Critical Viewing** How well does this shadow convey the idea that "Between the idea/And the reality/Between the motion/And the act/Falls the Shadow"? **[Evaluate]** ❶

II

[2] Eyes I dare not meet in dreams
In death's dream kingdom
These do not appear:
There, the eyes are
Sunlight on a broken column
There, is a tree swinging
And voices are
In the wind's singing
More distant and more solemn
Than a fading star.

Let me be no nearer
In death's dream kingdom
Let me also wear
[3] Such deliberate disguises
Rat's coat, crowskin, crossed staves
In a field[4]
Behaving as the wind behaves
No nearer—

Not that final meeting
In the twilight kingdom

III

This is the dead land
This is cactus land
[4] Here the stone images
Are raised, here they receive
[5] The supplication of a dead man's hand
Under the twinkle of a fading star.

Is it like this
In death's other kingdom
[6] Waking alone
At the hour when we are
[7] Trembling with tenderness
Lips that would kiss
Form prayers to broken stone.

4. crossed . . . field: Scarecrows.

◆ Build Vocabulary

supplication (sup′ lə kā′ shən) *n.*: Act of praying

Reinforce and Extend

3 Point out to students how the hollow men try to disguise themselves, perhaps to avoid judgment. When have students, or others they've observed, fashioned a specific presentation—even a disguise—of themselves for the world to see? *Students may mention descriptions given to new acquaintances, omitting or embellishing facts; clothing worn to blend in with or stand out from the crowd; views shared or unspoken to preserve others' good opinions.*

◆ Literary Focus

4 Modernism Point out the references to the "dead land" and the "dead man's hand." Discuss how these convey a sense of meaninglessness.

◆ Reading Strategy

5 Interpret Explain to students that one interpretation for "the fading star" is the lessening of religious faith during Eliot's time. The star refers to Christ; describing it as fading suggests Christianity is losing its power.

◆ Literary Focus

6 Modernism Ask students to describe the tone of these lines. Do they reflect the Modernist view of the world? *Students may say the lines suggest isolation, an aspect of the bleak Modernist world view. They may also note the possibility of hope, though, in the references to "death's other kingdom" and to "tenderness," and in the fact that this stanza is put as a question.*

◆ Grammar and Style

7 Adjectival Modifiers Have students identify and name the grammatical structure of the adjectival modifier in line 50. *The adjectival modifier is "that would kiss" and it forms an adjective clause modifying "lips."*

Beyond the Classroom

Career Connection

Ophthalmology/Optometry In this poem, the speakers are sightless and don't want to be seen. Doctors of ophthalmology and optometry help people improve their vision.

Using special instruments, these doctors look into and evaluate the shape and condition of the lenses inside a person's eyes. They can then design eyeglasses or contact lenses to correct any flaws. Ophthalmologists also perform corrective surgeries. Have interested students survey such doctors in your area, including those affiliated with retail vision-care stores. What services does each offer?

Community Connection

Services for the Blind Today, because of laws protecting the visually impaired, the hollow men would be able to navigate communities more easily. Have students brainstorm parts of your community—crowded areas, complex buildings, transportation systems, etc.—that would present difficult obstacles to the visually impaired. In pairs, have interested students travel some of these routes, observing features that may now exist to ease the challenges. For example, students may note Braille directories and elevator controls or auditory street crossing cues. If your community lacks these improvements, discuss where they might be most useful.

Customize for
Less Proficient Readers

Less proficient readers are unlikely to be familiar with the referenced texts, Dante's *Inferno* or Shakespeare's *Julius Caesar*. Invite students familiar with these works to summarize them briefly or do so yourself.

Customize for
English Language Learners

Remind these students that one feature of Modernist poetry is dreamlike jumps from topic to topic. Urge English language learners to regard Eliot's use of italics as signals of such jumps.

◆ Reading Strategy

❶ **Interpret** Discuss two interpretations for these lines: Only empty, hopeless men turn to religion OR religion is the only hope for empty men. Given Eliot's growing religious faith during his life, ask students which interpretation they find more plausible. Which interpretation is more meaningful to students? *Students will probably say the second interpretation is more plausible as Eliot's view, though they may personally believe in the first.*

◆ Literary Focus

❷ **Modernism** Point out the musical quality caused by repetition in these lines. Suggest additionally that the repetition, which both emphasizes the words' meaning while simultaneously causing the words to become chant-like and lose their meaning, evokes the Modernist view of a meaningless world where only art—words—can offer meaning.

IV

The eyes are not here
There are no eyes here
In this valley of dying stars
In this hollow valley
This broken jaw of our lost kingdoms

In this last of meeting places
We grope together
And avoid speech
Gathered on this beach of the tumid river[5]

Sightless, unless
The eyes reappear
As the perpetual star[6]
Multifoliate rose[7]
Of death's twilight kingdom
❶ The hope only
Of empty men.

V

Here we go round the prickly pear
Prickly pear prickly pear
Here we go round the prickly pear
At five o'clock in the morning.[8]

❷
Between the idea
And the reality
Between the motion
And the act[9]
Falls the Shadow

For Thine is the Kingdom[10]

Between the conception
And the creation
Between the emotion
And the response
Falls the Shadow

5. river: From Dante's *Inferno*, the river Acheron, which the dead cross on the way to Hell.

6. star: Traditional symbol for Christ.

7. Multifoliate rose: Rose with many leaves. Dante describes paradise as such a rose in his *Paradiso*. The rose is a traditional symbol for the Virgin Mary.

8. Here . . . morning: Adaptation of a common nursery rhyme. A prickly pear is a cactus.

9. Between . . . act: Reference to *Julius Caesar*, Act II, Scene i, 63–65: "Between the acting of a dreadful thing/And the first motion, all the interim is/Like a phantasma or hideous dream."

10. For . . . Kingdom: From the ending of the Lord's Prayer.

◆ Build Vocabulary

tumid (to͞o′ mid) *adj.*: Swollen

Cultural Connection

The religious images in this poem are almost exclusively Christian. Christianity is a monotheist religion, focused around the belief in one god. Judaism and Islam are both monotheistic as well, while Hinduism recognizes one supreme god amongst many lesser gods. Buddhists focus on human behavior rather than a god.

Despite differences amongst religions, they share many characteristics. Prayers, such as the Lord's Prayer alluded to by Eliot, are Judeo-Christian in origin; however, most religions include some form of prayer. This may include reciting words from a sacred book such as Islam's Koran or silent meditation. Many religions have important symbols as well, just as the star and rose are Christian symbols.

Have willing students share examples of prayer and symbols from religions they know. Discuss how these could be interchanged with Eliot's without losing the poet's central theme about the value of religion in human existence.

Life is very long[11]

Between the desire
And the spasm
Between the potency
And the existence
Between the essence
And the descent
Falls the Shadow

For Thine is the Kingdom

For Thine is
Life is
For Thine is the

This is the way the world ends
This is the way the world ends
This is the way the world ends
Not with a bang but a whimper.

11. **Life . . . long:** Quotation from Joseph Conrad's *An Outcast of the Islands*.

Guide for Responding

◆ Literature and Your Life

Reader's Response If you wanted to make a music video of this poem, what images from it would you use? Why?

Thematic Focus What do you think the hollow men fear in "death's dream kingdom"?

☑ Check Your Comprehension

1. What images describe the hollow men in the first ten lines?
2. Describe "death's dream kingdom" and "the dead land," the landscapes of this poem.
3. What is it that forever falls between idea and achievement, preventing the hollow men from accomplishing anything?
4. In the line, "Here we go round the prickly pear," what action is being described?
5. How does the poem's last line say the world will end?

◆ Critical Thinking

INTERPRET

1. What do the images of wind in parts I and II suggest about the hollow men? **[Infer]**
2. Why are Kurtz, a "hollow sham," and Guy Fawkes, a traitor, superior to the hollow men? **[Interpret]**
3. Why are the hollow men afraid of the "eyes" (lines 14, 19, 52)? **[Interpret]**
4. What do the fragments of prayer in the last part of the poem suggest about the hollow men? **[Draw Conclusions]**

EVALUATE

5. Is the nursery rhyme that Eliot uses in part V (lines 68–71, 95–98) effective in conveying the speakers' plight? Explain. **[Criticize]**

APPLY

6. What would you say makes someone a whole person rather than a hollow one? **[Apply]**

Beyond the Poems

FURTHER READING

Other Works by T.S. Eliot

"The Love Song of J. Alfred Prufrock"; *The Waste Land; The Four Quartets*

Other Works About Despair and Hope

"No Worst, There Is None," Gerard Manley Hopkins

"A Better Resurrection," Christina Rossetti

"Work Without Hope," Samuel Taylor Coleridge

We suggest that you preview these works before recommending them to students.

INTERNET

You and your students may find additional information about the T.S. Eliot on the Internet at the following sites. Please be aware, however, that sites may have changed since this information was published.

For more about Eliot, visit **http://killdevilhill.com/tseliotchat/wwwboard.html**

To consult a concordance of Eliot's works, visit **http:// www.missouri.edu/~enggf/tsebase.html**

We *strongly recommend* that you preview sites before you send students to them.

Reinforce and Extend

Customize for
Less Proficient Readers
Encourage less proficient readers to reread Eliot's difficult poems, explaining that the meaning of Modernist writing often reveals itself in layers. On subsequent readings, urge students to focus on the tone suggested by Eliot's chosen details and word arrangements.

Answers

◆ Literature and Your Life

Reader's Response Students may mention the images of hollow and eyeless men, scarecrows, the shadow, and arid desert landscapes.

Thematic Focus Students may say the hollow men fear judgment.

☑ Check Your Comprehension

1. Images include a headpiece filled with straw; dried voices; wind in dry grass; rats' feet over broken glass.
2. The first is sunlit and filled with singing; it is perhaps also the arid, desolate, and unproductive land in stanza III. "Death's other kingdom" is heaven; it is not described.
3. The Shadow, which may be interpreted as fear, falls between the idea and the achievement.
4. The dancing of children playing ring-around-the-rosy is described.
5. The world will end with a whimper (passively, quietly), not a bang (violently).

◆ Critical Thinking

1. Students may infer that the hollow men are without conviction, are hopeless and despairing, and want to hide in shame and be anonymous.
2. These individuals had a direction to their lives and were not afraid of dying.
3. They don't want to face judgment by the blessed because they know that judgment will find them lacking.
4. The hollow men cannot fully pray and therefore cannot improve their situation.
5. Eliot's use of the nursery rhyme effectively depicts the speakers as lost children chanting words that have lost their meaning.
6. A sense of purpose in life, whether from religious faith, commitment to excellence, or moral behavior, creates a whole person.

Answers

◆ Reading Strategy

1. Suggested response: Images of feet appear in each of the Preludes, perhaps suggesting that the modern world has cut off people's bodies (their feet) from their thinking and feeling heart and mind.
2. Suggested response: Repetition of the journey's difficulties suggests and emphasizes Eliot's meaning that spiritual reawakening is challenging but worthwhile.

◆ Build Vocabulary

Word Roots: *-fract-*

1. The law was broken.
2. It will take only a piece broken from your time; the rest remains.
3. The boys broke the rules.
4. The wrist bone is broken.
5. The clouds appear to be broken into pieces.

Using the Word Bank

1. b 2. a 3. a 4. c 5. c

◆ Literary Focus

1. Suggested response: Creating an image in readers' minds is more vivid and immediate than a simple statement of views. It makes the ideas personal for readers.
2. Suggested responses: Eliot uses images of the sounds, movements, and appearance of the hollow men; repetition contributes to musical language throughout; references to dead lands, cactus, broken and dried men, stone images, incomplete prayers all suggest a world without meaning.
3. Suggested response: By conveying the speaker's belief that spiritual reawakening may offer hope and direction, "Journey" suggests that faith may bring meaning to the world after all.

Guide for Responding *(continued)*

◆ Reading Strategy

Interpret

You can **interpret** Eliot's poetry by linking images, statements, or phrases in the poem and figuring out the meanings they suggest. For example, Eliot uses images of "eyes" throughout "The Hollow Men." In I, "Those who have crossed/With direct eyes, to death's other Kingdom" are unlike the hollow men. Then, in II, one of the hollow men talks of "Eyes I dare not meet in dreams." Again, in IV, "The eyes are not here," where the hollow men lead their "broken" existence. As a result, the hollow men are "Sightless."

These images suggest that the hollow men are unable to give or receive honest, direct looks. You might interpret this inability as evidence of their spiritual poverty.

Interpret these patterns from Eliot's poems:

1. Images in "Preludes" that focus on parts of bodies rather than whole people
2. In "Journey of the Magi," repetition of the journey's difficulties

◆ Build Vocabulary

Using the Word Root *-fract-*

Explain how the root *-fract-*, which means "to break," contributes to the meaning of each underlined word.

1. She was guilty of an infraction of the law.
2. This chore will take only a fraction of your time.
3. The fractious boys caused trouble at school.
4. Did you fall and fracture your wrist?
5. The fracto-stratus clouds were ragged and appeared in long, threadlike layers.

Using the Word Bank

On your paper, write the letter of the word that is closest in meaning to the first word.

1. galled: (a) stained, (b) sore, (c) bare
2. dispensation: (a) system, (b) trial, (c) exhaustion
3. supplication: (a) entreaty, (b) demand, (c) bribe
4. tumid: (a) dirty, (b) narrow, (c) swollen
5. refractory: (a) broken, (b) unable, (c) stubborn

◆ Literary Focus

Modernism

One of the founders of **Modernism,** T. S. Eliot uses images and musical language to depict a chaotic, directionless world. The final image of "Preludes" summarizes the whole Modernist perspective: "The worlds revolve like ancient women/Gathering fuel in vacant lots." He compares something once thought of as large, grand, and orderly—"The worlds"—to something shabby, insignificant, and wandering—old women gathering things to burn.

1. How is Eliot's image a more effective expression of Modernism than a direct statement would be?
2. Find examples of these Modernist qualities in "The Hollow Men": use of images; musical, suggestive language; a world without meaning.
3. Explain how "Journey of the Magi," a later poem than the others, represents a departure from Modernist despair. How does it suggest that the world might have meaning after all?

◆ Grammar and Style

Adjectival Modifiers

Adjectival modifiers—prepositional phrases, participial phrases, and adjective clauses that act as adjectives—are a key part of Eliot's style. Often he places them together to suggest a meaning. For example, in lines 11–12 of "The Hollow Men," he uses a series of prepositional phrases to suggest the ineffectiveness of the speakers: "Shape *without form*, shade *without color*, / . . . gesture *without motion*."

Practice On your paper, identify the adjectival modifiers in these lines and explain their effect:

1. "Preludes," lines 1–4
2. "Preludes," lines 19–23
3. "Journey of the Magi," lines 10–12
4. "The Hollow Men," lines 43–44
5. "The Hollow Men," lines 54–55

Writing Application Write a brief profile of the speaker in "Journey of the Magi," using a variety of adjectival modifiers to describe your subject. Experiment with series of modifiers, as Eliot does.

◆ Grammar and Style

1. Modifiers: "of steaks in passageways"; "of smoky days." These describe the setting as confining and smoky.
2. Modifiers: "that time resumes," "that are raising dingy shades." These portray the actions as repetitive and dreary.
3. Modifiers: "bringing sherbet," "cursing and grumbling," "running away," "wanting their liquor and women." These describe the girls and camel men, showing the comforts offered by the first and the second's irresponsibility.
4. Modifiers: "of a dead man's hand," "under the twinkle of a fading star." These suggest the hollow men's despair over their loss of faith.
5. Modifiers: "of dying stars." This repeated phrase emphasizes the barrenness of the landscape.

For additional instruction and practice, use the Writing Style unit of the **Language Lab CD-ROM,** and the section on phrases and clauses, pp. 27–33, in the *Writer's Solution Grammar Practice Book.*

Build Your Portfolio

Idea Bank

Writing

1. **Analysis of an Image** Select an image you like from one of Eliot's poems. Indicate the senses to which it appeals and explain why you think it is effective.

2. **Critical Evaluation** Rate the Eliot poems you have read. Then explain and justify your ranking system, quoting specific passages from the poems to support your points.

3. **Response to Criticism** Bernard Bergonzi writes that a number of Eliot's poems, including "The Hollow Men," "were all put together out of fragments . . ." Do the poems you have read show evidence of this method of composition? Explain.

Speaking and Listening

4. **Choral Reading** With a small group, perform "The Hollow Men." Different sections should be read by different individuals or groups. Use a nursery-rhyme rhythm to recite lines 68–71 and 95–98. **[Performing Arts Link]**

5. **Debate** Does Eliot's view of modern life have truth in it, or is it distorted? Divide into two teams and debate this question. **[Social Studies Link]**

Projects

6. **Imagism** Using a book of Ezra Pound's essays, find what he says about his version of Modernism—Imagism. Then report on whether Eliot's poems are Imagist works. **[Literature Link]**

7. **Modern Dance** Modernism transformed dance as well as poetry. Research and report on a leading creator of modern dance, like Isadora Duncan. Explain how she can be considered a Modernist. **[Performing Arts Link]**

Writing Mini-Lesson

Music Video Treatment

Modernist poetry conveys meaning largely through images, just as videos and movies do. Explaining the images you'll use, write a short descriptive plan (treatment) for a music video. Explain why you selected certain images and how you will coordinate them with the music. Draw on a variety of sources for your images.

Writing Focus: Variety of Sources

Many artistic expressions—from a Modernist poem to a music video—use a **variety of sources** to create fresh combinations of images. Here are some sources you might use to write your treatment:

- Music videos that you have enjoyed—what kinds of images do they use and how do they link them?
- Television commercials—what techniques of combining words and images do they use?
- Modern paintings—what strange combinations of images do they include?

Prewriting Research for images in a variety of sources. Then, with a flowchart like this one, show how you'll combine some of them:

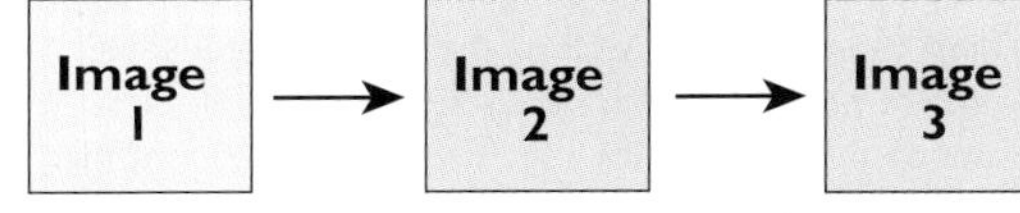

Drafting Start with a striking image to get the audience's attention. For imagery, look at your notes on sources and your flowchart. Describe how the images you've selected match the pace, rhythm, and words of the song.

Revising As you review your treatment, listen to the song again. Be sure that your plan captures the spirit of the music. If your plan doesn't work for a section of the song, go back to your sources and choose other images.

Idea Bank

Customizing for *Performance Levels*

Following are suggestions for matching Idea Bank topics with your students' performance levels:

Less Advanced Students: 1, 4
Average Students: 2, 5, 7
More Advanced Students: 3, 6

Customizing for *Learning Modalities*

Following are suggestions for matching Idea Bank topics with your students' learning modalities:

Verbal/Linguistic: 1, 2, 3, 4, 5
Interpersonal: 4, 5
Intrapersonal: 5
Bodily/Kinesthetic: 7

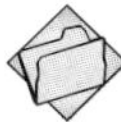

Writing Mini-Lesson

Refer students to the Writing Process Handbook, page 1189, for instruction on the writing process, and pages 1192–1193 for further information on creative writing.

Writing Lab CD-ROM

Have students write their treatments using the tutorial on Creative Writing. They should follow these steps:

1. View the author video segment in which Derek Walcott tells how he considers an audience.
2. View the interactive model on tone.
3. Draft on computer.
4. Revise, using the interactive self-evaluation checklists.
5. Complete the revision, using the revision checkers.

Sourcebook

Have students use Chapter 6, Creative Writing (pp. 166–195), for additional support.

✓ ASSESSMENT OPTIONS

Formal Assessment, Selection Test, pp. 233–235, and Assessment Resources Software. The selection test is designed so that it can be easily customized to the performance levels of your students.

Alternative Assessment, p. 47, includes options for less advanced students, more advanced students, logical/mathematical learners, verbal/linguistic learners, and visual/spatial learners.

PORTFOLIO ASSESSMENT

Use the following rubrics in the ***Alternative Assessment*** booklet to assess student writing:
Analysis of an Image: Literary Analysis Rubric, p. 113
Critical Evaluation: Literary Analysis Rubric, p. 113
Response to Criticism: Literary Analysis Rubric, p. 111
Writing Mini-Lesson: General Rubric, p. 94

Prepare and Engage

OBJECTIVES

1. To read, comprehend, and interpret poetry
2. To relate poetry to personal experience
3. To paraphrase poetry
4. To recognize a poem's theme
5. To build vocabulary in context and learn the word root *-top-*
6. To develop skill in using parallel structure
7. To write a poem about art, conveying a main impression
8. To respond to poetry through writing, speaking and listening, and projects

SKILLS INSTRUCTION

Vocabulary: Word Roots: *-top-*
Grammar: Parallel Structure
Reading Strategy: Paraphrase
Literary Focus: Theme
Writing: Conveying a Main Impression
Speaking and Listening: Museum Guide (teacher edition)
Critical Viewing: Interpret; Speculate

PORTFOLIO OPPORTUNITIES

Writing: Tribute; Essay; Response to Criticism
Writing Mini-Lesson: Poem About Art
Speaking and Listening: Museum Guide; Oral Interpretation
Projects: Art Exhibit; Family Background

More About the Author

W.H. Auden's distinctive blend of styles—his everyday, conversational tone mixed with bookish allusions, his use of concrete images as if they were abstract ideas, and of abstract ideas as if they were familiar friends—made him the voice of a generation. While his early poems reflect the social turmoil of his times, Auden found a renewed and staunch Christian faith later in life.

Stephen Spender, though infected with the despair and anxiety of the post-World War I era, was more optimistic than many Modernists. He wrote politically charged poetry reflecting an attempt to integrate his idealistic visions with the realities of society.

Louis MacNeice was not at all political in his poetry. He focused more on the craft, creating restrained and precise poetry. A Modernist, MacNeice took a somber and melancholy view of the world.

Guide for Interpreting

W. H. Auden *(1907–1973)*

Born in York, England, Wystan Hugh Auden had early dreams of becoming an engineer but, instead, he gravitated to poetry. In 1939, Auden left England for the United States, where he taught in a number of universities and became an American citizen in 1946. From 1956 to 1961, he returned to Oxford as Professor of Poetry.

Achievements in Poetry Auden's poems first appeared in *Oxford Poetry*, a series of annual collections of verse by the university's undergraduates. The volumes in which his poems appear also contain poems by Stephen Spender and Louis MacNeice. Auden's first published collection, entitled simply *Poems,* appeared in 1930. Innovative and eloquent, Auden's verse struck many readers of the day as strange, even impenetrable. His second collection, *On This Island* (1937), is more down-to-earth and generated greater enthusiasm. Auden won a Pulitzer Prize in 1948 for his poetry collection *The Age of Anxiety.*

A Versatile Poet Auden wrote equally well in the idiom of the street or in the archaic measures of *Beowulf.* His output is remarkable for its variety, originality, and craftsmanship. He has been called "the most provocative as well as the most unpredictable poet of his generation." With Yeats and Eliot, he is among the most highly regarded British poets of the first half of the twentieth century.

Stephen Spender *(1909–1995)*

No poet of the 1930's provided a more honest picture of the era between the wars than did Stephen Spender. Born in London and educated at Oxford, Spender's first important book, *Poems* (1933), was published while he was living in Germany.

Spender, a political activist, promoted antifascist propaganda in Spain during its Civil War (1936–1939). He later co-edited the literary magazine *Horizon* and the political, cultural, and literary review *Encounter.*

Louis MacNeice *(1907–1963)*

Louis MacNeice was born the son of a Protestant clergyman in Belfast, Northern Ireland. A gifted youth, he began to write poetry at age seven. His first collection of poems, *Blind Fireworks,* appeared in 1929, followed six years later by *Poems,* the volume that established his reputation. During the 1930's, MacNeice taught Classics at university. In 1941, he joined the British Broadcasting Corporation as a feature writer and producer.

A lyric and reflective poet, MacNeice was modest about the aims of poetry, doubting that it could truly change the world. Today, many consider MacNeice second only to Auden among the poets of his generation.

◆ Background for Understanding

LITERATURE: THE AUDEN CIRCLE—THE WORLD AS POETIC INSPIRATION

The 1930's was a decade poised between a worldwide economic depression and the impending devastation of World War II. The complexity of this period is reflected in the poems of the Auden circle, which consisted of Auden himself, Spender, MacNeice, and C. Day Lewis. The political urgency of the times shaped much of the poetry they wrote then. Yet each of these poets had, at the same time, a deep sense of a specifically "poetic" vocation—to make something happen in language.

Prentice Hall Literature Program Resources

REINFORCE / RETEACH / EXTEND

Selection Support Pages
Build Vocabulary: Word Roots: *-top-*, p. 231
Grammar and Style: Parallel Structure, p. 232
Reading Strategy: Paraphrase, p. 233
Literary Focus: Theme, p. 234

Strategies for Diverse Student Needs, p. 48

Beyond Literature
Social Studies Connection: The Great Depression, p. 48

Formal Assessment Selection Test, pp. 236–238; Assessment Resources Software

Alternative Assessment, p. 48

Resource Pro CD-ROM
"In Memory of W. B. Yeats," "Musée des Beaux Art," "Carrick Revisited," "Not Palaces"—includes all resource material and customizable lesson plan

Listening to Literature Audiocassettes
"In Memory of W. B. Yeats," "Musée des Beaux Art," "Carrick Revisited", "Not Palaces"

In Memory of W. B. Yeats ◆ Musée des Beaux Arts Carrick Revisited ◆ Not Palaces

◆ Literature and Your Life

Connect Your Experience

Things in life that make you pause and reflect—an object of exquisite beauty or a social injustice—might serve as sources of inspiration for creative pursuits such as art or music. The sources of inspiration for the following poems were world issues and events.

Journal Writing List a few memories, conversations, or events that might serve as inspiration for creative writing.

Thematic Focus: Waking From the Dream

Between the world wars, some poets woke from their "dreams" to demand social justice. As you read writers who came of age during this period, notice their ideas of the poet's place in society.

◆ Literary Focus

Theme

The **theme** of a literary work is its central idea, concern, or purpose. A poem's theme may be directly stated or it may be implied by the poet's choice of words, comparisons, and images.

For example, in "In Memory of W. B. Yeats," Auden explores the role of the writer as artist. There are direct clues to this theme, as in line 36 ("poetry makes nothing happen") and in lines 50–51, which state that time "Worships language and forgives/Everyone by whom it lives." The vivid imagery of the "dark cold day" on which Yeats died and the overall tone, or attitude, of the poem are indirect clues to the poem's theme.

As you read these poems, look for clues that reveal their themes.

◆ Reading Strategy

Paraphrase

To follow concentrated expressions of ideas and emotions in poetry, it is often helpful to **paraphrase**, restate the writer's words in your own words.

For example, you might paraphrase lines 4–6 of "In Memory of W. B. Yeats" this way: "It got colder as the day went on. There's no doubt that he died on a cold and dark day."

As you read these poems, check your understanding by choosing brief passages to paraphrase in your own words.

◆ Build Vocabulary

Word Roots: *-top-*

In "Carrick Revisited" you will encounter the word *topographical.* The Greek word root *-top-* means "place," and topographical means "relating to a map of the surface features of a place."

Word Bank

Before you read, preview this list of words from the poems.

- sequestered
- topographical
- affinities
- prenatal
- intrigues

◆ Grammar and Style

Parallel Structure

In both poetry and prose, writers create a natural rhythm and flow by using **parallel structure**; that is, they use the same grammatical form or pattern to express ideas of equal importance. In this example, Auden uses parallel pairs of prepositional phrases in the first and third lines:

In the deserts of the heart
Let the healing fountain
start,
In the prison of his days
Teach the free man how to
praise.

As you read the poems, look for other examples of parallel structure.

Hold up this textbook, or ask students to examine their own copies. Ask students to consider for a moment the art—poetry, fiction, drama, paintings—the book contains. Ask: What is the purpose of art? What does it do? Out of what impulses do people create it? In three very different ways, each of the poets in this section asks and perhaps answers these questions.

Customize for *Less Proficient Readers*

To help less proficient readers unravel the subtleties in these poems, urge them to read slowly. Tell them to pause at the end of each stanza and paraphrase for comprehension, rereading the stanza if necessary. Urge students to check their comprehension with a partner.

Customize for *More Advanced Students*

More advanced students can enhance their response to these poets by comparing the stylistic choices each poet makes. Urge students to look at tone, diction, and theme in their comparison.

Customize for *English Language Learners*

Guide English language learners to use the punctuation in the poetry to help them read in sentences for meaning.

Customize for *Visual/Spatial Learners*

Encourage these learners to use the selection illustrations as aids to comprehension. Have them preview the images on pages 924, 928, 931, and 933 and list emotions and ideas evoked by each image.

Preparing for Standardized Tests

Portions of some standardized tests require students to improve sentences or paragraphs by identifying the best revision from among several choices. For instance, students may be asked to analyze and respond to an item like the following:

Choose the best revision for the underlined portion.

At night the Himalayas can be freezing cold, <u>but they are often extremely hot in the day.</u> *(D)*

(A) NO CHANGE
(B) but the daytime is hotter.
(C) but it is hot in the daytime.
(D) but in the day they can be extremely hot.

The Grammar and Style lesson for this selection focuses on parallelism, one of the concepts students will need to successfully complete such items. For additional practice, use the page on Parallel Structure, p. 232, in ***Selection Support***.

Develop Understanding

One-Minute Insight This poem celebrates and honors the life of poet W.B. Yeats. Structured as an elegy, "In Memory . . ." sums up Yeats's lifetime accomplishments and crafts a vivid picture of the man. Part I describes his all-too-human death and the gap it will leave behind. In Part 2, Auden addresses Yeats directly to reassure him of poetry's enduring qualities. Part 3, addressed to both the Earth and to a generic poet, focuses on the nature of poetry. As a whole, the poem urges devotion to art as the path to moral and intellectual nourishment.

Customize for
Visual/Spatial Learners
Have students identify details in this photograph that give them a sense of the man Yeats is. *The many books behind him indicate a love of learning or an interest in literature, the dog at his side indicates a humane man who enjoys companionship, the surroundings appear to be comfortable, indicating a man who is relatively well-off.*

►Critical Viewing◄

❶ **Interpret** Encourage students to keep this question in mind while reading. After reading further, students may say that the photograph shows both aspects of Yeats, the old and frail man described in Part I and the writer—surrounded by books and papers—of Part 3.

◆ Literary Focus

❷ **Theme** Ask students to propose both a literal and a figurative interpretation of these lines. What do their interpretations suggest about the poem's theme? *Literally, Yeats died during the winter. Figuratively, when Yeats died, the world became a colder, more barren place for the speaker. The theme suggested is that Yeats's death leaves an emptiness in the world. Encourage more sophisticated readers to explore the implied contrast between the public spaces and objects (the airport, the statues, the instruments) and the private, solitary fact of Yeats's "disappearance." The poem will continue to question the relations between the poet and the world.*

In Memory of W. B. Yeats

W. H. AUDEN

Block Scheduling Strategies

Consider these suggestions to take advantage of extended class time:

- Introduce paraphrasing as a reading strategy. Encourage students to pause and paraphrase after Parts 1, 2, and 3 of this poem. After reading the poem, have students complete the Reading Strategy page on Paraphrasing, ***Selection Support,*** p. 233.
- Allow time for students to meet in small groups to discuss the Check Your Comprehension and other Guide for Responding questions.
- Have students listen to the selection poems on audiocassette. Discuss how hearing the poems affects students' interpretation of them.
- Have students complete the Writing Mini-Lesson (p. 935).
- Invite students to present and explain their Art Exhibitions (p. 935) to the class.

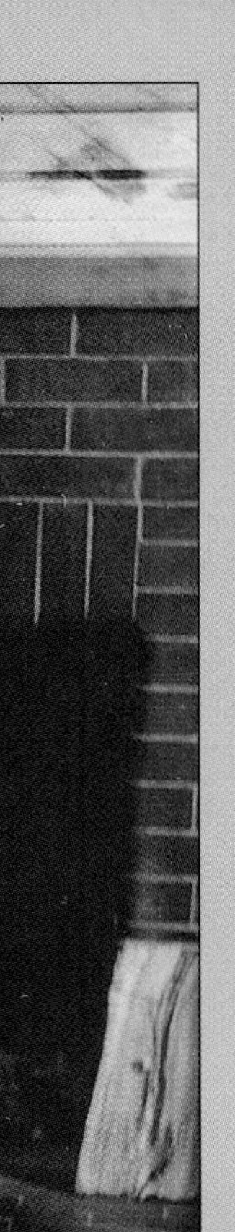

◀ Critical Viewing Does this photograph of Yeats present him as the man described in part 1 of Auden's poem or as the great writer eulogized in part 3? [Interpret] ❶

1

He disappeared in the dead of winter:
The brooks were frozen, the airports almost deserted,
And snow disfigured the public statues;
The mercury sank in the mouth of the dying day. ❷
O all the instruments agree
The day of his death was a dark cold day.

Far from his illness
The wolves ran on through the evergreen forests,
The peasant river was untempted by fashionable quays;[1]
By mourning tongues
The death of the poet was kept from his poems. ❸

But for him it was his last afternoon as himself,
An afternoon of nurses and rumors;
The provinces of his body revolted, ❹
The squares of his mind were empty, ❺
Silence invaded the suburbs,
The current of his feeling failed: he became his admirers. ❻

Now he is scattered among a hundred cities
And wholly given over to unfamiliar affections;
To find his happiness in another kind of wood
And be punished by another code of conscience.
The words of a dead man
Are modified in the guts of the living.

But in the importance and noise of tomorrow
When the brokers are roaring like beasts on the floor of the Bourse,[2]
And the poor have the sufferings to which they are fairly accustomed, ❼
And each in the cell of himself is almost convinced of his freedom;
A few thousand will think of this day ❽
As one thinks of a day when one did something slightly unusual.

O all the instruments agree
The day of his death was a dark cold day.

1. **quays** (kēz): Wharfs with facilities for loading or unloading ships.
2. **Bourse** (bo͝ors): Paris Stock Exchange.

◆ Critical Thinking

❸ **Interpret** Ask students who the "mourning tongues" represent, and what they do. *The mourning tongues are people who continue to read and recite Yeats's poetry. They keep the poems from dying as their author has—the poems live by being read.*

◆ Grammar and Style

❹ **Parallel Structure** Have students identify and explain the parallel structure in these lines. *The lines contain parallel prepositional phrases: "The provinces of his body"; "The squares of his mind."*

◆ Literary Focus

❺ **Theme** Encourage sophisticated readers to notice again the implied contrast or link between the public and private dimensions of the poet's being: His body (private) is like a country divided into provinces (places where many live).

◆ Critical Thinking

❻ **Interpret** In what sense has the poet "become his admirers"? *Though Yeats the man has died, Yeats the poet, a voice and a source of pleasure, lives on in his readers' enjoyment of his poems.*

◆ Critical Thinking

❼ **Infer** Ask students: What is the general reaction to Yeats' death? *The world is largely unmoved by Yeats' death.*

◆ Literature and Your Life

❽ Ask students to identify a public event that affected them enough that they remember what they were doing when they heard the news. *Examples may include the death of a popular musician or actor.*

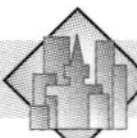

Beyond the Classroom

Career Connection

Meteorology In this poem, both Auden's observations and "the instruments" agree that the weather is very cold. In Auden's time, these instruments would have been much simpler than those used today to evaluate and predict weather.

Meteorologists now use computer modeling, satellite photographs, and sophisticated monitoring equipment. Have interested students learn more about these methods and share their findings with the class. Discuss how modern methods compare with human observations—such as Auden's—in measuring and predicting weather.

Community Connection

Local Climate Point out to students that the dead of winter is terribly cold in much of Europe, though it may not be in your community. Discuss how climate can frame a community's experiences. Have students monitor your community's climate for a set period of time, measuring, for example, temperature and precipitation. Then encourage students to describe the mood that climate would add to the day of an important person's death.

Customize for *Less Proficient Readers*

Point out to less proficient readers that in Part 2, the speaker is addressing Yeats directly, while in Part 1 he was speaking in the third person to a general audience. Explain that in Part 3 the speaker shifts again, addressing powers such as the Earth and the Poet (all poets or the poet in general).

Customize for *Musical/Rhythmic Learners*

Note with these students that the language in Part 3 is considerably more formal than either Parts 1 or 2. It is also comprised of rhyming couplets similar to those in a classical elegy. Have students read aloud Parts 2 and 3 before discussing the differences in rhyme and rhythm.

◆ Reading Strategy

❶ **Paraphrase** Invite students to restate lines 32–34 in their own words. *Sample paraphrase: You were human, and it was the pain of circumstances that brought you to write, but your poetry survives your flaws and those of your homeland.*

◆ Literary Focus

❷ **Theme** What did Yeats's poetry do to change Ireland? What place does poetry have in the world, according to these lines? *Yeats's poetry does nothing to change Ireland. Poetry "does" nothing; it is not the concern of those who get things done ("executives"); though born of isolation and grief, it "flows" beyond them and survives in its own right.*

◆ Critical Thinking

❸ **Evaluate** Ask students whether they agree or disagree with Auden's suggestion that an artist's talent outweighs his or her moral or political views. *Some students will say it makes sense to separate an artist's work from his or her personal views and behavior. Others will say the two are inextricably intertwined: An artist often uses art to express his or her views and beliefs. Sophisticated readers may note that here Auden may merely record a fact: Poets are remembered by their words, not for their views.*

2

You were silly like us: your gift survived it all;
❶ The parish of rich women, physical decay,
Yourself; mad Ireland hurt you into poetry.
Now Ireland has her madness and her weather still,
For poetry makes nothing happen: it survives
In the valley of its saying where executives
❷ Would never want to tamper; it flows south
From ranches of isolation and the busy griefs,
Raw towns that we believe and die in; it survives,
A way of happening, a mouth.

3

Earth, receive an honored guest;
William Yeats is laid to rest:
Let the Irish vessel lie
Emptied of its poetry.

Time that is intolerant
Of the brave and innocent,
And indifferent in a week
To a beautiful physique,

Worships language and forgives
❸ Everyone by whom it lives;
Pardons cowardice, conceit
Lays its honors at their feet.

Time with this strange excuse
Pardoned Kipling and his views,[3]
And will pardon Paul Claudel,[4]
Pardons him for writing well.

In the nightmare of the dark
All the dogs of Europe bark,
And the living nations wait,
Each sequestered in its hate;

3. **Kipling . . . views**: English writer Rudyard Kipling (1865–1936) was a supporter of imperialism.
4. **pardon Paul Claudel** (klō del′): French poet, dramatist, and diplomat. Paul Claudel (1868–1955) had antidemocratic political views, which Yeats at times shared.

◆ Build Vocabulary

sequestered (si kwes′ tərd) *v.*: Kept apart from others

Cross-Curricular Connection: Social Studies

The island of Ireland is occupied today by two political entities, the independent Republic of Ireland and Northern Ireland, a part of Great Britain. The island's Celtic heritage is rich in legend, mythology, and folklore. Part of the population also traces roots to England and its culture. The influence of Ireland's geography—the lushness of a rainy land and the cultural insulation of island life—is felt by all. Irish Gaelic is the national language and though not universally spoken, it is a required subject in the schools and has strongly influenced Irish literature with its character. All these factors contribute to a particularly fertile literary climate that has produced literary geniuses, including Jonathan Swift, James Joyce, and George Bernard Shaw.

Have students discuss how a cultural and physical setting can contribute to the development of literary talent.

Intellectual disgrace
Stares from every human face,
And the seas of pity lie
Locked and frozen in each eye.

Follow, poet, follow right
To the bottom of the night,
With your unconstraining voice
Still persuade us to rejoice;

With the farming of a verse
Make a vineyard of the curse,
Sing of human unsuccess
In a rapture of distress;

In the deserts of the heart
Let the healing fountain start,
In the prison of his days
Teach the free man how to praise.

Guide for Responding

◆ Literature and Your Life

Reader's Response The speaker hopes that poetry will teach people "how to praise." What do you think the main role of poetry is?

Thematic Focus In what ways does Auden contrast Yeats the man and Yeats the poet?

Notes for a Profile Jot down some of the specific facts about Yeats that a reader can learn from this poem.

☑ Check Your Comprehension

1. On what kind of day did Yeats die?
2. What kept the poet's death from killing his poems?
3. What was it that "hurt" Yeats into writing poetry?
4. According to the third section of the poem, to whom is time (a) intolerant? (b) indifferent?
5. Whom does time forgive?
6. What does the speaker ask the poet to teach people?

◆ Critical Thinking

INTERPRET

1. Twice in the first section, the speaker uses the words "all the instruments agree." What might he mean (a) in a literal sense? (b) in a metaphorical sense? **[Interpret]**
2. What do you think the poet means by stating in line 18 that Yeats is now "scattered among a hundred cities"? **[Interpret]**
3. Whom is the speaker addressing (a) in the second section? (b) in the third section? **[Analyze]**
4. (a) How does the speaker view the situation in Europe? (b) How does he think the poet should react to it? Give evidence for your answer. **[Draw Conclusions]**

EVALUATE

5. This work is an elegy, or poem of mourning, for William Butler Yeats. Yet, in a sense, it could be addressed to any poet, for Auden sets down the responsibilities and rewards he thinks belong to every poet. Does this generalization diminish the effectiveness of the poem? **[Evaluate]**

Cultural Connection

Different cultures value the voices of literature and creativity differently. Since 1668, England has had an official Poet Laureate. The role originally required the writing of commemorative verse, but since the term of William Wordsworth (beginning in 1843), it has served more to recognize poetic accomplishment. The United States also has Poet Laureates, including Rita Dove, who in 1993 became the first African American to hold the position. On an international level, the Nobel Prize in Literature honors the role of the literary artist. Begun in 1901, the Prize has been awarded to writers from countries such as Norway, India, Denmark, Chile, Iceland, Guatemala, and the United States.

Have students research to identify the current Poet Laureates of Great Britain and the United States, as well as the most recent Nobel Prize for Literature winner. Ask students what the works of these recipients suggest about the role of the poet in today's society.

◆ Literary Focus

4 Theme Ask students: What is the role of poetry in the times Auden describes? *Students may say that poets, by singing of even the darkest nights of humanity, teach us of the joy that is to be found in all that is.*

Reinforce and Extend

Customize for
Intrapersonal Learners
These students may appreciate Auden's recognition that art transcends one individual's experience and can affect people the artist has never met. Urge them to share in a group discussion the reasons they admire a contemporary artist.

Answers

◆ Literature and Your Life

Reader's Response Answers will probably include suggestions that poetry should have a social or moral purpose, or should entertain.

Thematic Focus Yeats the man is flawed; Yeats the poet is as large as those who love his verses.

☑ Check Your Comprehension

1. He died on a cold, winter day.
2. His mourners kept his poems alive, even after his death.
3. "Mad Ireland" hurt Yeats into writing poetry.
4. a) Time is intolerant of the brave and innocent and (b) indifferent to a beautiful physique.
5. Time forgives those who worship language.
6. The speaker asks the poet to teach people how to praise.

◆ Critical Thinking

1. (a) The literal instruments are thermometers and barometers.
   (b) Metaphorically the instruments are the minds and hearts of the poet's readers.
2. Yeats is in the minds of people in hundreds of cities.
3. Auden is addressing (a) Yeats in the second section and (b) the Earth and a generic poet in the third section.
4. (a) The speaker says that Europe is full of hatred. (b) He feels the poet should "persuade us to rejoice" and teach us how to praise.
5. The poem's effectiveness is enhanced by its universality.

Develop Understanding

One-Minute Insight This poem gives depth to the truism that "People suffer, yet the world moves on." Focusing on a painting by Pieter Brueghel, Auden points out how Brueghel's figures placidly ignore Icarus' tragic fall. The world of the painting is innocently indifferent to suffering, and Auden seems convinced that this indifference holds a profound truth. Perhaps it is a defiance—suffering cannot cancel the value of ordinary life. Perhaps we love the ordinary more for seeing it through the eyes of suffering. This indifference may even show us that there is something deeply private, even religious, about an individual's suffering that cannot be shared with others or directly depicted in art. Whatever the case, Brueghel's painting is not "wrong" about Icarus' suffering, precisely because it shows us what that suffering is *not.*

◆ Critical Thinking

❶ **Speculate** Ask students to suggest why the poet may have titled his poem with the name of an art museum. *Answers include: the paintings that he refers to in this poem hung there; the title may also refer to the view art as a whole offers of human life.*

▶Critical Viewing◀

❷ **Interpret** Students will note that the ploughman looks down, unaware of Icarus' plunge; the ship sails on, the shepherd doesn't glance Icarus' way and the sun shines on brightly.

Enrichment Daedalus, Icarus' father, designed the labyrinth in which King Minos of Crete imprisoned the Minotaur (a monster half-man, half-bull). Daedalus revealed the labyrinth's secret, enabling the hero Theseus to slay the Minotaur and escape with Minos' daughter Ariadne. When King Minos then imprisoned Daedalus and Icarus, Daedalus fashioned wings of wax and feathers, and he and Icarus flew off. Icarus flew too close to the sun; the wax on his wings melted, and he plummeted to his death.

❸ **Clarification** "The Old Masters" are distinguished painters of the 16th, 17th, and early 18th centuries.

❶

Musée des Beaux Arts[1]

W. H. AUDEN

❷ ▼ **Critical Viewing** In this poem, Auden comments on the indifference of humans to one another's misfortunes. How does this painting by Brueghel depict this indifference? **[Interpret]**

The Fall of Icarus, Pieter Brueghel, Musée Royaux des Beaux-Arts de Belgique, Bruxelles

Humanities: Fine Art

The Fall of Icarus by Pieter Brueghel.

This painting illustrates the last scene in the myth of Icarus, in which he falls into the sea. It is a visual depiction of the ideas Auden expresses in the poem.

Flemish painter Pieter Brueghel the Elder (he had a son Pieter Brueghel the Younger) served an artistic apprenticeship with Belgian artist Pieter Coecke van Aelst. As he developed his own style, Brueghel often roamed the countryside, making candid drawings of the landscape and its inhabitants for later use in his paintings. *The Fall of Icarus* could be one such painting, in which the everyday people are captured in exquisite detail.

Use these questions for discussion:

1. What specific elements from the painting does Auden describe? *He describes the ploughman, the sun shining, the white legs disappearing into the water, and the delicate ship sailing on.*
2. How do the attitudes of poet and painter toward human indifference compare? *Both draw a lesson about the nature of suffering.*

About suffering they were never wrong,
The Old Masters: how well they understood
Its human position; how it takes place
While someone else is eating or opening a window or just
  walking dully along;
How, when the aged are reverently, passionately waiting
For the miraculous birth, there always must be
Children who did not specially want it to happen, skating
On a pond at the edge of the wood:
They never forgot
That even the dreadful martyrdom must run its course
Anyhow in a corner, some untidy spot
Where the dogs go on with their doggy life and the
  torturer's horse
Scratches its innocent behind on a tree.

In Brueghel's *Icarus*,[2] for instance: how everything turns away
Quite leisurely from the disaster; the ploughman may
Have heard the splash, the forsaken cry,
But for him it was not an important failure; the sun shone
As it had to on the white legs disappearing into the green
Water; and the expensive delicate ship that must have seen
Something amazing, a boy falling out of the sky,
Had somewhere to get to and sailed calmly on.

1. **Musée des Beaux Arts:** Museum of Fine Arts in Brussels, Belgium, which contains Brueghel's *Icarus*.
2. **Brueghel's** (brü´ gəlz) ***Icarus*** (ik´ ə rəs): *The Fall of Icarus*, a painting by Flemish painter Pieter Brueghel (1525?–1599). In Greek mythology, Icarus flies too close to the sun. The wax of his artificial wings melts, and he falls into the sea.

Guide for Responding

◆ Literature and Your Life

Reader's Response Does the poem express a kind of optimism, or is it pessimistic? Explain.

Thematic Focus What is the reality of human experience to which the poem awakens us?

Alternate Art Draw or paint the fall of Icarus, with people showing concern over the disaster.

☑ Check Your Comprehension

1. Who are "The Old Masters"?
2. What do the Old Masters show "someone else" doing while suffering occurs?
3. (a) How does the ploughman react to the disaster? (b) How does the ship respond?

◆ Critical Thinking

INTERPRET

1. What do you think Auden intends the activities listed in line 4 to represent? **[Infer]**
2. What is the "miraculous birth" the aged are awaiting in line 6? **[Interpret]**
3. (a) What does Brueghel imply by calling his painting *The Fall of Icarus* but showing only Icarus's legs disappearing in the corner of the picture? (b) Does Auden's poem adhere to Brueghel's meaning? Explain. **[Analyze]**

APPLY

4. (a) In today's world what examples can you find of indifference to suffering? (b) What might Auden say about your examples? **[Relate]**

Cross-Curricular Connection: Art

Major museums usually house the works of artists from many different cultures. The Musée des Beaux Arts, or Museum of Fine Arts, in Brussels houses a collection representing artists from medieval times through the 20th century. Specialized museums may focus instead on displaying the works of a specific culture in greater depth. For example, the National Museum of the American Indian in New York City focuses on Native American arts while Egypt's Museum of Islamic Art turns its efforts toward Islamic art.

Have students contact museums, galleries, or public exhibition spaces such as libraries in your community or region to learn what cultures are represented there. View some works from one of these collections, in person or by photograph. Then ask students which works of art might inspire them to write poetry.

◆ Literary Focus

❹ **Theme** Ask students how Auden communicates his theme in these first few lines. *Auden attributes the theme to the works of the Old Masters—Dutch, Italian, and Belgian painters of the 13th through the 16th century. Auden states the theme almost directly: It is the nature of things and of suffering that the world goes on, even while individuals suffer.*

Reinforce and Extend

Customize for
Musical/Rhythmic Learners
The long sentences and varied line length in this poem can hinder an appreciation of the poem's rhyme. Help students hear the rhyme by playing the ***Listening to Literature Audiocassette*** while students read along.

Answers

◆ Literature and Your Life

Reader's Response The world's indifference to suffering may seem cruel to some readers, who will find the poem pessimistic. They should note, though, Auden's easy acceptance of it.

Thematic Focus The world is largely indifferent to suffering; one always suffers alone.

☑ Check Your Comprehension

1. The Old Masters are the painters whose work the speaker is viewing at the opening of the poem.
2. Those who are not suffering are doing commonplace things such as eating, walking, or opening a window.
3. (a) The ploughman ignores the sight and sound of Icarus' fall. (b) The ship sails on.

◆ Critical Thinking

1. The activities represent daily, ordinary, somewhat mindless tasks.
2. The miraculous birth is probably the birth of Christ, a favorite subject of the Old Masters.
3. (a) Brueghel implies that while Icarus' experience is an event of central importance, it is "outside" daily life. (b) Auden's poem adheres closely to Brueghel's message.
4. (a) Students can find examples of indifference to most types of human suffering such as hunger, disease, war. (b) He would say that such indifference is in the nature of things.

Develop Understanding

One-Minute Insight This poem takes readers on a journey back to the poet's birthplace in an effort to understand and define the influences on an artist's identity. The speaker—presumably MacNeice—describes Carrickfergus, with its castle and green hills, its familiar sights and sounds. As he tours the natural and human landscape, recalling the Carrick of his childhood, the poet acknowledges the irrefutable influence of Northern Ireland—a chance "Particular," neither the pure Irish of the west nor the pure English across the water—on his character.

◆ Background for Understanding

❶ Many Irish communities were dominated by a castle initially built by English settlers. MacNeice's mention of war may refer to the 1916 Easter Rising, a rebellion that ultimately led to the division of Ireland into independent Republic of Ireland and a British political entity, Northern Ireland. Despite these huge upheavals, MacNeice finds his birthplace largely unchanged.

◆ Literary Focus

❷ **Theme** Based on these lines, how can students define MacNeice's theme? *A poet's art derives at the same time from his or her history and from his or her wonder at having a history—at being here, not there.*

◆ Reading Strategy

❸ **Paraphrase** Invite students to restate this stanza in their own words. *Suggested paraphrase: The specifics of our personal history affect the way we view things; at the same time, we know that our view is only one of many possible views on the world.*

Carrick Revisited

Louis MacNeice

❶
Back to Carrick,[1] the castle as plumb assured
As thirty years ago—Which war was which?
Here are new villas, here is a sizzling grid
But the green banks are as rich and the lough[2] as hazily lazy
And the child's astonishment not yet cured.

❷
Who was—and am—dumbfounded to find myself
In a topographical frame—here, not there—
The channels of my dreams determined largely
By random chemistry of soil and air;
Memories I had shelved peer at me from the shelf.

Fog-horn, mill-horn, corncrake and church bell
Half-heard through boarded time as a child in bed
Glimpses a brangle of talk from the floor below
But cannot catch the words. Our past we know
But not its meaning—whether it meant well.

❸
Time and place—our bridgeheads into reality
But also its concealment! Out of the sea
We land on the Particular and lose
All other possible bird's-eye views, the Truth
That is of Itself for Itself—but not for me.

Torn before birth from where my fathers dwelt,
Schooled from the age of ten to a foreign voice,
Yet neither western Ireland nor southern England
Cancels this interlude; what chance misspelt
May never now be righted by my choice.

Whatever then my inherited or acquired
Affinities, such remains my childhood's frame
Like a belated rock in the red Antrim[3] clay
That cannot at this era change its pitch or name—
And the prenatal mountain is far away.

1. **Carrick:** Shortened form of Carrickfergus, a town in Northern Ireland.
2. **lough:** (läk): Lake, specifically Belfast Lough. Carrickfergus is situated on the northern shore of Belfast Lough.
3. **Antrim:** County in Northern Ireland in which Carrickfergus is located.

◆ Build Vocabulary

topographical (täp´ə graf´ i kəl) *adj.*: Relating to a map of the surface features of a region, including its elevations, rivers, mountains, and so on

affinities (ə fin´i tēz) *n.*: Family relationships; connections

prenatal (prē nāt´ əl) *adj.*: Before birth

Cross-Curricular Connection: Science

Memory is a complex process, involving the recall of both recent and distant data. New information enters the short-term memory, where it may remain until it is either transferred to long term memory or replaced by more current data. Research finds that items stored in long-term memory—such as Louis MacNeice's childhood memories—are more easily triggered by recognition than simple recall. In other words, visiting a place where you once lived will evoke many specific memories of experiences in that place, whereas simply being asked about that place and time may not.

Have students brainstorm to trigger each other's memories of earlier times spent together. Newcomers to the community may complete the activity with a family member.

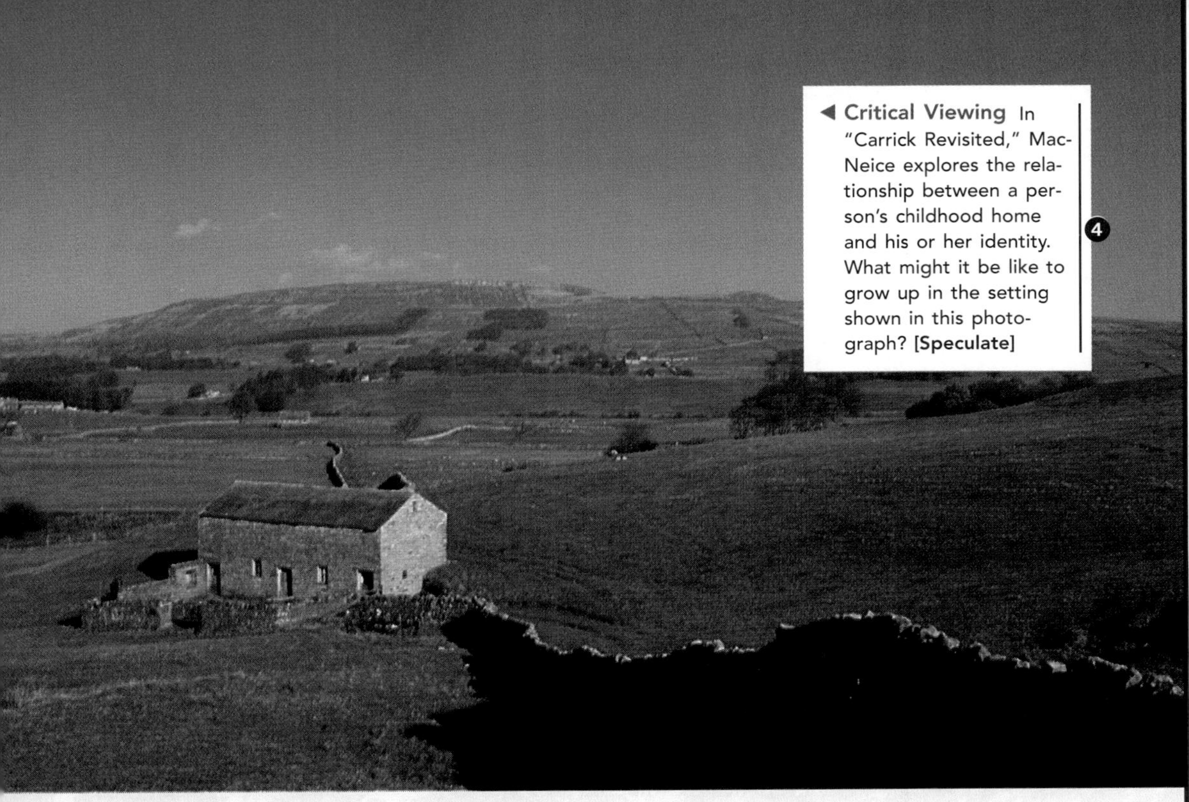

◀ Critical Viewing In "Carrick Revisited," MacNeice explores the relationship between a person's childhood home and his or her identity. What might it be like to grow up in the setting shown in this photograph? **[Speculate]** 4

Guide for Responding

◆ Literature and Your Life

Reader's Response The poet uses the words "astonishment" and "dumbfounded" to describe his reaction when returning to his birthplace. Do you find these feelings understandable? Explain.

Thematic Focus How does the speaker's visit to Carrick help him better understand the reality of his identity?

☑ Check Your Comprehension

1. (a) Where does the speaker find himself at the beginning of the poem? (b) According to the first stanza, how has the place changed, and how does it remain the same?

2. According to the speaker, what three things contribute to his identity?

◆ Critical Thinking

INTERPRET

1. What does the speaker mean by the line "Memories I had shelved peer at me from the shelf"? **[Interpret]**

2. What distinction does the speaker draw when he says, "Our past we know/But not its meaning—whether it meant well"? **[Infer]**

3. The speaker draws attention to the random, chance influences on his development. How does he view people's ability to control their own destinies? **[Draw Conclusions]**

APPLY

4. MacNeice's poem discusses issues of national identity—Irish-born, he was educated in England. Name two ways in which issues of identity are even more complex in our day. **[Relate]**

Speaking and Listening Mini-Lesson

Museum Guide

This mini-lesson supports the Speaking and Listening activity in the Idea Bank on page 935.

Introduce the Concept Have students exchange ideas about works of art they have viewed. Encourage students to share their emotional responses to the discussed works. You might point out that "The Musée des Beaux Arts" comes from W.H. Auden's responses to a work of art.

Develop Background Before students plan their presentation, have them review and consider the following suggestions:

- Use research to provide data about the artist's style.
- Draw clear links between the significance of the work and the emotional responses it engenders.

Apply the Information Assist students in noting significant points on note cards. Encourage students to practice their talks before presenting to the class.

Assess the Outcome Evaluate students' work based on evidence of preparation, support for original points, and clarity of presentation.

▶Critical Viewing◀

4 **Speculate** Students may note the isolation, physical beauty, distance from urban noise and crowds, and the rural surroundings. Students may see each of these factors as an advantage or disadvantage.

Reinforce and Extend

Customize for *Musical/Rhythmic Learners*

Urge these learners to read the poem aloud, paying particular attention to the sensory sound images. Ask students to describe how sounds trigger memory for them.

Answers

◆ Literature and Your Life

Reader's Response Suggested response: Yes, it makes sense that MacNeice is astonished by the strength of his memories. Many people are surprised by the intensity of reaction when returning to a place they knew in childhood.

Thematic Focus Suggested response: He realizes how much his Irish childhood has influenced his character, but that identity is ultimately a matter of chance.

☑ Check Your Comprehension

1. (a) He finds himself back at Carrickfergus, where he spent some childhood years. (b) The castle, green hills, and lake are the same while new houses and roads show change.
2. The speaker refers to the influence of his childhood home, of his education in England, and of "where my fathers dwelt" (western Ireland).

◆ Critical Thinking

1. Memories he thought forgotten now resurface.
2. We may recall events without full understanding of their context; whether the past "meant well" can only be decided by what we make of it.
3. MacNeice believes people cannot choose their own past, and that the past helps define who people are.
4. Many people are of mixed ethnic lineage, have relocated to new countries, or cannot trace their biological parents.

Develop Understanding

One-Minute Insight This poem contrasts the aesthetic values of art with its potential for social change. The poet discusses and rejects the idea that art should merely be a "palace"—a beautiful home for the imagination, remote from society. He calls emphatically instead for commitment to social action, asking artists to inspire change.

◆ Literary Focus

❶ **Theme** What clues does Spender offer about his theme in these lines? *Spender refers to what he will not build—a palace. Associated with the idea of a palace are certain ideas of history and society ("an era's crown," "people ordered like a single mind") and of the uses of art (to provide the imagination with a place to dwell, intrigue, and rest).*

◆ Reading Strategy

❷ **Paraphrase** Ask students to paraphrase these lines. *Suggested paraphrase: Use the energy of poetry to cause the change required by the times.*

❸ **Clarification** Spender here addresses each of the senses in turn.

◆ Literary Focus

❹ **Theme** Ask students how Spender expresses his theme here. *Spender uses direct, general imperatives, almost slogans, to indicate the goal of art.*

Customize for *Visual/Spatial Learners*
Ask these learners how the photograph on pages 932–933 evokes the feelings of aspiration in Spender's poem. *In lines 19–22, Spender alludes to skyscrapers as evidence of human will and capacity.*

Not Palaces

STEPHEN SPENDER

Not palaces, an era's crown
Where the mind dwells, intrigues, rests:
❶ Architectural gold-leaved flower
From people ordered like a single mind,
I build: this only what I tell:
It is too late for rare accumulation,
For family pride, for beauty's filtered dusts;
I say, stamping the words with emphasis,
Drink from here energy and only energy
❷ To will this time's change.
Eye, gazelle, delicate wanderer,
Drinker of horizon's fluid line;
❸ Ear that suspends on a chord
The spirit drinking timelessness;
Touch, love, all senses;
Leave your gardens, your singing feasts,
Your dreams of suns circling before our sun,
Of heaven after our world.
Instead, watch images of flashing glass
That strike the outward sense, the polished will,
Flag of our purpose which the wind engraves.
No spirit seek here rest. But this: No one
❹ Shall hunger: Man shall spend equally;
Our goal which we compel: Man shall be man.

◆ Build Vocabulary

intrigues (in trēgz´) *v.*: Plots or schemes secretly or underhandedly

Beyond the Classroom

Career Connection

Social Work Stephen Spender calls for social action through his poetry. One way such changes are enacted today is through the efforts of government and private social service agencies.

Social services agencies may offer information, training, and resources in regard to health care, employment, safety and nutrition, educational needs, and much more. Workers are often social workers or counselors trained to assist people sensitively in gaining the services they need. Have interested students learn about the social service agencies available in your community. How are these working to combat some of the problems Stephen Spender mentions?

Community Connection

Fund-Raising Events Point out to students that the money needed to solve social problems is often raised through donation. Fund-raising events enable people to support social causes of their choice in return for entertainment, products, or services. Have students brainstorm some recent fund-raising events in your community, especially any that are specifically affiliated with the place. For example, students may mention fund-raising annual sports events, seasonal festivals, or winter clothing drives. Then encourage students to discuss and list ways they could become involved in these or other social action efforts.

Guide for Responding

◆ Literature and Your Life

Reader's Response Do you agree with Spender's ideas about art? Explain.

Thematic Focus In what way does Spender urge his readers to wake from a dream—to abandon illusions or outdated ideas about art?

Artwork Sketch a drawing of which Stephen Spender might approve.

☑ Check Your Comprehension

1. In lines 1–7, what ideas about art is the speaker rejecting?
2. What does the speaker urge the poem's audience to do in lines 9–10?
3. What is the "gazelle" in line 11?
4. (a) What does the speaker tell "all senses" to leave in lines 16? (b) What should they attend to instead (lines 19–21)?

◆ Critical Thinking

INTERPRET

1. In what cultures or periods in history have people lived "ordered like a single mind"? **[Interpret]**
2. In line 9, what is meant by the word *energy*? **[Interpret]**
3. To what real-life events might the speaker be referring in lines 19–21? **[Infer]**
4. (a) What does Spender think the job of poetry once was? (b) What does he think the job of poetry should be now? **[Analyze]**

APPLY

5. Auden writes that, while "poetry makes nothing happen," it teaches us a kind of joy in what is. Spender writes as if poetry could incite social change. Can art serve either function in our time? Explain. **[Relate]**

Reinforce and Extend

Customize for
Less Proficient Readers

Less proficient readers may need help navigating Spender's poetic structure. Direct them to break down the sentences in the poem and read them, at first, according to punctuation only.

Answers

◆ Literature and Your Life

Reader's Response Some students may feel that socially responsible art is important, but that art for art's sake also has its place.

Thematic Focus He urges them to pay attention to ideals for the future, not the beauties of the past.

☑ Check Your Comprehension

1. He is rejecting the importance of building great and elaborate monuments or collecting rare objects from the past.
2. Readers should draw inspiration and motivation toward social action from modern art.
3. The gazelle is the eye, which wanders among sights and surveys the horizon.
4. (a) He urges them to leave gardens, feasts, and dreams. (b) He directs them toward images of flashing glass.

◆ Critical Thinking

1. Some students may suggest that the people of ancient Greek and Roman cultures had common beliefs and goals. Other students may point to dictatorships or totalitarian rule as producing people who live as one mind.
2. It means inspiration and motivation.
3. He may be referring to skyscrapers, which are visible examples of human ingenuity and will.
4. (a) He thinks it was once to provide a culture with its monuments or the imagination with a feast. (b) He asks it now to motivate people toward social change.
5. Art can serve both purposes in our time, rendering and rejoicing in what is or communicating poets' views about society.

Beyond the Selection

FURTHER READING

Other Works by the Poets

On This Island Auden, *Letters from Iceland,* MacNeice; *World Within World,* Spender

Other Works About Social Change

"Anecdote of the Jar," Wallace Stevens
"Two X," E.E. Cummings
"The Artist," Sir Walter Raleigh

We suggest that you preview these works before recommending them to students.

INTERNET

You and your students may find additional information about the poets at the following Web site. Please be aware, however, that the site may have changed since this information was published.

Auden: **http://redfrog.norconnect.no/~poems/mb/137.html**

We *strongly recommend* that you preview the site before you send students to it.

◆ Literary Focus

Theme

1. The ploughman's indifference to the disaster offers an example of the world's indifference to individual suffering.
2. (a) Art, in particular poetry, should serve the social purpose of improving the world. (b) It was stated both directly, in lines 9–10 and 23–25, and indirectly through reference to the past uses of art.
3. (a) The setting of the poet's birthplace points to an interest in his history. (b) The speaker's wonder and surprise suggest the enduring power of the past.

◆ Reading Strategy

Paraphrase

1. Suggested response: You were human but your poetry survives your flaws and that of your homeland. Poetry survives in itself, not by changing the world. (a) Paraphrasing aids comprehension of literal meaning. (b) Auden's craft enables him to state this message through vivid, suggestive, general images.
2. (a) Regardless of family traditions or the choices I have since made, my childhood experiences remain the same and exert a strong influence on who I am. (b) MacNeice's is more memorable for the rhythm, the flow of the words, and his strong images; students' own may be easier to remember because they are simply put.

◆ Build Vocabulary

Using the Word Root *-top-*

1. the common "place" shared by different opinions and ideas
2. Someone who maps the surface features of a place
3. A place without flaws

Using the Word Bank

1. b 2. a 3. c 4. c 5. c

◆ Grammar and Style

Parallel Structure

Practice

1. pardons
2. opening
3. admiring

Guide for Responding *(continued)*

◆ Literary Focus

Theme

The central idea, concern, or purpose of a literary work is its **theme,** which may be expressed directly or indirectly. Clues to the theme of a work include elements such as its title, setting, word choice, tone, and atmosphere or mood.

1. How does the ploughman's response to the disaster in "Musée des Beaux Arts" help convey the poem's theme?
2. (a) What might be the theme of "Not Palaces"? (b) Was the theme stated directly or indirectly, or both? Explain.
3. The theme of "Carrick Revisited," may be stated as "What creates an artist's identity?" (a) How does the setting of the poem help you identify the theme? (b) How does the speaker's attitude provide a clue to its theme?

◆ Reading Strategy

Paraphrase

By **paraphrasing,** restating a poet's words in your own words, you can ensure that you've understood the basic meaning of a poem. Once you've done that, you can interpret the poet's original work and appreciate how its language, imagery, and tone give it a deeper, more moving dimension.

For example, in "Musée des Beaux Arts" you can better understand the opening line by paraphrasing it as follows: "The Dutch painters of the sixteenth and seventeenth century were never wrong about suffering." When you reread the original line, however, you understand how Auden's word choice and phrasing make it sound like the speaker is musing aloud, and by putting the word *suffering* second, Auden emphasizes its importance.

1. Paraphrase lines 32–41 of "In Memory of W. B. Yeats." (a) How did paraphrasing help you to understand the basic meaning of the passage? (b) Looking back at the original lines, what appreciation do you have now for the poet's craft?
2. (a) How would you paraphrase the final stanza of "Carrick Revisited"? (b) Do you find your paraphrase or MacNeice's poetry more memorable? Explain.

◆ Build Vocabulary

Using the Word Root *-top-*

Knowing that the root *-top-* means "place," explain how it affects the meanings of these words.

1. topic **2.** topographer **3.** utopia

Using the Word Bank

Write the letter of the word or phrase whose meaning is closest to that of the first word.

1. sequestered: (a) convicted, (b) kept apart, (c) silent
2. intrigues: (a) schemes, (b) fails, (c) deceives
3. topographical: (a) representing a person's life, (b) atypical, (c) representing a place
4. affinities: (a) immensities, (b) ends, (c) attractions
5. prenatal: (a) natural, (b) naive, (c) before birth

◆ Grammar and Style

Parallel Structure

Poets at times may use **parallel structure**—repeated use of the same grammatical form or pattern—to make their writing memorable and effective. For example, lines 6–7 in "Not Palaces" contain parallel prepositional phrases.

It is too late *for rare accumulation,* /
For family pride, for beauty's filtered dusts.

Practice Rewrite each item in italics to make the sentence structure parallel.

1. Time worships language and is *pardoning* cowardice.
2. Suffering takes place while someone is likely to be eating or *opens* a window.
3. This is no time for collecting objects or *to admire* beautiful artifacts in museums.

Writing Application In your notebook, rewrite each sentence below, using parallel structure.

1. Auden and Brueghel both criticize people's self-centeredness and their being indifferent to the suffering of others.
2. The speaker in "Not Palaces" suggests that he is not interested in building palaces or the collection of rare objects.
3. Louis MacNeice tried his hand at various genres, including drama and translating in verse.

Writing Application

1. Auden and Brueghel criticize people's self-centeredness and their indifference to the suffering of others.
2. The speaker in "Not Palaces" suggests that he is not interested in building palaces or collecting rare objects.
3. Louis MacNeice tried his hand at various genres, including drama and verse translation.

Writer's Solution

For additional instruction and practice, use the Using Parallel Structure lesson in the *Sourcebook,* p. 127, and the page on Parallelism, p. 46, in the *Writer's Solution Grammar Practice Book.*

Build Your Portfolio

Idea Bank

Writing

1. Tribute In "In Memory of W. B. Yeats," Auden pays tribute to the late, great poet. Write a tribute of your own in praise of someone whose work you particularly admire.

2. Essay In "Musée des Beaux Arts," Auden finds relevance in art of old; in "Not Palaces," Spender finds it irrelevant. With whom do you agree? Write a persuasive essay defending your ideas.

3. Response to Criticism David Perkins said of Auden's poetry, "By lessening the distance between 'poetry' and ordinary speech, it widens the range of possible subject matters." Using examples from Auden's poetry, write an essay in which you explain this quotation.

Speaking and Listening

4. Museum Guide Auden finds a basic human truth in a painting by Brueghel. Choose a painting with which you're familiar, and give a short talk to the class in which you explain the artist's craft and the significance of the work. **[Art Link]**

5. Oral Interpretation Perform an oral interpretation of "Carrick Revisited" in which you highlight the poem's musical qualities. **[Performing Arts Link]**

Projects

6. Art Exhibition With a group, discuss the type of art of which Spender would approve and find examples that fit the description. Display copies of the art you've found. **[Art Link]**

7. Family Background Like MacNeice, explore your family background. Create a map or chart that shows regions from which your ancestors came and where you yourself have lived.

Writing Mini-Lesson

Poem About Art

Auden's poem "Musée des Beaux Arts" was inspired by Brueghel's painting *The Fall of Icarus.* Choose any painting or photograph that is reproduced in this book, and use the image as your inspiration for a poem. You may directly refer, as Auden does, to the specific work of art that serves as your inspiration, or you may choose to leave it unidentified.

Writing Skills Focus: Conveying a Main Impression

In "Not Palaces," Stephen Spender invokes "Eye . . . Ear . . . Touch, love, all senses." Heed his call as you write, and use sensory details to create a **main impression** of the art that inspired you. Rather than simply listing details in the painting, use details to capture the essence of the work.

No Main Impression: The painting is blue and yellow, with a large stripe in the middle . . .

Main Impression: A noisy, bold stripe down the center challenges the viewer to pick a side . . .

Prewriting Before you begin writing, study the art you have chosen. Freewrite for a few minutes about the feelings it prompts in you. Finally, jot down details that will help you to create a main impression for the reader.

Drafting As you draft your poem, you may decide to follow Auden's three-part structure, or you may choose another method of organization. Present your main idea in the most effective, vivid fashion.

Revising Exchange poems with a partner, and take turns reading them aloud. Showing each other the images you selected as inspiration may prompt helpful suggestions for revision. Display your poem along with the art that inspired it.

✓ ASSESSMENT OPTIONS

Formal Assessment, Selection Test, pp. 236–238, and Assessment Resources Software. The selection test is designed so that it can be easily customized to the performance levels of your students. ***Alternative Assessment,*** p. 48, includes options for less advanced students, more advanced students, logical/mathematical learners, musical/rhythmic learners, bodily/kinesthetic learners, and visual/spatial learners.

PORTFOLIO ASSESSMENT

Use the following rubrics in the ***Alternative Assessment*** booklet to assess student writing:
Tribute: Description Rubric, p. 98
Essay: Persuasion Rubric, p. 106
Response to Criticism: Literary Analysis Rubric, p. 113
Writing Mini-Lesson: Poetry Rubric, p. 109

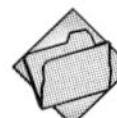

Idea Bank

Customizing for Performance Levels

Following are suggestions for matching Idea Bank topics with your students' performance levels:

- Less Advanced Students: 1, 5
- Average Students: 2, 6, 7
- More Advanced Students: 3, 4, 6, 7

Customizing for Learning Modalities

Following are suggestions for matching Idea Bank topics with your students' learning modalities:

- Visual/Spatial: 4, 6
- Logical/Mathematical: 7
- Verbal/Linguistic: 1, 2, 3, 5

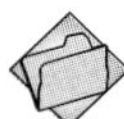

Writing Mini-Lesson

Refer students to the Writing Process Handbook, page 1189, for instruction on the writing process, and page 1192 for further information on poetry.

Writer's Solution

Writers at Work Videodisc

Have students view the videodisc segment on Creative Writing (Ch. 6) to consider Derek Walcott's ideas on how a poem "grows." Have students discuss his views.

Play frames 11452 to 13004

Writing Lab CD-ROM

Have students complete the tutorial on Creative Writing. They may follow these steps:

1. Choose descriptive words from Sensory Details and Rhyming Words Word Bins.
2. Explore the interactive examples of onomatopoeia, meter, figurative language, and rhyme scheme.
3. Review one another's work using the Peer Evaluation Checklist before completing a final draft.

Sourcebook

Have students use Chapter 6, Creative Writing (pp. 166–195), for additional support. The chapter includes instruction on gathering and using sensory details (p. 183).

Prepare and Engage

OBJECTIVES

1. To read, comprehend, and interpret an essay
2. To relate an essay to personal experience
3. To recognize the writer's attitudes to facilitate comprehension
4. To recognize irony
5. To build vocabulary in context and learn words about politics
6. To recognize and use restrictive and nonrestrictive participial clauses
7. To write a police report, using elaboration to give information
8. To respond to an essay through writing, speaking and listening, and projects

SKILLS INSTRUCTION

Vocabulary: Related Words: Words About Politics

Grammar: Participial Phrases: Restrictive and Nonrestrictive

Reading Strategy: Recognize the Writer's Attitudes

Literary Focus: Irony

Writing: Elaboration to Give Information

Speaking and Listening: Debate (teacher edition)

Critical Viewing: Make a Judgment; Analyze

PORTFOLIO OPPORTUNITIES

Writing: Profile; Film Treatment; Response to Criticism

Writing Mini-Lesson: Police Report

Speaking and Listening: Role Play; Debate

Projects: Orwell in Film; Biography

More About the Author
George Orwell's parents had little real wealth; their status in Indian society was based on race alone. So, too, George had little status while attending an extremely posh and prominent English boarding school. These formative experiences gave him the first insights into the life of the underdog—a perspective that informs much of Orwell's work.

Guide for Interpreting

George Orwell *(1903–1950)*

Many television news reports today are on-the-scene broadcasts, showing people in the middle of an event. They give us not just facts but close-up personal experience, and bestselling "nonfiction novels" do the same. George Orwell pioneered this personal kind of reporting, using nonfiction and novels to expose truths covered up by prejudice or dishonest politics.

Starting as Eric Blair Orwell was born Eric Blair in colonial India, was educated in England, then joined the Imperial Police in Burma. After five years, he became disillusioned with his job and resigned. His first novel, *Burmese Days* (1934), describes his bitter years (1922–1927) as an imperial police officer. "Shooting an Elephant," one of his most famous essays, is based on a memorable experience from this period.

Becoming George Orwell Orwell seemed to have a talent for immersing himself in difficult situations and then writing about them with extraordinary insight. Each book that emerged from an Orwell experience was a one-of-a-kind classic. In *Down and Out in Paris and London* (1933), for example, Orwell describes what it's like to be poor in two big cities. In a strange way, his experience of life's shabbiness gave him a stronger sense of identity. He now published, and lived, under a new name: George Orwell.

During the 1930's, Orwell gave himself to political causes. In *The Road to Wigan Pier* (1937), he wrote about English coal miners with whom he had lived.

Then, during the Spanish Civil War (1936–1939), he fought with anarchists and democratic, socialist Republicans and directly experienced the infighting among them that enabled the Fascists to win. In his book on the Spanish Civil War, *Homage to Catalonia* (1938), Orwell blamed the interference of the Soviet Union for undermining the Republican cause—a charge that made him unpopular with his fellow leftists. The book is a gripping adventure story, one in which the narrator has so much presence of mind that he can describe in precise detail his own experience of being wounded.

A Political Prophet During World War II, Orwell wrote political and literary journalism, and in 1945 he published *Animal Farm,* a satirical fable attacking both Fascism and Communism. In 1949 appeared his famous futuristic novel *1984,* in which a dictator controls all thought and language.

The year 1984 has passed, but George Orwell's lifelong commitment to political freedom and to the honest use of language is as relevant as ever.

◆ Background for Understanding

HISTORY: GEORGE ORWELL, AN ENGLISH POLICEMAN IN BURMA

George Orwell's Burmese experiences, on which this essay is based, were typical for a special group of young Englishmen. Recruited as police officers for the British empire, they had no experience of police work and no knowledge of the country they would police. Some of them were barely out of their teens.

Their training in Burma consisted of memorizing laws and procedures and learning the native languages. They lived apart from the Burmese, who deeply resented being ruled by the British.

These police officers were a small contingent in a native-born police force of 13,000. Among the ninety officers, Englishmen held almost all the top ranks—a few white men governing 13 million Asians.

Police officers were at risk in this tense political situation. With many large public protests, rebellion was a constant threat.

Prentice Hall Literature Program Resources

REINFORCE / RETEACH / EXTEND

Selection Support Pages
Build Vocabulary: Words About Politics, p. 235
Grammar and Style: Participial Phrases: Restrictive and Nonrestrictive, p. 236
Reading Strategy: Recognize the Writer's Attitudes, p. 237
Literary Focus: Irony, p. 238

Strategies for Diverse Student Needs, p. 49

Beyond Literature
Social Studies Connection: From Imperialism to Self-Rule in Burma, p. 49

Formal Assessment Selection Test, pp. 239–241; Assessment Resources Software

Alternative Assessment, p. 49

Writing and Language Transparencies

Resource Pro CD-ROM
"Shooting an Elephant"—includes all resource material and customizable lesson plan

Listening to Literature Audiocassettes
"Shooting an Elephant"

Shooting an Elephant

◆ Literature and Your Life

Connect Your Experience

One of the toughest things in the world is to put yourself on the line so that people can judge you. Even something as simple as giving an oral report at school can put you on the spot. Maybe you'll say something the wrong way or just say something silly.

In this essay, George Orwell describes a time when he had to perform in front of a crowd. Being a police officer for the British empire only made his situation more tense.

Journal Writing Describe how you would feel in Orwell's shoes—as a young police officer in a resentful country.

Thematic Focus: Waking From the Dream

As you read, notice how Orwell's experiences awaken him from the colonial dream of a stable empire.

◆ Build Vocabulary

Related Words: Words About Politics

Orwell uses words relating to political power, such as *imperialism,* in his essay. *Imperialism* refers to "the system by which a powerful country dominates less powerful ones."

Word Bank

Preview the list of words from the selection before you read.

prostrate
imperialism
despotic
squalid
dominion
senility

◆ Literary Focus

Irony

Orwell uses **irony**, a device that brings out surprising or amusing contradictions, to describe the difficult situation he faced. In **verbal irony**, the intended meaning of words clashes with their usual meaning (as when you sarcastically call a bully "kind"). In **irony of situation**, events contradict what you expect to happen.

Orwell uses both kinds of irony in "Shooting an Elephant"—but especially irony of situation—to capture his peculiar dilemma. Watch carefully as what he wants and expects to do clash ironically with what he *has* to do.

◆ Grammar and Style

Participial Phrases: Restrictive and Nonrestrictive

Orwell uses **participial phrases**—a group of words with a participle—to modify nouns and pronouns. Such phrases are **restrictive** when they are essential to the sentence's meaning. They are **nonrestrictive** when they provide additional, but not necessary, information. Nonrestrictive phrases are separated from the noun or pronoun by commas; restrictive phrases are not:

Restrictive: The wretched prisoners *huddling in the stinking cages of the lockups* . . . .

Nonrestrictive: Some more women followed, *clicking their tongues and exclaiming* . . . .

◆ Reading Strategy

Recognize the Writer's Attitudes

To understand what people say in a conversation, you must go beyond their words and recognize their attitudes. In the same way, to understand what you read, you must go beyond the words on the page and **recognize the writer's attitudes**.

Orwell's attitudes are not simple and clear-cut. For example, he feels that the Burmese are right, but at the same time, he hates them for tormenting him. Be aware of Orwell's clashing attitudes toward his situation as you read.

Have students imagine themselves in a tense situation in which they must make a quick decision. They want to act one way, but they're expected to act in another. Now have them imagine that their decision involves a potentially dangerous situation. What would go through their minds? What kinds of feelings would they have? Tell students that this is the situation in which the narrator of this essay finds himself.

Alternatively, discuss recent political events in which public figures have responded to charges of wrongdoing. What have these people said publicly about their own behavior? How might their private revelations differ?

Customize for *Less Proficient Readers*

Less proficient readers may miss some of Orwell's irony. Before they read, review and clarify the Literary Focus information on irony. Urge students to use questions such as "How does this action compare with Orwell's intentions or desires?" to identify irony.

Customize for *More Advanced Readers*

Encourage more advanced readers to enhance their comprehension of the essay by researching the historical context. Direct them to list questions about that context as they read, do the research to answer their own questions, and then reread for greater understanding.

Customize for *English Language Learners*

Some of Orwell's references may give English language learners difficulty. Direct them to look for familiar words nearby in the text that can help them figure out the meaning of difficult words and phrases.

Customize for *Bodily/Kinesthetic Learners*

Have these students look at the photograph on page 938. Ask them to mime the actions by which a human being might attempt to control an animal of the elephant's size.

Preparing for Standardized Tests

Reading and Vocabulary Both written stimuli and vocabulary items will often contain words related by content. Students' ability to recognize and distinguish these words by definition will enhance their performance on standardized tests. The Build Vocabulary lesson for this selection focuses on learning the meanings of words related to politics. Students can apply this skill on social studies or English portions of standardized tests. For additional practice, use the Build Vocabulary page in ***Selection Support***, p. 235.

Grammar and Language Some standardized test items require students to revise a sentence for meaning. Students may have to distinguish between items that are restrictive—necessary to meaning—and those that are nonrestrictive—not necessary—and punctuate accordingly. The Grammar and Style lesson for this selection focuses on this topic. For additional practice, use the Grammar and Style page on Participial Phrases: Restrictive and Nonrestrictive, p. 236, in ***Selection Support.***

Develop Understanding

One-Minute Insight This essay reveals the ambivalence a person may feel in a position of power. On the one hand, young George Orwell (then Eric Blair) sympathizes with the Burmese people, whom he feels are oppressed by the British colonists. On the other hand, Orwell, as a police officer, is committed to continuing and even defending that oppression. When an elephant goes wild in a Burmese marketplace, Orwell must act, making decisions more from his confused feelings than from common sense, and in the process demonstrating the intense human desire to avoid embarrassment.

◆ Literary Focus

❶ Point out to students that the speaker—George Orwell—must be important to be worth hating. Ask students to describe experiences in which they risk being the center of attention for a negative reason. *Students may mention competitive situations in which individual failure can affect a team, class, or school.*

◆ Build Vocabulary

❷ **Words About Politics** Point out the phrase *subdivisional police officer* to students. Have students use context to define the phrase and then explain how it relates to political power. *The phrase means a police officer in a subdivision, or smaller and less important section, of the police grid. It indicates that young Orwell was the local representative of a much larger system; however small his actual authority, his role had symbolic meaning.*

SHOOTING AN

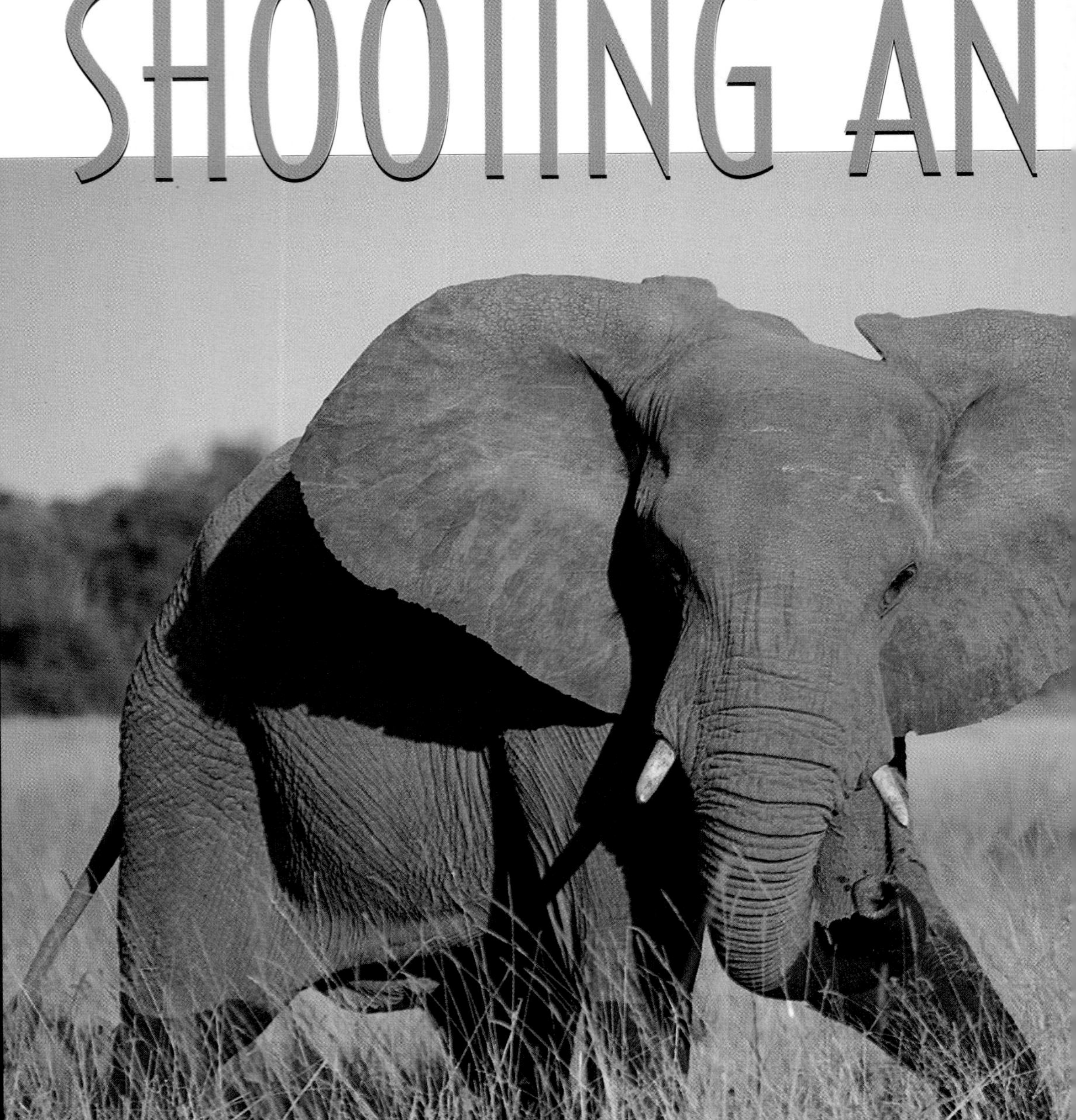

Block Scheduling Strategies

Consider these suggestions to take advantage of extended class time:

- Provide additional background by sharing with students the information provided in Cross-Curricular Connection on Social Studies (p. 940). Use the question provided to prompt a related discussion.
- Introduce the Literary Focus concept of irony on page 937. After students have read the essay, have them answer the Literary Focus questions on page 946.
- As a class, answer the Critical Thinking questions on page 945.
- Have students complete the Build Vocabulary and Build Grammar Skills exercises on page 946, working independently or in pairs.
- Have students undertake the Writing activity of their choice from the Idea Bank on page 947.
- Have the class stage the Speaking and Listening Debate. Use the Mini-Lesson on page 943 to develop the activity.
- To prepare students for the Orwell in Film project, show one of the pertinent films to the class.

ELEPHANT

George Orwell

In Moulmein, in lower Burma, I was hated by large numbers of people—the only time in my life that I have been important enough for this to happen to me. ❶ I was subdivisional police officer of the town, and in an aimless, petty kind of way anti-European feeling was very bitter. ❷ No one had the guts to raise a riot, but if a European woman went through the bazaars alone somebody would probably spit betel juice over her dress. As a police officer I was an obvious target and was baited whenever it seemed safe to do so. When a nimble Burman tripped me up on the football field and the referee (another Burman) looked the other way, the crowd yelled with hideous laughter. This happened more than once. In the end the sneering yellow faces of young men that met me everywhere, the insults hooted after me when I was at a safe distance, got badly on my nerves. ❸ The young Buddhist priests were the worst of all. There were several thousands of them in the town and none of them seemed to have anything to do except stand on street corners and jeer at Europeans.

All this was perplexing and upsetting. For at that time I had already made up my mind that imperialism was an evil thing and the sooner I chucked up my job and got out of it the better. Theoretically—and secretly, of course—I was all for the Burmese and all against their oppressors, the British. As for the job I was doing, I hated it more bitterly than I can

◆ **Reading Strategy** Identify some of Orwell's conflicting **attitudes** in these early paragraphs. ❹

◀ **Critical Viewing** Does this photograph depict a useful beast or a dangerous menace? Explain. **[Make a Judgment]** ❺

◆ Critical Thinking

❸ **Infer** Ask students: Why did the Burmese treat Orwell with contempt? *Students should recognize that the Burmese hated the British police; they realized that the police were afraid and could be taunted up to a point.*

◆ Reading Strategy

❹ **Recognize the Writer's Attitudes** Students should identify Orwell's sympathy for the Burmese, his dislike of imperialism, and his desire to leave his job. All of these attitudes conflict with his role as policeman, and with his bad treatment by the Burmese.

▶Critical Viewing◀

❺ **Make a Judgment** Students should recognize that the elephant has the potential to be either useful or dangerous, depending on the situation.

Beyond the Classroom

Career Connection

Police Officer The speaker in this essay is a police officer attempting to defuse a tense situation.

Police officers face duties ranging from monitoring political unrest to directing traffic around road construction. Depending on the area for which an officer is responsible, he or she may walk, ride a bicycle or horse, or drive a car. Have interested students inquire at a local police station about the types of police work done by that precinct and the related training officers receive in undertaking those duties. After reviewing those findings as a class, discuss the physical and emotional challenges police officers face in these various types of duty.

Workplace Skills

Coping with the Threat of Danger In this essay, George Orwell faces danger from both humans and animals. He comments that he feels no fear because he has been trained that fear is unacceptable in his situation. Have students brainstorm about the dangers present at jobs held by family members, friends, or adults in the community. Encourage them to propose physical or interpersonal training that might help workers cope with those dangers. For example, police officers might benefit from sensitivity training designed to help them view suspects as individuals rather than criminals.

Customize for
Less Proficient Readers
To help less proficient readers appreciate Orwell's conflicting attitudes, urge them to keep a list of phrases he uses to describe the British. Discuss the conflict one would have in representing a government and yet disagreeing with its politics.

◆ Critical Thinking

❶ **Connect** Ask students: What part does Orwell's age play in his ambivalent feelings towards the Burmese? *Students should note that as a young man, Orwell would not have fixed, ready ways of responding to the world, so his confusion would be greater than at an older age. He might be likely to sympathize with the less powerful, as he himself had little power. At the same time, as a young man, he might be more fearful of losing the limited status he had acquired.*

◆ Literary Focus

❷ **Irony** Point out to students the irony in Orwell's desire to kill a Buddhist monk. After all, he hates the British empire and sees the Burmese as oppressed.

❸ **Clarification** A *quarter* in this context refers to a neighborhood.

perhaps make clear. In a job like that you see the dirty work of Empire at close quarters. The wretched prisoners huddling in the stinking cages of the lockups, the gray, cowed faces of the long-term convicts, the scarred buttocks of the men who had been flogged with bamboos—all these oppressed me with an intolerable sense of guilt. But I could get nothing into perspective. I was young and ill educated and I had had to think out my problems in the utter silence that is imposed on every Englishman in the East. I did not even know that the British Empire is dying, still less did I know that it is a great deal better than the younger empires that are going to supplant it. All I knew was that I was stuck between my hatred of the empire I served and my rage against the evil-spirited little beasts who tried to make my job impossible. With one part of my mind I thought of the British Raj[1] as an unbreakable tyranny, as something clamped down, *in saecula saeculorum*,[2] upon the will of prostrate peoples; with another part I thought that the greatest joy in the world would be to drive a bayonet into a Buddhist priest's guts. Feelings like these are the normal byproducts of imperialism; ask any Anglo-Indian official, if you can catch him off duty.

One day something happened which in a roundabout way was enlightening. It was a tiny incident in itself, but it gave me a better glimpse than I had had before of the real nature of imperialism—the real motives for which despotic governments act. Early one morning the subinspector at a police station the other end of the town rang me up on the phone and said that an elephant was ravaging the bazaar. Would I please come and do something about it? I did not know what I could do, but I wanted to see what was happening and I got onto a pony and started out. I took my rifle, an old .44 Winchester and much too small to kill an elephant, but I thought the noise might be useful *in terrorem*.[3] Various Burmans stopped me on the way and told me about the elephant's doings. It was not, of course, a wild elephant, but a tame one which had gone "must."[4] It had been chained up, as tame elephants always are when their attack of "must" is due, but on the previous night it had broken its chain and escaped. Its mahout,[5] the only person who could manage it when it was in that state, had set out in pursuit, but had taken the wrong direction and was now twelve hours' journey away, and in the morning the elephant had suddenly reappeared in the town. The Burmese population had no weapons and were quite helpless against it. It had already destroyed somebody's bamboo hut, killed a cow and raided some fruit stalls and devoured the stock; also it had met the municipal rubbish van and, when the driver jumped out and took to his heels, had turned the van over and inflicted violences upon it.

The Burmese subinspector and some Indian constables were waiting for me in the quarter where the elephant had been seen. It was a very poor quarter, a labyrinth of squalid bamboo huts, thatched with palm leaf, winding all over a steep hillside. I remember that it was a cloudy, stuffy morning at the beginning of the rains. We began questioning the people as to where the ele-

1. **Raj** (räj): Rule.
2. ***in saecula saeculorum*** (in sē′ ko͞o lə sē′ ko͞o lôr′ əm): Forever and ever.
3. ***in terrorem:*** For terror.
4. **must:** Into a dangerous, frenzied state.
5. **mahout** (mə ho͞ot′): Elephant keeper and rider.

◆ Build Vocabulary

prostrate (präs′ trāt) *adj.*: Defenseless; in a prone or lying position

imperialism (im pir′ ē əl iz′əm) *n.*: Policy and practice of forming and maintaining an empire in seeking to control raw materials and world markets by the conquest of other countries, the establishment of colonies, and so on

despotic (de spät′ ik) *adj.*: Tyrannical

squalid (skwäl′ id) *adj.*: Miserably poor; wretched

Cross-Curricular Connection: Social Studies

British colonial rule began in Burma in 1886, after the British prevailed in the Third Anglo-Burmese War. To the surprise and dismay of the Burmese, the British made Burma a province of its own colony, India. The Burmese people, primarily Buddhists, had a long-standing prejudice against the Indians, in part because of that nation's Hindu caste system. The Burmese people never accepted British rule and continued to resist it politically, and occasionally through force, until the 1920's (the time of Orwell's essay). In 1923, the Burmese were given some additional constitutional protections, and in 1937 the colony was separated from India and became self-governing. It was not until 1947, however, that Burma was granted full independence.

Have students discuss how Burma's history would contribute to an atmosphere of daily tension.

4 ▲ **Critical Viewing** At the story's beginning, Orwell describes how, as a police officer, he was a target for ridicule and baited by the Burmese. Judging from the details in this photograph, what made Orwell (third from left in back row) and his fellow officers conspicuous? **[Analyze]**

phant had gone and, as usual, failed to get any definite information. That is invariably the case in the East; a story always sounds clear enough at a distance, but the nearer you get to the scene of events the vaguer it
5 becomes. Some of the people said that the elephant had gone in one direction, some said that he had gone in another, some professed not even to have heard of any elephant. I had almost made up my mind that the whole story was a pack of lies, when we heard yells a little distance away. There was a loud scandalized cry of "Go away, child!
6 Go away this instant!" and an old woman with a switch in her hand came round the corner of a hut, violently shooing away a 6
crowd of naked children. Some more women followed, clicking their tongues and exclaiming; evidently there was something that the children ought not to have seen. I rounded the hut and saw a man's dead body sprawling in the mud. He was an Indian, a black Dravidian[6] coolie,[7] almost naked, and he could not have been dead many minutes. The people said that the elephant had come suddenly upon him round the corner of the hut, caught him with its trunk, put its foot

6. **Dravidian** (drə vid′ ē ən): Belonging to the race of people inhabiting southern India.
7. **coolie:** Laborer.

▶**Critical Viewing**◀

4 **Analyze** Students may say that the officers' uniforms made them most obviously conspicuous. Also, they are mostly European white men, while the local citizens are Asian.

◆ Reading Strategy

5 **Recognize the Writer's Attitudes** What attitude does Orwell display towards the Burmese in these comments? *Students should note that this comment, while accepting the difference between the cultures, largely assumes the Burmese are at fault for inferior communication.*

◆ Grammar and Style

6 **Restrictive and Nonrestrictive Participial Phrases** Have students identify the participial phrase in this sentence and explain whether it is restrictive or nonrestrictive. *The participial phrase is "violently shooing away a crowd of naked children." It is nonrestrictive, since it provides additional, but not essential, information.*

Customize for
Visual/Spatial Learners

Direct these students to pay particular attention to the movements described in the essay. For example, a crowd of children and women burst on the scene just before the discovery of the corpse. Ask students how the kinetic activity in the essay affects the mood. *Students may say that there is a frenetic sense about the movement in the essay, which contributes to its building tension.*

Cultural Connection

Storytelling, whether of real or imaginary events, differs from culture to culture, though perhaps not in the way young George Orwell perceived. Many cultures, such as those of Native American peoples, passed their heritage along orally through stories. Their values were transmitted from one generation to the next through songs, chants, and narratives. In other cultures, storytellers known as *shanachies* (Irish), *skalds* (Norse), *griots* (African), and *troubadours* (French) were entertainers who gained social status through their efforts.

Have students discuss how the influences of culture might affect a person's recounting of specific events.

◆ Literary Focus

❶ **Irony** Point out to students the verbal irony in this description. Using the word *grinning*, usually associated with happiness, to describe the coolie's expression in death, produces an ironic effect by contrasting the reader's associations with the word with the ugly reality of death.

◆ Reading Strategy

❷ **Recognize the Writer's Attitudes** Ask students: Why does the crowd make Orwell "vaguely uneasy"? How else does it make him feel? Discuss how Orwell's reactions to the crowd mirror his conflicted feelings about his position in Burma. *Students may say that the crowd makes Orwell uneasy because he recognizes its restless unpredictability. It also makes him feel a fool because of its growing expectation that he will shoot the elephant, an action he isn't planning to pursue. Students should link these attitudes to Orwell's overall conflict, noting that he feels unpleasantly at the mercy of the Burmese crowd despite his sympathy for their situation.*

◆ Literature and Your Life

❸ Most students will say that they would counsel Orwell to spare the elephant because it isn't right to take a life merely to save oneself from embarrassment. Others may say that sparing the elephant might lead to a riot and greater loss of life; these students would counsel Orwell to kill the elephant.

Comprehension Check ☑

❹ Why do some countries selectively kill elephants? *Selective killing limits the number of elephants so that the natural food supply is sufficient and elephants needn't damage crops for food.*

Customize for *Visual/Spatial Learners*

Encourage these learners to enhance their appreciation of the essay by graphically plotting out key scenes. They might lay out the route of the elephant, Orwell, and the crowd through the marketplace or otherwise depict the interaction between cultures described in the essay.

on his back and ground him into the earth. This was the rainy season and the ground was soft, and his face had scored a trench a foot deep and a couple of yards long. He was lying on his belly with arms crucified and head sharply twisted to one side. His face was coated with mud, the eyes wide open, ❶ the teeth bared and grinning with an expression of unendurable agony. (Never tell me, by the way, that the dead look peaceful. Most of the corpses I have seen looked devilish.) The friction of the great beast's foot had stripped the skin from his back as neatly as one skins a rabbit. As soon as I saw the dead man I sent an orderly to a friend's house nearby to borrow an elephant rifle. I had already sent back the pony, not wanting it to go mad with fright and throw me if it smelled the elephant.

The orderly came back in a few minutes with a rifle and five cartridges, and meanwhile some Burmans had arrived and told us that the elephant was in the paddy fields[8] below, only a few hundred yards away. As I started forward practically the whole population of the quarter flocked out of the houses and followed me. They had seen the rifle and were all shouting excitedly that I was going to shoot the elephant. They had not shown much interest in the elephant when he was merely ravaging their homes, but it was different now that he was going to be shot. It was a bit of fun to them, as it would be to an English crowd; besides they wanted the meat. It made me vaguely uneasy. ❷ I had no intention of shooting the elephant—I had merely sent for the rifle to defend myself if necessary—and it is always unnerving to have a crowd following you. I marched down the hill, looking and feeling a fool, with the rifle over my shoulder and an ever-growing army of people jostling at my heels. At the bottom, when you got away from the huts, there was a metaled road[9] and beyond that a miry waste of paddy fields a thousand yards across, not yet plowed but soggy

◆ Literature and Your Life ❸

If you were Orwell's friend, what would you counsel him to do, kill the elephant or spare its life? Why?

8. **paddy fields:** Rice fields.

9. **metaled road:** Road in which the pavement is reinforced with metal strips.

Beyond Literature

Science Connection

Protecting Elephants Though elephants like the one in Orwell's memoir can be dangerous to people, people have turned out to be much more dangerous to elephants. By clearing land in forestry and for farming, and by hunting elephants for their valuable ivory tusks, human ❹ beings have brought the elephant into danger of extinction. Since the late 1970's and early 1980's, the elephant population in Africa has declined severely, dropping from 1.3 million to 600,000 in little more than a decade. Many countries have set aside parklands and preserves to protect elephants and other endangered species.

In 1989, the Convention on International Trade in Endangered Species of Wild Fauna and Flora (CITES) banned any trade in ivory. Illegal hunting continues, though. Some countries attempt to discourage poaching by turning profits from the use of wildlife—from tourism to sport hunting—to the benefit of local communities. They also practice culling—selectively killing individuals—to keep elephants from destroying people's crops in their quest for food. The hope is that local communities will come to view elephants as a more profitable resource when used according to a plan, rather than taken as booty.

Cross-Curricular Connection: Science

Elephants There are two types of elephant, the African and the Asian (Indian). African elephants are somewhat larger, weighing as much as six tons and standing more than ten feet tall. Asian elephants are more scarce than their African counterparts, with perhaps only 50,000 remaining in the wild. In southern and southeastern Asia, captured elephants are often used to do heavy logging work. They are also incorporated into rituals and ceremonies, both secular and spiritual. In India, the elephant-headed god Ganesh is one of the most popular and best loved of the Hindu gods.

Have student teams choose one the following elephant issues to research: the difference between Asian and African elephants, the belief that elephants have good memories, or the history of elephant hunting and the ivory trade.

from the first rains and dotted with coarse grass. The elephant was standing eight yards from the road, his left side toward us. He took not the slightest notice of the crowd's approach. He was tearing up bunches of grass, beating them against his knees to clean them, and stuffing them into his mouth.

I had halted on the road. As soon as I saw the elephant I knew with perfect certainty that I ought not to shoot him. It is a serious matter to shoot a working elephant—it is comparable to destroying a huge and costly piece of machinery—and obviously one ought not to do it if it can possibly be avoided. And at that distance, peacefully eating, the elephant looked no more dangerous than a cow. I thought then and I think now that his attack of "must" was already passing off; in which case he would merely wander harmlessly about until the mahout came back and caught him. Moreover, I did not in the least want to shoot him. I decided that I would watch him for a little while to make sure that he did not turn savage again, and then go home.

But at that moment I glanced round at the crowd that had followed me. It was an immense crowd, two thousand at the least and growing every minute. It blocked the road for a long distance on either side. I looked at the sea of yellow faces above the garish clothes—faces all happy and excited over this bit of fun, all certain that the elephant was going to be shot. They were watching me as they would watch a conjurer about to perform a trick. They did not like me, but with the magical rifle in my hands I was momentarily worth watching. And suddenly I realized that I should have to shoot the elephant after all. The people expected it of me and I had got to do it; I
5 could feel their two thousand wills pressing me forward, irresistibly. And it was at this moment, as I stood there with the rifle in my hands, that I first grasped the hollowness, the futility of the white man's dominion in the East. Here was I, the white man with his gun, standing in front of the unarmed native crowd—seemingly the leading actor of the piece; but in reality I was only an absurd puppet pushed to and fro by the will of those yellow faces behind. I perceived in this
moment that when the white man turns 5
tyrant it is his own freedom that he destroys. He becomes a sort of hollow, posing dummy, the conventionalized figure of a sahib.[10] For it is the condition of his rule that he shall spend his life in trying to impress the "natives," and so in every crisis he has got to do what the "natives" expect of him. He wears a mask, and his face grows to fit it. I had got to shoot the elephant. I had committed myself to doing it when I sent for the rifle. A sahib has got to act like a sahib; he has got to appear resolute, to know his own mind and do definite things. To come all that way, rifle in hand, with two thousand people marching at my heels, and then to trail feebly away, having done nothing—no, that was impossible. The crowd would laugh at me. And my whole life, every white man's life in the East, was one long struggle not to be laughed at.

◆ Literary Focus What ironic observation is shared here? 6

But I did not want to shoot the elephant. I watched him beating his bunch of grass against his knees with that preoccupied grandmotherly air that elephants have. It seemed to me that it would be murder to shoot him. At that age I was not squeamish about killing animals, but I had never shot an elephant and never wanted to. (Somehow it always seems worse to kill a *large* animal.) Besides, there was the beast's owner to be considered. Alive, the elephant was worth at least a hundred pounds, dead, he would only be worth the value of his tusks, five pounds, possibly. But I had got to act quickly. I turned to some experienced-looking Burmans who had been there when we

◆ Build Vocabulary

dominion (də min′ yən) *n.*: Rule or power to rule; a governed territory

10. **sahib** (sä′ ib): Indian word for European gentleman.

Reinforce and Extend

Customize for *Interpersonal and Bodily/Kinesthetic Learners* Invite these learners to role-play a situation in which a crowd is encouraging an individual toward a specific action. Afterwards, have them discuss the interpersonal dynamics of the situation.

◆ Reading Strategy

5 Recognize the Writer's Attitudes Challenge students to identify some of Orwell's attitudes about British imperialism in these lines. *Students should note that Orwell finally grasps the flaw in imperialism, though he has disliked its effects for some time. It is at this point that the tension in his attitudes—between his dislike for the taunting Burmese, and his simultaneous belief that they are oppressed—is finally crystallized. British tyranny subjects British officers to the tyranny of the native crowd, whom they must impress.*

◆ Literary Focus

6 Irony Orwell has discovered that to rule the natives is actually to be ruled by them, since his conduct is guided at every moment by the need to impress them.

Speaking and Listening Mini-Lesson

Debate

This mini-lesson supports the Speaking and Listening activity in the Idea Bank on page 947.

Introduce the Concept Have students share their initial emotional reactions to the debate proposition. Then refer them to the entry on debate on page 1201 in the Speaking and Listening Handbook to review debate structure.

Develop Background As students prepare to debate, have them follow these strategies:

- Research the impact of imperialism on at least two "Third World" peoples to support their position on the debate proposition.
- Organize debate arguments around the most important issues.
- Use the most compelling evidence—facts, reasons, examples—to support points.

Apply the Information Have debate teams work together to develop opening and closing arguments and rebuttals to likely opposing arguments. Remind students to be respectful debaters, listening and speaking politely. Hold the debate. You may moderate it, letting each team know when to present its arguments and rebuttals.

Assess the Outcome Assess the debate on the basis of the participants' preparedness, the strength of their support and examples, and their oral presentations. Then discuss as a class how young George Orwell would feel about the debate topic.

◆ *Literature and Your Life*

❶ Point out to students Orwell's lack of fear and the role of his training in maintaining that attitude. Ask students how training and previous experience influence their emotions and behavior in tense situations. *Students may say that they feel supported and reassured by training and prior experience, as in an athletic or dramatic performance.*

◆ Literary Focus

❷ **Irony** Ask students to identify and explain both the verbal irony and the irony of situation in these lines. *The verbal irony lies in the description of the crowd as happy theatergoers, when Orwell actually sees them as much more harmful. The irony of situation lies in their eagerness for entertainment, when the occasion involves death and danger.*

◆ Critical Thinking

❸ **Connect** Ask students: How does the elephant's death symbolize the fate of British imperialism in Burma? *Students may note that killing the elephant represents the British project of "civilizing" the East. While the project promises adventure and seems morally justified at the beginning, it collapses in a senile heap at the end.*

◆ Literary Focus

❹ **Irony** Ask students: What is the irony in this statement? What confusion does it reveal in Orwell's position? *The irony lies in the fact that Orwell comes to be glad of a man's death because it helps justify his actions legally, and helps conceal the real reason for his actions—to avoid looking silly. Orwell's conflicting attitudes are demonstrated by the fact that he really does value human life more highly, but at the same time his feelings follow the twisted logic of British colonial rule in Burma.*

arrived, and asked them how the elephant had been behaving. They all said the same thing: he took no notice of you if you left him alone, but he might charge if you went too close to him.

It was perfectly clear to me what I ought to do. I ought to walk up to within, say, twenty-five yards of the elephant and test his behavior. If he charged, I could shoot; if he took no notice of me, it would be safe to leave him until the mahout came back. But also I knew that I was going to do no such thing. I was a poor shot with a rifle and the ground was soft mud into which one would sink at every step. If the elephant charged and I missed him, I should have about as much chance as a toad under a steam-roller. But even then I was not thinking particularly of my own skin, only of the watchful yellow faces behind. For at that moment, with the crowd watching me, I was not afraid in the ordinary sense, as I would have been if I had been alone. A white man mustn't be frightened in front of "natives"; and so, in general, he isn't frightened. The sole thought in my mind was that if anything went wrong those two thousand Burmans would see me pursued, caught, trampled on, and reduced to a grinning corpse like that Indian up the hill. And if that happened it was quite probable that some of them would laugh. That would never do. There was only one alternative. I shoved the cartridges into the magazine and lay down on the road to get a better aim.

The crowd grew very still, and a deep, low, happy sigh, as of people who see the theater curtain go up at last, breathed from innumerable throats. They were going to have their bit of fun, after all. The rifle was a beautiful German thing with cross-hair sights. I did not then know that in shooting an elephant one would shoot to cut an imaginary bar running from ear hole to ear hole. I ought, therefore, as the elephant was sideways on, to have aimed straight at his ear-hole; actually I aimed several inches in front of this, thinking the brain would be further forward.

When I pulled the trigger I did not hear the bang or feel the kick—one never does when a shot goes home—but I heard the devilish roar of glee that went up from the crowd. In that instant, in too short a time, one would have thought, even for the bullet to get there, a mysterious, terrible change had come over the elephant. He neither stirred nor fell, but every line of his body had altered. He looked suddenly stricken, shrunken, immensely old, as though the frightful impact of the bullet had paralyzed him without knocking him down. At last, after what seemed a long time—it might have been five seconds, I dare say—he sagged flabbily to his knees. His mouth slobbered. An enormous senility seemed to have settled upon him. One could have imagined him thousands of years old. I fired again into the same spot. At the second shot he did not collapse but climbed with desperate slowness to his feet and stood weakly upright, with legs sagging and head drooping. I fired a third time. That was the shot that did for him. You could see the agony of it jolt his whole body and knock the last remnant of strength from his legs. But in falling he seemed for a moment to rise, for as his hind legs collapsed beneath him he seemed to tower upward like a huge rock toppling, his trunk reaching skyward like a tree. He trumpeted, for the first and only time. And then down he came, his belly toward me, with a crash that seemed to shake the ground even where I lay.

I got up. The Burmans were already racing past me across the mud. It was obvious that the elephant would never rise again, but he was not dead. He was breathing very rhythmically with long rattling gasps, his great mound of a side painfully rising and falling. His mouth was wide open—I could see far down into caverns of pale pink throat. I waited a long time for him to die, but his breathing did not weaken. Finally I fired my two remaining shots into the spot where I

◆ Build Vocabulary

senility (si nil′ ə tē) *n.*: Mental and physical decay due to old age

Cultural Connection

Hunting Today, hunting animals for sport or commerce is legally limited in much of the world. Throughout history, however, many cultures have relied on hunting for survival. For example, the earliest humans of the Stone Age were nomadic hunters, traveling continually in search of prey. Today, some Inuit people still hunt for food, traveling thousands of miles each year to hunting grounds.

Hunting for sport has a long history as well. The Romans staged battles between gladiators and animals, and in the Middle Ages, wealthy men and women hunted for sport. In Africa and Asia, big game hunting became popular among colonial Europeans, who hunted both for commercial gain and for sport.

Have students discuss how, if Orwell had shared modern attitudes about animals and the environment, the outcome of the essay would have changed.

thought his heart must be. The thick blood welled out of him like red velvet, but still he did not die. His body did not even jerk when the shots hit him, the tortured breathing continued without a pause. He was dying, very slowly and in great agony, but in some world remote from me where not even a bullet could damage him further. I felt that I had got to put an end to that dreadful noise. It seemed dreadful to see the great beast lying there, powerless to move and yet powerless to die, and not even to be able to finish him. I sent back for my small rifle and poured shot after shot into his heart and down his throat. They seemed to make no impression. The tortured gasps continued as steadily as the ticking of a clock.

In the end I could not stand it any longer and went away. I heard later that it took him half an hour to die. Burmans were bringing dahs[11] and baskets even before I left, and I was told they had stripped his body almost to the bones by the afternoon.

Afterward, of course, there were endless discussions about the shooting of the elephant. The owner was furious, but he was only an Indian and could do nothing. Besides, legally I had done the right thing, for a mad elephant has to be killed, like a mad dog, if its owner fails to control it. Among the Europeans opinion was divided. The older men said I was right, the younger men said it was a shame to shoot an elephant for killing a coolie, because an elephant was worth more than any Coringhee[12] coolie. And afterward I was very glad that the coolie had been killed; it put me legally in the right and it gave me a sufficient pretext for shooting the elephant. I often wondered whether any of the others grasped that I had done it solely to avoid looking a fool. 4

11. **dahs** (däz): Knives.

12. **Coringhee** (cor in′ gē): Southern Indian.

Guide for Responding

◆ *Literature and Your Life*

Reader's Response If you were in the narrator's position, would you give up your job? Why or why not?

Thematic Focus Did Britain eventually awaken from the imperialist dream that Orwell describes? Explain.

☑ Check Your Comprehension

1. (a) Why was Orwell hated in Burma? (b) What were the mixed ways in which he reacted to this hatred?
2. What grisly evidence of the elephant's rampage does Orwell encounter?
3. Why do the Burmese get excited when they see Orwell has a rifle?
4. What reasons does Orwell give for not wanting to shoot the elephant?
5. According to Orwell, why did he shoot the elephant?

◆ Critical Thinking

INTERPRET

1. Being "hated by large numbers of people" provokes a conflict in Orwell. (a) What is that conflict? (b) What does it show about his character? **[Analyze]**
2. How does the crowd's excitement make Orwell see his position is absurd? **[Analyze Causes and Effects]**
3. How does the end show that "when the white man turns tyrant it is his own freedom that he destroys"? **[Draw Conclusions]**

EVALUATE

4. Does Orwell judge himself too harshly? Explain. **[Make a Judgment]**

APPLY

5. If Orwell hadn't shot the elephant, would that change the meaning of the essay? **[Modify]**

Reinforce and Extend

Answers

◆ *Literature and Your Life*

Reader's Response Suggested responses: Quitting the job would provide an escape from its difficult choices. Staying on would enable one to influence and change the situation.

Thematic Focus Britain ultimately gave independence to most of its Asian and African colonies, some willingly and others through force.

☑ Check Your Comprehension

1. (a) He was European and a representative of British-Indian rule. (b) He sympathized with the Burmese cause but felt bullied by their taunts.
2. Orwell encounters a dead Indian coolie, squashed by the elephant.
3. They hope to watch him shoot the elephant.
4. The elephant is a costly working machine; it seems like murder, especially to shoot such a large animal; it's probably unnecessary for safety; the owner will lose a valuable animal.
5. He shoots the elephant to avoid looking foolish.

◆ Critical Thinking

1. (a) He sympathizes with their oppressed condition, but hates them for their treatment of him. (b) He is complex enough to have ambivalent feelings.
2. He sees that while he appears to have all the power, he really has very little power.
3. Orwell feels he has no choice but to shoot the elephant, thus his own freedom has been limited by the role he must play as "ruler."
4. Orwell's judgment may seem too harsh; in the situation, it would have taken tremendous courage to act differently.
5. Yes, not shooting the elephant would have emphasized Orwell's freedom to do as he saw fit. It would have suggested that British policy could be changed by individual actions.

Beyond the Essay

FURTHER READING

Other Works by George Orwell

Animal Farm; 1984; Down and Out in Paris and London

Other Works About Difficult Choices/ Social Conflict

The Endless Steppe, Esther Hautzig
Gandhi, Olivia Coolidge
To Kill a Mockingbird, Harper Lee

We suggest that you preview these works before recommending them to students.

INTERNET

You and your students may find additional information about George Orwell on the following Internet site. (Note: Site may have changed since this information was published.)

For the politcal writings of George Orwell, visit **http://www.resort.com/~prime8/Orwell**

We *strongly* recommend that you preview the site before recommending it to students.

Answers

◆ Reading Strategy

1. Orwell sympathizes with the situation of the Burmese and recognizes their cultural uniqueness. However, he resents their hostility, questions their intelligence, and is afraid of their power over him.
2. He disliked the humiliations to which the role exposed him and the requirements it placed upon him to use force. However, he embraced the role, meeting expectations that he be fearless and in control.
3. He quite reasonably wants to spare the elephant unless killing it is necessary for safety. Conversely, he doesn't want to be ridiculed for this position.
4. Imperialism creates a complex relationship between ruler and ruled in which each side "rules" the other but resents that interdependence.

◆ Literary Focus

1. Orwell dislikes the British empire, yet he works for it and thus contributes to its oppression of the Burmese.
2. Orwell may support the Burmese cause, but he disparages them and bitterly resents their resistance when it is directed at him.
3. Despite Orwell's perceived lack of choice in killing the elephant, *he* has the gun and the authority to do what he chooses.
4. "Red velvet" suggests luxury and privilege, yet Orwell's description otherwise emphasizes the ugly, sordid quality of the elephant's death.
5. The younger men disapprove of Orwell's deed, not out of sympathy with the elephant's owner or an understanding of Orwell's cowardice, but because they think the elephant is worth more than the person it killed.

◆ Grammar and Style

1. thatched with palm leaf; nonrestrictive; modifies "huts"
2. sprawling in the mud; restrictive; modifies "body"
3. looking and feeling a fool; nonrestrictive; modifies "I"
4. peacefully eating; nonrestrictive; modifies "elephant"
5. pushed to and fro by the will of those yellow faces; restrictive; modifies "puppet"

Guide for Responding *(continued)*

◆ Reading Strategy

Recognize the Writer's Attitudes

The contradictory **attitudes** reflected in Orwell's essay are a clue to its meaning. When the crowd views the slaughter of a huge animal as "a bit of fun," Orwell seems to tolerate this. As he feels their pressure to shoot the elephant, however, his attitude becomes one of uneasiness and resistance.

1. Describe Orwell's attitude toward the Burmese people.
2. What was Orwell's attitude toward being a police officer?
3. Describe Orwell's conflicting attitudes in the paragraph beginning "It was perfectly clear . . ."
4. What do Orwell's conflicting attitudes reveal about imperialism?

◆ Literary Focus

Irony

In this essay, Orwell reveals his conflicts through the surprising contradictions of **irony**: the clash between a word's meaning and its use (**verbal irony**) or between what is expected and what actually exists or occurs (**irony of situation**). Irony enables Orwell to describe a complex and contradictory experience. Without using this literary device, he would not have been able to write about these events with such insight and bitter humor.

Describing a supposedly dangerous elephant as "grandmotherly" is an amusing example of verbal irony. As for irony of situation, Orwell says that it isn't necessary to kill the elephant for safety. Then, ironically, he kills it to avoid embarrassment.

Indicate what is ironic about each of the following descriptions, facts, or occurrences:

1. Orwell's attitude toward the British empire
2. His attitude toward the Burmese he supported
3. His lack of choice about whether or not to kill the elephant
4. The comparison of the dying elephant's blood to "red velvet"
5. The attitude of "the younger men" toward the shooting of the elephant

◆ Grammar and Style

Participial Phrases: Restrictive and Nonrestrictive

Orwell uses **participial phrases**—groups of words with a participle—to modify nouns and pronouns. **Restrictive** participial phrases are essential to the meaning of the words they modify and aren't separated by commas. **Nonrestrictive** participial phrases are not essential and can be separated by commas.

Practice On your paper, underline the participial phrase in each sentence, say whether it is restrictive or nonrestrictive, and explain its effect.

1. It was a very poor quarter, a labyrinth of squalid bamboo huts, thatched with palm leaf . . .
2. I . . . saw a man's dead body sprawling in the mud.
3. I marched down the hill, looking and feeling a fool.
4. And at that distance, peacefully eating, the elephant looked no more dangerous than a cow.
5. . . . in reality I was only an absurd puppet pushed to and fro by the will of those yellow faces . . .

◆ Build Vocabulary

Using Words About Politics

Use your knowledge of the political words in this essay to answer these questions:

1. How was the relationship between Britain and Burma typical of *imperialism?*
2. Which nation had *dominion* over the other?
3. Name two specific examples of *despotic* power that Orwell mentions in the second paragraph.

Using the Word Bank

Replace each italicized word or phrase with a word from the Word Bank.

As a seasoned veteran of summer camps, I can tell you a few things about the *wretched* conditions under which *tyrannical* counselors force you to live. In their *governed territory*, they have philosophies of *total control* that leave some campers totally *defenseless* in their fear. Before *mental decay* sets in, I plan to write of my incredible summer experiences.

Writer's Solution

For additional instruction and practice, use the lesson on Writing Style: Using Phrases in the **Language Lab CD-ROM,** and the page on Participles and Participial Phrases, page 29 in the *Writer's Solution Grammar Practice Book.*

◆ Build Vocabulary

Using Words About Politics

1. Britain used its military and economic power to control Burmese society, resources, government, and economy.
2. Britain had dominion over Burma.
3. Answers include prisoners kept in horrible conditions; visible evidence of physical punishment.

Using the Word Bank

wretched: squalid
tyrannical: despotic
governed territory: dominion
total control: imperialism
defenseless: prostrate
mental decay: senility

Build Your Portfolio

Idea Bank

Writing

1. **Profile** Orwell reveals a great deal about himself in this essay. Use what you learn to write a profile of the author as a young man. Include both his ideas and his personal traits.

2. **Film Treatment** Write a memo to a director suggesting how Orwell's essay could be adapted for film. Explain how you would shoot some of the key scenes. **[Media Link]**

3. **Response to Criticism** Lionel Trilling said of Orwell, "He told the truth, and told it in an exemplary way, quietly, simply, with due warning to the reader that it was only one man's truth." Does this comment also apply to "Shooting an Elephant"? Why or why not?

Speaking and Listening

4. **Role Play** With several classmates, act out a scene in which Orwell recounts the shooting incident to some younger and older Englishmen. Have them react as Orwell describes in the essay. **[Performing Arts Link]**

5. **Debate** Reach your own conclusions about imperialism by having teams debate this proposition: It would have been better for "Third World" peoples if Europeans had never conquered their countries. **[Social Studies Link]**

Projects

6. **Orwell in Film** Orwell's books *1984* and *Animal Farm* have both inspired films. View one of these and report on it to the class. **[Media Link]**

7. **Biography** In 1991, a Burmese woman, Aung San Suu Kyi, won the Nobel Peace Prize. Research and report on her fight for freedom in Burma. **[Social Studies Link]**

Writing Mini-Lesson

Police Report

As a police officer, Orwell probably had to write a report on the incident he describes. Review the essay and write the police report that he might have filed. Briefly summarize what happened, explain the events in order, and justify the shooting of the elephant. However, don't include observations on imperialism or the role of Britain in Burma. The officer who reads your report will just want to know the key facts.

Writing Skills Focus: Elaboration to Give Information

In all kinds of writing, you have to **elaborate to give information**—to add details and comments that give the reader a fuller understanding of your subject. For your report, keep in mind the facts that a police administrator might want to know:

- What happened?
- Where and when did the events occur?
- Why did they occur? For example, what caused the elephant to run wild, and why did you decide to shoot it?

Prewriting Jot down notes in response to the key questions listed above. Then figure out a format for your report: the order in which you will present information, the titles you'll give to the various sections, and the space you'll devote to each.

Drafting Begin with a quick summary of events. Often, busy administrators like to have an overview of what occurred, especially if they don't have time to read further. As you draft your report, refer to your notes and include only the key facts.

Revising Review the story to see if you have left out any essential information. Then review your report to see if you have included unimportant details that could be left out. Be sure you have justified killing the elephant and that the format is clear.

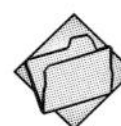

Idea Bank

Customizing for
Performance Levels
Following are suggestions for matching Idea Bank topics with your students' performance levels:

Less Advanced Students: 1, 4, 6
Average Students: 2, 4, 5, 6
More Advanced Students: 3, 5, 7

Customizing for
Learning Modalities
Following are suggestions for matching Idea Bank topics with your students' learning modalities:

Visual/Spatial: 2, 6
Verbal/Linguistic: 1, 3, 5, 7
Bodily/Kinesthetic: 4

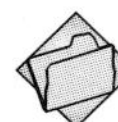

Writing Mini-Lesson

Refer students to the Writing Process Handbook, page 1189, for instruction on the writing process and to page 1191 for more about exposition.

Writing Lab CD-ROM
Have students complete the tutorial on Practical and Technical Writing. They may follow these steps:

1. Use the Chain of Events activity to gather details for their report.
2. Draft their reports on computer.
3. Use the Notecards Activity to elaborate on details.
4. Use revision checkers to help them revise their reports.

Sourcebook
Have students use Chapter 8, Practical and Technical Writing (pp. 230–264), for additional support.

✓ ASSESSMENT OPTIONS

Formal Assessment, Selection Test, pp. 239–241, and Assessment Resources Software. The selection test is designed so that it can be easily customized to the performance levels of your students.
Alternative Assessment, p. 49, includes options for less advanced students, more advanced students, interpersonal learners, verbal/linguistic learners, and visual/spatial learners.

PORTFOLIO ASSESSMENT
Use the following rubrics in the ***Alternative Assessment*** booklet to assess student writing:
Profile: General Rubric, p. 94
Film Treatment: General Rubric, p. 94
Response to Criticism: Literary Analysis/Interpretation Rubric, p. 113
Writing Mini-Lesson: Summary Rubric, p. 99

Prepare and Engage

OBJECTIVES

1. To read, comprehend, and interpret poetry
2. To relate poetry to personal experience
3. To build vocabulary in context and learn the language of grim reality
4. To connect poems to the theme of Waking From the Dream
5. To respond to the poems through writing, speaking and listening, and projects

SKILLS INSTRUCTION

Speaking and Listening: Persuasive Speech (teacher edition)

Critical Viewing: Connect; Compare and Contrast

PORTFOLIO OPPORTUNITIES

Writing: Narrative Essay; Personal Testament; Response to Criticism

Speaking and Listening: Persuasive Speech

Project: Historical Context

More About the Authors

Yehuda Amichai explores his own journey from Germany to Israel, from young man to middle age, in his autobiographical poem "Travels." Many of Amichai's other works, including his novel *Not of This Time, Not of This Place,* also struggle to define identity and to balance the author's German childhood and his knowledge of the Holocaust with his Israeli adult experiences.

Anna Akhmatova was linked with Russian Acmeism, a literary movement founded by her husband Nikolai Gumilev. Developed in opposition to Symbolism, Acmeism stressed the virtue of clarity and directness. Akhmatova's poems, with their simple language and everyday speech, demonstrate these characteristics.

Bei Dao resumed his literary education and career after Mao Zedong's death opened up China's cultural circles again. He is associated with the "Misty" school of Chinese poetry, which shares many characteristics of Western Modernist poetry. He is also known for editing *Today,* a publication linked to China's 1978 Democracy Movement.

CONNECTIONS TO WORLD LITERATURE

The Diameter of the Bomb — Yehuda Amichai

Everything Is Plundered — Anna Akhmatova

Testament — Bei Dao

Cultural Connection

Waking From the Dream

The writers in this section respond to the disconcerting, often violent, changes that mark the twentieth century. As their work shows, individuals caught up in these changes can feel as if they are trapped in a nightmare or are waking from an illusory dream to bitter disillusionment. Bowen, in "The Demon Lover," and Yeats, in "The Second Coming," stress the nightmarish aspects of war and of historical cycles. In "Preludes," T. S. Eliot portrays an awakening to a confused and fragmented world in which the soul suffers. Orwell depicts another kind of awakening in "To Shoot an Elephant." He shows how, as a young imperial police officer, he first understood the effects of colonialism on the oppressor and the oppressed alike.

"From starry bullet-holes"

Yehuda Amichai (yə ho͞o´ də ä´ mi khī), Anna Akhmatova (äk mä´tō və) and Bei Dao (bā dou) also respond to the century's grim realities. Akhmatova, writing just after a bitter civil war in Russia (1918–1920), describes both the "misery" she sees around her and the "miraculous" that she senses. Amichai, himself a veteran of Israel's wars, shows the devastating and far-reaching effects of an act of terrorism. Bei Dao writes the "Testament" of a prisoner about to be executed by the oppressive Chinese government. Though soon to die, this man holds out the possibility that his death will be a source of renewal: "From starry bullet-holes / The blood-red dawn will flow."

YEHUDA AMICHAI (1924–)

Born in Germany, Amichai emigrated to Palestine prior to the start of World War II. Since then he has fought in nearly all of Israel's wars and has written poetry that expresses the thoughts and feelings of a whole generation of Israelis. He has also skillfully combined—in Hebrew—biblical phrases and down-to-earth, everyday language.

ANNA AKHMATOVA (1889–1966)

Russian poet Anna Akhmatova began writing poems at eleven. During her long life, she experienced and wrote about a host of devastating events, from the Russian Revolution to Stalin's oppression. Stalin banned her work for a time. In 1940, however, the ban was lifted, and she continued to write and publish until her death.

BEI DAO (1949–)

Bei Dao is a Chinese poet whose work is—in the words of one of his translators, Bonnie S. McDougall—a "complex reaction to the pressures of a brutalized and corrupt society." He was traveling abroad during the Tiananmen Square massacre (June 4,1989), and since that time, he has lived in exile from China.

Prentice Hall Literature Program Resources

REINFORCE / RETEACH / EXTEND

Selection Support Pages
Build Vocabulary: The Language of Grim Reality, p. 239
Thematic Connection: Waking From the Dream, p. 240

Formal Assessment pp. 242–243; Assessment Resources Software

Resource Pro CD-ROM
"The Diameter of the Bomb," "Everything Is Plundered," "Testament"—includes all resource material and customizable lesson plan

Listening to Literature Audiocassettes
"The Diameter of the Bomb," "Everything Is Plundered," "Testament"

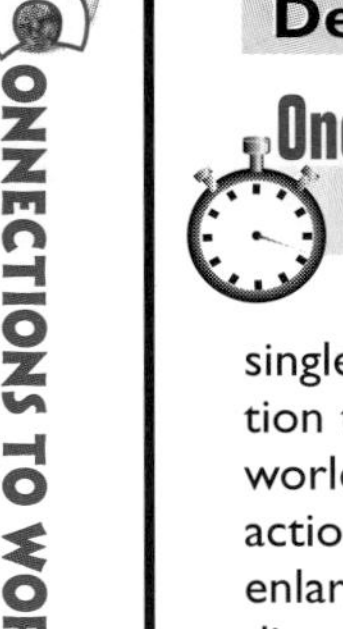

The Diameter of the Bomb

CONNECTIONS TO WORLD LITERATURE

Yehuda Amichai

Translated by Chana Bloch

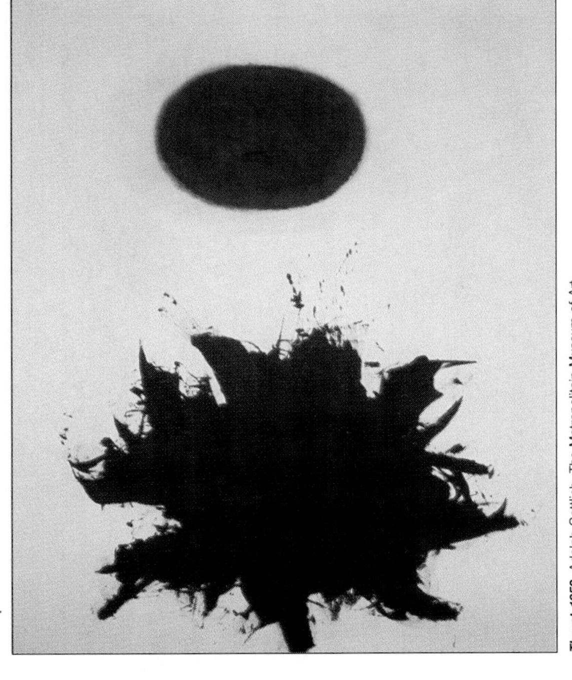

Thrust 1959, Adolph Gottlieb, The Metropolitan Museum of Art

❶ ▶ Critical Viewing
In what ways does this image illustrate Amichai's poem? **[Connect]**

The diameter of the bomb was thirty centimeters
and the diameter of its effective range about seven
meters,
with four dead and eleven wounded.
And around these, in a larger circle
of pain and time, two hospitals are scattered
and one graveyard. But the young woman
who was buried in the city she came from,
at a distance of more than a hundred kilometers,
enlarges the circle considerably,
❷ and the solitary man mourning her death
at the distant shores of a country far across the
sea
includes the entire world in the circle.
And I won't even mention the crying of orphans
that reaches up to the throne of God and
beyond, making
a circle with no end and no God.

Develop Understanding

One-Minute Insight

This poem vividly evokes the ripple effects of a single hostile action—of the devastation terrorism can wreak upon the world. The speaker traces that action, the detonation of a bomb, in enlarging concentric circles, from the diameter of the bomb itself, to the area of its damage, to the wounded and dead, to the grief of survivors, to the children orphaned or unborn because of death. By tracing the furthest consequences of this action, the poet is able to question the nature of a world that permits such suffering.

▶Critical Viewing◀

❶ **Connect** Students may link the oval above with the bomb and the splattered black paint below with the explosion.

Thematic Connection

❷ **Waking from the Dream**
How is this enlarged idea of the bomb's diameter a kind of awakening from a dream? *The belief that bombs target only the guilty and do not affect the innocent, or that their effects are only local, or that human suffering is a measurable quantity rather than an absolute wrong—these are dreams or illusions, from which the poem awakens us.*

Humanities: Art

Thrust, 1959, by Adolph Gottlieb.

This painting of a red oval and black splatter captures the images of a bomb and its explosion described by Amichai's poem.

American painter Adolph Gottlieb was born in New York City and studied there at the Art Students' League. He later studied at the Académie de la Grande Chaumière in Paris. Abstract Expressionist works such as *Thrust* are amongst Gottlieb's best-known works.

Use these questions for discussion:

1. How do the colors of the painting reflect the content of Amichai's poem? *The red reflects the fire of a bomb while the black suggests its destructive force.*
2. How does the painting's composition contrast with Amichai's theme of cause and effect? *The white background suggests that the depicted event is isolated while the poem stresses links between a single event and the entire world.*

Develop Understanding

One-Minute Insight Both the poems on these pages refer to the oppression that may follow in the wake of revolution. In "Everything Is Plundered," Anna Akhmatova answers despair with the mystery of nature and human resiliency. "Testament" honors its speaker's desire to be free even when condemned, and to die with grace. These poems demonstrate the strength of human spirit against despair.

▶Critical Viewing◀

❶ **Compare and Contrast** The woman depicted may seem too young and healthy to have suffered much; yet her relaxed, poised pose suggests Akhmatova's receptiveness to mystery.

Thematic Connection

❷ **Waking From the Dream** Ask students to connect "Everything is Plundered" to the Yeats's poetry. *Yeats too recognized a link between the wild, death, and the miraculous in "The Wild Swans at Coole."*

Customize for ***Verbal/Linguistic Learners*** Draw these students' attention to the kinetic verbs in "Everything Is Plundered." Ask how these verbs enlarge their appreciation of the poem.

Thematic Connection

❸ **Waking From the Dream** Ask students to contrast the picture of death in these lines with that in Eliot's "The Hollow Men." Which shows death to be an awakening, which a dream? *Eliot's "hollow men" live a life that is like a death—an unreal dream. Bei Dao envisions death as a morning, an awakening. This vision keeps him from the nightmare of despair.*

CONNECTIONS TO WORLD LITERATURE

Everything Is Plundered

Anna Akhmatova
Translated by Stanley Kunitz

◀ **Critical Viewing** Does the Anna Akhmatova depicted in the portrait seem as if she could have written this poem? Why or why not? **[Compare and Contrast]** ❶

Everything is plundered, betrayed, sold,
Death's great black wing scrapes the air,
Misery gnaws to the bone.
Why then do we not despair?

By day, from the surrounding woods,
❷ cherries blow summer into town;
at night the deep transparent skies
glitter with new galaxies.

And the miraculous comes so close
to the ruined, dirty houses—
something not known to anyone at all,
but wild in our breast for centuries.

Speaking and Listening Mini-Lesson

Persuasive Speech
This mini-lesson supports the Speaking and Listening activity in the Idea Bank on page 952.

Introduce the Concept Have students share examples of persuasive text, for example from political speeches or radio advertising. Discuss how poetry might function as persuasive text, suggesting by its mere existence a position of hope.

Develop Background Have students follow these guidelines:

- Organize speeches around a clearly stated central position.
- Present specific evidence such as quotations.
- Use formal language.

Apply the Information Direct students to prepare speeches of a specified length (2–5 minutes, for example). Encourage them to practice their delivery, working toward even but clear and audible speech. Remind students to check all direct quotations for accuracy. Finally, have them deliver their speeches.

Assess the Outcome Have all students rate the speeches for clarity, use of evidence, and overall persuasiveness. You might have them use the Self-Assessment for a Speech or the Peer Assessment for a Speaker/Speech, pages 118 and 119 in ***Alternative Assessment***. As follow-up, encourage students to discuss how poets in this section might respond to these speeches.

Testament[1]

Bei Dao

Translated by Donald Finkel and Xueliang Chen

CONNECTIONS TO WORLD LITERATURE

Perhaps the time has come.
I haven't left a will,
just one pen, for my mother.

I'm no hero, you understand.
This isn't the year for heroes.
I'd just like to be a man.

The horizon still divides
the living from the dead,
but the sky's all I need.

I won't kneel on the earth—
the firing squad might block
the last free breaths of air.

3 From starry bullet-holes
the blood-red dawn will flow.

1. **Testament** (Tes´ tə ment) *n.*: Will; also, a statement of one's beliefs.

Guide for Responding

◆ Literature and Your Life

Reader's Response Which poem did you find most disturbing? Which poem was most optimistic? Explain.

Thematic Connection What news of the twentieth century can you find in the work of these three poets?

☑ Check Your Comprehension

1. What does the circle include in Amichai's poem?
2. What sights help Akhmatova not "despair"?
3. Describe how the speaker in Bei Dao's poem pictures himself at his execution.

◆ Critical Thinking

INTERPRET

1. A paradox is an apparent contradiction. (a) What is paradoxical about the image in Amichai's poem of "a circle with no end"? (b) Why is a paradox well-suited to Amichai's ideas in this poem? **[Interpret]**
2. What is "the miraculous" Akhmatova refers to in line 9 of her poem? **[Interpret]**
3. What new insight about life does Akhmatova's poem reveal? **[Draw Conclusions]**
4. A testament is a will or a statement of belief. How do both meanings apply to "Testament"? **[Draw Conclusions]**

Beyond the Selection

FURTHER READING

Other Works by the Poets

Amen, Travels, Yehuda Amichai; *Rosary, Plantain,* Anna Akhmatova; *Forms of Distance, Old Snow,* Bei Dao

Other Works About Social Protest

"Girl Held Without Bail," Margaret Walker
"Song to the Men of England," Percy Bysshe Shelley
"Peace Walk," William Stafford

Preview the works before recommending them.

INTERNET

The following Internet sites provide additional information. (Note: Addresses may change or expire.)

Amichai: **http://israel-mfa.gov.il/facts/culture/lit/amichai.html**

Akhmatova: **http:/funnelweb.utcc.utk.edu/~jtdybka/akh.htm**

Bei Dao: **http://www.cstone.net/~poems/landsbe2.htm**

Always preview sites before recommending them.

Customize for
English Language Learners
To help language learners grasp the references in "Testament," discuss who the speaker is, referring to the background information given on page 948.

Reinforce and Extend

Answers

◆ Literature and Your Life

Reader's Response Possible answers: "The Diameter of the Bomb" is most disturbing because it lacks hope. "Plundered" is most optimistic because it offers hope in the face of despair.

Thematic Connection Students may mention the dropping of the atomic bomb, terrorist attacks, civil wars such as that in Bosnia, and political executions.

☑ Check Your Comprehension

1. The circle includes the bomb, its damage, four dead and eleven wounded, two hospitals and one graveyard, a dead woman's grieving survivor, her unborn and orphaned children, and the absence of God.
2. She is saved from despair by the summer scent of cherries and the glittering stars of the night sky.
3. He sees himself standing tall to breathe the last few breaths without obstacle; he imagines his death as a dawn.

◆ Critical Thinking

1. (a) A circle ends where it begins, but Amichai's circle is never complete. (b) The poem demonstrates that suffering links all people, yet only by destroying the links between them.
2. "The miraculous" may be nature's beauty and human hope.
3. She suggests that people have always longed for hope, have always cherished "the miraculous," no matter their situation.
4. Like a will, the poem disposes of the speaker's belongings (a pen) and leaves behind the hope for real change. It is also a statement of the the speaker's belief in freedom.

Answers
Thematic Connection

1. Amichai's language is detached, almost clinical, and he uses few images. Akhmatova uses figures of speech in her first stanza, images in her second, but finally turns to an abstract, allusive language in the third ("the miraculous," "something").
2. Auden requires the poet to follow us into the darkest night; Bei Dao finds a beautiful image in his own bullet-riddled corpse.
3. Possible response: The speaker might say that sometimes the only evidence of God is the deaths we die on the road to spiritual rebirth.
4. (a) Students may mention still popular songs from the 1960's or others of more recent acquaintance. (b) The songs may express hope for an end to war, sadness at the damage it causes, fear for loved ones, anger at "the other side," or devotion to a particular political cause.

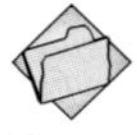

Idea Bank

Customizing for
Performance Levels

Following are suggestions for matching Idea Bank topics with your students' performance levels:

Less Advanced Students: 2
Average Students: 1, 5
More Advanced Students: 3, 4

Customizing for
Learning Modalities

Following are suggestions for matching Idea Bank topics with your students' learning modalities:

Verbal/linguistic: 1, 2, 3, 4
Intrapersonal: 5

Cultural Connection

Waking From the Dream

During the twentieth century, many writers in England and elsewhere had to find words to describe the realities of war and other upheavals. No longer could they rely on "poetic" language that depicted a dreamy, imaginary world.

1. How is the language that Amichai uses to describe the effects of a bomb different from that Akhmatova uses to describe the aftermath of a civil war?
2. Read Bei Dao's "Testament" together with part 3 of Auden's "In Memory of W. B. Yeats." Do you think that Bei Dao is—in Auden's terms—still persuading "us to rejoice"? Why or why not?
3. What do you think the speaker in Eliot's "Journey of the Magi" would say about the conclusion of Amichai's poem?
4. (a) Identify a contemporary song that deals with war or other political upheavals. (b) What thoughts and emotions does the song express?

Idea Bank

Writing

1. **Narrative Essay** In a narrative essay, describe a time when you woke up to a certain reality or became aware of a truth.
2. **Personal Testament** Bei Dao's "Testament" is not only a last will and testament, but also a statement of his beliefs. Write your own testament, explaining your most important beliefs.
3. **Response to Criticism** Akhmatova told Isaiah Berlin "that the unending ordeal of her country in her own lifetime had generated poetry of wonderful depth and beauty." Apply this observation to her own poem "Everything Is Plundered."

Speaking and Listening

4. **Persuasive Speech** Prepare and deliver a persuasive speech arguing that poetry can preserve hope in times of upheaval. To support your position, quote from poems that appear in this section of the book. **[Performing Arts Link]**

Project

5. **Historical Context** Research historical events that influenced one of these poets. One possible source, for instance, is the introduction to *The Complete Poems of Anna Akhmatova*, translated by Judith Hemschemeyer (Boston: Zephyr, 1992). Report on your findings to the class. **[Social Studies Link]**

✓ ASSESSMENT OPTIONS

ASSESSMENT OPTIONS

Formal Assessment, Selection Test, pp. 242–243, and Assessment Resources Software. The selection test is designed so that it can be easily customized to the performance levels of your students.

PORTFOLIO ASSESSMENT

Use the following rubrics in the ***Alternative Assessment*** booklet to assess student writing:
Narrative Essay: Narrative Based on a Personal Experience Rubric, p. 97
Personal Testament: Expression Rubric, p. 95
Response to Criticism: Literary Analysis Rubric, p. 113

Writing Process Workshop

Just as poets like T. S. Eliot quote other writers in their poems, you can use facts and ideas from different sources in your research paper. Use these sources to support a thesis statement, which presents one or more key points about a topic. Also, be sure your paper has an introduction, body, and conclusion. The introduction presents your thesis, and the body includes facts and arguments that support it, with source materials credited in footnotes, endnotes, or parenthetical notes. These skills will help you write your paper.

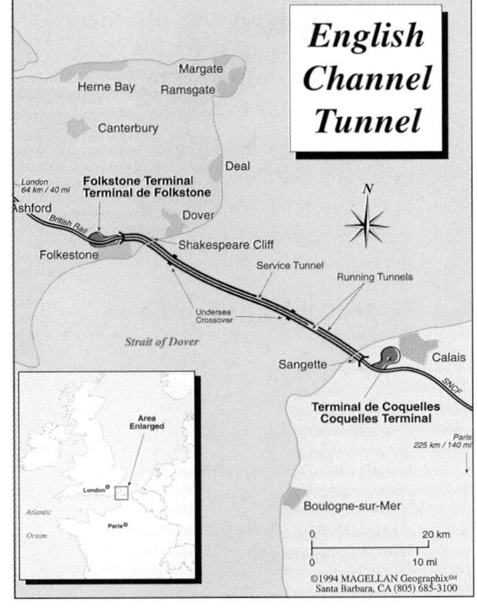

Writing Skills Focus

- **Choose a clear and logical organization** that matches the content and purpose of your paper. (See p. 895.)
- **Use details and language** that suit your readers and help you achieve your purpose. (See pp. 907, 935.)
- **Consult a variety of sources** when you gather information. (See p. 921.)
- **Elaborate** by including details that support your thesis. Details may be in chart, graph, or map form. (See p. 947.)

Student Model

from *The Chunnel: The Tunnel That Builds Bridges*
by Dan Mahoney, Darien High School, Darien, Connecticut

The rivalry between England and France stems from centuries of war between these two countries. Although they were allies in both world wars, the animosity between England and France remains.① . . . [S]ince the tunnel was opened in 1994, however, it has helped to bring these two great cultures a little closer together.②

The greater ease of travel between Britain and France . . . has led to an increase in tourism between these two nations. ③ This is largely due to the efficiency of the Channel Tunnel. High-speed trains traverse the 23.6-mile tunnel in 35 minutes (Schmidt, E4).④ The boost in tourism has, in turn, led to greater mutual understanding. . . .⑤

① The writer provides background information for readers.
② This statement reveals the writer's thesis.
③ The writer supports his thesis with this fact.
④ The writer acknowledges the source of this fact by using a parenthetical note.
⑤ The writer elaborates with a cause-and-effect statement.

Cross-Curricular Connection: Science

Explain to students that research is the backbone of the scientific community. While the format for reporting scientific findings varies somewhat from the research paper here, the research skills required are the same. Knowing how to use every facet of the library—especially the reference section, the computer catalog, and on-line services—is important to scientists, who must compare their findings with those published by others. Scientists must also do "hands-on" research in the laboratory, of course. They must plan experiments, draw logical conclusions from them, and present complete, accurate data. Ask students how these skills parallel those required for writing a research paper.

Prepare and Engage

Establish Writing Guidelines
Review the following key characteristics of a research paper:

- The paper supports a thesis with details from a variety of sources.
- Sources are cited for all details, either visual or verbal, quoted or paraphrased.
- The research paper concludes with a list of all sources used.

Share with students the criteria by which they will be evaluated. Show them the Scoring Rubric for Research Report/Paper (p. 107 in ***Alternative Assessment***). Suggestions on page 955 customize the rubric to this workshop.

Writing and Language Transparencies Use Writing Process Model 7: Research Report (pp. 57–69) to model the writing and revising process.

Connect to Literature To explain the difference between primary and secondary sources, compare Samuel Johnson's "Preface" (p. 505), a primary source, with James Boswell's *Life* (p. 510), a secondary source.

Writer's Solution

Writers at Work Videodisc
Play the videodisc segment on Research Writing (Ch. 5) featuring sportswriter Peter Ginsburg. Ask students how strong research skills benefit a writer like Ginsburg.

Play frames 3 to 7599

Writing Lab CD-ROM
Students can work in the Research Writing Tutorial to complete all or part of their research papers, following these steps:

1. Review the interactive models of research writing.
2. Narrow topics with a Topic Web and see tips on narrowing.
3. Consult interactive instructions for using library resources.
4. Study the interactive instruction on connecting citations with a bibliography.

Sourcebook
Students can find additional support in Research Writing (Ch. 5, pp. 131–165).

Develop Student Writing

Prewriting

Writing and Language Transparencies Depending on the organizational plan students choose, have them use an outline, comparison-and-contrast, or cause-and-effect graphic organizer (pp. 123–125, 115–117, 119–121) to help organize their thoughts.

Customize for *Visual/Spatial Learners*
Have these students tap their preference for visuals by encouraging them to include graphs, charts, maps, photos, and more in their research papers.

Writer's Solution

Writing Lab CD-ROM
In Organizing Information (in the Research Writing tutorial), students will find annotated instructions showing how to organize research into categories.

Drafting

Remind students that every bit of support for the points in their research paper must come from their sources and must be credited.

Applying Language Skills

Citing Sources You may want to assign the style of documentation you prefer students to use—parenthetical, footnote, or endnote—but remind them that all three forms are valid means of citing sources.

Writer's Solution Sourcebook
To compare parenthetical and footnote citations, refer to the models on pages 159–160 and 164–165 in the *Writer's Solution Sourcebook.*

Applying Language Skills: Citing Sources

Document your use of others' ideas or words with footnotes, endnotes, or parenthetical citations.

Text Citation: Footnote
Laura Wortley states, "The 'British' Impressionists translated the harsh facts of reality into a beautiful, fragile, fiction."[1]

Bottom of Page: Footnote
1. Laura Wortley, *British Impressionism: A Garden of Bright Images.* (London: The Studio Fine Art Publications, 1987) 285.

(For endnotes, number each cited passage like a footnote, but create a separate page for endnotes.)

Text Citation: Parenthetical
Laura Wortley states, "The 'British' Impressionists translated the harsh facts of reality into a beautiful, fragile, fiction" (Wortley 285).

Writing Application Refer to these examples as you document your sources.

Writer's Solution Connection
Writing Lab

For help with Internet research, complete the interactive instruction dealing with on-line services in the Gathering Information section of the Research Writing tutorial.

Prewriting

Choose a Topic If your teacher has not assigned a topic and you're having trouble finding interesting subjects, consider using one of these topic ideas:

Topic Ideas
- Weapons and tactics in World War I
- Picasso's early years in Paris

Selection-Related Topic Ideas
- The Easter Rising in Ireland (1916)
- The influence of Keats on Wilfred Owen
- Yeats's ideas about historical cycles

Consider Your Audience and Purpose Identify your audience (your readers) and purpose (your reason for writing) and gather details that will suit both.

Consult a Variety of Sources Collect information from a variety of credible sources, such as non-fiction books, almanacs, atlases, textbooks, anthologies, and personal interviews, when appropriate. On index cards, note the source (title, date, page number, author) from which each detail comes.

Organize Details Arrange your note cards in a clear and logical order. Here are some suggestions:

- **Chronological** Organize events in time order, especially if you will be giving a narrative account.
- **Order of importance** Organize details from least important to most important, or the other way around.
- **Cause and effect** Organize details according to causal relationships between them.
- **Pro and con** Arrange details in two categories, those that support an idea or point of view and those that contradict it.
- **Comparison and contrast** Arrange details in two categories, those showing similarities between two subjects and those showing differences between them.

Drafting

Draft a Thesis Statement Formulate a working thesis that can guide your writing. Modify this statement as you draft.

Work from Your Note Cards Work with prearranged note cards in front of you so that your thoughts are organized and you have facts at your fingertips to support your arguments.

Revising

Fact Check Review your draft, and highlight each fact you've used. Then verify each fact by checking it carefully against your sources.

Revision Tips Revise your research report, using the following tips to guide you:

- Check to be sure details and language are appropriate for your audience and purpose.
- Be sure you have maintained a consistent organization.
- Delete any details that do not support your thesis.
- Verify that you have properly credited sources for ideas and wording that are not your own.
- Proofread for errors in grammar, punctuation, capitalization, and spelling.

Revision Model

① , undisputed leader of the Modernist movement in poetry,
Thomas Stearns Eliot was born and educated in the United States. ~~His conversion to the Anglican Church in 1927 marked a new phase in his life and in his writing.~~ ② When
③ Eliot was studying at Oxford University, and he chose to remain in England, eventually acquiring British citizenship.
WWI broke out, ~~Eliot chose to remain in England.~~ In 1915, the year he married, Eliot published *The Love Song of*
④ , a bleak picture of a world fragmented by WWI and its aftermath.
J. Alfred Prufrock.

① This information strengthens the writer's purpose, which is to reveal the lasting influence Eliot has had on poetry.
② This statement must be deleted and moved because it is out of chronological order.
③ These details elaborate on the poet's background and nationality.
④ Taking into account the knowledge level of the reader, the author adds a brief description.

Publishing

- **Multimedia** Create a multimedia presentation that enhances the information in your report.
- **Internet** E-mail your work to interested people. For example, if you have written about Elizabethan clothing, send your paper to a site dedicated to costume design.

Applying Language Skills: Creating a Bibliography

Complete your paper by creating a bibliography of the works you have cited in your writing.

Book:
Fussell, Paul. *The Great War and Modern Memory*. New York: Oxford University Press, 1975.

Magazine or newspaper article:
Roach, Margaret. "Wedgwood." Martha Stewart Living, April 1997: 134–139.

Reference book:
"Imagery." *The Oxford Companion to the English Language*. 1992 ed.

CD-ROM:
"World Wonders: Eiffel Tower." Planet Earth, Macmillan Digital: 1996.

Electronic journals/newsletters:
Engle-Cox, Glen. "The Life and Times of Macintosh." Book Review Resources: 3pp. On line. Internet. 21 July 1996.

Videotape:
King Richard II. Dir. William Woodman. With David Birney and Paul Shenar. Bennett Video Group, 1982.

Writing Application Refer to these examples as you create a bibliography for your research report. List all the important sources you consulted in your research.

Revising

Discuss the Revision Model. Remind students that virtually every detail in the research paper should come from one of their sources. Using material without documentation can result in plagiarism.

Publishing

Students who interviewed sources about their topic may want to share a completed copy of the research paper with those people.

Applying Language Skills

Creating a Bibliography Discuss with students the importance of proper punctuation and capitalization in a bibliography. For additional details about documenting sources from the Internet, consult the Internet itself. Use any search engine, and search using the keyword *MLA* or *citations*.

Writer's Solution

For additional instruction and practice, use the practice pages on Understanding Research Papers and Writing a Research Paper (pp. 126–127 in the *Writer's Solution Grammar Practice Book*).

Reinforce and Extend

Analyzing the Writing Process
After students have completed their papers, ask them to identify the elements of research they found most difficult and explain how they finally resolved the difficulties.

ASSESSMENT		4	3	2	1
Use the rubric for Research Report/Paper (p. 107) to assess students' writing. Add these criteria to customize the rubric to this assignment.	**Research Process: Note Cards**	The writer shows evidence of thorough research with an extensive number of quality note cards.	The writer shows adequate research with an adequate number of quality note cards.	The writer shows inadequate research with only some quality note cards.	The writer shows little research with few quality note cards.
	Variety of Sources	The research paper shows extensive variety in sources, both primary and secondary.	The research paper shows an adequate variety of sources.	The research paper shows some variety of sources.	The research paper show little variety of sources.

Introduce the Strategy

Ask students to share their experiences seeking information on the Internet. Ask them to describe the appearance of various home pages and how that influenced their reactions to the information found there.

Customize for
Interpersonal Learners
Suggest that these students work in pairs or small groups to evaluate Web sites.

Apply the Strategy

Have students study the Web page reproduced here. You may want students to work in small groups to respond to the questions.

Answers

1. (a) The site is sponsored by Orwell fans. (b) They are partial to Orwell.
2. Since Orwell fans would be the majority of visitors to the Web site, a poll of visitors would give slanted results.
3. To verify the quotation, one could check a printed collection of Orwell's essays.

Evaluating Information on the Internet

Real-World Reading Skills Workshop

Strategies for Success

The Internet contains mountains of information—a great deal of it is accurate, but some pages include exaggerations or out-and-out falsehoods. Use extra caution when collecting facts from Internet sources.

Consider the Sponsor Every site on the Internet is sponsored by a group or an individual. When you find a site you want to use, find out who sponsored the site. Be wary if there's no author or sponsor listed. Think about why this site was created. Evaluating a sponsor's motivation will help you detect underlying bias. Consider these questions:

- ▶ What purpose might the sponsor have in maintaining this site?
- ▶ Which facts and details might be biased?
- ▶ Are generalizations on this page helpful or too sweeping?

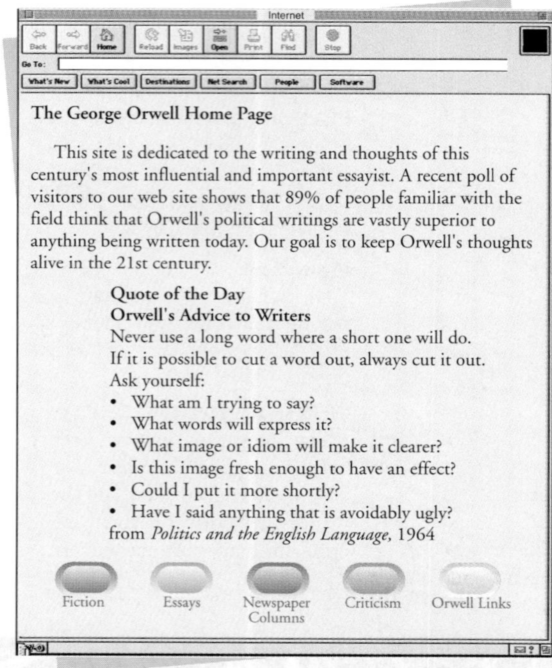

The George Orwell Home Page

This site is dedicated to the writing and thoughts of this century's most influential and important essayist. A recent poll of visitors to our web site shows that 89% of people familiar with the field think that Orwell's political writings are vastly superior to anything being written today. Our goal is to keep Orwell's thoughts alive in the 21st century.

Quote of the Day
Orwell's Advice to Writers
Never use a long word where a short one will do.
If it is possible to cut a word out, always cut it out.
Ask yourself:

- What am I trying to say?
- What words will express it?
- What image or idiom will make it clearer?
- Is this image fresh enough to have an effect?
- Could I put it more shortly?
- Have I said anything that is avoidably ugly?

from *Politics and the English Language,* 1964

Fiction | Essays | Newspaper Columns | Criticism | Orwell Links

Verify Data Remember that anyone can post anything to the Internet and claim it is factual. Whenever possible, verify information from a site by checking other Internet sources as well as reputable books and magazines.

Don't Be Fooled by Fancy Graphics An impressive, polished look is no guarantee of truthfulness. Art and design programs make it simple to create a web page that looks professional—but that doesn't mean that the editing and research were done carefully and thoroughly. Critical thinking skills and a healthy dose of skepticism will help you weed out web sites that are pretty but unreliable.

Apply the Strategy

You are conducting a research report on George Orwell. While surfing the Internet, you stumble onto this site, which is chock full of writing by and opinions about the author. You can use questions like the following to decide if the information is valid and useful.

1. (a) Who sponsored the site? (b) What biases might this organization have?
2. What is questionable about the poll results that are quoted?
3. How could you verify that Orwell actually wrote the advice to writers quoted on this page?

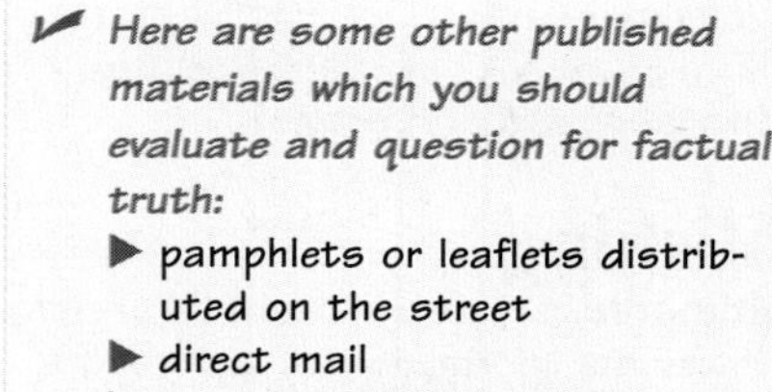

Here are some other published materials which you should evaluate and question for factual truth:

- ▶ pamphlets or leaflets distributed on the street
- ▶ direct mail
- ▶ posters and billboards

Cross-Curricular Connection: Social Studies

Because the Internet provides up-to-the-minute information, it is particularly valuable for keeping up with politics and world affairs. Government offices, political organizations, and newspapers maintain Web sites, some of which change hourly. Still, no one regulates what goes onto the Internet; political pundits have full reign at their own Web sites. Remind students to check not only the sponsoring organization and to consider any bias that group may have, but also to check authorship (names and credentials should appear at reputable sites) and the most recent update (usually posted at the bottom of the home page).

PART 2 Conflicts Abroad and at Home

A Balloon Site, Coventry, 1940
Dame Laura Knight, Imperial War Museum

Britain had its share of conflicts during the twentieth century. It fought in two world wars, which cost many lives. Writers who fought and sometimes died in these struggles expressed their sense of patriotism, horror, or compassion. Britain won both wars, yet by mid-century had lost nearly all of Ireland, India, and most of its empire.

Humanities: Fine Art

A Balloon Site, Coventry, 1940, by Dame Laura Knight.

This painting illustrates a group of female war workers launching a World War II defensive scouting balloon. It captures women's crucial participation in England's war effort at home.

The painter, British artist Dame Laura Knight, studied at the Nottingham School of Art. In peacetime, she was known for her paintings of circus life and ballet scenes. During World War II, the Air Ministry commissioned her to paint scenes of balloon fabric workers, like this one.

Use these questions for discussion:

1. What elements in the painting suggest the conflicts England faced? *The women's presence in the scene and the industrial evidence of war suggest the turmoil of war and changes in Britain's social structure and economy.*
2. How do the details of the painting suggest the contrast between nineteenth- and twentieth-century Britain? *The artificial sense of light and old-fashioned balloon suggest the idealism of the nineteenth century, while the female workers suggest the new realities of the twentieth century.*

One-Minute Planning Guide

The violence of two World Wars, as well as simmering conflicts at home and in British colonies abroad, left their mark on twentieth-century literature. In the work of the War Poets (Brooke, Sassoon, and Owen), students can get a sense of life in the trenches of World War I and witness the transformation of a generation's vigorous patriotism as it is dragged through mud and suffering. Courage in the face of conflict resounds in Churchill's and Gandhi's speeches—one calling on a nation's courage in an hour of common danger, the other displaying an individual's courage in standing up for his principles. Conflicts within a community raise questions of identity—for the working class, in Sillitoe's "The Fiddle," and for Ireland, in the work of Trevor, Heaney, and Boland. In the end, Lessing discovers, conflict always has many levels, as cultural conflict creates personal conflict in British-colonized Africa.

Customize for *Varying Student Needs*

When assigning selections in this part, keep in mind the following factors:

Brooke, Owen, and Sassoon

- Should be read as a group, to emphasize their contrasting responses to war. Musical/rhythmic learners will appreciate Brooke's language; Sassoon pictures reality more directly; Owen's sophistication will challenge advanced learners.

Churchill and Gandhi

- The speeches are formal, but the situation in which each was delivered was truly dramatic. Have less proficient readers paraphrase as they read.

Sillitoe

- Students may identify with the working class character's decision to improve his life—with a sacrifice.

Heaney and Boland

- Students may require background on the conflict in Ireland before reading the poems.

Lessing

- This short story poignantly reveals a cultural chasm between British family and African servants.

Prepare and Engage

OBJECTIVES

1. To read and interpret poems and an essay
2. To relate poems and an essay to personal experience
3. To make inferences while reading
4. To identify tone
5. To build vocabulary in context and learn the word root *-laud-*
6. To develop skill in using *who* and *whom* in adjective clauses
7. To write a historical letter, using transitions to show time
8. To respond to poems and an essay through writing, speaking and listening, and projects

SKILLS INSTRUCTION

Vocabulary: Word Roots: *-laud-*
Grammar: Use of *Who* and *Whom* in Adjective Clauses
Reading Strategy: Make Inferences
Literary Focus: Tone
Writing: Transitions to Show Time
Speaking and Listening: Skit (teacher edition)
Critical Viewing: Connect; Analyze; Draw Conclusions; Infer

PORTFOLIO OPPORTUNITIES

Writing: Interview Questions; Veterans Day; Critical Response
Writing Mini-Lesson: Historical Letter
Speaking and Listening: Debate; Skit
Projects: Timeline; Trench Warfare

More About the Authors

Rupert Brooke remarked, "There are three good things in this world. One is to read poetry, another is to write poetry, and the best of all is to *live* poetry." Brooke did all three in his short life, as he traveled in Europe, rambled the English countryside, and served in the Royal Navy.

Siegfried Sassoon came to hate the war so intensely that at one point he reportedly threw his Military Cross into the sea and would fight no more. Though his protests were treated as shell shock, Sassoon's pacifism found supporters among other soldiers.

Wilfred Owen refused to take a desk job, despite its safety and his deep hatred of war. As a poet, he felt that his experiences of war could reveal deep truths about war to the public.

Guide for Interpreting

Rupert Brooke *(1887–1915)*

Rupert Brooke had striking good looks, personal charm, and high intelligence. Before World War I began, Brooke had already established himself as a serious poet. In 1914, when war broke out, he joined the Royal Naval Division. Tragically, he died from blood poisoning while on a mission to defeat the Turks. Brooke's war sonnets, traditional and idealistic, were among the last from the soldier-poets of World War I that expressed unalloyed patriotism.

Siegfried Sassoon *(1886–1967)*

Born into a wealthy family in Kent, England, Sassoon published a number of pastoral poems and parodies while still in his twenties. In 1914, he joined the army and showed such reckless courage in battle that he earned the nickname "Mad Jack," along with a medal for gallantry. By 1917, though, Sassoon's attitude toward war had changed. He began to write starkly realistic "trench poems" about war's agonies. In 1918, he was mistakenly shot by a sentry and spent the rest of the war in a hospital. Although he lived for nearly fifty years more, he wrote little to match his wartime verses.

Wilfred Owen *(1893–1918)*

Always interested in literature, but unable to win a university scholarship, Wilfred Owen joined the army in 1915 and became a respected officer. He was wounded three times in 1917, and he won a medal for outstanding bravery in 1918. One week before the end of the war, he was killed in battle. Owen was influenced by Siegfried Sassoon after the two met in an army hospital. Having published only four poems during his lifetime, Owen was unknown as a poet until Siegfried Sassoon published a collection of his work, *Poems,* in 1920.

Saki (H. H. Munro) *(1870–1916)*

Despite an unhappy childhood, Saki was known for his witty and humorous short stories. While conventional in some aspects, many of Saki's stories contain dark humor and cynical attitudes, as evidenced in the famous story "The Open Window." When the Great War broke out, Saki refused a commission, preferring to serve as an enlisted man. He was killed in the Battle of the Somme two years after he volunteered for service.

◆ Background for Understanding

History: World War I

Called the "Great War," World War I was fought from 1914 to 1918. It began with the assassination of Archduke Ferdinand, heir to the throne of Austria, but quickly spread to nearly every country in the world. Nations fought either on the side of the Allies (Great Britain, France, Russia, and Italy) or with the Central Powers (Germany, Austria-Hungary, and the Ottoman Empire). The war was long, muddy, bloody, and complex, involving nationalist sentiments, hostile alliances, and arms races. By the time the Armistice, or peace treaty, was signed on November 11, 1918, about ten million people had been killed.

Prentice Hall Literature Program Resources

REINFORCE / RETEACH / EXTEND

Selection Support Pages
Build Vocabulary: Word Roots: *-laud-* p. 241
Grammar and Style: Use of *Who* and *Whom* in Adjective Clauses, p. 242
Reading Strategy: Make Inferences, p. 243
Literary Focus: Tone, p. 244

Strategies for Diverse Student Needs, p. 50

Beyond Literature, p. 50

Formal Assessment Selection Test, pp. 248–250; and Assessment Resources Software

Alternative Assessment, p. 50

Writing and Language Transparencies
Writing Process Model 2, pp. 13–18
Daily Language Practice, Week 33, p. 168
Art Transparency 20: *Troops Resting*

Resource Pro CD-ROM
Includes all resource material and customizable lesson plan for all selections.

Listening to Literature Audiocassettes
"The Soldier," "Wirers," "Anthem for Doomed Youth," "Birds on the Western Front"

The Soldier ◆ Wirers ◆ Anthem for Doomed Youth ◆ Birds on the Western Front

◆ Literature and Your Life

Connect Your Experience

You're thigh-deep in mud, trembling in the darkness, on the alert for the whine of a grenade. Supplies are low, half your friends have died, and disease is beginning to affect "uninjured soldiers." Three more countries have joined the war, and no end is in sight.

World War I's unprecedented devastation and slaughter inspired millions of words—patriotic, indignant, or disillusioned, depending on who wrote them. As you read, look for details about the effects of war on people, animals, and the land.

Thematic Focus: Conflicts Abroad and at Home

The writers of these works were participants in the Great War. As you read, identify each writer's attitude about war.

Journal Writing Jot down some ideas that spring to mind when you think of war.

◆ Literary Focus

Tone

The **tone** of a literary work is the writer's attitude toward the readers and toward the subject, which is primarily conveyed by his or her choice of words and details. In this passage, Rupert Brooke's recollection of England conveys a tone of patriotism and wistfulness:

Her sights and sounds; dreams happy as her day; / And laughter, learnt of friends; and gentleness, / In hearts at peace, under an English heaven.

◆ Build Vocabulary

Word Roots: *-laud-*

The word *laudable* comes from the Latin root *-laud-,* which means "praise." Knowing this, you can deduce that "laudable efforts," which Saki uses in his story, means "praiseworthy efforts."

Word Bank

Before you read, preview this list of words.

stealthy
desolate
mockeries
pallor
laudable
requisitioned
disconcerted

◆ Reading Strategy

Make Inferences

Because many elements of literature—tone, mood, theme—are implied, readers must **make inferences,** educated guesses based on clues within the text.

For example, in "The Soldier," the phrase "foreign field" is a clue that the speaker is away from his native country. Within the poem, there are four direct references to England, giving the poem a patriotic tone. Finally, its theme can be inferred from several clues, including the speaker's observation that his foreign grave would be "forever England."

As you read, make inferences based on clues like these.

◆ Grammar and Style

Use of *Who* and *Whom* in Adjective Clauses

Case is determined by the way a word is used. *Who,* in the subjective case, is used as a subject or a subject complement. *Whom,* in the objective case, is used as a direct object or as an object of a preposition. When *who* and *whom* are used in adjective clauses, the correct case is determined by the word's use in the clause.

Subject in Clause: What passing-bells for these *who die as cattle?*

Direct Object in Clause: A dust *whom England bore, shaped, made aware . . .*

Though students may see modern war in grisly detail on television, few will have heard firsthand accounts of war's battles, destruction, and horror. To prepare students for the emotional demands of this selection's writings, discuss students' sentiments about recent wars. If possible, display some photographs from World War I. Explain that the writers in this section, while perhaps against the war or affected by its horrors, took very seriously their patriotic duty to fight.

Customize for
Less Proficient Readers

Tone can be difficult to recognize, especially for less proficient readers. To assist these students, review with them the Literary Focus: Tone on page 959, and model some examples from the selection texts.

Customize for
More Advanced Students

Encourage more advanced students to use their knowledge of the historical background to expand their understanding of the selection texts. As students make inferences while reading, challenge them to incorporate contextual information into the explanation.

Customize for
Intrapersonal Readers

Urge these students to keep a readers' response log as they read, recording their thoughts and emotions. Also ask them to note examples of their own personal experiences or knowledge of war.

Preparing for Standardized Tests

Reading and Vocabulary Standardized tests contain literary passages that students will have to interpret. Knowing how to make inferences will help them to successfully answer questions about the passages' theme, meaning, and main idea. The Reading Strategy page in ***Selection Support,*** p. 243, focuses on making inferences.

Knowledge of word roots is one of the most successful preparations for deciphering words encountered on verbal reasoning or vocabulary items. The Build Vocabulary lesson for this selection focuses on learning word meaning through use of the word root *-laud-*. For additional practice, use the Build Vocabulary page in ***Selection Support,*** p. 241.

Grammar and Language On some standardized test items, students will be required to complete sentences with the words or phrases suited to a particular grammatical structure. For example, students may have to distinguish the appropriate use of *who* and *whom* in adjective clauses. The Grammar and Style lesson for this selection focuses on this topic. For additional practice, use the Grammar and Style page on Use of *Who* and *Whom* in Adjective Clauses, p. 242, in ***Selection Support.***

Develop Understanding

One-Minute Insight "The Soldier" records a soldier's love for his country and his wish to preserve all that he associates with that country. The speaker catalogs the features of beloved England that he will never see again should he die in battle. His portrait of the Englishness he embodies —the sights, sounds, and very air that have shaped him—poignantly demonstrates the strong bond that can exist between the individual and society.

Writing and Language Transparencies To set context for the selections, display Art Transparency 20: *Troops Resting*, p. 83, for students and have them speculate about the conditions of trench warfare.

◆ Critical Thinking

❶ Interpret Ask: What is "the corner of a foreign field / That is forever England"? *The speaker is referring to his grave on foreign soil.*

◆ Reading Strategy

❷ Make Inferences Ask students how these lines helps them infer the poem's theme. *Students should infer that the speaker feels that he carries England with him no matter where he goes.*

▶Critical Viewing◀

❸ Connect Students may say that the poster and poem express sentiments of patriotism and a longing to be home.

Customize for
Less Proficient Readers
Clarify with these students that Brooke is speaking metaphorically by describing himself as part of England.

Customize for
Verbal/Linguistic Learners
Encourage these students to appreciate Brooke's ability to evoke such powerful images with so few words. Point out the repetition of words such as "dust" and "England." How do these contribute to the overall effect? *Students may say that repetition creates an echo effect in readers' minds, such that these important words stand out.*

The Soldier

Rupert Brooke

❶ If I should die, think only this of me:
That there's some corner of a foreign field
That is forever England. There shall be
In that rich earth a richer dust concealed;
A dust whom England bore, shaped, made aware,
Gave, once, her flowers to love, her ways to roam,
A body of England's, breathing English air,
Washed by the rivers, blest by suns of home.

❷ And think, this heart, all evil shed away,
A pulse in the eternal mind, no less
Gives somewhere back the thoughts by England given;
Her sights and sounds; dreams happy as her day;
And laughter, learnt of friends; and gentleness,
In hearts at peace, under an English heaven.

❸ ▶ **Critical Viewing** How does the sentiment expressed in this poster relate to that in the poem? **[Connect]**

Beyond Literature

Community Connection

Showing Appreciation to War Veterans Citizens who fight in their nation's wars risk their own lives in the name of the entire community. Monuments are one important way that the community recognizes this sacrifice and expresses its gratitude to veterans. A monument may take any durable, public form, from plaques or statues to government buildings or opera houses to parks or museums. Usually there's a dedication to the veterans of a particular war. Often, memorials include a list of the names of the fallen, the most renowned of which is on the Vietnam War memorial in Washington.

If you were on a committee that had responsibility for paying tribute to returning soldiers, what would you suggest be done? What do you think is the best way of expressing gratitude to veterans?

Block Scheduling Strategies

Consider these suggestions to take advantage of extended class time:

- Introduce the context of the poems and essay by reading with students the Background for Understanding on page 958. Then have students read and discuss the questions in ***Beyond Literature*** feature on page 960.
- Introduce the Literary Focus on page 959 before students read the selections. Have students complete the Reading Strategy page on tone in ***Selection Support*** on page 244 and the Reading Strategy questions on page 968.
- Review the Grammar and Style lesson on page 959. Have students complete the exercises on page 968 when they've finished reading the selections. You may also want to display the ***Daily Language Practice,*** Week 33, p. 168, for students to complete before or after reading the selections.
- Allow students to work together or individually to complete one of the activities described in the Idea Bank on page 969.

"If ye break faith —
we shall not sleep"
BUY VICTORY BONDS

Guide for Responding

◆ Literature and Your Life

Reader's Response Do you find the speaker's patriotism touching or sentimental? Why?

Thematic Focus How do conflicts such as World War I affect people's ideas about patriotism?

Speech Write a short speech that might be delivered at the funeral of the speaker.

☑ Check Your Comprehension

1. How does the speaker ask his readers to remember him, should he die?

2. What three things has England given the speaker?

◆ Critical Thinking

INTERPRET

1. Why would the speaker go off to war, knowing he could be killed? **[Infer]**

2. What is the "richer dust" to which the speaker refers? **[Interpret]**

3. The speaker says his heart will become a "pulse in the eternal mind." Explain what he means. **[Interpret]**

EVALUATE

4. Brooke's attitude has been called a "ridiculous anachronism"—something outdated—in the face of modern warfare. Do you agree or disagree? **[Make a Judgment]**

Reinforce and Extend

Answers

◆ Literature and Your Life

Reader's Response Suggested responses: The speaker's patriotism is touching because although he is probably going to lose his life fighting for his country's cause, he still loves his country; the speaker's patriotism is sentimental because no one is truly that patriotic.

Thematic Focus Suggested response: Conflicts such as World War I inspire patriotism by providing a common cause that unites people of a country.

☑ Check Your Comprehension

1. The speaker asks the reader to think of him as being forever a part of England.
2. Suggested responses: England gave the speaker flowers to appreciate, paths to roam, air, water, sun, and the laughter of friends.

◆ Critical Thinking

1. Suggested response: He believed it was his duty and that England was worth defending.
2. The "richer dust" is the dust of the speaker's body and his English experiences.
3. Suggested response: The speaker's spirit has joined other heavenly spirits.
4. Suggested response: Some students will agree, saying that today's governments do not deserve such loyalty. Others will disagree, saying that patriotism is never outdated.

Humanities: Art

War Poster.

This poster depicts a soldier paying homage to a fallen comrade, perhaps the speaker of Rupert Brooke's poem.

During World War I and World War II, posters played an important part in communicating government instructions and propaganda to civilian and military communities. In graphic language, these posters urged people to support the war effort by enlisting, taking war jobs, buying bonds, conserving food, and above all, being patriotic. Like the soldier-poets, war posters spoke to citizens' emotions through their senses.

Use these questions for discussion:

1. How would Rupert Brooke feel about fellow soldiers visiting his foreign grave? *Suggested response: Brooke would be pleased, but he might think that it is unnecessary. He has faith in an "English heaven."*
2. What elements in the poster evoke the England described in the poem? *The flowers, the sunlight, the blue sky, and gentle roll of the land all suggest the much-loved place described in the poem.*

Develop Understanding

One-Minute Insight Both "Wirers" and "Anthem for Doomed Youth" focus on illustrating war's horrors. "Wirers" transports readers immediately into the experience of waiting out a battlefield night, watching with baited breath as the fence-menders risk almost-certain death. "Anthem for Doomed Youth" captures the sad despair of battlefield death that undergoes no loving rituals of peacetime mourning. Together, these poems convey the cynicism war often elicits.

▶Critical Viewing◀

❶ **Analyze** Students should note that the earthtones of the drawing lend a dreary and monotonous air to the scene. All the elements of the scene blend together, suggesting the physical messiness of war and the destruction of humanity's rules.

◆ Reading Strategy

❷ **Make Inferences** Ask students what inferences they can draw about the poet's feelings from the language of this poem. *Students should infer from language such as "unraveling," "twisting," "hammering," and "muffled thud" that the poet feels the war's chaos and is angered by it.*

◆ Literary Focus

❸ **Tone** Ask students to describe the tone of the poem's final lines. *Students should recognize that the tone is ironic. Sassoon creates the irony by trivializing the serious injury suffered by one of the wirers.*

◆ Reading Strategy

❹ **Make Inferences** Ask: Judging from the poem's first line, what can you infer about the poet's attitude toward war? *The poet is bitter about the realities of war.*

◆ Critical Thinking

❺ **Analyze** Ask students why the use of alliteration, such as the usage in this line, is particularly appropriate for this poem. *Alliteration creates a musical effect, which supports the poem's imagery of death services, with chanted prayers and choirs singing.*

Drawing of Tanks, World War I

◀ **Critical Viewing** How does the painter use color and line to convey the realities of war? **[Analyze]** ❶

Wirers[1]

Siegfried Sassoon

❷ "Pass it along, the wiring party's going out"—
And yawning sentries mumble, "Wirers going out."
Unraveling; twisting; hammering stakes with muffled thud,
They toil with <u>stealthy</u> haste and anger in their blood.

The Boche[2] sends up a flare. Black forms stand rigid there,
Stock-still like posts; then darkness, and the clumsy ghosts
Stride hither and thither, whispering, tripped by clutching
snare
Of snags and tangles.
Ghastly dawn with vaporous coasts
Gleams <u>desolate</u> along the sky, night's misery ended.

❸ Young Hughes was badly hit; I heard him carried away,
Moaning at every lurch; no doubt he'll die today.
But *we* can say the front-line wire's been safely mended.

1. **wirers:** Soldiers who were responsible for repairing the barbed-wire fences that protected the trenches in World War I.
2. **Boche** (bôsh): German soldier.

◆ Build Vocabulary

stealthy (stel´ thē) *adj.*: In a quiet, secretive way

desolate (des´ ə lit) *adj.*: Deserted; forlorn

mockeries (mäk´ ər ēz) *n.*: Ridicule; futile or disappointing efforts

pallor (pal´ ər) *n.*: Lack of color; paleness

Humanities: Art

Drawing of Tanks, World War I, c. 1914–1919, Artist unknown.

This drawing was made by an unknown World War I soldier-artist and depicts a battlefield perhaps like the one described in Sassoon's poem. When a country goes to war, artists and writers don soldiers' uniforms along with the other civilians and professional soldiers. This sketch is the work of one such soldier-artist. Its unglorified view of a battlefield shows the shocked and haggard faces of the troops as they follow the ominous shapes of the tanks. This brief and honest sketch is the work of someone who has experienced the horrors of war and paused to record that reality.

Use these questions for discussion:

1. What elements of this illustration capture the immediacy of Sassoon's poem? *Its sketchy, hurried nature suggests that the artist, like Sassoon, paused briefly from battle to record his impressions.*
2. What emotions do both the poem and drawing suggest? *The poem and drawing suggest despair, sadness, and fear.*

Anthem for Doomed Youth

Wilfred Owen

❹ What passing-bells for these who die as cattle?
Only the monstrous anger of the guns.
❺ Only the stuttering rifles' rapid rattle
Can patter out their hasty orisons.[1]
No mockeries for them from prayers or bells,
Nor any voice of mourning save the choirs—
The shrill, demented choirs of wailing shells;
And bugles calling for them from sad shires.[2]

What candles may be held to speed them all?
Not in the hands of boys, but in their eyes
Shall shine the holy glimmers of good-byes.
The pallor of girls' brows shall be their pall;
Their flowers the tenderness of patient minds,
And each slow dusk a drawing-down of blinds.

◀ **Critical Viewing** Does the compassion Owen shows in the poem come through in this photograph of him? Explain. [Analyze] ❻

1. **orisons** (ôr´ i zənz) *n.*: Prayers.
2. **shires** (shīrz) *n.*: Any of the counties of England.

Guide for Responding

◆ Literature and Your Life

Reader's Response Which poem conveys the horrors of war more effectively? Why?

Thematic Focus In times of conflict, what aspects of humanity are ignored?

☑ Check Your Comprehension

1. (a) What are the wirers getting ready to do at the beginning of the "Wirers"? (b) What happens when an enemy flare lights the scene?
2. What does the speaker in "Wirers" think will happen to the soldier named Hughes?
3. According to "Anthem for Doomed Youth," what are the only voices heard mourning the dying soldiers?
4. Where do the "holy glimmers of good-byes" shine in "Anthem for Doomed Youth"?

◆ Critical Thinking

INTERPRET

1. How do the soldiers in "Wirers" feel about the job they have to do? **[Infer]**
2. (a) Who is referred to as *we* in line 13 of "Wirers"? (b) What is the speaker's attitude towards this "we"? **[Draw Conclusions]**
3. Why does the speaker in "Anthem" refer to prayers and bells as mockeries? **[Interpret]**
4. (a) Name the four conventional signs of mourning in lines 9–14 of "Anthem." (b) What do Owen's suggested replacements for these signs have in common? **[Analyze]**
5. Explain how the last six lines of "Anthem" answer the first eight. **[Analyze]**

APPLY

6. Could the messages of these poems apply to other wars? Explain. **[Relate]**

Beyond the Selection

FURTHER READING

Other Works by Brooke/Sassoon/Owen

"The Old Vicarage, Grandchester"; *1914*, Rupert Brooke
The Path to Peace; Siegfried's Journey, Siegfried Sassoon
"Strange Meeting"; *Poems*, Wilfred Owen

Other Works About War

"Boots," Rudyard Kipling
"The Grenadiers," Heinrich Heine

We suggest that you preview these works before recommending them to students.

INTERNET

For more on these poets, go to the following Internet sites.
Rupert Brooke: **http://www.cc.emory.edu/ENGLISH/LostPoets/Brooke.html**
Siegfried Sassoon: **http://www.geocities.com/CapitolHill/8103**
Wilfred Owen: **http:// mason/gmu.edu/~mhuynh/frame.html**

We *strongly recommend* that you preview sites before you send students to them.

▶ **Critical Viewing** ◀

❻ **Analyze** Most students will say that Owen's face seems serious and caring.

Reinforce and Extend

Answers

◆ Literature and Your Life

Reader's Response Suggested responses: "Wirers" vividly conveys war's horrors through a soldier's view. "Anthem for Doomed Youth" conveys war's horrors by focusing on the unceremonial deaths of the soldiers.

Thematic Focus Suggested response: Rules about violence, concern for human emotion and rites of mourning all may be ignored.

☑ Check Your Comprehension

1. (a) The wirers are getting ready to mend barbed wire in no-man's-land. (b) The soldiers stand rigid to avoid being seen and shot.
2. The speaker thinks that Hughes will probably die that day.
3. The only "voices" are wailing shells and bugles calling.
4. The "holy glimmers of good-byes" shine in the eyes of the dead.

◆ Critical Thinking

1. They probably loathe their job and are afraid they will be killed.
2. (a) *We* refers literally to the entire British side but more specifically to its officers and leaders. (b) He wishes to distance himself from them; he condemns their behavior.
3. The speaker believes that prayers and bells would disguise the violent and unnecessary deaths of the soldiers.
4. (a) Signs include passing-bells, candles, drawn blinds, pall, flowers. (b) The replacements are less ceremonial and more human.
5. The sestet lists tender forms of mourning that contrast with the violent events in the octave.
6. Suggested response: Yes, war terrifies its participants, skews their values, and interrupts human rituals.

Develop Understanding

One-Minute Insight "Birds on the Western Front" throws the absurdity of war into sharp relief with a bitingly ironic tone. The narrator describes how battle has—and has not—affected the birds of the combat region. He catalogs the sturdy efforts of barn owls to withstand war's impact, the apparent immunity rooks and other birds have acquired to war's noises and destruction, and the surprising commitment the birds have to their surroundings. Using the birds as a possible metaphor for people, Saki suggests the stubborn determination of the human race to keep building as it is simultaneously destroying.

More About the Author Born in Burma, H. H. Munro, who adopted the pen name Saki, returned there after his English childhood to follow his father's footsteps in the Burma police. Journalism was Saki's second career and included stints as England's foreign correspondent to the Balkans, Russia, and Paris.

Perhaps the English years spent away from his parents and his many travels contributed to Saki's cynical view of the world.

◆ Literary Focus

1 Tone Have students use the details in the first paragraph to identify the tone of this piece. *Suggested response: By using verbs associated with war to describe the actions of bird life, Saki gives the essay a wry, humorous tone.*

Birds on the Western Front

Saki (H. H. Munro)

Considering the enormous economic dislocation which the war operations have caused in the regions where the campaign[1] is raging, there seems to be very little corresponding disturbance in the bird life of the same districts. Rats and 1
mice have mobilized and swarmed into the fighting line, and there has been a partial mobilization of owls, particularly barn owls, following in the wake of the mice, and making laudable efforts to thin out

1. **campaign:** Battles being fought against the Germans during World War I.

Cross-Curricular Connection: Art

War memorials throughout the world honor those who fought for their countries. The Vietnam Memorial in Washington, D.C., was designed by a young college student named Maya Lin. She submitted her idea as part of a national design competition held in 1980–1981. Lin's memorial is a large V-shaped sculpture built within the landscape of Constitution Gardens. Lin says the idea, "just popped into my head . . . while I was visiting the site." From a clay model, Lin envisioned the final polished granite structure. Today, visitors gather daily in front of the memorial to search the inscribed names for a loved one or to honor all those listed.

Have students identify and visit a war memorial in their own communities. What emotions do these stir? How do any words included in the memorials support their artistic intent?

▶ Critical Viewing ◀

❷ **Draw Conclusions** Students may say that the owl stands alone in the darkness, which emphasizes its separateness from human existence.

◀ Critical Viewing How does this photograph of an owl represent the separateness of nature from human existence that Saki stresses in this selection? [Draw Conclusions]

❶ their numbers. What success attends their hunting one cannot estimate; there are always sufficient mice left over to populate one's dug-out and make a parade-ground and race-course of one's face at night. In the matter of nesting accommodation the barn owls are well provided for; most of the still intact barns in the war zone are requisitioned for billeting[2] purposes, but there is a wealth of ruined houses, whole streets and clusters of them, such as can hardly have been available at any previous moment of the world's history since Nineveh and Babylon[3] became humanly desolate. Without human occupation and cultivation there can have been no corn, no refuse, and consequently very few mice, and the owls of Nineveh cannot have enjoyed very good hunting; here in Northern France the owls have desolation and mice at their disposal in ❸ unlimited quantities, and as these birds breed in winter as well as in summer, there should be a goodly output of war owlets to cope with the swarming generations of war mice.

Apart from the owls one cannot notice that the campaign is making any marked difference in the bird life of the country-side. The vast flocks of crows and ravens that one expected to find in the neighborhood of the fighting line are non-existent, which is perhaps rather a pity. ❹ The obvious explanation is that the roar and crash and fumes of high explosives have driven the crow tribe in panic from the fighting area; like many obvious explanations, it is not a correct one. The crows of the locality are not attracted to the battlefield, but they certainly are not scared away from it. The rook is normally so gun-shy and nervous where noise is concerned that the sharp banging of a barn door or the report of a toy pistol will sometimes set an entire rookery in commotion; out here I have seen him sedately busy among the refuse heaps of a battered village, with shells bursting at no great distance, and the impatient-sounding, snapping rattle of machine-guns going on all round him; for all the notice that he took he might have been in some peaceful English meadow on a sleepy Sunday afternoon. Whatever else German frightfulness may have done it has not frightened the rook of North-Eastern France; it has made his nerves steadier than they have ever been before, and future generations of small boys, employed in scaring rooks away from the sown crops in this region, will have to invent something in the way of super-frightfulness to achieve their purpose. ❺ Crows and magpies are nesting well within the shell-swept area, and over a small beech-copse I once saw a pair of crows engaged in hot combat with a pair of sparrow-hawks, while considerably higher in the sky, but almost directly above them, two Allied battle-planes were engaging an equal number of enemy aircraft.

◆ Literary Focus
What tone does Saki use in this description of the rook?

Unlike the barn owls, the magpies have had their choice of building sites considerably restricted by the ravages of war; the whole avenues of poplars, where they were accustomed to construct their nests, have been blown to bits, leaving nothing but dreary-looking rows of shattered and splintered trunks to show where once they stood. Affection for a particular tree has in one case induced a pair of magpies to build their bulky, domed nest in the battered remnants[4] of a poplar of which so little remained standing that the nest looked almost bigger than the tree; the effect rather suggested an archiepiscopal enthronement[5] taking place in the ruined remains of Melrose Abbey. The magpie, wary and suspicious in his wild state, ↓

2. **billeting** (bil′ it iŋ) *adj.*: Designated for sleeping by written order as soldiers' quarters.
3. **Nineveh** (nin′ ə və) **and Babylon** (bab′ ə lən): Two great and prosperous ancient civilizations that fell to ruin and desolation.

4. **remnants** (rem′ nənts) *n.*: Remainder; what is left over.
5. **archiepiscopal** (är′ kē ə pis′ kə pəl) **enthronement**: Ceremony during which the rank and duties of archbishop are conferred.

◆ **Build Vocabulary**

laudable (lôd′ ə bəl) *adj.*: Worthy of praise

requisitioned (rek′ wə zish′ ənd) *v.*: To have requested or applied for with a formal written order

◆ Reading Strategy

❸ **Make Inferences** Ask students: What can you infer about the narrator and his situation? *Students can infer that the narrator is a soldier or at least a firsthand observer in Northern France and that the situation in that region is very bleak.*

◆ Literature and Your Life

❹ Point out the link drawn between the presence of noise and pollution and the absence of natural wildlife. What observations have students made in their own communities of this causal relationship? *Students may mention animals once common but now scarce, specific open areas now occupied by buildings, or illness caused by pollution.*

◆ Literary Focus

❺ **Tone** Students may say Saki's tone is sarcastic and cynical as he notes with bitterness that the rooks have become inured to war's effects.

Speaking and Listening Mini-Lesson

Skit

This mini-lesson supports the Speaking and Listening activity in the Idea Bank on page 969.

Introduce the Concept Have students describe the tone and style of a recent casual chat with friends, perhaps over a meal or while passing the time at school. Discuss how such conversations can reveal the serious concerns and interests of participants, even though the structure is informal. Point out that the birds in the story, if they could talk, would snatch brief chats among the interruptions of war.

Develop Background Before students create and present their skit, urge them to consider the following tips:

- Consider carefully the impact of war on birds before developing dialogue content.
- Incorporate realistic details about bird behavior to create a more believable skit.
- Use dialogue and physical gesture to differentiate bird species and personalities.

Apply the Information Give students the option of including minimal sets, props, or costumes in their skits. Urge them to memorize the general thrust of the dialogue, even if they improvise specific wording. Allow groups some rehearsal time.

Assess the Outcome Evaluate the skits for their insightfulness and the creativity of their presentation. Ask students what Saki might have thought of the various skits.

Customize for
English Language Learners
The long and complex sentences of this essay may pose difficulty for English language learners. Direct them to use punctuation to identify meaningful sentence parts, paraphrase each of these, and then construct an overall paraphrase of the entire sentence or passage.

◆ Grammar and Style

❶ Use of *Who* and *Whom* in Adjective Clauses Point out the use of *who* in this sentence. Ask students to explain its grammatical function and defend its use in place of *whom*. *In this sentence,* who *functions as a subject complement and therefore should be in the subjective case.*

▶Critical Viewing◀

❷ Infer Students may say that the photograph suggests the soldiers are traveling through a destroyed wood. They are forced by their circumstances to ignore the harsh conditions of nature, or to treat it as camouflage or use it as a form of defense. Saki's essay makes a similar point as it describes how the birds adapt to their changed natural surroundings.

◆ Reading Strategy

❸ Make Inferences Students may infer that Saki feels saddened and angered by the effects of war on nature but that he also admires nature's endurance and resilience in the face of war.

1 must be rather intrigued at the change that has come over the erst-while[6] fearsome not-to-be-avoided human, stalking everywhere over the earth as its possessor, who now creeps about in screened and sheltered ways, as chary of showing himself in the open as the shyest of wild creatures.

The buzzard, that earnest seeker after mice, does not seem to be taking any war risks, at least I have never seen one out here, but kestrels[7] hover about all day in the hottest parts of the line, not in the least disconcerted, apparently, when a promising mouse-area suddenly rises in the air in a cascade of black or yellow earth. Sparrow-hawks are fairly numerous, and a mile or two back from the firing line I saw a pair of hawks that I took to be red-legged falcons, circling over the top of an oak-copse. According to investigations made by Russian naturalists, the effect of the war on bird life on the Eastern front has been more marked than it has been over here. "During the first year of the war rooks disappeared, larks no longer sang in the fields, the wild pigeon disappeared also." The skylark in this region has stuck tenaciously to the meadows and crop-lands that have been seamed and bisected with trenches and honeycombed with shell-holes. In the chill, misty hour of gloom that precedes a rainy dawn, when nothing seemed alive except a few wary waterlogged sentries[8] and many scuttling rats, the lark would suddenly dash skyward and pour forth a song of ecstatic jubilation that sounded horribly forced and insincere. It seemed scarcely possible that the bird could carry its insouciance[9] to the length of attempting to rear a brood in that desolate wreckage of shattered clods and gaping shell-holes, but once, having occasion to throw myself down with some abruptness on my face, I found myself nearly on the top of a brood of young larks. Two of them had already been hit by something, and were in rather a battered condition, but the survivors seemed as tranquil and comfortable as the average nestling.

At the corner of a stricken wood (which has had a name made for it in history, but shall be nameless here), at a moment when lyddite and shrapnel[10] and machine-gun fire swept and

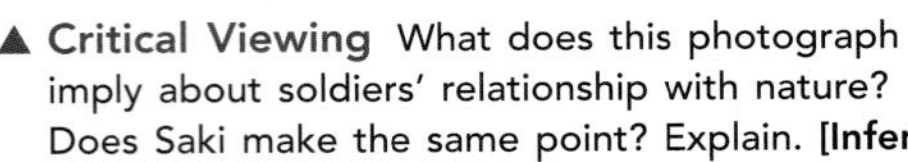

▲ **Critical Viewing** What does this photograph imply about soldiers' relationship with nature? Does Saki make the same point? Explain. **[Infer]** 2

◆ Reading Strategy
What can you infer about Saki's feelings about nature and war from his juxtaposition of images of peace and violence? 3

6. **erst-while** (ʉrst′hwīl) *adv.*: Formerly.
7. **kestrel** (kes′ trəl) *n.*: Either of two small reddish-gray European falcons.
8. **sentries** (sen′ trēs) *n.*: Men of military guard that are posted to warn others of danger.
9. **insouciance** (in sōō′sē əns) *n.*: The state of being calm and untroubled.
10. **lyddite** (lid′ it) **and shrapnel** (shrap′ nəl) *n.*: Lyddite is a powerful explosive, and shrapnel is a collection of fragments scattered by an exploding shell or bomb.

Cross-Curricular Connection: Science

Usually active at night, owls like the ones in the story feed on rodents such as mice and rats. They have highly developed eyesight but also rely on acute hearing to locate their prey, using it, for example, to catch mice in pitch-black spaces. Owls often live close to people, in abandoned or unused building areas.

Like the owl, both kestrels and buzzards are birds of prey. Buzzards, who feed on small reptiles in addition to rodents, survey the hunting ground from a high perch before swooping down to attack their prey on the ground. Kestrels often live in towns, undisturbed by human activities, and search for prey while in flight.

Have students observe the birds in your community. How do they interact with the human community?

raked and bespattered that devoted spot as though the artillery of an entire Division had suddenly concentrated on it, a wee hen-chaffinch flitted wistfully to and fro, amid splintered and falling branches that had never a green bough left on them. The wounded lying there, if any of them noticed the small bird,
4 may well have wondered why anything having wings and no pressing reason for remaining should have chosen to stay in such a place. There was a battered orchard alongside the stricken wood, and the probable explanation of the bird's presence was that it had a nest of young ones whom it was too scared to feed, too loyal to desert. Later on, a small flock of chaffinches blundered into the wood, which they were doubtless in the habit of using as a highway to their feeding-grounds; unlike the solitary hen-bird, they made no secret of their desire to get away as fast as their dazed wits would let them. The only other bird I ever saw there was a magpie, flying low over the wreckage of fallen tree-limbs; "one for sorrow," says the old superstition. There was sorrow enough in that wood.

The English gamekeeper, whose knowledge of wild life usually runs on limited and perverted lines, has evolved a sort of religion as to the nervous debility[11] of even the hardiest game birds; according to his beliefs a terrier trotting across a field in which a partridge is nesting, or a mouse-hawking kestrel hovering over the hedge, is sufficient cause to drive the distracted bird off its eggs and send it whirring into the next county.

The partridge of the war zone shows no signs of such sensitive nerves. The rattle and rumble of transport, the constant coming and going of bodies of troops, the incessant rattle of musketry and deafening explosions of artillery, the night-long flare and flicker of star-shells, have not sufficed to scare the local birds away from their chosen feeding grounds, and to all appearances they have not been deterred from raising their broods. Gamekeepers who are serving with the colors might seize the opportu- 5
nity to indulge in a little useful nature study.

11. **debility** (də bil′ ə tē) *n.*: Weakness or feebleness of body.

◆ Build Vocabulary

disconcerted (dis′ kən sʉrt′ əd) *adj.*: Embarassed and confused

Guide for Responding

◆ Literature and Your Life

Reader's Response Do you find the speaker's tone engaging? Why or why not?

Thematic Focus What effect does war have on wildlife?

Journal Writing How are humans and birds alike in their reactions to war? How do they differ?

☑ Check Your Comprehension

1. Where is the narrator? In what situation does he find himself?
2. How have the crows surprised the writer?
3. How does the war affect the birds in Russia?
4. What is the speaker's explanation of why the female chaffinch stayed on the battleground?

◆ Critical Thinking

INTERPRET

1. What effect has the "mobilization" of the rats and mice had on the owl population? **[Analyze Cause and Effect]**
2. (a) Describe the change that has occurred in human behavior, as witnessed by the magpie (paragraph 3). (b) What does this change imply about the state of humanity? **[Infer]**
3. What do you think is Saki's purpose in writing this description of wildlife in a war zone? **[Draw Conclusions]**

APPLY

4. How might various kinds of birds be affected by a modern war? **[Speculate]**

Beyond the Selection

FURTHER READING

Other Works by Saki (H. H. Munro)
The Chronicles of Clovis, Reginald in Russia, "The Open Window"

Other Works That Respond to War
Suddenly We Didn't Want to Die: Memoirs of a World War I Marine, Elson E. Mackin
All Quiet on the Western Front, Erich Maria Remarque

We suggest that you preview these works before recommending them to students.

INTERNET

You can find additional information about Saki on the Internet at the following sites.

To read an essay about Saki, go to **http: //crl.com/~subir/saki/bio.html**

For a bibliography of Saki's works, go to **http://ftp.cdrom.com/pub/obi/H.H.Munro**

We *strongly recommend* that you preview sites before you send students to them.

◆ Reading Strategy

4 Infer Ask students what they can infer from this sentence about Saki's attitude about war. *Saki, by observing that anyone with wings and sense would flee, reveals that he, too, would like to leave.*

◆ Literary Focus

5 Tone Ask students to explain the irony of this final sentence. *Saki creates irony by contrasting the activity of nature study, a normally peaceful activity, with the image of conducting that study during wartime.*

Reinforce and Extend

Answers

◆ Literature and Your Life

Reader's Response Some students will find the tone amusing; others will be put off by the complexity of the language.

Thematic Focus Suggested response: War damages wildlife habitats and endangers wildlife as it struggles to maintain habits and territory.

☑ Check Your Comprehension

1. The narrator is on the Western Front during World War I, in northern France.
2. The narrator is surprised by the crows' ability to nest and carry on with their lives despite the war.
3. They have been more seriously affected than those in Europe.
4. She has a nest nearby that she doesn't want to desert.

◆ Critical Thinking

1. It has increased the owls' food supply.
2. (a) Humans are now fearful, hiding out in trenches, rather than assuming ownership of nature. (b) Suggested response: Humanity has the ability to destroy itself.
3. Suggested response: Saki wants to share his ideas about human behavior and destructiveness.
4. Suggested response: The birds would see fewer humans in a modern war, but would be more affected by airplanes and bomb damage.

Answers

◆ Literary Focus

1. Suggested response: (a) The speaker is brusque but sympathetic. (b) The references to Hughes as "young," and "badly hit" suggest sympathy but the description of his "moaning at every lurch" suggests the speaker's impassive attitude.
2. Suggested response: Owen's tone is mournful and bitter.
3. Suggested response: (a) The tone is bitter and cynical. (b) A cynical tone helps the writer convey his disgust at war and inspire similar feelings in his readers.

◆ Reading Strategy

1. Suggested response: (a) The speaker is in a dangerous battle situation on foreign soil and suspects he may die. (b) He is discussing his own death and burial at the battle site, while reviewing his cherished memories of home.
2. Suggested response: (a) The soldiers "die as cattle." (b) The phrase helps make the contrast between peacetime mourning rituals and those of the battlefield, giving the poem a tone of bitter recognition.
3. Suggested response: (a) The tone is cynical and mocking. The tone emphasizes the folly and inhumanity of war.

◆ Build Vocabulary

Using the Word Root *-laud-*

1. To show approval by clapping hands or "praising"
2. A statement or action intended to "praise"

Using the Word Bank

Lying in the *desolate* trench, the wounded soldier's *pallor* became more pronounced. The *stealthy* approach of a medic *disconcerted* him. Although the medical supplies that had been *requisitioned* were *mockeries* of usable ones, the medic made *laudable* efforts to save the wounded soldier.

◆ Grammar and Style

1. who
2. whom
3. who

Guide for Responding *(continued)*

◆ Literary Focus

Tone

The **tone** in a work of literature is determined by the author's attitude toward the subject. Because a writer's tone is unstated or implied, examine the style of language and word choice to identify it. By identifying the tone, readers can understand and appreciate how it enhances the work or helps to convey the writer's purpose.

For example, after reading "The Soldier," you may identify the tone as patriotic, yet gentle and loving. Then, when you reflect about the poem's speaker, a soldier fighting on foreign soil, you gain a deeper understanding of the poignancy present in the speaker's tone.

1. (a) What is the speaker's attitude toward "Young Hughes" in "Wirers?" (b) How is this attitude revealed?
2. In "Anthem for Doomed Youth," Wilfred Owen contrasts customary funeral rituals with unceremonious death on the battlefield. In making this comparison, what tone does the poem take on?
3. (a) How would you describe the tone of "Birds on the Western Front"? (b) Explain how the tone reinforces the writer's purpose.

◆ Reading Strategy

Make Inferences

Make inferences as you read to identify a work's tone, mood, theme, and any unstated but useful details. For example, in "Wirers" there are several details that suggest that the wirers' missions were dangerous. Phrases such as "ghastly dawn" and "night's misery" help create a mood of misery. Finally, the last three lines of the poem are cynical and ironic, revealing an attitude or tone of disgust.

1. (a) What can you infer about the speaker's situation in "The Soldier"? (b) What details lead you to this conclusion?
2. (a) In "Anthem for Doomed Youth," who are "these who die as cattle"? (b) How does this phrase help to set the tone of the poem?
3. (a) What is the tone of "Birds on the Western Front"? (b) How does the tone reinforce the theme of the story?

◆ Build Vocabulary

Using the Word Root *-laud-*

With the knowledge that the root *-laud-* means "praise," define each of these words. Incorporate the definition of *-laud-* into each answer.

1. applaud **2.** plausible **3.** laudatory **4.** plaudit

Using the Word Bank

Replace each italicized word or phrase with a word from the Word List.

Lying in the *deserted* trench, the wounded soldier's *paleness* became more pronounced. The *secretive* approach of a medic *unnerved* him. Although the medical supplies that had been *ordered* were *cheap imitations* of usable ones, the medic made *praiseworthy* efforts to save the wounded soldier.

◆ Grammar and Style

Correct Use of *Who* and *Whom* in Adjective Clauses

When ***who*** and ***whom*** are used in ***adjective clauses,*** the correct case is determined by the word's use in the clause. *Who* is used for subjects and subject complements. *Whom* is used for objects of verbs and prepositions.

Practice In your notebook, write *who* or *whom* to complete each sentence.

1. Rupert Brooke, __?__ wrote a poem thought of as his own epitaph, died before seeing battle.
2. Siegfried Sassoon, without __?__ Wilfred Owen would be an unknown poet, was wounded twice in the war.
3. Wilfred Owen, __?__ wrote about "the pity of war," was killed a week before the war ended.

Writing Application Rewrite each pair of sentences as one sentence, using an adjective clause with *who* or *whom.*

1. Rupert Brooke was born in 1887. He was the son of a housemaster at Rugby School.
2. At school, Brooke became involved in amateur acting. He attended King's College, Cambridge.
3. Brooke was a poet of remarkable promise. He wrote the line, "Blow out, you bugles, over the rich Dead!"

Writing Application

Suggested answers:

1. Rupert Brooke, who was born in 1887, was the son of a housemaster at Rugby School.
2. Brooke, who attended Kings College, Cambridge, became involved in amateur acting.
3. Brooke, who was a poet of remarkable promise, wrote the line, "Blow out, you bugles, over the rich Dead!"

Writer's Solution

For additional instruction and practice, use the Pronoun Case lesson in the Nouns and Pronouns unit of the **Language Lab CD-ROM.**

Build Your Portfolio

Idea Bank

Writing

1. Interview Questions Prepare a set of questions about war that you'd like any of these writers to respond to.

2. Veterans Day Veterans Day is celebrated on the anniversary of the signing of the armistice that ended the First World War. In many places, there are no longer Veterans Day parades to honor war veterans. Write an editorial in which you express your views on such parades.

3. Critical Response Charles Sorley said of Rupert Brooke's patriotism, "He has clothed his attitude in fine words; but he has taken the sentimental attitude." Write an essay in response, using "The Soldier" to support your views. **[Literary Link]**

Speaking and Listening

4. Debate With three others, debate this statement: "Some issues are worth going to war over." Two people should take the pro side, and two take the con side. **[Social Studies Link]**

5. Skit If birds could talk, what would they say? Put on a skit in which talking birds discuss how a war between humans is interfering with their everyday lives. **[Performing Arts Link]**

Projects

6. Timeline With a group, create an illustrated timeline beginning with the assassination of Archduke Ferdinand in 1914. **[Social Studies Link]**

7. Trench Warfare Learn more about trench warfare during World War I, focusing on a soldier's daily life, and present your findings to your class. Consult Paul Fussell's *The Great War and Modern Memory.* **[Social Studies Link]**

Writing Mini-Lesson

Historical Letter

During World War I, soldiers maintained links with home by writing letters. In their letters, they no doubt talked about the past (their memories of home), the present (what it's like on the battlefront), and the future (how much they longed to get home). Put yourself in the place of a soldier at war, and write a letter home to a family member.

As you describe events, use transitions to show how these events are related in time.

Writing Skills Focus: Transitions to Show Time

All types of writing, from personal letters to legal documents, benefit from use of **transitions** to connect and clarify the relationship of events in time. As you write your letter, use transitions such as *first, then,* and *finally* to link events in time.

Follow these strategies as you write.

Prewriting Decide on your character (are you an officer, a pilot, a wirer, a foot-soldier?) and on the recipient of your letter (a sibling, a friend, a parent). Make a three-column table with these headings: *Past, Present, Future.* Under each heading, jot down a few ideas for your letter.

Drafting Using a standard letter format, draft your letter home, describing events your character has seen and expressing hopes for the future. Use transition words, such as *first, next, then, after that,* and *later* to indicate the order in which events happened or will happen.

Revising Show your letter to a classmate and ask whether the time transitions are clear and if any sections need better development. Add any details and transitions that might make your letter easier to understand.

Idea Bank

Customizing for *Performance Levels*

Following are suggestions for matching Idea Bank topics with your students' performance levels:

- Less Advanced Students: 1, 2, 6
- Average Students: 4, 5
- More Advanced Students: 3, 7

Customizing for *Learning Modalities*

Following are suggestions for matching Idea Bank topics with your students' learning modalities:

- Visual/Spatial: 6
- Verbal/Linguistic: 2, 3, 4, 7
- Interpersonal: 1, 4, 5

Writing Mini-Lesson

Refer students to the Writing Process Handbook, page 1189, for instruction on the writing process, and page 1191 for further information on description.

Writing and Language Transparencies Use Writing Process Model 2: Descriptive and Observational Writing, pp. 13–18, to model the drafting and revising process of a piece of descriptive writing.

Sourcebook

Have students use Chapter 1, Description, pp. 1–29, for additional support. The chapter includes an extensive instruction and tips for gathering descriptive details.

✓ ASSESSMENT OPTIONS

Formal Assessment, Selection Test, pp. 248–250, and Assessment Resources Software. The selection test is designed so that it can be easily customized to the performance levels of your students.

Alternative Assessment, p. 50, includes options for less advanced students, more advanced students, musical/rhythmic learners, verbal/linguistic learners, and visual/spatial learners.

PORTFOLIO ASSESSMENT

Use the following rubrics in the ***Alternative Assessment*** booklet to assess student writing:
Veterans Day: Persuasion Rubric, p. 106
Critical Response: Literary Analysis/Interpretation Rubric, p. 113
Writing Mini-Lesson: Description Rubric, p. 98

Prepare and Engage

OBJECTIVES

1. To read, comprehend, and interpret speeches
2. To relate speeches to personal experience
3. To identify main points and support while reading speeches
4. To identify the purpose behind and elements of a speech
5. To build vocabulary in context and learn the word root *-dur-*
6. To recognize and develop skill in using parallel structure
7. To write a press release, anticipating questions
8. To respond to speeches through writing, speaking and listening, and projects

SKILLS INSTRUCTION

Vocabulary: Word Roots: *-dur-*
Grammar: Parallel Structure
Reading Strategy: Identify Main Points and Support
Literary Focus: Speech
Writing: Anticipating Questions
Speaking and Listening: Speech (teacher edition)
Critical Viewing: Compare and Contrast; Draw Conclusions

PORTFOLIO OPPORTUNITIES

Writing: Reporting on a Speech; Dialogue; Comparison-and-Contrast Essay
Writing Mini-Lesson: Press Release
Speaking and Listening: Speech; Panel Discussion
Projects: Leaders on Film; Gandhi's Legacy

More About Churchill
Winston Churchill stood up to critics in the British government as staunchly as he later encouraged his people to resist Germany's invasion. Several times in and out of government service Churchill was often far from popular. He seemed to thrive on crises, all of which prepared him to lead his nation through its greatest crisis—World War II. (Further information about Gandhi appears on page 975.)

Guide for Interpreting

Winston Churchill *(1874–1965)*

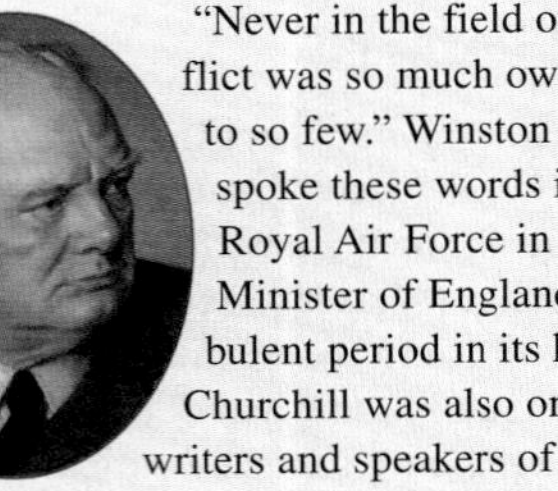

"Never in the field of human conflict was so much owed by so many to so few." Winston Churchill spoke these words in tribute to the Royal Air Force in 1940. Prime Minister of England during a turbulent period in its history, Churchill was also one of the finest writers and speakers of his time.

Churchill the Warrior Directly descended from the dukes of Marlborough, Churchill was educated at Harrow and the Royal Military College at Sandhurst. After serving in Cuba, India, and South Africa, he was first elected to Parliament in 1900 and went on to play an important role in the government during World War I. During the 1930's, Churchill vigorously criticized government policies, warning against the ominous ambitions of Nazi Germany. He became Prime Minister in May 1940, after World War II had broken out, and went on to play a key role in the eventual victory of the Allies.

Churchill the Writer Amazingly, Churchill found time to write even within a busy public career. During the 1930's, he produced a four-volume historical work on his ancestor, the first Duke of Marlborough. His monumental history entitled *The Second World War* (1948–1954) is now regarded as a classic. In 1953, he was awarded the Nobel Prize in literature.

Mohandas K. Gandhi *(1869–1948)*

Few leaders have had such a decisive impact on their country's destiny as Mohandas K. Gandhi. Although revered as a spiritual force, Gandhi was also a great political thinker and speaker.

Finding a Mission Born in the northwestern Indian state of Gujarat, Ghandi went to London to study law when he was eighteen years old. From 1893 to 1914, he worked for an Indian law firm in South Africa. His experiences there as a victim of racial discrimination led him to join and lead protest campaigns. When he returned to India, he fought for independence from Britain.

Passive Resistance Working fearlessly for the cause of independence, Gandhi gradually developed the principles of his philosophy of *satyagraha,* or nonviolent resistance, which was to have worldwide influence, notably on the American Civil Rights leader Martin Luther King, Jr., and on South African freedom fighter Nelson Mandela. Gandhi devoted himself to improving the lot of India's lowest castes, or classes, and he worked ceaselessly for harmony between the country's two major religions, Hinduism and Islam. India gained independence in August 1947, but to Gandhi's distress Pakistan was established as a separate nation. A little more than five months afterwards, Gandhi was assassinated by a Hindu fanatic.

◆ Background for Understanding

HISTORY: CHURCHILL AND WORLD WAR II

When Churchill gave his first radio address as Prime Minister, France was Britain's only ally in opposing German aggression. Germany had already overrun several other countries. Soon after this speech was delivered, France would surrender. Through the dark days that followed, Churchill's speeches contributed powerfully to British morale.

HISTORY: GANDHI AND BRITISH POLICY

In response to Indian resistance, the British Empire imposed a series of repressive measures, known as the Rowlatt Acts, in 1919. Gandhi urged all Indians to refuse to obey such "unjust, subversive laws." Protest against the Rowlatt Acts led to the Amritsar massacre, in which British troops fired on an unarmed crowd, killing 400 Indians.

Prentice Hall Literature Program Resources

REINFORCE / RETEACH / EXTEND

Selection Support Pages
Build Vocabulary: Word Roots: *-dur-,* p. 245
Grammar and Style: Parallel Structure, p. 246
Reading Strategy: Identify Main Points and Support, p. 247
Literary Focus: Speech, p. 248

Strategies for Diverse Student Needs, p. 51

Beyond Literature
Community Connection: Community Action Advocate, p. 51

Formal Assessment Selection Test, pp. 251–253; Assessment Resources Software

Alternative Assessment, p. 51

Writing and Language Transparencies
Problem/Solution Organizer, p. 107

Resource Pro CD-ROM "Wartime Speech," "Defending Nonviolent Resistance"—includes all resource material and customizable lesson plan

Listening to Literature Audiocassettes "Wartime Speech," "Defending Nonviolent Resistance"

◆ Wartime Speech ◆
Defending Nonviolent Resistance

◆ Literature and Your Life

Connect Your Experience

If you've ever stood up publicly for something you believed in, you took a risk. Even if you didn't risk injury, standing up for your beliefs—especially against prevailing opinion—could have caused you to lose popularity. In these selections, you'll see that the world leaders Churchill and Gandhi took substantial risks to assert their beliefs.

Journal Writing On a page in your notebook, freewrite about a person you admire, living or dead, who took a courageous stand for a cause or belief.

Thematic Focus: Conflicts Abroad and at Home

Notice what these speeches reveal about two of the most important conflicts Britain experienced during the twentieth century.

◆ Build Vocabulary

Word Roots: *-dur-*

You will find the word *endurance* in Churchill's wartime speech. The Latin root *-dur-* means "hard." A synonym for *endurance* would be "toughness," the ability to withstand pain, fatigue, or wear.

Word Bank

Before you read, preview this list of words from the speeches.

intimidated
endurance
formidable
invincible
retaliate
disaffection
diabolical
extenuating
excrescence

◆ Grammar and Style

Parallel Structure

Parallel structure is the use of the same grammatical form or pattern to express coordinate ideas. For example, Churchill uses parallel prepositional phrases early in his speech:

> I speak to you for the first time as Prime Minister in a solemn hour for the life *of our country, of our Empire, of our Allies,* and, above all, *of the cause of* Freedom.

Parallel structure contributes to clarity and smoothness in writing. These qualities, in turn, make parallel structures easy to remember and therefore especially effective in persuasive writing or speaking. Look for other examples of parallelism in these speeches.

◆ Literary Focus

Speech

The general purpose of a **speech**, whether it sets out to inform, entertain, or persuade, is to get and maintain the interest of an audience. Organization and clarity are paramount in achieving this goal. The speaker's delivery—pitch, rate, rhythm, and inflection—also plays an important role in audience response.

Winston Churchill delivered his wartime speech over the radio, while Gandhi spoke in a packed Indian courtroom. The purpose of each speech was to persuade. Notice the different strategies each speaker used to achieve this purpose.

◆ Reading Strategy

Identify Main Points and Support

Both Churchill and Gandhi deal with complex issues in their speeches. Both speakers, however, had a knack for presenting a few **main points** clearly and then using well-selected facts, examples, or reasons to **support** those points.

As you read these speeches, pause at the beginning of each paragraph to identify the speaker's main points. Then note the supporting details or arguments for each main idea.

Interest Grabber Present either or both of these scenarios to students:

(a) You're a leader of a country that's been at war for two years. Many casualties have been suffered, and the war is turning against you. The optimism with which your people began the war is fading fast, yet you need to persuade the people to fight on—to boost their morale. What do you say, and how do you say it?

(b) You're facing a long jail sentence for protesting mistreatment of your people. You are guilty of the crime but you want to make sure that people understand the cause for which you are fighting. You also hope to inspire your people to continue the fight while you're imprisoned. What do you say, and how do you say it?

Point out to students that both Churchill and Gandhi were impassioned, effective political speakers. Have students look for evidence of their oratorical skills as they read.

Customize for *Less Proficient Readers*

Less proficient readers may find the dense language and contextual references of these speeches difficult. Urge these students to decrease their reading pace as they read the material and to restate paragraphs in their own words for clarity.

Customize for *More Advanced Readers*

To help more advanced students appreciate the subtle persuasive techniques in these speeches, urge them to listen to and analyze the selection audiotapes. Have students identify ways in which variations in emphasis, tone, and cadence contribute to each speech's overall impact.

Preparing for Standardized Tests

Reading and Vocabulary Critical reading skills such as identifying the main points and support within a literary work will help students as they take standardized tests. For example, students may be required to read a passage and choose the main idea from an array of choices.

Students' ability to recognize and decipher unfamiliar words will improve their performance on vocabulary and analogy portions of standardized tests. The Build Vocabulary lesson for this selection focuses on learning word meaning through the use of the word root *-dur-*. Students can apply this skill to vocabulary, verbal reasoning, and reading comprehension items. For additional practice, use the Build Vocabulary page in ***Selection Support,*** p. 245.

Grammar and Language The ability to recognize parallel structures will help students to correctly complete fill-in-the-blank grammatical items. The Grammar and Style lesson for this selection focuses on parallel structure. For additional practice use the Grammar and Style page on Parallel Structure, p. 246, in ***Selection Support.***

Develop Understanding

One-Minute Insight This speech will captivate students with its dramatic call to bravery and unity. Delivered in May of 1940, when the Germans were rapidly advancing across France, Churchill's speech desperately sought to reassure and inspire the British armed services and general population. He cites his confidence in the skill and courage of both French and British services and his expectation of loyalty and sacrifice by citizens at home. By linking his belief in the possibility of success with the difficulty of the challenges ahead, Churchill demonstrates his extraordinary power of confident leadership.

◆ Grammar and Style

❶ **Parallel Structure** Ask students to identify the parallel phrases in this passage. Then ask them what effect this use of parallel structure has. *The phrases "of our country," "of our Empire," "of our Allies," and "of the cause of Freedom" are the parallel phrases. This parallel structure makes the sentiment memorable, and gives the listener a sense of infinite causes for which they may believe and fight.*

▶Critical Viewing◀

❷ **Compare and Contrast** Students should note that a radio speech makes no allowance for gesture or body language nor gives the speaker any emotional feedback from the audience.

◆ Reading Strategy

❸ **Identify Main Points and Support** Ask students to identify some of the evidence Churchill uses here to support his main point that the British and French armies can win. *Students may mention the gains French soldiers have made behind German lines; their genius for recovery and counterattack; the British endurance and determination.*

Wartime Speech

Winston Churchill

BBC, London, 19 May 1940

▲ Critical Viewing In what ways does the presentation of a radio speech, such as Churchill's, differ from a speech given in person? **[Compare and Contrast]** ❷

❶ I speak to you for the first time as Prime Minister in a solemn hour for the life of our country, of our Empire, of our Allies, and, above all, of the cause of Freedom. A tremendous battle is raging in France and Flanders.[1] The Germans, by a remarkable combination of air bombing and heavily armored tanks, have broken through the French defenses north of the Maginot Line,[2] and strong columns of their armored vehicles are ravaging the open country, which for the first day or two was without defenders. They have penetrated deeply and spread alarm and confusion in their track. Behind them there are now appearing infantry in lorries,[3] and behind them, again, the large masses are moving forward. The regroupment of the French armies to make head against, and also to strike at, this intruding wedge has been proceeding for several days, largely assisted by the magnificent efforts of the Royal Air Force.

We must not allow ourselves to be intimidated by the presence of these armored vehicles in unexpected places behind our lines. If they are behind our Front, the French are also at many points fighting actively behind theirs. Both sides are therefore in an extremely dangerous position. And if the French Army, and our own Army, are well handled, as I believe they will be; if the French retain that genius for recovery and counter-attack for which they have so long been famous; and if the British Army shows the dogged endurance and solid fighting power of which there have been so many exam- ❸

1. **Flanders** (flan´ dərz): Region in Northwest Europe, on the North Sea, includes Northwest France and the provinces of East Flanders and West Flanders in Belgium.
2. **Maginot** (mazh´ ə nō) **Line:** Heavy fortifications built before World War II on the Eastern frontier of France; it did not prevent invasion during World War II.
3. **lorries** (lôr´ ēz) *n.*: British for "trucks."

Block Scheduling Strategies

Consider these suggestions to take advantage of extended class time:

- Have students share journal entries from Literature and Your Life on page 971. Discuss the qualities common to most entries.
- Introduce the Reading Strategy page 971. Have students complete the Reading Strategy questions on page 980 after they've read the selections. Give students further practice by assigning the Reading Strategy page, p. 247, in ***Selection Support.***
- Have students listen to the selection audiotapes or to other recorded speeches given by either Churchill or Gandhi. Ask students how the persuasive techniques in each contributes to the impact of the speech.
- Teach the Literary Focus on page 971 and have students complete the Speaking and Listening Mini-Lesson on page 977 of the teacher edition.
- Have students answer the Critical Thinking questions on pages 974 and 979 after they read the selections.

3 ples in the past—then a sudden transformation of the scene might spring into being.

It would be foolish, however, to disguise the gravity of the hour. It would be still more foolish to lose heart and courage or to suppose that well-trained, well-equipped armies numbering three or four millions of men can be overcome in the space of a few weeks, or even months, by a scoop, or raid of mechanized vehicles, however formidable. We may look with confidence to the stabilization of the Front in France, and to the general engagement of the masses, which will enable the qualities of the French and British soldiers to be matched squarely against those of their adversaries. For myself, I have invincible confidence in the French Army and its leaders. Only a very small part of that splendid army has yet been heavily engaged; and only a very small part of France has yet been invaded. There is good evidence to show that practically the whole of the specialized and mechanized forces of the enemy have been already thrown into the battle; and we know that very heavy losses have been inflicted upon them. No officer or man, no brigade or division, which grapples at close quarters with the enemy, wherever encountered, can fail to
4 make a worthy contribution to the general result. The Armies must cast away the idea of resisting behind concrete lines or natural obstacles, and must realize that mastery can only be regained by furious and unrelenting assault. And this spirit must not only animate the High Command, but must inspire every fighting man.

In the air—often at serious odds—often at odds hitherto[4] thought overwhelming—we have been clawing down three or four to one of our enemies; and the relative balance of the British and German Air Forces is now considerably more favorable to us than at the beginning of the battle. In cutting down the German bombers, we are fighting our own battle as well as that of France. My confidence in our ability to fight it out to the finish with the German Air Force has been strengthened by the fierce encounters which have taken place and are taking place. At the same time, our heavy bombers are striking nightly at the taproot of German mechanized power, and have already inflicted serious damage upon the oil refineries on which the Nazi effort to dominate the world directly depends.

> ◆ **Reading Strategy** What is the **main point** of this paragraph? 5

We must expect that as soon as stability is reached on the Western Front, the bulk of that hideous apparatus of aggression which gashed Holland into ruin and slavery in a few days, will be turned upon us. I am sure I speak for all when I say we are ready to face it; to endure it; and to retaliate against it—to any extent that the unwritten laws of war permit. There will be many men, and many women, in this island who when the ordeal comes upon them, as come it will, will feel comfort, and even a pride—that they are sharing the perils of our lads at the Front—soldiers, sailors and airmen, God bless them—and are drawing away from them a part at least of the onslaught they have to bear. Is not this the appointed time for all to make the utmost exertions in their power? If the battle is to be won, we must provide our men with ever-increasing quantities of the 6
weapons and ammunition they need. We must have, and have quickly, more airplanes, more tanks, more shells, more guns. There is imperious need for these vital munitions. They increase our strength against the powerfully armed enemy. They replace the wastage of the obstinate struggle; and the knowledge that wastage will speedily be replaced enables us to draw more readily upon our reserves and throw them in now that everything counts so much.

Our task is not only to win the battle—but to win the War. After this battle in France abates[5] its force, there will come the battle for our island—for all that Britain is, and all that Britain

4. **hitherto** (hith′ ər to͞o) *adv.*: Until this time.

5. **abates** (ə bāts′) *v.*: Makes less in amount.

◆ Build Vocabulary

intimidated (in tim′ə dāt′ əd) *v.*: Made afraid, frightened

endurance (en door′ əns) *n.*: Ability to withstand pain or fatigue

formidable (fôr′ mə də bəl) *adj.*: Causing fear or dread

invincible (in vin′ sə bəl) *adj.*: Unconquerable

retaliate (ri tal′ ē āt′) *v.*: Return an injury or wrong

Customize for *Visual/Spatial Learners*

Show these students a map of Allied and Axis battlefield movements during 1940. Have them use the map to understand the status of Allied forces at the time of Churchill's speech.

◆ Literary Focus

4 Speech Ask students: What does Churchill want the armed forces to do? Which persuasive techniques does he employ in this passage? *Churchill wants every officer, unit, squadron, and brigade to actively engage the enemy forces in combat—to be more aggressive. Among the persuasive techniques used are strong word choices such as "inflicted," "grapple," "furious, unrelenting assault." He also uses a positive, forceful tone.*

◆ Reading Strategy

5 Identify Main Points and Support Students may say the main point is that Allied air forces are prevailing over the Germans.

◆ Literary Focus

6 Speech Discuss with students Churchill's goal of inspiring popular support for the war and its necessary sacrifices. Ask students how this paragraph serves that purpose. *Students should note that Churchill points out that many people will suffer hardship during the war, but that it is up to everyone to help in the war effort. He identifies for listeners specific ways that they can help. This engages their involvement, makes them feel part of the team.*

Beyond the Classroom

Media Connection

Wartime Communication When Winston Churchill gave his wartime speech, listeners saw no accompanying graphic images of war and destruction. There was no fax, e-mail, or live television broadcast to speed news instantly around the globe. As a result, a speaker could craft a particular description of the situation designed to serve his or her purpose. In Churchill's case, public knowledge of just how bad the Allied situation was would not have helped him reassure the public or inspire its dedication to the war cause.

Have interested students debate the issue that the media should expose wartime atrocities rather than withhold information that may compromise security or damage public morale.

Community Connection Mobilization of a community for war is an enormous and all-encompassing task. Churchill sought more than munitions and funds. Individual citizens were also asked to sacrifice or ration their use of materials needed for weapon production. Rationing restricted either the amount of a product an individual could use in a given period of time or the hours during which particular activities could take place.

Ask interested students to interview older adults about the gasoline rationing of the 1970's or about the broader rationing efforts of World War II. Discuss how these restrictions might both unite and divide a community.

◆ ***Literature and Your Life***

❶ Ask: When have students been asked or asked others to place a common goal above individual interests? *Students may mention athletic teams requiring coordinated efforts or social or political action in the interest of a community goal.*

◆ Literary Focus

❷ **Speech** Students should note the parallelism in "unless we conquer, as conquer we must; as conquer we shall."

Reinforce and Extend

Answers

◆ ***Literature and Your Life***

Reader's Response Suggested responses: Yes, his words exude confidence and stir listeners by including them in a common agenda; no, the language is too complex for a modern listener to follow.

Thematic Focus According to Churchill, Germany was the aggressor while Britain was defending itself.

☑ **Check Your Comprehension**

1. The Germans have broken through France's Maginot Line and are advancing.
2. Churchill mentions France's ability to recover and counterattack, the quality of their leaders, and the contributions of each soldier.
3. Churchill prepares them for Germany's attack on Great Britain.

◆ Critical Thinking

1. Weapons increase the army's fighting strength, replace wastage, and increase confidence.
2. (a) The tone is urgent and dramatic, but composed. (b) His commanding tone indicates that he isn't taking his people's support for granted.
3. (a) Suggested response: Examples include the coming German assault on Great Britain and the fate of peoples conquered by the Germans. (b) Churchill pits himself against the Germans along with British citizens. He uses religious language to stir citizens' consciences.
4. Possible responses: Politicians and coaches give rallying speeches.

means. That will be the struggle. In that supreme emergency we shall not hesitate to take every step, even the most drastic, to call forth from our people the last ounce and the last inch of effort of which they are capable. The interests of property, the hours of labor,
❶ are nothing compared with the struggle for life and honor, for right and freedom, to which we have vowed ourselves.

I have received from the Chiefs of the French Republic, and in particular from its indomitable Prime Minister, M. Reynaud, the most sacred pledges that whatever happens they will fight to the end, be it bitter or be it glorious. Nay, if we fight to the end, it can only be glorious.

Having received His Majesty's commission, I have found an administration of men and women of every party and of almost every point of view. We have differed and quarreled in the past; but now one bond unites us all—to wage war until victory is won, and never to surrender ourselves to servitude and shame, whatever the cost and the agony may be. This is one of the most awe-striking periods in the long history of France and Britain. It is also beyond doubt the most sublime. Side by side, unaided except by their kith and kin in the great Dominions and by the wide Empires which rest beneath their shield—side by side, the British and French peoples have advanced to rescue not only Europe but mankind from the foulest and most soul-destroying tyranny which has ever darkened and stained the pages of history. Behind them—behind us—behind the armies and fleets of Britain and France—gather a group of shattered States and bludgeoned races: the Czechs, the Poles, the Norwegians, the Danes, the Dutch, the Belgians—upon all of whom the long night of barbarism will descend, unbroken even by a star of hope, unless we conquer, as conquer we must; as conquer we shall.

> **◆ Literary Focus**
> What examples of parallelism can you find in the last sentence of this paragraph? ❷

Today is Trinity Sunday. Centuries ago words were written to be a call and a spur to the faithful servants of Truth and Justice; 'Arm yourselves, and be ye men of valor, and be in readiness for the conflict; for it is better for us to perish in battle than to look upon the outrage of our nation and our altar. As the Will of God is in Heaven, even so let it be.'

Guide for Responding

◆ ***Literature and Your Life***

Reader's Response Do Churchill's words still have the power to stir a listener? Explain.

Thematic Focus How clear were right and wrong in Britain's conflict with Germany? Explain.

☑ **Check Your Comprehension**

1. What new development in the war does Churchill report at the beginning of his speech?
2. What evidence does he use to support his confidence in the French?
3. For what future crisis does Churchill prepare his audience?

◆ Critical Thinking

INTERPRET

1. What arguments does Churchill use to support his call for more weapons? **[Analyze]**
2. (a) Describe the tone of this speech. (b) Judging from this tone, how confident is Churchill in his public support? Explain. **[Infer]**
3. (a) Give two examples in which Churchill describes the terror of war. (b) In each case, explain how his words work persuasively. **[Interpret]**

EXTEND

4. Name a career in which one gives speeches to rally the support of others. Explain your answer. **[Career Link]**

Beyond the Selection

FURTHER READING

Other Works by Winston Churchill

Onwards to Victory; My African Journey; The Second World War

Other Works Relating to World War II

Paris, Nathan Aaseng

London, Michael Kronenwetter

The Big Three: Churchill, Roosevelt, and Stalin in Peace and War, Deborah Dwork

We suggest that you preview these works before recommending them to students.

INTERNET

You can find additional information about Sir Winston Churchill at the following sites.

To read other speeches by Churchill, go to **http://www.empirenet.com/~rdaeley/authors/churchill.html**

For access to Churchill's archives, go to **http://www.ucalgary.ca/library/SpecColl/churchil.htm**

We *strongly recommend* that you preview sites before you send students to them.

Defending Nonviolent Resistance

Mohandas K. Gandhi

The following speech was given by Mohandas Gandhi before he was sentenced to six years in prison for stirring up rebellion. Gandhi, India's spiritual leader, worked to achieve political goals through nonviolent resistance. Through boycotts and passive refusal, he helped India gain freedom from British rule.

Before I read this statement, I would like to state that I entirely endorse the learned advocate general's remarks in connection with my humble self. I think that he was entirely fair to me in all the statements that he has made, because it is very true, and I have no desire whatsoever to conceal from this court the fact that to preach disaffection toward the existing system of government has become almost a passion with me; ❶ and the learned advocate general is also entirely in the right when he says that my preaching of disaffection did not commence with my connection with *Young India*, but that it commenced much earlier; and in the statement that I am about to read, it will be my painful duty to admit before this court that it commenced much earlier than the period stated by the advocate general. It is the most painful duty with me, but I have to discharge that duty knowing the responsibility that rests upon my shoulders, and I wish to endorse all the blame that the learned advocate general has thrown on my shoulders, in connection with the Bombay occurrences, Madras occurrences, and the Chauri Chaura occurrences. Thinking over these deeply and sleeping over them night after night, it is impossible for me to dissociate myself from the diabolical crimes of Chauri Chaura or the mad outrages of Bombay. He is quite right when he says that as a man of responsibility, a man having received a fair share of education, having had a fair share of experience of this world, I should have known the consequences of every one of my acts. I know that I was playing with fire. I ran the risk, and if I was set free, I would still do the same. I have felt it this morning that I would have failed in my duty, if I did not say what I said here just now. ❷

> ◆ **Reading Strategy**
> Review the first paragraph of the speech and then sum up Gandhi's **main point** in a sentence.

I wanted to avoid violence, I want to avoid violence. Nonviolence is the first article of my faith. It is also the last article of my creed. But

◆ Build Vocabulary

disaffection (dis´ə fek´ shun) *n.*: Discontent; disillusionment

diabolical (dī´ə bäl´ i kəl) *adj.*: Evil

Cross-Curricular Connection: Social Studies

The "occurrences" Gandhi mentions—Bombay, Madras, and Chauri Chaura—were only a few examples of the political unrest India experienced in 1918 and 1919. Under Gandhi's leadership, Indians were boycotting British products as well as institutions such as courts, offices, and schools. Thousands of Indians were willingly arrested as they pursued Gandhi's strategy of nonviolent resistance. Chauri Chaura, where violence did break out, persuaded Gandhi to end the mass protests. He was arrested soon thereafter.

Have students discuss the responsibility leaders have for the effects of protest strategies. How does that responsibility affect Gandhi as he negotiates the penalties he will pay personally?

Develop Understanding

This courtroom statement very calmly but effectively lays out the origin of Gandhi's beliefs and positions. He explains his journey from British supporter and public servant to prime motivator of Indian protest against the colonial presence. He credits experiences such as his time in South Africa where his Indian race made him socially inferior and events such as the massacre at Jallianwala Bagh for revolutionizing his views. Gandhi is proud to seek independence for his people, despite the need to break laws he had upheld, and thus shows his passionate love for his country.

More About the Author
Mohandas K. Gandhi was known as the Mahatma, meaning "great-souled." His legal training helped him in forging alliances and understanding between opposing groups, whether Indian and British or Hindu and Islamic. However, when negotiation failed to heal these rifts, Gandhi several times took a stand by fasting. His first fast in September 1932, while a British prisoner, inspired tremendous popular support. Later fasts in 1947 and 1948 were also effective in gaining political attention.

◆ Critical Thinking

❶ **Speculate** Ask: Why might Gandhi have chosen to begin his speech by calling the advocate general's remarks "entirely fair"? *Students may say that by opening his speech with this compliment, Gandhi means to show that he is reasonable and "entirely fair" himself.*

◆ Reading Strategy

❷ **Identify Main Points and Support** Sample summary: I admit that I have broken the law but I did so knowingly to pursue just goals.

◆ Literary Focus

❶ **Speech** Ask students why Gandhi asks several times to receive the harshest penalty available for his actions. *Students should recognize that Gandhi repeats these ideas for emphasis.*

▶Critical Viewing◀

❷ **Draw Conclusions** Students may note that Gandhi's expression is one of peaceful resignation. Also, he is wearing white, a traditional color of peace.

Customize for
Visual/Spatial Learners
Have these students envision Gandhi in a courtroom making his statement to the judge. Using the rendering on page 976 as a stimulus, challenge students to describe Gandhi's demeanor, tone of voice, and body language, as well as the overall mood he conveys. *Students may describe Gandhi as quiet but self-assured, speaking in an even but firm tone of voice, using very little body language, conveying a mood of peaceful defiance.*

▲ **Critical Viewing** How does this rendering of Gandhi reflect his beliefs about violence? **[Draw Conclusions]** ❷

I had to make my choice. I had either to submit to a system which I considered had done an irreparable harm to my country, or incur the risk of the mad fury of my people bursting forth, when they understood the truth from my lips. I know that my people have sometimes gone mad. I am deeply sorry for it, and I am therefore
❶ here to submit not to a light penalty but to the highest penalty. I do not ask for mercy. I do not plead any extenuating act. I am here, therefore, to invite and cheerfully submit to the highest penalty that can be inflicted upon me for what in law is a deliberate crime and what appears to ❶
me to be the highest duty of a citizen. The only course open to you, the judge, is, as I am just going to say in my statement, either to resign your post or inflict on me the severest penalty, if

you believe that the system and law you are assisting to administer are good for the people. I do not expect that kind of conversation, but by the time I have finished with my statement, you will perhaps have a glimpse of what is raging within my breast to run this maddest risk which a sane man can run.

I owe it perhaps to the Indian public and to the public in England to placate[1] which this prosecution is mainly taken up that I should explain why from a staunch loyalist and cooperator I have become an uncompromising disaffectionist and non-cooperator. To the court too I should say why I plead guilty to the charge of promoting disaffection toward the government established by law in India.

> ◆ Reading Strategy
> 3 What is the **main point** that Gandhi introduces in this section of the speech?

4 My public life began in 1893 in South Africa in troubled weather. My first contact with British authority in that country was not of a happy character. I discovered that as a man and as an Indian I had no rights. More correctly, I discovered that I had no rights as a man because I was an Indian.

But I was not baffled. I thought that this treatment of Indians was an excrescence upon a system that was intrinsically and mainly good. I gave the government my voluntary and hearty cooperation, criticizing it freely where I felt it was faulty but never wishing its destruction.

5 Consequently, when the existence of the empire was threatened in 1899 by the Boer challenge,[2] I offered my services to it, raised a volunteer ambulance corps, and served at several actions that took place for the relief of Ladysmith. Similarly in 1906, at the time of the Zulu revolt, I raised a stretcher-bearer party and served till the end of the "rebellion." On both these occasions I received medals and was even mentioned in dispatches. For my work in South Africa I was given by Lord Hardinge a Kaiser-i-Hind Gold Medal. When the war broke out in 1914 between England and Germany,[3] I raised a volunteer ambulance corps in London consisting of the then resident Indians in London, chiefly students. Its work was acknowledged by the authorities to be valuable. Lastly, in India, when a special appeal was made at the War Conference in Delhi in 1918 by Lord Chelmsford[4] for recruits, I struggled at the cost of my health to raise a corps in Kheda, and the response was being made when the hostilities ceased and orders were received that no more recruits were wanted. In all these efforts at service I was actuated by the belief that it was possible by such services to gain a status of full equality in the empire for my countrymen. 5

The first shock came in the shape of the Rowlatt Act,[5] a law designed to rob the people of all real freedom. I felt called upon to lead an intensive agitation against it. Then followed the Punjab horrors beginning with the massacre at Jallianwala Bagh[6] and culminating in crawling orders, public floggings, and other indescribable humiliations. I discovered too that the plighted word of the prime minister to the Mussulmans of India regarding the integrity of Turkey and the holy places of Islam was not likely to be fulfilled. But in spite of the forebodings and the grave warnings of friends, at the Amritsar Congress in 1919, I fought for cooperation and working with the Montagu-Chelmsford reforms,[7] hoping that the prime minister would redeem his promise to the Indian Mussulmans, that the Punjab wound would be healed, and that the re-

1. **placate** (plā´ kāt) *v.*: To stop from being angry.
2. **Boer challenge:** Rebellion in South Africa against British rule; the British suppressed the rebellion in 1902 after resorting to guerrilla warfare.
3. **the war . . . between England and Germany:** World War I.
4. **Lord Chelmsford:** Viceroy or governor as representative of Edwin Montagu, Secretary of State.
5. **Rowlatt Act:** Series of repressive acts that limited the powers of the Indian people.
6. **the massacre at Jallianwala Bagh:** Under orders of General R. H. Dyer, fifty British soldiers opened fire on a crowd of peaceful Indians, firing 1,650 rounds of ammunition. The general was dismissed from his duties.
7. **Montagu-Chelmsford reforms:** Formally known as The Government of India Act of 1919; an attempt to slowly place power in Indian hands.

◆ Build Vocabulary

extenuating (ek sten´ yo͞o āt´iŋ) *adj.*: Lessening the seriousness of; excusing

excrescence (eks kres´ əns) *n.*: Abnormal or disfiguring outgrowth

◆ Reading Strategy

3 Identify Main Points and Support Students should note that Gandhi introduces an explanation of his beliefs and how they evolved over time.

◆ Background for Understanding

4 Under the South African policy known as apartheid, peoples of different races were kept apart. Indians were grouped under the heading Asiastics. As non-whites, Asiastics were restricted from various occupations, could not vote, and were prohibited from marrying whites. After decades of pressure from within and without, apartheid finally ended in South Africa in the early 1990's.

◆ Reading Strategy

5 Identify Main Points and Support Ask students to note some of the details Gandhi uses to support this main point. *Students may mention any of the services Gandhi undertakes for the British government, either in South Africa or in India.*

Customize for *Less Proficient Readers*
Clarify with these students that while Gandhi is accepting, even inviting, a heavy penalty for breaking the law, he believes his actions were correct and justifiable. He isn't expressing contrition, rather he is accepting responsibility for his protests. Discuss how Gandhi's tone—of polite resignation—supports this position.

Speaking and Listening Mini-Lesson

Speech
This mini-lesson supports the Speaking and Listening activity on page 981.

Introduce the Concept Discuss with students the features of an effective speech, inviting them to cite recent examples from television or radio. Point out that effective speeches use persuasive techniques such as vivid language, parallel structure, clearly stated main ideas, and support or evidence that bolsters those ideas.

Develop Background Before students present their speeches, urge them to consider and review the following suggestions:

- Pacing and emphasis should derive from the speech text, using the main points as a structural outline. Main points should be supported with evidence.
- Devices such as repetition, rhetorical questions, allusions or other references, and parallel structure make speeches interesting and memorable.
- Effective speakers articulate clearly and audibly without shouting.

Apply the Information Encourage students to practice their speech presentations several times before a mirror or family audience, inviting feedback on style and impact.

Assess the Outcome Have all students evaluate speeches for effectiveness, clarity, and tone. Discuss how well speakers portrayed the characters of Churchill and Gandhi as history describes them.

Customize for

More Advanced Students

To enable more advanced students to appreciate the nature of Gandhi's concern about his fellow Indians, link his analysis to other world situations in which a people has become so accustomed to authoritarian rule that its members lose the ability to lead themselves. For example, point out the frequency with which colonial rule has been replaced by harsh native rule, whether military or civil. Invite students to research some examples from the continents of Africa or South America.

◆ Reading Strategy

❶ **Identify Main Points and Support** Ask students what main point Gandhi is making in this paragraph and how his evidence supports that point. *Students should note that Gandhi believes British rule is sapping India's strength. Supporting examples include using the nation's human and natural resources solely for British gain; enforcing a skewed legal system that stifles Indians' optimism; allowing incredible poverty to continue in regions in which the British presence has destroyed the local economy.*

◆ Grammar and Style

❷ **Parallel Structure** Have students identify the parallel structure in this passage. Ask them: How might this parallelism increase the impact of Gandhi's words? *The parallel structure surrounds the repeated use of "Little do" to begin sentences. Parallel structure makes the text more memorable and therefore more effective.*

◆ Literature and Your Life

❸ Point out Gandhi's understanding of his opponents' genuine convictions. Ask students whether they can appreciate and respect the commitment of those who have different views. *Students may acknowledge the difficulty in truly respecting others' commitment when highly emotional issues are at stake.*

forms, inadequate and unsatisfactory though they were, marked a new era of hope in the life of India.

But all that hope was shattered. The Khilafat promise was not to be redeemed. The Punjab crime was whitewashed, and most culprits went not only unpunished but remained in service and in some cases continued to draw pensions from the Indian revenue, and in some cases were even rewarded. I saw too that not only did the reforms not mark a change of heart, but they were only a method of further draining India of her wealth and of prolonging her servitude.

I came reluctantly to the conclusion that the British connection had made India more helpless than she ever was before, politically and economically. A disarmed India has no power of resistance against any aggressor if she wanted to engage in an armed conflict with him. So much is this the case that some of our best men consider that India must take generations before she can achieve the dominion status. She has become so poor that she has little power of resisting famines. Before the British advent, India spun and wove in her millions of cottages just the supplement she needed for adding to her meager agricultural resources. This cottage industry, so vital for India's existence, has been ruined by incredibly heartless
❶ and inhuman processes as described by English witnesses. Little do town dwellers know
❷ how the semistarved masses of India are slowly sinking to lifelessness. Little do they know that their miserable comfort represents the brokerage they get for the work they do for the foreign exploiter, that the profits and the brokerage are sucked from the masses. Little do they realize that the government established by law in British India is carried on for this exploitation of the masses. No sophistry,[8] no jugglery in figures can explain away the evidence that the skeletons in many villages present to the naked eye. I have no doubt whatsoever that both England and the town dwellers of India will have to answer, if there is a God above, for this crime against humanity which is perhaps unequaled in history. The law itself in this country has been used to serve the foreign exploiter. My unbiased examination of the Punjab Martial Law cases has led me to believe that at least 95 percent of convictions were wholly bad. My experience of political cases in India leads me to the conclusion that in nine out of every ten the condemned men were totally innocent. Their crime consisted in the love of their country. In ❶
ninety-nine cases out of a hundred justice has been denied to Indians as against Europeans in ❷
the courts of India. This is not an exaggerated picture. It is the experience of almost every Indian who has had anything to do with such cases. In my opinion, the administration of the law is thus prostituted consciously or unconsciously for the benefit of the exploiter.

The greatest misfortune is that Englishmen and their Indian associates in the administration of the country do not know that they are engaged in the crime I have attempted to describe. I am satisfied that many Englishmen and Indian officials honestly believe that they are administering one of the best systems de- ❸
vised in the world and that India is making steady though slow progress. They do not know that a subtle but effective system of terrorism and an organized display of force, on the one hand, and the deprivation of all powers of retaliation or self-defense, on the other, have emasculated the people and induced in them the habit of simulation. This awful habit has added to the ignorance and the self-deception of the administrators. Section 124-A, under which I am happily charged, is perhaps the prince among the political sections of the Indian Penal Code[9] designed to suppress the liberty of the citizen. Affection cannot be manufactured or regulated by law. If one has an affection for a person or system, one should be free to give the fullest expression to his disaffection, so long as he does not contemplate, promote, or incite to violence. But the section under which Mr. Banker [a colleague in nonviolence] and I are charged is one under which mere promotion of disaffection is a crime. I have studied some of the cases tried under it, and I know that some of the most loved of India's patriots have been convicted under it. I consider it a privilege, therefore, to be charged under that section. I have endeavored to give in their briefest outline

8. **sophistry** (säf´ is trē) *n.*: Unsound or misleading arguments.

9. **Section 124-A . . . Penal Code:** Gandhi was charged with sedition, inciting people to riot against British rule.

Cultural Connection

Conflict among religious groups in India was a contributing factor to the nation's colonization. Because Muslims, Sikhs, and Hindus were at odds, the British encountered a weakened nation. Hinduism and Islam have highly contrasting approaches to life. Hinduism, which originated in India nearly 5,000 years ago, is based upon the idea that the soul of every creature is reborn again and again. By improving that soul's spiritual state in each successive life, a soul can finally free itself of the cycle. Hindus worship many gods.

Islam, on the other hand, is monotheistic, like Judaism and Christianity. It was introduced to India much later when the Turks arrived in the 700's. Based on the teachings of Muhammad, Islam requires obedience to very specific rules of behavior.

Have students discuss the difficulty of uniting a people against an outside challenge when there is discord among themselves.

the reasons for my disaffection. I have no personal ill will against any single administrator, much less can I have any disaffection toward the king's person. But I hold it to be a virtue to be disaffected toward a government which in its totality has done more harm to India than any previous system. India is less manly under the British rule than she ever was before. Holding such a belief, I consider it to be a sin to have affection for the system. And it has been a precious privilege for me to be able to write what I have in the various articles, tendered in evidence against me.

In fact, I believe that I have rendered a service to India and England by showing in non-cooperation the way out of the unnatural state in which both are living. In my humble opinion, non-cooperation with evil is as much a duty as is cooperation with good. But in the past, non-cooperation has been deliberately expressed in violence to the evildoer. I am endeavoring to show to my countrymen that violent non-cooperation only multiplies evil and that as evil can only be sustained by violence, withdrawal of support of evil requires complete abstention from violence. Nonviolence implies voluntary submission to the penalty for non-cooperation with evil. I am here, therefore, to invite and submit cheerfully to the highest penalty that can be inflicted upon me for what in law is a deliberate crime and what appears to me to be the highest duty of a citizen. The only course open to you, the judge, is either to resign your post, and thus dissociate yourself from evil if you feel that the law you are called upon to administer is an evil and that in reality I am innocent, or to inflict on me the severest penalty if you believe that the system and the law you are assisting to administer are good for the people of this country and that my activity is therefore injurious to the public weal.[10]

◆ **Literary Focus**
In what tone of voice do you think Gandhi may have delivered this final paragraph of the speech? 4

10. weal (wēl) *n.*: Well-being; welfare.

Guide for Responding

◆ Literature and Your Life

Reader's Response If you had been the judge, what impression would Gandhi's speech have made on you?

Thematic Focus What fundamental conflict motivated Gandhi to take a stand against the government established by law in India?

☑ Check Your Comprehension

1. How does Gandhi plead to the charges?
2. What does Gandhi say is the first article of his faith?
3. What did Gandhi discover in South Africa?
4. Identify three reasons for Gandhi's "disaffection" toward the British system of rule in India.
5. What response to British rule does Gandhi advocate?

◆ Critical Thinking

INTERPRET

1. In his speech, why does Gandhi resist the strategy of protesting his innocence? **[Analyze]**
2. Taking into account his ideals, why does Gandhi consider it a privilege to be charged for "promotion of disaffection"? **[Draw Conclusions]**
3. Explain how Gandhi's request that the judge either punish him fully or resign supports the ideals expressed in this speech. **[Support]**

APPLY

4. Is *satyagraha,* nonviolent resistance, a good strategy to take against enemies? Explain. **[Generalize]**

EXTEND

5. Explain why Gandhi's speech would not have been necessary in a society that protected his civil liberties. **[Social Studies Link]**

Beyond the Selection

FURTHER READING

Other Works by Mohandas K. Gandhi
The Story of My Experiments with Truth
The Collected Works of Mahatma Gandhi
"Satyagraha in South Africa"

Other Works Relating to Social Action
The Movement and the Sixties, Terry H. Anderson
Long Walk to Freedom, Nelson Mandela

We suggest that you preview these works before recommending them to students.

INTERNET

You and your students may find additional information about Mohandas Gandhi on the Internet at the following sites. Please be aware, however, that sites may have changed since this information was published.

To read other writings by Gandhi, go to **http://home.earthlink.net/~whimsey/gand6.htm**

For essays about Gandhi, go to **http://www.ultranet.com/~craig/essays/ftwca/ftwca_8.html**

We *strongly recommend* that you preview sites before you send students to them.

◆ Literary Focus

4 Speech Students may say that Gandhi's tone of voice may have been determined and emphatic, but calm.

Reinforce and Extend

Answers

◆ Literature and Your Life

Reader's Response Some students will say that Gandhi's explanation of his "guilt" would convince them that he should go free; others may say that Gandhi admitted his guilt and should therefore be imprisoned.

Thematic Focus Suggested response: Gandhi believed British rule was undermining the Indian people and was fundamentally unfair.

☑ Check Your Comprehension

1. Gandhi pleads guilty as charged.
2. Nonviolence is the first article of Gandhi's faith.
3. He discovered that he was judged inferior and limited in his rights because of his Indian race.
4. British support of South African racial policies, British actions against Indian civilians at Punjab, and British exploitation of Indian workers and resources all explain Gandhi's disaffection.
5. Gandhi advocates nonviolent resistance.

◆ Critical Thinking

1. Suggested response: He wishes to keep the focus on the injustice of the laws he's broken, rather than on whether he has or has not broken them.
2. "Promotion of disaffection" is a badge of Gandhi's peaceful protest philosophy. It shows his desire to pursue his ideals by persuasion rather than force.
3. Suggested response: By asking the judge to adhere to the existing law, he is challenging the judge to acknowledge the law's injustice.
4. Suggested response: It is almost always preferable to violence, but it requires the participation of many people to be fully effective.
5. In a society protecting freedom of speech and ideas, Gandhi would be free to "promote disaffection" without penalty.

Answers

◆ Literary Focus

1. Suggested response: Churchill uses the reference to Trinity Sunday, an important religious day for most Britons of the 1940's and one focused on unity, to call his listeners to their task. He speaks to their belief in common goals of Truth and Justice. He emphasizes the importance of individual sacrifice and heroism. Finally, he suggests that all people who believe in a God must act together.
2. Suggested response: Gandhi's real audience is his fellow Indians and others around the world watching the struggle for independence. He is using the situation of his prominent arrest to gain attention for his cause.

◆ Build Vocabulary

Using the Word Root *-dur-*

1. Something which is tough enough to last a long time
2. Subject to hard or tough pressure
3. The ability to withstand difficult conditions

Using the Word Bank

1. b; frightened
2. a; toughness
3. c; fearsome
4. c; unconquerable
5. b; strike back
6. a; discontent
7. c; evil
8. b; excusing
9. b; abnormal growth

◆ Reading Strategy

Suggested response (for Churchill's speech):

1. The situation is grave.
   a. French defensive lines have been infiltrated.
   b. Allied armies are outnumbered.
2. We can still win the war.
   a. Allied armies have many strengths.
   b. Allied armies and nations are well led.
   c. Allied air forces are superior.
3. We must prepare for even tougher challenges in order to win.
   a. Citizens must support the army and its various needs.
   b. Citizens should expect a German attack and related hardships.
   c. Only unity among all citizens and Allied nations will make victory possible.

Guide for Responding *(continued)*

◆ Literary Focus

Speech

In a **speech,** a speaker addresses an audience with the purpose of informing, entertaining, or persuading. Churchill's and Gandhi's speeches have the dual purpose of informing ("The Germans . . . have broken through the French defenses north of the Maginot Line") and persuading ("Little do town dwellers know how the semi-starved masses of India are slowly sinking to lifelessness"). These purposes are strengthened by the fine writing and oratorical skills of these men—and by the passion that directs these skills.

1. Because Churchill spoke on radio, his listeners could not see him. Nevertheless, Churchill's capacity to forge a bond with his listeners became legendary. Analyze and comment upon his technique for emphasizing unity in the concluding paragraph of his speech.

2. On the surface, Gandhi addresses his statement to the court and the judge. Who is his real audience, in your opinion? Explain.

◆ Build Vocabulary

Using the Word Root *-dur-*

Knowing that the Latin root *-dur-* means "hard" or "tough," write definitions for each of these words:

1. durable **2.** duress **3.** endure

Using the Word Bank

On your paper, write the letter of the term closest in meaning to that of the first word.

1. intimidated: (a) hinted, (b) frightened, (c) risked
2. endurance: (a) toughness, (b) length, (c) stretch
3. formidable: (a) shapely, (b) bullying, (c) fearsome
4. invincible: (a) insane, (b) timely, (c) unconquerable
5. retaliate: (a) surrender, (b) strike back, (c) refute
6. disaffection: (a) discontent, (b) anger, (c) rebellion
7. diabolical: (a) transparent, (b) foolish, (c) evil
8. extenuating: (a) widening, (b) excusing, (c) diminishing
9. excrescence: (a) waste, (b) abnormal outgrowth, (c) delay

◆ Reading Strategy

Identify Main Points and Support

The **main points** of a speech or essay are often found in the topic sentence of a paragraph. Topic sentences usually occur at the beginning of paragraphs. This is often the case in a speech, since a speaker needs to be particularly clear about identifying the main idea for an audience of listeners.

As you read these speeches, you paused to check your understanding by identifying the main points and supporting details. Now choose one of the speeches and outline three of its main points. Under each main point in your outline, list supporting points or examples.

◆ Grammar and Style

Parallel Structure

Sometimes parallel structures follow correlative conjunctions: "Our task is *not only* to win the battle—*but* to win the War."

Parallel structure is the use of the same grammatical form or pattern to express similar ideas.

Practice In your notebook, rewrite each sentence below, correcting errors of faulty parallelism.

1. In Churchill's opinion, either to disguise the gravity of the hour or surrendering prematurely to despair would be a great mistake.
2. Churchill assembled an administration that represented every party and consisting of a complete spectrum of opinion.
3. Gandhi says that he faced the choice of submitting to a harmful system or to run the risk of his people's anger.
4. According to Gandhi, true affection cannot be manufactured or subjecting it to regulation by law.

Writing Application As the judge to whom Gandhi appeals, write a brief speech in response to his. Include two examples of parallel structures in your speech.

◆ Grammar and Style

1. In Churchill's opinion, either to disguise the gravity of the hour or to surrender prematurely to despair would be a great mistake.
2. Churchill assembled an administration that represented every party and consisted of a complete spectrum of opinion.
3. Gandhi says that he faced the choice of submitting to a harmful system or running the risk of his people's anger.
4. According to Gandhi, true affection cannot be manufactured or subjected to regulation by law.

For additional instruction and practice, use the Using Parallel Structures lesson in the Writing Styles unit of the **Language Lab CD-ROM**.

Build Your Portfolio

Idea Bank

Writing

1. **Reporting on a Speech** Write a newspaper report on Churchill's speech. Create a suitable headline and a lead paragraph stating the main point of the speech.

2. **Dialogue** Based on what you know of their beliefs, write a brief conversation between Churchill and Gandhi set at a peace conference.

3. **Comparison-and-Contrast Essay** Churchill's and Gandhi's speeches were both meant to rally support, but they arose from different circumstances. Compare and contrast them.

Speaking and Listening

4. **Speech** Rehearse a part of either Churchill's or Gandhi's speech, experimenting with pacing and emphasis. Deliver the speech to your class. **[Performing Arts Link]**

5. **Panel Discussion** With several classmates, prepare to discuss how Gandhi might have responded in Churchill's position. Choose a moderator, and hold your "discussion" in front of the class. **[Social Studies Link]**

Projects

6. **Leaders on Film** With a small group of classmates, screen a film documenting Churchill's or Gandhi's life. (You might view *Gandhi,* directed by Richard Attenborough.) Write a group evaluation of the film. **[Performing Arts Link]**

7. **Gandhi's Legacy** Research the influence of Gandhi's philosophy of nonviolent resistance on Dr. Martin Luther King, Jr. Write a brief report comparing how the two leaders used this tactic. **[Social Studies Link]**

Writing Mini-Lesson

Press Release

If you were a world leader like Churchill or Gandhi, you'd want your message to get out to the public accurately and in such a way as to encourage their support. To do this, you might write a **press release**—a statement to the news media.

Write a press release that announces a news development and how you are responding to it. The tone of your press release should reflect that you are in control of the situation and are acting on behalf of the people. Your press release should be brief and concise, yet answer any questions or comments you think the media might have.

Writing Skills Focus: Anticipating Questions

Anticipate questions by:
- presenting clear reasons that show you have considered all points of view.
- clearly refuting opposing arguments.
- conceding a point, if appropriate. Acknowledging the wisdom of opposing viewpoints establishes credibility with your audience.

Prewriting After you choose a real or imaginary news development and decide on your reaction, jot down questions the media would ask about your decision.

Drafting As you write your press release, keep in mind that your statement may be rapidly scanned or selectively summarized by reporters. Make every sentence count. Use devices like parallel structure where they are rhetorically effective.

Revising Read your statement aloud to a classmate. Encourage him or her to ask provocative or difficult questions. If your classmate comes up with a good question you haven't anticipated, revise your statement to address that question.

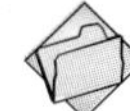

Idea Bank

Customizing for Performance Levels

Following are suggestions for matching Idea Bank topics with your students' performance levels:

Less Advanced Students: 4, 6
Average Students: 1, 2, 5
More Advanced Students: 3, 7

Customizing for Learning Modalities

Following are suggestions for matching Idea Bank topics with your students' learning modalities:

Verbal/Linguistic: 1, 2, 3, 7
Musical/Rhythmic: 4
Interpersonal: 5, 6

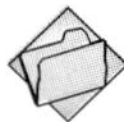

Writing Mini-Lesson

Refer students to the Writing Process Handbook, page 1189, for instruction on the writing process, and page 1191 for further information on expository writing like a press release.

Writing and Language Transparencies Display the Problem/Solution Organizer, p. 107, for students to copy and use as they anticipate questions for their press releases.

Writing Lab CD-ROM
Have students complete the tutorial on Exposition. Follow these steps:
1. Look at the video clip from *Cyrano de Bergerac* in the Audience and Purpose section to learn how different purposes can change the way someone presents information.
2. Use the interactive instruction on gathering details.
3. Create a draft on the computer.
4. Refer to a Proofreading Checklist.

Sourcebook
Have students use Chapter 3, Exposition, pp. 62–95, for additional support. The chapter includes audio-annotated models of a student's expository writing.

✓ ASSESSMENT OPTIONS

Formal Assessment, Selection Test, pp. 251–253, and Assessment Resources Software. The selection test is designed so that it can be easily customized to the performance levels of your students.
Alternative Assessment, p. 51, includes options for less advanced students, more advanced students, musical/rhythmic learners, verbal/linguistic learners, and visual/spatial learners.

PORTFOLIO ASSESSMENT
Use the following rubrics in the ***Alternative Assessment*** booklet to assess student writing:
Reporting on a Speech: Summary Rubric, p. 99
Dialogue: Drama Rubric, p. 110
Comparison-and-Contrast Essay: Comparison/Contrast Rubric, p. 104
Writing Mini-Lesson: Summary Rubric, p. 99

Prepare and Engage

Guide for Interpreting

OBJECTIVES

1. To read, comprehend, and interpret a short story
2. To relate a story to personal experience
3. To predict the effect of setting on characters and plot
4. To relate setting to atmosphere
5. To build vocabulary in context and learn the origin of the word *sublime*
6. To develop skill in varying sentence beginnings
7. To write a description of a favorite setting, using vivid details
8. To respond to the story through writing, speaking and listening, and projects

SKILLS INSTRUCTION

Vocabulary: Word Origins: Sublime

Grammar: Vary Sentence Beginnings

Reading Strategy: Predict Effect of Setting

Literary Focus: Setting and Atmosphere

Writing: Vivid Details

Speaking and Listening: Debate (teacher edition)

Critical Viewing: Analyze Cause and Effect; Speculate

PORTFOLIO OPPORTUNITIES

Writing: Journal Entry; Newspaper Report; Response to Criticism

Writing Mini-Lesson: Favorite Setting

Speaking and Listening: Debate; Music Discussion

Projects: Performing Arts; Coal Mining Report

More About the Author
Much of Alan Sillitoe's writing focuses on those who scratch out a living on the lowest rungs of society's ladder. His understanding of the effects of poverty is shown in this excerpt from his essay on the subject: "The very poor are too busy surviving to want to get on. To get on is something often dinned into them, handed down by the culture beneath which they exist. They are unable to take advantage of it, for to reach next week with clothes on your back, food still on the table, and enough life in your brain to face another week is the most they can do."

Alan Sillitoe *(1928–)*

Growing up poor left a permanent impression on Allan Sillitoe; much of his writing revolves around the struggles of the working poor, those whose labor leads to a hand-to-mouth existence.

A Short Military Career The son of an often unemployed tannery worker, Sillitoe grew up in Nottingham, an industrial city northwest of London. He left school at fourteen and worked in a bicycle plant and a plywood mill. At the same time, he enrolled in the Air Training Corps. World War II ended before he saw active duty, and after four years in the Royal Air Force, he was discharged because he had contracted tuberculosis. His illness entitled him to a pension, which he collected for thirteen years, lasting from age twenty-one until he was pronounced cured.

The Young Writer Sillitoe's small pension enabled him to survive without having to get a job. In his 1996 autobiography, *Life Without Armour*, he refers to this period in his life: "Such an extended period of cosseting merely for doing my duty turned into a much appreciated case of patronage." Sillitoe spent six years in France and Spain, writing and rewriting several books. He ended up scrapping the manuscripts of nine completed novels until he published *Saturday Night and Sunday Morning,* which met with instant success and was later made into a movie starring Albert Finney. For this work, Sillitoe was awarded the Author's Club Prize for the best English novel of 1958. Then, in 1959, he published the short story collection "The Loneliness of the Long Distance Runner,"—perhaps his most famous work. The title story—later adapted for film—tells of a young juvenile delinquent in an English reform school. Sillitoe's early works earned him a place among a group of writers known as the "Angry Young Men" who believed that British social and political traditions had become outmoded.

The scope of Sillitoe's subject matter has broadened to some extent in his later works, though he has remained primarily a chronicler of the working class. He is one of the more prolific British writers of our time, authoring more than forty books, including novels, short story collections, plays, a book of essays, books for children, and an autobiography.

The Story Behind the Story During his childhood, Alan Sillitoe lived for a time in a tiny cottage in Nottingham, England, near the River Leen. After a week of rain, the Sillitoes' cottage was flooded and had to be abandoned. The River Leen and the cottages on its banks make up the setting of "The Fiddle." Perhaps the people living in the houses served as inspiration for its characters.

◆ Background for Understanding

CULTURE: SILLITOE'S SETTING, THE COAL-MINING LIFE

This story is set in a town that revolves around coal-mining. The coal industry has been crucial to the British economy for generations, and the conditions in which miners work has been of concern. When coal mining began in England, working conditions were extremely dangerous. Until the mid-1600's, miners were often serfs or paroled convicts whose safety was of little concern to mine operators. The work was done entirely by hand; men crouched in narrow mine seams, digging the coal with picks. Women and children dragged the coal to the surface in baskets. Whole families settled near the mines and earned just enough to get by. In more recent years, both working conditions and wages have improved for miners. Yet, as this story reveals, the miners and their families still led difficult lives.

Prentice Hall Literature Program Resources

REINFORCE / RETEACH / EXTEND

Selection Support Pages
Build Vocabulary: Word Origins: *Sublime,* p. 249
Grammar and Style: Vary Sentence Beginnings, p. 250
Reading Strategy: Predict Effect of Setting, p. 251
Literary Focus: Setting and Atmosphere, p. 252

Strategies for Diverse Student Needs, p. 52

Beyond Literature
Science Connection: Coal, p. 52

Formal Assessment Selection Test, pp. 254–256; Assessment Resources Software

Alternative Assessment, p. 52

Writing and Language Transparencies
Descriptive and Observational Writing, pp. 13–16

Resource Pro CD-ROM
"The Fiddle"—includes all resource material and customizable lesson plan

Listening to Literature Audiocassettes
"The Fiddle"

The Fiddle

◆ Literature and Your Life

CONNECT YOUR EXPERIENCE

Do you feel especially carefree on a sunny spring day—or especially gloomy when you pass down a particular dark side street? Some settings, such as the bleak coal mines in which a character in this story works, can have a profound effect on a person's outlook on life. As you read, think about how the setting of this story would affect *your* outlook on life.

Journal Writing Jot down the titles of some literary works with memorable settings. What moods do they evoke?

THEMATIC FOCUS: CONFLICTS ABROAD AND AT HOME

As you read, compare the conflicts faced by English laborers with those faced by laborers in the United States today.

◆ Reading Strategy

PREDICT EFFECT OF SETTING

A story's setting often has a major impact on the characters and the plot. The setting is likely to shape the characters' personalities and outlooks, and may affect or limit the courses of action that characters can consider. As you read this story, predict how the **setting**—an English coal-mining town in the 1930's—will affect the characters' lives and shape the options they have available. You can use a chart like this to note your observations and your predictions.

Details of Setting	Effect on Characters	Predictions

◆ Build Vocabulary

WORD ORIGINS: *SUBLIME*

In his story, Sillitoe uses the expression "from ridiculousness to sublimity." The word *sublimity* is formed by combining the Latin roots *sub-*, meaning "up to" and *-limen-*, meaning "lintel," the piece of timber or stone over a door. *Sublimity* is therefore "the quality of being uplifted or noble."

WORD BANK

Before you read, preview these words from the story.

persistent
obliterate
sublimity
harried

◆ Literary Focus

SETTING AND ATMOSPHERE

The hardships faced by the characters in this story are directly related to the **setting,** or the time and place in which the characters live. In turn, the setting contributes to the **atmosphere**—the overall feeling or mood of a work. When Sillitoe describes the cottages as being "in a ruinous condition" and "isolated," he uses setting to evoke a bleak atmosphere. Be aware, as you read, of other details of setting that contribute to the atmosphere of this story.

◆ Grammar and Style

VARY SENTENCE BEGINNINGS

To make sentences flow together smoothly and to avoid monotony, good writers vary the way in which they begin their sentences. Look at some of the different ways Sillitoe begins his sentences:

Introductory Adverb *Sometimes* they could almost paddle.

Introductory Phrase *In that case* there was no telling where you'd end up.

Introductory Clause *When they did get Ted Griffin . . .*

Tell students that some authors, Sillitoe among them, use setting as if it were a character in their stories. Ask them to consider their own environment—the region, the neighborhood, the school, their home—and think about its effect on a story they might write. Have students write ten sentences about the local environment to show the impact its features would have on their piece. Invite students to share their ideas.

Customize for
Less Proficient Readers

Help readers to clarify the meanings of the several "Briticisms" Sillitoe uses that are not already defined beneath the text, such as *brilliantined, wash-copper, quid, slice of bluff, collier,* and *queue*.

Customize for
More Advanced Students

Guide students to look for the symbolic meaning of things and places in this story. They can notice, for example, that the fiddle symbolizes beauty and that the River Leen represents freedom, a link to the unknown outside world.

Customize for
English Language Learners

Students may find the slang-filled snatches of dialogue hard to follow. To help students grasp the gist of conversations in the story, read them aloud in your best working-class British accent (or invite a student to do so). Then go over the conversations with students, defining terms or giving synonyms, as needed.

Customize for
Visual/Spatial Learners

Have students imagine the setting in and around Harrison's Row. They can picture the sameness of the drab row houses and dirty coal-blackened workers trudging back from the unsightly coal mines. Help them imagine the commanding presence of huge and grim factories for coal processing, with their smokestacks and railroad sidings.

Preparing for Standardized Tests

Reading and Vocabulary Predicting the effect of setting will enable students to improve their understanding of literature they read. This in turn will improve their performance on critical-reading items on standardized tests. Have students examine how setting enables them to predict the outcome of events by answering the Reading Strategy questions on page 990. For additional practice, use the Reading Strategy page in ***Selection Support,*** p. 251.

Grammar and Language Portions of some standardized tests, such as state achievement tests, require students to write an essay. By varying sentence beginnings, students can make their essays livelier, emphasize relationships among ideas, and make sentences flow smoothly, thereby improving their test scores. The Grammar and Style lesson for this selection focuses on this varying sentence beginnings. For additional practice, use the Grammar and Style page in ***Selection Support,*** p. 250.

Develop Understanding

One-Minute Insight In "The Fiddle" Alan Sillitoe describes the bleak physical setting of Harrison's Row in the coal-mining town of Radford, the views of its inhabitants, and the activities that take place there. In particular, he describes the sacrifice one man makes to successfully escape the misery of the miner's life, and the impact of his decision on his neighbors.

◆ Reading Strategy

❶ **Predict Effect of Setting** Have students imagine the impact of this dreary setting on the people who live there. *Students may say that the sameness of the "ruinous" cottages, the shared backyards, and the monotonous and degrading routines could rob tenants of individuality, curiosity, and hope for a better life.*

❷ **Clarification** Point out to students that the Great Depression that rocked the United States in the years following the stock market crash of 1929 was a worldwide calamity. Money and opportunity were in short supply in Britain and all over Europe.

◆ Literary Focus

❸ **Setting and Atmosphere** Ask students to explain why the author describes the views from behind Harrison's Row. *Students may suggest that he does so to suggest the isolation of the place and to show that the poor can see evidence of wealth just across the river, but cannot attain it.*

◆ Critical Thinking

❹ **Connect** Ask students how the behavior of the river contributes to the sense of trapped isolation in Harrison's Row. *After heavy rains, the river's swift currents make it an impassable barrier.*

❺ **Clarification** Inform students that *district* is an official term for "neighborhood" in Great Britain.

The FIDDLE

Alan Sillitoe

On the banks of the sinewy River Leen, where it flowed through Radford, stood a group of cottages called Harrison's Row. There must have been six to eight of them, all in a ruinous condition, but lived in nevertheless.

They had been put up for stockingers[1] during the Industrial Revolution a hundred years before, so that by now the usual small red English housebricks had become weatherstained and, in some places, almost black.

Harrison's Row had a character all of its own, both because of its situation, and the people
❶ who lived there. Each house had a space of pebbly soil rising in front, and a strip of richer garden sloping away from the kitchen door down to the diminutive River Leen at the back. The front gardens had almost merged into one piece of common ground, while those behind had in most cases retained their separate plots.

As for the name of the isolated row of cottages, nobody knew who Harrison had been, and no one was ever curious about it. Neither did they know where the Leen came from, though some had a general idea as to where it finished up.

A rent man walked down cobblestoned Leen Place every week to collect what money he could. This wasn't much, even at the best of
❷ times which, in the "thirties," were not too good —though no one in their conversation was able to hark back to times when they had been any better.

❸ From the slight rise on which the houses stood, the back doors and windows looked across the stream into green fields, out towards the towers and pinnacles of Wollaton Hall in one direction, and the woods of Aspley Manor in the other.

After a warm summer without much rain the children were able to wade to the fields on the other side. Sometimes they could almost paddle. But after a three-day downpour when the air was still heavy with undropped water, and colored a menacing gun-metal blue, it was best not to go anywhere near the river, for one false slip and you would get sucked in, and be dragged by the powerful current along to the Trent some miles away. In that case there was no telling where you'd end up. The water
seemed to flow into the River Amazon[2] itself, indicated by the fact that Frankie Buller swore ❹
blind how one day he had seen a crocodile snapping left and right downstream with a newborn baby in its mouth. You had to be careful—and that was a fact. During the persistent rain of one autumn water came up over the gardens and almost in at the back doors.

Harrison's Row was a cut-off place in that not many people knew about it unless they were
familiar with the district. You went to it along ❺
St. Peter's Street, and down Leen Place. But it was delightful for the kids who lived there because out of the back gardens they could go straight into the stream of the Leen. In summer an old tin hip bath would come from one of the

1. **stockingers** *n.*: Stocking weavers.

2. **River Amazon:** Largest, most powerful river in South America.

Block Scheduling Strategies

Consider these suggestions to take advantage of extended class time:

- Introduce the Literary Focus with the note on Setting and Atmosphere (p. 983). After students have read the story, have them answer the Literary Focus questions (p. 990) and complete the practice page in ***Selection Support*** (p. 252).
- Ask students to complete the journal activity in Literature and Your Life (p. 983) and discuss their entries in small groups. Alternatively, students may draw on their own experience by doing the Personal Setting activity in ***Alternative Assessment*** (p. 52).
- Instruct students to complete the Science Connection: Coal page in ***Beyond Literature*** (p. 52). Students may also create a bar graph on coal production, as suggested in ***Alternative Assessment*** (p. 52).
- Organize discussion groups in which students answer the Critical Thinking questions (p. 989).
- Students may work on the writing activity of their choice in Build Your Portfolio (p. 991).

Hillside in Wales, *(detail), L. S. Lowry,* The Tate Gallery, London

◀ Critical Viewing What effect do you think this setting would have on residents? [Analyze Cause and Effect] 8

houses. Using it for a boat, and stripped to their white skins, the children were happy while sun and weather lasted.

The youths and older kids would eschew this fun and set out in a gang, going far beyond, to
6 a bend of the canal near Wollaton Pit where the water was warm—almost hot—due to some outlet from the mine itself. This place was known as "'otties," and they'd stay all day with a bottle of lemonade and a piece of bread, coming back late in the evening looking pink and tired as if out of a prolonged dipping in the ritual bath. But a swim in 'otties was only for the older ones, because a boy of four had once been drowned there.

Harrison's Row was the last of Nottingham where it met the countryside. Its houses were at the very edge of the city, in the days before those numerous housing estates had been built beyond. The line of dwellings called Harrison's Row made a sort of outpost bastion before the country began.

Yet the houses in the city didn't immediately start behind, due to gardens and a piece of wasteground, which gave to Harrison's Row a feeling of isolation. It stood somewhat on its own, as if the city intended one day to leapfrog
7 over it and obliterate the country beyond.

On the other hand, any foreign army attacking from the west, over the green fields that glistened in front, would first have to flatten Harrison's Row before getting into the innumerable streets of houses behind.

Across the Leen, horses were sometimes to be seen in the fields and, in other fields beyond, the noise of combine harvesters could be heard at work in the summer. Children living there, and adults as well, had the advantage of both town and country. On a fine evening late in August one of the unemployed husbands might be seen looking across at the noise of some machinery working in a field, his cap on but wearing no shirt, as if wondering why he was here and not over there, and why in fact he had ever left those same fields in times gone by to be forced into this bit of a suburb where he now had neither work nor purpose in life. He was not bitter, and not much puzzled perhaps, yet he couldn't help being envious of those still out there in the sunshine.

◆ Literary Focus What mood is created through these details or the setting? 9

In my visions of leaving Nottingham for good—and they were frequent in those days—I never reckoned on doing so by the high road or railway. Instead I saw myself wading or swimming the Leen from Harrison's Row, and setting off west once I was on the other side. 10

A tale remembered with a laugh at that time told about how young Ted Griffin, who had just started work, saw two policemen one day walking down Leen Place towards Harrison's Row.

◆ **Build Vocabulary**

persistent (pər sis′ tənt) *adj.*: Continuing

obliterate (ə blit′ ə rāt) *v.*: Destroy utterly

Humanities: Art

Hillside in Wales (detail), by L. S. Lowry.

Lawrence Stephen Lowry (1887–1976) is best known for his simple and highly personal industrial landscapes populated with antlike figures. He was educated at the Municipal College of Art in Manchester and the Salford School of Art. This detail, representing Harrison's Row in the story, is from a painting that presents a full panoramic, detached view of a countryside.

Use these questions for discussion:

1. What is the effect of the naive style of the painting? *Students may say that it emphasizes the mechanical, dehumanizing nature of industrial society.*
2. What view of society does the painting appear to present? *Students may say that it presents society as distant, impersonal, and imposing conformity.*

6 **Clarification** Tell students that Wollaton Pit is a coal mine; one meaning of *pit* is "mine."

◆ Reading Strategy

7 **Predict Effect of Setting** Guide students to notice the foreboding tone here in the description of the isolation and vulnerability of Harrison's Row. Ask students: What does the author say would happen to Harrison's Row if the city invaded the countryside? If the city were attacked from the countryside? *Either way, Harrison's Row would be the first thing destroyed.* Ask students to speculate about what might happen to Harrison's Row. *Some students may suggest that the houses will be demolished or that they will face ruin in some other fashion.*

▶Critical Viewing◀

8 **Analyze Cause and Effect** Students may suggest that the sameness and closeness of the flats could cause the inhabitants to know each other's business and to develop a sameness in outlook and lifestyle; that neighbors would have a unique camaraderie as a result of the cramped quarters and lack of privacy; or that the bleak, claustrophobic setting might cause residents to feel trapped and despairing.

◆ Literary Focus

9 **Setting and Atmosphere** Students may say that the details create a mood of resignation, or perhaps of hopelessness and depression.

◆ Critical Thinking

10 **Analyze** Ask students to explain the effect of the revelation that the narrator is or was a resident of Harrison's Row. *Students may say that he would have an intimate knowledge of the effects of the place on the people living there and that his knowledge of the people and his opinions of Harrison's Row come from firsthand experience.*

▶Critical Viewing◀

❶ **Speculate** Students may say that a fiddle might be a means for providing its player with beautiful music, a sense of accomplishment and pride, or a way to relax.

Customize for
English Language Learners

❷ Clarify the meanings of the unfamiliar regional or unusual terms in this passage. Explain that Ted Griffin probably broke the gas, water, or electric meter in his house to avoid paying his bills and then sped from the scene like a racehorse. Explain that *poaching* is trespassing and stealing, and here probably refers to the theft of fish, game, or eggs.

◆ Critical Thinking

❸ **Evaluate** Ask students to explain the irony in Ted Griffin's arrest. *Ted performed a perfect escape when he didn't need to. When the police did come for him, they caught him by surprise, and he had no opportunity to escape.*

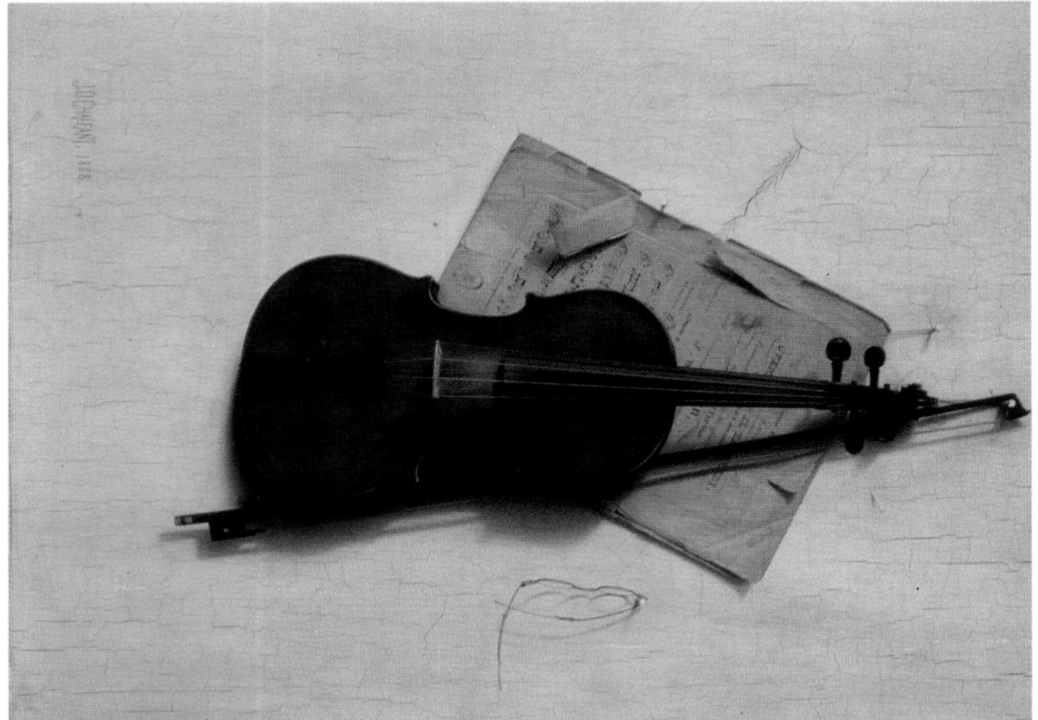
The Old Fiddle, Jefferson David Chalfant

❶ ▲ Critical Viewing Why might a fiddle like this one be a cherished possession? **[Speculate]**

Convinced they had come to arrest him for meter-breaking, he ran through the house and garden, went over the fence, jumped into the Leen—happily not much swollen—waded across to the field, then four-legged it over the railway, ❷ and made his way to Robins Wood a mile or so beyond. A perfect escape route. He stayed two days in hiding, and then crept home at night, famished and soaked, only to find that the police had not come for him, but to question Blonk next door, who was suspected of poaching. When they did get Ted Griffin he was pulled out of bed one morning even before he'd ❸ had time to open his eyes and think about a spectacular escape across the Leen.

Jeff Bignal was a young unmarried man of twenty-four. His father had been killed in the Great War,[3] and he lived with his mother at Number Six Harrison's Row, and worked down nearby Radford Pit. He was short in height, and plump, his white skin scarred back and front with livid blue patches where he had been knocked with coal at the mine face. When he went out on Saturday night he brilliantined his hair.

After tea in summer while it was still light and warm he would sit in his back garden playing the fiddle, and when he did everybody else came out to listen. Or they opened the doors and windows so that the sound of his music drifted in, while the woman stayed at the sink or wash-copper, or the man at his odd

3. **Great War:** World War I.

Humanities: Media

An Alan Sillitoe Film Festival.
Two of Alan Sillitoe's angry works about working-class life in twentieth-century Great Britain were made into powerful films. The adaptation of his novel *Saturday Night and Sunday Morning* (1958) appeared in 1960, directed by Karel Reisz and starring Albert Finney. Sillitoe himself wrote the screenplay. He also wrote the screenplay for the film of *The Loneliness of the Long Distance Runner* (story: 1959; film: 1962). Tom Courtney and Michael Redgrave starred in this highly acclaimed film, directed by Tony Richardson. Invite students to view either or both of these films; each is available in video. Use the following questions for discussion:

1. How would you describe the view of life each film expresses? *Students should focus on the dreary, grim, demoralized lives of the working classes.*
2. In what ways does the environment influence the characters' actions in the film? *The grim environment lowers the protagonist's expectations and increases his dissatisfactions.*

jobs. Anyone with a wireless would turn it down or off.

Even tall dark sallow-faced elderly Mrs. Deaffy (a kid sneaked into her kitchen one day and thieved her last penny-packet of cocoa and she went crying to tell Mrs. Atkin who, when her youngest came in, hit him so hard with her elbow that one of his teeth shot out and the blood
4 washed away most of the cocoa-stains around his mouth)—old Mrs. Deaffy stood by her back door as if she weren't stone deaf any more and could follow each note of Jeffrey Bignal's exquisite violin. She smiled at seeing everyone occupied, fixed or entranced, and therefore no torment to herself, which was music enough to her whether she could hear it or not.

And Blonk, in the secretive dimness of the kitchen, went on mending his poaching nets before setting out with Arthur Bede next door on that night's expedition to Gunthorpe by the banks of the Trent, where the green escarpment between there and Kneeton was riddled with warrens and where, so it was said, if you stood sufficiently still the rabbits ran over your feet, and it was only necessary to make a quick grab to get one.

Jeff sat on a chair, oblivious to everybody, fed up with his day's work at the pit and only wanting to lose himself in his own music. The kids stopped splashing and shouting in the water, because if they didn't they might get hauled in and clouted with just the right amount of viciousness to suit the crime and the occasion. It had happened before, though Jeff had always been too far off to notice.

His face was long, yet generally cheerful—contrary to what one would expect—a smile settling on it whenever he met and passed anybody on the street, or on his way to the group of shared lavatories at the end of the Row. But his face was almost down and lost to the world as he sat on his chair and brought forth his first sweet notes of a summer's evening.

It was said that a neighbor in the last place they had lived had taught him to play like that. Others maintained it was an uncle who had
5 shown him how. But nobody knew for sure because when someone asked directly he said that if he had any gift at all it must have come from God above. It was known that on some Sundays
of the year, if the sun was out, he went to the 5
Methodist chapel on St. Peter's Street.

He could play anything from "Greensleeves" to "Mademoiselle from Armentières." He could do a beautiful heart-pulling version of Handel's *Largo,* and throw in bits from *The Messiah* as well. He would go from one piece to another with no rhyme or reason, from ridiculousness to sublimity, with almost shocking abruptness, but as the hour or so went by it all appeared easy and natural, part of a long piece coming from Jeff Bignal's fiddle while the ball of the sun went down behind his back.

To a child it seemed as if the songs lived in the hard collier's muscle at the top of his energetic arm, and that they queued one by to get
out. Once free, they rushed along his flesh from 6
which the shirtsleeves had been rolled up, and split into his fingertips, where they were played out with ease into the warm evening air.

The grass in the fields across the stream was livid and lush, almost blue, and a piebald horse stood with bent head, eating oats out of a large old pram whose wheels had long since gone. The breeze wafted across from places farther out, from Robins Wood and the Cherry Orchard, Wollaton Roughs and Bramcote Hills and even, on a day that was not too hot, from the tops of the Pennines in Derbyshire.

Jeff played for himself, for the breeze against his arm, for the soft hiss of the flowing Leen at the end of the garden, and maybe also for the horse in the field, which took no notice of anything and which, having grown tired of its oats in the pram, bent its head over the actual grass and began to roam in search of succulent pastures.

In the middle of the winter Jeff's fiddling was forgotten. He went into the coal mine before it was light, and came up only after it had got
dark. Walking down Leen Place, he complained 7
to Blonk that it was hard on a man not to see daylight for weeks at a time.

◆ Build Vocabulary

sublimity (sə blim′ ə tē) *n.*: Quality of being majestic or noble

◆ Literary Focus

4 Setting and Atmosphere Ask students to describe the effect of the parenthetical anecdote on their understanding of the setting. *The anecdote reveals a casual, matter-of-fact attitude towards violence that makes the setting even bleaker. The anecdote also shows how intertwined all lives are in Harrison's Row.* Have them explain why Mrs. Deaffy enjoyed Jeff's music so much. *Even though she is deaf, Mrs. Deaffy enjoys the music because it keeps people calm and occupied, which means that they are not interacting with, and thereby annoying, her.*

◆ Critical Thinking

5 Infer Ask students to tell what they can infer about Jeff from this passage. *Students may say that he is modest, reserved, and independent.*

◆ Literary Focus

6 Setting and Atmosphere Ask students to explain why this image of how Jeff's music is produced is a reasonable one for children of this district to have. *Students may say that their limited experience and their collective lack of curiosity make the children's image an appropriate one.*

◆ Grammar and Style

7 Vary Sentence Beginnings Point out that each of the three sentences in this paragraph has a different kind of beginning: the first one begins with an introductory phrase; the second, with a subject; and the third, with an introductory clause.

Cross-Curricular Connection: Social Studies

"The Fiddle" presents a vivid look at what life is like for people living and working in a coal-mining town. Students can appreciate the way things stayed the same for the inhabitants of Harrison's Row despite progress and the passage of time. They may assume that life in Harrison's Row is indicative of life in other coal-mining towns throughout Great Britain. Is it indicative of life in mining towns in America? Have students find out.

Ask students to form groups. Each group should choose a mining town from a different part of the United States. They can, for example, find coal-mining towns in Pennsylvania, copper-mining towns in Arizona, silver-mining towns in Colorado and Nevada, and gold-mining towns in California and Alaska. Each group should research life in a mining town, now or in the past, comparing and contrasting it with life in Harrison's Row. What did miners think about their lives? Did they have enough money? Was the population transient or did people stay put? Did the towns change in any way, and if so, how? Were neighbors' lives interconnected? Have groups present their findings.

Customize for
English Language Learners

❶ Read this sentence aloud so that students can hear the accent as written in the dialogue. Explain that *bleddy* is how "bloody" sounds in dialect. Point out that *bloody* is a vulgar British term that means "cursed" or "damned."

◆ Reading Strategy

❷ **Predict Effect of Setting** Students may suggest that Jeff's options are limited in Harrison's Row. Not knowing anything about the availability of jobs beyond work in the coal mines, they might guess that he will leave the region, perhaps to become a musician.

◆ Reading Strategy

❸ **Predict Effect of Setting** Ask students to explain what the reaction to Jeff's news reveals about the people in Harrison's Row. *Students may say that their amazement over Jeff's relatively modest amount of spunk indicates how resigned they are to their lot in life and how low their expectations are.*

❹ **Clarification** Inform students that "chitterlings" are fried pieces of the small intestines of a pig or other edible animal, and that "black pudding" is a savory dish made with blood. Point out that both are considered delicacies by some segments of the British population.

◆ Literary Focus

❺ **Setting and Atmosphere** Ask students to explain how the demolition of Harrison's Row relates to Jeff Bignal's act of selling his fiddle. *Students may suggest that the people of Harrison's Row are set in their ways and resigned to their fate. Despite changes around them, such as Jeff Bignal selling his fiddle or the old houses being torn down, they continue to live lives trapped in dreary poverty.*

❶ "That's why I wain't go anywhere near the bleddy pit," Blonk said vehemently, though he had worked there from time to time, and would do so again when harried by his wife and children. "You'd do better to come out on a bit o' poaching with me and Arthur," he suggested.

It was virtually true that Jeff saw no daylight, because even on Sunday he stayed in bed most of the day, and if it happened to be dull there was little enough sky to be seen through his front bedroom window, which looked away from the Leen and up the hill.

The upshot of his complaint was that he would do anything to change such a situation. A man was less than an animal for putting up with it.

> ◆ **Reading Strategy**
> ❷ What choice does Jeff have? Predict what he might do.

"I'd do anything," he repeated to his mother over his tea in the single room downstairs.

"But what, though?" she asked. "What can you do, Jeff?"

"Well, how do I know?" he almost snapped at her. "But I'll do summat,[4] you can be sure of that."

He didn't do anything till the weather got better and life turned a bit sweeter. Maybe this improvement finally got him going, because it's hard to help yourself towards better things when you're too far down in the dumps.

On a fine blowy day with both sun and cloud in the sky Jeff went out in the morning, walking up Leen Place with his fiddle under his arm. The case had been wiped and polished.

In the afternoon he came back without it.

"Where's your fiddle?" Ma Jones asked.

He put an awkward smile on to his pale face, and told her: "I sold it."

"Well I never! How much for?"

He was too shocked at her brazen question not to tell the truth: "Four quid."

"That ain't much."

"It'll be enough," he said roughly.

"Enough for what, Jeff?"

He didn't say, but the fact that he had sold his fiddle for four quid rattled up and down the line of cottages till everybody knew of it. Others swore he'd got ten pounds for it, because something that made such music must be worth more than a paltry four, and in any case Jeff would never say how much he'd really got for it, for fear that someone would go in and rob him.

They wondered why he'd done it, but had to wait for the answer, as one usually does. But there was nothing secretive about Jeff Bignal, and if he'd sold his music for a mess of pottage he saw no point in not letting them know why. They'd find out sooner or later, anyway.

All he'd had to do was make up his mind, and he'd done that lying on his side at the pit face while ripping coal out with his pick and shovel. Decisions made like that can't be undone, he knew. He'd brooded on it all winter, till the fact of having settled it seemed to have altered the permanent expression of his face, and given it a new look which caused people to wonder whether he would ever be able to play the fiddle again anyway—at least with his old spirit and dash. ❸

With the four quid he paid the first week's rent on a butcher's shop on Denman Street, and bought a knife, a chopper, and a bit of sharpening stone, as well as a wooden block. Maybe he had a quid or two more knocking around, though if he had it couldn't have been much, but with four quid and a slice of bluff he got enough credit from a wholesaler at the meat market downtown to stock his shop with mutton and beef, and in a couple of days he was in trade. The people of Harrison's Row were amazed at how easy it was, though nobody had ever thought of doing it themselves.

Like a serious young man of business Mr. Bignal—as he was now known—parted his hair down the middle, so that he didn't look so young any more, but everyone agreed that it was better than being at Radford Pit. They'd seen how he had got fed up with selling the

◆ **Build Vocabulary**

harried (har´ ēd) *v.*: Harassed

4. **summat:** Something.

Speaking and Listening Mini-Lesson

Debate

This mini-lesson supports the Speaking and Listening activity in the Idea Bank on page 991.

Introduce the Concept Explain that a debate is a formal contest in reasoned argument between two teams. The affirmative side presents its view, or argument, which consists of contentions supported by evidence. Then the negative side presents its argument. Each team then gets to respond to its opponent's argument, with the negative side going first. During this round, the teams can present new evidence, but cannot introduce new contentions.

Develop Background Write the resolution on the chalkboard. Have students form teams of two. Guide students to identify and discuss the pertinent issues. Point out that they should be prepared to argue the issue from either side. Remind students to rely on logic to build and present their points.

Apply the Information Pair up teams. The winner of a coin toss decides which side to argue.

Assess the Outcome Assess students' efforts according to how well they demonstrate an understanding of the lives of the people in Harrison's Row and the issues involved in urban renewal. Judge according to how well they demonstrate an understanding of the issues involved, and how well they support their opinions.

sweat of his brow.

No one could say that he prospered, but they couldn't deny that he made a living. And he didn't have to suffer the fact of not seeing daylight for almost the whole of the winter.

Six months after opening the shop he got married. The reception was held at the chapel on St. Peter's Street, which seemed to be a sort of halfway house between Harrison's Row on the banks of the Leen and the butcher's shop on Denman Street farther up.

Everybody from Harrison's Row was invited for a drink and something to eat; but he knew them too well to let any have either chops or
4 chitterlings (or even black puddings) on tick[5] when they came into his shop.

The people of Harrison's Row missed the sound of his fiddle on long summer evenings, though the children could splash and shout with their tin bathtub undisturbed, floundering through shallows and scrambling up to grass on the other bank, and wondering what place they'd reach if they walked without stopping till it got dark.

Two years later the Second World War began, and not long afterwards meat as well as nearly everything else was put on the ration. Apart from which, Jeff was only twenty-six, so got called up into the army. He never had much chance to make a proper start in life, though people said that he came out all right in the end.

The houses of Harrison's Row were condemned as unfit to live in, and a bus depot stands on the site.

The packed mass of houses on the hill behind—forty years after Jeff Bignal sold his violin—is also vanishing, and high-rise hencoops (as the people call them) are put in their place. The demolition crew knock down ten houses a day—though the foreman told me there was still work for another two years.

Some of the houses would easily have lasted 5
a few more decades, for the bricks were perfect, but as the foreman went on: "You can't let them stand in the way of progress"—whatever that means.

The people have known each other for generations but, when they are moved to their new estates and blocks of flats,[6] they will know each other for generations more, because as I listen to them talking, they speak a language which, in spite of everything and everyone, never alters.

5. **tick:** Credit.

6. **flats:** Apartments.

Guide for Responding

◆ *Literature and Your Life*

Reader's Response What advice would you have given Jeff about his decision?

Thematic Focus Is there always a conflict between pleasure and getting ahead?

☑ Check Your Comprehension

1. In what era does the story take place?

2. Tell the events that preceded Ted Griffin's arrest.

3. How did people react to Jeff's music?

4. (a)What does Jeff finally do with his fiddle? (b) For what purpose does he do this?

◆ Critical Thinking

INTERPRET

1. How is Jeff's attitude about the coal mines different from his friend's? **[Compare and Contrast]**

2. What is the connection between Jeff's fiddle and his standing in the town? **[Connect]**

3. (a) What does the fiddle symbolize? (b) How does this symbol reveal the story's theme? **[Draw Conclusions]**

EVALUATE

4. Do you think Jeff's decision to give up music is a good one? Explain. **[Make a Judgment]**

Reinforce and Extend

Answers

◆ *Literature and Your Life*

Reader's Response Students may support Jeff in his decision but also advise him to buy his fiddle back when he can afford to.

Thematic Focus Students may suggest that, except for the fortunate few, getting ahead demands a focus on one's goal and, therefore, a deemphasis on time spent for pleasure.

☑ Check Your Comprehension

1. The story takes place during the Depression, in the 1930's.
2. Ted Griffin had tinkered with the meters. When he saw police officers walking toward Harrison's Row, he assumed they were coming for him. That time they were not, but soon they did come back to arrest him.
3. People stopped what they were doing and listened to Jeff's music.
4. (a) He sells his fiddle for four quid. (b) He uses the money to set himself up as a butcher.

◆ Critical Thinking

1. Jeff, like all the other workers, detests the life of a coal miner, but only he is willing and determined to do something to change his life.
2. Jeff's fiddle playing makes him an integral part of the small community and earns him the respect of his neighbors.
3. (a) The fiddle symbolizes the manifestation of beauty in an otherwise dreary environment. (b) It emphasizes the sacrifice that the protagonist makes to make a living.
4. Students are likely to applaud Jeff's rebellion against his situation in life, but wish he had done so without sacrificing his music.

Beyond the Selection

FURTHER READING

Other Works by Alan Sillitoe

Saturday Night and Sunday Morning
The Loneliness of the Long Distance Runner
The Ragman's Daughter

Other Works About Life in a Coal-Mining Town

Union Dues, John Sayles
How Green Was My Valley, Richard Llewellyn

We suggest that you preview these works before recommending them to students.

INTERNET

You and your students may find additional information about Alan Sillitoe on the Internet at the following site. Please be aware that sites may have changed since this information was published.

For biographical information, a bibliography, and synopses of some of Sillitoe's works, go to **http://educeth.ethz.ch/english/readinglist/sillitoe,alan.html**

We *strongly recommend* that you preview sites before you send students to them.

Guide for Responding *(continued)*

◆ Literary Focus

Setting and Atmosphere

When a **setting** plays an important role in a story, as it does in "The Fiddle," it often evokes a certain **atmosphere**—a mood or feeling you get when you read the story. Sillitoe creates a forbidding atmosphere in this passage:

> But after a three-day downpour when the air was still heavy with undropped water and colored a menacing gun-metal blue, it was best not to go anywhere near the river, for one false step and you would get sucked in, and be dragged by the powerful current along to the Trent some miles away.

1. Find two examples from the story in which a description of the setting creates an ominous or depressing atmosphere. Explain each of your choices, citing individual words that contribute to the atmosphere.
2. Explain the effect the River Leen has on the atmosphere of this story. Support your explanation with examples from the story.
3. Describe the effect of the violin—an element of setting—on the atmosphere in this story, including how it changes the atmosphere at specific points.

◆ Reading Strategy

Predict Effect of Setting

The more you know about the setting of a particular story, the more accurately you may be able to **predict** the outcome of events.

The job of knowing about setting is a collaboration between the author and you; the author provides information and descriptions and you add to that what you already know. For example, if you know about the difficulties of life in a coal-mining district, you can better appreciate Jeff Bignal's efforts to better his life in this story.

1. What effect did the violin, an important detail of setting, have on the outcome of events?
2. What was the effect of World War II, barely alluded to, on the outcome of events in this story?
3. Which elements of setting pointed most strongly to a particular outcome in this story? Why?

◆ Build Vocabulary

Using the Word Origin *Sublime*

The word *sublime* comes from roots meaning "up to" and "lintel." Use this knowledge to help you define these words.

1. sublimity **2.** sublimate **3.** sublimation

Using the Word Bank

Review the Build Vocabulary boxes at the bottom of the selection pages. Then, in your notebook, write the vocabulary word that best completes each of the following sentences.

1. The world would be a better place if we could __?__ poverty from coal miners' lives forever.
2. When labor conditions are poor, workers must be __?__ in their pursuit of safe conditions and decent wages.
3. It's hard to make plans to improve your life when you are so __?__ working to fulfill your daily needs.
4. For a while, the __?__ of the violin music transported the residents of Harrison's Row away from their grim existence.

◆ Grammar and Style

Vary Sentence Beginnings

One way that writers sustain a reader's interest and establish a flow in their writing is by varying sentence beginnings.

Practice In your notebook, identify each of the italicized sentence beginnings as subject, introductory adverb, or introductory phrase or clause.

1. *Alan Sillitoe* grew up in Nottingham, England.
2. *By age fourteen*, he was earning enough to help his family.
3. *Fortunately*, he passed the necessary tests to join the Royal Air Force.
4. *When he was twenty-one*, he knew he wanted to be a writer.

Writing Application In your notebook, rewrite each Practice sentence so that it begins with a new part of speech, picked from the following:
1. an adverb **2.** a subject **3.** a clause **4.** a phrase

Reinforce and Extend

Answers

◆ Literary Focus

1. The paragraph about rent collecting points out that no one could recall a better time. This helps create an atmosphere of sameness, hopelessness, and resignation. The paragraph that describes how Harrison's Row would be the first neighborhood to suffer the effects of an invading army points to the isolation and helplessness of the place.
2. Students may say that the fact that no one knew where the Leen came from suggests that people have lost interest in life. They may say that the river's forbidding nature contributes to an atmosphere of hopelessness, as it represents a barrier to possibilities and outside opportunities.
3. The violin is a symbol of beauty in an otherwise dreary setting. When Jeff plays, the music awakens his neighbors to a moment of pleasure, a brief respite from their downtrodden lives.

◆ Reading Strategy

1. By selling the violin, Jeff was able to escape his dismal life in the mines, but for the others in Harrison's Row, life went on as it had before.
2. World War II did not change the prospects for people on Harrison's Row. The upturn in the economy and the building boom that followed in the wake of the war simply resulted in the demolition of old slums and the construction of new ones. People from Harrison's Row were no better off. Jeff went back to his butcher shop; others went back to the mine.
3. Students may say that the isolation of Harrison's Row and the bleak outlook of the people leading dreary lives there were the strongest contributors to the continuation of hopelessness.

◆ Build Vocabulary

Using the Word Origins of *Sublime*

1. the state or quality of being sublime, majestic, noble; 2. to have a purifying or ennobling influence or effect on; 3. the act or experience of being purified or ennobled

Using the Word Bank

1. obliterate; 2. persistent; 3. harried; 4. sublimity

◆ Grammar and Style

Practice

1. subject; 2. introductory phrase; 3. adverb; 4. introductory clause

Writing Application

Student sentences may resemble the following:

1. In Nottingham, England, Alan Sillitoe grew up.
2. Eventually, by the age of fourteen, he was earning enough to help his family.
3. After passing the necessary tests, he joined the Royal Air Force.
4. He knew at age twenty-one that he wanted to be a writer.

Writer's Solution

For additional instruction and practice, use the lesson on Varying Sentence Structure in the **Language Lab CD-ROM** and the page on Using Different Sentence Openers and Structures, in the *Writer's Solution Grammar Practice Book*, p. 105.

Build Your Portfolio

Idea Bank

Writing

1. **Journal Entry** Put yourself in Jeff's place, and write a journal entry describing how you feel about having to sell your fiddle.

2. **Newspaper Report** As a reporter on the crime beat, write about Ted Griffin being pulled out of bed and arrested for meter-breaking. Tell who, what, when, where, and why.

3. **Response to Criticism** Critic Clancy Sigal has said no living English writer "can match Alan Sillitoe's sharp instinct for the grinding pain and convulsive joys of working-class life." Support or refute this view, using details from "The Fiddle."

Speaking and Listening

4. **Debate** Should the houses near Harrison's Row have been torn down so they wouldn't "stand in the way of progress?" In two teams of classmates, debate this issue. **[Social Studies Link]**

5. **Music Discussion** Preview various kinds of fiddle (violin) music, and select a few pieces with very different sounds. Present them to the class, and lead a discussion about the atmosphere that each piece creates. **[Music Link]**

Projects

6. **Performing Arts** With a group, write a script based on any scene in the story. Then rehearse it and perform it. **[Performing Arts Link]**

7. **Coal Mining Report** Research and report on current conditions in the coal mining industry in Great Britain. Broadly explain how coal is mined and cover labor union or management's efforts to protect the safety and quality of life of coal miners. **[Social Studies Link; Health Link]**

Writing Mini-Lesson

Favorite Setting

Alan Sillitoe creates a memorable impression of of Harrison's Row and the surrounding area. His description of this setting just seems to ring true.

Whether the realistic setting in a story comes from the writer's memory or from his or her imagination, it must rely upon vivid details and clear, accurate description. Choose a favorite setting, and write a description of it. The setting could be one you come in contact with every day, one you remember, or just a place you've passed and admired. Following Sillitoe's example, use vivid details to describe this favorite setting.

Writing Skills Focus: Vivid Details

Once you've decided on a setting, you'll need to gather **vivid details** to capture how it looks, smells, sounds, tastes, and feels. To evoke these sensations:

- Choose exact nouns.
- Use vivid verbs, ones that suggest as closely as possible the action being described.
- Use strong, precise modifiers to help your reader envision the scene.

Prewriting Make a five-column table like this one. Under the appropriate heading, jot down the first few sensory details that come to mind.

Sight	Smell	Taste	Hearing	Touch

Drafting Choose an organizing principle for your description. You might organize your details in spatial order or order of importance. You might even mix organizing principles, such as organizing details by the sense to which they appeal, then showing these in order of importance.

Revising Show your description to a classmate and ask for a reaction. Can your classmate picture the setting clearly? Add any details that might help your reader envision the setting.

✓ ASSESSMENT OPTIONS

Formal Assessment, Selection Test, pp. 254–256, and Assessment Resources Software. The selection test is designed so that it can be easily customized to the performance levels of your students. ***Alternative Assessment,*** p. 52, includes options for less advanced students, more advanced students, logical/mathematical learners, visual/spatial learners, intrapersonal learners, and verbal/linguistic learners.

PORTFOLIO ASSESSMENT
Use the following rubrics in the ***Alternative Assessment*** booklet to assess student writing:
Journal Entry: Expression Rubric, p. 95
Newspaper Report: Summary Rubric, p. 99
Response to Criticism: Literary Analysis/Interpretation Rubric, p. 113
Writing Mini-Lesson: Description Rubric, p. 98

Idea Bank

Customizing for
Performance Levels
Following are suggestions for matching Idea Bank topics with your students' performance levels:
Less Advanced Students: 1, 5
Average Students: 2, 4, 6
More Advanced Students: 3, 7

Customizing for
Learning Modalities
Following are suggestions for matching Idea Bank topics with your students' learning modalities:
Logical/Mathematical: 4
Bodily/Kinesthetic: 6
Intrapersonal: 1
Interpersonal: 4, 6
Musical/Rhythmic: 5

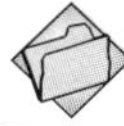

Writing Mini-Lesson

Refer students to the Writing Handbook, page 1189, for instruction on the writing process, and page 1191 for further information on description.

Writer's Solution

Writers at Work Videodisc
Have students view the videodisc segment (Ch. 1) featuring travel writer Guy Garcia to see how he shares his travel experiences with readers. Have students discuss how vivid details help to bring a description of a place to life.

Play frames 335 to 10062

Writing Lab CD-ROM
Have students complete the tutorial on Description. Follow these steps:

1. View the audio-annotated writing models for audience and purpose.
2. Use the notecards activity to gather details.
3. Draft on the computer, referring as needed to the Word Bins of sensory details, places, and modifiers.
4. To aid in revision, use the revision checker for vague adjectives.

Sourcebook
Have students use Chapter 1, Description (pp. 1–29), for additional support. The chapter includes model from literature of a description of a place (pp. 5, 28–29), in-depth instruction on Gathering Details (pp. 18–19), Organizing a Description (pp. 19–20) and Using Modifiers (p. 27).

Prepare and Engage

OBJECTIVES

1. To read, comprehend, and interpret a short story
2. To relate a story to personal experience
3. To identify causes and effects while reading
4. To analyze social conflict
5. To build vocabulary in context and learn the suffix: *-ity (-ty)*
6. To recognize and correctly punctuate restrictive and nonrestrictive adjective clauses
7. To write a persuasive letter with brevity and clarity
8. To respond to the story through writing, speaking and listening, and projects

SKILLS INSTRUCTION

Vocabulary:
Suffixes: *-ity (-ty)*

Grammar:
Restrictive and Nonrestrictive Adjective Clauses

Reading Strategy:
Cause and Effect

Literary Focus:
Social Conflict

Writing:
Brevity and Clarity

Speaking and Listening:
Eulogy (teacher edition)

Critical Viewing:
Apply; Analyze

PORTFOLIO OPPORTUNITIES

Writing: Obituary; Poem; Literary Analysis
Writing Mini-Lesson: Persuasive Letter
Speaking and Listening: Eulogy; Interview
Projects: Portfolio; A Celebration of Irish Culture

More About the Author
Before embarking on a career as a writer, William Trevor was an art teacher and a history teacher at a school in Armagh, Northern Ireland. He was also an advertising copywriter. He turned to writing fiction, he said, because he found that he could not express humanity in sculpture. Trevor used his art background to help describe the craft of writing. He wrote: "A short story is like an impressionist painting. You cut down everything enormously and you get the effects from one big splash or explosion. You have to cut to the very edge. What excites me is to go as far as I can."

Guide for Interpreting

William Trevor *(1928–)*

Like his protagonists in "The Distant Past," William Trevor was born into a Protestant family in the largely Catholic Republic of Ireland. This experience of being outside the dominant culture—and the fact that his parents moved around constantly during his youth—gave him a sympathy for the outsiders about whom he writes in his short stories and novels. Trevor himself has said:

"I think the feeling of not belonging is very strong in me. In order to write about people, you have got actually to stand back quite a distance."

Trevor admits that his view of life is pessimistic. The "villain" in his stories is usually circumstance. People's lives are troubled through no fault of their own.

Finding a Career Trevor attended Trinity College in Dublin and afterwards taught school to support his wife and young family while devoting his creative energies to sculpture. Eventually his sculpture became too abstract to interest him. "There weren't any people in it anymore, and I didn't like it," he says.

After abandoning sculpture, he took up writing, and became an immediate success, publishing short stories in magazines as fast as he could write them.

Acclaim Today William Trevor is recognized as one of the greatest living writers of short stories in the English language. In fact, critics have compared his stories to those of Anton Chekhov, Muriel Spark, and James Joyce. He has been praised for the "gritty detail" of his stories, his lack of sentimentality, and the subtle sense of humor that infuses his work.

◆ Background for Understanding

HISTORY: TROUBLE IN IRELAND

Between 1968 and 1994, in Northern Ireland—which has a population of about 1.6 million people—more than 40,000 people were wounded and 3,100 were killed in shootings and bombings as a result of a political dispute between Catholics and Protestants. Though 1968 is given as the starting date of "the Troubles," the source of the violence goes back about three hundred years to when the British government encouraged thousands of Scottish Protestants to emigrate to the north of Ireland and allowed them to confiscate land owned by Catholics. By 1703, Protestants owned 95 percent of the land in the six counties that make up present-day Northern Ireland. For the next two hundred years there was periodic violence between the two groups. More importantly, many Catholics left the six counties for the South and West of Ireland, where they joined others in agitating for independence from Britain.

When the Irish people finally won home rule in 1922, the six northern counties, with a firm majority of Protestants, remained part of Britain. The Catholics who still lived in the North experienced political and economic discrimination. In 1969 an incident occurred in which police fired on a group of Catholic demonstrators. Before long the troubles had escalated, leading to almost thirty years of violence between Catholics and Protestants and British troops, who were generally supportive of the Protestants. It wasn't until 1996 that a cease-fire was declared and negotiations began between the two parties in hope of resolving the conflict.

992 ◆ *A Time of Rapid Change (1901–Present)*

Prentice Hall Literature Program Resources

REINFORCE / RETEACH / EXTEND

Selection Support Pages
Build Vocabulary: Suffixes: *-ity (-ty),* p. 253
Grammar and Style: Restrictive and Nonrestrictive Adjective Clauses, p. 254
Reading Strategy: Cause and Effect, p. 255
Literary Focus: Social Conflict, p. 256

Strategies for Diverse Student Needs, p. 53

Beyond Literature
Career Connection: Screenwriter, p. 53

Formal Assessment Selection Test, pp. 257–259; Assessment Resources Software

Alternative Assessment, p. 52

ResourcePro CD-ROM
"The Distant Past"—includes all resource material and customizable lesson plan

Listening to Literature Audiocassettes
"The Distant Past"

The Distant Past

◆ Literature and Your Life

CONNECT YOUR EXPERIENCE

Perhaps you'll soon join a political party and vote for its candidates. Joining a party means taking a stand with others, but it also means separating yourself from those who belong to a different party. In "The Distant Past," a brother and sister find themselves the only representatives of a very unpopular political viewpoint in the town in which they live.

Journal Writing How would you feel about being the only supporter of an unpopular political position in your school? Jot down your thoughts.

THEMATIC FOCUS: CONFLICTS AT HOME AND ABROAD

As you read, notice how people's alliances in the political conflict in Ireland affect their feelings toward one another.

◆ Literary Focus

SOCIAL CONFLICT

Conflict—a struggle between opposing forces—is at the heart of most stories. Some conflicts between people are individual and personal; others are on a larger scale. **Social conflict** refers to a struggle between those with opposing views about the society they live in. In "The Distant Past," notice how social conflict separates the two main characters from everyone else.

◆ Build Vocabulary

SUFFIXES: *-ity (-ty)*

In "The Distant Past," two characters experience *adversity* ("misfortune") because they insist on the *sovereignty* ("ruling power") of the British crown. Both words contain the suffix *-ity* (or *-ty*), meaning "the state of" or "the quality of."

WORD BANK

Preview these words from the story.

countenance
adversity
sovereignty
anachronism
internment

◆ Reading Strategy

CAUSE AND EFFECT

For years, a brother and sister are accepted as harmless eccentrics. Then suddenly they became outcasts. Why? Asking the question *why* is looking for a **cause**, the reason that something happens. An **effect** is the thing that happens as a result of the cause. When something unexpected happens in a story, ask yourself, *why*. Sometimes the author will explain. Other times, you will have to use your detective skills and examine events that come before and after the one in question for clues. Looking for causes and effects will make you more aware of the meaning behind the events in a story.

◆ Grammar and Style

RESTRICTIVE AND NONRESTRICTIVE ADJECTIVE CLAUSES

An adjective clause is a subordinate clause (a group of words that contains a subject and a verb but can't stand alone as a sentence) that modifies a noun or pronoun. A **restrictive adjective clause** contains information necessary to the meaning of the sentence. It is not separated by commas. A **nonrestrictive adjective clause** contains information that isn't necessary to the meaning of the sentence. It is separated by commas.

Nonrestrictive: Fat Driscoll, *who kept the butcher shop*, used even to joke about the past. . .

Restrictive: Mr. Healey doubled the number of girls *who served as waitresses in his dining room*. . .

Preparing for Standardized Tests

Grammar and Language The Improving Sentences portion of some standardized tests requires students to identify a mechanics error from among several choices. Students may be asked to choose the correct way to punctuate a sentence, as in the following example. *(B)*

A. Driscoll, who was a butcher began to ignore the Middletons.

B. Driscoll, who was a butcher, began to ignore the Middletons.

C. Driscoll who was a butcher, began to ignore the Middletons.

D. Driscoll who was a butcher began to ignore the Middletons.

The Grammar and Style lesson for this selection focuses on recognizing restrictive and nonrestrictive adjective clauses and their punctuation. For additional practice, use the Grammar and Style page on Restrictive and Nonrestrictive Adjective Clauses, p. 254, in ***Selection Support.***

Invite a popular teacher or student to your classroom to pitch an *unpopular* idea. Then ask that person to leave. Have students debate the point of view. Then ask them if their view of the person who made the pitch has changed because of his or her opinion. At the conclusion, clarify that the visit was an act. Tell students that in "The Distant Past," people's unpopular political opinions lead to conflict.

Customize for
Less Proficient Readers

Explain to students that it is possible for families that once had great wealth to be left with only the trappings—land, a stately home, servants. Guide them to understand that the circumstances of the Middletons is not so uncommon; wealth can be squandered as easily as it can be accumulated. Tell them that the Middletons have very little income despite having inherited the house and the property and all the prestige they afford.

Customize for
More Advanced Students

Discuss with students that characters in realistic fiction are sometimes shaped by historical events that occur during the period in which the story is set. Guide them to look for ways that history affects the characters in this story, how it makes them change, and how it makes others see them differently.

Customize for
English Language Learners

Help students make sense of any unfamiliar language Trevor uses that isn't otherwise identified and defined. Assist students to find definitions or synonyms of words or expressions such as *part and parcel, stout, ruffians, union jack, family crest, internment,* and so on. Guide them to use context clues and a dictionary.

Customize for
Musical/Rhythmic Learners

The Irish rock group U2 has recorded several songs that deal with the continuing Catholic-Protestant turmoil. As a way of introducing this short story, you may wish to play their song "Sunday, Bloody Sunday" and get student reactions.

Develop Understanding

One-Minute Insight "The Distant Past" explores the effects of historical events and social change on relationships among neighbors in a village. When economic times are good and conflict between the Irish Catholics and the British government is eased, a once-wealthy British family living in Ireland is thought odd by villagers, but accepted nonetheless. When that conflict flares up again, the villagers' reaction to the family illustrates that social and political forces can have a profound impact on personal relationships.

❶ **Enrichment** Point out that, unlike many contemporary short stories, this one begins with an exposition, in which the author provides background information.

Customize for
More Advanced Students
❷ Discuss with students that the decay in the fortunes of the Middletons can be seen as a metaphor for the decline in the fortunes of the British Empire. Point out that in the period following World War I, some British colonies demanded and achieved their independence.

◆ Reading Strategy

❸ **Cause and Effect** Guide students to recognize that, although the Middletons blame their financial troubles on the Catholic woman with whom their father was involved, and on the new national regime, neither is responsible for the decline of their fortunes. Their adversity is due to their father's poor judgment and irresponsible lifestyle.

◆ Literary Focus

❹ **Social Conflict** Students may respond that the social conflict established here is that a patriotic English Protestant family, down on its luck but still very attached to the British crown, resides among Catholics in an Irish village.

William Trevor

In the town and beyond it they were regarded as harmlessly peculiar. Odd, people said, and in time this reference took on a burnish of affection.

They had always been thin, silent with one another, and similar in appearance: a brother and sister who shared a family face. It was a
❶ bony countenance, with pale blue eyes and a sharp, well-shaped nose and high cheekbones. Their father had had it too, but unlike them their father had been an irresponsible and careless man, with red flecks in his cheeks that they didn't have at all. The Middletons of Carraveagh the family had once been known as, but now the brother and sister were just the Middletons, for Carraveagh didn't count any more, except to them.

They owned four Herefords,[1] a number of hens, and the house itself, three miles outside the town. It was a large house, built in the reign of George II,[2] a monument that reflected in its glory and later decay the fortunes of a family.
❷ As the brother and sister aged, its roof increasingly ceased to afford protection, rust ate at its gutters, grass thrived in two thick channels all along its avenue. Their father had mortgaged his inherited estate, so local rumor claimed, in order to keep a Catholic Dublin woman in brandy and jewels. When he died, in 1924, his two children discovered that they possessed only a dozen acres. It was locally said also that this adversity hardened their will and that because of it they came to love the remains of Carraveagh more than they could ever have loved a husband or a wife. ❷ They blamed for their ill-fortune the Catholic Dublin woman whom they'd never met and they blamed as well the new national regime, contriving in their eccentric way to relate the two. ❸ In the days of the union jack[3] such women would have known their place—wasn't it all part and parcel?

Twice a week, on Fridays and Sundays, the Middletons journeyed into the town, first of all in a trap[4] and later in a Ford Anglia car. In the shops and elsewhere they made, quite gently, no secret of their continuing loyalty to the past. They attended on Sundays St. Patrick's Protestant Church, a place that matched their mood, for prayers were still said there for the King whose sovereignty their country had denied. ❹ The revolutionary regime would not last, they quietly informed the Reverend Packham—what sense was there in green-painted pillar boxes[5] and a language that nobody understood?

> **◆ Literary Focus**
> What social conflict is established in the opening paragraphs?

On Fridays, when they took seven or eight

1. **Herefords** *n.*: Breed of cattle.
2. **reign of George II:** 1727–1760.
3. **union jack:** British flag; symbol of British rule.
4. **trap** *n.*: Two-wheeled, horse-drawn carriage.
5. **pillar boxes:** Mail collection boxes.

Block Scheduling Strategies

Consider these suggestions to take advantage of extended class time:

- Introduce the selection by having students read and discuss the Background for Understanding (p. 992).
- Before students read the selection, introduce the Reading Strategy. Have students keep notes about causes and effects as they read the story. Allow time for students to meet and discuss causes and effects. Then have students work independently to complete the Reading Strategy page on Cause and Effect, in ***Selection Support,*** p. 255.
- Organize discussion groups in which students can answer the Critical Thinking questions (p. 1000).
- Assign the writing Mini-Lesson (p. 1001). Before students begin, discuss the characteristics of persuasive writing, including the effectiveness of writing clearly and of being brief.

dozen eggs to the town, they dressed in pressed tweeds and were accompanied over the years by a series of red setters, the breed there had always been at Carraveagh. They sold the eggs in Keogh's grocery and then had a drink with Mrs. Keogh in the part of her shop that was devoted to the consumption of refreshment. They enjoyed the occasion, for they liked Mrs. Keogh and were liked by her in return. Afterwards they shopped, chatting to the shopkeepers about whatever news there was, and then they went to Healy's Hotel for a few more drinks before driving home.

. . . In spite of their loyalty to the past, they built up convivial relationships with the people of the town. Fat Driscoll, who kept the butcher's shop, used even to joke about the past when he stood with them in Healy's Hotel or stood behind his own counter cutting their slender
5 chops or thinly slicing their liver. "Will you ever forget it, Mr. Middleton? I'd ha' run like a rabbit if you'd lifted a finger at me." Fat Driscoll would laugh then, rocking back on his heels with a glass of stout in his hand or banging their meat on to his weighing-scales. Mr. Middleton would smile. "There was alarm in your eyes, Mr. Driscoll," Miss Middleton would murmur, smiling also at the memory of the distant occasion.

▲ **Critical Viewing** How does the image of the house illustrate the Middletons' relationship with the townspeople? **[Apply]** 6

Fat Driscoll, with a farmer called Maguire and another called Breen, had stood in the hall of Carraveagh, each of them in charge of a shotgun. The Middletons, children then, had been locked with their mother and father and an aunt into an upstairs room. Nothing else had happened: the expected British soldiers had not, after all, arrived and the men in the hall had eventually relaxed their vigil. "A massacre they wanted," the Middletons' father said after they'd gone. . . . "Bloody ruffians."

◆ **Reading Strategy** Why was the family locked up? 7

◆ Build Vocabulary

countenance (koun′ tə nəns) *n.*: Face; facial features
adversity (ad vur′ sə tē) *n.*: Misfortune
sovereignty (säv′ rən tē) *n.*: Supreme political authority

◆ Reading Strategy

5 Cause and Effect Ask students to explain why Driscoll would have run away from the Middleton house, even though he was armed. *Students may say that he would have done so out of respect for the upper-class status of the Middleton family, who had been landed gentry in the region for three hundred years.*

▶Critical Viewing◀

6 Apply Students may suggest that the image shows the house set apart from and inaccessible to outsiders. The Middletons were once set apart by their wealth and status, now by their religion and loyalty to the crown.

◆ Reading Strategy

7 Cause and Effect Some students may say that the family was locked up because they were viewed as temporary prisoners or hostages in a time of war. Others may suggest that they were detained for their own protection.

Cross-Curricular Connection: Social Studies

Social conflict separated the Middletons from everyone else in their community; they were British patriots living in Ireland. Tell students that in the Irish struggle for independence in the early part of this century, as in any highly charged socio-political movement, there were conflicts not only between people on opposing sides, but between people within a side. Rebellion leaders Michael Collins and Eamon de Valera became antagonists, although they fought for the same goals. For a dynamic look at the issues in the conflict between the rebel leaders and the British government, and among the factions within the rebel movement itself, students can view the film *Michael Collins* (1996; directed by Neil Jordan).

◆ Literary Focus

1 Social Conflict Guide students to appreciate why the Middletons were regarded as anachronisms: They were non-working minor royalty, of the "wrong" political affiliation and religion, unmarried, and living in a crumbling manor on an ancient estate. To the members of the community, the Middletons represented the past.

◆ Background for Understanding

2 History: Trouble in Ireland Inform students that the changes in the church reflect the ongoing changes in society as a whole. Point out that the Irish Free State had become increasingly detached from Great Britain and, in 1949, severed all ties with Britain and renamed itself the Republic of Ireland.

3 Clarification Inform students that Queen Elizabeth II, was crowned in 1952, three years after Ireland officially severed its ties with Great Britain. Tell them that "God Save the King (or Queen)" is the British national anthem and that it has the same melody as "America" ("My Country 'Tis of Thee").

Customize for
Logical/Mathematical Learners

4 Point out that in 1961, twenty-two thousand pounds would have been worth about sixty-six thousand dollars.

◆ Critical Thinking

5 Predict Ask students to predict how the Middletons will react to the change in their lifestyle. *Some students may say they will become friendlier with the "common folk" because the distinctions are less clear now. Other students may feel that the Middletons will resent the decline in their lifestyle and withdraw from the community.*

The Second World War took place. Two Germans, a man and his wife called Winkelmann who ran a glove factory in the town, were suspected by the Middletons of being spies for the Third Reich.[6] People laughed, for they knew the Winkelmanns well and could lend no credence to the Middletons' latest fantasy—typical of them, they explained to the Winkelmanns, who had been worried. Soon after the War the Reverend Packham died and was replaced by the Reverend Bradshaw, a younger man who laughed also and regarded the Middletons as
1 an <u>anachronism</u>. They protested when prayers were no longer said for the Royal Family in St. Patrick's, but the Reverend Bradshaw considered that their protests were as absurd as the
2 prayers themselves had been. Why pray for the monarchy of a neighboring island when their own island had its chosen President now? The Middletons didn't reply to that argument. In the Reverend Bradshaw's presence they rose to their feet when the BBC played "God Save the King," and on the day of the coronation of Queen Elizabeth II they drove into the town with a small union jack propped up in the back window of their Ford Anglia. "Bedad, you're a holy terror, Mr. Middleton!" Fat Driscoll laughingly exclaimed, noticing the flag as he lifted a
3 tray of pork steaks from his display shelf. The Middletons smiled. It was a great day for the Commonwealth of Nations, they replied, a remark which further amused Fat Driscoll and which he later repeated in Phelan's public house. "Her Britannic Majesty," guffawed his friend Mr. Breen.

Situated in a valley that was noted for its beauty and with convenient access to rich rivers and bogs over which gamebirds flew, the town benefited from post-war tourism. Healy's Hotel changed its title and became, overnight, the New Ormonde. Shopkeepers had their shopfronts painted and Mr. Healy organized an annual Salmon Festival. Even Canon Kelly, who had at first commented severely on the habits of the tourists, and in particular on the summertime dress of the women, was in the end obliged to confess that the morals of his flock remained unaffected. "God and good sense," he proclaimed, meaning God and his own teaching. In time he even derived pride from the fact that people with other values came briefly to the town and that the values esteemed by his parishioners were in no way diminished. . . .

From the windows of their convent the Loretto nuns observed the long, sleek cars with G.B. plates; English and American accents drifted on the breeze to them. Mothers cleaned up their children and sent them to the Golf Club to seek employment as caddies. Sweet shops sold holiday mementoes. The brown, soda and currant breads of Murphy-Flood's bakery were declared to be delicious. Mr. Healy doubled the number of local girls who served as waitresses in his dining room, and in the winter of 1961 he had the builders in again, working on an extension for which the Munster and Leinster Bank had lent him twenty-two thou- 4
sand pounds.

But as the town increased its prosperity Carraveagh continued its decline. The Middletons were in their middle sixties now and were reconciled to a life that became more uncomfortable with every passing year. Together they roved the vast lofts of their house, placing old paint tins and flowerpot saucers beneath the drips from the roof. At night they sat over their thin chops in a dining room that had once been gracious and which in a way was gracious still, except for the faded appearance of furniture that was dry from lack of polish and of a wall- 5
paper that time had rendered colorless. In the hall their father gazed down at them, framed in ebony and gilt, in the uniform of the Irish Guards. He had conversed with Queen Victoria, and even in their middle sixties they could still hear him saying that God and Empire and Queen formed a trinity unique in any worthy soldier's heart. In the hall hung the family crest, and on ancient Irish linen the Cross of St. George.[7]

The dog that accompanied the Middletons now was called Turloch, an animal whose death they dreaded for they felt they couldn't

◆ Build Vocabulary

anachronism (ə nak′ rə niz′ əm) *n.*: Something out of its proper time in history

6. **Third Reich** (rīk): German government under the Nazis (1933–1945).

7. **St. George:** Patron saint of England.

Cultural Connection

Nobel-Prize winning Irish poet William Butler Yeats (1865–1939) took an active role in political movements bent on achieving Ireland's independence from England. In 1922, he was appointed a senator of the new Irish Free State. In some of his poems, Yeats celebrated the efforts of the early fighters and martyrs for Irish freedom, and referred to some of the bloody historical events that paved the way for the eventual success of the rebellion. Invite students to look through Yeats's work for poems that reflect his political views about the struggle for Irish nationalism. Have them choose some to read aloud to classmates.

◄ **Critical Viewing** What do these flags symbolize to the characters in the story? **[Analyze]** 6

manage the antics of another pup. Turloch, being thirteen, moved slowly and was blind and a little deaf. He was a reminder to them of their own advancing years and of the effort it had become to tend the Herefords and collect the weekly eggs. More and more they looked forward to Fridays, to the warm companionship of Mrs. Keogh and Mr. Healy's chatter in the hotel. They stayed longer now with Mrs. Keogh and in the hotel, and idled longer in the shops, and drove home more slowly. Dimly, but with no less loyalty, they still recalled the distant
7 past and were listened to without ill-feeling when they spoke of it and of Carraveagh as it had been, and of the Queen whose company their careless father had known.

The visitors who came to the town heard about the Middletons and were impressed. It was a pleasant wonder, more than one of them remarked, that old wounds could heal so completely, that the Middletons continued in their loyalty to the past and that, in spite of it, they were respected in the town. When Miss Middleton had been ill with a form of pneumonia in 1958 Canon Kelly had driven out to Carraveagh twice a week with pullets and young ducks that his housekeeper had dressed. "An upright couple," was the Canon's public opinion of the Middletons, and he had been known to add that eccentric views would hurt you less than malice. "We can disagree without guns in this town," Mr. Healy pronounced in his cocktail room, and his visitors usually replied that as far as they could see that was the result of living in a Christian country. That the Middletons bought their meat from a man who had once locked them into an upstairs room and had then waited to shoot soldiers in their hall was a fact that amazed the seasonal visitors. You lived and learned, they remarked to Mr. Healy.

The Middletons, privately, often considered that they led a strange life. Alone in their two beds at night they now and again wondered why they hadn't just sold Carraveagh forty-eight years ago when their father had died—why had the tie been so strong and why had they in perversity encouraged it? They
didn't fully know, nor did they attempt to dis- 8
cuss the matter in any way. Instinctively they had remained at Carraveagh, instinctively feeling that it would have been cowardly to go. Yet often it seemed to them now to be no more than a game they played, this worship of the distant past. And at other times it seemed as real and as important as the remaining acres of land, and the house itself.

"Isn't that shocking?" Mr. Healy said one day
in 1967. "Did you hear about that, Mr. Middle- 9
ton, blowing up them post offices in Belfast?"

Mr. Healy, red-faced and short-haired, spoke casually in his Cocktail Room, making midday conversation. He had commented in much the same way at breakfast-time, looking up from the *Irish Independent*. Everyone in the town had said it too: that the blowing up of sub-post offices in Belfast was a shocking matter.

"A bad business," Fat Driscoll remarked, wrapping the Middletons' meat. "We don't want that old stuff all over again."

"We didn't want it in the first place," Miss Middleton reminded him. He laughed, and she laughed, and so did her brother. Yes, it was a game, she thought—how could any of it be as real or as important as the afflictions and problems of the old butcher himself, his rheumatism and his reluctance to retire? Did her

►Critical Viewing◄

❻ **Analyze** Some students may say that the flags symbolize the divided loyalty of the Middletons; they are loyal both to Great Britain and to their home and community in Ireland. Others might point to the conflict caused by living under one flag while remaining loyal to another.

◆ Reading Strategy

❼ **Cause and Effect** Ask students to identify the reason the Middletons seek out the companionship of their neighbors. *As old age approaches and English influence in Ireland declines, the Middletons feel more and more isolated. In response, they seek out the companionship of those who are nearby. Some students may point out that the passage of time helps to smooth past difficulties.*

◆ Critical Thinking

❽ **Analyze** Ask students to explain how the Middletons' personalities are revealed through descriptions of their thoughts and actions. *Students may say that their thoughts and actions indicate that the Middletons are confused about the very nature of their being; that they are passive, fearful, directionless, and incommunicative.*

◆ Background for Understanding

❾ **History: Trouble in Ireland** Inform students that, at first, the bombings of post offices in Belfast were attributed to the Irish Republican Army, but that later it was determined that the explosions were the work of a Protestant paramilitary group keen on removing the prime minister from office.

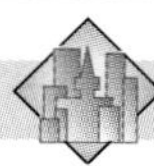

Beyond the Classroom

Career Connection

Travel Agent Times are considerably better now for tourism in Ireland than they were in the Middletons' later years. Have groups of students imagine that they are travel agents specializing in creative theme tours of the Republic of Ireland. Invite them to choose a specific theme and plan a trip accordingly, presenting their efforts in a travel brochure. For instance, one group can choose "Sights and Sounds of the Rebellion," while others may select "Irish Castles and Great Homes," "Irish Literary Landmarks," "Irish Music and Dance," "Crafts of Ireland," and so on. To gather ideas for their brochures, groups can contact tourist offices, visit the library and bookstores, look at travel videos, browse the Internet, and talk with people who have visited or lived in Ireland. Have groups contribute their polished brochures to a class Irish travel center or to the school library.

Customize for
Less Proficient Readers

1 This is a concrete example to help these students understand the difference between the past and the present. Ask students to describe how Driscoll's attitude has changed, based on his reaction to the Middletons' dog. *Students should note that he now gives treats to their dog, where as in the past, he locked their dog up in fear. This change in attitude reflects a general change from fear to friendliness.*

◆ Background for Understanding

2 History: Trouble in Ireland
Inform students that Belfast is the capital of Northern Ireland and that Derry, or Londonderry, is a seaport there. Tell them that in 1969, following bloody riots in those two cities, British troops were sent into Northern Ireland. In 1972, as the violence continued, the British government took over direct control of the country.

◆ Literary Focus

3 Social Conflict Ask students to describe how the Middletons' relationship with their neighbors is affected by the early stages of the new conflict. *At first, it seems as if they will maintain their friendly attitudes toward each other. This is illustrated by Mr. Healy's attempt to commiserate with Middleton over the tourist situation.*

◆ Reading Strategy

4 Cause and Effect Students may suggest that tourism ground to a halt for fear of the bloodshed that might occur. They also may say that British travelers avoided the region for fear that they would not be well treated.

◆ Critical Thinking

5 Draw Conclusions Have students explain why they think the villagers' attitudes are changing. *The villagers are feeling the pressure of the conflict. Since the Middletons represent the power that is killing their trade and tourism, the villagers resent them.*

◆ Grammar and Style

6 Restrictive and Nonrestrictive Adjective Clauses
Guide students to see that the adjective clause in this sentence is nonrestrictive because it is not necessary to the meaning of the sentence.

---

brother, she wondered, privately think so too?

"Come on, old Turloch," he said, stroking the flank of the red setter with the point of his shoe, and she reflected that you could never tell what he was thinking. Certainly it wasn't the kind of thing you wanted to talk about.

"I've put him in a bit of mince," Fat Driscoll said, which was something he often did these days, pretending the mince would otherwise be
1 thrown away. There'd been a red setter about the place that night when he waited in the hall for the soldiers; Breen and Maguire had pushed it down into a cellar, frightened of it.

"There's a heart of gold in you, Mr. Driscoll," Miss Middleton murmured, nodding and smiling at him. He was the same age as she was, sixty-six—he should have shut up shop years ago. He would have, he'd once told them, if there'd been a son to leave the business to. As it was, he'd have to sell it and when it came to the point he found it hard to make the necessary arrangements. "Like us and Carraveagh," she'd said, even though on the face of it it didn't seem the same at all.

Every evening they sat in the big old kitchen, hearing the news. It was only in Belfast and Derry, the wireless said; outside Belfast and Derry you wouldn't know anything was hap-
2 pening at all. On Fridays they listened to the talk in Mrs. Keogh's bar and in the hotel. "Well, thank God it has nothing to do with the South," Mr. Healy said often, usually repeating the statement.

The first British soldiers landed in the North of Ireland, and soon people didn't so often say that outside Belfast and Derry you wouldn't know anything was happening. There were incidents in Fermanagh and Armagh, in border villages and towns. One Prime Minister resigned and then another one. The troops were unpopular, the newspapers said; <u>internment</u> became part of the machinery of government. In the town, in St. Patrick's Protestant Church and in the Church of the Holy Assumption, prayers for peace were offered, but no peace came.

"We're hit, Mr. Middleton," Mr. Healy said one
3 Friday morning. "If there's a dozen visitors this summer it'll be God's own stroke of luck for us."

"Luck?"

"Sure, who wants to come to a country with all that malarkey in it?"

"But it's only in the North."

"Tell that to your tourists, Mr. Middleton."

The town's prosperity ebbed. The border was more than sixty miles away, but over that distance had spread some wisps of the fog of war. As anger rose in the town at the loss of fortune so there rose also the kind of talk there had been in the distant past. There was talk of atrocities and counteratrocities, and of guns and gelignite[8] and the rights of people. There was bitterness suddenly in Mrs. 4
Keogh's bar because of the lack of trade, and in the empty hotel there was bitterness also.

> **◆ Reading Strategy**
> Why have tourists stopped coming to the town?

On Fridays, only sometimes at first, there was a silence when the Middletons appeared. It was as though, going back nearly twenty years, people remembered the union jack in the window of their car and saw it now in a different light. It wasn't something to laugh at any more, nor were certain words that the Middletons had gently spoken, nor were they themselves just 5
an old, peculiar couple. Slowly the change crept about, all around them in the town, until Fat Driscoll didn't wish it to be remembered that he had ever given them mince for their dog. He had stood with a gun in the enemy's house, waiting for soldiers so that soldiers might be killed—it was better that people should remember that.

One day Canon Kelly looked the other way when he saw the Middletons' car coming and they noticed this movement of his head, although he hadn't wished them to. And on another day Mrs. O'Brien, who had always been 6
keen to talk to them in the hotel, didn't reply when they addressed her.

The Middletons naturally didn't discuss these rebuffs but they each of them privately knew that there was no conversation they could have at this time with the people of the town. The stand they had taken and kept to for so many years no longer seemed ridiculous in the town. Had they driven with a union jack now they would, astoundingly, have been shot.

◆ Build Vocabulary

internment (in turn′ mənt) *n.*: Confinement during war

---

8. **gelignite** *n.*: Explosive.

Speaking and Listening Mini-Lesson

Eulogy

This mini-lesson supports the Speaking and Listening activity in the Idea Bank on page 1001.

Introduce the Concept Tell students that they are going to write and present a eulogy, a formal speech of praise, that Mr. Driscoll might give at the funeral of Miss Middleton.

Develop Background Discuss the concept of eulogies. If possible, students should read actual eulogies to get a better appreciation of their style and tone. Then have them gather information about Miss Middleton, about Driscoll, and about their friendship, rereading parts of the story as necessary to check the details.

Apply the Information Have students write and edit their eulogies and then practice their delivery prior to presenting them to the class.

Assess the Outcome Evaluate the eulogies according to how accurately they express Driscoll's relationship with Miss Middleton. The speeches should reflect a clear understanding of both characters, and should have a respectful tone.

"It will never cease." He spoke disconsolately one night, standing by the dresser where the wireless was.

She washed the dishes they'd eaten from, and the cutlery. "Not in our time," she said.

"It is worse than before."

"Yes, it is worse than before."

They took from the walls of the hall the portrait of their father in the uniform of the Irish Guards because it seemed wrong to them that at this time it should hang there. They took down also the crest of their family and the Cross of St. George, and from a vase on the drawing-room mantelpiece they removed the small union jack that had been there since the coronation of Queen Elizabeth II. They did not remove these articles in fear but in mourning for the *modus vivendi* [9] that had existed for so long between them and the people of the town. They had given their custom to a butcher who had planned to shoot down soldiers in their
7 hall and he, in turn, had given them mince for their dog. For fifty years they had experienced, after suspicion had seeped away, a tolerance that never again in the years that were left to them would they know.

9. ***modus vivendi*** (vi ven′ dī): Manner of getting along.

One November night their dog died and he said to her after he had buried it that they must not be depressed by all that was happening. They would die themselves and the house would become a ruin because there was no one to inherit it, and the distant past would be set to rest. But she disagreed: the *modus vivendi* had been easy for them, she pointed out, because they hadn't really minded the dwindling of their fortunes while the town prospered. It had given them a life, and a kind of dignity: you could take a pride out of living in peace.

He did not say anything and then, because of the emotion that both of them felt over the death of their dog, he said in a rushing way that they could no longer at their age hope to make a living out of the remains of Carraveagh. They must sell the hens and the four Herefords. As he spoke, he watched her nodding, agreeing with the sense of it. Now and again, he thought, he would drive slowly into the town, to buy groceries and meat with the money they had saved, and to face the silence that would sourly thicken as their own two deaths came closer and death increased in another part of their island. She felt him thinking that and she knew that he was right. Because of the distant past they would die friendless. It was worse than being murdered in their beds.

Guide for Responding

◆ Literature and Your Life

Reader's Response Would you describe the Middletons as odd, foolish, courageous, or with some other adjective? Explain.

Thematic Focus In this story, how does the "distant past" cause conflicts in the present?

Role-Play With a partner, role-play a scene in which Miss Middleton discusses openly and honestly with Fat Driscoll her feelings about how she and her brother are being treated.

☑ Check Your Comprehension

1. (a) Who is responsible for the Middletons' reduced economic position? (b) Whom do they blame?
2. Describe two ways in which the Middletons show their loyalty to the "distant past."
3. What kind of relationships do the Middletons have with the townspeople?
4. What changes occur in the town after World War II?
5. How is the town affected by the violence in the North?

Beyond the Selection

FURTHER READING

Other Works by William Trevor

A Standard of Behavior
Angels at the Ritz, and Other Stories
Family Sins

Other Works About the Experience of Alienation

The Dangling Man, Saul Bellow
The Invisible Man, Ralph Ellison

We suggest that you preview these works before recommending them to students.

INTERNET

You may find additional information about William Trevor on the Internet at the following site. Please be aware, however, that sites may have changed since this information was published.

For biographical information and synopses of and brief critical comments on some of his works, go to **http://www.futurenet.co.uk/penguin/books/0670841293.html**

We *strongly recommend* that you preview sites before you send students to them.

◆ Grammar and Style

7 Restrictive and Nonrestrictive Adjective Clauses Guide students to see that the adjective clause in this sentence is restrictive because it adds information necessary to the meaning of the sentence. That is, it specifically indicates to which butcher the Middletons refer.

◆ Critical Thinking

Speculate Ask students to think about and discuss why the Middletons do not consider leaving a place that has become inhospitable to them. *Most students will say that the Middletons feel too old to move or that they do not have the resources to move. Some students may feel that in an ironic twist, the Middletons are again refusing to let go of the past, only this time, of an Irish past rather than a British one.*

Reinforce and Extend

Answers

◆ Literature and Your Life

Reader's Response Some students may describe the Middletons as naive because they don't understand how outside conflicts can affect their lives and those of the people around them. Others may think they are simply stuck in the past, detached from and oblivious to change.

Thematic Focus Students may respond that the Middletons' loyalty to the British crown at a time when many in Ireland are openly hostile to the English leads to conflict.

☑ Check Your Comprehension

1. (a) The father is responsible, but (b) the Middletons blame his girlfriend and the new government.
2. They attend a Protestant church where prayers for the British king are still said, and they display a union jack in their car.
3. Up until the renewal of anti-British sentiment, they had enjoyed cordial relationships with the townspeople, who regarded them as eccentric, but harmless.
4. After World War II there is an economic boom that brings a surge of tourism and prosperity for the town.
5. As violence erupts in the North, tourism declines in the town.

◆ Critical Thinking

1. The Middletons were running out of money and influence, and their property was deteriorating at about the same time the British Empire was dwindling through the loss of many of its colonies.
2. As long as the town prospered, the Middletons were respected, even though they were at political odds with the villagers.
3. Students may say that deeply felt loyalties never change and that old wounds never heal.
4. Students may say that economic adversity can create bitterness and cruelty, or that in good times, people are more likely to accept differences than they are in hard times. When the town was prosperous, the Middletons were considered odd, but accepted; when the town fell on hard times, they were outcasts.
5. Students may say that the Middletons are responsible because they buried their heads in the past. Others may feel that they are the undeserving target of the townspeople's anger at their declining tourism and trade.

◆ Reading Strategy

Cause and Effect

1. . . . they were ardent supporters of the British Crown, and proud of it.
2. . . . prosperity came to an end in the Republic of Ireland and old wounds surfaced.
3. . . . they blamed the British, and the Middletons by association, for the drop-off in tourism.

◆ Literary Focus

Social Conflict

1. The Middletons see Ireland as part of Great Britain; the villagers recognize that they are part of the Republic of Ireland.
2. When the town was prosperous, people found the Middletons' views more curious than distasteful.
3. The events in Northern Ireland and the resulting downturn in the local economy caused the social conflict to escalate.
4. To demonstrate his loyalty to the cause of Irish freedom, Driscoll shuns the Middletons, keeping his friendship with them hidden from his neighbors.

Guide for Responding *(continued)*

◆ Critical Thinking

INTERPRET

1. How does the decline in the Middletons' fortunes parallel the decline of the British Empire? **[Connect]**

2. What is ironic about the fact that throughout most of the story the townspeople respect the Middletons? **[Analyze]**

3. What does the change in the townspeople's attitude toward the Middletons reveal about human nature? **[Draw Conclusions]**

4. What message does this story convey? Support your answer. **[Draw Conclusions]**

EVALUATE

5. Are the Middletons to blame for their isolation at the end of the story? **[Make a Judgment]**

◆ Reading Strategy

CAUSE AND EFFECT

Noticing **cause and effect**—the reasons why things happen—can help you understand the theme of a story. Complete each sentence with a cause or an effect.

1. The Middletons displayed a union jack because . . .

2. As a result of the violence in the north, . . .

3. The townspeople began to shun the Middletons because . . .

◆ Literary Focus

SOCIAL CONFLICT

The plot of "The Distant Past" rises and falls around a central **social conflict,** a struggle between two different political views. Though the political events occur offstage, so to speak, they have a major effect on the characters in the story.

1. How is the Middletons' view of society different from that of everyone around them?

2. Why is the social conflict very mild at first?

3. What causes the social conflict to escalate?

4. How does the changing relationship between Fat Driscoll and the Middletons reflect the larger social conflict?

5. What connection is there between the social conflict and the theme of the story?

◆ Build Vocabulary

USING THE SUFFIX *-ity*

In your notebook, add *-ity* to each word and insert the new word in the sentence where it fits.

a. serene **b.** civil **c.** adverse

1. Though feelings ran high, the opposing factions maintained their __?__ during negotiations.

2. The campers encountered one __?__ after another, from ants to torrential rains.

3. The soothing music established a mood of __?__ in the room.

USING THE WORD BANK

In your notebook, write the word from the word bank that best completes each sentence.

1. The townspeople regarded the brother and sister as an __?__.

2. They did not question the __?__ of the English king.

3. Financial __?__ bore down on them after their father's death.

4. Kindly eyes sparkled from the sister's careworn __?__.

5. They shuddered at news of the unjust __?__ of innocent citizens.

◆ Grammar and Style

RESTRICTIVE AND NONRESTRICTIVE ADJECTIVE CLAUSES

A **restrictive adjective clause** is not separated from the rest of the sentence by commas. A **nonrestrictive adjective clause** is set off by commas.

Practice Rewrite the sentences, underlining each adjective clause and adding commas where needed.

1. The Middletons who had lived comfortably found themselves impoverished.

2. Twice a week they rode to town where they had friendly encounters with the townspeople.

3. The dog that accompanied them was always a red setter.

4. The shopkeepers with whom they did business considered them odd.

5. After a convivial afternoon, they made the trip back to their rundown home which they called Carraveagh.

5. The social conflict reflects the ebbs and flows of the larger political conflict between Great Britain and the Irish people.

◆ Build Vocabulary

Using the Suffix *-ity*

1. civility; 2. adversity; 3. serenity

Using the Word Bank

1. anachronism; 2. sovereignty; 3. adversity; 4. countenance; 5. internment

◆ Grammar and Style

Restrictive and Nonrestrictive Adjective Clauses

1. The Middletons, who had lived comfortably, found themselves impoverished.
2. Twice a week they rode to town, where they had friendly encounters with the townspeople.
3. The dog that accompanied them was always a red setter.
4. The shopkeepers with whom they did business considered them odd.
5. After a convivial afternoon, they made the trip back to their rundown home, which they called Carraveagh.

Build Your Portfolio

Idea Bank

Writing

1. Obituary Write an obituary for either of the Middletons to appear in the local newspaper. Summarize the details of his or her life and comment on his or her position in the community.

2. Poem Write a poem that expresses the same theme as "The Distant Past." Your poem may be about the Middletons or any other topic that shows the effect of social conflict on individuals.

3. Literary Analysis Write an essay in which you analyze the effect of the story's social conflict on the characters. Support your points with details from the story.

Speaking and Listening

4. Eulogy Miss Middleton has died. As Fat Driscoll, give the eulogy at the funeral service. Present an honest portrait of the deceased and your relationship with her. **[Performing Arts Link]**

5. Interview With a group of classmates, stage an interview between a news reporter and the Middletons about how the troubles in Northern Ireland affected their lives. **[Media Link]**

Projects

6. Portfolio Create a series of sketches of the Middletons through the years. Put Carraveagh in the background and include a red setter, a trap or Ford Anglia, or other items that reflect the changes in their lives. **[Art Link]**

7. A Celebration of Irish Culture Stage a celebration of Irish culture that includes music, food, and storytelling. Tape Irish music, write out recipe cards for Irish dishes, and prepare Irish stories to tell. **[Social Studies Link; Music Link]**

Writing Mini-Lesson

Persuasive Letter

The political struggles in Northern Ireland is just one of many major social conflicts that have occurred in recent years. Think of a current social conflict—local, national, or international—about which you are concerned. Then write a persuasive letter to parties involved in the conflict, offering suggestions about how the conflict can be resolved.

Writing Skills Focus: Brevity and Clarity

To be effective, a persuasive letter must be **brief**—saying only what needs to be said—and **clear**—stating exactly what you propose.

- State your proposal for resolving the conflict in your introductory paragraph.
- Follow with a series of concise paragraphs supporting your opinion.
- Be as exact as possible when choosing words to present your case.
- Leave out any words or details that don't advance your argument.

Prewriting Start by charting out the causes and effects of the conflict. Then come up with possible solutions. List reasons you think the solutions would work. Review your notes and decide on the strongest possible solutions.

Drafting In your opening paragraph, use some of the effects of the conflict to demonstrate why it is essential for the conflict to be resolved. Then present your ideas for resolving the conflict. Follow with a series of paragraphs that each focus on a single main point. End with a strong appeal to both parties to follow your advice.

Revising Show your letter to a classmate. Ask for suggestions about how you can make it more convincing and more direct. Use your peer's suggestions to help direct your revisions.

ASSESSMENT OPTIONS

Formal Assessment, Selection Test, pp. 257–259, and Assessment Resources Software. The selection test is designed so that it can be easily customized to the performance levels of your students.

Alternative Assessment, p. 53, includes options for less advanced students, more advanced students, musical/rhythmic learners, verbal/linguistic learners, and visual/spatial learners.

PORTFOLIO ASSESSMENT

Use the following rubrics in the ***Alternative Assessment*** booklet to assess student writing:
Obituary: Expression Rubric, p. 95
Poem: Expression Rubric, p. 95
Literary Analysis: Literary Analysis Rubric, p. 113
Writing Mini-Lesson: Persuasion Rubric, p. 106

Idea Bank

Customizing for *Performance Levels*

Following are suggestions for matching Idea Bank topics with your students' performance levels:

Less Advanced Students: 1, 4, 6
Average Students: 2, 5, 6
More Advanced Students: 3, 7

Customizing for *Learning Modalities*

Following are suggestions for matching Idea Bank topics with your students' learning modalities:

Verbal/Linguistic: 4, 5
Interpersonal: 5
Visual/Spatial: 6, 7
Bodily/Kinesthetic: 7

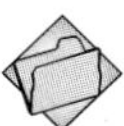

Writing Mini-Lesson

Refer students to the Writing Process Handbook, page 1189, for instruction on the writing process, and page 1192 for further information on Persuasion.

Writers at Work Videodisc

Have students view the videodisc segment on Persuasion (Ch. 4) featuring Cary Bricker to get tips on revising a draft.

Play frames 39870 to 40926

Writing Lab CD-ROM

Have students complete the tutorial on Persuasion. Follow these steps:

1. Tell students to use the interactive instruction on identifying an audience.
2. Encourage students to use the audience profile tool.
3. Allow time for students to draft on the computer.
4. Have students take advantage of the Revision Checker for Language Variety.

Sourcebook

Have students use Chapter 4, Persuasion (pp. 96–129), for additional support. The chapter includes questions to guide self-revision (p. 121).

OBJECTIVES

1. To read, comprehend, and interpret poetry
2. To relate poetry to personal experience
3. To summarize in order to facilitate comprehension
4. To analyze diction and style
5. To build vocabulary in context and learn the word root *-mort-*
6. To recognize how use of concrete and abstract nouns affects a writer's style
7. To write conflict-resolution guidelines, including a clear explanation of procedures
8. To respond to poetry through writing, speaking and listening, and projects

SKILLS INSTRUCTION

Vocabulary: Word Roots: *-mort-*

Grammar: Concrete and Abstract Nouns

Reading Strategy: Summarize

Literary Focus: Diction and Style

Writing: Clear Explanation of Procedures

Speaking and Listening: Monologue (teacher edition)

Critical Viewing: Evaluate; Compare and Contrast; Analyze

PORTFOLIO OPPORTUNITIES

Writing: Book Blurb; Comparison and Contrast; Response to Criticism

Writing Mini-Lesson: Conflict-Resolution Guidelines

Speaking and Listening: Monologue; Oral Interpretation

Projects: Irish Folk Music; The History of the "Troubles"

More About the Authors

Seamus Heaney's poetry arises from an intersection of two histories—his Irish Catholic upbringing on a farm and his British education. In his poetry, Heaney sometimes confronts personal and literary ghosts; at other times, he seems to celebrate his history.

Eavan Boland published her first collection of poems, *23 Poems,* with money she earned working as a hotel housekeeper in Dublin. She later resigned a position as a lecturer at Dublin's Trinity College when she found that it interfered with her writing. In that writing, Boland explores what she calls "a transaction" between strong emotions and lyric tone.

Guide for Interpreting

Seamus Heaney *(1939–)*

Born in County Derry, Northern Ireland, Seamus Heaney has devoted much of his poetry to the life and history of his homeland. He is a gifted traditionalist whom the American poet Robert Lowell called "the most important Irish poet since Yeats." Heaney has earned that high praise with visionary books of poetry like *Seeing Things* (1991) and *The Spirit Level* (1996), and with his brilliant lectures on poetry in *The Redress of Poetry* (1995).

The eldest of nine children, Heaney spent a happy childhood on a farm that had been in his family for generations. He has said that his deep regard for tradition and the past grew from his early experiences in the countryside.

He first published as an undergraduate at Queen's University in Belfast. Somewhat later, having struggled with the role of the artist in Northern Ireland's troubled political climate, he left Northern Ireland and settled in the Irish Republic in 1972. His departure was called by some an artistic necessity and by others, a betrayal. Heaney nevertheless remains the leading Irish poet, Republican or Northern.

Since 1984, he has been Boylston Professor of Rhetoric and Poetry at Harvard, and from 1989 to 1994 he held the chair of Professor of Poetry at Oxford. In 1995, Seamus Heaney received the Nobel Prize for Literature.

Eavan Boland *(1944–)*

Eavan Boland was born in Dublin, the capital of the Irish Republic. Her father was a diplomat who, she says, "recognized the importance of poetry to civilization." Her mother was a painter, who also "was totally in tune with what poetry tried to do."

During much of Boland's early life, she was away from Ireland. While her father was ambassador to Great Britain in the 1950's, she experienced anti-Irish hostility and felt "a great sense of isolation." Returning to Ireland in 1959, she found "a great imaginative release." Since 1967 she has published several acclaimed volumes of poetry, including *The War Horse, In Her Own Image, Night Feed,* and *Beyond History.*

Married to a novelist and the mother of two daughters, Boland often writes about domestic life, but she shuns the label "woman poet." She says poetry should create only statements that are "bound to be human."

◆ Background for Understanding

History: Heaney in the Context of Northern Ireland

For about 800 years before the twentieth century Ireland was, with the exception of a few brief periods, under English control. Since the 1920's, Ireland has been partitioned into the Irish Republic in the South and Ulster, or Northern Ireland, which remains allied with Great Britain.

Ulster has been a focus of conflict between Protestants and Catholics. The Ulster Protestants generally support British rule of Northern Ireland. For the most part, Northern Irish Catholics want "the British out" and Ireland united.

From the early 1970's on, this conflict has produced terrorism by Catholics and Protestants, with occasional cease-fires. It was just this strife—and the pressure it created to take sides—that Seamus Heaney turned from when he settled in the Irish Republic in 1972. In his poem "Two Lorries," he refers to a bombing incident from this struggle.

Prentice Hall Literature Program Resources

REINFORCE / RETEACH / EXTEND

Selection Support Pages
Build Vocabulary: Word Roots: *-mort-*, p. 257
Grammar and Style: Concrete and Abstract Nouns, p. 258
Reading Strategy: Summarize, p. 259
Literary Focus: Diction and Style, p. 260

Strategies for Diverse Student Needs, p. 54

Beyond Literature, p. 54

Formal Assessment Selection Test, pp. 260–262; Assessment Resources Software

Activities for Alternative Assessment, p. 54

Writing and Language Transparencies
Branching Organizer, p. 95

Resource Pro CD-ROM
Includes all resource material and customizable lesson plan for all selections

Listening to Literature Audiocassettes
"Follower," "Two Lorries," "Outside History"

Looking at Literature Videodisc Chapter 11, "Eavan Boland on Appreciating Literature"

Follower ◆ Two Lorries ◆ Outside History

◆ Literature and Your Life

CONNECT YOUR EXPERIENCE

Try to go through a day without making a choice—it's impossible. Even if you spent the day in bed, under the covers, your mind would be roaming around the world—making choices.

These two Irish poets think about choices, and make them, in poems. "Deciding" in poetry lets these poets bring their deepest thoughts and feelings to their choices.

Journal Writing Briefly describe an important choice you made that turned out well.

THEMATIC FOCUS: CONFLICTS ABROAD AND AT HOME

What do these poets have to say, directly or indirectly, about the conflicts in Northern Ireland?

◆ Build Vocabulary

WORD ROOTS: *-mort-*

In "Outside History," Boland speaks about being *mortal,* meaning "subject to death." This word contains the root *-mort-,* which means "death." The same root appears in words like *mortuary,* "a funeral home."

WORD BANK

Preview this list of words before you read the poems.

furrow
nuisance
inklings
mortal
ordeal

◆ Literary Focus

DICTION AND STYLE

Diction refers to a writer's typical choice of words—formal or informal, down-to-earth or intellectual. Word choice is an important part of **style**, which takes in a writer's whole manner of expression. Style also includes a poet's use of forms and rhythms (traditional or otherwise) and his or her typical themes and images.

Heaney's style is marked by his use of traditional forms like the **sestina** ("Two Lorries"), which recycles six words to end each line. He also has a love of precise and down-to-earth language. A farmer's son, he handles words as if they had the heft of potatoes.

◆ Grammar and Style

CONCRETE AND ABSTRACT NOUNS

Both poets use **concrete nouns,** which name things that can be sensed, and **abstract nouns,** which name general things, like ideas and qualities. However, they use these two types of nouns in different proportions.

Heaney, as a farmer's son, fills his work with down-to-earth, concrete nouns—*shafts, furrow, horses.* Boland, at least in "Outside History," uses a greater proportion of abstract nouns, like *history* and *myth.*

As you read Heaney's and Boland's poems, notice the ratio of concrete to abstract nouns. This ratio is one measure of a writer's style.

◆ Reading Strategy

SUMMARIZE

No matter how you respond to individual images in a poem, when you reach the last line, it may seem as if you are left with nothing to hold onto. **Summarizing** a poem—briefly restating its key points—can help you hold it in your mind. You can even summarize individual stanzas like this one:

I wanted to grow up and plow,
To close one eye, stiffen my arm.
All I ever did was follow
In his broad shadow round the farm. ("Follower")

Summary I wanted to be a farmer, like my father.

Ask the class to brainstorm for television shows, cartoon shows, rock groups, and fads that were popular when they were around eight years old. List responses on the chalkboard. Then ask students to observe how they now view the things listed. For example, do the shows seem silly. Also ask students what they learned from those past entertainments.

Then tell students that the poems in this section all deal with how the poets' pasts form part of their present.

Customize for
Less Proficient Readers
Encourage less proficient readers to engage all their senses in reading the poems. By responding through the senses, readers will be able to enjoy the poetry even when literal comprehension is challenging.

Customize for
More Advanced Students
Have more advanced students use the summarizing strategy to analyze the figurative language in these poems. By comparing the summary with the poet's original work, students can comprehend the depth and layers of meaning in the original.

Customize for
English Language Learners
Heaney's use of regional and technical words may pose difficulties for these students. Ask them to identify unusual words in these poems—words they have never seen before. Have them look up the definition of each, then note what special significance each word has related to the topic of the poem.

Customize for
Verbal/Linguistic Learners
To help verbal/linguistic learners appreciate these poems' carefully crafted language, have them identify and define particularly evocative words. How do the connotative meanings of these words contribute to the poems' overall effect?

Preparing for Standardized Tests

Reading and Vocabulary Learning word roots is a useful test preparation strategy, enabling students to improve performance on vocabulary, spelling, sentence completion, and reading comprehension items. The Build Vocabulary lesson for this selection focuses on learning word meanings through the use of the word root *-mort-.* For additional practice, use the Build Vocabulary page in ***Selection Support,*** p. 257.

Grammar and Language When students are asked to complete open-ended written responses, incorporating a range of language and stylistic techniques will contribute to improved results. For example, using both concrete and abstract nouns will enable students to craft a variety of moods and tones in their writing. The Grammar and Style lesson for this selection focuses on this topic. For additional practice, use the Grammar and Style page on Concrete and Abstract Nouns, p. 258, in ***Selection Support.***

Develop Understanding

One-Minute Insight Both of Seamus Heaney's poems refer to his relationship with his parents and, by extension, with his Irish homeland. "Follower" focuses on the personal interaction between a small boy and his farmer father, poignantly conveying how the roles of parent and child shift as they age. In "Two Lorries," the poet laments the threat of Irish terrorism, contrasting a terrorist's truck bomb with a flirtatious delivery-truck driver—both might have taken his mother away from him, and both involve a "cheap," unreal passion. Each poem shows the two faces of Ireland, one turned towards the past, the other towards the present; the strong emotions tying the Irish to their land; and the powerful ability of memories from daily life to focus those emotions.

Customize for *Visual/Spatial Learners* Invite these learners to bring in pictures of families from magazines or other sources. How do the images in these photographs compare with those in "Follower"?

◆ Literary Focus

1 Diction and Style Ask students how the language Heaney uses in this stanza gives an impression of his father's expertise. *Terminology such as* steel-pointed sock *and* headrig *convey that his father had a job requiring skill and knowledge.*

◆ Critical Thinking

2 Connect Discuss with students how the poem shifts here from a view of the father to a view of the speaker. Ask students: Is each section of the poem exclusively about either the father or the son? What other contrast exists between these lines and lines 1–12? *Students should note that the first part, while about the father on its surface, describes the son's perceptions of his father. The second part, while focused largely on the son's experience, includes the father's actions. Lines 1–12 focus on the father's expertise while lines 13–14 describe the son's clumsiness.*

FOLLOWER

Seamus Heaney

My father worked with a horse plow,
His shoulders globed like a full sail strung
Between the shafts and the furrow.
The horses strained at his clicking tongue.

(1) An expert. He would set the wing
And fit the bright steel-pointed sock.
The sod rolled over without breaking.
At the headrig, with a single pluck

Of reins, the sweating team turned round
And back into the land. His eye
Narrowed and angled at the ground,
Mapping the furrow exactly.

(2) I stumbled in his hobnailed wake,
Fell sometimes on the polished sod;
Sometimes he rode me on his back
Dipping and rising to his plod.

I wanted to grow up and plow,
To close one eye, stiffen my arm.
All I ever did was follow
In his broad shadow round the farm.

(3) I was a nuisance, tripping, falling,
Yapping always. But today
(4) It is my father who keeps stumbling
Behind me, and will not go away.

◆ Build Vocabulary

furrow (fur′ ō) *n.*: Narrow groove made in the ground by a plow

nuisance (no͞o′ səns) *n.*: Act, thing, or condition causing trouble

Block Scheduling Strategies

Consider these suggestions to take advantage of extended class time:

- Introduce the Reading Strategy on p. 1003. Have students practice using the Reading Strategy page in ***Selection Support,*** p. 259.
- Introduce the selections with the Interest Grabber provided in the ATE, p. 1003.
- As a class, discuss and answer the Guide for Responding questions on pp. 1007 and 1009.
- Introduce the Literary Focus (Diction and Style). Have students work in pairs to analyze diction and style in the poems and answer the related questions on page 1010.
- Have students use the Internet or library sources to gather additional data on one of these poets, then have them begin the Book Blurb activity (p. 1011).

◀ Critical Viewing How does this photograph reveal the two sides of the father-son relationship that Heaney describes in his poem? How is it different? **[Evaluate]** ❺

◆ Grammar and Style

❸ Concrete and Abstract Nouns Challenge students to categorize the noun *nuisance* as concrete or abstract. *Nuisance is concrete because it carries vivid associations with particular sounds and sights and behavior.*

◆ Literary Focus

❹ Diction and Style Ask students how the language Heaney uses in the final stanza helps him express a central theme in the poem. *Students should note that the language describing the boy and the father operates on two levels—literal and figurative. This meaning can then be extended to arrive at the poem's theme: how the past and future conflict and intertwine.*

▶Critical Viewing◀

❺ Evaluate Students may note that the father, while older, appears here to be following the son—a reversal of the relationship in the poem. At the same time, the boy seems to be looking to his father for guidance. Together, these facts show the two sides to the relationship.

◆ Background for Understanding

Heaney in the Context of Northern Ireland Point out to students that Heaney made a significant choice about his relation to his own past when he settled in the Irish Republic in 1972. His own disquiet about living away from the continued conflict in Northern Ireland (his birthplace) might, for Heaney, be compared to the father who follows him, stumbling.

Customize for
Musical/Rhythmic Learners
Have these students listen to the selection audiotape in order to appreciate how the poem evokes elements of the traditional ballad.

Speaking and Listening Mini-Lesson

Monologue

This mini-lesson supports the Speaking and Listening activity in the Idea Bank on page 1011.

Introduce the Concept Point out that "Follower" shows the adult Heaney looking back at his childhood. At the same time, his father may also have looked back on Heaney's childhood after Heaney had grown up. Ask students to discuss how adults perceive children, and how they adjust once their children become adults.

Develop Background Before students create their monologues, have them review and discuss the following strategies:

- Study "Follower" carefully for clues about Heaney's father.
- Analyze the character's personal background before adopting his perspective.
- Include details about the relationship to lend authenticity to the monologue.

Apply the Information Urge students to experiment with different approaches before finalizing their monologue. Suggest that, once they have drafted their monologue, they experiment with delivery, practicing in front of a mirror or family audience.

Assess the Outcome Evaluate students' monologues for plausibility, insight into the father's character, and creativity in presentation.

Customize for
More Advanced Students
Challenge more advanced students to study the sestina form Heaney employs in this poem. Ask them to name the six recycled words and point out the variations Heaney uses to match the poem's content with its form.

Customize for
English Language Learners
Have these students locate four words in the poem that are made up of two words (many are hyphenated). Ask them to define each part of the compound before building an overall definition. Explain that poets sometimes create original compounds to accurately convey a particular image.

❶ **Clarification** Belfast is a city in Northern Ireland. Much of the violence in Northern Ireland has taken place in Belfast.

▶Critical Viewing◀

❷ **Compare and Contrast** The pictures show a lorry or truck exploding. In the poem, one of the lorries is rigged with explosives and is detonated in a terrorist attack.

◆ Grammar and Style

❸ **Concrete and Abstract Nouns** Have students identify the concrete and abstract nouns in these lines. How does the relationship between the two mirror the poem's overall contrast? *Concrete nouns include* films, coalman, lead, paper, mother. *Abstract nouns include* conceit. *Students should note that the abstract noun is linked to the coalman, who will reappear later as a figure of death (line 28), while all the nouns linked to his mother and her everyday life are concrete.*

◆ Reading Strategy

❹ **Summarize** Ask students to summarize this scene, focusing on the mother's reaction. *All business, the mother dismisses the coalman's flirtation with a few words, then returns to the business of polishing the stove.*

Two Lorries

Seamus Heaney

It's raining on black coal and warm wet ashes.
There are tire-marks in the yard, Agnew's old lorry[1]
Has all its cribs down and Agnew the coalman
❶ With his Belfast accent's sweet-talking my mother.
Would she ever go to a film in Magherafelt?
But it's raining and he still has half the load

To deliver farther on. This time the lode
Our coal came from was silk-black, so the ashes
Will be the silkiest white. The Magherafelt
(Via Toomebridge) bus goes by. The half-stripped lorry
With its emptied, folded coal-bags moves my mother:
The tasty ways of a leather-aproned coalman!

And films no less! The conceit of a coalman . . .
She goes back in and gets out the black lead
❸ And emery paper, this nineteen-forties mother,
All business round her stove, half-wiping ashes
❹ With a backhand from her cheek as the bolted lorry
Gets revved and turned and heads for Magherafelt

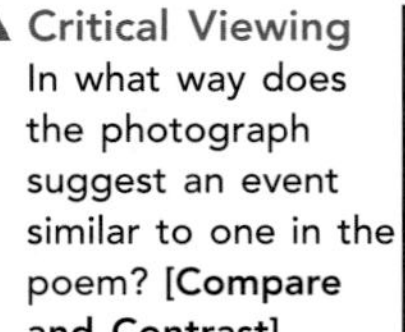

▲ **Critical Viewing** In what way does the photograph suggest an event similar to one in the poem? **[Compare and Contrast]** ❷

1. **lorry:** Truck.

Cross-Curricular Connection: Social Studies

Northern Ireland and The Republic of Ireland The strife in Ireland, while often polarized around religious differences between Protestants and Catholics, has socio-economic causes as well. When the largely Protestant English ruled Ireland, the English aristocrats seized ownership of much of the land and instituted a feudal system. The Irish peasantry, largely Catholic, became dependent on foreign landowners and thus became less educated and poorer, losing socio-economic power.

When the Irish Free State was established in 1921, the British kept the mainly Protestant counties of northeastern Ireland under British rule. These counties form Northern Ireland. Approximately two-thirds of its inhabitants are Protestants of English or Scots descent. The Catholics of Northern Ireland claim that they suffer oppression under the Protestant majority, and the Protestants fear Catholic Irish attempts to join Northern Ireland with the Republic of Ireland.

Have students discuss how the socio-economic balance of groups in society can contribute to tensions among individual members.

And the last delivery. Oh, Magherafelt!
Oh, dream of red plush and a city coalman
As time fastforwards and a different lorry
Groans into shot, up Broad Street, with a payload
That will blow the bus station to dust and ashes . . .
After that happened, I'd a vision of my mother, ❺

A revenant on the bench where I would meet her
In that cold-floored waiting-room in Magherafelt,
Her shopping bags full up with shoveled ashes.
Death walked out past her like a dust-faced coalman
Refolding body-bags, plying his load
Empty upon empty, in a flurry

Of motes and engine-revs, but which lorry
Was it now? Young Agnew's or that other,
Heavier, deadlier one, set to explode
In a time beyond her time in Magherafelt . . .
So tally bags and sweet-talk darkness, coalman.
Listen to the rain spit in new ashes

As you heft a load of dust that was Magherafelt,
Then reappear from your lorry as my mother's
Dreamboat coalman filmed in silk-white ashes.

Guide for Responding

◆ Literature and Your Life

Reader's Response Have you ever felt about an adult the way the speaker feels about his father in "Follower"? Explain.

Thematic Focus What is the conflict between the world of each lorry? Explain.

☑ Check Your Comprehension

1. In "Follower," what is the father doing?
2. In "Follower," what does the speaker want to do in the future?
3. What are the two different incidents described in "Two Lorries"?
4. Which incident in "Two Lorries" comes before the other?

◆ Critical Thinking

INTERPRET

1. In "Follower," why does the boy want "To close one eye" and "stiffen" his "arm"? **[Interpret]**
2. Explain the reversal that occurs in lines 23–24 of "Follower." **[Draw Conclusions]**
3. Why does Heaney combine the two different incidents in "Two Lorries"? **[Interpret]**
4. From "Two Lorries," how would you describe Heaney's attitude toward violence in the Irish conflicts? **[Draw Conclusions]**

APPLY

5. "Follower" suggests that children never outgrow their parents. Do people's relations with their parents always leave lasting marks or burdens? Explain. **[Generalize]**

Beyond the Selection

FURTHER READING

Other Works by Seamus Heaney and Eavan Boland

Door into the Dark, Heaney
"The Achill Woman," Boland

Other Works With the Themes of Artistic Identity and Terrorism

"Nails," Brendan Kennelly
"The Author to Her Book," Anne Bradstreet

We suggest that you preview these works before recommending them to students.

INTERNET

You may find additional information about Seamus Heaney on the Internet at the following site. Please be aware, however, that the site may have changed since this information was published.

To read Seamus Heaney's Nobel Prize Lecture and a biography, visit **http://sunsite.unc.edu/ipa/heaney**

We *strongly recommend* that you preview sites before you send students to them.

◆ Reading Strategy

❺ **Summarize** Ask students to summarize the events of these lines. *Suggested summary: After a truck explodes in the recent past and destroys the Magherafelt bus station, Heaney imagines his mother (now a ghost), sitting in the bus station, while the coalman, now a figure of death, walks past her.*

Reinforce and Extend

Answers

◆ Literature and Your Life

Reader's Response Some students may recall admiring an adult, then later experiencing a role reversal.

Thematic Focus One lorry exists in the everyday world of coal deliveries while the other occupies a world of violence.

☑ Check Your Comprehension

1. He is plowing his farm fields.
2. He wants to be a farmer like his father.
3. In the first incident, the coal delivery man asks Heaney's mother for a date to the movies. In the second incident, a bomb-carrying truck explodes, destroying a city bus station.
4. The dialogue between the coal driver and Heaney's mother comes first.

◆ Critical Thinking

1. The boy wants to imitate his father's expertise and mastery in every detail.
2. Heaney has become an adult. He can no longer find sure answers and ideals such as his father once provided (his father now stumbles); Heaney is not reconciled to this loss (his father will not go away).
3. He wants to contrast the ordinary world with the world of terrorism, and perhaps to show that terrorism, like a sweet-talking coalman's fantasy, is not based in true love of country.
4. Suggested response: He dislikes it for threatening to take away what he loves in Ireland, even as a sweet-talking coalman tried to steal away his mother.
5. Suggested response: Parents can serve as their children's models into adulthood. Sometimes, living up to these ideals is a burden.

Develop Understanding

One-Minute Insight This poem poses the choice between immortality—a place outside human history—and participation in the struggles of flawed life. The poet presents the stars as the symbol of immortality, a landscape impervious to history's pain. Against this image, she contrasts the many dead Irish whose memory clots the Earth's landscape. In choosing to join history, Boland engages in the fight to relieve pain and injustice, but knows she will always be too late.

Enrichment Eavan Boland, like many writers, has a creative routine. She writes in longhand in ledger-type notebooks, begun anew each year. With a ballpoint pen, Boland fills only one side of the paper. After completing a draft, Boland considers either revision—"reshaping lines, and language"—or rewriting—almost literally writing again. She rarely shows her work to anyone until it is finished.

▶Critical Viewing◀

❶ **Analyze** Students should note that the stars and water can stand for unchanging elements standing outside history; the people and shore lights are the elements inside history.

◆ Literary Focus

❷ **Diction and Style** Note to students that the poem uses words, such as *outsiders,* that seem concrete, but are not, to create a generalized, mythical scene.

❸ **Clarification** In these lines, Boland refers to scientific fact—astronomical distances are so great that the light of the stars we see in the night sky actually left those stars thousands of years ago and is only now arriving at Earth.

◆ Reading Strategy

❹ **Summarize** Ask students to summarize lines 7–11. *Suggested summary: The stars shine outside the pain and limitations of human life. By contrast, human beings suffer, choose, and die. We must choose whether or not to engage with the frustrating pursuit of justice on Earth.*

Outside History

Eavan Boland

Starry Night Over the Rhone River, Vincent van Gogh, Musée d'Orsay, Paris, France

❶ ▲ **Critical Viewing** How does this image depict outside and inside history as Boland does in her poem? **[Analyze]**

Humanities: Art

Starry Night Over the Rhone River, 1888, by Vincent van Gogh.

Vincent van Gogh, though virtually unknown and often impoverished in his lifetime, is today one of the best-known Post-Impressionist painters. Born in Holland, Van Gogh turned to painting late in life, around 1880, studying on his own as well as with other painters. Though he experienced periods of deep unhappiness and mental instability, Van Gogh's short career was highly productive.

Ask the following to promote discussion.

(a) What parts of the painting are most intense and alive? (b) Describe the manner in which the people are painted. (c) From these facts, speculate about how Van Gogh would respond to Boland's decision to move "inside" history. *(a) The orange-yellow lights along the shore and their reflections in the water are the most intense and alive part. (b) The people seem insubstantial, scraped together out of paint. (c) He might respond that life within history is insubstantial unless a light burns through from outside.*

There are outsiders, always. These stars—
these iron inklings of an Irish January,
whose light happened

thousands of years before
our pain did: they are, they have always been
outside history.

They keep their distance. Under them remains
a place where you found
you were human, and

a landscape in which you know you are mortal.
And a time to choose between them.
I have chosen:

Out of myth into history I move to be
part of that ordeal
whose darkness is

only now reaching me from those fields,
those rivers, those roads clotted as
firmaments[1] with the dead.

How slowly they die
as we kneel beside them, whisper in their ear.
And we are too late. We are always too late.

1. **firmaments** *n.*: The heavens.

◆ **Build Vocabulary**

inklings (iŋk′ liŋz) *n.*: Indirect suggestions

mortal (môr′ təl) *adj.*: That which must eventually die

ordeal (ôr dēl′) *n.*: Any difficult or painful experience

Guide for Responding

◆ Literature and Your Life

Reader's Response Is Boland too pessimistic when she writes, "We are always too late"? Explain.

Thematic Focus How might Boland's early years away from Ireland have contributed to the poem?

☑ Check Your Comprehension

1. What are the "iron inklings of an Irish January"?
2. What does the speaker learn under the stars?
3. What do the fields, rivers, and roads hold?
4. What does the speaker choose in this poem?
5. Whom does the poet "kneel beside" at the end of the poem?

◆ Critical Thinking

INTERPRET

1. Why are stars "outside" history? **[Interpret]**
2. What is the "ordeal" in line 14? **[Interpret]**
3. Who are "the dead" in line 18? **[Interpret]**
4. What does it mean to choose between myth and history? **[Draw Conclusions]**

EVALUATE

5. Does Boland really become part of a larger "ordeal," or is that itself a myth? Explain. **[Evaluate]**

APPLY

6. Defend the right to stay uninvolved in a conflict. **[Defend]**

Cultural Connection

Science Connection

The Stars The stars of which Boland speaks number in the billions. They range from stars as big as the Sun to giant stars that would cover the distance from the Earth to the Sun. Each emits light from the nuclear furnace at its center, in which atoms are continually fused to release intense, radiant energy. On Earth we see this light many centuries after it first leaves the star.

Stars are born, shine for a period of time, and then slowly die. Larger stars burn the brightest but more briefly; perhaps for only 10 million years. Though they appear as mere sparkles in the sky, stars have colors, ranging from white to yellow, blue, or red.

Have students locate data about the number of light years it takes light from each of ten stars to reach Earth. After making a chart with the data, ask students to calculate the Earth year in which the light reaching us today first left each star.

Reinforce and Extend

Looking at Literature Videodisc Play Chapter 11 for students, in which Eavan Boland discusses various ways to respond to literature. Then initiate a discussion with students in which they offer responses to "Outside History."

Chapter 11

Answers

◆ Literature and Your Life

Reader's Response Responses include: No, we cannot "erase" past suffering; yes, we can prevent the same injustices from occuring in the future.

Thematic Focus Living away from Ireland gave Boland a special perspective on the role of outsider and on Irish history.

☑ Check Your Comprehension

1. The stars are the "iron inklings of an Irish January."
2. The speaker learns that she is human and mortal.
3. They hold memories of generations of the dead.
4. The speaker chooses to acknowledge a responsibility to the past.
5. The poet kneels beside the many who have died throughout history, taking responsibility for their cause.

◆ Critical Thinking

1. It takes thousands of years for a star's light to reach Earth.
2. The ordeal is the collective struggle of a people or of humanity.
3. "The dead" are those who have fallen, perhaps for a cause.
4. Choosing myth might mean accepting things as they are ("as the gods will"); choosing history means acknowledging responsibility to remedy the past.
5. Every human being exists only in his or her own particular time. In this sense, Boland's decision to "participate" in history is based on her own myth of the continuity of the ordeal.
6. Students may point out that life is too short to engage in conflict; others may argue that it's impossible to stay uninvolved.

Answers

◆ Reading Strategy

1. Stanzas 3–5 summarize the poem's meaning, noting the star's outsider position and the poet's choice to join history and leave both immortality and myth behind.
2. People have a choice as to whether or not to engage in conflicts stemming from the past. In choosing to participate in Ireland's painful history, the poet accepts that her efforts cannot really undo the losses suffered in the past.
3. In the first incident, the poet's mother chats with the coal deliveryman who invites her to see a film. She declines; the coalman drives off to the city. In the second incident, a terrorist-driven truck explodes, destroying the bus station in which the poet used to meet his mother. In a vision, the poet sees his mother's ghost at the station, attended by the coalman as a figure of Death.

◆ Build Vocabulary

Using the Word Root *-mort-*

1. Someone who prepares the dead for burial
2. The incidence of death
3. Immune to death
4. Causing death

Using the Word Bank

1. nuisance; 2. furrow; 3. ordeal; 4. inklings; 5. mortal

◆ Literary Focus

1. That Boland is not as traditionalist as Heaney is evidenced by her more abstract language (*e.g.*, "outside history") and unrhymed, free verse. Heaney writes rhyming poetry in old forms such as the ballad ("Follower") and the sestina ("Two Lorries").
2. Heaney offers an intimate view of Irish life, rich in specific details, such as "the polished sod," "the Magherafelt/(Via Toomebridge) bus." Boland pictures Ireland as an "ordeal" in which she is morally bound to participate—not as a storehouse of warm memories.

Guide for Responding *(continued)*

◆ Reading Strategy

SUMMARIZE

It is often more difficult to **summarize** a poem, briefly restating its main idea, than to summarize an essay. However, it *is* possible to capture the essence of a poem while leaving out its many details and images. Sometimes a line or two near the end of a poem will point you toward a summary.

In "Follower," for example, the last two stanzas seem to sum up the many details from the poet's childhood relationship with his father: As a child, he followed his father as a hero, but now his aging or dead father follows him, as a memory.

1. Which three stanzas in "Outside History" seem to summarize the meaning of the poem?
2. Basing your answer on the stanzas you found but using your own words, summarize "Outside History."
3. A summary of "Two Lorries" would involve a brief comparison of the two incidents the poet recalls. Write such a summary.

◆ Build Vocabulary

USING THE WORD ROOT *-mort-*

Keeping in mind that the word root *-mort-* means "death," briefly define the italicized words.

1. The head of the funeral home was a *mortician*.
2. The *mortality* rate for smokers is usually higher than it is for nonsmokers.
3. Some performers think that fame will make them *immortal*.
4. In sufficient amounts, arsenic is *mortiferous*.

USING THE WORD BANK

On your paper, fill in each blank with the most appropriate word from the Word Bank. Use each word only once.

When, as a child, Seamus Heaney followed his father around the farm, he may have made a __?__ of himself. However, young Seamus's tripping over a __?__ was probably more of a source of amusement than an __?__ for his father. One thing is sure, that young Seamus Heaney had no __?__ that his father was __?__ .

◆ Literary Focus

DICTION AND STYLE

In poetry, **style** is a little word with a large meaning: It includes everything that is unique about a poet's **diction** (word choice), imagery, rhythms, forms, and themes. You can begin to understand these two poets' styles by comparing how they handle these elements. Be aware, however, that a style comparison based on a few poems is just a start.

Heaney tends to use images that help tell a story, and his diction is conversational and informal. He also uses well-crafted poetic forms: regular stanzas that rhyme *abab* ("Follower") and a sestina, built around six line-ending words ("Two Lorries").

By contrast, Boland uses an improvised, free-verse rhythm and only one partial rhyme ("found/ "and") in "Outside History." Her diction is abstract at first and then more concrete as she decides to become involved in the pain of life.

Use passages from the poems to help prove or disprove these claims about the poets' styles:

1. Boland is more of a gifted traditionalist than Heaney.
2. Of these two gifted poets, Heaney writes more as the Irish insider and Boland as the outsider.

◆ Grammar and Style

CONCRETE AND ABSTRACT NOUNS

Both poets use **concrete nouns,** which name specific things, and **abstract nouns,** which name general things. In moving from abstract nouns like *myth* to concrete nouns like *fields,* Boland expresses her initial detachment from Irish suffering and her later acceptance of it. Heaney in "Two Lorries" makes concrete nouns gradually take on abstract meaning, as when the word *dust* changes its meaning from "coal-dust" into a noun referring to "death."

Practice On your paper, identify which italicized nouns are concrete and which are abstract.

1. My father worked with a *horse-plough* . . .
2. . . . the sweating *team* turned round . . .
3. The *conceit* of a coalman . . .
4. Dreamboat *coalman* filmed in silk-white ashes.
5. I move to be / part of that *ordeal* . . .

◆ Grammar and Style

Concrete and Abstract Nouns

1. *horse-plough:* concrete
2. *team:* concrete
3. *conceit:* abstract
4. *coalman:* concrete
5. *ordeal:* abstract

Writer's Solution

For additional instruction and practice, use the Choosing Precise Nouns and Vivid Verbs lesson in the Writing Style unit of the **Language Lab CD-ROM**, and the pages on Using Words Effectively, pp. 99–101, in the *Writer's Solution Grammar Practice Book.*

Build Your Portfolio

Idea Bank

Writing

1. Book Blurb Write a book blurb to appear on the jacket of a book by one of these poets. Describe the poet and the work in a way that will interest readers.

2. Comparison and Contrast Compare and contrast the styles of Heaney and Boland. Consider such elements as word choice, imagery, poetic form, and theme.

3. Response to Criticism Dillon Johnston writes that Heaney's "poetry immediately attracts the reader: the images are vivid and precise; the speaking voice is reassuring . . ." Comment on this remark, citing passages from the poems.

Speaking and Listening

4. Monologue As Heaney's father, improvise a monologue in answer to the poem "Follower." Give your perspective on the experience described by your "son." **[Performing Arts Link]**

5. Oral Interpretation Choose a poem by Heaney or Boland, rehearse it, then recite for the class. Be sure you know how to pronounce all the words, and note where you will pause. **[Performing Arts Link]**

Projects

6. Irish Folk Music Listen to recordings of Irish folk music made by groups like The Chieftains. Give an oral report on the recordings to your classmates, playing the music and explaining historical references in the songs. **[Music Link]**

7. The History of the "Troubles" Using books on recent Irish history, research and report on the causes of the strife in Northern Ireland. **[Social Studies Link]**

Writing Mini-Lesson

Conflict-Resolution Guidelines

Both Heaney and Boland refer to conflicts in Northern Ireland. You may not be able to suggest ways for settling that dispute, but you can probably give valuable advice for resolving conflicts in your own school. Work your ideas into a set of guidelines that students and teachers can follow in settling disagreements. Include specific procedures for putting your guidelines into action.

Writing Skills Focus: Clear Explanation of Procedures

Whether you're writing a manual for assembling a VCR or guidelines for settling conflicts, it's important to **explain procedures clearly**. Be sure that you give step-by-step instructions for part of the process you describe.

Prewriting Consider these questions: What kinds of conflicts arise in your school? Who, if anyone, tries to settle them? If necessary, create a new conflict-resolution group and diagram its authority using an organizational chart like this one:

Drafting Devise and spell out step-by-step instructions for identifying, discussing, and resolving conflicts. Specify the rights and responsibilities of the disputing parties at each stage of the process.

Revising Test your procedures with several classmates by staging a mock conflict resolution. Note where procedures seem weak and brainstorm with your classmates to strengthen them.

✓ ASSESSMENT OPTIONS

Formal Assessment, Selection Test, pp. 260–262, and Assessment Resources Software. The selection test is designed so that it can be easily customized to the performance levels of your students.

Alternative Assessment, p. 54, includes options for less advanced students, more advanced students, interpersonal learners, verbal/linguistic learners, and visual/spatial learners.

PORTFOLIO ASSESSMENT

Use the following rubrics in the ***Alternative Assessment*** booklet to assess student writing:
Book Blurb: Summary Rubric, p. 99
Comparison and Contrast: Comparison/Contrast Rubric, p. 104
Response to Criticism: Literary Analysis/Interpretation Rubric, p. 113
Writing Mini-Lesson: How-to/Process Explanation Rubric, p. 101

Idea Bank

Customizing for *Performance Levels*

Following are suggestions for matching Idea Bank topics with your students' performance levels:

Less Advanced Students: 1, 5
Average Students: 2, 6
More Advanced Students: 3, 4, 7

Customizing for *Learning Modalities*

Following are suggestions for matching Idea Bank topics with your students' learning modalities:

Verbal/Linguistic: 1, 2, 3, 4, 5, 7
Musical/Rhythmic: 5, 6

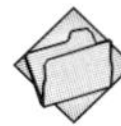

Writing Mini-Lesson

Refer students to the Writing Process Handbook, page 1189, for instruction on the writing process, and page 1193, for further information on Practical and Technical Writing.

Writing and Language Transparencies Display the Branching Organizer, p. 95, on an overhead. Encourage students to copy and use it as they gather details for their writing.

Writer's Solution

Writers at Work Videodisc

Have students view the videodisc segment on Practical and Technical Writing (Ch. 8), featuring Jeff Christian, to see how he organizes his ideas.

Play frames 37727 to 39423

Writing Lab CD-ROM

Have students complete the tutorial on Practical and Technical Writing. Follow these steps:

1. Refer to the Details Checklist as they gather details.
2. Organize their information using the Cluster Diagram.
3. Study the interactive examples on format and special type.

Sourcebook

Have students use Chapter 8, Practical and Technical Writing (pp. 230–264), for additional support. The chapter includes an annotated student model of a process explanation (p. 259).

Prepare and Engage

OBJECTIVES

1. To read, comprehend, and interpret a short story
2. To relate a short story to personal experience
3. To analyze cultural differences to better understand a story
4. To identify and trace cultural conflict within a story
5. To build vocabulary in context and to learn forms of *skeptical*
6. To develop skill in the correct use of *like* and *as*
7. To write a problem-and-solution essay, using elaboration to enhance understanding
8. To respond to the short story through writing, speaking and listening, and projects

SKILLS INSTRUCTION

Vocabulary: Related Words: Forms of *Skeptical*
Grammar: Correct Use of *Like* and *As*
Reading Strategy: Analyze Cultural Differences
Literary Focus: Cultural Conflict
Writing: Elaboration to Enhance Understanding
Speaking and Listening: Debate (teacher edition)
Critical Viewing: Predict; Evaluate

PORTFOLIO OPPORTUNITIES

Writing: Review; Proposal; Critical Response
Writing Mini-Lesson: Problem-and-Solution Essay
Speaking and Listening: Debate; Dramatic Scene
Projects: Book Cover Design; Comparison Report

More About the Author
Doris Lessing left school at the age of fifteen and held a range of jobs, including nursemaid, telephone operator, and shorthand-typist. In 1949, she moved to England, where she published her first novel, *The Grass is Singing*. In an interview in 1962, Lessing reflected, "I feel the best thing that ever happened to me was that I was brought up out of England. I took for granted kinds of experiences that would be impossible to a middle-class girl here."

Guide for Interpreting

Doris Lessing *(1919–)*

Freely admitting her desire to influence others through her fiction, Doris Lessing has said that publishing a story or novel is "an attempt to impose one's personality and beliefs on other people. If a writer accepts this responsibility, he must see himself . . . as an architect of the soul."

Exposing Injustice One of the ways that Doris Lessing fulfills this responsibility is by writing about social injustice. Her own experiences give her a unique perspective on the problems caused when cultures conflict.

She was born in Persia (now Iran), the daughter of a British bank clerk. When she was five, her family moved to the British colony of Rhodesia (now the independent country of Zimbabwe) in south-central Africa. Her memoir *Under My Skin* (1994) describes some ways in which Europeans mistreated the Africans, displacing them from their lands and ignoring their deeply held beliefs and traditions. Lessing's awareness of such injustice is reflected in her first novel, *The Grass is Singing* (1950), and in *African Stories* (1964).

Personal and Political Lessing's stories and novels often focus on how personal decisions can reflect and alter society. Martha Quest, the heroine of a five-novel series called *Children of Violence* (1952–1969), faces private battles that reflect global conflicts.

For Doris Lessing, the actions that people take every day are as political as government maneuvers.

Lessing's best-known novel, *The Golden Notebook* (1962), highlights the social relevance of one woman's persistent search for identity. The dominant theme is that of the free woman who struggles for individuality and equality despite social and psychological conditioning.

Throughout her writing career, Doris Lessing has honored her responsibility to her audience. Her short stories and novels have explored the roles of women in modern society, the evils of racism, and the limits of idealism in solving the problems facing society. Her vision is broad and her voice is direct and challenging.

◆ Background for Understanding

History: Lessing and the British Household in Rhodesia

In 1890, a team of British explorers, settlers, hunters, and missionaries came to Africa seeking to expand the British Empire. Many of the British immigrants felt that colonization would be "good for Africa." Lessing suggests that this kind of idealism is enough to make us "wonder which of the idealisms that make our hearts beat faster will seem wrong-headed to people a hundred years from now."

By 1924, when Lessing's family moved to Rhodesia, the country had been under British rule for many years. Two cultures had met, clashed, and achieved an unequal balance. The British settlers were home-owners; native Africans became their servants. Although they were paid wages, salaries were so low they could not afford independence.

Christian missionaries converted many Africans in Rhodesia, but these conversions reflected the uneasy juxtapositions of widely divergent cultures. Many Africans incorporated a belief in Jesus Christ into their religious life without altering their traditional beliefs.

In "No Witchcraft for Sale," you will encounter native Africans who work for privileged British settlers. You'll also encounter two cultures, native and European, that coexist uneasily.

Prentice Hall Literature Program Resources

REINFORCE / RETEACH / EXTEND

Selection Support Pages
Build Vocabulary: Related Words: Forms of *Skeptical*, p. 201
Grammar and Style: Correct Use of *Like* and *As*, p. 202
Reading Strategy: Analyze Cultural Differences, p. 203
Literary Focus: Cultural Conflict, p. 204

Strategies for Diverse Student Needs, p. 55

Beyond Literature
Science Connection: Alternative Medicine, p. 55

Formal Assessment Selection Test, pp. 263–265; Assessment Resources Software

Alternative Assessment, p. 55

Writing and Language Transparencies
Problem/Solution Organizer, p. 107

Resource Pro CD-ROM
"No Witchcraft for Sale"—includes all resource material and customizable lesson plan

Listening to Literature Audiocassettes
"No Witchcraft for Sale"

No Witchcraft for Sale

◆ Literature and Your Life

Connect Your Experience

An anthropologist once described his nervousness as a foreigner approached him and, standing less than a foot away, started talking. The anthropologist became angrier and angrier at what he regarded as an invasion of his space. This incident shows how differences in the unwritten rules of cultures can spark a conflict.

In this story, Doris Lessing writes about a cultural conflict that arises between an English family and their African servant.

Journal Writing Jot down some unwritten cultural "rules" about matters like personal distance, privacy, or smiling.

Thematic Focus: Conflicts Abroad and at Home

As you read this story, consider what it suggests about the types of conflicts that arose in British colonies.

◆ Build Vocabulary

Related Words: Forms of *Skeptical*

A character in this story smiles "with skeptical good humor." The word *skeptical* means "inclined to doubt or question." Other forms of this word include the nouns *skeptic* ("a person who doubts or disbelieves") and *skepticism* ("the tendency to doubt or disbelieve") and the adjective *skeptical* ("not believing readily").

Word Bank

Before you read, preview these words from the story.

reverently
defiantly
efficacy
incredulously
skeptical

◆ Grammar and Style

Correct Use of *Like* and *As*

Lessing correctly uses the subordinating conjunctions *as* or *as if* to introduce a subordinate clause, which has a subject and a verb. She uses the preposition *like* to introduce a prepositional phrase, which consists of an object and any words that modify it.

as if: subordinate clause
They congratulated Mrs. Farquar *as if she had achieved a very great thing.*

like: prepositional phrase
He spoke to Mr. Farquar *like an unwilling servant.*

◆ Literary Focus

Cultural Conflict

By bringing different peoples together, colonialism provided a new focus for writers: the **cultural conflicts** arising from differences in customs, beliefs, and values. Such conflicts could lead to misunderstandings, tension, and even violent confrontations.

In "No Witchcraft for Sale," Lessing helps you understand a cultural conflict by allowing you to see it from two different sides. Trace the conflict as it arises, and predict whether or not it will be resolved. You can even propose resolutions of your own.

◆ Reading Strategy

Analyze Cultural Differences

You can better understand a story involving cultural conflicts by analyzing the **cultural differences** that create the problem in the first place.

To analyze the cultural differences in this story, use a diagram like the one below to compare the Farquars and Gideon. Where the circles intersect, jot down similarities in thinking. Where the circles are separate, jot down differences.

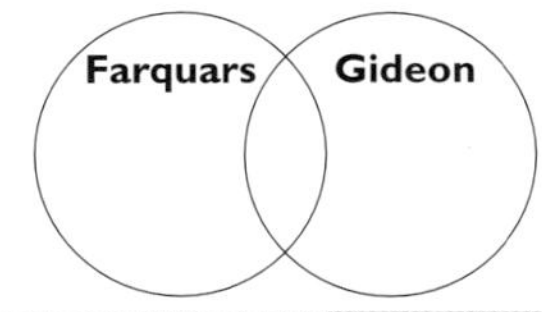

Interest Grabber Before introducing this story, compile a list of folk remedies. Examples include currant tea for sore throats, cranberries to cure blood poisoning, raw meat to reduce swelling, crushed garlic or sour cream to soothe stings, sugar to stop hiccups, fennel to sharpen eyesight, strawberries to curb gout, papaya for indigestion, parsley for clean breath, and okra paste to ease muscle pain. Write substances in one column and ailments, in mixed order, in another. Have students try to pair a substance with what it treats or cures. As you reveal the correct matches, invite discussion of which remedies, if any, students have heard of or used. Then tell them that in the story they will read, folk medicine plays a key role.

Customize for
More Advanced Students
Challenge students to find examples of cultural balance as well as bias on the part of the author. Encourage them to analyze passages to decide whose side the narrator seems to take, and point to evidence that supports their view. For example, they might determine moments when the Farquars are sympathetic toward Gideon, and others, when they seem to turn on him.

Customize for
Intrapersonal Learners
Ask students, as they read, to put themselves in Gideon's place to try to understand his feelings: his pride, his sense of betrayal, his resignation to his role as a black African man working on a white, Eurocentric homestead, and so on. Challenge students not to judge Gideon, as the Farquars do, but to grasp his point of view.

Preparing for Standardized Tests

Reading and Vocabulary Vocabulary development in context will help students improve their performance on the verbal portions of tests in reading comprehension, vocabulary, and analogy items. For additional practice, use the Build Vocabulary page in ***Selection Support,*** p. 201.

Grammar and Language Portions of some standardized tests require students to identify the correct use of *like* and *as*. Students may be asked to pick the best choice for an underlined subordinating conjunction, as in the following:

We regarded the doctor like she was a wizard. (C)

(A) NO CHANGE
(B) like as
(C) as if
(D) like

The Grammar and Style lesson for this selection focuses on this topic. For additional practice, use the Grammar and Style page on Correct Use of *Like* and *As,* p. 202, in ***Selection Support.***

Develop Understanding

One-Minute Insight The Farquars, a white family living on a homestead in Africa, employ Gideon, a local man, as their cook. He is kind and loving toward their young son, Teddy, but never forgets his place as a servant. When a medical emergency causes Gideon to use his traditional healing skills to restore Teddy's eyesight, the family is deeply grateful. But the incident leads to a cultural clash when the Farquars misunderstand Gideon's tribal position as a healer. The standoff between Gideon and the Farquars underscores a cultural gap that cannot be bridged.

▶Critical Viewing◀

❶ **Predict** Students may predict the story will be about poisonous snakes or plants, stinging insects, animals or birds that might attack humans, quicksand, strangling vines, or unfriendly locals.

◆ Reading Strategy

❷ **Analyze Cultural Differences** Ask students to identify the hints of future conflict within the opening paragraph. *The servants humor Mrs. Farquar, privately thinking she is silly; Mrs. Farquar is too dense to sense their attitude and she is condescendingly grateful to the servants for their kindness.*

◆ Critical Thinking

❸ **Analyze** Ask: What is Mrs. Farquar's attitude toward Gideon? What does this indicate about her character? *Students should recognize that Mrs. Farquar "likes" Gideon because of his fondness for her son Teddy. Mrs. Farquar is extremely self-centered; she likes people only for what they can do for her.*

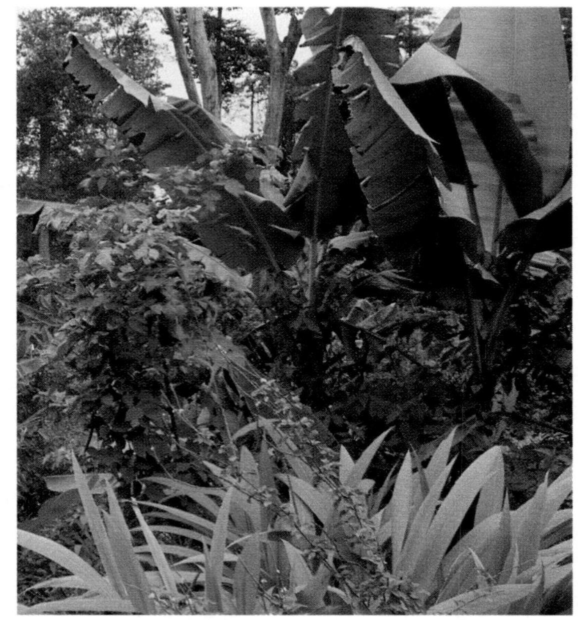

◀ Critical Viewing Using this picture and the title, predict what this story will be about. **[Predict]** ❶

NO WITCHCRAFT FOR SALE

Doris Lessing

❷ The Farquars had been childless for years when little Teddy was born; and they were touched by the pleasure of their servants, who brought presents of fowls and eggs and flowers to the homestead when they came to rejoice over the baby, exclaiming with delight over his downy golden head and his blue eyes. They congratulated Mrs. Farquar as if she had achieved a very great thing, and she felt that she had—her smile for the lingering, admiring natives was warm and grateful.

Later, when Teddy had his first haircut, Gideon the cook picked up the soft gold tufts from the ground, and held them reverently in his hand. Then he smiled at the little boy and said: "Little Yellow Head." That became the native name for the child. Gideon and Teddy were great friends from the first. When Gideon had finished his work, he would lift Teddy on his shoulders to the shade of a big tree, and play with him there, forming curious little toys from twigs and leaves and grass, or shaping animals from wetted soil. When Teddy learned to walk it was often Gideon who crouched before him, clucking encouragement, finally catching him when he fell, tossing him up in the air till they both became breathless with laughter. Mrs. Farquar was fond of the old cook because of his love for her child. ❸

There was no second baby; and one day Gideon said: "Ah, missus, missus, the Lord above sent this one; Little Yellow Head is the most good thing we have in our house." Because of that "we" Mrs. Farquar felt a warm impulse toward her cook; and at the end of the month she raised his wages. He had been with her now for several years; he was one of the few natives who had his wife and children in the compound and never wanted to go home to his kraal,[1] which was some hundreds of miles away.

1. **kraal** (kräl): Village of South African natives, usually fenced in with a stockade.

Block Scheduling Strategies

Consider these suggestions to take advantage of extended class time:

- Review with students the Background for Understanding on page 1012. Then hold a discussion with students about colonialism.
- Discuss the Literary Focus on page 1013 and have students answer the questions on page 1020 when they've finished the story. You may also want to give students additional practice by assigning the Literary Focus page in ***Selection Support*** on page 204.
- Introduce and teach the Grammar and Style lesson on page 1013. Then have students complete the Grammar and Style exercises on page 1020.
- To extend the ideas in this story and to help students make inferences about the issues of colonialism in general, assign the Debate activity in the Idea Bank on page 1021. Also use the Speaking and Listening Mini-Lesson on page 1018 in the teacher edition to give students further guidance.
- Provide an alternative activity, found in ***Alternative Assessment,*** p. 54, to evaluate the progress of students of various performance levels or learning modalities.

Sometimes a small piccanin who had been born the same time as Teddy, could be seen peering from the edge of the bush, staring in awe at the little white boy with his miraculous fair hair and Northern blue eyes. The two little children would gaze at each other with a wide, interested gaze, and once Teddy put out his hand curiously to touch the black child's cheeks and hair.

4 Gideon, who was watching, shook his head wonderingly, and said: "Ah, missus, these are both children, and one will grow up to be a baas, and one will be a servant"; and Mrs. Farquar smiled and said sadly, "Yes, Gideon, I was thinking the same." She sighed. "It is God's will," said Gideon, who was a mission boy. The Farquars were very religious people; and this shared feeling about God bound servant and masters even closer together.

Teddy was about six years old when he was given a scooter, and discovered the intoxications of speed. All day he would fly around the homestead, in and out of flowerbeds, scattering squawking chickens and irritated dogs, finishing with a wide dizzying arc into the kitchen door. There he would cry: "Gideon, look at me!" And Gideon would laugh and say: "Very clever, Little Yellow Head." Gideon's youngest son, who was now a herdsboy, came especially up from the compound to see the scooter. He was afraid to come near it, but Teddy showed off in front of him. "Piccanin," shouted Teddy, "get out of my way!" And he raced in circles around the black child until he was frightened, and fled back to the bush.

"Why did you frighten him?" asked Gideon, gravely reproachful.[2]

5 Teddy said defiantly: "He's only a black boy," and laughed. Then, when Gideon turned away from him without speaking, his face fell. Very soon he slipped into the house and found an orange and brought it to Gideon, saying: "This is for you." He could not bring himself to say he was sorry; but he could not bear to lose Gideon's affection either. Gideon took the orange unwillingly and sighed. "Soon you will be going away to school, Little Yellow Head," he said wonderingly, "and then you will be grown up." He shook his head gently and said, "And that is how our lives go." He seemed to be putting a distance between himself and Teddy, not because of resentment, but in the way a person accepts something inevitable. The baby had lain in his arms and smiled up into his face: the tiny boy had swung from his shoulders and played with him by the hour. Now Gideon would not let his flesh touch the flesh of the white child. He was kind, but there was a grave formality in his voice that made Teddy pout and sulk away. Also, it made him into a man: with Gideon he was polite, and carried himself formally, and if he came into the kitchen to ask for something, it was in the way a white man uses toward a servant, expecting to be obeyed.

But on the day that Teddy came staggering into the kitchen with his fists to his eyes, shrieking with pain, Gideon dropped the pot full of hot soup that he was holding, rushed to the child, and forced aside his fingers. "A snake!" he exclaimed. Teddy had been on his scooter, and had come to a rest with his foot on the side of a big tub of plants. A tree-snake, hanging by its tail from the roof, had spat full into his eyes. Mrs. Farquar came running when she heard the commotion. "He'll go blind," she sobbed, holding Teddy close against her. "Gideon, he'll go blind!" Already the eyes, with perhaps half an hour's sight left in them, were swollen up to the size of fists: Teddy's small white face was distorted by great purple oozing protuberances.[3] Gideon said: "Wait a minute, missus, I'll get some medicine." He ran off into the bush. 6

2. **reproachful** (ri prōch´ fəl) *adj.*: Expressing blame.

3. **protuberances** (prō to͞o´ bər əns iz) *n.*: Bulges; swellings.

◆ Build Vocabulary

reverently (rev´ ər ənt lē) *adv.*: Respectfully

defiantly (di fī´ ənt lē) *adv.*: Disobediently; with resistance

◆ Critical Thinking

4 Infer Ask students what this passage indicates about religion and destiny for blacks and whites in this colony. *Both blacks and whites believe in God and destiny. However, the black Christians believe they are born to serve, and white colonists believe they're born to rule.*

◆ Literary Focus

5 Cultural Conflict Ask students to explain why this childish incident has such a strong impact upon Gideon and then on Teddy. *Students may say that Teddy's callow remark was not only racist, but that it reminded Gideon that they are not one family, and that sooner or later they will have to find their own destinies in two separate worlds. Gideon is wise enough to know that this rift would come eventually, but he may feel upset that it is coming sooner rather than later. Teddy may be beginning to realize that he and Gideon will never be able to maintain their closeness.*

◆ Reading Strategy

6 Analyze Cultural Differences Guide students to see that here, roles are reversed: Mrs. Farquar, the master, is reduced to helplessness, while Gideon, the servant, is master of the situation. Ask students to explain where they think Gideon plans to go. *Students may say that he will get medicine from a local source: a neighbor, friend, or healer, or try to find a natural remedy he knows will work.*

Cross-Curricular Connection: Science

In this story, young Teddy Farquar's vision is threatened when a startled tree-snake spits a poisonous substance into the boy's eyes. Many parts of the world are home to species of venomous snakes, insects, reptiles, or fish, whose contact with humans can cause a range of problems, from minor rashes to grave illness, disability, or death.

Have interested students select a kind of venomous creature to research. They should determine the natural habitat of the creatures, find out how and when they uses their venom, who or what are their usual victims, what, if any, known antidotes exist, and how people can protect themselves when traveling in areas these creatures inhabit. Students can present their findings in the form of a safety pamphlet or a multimedia presentation for travelers.

1 Clarification Permanganate is a chemical salt, $KMnO_4$, also known as potassium permanganate, that has been used since the mid-nineteenth century as a disinfectant.

◆ Critical Thinking

2 Analyze Guide students to express any insights they have gained about Gideon from his behavior in this scene. *Students should recognize that Gideon is more than a cook; he is a healer who knows exactly how to counteract the ill effects of snake spit in the eyes and responds to the urgent situation with calm, focused intensity.*

◆ Reading Strategy

3 Analyze Cultural Differences In their Venn diagrams, students may use terms for Mrs. Farquar such as *hysterical, fearful, freaked out,* or *ineffective;* for Gideon they might write *knowledgeable, focused, calm, experienced,* or *reassuring.* Words that might apply to both can include *concerned, loving,* and *worried.*

◆ Grammar and Style

4 Correct Use of *Like* and *As* Ask students to justify the use of *like* in this sentence. *Like is the correct word because it introduces a prepositional phrase.*

Mrs. Farquar lifted the child into the house
1 and bathed his eyes with permanganate.[4] She had scarcely heard Gideon's words; but when she saw that her remedies had no effect at all, and remembered how she had seen natives with no sight in their eyes, because of the spitting of a snake, she began to look for the return of her cook, remembering what she heard of the efficacy of native herbs. She stood by the window, holding the terrified, sobbing little boy in her arms, and peered helplessly into the bush. It was not more than a few minutes before she saw Gideon come bounding back, and in his hand he held a plant.

"Do not be afraid, missus," said Gideon, "this will cure Little Yellow Head's eyes." He stripped the leaves from the plant, leaving a small white fleshy root. Without even washing it, he put the root in his mouth, chewed it vigorously, and then held the spittle there while he took the child forcibly from Mrs. Farquar. He gripped Teddy down between his knees, and pressed the balls of his thumbs into the swollen eyes,
2 so that the child screamed and Mrs. Farquar cried out in protest: "Gideon, Gideon!" But Gideon took no notice. He knelt over the writhing child, pushing back the puffy lids till chinks of eyeball showed, and then he spat hard, again and again, into first one eye, and then the other. He finally lifted Teddy gently into his mother's arms, and said: "His eyes will get better." But Mrs. Farquar was weeping with terror, and she could hardly thank him: it was impossible to believe that Teddy could keep his sight. In a couple of hours the swellings were gone: the eyes were inflamed and tender but Teddy could see. Mr. and Mrs. Farquar went to Gideon in the kitchen and thanked him over and over again. They felt helpless because of their gratitude: it seemed they could do nothing to express it. They gave Gideon presents for his wife and children, and a big increase in wages, but these things could not pay for Teddy's now completely cured eyes. Mrs. Farquar said: "Gideon, God chose you as an instrument for His goodness," and Gideon said: "Yes, missus, God is very good."

> **◆ Reading Strategy**
> When Teddy is injured, how do Gideon and Mrs. Farquar react differently? 3
> Jot your ideas in the diagram you are using to analyze cultural differences.

Now, when such a thing happens on a farm, it cannot be long before everyone hears of it. Mr. and Mrs. Farquar told their neighbors and the story was discussed from one end of the district to the other. The bush is full of secrets. No one can live in Africa, or at least on the veld,[5] without learning very soon that there is an ancient wisdom of leaf and soil and season—and, too, perhaps most important of all, of the darker tracts of the human mind—which is the black man's heritage. Up and down the district people were telling anecdotes, reminding each other of things that had happened to them.

"But I saw it myself, I tell you. It was a puff-adder bite. The kaffir's[6] arm was swollen to the
elbow, like a great shiny black bladder. He was 4
groggy after half a minute. He was dying. Then suddenly a kaffir walked out of the bush with his hands full of green stuff. He smeared something on the place, and next day my boy was back at work, and all you could see was two small punctures in the skin."

This was the kind of tale they told. And, as always, with a certain amount of exasperation, because while all of them knew that in the bush of Africa are waiting valuable drugs locked in bark, in simple-looking leaves, in roots, it was impossible to ever get the truth about them from the natives themselves.

The story eventually reached town; and perhaps it was at a sundowner party, or some such function, that a doctor, who happened to be there, challenged it. "Nonsense," he said. "These things get exaggerated in the telling. We are always checking up on this kind of story, and we draw a blank every time."

Anyway, one morning there arrived a strange

4. **permanganate** (pər maŋ´ gə nāt´): Salt of permanganic acid.

5. **veld:** In South Africa, open grassy country, with few bushes and almost no trees.

6. **kaffir's:** Belonging to a black African; in South Africa, a contemptuous term.

Beyond the Classroom

Career Connection

Ethnobotanist Most students know that *botany* is the scientific study of plants. A special area of botany that combines science with folk culture is *ethnobotany*. Ethnobotanists study the plant lore of a region or group of people and learn the ways indigenous people use the plants for food, medicine, commerce, art, or any other purpose. Unlike the arrogant scientist in the story, ethnobotanists are trained in botany *and* in cultural anthropology. They know to respect the ancient lore and knowledge local people possess and to analyze their remedies scientifically.

Have students find out more about the field of ethnobotany. Students who are ecologically minded may be interested to know that some ethnobotanists live and work with rain forest peoples to learn more about the local uses of the unique plants of that environment. This kind of research can lead to discoveries of ways to synthesize compounds in the lab without defoliating forests.

car at the homestead, and out stepped one of the workers from the laboratory in town, with cases full of test-tubes and chemicals.

Mr. and Mrs. Farquar were flustered and pleased and flattered. They asked the scientist to lunch, and they told the story all over again, for the hundredth time. Little Teddy was there too, his blue eyes sparkling with health, to prove the truth of it. The scientist explained how humanity might benefit if this new drug could be offered for sale; and the Farquars were even more pleased: they were kind, simple people, who liked to think of something good com-
5 ing about because of them. But when the scientist began talking of the money that might result, their manner showed discomfort. Their feelings over the miracle (that was how they thought of it) were so strong and deep and religious, that it was distasteful to them to think of money. The scientist, seeing their faces, went back to his first point, which was the advancement of humanity. He was perhaps a trifle perfunctory:[7] it was not the first time he had come salting the tail of a fabulous bush secret.[8]

Eventually, when the meal was over, the Farquars called Gideon into their living room and explained to him that this baas, here, was a Big Doctor from the Big City, and he had come all that way to see Gideon. At this Gideon seemed afraid; he did not understand; and Mrs. Farquar explained quickly that it was because of the wonderful thing he had done with Teddy's eyes that the Big Baas had come.

Gideon looked from Mrs. Farquar to Mr. Farquar, and then at the little boy, who was showing great importance because of the occasion.
6 At last he said grudgingly: "The Big Baas want to know what medicine I used?" He spoke incredulously, as if he could not believe his old friends could so betray him. Mr. Farquar began explaining how a useful medicine could be made out of the root, and how it could be put on sale, and how thousands of people, black and white, up and down the continent of Africa, could be saved by the medicine when that spitting snake filled their eyes with poison. Gideon listened, his eyes bent on the ground, the skin of his forehead puckering in discomfort. When Mr. Farquar had finished he did not reply. The scientist, who all this time had been leaning back in a big chair, sipping his coffee and smiling with skeptical good humor,

▲ Critical Viewing In what ways does this man's
expression and appearance illustrate the wisdom of 7
Gideon's generation? **[Evaluate]**

7. **perfunctory** (pər fuŋk´ tə rē) *adj.*: Done without care or interest.
8. **salting . . . bush secret:** Allusion to the humororus and ironic advice given to children about how to catch a bird—by putting salt on its tail. In other words, the scientist does not really expect to capture a valuable bit of information.

◆ Build Vocabulary

efficacy (ef´ i kə sē) *n.*: Power to produce effects

incredulously (in krej´ oo ləs lē) *adv.*: In a doubting manner

skeptical (skep´ ti kəl) *adj.*: Not easily persuaded

◆ Literary Focus

5 Cultural Conflict Ask students to identify the ways in which the Farquars get caught between two cultures. *Students may say that they bridge a chasm between modern western science and technology and the ancient natural world of Gideon and the native African healers.*

◆ Reading Strategy

6 Analyze Cultural Differences Talk with students about why Gideon feels so betrayed. *Students may say that Gideon believes that he possesses the gift of healing; he helped Teddy for love and because it was the right thing to do; now he feels so uncomfortable because the white colonials regard him as some kind of magician with a secret they want to pry out of him.*

▶Critical Viewing◀

7 Evaluate Students may say that his gray hair and weathered face suggest the experience and wisdom of age, and that his long stare can represent a concern for those around him or a wariness of strangers.

Cultural Connection

Folk Medicine Long before people could obtain synthetic medicines and compounds from doctors or pharmacies, people all over the world relied on the natural materials of their environment to battle illness and injury. For example, we now know that an aspirin tablet contains salicylic acid, which can relive pain and reduce fever. But for centuries, Native Americans chewed on willow bark for the same purpose. Scientists now know that willow bark contains that compound.

Some folk remedies use local plants or herbs for soothing teas or poultices. Others combine crushed minerals or animal by-products with plant substances to form compounds that cure various ailments.

Invite interested students to research folk medicine in any culture of their choosing. They can present their findings in the form of an oral or written report, with sketches or diagrams to support their research.

◆ Literary Focus

❶ **Cultural Conflict** Ask students to describe the nature of the realization the Farquars make here. *At this point, the Farquars recognize that he will never give in to their demands; that he possesses true power and wisdom they will never pry out of him no matter how hard they try; and that Gideon, like other native healers, will keep his knowledge inside himself, to use only as needed.*

◆ Literary Focus

❷ **Cultural Conflict** Students may cite *exasperating, seemed not to care, rude, stubborn, ignorant, perversely obstinate,* and *stupid refusals* to show the level of frustration the Farquars feel and their lack of understanding of Gideon's feelings on this subject.

◆ Critical Thinking

❸ **Analyze** Ask students to identify the point of view and bias of the narrator here. *The narrator uses a third-person limited point of view with a Eurocentric bias because none of Gideon's thoughts are revealed and the description is slanted to the colonial viewpoint. It is unlikely that Gideon would judge the day as "... fit only for reclining on a verandah with iced drinks ..."*

◆ Reading Strategy

❹ **Analyze Cultural Differences** Ask students why they think Gideon and the Farquars would ever return to liking each other at all. *Students may say that they must find a way to get along.*

❺ **Clarification** During the colonial period, white masters often referred to adult African male servants as "boys" to reinforce their subservience.

chipped in and explained all over again, in different words, about the making of drugs and the progress of science. Also, he offered Gideon a present.

There was silence after this further explanation, and then Gideon remarked indifferently that he could not remember the root. His face was sullen and hostile, even when he looked at the Farquars, whom he usually treated like old friends. They were beginning to feel annoyed; and this feeling annulled[9] the guilt that had been sprung into life by Gideon's accusing ❶ manner. They were beginning to feel that he was unreasonable. But it was at that moment that they all realized he would never give in. The magical drug would remain where it was, unknown and useless except for the tiny scattering of Africans who had the knowledge, natives who might be digging a ditch for the municipality in a ragged shirt and a pair of patched shorts, but who were still born to healing, hereditary healers, being the nephews or sons of the old witch doctors whose ugly masks and bits of bone and all the uncouth[10] properties of magic were the outward signs of real power and wisdom.

The Farquars might tread on that plant fifty times a day as they passed from house to garden, from cow kraal to mealie field, but they would never know it.

But they went on persuading and arguing, with all the force of their exasperation; and Gideon continued to say that he could not remember, or that there was no such root, or that it was the wrong season of the year, or that it wasn't the root itself, but the spit from his mouth that had cured Teddy's eyes. He said all these things one after another, and seemed not to care they were contradictory. He was rude and stubborn. The Farquars could hardly recognize their gentle, lovable old servant in this ignorant, perversely obstinate African, standing there in front of them with lowered eyes, his hands twitching his cook's apron, repeating over and over whichever one of the stupid refusals that first entered his head.

> ❷ **◆ Literary Focus**
> What emotionally charged words does Lessing use to describe this scene? How do these words help her portray cultural conflict?

And suddenly he appeared to give in. He lifted his head, gave a long blank angry look at the circle of whites, who seemed to him like a circle of yelping dogs pressing around him, and said: "I will show you the root."

They walked single file away from the homestead down a kaffir path. It was a blazing December afternoon, with the sky full of hot rain clouds. Everything was hot: the sun was like a bronze tray whirling overhead, there was a heat shimmer over the fields, the soil was scorching ❸ underfoot, the dusty wind blew gritty and thick and warm in their faces. It was a terrible day, fit only for reclining on a verandah with iced drinks, which is where they would normally have been at that hour.

From time to time, remembering that on the day of the snake it had taken ten minutes to find the root, someone asked: "Is it much further, Gideon?" And Gideon would answer over his shoulder, with angry politeness: "I'm looking for the root, baas." And indeed, he would frequently bend sideways and trail his hand among the grasses with a gesture that was insulting in its perfunctoriness. He walked them through the bush along unknown paths for two hours, in that melting destroying heat, so that the sweat trickled coldly down them and their heads ached. They were all quite silent: the Farquars because they were angry, the scientist because he was being proved right again; there was no such plant. His was a tactful[11] silence.

At last, six miles from the house, Gideon suddenly decided they had had enough; or perhaps his anger evaporated at that moment. He picked up, without an attempt at looking anything but casual, a handful of blue flowers from the grass, flowers that had been growing plentifully all down the paths they had come.

He handed them to the scientist without looking at him, and marched off by himself on the way home, leaving them to follow them if they chose.

9. **annulled** (ə nuld´) *v.*: Did away with.
10. **uncouth** (un ko͞oth´) *adj.*: Uncultured; crude; strange.
11. **tactful** (takt´ fəl) *adj.*: Polite.

Speaking and Listening Mini-Lesson

Debate

This mini-lesson supports the Speaking and Listening activity on page 1021.

Introduce the Concept Tell students that this activity will involve learning about the economic, cultural, and medical effects of colonialism in order to debate its pros and cons. Tell students that they must support their arguments not only with facts, but also with their speaking and listening skills. They should listen closely to questions asked or arguments made by opponents. Then they should speak clearly and confidently to answer questions and refute arguments.

Develop Background Divide the class into debate teams. Assign each team a side to debate. Then give teams time to prepare their arguments in advance of the actual debate. Go over the rules of debate to establish uniform guidelines for behavior. Have them prepare notecards on which they record statistics, quotations, and other facts that would be useful to cite during the debate.

Apply the Information Hold the debates in front of the classes. You may act as moderator, who times the debate and asks questions, or you may appoint a student to act as moderator.

Assess the Outcome Evaluate students in terms of the coherence of their arguments, ability to support or refute contentions, ability to offer cogent rebuttals, and the overall effectiveness of the team.

When they got back to the house, the scientist went to the kitchen to thank Gideon: he was being very polite, even though there was an amused look in his eyes. Gideon was not there. Throwing the flowers casually into the back of his car, the eminent visitor departed on his way back to his laboratory.

4 Gideon was back in his kitchen in time to prepare dinner, but he was sulking. He spoke to Mr. Farquar like an unwilling servant. It was days before they liked each other again.

The Farquars made inquiries about the root from their laborers. Sometimes they were answered with distrustful stares. Sometimes the natives said: "We do not know. We have never heard of the root." One, the cattle boy, who had been with them a long time, and had grown to
5 trust them a little, said: "Ask your boy in the kitchen. Now, there's a doctor for you. He's the son of a famous medicine man who used to be in these parts, and there's nothing he cannot
6 cure." Then he added politely: "Of course, he's not as good as the white man's doctor, we know that, but he's good for us." 6

After some time, when the soreness had gone from between the Farquars and Gideon, they began to joke: "When are you going to show us the snake-root, Gideon?" And he would laugh and shake his head, saying, a little uncomfortably: "But I did show you, missus, have you forgotten?"

Much later, Teddy, as a schoolboy, would come into the kitchen and say: "You old rascal, Gideon! Do you remember that time you tricked us all by making us walk miles all over the veld for nothing? It was so far my father had to carry me!" 7

> ◆ **Literary Focus** Is the cultural conflict resolved? Why or why not?

And Gideon would double up with polite laughter. After much laughing, he would suddenly straighten himself up, wipe his old eyes, and look sadly at Teddy, who was grinning mischievously at him across the kitchen: "Ah, Little Yellow Head, how you have grown! Soon you will be grown up with a farm of your own . . ."

Guide for Responding

◆ Literature and Your Life

Reader's Response Do you think Gideon is right to be so stubborn? Why or why not?

Thematic Focus What specific effects of colonial rule are demonstrated in this story?

Journal Writing When two cultures meet, is conflict inevitable? Write down your instinctive response and a few ideas that back it up.

☑ Check Your Comprehension

1. Who is "Little Yellow Head"?
2. How does Gideon save Teddy's sight?
3. Why does a scientist visit the Farquar's farm?
4. How does Gideon respond to the scientist's request?

◆ Critical Thinking

INTERPRET

1. Why are Teddy and Gideon closest during the period Teddy is under the age of six? **[Infer]**
2. Analyze the ultimate effect of the scientist's visit on the relationship between the Farquars and Gideon. **[Analyze Cause and Effect]**
3. Explain how the term "Little Yellow Head" gathers meaning as it reappears at different points. **[Interpret]**
4. Think about Gideon's last words to Teddy. What might they mean? **[Draw Conclusions]**

EXTEND

5. In what other countries or times could a story with the same theme be set? **[Social Studies Link]**

Beyond the Selection

FURTHER READING

Other Works by Doris Lessing

Martha Quest
Memoirs of a Survivor
The Fifth Child

Other Works About Cultural Conflict

Cry, The Beloved Country, Alan Paton
A Passage to India, E. M. Forster
Burger's Daughter, Nadine Gordimer

We suggest that you preview these works before recommending them to students.

INTERNET

You may find additional information about Doris Lessing on the Internet at the following site.

For biographical information about Doris Lessing go to **http://tile.net:2001/lessing/**

You may also find related information on Doris Lessing and colonialism on the Internet.

We *strongly recommend* that you preview sites before you send students to them.

◆ Critical Thinking

6 Infer Ask students if they think the cattle boy really means this remark. *He probably does not mean this, but he knows that it's not "his place" to praise a black man so highly.*

◆ Literary Focus

7 Cultural Conflict Although the anger between the Farquars and Gideon has passed, the Farquars will never understand the servants, and the servants will never understand the Farquars.

Reinforce and Extend

Answers

◆ Literature and Your Life

Reader's Response Yes, he should hold his heritage in respect; no, he should pass his knowledge along to help people.

Thematic Focus Africans are held subservient and deferential to the colonial masters; most of the Africans live away from the colonial compound and have converted to Christianity.

☑ Check Your Comprehension

1. "Little Yellow Head" is the native name given to Teddy Farquar.
2. Gideon uses a folk remedy to save Teddy's sight.
3. The scientist hopes Gideon will show him the plant he used to save Teddy's eyesight.
4. Gideon refuses to reveal the plant, but he pretends to look for it.

◆ Critical Thinking

1. Young Teddy has no understanding of the different roles he and Gideon are destined to play in life.
2. When the scientist tried to get Gideon to reveal his secret, the Farquars did not understand Gideon's reluctance; that misunderstanding forced a wedge into their otherwise amicable relationship.
3. At first, "Little Yellow Head" is a term of affection. Once Teddy has grown, the term brings sadness at the loss of innocence, and reinforces the fact that Gideon and Teddy have vastly different lives and positions.
4. Gideon realizes that soon Teddy will become a white master over other black servants.
5. Possible response: India in the late nineteenth century.

Answers

◆ Literary Focus

1. The Farquars do not understand Gideon's refusal to identify for western scientists the flower he used to save Teddy's eyesight. Gideon and the other native residents believe that the healing methods are sacred and not to be divulged to outsiders.
2. The conflict is resolved in that life eventually goes back to normal for Gideon and the Farquars. But it is unresolved in that neither Gideon nor the Farquars ever completely understands the other's viewpoint.
3. Students may say that Lessing tries for an even-handed portrayal of the conflict. She gives evidence of Gideon's pride in his heritage and acknowledges that others praise his skills. She also presents logical arguments from the scientist that, when divorced from his arrogance, hold western appeal.
4. (a) Students may say that an essay or journal article might be too full of scientific or philosophical rhetoric to engage readers. (b) Whereas a story can address the heart of a matter in empathic, emotional, and creative ways, an article would probably be more objective and less moving.

◆ Reading Strategy

1. (a) When Teddy frightens Gideon's son, he is childishly imitating racist behavior he has observed in others, including his parents. (b) By inviting the scientist to lunch without consulting with Gideon first, the Farquars act without forethought and insight. They view Gideon's actions as a lucky miracle and don't stop to think of his willingness to share his medical skills.
2. Both cultures celebrate their children and have strong religious faith.
3. The Farquars know to trust Gideon to work for them and care for their son, yet they are ignorant of his standing among his own people.
4. The farm represents western culture—it is run according to western beliefs and traditions. The bush seems wild and foreign to the Farquars; it is there that Teddy is injured.
5. The title suggests that to Gideon, the vast and ancient wealth of his folk medicine tradition can never be bought or sold; to the colonials, his medical knowledge is "witchcraft," and should be as available as any other remedy.

Guide for Responding *(continued)*

◆ Literary Focus

Cultural Conflict

In Lessing's short story, a **cultural conflict** arises when the Farquars want to use Gideon's medicine to benefit "thousands of people." They are surprised when Gideon feels betrayed by their efforts. The cultural conflict between the Farquars and Gideon stems from differing ideas about the way knowledge of medicines should be preserved and transmitted.

1. Summarize the point of view of each side in this cultural conflict.
2. In what way is this cultural conflict both resolved and not resolved?
3. In describing the conflict, does Lessing seem to assign blame to either side? Explain.
4. Journalists and nonfiction writers also write about cultural conflict. (a) Do you think that Lessing could have communicated the same message in a newspaper article or essay? Why or why not? (b) In what ways would a feature article on the incident with the snake differ from Lessing's story?

◆ Reading Strategy

Analyze Cultural Differences

Lessing indicates **cultural differences** both in her portrayal of characters and in her description of the setting. For example, although the Farquars and Gideon share a "feeling about God," the Farquars seem to believe that their culture and ways are generally superior to Gideon's.

1. Explain how each of these episodes reveals the Farquars' sense of superiority over Gideon: (a) Teddy's frightening of Gideon's son, and (b) the Farquars' bringing the scientist to lunch.
2. In what ways do the Farquars and Gideon share universal human values?
3. How do the Farquars both know and fail to know Gideon?
4. In what ways does Lessing use the Farquars' farm and the bush to stand for different cultures and different values?
5. Considering the cultural differences this story brings out, explain the meaning of the story's title.

◆ Build Vocabulary

Using Forms of *Skeptical*

The word *skeptical* means "doubting" or "not easily persuaded." Think about this definition as you answer each of the following questions.

1. In ancient Greece, some philosophers called themselves Skeptics. What do you think they believed about human knowledge?
2. Is skepticism an attitude appropriate for a modern scientist? Why or why not?
3. What might a *skeptical* store owner do when offered a personal check by a stranger?

Word Bank

In your notebook, write the letter of the word that is the best synonym for the first word.

1. reverently: (a) politely, (b) respectfully, (c) shyly
2. defiantly: (a) disobediently, (b) wryly, (c) strongly
3. efficacy: (a) strength, (b) stamina, (c) effectiveness
4. incredulous: (a) disbelieving, (b) sincere, (c) flip
5. skeptical: (a) trusting, (b) angry, (c) suspicious

◆ Grammar and Style

Correct Use of *Like* and *As*

Writers use the words *like* and *as* or *as if* to compare things and ideas. In making comparisons, however, don't confuse *like* with forms of *as*. *As, as if,* and *as though* are subordinating conjunctions. They introduce a clause with a subject and a verb. *Like* is a preposition, and it takes a noun or a pronoun as an object. Do not use *like* in place of *as*.

Practice In your notebook, complete each comparison with *as, as if, as though* or *like*.

1. Teddy's hair was colored __?__ straw.
2. At first, Gideon stared __?__ he didn't understand.
3. The scientist looked __?__ he were skeptical.
4. The sun was __?__ a bronze tray whirling overhead.
5. Teddy laughed __?__ he had said something clever.

Writing Application In your notebook, write a paragraph describing Gideon's behavior during the medical crisis. Use *like* and *as* to make comparisons.

◆ Build Vocabulary

Related Words: Forms of *Skeptical*

1. Skeptics probably believed that human knowledge was limited and unreliable.
2. Yes, to be a successful scientist, you must question and test every result; no, to be a scientist, you must believe in the "impossible."
3. The store owner would insist on several forms of identification before accepting the check.

Using the Word Bank

1. b; respectfully
2. a; disobediently
3. c; effectiveness
4. a; disbelieving
5. c; suspicious

◆ Grammar and Style

1. like; 2. as if; 3. as if;
4. like; 5. as if

Build Your Portfolio

Idea Bank

Writing

1. Review For a class critic's file, write a review of "No Witchcraft for Sale." Prepare readers without giving away too much of the story.

2. Proposal Write a proposal for adapting this story as a short film. Explain which scenes would be particularly effective in a movie and why.

3. Critical Response Lessing has said that a responsible writer "must be a humanist, and must feel himself as an instrument of change for good or for bad." In an essay, explain how she meets or fails to meet this challenge in her story.

Speaking and Listening

4. Debate With two teams of classmates, debate the pros and cons of colonialism. Consider the economic, cultural, and medical effects of colonial rule. Use ideas from the story to support your main points. **[Social Studies Link]**

5. Dramatic Scene Create and produce a scene in which Gideon tells his family about a major event from the story. Include details that reflect Gideon's unique point of view. **[Performing Arts Link]**

Projects

6. Book Cover Design By hand or with a computer, create a book jacket for a collection that includes "No Witchcraft for Sale" and other stories about cultural conflict. Choose a title and cover design that reflect the content. **[Art Link]**

7. Comparison Report Pick an African nation, like Zimbabwe, and prepare a report on the aftermath of colonialism there. **[Social Studies Link]**

Writing Mini-Lesson

Problem-and-Solution Essay

Lessing's character Gideon knows many remedies. What is the most effective home remedy you and your family use? Your remedy might be a food, (like chicken soup) or a method (like curing hiccups by holding your breath or taking steam baths to cure a cough). Write a problem-and-solution essay in which you state a problem (on illness or injury) and give a solution (a remedy with exact steps). Elaborate to give precise instructions.

Writing Skills Focus: Elaboration to Enhance Understanding

Elaborate to add information that will enhance a reader's understanding of the remedy you describe. Follow these steps to make sure readers will follow your explanations:

- Introduce the type and purpose of the remedy you're proposing, and elaborate with details so your reader will have no doubt *what* he or she is using and *why*.
- Be exact. Replace vague words with precise terms that describe your remedy exactly.
- Anticipate difficulties a reader might face and provide information to overcome them.
- Provide step-by-step instructions.

Prewriting Brainstorm for a list of home remedies you might write about. Choose two potential cures and write notes in support of each. Once you make a final decision, sketch out the steps you will describe.

Drafting Identify the remedy and its purpose. Then describe the materials needed and list the steps to follow in order. Use transition words, such as *first, then, next,* and *finally,* to clearly signal the order. End with a discussion of problems people might encounter as well as possible solutions.

Revising Ask a classmate to read your description and tell you where your directions are unclear. Elaborate the details in those sections.

✓ ASSESSMENT OPTIONS

Formal Assessment, Selection Test, pp. 263–265, and Assessment Resources Software. The selection test is designed so that it can be easily customized to the performance levels of your students.

Alternative Assessment, p. 55, includes options for less advanced students, more advanced students, musical/rhythmic learners, verbal/linguistic learners, and visual/spatial learners.

PORTFOLIO ASSESSMENT

Use the following rubrics in the ***Alternative Assessment*** booklet to assess student writing:
Review: Evaluation/Review Rubric, p. 105
Proposal: Drama Rubric, p. 110
Critical Response: Literary Analysis/Interpretation Rubric, p. 113
Writing Mini-Lesson: How-to/Process Explanation Rubric, p. 101

Customizing for *Performance Levels*

Following are suggestions for matching Idea Bank topics with your students' performance levels:

Less Advanced Students: 1, 6
Average Students: 2, 5, 7
More Advanced Students: 3, 4

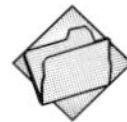

Idea Bank

Customizing for *Learning Modalities*

Following are suggestions for matching Idea Bank topics with your students' learning modalities:

Visual/Spatial: 2, 6
Verbal/Linguistic: 1, 3, 4, 5, 7
Interpersonal: 4

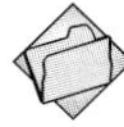

Writing Mini-Lesson

Refer students to the Writing Process Handbook, page 1189, for instruction on the writing process, and page 1191 for further information on expository writing.

Writing and Language Transparencies Display on an overhead the Problem/Solution Organizer, p. 107. Allow students to copy and use this organizer to help students prepare their problem-and-solution essays.

Writing Lab CD-ROM

Have students complete the tutorial on Exposition. Follow these steps:

1. Look at the audio-annotated model of a how-to essay.
2. Complete the Questionnaire designed to help students gather details for a problem-and-solution essay.
3. Create a draft on the computer.
4. Use a Revision Checker for Unity and Coherence.

Sourcebook

Have students use Chapter 3, Exposition, pp. 62–95, for additional support. The chapter includes extensive tips for organizing a how-to or problem-and-solution essay.

Prepare and Engage

OBJECTIVES

1. To read, comprehend, and interpret a speech
2. To relate a speech to personal experience
3. To connect a speech to the theme of conflicts at home and abroad
4. To respond to a speech through writing, speaking and listening, and a project

PORTFOLIO OPPORTUNITIES

Writing: Campaign Poster; Persuasive Essay; Problem-Solution Essay
Speaking and Listening: Global Village Meeting
Project: Taking Responsibility

More About the Author
A popular and enthusiastic speaker, Tony Blair has been winning elections since the early 1980's. His move to political prominence has been built in part on a strong ability to resolve conflicts and find a middle ground between divergent views. The changes Blair made as Labor Party leader—developing policies seeking lower taxes, carefully controlled social spending, and balanced power for labor and management, for example—brought his Party closer to the political center and made it more acceptable to business leaders.

Enrichment

The Labor Party and The Fabian Society From Lord Byron to William Morris (a friend of the Pre-Raphaelites) to George Bernard Shaw to Stephen Spender, many British writers sympathized with the plight of workers. Some advocated socialism (the use of society's wealth for the benefit of all). George Bernard Shaw, the Irish dramatist, helped lead a socialist movement called the Fabian Society, founded in 1884. Together with trade unionists, the Fabian Society was key to the founding of the Labor Party.

CONNECTIONS TO TODAY'S WORLD

The Rights We Enjoy, the Duties We Owe

from New Britain: My Vision of a Young Country

Tony Blair

Thematic Connection

CONFLICTS AT HOME AND ABROAD

In his speech "The Rights We Enjoy, the Duties We Owe," prime minister of England Tony Blair calls for a moral approach to social issues. As the writers in this section demonstrate, moral and social values have been tested by the many conflicts Britain has experienced in the twentieth century. The soldier-poets Siegfried Sassoon and Wilfred Owen, for example, show how traditional notions of patriotism were called into question by the horrors of trench warfare in World War I. Later, in World War II, Winston Churchill rallied the English to their traditional values in order to oppose the fascist tyranny of Hitler.

British belief in the value and permanence of empire was also tested during the twentieth century. Gandhi's speech illustrates the struggles of Indians to assert their own national identity in the face of British oppression. Also, stories by Lessing and Trevor and poems by Heaney and Boland address conflicts in South Africa and Ireland arising from the injustices of imperial rule.

A NEW BRITAIN

With many of Britain's major external conflicts settled, Tony Blair has expressed a new vision of British citizenship. Rejecting both the notion of doing one's "own thing" and the urge to look out only for oneself, he reaffirms the importance of rights and responsibilities. He argues for "practical policies" guided by "values" that stress "the good of all."

TONY BLAIR
(1953–)

Tony Blair, Britain's youngest prime minister in the twentieth century, is a skillful orator and speech writer. Educated as an attorney, he became a member of Parliament in 1983. He went on to become leader of the Labor Party in 1994, transforming it into what became known as the "New Labor Party" In May 1997, Blair became the first Labor Party prime minister elected in eighteen years. He is also the first prime minister not to live at 10 Downing Street, traditional residence of the country's leader, because the home was too small to accommodate his wife and three young children.

Prentice Hall Literature Program Resources

REINFORCE / RETEACH / EXTEND

Selection Support Pages
Build Vocabulary: The Language of Building a New Society, p. 265
Thematic Connection: Conflicts at Home and Abroad, p. 266

Formal Assessment, pp. 266–267

Resource Pro CD-ROM
"The Rights We Enjoy, the Duties We Owe"—includes all resource material and customizable lesson plan

Listening to Literature Audiocassettes
"The Rights We Enjoy, the Duties We Owe"

The Rights We Enjoy, *The* Duties We Owe

TONY BLAIR

from New Britain: My Vision of a Young Country

CONNECTIONS TO TODAY'S WORLD

Individuals prosper best within a strong and cohesive society. Especially in a modern world, we are interdependent. Unless we act together to provide common services, prepare our industry and people for industrial and technological challenge, and guarantee a proper system of law and government, we will
❶ be worse off as individuals. In particular, those without the best start in life through birth are unlikely to make up for it without access to the means of achievement. Furthermore—though this may be more open to debate—a society which is fragmented and divided, where people feel no sense of shared purpose, is unlikely to produce well-adjusted and responsible citizens.

But a strong society should not be confused with a strong state, or with powerful collectivist institutions. That was the confusion of early Left[1] thinking. It was compounded by a belief that the role of the state was to grant rights, with the language of responsibility spoken far less fluently. In a further strain of thinking, connected with the libertarian Left, there was a kind of social individualism espoused,[2] where you "did your own thing." In fact this had very little to do with any forms of left-of-center philosophy recognizable to the founders of the Labor Party.[3]

The reaction of the Right,[4] after the advent of Mrs. Thatcher, was to stress the notion of the individual as against the state. Personal responsibility was extolled.[5] But then a curious thing happened. In a mirror-image of the Left's confusion, the Right started to define personal responsibility as responsibility not just for yourself but to yourself. Outside of a duty not to break the law, responsibility appeared to exclude the broader notion of duty to others. It became narrowly acquisitive[6] and rather destructive. The economic message of enterprise—of the early 1980s—became a philosophy of "Get what you can."

All over the Western world, people are searching for a new political settlement which starts with the individual but sets him or her within the wider society. People don't want an overbearing state, but they don't want to live in a social vacuum either. It is in the search for this different, reconstructed, relationship between individual and society that ideas about "community" are found. "Community" implies a recognition of interdependence, but not overweening[7] government power. It accepts that we are better equipped to meet the forces of change and insecurity through working together. It provides a basis for the elements of our character that are cooperative as well as competitive, as part of a more enlightened view of self-interest.

People know they face a greater insecurity than ever before: a new global economy; massive and rapid changes in technology; a labor market where half the workers are women; a family life that has been altered drastically; telecommunications and media that visit a common culture upon us and transform our expectations and behavior.

This insecurity is not just about jobs or mortgages—though of course these are serious problems. It is about a world that in less than a lifetime has compressed the historical change

1. **Left:** Term used to describe liberal political views.
2. **espoused** (e spouzd´) *v.*: Supported a cause.
3. **Labor Party:** British political party.
4. **Right:** Term used to describe conservative political views.
5. **extolled** (eks tōld´) *v.*: Praised highly.
6. **acquisitive** (ə kwiz´ə tiv) *adj.*: Eager to acquire.
7. **overweening** (ō´vər wēn´ iŋ) *adj.*: Arrogant; excessively proud.

Develop Understanding

Students will find this speech reasonable or reactionary, depending on their political views, but almost certainly engaging. Prime Minister Blair advocates practical morality—rules of behavior for citizens and businesses that acknowledge duty to society, individual rights, and legitimate self-interest. In examining preconceptions about his Labor Party's views, Blair constructs a new view of the "strong society" in which modern insecurity is met with definable rules and expectations, duty is viewed as healthy, and all policies are required to be both moral and practical.

Customize for *Less Proficient Readers*
Encourage these students to read slowly, to pause frequently to paraphrase, and to note confusing passages, to which they should later return for additional analysis.

Customize for *More Advanced Students*
To extend the selection for these students, have them locate and read Britain's Conservative Party's responses to Blair's positions.

Thematic Connection

❶ Conflicts at Home and Abroad Ask students whether Blair's view of the individual's relation to society could have been applied by the soldier-poets to their situation or by Winston Churchill to his. What can they conclude about the limitations of Blair's view? *Blair stresses the possibility of balancing both rights in and duties to society. Sassoon and Owen discovered that social duty (the duty to serve in war) was counterbalanced, not by individual rights, but by the irrationality and ugliness of what society asked for—which was war. Churchill's times demanded an extensive subjugation of individual rights to the common good—no balance between the two was possible. Students may conclude that Blair's views cannot apply in times of crisis.*

Beyond the Classroom

Career Connection

Public Servant This speech was made by England's Prime Minister, the leader of the party holding the majority of votes in Parliament. Members of Parliament represent a district or geographic area in national government and face reelection at regular intervals, just as members of Congress do in the United States. Have interested students learn about their community's current representatives to national government. Discuss how these individuals view the balance between rights and duties.

Workplace Skills Tony Blair advocates voluntary individual duty to the community or the group. In the workplace, this means each worker, no matter his or her individual role, must consider and value the overall business goals. In so doing, goes the theory, he or she will also benefit individually. Ask interested students to discuss local businesses with this model in mind. Which businesses might benefit from the Blair approach? Are there any business situations in which Blair's model might be counterproductive?

▶Critical Viewing◀

❶ **Evaluate** Students may say Blair dresses neatly and formally, has confident body language, and an assured expression.

Customize for
English Language Learners
Language learners may need help overcoming the hurdle of Blair's dense and difficult language in order to reach his relatively straightforward positions. You may want to summarize the speech for these students *before* they read it, as a comprehension aid.

Thematic Connection

❷ **Conflicts at Home and Abroad** Ask students how Gandhi saw the relation of the individual to these rules. Then ask them to contrast this view with Blair's. *Gandhi puts individual conscience outside, but not above, the rules. Law and conscience are separate domains: the judge must either punish Gandhi fully (follow the rules), or resign (follow conscience). By contrast, Blair holds out for a world in which rules can always be revised to serve both society and self-interest.*

◆ *Literature and Your Life*

❸ Invite a student to read these lines aloud. Discuss as a class what they mean. Then ask students to offer examples from their own lives of citizenship duties and rights. *Students may mention duties to others in the community, such as the elderly or disabled; work to protect the environment for all; obligations to team and family members. Rights might include access to educational and employment opportunities; a safe and supportive home and school environment.*

CONNECTIONS TO TODAY'S WORLD

◀ Critical Viewing In what ways does Tony Blair present himself as a leader? **[Evaluate]** ❶

of epochs. It is bewildering. Even religion—once a given—is now an exception. And of course the world has the nuclear weapons to destroy itself many times over. Look at our children and the world into which they are growing. What parent would not feel insecure?

❷ People need rules which we all stand by, fixed points of agreement which impose order on chaos. That does not mean a return to the old hierarchy of deference. That is at best nostalgia, at worst reactionary. We do not want old class structures back. We do not want women chained to the sink. We do not want birth rather than merit to become once again the basis of personal advancement. Nor does it mean bureaucracy and regulation. Bad and foolish rules are bad and foolish rules, but they do not invalidate the need to have rules.

Duty is the cornerstone of a decent society. It recognizes more than self. It defines the context in which rights are given. It is personal; but it is also owed to society. Respect for others—responsibility to them—is an essential prerequisite of a strong and active community. It is the method through which we can build a society that does not subsume our individuality but allows it to develop healthily. It accords instinct with common sense. It draws on a broader and therefore more accurate notion of human nature than one formulated on insular[8] self-interest. The rights we receive should reflect the duties we owe. With power should come responsibility. ❸

Duty is a Labor Value

The assertion that each of us is our brother's keeper has motivated the Labor movement since the mid nineteenth century. It is time to reassert what it really means.

The Left has always insisted that it is not enough to argue that our only duty is not to infringe on the lives and rights of others—what might be called negative duty. A minimal community creates a society of minimal citizens. It is a broader notion of duty that gives substance to the traditional belief of the Left in solidarity. This was well understood by the early pioneers of socialism. William Morris[9] put it colorfully: "Fellowship is life, and lack of fellowship is death."

But solidarity[10] and fellowship are the start of the story, and not the end, because they will be achieved only on the basis of both social equality and personal responsibility.

The historians of *English Ethical Socialism*, Norman Dennis and A.H. Halsey, argue that William Cobbett,[11] who lived before the word "socialism" achieved common currency, took it for granted that people stood a better chance of having a happy life if they were not selfish. They write that "a person matching Cobbett's ideal, therefore, was one who enjoyed the rights and performed the duties of citizenship."

Early socialists like Robert Owen understood very clearly that a society which did not encour-

8. **insular** (in´ sə lər) *adj.*: Detached or isolated.
9. **William Morris** Early English socialist (1834–1896).
10. **solidarity** (säl´ə dar´ə tē) *n.*: Combination or agreement of all elements or individuals.
11. **William Cobbett** (käb´ it): English journalist and reformer (1762–1835).

Speaking and Listening Mini-Lesson

Global Village Meeting
This mini-lesson supports the Speaking and Listening activity in the Idea Bank on page 1026.

Introduce the Concept Have students discuss some global problems from recent media coverage. Point out that many of these issues affect nations around the globe, while others are specific to a particular region. Note that the problems facing Britain, according to Tony Blair, are similar to those facing the United States.

Develop Background Before students begin their meeting, urge them to review and consider these research and discussion strategies:

- Use current sources such as newspaper and Internet articles to identify and research a nation's pressing problems.
- Individuals representing a nation must consider that nation's needs, rather than their own personal views.

Apply the Information Assist students in preparing for the meeting. Ask the group to agree on a discussion structure. Students should then be able to stage a successful meeting. Remind them to be courteous listeners.

Assess the Outcome Invite students to comment on the success of the meeting. Were participants prepared and professional?

age people voluntarily to carry out their responsibilities to others would always be in danger of slipping either into the anarchy[12] of mutual indifference—and its corollary, the domination of the powerless by the powerful—or the tyranny of collective coercion, where the freedom of all is denied in the name of the good of all.

Ethical socialists have long asserted that there was and is a distinctive socialist view of both human nature and social morality. R.H. Tawney[13] put it clearly in the 1920s: "Modern society is sick through the absence of a moral ideal," he wrote. "What we have been witnessing . . . both in international affairs and in industry, is the breakdown of society on the basis of rights divorced from obligations." And G.D.H Cole said that "A socialist society that is to be true to its egalitarian principles of human brotherhood must rest on the widest possible diffusion of power and responsibility, so as to enlist the active participation of as many of its citizens in the tasks of democratic self-government."

In his book *Liberals and Social Democrats*, the historian Peter Clarke drew a distinction between "moral reformers" and "mechanical reformers." The moral reformers were the ethical socialists like Tawney and Morris. They looked around the communities in which they lived, and called for a new moral impulse to guide them. The mechanical reformers, on the other hand, concentrated on the technicalities of social and economic reform. They were severely practical in their outlook.

Values without practical policies are useless; but policies without a set of values guiding them give no sense of meaning or direction to public life.

12. anarchy (an´ ər kē) *n.*: Complete absence of government.
13. Robert Tawney (tô´ nē): ; British economic historian (1880–1962).

Guide for Responding

◆ Literature and Your Life

Reader's Response After reading this selection, did you feel optimistic or pessimistic about Britain's ability to solve its own problems? Explain.

Thematic Focus Do you see yourself as a member of a global community? Why or why not?

Journal Writing List some values that will help individuals and governments to achieve a just society.

Check Your Comprehension

1. What are two beliefs of the Left that Blair rejects?
2. What is a "mirror-image" belief of the Right that Blair also rejects?
3. What changes in the world does Blair see as contributing to a sense of insecurity?
4. Blair sees solidarity and fellowship as dependent upon what two social principles?

◆ Critical Thinking

INTERPRET

1. This essay is entitled "The Rights We Enjoy, The Duties We Owe." (a) Do you think this title is appropriate? (b) What statements by Blair support or contradict the title of this selection? **[Support]**
2. Would you describe Blair as a "moral reformer," "mechanical reformer," or a combination of both? Explain. **[Analyze]**
3. (a) Explain what Tawney means by his statement "what we have been witnessing . . . is the breakdown of society on the basis of rights divorced from obligations." (b) Why would Blair have included this reference? **[Draw Conclusions]**

EVALUATE

4. How convincing and effective is Blair in getting his points across? **[Evaluate]**

Beyond the Selection

FURTHER READING

Other Works by Tony Blair

"The Welfare Reform Address," *Vital Speeches of the Day*, 6/2/97

"Far More Carrot Than Stick," *London Times Educational Supplement*, 1/19/96

Other Works About Citizenship

Culture Wars, Fred Whitehead

What Can I Do to Make a Difference? A Positive Action Sourcebook, Richard Zimmerman

Preview works before recommending them.

INTERNET

You may find additional information about Tony Blair on the Internet at the following sites.

For information and opinions about Blair, visit **http://www.geocities.com/~journo/blair.html**

To read another speech by Blair, visit **http://www.oxfe.ac.uk/Ruskin/blairsp.htm**

You may also find related information on the Labor Party on the Internet. We *strongly recommend* that you preview sites before you send students to them.

Reinforce and Extend

Answers

◆ Literature and Your Life

Reader's Response Students may respond that they are optimistic, because Blair is realistic about both social values and individual interests.

Thematic Focus Students may respond that complex economic interdependence binds them to the global community, even while the extreme disparity between life in the United States and life elsewhere isolates them.

Check Your Comprehension

1. He rejects a strong state that grants rights without responsibilities, and "individualism."
2. This "mirror-image" is an idea of personal responsibility that excludes duty to others.
3. He mentions global economy, technological changes, women in the labor market, altered family life, cultural change through mass media, the rapidness of change, the loss of religion, and nuclear weapons.
4. They are dependent on both social equality and personal responsibility.

◆ Critical Thinking

1. (a) Most students will recognize that the title conveys the main idea of the speech. (b) "Duty is the cornerstone of a decent society" supports the title; at the same time, the speech suggest that rights and duties are not properly "enjoyed" or "owed" in today's world.
2. Blair is a combination of moral and mechanical reformer; he wants both to elevate citizens' morality and to make public policy more practical.
3. (a) Society treats rights as a given, rather than as part of responsible participation in society. (b) Blair's emphasis on duty departs from his party's recent ideology; he therefore needs to assert continuity with the larger tradition of the Left.
4. Students may respond that his use of scholarly references along with accessible, human appeals is convincing; others may say that his speech would be more effective if it were written in simpler language.

Answers

Thematic Connection

1. Blair believes Britain is entering a new phase in its development, and thus is young again.
2. Blair's speech is more measured, more careful to balance both sides of the issues, than either Gandhi's or Churchill's speeches. Both the historical speeches advocate specific actions, while Blair's is more focused on formulating a philosophical approach to problems. Where Gandhi and Churchill faced clearly defined conflicts, Blair responds to a sense of uncertainty and directionlessness.
3. Britain may take a more balanced approach to social responsibility, seeking to care for its less fortunate without an overly strong government and to form a national community with a place for all.

Idea Bank

Customizing for
Performance Levels

Following are suggestions for matching Idea Bank topics with your students' performance levels:

Less Advanced Students: 1
Average Students: 2, 4
More Advanced Students: 3, 5

Customizing for
Learning Modalities

Following are suggestions for matching Idea Bank topics with your students' learning modalities:

Visual/Spatial: 1
Verbal/Linguistic: 2, 4, 5
Interpersonal: 4

Thematic Connection

Conflicts at Home and Abroad

Many of the poems and stories in this section deal with social and political conflicts that were resolved at great cost—or that have not yet been resolved. By contrast with the solemn, defiant, or pessimistic moods of these works, this speech by Tony Blair strikes a note of optimism. Blair seems to believe that, with rights and responsibilities in balance, Great Britain can meet the global challenges of a new century.

1. Why do you think Blair subtitles his speech "My Vision of a Young Country"?
2. Compare and contrast Blair's speech with those of Churchill and Gandhi. Pay special attention to tone, historical circumstances, and key ideas.
3. What do you think the election of Tony Blair suggests about the direction Britain will take in the twenty-first century?

Idea Bank

Writing

1. **Campaign Poster** Using Tony Blair's key ideas, design a campaign poster that will help him in a future election.
2. **Persuasive Essay** Blair states that "The rights we receive should reflect the duties we owe." Write a persuasive essay in which you explain how this notion has relevance in your home, at work and school, and in your local community.
3. **Problem-Solution Essay** Apply Tony Blair's ideas about rights and responsibilities to resolve a conflict addressed in one of the stories and poems of this section.

Speaking and Listening

4. **Global Village Meeting** Stage a global village meeting with your classmates. Each student should choose a country and come to the meeting prepared to discuss that country's most pressing problems. **[Social Studies Link]**

Project

5. **Taking Responsibility** Many organizations, from local food banks to the International Red Cross, take responsibility for those who are less fortunate. Select one of these organizations and learn about how it functions. Present your findings in an article for your school newspaper. **[Social Studies Link]**

✓ Assessment Options

Formal Assessment, Selection Test, pp. 266–267, and Assessment Resources Software. The selection test is designed so that it can be easily customized to the performance levels of your students.

PORTFOLIO ASSESSMENT

Use the following rubrics in the ***Alternative Assessment*** booklet to assess student writing:
Campaign Poster: Persuasion Rubric, p. 106
Persuasive Essay: Persuasion Rubric, p. 106
Problem-Solution Essay: Problem-Solution Rubric, p. 102

Writing Process Workshop

How-to Essay

Literature inspired by World War I is intense and shocking. Writers who unflinchingly described trench warfare may have wished they could have given the world instructions on how to avoid warfare in the first place.

Choose a simpler process than solving global conflict, and write a traditional how-to essay in which you explain the ways in which readers can accomplish a specific task. After stating the task and giving necessary background information, take readers step by step through the process.

Use the following skills to guide you as you write:

Writing Skills Focus

- **Anticipate reader's questions** by considering what your readers will want or need to know, and providing adequate information. (See p. 981.)
- **Choose vivid, specific details** to clarify the steps in the process. (See p. 991.)
- **Maintain brevity and clarity** by providing information in the form of charts, outlines, or pictures. (See p. 1001.)
- **Elaborate to enhance understanding** by providing necessary details and explanations for each procedure. (See p. 1021.)

Workplace Writing Model

from "In Praise of the Kitchen Garden,"
Gardening How-To, May/June 1997

The history of the kitchen garden goes way back, as witnessed by this late-nineteenth-century walled kitchen garden in England. ① The walls kept predators at bay and created a microclimate ② more conducive to growing vegetables. To create your own special kitchen garden, follow these basic guidelines. Your kitchen garden should be: ③

1. Close to your house, preferably right next to your kitchen door. . . . It will be handiest there; besides, it will look wonderful④. . . .

① Historical background creates interest and explains the origins of the task.

② The word *microclimate* is vivid and specific.

③ A numbered list, rather than a paragraph, keeps the explanation brief and clear.

④ The author anticipates and answers the reader's question, "Why next to the door?"

Beyond the Classroom

Workplace Skills

Instruction Manuals Every piece of equipment—from videodisc players to dishwashers to automobiles—comes with instructions. These how-to booklets usually include diagrams and step-by-step instructions, and somebody was paid, probably quite well, to write those instructions.

Ask students to brainstorm for a list of instruction manuals they find at home or at work. Ask what problems they may have encountered in following the instructions and what caused the problems. Have students discuss what their experiences suggest about writing effective how-to essays.

Prepare and Engage

Establish Writing Guidelines
Review the following key characteristics of a how-to essay:

- A how-to essay explains the steps of a specific task.
- It provides adequate instruction so that the reader can complete the task.
- Ample transitions enhance organization.

Before students begin, you may want to share with them the Scoring Rubric for How-to/Process Explanation (p. 101 in ***Alternative Assessment***) so that students see the criteria by which they will be evaluated. Suggestions on page 1029 customize the rubric to this workshop.

Connect to Literature Refer students to Jane Austen's "On Making an Agreeable Marriage" on page 716 in Unit 4. Have students review the piece for Austen's steps. Ask how this essay differs from one on, for instance, building a birdhouse.

Writer's Solution

To help students distinguish a how-to essay from other expository writing, play the videodisc segment on Exposition to hear film critic Anne Billson. Ask students how the expository elements will apply to the how-to essay.

Play frames 22650 to 31677

Writing Lab CD-ROM
If students have access to computers, have them work in the tutorial on Exposition to complete all or part of their how-to essay. Follow these steps:

1. Students can review an audio-annotated example of how-to instructions.
2. Have students use the Sunburst Diagram to help choose a topic.
3. Have students consult the Transition Word Bin to show chronology.
4. Have students use the Revision Checker for Unity and Coherence to refine their essays.

Sourcebook
Students can study a workplace writing model of a how-to essay in Exposition (Ch. 3, p. 68).

Develop Student Writing

Prewriting

Writing and Language Transparencies Since how-to essays must follow a chronological organization, you may want students to use a Cubing Organizer (***Writing and Language Transparencies,*** p. 100) to organize their thoughts.

Customize for
Visual/Spatial Learners
Encourage these students to serve as peer advisors to their classmates as they develop visuals for the how-to essays.

Writer's Solution

Writing Lab CD-ROM
To help students focus on audience, have them study the audio-annotated writing models (in Considering Audience and Purpose in the Exposition tutorial) that show two how-to essays on the same topic but for different audiences.

Drafting

As they write, have students highlight transitional words, phrases, or sentences to focus attention on their importance.

Applying Language Skills

Avoiding Run-on Sentences
Remind students that to achieve clarity, each step in a how-to essay must appear in its own sentence. Run-on sentences will muddy the message.

Answers
Possible student response:
To make linen by the traditional method, watch flax blooms carefully for the right moment to harvest them. Pull mature plants up by the roots, and bundle them loosely to dry. Soak the dry flax until the fibers separate. When the flax is dry again, crush, scrape, comb, and split the stems. Wind the long fibers onto a distaff, ready for spinning.

APPLYING LANGUAGE SKILLS:
Avoiding Run-on Sentences

It is important to avoid confusing run-on sentences in how-to essays. Use the following strategies to correct run-on sentences.

- Form two sentences.

  Draft: Scrub the pot, pat it dry.

  Revision: Scrub the pot. Pat it dry.
- Separate independent clauses with a semicolon.

  Draft: Allow the paint to dry it should take two days.

  Revision: Allow the paint to dry; it should take two days.
- Use a comma and a coordinating conjunction to join the two sentences.

  Draft: Set the plant in the shelf give it lots of light.

  Revision: Set the plant in the shelf, and give it lots of light.

Practice Revise the following paragraph by correcting the run-on sentences.

To make linen by the traditional method, watch flax blooms carefully for the right moment to harvest them pull mature plants up by the roots. Bundle them loosely to dry soak the dry flax until the fibers separate. When the flax is dry again crush scrape, comb and split the stems wind the long fibers onto a distaff, ready for spinning.

Prewriting

Choose a Topic To choose a topic for a how-to essay, think about your areas of interest and expertise, anything from aerobics to guitar playing. Here are more ideas for topics:

Topic Ideas
- Training a dog to roll over
- Playing a computer game

Selection-Related Topic Ideas
- Playing a fiddle
- Bird-watching basics

List Vivid, Specific Details Gather precise, specific details about materials and tools needed to complete the project. Also, sketch or obtain any visual aids such as maps, charts, and diagrams that you plan to include in your how-to essay.

Vague:	a saw	oil	fabric
Specific:	a hacksaw	olive oil	raw silk

Develop Details by Anticipating Questions Jot down some questions your readers might ask, and gather information that will answer them. For example, if you are explaining how to brew herbal tea by infusion, provide answers to questions like the following:

- What types of kettles are best?
- How long should the herbs steep?
- What types of herbs can be blended?

Drafting

Provide Background Information At the beginning of your essay, engage readers by briefly noting the origins, historical significance, or relevance of the task you are explaining.

Provide Transitions As you draft, present the steps in time order. Use transitions such as *before*, *after*, *during*, and *next* to indicate the order in which steps should be performed.

Elaborate Details If you think of additional information that will enhance readers' understanding of the process you're describing, include it at this point.

Create Visual Aids Create graphs, diagrams, and charts to convey complex information in an easy-to-understand form. For example, diagrams can convey assembly instructions more effectively than numbered lists can.

Writer's Solution

For additional explanation and practice on how to avoid run-on sentences, have students use the **Language Lab CD-ROM**, Sentence Errors, Fragments and Run-on Sentences.

You may also use page 43 on Fragments and Run-ons in *Writer's Solution Grammar Practice Book.*

Revising

Test-Run Ask a classmate to use your instructions to accomplish the task. Your classmate should use the following guidelines for reviewing:

- ▶ Does the background information help the reader better understand the task?
- ▶ Are any of the details vague and unspecific?

Revision Model

Mrs. McCabe is the "uncrowned queen of the castle bakehouse" at Brodick Castle ① on the Isle of Arran, Scotland. She bakes for the 50,000 annual visitors to the Castle. Here is one of her recipes:

~~Place ten ounces of self rising flour in a bowl and make a well in the center. Put three ounces of sugar and four ounces of margarine in the well. . .~~ ② 10 oz self-rising flour, 4 oz margarine, 3 oz sugar, 1 pt. milk

1. ~~Before mixing dough, generously grease a cookie sheet and~~ Preheat oven to 375 degrees.
2. ③ Generously grease a cookie sheet.
3. Place 10 oz flour in a bowl and make a well ④ in the center.
4. ~~Mix~~ ⑤ Roughly combine margarine and sugar . . .

① The author adds information to answer the question, "Where is Brodick Castle?"
② The author substitutes an ingredient list for a wordy and difficult-to-follow paragraph.
③ These steps were confusing and in the wrong order.
④ This detail is important for beginners to know.
⑤ The vague term *mix* was replaced by a more specific phrase.

Publishing

- ▶ **How-to Fair** Organize a fair at which classmates can teach one another the procedures they have written about. Ask classmates to distribute copies of their essays at the fair.
- ▶ **Workshop** Use your how-to essay as the basis for a workshop. Teach friends and classmates the process you have explained.

Applying Language Skills: Formatting Instructions

Maintain consistency as you format your instructions. Below is a list of tips.

- ▶ **Boldface:** Used for important information and warnings.
- ▶ **Capital letters:** Good for headings.
- ▶ **Italics:** Often used in chart labels.
- ▶ **Numbered Lists:** Organizes steps that should be performed in time order.
- ▶ **Bulleted Lists:** Handy way to list items or ingredients.

Practice Format the following directions.

When you determine you will need a passport, have a small picture made of yourself. You can call your local post office to get information on the cost and requirements. Take your materials to the post office and apply for the passport. Write a check and obtain a receipt. Bring forms of ID!

Writer's Solution Connection Writing Lab

For help in revising your essay, use the Revision checker for transition words in the Revising and Editing section of the tutorial on Exposition.

Revising

Discuss with students the Revision Model. In addition to the test run suggested in the text, you may want peer editors to look for any additional need for visuals or any helpful changes in formatting.

Writer's Solution

To help students complete a self-evaluation or to help peer editors respond, have students use the interactive self-evaluation checklist for how-to instructions (Revising and Editing segment in Exposition tutorial).

Publishing

Suggest that students submit their essays to appropriate magazines. Have them consult the current issue of *Writer's Market* (available in most libraries) for suggested markets.

Applying Language Skills

Formatting Instructions

Have students examine this page and discuss the importance of formatting here. Ask them to look for boldface, capital letters, italics, and bulleted and numbered lists and discuss how these affect the reader.

Answers

Possible student response:

When you determine that you will need a passport, follow these steps:

1. Have a small picture made of yourself.
2. Call the local post office to verify cost and requirements.
3. Gather the necessary forms of ID.
4. Take your photo and ID forms to the post office and complete the application.
5. Pay by check and obtain a receipt.

✓ ASSESSMENT		4	3	2	1
PORTFOLIO ASSESSMENT Use the rubric on How-to/ Process Explanation (p. 101) to assess student writing. Add these criteria to customize the rubric to this assignment.	**Background Information**	The how-to essay includes ample background information to engage readers.	The essay includes some background information.	The essay includes little background information.	The essay includes no background information.
	Visual Aids	The how-to essay includes ample and appropriately varied visual aids.	The essay includes some various visual aids.	The essay includes few visual aids or little appropriate variety in visual aids.	The essay includes no visual aids.

Introduce the Strategy

Point out to students that reading directions is part of everyday life—taking tests in school, filling out income tax forms, applying for a loan, completing a job application, and so on. Discuss with students the three key strategies and their importance.

Customize for
English Language Learners
Help these students identify the many synonyms or near-synonyms that ask for the same results. For instance, in directions on an essay test, *explain* may mean nearly the same as *enumerate or describe*. Have students compile a list of similar words and discuss the meanings.

Apply the Strategy

Have students read the directions first. Then ask them to respond to the three questions, reviewing the directions as necessary.

Answers

1. Follow the directions one step at a time and try a test run.
2. They are numbered by step.
3. Recheck the *Before You Begin* list.

Following Directions

Real-World Reading Skills Workshop

Strategies for Success

Instructions are meant to be followed—carefully and step by step. Don't try to cut corners by skimming directions or "winging it"—you'll lose time when you have to go back and start again. Remembering a few simple strategies can help guarantee success.

Read Before You Start Always read what you're going to do *before* you do anything. Make sure that each step makes sense. Often, a set of directions begins with a list of the materials you'll need to complete the project. Take time to collect each item. Review all diagrams carefully, making sure you can identify each part shown. You can even try acting out what you plan to do.

Recording A Television Program While You Watch

Before You Begin:

Check all connections.

Make sure VCR is plugged in.

Check that TV is on and set to channel 3 or 4 (see p. 12)

Buttons You Will Use:

Step 1) Insert a video cassette. (VCR power will turn on if it is off.)

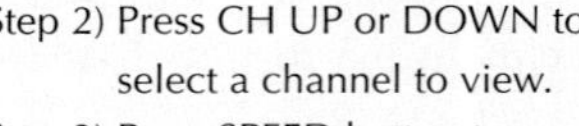

Step 2) Press CH UP or DOWN to select a channel to view.

Step 3) Press SPEED button to choose a recording speed:
SP (standard play),
LP (long play) or
EP (extended play).

Step 4) Press RECORD button to start recording.

Step 5) Press STOP button to stop recording.

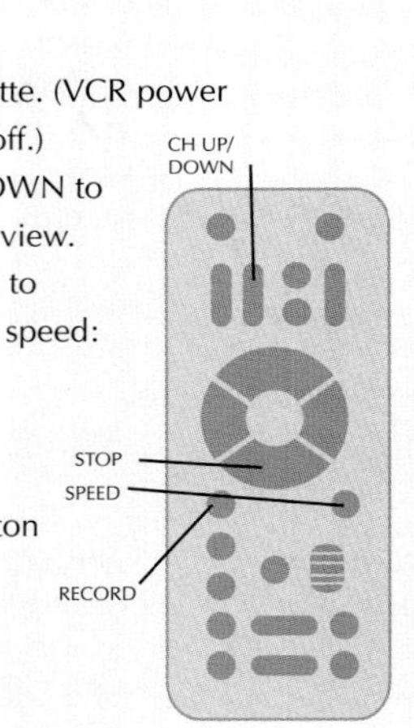

Pay Attention to Signal Words and Precise Details When reading directions, look for signal words and words that give precise information. Signal words such as *before*, *next*, *then*, and *finally* indicate chronology. Others, such as *next to*, *inside*, *right*, *left*, and *beside*, show placement. Pay attention to detailed descriptions—if you use the 3/8" nails when you should have used the 15/16" screws, your project could fall apart before you know it.

Use Troubleshooting Advice Often directions include troubleshooting advice to help readers out of the most common difficulties. If you run into a problem, look for information that will help you. If the directions are incomplete, look for a customer support number and contact the manufacturer directly.

Apply the Strategy

Your family bought a VCR and plans to record a program this evening. You're in charge, so you're reviewing the manual for information.

1. Describe two strategies you can follow to make sure that you record the program correctly.
2. How do the directions indicate the order in which you must perform the actions described?
3. Suppose that during a test run, the VCR power does not turn on. What can you do?

Here are some other types of writing that contain directions:
- Assembly instructions
- Recipes
- Navigational guides

PART 3

Focus on Literary Forms: The Short Story

The Snack Bar, 1930, Edward Burra, Tate Gallery, London

The short story was the perfect form for a century in a hurry. It had all the elements of a novel—plot, setting, character, theme—but on a smaller scale. It could take you to the house next door, to Ireland, or to Southeast Asia, but wherever you went you got back quickly. It could also display the latest fictional techniques, sometimes taking you into a character's stream of thoughts.

Humanities: Art

The Snack Bar 1930, by Edward Burra.

British painter and theatrical designer Edward Burra (1905–1976) was deeply interested in human vitality and style. As a boy, he endured chronic illness that prevented him from completing school and enjoying an active life. With his family's support, he turned to art. He became fascinated by life at the edge of society and delighted in the grotesque and flamboyant.

His oil painting "The Snack Bar" shows how he intensifies unremarkable elements to increase their impact. He also emphasizes external details such as hats, hair, and clothes.

Use this question for discussion:

In what ways does this picture tell a story? *The artist makes viewers wonder what the counterman and the woman at the counter are thinking. The artist's exaggeration of their features makes them into interesting "characters."*

One-Minute Planning Guide

The short stories in this section allow students to explore a variety of fictional techniques and topics. "The Lagoon" tells a story within a story, taking students to Malaysia. The main character in "Araby" stays close to home, but learns so much about himself that he feels as if he has traveled far. "The Lady in the Looking Glass" captures the fragmentary quality life sometimes seems to have by exploring the random thoughts in one character's mind. In "The First Year of My Life," Muriel Spark's narrator is a baby who is able to comment on the events of World War I, and who knows "everything . . . going on everywhere in the world." "The Rocking Horse Winner" is the story of a family desperate to improve its social position. "A Shocking Accident" highlights life's absurdity. "The Book of Sand" is a fantastic story filled with symbolism and told by a first-person narrator.

Customize for *Varying Student Needs*

When assigning the selections in Part 3 to your students, keep in mind the following factors:

"The Lagoon," "Araby"

- Cultural differences may make these selections difficult for some students to understand.

"The Lady in the Looking Glass: A Reflection" and "The First Year of My Life"

- Some students may need help working through the unconventional structures and techniques used in these stories.
- The vocabulary in these stories is challenging.

"The Rocking-Horse Winner" and "A Shocking Accident"

- Most students will find the subjects of these stories and the traditional narrative style easy to understand.

"The Book of Sand"

- The mysterious quality of this story will capture students' interest.
- Less advanced students may need help with the moderately challenging vocabulary in this story.
- More advanced students can explore the complexities of the story's theme.

Prepare and Engage

OBJECTIVES

1. To read, comprehend, and interpret short stories
2. To relate a short story to personal experience
3. To envision action and situation while reading
4. To analyze plot devices
5. To build vocabulary in context and learn the word root *-vinc-*
6. To recognize and use adverb clauses
7. To write a personal essay using elaboration
8. To respond to the short stories through writing, speaking and listening, and projects

SKILLS INSTRUCTION

Build Vocabulary: Word Roots: *-vinc-*
Grammar: Adverb Clauses
Reading Strategy: Envision Action and Situation
Literary Focus: Plot Devices
Writing: Elaboration to Entertain
Speaking and Listening: Courtroom; Panel Discussion (teacher edition)
Critical Viewing: Make a Judgment; Deduce; Assess; Infer

PORTFOLIO OPPORTUNITIES

Writing: Recollection; Extending a Story; Essay
Writing Mini-Lesson: Personal Essay
Speaking and Listening: Courtroom; Panel Discussion
Projects: Poster; Report on Colonialism

More About the Authors

Joseph Conrad (Jozef Teodor Konrad Nalecz Korzeniowski) was the son of a Polish poet and patriot whose political sympathies forced the family into exile in northern Russia. Growing up in the Ukraine, young Conrad was isolated—by culture, language, and customs—from those around him.

James Joyce's biographer Richard Ellmann wrote: "The surface of the life Joyce lived seemed always erratic and provisional. But its central meaning was directed as consciously as his work. . . . In whatever he did, his two profound interests—his family and his writings—kept their place. . . ."

Guide for Interpreting

Joseph Conrad *(1857–1924)*

It is accomplishment enough to become one of the most distinguished novelists in your age, but to do so in your third language is a true feat. Born in Poland, Joseph Conrad mastered English after his native language, Polish, and his second language, Russian.

At Sea in the World Orphaned at the age of eleven, Conrad fled his Russian-occupied homeland to France when he was seventeen (and later, to England), and spent the next six years as an apprentice seaman. The voyages he made to Asia, Africa, and South America became the vivid settings of much of his fiction. In 1886 Conrad became a master mariner and an English citizen.

A Storytelling Life Conrad published his first novel, *Almayer's Folly*, in his late thirties. In 1897, *The Nigger of the Narcissus* appeared. Three masterpieces followed: *Lord Jim* (1900); *Youth*, a collection of shorter pieces that includes his famous "Heart of Darkness" (1902); and *Nostromo* (1904).

Almost invariably, the notion of "voyage" in a tale by Conrad translates to a voyage of self-discovery. The menacing jungles, vast oceans, and exotic people that confront the characters become metaphors for the hidden depths of the self.

James Joyce *(1882–1941)*

The Dublin writer James Joyce's innovations in plot, character, and language make him one of the most radically challenging writers of the twentieth century.

Experimentation His family and teachers wanted him to become a priest. However, in 1907 he answered his true calling of writer by publishing the poetry collection *Chamber Music*.

Joyce moved to Zurich, Switzerland in 1915, a year after the appearance of his landmark *Dubliners*, a short story collection. Each of the main characters experiences a growth in self-awareness that leads to a climactic peak in the story. Joyce developed this process further in *A Portrait of the Artist as a Young Man* (1916), a fictionalized account of his life.

Mature Fiction A heightened awareness of language and a deep immersion in the minds of characters were carried forward in *Ulysses* (1922). This stream-of-consciousness novel, originally banned in England and the United States, roughly parallels Homer's *Odyssey.* It presents a single day in the life of three Dubliners. Joyce's final novel, *Finnegans Wake* (1939), written in what one scholar terms "a dream language of Joyce's own invention," explores the author's view of human existence and its cycles.

◆ Background for Understanding

CULTURE: MALAY SETTING

Between 1883 and 1888, Conrad sailed the Far East in British merchant ships. He used his knowledge of Malay language, details of setting, and facts about local people and customs to enrich his Far East tales. It is likely that Captain William Lingard, revered as a spellbinding storyteller among sailors of the Malay settlements, was the model for Marlow, who appears in many Conrad tales.

CULTURE: ANGLO-IRISH RELATIONS

James Joyce grew up at a turbulent time in Ireland, with demands for Irish home rule becoming ever louder. One of Ireland's most popular leaders was Charles Stewart Parnell (1846–1891), a Protestant who led the Irish members of the British House of Commons in the fight for Irish self-government. Home rule for the Irish Republic was achieved in 1922.

Prentice Hall Literature Program Resources

REINFORCE / RETEACH / EXTEND

Selection Support Pages
Build Vocabulary: Word Roots: *-vinc-*, p. 267
Grammar and Style: Adverb Clauses, p. 268
Reading Strategy: Envision, p. 269
Literary Focus: Plot Devices, p. 270

Strategies for Diverse Student Needs,
Use Senses to Appreciate Setting, p. 56

Beyond Literature
Humanities Connection: Fine Art, p. 56

Formal Assessment Selection Test, pp. 271–271; Assessment Resources Software

Alternative Assessment, p. 56

Writing and Language Transparencies
Writing Process Model 3 Personal Narrative, pp. 17–23; Art Transparency 13, *The Bridge*

Resource Pro CD-ROM
"The Lagoon," "Araby"— includes all resource material and customizable lesson plan

Listening to Literature Audiocassettes
"The Lagoon," "Araby"

The Lagoon ◆ Araby

◆ Literature and Your Life

CONNECT YOUR EXPERIENCE

If you've ever had a sudden rush of insight—a moment when reasons for your behavior or basic truths about life seem to coalesce before your eyes—you know that gaining insight is an important part of growing up. Yet attaining these insights can be difficult or even painful—as these stories reveal.

Journal Writing Logan Pearsall Smith wrote, "All mirrors are magical mirrors; never can we see our faces in them." Write down your ideas about this in your journal.

THEMATIC FOCUS: CONFLICTS ABROAD AND AT HOME

These stories were influenced by the studies of Sigmund Freud and others who opened new frontiers by probing the human unconscious. As you read, notice how Conrad and Joyce explore conflicts and realizations within the protagonists' minds.

◆ Literary Focus

PLOT DEVICES

Both Conrad and Joyce use **plot devices** in these stories to achieve innovative effects. In "The Lagoon," Conrad uses a **story within a story**—a tale told by a character in a fictional narrative—to evoke the multi-faceted aspect of an experience. By using two or more fictional narrators, Conrad suggests various perspectives on the same events. In "Araby," Joyce employs an **epiphany**—a character's profound revelation—to heighten the climax of the story. This device generally occurs in stories that operate on a psychological level.

◆ Reading Strategy

ENVISION ACTION AND SITUATION

In modernist fiction, what characters *think* is often more important than what they *do*. To understand and appreciate this kind of storytelling, pause to **envision the action and situation** at different points in the narrative. Give at least equal weight to the characters' emotional state as you do to what is occurring at a given moment.

In "The Lagoon," for example, as you picture what is happening to Arsat during the last part of his journey with his brother and Diamelen, think about what is happening inside his mind.

◆ Build Vocabulary

WORD ROOTS: *-vinc-*

Early in Conrad's "The Lagoon," you'll find the word *invincible*. The word root *-vinc-* comes from a Latin verb *vincere*, meaning "to conquer." Something *invincible* is not able to be conquered.

WORD BANK

Before you read, preview this list of words from the stories.

portals
invincible
propitiate
conflagration
august
imperturbable
litanies
garrulous
derided

◆ Grammar and Style

An **adverb clause** is a subordinate clause that modifies a verb, an adjective, or an adverb. For example, Conrad uses this sentence to describe a sound:

> Astern of the boat the repeated call of some bird, a cry discordant and feeble, skipped along over the smooth water and lost itself, *before it could reach the other shore, in the breathless silence of the world.*

The adverb clause in italics modifies the verb *lost*. Like many other adverbs, it answers the question, *When?*

Look for other adverb clauses that add precision and vivid detail to these narratives.

Preparing for Standardized Tests

Grammar and Language The improving paragraphs portion of some standardized tests asks students to identify the best way to combine sentences. Understanding adverb clauses will help students recognize when to use them in combining sentences.

Reading and Vocabulary Knowledge of word roots will help students infer the meaning of unfamiliar words in the reading comprehension section of standardized tests. Such knowledge will also help students do well in the vocabulary section of tests. The vocabulary lesson that goes with these selections will teach students the meaning of the word root *-vinc-*.

The Grammar and Style lesson for this selection focuses on adverb clauses. For additional practice, use the Build Grammar Skills page on Adverb Clauses, p. 268, in ***Selection Support.***

Before assigning "The Lagoon" or "Araby," play the Carly Simon song "Anticipation." Then have students think back on something they eagerly anticipated, such as a vacation or a special event. Have them share their recollections about which was better: the event itself or the build-up to it. Then tell students that in "The Lagoon" and "Araby," the main character's sense of anticipation plays a key role in the story.

Customize for
Less Proficient Readers

To appreciate "The Lagoon," students must be able to follow the story within the story and identify shifts in point of view. Guide them to ask themselves, as they read, who is telling the story at any point: is it the third-person omniscient narrator or is it Arsat?

In both stories, assist less proficient readers in clarifying unfamiliar cultural details.

For either story, students can follow along in their text as they listen to the audio-taped version.

Listening to Literature
"The Lagoon," "Araby"

Customize for
More Advanced Students

For "The Lagoon," students can analyze the role of Arsat's friend as a bridge between the particular story of Arsat and the universal human truths his story represents.

For "Araby," challenge students to look for the use of opposites in Joyce's descriptive writing: dark/light, light/shadow, colorful/dull, bright/dim, and so on. Ask them to interpret the effect this technique has on the story and on their understanding of the mood and mind of the narrator.

Customize for
English Language Learners

"The Lagoon" contains a number of boating terms that may be unfamiliar to students learning English. Examples include *stern, steersman, wake, upstream,* and *prow*. Display illustrations to help students grasp the meaning of these terms.

Develop Understanding

One-Minute Insight Two old comrades—a Malay and a white man—meet near a Malaysian lagoon landscape. As his beloved lies dying inside the hut, Arsat, the Malay, tells how he betrayed his own brother, impelled by passion for the woman now dying. In leaving Arsat to his misery, the white man seems to commit a betrayal as well.

◆ Literary Focus

1 Plot Devices Guide students to notice that the story starts out by telling readers that the group is headed to Arsat's clearing. Tell students to jot down questions they have at this point. *Students might wonder "Who is Arsat?" "Who is the white man?" "How do they know each other?"*

◆ Reading Strategy

2 Envision Action and Situation Ask students to identify details that help them envision the action and situation. *The almost silent progress of the boat is brought to life by envisioning details like the Malay boatman's grunted response, his fixed gaze, the regular motion of the oars, the sun glinting off the oars, and the eddies of water the boat leaves in its wake.*

Customize for
More Advanced Students
3 Ask more advanced students to identify the significance of this description. *Portals to a land without the memory of motion suggest doorways or entrances into a place completely cut off from progress—a place suspended in time where the internal life of a character is more "real" than the external world.*

◆ Reading Strategy

4 Envision the Action and the Situation Ask students to describe their mental picture of what is happening in this passage. *The boat that has calmly carried the men into this place of suspended time makes a sudden and sharp turn.*

Customize for
English Language Learners
Help these students envision the action by guiding them to act out the steersman's actions.

The Lagoon

Joseph Conrad

The white man, leaning with both arms over the roof of the little house in the stern of the
1 boat, said to the steersman—

"We will pass the night in Arsat's clearing. It is late."

The Malay[1] only grunted, and went on looking fixedly at the river. The white man rested his chin on his crossed arms and gazed at the wake of the boat. At the end of the straight avenue of forests cut by the intense glitter of the river, the sun appeared unclouded and dazzling, poised low over the water that shone smoothly like a band of metal. The forests, somber and dull, stood motionless and silent on each side of the broad stream. At the foot of big, towering trees trunkless nipa palms rose from the mud of the bank, in bunches of leaves
2 enormous and heavy, that hung unstirring over the brown swirl of eddies. In the stillness of the air every tree, every leaf, every bough, every tendril of creeper and every petal of minute blossoms seemed to have been bewitched into an immobility perfect and final. Nothing moved on the river but the eight paddles that rose flashing regularly, dipped together with a single splash; while the steersman swept right and left with a periodic and sudden flourish of his blade describing a glinting semicircle above his head. The churned-up water frothed alongside with a confused murmur. And the white man's canoe, advancing up stream in the short-lived disturbance of its own making, seemed to enter
the portals of a land from which the very mem- 3
ory of motion had forever departed.

The white man, turning his back upon the setting sun, looked along the empty and broad expanse of the sea-reach. For the last three miles of its course the wandering, hesitating river, as if enticed irresistibly by the freedom of an open horizon, flows straight into the sea, flows straight to the east—to the east that harbors both light and darkness. Astern of the boat the repeated call of some bird, a cry discordant and feeble, skipped along over the smooth water and lost itself, before it could reach the other shore, in the breathless silence of the world.

The steersman dug his paddle into the stream, and held hard with stiffened arms, his body thrown forward. The water gurgled aloud; and suddenly the long straight reach seemed to pivot on its center, the forests swung in a semicircle, and the slanting beams of sunset touched the broadside of the canoe with a fiery
glow, throwing the slender and distorted shad- 4
ows of its crew upon the streaked glitter of the river. The white man turned to look ahead. The course of the boat had been altered at right-angles to the stream, and the carved dragonhead of its prow was pointing now at a gap in the fringing bushes of the bank. It glided through, brushing the overhanging twigs, and disappeared from the river like some slim and

1. **Malay** (mā′ lā): Native of the Malay peninsula in Southeast Asia.

Block Scheduling Strategies

Consider these suggestions to take advantage of extended class time:

- Prepare students for reading "The Lagoon" by discussing the Literature and Your Life feature (p. 1033). Have them complete the Journal Writing activity and discuss their entries in small groups.
- Introduce the Literary Focus and Reading Strategy for this selection. You may wish to use the Reading Strategy Literary Focus and/or practice pages in ***Skills Support,*** pp. 269 and 270.
- Have students read the story or listen to it on tape. They can discuss the Check Your Comprehension questions in small groups; then assign pairs of students to work together on the Critical Thinking questions (p. 1043).
- Provide time for groups to prepare and perform the Courtroom project, as described in the Speaking and Listening Mini-Lesson (p. 1051).
- Assign the multiple-choice portion of the Selection Test, found in the ***Formal Assessment*** booklet. Students may complete a test essay in class or for homework.

amphibious creature leaving the water for its lair in the forests.

The narrow creek was like a ditch: tortuous, fabulously deep; filled with gloom under the thin strip of pure and shining blue of the heaven. Immense trees soared up, invisible behind the festooned draperies of creepers. Here and there, near the glistening blackness of the water, a twisted root of some tall tree showed amongst the tracery of small ferns, black and
5 dull, writhing and motionless, like an arrested snake. The short words of the paddlers reverberated loudly between the thick and somber walls of vegetation. Darkness oozed out from between the trees, through the tangled maze of the creepers, from behind the great fantastic and unstirring leaves; the darkness, mysterious and invincible; the darkness scented and poisonous of impenetrable forests.

The men poled in the shoaling[2] water. The creek broadened, opening out into a wide sweep of a stagnant lagoon. The forests receded from the marshy bank, leaving a level strip of bright green, reedy grass to frame the reflected blueness of the sky. A fleecy pink cloud drifted high above, trailing the delicate coloring of its image under the floating leaves and the silvery blossoms of the lotus. A little house, perched on high piles, appeared black in the distance. Near it, two tall nibong palms, that seemed to have come out of the forests in the background, leaned slightly over the ragged roof, with a suggestion of sad tenderness and care in the droop of their leafy and soaring heads.

The steersman, pointing with his paddle,
6 said, "Arsat is there. I see his canoe fast between the piles."

The polers ran along the sides of the boat glancing over their shoulders at the end of the day's journey. They would have preferred to
7 spend the night somewhere else than on this lagoon of weird aspect and ghostly reputation. Moreover, they disliked Arsat, first as a stranger, and also because he who repairs a ruined house, and dwells in it, proclaims that he is not afraid to live amongst the spirits that haunt the places abandoned by mankind. Such a man can disturb the course of fate by glances or words; while his familiar ghosts are not easy to propitiate by casual wayfarers upon whom
they long to wreak the malice of their human master. White men care not for such things, 7
being unbelievers and in league with the 8
Father of Evil, who leads them unharmed through the invisible dangers of this world. To the warnings of the righteous they oppose an offensive pretense of disbelief. What is there to be done?

So they thought, throwing their weight on the end of their long poles. The big canoe glided on swiftly, noiselessly, and smoothly, toward Arsat's clearing, till, in a great rattling of poles thrown down, and the loud murmurs of "Allah[3] be praised!" it came with a gentle knock against the crooked piles below the house.

The boatmen with uplifted faces shouted discordantly, "Arsat! O Arsat!" Nobody came. The white man began to climb the rude ladder giving access to the bamboo platform before
the house. The juragan[4] of the boat said sulk- 9
ily, "We will cook in the sampan,[5] and sleep on the water."

"Pass my blankets and the basket," said the white man curtly.

He knelt on the edge of the platform to receive the bundle. Then the boat shoved off, and the white man, standing up, confronted Arsat, who had come out through the low door of his hut. He was a man young, powerful, with a broad chest and muscular arms. He had

2. **shoaling:** Shallow.

3. **Allah** (al′ ə): Muslim name for God.
4. **juragan** (jo͞o rä′ gän): Captain or master.
5. **sampan:** Small flat-bottomed boat with a cabin formed by mats.

◆ Build Vocabulary

portals (pôr′ təlz) *n.*: Doors; gateways

invincible (in vin′ sə bəl) *adj.*: Unconquerable

propitiate (prə pish′ ē āt) *v.*: Win the good will of; appease

◆ Reading Strategy

5 Envision Action and Situation Ask a volunteer to read this paragraph aloud or play the portion of the **Listening to Literature Audiocassettes** so students can better sense the mood Conrad means to convey. Have students identify details that create this mood. *Students may describe the mood as creepy, gloomy, stagnant, and foreboding, based on Conrad's use of words like* tortuous, twisted, writhing, arrested, somber, unstirring, mysterious, invincible, poisonous, *and* impenetrable.

Customize for
English Language Learners

6 Point out that the word *fast,* as used here, is not the opposite of *slow,* as students learning English might assume. Rather, it means *secure.* Take this opportunity to assist with other words that they may find challenging such as *fleecy, shallow, reverberated,* and *discordantly.* If possible, demonstrate with concrete examples.

◆ Reading Strategy

7 Envision Action and Situation The locals mistrust Arsat and want nothing to do with him or his lagoon. Have students describe how they might feel if they were on the boat. *Students should note the fear and mistrust the people on the boat have for Arsat. As they must enter Arsat's lagoon, the situation becomes more tense and mysterious.*

◆ Literary Focus

8 Plot Devices Point out to students that from what they have read so far, they know more about Arsat than they do about the white man on the boat. In fact, the white man is not even identified by name. Ask students why Conrad may be revealing information in this way. *Students may have guessed by now that Arsat's story, when revealed, will overshadow the story of the white man's journey.*

◆ Reading Strategy

9 Envision Action and Situation Ask students to describe what is happening and how it affects the situation. *The white man is being left at this mysterious hut where no one answers. The mental image of him climbing the ladder as the boat moves away creates a sense of isolation.*

Cross-Curricular Connection: Social Studies

Malaysia Malaysia, with a population of approximately twenty million people, has had a variety of inhabitants from many cultures. Most of the people live on Peninsular Malaysia, the southern part of the Malay Peninsula. This region is covered with thick tropical rain forests like the one described in this story. Although the official language is Malay, languages like English, Indian, and Chinese are also spoken there. The people observe Muslim, Hindu, Buddhist, Confucianist, and Christian religions, and many also practice local religions.

Have students conduct research on Malaysia to learn more about its long history, colonial occupation, struggles for freedom, and current political situation. Some students might concentrate on the period around 1867, when Britain established control there, or the 1880's, when Joseph Conrad spent time there as a British merchant seaman. Invite students to present their findings orally or in the form of written reports.

◆ Reading Strategy

❶ Envision Action and Situation Students should use details from the vivid description of Arsat and the description of the setting to envision the characters and situation: *Arsat is "young" and "muscular." He wears a sarong, and his eyes are "big" and "soft." The setting is a hut on stilts above the water, surrounded by jungle. The white man gets to his feet to meet Arsat, who is coming "through the low door of his hut."*

◆ Background for Understanding

❷ Culture *Tuan* is a Malay term of respect. The term *tuan* was probably used to describe Captain William Lingard, a local hero at the time Conrad sailed through Malaysia. According to Conrad's biographer, Frederick Karl, Lingard was also known as "Rajah Laut" or "King of the Sea," for his ". . . shrewdness as a trader, daring as a contender with sea pirates for routes and goods, and expertise as a handler of sailing vessels." Men like Arsat probably worked with and fought beside Lingard in a number of his daring adventures.

◆ Reading Strategy

❸ Envision Action and Situation Discuss with students the thoughts that might be going through each man's mind, to help them appreciate the intensity of this moment. *Students may say that Tuan is shocked and saddened and feels bad that he cannot help the sick woman, but that Arsat is stunned and grasps at any possible hope Tuan might bring. The gravity of the situation makes both men stand in silence.*

◆ Literary Focus

❹ Plot Devices Ask students to identify the significance of Arsat's question about the woman. *Her fight against death seems to be central to the story.*

▶Critical Viewing◀

❺ Make a Judgment Students may say that the thick foliage, dark shadows, and wide waterways would probably make escape possible for someone well acquainted with that region.

---

nothing on but his sarong.[6] His head was bare. His big, soft eyes stared eagerly at the white man, but his voice and demeanor were composed as he asked, without any words of greeting—

> **◆ Reading Strategy** As Arsat and the white man meet for the first time in the story, envision the characters and the situation as vividly as you can. ❶

"Have you medicine, Tuan?"[7] ❷

"No," said the visitor in a startled tone. "No. Why? Is there sickness in the house?"

"Enter and see," replied Arsat, in the same calm manner, and turning short round, passed again through the small doorway. The white man, dropping his bundles, followed.

❸ In the dim light of the dwelling he made out on a couch of bamboos a woman stretched on her back under a broad sheet of red cotton cloth. She lay still, as if dead; but her big eyes, wide open, glittered in the gloom, staring upward at the slender rafters, motionless and unseeing. She was in a high fever, and evidently unconscious. Her cheeks were sunk slightly, her lips were partly open, and on the young face there was the ominous and fixed expression—the absorbed, contemplating expression of the unconscious who are going to die. The two men stood looking down at her in silence.

❹ "Has she been long ill?" asked the traveler.

"I have not slept for five nights," answered the Malay, in a deliberate tone. "At first she heard voices calling her from the water and struggled against me who held her. But since the sun of today rose she hears nothing—she hears not me. She sees nothing. She sees not me—me!"

He remained silent for a minute, then asked softly—

"Tuan, will she die?"

"I fear so," said the white man sorrowfully. He had known Arsat years ago, in a far country in times of trouble and danger, when no friendship is to be despised. And since his Malay friend had come unexpectedly to dwell in the hut on the lagoon with a strange woman, he had slept many times there, in his journeys up and down the river. He liked the man who knew how to keep faith in council and how to fight without fear by the side of his white friend. He liked him—not so much perhaps as a man likes his favorite dog—but still he liked him well enough to help and ask no questions, to think sometimes vaguely and hazily in the midst of his own pursuits, about the lonely man and the long-haired woman with audacious face and triumphant eyes, who lived together by the forests—alone and feared.

▲ **Critical Viewing** Judging from this photograph, would it be difficult to escape from an enemy in jungle territory? **[Make a Judgment]** ❺

6. **sarong:** Long, brightly colored strip of cloth worn like a skirt.
7. **Tuan** (twan): Malayan for "sir."

Cross-Curricular Connection: Social Studies

Write this old saying on the chalkboard: "The sun never sets on the British Empire." Explain that at one time in British history, the British Empire was so large that it extended to all parts of the globe, including North, Central, and South America, the Caribbean, the Middle East, Asia, Africa, and the South Pacific.

Point out that Malaysia, where this story is set, was a British colony. Invite students to select Malaysia or another country that was once a British colony, such as India, Belize, the Bahamas, Kenya, or Guyana, to name a few. Challenge them to find out about Britain's colonization in that area, and the process by which the region gained independence. Students might also investigate authors from these places—such as Ngugi wa Thiong'o from Kenya—who have written about their country's struggles. You might display a world map with information about former British colonies.

The white man came out of the hut in time to see the enormous conflagration of sunset put out by the swift and stealthy shadows that, rising like a black and impalpable vapor above the treetops, spread over the heaven, extinguishing the crimson glow of floating clouds and the red brilliance of departing daylight.
6 In a few moments all the stars came out above the intense blackness of the earth, and the great lagoon gleaming suddenly with reflected lights resembled an oval patch of night sky flung down into the hopeless and abysmal night of the wilderness. The white man had some supper out of the basket, then collecting

a few sticks that lay about the platform, made up a small fire, not for warmth, but for the sake of the smoke, which would keep off the mosquitos. He wrapped himself in his blankets and sat with his back against the reed wall of the house, smoking thoughtfully.

Arsat came through the doorway with noiseless steps and squatted down by the fire. The white man moved his outstretched legs a little.

"She breathes," said Arsat in a low voice, anticipating the expected question. "She breathes and burns as if with a great fire. She speaks not; she hears not—and burns!"

He paused for a moment, then asked in a quiet, incurious tone—

"Tuan . . . will she die?"

The white man moved his shoulders uneasily, and muttered in a hesitating manner—

"If such is her fate."

"No, Tuan," said Arsat calmly. "If such is my fate. I hear, I see, I wait. I remember . . . Tuan, do you remember the old days? Do you remember my brother?"

"Yes," said the white man. The Malay rose suddenly and went in. The other, sitting still outside, could hear the voice in the hut. Arsat 7 said: "Hear me! Speak!" His words were succeeded by a complete silence. "O Diamelen!" he cried suddenly. After that cry there was a deep sigh. Arsat came out and sank down again in his old place.

They sat in silence before the fire. There was no sound within the house, there was no sound near them; but far away on the lagoon they could hear the voices of the boatmen ringing fitful and distinct on the calm water. The fire in the bows of the sampan shone faintly in 8 the distance with a hazy red glow. Then it died out. The voices ceased. The land and the water slept invisible, unstirring and mute. It was as though there had been nothing left in the world but the glitter of stars streaming, ceaseless and vain, through the black stillness of the night.

The white man gazed straight before him into the darkness with wide-open eyes. The fear and fascination, the inspiration and the wonder of death—of death near, unavoidable,

◆ Build Vocabulary

conflagration (kän′ flə grā′ shən) *n.*: Great fire

◆ Critical Thinking

6 Connect Lead students to recognize that the physical environment echoes the desperate situation in the hut. Have students discuss the parallels. *Students may say that the vivid sunset suggests the departure of the woman's spirit; the "swift and stealthy shadows" suggest the approach of death; the "hopeless and abysmal night" suggests Arsat's despair at the hopeless situation.*

◆ Literary Focus

7 Plot Devices Ask students what new questions they have. How do these questions indicate that a new story might be beginning? *Students probably have questions about Arsat's brother and the events from the "old days" that he wants the white man to remember. Students may wonder how these events relate to Diamelen, the dying woman.*

Customize for
Less Proficient Readers

8 Guide these students in summarizing the events to this point. *A white man has entered a lagoon and arrived at the home of a feared and mysterious man, Arsat. It turns out that the white man and Arsat already know each other. Inside Arsat's hut, a woman Arsat loves lies dying. While they wait for her condition to resolve itself one way or another, the two men sit outside the hut. Arsat indicates that something in his past is troubling him.* Then point out how Conrad uses images of isolation here, as he did earlier, to set the stage for a tale.

◆ Reading Strategy

1 Enrichment During the early part of the twentieth century, the writings of Sigmund Freud and others who studied the human unconscious deeply influenced Conrad. As at the end of this passage Conrad's writing shows a fascination for the workings of the unconscious mind.

◆ Literary Focus

2 Plot Devices Students may say that the ellipses indicate a narrative shift to Arsat. The narration is now in the first person, and the speaker addresses the white man directly: "You, Tuan, know . . ."

◆ Critical Thinking

3 Infer Ask students what they can infer about the tale Arsat will tell based on these words. *Students can infer from Arsat's opening words about the heaviness of trouble that the story will be a sad one. Since Arsat reminds Tuan that he, Arsat, has known danger and has not fled from it, students can infer that the tale will involve some danger, some test of courage.*

◆ Literary Focus

4 Plot Devices Conrad's use of the story within a story is an ancient device. Roman writer Apuleius wrote a novel in which various characters tell stories. Conrad employs this device to evoke the many-sidedness of an experience.

Customize for *Less Proficient Readers*

5 These students may need help understanding the figurative language in this passage. Help them recognize the images of peace and prosperity at the beginning of the passage. Help students understand Arsat's statement that his "eyes could see nothing in the past, because they had looked upon the one who is dying there." *When Arsat met Diamelen, he fell in love and forgot everything else.*

◆ Background for Understanding

6 Culture: Malay Setting Conrad used facts about local people to enrich his stories. Inchi Midah was a local woman married to a chief of Perak. The princess of Perak, described as "light, spare and a little witch like," was probably the model for Conrad's Inchi Midah.

and unseen, soothed the unrest of his race and stirred the most indistinct, the most intimate of his thoughts. The ever-ready suspicion of evil, the gnawing suspicion that lurks in our hearts, flowed out into the stillness round him—into the stillness profound and dumb, and made it appear untrustworthy and infamous, like the placid and impenetrable mask of an unjustifi-
1 able violence. In that fleeting and powerful disturbance of his being the earth enfolded in the starlight peace became a shadowy country of inhuman strife, a battlefield of phantoms terrible and charming, august or ignoble, struggling ardently for the possession of our helpless hearts. An unquiet and mysterious country of inextinguishable desires and fears.

A plaintive murmur rose in the night; a murmur saddening and startling, as if the great solitudes of surrounding woods had tried to whisper into his ear the wisdom of their immense and lofty indifference. Sounds hesitating and vague floated in the air round him, shaped themselves slowly into words; and at last flowed on gently in a murmuring stream of soft and monotonous sentences. He stirred like a man waking up and changed his position slightly. Arsat, motionless and shadowy, sitting with bowed head under the stars, was speaking in a low and dreamy tone—

> **◆ Literary Focus**
> 2 What clues let you know that a story within a story begins here?

"... for where can we lay down the heaviness of our trouble but in a friend's heart? A man must speak of war and of love. You, Tuan, know what war is, and you have seen me in time of danger seek death as other
3 men seek life! A writing may be lost; a lie may be written; but what the eye has seen is truth and remains in the mind!"

"I remember," said the white man quietly. Arsat went on with mournful composure—

"Therefore I shall speak to you of love. Speak in the night. Speak before both night and love
4 are gone—and the eye of day looks upon my sorrow and my shame; upon my blackened face; upon my burnt-up heart."

A sigh, short and faint, marked an almost imperceptible pause, and then his words flowed on, without a stir, without a gesture.

"After the time of trouble and war was over and you went away from my country in the pursuit of your desires, which we, men of the islands, cannot understand, I and my brother became again, as we had been before, the sword bearers of the Ruler. You know we were men of family, belonging to a ruling race, and more fit than any to carry on our right shoulder the emblem of power. And in the time of prosperity Si Dendring showed us favor, as we, in time of sorrow, had showed to him the faithfulness of our courage. It was a time of peace. A time of deer hunts and cock fights; of idle talks and foolish squabbles between men whose bellies are full and weapons are rusty. But the sower watched the young rice shoots grow up without fear, and the traders came and went, departed lean and returned fat into the river of peace. They brought news too. Brought lies and truth mixed together, so that no man knew
when to rejoice and when to be sorry. We heard 5
from them about you also. They had seen you here and had seen you there. And I was glad to hear, for I remembered the stirring times, and I always remembered you, Tuan, till the time came when my eyes could see nothing in the past, because they had looked upon the one who is dying there—in the house."

He stopped to exclaim in an intense whisper, "O Mara bahia! O Calamity!" then went on speaking a little louder.

"There's no worse enemy and no better friend than a brother, Tuan, for one brother knows another, and in perfect knowledge is strength for good or evil. I loved my brother. I went to him and told him that I could see nothing but one face, hear nothing but one voice. He told
me: 'Open your heart so that she can see what 6
is in it—and wait. Patience is wisdom. Inchi Midah may die or our Ruler may throw off his fear of a woman!'. . . I waited! . . . You remember the lady with the veiled face, Tuan, and the fear of our Ruler before her cunning and temper. And if she wanted her servant, what could

Humanities: Fine Art

Conrad is sometimes termed an impressionistic writer because he seeks to capture the atmosphere and texture of reality as well as the complexity of subjective experience. Originally, the term *Impressionism* was applied to the work of a group of nineteenth-century painters in Paris. These painters tried to show in their paintings impressions gained from direct observation of nature, rather than precise representations. They painted with dabs of discontinuous color, allowing the viewer's eye to recombine the colors into an image. While it is not strictly speaking an Impressionist work, Yuan Lee's *The Reflection in the Store Window Glass,* Art Transparency 18, may provide students with a visual analog for Conrad's impressionistic writing style. Point out to students how Lee gives viewers impressionistic "slices" of a scene as it is reflected in the glass of a store window. As with Conrad, the result is an atmospheric rendering of reality rather than a "snapshot" of it.

I do? But I fed the hunger of my heart on short glances and stealthy words. I loitered on the path to the bath houses in the daytime, and when the sun had fallen behind the forest I crept along the jasmine hedges of the women's courtyard. Unseeing, we spoke to one another through the scent of flowers, through the veil of leaves, through the blades of long grass that stood still before our lips; so great was our prudence, so faint was the murmur of our great longing. The time passed swiftly . . . and there were whispers amongst women—and our enemies watched—my brother was gloomy, and I began to think of killing and of a fierce death. . . . We are of a people who take what they want—like you whites. There is a time when a man should forget loyalty and respect. Might and authority are given to rulers, but to all men is given love and strength and courage. My brother said, 'You shall take her from their midst. We are two who are like one.' And I answered, 'Let it be soon, for I find no warmth
7 in sunlight that does not shine upon her.' Our time came when the Ruler and all the great people went to the mouth of the river to fish by torchlight. There were hundreds of boats, and on the white sand, between the water and the forests, dwellings of leaves were built for the households of the Rajahs.[8] The smoke of cooking fires was like a blue mist of the evening, and many voices rang in it joyfully. While they were making the boats ready to beat up the fish, my brother came to me and said, 'Tonight!' I looked to my weapons, and when the time came our canoe took its place in the circle of boats carrying the torches. The lights blazed on the water, but behind the boats there was darkness. When the shouting began and the excitement made them like mad we dropped out. The water swallowed our fire, and we floated back to the shore that was dark with only here and there the glimmer of embers. We could hear the talk of slave girls amongst the sheds. Then we found a place deserted and silent. We waited there. She came. She came running along the shore, rapid and leaving no trace, like a leaf driven by the wind into the sea. My brother said gloomily, 'Go and take her; carry her into our boat.' I lifted her in my arms. She panted. Her heart was beating against my breast. I said, 'I take you from those people. You came to the cry of my heart, but my arms take you into my boat against the
will of the great!' 'It is right,' said my brother. 8
'We are men who take what we want and can hold it against many. We should have taken her in daylight.' I said, 'Let us be off'; for since she was in my boat I began to think of our Ruler's many men. 'Yes. Let us be off,' said my brother. 'We are cast out and this boat is our country now—and the sea is our refuge.' He lingered with his foot on the shore, and I entreated him to hasten, for I remembered the strokes of her heart against my breast and thought that two men cannot withstand a hundred. We left, paddling downstream close to the bank; and as we passed by the creek where they were fishing, the great shouting had ceased, but the murmur of voices was loud like the humming of insects flying at noonday. The boats floated, clustered together, in the red
light of torches, under a black roof of smoke; 9
and men talked of their sport. Men that boasted, and praised, and jeered—men that would have been our friends in the morning, but on that night were already our enemies. We paddled swiftly past. We had no more friends in the country of our birth. She sat in the middle of the canoe with covered face; silent as she is now; unseeing as she is now—and I had no regret at what I was leaving because I could hear her breathing close to me—as I can hear her now."

He paused, listened with his ear turned to the doorway, then shook his head and went on.

"My brother wanted to shout the cry of challenge—one cry only—to let the people know we 10
were freeborn robbers who trusted our arms

8. **Rajahs** (rä′ jəz): Malayan chiefs.

◆ Build Vocabulary

august (ô gust′) *adj.*: Worthy of great respect

Customize for
More Advanced Students

7 Encourage these students to relate Arsat and Diamelen's situation to that of other "star-crossed lovers" in literature. *You might suggest that students look for parallels in Shakespeare's* Romeo and Juliet, *the opera* Aïda, *or the novel* Wuthering Heights.

◆ Critical Thinking

8 Analyze Ask students to identify how Arsat felt when the event took place. *Diamelen came to him of her own free will, but he knew he was kidnapping her. The brothers were gloomy, realizing the enormity of their crime. They knew they were committing a disloyal act that could leave them no refuge.*

◆ Critical Thinking

9 Draw Conclusions Ask students whether they think Arsat has any regrets now. *Arsat's deep love for Diamelen may prompt students to conclude that he still does not regret leaving behind his friends and country. Other clues in the story, however, indicate that something about this past event still troubles Arsat.*

◆ Critical Thinking

10 Speculate Have students suggest reasons why the brother would have wanted to shout a cry of challenge instead of escaping silently. *He may have felt that leaving silently was cowardly; he may have felt pride in his ability to outwit his enemies and wanted to let them know they had been tricked.*

Humanities: Media

A Joseph Conrad Film Festival.

There have been many films whose ideas come from the writings of Joseph Conrad. Some of the films are fairly literal versions of the literature.

Invite interested students to get together to view some of the available films based on Conrad's writings: *Victory* (1940), *Outcast of the Islands* (1951), *Lord Jim* (1965), and *Heart of Darkness* (1994). However, we suggest that you preview films before showing them to students.

Use these questions for discussion:

1. In what ways does this film remind you of "The Lagoon"? *Answers may refer to similarities in locale, characters, mood, tension, and so on.*
2. How is Conrad's interest in a person's voyage of self-discovery shown in this film? *Ask students to cite specific examples of events or character's behavior or thoughts that suggest a journey of self-discovery.*

◆ Literary Focus

1 Plot Devices Ask students to identify how the pauses affect their reaction to the story within a story. *In the pauses, Arsat listens to Diamelen, or sighs or exclaims. Arsat's present emotions concerning Diamelen, who also figures in the story, highten the suspense.*

Customize for
More Advanced Students

2 Have your more advanced students identify the irony in this passage. *Arsat thought his love could take him to a country where death was unknown. However, at the very moment he is speaking, Diamelen is dying.*

◆ Reading Strategy

3 Envision Action and Situation Ask students to describe the characters' positions in the boat. *Diamelen is in the middle of the canoe, probably lying down. Arsat is paddling in the front of the boat, facing forward, while his brother is sitting in the rear of the boat, acting as a paddler and steersman. His brother is also facing forward.*

▶Critical Viewing◀

4 Deduce Based on details in the picture, students may say that the place is too small, too isolated, and too exposed to the open sea.

◆ Literary Focus
Notice that the reader experiences the story within a story the same way the white man does, with pauses that allow a listener to observe changes in Arsat's emotional state.

1 and the great sea. And again I begged him in the name of our love to be silent. Could I not hear her breathing close to me? I knew the pursuit would come quick enough. My brother loved me. He dipped his paddle without a splash. He only said, 'There is half a man in you now—the other half is in that woman. I can wait. When you are a whole man again, you will come back with me here to shout defiance. We are sons of the same mother.' I made no answer. All my strength and all my spirit were in my hands that held
2 the paddle—for I longed to be with her in a safe place beyond the reach of men's anger and of women's spite. My love was so great, that I thought it could guide me to a country where death was unknown, if I could only escape from Inchi Midah's fury and from our Ruler's sword. We paddled with haste, breathing through our teeth. The blades bit deep into the smooth water. We passed out of the river; we flew in clear channels amongst the shallows. We skirted the black coast; we skirted the sand beaches where the sea speaks in whispers to the land; and the gleam of white sand flashed back past our boat, so swiftly she ran upon the water. We spoke not. Only once I said, 'Sleep, Diamelen, for soon you may want all your strength.' I heard the sweetness of her voice, but I never
3 turned my head. The sun rose and still we went on. Water fell from my face like rain from a cloud. We flew in the light and heat. I never looked back, but I knew that my brother's eyes, behind me, were looking steadily ahead, for the boat went as straight as a bushman's dart, when it leaves the end of the sumpitan.[9] There was no better paddler, no better steersman than my brother. Many times, together, we had won races in that canoe. But we never had put out our strength as we did then—then, when for the last time we paddled together! There was no braver or stronger man in our country than my brother. I could not spare the strength to turn my head and look at him, every moment I heard the hiss of his breath getting louder behind me. Still he did not speak. The sun was high. The heat clung to my back like a flame of fire. My ribs were ready to burst, but I could no longer get enough air into my chest. And then I felt I must cry out with my last breath. 'Let us rest!' . . . 'Good!' he answered; and his voice was firm. He was strong. He was brave. He knew not fear and no fatigue . . . My brother!" 3

▲ **Critical Viewing** Why might a peninsula or an island such as this one be a bad choice as a hiding place? **[Deduce]** 4

9. **sumpitan** (sump´ ə tän): Malayan blowgun which discharges poisonous darts.

5 A murmur powerful and gentle, a murmur vast and faint; the murmur of trembling leaves, of stirring boughs, ran through the tangled depths of the forests, ran over the starry smoothness of the lagoon, and the water between the piles lapped the slimy timber once with a sudden splash. A breath of warm air touched the two men's faces and passed on with a mournful sound—a breath loud and short like an uneasy sigh of the dreaming earth.

Arsat went on in an even, low voice:

"We ran our canoe on the white beach of a little bay close to a long tongue of land that seemed to bar our road; a long wooded cape going far into the sea. My brother knew that place. Beyond the cape a river has its entrance, and through the jungle of that land there is a narrow path. We made a fire and cooked rice. Then we lay down to sleep on the soft sand in the shade of our canoe, while she watched. No 6 sooner had I closed my eyes than I heard her cry of alarm. We leaped up. The sun was halfway down the sky already, and coming in sight in the opening of the bay we saw a prau[10] manned by many paddlers. We knew it at once; it was one of our Rajah's praus. They were watching the shore, and saw us. They beat the gong, and turned the head of the prau into the bay. I felt my heart become weak within my breast. Diamelen sat on the sand and covered her face. There was no escape by sea. My brother laughed. He had the gun you had given him, Tuan, before you went away, but there was only a handful of powder. He spoke to me quickly: 'Run with her along the path. I shall keep them back, for they have no firearms, and landing in the face of a man with a gun is certain death for some. Run with her. On the other side of that wood there is a fisherman's house—and a canoe. When I have fired all the 7 shots I will follow. I am a great runner, and before they can come up we shall be gone. I will hold out as long as I can, for she is but a woman—that can neither run nor fight, but she has your heart in her weak hands.' He dropped behind the canoe. The prau was coming. She and I ran, and as we rushed along the path I heard shots. My brother fired—once—twice—and the booming of the gong ceased. There was silence behind us. That neck of land is narrow. Before I heard my brother fire the third shot I saw the shelving shore, and I saw the water again: the mouth of a broad river. We crossed a grassy glade. We ran down to the water. I saw a low hut above the black mud, and a small canoe hauled up. I heard another shot behind me. I thought, 'That is his last charge.' We rushed down to the canoe; a man came running from the hut, but I leaped on him, and we rolled together in the mud. Then I got up, and he lay still at my feet. I don't know whether I

10. **prau** (prou): Swift Malayan boat with a large sail.

◆ Literary Focus

5 Plot Devices Ask students to explain how they recognize the shift in this passage from Arsat's story-within-a-story to the third-person narrator's larger story. What purpose does this shift serve? *Arsat's story is taking place in the blazing heat of the day; the shift to nighttime is identifiable because Conrad describes the starry reflection in the lagoon. The return to the lagoon in the middle of Arsat's story reinforces the concept of isolation—a concept that will become increasingly important in Arsat's story.*

◆ Grammar in Action

6 Adverb Clauses Ask students to identify the adverb clause in this sentence and the word it modifies. Tell students to notice how Conrad uses many adverb clauses in the upcoming passage to indicate when events happened. *The adverb clause is "while she watched;" it modifies lay. In the upcoming passages, students will come across these adverb phrases: "before you went away," "before they can come up," "as we rushed along the path," and "Before I heard my brother fire the third shot."*

Customize for *Less Proficient Readers*

7 Have students summarize the strategy Arsat's brother proposes for the escape. Ask whether they think the plan will work. *Arsat's brother will use his gun to hold off the pursuers while Arsat and Diamelen run to get a canoe from a nearby fisherman; the brother will join them once he has fought off the pursuers, and the three will row off to safety together. Students may predict that the plan is doomed because the brother won't be able to hold off all the pursuers.*

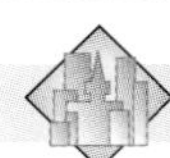

Beyond the Classroom

WorkPlace Skills Connection

Being a Good Listener In "The Lagoon," the white man plays no role in the dramatic story Arsat tells. Rather, his presence serves as a vehicle to allow Arsat to share the tale. The white man never judges, interrupts, or injects his own opinions or comments, but acts as a good listener so Arsat can pour out his heart.

Being a good listener is important in a friend, but there are also many jobs for which being a good listener is a requirement. Brainstorm with students for a list of jobs in which the ability to be a good listener is a significant job requirement. Examples might include customer service representative, guidance counselor, therapist, public opinion pollster, personnel manager, or journalist. Discuss with students ways to improve one's ability to be a good listener, such as concentrating, taking notes, making eye contact, or asking pertinent questions. Students might interview workers they know for whom listening is a significant part of their job.

◆ **Reading Strategy**

❶ **Envision the Action and Situation** Be sure students understand the nature of the terrible decision Arsat has to make. *Arsat is trying to escape with Diamelen, but the pursuers are closing in on his brother. If he pushes off in the canoe with Diamelen, he will have to abandon his brother; but if he tries to help his brother, all three of them may die.*

◆ **Reading Strategy**

❷ **Envision the Action and Situation** Students may imagine that Arsat has a look of pain, resignation, or sorrow on his face, and that Tuan looks serious, thoughtful, and troubled, but also sympathetic.

◆ **Critical Thinking**

❸ **Assess** Discuss with students the price Arsat has paid for his desires. *Some students may say that the price was too high, that his guilt has followed him all his life. Others may point out that he thought he could flee death itself, yet now Diamelen is dying.*

Customize for
More Advanced Students

❹ Direct students' attention to the description of the white eagle. Ask them what they think it symbolizes. *Students may say that it symbolizes Diamelen's spirit leaving her body and flying off into eternity.*

had killed him or not. I and Diamelen pushed the canoe afloat. I heard yells behind me, and I saw my brother run across the glade. Many men were bounding after him. I took her in my arms and threw her into the boat, then leaped in myself. When I looked back I saw that my brother had fallen. He fell and was up again, but the men were closing round him. He shouted, 'I am coming!' The men were close to him. I looked. Many men. Then I looked at her. Tuan, I pushed the canoe! I pushed it into deep water. She was kneeling forward looking at me, and I said, 'Take ❶ your paddle,' while I struck the water with mine. Tuan, I heard him cry. I heard him cry my name twice; and I heard voices shouting, 'Kill! Strike!' I never turned back. I heard him calling my name again with a great shriek, as when life is going out together with the voice—and I never turned my head. My own name! . . . My brother! Three times he called—but I was not afraid of life. Was she not there in that canoe? And could I not with her find a country where death is forgotten—where death is unknown!"

> ◆ **Reading Strategy** ❷
> What expression do you think is on each character's face at the end of the story within a story?

The white man sat up. Arsat rose and stood, an indistinct and silent figure above the dying embers of the fire. Over the lagoon a mist drifting and low had crept, erasing slowly the glittering images of the stars. And now a great expanse of white vapor covered the land; it flowed cold and gray in the darkness, eddied in noiseless whirls round the tree-trunks and about the platform of the house, which seemed to float upon a restless and impalpable illusion of a sea. Only far away the tops of the trees stood outlined on the twinkle of heaven, like a somber and forbidding shore—a coast deceptive, pitiless and black.

Arsat's voice vibrated loudly in the profound peace.

"I had her there! I had her! To get her I would have faced all mankind. But I had her—and—"

His words went out ringing into the empty distances. He paused, and seemed to listen to them dying away very far—beyond help and beyond recall. Then he said quietly—

"Tuan, I loved my brother."

A breath of wind made him shiver. High above his head, high above the silent sea of mist the drooping leaves of the palms rattled together with a mournful and expiring sound. The white man stretched his legs. His chin ❸ rested on his chest, and he murmured sadly without lifting his head—

"We all love our brothers."

Arsat burst out with an intense whispering violence—

"What did I care who died? I wanted peace in my own heart."

He seemed to hear a stir in the house —listened—then stepped in noiselessly. The white man stood up. A breeze was coming in fitful puffs. The stars shone paler as if they had retreated into the frozen depths of immense space. After a chill gust of wind there were a few seconds of perfect calm and absolute silence. Then from behind the black and wavy line of the forests a column of golden light shot up into the heavens and spread over the semicircle of the eastern horizon. The sun had risen. The mist lifted, broke into drifting patches, vanished into thin flying wreaths; and the unveiled lagoon lay, polished and black, in the heavy shadows at the foot of the wall of trees. A white eagle rose over it with a slanting and ponderous flight, reached the clear sunshine and appeared dazzlingly brilliant for a moment, then soaring higher, became a dark ❹ and motionless speck before it vanished into the blue as if it had left the earth forever. The white man, standing gazing upward before the doorway, heard in the hut a confused and broken murmur of distracted words ending with a loud groan. Suddenly Arsat stumbled out with outstretched hands, shivered, and stood still for some time with fixed eyes. Then he said—

"She burns no more."

Before his face the sun showed its edge above the treetops, rising steadily. The breeze freshened; a great brilliance burst upon the lagoon, sparkled on the rippling water. The

Speaking and Listening Mini-Lesson

Courtroom

This mini-lesson supports the Speaking and Listening activity in the Idea Bank on page 1051.

Introduce the Concept In this activity, students will role-play a courtroom scene in which Arsat stands trial for the death of his brother. An effective presentation will require students to take time to build cases for the prosecution and the defense, gather evidence from the story and from "witnesses," prepare questions, and plan a courtroom strategy.

Develop Background Review the basic facts of the case: Arsat's brother died during his attempt to help Arsat and Diamelen escape from the ruler's guards. Review the function of the prosecution and the defense in bringing out pertinent facts. You might have some students serve as jury members, reporters, or others who can take active roles in this simulation.

Apply the Information Allow groups time to prepare their cases, gather details, and practice their presentations. Hold the mock trial, and have the jury return a verdict based on the evidence presented.

Assess the Outcome Evaluate participants in terms of how clearly they present the case, how thoroughly they use the known details from the story, how effectively they argue their side, and how persuasively they present closing arguments.

❺ forests came out of the clear shadows of the morning, became distinct, as if they had rushed nearer—to stop short in a great stir of leaves, of nodding boughs, of swaying branches. In the merciless sunshine the whisper of unconscious life grew louder, speaking in an incomprehensible voice round the dumb darkness of that human sorrow. Arsat's eyes wandered slowly, then stared at the rising sun.

❻ "I can see nothing," he said half aloud to himself.

❼ "There is nothing," said the white man, moving to the edge of the platform and waving his hand to his boat. A shout came faintly over the lagoon and the sampan began to glide toward the abode of the friend of ghosts.

> ◆ Reading Strategy
> What tone of voice do you think each character uses at this point?

"If you want to come with me, I will wait all the morning," said the white man, looking away upon the water.

"No, Tuan," said Arsat softly. "I shall not eat or sleep in this house, but I must first see my road. Now I can see nothing—see nothing! There is no light and no peace in the world; but there is death—death for many. We were sons of the same mother—and I left him in the midst of enemies; but I am going back now."

He drew a long breath and went on in a dreamy tone:

"In a little while I shall see clear enough to strike—to strike. But she has died, and . . . now . . . darkness."

He flung his arms wide open, let them fall along his body, then stood still with unmoved face and stony eyes, staring at the sun. The white man got down into his canoe. The polers ran smartly along the sides of the boat, looking over their shoulders at the beginning of a weary journey. High in the stern, his head muffled up in white rags, the juragon sat moody, letting his paddle trail in the water. The white man, leaning with both arms over the grass roof of the little cabin, looked back at the shining ripple of the boat's wake. Before the sampan passed out of the lagoon into the creek he lifted his eyes. Arsat had not moved. He stood lonely in the searching sunshine; and he looked beyond the great light of a cloudless day into the darkness of a world of illusions.

Guide for Responding

◆ Literature and Your Life

Reader's Response Do you think "The Lagoon" effectively dramatizes the idea that life is a "world of illusions"? Explain your view.

Thematic Focus What internal conflict rages within Arsat?

☑ Check Your Comprehension

1. Why do the members of the white man's crew want nothing to do with Arsat?
2. Why does Arsat ask the white man if he has medicine?
3. What happened to Arsat's brother?
4. At the end of the story, what does Arsat intend to do?

◆ Critical Thinking

INTERPRET

1. Compare and contrast the white man and Arsat. **[Compare and Contrast]**
2. Arsat abandons his brother to his death. (a) What motivates him to flee? (b) How else could he have responded, and what would have been the results? **[Analyze Cause and Effect]**
3. Following Diamelen's death, Arsat says, "I can see nothing," and the white man replies, "There is nothing." (a) What does each mean? (b) How might this dialogue relate to the story's final line? **[Infer]**
4. (a) Does Conrad present love or loyalty, or neither, as the worthier motive? Explain. (b) How would Conrad recommend people deal with past mistakes or regrets? Explain. **[Draw Conclusions]**

Beyond the Selection

FURTHER READING

Other Works by Joseph Conrad

Lord Jim; Nostromo; Under Western Eyes

Other Works About Illusion and Transformation

"Tears, Idle Tears," Alfred, Lord Tennyson
"A Voyage to Cythera," Margaret Drabble
"Across the Bridge," Graham Greene

We suggest that you preview these works before recommending them to students.

INTERNET

Students will find a chronology of Conrad's life and general biographical information at the following Internet address: **http://www.nyu.edu/classes/garcia/conrad/page9.htm** Please be aware, however, that the site may have changed since this information was published.

We strongly recommend that you preview sites before you send students to them.

◆ Critical Thinking

❺ **Connect** Ask students to explain the connection between the sunrise and Diamelen's death. *The merciless sunshine highlights nature's indifference to suffering.*

◆ Critical Thinking

❻ **Interpret** Have students explain the men's statements. *Arsat is saying he doesn't "see" the reasons for the tragedies in his life. The white man is saying there is no grand plan to understand.*

◆ Reading Strategy

❼ **Envision Action and Situation** Students may imagine Arsat speaking in a mumble or near-whisper. Tuan probably speaks with a flat tone.

Reinforce and Extend

Answers

◆ Literature and Your Life

Reader's Response Conrad shows that Arsat's decisions were based on illusion.

Thematic Focus Arsat is torn by guilt for acting out of passion and for causing his brother's death.

☑ Check Your Comprehension

1. They fear Arsat because he does not respect the spirits.
2. He hopes the white man can cure Diamelen.
3. He got killed by the Ruler's henchmen after Arsat deserted him.
4. He plans to strike back at the enemies who killed his brother.

◆ Critical Thinking

1. The white man is dispassionate and objective; Arsat is passionate and conflicted. Both have known danger and isolation.
2. (a) Arsat is desperate to escape with Diamelen. (b) He might have urged Diamelen to escape and gone back to help his brother. Then both brothers might have died.
3. (a) To Arsat, life means nothing now that Diamelen is dead. The white man means that there are no more illusions to cling to. (b) Conrad is saying that all human life is illusion.
4. (a) Possible answer: Arsat's brother seems nobler than Arsat. (b) Conrad might say that a person must struggle to see through illusions to understand.

Develop Understanding

One-Minute Insight A boy has a deep crush on the older sister of a neighborhood friend. He watches her and dreams of their romantic future. Late one night he goes on a mission to a bazaar called "Araby" to get her a gift, only to realize that Araby is not the exotic world he had imagined. In the darkness of the closing bazaar, he has a sudden vision of himself "as a creature driven and derided by vanity." This vision, provoking "anguish and anger," seems to take in his imaginary relationship with the girl and all his illusions.

Customize for
Less Proficient Readers
Remind these students to use context clues to aid comprehension. For instance, if students understand from context that *The Abbot* and *The Devout Communicant* are books, they may choose not to stop reading to get specific information from the footnote.

Customize for
More Advanced Readers
Tell students to consider the significance of specific references to gain an even greater understanding of Joyce's message and wry humor. For example, why might the three books mentioned be important? *The boy's preference for the memoirs of a French adventurer, based on the paper's color, foreshadows his own penchant for romance and his tendency to judge things on their appearances.*

Customize for
Visual/Spatial Learners
Help these students map out the relationship between the houses on the street. This will allow students to envision the action in the street throughout the rest of the story.

❶ **Clarification** *Araby* is a poetic form of *Arabia*. During Joyce's time, Arabia was seen as an exotic and seductive land. To name a bazaar *Araby*, with its mystical connotations, amounts to an advertising ploy.

◆ Critical Thinking

❷ **Analyze** Ask students to identify the figurative technique Joyce uses in this passage, and tell how it helps set the scene. *Joyce personifies the houses as if they gazed at one another and judged the behavior of the inhabitants.*

❶ 

❷ North Richmond Street, being blind,[1] was a quiet street except at the hour when the Christian Brothers' School set the boys free. An uninhabited house of two stories stood at the blind end, detached from its neighbors in a square ground. The other houses of the street, conscious of decent lives within them, gazed at one another with brown imperturbable faces.

The former tenant of our house, a priest, had died in the back drawing room. Air, musty from having been long enclosed, hung in all the rooms, and the waste room behind the kitchen was littered with old useless papers. Among these I found a few paper-covered books, the pages of which were curled and damp: *The Abbot*, by Walter Scott, *The Devout Communicant* and *The Memoirs of Vidocq*.[2] I liked the last best because its leaves were yellow. The wild garden behind the house contained a central apple tree

1. **blind:** Dead end.

2. ***The Abbot . . . Vidocq:*** A historical tale, a religious manual, and the remembrances of a French adventurer, respectively.

Block Scheduling Strategies

Consider these suggestions to take advantage of extended class time:

- Discuss the biographical material about James Joyce (p. 1032) with the class. Provide additional information about the author (ATE, p. 1032) to help them appreciate his standing in the literary world. Display a copy of *The Dubliners*, the collection of stories from which "Araby" is taken.
- Working individually or in small groups, students can preview the Word Bank vocabulary they will encounter in this story.
- Introduce the literary concept of epiphany. Review the instruction on page 1033 then use the Literary Focus page on plot devices, page 270 in ***Selection Support***. After reading the selection, students can complete the Literary Focus questions on page 1050.
- Before reading, review the Reading Strategy of envisioning action and situation. Then have students preview the Reading Strategy assignment on page 1050. Encourage students to keep the assignment in mind as they read.

ENGLISH MONEY.

English or Sterling Money is the currency of Great Britain.

TABLE.

4 farthings (far. or qr.)	make	1 penny,	marked d.
12 pence	"	1 shilling,	" s.
20 shillings	"	1 pound or sovereign, £, sov.	
21 shillings	"	1 guinea, marked guin.	

COINS.—The gold coins are the *sovereign* (£1), and the *half-sovereign* (10s.).

The silver coins are the *crown* (5s.), the *half-crown* (2s. 6d.), the *florin* (2s.), the *shilling* (12d.), *sixpenny-piece* (6d.), and *threepenny-piece* (3d.).

▶ **Critical Viewing** The narrator enters Araby at the shilling gate. Use this
3 table to determine how many times less the price of entrance at the sixpence gate would be. **[Assess]**

and a few straggling bushes under one of
which I found the late tenant's rusty bicycle
pump. He had been a very charitable priest: in
his will he had left all his money to institutions
and the furniture of his house to his sister.

When the short days of winter came dusk
fell before we had well eaten our dinners. When
we met in the street the houses had grown
somber. The space of sky above us was the
color of ever-changing violet and toward it the
4 lamps of the street lifted their feeble lanterns.
5 The cold air stung us and we played till our
bodies glowed. Our shouts echoed in the silent
street. The career of our play brought us
through the dark muddy lanes behind the
houses where we ran the gantlet of the rough
tribes from the cottages, to the back doors of
the dark dripping gardens where odors arose
from the ashpits, to the dark odorous stables 4
where a coachman smoothed and combed the
horse or shook music from the buckled har- 5
ness. When we returned to the street, light
from the kitchen windows had filled the areas.
If my uncle was seen turning the corner we
hid in the shadow until we had seen him safely
housed. Or if Mangan's sister came out on the
doorstep to call her brother in to his tea we
watched her from our shadow peer up and
down the street. We waited to see whether she

◆ Build Vocabulary

imperturbable (im´ pər tur´ bə bəl) *adj.*: Calm; not easily ruffled

▶Critical Viewing◀

3 Assess A shilling is worth twelve pence, so it would cost twice as much to enter at a shilling gate than at a sixpence gate.

◆ Reading Strategy

4 Envision Action and Situation Have students describe the kind of childhood the narrator has and guess how old the boys are. *Students may say that he lives in a quiet, modest, old neighborhood where many other families live. The conditions are spare and not modern. The boys may be about twelve to fourteen years old: old enough to describe their get-togethers as "play" and to be out after dark, but young enough to run home to the comfort of a warm kitchen.*

5 Clarification The expression "ran the gantlet" is an expression that describes an old method of determining someone's guilt or innocence. The person in question runs between two rows of people who have sticks; they try to beat the accused as he or she runs by. The reaction of the accused to the ordeal would indicate that person's guilt or innocence. Joyce refers here to the boys having to endure similar treatment from the local bullies.

Cultural Connection

In the works of James Joyce, an *epiphany* is a profound revelation experienced by a main character. The term was used in Greek mythology to describe an occasion when a god or goddess would suddenly reveal his or her true identity to a mortal. The word *epiphany* also has an ecclesiastical meaning. The Epiphany, or Twelfth Night, is a Christian holiday celebrated twelve days after Christmas, on January 6. It commemorates the day that the Magi arrived to visit the Christ child and the beasts in the stable were able to talk. Religious symbols and references are common in the works of Joyce.

Challenge students to think back on works they have read in which a character experiences a moment of epiphany, either in the Joycean sense of a sudden awareness, or in the more literal, mythological sense of a character who suddenly reveals his or her true identity. Compile a list of these characters from diverse cultures and literary traditions.

◆ Critical Thinking

❶ Infer Students can infer the narrator's age from this passage. Guide them to notice that since the boy lacks the composure to approach Mangan's sister, he must be fairly young.

◆ Reading Strategy

❷ Envision Action and Situation Students may cite the sights of crowds and shop fronts, but most of the details in this passage appeal to the sense of hearing: the voices of bargaining women, the voices of the shop-boys singing out their wares, and the chanting of the street singers.

◆ Critical Thinking

❸ Connect Have students scan the passage for other words with religious connotations, such as *chalice, prayers, praises,* and *adoration.* Discuss how this imagery affects the mood of "Araby" and echoes the narrator's feelings about Mangan's sister. *Students may say that the religious imagery suggests that the narrator has an almost religious adoration for Mangan's sister.*

Customize for
Less Proficient Readers

❹ Guide these students to recognize how the boy makes more of the moment with Mangan's sister than it actually is. He imagines that they have established a relationship in which his promise means something to her. This promise creates the conflict that drives the rest of the story.

◆ Literary Focus

❺ Plot Devices Ask students to consider how the narrator's meeting with Mangan's sister may be related to his epiphany, which will come at the end of the story. *Students may predict that the epiphany will have something to do with his feelings toward her and his interpretation of what they mean to each other.*

◆ Critical Thinking

❻ Relate Encourage students to relate the narrator's anticipation of the bazaar to an event that they have anticipated. *Students may suggest that they have felt similar excitement and anxiety looking forward to a dance, a big game or an awards ceremony.*

would remain or go in and, if she remained, we left our shadow and walked up to Mangan's steps resignedly. She was waiting for us, her figure defined by the light from the half-opened door. Her brother always teased her before he obeyed and I stood by the railings looking at her. Her dress swung as she moved her body and the soft rope of her hair tossed from side to side.

Every morning I lay on the floor in
❶ the front parlor watching her door. The blind was pulled down to within an inch of the sash so that I could not be seen. When she came out on the doorstep my heart leaped. I ran to the hall, seized my books and followed her. I kept her brown figure always in my eye and, when we came near the point at which our ways diverged, I quickened my pace and passed her. This happened morning after morning. I had never spoken to her, except for a few casual words, and yet her name was like a summons to all my foolish blood.

❷ **◆ Reading Strategy** Which vivid details in this passage help you to form a mental picture of the scene?

Her image accompanied me even in places the most hostile to romance. On Saturday evenings when my aunt went marketing I had to go to carry some of the parcels. We walked through the flaring streets, jostled by drunken men and bargaining women, amid the curses of laborers, the shrill litanies of shop-boys who stood on guard by the barrels of pigs' cheeks, the nasal chanting of street singers, who sang a *come-all-you* about O'Donovan Rossa,[3] or a ballad about the troubles in our native land. These noises converged in a single sensation of life for me: I imagined that I bore my chalice safely through a throng of foes. Her name sprang to my lips at moments in strange prayers and praises which I myself did not
❸ understand. My eyes were often full of tears (I could not tell why) and at times a flood from my heart seemed to pour itself out into my bosom. I thought little of the future. I did not know whether I would ever speak to her or not or, if I spoke to her, how I could tell her of my confused adoration. But my body was like a harp and her words and gestures were like fingers running upon the wires.

One evening I went into the back drawing room in which the priest had died. It was a dark rainy evening and there was no sound in the house. Through one of the broken panes I heard the rain impinge upon the earth, the fine incessant needles of water playing in the sodden beds. Some distant lamp or lighted window gleamed below me. I was thankful that I could see so little. All my senses seemed to desire to veil themselves and, feeling that I was about to slip from them, I pressed the palms of my hands together until they trembled, murmuring: *"O love! O love!"* many times.

At last she spoke to me. When she addressed the first words to me I was so confused that I did not know what to answer. She asked me was I going to *Araby.* I forget whether I answered yes or no. It would be a splendid bazaar, she said; she would love to go.

"And why can't you?" I asked.

While she spoke she turned a silver bracelet round and round her wrist. She could not go, she said, because there would be a retreat[4] that week in her convent.[5] Her brother and two other boys were fighting for their caps and I was alone at the railings. She held one of the spikes, bowing her head towards me. The light from the lamp opposite our door caught the white curve of her neck, lit up her hair that rested there and, falling, lit up the hand upon the railing. It fell over one side of her dress and caught the white border of a petticoat, just visible as she stood at ease.

"It's well for you," she said.

"If I go," I said, "I will bring you something."

What innumerable follies laid waste my waking and sleeping thoughts after that evening! I wished to annihilate the tedious intervening days. I chafed against the work of school. At
night in my bedroom and by day in the class- ❻
room her image came between me and the page I strove to read. The syllables of the word *Araby* were called to me through the silence in which my soul luxuriated and cast an Eastern

3. **come-all-you . . . Rossa:** Opening of a ballad about an Irish hero.

4. **retreat** *n.*: Period of retirement or seclusion for prayer, religious study, and meditation.
5. **convent** *n.*: School run by an order of nuns.

Cross-Curricular Connection: Social Studies

People in the West have long had a fascination for the East. This phenomenon goes back at least to the 1200's, when Italian trader Marco Polo returned from China and central Asia and wrote a book about his fabulous adventures. In the 1880's *The Arabian Nights,* a collection of two hundred folk tales from Arabia, Egypt, India, and Persia, was translated into English by the explorer and scholar Richard Francis Burton. The book, which became an instant classic in the West, reinforced people's impression of the East as an exotic land of genies and flying carpets.

Discuss with students some of the stories they may remember from *The Arabian Nights.* Ask them how these stories might have created a false impression in the West about the people and cultures of the Middle East and Far East. You might have students read some of the works of modern Eastern writers, such as Anita Desai, Amos Oz, or R. K. Narayan, to analyze how writers portray their countries and cultures today.

7 enchantment over me. I asked for leave to go to the bazaar on Saturday night. My aunt was surprised and hoped it was not some Freemason[6] affair. I answered few questions in class. I watched my master's face pass from amiability to sternness; he hoped I was not beginning to idle. I could not call my wandering thoughts together. I had hardly any patience with the serious work of life which, now that it stood between me and my desire, seemed to me child's play, ugly monotonous child's play.

On Saturday morning I reminded my uncle that I wished to go to the bazaar in the evening. He was fussing at the hallstand, looking for the hat brush, and answered me curtly:

"Yes, boy, I know."

As he was in the hall I could not go into the front parlor and lie at the window. I left the house in bad humor and walked slowly toward the school. The air was pitilessly raw and already my heart misgave me.

9 When I came home to dinner my uncle had not yet been home. Still it was early. I sat staring at the clock for some time and, when its ticking began to irritate me, I left the room. I mounted the staircase and gained the upper part of the house. The high cold empty gloomy rooms liberated me and I went from room to room singing. From the front window I saw my companions playing in the street. Their cries reached me weakened and indistinct and, leaning my forehead against the cool glass, I looked over at the dark house where she lived. I may have stood there for an hour, seeing nothing but the brown-clad figure cast by my imagination, touched discreetly by the lamplight at the curved neck, at the hand upon the railings and at the border below the dress.

When I came downstairs again I found Mrs. Mercer sitting at the fire. She was an old garrulous woman, a pawnbroker's widow, who collected used stamps for some pious purpose. I had to endure the gossip of the tea table. The meal was prolonged beyond an hour and still my uncle did not come. Mrs. Mercer stood up to go: she was sorry she couldn't wait any longer, but it was after eight o'clock and she did not like to be out late, as the night air was bad for her. When she had gone I began to walk up and down the room, clenching my fists. My aunt said:

"I'm afraid you may put off your bazaar for this night of Our Lord."

At nine o'clock I heard my uncle's latchkey in the hall door. I heard him talking to himself and heard the hallstand rocking when it had received the weight of his overcoat. I could interpret these signs. When he was midway through his dinner I asked him to give me the money to go to the bazaar. He had forgotten.

"The people are in bed and after their first sleep now," he said.

I did not smile. My aunt said to him energetically:

"Can't you give him the money and let him go? You've kept him late enough as it is."

My uncle said he was very sorry he had forgotten. He said he believed in the old saying: *All work and no play makes Jack a dull boy.* He asked me where I was going and, when I had told him a second time he asked me did I know *The Arab's Farewell to His Steed.*[7] When I left the kitchen he was about to recite the opening lines of the piece to my aunt.

I held a florin[8] tightly in my hand as I strode down Buckingham Street toward the station. The sight of the streets thronged with buyers and glaring with gas recalled to me the purpose of my journey. I took my seat in a third-class carriage of a deserted train. After an intolerable delay the train moved out of the

> ◆ **Reading Strategy**
> How do you envision the uncle, given the details in the paragraph above? 10

6. **Freemason:** Free and Accepted Masons, an international secret society.

7. ***The Arab's . . . His Steed:*** Popular nineteenth-century poem.
8. **florin:** Two-shilling coin of the time.

◆ Build Vocabulary

litanies (lit´ən ēz) *n.*: Forms of prayer in which a congregation repeats a fixed response

garrulous (gar´ ə ləs) *adj.*: Talking continuously

◆ Critical Thinking

7 Compare and Contrast Have students contrast how the narrator feels about the bazaar with his aunt's view of it. How might her opinion foreshadow the outcome of the story? *She is suspicious of the event and appears not in favor of it.*

◆ Critical Thinking

8 Analyze Guide students to analyze the narrator's state of mind here, noting how he tries to distance himself from his boyhood companions as his imagination runs wild. *The boy's illusions lead him to see himself as separate from the things he once considered important. His distance from these activities and responsibilities is an illusion, as they are appropriate for someone his age.*

◆ Reading Strategy

9 Envision Action and Situation Ask students to describe the effect of the details in this passage. *The many details and minor events that the author includes should help students to appreciate the boy's feelings of impatience and building anxiety.*

◆ Reading Strategy

10 Envision Action and Situation Students may say that the uncle is detached, somewhat self-absorbed, and has little appreciation of his nephew's state of mind.

Speaking and Listening Mini-Lesson

Panel Discussion

This mini-lesson supports the Speaking and Listening activity in Idea Bank on page 1051.

Introduce the Concept This activity asks students to hold a panel discussion to explore the role of loyalty in "The Lagoon" and in "Araby." Tell students that you will judge them not on their personal opinions, but on how effectively they support their views with details from the two stories.

Develop Background Suggest that students reread "The Lagoon" and "Araby" with the concept of loyalty in mind. They might use self-stick notes to highlight passages that address this idea. Encourage students to formulate their own opinion on this issue and to identify relevant passages that support their views, so they can cite them during the discussion.

Apply the Information Hold panel discussions. You can have four to six students conduct their discussion before the class, or you can have a series of smaller panels with peer judges and questioners for each. In the latter case, students who are in the audience should prepare peer evaluations.

Assess the Outcome Evaluate the participants in terms of their ability to express and support their opinions. Have audience members who make these evaluations use the Peer Assessment: Speakers–Speech, p. 119, in the ***Alternative Assessment*** booklet.

▶Critical Viewing◀

❶ **Infer** Students may say that the allure of an exotic, romantic bazaar would be a welcome contrast to the bleak, squalid conditions of the neighborhood.

Customize for
Less Proficient Readers

❷ Direct students to envision the narrator sitting alone in the empty carriage. Ask them what this might foreshadow about the bazaar itself. *Students may say that it really is too late, or that if a special car for the bazaar is empty, then few people share the narrator's enthusiasm for it, which, in turn, suggests that Araby may not live up to his expectations.*

◆ Reading Strategy

❸ **Envision Action and Situation** Be sure students understand that because the narrator was so eager to get to the bazaar, he went in at a full-price entrance rather than at a sixpenny gate, which probably was a children's entrance. Ask students whether the narrator's first glimpse of the bazaar lives up to their own expectations of what Araby would be like. *If students expected a lively, exotic environment, they may be surprised, even disappointed, that the hall is nearly empty and that most of it is dark and closed.*

❶ ▶ **Critical Viewing** Why might the prospect of a fair or bazaar be appealing to someone who lived in a setting such as this? **[Infer]**

St. Patrick's Close, Walter Osborne, Courtesy of the National Gallery of Ireland

❷ station slowly. It crept onward among ruinous houses and over the twinkling river. At Westland Row Station a crowd of people pressed to the carriage doors; but the porters moved them back, saying that it was a special train for the bazaar. I remained alone in the bare carriage. In a few minutes the train drew up beside an improvised wooden platform. I passed out onto the road and saw by the lighted dial of a clock that it was ten minutes to ten. In front of me was a large building which displayed the magical name.

I could not find any sixpenny entrance and, fearing that the bazaar would be closed, I passed in quickly through a turnstile, handing a shilling to a weary-looking man. I found myself in a big hall girdled at half its height by a gallery. Nearly all the stalls were closed and the greater part of the hall was in darkness. ❸
I recognized a silence like that which pervades

Humanities: Art

St. Patrick's Close by Walter Osborne.

Walter Frederick Osborne (1859–1903) was an English landscape painter who lived in Ireland and received his art training there, at the Royal Hibernian Academy. His paintings generally portray urban scenes with a special focus on children. He painted the area around St. Patrick's Cathedral in Dublin many times.

This painting shows the poverty and squalor of the neighborhood surrounding the cathedral. The placement of the children leads the eye into the picture plane, allowing it to go from one bleak scene to another. It is an effective portrayal of the indifference of children to the poverty around them.

Use these questions for discussion:

1. Is the artist observing the scene or judging it? *Some students might say that his realistic representation suggests he is an observer. Others may say he makes a judgment through his decision to depict the dull eyes of the boy playing the flute.*
2. Compare and contrast this scene with the description of North Richmond Street in Joyce's story. *Students may say that, like Joyce's street, this street has low attached row houses with brown facades. In the story, North Richmond Street is a quiet dead end. However, this street is dominated by the cathedral.*

> ◆ **Literary Focus**
> In the remainder of this paragraph, Joyce leads directly to the epiphany of the story. What realization do you think the narrator is about to experience about himself and his situation? ❹

a church after a service. I walked into the center of the bazaar timidly. A few people were gathered about the stalls which were still open. Before a curtain, over which the words *Café Chantant*[9] were written in colored lamps, two men were counting money on a salver.[10] I listened to the fall of the coins.

Remembering with difficulty why I had come I went over to one of the stalls and examined porcelain vases and flowered tea sets. At the door of the stall a young lady was talking and laughing with two young gentlemen. I remarked their English accents and listened vaguely to their conversation.

"O, I never said such a thing!"

"O, but you did!"

"O, but I didn't!"

"Didn't she say that?"

"Yes. I heard her."

"O, there's a . . . fib!"

Observing me the young lady came over and asked me did I wish to buy anything. The tone of her voice was not encouraging; she seemed to have spoken to me out of a sense of duty. I looked humbly at the great jars that stood like Eastern guards at either side of the dark entrance to the stall and murmured:

"No, thank you."

The young lady changed the position of one of the vases and went back to the two young men. They began to talk of the same subject. Once or twice the young lady glanced at me over her shoulder.

I lingered before her stall, though I knew my stay was useless, to make my interest in her wares seem the more real. Then I turned away slowly and walked down the middle of the bazaar. I allowed the two pennies to fall against the sixpence in my pocket. I heard a voice call from one end of the gallery that the light was out. The upper part of the hall was now completely dark.

Gazing up into the darkness I saw myself as a creature driven and derided by vanity; and my eyes burned with anguish and anger. ❺

9. ***Café Chantant:*** Café with musical entertainment.
10. **salver** *n.:* Tray usually used for the presentation of letters or visiting cards.

◆ Build Vocabulary

derided (di rīd′ id) *v.:* Made fun of; ridiculed

Guide for Responding

◆ Literature and Your Life

Reader's Response Like the narrator in this story, do you ever have doubts or ambivalent feelings about a promise you've made?

Thematic Focus Why does the narrator feel conflict about the change he is experiencing?

☑ Check Your Comprehension

1. Why is going to the bazaar so important to the narrator?
2. Why is the narrator late getting to Araby?
3. Describe the narrator's experience at Araby.
4. How does the narrator feel at the end of the story?

◆ Critical Thinking

INTERPRET

1. What might have been the author's reason for not giving Mangan's sister a name? **[Analyze]**
2. Does Araby live up to the narrator's expectations? Describe his mood as he walks around Araby, and give reasons for that mood. **[Analyze Causes and Effects]**
3. (a) Why do you think the author chose "Araby" as the name for the bazaar? (b) As a title for the story? (c) How does this name relate to the narrator's experiences? **[Draw Conclusions]**

APPLY

4. Can reality ever live up to a person's dreams? Explain. **[Apply]**

◆ Literary Focus

❹ Plot Devices Students may predict that the narrator will come to realize that, just as Araby was not all he expected, he too is not the romantic hero he imagined.

◆ Literary Focus

❺ Plot Devices Ask students to describe how the narrator feels at this moment of epiphany. *Students may say that he feels ashamed, and ridiculous. He has lost an illusion that can never be regained, but he now has a more realistic image of himself.*

Reinforce and Extend

Answers

◆ Literature and Your Life

Reader's Response Most students will identify with such feelings.

Thematic Focus The narrator enjoyed the romantic fantasy he had woven, yet when he realizes how foolish he was, he feels ridiculous.

☑ Check Your Comprehension

1. He wants to buy a gift for Mangan's sister.
2. His uncle was late in giving him the money to go.
3. He overpays, finds almost nobody there, and the people he encounters seem bored.
4. He feels upset by his foolishness.

◆ Critical Thinking

Interpret

1. Her lack of a name makes her seem remote. It also shows how little the narrator knows her.
2. Araby is a disappointment. The narrator's mood is as dark and gloomy as the setting.
3. (a) It makes the bazaar sound exotic and mysterious. (b) It makes the story sound like it will take readers to an exotic or romantic place. (c) The narrator was seduced by his own romantic fantasies; the image of Arabia then was one of an alluring, tempting place of delights.
4. Students may say that dreams and reality often clash. Some may assert that it's important nevertheless to have goals and dreams.

Beyond the Selection

FURTHER READING

Other Works by James Joyce
"The Dead"; "The Boarding House"; "A Painful Case"

Other Works About Self-Realization
"B. Wordsworth," V. S. Naipaul
"An Essay on Man," Alexander Pope
"The Hollow Men," T. S. Eliot

We suggest that you preview these works before recommending them to students.

INTERNET

Students can find information about Joyce at the following Web site. **http://www2.lucidcafe.com/lucidcafe/library/96feb/joyce.html**

Please be aware that the site may have changed since this information was published.

We *strongly recommend* that you preview the site before you send students to it.

Develop Understanding

◆ Literary Focus

1. You would not know the antagonism the locals felt toward him or the sense of mystery that surrounds him.
2. Arsat can dramatize the story with his own emotions.
3. The epiphany occurs at the bazaar when the narrator's illusions are shattered.
4. The narrator realizes that his "romance" with Mangan's sister is as imaginary as the romance of the Araby bazaar.

◆ Grammar and Style

Practice

1. slept; 2. lifted; 3. had grown

Writing Application

1. Since nothing moved on the river, the steersman swept right and left with periodic flourishes of his blade.
2. After the sun had fallen behind the forest, I crept along the jasmine hedges.
3. While we played during the cold late afternoons, our bodies glowed.

◆ Build Vocabulary

Using the Word Root *-vinc-*

1. to overcome by good arguments; so, to conquer your opponent with the strength of your opinion
2. to show clearly or reveal; from a Latin word meaning "conquer, elicit by argument, prove" (students probably won't know this and may say that showing is a form of conquest)
3. inability to be beaten; so, not able to be conquered

Using the Word Bank

1. b 2. a 3. a 4. c 5. c
6. b 7. b 8. a 9. b

◆ Reading Strategy

Sample paragraph: In "The Lagoon," when Arsat stumbles out of the hut and says "She burns no more," it sends a chill down the spine. Arsat must announce the death of his beloved to the white man. I see him with his lips tight but trembling and a sad, distant look in teary eyes. I hear a long, low sigh from his chest as he searches the sky for help. The white man is silent, knowing that there is nothing he can say to comfort his friend, knowing that it is time to show quiet respect. The scene is still, tense, and too silent. This moment is accompanied by a brilliant sunrise that mocks Arsat's grief but also represents that he now knows what he must do.

For additional instruction and practice, use the page on adverb clauses, p. 32, in the *Writer's Solution Grammar Practice Book*

Guide for Responding *(continued)*

◆ Literary Focus

Plot Devices

A **story within a story** is a tale told by a character in a fictional narrative. Conrad uses this device in "The Lagoon" to enhance the meaning of Arsat's tale. The outer narrative provides a framework for Arsat's story.

An **epiphany** is a sudden recognition of an important truth by a character in a fictional work. An epiphany usually unmasks a truth that was present all along in a character's mind.

1. What specific information would you lack if "The Lagoon" had been narrated entirely by Arsat?
2. Why do you think Conrad chose to have Arsat narrate his own story?
3. Where in "Araby" does the epiphany occur?
4. What does the hero in "Araby" suddenly realize?

◆ Grammar and Style

Adverb Clauses

Joseph Conrad and James Joyce often use **adverb clauses**—subordinate clauses that modify verbs, adjectives, and adverbs. As modifiers, adverb clauses add specificity and interest to writing.

Practice In your notebook, identify the word(s) that each adverb clause modifies.

1. And *since his Malay friend had come unexpectedly to dwell in the hut on the lagoon with a strange woman,* he had slept many times there.
2. *Before the sampan passed out of the lagoon into the creek* he lifted his eyes.
3. *When we met in the street* the houses had grown somber.

Writing Application Rewrite each of the following items, using an adverb clause to combine the sentences.

1. Nothing moved on the river. The steersman swept right and left with periodic flourishes of his blade.
2. The sun had fallen behind the forest. I crept along the jasmine hedges.
3. We played during the cold, late afternoons. Our bodies glowed.

◆ Build Vocabulary

Using the Word Root *-vinc-*

Knowing that the Latin root *-vinc-* means "conquer," write definitions for the following words. Within the definition, explain how the root's meaning affects the word's meaning.

1. convince
2. evince
3. invincibility

Using the Word Bank

In your notebook, write the letter of the word whose meaning is closest to that of the first word.

1. portals: (a) arteries, (b) doorways, (c) furniture
2. invincible: (a) unconquerable, (b) warrior-like, (c) facile
3. propitiate: (a) appease, (b) refuse, (c) resign
4. conflagration: (a) battle, (b) dispute, (c) fire
5. august: (a) portly, (b) virtuous, (c) awe-inspiring
6. imperturbable: (a) indifferent, (b) calm, (c) ruthless
7. litanies: (a) lawsuits, (b) prayers, (c) harangues
8. garrulous: (a) talkative, (b) extravagant, (c) suspicious
9. derided: (a) ejected, (b) ridiculed, (c) exaggerated

◆ Reading Strategy

Envision Action and Situation

Your understanding of a story will be improved if you **envision its action and characters' situations.** In modernist fiction like Conrad's and Joyce's, it's also helpful to focus in on the characters' internal responses to their situations.

Choose a moment in either "The Lagoon" or "Araby" in which the characters are involved in an especially intense or suspenseful dialogue. "Freeze" this moment in your mind's eye. Then write a paragraph in which you describe as vividly as you can your impression of what is happening, what each character looks like, and particularly any gestures, tones of voice, or facial expressions that are revealing of that character's inner thoughts or conflicts. Also describe changes in setting—in location or weather—that reflect the characters' inner states.

Build Your Portfolio

Idea Bank

Writing

1. Recollection In Conrad's story, Arsat reveals a confidence to the narrator. Write several paragraphs recalling a time you either (a) revealed a confidence or (b) listened to a confidence. Address your inner thoughts at the time.

2. Extending a Story Choose an episode from Joyce's "Araby" involving the narrator and Mangan's sister. Going beyond the events of the story, write a meaningful dialogue around this episode.

3. Essay A lagoon is a pool of brackish water separated from the sea by sandbars and reefs. In an essay, answer these questions: What does the lagoon represent in Conrad's story? What does a voyage to and from the lagoon symbolize?

Speaking and Listening

4. Courtroom Is Arsat in Conrad's "The Lagoon" responsible for the death of his brother? With a peer, argue for the defense and the prosecution. You may present your arguments to the class as "jury" and have them return a verdict.

5. Panel Discussion In "The Lagoon," Arsat betrays his brother, while in "Araby" the narrator's uncle breaks faith with him. With a panel of classmates, discuss the role of loyalty in these stories.

Projects

6. Poster Make a poster for the Araby bazaar. Research the design of turn-of-the century posters. Then design, write copy for, and illustrate your poster. **[Art Link]**

7. Report on Colonialism Choose a country that was formerly a British colony, such as India, Burma, or Malaysia. Investigate Britain's colonization in this area and the country's fight for independence. Present your findings to the class.

Writing Mini-Lesson

Personal Essay

The term *epiphany* was introduced by James Joyce to describe a moment of revelation or insight in which a literary character recognizes a truth. However, you've probably had an epiphany in your own life—a moment in which aspects of your experience just seem to come together in a sweep of truth or a charge of meaning.

Write a personal essay in which you describe an epiphany you've experienced. Use elaboration to build up to your final insight.

Writing Skills Focus: Elaboration to Entertain

To make your essay entertaining and suspenseful, work up gradually to the climactic moment at which you experienced your realization.

Joyce carefully builds towards his character's epiphany, fleshing out his situation by elaborating details. For instance, he does not begin the story with Mangan's sister; he leads up to her by first introducing the neighborhood boys. When he describes the narrator's crush on her, he elaborates by showing how the crush affects every part of the narrator's life, from the mornings he spends watching for her to the Saturday evenings he pretends to be carrying a "chalice" for her through the market crowd.

Prewriting Identify the situation that led to your epiphany, and then jot down the aspects of this situation that directly relate to the epiphany.

Drafting As you draft your essay, use vivid language and sensory details. Help your friend "see" your epiphany, then let him or her know how it changed your outlook.

Revising Read your essay aloud. Make sure it is clearly narrated and that it does not include irrelevant details. Be sure the written version of your essay corresponds to the way you would tell the story orally to a good friend.

✓ ASSESSMENT OPTIONS

Formal Assessment, Selection Test, pp. 271–273, and Assessment Resources Software. The selection test is designed so that it can be easily customized to the performance levels of your students. ***Alternative Assessment,*** p. 56, includes options for less advanced students, more advanced students, musical/rhythmic learners, bodily/kinesthetic learners, and visual/spatial learners.

PORTFOLIO ASSESSMENT

Use the following rubrics in the ***Alternative Assessment*** booklet to assess student writing:

1. Scoring Rubric for Narrative Based on Personal Experience
2. Scoring Rubric for Fictional Narrative
3. Scoring Rubric for Literary Interpretation Writing Mini-Lesson: Scoring Rubric for Narrative Based on Personal Experience

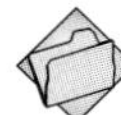

Idea Bank

Customizing for *Performance Levels*

Following are suggestions for matching Idea Bank topics with your students' performance levels:

Less Advanced Students: 1, 5, 7
Average Students: 2, 4, 5, 6, 7
More Advanced Students: 3, 4, 7

Customizing for *Learning Modalities*

Following are suggestions for matching Idea Bank topics with your students' learning modalities:

Visual/Spatial: 6
Verbal/Linguistic: 1, 2, 3, 4, 5,7
Interpersonal:4, 5
Intrapersonal: 1

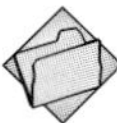

Writing Mini-Lesson

Refer students to the Writing Process Handbook, page 1189, for instruction on the writing, and page 1191 for further information on description.

Writing and Language Transparencies Use Writing Process Model 3, Personal Narrative, to model for students the stages of writing a personal essay.

Writer's Solution

Writing Lab CD-ROM

Have students complete the tutorial on Narration. Have students follow these steps:

1. Have students preview the Evaluation Guidelines.
2. Encourage students to use the Interactive Word Bins to select transition words and sensory words.
3. Allow time for students to draft on the computer.
4. Tell students to revise using the interactive revision checkers for transitions, language variety, and vague adjectives.

Sourcebook

Have students use Chapter 2, Narration (pp. 30–61), for additional support. The chapter includes a writing model for three different purposes.

Prepare and Engage

OBJECTIVES

1. To read, comprehend, and interpret a short story
2. To relate a story to personal experience
3. To ask questions as you read
4. To analyze different point-of-view techniques
5. To build vocabulary in context and learn the word root *-trans-*
6. To make verbs agree with their subjects in inverted sentences
7. To write a narrative from an unusual perspective and create suspense
8. To respond to the stories through writing, speaking and listening, and projects

SKILLS INSTRUCTION

Vocabulary: Word Roots: *-trans-*
Grammar: Subject-Verb Agreement in Inverted Sentences
Reading Strategy: Question
Literary Focus: Point of View: Modern Experiments
Writing: Suspense
Speaking and Listening: Oral Interpretation (teacher edition)
Critical Viewing: Interpret; Infer; Evaluate

PORTFOLIO OPPORTUNITIES

Writing: Letter to the Author; Stream-of-Consciousness Narrative; Response to Criticism
Writing Mini-Lesson: Narrative From an Unusual Perspective
Speaking and Listening: Poetry Reading; Oral Interpretation
Projects: Report on World War I; Freudian Psychology and Fiction

Guide for Interpreting

Virginia Woolf *(1882–1941)*

Virginia Woolf revolutionized modern fiction by pioneering the use of the stream-of-consciousness technique. This device allows readers to tune in directly to the random flow of thoughts and images in a character's mind.

A Literary Life Woolf was a pioneer writer who came from a prim and proper Victorian family. Her father, the renowned editor Leslie Stephen, made sure his daughter grew up surrounded by books. This literary atmosphere had a strong effect. At the age of twenty-three, Woolf began contributing reviews to the *Times* of London. Later, she and her husband, Leonard, made their house in the Bloomsbury section of London, a meeting place for writers. This circle of thinkers became known as the Bloomsbury Group.

Revolutionizing Fiction Woolf's first two novels were not unusual, but *Jacob's Room* (1922) shattered the conventions of fiction by telling the story of a young man's life entirely through an examination of his room. (She also uses this device in "The Lady in the Looking Glass: A Reflection.") Woolf continued to refine her fluid, inward-looking style with three more stream-of-consciousness novels—*Mrs. Dalloway* (1925), *To the Lighthouse* (1927), and *The Waves* (1931). In her more revolutionary works, she virtually abolished the traditional concept of plot, preferring to concentrate on what she called "an ordinary mind on an ordinary day."

Depression and Tragedy Woolf suffered episodes of severe depression brought on by poor health and the turmoil of war. In 1941, two years after the outbreak of World War II, she drowned. Today she is recognized, along with James Joyce, as one of the shapers of modern fiction.

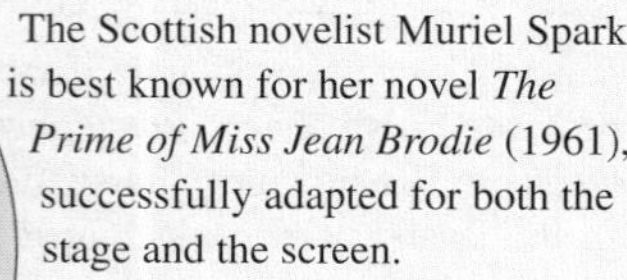

Muriel Spark *(1918–)*

The Scottish novelist Muriel Spark is best known for her novel *The Prime of Miss Jean Brodie* (1961), successfully adapted for both the stage and the screen.

A Prolific Career Born and educated in Edinburgh, Scotland, Spark began her literary career as an editor and biographer. She began to write fiction after she won a short story competition sponsored by the *Observer*, a Sunday newspaper.

In 1958, she published *The Go-Away Bird*, a collection of short stories. Some of these stories were set in central Africa, where she had spent several years in her youth. Her novels include *The Mandelbaum Gate* (1965), *Territorial Rights* (1979), and *The Only Problem* (1984).

Carefully crafted, suspenseful, and witty, Spark's fiction often raises serious moral issues. You will see all these qualities in "The First Year of My Life."

◆ Background for Understanding

HISTORY: SPARK'S ALLUSIONS TO WORLD WAR I

The title of Spark's story "The First Year of My Life" refers to 1918, the final year of World War I. For over three years, the nations of Europe had been locked in the bloodiest combat in history. Britain, allied with France, Italy, Russia, and the United States, fought against Germany, Austria-Hungary, and Turkey. Spark's story alludes to events in the final year of that war, like the collapse of the Russian effort on the Eastern Front and the German Spring Offensive, halted just short of Paris. British political leaders mentioned include Prime Ministers Herbert Asquith and David Lloyd George.

Prentice Hall Literature Program Resources

REINFORCE / RETEACH / EXTEND

Selection Support Pages
Build Vocabulary: Word Roots: *-trans-*, p. 271
Grammar and Style: Subject-Verb Agreement in Inverted Sentences, p. 272
Reading Strategy: Question, p. 273
Literary Focus: Point of View, p. 274

Strategies for Diverse Student Needs, p. 57

Beyond Literature
Cross-Curricular Connection: Science, p. 57

Formal Assessment Selection Test, pp. 274–276; Assessment Resources Software

Alternative Assessment, p. 57

Writing and Language Transparencies
Virginia Woolf: Stream of Consciousness, p. 165

Resource Pro CD-ROM
"The Lady in the Looking Glass: A Reflection," "The First Year of My Life"—includes all resource material and customizable lesson plan

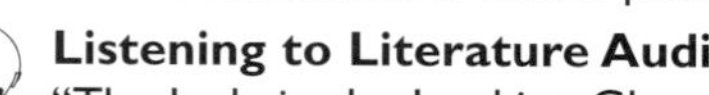

Listening to Literature Audiocassettes
"The Lady in the Looking Glass: A Reflection," "The First Year of My Life"

More About the Authors

The famous intellectual discussions in Bloomsbury brought fresh ideas and attitudes to **Virginia Woolf**, helping to free her from the reserve of her Victorian upbringing. She resented the sexism and corruption of English universities and other aspects of male-dominated Victorian England, and she refused honorary degrees from several universities.

Dame **Muriel Spark** wrote several novels which, for the most part, are short, eccentric, and sophisticated. Many are distinguished by her use of the omniscient narrator. Several have the qualities of fables or parables.

The Lady in the Looking Glass: A Reflection ◆ The First Year of My Life ◆

◆ Literature and Your Life

Connect Your Experience

As you sit waiting in the dentist's office, you glance at a magazine cover featuring a model who looks like the woman who serves food in the cafeteria where you had an argument with your best friend yesterday who just got into college and, oh, no, did I forget to mail my application? The mind flows by such associations, which Virginia Woolf captures in her stream-of-consciousness narration.

Journal Writing Quickly jot down a series of linked thoughts as they enter your mind.

Thematic Focus: Waking From the Dream

As you read, notice how both these stories end with a moment of disillusion, a waking into an unpleasant reality.

◆ Literary Focus

Point of View: Modern Experiments

To capture the fragmentary quality of modern life, writers experimented with **point of view**, the perspective from which a story is told. **Stream-of-consciousness** narration, for example, reflects the random flow of thoughts in a character's mind. Other experiments involved surprising versions of **omniscient** narration, in which a narrator knows every character's thoughts.

Virginia Woolf pioneered the use of the stream-of-consciousness technique. As you read her story, don't confuse the narrator with Isabella Tyson. Muriel Spark plays with the traditional idea of the omniscient narrator. She pretends that, as a baby, her mind knew "everything . . . going on everywhere in the world."

◆ Reading Strategy

Question

Experimental works, like Woolf's and Spark's, offer great rewards but also place great demands on readers. You must continually **ask questions** as you read, to find your way in the story.

In reading Woolf's story, ask how one thought leads to the next. Also ask: Who is the narrator and what is the reality mirrored in this character's mind? In reading Spark's story, ask why she combines her own early development with the events of World War I.

◆ Build Vocabulary

Word Roots: *-trans-*

You'll find the word *transient* in Woolf's story. This word, which means "passing through quickly," is built on the Latin root *-trans-*, meaning "through or across." A frequently used word with this same root is *transit*, as in *mass transit.*

Word Bank

Before you read, preview this list of words from the stories.

- suffused
- transient
- upbraidings
- evanescence
- reticent
- omniscient
- authenticity
- discerned

◆ Grammar and Style

Subject-Verb Agreement in Inverted Sentences

Verbs must **agree** in number with subjects even when the verb precedes the subject, as it does in sentences beginning with *here* or *there*. In the following example, from "The Lady in the Looking Glass," the verb *were* precedes the plural subject and agrees with it in number:

> There *were* her gray-green *dress*, and her *long shoes*, her *basket*, and *something* sparkling at her throat.

As you read these stories, note subject-verb agreement in other inverted sentences.

Before students read the story by Virginia Woolf, bring in 6–10 unrelated objects and place them together on a table in full view of students. Challenge pairs of students to do one of two things: describe the type of character to whom these things belong or contrive some connection between all these items. After students have had time to share their ideas, tell them that in "The Lady in the Looking Glass" the narrator tries to understand a character by viewing her possessions. In "The First Year of My Life" the narrator tries to understand a series of seemingly unrelated events and make sense of the connections among them.

Customize for *Less Proficient Readers*

"The Lady in the Looking Glass: A Reflection" contains several lengthy sentences. Guide readers to identify the subjects in those long sentences and then break the sentences down into smaller parts. Also, encourage students to reread all or parts of the story, as needed, for comprehension.

Customize for *More Advanced Students*

Encourage students to get the most out of these stories by investigating some of the information the authors introduce. For example, they can look up the flowers named in the Woolf story to see what they look like. They can consult a dictionary to fully understand what Woolf means by describing furniture legs as "hieroglyphic." They can also do research to familiarize themselves with the many people and events Muriel Spark mentions.

Customize for *English Language Learners*

Help students to understand the meanings of common words or expressions that are used in these stories in less familiar ways. Examples include *prize* as in prize something open and *fix* as in fix ones mind on something.

Customize for *Visual/Spatial Learners*

Invite students to visualize, and perhaps diagram, the room, house, and garden in Woolf's story. They can also create a World War I timeline to help them track the events referred to in Spark's story.

Preparing for Standardized Tests

Reading and Vocabulary Vocabulary development will enable students to improve performance on the verbal portions of tests. A knowledge of word roots will help students make educated guesses about unfamiliar words they encounter on tests, thereby improving their scores. The Build Vocabulary Skills lesson focuses on the word root: *-trans-*. For additional practice with this root, use the Build Vocabulary page in ***Selection Support,*** p. 271.

Grammar and Language Portions of some standardized tests require students to identify and correct sentence errors, including errors in subject-verb agreement. Students may be asked to determine whether subjects and verbs agree in a given sentence and, if they do not, to choose a correct version.

The Grammar and Style lesson for this selection focuses on subject-verb agreement in inverted sentences. For additional practice, use the Grammar and Style page on subject-verb agreement, p. 272, in ***Selection Support.***

Develop Understanding

One-Minute Insight Isabella, a wealthy woman living alone, is in her garden. The narrator forms a concept of her by examining the objects in her home partly as they appear in a mirror, and by imagining Isabella in the garden. To the narrator, Isabella's wealth and possessions are signs of happiness and success; her silence implies mystery and passion. When Isabella returns from the garden and appears in the mirror, the true loneliness and emptiness of her life are revealed. Her letters, which seemed so mysterious, turn out to be only a collection of bills.

Customize for
English Language Learners

❶ Tell students that a looking glass is a mirror. Then discuss the double meaning of "A Reflection," pointing out that it is an expression of a mental process as well as a visual one.

◆ Literary Focus

❷ **Point of View: Modern Experiments** Guide students to understand their responsibility when reading a stream-of-consciousness narrative: they must become actively involved in the work and try to piece together a meaningful whole from unconnected thoughts and emotions.

◆ Reading Strategy

❸ **Question** Students may say that the narrator is keenly observant, like a naturalist. They may suggest that the subject of the story is like one of the creatures the narrator describes.

◆ Reading Strategy

❹ **Question** Have students begin to consider who the narrator might be. Have them jot down clues as they read. *Based on the narrator's level of knowledge about Isabella, he or she is probably a friend or acquaintance, rather than a family member.*

Customize for
Visual/Spatial Learners

❺ Display pictures of these flowers to give students a sense of what the descriptions imply about Isabella.

❶ The Lady in the Looking Glass: A Reflection

Virginia Woolf

People should not leave looking glasses hanging in their rooms any more than they should leave open checkbooks or letters confessing some hideous crime. One could not help looking, that summer afternoon, ❷ in the long glass that hung outside in the hall. Chance had so arranged it. From the depths of the sofa in the drawing room one could see reflected in the Italian glass not only the marble-topped table opposite, but a stretch of the garden beyond. One could see a long grass path leading between banks of tall flowers until, slicing off an angle, the gold rim cut it off.

> ◆ **Reading Strategy** ❸ What does this description reveal about the narrator? About the person the story is about?

The house was empty, and one felt, since one was the only person in the drawing room, like one of those naturalists who, covered with grass and leaves, lie watching the shyest animals—badgers, otters, king-fishers—moving about freely, themselves unseen. The room that afternoon was full of such shy creatures, lights and shadows, curtains blowing, petals falling—things that never happen, so it seems, if someone is looking. The quiet old country room with its rugs and stone chimney pieces, its sunken bookcases and red and gold lacquer cabinets, was full of such nocturnal creatures. They came pirouetting across the floor, stepping delicately with high-lifted feet and spread tails and pecking allusive beaks as if they had been cranes or flocks of elegant flamingoes whose pink was faded, or peacocks whose trains were veiled with silver. And there were obscure flushes and darkening too, as if a cuttlefish had suddenly suffused the air with purple; and the room had its passions and rages and envies and sorrows coming over it and clouding it, like a human being. Nothing stayed the same for two seconds together.

But, outside, the looking glass reflected the hall table, the sunflowers, the garden path so accurately and so fixedly that they seemed held there in their reality unescapably. It was a strange contrast—all changing here, all stillness there. One could not help looking from one to the other. Meanwhile, since all the doors and windows were open in the heat, there was a perpetual sighing and ceasing sound, the voice of the transient and the perishing, it seemed, coming and going like human breath, while in the looking glass things had ceased to breathe and lay still in the trance of immortality.

Half an hour ago the mistress of the house, Isabella Tyson, had gone down the grass path in her thin summer dress, carrying a basket, and ❹ had vanished, sliced off by the gilt rim of the looking glass. She had gone presumably into the lower garden to pick flowers; or as it seemed more natural to suppose, to pick something light and fantastic and leafy and trailing, traveler's-joy, or one of those elegant sprays of convolvulus that twine round ugly walls and burst here and there into white and violet blossoms. She suggested the fantastic and the tremulous convolvulus rather than the upright aster, the starched zinnia, or her own burning roses alight like lamps on the straight posts of their rose ❺ trees. The comparison showed how very little, after all these years, one knew about her; for it is impossible that any woman of flesh and blood

Block Scheduling Strategies

Consider these suggestions to take advantage of extended class time:

- Introduce the selection with the Interest Grabber activity provided in the Annotated Teacher's Edition. Then introduce and discuss the Reading Strategy: Question.
- Introduce the Literary Focus: Point of View: Modern Experiments to acquaint students with stream-of-consciousness and omniscient narration. Follow up with the Literary Focus page in ***Selection Support,*** p. 274
- Organize discussion groups in which students can answer the Critical Thinking questions (pp. 1057 and 1063).
- Assign the Idea Bank writing activity: Letter to the Author (p. 1065).
- Provide an alternate activity, found in ***Alternate Assessment,*** p. 57, to assess the progress of students with varying performance levels or learning modalities.

of fifty-five or sixty should be really a wreath or a tendril. Such comparisons are worse than idle and superficial—they are cruel even, for they come like the convolvulus itself trembling between one's eyes and the truth. There must be truth; there must be a wall. Yet it was strange that after knowing her all these years one could not say what the truth about Isabella was; one still made up phrases like this about convolvulus and traveler's-joy. As for facts, it was a fact that
6 she was a spinster; that she was rich; that she had bought this house and collected with her own hands—often in the most obscure corners of the world and
7 at great risk from poisonous stings and Oriental diseases—the rugs, the chairs, the cabinets which now lived their nocturnal life before one's eyes. Sometimes it seemed as if they knew more about her than we, who sat on them, wrote at them, and trod on them so carefully, were allowed to know. In each of these cabinets
8 were many little drawers, and each almost certainly held letters, tied with bows of ribbon, sprinkled with sticks of lavender or rose leaves. For it was another fact—if facts were what one wanted—that Isabella had known many people, had had many friends; and thus if one had the audacity to open a drawer and read her letters, one would find the traces of many agitations, of appointments to meet, of upbraidings for not having met, long letters of intimacy and affection, violent letters of jealousy and reproach, terrible final words of parting—for all those interviews and assignations had led to nothing—that is, she had never married, and yet, judging from the masklike indifference of her face, she had gone through twenty times more of passion and experience than those whose loves are trumpeted forth for all the world to hear. Under the stress of thinking about Isabella, her room became more shadowy and symbolic; the corners seemed darker, the legs of 10
chairs and tables more spindly and hieroglyphic.

Suddenly these reflections were ended violently and yet without a sound. A large black form loomed into the looking glass; blotted out everything, strewed the table with a packet of marble tablets veined with pink and gray, and was gone. But the picture was entirely altered. For the moment it was unrecognizable and irrational and entirely out of focus. One could not relate these tablets to any human purpose. And then by degrees some logical process set to work on them and

The Garden of Love, (detail), Walter Richard Sickert, The Fitzwilliam Museum, Cambridge

9 ▲ **Critical Viewing** This story is a stream-of-consciousness narrative, in which thoughts, dreams, and ideas blend together to reveal a story. What aspects of this painting mirror this style of writing? **[Interpret]**

◆ Build Vocabulary

suffused (sə fyo͞ozd′) *v.*: Filled

transient (tran′ shənt) *adj.*: Temporary; passing through quickly

upbraidings (up brād′ iŋz) *n.*: Stern words of disapproval for an action

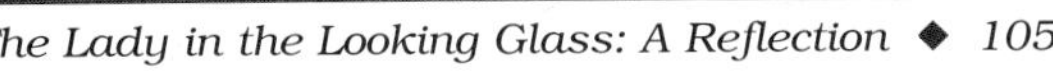

❻ **Clarification** Point out the term *spinster,* which is not currently in favor, refers to a woman, usually middle-aged, who has never married.

◆ Reading Strategy

❼ **Question** Discuss with students what one can learn about a person by examining his or her possessions. *Students may say that possessions can reveal something about a person's background, interests, education, financial status, or taste.*

◆ Literary Focus

❽ **Point of View: Modern Experiments** Discuss with students that, previously, Virginia Woolf gave the room human emotions, writing that it "had its passions and rages and envies and sorrows. . . ." Now, in this passage, she personifies it again, poignantly suggesting that the furniture knew Isabella better than people did.

▶Critical Viewing◀

❾ **Interpret** Students may say that the painting has the same playful, scattered quality as stream-of-consciousness narrative, referring to the interplay of light and shadow and the contrast between hard edges and curves. They may say that their eyes are drawn all over the canvas, even off its edge, since only some of the objects shown appear in full view.

◆ Reading Strategy

❿ **Question** Have students ask themselves what the writer means by this description of the changes in the room. *Students may suggest that under closer observation, the items in the room really do not appear to present a clear picture of Isabella. Be sure students know that "hieroglyphic" means symbolic in a way that's "hard to read or understand."*

Humanities: Art

The Garden of Love by Walter Sickert.

Walter Richard Sickert (1860–1924) was born in Munich, Germany, but became a British subject. He studied at the Slade School of Fine Art in London, but, discouraged by the strict academic atmosphere, left to work and study with James McNeil Whistler. Later, in Paris, he studied with the French painter Edgar Degas. Sickert's greatest contribution to British art was his willingness to experiment with, teach, and defend new ideas in art.

Use these questions for discussion:

1. How does *The Garden of Love* show the effects of different types of light on colors? *Students may say that the sun-bleached pastels in the garden contrast with the cool dark of the shaded areas.*
2. How does the garden in the painting compare with the garden in the story? *Students may say that in the story the garden, described as the "lower garden," is more dense with flowers and plants, and has a path.*

Customize for
Less Proficient Readers

❶ Point out to these students that at the time this story was written, letter-writing was an important way in which people communicated; a person's letters could provide a rich source of information about him or her.

◆ Literary Focus

❷ **Point of View: Modern Experiments** Guide students to notice the stream-of-consciousness style of narration here: from speaking figuratively about putting oneself in Isabella's shoes, to imagining seeing those shoes and Isabella in them.

Customize for
English Language Learners

❸ These students may not easily understand that mundane activities are being contrasted with the deeper interior life of a character. Help these students to identify obligations and responsibilites that are as trivial as ordering a strawberry net or seeing the neighbor's new home.

Customize for
Less Proficient Readers

❹ Paraphrase this paragraph for students to help them grasp that the profound understanding and complex emotions the narrator attributes to Isabella may be the narrator's own thoughts.

began ordering and arranging them and bringing them into the fold of common experience. One realized at last that they were merely letters. The man had brought the post.

There they lay on the marble-topped table, all dripping with light and color at first and crude and unabsorbed. And then it was strange to see how they were drawn in and arranged and composed and made part of the picture and granted that stillness and immortality which the looking glass conferred. They lay there invested with a new reality and significance and with a greater heaviness, too, as if it would have needed a chisel to dislodge them from the table. And, whether it was fancy or
1 not, they seemed to have become not merely a handful of casual letters but to be tablets graven with eternal truth—if one could read them, one would know everything there was to be known about Isabella, yes, and about life, too. The pages inside those marble-looking envelopes must be cut deep and scored thick with meaning. Isabella would come in, and take them, one by one, very slowly, and open them, and read them carefully word by word, and then with a profound sigh of comprehension, as if she had seen to the bottom of everything, she would tear the envelopes to little bits and tie the letters together and lock the cabinet drawer in her determination to conceal what she did not wish to be known.

The thought served as a challenge. Isabella did not wish to be known—but she should no longer escape. It was absurd, it was monstrous. If she concealed so much and knew so much one must prize her open with the first tool that came to hand—the imagination. One must fix one's mind upon her at that very moment. One must fasten her down there. One must refuse to be put off any longer with sayings and doings such as the moment brought forth—with dinners and visits and polite conversations. One must put oneself in her shoes. If one took the phrase literally, it was easy to see the shoes in which she stood, down in the lower garden, at this moment. They were very narrow and long and fashionable —they were made of the softest and most flexible leather. Like everything she wore, they were exquisite. And she would be standing under the high hedge in the lower part of the garden, raising the scissors that were tied to her waist to cut some dead flower, some overgrown branch. The sun would beat down on her face, into her eyes; but no, at the critical moment a veil of cloud covered the sun, making the expression of her eyes doubtful—was it mocking or tender, brilliant or dull? One could only see the indeterminate outline of her rather faded, fine face looking at the sky. She was thinking, perhaps, that she must order a new net for the strawberries; that she must send flowers to Johnson's widow; that it was time she drove over to see the Hippesleys in their new house. Those were
the things she talked about at dinner certainly. 3
But one was tired of the things that she talked about at dinner. It was her profounder state of being that one wanted to catch and turn to words, the state that is to the mind what breathing is to the body, what one calls happiness or unhappiness. At the mention of those words it became obvious, surely, that she must be happy. She was rich; she was distinguished; she had many friends; she traveled—she bought rugs in Turkey and blue pots in Persia. Avenues of pleasure radiated this way and that from where she stood with her scissors raised to cut the trembling branches while the lacy clouds veiled her face.

> **◆ Literary Focus**
> 2 What elements in this paragraph reveal that the author uses a stream-of-consciousness technique?

Here with a quick movement of her scissors she snipped the spray of traveler's-joy and it fell to the ground. As it fell, surely some light came in too, surely one could penetrate a little farther into her being. Her mind then was filled with tenderness and regret. . . . To cut an overgrown branch saddened her because it had once lived, and life was dear to her. Yes, and at the same time the fall of the branch would suggest to her how she must die herself and all the futility and evanescence of things. And then
4 again quickly catching this thought up, with her instant good sense, she thought life had treated her well; even if fall she must, it was to lie on the earth and molder sweetly into the roots of violets. So she stood thinking. Without making any thought precise—for she was one of those reticent people whose minds hold their thoughts enmeshed in clouds of silence—she was filled with thoughts. Her mind was like her room, in which lights advanced and retreated, came pirouetting and stepping delicately, spread

Humanities: Art

For centuries mirrors were rare and expensive. The first mirrors were made of polished metal; in the Middle Ages the idea of using glass with a metal backing was introduced. Venice, known for the art of glass blowing during the fifteenth century, was also a center for making mirrors.

The use of mirrors in the main rooms at the Palace of Versailles in France is one reason that observers consider it so magnificent. Built for Louis XIV in the seventeenth century, Versailles has a famous Hall of Mirrors named for the huge mirrors that face each window.

Ask students to find out more about the use of mirrors in the architecture and design of different cultures. What famous uses have been made of reflecting surfaces? What do these uses say about the cultures in which they appear?

their tails, pecked their way; and then her whole being was suffused, like the room again, with a cloud of some profound knowledge, some unspoken regret, and then she was full of locked drawers, stuffed with letters, like her cabinets.
4 To talk of "prizing her open" as if she were an oyster, to use any but the finest and subtlest and most pliable tools upon her was impious and absurd. One must imagine—here was she in the looking glass. It made one start.

She was so far off at first that one could not see her clearly. She came lingering and pausing, here straightening a rose, there lifting a pink to smell it, but she never stopped; and all the time she became larger and larger in the looking glass, more and more completely the person into whose mind one had been trying to penetrate. One verified her by degrees—fitted the qualities one had discovered into this visible body. There were her gray-green dress, and her long shoes, her basket, and something sparkling at her throat. She came so gradually that she did not seem to derange the pattern in the glass, but only to bring in some new element which gently moved and altered the other objects as if asking them, courteously, to make room for her. And the letters and the table and the grass walk and the sunflowers which had been waiting in the looking glass separated and opened out so that she might be received among them. At last there she was, in the hall. She stopped dead. She stood by the table. She stood perfectly still. At once the looking glass began to pour over her a light that seemed to fix her; that seemed like some acid to bite off the unessential and superficial and to leave only the truth. It was an enthralling spectacle. Everything dropped from her—clouds, dress, basket, diamond—all that one had called the creeper and convolvulus. Here was the hard wall beneath. Here was the woman herself. She stood naked in that pitiless light. And there was nothing. Isabella was perfectly empty. She had no thoughts. She had no friends. She cared for nobody. As for her letters, they were all bills. Look, as she stood there, old and angular, veined and lined, with her high nose and her wrinkled neck, she did not even trouble to open them.

People should not leave looking glasses hanging in their rooms.

◆ **Reading Strategy**
What is happening here? How does this description reveal the story's theme? 5

◆ Build Vocabulary

evanescence (ev´ ə nes´ əns) *n.*: Gradual disappearance, especially from sight

reticent (ret´ ə sənt) *adj.*: Silent; reserved

Guide for Responding

◆ Literature and Your Life

Reader's Response Do you think that knowledge about someone's true nature can be firmly "fastened down"? Explain.

Thematic Focus In what way does the narrator waken from a dream at the end of this story?

Sketch Do a quick drawing of the room described in the story.

☑ Check Your Comprehension

1. What has Isabella Tyson gone to do?
2. What arrives while she is out?
3. Briefly describe the room in the story.
4. What conclusion does the narrator reach about Isabella at the end of the story?

◆ Critical Thinking

INTERPRET

1. Who do you think the narrator is? **[Infer]**
2. (a) How does the looking glass "lead" the narrator to an understanding of Isabella? (b) What does the last sentence of the story, repeated from the beginning, mean? **[Interpret]**
3. In the story, what is the relation between imagination and "the hard wall" of the truth? **[Draw Conclusions]**

EVALUATE

4. Does Woolf succeed in creating a vivid portrait of Isabella? Why or why not? **[Criticize]**

EXTEND

5. How might free association give a psychologist insight into a patient's problems? **[Science Link]**

Beyond the Selection

FURTHER READING

Other Works by Virginia Woolf
"The Voyage Out"; "Jacob's Room"
"The Waves"; "A Room of One's Own"

Other Works With Stream-of-Consciousness Narration
"The Jilting of Granny Weatherall," Katherine Anne Porter
Ulysses, James Joyce

We suggest that you preview these works before recommending them to students.

INTERNET

Students can find additional information about Virginia Woolf at the following Web site:
http://www.aianet.or.jp/~orlando/vvw/english.html

Please be aware, however, that sites may have changed since this information was published.

We *strongly recommend* that you preview the site before you send students to it.

◆ Reading Strategy

5 Question Students may say that when Isabella appears in the mirror, readers learn that the reality of her life is nothing like the picture the narrator has presented; Isabella is lonely, isolated, and uncaring.

Answers

◆ Literature and Your Life

Reader's Response Most students will indicate that no one can know everything that another person thinks and feels.

Thematic Focus The narrator sees Isabella for who she really is rather than romanticizing her.

☑ Check Your Comprehension

1. She has gone into her garden to pick and cut some flowers.
2. The mail arrives in her absence.
3. The room is richly furnished and filled with Isabella's impressive possessions.
4. At the end of the story, the narrator realizes that Isabella's life is empty, void of friendship and thought.

◆ Critical Thinking

1. Some students may say that the narrator is someone well acquainted with the superficial aspects of Isabella's life, perhaps a longtime but not very close friend.
2. (a) At first, the looking glass provides a view of Isabella's life through her possessions. When Isabella herself appears in the looking glass, the narrator sees the true emptiness of her life. (b) It means that the reflections in the mirror and the mental reflections they lead to can be dangerously revealing.
3. The hard wall of reality is in conflict with the imagination's version of reality.
4. Students may say that Woolf presents a vivid portrait of who Isabella appears to be. They may say that her description of who she really is is limited.
5. A psychologist might see connections among seemingly unrelated thoughts and actions, and thereby uncover a pattern in the patient's behavior or in the issues that deeply affect the patient.

Develop Understanding

One-Minute Insight Using the improbable and comical idea of an omniscient infant, Spark presents her amusing, yet perceptive and poignant views on the state of the world as it was in 1918, the year of her birth. Like a fly on the wall, the narrator witnesses key events and eavesdrops on the conversations of politicians and writers. The effect is a devastating attack on the insanities of World War I and the leaders who supported the war.

Customize for
More Advanced Students
Encourage students to take the time to carefully read all the footnotes to get a fuller understanding of the points the author makes and the issues that concern her.

◆ Literary Focus

1 Point of View: Modern Experiments Guide students to understand that the author is joking, that the idea of a baby's omniscience is simply a narrative device that allows her to present her own fresh look at events in an engaging way. Also point out that a first-person narrator is usually not omniscient.

◆ Reading Strategy

2 Question Students may wonder why the baby's condition is presented in such an unappealing way when, generally speaking, an infant's helpless condition is equated with cuteness. *Some students may suggest that this particular baby has been infused with the wisdom of the ages; its frailties, therefore, are described as one might describe those of a very elderly person.*

The First Year of My Life

Muriel Spark

I was born on the first day of the second month of the last year of the First World War, a Friday. Testimony abounds that during the first year of my life I never smiled. I was known as the baby whom nothing and no one could make smile. Everyone who knew me then has told me so. They tried very hard, singing and bouncing me up and down, jumping around, pulling faces. Many times I was told this later by my family and their friends; but, anyway, I knew it at the time.

1 You will shortly be hearing of that new school of psychology, or maybe you have heard of it already, which after long and far-adventuring research and experiment has established that all of the young of the human species are born omniscient. Babies, in their waking hours, know everything that is going on everywhere in the world; they can tune in to any conversation they choose, switch on to any scene. We have all experienced this power. It is only after the first year that it was brainwashed out of us; for it is demanded of us by our immediate environment that we grow to be of use to it in a practical way. Gradually, our know-all brain-cells are blacked out, although traces remain in some individuals in the form of E.S.P., and in the adults of some primitive tribes.

It is not a new theory. Poets and philosophers, as usual, have been there first. But scientific proof is now ready and to hand. Perhaps the final touches are being put to the new manifesto[1] in some cell at Harvard University. Any day now it will be given to the world, and the world will be convinced.

2 Let me therefore get my word in first, because I feel pretty sure, now, about the authenticity of my remembrance of things past. My autobiography, as I very well perceived at the time, started in the very worst year that the world had ever seen so far. Apart from being born bedridden and toothless, unable to raise myself on the pillow or utter anything but farmyard squawks or police-siren wails, my bladder and my bowels totally out of control, I was further depressed by the curious behavior of the two-legged mammals around me. There were those black-dressed people, females of the species to which I appeared to belong, saying they had lost their sons. I slept a great deal. Let them go and find their sons. It was like the special pin for my nappies[2] which my mother or some other hoverer dedicated to my care was always losing. These careless women in black lost their husbands and their brothers. Then they came to visit my mother and clucked and crowed over my cradle. I was not amused.

"Babies never really smile till they're three months old," said my mother. "They're not *supposed* to smile till they're three months old."

My brother, aged six, marched up and down

1. **manifesto** (man´ə fes´ tō) *n.*: Public declaration of motives and intentions.
2. **nappies** (nap´ ēz) *n.*: British term for diapers.

Cross-Curricular Connection: Social Studies

World War I In 1914, a Serbian Nationalist assinated Archduke Francis Ferdinand, of Austro-Hungary, which ruled a restless Serbia struggling for independence. Following the assassination, Austria sent Serbia an ultimatum. Serbia's refusal to comply led Austria, backed by Germany, to declare war. Although at first it seemed this would be a short-lived European war, it was actually the start of World War I. Serbia sought the aid of Russia; Germany declared war on Russia and France, which wanted to avenge its defeat in the Franco-Prussian War. When Germany violated a treaty by invading Belgium, Britain joined the conflict as well. German submarine attacks on merchant and passenger ships traveling in the Atlantic led the United States to enter the war in 1917. The human cost of this war was staggering. Approximately 10 million people died. Double that number had been wounded, many handicapped for life. (Note that Spark's figures on p. 1061 vary somewhat.) The devastation was made even worse by a deadly influenza epidemic that swept the world in 1918, killing more than 20 million people.

with a toy rifle over his shoulder:

The grand old Duke of York
He had ten thousand men;
He marched them up to the top of the hill
And he marched them down again.

3 And when they were up, they were up.
And when they were down, they were down.
And when they were neither down nor up
They were neither up nor down.

"Just listen to him!"

"Look at him with his rifle!"

I was about ten days old when Russia stopped fighting. I tuned in to the Czar,[3] a prisoner, with the rest of his family, since evidently the country had put him off his throne and there had been a revolution not long before I was born. Everyone was talking about it. 4 I tuned in to the Czar. "Nothing would ever induce me to sign the treaty of Brest-Litovsk,"[4] he said to his wife. Anyway, nobody had asked him to.

At this point I was sleeping twenty hours a day to get my strength up. And from what I discerned in the other four hours of the day I knew I was going to need it. The Western Front on my frequency was sheer blood, mud, dismembered bodies, blistered crashes, hectic flashes of light in the night skies, explosions, total terror. Since it was plain I had been born into a bad moment in the history of the world, the future bothered me, unable as I was to raise my head from the pillow and as yet only twenty inches long. 5 "I truly wish I were a fox or a bird," D. H. Lawrence[5] was writing to somebody. . . . I fell asleep.

Red sheets of flame shot across the sky. It was 21 March, the fiftieth day of my life, and the German Spring Offensive[6] had started before my morning feed. Infinite slaughter. I scowled at the scene, and made an effort to kick out. But the attempt was feeble. Furious, and impatient for some strength, I wailed for my feed. After which I stopped wailing but continued to scowl.

The grand old Duke of York
He had ten thousand men . . .

They rocked the cradle. I never heard a sillier song. Over in Berlin and Vienna the people were starving, freezing, striking, rioting and yelling in the streets. In London everyone was bustling to work and muttering that it was time the whole . . . business was over.

The big people around me bared their teeth; that meant a smile, it meant they were pleased or amused. They spoke of ration cards[7] for meat and sugar and butter.

◆ Literary Focus
What elements of omniscient narration can you find in this passage? 6

"Where will it all end?"

I went to sleep. I woke and tuned into Bernard Shaw[8] who was telling someone to shut up. I switched over to Joseph Conrad[9] who, strangely enough, was saying precisely the same thing. I still didn't think it worth a smile, although it was expected of me any day now. I got on to Turkey. Women draped in black huddled and chattered in their harems; yak-yak-yak. This was boring, so I came back to home base.

In and out came and went the women in British black. My mother's brother, dressed in

3. **Czar:** Czar Nicholas II of Russia, who was removed from power during the Russian Revolution of 1917.
4. **treaty of Brest-Litovsk:** Treaty in which Russia's new Communist government made peace with Germany and withdrew from WWI eight months before its end.
5. **D. H. Lawrence:** (1885–1930) English novelist and poet.
6. **German Spring Offensive:** After signing the peace treaty with Russia in March of 1918, Germany began to push to win the war along the western front.
7. **ration cards:** Used to limit individuals' purchases of goods that were in short supply during the war.
8. **Bernard Shaw:** George Bernard Shaw (1856–1950), British dramatist and critic, born in Ireland.
9. **Joseph Conrad:** (1857–1924) English novelist, born in Poland.

◆ Build Vocabulary

omniscient (äm nish´ ənt) *adj.*: Having infinite knowledge; knowing all things

authenticity (ô´ thən tis´ə tē) *n.*: Quality or state of being authentic; genuineness

discerned (di zurnd´) *v.*: Recognized as separate or different

◆ Reading Strategy

3 Question Ask students to explain why Spark has included this song here. *Students may suggest that she is poking fun at one of the follies of war. Like many previous wars, World War I was characterized by the inefficient, even negligent, command of armies by upper-class gentlemen officers who knew little about soldiering and military tactics.*

4 Clarification Make sure students understand that the narrator, in her omniscience, "visits" people and places around the world at will.

◆ Reading Strategy

5 Question Ask students to explain why Spark uses this quotation from D. H. Lawrence here. *Students may suggest that she thinks Lawrence had the right idea: foxes and birds had it better than people during the catastrophe of war, for they could escape it.*

◆ Literary Focus

6 Point of View: Modern Experiments Students may point to the way the narrator jumps back and forth from what is happening within sight of her crib to events taking place all over the world. She seems able to go anywhere and "tune in" on everything.

Cross-Curricular Connection: Social Studies

Child Development
In the story, the all-knowing infant is as astute as the most clever social critic or political columnist. This imagined mental activity is set against a backdrop of realistic developmental stages. While development does vary from individual to individual, psychologists have identified sequential stages of development, and an approximate age range at which they occur. Have students do research to identify these stages and create a chart illustrating the information. Students can present their charts along with a brief oral report outlining how this information might apply to the story.

◆ Literary Focus

❶ **Point of View: Modern Experiments** Guide students to notice that the omniscient point of view allows Spark to contrast the baby's development with events taking place around the world.

◆ Reading Strategy

❷ **Question** Encourage students to ask themselves the following questions: Why do the sentries use dead bodies as barricades? Why does the baby fall asleep listening to the House of Commons? Why does this passage include trivial details about current plays as well as horrifying details from the front? *The sentries use bodies because the dead are so numerous; the speeches in the House of Commons are probably boring; the trivial details show the contrast between what's happening at the front and what people are doing at home.*

▶Critical Viewing◀

❸ **Infer** Students may suggest that the soldiers look both weary and numb. You may wish to point out that this photograph is from 1914, when the full horrors of war were as yet unknown to many; the soldiers' exhaustion may have resulted from a long march rather than from combat.

his uniform, came coughing. He had been poison-gassed in the trenches. *"Tout le monde à la bataille!"*[10] declaimed Marshal Foch[11] the old swine. He was now Commander-in-Chief of the Allied Forces. My uncle coughed from deep within his lungs, never to recover but destined to return to the Front. His brass buttons
❶ gleamed in the firelight. I weighed twelve pounds by now; I stretched and kicked for exercise, seeing that I had a lifetime before me, coping with this crowd. I took six feeds a day and kept most of them down by the time the *Vindictive* was sunk in Ostend harbor,[12] on which day I kicked with special vigor in my bath.

In France the conscripted[13] soldiers leapfrogged over the dead on the advance and littered the fields with limbs and hands, or drowned in the mud. The strongest men on all fronts were dead before I was born. Now the sentries[14] used bodies for barricades and the fighting men were unhealthy from the start. I checked my toes and fingers, knowing I was going to need them. *The Playboy of the Western*
❷ *World* was playing at the Court Theatre in London, but occasionally I beamed over to the House of Commons[15] which made me drop off gently to sleep. Generally, I preferred the Western Front[16] where one got the true state of affairs. It was essential to know the worst, blood and explosions and all, for one had to be prepared, as the boy scouts said. Virginia Woolf[17] yawned and reached for her diary. Really, I preferred the Western Front.

In the fifth month of my life I could raise my head from my pillow and hold it up. I could grasp the objects that were held out to me. Some of these things rattled and squawked. I gnawed on them to get my teeth started. "She hasn't smiled yet?" said the dreary old aunties. My mother, on the defensive, said I was probably one of those late smilers. On my wavelength Pablo Picasso[18] was getting married and early in that month of July the Silver Wedding of King George V and Queen Mary was celebrated in joyous pomp at St. Paul's Cathedral. They drove

▲ **Critical Viewing** This story takes place in 1918, the last year of World War I. Judging by this photograph, would you say the soldiers pictured were excited, weary, or numb? **[Infer]** ❸

10. ***Tout le monde à la bataille*** (tōō lə mônd′ ä lä bä tē′): The whole world into the battle!
11. **Marshal Foch** (fôsh): Ferdinand Foch, a French general who, after March 1918, became commander of all Allied forces on the Western Front.
12. ***Vindictive* was sunk in Ostend harbor:** Referring to a ship sunk in May 1918, by Allied forces, to block the harbor of Ostend, Belgium, used by the Germans as a submarine base.
13. **conscripted** (kən skript′ əd) *adj.*: Enrolled for compulsory service in the armed service.
14. **sentries** (sen′ trēs) *n.*: Men of the military guard.
15. **House of Commons:** Lower house of British Parliament.
16. **Western Front:** 450-mile-long battlefront starting in Belgium and moving across France. This line is where the allies and Germany engaged in trench warfare from 1914 to 1918.
17. **Virginia Woolf:** (1882–1941) English novelist and critic.
18. **Pablo** (pä′ blō) **Picasso** (pi kä′ sō): (1881–1973) Spanish painter and sculptor.

Humanities: Media

War in the Movies

Novelists, poets, and painters were not the only artists who attempted to make some sense of the catastrophe of World War I. Without a single battle scene, Jean Renoir's masterpiece *Grand Illusion* powerfully captures the futility and demoralizing features of the conflict. Other powerful films about the war include *All Quiet on the Western Front* (1930, directed by Lewis Milestone) and *Gallipoli* (1981, directed by Peter Weir). *Gallipoli,* which stars a young Mel Gibson, offers a striking feel for period detail in its depiction of one of the war's most devastating battles. Guide a discussion of how war is portrayed in the media by asking the following question:

What other movies have students seen that depict war? How is war portrayed? *Students may suggest films such as* The Deerhunter, Full Metal Jacket, Glory, *or* In Love and War. *Most of these films portray the horrors of war, but students may also suggest films that portray the glory of war or the loyalties and friendships formed during war.*

through the streets of London with their children. Twenty-five years of domestic happiness. A lot of fuss and ceremonial handing over of swords went on at the Guildhall where the King and Queen received a check for £53,000 to dispose of for charity as they thought fit. *Tout le monde à la bataille!* Income tax in England had reached six shillings in the pound. Everyone was talking about the Silver Wedding; yak-yak-yak, and ten days later the Czar and his family, now in Siberia, were invited to descend to a
4 little room in the basement. Crack, crack, went the guns; screams and blood all over the place, and that was the end of the Romanoffs.[19] I flexed my muscles. "A fine healthy baby," said the doctor; which gave me much satisfaction.

19. **Romanoff** (rō mə nôf′): Name of the ruling family of Russia from 1613 to 1917.

Tout le monde à la bataille! That included my gassed uncle. My health had improved to the point where I was able to crawl in my playpen. Bertrand Russell[20] was still cheerily in prison for writing something seditious about pacifism. Tuning in as usual to the Front Lines it looked as if the Germans were winning all the battles yet losing the war. And so it was. The upper-income people were upset about the income tax at six shillings to the pound. But all women over thirty got the vote. "It seems a long time to wait," said one of my drab old aunts, aged twenty-two. The speeches in the House of Commons always sent me to sleep which was why I missed, at the actual time, a certain
oration by Mr. Asquith[21] following the armistice 6
on 11 November.[22] Mr. Asquith was a greatly esteemed former prime minister later to be an Earl, and had been ousted by Mr. Lloyd George.[23] I clearly heard Asquith, in private, refer to Lloyd George as "that . . . Welsh goat."

◆ **Reading Strategy** How would you describe the narrator's tone up to this point in the story? 5

The armistice was signed and I was awake for that. I pulled myself on to my feet with the aid of the bars of my cot. My teeth were coming through very nicely in my opinion, and well worth all the trouble I was put to in bringing them forth. I weighed twenty pounds. On all the world's fighting fronts the men killed in action or dead of wounds numbered 8,538,315 and the warriors wounded and maimed were
21,219,452. With these figures in mind I sat 7
up in my high chair and banged my spoon on the table. One of my mother's black-draped friends recited:

I have a rendezvous with Death
At some disputed barricade,
When spring comes back with rustling shade
And apple blossoms fill the air—
I have a rendezvous with Death.[24]

20. **Bertrand Russell:** (1872–1970) British philosopher, mathematician, and writer.
21. **Mr. Asquith** (as′kwith): Henry Herbert Asquith (1852–1928), Prime Minister of Britain from 1908–1916.
22. **armistice on 11 November:** The agreement that brought World War I to an end.
23. **Mr. Lloyd George:** David Lloyd George (1863–1945), British Prime Minister from 1916 to 1922.
24. ***I . . . Death***: From the poem "I Have a Rendezvous with Death" by American poet Alan Seeger, killed in war.

◆ Background for Understanding

4 History: Spark's Allusions to World War I Inform students that the event described here is the assassination by the Bolsheviks of Czar Nicholas II and his family. The murderers then burned the bodies and buried them in a nearby forest. It was not until 1994 that the remains of the Romanoffs were positively identified.

◆ Reading Strategy

5 Question Students may suggest that the narrator's tone is deliberately light and humorous, making what is grim seem almost comical.

◆ Background for Understanding

6 History: Spark's Allusions to World War I Point out to students that November 11, once known as Armistice Day, now is called Veteran's Day.

◆ Reading Strategy

7 Question Have students ask themselves why Spark talks about these enormous casualties just after giving her own weight. *The odd contrast between these two statistics points up the horror of the war. It emphasizes how opposed to life and normal development war is.*

Cross-Curricular Connection: Math

Statistical Analysis Muriel Spark presents the staggering casualty totals for World War I: about 8.5 million dead and 21 million wounded. (These vary somewhat from figures given in other sources.) Have groups of students do research to verify these figures compare them to the totals for World War II and for other wars in which American troops participated, such as the Vietnam War, the Korean War, and the American Civil War. In addition, have them find out the number of American casualties in all these wars.

Have groups record and analyze their data, compare their data using graphs and charts, and then present and summarize their findings. *Students may be surprised to learn that more Americans died in the Civil War than in all the other wars put together. They will learn that European losses, particularly on the part of Russia and Germany, dwarfed American losses in both world wars.*

▶Critical Viewing◀

❶ **Evaluate** Students may say that the one-year-old seems babylike in that she sits on a table, is dressed like a baby, and is fascinated by a cake with a candle in it. They may suggest that she is adult-like in that she does not grab for the cake.

◆ Literary Focus

❷ **Point of View: Modern Experiments** Guide students to notice the omniscient narration here, as the scene moves from the narraror's birthday party to distant social events attended by Mr. Asquith. Ask students what they think Spark intends by this technique. *Spark does not portray Mr. Asquith in a favorable light. He seems to behave no better than a child at parties, in spite of the responsibility he carries.*

◀ **Critical Viewing** This story is narrated by a one-year-old girl who has an adult attitude about the bloodshed and devastation caused by World War I. Does the one-year-old in this photograph seem babylike or mature to you? Explain. **[Evaluate]** ❶

Most of the poets, they said, had been killed. The poetry made them dab their eyes with clean white handkerchiefs.

Next February on my first birthday, there was a birthday-cake with one candle. Lots of children and their elders. The war had been over two months and twenty-one days. "Why doesn't she smile?" My brother was to blow out the candle. The elders were talking about the war and the political situation. Lloyd George and Asquith, Asquith and Lloyd George. I remembered recently having switched on to Mr. Asquith at a private party where he had been ❷ drinking a lot. He was playing cards and when he came to cut the cards he tried to cut a large box of matches by mistake. On another occasion I had seen him putting his arm around a lady's shoulder in a Daimler motor car, and generally behaving towards her in a very friendly fashion. Strangely enough she said, "If you don't stop this nonsense immediately, I'll order the chauffeur to stop and I'll get out." Mr. Asquith replied, "And pray, what reason will you give?" Well anyway it was my feeding time.

The guests arrived for my birthday. It was so sad, said one of the black widows, so sad about Wilfred Owen[25] who was killed so late in the war, and she quoted from a poem of his: ❷

What passing-bells for these who die
as cattle?
Only the monstrous anger of the guns.[26]

The children were squealing and toddling around. One was sick and another wet the floor and stood with his legs apart gaping at the puddle. All was mopped up. I banged my spoon on the table of my high chair.

But I've a rendezvous with Death
At midnight in some flaming town;
When spring trips north again this year,
And I to my pledged word am true,
I shall not fail that rendezvous.

25. Wilfred Owen: (1893–1918) English poet.

***26. What . . . guns*:** From Wilfred Owen's "Anthem for Doomed Youth" (see p. 963).

Speaking and Listening Mini-Lesson

Oral Interpretation

This mini-lesson supports the Speaking and Listening activity in the Idea Bank on p. 1065.

Introduce the Concept Tell students that they are to select one of the two stories and read all or part of it aloud to the class. Inform them that their presentations will be judged according to how well they express the author's style and message. Guide them to pay particular attention to volume, rate, pitch, and tone of voice when determining how to offer the most effective presentation.

Develop Background Have students select the story or part of a story to read. Guide them to figure out how the author herself would present it, noting the distinct differences between the dry wit of the omniscient infant in the Spark story and the detached narration of whoever is looking in the mirror in the Woolf piece. Have students practice their delivery. Invite them to do so in front of others to get reactions. Students may benefit from taping themselves and listening critically to the recording.

Apply the Information Ask students to make their presentations. Guide listeners to be polite, respectful, and supportive, much as theatergoers would be.

Assess the Outcome Have students assess the oral interpretations by using the Peer Assessment: Oral Interpretation Rubric, p. 120, in the ***Alternative Assessment*** booklet.

> **◆ Reading Strategy**
> Why do you think the narrator quotes from this poem again?

3 More parents and children arrived. One stout man who was warming his behind at the fire, said, "I always think those words of Asquith's after the armistice were so apt. . . ."

They brought the cake close to my high chair for me to see, with the candle shining and flickering above the pink icing. "A pity she never smiles."

"She'll smile in time," my mother said, obviously upset.

"What Asquith told the House of Commons just after the war," said that stout gentleman with his backside to the fire, "—so apt, what Asquith said. He said that the war has cleansed and purged the world. . . . I recall his actual words: 'All things have become new. In this great cleansing and purging it has been the privilege of our country to play her part. . . .'"

That did it. I broke into a decided smile and everyone noticed it, convinced that it was provoked by the fact that my brother had blown out the candle on the cake. "She smiled!" my mother exclaimed. And everyone was clucking away about how I was smiling. For good measure I crowed like a demented raven. "My baby's smiling," said my mother. 4

"It was the candle on her cake," they said.

. . . . Since that time I have grown to smile quite naturally, like any other healthy and house-trained person, but when I really mean a smile, deeply felt from the core, then to all intents and purposes it comes in response to the words uttered in the House of Commons after the First World War by the distinguished, the immaculately dressed and the late Mr. Asquith.

Guide for Responding

◆ Literature and Your Life

Reader's Response Did you find this story amusing, sad, or a combination of the two? Explain.

Thematic Focus In what way does Mr. Asquith's speech about the war reveal that he has not woken from a dream?

Interview Interview a classmate about his or her first year of life. Encourage your classmate to sort out what he or she has been told from actual recollections. Then reverse roles.

☑ Check Your Comprehension

1. What worldwide crisis corresponds with the first year of the narrator's life?
2. What special power does the narrator possess?
3. Briefly describe two examples that show the narrator's power.
4. (a) When does the narrator smile for the first time? (b) How do the guests explain this smile? (c) What is it that actually causes the narrator to smile?

◆ Critical Thinking

INTERPRET

1. (a) Sum up what you learn about the war from the narrator's "news briefs." (b) What do you learn about the war from the poems? **[Infer]**
2. Given the state of the world, what is amusing or surprising about the concern over the narrator's smile? **[Connect]**
3. What statement is the narrator making with her smile at the end of the story? **[Interpret]**
4. Summarize the central message of this story. **[Draw Conclusions]**

APPLY

5. How would the story have been different if it had been told by an adult? **[Speculate]**

EXTEND

6. Do you think the message about war in this story is relevant today? Explain. **[Social Studies Link]**

Beyond the Selection

FURTHER READING

Other Works by Muriel Spark

The Comforters; The Prime of Miss Jean Brodie; The Girls of Slender Means; The Mandelbaum Gate

Other Works About World War I

All Quiet on the Western Front, Erich Maria Remarque
The Guns of August, Barbara Tuchman
The Great War and Modern Memory, Paul Fussell
"Anthem for Doomed Youth," Wilfred Owen

INTERNET

For biographical information on Muriel Spark and brief synopses of her works, go to **http://www. futurenet.co.uk/penguin/books/0140123113.html**

Please be aware, however, that sites may have changed since this information was published. We *strongly recommend* that you preview sites before you send students to them.

◆ Reading Strategy

3 Question She quotes again from Alan Seeger's poem to express her feelings about the horrors of war.

◆ Reading Strategy

4 Question Have students ask, "Why does the baby smile?" *The baby smiles at the foolishness and irony of the politician's words.*

Reinforce and Extend

Answers

◆ Literature and Your Life

Reader's Response Students are likely to respond that the story is both amusing and sad. Have them cite details to support their points.

Thematic Focus Asquith's words show that he is still deluding himself about the effects of the war.

☑ Check Your Comprehension

1. World War I is in its final year.
2. The narrator can "tune in" on what is happening everywhere.
3. The narrator can view events as diverse as the German Spring Offensive and the offensive party behavior of Asquith.
4. (a) She smiles at her first birthday party. (b) The guests think she smiles at the candle on her cake. (c) Asquith's ludicrous remarks cause her to smile.

◆ Critical Thinking

1. (a) From the news briefs, we learn how the war is affecting soldiers and civilians alike. (b) From the poems we learn of the terror and the inevitability of death on the battlefield.
2. Given the sorry state of the world, that concern is ludicrous but perhaps understandable.
3. The narrator realizes that the Prime Minister's foolish remarks prove that nothing has been gained by all the destruction.
4. War is both horrible and futile and the lack of understanding of its causes and effects dooms humankind to suffer it interminably.
5. If told by an adult the story may have lacked the effective contrasts between a child's development and war's destruction. Students should recognize that Spark's message about war's horrors is still relevant.

◆ Literary Focus

Point of View: Modern Experiments

1. The narrator notices one of Isabella's possessions after the next and, in a stream-of-consciousness manner, makes inferences about her from them. In one passage, for example, she presents a picture of Isabella gleaned from looking at her rugs, chairs, and cabinets. When the mail is delivered, the narrator reflects on that.
2. (a) The narrator's fanciful reflections on Isabella's character end suddenly as Isabella appears in the mirror. (b) The climax reveals that Isabella is nothing like the person the narrator has imagined her to be; she is devoid of feeling, lonely, and unattached to anyone or anything.
3. Spark gets readers to accept her unusual point of view with her wit; she humorously claims that research has verified infant omniscience.
4. Sample answer: When she is ten days old, Russia stops fighting the Germans, its internal struggle intensifies; when her weight reaches twenty pounds, she presents the "heavy" casualty figures from the war.

◆ Reading Strategy

Question

1. One might ask precisely who the narrator is, why she is in Isabella's house, and what relationship she has to Isabella.
2. (a) Students might wonder what exactly the Prime Minister means by his remark and why it is that these comments cause the narrator to smile for the first time. (b) By examining Asquith's statement and the narrator's reaction to it, students can appreciate the author's message about the folly and futility of war.

Guide for Responding (continued)

◆ Literary Focus

Point of View: Modern Experiments

These authors experiment with **point of view**, the perspective from which they tell their stories, in order to surprise you into new insights. By immersing you in a narrator's **stream of consciousness**, Woolf makes you aware of your own random flow of thoughts. She also contrasts the fullness of the narrator's speculations about Isabella with the emptiness of Isabella's own mind. Reflected in the mirror of the narrator's thoughts, Isabella's material wealth becomes a sign of inner poverty.

Spark gets you to think about the war differently by reinventing herself as an **omniscient** baby who knows "everything." This device allows her to contrast the normal development of a baby with the abnormal destruction of war.

1. Using specific examples, show how Woolf's narrative is more a series of mental impressions than a chain of events in a normal plot.
2. (a) How does the literal reflection of Isabella in the mirror serve as a climax for the narrator's mental reflections? (b) What does this climax reveal about Isabella?
3. At the beginning of her story, how does Spark get you to accept her unusual point of view?
4. Find two examples in Spark's story where the baby's healthy development underscores the death and destruction going on in the world.

◆ Reading Strategy

Question

Pausing to **question** as you read will help you understand works of literature, especially experimental stories like Woolf's or Spark's. Two types of questions relate to *who* is narrating a story and *why* the narrator emphasizes an incident. The first type of question helps you orient yourself in a story and the second points you toward its meaning.

1. In Woolf's story, what questions about the narrator might you ask after reading the beginnings of the second and fourth paragraphs?
2. (a) What questions arise from the final paragraph of Spark's story? (b) Show how these questions lead you toward the story's meaning.

◆ Build Vocabulary

Using the Word Root *-trans-*

Use your knowledge of the Latin root *-trans-* ("through or across") to guess what each of these companies or organizations does:

1. Transatlantic Shipping
2. City of Boston Mass Transit
3. Transitions to New Careers
4. Translations: German-English, English-German
5. Hotel for Transients

Using the Word Bank

On your paper, fill in each blank with the most suitable word from the Word Bank.

The ___?___ baby in Spark's story knew about everything. She may have been ___?___ with regard to her power, not telling the adults, but there is no doubt as to the ___?___ of her abilities. She could ___?___ events on remote battlefields, no matter how ___?___ they were. The ___?___ of human interactions, whether kisses or ___?___, did not protect them from her knowledge. She ___?___ with joy as she exercised her powers.

◆ Grammar and Style

Subject-Verb Agreement in Inverted Sentences

In inverted sentences, which often begin with *here* or *there*, the verb precedes the subject. However, the verb must still **agree** in number with its subject. Don't be misled into thinking that the subject is *here, there*, or any of the nouns or pronouns preceding the verb.

Practice On your paper, identify the subject in each sentence and choose the correct verb for it.

1. There (was, were) a perpetual sighing and ceasing sound.
2. In each of these cabinets (was, were) many little drawers.
3. There (was, were) her gray-green dress, and her long shoes, her basket, and something sparkling at her throat.
4. There (was, were) those people in black.
5. Next February on my first birthday, there (was, were) a birthday cake with one candle.

◆ Build Vocabulary

Using the Word Root *-trans-*

1. It delivers goods by boat across the Atlantic Ocean.
2. It handles bus, subway, train, and other public means of travel through the city of Boston.
3. It helps people cross from one career to another.
4. It provides English versions of German texts and German versions of English texts (taking meanings across languages).
5. It houses people who are just passing through and will quickly move on.

Using the Word Bank

omniscient; reticent; authenticity; discern; evanescent; transience; upbraidings; suffused

◆ Grammar and Style

Subject-Verb Agreement in Inverted Sentences

1. was; 2. were; 3. were; 4. were; 5. was

Writer's Solution

For additional instruction and practice, use the Agreement in Number and Special Problems in Agreement units in the **Language Lab CD-ROM,** and the page on Subject-Verb Agreement, p. 63, in the *Writer's Solution Grammar Practice Book.*

Build Your Portfolio

Idea Bank

Writing

1. **Letter to the Author** Write a letter to either author responding to the unusual point of view in her story. Let her know your impressions of her narrative technique.
2. **Stream-of-Consciousness Narrative** List the contents of your own or a fictional character's room. Then write a brief stream-of-consciousness narrative about the room and its owner.
3. **Response to Criticism** Woolf has said, "The mind receives a myriad of impressions—trivial, fantastic, evanescent, or engraved with the sharpness of steel." In an essay, discuss how this observation relates to "The Lady in the Looking Glass."

Speaking and Listening

4. **Poetry Reading** Read aloud some poems that focus on World War I. Include poems by Alan Seeger and Wilfred Owen, whose work appears in Spark's story. **[Performing Arts Link]**
5. **Oral Interpretation** Choose one of these stories, and practice reading part or all of it aloud. Pay special attention to volume, rate, pitch, and tone of voice. Perform your oral interpretation for classmates. **[Performing Arts Link]**

Projects

6. **Report on World War I** Research the last year of World War I, referred to in Spark's story. Using maps, report to your classmates on the key developments of this year. **[Social Studies Link]**
7. **Freudian Psychology and Fiction** Freud used free association in therapy before Woolf wrote her stream-of-consciousness narratives. Research Freud's method, then compare and contrast it with Woolf's device. **[Science Link]**

Writing Mini-Lesson

Narrative From an Unusual Perspective

In Muriel Spark's story, the omniscient infant narrator can "tune in" to people and events all over the world. Imitate Spark and write a narrative from the perspective of an omniscient one-year-old, either yourself or a fictional character. Like Spark, combine realistic details of a baby's life with current events of the time. Keep readers involved by creating suspense about the outcome of your "autobiography."

Writing Skills Focus: Suspense

Suspense is a feeling of growing curiosity or anxiety about the outcome of events in a narrative. To create suspense, writers play a cat-and-mouse game with readers. Spark, for example, keeps you guessing about whether the baby will smile. She finally answers the question, but with a surprising twist. You can also plant questions in the reader's mind about the outcome. Further, you can hint at the ending without giving it away—just enough to make readers nervous about it.

Prewriting Picture babies you know. What physical limitations and communication barriers will the baby-narrator encounter? Think of a realistic goal the narrator can strive for, one that will keep readers in suspense. Also, include suspenseful world events from the first year of this baby's life.

Drafting Remember that a good narrative involves a conflict (the war in Spark's tale) and rises to a climax, or turning point (the birthday party in Spark's story). Keep readers in suspense until the climax, and alternate between descriptions of the baby's life and accounts of outside events.

Revising Have a friend who knows about babies review your account and suggest ways to make it more realistic. Also, rewrite or remove any passages that reveal too much of the outcome before the climax. Only hints at the ending should remain.

✓ ASSESSMENT OPTIONS

Formal Assessment, Selection Test, pp. 274–276, and Assessment Resources Software. The selection test is designed so that it can be easily customized to the performance levels of your students.

Alternative Assessment, p. 57, includes options for less advanced students, more advanced students, musical/rhythmic learners, verbal/linguistic learners, and visual/spatial learners.

PORTFOLIO ASSESSMENT

Use the following rubrics in the ***Alternative Assessment*** booklet to assess student writing:
Letter to the Author: Response to Literature Rubric, p. 111
Stream-Of-Consciousness Narrative: Fictional Narrative Rubric, p. 96
Response to Criticism: Literary Analysis Rubric, p. 113
Writing Mini-Lesson: Fictional Narrative Rubric, p. 96

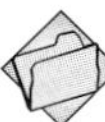

Idea Bank

Customizing for
Performance Levels

Following are suggestions for matching Idea Bank topics with your students' performance levels:
- Less Advanced Students: 1, 4
- Average Students: 2, 5, 6
- More Advanced Students: 3, 5, 6, 7

Customizing for
Learning Modalities

Following are suggestions for matching Idea Bank topics with your students' learning modalities:
- Visual/Spatial: 6
- Verbal Linguistic: 1, 2, 3, 4, 5, 7
- Intrapersonal: 1, 2, 4

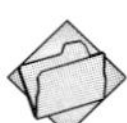

Writing Mini-Lesson

Refer students to the Writing Process Handbook, page 1189, for instruction on the writing process, and page 1191 for further information on Narration.

Writer's Solution

Writers at Work Videodisc
Have students view the videodisc segment Narration (Ch. 2), featuring James Berry, to see how he develops narrative elements.

Play frames 15185 to 17838

Writing Lab CD-ROM
Have students complete the tutorial on Narration. Follow these steps:
1. Have students use the interactive Story Line Diagram to outline the key events of their narratives.
2. Encourage students to view the audio-annotated Literary Models showing different points of view.
3. Allow time for students to draft on the computer.
4. Suggest that students use the tips for publishing a class anthology.

Sourcebook
Have students use Chapter 2, Narration (pp. 30–61), for additional support. The chapter includes in-depth instruction on developing a point of view and writing a specialized narrative (pp. 49–50).

Prepare and Engage

OBJECTIVES

1. To read, comprehend, and interpret short stories
2. To relate short stories to personal experience
3. To identify with a character in a short story
4. To analyze theme
5. To build vocabulary in context and learn the prefix *ob-*
6. To develop skill in using the subjunctive mood
7. To write a product description
8. To respond to the short stories through writing, speaking and listening, and projects

SKILLS INSTRUCTION

Vocabulary:
Prefixes: *ob-*

Grammar:
Subjunctive Mood

Reading Strategy:
Identify With a Character

Literary Focus:
Theme

Writing:
Climax and Resolution

Speaking and Listening:
Soliloquy (teacher edition)

Critical Viewing:
Interpret; Classify; Evaluate

PORTFOLIO OPPORTUNITIES

Writing: Notes for a Screenplay; Retelling a Passage; Response to Criticism

Writing Mini-Lesson: Product Description

Speaking and Listening: Soliloquy; Discussion Group

Projects: Social Research; Multimedia Travelogue

More About the Authors

D. H. Lawrence was known to have had a stormy temperament, which may have developed during a childhood marked by illness, poverty, constant bickering between his ill-suited parents, and his mother's driving ambition to keep her son in school and away from mining.

Novelist and playwright **Henry Graham Greene** was fascinated by danger and the contradictions he imagined on the seedy edges of society: a tender killer or an honest robber, for example. Yet, despite his absorption with weighty issues, he demonstrated a playful sense of humor and was an active practical joker all of his life.

Guide for Interpreting

D. H. Lawrence *(1885–1930)*

During his lifetime, D. H. Lawrence's literary achievements were overshadowed by explosive controversy. Like Shelley and Byron in their day, Lawrence took unorthodox positions on politics, society and morality.

Early Years David Herbert Lawrence was born in Eastwood, Nottinghamshire, the son of a coal miner. After attending local schools, Lawrence spent several years as a teacher. In 1913, he published his first major novel, *Sons and Lovers,* a thinly disguised autobiography. Two years later, *The Rainbow* (1915) was published.

Travels Abroad At the end of World War I, Lawrence and his wife, Frieda, traveled to Italy, Ceylon, Australia, Mexico, and the United States, and he later used many of these locales in his fiction. In 1921, while away from England, one of his greatest novels, *Women in Love,* was finally published. Ill from tuberculosis, Lawrence completed *Lady Chatterley's Lover* (1928), while living in Italy.

In over half a century since his death, society's views on Lawrence's writings have changed profoundly. Today his fiction is universally admired for its vivid settings, fine craftsmanship, and psychological insight.

Graham Greene *(1904–1991)*

The search for a source of inner peace, launched by such poets as Yeats and Eliot, continues in the novels and short stories of Graham Greene. A religious convert like Eliot, Greene wrote of pain, fear, despair, and alienation.

Reporting and Travel The son of a schoolmaster, Greene was born in Berkhamsted in Hertfordshire. Much of his early life was spent as a journalist and travel writer, and he developed the powers of observation, sensitivity to atmosphere, and simplicity of language that became hallmarks of his fiction. His trips to Africa inspired travelogues as well as two novels, *The Heart of the Matter* (1948) and *A Burnt-Out Case* (1961).

Psychological Insight Greene wrote children's books, as well as adventure stories, thrillers, and film scripts. However, his literary fiction focuses on the psychology of human character, rather than on plot. Many of his protagonists are people without roots or beliefs—people in pain. The characters in a Greene story are often unlikeable, but they almost always excite the reader's curiosity and pity—and, almost always, Greene treats them with compassion.

◆ Background for Understanding

CULTURE: WEALTH AND SOCIAL STATUS

The stories that follow touch on the subject of wealth. The British elite maintained their position by living at the "right addresses," attending the "right schools," and having the "right friends."

In "The Rocking-Horse Winner," Lawrence emphasizes the mother's persistent drive to live in style, despite the family's modest income. This need for wealth turns the house into a whispering gallery of voices: "There *must* be more money!"

Greene's "A Shocking Accident" concerns the fate of Jerome, whom we meet at "a rather expensive preparatory school." Because of the ludicrous way in which his father dies, Jerome faces ridicule from classmates and, later, from others who will not tolerate such abnormal occurrences.

Lawrence's story features "old money" and Greene's features more newly-acquired wealth, but, in both stories, money determines fate.

Prentice Hall Literature Program Resources

REINFORCE / RETEACH / EXTEND

Selection Support Pages
Build Vocabulary: Prefixes: *ob-*, p. 275
Grammar and Style: Subjunctive Mood, p. 276
Reading Strategy: Identify With a Character, p. 277
Literary Focus: Theme, p. 278

Strategies for Diverse Student Needs, p. 58

Beyond Literature
Humanities Connection: Greek Notion of Fate, p. 58

Formal Assessment Selection Test, pp. 277–279; Assessment Resources Software

Alternative Assessment, p. 58

Writing and Language Transparencies
Writing Process Model 2: Descriptive and Observational Writing

Resource Pro CD-ROM
"The Rocking-Horse Winner," "A Shocking Accident"—includes all resource material and customizable lesson plan

Listening to Literature Audiocassettes
"The Rocking-Horse Winner"; "A Shocking Accident"

The Rocking-Horse Winner
◆ A Shocking Accident ◆

◆ Literature and Your Life

CONNECT YOUR EXPERIENCE

Have you ever had a relationship with someone who understood you completely? In each of these stories, the protagonist finds such a relationship. Paul in "The Rocking-Horse Winner" enjoys a special alliance with the gardener, and Jerome in "A Shocking Accident" discovers the healing power of having a true soul mate.

Journal Writing On a page in your journal, list several qualities that you value in a friend.

THEMATIC FOCUS: CONFLICTS AT HOME AND ABROAD

Although much of early twentieth-century literature is about war and its effects, some writers, like D. H. Lawrence and Graham Greene, explored conflicts at home in stories such as the following.

◆ Literary Focus

THEME

Most short stories contain a **theme,** or central idea, that the writer explores. One way in which a theme can be revealed is through symbols. A **symbol** is anything that represents something else. For example, a mask may symbolize deception or falsehood. As you read Lawrence's story, think about the symbolic meaning of the rocking horse.

Greene's "A Shocking Accident" highlights life's **absurdity**—the notion that human existence is irrational or meaningless. As you read the story, notice the ways in which Greene conveys his belief that life is absurd.

◆ Reading Strategy

IDENTIFY WITH A CHARACTER

In order to understand the author's purpose and the overall theme of a literary work, it helps to **identify with a character**—to put yourself in that character's place so you can truly understand his or her thoughts, feelings, problems, and motivations. When you identify with a character, you may feel as if you *are* that character. As you read these stories, for example, you may feel the anxiety of Paul in "The Rocking-Horse Winner" or the distress and embarrassment of Jerome in "A Shocking Accident."

◆ Build Vocabulary

PREFIXES: *ob-*

In "The Rocking-Horse Winner," you will encounter the word *obstinately.* The word contains the Latin prefix *ob-* which means "against, to, before, or on account of." *Obstinately* means "as if standing against" or "in an opposing manner"—"stubbornly."

WORD BANK

Before you read, preview this list of words from the stories.

discreet
brazening
careered
obstinately
uncanny
remonstrated
apprehension
embarked
intrinsically

◆ Grammar and Style

SUBJUNCTIVE MOOD

The **subjunctive mood** of a verb is used to state a wish or condition contrary to fact. It is most commonly expressed using the verb *were.* For example, in "The Rocking-Horse Winner," Paul's mother says to her son:

> If you *were* me and I *were* you . . . I wonder what we should do!

As you read, look for other examples of the subjunctive mood.

Preparing for Standardized Tests

Reading and Vocabulary Building vocabulary by using word parts to infer the meanings of unfamiliar words can help students to improve performance on the verbal portions of tests—both reading comprehension and vocabulary items. The Build Vocabulary Skills lesson focuses on the prefix *ob-*. Students can use this prefix to determine the meaning of words—such as *obdurate, obligatory, obliteration; obloquy,* or *obviate*—they encounter in critical reading passages. For additional practice, use the Build Vocabulary page in ***Selection Support,*** p. 275.

Grammar and Language Portions of some standardized tests require students to choose the best way to express a thought or idea. Being able to identify and correctly use the subjunctive mood will help students on questions like the following: B

Paul rode him as if <u>he was</u> a thoroughbred.

A. NO CHANGE C. he is
B. he were D. he be

The Grammar and Style lesson for this selection focuses on this topic. For additional practice, use the Grammar and Style page on subjunctive mood, p. 276, in ***Selection Support.***

Interest Grabber Before assigning the D. H. Lawrence story, write down a number between one and ten without letting students see your choice. Then ask students to guess the number you selected and record their guess on a slip of paper. Collect the slips and tally all responses on the chalkboard. Then reveal the number you wrote. How many guessed correctly? If any did, have them tell how they made their choice—luck? intuition? chance? Lead a discussion in which students share their ideas about the role of luck and chance in their lives. Then tell students that luck and chance play a very important role in these two stories.

Customize for
Less Proficient Readers
These students may need assistance with unfamiliar cultural references. In addition, you may need to guide these students to understand that the whispering is not really in the house but in the children's minds.

Customize for
More Advanced Students
Throughout his story, Lawrence describes changes in Paul's eyes. Guide students to look for these descriptions and for the ways in which they mirror emotional or psychological changes in the character.

Customize for
English Language Learners
You may want to prepare these students by giving them the meanings of unfamiliar words or familiar words used in unfamiliar ways. Examples are *Mad* (crazy), p1070, col. 2; and *go down* (lose), p.1073, col. 2; *writs* ("legal documents ordering the payment of debts"), p. 1074, col. 1.

Customize for
Logical/Mathematical Learners
In the Lawrence story, a small boy has the uncanny power of being able to choose a winner; to "play the odds." Have students calculate the odds of choosing the winning horse in a field of ten, completely by chance.

Develop Understanding

One-Minute Insight In this parable about the ill effects of greed, a family is in constant need of money; at least that is what the cold and greedy mother tells her impressionable son. She says that having money is a matter of being lucky. Eager to please his mother and help her obtain the wealth she desires, the boy sets out to prove that he is lucky. His ability to choose winning race horses, and the price he pays for this ability, will lead students to analyze their own ideas about luck and money.

◆ Literary Focus

❶ **Theme** Point out that the opening of this story resembles the conventional opening of a fairy tale. Ask students to predict the lesson that will be taught. *Some students may guess that a mother who doesn't love her children will experience some kind of setback, that she will not be the "winner" referred to in the title.*

◆ Reading Strategy

❷ **Identify With a Character** Ask students to tell how the children know their mother doesn't love them. *Students may say that children can sense things, even unspoken feelings.*

◆ Background for Understanding

❸ **Culture: Wealth and Social Status** Guide students to understand that the "small income" each parent receives is an annuity, the result of being born into families of wealth. The mother yearns for the trappings of wealth and believes they are her due.

◆ Critical Thinking

❹ **Infer** Have students discuss what they have inferred about this family so far. *They can infer that the parents, the mother in particular, are greedy social snobs from wealthy families, but are not financially successful on their own.*

The Rocking-Horse Winner

D. H. Lawrence

There was a woman who was beautiful, who started with all the advantages, yet she had no luck. She
❶ married for love, and the love turned to dust. She had bonny children, yet she felt they had been thrust upon her, and she could not love them. They looked at her coldly, as if they were finding fault with her. And hurriedly she felt she must cover up some fault in herself. Yet what it was that she must cover up she never knew. Nevertheless, when her children were present, she always felt the center of her heart go hard. This troubled her, and in her manner she was all the more gentle and anxious for her children, as if she loved them very much. Only she herself knew that at the center of her heart was a hard little place that could not feel love, no, not for anybody. Everybody else said of her: "She is such a good mother. She adores her children." Only she herself, and her children themselves,
❷ knew it was not so. They read it in each other's eyes.

There were a boy and two little girls. They lived in a pleasant house, with a garden and they had discreet servants, and felt themselves superior to anyone in the neighborhood.

Although they lived in style, they felt always an anxiety in the house. There was never enough money. The mother had a small income
and the father had a small income, but not ❸
nearly enough for the social position which they had to keep up. The father went into town to some office. But though he had good prospects, these prospects never materialized. There
was always the grinding sense of the ❹
shortage of money, though the style was always kept up.

At last the mother said, "I will see if *I* can't make something." But she did not know where to begin. She racked her brains, and tried this thing and the other, but could not find anything successful. The failure made deep lines come into her face. Her children were growing up, they would have to go to school. There must be more money, there must be more money. The father, who was

◆ Build Vocabulary

discreet (dis krēt′) *adj.*: Wise; prudent

Block Scheduling Strategies

Consider these suggestions to take advantage of extended class time:

- Introduce the story with the Interest Grabber provided in the ATE (p. 1067) and discuss the role of chance, luck, and intuition in making a good guess.
- Discuss the Reading Strategy (p. 1067) with students to prepare them for the story. Tell students to apply the strategy as they read, then assign the Reading Strategy page in ***Selection Support*** (p. 277).
- Have students work in discussion groups to answer the Critical Thinking questions (p. 1077).
- Allow time for interested students to research D. H. Lawrence on the Internet either before or after their read.
- Have students work in small groups to complete one of the projects or speaking and listening activities listed on page 1083.

always very handsome and expensive in his tastes, seemed as if he never *would* be able to do anything worth doing. And the mother, who had a great belief in herself, did not succeed any better, and her tastes were just as expensive.

And so the house came to be haunted by the unspoken phrase: *There must be more money! There must be more money!* The children could hear it all the time, though nobody said it aloud. They heard it at Christmas, when the expensive and splendid toys filled the nursery. Behind the shining modern rocking horse, behind the smart doll's house, a voice would start whispering: "There *must* be more money! There *must* be
5 more money!" And the children would stop playing, to listen for a moment. They would look into each other's eyes to see if they had all heard. And each one saw in the eyes of the other two that they too had heard. "There *must* be more money! There *must* be more money!"

It came whispering from the springs of the still-swaying rocking horse, and even the horse, bending his wooden, champing head, heard it. The big doll, sitting so pink and smirking in her new pram,[1] could hear it quite plainly, and seemed to be smirking all the more self-consciously because of it. The foolish puppy, too, that took the place of the teddy bear, he was looking so extraordinarily foolish for no other reason but that he heard the secret whisper all over the house: "There *must* be more money."

Yet nobody ever said it aloud. The whisper was everywhere, and therefore no one spoke it. Just as no one ever says: "We are breathing!" in spite of the fact that breath is coming and going all the time.

"Mother!" said the boy Paul one day. "Why don't we keep a car of our own? Why do we always use uncle's, or else a taxi?"

"Because we're the poor members of the family," said the mother.

"But why *are* we, mother?"

"Well—I suppose," she said slowly and
bitterly, "it's because your father has no luck." 6

The boy was silent for some time.

"Is luck money, mother?" he asked, rather timidly.

▲ **Critical Viewing** Lawrence's story comments on the unseen conflicts at work within a seemingly happy family. What aspects of this photograph seem too good to be true? **[Interpret]** 7

1. **pram:** Baby carriage.

◆ Literary Focus

5 Theme Discuss with students that the whispering is a sign of the family's desperation, but may also be seen as symbolic of the downturn in the fortunes of the vast but overextended British Empire.

◆ Reading Strategy

6 Identify With a Character Have students put themselves in the mother's place for a moment. Ask them to explain why she is so bitter. *Students may suggest that because she grew up living in a certain style, it is difficult for her to adjust to a more modest financial status.*

▶Critical Viewing◀

7 Interpret Students may suggest that although this appears to be a candid shot, it is unlikely that both small children would be so neatly dressed with hair combed and smiling faces if they had not been prepared for this shot. Other students may notice that it can't be coincidence that each face is framed in a pane of glass; no one's face is obscured by the wood casings.

◆ *Literature and Your Life*

❶ Have students respond to the mother's definition of luck. Ask them if they agree. *Students should support their answers with reasons and examples from life, literature, movies, or current events.*

◆ Reading Strategy

❷ **Identify With a Character** Most students will probably feel that a child will take this exchange to heart and look for ways to bring luck to his family.

◆ Critical Thinking

❸ **Predict** Ask students to consider the information Paul has just received from his mother and predict what he will do. *Students may predict that Paul will do something to prove that he is lucky, or to get money somehow.*

◆ Reading Strategy

❹ **Identify With a Character** Discuss with students what we can infer from Paul's frenzied riding. Ask them why he so badly wants to find luck. *Students may say that Paul believes deeply that it is his responsibility to get money for his mother, and therefore he needs to prove that he is lucky. Some may suggest that Paul desperately wants his mother to love him and believes that she will if he is lucky.*

"No, Paul! Not quite. It's what causes you to have money."

"Oh!" said Paul vaguely. "I thought when Uncle Oscar said *filthy lucker*, it meant money."

"*Filthy lucre* does mean money," said the mother. "But it's lucre, not luck."

❶ "Oh!" said the boy. "Then what *is* luck, mother?"

"It's what causes you to have money. If you're lucky you have money. That's why it's better to be born lucky than rich. If you're rich, you may lose your money. But if you're lucky, you will always get more money."

"Oh! Will you! And is father not lucky?"

"Very unlucky, I should say," she said bitterly.

The boy watched her with unsure eyes.

"Why?" he asked.

"I don't know. Nobody ever knows why one person is lucky and another unlucky."

"Don't they? Nobody at all? Does *nobody* know?"

> ◆ **Reading Strategy**
> ❷ What impact might this exchange have on a young child? In what way does Paul's confusion evoke the reader's sympathy?

"Perhaps God! But He never tells."

"He ought to, then. And aren't you lucky either, mother?"

"I can't be, if I married an unlucky husband."

"But by yourself, aren't you?"

"I used to think I was, before I married. Now I think I am very unlucky indeed."

"Why?"

"Well—never mind! Perhaps I'm not really," she said.

❸ The child looked at her, to see if she meant it. But he saw, by the lines of her mouth, that she was only trying to hide something from him.

"Well, anyhow," he said stoutly, "I'm a lucky person."

"Why?" said his mother, with a sudden laugh.

He stared at her. He didn't even know why he had said it.

"God told me," he asserted, brazening it out.

"I hope He did, dear!" she said, again with a laugh, but rather bitter.

"He did, mother!"

"Excellent!" said the mother, using one of her husband's exclamations.

The boy saw she did not believe him; or rather, that she paid no attention to his assertion. This angered him somewhere, and made him want to compel her attention.

He went off by himself, vaguely, in a childish way, seeking for the clue to "luck." Absorbed, taking no heed of other people, he went about with a sort of stealth, seeking inwardly for luck. He wanted luck, he wanted it, he wanted it. When the two girls were playing dolls, in the nursery, he would sit on his big rocking horse, charging madly into space, with a frenzy that made the little girls peer at him uneasily. Wildly the horse careered, the waving dark hair of the boy tossed, his eyes had a strange glare in them. The little girls dared not speak to him.

When he had ridden to the end of his mad little journey, he climbed down and stood in front of his rocking horse, staring fixedly into its lowered face. Its red mouth was slightly open, its big eye was wide and glassy bright. ❹

"Now!" he would silently command the snorting steed. "Now take me to where there is luck! Now take me!"

And he would slash the horse on the neck with the little whip he had asked Uncle Oscar for. He *knew* the horse could take him to where there was luck, if only he forced it. So he would mount again, and start on his furious ride, hoping at last to get there. He knew he could get there.

"You'll break your horse, Paul!" said the nurse.

"He's always riding like that! I wish he'd leave off!" said his elder sister Joan.

But he only glared down on them in silence. Nurse gave him up. She could make nothing of him. Anyhow he was growing beyond her.

One day his mother and his Uncle Oscar came in when he was on one of his furious rides. He did not speak to them.

"Hallo! you young jockey! Riding a winner?" ❺ said his uncle.

"Aren't you growing too big for a rocking

◆ Build Vocabulary

brazening (brā′ zən iŋ) *v.*: Daring boldly or shamelessly

careered (kə rird′) *v.*: Rushed wildly

Beyond the Classroom

Career Connection

Financial Planning Paul's mother and father can't seem to manage their money. Today, professional financial planners help people to invest their money wisely. Career possibilities in the field of financial planning have grown dramatically. Job opportunities abound as so many more kinds of investments become available, as companies grow and expand here and overseas, as computers process and provide information on a global scale, and as individuals become more savvy about saving or investing money and more interested in preparing for longer lives. More people are needed to design tools, to record, interpret, and manage the data, to identify trends, and to develop strategies to advise and direct investors.

Have students look further into opportunities in this field. Invite a professional who is knowledgeable about the field to address the class and answer their questions about what opportunities await them.

horse? You're not a very little boy any longer, you know," said his mother.

But Paul only gave a blue glare from his big, rather close-set eyes. He would speak to nobody when he was in full tilt. His mother watched him with an anxious expression on her face.

At last he suddenly stopped forcing his horse into the mechanical gallop, and slid down.

"Well, I got there!" he announced fiercely, his
5 blue eyes still flaring, and his sturdy long legs straddling apart.

"Where did you get to?" asked his mother.

"Where I wanted to go to," he flared back at her.

"That's right, son!" said Uncle Oscar. "Don't you stop till you get there. What's the horse's name?"

"He doesn't have a name," said the boy.

"Gets on without all right?" asked the uncle.

"Well, he has different names. He was called Sansovino last week."

"Sansovino, eh? Won the Ascot.[2] How did you know his name?"

"He always talks about horse races with Bassett," said Joan.

The uncle was delighted to find that his small nephew was posted with all the racing news. Bassett, the young gardener who had been wounded in the left foot in the war, and had got his present job through Oscar Cresswell, whose batman[3] he had been, was a perfect blade of the "turf."[4] He lived in the racing events, and the small boy lived with him.

Oscar Cresswell got it all from Bassett.

"Master Paul comes and asks me, so I can't do more than tell him, sir," said Bassett, his
6 face terribly serious, as if he were speaking of religious matters.

"And does he ever put anything on a horse he fancies?"

"Well—I don't want to give him away—he's a
7 young sport, a fine sport, sir. Would you mind asking him yourself? He sort of takes a pleasure in it, and perhaps he'd feel I was giving 7
him away, sir, if you don't mind."

Bassett was serious as a church.

The uncle went back to his nephew, and took him off for a ride in the car.

"Say, Paul, old man, do you ever put anything on a horse?" the uncle asked.

The boy watched the handsome man closely.

"Why, do you think I oughtn't to?" he parried.

"Not a bit of it! I thought perhaps you might give me a tip for the Lincoln."[5]

The car sped on into the country, going down to Uncle Oscar's place in Hampshire.

"Honor bright?" said the nephew.

"Honor bright, son!" said the uncle.

"Well, then, Daffodil."

"Daffodil! I doubt it, sonny. What about Mirza?"

"I only know the winner," said the boy. "That's Daffodil!"

"Daffodil, eh?"

There was a pause. Daffodil was an obscure
horse comparatively. 8

"Uncle!"

"Yes, son?"

"You won't let it go any further, will you? I promised Bassett."

"Bassett be hanged, old man! What's he got to do with it?"

"We're partners! We've been partners from the first! Uncle, he lent me my first five shillings, which I lost. I promised him, honor bright, it was only between me and him: only you gave me that ten-shilling note I started winning with, so I thought you were lucky. You won't let it go any further, will you?"

> ◆ **Reading Strategy**
> What does this exchange indicate about Paul's sense of loyalty? 9

The boy gazed at his uncle from those big, hot, blue eyes, set rather close together. The uncle stirred and laughed uneasily.

"Right you are, son! I'll keep your tip private. Daffodil, eh! How much are you putting on him?"

"All except twenty pounds," said the boy. "I keep that in reserve."

The uncle thought it a good joke.

"You keep twenty pounds in reserve, do you,

2. **Ascot:** Major English horse race.
3. **batman:** British military officer's orderly.
4. **blade . . . "turf":** Horse-racing fan.
5. **Lincoln:** Major English horse race.

Customize for *More Advanced Students*

5 Guide students to notice that Uncle Oscar is always joking, that he supplies Paul with the whip for his rocking horse, and gives him the incentive to keep wagering. Tell them that Uncle Oscar may be an allusion to Oscar Wilde, who prefaced his Gothic novel *The Picture of Dorian Gray* with "there is no such thing as a moral or immoral book." The character Uncle Oscar echoes Wilde's individualism and his ideas on morality. The "changeable" name of Paul's horse suggests a reference to Wilde's pen name, Speranza. Just as Wilde firmly believed that art must stand apart from life, Uncle Oscar, like the story's omniscient narrator, stays emotionally aloof.

◆ Grammar and Style

6 **Subjunctive Mood** Point out Lawrence's use here of the subjunctive mood to state a condition contrary to fact: talking about horse racing is *not* the same as having a religious discussion.

◆ Reading Strategy

7 **Identify With a Character** Ask students to explain how they might feel in Bassett's place. *Most students will be able to relate to the feeling of not wanting to betray a friend's confidence.*

◆ Build Vocabulary

8 **Prefixes: *ob-*** Point out that the word *obscure* is formed by combining the prefix *ob-* and the root *skuro,* which means "to conceal or cover." By definition, something that is obscure lacks light, is dark, and is not easily perceived. *Daffodil* is what is known as a "dark horse," the unforeseen winner of a race.

◆ Reading Strategy

9 **Identify With a Character** Students may say that Paul, like Bassett, is loyal and intends to honor their partnership.

Cross-Curricular Connection: Art/Social Studies

Horse Racing Tell students that horseracing dates back to ancient times. For example, evidence of such races appears in Egypt in 1500 B. C. Also, saddle-horse races were a part of the ancient Olympic games held in Greece. Romans were particularly fond of chariot races, in which teams of horses pulled small carriages, each with a skilled driver. In the MGM movie *Ben Hur* (1959), there is a vivid re-enactment of an ancient Roman chariot race.

It is appropriate that this story involving horse racing is set in England because modern racing began in that country during the twelfth century. The sport was favored by royalty, and most of the thoroughbred horses of today are descendants of English horses. As early as the 1500's winners received prizes. Horse racing was introduced into France by King Louis XIV. It was also popular among wealthy citizens in the American colonies.

Customize for
Less Proficient Readers

❶ Point out to students that in the early twentieth century, three hundred pounds would have been a very considerable sum of money; it is a large sum today.

◆ Reading Strategy

❷ **Identify With a Character** Ask students to explain how Uncle Oscar must be feeling about this wager. *He is probably torn between wanting to protect his nephew from losing money and curosity about the outcome of the bet.*

◆ Literary Focus

❸ **Theme** Paul seems eager to share his good fortune with others. Ask students how this information contributes to their understanding of the theme. *Students may say that this lack of greed is as responsible for his success as is luck. This may lead students to surmise that the author is saying that since greedy people are never satisfied, they will never feel lucky. Others, who are not greedy, will feel lucky because they are satisfied with what they get.*

◆ Critical Thinking

❹ **Speculate** Discuss with students what makes Paul "sure" sometimes, and why Bassett is in awe of him. *Students may say that Paul sometimes mysteriously comes up with the winner of the race, perhaps after riding on his rocking horse. Bassett cannot possibly understand how Paul gets his information, but he doesn't turn his back on success.*

you young romancer? What are you betting, then?"

❶ "I'm betting three hundred," said the boy gravely. "But it's between you and me, Uncle Oscar! Honor bright?"

The uncle burst into a roar of laughter.

"It's between you and me all right, you young Nat Gould,"[6] he said, laughing. "But where's your three hundred?"

"Bassett keeps it for me. We're partners."

"You are, are you! And what is Bassett putting on Daffodil?"

"He won't go quite as high as I do, I expect. Perhaps he'll go a hundred and fifty."

"What, pennies?" laughed the uncle.

"Pounds," said the child, with a surprised look at his uncle. "Bassett keeps a bigger reserve than I do."

Between wonder and amusement, Uncle Oscar was silent. He pursued the matter no further, but he determined to take his nephew with him to the Lincoln races.

"Now, son," he said, "I'm putting twenty on Mirza, and I'll put five for you on any horse you fancy. What's your pick?"

❷ "Daffodil, uncle!"

"No, not the fiver on Daffodil!"

"I should if it was my own five," said the child.

"Good! Good! Right you are! A fiver for me and a fiver for you on Daffodil."

The child had never been to a race meeting before, and his eyes were blue fire. He pursed his mouth tight, and watched. A Frenchman just in front had put his money on Lancelot. Wild with excitement, he flayed his arms up and down, yelling *"Lancelot! Lancelot!"* in his French accent.

Daffodil came in first, Lancelot second, Mirza third. The child, flushed and with eyes blazing, was curiously serene. His uncle brought him five five-pound notes: four to one.

"What am I to do with these?" he cried, waving them before the boy's eyes.

"I suppose we'll talk to Bassett," said the boy. "I expect I have fifteen hundred now; and twenty in reserve; and this twenty."

His uncle studied him for some moments.

"Look here, son!" he said. "You're not serious about Bassett and that fifteen hundred, are you?"

"Yes, I am. But it's between you and me, uncle! Honor bright!"

"Honor bright all right, son! But I must talk to Bassett."

"If you'd like to be a partner, uncle, with Bassett and me, we could all be partners. Only you'd have to promise, honor bright, uncle, not to let it go beyond us three. Bassett and I are lucky, and you must be lucky, because it was your ten shillings I started winning with. . . ." ❸

Uncle Oscar took both Bassett and Paul into Richmond Park for an afternoon, and there they talked.

"It's like this, you see, sir," Bassett said. "Master Paul would get me talking about racing events, spinning yarns, you know, sir. And he was always keen on knowing if I'd made or if I'd lost. It's about a year since, now, that I put five shillings on Blush of Dawn for him—and we lost. Then the luck turned, with that ten shillings he had from you, that we put on Singhalese. And since that time, it's been pretty steady, all things considering. What do you say, Master Paul?"

"We're all right when we're *sure*," said Paul. "It's when we're not quite sure that we go down."

"Oh, but we're careful then," said Bassett.

"But when are you *sure*?" smiled Uncle Oscar. ❹

"It's Master Paul, sir," said Bassett, in a secret, religious voice. "It's as if he had it from heaven. Like Daffodil now, for the Lincoln. That was as sure as eggs."

"Did you put anything on Daffodil?" asked Oscar Cresswell.

"Yes, sir. I made my bit."

"And my nephew?"

Bassett was obstinately silent, looking at Paul.

"I made twelve hundred, didn't I, Bassett? I told uncle I was putting three hundred on Daffodil."

6. **Nat Gould:** Famous English sportswriter and authority on horse racing.

◆ Build Vocabulary

obstinately (äb´ stə nət lē) *adv.*: In a determined way; stubbornly

Enrichment

"The Rocking Horse Winner," like much of Lawrence's work and like the works of other established writers, has sparked a huge output of critical commentary. In an article entitled "A Rocking-Horse: The Symbol, the Pattern, the Way to Live," critic W. D. Snodgrass examines the names of the horses on which Paul, Bassett, and Oscar gamble. He notes that the first winner, Singhalese, and his last, Malabar, have names that refer to former British colonial regions in India. He sees in another name, Mirza, the suggestion of a third colony, Mirzapur. Snodgrass suggests that Lawrence deliberately selected these names, and that he sees a parallel between Paul's fate and the fate of the British Empire.

Invite students to give their opinions of Snodgrass's theory. Ask them to explain why they do or do not agree with the critic's equating Paul's fate and that of the British Empire. *In their responses, students may point out that the colonies were "winners" for the British Empire for many years and that the British had very limited direct contact with the people and materials they controlled.*

"That's right," said Bassett, nodding.

"But where's the money?" asked the uncle.

"I keep it safe locked up, sir. Master Paul, he can have it any minute he likes to ask for it."

"What, fifteen hundred pounds?"

"And twenty! And *forty*, that is, with the twenty he made on the course."

"It's amazing!" said the uncle.

5 "If Master Paul offers you to be partners, sir, I would, if I were you; if you'll excuse me," said Bassett.

Oscar Cresswell thought about it.

"I'll see the money," he said.

They drove home again, and sure enough, Bassett came round to the garden house with fifteen hundred pounds in notes. The twenty pounds reserve was left with Joe Glee, in the Turf Commission deposit.

"You see, it's all right, uncle, when I'm *sure*! Then we go strong, for all we're worth. Don't we, Bassett?"

"We do that, Master Paul."

"And when are you sure?" said the uncle, laughing.

"Oh, well, sometimes I'm *absolutely* sure, like about Daffodil," said the boy, "and sometimes I have an idea; and sometimes I haven't even an idea, have I, Bassett? Then we're careful, because we mostly go down." 7

"You do, do you! And when you're sure, like about Daffodil, what makes you sure, sonny?"

"Oh, well, I don't know," said the boy uneasily. "I'm sure, you know, uncle; that's all."

"It's as if he had it from heaven, sir," Bassett reiterated.

"I should say so!" said the uncle.

But he became a partner. And when the Leger was coming on, Paul was "sure" about Lively Spark, which was a quite inconsiderable horse. The boy insisted on putting a thousand on the horse, Bassett went for five hundred, and Oscar Cresswell two hundred. Lively Spark came in first, and the betting had been ten to one against him. Paul had made ten thousand.

"You see," he said. "I was absolutely sure of him."

Even Oscar Cresswell had cleared two thousand.

"Look here, son," he said, "this sort of thing makes me nervous."

"It needn't, uncle! Perhaps I shan't be sure again for a long time."

"But what are you going to do with your money?" asked the uncle. 8

6 ▲ **Critical Viewing** Although Paul, the young protagonist of the story, rides a rocking horse, he acts years older than he is. Which elements in this photograph make the child seem old and serious? Which elements emphasize the child's youth? **[Classify]**

◆ Background for Understanding

5 Culture: Wealth and Social Status Point out Bassett's use of the expression "If you'll excuse me." Inform students that, in keeping with the social standards of the time, he would not presume to give advice to a gentleman, such as his former officer, Uncle Oscar.

▶Critical Viewing◀

6 Classify Students may suggest that the child's expression makes him look older, while his clothing emphasizes his young age. Students may also say that the child pictured here is much younger than Paul, who may be reasonably pictured as a boy from nine to twelve years old.

◆ Reading Strategy

7 Identify With a Character Ask students to explain how Paul's confusion about his ability reflects larger issues in his life. *Paul's absolute faith in some of his choices seems to reflect his desperate need to be lucky and loved. His unsureness about other choices may stem from his feeling of being unloved.*

◆ Reading Strategy

8 Identify With a Character Ask students to answer the question Uncle Oscar asks: What is Paul going to do with the money? *Students may say that Paul is stashing it away and plans to give it to his mother.*

Thematic Focus

1 Conflicts Abroad and at Home Discuss with students that Paul, by betting on the horses in tandem with Bassett and Uncle Oscar, hopes to alleviate the conflict at home, which is one between his mother's desire to have a certain lifestyle and the family's inability to pay for it. Have students link this conflict with Britain's struggle to maintain its empire.

◆ Critical Thinking

2 Evaluate Ask students to evaluate Paul's plan, based on what they know about his mother. *Most students will point out that no matter how much Paul wins, the house won't stop whispering because his mother will always want more.*

◆ Reading Strategy

3 Identify With a Character Ask students to explain how this comment demonstrates Oscar's understanding of his sister's attitude toward money. *Students may say that Oscar realizes that his sister spends freely and that she may make better use of the money if he monitors the rate at which she receives it.*

◆ Background for Understanding

4 Culture: Wealth and Social Status Guide students to understand that in households like this one, parents were relieved of the "burden" of messy meals with their small children. Paul is now at an age when he may dine with the grownups.

◆ Literary Focus

5 Theme Ask students how this passage gives them information that helps them interpret the theme. *Here, Lawrence reveals that the mother's greed and dissatisfaction stem from more than just a want of money. Her life is driven by the need to be better than or above others.*

◆ Critical Thinking

6 Respond Ask students to respond to the way the mother reacts to the receipt of the money. *Students may say that her reaction is somewhat surprising; her immediate thoughts are not about her unanticipated good fortune, as Paul might have hoped, but about how she can get more money sooner.*

---

1 "Of course," said the boy, "I started it for mother. She said she had no luck, because father is unlucky, so I thought if *I* was lucky, it might stop whispering."

"What might stop whispering?"

"Our house! I *hate* our house for whispering."

"What does it whisper?"

"Why—why"—the boy fidgeted—"why, I don't know! But it's always short of money, you know, uncle."

"I know it, son, I know it."

"You know people send mother writs, don't you, uncle?"

"I'm afraid I do," said the uncle.

"And then the house whispers like people laughing at you behind your back. It's awful, that is! I thought if I was lucky . . ."

2 "You might stop it," added the uncle.

The boy watched him with big blue eyes, that had an uncanny cold fire in them, and he said never a word.

"Well then!" said the uncle. "What are we doing?"

"I shouldn't like mother to know I was lucky," said the boy.

"Why not, son?"

"She'd stop me."

"I don't think she would."

"Oh!"—and the boy writhed in an odd way—"I *don't* want her to know, uncle."

"All right, son! We'll manage it without her knowing."

They managed it very easily. Paul, at the other's suggestion, handed over five thousand pounds to his uncle, who deposited it with the family lawyer, who was then to inform Paul's mother that a relative had put five thousand
3 pounds into his hands, which sum was to be paid out a thousand pounds at a time, on the mother's birthday, for the next five years.

"So she'll have a birthday present of a thousand pounds for five successive years," said Uncle Oscar. "I hope it won't make it all the harder for her later."

Paul's mother had her birthday in November. The house had been "whispering" worse than ever lately, and even in spite of his luck, Paul could not bear up against it. He was very anxious to see the effect of the birthday letter, telling his mother about the thousand pounds.

When there were no visitors, Paul now took his meals with his parents, as he was beyond the nursery control. 4 His mother went into town nearly every day. She had discovered that she had an odd knack of sketching furs and dress materials, so she worked secretly in the studio of a friend who was the chief "artist" for the leading drapers. She drew the figures of ladies in furs and ladies in silk and sequins for the newspaper advertisements. This young woman artist earned several thousand pounds a year, but Paul's mother only made several hundreds, and she was again dissatisfied. 5 She so wanted to be first in something, and she did not succeed, even in making sketches for drapery advertisements.

She was down to breakfast on the morning of her birthday. Paul watched her face as she read her letters. He knew the lawyer's letter. As his mother read it, her face hardened and became more expressionless. Then a cold, determined look came on her mouth. She hid the letter under the pile of others, and said not a word about it.

"Didn't you have anything nice in the post for your birthday, mother?" said Paul.

"Quite moderately nice," she said, her voice cold and absent.

She went away to town without saying more. 6

But in the afternoon Uncle Oscar appeared. He said Paul's mother had had a long interview with the lawyer, asking if the whole five thousand could not be advanced at once, as she was in debt.

"What do you think, uncle?" said the boy.

"I leave it to you, son."

"Oh, let her have it, then! We can get some more with the other," said the boy.

"A bird in the hand is worth two in the bush, laddie!" said Uncle Oscar.

"But I'm sure to *know* for the Grand National; or the Lincolnshire; or else the Derby.[7] I'm sure to know for *one* of them," said Paul.

So Uncle Oscar signed the agreement, and Paul's mother touched the whole five thousand. Then something very curious happened. The voices in the house suddenly went mad, like a chorus of frogs on a spring evening. There were

7. **Grand National . . . Derby:** Major English horse races.

Cross-Curricular Connection: Mathematics

When Paul picks his winners, he pays no attention to which horses are favored and which are "dark horses." For him, the choice of a winner is based on a mysterious process of intuition, not on science or mathematics. The mathematical study of probability deals with the likelihood that events will occur. This field of study can be quite complex. A simple example of probability, however, involves the tossing of a die with six faces. The probability of one face appearing is equal to the ratio of that event (1) over the number of *possible* events (6). Therefore, the probability of throwing a die and having a particular face come up is 1/6.

However, here is a point about probability that people often don't understand. The die has no memory. You might think that having thrown a particular face four times in succession, it is less likely to appear on the next throw. This is wrong. The probability of throwing it again is still 1/6.

◆ **Literary Focus**
In what way does the personification of the house help you to identify the theme of the story?

7 certain new furnishings, and Paul had a tutor. He was *really* going to Eton,[8] his father's school, in the following autumn. There were flowers in the winter, and a blossoming of the luxury Paul's mother had been used to. And yet the voices in the house, behind the sprays of mimosa and almond blossom, and from under the piles of iridescent cushions, simply trilled and screamed in a sort of ecstasy: "There *must* be more money! Oh-h-h! There *must* be more money! Oh, now, now-w! now-w-w—there *must* be more money!—more than ever! More than ever!"

It frightened Paul terribly. He studied away at his Latin and Greek with his tutors. But his intense hours were spent with Bassett. The Grand National had gone by: he had not "known," and had lost a hundred pounds. Summer was at hand. He was in agony for the Lincoln. But even for the Lincoln he didn't "know," and he lost fifty pounds. He became wild-eyed and strange, as if something were going to explode in him.

"Let it alone, son! Don't you bother about it!" urged Uncle Oscar. But it was as if the boy couldn't really hear what his uncle was saying.

"I've got to know for the Derby! I've *got* to know for the Derby!" the child reiterated, his big blue eyes blazing with a sort of madness.

His mother noticed how overwrought he was.

"You'd better go to the seaside. Wouldn't you like to go now to the seaside, instead of waiting? I think you'd better," she said, looking
8 down at him anxiously, her heart curiously heavy because of him.

But the child lifted his uncanny blue eyes.

"I couldn't possibly go before the Derby, mother!" he said. "I couldn't possibly!"

"Why not?" she said, her voice becoming heavy when she was opposed. "Why not? You can still go from the seaside to see the Derby with your Uncle Oscar, if that's what you wish. No need for you to wait here. Besides, I think you care too much about these races. It's a bad sign. My family has been a gambling family, and you won't know till you grow up how much damage it has done. But it has done damage. I shall have to send Bassett away, and ask Uncle Oscar not to talk racing to you, unless you promise to be reasonable about it; go away to the seaside and forget it. You're all nerves!"

"I'll do what you like, mother, so long as you don't send me away till after the Derby," the boy said.

"Send you away from where? Just from this house?"

"Yes," he said, gazing at her.

"Why, you curious child, what makes you care about this house so much, suddenly? I never knew you loved it!"

He gazed at her without speaking. He had a secret within a secret, something he had not divulged, even to Bassett or to his Uncle Oscar.

But his mother, after standing undecided and a little bit sullen for some moments, said:

"Very well, then! Don't go to the seaside till after the Derby, if you don't wish it. But promise me you won't let your nerves go to pieces! Promise you won't think so much about horse racing and *events*, as you call them!"

"Oh, no!" said the boy, casually. "I won't think much about them, mother. You needn't worry. I wouldn't worry, mother, if I were you."

"If you were me and I were you," said his mother, "I wonder what we *should* do!"

"But you know you needn't worry, mother, don't you?" the boy repeated.

"I should be awfully glad to know it," she said wearily.

"Oh, well, you *can*, you know. I mean you *ought* to know you needn't worry!" he insisted.

"Ought I? Then I'll see about it," she said.

Paul's secret of secrets was his wooden horse, that which had no name. Since he was emancipated from a nurse and a nursery governess, he had had his rocking horse removed 9
to his own bedroom at the top of the house.

"Surely you're too big for a rocking horse!" his mother had remonstrated.

"Well, you see, mother, till I can have a *real* horse, I like to have *some* sort of animal

8. **Eton:** Prestigious private school in England.

◆ **Build Vocabulary**

uncanny (un kan´ ē) *adj.*: Mysterious; hard to explain

remonstrated (ri män´ strāt id) *v.*: Objected strongly

◆ Literary Focus

7 Theme Students may say that the personification of the house supports the idea that greed is insatiable and feeds on itself.

Thematic Focus

8 Conflicts Abroad and At Home Help students understand the conflicts expressed here. Paul seems unwell but his mother, rather than showing concern over the causes of his condition or trying any meaningful way to alleviate it, simply suggests a trip to the shore for some sea air, something she might do herself when feeling ill. Paul, on the other hand, wants to stay put to stop the whispering in the house by finding the winner for the Derby.

Customize for
Less Proficient Readers
9 Guide students to understand that Paul's secret is that he finds his winners by riding furiously on the rocking horse.

Humanities: Media

The Rocking Horse Winner, 1949, directed by Anthony Pelissier.

The director wrote the screenplay for this beautifully done adaptation, which is in black and white. Show the film and invite students to compare and contrast it with Lawrence's story.

Use these questions for discussion:

1. Are the characters in the film faithful to the story? Explain. *Students may point to the more sympathetic portrayal of the mother in the film and to the fact that the boy is portrayed as being much older than the very young child shown in the photo that accompanies the text.*
2. How do the visual images in the film compare with the mental images you formed when reading the story? *One thing students may notice is that the movie version takes place much later, perhaps in the 1930's or 1940's, and that the family's home is more opulent than they might have envisioned.*
3. Which version is more effective? Why? *Opinions will vary, but students who respond better to visual images than to the written word may find the film more accessible.*

◆ Build Vocabulary

1 Prefixes: *ob-* Discuss with students that Paul is *obsessed* with finding the Derby winner. Define *obsession* as "a persistent preoccupation with an idea or emotion." Point out the derivation of the word, from the Latin *ob-* meaning "toward, over, or against" and *sedére,* meaning "to sit." This derivation suggests that when you are obsessed, an idea sits over you or besieges you. Have students apply this definition to Paul's situation.

◆ Reading Strategy

2 Identify With a Character Have students imagine what the mother is thinking and feeling now. *Students can recognize that she is experiencing a deep inner fear, a recognition that something awful has befallen her son. They may be surprised that she feels this so strongly, considering how minimally she has expressed affection for him or worried about him previously.*

◆ Critical Thinking

3 Deduce Ask students how they know who Malabar is. *By connecting to earlier hints that the rocking horse has something to do with his choices, and with Paul's obsession with staying in the house until the Derby, students can deduce that Malabar will be the Derby winner.*

◆ Reading Strategy

4 Identify With a Character Ask students why the author says Oscar placed the bet "in spite of himself." *Students should be able to identify Oscar's feelings of guilt about taking advantage of Paul's ability when the boy is so sick.*

about," had been his quaint answer.

"Do you feel he keeps you company?" she laughed.

"Oh, yes! He's very good, he always keeps me company, when I'm there," said Paul.

So the horse, rather shabby, stood in an arrested prance in the boy's bedroom.

The Derby was drawing near, and the boy grew more and more tense. He hardly heard
1 what was spoken to him, he was very frail, and his eyes were really uncanny. His mother had sudden strange seizures of uneasiness about him. Sometimes, for half an hour, she would feel a sudden anxiety about him that was al-
2 most anguish. She wanted to rush to him at once, and know he was safe.

Two nights before the Derby, she was at a big party in town, when one of her rushes of anxiety about her boy, her firstborn, gripped her heart till she could hardly speak. She fought with the feeling, might and main, for she believed in common sense. But it was too strong. She had to leave the dance and go downstairs to telephone to the country. The children's nursery governess was terribly surprised and startled at being rung up in the night.

"Are the children all right, Miss Wilmot?"

"Oh yes, they are quite all right."

"Master Paul? Is he all right?"

"He went to bed as right as a trivet.[9] Shall I run up and look at him?"

"No!" said Paul's mother reluctantly. "No! Don't trouble. It's all right. Don't sit up. We shall be home fairly soon." She did not want her son's privacy intruded upon.

"Very good," said the governess.

It was about one o'clock when Paul's mother and father drove up to their house. All was still. Paul's mother went to her room and slipped off her white fur cloak. She had told her maid not to wait up for her. She heard her husband downstairs, mixing a whisky-and-soda.

And then, because of the strange anxiety at her heart, she stole upstairs to her son's room. Noiselessly she went along the upper corridor. Was there a faint noise? What was it?

She stood, with arrested muscles, outside his door, listening. There was a strange, heavy, and yet not loud noise. Her heart stood still. It was a soundless noise, yet rushing and powerful. Something huge, in violent, hushed motion. What was it? What in God's name was it? She ought to know. She felt that she *knew* the noise. She knew what it was.

Yet she could not place it. She couldn't say what it was. And on and on it went, like madness.

Softly, frozen with anxiety and fear, she turned the door handle.

The room was dark. Yet in the space near the window, she heard and saw something plunging to and fro. She gazed in fear and amazement.

Then suddenly she switched on the light, and saw her son, in his green pajamas, madly surging on his rocking horse. The blaze of light suddenly lit him up, as he urged 3
the wooden horse, and lit her up, as she stood, blond, in her dress of pale green and crystal, in the doorway.

"Paul!" she cried. "Whatever are you doing?"

"It's Malabar!" he screamed, in a powerful, strange voice. "It's Malabar!"

His eyes blazed at her for one strange and senseless second, as he ceased urging his wooden horse. Then he fell with a crash to the ground, and she, all her tormented motherhood flooding upon her, rushed to gather him up.

But he was unconscious, and unconscious he remained, with some brain fever. He talked and tossed, and his mother sat stonily by his side.

"Malabar! It's Malabar! Bassett, Bassett, I *know* it's Malabar!"

So the child cried, trying to get up and urge the rocking horse that gave him his inspiration.

"What does he mean by Malabar?" asked the heart-frozen mother.

"I don't know," said the father, stonily.

"What does he mean by Malabar?" she asked her brother Oscar.

"It's one of the horses running for the Derby," was the answer.

And, in spite of himself, Oscar Cresswell
spoke to Bassett, and himself put a thousand 4
on Malabar: at fourteen to one.

The third day of the illness was critical: they were watching for a change. The boy, with his rather long, curly hair, was tossing ceaselessly on the pillow. He neither slept nor regained consciousness, and his eyes were like blue

9. **right as a trivet:** Perfectly right.

stones. His mother sat, feeling her heart had gone, turned actually into a stone.

In the evening, Oscar Cresswell did not come, but Bassett sent a message, saying could he come up for one moment, just one moment? Paul's mother was very angry at the intrusion, but on second thoughts she agreed. The boy was the same. Perhaps Bassett might bring him to consciousness.

5 The gardener, a shortish fellow with a little brown moustache and sharp little brown eyes, tiptoed into the room, touched his imaginary cap to Paul's mother, and stole to the bedside, staring with glittering, smallish eyes at the tossing, dying child.

"Master Paul!" he whispered. "Master Paul! Malabar came in first all right, a clean win. I did as you told me. You've made over seventy thousand pounds, you have; you've got over eighty thousand. Malabar came in all right, Master Paul."

"Malabar! Malabar! Did I say Malabar, mother? Did I say Malabar? Do you think I'm lucky, mother? I knew Malabar, didn't I? Over eighty thousand pounds! I call that lucky, don't you, mother? Over eighty thousand pounds! I knew, didn't I know I knew? Malabar came in all right. If I ride my horse till I'm sure, then I tell you, Bassett, you can go as high as you like. Did you go for all you were worth, Bassett?"

"I went a thousand on it, Master Paul."

"I never told you, mother, that if I can ride my horse, and *get there*, then I'm absolutely sure—oh, absolutely! Mother, did I ever tell you? I *am* lucky!"

"No, you never did," said the mother.

But the boy died in the night.

And even as he lay dead, his mother heard her brother's voice saying to her: "My God, Hester, you're eighty-odd thousand to the good, and a poor devil of a son to the bad. But, poor devil, poor devil, he's best gone out of a life where he rides his rocking horse to find a winner." 6

Guide for Responding

◆ Literature and Your Life

Reader's Response What is your impression of Paul's relationship with (a) his mother? (b) his Uncle Oscar?

Thematic Focus To what extent do you think that the family problems that Lawrence addresses in this story—lack of communication, social snobbery, and greed—reflect conflicts in the larger world? Explain your answer.

☑ Check Your Comprehension

1. Why is the family in the story always short of money?
2. How does Paul try to change the family's luck?
3. Why is Paul sometimes "careful" when he bets on horses?
4. (a) What secret birthday present does Paul give his mother? (b) How does she react to it?
5. What does Paul's mother discover upon returning from the big party?

◆ Critical Thinking

INTERPRET

1. (a) What do you think Paul's mother means when she describes her husband as unlucky? (b) What does the description reveal about her as a person? **[Infer]**
2. (a) Over the course of the story, how is Paul affected by the house's "whispers?" (b) Why is he affected as he is? **[Analyze Cause and Effect]**
3. What comment about life do you think the author is suggesting by Uncle Oscar's statement on Paul's death at the story's close? **[Draw Conclusions]**

APPLY

4. (a) Identify Lawrence's theme in this story. (b) Do you think the theme is still relevant today? Explain. **[Relate]**

EXTEND

5. What other stories do you know of in which a perceived lack of money has driven characters to extremes? Explain. **[Literature Link]**

Beyond the Selection

FURTHER READING

Other Works by D. H. Lawrence

The White Peacock; The Lost Girl
Aaron's Rod; The Plumed Serpent

Other Works With the Theme of Obsession

"The Lagoon," Joseph Conrad
Rebecca, Daphne du Maurier
Of Human Bondage, Somerset Maugham
Othello, William Shakespeare

We suggest that you preview these works before recommending them to students.

INTERNET

For information about D. H. Lawrence, go to **http://www.eastwood.co.uk /dhl/dhllivin.htm**

To take a virtual 3.5 km walk through Eastwood, Lawrence's home town, which includes visits to his birthplace and other key sites, go to **http://www.eastwood.co.uk/dhl/dhllivin.htm**

Please be aware that sites may have changed since this information was published. We *strongly recommend* that you preview sites before you send students to them.

◆ Reading Strategy

5 Identify With a Character Ask students to explain why Bassett wants to see Paul. *Some may say that Bassett really cares for the boy.*

◆ Literary Focus

6 Theme Ask students to explain how this last passage reinforces the theme of the story. *The boy has been sacrificed to his family's greed.*

Reinforce and Extend

Answers

◆ Literature and Your Life

Reader's Response (a) Students may say that Paul cares more about his mother than she does for him. (b) Some may say that Paul and his uncle have a warm and trusting relationship, while others may suggest that Oscar should have been more sensitive to the boy's emotional state.

Thematic Focus Students should support their answers with details.

☑ Check Your Comprehension

1. Neither parent makes much, yet the family spends a lot.
2. Paul tries to win money.
3. Sometimes he is not certain of the winner.
4. (a) He arranges for her to receive yearly sums of money. (b) She quickly attempts to get the entire sum at once rather than in five installments.
5. She discovers Paul in a frenzied state and learns about his wagering.

◆ Critical Thinking

1. (a) She may mean that he does not know how to make a lot of money. (b) She thinks that people's lives are fated.
2. (a) The continuing whispers fuel his frenzied attempts to find luck. (b) He wants to help his mother so she'll love him.
3. Oscar's comment points to how desperate we are for love in a greedy world.
4. (a) Lawrence's theme is that in the modern world, unbridled greed coupled with a lack of affection and an absence of communication will lead inevitably to destruction. (b) Students' answers will vary, but are likely to support Lawrence's views.
5. Students should explain their choices.

Develop Understanding

One-Minute Insight In this story about the absurdities of life, a prep school boy learns that his father, whom he hardly knows and whom he has romanticized, has died in an abrupt, embarrassing manner: a pig fell on him. The bizarre nature of this accident haunts the young man as he grows up, making him feel isolated and odd. In a surprising twist at the end of the story, his bride doesn't laugh when hearing the story for the first time. Her sympathetic response shows that even in the face of absurdity, people can find comfort and a measure of stability. Ironically, his sense of humiliation ends when another person appreciates the ghastliness of his father's absurd death.

❶ **Clarification** Inform students that here the author is describing routines in one of England's private boarding schools. These preparatory schools, which are largely the domain of the wealthy, are called "public schools."

◆ Reading Strategy

❷ **Identify With a Character** Students may suggest that Jerome, a boarding school student who doesn't have a close relationship with his father, may romanticize what his father does to explain why his father pays so little attention to him. The job is just too important to give the man time for Jerome.

Customize for *Less Proficient Readers*

❸ Guide students to understand the conflict here: the headmaster is trying to give Jerome the bad news, but the boy is still busy working on his fantasy.

A Shocking Accident

Graham Greene

1

❶ Jerome was called into his housemaster's room in the break between the second and the third class on a Thursday morning. He had no fear of trouble, for he was a warden—the name that the proprietor and headmaster of a rather expensive preparatory school had chosen to give to approved, reliable boys in the lower forms (from a warden one became a guardian and finally before leaving, it was hoped for Marlborough or Rugby, a crusader). The housemaster, Mr. Wordsworth, sat behind his desk with an appearance of perplexity and apprehension. Jerome had the odd impression when he entered that he was a cause of fear.

"Sit down, Jerome," Mr. Wordsworth said. "All going well with the trigonometry?"

"Yes, sir."

"I've had a telephone call, Jerome. From your aunt. I'm afraid I have bad news for you."

"Yes, sir?"

"Your father has had an accident."

"Oh."

Mr. Wordsworth looked at him with some surprise. "A serious accident."

"Yes, sir?"

❷ **◆ Reading Strategy** Why might a character like Jerome romanticize his absent father's job?

Jerome worshipped his father: the verb is exact. As man re-creates God, so Jerome re-created his father—from a restless widowed author into a mysterious adventurer who traveled in far places—Nice, Beirut, Majorca, even the Canaries. The time had arrived about his eighth birthday when Jerome believed that his father either "ran guns" or was a member of the British Secret Service. Now it occurred to him that his father might have been wounded in "a hail of machine-gun bullets."

Mr. Wordsworth played with the ruler on his desk. He seemed at a loss how to continue. He said, "You knew your father was in Naples?"

"Yes, sir."

"Your aunt heard from the hospital today."

"Oh."

Mr. Wordsworth said with desperation, "It was a street accident."

"Yes, sir?" It seemed quite likely to Jerome that they would call it a street accident. The police, of course, had fired first; his father would not take human life except as a last resort. ❸

"I'm afraid your father was very seriously hurt indeed."

"Oh."

"In fact, Jerome, he died yesterday. Quite without pain."

"Did they shoot him through the heart?"

"I beg your pardon. What did you say, Jerome?"

"Did they shoot him through the heart?"

◆ Build Vocabulary

apprehension (ap´ rē hen´ shən) *n.*: Anxious feeling of foreboding; dread

embarked (em bärkt´) *v.*: Engaged in conversation

Block Scheduling Strategies

Consider these suggestions to take advantage of extended class time:

- Spend some time discussing the Literary Focus for this selection: Theme. Have students complete the Journal Writing activity in Literature and Your Life (p. 1067) and discuss their entries in groups.
- Emphasize the importance of the Reading Strategy: Identify With a Character, before you assign the story. Then have students read the story independently, or listen to it on audiocassette.
- Invite students to select an activity or project from the Idea Bank. Remind them to apply the steps of the writing process as applicable.
- Use the Scoring Rubric: Description, p. 98 in ***Alternative Assessment,*** to help you evaluate students' writing.

"Nobody shot him, Jerome. A pig fell on him." An inexplicable convulsion took place in the nerves of Mr. Wordsworth's face; it really looked for a moment as though he were going to laugh. He closed his eyes, composed his features, and said rapidly, as though it were necessary to expel the story as rapidly as possible, "Your father was walking along a street in Naples when a pig fell on him. A shocking accident. Apparently in the poorer quarters of Naples they keep pigs on their balconies. This one was on the fifth floor. It had grown too fat. The balcony broke. The pig fell on your father."

4 ◆ Literary Focus
How does the manner in which Jerome's father died convey the idea that life is absurd?

Mr. Wordsworth left his desk rapidly and went to the window, turning his back on Jerome. He shook a little with emotion.

5 Jerome said, "What happened to the pig?"

2

This was not callousness on the part of Jerome as it was interpreted by Mr. Wordsworth to his colleagues (he even discussed with them whether, perhaps, Jerome was not yet fitted to be a warden). Jerome was only attempting to visualize the strange scene and to get the details right. Nor was Jerome a boy who cried; he was a boy who brooded, and it never occurred to him at his preparatory school that the circumstances of his father's death were comic—they were still part of the mystery of life. It was later in his first term at his public school, when he told the story to his best friend, that he began to realize how it affected others. Naturally, after that disclosure he was known, rather unreasonably, as Pig.

Unfortunately his aunt had no sense of humor. There was an enlarged snap-shot of his father on the piano: a large sad man in an unsuitable dark suit posed in Capri with an umbrella (to guard him against sunstroke), the Faraglioni rocks forming the background. By the age of sixteen Jerome was well aware that the portrait looked more like the author of *Sunshine and Shade* and *Rambles in the Balearics* than an agent of the Secret Service. All the same, he loved the memory of his father: he still possessed an album filled with picture-postcards (the stamps had been soaked off long ago for his other collection), and it pained him when his aunt <u>embarked</u> with strangers on the story of his father's death. 7

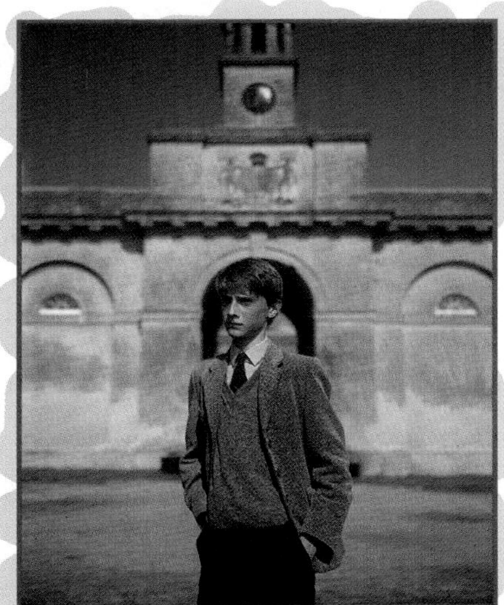

6 ▲ **Critical Viewing** In this story, Jerome becomes orphaned and suffers humiliation because of the way in which his father died. How well does this photograph convey a young man's loneliness and sadness? **[Evaluate]**

"A shocking accident," she would begin, and the stranger would compose his or her features into the correct shape for interest and commiseration. Both reactions, of course, were false, but it was terrible for Jerome to see how suddenly, midway in her rambling discourse, the interest would become genuine. "I can't think how such things can be allowed in a civilized country," his aunt would say. "I suppose one has to regard Italy as civilized. One is prepared for all kinds of things abroad, of course, and my brother was a great traveler. He always carried a water-filter with him. It was far less expensive, you know, than buying all those bottles of mineral water. My brother always said that his filter paid for his dinner wine. You can see from that what a careful man he was, but who could possibly have expected when he was walking along the Via Dottore Manuele Panucci on his way to the Hydrographic Museum that a pig would fall on him?" That was the moment when the interest became genuine.

Jerome's father had not been a distinguished writer, but the time always seems to

◆ Literary Focus

4 Theme Students may say that the absurdity lies in the fact that contrary to the boy's heroic notion of how his father must have died, the man met his end as a result of a ridiculous accident.

◆ Reading Strategy

5 Identify With a Character Ask students to explain why Jerome asked this unlikely question. *Jerome's question indicates he wants to visualize the accident clearly. He asks about the pig's fate the way someone might ask what happened to another person in an accident.*

▶Critical Viewing◀

6 Evaluate Students may say that although this photograph does not distinctly evoke sadness and loneliness, the boy has a distant look in his eye and stands alone in a large stately courtyard.

◆ Reading Strategy

7 Identify With a Character Ask students to explain why Jerome is so pained by his aunt's retelling of the story of his father's death. *Students may say that Jerome preferred to romanticize the memory of his father. The aunt's story makes the father seem a fool; it is preposterous to die from a falling pig.*

Beyond the Classroom

Career Connection

Travel Writer Jerome's father was neither a Secret Service agent nor a mysterious adventurer. He did, in fact, have a job that many people would envy: travel writer. Have students imagine a life that consists of exploring the world's exciting regions, acquainting oneself with the bounties of its cultures, tasting different foods, meeting all kinds of people, and staying in its finest or most unique hotels and inns. Is travel writing a job students would want to have? Have them brainstorm for a list of the pros and cons of such an occupation. Students can verify their suggestions by contacting and interviewing a travel writer, or by reading travel writings.

Invite interested students to examine travel books at a local bookstore, at the library, or on the Internet. Ask them to suggest ways that they, as future travel writers, would distinguish themselves in the field. What aspects of travel would they focus on? What would they de-emphasize? How would they improve upon the efforts they have seen? How would their books be different and unique? Have students share their responses in groups.

◆ Reading Strategy

❶ **Identify With a Character** Ask students why a person might want to rehearse telling a story like the one Jerome must tell. *Students should recognize that when a person is embarrassed by a story, as Jerome is, they might rehearse ways of telling it to minimize the embarrassing details.*

◆ *Literature and Your Life*

❷ Although students may not be comfortable sharing the details of the story they rehearsed, they might share the general reasons a person might rehearse a sad or troubling story.

Customize for *Verbal/Linguistic Learners*

❸ Point out to students that a *Neapolitan* is a person from Naples. Ask students to suggest other somewhat unexpected ways that people from different cities, states, or countries are identified. For instance, a person from Denmark is a *Dane* and an inhabitant of Glasgow, Scotland, is a *Glaswegian.*

❹ **Clarification** Tell students that Hugh Walpole was a British novelist whose popular and, perhaps, old-fashioned works set a pattern for books and plays about schoolmasters. This allusion adds to the impression of Sally as an unremarkable, conventional girl.

◆ Grammar and Style

❺ **Subjunctive Mood** Guide students to notice the use of the subjunctive voice in this sentence. It indicates that Jerome would be hurt if Sally behaved insensitively.

come, after an author's death, when somebody thinks it worth his while to write a letter to *The Times Literary Supplement* announcing the preparation of a biography and asking to see any letters or documents or receive any anecdotes from friends of the dead man. Most of the biographies, of course, never appear—one wonders whether the whole thing may not be an obscure form of blackmail and whether many a potential writer of a biography or thesis finds the means in this way to finish his education at Kansas or Nottingham. Jerome, however, as a chartered accountant, lived far from the literary world. He did not realize how small the menace really was, nor that the danger period for someone of his father's obscurity had long passed. Sometimes he rehearsed the method of recounting his father's death so as to reduce the comic element to its smallest dimensions—
❶ it would be of no use to refuse information, for in that case the biographer would undoubtedly visit his aunt, who was living to a great old age with no sign of flagging.

It seemed to Jerome that there were two possible methods—the first led gently up to the accident, so well prepared that the death came really as an anticlimax. The chief danger of laughter in such a story was always surprise. When he rehearsed this method Jerome began boringly enough.

> ◆ *Literature and Your Life*
>
> ❷ Have you ever rehearsed before telling someone sad or bad news?

"You know Naples and those high tenement
❸ buildings? Somebody once told me that the Neapolitan always feels at home in New York just as the man from Turin feels at home in London because the river runs in much the same way in both cities. Where was I? Oh, yes, Naples, of course. You'd be surprised in the poorer quarters what things they keep on the balconies of those skyscraping tenements—not washing, you know, or bedding, but things like livestock, chickens or even pigs. Of course the pigs get no exercise whatever and fatten all the quicker." He could imagine how his hearer's eyes would have glazed by this time. "I've no idea, have you, how heavy a pig can be, but those old buildings are all badly in need of repair. A balcony on the fifth floor gave way under one of those pigs. It struck the third-floor balcony on its way down and sort of ricocheted into the street. My father was on the way to the Hydrographic Museum when the pig hit him. Coming from that height and that angle it broke his neck." This was really a masterly attempt to make an intrinsically interesting subject boring.

The other method Jerome rehearsed had the virtue of brevity.

"My father was killed by a pig."

"Really? In India?"

"No, in Italy."

"How interesting. I never realized there was pig-sticking in Italy. Was your father keen on polo?"

In course of time, neither too early nor too late, rather as though, in his capacity as a chartered accountant, Jerome had studied the statistics and taken the average, he became engaged to be married: to a pleasant fresh-faced girl of twenty-five whose father was a doctor in Pinner. Her name was Sally, her favorite author was still Hugh Walpole, and ❹
she had adored babies ever since she had been given a doll at the age of five which moved its eyes and made water. Their relationship was contented rather than exciting, as became the love affair of a chartered accountant; it would never have done if it had interfered with the figures.

One thought worried Jerome, however. Now that within a year he might himself become a father, his love for the dead man increased; he realized what affection had gone into the picture-postcards. He felt a longing to protect his memory, and uncertain whether this quiet love of his would survive if Sally were so insensitive as to laugh when she heard the story of his father's death. ❺ Inevitably she would hear it when Jerome brought her to dinner with his aunt. Several times he tried to tell her himself, as she was naturally anxious to know all she could that concerned him.

"You were very small when your father died?"

"Just nine."

"Poor little boy," she said.

◆ Build Vocabulary

intrinsically (in trin′ sik lē) *adv.*: At its core; inherently; innately

Speaking and Listening Mini-Lesson

Soliloquy

This mini-lesson supports the Speaking and Listening activity in the Idea Bank on page 1083.

Introduce the Concept Tell students that they will be delivering a soliloquy, as Jerome, that focuses on others' reactions to his father's death. Tell them that the soliloquy should reflect Jerome's experiences and responses. Review the definition of soliloquy and discuss elements that distinguish soliloquies from other literary speeches.

Develop Background Guide students to gather on one hand all the responses presented in the story—from the laughter of some to the sympathy of Sally. On the other, they can list all they know about Jerome's reactions to them. Guide them to assess Jerome's character to determine a tone for the speech. If possible, have students listen to one or two soliloquies to gain a better appreciation of this style of speaking.

Apply the Information Have students write and edit their soliloquies. Encourage them to practice their deliveries several times prior to giving them in class. Invite students to tape themselves to see where improvements are needed.

Assess the Outcome Have students evaluate each others' performances, using the Peer Assessment: Dramatic Performance, p. 121 in the ***Alternative Assessment*** booklet.

"I was at school. They broke the news to me."

"Did you take it very hard?"

"I can't remember."

"You never told me how it happened."

"It was very sudden. A street accident."

"You'll never drive fast, will you, Jemmy?" (She had begun to call him "Jemmy.") It was too late then to try the second method—the one he thought of as the pig-sticking one.

They were going to marry quietly at a registry-office and have their honeymoon at Torquay. He avoided taking her to see his aunt until a week before the wedding, but then the night came, and he could not have told himself whether his apprehension was more for his father's memory or the security of his own love.

The moment came all too soon. "Is that Jemmy's father?" Sally asked, picking up the portrait of the man with the umbrella.

"Yes, dear. How did you guess?"

"He has Jemmy's eyes and brow, hasn't he?"

"Has Jerome lent you his books?"

"No."

"I will give you a set for your wedding. He wrote so tenderly about his travels. My own favorite is *Nooks and Crannies*. He would have had a great future. It made that shocking accident all the worse."

"Yes?"

How Jerome longed to leave the room and not see that loved face crinkle with irresistible amusement.

"I had so many letters from his readers after the pig fell on him." She had never been so abrupt before.

And then the miracle happened. Sally did not laugh. Sally sat with open eyes of horror while his aunt told her the story, and at the end, "How horrible," Sally said. "It makes you think, doesn't it? Happening like that. Out of a clear sky."

Jerome's heart sang with joy. It was as though she had appeased his fear forever. In the taxi going home he kissed her with more passion than he had ever shown, and she returned it. There were babies in her pale blue pupils, babies that rolled their eyes and made water.

"A week today," Jerome said, and she squeezed his hand. "Penny for your thoughts, my darling."

"I was wondering," Sally said, "what happened to the poor pig?" "They almost certainly had it for dinner," Jerome said happily and kissed the dear child again.

◆ **Literary Focus**
How does Sally's reaction to this news support the story's theme that life is absurd? ❻

Guide for Responding

◆ *Literature and Your Life*

Reader's Response Did you anticipate the way in which this story ended? Why or why not?

Thematic Focus After the "shocking accident" occurred to Jerome's father, what conflicts does Jerome experience?

☑ Check Your Comprehension

1. What roles in life does Jerome assign his father in his imagination?
2. What is the "accident" of the title?
3. (a) How does Sally react when she hears the story about the accident? (b) How does Sally's reaction affect her relationship with Jerome?

◆ Critical Thinking

INTERPRET

1. Keeping in mind that Jerome worshiped his father, explain his reaction to news of his father's death—"What happened to the pig?" **[Interpret]**
2. Compare and contrast Jerome's attitude towards the circumstances of his father's death with that of his aunt. Support your points with examples from the story. **[Compare and Contrast]**
3. (a) What are some inner conflicts Jerome experiences after his father's death? (b) Are Jerome's conflicts resolved at the end of the story? Why or why not? **[Draw Conclusions]**

Beyond the Selection

FURTHER READING

Other Works by Graham Greene
A Sort of Life
The Power and the Glory
Our Man in Havana

Other Works About the Absurdity of Life
"The Night the Ghost Got In," James Thurber
Waiting for Godot, Samuel Beckett
The Bald Soprano, Eugene Ionesco

We suggest that you preview these works before recommending them to students.

INTERNET

You and your students may find additional information about Graham Greene at the following Web sites:

http://www.cyber-nation.com/victory/quotations/authors/quotes_greene_graham.html

http://www.umsl.edu/~S1006642/

Please be aware, however, that sites may have changed since this information was published.

We *strongly recommend* that you preview sites.

◆ Literary Focus

❻ Theme Students may say that Sally's response is completely unexpected, that the question was odd enough when Jerome asked it as a nine-year-old. They may suggest that life is full of surprises.

Reinforce and Extend

Answers

◆ *Literature and Your Life*

Reader's Response Some students may not have expected Sally's perfect response while others might have predicted the absurdity of the ending.

Thematic Focus Jerome needs to come to terms with the gap between his romanticized vision of his father's life and the absurdity of the way he died. He struggles to find a satisfactory way to tell people about the accident and to respond to their reactions.

☑ Check Your Comprehension

1. Jerome sees his father as a valiant member of the Secret Service or as a worldly adventurer.
2. The father is killed when a pig falls on him.
3. (a) Sally takes the news very seriously; she responds to the absurdity as if it were commonplace. (b) Her reaction pleases Jerome and cements their relationship.

◆ Critical Thinking

1. Jerome soberly and calmly asks questions for the purpose of understanding what befell his father in full detail. Students may suggest that Jerome is trying to visualize the scene to get it right in his mind.
2. His aunt relishes the absurdity while Jerome is embarrassed by it. His aunt enjoys telling the story to strangers. He dreads telling it.
3. (a) Jerome wants to protect his father's memory and wonders whether his fiancée, Sally, will be sensitive to his feelings about his father when he tells her about the accident. (b) His conflicts are resolved when he tells Sally about the event and her reaction shows her understanding, concern, and sympathy.

◆ Literary Focus

Theme

1. Students may say that Paul's rocking horse and his attachment to it symbolize his obsession with satisfying his mother's needs, an obsession that, like the rocking horse, takes him nowhere.
2. The symbolism reveals that Paul's family, and English society, are greedy and desperate to be "lucky." Like the rocking horse, however, the family and the society are going nowhere.
3. Students may point to the absurd manner in which Jerome's father died, to Jerome's reaction to the news, and, finally, to Sally's response, which mirrors Jerome's.

◆ Build Vocabulary

Using the Prefix *ob-*

1. object: to speak out against
2. obstacle: anything that gets in the way or hinders; a thing that is against forward motion
3. obligation: the action of binding oneself, legally or morally, to a course of action
4. obstruction: an act against forward motion; the condition of being closed or blocked
5. obnoxious: disgustingly objectionable; harmful to good taste or manners

Using the Word Bank

1. b 2. a 3. c 4. c 5. a
6. b 7. c 8. b 9. b

◆ Reading Strategy

1. Students may say that, as Paul, they would try even harder or try another strategy.
2. Some students may have reacted like Jerome; others may feel he was overreacting.
3. Answers should be supported by examples from the story and by an explanation of their own view of things.

◆ Grammar and Style

Practice

1. go; 2. be; 3. weren't; 4. were; 5. were

Writer's Solution

For additional instruction and practice, use the page on subjunctive mood, p. 55, in the *Writer's Solution Grammar Practice Book.*

Guide for Responding *(continued)*

◆ Literary Focus

Theme

Most short stories revolve around a single **theme**, which conveys a main idea or message about life to the reader.

A **symbol** in a literary work may often enhance that work's theme by suggesting multiple meanings, references, and associations. Similarly, the notion of **absurdity**, or the belief that human existence is irrational or meaningless, is another literary element that adds dimension to the theme of a literary work.

1. What do you think Paul's rocking horse and his attachment to it may symbolize in Lawrence's story?
2. What does this symbolism reveal about Paul's family and the society in which Paul and his family live? Explain.
3. In "A Shocking Accident," what events suggest that life is fundamentally absurd? Explain your choices.

◆ Build Vocabulary

Using the Prefix *ob-*

The Latin prefix *ob-* means "against, to, before, or on account of." Write definitions for the following words.

1. object (verb)
2. obstacle
3. obligation
4. obstruction
5. obnoxious

Using the Word Bank

On your paper, write the letter of the word that is the best antonym of the first word.

1. discreet: (a) multiple, (b) imprudent, (c) invisible
2. brazening: (a) flinching, (b) shouting, (c) insisting
3. obstinately: (a) boldly, (b) concisely, (c) agreeably
4. uncanny: (a) eerie, (b) funny, (c) explainable
5. remonstrated: (a) praised, (b) scolded, (c) scorned
6. apprehension: (a) turmoil, (b) confidence, (c) fear
7. embark: (a) emphasize, (b) hesitate, (c) conclude
8. intrinsically: (a) emphatically, (b) uncharacteristically, (c) richly
9. careered: (a) advanced, (b) stayed still, (c) tipped over

◆ Reading Strategy

Identify with a Character

Understanding a story is often easier if you **identify with characters** by putting yourself in their situation and "trying it on for size." By doing this, you sympathize with their struggles and experiences and get an idea how you might respond in their circumstances.

1. In "The Rocking-Horse Winner," Paul hears his house's desperate but silent plea, "There *must* be more money!" What might you do in response to such a message?
2. In "A Shocking Accident," Jerome feels the degradation of having his father's death ridiculed. How would you respond if you found yourself in a similar position?
3. Did you identify with any other character? If so, which actions and events led you to identify with that character?

◆ Grammar and Style

Subjunctive Mood

To state a wish or condition contrary to fact, writers use the **subjunctive mood.** They also use the subjunctive in *that* clauses of recommendation, command, or demand. The subjunctive form, used with third-person singular subjects, is the present form of the verb without *s*. For the verb *to be*, the present subjunctive form is *be* and the past is *were*.

Recommendation: It is important that he *speak* up.
Demand: The teacher insisted that students *be* on time.

Practice In your notebook, write the correct verb for each sentence.

1. Paul's mother insisted that the child (goes, go) to a first-class boarding school.
2. Bassett and Paul thought it essential that they (are, be) sure of a winner before placing a bet.
3. Paul often wished that his mother (wasn't, weren't) so worried.
4. It really looked for a moment as though he (was, were) going to laugh.
5. Jerome thought that, if Sally (was, were) insensitive, their engagement might end.

Build Your Portfolio

Idea Bank

Writing

1. **Notes for a Screenplay** Make some notes for a screenplay based on "A Shocking Accident." Your notes might include a list of settings, costume descriptions, and casting suggestions.

2. **Retelling a Passage** Select a portion of "The Rocking-Horse Winner" and retell it from Paul's perspective. Maintain a consistent point of view.

3. **Response to Criticism** E. M. Forster called Lawrence "the only prophetic novelist" writing at that time. Keeping in mind the meaning of "prophetic," write a response, evaluating whether or not you find Lawrence's story prophetic.

Speaking and Listening

4. **Soliloquy** A play has been made of "A Shocking Accident," and you are playing Jerome. Deliver a soliloquy—a speech made by a character who is alone—about other people's reactions to your father's death. **[Performing Arts Link]**

5. **Discussion Group** Together with a small group, find and screen the film *The Rocking-Horse Winner* (1949). Then present a round table discussion in which you compare and contrast the film with Lawrence's story. **[Media Link]**

Projects

6. **Social Research** At the time these stories were set, the British class system was rigidly stratified. Research the classes and their effect on British society in general. Present your findings in a report to the class. **[Social Studies Link]**

7. **Multimedia Travelogue** Research Graham Greene's travels. Compile your results in a multimedia exhibit that guides your audience in the footsteps of the novelist. **[Social Studies Link]**

Writing Mini-Lesson

Product Description

From the moment it is first mentioned as an example of the "expensive and splendid toys [that] filled the nursery," the rocking horse in Lawrence's tale occupies a central role in the narrative.

In their own way, many toys *do* possess a magical dimension for children. Write a description of an amazing toy. Think of it as a product description intended to sell the toy. Try to convey the wonder and happiness that this toy inspires in children.

Writing Skills Focus: Climax and Resolution

Even a product description can build to a high point of interest, a **climax,** and present a **resolution**—the point at which all pieces of description come together. To achieve this:

- Present your points in order of interest. Start by describing what a customer would *expect* of this particular toy, then present increasingly amazing details about it.
- Conclude with an irresistible argument as to why your reader should buy your toy. Restate your strongest points and leave no question in your reader's mind that your toy possesses unique qualities.

Prewriting Before you begin your description, visualize your toy. Sketch it, and make notes about its size, sounds, color, texture, moving parts, as well as its function.

Drafting As you draft, remember that the aim of your description is to sell the toy. Your audience is children and their parents. Describe the amazing features of your toy, but make the description believable, too.

Revising Exchange description with a partner. Ask: Do my points build to a peak of interest? Is my description persuasive? Did I do an effective job of making my toy seem like an object of wonder?

✓ ASSESSMENT OPTIONS

Formal Assessment, Selection Test, pp. 277–279, and Assessment Resources Software. The selection test is designed so that it can be easily customized to the performance levels of your students. ***Alternative Assessment,*** p. 58, includes options for less advanced students, more advanced students, logical/mathematical learners, visual/spatial learners, interpersonal learners, intrapersonal learners, musical/rhythmic learners, verbal/linguistic learners, and visual/spatial learners.

PORTFOLIO ASSESSMENT
Use the following rubrics in the ***Alternative Assessment*** booklet to assess student writing:
Notes for a Screenplay: General Rubric, p. 94
Retelling a Passage: Summary Rubric, p. 99
Response to Criticism: Literary Analysis/Interpretation Rubric, p. 113
Writing Mini-Lesson: Description Rubric, p. 98

Idea Bank

Customizing for *Performance Levels*
Following are suggestions for matching Idea Bank topics with your students' performance levels:
Less Advanced Students: 1, 5
Average Students: 2, 4, 5,
More Advanced Students: 3, 4, 5, 6, 7

Customizing for *Learning Modalities*
Following are suggestions for matching Idea Bank topics with your students' learning modalities:
Visual/Spatial: 7
Intrapersonal: 4
Interpersonal: 5
Verbal/Linguistic: 1, 2, 3, 4, 5, 6

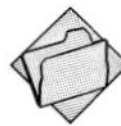

Writing Mini-Lesson

Refer students to the Writing Process Handbook, page 1189, for instruction on the writing process, and page 1191 for further information on description.

Writing and Language Transparencies Use the Writing Process Model 2: Descriptive and Observational Writing to guide students in descriptive writing.

Writers at Work Videodisc
Have students view the videodisc segment on description (Ch. 1) featuring Guy Garcia who explains the dangers of using too many adjectives.

Play frames 5648 to 8620

Writing Lab CD-ROM
Have students complete the tutorial on Description. Follow these steps:

1. Encourage students to brainstorm for descriptive details using the interactive Cluster Diagram.
2. Allow time for students to draft on the computer.
3. Encourage students to consider the tips for presenting their descriptions as multimedia presentations.

Sourcebook
Have students use Chapter 1, Description (pp. 1–29), for additional support. The chapter includes a sample of a cluster diagram and a model of how to effectively use it.

Prepare and Engage

OBJECTIVES

1. To read, comprehend, and interpret a short story
2. To relate a short story to personal experience
3. To identify thematic and literary connections: the short story
4. To respond to the short story through writing, speaking and listening, and projects

PORTFOLIO OPPORTUNITIES

Writing: New Ending; Comparison and Contrast; Response to Criticism

Projects: Model of "The Book of Sand"; Geometry and the Short Story

More About the Author
Born in Argentina, Jorge Luis Borges was educated in Switzerland and lived in Spain before returning to his native land. Because his family was of British ancestry, he learned to speak English before he learned Spanish.

Play this mathematical game with students to give them an appreciation of the concept of infinity: Choose a student and have him or her come up with a number as close as possible—but not equal to—one. When that student chooses a number, go around the room asking successive students to come up with numbers closer to one than the previous number mentioned. After a while, ask students how long this game can go on. The answer is that it can continue for an infinite amount of time. Then tell students that this story is about infinity.

CONNECTIONS TO WORLD LITERATURE

The Book of Sand

Jorge Luis Borges

Literary Connection

THE SHORT STORY

A short story is a brief work of fiction; it resembles the longer novel but generally has a simpler plot and setting. In addition, a short story tends to reveal character at a crucial moment rather than develop it through many incidents. The writers in this section helped make the story an important literary form in the twentieth century, and they pioneered the use of bold new fictional techniques.

MASTERS OF STORYTELLING

In "The Lagoon" Conrad uses elements that appear in much of his fiction: a tale of betrayal set in an exotic, dreamlike place and a story-within-a-story narrative. As in many of his other stories, Joyce builds to an epiphany in "Araby"—a character's flash of awareness that illuminates the story's meaning. In their stories, Woolf and Spark use unusual narrative devices—a stream-of-consciousness narration that mirrors the random thoughts in a character's mind and an omniscient point of view attributed to an infant!

Argentine writer Jorges Luis Borges's uses story-telling techniques as original as those of the early twentieth-century English writers. His tale "The Book of Sand," for example, is a fantastic story filled with symbolism and inspired by philosophical ideas. Told by a first-person narrator, it gains in strangeness what it lacks in conventional action. It may be brief, but it will cause you to think about its narrator's discovery and dilemma for a long time.

JORGE LUIS BORGES

(1899 – 1986)

Jorge Luis Borges (hōr´ he lo͞o ēs´ bōr´ hes) is an Argentine writer known for his inventive, poetic, and fantastic short stories and poetry. The strangeness of his tales recalls the fiction of Edgar Allan Poe. Despite their strangeness, however, these stories deal with universal themes like the meaning of time and infinity, and the nature of personal identity. Often Borges de-emphasizes the usual fictional elements of plot and character as he pursues meaning and fantastic effects. For many years, his work was not widely known. However, he received the International Publisher's Prize in 1961, finally gaining the recognition he deserved. His book Labyrinths (1962), which contains a number of his best stories, has influenced the work of many American writers.

Customize for
English Language Learners
The author uses several terms that describe books or parts of them: *octavo, spine, versicles,* and *flyleaf.* Bring in an octavo-sized (approximately 6 inches by 9 inches) book you can use to identify these parts.

Customize for
Logical/Mathematical Learners
This piece explores the concept of infinity. Ask students to think about the meaning of infinity in a mathematical sense, and to apply their understanding of it to appreciate "The Book of Sand" as a metaphor for something that defies explanation.

Prentice Hall Literature Program Resources

REINFORCE / RETEACH / EXTEND

Selection Support Pages
Build Vocabulary: The Language of Philosophical Ideas, p. 279
Literary Connection: The Short Story, p. 280

Formal Assessment Selection Test, pp. 280–281; Assessment Resources Software

Resource Pro CD-ROM
"The Book of Sand"—includes all resource material and customizable lesson plan

Listening to Literature Audiocassettes from "The Book of Sand"

The Book of Sand

JORGE LUIS BORGES

Translated by Norman Thomas Di Giovanni

❶ **Thy rope of sands . . . —George Herbert**

The line is made up of an infinite number of points; the plane of an infinite number of lines; the volume of an infinite number of planes; the hypervolume of an infinite number of volumes. . . .
❷ No, unquestionably this is not—*more geometrico*[1]—the best way of beginning my story. To claim that it is true is nowadays the convention of every made-up story. Mine, however, is true.

I live alone in a fourth-floor apartment on Belgrano Street, in Buenos Aires.[2] Late one evening, a few months back, I heard a knock at my door. I opened it and a stranger stood there. He was a tall man, with nondescript features—or perhaps it was my myopia[3] that made them seem that way. Dressed in gray and carrying a gray suitcase in his hand, he had an unassuming look about him. I saw at once that he was a foreigner. At first, he struck
❸ me as old; only later did I realize that I had been misled by his thin blond hair, which was, in a Scandinavian sort of way, almost white. During the course of our conversation, which was not to last an hour, I found out that he came from the Orkneys.[4]

▲ ❹ **Critical Viewing** What words would you use to describe the books in this photograph? **[Interpret]**

I invited him in, pointing to a chair. He paused awhile before speaking. A kind of gloom emanated from him—as it does now from me.

"I sell Bibles," he said.

Somewhat pedantically,[5] I replied, "In this house are several English Bibles, including the first—John Wiclif's.[6] I also have Cipriano de Valera's, Luther's—which, from a literary viewpoint, is the worst—and a Latin copy of the Vulgate.[7] As you see, it's not exactly Bibles I stand in need of."

After a few moments of silence, he said, "I don't only sell Bibles. I can show you a holy book I came across on the outskirts of Bikaner.[8] It may interest you."

He opened the suitcase and laid the book on a table. It was an octavo volume, bound in cloth. There was no doubt that it had passed through many hands. Examining it, I was surprised by its unusual weight. On the spine were the words "Holy Writ" and, below them, "Bombay.[9]"

"Nineteenth century, probably," I remarked.

"I don't know," he said. "I've never found out."

1. ***more geometrico*** (môr´ ā gā´ ō me´ tri cō): By the method of geometry; a learned Latin phrase.
2. **Buenos Aires** (bwā´ nəs er´ ēz): Capital of Argentina.
3. **myopia** (mī ō´ pē ə) *n.*: Abnormal eye condition in which objects are not seen distinctly; nearsightedness.
4. **Orkneys** (ôrk´ nēs): Orkney Islands; group of islands north of Scotland.
5. **pedantically** (pe dan´ ti clklē) *adv.*: Putting unnecessary stress on minor or trivial points of learning.
6. **John Wiclif** (wīk´ lif): (1330–1380) English religious reformer who made the first translation of the Bible into English from the Vulgate, a Latin version of the Bible authorized as the official Bible in the fourth century.
7. **Capriano de Valera's, Luther's . . . Vulgate:** Different translations of the Holy Bible.
8. **Bikaner** (bē kə nir´): City in Northwest India.
9. **Bombay** (bäm´ bā): Seaport in West India.

Develop Understanding

One-Minute Insight

In this fantastical allegory about time and life, a book collector receives an unexpected visit from a stranger, who wishes to sell him a rare book from India. At first, the book looks like any old volume, but the book's strange properties tempt the man. For example a page once seen will never be seen again. He buys the book, which comes to preoccupy his thoughts. At last, he rids himself of the book to preserve his sanity. His experience suggest that no one can master the infinite mysteries of the universe.

❶ **Clarification** George Herbert (1593–1633) was a metaphysical poet noted for his steadfast religious devotion and his use of allegory. Borges chose to open the story with a brief quotation from Herbert's writings. "The Book of Sand" is an allegory—a work that can be interpreted on two or more levels, and thus conveys a veiled moral or spiritual meaning. As students read, challenge them to explain the allegorical meaning of the peculiar book.

Literary Connection

❷ **The Short Story** Have students identify the point of view used in this story. *It is told in the first person, which will offer a limited point of view.* Discuss the tone of the opening paragraph, and ask students if it generates questions in their minds. *Students may infer that the narrator offers statements of mathematical logic to introduce what may be an illogical story. They might question why the narrator is so insistent that the tale is true.*

◆ Critical Thinking

❸ **Analyze** Ask students why the author may have included these details. *By supplying these details, the author makes the story seem more realistic.*

▶Critical Viewing◀

❹ **Interpret** Students might use words such as *musty, illuminated, worn, ornate, hand-bound, thick, rare, sacred, dog-eared,* or *antique.*

Beyond the Classroom

Community Connection

Rare or Used Books Some communities are home to special museums, libraries, antiquarian book dealers, historical societies, or private collections that attract bibliophiles. Have students research the availability of this kind of resource in your area to learn where people can see, examine, or purchase rare or used books. They might find out what rare books specific to your area are housed locally, such as regional histories, old diaries or journals, or one-of-a-kind manuscripts by area authors. Others might find out about the procedures technicians can apply to restore or preserve fragile books, and if any such workshops exist in your area.

Customize for
Less Proficient Readers
❶ Ask students to paraphrase the information the stranger gives in this passage to ensure that they understand how he came to have the book. *The stranger traded a small amount of money and a Bible for the book. It came from a lower-class illiterate man who was relieved to be able to get something valuable in exchange for this strange book.*

Customize for
Logical/Mathematical Learners
❷ Discuss the meaning of *infinite*. One mathematical definition of infinite, with respect to a set of things, is that it is unlimited in number, or unbounded in space or magnitude. Challenge students to consider a symbolic meaning for a book that has an infinite number of pages. *Students may suggest that it represents time, the universe, or the ongoing cycle of life.*

◆ Critical Thinking
❸ **Hypothesize** Ask students to imagine why the stranger's speculations irritated the narrator. *Students may say that the musings about infinity were wasting the narrator's time, or that he felt that the stranger was trying to engage him in a philosophical discussion when the narrator really wanted details about the book.*

Literary Connection
❹ **The Short Story** Ask students how this fact foreshadows upcoming events. *It suggests that the book is troublesome, that the man wanted to get rid of it, and that the narrator will have trouble with it.*

I opened the book at random. The script was strange to me. The pages, which were worn and typographically poor, were laid out in double columns, as in a Bible. The text was closely printed, and it was ordered in versicles. In the upper corners of the pages were Arabic numbers. I noticed that one left-hand page bore the number (let us say) 40,514 and the facing right-hand page 999. I turned the leaf; it was numbered with eight digits. It also bore a small illustration, like the kind used in dictionaries—an anchor drawn with pen and ink, as if by a schoolboy's clumsy hand.

It was at this point that the stranger said, "Look at the illustration closely. You'll never see it again."

I noted my place and closed the book. At once, I reopened it. Page by page, in vain, I looked for the illustration of the anchor. "It seems to be a version of Scriptures in some Indian language, is it not?" I said to hide my dismay.

"No," he replied. Then, as if confiding a secret, he lowered his voice. "I acquired the book in a town out on the plain in exchange for a handful of rupees and a Bible. Its owner did not know how to read. I suspect that he saw
❶ the Book of Books as a talisman. He was of the lowest caste;[10] nobody but other untouchables could tread his shadow without contamination. He told me his book was called the Book of Sand, because neither the book nor the sand has any beginning or end."

The stranger asked me to find the first page.

I laid my left hand on the cover and, trying to put my thumb on the flyleaf, I opened the book. It was useless. Every time I tried, a number of pages came between the cover and my thumb. It was as if they kept growing from the book.

"Now find the last page."

Again I failed. In a voice that was not mine, I barely managed to stammer, "This can't be."

Still speaking in a low voice, the stranger said, "It can't be, but it *is*. The number of pages in this book is no more or less than infinite.
❷ None is the first page, none the last. I don't know why they're numbered in this arbitrary way. Perhaps to suggest that the terms of an infinite series admit any number."

Then, as if he were thinking aloud, he said, "If space is infinite, we may be at any point in space. If time is infinite, we may be at any point in time."

His speculations irritated me. "You are religious, no doubt?" I asked him. ❸

"Yes, I'm a Presbyterian. My conscience is clear. I am reasonably sure of not having cheated the native when I gave him the word of God in exchange for his devilish book."

I assured him that he had nothing to reproach himself for, and I asked if he were just passing through this part of the world. He replied that he planned to return to his country in a few days. It was then that I learned that he was a Scot from the Orkney Islands. I told him I had a great personal affection for Scotland, through my love of Stevenson[11] and Hume.[12]

"You mean Stevenson and Robbie Burns,"[13] he corrected.

While we spoke, I kept exploring the infinite book. With feigned indifference, I asked, "Do you intend to offer this curiosity to the British Museum?"

"No. I'm offering it to you," he said, and he stipulated a rather high sum for the book.

I answered, in all truthfulness, that such a sum was out of my reach, and I began thinking. After a minute or two, I came up with a scheme.

"I propose a swap," I said. "You got this book for a handful of rupees and a copy of the Bible. I'll offer you the amount of my pension check, which I've just collected, and my black-letter Wiclif Bible. I inherited it from my ancestors."

"A black-letter Wiclif!" he murmured.

I went to my bedroom and brought him the money and the book. He turned the leaves and studied the title page with all the fervor of a true bibliophile.[14]

"It's a deal," he said.

It amazed me that he did not haggle. Only later was I to realize that he had entered my house with his mind made up to sell the book. ❹ Without counting the money, he put it away.

We talked about India, about Orkney, and

10. **lowest caste** (kast) *n.*: Member of the lowest social class; an "untouchable."

11. **Stevenson:** Robert Louis Stevenson, (1850–1894); Scottish novelist, poet, and essayist.

12. **Hume** (hyo͞om): David Hume, (1711–1776); Scottish philosopher and historian.

13. **Robbie Burns:** Robert Burns, (1759–1796); Scottish poet.

14. **bibliophile** (bib´ lē ə fil´) *n.*: Person who loves or admires books.

Cultural Connection

Sacred Books Almost every culture has one or more sacred books that express its teachings, beliefs, myths, legends, laws, or philosophies. One example is the *Qur'an* (Koran), the sacred Islamic scripture that Muslims accept as the infallible Word of God, revealed over a twenty-year period to the Prophet Muhammad. The *Bhagavadgita* (Sanskrit for "Song of the Lord") is one of the great Hindu scriptures. It forms Book IV of the Indian epic the *Mahabharata;* its verses consider, among other things, the nature of God and how mortals can know Him.

Invite interested students to learn about a sacred book of a culture of their choosing. It can be a book, a manuscript, something in picture writing, or any form appropriate to that culture. Have them find out when and where the work was composed, where the original is kept, and how it expresses its principal philosophical or ethical precepts.

about the Norwegian jarls[15] who once ruled it. It was night when the man left. I have not seen him again, nor do I know his name.

5 I thought of keeping the Book of Sand in the space left on the shelf by the Wiclif, but in the end I decided to hide it behind the volumes of a broken set of The Thousand and One Nights. I went to bed and did not sleep. At three or four in the morning, I turned on the light. I got down the impossible book and leafed through its pages. On one of them I saw engraved a mask. The upper corner of the page carried a number, which I no longer recall, elevated to the ninth power.

6 I showed no one my treasure. To the luck of owning it was added the fear of having it stolen, and then the misgiving that it might not truly be infinite. These twin preoccupations intensified my old misanthropy.[16] I had only a few friends left; I now stopped seeing even them. A prisoner of the book, I almost never went out anymore. After studying its frayed spine and covers with a magnifying glass, I rejected the possibility of a contrivance of any sort. The small illustrations, I verified, came two thousand pages apart. I set about listing them alphabetically in a notebook, which I was not long in filling up. Never once was an illustration repeated. At night, in the meager intervals my insomnia granted, I dreamed of the book.

Summer came and went, and I realized that the book was monstrous. What good did it do me to think that I, who looked upon the volume with my eyes, who held it in my hands, was any less monstrous? I felt that the book was a nightmarish object, an obscene thing that affronted and tainted reality itself.

I thought of fire, but I feared that the burning of an infinite book might likewise prove infinite and suffocate the planet with smoke. Somewhere I recalled reading that the best place to hide a leaf is in a forest. Before retirement, I worked on Mexico Street, at the Argentine National Library, which contains nine hundred thousand volumes. I knew that to the right of the entrance a curved staircase leads down into the basement, where books and maps and periodicals are kept. One day I went there and, slipping past a member of the staff and trying not to notice at what height or distance from the door, I lost the Book of Sand on one of the basement's musty shelves.

15. **jarls** (yärlz) *n.*: In early Scandinavia, a chieftain or nobleman.
16. **misanthropy** (mis an′thrə pē) *n.*: Hatred or distrust of all people.

Guide for Responding

◆ Literature and Your Life

Reader's Response Do you believe that a chance encounter, like the one in the story, can change a person's life? Why or why not?

Thematic Focus In what ways does the character's experience have a dreamlike quality?

☑ Check Your Comprehension

1. How did the Bible salesman acquire the Book of Sand?
2. Name everything that is unique about the Book of Sand.
3. How does the main character dispose of the Book of Sand?

◆ Critical Thinking

INTERPRET

1. (a) What is the meaning of the title of the story? (b) What does it suggest about the book? **[Interpret]**
2. How does owning the Book of Sand change the narrator's life? **[Analyze]**
3. (a) In what way is the book "devilish"? (b) How does the book affront and taint reality? **[Draw Conclusions]**

EVALUATE

4. Does Borges effectively blend elements of fantasy and elements of reality? Explain. **[Evaluate]**

Beyond the Selection

FURTHER READING

Other Works by Jorge Luis Borges
A Universal History of Infamy
Other Inquisitions
The Book of Imaginary Beings

We suggest that you preview these works before recommending them to students.

INTERNET

You and your students may find additional information about Jorge Luis Borges on the Internet. We suggest the following site. Please be aware, however, that the site may have changed since this information was published.

For a biographical sketch and a timeline of Borges's life and writings, visit **http://www.rpg.net/quail/labyrinth/borges.bio.html**

We *strongly recommend* that you preview the site before you send students to it.

◆ Critical Thinking

5 Connect Remind students that *The Thousand and One Nights* is a book of tales told by the wife of a cruel king. She prevents her husband from killing her by telling him a story each night. Like her stories, the Book of Sand seems to go on and on.

◆ Critical Thinking

6 Speculate Ask students to explain why they think the Book of Sand so consumes the narrator. *He becomes obsessed with trying to understand the book.*

Reinforce and Extend

Answers

◆ Literature and Your Life

Reader's Response It can change a person's life if the encounter is significant enough.

Thematic Focus Students may cite the mysteries of the encounter, the puzzles of the book, and the odd way the book comes to and goes from the man's life.

☑ Check Your Comprehension

1. He traded a Bible and some rupees for it.
2. The Book of Sand has no beginning or end, its pages are numbered out of order, new pages appear when the book is opened, and it is impossible to return to a page once it is passed.
3. He sneaks it into the Argentine National Library.

◆ Critical Thinking

1. Students may say that "The Book of Sand," like sand at the edge of the sea, is ever-changing and endless. It suggests that the book may hold secrets of life, but that, like sand, they slip away when a person tries to grasp them.
2. He becomes obsessed with it.
3. (a) It is devilish because it is out of control, because it taunts the narrator, and because it seems to be monstrous and evil. (b) It defies all the laws of books, knowledge, and nature that the narrator knows.
4. Students may say that Borges effectively combines fantasy and reality because the details are very straightforward, yet the nature of the book defies logic.

Answers

Thematic Connection

The Short Story

1. Answers will depend on each student's opinion of the authors' effective use of symbolism. Look for specific details from the selections to support the student's evaluation.
2. Students' answers should include concrete ideas on how the chosen symbol would be used, and on the message it would convey.
3. Answers will vary, based on students' opinions. Some students may suggest a decline in the genre along with a rise in non-print media; others may suggest that the short story will flourish as a way to examine social issues of the day; still others may say that the brevity of the short story will help it surpass the novel in popularity as people's lives get busier and they have less time to read.

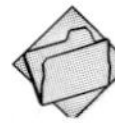

Idea Bank

Customizing for *Performance Levels*

Following are suggestions for matching Idea Bank topics with your students' performance levels:

Less Advanced Students: 1, 4
Average Students: 2, 4,
More Advanced Students: 3, 4, 5

Customizing for *Learning Modalities*

Following are suggestions for matching Idea Bank topics with your students' learning modalities:

Verbal/Linguistic: 1, 2, 3
Visual/Spatial: 4
Bodily/Kinesthetic: 4
Logical/Mathematical: 5

Literary Connection

The Short Story

Short story writers often use the shorthand of symbolism to convey their meaning in a brief work of fiction. For D. H. Lawrence, a child's rocking horse becomes a means of summing up and criticizing a whole society's materialism. For Virginia Woolf, a looking glass symbolizes the skin-deep, superficial personality of a character. Like these authors, Borges centers his narrative on a single symbolic object. For him it is a mysterious book that appears to sum up life's infinite meaning and possibility.

1. Which writer is more effective in using symbolism—Woolf, Lawrence, or Borges? Why?
2. If you were to write story about a symbolic object, what would it be? Explain.
3. Do you think that in the next hundred years, the short story will continue to be as important a literary form as it has been in the last hundred years? Why or why not?

Idea Bank

Writing

1. **New Ending** How would you end this story if you were its author? Continue the story and develop a new ending. However, maintain Borges's use of suspense and the fantastic.
2. **Comparison and Contrast** Compare and contrast this story with one of the British stories from this section. Consider such elements as point of view, setting, plot, and theme.
3. **Response to Criticism** James E. Irby writes of Borges's tales that "The insight they provide is ironic, pathetic: a painful sense of inevitable limits that block total aspirations." Is this remark true of "The Book of Sand"? Why or why not?

Projects

4. **Model of the Book of Sand** Scan the story for descriptions of The Book of Sand. Then, using the details you find, create a model of the book that you can display in your classroom. **[Art Link]**
5. **Geometry and the Short Story** Borges begins the story with geometric principles. Research those principles and then apply them in order to understand the story. Write a brief essay, with mathematical diagrams, in which you present your conclusions to the class. **[Math Link]**

✓ ASSESSMENT OPTIONS

Formal Assessment, Selection Test, pp. 280–281, and Assessment Resources Software. The selection test is designed so that it can be easily customized to the performance levels of your students.

PORTFOLIO ASSESSMENT

Use the following rubrics in the ***Alternative Assessment*** booklet to assess student writing:
New Ending: Fictional Narrative Rubric, p. 96
Comparison and Contrast: Critical Review Rubric, p. 112
Response to Criticism: Literary Analysis/Interpretation Rubric, p. 113

Writing Process Workshop

Short Story

During the twentieth century, the short story came into its own as a literary form. Its brevity and its focus on a few characters and settings were appropriate for an intense and fast-paced world.

Write a short story of your own. Your brief fictional narrative should include a limited number of characters and settings, with a plot centered on a conflict involving the main character. The narrator who tells your story may or may not be a character in the story. If possible, your story should convey a central message about life or human nature.

These writing skills, introduced in the Mini-Lessons in this section, will help you write your story.

Joseph Conrad

Writing Skills Focus

- ▶ **Elaborate to entertain** by including interesting and unusual details. (See p. 1051.)
- ▶ **Create suspense** by raising questions in the mind of your reader; create a feeling of growing curiosity. (See p. 1065.)
- ▶ **Develop the story to a climax and resolution** by advancing the conflict to a high point, then explaining how it is resolved. (See p. 1083.)

This brief passage from Conrad's "The Lagoon" contains or suggests many elements of a short story.

Model From Literature

from "The Lagoon" by Joseph Conrad

Arsat went on in an even, low voice ①: "We ran our canoe on the white beach of a little bay close to a long tongue of land that seemed to bar our road; a long wooded cape going far into the sea. ② My brother knew that place. . . . No sooner had I closed my eyes than I heard her cry of alarm ③. We leaped up. . . and coming in sight in the opening of the bay we saw a prau manned by many paddlers. We knew it at once; it was one of our Rajah's praus."④

① The action and dialogue in this passage are building to a high point.

② This sentence creates suspense. It makes the reader wonder what will happen next.

③ This detail heightens the suspense.

④ An unusual detail, the Malayan boat, adds interest to the story.

Prepare and Engage

Establish Writing Guidelines
Review the following key characteristics of a short story:

- A short story relies on only a few characters to convey its theme.
- The conflict involves the main character.
- The narrator may or may not be a character in the story.

Before students begin, you may want to share with them the Scoring Rubric for Fictional Narrative (p. 96 in ***Alternative Assessment***) so that students see the criteria by which they will be evaluated. Suggestions on page 1091 customize the rubric for this workshop.

Connect to Literature You may want students to review Edgar Allan Poe's "The Oval Portrait" (Unit 4, p. 605). Ask students how Poe's treatment of the genre differs from that by British authors.

Writer's Solution

Writers at Work Videodisc
To review key elements and to hear fiction writer James Berry discuss narration, play the videodisc segment on Narration (Ch. 2).

Play frames 11464 to 21147

Writing Lab CD-ROM
If students have access to computers, have them work in the Narration tutorial to complete all or part of their short stories. Follow these steps:

1. Students can review an audio-annotated literary model.
2. Have students use Story Wheels to help create characters and conflicts.
3. Have students work interactively with Developing Narrative Elements.
4. After drafting, students can improve their writing by selecting words or phrases from Character Traits or Sensory Details Word Bins.

Sourcebook
In Chapter 2, Narration (pp. 31–61), students can find additional support, including topic ideas, suggestions for developing narrative elements, and models written from different points of view.

Cross-Curricular Connection: Science

Remind students that the setting of a story must maintain scientific accuracy. No gangster, no matter how sinister, can be hanged from a sycamore tree high on a mountain. Sycamores grow in lowlands, near streams and rivers. No Montana damsel in distress can hear the melodious song of a cardinal. Cardinals live east of there. No Louisiana orphan can disappear into a dark, mysterious bog. Bogs develop in the north. Thus, scientific details, even in a fictional short story, must be accurate. Ask students to discuss how they might verify the scientific accuracy of their settings.

Develop Student Writing

Prewriting

Writing and Language Transparencies
You may want to have students use a Story Map graphic organizer (***Writing and Language Transparencies,*** p. 126) to help organize their thoughts.

Customize for
Bodily/Kinesthetic Learners
To help these students develop their stories, encourage them to act out scenes with a partner or in front of a mirror. Then they can incorporate these scenes into their narratives.

Writer's Solution

Writing Lab CD-ROM
The audio-annotated Writing Model about plot in the Developing Narrative Elements section of the Narration tutorial shows students examples of exposition, rising action, climax, falling action, and resolution.

Drafting

Remind students to include sights and sounds that establish the historical time period, like a satellite drifting across a star-lit sky or the low hiss of gas lamps along the street.

Applying Language Skills

Writing Dialogue
Ask students to review stories in this unit to find examples of dialogue that enhance setting, advance the plot, or create a mood.

Answers

Possible response:

The storm drew near and Gerry's mother called to him, "Gerry? Gerry, it's time to come in now."

Gerry ignored the call. "That game was so exciting that. . . ." The lightning bolt cut off his sentence and sent Jack flying. "Mom!" Gerry screamed. "Mom, get help! Jack's hurt!"

Writer's Solution

For additional instruction and practice, use the practice pages on Understanding Short Stories and Writing a Story, pp. 136–138, in the *Writer's Solution Grammar Practice Book.*

Applying Language Skills: Writing Dialogue

Through dialogue, a character's own words reveal his or her personality. Dialogue can also do the following:

- **Enhance setting.**
  Narration: It was a starry night.
  Dialogue: "I've never seen so many stars in the sky."
- **Advance the plot.**
  Narration: She sent Charlie to get the police.
  Dialogue: "Charlie! Get the police!"
- **Create a mood.**
  Narration: The team felt depressed and grim.
  Dialogue: "Who cares, anymore?"

Practice Rewrite the following, using dialogue.

It was a stormy night. Gerry's mother called for him to come inside. Gerry pretended not to hear and continued telling his friend Jack about last night's big game. Suddenly, a bolt of lighting struck near them and sent Jack flying. Gerry screamed to his mother to get help.

Writer's Solution Connection
Writing Lab

For help in finding story ideas, use the Story Wheel in the Choosing a Topic section of the Narration tutorial.

Prewriting

Choose a Topic Using a real series of events or your own imagination as inspiration, decide on a character and a situation for your short story. If you're having trouble coming up with ideas, try one of these:

Topic Ideas

- A servant is accused of stealing.
- A series of misunderstandings occurs.

Selection-Related Topic Ideas

- A person comes to a painful realization.
- A mysterious woman appears.
- A boy develops special abilities.

Develop Character Decide on the characters for your story and take notes about their personalities, habits, desires, as well as about their appearance, income level, and background.

Plot Diagram Rough out the events for your short story by filling in a plot diagram such as this one. Identify the major events that form the story's exposition, the events that build conflict, the climax, and the resolution of the conflict.

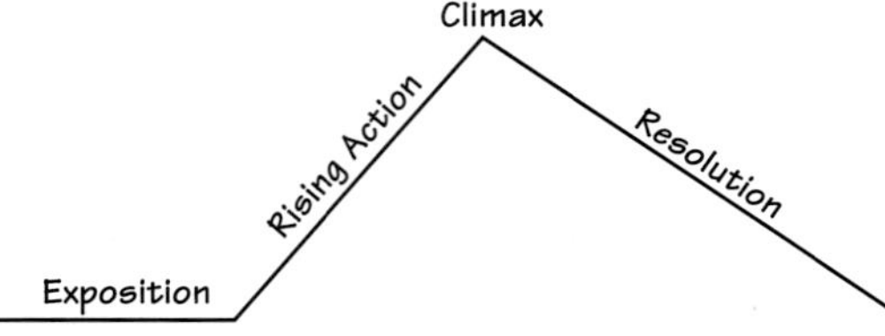

Drafting

Draft the Climax and Resolution Some writers find it easier to write the high point of the story first, then backtrack to the exposition. With your story ending in place, you can focus on creating suspense and interest.

Develop Setting Although most short stories contain only one setting, that setting may have a significant impact on the story and help to create mood and atmosphere. As you draft your story, bring the setting to life through vivid descriptions or dialogue.

Revising

Follow these Tips for Revising:

- ▶ **Character** Give a boring character a quirk or endearing habit to make him or her more interesting. Revise dialogue to make your characters more believable and sympathetic. Eliminate unnecessary characters from the story.
- ▶ **Plot** Examine plot events to ensure that they make sense and build suspense. To build suspense, try hinting at an ominous event before it happens.
- ▶ **Setting** Make the setting a part of the story by adding vivid sensory details to enhance your description. Consider using details from the setting to hint at the story's outcome.

Revision Model

The sun ~~shone down on me~~ ① glowered at me as I biked down the desert highway. Head down, I hunched my shoulders and felt the sweat trickle down my back. ② "Nobody but me in this crazy old world," I suddenly shouted at the top of my lungs. No one looked at me or yelled back because there was no one. ③ Literally. ④ With a loud squawk and a battering of wings, a desert bird flew directly over my shoulder and headed for the sun. It turned around in midair and poised as if to attack, then, silently and suddenly, it dropped like a stone out of the sky and smashed to the ground.

① To make the setting more dynamic, the verb *glowered* replaced a standard descriptive phrase.

② This dialogue reveals the character's situation and his attitude.

③ This fragment adds interest and will make readers feel slightly uneasy.

④ This passage was added to foreshadow the danger that is to come.

Publishing

- ▶ **Festival** Hold a storytelling festival in which students read their short stories to an invited audience.
- ▶ **Videotape** Adapt your short story for film. Create a video-script and ask your classmates to serve as the cast and crew.
- ▶ **Contest** Enter a student fiction contest, for example, the *Seventeen Magazine* Fiction Contest. Ask your teacher or librarian for contest information.

Applying Language Skills: Using Active Voice

Your short story will be more exciting if you use the active voice. The active voice indicates that the subject of the sentence performs an action; the passive voice indicates that the subject receives the action, or is acted upon.

Passive Voice:
The candle was lit by Brian.

Active Voice:
Brian lit the candle.

Practice Rewrite this paragraph, using the active voice.

After the award was won by Stephanie, she was given a ride home by her friend, Marvin. The car ride was felt by them to be too bumpy. The car was then stopped by Marvin and Stephanie was asked by him to get out and see if the tires were okay.

Writing Application As you revise your story, replace the passive voice with the active voice—unless you want to disguise who or what performed an action.

Writer's Solution Connection Writing Lab

For help in punctuating dialogue, complete the Semicolons, Colons, and Quotation Marks lesson in the Punctuation unit.

Revising

Discuss the Revision Model with the class. Then you may want to have students work with a peer editor to improve their stories. Ask students to refer again to the scoring rubrics and to use them now as a peer editing guide.

Publishing

Share audio or videotapes of short stories with nursing home residents or other community groups.

Applying Language Skills:

Using Active Voice

Explain that while active voice is strong, passive voice is essential in mysteries when the doer is unknown. For example, *During the night, his wrists were slit* is in passive voice since readers don't know who the murderer is.

Answers

Possible response: After Stephanie won the award, Marvin, her friend, gave her a ride home. They felt the ride was too bumpy, so Marvin stopped and asked Stephanie to get out and see if the tires were okay.

Writer's Solution

For additional instruction and practice, use the **Language Lab CD-ROM** section on Writing Style and/or the practice page on Voice, p. 56, in the *Writer's Solution Grammar Practice Book.*

Reinforce and Extend

Applying Knowledge

After students have completed their short stories, ask them to discuss in what ways the experience affected their appreciation of short stories by other writers.

ASSESSMENT		4	3	2	1
PORTFOLIO ASSESSMENT Use the rubric on Fictional Narrative (p. 96) to assess student writing. Add these criteria to customize the rubric to this assignment.	**Dialogue**	Dialogue regularly enhances setting and plot and/or helps establish mood.	Dialogue often enhances setting and plot and/or helps establish mood.	Dialogue sometimes enhances setting and plot and/or helps establish mood.	Dialogue rarely enhances setting and plot or helps establish mood.
	Active Voice	The writer tells the story entirely in active voice except when the doer is unknown.	The writer tells the story mostly in active voice except when the doer is unknown.	The writer tells the story mostly in passive voice.	The writer tells the story mostly in passive voice.

Introduce the Strategy

Ask students to brainstorm for a list of manuals they have seen in the last year at home, school, or work. Discuss the remark, "When all else fails, read the manual." Have students recount their experiences with not reading manuals.

Customize for
Visual/Spatial Learners
Ask these students to examine manuals for helpful visuals. Ask them to discuss what generalizations they can make about the importance of visuals in any practical or technical writing.

Apply the Strategy

Have students study the table of contents page of the computer program manual. Ask students what they might expect to find under "Troubleshooting" or in the index. Then ask students to answer the four questions.

Answers

Responses might include these:

1. Monthly calendar details are in part II.
2. Part I gives general background; II deals with the monthly calendar; III with the daily calendar; IV with customizing.
3. I might want to use it only for weekly or daily planning.
4. I might want to make a weekly calendar.

Reading Manuals
Real-World Reading Skills Workshop

Strategies for Success

People sometimes jokingly remark, "When all else fails, read the manual." This statement really means that it's probably smart to read the manual before *anything* fails. You may not need to read a manual cover-to-cover before you use a product, but you can save yourself a great deal of time and confusion if you learn to use manuals wisely.

Preview the Manual Start by conducting a thorough preview of the manual. Begin with the table of contents—look at the headings to see what the product does and how information about it is organized. The introduction will usually provide a general overview.

DayMaker 2.1
Table of Contents

Read All Relevant Sections Use your preview to identify sections that you want to read. You'll probably want to read the first few sections straight through; however, you can postpone reading supplementary material in the back until you need specific information. Use a bookmark to show where you left off reading so that you can return to the spot later when you want more information.

Use the Index to Locate Details Keep manuals handy while using a product. You may want to refer to sections you have already explored or to look up new topics as you become familiar with a product. The index is the place to start when you need to locate a specific piece of information.

Apply the Strategy

The computer lab in your school has a program called DayMaker. You're planning to use the program to create a calendar that will schedule your time. Reading the table of contents will help you use the manual wisely.

1. Where would you look for information about setting up a monthly calendar?
2. Describe the information found in each of the four sections of the manual.
3. Explain why you might want to read section III before section II.
4. Describe one situation in which you would use the index instead of the table of contents.

Here are some other situations in which you may need to read manuals:
- *learning to drive*
- *using a word processor*
- *setting up an audio system*

Beyond the Classroom

Workplace Skills Connection

Being an Autonomous Learner While business and industry offer on-the-job training, the worker who learns on his own gets ahead. Knowing how and where to find information and knowing how to study, understand, and apply that information gives a worker a distinct advantage over his peers. Manuals are the usual mode by which autonomous learners gain job-related information. Suggest that students borrow manuals from someone they know in the workplace and share them with the class. Ask how strategies they have learned here would help them use and understand the manuals that are available to workers and to the general public.

Part 4

From the National to the Global

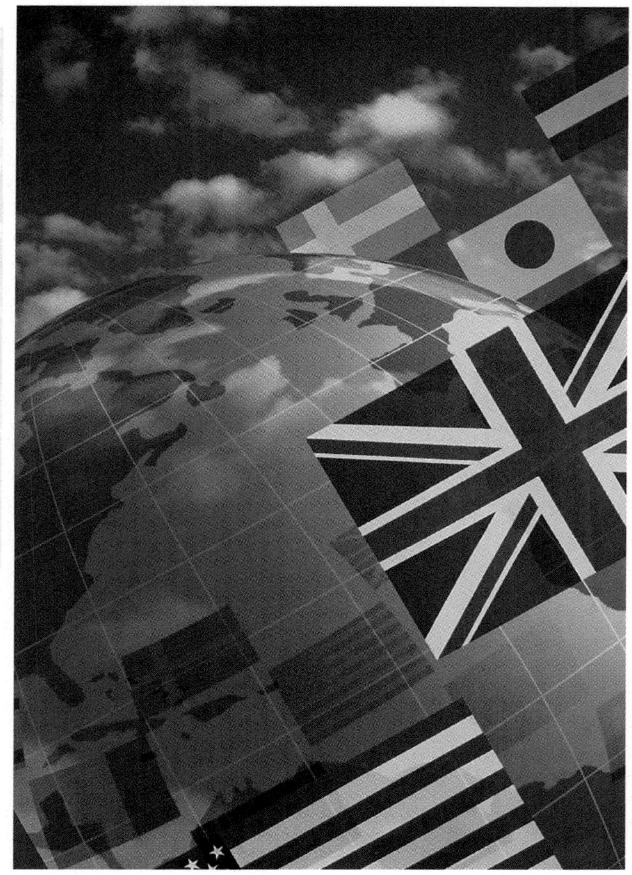

Political World, Kenneth Eward

Humanities: Art

Political World, by Kenneth Eward.

This painting depicts a world that is dominated by political concerns. Have students link the art to the focus of Part 4, "From the National to the Global," by answering the following questions:

1. Which nations are represented by flags in this painting? *From the lower left are shown, the flag of the United States, Britain's Union Jack, the Swedish flag, the Japanese flag, and the red and white Austrian flag.*
2. What countries are represented by land masses? *Students should be able to identify the United States' and Canada's eastern seaboards, Greenland, the Caribbean islands, and to the east, the British Isles, Spain, and France.*
3. What point about the struggle between national and global concerns does the artist make? *Sample answers: The artist makes the flags disproportionately large, suggesting that individual national interests can be blown out of proportion and so blind us to world problems.*

One-Minute Planning Guide

The selections in this part are by modern writers nurtured in the British tradition. Poets Dylan Thomas, Ted Hughes, Philip Larkin, Peter Redgrove, and Stevie Smith are modern writers redefining that tradition. Writers V. S. Naipaul, Nadine Gordimer, Derek Walcott, and Anita Desai are leading voices of cultures once dominated by the British Empire, cultures with unique world views. Science-fiction writer Arthur C. Clarke addresses the the daunting prospect of conquering space.

Customize for
Varying Student Needs

When assigning the selections in this part to your students, keep in mind the following factors:

"Do Not Go Gentle into That Good Night" / "Fern Hill"
- Short, accessible poems about grief and innocence lost

"The Horses" / "The Rain Horse"
- Poem about the beauty of nature
- Thrilling short story about a horse gone mad

"An Arundel Tomb" / "The Explosion"
- In two short poems, Larkin muses about the prospects of immortality

"On the Patio"
- Short poem that captures a moment in a rainstorm

"Not Waving but Drowning"
- Short poem that is grimly amusing

"B. Wordsworth"
- Short story about the plight of artists and poets in Trinidad

"The Train from Rhodesia"
- Short story that addresses apartheid; students may be confused by unpunctuated dialogue

from "Midsummer XXXIII" / from *Omeros*, "Chapter XXVIII"
- Difficult allusions in "Midsummer"
- from Omeros, "Chapter XXVIII" is a poignant, readable poem about ordeals of those captured by slavers

"From Lucy: Englan' Lady"
- Dialect in this poem may be challenging to some readers

"A Devoted Son"
- Short story contains many references to life in modern India

"We'll Never Conquer Space"
- High-interest futurist essay by science-fiction writer Arthur C. Clarke

Prepare and Engage

OBJECTIVES

1. To read, comprehend, and interpret poems and a short story
2. To relate poems and a story to personal experience
3. To judge a writer's message
4. To recognize a writer's voice
5. To build vocabulary in context and learn the word root *-vol-*
6. To identify adverb clauses and use them to add variety to sentence beginnings
7. To write an entry for a nature journal, using specific details
8. To respond to the poems and the story through writing, speaking and listening, and projects

SKILLS INSTRUCTION

Vocabulary: Word Roots: *-vol-*
Grammar: Sentence Beginnings: Adverb Clauses
Reading Strategy: Judge the Message
Literary Focus: Voice
Writing: Use of Specific Details
Speaking and Listening: Anecdote (teacher edition)
Critical Viewing: Analyze; Compare and Contrast; Apply

PORTFOLIO OPPORTUNITIES

Writing: Description; Reflective Essay; Response to Criticism
Writing Mini-Lesson: Nature Journal
Speaking and Listening: Oral Interpretation; Anecdote
Projects: The Laureateship; The Voice of Dylan Thomas

More About the Authors

Dylan Thomas's poetry is known for the richness of its sounds as well as the richness of its imagery. According to critic Tim Reynolds, from the earliest works on, Thomas revealed his "obsession with . . . the sound of words."

One of **Ted Hughes's** chief themes is the modern world's overdependence on rational thinking and the toll that such a way of life takes on instinct and creativity. Critic Keith Sagar has observed that much of his work explores "the lost sense of the sacredness of nature."

Guide for Interpreting

Dylan Thomas (1914–1953)

Playful with language and exuberant about life, Thomas also had a darker side, evident in his poems of death and the loss of childhood innocence.

Dylan Thomas was born in Swansea, Wales, and wrote many of his best-known poems before he turned twenty. As a teenager he also produced source books of ideas that served as a basis for later works.

Visits to America At the age of twenty, Thomas went to London where he worked in journalism, broadcasting, and filmmaking. In 1950, he made the first of four trips to the United States. Audiences here embraced him not only for his theatrical readings of his poems but for the freshness of his poetic voice.

An Artist's Problems Though acclaimed at an early age, Thomas struggled with poverty and alcoholism. In later years, he had difficulty achieving the focus needed to write poetry and turned instead to prose, producing two of the works for which he is best known, *Under Milkwood*, a play for voices, and *A Child's Christmas in Wales*, a memoir. Dylan Thomas died while on a trip to the United States, where he planned to collaborate on an opera with Igor Stravinsky.

Ted Hughes (1930–)

Born in rural West Yorkshire, Hughes spent much of his youth hunting and fishing with his brother. These experiences contributed to his lifelong interest in the beauty and violence of nature, recurring themes in his work.

Hughes and His Father It would be a mistake, however, to ignore the violence of World War I as an influence on Hughes. He was born well after that war, but his father had had terrible experiences in it. Hughes once said that, as a child, he was strongly affected by his father's silence about those experiences.

Hughes himself served in the Royal Air Force and then studied archaeology and anthropology at Pembroke College, Cambridge, where he met the American poet Sylvia Plath. He married Plath in 1956, but they later separated.

A Variety of Work Best known for volumes of poetry like *Hawk in the Rain*, *Crow*, and *Moortown*, Hughes has written a variety of works. These include books for children, a play in an invented language, and fiction like "The Rain Horse." In 1984, he was named poet laureate of England.

◆ Background for Understanding

LITERATURE: THOMAS, HUGHES, AND WRITERS' ATTITUDES TOWARD NATURE

Is nature an arena of bloody competition, "red in tooth and claw," as Tennyson writes? Is it something in which we can trust, as Wordsworth suggests: "Nature never did betray/The heart that loved her"? The answer is that different poets "see" different things in the natural world.

Dylan Thomas was fascinated by nature's double face: life and death. He refers to both creation and destruction in the title of one of his most famous poems, "The Force That Through the Green Fuse Drives the Flower." The color green suggests life and vitality, but the word *fuse*—a figure of speech for the flower's stem—suggests a bomb's fuse. In "Fern Hill," the double face of nature is also evident: "Time held me green and dying." Through most of the poem, however, Thomas stresses nature's sweet greenness, associated with childhood.

Ted Hughes is attuned to nature's violence. In "Hawk Roosting," a poem not included here, he has the hawk say, "I kill where I please . . ." This violence may be present in "The Rain Horse," but does it come from nature or from the human mind?

Prentice Hall Literature Program Resources

REINFORCE / RETEACH / EXTEND

Selection Support Pages
Build Vocabulary: Word Roots: *-vol-*, p. 281
Grammar and Style: Sentence Beginnings: Adverb Clauses, p. 282
Reading Strategy: Judge the Message, p. 283
Literary Focus: Voice, p. 284

Strategies for Diverse Student Needs, p. 59

Beyond Literature, p. 59

Formal Assessment Selection Test, pp. 285–287; Assessment Resources Software

Alternative Assessment, p. 59

Writing and Language Transparencies
Writing Process Model 2: Descriptive and Observational Writing, pp. 13–16

Resource Pro CD-ROM
Includes all resource material and customizable lesson plan for all selections

Listening to Literature Audiocassettes
"Do Not Go Gentle into That Good Night," "Fern Hill," "The Horses," "The Rain Horse"

Do Not Go Gentle into That Good Night
Fern Hill ◆ The Horses ◆ The Rain Horse

◆ *Literature and Your Life*

Connect Your Experience

Maybe you live on a mountain and can step out your door into a glorious sunset or sunrise. Perhaps you live in the suburbs, where houses have neat lawns but crows, raccoons, and deer are shy or feisty neighbors. Maybe you're a big-city person who finds nature in a park—pigeons, squirrels, and starlings—but can occasionally spot a peregrine falcon mistaking a church for a cliff. Wherever you live, nature is all around you. In fact, it's your home.

These poets reflect on what a strangely familiar home nature is, rocking us *awake* in its cradle or haunting us with memories.

Journal Writing Describe a memorable encounter you had with nature. Include as many specific details as you can.

Thematic Focus: From the National to the Global

Notice how these writers describe scenes that are local but address concerns that are universal.

◆ Literary Focus

Voice

In the same way you recognize a friend's voice, you can recognize the **voices** of different poets, their "sound" on the page. This distinctive voice is based on word choice and combinations, sound devices, pace of "speaking," attitude, and even patterns of vowels and consonants.

Dylan Thomas, for example, tends to tumble words out, "speaking" in a rush: "All the sun long it was running, it was lovely . . ." Hughes, however, speaks in a different voice, giving you little separate blips of images: "Not a leaf, not a bird." People who know him claim that he really does speak that way!

◆ Grammar and Style

Sentence Beginnings: Adverb Clauses

To add variety to their writing, Dylan Thomas and Ted Hughes sometimes begin sentences with **adverb clauses**, subordinate clauses that modify verbs, adverbs, and adjectives, and answer the questions *when*, *why*, or *under what conditions*.

Example: *As he watched it*, the horse ran up to that crest . . .

◆ Reading Strategy

Judge the Message

Reading involves not only understanding a **writer's message** but also **judging** it. In this process, you test what a writer says against your own experience and from past reading. Such testing helps you to keep and use ideas that make sense to you and to discard ones that don't.

The message of "Do Not Go Gentle into That Good Night" is that dying people should fight against death. Don't simply ignore this idea or accept it blindly. Use what you know to judge it. Would you give Thomas's advice to a person, real or imaginary, who was very sick? Why or why not?

◆ Build Vocabulary

Word Roots: *-vol-*

In "The Rain Horse," the narrator suspects the horse of having malevolent intentions. The word *malevolent* contains the root *-vol-*, meaning "wish." Combined with the prefix *mal-*, meaning "evil," the root offers a clue to the word's definition, "wishing evil."

Word Bank

Before you read, preview this list of words from the poems.

grieved
transfiguring
exasperated
nondescript
malevolent

Begin a class chart by writing the general heading *Nature* and then creating two columns headed *creative power* and *destructive power*. Invite students to brainstorm for phenomena that fit each category. After discussing such contrasting entries as "plant growth" and "hurricanes," let students know that the works in this selection will help them further explore both aspects of nature's awesome power.

Customize for
Less Proficient Readers

To help students grasp the message of Dylan Thomas's poetry, remind them that poets sometimes "break the rules" of conventional sentence structure. Encourage them to approach the poems as conversations of a daringly original poetic voice.

Customize for
More Advanced Students

Invite more advanced students to consider and discuss these questions as they read the four works: Which message did you find most persuasive? Which message was expressed most effectively?

Customize for
English Language Learners

To help students understand the different symbolic roles that horses play in "The Horses" and "The Rain Horse," have them create a chart in which they list the animals' characteristics in each work. Then discuss how the different kinds of horses helped Hughes express two different messages about nature.

Customize for
Musical/Rhythmic Learners

Have these students read aloud excerpts from two or more of the works. The readers can then lead a discussion about how the various voices differ from one another.

Preparing for Standardized Tests

Reading and Vocabulary The Reading Strategy for this selection focuses on determining and judging a writer's message, a skill that will help students improve their performance on reading comprehension items. Students may be asked to read a poem or portion of one and identify the poet's message. Following is an example:

Read the following stanza and identify the poet's message from the listed choices. *(B)*

Do not go gentle into that good night,
Old age should burn and rave at close of day:
Rage, rage against the dying of the light.

(A) Do not venture out into a stormy situation.
(B) Don't accept death meekly; resist it.
(C) It's best to die quietly, at day's end.
(D) Before going to sleep, you should engage in mental exercise.
(E) Combat blindness and ignorance around you.

To provide students with practice in this skill, have them apply the strategy to the selection as they read. Follow up with the Reading Strategy page in ***Selection Support,*** p. 283.

Develop Understanding

One-Minute Insight The speaker urges an old person, identified in the last stanza as his father, to resist death, or "Do not go gentle into that good night." In stanzas 2–5, he offers examples of different kinds of people who "raged against the dying of the light," suggesting that the urge to resist death is as much a part of the human condition as death itself.

Customize for
More Advanced Students
Point out that Thomas's poem is an example of a villanelle, a verse form of French poetry dating from the sixteenth-century. Encourage these students to define the verse form based on Thomas's poem and to find other examples of the form in English or French. *Students should note that the first and third lines serve as refrains repeated alternately following each tercet and forming the last two lines of the poem. Another famous example of this form in English is E. A. Robinson's "House on the Hill."*

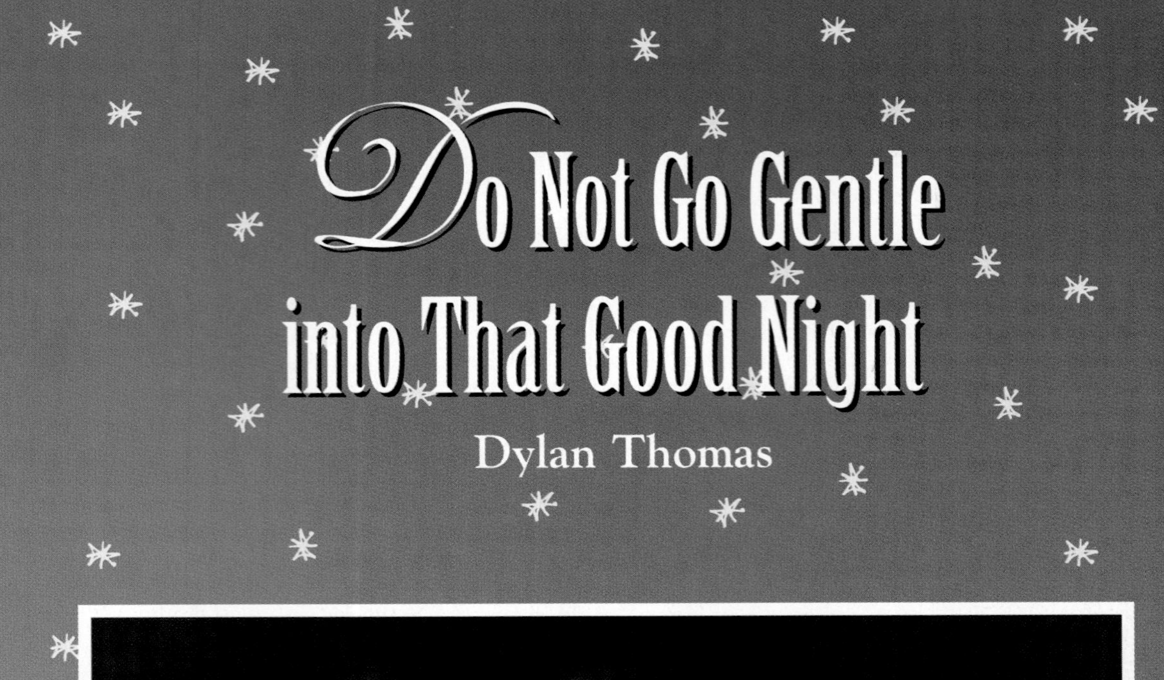

Do Not Go Gentle into That Good Night

Dylan Thomas

Fisherman at Sea off the Needles, J. M. W. Turner, Tate Gallery

Block Scheduling Strategies

Consider these suggestions to take advantage of extended class time:

- Encourage students to complete the Journal Writing activity on page 1095 before they read, and then revisit their entries after they have read the selections.
- Introduce the concept of judging a writer's message by having students read the information and examples in Reading Strategy, p. 1095. After students have read through the poems and the story, have them form small groups to identify and discuss the message of each work and then complete the activities on page 1108.
- Have students listen to each of the poems and to all or part of the story on the Listening to Literature audiocassettes. Have them discuss how hearing the works read aloud helped them appreciate each author's distinctive voice.
- To give students an opportunity to gather and record their own observations about nature, have them complete the Writing Mini-Lesson on page 1109.
- Have students explore the issue of wilderness preservation with the Community Connection: Preservation of Wilderness Lands page in ***Beyond Literature,*** p. 59.

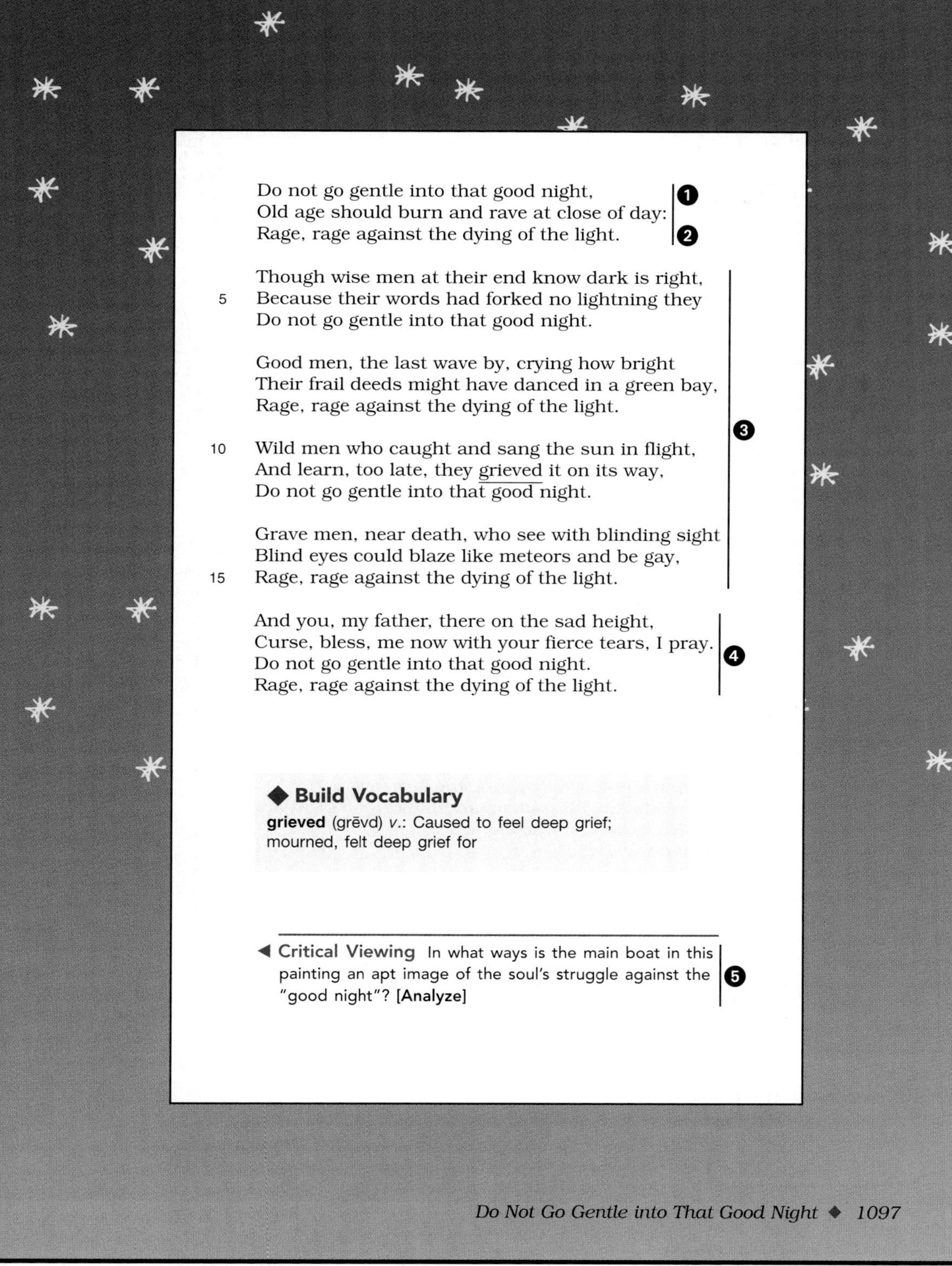

Do not go gentle into that good night,
Old age should burn and rave at close of day:
Rage, rage against the dying of the light. ❶ ❷

Though wise men at their end know dark is right,
Because their words had forked no lightning they
Do not go gentle into that good night.

Good men, the last wave by, crying how bright
Their frail deeds might have danced in a green bay,
Rage, rage against the dying of the light. ❸

Wild men who caught and sang the sun in flight,
And learn, too late, they grieved it on its way,
Do not go gentle into that good night.

Grave men, near death, who see with blinding sight
Blind eyes could blaze like meteors and be gay,
Rage, rage against the dying of the light.

And you, my father, there on the sad height,
Curse, bless, me now with your fierce tears, I pray.
Do not go gentle into that good night.
Rage, rage against the dying of the light. ❹

◆ Build Vocabulary

grieved (grēvd) *v.*: Caused to feel deep grief; mourned, felt deep grief for

◀ Critical Viewing In what ways is the main boat in this painting an apt image of the soul's struggle against the "good night"? **[Analyze]** ❺

Humanities: Art

Fishermen at Sea off the Needles by Joseph Mallord William Turner.

Along with John Constable, J.M.W. Turner is one of the two most celebrated English landscape painters of the Romantic era. The dramatic sky seen in *Fisherman at Sea* is one of the hallmarks of Turner's style, characterized by dramatic lighting and dazzling pagentries.

Use these questions for discussion:

1. What message about nature does this painting convey? In what way is this similar to the poem's message? *The painting suggests that nature is mighty and has the power to destroy human lives; the poem deals with the human struggle against nature's destructive power in the form of death.*
2. What specific elements in the painting convey the power of nature? *Students may point out the dark, ominous sky, the buffeting waves, and the smallness of the human figures.*

Comprehension Check ☑

❶ Have students explain what the images "that good night," "close of day," and "the dying of the light" in lines 1–3 represent. What is the speaker urging in this stanza? *The images represent death; the speaker is urging someone who is dying to "rage against," or fight, death.*

◆ Literary Focus

❷ **Voice** Have a volunteer read this stanza aloud. Then encourage students to characterize the voice that Thomas establishes for the poem. *Students may describe the voice as being dynamic, dramatic, or musical.*

◆ Critical Thinking

❸ **Analyze** Have students identify the parallel elements in these four stanzas. Encourage them to comment on the message that these stanzas convey when considered together. *Students should note that each stanza names a different human type and then describes how each type of man does not feel ready to die when the time comes and consequently fights against death. The overall message is that the urge to struggle against rather than accept death is natural and universal.*

◆ Reading Strategy

❹ **Judge the Message** Ask students whether they agree with Thomas's message that people should "rage against the dying of the light." Have them explain their opinions. *Some students may say they agree, citing Thomas's position that it is part of human nature to resist death; others may disagree, saying that death is a natural part of life and must ultimately be accepted.*

▶Critical Viewing◀

❺ **Analyze** Sample answer: The boat, representing the soul, struggles to stay afloat as it resists the forces of the dark and powerful sea, which represent death.

One-Minute Insight

From the perspective of adulthood, the speaker recalls the carefree and magical days he spent on a farm during his childhood—days when "Time let me play and be/Golden in the mercy of his means." At the end of the poem, he contrasts his former innocence with his present knowledge of the tyranny of time. He now knows that during childhood "Time held me green and dying/ Though I sang in my chains like the sea."

◆ Literary Focus

❶ **Voice** Encourage students to think of words that describe Thomas's voice in this poem. Then have them identify specific features that helped create their impressions. *Students may describe Thomas's voice as rich, lavish, magical, or musical; in support, they may point to such features as his long, tumbling sentences; the overall wealth of images; and particular images such as "prince of the apple towns" and "huntsman and herdsman," which are reminiscent of folktales and fairy tales.*

◆ Critical Thinking

❷ **Interpret** Draw students' attention to Thomas's use of the words *green* and *golden* in lines 2, 5, 10, 14, and 15. Encourage them to comment on the meaning and significance of these two colors. *Responses may include the following: Green is associated not only with nature and growth but also with the speaker's state of being young and carefree. Golden is associated with the speaker's privileged and almost god-like status when young.*

Comprehension Check ☑

❸ To what does the speaker compare each new day to which he awakened on the farm? *He compares each new day to the creation of the Earth and the garden of Eden, as described in the Bible.*

Fern Hill

Dylan Thomas

Now as I was young and easy under the apple boughs
About the lilting house and happy as the grass was green,
The night above the dingle starry,
Time let me hail and climb
Golden in the heydays of his eyes,
And honored among wagons I was prince of the apple towns
And once below a time I lordly had the trees and leaves
Trail with daisies and barley
❶ Down the rivers of the windfall light.

❷ And as I was green and carefree, famous among the barns
About the happy yard and singing as the farm was home,
In the sun that is young once only,
Time let me play and be
Golden in the mercy of his means,
And green and golden I was huntsman and herdsman, the calves
Sang to my horn, the foxes on the hills barked clear and cold,
And the sabbath rang slowly
In the pebbles of the holy streams.

All the sun long it was running, it was lovely, the hay
Fields high as the house, the tunes from the chimneys, it was air
And playing, lovely and watery
And fire green as grass.
And nightly under the simple stars
As I rode to sleep the owls were bearing the farm away,
All the moon long I heard, blessed among stables, the nightjars[1]
Flying with the ricks,[2] and the horses
Flashing into the dark.

And then to awake, and the farm, like a wanderer white
With the dew, come back, the cock on his shoulder; it was all
Shining, it was Adam and maiden,
❸ The sky gathered again
And the sun grew round that very day.
So it must have been after the birth of the simple light
In the first, spinning place, the spellbound horses walking warm
Out of the whinnying green stable
On to the fields of praise.

---

1. **nightjars** *n.*: Common nocturnal birds, named for the whirring sound that the male makes.
2. **ricks** *n.*: Haystacks.

1098 ◆ A Time of Rapid Change (1901–Present)

Cross-Curricular Connection: Social Studies

In "Fern Hill," as in many of his works, Dylan Thomas evokes the charmed landscape and atmosphere of his native Wales.

Tell students that Wales is a small country (about the size of the state of Massachusetts) west of England. Together, Wales, England, Northern Ireland, and Scotland make up the larger country known as the United Kingdom of Great Britain and Northern Ireland. Two official languages, English and Welsh, are spoken in Wales.

Have groups of students do research to learn more about the geography, history, and culture of Wales. To raise students' interest in the Welsh language, you might write this word on the board: *Llanfairpwllgwyngyllgogerychwyrndrobwllllantysiliogogogoch.* Explain that this is the name of a village in Wales, famous for having the longest name of any place in Great Britain.

And honored among foxes and pheasants by the gay house
Under the new made clouds and happy as the heart was long,
In the sun born over and over,
I ran my heedless ways,
My wishes raced through the house-high hay
And nothing I cared, at my sky blue trades, that time allows
In all his tuneful turning so few and such morning songs
Before the children green and golden
Follow him out of grace,

Nothing I cared, in the lamb white days, that time would take me
Up to the swallow thronged loft by the shadow of my hand,
In the moon that is always rising,
Nor that riding to sleep
I should hear him fly with the high fields
And wake to the farm forever fled from the childless land.
Oh as I was young and easy in the mercy of his means,
Time held me green and dying
Though I sang in my chains like the sea. ❹

Guide for Responding

◆ Literature and Your Life

Reader's Response Which poem do you like better? Why?

Thematic Focus Does Thomas succeed in moving beyond his own personal concerns in these poems? Explain.

☑ Check Your Comprehension

1. (a) What is the "good night" mentioned in the title of "Do Not Go Gentle into That Good Night"? (b) Who are the four kinds of men the poet describes in the poem?
2. (a) To whom is the "Do not go gentle" addressed? (b) What does the poet tell the person he is addressing?
3. Use Thomas's images in "Fern Hill" to describe the farm he used to visit there.
4. In "Fern Hill," what two colors does the speaker use to describe himself in his youth?
5. In the last stanza of "Fern Hill," where does the speaker suggest that time has taken him?

◆ Critical Thinking

INTERPRET

1. (a) In "Fern Hill," how would you describe the speaker's feelings about his childhood? (b) What are some of the words and phrases that convey this feeling? **[Analyze]**
2. The mood in the last stanza of "Fern Hill" changes from that in the preceding stanzas. (a) What is the change? (b) What lines or phrases earlier in the poem foreshadow that change? **[Interpret]**
3. In "Do Not Go Gentle into That Good Night," why do you think Thomas wants his father to "rage against the dying of the light"? **[Infer]**
4. Basing your answer on these two poems and using your own words, summarize Thomas's attitudes toward the different stages of life. **[Draw Conclusions]**

APPLY

5. Which of the four kinds of men mentioned in "Do Not Go Gentle into That Good Night" do you think Thomas saw himself as? Why? **[Speculate]**

◆ Critical Thinking

1. Sample answer: (a) The speaker feels that his childhood was a charmed and almost mythical time. (b) Phrases include "happy as the grass was green," "I was the prince of the apple towns," and "it was Adam and the maiden."
2. (a) The mood changes from one of joy and celebration to one of sadness and loss. (b) Lines 42–45 foreshadow the change.
3. Responses may include the following: He feels that it is not natural to accept death meekly; he does not want his father to die.
4. Sample answer: He feels that childhood is a time of joy and innocence; that adulthood is a time of greater knowledge and sadness; and that old age, a time of struggle, requires spirit and courage.
5. Based on Thomas's biography, students may say that he saw himself as a "wild man."

◆ Critical Thinking

❹ **Contrast** Have students identify and explain the contrasts that Thomas presents in these lines. *Responses may include the following: He contrasts the images "green" and "dying" and the images of singing and being in chains. These contrasting images express the contrast between youth and age and between innocence and knowledge.*

Reinforce and Extend

Answers

◆ Literature and Your Life

Reader's Response Students may more easily respond to "Do Not Go Gentle . . ." because of its accessible message. Encourage students to appreciate the music and language of "Fern Hill" as well.

Thematic Focus Sample answers: Yes, in both poems he reflects on the meaning of mortality and death, which are universal concerns; no, in the first poem he refers to his father, and in the second, he describes his own experiences.

☑ Check Your Comprehension

1. (a) The "good night" is death. (b) The poet describes "wise men," "good men," "wild men," and "grave men."
2. (a) It is addressed to the speaker's father. (b) He tells his father to "rage" and fight against death.
3. Sample answer: The pleasant, "lilting" farmhouse is surrounded by apple orchards, fields of green grass, tall hay fields, and clear streams. Barns and stables house calves and horses. Other animals on and around the farm include foxes, pheasants, owls, and nightjars.
4. He describes himself as being "green and golden."
5. It has taken him to a point where he can no longer be innocent about aging and death.

Develop Understanding

One-Minute Insight The speaker vividly describes an encounter with nature as well as the sense of awe that accompanied it: First in the predawn darkness and then as the morning breaks, he observes a group of horses, "Huge . . . ten together." He hopes that the image of these statue-like horses, stalwart and unflinching in a desolate landscape, will remain with him through the years, even when he is far from the place where he caught sight of the horses.

◆ Critical Thinking

❶ **Support** Have students identify the qualities or ideas that the horses represent. Have them cite specific images or phrases to support their responses. *Sample responses: The horses represent the strength, beauty, and dignity of nature; these qualities are conveyed by the image "Huge in the dense gray," by the image of their "draped manes and tilted hind-hooves," and by the phrase "not one snorted or jerked its head." The horses also represent the timelessness of nature; the phrases "Megalith still" and "Gray silent fragments / Of a gray silent world" link them to ancient times.*

◆ Literary Focus

❷ **Voice** Have students describe Hughes's voice in these lines and name the features that help them characterize it. *Students may describe Hughes's voice as being slow in pace, thoughtful, or deliberate. They may point to such features as the unexpected pauses, the alliteration, and the internal rhyme in the line "Silently, and splitting to its core tore and flung cloud"; and the clipped precision in the lines "Then the sun / Orange, red, red, erupted / Silently," describing the burst of sunlight over the scene.*

The Horses

Ted Hughes

I climbed through woods in the hour-before-dawn dark.
Evil air, a frost-making stillness,

Not a leaf, not a bird—
A world cast in frost. I came out above the wood

Where my breath left tortuous statues in the iron light.
But the valleys were draining the darkness

Till the moorline—blackening dregs of the brightening gray—
Halved the sky ahead. And I saw the horses:

Huge in the dense gray—ten together—
Megalith-still.[1] They breathed, making no move,

❶ With draped manes and tilted hind-hooves,
Making no sound.

I passed: not one snorted or jerked its head.
Gray silent fragments

Of a gray silent world.

I listened in emptiness on the moor-ridge.
The curlew's[2] tear turned its edge on the silence.

Slowly detail leafed from the darkness. Then the sun
❷ Orange, red, red erupted

Silently, and splitting to its core tore and flung cloud,
Shook the gulf open, showed blue,

And the big planets hanging—
I turned

Stumbling in the fever of a dream, down towards
The dark woods, from the kindling tops.

1. **Megalith-still:** Still as the huge stones left by ancient peoples, such as those at Stonehenge.
2. **curlew** (kur´ lo͞o) *n.*: Large, brownish wading bird with long legs.

Cross-Curricular Connection: Science

Although the horses in both Ted Hughes's poem and short story symbolize the timeless and untamed energies of nature, horses are in fact domesticated animals, as are dogs, cats, cows, and sheep. Encourage interested students to learn about the history and "family tree" of the domestic horse—whose scientific name is *Equus caballus*—and share their findings with the class. Among the questions students might research: When did people first domesticate the horse? What species represent the horse's wild "cousins"? Where in the world are there populations of domestic horses that have reverted to living in the wild?

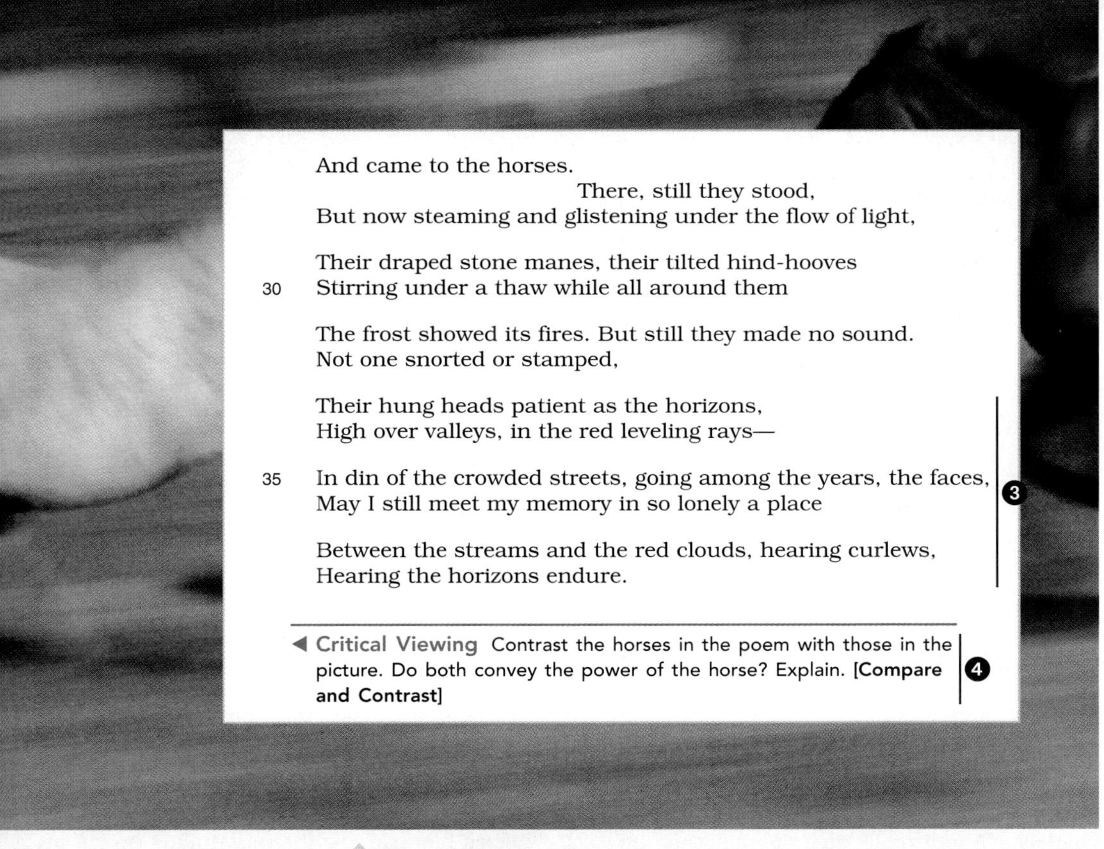

And came to the horses.
There, still they stood,
But now steaming and glistening under the flow of light,

Their draped stone manes, their tilted hind-hooves
Stirring under a thaw while all around them

The frost showed its fires. But still they made no sound.
Not one snorted or stamped,

Their hung heads patient as the horizons,
High over valleys, in the red leveling rays—

In din of the crowded streets, going among the years, the faces,
May I still meet my memory in so lonely a place

Between the streams and the red clouds, hearing curlews,
Hearing the horizons endure.

◀ **Critical Viewing** Contrast the horses in the poem with those in the picture. Do both convey the power of the horse? Explain. **[Compare and Contrast]**

Guide for Responding

◆ *Literature and Your Life*

Reader's Response What kind of place or scene would you like to remember later, in "the crowded streets, going among the years"? Why?

Thematic Focus In what way does this poem touch upon issues that ecologists discuss?

Sketch Briefly sketch one of the scenes that Hughes describes in the poem.

☑ Check Your Comprehension

1. What is the setting of the poem (time, place, weather)?
2. What are the horses doing?
3. What wish does the speaker make near the end of the poem?

◆ Critical Thinking

INTERPRET

1. Compare and contrast the horses in the first and second sighting. **[Compare and Contrast]**
2. (a) What figure of speech is found in line 33? (b) How do you explain the comparison? **[Analyze]**
3. What view of nature does this poem express? **[Draw Conclusions]**

EVALUATE

4. Are horses a good symbol for what the poet is expressing about nature? Explain. **[Criticize]**

APPLY

5. What are some of the reasons people might have for cherishing memories of solitary experiences? **[Generalize]**

◆ Critical Thinking

❸ **Draw Conclusions** Have students reread this passage, paying special attention to Hughes's use of the word *horizons* in lines 33 and 38. With what words is *horizons* associated? What conclusions can students draw about the poem's meaning from Hughes's choice of words? *Elicit the following responses: In line 33, the horses' "hung heads" are compared to the horizon, and both are characterized as being "patient"; in line 38, the speaker expresses his wish to hear once again the horizons "endure." Both the horizons and the horses are symbolic of nature's enduring power and presence.*

▶Critical Viewing◀

❹ **Compare** The horses in the photo are running, while the horses in the poem are still. Both convey power but in different ways—the horses in the photo convey released energy, whereas those in the poem are filled with tension and potential energy.

Reinforce and Extend

Answers

◆ *Literature and Your Life*

Reader's Response Students should offer reasons to explain their choices.

Thematic Focus Sample answer: At the end of the poem, Hughes contrasts cities and their crowded streets with the "lonely" place where he saw the horses. Ecologists stress the importance of preserving open spaces and natural habitats.

☑ Check Your Comprehension

1. The poem is set in the woods in the hour before dawn. The weather is frosty.
2. The horses are standing still.
3. He wishes to retain the memory of his encounter with the horses.

◆ Critical Thinking

1. In the first, predawn sighting, the horses appear gray and stonelike, whereas in the second sightings, they "steam" and "glisten" in the morning light. In both sightings, the horses are powerful, mysterious, silent, and still.
2. (a) The figure of speech is a simile. (b) By comparing the horses to "horizons," which are "patient" (line 33) and which "endure" (line 38), Hughes endows them with a timeless quality.
3. The poem suggests that nature is beautiful, powerful, and timeless.
4. Sample answer: Horses are a good symbol because they are beautiful and powerful animals and have been depicted as such by many cultures, going back to ancient times.
5. Sample answer: In our busy, overcrowded modern world, many people find solitary experiences soothing and refreshing.

Develop Understanding

One-Minute Insight In a story laden with symbolism, the weather and a rogue horse conspire to make a man miserable and frightened as he visits the farmland where he grew up. The man has come to the scene seeking to recapture an image that he held in his imagination from the past. Instead he finds himself in an unfamiliar, hostile landscape that threatens his very life as well as his lost memories.

◆ Critical Thinking

❶ **Infer** Have students identify the situation that Hughes describes in this opening passage. Then encourage them to make inferences about the young man, based on the way he is dressed and his reaction to the situation. *Students should note that the man is walking through some once-familiar farmland; it is a cold, rainy day. They can infer that the man does not now live in the area—he is wearing a suit and is apparently unprepared for the weather and the terrain.*

Comprehension Check ☑

❷ What important facts about the man's background do we learn in this passage? *He had lived in the area as a boy twenty years ago, but moved away twelve years ago.*

◆ Reading Strategy

❸ **Judge the Message** Responses may include the following: *The man feels alienated from the land, despite the fact that he grew up there. The horse, which seems to be "up to no good," confirms his feeling that his surroundings are hostile to him. The phrase "nightmarish leopard" suggests that the horse has hostile intentions.*

The Rain Horse

Ted Hughes

As the young man came over the hill the first thin blowing of rain met him. He turned his coat-collar up and stood on top of the shelving rabbit-riddled hedgebank, looking down into the valley.

He had come too far. What had set out as a walk along pleasantly-remembered tarmac[1] ❶ lanes had turned dreamily by gate and path and hedge-gap into a cross-ploughland trek, his shoes ruined, the dark mud of the lower fields inching up the trouser legs of his gray suit where they rubbed against each other. And now there was a raw, flapping wetness in the air that would be downpour again at any minute. He shivered, holding himself tense against the cold.

This was the view he had been thinking of. Vaguely, without really directing his walk, he had felt he would get the whole thing from this point. For twelve years, whenever he had recalled this scene, he had imagined it as it looked from here. Now the valley lay sunken in front of him, utterly deserted, shallow, bare fields, black and sodden as the bed of an ancient lake after the weeks of rain.

Nothing happened. Not that he had looked forward to any very transfiguring experience. But he had expected something, some pleasure, some meaningful sensation, he didn't quite know what.

So he waited, trying to nudge the right feelings alive with the details—the surprisingly familiar curve of the hedges, the stone gate- ❷ pillar and iron gatehook let into it that he had used as a target, the long bank of the rabbit-warren on which he stood and which had been the first thing he ever noticed about the hill when twenty years ago, from the distance of the village, he had said to himself "That looks like rabbits."

❷ Twelve years had changed him. This land no longer recognized him, and he looked back at it coldly, as at a finally visited home-country, known only through the stories of a grandfather; felt nothing but the dullness of feeling nothing. Boredom. Then, suddenly, impatience, with a whole exasperated swarm of little anxieties about his shoes, and the spitting rain and his new suit and that sky and the two-mile trudge through the mud back to the road.

It would be quicker to go straight forward to the farm a mile away in the valley and behind which the road looped. But the thought of meeting the farmer—to be embarrassingly remembered or shouted at as a trespasser—deterred him. He saw the rain pulling up out of the distance, dragging its gray broken columns, smudging the trees and the farms.

A wave of anger went over him: anger against himself for blundering into this mud-trap and anger against the land that made him feel so outcast, so old and stiff and stupid. He wanted nothing but to get away from it as quickly as possible. But as he turned, something moved in his eye-corner. All his senses startled alert. He stopped.

Over to his right a thin, black horse was running across the ploughland towards the hill, its head down, neck stretched out. It seemed to be running on its toes like a cat, like a dog up to no good.

> **◆ Reading Strategy**
> Here the author begins to set up his message. What is the man's relation to the land? In what way ❸ is the horse an "answer" to his anger and impatience? What does the phrase "nightmarish leopard" suggest?

1. **tarmac:** Material used for paving.

Speaking and Listening Mini-Lesson

Anecdote

This mini-lesson supports the Speaking and Listening activity in the Idea Bank on page 1109.

Introduce the Concept Explain that an anecdote is a short, personal account of an incident that actually happened.

Develop Background Suggest that students do the following as they prepare their versions of the anecdote that the story's main character might tell:

- Review the story for the main events that will shape the anecdote. Jot down any striking words or phrases that you might want to incorporate into your first-person account.
- Reread the ending of the story to determine the man's attitude toward the events just after they happened. Decide whether you will relate the anecdote from a perspective that has stayed the same or one that has changed over the years.

Apply the Information Allow time for students to practice and deliver their anecdotes. Remind them to keep the speeches brief, natural, and true to character.

Assess the Outcome To evaluate the presentations, have students complete the Self-Assessment: Speech page in ***Alternative Assessment,*** p. 118.

From the high point on which he stood the hill dipped slightly and rose to another crested point fringed with the tops of trees, three hundred yards to his right. As he watched it, the horse ran up to that crest, showed against the sky—for a moment like a nightmarish leopard—and disappeared over the other side.

For several seconds he stared at the skyline, stunned by the unpleasantly strange impression the horse had made on him. Then the plastering beat of icy rain on his bare skull
4 brought him to himself. The distance had vanished in a wall of gray. All around him the fields were jumping and streaming.

Holding his collar close and tucking his chin down into it he ran back over the hilltop towards the town-side, the lee-side, his feet sucking and splashing, at every stride plunging to the ankle.

This hill was shaped like a wave, a gently rounded back lifting out of the valley to a sharply crested, almost concave front hanging over the river meadows towards the town. Down this front, from the crest, hung two small woods separated by a fallow field. The near wood was nothing more than a quarry, circular, full of stones and bracken,[2] with a few thorns and nondescript saplings, foxholes and rabbit holes. The other was rectangular, mainly a planting of scrub oak trees.
5 Beyond the river smoldered the town like a great heap of blue cinders.

He ran along the top of the first wood and finding no shelter but the thin, leafless thorns of the hedge, dipped below the crest out of the wind and jogged along through thick grass to the wood of oaks. In blinding rain he lunged through the barricade of brambles at the wood's edge. The little crippled trees were small choice in the way of shelter, but at a sudden fierce thickening of the rain he took one at random and crouched down under the leaning trunk.

Still panting from his run, drawing his knees up tightly, he watched the bleak lines of rain, gray as hail, slanting through the boughs into the clumps of bracken and bramble. He felt hidden and safe. The sound of the rain as it rushed and lulled in the wood seemed to seal him in. Soon the chilly sheet lead of his suit became a tight, warm mold, and gradually he sank into a state of comfort that was all but trance, though the rain beat steadily on his exposed shoulders and trickled down the oak trunk on to his neck.

All around him the boughs angled down, glistening, black as iron. From their tips and elbows the drops hurried steadily, and the channels of the bark pulsed and gleamed. For a time he amused himself calculating the variation in the rainfall by the variations in a dribble of water from a trembling twig-end two feet in front of his nose. He studied the twig, bringing dwarfs and continents and animals out of its

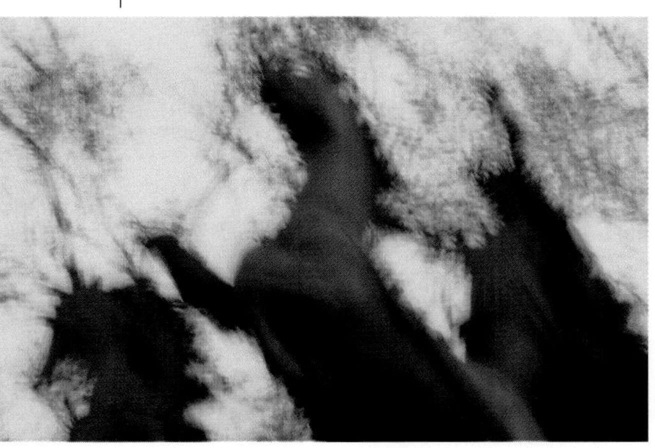

Rearing Horse, Kazuyuki Hashimoto

▲ **Critical Viewing** The horse in the photograph, like the horse in the story, is a symbol of untamed natural power. How does the photographer emphasize the energy and wildness of horses? **[Apply]** 6

2. **bracken:** Large, coarse ferns.

◆ Build Vocabulary

transfiguring (trans fig´ yər iŋ) *adj.*: Changing the appearance of a thing or person, especially so as to glorify it

exasperated (eg zas´ pər āt´ id) *adj.*: Extremely annoyed; out of patience

nondescript (nän´ di skript´) *adj.*: Lacking identifying characteristics; bland

◆ Critical Thinking

4 **Speculate** Ask students what kind of weather conditions Hughes describes in this passage. Then have them speculate about the role this type of weather might play in the story. *Responses may include the following: The "wall of gray," or rain, gives the weather an animate quality; the torrential rain will distort the sights the young man will encounter.*

◆ Reading Strategy

5 **Judge the Message** Call students' attention to the way in which the story's narrator describes the nearby town. In what way might this description provide a clue to Hughes's message about nature? *Students should note that the town is described as "smoldering" "like a great heap of blue cinders." They may say that this image carries negative connotations, as it suggests smoke, industry, and pollution. They may further conclude that Hughes himself is sympathetic rather than hostile to nature and the natural landscape.*

▶Critical Viewing◀

6 **Apply** Sample answer: By blurring the horse's silhouette, the photographer creates a sense of movement and mystery, thus emphasizing the qualities of energy and movement.

◆ Critical Thinking

❶ **Speculate** Have students identify the coincidence that occurs in this passage. Then encourage them to speculate about its significance. *Just after the man thinks of the horse, he turns around and finds it watching him. Some students may interpret this to mean that the horse is in fact "stalking" the man as a leopard might. Others may say that the coincidence suggests that the horse is a hallucination—a product of the man's fear and imagination.*

◆ *Literature and Your Life*

❷ Some students may recall being alarmed by an animal's sudden appearance. Others may tell about inadvertently alarming an animal by coming upon it suddenly and causing it to flee or hide.

Comprehension Check ☑

❸ What sudden event frightens the man? *The horse charges toward him and almost bites him.*

◆ Reading Strategy

❹ **Judge the Message** Encourage students to discuss what this detail reveals about the story's theme and message. *Students should note that the detail reinforces the fact that the man is mismatched to his surroundings, both in terms of his dress and his attitude; the detail also introduces the idea of a deeper and more elemental fear and distrust of nature.*

◆ Grammar and Style

❺ **Sentence Beginnings: Adverb Clauses** Have students identify the adverb clause that begins this sentence. What word does the clause modify? What question does it answer? *Students should identify the clause "As he went." It modifies the verb* broke *and answers the question: "When did he break a yard length of . . . branch from one of the oaks"?*

scurfy bark. Beyond the boughs the blue shoal of the town was rising and falling, and darkening and fading again, in the pale, swaying backdrop of rain.

He wanted this rain to go on forever. Whenever it seemed to be drawing off he listened anxiously until it closed in again. As long as it lasted he was suspended from life and time. He didn't want to return to his sodden shoes and his possibly ruined suit and the walk back over that land of mud.

All at once he shivered. He hugged his knees to squeeze out the cold and found himself thinking of the horse. The hair on the nape of his neck prickled slightly. He remembered how it had run up to the crest and showed against the sky.

He tried to dismiss the thought. Horses wander about the countryside often enough. But the image of the horse as it had appeared against the sky stuck in his mind. It must have come over the crest just above the wood in which he was now sitting. To clear his mind, ❶ he twisted around and looked up the wood between the tree stems, to his left.

At the wood top, with the silvered gray light coming in behind it, the black horse was standing under the oaks, its head high and alert, its ears pricked, watching him.

A horse sheltering from the rain generally goes into a sort of stupor, tilts a hind hoof and hangs its head and lets its eyelids droop, and so it stays as long as the rain lasts. This horse was nothing like that. It was watching him intently, standing perfectly still, its soaked neck and flank shining in the hard light.

❷ **◆ *Literature and Your Life***
Think of a moment when you were alone and suddenly came upon an animal. How did it behave? Were you alarmed?

He turned back. His scalp went icy and he shivered. What was he to do? Ridiculous to try driving it away. And to leave the wood, with the rain still coming down full pelt, was out of the question. Meanwhile the idea of being watched became more and more unsettling until at last he had to twist around again, to see if the horse had moved. It stood exactly as before.

This was absurd. He took control of himself and turned back deliberately, determined not to give the horse one more thought. If it wanted to share the wood with him, let it. If it wanted to stare at him, let it. He was nestling firmly into these resolutions when the ground shook and he heard the crash of a heavy body coming down the wood. Like lightning his legs bounded him upright and about face. The horse was almost on top of him, its head stretching forwards, ❸ ears flattened and lips lifted back from the long yellow teeth. He got one snapshot glimpse of the red-veined eyeball as he flung himself backwards around the tree. Then he was away up the slope, whipped by oak twigs as he leapt the brambles and brushwood, twisting between the close trees till he tripped and sprawled. As he fell the warning flashed through his head that he must at all costs keep his suit out of the leaf-mold, but a more urgent ❹ instinct was already rolling him violently sideways. He spun around, sat up and looked back, ready to scramble off in a flash to one side. He was panting from the sudden excitement and effort. The horse had disappeared. The wood was empty except for the drumming, slant gray rain, dancing the bracken and glittering from the branches.

He got up, furious. Knocking the dirt and leaves from his suit as well as he could he looked around for a weapon. The horse was evidently mad, had an abscess on its brain or something of the sort. Or maybe it was just spiteful. Rain sometimes puts creatures into queer states. Whatever it was, he was going to get away from the wood as quickly as possible, rain or no rain.

Since the horse seemed to have gone on down the wood, his way to the farm over the hill was clear. As he went, he broke a yard length of wrist-thick dead branch from one of the oaks, but immediately threw it aside and ❺ wiped the slime of rotten wet bark from his hands with his soaked handkerchief. Already he was thinking it incredible that the horse could have meant to attack him. Most likely it was just going down the wood for better shelter and had made a feint[3] at him in passing—as much out of curiosity or playfulness as anything. He recalled the way horses menace each other when they are galloping around in a paddock.

3. **feint:** Pretend attack.

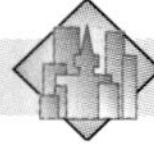

Beyond the Classroom

Community Connection

Connecting With Nature While students may agree with Ted Hughes's message that many people in the modern world feel cut off from nature, they are also likely to agree that many people are taking action to protect the earth's environment and to raise awareness about environmental issues. Encourage students to report on environmental projects and activities that they have been directly involved in or that they have heard about. Also have students use newspapers, bulletins, and other local resources to learn of additional hands-on projects and educational programs in their community that are ongoing. Students might compile their findings into a directory of community events focusing on nature and the environment.

The wood rose to a steep bank topped by the hawthorn hedge that ran along the whole ridge of the hill. He was pulling himself up to a thin place in the hedge by the bare stem of one of the hawthorns when he ducked and shrank down again. The swelling gradient of fields lay in front of him, smoking in the slowly crossing rain. Out in the middle of the first field, tall as a statue, and a ghostly silver in the under-cloud light, stood the horse, watching the wood.

He lowered his head slowly, slithered back down the bank and crouched. An awful feeling of helplessness came over him. He felt certain the horse had been looking straight at him.
6 Waiting for him? Was it clairvoyant?[4] Maybe a mad animal can be clairvoyant. At the same time he was ashamed to find himself acting so inanely, ducking and creeping about in this way just to keep out of sight of a horse. He tried to imagine how anybody in their senses would just walk off home. This cooled him a little, and he retreated farther down the wood. He would go back the way he had come, along under the hill crest, without any more nonsense.

The wood hummed and the rain was a cold weight, but he observed this rather than felt it. The water ran down inside his clothes and squelched in his shoes as he eased his way carefully over the bedded twigs and leaves. At every instant he expected to see the prick-eared black head looking down at him from the hedge above.

At the woodside he paused, close against a tree. The success of this last manoeuvre was restoring his confidence, but he didn't want to venture out into the open field without making sure that the horse was just where he had left it. The perfect move would be to withdraw quietly and leave the horse standing out there in the rain. He crept up again among the trees to the crest and peeped through the hedge.

The gray field and the whole slope were empty. He searched the distance. The horse was quite likely to have forgotten him altogether and wandered off. Then he raised himself and leaned out to see if it had come in close to the hedge. Before he was aware of any-
7 thing the ground shook. He twisted around wildly to see how he had been caught. The black shape was above him, right across the light. Its whinnying snort and the spattering whack of its hooves seemed to be actually inside his head as he fell backwards down the bank, and leapt again like a madman, dodging among the oaks, imagining how the buffet would come and how he would be knocked headlong. Half-way down the wood the oaks gave way to bracken and old roots and stony rabbit diggings. He was well out into the middle of this 8 before he realized that he was running alone.

> **◆ Literary Focus**
> Consider the writer's use of phrases such as "whinnying snort" and "spattering whack." Describe the voice such word choices create—is it distant or engaged, slow or rapid?

Gasping for breath now and cursing mechanically, without a thought for his suit he sat down on the ground to rest his shaking legs, letting the rain plaster the hair down over his forehead and watching the dense flashing lines disappear abruptly into the soil all around him as if he were watching through thick plate glass. He took deep breaths in the effort to steady his heart and regain control of himself. His right trouser turn-up was ripped at the seam and his suit jacket was splashed with the yellow mud of the top field.

Obviously the horse had been farther along the hedge above the steep field, waiting for him to come out at the woodside just as he had intended. He must have peeped through the hedge—peeping the wrong way—within yards of it.

However, this last attack had cleared up one thing. He need no longer act like a fool out of mere uncertainty as to whether the horse was simply being playful or not. It was definitely after him. He picked up two stones about the size of goose eggs and set off towards the bottom of the wood, striding carelessly.

A loop of the river bordered all this farmland. If he crossed the little level meadow at
9 the bottom of the wood, he could follow the three-mile circuit, back to the road. There were deep hollows in the river-bank, shoaled with pebbles, as he remembered, perfect places to defend himself from if the horse followed him out there.

The hawthorns that choked the bottom of the wood—some of them good-sized trees—

4. **clairvoyant:** Having the supernatural ability to see what is not present or to read minds.

◆ Critical Thinking

6 Compare Encourage students to compare the man's feelings about his surroundings to his feelings about the horse. *The rural surroundings threaten and disorient the man; the horse and its behavior make the man feel helpless, foolish, and uncomfortable.*

◆ Grammar and Style

7 Sentence Beginnings: Adverb Clauses Have students identify the adverb clause that begins this sentence *Students should identify the clause "Before he was aware of anything."* You might point out that this clause would be set off by a comma in standard American English.

◆ Literary Focus

8 Voice Sample answer: The voice in this passage is fast-paced and immediate, reflecting the intense physical action that is taking place.

◆ Grammar and Style

9 Sentence Beginnings: Adverb Clauses Point out the adverb clause "If he crossed the little level meadow at the bottom of the wood," which begins this sentence. What word or words does the clause modify? What question does it answer? *It modifies the verb phrase "could follow" and answers the question "Under what conditions could he follow the three-mile circuit?"*

Customize for
Less Proficient Readers
Have students summarize the behavior of the horse so far in the story. *Summaries should include the following points: The horse first appeared at a distance and left an eerie impression on the man. It reappeared after the man moved through the woods, as if it were following and watching him. After the man continued on his way, it appeared again and charged him.*

◆ Critical Thinking

❶ **Analyze** How does the description of the weather reinforce the action that takes place in this passage? *Just as the weather becomes more threatening, the horse's behavior becomes more threatening.*

◆ Grammar and Style

❷ **Sentence Beginnings: Adverb Clauses** Have students identify the adverb clause that begins this sentence. Also have them identify the question that it answers. *Students should identify the clause "As it dropped back on its fore-feet." The clause answers the question "When did he fling his second stone?"*

◆ Reading Strategy

❸ **Judge the Message** Tell students that in his writings, Hughes often explores modern humanity's alienation from the natural world and that Hughes's work is known for its powerful use of myth and symbol. Encourage students to relate these ideas to the man's confrontation with the horse. *Students may observe that the man embodies the trait of being in disharmony with nature; the horse symbolizes the untamed and unpredictable aspects of nature that the man fears.*

knitted into an almost impassable barrier. He had found a place where the growth thinned slightly and had begun to lift aside the long spiny stems, pushing himself forward, when he stopped. Through the bluish veil of bare twigs he saw the familiar shape out in the field below the wood.

But it seemed not to have noticed him yet. It was looking out across the field towards the river. Quietly, he released himself from the thorns and climbed back across the clearing towards the one side of the wood he had not yet tried. If the horse would only stay down there he could follow his first and easiest plan, up the wood and over the hilltop to the farm.

Now he noticed that the sky had grown much darker. The rain was heavier every second, pressing down as if the earth had to be flooded before nightfall. The oaks ahead blurred and the ground drummed. He began to run. And as he ran he heard a deeper sound
1 running with him. He whirled around. The horse was in the middle of the clearing. It might have been running to get out of the terrific rain except that it was coming straight for him, scattering clay and stones, with an immensely supple and powerful motion. He let out a tearing roar and threw the stone in his right hand. The result was instantaneous. Whether at the roar or the stone the horse reared as if against a wall and shied to the left. As it dropped back on its fore-feet he flung his second stone, at ten yards' range, and saw a
2 bright mud blotch suddenly appear on the glistening black flank. The horse surged down the wood, splashing the earth like water, tossing its long tail as it plunged out of sight among the hawthorns.

He looked around for stones. The encounter had set the blood beating in his head and given him a savage energy. He could have killed the horse at that moment. That this brute should pick him and play with him in this malevolent fashion was more than he could bear. Whoever owned it, he thought, deserved to have its neck broken for letting the dangerous thing loose.

He came out at the woodside, in open battle now, still searching for the right stones. There were plenty here, piled and scattered where they had been ploughed out of the field. He selected two, then straightened and saw the horse twenty yards off in the middle of the steep field, watching him calmly. They looked at each other.

"Out of it!" he shouted, brandishing his arm. "Out of it! Go on!" The horse twitched its pricked ears. With all his force he threw. The stone soared and landed beyond with a soft thud. He re-armed and threw again. For several minutes he kept up his bombardment without a single hit, working himself into a despair and throwing more and more wildly, till his arm began to ache with the unaccustomed exercise. Throughout the performance the horse watched him fixedly. Finally he had to stop and ease his shoulder muscle. As if the horse had been waiting for just this, it dipped its head twice and
came at him. 3

He snatched up two stones and roaring with all his strength flung the one in his right hand. He was astonished at the crack of the impact. It was as if he had struck a tile—and the horse actually stumbled. With another roar he jumped forward and hurled his other stone. His aim seemed to be under superior guidance. The stone struck and rebounded straight up into the air, spinning fiercely, as the horse swirled away and went careering down towards the far bottom of the field, at first with great, swinging leaps, then at a canter,[5] leaving deep churned holes in the soil.

It turned up the far side of the field, climbing till it was level with him. He felt a little surprise of pity to see it shaking its head, and once it paused to lower its head and paw over its ear with its fore-hoof as a cat does.

"You stay there!" he shouted. "Keep your distance and you'll not get hurt."

And indeed the horse did stop at that moment, almost obediently. It watched him as he climbed to the crest.

The rain swept into his face and he realized that he was freezing, as if his very flesh were sodden. The farm seemed miles away over the dreary fields. Without another glance at the horse—he felt too exhausted to care now what it did—he loaded the crook of his left arm with stones and plunged out on to the waste of mud.

He was half-way to the first hedge before the horse appeared, silhouetted against the sky at

5. **canter:** Gait like a slow gallop.

the corner of the wood, head high and attentive, watching his laborious retreat over the three fields.

The ankle-deep clay dragged at him. Every stride was a separate, deliberate effort, forcing him up and out of the sucking earth, burdened as he was by his sogged clothes and load of stone and limbs that seemed themselves to be turning to mud. He fought to keep his breathing even, two strides in, two strides out, the air ripping his lungs. In the middle of the last field he stopped and looked around. The horse, tiny on the skyline, had not moved.

At the corner of the field he unlocked his clasped arms and dumped the stones by the gatepost, then leaned on the gate. The farm was in front of him. He became conscious of the rain again and suddenly longed to stretch out full-length under it, to take the cooling, healing drops all over his body and forget himself in the last wretchedness of the mud. Making an effort, he heaved his weight over the gate-top. He leaned again, looking up at the hill.

Rain was dissolving land and sky together like a wet water-color as the afternoon darkened. He concentrated raising his head, searching the skyline from end to end. The horse had vanished. The hill looked lifeless and desolate, an island lifting out of the sea, awash with every tide.

Under the long shed where the tractors, plough, binders and the rest were drawn up, waiting for their seasons, he sat on a sack thrown over a petrol drum, trembling, his lungs heaving. The mingled smell of paraffin, creosote,[6] fertilizer, dust—all was exactly as he had left it twelve years ago. The ragged swallows' nests were still there tucked in the angles of the rafters. He remembered three dead foxes hanging in a row from one of the beams, their teeth bloody.

The ordeal with the horse had already sunk from reality. It hung under the surface of his mind, an obscure confusion of fright and shame, as after a narrowly-escaped street accident. There was a solid pain in his chest, like a spike of bone stabbing, that made him wonder if he had strained his heart on that last stupid burdened run. Piece by piece he began to take off his clothes, wringing the gray water out of them, but soon he stopped that and just sat staring at the ground, as if some important part had been cut out of his brain.

> ◆ **Reading Strategy**
> What does the man's "victory" over the horse signify? Explain why you agree or disagree with Hughes's message about nature. ❹

◆ **Build Vocabulary**

malevolent (mə lev′ ə lent) *adj.*: Wishing harm to others

6. **petrol . . . paraffin, creosote** (krē′ ə sōt′): Petrol is gasoline; paraffin, wax; creosote, an oily liquid made from tar and used to preserve wood.

Guide for Responding

◆ *Literature and Your Life*

Reader's Response Describe a time when you have seen an animal behave as the "rain horse" does.

Thematic Focus What elements of this story are purely English? Which are universal?

☑ Check Your Comprehension

1. (a) What expectations does the man have when he starts the walk? (b) What are his reactions when he arrives at his destination?
2. What is the man's first impression of the horse?
3. Briefly describe what the horse does and how the man finally gets free of it.

◆ Critical Thinking

INTERPRET

1. What do you learn about the man? **[Analyze]**
2. Why is the weather significant? **[Analyze]**
3. (a) What is the relationship between the behavior of the horse and the man's feelings about nature? (b) What is the meaning of the last line of the story? **[Connect]**
4. Has the man been imagining the horse? Why or why not? **[Draw Conclusions]**

Beyond the Selection

FURTHER READING

Other Works by the Authors

"Poem in October"; "The Force That Through the Green Fuse Drives the Flower," Dylan Thomas

Moortown; Crow; River, Ted Hughes

Other Poems on the Theme of the Power of Nature

"My Heart Leaps Up," William Wordsworth

"On the Sea," John Keats

We suggest that you preview these works before recommending them to students.

INTERNET

You can find additional information about Dylan Thomas and Ted Hughes on the Internet at these sites. For information on and poetry of Ted Hughes, go to **http://www12yahoo.com/text/headlines/970905/entertainment/stories**

For information about and poetry by Dylan Thomas, go to **http.//www.uslink.net/~snoopy/dylan.html**

We *strongly recommend* that you preview the sites before you send students to them.

◆ Reading Strategy

❹ **Judge the Message** Students may say that the man's victory over the horse represents the persistence of his desire to escape from or control nature. Some students may agree with Hughes's overt message about modern civilization's alienation from nature, while others may say that they find it overly pessimistic.

Reinforce and Extend

Answers

◆ *Literature and Your Life*

Reader's Response Students' descriptions should reflect their understanding that the "rain horse" is aggressive and unpredictable.

Thematic Focus Only a few details, such as the reference to the "petrol" drum, are purely English. The main themes are universal.

☑ Check Your Comprehension

1. (a) He expects to have a pleasant walk on a paved path. (b) He is disappointed and annoyed.
2. His first impression is that it is strange and up to no good.
3. The horse follows him, seems to watch and charges at him several times. The man finally gets away by pelting it with stones and then running to the gate.

◆ Critical Thinking

1. We learn that the man grew up on the farm and that he has not been back for twelve years. Also, he seems unused to and unprepared for the weather and the terrain.
2. The weather is unpleasant and threatening. It mirrors the hostile threat presented by the horse.
3. (a) The man feels hostile toward nature, just as the horse behaves in a hostile manner toward him. (b) Sample answer: In beating back nature's forces, the man has lost an important aspect of himself—the part that is in tune with the natural world.
4. There is considerable evidence that the horse is real, although the man's fears may have projected more hostility onto its behavior than exists in fact.

Answers

◆ Reading Strategy

1. (a) Sample answer: He was "green" in that he was young and full of life, and he was "dying" in that he was bound to grow older and die, as all living things are. (b) Sample answer: It means that the speaker felt and acted as if he would live and be happy forever, even though he wore the "chains" of mortality.
2. Students' responses should reflect an understanding of the meanings of the images of singing and of chains.

◆ Literary Focus

1. Sample answers: Thomas uses *rhyme* throughout "Do Not Go Gentle into That Good Night;" the last word of each line rhymes with either "night" or "day." Two examples of *alliteration*—"green and golden" and "huntsman and herdsman"—can be found in line 11 of "Fern Hill." Examples of *assonance* in "Fern Hill" include "green and carefree" (line 10) and "fly with the high fields" (line 50). An example of "speaking in a rush" can be found in each stanza of "Fern Hill"; each of these stanzas is made up of one long, image-filled sentence.
2. Students should identify the voice as that of Hughes. They might point to such characteristic features as short, staccato phrases and the use of dashes to indicate pauses when explaining their choice.

◆ Build Vocabulary

Using the Word Root *-vol-*

Sample answers:

1. Wishing good—wishing ill
2. In accord with one's wishes—against one's wishes
3. One who fights in a war because he or she wishes to do so—one who fights in a war because he or she was called upon to do so
4. Happening because of one's wishes—happening because of the forces of destiny

Using the Word Bank

exasperated; nondescript; malevolent; transfiguring; grieved

Guide for Responding *(continued)*

◆ Reading Strategy

Judge the Message

A final step in reading a poem is using your own experience and knowledge to **judge its message.** Poets don't always neatly sum up their messages, but Thomas offers a kind of summary at the end of "Fern Hill": "Time held me green and dying/Though I sang in my chains like the sea."

1. (a) Explain how, as a child, the poet was both "green and dying." (b) What is the meaning of the poem's final line?
2. Use your knowledge of children and of your own childhood to judge the poet's message. Do children "sing" while unaware they are in "chains"?

◆ Literary Focus

Voice

A poet's **voice** is the distinct "sound" of his or her work. Once you know a poet's writing, you can identify this sound even if the author's name is missing—just as you can identify a friend's voice in a crowd. For example, imagine coming across lines 1–15 of "The Horses" without a name or title attached. The clipped couplets, spoken as if through held breath, might suggest you were "hearing" Hughes's voice. Also typical of his voice is the sense of wonder at nature, an almost whispered reverence. Still another sign is the use of phrases and fragments to give information: "Huge in the dense gray—ten together—/Megalith-still."

1. One sign of Thomas's voice is his use of sound devices like rhyme, alliteration (repetition of initial consonant sounds), and assonance (repetition of vowel sounds). Also, he "speaks" in a rush, crowding together images and perceptions even as he uses complex poetic forms. Find an example to demonstrate each of these qualities.
2. Identify the voice in this passage as belonging to Thomas or Hughes and explain your choice:

> Dawn—a smoldering fume of dry frost,
> Sky-edge of red-hot iron.
> Daffodils motionless—some fizzled out.
> The birds—earth-brim simmering.
> Sycamore buds unsticking—the leaf out-crumpling, purplish . . .

◆ Build Vocabulary

Using the Word Root *-vol-*

Use your knowledge of the word root *-vol-* ("wish") to define each word in these pairs of antonyms.

1. benevolent—malevolent
2. voluntary—involuntary
3. volunteer—conscript
4. volitional—fated

Using the Word Bank

On your paper, write the word from the Word Bank that best fits in each blank.

At first the young man walking in the rain was merely ___?___ . His clothes were soaked and the meadow was dull and ___?___—that is, until the moment the ___?___ horse showed up and tried to attack him. His flight from the "rain horse" became a disturbing experience but also a(n) ___?___ one. As he thought about it later, he ___?___. Nature, once friendly toward him, had become hostile.

◆ Grammar and Style

Sentence Beginnings: Adverb Clauses

Both Hughes and Thomas employ **adverb clauses** at the beginning of sentences to increase sentence variety.

Practice In your notebook, combine each pair of sentences to create a single sentence that begins with an adverb clause. Add subordinating conjunctions like *as, as if, after, because, when,* and *since.* Insert a comma after the adverb clause to separate it from the main clause. If necessary, use pronouns to avoid repeating nouns.

1. The young man came over the hill. The first thin blowing of rain met him.
2. He went. He broke a yard length of wrist-thick dead branch from one of the oaks.
3. The horse seemed to have gone on down the wood. His way to the farm was clear.
4. He fell. The warning flashed through his head that he must keep his suit out of the leaf-mold.
5. The horse had been waiting for just this. It dipped its head twice and came at him.

◆ Grammar and Style

Suggested answers:

1. As the young man came over the hill, the first thin blowing of rain met him.
2. As he went, he broke a yard length of wrist-thick dead branch from one of the oaks.
3. Since the horse seemed to have gone on down the wood, his way to the farm was clear.
4. As he fell, the warning flashed through his head that he must keep his suit out of the leaf-mold.
5. As if the horse had been waiting for just this, it dipped its head twice and came at him.

Writer's Solution

For additional instruction and practice, use the lesson on Varying Sentence Structure in the **Language Lab CD-ROM,** and the page on Adverb Clauses, p. 32 in the *Writer's Solution Grammar Practice Book.*

Build Your Portfolio

Idea Bank

Writing

1. **Description** Describe a place you went as a child or a scene from nature that has haunted your memory. Use language that appeals to a variety of senses, as Hughes and Thomas do.

2. **Reflective Essay** Both Thomas and Hughes describe memories that are important to them. Using their poems as examples, write a reflective essay on memory and the gifts it gives us.

3. **Response to Criticism** William York Tindall writes of "Fern Hill": "Waking to death, the poet still sings green and golden songs." Comment on the truth of this remark, citing specific passages from the poem.

Speaking and Listening

4. **Oral Interpretation** Read one of these poems aloud to the class. As part of your rehearsal, listen to a recorded reading of the poem. Note instances in which the speaker pauses or emphasizes words. **[Performing Arts Link]**

5. **Anecdote** As the young man in "The Rain Horse," tell someone about this strange experience several years afterward. Remember that passing time might give you a different perspective on the events. **[Performing Arts Link]**

Projects

6. **The Laureateship** Ted Hughes is the poet laureate of England. Research his duties and compare and contrast them with those of the American poet laureate. **[Literature Link]**

7. **The Voice of Dylan Thomas** Thomas's poetry readings made him a star. Treat classmates to recordings of his performances. Then lead a discussion on what makes his readings so powerful. **[Performing Arts Link]**

Writing Mini-Lesson

Nature Journal

Dylan Thomas and Ted Hughes are both keen observers of nature, and it shows in their writing. Train your powers of observation by writing an entry for a nature journal. Choose a place to observe and record your observations. You may write one long entry or several shorter ones showing changes over time. Whether you observe nature in the city, the suburbs, or the country, be sure to describe specific details in your journal entry.

Writing Skills Focus: Use of Specific Details

A nature journal is a record of fleeting moments. The more **specific details** you use, the more readers can experience those moments. "A beautiful day" tells almost nothing. Was it blazing hot, steamy and muggy, or cool and crisp? Did a butterfly flit, float, or flutter? Notice the specific details that Ted Hughes includes in this description from "The Rain Horse":

Model From Literature

The horse was almost on top of him, its head stretching forwards, ears flattened and lips lifted back from the long yellow teeth.

Prewriting Choose a place to observe and make yourself inconspicuous. If you are noisy or obvious, you may frighten animals and distract yourself from what you want to see. Be prepared to take notes so that you don't forget specific details.

Drafting Refer to the notes you took and organize them systematically: chronologically, from earliest to latest; spatially, from top to bottom or left to right; or by order of importance.

Revising Check to be sure you've included details that appeal to the senses of touch, smell, and taste, which are often neglected. If you haven't, add them. Replace general words like *beautiful* with more specific ones like *purple-and-yellow striped.*

✓ ASSESSMENT OPTIONS

Formal Assessment, Selection Test, pp. 285–287, and Assessment Resources Software. The selection test is designed so that it can be easily customized to the performance levels of your students. ***Alternative Assessment,*** p. 59, includes options for less advanced students, more advanced students, intrapersonal learners, verbal/linguistic learners, visual/spatial learners and logical/mathematical learners.

PORTFOLIO ASSESSMENT

Use the following rubrics in the ***Alternative Assessment*** booklet to assess student writing:
Description: Description Rubric, p. 98
Reflective Essay: Expression Rubric, p. 95
Response to Criticism: Literary Analysis/Interpretation Rubric, p. 113
Writing Mini-Lesson: Description Rubric, p. 98

Idea Bank

Customizing for *Performance Levels*

Following are suggestions for matching Idea Bank topics with your students' performance levels:

Less Advanced Students: 1, 4, 7
Average Students: 2, 5, 7
More Advanced Students: 3, 6

Customizing for *Learning Modalities*

Following are suggestions for matching Idea Bank topics with your students' learning modalities:

Verbal/Linguistic: 1, 2, 3, 4, 5, 6
Musical/Rhythmic: 4, 7
Intrapersonal: 1,2

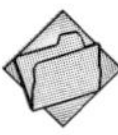

Writing Mini-Lesson

Refer students to the Writing Process Handbook, page 1189, for instruction on the writing process, and page 1191 for further information on description.

Writing and Language Transparencies Use the Writing Process Model 2: Descriptive and Observational Writing, pp. 13–17, to guide students through the process of writing and revising their nature journals.

Writer's Solution

Writing Lab CD-ROM

Have students complete the tutorial on Description. Follow these steps:

1. Refer students to the Audio-Annotated Literary Model of an observation of a natural phenomenon.
2. Have students draw descriptive words from the Word Bins.
3. Students should draft on the computer.
4. Suggest that students use the Proofreading Checklist as they revise their drafts.

Allow approximately 90 minutes of class time to complete these steps.

Sourcebook

Have students use Chapter 1, Description (pp. 1–29), for additional support. The chapter includes a Model From Literature of an Observation (p. 6).

Prepare and Engage

OBJECTIVES

1. To read, comprehend, and interpret poems
2. To relate poems to personal experience
3. To read in sentences to improve comprehension
4. To identify free verse and meter
5. To build vocabulary in context and learn the word root *-fid-*
6. To use correct sequence of tenses
7. To write a how-to guide for an interview, using elaboration to prove a point
8. To respond to poetry through writing, speaking and listening, and projects

SKILLS INSTRUCTION

Vocabulary: Word Roots: *-fid-*

Grammar: Sequence of Tenses

Reading Strategy: Read in Sentences

Literary Focus: Free Verse and Meter

Speaking and Listening: Eulogy (teacher edition)

Critical Viewing: Relate; Evaluate

PORTFOLIO OPPORTUNITIES

Writing: Description; Comparison and Contrast; Response to Criticism

Writing Mini-Lesson: How-to Guide for an Interview

Speaking and Listening: Eulogy, Poetry Reading

Projects: Pantomime; Film Review

More About the Authors

Philip Larkin liked to portray himself as isolated and uncomfortable with the modern world. Many critics, however, see this more as the stance of his narrators than as the position of the poet himself. These critics point to Larkin's tongue-in-cheek humor and effective use of modern speech as evidence of the poet's shrewd understanding of contemporary life.

Stevie Smith was known for her ability to write about serious topics in a bright, humorous tone. However, much of her poetry deals in profound and disturbing ways with loneliness and other painful topics.

In addition to his several volumes of poetry, **Peter Redgrove** has published novels, romances, and volumes of plays and radio scripts.

Guide for Interpreting

Philip Larkin *(1922–1985)*

Larkin turned what could have been a discouragement into a reason for developing poetic skill and emotional restraint. As a child in Coventry, England, his home life was dominated by a father who held him accountable to rigid standards. Larkin escaped from these pressures by building a private childhood world, rich in creativity and imagination. He began a lifelong interest in jazz, which he came to love "even more than poetry." However, it was his clear-eyed, honest poetry, combining conversational language with well-crafted forms, that won him international fame. His poetry speaks of everyday realities, sometimes discouragingly, but is quietly haunted by realities beyond everyday life.

Stevie Smith *(1902–1971)*

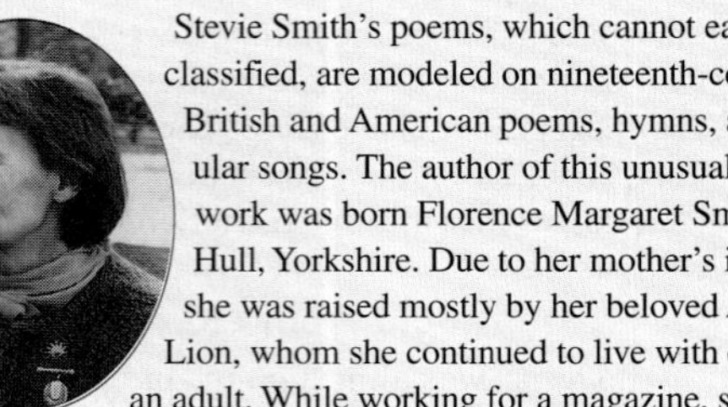

Stevie Smith's poems, which cannot easily be classified, are modeled on nineteenth-century British and American poems, hymns, and popular songs. The author of this unusual body of work was born Florence Margaret Smith in Hull, Yorkshire. Due to her mother's ill health, she was raised mostly by her beloved Auntie Lion, whom she continued to live with even as an adult. While working for a magazine, she wrote three novels and more than ten collections of poetry.

Peter Redgrove *(1932–)*

Like William Blake, a visionary poet with whom he is sometimes compared, Peter Redgrove does not fit into the usual categories. He lives at a distance from the literary hub of London—in Falmouth, Cornwall, the southwestern tip of England. He lives at an imaginative distance from London as well, rejecting the drab dailiness so prevalent in many post-World War II British poems. In his own poems, novels, television scripts, and nonfiction works, he celebrates our power to reimagine and transform our lives. His poems of celebration have been widely acclaimed in England, and he is the recipient of the 1996 Queen's Medal for Poetry, an honor that was also accorded the late Philip Larkin.

◆ Background for Understanding

SCIENCE: BODY LANGUAGE

In the past two centuries, scientists have discovered much about the role of body language in communication. Biologists have studied how animals use different postures to communicate messages like "threat" and "submission." Also, anthropologists have examined differences in human body language from culture to culture.

For example, people from Latin American and Arab cultures generally stand closer together when they talk than do people from the United States. In addition, people from Japanese and Native American cultures consider it disrespectful to look a person in the eye in some situations. Finally, if you "read" body language, you can occasionally detect differences between what people say with words and what they say with posture and gestures.

Poets have long recognized the importance of body language. Each of these poems includes a gesture that "comments" on what is happening. In Larkin's "Explosion," wives who are remembering an explosion that killed their husbands imagine one man holding miraculously "unbroken" eggs in his outstretched hand. Stevie Smith, in "Not Waving but Drowning," shows how a misinterpreted gesture can tell the story of a person's life. Meanwhile, Redgrove sums up a whole attitude toward life in a single gesture.

Read these poems for their body language as well as for their words.

Prentice Hall Literature Program Resources

REINFORCE / RETEACH / EXTEND

Selection Support Pages
Build Vocabulary: Word Roots: *-fid-*, p. 285
Grammar and Style: Sequences of Tenses, p. 286
Reading Strategy: Read in Sentences, p. 287
Literary Focus: Free Verse and Meter, p. 288

Strategies for Diverse Student Needs, p. 60

Beyond Literature
Cross-Curricular Connection: Social Studies
Coal Mining in England, p. 60

Formal Assessment Selection Test, pp. 288–290; Assessment Resources Software

Alternative Assessment, p. 60

Writing and Language Transparencies
Outline, pp. 123–125

Resource Pro CD-ROM
"An Arundel Tomb," "The Explosion," "On the Patio," "Not Waving but Drowning"— includes all resource material and customizable lesson plan

Listening to Literature Audiocassettes
"An Arundel Tomb," "The Explosion," "On the Patio," "Not Waving but Drowning"

An Arundel Tomb ◆ The Explosion On the Patio ◆ Not Waving but Drowning

◆ Literature and Your Life

Connect Your Experience

You look at your friend's tense shoulders and clenched fist and know immediately that something is wrong. However, when you ask what it is, your friend denies that there is a problem, claiming that he or she couldn't be in a better mood.

There are many reasons for hiding feelings, but in some cases, our body language betrays the truth. These poems play on body language as an essential indicator of human thought and emotion. In each case, a striking gesture stands out, offering itself as the central image of the poem, holding the secret to the poem's meaning.

Journal Writing Describe a scene from a movie or from life in which body language revealed a person's true feelings.

Thematic Focus: From the National to the Global

As you read these poems, notice how they go beyond specific settings and situations to arrive at universal meanings.

◆ Build Vocabulary

Word Roots: *-fid-*

Larkin uses the word *fidelity* in "An Arundel Tomb." It means "faithfulness" and contains the root *-fid-*, based on a word that means "faith." Think about other words that use this root, like *confide*.

Word Bank

Before you read, preview this list of words from the poems.

effigy
supine
fidelity
larking

◆ Grammar and Style

Sequence of Tenses

These poets use different **verb tenses** to show the relationship of events in time. The present tense indicates events in the present or ongoing conditions. The past tense shows events that occurred and ended in the past, while the present perfect tense shows events that began in the past and have continued into the present. Following are examples from Larkin's "An Arundel Tomb," which describes a sculpture of an "earl and countess":

Present Tense: The earl and countess *lie* in stone.
Past Tense: Rigidly they/*Persisted*, *linked* . . .
Present Perfect Tense: Time *has transfigured* them . . .

◆ Literary Focus

Free Verse and Meter

Free verse is rhymed or unrhymed poetry without any of the regular rhythms called **meter**. Widely used in twentieth-century poetry, free verse has lines of different lengths and an invented rhythm that suits its meaning.

Smith and Redgrove use varying free-verse rhythms to reinforce their meanings. Larkin uses trochaic tetrameter in "The Explosion" and iambic tetrameter in "An Arundel Tomb" (a trochee is a stressed followed by an unstressed syllable ´˘; an iamb is an unstressed followed by a stressed syllable ˘´; and *tetrameter* means four feet per line):

On the day of the explosion
("The Explosion")

Untruth the stone fidelity
("An Arundel Tomb")

◆ Reading Strategy

Read in Sentences

Poets often run sentences past the ends of lines. Therefore, when you're reading a poem for meaning, rather than for rhyme or sound devices, **read sentences** and not lines.

If you stop after the first line of "The Explosion," for example—"On the day of the explosion"—you don't find out *what* happened on that day.

Interest Grabber Invite volunteers to use body language to convey an emotion, encouraging the rest of the class to guess the emotion. Then have some students work in pairs to convey a relationship through the use of body language and gesture, with the class guessing. Finally, discuss why body language is such a powerful tool in communication. Together, make a list of situations in which it is important to read body language (e.g., when caring for a child, when someone is angry or upset, when encountering a stranger in a deserted place). Tell students to watch for examples of "telling" body language in the following poems.

Customize for
Less Proficient Readers
"An Arundel Tomb" is difficult to follow even for experienced readers. Work with students to paraphrase what is being described. Encourage two students to demonstrate the pose of the couple in effigy, perhaps providing them with a glove or a paper bag to represent the left-hand "gauntlet."

Customize for
More Advanced Students
Invite these students to discuss Larkin's and Smith's brilliant use of rhyme to comment on the action they describe and to convey a sense of irony.

Customize for
Bodily/Kinesthetic Learners
These students might demonstrate the poses or central gestures in each poem. This will help them appreciate the poetry and assist their classmates in visualizing the poems' action.

Preparing for Standardized Tests

Reading and Vocabulary Many standardized tests require students to demonstrate their mastery of vocabulary, including words that come from the root *-fid-*. Sometimes students may be asked to choose accurate definitions or synonyms, as in this example:

Confide means *(A)*
(A) share a secret (B) develop a plan
(C) cheat (D) ignore

Sometimes students may be asked to complete analogies correctly to demonstrate their understanding of a word's meaning:

CONFIDENTIAL : PRIVATE : : CONSPIRACY : *(B)*
(A) confession (B) plot
(C) conclusion (D) pastime

The Build Vocabulary lesson helps students learn a number of words with the root *-fid-* as well as provides a mnemonic device to help students remember word meanings. For more practice, have students complete the Build Vocabulary page in ***Selection Support,*** p. 285.

Develop Understanding

One-Minute Insight Both of these poems deal with death and its effect on those who survive. In "An Arundel Tomb," Larkin points out an amusing misconception on the part of the tomb's visitors: Whereas those who view the effigy are comforted by the thought of love's enduring the centuries, the actual couple buried in the tomb had no intention of conveying such a message or serving as such an ideal.

In "The Explosion," Larkin vividly depicts the fatal suddenness of a coal mine's explosion and how it affects the town's women—the survivors.

◆ Critical Thinking

❶ **Infer** Ask students to demonstrate the gesture described here and then to tell what it conveys. *Students should understand that a man has taken his left hand out of his gauntlet so that he can hold his wife's hand in his own bare hand; the gesture conveys love.*

◆ Critical Thinking

❷ **Compare and Contrast** Ask students how death might be compared to a "supine stationary voyage." *Students should see that in death, people may lie supine, without moving, yet be on a "voyage" to another physical state.*

◆ Build Vocabulary

❸ **Word Roots: *-fid-*** Draw students' attention to the word *fidelity* and ask how it relates to its root, *-fid-*. Then invite them to supply other words with this root. *Students should see that -fid-, "faith," shapes the meaning of* fidelity*: "faithfulness." They might suggest the words* confide, confidential, *and* confidence.

▶Critical Viewing◀

❹ **Relate** Some students may say that an engraved image always becomes an "untruth" because later viewers can never see the original image as it was seen by people of the time. Other students may say that the passage of time offers new opportunities to see more truly.

An Arundel Tomb

Philip Larkin

Side by side, their faces blurred,
The earl and countess lie in stone,
Their proper habits vaguely shown
As jointed armour, stiffened pleat,
And that faint hint of the absurd—
The little dogs under their feet.

Such plainness of the pre-baroque
Hardly involves the eye, until
It meets his left-hand gauntlet,[1] still
❶ Clasped empty in the other; and
One sees, with a sharp tender shock,
His hand withdrawn, holding her hand.

They would not think to lie so long.
Such faithfulness in effigy
Was just a detail friends would see:
A sculptor's sweet commissioned grace
Thrown off in helping to prolong
The Latin names around the base.

They would not guess how early in
❷ Their supine stationary voyage
The air would change to soundless damage,
Turn the old tenantry[2] away;
How soon succeeding eyes begin
To look, not read. Rigidly they

Persisted, linked, through lengths and breadths
Of time. Snow fell, undated. Light
Each summer thronged the glass. A bright
Litter of birdcalls strewed the same
Bone-riddled ground. And up the paths
The endless altered people came,

Washing at their identity.
Now, helpless in the hollow of
An unarmorial age, a trough
Of smoke in slow suspended skeins[3]
Above their scrap of history,
Only an attitude remains:

Time has transfigured them into
❸ Untruth. The stone fidelity
They hardly meant has come to be
Their final blazon,[4] and to prove
Our almost-instinct almost true:
What will survive of us is love.

1. **gauntlet:** Armored glove.
2. **tenantry:** Peasants farming the nobles' land.
3. **skeins:** Loosely coiled bunches of thread or yarn.
4. **blazon:** Coat of arms; a noble family's symbol.

Tombstones of Tiberius Julius Rufus and his son Petronius Rufus and their wives.

▲ **Critical Viewing** Do engraved images and messages such as the ones on these tombstones always become an "untruth" in relation to life—as Larkin's poem seems to claim? Explain. **[Relate]** ❹

◆ Build Vocabulary

effigy (ef′ i jē) *n.*: Image of a person

supine (so͞o pīn′) *adj.*: Lying on the back

fidelity (fə del′ ə tē) *n.*: Faithfulness

Block Scheduling Strategies

Consider these suggestions to take advantage of extended class time:

- Have students complete the journal activity in Literature and Your Life (p. 1111).
- Introduce the Reading Strategy of Read in Sentences (p. 1111). Model, or have students model, various ways of reading poetry aloud: with no regard for line endings or sentences, stopping mechanically at the end of each line, and focusing on the sentences. Discuss the advantages of reading in sentences.
- Introduce the Literary Focus on Free Verse and Meter. Model, or have students model, ways of reading aloud these four poems that help bring out the meter or rhythm of each.
- Use the **Listening to Literature Audiocassettes** to help students hear one possible way of reading these poems aloud. Then encourage interested students to develop alternate readings and to share them with the class as they complete the Speaking and Listening activity on page 1117.

Philip Larkin

On the day of the explosion
Shadows pointed towards the pithead:
In the sun the slagheap slept.

Down the lane came men in pitboots
Coughing oath-edged talk and pipe-smoke,
Shouldering off the freshened silence.

One chased after rabbits; lost them;
Came back with a nest of lark's eggs;
Showed them; lodged them in the grasses.

So they passed in beards and moleskins,[1]
❺ Fathers, brothers, nicknames, laughter,
Through the tall gates standing open.

At noon, there came a tremor; cows
Stopped chewing for a second; sun,
Scarfed as in a heat-haze, dimmed.

The dead go on before us, they
❻ *Are sitting in God's house in comfort,*
We shall see them face to face—

Plain as lettering in the chapels
It was said, and for a second
Wives saw men of the explosion

Larger than in life they managed—
Gold as on a coin, or walking
Somehow from the sun towards them,

One showing the eggs unbroken.

1. **moleskins:** Garments, especially trousers, of heavy cotton.

Guide for Responding

◆ *Literature and Your Life*

Reader's Response Which of these poems do you prefer? Why?

Thematic Focus Larkin has sometimes been called an especially British poet. (a) What, if anything, is British about these poems? (b) What, if anything, has universal meaning?

☑ Check Your Comprehension

1. (a) In "An Arundel Tomb," what is the sculpture on the tomb? (b) What detail of the sculpture catches the eye?
2. What is the "final blazon" of the couple on the tomb?
3. (a) Where is "The Explosion" set? (b) What immediate effect does the explosion have on life above ground?
4. What do the widows of the miners see "for a second" at the funeral service?

◆ Critical Thinking

INTERPRET

1. (a)In "An Arundel Tomb," what is the "supine stationary voyage" of the couple? (b) How has time "transfigured them into / Untruth"? **[Interpret]**
2. What two things in "The Explosion" last "for a second"? **[Connect]**
3. (a) How does the final gesture in the poem seem to "undo" everything? (b) Does it really "undo" everything? Explain. **[Draw Conclusions]**
4. Each of these poems has a central gesture. (a) Compare and contrast those gestures. (b) What does each symbolize? **[Draw Conclusions]**

APPLY

5. (a) How do these poems show the imagination ranging freely in time, zeroing in on an instant or observing the effects of centuries? (b) What gives the imagination this power? **[Generalize]**

◆ Literary Focus

❺ **Free Verse and Meter** Ask students why Larkin uses a regular meter here. *Students may say that regular meter creates a sense of ceremony.*

◆ Grammar and Style

❻ **Sequence of Tenses** Ask students why Larkin chose in this verse to shift to the present and future tenses. *The shift in tense is a reminder that death is always with us and before us.*

Reinforce and Extend

Answers

◆ *Literature and Your Life*

Reader's Response Students may find "The Explosion" more accessible.

Thematic Focus (a) Larkin's language is especially British; also, the stone effigies he describes are more common in Britain than elsewhere. (b) His poems have universal meaning.

☑ Check Your Comprehension

1. (a) The sculpture is of a husband and wife. (b) The image of the man's bare hand holding his wife's hand catches the eye.
2. Love is the "final blazon."
3. (a) The poem is set in a mining town. (b) The ground trembles, cows pause, and the sun dims.
4. They see their men as they lived before the explosion.

◆ Critical Thinking

1. (a) The "voyage" is death. (b) Their love is more in the eye of the beholder than actual "truth."
2. The explosion and the vision of the men at the funeral service last "for a second."
3. (a) Portraying the men alive seems to "undo" their deaths. (b) No, the deaths are final.
4. (a) The hand-holding of the effigies and the envisioning of the dead men as they lived both convey love's triumph over death. (b) Each gesture symbolizes love.
5. (a) "An Arundel Tomb" compares present ideas with past truths. "The Explosion" focuses on two instants: an explosion and the moment of survivors "seeing" their loved ones restored to life. (b) Students may say that the ability to perceive deeper meanings gives the imagination its power.

Speaking and Listening Mini-Lesson

Eulogy

This mini-lesson supports the Speaking and Listening activity on page 1117.

Introduce the Concept A eulogy is a speech delivered to help survivors remember and honor someone who has died.

Develop Background As a class, discuss what elements make a good eulogy. What personal qualities are appropriate to mention in a eulogy? What will bring most comfort to survivors? What is important to honor about a person's life?

Apply the Information Encourage students to create a eulogy for the miners, drawing both on the information in the poem and on their own imaginations. Provide time for students to deliver their eulogies to the class.

Assess the Outcome Have the class evaluate the eulogies based on appropriateness, clarity, and effectiveness.

Develop Understanding

One-Minute Insight Both of these poems use images of water, but in strikingly different ways. "On the Patio" uses the image of the poet draining a glass and allowing the thunderstorm to refill it as a symbol of a person willing to be open to nature and its bounty, someone who wants to get the most out of life, "draining" life's glass and coming back for a "refill." "Not Waving but Drowning" uses the water that killed a drowned man as a symbol of the coldness and isolation that plagued him his whole life—and finally led to his death.

◆ Reading Strategy

❶ **Read in Sentences** Encourage students to read this passage aloud in two ways: first pausing at the end of each line, then focusing on the continuity of the sentence. Ask students to contrast the two ways of reading. *Students should see that reading in sentences helps them to follow the author's ideas.*

◆ Critical Thinking

❷ **Interpret** Ask students to describe the final gesture of the poem in their own words. Then ask what might be symbolized by the words "drain" and "refill." *Students should describe a person quickly drinking a full glass and putting it out in the rain to be filled again. "Drain" might symbolize getting the most out of life; "refill" might symbolize wanting to experience still more.*

◆ Critical Thinking

❸ **Connect** Ask students to suggest other ordinary moments or gestures that might take on symbolic value. *Students might suggest unlocking a door, dancing for joy, or kneeling in prayer.*

▶Critical Viewing◀

❹ **Evaluate** Students should focus on the strong visual elements of the photograph: the slanting lines of the falling rain and the explosive profusion of the fallen drops.

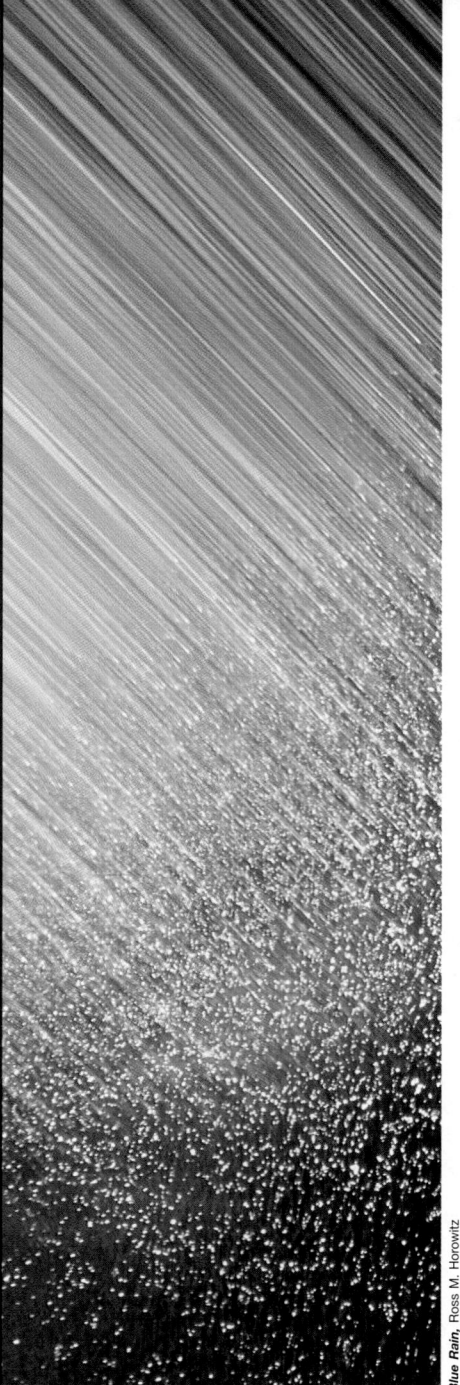

Blue Rain, Ross M. Horowitz

On the Patio

Peter Redgrove

❶ A wineglass overflowing with thunderwater
Stands out on the drumming steel table

Among the outcries of the downpour
Feathering chairs and rethundering on the awnings.

How the pellets of water shooting miles
Fly into the glass of swirl, and slop

Over the table's scales of rust
Shining like chained sores,

Because the rain eats everything except the glass
Of spinning water that is clear down here

But purple with rumbling depths above, and this cloud
Is transferring its might into a glass

In which thunder and lightning come to rest,
The cloud crushed into a glass.

Suddenly I dart out into the patio,
❷ Snatch the bright glass up and drain it,

❸ Bang it back down on the thundery steel table for a refill.

❹ ◀ **Critical Viewing** Does this photograph convey the power of the "thunderwater" in the poem? Explain your answer. **[Evaluate]**

Humanities: Art

Blue Rain, (detail), by Ross M. Horowitz.

This photograph suggests the wild profusion of rain during a thunderstorm as described by Peter Redgrove in "On the Patio." It is easy to imagine the rain portrayed in this picture as filling up a glass left out in the rain. The picture also conveys the "might" of the storm.

Use these questions for discussion:

1. The poet refers to the "cloud . . . transferring its might into a glass." What elements of this photograph convey that "might"? *The slanting lines of the rain and the sheer profusion of the dot-like raindrops convey the sense of an explosion, a huge force that cannot be contained.*
2. Imagine drinking a glass full of the rain portrayed in this photograph. What emotions might you feel and why? *It might be exhilarating, joyful, or even a little frightening to drink the results of such a powerful, explosive event.*

Not Waving but Drowning

Stevie Smith

Nobody heard him, the dead man,
But still he lay moaning:
I was much further out than you thought
And not waving but drowning.

Poor chap, he always loved larking
And now he's dead
It must have been too cold for him his heart gave way, ❺
They said.

Oh, no no no, it was too cold always
(Still the dead one lay moaning)
I was much too far out all my life
And not waving but drowning.

◆ **Build Vocabulary**

larking (lark´ iŋ) *n.*: Free-spirited, whimsical fun

Guide for Responding

◆ Literature and Your Life

Reader's Response When have you seen a gesture completely misinterpreted, as in "Not Waving but Drowning"?

Thematic Focus Does the way in which these poems focus on gestures make them accessible to a wider audience? Why or why not?

Danger Signals If you know special signs or signals for danger, draw or perform them for a group of classmates.

☑ Check Your Comprehension

1. Describe the scene in "On the Patio."
2. At the end of "On the Patio," what does the speaker do?
3. In "Not Waving but Drowning," what do "They" say about "the dead man"?
4. What does "the dead man" say about himself?

◆ Critical Thinking

INTERPRET

1. What do you think is the meaning of Redgrove's gesture in "On the Patio"? **[Interpret]**
2. How does "On the Patio" transform the ordinary into the extraordinary? **[Draw Conclusions]**
3. In "Not Waving but Drowning," how do "They" misinterpret the gesture and the whole life of "the dead man"? **[Interpret]**
4. (a) What does "the dead man" in "Not Waving but Drowning" mean by the statement in line 11? (b) In what way is the "drowning" in the poem a figure of speech? **[Draw Conclusions]**

EXTEND

5. To what extent can animals and humans communicate by gesture? **[Science Link]**

Beyond the Selection

FURTHER READING

Other Works by the Authors

The Collected Poems, Philip Larkin

Man Named East and Other New Poems, Peter Redgrove

Novel on Yellow Paper, Stevie Smith

We suggest that you preview these works before recommending them to students.

INTERNET

You may find additional information about these poets on the Internet at the following sites.

For Philip Larkin, go to **http://http.c.s.berkeley.edu/~angup/other/larkin.html/**

For Stevie Smith, see **http://www.magic.mb.ca/~annemari/el64C.html**

We *strongly recommend* that you preview sites before you send students to them.

◆ Literary Focus

❺ **Free Verse and Meter** Invite students to read this verse aloud and to say why the poet chose an irregular rhythm here. *Students should see that the abrupt, short lines convey how unsatisfying these comments are. To match the rhythm of the first and third lines, the readers expect something more—but do not get it.*

Reinforce and Extend

Answers

◆ **Literature and Your Life**

Reader's Response Sample response: When signaling for a check, the waiter brought a pen instead.

Thematic Focus Yes, the poems are accessible, since we all interpret body language every day; no, the poems' language makes it difficult to visualize the gestures described, rendering the poems less accessible.

Comprehension Check ☑

1. A wineglass has been left out on a table on a patio during a thunderstorm and is filling up with water.
2. He drinks the glass of rainwater and puts it back to fill up again.
3. "They" say that the man always loved "larking"—having a whimsical good time—and imagine that the cold water killed him.
4. The dead man says that all his life, he was "too cold," "too far out," and "drowning."

◆ **Critical Thinking**

1. The gesture symbolizes getting the most that life has to offer.
2. An ordinary rainstorm and gesture take on an extraordinary meaning.
3. "They" see the man as having whimsical fun, rather than as desperately calling for help.
4. (a) He might mean that he took risks that separated him from his society. (b) Drowning is a metaphor for being unable to cope with life.
5. Students might mention ways that humans use hand gestures and voice to communicate with dogs, horses, and trained circus animals.

Guide for Responding *(continued)*

◆ Reading Strategy

Read in Sentences

Even in poetry, where line breaks and rhymes can distract your eye and ear, the sentence is the unit of meaning. When you read a poem for meaning, therefore, you must **read in sentences.** Train your eye to continue past line endings where there are no marks of punctuation. Also, identify the sentences in a poem, noticing how they fall in relation to lines and stanzas. The first stanza of "The Explosion," for example, is one complete sentence.

1. (a) How many other stanzas in this poem represent complete sentences? (b) Where does the last sentence in the poem begin and end? (c) What is the relation of its length to the pace of the poem?

2. (a) How many complete sentences are there in "On the Patio"? (b) Which sentence describes a scene, which elaborates on the description, and which describes an action?

◆ Literary Focus

Free Verse and Meter

Smith and Redgrove use **free verse**, improvising the rhythms and line lengths that will best convey their meanings. Larkin uses regular **meters**, the set rhythms of trochaic tetrameter ("The Explosion") and iambic tetrameter ("An Arundel Tomb"). However, he varies these meters to suit his meanings. For example, the downbeat of trochaic tetrameter creates the feeling of a measured procession: "Down the lane came men in pitboots." However, Larkin introduces variations in this rhythm at key points: "One showing the eggs unbroken."

1. (a) What is the effect of breaking the rhythm for this final image and gesture? (b) What is the relation between the rhythmic variation in lines 13–14 and the event being described?

2. In lines 5–9 of "Not Waving but Drowning," how do the alternating long and short lines (a) first stress the finality of the death, (b) then seem to bring "the dead man" back to life?

3. How do the sometimes long free-verse lines of "On the Patio" relate to the setting?

◆ Build Vocabulary

Using the Word Root *-fid-*

Use your knowledge of the word root *-fid-* ("faith") to paraphrase this paragraph:

In "An Arundel Tomb," Larkin <u>confides</u> to us that the <u>fidelity</u> of the earl and countess is a facade. Their loving gesture, which at first seems <u>bona fide</u>, is revealed as a sculptor's invention.

Using the Word Bank

On your paper, write the word from the Word Bank that is opposite to each numbered word.

1. original
2. standing
3. working
4. treachery

◆ Grammar and Style

Sequence of Tenses

Like all writers, these poets use **verb tenses** to to show the relationship of events in time. Further, the skillful use of tenses by these expert writers produces desirable stylistic effects.

Stevie Smith, for example, uses the past tense to describe the mysterious "moaning" of an already "dead man" and the discussion of his life by a mysterious "They." However, her use of the present participle *moaning* gives the dead man's complaint the sense of an ongoing action. This moaning mysteriously continues even though someone says, shifting to the present tense, "now *he's* dead" (line 6).

Practice Answer these questions about tenses on your paper.

1. (a) What tense does Larkin use in lines 1–12 of "An Arundel Tomb"? (b) How does this tense help put you face to face with the sculpture?

2. (a) Where in "An Arundel Tomb" does Larkin use the past tense to describe what happened to the sculpture over the years? (b) In which line does the poem shift from past back to present? (c) How does the use of the present perfect tense in lines 37–39 help Larkin sum up his message?

3. (a) Which tense does Redgrove use in "On the Patio"? (b) Why is this tense a good choice for the poem?

◆ Reading Strategy

1. (a) Four stanzas are complete sentences. (b) It begins with *"The dead go on"* (line 16) and ends at the poem's ending. (c) The longer final sentence speeds up the poem's pace considerably.
2. (a) There are three complete sentences. (b) The first describes the scene, the second elaborates on the description, and the third describes an action.

◆ Literary Focus

1. (a) The break in rhythm slows down the last line in a sudden and dramatic way, highlighting the power of the image to the women who saw it as well as to us, the readers. (b) The break between lines 13 and 14 represents the break in the town's life caused by the explosion.
2. (a) The sudden short lines seem to convey the finality of death. (b) The long, "empty" space after "They said," where we expect syllables to match the length of the previous line, might be seen as giving the dead man space to "come back to life."
3. The long free-verse lines of "On the Patio" convey the continuous drumming of the rain on the steel table and the profusion of water pouring out of the clouds.

◆ Build Vocabulary

Using the Word Root *-fid-*

Sample response:

In "An Arundel Tomb," Larkin *shares* with us that the *faithfulness* of the effigies is false. Their hand-holding, which seems *true to life,* is actually an artist's creation.

Using the Word Bank

1. effigy; 2. supine;
3. larking; 4. fidelity

◆ Grammar and Style

1. (a) He uses present tense. (b) By reading in the present tense, we imagine ourselves in the poet's place, looking at the sculpture.
2. (a) The sentence that begins in line 24 begins the poet's use of past tense. (b) The poem shifts back to the present in line 32 (although the verb of that sentence appears in line 36). (c) The present perfect tense conveys an action beginning in the past and continuing into the present. This movement is central to the meaning of the poem.
3. (a) He uses present tense. (b) The present tense conveys the immediacy of the events. The poet is urging us to respond with immediacy in our own lives.

Writer's Solution

For additional instruction and practice, use the Correct and Effective Use of Verbs lesson in the Using Verbs unit of the **Language Lab CD-ROM,** and the page on The Correct Use of Tenses, p. 53, in the *Writer's Solution Grammar Practice Book.*

Build Your Portfolio

Idea Bank

Writing

1. Description Each of these poems focuses on a gesture. In your own words, describe these four different gestures.

2. Comparison and Contrast Compare and contrast poems by two of these poets. Consider such elements as rhythm, form, imagery, and theme.

3. Response to Criticism David Perkins describes Larkin's "pervading emotional state . . . as low-grade psychological depression." In an essay, explain whether "The Explosion" and "An Arundel Tomb" confirm that description.

Speaking and Listening

4. Eulogy Drawing on images and descriptions from "The Explosion," deliver a speech in praise of the miners killed in the accident. **[Performing Arts Link]**

5. Poetry Reading With a small group, organize a reading of these poems for your class. Remember not to pause automatically at line endings as you read a poem aloud. **[Performing Arts Link]**

Projects

6. Pantomime of a Poem Create a series of gestures without words to capture the action, spirit, and meaning of one of these poems. Then perform your pantomime for the class. **[Performing Arts Link]**

7. Film Review View the film *Stevie,* which is based on the life of poet Stevie Smith, and report on it to the class. Consider reading a biography about Smith so you can explain whether the film is accurate. **[Media Link]**

Writing Mini-Lesson

How-to Guide for an Interview

The poems you have read show the importance of body language. Gesture and posture can also be important in everyday situations. When you interview for a job or for a college, your body language can convey confidence or insecurity, honesty or evasiveness. Write a how-to guide for students going on interviews, explaining how to read and control body language. Support the points you make with stories, facts, and examples.

Writing Skills Focus: Elaboration to Prove a Point

In writing a how-to guide or a critical evaluation, you must **elaborate to prove the points** you make. A guide, for example, should do more than mention the steps of a process. It should support what it says with anecdotes, facts, examples, and statistics. This elaboration will help readers understand the *why* behind the *how*.

Prewriting Jot down some typical body language mistakes that occur at interviews. What gives the interviewer a clue that you are nervous? Uninterested? Also, freewrite about your own interview experiences and those you have heard about from others. Note some of the lessons that these experiences teach.

Drafting Use humor to engage readers and support the points you make about body language. Draw on your prewriting notes to give some purposely exaggerated examples of what *not* to do. Consider including sketches of postures and gestures as part of your elaboration.

Revising Have several classmates use your how-to guide to stage a mock job or college interview. As you watch them, you may think of additional negative examples, anecdotes, or statistics that you can include to support your points.

✓ ASSESSMENT OPTIONS

Formal Assessment, Selection Test, pp. 288–290, and Assessment Resources Software. The selection test is designed so that it can be easily customized to the performance levels of your students. ***Alternative Assessment,*** p. 60, includes options for less advanced students, more advanced students, visual/spatial learners, intrapersonal learners, and verbal/linguistic learners.

PORTFOLIO ASSESSMENT

Use the following rubrics in the ***Alternative Assessment*** booklet to assess student writing:
Description: Description Rubric, p. 98
Comparison and Contrast: Comparison/Contrast Rubric, p. 104
Response to Criticism: Literary Analysis/Interpretation Rubric, p. 113
Writing Mini-Lesson: How-to/Process Explanation Rubric, p. 101

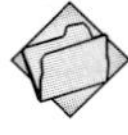

Idea Bank

Customizing for *Performance Levels*

Following are suggestions for matching Idea Bank topics with your students' performance levels:

- Less Advanced Students: 1, 5, 6
- Average Students: 2, 7
- More Advanced Students: 3, 4

Customizing for *Learning Modalities*

Following are suggestions for matching Idea Bank topics with your students' learning modalities:

- Verbal/Linguistic: 1, 2, 3, 4, 5, 7
- Bodily/Kinesthetic: 6
- Visual/Spatial: 7
- Musical/Rhythmic: 4

Writing Mini-Lesson

Refer students to the Writing Process Handbook, page 1189, for instruction on the writing process, and page 1191 for further information on exposition.

Writing and Language Transparencies Display the transparency Outline, p. 123, and have students use it to organize their How-to Guides.

Writer's Solution

Writing Lab CD-ROM

Have students complete the tutorial on Exposition. Follow these steps:

1. Complete the Personal Profile to generate ideas.
2. View the Audio-annotated Writing Models of how-to essays, targeting different audiences.
3. Use the Chain of Events activity to organize ideas.
4. Create a draft on the computer.
5. Use the Revision Checker for Unity and Coherence.

Allow approximately 90 minutes of class time to complete these steps.

Sourcebook

Have students use Chapter 3, Exposition (pp. 62–95), for additional support. The chapter includes a workplace writing model of a How-to Essay (p. 68).

Prepare and Engage

OBJECTIVES

1. To read, comprehend, and interpret a short story
2. To relate a short story to personal experience
3. To respond to character while reading
4. To recognize a first-person narrator
5. To build vocabulary in context and learn forms of *patron*
6. To use correct pronoun case in compound constructions
7. To write a description of a person supported by the use of details
8. To respond to a short story through writing, speaking and listening, and projects

SKILLS INSTRUCTION

Vocabulary: Related Words: Forms of *Patron*

Grammar: Pronoun Case in Compound Constructions

Reading Strategy: Respond to Character

Literary Focus: First-Person Narrator

Writing: Types of Support—Details

Speaking and Listening: Poetry Reading; Music Appreciation (teacher edition)

Critical Viewing: Compare and Contrast; Analyze

PORTFOLIO OPPORTUNITIES

Writing: Memorial Plaque; First-Person Narrative; Critical Evaluation

Writing Mini-Lesson: Description of a Person

Speaking and Listening: Poetry Reading; Music Appreciation

Projects: Exhibit; Fashion Design

More About the Author

In his writing, V. S. Naipaul has frequently focused on re-creating the voices of those who are forgotten or ignored by the dominant cultures within which they live. The book that made him famous, *A House for Mr. Biswas (1961)*, portrayed three generations of Trinidadians, but its main attention was given to Mr. Biswas, whose difference from the society around him is marked by the fact of his having six fingers. Naipaul's Booker Prize-winning work, *A Bend in the River* (1979), portrays the experience of living under an African dictatorship.

Guide for Interpreting

V. S. Naipaul *(1932–)*

Do you live in the country of your ancestors? Can you feel removed from the government in power and still be part of that country? These questions of cultural identification are central to the writing of V. S. Naipaul; he explores them in novels and his nonfiction works about India.

A "Many-Sided Background"

Naipaul, whose family came from India, was born in Trinidad, then a part of the British West Indies. There he grew up in the Hindu culture and attended British schools. These experiences, combined with the experience of living in England as a young man and traveling all over the world since, make up what Naipaul calls his "many-sided background."

An excellent writer even as a student, he won a scholarship to Oxford University. When his father died, his family wanted him to return to Trinidad, but Naipaul decided to remain in Britain. Yet his choice of subject matter clearly indicates his strong ties to the country where he was raised. Few writers are better suited than Naipaul to examine the results of British colonialism.

Explorations in Writing

In his 1959 collection of short stories, *Miguel Street*, a young narrator's tales celebrate the comic and absurd elements of growing up in the West Indies. Comedy remains a key element in *A House for Mr. Biswas* (1961), but Naipaul adds poignant and universal themes to this story of a man similar to his father, a popular journalist with the main Trinidadian newspaper. Naipaul returns to his own youth in the novelistic memoir *A Way in the World* (1994).

Reports on Rootlessness

Naipaul is drawn to writing about people living on the margins of the modern world, people who have to struggle against rootlessness and overwhelming change. His 1971 novel *In a Free State*, about self-exiles who meet in Africa, won the prestigious Booker Prize.

Naipaul has written several books detailing his changing feelings about India. *An Area of Darkness* (1964) has a light, confident tone while *India: A Wounded Civilization* (1977) darkens toward pessimism. Naipaul's doubt reverses again into optimism in *India: A Million Mutinies Now* (1990).

◆ Background for Understanding

CULTURE: NAIPAUL'S EXPERIENCE AS RESIDENT IN A BRITISH COLONY

Imagine that a foreign country takes control of your country, changes the language spoken, the holidays celebrated, and the religion observed. How would you feel? These changes occurred in British colonies, creating feelings of alienation in the native people of each colonized region.

Naipaul recognizes the feelings of displacement caused by unjust colonialism. Writing about displaced Indians in Trinidad, Naipaul says "they were people who had been, as in a fairy story, lifted up from the peasantry of India and set down thousands of miles away . . ."

Writers living in former British colonies, such as Indian writers R. K. Narayan, Anita Desai, and Salman Rushdie, have explored how people have adjusted to post-colonial life, and Nobel-Prize-winning poet Derek Walcott often deals with the Jamaicans' struggle for identity. Naipaul feels that the key post-colonial challenge is to find a way to accept the past and continue to grow.

As you read "B. Wordsworth," keep in mind that the characters are living their daily lives against the ever-present feelings of displacement brought about by colonialism.

Prentice Hall Literature Program Resources

REINFORCE / RETEACH / EXTEND

Selection Support Pages
Build Vocabulary: Related Words: Forms of *Patron,* p. 289
Grammar and Style: Pronoun Case in Compound Constructions, p. 290
Reading Strategy: Respond to Character, p. 291
Literary Focus: First-Person Narrator, p. 292

Strategies for Diverse Student Needs, p. 61

Beyond Literature
Career Connection: Astronomer, p. 61

Formal Assessment Selection Test, pp. 291–293; Assessment Resources Software

Alternative Assessment, p. 61

Writing and Language Transparencies
Writing Process Model 2: Descriptive and Observational Writing," pp. 13–16

Resource Pro CD-ROM
"B. Wordsworth"—includes all resource material and customizable lesson plan

Listening to Literature Audiocassettes
"B. Wordsworth"

B. Wordsworth

◆ Literature and Your Life

CONNECT YOUR EXPERIENCE

What does your name say about you? Many names come from Latin, Greek, and Hebrew, and they have specific meanings. For example, *Richard* means "strong." If you could choose a name for yourself, what would it be? A character in "B. Wordsworth" chooses a name for himself, taking inspiration from a famous British poet.

Journal Writing Jot down four names you might choose if you decided to change your name. Add a few notes about what inspired you to select each name.

THEMATIC FOCUS: FROM THE NATIONAL TO THE GLOBAL

Although Trinidad gained its independence in 1962, the events in "B. Wordsworth" take place in a British-ruled Trinidad. As you read, imagine what it would be like to come under the rule of a such a geographically and culturally removed "mother country."

◆ Literary Focus

FIRST-PERSON NARRATOR

When you read a story, consider the point of view from which the story is told. A **first-person narrator** is one who participates in the events described in a story and is identified by the first-person pronoun *I*. However, an *I* narrator, just as a *he* or *she* third-person narrator, is a fictional creation and does not necessarily express the author's views or experiences.

In "B. Wordsworth," Naipaul uses a first-person narrator to recreate an environment he knows well from his own childhood—Trinidad in the 1940's. Why might Naipaul have chosen as narrator a boy roughly Naipaul's own age at the time?

◆ Grammar and Style

PRONOUN CASE IN COMPOUND CONSTRUCTIONS

When writers use pronouns in compound constructions, such as compound objects of prepositions, they use the case that would be correct if the pronoun were used alone. Notice the **pronoun case** in these compound constructions that the narrator of "B. Wordsworth" uses:

Subjective Case: We became friends, B. Wordsworth and *I*.
(appositive of subject, *we*)

Objective Case: This is just between you and *me*, remember.
(object of preposition *between*)

◆ Build Vocabulary

RELATED WORDS: FORMS OF *PATRON*

A character in "B. Wordsworth" asks "Which café shall we patronize?" *Patronize* means "to be a customer of a store or merchant." It contains the word *patron,* meaning "customer." Other related words include *patronage*, "the support of a customer," and *patronizing,* "to treat as a customer of" or "condescending to."

WORD BANK

Preview this list of words from the story before you read.

rogue
patronize
distill
keenly

◆ Reading Strategy

RESPOND TO CHARACTER

It will help you be an active reader, one who fully envisions the word created by a writer, if you **respond to character** as you read. For example, when the title character first appears in "B. Wordsworth," he is a stranger with an odd request: He wants to watch bees in the narrator's yard. How do you feel about this unusual request? As you continue to read, jot down your personal responses to the behavior and comments of each of the main characters.

Preparing for Standardized Tests

Grammar and Language Many standardized tests require students to correct sentences that contain errors in the use of pronoun case, including pronoun use in compound constructions. For example, students might be asked to identify the error in a sentence like the following:

Brian didn't ask Tanya or I why we had left. *(B)*
(A) Tanya or I
(B) Tanya or me
(C) Tanya or myself

The Grammar and Style lesson for this selection teaches students how to analyze a compound construction so as to determine the case of the pronoun in question. For additional practice, use the Grammar and Style page in ***Selection Support,*** p. 290.

Reading and Vocabulary Questions on the reading comprehension passages of standardized tests often ask students to evaluate or interpret characters. The Reading Strategy, Response to Character, focuses on this skill. For more practice, use the Respond to Character practice page in ***Selection Support,*** p. 291.

Interest Grabber Ask students to define "poet" and "poem." Elicit the broader meanings of "poet" (someone who has profound insights into the world and who expresses these insights in meaningful, provocative ways), and "poem" (an expression of beauty or deep feeling, through use of words). Tell students that the main character in this story will help them further define the concept of a poet or a poem.

Customize for
Less Proficient Readers
Point out to these students that the story is set in Trinidad, a former colony of Great Britain. Invite students to speculate on what effect the British colonization might have had on Trinidadians, and to guess why a poet of Trinidad might name himself "Black Wordsworth," the so-called brother of the British poet, "White Wordsworth."

Customize for
More Advanced Students
Invite these students to note the use of dialect in the story. Have them discuss ways in which the dialect contributes to the effect of the story.

Customize for
English Language Learners
Preview the basic premise of the story: A young, uneducated boy in a colonial society meets an educated poet who helps him appreciate the beauty in life and the injustice in his own society. To help these students read the dialect in the story, have them restate each passage in standard English.

Customize for
Musical/Rhythmic Learners
Help these students find recorded examples of British and West Indian accents. Then encourage them to prepare dramatic readings of parts of the story's dialogue, contrasting the narrator's and B. Wordsworth's ways of speaking.

Develop Understanding

One-Minute Insight This story expresses the pain of life in colonial society by dramatizing the ways in which a Trinidadian poet is excluded from his oppressive culture. An innocent narrator—a young boy—at first takes the poet at face value, noticing only his wondrous way of appreciating life's beauty. Gradually, however, the boy realizes the ways the poet's life has been limited, so that his ability to produce written work has been stunted. By the story's end, the boy is brought to tears, not only by the poet's approaching death, but by society's restrictions and life's tragedy: "I . . . ran home crying, like a poet, for everything I saw."

◆ Critical Thinking

❶ Analyze Ask students to point to a clue that tells about the story's setting. Then have them explain what this clue reveals. *Students should note that the descriptions of beggars reveal the setting's poverty.*

◆ Literary Focus

❷ First-Person Narrator Point out the use of the first-person narrator in this passage. Have students tell what they know about him from what he says and from what he observes. *Students can note that he is young, obedient, uneducated, and sensitive to feelings.*

❸ Clarification William Wordsworth was a Romantic poet who also loved nature. Students may want to draw further parallels between the "brothers" by reading W. Wordsworth's poem "The World Is Too Much with Us," p. 624.

◆ Reading Strategy

❹ Respond to Character Ask students to describe their personal responses to B. Wordsworth's comment. *Sample response: Wordsworth seems to be kind, but eccentric.*

B. Wordsworth

V. S. Naipaul

❶ Three beggars called punctually every day at the hospitable houses in Miguel Street. At about ten an Indian came in his dhoti[1] and white jacket, and we poured a tin of rice into the sack he carried on his back. At twelve an old woman smoking a clay pipe came and she got a cent. At two a blind man led by a boy called for his penny.

Sometimes we had a rogue. One day a man called and said he was hungry. We gave him a meal. He asked for a cigarette and wouldn't go until we had lit it for him. That man never came again.

The strangest caller came one afternoon about four o'clock. I had come back from school and was in my home-clothes. The man said to me, "Sonny, may I come inside your yard?"

He was a small man and he was tidily dressed. He wore a hat, a white shirt and black trousers.

❷ I asked, "What do you want?"

He said, "I want to watch your bees."

We had four small gru-gru palm trees[2] and they were full of uninvited bees.

I ran up the steps and shouted, "Ma, it have a man outside here. He say he want to watch the bees."

My mother came out, looked at the man and asked in an unfriendly way, "What you want?"

The man said, "I want to watch your bees."

His English was so good, it didn't sound natural, and I could see my mother was worried.

She said to me, "Stay here and watch him while he watch the bees."

The man said, "Thank you, Madam. You have done a good deed today."

He spoke very slowly and very correctly as though every word was costing him money.

We watched the bees, this man and I, for about an hour, squatting near the palm trees.

The man said, "I like watching bees. Sonny, do you like watching bees?"

I said, "I ain't have the time."

He shook his head sadly. He said, "That's what I do, I just watch. I can watch ants for days. Have you ever watched ants? And scorpions, and centipedes, and congorees[3]—have you watched those?"

I shook my head.

I said, "What you does do, mister?"

He got up and said, "I am a poet."

I said, "A good poet?"

He said, "The greatest in the world."

❸ "What your name, mister?"

"B. Wordsworth."

"B for Bill?"

"Black. Black Wordsworth. White Wordsworth[4] was my brother. We share one heart. I can watch a small flower like the morning glory and cry."

I said, "Why you does cry?"

❹ "Why, boy? Why? You will know when you grow up. You're a poet, too, you know. And when you're a poet you can cry for everything."

I couldn't laugh.

He said, "You like your mother?"

"When she not beating me."

He pulled out a printed sheet from his

1. **dhoti** (dō´ tē): Traditional loincloth worn by Hindu men.
2. **gru-gru** (grōō´ grōō´) **palm trees**: West Indian palms that yield edible nuts.
3. **congorees** (käŋ´ gər ēz): Conger or Congo eels; large, scaleless eels found in the warm waters of the West Indies.
4. **White Wordsworth:** English Romantic poet William Wordsworth (1770–1850).

Block Scheduling Strategies

Consider these suggestions to take advantage of extended class time:

- Suggest that students complete the Journal Activity in Literature and Your Life (p. 1119).
- Assign the Daily Language Practice for Week 36, p. 76, on the creative process of artists. Compare the information in these sentences to students' definitions of *poet* and *poem* from the Interest Grabber activity on page 1119.
- Introduce the Reading Strategy, (p. 1119). When students have read the selection, have them answer the Reading Strategy questions on page 1126.
- Introduce the Literary Focus on First-Person Narrator (p. 1119). Discuss why authors might use first-person rather than third-person narrators.
- Use the Career Connection: Astronomer page in ***Beyond Literature,*** p. 61. You may also suggest that students explore the same questions in light of a career connection to "poet."

Man From the Village, Carlton Murrell

◀ Critical Viewing Compare the attitude of the man in the painting with that of B.
Wordsworth. How might the 6
man in the painting appear to a young boy such as the narrator? **[Compare and Contrast]**

hip-pocket and said, "On this paper is the greatest poem about mothers and I'm going to sell it to you at a bargain price. For four cents."

I went inside and I said, "Ma, you want buy a poetry for four cents?"

My mother said, "Tell that blasted man I haul his tail away from my yard, you hear."

5 I said to B. Wordsworth, "My mother say she ain't have four cents."

B. Wordsworth said, "It is the poet's tragedy."

And he put the paper back in his pocket. He didn't seem to mind.

I said, "Is a funny way to go round selling poetry like that. Only calypsonians[5] do that sort of thing. A lot of people does buy?"

He said, "No one has yet bought a single copy."

"But why you does keep on going round, then?"

He said, "In this way I watch many things, and I always hope to meet poets."

I said, "You really think I is a poet?" 7

"You're as good as me," he said.

And when B. Wordsworth left, I prayed I would see him again.

About a week later, coming back from school one afternoon, I met him at the corner of Miguel Street.

5. **calypsonians** (kə lip sō′ nē ənz): Those who sing songs, the characteristic satirical street singers of Trinidad.

◆ Build Vocabulary

rogue (rōg) *n.:* Scoundrel; wandering beggar

◆ Literary Focus

5 First-Person Narrator Remind students that Naipaul himself was a boy in Trinidad roughly the narrator's age at the time this story is set. Today, however, Naipaul is an educated writer. Invite students to speculate on the relationship between the colloquial speech of the boy and his mother and the standard English of the narrator. *Students might suggest that today, Naipaul writes and talks like the narrator, although he still recalls a childhood in which he—and his mother—spoke like the characters in this passage.*

▶Critical Viewing◀

6 Compare and Contrast Students might say that both B. Wordsworth and the man in the painting have a quiet dignity, a serene air, and a strong relationship to their environments. Students might speculate that a young boy such as the narrator would see the man in the painting as quite old—almost ancient—and as a somewhat intriguing, mysterious figure.

◆ Critical Thinking

7 Make a Judgment Invite students to say whether they agree or disagree with B. Wordsworth's comment that the boy is as good a poet as he is, and to explain their judgments. *Students who agree might say that B. Wordsworth isn't a real poet, so the boy may well be "as good as" him; some may say that the boy's insight qualifies him as "poet." Students who disagree might say that a boy can't possibly be as good a poet as a grown man; that the boy has shown no special, "poetic" qualities; or that the boy doesn't seem to have written any poetry.*

Humanities: Art

Man From the Village, (detail), by Carlton Murrell.

Murrell was born in Bridgetown, Barbados, in 1945, and now lives in Brooklyn, New York. His work has been shown throughout the United States and the Caribbean. This award-winning painting was done by the artist on one of his yearly trips to Barbados. One night, Murrell saw this retired fisherman and was struck by the man's dignity, despite his obvious poverty.

Murrell's title, his use of composition, and his choice of color all work together to relate the man in the picture to the village from which he comes. Murrell focuses our attention on the man's relationship to his environment, which he reinforces by choosing warm blues and browns for both the man and the background against which he stands. These colors, as well as the man's blurry outline, suggest that the man is literally emerging from the village behind him.

Use these questions for discussion:

1. How is this man's relationship to his village like that of B. Wordsworth's? How is it different? *Both figures are shaped by their environments, but B. Wordsworth departs from his environment through his careful, educated speech and poetic aspirations.*
2. What characteristics of this man suggest the character B. Wordsworth? *The man in the painting suggests a quiet dignity despite his impoverished surroundings.*

1 Clarification Alberto Street is on the southwest side of town and ends at the ocean.

2 Clarification St. Clair is an east-west street. Queen's Park Savannah, originally a 200-acre park but now only 80 acres on the north side of town, includes the rock gardens referred to later.

◆ Literary Focus

3 First-Person Narrator Invite students to tell what the author gains by using a first-person narrator here. *The narrator's personal description of how much the star-gazing meant to him is more immediate and intense because of the first-person voice, which helps readers to identify with this reaction and to view B. Wordsworth through the boy's admiring, grateful eyes.*

▶Critical Viewing◀

4 Analyze Students might point out the many shuttered windows, the turned back of the person entering the house, and the painting's soft, glowing colors.

◆ Literary Focus

5 First-Person Narrator Ask what emotional impact this passage has on the reader. *Students might say that the narrator's forgetting what he has learned evokes a sense of loss and a realization of how far away he now is from the young boy of the story.*

Comprehension Check ☑

6 Explain the humor in Wordsworth's reply. *The policeman is asking a literal question. B. Wordsworth answers as though the policeman had asked a philosophical question—"What are you doing here on earth?"*

◆ Reading Strategy

7 Respond to Character
Students might admire B. Wordsworth for comforting the boy and for broadening his perspective; they might also note B. Wordsworth's love of nature and knowledge of the stars and enjoy his sense of humor.

He said, "I have been waiting for you for a long time."

I said, "You sell any poetry yet?"

He shook his head.

He said, "In my yard I have the best mango tree in Port-of-Spain.[6] And now the mangoes are ripe and red and very sweet and juicy. I have waited here for you to tell you this and to invite you to come and eat some of my mangoes."

He lived in Alberto Street in a one-roomed
1 hut placed right in the center of the lot. The yard seemed all green. There was the big mango tree. There was a coconut tree and there was a plum tree. The place looked wild, as though it wasn't in the city at all. You couldn't see all the big concrete houses in the street.

He was right. The mangoes were sweet and juicy. I ate about six, and the yellow mango juice ran down my arms to my elbows and down my mouth to my chin and my shirt was stained.

My mother said when I got home, "Where you was? You think you is a man now and could go all over the place? Go cut a whip for me."

She beat me rather badly, and I ran out of the house swearing that I would never come back. I went to B. Wordsworth's house. I was so angry, my nose was bleeding.

B. Wordsworth said, "Stop crying, and we will go for a walk."

I stopped crying, but I was breathing short. We went for a walk. We walked down St. Clair
2 Avenue to the Savannah and we walked to the race-course.

B. Wordsworth said, "Now, let us lie on the grass and look up at the sky, and I want you to think how far those stars are from us."

3

I did as he told me, and I saw what he meant. I felt like nothing, and at the same time I had never felt so big and great in all my life. I forgot all my anger and all my tears and all the blows.

When I said I was better, he began telling me
5 the names of the stars, and I particularly remembered the constellation of Orion the Hunter,[7] though I don't really know why. I can spot Orion even today, but I have forgotten the rest. 5

6. **Port-of-Spain:** Seaport capital of Trinidad and Tobago.

▶ **Critical Viewing** The house in the painting, like B. Wordsworth's hut, seems to be a world of its own; our attention is focused on the question of what is inside. What methods does the artist use to achieve this effect? **[Analyze]** 4

Then a light was flashed into our faces, and we saw a policeman. We got up from the grass.

The policeman said, "What you doing here?"

B. Wordsworth said, "I have been asking myself the same question for forty years." 6

◆ **Reading Strategy** Describe how the star-gazing scene contributes to your response to B. Wordsworth. 7

We became friends, B. Wordsworth and I. He told me, "You must never tell anybody about me and about the mango tree and the coconut tree and the plum tree. You must keep that a secret. If you tell anybody, I will know, because I am a poet."

I gave him my word and I kept it.

I liked his little room. It had no more furniture than George's front room,[8] but it looked cleaner and healthier. But it also looked lonely.

One day I asked him, "Mister Wordsworth, why you does keep all this bush in your yard? Ain't it does make the place damp?"

He said, "Listen, and I will tell you a story. Once upon a time a boy and girl met each other and they fell in love. They loved each other so much they got married. They were both poets. He loved words. She loved grass and flowers and trees. They lived happily in a single room,
and then one day, the girl poet said to the boy 8
poet, 'We are going to have another poet in the family.' But this poet was never born, because the girl died, and the young poet died with her, inside her. And the girl's husband was very sad, and he said he would never touch a thing in the girl's garden. And so the garden

7. **Constellation of Orion** (ō rī´ ən) **the Hunter:** Group of stars named after a mythological giant who was killed accidentally by the goddess of hunting, Diana.

8. **George's front room:** George is a character in one of the companion stories in Naipaul's book, *Miguel Street.*

Speaking and Listening Mini-Lesson

Poetry Reading

This mini-lesson supports the Speaking and Listening activity in the Idea Bank on page 1127.

Introduce the Concept A poetry reading is an event in which one or more people read poems aloud, often for a special occasion or to illustrate a particular theme.

Develop Background As a class, discuss the elements of an effective oral reading of poetry:

- to convey a thorough understanding of the poem's meaning
- to bring out rhythm, rhyme, and musical devices
- to convey a strong emotional response through tone of voice

Apply the Information Remind students to choose poems that B. Wordsworth would enjoy and rehearse reading the poems aloud.

Assess the Outcome Have students evaluate the readings using the criteria outlined in Develop Background and consider whether B. Wordsworth would have liked them.

The Red House, Carlton Murrell

◆ Literary Focus

8 Respond to Character Have students discuss how B. Wordsworth's story makes them feel about the character. *Some students may say they feel sympathetic to one who has experienced such a tragic loss; others may note the simple, fairy-tale quality of the story and think B. Wordsworth is making it all up.*

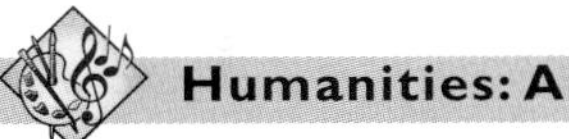

Humanities: Art

The Red House, by Carlton Murrell.

Artist Murrell returns to his native Barbados once or twice a year and tries to document a way of life that is rapidly changing. *The Red House* is a painting of a chattel house, a type of residence that is being phased out in the islands. The sides of the house can be taken off, moved to another location, and reassembled.

This painting conveys the colors, scenery, and mood of a tropical culture. The unassuming wooden house, the lofty palm trees, and the simple clothes of the man entering the house combine to suggest a certain amount of poverty within a lovely natural setting.

Use these questions for discussion:

1. The boy in the story describes B. Wordsworth's home as "lonely." What feelings do you have looking at this painting? Summarize those feelings into "one good line." *Students may observe that there is peace and beauty in the loneliness of the house.*
2. Ask students: Which character in the story might live in this house? *Some students might suggest that the cramped, narrow house could be the home of the narrator and his mother, who seem to live in a rather confined world until B. Wordsworth offers the narrator a broader view. Others might say that the private, mysterious world of the house evokes B. Wordsworth's unique and special world.*

Speaking and Listening Mini-Lesson

Music Appreciation

This mini-lesson supports the Speaking and Listening activity in the Idea Bank on page 1127.

Introduce the Concept Calypso is a traditional form of Trinidadian music: satirical, topical ballads sung in a lively, syncopated rhythm. Harry Belafonte was the first singer to popularize this musical form in the United States.

Develop Background As a class, discuss why people living in the society described in this short story might enjoy songs that satirized current events and made fun of prominent people.

Apply the Information Remind students that liner notes on record albums, tapes, and CDs often include information that can help them better understand the music and musicians they are listening to. Encourage students to share this information with classmates.

Assess the Outcome Have students identify what they learned about calypso music and about Trinidadian culture from this project.

◆ Literary Focus

❶ **First-Person Narrator** Why does the author include this observation? *Students should note that the narrator assumes B. Wordsworth's story is a parable of his own life. As readers, however, they can interpret the story differently.*

❷ **Clarification** The city is surrounded by the foothills of the Northern Range. Chancellor Hill is one of them.

◆ Critical Thinking

❸ **Analyze** Ask students how a person who did "everything as though he were doing it for the first time in his life" might feel. *Students might say that this person would feel enthusiastic and awe-struck, and even a bit nervous.*

◆ Build Vocabulary

❹ **Forms of *Patron*** Invite students to relate the word *patronize* to the word *patron*, which means "customer." *Patronize means "be a customer."*

◆ Critical Thinking

❺ **Analyze** Ask students what B. Wordsworth might enjoy about spending time with the boy. *B. Wordsworth enjoys spending time with the boy because he is impressionable and an enthusiastic fan of his poetry.*

◆ Literary Focus

❻ **First-Person Narrator** Students should realize that using a first-person narrator allows the author to achieve several effects that he could not achieve as easily with a third-person narrator: We see B. Wordsworth through the boy's eyes; we identify with the narrator's growth and with his loss of innocence; we feel the difference between the narrator now and the narrator as a small boy.

◆ Reading Strategy

❼ **Respond to Character** Invite students to share the ways in which this passage affects their responses to B. Wordsworth. *Some students may feel sympathy for the man; others may feel angry at the waste of his potential; still others may feel upset that he is unable to protect the boy from this view of death.*

remained, and grew high and wild."

❶ I looked at B. Wordsworth, and as he told me this lovely story, he seemed to grow older. I understood his story.

❷ We went for long walks together. We went to the Botanical Gardens and the Rock Gardens. We climbed Chancellor Hill in the late afternoon and watched the darkness fall on Port-of-Spain, and watched the lights go on in the city and on the ships in the harbor.

❸ He did everything as though he were doing it for the first time in his life. He did everything as though he were doing some church rite.

He would say to me, "Now, how about having some ice cream?"

❹ And when I said, yes, he would grow very serious and say, "Now, which café shall we patronize?" As though it were a very important thing. He would think for some time about it, and finally say, "I think I will go and negotiate the purchase with that shop."

The world became a most exciting place.

One day, when I was in his yard, he said to me, "I have a great secret which I am now going to tell you."

I said, "It really secret?"

"At the moment, yes."

I looked at him, and he looked at me. He said, "This is just between you and me, remember. I am writing a poem."

"Oh." I was disappointed.

He said, "But this is a different sort of poem. This is the greatest poem in the world."

❺ I whistled.

He said, "I have been working on it for more than five years now. I will finish it in about twenty-two years from now, that is, if I keep on writing at the present rate."

"You does write a lot, then?"

He said, "Not any more. I just write one line a month. But I make sure it is a good line."

I asked, "What was last month's good line?"

He looked up at the sky, and said, *"The past is deep."*

I said, "It is a beautiful line."

B. Wordsworth said, "I hope to distill the experiences of a whole month into that single line of poetry. So, in twenty-two years, I shall have written a poem that will sing to all humanity."

I was filled with wonder.

Our walks continued. We walked along the sea-wall at Docksite one day, and I said, "Mr. Wordsworth, if I drop this pin in the water, you think it will float?"

> **◆ Literary Focus**
> Would the story have the same impact if told by a third-person narrator? Explain. ❻

He said, "This is a strange world. Drop your pin, and let us see what will happen."

The pin sank.

I said, "How is the poem this month?"

But he never told me any other line. He merely said, "Oh, it comes, you know. It comes."

Or we would sit on the sea-wall and watch the liners come into the harbor.

But of the greatest poem in the world I heard no more.

I felt he was growing older.

"How you does live, Mr. Wordsworth?" I asked him one day.

He said, "You mean how I get money?"

When I nodded, he laughed in a crooked way.

He said, "I sing calypsoes in the calypso season."

"And that last you the rest of the year?"

"It is enough."

"But you will be the richest man in the world when you write the greatest poem?"

He didn't reply.

One day when I went to see him in his little house, I found him lying on his little bed. He looked so old and so weak, that I found myself wanting to cry.

He said, "The poem is not going well."

He wasn't looking at me. He was looking through the window at the coconut tree, and he was speaking as though I wasn't there. He said, "When I was twenty I felt the power within myself." Then, almost in front of my eyes, I could see his face growing older and more tired. He said, "But that—that was a long time ago." ❼

And then—I felt it so keenly, it was as though I had been slapped by my mother. I could see it clearly on his face. It was there for everyone to see. Death on the shrinking face.

He looked at me, and saw my tears and sat up.

Cross-Curricular Connection: Music

When asked what he does for a living, B. Wordsworth says that he sings calypsos. Explain to students that calypso is a type of music that originated on the island of Trinidad in the Caribbean and combines features of African and Spanish music with American jazz and blues. Calypso is often sung in French Creole dialect as well as in English. The songs are accompanied by such instruments as maracas, which are pairs of rattles traditionally made of dried gourds containing loose seeds; the cuatro—a stringed instrument; and guitars, flutes, and saxophones. Calypso songs may also be accompanied by a steel band, a group of drums made from steel oil containers and played with sticks. The lyrics of calypso songs convey a variety of messages as they express the personal point of view of the singer-poet. The calypso season mentioned by B. Wordsworth takes place during carnival time beginning in January and ending at the start of Lent.

Students doing the Speaking and Listening activity on Music Appreciation (p. 1127) should find out more about the calypso tradition. Can they name other popular calypso singers besides Harry Belafonte?

He said, "Come." I went and sat on his knees.

He looked into my eyes, and he said, "Oh, you can see it, too. I always knew you had the poet's eye."

He didn't even look sad, and that made me burst out crying loudly.

He pulled me to his thin chest, and said, "Do you want me to tell you a funny story?" and he smiled encouragingly at me.

But I couldn't reply.

He said, "When I have finished this story, I
8 want you to promise that you will go away and
never come back to see me. Do you promise?"

I nodded.

He said, "Good. Well, listen. That story I told you about the boy poet and the girl poet, do you remember that? That wasn't true. It was something I just made up. All this talk about poetry and the greatest poem in the world, that wasn't true, either. Isn't that the funniest thing you have heard?"

But his voice broke.

I left the house, and ran home crying, like a poet, for everything I saw.

I walked along Alberto Street a year later, but I could find no sign of the poet's house. It hadn't vanished, just like that. It had been pulled down, and a big, two-storied building had taken its place. The mango tree and the plum tree and the coconut tree had all been cut down, and there was brick and concrete everywhere.

It was just as though B. Wordsworth had never existed.

◆ Build Vocabulary

patronize (pā´ trə nīz) *v.*: To be a customer of a particular merchant or store

distill (dis til´) *v.*: To obtain the essential part

keenly (kēn´ lē) *adv.*: Sharply; intensely

Guide for Responding

◆ Literature and Your Life

Reader's Response What simple things make the world a more exciting place for you? Why?

Thematic Focus In what way does the title of the story reflect the challenge of developing an identity in a colonial society?

Journal Writing Note down a few ideas you have for stories you could write based on your own childhood. Jot down details about specific settings, people, and events you'd like to write about.

☑ Check Your Comprehension

1. What reason does B. Wordsworth give for wanting to come into the boy's yard?
2. What does the "B" in the title character's name stand for?
3. How does B. Wordsworth explain his overgrown yard?
4. What happens to B. Wordsworth's house?

◆ Critical Thinking

INTERPRET

1. What does the opening description tell you about the city in which the story is set? **[Infer]**
2. How is B. Wordsworth different from the other visitors described? **[Compare and Contrast]**
3. B. Wordsworth says that he thinks the boy is a "poet." How do you think he would define that term? **[Interpret]**
4. What is B. Wordsworth's motivation for spending time with the boy? **[Infer]**
5. Why does B. Wordsworth ask the boy to promise not to return after their last visit? **[Infer]**
6. B. Wordsworth "did everything as though he was doing it for the first time." What does this mean? **[Draw Conclusions]**

EVALUATE

7. Why did Naipaul choose the character of B. Wordsworth as the focal point of a story? **[Evaluate]**

◆ Critical Thinking

8 Analyze Ask students what B. Wordsworth is trying to avoid by asking the boy to promise not to come back. *Students may suggest that the poet does not want to be seen when he is weak and helpless, or that he is trying to spare the boy the knowledge of his death.*

Reinforce and Extend

Answers

◆ Literature and Your Life

Reader's Response Students might refer to aspects of nature, relationships with people, or favorite types of entertainment.

Thematic Focus Students should point out that the title refers both to the society's British heritage—the poet William Wordsworth—and to its difference from Britain—the original Wordsworth was white. Understanding one's similarities to and differences from the colonizing society is part of the challenge of developing an identity in a colonial society.

☑ Check Your Comprehension

1. He wants to watch the bees.
2. "B" stands for "Black."
3. He tells a story about a man who loses his wife and does not then want to change or even touch the garden that she created.
4. It is pulled down and replaced by a two-story building.

◆ Critical Thinking

1. The details about beggars tell you that the city is poor.
2. Wordsworth is polite, well-dressed, educated; unlike the others, he doesn't ask for money.
3. He might define "poet" as anyone who sees and feels deeply.
4. He seems to want to nurture another young poet, and possibly to have an admiring audience for himself.
5. He probably does not want the boy to see him die.
6. He finds the world constantly surprising and delightful.
7. Possible response: Naipaul, a writer, is fascinated by someone struggling to be a poet in colonial society.

Beyond the Selection

FURTHER READING

Other Works by V. S. Naipaul

Miguel Street
Finding the Centre
A Way in the World
In a Free State
A House for Mr. Biswas

We suggest that you preview these works before recommending them to students.

INTERNET

You may find additional information about Naipaul on the Internet at the following site. Please be aware, however, that the site may have changed since this information was published.

For information about Naipaul and his work, go to **http://kali.murdoch.edu.au/~cntinuum/lttserv/SPAN/34/pointon.html**

We *strongly recommend* that you preview the site before you send students to it.

Guide for Responding (continued)

◆ Literary Focus

First-Person Narrator

A **first-person narrator** conveys a limited perspective. We know only what the narrator knows. For example, when the narrator describes the beggars, we believe him because he presents himself as an eyewitness. However, when B. Wordsworth tells the narrator that he earns a living as a calypso singer, neither we nor the boy think that this is true.

1. How would the story be different if it were told from B. Wordsworth's point of view?
2. What would you like to know about events in this story that the first-person narrator, with his limited viewpoint, cannot convey?
3. (a) How is the narrator's voice different from the boy's dialogue? (b) Explain how this difference emphasizes B. Wordsworth's effect on the boy.

◆ Reading Strategy

Respond to Character

After finishing a story, reflect on your **response to the characters.** Think about the qualities and behaviors they display. Then note how *other* characters respond to them. For example when the narrator reflects that B. Wordsworth "did everything as though he were doing it for the first time," he is revealing an important part of B. Wordsworth's character—an insight that will ultimately help you respond to him.

Once you have looked at a character from all angles, including other characters' reactions to him or her, draw from your own experience and set of values to respond personally to that character—as if he or she were entering your life for the first time.

1. Based on your observations about him, how do you think B. Wordsworth would sum up his philosophy of life?
2. Why do you think B. Wordsworth repeatedly tells the narrator that he, too, is a poet?
3. Which of the two main characters do you identify with more strongly? Why?

◆ Build Vocabulary

Using Forms of *Patron*

The word *patronize* means "be a customer of." Use this knowledge to help you complete each sentence using one of the following words.

patron   patronage   patronizing

1. The continued __?__ of a core group of loyal customers helped to keep the small bookstore in business.
2. I enjoy __?__ that fruit store because its owner has a wonderful sense of humor.
3. Every time I go to that restaurant some loud and obnoxious __?__ makes a scene.

Using the Word Bank

In your notebook, answer the following.

1. Would a *keenly* observant poet be more likely to describe, or gloss over, details?
2. If you *distill* the meaning in a passage, do you concentrate it or expand upon it?
3. Does a *rogue* ignore or promote society's rules?
4. Would you *patronize* a forest or a cafe?

◆ Grammar and Style

Pronoun Case in Compound Constructions

In a compound construction, use the **correct pronoun case,** depending on the pronoun's function in the sentence. For example, because the pronoun *I* is an appositive of the subject "We," the subjective case is used in the compound construction: "We watched the bees, this man and *I*, for about an hour."

Practice In your notebook, write each sentence, using the correct pronoun.

1. The poet and (I/me) shared a mango.
2. It was a secret between (he/him) and (I/me).
3. It was as if the stars glowed for (he/him) and (I/me).
4. A calypsonian sang my friend and (I/me) a song.

Writing Application In your notebook, write a paragraph featuring the adventures of you and a friend. Use the subjective and objective cases one time each in compound constructions.

◆ Literary Focus

1. If B. Wordsworth told the story, the aura of mystery that is central to the main character in the story would not be as evident.
2. Students might want to know more about B. Wordsworth's past, about whether he ever writes any actual poetry, and about what becomes of him.
3. (a) The narrator uses standard English, whereas the boy's dialogue is written in colloquial West Indian speech. (b) We can imagine that, because of knowing B. Wordsworth, the boy grew up to become an educated man and a writer.

◆ Reading Strategy

1. Students might imagine that B. Wordsworth's philosophy would be "Appreciate every aspect of the world around you and then translate that appreciation into poetry"
2. Students might suggest that B. Wordsworth appreciates the boy's sensitivity and ability to appreciate the world; that he is encouraging a young man to take himself seriously and believe in himself; or that he has a special ability to perceive poetic talent in others—since the boy does in fact grow up to be the poetic narrator of this story.
3. Some students will identify with the boy because of his appreciation of an older mentor and because of his sense of loss when that mentor dies. Others will identify with B. Wordsworth, perhaps because of his status as an outsider and because his society fails to appreciate him.

◆ Build Vocabulary

Using Forms of Patron

1. patronage; 2. patronizing; 3. patron

Using the Word Bank

1. He would be more likely to describe details.
2. You concentrate it.
3. He ignores them.
4. You would patronize a cafe.

◆ Grammar and Style

1. I; 2. him, me; 3. him, me; 4. me

Writer's Solution

For additional instruction and practice, use the lesson on Pronoun Case in the **Language Lab CD-ROM,** and the pages on Pronoun Case, pp. 57–58 in the *Writer's Solution Grammar Practice Book.*

Build Your Portfolio

Idea Bank

Writing

1. **Memorial Plaque** Write the text of a memorial plaque that the narrator of "B. Wordsworth" might have created to honor his friend. Consider using a quotation from the story on your plaque.

2. **First-Person Narrative** Write a story using a first-person narrator. You may use a series of events that you actually experienced, but choose a narrator who is different from you.

3. **Critical Evaluation** Naipaul once said, "I think I look for the seeds of regeneration in a situation; I long to find what is good and hopeful . . ." Write an essay in which you explain whether or not this philosophy is reflected in "B. Wordsworth."

Speaking and Listening

4. **Poetry Reading** Select three poems from British literature that you think B. Wordsworth would enjoy. Read the poems aloud to the class and explain why you chose each selection.

5. **Music Appreciation** Find and play for the class several calypso songs. As a class, discuss your responses to the Trinidadian music. **[Music Link]**

Projects

6. **Exhibit** Investigate the history of the British colonialism in the West Indies through Independence. Create a classroom exhibit that reflects the British influence on the West Indies. **[Social Studies Link]**

7. **Fashion Design** Research traditional Indian clothing such as *saris* and *dhotis*. Then choose an article of clothing to design. You can just sketch it, or carry your design from sketch through pattern and finished piece. **[Art Link]**

Writing Mini-Lesson

Description of a Person

The narrator of Naipaul's story will never forget B. Wordsworth for his remarkable qualities. Think about the most remarkable person you have ever met and write a description in which you share your perceptions of this person with your readers. Your goal is to make readers feel as if they actually know this outstanding person.

Writing Skills Focus: Types of Support—Details

Choose **specific details** that show readers why this person is so memorable.

- Choose details that are unique to the person you are describing.
- Support generalizations with specific, precise details.
- Use figurative language to create fresh details that will capture your readers' attention.
- Use a variety of sensory details to create a full portrait.
- Bring your character to life by writing dialogue appropriate to his or her personality.

Prewriting Think about the traits and actions that make this person special, and choose a situation to describe in which your character displays his or her memorable personality. Then brainstorm for sensory words and phrases that apply to your character. Also, jot down ideas for dialogue that capture the character's manner of talking.

Drafting As you draft, weave together the details you've gathered to create a memorable portrait.

Revising Review your description critically. Replace vague, generalized details with ones specific to the person you're describing. Add dialogue whenever the description seems flat or unlively. Read your description aloud to a friend to get more suggestions for revision.

✓ ASSESSMENT OPTIONS

Formal Assessment, Selection Test, pp. 291–293, and Assessment Resources Software. The selection test is designed so that it can be easily customized to the performance levels of your students. ***Alternative Assessment,*** p. 61, includes options for less advanced students, more advanced students, verbal/linguistic learners, logical/mathematical learners, visual/spatial learners, and interpersonal learners.

PORTFOLIO ASSESSMENT

Use the following rubrics in the ***Alternative Assessment*** booklet to assess student writing:
Memorial Plaque: Summary Rubric, p. 99
First-Person Narrative: Fictional Narrative Rubric, p. 96
Critical Evaluation: Response to Literature Rubric, p. 111
Writing Mini-Lesson: Description Rubric, p. 98

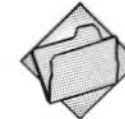

Idea Bank

Customizing for *Performance Levels*

Following are suggestions for matching Idea Bank topics with your students' performance levels:

Less Advanced Students: 1, 4, 5
Average Students: 2, 6
More Advanced Students: 3, 7

Customizing for *Learning Modalities*

Following are suggestions for matching Idea Bank topics with your students' learning modalities:

Verbal/Linguistic: 1, 2, 3, 4
Musical/Rhythmic: 4, 5
Visual/Spatial: 6, 7

Writing Mini-Lesson

Refer students to the Writing Process Handbook, page 1189, for instruction on the writing process, and page 1191 for further information on description.

Writing and Language Transparencies Use the Writing Process Model 2: Descriptive and Observational Writing," pp. 13–16, to guide students through the process of drafting and revising a description.

Writer's Solution

Writing Lab CD-ROM

Have students complete the tutorial on Description. Follow these steps:

1. Use the Word Bins activity to spark topic ideas for writing about fascinating people.
2. Use the Notecards activity to gather and organize details.
3. Use the Word Bins of character traits and sensory details.
4. Create a draft on the computer.
5. Suggest that they use the Evaluation Checklist to help in revising their drafts.

Allow approximately 90 minutes of class time to complete these steps.

Sourcebook

Have students use Chapter 1, Description (pp. 1–29), for additional support. The chapter includes a model from literature of a Character Profile (p. 7).

Prepare and Engage

OBJECTIVES

1. To read, comprehend, and interpret a short story
2. To relate a story to personal experience
3. To read between the lines
4. To identify conflict and theme
5. To build vocabulary in context and learn the prefix *a-*
6. To identify absolute phrases
7. To write a wedding speech, using a particular level of formality
8. To respond to the story through writing, speaking and listening, and projects

SKILLS INSTRUCTION

Vocabulary: Prefixes: *a-*

Grammar: Absolute Phrases

Reading Strategy: Read Between the Lines

Literary Focus: Conflict and Theme

Writing: Level of Formality

Speaking and Listening: Debate (teacher edition)

PORTFOLIO OPPORTUNITIES

Writing: Letter of Advice; Interpretation; Evaluation

Writing Mini-Lesson: Wedding Speech

Speaking and Listening: Debate; Nobel Prize Address

Projects: Retelling; African Art

More About the Author

Many of Nadine Gordimer's stories, including "The Train from Rhodesia," explore the place of the European in Africa. Gordimer firmly believes that "politics is character" in Africa, and so observes the personal in order to evoke a larger political reality. Her decision to remain in South Africa during the time of apartheid, even though many of her books were banned by the government, reveals the strength of her desire to see an end to the repressive system—an end that, at last, she has witnessed.

Guide for Interpreting

Nadine Gordimer *(1923–)*

The fiction of Nadine Gordimer has been shaped by her life in South Africa and by her firm opposition to the former government's policy of apartheid (ə pär´ tīd´)—racial separation and prejudice. Initially honored for her short fiction, she says that in time she found the short story "too delicate for what I have to say." In her longer works, and in short stories as well, she has had a great deal to say about racial prejudice and its harmful effects on oppressed and oppressor alike.

Born in a Small Town Gordimer was born in Springs, South Africa, a small town near Johannesburg. Her mother took her out of the local private school when she was eleven, and from then until she was sixteen, she "read tremendously," wrote much fiction, and published her first adult short story, "Come Again Tomorrow," when she was fifteen. She studied for a year at the University of Witwatersrand, continuing to write short stories.

Literary Successes *The Soft Voice of the Serpent* (1952) was the first collection of her stories to be published in the United States. Following the critical success of that book, Gordimer's stories began appearing in well-known American magazines. These stories often describe the entrapment of whites who have inherited power in South Africa's closed society. Frequently, as in "The Train from Rhodesia," she builds a tale around a fleeting but sharply focused moment of insight.

Compassionate Observer In all her fiction—including novels like *A Guest of Honor* (1970), *The Conservationist* (1974), and *Burger's Daughter* (1979)—she shows an ability to write from different vantage points. She portrays the Anglos (South Africans of English ancestry), Afrikaners (South Africans of Dutch ancestry), and black South Africans, describing her characters in a variety of economic and social settings. She writes as a compassionate observer, stressing the themes of understanding, adjustment, and forgiveness.

"Luminous Symbol" Until she was thirty, Gordimer had never been outside South Africa. Since then, however, she has traveled widely and lectured in a number of universities. She has also won a great many literary awards, including the Nobel Prize for Literature in 1991. Called "a luminous symbol of at least one white person's understanding of the black man's burden," she is also one of the leading novelists writing in English.

◆ Background for Understanding

HISTORY: GORDIMER, COLONIALISM, AND APARTHEID

This story takes place at a small train station somewhere on the line from Rhodesia (now the African nation of Zimbabwe) to South Africa. It occurs at a time when South Africa, and Rhodesia to its north, were dominated by policies of racial separation and prejudice called apartheid. This word itself means "apartness" in Afrikaans, the language of Dutch South Africans.

Racial prejudice and apartheid were a legacy of European colonial domination of Africa. In the late nineteenth century, the major European powers carved up the African continent for their own economic and political gain: Much of Central Africa was controlled by the Belgians, North and Northwestern Africa by the French, and Eastern and Southern Africa by the British.

Whites lived as privileged rulers in Rhodesia and South Africa, as they did elsewhere in the continent. The native black people, however, lived for the most part in poverty.

Prentice Hall Literature Program Resources

REINFORCE / RETEACH / EXTEND

Selection Support Pages
Build Vocabulary: Prefixes: *a-*, p. 293
Grammar and Style: Absolute Phrases, p. 294
Reading Strategy: Read Between the Lines, p. 295
Literary Focus: Conflict and Theme, p. 296

Strategies for Diverse Student Needs, p. 62

Beyond Literature
Cross-Curricular Connection: Social Studies Cultural Attitudes, p. 62

Formal Assessment Selection Test, pp. 294–296; Assessment Resources Software

Alternative Assessment, p. 62

Writing and Language Transparencies
Writing Process Model 3: Personal Narrative, pp. 17–24

Resource Pro CD-ROM
"The Train from Rhodesia"—includes all resource material and customizable lesson plan

Listening to Literature Audiocassettes
"The Train from Rhodesia"

The Train from Rhodesia

◆ Literature and Your Life

Connect Your Experience

You've seen movies in which a honeymoon, instead of bringing a couple together, reveals the differences that will eventually tear them apart. Often the clue to these differences is something small, a single harsh word or even a false gesture.

The woman in this story seems to be coming back from her honeymoon. Her train stops at a station in the middle of nowhere, and a minor incident occurs—or is it minor?

Journal Writing Describe a movie you've seen or a story you've read in which a small difference of opinion revealed a major difference in personality or belief.

Thematic Focus: From the National to the Global

As you read this story, consider the global importance of an incident at an out-of-the-way train station.

◆ Build Vocabulary

Prefixes: *a-*

The word *atrophy*, which appears in this story, means "waste away." It combines the prefix *a-*, meaning "without or not," with a word that means "to nourish." As you can see from this example, the prefix negates the root it precedes, like a negative sign in front of a number.

Word Bank

Before you read, preview this list of words from the story.

impressionistic
elongated
segmented
splaying
atrophy

◆ Grammar and Style

Absolute Phrases

Throughout her story, Gordimer piles up details so that you can experience the tension of the situation. One grammatical device she uses to create this effect is the **absolute phrase**, a group of words containing a participle and the words the participle modifies. An absolute phrase does not have a grammatical link with any single word in the sentence. Instead, it modifies the whole clause to which it is attached:

"The old native stood, *breath blowing out the skin between his ribs . . .*"

As you come across absolute phrases, delete them in your mind and see how tension and immediacy drain from the description.

◆ Literary Focus

Conflict and Theme

Writers often dramatize their **themes**, their central insights, by showing a character in the midst of a **conflict**, an inner or outer struggle. The way in which the character resolves, or fails to resolve, this conflict helps communicate the writer's message.

In this story, a young woman reacts to a conflict as if she were focusing a lens. At first the conflict is totally out of focus. Gradually, however, she turns a dial in her mind and the conflict becomes clearer. By the end of the story, the conflict and its meaning will be painfully clear—to her and to you.

◆ Reading Strategy

Read Between the Lines

In fiction, characters sometimes react to things without understanding them. You have to **read between the lines** in order to make the connections that the character is missing.

In Gordimer's story, for example, a young woman wants to buy a carved lion. However, she does not understand at first the powerful effect of a seemingly insignificant object: The lion's mouth "opened in an endless roar too terrible to be heard." You can read between the lines by asking yourself what is so "terrible" about the lion or the situation in which the woman finds herself.

Preparing for Standardized Tests

Grammar and Language Portions of standardized tests, such as the Sentence Structure section of the ACT, may ask students to identify absolute phrases in a sentence. The Grammar and Style lesson for this selection focuses on this topic and can help students better understand the role of these phrases in writing. For more practice, use the Grammar and Style page on Absolute Phrases in ***Selection Support,*** page 294.

Reading and Vocabulary The Critical Reading section of the SAT may ask students to read a passage and answer questions based on what is implied in the passage. The Reading Strategy lesson for this selection focuses on reading between the lines, a skill that can help students identify implied information. For more practice, direct students to the Reading Strategy page in ***Selection Support,*** page 295.

Interest Grabber Ask students to think of a moment in their own lives when a person they had admired, trusted, or loved said or did something that shocked them or caused them to think differently about the person. Point out that the moment of revelation might have been a minor incident, but one that revealed a great character flaw. Read this passage from the story aloud:

> But how could you, she said. He was shocked by the dismay of her face.
>
> Good heavens, he said, what's the matter?

Have students use these lines to predict what might be wrong between the two characters. Then have them read the story to find out.

Customize for *Less Proficient Readers*
Remind less proficient readers that the story is set in the time of apartheid, a political situation that the writer did not support. Help them to see that the chasm between the husband and wife on the train reflects the chasm between the Africans and the Europeans in Africa.

Customize for *More Advanced Students*
Advanced readers can be challenged to read between the lines to identify the role of the train in the story. Point out that the railroads were built with native African labor for the social and economic convenience of the European colonists. Have these students interpret the symbolic function of the train in the story.

Customize for *English Language Learners*
English language learners might be confused by the lack of quotation marks surrounding dialogue in the story. Encourage them to look for speaker tags to identify who is speaking.

Customize for *Interpersonal Learners*
Interpersonal learners might benefit by imagining themselves in the place of the young woman on the train. Encourage them to jot down thoughts she might have as the conflict with her husband intensifies.

Develop Understanding

One-Minute Insight The story "The Train from Rhodesia" illustrates how a moment in time can change and define a life. Though the incident described takes only an instant, it is an instant that not only shapes a marriage, but reflects the social and political situation of a whole continent. On the surface, the incident is nothing more than a bargain sought and made over a carving, but below that surface, basic emotions and conflicts stir, struggle, and finally emerge for a brief moment of both despair and clarity.

◆ Critical Thinking

❶ **Analyze** Ask students how this image of the train reflects its impact on the people waiting for it. *The train is described as powerful and almost weapon-like, reflecting the tremendous impact it can have on the lives of those waiting.*

◆ Critical Thinking

❷ **Infer** Urge students to reflect on how this image of the children's feet reveals the writer's feelings about apartheid. *The fact that their feet leave no imprint shows that the writer feels the African children have no impact on or importance in the Africa of her time.*

Warp-printed cotton, Arthur Sanderson & Sons, 1930, The Victoria and Albert Museum, London

The Train from Rhodesia[1]

Nadine Gordimer

❶ The train came out of the red horizon and bore down toward them over the single straight track.

The stationmaster came out of his little brick station with its pointed chalet roof, feeling the creases in his serge uniform in his legs as well. A stir of preparedness rippled through the squatting native vendors waiting in the dust; the face of a carved wooden animal, eternally surprised, stuck out of a sack. The stationmaster's barefoot children wandered over. From the gray mud huts with the untidy heads that stood within a decorated mud wall, chickens, and dogs with their skin stretched like parchment over their bones, followed the piccanins[2] down to the track. The flushed and perspiring west cast a reflection, faint, without heat, upon the station, upon the tin shed marked "Goods," upon the walled kraal,[3] upon the gray tin house of the stationmaster and upon the sand, that lapped all around, from sky to sky, cast little rhythmical cups of shadow, so that the sand became the sea, and closed over the children's black feet softly and without imprint. ❷

The stationmaster's wife sat behind the mesh of her veranda. Above her head the hunk of a sheep's carcass moved slightly, dangling in a current of air.

They waited.

The train called out, along the sky; but there was no answer; and the cry hung on: I'm coming . . . I'm coming . . .

The engine flared out now, big, whisking a dwindling body behind it; the track flared out to let it in.

Creaking, jerking, jostling, gasping, the train filled the station.

Here, let me see that one—the young woman curved her body further out of the corridor window. Missus? smiled the old boy, looking at the creatures he held in his hand. From a piece of string on his gray finger hung a tiny woven basket; he lifted it, questioning. No, no, she urged, leaning down toward him, across the height of the train, toward the man in the piece of old rug; that one, that one, her hand commanded. It was a lion, carved out of soft dry wood that looked like spongecake; heraldic, black and, white, with impressionistic detail

1. **Rhodesia** (rō dē′ zhə): Former name of Zimbabwe (zim bä′ bwā), a country in southern Africa.
2. **piccanins** *n.*: Native children.
3. **kraal** (kräl) *n.*: Fenced-in enclosure for cattle or sheep.

Block Scheduling Strategies

Consider these suggestions to take advantage of extended class time:

- Introduce the Reading Strategy concept of reading between the lines. Encourage students to consider, as they read, what the story reveals about the characters that the characters might not know themselves. After they finish the story, have them answer the Reading Strategy questions on page 1134. For more practice, assign the Reading Strategy page in ***Selection Support,*** page 295.
- Have students explore the Background for Understanding passage on page 1128. Encourage them to look into the present-day situation in South Africa and to note any information in their local newspapers about ongoing trials of South Africans who were part of apartheid.
- Ask students to form groups to discuss conflict and theme in the story before they complete the Literary Focus activity on page 1134. Then direct them to the Literary Focus page in ***Selection Support,*** page 296.
- Students can work in pairs to complete the Evaluation exercise in the Idea Bank on page 1135. Encourage one student to approach the story as pessimistic and the other to approach it as optimistic.

burnt in. The old man held it up to her still
3 smiling, not from the heart, but at the customer. Between its Vandyke[4] teeth, in the mouth opened in an endless roar too terrible to be heard, it had a black tongue. Look, said the young husband, if you don't mind! And
4 round the neck of the thing, a piece of fur (rat? rabbit? meerkat?); a real mane, majestic, telling you somehow that the artist had delight in the lion.

> ◆ **Reading Strategy**
> 5 What conflict is suggested by the contrast between the "bent" artists, moving like performing animals, and the "elongated" statues of lion-hunting warriors?

All up and down the length of the train in the dust the artists sprang, walking bent, like performing animals, the better to exhibit the fantasy held toward the faces on the train. Buck, startled and stiff, staring with round black and white eyes. More lions, standing erect, grappling with strange, thin, elongated warriors who clutched spears and showed no fear in their slits of eyes. How much, they asked from the train, how much?

Give me penny, said the little ones with nothing to sell. The dogs went and sat, quite still, under the dining car, where the train breathed out the smell of meat cooking with onion.

A man passed beneath the arch of reaching arms meeting gray-black and white in the exchange of money for the staring wooden eyes, the stiff wooden legs sticking up in the air; went along under the voices and the bargaining, interrogating the wheels. Past the dogs; glancing up at the dining car where he could stare at the faces, behind glass, drinking beer, two by two, on either side of a uniform railway vase with its pale dead flower. Right to the end, to the guard's van, where the stationmaster's children had just collected their mother's two loaves of bread; to the engine itself, where the stationmaster and the driver stood talking against the steaming complaint of the resting beast.

The man called out to them, something loud and joking. They turned to laugh, in a twirl of steam. The two children careered over the sand, clutching the bread, and burst through the iron gate and up the path through the garden in which nothing grew.

Passengers drew themselves in at the corridor windows and turned into compartments to fetch money, to call someone to look. Those sitting inside looked up: suddenly different, caged faces, boxed in, cut off, after the contact of outside. There was an orange a piccanin would like. . . . What about that chocolate? It wasn't very nice. . . .

A young girl had collected a handful of the hard kind, that no one liked, out of the chocolate box, and was throwing them to the dogs, over at the dining car. But the hens darted in, and swallowed the chocolates, incredibly quick and accurate, before they had even dropped in the dust, and the dogs, a little bewildered, looked up with their brown eyes, not expecting anything.

—No, leave it, said the girl, don't take it. . . .

Too expensive, too much, she shook her head and raised her voice to the old boy, giving up the lion. He held it up where she had handed it to him. No, she said, shaking her head. Three-and-six?[5] insisted her husband, loudly. Yes baas! laughed the boy. *Three-and-six?*—the young man was incredulous. Oh leave it—she said. The young man stopped. Don't you want it? he said, keeping his face closed to the boy. No, never mind, she said, leave it. The old native kept his head on one side, looking at them sideways, holding the lion. Three-and-six, he murmured, as old people repeat things to themselves. 6

The young woman drew her head in. She went into the coupé[6] and sat down. Out of the

4. **Vandyke** (van dīk′) *adj.*: Tapering to a point, like a Vandyke beard.

5. **three-and-six:** Three shillings and sixpence.

6. **coupé** (ko͞o pā′) *n.*: Half-compartment at the end of a train, with seats on only one side.

◆ Build Vocabulary

impressionistic (im presh′ ə nis′ tik) *adj.*: Conveying a quick, overall picture

elongated (i lôŋ′ gāt id) *adj.*: Lengthened; stretched

◆ Reading Strategy

3 Read Between the Lines Ask students: What does this sentence mean? What is the difference between smiling "from the heart" and "at the customer"? *Students should note that a smile "at the customer" denotes courtesy rather than warmth or emotional feeling.*

◆ Critical Thinking

4 Draw Conclusions Ask students why they think the fur of the mane is important to the young woman. *The fur makes the lion more realistic and shows that the artist really cared about creating it, both of which make it more representative of Africa for her.*

◆ Reading Strategy

5 Read Between the Lines *The artists are treated like animals in a zoo or circus, while the carved warriors carry themselves with nobility and pride, a pride the Europeans no longer allow the Africans to feel.*

◆ Literary Focus

6 Conflict and Theme Ask students what the young man's "closed" face reveals about the conflict between him and the artists outside the train. *He is unable to react to them as real human beings and closes himself off to them, revealing his belief that they are not his equals.*

Speaking and Listening Mini-Lesson

Debate

This mini-lesson supports the Speaking and Listening activity in the Idea Bank on page 1135.

Introduce the Concept Remind students that a debate is a structured argument between two groups on opposite sides of an issue. Each group is allowed to argue its points for a predetermined amount of time; the other side may rebut each point. Each side may sum up its position at the end.

Develop Background Have students divide into two teams. Each team can research its side of the issue. Encourage them to find statistics, examples, and reasons to support their arguments. Have the teams explore these points:

- What was African society like before colonialism?
- What technological and social changes did colonialism bring to Africa?
- How did the changes affect the native Africans?

Apply the Information Have students present their debate. Those members of the class who are not on teams can listen to the arguments and prepare to judge the outcome.

Assess the Outcome Students can evaluate the effectiveness of each team's arguments and can declare a winner, based on which team presented the most convincing statistics, facts, examples and delivery.

◆ Reading Strategy

❶ **Read Between the Lines** Ask students what this passage reveals about the young woman's feelings for her husband. *She does not know him very well and dreads the beginning of their real life together.*

◆ Critical Thinking

❷ **Compare and Contrast** Ask students: How does this description of the train compare to the description at the beginning of the story? *Students should note that the train is a helpless victim here, rather than a threatening weapon.*

◆ Reading Strategy

❸ **Read Between the Lines** Ask students what they think the young woman sees when she looks at the lion. *She may be seeing a hint of what life with her new husband will be like.*

◆ Grammar and Style

❹ **Absolute Phrases** Have students identify the absolute phrase in this passage and explain its effect. *The phrase is "his hands hanging at his sides." It reveals the young man's absolute helplessness and lack of understanding in the face of his wife's anger.*

window, on the other side, there was nothing; sand and bush; a thorn tree. Back through the open doorway, past the figure of her husband in the corridor, there was the station, the voices, wooden animals waving, running feet. Her eye followed the funny little valance of scrolled wood that outlined the chalet roof of the station; she thought of the lion and smiled. That bit of fur round the neck. But the wooden buck, the hippos, the elephants, the baskets that already bulked out of their brown paper under the seat and on the luggage rack! How will they look at home? Where will you put them? What will they mean away from the places you found them? Away from the unreality of the last few weeks? The man outside. But he is not part of the unreality; he is for good now. Odd . . . somewhere there was an idea that he, that living with him, was part of the holiday, the strange places. ❶

Outside, a bell rang. The stationmaster was leaning against the end of the train, green flag rolled in readiness. A few men who had got down to stretch their legs sprang on to the train, clinging to the observation platforms, or perhaps merely standing on the iron step, holding the rail; but on the train, safe from the one dusty platform, the one tin house, the empty sand.

There was a grunt. The train jerked. Through the glass the beer drinkers looked out, as if they could not see beyond it. Behind the flyscreen, the stationmaster's wife sat facing back at them beneath the darkening hunk of meat.

There was a shout. The flag drooped out. Joints not yet coordinated, the segmented body of the train heaved and bumped back against itself. It began to move; slowly the scrolled chalet moved past it, the yells of the natives, running alongside, jetted up into the air, fell back at different levels. Staring wooden faces waved drunkenly, there, then gone, questioning for the last time at the windows. Here, one-and-six baas!—As one automatically opens a hand to catch a thrown ball, a man fumbled wildly down his pocket, brought up the shilling and sixpence and threw them out; the old native, gasping, his skinny toes splaying the sand, flung the lion.

The piccanins were waving, the dogs stood, tails uncertain, watching the train go: past the mud huts, where a woman turned to look, up from the smoke of the fire, her hand pausing on her hip.

The stationmaster went slowly in under the chalet.

The old native stood, breath blowing out the skin between his ribs, feet tense, balanced in the sand, smiling and shaking his head. In his opened palm, held in the attitude of receiving, was the retrieved shilling and sixpence.

The blind end of the train was being pulled helplessly out of the station. ❷

The young man swung in from the corridor, breathless. He was shaking his head with laughter and triumph. Here! he said. And waggled the lion at her. One-and-six!

What? she said.

He laughed. I was arguing with him for fun, bargaining—when the train had pulled out already, he came tearing after. . . . One-and-six baas! So there's your lion.

She was holding it away from her, the head with the open jaws, the pointed teeth, the black tongue, the wonderful ruff of fur facing her. She was looking at it with an expression of not seeing, of seeing something different. Her face was drawn up, wryly, like the face of a discomforted child. Her mouth lifted nervously at the corner. Very slowly, cautious, she lifted her finger and touched the mane, where it was joined to the wood. ❸

But how could you, she said. He was shocked by the dismay of her face.

Good heavens, he said, what's the matter?

If you wanted the thing, she said, her voice rising and breaking with the shrill impotence of anger, why didn't you buy it in the first place? If you wanted it, why didn't you pay for it? Why didn't you take it decently, when he offered it? Why did you have to wait for him to run after the train with it, and give him one-and-six? One-and-six!

She was pushing it at him, trying to force him to take it. He stood astonished, his hands hanging at his sides. ❹

Beyond the Classroom

Community Connection

Local Trains Point out that the social and economic activity of the town in the story seems centered on the train station. Explain that in many areas, trains are the main mode of transportation. Africa, especially, has a poor road system due to problems of topography and climate. In the south, where the story is set, railroad development has been vital to the economy. Ask students if their community is served by a railroad, or if it was in the past. If so, have them explore how the coming of the railroad affected the community and, if it has stopped running, how its passing affected the area.

But you wanted it! You liked it so much?

—It's a beautiful piece of work, she said fiercely, as if to protect it from him.

> ◆ **Literary Focus**
> 5 Analyze the conflict between the husband and wife. What connections does the man see between "liking," "wanting," and "buying"? What connections does the woman see?

You liked it so much! You said yourself it was too expensive—

Oh *you*—she said, hopeless and furious. *You* . . . . She threw the lion onto the seat.

He stood looking at her.

She sat down again in the corner and, her face slumped in her hand, stared out of the window. Everything was turning around inside her. One-and-six. One-and-six. One-and-six for the wood and the carving and the sinews of the legs and the switch of the tail. The mouth open like that and the teeth, the black tongue, rolling, like a wave. The mane round the neck. To give one-and-six for that. The heat of shame mounted through her legs and body and sounded in her ears like the sound of sand pouring, pouring, pouring. She sat there, sick. A weariness, a tastelessness, the discovery of a void made her hands slacken their grip, atrophy emptily, as if the hour was not worth their grasp. She was feeling like this again. She had thought it was something to do with singleness, with being alone and belonging too much to oneself.

She sat there not wanting to move or speak, or to look at anything, even; so that the mood should be associated with nothing, no object, word or sight that might recur and so recall the feeling again. . . . Smuts blew in grittily, settled on her hands. Her back remained at exactly the same angle, turned against the young man sitting with his hands drooping between his sprawled legs, and the lion, fallen on its side in the corner. 6

The train had cast the station like a skin. It called out to the sky, I'm coming, I'm coming; and again, there was no answer.

◆ **Build Vocabulary**

segmented (seg´ ment id) *adj.*: Separated into parts

splaying (splā´ iŋ) *v.*: Spreading

atrophy (a´ trə fē) *v.*: Waste away

Guide for Responding

◆ *Literature and Your Life*

Reader's Response What do you think of the bargaining custom described in the story? Is it an example of exploitation? Explain.

Thematic Focus Suppose you are an American television reporter on vacation, and you witness the scene in the station. Would you report it as a local incident or one that reflects global issues?

Travel Anecdotes In a small group, share stories about your travel experiences. Tell about times when you saw how very different people interacted with each other.

☑ Check Your Comprehension

1. Who comes to meet the train from Rhodesia?
2. (a) How much money does the vendor want for the carved lion? (b) How much does he finally accept?
3. Describe what kinds of things the young couple have already bought on their holiday.
4. How does the "old native" get paid by the young man as the train pulls away?
5. Briefly summarize the interaction between the young woman and her husband at the end of the story.

Beyond the Selection

FURTHER READING

Other Works by Nadine Gordimer

July's People
Burgher's Daughter
Something Out There

Other Works With the Theme of National to Global Impact

The House of the Spirits, Isabelle Allende
Cry the Beloved Country, Alan Paton

We suggest that you preview these works before recommending them to students.

INTERNET

You may find additional information about Nadine Gordimer on the Internet at the following site. Please be aware, however, that the site may have changed since this information was published.

For information about Nadine Gordimer, go to **http://www/stg.brown.edu/projects/hypertext/landow/post/gordimer/go**

We *strongly recommend* that you preview the site before you send students to it.

◆ **Literary Focus**

5 Conflict and Theme The man believes that "liking" and "wanting" should be satisfied by "buying" whenever possible, and as *economically* as possible. The wife believes that "liking" and "wanting" should not be satisfied by "buying" if it means taking advantage of another person.

◆ **Reading Strategy**

6 Read Between the Lines Have students determine why the young woman does not want anything to be associated with her mood. *She does not want any future trigger that might make her remember how she felt because she knows she will be unable to live with the feeling.*

Reinforce and Extend

Answers

◆ *Literature and Your Life*

Reader's Response Sample answer: Although bargaining is a custom, in this case it is exploitative because the artists are very poor and rely on sales to white travelers who come by train.

Thematic Focus Sample answers: It as a global incident because it reflects the unthinking attitude of the wealthy toward the poor; it is a local incident concerning an incident at a train depot.

☑ **Check Your Comprehension**

1. Native Africans who hope to make money begging or selling homemade goods meet the train.
2. (a) The artist wants three shillings and sixpence. (b) He takes one shilling and sixpence.
3. The couple has bought a wooden deer, hippos, elephants, and baskets.
4. The young man throws the money on the ground.
5. The woman is appalled at her husband's treatment of the artist; he is bewildered at her response, and they realize there is a gulf between them.

Guide for Responding (continued)

◆ Critical Thinking

Interpret

1. Why is the arrival of the train important to the people of the town? **[Infer]**

2. Why do you think the young woman wants the carved lion? **[Analyze]**

3. Why is the young woman angry when her husband bargains for and obtains the lion at a low price? **[Interpret]**

4. How does the final description of the train help disclose the story's meaning? **[Draw Conclusions]**

Evaluate

5. Do you think the woman is being too harsh on her husband? Explain. **[Make a Judgment]**

Apply

6. What issues would this couple have to discuss to reconcile their differences? **[Resolve]**

◆ Reading Strategy

Read Between the Lines

Because Gordimer doesn't spell out the underlying conflict between blacks and whites, you must **read between the lines** to discover it. Find evidence of this conflict between the lines of the following descriptions:

1. "...the artists sprang, walking bent, like performing animals, the better to exhibit the fantasy held toward the faces on the train."

2. "A man passed beneath the arch of reaching arms meeting gray-black and white in the exchange of money ..."

◆ Build Vocabulary

Using the Prefix *a-*

Use your knowledge of the prefix *a-* to explain each of these terms:

1. *atypical* situation
2. *asymmetrical* design
3. *amoral* person
4. *atonal* music

Using the Word Bank

As the woman in the story, write a diary entry about the incident at the station. Use all the words from the Word Bank in your entry.

◆ Literary Focus

Conflict and Theme

As the **conflicts** in the story become clearer—the woman's inner struggle and her struggle with her husband—so does its central idea, its **theme**. You can trace the stages by which the woman understands her conflicts and their meaning. First she vaguely senses something "terrible" about the unheard roar of the carved lion. Then she is dimly aware that her relationship with her husband has an "unreality ... that living with him ... was part of the holiday, the strange places."

1. Why does her conflict with her husband flare up when he buys the lion so cheaply?

2. (a) How does the "shame" she feels relate to an inner conflict? (b) Why might she explain her inner "void" differently from the way she once did?

3. Are the woman's conflicts resolved at the end of the story? Why or why not?

4. In a thematic statement, explain the link between the woman's conflicts and those in the society.

◆ Grammar and Style

Absolute Phrases

Gordimer uses **absolute phrases,** which contain a participle and the word the participle modifies, to add details to descriptions. These details bring scenes to life, heighten suspense, and point out conflicts.

Practice On your paper, identify the absolute phrase in each sentence and describe its effect.

1. A man passed beneath the arch of reaching arms meeting ... in the exchange of money for the staring wooden eyes, the stiff wooden legs sticking up in the air.

2. The stationmaster was leaning against the end of the train, green flag rolled in readiness.

3. Joints not yet coordinated, the segmented body of the train ... bumped back against itself.

4. If you wanted the thing, she said, her voice rising and breaking with the shrill impotence of anger, why didn't you buy it in the first place?

5. She sat down again in the corner and, her face slumped in her hand, stared out of the window.

◆ Critical Thinking

1. The arrival of the train is an opportunity for the townspeople to make money.
2. The carved lion is a work of art. It also represents something wild and free that is missing from her life.
3. The woman feels it is degrading to the artist—and to Africa as a whole—to be paid so little for something that is representative of the country's spirit.
4. The train calling to the sky reflects the longing the woman feels to move beyond the confines of her class, race, and position. The fact that the sky does not answer reveals her isolation.
5. Sample answers: Yes, she is too harsh, because her husband is simply revealing attitudes he was raised with and has never questioned; no, she is not too harsh, because his behavior was very unthinking and insulting.
6. Sample answer: They have to discuss their differences on the issues of racism and class distinction.

◆ Reading Strategy

1. This quotation reveals that the artists must demean themselves in order to sell their wares, setting up a conflict between them and the whites who buy the art.
2. The image of the arch of hands presents the exchange of money between blacks and whites as a tangible, dehumanizing institution.

◆ Build Vocabulary

Using the Prefix *a-*

1. not a typical situation
2. a design without symmetry
3. someone who has no morals
4. music in which tones do not go together in a traditional fashion

◆ Literary Focus

1. The purchase of the lion reveals the deep rift between the couple's basic beliefs and feelings.
2. (a) Her shame reveals the conflict within her between the way she lives and acts and the way she feels she should live and act.
(b) While she previously felt her inner void was the result of being single, she now sees that her isolation is unrelated to her matrimonial state.
3. Her conflicts are not resolved, but she has determined not to resolve them.
4. The woman recoils from, and is shamed by, a sense of entitlement that comes from being a European in Africa, while society is split between those who have that sense of entitlement and those who are exploited.

◆ Grammar and Style

1. The phrase "the stiff wooden legs sticking up in the air" makes the items for sale sound ghastly and lifeless.
2. The phrase "green flag raised in readiness" gives his attitude of readiness a feeling of mechanical obedience.
3. The phrase "joints not yet coordinated" makes the train sound like an awkward living creature.
4. The phrase "her voice rising and breaking" reveals how upset she is.
5. The phrase "her face slumped in her hand" shows her hopelessness.

For additional practice, use the practice pages on Verbals and Verbal Phrases, pp. 29–30, in the *Writer's Solution Grammar Practice Book.*

Build Your Portfolio

Idea Bank

Writing

1. **Letter of Advice** Suppose you are a friend of the young woman in the story. Write her a letter advising her what to do about her new feelings of "shame" and "weariness."

2. **Interpretation** Why does Gordimer say at the end, "The train had cast the station like a skin"? Explain the meaning of this image by connecting it to other passages in the story.

3. **Evaluation** Do you think the story is pessimistic or optimistic about the relations of blacks and whites in Southern Africa? Use specific passages to support the points you make.

Speaking and Listening

4. **Debate** Divide into teams and debate this proposition: Colonialism brought little or nothing of value to the native peoples of Africa. **[Social Studies Link]**

5. **Nobel Prize Address** Find the speech that Gordimer made on receiving the Nobel Prize for Literature in 1991. Then rehearse it, choosing the words you will emphasize, and present it to the class. **[Literature Link; Performing Arts Link]**

Projects

6. **Retelling** Find a book or a recording of folk tales that come from Southern Africa. Choose one of these and retell it to the class. Keep the main story line, but add details if you like. **[Performing Arts Link; Social Studies Link]**

7. **African Art** What might the carved lion in the story look like? In an art book, find examples of sculpture from Southern Africa. Show the class pictures of this sculpture, and share what you've learned about it. **[Art Link]**

Writing Mini-Lesson

Wedding Speech

In "The Train from Rhodesia," Gordimer uses a minor incident to reveal the personalities of her characters. You can use the same device to reveal a friend's personality. Imagine that you must write and deliver a speech about a friend at his or her wedding. To help people appreciate your friend, focus on an incident that discloses the real person. Be sure to use the right level of formality for the occasion.

Writing Skills Focus: Level of Formality

No matter what you write, you can decide on the **level of formality** to use by considering your audience. You can be very casual in a letter to a good friend. However, in speaking to a wedding crowd, you will be addressing a variety of people who know your friend in different ways. It is therefore appropriate to be a bit more formal than you would in a letter to someone who knows you well. However, you can be conversational and humorous.

Prewriting To bring to mind your friend's traits and stories that illustrate them, fill in a cluster diagram like this one:

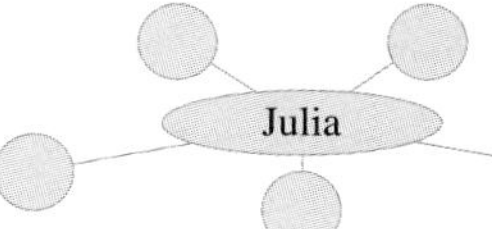

Drafting Choose one story that illustrates your friend's personality. Before telling it, introduce yourself, describe your relationship with your friend, and provide any background that listeners will need to understand the story. As you tell the anecdote, help yourself reach the right level of formality by picturing your audience in front of you.

Revising Read your speech aloud to several friends who know your subject. If they think passages are too informal, take out slang and colloquial phrases. If passages are too formal, add humorous details.

✓ ASSESSMENT OPTIONS

Formal Assessment, Selection Test, pp. 294–296, and Assessment Resources Software. The selection test is designed so that it can be easily customized to the performance levels of your students. ***Alternative Assessment,*** p. 62, includes options for less advanced students, more advanced students, visual/spatial learners, logical/mathematical learners, interpersonal learners, and verbal/linguistic learners.

PORTFOLIO ASSESSMENT

Use the following rubrics in the ***Alternative Assessment*** booklet to assess student writing:
Letter of Advice: Expression Rubric, p. 95
Interpretation: Literary Analysis/Interpretation Rubric, p. 113
Evaluation: Response to Literature Rubric, p. 111
Writing Mini-Lesson: Narrative Based on Personal Experience Rubric, p. 97

Idea Bank

Customizing for *Performance Levels*

Following are suggestions for matching Idea Bank topics with your students' performance levels:

- Less Advanced Students: 1, 5, 7
- Average Students: 2, 4, 6
- More Advanced Students: 3

Customizing for *Learning Modalities*

Following are suggestions for matching Idea Bank topics with your students' learning modalities:

- Verbal/Linguistic: 1, 2, 3, 4, 5, 6,
- Visual/Spatial: 7
- Interpersonal: 1, 7

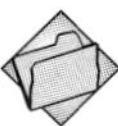

Writing Mini-Lesson

Refer students to the Writing Process Handbook, page 1189, for instruction on the writing process, and page 1191 for further information on narration.

Writing and Language Transparencies Use the Writing Process Model 3: Personal Narrative, pp. 17–23, to guide students through the process of writing and revising a personal narrative.

Writer's Solution

Writing Lab CD-ROM

Have students complete the tutorial on Narration. Follow these steps:

1. Use the Personal Experience Wheel to spark ideas for their narratives.
2. Complete the Audience Profile to focus on their intended audience.
3. Refer to the Character Traits Word Bin.
4. Create a draft on the computer.
5. Review the audio-annotated student model of a personal narrative.

Allow approximately 120 minutes of class time to complete these steps.

Sourcebook

Have students use Chapter 2, Narration (pp. 30–61), for additional support. The chapter includes a model from literature of a firsthand biography (p. 36).

Prepare and Engage

OBJECTIVES

1. To read, comprehend, and interpret poems
2. To relate poems to personal experience
3. To apply background information to understand a poem
4. To analyze the theme and context of poems
5. To build vocabulary in context and learn the word root *-duc-*
6. To use the commonly confused words *affect* and *effect* correctly
7. To write a pro-and-con editorial using transitions to show comparison
8. To respond to the poems through writing, speaking and listening, and projects

SKILLS INSTRUCTION

Vocabulary: Word Roots *-duc-*
Grammar: Commonly Confused Words: *Affect* and *Effect*
Reading Strategy: Apply Background Information
Literary Focus: Theme and Context
Writing: Transitions to Show Comparisons
Speaking and Listening: Debate (teacher edition)
Critical Viewing: Compare and Contrast; Analyze

PORTFOLIO OPPORTUNITIES

Writing: Personal Letter; Literary Analysis; Response to Criticism
Writing Mini-Lesson: Pro-and-Con Editorial
Speaking and Listening: Oral Interpretation of Dialect; Debate
Projects: Black Roots; Caribbean Festival

More About the Authors

Complicating **Derek Walcott's** conflicting loyalties is his great love of the English language and its literature. In one of his poems he says, "How choose/Between this Africa and the English tongue I love?"

James Berry is known as a popular performer of his own poetry. He also works in multicultural education and as an editor of other writers.

Guide for Interpreting

Derek Walcott (1930–)

Both Derek Walcott's grandmothers were descended from African slaves, and both of his grandfathers were white. Throughout his life, the poet has had to reflect upon these contrasting elements in his heritage. These reflections have propelled his poems, which may lead the reader from Trinidad to ancient Greece, sometimes in a single line of poetry.

Early Success Walcott was born on the Caribbean Island of St. Lucia and attended university in Jamaica, where he now lives. He published the first of his many books of poetry, *Twenty-five Poems*, when he was just a teenager. His subsequent books of poetry include, among others, *The Gulf* (1970), *Sea Grapes* (1976), and *Collected Poems* 1948–1984 (1986).

Playwright In addition to being a poet, Walcott is also an accomplished playwright. He was the founding director of the Trinidad Theatre Workshop (1959), which staged a number of his plays. In these dramas, he explores his Caribbean roots even more deeply than he does in his poetry. His most famous play is *Dream on Monkey Mountain*, which won an Obie award (1971) when it was produced in New York. Walcott recently collaborated with composer Paul Simon on a Broadway musical, *The Capeman* (1997).

Walcott has taught at a number of American colleges, including Boston University, and is just as at home in the United States as he is in the Caribbean.

Most critics agree that it was his 1990 book, *Omeros*, which draws on the epics of the ancient Greek poet Homer, that ensured his winning the Nobel Prize for Literature in 1992. The Swedish Academy granting the award concluded that "West Indian culture has found its great poet."

James Berry (1925–)

Born in a small village in Jamaica and finally settling in Britain, Berry draws upon the imagery and rhythms of his rural West Indian background as well as the excitement and personal freedom of urban London.

Experiences of Poverty Berry's childhood experiences of poverty are common in the West Indies. He had to leave school at age fourteen to help support his family. During World War II, he left Jamaica for the United States to find work. After living in several places, including Harlem, he returned to Jamaica, discouraged by the prejudice he encountered. Then, in 1948, he left for England and began to write.

His books include collections of stories for children like *A Thief in the Village*, which was a Coretta Scott King Honor Book in 1989. Among his volumes of poetry are *Fractured Circles* (1979) and *Lucy's Letters and Loving* (1982), from which "From Lucy: Englan' Lady" comes.

◆ Background for Understanding

HISTORY: WALCOTT, BERRY, AND THE BRITISH EMPIRE

Several island groups in the West Indies were part of the British Empire, and colonial settlers brought enslaved Africans to work on their plantations. These slaves were set free in the 1830's and, in the 1960's and 1970's, the islands won their political independence. A lasting legacy of British rule, however, is a British system of education and the use of the English language. Because of that legacy, Walcott and Berry write in English but bring a Caribbean flavor and perspective to their work.

Many West Indians, including Berry, have emigrated to the United Kingdom in search of a better life. West Indians in Britain have suffered from racial prejudice and economic hardship. Sometimes frustrations erupt in violence, as in the April 1981 riots in the West Indian neighborhood of Brixton.

Prentice Hall Literature Program Resources

REINFORCE / RETEACH / EXTEND

Selection Support Pages
Build Vocabulary: Word Roots *-duc-*, p. 297
Grammar and Style: *Affect* and *Effect*, p. 298
Reading Strategy: Apply Background, p. 299
Literary Focus: Theme and Context, p. 300

Strategies for Diverse Student Needs, p. 63

Beyond Literature
Cross-Curricular Connection: Social Studies
British Royalty, p. 63

Formal Assessment Selection Test, pp. 297–299; Assessment Resources Software

Alternative Assessment, p. 63

Writing and Language Transparencies
Argument Organizer, pp. 103–106
Writing Process Model 5: pp. 37–44

Resource Pro CD-ROM
from *Midsummer;* from *Omeros,* "Lucy"

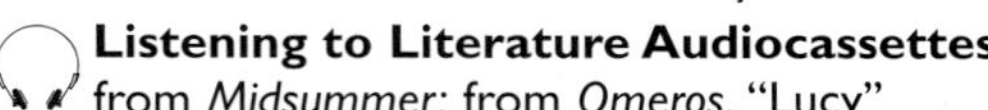

Listening to Literature Audiocassettes
from *Midsummer;* from *Omeros,* "Lucy"

Looking at Literature Videodisc
The Music and Rhythm of Writing, Chapter 12

from Midsummer, XXIII ◆ *from* Omeros, *from* Chapter XXVIII ◆ From Lucy: Englan' Lady

◆ Literature and Your Life

CONNECT YOUR EXPERIENCE

Like Walcott's St. Lucia and Berry's Jamaica, the United States was once a British colony. In its struggle for independence, it adopted British principles and gave them eloquent expression in *The Declaration of Independence*.

Walcott and Berry, whose island nations won independence in their lifetimes, are also giving gifts to the English language, infusing it with a new Caribbean vision.

THEMATIC FOCUS: FROM THE NATIONAL TO THE GLOBAL

As you read, find the new words, rhythms, and perspectives that Walcott and Berry are contributing to the language.

◆ Literary Focus

THEME AND CONTEXT

The central insight expressed in a literary work is its **theme**. Often such insights are universal, applying to people who live in different places and times. No matter how global a theme is, however, you can better understand it by appreciating the local conditions from which it comes, its **context**.

The context of these poems is the colonial history of the Caribbean region and the experience of Caribbean immigrants in Britain. As a result, the insights these poets express come from a dialogue between British culture and Afro-Caribbean culture.

Journal Writing Jot down some interesting cultural combinations you have observed, in food, language, or customs.

◆ Grammar and Style

COMMONLY CONFUSED WORDS: *AFFECT* AND *EFFECT*

Two commonly confused words are *affect* and *effect*. In a poem that re-creates Jamaican English, Berry abbreviates the verb *affect*, which means "influence": "She *affec'* the place / like the sun." Keep these definitions in mind:

Affect most often means "to influence" (verb); it can also mean "mood; feeling" (noun).

Effect most often means "result" (noun); it can also mean "bring about" (verb).

◆ Reading Strategy

APPLY BACKGROUND INFORMATION

Sometimes you must **apply background information** to understand a poem. For example, the more you know about the history of the West Indies and the lives of Walcott and Berry, the better you will understand the language and attitudes of these poets.

It's especially helpful to apply background information to the excerpts from Walcott's *Midsummer* and *Omeros*. You can find this information on p. 1136 and in the footnotes to the poems. Also, keep in mind Walcott's mixed European and African heritage. This key detail helps explain his guilt and anger at the Brixton riots (*Midsummer*) and his fascination with his African roots (*Omeros*).

◆ Build Vocabulary

WORD ROOTS: *-duc-*

In Walcott's *Midsummer*, you'll encounter the verb *inducted*, which means "to bring or lead formally into a group." Its root, *-duc-*, which means "to lead," appears in such words as *conduct* and *education*.

WORD BANK

Before you read, preview this list of words from the poems.

antic
rancor
eclipse
inducted

To prepare students for these poems about West Indians adapting to European culture, have them share memories of times they visited a place very different from their own home—a different country, region, or neighborhood unlike the place they live. What differences did they find in the way people talked, dressed, ate, and behaved? How did they cope? The conditions they experienced are the *context* of their story. Then ask whether they enjoyed their visit, and why. Tell them that what they got out of their trip could be the *theme* of their story.

Customize for
Less Proficient Readers
These students may have difficulty with the plant imagery, shifting speakers, and time shifts in the excerpt from Walcott's *Omeros*. Explain these aspects of the poem before students read. After they read, use the annotations accompanying the poem to guide these students.

Customize for
More Advanced Students
These students may enjoy researching more information about the slave trade and the colonial history of the Caribbean region. Encourage them to do the Black Roots project in the Idea Bank on page 1145.

Customize for
English Language Learners
These students may respond strongly to the themes of these selections. Encourage them to participate in the debate on assimilation in the Idea Bank on page 1145.

Customize for
Interpersonal Learners
These poems may inspire your interpersonal learners to explore how different ethnic groups interact in your own community. Encourage them to learn about and join local organizations that foster multicultural tolerance and understanding.

Preparing for Standardized Tests

Grammar The Grammar and Style lesson for this selection gives students practice in using the commonly confused words *affect* and *effect* correctly. Students might encounter such usage issues in the Writing Skills portion of standardized tests, where they must identify errors: *(B)*

One of the scientists is studying (A) the affect (B) that ultraviolet light and other radiation has (C) on this kind (D) of plant.

(A) is studying
(B) affect
(C) has
(D) this kind
(E) No error

Use the Grammar and Style exercise on page 1144 to help students practice this skill. If students need more reinforcement, use the Grammar and Style page on Commonly Confused Words: *Affect* and *Effect*, p. 298, in ***Selection Support.***

Develop Understanding

One-Minute Insight Derek Walcott wrestles with his conflicting loyalties as a black Caribbean poet accepted in white British society. He explores his anger and guilt at the treatment of other Caribbeans in England at the time of the 1981 riot in the Brixton area of London.

Looking at Literature Videodisc To introduce students to Walcott's poetry, play Chapter 12 of the videodisc "The Music and Rhythm of Writing," featuring Derek Walcott.

Chapter 12

◆ Literary Focus

❶ Theme and Context Ask students how Walcott develops both a specific context and the beginning of a universal theme in the first five lines of the poem. *His description of the Brixton riot establishes a specific context for the poem, while the statement "it is in their nature,/being men as well as leaves, to die for the sun" begins to establish a universal theme about the quest of all people for light and a meaningful life.*

◆ Reading Strategy

❷ Apply Background Information Ask students what relevance these references to the Boer War and apartheid have to the context and theme of the poem. *Although it was the Dutch Boers who actually established the system of apartheid, or racial separation, in South Africa, Walcott suggests that the British "Tory whips" cooperated with, or did not resist, the Boer plan for oppressing blacks, and that the position of blacks in England today is like the radical racial segregation of society under apartheid.*

❸ Clarification Lines 16 and 19 contain allusions to the work of Shakespeare. "[T]he Sonnets" are Shakespeare's poems. "The Moor's eclipse" refers to the betrayal of Othello. Caliban is the deformed slave in *The Tempest*, a play set on a magical island inspired by the 1609 discovery of Bermuda. He represents the bestial urges of humanity.

from

Midsummer XXIII

Derek Walcott

With the stampeding hiss and scurry of green lemmings,
midsummer's leaves race to extinction like the roar
❶ of a Brixton riot[1] tunneled by water hoses;
they seethe towards autumn's fire—it is in their nature,
being men as well as leaves, to die for the sun.
The leaf stems tug at their chains, the branches bending
❷ like Boer cattle under Tory whips that drag every wagon
nearer to apartheid.[2] And, for me, that closes
the child's fairy tale of an antic England—fairy rings,
thatched cottages fenced with dog roses,
a green gale lifting the hair of Warwickshire.
I was there to add some color to the British theater.
"But the blacks can't do Shakespeare, they have no experience."
This was true. Their thick skulls bled with rancor
when the riot police and the skinheads exchanged quips
you could trace to the Sonnets, or the Moor's eclipse.
❸ Praise had bled my lines white of any more anger,
and snow had inducted me into white fellowships,
while Calibans howled down the barred streets of an empire
that began with Caedmon's raceless dew,[3] and is ending
in the alleys of Brixton, burning like Turner's ships.[4]

1. **Brixton riot:** Residents of the South London district of Brixton rioted in April 1981 to protest racial prejudice and economic disadvantage.
2. **Boer** (boor) **cattle . . . apartheid:** In the seventeenth century, the Boers, people of Dutch descent, colonized a portion of what is now South Africa. The Tories, members of a political party in Britain, held power when the Boer War (1899–1902) resulted in British control of South Africa. The system of apartheid was established by the Boers when South Africa became a republic.
3. **Caedmon's:** (kad´ mən) **raceless dew:** Poetry written by the earliest known English poet, Caedmon, who lived in the seventh century.
4. **Turner's ships:** British artist J.M.W. Turner (1775–1851) painted atmospheric canvases of ships burning in battle.

◆ Build Vocabulary

antic (an´ tik) *adj.*: Odd and funny

rancor (raŋ´ kər) *n.*: Continuing, bitter hate or ill will

eclipse (ē klips´) *n.*: Dimming or extinction of fame or glory

inducted (in dukt´ id) *v.*: Brought formally into a society or organization; provided with knowledge or experience of something

Block Scheduling Strategies

Consider these suggestions to take advantage of extended class time:

- Introduce the Literary Focus concepts of Theme and Context (p. 1137). Then use the Interest Grabber activity to help students identify the context and theme of their own personal narratives. Point out that two stories can have the same context but different themes or different contexts but the same theme. Give examples from popular movies. After students read the poems, use the Literary Focus exercise on page 1144 and the Literary Focus page on Theme and Context in ***Selection Support***, p. 300, to reinforce these important concepts. The Caribbean Festival project on page 1145 can also help students understand more about the context from which West Indian writers emerged.
- Have students work on their pro-and-con editorials on the British royal family. Before students begin, use the Cross-Curricular Connection: Social Studies page on British Royalty in ***Beyond Literature***, p. 63, to help build background on this issue.

Revolution Is Change, Change Is Life, 1988, Jean Patrick Icart-Pierre, The Bronx Museum of the Arts, New York

◀ **Critical Viewing** How does the painter suggest violence similar to "the roar/of a Brixton riot"? What details suggest that the rage of "Calibans" might express the desire for a more meaningful existence? **[Compare and Contrast]** 4

Guide for Responding

◆ Literature and Your Life

Reader's Response Does the tone and language of this poem make you feel as if you were listening to a British or West Indian person? Explain.

Thematic Focus What makes the issues Walcott discusses in this poem global rather than national?

☑ Check Your Comprehension

1. To what things does Walcott compare midsummer's leaves?
2. (a) What references to British history does Walcott make? (b) What event, recent at the time, does he include in those references?

◆ Critical Thinking

INTERPRET

1. What "closes" for the speaker "the child's fairy tale of an antic England"? Why? **[Interpret]**
2. What does the speaker mean when he says that the "empire . . . is ending / in the alleys of Brixton"? **[Draw Conclusions]**

EVALUATE

3. From reading this poem, would you say that Walcott has come to terms with his dual heritage? Why or why not? **[Make a Judgment]**

APPLY

4. How does this poem affect your attitude toward racial prejudice? **[Relate]**

Humanities: Art

Revolution Is Change, Change Is Life, 1988, by Jean Patrick Icart-Pierre.

This emotional scene of people protesting the conditions of their lives and fighting for change will help students understand Walcott's emotional response to the Brixton riot, as described in the excerpt from *Midsummer.*

Use these questions for discussion:

1. Which lines from the poem could serve as captions for this piece of art? *Suggested responses: "Their thick skulls bled with rancor/when the riot police and the skinheads exchanged quips/you could trace to the Sonnets, or the Moor's eclipse" (lines 14–16) or "while Calibans howled down the barred streets of an empire" (line 19).*
2. If you were an educated, relatively privileged black person, like Derek Walcott, how might you respond to seeing a scene such as the one shown in the picture? *Students might say they would feel guilty for their relative ease in white society, or they might feel embarrassed or angry.*

▶Critical Viewing◀

4 Compare and Contrast The painter suggests violence by the raised fists, open mouths, and swirls of contrasting colors such as purple and yellow. The desire for a more meaningful existence is suggested by the anguished expressions on the faces, the closed eyes, and the fact that many of the faces are raised to the sky (as if in prayer).

Reinforce and Extend

Answers

◆ Literature and Your Life

Reader's Response The educated style, the references to Shakespeare, and the use of *they* and *their* suggest a British person. The angry descriptions of British oppression suggest a West Indian.

Thematic Focus The issues of immigration and racism arise from the historical ties between different parts of the world.

☑ Check Your Comprehension

1. He compares midsummer's leaves to "green lemmings" and "the roar of a Brixton riot."
2. (a) He refers to the Boer War and the establishment of apartheid in South Africa. (b) He refers to the Brixton riot.

◆ Critical Thinking

1. The violence of the Brixton riots ends the speaker's romantic picture of England; the riots show that Britain is a troubled, divided, and violent society.
2. West Indians were once ruled by the British; West Indian immigration to Britain is an after-effect or even continuation of the empire; the riots are a response to the continuing oppression of West Indians.
3. Suggested response: The speaker seems torn between identifying with his oppressed countrymen and enjoying the praise and acceptance of British critics.
4. Students may say that the poem helps them understand the conflict experienced by even a successful person from a racial minority as he attempts to assimilate.

Develop Understanding

One-Minute Insight This excerpt from Chapter XXVIII of Walcott's epic poem focuses on the painful legacies of the trade that brought enslaved Africans to America and the Caribbean. A West African griot, or storyteller, describes the Africans' experiences on the slave ships and another speaker then comments on the legacy of those experiences.

◆ Critical Thinking

❶ **Infer** Have students explain when the poem switches from one speaker to another. *In the first stanza of the poem, the first speaker introduces the griot, or West African storyteller. The griot tells the story of slavery from lines 4–19. Later, the first speaker will return to sum up the meaning of the story the griot has told.*

◆ Reading Strategy

❷ **Apply Background Information** Have students reread the Background for Understanding information on page 1136 to help them interpret this stanza. Ask what the speaker means when he says "these shadows are reprinted now on the white sand/of antipodal coasts." *Enslaved Africans were brought to the Caribbean to work on plantations far away from their home—on "antipodal coasts." The descendants of these Africans—the black "shadows"—still live in the Caribbean today.*

◆ Literary Focus

❸ **Theme and Context** Ask students why the speaker might have decided to use plant imagery such as "seeds," "pods," "tubers," and "dried fronds" to describe the enslaved Africans. *The plant imagery places the Africans in the context from which they were taken—a region of palm trees where much of the diet is based on tubers such as yams. It suggests the closeness that existed between the people and their natural environment.*

from Omeros

from Chapter XXVIII

Derek Walcott

Now he heard the griot[1] muttering his prophetic song
of sorrow that would be the past. It was a note, long-drawn
and endless in its winding like the brown river's tongue:

❶

"We were the color of shadows when we came down
with tinkling leg-irons to join the chains of the sea,
for the silver coins multiplying on the sold horizon,

and these shadows are reprinted now on the white sand
❷ of antipodal[2] coasts, your ashen ancestors
from the Bight of Benin, from the margin of Guinea.[3]

There were seeds in our stomachs, in the cracking pods
of our skulls on the scorching decks, the tubers[4]
withered in no time. We watched as the river-gods

❸

changed from snakes into currents. When inspected,
our eyes showed dried fronds[5] in their brown irises,
and from our curved spines, the rib-cages radiated

1. **griot** (grē′ ō) *n.*: In West African cultures, a poet/historian/performer who preserves and passes on the oral tradition.
2. **antipodal** (an tip′ ə dəl) *adj.*: Situated on opposite sides of the earth.
3. **the Bight** (bīt) **of Benin** (be nēn′) **. . . Guinea** (gin′ ē): Area of west central Africa that came to be known as the Slave Coast.
4. **tubers** (to͞o′ bərz) *n.*: Thick, fleshy parts of underground stems, such as potatoes.
5. **fronds** (frändz) *n.*: Leaves of a palm; also the leaflike parts of seaweed.

Cross-Curricular Connection: Social Studies

A bight is a bay formed by a curve in a coastline. The Bight of Benin is one of two bays on the West Coast of Africa that together form the Gulf of Guinea. The land along the Bight of Benin was once home to the great Kingdom of Benin, which existed from the thirteenth to the nineteenth century. The residents of Benin were great traders, and their king ruled from an affluent court known for its beautiful brass and bronze sculptures. The first Europeans to visit Benin were the Portuguese in 1485. The king of Benin actually sent armies to raid rival villages to capture slaves to sell to European traders.

Today Benin is a small country in west Africa located between Nigeria and Togo. It was once known as Dahomey. Benin is one of the poorest countries in West Africa, and most people there are subsistence farmers. Their crops include palm kernels, yams, and peanuts.

Have interested students do more research on Benin and other great kingdoms of west Africa, from which many enslaved Africans were taken.

like fronds from a palm-branch. Then, when the dead
palms were heaved overside, the ribbed corpses
floated, riding, to the white sand they remembered,

to the Bight of Benin, to the margin of Guinea.
So, when you see burnt branches riding the swell,
trying to reclaim the surf through crooked fingers,

after a night of rough wind by some stone-white hotel, ❹
past the bright triangular passage of the windsurfers,
remember us to the black waiter bringing the bill."

But they crossed, they survived. There is the epical splendor.
Multiply the rain's lances, multiply their ruin,
the grace born from subtraction as the hold's iron door

rolled over their eyes like pots left out in the rain, ❺
and the bolt rammed home its echo, the way that thunder-
claps perpetuate their reverberation.

So there went the Ashanti one way, the Mandingo another,
the Ibo another, the Guinea.[6] Now each man was a nation
in himself, without mother, father, brother.

---

6. **the Ashanti** (ə shan´ tē) . . . **the Mandingo** (man diŋ´ gō) . . . **the Ibo** (ē´ bō´) . . . **the Guinea** (gin´ ē): Names of West African peoples.

Guide for Responding

◆ Literature and Your Life

Reader's Response How does the tone of this poem affect you? Explain.

Thematic Focus What other factors besides nationality determine people's identity, according to the griot?

Group Activity In the excerpt from *Omeros*, Walcott refers to the slave trade. With several classmates, discuss what you know about the process that brought enslaved Africans to America and the Caribbean islands.

☑ Check Your Comprehension

1. In this excerpt from *Omeros*, what does the speaker describe in lines 4 through 24?
2. What happens to members of the different West African peoples once they cross the sea?

◆ Critical Thinking

INTERPRET

1. In this excerpt from *Omeros*, who is speaking in lines 4 through 24? **[Infer]**
2. What does Walcott mean when he says, "Now each man was a nation / in himself"? **[Interpret]**
3. Does anything positive come from the suffering caused by the slave trade? Explain. **[Draw Conclusions]**

EVALUATE

4. Would you say that Walcott has effectively portrayed the condition of the enslaved peoples? Explain. **[Assess]**

APPLY

5. What movies or television presentations have you seen that explore the history of slavery? **[Relate]**

◆ Literary Focus

❹ **Theme and Context** Ask students how the context of the poem suddenly switches. *The griot switches from the past time of slavery to the present conditions in the Caribbean.*

◆ Critical Thinking

❺ **Draw Conclusions** Ask students what message the first speaker seems to derive from the griot's story. *The first speaker finds there was an "epical splendor" and "grace" in the enslaved African's survival.*

Reinforce and Extend

Answers

◆ Literature and Your Life

Reader's Response Students may say that the sad, angry tone inspires compassion.

Thematic Focus Sample answer: Each enslaved African was stripped of his or her ties to family and community.

☑ Check Your Comprehension

1. The speaker describes the experiences of enslaved Africans as they were taken from Africa to America.
2. They are separated and sent to different parts of the world.

◆ Critical Thinking

1. The griot, a West African poet/historian/performer, is speaking of the history of his people.
2. Separated from homeland, community, countrymen, and centuries of tradition, each enslaved African now had to struggle on his own to survive and create a new identity.
3. Born from extreme deprivation came a kind of "grace" that taught the enslaved how to endure.
4. Sample answer: Yes, Walcott has effectively portrayed the suffering through such imagery as "the cracking pods/of our skulls on the scorching decks," "the ribbed corpses floated," and "the bolt rammed home its echo."
5. Students may mention the television mini-series *Roots* and the film *Amistad*.

Cross-Curricular Connection: Social Studies

The Ashanti, or Asante, are a West African group united by a common language. Many Ashanti still inhabit areas of Ghana, Togo, and the Ivory Coast in West Africa today. They live by farming and the trading of handmade crafts.

The Ashanti established a powerful, wealthy empire built on trade in Central Guinea during the seventeenth and eighteenth centuries. When English officials visited the Ashanti capital of Kumasi in 1817, they were amazed to find long, wide streets and a great city. One of the officials wrote: "An area of nearly a mile in circumference was crowded with magnificence and novelty. The king, his chiefs, and captains, were splendidly dressed and were surrounded by attendants of every kind. More than a hundred bands broke into music on our arrival."

Have students discuss their reactions to this vivid description of a nineteenth-century African city. Did they find the wealth and culture of the Ashanti city surprising? Why or why not?

Develop Understanding

One-Minute Insight In this poem a Jamaican immigrant woman living in London expresses her thoughts about Queen Elizabeth in a letter to a friend back home. In Jamaican dialect, she wonders, in a half-amused, bittersweet tone, whether the queen doesn't find her life as a royal celebrity lonely.

◆ Grammar and Style

❶ **Commonly Confused Words: *Affect* and *Effect*** Ask students if they can paraphrase the idea in lines 3 and 4 in a sentence that uses the word *effect*, rather than *affect*, correctly. *Suggested response: "She has an effect like that of the sun."*

◆ Literary Focus

❷ **Theme and Context** Ask students how they can tell that Lucy is not used to living in a big European city and feels out of place there. *Lucy is awed by the size and age of London and impressed by all the streets and buildings.*

◆ Critical Thinking

❸ **Draw Conclusions** Ask students what Lucy's statement here suggests about her character. *Lucy seems compassionate, perceptive, and wise about human nature, rather than unthinkingly envious of the queen's wealth and privileges.*

▶Critical Viewing◀

❹ **Analyze** To help students answer this question, you may want to have them compare the queen's posture and expression in this photo with those she displays in the more relaxed photo on page 1143. Students may say that the queen's posture in this photo looks stiff and that her smile looks frozen and artificial, reflecting the "strain" referred to in the poem.

From Lucy: Englan' Lady

James Berry

You ask me 'bout the lady. Me dear,
old center here still shine
❶ with Queen. She affec' the place
like the sun: not comin' out oft'n
an' when it happ'n everybody's out
smilin' as she wave a han'
like a seagull flyin' slow slow.

An' you know she come from
dust free rooms an' velvet
an' diamond. She make you feel
this on-an'-on[1] town, London,
where long long time deeper than mind.[2]
❷ An' han's after han's[3] die away,
makin' streets, putt'n' up bricks,
a piece of brass, a piece of wood
an' plantin' trees: an' it give
a car a halfday job gett'n' through.

An' Leela, darlin', no, I never
❸ meet the Queen in flesh. Yet
sometimes, deep deep, I sorry for her.

1. **on-an'-on:** Extraordinary.
2. **deeper . . . mind:** More than can be comprehended.
3. **han's after han's:** Many generations.

Elizabeth II

▲ **Critical Viewing** Does Queen Elizabeth show the "strain keepin' good graces" referred to in the poem? Explain. **[Analyze]** ❹

Speaking and Listening Mini-Lesson

Debate

This mini-lesson supports the Speaking and Listening activity in the Idea Bank on p. 1145.

Introduce the Concept Explain that a debate is an organized, reasoned argument in which two groups present opposing sides of an issue.

Develop Information Organize two groups of five students each. One side should research information that supports assimilation for immigrants. The other side should research facts that support the benefits of holding onto ethnic traditions. Encourage students on both sides to interview recent immigrants in your community.

Apply the Information Each side should present a summary of their main arguments first. Then each side can take turns presenting specific reasons for their view, followed by a rebuttal by the other side.

Assess the Outcome Use the Scoring Rubric: in ***Alternative Assessment,*** p. 106, to help evaluate each side's performance.

Everybody expec' a show
from her, like she a space touris'
on earth. An' darlin', unless
(5) you can go home an' scratch up[4]
you' husban', it mus' be hard
strain keepin' good graces for
all hypocrite faces.

Anyhow, me dear, you know what
ole time people say,
"Bird sing sweet for its nest."[5]

---

4. **scratch up:** Lose your temper at.
5. **"Bird . . . nest":** Jamaican proverb, referring to the nightingale's habit of singing loudest near its nest. It means, "Those closest to home are the most contented."

Elizabeth II at Age 18 at Sandringham

▲ Critical Viewing What details in this photograph suggest the "human" side of the queen, the side alluded to by the poem's speaker? **[Analyze]**

Guide for Responding

◆ Literature and Your Life

Reader's Response How did you react to Lucy's description of Queen Elizabeth?

Thematic Focus What is distinctively Jamaican about Lucy's comments on the Queen?

Proverbs and Sayings Lucy closes her letter with a Jamaican proverb. In a small group, brainstorm to come up with other proverbs similar to Lucy's.

☑ Check Your Comprehension

1. Where is the speaker of this poem?
2. To whom is the poem addressed?
3. According to Lucy, how is the Queen like the sun?

◆ Critical Thinking

INTERPRET

1. What problems does Lucy think the Queen has as a result of her position? **[Interpret]**
2. What perception of the Queen does Lucy illustrate by quoting the proverb in line 30? **[Connect]**
3. What can you infer about Lucy's character from her "letter"? **[Draw Conclusions]**

EVALUATE

4. Is this poem effective in conveying the rhythm and feel of Jamaican dialect? Explain. **[Evaluate]**

APPLY

5. How do you think Lucy would react to life in the United States? **[Hypothesize]**

Beyond the Selection

FURTHER READING

Other Works by the Authors

"A Far Cry from Africa"; "Another Life," Derek Walcott

Lucy's Letter, Chain of Days, James Berry

Other Works on the Theme

"Where Is My Country?" Nellie Wong

"Immigrants," Pat Mora

"Ka' Ba," Amiri Baraka

We suggest that you preview these works before recommending them to students.

INTERNET

You and your students may find additional information about Derek Walcott and James Berry on the Internet. We suggest the following sites. (Note: Addresses expire without notice.)

For information about Nobel Laureates go to **http://www.nobel.se/laureates/literature-1992-press.html**. For information about James Berry go to **http://www.futurenet.co.uk/Penguin/Authors/1060.html**.

We *strongly recommend* that you preview sites.

◆ Literature and Your Life

(5) Ask students if they agree with Lucy's view of celebrity. *Students may base their responses on information about American media and performing arts celebrities.*

▶Critical Viewing◀

(6) **Analyze** Students might cite her casual clothes, disheveled hair, relaxed pose and facial expression, as well as the fact that she is in the country with her horse.

Reinforce and Extend

Answers

◆ Literature and Your Life

Reader's Response Some may have found the description amusing; others may have found it sad.

Thematic Focus The description is made in a Jamaican dialect, from the point of view of an outsider.

☑ Check Your Comprehension

1. The speaker is in London.
2. The poem is addressed to a friend back in Jamaica, the speaker's home.
3. Like the sun in England, the queen doesn't come out often; when she does, she makes everyone smile.

◆ Critical Thinking

1. Lucy thinks the queen can never really relax or lose her temper because she is always "on stage."
2. Lucy illustrates the perception that it must be lonely to be such a public person and not even have privacy in one's own home.
3. Sample answer: Lucy's down-to-earth simplicity makes her perceptive and allows her to feel compassion.
4. Some students may feel that Jamaican expressions such as "on-an'-on town," as well as the dropped consonants at the ends of many words, convey the feel of the dialect.
5. Lucy might feel sorry for American celebrities who lead public lives similar to the queen's.

Answers

◆ Reading Strategy

1. In *Omeros* Walcott modifies a traditional British form of poetry to describe his African heritage.
2. Berry's perspective as an outsider in London as well as his roots in the dialect of Jamaica are reflected in the speaker Lucy's voice in "From Lucy: Englan' Lady."

◆ Literary Focus

1. As a beneficiary of Britain's admiration and praise for his dramatic and literary success, Walcott feels a sense of disloyalty to his people in light of the riots of South London's black population.
2. (a) The conflict is between the African culture expressed by the voice of the griot and the plight of the contemporary black worker, represented by "the black waiter bringing the bill." (b) Walcott's internal conflict is reflected in the rootlessness of the image "each man was a nation/in himself."
3. (a) Lucy is impressed by the opulence and cleanliness of the Queen's environment and with the age of the town of London. (b) To a New World resident, the historical age of European cities is impressive; coming from an impoverished nation, Lucy would be impressed by the opulence of royal wealth.
4. (a) Comparing the Queen's wave to that of a seagull and her appearances to a visit by a "space tourist" adds a touch of Jamaican humor to Lucy's descriptions. (b) Lucy appears to appreciate the history and traditions of British culture, although she penetrates beyond the pageantry to ask about its human cost.

◆ Build Vocabulary

Using the Word Root *-duc-*

Sample responses:

1. conduct: "lead"; educational: "leading knowledge out of"; ducts: "pipes that lead fluid from one place to another"; products: "goods led forth from the land"; Duchess: "one who leads"; induce: "lead into"

Using the Word Bank

1. b 2. a 3. a 4. c

Guide for Responding *(continued)*

◆ Reading Strategy

Apply Background Information

By **applying background information** from the writers' biographies, the Background for Understanding, and the footnotes, you can better understand the poems. For example, Walcott's divided heritage—part European, part African—explains why he seems to accuse himself of not sharing the rioters' fury: "Praise had bled my lines white of any more anger." It's as if he's saying that his own white heritage and British "praise" for his work have led him to betray his African origins.

1. If Walcott expresses the conflict of a divided heritage in *Midsummer*, how does he deal with that heritage in the excerpt from *Omeros*?
2. How do Berry's rural Jamaican background and longtime residence in London help explain the word choice, form, and subject matter of his poem?

◆ Literary Focus

Theme and Context

The **themes** of these poems, their central insights, cannot be separated from their **context**: the history of British colonization in the Caribbean and the recent immigration of West Indians to Britain. Because of this history, the key ideas in these poems relate to the collision of cultures. In *Midsummer,* XXIII, that collision sparks a riot, while in "From Lucy: Englan' Lady," it lights a twinkle in the eye of a Jamaican woman.

1. Explain how, in *Midsummer*, a clash between cultures ignites a conflict in the poet's mind.
2. (a) What is the conflict between cultures that Walcott brings to life in the excerpt from *Omeros?* (b) Is there also an internal conflict? Why or why not?
3. (a) In Berry's poem, what does Lucy find impressive about London, her new home? (b) As a rural Jamaican, why might she be especially impressed by this aspect of London?
4. (a) Identify two ways in which Lucy brings a humorous Jamaican twist to her observations of an English queen. (b) Overall, would you say that Lucy appreciates British culture? Explain.

◆ Build Vocabulary

Using the Word Root *-duc-*

Briefly explain how the meaning of the root *-duc-* ("to lead") contributes to the definition of each underlined word:

I'm here to <u>conduct</u> the tour of a typical West Indian sugar plantation that will be very <u>educational</u>. Please, don't bump into the <u>ducts</u> that transport the juice from the pressed sugarcane stalks. In this room, the juice is concentrated by evaporation into a dark, sticky sugar, a <u>product</u> that can be sold locally —it can be further refined by eliminating nonsugar elements. Under British colonialism, the plantation was owned by the <u>Duchess</u> of Devonshire. Perhaps I can <u>induce</u> you to donate to our museum on the way out.

Using the Word Bank

On your paper write the lettered word closest in meaning to the first word.

1. rancor: (a) pleasure, (b) hate, (c) music
2. inducted: (a) initiated, (b) cried, (c) lost
3. antic: (a) zany, (b) dangerous, (c) helpful
4. eclipse: (a) burst, (b) fire, (c) extinction

◆ Grammar and Style

Commonly Confused Words: *Affect* and *Effect*

You can usually avoid confusing ***affect*** and ***effect*** by deciding if you want a verb meaning "to influence" (*affect*) or a noun meaning "result" (*effect*). Other forms of these words—*affect* as a noun ("mood") and *effect* as a verb ("bring about") are less common.

Practice On your paper, insert the correct word.

1. Berry's stay in Harlem had a great (affect/effect) upon his ideas about prejudice.
2. Walcott's multiracial background has (effected/ affected) the kind of poetry he writes.
3. The (affect/effect) of Berry's poetry is to change the way West Indians view themselves.
4. Was Walcott less (effected, affected) by the Brixton riot when it happened than he was later?
5. Readers respond strongly to the (effect/affect) of Berry's use of Jamaican dialect in his Lucy poems.

◆ Grammar and Style

1. effect; 2. affected; 3. effect; 4. affected; 5. effect

Writer's Solution

For additional instruction and practice, use the page on One Hundred Common Usage Problems, p. 75 in the *Writer's Solution Grammar Practice Book.*

Build Your Portfolio

Idea Bank

Writing

1. Personal Letter Write a letter to Lucy giving her some recent news about the queen and other members of Britain's royal family. Respond to some of the ideas she expresses in her letter.

2. Literary Analysis Choose one of these poems and show how its author brings Caribbean language, rhythms, and perspectives to English.

3. Response to Criticism Louis James writes that in *Midsummer*, Derek Walcott tries "to reconcile his divided heritage." Show how Walcott makes this attempt in *Midsummer*, XXIII.

Speaking and Listening

4. Oral Interpretation of Dialect Perform Berry's dialect poem for the class. In rehearsing, follow the poet's own advice for reading a poem in Jamaican dialect: "Feel out the rhythms. . . . Then express it with your own easy natural voice." **[Performing Arts Link]**

5. Debate Are Caribbean immigrants better off shedding their culture and adapting fully to their new British home, or is there value in holding on to traditions? Organize a debate about the issue. **[Social Studies Link]**

Projects

6. Black Roots What happened to the Ashanti and other African cultures transplanted to the Caribbean by slavery? Research the answer in books on Caribbean history and write a report on your findings. **[Social Studies Link]**

7. Caribbean Festival Prepare a festival of Caribbean culture. Highlight the language, food, and music of Jamaica, St. Lucia, and other countries in the region. **[Social Studies Link]**

Writing Mini-Lesson

Pro-and-Con Editorial

"From Lucy: Englan' Lady" offers a humorous, endearingly biased portrait of the Queen. Today, however, the royal family is a controversial issue. Some think it is an expensive symbol of the past that should be eliminated. Others think it is an important tradition that must be maintained. Discuss this subject in an editorial written for a local newspaper. Give the arguments on both sides, the pros and cons, before expressing your own opinion.

Writing Skills Focus: Transitions to Show Comparisons

In giving pro-and-con arguments, you'll want to use **transitions to show comparisons**. Such transitions help readers find their way among different arguments. Following are some commonly used transitions:

on the one hand	however
on the other hand	nevertheless
while	

Prewriting Jot down a sentence or phrase that sums up the main point of your editorial. Under it, summarize arguments for and against your point of view.

Drafting Begin with a question, image, or anecdote that will surprise readers, get their attention, and possibly even support your main point. As you move from arguments for to arguments against, use transitions to show comparisons.

Revising If possible, choose as a peer editor someone who has taken the opposite point of view. Have this person carefully read your editorial and suggest any strong arguments against your position that you may have left out. Include and respond to these arguments, making sure you use transitions to show comparisons.

✓ ASSESSMENT OPTIONS

Formal Assessment, Selection Test, pp. 297–299, and Assessment Resources Software. The selection test is designed so that it can be easily customized to the performance levels of your students. ***Alternative Assessment,*** p. 63, includes options for less advanced students, more advanced students, musical/rhythmic learners, visual/spatial learners, interpersonal learners, and verbal/linguistic learners.

PORTFOLIO ASSESSMENT
Use the following rubrics in the ***Alternative Assessment*** booklet to assess student writing:
Personal Letter: Expression Rubric, p. 95
Literary Analysis: Literary Analysis/Interpretation Rubric, p. 113
Response to Criticism: Response to Literature Rubric, p. 111
Writing Mini-Lesson: Persuasion Rubric, p. 106

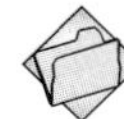

Idea Bank

Customizing for *Performance Levels*
Following are suggestions for matching Idea Bank topics with your students' performance levels:
Less Advanced Students: 1, 4, 6
Average Students: 2, 5, 7
More Advanced Students: 3, 7

Customizing for *Learning Modalities*
Following are suggestions for matching Idea Bank topics with your students' learning modalities:
Verbal/Linguistic: 1, 2, 3, 4, 5, 6
Musical/Rhythmic: 7

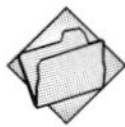

Writing Mini-Lesson

Refer students to the Writing Process Handbook, page 1189, for instruction on the writing process, and page 1192 for further information on persuasion.

Writing and Language Transparencies Students may use the Argument Organizer, pp. 103–106, to organize their editorials. Use Writing Process Model 5, pp. 37–44, to guide students through drafting and revising.

Writer's Solution

Writers at Work Videodisc
Have students view the videodisc segment on Persuasion (Ch. 4) featuring Cary Bricker to see how she gathers information for her persuasive writing.

Play frames 37854 to 38686

Writing Lab CD-ROM
Have students complete the tutorial on Persuasion, following these steps:

1. Use the Issues Wheel to spark writing ideas.
2. Use the Pros and Cons Chart to evaluate arguments.
3. Draft on computer.
4. Use the Interactive Self-Evaluation Checklist for revising.

Sourcebook
Have students use Chapter 4, Persuasion (pp. 96–129), for additional support. The chapter includes an annotated student model of a position paper on the British Monarchy (pp. 124–125).

Prepare and Engage

OBJECTIVES

1. To read, comprehend, and interpret a short story
2. To relate a story to personal experience
3. To evaluate characters' decisions
4. To analyze static and dynamic characters
5. To build vocabulary in context and learn the word root *-fil-*
6. To analyze the variety of sentences used in a short story and to practice using a variety of sentence types
7. To write a proposal for improving relationships with elders, using words with positive connotations
8. To respond to the poems through writing, speaking and listening, and projects

SKILLS INSTRUCTION

Vocabulary: Word Roots *-fil-*

Grammar: Sentence Variety

Reading Strategy: Evaluate Characters' Decisions

Literary Focus: Static and Dynamic Characters

Writing: Connotations

Speaking and Listening: Panel Discussion (teacher edition)

Critical Viewing: Speculate; Interpret

PORTFOLIO OPPORTUNITIES

Writing: Character Sketch; Memorial Tribute; Response to Criticism

Writing Mini-Lesson: Proposal

Speaking and Listening: Role-Play; Panel Discussion

Projects: India's Public Health; Cross-Cultural Survey

More About the Author
Critic A. G. Mojtakai has described the advantages of Anita Desai's broad cultural awareness: "Anita Desai . . . stands in a complicated but advantageous relation to India. Insiders rarely notice this much; outsiders cannot have this ease of reference."

Guide for Interpreting

Anita Desai *(1937–)*

Anita Desai's unusual heritage—her father was Indian and her mother German—may have contributed to her understanding of people from different cultures. She displays that understanding in finely-crafted novels and short stories about conflicts among people of different generations and backgrounds. These works of fiction have gained her a reputation as one of the most gifted Indian novelists writing in English.

Early Life Desai was born in the northern Indian town of Mussoorie, located at the foot of the Himalayan mountains. She grew up in a large house in the old section of Delhi, India's capital city.

> *"There were a great many books in the house and we were all bookworms," Desai recalls.*

Because of her unique heritage, her family spoke three languages—Hindi, English, and German. However, English became Desai's literary language.

Early Work and Recognition After graduating from Delhi University, Desai, newly married, joined the Writers Workshop in Calcutta. In 1963, she published her first novel, *Cry the Peacock*, a portrayal of the despair of a young married woman. This novel was followed by *Bye-Bye, Blackbird* (1968), *Fire on the Mountain* (1977), and *Clear Light of Day* (1980). This last novel, a study of complex family relationships, was nominated for England's prestigious Booker Prize. The critic Victoria Glendinning said of this work, "Quiet writing, like Anita Desai's, can be more impressive than stylistic fireworks."

Teaching Career After winning success as a writer, Desai pursued a teaching career, too. She has taught, for example, at Cambridge University in England and at Smith College in Massachusetts.

Recent Fiction In her recent novels, Desai examines the gulf between reality and the delusions of her characters. Another theme of her work, evident in *Baumgartner's Bombay* (1989) and in *Journey to Ithaca* (1995), is the contrast between Indian and modern European perspectives. *Journey to Ithaca*, for example, features a European couple who travel to India on a quest for spiritual meaning. "A Devoted Son," which first appeared in the collection of short stories *Games at Twilight* (1978), also shows a clash between modern and traditional Indian values.

◆ Background for Understanding

CULTURE: DESAI'S PORTRAIT OF INDIA, OLD AND NEW

Ever since India won its independence from Britain in 1947, increasing modernization has resulted in dramatic contrasts between the old and the new. For example, it's not unusual to see a camel pulling a cart filled with brand-new motorcycles or a fax sign at a traditional marketplace.

In her story, Anita Desai alludes to traditional customs of Indian family life, as when children show their father respect by touching his feet. Desai also shows the customary way in which several generations live in the same household.

However, Desai contrasts these traditions with features of the new India: travel for study in the United States, a scientific attitude toward public health, and a challenge to the older generation's household authority. The title "A Devoted Son" is, therefore, a bit ironic. It suggests the India of old, while the story captures the poignant contradictions of old and new. In the new India, devotion may not be all that it seems.

Prentice Hall Literature Program Resources

REINFORCE / RETEACH / EXTEND

Selection Support Pages
Build Vocabulary: Word Roots: *-fil-*, p. 301
Grammar and Style: Sentence Variety, p. 302
Reading Strategy: Evaluate Characters' Decisions, p. 303
Literary Focus: Static and Dynamic Characters, p. 304

Strategies for Diverse Student Needs, p. 64

Beyond Literature
Cross-Curricular Connection: Physical Education: Cricket, p. 64

Formal Assessment Selection Test, pp. 300–302; Assessment Resources Software

Alternative Assessment, p. 64

Writing and Language Transparencies
Problem-Solution Organizer, pp. 107–110

Resource Pro CD-ROM
"A Devoted Son"—includes all resource material and customizable lesson plan

Listening to Literature Audiocassettes
"A Devoted Son"

A Devoted Son

◆ Literature and Your Life

Connect Your Experience

Computers, VCR's, cellular phones, the Internet, fax machines: Are you more "plugged in" to the latest technology than your parents are? When it comes to gadgets, do you feel that the older generation is just a little slow to pick up on things?

In "A Devoted Son," a major theme is the difference between generations, especially in their reactions to what is new.

Journal Writing Freewrite about some of the ways in which your generation differs from your parents' generation.

Thematic Focus: From the National to the Global

As you read this story, notice that Desai is not simply a "regional" author. The conflicts she depicts are universal.

◆ Literary Focus

Static and Dynamic Characters

A **static character** is a figure in a literary work who does not change. In contrast, a figure who undergoes significant change is called a **dynamic character**. Often readers feel that a dynamic character is more lifelike—the basis of life is change—and therefore more appealing.

In "A Devoted Son," only one character is dynamic. Consider whether the character who changes is someone who *believes* in change or someone who is committed to traditional ways.

◆ Grammar and Style

Sentence Variety

Sentence variety makes for lively, interesting writing. Sentences can vary by length, type (declarative, interrogative, imperative), structure (simple, compound, complex), and placement of elements like appositives and participial phrases.

Notice how Desai uses sentence variety in the fourth paragraph of her story to dramatize a family's joy. Two short, simple sentences are followed by a longer sentence and then by a very long sentence, with parallel phrases and clauses, ending with the words "golden and glorious." Be alert to other passages in which sentence variety heightens the suspense or drama.

◆ Reading Strategy

Evaluate Characters' Decisions

Like people in life, characters in literary works make choices. You can **evaluate** their choices just as you would assess your own decisions: Was the decision based on logic or emotion? Were the results worth the risks, and why? Also, just as you might celebrate or regret a decision you have made, you can respond emotionally to the choices that literary characters make.

Each time a character in this story makes a choice, evaluate it and trace its effects on future actions. In making such judgments, however, don't forget to mourn and rejoice with characters as they live out the results of their decisions.

◆ Build Vocabulary

Word Roots: *-fil-*

In "A Devoted Son," you will find the word *filial*. This word contains the Latin root *-fil-*, meaning "son or daughter," and means "suitable to, or due from, a son or daughter." Look for other words with this root, like *affiliation*.

Word Bank

Before you read, preview this list of words from the story.

exemplary
filial
encomiums
complaisant
fathom

Interest Grabber Ask students what they know of care for the elderly in the United States today. Students may share experiences of grandparents with Alzheimer's or elderly relatives living in their homes. Ask: To what extent are children responsible for their parents' care in their later years? What problems arise from this intergenerational interaction? Tell students that in this story a conflict arises over a son's attempts to control his elderly father's diet and medical care at the end of his life. Have students reevaluate their opinions on this subject after they have read the story.

Customize for
Less Proficient Readers
These students may have difficulty with the many long, complicated sentences Desai uses. Some of these passages are annotated under the heading Grammar and Style. Read these passages aloud for students and help them interpret and analyze them.

Customize for
More Advanced Students
Encourage these students to do their own research on different aspects of Indian society. They may enjoy preparing the Panel Discussion on Indian family arrangements in the Idea Bank on page 1157.

Customize for
English Language Learners
These students may find much to identify with in this story of a clash between generations, in which the young embrace the modern world, while older relatives cling to traditional ways. The issue of filial devotion may also be an important one for them. Involve these students in discussions of these issues.

Customize for
Bodily/Kinesthetic Learners
This story begins with an important act of filial devotion: a successful son's bowing down to touch his father's feet. As these students read, encourage them to notice how characters use body language and facial expressions to express their feelings for each other. Encourage them to try the Role-Play suggested in the Idea Bank (p. 1157).

Preparing for Standardized Tests

Vocabulary The Build Vocabulary lesson for this selection focuses on the word root *-fil-*, meaning "son or daughter." Understanding the meaning of this root will help students remember the meanings of related words such as *affiliate* and can also help them with the synonyms, antonyms, and analogies in the vocabulary section of standardized tests. For example, students might encounter an analogy such as the following:

son : father :: _________ : paternal *(B)*
(A) maternal
(B) filial
(C) familial
(D) parental
(E) ancestral

Understanding that the word *filial* means "due from a son or daughter" will help students choose this word correctly to complete the analogy. Use the Build Vocabulary exercise on page 1156, as well as the Build Vocabulary page in **Selection Support**, p. 301, to help students master this word root.

Develop Understanding

One-Minute Insight In this ironically titled story, an Indian family sacrifices everything to send their son Rakesh to medical school. Rakesh's father is proud of his son's success and devotion—until the son begins applying his modern medical knowledge and devotion to a strict control of his aging father's diet. The father's decline in body and spirit, and his growing regret at the estrangement that a modern education has caused between him and his son make for a poignant story with a universal theme of generational conflict.

◆ Reading Strategy

❶ **Evaluate Characters' Decisions** Ask how the family feels at the beginning of the story about their decision to make sacrifices to educate their son. Then ask students if they think the family did the right thing. Have them give reasons for their answers. *At the beginning of the story the family feels that all of their sacrifices have been worth it, because Rakesh has brought honor and glory to them through his achievement. Some students may question the fairness of a family sacrificing everything for the sake of one sibling.*

◆ Critical Thinking

❷ **Draw Conclusions** Ask students how they can tell that touching a father's feet is an important sign of a devoted son in Indian culture. *Students can tell that this behavior is important by the father's bragging about it to his friends and by the reaction of the other parents to this news: The mothers are moved to tears, and the fathers shake their heads "in wonder and approval."*

When the results appeared in the morning papers, Rakesh scanned them barefoot and in his pajamas, at the garden gate, then went up the steps to the verandah where his father sat sipping his morning tea and bowed down to touch his feet.

"A first division, son?" his father asked, beaming, reaching for the papers.

"At the top of the list, papa," Rakesh murmured, as if awed. "First in the country."

Bedlam broke loose then. The family whooped and danced. The whole day long visitors streamed into the small yellow house at the end of the road to congratulate the parents of this *Wunderkind,*[1] to slap Rakesh on the back and fill the house and garden with the sounds and colors of a festival. There were garlands and halwa,[2] party clothes and gifts (enough fountain pens to last years, even a watch or two), nerves and temper and joy, all in a multicolored whirl of pride and great shining vistas newly opened: Rakesh was the first son
❶ in the family to receive an education, so much had been sacrificed in order to send him to school and then medical college, and at last the
fruits of their sacrifice had arrived, golden and glorious. ❶

To everyone who came to him to say "*Mubarak,* Varmaji, your son has brought you glory," the father said, "Yes, and do you know what is the first thing he did when he saw the results this morning? He came and touched my feet. He bowed down and touched my feet." This moved many of the women in the crowd so much that they were seen to raise the ends of
their saris and dab at their tears while the men ❷
reached out for the betel-leaves[3] and sweetmeats that were offered around on trays and shook their heads in wonder and approval of such exemplary filial behavior. "One does not often see such behavior in sons any more," they all agreed, a little enviously perhaps. Leaving the house, some of the women said, sniffing, "At least on such an occasion they might have served pure *ghee*[4] sweets," and some of the men said, "Don't you think old Varma was giving himself airs? He needn't think we don't remember that he comes from the vegetable

1. ***Wunderkind:*** Person who achieves remarkable success at an early age.
2. **halwa (also halva):** Middle Eastern sweet confection made of sesame flour and honey.
3. **betel-leaves:** Leaves of a climbing evergreen shrub which are chewed in the East with betel nut parings and a little lime.
4. ***ghee:*** Clarified butter, often used in Indian cooking.

Block Scheduling Strategies

Consider these suggestions to take advantage of extended class time:

- This selection is rich in opportunities for literary analysis, improving students' writing style, research projects, and community action. You may want to have students first analyze the characters and style of the work itself and then encourage them to practice using sentence variety in their own writing. Use the Grammar and Style exercise on page 1156 to work on this skill, as well as the Grammar and Style page in ***Selection Support,*** p. 302.
- Allow class time for students to focus on projects related to this selection. The Panel Discussion and the presentations on India's Public Health and the Cross-Cultural Survey (p. 1157) will enhance students' understanding of and appreciation for the story.
- The Writing Mini-Lesson offers an opportunity for students to produce writing with a specific, practical purpose and audience in mind and to create a real program for improving contact between teenagers and elders. Before students begin, invite the director of a local residence for elders to speak to the class about current volunteer needs at the residence.

market himself, his father used to sell vegetables, and he has never seen the inside of a school." But there was more envy than rancor[5] in their voices and it was, of course, inevitable—not every son in that shabby little colony at the edge of the city was destined to shine as Rakesh shone, and who knew that better than the parents themselves?

And that was only the beginning, the first step in a great, sweeping ascent to the radiant heights of fame and fortune. The thesis he wrote for his M.D. brought Rakesh still greater glory, if only in select medical circles. He won a scholarship. He went to the USA (that was what his father learnt to call it and taught the whole family to say—not America, which was what the ignorant neighbors called it, but, with a grand familiarity, "the USA") where he pursued his career in the most prestigious of all hospitals and won <u>encomiums</u> from his American colleagues which were relayed to his admiring and glowing family. ❸ What was more, he came *back*, he actually returned to that small yellow house in the once-new but increasingly shabby colony, right at the end of the road where the rubbish vans tipped out their stinking contents for pigs to nose in and rag-pickers to build their shacks on, all steaming and smoking just outside the neat wire fences and well-tended gardens. To this Rakesh returned and the first thing he did on entering the house was to slip out of the embraces of his sisters and brothers and bow down and touch his father's feet.

As for his mother, she gloated chiefly over the strange fact that he had not married in America, had not brought home a foreign wife as all her neighbors had warned her he would, for wasn't that what all Indian boys went abroad for? Instead he agreed, almost without ❹ argument, to marry a girl she had picked out for him in her own village, the daughter of a childhood friend, a plump and uneducated girl, it was true, but so old-fashioned, so placid, so <u>complaisant</u> that she slipped into the household and settled in like a charm, seemingly too lazy and too good-natured to even try and make Rakesh leave home and set up independently, as any other girl might have done. What was more, she was pretty—really pretty, in a plump, pudding way that only gave way to fat—soft, spreading fat, like warm wax—after the birth of their first baby, a son, and then what did it matter?

For some years Rakesh worked in the city hospital, quickly rising to the top of the administrative organization, and was made a director before he left to set up his own clinic. He took his parents in his car—a new, sky-blue Ambassador with a rear window full of stickers and charms revolving on strings—to see the clinic when it was built, and the large sign-board over the door on which his name was printed in letters of red, with a row of degrees and qualifications to follow it like so many little black slaves of the regent.[6] Thereafter his fame seemed to grow just a little dimmer—or maybe it was only that everyone in town had grown accustomed to it at last—but it was also the beginning of his fortune for he now became known not only as the best but also the richest doctor in town.

> **◆ Reading Strategy** What seems to be guiding the decisions Rakesh is making about his life? What kind of character do these decisions show him to be? ❺

However, all this was not accomplished in the wink of an eye. Naturally not. It was the achievement of a lifetime and it took up Rakesh's whole life. At the time he set up his clinic his father had grown into an old man and retired from his post at the kerosene dealer's depot at which he had worked for forty

5. **rancor:** Bitter, lasting hate.

6. **regent:** Ruler; governor.

◆ Build Vocabulary

exemplary (eg zem´ plə rē) *adj*.: Serving as a model or example; of that which should be imitated

filial (fil´ ē əl) *adj*.: Suitable to, of, or from a son or daughter

encomiums (en kō´ mē əmz) *n*.: Formal expressions of great praise

complaisant (kəm plā´ zənt) *adj*.: Agreeable; willing to please

◆ Grammar and Style

❸ **Sentence Variety** Have students contrast the short, simple sentence that announces Rakesh's scholarship with the long, complex sentences that describe his family's reaction to his success and devotion. Ask what the long, rambling sentences convey about the family's reaction to Rakesh's success. *Suggested response: The rest of the family is overflowing with pride and excitement at Rakesh's success. They can't stop marveling at it and rambling on about every detail of his devotion and achievement.*

◆ Critical Thinking

❹ **Compare and Contrast** Ask students in what way Rakesh's mother measures her son's devotion by different standards than his father does. Then ask in what way their standards are similar. *To his father, Rakesh's devotion is measured by his career success, while his mother measures it according to Rakesh's choice of a wife. To both parents, humility and submission to parental wishes are important measures of devotion.*

◆ Reading Strategy

❺ **Evaluate Characters' Decisions** Students may say that Rakesh bases his decisions on his desire for success and his desire to please his parents. Others may see him as spineless and empty, doing everything just to fulfill his parents' expectations.

Beyond the Classroom

Career Connection

Training for Physicians The conflict in this story involves the sacrifices a family makes to send a son to medical school. Tell students that in the United States most students who wish to become physicians first complete four years of college, followed by four years of medical school. For the first two years, students study anatomy, physiology, pathology, and other related subjects. During the last two years students have a clinical internship, in which they work, under supervision, with patients. After graduating from medical school, most doctors then do a residency in a specialty such as emergency medicine, pediatrics, or surgery. This training may last two to seven years, during which time the physician must pass a state exam and obtain a license to practice medicine.

Invite a medical student, intern, or resident physician to speak to the class about their training and the sacrifices and rewards of their career.

Community Connection

Students interested in working on a proposal for contact between teenagers and the elderly (Writing Mini-Lesson, p. 1157) may enjoy visiting a residence for elders before brainstorming ideas for their proposals. Help them set up an appointment to interview the staff, meet elders, and observe the routine of the residence.

◆ Grammar and Style

1 Sentence Variety Have students contrast the sentences in the long paragraph with the first sentence in the next paragraph. Ask what effect the contrast has. *The long paragraph is made up of only two sentences. The second sentence takes up the rest of the paragraph. The first sentence of the next paragraph, although complex, is short by comparison. The contrast gives dramatic emphasis to this sentence, which is a surprising conclusion to the description of Rakesh's success.*

◆ Literary Focus

2 Static and Dynamic Characters Ask students what hints the author gives here that the father may be a dynamic character in the story. *Varma's character is beginning to change: He is "falling apart."*

◆ Grammar and Style

3 Sentence Variety Ask students why the author ends the paragraph with a sentence fragment. *The fragment tells how Rakesh reacts differently from others. The contrast in sentence structure matches the contrast in behavior.*

◆ Critical Thinking

4 Analyze Character Ask students how Rakesh continues to show devotion to his father. *Rakesh brings his father his tea in the man's favorite tumbler, sits on the old man's bed and reads to him, encourages him to spend his summer evenings outdoors, and even soothes him to sleep.*

Comprehension Check ☑

5 Have students note the transition that these sentences introduce. *All of the son's devotion has so far been "very gratifying to the old man." Supervising his father's diet is not "gratifying."*

years, and his mother died soon after, giving up the ghost with a sigh that sounded positively happy, for it was her own son who ministered to her in her last illness and who sat pressing her feet at the last moment—such a son as few women had borne.

For it had to be admitted—and the most unsuccessful and most rancorous of neighbors eventually did so—that Rakesh was not only a devoted son and a miraculously good-natured man who contrived somehow to obey his parents and humor his wife and show concern equally for his children and his patients, but there was actually a brain inside this beautifully polished and formed body of good manners and kind nature and, in between ministering to his family and playing host to many friends and coaxing them all into feeling
1 happy and grateful and content, he had actually trained his hands as well and emerged an excellent doctor, a really fine surgeon. How one man—and a man born to illiterate parents, his father having worked for a kerosene dealer and his mother having spent her life in a kitchen—had achieved, combined and conducted such a medley of virtues, no one could fathom, but all acknowledged his talent and skill.

It was a strange fact, however, that talent and skill, if displayed for too long, cease to dazzle. It came to pass that the most admiring of all eyes eventually faded and no longer blinked at his glory. Having retired from work and having lost his wife, the old father very quickly went to pieces, as they say. He developed so many complaints and fell ill so frequently and with such mysterious diseases that even his son could no longer make out when it was
2 something of significance and when it was merely a peevish whim. He sat huddled on his string bed most of the day and developed an exasperating habit of stretching out suddenly and lying absolutely still, allowing the whole family to fly around him in a flap, wailing and weeping, and then suddenly sitting up, stiff and gaunt, and spitting out a big gob of betel-juice as if to mock their behavior.

He did this once too often: there had been a big party in the house, a birthday party for the youngest son, and the celebrations had to be suddenly hushed, covered up and hustled out of the way when the daughter-in-law discovered, or thought she discovered, that the old man, stretched out from end to end of his string bed, had lost his pulse; the party broke
up, dissolved, even turned into a band of 3
mourners, when the old man sat up and the distraught daughter-in-law received a gob of red spittle right on the hem of her organza sari.[7] After that no one much cared if he sat up crosslegged on his bed, hawking and spitting, or lay down flat and turned gray as a corpse. Except, of course, for that pearl amongst pearls, his son Rakesh.

It was Rakesh who brought him his morning tea, not in one of the china cups from which the rest of the family drank, but in the old man's favorite brass tumbler, and sat at the edge of his bed, comfortable and relaxed with the string of his pajamas dangling out from under his fine lawn night-shirt, and discussed or, rather, read out the morning news to his father. It made no difference to him that his father made no response apart from spitting. It was
Rakesh, too, who, on returning from the clinic 4
in the evening, persuaded the old man to come out of his room, as bare and desolate as a cell, and take the evening air out in the garden, beautifully arranging the pillows and bolsters on the *divan* in the corner of the open veranda. On summer nights he saw to it that the servants carried out the old man's bed onto the lawn and himself helped his father down the steps and onto the bed, soothing him and settling him down for a night under the stars.

All this was very gratifying for the old man.
What was not so gratifying was that he even 5
undertook to supervise his father's diet. One day when the father was really sick, having

◆ Build Vocabulary

fathom (fath′ əm) *v.*: To understand thoroughly

7. **organza sari:** Saris are traditional garments worn by Indian women, consisting of lengths of cotton, silk, or other cloth wrapped around the waist and draped over one shoulder; organza is a sheer, stiffened fabric.

Speaking and Listening Mini-Lesson

Panel Discussion

This mini-lesson supports the Speaking and Listening activity in the Idea Bank on page 1157.

Introduce the Concept Explain that a panel discussion offers an opportunity to share information on both sides of an issue without the formal structure or competitive focus of a debate.

Develop Information Encourage students to interview people who have lived in a multigenerational family situation. Have different students explore different aspects of such families: advantages and disadvantages for children, parents, and grandparents.

Apply the Information Choose a moderator to make sure each participant in the panel has a chance to present his or her information and to make sure that panel members treat each other respectfully.

Assess the Outcome To assess both speakers and listeners after the panel discussion, have students complete the Peer Assessment: Speaker/Speech page and the Listening: Self-Assessment page in ***Alternative Assessment,*** pp. 119 and 122. Students can also sum up the information by making a list of advantages and conflicts of extended families living together. Have students compare their lists and discuss what they have learned from the panel.

ordered his daughter-in-law to make him a dish of *soojie halwa* and eaten it with a saucerful of cream, Rakesh marched into the room, not with his usual respectful step but with the confidant and rather contemptuous stride of the famous doctor, and declared, "No more

6 *halwa* for you, papa. We must be sensible, at your age. If you must have something sweet, Veena will cook you a little *kheer*,[8] that's light, just a little rice and milk. But nothing fried, nothing rich. We can't have this happening again."

> **◆ Literary Focus**
> Does Rakesh's "rather contemptuous stride" show a
> 7 change in his character? In what way is he still the ideal son in this scene?

The old man who had been lying stretched out on his bed, weak and feeble after a day's illness, gave a start at the very sound, the tone of these

8. **kheer:** Rice pudding traditionally served as a dessert in Southern India.

▲ **Critical Viewing** How comfortable do you imagine it is for a man such as Rakesh or the businessman in the photograph to dwell among those less fortunate than themselves? **[Speculate]** 8

words. He opened his eyes—rather, they fell open with shock—and he stared at his son with disbelief that darkened quickly to reproach. A son who actually refused his father the food he craved? No, it was unheard of, it was incredible. But Rakesh had turned his back to him and was cleaning up the litter of bottles and packets on the medicine shelf and did not notice while Veena slipped silently out 9 of the room with a little smirk that only the old man saw, and hated.

Halwa was only the first item to be crossed off the old man's diet. One delicacy after the other went—everything fried to begin with, then everything sweet, and eventually everything, everything that the old man enjoyed. The meals that arrived for him on the shining

Cross-Curricular Connection: Health

In this story a conflict arises over a son's attempts to control his father's diet, particularly the father's intake of fat and sugar. As societies become more affluent, people tend to consume fewer complex carbohydrates and more fats and animal proteins. In the United States, for example, about forty percent of the calories people consume come from fats and about twenty percent come from sugar. High consumption of foods containing saturated fats and cholesterol is related to an increase in heart disease.

Have some students research information about high-density lipoprotein (HDL), or "good cholesterol," and low-density lipoprotein (LDL), or "bad cholesterol," and report their findings to the class. Have other students research the low fat/ high carbohydrate "food pyramid" diet currently recommended by doctors as a healthy diet.

Customize for
Bodily/Kinesthetic Learners
The scene on this page is a good one for bodily/kinesthetic learners to role-play, as described in the Speaking and Listening activity in the Idea Bank on page 1157. Have them pay attention to how the author describes the facial expressions and body language of Rakesh, Varma, and Veena and to use these examples of nonverbal communication to express the emotions of the characters in the role-play.

◆ Critical Thinking

6 Evaluate Ask students: Why is Rakesh refusing to serve his father the old man's favorite food? *Rakesh is a doctor and knows that sweet and fried foods are not good for his father's health.*

◆ Literary Focus

7 Static and Dynamic Characters Suggested response: Although Rakesh is acting more assertively than in the past and seems less concerned about pleasing his father, he is still an ideal, devoted son because he wants to do everything possible to keep his father alive and healthy. He is willing to risk his father's anger in order to save his father's life.

▶Critical Viewing◀

8 Speculate Sample response: Such people probably feel very uncomfortable, and perhaps guilty, about the contrasts between their own opportunities and comforts and those available to most other people in their society, especially if those other people are family members and childhood friends.

◆ Reading Strategy

9 Evaluate Characters' Decisions Ask students if they think Rakesh does the right thing by controlling his father's diet so strictly. *Some students may feel Rakesh does the right thing because he is trying to keep his father alive; others may feel Rakesh makes a mistake by not allowing his father the small pleasures that mean so much to him and by alienating himself from the old man at the end of his life.*

▶Critical Viewing◀

❶ **Interpret** Suggested response: The billboard in English tells about computer courses that lead to a degree from an American university, which shows the appeal being made to young Indians to be modern and ambitious. The sign on the buildings advertises modern air travel in both English and Indian characters, but the Indian characters are fading. The cow is a sign of India's traditional Hindu religion, in which cows are considered sacred animals and are protected, rather than killed and eaten.

◆Critical Thinking

❷ **Analyze** Ask students to explain the conflict between Rakesh and his father. Then ask which man seems to have the upper hand in the conflict at this point. *The conflict is over opposing views of what foods the father should be eating. Rakesh has the upper hand because his wife prepares and serves the meals and because he has now assumed control over the household. Varma is reduced to bribing his grandchildren to buy him sweets, but when Rakesh finds out, he puts and end to the practice and scolds his father.*

◀ **Critical Viewing** ❶ Name three details in this photograph that illustrate the story's theme of ambition and the conflict between the modern and the traditional. **[Interpret]**

stainless steel tray twice a day were frugal to say the least—dry bread, boiled lentils, boiled vegetables and, if there were a bit of chicken or fish, that was boiled too. If he called for another helping—in a cracked voice that quavered theatrically—Rakesh himself would come to the door, gaze at him sadly and shake his head, saying, "Now, papa, we must be careful, we can't risk another illness, you know," and although the daughter-in-law kept tactfully out of the way, the old man could just see her smirk sliding merrily through the air. He tried to bribe his grand-children into buying him sweets (and how he missed his wife now, that generous, indulgent and illiterate cook), ❷ whispering, "Here's fifty paise," as he stuffed the coins into a tight, hot fist. "Run down to the shop at the crossroads and buy me thirty paise worth of *jalebis*,[9] and you can spend the remaining twenty paise on yourself. Eh? Understand? Will you do that?" He got away with it once or twice but then was found out, the conspirator was scolded by his father and smacked by his mother and Rakesh came storming into the room, almost tearing his hair as he shouted through compressed lips, "Now papa, are you

9. **jalebis:** Indian sweet made by frying a coil of batter and then soaking it in syrup.

Cultural Connection

To help explain the significance of the grazing cow in the photo on this page, tell students that over eighty percent of the Indian population practices the religion of Hinduism. Among the characteristics of Indian society traceable to Hinduism are the Indian caste system, the concepts of dharma, karma, and reincarnation, the practice of yoga, and the veneration of cows as sacred animals. For Hindus, the cow represents life because it provides for human beings in so many ways. Cows are honored and protected in Indian society, and, at one time, killing a cow was considered a capital offense.

trying to turn my little son into a liar? Quite apart from spoiling your own stomach, you are spoiling him as well—you are encouraging him to lie to his own parents. You should have heard the lies he told his mother when she saw him bringing back those jalebis wrapped up in filthy newspaper. I don't allow anyone in my house to buy sweets in the bazaar, papa, ❸ surely you know that. There's cholera in the city, typhoid, gastroenteritis[10]—I see these cases daily in the hospital, how can I allow my own family to run such risks?" The old man sighed and lay down in the corpse position. But that worried no one any longer.

There was only one pleasure left in the old man now (his son's early morning visits and readings from the newspaper could no longer be called that) and those were visits from elderly neighbors. These were not frequent as his contemporaries were mostly as decrepit and helpless as he and few could walk the length of the road to visit him any more. Old Bhatia, next door, however, who was still spry enough to refuse, adamantly, to bathe in the tiled bathroom indoors and to insist on carrying out his brass mug and towel, in all seasons and usually at impossible hours, into the yard and bathe noisily under the garden tap, would look over the hedge to see if Varma were out on his ❹ verandah and would call to him and talk while he wrapped his *dhoti*[11] about him and dried the sparse hair on his head, shivering with enjoyable exaggeration. Of course these conversations, bawled across the hedge by two rather deaf old men conscious of having their entire households overhearing them, were not very satisfactory but Bhatia occasionally came out of his yard, walked down the bit of road and came in at Varma's gate to collapse onto the stone plinth built under the temple tree. If Rakesh was at home he would help his father down the steps into the garden and arrange him on his night bed under the tree and leave the two old men to chew betel-leaves and discuss the ills of their individual bodies with combined passion. ❹

"At least you have a doctor in the house to look after you," sighed Bhatia, having vividly described his martyrdom to piles.

"Look after me?" cried Varma, his voice cracking like an ancient clay jar. "He—he does not even give me enough to eat."

"What?" said Bhatia, the white hairs in his ears twitching. "Doesn't give you enough to eat? Your own son?"

"My own son. If I ask him for one more piece of bread, he says no, papa, I weighed out the *ata* myself and I can't allow you to have more than two hundred grams of cereal a day. He *weighs* the food he gives me, Bhatia—he has scales to weigh it on. That is what it has come to."

"Never," murmured Bhatia in disbelief. "Is it possible, even in this evil age, for a son to refuse his father food?"

"Let me tell you," Varma whispered eagerly. "Today the family was having fried fish—I could smell it. I called to my daughter-in-law to bring me a piece. She came to the door and said no. . . ."

"Said no?" It was Bhatia's voice that cracked. A *drongo*[12] shot out of the tree and sped away. *"No?"*

"No, she said no, Rakesh has ordered her to give me nothing fried. No butter, he says, no ❺ oil. . . ."

"No butter? No oil? How does he expect his father to *live?*"

Old Varma nodded with melancholy triumph. "That is how he treats me—after I have brought him up, given him an education, made him a great doctor. Great doctor! This is the way great doctors treat their fathers, Bhatia," ❻ for the son's sterling personality and character now underwent a curious sea change. Outwardly all might be the same but the interpretation had altered: his masterly efficiency was nothing but cold heartlessness, his authority was only tyranny in disguise.

There was cold comfort in complaining to neighbors and, on such a miserable diet,

---

10. **cholera...typhoid, gastroenteritis:** Dangerous infectious diseases causing fever or intestinal problems.
11. ***dhoti:*** Cloth worn by male Hindus, the ends being passed through the legs and tucked in at the waist.
12. ***drongo:*** Any of several black birds with long forked tails, native to Africa, Southern Asia, and Australia.

◆ Reading Strategy

❸ Evaluate Characters' Decisions Ask students if Rakesh's decision banning sweets from the bazaar is based on logic or emotion. Then ask what consequences this decision has on Rakesh's relationship with his father. *Though his desire to protect his family involves some emotion, Rakesh's decision is based mainly on logic: Buying sweets from the bazaar carries some risk of disease, so there will be no sweets bought, no matter how happy they make his father. Rakesh's severe control of Varma's diet causes the relationship between father and son to deteriorate: Visits from Rakesh are no longer a pleasure for Varma.*

◆ Literary Focus

❹ Static and Dynamic Characters Ask students what evidence this page offers that Rakesh remains a devoted son, despite the conflict over his father's diet. *Rakesh continues to help his father get outside, so that Varma can spend time with an old friend.*

❺ Clarification Tell students that the traditional Indian diet is full of foods fried in oil and butter, from breads and curries to sweets. To the old men, it is not worth being alive if they are deprived of these staples of the traditional Indian diet.

◆ Reading Strategy

❻ Evaluate Characters' Decisions Ask students how Varma's evaluation of his decision to educate his son has changed. Then ask students if their own evaluation of the decision has changed from the beginning of the story. Have them give reasons for their answer. *Varma now regrets the decision to educate his son, because he believes his son has become heartlessly efficient and tyrannical as a result of his medical training and success. Students' own evaluation of the decision will vary. Some may still feel that the decision is wise because Rakesh can now protect and provide for his family. Others may feel the decision was unwise because it has disrupted the relationship between father and son and has made the final years of the father's life miserable.*

Cross-Curricular Connection: Science

Cholera and Typhoid Fever Cholera, an infectious disease caused by drinking water that has been contaminated with bacteria, is widespread in India. The disease causes severe diarrhea, which leads to loss of body fluids and salts. If the fluids are not replaced promptly, the victim can lapse into a coma and die within twenty-four hours. Vaccines against the disease offer limited protections, and the best way to prevent the spread of disease in India is by cleaning up its supply of drinking water.

Typhoid fever is also caused by bacteria. It can be spread by food handlers who are carriers of the disease, one reason for requiring workers in restaurants to wash their hands. Typhoid can now be treated with antibiotics.

Have students research cholera and typhoid epidemics that have occurred in American history and find out whether any outbreaks still occur in the United States today.

Customize for
Bodily/Kinesthetic Learners
The final scenes of the story, beginning here, are dramatic confrontations between Rakesh and Varma, which are ideal for these students to act out. After the role-plays, ask the students playing Varma and Rakesh to analyze the emotions they think each character was experiencing in the scenes.

◆ Literature and Your Life

❶ Ask students if older people in American society ever experience conflicts similar to the one Varma is undergoing. Then ask if students think older people should have the right to refuse excessive medical treatment at the end of their lives and have their wishes to die comfortably respected.

◆ Reading Strategy

❷ **Evaluate Characters' Decisions** Ask students why, in their opinion, Rakesh keeps insisting that his father be taken out into the night air and be made to sit up, even though the experience is now nothing but agony for Varma. Ask students to evaluate the wisdom of Rakesh's insistence on continuing this practice. *Suggested response: As a doctor, Rakesh knows that fresh air is good for his patient, and sitting up will help Varma's body function better, but Rakesh's insistence on continuing this practice, which now only makes his father suffer, shows extreme insensitivity to his father's emotional needs and physical comfort.*

◆ Literary Focus

❸ **Static and Dynamic Characters** The once proud, tyrannical ruler of the household has now become a weak, vulnerable, terrified old man whose wishes are ignored and who is totally under the thumb of his son. He now seems victimized by the rest of the family, and the reader feels sorry for him.

Varma found himself slipping, weakening and soon becoming a genuinely sick man. Powders and pills and mixtures were not only brought in when dealing with a crisis like an upset stomach but became a regular part of his diet—became his diet, complained Varma, supplanting the natural foods he craved. There were pills to regulate his bowel movements, pills to bring down his blood pressure, pills to deal with his arthritis and, eventually, pills to keep his heart beating. In between there were panicky rushes to the hospital, some humiliating experience with the stomach pump and enema, which left him frightened and helpless. He cried easily, shriveling up on his bed, but if he complained of a pain or even a vague, gray fear in the night, Rakesh would simply open another bottle of pills and force him to take one. "I have my duty to you papa," he said when his father begged to be let off.

"Let me be," Varma begged, turning his face away from the pills on the outstretched hand. "Let me die. It would be better. I do not want to live only to eat your medicines."

"Papa, be reasonable."

"I leave that to you," the father cried with sudden spirit. "Leave me alone, let me die now, I cannot live like this."

"Lying all day on his pillows, fed every few hours by his daughter-in-law's own hand, visited by every member of his family daily—and then he says he does not want to live 'like this,'" Rakesh was heard to say, laughing, to someone outside the door.

❶ "Deprived of food," screamed the old man on the bed, "his wishes ignored, taunted by his daughter-in-law, laughed at by his grand-children—*that* is how I live." But he was very old and weak and all anyone heard was an incoherent croak, some expressive grunts and cries of genuine pain. Only once, when old Bhatia had come to see him and they sat together under the temple tree, they heard him cry, "God is calling me—and they won't let me go."

The quantities of vitamins and tonics he was made to take were not altogether useless. They kept him alive and even gave him a kind of strength that made him hang on long after he ceased to wish to hang on. It was as though he were straining at a rope, trying to break it, and it would not break, it was still strong. He only hurt himself, trying.

In the evening, that summer, the servants would come into his cell, grip his bed, one at each end, and carry it out to the verandah, there sitting it down with a thump that jarred every tooth in his head. In answer to his agonized complaints they said the doctor sahib had told them he must take the evening air and the evening air they would make him take— ❷
thump. Then Veena, that smiling, hypocritical pudding in a rustling sari, would appear and pile up the pillows under his head till he was propped up stiffly into a sitting position that made his head swim and his back ache.

"Let me lie down," he begged. "I can't sit up any more."

"Try, papa, Rakesh said you can if you try," she said, and drifted away to the other end of the verandah where her transistor radio vibrated to the lovesick tunes from the cinema that she listened to all day.

So there he sat, like some stiff corpse, terrified, gazing out on the lawn where his grandsons played cricket,[13] in danger of getting one of their hard-spun balls in his eye, and at the gate that opened onto the dusty and rubbish-heaped lane but still bore, proudly, a newly touched-up signboard that bore his son's name and qualifications, his own name having vanished from the gate long ago.

> **◆ Literary Focus** ❸
> Compare the father's character at the end of the story with the proud father and the betel-juice spitter of earlier scenes. Is he more sympathetic? Explain.

At last the sky-blue Ambassador arrived, the cricket game broke up in haste, the car drove in smartly and the doctor, the great doctor, all in white, stepped out. Someone ran up to take his bag from him, others to escort him up the steps. "Will you have tea?" his wife called, turning down the transistor set. "Or a Coca-Cola? Shall I fry you some *samosas?*"[14] But he did not reply or even

---

13. **cricket:** Open-air game played between two teams and utilizing a ball, bats, and wicket.

glance in her direction. Ever a devoted son, he went first to the corner where his father sat gazing, stricken, at some undefined spot in the dusty yellow air that swam before him. He did not turn his head to look at his son. But he stopped gobbling air with his uncontrolled lips and set his jaw as hard as a sick and very old man could set it.

"Papa," his son said, tenderly, sitting down on the edge of the bed and reaching out to press his feet.

Old Varma tucked his feet under him, out of the way, and continued to gaze stubbornly into the yellow air of the summer evening.

"Papa, I'm home."

Varma's hand jerked suddenly, in a sharp, derisive movement, but he did not speak.

"How are you feeling, papa?"

Then Varma turned and looked at his son. His face was so out of control and all in pieces, that the multitude of expressions that crossed it could not make up a whole and convey to the famous man exactly what his father thought of him, his skill, his art.

"I'm dying," he croaked. "Let me die, I tell you."

---

14. samosas: Triangular pastries fried in clarified butter or oil, containing spiced vegetables or meat.

"Papa, you're joking," his son smiled at him, lovingly. "I've brought you a new tonic to make you feel better. You must take it, it will make you feel stronger again. Here it is. Promise me you will take it regularly, papa."

Varma's mouth worked as hard as though he still had a gob of betel in it (his supply of betel had been cut off years ago). Then he spat out some words, as sharp and bitter as poison, into his son's face. "Keep your tonic—I want none—I want none—I won't take any more of—of your medicines. None. Never," and he swept the bottle out of his son's hand with a wave of his own, suddenly grand, suddenly effective.

His son jumped, for the bottle was smashed and thick brown syrup had splashed up, staining his white trousers. His wife let out a cry and came running. All around the old man was hubbub once again, noise, attention.

He gave one push to the pillows at his back and dislodged them so he could sink down on his back, quite flat again. He closed his eyes and pointed his chin at the ceiling, like some dire prophet, groaning, "God is calling me—now let me go."

◆ **Reading Strategy** How does the father's situation at the end of the story reflect on the family's decision, referred to at the beginning, to educate Rakesh? ❹

Guide for Responding

◆ Literature and Your Life

Reader's Response At the end of the story, with whom do you sympathize more—Rakesh or his father? Explain your answer.

Thematic Focus Would you consider Anita Desai to be a British author, an Indian author, or a combination of the two? Explain.

Monologue Improvise a brief monologue in which the elderly Varma expresses his deepest feelings about his son and about his own future.

☑ Check Your Comprehension

1. According to the father's boast, what is the first thing Rakesh did when he saw the exam results?
2. Why does Rakesh's marriage surprise his family?
3. By the time his father has grown old, what has Rakesh achieved in his professional career?
4. What does Rakesh's father complain of to Bhatia, the neighbor?
5. At the end of the story, what does Varma do when his son tries to persuade him to take a new medicine?

Beyond the Selection

FURTHER READING

Other Works by Anita Desai

Games at Twilight, Clear Light of Day, In Custody

Other Works With the Theme of From the National to the Global

"Dead Man's Path," Chinua Achebe

"The Kabuliwallah," Rabindranath Tagore

"On the Ferry," N.V.M. Gonzalez

"The Quarry," Alan Paton

We suggest that you preview these works before recommending them to students.

INTERNET

You and your students may find additional information about Anita Desai at the following Internet sites. Please be aware that sites may have changed since this information was published. **http://www.cis.upenn.edu/~anoop/desai/desai.html** and **http://www.stg.brown.edu/projects/hypertext/landow/post/desai/desaiov.html**

You may also find related information on Indian culture at **http://www.webpage.com/indiapages**

Always preview sites before recommending them.

◆ Reading Strategy

❹ Evaluate Characters' Decisions The father now regrets educating his son, because his son is a doctor who will not let the father die in peace or enjoy the end of his life. From the family's point of view, perhaps it was a mistake to educate their son.

Reinforce and Extend

Answers

◆ Literature and Your Life

Reader's Response Many students may say they sympathize with the father because he is in such a weak, pitiable condition, while the son refuses to consider his father's point of view. Others may sympathize with the son because he is trying to give his father the best possible medical care.

Thematic Focus Students may say that Desai's intimate, extensive knowledge of Indian customs and attitudes could come only from someone who was Indian herself, while her objective consideration of both generations' point of view marks her as an outsider, one who has lived away from Indian society.

☑ Check Your Comprehension

1. Rakesh bows down to touch his father's feet.
2. Instead of finding a wife in the United States while studying there, as many Indian men do, Rakesh agrees to marry an old-fashioned, uneducated girl of his mother's choice, someone very different from himself.
3. Rakesh has become director of the city hospital and then left to set up his own clinic. He has become the richest doctor in town.
4. The father complains that Rakesh does not give him enough to eat because his son has put him on a strict low-fat, low-sugar diet, which does not allow any butter or oil.
5. Varma refuses to take any more medicine and smashes the bottle by sweeping it from his son's hand.

Guide for Responding *(continued)*

◆ Critical Thinking

INTERPRET

1. Name three things that qualify Rakesh as a devoted son. **[Classify]**

2. (a) What is the central conflict of this story? (b) Is this conflict a struggle between different generations? Explain. **[Interpret]**

3. In what ways is the conflict in this story specifically Indian and in what ways is it universal? **[Distinguish]**

EVALUATE

4. Do you think the title of this story is suitable and effective? Why or why not? **[Criticize]**

EXTEND

5. From the evidence presented in this story, how would you describe attitudes toward the elderly in India? **[Social Studies Link]**

◆ Reading Strategy

EVALUATE CHARACTERS' DECISIONS

Evaluate the wisdom of each of the following choices by considering whether it was based on emotion or logic, sympathy or selfishness. Also consider the consequences or later effects of the choice as you make your evaluation.

1. The family sacrifices for Rakesh's education.
2. Rakesh marries a young woman from the village.
3. Rakesh supervises his father's diet.

◆ Build Vocabulary

USING THE WORD ROOT *-fil-*

Explain how the Latin root *-fil-* ("son or daughter") contributes to the meanings of these words:

1. filial **2.** affiliate (noun) **3.** affiliate (verb)

USING THE WORD BANK

On your paper, write the word from the Word Bank that fits best in each sentence.

1. Rakesh won __?__ for his superior talents.
2. Rakesh felt he had fulfilled his __?__ obligations.
3. The town considered Rakesh an __?__ son.
4. Varma could not __?__ the change in his relationship with Rakesh.
5. People who are __?__ aim to please.

◆ Literary Focus

STATIC AND DYNAMIC CHARACTERS

Desai's use of **static** and **dynamic characters**, characters who remain the same and those who change, is essential to her theme. Strangely, it is the tradition-bound father who is dynamic while his forward-looking son is static. Varma is dynamic even in his defeat, as his attitude toward Rakesh changes. Varma sees that, by sacrificing to create a "modern" son, he has lost in old age all that he hoped to gain.

1. After the conversation between Old Bhatia and Varma, Desai summarizes in a paragraph how Varma has changed. In what way has Varma developed a new perspective on his "devoted son"?
2. Cite evidence from the story to support the idea that Rakesh is a static character.
3. What does the relationship between dynamic father and static son reveal about the fate of traditional beliefs in the modern world?

◆ Grammar and Style

SENTENCE VARIETY

Desai uses **sentence variety**—sentences of different lengths, types, and structures—to heighten drama and reinforce meanings. For example, in the paragraph beginning "However, all this was not accomplished . . ." Desai sums up Rakesh's achievements with a simple sentence, a fragment, and a compound sentence, all of which are brief. By contrast, she uses a long compound-complex sentence to describe his father's retirement and his mother's death. This contrast suggests the emptiness of Rakesh's life, even though it is filled with triumphs, and the fullness of his mother's feelings about him.

Practice On your paper, vary these sentences to make them more lively and interesting.

Rakesh's mother gloated over his decision to marry an Indian village girl. Rakesh was not like most Indian boys who went abroad, she thought. He agreed almost without argument to his mother's choice of bride. The new wife was the daughter of a childhood friend. She was old-fashioned, placid, and complaisant. She was too good-natured to make Rakesh leave home and set up independently.

◆ Critical Thinking

1. He makes his parents proud by getting a good education, becoming successful, and continuing to honor his parents, respecting their wishes.
2. (a) The conflict is between two different ideas of the value of life: the Western, emphasizing only the "quantity" of life without regard to tradition and warmth, and the traditional. (b) Rakesh, although devoted in a traditional sense, represents a younger generation that has adopted Western values.
3. The conflict focuses on the traditional Indian diet and Indian ideas about what makes a devoted son. It is universal because it questions the value of scientific reason in life.
4. Some students may say that the title is suitable because it focuses on the central irony of the story: In the end, the same education and accomplishments that made Rakesh seem such a devoted son destroy his relationship with his father.
5. As younger generations become more educated, they are assuming more power in family life, and the traditional power of the elderly is receding.

◆ Reading Strategy

1. The family's sacrifice is both logical, since it benefits them, and emotional, since it satisfies their pride.
2. The dutiful decision has ensured Rakesh's happiness: His wife never criticizes anything he does.
3. Rakesh apparently feels he is being a dutiful son, even if it means going against his father's wishes.

◆ Build Vocabulary

Using the Word Root *-fil-*

1. filial: relating to a son or daughter
2. affiliate (*n.*): one who is related to another
3. affiliate (v.): to relate to another person or thing

Using the Word Bank

1. encomiums; 2. filial; 3. exemplary; 4. fathom; 5. complaisant

◆ Literary Focus

1. Varma has reevaluated the son's "masterly efficiency" as "cold heartlessness" and his "authority" as "tyranny in disguise."
2. Rakesh continues the same dutiful behavior, even when he is rebuffed for doing so.
3. The "enlightened" modern attitude is static: It has less insight into tradition than tradition has into modern attitudes.

◆ Grammar and Style

Sample response: Rakesh's mother gloated over his decision to marry an Indian village girl. Rakesh is not like other Indian boys who went abroad, she thought. Instead, he agreed to marry the daughter of her childhood friend. The new wife was old fashioned, placid, complaisant, and too good natured to make Rakesh leave home and set up independently.

Writer's Solution

For additional instruction and practice, use the Varying Sentence Structure lesson in the Writing Style unit of the **Language Lab CD-ROM**, and the pages on Improving Your Sentences, pp. 103–105 in the *Writer's Solution Grammar Practice Book*.

Build Your Portfolio

Idea Bank

Writing

1. **Character Sketch** Write a character sketch of Rakesh or his father. Include information on your subject's appearance, opinions, and habits.

2. **Memorial Tribute** Write a memorial tribute—a speech in praise of someone who has died—that Rakesh might deliver for his father.

3. **Response to Criticism** Desai has said she's interested in discovering "the truth that is nine-tenths of the iceberg that lies submerged beneath the one-tenth visible portion we call Reality." Write an essay discussing how this statement relates to "A Devoted Son."

Speaking and Listening

4. **Role-Play** Choose a scene from the story. Together with a partner, role-play the scene for an audience of classmates, adding dialogue where necessary. **[Performing Arts Link]**

5. **Panel Discussion** In India, elderly parents often live with the family of one of their children. In a panel with classmates, discuss the potential advantages and conflicts of such an arrangement. **[Social Studies Link]**

Projects

6. **India's Public Health** Rakesh mentions cholera and typhoid as infectious diseases in India. Research India's major infectious diseases and the ways doctors are treating them. Present your findings to the class. **[Health Link]**

7. **Cross-Cultural Survey** Research and compare how India and two other countries provide for their elderly. Present your findings to the class, using graphs to illustrate comparative statistics. **[Social Studies Link; Math Link]**

Writing Mini-Lesson

Proposal

As Anita Desai's story shows, people are often blind or indifferent to the feelings of elders. Help remedy that situation. Write a proposal to your principal in which you plan for regular student contact with elders. First, state two or three major objectives for your program. Then develop a specific program calling for visits to elders. Such visits might include socializing, conducting oral-history interviews, and giving performances. In writing your proposal, use language that will help "sell" your idea.

Writing Skills Focus: Connotations

The associations that words have beyond their dictionary meaning, their **connotations**, create an emotional "music." If you're tone-deaf to this music, you may be playing sour notes that spoil the effects of your good ideas. One such sour note is the term *old folks' home,* which has depressing associations and is condescending to the residents. A term that's more on key is *residence for elders*, which suggests a more positive environment. Throughout the writing process, be sure the emotional music of your words supports your message.

Prewriting Brainstorm with a group about the benefits that a program for visiting elders might offer to *everyone* concerned. Including benefits to students and to the school will help convince your most important reader, the principal.

Drafting Be especially careful in drafting your objectives. Use active verbs with positive associations, like *broaden*, *teach*, and *serve*. Also, include upbeat quotations from students and elders enthusiastic about your project.

Revising Trade papers with a classmate and read over each other's proposals. Watch out for—and replace—words that sour your positive tune or that suggest the benefits are all one way.

✓ ASSESSMENT OPTIONS

Formal Assessment, Selection Test, pp. 300–302, and Assessment Resources Software. The selection test is designed so that it can be easily customized to the performance levels of your students.
Alternative Assessment, p. 64, includes options for less advanced students, more advanced students, intrapersonal learners, musical/rhythmic learners, visual/spatial learners, and interpersonal learners.

PORTFOLIO ASSESSMENT
Use the following rubrics in the ***Alternative Assessment*** booklet to assess student writing:
Character Sketch: Description Rubric, p. 98
Memorial Tribute: Narrative Based on Personal Experience Rubric, p. 97
Response to Criticism: Literary Analysis/Interpretation Rubric, p. 113
Writing Mini-Lesson: Persuasion Rubric, p. 106

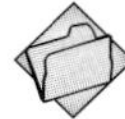

Idea Bank

Customizing for
Performance Levels
Following are suggestions for matching Idea Bank topics with your students' performance levels:
- Less Advanced Students: 1, 4, 6
- Average Students: 2, 5, 6
- More Advanced Students: 3, 7

Customizing for
Learning Modalities
Following are suggestions for matching Idea Bank topics with your students' learning modalities:
- Verbal/Linguistic: 1, 2, 3, 5, 6
- Bodily/Kinesthetic: 4
- Visual/Spatial: 7

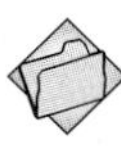

Writing Mini-Lesson

Refer students to the Writing Process Handbook, page 1189, for instruction on the writing process, and page 1192 for further information on persuasion.

Writing and Language Transparencies Have students use the Problem-Solution Organizer, pp. 107–110, to develop supporting reasons for their proposals.

Writer's Solution

Writing Lab CD-ROM
Have students complete the tutorial on Persuasion. Follow these steps:
1. Have students complete the Audience Profile to help them focus on their intended audience.
2. Refer them to the interactive instruction on evaluating facts and opinions.
3. Suggest they use the interactive instruction in avoiding faulty logic and unreasonable appeals.
4. Students should draft on computer.
5. Have them use the Proofreading Checklist in revising and checking their drafts.

Allow approximately 90 minutes to complete these steps.

Sourcebook
Have students use Chapter 4, Persuasion (pp. 96–129), for additional support. The chapter includes a writing model of a grant proposal (p. 101).

Prepare and Engage

OBJECTIVES

1. To read, comprehend, and interpret an essay
2. To relate an essay to personal experience
3. To challenge the text to improve comprehension
4. To identify a prophetic essay
5. To build vocabulary in context and learn the suffixes *-ible* and *-able*
6. To identify linking verbs and subject complements
7. To write an astronaut's diary using consistent perspective
8. To respond to the essay through writing, speaking and listening, and projects

SKILLS INSTRUCTION

Vocabulary: Suffixes: *-ible* and *-able*
Grammar: Linking Verbs and Subject Complements
Reading Strategy: Challenge the Text
Literary Focus: Prophetic Essay
Writing: Consistent Perspective
Speaking and Listening: Panel Discussion (teacher edition)
Critical Viewing: Make a Judgment; Analyze

PORTFOLIO OPPORTUNITIES

Writing: E-mail Response; Reflective Essay; Literary Analysis
Writing Mini-Lesson: Astronaut's Diary
Speaking and Listening: Panel Discussion; Introduction
Projects: Film Review; Museum Exhibit

More About the Author
Arthur Clarke's scientific interest in and knowledge of space contributed to his role as one of the CBS broadcasters for the Apollo 11, 12, and 15 space missions. In a personal attempt to experience the weightlessness of space, Clarke took up scuba diving. His love for the underwater world took him to Sri Lanka, where he has lived and dived for 40 years.

Guide for Interpreting

Arthur C. Clarke *(1917–)*

With more than one hundred million copies of his books in print worldwide, Arthur C. Clarke may be the most successful science fiction writer of all time. The appeal of his books may result from the way he combines technical expertise with touches of poetry.

Early Career Clarke discovered science fiction at the age of twelve when he started to read a mass-circulation magazine called *Amazing Stories*. His interest in scientific matters led to his service as a radar instructor in the Royal Air Force during World War II.

After the war, he graduated from the University of London with honors in science. Even before he graduated, he had published a prophetic article exploring the possibility of a communications satellite.

Success as a Writer Since the early 1950's, Clarke has worked full-time as a writer producing more than seventy works of fiction and nonfiction. Among his famous novels are *Childhood's End* (1953) and *The City and the Stars* (1956).

His story "The Sentinel" served as the basis for the epic film *2001: A Space Odyssey* (1968). Clarke worked on this film with British director Stanley Kubrick.

Clarke and Science Fiction Like his distinguished contemporaries Isaac Asimov and Ray Bradbury, Clarke has established credibility with his audience by means of an impressive command of aeronautics, astronautics, and undersea exploration. Clarke has also contributed a lyrical, romantic element to science-fiction.

Not Escapism Challenging the concept that science fiction is escapism, Clarke has asserted that the genre is "virtually the only kind of writing that's dealing with real problems and possibilities. . . ."

◆ Background for Understanding

HISTORY: A TIMELINE OF SPACE EXPLORATION
In reading Arthur C. Clarke's assessment of the future of space travel, keep these milestones in mind.

1997 Landing of *Pathfinder* on Mars

1995 Docking of American space shuttle *Atlantis* with Russian space station *Mir*

1981 First space shuttle flight

1976 Missions of *Viking 1* and *Viking 2* to Mars

1969 First landing of men on moon

1961 Alan Shepard is first American in space

1957 *Sputnik* launched by former USSR

1945 Clarke's essay predicting space satellites

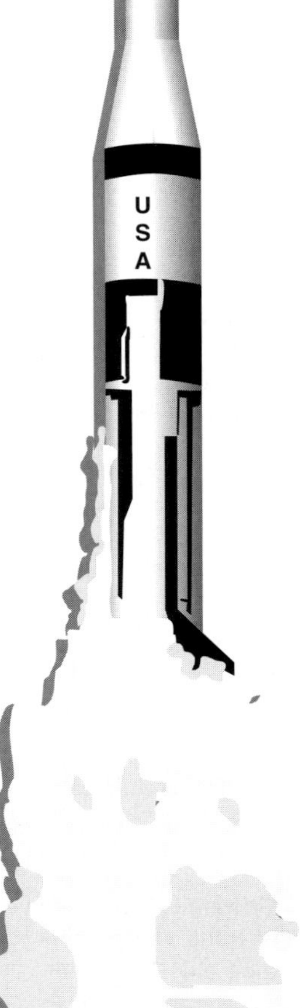

Prentice Hall Literature Program Resources

REINFORCE / RETEACH / EXTEND

Selection Support Pages
Build Vocabulary: Using the Suffixes *-ible* and *-able*, p. 305
Grammar and Style: Linking Verbs and Subject Complements, p. 306
Reading Strategy: Challenge the Text, p. 307
Literary Focus: Prophetic Essay, p. 308

Strategies for Diverse Student Needs, p. 65

Beyond Literature
Cross-Curricular Connection: Science: The Theory of Relativity, p. 65

Formal Assessment Selection Test, pp. 303–305; Assessment Resources Software

Alternative Assessment, p. 65

Writing and Language Transparencies
Writing Process Model 9: Technical Writing: Status Report, pp. 81–84

Resource Pro CD-ROM
"We'll Never Conquer Space"—includes all resource material and customizable lesson plan

Listening to Literature Audiocassettes
"We'll Never Conquer Space"

from We'll Never Conquer Space

◆ Literature and Your Life

Connect Your Experience

Focus on an object that is five feet away from you. Then imagine that there is no other object for a thousand miles, about the distance from New York City to Kansas City, Missouri. You have just formed a picture of the distance to the nearest planet, as compared with the distance to the nearest star.

Arthur C. Clarke uses such comparisons to help you picture the vastness of the universe. Because the universe will be "forever too large," he argues, "We'll Never Conquer Space."

Journal Writing Briefly freewrite about your fantasies, associations, or opinions on the conquest of space.

Thematic Focus: From the National to the Global

Notice how Clarke gives his own twist to the theme of the shrinking globe as he discusses an unshrinkable universe.

◆ Literary Focus

Prophetic Essay

All of us make guesses about the future. In a **prophetic essay**, however, a writer uses a brief work of nonfiction to make bold statements about the future of a nation or of our entire planet. Like the statements of prophets in the Bible, these predictions can serve as a kind of warning.

The title of the prophetic essay "We'll Never Conquer Space" contains a prediction that is also a warning against overconfidence.

◆ Grammar and Style

Linking Verbs and Subject Complements

Clarke often uses **linking verbs** like *seem* or *be* to connect the subject of a sentence with nouns, pronouns, or adjectives that are called **subject complements**. The connection between a subject and a subject complement is so close that the sentence is like an equation: the subject = the complement. This grammatical device helps Clarke to make definite statements that will convince you of his predictions:

subject linking verb subject complement

. . . the vastness of the earth *was* a dominant fact.

◆ Build Vocabulary

Suffixes: *-ible* and *-able*

In Clarke's essay, you will find the words *incredible* and *irrevocable*. The suffixes of these words, *-ible* and *-able,* both mean "able to, having qualities of, worthy of, or capable of." Something that is *incredible* is "not able to be believed." Something that is *irrevocable* is "not able to be altered."

Word Bank

Preview this list of words before you read the essay.

- ludicrous
- irrevocable
- instantaneous
- enigma
- inevitable
- zenith

◆ Reading Strategy

Challenge the Text

By **challenging a text**, you call into question the statements it makes. You treat it like a friend you can argue with rather than like an authority whose words you must accept. As a result, you will start to feel more friendly toward what you read.

Don't be bullied by the definite statements that Clarke makes, including the assertion in his title: "We'll Never Conquer Space." Be suspicious of generalizations with *never* and *always*—just one counterexample proves them wrong. Check to see that his comparisons really prove what he says they do.

Students may be familiar with such science fiction films as *2001: A Space Odyssey* and the *Star Trek* television series in which space travel is a basic premise. Have students discuss the extent to which they believe that people will make themselves at home in space in their lifetime. Then tell them that the essay they will read by a noted science fiction writer may qualify some of the ideas they have about life in the Space Age.

Customize for
Less Proficient Readers

These students may find some of the scientific ideas in this selection confusing. Encourage them to create a main idea and details chart for each section of the essay, breaking down Clarke's ideas and supporting details into manageable form.

Customize for
More Advanced Students

Advanced readers may benefit from finding statements in the text that they would like to challenge and refuting them.

Customize for
English Language Learners

Students learning English may have difficulty with some of the technical terms in the selection. Go over words and phrases such as *suspended animation, solar space, stellar space, solar system, galaxy,* and *light-year* to help students understand their meaning.

Customize for
Visual/Spatial Learners

These students may find it helpful to have an image or map of the galaxy at hand as they read. They can use the map to locate some of the stars and systems the writer mentions.

Preparing for Standardized Tests

Reading Standardized tests often include Critical Reading questions that ask students to evaluate an author's assumptions. By challenging the text, students will be better able to evaluate how convincing an author's arguments are. Students may be asked to evaluate a passage such as the following:

> The only way to control the Greenhouse Effect is to control emissions of carbon dioxide into our atmosphere. Though the atmospheric blanket that traps the heat of sunlight is 98 percent water vapor, the 2 percent made of carbon dioxide is probably the real danger. As that percentage rises, so do our temperatures. As temperatures rise, the polar ice caps melt, and ocean levels rise. Without a significant reduction in greenhouse gases, climate will change dramatically. Coastlines will erode; interior plains will turn to desert; and flooding, famine, and disease will result.

Which of the following statements is the author's weakest point? (B)

(A) The atmospheric blanket is 98 percent water vapor.
(B) The real danger is probably that 2 percent of the atmosphere is carbon dioxide.
(C) Coastlines will erode.
(D) Polar ice caps will melt

The Reading Strategy lesson will help students realize that (B) is the correct answer. For more practice in challenging the text, use the Reading Strategy page in ***Selection Support,*** page 307.

Develop Understanding

One-Minute Insight In this essay, Arthur C. Clarke challenges the idea that we may ever truly "conquer" space. He stresses the improbability that humans will ever travel fast enough to make space exploration feasible. Beyond that, he points out that even if we conquer the problem of time, the physical limitations on communication would separate humanity from itself, rendering its journeys meaningless.

▶Critical Viewing◀

❶ **Make a Judgment** Sample answer: It supports Clarke's argument. The suit is bulky and surrounds the astronaut completely, adding to his or her isolation and limiting his or her ability to maneuver. "Conquering" space—that is, truly being at home there—in such a suit seems unlikely.

◆ Literary Focus

❷ **Prophetic Essay** Ask students what Clarke is warning of in this passage. *He is warning against generalizing from our triumphs on the surface of the Earth to our prospects in space.*

We'll Never Conquer Space

Arthur C. Clarke

Astronaut Buzz Aldrin on moon near lunar module, during Apollo 11, NASA

◀ **Critical Viewing** In your estimation, does the suit worn by astronauts support or detract from Clarke's argument that space cannot be "conquered"? Explain. **[Make a Judgment]** ❶

Man will never conquer space. Such a statement may sound ludicrous, now that our rockets are already 100 million miles beyond the moon and the first human travelers are preparing to leave the atmosphere. Yet it expresses a truth which our forefathers knew, one we have forgotten—and our descendants must learn again, in heartbreak and loneliness.

Our age is in many ways unique, full of events and phenomena which never occurred before and can never happen again. They distort our thinking, making us believe that what is true now will be true forever, though perhaps on a larger scale. Because we have annihilated distance on this planet, we imagine that we can do it once again. The facts are far otherwise, and we will see them more clearly if we forget the present and turn our minds towards the past. ❷

Block Scheduling Strategies

Consider these suggestions to take advantage of extended class time:

- Go over the Background for Understanding section on History: A Timeline of Space Exploration (p. 1158) with students. Encourage them to add any important space dates they can think of to the timeline.
- Encourage students to complete the Cross-Curricular Connection: Science worksheet on the Theory of Relativity in ***Beyond Literature,*** page 65, before they begin reading.
- Read students the information on Prophetic Essays on page 1159 and have them complete the Literary Focus activity on page 1166. Then ask them to consider prophetic essays further by completing the Literary Focus worksheet in ***Selection Support,*** page 308.
- Encourage students to challenge the text as they read. They can write down questions or problems they have with passages in the essay. Have them complete the Reading Strategy activity on page 1166 and use their questions and challenges to write the E-Mail Response from the Idea Bank on page 1167.
- Ask students to work in pairs or small groups to write the Film Review from the Idea Bank on page 1167. Students can expand the review to include the movie's sequel, *2010: Odyssey Two.*

To our ancestors, the vastness of the earth was a dominant fact controlling their thoughts and lives. In all earlier ages than ours, the world was wide indeed, and no man could ever see more than a tiny fraction of its immensity. A few hundred miles—a thousand, at the most—was infinity. Only a lifetime ago, parents waved farewell to their emigrating children in the virtual certainty that they would never meet again.

And now, within one incredible generation, all this has changed. Over the seas where Odysseus wandered for a decade, the Rome-Beirut Comet whispers its way within the hour. And above that, the closer satellites span the distance between Troy and Ithaca[1] in less than a minute.

Psychologically as well as physically, there are no longer any remote places on earth. When a friend leaves for what was once a far country, even if he has no intention of returning, we cannot feel that same sense of irrevocable separation that saddened our forefathers. We know that he is only hours away by jet liner, and that we have merely to reach for the telephone to hear his voice.

> ◆ **Reading Strategy**
> ❸ Name an event or trend in the contemporary world that you could use in challenging Clarke's statement that the world is "shrinking." (Think of things that separate people besides distance.)

In a very few years, when the satellite communication network is established, we will be able to see friends on the far side of the earth as easily as we talk to them on the other side of the town. Then the world will shrink no more, for it will have become a dimensionless point.

Forever Too Large

But the new stage that is opening up for the human drama will never shrink as the old one has done. We have abolished space here on the little earth; we can never abolish the space that yawns between the stars. Once again we are face to face with immensity and must accept its grandeur and terror, its inspiring possibilities and its dreadful restraints. From a world that has become too small, we are moving out into one that will be forever too large, whose frontiers will recede from us always more ❹ swiftly than we can reach out towards them.

Consider first the fairly modest solar, or planetary, distances which we are now preparing to assault. The very first Lunik[2] made a substantial impression upon them, traveling more than 200 million miles from the earth—six times the distance to Mars. When we have harnessed nuclear energy for spaceflight, the solar system will contract until it is little larger than the earth today. The remotest of the planets will be perhaps no more than a week's travel from the earth, while Mars and Venus will be only a few hours away.

This achievement, which will be witnessed within a century, might appear to make even the solar system a comfortable, homely place, with such giant planets as Saturn and Jupiter playing much the same role in our thoughts as do Africa or Asia today. (Their qualitative differences of climate, atmosphere and gravity, fundamental though they are, do not concern us at the moment.) To some extent this may be true, yet as soon as we pass beyond the orbit of the moon, a mere quarter-million miles away, we will meet the first of the barriers that will separate the earth from her scattered children.

The marvelous telephone and television network that will soon enmesh the whole world, making all men neighbors, cannot be extended into space. It will never be possible to converse with anyone on another planet.

Do not misunderstand this statement. Even with today's radio equipment, the problem of sending speech to the other planets is almost ❺ trivial. But the messages will take minutes—sometimes hours—on their journey, because radio and light waves travel at the same limited speed of 186,000 miles a second.

1. **Odysseus . . . Troy and Ithaca:** Odysseus was the King of Ithaca and hero of Homer's *Odyssey*. The distance between Troy and Ithaca, the cities marking the beginning and end of Odysseus' wanderings in the Odyssey, are about equal to the route flown by the Comet airplane between Rome and Beirut.

2. **Lunik:** Name given by American journalists to Luna I, an unmanned Soviet space probe of 1959.

◆ Build Vocabulary

ludicrous (lo͞o′ di krəs): Absurd; ridiculous

irrevocable (ir rev′ ə kə bəl): That which cannot be undone or canceled

◆ Reading Strategy

❸ **Challenge the Text** Terrorist activity, civil war, and poor youth without hope all point to significant, perhaps unbridgeable, distances between people.

◆ Literary Focus

❹ **Prophetic Essay** Ask students what Clarke, in this passage, is suggesting that humans do. *He is suggesting that humans accept the idea that space is too big for us to dominate.*

◆ Critical Thinking

❺ **Draw Conclusions** Have students determine how the time lag in messages sent to another planet might affect conversations between people. *Because receipt and reply would not be instantaneous, as they are now, people would be simply transmitting messages rather than conversing back and forth.*

Cross-Curricular Connection: Science

Artificial Satellites Point out to students that there are over 2,000 artificial satellites orbiting the earth right now. There are six different types of satellites. (1) Earth-observation satellites take pictures of the earth that are then analyzed by computers to study the location of mineral and water deposits, the effects of pollution, and the spread of crop and forest disease. (2) Communications satellites, used primarily by television and telephone companies, receive radio signals and transmit them to other locations. (3) Scientific research satellites gather information about space, the planets, and Earth's atmosphere. (4) Weather satellites observe and relay information about weather patterns. (5) Navigation satellites aid vehicles on land, sea, and in the air to determine their exact locations by sending out signals picked up by a transmitter on the vehicle. (6) Finally, military satellites are used for military purposes such as noting the location of weapons and the movement of troops.

Have students discuss the types of satellites that might have an impact on Clarke's argument.

◆ Reading Strategy

❶ **Challenge the Text** Conversation is perhaps not as important as Clarke seems to think: People could conduct business over the long term, sending messages, as they did in the days of the American frontier.

◆ Build Vocabulary

❷ **Suffixes: *-ible* and *-able*** Ask students to determine the meaning of the word with the suffix *-ible* or *-able* in this passage. Intolerable *means "not able to be tolerated."*

◆ Grammar and Style

❸ **Linking Verbs and Subject Complements** Have students identify the linking verb and subject complement in this sentence and determine how the writer uses them to stress his point. *The use of the verb "is" with the complement "the ultimate speed limit" helps to reinforce the idea that, according to the theory of Relativity, nothing can go faster than the speed of light.*

◆ Literary Focus

❹ **Prophetic Essay** Ask students what warning the writer is giving readers in this sentence. *He is warning that the exploration of deep space will require a sacrifice of immediate communications that may prove too great a strain for human relations.*

Twenty years from now you will be able to listen to a friend on Mars, but the words you hear will have left his mouth at least three minutes earlier, and your reply will take a corresponding time to reach him. In such circumstances, an exchange of verbal messages is possible—but not a conversation.

> ◆ **Reading Strategy**
> How important do you judge conversation to be in conducting human affairs across a distance?

❶ ❷ Even in the case of the nearby moon, the 2½ second time-lag will be annoying. At distances of more than a million miles, it will be intolerable.

"Time Barrier"

To a culture which has come to take instantaneous communication for granted, as part of the very structure of civilized life, this "time barrier" may have a profound psychological impact. It will be a perpetual reminder of universal laws and limitations against which not all our technology can ever prevail. For it seems as certain as anything can be that no signal—still less any material object—can ever travel faster than light. ❸ The velocity of light is the ultimate speed limit, being part of the very structure of space and time. Within the narrow confines of the solar system, it will not handicap us too severely, once we have accepted the delays in communication which it involves. At the worst, these will amount to 20 hours—the time it takes a radio signal to span the orbit of Pluto, the outermost planet.

Between the three inner worlds the earth, Mars, and Venus, it will never be more than 20 minutes—not enough to interfere seriously with commerce or administration, but more than sufficient to shatter those personal links of sound or vision that can give us a sense of direct contact with friends on earth, wherever they may be.

It is when we move out beyond the confines of the solar system that we come face to face with an altogether new order of cosmic reality. Even today, many otherwise educated men—like those savages who can count to three but lump together all numbers beyond four—cannot grasp the profound distinction between solar and stellar space. The first is the space enclosing our neighboring worlds, the planets; the second is that which embraces those distant suns, the stars, and it is literally millions of times greater.

There is no such abrupt change of scale in terrestrial affairs. To obtain a mental picture of the distance to the nearest star, as compared with the distance to the nearest planet, you must imagine a world in which the closest object to you is only five feet away—and then there is nothing else to see until you have traveled a thousand miles.

Many conservative scientists, appalled by these cosmic gulfs, have denied that they can ever be crossed. Some people never learn; those who 60 years ago scoffed at the possibility of flight, and ten (even five!) years ago laughed at the idea of travel to the planets, are now quite sure that the stars will always be beyond our reach. And again they are wrong, for they have failed to grasp the great lesson of our age—that if something is possible in theory, and no fundamental scientific laws oppose its realization, then sooner or later it will be achieved.

One day, it may be in this century, or it may be a thousand years from now, we shall discover a really efficient means of propelling our space vehicles. Every technical device is always developed to its limit (unless it is superseded by something better) and the ultimate speed for spaceships is the velocity of light. They will never reach that goal, but they will get very close to it. And then the nearest star will be less than five years' voyaging from the earth.

Our exploring ships will spread outwards from their home over an ever-expanding sphere of space. It is a sphere which will grow at almost—but never quite—the speed of light. Five years to the triple system of Alpha Centauri, 10 to the strangely-matched doublet Sirius A and B, 11 to the tantalizing enigma of 61 Cygni,[3] the first star suspected to possess a planet. These journeys are long, but they are not impossible. Man has always accepted whatever price was necessary for his explorations and discoveries, *and the price of Space is Time.* ❹

3. **Alpha Centauri . . . 61 Cygni:** Alpha Centauri is a system of three stars in the constellation of the Centaur; one of these, Proxima Centauri, is the star closest to Earth besides the sun. Sirius, known as the Dog Star, is the brightest star in Earth's sky; it is actually two stars orbiting each other, one of which (Sirius B), is only as big as the earth. 61 Cygni is a binary star in the constellation Cygnus, the Swan.

Beyond the Classroom

Career Connection

Astronaut An astronaut, or "sailor of the stars," is chosen and trained by the National Aeronautics and Space Administration (NASA). The early astronauts were military test pilots, all with degrees or experience in science or engineering. They were under 40 and, because of the small size of the rocket capsules, less that five feet eleven inches. The first women astronauts were chosen in 1973, and like the others had to undergo rigorous training. This training includes studies in aerodynamics, astronomy, navigation, computer science, communications, mechanics, and physiology. Flight simulation and emergency condition simulation are a big part of training as well. Discuss with students what additional training might help astronauts deal with some of the problems Clarke discusses in his essay.

5 Even voyages which may last for centuries or millennia will one day be attempted. Suspended animation has already been achieved in the laboratory, and may be the key to interstellar travel. Self-contained cosmic arks which will be tiny traveling worlds in their own right may be another solution, for they would make possible journeys of unlimited extent, lasting generation after generation.

The famous Time Dilation effect predicted by the Theory of Relativity,[4] whereby time appears to pass more slowly for a traveler moving at almost the speed of light, may be yet a third. And there are others.

Looking far into the future, therefore, we must picture a slow (little more than half a billion miles an hour!) expansion of human activities outwards from the solar system, among the suns scattered across the region of the galaxy in which we now find ourselves. These suns are on the average five light-years apart; in other words, we can never get from one to the next in less than five years.

To bring home what this means, let us use a down-to-earth analogy. Imagine a vast ocean, sprinkled with islands—some desert, others perhaps inhabited. On one of these islands an energetic race has just discovered the art of building ships. It is preparing to explore the ocean, but must face the fact that the very nearest island is five years' voyaging away, and that no possible improvement in the technique of ship-building will ever reduce this time.

In these circumstances (which are those in which we will soon find ourselves) what could the islanders achieve? After a few centuries, they might have established colonies on many of the nearby islands and have briefly explored many others. The daughter colonies might themselves have sent out further pioneers, and so a kind of chain reaction would spread the original culture over a steadily expanding area of the ocean.

But now consider the effects of the inevitable, unavoidable time-lag. There could be only the most tenuous contact between the home island and its offspring. Returning messengers could report what had happened on the nearest colony—five years ago. They could never bring information more up to date than

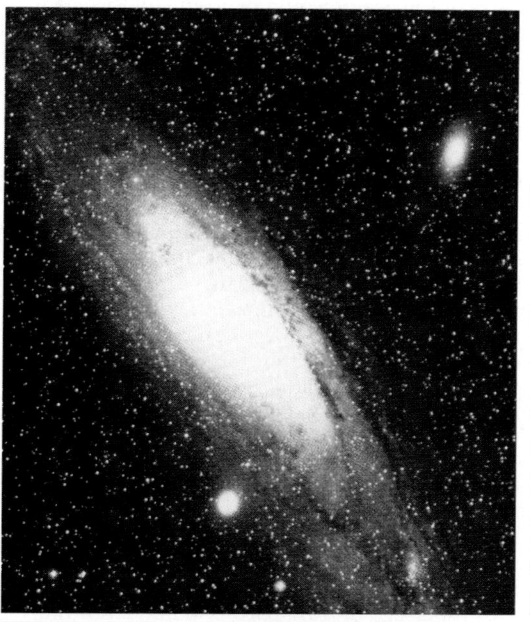
Large spiral galaxy, Andromeda with two small companion galaxies, NASA

▲ Critical Viewing Think about your reponse to Clarke's comparison of distances within the solar system to galactic distance. Does this picture convey a sense of these immense distances as clearly as Clarke's prose? Explain. **[Analyze]** 6

◆ **Reading Strategy**
In his arguments about information-lag, what is Clarke quietly assuming about the length of human life? Formulate a challenge to his argument by making the opposite assumption. 7

4. **Theory of Relativity:** In physics, the theory that measurements of an object's physical properties (and thus the measurement of time) will vary depending on the relative motion of the observer and the observed object—only the speed of light is constant when measured in any frame of reference. One of the consequences of the theory is that speeds faster than the speed of light are impossible.

◆ Build Vocabulary

instantaneous (in' stən tā' nē əs) *adj.*: Done or happening in an instant

enigma (e nig' mə) *n.*: Riddle; a perplexing statement, person, or situation

inevitable (in ev' i tə bəl) *adj.*: Unavoidable; certain to happen

◆ Literature and Your Life

5 Ask students whether they think they will see "self-contained cosmic arks" in their lifetime and, if so, what problems may arise from them. *Sample answer: yes, we may, but the loneliness and isolation that voyagers will feel in them may be too extreme to deal with.*

▶Critical Viewing◀

6 **Analyze** Because the picture is on such a small scale, it doesn't give a sense of the great distances in space. It doesn't relate to anything we know, whereas Clarke's analogy to ocean islands is dramatic and convincing.

◆ Reading Strategy

7 **Challenge the Text** Clarke is assuming that we will not extend our lifetimes appreciably. If we do, however, the lag in time in communications may mean far less to us that it would today.

Cross-Curricular Connection: Science

Space Station Mir Clarke's mention of "self-contained cosmic arks" may bring to mind the Russian space station Mir. Mir, meaning "peace," was launched in February of 1986 by the former Soviet Union. It is a core module with two docking ports and four other hatches designed to hook up with laboratory modules. Scientists on Mir are able to study many aspects of space as well as the effects of long-term stays in space on humans—some of the crew members have stayed on board for over a year at a time. Now that Mir is over a decade old, it has developed some serious technical problems, including several power losses. However, the space station is still staffed by cosmonauts, joined at times by astronauts from other countries including the United States.

Encourage students to research information about Mir and other proposed space-station projects and to report their findings to the class.

◆ Build Vocabulary

❶ **Suffixes: *-ible* and *-able*** Ask students to locate the word with the suffix *-able* in the sentence and to define the word. *The word inviolably means "in such a manner as to be impossible to violate."*

◆ Literary Focus

❷ **Prophetic Essay** Now that Clarke has put aside his argument about the time that space travel would take, ask students what aspect of the universe he is now warning about. *He is now warning that the complexity of the universe is an even more daunting deterrent to conquest than its size.*

◆ Reading Strategy

❸ **Challenge the Text** Ask students if they can envision a time in the future when 10^{20} (the number of stars) would be a number that humans could grasp easily. *Sample answer: Yes, because as our lives have become incalculably more complex over history, we have been able to grasp numbers that in earlier epochs would have been difficult to comprehend.*

that, and dispatches from the more distant parts of the ocean would be from still further in the past—perhaps centuries behind the times. There would never be news from the other islands, but only history.

Independent "Colonies"

All the star-borne colonies of the future will be independent, whether they wish it or not. ❶ Their liberty will be inviolably protected by Time as well as Space. They must go their own way and achieve their own destiny, with no help or hindrance from Mother Earth.

At this point, we will move the discussion on to a new level and deal with an obvious objection. Can we be sure that the velocity of light is indeed a limiting factor? So many "impassible" barriers have been shattered in the past; perhaps this one may go the way of all the others.

We will not argue the point, or give the reasons why scientists believe that light can never be outraced by any form of radiation or any material object. Instead, let us assume the contrary and see just where it gets us. We will even take the most optimistic possible case and imagine that the speed of transportation may eventually become infinite.

Picture a time when, by the development of techniques as far beyond our present engineering as a transistor is beyond a stone axe, we can reach anywhere we please instantaneously, with no more effort than by dialing a number. This would indeed cut the universe down to size and reduce its physical immensity to nothingness. What would be left?

❷ Everything that really matters. For the universe has two aspects—its scale, and its overwhelming, mind-numbing complexity. Having abolished the first, we are now face-to-face with the second.

What we must now try to visualize is not size, but quantity. Most people today are familiar with the simple notation which scientists use to describe large numbers; it consists merely of counting zeroes, so that a hundred becomes 10^2, a million, 10^6, a billion, 10^9 and so on. This useful trick enables us to work with quantities of any magnitude, and even defense budget totals look modest when expressed as $5.76 x 10^9 instead of $5,760,000,000.

The number of other suns in our own galaxy (that is, the whirlpool of stars and cosmic dust of which our sun is an out-of-town member, lying in one of the remoter spiral arms) is estimated at about 10^{11}—or written in full, 100,000,000,000. Our present telescopes can observe something like 10^9 other galaxies, and they show no sign of thinning out even at the extreme limit of vision.

There are probably at least as many galaxies in the whole of creation as there are stars in our own galaxy, but let us confine ourselves to those we can see. They must contain a total of about 10^{11} times 10^9 stars, or 10^{20} stars altogether. 1 followed by 20 other digits is, of course, a number beyond all understanding. ❸

Before such numbers, even spirits brave enough to face the challenge of the light-years must quail. The detailed examination of all the grains of sand on all the beaches of the world

Beyond Literature

Technology Connection

Clarke and COMSAT Arthur C. Clarke is one of the few writers to have had the pleasure of making the future happen even as they predict it. At end of World War II, Clarke combined his wartime experience of radar operation with his passion for space and wrote an article for *Wireless World* magazine. The piece, entitled "Extra Terrestrial Relays," explained how television and telephone signals could be bounced off relay stations—satellites—sent into orbit by rocket. Clarke described, in essence, the methods used to this day for television and other broadcasting. Nearly twenty years later, in 1962, the Communications Satellite Corporation (COMSAT) was authorized by Congress to manage commercial communication satellite systems. Clarke modestly believed that the article advanced telecommunications by "15 minutes." Even a genius can be wrong about his own work, though. Many consider Clarke "the godfather of global communications."

Make your own prediction about communications in the future. What contemporary trends support your prediction?

Speaking and Listening Mini-Lesson

Panel Discussion

This mini-lesson supports the Speaking and Listening activity in the Idea Bank on p. 1167.

Introduce the Concept Explain that a panel discussion usually involves people who are experts in various fields getting together to discuss events or ideas.

Develop Background Have students choose an area of expertise and find out as much as they can on the topic as it applies to Clarke's essay. Some possible areas to explore are Einstein's Theory of Relativity, communications technology, space travel, and space exploration. Each student should consider these points:

- How does my topic relate to the idea that space will never be conquered?
- How can my topic help explain how space exploration can benefit humankind?

Apply the Information With the answers to these questions in mind, students can discuss the implications of the essay. Encourage them to try to reach a conclusion that all the "experts" can support.

Assess the Outcome Have the students determine how well their group worked together to arrive at a conclusion and how well each member was prepared to discuss his or her area of expertise. Encourage them to complete the Self-Assessment: Speaking and Listening Progress page in ***Alternative Assessment*** (p. 123) to gauge their progress.

is a far smaller task than the exploration of the universe.

And so we return to our opening statement. Space can be mapped and crossed and occupied without definable limit; but it can never be conquered. When our race has reached its ultimate achievements, and the stars themselves are scattered no more widely than the seed of Adam, even then we shall still be like ants crawling on the face of the earth. The ants have covered the world but have they conquered it—for what do their countless colonies know of it, or of each other?

4 So it will be with us as we spread outwards from Mother Earth, loosening the bonds of kinship and understanding, hearing faint and belated rumors at second—or third—or thousandth-hand of an ever-dwindling fraction of the entire human race.

Though Earth will try to keep in touch with her children, in the end all the efforts of her archivists and historians will be defeated by time and distance, and the sheer bulk of material. For the number of distinct societies or nations, when our race is twice its present age, may be far greater than the total number of all the men who have ever lived up to the present time.

We have left the realm of human comprehension in our vain effort to grasp the scale of the universe; so it must always be, sooner rather than later.

When you are next outdoors on a summer night, turn your head towards the zenith. Almost vertically above you will be shining the brightest star of the northern skies—Vega of the Lyre,[5] 26 years away at the speed of light, near enough the point-of-no-return for us short-lived creatures. Past this blue-white beacon, 50 times as brilliant as our sun, we may send our minds and bodies, but never our hearts.

For no man will ever turn homewards from beyond Vega, to greet again those he knew and loved on the earth.

◆ Literary Focus
In what ways is this a prophetic statement? 5

◆ Build Vocabulary
zenith (zē′ nəth) *n.*: Highest point of something, especially of the sky or celestial sphere

5. **Vega of the Lyre:** Star in the northern constellation, Lyra. Fourth brightest of the stars in Earth's night sky.

Guide for Responding

◆ Literature and Your Life

Reader's Response What questions would you like to ask the author of this essay?

Thematic Focus In what ways is our world still vast? In what ways is it small?

Check Your Comprehension

1. Why will it never be possible to have a true conversation with someone on another planet?
2. What is the ultimate speed limit, which is part of the very structure of space and time?
3. What achievement will be reached within a century, according to Clarke?

◆ Critical Thinking

INTERPRET

1. (a) What distinction does Clarke make between exchanging verbal messages and having a conversation? (b) Why is this distinction crucial to his thesis? **[Classify; Draw Conclusions]**
2. At the end of "Time Barrier," why does Clarke use the analogy of an ocean sprinkled with islands? **[Compare and Contrast]**
3. What implications does Clarke seem to suggest conquering space would have for human relations? **[Infer]**

EVALUATE

4. Has Clarke made a persuasive argument about the impossibility of conquering space? Explain. **[Assess]**

Beyond the Selection

FURTHER READING

Other Works by Arthur C. Clarke
The Exploration of Space; Childhood's End; 2001: A Space Odyssey

Other Works With the Theme of the National to the Global
Fahrenheit 451, Ray Bradbury
Stranger in a Strange Land, Robert Heinlein
A Canticle for Liebowitz, Walter M. Miller

We suggest that you preview these works before recommending them to students.

INTERNET

You and your students may find additional information about Arthur C. Clarke and his work on the Internet. We suggest the following site. Please be aware, however, that the site may have changed since this information was published. For information about Clarke's writings, go to **http://www.lsi.usp.br~rbianchi/clarke/**.

We *strongly recommend* that you preview the site before you send students to it.

◆ Critical Thinking

4 Compare and Contrast Ask students what Clarke's analogy suggests about the current status of human achievement. *Clarke observes that ants have not in fact "conquered" the Earth, even if they have "covered" it; he argues the same will be true of humans in space.*

◆ Literary Focus

5 Prophetic Essay It prophesies that humans will probably never truly inhabit space; if they do, they will be irrevocably separated from Earth.

Reinforce and Extend

Answers

◆ Literature and Your Life

Reader's Response Students might ask whether Clarke is pleased or disappointed that humans will never conquer space.

Thematic Focus Our world is still vast in the sense that people still don't understand or relate well to each other. It is small because it takes little time to travel or communicate across great distances.

Check Your Comprehension

1. The time lag between remarks would be too great for real conversation.
2. The ultimate speed limit is the speed of light.
3. Within a century we will harness nuclear energy for space travel.

◆ Critical Thinking

1. (a) A conversation requires a timely response between speakers. A verbal message does not require a response. (b) Clarke feels that the time lag between conversants would make true dialogue impossible, eroding understanding.
2. Clarke uses a familiar image to make the situation he envisions understandable and convincing.
3. Clarke suggests that humans spreading through space would not be able to maintain "real-time" relationships.
4. Sample answers: Yes, given his assumptions about the limits on communication; or no, Clarke doesn't allow for the possibility of great technological leaps.

Answers

◆ **Literary Focus**

1. Sample answers:
   "When our race has reached its ultimate achievements, and the stars themselves are scattered no more widely than the seed of Adam, even then we shall still be like ants crawling on the face of the earth." This sentence is effective because it seems almost Biblical in its language.
   "For no man will ever turn homewards from beyond Vega, to greet again those he knew and loved on earth." This sentence is effective because it speaks of the emotional distance that will arise between humans.
2. Sample answer: Clarke compares the number of stars in our galaxy, which seems almost infinite, to the number of galaxies in the universe. This suggests a number beyond imagining.
3. (a) Sample answer: I agree, because I think that as humans race toward the technological frontier they neglect the links and emotions that define their humanity. (b) Yes; Clarke points out that humans still have a lot to learn about successfully coexisting on planet Earth.

◆ **Reading Strategy**

1. "It will never be possible to converse with anyone on another planet." I think that at some point in the future, we will be able to bypass the problem with the speed of messages and will be able to arrange conversations.
2. Clarke guesses that "in a few years" we will be able to see friends around the globe via satellite. He did not predict that satellite television broadcasting would be dominated by entertainment companies, and that "videophones" would not become widespread even as satellite technology became more sophisticated.

Guide for Responding *(continued)*

◆ Literary Focus

Prophetic Essay

In his **prophetic essay**, Clarke predicts that humans will never dominate outer space as we have dominated the Earth. As is often true in prophetic essays, his prediction may also suggest a moral lesson: We need to be more humble about ourselves and our place in the universe.

To convince you of his prediction, Clarke includes such pieces of information as the speed of light and a description of the Lunik space probe. However, he also uses two effective persuasive devices. First, he writes in memorable phrases and sentences, like "... the price of Space is Time." Second, he uses comparisons to help you visualize the vastness of space.

1. Find two memorable phrases or sentences in the essay, and explain why they are effective.
2. Identify a comparison Clarke uses, and tell why it does or does not help you "see" the point he is making.
3. (a) Do you agree or disagree with Clarke's prophecy concerning space travel? Explain.
(b) Do you think that Clarke is asking readers to rethink their behavior or attitudes? Why or why not?

◆ Reading Strategy

Challenge the Text

Challenging a text means giving yourself the freedom to argue with it as you would with a friend. Often key words like *always*, *never*, *ever*, or *may* give you a clue about which statements to test against your own knowledge. *Never*, *always*, or *ever* signal a sweeping generalization: "Man has *always* accepted whatever price was necessary for his explorations." You can challenge such generalizations by looking for a single exception that would disprove them.

Also, look for the word *may*, which indicates that Clarke is guessing rather than giving facts: "this 'time barrier' *may* have a profound psychological impact." Test such statements by determining whether they suggest other results or explanations.

1. Find another *always* or *never* statement, challenge it, and then decide whether you agree with it.
2. Find and challenge one of Clarke's guesses.

◆ Build Vocabulary

Using the Suffixes *-ible* and *-able*

Use the suffixes *-ible* and *-able* to form words with the following definitions:

1. able to be defined **3.** showing hospitality
2. able to be tolerated **4.** able to be resisted

Using the Word Bank

On your paper, write the letter of the word or words closest in meaning to the first word.

1. ludicrous: (a) frisky, (b) fun-loving, (c) absurd
2. irrevocable: (a) rapid, (b) unalterable, (c) fickle
3. instantaneous: (a) immediate, (b) faulty, (c) risky
4. enigma: (a) beverage, (b) riddle, (c) archive
5. inevitable: (a) unavoidable, (b) incomprehensible, (c) direct
6. zenith: (a) point on the horizon, (b) point directly overhead, (c) bending of light rays

◆ Grammar and Style

Linking Verbs and Subject Complements

Clarke uses **linking verbs** like *seem* or *be* to equate subjects with their **complements**, nouns, pronouns, or adjectives that describe them. The effect of this grammatical structure is to make sentences seem like equations that must be true.

Practice In your notebook, identify the linking verb and subject complement in each sentence.

1. Our age is in many ways unique.
2. To our ancestors, the vastness of the Earth was a dominant fact.
3. A few hundred miles was infinity.
4. The problem of sending speech to other planets is almost trivial.
5. The detailed examination of all the grains of sand on all the beaches of the world is a far smaller task than the exploration of the universe.

Writing Application Find five well-known proverbs or sayings, like "Home is where the heart is," and determine whether or not they use linking verbs and subject complements. If you find that many of them do have this grammatical structure, explain why this might be so.

◆ **Build Vocabulary**

Using the Suffixes *-ible* and *-able*
1. definable; 2. tolerable; 3. hospitable; 4. resistible

Using the Word Bank
1. c 2. b 3. a 4. b 5. a 6. b

◆ **Grammar and Style**

1. Linking verb: *is*; subject complement: "in many ways unique"
2. Linking verb: *was*; subject complement: "a dominant fact"
3. Linking verb: *was*; subject complement: "infinity"
4. Linking verb: *is*; subject complement: "almost trivial"
5. Linking verb: *is*; subject complement: "a far smaller task than the exploration of the universe"

Writing Application
Students should point out that the grammatical structure of linking verbs and subject complements suggests that these sayings are always true.

Writer's Solution

For additional instruction and practice, use the Writing With Nouns and Verbs lesson in the Writing Style unit of the **Language Lab CD-ROM**, and the page on Complements, p. 21 in the *Writer's Solution Grammar Practice Book.*

Build Your Portfolio

Idea Bank

Writing

1. E-mail Response Write an e-mail message to Arthur C. Clarke responding to his message in "We'll Never Conquer Space." Tell him about passages you liked or disliked and ask him any questions you may have.

2. Reflective Essay Using Clarke's piece as a launching pad, write your own reflective essay on space exploration. Speculate about future developments and what they might teach us.

3. Literary Analysis Clarke is known for combining scientific knowledge with a philosophical outlook. Write a literary analysis of "We'll Never Conquer Space," finding evidence of both these qualities.

Speaking and Listening

4. Panel Discussion In a small group, discuss the implications of Clarke's essay. If Clarke is correct that space will never be conquered, what are the practical and philosophical uses of space exploration? **[Science Link]**

5. Introduction Arthur C. Clarke is appearing on your television talk show to discuss "We'll Never Conquer Space." Using the biographical information on page 1158, introduce him to viewers. **[Media Link; Performing Arts Link]**

Projects

6. Film Review View *2001: A Space Odyssey* and write a review of it for your classmates. Focus on its plot, music, and special effects. **[Media Link]**

7. Museum Exhibit Create a museum exhibit that will dramatize Clarke's ideas about space for high-school students. Contact your local science museum or university for advice. **[Science Link]**

Writing Mini-Lesson

Astronaut's Diary

Arthur C. Clarke is convinced that we will continue to explore space, although we can never conquer it. Imagine that you are an astronaut on a mission of exploration and discovery sometime in the future. Write a series of diary entries recording your experiences. Be consistent in giving your impressions from an astronaut's perspective.

Writing Skills Focus: Consistent Perspective

In writing diary entries, and other types of narration and description, you should keep a **consistent perspective.** Your astronaut should always refer to himself or herself as "I." Also, avoid having your astronaut describe scenes that he or she could not have actually seen. Still another way to maintain consistency is to keep the details of the mission the same in all your entries. Such details might include the ones in the chart below.

Prewriting Review Clarke's essay for information you can use for diary entries. Then make a prewriting chart like this one, listing items that you can refer to for consistency:

Purpose of Mission	Duration	Type of ship	Gear and clothing

Drafting Imagine the day-to-day concerns your astronaut would have, even in outer space, and incorporate these into the entries. In addition, always write from your astronaut's point of view and refer to your chart so that details remain consistent.

Revising Have a peer editor review your entries and suggest where you can include more sensory details to bring descriptions to life. Also have your editor check for consistency in the use of the pronoun "I" and in descriptions of details.

✓ ASSESSMENT OPTIONS

Formal Assessment, Selection Test, pp. 303–305, and Assessment Resources Software. The selection test is designed so that it can be easily customized to the performance levels of your students. ***Alternative Assessment,*** p. 65, includes options for less advanced students, more advanced students, verbal/linguistic learners, visual/spatial learners, and logical/mathematical learners.

PORTFOLIO ASSESSMENT
Use the following rubrics in the ***Alternative Assessment*** booklet to assess student writing:
E-mail Response: Response to Literature Rubric, p. 111
Reflective Essay: Expression Rubric, p. 95
Literary Analysis: Literary Analysis/Interpretation Rubric, p. 113
Writing Mini-Lesson: Fictional Narrative Rubric, p. 96

Idea Bank

Customizing for *Performance Levels*
Following are suggestions for matching Idea Bank topics with your students' performance levels:
Less Advanced Students: 1, 5, 6
Average Students: 2, 4, 6
More Advanced Students: 3, 7

Customizing for *Learning Modalities*
Following are suggestions for matching Idea Bank topics with your students' learning modalities:
Verbal/Linguistic: 1, 2, 3 ,4, 5
Visual/Spatial: 6, 7

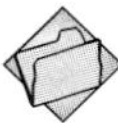

Writing Mini-Lesson

Refer students to the Writing Process Handbook, page 1189, for instruction on the writing process, and page 1191 for further information on narration.

Writing and Language Transparencies Use the Writing Process Model 9: Technical Writing: Status Report, pp. 81–84 in the **Writing and Language Transparencies** to model a format for students' Astronaut's Diary.

Writer's Solution

Writing Lab CD-ROM
Have students complete the tutorial on Narration. Follow these steps:

1. Complete the Setting Profile to clarify information to include in the diary entries.
2. Use the Audio-annotated Literary Models of point of view to help define the first-person narrator.
3. Students should draft on computer.
4. Refer them to the interactive guidelines for peer revision for help in revising their drafts.

Allow approximately 75 minutes of class time to complete these steps.

Sourcebook
Have students use Chapter 2, Narration (pp. 30–61), for additional support. The chapter contains a Writing Hint for Developing a Specialized Narrative (p. 50).

Prepare and Engage

Establish Writing Guidelines
Review the following key characteristics of a critical evaluation:

- A critical evaluation addresses positive and negative characteristics of a literary work.
- It examines the literary elements and shows how they fit together.
- It uses specific examples from the literary work to support the thesis.

Before students begin, you may want to share with them the Scoring Rubric for Literary Analysis/Interpretation (p. 113 in ***Alternative Assessment***) so that students see the criteria by which they will be evaluated. Suggestions on page 1170 customize the rubric to this workshop.

Connect to Literature You might refer students to *The London Times* article "Elizabeth II: A New Queen" (p. 131) in Unit 1. This news article analyzes an event. Ask students to review the article and discuss how it is like and unlike a critical evaluation of literature.

Writer's Solution

Writer's at Work Videodisc
To review the key elements of critical evaluation, play the videodisc segment on Response to Literature (Ch. 7). Ask students in what way critic Eavan Boland responds to literature.

Play frames 21571 to 31063

Writing Lab CD-ROM
Have students work in the Response to Literature tutorial to complete their critical evaluations. They may follow these steps:

1. Review an audio-annotated model of a critical review.
2. Study interactive models of broad and focused topics for literary responses.
3. Use the Transition Word Bin to draft effective connections.
4. Use the Revision Checker for Vague Language to replace vague language with precise words.

Sourcebook
Students can find additional support, including topic ideas, models, and a list of transitional words and phrases, in Chapter 7, Response to Literature (pp. 196–229).

Critical Evaluation

Writing Process Workshop

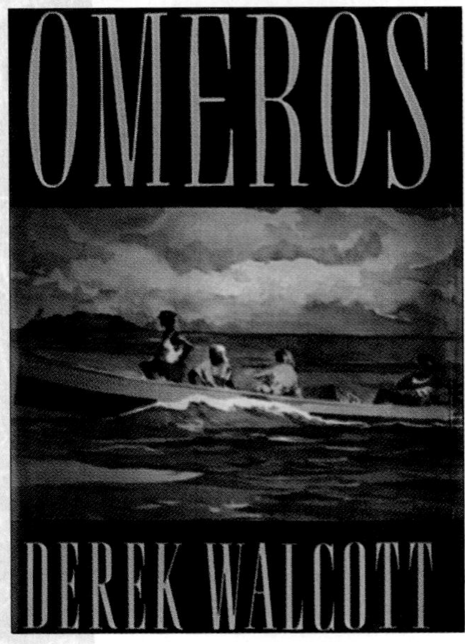

The works of modern writers, like the ones in this section, have yet to stand the test of time. However, they have undergone, and will continue to undergo, evaluation—by literary scholars, historians, students, and everyday people who discuss books in informal groups. Write a critical evaluation in which you focus on the positive and negative characteristics of a literary work. In your evaluation, include an examination of various literary elements, with specific examples, and a summary of the work. The writing-skills focus points, introduced in Mini-Lessons in this section, will help you write your evaluation.

Writing Skills Focus

- **Use specific examples** by including direct quotations from the work that support your opinion. (See p. 1109.)
- **Maintain a level of formality** that suits a critical evaluation. (See p. 1135.)
- **Use transitions to show comparisons** and connections among your ideas and details. (See p. 1145.)
- **Choose words with positive and negative connotations** to help convey your purpose. (See p. 1157.)

The following passage from a critical evaluation contains many elements appropriate to this type of writing.

Model From Literature

from A Critical Evaluation of *Omeros* by John Figueroa

In *Omeros* the grand names are given to simple folk, some of whom had the kind of problems the noble heroes had in Homer's poems. With these problems they struggled, as with the "loud sounding sea," with no less dignity and humanity ① than all the heroes in the bloody wars . . . . But what is common to ② Homer and *Omeros* is not only struggle and coming to terms with death and violence and separation from home, but the sea . . . and its moods and sounds. ③

① The positive connotations of *dignity* and *humanity* convey the writer's approval of Walcott's work.

② The transition *what is common to* introduces a similarity between *Omeros* and the ancient work that inspired it.

③ The writer uses appropriately formal language throughout his evaluation.

Cross-Curricular Connection: Science

Scientists know that the articles they write for publication in scientific journals will be critically evaluated by their colleagues. Whether scientists do research in medicine or about outer space, their literature is thoroughly scrutinized. Scientific writers rely on this critical evaluation of their literature in order to bring the best thinking and most careful analysis to every issue. Scientific critical evaluations involve the same skills as a literary critique. Both are formal, address specific examples from other texts, make comparisons, and evaluate both negative and positive characteristics. Discuss with students why such critical evaluation is important to people outside the scientific community.

Prewriting

Choose a Topic To find a topic for your critical evaluation, think about books or poems you've read, such as a current best seller, something you read for class, or even a children's book. Following are additional topic ideas:

Topic Ideas

- A drama you loved
- A short story you hated

Selection-Related Topic Ideas

- "From Lucy: Englan' Lady" by James Berry
- A work by Arthur C. Clarke

Support Your Ideas with Specific Examples Write your thesis statement, then list specific references from the work that support your point. You may use specific words, lines, or entire stanzas to support your arguments.

Experiment with Connotations Think of the words you might use in your evaluation. Then use a thesaurus or dictionary to identify similar words with slightly different meanings. The following sentences convey different ideas because of the different connotations of the underlined words.

- ▶ The poetry of Ted Hughes reveals a *fascination* with nature.
- ▶ The poetry of Ted Hughes reveals an *over-absorption* with nature.
- ▶ The poetry of Ted Hughes reveals a *fondness* for nature.

Drafting

Develop a Consistent Level of Formality A scholarly work, such as a critical evaluation, should be formal and serious in tone. As you draft, maintain this tone by choosing formal vocabulary and creating balanced and complex sentences.

- ▶ **Informal:** *The story really rocks.*
- ▶ **Formal:** *The narrative is gripping and involving.*

Connect Your Ideas and Examples While drafting, use transitions to connect your ideas and examples. Refer to the following word list for suggestions:

Transitions: all, alike, both, most, similar, either, neither, equal, identical, same, like, other, closely related, common to, also, likewise, too, similarly, therefore, however, thus.

Applying Language Skills: Avoiding Incomplete and Illogical Comparisons

Critical evaluation often involves comparing works. Avoid illogical comparisons that do not match similar items.

Example:
Walcott's hero Achille is very different from the *Iliad.*

Revision:
Walcott's hero Achille is very different from the hero Achilleus in the *Iliad.*

Avoid incomplete comparisons by clearly indicating the group of items with which you are comparing a work.

Example:
Dylan Thomas's work is more powerful than others.

Revision:
Dylan Thomas's work is more powerful than that of any other modern poet.

Practice Rewrite the following sentences to make the comparisons logical and complete.

1. Derek Walcott's *Omeros* has more precise sea imagery.
2. The dialect in Berry's work is more accurate than Walcott's poetry.
3. The imagery in Walcott's *Omeros* is more convincing.

Develop Student Writing

Prewriting

Writing and Language Transparencies You may want students to use an Analysis Map, pp. 111–114 in the ***Writing and Language Transparencies,*** to organize their thoughts.

Customize for
Less Advanced Students
Have these students work in pairs or small groups to find a topic and gather and organize details. Then each will be better prepared to write his or her own critical evaluation.

Writing Lab CD-ROM
To help students focus their critical evaluations, suggest they use the interactive Literary Elements Chart in the Focusing Your Response section of the Response to Literature tutorial.

Drafting

As they write, encourage students to use mature sentence structures, including phrases and clauses to create compound-complex sentences. The mature sentence structure will enhance the level of formality.

Applying Language Skills

Avoiding Incomplete and Illogical Comparisons
Suggest to students for whom comparisons are particularly difficult that they put comparisons into a simple chart and then make sure their sentences say what the chart shows.

Answers
Possible responses:

1. Derek Walcott's *Omeros* has more precise sea imagery than Berry's work does.
2. The dialect in Berry's work is more accurate than that in Walcott's poetry.
3. The imagery in Walcott's *Omeros* is more convincing than that in Berry's work.

For additional practice, use the Clear Comparisons worksheet, p. 70, in the *Writer's Solution Grammar Practice Book.*

Revising

Discuss the Revision Model with the class. Then ask students to work with a peer editor to respond to the Revision Checklist.

Writer's Solution

Writing Lab CD-ROM
Have students use the Self-Evaluation Checklist in the Revising and Editing section of the Response to Literature tutorial to determine the effectiveness of their critical evaluations.

Publishing

You may want to have students publish a magazine of critical evaluations to put in the school library.

Applying Language Skills

Avoiding Clichés
Phrases like *the best thing since sliced bread* and *as dull as watching paint dry* have probably been replaced by students with other clichés. Ask them to brainstorm a list of clichés from their daily conversations.

Answers

Possible responses:

1. crescendos
2. hours disappear as fast as minutes
3. worth a whole roll of film

Reinforce and Extend

Reflect on the Writing Process
After students have completed their critical evaluations, ask them to discuss how principles learned here can apply to writing college or scholarship applications.

Applying Language Skills: Avoiding Clichés

Clichés are expressions that were once fresh and vivid but through overuse now lack force and appeal. Replace any clichés you find with original observations.

First Draft:
Until I studied British history, I found reading poetry to be as dull as dishwater.

Revision:
Until I studied British history, I found reading poetry to be as tedious as counting out pennies.

Practice Rewrite the following statements, using fresh, interesting images in place of the highlighted clichés.

1. In her story, the train *roars like thunder* through the countryside.
2. According to A. E. Housman, *time flies.*
3. The leading character is *as pretty as a picture.*

Writing Application Search for and delete clichés in your own writing.

Writer's Solution Connection
Language Lab

For help in using quotation marks in titles of literary works or in punctuating passages from literature, see the Semicolons, Colons, and Quotation Marks lesson in the Punctuation unit.

Revising

Revision Checklist Use the following questions to develop a revision checklist:

- Is the level of formality consistent throughout?
- What words can you replace to clarify your meaning?
- Have you used transitions to connect details and ideas?
- What details from the work can you add as support?

Revision Model

① In comparison to descriptions in other poetry,
the description of an event from three perspectives distinguishes "Not Waving but Drowning." Stevie Smith uses a literary element, point of view, to create depth. ② Notice the unusual shift in perspective from line two to line three: "But still he lay moaning: /I was much further out than you thought . . ." ~~When you read this simple poem,~~ ③ On first reading the deceptively simple piece, the reader might be confused by the change in speaker, but Smith uses this ~~deception~~ ④ stratagem to force the reader to read again. It is in the careful, subsequent readings that one moves beyond the apparent meanings to the metaphorical meanings.

① This transition signals to the reader that the writer is linking this piece to poetry in general.

② By adding a direct quotation from the poem, the writer supports his prior statement.

③ This phrase was revised to better match the formal, academic tone set in the rest of the evaluation.

④ Because the word *deception* creates a negative connotation that was unintended by the writer, the word *stratagem* was substituted.

Publishing

- **Discussion** Organize a literary discussion group. Let members read and discuss the critical evaluations they have written.
- **Internet** Submit your work to an Internet site that is dedicated to literary reviews.

☑ ASSESSMENT		4	3	2	1
PORTFOLIO ASSESSMENT Use the rubric on Literary Analysis/Interpretation in ***Alternative Assessment*** (p. 113) to assess student writing. Add these criteria to customize the rubric to this assignment.	**Positives and Negatives**	The critical evaluation extensively addresses both positive and negative characteristics of the work.	It adequately addresses both positive and negative characteristics of the work.	It inadequately addresses both positive and negative characteristics of the work.	It addresses only positive or negative characteristics of the work.
	Level of Formality	The critical evaluation consistently maintains a formal level.	The critical evaluation usually maintains a formal level.	The critical evaluation sometimes maintains a formal level.	The critical evaluation is informal.

Real-World Reading Skills Workshop

Using Heads and Text Structure

Strategies for Success

Magazine articles and other nonfiction pieces aren't just long blocks of prose. They use special features like heads, bulleted lists, and pull-out quotations to draw a reader in and get the main points across. Learn to use these features to analyze what you read.

Read and Evaluate Heads A newspaper headline catches your eye and tells you what a story is about; the headings in a magazine article have the same purpose. They also tell you when a new topic is being introduced. Use heads to guide your reading rate.

- ▶ Read a head at the beginning of a section and think about what it means.
- ▶ When you come to the end of the section, reconsider the head. Does it match what you learned in the section?

MULTIPLE-CHOICE QUESTIONS

Multiple-choice questions require specific test-taking strategies. The following strategies will help you succeed on tests with this kind of question.

Guess Smart Most standardized tests give five answer choices per question. If you just filled in blank circles without reading the questions, you'd probably get 20% right—not a very good score. But if you read carefully, you can almost always eliminate a few answer choices. Unless there's a penalty for wrong answers, it's always best to make a guess. These hints can help you:

- If two answers are similar, choose one of them.
- If two answers have opposite meanings, choose one of them.
- Choose the longest answer.
- If all else fails, choose answer b. If people generate the answers instead of computers, that's the most common answer choice.

Caution: Trigger Words Many multiple choice answers contain "trigger" words that make an answer false. These words can be negatives, such as *not* or *no*, or superlative adverbs, such as *never*, *always*, or *necessarily*. Think twice before choosing an answer with one of these trigger words—are you sure the statement is correct?

Additional Strategies These hints can help improve your scores:

- Try to answer the questions before reading the answers. Then look for the right answer.
- Answer questions you know first. Mark the others and come back to them later.
- Your gut response is probably correct. Don't change an answer unless you're sure it's wrong.

Identify Text Structure The heads in an article or chapter help you understand how an author's ideas are organized. Heads often come in two kinds—main heads and subheads. As you read, remember that each subhead is directly related to the main head under which it falls. If you're taking notes on what you read, create an outline using the heads and subheads, adding your own notes under each one.

Look for Special Features Articles often contain other text formats designed to aid comprehension. Bulleted lists call attention to a group of related ideas. Pull-out quotations are important sentences or phrases from the piece that are reprinted in larger type. They are often used to get a reader's interest. When you review your reading, refer to the pull-quotes to help crystallize your personal response.

Apply the Strategy

Many nonfiction books use headings to organize information. Read this page from a book on taking tests successfully.

1. Describe how the text is organized on the page.
2. Identify each subhead and the new topic it introduces.
3. What is similar about the points on each bulleted list?
4. Think of two subheads that you might find under another main heading: *True-False Questions.*

Here are other types of material to which these strategies apply:

- ▶ *extended encyclopedia entries*
- ▶ *textbooks*
- ▶ *World Wide Web pages*

Introduce the Strategy

Ask students, without reading, to discuss the layout of this page. Have them discuss how headings and the placement of page features affect understanding. Next, ask them to read only the five heads in the text. From those, ask what they know or can deduce about the text.

Customize for
English Language Learners
These students can improve their comprehension by putting into daily practice the procedure described above in Introduce the Strategy.

Apply the Strategy

Have students study the sample page, reading first only the heads. Then have them answer questions 1–2. Next have students read the two sets of bulleted items and answer question 3. Using what they have discovered about the organization of this page, have them answer question 4.

Answers

Suggested responses:

1. It is organized by strategy.
2. Guess Smart, Caution: Trigger Words, and Additional Strategies are the three subheads.
3. Each gives hints of equal weight.
4. Two subheads might be Guess Smart and Caution: Trigger Words.

Introduce the Strategy

Remind students that conflict is part of daily life. Even in the workplace conflicts can arise that become stumbling blocks to productivity. When that happens, one or all parties may soon be unemployed. Thus, knowing how to resolve conflict is essential to success. You may want to ask students to cite examples of typical conflicts at home, school, or work.

Apply the Strategy

Give partners time to plan their role-play for one or the other of the situations. You may want to videotape the role-play for follow-up discussion and then apply the four steps of conflict resolution.

Speaking and Listening Workshop

Conflict Resolution

Strategies for Success

Use communication skills to avoid or resolve conflicts. Speaking carefully, saying what you mean, and really listening when other people talk can help you stay in tune with others. When conflicts do occur, consider these four steps to conflict resolution.

Identify the Problem The first thing you need to do is understand the problem. State the problem in a brief, straightforward way that isn't biased or emotional. Sometimes it can be helpful to review the causes of the problem, outlining the steps that led to the current difficulty.

Devise a Plan Next, you need to work together to create a plan that will resolve the conflict. Remember that a conflict that has been building for days or weeks may take time to settle. Make sure your plan is realistic and allows enough time for the gradual and complete resolution of the conflict. As always, discussion and careful listening will help you find a plan that's fair and effective.

Evaluate Progress Plans don't run themselves. All people involved in the conflict need to monitor the plan and assess how well it is working. You might ask an unbiased third party to help you evaluate your progress.

Make Necessary Revisions Your plan for resolving the conflict should be flexible, not rigid. As you work toward your goal, you may think of better ideas or strategies. When you adjust the plan, make sure that everyone involved understands and accepts the changes.

Apply the Strategies

Use the four steps of conflict resolution as you role-play these situations with a partner.

1. One neighbor thinks that another is playing music too loudly. Pretending to be the neighbors, work together to resolve your dispute.
2. Suppose you represent groups that want to use the same classroom space after school. No other space is available for use, and both groups feel they need the space at least four days a week.

Tips for Resolving Conflicts

✔ *Strong communication skills will always help you resolve conflicts. Remember these strategies when trying to settle a dispute.*

- Use "I" statements that describe how you feel.
- Avoid "you" statements that can lead to name-calling and finger-pointing.
- Remain calm and speak carefully. Don't let emotions encourage you to say things you don't mean.

Beyond the Classroom

Career Connection

Counselor Some people have keen insight into others' motives and reactions. They know how to read body language. They understand negotiation. They know how to resolve conflict. In short, they have the skills that make superior counselors.

Other people can learn the same skills but need someone to help them learn. Counselors can do that. Remind students that besides in schools, counselors work in business and industry and establish private practices to work with individuals. Suggest that interested students explore the opportunities in this career field.

Extended Reading Opportunities

These twentieth century works reflect the rapid changes that occurred during this period. The British Empire fell, the world survived two world wars, and all traditional social norms were turned upside down.

Suggested Titles

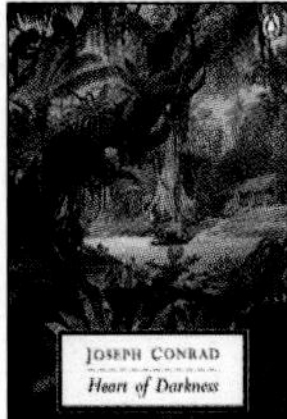

Heart of Darkness
Joseph Conrad

Conrad explores the human mind and the effects of colonialism in this great novel that has inspired many other writers. Conrad's narrator, the river steamer captain Marlow, tells a group of friends about an ominous journey into the heart of the African jungle. Mysterious, grotesque tales about the white ivory trader Kurtz pale in comparison to the reality Marlow finds when he meets the man. In Conrad's classic tale, the "heart of darkness" is both the human heart and the oppressive colonial system.

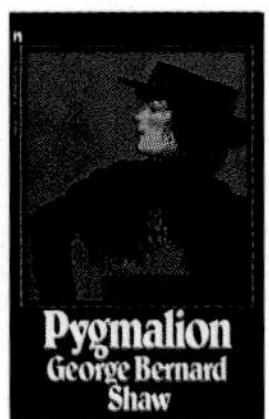

Pygmalion
George Bernard Shaw

Like his professor of phonetics, Henry Higgins, Shaw believed in the power of language to break down class barriers. In Shaw's play, the overbearing Higgins transforms Eliza Doolittle, a cockney flower girl, into an elegant woman. Neither character foresees, however, that falling in love may complicate the process of Eliza's transformation. Nearly half a century after it was written, Shaw's comedy became the basis of the enormously successful musical *My Fair Lady* and still has the power to entertain and educate.

A Passage to India
E. M. Forster

Forster's novel is a classic portrayal of clashing cultures. Adela Quested, a young British visitor to India, falsely accuses Aziz, a likable Indian doctor, of assaulting her on a tour of the Malabar Caves. As the British and Indian characters react to this accusation, the reader sees the cultural differences between them. Forster shows that in a colonial situation, these differences inevitably lead to misunderstandings. Forster's descriptions are so skillful that even the setting seems to take on the role of a character.

Other Possibilities

British

A Portrait of the Artist as a Young Man	James Joyce
A House for Mr. Biswas	V. S. Naipaul
The Golden Notebook	Doris Lessing

World

The Plague	Albert Camus

Planning Students' Extended Reading

The works featured on this page focus on the rapidly changing social norms and traditions of the twentieth century. The following information may help you choose which work to assign.

Customize for *Varying Student Needs and Interests*

When assigning these works to students, keep in mind the following factors.

- *Heart of Darkness* will be of high interest to students, but interpreting the psychological aspects of the story that result from colonization may present difficulty for some students. Have students re-read the introductions to Unit 5 (pages 740–745) and Unit 6 (pages 878–883) for historical background on colonization, which they can then apply to understanding the story.
- *Pygmalion* is a play that students may enjoy reading aloud in class or performing scenes as group projects. Students will better understand the play if you review the traditional social structure of England and how it was changed by the emergence of the middle class.
- *A Passage to India* requires understanding of British involvement in India. Review with students background on the colonization and independence of India before they read.
- Students may be interested in knowing that each of the works spurred media creations. The famous movie *Apocolypse Now* was based on *Heart of Darkness*. The hit musical *My Fair Lady*, which was first run in 1956, and became a movie in 1964, evolved from *Pygmalion*. *A Passage to India* was also produced as a movie, which is known for its breathtaking scenery.

Sensitive Issues

- Both *Heart of Darkness* and *A Passage to India* contain issues and references that you may find sensitive in your classroom.
- Some students may be disturbed by the strong language, violence, and inhumanity of colonization as presented in *Heart of Darkness*. Stress to students that Conrad uses this strong treatment to accentuate the oppressive aspects of the colonial system.
- *A Passage to India* deals with class and racial prejudice and also alludes to a rape.

Resources for Teaching Novels, Plays, and Literature Collections

This resource includes graphic organizers, teaching strategies, and transparencies that are invaluable in teaching these novels.

Customize for *Special Needs*

To meet the needs of your special needs students, you may want to consider using *Heart of Darkness* from Globe Fearon's Pacemaker Classics series.

Access Guide to Vocabulary

KEY TO PRONUNCIATION SYMBOLS USED

Symbol	*Key Words*						
		i	is, hit, mirror	yo͞o	use, cute, few	ə	**a** in ago
a	asp, fat, parrot	ī	ice, bite, high	yo͝o	united, cure, globule		**e** in agent
ā	ape, date, play	ō	open, tone, go	oi	oil, point, toy		**i** in sanity
ä	ah, car, father	ô	all, horn, law	ou	out, crowd, plow		**o** in comply
e	elf, ten, berry	o͞o	ooze, tool, crew	u	up, cut, color		**u** in focus
ē	even, meet, money	o͝o	look, pull, moor	ʉr	urn, fur, deter	ər	perhaps, murder

Symbol	*Key Words*						
		k	kill, tackle, bake	t	top, cattle, hat	th	thin, nothing, truth
b	bed, fable, dub	l	let, yellow, ball	v	vat, hovel, have	*th*	then, father, lathe
d	dip, beadle, had	m	met, camel, trim	w	will, always, swear	zh	azure, leisure
f	fall, after, off	n	not, flannel, ton	y	yet, onion, yard	ŋ	ring, anger, drink
g	get, haggle, dog	p	put, apple, tap	z	zebra, dazzle, haze		
h	he, head, hotel	r	red, port, dear	ch	chin, catcher, arch		
j	joy, agile, badge	s	sell, castle, pass	sh	she, cushion, dash		

Foreign Sounds

à This symbol, representing the *a* in French *salle*, can best be described as intermediate between (a) and (ä).

ë This symbol represents the sound of the vowel cluster in French *coeur* and can be approximated by rounding the lips as for (ō) and pronouncing (e).

ö This symbol variously represents the sound of *eu* in French *feu*, or of ö or *oe* in German *blöd* or *Geothe,* and can be approximated by rounding lips as for (ō) and pronouncing (ā).

ô This symbol represents a range of sounds between (ô) and (u); it occurs typically in the sound of the *o* in French *tonne* or German *korrekt*; in Italian *poco* and Spanish *torero*, it is almost like English (ô), as in *horn*.

ü This symbol variously represents the sound of *u* in French *duc* and in German *grun* and can be approximated by rounding the lips as for (ō) and pronouncing (ē).

kh This symbol represents the voiceless velar or uvular fricative as in the ch of German *doch* or Scots English *loch*. It can be approximated by placing the tongue as for (k) but allowing the breath to escape in a stream, as in pronouncing (h).

H This symbol represents a sound similiar to the preceding but formed by friction against the forward part of the palate, as in German *ich*. It can be made by placing the tongue as for English (sh) but with the tip pointing downward.

n This symbol indicates that the vowel sound immediately preceding it is nasalized; that is, the nasal passage is left open so that the breath passes through both the mouth and nose in voicing the vowel, as in French *mon* (mōn). The letter *n* itself is not pronounced unless followed by a vowel.

r This symbol represents any of the various sounds used in languages other than English for the consonant *r*. It may represent the tongue-point trill or uvular trill of the *r* in French *reste* or *sur*, German *Reuter*, Italian *ricotta*, Russian *gorod,* etc.

' The apostrophe is used after final *l* and *r*, in certain French pronunciations, to indicate that they are voiceless after an unvoiced consonant as in lettre (let′r'). In Russian words the "soft sign" in Cyrillic spelling is indicated by (y'). The sound can be approximated by pronouncing an unvoiced (y) directly after the consonant involved, as in *Sevastopol* (se′väs tô′pel y').

LITERARY TERMS HANDBOOK

ALLEGORY A literary work with two or more levels of meaning—one literal level and one or more symbolic levels. The events, settings, objects, or characters in an allegory—the literal level—stand for ideas or qualities such as goodness, tyranny, salvation, and so on. Allegorical writing was common in the Middle Ages. Spenser revived the form in *The Faerie Queene*, and John Bunyan revived it yet again in *The Pilgrim's Progress*. Some modern novels, such as George Orwell's *Animal Farm*, can be read as allegories.

ALLITERATION The repetition of initial consonant sounds in accented syllables. Coleridge uses the alliteration of both *b* and *f* sounds in this line from the *Rime of the Ancient Mariner*:

> The fair *b*reeze *b*lew, the white *f*oam *f*lew.

Alliteration is often used, especially in poetry, to emphasize and to link words as well as to create pleasing, musical sounds.

See Anglo-Saxon Poetry.

ALLUSION A reference to a well-known person, place, event, literary work, or work of art.

ANAPEST *See* Meter.

ANGLO-SAXON POETRY The rhythmic poetry composed in the Old English language before A.D. 1100. It generally has four accented syllables and an indefinite number of unaccented syllables in each line. Each line is divided in half by a caesura, or pause, and the halves are linked by the alliteration of two or three of the accented syllables. The following translation from "Wulf and Eadwacer" shows the alliteration and caesuras used in Anglo-Saxon poetry:

> I waited for my Wulf // with far-Wandering yearnings,
>
> When it was rainy weather // and I sat weeping.

Anglo-Saxon poetry was sung or chanted to the accompaniment of a primitive harp; it was not written, but was passed down orally.

See Alliteration, Caesura, *and* Kenning.

ASSONANCE The repetition of vowel sounds in stressed syllables containing dissimilar consonant sounds. Robert Browning uses assonance in this line in "Andrea del Sarto":

> Ah, but man's reach should exceed his grasp

The long e sound is repeated in the words *reach* and *exceed*. The syllables containing these sounds are stressed, and contain different consonants: *r-ch* and *c-d*.

See Consonance.

BALLAD A song that tells a story, often dealing with adventure or romance, or a poem imitating such a song. Most ballads are divided into four- or six-line stanzas, are rhymed, use simple language, and depict dramatic action. Many ballads employ a repeated refrain. Some use incremental repetition, in which the refrain is varied slightly each time it appears.

Folk ballads are songs that originated among illiterate peoples and were passed from singer to singer by word of mouth. Literary ballads are written by more sophisticated writers and are not usually set to music. "Barbara Allan," on page 176, is a folk ballad. Samuel Taylor Coleridge's *The Rime of the Ancient Mariner*, on page 630, is a literary ballad.

BLANK VERSE Unrhymed poetry written in iambic pentameter (*see* Meter). Usually, occasional variations in rhythm are introduced in blank verse to create emphasis, variety, and naturalness of sound. Because blank verse sounds much like ordinary spoken English, it is often used in drama, as by Shakespeare, and in poetry. The following lines come from Wordsworth's blank-verse poem "Lines Composed a Few Miles Above Tintern Abbey," on page 616:

> For thǒu / árt with / mě hére / ŭpón / thě bánks
>
> Ŏf thís / făir rív / ĕr; thóu / mў déar / ĕst Fríend

See Meter.

CAESURA A natural pause, or break, in the middle of a line of poetry. In Anglo-Saxon poetry a caesura divides each four-stress line in half and thus is essential to the rhythm.

See Anglo-Saxon Poetry.

CARPE DIEM A Latin phrase meaning "seize the day," or "make the most of passing time." Many great literary works have been written with the carpe diem theme, presenting arguments for enjoying life in the present. One of the best-known poems on this theme is Robert Herrick's "To the Virgins, to Make Much of Time," on page 416.

CHARACTER A person (though not necessarily a human being) who takes part in the action of a literary work. Characters can be classified in different ways:

1. In terms of their significance: A character who plays an important role is called a *major character.* A character who does not play an important role is called a *minor character.*
2. In terms of their roles: A character who plays the central role in a story is called the *protagonist.* A character who opposes the protagonist is called the *antagonist.*
3. In terms of their complexity: A character with many aspects to his or her personality, possibly including internal conflicts, is called *round;* a character defined by only a few qualities is called *flat.*
4. In terms of the degree to which they change: A character who changes is called *dynamic*; a character who does not change is called *static.*

Character types that readers recognize easily, such as the hard-boiled detective or the wicked stepmother, are called *stereotypes,* or *stock characters.*

See Characterization.

CHARACTERIZATION The act of creating and developing a character. A writer uses *direct characterization* when he or she describes a character's traits explicitly. Writers also use *indirect characterization.* A character's traits can be revealed indirectly by means of what he or she says, thinks, or does; by means of a description of his or her appearance; or by means of the statements, thoughts, or actions of other characters.

See Character.

CLIMAX The high point of interest or suspense in a literary work. Often the climax is also the *crisis* in the plot, the point at which the protagonist changes his or her understanding or situation. Sometimes the climax coincides with the *resolution,* the point at which the central conflict is ended. In a story the climax generally occurs near the end. In a play the climax often falls close to the middle, marking the end of the rising action and the beginning of the falling action.

See Plot.

COMEDY A literary work, especially a play, that has a happy ending, often marked by a marriage. Comedies often show ordinary characters in conflict with their societies. These conflicts are resolved through misunderstandings, deceptions, and concealed identities, which result in the correction of moral faults or social wrongs. Types of comedy include *romantic comedy,* which involves problems among lovers, and the *comedy of manners,* which satirically challenges the social customs of a sophisticated society. Comedy is often contrasted with tragedy, in which the protagonist meets an unfortunate end.

See Drama *and* Tragedy.

CONCEIT An unusual and surprising comparison between two very different things. This special kind of metaphor or complicated analogy is often the basis for a whole poem. During the Elizabethan period, sonnets commonly included *Petrarchan conceits.* Petrarchan conceits make extravagant claims about the beloved's beauty or the speaker's suffering, making comparisons to divine beings, powerful natural forces, and objects that contain a given quality in the highest degree. Spenser uses a Petrarchan conceit when he claims in Sonnet 1 on page 209 that the "starry light" of his beloved's eyes will make his book happy when she reads it.

Seventeenth-century metaphysical poets were fond of elaborate, unusual, highly intellectual conceits. For example, in "Valediction: Forbidding Mourning," on page 398, John Donne compares two separated lovers to the two legs of a drawing compass, which are united even when they are apart.

See Metaphor.

CONFLICT A struggle between opposing forces. Sometimes this struggle is internal, or within a character. At other times the struggle is external, or between the character and some outside force. The outside force may be another character, nature, or some element of society such as a custom or a political institution. Often the conflict in a work combines several of these possibilities. For example, in Shakespeare's *Macbeth*, beginning on page 270, Macbeth struggles against the better parts of his own nature, against Banquo and Fleance, against fate, and against the forces led by Malcolm, Macduff, and Siward.

See Plot.

CONNOTATION Associations that a word calls to mind in addition to its dictionary meaning. For example, the words *home* and *domicile* have the same dictionary meaning. However, the first has positive connotations of warmth and security while the second does not.

See Denotation.

CONSONANCE The repetition of final consonant sounds in stressed syllables containing dissimilar vowel sounds. Samuel Taylor Coleridge uses consonance in these lines from *The Rime of the Ancient Mariner* on page 645:

a frightful fiend / Doth close behind him tread.

Fiend and the stressed syllable in *behind* have the same final consonant sounds but different vowel sounds.

See Assonance.

COUPLET A pair of rhyming lines written in the same meter. A *heroic couplet* is a rhymed pair of iambic pentameter lines. In a *closed couplet*, the meaning and grammar is completed within the two lines. These lines from Alexander Pope's *An Essay on Criticism* illustrate the closed heroic couplet:

True ease in writing comes from art, not chance,
As those move easiest who have learned to dance.

Sonnets written in the English, or Shakespearean, style usually end with heroic couplets.

See Sonnet.

DACTYL See Meter.

DENOTATION The objective meaning of a word; that to which the word refers, independent of other associations the word calls to mind. Dictionaries list the denotative meanings of words.

See Connotation.

DIALECT The form of a language spoken by people in a particular region or group. Dialects differ from one another in grammar, vocabulary, and pronunciation. Robert Burns used a Scots dialect in poems like "Auld Lang Syne":

Should auld acquaintance be forgot,
And never brought to min'?
Should auld acquaintance be forgot,
And days o' lang syne?

Dialect is sometimes used as a part of characterization, as in V. S. Naipul's "B. Wordsworth," on page 1118, in which B. Wordsworth's "educated" English contrasts with the island dialect of other characters.

DIALOGUE A conversation between characters. Writers use dialogue to reveal character, to present events, to add variety to narratives, and to interest readers. The dialogue in a story or play is usually set off by quotation marks and paragraphing. The dialogue in a play script generally follows the characters' names.

DIARY A personal record of daily events, usually written in prose. Most diaries are not written for publication; sometimes, however, interesting diaries or diaries by influential people do find their way into print. One example of a published diary is that of Samuel Pepys, a selection from which appears on page 462.

See Journal.

DICTION Word choice. A writer's diction can be a major determinant of his or her style. Diction can be described as formal or informal, abstract or concrete, plain or ornate, ordinary or technical.

See Style.

DIMETER See Meter.

DRAMA A story written to be performed by actors. It may consist of one or more large sections called acts, which are made up of any number of smaller sections called scenes.

Drama originated in the religious rituals and symbolic re-enactments of primitive peoples. The ancient Greeks developed drama into a sophisticated art and created such dramatic forms as tragedy and comedy.

The first dramas in England were the miracle plays and morality plays of the Middle Ages. Miracle plays told Biblical stories. Morality plays, such as *Everyman*, were allegories dealing with personified virtues and vices. The English Renaissance saw a great flowering of drama in England, culminating in the works of William Shakespeare, who wrote many of the world's greatest comedies, tragedies, histories, and romances. During the Neoclassical Age, English drama turned to witty, satirical comedies of manners that probed the virtues of upper-class society, such as Goldsmith's *She Stoops to Conquer* and Congreve's *The Way of the World*. The Romantic and Victorian ages were not great periods for drama in England. However, a few good verse plays were written, including Percy Bysshe Shelley's *The Cenci* and *Prometheus Unbound* and Robert Browning's *Pippa Passes*. The end of the nineteenth and beginning of the twentieth centuries saw a resurgence of the drama in England and throughout the English-speaking world. Great plays of the Modern Period include plays by Bernard Shaw, William Butler Yeats, John Millington Synge, Christopher Fry, T. S. Eliot, Harold Pinter, and Samuel Beckett.

DRAMATIC MONOLOGUE A poem in which an imaginary character speaks to a silent listener. During the monologue, the speaker reveals his or her personality, usually at a moment of crisis. Examples of dramatic monologues in this text are Robert Browning's "My Last Duchess," on page 766 and Alfred, Lord Tennyson's "Ulysses," on page 757.

ELEGY A solemn and formal lyric poem about death. It may mourn a particular person or reflect on a serious or tragic theme, such as the passing of youth, beauty, or a way of life. See Thomas Gray's "Elegy Written in a Country Churchyard," on page 520.

See Lyric Poem.

END-STOPPED LINE A line of poetry concluding with a break in the meter and in the meaning. This pause at the end of a line often is punctuated by a period, comma, dash, or semicolon. These lines from "Away, Melancholy," by Stevie Smith, are end-stopped:

Are not the trees green,
The earth as green?
Does not the wind blow,
Fire leap and the rivers flow?
Away melancholy.

See Run-on Line.

EPIC A long narrative poem about the adventures of gods or of a hero. *Beowulf,* on page 40, is a *folk epic,* one that was composed orally and passed from storyteller to storyteller. The ancient Greek epics attributed to Homer—the *Iliad* and the *Odyssey*—are also folk epics. The *Aeneid*, by the Roman poet Virgil, and *The Divine Comedy*, by the Italian poet Dante Alighieri, are examples of literary epics from the Classical and Medieval periods, respectively. John Milton's *Paradise Lost*, a selection from which appears on page 434, is also a literary epic. Milton's goal in creating *Paradise Lost* was to write a Christian epic similar in form and equal in value to the great epics of antiquity. Serious and wide-ranging, an epic presents an encyclopedic portrait of the culture in which it was produced.

Epic conventions are traditional characteristics of epic poems, including an opening statement of the theme; an appeal for supernatural help in telling the story (an invocation); a beginning *in medias res* (Latin: "in the middle of things"); long lists, or catalogs, of people and things; accounts of past events; and descriptive phrases such as kennings, Homeric similes, and Homeric epithets (a word or phrase that states a characteristic quality of a person or thing, such as "wide-wayed city" or "clear-voiced heralds" in the *Iliad*).

See Kenning.

EPIGRAM A brief, pointed statement in prose or in verse. The concluding couplet in an English sonnet may be epigrammatic. An essay may be written in an epigrammatic style, one characterized by use of epigrams.

EPIPHANY A term introduced by James Joyce to describe a moment of insight in which a character recognizes some truth. In Joyce's "Araby," beginning on page 1042, the boy's epiphany comes at the end of the story, when he recognizes the falsity of his dream.

EPITAPH An inscription written on a tomb or burial place. In literature, epitaphs include serious or humorous lines written as if intended for such use. An example is the epitaph in Thomas Gray's "Elegy Written in a Country Churchyard," on page 520.

EPITHET *See* Epic.

ESSAY A short, nonfiction work about a particular subject. Essays are of many types but may be classified by tone or style as formal or informal. Addison's breezy style and tongue-in-cheek descriptions make "The Aims of the Spectator," on page 550, an instance of an informal essay. An essay is often classed by its main purpose as descriptive, narrative, expository, argumentative, or persuasive. Jonson's "On Spring,"on page 546, mixes a variety of purposes, but is in the end an attempt to persuade us about one means to happiness.

EXTENDED METAPHOR *See* Metaphor.

FICTION Prose writing about imaginary characters and events. Some writers of fiction base their stories on real people and events, while others rely solely on their imaginations.

See Narration *and* Prose.

FIGURATIVE LANGUAGE Writing or speech not meant to be interpreted literally. Poets and other writers use figurative language to create vivid word pictures, to make their writing emotionally intense and concentrated, and to state their ideas in new and unusual ways that satisfy readers' imaginations.

Among the figures of speech making up figurative language are apostrophe, hyperbole, irony, metaphor, metonymy, oxymoron, paradox, personification, simile, and synecdoche.

See also the entries for individual figures of speech.

FOLKLORE The stories, legends, myths, ballads, riddles, sayings, and other traditional works produced orally by illiterate or semi-literate peoples. Folklore influences written literature in many ways. Examples include the beheading contest in *Sir Gawain and the Green Knight,* on page 142, and the fiancé in Elizabeth Bowen's "The Demon Lover," on page 887, a creation inspired by the ghostly lover in the old ballad of the same title.

FOOT See Meter.

FREE VERSE Poetry not written in a regular rhythmical pattern or meter. Instead of having metrical feet and lines, free verse has a rhythm that suits its meaning and that uses the sounds of spoken language in lines of different lengths. Free verse has been widely used in twentieth-century poetry. An example is "The Galloping Cat," by Steve Smith:

> All the same I
> Intend to go on being
> A cat that likes to
> Gallop about doing good
> So
> Now with my bald head I go,
> Chopping the untidy flowers down, to and fro.

GOTHIC A term used to describe literary works that make extensive use of primitive, medieval, wild, mysterious, or natural elements. Gothic novels, such as Mary Wollstonecraft Shelley's *Frankenstein*, a selection from which appears on page 579, are often set in gloomy castles where horrifying events take place.

HEPTAMETER See Meter.

HEXAMETER See Meter.

HYPERBOLE Deliberate exaggeration or overstatement. In "Song," John Donne uses this figure of speech:

> When thou sigh'st, thou sigh'st not wind,
> but sigh'st my soul away

However much pain his beloved's unhappiness causes him—and however intertwined their fates are by love—her sighs surely do not bring him near death. Such an excessive claim is an example of hyperbole.

See Figurative Language.

IAMBIC PENTAMETER See Meter.

IMAGE A word or phrase that appeals to one or more of the senses—sight, hearing, touch, taste, or smell. In a famous essay on Hamlet, T. S. Eliot explained how a group of images can be used as an "objective correlative." By this phrase Eliot meant that a complex emotional state can be suggested by images that are carefully chosen to evoke this state.

See Imagery.

IMAGERY The descriptive language used in literature to re-create sensory experiences. Imagery enriches writing by making it more vivid, setting a tone, suggesting emotions, and guiding a reader's reactions.

IRONY The general name given to literary techniques that involve surprising, interesting, or amusing contradictions. In *verbal irony,* words are used to suggest the opposite of their usual meaning. In *dramatic irony,* there is a contradiction between what a character thinks and what the reader or audience knows to be true. In *irony of situation,* an event occurs that directly contradicts expectations.

JOURNAL A daily autobiographical account of events and personal reactions. Daniel Defoe adapted this form to fictional use in his *A Journal of the Plague Year*, an excerpt from which appears on page 468.

See Diary.

KENNING A metaphorical phrase, used in Anglo-Saxon poetry to replace a concrete noun. In "The Seafarer," on page 15, the cuckoo is called "summer's sentinel" and the sea "the whale's home."

See Anglo-Saxon Poetry *and* Epic.

LEGEND A widely told story about the past that may or may not be based in fact. A legend often reflects a people's identity or cultural values, generally with more historical truth than in a myth. English legends include the stories of King Arthur (retold in the *Morte d'Arthur*, a selection from which appears on page 156) and Robin Hood.

See Myth.

LYRIC POEM A poem expressing the observations and feelings of a single speaker. Unlike a narrative poem, it presents an experience or a single effect, but it does not tell a full story. Types of lyrics include the elegy, the ode, and the sonnet. The lyric flourished in the songs and sonnets of the Renaissance, was revived by the Romantic poets, and remained the most common poetic form in the nineteenth and twentieth centuries. Alfred, Lord Tennyson; Robert Browning; Elizabeth Barrett Browning; Matthew Arnold; William Butler Yeats; W. H. Auden; Dylan Thomas; and Stevie Smith all wrote great lyric poems.

MEMENTO MORI A Latin phrase meaning "remember that you must die." Many literary works have dealt with the *memento mori* theme, including Marvell's "To His Coy Mistress," on page 414, and Gray's "Elegy Written in a Country Churchyard," on page 520.

METAPHOR A figure of speech in which one thing is spoken of as though it were something else, as in "death that long sleep." Through this identification of dissimilar things, a comparison is suggested or implied. Emily Brontë uses the following metaphor in her poem "Remembrance" on page 846: "my thoughts no longer hover . . . resting their wings." The metaphor suggests similarities between the speaker's thoughts and the wings of a bird.

An *extended metaphor* is developed at length and involves several points of comparison. A *mixed metaphor* occurs when two metaphors are jumbled together. For example, thorns and rain are illogically mixed in "The thorns of life rained down on him."

A *dead metaphor* is one that has been so overused that its original metaphorical impact has been lost. Examples of dead metaphors include "the foot of the bed" and "toe the line."

See Figurative Language.

METAPHYSICAL POETRY The term used to describe the works of such seventeenth-century English poets as Richard Crashaw, John Donne, George Herbert, Andrew Marvell, Thomas Traherne, and Henry Vaughan. The term was first used by Samuel Johnson in an attack on writers who fill their works with far-fetched conceits and who make poetry a vehicle for displays of learning. Characteristic features of metaphysical poetry include intellectual playfulness, argument, paradoxes, irony, elaborate and unusual conceits, incongruity, and the rhythms of ordinary speech. Examples of metaphysical poems in this text include Donne's "Song," on page 396, and Marvell's "To His Coy Mistress," on page 414.

METER The rhythmical pattern of a poem. This pattern is determined by the number and types of stresses, or beats, in each line. To describe the meter of a poem, you must scan its lines. Scanning involves marking the stressed and unstressed syllables, as follows:

> I ween / that, when / the grave's / dark wall
> Did first / her form / retain,
> They thought / their hearts / could ne'er / recall
> The light / of joy / again.
> —Emily Brontë, "Song"

As you can see, each stressed syllable is marked with a slanted line (´) and each unstressed syllable with a horseshoe symbol (˘). The stresses are then divided by vertical lines into groups called feet. The following types of feet are common in English poetry:

1. *Iamb:* a foot with one unstressed syllable followed by one stressed syllable, as in the word "afraid"
2. *Trochee:* a foot with one stressed syllable followed by one unstressed syllable, as in the word "heather"
3. *Anapest:* a foot with two unstressed syllables followed by one stressed syllable, as in the word "disembark"
4. *Dactyl:* a foot with one stressed syllable followed by two unstressed syllables, as in the word "solitude"
5. *Spondee:* a foot with two stressed syllables, as in the word "workday"
6. *Pyrrhic:* a foot with two unstressed syllables, as in the last foot of the word "unspeak / ably"
7. *Amphibrach:* a foot with an unstressed syllable, one stressed syllable, and another unstressed syllable, as in the word "another"
8. *Amphimacer:* a foot with a stressed syllable, one unstressed syllable, and another stressed syllable, as in "up and down"

A line of poetry is described as *iambic, trochaic, anapestic,* or *dactylic* according to what kind of foot appears most often in the line.

Lines are also described in terms of the number of feet that occur in them, as follows:

1. *Monometer:* verse written in one-foot lines:

> Sound the Flute!
> Now it's mute.
> Birds delight
> Day and Night.
> —William Blake, "Spring"

2. *Dimeter:* verse written in two-foot lines:

> O Rose / thou art sick.
> The invis / ible worm.
> That flies / in the night
> In the how / ling storm:
> Has found / out thy bed
> Of crim / son joy:
> And his dark / secret love
> Does thy life / destroy.
> —William Blake, "The Sick Rose"

3. *Trimeter:* verse written in three-foot lines:

Ĭ wént / tŏ thĕ Gárd / ĕn ŏf Lóve
Ănd sáw / whăt Ĭ név / ĕr hăd séen:
Ă Cháp / ĕl wăs búilt ĭn thĕ mídst,
Whĕre Ĭ úsed / tŏ pláy / ŏn thĕ gréen.
—William Blake, "The Garden of Love"

4. *Tetrameter:* verse written in four-foot lines:

Ĭ wánd / ĕr thró' / ĕach chárt / ĕr'd stréet
Néar whĕre / thĕ chárt / ĕr'd Thámes / dŏes flów
Ănd márk / ĭn év / ĕry fáce / Ĭ méet
Márks ŏf / wéaknĕss, / márks ŏf / wóe.
—William Blake, "The Little Black Boy"

A six-foot line is called a hexameter. A line with seven feet is a heptameter.

A complete description of the meter of a line tells both how many feet there are in the line and what kind of foot is most common. Thus the stanza from Emily Brontë's poem, quoted at the beginning of this entry, would be described as being made up of alternating iambic tetrameter and iambic trimeter lines. Poetry that does not have a regular meter is called free verse.

See Free Verse.

METONYMY A figure of speech that substitutes something closely related for the thing actually meant. In the opening line of "The Lost Leader," Robert Browning says, "Just for a handful of silver he left us," using silver to refer to money in the form of a government grant.

See Figurative Language.

MIRACLE PLAY See Drama.

MOCK EPIC A poem about a trivial matter written in the style of a serious epic. The incongruity of style and subject matter produces comic effects. Alexander Pope's *The Rape of the Lock*, on page 488, is a mock epic.

See Epic.

MODERNISM An international movement in the arts of the early twentieth century. Modernists rejected old forms and experimented with the new, which often led to controversy. Literary modernists such as James Joyce, W. B. Yeats, and T. S. Eliot used images as symbols. They presented human experiences in fragments, rather than as a coherent whole, which led to new experiments in the forms of poetry and fiction. Often, Modernists took on trivial or shocking subject matter—subject matter not traditionally the focus of art.

MONOLOGUE A speech or performance given entirely by one person or by one character.

See Dramatic Monologue *and* Soliloquy.

MOOD *Atmosphere;* the feeling created in the reader by a literary work or passage. Mood may be suggested by the writer's choice of words, by events in the work, or by the physical setting. Nadine Gordimer begins "The Train from Rhodesia," on page 1128, with a mood-evoking description of the brick, mud, and tin buildings at the hot, sandy train station. Everyone there awaits the train, the only relief in this inactive and restricted environment.

See Setting *and* Tone.

MORALITY PLAY See Drama.

MYTH A fictional tale, originally with religious significance, that explains the actions of gods or heroes, the causes of natural phenomena or both. Allusions to characters and motifs from Greek, Roman, Norse, and Celtic myths are common in English literature. In addition, mythological stories are often retold or adapted.

See Legend.

NARRATION Writing that tells a story. The act of telling a story is also called narration. The *narrative,* or story, is told by a storyteller called the *narrator.* Narration is one of the major forms of discourse and appears in many guises. Biographies, autobiographies, journals, reports, novels, short stories, plays, narrative poems, anecdotes, fables, parables, myths, legends, folk tales, ballads, and epic poems are all narratives, or types of narration.

See Point of View.

NARRATIVE POEM A poem that tells a story in verse. Three traditional types of narrative poems include ballads, such as "Barbara Allan," on page 176; epics, such as *Beowulf,* on page 40; and metrical romances, such as *Sir Gawain and the Green Knight*, on page 142. Other narrative poems in this text include the selection from Milton's *Paradise Lost*, on page 434; Coleridge's *The Rime of the Ancient Mariner* on page 630; and Tennyson's "The Lady of Shalott," on page 752.

NATURALISM A literary movement among writers at the end of the nineteenth century and during the early decades of the twentieth century. The Naturalists depicted life in its grimmer details and tended to view people as hopeless victims of immutable natural laws.

See Realism.

NEOCLASSICISM A literary movement of the Restoration and the eighteenth century in which writers turned to classical Greek and Roman literary models and standards. Like the ancients, Neoclassicists, such as Alexander Pope, stressed order, harmony, restraint, and the ideal. Much Neoclassical literature dealt with themes related to proper human conduct. The most popular literary forms of the day—essays, letters, early novels, epigrams, parodies, and satires—reflected this emphasis on society as a subject. Just as the Neoclassicists rejected the individualism and extravagance of the Renaissance in favor of classical restraint, so the nineteenth-century Romantics rejected Neoclassicism in favor of imagination, emotion, and the individual.

See Romanticism.

NOVEL An extended work of fiction. A novel often has a complicated plot, many major and minor characters, a unifying theme, and several settings. Novels can be grouped in many ways based on the historical periods in which they are written (such as Romantic or Victorian), on the subjects and themes that they treat (such as Gothic or regional) on the techniques used in them (such as stream-of-consciousness), or on their debts to literary movements (such as Naturalism or Realism). Among early novels were Samuel Richardson's works *Pamela* and *Clarissa*, and Henry Fielding's *Tom Jones*. Other classic English novels include Jane Austen's *Pride and Prejudice*, Sir Walter Scott's *Waverley*, Charles Dickens's *David Copperfield*, and George Eliot's *The Mill on the Floss*. Major twentieth-century novelists include James Joyce, Virginia Woolf, D. H. Lawrence, Henry James, Graham Greene, and Patrick White. A *novella,* for example, Joseph Conrad's *Heart of Darkness*, is not as long as a novel but is longer than a short story.

OBJECTIVE CORRELATIVE *See* Image.

OCTAVE *See* Stanza.

ODE A long, formal lyric poem with a serious theme. It may have a traditional structure with three alternating stanza patterns called the *strophe,* the *antistrophe,* and the *epode.* An ode may be written for a private occasion, as was John Keats's "Ode to a Nightingale" on page 686, or it may be prepared for a public ceremony. Odes often honor people, commemorate events, or respond to natural scenes.

See Lyric Poem.

ONOMATOPOEIA The use of words that imitate sounds. Examples of such words are *buzz, hiss, murmur,* and *rustle*. Seamus Heaney uses onomatopoeia in "Churning Day" to suggest the sounds of making butter:

> My mother took first turn, set up rhythms
> that slugged and thumped for hours. Arms
> ached.
> Hands blistered. Cheeks and clothes were
> splattered
> with flabbymilk.

Onomatopoeia is used to create musical effects and to reinforce meaning.

ORAL TRADITION A body of songs, stories, and poems, preserved by being passed from generation to generation by word of mouth. Among the many materials composed or preserved through oral tradition in Great Britain are *Beowulf*, on page 40, and the folk ballads on pages 170–176. In his *Morte d'Arthur*, a selection from which appears beginning on page 156, Sir Thomas Malory drew on written French sources and on Arthurian legends from the oral tradition. Shakespeare drew on materials from the oral tradition to create the sprites and fairies of *A Midsummer Night's Dream*, and the witches of *Macbeth*, on page 270. Folk epics, ballads, myths, legends, folk tales, folk songs, proverbs, nursery rhymes—all such products of the oral tradition were originally spoken or sung rather than written down.

See Ballad, Folklore, Legend, *and* Myth.

OXYMORON A figure of speech that fuses two contradictory or opposing ideas. An oxymoron, such as "freezing fire" or "happy grief," thus suggests a paradox in just a few words. In Book I of *Paradise Lost*, which begins on page 434, Milton uses the oxymoron "darkness visible" to describe the pit into which Satan and the other rebellious angels have been thrown.

See Figurative Language *and* Paradox.

PARABLE A short, simple story from which a moral or religious lesson can be drawn. The most famous parables are those in the New Testament, an example of which appears on page 248.

PARADOX A statement that seems to be contradictory but that actually presents a truth. In "Love's Growth," John Donne presents the following paradox:

> Methinks I lied all winter, when I swore
> My love was infinite, if spring make it more.

Because a paradox is surprising or even shocking, it draws the reader's attention to what is being said.

See Figurative Language *and* Oxymoron.

PASTORAL The quality of literary works that deal with the pleasures of a simple, rural life or with escape to a simpler place and time. The tradition of pastoral literature began in ancient Greece with the poetic idylls of Theocritus. Theocritus wrote about the simple lives of shepherds and goatherds. The Roman poet Virgil also wrote a famous collection of pastoral poems, the *Eclogues,* in imitation of Theocritus. Virgil's characters were also idealized rustics.

During the European Renaissance, pastoral writing became quite popular. One famous example of the genre is *The Countess of Pembroke's Arcadia*, by Sir Phillip Sidney. Another example is Christopher Marlowe's "The Passionate Shepherd to His Love," on page 217.

Today the term pastoral is commonly applied to any work in which a speaker longs to escape to simpler, rural life. By this definition both William Wordsworth's "The World Is Too Much with Us," on page 624, and William Butler Yeats's "The Lake Isle of Innisfree," on page 897, are pastoral poems.

PENTAMETER *See* Meter.

PERSONIFICATION A figure of speech in which a nonhuman subject is given human characteristics. Percy Bysshe Shelley uses personification in these lines from "To Night":

> Swiftly walk o'er the western wave,
> Spirit of the Night!
> Out of the misty eastern cave
> Where, all the long and lone daylight
> Thou wovest dreams of joy and fear,
> Which makes thee terrible and dear,
> Swift be thy flight!

Effective personification of things or ideas makes them vital, as if they were human.

See Figurative Language *and* Metaphor.

PLOT The sequence of events in a literary work. The two primary elements of any plot are characters and a conflict. Most plots can be analyzed into many or all of the following parts:

1. The *exposition* introduces the setting, the characters, and the basic situation.
2. The *inciting incident* introduces the central conflict.
3. During the *development,* the conflict runs its course and usually intensifies.
4. At the *climax,* the conflict reaches a high point of interest or suspense.
5. At the *resolution,* the conflict is ended.
6. The *denouement* ties up loose ends that remain after the resolution of the conflict.

There are many variations on the standard plot structure. Some stories begin *in medias res* ("in the middle of things"), after the inciting incident has already occurred. In some stories the expository material appears toward the middle, in flashbacks. In many stories there is no denouement. Occasionally, though not often, the conflict is left unresolved.

POETRY One of the three major types, or genres, of literature, the others being prose and drama. Poetry defies simple definition because there is no single characteristic that is found in all poems and not found in all non-poems.

Often poems are divided into lines and stanzas. Poems such as sonnets, odes, villanelles, and sestinas are governed by rules regarding the number of lines, the number and placement of stressed syllables in each line, and the rhyme scheme. In the case of villanelles and sestinas, the repetition of words at the ends of lines or of entire lines is required. (An example of a sestina, Seamus Heaney's "Two Lorries," appears on page 1004. An example of a villanelle, Dylan Thomas's "Do Not Go Gently into that Dark, Dark Night," appears on page 1094.) However, some poems are written in free verse. Most poems make use of highly concise, musical, and emotionally charged language. Many also use imagery, figurative language, and devices of sound like rhyme.

Types of poetry include *narrative poetry* (ballads, epics, and metrical romances), *dramatic poetry* (dramatic monologues and dramatic dialogues), *lyrics* (sonnets, odes, elegies, and love poems), and *concrete poetry* (a poem presented on the page in a shape that suggests its subject).

POINT OF VIEW The perspective, or vantage point, from which a story is told. If a character within the story tells the story, then it is told from the *first-person point of view*. If a voice from outside the story tells it, then the story is told from the *third-person point of view*. If the knowledge of the storyteller is limited to the internal states of one character, then the storyteller has a *limited point of view*. If the storyteller's knowledge extends to the internal states of all of the characters, then the storyteller has an *omniscient point of view*. The point of view from which a story is told determines what view of events will be presented.

PROSE The ordinary form of written language and one of the three major types of literature. Most writing that is not poetry, drama, or song is considered prose. Prose occurs in two major forms: fiction and nonfiction.

PSALM A song or hymn of praise, like those in the Book of Psalms in the Bible.

PYRRHIC See Meter.

QUATRAIN See Stanza.

REALISM The presentation in art of details from actual life. Another term for Realism, one that derives from Aristotle's *Poetics*, is *mimesis*, the Greek word for "imitation." During the last part of the nineteenth century and the first part of the twentieth, Realism enjoyed considerable popularity among writers in the English-speaking world. Novels often dealt with grim social realities and presented realistic portrayals of the psychological states of characters. The most common sort of stage setting during this period was one in which a room was presented as though one wall had been removed and the audience were peering inside.

REFRAIN A regularly repeated line or group of lines in a poem or song.

See Ballad.

REGIONALISM Regionalism is the tendency to confine one's writing to the presentation of materials drawn from a particular geographical area. For example, the Brontës wrote about Yorkshire, Thomas Hardy wrote about Dorset and Wessex, and D. H. Lawrence wrote about Nottinghamshire. A Regionalist writer presents the distinct culture of an area, including its speech, customs, landscape, and history.

RHYME The repetition of sounds at the ends of words. *End rhyme* occurs when rhyming words appear at the ends of lines. *Internal rhyme* occurs when rhyming words fall within a line. *Exact rhyme* is the use of identical rhyming sounds, as in *love* and *dove*. *Approximate*, or *slant rhyme*, is the use of sounds that are similar but not identical, as in *prove* and *glove*.

RHYME SCHEME A regular pattern of rhyming words in a poem or stanza. To indicate a rhyme scheme, assign each final sound in the poem or stanza a different letter. The following lines from Charlotte Brontë's "On the Death of Anne Brontë " have been marked:

There's little joy in life for me, *a*
And little terror in the grave; *b*
I've lived the parting hour to see *a*
Of one I would have died to save. *b*

The rhyme scheme of this stanza is *abab*.

RHYTHM See Meter.

ROMANCE A story that presents remote or imaginative incidents rather than ordinary realistic experience. The term romance was originally used to refer to medieval tales of the deeds and loves of noble knights and ladies. These early romances, or tales of chivalry and courtly love, are exemplified by *Sir Gawain and the Green Knight*, on page 142, and by Malory's *Morte d'Arthur*, on page 156. During the Renaissance in England, many writers, such as Edmund Spenser in his *The Faerie Queene*, drew heavily on the romance tradition. From the eighteenth century on, the term *romance* has been used to describe sentimental novels about love.

ROMANTICISM A literary and artistic movement of the eighteenth and nineteenth centuries. In reaction to Neoclassicism, the Romantics emphasized imagination, fancy, freedom, emotion, wildness, the beauty of the untamed natural world, the rights of the individual, the nobility of the common man, and the attractiveness of pastoral life. Important figures in the Romantic movement included William Wordsworth; Samuel Taylor Coleridge; Percy Bysshe Shelley; John Keats; and George Gordon, Lord Byron.

RUN-ON LINE A line that does not contain a pause or a stop at the end. A run-on line ends in the middle of a statement and of a grammatical unit, and the reader must read the next line to find the end of the statement and the completion of the grammatical unit. The beginning of Molly Holden's "The Double Nature of White" illustrates the run-on line:

White orchards are the earliest, stunning
the spirit resigned to winter's black, white thorn
sprays first the bare wet branches of the hedge.

See End-Stopped Line.

SATIRE Writing that ridicules or holds up to contempt the faults of individuals or of groups. A satirist may use a sympathetic tone or an angry, bitter tone. Some satire, like Jonathan Swift's *Gulliver's Travels*, an excerpt from which appears beginning on page 476, is written in prose. Other satire, such as Alexander Pope's *The Rape of the Lock*, on page 488, is written in poetry. Although a satire is often humorous, its purpose is not simply to make readers laugh but also to correct the flaws and shortcomings that it points out.

SCANSION The process of analyzing the metrical pattern of a poem.

See Meter.

SERMON A speech offering religious or moral instruction. Given by Jesus on a mountainside in Galilee, the Sermon on the Mount, on page 247, contains the basic teachings of Christianity.

SESTET *See* Stanza.

SETTING The time and place of the action of a literary work. A setting can serve many different purposes. It can provide a backdrop for the action. It can be the force that the protagonist struggles against and thus the source of the central conflict. It can also be used to create an atmosphere. In many works the setting symbolizes a point that the author wishes to emphasize.

See Mood *and* Symbol.

SHORT STORY A brief work of fiction. The short story resembles the longer novel but generally has a simpler plot and setting. In addition, a short story tends to reveal character at a crucial moment rather than to develop it through many incidents.

SIMILE A figure of speech that compares two apparently dissimilar things by using a key word such as *like* or *as*. Christina Rossetti uses simile in "Goblin Market" to describe two sisters:

> Like two blossoms on one stem,
> Like two flakes of new-fallen snow,
> Like two wands of ivory
> Tipped with gold for awful kings.

By comparing apparently dissimilar things, the writer of a simile surprises the reader into an appreciation of the hidden similarities of the things being compared.

See Figurative Language.

SOLILOQUY A long speech in a play or in a prose work made by a character who is alone and thus reveals his or her private thoughts and feelings to the audience or reader. William Shakespeare opens Act III of *Macbeth* with a soliloquy in which Banquo speculates on Macbeth's reaction to the witches' prophecy.

See Monologue.

SONNET A fourteen-line lyric poem with a single theme. Sonnets vary but are usually written in iambic pentameter, following one of two traditional patterns.

The *Petrarchan* or *Italian sonnet* is divided into two parts, an eight-line octave and a six-line sestet. The octave rhymes *abba abba*, while the sestet generally rhymes *cde cde* or uses some combination of *cd* rhymes. The two parts of this sonnet work together. The octave raises a question, states a problem, or presents a brief narrative, and the sestet answers the question, solves the problem, or comments on the narrative.

The *Shakespearean* or *English sonnet* has three four-line quatrains plus a concluding two-line couplet. The rhyme scheme of such a sonnet is usually *abab cdcd efef gg*. Each of the three quatrains usually explores a different variation of the main theme. Then the couplet presents a summarizing or concluding statement.

See Lyric Poem *and* Sonnet Sequence.

SONNET SEQUENCE A series or group of sonnets written to one person or on one theme. Although each sonnet can stand alone as a separate poem, the sequence lets the poet trace the development of a relationship or examine different aspects of a single subject. Examples of sonnet sequences are Sir Philip Sidney's *Astrophel and Stella*, Edmund Spenser's *Amoretti*, and Elizabeth Barrett Browning's *Sonnets from the Portuguese*.

See Sonnet.

SPEAKER The imaginary voice assumed by the writer of the poem; the character who "tells" the poem. This character is often not identified by name. The title of William Blake's poem "The Chimney Sweeper" on page 600 identifies the speaker, a child who gives an account of his life. The child tells us in the poem, for instance, that "When my mother died I was very young."

Although this speaker matter-of-factly accepts his life, the poem is ironic because the poet expects readers to have a different view of the child's situation. Recognizing the speaker and thinking about his or her characteristics are often central to interpreting a lyric poem.

See Point of View.

SPONDEE *See* Meter.

SPRUNG RHYTHM The term used by Gerard Manley Hopkins to describe the idiosyncratic meters of his poems. Discovering the underlying metrical pattern of a poem written in sprung rhythm is difficult. The rhythm is quite varied and contains such violations of traditional metrical rules as several strong stresses in a row or feet containing more than two weak stresses.

STANZA A group of lines in a poem, seen as a unit. Many poems are divided into stanzas that are separated by spaces. Stanzas often function like paragraphs in prose. Each stanza states and develops one main idea.

Stanzas are commonly named according to the number of lines found in them, as follows:

1. *Couplet:* a two-line stanza
2. *Tercet:* a three-line stanza
3. *Quatrain:* a four-line stanza
4. *Cinquain:* a five-line stanza
5. *Sestet:* a six-line stanza
6. *Heptastich:* a seven-line stanza
7. *Octave:* an eight-line stanza

See Sonnet.

STYLE A writer's typical way of writing. Determinants of a writer's style include formality, use of figurative language, use of rhythm, typical grammatical patterns, typical sentence lengths, and typical methods of organization. John Milton is noted for a grand, heroic style that contrasts with John Keats's rich, sensory style and with T. S. Eliot's allusive, ironic style.

See Diction.

SYMBOL A sign, word, phrase, image, or other object that stands for or represents something else. Thus a flag can symbolize a country, a spoken word can symbolize an object, a fine car can symbolize wealth, and so on. In literary criticism a distinction is often made between *traditional* or *conventional symbols*—ones that are part of our general cultural inheritance—and personal symbols—ones that are created by particular authors for use in particular works. For example, the lamb in William Blake's poem "The Lamb" on page 598 is a conventional symbol for peace, gentleness, and innocence, one that Blake inherited from the Bible and from the pastoral tradition. However, the tiger in Blake's poem "The Tyger" on page 599 is not a conventional or inherited symbol. Blake created this symbol specifically for this poem.

Conventional symbolism is often based on elements of nature. For example, youth is often symbolized by greenery or springtime, middle age by summer, and old age by autumn or winter. Conventional symbols are also borrowed from the spheres of religion and politics. For example, a cross may be a symbol of Christianity or the color red a symbol of Marxist ideology.

SYNECDOCHE A figure of speech in which a part of something is used to stand for the whole. In the preface to his long poem entitled *Milton,* William Blake includes these lines: "And did those feet in ancient time/ Walk upon England's mountains green?" The feet stand for the whole body, and "England's mountains green" stand for England generally.

See Figurative Language.

TETRAMETER *See* Meter.

THEME A central idea, concern, or purpose in a literary work. In an essay, the theme might be directly stated in what is known as a thesis statement. In a serious literary work, the theme is usually expressed indirectly rather than directly. A light work, one written strictly for entertainment, may not have a theme.

TONE The writer's attitude toward the readers and toward the subject. A writer's tone may be formal or informal, friendly or distant, personal or pompous. For example, John Keats's tone in his poem "On First Looking into Chapman's Homer," on page 684, is earnest and respectful, while James Boswell's tone in *The Life of Samuel Johnson*, which begins on page 510, is familiar and engaging.

See Mood.

TRAGEDY A type of drama or literature that shows the downfall or destruction of a noble or outstanding person, traditionally one who possesses a character weakness called a *tragic flaw.* Macbeth, for example, is a brave and noble figure led astray by ambition. The *tragic hero* is caught up in a sequence of events that inevitably results in disaster. Because the protagonist is neither a wicked villain nor an innocent victim, the audience reacts with mixed emotions—both pity and fear, according to the Greek philosopher Aristotle, who defined tragedy in the *Poetics.* The outcome of a tragedy, in which the protagonist is isolated from society, contrasts with the happy resolution of a comedy, in which the protagonist makes peace with society.

See Comedy *and* Drama.

TRIMETER *See* Meter.

TROCHEE *See* Meter.

WRITING PROCESS HANDBOOK

THE WRITING PROCESS

A polished piece of writing can seem to have been effortlessly created, but most good writing is the result of a process of writing, rethinking, and rewriting. The process can be roughly divided into stages: prewriting, drafting, revising, editing, proofreading, and publishing.

It's important to remember that the writing process is one that moves backward as well as forward. Even while you are moving forward in the creation of your composition, you may still return to a previous stage—to rethink or rewrite.

Following are stages of the writing process, with key points to address during each stage.

Prewriting

In this stage you plan out the work to be done. You prepare to write by exploring ideas, gathering information, and working out an organization. Following are the key steps to take at this stage:

Step 1: Analyze the writing situation. Start by clarifying your assignment, so that you know exactly what you are supposed to do.

- *Focus your topic.* If you need to, narrow the topic—the subject you are writing about—so that you can write about it fully in the space you have.
- *Know your purpose.* What is your goal for this paper? What do you want to accomplish? Your purpose will determine what you include in the paper.
- *Know your audience.* Knowing who will read your paper should influence what you say and how you say it.

Step 2: Gather ideas and information. You can do this in a number of ways:

- *Brainstorm.* Brainstorm, either alone or with others, to come up with possible ideas to use in your paper. Not all of the ideas that occur to you will be useful or suitable. You'll need to evaluate them later.
- *Consult other people about your subject.* Speaking informally with others may suggest an idea or approach you did not see at first.
- *Make a list of questions about your topic.* Then find the answers to your questions.
- *Do research.* Your topic may require information that you don't have, so you will need to go to other sources to find information. There are numerous ways to find information on a topic. See the Research Handbook, p. 1202, for suggestions.

The ideas and information you gather will become the content of your paper. Not all of the information you gather will be needed. As you develop and revise your paper, you will make further decisions about what to include and what to leave out.

Step 3: Organize. First, make a rough plan for presenting your information. Sort your ideas and notes; decide what goes with what, and which points are the most important. You can make an outline to show the order of ideas, or you can use some other organizing plan that works for you.

There are many ways in which you can organize and develop your material. Use a method that works for your topic. Following are common methods of organizing information in the development of a paper.

- *Chronological Order* You can present events in the order in which they occurred. This organization works best for presenting narrative material or explaining a process in a "how to."
- *Spatial Order* You can present details as they appear in space, for example, from left to right or from foreground to background. This order helps in descriptive writing.
- *Order of Importance* By presenting ideas from most to least important or from least to most important, you help your reader grasp your priorities.
- *Main Idea and Details* This logical organization works well to support an idea or opinion.

Drafting

When you draft, you put down your ideas on paper in rough form. Working from your prewriting notes and your outline or plan, you develop and present your ideas in sentences and paragraphs.

Don't worry about getting everything perfect at the drafting stage. Concentrate on getting your ideas down.

Draft in a way that works for you. Some writers work best by writing a quick draft—putting down all their ideas without stopping to evaluate them. Other writers prefer to develop each paragraph carefully and thoughtfully, making sure each main idea is supported by details.

As you are developing a draft, keep in mind your purpose and your audience. These determine what you say and how you say it.

Don't be afraid to change your original plans during drafting. Some of the best ideas are those that were not planned at the beginning. Write as many drafts as you like. You can draft over and over until you're happy with the results.

Most papers, regardless of the topic, are developed with an introduction, a body, and a conclusion. Here are tips for developing these parts.

Introduction In the introduction to a paper, you want to engage your readers' attention and let them know the purpose of your paper. You may use the following strategies in your introduction:

- State your main idea.
- Use an anecdote.
- Startle your readers.
- Take a stand.
- Quote someone.

Body of the paper In the body of your paper, you present your information and make your points. Your **organization** is an important factor in leading readers through your ideas. Your elaboration on your main ideas is also important. **Elaboration** is the development of ideas to make your written work precise and complete. You can use the following kinds of details to elaborate your main ideas:

- Facts and statistics
- Sensory details
- Explanation and definition
- Anecdotes
- Examples
- Quotations

Conclusion The ending of your paper will determine the final impression you leave with your readers. Your conclusion should give readers the sense that you have pulled everything together. Following are some effective ways to end your paper:

- Summarize and restate.
- State an opinion.
- Call for action.
- Ask a question.
- Tell an anecdote.

Revising

Once you have a draft, you can look at it critically or have others review it. This is the time to make changes—on many levels. Revising is the process of reworking what you have written to make it as good as it can be. You may change some details so that your ideas flow smoothly and are clearly supported. You may discover that some details don't work and you'll need to discard them. Two strategies may help you start the revising process:

1. Read your work aloud. This is an excellent way to catch any ideas or details that have been left out and to notice errors in logic.
2. Ask someone else to read your work. Choose someone who can point out its strengths as well as suggest how to improve it.

How do you know what to check for and what to change? Here is a checklist of major writing issues. If the answer to any of these questions is "no," then that is an area that needs revision.

1. Does the writing achieve your purpose?
2. Does the paper have unity? That is, does it have a single focus, with all details and information contributing to that focus?
3. Is the arrangement of information clear and logical?
4. Have you elaborated enough to give your audience sufficient information?

Editing

When you edit, look more closely at the language you have used to ensure that the way you express your ideas is most effective.

- Replace dull language with vivid, precise words.
- Cut or change redundant expressions (unnecessary repetition).
- Cut empty words and phrases (those that do not add anything to the writing).
- Check for passive voice. Usually active voice is more effective.
- Replace wordy expressions with shorter, more precise ones.

Proofreading

After you finish your final draft, you must proofread it, either on your own or with the help of a partner.

It's useful to have handy both a dictionary and a usage handbook to help you check for correctness. Here are the tasks in proofreading:

- Correct errors in grammar and usage.
- Correct errors in punctuation and capitalization.
- Correct errors in spelling.

Publishing

Now your paper is ready to be shared by others.

The Modes of Writing

Description

Description is writing that creates a vivid picture, draws readers into a scene, and makes readers feel as if they are meeting a character or experiencing an event firsthand. A description may stand on its own or be part of a longer work, such as a short story.

When you write a description, bring it to life with sensory details, which tell how your subject looks, smells, sounds, tastes, or feels. You'll want to choose your details carefully so that you create a single main impression of your subject. Avoid language and details that don't contribute to this main impression. Keep these guidelines in mind whenever you are assigned one of the following types of description:

Observation In an observation, you describe an event that you have witnessed firsthand, often over an extended period of time. You may focus on an aspect of daily life or on a scientific phenomenon, such as a storm or an eclipse.

Remembrance When you write a remembrance, you use vivid descriptive details to bring to life memorable people, places, or events from your past.

Reflective Essay A reflective essay is more than just a description of personal experiences or pivotal events from your life; it also describes your thoughts and feelings about the significance of those events.

Character Profile In a character profile, you capture a person's appearance and personality traits and reveal information about his or her life. Your subject may be a real person or a fictional character.

Travel Brochure Present details about culture, architecture, food, and scenery to describe a vacation destination in a way that appeals to potential visitors.

Narration

Whenever writers tell any type of story, they are using **narration**. While there are many kinds of narration, most narratives share certain elements—characters, a setting, a sequence of events (or plot, in fiction), and, often, a theme. You might be asked to try your hand at one of these types of narration:

Personal Narrative A personal narrative is a true story about a memorable experience or period in your life. In a personal narrative, your feelings about events shape the way you tell the story—even the way you describe people and places.

Historical Narrative A historical narrative recounts an event or series of events from the past. It may be partially fictional, as when a writer creates a character who witnesses the actions of real historical characters from up close. In your historical narrative, you draw on research to create accurate settings and authentic characters from the time.

Firsthand Biography A firsthand biography tells about the life (or a period in the life) of someone whom you know personally. Use your close relationship with the person to help you include insights not found in biographies based solely on research.

Short Story Short stories are brief fictional, or made-up, narratives in which a main character faces a conflict that is resolved by the end of the story. In planning a short story, you focus on developing the plot, the setting, and the characters. You must also decide on a point of view: Will your story be told by a character who participates in the action, or by someone who describes the action as an outside observer?

Exposition

Exposition is writing that informs or explains. The information you include in expository writing is factual or (when you're expressing an opinion) based on fact.

Your expository writing should reflect a well-thought-out organization—one that includes a clear introduction, body, and conclusion and is appropriate for the type of exposition you are writing. Here are some types of exposition you may be asked to write:

Cause-and-Effect Essay In a cause-and-effect essay, you consider the reasons something did happen or might happen. You may examine several causes of a single effect or several effects of a single cause.

Comparison-and-Contrast Essay When you write a comparison-and-contrast essay, you consider the similarities and differences between two or more subjects. You may organize your essay point by point—moving from one aspect of your subjects to the next—or subject by subject—discussing the qualities of one subject first, then the qualities of the next subject.

Problem-and-Solution Essay In a problem-and-solution essay, you identify a conflict or problem and offer a resolution. Begin by clearly stating the problem, then present a reasoned path to a solution.

How-To Essay A how-to essay provides explicit instructions for accomplishing a specific task. To aid readers, provide background (such as a list of materials) at the beginning of your piece, then break down the task into smaller logical steps. Use diagrams, photographs, and other visual aids where needed for clarity.

Consumer Report A consumer report presents up-to-date information and relevant statistical data about one or more products in a given category. You might also rate the product or products you profile, and discuss the advantages or disadvantages of each.

Persuasion

Persuasion is writing or speaking that attempts to convince people to agree with a position or take a desired action. When used effectively, persuasive writing has the power to change people's lives. As a reader and a writer, you will find yourself engaged in many forms of persuasion. Here are a few of them:

Persuasive Essay In writing a persuasive essay, you build an argument, supporting your opinions with a variety of evidence: facts, statistics, examples, statements from experts. You also anticipate and develop counter-arguments to opposing opinions.

Advertisement Advertisements are probably the most common type of persuasion. When you write an advertisement, you present information in an appealing way to make the product or service seem desirable.

Position Paper In a position paper, you try to persuade readers to accept your views on a controversial issue. Most often, your audience will consist of people who have some power to shape policy related to the issue. Your views in a position paper should be supported with evidence.

Persuasive Speech A persuasive speech is a piece of persuasion that you present orally instead of in writing. As a persuasive speaker, you use a variety of techniques, such as repetition of key points, to capture your audience's interest and to add force to your argument.

Editorial An editorial expresses an opinion or position on a current issue or concern. When you write an editorial, you state and then defend your opinion with logical reasons, facts, examples, and other details.

Research Writing

Writers often use outside research to gather information and explore subjects of interest. The product of that research is called **research writing**. In connection with your reading, you may occasionally be assigned one of the following types of research writing:

Research Paper A research paper uses information gathered from a variety of outside sources to explore a topic. In your research paper, you will usually include an introduction, in which you state your thesis, or main point; a body, in which you present support for the thesis; and a conclusion that summarizes, or restates, your main points. You should credit the sources of information, using footnotes or other types of citation, and include a bibliography, or general list of sources, at the end.

Multimedia Presentation In preparing a multimedia presentation, you will gather and organize information in a variety of media, or means of communication. You may present your information using written materials, slides, videos, audio cassettes, sound effects, art, photographs, models, charts, and diagrams.

Annotated Bibliography An annotated bibliography is a list of materials about a certain topic. For each entry, you must provide source information (title, author, date of publication, etc.), as well as a summary of the material that includes your personal review or comments.

Statistical Report A statistical report uses numbers to support a thesis, or main idea. Before drafting your report, you must first interpret and draw conclusions from the numerical data you've gathered. Then present and support your findings in the report.

Creative Writing

Creative writing blends imagination, ideas, and emotions, and allows you to present your own unique view of the world. Poems, plays, short stories, dramas, and even some cartoons are examples of creative writing. Many are found in this anthology; use them as an inspiration to produce your own creative works, such as the following:

Poem In a poem, you use sensory images, figurative language, and sound devices to communicate ideas, tell a story, describe feelings, or create a mood. Using exact and highly charged language will help you convey meaning and create vivid images for your readers.

Drama When you write a drama or a dramatic scene, you are writing a story that is intended to be performed. Since a drama consists largely of the words and actions of the characters, be sure to write dialogue that clearly shows the characters' personalities, thoughts, and emotions, and stage directions that convey your ideas about sets, props, sound effects, and the speaking style and movements of the characters.

Monologue A monologue is a speech delivered by a single character. You may create a monologue within the context of a longer drama, or as a work to be read or performed in its own right.

Video Script A video script or screenplay is a drama written for television, film, or video production. In addition to dialogue and stage directions, you must also include detailed stage and camera directions in your video script. These instructions indicate the specific actions or effects necessary to telling the story clearly.

Imitation of an Author's Style In this type of creative writing, you take the recognizable elements of an author's style and use them to create your own piece of writing. You may write your imitation in a true attempt to replicate a writer's style, or in the spirit of a humorous parody.

Response to Literature

In a **response to literature**, you express your thoughts and feelings about a work and often, in so doing, gain a better understanding of what the work is all about. Your response to literature can take many forms—oral or written, formal or informal. During the course of your reading, you may be asked to respond to a work of literature in one of these forms:

Critical Review In a critical review of a literary work, you discuss various elements in the work and offer opinions about them. You may also give a summary of the work and a recommendation to readers.

Comparative Analysis of Two Literary Works A comparative analysis shows the similarities and differences between several elements—such as characters and plot—of two literary works. You might compare the works on a point-by-point basis, or analyze one work before moving on to the next. Use quotations and specific details from the works to support your points.

Response to a Short Story In your response to a short story, you present your reactions to elements of the story—such as the setting, a particular character, or a plot twist—that made a strong impression on you. Include supporting quotations from the story, as well as a brief summary and personal evaluation of the work.

Literary Analysis In a literary analysis, you take a critical look at various important elements in the work. You then attempt to explain how the author has used those elements and how they work together to convey the author's message.

Parody A parody is a piece imitating the style of another work in a humorous or satirical manner. You can often get a good start on a parody by applying an author's serious style to an inappropriate subject.

Practical and Technical Writing

Practical writing is fact-based writing that people do in the workplace or in their day-to-day lives. Business letters, memos, school forms, and job applications are examples of practical writing. **Technical writing,** which is also based on facts, explains procedures, provides instructions, or presents specialized information. You encounter technical writing every time you read a manual or a set of instructions.

In the following descriptions, you'll find tips for tackling several types of practical and technical writing.

Résumé A résumé is a written summary of your educational background, work experience, and job qualifications presented in a concise, consistent format. Keep your descriptions brief and to-the-point. A résumé should be limited to one page. Each section should be appropriately labeled. Include a centered heading giving your name, address, and phone number.

Cover and Follow-up Letters Accompany a résumé with a cover letter in which you introduce yourself and briefly explain your qualifications for the position. It's also a good idea to send a brief thank-you letter to follow up an interview. Use proper business letter format for both types of correspondence.

College-Application Essay College applications usually ask for an essay. The question can require a descriptive, narrative, or expository approach. Often, these essays give you the chance to describe an experience that had a profound effect on who you are. Since the point of such essays is to give the college admissions staff a little insight into who you are, make sure that your introduction captures their attention and that your conclusion is memorable. Focus on a subject that is of genuine interest to you. Your own enthusiasm or concern for your subject will help you find words your readers will remember.

Test Essay Good organization is the key to writing an effective essay under test conditions. Adhering to an organizational plan will help you create a coherent essay, even under tight time restrictions. Your introduction should include a thesis statement, a one-sentence summary of your response to the test essay question. Make sure that each paragraph in the body of the essay supports this main idea, and conclude with a restatement of the thesis and a summary of your main points.

Grammar and Mechanics Handbook

Summary of Grammar

Nouns A **noun** names a person, place, or thing. A **common noun** such as *country*, names any one of a class of people, places, or things. A **proper noun,** such as *Great Britain*, names a specific person, place, or thing.

Pronouns **Pronouns** are words that stand for nouns or for words that take the place of nouns. **Personal pronouns** refer to the person speaking; the person spoken to; or the person, place, or thing spoken about.

	Singular	**Plural**
First Person	I, me, my, mine	we, us, our, ours
Second Person	you, your, yours	you, your, yours
Third Person	he, him, his, she, her, hers, it, its	they, them, their, theirs

A **reflexive pronoun** ends in *-self* or *-selves* and names the person or thing receiving an action, when that person or thing is the same as the one performing the action.

I pray you, school *yourself.* (Shakespeare, p. 334)

An **intensive pronoun** also ends in *-self* or *-selves.* It adds emphasis to a noun or pronoun.

The raven *himself* is hoarse
That croaks the fatal entrance of Duncan
Under my battlements. (Shakespeare, p. 285)

Demonstrative pronouns, such as *this, that, these,* and *those*, single out specific people, places, or things.

A **relative pronoun** begins a subordinate clause and connects it to another idea in the sentence.

Annoyed, she picked up the letter, *which* bore no stamp. (Bowen, p. 890)

Interrogative pronouns are used to begin questions.

Who casts not up his eye to the sun when it rises? (Donne, p. 394)

Indefinite pronouns refer to people, places, or things, often without specifying which ones.

Nought's had, *all's* spent,
Where our desire is got without content: . . .
(Shakespeare, p. 314)

Verbs A **verb** is a word or group of words that expresses an action, a condition, or the fact that something exists, while indicating the time of the action, condition, or fact. An **action verb** tells what action someone or something is performing. An action verb is **transitive** if it directs action toward someone or something named in the same sentence.

Gather ye rosebuds while ye may, . . . (Herrick, p. 416)

An action verb is **intransitive** if it does not direct action toward something or someone named in the same sentence.

The thought *served* as a challenge. (Woolf, p. 1056)

A **linking verb** expresses its subject's condition by connecting the subject with another word.

But after some time that order *was* more necessary, . . . (Defoe, p. 470)

Helping verbs are verbs added to another verb to make a single verb phrase. They indicate the time at which an action takes place, or whether it actually happens, could happen, or should happen.

Nothing but an extreme love of truth *could have* hindered me from concealing this part of my story. (Swift, p. 482)

Adjectives An **adjective** is a word used to describe what is named by a noun or pronoun or to give a noun or pronoun a more specific meaning. Adjectives answer these questions:

What kind? *purple* hat, *happy* face

Which one? *this* bowl, *those* cameras

How many? *three* cars, *several* dishes

How much? *less* attention, *enough* food

The **articles** *the, a,* and *an* are adjectives. *An* is used before a word beginning with a vowel sound. *This, that, these,* and *those* are used as **demonstrative adjectives** when they appear directly before a noun.

Perhaps he for whom *this* bell tolls may be so ill as that he knows not it tolls for him. . . . (Donne, p. 393)

A noun may sometimes be used as an adjective:

language lesson *chemistry* book

Adverbs An **adverb** is a word that modifies a verb, an adjective, or another adverb. Adverbs answer the questions *Where? When? How? To what extent?*

She will answer *soon.* [modifies verb *will answer*]

I was *extremely* sad. [modifies adjective *sad*]

You called *more* often than I. [modifies adverb *often*]

Prepositions A **preposition** is a word that relates a noun or pronoun that appears with it to another word in the sentence. It can indicate relations of time, place, causality, responsibility, and motivation. Prepositions are almost always followed by nouns or pronouns.

around the fire　　*for* us

in sight　　*till* sunrise

Conjunctions A conjunction is used to connect other words or groups of words.

Coordinating conjunctions connect similar kinds or groups of words:

bread *and* wine

brief *but* powerful

Correlative conjunctions are used in pairs to connect similar words or groups of words:

both Luis *and* Rosa

neither you *nor* I

Subordinating conjunctions indicate the connection between two ideas by placing one below the other in rank or importance:

The Count your master's known munificence
Is ample warrant *that* no one just pretense
Of mine for dowry will be disallowed; . . .
(Browning, p. 770)

Interjections An **interjection** is a word or phrase that expresses feeling or emotion and functions independently of a sentence.

Ah, love, let us be true
To one another! . . . . (Arnold, p. 793)

Sentences A **sentence** is a group of words with a subject and predicate expressing a complete thought.

Phrases A **phrase** is a group of words, without subject and verb, that functions as one part of speech. A **prepositional phrase** is a group of words that includes a preposition and a noun or pronoun.

before dawn　　*on account of* the rain

An **adjective phrase** is a prepositional phrase that modifies a noun or pronoun.

The space of sky above us was the color *of ever-changing violet*. . . . (Joyce, p. 1045)

An **adverb phrase** is a prepositional phrase that modifies a verb, an adjective, or an adverb.

Arsat came *through the doorway with noiseless steps* . . . (Conrad, p. 1037)

An **appositive phrase** is a noun or pronoun with modifiers, placed next to a noun or pronoun to add information and details.

How soon hath Time, *the subtle thief of youth,*
Stolen on his wing my three and twentieth year.
(Milton, p. 432)

A **participial phrase** is a participle that is modified by an adjective or adverb phrase or that has a complement (a group of words that completes the participle's meaning). The entire phrase acts as an adjective.

The boy gazed at his uncle from those big, hot, blue eyes, *set rather close together.* (Lawrence, p. 1071)

A **gerund** is a noun formed from the present participle of a verb (ending in *-ing*). A **gerund phrase** is a gerund with modifiers or a complement (words that complete its meaning), all acting together as a noun.

Neither can we call this *a begging of misery* or *a borrowing of misery* . . . (Donne, p. 394)

An **infinitive phrase** is an infinitive with modifiers, complements (words completing its meaning), or a subject, all acting together as a single part of speech.

. . . let baser things devise To die in dust . . .
(Spenser, p. 211)

Clauses A **clause** is a group of words with its own subject and verb. An **independent clause** can stand by itself as a complete sentence. A **subordinate clause** cannot stand by itself as a complete sentence.

Mr. Thomas Davies the actor, *who then kept a bookseller's shop in Russell Street, Covent Garden,* told me that Johnson was very much his friend . . . .
(Boswell, p. 510)

An **adjective clause** is a subordinate clause that modifies a noun or pronoun by telling what kind or which one.

. . . coffins were not to be had for the prodigious numbers *that fell in such a calamity as this.*
(Defoe, p. 471)

Subordinate adverb clauses modify verbs, adjectives, adverbs, or verbals by telling where, when, in what manner, to what extent, under what condition, or why.

As soon as I saw the dead man I sent an orderly to a friend's house nearby . . . (Orwell, p. 942)

Subordinate noun clauses act as nouns.

To confirm *what I have now said,* . . . I shall here insert a passage which will hardly obtain belief.
(Swift, p. 482)

Summary of Capitalization and Punctuation

Capitalization

Capitalize the first word in sentences, interjections, and complete questions. Also capitalize the first word in a quotation if the quotation is a complete sentence.

I asked, "What do you want?" (Naipul, p. 1120)

Capitalize all proper nouns and adjectives.

Trinidadian   Thames River

Capitalize titles showing family relationships when they refer to a specific person unless they are preceded by a possessive noun or pronoun.

Uncle Oscar   Mangan's sister

Capitalize the first word and all other key words in the titles of books, periodicals, poems, stories, plays, songs, and other works of art.

Frankenstein   "Shooting an Elephant"

Punctuation

End Marks Use a **period** to end a declarative sentence, imperative sentence, an indirect question, and most abbreviations.

This tale is true, and mine. ("The Seafarer," p. 15)

Let me not to the marriage of true minds
Admit impediments. (Shakespeare, p. 222)

She asked me was I going to Araby. (Joyce, p. 1046)

Mrs. Drover

Use a **question mark** to end an interrogative sentence or an incomplete question.

Sent he to Macduff? (Shakespeare, p. 325)

what ignorance of pain? (Shelley, p. 678)

Use an **exclamation mark** after an exclamatory sentence, a forceful imperative sentence, or an interjection expressing strong emotion.

"Hold off! unhand me, graybeard loon!" (Coleridge, p. 630)

Commas Use a **comma** before the conjunction to separate two independent clauses in a compound sentence.

My heart aches, and a drowsy numbness pains
My sense, . . . (Keats, p. 686)

Use commas to separate three or more words, phrases, or clauses in a series.

Daffodil came in first, Lancelot second, Mirza third. (Lawrence, p. 1072)

Use commas to separate adjectives unless they must stay in a specific order.

His *big, soft* eyes stared . . . (Conrad, p. 1036)

And *each slow* dusk a drawing-down of blinds. (Owen, p. 963)

Use a comma after an introductory word, phrase, or clause.

When I nodded, he laughed in a crooked way. (Naipul, p. 1124)

Use commas to set off nonessential expressions.

"Only you'd have to promise, *honor bright, uncle,* not to let it go beyond us three." (Lawrence, p. 1072)

Use commas with places, dates, and titles.

Coventry, England

September 1, 1939

Reginald Farrars, M. P.

Use commas after items in addresses, after the salutation in a personal letter, after the closing in all letters, and in numbers of more than three digits.

Hull Crescent, Dorchester

Dear Randolph,

Yours faithfully,

9,744

Use a comma to indicate words left out of parallel clauses, to set off a direct quotation, and to prevent a sentence from being misunderstood.

In Tennyson's poetry, I admire the music; in Browning's, the sentiments.

"Well—I suppose," she said slowly and bitterly, "it's because your father has no luck." (Lawrence, p. 1069)

Semicolons Use a **semicolon** to join independent clauses that are not already joined by a conjunction.

He had been a very charitable priest; in his will he had left all his money to institutions . . . . (Joyce, p. 1045)

Use semicolons to avoid confusion when independent clauses or items in a series already contain commas.

The Emperor concluded me to be drowned, and that the enemy's fleet was approaching in a hostile manner; but he was soon eased of his fears; for, the channel growing shallower every step I made, I came in a short time within hearing, . . . (Swift, p. 479)

Colons Use a **colon** before a list of items following an independent clause.

Notable Victorian poets include the following: Tennyson, Browning, Arnold, Housman, and Hopkins.

Use a colon to introduce a formal or lengthy quotation.

And on the pedestal these words appear:
"My name is Ozymandias, king of kings: . . ."
(Shelley, p. 670)

Use a colon to introduce an independent clause that summarizes or explains the sentence before it.

The third day of the illness was critical: they were waiting for a change. (Lawrence, p. 1076)

Quotation Marks A **direct quotation** represents a person's exact speech or thoughts and is enclosed within quotation marks.

"If I go," I said, "I will bring you something." (Joyce, p. 1046)

An **indirect quotation** reports only the general meaning of what a person said or thought and does not require quotation marks.

Mother said he never considered me. (Bowen, p. 892)

Always place a comma or a period inside the final quotation mark.

"We will each write a ghost story," said Lord Byron . . . (Shelley, p. 580)

Always place a question mark or an exclamation mark inside the final quotation mark if the end mark is part of the quotation; if it is not part of the quotation, place it outside the final quotation mark.

The man said to me, "Sonny, may I come inside your yard?" (Naipul, p. 1120)

Use single quotation marks for a quotation within a quotation.

"Lying all day on his pillows, . . . and then he says he does not want to live 'like this,'" Rakesh was heard to say . . . . (Desai, p. 1154)

Italicize the titles of long written works, movies, television and radio shows, lengthy works of music, paintings, and sculptures. Also italicize foreign words not yet accepted into English and words you wish to stress. Underline such titles and words.

Howards End *60 Minutes*
Guernica *déjà vu*

Use quotation marks around the titles of short written works, episodes in a series, songs, and titles of works mentioned as parts of collections.

"The Lagoon" "Boswell Meets Johnson"

Parentheses Use **parentheses** to set off asides and explanations only when the material is not essential or when it consists of one or more sentences.

My eyes were often full of tears (I could not tell why) and at times a flood from my heart seemed to pour itself out into my bosom. (Joyce, p. 1046)

Hyphens Use a **hyphen** with certain numbers, after certain prefixes, with two or more words used as one word, with a compound modifier and within a word when a combination of letters might otherwise be confusing.

twenty-nine re-create
pre-Romantic brother-in-law

Apostrophe Add an **apostrophe** and an *s* to show the possessive case of most singular nouns and of plural nouns that do not end in *-s* or *-es*.

Blake's poems the mice's whiskers

Add an apostrophe to show the possessive case of plural nouns ending in *-s* and *-es*.

the girls' songs the Ortizes' car

Use an apostrophe in a contraction to indicate the position of the missing letter or letters.

His English was so good, it *didn't* seem natural. . . . (Naipul, p. 1120)

Use an apostrophe and an -s to write the plurals of numbers, symbols, letters, and words used to name themselves.

the 1890's no *if*'s or *but*'s
five *a*'s

Glossary of Common Usage

among, between

Among is generally used with three or more items. *Between* is generally used with only two items.

> *Among* Chaucer's characters, my favorite has always been the Wife of Bath.
>
> The ballad "Get Up and Bar the Door" consists largely of a dialogue *between* a man and his wife.

amount, number

Amount refers to quantity or a unit, whereas *number* refers to individual items that can be counted. *Amount* generally appears with a singular noun, and *number* appears with a plural noun.

> The *amount* of attention that great writers have paid to the Faust legend is remarkable.
>
> A considerable *number* of important English writers have been fascinated by the legend of King Arthur.

as, because, like, as to

To avoid confusion, use *because* rather than *as* when you want to indicate cause and effect.

> *Because* the narrator of Joyce's "Araby" is infatuated with Mangan's sister, he cannot see that he is driven by vanity.

Do not use the preposition *like* to introduce a clause that requires the conjunction *as.*

> *As* we might expect in a story by Joseph Conrad, there are two narrators in "The Lagoon."

The use of *as to* for *about* is awkward and should be avoided.

bad, badly

Use the predicate adjective *bad* after linking verbs such as *feel, look,* and *seem.* Use *badly* when an adverb is required.

> In "My Last Duchess," the Duke of Ferrara does not seem to feel *bad* about the death of his wife.
>
> The announcement of Lady Macbeth's death *badly* unnerves Macbeth.

because of, due to

Use *due to* if it can logically replace the phrase *caused by.* In introductory phrases, however, *because of* is better usage than *due to.*

> The classical allusions in *Paradise Lost* may be *due to* the poet's ambition to imitate the epics of Homer and Virgil.
>
> *Because of* the expansion of the reading public, eighteenth-century writers became less dependent on wealthy patrons.

compare, contrast

The verb *compare* can involve both similarities and differences. The verb *contrast* always involves differences. Use *to* or *with* after compare. Use *with* after contrast.

> Denise's report compared Shelley's style in "To a Skylark" *with* that of Keats in "Ode to a Nightingale."
>
> In Conrad's "The Lagoon," Arsat's point of view in the narration of his "story within a story" contrasts *with* the more detached, third-person point of view that the author uses for the rest of the tale.

continual, continuous

Continual means "occurring again and again in succession," while *continuous* means "occurring without interruption".

> In "The Seafarer" the speaker describes *continual* hailstorms at sea.
>
> The white-hot fervor of "Ode to the West Wind" suggests that Shelley wrote the poem in a single *continuous* burst of inspiration.

different from, different than

The preferred usage is *different from.*

> In its simple, precise language, Housman's style is *different from* that of many other Victorian poets, including Tennyson and Hopkins.

farther, further

Use *farther* when you refer to distance. Use *further* when you mean "to a greater degree" or "additional."

> Although the sexton tries to persuade him to go no *farther,* Defoe is determined to enter the churchyard.
>
> Boswell *further* illustrates Johnson's conversation by quoting his opinions of Sheridan and Derrick.

fewer, less

Use *fewer* for things that can be counted. Use *less* for amounts or quantities that cannot be counted.

> Wordsworth uses *fewer* end-stopped lines than Pope does.
>
> At the beginning of Luke's parable, the prodigal son shows *less* respect than the older son for the father.

just, only

Only should appear directly before the word it modifies. *Just,* used as an adverb meaning "no more than," also belongs directly before the word it modifies.

> The form of the villanelle allows a poet to use *just* two rhymes.
>
> John Keats was *only* twenty-four when he wrote some of his greatest poems.

lay, lie

Lay is a transitive verb meaning "to set or put something down." Its principal parts are *lay, laying, laid, laid. Lie* is an intransitive verb meaning "to recline." Its principal parts are *lie, lying, lay, lain.*

> Coleridge implies that the mariner's reckless act of killing the albatross *lays* a curse on the crew.
>
> As Paul *lies* dead at the end of D. H. Lawrence's story, his Uncle Oscar sadly comments that the boy may be better off.

plurals that do not end in -s

The plurals of certain nouns from Greek and Latin are formed as they were in their original language. Words such as *criteria, media,* and *phenomena* are plural and should be treated as such. Each has its own distinctive singular form: *criterion, medium, phenomenon.*

> Are the electronic *media* of the twentieth century contributing to the death of literature?

raise, rise

Raise is a transitive verb that usually takes a direct object. *Rise* is intransitive and never takes a direct object.

> In "Musée des Beaux Arts," W. H. Auden *raises* the question of our insensitivity to suffering.
>
> In Tennyson's poem, when Lancelot passes, the Lady of Shallot *rises* from her loom and paces.

that, which, who

Use the relative pronoun *that* to refer to things or people. Use *which* only for things and *who* only for people. Use *that* when introducing a subordinate clause that singles out a particular thing or person,.

> The contemporary poet *that* I most enjoy reading is James Berry.

Which is usually used to introduce a subordinate clause that is not essential to identifying the thing or person in question:

> "Fern Hill," *which* reflects Dylan Thomas's brilliant ability to evoke emotional response, plays on the connotations of words.

Who can be used to introduce either essential or non-essential subordinate clauses:

> Two writers *who* helped redefine the essay are Addison and Steele. [essential]
>
> Addison and Steele, *who* were close friends for most of their lives, had very different personalities and careers. [non-essential]

when, where

Do not directly follow a linking verb with *when* or *where.* Also be careful not to use *where* when your context requires *that.*

> Evaluation is ~~when you make~~ *the process of making* a judgment about the quality or value of something.
>
> Sandy read ~~where~~ *that,* after the Brownings eloped to Italy, they spent most of their married life in Florence.

who, whom

Remember to use *who* only as a subject in clauses and sentences and *whom* only as an object.

> V. S. Naipul, who wrote "B. Wordsworth," has also written some well-received novels.
>
> V. S. Naipaul, whom many critics have praised as one of the best contemporary writers in English, was born and raised in Trinidad.

Speaking and Listening Handbook

Language is both spoken and written. The literature in this book is written, which is one form of communication, but most of your communication is probably oral. Oral communication involves both speaking and listening. Having strong speaking and listening skills benefits you both in your school life and your life outside of school.

Many of the assignments accompanying the literature in this textbook involve speaking and listening. This handbook identifies some of the terminology related to speaking and listening, both the oral communication you experience every day and the assignments you may do in conjunction with the literature in this book.

Oral Communication

You use many different kinds of oral communication each day. When you communicate with your friends, when you communicate with your teachers or your parents, when you interact with a cashier in a store, you are communicating orally. In addition to ordinary, everyday conversation, oral communication includes class discussions, speeches, interviews, presentations, debates. When you communicate face to face, you usually use more than your voice to get your message across. If you communicate by telephone, however, you must rely solely on your verbal skills.

The following terms will give you a better understanding of the many elements that are part of oral communication.

ARTICULATION is the process of forming sounds into words; it is the way in which the tongue, teeth, lower jaw, and soft palate are used to produce speech sounds.

BODY LANGUAGE refers to the use of facial expressions, eye contact, gestures, posture, and movement to communicate a feeling or idea.

CONNOTATION is the set of associations a word calls to mind. The connotations of the words you choose influence the message you send. For example, most people respond more favorably to being described as "slim" rather than as "skinny." The connotation of *slim* is more appealing than that of *skinny.*

EYE CONTACT is direct visual contact with another person's eyes.

FEEDBACK is the set of verbal and nonverbal reactions that indicate to a speaker that a message has been received and understood.

GESTURES are the movements made with arms, hands, face, and fingers to communicate.

INFLECTION refers to the rise and fall in the pitch of the voice in speaking; it is also called **intonation.**

LISTENING is understanding and interpreting sound in a meaningful way. You listen differently for different purposes.

Listening for key information: For example, when a teacher gives an assignment, or when someone gives you directions to a place, you listen for key information.

Listening for main points: In a classroom exchange of ideas or information, or while watching a television documentary, you listen for main points.

Listening critically: When you evaluate a performance, song, or a persuasive or political speech, you listen critically, questioning and judging the speaker's message.

NONVERBAL COMMUNICATION is communication without the use of words. People communicate nonverbally through gestures, facial expressions, posture, and body movements. Sign language is an entire language based on nonverbal communication.

PROJECTION is speaking in such a way that the voice carries clearly to an audience. It's important to project your voice when speaking in a large space like a classroom or auditorium.

VOCAL DELIVERY is the way in which you present a message. Your vocal delivery involves all of the following elements:

Volume: the loudness or quietness of your voice
Pitch: the high or low quality of your voice
Rate: the speed at which you speak; also called pace
Stress: the amount of emphasis placed on different syllables in a word or on different words in a sentence

All of these elements individually, and the way in which they are combined, contribute to the meaning of a spoken message.

Speaking and Listening Situations

The following are some of the many types of situations in which your speaking and listening skills apply.

AUDIENCE Your audience is the person or persons to whom you direct your message. An audience can be a group of people sitting in a classroom observing a performance or just one person to whom you address a comment. When preparing for any speaking situation, analyze your audience so you can tailor your message to their background, interests, and attitudes.

DEBATE A debate is a formal event in which participants prepare and present arguments on opposing sides of a question, stated as a **proposition**. The proposition must be controversial: It must concern an issue on which there are two serious positions.

The two sides in a debate are the *affirmative* (pro) and the *negative* (con). The affirmative side begins the debate. The opposing sides take turns presenting their arguments, and each side has an opportunity for *rebuttal,* in which they may challenge or question the other side's argument.

GROUP DISCUSSION results when three or more people meet to solve a common problem, arrive at a decision, or answer a question of mutual interest. Group discussion is one of the most widely used forms of interpersonal communication in modern society.

INTERVIEW An interview is a form of interaction in which one person, the interviewer, asks questions of another person, the interviewee. Interviews may take place for many purposes: to obtain information, to discover a person's suitability for a job or a college, or to inform the public of a notable person's opinions.

ORAL INTERPRETATION is the reading or speaking of a piece of literature aloud for an audience. Oral interpretation involves giving expression to the ideas, meaning, or even the structure of a piece of literature. The speaker interprets the piece through his or her vocal delivery. **Storytelling,** in which a speaker reads or tells a story, is a form of oral interpretation.

PANEL DISCUSSION is a group discussion on a topic of interest common to all members of a panel and to a listening audience. A panel is usually composed of four to six experts on a particular topic who are brought together to share information and opinions.

PANTOMIME is a nonverbal performance in which an idea or a story is communicated completely through the use of gesture and facial expressions.

PARLIAMENTARY PROCEDURE refers to the set of rules used to conduct a meeting in an orderly manner. Parliamentary procedure makes discussions at meetings more efficient and productive, and protects the rights of individuals attending the meeting.

All of the business conducted according to parliamentary procedure is handled through motions. **Motions** are proposals for action made by participants. For example, beside main motions that set forth the items of business that will be considered, a motion can be made to adjourn (end the meeting) or to amend (alter the wording of) another motion.

The following are the main principles of parliamentary procedure:

1. Only one item of business may be considered at a time.
2. Everyone has a right to express an opinion.
3. Every member of the group has the right to vote, and each vote is counted as equal.
4. The group follows the decision of the majority.

READERS THEATER is a dramatic reading of a piece of literature in which participants take parts from a story or play and read aloud in expressive voices. Sets and costumes are not part of the performance, and the participants remain seated as they deliver their lines.

ROLE PLAY To role play is to act out a part in a given situation, speaking, acting, and responding in the manner of a particular person or character.

SPEECH A speech is a talk or address given to an audience. A speech may be **impromptu**—delivered on the spur of the moment with no preparation—or formally prepared and delivered for a specific purpose or occasion.

- *Purposes:* The most common purposes of speeches are to persuade, to entertain, to explain, and to inform.
- *Occasions:* The following are common occasions for speeches.

  Introduction: Introducing a speaker or presenter at a meeting or assembly

  Presentation: Giving an award or acknowledging the contributions of someone

  Acceptance: Accepting an award or tribute

  Keynote: Giving an inspirational address at a large meeting or convention

  Commencement: Honoring the graduates of a school or university

RESEARCH HANDBOOK

Many of the assignments and activities in this literature book require you to find out more about your topic. Whenever you need ideas, details, or information, you must conduct research. You can find information by using library resources and computer resources, as well as by interviewing experts in a field.

Before you begin, create a research plan that lists the questions you want answered about your topic. Then decide which sources will best provide answers to those questions. When gathering information, it is important to use a variety of sources and not to rely on one main source of information. It is also important to document where you find different pieces of information you use so that you can cite those sources in your work.

The suggestions that follow can help you locate your sources.

Library Resources

Libraries contain many sources of information in both print and electronic form. You'll save time if you plan your research before actually going to the library. Make a list of the information you think you will need, and for each item list possible sources for the information. Here are some sources to consider:

NONFICTION BOOKS An excellent starting point for researching your topic, nonfiction books can provide either broad coverage or specific details, depending on the book. To find appropriate nonfiction books, use the library catalog, which may be in card files or in electronic form on computers. In either case, you can search by author, title, or subject; in a computer catalog, you can also search by key word. When you find the listing for a book you want, print it out or copy down the title, author, and call number. The call number, which also appears on the book's spine, will help you locate the book in the library.

NEWSPAPERS AND MAGAZINES Books are often not the best places for finding up-to-the-minute information. Instead, you might try newspapers and magazines. To find information about an event that occurred on a specific date, go directly to newspapers and magazines for that date. To find articles on a particular topic, use indexes like the *Readers' Guide to Periodical Literature*, which lists magazine articles under subject headings. For each article that you want, jot down the title, author (if given), page number or numbers, and the name and date of the magazine in which the article appears. If your library does not have the magazine you need, either as a separate issue or on microfilm, you may still be able to obtain photocopies of the article through an interlibrary loan.

REFERENCE WORKS The following important reference materials can also help you with your research.

- ***General encyclopedias*** have articles on thousands of topics and are a good starting point for your research, although they shouldn't be used as primary sources.
- ***Specialized encyclopedias*** contain articles in particular subject areas, such as science, music, or art.
- ***Biographical dictionaries and indexes*** contain brief articles on people and often suggest where to find more information.
- ***Almanacs*** provide statistics and data on current events and act as a calendar for the upcoming year.
- ***Atlases***, or books of maps, usually include geographical facts and may also include information like population and weather statistics.
- ***Indexes and bibliographies***, such as the *Readers' Guide to Periodical Literature*, tell you in what publications you can find specific information, articles, or shorter works (such as poems or essays).
- ***Vertical files*** (drawers in file cabinets) hold pamphlets, booklets, and government publications that often provide current information.

Computer Research

The Internet Use the Internet to get up-to-the-minute information on virtually any topic. The Internet provides access to a multitude of resource-rich sources such as news media, museums, colleges and universities, and government institutions. There are a number of indexes and directories organized by subject to help you locate information on the Internet, including Yahoo!, the World Wide Web Virtual Library, the Kids Web, and the Webcrawler. These indexes and directories will help you find direct links to information related to your topic.

Internet Sources and Addresses

- ***Yahoo! Directory*** allows you to do word searches or link directly to your topic by clicking on such subjects as the arts, computers, entertainment, or government.
  http://www.yahoo.com
- ***World Wide Web Virtual Library*** is a comprehensive and easy-to-use subject catalog that provides direct links to academic subjects in alphabetical order.
  http://celtic.stanford.edu/vlib/Overview.html
- ***Kids Web*** supplies links to reference materials, such as dictionaries, *Bartlett's Familiar Quotations*, a thesaurus, and a world fact book.
  http://www.npac.syr.edu/textbook/kidsweb/
- ***Webcrawler*** helps you to find links to information about your topic that are available on the Internet when you type in a concise term or key word.
  http://www.webcrawler.com

CD-ROM References

Other sources that you can access using a computer are available on CD-ROM. The Wilson Disk, Newsquest, the *Readers' Guide to Periodical Literature*, and many other useful indexes are available on CD-ROM, as are encyclopedias, almanacs, atlases, and other reference works. Check your library to see which are available.

Interviews as Research Sources

People who are experts in their field or who have experience or knowledge relevant to your topic are excellent sources for your research. If such people are available to you, the way to obtain information from them is through an interview. Follow these guidelines to make your interview successful and productive:

- Make an appointment at a time convenient to the person you want to interview, and arrange to meet in a place where he or she will feel comfortable talking freely.
- If necessary, do research in advance to help you prepare the questions you will ask.
- Before the interview, list the questions you will ask, wording them so that they encourage specific answers. Avoid questions that can be answered simply with *yes* or *no*.
- Make an audiotape or videotape of the interview if possible. If not, write down the answers as accurately as you can.
- Include the date of the interview at the top of your notes or on the tape.
- Follow up with a thank-you note or phone call to the person you interviewed.

Sources for a Multimedia Presentation

When preparing a multimedia presentation, keep in mind that you'll need to use some of your research findings to illustrate or support your main ideas when you actually give the presentation. Do research to find media support, such as visuals, CD's, and so on—in addition to those media you might create yourself. Here are some media that may be useful as both sources and illustrations:

- Musical recordings on audiocassette or compact disc (CD) (often available at libraries)
- Videos that you prepare yourself
- Fine art reproductions (often available at libraries and museums)
- Photographs that you or others have taken
- Computer presentations using slide shows, graphics, and so on
- Video or audiocassette recordings of interviews that you conduct.

Crediting Sources

Whatever form you use to present your research results, remember to credit your sources for any ideas you use that are not common knowledge and are not your own. In addition, be sure that you acknowledge passages or distinctive phrases that come from a source. In written work, credit others' ideas or words with footnotes, endnotes, or parenthetical notes.

Failure to credit sources properly is **plagiarism,** the presenting of someone else's words or ideas as your own. Plagiarism is a form of stealing. Words and ideas may not seem as tangible as physical property, but they are forms of intellectual property. As you know from your own experience, it takes hard work to formulate a new idea or to find just the right phrase to describe something. Acknowledge this work.

College and Career Handbook

BEYOND GRADUATION

Deciding what to do after high school is one of the most important decisions of your life. You probably have definite ideas about what you are interested in and whether you would like to pursue a college education or jump directly into the job market. The challenge you face is getting admitted to the right college or landing the right job. The following tips can help you prepare for life after high school.

Tips for the College-Bound

CHOOSING A COLLEGE

To create a list of schools to which to apply, narrow your choices step by step. You will find helpful information in guidebooks such as *Barron's, Lovejoy's,* and *Peterson's.* Make an appointment with your guidance counselor to match your interests and high school record with the most likely college choices. Draw up a list of schools, then start narrowing them down.

Step 1: Identify Your Options

- ***Be realistic.*** Focus on schools that are in the range of competitiveness—and expense—suited to you.

If you are in the top quarter of your high school class and have combined SAT scores of at least 1000 or ACT scores starting at 25, you have a good chance of being accepted at a very selective college. If your scores and standing are lower, you are better off focusing your application efforts on less selective schools.

- ***Identify a "safety" school.*** The college admissions process is affected by many factors, and schools turn down many qualified candidates. To ensure that you can start college when you plan to, apply to at least one less competitive school.

- ***Identify a "wish list" school.*** Even if your academic performance is not outstanding, you may have other assets that a highly competitive school finds valuable. Apply to a "wish list" school that you would enjoy attending if you were accepted.

Step 2: Identify Your Needs

- ***Special interests*** Not every college has the same academic strengths. If you think you will end up specializing in a particular field, look for schools with a strong department in that field.

- ***General experience*** Consider the kind of life a college can offer you. Will you be happier amid the bustle of a large university in a big city or the intimate atmosphere of a small college in a quiet town? Do you want to live in a dorm or off-campus? Keep your answers to these questions in mind as you narrow your list.

Step 3: Evaluate Your Choices

Once you have narrowed your list down to about half a dozen choices, write or call the admissions office of each school to request an application and catalogue. The catalogues, along with the college guidebooks you consult, will give you the information you need to evaluate your choices. In addition to general rankings of colleges, pay attention to the following:

- ***Facilities*** Consider the athletic facilities, computer labs, libraries, and other facilities at the school. What hours do they keep? How up-to-date are they?

- ***Special areas of study*** If you are interested in a special area of study, find out the size of the department in that area. What degrees do the teachers have? What courses are required to major in that area?

Step 4: Reality Check

After you have looked through the catalogues of promising schools, consider paying them a visit.

- ***Visit when school is in session.*** Pick up the school newspaper, look at the bulletin boards, talk to students in the cafeteria. Are there activities on campus in which you are interested? Do you think you will fit in with the other students? If there is a special subject you are interested in, speak to one of the professors teaching in that area and sit in on a class.

- ***Speak to alumni.*** Talk to alumni—graduates of the school—about their experiences. The school may be able to provide the names of alumni in your area.

APPLYING TO SCHOOLS

The College Application

There are usually two parts to a college application. The first includes basic questions about who you are, with special attention to your educational background and outside interests. Keep your answers to these questions accurate, specific, and clear.

The essay portion of the application often asks you to describe an experience that played an important role in shaping your character. To help your essay stay in the reader's mind, write from your heart—from what interests or excites you.

It's a good idea to make a photocopy of the blank application, and draft your answers on the photocopy. Save the original for your final draft.

For more tips, see the Real-World Reading Skills Workshop on "Reading a Job Application" on page 138 and the Writing Process Workshop on the College-Application Essay" on page 135.

Interviewing

An interview with a school representative is a good chance for you to learn more about the school, as well as to make a good impression. Expect questions about your in-school and extracurricular interests and activities, your strengths and weaknesses (both academic and personal), and what makes you a good candidate for admission.

Recommendations

Written recommendations are a required part of your application. Look to family friends, co-workers, and community leaders as well as teachers for recommendations. People are often happy to write on behalf of others. Indicate to your recommendation writers what qualities, interests, or accomplishments of yours you feel are worth emphasizing.

SUCCESS IN COLLEGE

Once you have chosen and been accepted by a college, you face a new challenge—surviving the next four years. The following two tips may help you orient yourself in your new life.

- ***Get the most out of your classes.*** Arrive to class on time, prepared to participate actively. Consistent lateness is a sign of disrespect, and participation is often weighed as part of your grade.

Getting the most out of class also means meeting with your instructors during their office hours or by appointment to clarify difficult concepts, to get project ideas approved, and to resolve any questions you may have about your grades.

- ***Manage your time.*** At college, you will have large amounts of time that you must manage for yourself. Maintain a weekly schedule. Note which activities in your routine cannot change, then plan study and social time around them.

Many college courses require long-term assignments. Keep a calendar on which you mark the due date for each paper or project. Begin researching your topic choices early on.

A schedule should not imprison you; rather, it should give your life a healthy rhythm. Leave enough time open to stay flexible. Successful scheduling will help you avoid long periods of little work followed by frantic "all-nighters"—an unnecessary source of stress.

Tips for a Career Search

You may decide that, after high school, you want to move directly into the job market. Your first step is to identify your skills and interests and try to match them to an appropriate job. For example, if you have excellent interpersonal skills, don't apply for a job that will keep you alone in an office doing paperwork.

FINDING WORK

- ***Check job listings.*** The "Help Wanted" section of a newspaper is a good place to start. If you want to move, call the papers in the area you are considering and ask if they will send you copies of their want ads. Some towns sponsor career centers that post information about jobs. You may want to find out more about training programs that are available for specific kinds of work, such as computer support or clerical jobs.

- ***Send out your résumé to companies in your field.*** Even if they have no job openings when they receive your résumé, businesses may keep it on file for a period of time and contact candidates when an opportunity does arise.

- ***Network.*** Many people report that they got their jobs by talking to a neighbor, a family friend, a person they caddied for on the golf course, a teacher, or a business associate of their mother's—a person who knew someone in the business.

Make a list of people you can contact. Call them and let them know that you are looking for a job of a particular sort. Ask if they know of anyone in that line of work, and if they would be willing to give you that person's name and number. When you call these new contacts, mention who gave you their name and explain your reason for calling. Even though you are a stranger, the person you call may be quite helpful.

THE RÉSUMÉ

Assembling a polished, professional résumé and cover letter is the most important part of your job search. The following tips can help:

- ***Limit your résumé to one page.*** Employers must review hundreds of résumés and will not have time to read lengthy documents.

- ***Format your résumé.*** Allow employers to find important facts easily. Use boldface, capitalization, bullets, underlining and other devices to highlight your résumé's organization. For professional effect, though, do not use different typefaces or sizes.

- ***Clearly indicate the contents.*** Your résumé should begin with a heading, centered in the middle of the top of the page, and should include your name, address, and phone number near the top. It should also include the following sections, each with an appropriate label:

Objective: In a single phrase, let your prospective employer know what position you are interested in.

Employment History: List jobs and the dates between which you held them. Include a description of the responsibilities that you held in each position, emphasizing those that would make you an excellent candidate for the new job.

Education: Include your educational history up to this point. List any special training you have received that would make you a desirable candidate for the position for which you are applying.

Skills and Talents; Clubs and Organizations: List any additional skills that may be helpful in the new job, such as computer knowledge or fluency in a language. Your membership in clubs and other organizations indicates social skills and an ability to work well with people.

For more tips, see the Writing Process Workshop on the "Job Portfolio," on page 730.

THE COVER LETTER

A cover letter, tailored to the specific job for which you are applying, should accompany each résumé you send out. It should be as brief as possible; the recipient can read the enclosed résumé for more details. If possible, find out who will be reviewing your résumé and address the letter to that person.

- ***Use a standard business letter form.*** The body of your letter may be divided as follows:

First paragraph: The letter should start by explaining how you came to apply for a job with that particular company. If you are answering an ad, refer to its place and date of appearance. If you are sending out résumés "cold," explain how the company came to your attention.

Second paragraph: The next paragraph should briefly and forcefully explain how your experience, qualities, and skills fit the employer's needs.

Third paragraph: In the third and last paragraph, thank the reader, note that you are available for an interview at his or her convenience, and mention that you look forward to a meeting.

For more tips, see the Writing Process Workshop on the "Job Portfolio," on page 730.

THE INTERVIEW

Once you get an appointment for an interview, prepare yourself with answers and questions for your interviewer.

- ***Practice answering questions.*** Your interviewer will ask about your work experience, skills and talents, strengths and weaknesses, and desire for the job. Practice answering such questions with a friend.

- ***List questions you want to ask.*** Asking questions based on your knowledge of the company shows your interest in the job.

- ***Dress appropriately.*** Arrive neatly groomed.

- ***Speak clearly, politely, grammatically, and loudly enough to be heard.*** If you are asked an unexpected question, relax and give yourself time to think.

After your interview, write your interviewer a follow-up letter mentioning that you enjoyed your conversation and thanking him or her for the opportunity.

For more tips, see the Speaking and Listening Workshop on "Handling a Job Interview," on page 734.

Index of Authors and Titles

INDEX OF SKILLS

LITERARY TERMS

READING STRATEGIES

GRAMMAR AND STYLE

VOCABULARY

CRITICAL THINKING AND VIEWING

WRITING

Writing Opportunities

Writing Skills

SPEAKING AND LISTENING

LIFE AND WORK SKILLS

BACKGROUND FOR UNDERSTANDING

PROJECTS

Index of Fine Art

ACKNOWLEDGMENTS (continued)

Carol Publishing Group
"The Lorelei" by Heinrich Heine from *The Poetry and Prose of Heinrich Heine,* edited by Frederic Ewen. Copyright © 1948, 1976 by The Citadel Press. Used by arrangement with Carol Publishing Group.

Cassell PLC
"Be Ye Men of Valor" (retitled Wartime Speech), BBC, London, May 19, 1940, from *Blood, Toil, Tears and Sweat: The Speeches of Winston Churchill,* edited and with an Introduction by David Cannadine. Speeches Copyright © 1989 by Winston Churchill, MP. All rights reserved.

Darhansoff & Verrill Literary Agency
"Everything Is Plundered" by Anna Akhmatova, from *Poems of Akhmatova,* selected, translated and introduced by Stanley Kunitz and Max Hayward. Copyright © 1967, 1968, 1972, 1973 by Stanley Kunitz and Max Hayward. Reprinted by permission of Darhansoff & Verrill Literary Agency.

Doubleday & Company, Inc.
"The Tyger" by William Blake from *The Poetry and Prose of William Blake,* edited by David V. Erdman, published by Doubleday & Company, Inc. "The Lagoon" from *Tales of Unrest* by Joseph Conrad (Doubleday, Page & Company). Reprinted by permission of Doubleday & Company, Inc. "Poverty's child" and "Clouds come from time to time" by Bashō, translated by Harold G. Henderson, from *An Introduction to Haiku* by Harold G. Henderson. Copyright © 1958 by Harold G. Henderson. Used by permission of Doubleday, a division of Bantam Doubleday Dell Publishing Group, Inc.

Dutton Signet, a division of Penguin Books USA Inc.
"The Book of Sand," from *The Book of Sand,* by Jorge Luis Borges, translated by Norman Thomas di Giovanni. Translation copyright © 1971, 1975, 1976, 1977 by Emece Editores, S.A., and Norman Thomas di Giovanni. From *Beowulf* by Burton Raffel, translator. Translation copyright © 1963 by Burton Raffel, Afterword © 1963 by New American Library. Used by permission of Dutton Signet, a division of Penguin Books USA Inc.

Faber and Faber Ltd.
"The Horses" from *New Selected Poems* by Ted Hughes from *Wodwo* Copyright © 1957, 1960 by Ted Hughes. "The Rain Horse" by Ted Hughes from Copyright © 1967. "Not Palaces" by Stephen Spender from *Collected Poems* 1928–1985. Copyright © 1986 by Stephen Spender.

Farrar, Straus & Giroux, Inc.
Excerpt from *Omeros* by Derek Walcott. Copyright © 1990 by Derek Walcott. Excerpt from "Midsummer" from *Collected Poems* 1948–1984 by Derek Walcott. Copyright © 1986 by Derek Walcott. Excerpt from *Gilgamesh: A New Rendering in English Verse* by David Ferry. Copyright © 1992 by David Ferry. Reprinted by permission of Farrar, Straus & Giroux, Inc.

Farrar, Straus & Giroux, Inc., and Faber and Faber, Ltd.
"The Explosion" from *Collected Poems* by Philip Larkin. Copyright © 1988, 1989 by the Estate of Philip Larkin. "An Arundel Tomb" from *Collected Poems* by Philip Larkin. Copyright © 1988, 1989 by the Estate of Philip Larkin. "Follower" from *Poems* 1965–1975 by Seamus Heaney. Copyright © 1980 by Seamus Heaney. Published in London in *Death of a Naturalist* by Seamus Heaney. "Two Lorries" from *The Spirit Level* by Seamus Heaney. Copyright © 1996 by Seamus Heaney. Reprinted by permission.

Angel Flores
"Eternity" by Arthur Rimbaud, translated by Francis Golffing, from *An Anthology of French Poetry From Nerval to Valéry in English Translation With French Originals,* edited by Angel Flores.

Fourth Estate Ltd.
"The Rights We Enjoy, the Duties We Owe" reprinted by permission of Fourth Estate Ltd. from *New Britain: My Vision of a Young Country* by Tony Blair © 1996 by The Office of Tony Blair.

Gardening: How-to
From "In Praise of the Kitchen Garden" from *Gardening: How-To,* May/June 1997, published by the National Home Gardening Club. Used by permission of *Gardening: How-To* magazine.

Hal Leonard Corporation
"New Beginning," words and music by Tracy Chapman. © 1996 EMI April Music Inc. and Purple Rabbit Music. All rights controlled and administered by EMI April Music Inc. All Rights Reserved. International copyright secured. Used by permission.

Harcourt Brace & Company
"L'Invitation au Voyage" by Charles Baudelaire, translated by Richard Wilbur, from *Things of This World,* copyright © 1956 and renewed 1984 by Richard Wilbur. Reprinted by permission of Harcourt Brace & Company.

Harcourt Brace & Company, the Executors of the Virginia Woolf Estate, and the Hogarth Press
"The Lady in the Looking Glass: A Reflection" from *A Haunted House and Other Short Stories* by Virginia Woolf, copyright 1944 and renewed 1972 by Harcourt Brace & Company. Reprinted by permission.

Harcourt Brace & Company, and Faber and Faber Ltd.
"The Hollow Men," "Preludes" and "Journey of the Magi" from *Collected Poems 1909–1962* by T. S. Eliot, copyright 1936 by Harcourt Brace & Company, copyright © 1964, 1963 by T. S. Eliot. Reprinted by permission of the publishers, Harcourt Brace & Company, and Faber and Faber Limited.

Harcourt Brace & Company, and A. M. Heath & Co. Ltd.
"Shooting an Elephant" from *Shooting an Elephant and Other Essays* by George Orwell, copyright 1950 by Sonia Brownell Orwell and renewed 1978 by Sonia Pitt-Rivers. Copyright © Mark Hamilton as the Literary Executor of the Estate of the Late Sonia Brownell Orwell and Martin Secker and Warburg Ltd. Reprinted by permission of Harcourt Brace & Company and A. M. Heath & Co. Ltd.

Harlan Davidson/Forum Press Inc.
Excerpt from "Book I" of *Utopia* by Thomas More, edited and translated by H. V. S. Ogden, pp. 21, 22 (Crofts Classics Series). Copyright © 1949 by Harlan Davidson, Inc. Reprinted by permission.

HarperCollins Publishers, Inc., and Rogers, Coleridge & White Ltd.
"The Devoted Son" from *Games at Twilight and Other Stories* by Anita Desai. Copyright © 1978 by Anita Desai. Reprinted by permission of HarperCollins Publishers, Inc., and the author c/o Rogers, Coleridge & White Ltd., 20 Powis Mews, London W11 1JN.

David Higham Associates
"On the Patio" from *Poems 1954–1987* by Peter Redgrove. Copyright © Peter Redgrove, 1959, 1961, 1963, 1966, 1972, 1973, 1975, 1977, 1979, 1981, 1985, 1986, 1987. All rights reserved. Reprinted by permission.

Henry Holt & Co., Inc.
"To an Athlete Dying Young" from "A Shropshire Lad"- Authorized edition, and "When I Was One-and-Twenty" from *The Collected Poems of A. E. Housman* by A. E. Housman. Copyright 1939, 1940, © 1965 by Henry Holt and Company, Inc., © 1967, 1968 by Robert E. Symons. Reprinted by permission of Henry Holt and Company, Inc.

Houghton Mifflin Company
From "Childe Harold's Pilgrimage" ("Apostrophe to the Ocean"), lines from "Don Juan" and "She Walks in Beauty," reprinted from *The Complete Poetical Words of Lord Byron.* From "A Voyage to Brobdingnag" and from "A Voyage to Lilliput" reprinted from *Gulliver's Travels and Other Writings* by Jonathan Swift, edited by Louis A. Landa. Riverside Edition. Copyright © 1960 by Houghton Mifflin Company. Used by permission.

Jonathan Cape Ltd.
Emilia Lanier: "Eves Apologie" from *The Poems of Shakespeare's Dark Lady: Salve Deus Rex Judaeorum* by Emilia Lanier, introduced by A. L. Rowse. Reprinted by permission of Jonathan Cape Ltd.

Alfred A. Knopf, Inc.
"The Demon Lover" from *Collected Stories* by Elizabeth Bowen. Copyright 1946 and renewed 1974 by Elizabeth Bowen. Reprinted by permission of Alfred A. Knopf, Inc.

L. R. Lind
From *Ovid: Tristia* translated by L. R. Lind. Published by The University of Georgia Press. Copyright © 1975 by L. R. Lind. All rights reserved.

Methuen & Company Ltd.
Lines from "An Essay on Man," Canto III and lines from Canto V from *The Rape of the Lock,* reprinted from *The Poems of Alexander Pope* edited by John Butt. Published by Methuen & Co., Ltd, London.

New Beacon Books Ltd.
"From Lucy: Englan' Lady" from *Lucy's Letters and Loving* by James Berry. © 1982 by James Berry. Reprinted by permission of the publisher, New Beacon Books Ltd.

New Directions Publishing Co.
"Not Waving but Drowning" from Stevie Smith, *The Collected Poems of Stevie Smith.* Copyright © 1972 by Stevie Smith. "Far Corners of the Earth" by Tu Fu, translated by David Hinton, from *The Selected Poems of Tu Fu.* Copyright ©1989 by David Hinton. "Anthem for Doomed Youth" by Wilfred Owen, from *The Collected Poems of Wilfred Owen,* edited by C. Day Lewis. Copyright © Chatto & Windus Ltd. 1946, 1963. Reprinted by permission of New Directions Publishing Co.

New Directions Publishing Corporation, and David Higham Associates Ltd.
"Do Not Go Gentle into That Good Night" by Dylan Thomas, from *The Poems of Dylan Thomas.* Copyright © 1952 by The Trustees for the Copyrights of Dylan Thomas. "Fern Hill" by Dylan Thomas, from *The Poems of Dylan Thomas.* Copyright © 1945 by The Trustees for the Copyrights of Dylan Thomas. Reprinted by permission of New Directions Publishing Corporation, and David Higham Associates Ltd.

Newmarket Press
From *The Sense and Sensibility Screenplay & Diaries,* by Emma Thompson. Screenplay Copyright © 1995 Columbia Pictures Industries, Inc. All Rights Reserved. Reprinted by permission of Newmarket Press, 18 East 48th Street, New York, NY 10017.

News International Syndication
Articles "Death of a King" and "The New Queen" reprinted from Times Newspapers Limited, 7 February 1952. Copyright © Times Newspapers Limited, 1952. Used by permission of News International Syndication.

North Point Press, a division of Farrar, Straus & Giroux, Inc.
"Testament" by Bei Dao from *A Splintered Mirror: Chinese Poetry From the Democracy Movement,* translated by Donald Finkel. Translation copyright © 1991 by Donald Finkel. Reprinted by permission of North Point Press, a division of Farrar, Straus & Giroux, Inc.

W. W. Norton & Company, Inc.
"Sonnet 35" by Edmund Spenser, from *Edmund Spenser's Poetry: Authoritative Texts Criticism,* selected and edited by Hugh Maclean, copyright © 1968 by W. W. Norton & Company, Inc. "Outside History" reprinted from *Outside History, Selected Poems, 1980–1990,* by Eavan Boland, by permission of W. W. Norton & Company, Inc. Copyright © 1990 by Eavan Boland. Reprinted from *Sir Gawain and the Green Knight: A New Verse Translation* by Marie Borroff, translator. Copyright © 1967 by W. W. Norton & Company, Inc. Reprinted by permission of W. W. Norton & Company, Inc.

Oxford University Press, Inc.
From "The Wanderer," translated by Charles W. Kennedy, from *An Anthology of Old English Poetry.* Copyright © 1960 by Charles W. Kennedy. Used by permission of Oxford University Press, Inc.

Oxford University Press, London
"God's Grandeur" and "Spring and Fall" from *Poems of Gerard Manley Hopkins,* 4th edition, edited by W. H. Gardner and N. H. MacKenzie. "The Lamb," "The Chimney Sweeper," and "Infant Sorrow" from *The Poetical Works of William Blake,* edited by John Sampson. "Sonnet 43" from *The Poetical Works of Elizabeth Barrett Browning,* Oxford Edition. "To Althea" and "To Lucasta, on Going to the Wars" from *The Poems of Richard Lovelace,* edited by C. H. Wilkinson, copyright © 1953. "Kubla Khan" and "The Rime of the Ancient Mariner" from *The Poems of Samuel Taylor Coleridge.* Lines from "In Memoriam, A. H. H.," "Tears, Idle Tears," "The Lady of Shalott," lines from "The Princess," and "Ulysses" from *Alfred Tennyson: Poetical Works.* "To the Virgins, to Make Much of Time" from *The Poems of Robert Herrick,* edited by L. C. Martin. From "The Life of Samuel Johnson" in *Boswell's Life of Johnson* by James Boswell, edited by C. B. Tinker. "Sonnet 31" and "Sonnet 39" from *The Poems of Sir Philip Sidney,* edited by William A. Ringler, Jr. "The Passionate Shepherd to His Love" from *Marlow's Poems,* edited by Roma Gill, Volume 1, © Roma Gill 1987, Clarendon Press, Oxford. Reprinted by permission of the publisher, Oxford University Press. "Sonnet 1" and "Sonnet 75" from *The Poetical Works of Edmund Spenser,* edited by J. C. Smith and E. de Selincourt. "On Making an Agreeable Marriage" from *Jane Austen's Letters,* collected and edited by Deirdre Le Faye, copyright Deirdre Le Faye 1995. Permission granted by the publisher, Oxford University Press Ltd.

Penguin Books Ltd.
"How Siegfried Was Slain" from *The Nibelungenlied,* translated by A. T. Hatto (Penguin Classics, Revised Edition, 1969), copyright © A. T. Hatto, 1965, 1969. From *A History of the English Church and People* by Bede, translated by Leo Sherley-Price, revised by R. E. Latham (Penguin Classics 1955, Revised edition 1968). Copyright © Leo Sherley-Price, 1955, 1968. "The Nun's Priest's Tale" and "The Prologue" to *The Canterbury Tales* by Geoffrey Chaucer, translated by Nevill Coghill (Penguin

Classics 1951, fourth revised edition 1977), copyright © 1951 by Coghill Nevill. Copyright ©, 1958, 1960, 1975, 1977. Reprinted by permission of Penguin Books Ltd.

Phoebe Phillips Editions
Excerpt from *The Anglo-Saxon Chronicle,* translated and collated by Anne Savage. Copyright © 1983 by Phoebe Phillips. All rights reserved.

Random House, Inc.
From "That English Weather" from *Parodies: An Anthology from Chaucer to Beerbohm—and After,* edited by Dwight Macdonald. © Copyright, 1960, by Dwight Macdonald. From *War and Peace* by Leo Tolstoy, translated from the Russian by Constance Garnett, published by Modern Library, Random House, Inc. "Holy Sonnet 10", "A Valediction: Forbidding Mourning," "Meditation 17," and "Song" from *Complete Poetry and Selected Prose of John Donne* by John Donne, edited by John Hayward. "Musée des Beaux Arts" and "In Memory of W. B. Yeats" from *W. H. Auden: Collected Poems* by W. H. Auden, edited by Edward Mendelson. Copyright 1940 and renewed 1968 by W. H. Auden. "Homeless" from *Living Out Loud* by Anna Quindlen. Copyright © 1987 by Anna Quindlen. Reprinted by permission of Random House, Inc.

Random House, Inc., and Heinemann Educational Publishers, a division of Reed Educational & Professional Publishing Limited
From *A Man For All Seasons* by Robert Bolt, published by Heinemann Educational Books. Copyright © 1960, 1962 by Robert Bolt; copyright renewed 1988, 1990 by Robert Bolt. Reprinted by permission of Random House, Inc. and Heinemann Educational Publishers, a division of Reed Educational & Professional Publishing Limited.

Tessa Sayle Agency
"The Fiddle" from The *Second Chance and Other Stories* by Alan Sillitoe. Copyright © 1981 by Alan Sillitoe. First appeared in The Nottingham Press.

Scovil Chichak Galen Literary Agency, Inc.
"We'll Never Conquer Space" by Arthur C. Clarke, published in *Science Digest,* June 1960, © 1960 by Popular Mechanics Company. Reprinted by permission of the author and the author's agents, Scovil Chichak Galen Literary Agency, Inc., New York.

Simon & Schuster, Inc.
"Ah, Are You Digging on My Grave?" and "The Darkling Thrush" from *The Complete Poems of Thomas Hardy,* edited by James Gibson (New York: Macmillan, 1978). This collection was published outside the U.S. by Macmillan (London) Ltd. in 1976. Reprinted with permission of Simon & Schuster, Inc. from *The Poems of W. B. Yeats: A New Edition,* edited by Richard J. Finneran: "The Lake Isle at Innisfree," "When You are Old" and "The Wild Swans at Coole," copyright 1919 by Macmillan Publishing Company, renewed 1947 by Bertha Georgie Yeats; "The Second Coming," copyright © 1924 by Macmillan Publishing Company, renewed 1952 by Bertha Georgie Yeats; "Sailing to Byzantium," copyright 1928 by Macmillan Publishing Company, copyright renewed © 1956 by Bertha Georgie Yeats.

Simon & Schuster, Inc. and Jonathan Clower Ltd.
"No Witchcraft for Sale" from *African Short Stories* by Doris Lessing. Copyright © 1951, 1953, 1954, 1957, 1958, 1962, 1963, 1964, 1965, 1972, 1981 by Doris Lessing. Used by permission.

Simon & Schuster, and HarperCollins Publishing Ltd.
Excerpts from *The Analects of Confucius,* translated and annotated by Arthur Waley, is reprinted with the permission of Simon & Schuster and HarperCollins Publishing Ltd. Copyright © 1938 by George Allen and Unwin Ltd.

University of California Press
Excerpts from "An Essay on Dramatic Poesy" by John Dryden, from *The Works of John Dryden, Prose 1668–1691,* General Editor H. T. Swedenberg, Jr. Copyright © 1971 by The Regents of the University of California. "You Know the Place, Then" from *Sappho: A New Translation* by Mary Barnard. Copyright © 1958 The Regents of the University of California; © renewed 1984 Mary Barnard. "The Diameter of the Bomb," translated by Chana Bloch, from *The Selected Poetry of Yehuda Amichai,* translated/edited by Chana Bloch and Stephen Mitchell. Translation Copyright © 1986 by Chana Bloch and Stephen Mitchell. Reprinted by permission of the University of California Press.

University of Chicago Press
From "Oedipus the King," Sophocles, translated by David Grene, from *Complete Greek Tragedies,* edited by David Grene and Richmond Lattimore. Copyright 1954 by The University of Chicago. Excerpt from *The Iliad of Homer,* translated by Richmond Lattimore. Copyright © 1951, The University of Chicago. Reprinted by permission of the publisher, University of Chicago Press.

University of Texas Press
"Sonnet LXXXIX" on page 189 and "Sonnet LXIX" on page 147 from *100 Love Sonnets: Cien Sonetos de Amor,* by Pablo Neruda, translated by Stephen Tapscott. © Pablo Neruda, 1959. Copyright © 1986 by The University of Texas Press. Reprinted by permission.

Viking Penguin, a division of Penguin Books USA Inc.
"Birds on the Western Front" from *The Complete Works of Saki* by H. H. Munro, published by Barnes & Noble by arrangement with Doubleday & Company, Inc. "Araby," from *Dubliners,* by James Joyce. Copyright 1916 by B. W. Heubsch. Definitive text copyright © 1967 by The Estate of James Joyce. "The Rocking-Horse Winner" by D. H. Lawrence. Copyright © 1933 by the Estate of D. H. Lawrence, renewed © 1961 by Angelo Ravagli and C. M. Weekley, Executors of the Estate of Frieda Lawrence, from *Complete Short Stories of D. H. Lawrence* by D. H. Lawrence. "The Train from Rhodesia," copyright 1952 by Nadine Gordimer, from *Selected Stories* by Nadine Gordimer. Used by permission of Viking Penguin, a division of Penguin Books USA Inc.

Viking Penguin, a division of Penguin Books USA Inc., and John Johnson (Author's Agent) Limited
"The Distant Past" from *Angels at the Ritz and Other Stories* by William Trevor. Copyright © 1975 by William Trevor, published in England by The Bodley Head. Used by permission.

Viking Penguin, a division of Penguin Books USA Inc., and George Sassoon
"Wirers" from *Collected Poems of Siegfried Sassoon* by Siegfried Sassoon. Copyright 1918, 1920 by E. P. Dutton. Copyright 1936, 1946, 1947, 1948 by Siegfried Sassoon. Reprinted by permission.

Viking Penguin, a division of Penguin Books USA Inc., and Aitken and Stone
"B. Wordsworth" by V. S. Naipaul, from *Miguel Street* by V. S. Naipaul. Copyright © 1959 by V. S. Naipaul. Used by permission of Viking Penguin, a division of Penguin Books USA Inc., and The Wylie Agency.

Viking Penguin, a division of Penguin Books USA Inc. and David Higham Associates Ltd.
"A Shocking Accident," copyright © 1957 by Graham Greene. In the USA from *Collected Stories of Graham Greene* by Graham Greene. In England from *Twenty-One Stories* by Graham Greene. Used by permission of Viking Penguin, a division of

Penguin Books USA Inc. and David Higham Associates Ltd.

Vital Speeches of the Day
From "The New Atlantic Initiative" by Margaret Thatcher, delivered at the John Findley Green Foundation Lecture, Westminster College, Fulton, Mo., March 9, 1996. Used by permission.

Wake Forest University Press
"Carrick Revisited" from *Selected Poems of Louis MacNeice*, edited by Michael Longley. © Wake Forest University Press, 1990. Reprinted by permission of Wake Forest University Press.

Warner Chappell Music
"Freeze Tag" written by Suzanne Vega. Song copyright © 1985 by Waifersongs Ltd. and AGF Music Ltd. (ASCAP).

The Wylie Agency, Inc.
Excerpt from "Chatwin Revisited" by Paul Theroux. First published in *Granta*. Copyright © 1993 by Paul Theroux. Printed with the permission of The Wylie Agency, Inc.

Yale University Press
"The Seafarer" from *Poems From the Old English,* translated by Burton Raffel. Copyright © 1960, 1964; renewed 1988, 1992 by the University of Nebraska Press. Copyright © 1994 by Burton Raffel. Reprinted by permission of Yale University Press.

Note: Every effort has been made to locate the copyright owner of material reprinted in this book. Omissions brought to our attention will be corrected in subsequent editions.

ART CREDITS

Cover: Leo de Wys, Inc.; **vii:** (top) *Susanna in Bath (detail),* Albrecht Altdorfer, Wasserholendes, Madchen, Munchen, Alte Pinakothek, Munich. Photo: Blauel/Artothek; (bottom) *Golden Horn* (detail), The National Museet, Copenhagen, Photo by Lennart Larsen; **viii:** The Granger Collection, New York; **x:** Photofest; **xii:** Corel Professional Photos CD-ROM™; **xiv:** Greek Vase, Terracotta c. 460 B.C., Attributed to the Orchard Painter, Column Krater (called the "Orchard Vase"), Side A: *Women Gathering Apples,* The Metropolitan Museum of Art, Rogers Fund, 1907, (07.286.74) **xvi:** Springer/Corbis-Bettmann; **xvii:** ©Gregory C. Dimijian/Photo Researchers, Inc.; **xix:** Grace Davies/Omni-Photo Communications, Inc.; **xx–1:** *Sir Gawain and the Green Knight,* MS Douce 199, folio 157 verso, Bodleian Library, Oxford; **2:** (449) Richard Nowitz/Corbis; (552) Art Resource, NY; (771) *King Charlemagne – Jewelled Gold Reliquary Bust,* c.1350, Domschatz, Aachen, Art Resource, NY; (792) *Arrival of William at Penvesy* (detail from Bayeux Tapestry), Giraudon/Art Resource, NY; (871) Michael Nicholson/Corbis; (1066)The Granger Collection, New York; **3:** (1170) & (1348) & (1408) The Granger Collection, New York; (1327) Art Resource, NY; (1386) Superstock; **4:** (top) Richard Nowitz/ Corbis; (bottom) The Granger Collection, New York; **6:** (top) Art Resource, NY; (bottom) *Viking Sword, Iron, Copper, and Silver,* The Metropolitan Museum of Art, Rogers Fund, 1955, © Copyright 1980/87 By The Metropolitan Museum of Art; **8:** (top) & (bottom) The Granger Collection, New York; **9:** (top) Lauros-Giraudon/Art Resource, NY; (bottom) The Granger Collection, New York; 10: *Sampler,* (detail) 1797 by Mary Wiggin. 18x 21 1/2." Philadelphia Museum of Art, Whitman Sampler Collection/Given by Pet, Incorportaed.:**11:** *Arrival of William at Penvesy* (detail from Bayeux Tapestry), Giraudon/Art Resource, NY; **12:** Corel Professional Photos CD-ROM™; **15:** *Ships with Three Men, Fish,* Ms. Ashmole, 1511, Folio 86 verso, Bodleian Library, Oxford; **18:** *Arthur Going to Avalon for "The High Kings"* (detail), George Sharp, Courtesy of the artist; **20:** The Granger Collection, New York; **24:** *Susanna in Bath,* detail, Albrecht Altdorfer, Wasserholendes, Madchen, Munchen, Alte Pinakothek, Munich. Photo: Blauel/Artothek; **28:** (background) NASA; (top) Corbis-Bettmann; (bottom) New York Public Library Picture Collection; **30:** The Granger Collection, New York; **31:** Fan mounted as an album leaf: *Evening in Spring Hills,* Ink and color on silk. H. 9-3/4 in. W. 10-1/4 in. (24.8 x 26.1 cm.) Chinese, The Metropolitan Museum of Art, Gift of John M. Crawford, Jr., in honor of Alfreda Murck, 1986, (1986.493.1) Photograph © 1987 The Metropolitan Museum of Art; **32:** (background) NASA; **33:** Corel Professional Photos CD-ROM™; **36:** Cotton Ms. Tiberius C II Folio 5 Verso Page of Bede's History, Courtesy of the Trustees of British Library; **37:** The Granger Collection, New York; **38:** (top) Statens Historiska Museet, Stockholm, Werner Forman Archive/Art Resource, NY; (bottom) Werner Forman Archive, National Museum, Copenhagen, Art Resource, NY; **41:** *Grendel, Frontispiece from Beowulf,* 1908, Patten Wilson, Courtesy of the Trustees of British Library; **44:** Werner Forman Archive, Viking Ship Museum, Bygdoy, Oslo, Art Resource, NY; **46:** Werner Forman Archive, Statens Historiska Museet, Stockholm, Art Resource, NY; **50:** *Golden Horn* (detail), The National Museet, Copenhagen, Photo by Lennart Larsen; **52:** Silver Pendant Showing the Helmet of the Vendel, 10th century, Swedish-Ostergotland, Viking, Werner Forman Archive, Statens Historiska Museet, Stockholm, Art Resource, NY; **55:** Courtesy of the artist; **56:** Werner Forman Archive, National Museum, Copenhagen, Art Resource, NY; **57:** Gilt-Bronze Winged Dragon-Bridle Mounting, 8th century, Swedish Artifact, Statens Historiska Museet, Stockholm, Werner Forman Archive/Art Resource, NY; **60:** Head of Carved Post from the Ship Burial at Oseberg, Werner Forman Archive/Art Resource, NY; **64:** (background) NASA; (bl) © British Museum; (br) Corbis-Bettmann; **65:** The Granger Collection, New York; **67–69:** (background) Red-figured crater, Eucharides Painter, *Running warriors with shields and spears.* Louvre, Paris, France, Erich Lessing/ Art Resource, NY; **69:** (tl) The Granger Collection, New York; **70:** (background) NASA; **71:** Culver Pictures, Inc.; **75:** *Four Kings of England* (left to right): Henry II, Richard I, John, Henry III, from Historia Anglorum, 13th c. Roy 14 C VII f. 9. British Library, London, Great Britain, Bridgeman/ Art Resource, NY; **76:** Snark/ Art Resource, NY; **79:** Cotton Ms. Tiberius C II Folio 5 Verso Page of Bede's History, Courtesy of the Trustees of British Library; **80:** *Monks,* Ms. University College 165 pii, Bodleian Library, Oxford; **86:** Image Select/Art Resource, NY; **89:** *The Tabard Inn,* Arthur Szyk for *The Canterbury Tales;* **91:** *The Yeoman,* Arthur Szyk for *The Canterbury Tales,* The George Macy Companies; **93:** *The Monk,* Arthur Szyk for *The Canterbury Tales,* The George Macy Companies; **96:** *The Student,* Arthur Szyk for *The Canterbury Tales,* The George Macy Companies; **100:** *The Wife of Bath,* Arthur Szyk for *The Canterbury Tales,* The George Macy Companies; **106:** *The Pardoner,* Arthur Szyk for *The Canterbury Tales,* The George Macy Companies; **114:** Courtesy of the Trustees of British Library; **117:** *Woman Feeding Chickens,* From an Italian Manuscript (c. 1385), Osterreichische National Bibliothek, Vienna; **121:** *Chaucer Reciting Troilus and Cressida Before a Court Gathering* (Frontispiece), Corpus Christi College; **122:** *The Nun's Priest* (detail), from The Ellesmere Manuscript, Chaucer's *The Canterbury Tales,* The Hunington Library, San Marino, California; **124:** *Chaucer's Canterbury Pilgrims,* by William Blake, The Huntington Library, San Marino, California; **130:** (background) NASA; (tr) C. Beaton/Camera Press London; **134:** (background) NASA; **135:** Bob Daemmrich/Stock, Boston; **139:** *St. George and the Dragon,* c. 1506, Raphael, oil on panel, 11 1/8 x 8 1/2" © Board of Trustees, National Gallery of Art, Washington, D.C. Andrew W. Mellon Collection; **143:** From *The Romance of King Arthur and His Knights of the Round Table,* Arthur Rackham, Weathervane Books; **145:** *Three Knights Returning from a Tournament.* French miniature from "Recueil de Traites de Devotion." Ms. 137/1687, fol. 144 r.c.1371-78, Giraudon/Art Resource, NY; **149:** *Sir Gawain and the Green Knight,* MS Douce 199, folio 157 verso, Bodleian Library, Oxford; **154:** *Gawain Receiving the Green Girdle,* Fritz Kredel, Woodcut, From John Gardner's *The Complete Works of the Gawain Poet,* © 1965, The University of Chicago; **157:** Art Resource, NY; **158:** *The Nine Heroes Tapestries: Christian Heroes: Arthur* (Detail), Probably Nicolas Bataille, Paris, The Metropolitan Museum of Art; **167:** Nicholas Sapieha/Stock, Boston; **168:** (tr) & (bl) Culver Pictures, Inc.; **171 & 172:** The Granger Collection, New York; **175:** ©Michael Giannechini/ Photo Researchers, Inc.; **177:** *Veronica Veronese,* Dante Gabriel Rossetti, Delaware Art Museum, Samuel and Mary Bancroft Memorial Collection; **180:** (background) NASA; **182:** The Granger Collection, New York; **185:** *Siegfried's Death,* Handschriftenabteilung, Staatsbibliothek Preussischer Kulturbesitz, Berlin, photo Bildarchiv Preussischer Kulturbesitz; **187:** (background) NASA; **188:** UPI/ Corbis-Bettmann; **192:** Ken Karp Photography; **193:** (left) Vintage Books, Illustrated by Emil Antonucci; (center) Cover of "The Once and Future King" by T. H. White. Reproduced by arrangement with The Berkley Publishing Group, a member of Penguin Putnam, Inc. All rights reserved.; (right) Book cover from "Murder in the Cathedral" by T. S. Eliot. Copyright 1935 by Harcourt Brace & Company. Copyright renewed 1963 by T. S. Eliot. Reproduced by permission of Harcourt Brace Jovanovich, Inc.; **194:** The Granger Collection, New York; **196:** (1503) Scala/ Art Resource, NY; (1532) & (1534) & (1535) & (1564) The Granger Collection, New York; (1558) National Portrait Gallery, London/Superstock; **197:** (1558) & (1594) & (1611) & (1620) The Granger Collection, New York; (1582) Library of Congress/Corbis; (1609) Scala/Art Resource, NY; **198:** Hornbook dating from Shakspeare's lifetime, by permission of the Folger Shakespeare Library; **199:** (top) Marquess of Bath Collection, Longleat House, Wilts/ET Archive, London/ Superstock; (center) & (bottom) The Granger Collection, New York; **200:** (top) The Granger Collection, New York; (bottom) *The Hireling Shepherd,* William Holman Hunt, The Manchester City Art Galleries; **201:** (top) National Trust/Art Resource, NY; (bottom) National Portrait Gallery, London/Superstock; **202:** (top) Corbis-Bettmann; (bottom) The Granger Collection, New York; **203:** (top) *The Launching of Fireships Against the Spanish Armada* (detail), National Maritime Museum, Greenwich, England; (bottom) Collection of Plymouth City Museum and Art Gallery; **204**: *Sampler*, (detail) 1797 by Mary Wiggin. 18x 21 1/2." Philadelphia Museum of Art, Whitman Sampler Collection/ Given by Pet, Incorporated.; **205:** Victoria and Albert Museum/Art Resource, NY; **206:** (left) The Granger Collection, New York; (right) *Sir Philip Sidney* (detail), c.1576, Artist Unknown, by courtesy of the National Portrait Gallery, London; **209 & 211:** Corel Professional Photos CD-ROM™; **212:** Chad Ehlers, 1987/PNI; **216:** (left) & (right) The Granger Collection, New York; **218:** *William Shakespeare,* (detail), Artist Unknown, by courtesy of the National Portrait Gallery, London; **219:** Corel Professional Photos CD-ROM™; **220:** *Autumn,* 1865, Frederick Walker, Victoria & Albert Museum/Art Resource, NY; **222:** Corel Professional Photos CD-ROM™; **226:** (background) NASA; (top) The Granger Collection, New York; (bottom) Sergio Larrain/Magnum Photos, Inc.; **227:** *Portrait of Laura,* Biblioteca Laurenziana, Firenze, Scala/Art Resource, NY; **229:** *Man and Woman,* 1981, Rufino Tamayo, Tate Gallery, London/Art Resource, NY; **230:** NASA; **231:** Ken Karp/ Omni-Photo Communications, Inc.; **235:** (left) & (right) The Granger Collection, New York; (bottom) Scala/Art Resource, NY; **236:** (left) The Granger Collection, New York; (right) North Wind Picture Archives; **237:** Petrified Colle/The Image Bank; **238–239:** *Gardens at Llanerch, Denbigshire,* c. 1662–72, British School, 17th c., oil on canvas, 45 x 59 3/4 in. (114.1 x 151.7 cm) B1976.7.115. Yale Center for British Art, New Haven, Connecticut, Paul Mellon Collection; **240:** *Portrait of Queen Elizabeth I,* Bridgeman/Art Resource, NY; **241:** "Dangers Averted" medal celebrating the defeat of the Spanish Armada, © 1589, gold cast and chased by Nicholas Hilliard (1537–1619), Fitzwilliam Museum, University of Cambridge/The Bridgeman Art Library International Ltd., London/ New York; **244:** © Mark N. Boulton/Photo Researchers, Inc.; **246:** The Folger Shakespeare Library, Washington, D.C.; **252:** (background) NASA; (br) AP/Wide World Photos; **254–255:** Photofest; **258:** NASA; **259:** *Portrait of Queen Elizabeth I,* Bridgeman/Art Resource, NY; **263 & 265:** The Granger Collection, New York; **266:** (tl) Hulton-Deutsch/Corbis; (rc) Photofest; (bl) New York Public Library at Lincoln Center; **267:** (tl) *Mrs. Siddons as Lady Macbeth,* (detail), G.H. Harlow, Garrick Club/ET Archive; (rc) *Ellen Terry (as Lady Macbeth),* 1889, oil on canvas, 87 x 45," Tate Gallery on loan to National Portrait Gallery London, Art Resource, NY; (bl) Photofest; **268:** *William Shakespeare,* (detail), Artist Unknown, by courtesy of the National Portrait Gallery, London; **273:** *The Three Witches,* 1783, Henry Fuseli, oil on canvas, 65 x 91.5 cm, Kunsthaus Zurich © 1997 Copyright Kunsthaus Zurich. All rights reserved.; **277:** *Macbeth and the Witches,* Clarkson Stanfield, Leicestershire Museums, Art Galleries and Records Service; **283:** Anne Van De Vaeken/The Image Bank; **287:** Photofest; **289:** Hans Neleman/The Image Bank; **297:** *Ellen Terry (as Lady Macbeth),* 1889, oil on canvas, 87x45," Tate Gallery on loan to National Portrait Gallery London, Art Resource, NY; **304:** *Lady Macbeth Seizing the Daggers,* Henry Fuseli, The Tate Gallery, London/Art Resource, NY; **315:** *Mrs. Siddons as Lady Macbeth,* G.H. Harlow, Garrick Club/ET Archive; **321:** *Scene from Macbeth and the Witches,* Cattermole, The Folger Shakespeare Library, Washington, D.C.; **329:** e.t.archive; **337:** The Granger Collection, New York; **349:** *Lady Macbeth Sleepwalking,* Henry Fuseli, Louvre, Paris, Scala/Art Resource, NY; **364:** (background) NASA; (br) Vatican Museum/Scala/Art Resource, NY; **367 & 368:** Photofest; **371:** NASA; **372:** The Granger Collection, New York; **376:** ©Bill Losh/FPG International Corp.; **377:** (right) Jacket illustration from ELIZABETH AND ESSEX, copyright ©1928 by Lytton Strachey, copyright renewed 1956 by James Strachey, reprinted by permission of Harcourt Brace & Company; **378–379:** The Granger Collection, New York; **380:** (1600) & (1614) & (1627) & (1649) & (1650) The Granger Collection, New York; (1644) Chinese Porcelain Jar Hsuan-te (Xuande) Period, 1426–1435. Ming dynasty porcelain painted in underglaze blue, 19 inches in height. The Metropolitan Museum of Art, Gift of Robert E. Tod, 1937. (37.191.1); (1661) Dave G. Houser/Corbis; (1663) Historical Picture Archive/Corbis; (1667) Corbis-Bettmann; **381:** (1680) Erich Lessing/Art Resource, NY; (1690) & (1721) & (1773) The Granger Collection, New York; (1719) *Marylebone Cricket Club,* London/The Bridgeman Art Library, London; (1775) *Mrs. Siddons,* Thomas Gainsborough, National Gallery, London/The Bridgeman Art Library, London; **382:** (top) & (bottom) The Granger Collection, New York; **383 & 384:** (bottom) Archiv für Kunst und Geschichte, Berlin; **384:** (top) *Haycarting* by George Stubbs, 1785, Board of Trustees of the National Museums and Galleries on Merseyside (Lady Lever Art Gallery, Port Sunlight); **385:** (top) The Granger Collection, New York; (bottom) (©)British Museum; **386:** (top) Corbis-Bettmann; (tl) Archiv für Kunst und Geschichte, Berlin; (tr) Burghley House Collection, Lincolnshire/ The Bridgeman Art Library International Ltd., London/New York; (lc) Philip Mould, Historical Portraits, Ltd./The Bridgeman Art Library International Ltd., London/ New York; (rc) Division of Rare and Manuscript Collections, Carl A. Kroch Library, Cornell University; (bl) © Roger-Viollet; (br) © Editions Tallandier; **387:** (top) *Marriage à la Mode: The Marriage Contract,* 1743, William Hogarth, Reproduced by courtesy of the Trustees, National Gallery of Art, London; (bottom) *The River Dee Near Eaton Hall,* Richard Wilson, The Barber Institute of Fine Arts, The University of Birmingham; **388:** *Sampler*, (detail) 1797 by Mary Wiggin. 18x 21 1/2." Philadelphia Museum of Art, Whitman Sampler Collection/ Given by Pet, Incorporated.; **389:** *A Musical Garden Party* (detail), colored silk on canvas, very fine tent stitch. H.13 in. W. 20-1/2 in. Metropolitan Museum of Art, Gift of Irwin Untermyer, 1964. (64.101.1314) Photograph Copyright © 1991 By the Metropolitan Museum of Art; **390:** The Granger Collection, New York;

391: Corel Professional Photos CD-ROM ™; **393:** Romilly Lockyer/The Image Bank; **397:** *Fair is My Love* (detail), Edwin A. Abbey, Harris Museum and Art Gallery, Preston; **399:** The Granger Collection, New York; **401:** *Sir Thomas Aston at the Deathbed of his Wife,* John Souch, Manchester City Art Galleries; **404:** The Granger Collection, New York; **409:** *The Interrupted Sleep,* oil on canvas. Oval, 29-1/2 x 25-1/2 in., Francois Boucher, The Metropolitan Museum of Art, The Jules Bache Collection, 1949. (49.7.46) Photograph © 1984 The Metropolitan Museum of Art; **412:** (top) & (bottom) The Granger Collection, New York; (center) New York Public Library; **416:** *Three Ladies Adorning a Term of Hymen,* 1773, Sir Joshua Reynolds, The Tate Gallery, London/Art Resource, NY; **420:** (background) NASA; (top) Jane Bowr/ Camera Press London/Globe Photos; (bottom) AP/ Wide World Photos; **421:** Jules Zalon/The Image Bank; **422–423:** (background) Corel Professional Photos CD-ROM™; **424:** (background) NASA; **425:** Bill Bachmann/PNI; **429:** *Whitehall, January 30th, 1649 (Execution of Charles I),* Ernest Crofts, Forbes Magazine Collection, Bridgeman/ Art Resource, NY; **430:** Corbis-Bettmann; **433:** The Granger Collection, New York; **437 & 440:** *Paradise Lost,* 1688, John Milton, British Library; **444:** The Granger Collection, New York; **446:** *Dorothy Seton—A Daughter of Eve,* 1903, James McNeil Whistler, oil on canvas, 20 3/8 x 12 1/2" Hunterian Art Gallery, University of Glasgow, Scotland; **448:** *Going to the Battle,* 1858, Edward Burne-Jones, Fitzwilliam Museum, Cambridge; **452:** (background) NASA; (br) Henrieta Butler/ Globe Photos; **454:** (background) NASA; **455 & 459 & 460 & 463:** The Granger Collection, New York; **464:** Last page of Samuel Pepys's Diary 31 May 1669, Pepys Library, Magdalene College, Cambridge, England; **466–467:** *The Great Fire,* 1666, (coloured engraving) by Marcus Willemsz Doornik, (17th century), Guildhall Library, Corporation of London/ Bridgeman Art Library International Ltd., London/New York; **468:** *Journal of the Plague Year: the Dead Cart,* The British Library; **474 & 477 & 478 & 481 & 486:** The Granger Collection, New York; **489:** *The Barge, (detail)* 1895–1896, Aubrey Beardsley, from "The Rape of the Lock," Smithers, 1896 from *The Best of Beardsley,* Collected and edited by R.A. Walker, ©1948 by The Bodley Head, Published in the U.S.A. by Excalibur Books, plate 63; **491:** *The Rape of the Lock,* 1895–1896, Aubrey Beardsley, from "The Rape of the Lock," Smithers, 1896, from *The Best of Beardsley,* Collected and edited by R.A. Walker, ©1948 by The Bodley Head, Published in the U.S.A. by Excalibur Books, plate 64; **493:** *The Battle of the Beaux and Belles,* Aubrey Beardsley, The Barber Institute of Fine Arts, The University of Birmingham; **498–499:** Corel Professional Photos CD-ROM™; **502 & 504:** The Granger Collection, New York; **513:** *Johnson and Boswell,* ©Trustees of the British Museum; **518:** (left) & (right) The Granger Collection, New York; **520–521:** Lenore Weber/ Omni-Photo Communications, Inc.; **526–527:** Alan Becker/The Image Bank; **528:** *Cottage and Pond, Moonlight,* Thomas Gainsborough, Art Resource, NY/ Victoria and Albert Museum, London; **532:** (background) NASA; (top) AP/Wide World Photos; (bottom) The Granger Collection, New York; **533:** *The Thirteen Emperors,* (view: overall of 7th emperor) second half of 7th century (with later replacement), Yan Liben (attributed to) d. 673, China, Tang Dynasty, handscroll; ink and color on silk 51.3x531.0 cm (pictorial section), Denman Waldo Ross Collection, Courtesy, Museum of Fine Arts, Boston; **536:** *Thomas Jefferson,* Gilbert Stuart, National Portrait Gallery, Smithsonian Institution; gift of the Regents of the Smithsonian Institution, the Thomas Jefferson Memorial Foundation, and the Enid and Crosby Kemper Foundation; owned jointly with Monticello, Art Resource, NY; **538:** (background) NASA; **539:** The Granger Collection, New York; **543:** *Girl Writing by Lamplight,* © 1850, by William Henry Hunt, (1790–1864), The Maas Gallery London/ Bridgeman Art Library, London; **544:** The Granger Collection, New York; **546–549:** Corel Professional Photos CD-ROM™; **554:** (br) John Barrett/Globe Photos; **556:** Joan Slatkin/ Omni-Photo Communications, Inc.; **557:** (background) NASA; **558:** Gayna Hoffman/ PNI; **562:** Ken Karp Photography; **563:** (left) From *Robinson Crusoe* (Jacket Cover) by Daniel Defoe. Used by permission of Bantam Books, a division of Bantam Doubleday Dell Publishing Group, Inc.; (center) "Cover" from *Gulliver's Travels* by Jonathan Swift. Foreword by Marcus Cunliffe. Copyright © 1960 Foreword by New American Library. Used by permission of Dutton Signet, a division of Penguin Books USA Inc.; (right) Cover from *Tom Jones* by Henry Fielding. Published by Penguin Books Ltd.; Cover image WLN1576 Westcombe House, Blackheath by George Lambert (1700-65), Collection of the Earl of Pembroke, Wilton House/ Bridgeman Art Library, London/New York; **564–565:** *Two Men Observing the Moon,* Caspar David Friedrich, oil on canvas, 35 x 44.5 cm, (1819-1820), Staatl, Kunstsammlungen, Neue Meister, Dresden, Germany, Erich Lessing/ Art Resource, NY; **566:** (1799) Art Resource, NY; (1801) Corel Professional Photos CD-ROM™; (1802) Gianni Dagli Orti/ Corbis; (1805) & (1807) & (1813) & (1814) The Granger Collection, New York; **567:** (1818) ©Barson Collection/Archive Photos; (1819) ©Archive Photos; (1825) ©Brian Yarvin, 1994/ PNI; (1830) & (1831) The Granger Collection, New York; **568** (top) **&** (bottom) **569:** (top) The Granger Collection, New York; **570:** (top) Christie's, London/SuperStock; (bottom) Private Collection/The Bridgeman Art Library, London; **571:** (top) The Granger Collection, New York; **572:** (top) SEF/Art Resource, NY; (bottom) IBM; **573:** (top) & (bottom) The Granger Collection, New York; **574 (top):** *Sampler,* (detail)1797 by Mary Wiggin. 18x21 1/2." Philadelphia Museum of Art, Whitman Sampler Collection/ Given by Pet, Incorporated.; **575:** *Hummingbird Hunters,* 1884, James Farrington Gookins, Collection of the Shelden Swope Art Museum, Terre Haute, Indiana; **576:** (top) *Mary Shelley* (detail), c.1840, Richard Rothwell, by courtesy of the National Portrait Gallery, London; (bottom) John Lei/Omni-Photo Communications, Inc.; **577:** Photofest; **580–581:** *A View of Chamonix and Mt. Blanc,* Julius Schnon von Carolsfeld, Austrian Gallery, Vienna; **586:** (top) *Robert Burns,* A. Nasmyth, by courtesy of the National Portrait Gallery, London; (bottom) The Granger Collection, New York; **589:** ©R. J. Erwin/ Photo Researchers, Inc.; **590:** Warrington Museum & Art Gallery, Great Britain, Bridgeman/Art Resource, NY; **592:** *The Village Wedding,* detail, Sir Luke Fildes, (1844–1927) Christopher Wood Gallery, London/The Bridgeman Art Library/ London; **596:** The Granger Collection, New York; **598:** From a Manuscript of "The Lamb" by William Blake, Lessing J. Rosenwald Collection, Courtesy of the Library of Congress, Washington, D.C.; **599:** *The Tiger,* A Page from "Songs of Innocence and Experience," William Blake, The Metroplitan Museum of Art, Rogers Fund, 1917 © Copyright 1984 By The Metropolitan Museum of Art; **600–601:** The Granger Collection, New York; **604:** (background) NASA; (br) Corbis-Bettmann; **605:** *Elizabeth Beale Bordley,* ca. 1797, Gilbert Stuart, Oil on canvas, 29 1/4 x 24", 1886.2, Courtesy of the Museum of American Art of the Pennsylvania Academy of the Fine Arts, Philadelphia. Bequest of Elizabeth Mifflin; **608:** (background) NASA; **609:** Superstock; **613:** *The Wanderer over the Sea of Clouds,* 1818, by Caspar-David Friedrich, (1774-1840) Kunsthalle, Hamburg/ Bridgeman Art Library, London; **614:** The Granger Collection, New York; **616–617:** The Granger Collection, New York; **618:** (tc) *Tintern Abbey,* J.M.W. Turner, Courtesy of the Trustees of the British Museum; **618– 619 & 620:** (background) The Granger Collection, New York; **622:** *Storming of the Bastille 14 July 1789,* Anonymous, Chateau, Versailles, France; **623:** *Execution of King Louis XVI on January 21, 1793,* Musee de la Ville de Paris, Musee Carnavalet, Paris, France, Erich Lessing/ Art Resource, NY; **624:** Corel Professional Photos CD-ROM™; **628:** *Samuel Taylor Coleridge* (detail), by courtesy of the National Potrait Gallery, London; **633, 635, 636, 642:** Engraving by Gustáve Doré for *The Rime of the Ancient Mariner* by Samuel Taylor Coleridge, ©1970 by Dover Publications, Inc.; **646 & 649:** The Granger Collection, New York; **652:** *Box and Cover,* Ming Dynasty, first half of 16th century, lacquer, black; mother-of-pearl; wood; fabric. H. 4 in. The Seattle Art Museum, Gift of Mr. and Mrs. Louis Brechemin, Photo by Paul Macapia; **656:** The Granger Collection, New York; **659:** *In the Garden* (detail), ca. 1889, Thomas Wilmer Dewing, oil on canvas, 20 5/8 x 35", National Museum of American Art, Washington, D.C./Art Resource, NY; **660–661:** *Shipwreck*, J.C.C. Dahl, Munich Neue Pinakothek/Kavaler/Art Resource, NY; **663, 664, 665:** *Lord Byron, shaking the dust of England from his shoes,* from "The Poet's Corner" pub. by William Heinemann, 1904 (engraving) by Max Beerbohm (1872–1956), Central Saint Martins College of Art and Design/ The Bridgeman Art Library International Ltd., London/New York; **668:** The Granger Collection, New York; **671:** © Diane Rawson/Photo Researchers, Inc.; **673:** *Cirrus Cloud Study,* John Constable, Victoria and Albert Museum Trustees/Art Resource, NY; **676:** *Cloud Study,* 1821, John Constable, Yale Center for British Art, Paul Mellon Collection; **682:** (top) The Granger Collection, New York; (bottom) Greek Vase, Terracotta c. 460 B.C., Attributed to the Orchard Painter, Column Krater (called the "Orchard Vase"), Side A: *Women Gathering Apples,* The Metropolitan Museum of Art, Rogers Fund, 1907, (07.286.74) **684:** Frontspiece, Homer's *Iliad* and *Odyssey,* 1612, William Hole, By permission of the British Library; **685:** *John Keats,* 1821, Joseph Severn, by courtesy of the National Portrait Gallery, London; **687:** *Small Bird on a Flowering Plum Branch,* attributed to Ma Lin, The Goto Museum; **690–691:** Greek Vase, Terracotta c. 460 B.C., Attributed to the Orchard Painter, Column Krater (called the "Orchard Vase"), Side A: *Women Gathering Apples,* The Metropolitan Museum of Art, Rogers Fund, 1907, (07.286.74) **694:** (background) NASA; (top) Corbis-Bettmann; (center) The Granger Collection, New York; (bottom) Yosa Buson, Heibonsha/Pacific Press Service; **696:** *Crows Taking Flight through Spring Haze,* (1782–1846) hanging scroll, Edo period, dated 1841; Toyama Kinenkan, Saitama prefecture, Okada Hanko, Foundation Toyama Memorial Museum; **698:** (background) NASA; **699:** Chris Steele-Perkins/PNI; **703:** *Forging the Anchor,* 1831, William James Muller, (1812–45) City of Bristol Museum and Art Gallery/Bridgeman Art Library, London; **704:** The Granger Collection, New York; **709:** *The Workshops at the Gobelins Factory, 1840,* Jean-Charles Develly, (1876– 1958) watercolor, Musée Carnavalet, Paris/Giraudon/ Bridgeman Art Library, London; **710:** © British Museum; **714:** (top) Jane Austen (detail), c. 1801 – C. Auston., by courtesy of the National Portrait Gallery, London; (bottom) The Granger Collection, New York; **716–717:** *Marriage à la Mode: The Marriage Contract,* 1743, William Hogarth, Reproduced by courtesy of the Trustees, National Gallery of Art, London; **724:** (background) NASA; (br) Globe Photos; **726:** Photofest; **729:** (background) NASA; **730:** Bob Daemmrich/ Stock, Boston; **735:** (left) From *Frankenstein* (jacket cover) by Mary Shelley. Cover illustration, *A Physician* by T. Bigot, Ashmolean Museum, Oxford. Used by permission of Oxford University Press Inc.; (right) From EMMA (JACKET COVER) by Jane Austen. Used by permission of Bantam Books, a division of Bantam Doubleday Dell Publishing Group, Inc.; **736-737:** *The Railway Station, 1862,* by William Powell Frith (1819–1909), Royal Holloway and Bedford New College, Surrey/Bridgeman Art Library International Ltd., London/ New York; **738:** (1837) © British Museum; (1844) Corbis-Bettmann; (1845) Illustrated London News/Corbis; (1854) The Granger Collection, New York; (1860) Library of Congress/ Corbis; (1861) Chicago Historical Society, 1920.691; **739:** (1865–Alice) & (1880) & (1888) The Granger Collection, New York; (1865–Stamp) Gary J. Shulfer; (1876) Corbis-Bettmann; (1898) National Institutes of Health/Corbis; **740:** The Royal Collection © Her Majesty Queen Elizabeth II; **741:** (bottom) Hulton-Deutsch Collection/ Corbis; **742:** (top) The Granger Collection, New York; (bottom) London Musuem/E.T. Archive; **743:** (top) © Museum of London; (bottom) *Bayswater Omnibus,* G.W. Joy, Museum of London; **744:** (top) *Edwardian London,* 1901, Eugene Joseph McSwiney, Chris-topher Wood Gallery, London/The Bridgeman Art Library, London; (bottom) Science Museum, London/The Bridgeman Art Library, London; **745:** (top) Erich Lessing/Art Resource, NY; (bottom) Historical Picture Archive/Corbis; **746:** *Sampler,* (detail) 1797 by Mary Wiggin. 18x 21 1/2." Philadelphia Museum of Art, Whitman Sampler Collection/ Given by Pet, Incorporated.; **747:** *Faustine,* 1904, Maxwell Armfield, Museé d'Orsay, Paris, France/ Erich Lessing/ Art Resource, NY; **748:** *Alfred Lord Tennyson* (detail), c.1840, S. Laurence, by courtesy of the National Portrait Gallery, London; **751:** *The Stages of Life* by Caspar-David Friedrich (1774–1840), Museum der Bildenden Kunst, Leipzig/Bridgeman Art Library International Ltd., London/New York; **755:** *The Lady of Shalott* by John W. Waterhouse, Tate Gallery, London/ E.T. Archive, London/ SuperStock; **760:** *Ulysses Mourning for Home,* carved gem of light brown sardonyx, Roman 3rd to 2nd century B.C., Staatliche Museen zu Berlin; **762:** *Beach at Heist (Belgium),* 1891–1892, Georges Lemmen, Musée d'Orsay, Paris, France/Erich Lessing/Art Resource, NY; **766:** The Granger Collection, New York; **769:** *Antea (Portrait of a Lady),* Parmigianino, Museo Nazionale di Capodimonte, Naples/Art Resource, NY; **771:** Culver Pictures, Inc.; **772:** Victoria and Albert Museum/ Art Resource, NY; **773 & 774–775:** Corel Professional Photos CD-ROM™; **776:** Corbis-Bettmann; **777:** Archive Photos; **780:** (background) NASA; (top) & bottom) Corbis-Bettmann; **781:** Walters Art Gallery, Baltimore; **782:** *Marine,* Marcel Mouillot, Galleria d'arte Moderna, Nancy/Art Resource, NY; **785:** Jean-Philippe Varin/JACANA/ Photo Researchers, Inc.; **789:** e.t.archive; **790:** (left) *Matthew Arnold* (detail), 1888, G.J. Watts, by courtesy of the National Portrait Gallery, London; (right) *Rudyard Kipling* (detail), 1899, P. Burne Jones, by courtesy of the National Portrait Gallery, London; **792:** Andrea Pistolesi/The Image Bank; **794:** The Granger Collection, New York; **796:** Culver Pictures, Inc.; **802:** *Woman Begging at Clonakilty,* James Mahony, *The Illustrated London News,* 1847. Photo by Grace Davies/Omni-Photo Communications, Inc.; **805 & 806:** Culver Pictures, Inc.; **810:** (left) NASA; (br) Derek Speirs/Report Ltd.; **812:** Derek Speirs/ Report Ltd.; **814:** (left) NASA; **815:** The Granger Collection, New York; **819:** *Music and Literature,* 1878, William M. Harnett, oil on canvas, 24 x 32-1/8," Albright-Knox Art Gallery Buffalo, New York, Gift of Seymour H. Knox, 1941; **820 & 823:** The Granger Collection, New York; **824:** "Horses" design #5, page 301 from the book *Textile Designs,* © The Design Library, New York; **831:** Springer/Corbis-Bettmann; **836:** (background) NASA; (br) *L. N. Tolstoi,* I. E. Repin, Sovfoto/ Eastfoto; **838:** *Portrait of Koutouzov, Prince of Smolensk,* George Dawe, Hermitage, St. Petersburg, Russia/Giraudon/Art

Resource, NY; **841:** The Granger Collection, New York; **845:** *Past and Present (no. 2),* Augustus Leopold Egg, Tate Gallery, London/Art Resource, NY; **846:** (top) The Granger Collection, New York; (bottom) *Thomas Hardy* (detail), R.G. Eres, by courtesy of the National Portrait Gallery, London; **848:** *My Sweet Rose,* John William Watehouse, Roy Miles Gallery, London/ Bridgeman/ Art Resource, NY; **850–851:** © Gregory K. Scott/Photo Researchers, Inc.; **852 & 853:** Lenore Weber/ Omni-Photo Communications, Inc.; **856:** (left) *Gerard Manley Hopkins* (detail), 1859, A.E. Hopkins, by Courtesy of the National Portrait Gallery, London; (right) The Granger Collection, New York; **858:** *Bird's Nest,* Ros W. Jenkins. Warrington Museum and Art Gallery, Bridgeman/Art Resource, NY; **860–861:** Springer/Corbis-Bettmann; **864:** (left) NASA; (br) Art Resource, NY; **865 & 866:** Corel Professional Photos CD-ROM™; **872:** Costa Manos/PNI; **874–875:** *The City Rises,* 1911 (tempera on card), Umberto Boccioni (1882–1916), Jesi Collection, Milan/The Bridgeman Art Library International Ltd., London/New York; **876:** (1905) UPI/Corbis-Bettmann; (1914) Imperial War Museum, London; (1927) Wood River Gallery/ PNI; (1939) The National Archives/Corbis; (1945) SuperStock; (1949) Corel Professional Photos CD-ROM™; (1954) Corbis-Bettmann; **877:** (1969) NASA; (1975) Michael St. Maur Shell/ Corbis; (1979) © Peter Marlow/Sygma (1989) © Reggis Bossu/ Sygma; **878:** (top) Corel Professional Photos CD-ROM™; (bottom) Musée de Verdun/ Luc Joubert/ Tallandier; **879:** (top) Culver Pictures, Inc.; (bottom) UPI/Corbis-Bettmann; **880:** (top) Domenica del Corriere/ET Archive, London/ SuperStock; (center) & (bottom) AP/Wide World Photos; **881:** (top) AP/Wide World Photos; (bottom) UPI/Corbis-Bettmann; **882:** (top) Culver Pictures, Inc.; (bottom) Erik Schaffer; Ecoscene/ Corbis; **883:** (top) David Hockney Studio; (bottom) Martin Jones/ Corbis; **884 (top):** *Sampler,* (detail) 1797 by Mary Wiggin. 18x 21 1/2." Philadelphia Museum of Art, Whitman Sampler Collection/ Given by Pet, Incorporated.; **885:** *The Children Enter the Palace of Luxury,* probably from "The Bluebird" by Maeterlinck, 1911 (oil on card) by Frederick Cayley Robinson (1862–1927), The Fine Art Society, London/Bridgeman Art Library International Ltd., London/New York; **886:** (top) Alfred A. Knopf; (bottom) Hulton-Deutsch Collection/Corbis; **892:** *Ox House, Shaftsbury,* 1932, John R. Biggs, Wood Engraving; **896:** The Granger Collection, New York; **898:** *Her Signal,* c. 1892, Norman Garstin, (1847–1926) The Royal Cornwall Museum, Truro/Bridgeman Art Library International Ltd., London/New York; **901:** Dennis Stock/ Magnum Photos, Inc.; **902:** *Man in the World,* P. Filonov, Russian State Museum, St. Petersburg, Russia/Superstock; **905:** The Granger Collection, New York; **908:** *T. S. Eliot* (detail), 1888–1965, Sir Gerald Kelly, National Portrait Gallery, Smithsonian Institution, Art Resource, New York; **911:** *Bolton,* 1938 (detail), William Coldstream, The National Gallery of Canada, Ottawa, Gift of the Massey Foundation, 1946; **913:** Clasen/The Image Bank; **914 & 915:** T. Sawada/Photonica; **916:** Harald Sund/The Image Bank; **922:** (tl) BBC Hulton/Corbis-Bettmann; (tr) The Granger Collection, New York; (br) *Louis MacNeice* (detail) H. Loster, by Courtesy of the National Portrait Gallery, London; **924:** The Granger Collection, New York; **928:** *The Fall of Icarus,* Pieter I. Brueghel, Musées Royaux des Beaux-Arts de Belgique, Bruxelles; **931:** Simon Wilkinson/The Image Bank; **932–933:** Richard Nowitz/Corbis; **936:** The Granger Collection, New York; **938–939:** © Gregory C. Dimijian/Photo Researchers, Inc.; **941:** © Orwell Archive; **948:** (background) NASA; (tl) Inge Morath/ Magnum Photos, Inc.; (tr) The Granger Collection, New York; (bottom) Dorothy Alexander; **949:** *Thrust,* 1959, Adolph Gottlieb, The Metropolitan Museum of Art, George A. Hearn Fund, 1959, Photography by Malcolm Varon, © 1987/1989 Copyright by the Metropolitan Museum of Art; **950:** The Granger Collection, New York; **952:** (background) NASA; **953:** Corbis; **957:** *A Balloon Site, Coventry,* 1940, Dame Laura Knight, Imperial War Museum, London; **958:** (tl) & (tr) & (br) The Granger Collection, New York; (bl) *Siefried Sassoon* (detail), Bassano, by Courtesy of the National Portrait Gallery, London; **961 & 962:** Photri; **963:** The Granger Collection, New York; **964:** © S.C. Fried/Photo Researchers, Inc.; **966:** Corbis-Bettmann; **970:** (left) *Winston Churchill* (detail), National Portrait Gallery, Smithsonian Institution, Washington, D.C./Art Resource, NY; (right) The Granger Collection, New York; **972:** Snark/Art Resource, NY; **976:** Culver Pictures, Inc.; **982:** Hulton Getty/Tony Stone Images; **985:** *Hillside in Wales* (detail), L.S. Lowry, The Tate Gallery, London/ Art Resource, New York; **986:** The Granger Collection, New York; **992:** Mark Carson Geson Photography; **995:** Nicholas Devore/ Bruce Coleman, Inc.; **997:** (tl) Patrick Ward/ Stock, Boston; (center) The Granger Collection, New York; **1002:** (top) Thomas Victor; (bottom) The Irish Times; **1004–1005:** D'Lynn Waldron/The Image Bank; **1006:** Geoffrey Gove/The Image Bank; **1008:** *Starry Night over the Rhone River,* Vincent van Gogh, Musee d'Orsay, Paris, France/Art Resource, NY; **1012:** Thomas Victor; **1014:** Peter Dublin/Stock, Boston; **1017:** Terry Madison/The Image Bank; **1022:** (background) NASA; (br) © Richard Smith/Sygma; **1024:** © Richard Smith/ Sygma; **1026:** (background) NASA; **1027:** Corel Professional Photos CD- ROM™; **1031:** *The Snack Bar,* 1930, Edward Burra, Tate Gallery, London/Art Resource, NY; **1032:** (left) *Joseph Conrad* (detail), Walter Tittle, by Courtesy of the National Portrait Gallery, London; (right) The Granger Collection, New York; **1036–1037:** Dieter & Mary Plage/Bruce Coleman, Inc.; **1040–1041:** Michael Freidel/Woodfin Camp & Associates; **1045:** Culver Pictures, Inc.; **1048:** *St. Patrick's Close,* Walter Osborne, Courtesy of the National Gallery of Ireland; **1052:** (top) The Granger Collection, New York; (bottom) Photo by Jerry Bauer; **1055:** *The Garden of Love,* Walter Richard Sickert, Fitzwilliam Museum, Cambridge; **1060–1061:** The Granger Collection, New York; **1062:** Culver Pictures, Inc.; **1066:** (left) *D. H. Lawrence* (detail), Jan Juta, by Courtesy of the National Portrait Gallery, London; (right) The Granger Collection, New York; **1069:** Corbis-Bettmann; **1073:** Culver Pictures, Inc.; **1079:** Hans Neleman/ The Image Bank; **1084:** (background) NASA; (br) Susan Meiselas/Magnum Photos, Inc.; **1085:** Steve Dunwell/The Image Bank; **1088:** (background) NASA; **1089:** *Joseph Conrad* (detail), Walter Tittle, by Courtesy of the National Portrait Gallery, London; **1093:** © Kenneth Eward/BioGrafz —Science Source/Photo Researchers, Inc.; **1094:** (left) Corbis-Bettmann; (right) Thomas Victor; **1096:** *Fishermen at Sea off the Needles,* J.M.W. Turner, Tate Gallery (on loan)/e.t.archive; **1100-1101:** Dann Coffey/ The Image Bank; **1103 & 1105:** (right) **& 1107:** (right) Kazuyuki Hashimoto/Photonica; **1110:** (top) *Philip Larkin* (detail), Humphrey Ocean, by Courtesy of the National Portrait Gallery, London; (center) *Stevie Smith* (detail), Godfrey Argent, by Courtesy of the National Portrait Gallery, London; (bottom) Nicolas Elder/Globe Photos; **1112:** (right) & (inset) Tombstones of Tiberius Julius Rufus and his son, Petronius Rufus and their wives, Erich Lessing/Art Resource, NY; **1114:** Ross M. Horowitz/ The Image Bank; **1118:** Ian Berry/Magnum Photos, Inc.; **1121:** *Man from the Village,* Carlton Murrell, Courtesy of the artist; **1123:** *The Red House,* Carlton Murrell, Courtesy of the artist; **1128:** Thomas Victor; **1130–1133:** Warp-printed cotton, Arthur Sanderson & Sons, 1930, The Victoria and Albert Museum, London/Art

Resource, NY; **1136:** (top) Eugene Richards/Magnum Photos, Inc.; (bottom) Camera Press/Globe Photos; **1139:** *Revolution Is Change, Change Is Life,* 1988, Jean Patrick Icart-Pierre, Soft pastel on stretched paper, Collection of the artist, Photo by Tony Velez, Courtesy The Bronx Museum of the Arts, New York; **1142 & 1143:** UPI/Corbis-Bettmann; **1146:** Thomas Victor; **1151:** Dinodia/Omni-Photo Communications, Inc.; **1152:** Grace Davies/Omni-Photo Communications, Inc.; **1158:** (left) UPI/Corbis-Bettmann; **1160 & 1163:** NASA/Omni-Photo Communications, Inc.; **1168:** Cover painting by Derek Walcott from OMEROS by Derek Walcott. Copyright© 1990 by Derek Walcott. Reprinted by permission of Farrar, Straus and Giroux, Inc.; **1172:** © Dennis Brack, 1993/PNI; **1173:** (left) Cover from *Heart of Darkness* by Joseph Conrad. Copyright © 1995. Published by the Penguin Group, a division of Penguin Books USA Inc.; (center) Reprinted with the permission of Pocket Books, a division of Simon & Schuster from Pygmalion by George Bernard Shaw. Copyright © 1973 by Simon & Schuster, a publication of Washington Square Press.; (right) Book cover from *Passage to India* by E. M. Forester. Copyright 1924 by Harcourt Brace & Company. Copyright renewed 1952 by E. M. Forester. Reproduced by permission of Harcourt Brace Jovanovich, Inc., Front photograph copyright © 1984 by Columbia Pictures Industries, Inc.

ADDITIONAL CREDITS

Editorial: Tim Callahan, Elaine Goldman, Gregory Lynch, Laura Ring

Media Resources: Diane Alimena, Katty Gavilanes, Suzi Myers

Permissions: Rosalyn Arcilla, Jeanette Myers

Photo Research Service: Omni-Photo Communications, Inc.

PrePress Production: James D. Gwyn

Production: Claudia Dukeshire, Deborah O'Connell

Design and Page Layout: Ernest Albanese, Robert Aleman, Jane Alexander, Lisa Ann Arcuri, Penelope Baker, Anthony Barone, Linda Berniak, Elizabeth Bostwick, Emily Buckley, Chris Callaway, Rui Camarinha, Tara Campbell, Carlos Crespo, Thomas Davidson, Paul DelSignore, Robert Dobasczewski, Irene Ehrmann, Jeffrey Engel, Frederic Joe Galka, Diane Gerard, Pat Gilbanks, Florrie Gladson, Julie Goldstein, Alison Grabow, Leslie Greenberg, Greg Harrison, Ralph Henriquez, Kathleen Kennedy, Gregory Ludwig, Laura Maggio, Lynn Mandarino, John McClure, Deirdre Mitchell, Thomas Mitchell, Rebecca Myers, Karolyn Necco, Evelyn O'Shea, Harry Phillips, Linda Punskovsky, Ken Rosenblat, David Rosenthal, Phyllis Rosinsky, Janelle Roth, Irene Schwartz, Jan Schwartz, Rose Sievers, Dakota Smith, Scott Steinhardt, Tom Tedesco, Frances Turcott, Karen Vignola, Wendy Wolf